Standard & Poor's®
500 Guide

2010 Edition

Standard & Poor's

New York   Chicago   San Francisco
Lisbon   London   Madrid   Mexico City
Milan   New Delhi   San Juan   Seoul
Singapore   Sydney   Toronto

FOR STANDARD & POOR'S

Managing Director, Equity Research Services: Robert Barriera
Publisher: Frank LoVaglio

The **McGraw·Hill** Companies

1 2 3 4 5 6 7 8 9 0   CUS/CUS   0 1 0

ISBN-   978-0-07-170336-9
MHID-   0-07-170336-5

This book is printed on acid-free paper.

This publication is designed to provide accurate and authoritative information in regard to the subject matter covered. It is sold with the understanding that the publisher is not engaged in rendering legal, accounting, or other professional service. If legal advice or other expert assistance is required, the services of a competent professional person should be sought.

—From a declaration of principles jointly adopted by a committee of the
American Bar Association and a committee of publishers

The companies contained in this handbook represented the components of the S&P 500 Index as of November 30, 2009.
Additions to or deletions from the Index will cause its composition to change over time.
Company additions and company deletions from the Standard & Poor's equity indexes do not in any way reflect an opinion on the investment merits of the company.

ABOUT THE AUTHOR

Standard & Poor's Financial Services LLC, a subsidiary of The McGraw-Hill Companies, Inc., is the nation's leading securities information company. It provides a broad range of financial services, including the respected Standard & Poor's ratings and stock rankings, advisory services, data guides, and the most closely watched and widely reported gauges of stock market activity—the S&P 500, S&P MidCap 400, S&P SmallCap 600, and the S&P Composite 1500 stock price indexes. Standard & Poor's products are marketed around the world and used extensively by financial professionals and individual investors.

Introduction

by **David M. Blitzer, Ph.D.**
Managing Director & Chairman of the Index Committee
Standard & Poor's

The S&P 500

Any Web site, television news program, newspaper, or radio report covering the stock market gives the latest results of a handful of stock indices, including the Dow Industrials, the NASDAQ, and the S&P 500. The Dow is the oldest, extending back over 100 years, and has covered only 30 stocks since shortly before the crash of 1929. The NASDAQ came to fame in the tech boom but ignores all the companies listed on the New York Stock Exchange. The S&P 500 is the index used by market professionals and institutional investors when they need to know what the stock market is doing. While there are several thousand stocks traded in the U.S. market, the S&P 500 covers the most significant ones, representing some three-quarters of the total value of all U.S. equities. Over $1.5 trillion invested through mutual funds, pensions, and exchange-traded funds track the S&P 500. These funds mimic what the index does—if the index rises, so do the funds. Further, when a stock is added to or dropped from the index, these trillions of dollars of funds buy, or sell, the stock. The S&P 500 is also the way the market and its condition is measured—for Wall Street, corporate earnings are the earnings per share calculated for the S&P 500, and the market's valuation is gauged by the price-earnings ratio on the S&P 500.

The S&P 500 and You, the Investor

If you picked up this book, you are probably interested in the stock market or stocks you might invest in; you may be wondering why institutional investors and market professionals focus so much attention on the 500 or what you can learn from the index. So, what can the index do? It can:

- Give you a benchmark for investment performance
- Tell you what kinds of stocks performed well or poorly in the past
- Let you see if today's valuations are higher or lower than in the past
- Help you compare one company or industry to another

We will look at these in turn before describing what's inside the S&P 500 and how S&P maintains the index.

Benchmarks: Monitoring investment performance—keeping score—is what separates occasional stock pickers from serious investors. People who chat about stocks with fellow workers or around the backyard barbeque rarely maintain records beyond the minimum level required to file their taxes. For these investors, stocks that go up are good and stocks that go down are disappointing; there is no serious analysis of what makes stocks move. Serious investors, whether institutional investors or individuals committed to managing their investments, know that understanding whether your stock selections work out requires knowing what the market did and how your portfolio compares to the market. This is where an index benchmark is essential.

The first question most investors have about their success is whether they are beating the market. A rough and ready answer can be found by comparing your portfolio's results to the S&P 500. More in-depth answers would either include dividends as well as price changes or would adjust for investment risks, or both. All the necessary data are widely available for the S&P 500 as well as being included in some brokerage statements and most mutual fund reports.

What went up and what went down: Simply looking at whether the market—the index—gained or lost can tell you a lot about what happened to your portfolio. For most portfolios and most stocks, the largest factor in their movements is how the overall market did. The second largest factor is often how similar stocks—in the same economic sector or industry—behaved. Because the S&P 500 covers 75 percent of the total value of the U.S. equity market, it is a very good indication of what the market did. The stocks in the index are all classified into sectors and industries, so you can use these segments of the index to see if your stocks did better or worse than others in the same sector.

There are 10 economic sectors that classify all the stocks in the S&P 500; the table following lists these sectors, the number of stocks in each, and the weight (based on market values) of each sector in the index. The performance of different sectors can be very different. Looking at the period from the recent low on March 9, 2009, to the end of November 2009, the financial sector gained 135%, materials and industrials each rose about 81% while telecommunication services gained "only" 24%. Before someone decides financial stocks are the all-time best remember that from the record high on October 9, 2007, to March 9th financials fell 59%, far more than any other sector. One comment heard from time to time is that no sector holds the leadership in the S&P 500 forever. Indeed, technology and financials have been trading the leadership back and forth for some 20 years. So be wary of anything that seems to overstay its welcome at the top of the list.

There are other classifications of stocks in the S&P 500. Not only are stocks assigned to an economic sector. They are also assigned to an industry group, an industry, and a sub-industry, using a classification standard called GICS® or the Global Industry Classification Standard.[1] There are 10 sectors, about 25 industry groups, some 60 industries, and about 150 sub-industries. Separately from GICS, stocks are classified as growth or value stocks. Traditionally, growth stocks are those with fast-growing earnings, which offer investors the promise of higher earnings in the future. Value stocks are stocks believed to offer unrecognized values that are not reflected in the stock price. The classification is based on a number of financial ratios and measures, including earnings growth, price/earnings ratios, dividend yields, and similar measures. Although most investors hunt for growth stocks, value stocks tend to perform better over the long run. During periods of a few years or less, either one can easily outperform the other. Investors aren't the only people seeking growth; few if any companies want to be known as value stocks, and all want to be called growth stocks.

Market Valuations: The last few years certainly proved that there are times when markets go both up and down, sometimes by large amounts. The last 10 years of market moves are likely to be remembered for a long, long time. Through it all, what we really want to know is if stocks are really cheap and the market is likely to rise, or if stocks are overpriced and the market will tumble.

Economics tells us that a stock's value lies in the future earnings and dividends. Two convenient measures of how stock prices compare to earnings and dividends are the ratio of the price to earnings (P/E) and the dividend yield or percentage that the dividend is of the stock's price. Just as these are used for individual stocks, they are also used for the overall market by calculating these measures for the S&P 500. As of November 2009, the figures for the index were a P/E of 19.4 and a dividend yield of 2.3 percent. These numbers change as the market rises or falls and as company earnings and dividends change. Up-to-date numbers are published by Standard & Poor's on the Web at www.indices.standardandpoors.com and by various newspapers, magazines, and financial and investing Web sites.

---

[1]GICS(®) is maintained jointly by Standard & Poor's and MSCIBarra. Standard & Poor's Financial Services LLC is a subsidiary of the McGraw-Hill Companies, Inc.

A P/E of 19.4 for the index is virtually the same as the average since 1988 of 19.5. Since 1988 the range of the P/E ratio is 11.5 to 30; going farther back, the P/E ranges from a low of about eight to a high in the mid to upper thirties. Many investors see a P/E below average as a sign that stocks are undervalued and that there are buying opportunities while a P/E far above the average is a caution sign. Earnings move up and down just as stock prices do, so both can affect the P/E ratio. Corporate earnings tend to fall in recessions and rise in good times, and these movements could distort P/E ratios.

Dividends have dropped out of fashion in the last two decades, and fewer investors seem to watch dividend yields. However, about 375 of the 500 stocks in the S&P 500 pay dividends, so the current dividend yield of 2.3 percent may tell us something about the market. Since the 1950s, the dividend yield on the S&P 500 has almost always been lower than the yield on U.S. treasury or high-grade corporate bonds. The bonds may be attractive for their safety, but they don't offer any opportunity for growth, although companies often raise their dividends as their earnings grow. In late 2008, this pattern reversed for awhile; the dividend yield of 2.3 percent topped the yield on 10-year U.S. treasuries.

Following the gyrations of 2008 another version of the P/E ratio has become popular with some analysts. Instead of looking at one year, the idea is to look at a longer period so that sharp short-term swings don't warp the figures. This approach, originally due to two academic economists[2] is to divide the current price by a 10-year average of earnings after the earnings' figures are adjusted for inflation. This figure gives a sense of the market's long-term relative value and long-run prospects that are less affected by recent economic and market gyrations. In March 2009, when the market made a deep low, this 10-year P/E was about 13 compared to a long-run average around 19 and it suggested stocks were cheap. At the end of November 2009, it was back to 20, a touch above the average and stocks didn't look so cheap.

Both these measures may give some sense of whether the market is over- or underpriced. However, neither of these is even close to being a fail-safe guide to the stock market in any time period. Moreover, the wide price swings seen in 2007 through 2009 should remind all investors that the market constantly changes and evolves and must be approached with both care and respect.

Comparing One Company to Another: Suppose you neighbor or a coworker tells you about a stock you "have to own" because the P/E is only 10, a quarter less than the overall market. Is it a buy? Maybe, or maybe not. The index and its components can tell you a lot about the stocks in the index as well as about the market. Stocks in the same industry or industry group often rise and fall together because the economic events and factors that affect one stock in an industry will affect others as well. When oil prices rise, most oil company stocks tend to do well. Rumors of changes in Medicare and other health care programs may affect all pharmaceutical stocks at once. One can compare data about a stock to the same information for similar stocks, to the industry or economic sector, and to the whole market. The S&P 500 and information about the stocks in it make this possible.

How does this help decide if a stock is cheap? Suppose the market's P/E as measured by the S&P 500 is 19 and the stock's P/E is 25, so it looks to be overpriced. Before forgetting about it, compare the data on the stock—P/E ratios, dividend yields, or other statistics—to similar stocks. The easiest way to find similar stocks is to use the sector and industry classifications from the S&P 500, as shown on the stock reports. As you do this with various stocks, you will begin to see that some sectors or industries seem to always have P/Es higher than the market while other sectors have low P/Es. Some sectors focus on growth stocks, which have high P/Es, while others focus on value stocks. You will notice similar patterns if you compare dividend yields. In fact, even looking for stocks that pay dividends will reveal some patterns.

---

[2]John Y. Campbell and Robert J. Shiller, "Valuation Ratios and the Long-Run Stock Market Outlook", *Journal of Portfolio Management*, winter 1998. Figures used in the text from www.dshort.com.

The stock market is shifting all the time, with some sectors becoming relatively more expensive and others fading from popularity. Within a sector there are similar movements among stocks as some move up faster while others may fade. It is useful to know how a stock compares to its peers in the same industry or sector as well as to understand how it compares to the entire market. Using the S&P 500 and the data shown on the stock reports, one can see these shifts and comparisons.

What's in the S&P 500

The S&P 500 Index consists of 500 stocks selected by Standard & Poor's to represent the U.S. stock market and, through the market, the U.S. economy. It is not the 500 "largest" stocks in the market. Rather, it is sometimes described as containing the leading stocks in leading industries. The stocks are selected based on published guidelines; all members of the S&P 500 must be U.S. companies. When they join the index, they must have market values of at least $3 billion, trade with reasonable liquidity, be profitable, and have at least half their shares available to investors. The selection of companies also considers the balance of economic sectors in the market and the index so that the index is a fair representation of the market as a whole.

The S&P 500 index is reported on television, Web sites and newspapers very widely. Data are also published on S&P Web site at www.indices.standardandpoors.com. Many investors and investment analysts use the S&P 500 to help choose stocks, as described above. However it has many other investment uses: index mutual funds, exchange-traded funds (ETFs), futures, and options. Index mutual funds are mutual funds that track an index. The first funds, and the largest index funds today, track the S&P 500. Exchange-traded funds have grown in popularity in recent years. These are similar to index mutual funds except that they trade on an exchange and can by bought and sold at any time of day whereas mutual funds are only sold at prices based on the market close. The first U.S. ETF was based on the S&P 500; there are two large ETFs based on the S&P 500. In addition, numerous pension funds, endowments, and other institutional investments track the S&P 500. As of the end of 2007, over $1.5 trillion was invested in various investments that track the S&P 500 as closely as possible. This means that the fund tries to mimic the index, adding stocks when they are added to the index and matching any other adjustments in the index.

There are relatively few changes in the index; most of these changes are caused by mergers, acquisitions, and other corporate actions that remove companies from the index. Over the last several years, the index has seen about 30 changes each year where a "change" is one company added and one dropped. If one thinks of the index as a portfolio, it is amazingly stable compared to most mutual funds—the turnover in the S&P 500 is about 5 to 10 percent of its value each year, whereas mutual funds can see a turnover of over 100 percent in a single year. A typical change in the index occurs when a company is acquired and is dropped from the index and replaced with another company. At times, especially recently with the turmoil in the markets, companies in the index are removed because of bankruptcy.

While changes to the index don't occur every day, they can be important to some traders. Because so much money tracks the index, about 10 percent of the outstanding stock of any company in the index is bought by index funds, ETFs, and other index investors when a stock is added to the index. Further, this buying occurs over a relatively short period of time—a few weeks or less. The result is that stocks added to the S&P 500 often see their prices rise when they go into the index.

The S&P 500 index was created and is maintained by S&P. There is an Index Committee of S&P professional staff who oversee the index and are responsible for making necessary changes to assure that the index will be an accurate reflection of the U.S. equity markets. Because changes in the index can move the market, all the work done by the Index Committee is confidential until any changes to the index are announced. Moreover, because the changes can move the market, the announcements are made available to the public, and no one gets any advance notice before the public announcements on S&P's Web site.

Beyond various kinds of index funds and ETFs, there are other investment uses of the index—futures and options. These are derivatives based on the value of the index that offer investors—mostly institutional investors, but some individuals as well—opportunities to either hedge their positions or to easily establish a leveraged position in the index. Futures and options are usually seen as more complex and often riskier than buying stocks. Just as successful stock investing requires research and understanding, successful use of futures and options demands a solid understanding of how the instruments work and what the risks are. At times these can magnify the impact of shifts in the index. Furthermore, unlike stocks, futures and options have firm expiration dates that must be considered in any investment plan.

History

The S&P 500 celebrated its fiftieth anniversary in March 2007. However, its forebears go farther back. The S&P 500 is not the oldest index, an honor which goes to the Dow Jones Industrials. The 500 traces its lineage back to an index of 233 companies published weekly by The Standard Statistics Company beginning in 1923. That index was one of the first to have industry classifications to support investment analysis. In 1926, Standard Statistics began a daily index of 90 stocks. A decade and a half later, in 1941, Standard Statistics merged with Poor's Publishing to form S&P. In 1957 the indices were combined and gave us the S&P 500. A small number of companies in the current S&P 500 can trace their membership back to the 1920s, over 50 were members in 1957.

The index has seen various changes over the years as it kept up with the times and with developments in the market. Different industries have come and gone. Some of today's leading sectors were barely present or nonexistent in 1957. Technology is now a much bigger part of the index. Investment banks and brokerage houses were all private partnerships in 1957 and didn't begin to enter the index until the 1970s. In many ways the index's history is the history of the U.S. stock market.

Many investors, especially those who consider mutual funds, have seen data on the history of the U.S. stock market since 1926. That history is the S&P 500 and the 90 stock index that preceded the 500. Mutual funds and other investment products often compare their performance to the market; the market is the S&P 500. You might think that 500 stocks chosen simply to represent the market without any attempt to select "good" stocks that will beat the market might be an easy target to outperform. Actually, it is not; in fact, it is *very* difficult to consistently outperform the S&P 500 or most other broad-based indices. Research by Standard & Poor's and by various others shows that in a typical period of three or more years, fewer than one-third of mutual funds outperform the index. Further, a fund that managed to be in the lucky third that beat the index in the last three years has only a one-in-three chance of beating the index in the next three years. Why? First, index funds and ETFs are cheap, with very low expenses. Second, since it is very hard to know which stocks will go up first, it helps to own a lot of stocks.[3]

Today Standard & Poor's publishes literally hundreds of thousands of indices, covering over 80 stock markets in almost every country where there is a stock market. The largest indices have several times more stocks than the 500, including a global equity index with over 11,000 securities. At the other extreme there are narrow indices focused on a small sub-industry in one country. All these indices are used by investors, often in the same way the 500 can be used, as described here.

[3]On index results vs. mutual funds, see S&P's SPIVA reports on S&P's Web site or books by John Bogle or Burton Malkiel.

In conclusion

When you want to know how the market did, what went up or down, or whether your stock picks beat the market, the best place to look is the S&P 500.

S&P 500 Global Industry Classification Standard (GICS) Sectors
As of November 30, 2009

	Number of Companies	Percent of Market Capitalization
Consumer Discretionary	79	9.27
Consumer Staples	41	11.74
Energy	40	12.05
Financials	79	14.42
Health Care	52	12.87
Industrials*	59	10.38
Information Technology	76	18.95
Materials	30	3.58
Telecommunication Services	9	3.11
Utilities	35	3.64

What You'll Find in This Book

In the pages that follow you will find an array of text and statistical data on 500 different companies spanning 154 sub-industries. This information, dealing with everything from the nature of these companies' basic businesses, recent corporate developments, current outlooks, and select financial information relating to revenues, earnings, dividends, margins, capitalization, and so forth, might initially seem overwhelming. However, it's not that difficult. Just take a few moments to familiarize yourself with what you'll find on these pages.

Following is a glossary of terms and definitions used throughout this book. Please refer to this section as you encounter terms which need further clarification.

Glossary

S&P STARS – Since January 1, 1987, Standard & Poor's Equity Research Services has ranked a universe of common stocks based on a given stock's potential for future performance. Under proprietary STARS (STock Appreciation Ranking System), S&P equity analysts rank stocks according to their individual forecast of a stock's future total return potential versus the expected total return of a relevant benchmark (e.g., a regional index (S&P Asia 50 Index, S&P Europe 350 Index or S&P 500 Index), based on a 12-month time horizon. STARS was designed to meet the needs of investors looking to put their investment decisions in perspective.

S&P 12-Month Target Price – The S&P equity analyst's projection of the market price a given security will command 12 months hence, based on a combination of intrinsic, relative, and private market valuation metrics.

Investment Style Classification – Characterizes the stock as either a growth-or value-oriented investment, and, indicates the market value (size) of the company as large-cap, mid-cap or small-cap. Growth stocks typically have a higher price-to-earnings and price-to-cash flow ratio, that represents the premium that is being paid for the expected higher growth. Value stocks typically have higher dividends and more moderate P/E ratios consistent with their current return policies.

Qualitative Risk Assessment – The S&P equity analyst's view of a given company's operational risk, or the risk of a firm's ability to continue as an ongoing concern. The Qualitative Risk Assessment is a relative ranking to the S&P U.S. STARS universe, and should be reflective of risk factors related to a company's operations, as opposed to risk and volatility measures associated with share prices.

Quantitative Evaluations – In contrast to our qualitative STARS recommendations, which are assigned by S&P analysts, the quantitative evaluations described below are derived from proprietary arithmetic models. These computer-driven evaluations may at times contradict an analyst's qualitative assessment of a stock. One primary reason for this is that different measures are used to determine each. For instance, when designating STARS, S&P analysts assess many factors that cannot be reflected in a model, such as risks and opportunities, management changes, recent competitive shifts, patent expiration, litigation risk, etc.

S&P Quality Rankings (also known as **S&P Earnings & Dividend Rankings**) – Growth and stability of earnings and dividends are deemed key elements in establishing S&P's Quality Rankings for common stocks, which are designed to capsulize the nature of this record in a single symbol. It should be noted, however, that the process also takes into consideration certain adjustments and modifications deemed desirable in establishing such rankings. The final score for each stock is measured against a scoring matrix determined by analysis of the scores of a large and representative sample of stocks. The range of scores in the array of this sample has been aligned with the following ladder of rankings:

A+	Highest	B−	Lower
A	High	C	Lowest
A−	Above Average	D	In Reorganization
B+	Average	NR	Not Ranked
B	Below Average		

S&P Fair Value Rank – Using S&P's exclusive proprietary quantitative model, stocks are ranked in one of five groups, ranging from Group 5, listing the most undervalued stocks, to Group 1, the most overvalued issues. Group 5 stocks are expected to generally outperform all others. A positive (+) or negative (−) Timing Index is placed next to the Fair Value ranking to further aid the selection process. A stock with a (+) added to the Fair Value Rank simply means that this stock has a somewhat better chance to outperform other stocks with the same Fair Value Rank. A stock with a (−) has a somewhat lesser chance to outperform other stocks with the same Fair Value Rank. The Fair Value rankings imply the following: 5-Stock is significantly undervalued; 4-Stock is moderately undervalued; 3-Stock is fairly valued; 2-Stock is modestly overvalued; 1-Stock is significantly overvalued.

S&P Fair Value Calculation – The price at which a stock should trade at, according to S&P's proprietary quantitative model that incorporates both actual and estimated variables (as opposed to only actual variables in the case of S&P Quality Ranking). Relying heavily on a company's actual return on equity, the S&P Fair Value model places a value on a security based on placing a formula-derived price-to-book multiple on a company's consensus earnings per share estimate.

Insider Activity – Gives an insight as to insider sentiment by showing whether directors, officers and key employees who have proprietary information not available to the general public, are buying or selling the company's stock during the most recent six months.

Investability Quotient (IQ) – The IQ is a measure of investment desirability. It serves as an indicator of potential medium- to long-term return and as a caution against downside risk. The measure takes into account variables such as technical indicators, earnings estimates, liquidity, financial ratios and selected S&P proprietary measures.

Volatility – Rates the volatility of the stock's price over the past year.

Technical Evaluation – In researching the past market history of prices and trading volume for each company, S&P's computer models apply special technical methods and formulas to identify and project price trends for the stock.

Relative Strength Rank – Shows, on a scale of 1 to 99, how the stock has performed versus all other companies in S&P's universe on a rolling 13-week basis.

Global Industry Classification Standard (GICS) – An industry classification standard, developed by Standard & Poor's in collaboration with Morgan Stanley Capital International (MSCI). GICS is currently comprised of 10 sectors, 25 industry groups, 60 industries, and about 150 sub-industries.

S&P Core Earnings – Standard & Poor's Core Earnings is a uniform methodology for adjusting operating earnings by focusing on a company's after-tax earnings generated from its principal businesses. Included in the Standard & Poor's definition are employee stock option grant expenses, pension costs, restructuring charges from ongoing operations, write-downs of depreciable or amortizable operating assets, purchased research and development, M&A related expenses and unrealized gains/losses from hedging activities. Excluded from the definition are pension gains, impairment of goodwill charges, gains or losses from asset sales, reversal of prior-year charges and provision from litigation or insurance settlements.

S&P Issuer Credit Rating – A Standard & Poor's Issuer Credit Rating is a current opinion of an obligor's overall financial capacity (its creditworthiness) to pay its financial obligations. This opinion focuses on the obligor's capacity and willingness to meet its financial commitments as they come due. It does not apply to any specific financial obligation, as it does not take into account the nature of and provisions of the obligation, its standing in bankruptcy or liquidation, statutory preferences, or the legality and enforceability of the obligation. In addition, it does not take into account the creditworthiness of the guarantors, insurers, or other forms of credit enhancement on the obligation. The Issuer Credit Rating is not a recommendation to purchase, sell, or hold a financial obligation issued by an obligor, as it does not comment on market price or suitability for a particular investor. Issuer Credit Ratings are based on current information furnished by obligors or obtained by Standard & Poor's from other sources it considers reliable. Standard & Poor's does not perform an audit in connection with any Issuer Credit Rating and may, on occasion, rely on unaudited financial information. Issuer Credit Ratings may be changed, suspended, or withdrawn as a result of changes in, or unavailability of, such information, or based on other circumstances.

Standard & Poor's Equity Research Services – Standard & Poor's Equity Research Services U.S. includes Standard & Poor's Investment Advisory Services LLC; Standard & Poor's

Equity Research Services Europe includes Standard & Poor's LLC- London; Standard & Poor's Equity Research Ser-vices Asia includes Standard & Poor's LLC's offices in Hong Kong and Singapore, Standard & Poor's Malaysia Sdn Bhd, and Standard & Poor's Information Services (Australia) Pty Ltd.

<u>Abbreviations Used in S&P Equity Research Reports</u>
CAGR – Compound Annual Growth Rate
CAPEX – Capital Expenditures
CY – Calendar Year
DCF – Discounted Cash Flow
EBIT – Earnings Before Interest and Taxes
EBITDA – Earnings Before Interest, Taxes, Depreciation and Amortization
EPS – Earnings Per Share
EV – Enterprise Value
FCF – Free Cash Flow
FFO – Funds From Operations
FY – Fiscal Year
P/E – Price/Earnings
PEG Ratio – P/E-to-Growth Ratio
PV – Present Value
R&D – Research & Development
ROA – Return on Assets
ROE – Return on Equity
ROI – Return on Investment
ROIC – Return on Invested Capital
SG&A – Selling, General & Administrative Expenses
WACC – Weighted Average Cost of Capital
Dividends on American Depository Receipts (ADRs) and American Depository Shares (ADSs) are net of taxes (paid in the country of origin).

REQUIRED DISCLOSURES

S&P Global STARS Distribution

In North America
As of September 30, 2009, research analysts at Standard & Poor's Equity Research Services North America recommended 28.6% of issuers with buy recommendations, 57.6% with hold recommendations and 13.8% with sell recommendations.

In Europe
As of September 30, 2009, research analysts at Standard & Poor's Equity Research Services Europe recommended 33.8% of issuers with buy recommendations, 45.3% with hold recommendations and 20.9% with sell recommendations.

In Asia
As of September 30, 2009, research analysts at Standard & Poor's Equity Research Services Asia recommended 32.2% of issuers with buy recommendations, 52.5% with hold recommendations and 15.3% with sell recommendations.

Globally
As of September 30, 2009, research analysts at Standard & Poor's Equity Research Services globally recommended 29.7% of issuers with buy recommendations, 55.2% with hold recommendations and 15.1% with sell recommendations.

5-STARS (Strong Buy): Total return is expected to outperform the total return of a relevant benchmark, by a wide margin over the coming 12 months, with shares rising in price on an absolute basis.

4-STARS (Buy): Total return is expected to outperform the total return of a relevant benchmark over the coming 12 months, with shares rising in price on an absolute basis.

3-STARS (Hold): Total return is expected to closely approximate the total return of a relevant benchmark over the coming 12 months, with shares generally rising in price on an absolute basis.

2-STARS (Sell): Total return is expected to underperform the total return of a relevant benchmark over the coming 12 months, and the share price not anticipated to show a gain.

1-STAR (Strong Sell): Total return is expected to underperform the total return of a relevant benchmark by a wide margin over the coming 12 months, with shares falling in price on an absolute basis.
Relevant benchmarks: In North America, the relevant benchmark is the S&P 500 Index, in Europe and in Asia, the relevant benchmarks are generally the S&P Europe 350 Index and the S&P Asia 50 Index.

For All Regions:
All of the views expressed in this research report accurately reflect the research analyst's personal views regarding any and all of the subject securities or issuers. No part of analyst compensation was, is, or will be directly or indirectly, related to the specific recommendations or views expressed in this research report.

Additional information is available upon request.
Other Disclosures

This report has been prepared and issued by Standard & Poor's and/or one of its affiliates. In the United States, research reports are prepared by Standard & Poor's Investment Advisory Services LLC ("SPIAS"). In the United States, research reports are issued by Standard & Poor's ("S&P"); in the United Kingdom by Standard & Poor's LLC ("S&P LLC"), which is authorized and regulated by the Financial Services Authority; in Hong Kong by Standard & Poor's LLC, which is regulated by the Hong Kong Securities Futures Commission; in Singapore by Standard & Poor's LLC, which is regulated by the Monetary Authority of Singapore; in Malaysia by Standard & Poor's Malaysia Sdn Bhd ("S&PM"), which is regulated by the Securities Commission; in Australia by Standard & Poor's Information Services (Australia) Pty Ltd ("SPIS"), which is regulated by the Australian Securities & Investments Commission; and in Korea by SPIAS, which is also registered in Korea as a cross-border investment advisory company.

The research and analytical services performed by SPIAS, S&P LLC, S&PM, and SPIS are each conducted separately from any other analytical activity of Standard & Poor's.

Standard & Poor's or an affiliate may license certain intellectual property or provide pricing or other services to, or otherwise have a financial interest in, certain issuers of securities, including exchange-traded investments whose investment objective is to substantially replicate the returns of a proprietary Standard & Poor's index, such as the S&P 500. In cases where Standard & Poor's or an affiliate is paid fees that are tied to the amount of assets that are invested in the fund or the volume of trading activity in the fund, investment in the fund will generally result in Standard & Poor's or an affiliate earning compensation in addition to the subscription fees or other compensation for services rendered by Standard & Poor's. A reference to a particular investment or security by Standard & Poor's and/or one of its affiliates is not a recommendation to buy, sell, or hold such investment or security, nor is it considered to be investment advice.

Indexes are unmanaged, statistical composites and their returns do not include payment of any sales charges or fees an investor would pay to purchase the securities they represent. Such costs would lower performance. It is not possible to invest directly in an index. Standard & Poor's and its affiliates provide a wide range of services to, or relating to, many organizations, including issuers of securities, investment advisers, broker-dealers, investment banks, other financial institutions and financial intermediaries, and accordingly may receive fees or other economic benefits from those organizations, including organizations whose securities or services they may recommend, rate, include in model portfolios, evaluate or otherwise address.

For a list of companies mentioned in this report with whom Standard & Poor's and/or one of its affiliates has had business relationships within the past year, please go to: http://www2.standardandpoors.com/portal/site/sp/en/us/page.article/2,5,1,0,1145719 622102.html

Disclaimers

This material is based upon information that we consider to be reliable, but neither S&P nor its affiliates warrant its completeness, accuracy or adequacy and it should not be relied upon as such. With respect to reports issued to clients in Japan and in the case of inconsistencies between the English and Japanese version of a report, the English version prevails. Neither S&P nor its affiliates guarantee the accuracy of the translation. Assumptions, opinions and estimates constitute our judgment as of the date of this material and are subject to change without notice. Neither S&P nor its affiliates are responsible for any errors or omissions or for results obtained from the use of this information. Past performance is not necessarily indicative of future results.

This material is not intended as an offer or solicitation for the purchase or sale of any security or other financial instrument. Securities, financial instruments or strategies mentioned herein may not be suitable for all investors. Any opinions expressed herein are given in good faith, are subject to change without notice, and are only correct as of the stated date of their issue. Prices, values, or income from any securities or investments mentioned in this report may fall against the interests of the investor and the investor may get back less than the amount invested. Where an investment is described as being likely to yield income, please note that the amount of income that the investor will receive from such an investment may fluctuate. Where an investment or security is denominated in a different currency to the investor's currency of reference, changes in rates of exchange may have an adverse effect on the value, price or income of or from that investment to the investor. The information contained in this report does not constitute advice on the tax consequences of making any particular investment decision. This material is not intended for any specific investor and does not take into account your particular investment objectives, financial situations or needs and is not intended as a recommendation of particular securities, financial instruments or strategies to you. Before acting on any recommendation in this material, you should consider whether it is suitable for your particular circumstances and, if necessary, seek professional advice.

For residents of the U.K. – this report is only directed at and should only be relied on by persons outside of the United Kingdom or persons who are inside the United Kingdom and who have professional experience in matters relating to investments or who are high net worth persons, as defined in Article 19(5) or Article 49(2) (a) to (d) of the Financial Services and Markets Act 2000 (Financial Promotion) Order 2005, respectively.

For residents of Singapore - Anything herein that may be construed as a recommendation is intended for general circulation and does not take into account the specific investment objectives, financial situation or particular needs of any particular person. Advice should be sought from a financial adviser regarding the suitability of an investment, taking into account the specific investment objectives, financial situation or particular needs of any person in receipt of the recommendation, before the person makes a commitment to purchase the investment product.

For residents of Malaysia, all queries in relation to this report should be referred to Alexander Chia, Desmond Ch'ng, or Ching Wah Tam.

This investment analysis was prepared from the following sources: S&P MarketScope, S&P Compustat, S&P Industry Reports, I/B/E/S International, Inc.; Standard & Poor's, 55 Water St., New York, NY 10041.

Key Stock Statistics

Market Cap.—The stock price multiplied by the number of shares outstanding, based on market value calculated at the issue level.

Institutional Holdings—Shows the percent of total common shares held by financial institutions. This information covers some 2,500 institutions and is compiled by Vickers Stock Research Corporation, 226 New York Avenue, Huntington, N.Y. 11743

Value of $10,000 Invested 5 years ago—The value today of a $10,000 investment in the stock made 5 years ago, assuming year-end reinvestment of dividends.

Beta—The beta coefficient is a measure of the volatility of a stock's price relative to the S&P 500 Index (a proxy for the overall market). An issue with a beta of 1.5 for example, tends to move 50% more than the overall market, in the same direction. An issue with a beta of 0.5 tends to move 50% less. If a stock moved exactly as the market moved, it would have a beta of 1.0. A stock with a negative beta tends to move in a direction opposite to that of the overall market.

Per Share Data ($) Tables

Cash Flow—Net income plus depreciation, depletion, and amortization, divided by shares used to calculate earnings per common share. (See also: "Cash Flow" under Industrial Companies.)

Dividends—Generally total cash payments per share based on the ex-dividend dates over a 12-month period. May also be reported on a declared basis where this has been established to be a company's payout policy.

Earnings—The amount a company reports as having been earned for the year on its common stock based on generally accepted accounting standards. Earnings per share are presented on a "diluted" basis pursuant to FASB 128, which became effective December 15, 1997, and are generally reported from continuing operations, before extraordinary items. This reflects a change from previously reported *primary earnings per share*. Insurance companies report *operating earnings* before gains/losses on security transactions and *earnings* after such transactions.

Net Asset Value—Appears on investment company reports and reflects the market value of stocks, bonds, and net cash divided by outstanding shares. The % difference indicates the percentage premium or discount of the market price over the net asset value.

Payout Ratio—Indicates the percentage of earnings paid out in dividends. It is calculated by dividing the annual dividend by the earnings. For insurance companies, *earnings* after gains/losses on security transactions are used.

P/E Ratio High/Low—The ratio of market price to earnings—essentially indicates the valuation investors place on a company's earnings. Obtained by dividing the annual earnings into the high and low market price for the year. For insurance companies, *operating earnings* before gains/losses on security transactions are used.

Portfolio Turnover—Appears on investment company reports and indicates percentage of total security purchases and sales for the year to overall investment assets. Primarily mirrors trading aggressiveness.

Prices High/Low—Shows the calendar year high and low of a stock's market price.

Tangible Book Value; Book Value (See also: "Common Equity" under Industrial Companies)—Indicates the theoretical dollar amount per common share one might expect to receive from a company's tangible "book" assets should liquidation take place. Generally, book value is determined by adding the stated value of the common stock, paid-in capital and retained earnings and then subtracting intangible assets (excess cost over equity of acquired companies, goodwill, and patents), preferred stock at liquidating value and unamortized debt discount. Divide that amount by the outstanding shares to get book value per common share.

Income/Balance Sheet Data Tables

Banks

Cash—Mainly vault cash, interest-bearing deposits placed with banks, reserves required by the Federal Reserve, and items in the process of collection—generally referred to as float.

Commercial Loans—Commercial, industrial, financial, agricultural loans and leases, gross.

Common Equity—Includes common/capital surplus, undivided profits, reserve for contingencies and other capital reserves.

Deposits—Primarily classified as either *demand* (payable at any time upon demand of depositor) or *time* (not payable within 30 days).

Deposits/Capital Funds—Average deposits divided by average capital funds. Capital funds include capital notes/debentures, other long-term debt, capital stock, surplus, and undivided profits. May be used as a "leverage" measure.

Earning Assets—Assets on which interest is earned.

Effective Tax Rate—Actual income tax expense divided by net before taxes.

Gains/Losses on Securities Transactions—Realized losses on sales of securities, usually bonds.

Government Securities—Includes United States Treasury securities and securities of other U.S. government agencies at book or carrying value. A bank's major "liquid asset."

Investment Securities—Federal, state, and local government bonds and other securities.

Loan Loss Provision—Amount charged to operating expenses to provide an adequate reserve to cover anticipated losses in the loan portfolio.

Loans—All domestic and foreign loans (excluding leases), less unearned discount and reserve for possible losses. Generally considered a bank's principal asset.

Long-Term Debt—Total borrowings for terms beyond one year including notes payable, mortgages, debentures, term loans, and capitalized lease obligations.

Money Market Assets—Interest-bearing interbank deposits, federal funds sold, trading account securities.

Net Before Taxes—Amount remaining after operating expenses are deducted from income, including gains or losses on security transactions.

Net Income—The final profit before dividends (common/preferred) from all sources after deduction of expenses, taxes, and fixed charges, but before any discontinued operations or extraordinary items.

Net Interest Income—Interest and dividend income, minus interest expense.

Net Interest Margin—A percentage computed by dividing net interest income, on a taxable equivalent basis, by average earning assets. Used as an analytical tool to measure profit margins from providing credit services.

Noninterest Income—Service fees, trading, and other income, excluding gains/ losses on securities transactions.

Other Loans—Gross consumer, real estate and foreign loans.

% Equity to Assets—Average common equity divided by average total assets. Used as a measure of capital adequacy.

% Equity to Loans—Average common equity divided by average loans. Reflects the degree of equity coverage to loans outstanding.

% Expenses/Op. Revenues—Noninterest expense as a percentage of taxable equivalent net interest income plus noninterest income (before securities gains/losses). A measure of cost control.

% Loan Loss Reserve—Contra-account to loan assets, built through provisions for loan losses, which serves as a cushion for possible future loan charge-offs.

% Loans/Deposits—Proportion of loans funded by deposits. A measure of liquidity and an indication of bank's ability to write more loans.

% Return on Assets—Net income divided by average total assets. An analytical measure of asset-use efficiency and industry comparison.

% Return on Equity—Net income (minus preferred dividend requirements) divided by average common equity. Generally used to measure performance.

% Return on Revenues—Net income divided by gross revenues.

State and Municipal Securities—State and municipal securities owned at book value.

Taxable Equivalent Adjustment—Increase to render income from tax-exempt loans and securities comparable to fully taxed income.

Total Assets—Includes interest-earning financial instruments—principally commercial, real estate, consumer loans and leases; investment securities/ trading accounts; cash/money market investments; other owned assets.

Industrial Companies

Following data is based on Form 10K Annual Report data as filed with SEC.

Capital Expenditures—The sum of additions at cost to property, plant and equipment, and leaseholds, generally excluding amounts arising from acquisitions.

Cash—Includes all cash and government and other marketable securities.

Cash Flow—Net income (before extraordinary items and discontinued operations, and after preferred dividends) plus depreciation, depletion, and amortization.

Common Equity [See also "Tangible Book Value" under Per Share Data($) Tables]—Common stock plus capital surplus and retained earnings, less any difference between the carrying value and liquidating value of preferred stock.

Current Assets—Those assets expected to be realized in cash or used up in the production of revenue within one year.

Current Liabilities—Generally includes all debts/obligations falling due within one year.

Current Ratio—Current assets divided by current liabilities. A measure of liquidity.

Depreciation—Includes noncash charges for obsolescence, wear on property, current portion of capitalized expenses (intangibles), and depletion charges.

Effective Tax Rate—Actual income tax charges divided by net before taxes.

Interest Expense—Includes all interest expense on short/long-term debt, amortization of debt discount/premium, and deferred expenses (e.g., financing costs).

Long-Term Debt—Debts/obligations due after one year. Includes bonds, notes payable, mortgages, lease obligations, and industrial revenue bonds. Other long-term debt, when reported as a separate account, is excluded. This account generally includes pension and retirement benefits.

Net Before Taxes—Includes operating and nonoperating revenues (including extraordinary items not net of taxes), less all operating and nonoperating expenses, except income taxes and minority interest, but including equity in nonconsolidated subsidiaries.

Net Income—Profits derived from all sources after deduction of expenses, taxes, and fixed charges, but before any discontinued operations, extraordinary items, and dividends (preferred/common).

Operating Income—Net sales and operating revenues less cost of goods sold and operating expenses (including research and development, profit sharing, exploration and bad debt, but excluding depreciation and amortization).

% Long-Term Debt of Invested Capital—Long-term debt divided by total invested capital. Indicates how highly "leveraged" a business might be.

% Operating Income of Revenues—Net sales and operating revenues divided into operating income. Used as a measure of operating profitability.

% Net Income of Revenues—Net income divided by sales/operating revenues.

% Return on Assets—Net income divided by average total assets on a per common share basis. Used in industry analysis and as a measure of asset-use efficiency.

% Return on Equity—Net income less preferred dividend requirements divided by average common shareholders' equity on a per common share basis. Generally used to measure performance and industry comparisons.

Revenues—Net sales and other operating revenues. Includes franchise/ leased department income for retailers, and royalties for publishers and oil and mining companies. Excludes excise taxes for tobacco, liquor, and oil companies.

Total Assets—Current assets plus net plant and other noncurrent assets (intangibles and deferred items).

Total Invested Capital—The sum of stockholders' equity plus long-term debt, capital lease obligations, deferred income taxes, investment credits, and minority interest.

Insurance Companies

Life Insurance In Force—The total value of all life insurance policies including ordinary, group, industrial and credit. Generally the figure is reported before any amounts ceded, or the portions placed with other insurance companies.

Premium Income—The amount of premiums earned during the year is generally equal to the net premiums written plus any increase or decrease in earned premiums. The categories are divided into Life, Accident & Health, Annuity and Property & Casualty.

Net Investment Income—Income received from investment assets (before taxes) including bonds, stocks, loans and other investments (less related expenses).

Total Revenues—Includes premium income, net investment income and other income.

Property & Casualty Underwriting Ratios— Includes: Loss Ratio—losses and loss adjustment expenses divided by premiums earned; Expense Ratio—underwriting expenses divided by net premiums written; Combined Loss-Expense Ratio—Measures claims, losses and operating expenses against premiums. The total of losses and loss expenses, before policyholders' dividends, to premiums earned, e.g., at 106.0%, equivalent to a loss of six cents of every premium dollar before investment income and taxes.

Net Before Taxes—Total operating income before income taxes and security gains or losses. Generally will include any equity in income of subsidiaries.

Net Operating Income—Includes income from operations, before security gains or losses, and before results of discontinued operations and special items.

Net Income—Includes income from operations, after security gains or losses, and before results of discontinued operations and special items.

% Return On Revenues—Is the net operating income divided by the total revenues.

% Return On Assets—Is the net operating income divided by the mean/ average assets.

% Return On Equity—Is obtained by dividing the average common equity for the year into the net operating income, less any preferred stock dividend requirements.

Cash & Equivalent—Includes cash, accrued investment income and short- term investments (except when classified as investments by the company).

Premiums Due—Generally includes premiums owed but uncollected, agent's balances receivable and earned and unbilled premiums receivable.

Investment Assets—Includes all investments shown under the company's investment account. Bonds, values at cost, includes bonds and notes, debt obligations and any short-term investments. Stocks, values at market, includes common and preferred stocks in the investment portfolio. Loans, includes mortgage, policy and other loans.

% Investment Yield—Is the return received on the company's investment assets, and is obtained by dividing the average investment assets into the net investment income, before applicable income taxes.

Deferred Policy Costs—Reflect certain costs of acquiring insurance business which have been deferred. These costs are primarily related to the production of business such as commissions, expenses in issuing policies and certain agency expenses.

Total Assets—Includes total investments, cash and cash items, accrued investment income, premiums due, deferred policy acquisition costs, property and equipment, separate accounts and other assets.

Debt—Includes bonds, debentures, notes, loans and mortgages payable.

Common Equity—Consists of common stock, additional paid in capital, net unrealized capital gains or losses on investments, retained earnings—less treasury stock at cost.

Investment Companies

Total Investment Income—The sum of income received from dividends and interest on portfolio holdings.

Net Investment Income—The amount of income remaining after operating expenses are deducted from total investment income. The per share figure is generally reported by the company, or may be obtained by dividing the net investment income by the shares outstanding. This amount is available for the payment of distributions.

Realized Capital Gains—Represents the net gain realized on the sale of investments, as reported by the company in the statement of changes in net assets. Divide amount by shares outstanding to obtain per share figure.

% Net Investment Income/Net Assets—Measures return on net assets. Percentage is obtained by dividing net investment income by average net assets.

% Expenses/Net Assets—Generally measures cost control. Percentage is obtained by dividing operating expenses by average net assets.

% Expenses/Investment Income—Indicates the amount of income absorbed by expenses. Percentage is obtained by dividing operating expenses by total investment income.

Net Assets—Represents the total market value of portfolio securities, including net cash, short-term investments, and stocks and bonds at market.

% Change S&P "500"—Measures the percentage change in Standard & Poor's 500 stock price index, before reinvestment of dividends, and is a general indicator of overall stock market performance.

% Change AAA Bonds—Measures the percentage change in the Standard & Poor's high grade bond index, before reinvestment of interest, and is a measure of AAA bond price movements.

% Net Asset Distribution—Indicates the percentage breakdown of net assets in the following categories: a) net cash (cash receivables and other assets, less liabilities); b) short-term obligations (U.S. Government securities, commercial paper and certificates of deposit); c) bonds and preferred stocks; d) common stocks. To calculate the % net asset distribution, divide net assets into each of the above categories.

Real Estate Investment Trusts and Savings & Loans

Rental Income—Primarily income received from rental property.

Mortgage Income—Primarily income derived from mortgages.

Total Income—Includes rental and mortgage income, gains on sale of real estate and other.

General Expenses—Includes property operating expenses, real estate taxes, depreciation & amortization, administrative expenses and provision for losses.

Interest Expense—Includes interest paid on mortgage debt, convertible debentures, other debt obligations and short-term debt.

% Expenses/Revenues—Total expenses divided by revenues. The result represents the percentage of revenues (or the number of cents per dollar of income) absorbed by expenses.

Provision for Losses—Reserve charged to income for possible real estate losses.

Net Income—Profits for the year. This would include any gains/losses on the sale of real estate but exclude extraordinary items.

% Earnings & Depreciation/Assets—Obtained by dividing average assets into the sum of net income and depreciation expense (a measure of "cash flow" for REITs).

Total Assets—The sum of net investments in real estate and other assets.

Real Estate Investments—The sum of gross investments in real estate, construction in process and mortgage loans and notes before allowances for losses and accumulated depreciation.

Loss Reserve—Reserves set aside for possible losses on real estate investments.

Net Investment—Real estate investments less accumulated depreciation and loss reserves.

Cash—Cash on hand, cash in escrow and short-term investments.

S T Debt—Short-term obligations due and payable within one year of balance sheet date. This would include the current portion of long-term debt, mortgages and notes, bank loans and commercial paper.

Debt—Includes debentures, mortgages and other long-term debt due after one year of balance sheet date.

Equity—Represents the sum of shares of beneficial interest or common stock, convertible preferred stock when included as equity, capital surplus and undistributed net income.

Total Capitalization—Is the sum of the stated values of a company's total shareholders' equity including preferred, common stock and debt obligations.

Price Times Book Value Hi Lo—Indicates the relationship of a stock's market price to book value. Obtained by dividing year-end book values into yearly high/low range.

Utilities

Capital Expenditures—Represents the amounts spent on capital improvements to plant and funds for construction programs.

Capitalization Ratios—Reflect the percentage of each type of debt/equity issues outstanding to total capitalization. % DEBT is obtained by dividing total debt by the sum of debt, preferred, common, paid-in capital and retained earnings. % PREFERRED is obtained by dividing the preferred stocks outstanding by total capitalization. % COMMON, divide the sum of common stocks, paid-in capital and retained earnings by total capitalization.

Construction Credits—Credits for interest charged to the cost of constructing new plant. A combination of allowance for equity funds used during construction and allowance for borrowed funds used during construction—credit.

Depreciation—Amounts charged to income to compensate for the decline in useful value of plant and equipment.

Effective Tax Rate—Actual income tax expense divided by the total of net income and actual income tax expense.

Fixed Charges Coverage—The number of times income before interest charges (operating income plus other income) after taxes covers total interest charges and preferred dividend requirements.

Gross Property—Includes utility plant at cost, plant work in progress, and nuclear fuel.

Long-Term Debt—Debt obligations due beyond one year from balance sheet date.

Maintenance—Amounts spent to keep plants in good operating condition.

Net Income—Amount of earnings for the year which is available for preferred and common dividend payments.

Net Property—Includes items in gross property less provision for depreciation.

Operating Revenues—Represents the amount billed to customers by the utility.

Operating Ratio—Ratio of operating costs to operating revenues or the proportion of revenues absorbed by expenses. Obtained by dividing operating expenses including depreciation, maintenance, and taxes by revenues.

% Earned on Net Property—Percentage obtained by dividing operating income by average net property for the year. A measure of plant efficiency.

% Return on Common Equity—Percentage obtained by dividing income available for common stock (net income less preferred dividend requirements) by average common equity.

% Return on Invested Capital—Percentage obtained by dividing income available for fixed charges by average total invested capital.

% Return on Revenues—Obtained by dividing net income for the year by revenues.

Total Capitalization—Combined sum of total common equity, preferred stock and long-term debt.

Total Invested Capital—Sum of total capitalization (common-preferred-debt), accumulated deferred income taxes, accumulated investment tax credits, minority interest, contingency reserves, and contributions in aid of construction.

Finally, at the very bottom of the right-hand page, you'll find general information about the company: its address and telephone number, the names of its senior executive officers and directors (usually including the name of the investor contact), and the state in which the company is incorporated.

How to Use This Book to Select Investments

And so, at last, we come to the $64,000 question: Given this vast array of data, how might a businesswoman seeking to find out about her competition, the marketing manager looking for clients, a job seeker, and the investor use it to best serve their respective purposes?

If you are like one of the first three of these individuals—a businesswoman, the marketing manager, or the job seeker—your task will be arduous, to be sure, but this book will provide you with an excellent starting point and your payoff can make it all worthwhile. You will have to go through this book page by page, looking for those companies that are in the industries in which you are interested, that are of the size and financial strength that appeal to you, that are located geographically in your territory or where you're willing to relocate, that have been profitable and growing, and so forth. And then you will have to read about just what's going on at those companies by referring to the appropriate "Highlights" and "Business Summary" comments in these reports.

Of course, this book won't do it *all* for you. It is, after all, just a starting point, not a conclusive summary of everything you might need to know. It is designed to educate, not to render advice or provide recommendations. But it will get you pointed in the right direction.

Finally, what about the investor who wants to use this book to find good individual investments from among the 500 stocks in the S&P 500 Index? If you fall into that category, what should you do?

Well, you can approach your quest the same way that the businesswoman looking for information about her competitors, the marketing manager, and the job seeker approached theirs—by thumbing through this book page by page, looking for companies with high historical growth rates, generous dividend payout policies, wide profit margins, A+ Standard & Poor's Quality Rankings, or whatever other characteristics you consider desirable in stocks in which you might invest. In this case, however, we have made your job just a little bit easier.

We have already prescreened the 500 companies in this book for several of the stock characteristics in which investors generally are most interested, including Standard & Poor's Quality Rankings, growth records, and dividend payment histories, and we're pleased to present on the next several pages lists of those companies which score highest on the bases of these criteria. So if you, like most investors, find these characteristics important in potential investments, you might want to turn first to the companies on these lists in your search for attractive investments.

Good luck and happy investment returns!

Companies With Five Consecutive Years of Earnings Increases

This table, compiled from a computer screen of the stocks in this handbook, shows companies that have recorded rising per-share earnings for five consecutive years, have estimated 2009 EPS above those reported for 2008, pay dividends, and have Standard & Poor's Quality Rankings of A– or better.

Company	Business	S&P Quality Ranking	Fiscal year End	EPS $ 2008 Act.	EPS $ 2009 Est.	5 Yr. EPS% Growth	Price	P/E on 2009 Est.	% Yield
C.H. Robinson Worldwide	Motor freight transportat'n	A+	Dec	2.08	2.16	21	58.19	26.9	1.7
Hudson City Bancorp	Savings bank,New Jersey	A	Dec	0.90	1.07	21	13.48	12.6	4.5
Stryker Corp	Specialty medical devices	A+	Dec	2.78	2.95	19	50.50	17.1	1.2
CVS Caremark Corp	Oper drug/health stores	A+	Dec	2.18	2.62	16	31.18	11.9	1.0
Genl Dynamics	Armored/space launch vehicles	A+	Dec	6.17	6.20	16	68.24	11.0	2.2
Polo Ralph Lauren 'A'	Retail apparel/home prd	A+	Mar+	4.01	4.30	15	79.71	18.5	0.5
Praxair Inc	Ind'l gases/spcl coatings	A+	Dec	3.80	3.98	13	80.28	20.2	2.0
TJX Companies	Off-price specialty stores	A+	Jan+	1.99	2.62	13	36.78	14.0	1.3
Yum Brands	Oper family style restaurants	A–	Dec	1.96	2.14	13	34.51	16.1	2.4
Sigma-Aldrich	Specialty chem prod	A+	Dec	2.65	2.76	10	51.33	18.6	1.1

+Fiscal 2009 and 2010, P/E based on 2010 estimate.

Chart based on data at the close of December 18, 2009.

[NOTE]: All earnings estimates are Standard & Poor's projections.

S&P 500 STOCK SCREENS

Stocks With A+ Rankings

Based on the issues in this handbook, this screen shows stocks of all companies with Standard & Poor's Quality Rankings of A+.

Company	Business	Company	Business
3M Co	Scotch tapes: coated abrasives	NIKE, Inc 'B'	Athletic footwear
Automatic Data Proc	Computer services	Omnicom Group	Major int'l advertising co
C.H. Robinson Worldwide	Motor freight transportat'n	Paychex Inc	Computer payroll acctg svcs
Caterpillar Inc	Earthmoving mchy: diesel eng	PepsiCo Inc	Soft drink:snack foods
Colgate-Palmolive	Household & personal care	Praxair Inc	Ind'l gases/spcl coatings
CVS Caremark Corp	Oper drug/health stores	Procter & Gamble	Hshld, personal care,food prod
Danaher Corp	Mfr hand tools,auto parts	Sigma-Aldrich	Specialty chem prod
Ecolab Inc	Comm'l cleaning&sanitizing	Smucker (J.M.)	Preserves: jellies & fillings
Expeditors Intl,Wash	Int'l air freight forward'g	Stryker Corp	Specialty medical devices
Exxon Mobil	World's leading oil co	Sysco Corp	Food distr & service systems
Family Dollar Stores	Self-service retail stores	Target Corp	Depart/disc/spec stores
Genl Dynamics	Armored/space launch vehicles	TJX Companies	Off-price specialty stores
Grainger (W.W.)	Natl dstr indus/comm'l prod	United Technologies	Aerospace, climate ctrl sys
Hormel Foods	Meat & food processing	UnitedHealth Group	Manages health maint svcs
Johnson & Johnson	Health care products	Wal-Mart Stores	Operates discount stores
McCormick & Co	Spices, flavoring, tea, mixes	Walgreen Co	Major retail drug chain

Table based on data at the close of December 18, 2009.

S&P 500 STOCK SCREENS

Rapid Growth Stocks

The stocks listed below have shown strong and consistent earnings growth. Issues of rapidly growing companies tend to carry high price-earnings ratios and offer potential for substantial appreciation. At the same time, though, the stocks are subject to strong selling pressures should growth in earnings slow. Five-year earnings growth rates have been calculated for fiscal years 2004 through 2008 and the most current 12-month earnings.

Company	Business	Fiscal Year End	5 Yr. EPS Growth Rate %	EPS $ 2008 Act.	EPS $ 2009 Est.	S&P Quality Rank	Price	P/E on 2009 Est.	% Yield
Abbott Laboratories	Diversified health care prod	Dec	14	3.12	3.70	A–	53.34	14.4	3.0
Amazon.com Inc	Online book retailer	Dec	11	1.49	1.99	B–	128.48	64.6	0.0
Apollo Group 'A'	Adult higher education svcs	Aug#	27	2.87	3.75	B+	58.40	15.6	0.0
Apple Inc	Personal computer systems	Sep#	70	5.36	6.29	B	195.43	31.1	0.0
AutoZone Inc	Retail auto parts stores	Aug#	12	10.05	11.73	B+	158.29	13.5	0.0
Baxter Intl	Mfr,dstr hospital/lab prod	Dec	37	3.16	3.80	A–	57.60	15.2	2.0
Cognizant Tech Solutions 'A'	Computer software & svcs	Dec	36	1.44	1.77	B+	44.45	25.1	0.0
Colgate-Palmolive	Household & personal care	Dec	13	3.66	4.32	A+	82.62	19.1	2.1
DeVry Inc	Tech'l/MBA degree schools	Jun#	49	1.73	2.28	B	56.48	24.8	0.4
Gilead Sciences	Nucleotide pharmaceut'l R&D	Dec	81	2.10	2.82	B–	42.83	15.2	0.0
Medco Health Solutions	Managed pharmac'l svcs	Dec	24	2.13	2.82	NR	63.09	22.4	0.0
priceline.com Inc	Internet based buy/sell svcs	Dec	45	3.98	7.15	B–	216.39	30.3	0.0
Red Hat Inc	Computer software & svcs	Feb+	9	0.39	0.49	B–	29.27	59.7	0.0
salesforce.com inc	Customer info to businesses	Jan+	51	0.35	0.62	NR	67.88	109.5	0.0
Stericycle Inc	Environmental mgmt svcs	Dec	21	1.68	2.08	B+	55.16	26.5	0.0
Thermo Fisher Scientific	Eng'd ind'l pr: environ instr	Dec	6	2.29	3.03	B–	48.31	15.9	0.0
TJX Companies	Off-price specialty stores	Jan+	13	1.99	2.62	A+	36.78	14.0	1.3
Watson Pharmaceuticals	Mfr off-patent medications	Dec	52	2.09	2.55	B–	38.09	14.9	0.0

#Actual 2009 EPS; P/E based on actual 2009 EPS.
+Fiscal 2009 and 2010, P/E based on 2010 estimate.
Chart based on data at the close of December 18, 2009.
NOTE: All earnings estimates are Standard & Poor's projections.

S&P 500 STOCK SCREENS

Fast-Rising Dividends

Based on the issues in this handbook, the companies below were chosen on the basis of their five-year annual growth rate in dividends to the current 12-month indicated rate. All have increased their dividend payments each calendar year from 2004 to their current 12-month indicated rate.

Company	$ Divd. Paid 2004	Paid 2008	†Ind. Divd. Rate	*Divd. Growth Rate%	Price	%Yield
Century Tel Inc	0.23	2.80	2.80	76.59	35.09	8.0
Amerisource Bergen Corp	0.03	0.16	0.32	68.62	26.03	1.2
Darden Restaurants	0.08	0.76	1.00	59.78	35.13	2.8
XTO Energy	0.05	0.48	0.50	56.78	46.68	1.1
Stryker Corp	0.07	0.33	0.60	54.97	50.50	1.2
Yum Brands	0.10	0.68	0.84	52.54	34.51	2.4
Noble Energy	0.10	0.66	0.72	52.52	71.48	1.0
Microchip Technology	0.17	1.33	1.36	48.38	28.42	4.8
Texas Instruments	0.09	0.41	0.48	46.50	25.46	1.9
Cardinal Health	0.12	0.52	0.70	42.26	32.14	2.2
Lowe's Cos	0.07	0.33	0.36	41.87	23.62	1.5
Molex Inc	0.11	0.49	0.61	41.15	20.80	2.9
EOG Resources	0.12	0.47	0.58	40.46	92.95	0.6
CSX Corp	0.20	0.77	0.88	39.81	48.47	1.8
Pepsi Bottling Group	0.12	0.62	0.72	39.24	37.17	1.9
Valero Energy	0.14	0.57	0.60	36.41	16.69	3.6
C.H. Robinson Worldwide	0.24	0.88	1.00	35.72	58.19	1.7
Williams Cos	0.08	0.43	0.44	34.11	20.68	2.1
Harris Corp	0.22	0.70	0.88	33.05	45.06	2.0
McDonald's Corp	0.55	1.62	2.20	33.05	62.17	3.5
Airgas Inc	0.17	0.52	0.72	32.37	46.60	1.5
Monsanto Co	0.28	0.83	1.06	32.09	80.52	1.3
Xilinx Inc	0.15	0.54	0.64	32.04	24.65	2.6
QUALCOMM Inc	0.15	0.60	0.68	31.30	44.57	1.5
Hasbro Inc	0.21	0.76	0.80	31.10	31.62	2.5
L-3 Communications Hldgs	0.40	1.20	1.40	29.98	84.26	1.7
Republic Services	0.20	0.70	0.76	29.83	27.83	2.7
Analog Devices	0.22	0.78	0.80	28.57	30.88	2.6
Expeditors Intl, Wash	0.11	0.32	0.38	28.27	34.69	1.1
Intl Bus. Machines	0.70	1.90	2.20	28.24	127.91	1.7
Intel Corp	0.16	0.55	0.63	27.79	19.63	3.2
Norfolk Southern	0.46	1.22	1.36	27.72	52.04	2.6
Tiffany & Co	0.22	0.64	0.68	27.08	42.32	1.6
AFLAC Inc	0.38	0.96	1.12	26.11	46.16	2.4
Gap Inc	0.11	0.34	0.34	25.62	20.89	1.6
Linear Technology Corp	0.32	0.84	0.88	23.78	29.25	3.0
Staples Inc	0.13	0.33	0.37	23.65	24.59	1.5
Paychex Inc	0.49	1.22	1.24	23.63	30.92	4.0
Moody's Corp	0.15	0.40	0.42	23.28	26.78	1.6
TJX Companies	0.17	0.42	0.48	23.17	36.78	1.3
Praxair Inc	0.60	1.50	1.60	23.15	80.28	2.0
Danaher Corp	0.06	0.12	0.16	22.77	75.16	0.2
Walgreen Co	0.19	0.41	0.55	22.77	36.64	1.5
Assurant Inc	0.21	0.54	0.60	22.51	29.48	2.0
NIKE, Inc 'B'	0.40	0.92	1.08	22.04	64.42	1.7
Lockheed Martin	0.91	1.83	2.52	21.87	76.34	3.3
Burlington Northn Santa Fe	0.62	1.36	1.60	21.86	98.32	1.6
Illinois Tool Works	0.50	1.15	1.24	21.53	47.57	2.6
Automatic Data Proc	0.56	1.16	1.36	21.16	42.36	3.2
Hudson City Bancorp	0.22	0.45	0.60	21.12	13.48	4.5
Medtronic, Inc	0.31	0.62	0.82	20.78	43.22	1.9
Murphy Oil	0.42	0.88	1.00	20.49	53.40	1.9
VF Corp	1.05	2.33	2.40	20.49	72.34	3.3
Robert Half Intl	0.18	0.44	0.48	20.35	26.12	1.8

† 12-month indicated rate.   *Five-year annual compounded growth rate.   Chart based on data at the close of December 18, 2009.

S&P 500 STOCK SCREENS

Stock Reports

In using the Stock Reports in this handbook, please pay particular attention to the dates attached to each evaluation, recommendation, or analysis section. Opinions rendered are as of that date and may change often. It is strongly suggested that before investing in any security you should obtain the current analysis on that issue.

To order the latest Standard & Poor's Stock Report on a company, for as little as $3.00 per report, please call:

S&P Reports On-Demand at 1–800–292–0808.

Abbott Laboratories

STANDARD &POOR'S

S&P Recommendation	BUY ★★★★☆	Price $54.08 (as of Nov 27, 2009)	12-Mo. Target Price $58.00	Investment Style Large-Cap Growth

GICS Sector Health Care
Sub-Industry Pharmaceuticals

Summary This diversified life science company is a leading maker of drugs, nutritional products, diabetes monitoring devices, and diagnostics.

Key Stock Statistics (Source S&P, Vickers, company reports)

52-Wk Range	$57.39–41.27	S&P Oper. EPS 2009**E**	3.70	Market Capitalization(B)	$83.648	Beta		0.19
Trailing 12-Month EPS	$3.69	S&P Oper. EPS 2010**E**	4.15	Yield (%)	2.96	S&P 3-Yr. Proj. EPS CAGR(%)		11
Trailing 12-Month P/E	14.7	P/E on S&P Oper. EPS 2009**E**	14.6	Dividend Rate/Share	$1.60	S&P Credit Rating		AA
$10K Invested 5 Yrs Ago	$14,496	Common Shares Outstg. (M)	1,546.7	Institutional Ownership (%)	68			

Price Performance

30-Week Mov. Avg. ···· 10-Week Mov. Avg. – – **GAAP Earnings vs. Previous Year**   Volume Above Avg. |||| STARS
12-Mo. Target Price — Relative Strength — ▲ Up ▼ Down ► No Change   Below Avg. |||| ★

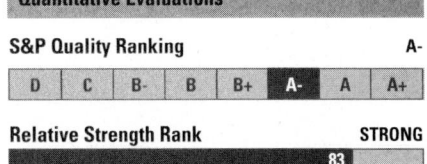

Options: ASE, CBOE, P, Ph

Analysis prepared by **Herman B. Saftlas** on October 29, 2009, when the stock traded at **$ 50.40**.

Highlights

▶ We see revenues rising to about $33 billion in 2010, from an indicated $30.5 billion in 2009, lifted by gains in key existing product franchises (excluding an estimated $3 billion from the planned purchase of a pharmaceuticals business from Solvay Group). We forecast continued strength in Humira, which continues to grow faster than the overall self-injectable anti-TNF market. The new Xience drug-eluting coronary stent should continue to bolster vascular sales, while new products should support growth in nutritional and diagnostic products.

▶ We expect gross margins to be well maintained, helped by manufacturing efficiencies. SG&A spending as a percentage of total sales is expected to decline somewhat as a result of cost streamlining measures. R&D expenses will probably increase in the high single digits.

▶ After a projected effective tax rate of about 19%, versus an indicated 18% for 2009, we forecast operating EPS of $4.15 for 2010, up from an estimated $3.70 for 2009. We expect the planned acquisition of Solvay drugs (if completed) to add about $0.10 to our 2010 EPS estimate.

Investment Rationale/Risk

▶ In late September 2009, ABT agreed to acquire the pharmaceuticals unit of Belgium-based Solvay SA for $6.6 billion in cash. We view this deal positively, as it gives ABT full rights to cholesterol drugs Tricor and Trilipix, and allows it to expand in vaccines and emerging foreign markets. The deal should also diversify ABT away from its reliance on Humira. ABT plans to fund the deal, which should be completed in the first quarter of 2010 (subject to customary approvals), with cash on hand. The deal should add over $3 billion in annual sales and boost EPS by $0.10 in 2010 and $0.20 in 2011.

▶ Risks to our recommendation and target price include failure to complete the Solvay purchase, lower-than-expected Humira sales, and possible pipeline setbacks.

▶ Our 12-month target price of $58 applies a premium-to-peers 14X multiple to our 2010 EPS estimate. We think this valuation is warranted in light of ABT's rapidly growing franchises in diversified health care markets. Our DCF model, which assumes a WACC of about 8.3% and terminal growth of 2%, also implies intrinsic value of $58.

Qualitative Risk Assessment

LOW	MEDIUM	HIGH

Our risk assessment reflects Abbott's operations in competitive markets and its exposure to the potential for generic competition. However, we believe the company has a relatively strong new product pipeline, with possible significant launches in both the medical device and pharmaceutical areas. In our opinion, the company is financially sound, with a strong balance sheet.

Quantitative Evaluations

S&P Quality Ranking A-

D	C	B-	B	B+	A-	A	A+

Relative Strength Rank STRONG

83

LOWEST = 1   HIGHEST = 99

Revenue/Earnings Data

Revenue (Million $)

	1Q	2Q	3Q	4Q	Year
2009	6,718	7,495	7,761	--	--
2008	6,766	7,314	7,498	7,950	29,528
2007	5,290	6,371	6,377	7,221	25,914
2006	5,183	5,501	5,574	6,218	22,476
2005	5,383	5,524	5,384	6,047	22,338
2004	4,641	4,703	4,682	5,654	19,680

Earnings Per Share ($)

2009	0.92	0.83	0.95	E1.16	E3.70
2008	0.60	0.85	0.69	0.89	3.03
2007	0.41	0.63	0.46	0.77	2.31
2006	0.56	0.40	0.46	-0.31	1.12
2005	0.53	0.56	0.44	0.63	2.16
2004	0.52	0.40	0.51	0.62	2.02

Fiscal year ended Dec. 31. Next earnings report expected: Late January. EPS Estimates based on S&P Operating Earnings; historical GAAP earnings are as reported.

Dividend Data (Dates: mm/dd Payment Date: mm/dd/yy)

Amount ($)	Date Decl.	Ex-Div. Date	Stk. of Record	Payment Date
0.360	12/12	01/13	01/15	02/15/09
0.400	02/20	04/13	04/15	05/15/09
0.400	06/12	07/13	07/15	08/15/09
0.400	09/17	10/13	10/15	11/15/09

Dividends have been paid since 1926. Source: Company reports.

Please read the Required Disclosures and Analyst Certification on the last page of this report.

The McGraw·Hill Companies

Abbott Laboratories

STANDARD
&POOR'S

Business Summary October 29, 2009

CORPORATE OVERVIEW. Abbott Laboratories is a leading player in several growing health care markets. Through acquisitions, product diversification and R&D programs, ABT offers a wide range of prescription pharmaceuticals, infant and adult nutritionals, diagnostics, and medical devices.

During 2008, pharmaceuticals accounted for 57% of operating revenues, while nutritionals represented 17%, diagnostics contributed 11%, and vascular represented 8%. Sales of other products represented 7% of 2008 sales. Foreign sales accounted for 52% of total sales in 2008.

ABT's Pharmaceutical Products Group markets a wide array of human therapeutics. Major products include: Humira to treat rheumatoid arthritis and psoriatic arthritis ($4.5 billion in 2008 sales); Kaletra, an anti-HIV medication ($1.5 billion); Depakote, an anti-epileptic and bipolar disorder drug ($1.4 billion); TriCor/Trilipix, cholesterol treatments ($1.3 billion); Ultane, a general inhalation anesthetic ($787 million); and Niaspan, a niacin-based cholesterol treatment.

Nutritionals fall under U.S.-based Ross Products and Abbott Nutrition International. Products include leading infant formulas sold under the Similac and

Isomil names, as well as adult nutritionals, such as Ensure and ProSure for patients with special dietary needs, including cancer and diabetes patients. ABT also markets enteral feeding items.

Abbott Diabetes Care markets the Precision and FreeStyle lines of hand-held glucose monitors for diabetes patients. This division also markets data management and point-of-care systems, insulin pumps and syringes, and Glucerna shakes and nutrition bars tailored for diabetics.

Abbott Vascular markets coronary and carotid stents, catheters and guide wires, and products used for surgical closure. The principal product is the new Xience drug-eluting stent (DES), which was launched in July 2008 and is presently the leading product in the domestic DES market. Boston Scientific markets the Xience stent manufactured by Abbott under the Promus name, pursuant to an agreement with ABT.

Company Financials Fiscal Year Ended Dec. 31

Per Share Data ($)	2008	2007	2006	2005	2004	2003	2002	2001	2000	1999
Tangible Book Value	1.51	1.24	NM	2.89	2.22	2.90	1.93	1.14	4.54	3.78
Cash Flow	4.21	3.50	2.13	3.02	2.84	2.56	2.52	1.74	2.31	2.10
Earnings	3.03	2.31	1.12	2.16	2.02	1.75	1.78	0.99	1.78	1.57
S&P Core Earnings	2.86	2.31	1.16	2.01	1.90	1.95	1.62	0.77	NA	NA
Dividends	1.41	1.27	1.16	1.09	1.03	0.97	0.92	0.82	0.74	0.66
Payout Ratio	46%	55%	104%	50%	51%	55%	51%	83%	42%	42%
Prices:High	61.09	59.50	49.87	50.00	47.63	47.15	58.00	57.17	56.25	53.31
Prices:Low	45.75	48.75	39.18	37.50	38.26	33.75	29.80	42.00	29.38	33.00
P/E Ratio:High	20	26	45	23	24	27	33	58	32	34
P/E Ratio:Low	15	21	35	17	19	19	17	42	16	21

Income Statement Analysis (Million $)										
Revenue	29,528	25,914	22,476	22,338	19,680	19,681	17,685	16,285	13,746	13,178
Operating Income	8,316	7,378	6,419	5,738	5,187	4,597	4,815	3,062	4,228	3,977
Depreciation	1,839	1,855	1,559	1,359	1,289	1,274	1,177	1,168	827	828
Interest Expense	528	593	416	241	200	146	239	307	114	81.8
Pretax Income	5,856	4,479	2,276	4,620	4,126	3,734	3,673	1,883	3,816	3,397
Effective Tax Rate	19.2%	19.3%	24.6%	27.0%	23.0%	26.3%	23.9%	17.7%	27.0%	28.0%
Net Income	4,734	3,606	1,717	3,372	3,176	2,753	2,794	1,550	2,786	2,446
S&P Core Earnings	4,473	3,609	1,787	3,158	2,972	2,971	2,561	1,233	NA	NA

Balance Sheet & Other Financial Data (Million $)										
Cash	5,080	2,821	521	2,894	1,226	995	704	657	914	608
Current Assets	17,043	14,043	11,282	11,386	10,734	10,290	9,122	8,419	7,376	6,420
Total Assets	42,419	39,714	36,178	29,141	28,767	26,715	24,259	23,296	15,283	14,471
Current Liabilities	11,592	9,103	11,951	7,416	6,826	7,640	7,002	7,927	4,298	4,517
Long Term Debt	8,713	9,488	7,010	4,572	4,788	3,452	4,274	4,335	1,076	1,337
Common Equity	17,480	17,779	14,054	14,415	14,326	13,072	10,665	9,059	8,571	7,428
Total Capital	26,193	27,266	21,064	19,570	19,334	16,525	14,939	13,395	9,647	9,046
Capital Expenditures	1,288	1,656	1,338	1,207	1,292	1,247	1,296	1,164	1,036	217
Cash Flow	6,573	5,461	3,276	4,731	4,465	4,027	3,971	2,718	3,613	3,274
Current Ratio	1.5	1.5	0.9	1.5	1.6	1.3	1.3	1.1	1.7	1.4
% Long Term Debt of Capitalization	33.3	34.8	33.3	23.4	24.8	20.9	28.6	32.4	11.2	14.8
% Net Income of Revenue	16.0	13.9	7.6	15.1	16.1	14.0	15.8	9.5	20.3	18.6
% Return on Assets	11.5	9.5	5.3	11.6	11.6	10.8	11.7	8.0	18.7	17.6
% Return on Equity	26.9	22.7	12.1	23.5	23.2	23.2	28.3	17.6	34.8	37.2

Data as orig reptd.; bef. results of disc opers/spec. items. Per share data adj. for stk. divs.; EPS diluted. E-Estimated. NA-Not Available. NM-Not Meaningful. NR-Not Ranked. UR-Under Review.

Office: 100 Abbott Park Road, Abbott Park, IL 60064-6400.
Telephone: 847-937-6100.
Website: http://www.abbott.com
Chrmn & CEO: M.D. White

EVP & CFO: T.C. Freyman
EVP, Secy & General Counsel: L.J. Schumacher
Chief Acctg Officer & Cntlr: G.W. Linder
Treas: R.E. Funck

Investor Contact: L. Peepo (847-935-6722)
Board Members: R. J. Alpern, R. S. Austin, W. M. Daley, W. J. Farrell, H. L. Fuller, A. J. Higgins, W. A. Osborn, D. A. Owen, W. A. Reynolds, R. S. Roberts, S. C. Scott, III, W. D. Smithburg, G. F. Tilton, M. D. White

Founded: 1888
Domicile: Illinois
Employees: 69,000

Abercrombie & Fitch Co.

STANDARD
&POOR'S

S&P Recommendation	HOLD ★★★☆☆	Price $39.97 (as of Nov 27, 2009)	12-Mo. Target Price $45.00	Investment Style Large-Cap Growth

GICS Sector Consumer Discretionary
Sub-Industry Apparel Retail

Summary This apparel retailer, which specializes in lifestyle branding, operates over 1,100 retail apparel stores across five brands.

Key Stock Statistics (Source S&P, Vickers, company reports)

52-Wk Range	$42.31– 15.30	S&P Oper. EPS 2010E	1.10	Market Capitalization(B)	$3.516	Beta	1.43
Trailing 12-Month EPS	$0.24	S&P Oper. EPS 2011E	2.40	Yield (%)	1.75	S&P 3-Yr. Proj. EPS CAGR(%)	5
Trailing 12-Month P/E	NM	P/E on S&P Oper. EPS 2010E	36.3	Dividend Rate/Share	$0.70	S&P Credit Rating	NA
$10K Invested 5 Yrs Ago	$9,234	Common Shares Outstg. (M)	88.0	Institutional Ownership (%)	NM		

Price Performance

30-Week Mov. Avg. ···· 10-Week Mov. Avg. - - GAAP Earnings vs. Previous Year Volume Above Avg. STARS
12-Mo. Target Price — Relative Strength — ▲ Up ▼ Down ▶ No Change Below Avg.

Options: ASE, CBOE, P, Ph

Analysis prepared by **Marie Driscoll, CFA** on November 17, 2009, when the stock traded at **$ 41.27**.

Highlights

► We believe the worst is behind ANF, in part due to easy comparisons, but also reflecting its growing international presence. In the first nine months of FY 10 (Jan.), sales were down 20% on a -27% comp with online sales off 8% to $162 million; in the October quarter, sales were off 5%, with a -15% comp and ecommerce up 24%. We see a 1% sales decline in the final quarter of FY 10, for a 15% annual decline, and we look for a resumption of sales growth in FY 11, to 7%.

► We estimate 200 basis points (bps) of gross margin contraction to 64.7% in FY 10, with reduced initial markups as ANF attempts to lower price and maintain quality as it navigates weakened consumer demand. We see deleveraging of store and distribution and marketing expenses and project a 740 bps EBIT margin contraction, to 5% of sales.

► We expect the absence of Ruehl, an improved value proposition, and the ramp-up of international store expansion to drive 520 bps of EBIT margin expansion in FY 11.

Investment Rationale/Risk

► We see FY 09-FY 10 as an investment period for ANF -- brand building, international expansion, and flagship locations, to prepare the company for the next decade. U.K. expansion is posting strong results, beating U.S. flagship locations, and ANF sees an opportunity for about 30 Hollister U.K. locations near term and is negotiating for continental European store sites. An adult A&F store recently opened in Milan to early accolades, and we expect focus in the next five years to be abroad while rigor on brand positioning is maintained.

► Risks to our recommendation and target price include a longer and deeper global recession that we currently project, negative same-store sales trends, and fashion and inventory risk. In terms of corporate governance, the presence of affiliated outsiders on the board is not best practices, in our opinion.

► Our 12-month target price of $45 is about 19X our FY 11 EPS estimate, in line with apparel retail peers. We believe operating performance will be at a cyclical low in FY 10, but that the strong and growing global appeal of ANF brands will drive improved operating metrics and margin recovery in FY 11.

Qualitative Risk Assessment

LOW	MEDIUM	HIGH

Our risk assessment reflects our view of ANF's strong balance sheet and cash flows, offset by a consumer base whose tastes change constantly.

Quantitative Evaluations

S&P Quality Ranking B+

D	C	B-	B	B+	A-	A	A+

Relative Strength Rank STRONG

92

LOWEST = 1 HIGHEST = 99

Revenue/Earnings Data

Revenue (Million $)

	1Q	2Q	3Q	4Q	Year
2010	612.1	648.5	765.4	--	--
2009	800.2	845.8	896.3	998.0	3,540
2008	742.4	804.5	973.9	1,229	3,750
2007	657.3	658.7	863.5	1,139	3,318
2006	546.8	571.6	704.9	961.4	2,785
2005	411.9	401.4	520.7	687.3	2,021

Earnings Per Share ($)

2010	-0.68	-0.30	0.44	E1.07	E1.10
2009	0.69	0.87	0.72	0.78	3.05
2008	0.65	0.87	1.29	2.40	5.20
2007	0.62	0.72	1.11	2.14	4.59
2006	0.45	0.63	0.79	1.80	3.66
2005	0.30	0.44	0.42	1.15	2.28

Fiscal year ended Jan. 31. Next earnings report expected: Mid February. EPS Estimates based on S&P Operating Earnings; historical GAAP earnings are as reported.

Dividend Data (Dates: mm/dd Payment Date: mm/dd/yy)

Amount ($)	Date Decl.	Ex-Div. Date	Stk. of Record	Payment Date
0.175	02/13	02/25	02/27	03/17/09
0.175	05/15	05/27	05/29	06/16/09
0.175	08/14	08/26	08/28	09/15/09
0.175	11/13	11/24	11/27	12/15/09

Dividends have been paid since 2004. Source: Company reports.

Please read the Required Disclosures and Analyst Certification on the last page of this report.

The McGraw-Hill Companies

Abercrombie & Fitch Co.

STANDARD &POOR'S

Business Summary November 17, 2009

CORPORATE OVERVIEW. Abercrombie & Fitch, established in 1892, operates five branded retail concepts: Abercrombie & Fitch (356 stores as of January 2009), abercrombie kids (212), Hollister Co. (515), Ruehl (28), and Gilly Hicks (14) and e-commerce sites for each concept. Each targets a different age demographic, minimizing cannibalization, and all employ casual luxury positioning. In June 2009, ANF announced the planned closure of Ruehl in the current year at a projected cost of $115 million.

MARKET PROFILE. The company participates in the specialty apparel retail market targeted at youth, spanning the tween to young adult demographic. While the U.S. apparel market is considered mature, with demand mirroring population growth and a modicum related to fashion, the youth marketplace is generally considered attractive based on its spending clout. According to NPD consumer data, collectively, this group accounts for approximately 35% of total apparel spending, with the "sweet spot" being teenagers, who represent about 20%.

COMPETITIVE LANDSCAPE. The retail landscape is consolidating, with share accruing to the mass merchants and specialty chains while the traditional department store is losing ground. Specialty chains compete on customer knowledge garnered from daily interactions, focus groups and marketing in-

telligence, and this knowledge is often combined with high customer service levels to result in an attractive price/value equation for the consumer. ANF's target demographic is attracted to strong brands, as well as fashion and value, when determining apparel selections. The specialty channel holds the largest share of the apparel market at about 30% according to NPD Group and the sub-segment serving the youth demographic represents about 3% of total retail sales. With barriers to entry minimal (capital investment in merchandise, rent and labor expense) and potential returns on investment high and quick (four wall return on investment exceed 40% in 12 months for many specialty retailers), there was a steady flow of new industry participants through most of this decade, but more recently we've seen more store closures and slowed expansion plans. In addition to competing with other apparel retailers, regardless of channel, for youth discretionary spending, ANF competes with merchandise and services, especially consumer electronics and entertainment services.

Company Financials Fiscal Year Ended Jan. 31

Per Share Data ($)	2009	2008	2007	2006	2005	2004	2003	2002	2001	2000
Tangible Book Value	21.06	23.45	19.17	11.34	7.78	9.21	7.71	6.02	4.28	3.05
Cash Flow	5.57	7.21	6.18	5.02	3.39	2.73	2.50	2.05	1.85	1.65
Earnings	3.05	5.20	4.59	3.66	2.28	2.06	1.94	1.65	1.55	1.39
S&P Core Earnings	3.15	5.20	4.59	3.38	2.32	1.81	1.70	1.45	1.35	NA
Dividends	0.70	0.70	0.60	0.50	0.50	Nil	Nil	Nil	Nil	Nil
Payout Ratio	23%	13%	13%	14%	22%	Nil	Nil	Nil	Nil	Nil
Calendar Year	2008	2007	2006	2005	2004	2003	2002	2001	2000	1999
Prices:High	82.06	85.77	79.42	74.10	47.45	33.65	33.85	47.50	31.31	50.75
Prices:Low	13.66	67.72	49.98	44.17	23.07	20.65	14.97	16.21	8.00	21.00
P/E Ratio:High	27	16	17	20	21	16	17	29	20	37
P/E Ratio:Low	4	13	11	12	10	10	8	10	5	15

Income Statement Analysis (Million $)	2009	2008	2007	2006	2005	2004	2003	2002	2001	2000
Revenue	3,540	3,750	3,318	2,785	2,021	1,708	1,596	1,365	1,238	1,042
Operating Income	686	912	794	661	453	398	370	313	284	270
Depreciation	225	184	146	124	106	66.6	56.9	41.2	30.7	27.7
Interest Expense	3.40	Nil	Nil	Nil	Nil	Nil	Nil	Nil	Nil	Nil
Pretax Income	451	759	672	549	353	335	316	277	261	249
Effective Tax Rate	39.6%	37.4%	37.2%	39.2%	38.7%	38.8%	38.4%	39.0%	39.5%	40.0%
Net Income	272	476	422	334	216	205	195	169	158	150
S&P Core Earnings	281	476	422	312	220	180	170	148	138	NA

Balance Sheet & Other Financial Data (Million $)	2009	2008	2007	2006	2005	2004	2003	2002	2001	2000
Cash	522	649	530	462	350	521	401	239	138	194
Current Assets	1,085	1,140	1,092	947	652	753	601	405	304	300
Total Assets	2,848	2,568	2,248	1,790	1,348	1,199	995	771	588	458
Current Liabilities	450	543	511	492	414	280	211	164	155	138
Long Term Debt	100	Nil	Nil	Nil	Nil	Nil	Nil	Nil	Nil	Nil
Common Equity	1,846	1,618	1,405	995	669	871	750	595	423	311
Total Capital	1,980	1,641	1,436	1,034	725	891	770	597	423	311
Capital Expenditures	368	403	403	256	185	99.1	93.0	127	153	83.8
Cash Flow	498	659	568	458	322	272	252	210	189	177
Current Ratio	2.4	2.1	2.1	1.9	1.6	2.7	2.8	2.5	2.0	2.2
% Long Term Debt of Capitalization	5.1	Nil	Nil	Nil	Nil	Nil	Nil	Nil	Nil	Nil
% Net Income of Revenue	7.7	12.7	12.7	12.0	10.7	12.0	12.2	12.4	12.8	14.4
% Return on Assets	10.1	19.8	20.9	21.0	15.8	18.5	22.1	24.8	30.2	38.5
% Return on Equity	15.7	31.5	35.2	40.1	28.3	25.3	29.0	33.1	43.1	60.2

Data as orig reptd.; bef. results of disc opers/spec. items. Per share data adj. for stk. divs.; EPS diluted. E-Estimated. NA-Not Available. NM-Not Meaningful. NR-Not Ranked. UR-Under Review.

Office: 6301 Fitch Path, New Albany, OH 43054.
Telephone: 614-283-6500.
Email: investor_relations@abercrombie.com
Website: http://www.abercrombie.com

Chrmn & CEO: M.S. Jeffries
EVP, CFO & Chief Acctg Officer: J.E. Ramsden
SVP, Secy & General Counsel: D.S. Cupps
Investor Contact: T.D. Lennox (614-283-6751)

Cntlr: B.P. Logan
Board Members: J. B. Bachmann, L. J. Brisky, A. M. Griffin, M. S. Jeffries, J. W. Kessler, E. Limato, R. A. Rosholt, C. R. Stapleton

Founded: 1892
Domicile: Delaware
Employees: 83,000

The McGraw-Hill Companies

STANDARD &POOR'S

Adobe Systems Inc

S&P Recommendation **HOLD** ★★★☆☆	Price	12-Mo. Target Price	Investment Style
	$35.38 (as of Nov 27, 2009)	$36.00	Large-Cap Growth

GICS Sector Information Technology
Sub-Industry Application Software

Summary This company provides software for multimedia content creation, distribution, and management.

Key Stock Statistics (Source S&P, Vickers, company reports)

52-Wk Range	$37.15– 15.70	S&P Oper. EPS 2009**E**	1.29	Market Capitalization(B)	$18.531	Beta	1.82
Trailing 12-Month EPS	$1.25	S&P Oper. EPS 2010**E**	1.43	Yield (%)	Nil	S&P 3-Yr. Proj. EPS CAGR(%)	14
Trailing 12-Month P/E	28.3	P/E on S&P Oper. EPS 2009**E**	27.4	Dividend Rate/Share	Nil	S&P Credit Rating	NA
$10K Invested 5 Yrs Ago	$11,670	Common Shares Outstg. (M)	523.8	Institutional Ownership (%)	88		

Price Performance

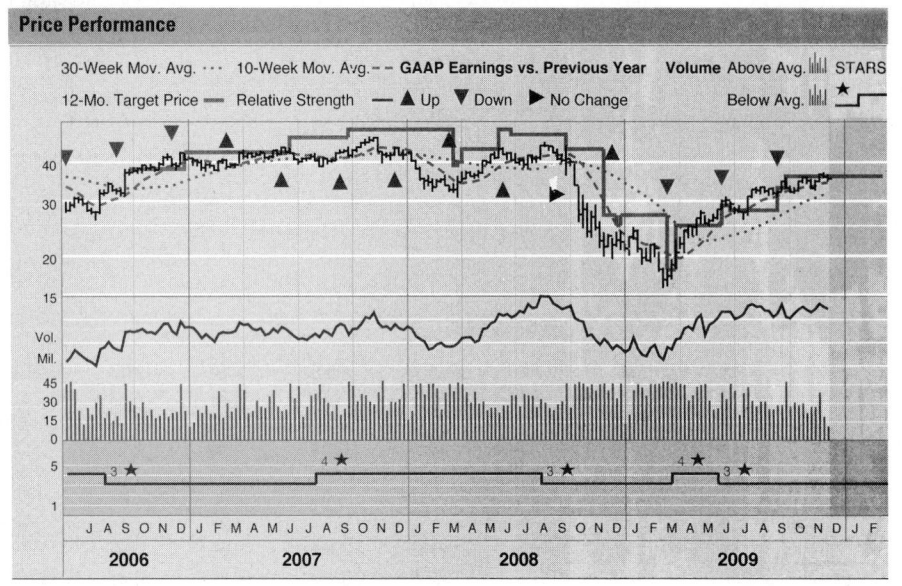

30-Week Mov. Avg. · · · 10-Week Mov. Avg. - - **GAAP Earnings vs. Previous Year** Volume Above Avg. STARS
12-Mo. Target Price — Relative Strength ▲ Up ▼ Down ▶ No Change Below Avg.

Options: ASE, CBOE, P, Ph

Analysis prepared by **Zaineb Bokhari** on September 25, 2009, when the stock traded at **$ 32.19**.

Highlights

► We estimate that sales will fall 18% in FY 09 (Nov.), reflecting our outlook for weak product revenues, for which we project a 19% decline. ADBE has seen weak sales for its Creative Solutions and Business Productivity Solutions segments, due to weak economic conditions, although the pace of the decline seems to be slowing. We see sales rising by about 5% in FY 10. Our forecast does not include pending acquisition of Omniture (OMTR: hold $22), which is subject to conditions, but we expect it to add to FY 10 sales after the transaction closes.

► We expect gross margins of approximately 90% in FY 09, comparable to levels seen in FY 08, despite lower product revenues. We think FY 09 non-GAAP operating margins will narrow to approximately 35% from 40% in FY 08, based on our outlook for lower sales for the year. We expect ADBE to remain focused on costs in FY 09 as demand remains weak. We look for expenses to trend higher in FY 10 as new products are launched, but think operating margins will widen modestly.

► Our operating EPS estimate is $1.29 for FY 09, rising to $1.43 in FY 10 (our GAAP estimates are $1.07 and $1.20, respectively).

Investment Rationale/Risk

► Global economic weakness has impacted growth prospects for Creative Suite 4 and other products, however, we still consider ADBE to be well-positioned to benefit from growth in rich Internet applications, websites, and related web-based graphics and video creation. We think ADBE's lack of a significant maintenance revenue stream makes it more vulnerable in a downturn than peers, but we think efforts to manage expenses will help its operating margins stabilize at a lower level until growth resumes. Low uptake of CS4 may help create pent-up demand for the next version of Creative Suite, although we think prevailing economic conditions will play a role.

► Risks to our recommendation and target price include weaker-than-expected demand for ADBE's CS4 and subsequent products, loss of share to competing products from larger vendors such as Microsoft, as well as increased competition for the Acrobat franchise from lower-cost PDF creation software.

► We derive our 12-month target price of $36 by applying a 25X P/E multiple, within the three-year average range we calculate for the shares of 17X-31.2X, to our FY 10 EPS estimate.

Qualitative Risk Assessment

LOW	MEDIUM	HIGH

Our risk assessment reflects the regularly changing nature of the software industry and our outlook for weak demand resulting from the global economic environment. These factors are only partially offset by our view of the company's size and market leadership, strong operating history, and solid balance sheet.

Quantitative Evaluations

S&P Quality Ranking B+

D	C	B-	B	B+	A-	A	A+

Relative Strength Rank STRONG

71

LOWEST = 1 HIGHEST = 99

Revenue/Earnings Data

Revenue (Million $)

	1Q	2Q	3Q	4Q	Year
2009	786.4	704.7	697.5	--	--
2008	890.5	886.9	887.3	915.3	3,580
2007	649.4	745.6	851.7	911.2	3,158
2006	655.5	635.5	602.2	682.2	2,575
2005	472.9	496.0	487.0	510.4	1,966
2004	423.3	410.1	403.7	429.5	1,667

Earnings Per Share ($)

	1Q	2Q	3Q	4Q	Year
2009	0.30	0.24	0.26	E0.32	E1.29
2008	0.38	0.41	0.35	0.46	1.59
2007	0.24	0.25	0.35	0.38	1.21
2006	0.17	0.20	0.16	0.30	0.83
2005	0.30	0.29	0.29	0.31	1.19
2004	0.25	0.22	0.21	0.23	0.91

Fiscal year ended Nov. 30. Next earnings report expected: Mid December. EPS Estimates based on S&P Operating Earnings; historical GAAP earnings are as reported.

Dividend Data

No cash dividends have been paid since 2005.

The McGraw·Hill Companies

Adobe Systems Inc

STANDARD
&POOR'S

Business Summary September 25, 2009

CORPORATE OVERVIEW. Adobe Systems (founded in 1982) is one of the world's largest software companies. It offers creative, business and mobile software and services used by consumers, artistic professionals, designers, knowledge workers, original equipment manufacturers, developers and enterprises for producing, managing, delivering and experiencing content across multiple operating systems, devices and media. Its cornerstone products include Acrobat (for document creation, distribution and management), Illustrator (to make graphic artwork), and Photoshop (for photo design, enhancement and editing). In December 2005, ADBE acquired Macromedia, a leading developer of software that enables the creation and consumption of digital content, for $3.5 billion in stock and related costs. We believe this was an extremely important transaction for the company through which ADBE gained Macromedia's significant products included Dreamweaver (Web development) and Flash (which provides an environment to produce dynamic digital content). Subsequent acquisitions have been minor; during FY 07 (Nov.), ADBE acquired two businesses and completed one asset acquisition for about $77 million. In FY 08, ADBE completed one business combination for $4.3 million.

In FY 08, the company categorized its products into four businesses: Creative Solutions, Business Productivity Solutions (including the Knowledge Worker and Enterprise and Developer segments), Mobile and Device Solutions, and Other (including the Platform and Printing and Publishing segments). In the first quarter of FY 09, ADBE moved Mobile Device Solutions into its Platform segment, leading to a structure with five segments: Creative Solutions, Knowledge Worker, Enterprise, Platform, and Print and Publishing.

CORPORATE STRATEGY. ADBE's indicated strategy is to address the needs of a variety of customers with offerings that support industry standards and can be deployed in a variety of contexts. We believe ADBE is focused on leveraging its market-leading software franchises with bundles and enhancements. Selling multiple products together has enabled ADBE to gain market share, increase penetration with existing customers, and expand its overall customer base, in our view. The Creative Suite is the company's flagship bundled offering. Macromedia was acquired to further this strategy.

We believe the purchase of Macromedia was an excellent strategic move for ADBE because it contributed technologies and products that have achieved notable adoption in the areas of dynamic digital content creation, and mobile platforms. In our opinion, the acquisition significantly bolstered ADBE's offerings in these areas.

Company Financials Fiscal Year Ended Nov. 30

Per Share Data ($)	2008	2007	2006	2005	2004	2003	2002	2001	2000	1999
Tangible Book Value	3.74	3.67	4.25	3.54	2.68	2.08	1.24	1.23	1.45	1.01
Cash Flow	2.09	1.74	1.33	1.31	1.03	0.65	0.52	0.53	0.65	0.56
Earnings	1.59	1.21	0.83	1.19	0.91	0.55	0.40	0.42	0.57	0.46
S&P Core Earnings	1.57	1.21	0.76	1.01	0.69	0.18	0.05	0.11	NA	NA
Dividends	Nil	Nil	Nil	0.01	0.03	0.03	0.03	0.03	0.03	0.03
Payout Ratio	Nil	Nil	Nil	1%	3%	5%	6%	6%	6%	5%
Prices:High	46.44	48.47	43.22	39.48	32.24	23.19	21.66	30.81	43.66	19.75
Prices:Low	19.49	37.20	25.98	25.80	17.15	12.29	8.25	11.10	13.36	4.71
P/E Ratio:High	29	40	52	33	35	42	55	74	77	43
P/E Ratio:Low	12	31	31	22	19	22	21	27	24	10
Income Statement Analysis (Million $)										
Revenue	3,580	3,158	2,575	1,966	1,667	1,295	1,165	1,230	1,266	1,015
Operating Income	1,328	1,173	870	793	653	428	368	447	457	337
Depreciation	268	315	308	64.3	60.8	49.0	63.5	56.6	43.3	50.8
Interest Expense	10.0	Nil	Nil	Nil	Nil	Nil	Nil	Nil	Nil	Nil
Pretax Income	1,079	947	680	766	609	380	285	307	444	374
Effective Tax Rate	19.2%	23.5%	25.6%	21.3%	26.0%	30.0%	32.8%	33.0%	35.1%	36.5%
Net Income	872	724	506	603	450	266	191	206	288	238
S&P Core Earnings	860	721	466	515	343	86.7	20.6	51.7	NA	NA
Balance Sheet & Other Financial Data (Million $)										
Cash	2,019	946	772	421	376	190	184	219	237	171
Current Assets	2,735	2,573	2,884	2,009	1,551	1,329	814	767	878	623
Total Assets	5,822	5,714	5,963	2,440	1,959	1,555	1,052	931	1,069	804
Current Liabilities	763	852	677	480	451	437	377	314	315	268
Long Term Debt	350	Nil	Nil	Nil	Nil	Nil	Nil	Nil	Nil	Nil
Common Equity	4,410	4,650	5,152	1,864	1,423	1,101	674	617	753	512
Total Capital	4,878	4,799	5,223	1,943	1,502	1,119	674	617	755	536
Capital Expenditures	112	132	83.3	48.9	63.2	39.5	31.6	46.6	29.8	42.2
Cash Flow	1,140	1,039	814	667	511	315	255	262	331	289
Current Ratio	3.6	3.0	4.3	4.2	3.4	3.0	2.2	2.4	2.8	2.3
% Long Term Debt of Capitalization	7.2	Nil	Nil	Nil	Nil	Nil	Nil	Nil	Nil	Nil
% Net Income of Revenue	24.4	22.9	19.6	30.7	27.0	20.6	16.4	16.7	22.7	23.4
% Return on Assets	15.1	12.3	12.0	27.4	25.6	20.4	19.3	20.6	30.7	30.3
% Return on Equity	19.2	14.7	14.4	36.7	35.7	30.0	29.6	30.0	45.5	46.2

Data as orig reptd.; bef. results of disc opers/spec. items. Per share data adj. for stk. divs.; EPS diluted. E-Estimated. NA-Not Available. NM-Not Meaningful. NR-Not Ranked. UR-Under Review.

Office: 345 Park Avenue, San Jose, CA, USA 95110-2704.
Telephone: 408-536-6000.
Email: ir@adobe.com
Website: http://www.adobe.com

Co-Chrmn: J. Warnock
Co-Chrmn: C. Geschke
Pres & CEO: S. Narayen
EVP & CFO: M. Garrett

SVP & CTO: K. Lynch
Board Members: C. M. Baldwin, E. W. Barnholt, R. K. Burgess, M. R. Cannon, J. E. Daley, C. Geschke, S. Narayen, D. L. Rosensweig, R. Sedgewick, J. Warnock

Founded: 1983
Domicile: Delaware
Employees: 7,544

Advanced Micro Devices Inc

S&P Recommendation **HOLD** ★★★☆☆	Price $6.85 (as of Nov 27, 2009)	12-Mo. Target Price $7.00	Investment Style Large-Cap Value

GICS Sector Information Technology
Sub-Industry Semiconductors

Summary This company is a leading producer of semiconductors that are used principally in computers and related products.

Key Stock Statistics (Source S&P, Vickers, company reports)

52-Wk Range	$7.33–1.86	S&P Oper. EPS 2009E	-1.52	Market Capitalization(B)	$4.592	Beta	2.13
Trailing 12-Month EPS	$-3.52	S&P Oper. EPS 2010E	-0.65	Yield (%)	Nil	S&P 3-Yr. Proj. EPS CAGR(%)	NM
Trailing 12-Month P/E	NM	P/E on S&P Oper. EPS 2009E	NM	Dividend Rate/Share	Nil	S&P Credit Rating	B-
$10K Invested 5 Yrs Ago	$3,180	Common Shares Outstg. (M)	670.3	Institutional Ownership (%)	48		

Price Performance

30-Week Mov. Avg. · · · 10-Week Mov. Avg. — **GAAP Earnings vs. Previous Year**   Volume Above Avg. ▮▮▮ STARS
12-Mo. Target Price — Relative Strength — ▲ Up ▼ Down ▶ No Change   Below Avg. ▮▮▮ ★

Options: ASE, CBOE, P, Ph

Analysis prepared by **Clyde Montevirgen** on October 16, 2009, when the stock traded at **$ 5.74**.

Highlights

► We expect revenues to rise around 13% in 2010, following a projected 10% drop in 2009, reflecting our view of increasing computer sales, higher inventory levels in the supply chain, and market share gains in certain microprocessor segments. We think AMD will be able to further penetrate lower-end markets and improve sales of its quad-core and graphics chips, which should support growth. We believe PC makers prefer to have more than one microprocessor supplier and will try to support AMD as long as financially feasible.

► We see AMD's gross margin widening in coming quarters, as utilization improves at its joint venture and manufacturing arm Globalfoundries. We also think margins will be aided by benefits from production shifts to smaller linewidths and traction of new chip offerings. Consequently, we see operating margins improving to around breakeven in 2010 from an anticipated -13% in 2009, also reflecting tighter expense management and fewer non-recurring items.

► Reflecting substantial financial leverage, we think AMD's interest payments will continue to weigh on its bottom line.

Investment Rationale/Risk

► We think AMD's new line of quad-core microprocessors has kept it in the microprocessor race against Intel, and believe demand for these chips will help near-term sales and aid ASPs. Also, the company's new graphics chips have been competitive and should help profitability. Furthermore, AMD unveiled a new manufacturing strategy that we think will help reduce business risk and strengthen its balance sheet over the long-term. However, we believe AMD has lost its technological edge and has become more vulnerable to share losses in lucrative high-end markets, and we expect Intel's upcoming chip launches to pose more challenges.

► Risks to our recommendation and target price include less-than-anticipated demand for computers, greater market share losses, and notable financial risk.

► Our 12-month target price of $7 is derived by applying a price-to-sales ratio of about 0.8X, at the low end of the historical range to account for our weak sales outlook, to our forward 12-month sales per share estimate.

Qualitative Risk Assessment

LOW	MEDIUM	**HIGH**

AMD is subject to the cyclical swings of the semiconductor industry, demand fluctuations for computer end-products, vacillation in average selling prices for chips, and strong competition from Intel, which is a much larger rival in microprocessors.

Quantitative Evaluations

S&P Quality Ranking   C

D	**C**	B-	B	B+	A-	A	A+

Relative Strength Rank   **STRONG**

96

LOWEST = 1   HIGHEST = 99

Revenue/Earnings Data

Revenue (Million $)

	1Q	2Q	3Q	4Q	Year
2009	1,177	1,184	1,396	--	--
2008	1,487	1,362	1,797	1,162	5,808
2007	1,233	1,378	1,632	1,770	6,013
2006	1,332	1,216	1,328	1,773	5,649
2005	1,227	1,260	1,523	1,838	5,848
2004	1,236	1,262	1,239	1,264	5,001

Earnings Per Share ($)

	1Q	2Q	3Q	4Q	Year
2009	-0.65	-0.49	-0.18	E-0.20	E-1.52
2008	-0.54	-1.14	-0.04	-2.32	-3.98
2007	-1.11	-1.09	-0.71	-3.06	-6.06
2006	0.38	0.18	0.27	-1.08	-0.34
2005	-0.04	0.03	0.18	0.21	0.40
2004	0.12	0.09	0.12	-0.08	0.25

Fiscal year ended Dec. 31. Next earnings report expected: Late January. EPS Estimates based on S&P Operating Earnings; historical GAAP earnings are as reported.

Dividend Data

No cash dividends have been paid.

Advanced Micro Devices Inc

STANDARD &POOR'S

Business Summary October 16, 2009

CORPORATE OVERVIEW. Advanced Micro Devices makes digital integrated circuits, including microprocessors for computers, embedded microprocessors for personal connectivity devices and, as a result of the company's acquisition of ATI Technologies in October 2006, 3D graphics, video, and multimedia products for various computing products. AMD also makes processors for consumer electronic devices such as mobile phones, digital televisions, and game consoles.

The company has three reportable segments: Computing Solutions, Graphics, and All Other. The Computing Solutions segment (79% of 2008 total revenues) includes sales of microprocessors, chipsets, and embedded processors. The Graphics segment (20%) includes graphics, video and multimedia products. The All Other segment (1%) includes expenses and credits that are not allocated to any of the operating segments.

COMPETITIVE LANDSCAPE. AMD generally competes in three main chip markets: microprocessor, graphics, and consumer electronics. The microprocessor is the central processing unit (CPU), or the "brains" of a computer. The microprocessor market is highly competitive, with competitors focusing on mi-

croprocessor performance as a way to gain market share, in our opinion. The company notes work-per-cycle, clock speed, power consumption, number of cores, bit ratings, memory size, and data access speed as key indicators or factors of processor performance.

The semiconductor graphics market addresses the need for visual processing in various computing computers. The primary product in this space is the graphics processor unit (GPU), which off-loads the burden of graphics processing from the CPU. More broadly characterized, the consumer electronics semiconductor market includes video, graphics and media processors in consumer electronics products that address the need for enhancing the visual experience. Similar to the microprocessor market, competitors in the GPU and consumer electronic chip markets focus on speed and performance as a means to improve multimedia functions in devices.

Company Financials Fiscal Year Ended Dec. 31

Per Share Data ($)	2008	2007	2006	2005	2004	2003	2002	2001	2000	1999
Tangible Book Value	NM	0.82	2.49	7.70	7.68	6.96	7.16	10.64	10.09	6.66
Cash Flow	-1.96	-3.72	1.36	3.14	3.54	2.08	-1.60	1.69	4.53	1.45
Earnings	-3.98	-6.06	-0.34	0.40	0.25	-0.79	-3.81	-0.18	2.95	-0.30
S&P Core Earnings	-2.32	-6.08	-0.35	0.38	-0.19	-1.08	-4.24	-0.49	NA	NA
Dividends	Nil	Nil	Nil	Nil	Nil	Nil	Nil	Nil	Nil	Nil
Payout Ratio	Nil	Nil	Nil	Nil	Nil	Nil	Nil	Nil	Nil	Nil
Prices:High	8.08	20.63	42.70	31.84	24.95	18.50	20.60	34.65	48.50	16.50
Prices:Low	1.62	7.26	16.90	14.08	10.76	4.78	3.10	7.69	13.56	7.28
P/E Ratio:High	NM	NM	NM	80	NM	NM	NM	NM	16	NM
P/E Ratio:Low	NM	NM	NM	35	NM	NM	NM	NM	5	NM

Income Statement Analysis (Million $)	2008	2007	2006	2005	2004	2003	2002	2001	2000	1999
Revenue	5,808	6,013	5,649	5,848	5,001	3,519	2,697	3,892	4,644	2,858
Operating Income	255	94.0	1,238	1,451	1,452	748	-139	654	1,468	233
Depreciation	1,223	1,305	837	1,219	1,224	996	756	623	579	516
Interest Expense	375	390	126	105	112	110	71.3	61.4	60.0	69.3
Pretax Income	-2,313	-3,321	-115	33.7	116	-316	-1,258	-75.0	1,263	78.4
Effective Tax Rate	NM	NM	NM	NM	5.05%	NM	NM	NM	20.3%	NM
Net Income	-2,414	-3,379	-166	165	91.2	-274	-1,303	-60.6	1,006	-88.9
S&P Core Earnings	-1,401	-3,391	-170	155	-68.2	-373	-1,450	-161	NA	NA

Balance Sheet & Other Financial Data (Million $)	2008	2007	2006	2005	2004	2003	2002	2001	2000	1999
Cash	1,096	1,889	1,380	633	918	968	429	427	591	294
Current Assets	2,379	3,816	3,963	3,559	3,228	2,900	2,020	2,353	2,658	1,410
Total Assets	7,675	11,550	13,147	7,288	7,844	7,094	5,619	5,647	5,768	4,378
Current Liabilities	2,226	2,625	2,852	1,822	1,846	1,452	1,372	1,314	1,224	911
Long Term Debt	4,702	5,031	3,672	1,327	1,628	1,900	1,780	673	1,168	1,427
Common Equity	-82.0	2,990	5,785	3,352	3,010	2,438	2,467	3,555	3,172	1,979
Total Capital	4,880	8,292	9,778	5,006	5,583	5,213	4,247	4,333	4,544	3,467
Capital Expenditures	624	1,685	1,857	1,513	1,440	570	705	679	805	620
Cash Flow	-1,191	-2,074	671	1,385	1,315	721	-547	562	1,585	427
Current Ratio	1.1	1.5	1.4	2.0	1.7	2.0	1.5	1.8	2.2	1.5
% Long Term Debt of Capitalization	96.4	60.7	37.6	26.5	29.2	36.4	41.9	15.5	25.7	41.2
% Net Income of Revenue	NM	NM	NM	2.8	1.8	NM	NM	NM	21.7	NM
% Return on Assets	NM	NM	NM	2.2	1.2	NM	NM	NM	19.8	NM
% Return on Equity	NM	NM	NM	5.2	3.3	NM	NM	NM	39.1	NM

Data as orig reptd.; bef. results of disc opers/spec. items. Per share data adj. for stk. divs.; EPS diluted. E-Estimated. NA-Not Available. NM-Not Meaningful. NR-Not Ranked. UR-Under Review.

Office: One AMD Place, Sunnyvale, CA 94088.
Telephone: 408-749-4000.
Email: investor.relations@amd.com
Website: http://www.amd.com

Chrmn: B.L. Claflin
Pres & CEO: D.R. Meyer
COO, EVP & Chief Admin Officer: R.J. Rivet
SVP & CFO: T. Seifert

SVP & General Counsel: H.A. Wolin
Investor Contact: R. Cotter (408-749-3887)
Board Members: W. A. Al Muhairi, W. M. Barnes, J. E. Caldwell, B. L. Claflin, F. M. Clegg, C. Conway, H. P. Eberhart, D. R. Meyer, R. B. Palmer

Founded: 1969
Domicile: Delaware
Employees: 14,700

AES Corporation (The)

STANDARD &POOR'S

| S&P Recommendation **BUY** ★★★★☆ | Price $12.78 (as of Nov 27, 2009) | 12-Mo. Target Price $18.00 | Investment Style Large-Cap Growth |

GICS Sector Utilities
Sub-Industry Independent Power Producers & Energy Traders

Summary The world's largest independent power producer, AES produces and distributes electricity in international and domestic markets.

Key Stock Statistics (Source S&P, Vickers, company reports)

52-Wk Range	$15.44– 4.80	S&P Oper. EPS 2009**E**	1.09	Market Capitalization(B)	$8.532	Beta	1.52
Trailing 12-Month EPS	$0.99	S&P Oper. EPS 2010**E**	1.21	Yield (%)	Nil	S&P 3-Yr. Proj. EPS CAGR(%)	17
Trailing 12-Month P/E	12.9	P/E on S&P Oper. EPS 2009**E**	11.7	Dividend Rate/Share	Nil	S&P Credit Rating	BB-
$10K Invested 5 Yrs Ago	$10,008	Common Shares Outstg. (M)	667.6	Institutional Ownership (%)	83		

Price Performance

30-Week Mov. Avg. ··· 10-Week Mov. Avg.- - **GAAP Earnings vs. Previous Year** Volume Above Avg. STARS
12-Mo. Target Price — Relative Strength ▲ Up ▼ Down ► No Change Below Avg.

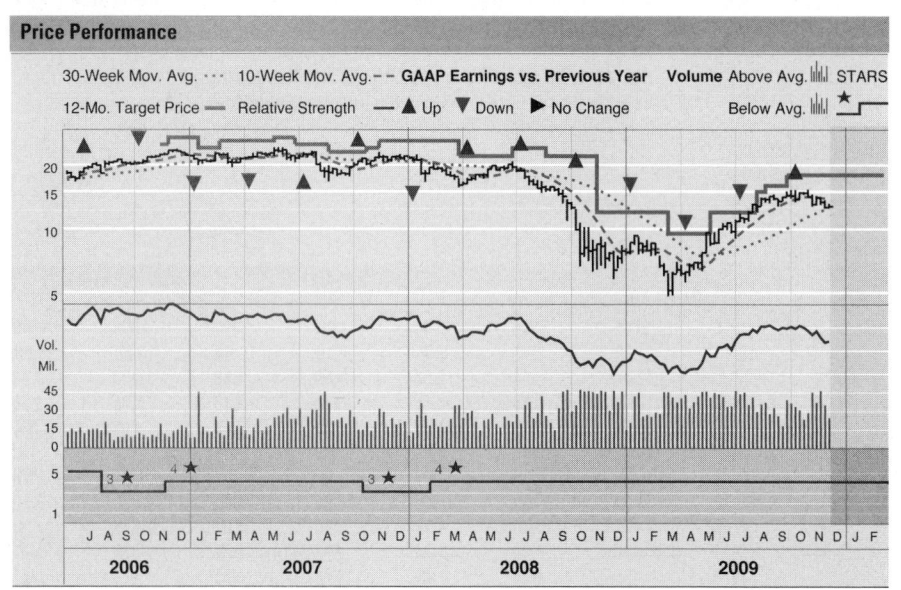

Options: ASE, CBOE, P, Ph

Analysis prepared by **Christopher B. Muir** on September 24, 2009, when the stock traded at **$ 14.92**.

Highlights

► We see revenues falling 12% in 2009 and rising 4.9% in 2010. We project revenue contraction in 2009 mostly in unregulated operations due to lower commodity prices, partly offset by new projects and acquisitions. We also anticipate a fall in regulated revenues, also hurt by lower commodity prices and a weaker global economy. We believe 2010 will be helped by stabilizing commodity prices and a weaker US dollar.

► Our operating margin forecasts are 21.8% for 2009 and 22.9% for 2010, versus 20.7% in 2008. In 2009, we expect lower per-revenue unregulated cost of sales, partly offset by higher per-revenue selling & administrative expenses and regulated cost of sales. Our pretax margin forecasts are 15.1% in 2009 and 16.9% in 2010, up from 12.9% in 2008, reflecting higher non-operating income in 2009 and lower net interest expense in 2009 and 2010.

► We estimate 2009 operating EPS, excluding $0.15 in nonrecurring gains, of $1.05, a 27% increase from operating EPS in 2008 of $0.83, which excludes nonrecurring gains of $0.93. Our 2010 EPS forecast is $1.17, up an additional 11%.

Investment Rationale/Risk

► We believe AES is a superior independent power producer. We think it should see above-average earnings growth and an improving balance sheet over the next couple of years, partly due to expansion projects. Results should also be helped by cost controls and strategic growth initiatives, which include 6 gigawatts (GW) of traditional and 3 GW of wind generation capacity additions between 2009 and 2012. We like AES's investments in renewable generation with 0.6 GW scheduled to be completed in 2009.

► Risks to our recommendation and target price include financial statement revisions, currency fluctuations, political and regulatory uncertainty regarding utility rates and U.S. power margins, and counterparty default risk.

► The stock recently traded at 13.0X our 2010 EPS estimate, or a 12% premium to independent power producer peers. Our 12-month target price of $18 is 15.4X our 2010 EPS estimate, a 19% premium to our peer target, as we see solid operations, growth opportunities, and favorable currency movements.

Qualitative Risk Assessment

| LOW | MEDIUM | HIGH |

Our risk assessment reflects the company's relatively large capitalization and mix of lower-risk regulated utility businesses in North America, offset by higher-risk merchant power operations and utility operations in emerging markets in South America, Eastern Europe, Central America and Asia.

Quantitative Evaluations

S&P Quality Ranking   B

| D | C | B- | **B** | B+ | A- | A | A+ |

Relative Strength Rank   WEAK

27

LOWEST = 1   HIGHEST = 99

Revenue/Earnings Data

Revenue (Million $)

	1Q	2Q	3Q	4Q	Year
2009	3,378	3,495	3,838	--	--
2008	4,081	4,126	4,319	3,544	16,070
2007	3,121	3,344	3,471	3,673	13,588
2006	2,973	3,044	3,135	3,147	12,299
2005	2,663	2,668	2,782	2,973	11,086
2004	2,257	2,263	2,423	2,543	9,486

Earnings Per Share ($)

	1Q	2Q	3Q	4Q	Year
2009	0.33	0.45	0.28	E0.19	E1.09
2008	0.35	1.31	0.22	-0.10	1.80
2007	0.18	0.41	0.14	0.01	0.73
2006	0.53	0.33	-0.51	0.07	0.43
2005	0.19	0.13	0.37	0.27	0.95
2004	0.12	0.10	0.20	0.14	0.57

Fiscal year ended Dec. 31. Next earnings report expected: Late February. EPS Estimates based on S&P Operating Earnings; historical GAAP earnings are as reported.

Dividend Data

No cash dividends have been paid.

Please read the Required Disclosures and Analyst Certification on the last page of this report.

The McGraw-Hill Companies

AES Corporation (The)

STANDARD &POOR'S

Business Summary September 24, 2009

CORPORATE OVERVIEW. AES Corporation (AES) owns and operates a portfolio of electricity generation and distribution business in 29 countries through its subsidiaries and affiliates. The company has two principal businesses: generation and regulated utilities.

The generation business provides power for sale to utilities and other wholesale customers while the regulated utilities business distributes power to retail, commercial, industrial, and governmental customers. In 2008, the generation unit contributed 48% of total revenues. It primarily sells electricity to utilities or other wholesale customers under power purchase agreements that are generally for five years or longer. We are positive on AES usually retaining 75% or more of a given customer's total capacity needs. The generation business also sells electricity to wholesale customers through competitive markets.

The remaining 52% of total revenues in 2008 came from the regulated utilities business. It markets electricity to residential, business, and government customers through integrated transmission and distribution systems.

The company also reports results geographically by segment. Latin American operations accounted for 65% of revenues, North American operations for 21%, European and African operations for 12%, Middle Eastern and Asian operations for 8% and corporate activities for -6%. The company's largest exposures geographically are to Brazil (34%), the U.S. (17%), Chile (8%) and Argentina (6%).

CORPORATE STRATEGY. AES pursues both a global and a local growth strategy to increase its business. The company's global strategy focuses on large-scale projects and pursues strategic initiatives. It concentrates on mergers and acquisitions, exploring opportunities in the climate change business such as the production of greenhouse gas reduction activities and related industries that involve environmental issues. The company also aims to mitigate exposure to price swings. In 2008, 61% of the revenues from its generation business was from plants that operate under PPAs of five years or longer for at least 75% of their output capacity.

Company Financials Fiscal Year Ended Dec. 31

Per Share Data ($)	2008	2007	2006	2005	2004	2003	2002	2001	2000	1999
Tangible Book Value	2.64	1.91	1.97	NM	NM	NM	NM	2.87	5.21	3.88
Earnings	1.80	0.73	0.43	0.95	0.57	0.56	-4.81	0.87	1.42	0.63
S&P Core Earnings	0.53	0.65	0.78	1.04	0.51	0.94	-3.66	0.74	NA	NA
Dividends	Nil	Nil	Nil	Nil	Nil	Nil	Nil	Nil	Nil	Nil
Payout Ratio	Nil	Nil	Nil	Nil	Nil	Nil	Nil	Nil	Nil	Nil
Prices:High	22.48	24.24	23.85	18.13	13.71	9.50	17.92	60.15	72.81	38.19
Prices:Low	5.80	16.69	15.63	12.53	7.56	2.63	0.92	11.60	34.25	16.41
P/E Ratio:High	12	33	55	19	24	17	NM	69	51	61
P/E Ratio:Low	3	23	36	13	13	5	NM	13	24	26

Income Statement Analysis (Million $)	2008	2007	2006	2005	2004	2003	2002	2001	2000	1999
Revenue	16,070	13,588	12,299	11,086	9,486	8,415	8,632	9,327	6,691	3,253
Depreciation	960	942	933	889	841	781	837	859	582	278
Maintenance	NA	NA	NA	NA	NA	NA	NA	NA	NA	NA
Fixed Charges Coverage	2.12	1.90	1.94	1.73	1.30	1.38	0.34	1.42	1.80	NA
Construction Credits	NA	NA	NA	NA	NA	NA	NA	NA	NA	NA
Effective Tax Rate	27.8%	42.4%	31.0%	31.9%	28.2%	30.3%	NM	28.7%	24.7%	26.4%
Net Income	1,216	495	286	632	366	336	-2,590	467	648	245
S&P Core Earnings	344	447	526	693	332	564	-1,970	394	NA	NA

Balance Sheet & Other Financial Data (Million $)	2008	2007	2006	2005	2004	2003	2002	2001	2000	1999
Gross Property	28,908	27,522	26,053	24,741	24,141	23,098	23,050	26,748	19,150	NA
Capital Expenditures	2,840	2,425	1,460	1,143	892	1,228	2,116	3,173	2,150	918
Net Property	21,393	20,020	19,074	18,654	18,788	18,505	18,846	23,434	17,846	NA
Capitalization:Long Term Debt	16,863	16,629	14,892	36,674	16,823	16,792	17,684	20,564	16,927	NA
Capitalization:% Long Term Debt	82.1	84.0	83.1	95.7	91.1	96.3	102.0	78.8	77.9	75.9
Capitalization:Preferred	Nil	Nil	Nil	Nil	Nil	Nil	Nil	Nil	NA	NA
Capitalization:% Preferred	Nil	Nil	Nil	Nil	Nil	Nil	Nil	Nil	NA	NA
Capitalization:Common	3,669	3,164	3,036	1,649	1,645	645	-341	5,539	4,811	2,637
Capitalization:% Common	17.9	16.0	16.9	4.30	8.91	3.70	-1.97	21.2	22.1	NA
Total Capital	25,082	24,282	21,818	40,655	20,758	19,293	19,142	29,537	24,752	17,708
% Operating Ratio	84.1	83.7	83.8	85.5	84.2	84.5	88.5	89.7	88.3	NA
% Earned on Net Property	16.1	15.5	23.0	20.9	18.5	17.0	14.3	13.6	14.0	NA
% Return on Revenue	7.6	3.6	2.3	5.7	3.9	4.0	NM	5.0	9.7	7.5
% Return on Invested Capital	12.7	16.7	16.3	7.0	13.6	13.6	21.6	7.3	9.8	NA
% Return on Common Equity	35.6	15.9	12.3	48.5	33.4	221.1	NM	8.4	17.4	11.1

Data as orig reptd.; bef. results of disc opers/spec. items. Per share data adj. for stk. divs.; EPS diluted. E-Estimated. NA-Not Available. NM-Not Meaningful. NR-Not Ranked. UR-Under Review.

Office: 4300 Wilson Blvd Ste 1100, Arlington, VA 22203-4167.
Telephone: 703-522-1315.
Email: invest@aes.com
Website: http://www.aes.com

Chrmn: P.A. Odeen
Pres & CEO: P. Hanrahan
COO & EVP: A.R. Weilert
EVP & CFO: V.D. Harker

EVP, Secy & General Counsel: B.A. Miller
Investor Contact: A. Pasha (703-682-6552)
Board Members: S. W. Bodman, III, P. Hanrahan, T. Khanna, J. A. Koskinen, P. Lader, S. O. Moose, J. B. Morse, Jr., P. A. Odeen, C. O. Rossotti, S. Sandstrom

Founded: 1981
Domicile: Delaware
Employees: 25,000

Aetna Inc.

STANDARD &POOR'S

S&P Recommendation **BUY** ★★★★☆	Price $29.44 (as of Nov 27, 2009)	12-Mo. Target Price $32.00	Investment Style Large-Cap Blend

GICS Sector Health Care
Sub-Industry Managed Health Care

Summary This company is a leading U.S. provider of health care, dental, pharmacy, group life, disability and long-term care benefits.

Key Stock Statistics (Source S&P, Vickers, company reports)

52-Wk Range	$34.87– 18.66	S&P Oper. EPS 2009**E**	2.75	Market Capitalization(B)	$12.762	Beta	1.29
Trailing 12-Month EPS	$2.86	S&P Oper. EPS 2010**E**	3.15	Yield (%)	0.14	S&P 3-Yr. Proj. EPS CAGR(%)	-4
Trailing 12-Month P/E	10.3	P/E on S&P Oper. EPS 2009**E**	10.7	Dividend Rate/Share	$0.04	S&P Credit Rating	A-
$10K Invested 5 Yrs Ago	$10,190	Common Shares Outstg. (M)	433.5	Institutional Ownership (%)	91		

Price Performance

- 30-Week Mov. Avg. ···· 10-Week Mov. Avg. - - **GAAP Earnings vs. Previous Year** Volume Above Avg.▪▪▪ STARS
- 12-Mo. Target Price — Relative Strength — ▲ Up ▼ Down ▶ No Change Below Avg.▪▪▪ ★

Options: ASE, CBOE, P, Ph

Analysis prepared by **Phillip M. Seligman** on November 10, 2009, when the stock traded at **$ 29.80.**

Qualitative Risk Assessment

LOW	MEDIUM	HIGH

Our risk assessment reflects AET's leadership in the highly fragmented managed care market. We see competition intensifying as consolidation has led the largest companies, including AET, to bump up against one another in more markets and geographies. Still, we believe AET's expanding product, market and geographic diversity will permit stable operational performance over the longer term.

Quantitative Evaluations

S&P Quality Ranking B+

D	C	B-	B	B+	A-	A	A+

Relative Strength Rank STRONG

78

LOWEST = 1   HIGHEST = 99

Revenue/Earnings Data

Revenue (Million $)

	1Q	2Q	3Q	4Q	Year
2009	8,615	8,671	8,722	--	--
2008	7,739	7,828	7,625	7,759	30,951
2007	6,700	6,794	6,961	7,144	27,600
2006	6,235	6,252	6,300	6,360	25,146
2005	5,427	5,497	5,701	5,867	22,492
2004	4,821	4,875	5,040	5,168	19,904

Earnings Per Share ($)

2009	0.95	0.77	0.73	E0.40	E2.75
2008	0.85	0.97	0.58	0.42	2.83
2007	0.81	0.85	0.95	0.87	3.47
2006	0.65	0.67	0.85	0.80	2.96
2005	0.70	0.68	0.63	0.71	2.70
2004	0.51	0.45	0.48	0.49	1.94

Fiscal year ended Dec. 31. Next earnings report expected: Mid February. EPS Estimates based on S&P Operating Earnings; historical GAAP earnings are as reported.

Highlights

▶ We forecast health care operating revenue growth of over 10% in 2009, to about $31.6 billion, from 2008's $28.7 billion. Drivers we see include net enrollment growth of under 1.3 million members by year end from large-customer wins and gains in Medicare, offset by disenrollment amid rising unemployment. We project these revenues to grow 2.3% in 2010, to $32.4 billion, as higher commercial pricing is partly offset by further disenrollment.

▶ Given higher claims intensity, rising COBRA membership, the H1N1 flu, and unfavorable prior period reserve development (PPRD), we forecast that the commercial medical loss ratio (MLR) will rise 440 basis points (bps) in 2009, but with repricing and assuming no PPRD, decline 60 bps in 2010. We expect the firmwide MLR to rise through 2010 on higher Medicare and Medicaid premium revenues in the mix, while the SG&A cost ratio rises on IT initiatives and preparation for TRICARE.

▶ We project operating EPS of $2.75 before $0.11 of one-time and net realized capital gains in 2009, versus 2008's $3.93 before $1.10 of realized investment losses and one-time costs, and $3.15 in 2010.

Investment Rationale/Risk

▶ We recently upgraded the shares to buy, from hold, on valuation. We remain encouraged by AET's focus on new markets and products, which we believe helped it garner industry-leading membership gains thus far in 2009, particularly amid the weak economy. Nonetheless, we think it may have underpriced its premiums for competitive reasons, while its recent string of negative PPRDs suggests to us that it had under-reserved for rising medical cost trends. However, it recently increased prices in the commercial risk business for 2010, and we think that and intensified medical management should help reduce the commercial MLR. Meanwhile, we are encouraged by its win of a TRICARE contract from the Defense Dept. to provide managed care support. We expect a start date in the fourth quarter of 2010 amid government review of the protests from insurers that lost the accounts.

▶ Risks to our recommendation and target price include intensified competition, a weaker economy, and adverse medical cost trends.

▶ We apply a peer-level multiple of 10X to our 2010 EPS estimate to derive our 12-month target price of $32.

Dividend Data (Dates: mm/dd Payment Date: mm/dd/yy)

Amount ($)	Date Decl.	Ex-Div. Date	Stk. of Record	Payment Date
0.040	09/26	11/10	11/13	11/28/08
0.040	09/25	11/10	11/13	11/30/09

Dividends have been paid since 2001. Source: Company reports.

Please read the Required Disclosures and Analyst Certification on the last page of this report.

The McGraw·Hill Companies

Aetna Inc.

STANDARD
&POOR'S

Business Summary November 10, 2009

CORPORATE OVERVIEW. In December 2000, Aetna sold its financial services and international operations for $5 billion ($35.33 a share, not adjusted) and the assumption of $2.7 billion of debt. AET shareholders received $35.33 a share in cash, plus one share of a new health care company named Aetna. Revenue contributions (excluding net investment and other income) from the company's business operations in 2008 were: Health Care 93.5%; Group Insurance 5.8%; and Large Case Pensions 0.7%.

The Health Care segment offers health maintenance organization (HMO), point-of-service (POS), preferred provider organization (PPO) and indemnity benefit products. The company had total health plan enrollment of 19,027,000 lives at September 30, 2009, up from 17,701,000 at December 31, 2008. Commercial risk enrollment was 5,676,000 lives, versus 5,595,000, while commercial administrative services (ASC; fee-based, self-funded accounts) was 11,906,000 lives, versus 10,893,000. Medicare enrollment was 428,000 lives, versus 366,000, while Medicaid enrollment was 1,017,000 lives, versus 847,000. The company also provided dental benefits to 14,183,000 members, versus

14,124,000, and pharmacy benefits to 11,155,000 members, versus 11,098,000.

Group Insurance provides group life, disability, and long-term care products. Group life contracts and group conversion policies totaled 41,673,000 at December 31, 2008, up from 42,402,000 at December 31, 2007.

Large Case Pensions manages various retirement products, including pension and annuity products, for defined benefit and defined contribution plans. Aetna has not marketed its Large Case Pensions products since 1993, but continues to manage the run-off of existing business. At December 31, 2008, assets under management totaled $10.7 billion, up from $24.2 billion at December 31, 2007.

Company Financials Fiscal Year Ended Dec. 31

Per Share Data ($)	2008	2007	2006	2005	2004	2003	2002	2001	2000	1999
Tangible Book Value	5.33	8.46	7.46	8.57	8.42	6.15	4.69	4.51	4.25	NA
Cash Flow	3.61	4.08	2.96	3.04	2.22	1.79	1.14	0.54	0.82	NA
Earnings	2.83	3.47	2.96	2.70	1.94	1.48	0.64	-0.51	-0.23	0.84
S&P Core Earnings	3.17	3.39	2.96	2.55	1.71	1.51	0.19	-1.12	NA	NA
Dividends	0.04	0.04	0.04	0.02	0.01	0.01	0.01	0.01	Nil	NA
Payout Ratio	1%	1%	1%	NM	NM	1%	2%	NM	Nil	NA
Prices:High	59.80	60.00	52.48	49.68	31.89	17.56	12.98	10.67	10.59	NA
Prices:Low	14.21	39.02	30.94	29.93	16.41	9.98	7.48	5.75	8.23	NA
P/E Ratio:High	21	17	18	18	16	12	20	NM	NM	NA
P/E Ratio:Low	5	11	10	11	8	7	12	NM	NM	NA

Income Statement Analysis (Million $)										
Revenue	30,951	27,600	25,146	22,492	19,904	17,976	19,879	25,191	26,819	22,110
Operating Income	2,765	3,234	2,983	2,807	2,184	1,596	1,119	460	1,104	NA
Depreciation	378	322	270	204	182	200	302	598	588	488
Interest Expense	236	181	148	123	105	103	120	143	248	NA
Pretax Income	2,174	2,796	2,587	2,547	1,899	1,442	545	-379	-39.0	745
Effective Tax Rate	36.3%	34.5%	34.8%	35.8%	36.0%	35.2%	27.8%	NM	NM	46.4%
Net Income	1,384	1,831	1,686	1,635	1,215	934	393	-292	-127	399
S&P Core Earnings	1,551	1,792	1,682	1,542	1,072	957	140	-639	NA	NA

Balance Sheet & Other Financial Data (Million $)										
Cash	1,180	2,078	880	1,378	1,595	1,655	2,017	1,631	2,204	1,629
Current Assets	4,918	5,288	18,304	18,235	19,516	19,557	19,349	18,751	19,768	NA
Total Assets	35,853	50,725	47,626	44,365	42,134	40,950	40,048	43,255	47,446	52,422
Current Liabilities	7,555	7,675	7,103	7,617	7,011	7,368	7,719	8,139	10,003	NA
Long Term Debt	3,638	3,269	2,442	1,156	1,610	1,614	1,633	1,591	Nil	2,094
Common Equity	8,186	10,038	11,009	12,167	9,081	7,924	6,980	9,890	10,127	10,703
Total Capital	11,825	13,323	11,587	13,338	10,691	9,538	8,613	11,481	10,127	12,797
Capital Expenditures	447	400	291	272	190	211	156	143	36.9	58.1
Cash Flow	1,762	2,153	1,686	1,839	1,397	1,133	695	306	461	NA
Current Ratio	0.7	0.7	2.6	2.4	2.8	2.7	2.5	2.3	2.0	2.0
% Long Term Debt of Capitalization	30.8	23.8	18.2	8.7	15.1	16.9	19.0	13.9	Nil	16.4
% Net Income of Revenue	4.5	6.6	6.7	7.6	6.4	5.2	2.0	NM	NM	1.8
% Return on Assets	3.2	3.7	3.7	3.8	2.9	2.3	0.9	NM	NM	0.8
% Return on Equity	15.2	19.1	14.5	14.0	14.3	12.5	4.7	NM	NM	3.6

Data as orig reptd.; bef. results of disc opers/spec. items. Per share data adj. for stk. divs.; EPS diluted. E-Estimated. NA-Not Available. NM-Not Meaningful. NR-Not Ranked. UR-Under Review.

Office: 151 Farmington Avenue, Hartford, CT 06156-0002.
Telephone: 860-273-0123.
Email: investorrelations@aetna.com
Website: http://www.aetna.com

Chrmn & CEO: R.A. Williams
Pres & COO: M.T. Bertolini
EVP & CFO: J. Zubretsky
SVP & General Counsel: W.J. Casazza

SVP & CIO: M. McCarthy
Investor Contact: J. Chaffkin (860-273-7830)
Board Members: L. Abramson, F. M. Clark, Jr., B. Z. Cohen, M. J. Coye, R. N. Farah, B. H. Franklin, J. E. Garten, E. G. Graves, G. Greenwald, E. M. Hancock, R. J. Harrington, E. J. Ludwig, A. Misher, J. Newhouse, D. B. Soll, R. A. Williams

Founded: 1982
Domicile: Pennsylvania
Employees: 35,500

Affiliated Computer Services Inc.

STANDARD &POOR'S

S&P Recommendation	HOLD ★★★☆☆	Price	12-Mo. Target Price	Investment Style
		$55.54 (as of Nov 27, 2009)	$64.00	Large-Cap Growth

GICS Sector Information Technology
Sub-Industry Data Processing & Outsourced Services

Summary This company, which provides a full range of information technology services, including technology outsourcing, business process outsourcing, and professional services, has agreed to be acquired by Xerox Corp.

Key Stock Statistics (Source S&P, Vickers, company reports)

52-Wk Range	$56.27– 36.79	S&P Oper. EPS 2010E	4.20	Market Capitalization(B)	$5.059	Beta	0.55
Trailing 12-Month EPS	$3.42	S&P Oper. EPS 2011E	4.76	Yield (%)	Nil	S&P 3-Yr. Proj. EPS CAGR(%)	10
Trailing 12-Month P/E	16.2	P/E on S&P Oper. EPS 2010E	13.2	Dividend Rate/Share	Nil	S&P Credit Rating	BB
$10K Invested 5 Yrs Ago	$9,291	Common Shares Outstg. (M)	97.7	Institutional Ownership (%)	85		

Price Performance

30-Week Mov. Avg. · · · 10-Week Mov. Avg. - - GAAP Earnings vs. Previous Year Volume Above Avg. STARS
12-Mo. Target Price — Relative Strength — ▲ Up ▼ Down ▶ No Change Below Avg.

Options: ASE, CBOE, P, Ph

Analysis prepared by **Dylan Cathers** on October 26, 2009, when the stock traded at **$ 53.39**.

Highlights

▶ We expect revenues for stand-alone ACS to increase 7.5% in FY 10 (Jun.). While we think growth this fiscal year will be stronger in the government segment, with gains in electronic payments and education solutions, we note September-quarter new business signings were heavily slanted towards the commercial segment. Therefore, we expect growth in the healthcare payer, and communications and consumer goods verticals. Contract signings of $212 million in the September quarter were up over 4% year over year. In FY 11, we look for sales growth of 6%.

▶ After widening in FY 09, we think operating margins will be roughly flat in FY 10. We expect higher sales of low-margin work, increased employee levels (including both staff for contracts and sales personnel), and contract start-up costs to offset operational efficiencies and cost cuts.

▶ Our FY 10 operating EPS estimate of $4.20 excludes acquisition-related expenses, after operating EPS of $3.73 in FY 09, which includes items related to an internal options investigation. In FY 11, we see EPS of $4.76.

Investment Rationale/Risk

▶ Xerox (XRX 7, Buy) recently agreed to acquire ACS. The terms of the proposed deal call for XRX to pay $18.60 in cash and 4.935 shares of XRX stock for each ACS share outstanding for a total value of $6.4 billion. XRX would also assume $2 billion in ACS debt and issue $300 million of convertible preferred shares to Chairman Darwin Deason, ACS's class B shareholder. The deal is expected to close in the first quarter of 2010, and is subject to customary closing conditions and approvals.

▶ Risks to our recommendation and target price include deterioration of XRX's share price, which makes up a large portion of the total compensation to ACS shareholders in the proposed acquisition, and the possibility of the deal falling through. More generally, risks include rising competition in the business process outsourcing arena and ongoing expenses related to shareholder lawsuits.

▶ Our 12-month target price of $64 reflects XRX's offer price (based on prices before the announcement) and represents a roughly peer-average P/E of 14.3X our calendar 2010 EPS estimate of $4.48.

Qualitative Risk Assessment

LOW	MEDIUM	HIGH

Our risk assessment reflects what we see as the highly competitive nature of the IT outsourcing and business process outsourcing markets, the company's recently increased debt load, and the SEC's informal investigation surrounding the timing of ACS's stock options.

Quantitative Evaluations

S&P Quality Ranking B+

D	C	B-	B	B+	A-	A	A+

Relative Strength Rank STRONG

81

LOWEST = 1 HIGHEST = 99

Revenue/Earnings Data

Revenue (Million $)

	1Q	2Q	3Q	4Q	Year
2010	1,677	--	--	--	--
2009	1,604	1,612	1,610	1,696	6,523
2008	1,493	1,511	1,542	1,614	6,161
2007	1,385	1,427	1,441	1,520	5,772
2006	1,311	1,348	1,314	1,381	5,354
2005	1,046	1,027	1,063	1,214	4,351

Earnings Per Share ($)

	1Q	2Q	3Q	4Q	Year
2010	0.70	E1.00	E1.07	E1.18	E4.20
2009	0.85	0.77	0.95	0.99	3.57
2008	0.65	0.81	0.85	1.01	3.32
2007	0.59	0.72	0.82	0.37	2.49
2006	0.73	0.81	0.61	0.73	2.87
2005	0.72	0.73	0.88	0.87	3.19

Fiscal year ended Jun. 30. Next earnings report expected: Late January. EPS Estimates based on S&P Operating Earnings; historical GAAP earnings are as reported.

Dividend Data

No cash dividends have been paid.

Please read the Required Disclosures and Analyst Certification on the last page of this report.

The McGraw-Hill Companies

Affiliated Computer Services Inc.

STANDARD &POOR'S

Business Summary October 26, 2009

CORPORATE OVERVIEW. Affiliated Computer Services (ACS) provides business process and information technology outsourcing solutions to commercial and government clients. In the commercial sector, the company provides business outsourcing, systems integration services and technology outsourcing to a variety of clients. The business process outsourcing division provides services such as claims processing, finance and accounting, and loan processing. The technology outsourcing division offers the delivery of information processing services on a remote basis from host data centers that provide processing capacity, network management, and desktop support. The systems integration services unit offers application development and implementation, applications outsourcing, technical support and training, network design and installation.

In the federal government sector, ACS offers business process outsourcing and systems integration services. The business process outsourcing unit consists primarily of loan servicing and human resource services for federal agencies. Within the state and local government sector, ACS designs, implements and operates large-scale health and human services programs and the supporting information technology solutions. ACS also provides child support and payment processing with high volume remittance processing and service center operations.

CORPORATE STRATEGY. Key elements of the company's business strategy include developing long-term relationships with new clients, expanding existing customer relationships, building recurring revenue streams, investing in technology, and completing strategic and tactical acquisitions. ACS provides a full range of information technology services to clients with time critical, transaction intensive business and information processing needs. Its services are designed to enable businesses and government agencies to focus on core operations, respond to rapidly changing technologies, and reduce expenses.

Company Financials Fiscal Year Ended Jun. 30

Per Share Data ($)	2009	2008	2007	2006	2005	2004	2003	2002	2001	2000
Tangible Book Value	NM	NM	NM	NM	0.30	2.64	1.94	0.11	0.90	0.44
Cash Flow	7.60	7.17	5.90	5.19	4.98	5.11	3.20	2.47	1.96	1.74
Earnings	3.57	3.32	2.49	2.87	3.19	3.83	2.20	1.76	1.23	1.04
S&P Core Earnings	3.52	3.31	2.45	2.70	3.03	2.48	2.11	1.73	1.11	NA
Dividends	Nil	Nil	Nil	Nil	Nil	Nil	Nil	Nil	Nil	Nil
Payout Ratio	Nil	Nil	Nil	Nil	Nil	Nil	Nil	Nil	Nil	Nil
Prices:High	56.27	57.40	61.67	63.66	61.16	61.23	56.56	57.05	53.63	31.31
Prices:Low	42.10	34.84	39.46	46.50	45.81	46.01	40.01	32.70	26.81	15.50
P/E Ratio:High	16	17	25	22	19	16	26	32	44	30
P/E Ratio:Low	12	10	16	16	14	12	18	19	22	15

Income Statement Analysis (Million $)	2009	2008	2007	2006	2005	2004	2003	2002	2001	2000
Revenue	6,523	6,161	5,772	5,354	4,351	4,106	3,787	3,063	2,064	1,963
Operating Income	1,081	1,035	960	926	887	742	671	511	317	265
Depreciation	395	381	346	290	233	184	152	110	93.6	84.8
Interest Expense	130	162	183	68.4	18.6	17.0	25.2	30.6	23.7	24.0
Pretax Income	554	496	383	558	641	829	491	360	221	195
Effective Tax Rate	36.9%	33.7%	34.0%	35.7%	35.1%	36.1%	37.5%	36.3%	39.3%	44.0%
Net Income	350	329	253	359	416	530	307	230	134	109
S&P Core Earnings	346	328	249	337	393	339	291	225	119	NA

Balance Sheet & Other Financial Data (Million $)	2009	2008	2007	2006	2005	2004	2003	2002	2001	2000
Cash	731	462	307	101	62.7	76.9	51.2	33.8	242	44.5
Current Assets	2,415	2,103	1,811	1,529	1,244	1,044	979	874	810	772
Total Assets	6,901	6,469	5,982	5,502	4,851	3,907	3,699	3,404	1,892	1,656
Current Liabilities	1,486	1,085	971	825	838	638	557	486	281	358
Long Term Debt	2,042	2,358	2,342	1,614	750	372	498	708	649	526
Common Equity	2,622	2,308	2,066	2,456	2,838	2,590	2,429	2,095	886	711
Total Capital	5,134	5,078	4,776	4,402	3,829	3,197	3,104	2,899	1,590	1,272
Capital Expenditures	320	268	317	394	253	225	206	144	99.1	71.5
Cash Flow	745	710	599	649	649	714	459	340	228	194
Current Ratio	1.6	1.9	1.9	1.9	1.5	1.6	1.8	1.8	2.9	2.2
% Long Term Debt of Capitalization	39.8	46.4	49.0	36.7	19.6	11.6	16.1	24.4	40.8	41.3
% Net Income of Revenue	5.4	5.3	4.4	6.7	9.6	12.9	8.1	7.5	6.5	5.6
% Return on Assets	5.2	5.3	4.4	6.9	9.5	13.9	8.6	8.7	7.6	7.6
% Return on Equity	14.2	15.0	11.2	13.6	15.3	21.1	13.6	15.4	16.8	16.6

Data as orig reptd.; bef. results of disc opers/spec. items. Per share data adj. for stk. divs.; EPS diluted. E-Estimated. NA-Not Available. NM-Not Meaningful. NR-Not Ranked. UR-Under Review.

Office: 2828 North Haskell Avenue, Dallas, TX 75204-2988.
Telephone: 214-841-6111.
Email: info@acs-inc.com
Website: http://www.acs-inc.com

Chrmn: D. Deason
Pres & CEO: L. Blodgett
COO & EVP: T. Burlin
EVP & CFO: K. Kyser

EVP, Secy & General Counsel: T. Panos
Investor Contact: J. Puckett (214-841-8281)
Board Members: L. Blodgett, D. Deason, R. Druskin, K. Krauss, T. B. Miller, Jr., P. E. Sullivan, F. A. Varasano

Founded: 1971
Domicile: Pennsylvania
Employees: 74,000

AFLAC Inc

STANDARD &POOR'S

S&P Recommendation HOLD ★★★☆☆	Price $43.65 (as of Nov 27, 2009)	12-Mo. Target Price $44.00	Investment Style Large-Cap Growth

GICS Sector Financials
Sub-Industry Life & Health Insurance

Summary AFL provides supplemental health and life insurance in the U.S. and Japan. Products are marketed at worksites and help fill the gaps in primary insurance coverage. Approximately 75% of revenues comes from Japan and 25% from the U.S.

Key Stock Statistics (Source S&P, Vickers, company reports)

52-Wk Range	$47.88– 10.83	S&P Oper. EPS 2009E	4.78	Market Capitalization(B)	$20.424	Beta	1.79
Trailing 12-Month EPS	$3.08	S&P Oper. EPS 2010E	5.22	Yield (%)	2.57	S&P 3-Yr. Proj. EPS CAGR(%)	16
Trailing 12-Month P/E	14.2	P/E on S&P Oper. EPS 2009E	9.1	Dividend Rate/Share	$1.12	S&P Credit Rating	A-
$10K Invested 5 Yrs Ago	$12,670	Common Shares Outstg. (M)	467.9	Institutional Ownership (%)	67		

Price Performance

- 30-Week Mov. Avg. · · · 10-Week Mov. Avg. - - **GAAP Earnings vs. Previous Year**   Volume Above Avg. STARS
- 12-Mo. Target Price — Relative Strength — ▲ Up ▼ Down ▶ No Change   Below Avg. ★

Options: ASE, CBOE, Ph

Analysis prepared by **Bret Howlett** on November 02, 2009, when the stock traded at **$ 40.79**.

Highlights

► We expect total revenues to rise 10% in 2010, reflecting contributions from additional distribution outlets, improved persistency, introduction of new products, and conversions and upgrades of older insurance policies. While AFL has not given its sales growth goal in Japan, we forecast growth of 3%, and expect sales to ramp up in the bank channel and think AFL's partnership with Japan Post will contribute to increased sales as well. We expect the benefit ratio in Japan to improve, since hospital stays continue to shorten and new products such as EVER have a lower average benefit ratio.

► AFL's U.S. sales have declined sharply in 2009 due to the weak economy. Although economic conditions for the industry should remain weak in 2010, we think U.S. sales will rise 5% due to agent recruitment efforts, increased payroll accounts, low product penetration, and improved persistency. We believe investment income will decline as AFL invest more in yen denominated securities.

► We estimate operating EPS growth of 16% in 2009, to $4.78. We estimate operating EPS of $5.22 in 2010. Our estimates exclude realized investment gains and losses.

Investment Rationale/Risk

► We believe AFL is fairly valued, recently trading at a significant premium to its book value per share. We think AFL is overexposed to the financial service sector due to its sizable holdings of European bank hybrid bonds. While we think significant losses stemming from its hybrid portfolio are unlikely, we believe lower credit ratings on these hybrids could pressure AFL's capital position, as the financial positions of many banks is stressed. However, AFL mainly invests in high-quality corporate debt, has no subprime holdings, and has low CMBS, RMBS, and equity exposure. We also believe AFL maintains a solid capital position and generates strong statutory earnings. We expect new distribution channels in Japan to drive sales.

► Risks to our recommendation and target price include investment losses, unfavorable movements in the yen/dollar exchange rate, less organic premium growth than anticipated, higher-than-projected operating expenses, and agent recruiting difficulties.

► Our 12-month target price is $44, or roughly 2.6X our 2009 book value per share estimate, below historical multiples.

Qualitative Risk Assessment

LOW	MEDIUM	HIGH

Our risk assessment for AFL reflects the potential for sizable investment losses given AFL's large exposure to financial services companies, particularly European banks, partly offset by its strong market share position and solid risk-based capital ratio, and the company's consistent track record of share repurchases and dividend increases.

Quantitative Evaluations

S&P Quality Ranking   A

D	C	B-	B	B+	A-	A	A+

Relative Strength Rank   MODERATE

67

LOWEST = 1   HIGHEST = 99

Revenue/Earnings Data

Revenue (Million $)

	1Q	2Q	3Q	4Q	Year
2009	4,818	4,313	4,526	--	--
2008	4,267	4,336	3,691	4,260	16,554
2007	3,751	3,764	3,861	4,018	15,393
2006	3,559	3,697	3,672	3,687	14,616
2005	3,559	3,567	3,669	3,567	14,363
2004	3,280	3,233	3,321	3,448	13,281

Earnings Per Share ($)

	1Q	2Q	3Q	4Q	Year
2009	1.22	0.67	0.77	E1.15	E4.78
2008	0.98	1.00	0.21	0.42	2.62
2007	0.84	0.84	0.85	0.78	3.31
2006	0.74	0.81	0.73	0.67	2.95
2005	0.64	0.66	0.90	0.72	2.92
2004	0.61	0.51	0.58	0.81	2.52

Fiscal year ended Dec. 31. Next earnings report expected: Early February. EPS Estimates based on S&P Operating Earnings; historical GAAP earnings are as reported.

Dividend Data (Dates: mm/dd Payment Date: mm/dd/yy)

Amount ($)	Date Decl.	Ex-Div. Date	Stk. of Record	Payment Date
0.280	10/23	02/13	02/18	03/02/09
0.280	04/29	05/18	05/20	06/01/09
0.280	07/29	08/17	08/19	09/01/09
0.280	10/28	11/16	11/18	12/01/09

Dividends have been paid since 1973. Source: Company reports.

Please read the Required Disclosures and Analyst Certification on the last page of this report.

The McGraw-Hill Companies

AFLAC Inc

STANDARD
&POOR'S

Business Summary November 02, 2009

CORPORATE OVERVIEW. Aflac provides supplemental health and life insurance in the U.S. and Japan. Most of Aflac's policies are individually underwritten and marketed at work sites through independent agents, with premiums paid by the employee. As of the end of 2008, Aflac believed it was the world's leading underwriter of individually issued policies marketed at work sites.

In 2008, Aflac Japan accounted for 72% of total revenues, compared to 71% in 2007. At December 31, 2008, Aflac Japan accounted for 87% of total company assets, up from 82% at year-end 2007. As of year-end 2008, Aflac Japan ranked first in terms of individual insurance policies in force, surpassing Nippon Life in March 2003.

Aflac Japan's insurance products are designed to help pay for costs that are not reimbursed under Japan's national health insurance system. Products include cancer life plans (34% of total Japanese sales in 2008; 23% in 2007); Rider MAX (5%; 7%), a rider for cancer life policies that provides accident and

medical/sickness benefits; and EVER (34%; 33%), a stand-alone whole life medical plan. Aflac Japan also offers ordinary life products (23%; 22%) and other products such as living benefit life plans and care products.

During 2008, the number of licensed sales associates rose to approximately 107,458 compared with 100,810 at December 31, 2007. The growth in licensed sales associates resulted primarily from individual agency recruitment.

Aflac U.S. sells cancer plans (19% of total U.S. sales in 2008; 18% in 2007) and various types of health insurance, including accident and disability (49%; 51%), fixed-benefit dental (5%; 6%), and hospital indemnity (16%; 14%). Other products include long-term care, short-term disability, and ordinary life policies (11%; 11%).

Company Financials Fiscal Year Ended Dec. 31

Per Share Data ($)	2008	2007	2006	2005	2004	2003	2002	2001	2000	1999
Tangible Book Value	13.78	27.97	25.32	15.89	15.03	13.03	12.41	10.39	8.87	7.28
Operating Earnings	NA	NA	NA	NA	NA	NA	1.56	1.34	1.21	1.00
Earnings	2.62	3.31	2.95	2.92	2.52	1.52	1.55	1.28	1.26	1.04
S&P Core Earnings	3.98	3.27	2.86	2.60	2.47	1.85	1.49	1.25	NA	NA
Dividends	0.96	0.80	0.55	0.44	0.38	0.30	0.23	0.19	0.17	0.15
Payout Ratio	366%	24%	19%	15%	15%	20%	15%	15%	13%	14%
Prices:High	68.81	63.91	49.40	49.65	42.60	36.91	33.45	36.09	37.47	28.38
Prices:Low	29.68	45.18	41.63	35.50	33.85	28.00	23.10	23.00	16.78	19.50
P/E Ratio:High	26	19	17	17	17	24	22	28	30	27
P/E Ratio:Low	11	14	14	12	13	18	15	18	13	19

Income Statement Analysis (Million $)										
Life Insurance in Force	NA	NA	NA	80,610	80,496	69,582	56,680	46,610	51,496	44,993
Premium Income:Life	NA	NA	NA	1,139	1,031	876	761	697	716	625
Premium Income:A & H	NA	NA	NA	10,851	10,271	9,052	7,839	7,366	7,523	6,639
Net Investment Income	2,578	2,333	2,171	2,071	1,957	1,787	1,614	1,550	1,550	1,369
Total Revenue	16,554	15,393	14,616	14,363	13,281	11,447	10,257	9,598	9,720	8,640
Pretax Income	1,914	2,499	2,264	2,226	1,807	1,225	1,259	1,081	1,012	778
Net Operating Income	NA	NA	NA	NA	NA	NA	825	720	657	550
Net Income	1,254	1,634	1,483	1,483	1,299	795	821	687	687	571
S&P Core Earnings	1,903	1,616	1,438	1,321	1,274	962	791	670	NA	NA

Balance Sheet & Other Financial Data (Million $)										
Cash & Equivalent	1,591	2,523	2,036	1,781	4,308	1,508	1,793	1,233	989	985
Premiums Due	920	732	535	479	417	547	435	347	301	270
Investment Assets:Bonds	67,495	55,410	50,686	47,551	48,024	42,893	37,483	31,677	31,305	31,175
Investment Assets:Stocks	27.0	22.0	25.0	84.0	77.0	73.0	258	245	236	215
Investment Assets:Loans	Nil	Nil	Nil	Nil	Nil	Nil	Nil	Nil	Nil	Nil
Investment Assets:Total	67,609	57,056	50,769	47,692	48,142	42,999	37,768	31,941	31,558	31,408
Deferred Policy Costs	8,237	6,654	6,025	5,590	5,595	5,044	4,277	3,645	3,685	3,692
Total Assets	79,331	65,805	59,805	56,361	59,326	50,964	45,058	37,860	37,232	37,041
Debt	1,721	1,465	1,420	1,050	1,141	1,409	1,312	1,000	956	931
Common Equity	6,639	8,795	8,341	7,927	7,573	6,646	6,394	5,425	4,694	3,868
% Return on Revenue	7.6	10.6	10.1	10.4	9.8	6.9	8.0	7.2	7.1	6.6
% Return on Assets	1.7	2.6	2.6	2.6	2.4	1.7	2.0	1.8	1.8	1.7
% Return on Equity	16.3	19.1	18.2	19.1	18.3	12.2	13.9	13.6	16.0	15.0
% Investment Yield	4.2	4.3	4.4	4.3	4.3	4.4	4.6	4.9	4.9	4.7

Data as orig reptd.; bef. results of disc opers/spec. items. Per share data adj. for stk. divs.; EPS diluted. E-Estimated. NA-Not Available. NM-Not Meaningful. NR-Not Ranked. UR-Under Review.

Office: 1932 Wynnton Road, Columbus, GA 31999.
Telephone: 706-323-3431.
Email: ir@aflac.com
Website: http://www.aflac.com

Chrmn & CEO: D.P. Amos
Pres, EVP, CFO & Treas: K. Cloninger, III
EVP & Chief Admin Officer: R.C. Davis
EVP, Secy & General Counsel: J.M. Loudermilk

SVP & Chief Acctg Officer: R.A. Rogers, Jr.
Investor Contact: K.S. Janke, Jr. (706-596-3264)
Board Members: D. P. Amos, J. S. Amos, II, P. S. Amos, II, Y. Aoki, M. H. Armacost, K. Cloninger, III, J. F. Harris, E. J. Hudson, K. S. Janke, D. W. Johnson, R. B. Johnson, C. B. Knapp, E. S. Purdom, B. K. Rimer, M. R. Schuster, D. G. Thompson, R. L. Wright

Founded: 1973
Domicile: Georgia
Employees: 7,949

The *McGraw-Hill* Companies

Agilent Technologies Inc.

STANDARD &POOR'S

S&P Recommendation	BUY ★★★★☆	Price	12-Mo. Target Price	Investment Style
		$28.85 (as of Nov 27, 2009)	$32.00	Large-Cap Blend

GICS Sector Information Technology
Sub-Industry Electronic Equipment Manufacturers

Summary This Hewlett-Packard (HPQ) spin-off is a diversified global manufacturer of test and measurement instruments, and life sciences and chemical analysis instruments.

Key Stock Statistics (Source S&P, Vickers, company reports)

52-Wk Range	$29.71–12.02	S&P Oper. EPS 2010**E**	1.43	Market Capitalization(B)	$9.956	Beta	1.34
Trailing 12-Month EPS	$-0.09	S&P Oper. EPS 2011**E**	1.72	Yield (%)	Nil	S&P 3-Yr. Proj. EPS CAGR(%)	19
Trailing 12-Month P/E	NM	P/E on S&P Oper. EPS 2010**E**	20.2	Dividend Rate/Share	Nil	S&P Credit Rating	BBB-
$10K Invested 5 Yrs Ago	NA	Common Shares Outstg. (M)	345.1	Institutional Ownership (%)	79		

Price Performance

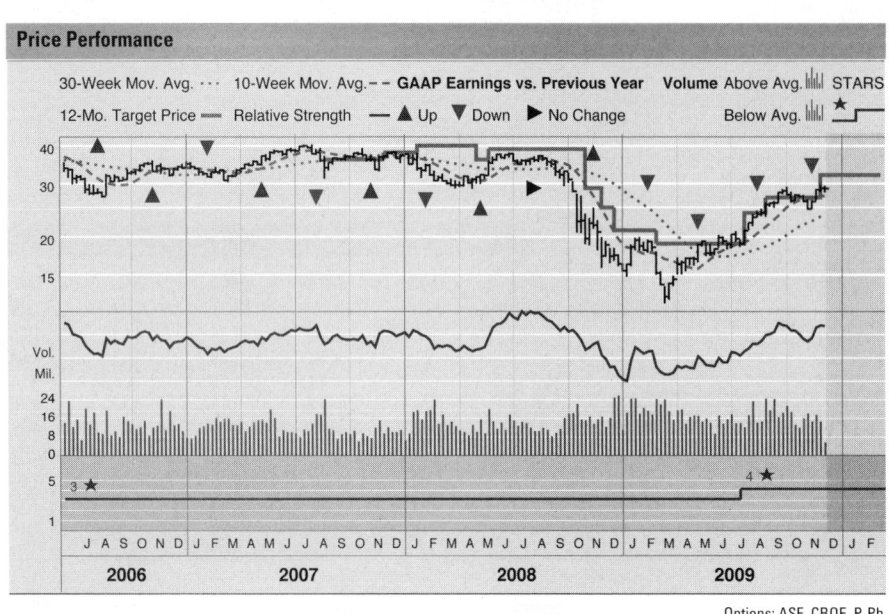

30-Week Mov. Avg. · · ·   10-Week Mov. Avg. – –   GAAP Earnings vs. Previous Year   Volume Above Avg. STARS
12-Mo. Target Price —   Relative Strength —   ▲ Up ▼ Down ▶ No Change   Below Avg.

Options: ASE, CBOE, P, Ph

Analysis prepared by **Angelo Zino** on November 16, 2009, when the stock traded at **$ 29.06**.

Highlights

► Following a revenue decline of 22% in FY 09 (Oct.), we project sales to increase 5% in FY 10 and 4% in FY 11, reflecting improving sales across most business segments, especially A's more cyclical electronic measurement end markets. We see the bio-analytical segment benefiting from higher food and safety orders and improvement in the pharmaceutical market. We expect rising semiconductor-related orders, but see communications sales constrained by excess test capacity.

► We project annual gross margins of 55% in FY 10 and 56% in FY 11, compared with 51% in FY 09, benefiting from higher volume and cost-cutting efforts. We view positively cost-reduction moves aimed at achieving $525 million of annualized cost savings by the middle of FY 10, reflecting the restructuring of A's electronic measurement and semiconductor and board test segments.

► We estimate FY 10 operating EPS of $1.43 and $1.72 for FY 11. We think A's intent to acquire Varian (VARI 51, NR) would expand it into high-growth adjacent markets, such as environmental analysis, and expand its already strong presence in the life science market.

Investment Rationale/Risk

► We have a favorable view of the company's diversified end-market mix, with exposure to the non-cyclical life sciences and chemical analysis markets as well as cyclical electronic measurement markets. Over the longer term, we expect Agilent to focus on expanding aggressively through new product offerings in high-growth industries, complemented by opportunistic acquisitions in core markets. We forecast more stable demand and higher market share in both the chemical analysis and life science end markets, with growth potential in areas such as food and safety as well as academic and government.

► Risks to our recommendation and target price include a weaker-than-expected global economy, narrower margins than we project, and weaker-than-anticipated traction for new product introductions.

► Our 12-month target price of $32 is based on our discounted cash flow analysis, which assumes a weighted average cost of capital of 10% and a terminal growth rate of 3%. Our target price is supported by a price-to-sales (P/S) ratio of 2.36X our FY 10 sales per share estimate, near A's five-year historical average.

Qualitative Risk Assessment

LOW	**MEDIUM**	HIGH

Our risk assessment reflects the variability of Agilent's results in the past, offset by recent efforts to streamline its businesses and divest parts of its portfolio that contributed to this variability.

Quantitative Evaluations

S&P Quality Ranking   B-

D	C	**B-**	B	B+	A-	A	A+

Relative Strength Rank   STRONG

84

LOWEST = 1   HIGHEST = 99

Revenue/Earnings Data

Revenue (Million $)

	1Q	2Q	3Q	4Q	Year
2009	1,166	1,091	1,057	1,167	4,481
2008	1,393	1,456	1,444	1,481	5,774
2007	1,280	1,320	1,374	1,446	5,420
2006	1,167	1,239	1,239	1,328	4,973
2005	1,212	1,688	1,242	1,407	5,139
2004	1,643	1,831	1,885	1,822	7,181

Earnings Per Share ($)

	1Q	2Q	3Q	4Q	Year
2009	0.18	-0.29	-0.06	0.07	-0.09
2008	0.31	0.47	0.45	0.64	1.87
2007	0.36	0.30	0.45	0.46	1.57
2006	2.03	0.28	0.51	0.31	3.26
2005	0.10	0.11	0.10	-0.03	0.28
2004	0.14	0.21	0.20	0.15	0.71

Fiscal year ended Oct. 31. Next earnings report expected: Mid February. EPS Estimates based on S&P Operating Earnings; historical GAAP earnings are as reported.

Dividend Data

No cash dividends have been paid.

Agilent Technologies Inc.

STANDARD &POOR'S

Business Summary November 16, 2009

CORPORATE OVERVIEW. Agilent Technologies, which was spun off from Hewlett-Packard (HPQ) in 1999, provides investors with exposure to the communications, electronics, life sciences and chemical analysis industries. Agilent's revenues during FY 08 (Oct.) came from two business segments: electronic measurement 60% (63% in FY 07) and bio-analytical measurement 40% (37%). Starting in FY 09 (Oct.), Agilent will report results in three separate business segments comprised of the electronic measurement business, the bio-analytical measurement business and the semiconductor and board test business. The semiconductor and board test segment will combine laser interferometer, parametric test and printed circuit board manufacturing test equipment.

The company's electronic measurement products compete in the communications test market and the general test market, which represented 42% and 58% of FY 08 segment revenues, respectively. The communications test market includes handset manufacturers, network equipment manufacturers and communications service providers. Agilent has a suite of fiber optic, broadband and data and wireless communications and microwave network products. General purpose test products and services are sold to the electronics industry and other industries with significant electronic content, such as the aerospace and defense, computer and semiconductor industries. It sells electronic measurement products that are used for electronics manufacturing testing, parametric testing, and flat panel display (FPD) markets.

Agilent's bio-analytical measurement business products include microarrays, microfluidics, gas chromatography, liquid chromatography, mass spectrometry, software and informatics, and related consumables and services used in pharmaceutical analysis, the proteomics and gene expression markets, as well as the petrochemical and environmental markets, among others. Applications include measuring octane levels in gasoline, and analyzing pesticide levels in drinking water. Customers span the hydrocarbon-processing, environmental, pharmaceutical and bioscience markets. In the pharmaceutical and biopharmaceutical markets, Agilent's instruments help lower the cost of discovering and developing new drugs. Agilent's chemical analysis markets accounted for 55% of revenue from the bio-analytical measurement business in FY 08. Chemical analysis focuses primarily on the following areas: petrochemical, environmental, homeland security and forensics, bioagriculture and food safety, and material science.

Company Financials Fiscal Year Ended Oct. 31

Per Share Data ($)	2009	2008	2007	2006	2005	2004	2003	2002	2001	2000
Tangible Book Value	NA	4.81	6.75	7.79	7.39	6.42	5.09	8.44	9.95	10.37
Cash Flow	NA	2.35	2.04	3.64	0.65	1.31	-3.02	-0.62	0.72	2.75
Earnings	-0.09	1.87	1.57	3.26	0.28	0.71	-3.78	-2.20	-0.89	1.66
S&P Core Earnings	NA	1.51	1.52	1.59	-0.11	0.27	-5.70	-3.10	-2.63	NA
Dividends	Nil	Nil	Nil	Nil	Nil	Nil	Nil	Nil	Nil	Nil
Payout Ratio	Nil	Nil	Nil	Nil	Nil	Nil	Nil	Nil	Nil	Nil
Prices:High	29.71	38.00	40.42	39.54	36.10	38.80	29.42	38.00	68.00	162.00
Prices:Low	12.02	14.76	30.26	26.96	20.11	19.51	18.35	10.50	18.00	38.06
P/E Ratio:High	NM	20	26	12	NM	55	NM	NM	NM	98
P/E Ratio:Low	NM	8	19	8	NM	27	NM	NM	NM	23

Income Statement Analysis (Million $)										
Revenue	4,481	5,774	5,420	4,973	5,139	7,181	6,056	6,010	8,396	10,773
Operating Income	NA	974	775	680	367	678	-363	-872	-44.0	1,548
Depreciation	162	179	191	170	186	292	362	735	734	495
Interest Expense	NA	123	91.0	69.0	27.0	36.0	Nil	Nil	Nil	Nil
Pretax Income	7.00	815	670	1,528	306	440	-690	-1,547	-477	1,164
Effective Tax Rate	542.9%	15.0%	4.70%	5.96%	50.7%	20.7%	NM	NM	NM	35.0%
Net Income	-31.0	693	638	1,437	141	349	-1,790	-1,022	-406	757
S&P Core Earnings	NA	561	615	701	-55.1	137	-2,695	-1,438	-1,202	NA

Balance Sheet & Other Financial Data (Million $)										
Cash	2,493	1,429	1,826	2,262	2,251	2,315	1,607	1,844	1,170	996
Current Assets	NA	3,208	3,671	3,958	4,447	4,577	3,889	4,880	4,799	5,655
Total Assets	7,612	7,437	7,554	7,369	6,751	7,056	6,297	8,203	7,986	8,425
Current Liabilities	NA	1,325	1,663	1,538	1,936	1,871	1,906	2,181	2,002	2,758
Long Term Debt	2,904	2,125	2,087	1,500	Nil	1,150	1,150	1,150	Nil	Nil
Common Equity	2,506	2,559	3,234	3,648	4,081	3,569	2,824	4,627	5,659	5,265
Total Capital	5,410	4,684	5,321	5,341	4,081	4,719	3,974	5,777	5,659	5,265
Capital Expenditures	128	154	154	185	139	118	205	301	881	824
Cash Flow	NA	872	829	1,607	327	641	-1,428	-287	328	1,252
Current Ratio	3.5	2.4	2.2	2.6	2.3	2.4	2.0	2.2	2.4	2.1
% Long Term Debt of Capitalization	53.7	45.4	39.2	29.1	Nil	24.4	28.9	19.9	Nil	Nil
% Net Income of Revenue	NM	12.0	11.7	28.9	2.7	4.9	NM	NM	NM	7.0
% Return on Assets	NM	9.3	8.5	20.4	2.0	5.2	NM	NM	NM	10.9
% Return on Equity	NM	23.9	18.5	37.2	3.7	10.9	NM	NM	NM	17.5

Data as orig reptd.; bef. results of disc opers/spec. items. Per share data adj. for stk. divs.; EPS diluted. E-Estimated. NA-Not Available. NM-Not Meaningful. NR-Not Ranked. UR-Under Review.

Office: 5301 Stevens Creek Blvd, Santa Clara, CA 95051-7201.
Telephone: 408-553-7777.
Email: investor_relations@agilent.com
Website: http://www.agilent.com

Chrmn: J.G. Cullen
Pres & CEO: W.P. Sullivan
SVP & CTO: D.J. Solomon
SVP, Secy & General Counsel: M.O. Huber

CFO & Chief Admin Officer: A.T. Dillon
Investor Contact: R. Gonsalves (408-345-8948)
Board Members: K. Boon Hwee, P. N. Clark, J. G. Cullen, H. Fields, R. J. Herbold, R. L. Joss, D. M. Lawrence, A. B. Rand, W. P. Sullivan

Founded: 1999
Domicile: Delaware
Employees: 19,600

The McGraw-Hill Companies

Airgas Inc.

STANDARD &POOR'S

| S&P Recommendation | HOLD ★★★☆☆ | Price $46.12 (as of Nov 27, 2009) | 12-Mo. Target Price $48.00 | Investment Style Large-Cap Growth |

GICS Sector Materials
Sub-Industry Industrial Gases

Summary This leading distributor of industrial, medical and specialty gases and related equipment also distributes safety and other disposable supplies through its network of stores.

Key Stock Statistics (Source S&P, Vickers, company reports)

52-Wk Range	$51.00–26.29	S&P Oper. EPS 2010E	2.67	Market Capitalization(B)	$3.787	Beta	1.41
Trailing 12-Month EPS	$2.76	S&P Oper. EPS 2011E	3.15	Yield (%)	1.56	S&P 3-Yr. Proj. EPS CAGR(%)	13
Trailing 12-Month P/E	16.7	P/E on S&P Oper. EPS 2010E	17.3	Dividend Rate/Share	$0.72	S&P Credit Rating	BBB
$10K Invested 5 Yrs Ago	$18,406	Common Shares Outstg. (M)	82.1	Institutional Ownership (%)	79		

Price Performance

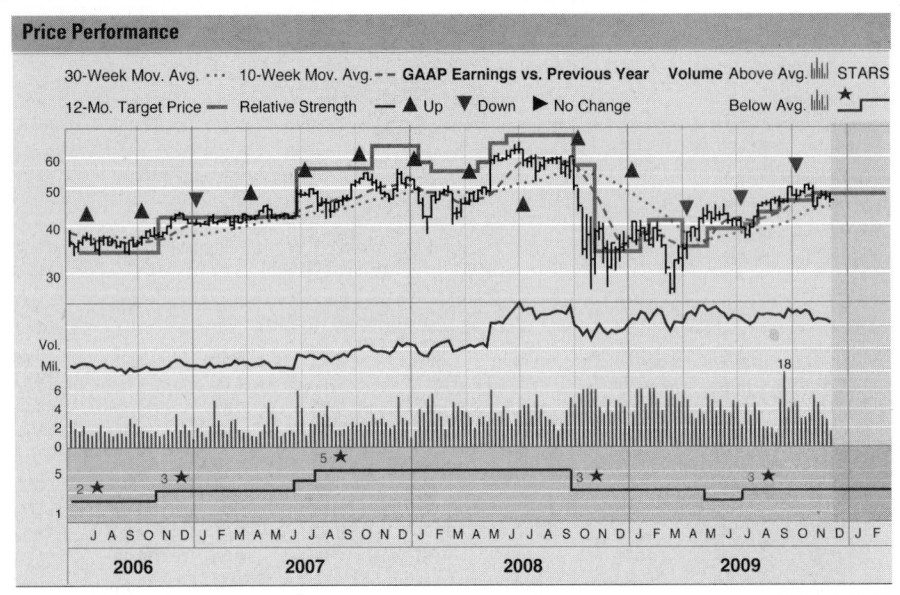

30-Week Mov. Avg. ··· 10-Week Mov. Avg. -- GAAP Earnings vs. Previous Year Volume Above Avg. STARS
12-Mo. Target Price — Relative Strength ▲ Up ▼ Down ► No Change Below Avg.

Options: CBOE, Ph

Analysis prepared by **Mathew Christy, CFA** on November 04, 2009, when the stock traded at **$ 45.12**.

Highlights

► We see FY 10 (Mar.) sales falling 9.5%, primarily on lower volumes, pricing and same-store sales, as demand for industrial gas falls, offset somewhat by continued acquisitions. Our forecast is based on much lower revenue in the first half of the fiscal year that is only partially offset by somewhat better results in the back half. However, we forecast that FY 11 revenue will rise somewhat more than 4%, and we see better results on improved demand, volumes and pricing resulting from an improving economic outlook.

► We believe operating margins will fall in FY 10. Our forecast is based on lower operating leverage on reduced volumes and capacity utilization, partially offset by recently announced cost-cutting efforts, including salary freezes. In FY 11, we forecast a moderate increase in the operating margin due to better operating leverage as volumes and demand improve and due to lower SG&A expenses as a percentage of sales.

► With our forecast for flat tax rates, we expect operating EPS of $2.67 in FY 10 and $3.15 in FY 11.

Investment Rationale/Risk

► We expect the slowing economy to lead to overall lower volumes, some pricing declines, and reduced same-store sales in FY 10, and we forecast that revenues will fall more than 9%. In addition, we expect reduced operating leverage, partially offset by cost-cutting efforts, to lead to somewhat reduced operating margins. However, we expect ARG to continue to consolidate in this highly fragmented industry and achieve some growth and margin benefits from ongoing acquisitions. We view the shares, trading recently at 15X our calendar 2010 EPS estimate, as appropriately valued.

► Risks to our recommendation and target price include lower-than-expected demand, lower-than-expected prices, and higher commodity or transportation costs.

► Our 12-month target price of $48 represents a blend of two valuation metrics. Our DCF model, which assumes a 3% perpetual growth rate and a 9.7% discount rate, indicates intrinsic value of about $47. For relative valuation, we apply a multiple of 16.2X to our calendar 2010 EPS estimate of $3.03, a discount to peers, which suggests a $49 value.

Qualitative Risk Assessment

| LOW | MEDIUM | HIGH |

Our risk assessment for Airgas reflects the company's acquisition strategy, its significant proportion of sales to the cyclical industrial manufacturing industry, and what we consider a relatively high level of debt.

Quantitative Evaluations

S&P Quality Ranking A-

| D | C | B- | B | B+ | A- | A | A+ |

Relative Strength Rank MODERATE

40

LOWEST = 1   HIGHEST = 99

Revenue/Earnings Data

Revenue (Million $)

	1Q	2Q	3Q	4Q	Year
2010	979.3	962.3	--	--	--
2009	1,117	1,162	1,079	992.1	4,349
2008	915.1	1,007	1,008	1,087	4,017
2007	773.0	790.8	787.4	853.9	3,205
2006	690.7	714.4	702.4	746.9	2,830
2005	544.0	599.8	611.5	656.1	2,411

Earnings Per Share ($)

	1Q	2Q	3Q	4Q	Year
2010	0.66	0.65	E0.66	E0.70	E2.67
2009	0.81	0.86	0.76	0.68	3.12
2008	0.63	0.60	0.67	0.76	2.66
2007	0.48	0.49	0.40	0.54	1.92
2006	0.38	0.38	0.41	0.45	1.62
2005	0.29	0.30	0.30	0.31	1.20

Fiscal year ended Mar. 31. Next earnings report expected: Late January. EPS Estimates based on S&P Operating Earnings; historical GAAP earnings are as reported.

Dividend Data (Dates: mm/dd Payment Date: mm/dd/yy)

Amount ($)	Date Decl.	Ex-Div. Date	Stk. of Record	Payment Date
0.160	02/05	03/11	03/13	03/31/09
0.180	05/19	06/11	06/15	06/30/09
0.180	08/18	09/11	09/15	09/30/09
0.180	11/05	12/11	12/15	12/31/09

Dividends have been paid since 2003. Source: Company reports.

Please read the Required Disclosures and Analyst Certification on the last page of this report.

The McGraw·Hill Companies

Airgas Inc.

STANDARD &POOR'S

Business Summary November 04, 2009

CORPORATE OVERVIEW. Airgas has completed over 400 acquisitions in the past 25 years to become the largest U.S. distributor of packaged gases and welding, safety and related products, with an average market share of 25% based on the company's data. ARG operated an integrated network of over 1,100 locations and 14,000 employees as of March 2009, and markets its products and services through sales representatives, retail stores, and electronic, catalog and telesales channels. Competitors in the packaged gas market include independent distributors (50% of the market), through a fragmented distribution network, as well as large distributors (25%), including Praxair, Linde AG, Air Liquide, Matheson Trigas and Valley National.

The distribution segment (90.1% of FY 09 (Mar.) total sales, 89.5% of earnings before interest and taxes (EBIT), and nearly 12% EBIT margins) purchases and distributes industrial, medical and specialty gases, process chemicals and hardgoods. Products include industrial, specialty and medical gases, and welding, safety and related products. Gas and rent revenues accounted for 57% of segment sales in FY 09, with hardgoods providing the remaining 43%. Industry segments served include manufacturing, service, construction, retail consumer establishments, transportation and utilities, and agriculture and mining.

The other operations segment (10%, 10.5%, 12%) produces and distributes certain gas products, principally dry ice, carbon dioxide, specialty gases, and nitrous oxide. The segment also includes the results of the company's National Welders, a producer and distributor of industrial gases. Customers include food processors, food services, pharmaceutical and biotech industries, and wholesale trade and grocery outlets.

The company has a fairly broad exposure to the overall U.S. economy, as it serves over 800,000 customers in multiple industries. As a percentage of total net sales, ARG estimates sales to the repair and maintenance segment accounted for 27%; industrial manufacturing 25%; non-residential construction 13%; medical 9%; petrochemical 7%; food products 6%; wholesale trade 4%; analytical 2%; utilities and mining 2%; transportation 2%; and other 3%.

Company Financials Fiscal Year Ended Mar. 31

Per Share Data ($)	2009	2008	2007	2006	2005	2004	2003	2002	2001	2000
Tangible Book Value	3.59	3.59	2.93	4.59	3.76	2.22	1.84	0.95	0.87	NM
Cash Flow	5.75	4.90	3.66	3.14	2.64	2.25	2.05	1.74	1.71	1.82
Earnings	3.12	2.66	1.92	1.62	1.20	1.07	0.94	0.69	0.42	0.55
S&P Core Earnings	3.12	2.66	1.92	1.52	1.11	0.99	0.86	0.64	0.34	NA
Dividends	0.39	0.28	0.24	0.18	0.16	Nil	Nil	Nil	Nil	Nil
Payout Ratio	13%	11%	12%	11%	13%	Nil	Nil	Nil	Nil	Nil
Calendar Year	2008	2007	2006	2005	2004	2003	2002	2001	2000	1999
Prices:High	65.45	55.89	43.43	33.79	27.19	21.75	20.74	15.85	10.19	14.00
Prices:Low	27.09	39.00	31.65	21.15	19.82	15.27	11.75	6.38	4.63	7.88
P/E Ratio:High	21	21	22	21	23	20	22	23	24	25
P/E Ratio:Low	9	15	16	13	17	14	13	9	11	14

Income Statement Analysis (Million $)										
Revenue	4,349	4,017	3,205	2,830	2,411	1,895	1,787	1,636	1,629	1,542
Operating Income	746	676	489	396	315	255	238	198	198	193
Depreciation	221	190	147	128	112	88.0	79.8	72.9	86.8	89.3
Interest Expense	87.1	61.4	62.1	55.7	52.8	43.0	47.3	48.0	61.4	58.7
Pretax Income	429	371	257	208	148	128	109	78.4	48.9	70.4
Effective Tax Rate	39.2%	38.9%	38.8%	37.4%	36.8%	37.1%	37.7%	38.0%	42.3%	44.8%
Net Income	261	223	154	128	92.0	80.2	68.1	48.6	28.2	38.9
S&P Core Earnings	261	223	154	119	84.9	74.2	61.8	44.5	23.3	NA

Balance Sheet & Other Financial Data (Million $)										
Cash	47.2	43.1	25.9	35.0	32.6	Nil	Nil	Nil	Nil	Nil
Current Assets	718	639	550	459	466	327	271	304	334	409
Total Assets	4,400	3,979	3,333	2,474	2,292	1,931	1,700	1,717	1,583	1,739
Current Liabilities	432	506	428	476	333	242	209	221	282	220
Long Term Debt	1,750	1,540	1,310	636	802	683	658	764	621	857
Common Equity	1,572	1,413	1,125	947	814	692	597	503	497	473
Total Capital	3,888	2,993	2,866	1,968	1,934	1,668	1,464	1,465	1,279	1,491
Capital Expenditures	352	267	244	214	168	93.7	68.0	58.3	65.9	65.2
Cash Flow	482	413	302	255	204	168	148	122	115	128
Current Ratio	1.7	1.3	1.3	1.0	1.4	1.3	1.3	1.4	1.2	1.9
% Long Term Debt of Capitalization	45.0	51.4	52.6	32.3	41.4	40.9	44.9	52.1	48.5	57.5
% Net Income of Revenue	6.0	5.6	4.8	4.5	3.8	4.2	3.8	3.0	1.7	2.5
% Return on Assets	6.2	6.1	5.3	5.4	4.3	4.4	4.0	2.9	1.7	2.3
% Return on Equity	17.5	17.6	14.9	14.5	12.2	12.4	12.4	9.7	5.8	8.2

Data as orig reptd.; bef. results of disc opers/spec. items. Per share data adj. for stk. divs.; EPS diluted. E-Estimated. NA-Not Available. NM-Not Meaningful. NR-Not Ranked. UR-Under Review.

Office: 259 North Radnor-Chester Road, Radnor, PA 19087-5283.
Telephone: 610-687-5253.
Email: investor@airgas.com
Website: http://www.airgas.com

Chrmn, Pres & CEO: P. McCausland
COO & EVP: M.L. Molinini
SVP & CFO: R.M. McLaughlin
SVP, Secy & General Counsel: R.H. Young, Jr.

SVP & CIO: R.A. Dougherty
Investor Contact: J. Worley (610-902-6206)
Board Members: W. T. Brown, J. W. Hovey, R. C. III, P. McCausland, P. A. Sneed, D. Stout, L. M. Thomas, E. C. Wolf, J. C. van Roden, Jr.

Founded: 1986
Domicile: Delaware
Employees: 14,000

The McGraw-Hill Companies

Air Products and Chemicals Inc.

STANDARD
&POOR'S

S&P Recommendation	HOLD ★★★☆☆	Price	12-Mo. Target Price	Investment Style
		$82.11 (as of Nov 27, 2009)	$85.00	Large-Cap Blend

GICS Sector Materials
Sub-Industry Industrial Gases

Summary This major producer of industrial gases and electronics and specialty chemicals also has interests in environmental and energy-related businesses.

Key Stock Statistics (Source S&P, Vickers, company reports)

52-Wk Range	$85.44– 43.00	S&P Oper. EPS 2010**E**	4.75	Market Capitalization(B)	$17.250	Beta		1.16
Trailing 12-Month EPS	$2.96	S&P Oper. EPS 2011**E**	NA	Yield (%)	2.19	S&P 3-Yr. Proj. EPS CAGR(%)		NA
Trailing 12-Month P/E	27.7	P/E on S&P Oper. EPS 2010**E**	17.3	Dividend Rate/Share	$1.80	S&P Credit Rating		A
$10K Invested 5 Yrs Ago	$16,137	Common Shares Outstg. (M)	210.1	Institutional Ownership (%)	83			

Price Performance

30-Week Mov. Avg. · · · 10-Week Mov. Avg. – – GAAP Earnings vs. Previous Year   Volume Above Avg. STARS
12-Mo. Target Price — Relative Strength — ▲ Up ▼ Down ► No Change   Below Avg.

Options: CBOE, P, Ph

Analysis prepared by **Richard O'Reilly, CFA** on October 22, 2009, when the stock traded at **$ 83.09**.

Highlights

► Sales in FY 09 (Sep.) declined 8%, excluding unfavorable currency exchange and the pass-through of lower energy costs totaling 13%, and operating EPS fell 20% to $4.06. We expect a modest rise in sales in FY 10 and a partial recovery in EPS to $4.75, boosted by cost reductions implemented since late 2008. Currency exchange rates should become a tailwind.

► We believe the industrial gases businesses will begin to post volume gains in calendar 2010 assuming growth in global manufacturing activity and boosted by the start-up of new plants. We expect continued positive volume comparisons for hydrogen gas in FY 10 driven by its growing use in petroleum refining. We also project a recovery in the results of the electronics business where APD is implementing a restructuring.

► We project equipment unit profits in FY 10 to be similar to the $42 million in FY 09 despite a recent decline in the order backlog. Currency impact should be favorable, versus a negative effect in FY 09, but we expect higher pension expense in FY 10. Reported EPS for FY 09 includes special charges of $1.06, mainly for cost reductions.

Investment Rationale/Risk

► Our hold opinion on the shares is based on valuation. We believe that APD may be less recession-resistant than generally thought by investors. However, we also think the company has a strong backlog of industrial gases projects, which should enhance long-term sales growth, while profits in FY 10 should be boosted from recent cost reductions and restructuring actions.

► Risks to our recommendation and target price include weaker-than-expected growth in U.S. industrial activity and in the global electronics materials industry, higher-than-forecast raw material and energy prices, and inability by APD to achieve planned cost reductions.

► The shares recently traded at a P/E of about 17X our FY 10 EPS estimate, above the level of the S&P 500 (15X). Based on a P/E of about 18X, similar to that of APD's industrial gases peer group, applied to our FY 10 EPS estimate, our 12-month target price is $85. The dividend was raised in 2009 for the 27th consecutive year, a record that we see being extended.

Qualitative Risk Assessment

LOW	MEDIUM	HIGH

Our risk assessment reflects the stable growth of the industrial gases industry versus commodity chemicals, and what we see as the company's relatively strong balance sheet, offset by volatile raw material cost exposure in the chemical segment.

Quantitative Evaluations

S&P Quality Ranking   A

D	C	B-	B	B+	A-	A	A+

Relative Strength Rank   STRONG

71

LOWEST = 1   HIGHEST = 99

Revenue/Earnings Data

Revenue (Million $)

	1Q	2Q	3Q	4Q	Year
2009	2,195	1,955	1,976	2,129	8,256
2008	2,474	2,605	2,808	2,715	10,415
2007	2,410	2,451	2,574	2,603	10,038
2006	2,016	2,230	2,246	2,359	8,850
2005	1,991	2,003	2,078	2,071	8,144
2004	1,685	1,857	1,893	1,978	7,411

Earnings Per Share ($)

2009	0.42	0.89	0.54	1.14	3.00
2008	1.16	1.16	0.23	1.26	4.98
2007	1.03	1.02	1.28	1.35	4.67
2006	0.80	0.89	--	0.73	3.29
2005	0.72	0.75	0.82	0.79	3.08
2004	0.58	0.62	0.71	0.73	2.64

Fiscal year ended Sep. 30. Next earnings report expected: Late January. EPS Estimates based on S&P Operating Earnings; historical GAAP earnings are as reported.

Dividend Data (Dates: mm/dd Payment Date: mm/dd/yy)

Amount ($)	Date Decl.	Ex-Div. Date	Stk. of Record	Payment Date
0.450	03/19	03/30	04/01	05/11/09
0.450	05/21	06/29	07/01	08/10/09
0.450	09/17	09/29	10/01	11/09/09
0.450	11/19	12/30	01/04	02/08/10

Dividends have been paid since 1954. Source: Company reports.

Air Products and Chemicals Inc.

STANDARD
&POOR'S

Business Summary October 22, 2009

CORPORATE OVERVIEW. Air Products & Chemicals is one of the largest global producers of industrial gases, and has a large specialty chemicals business. APD focuses on several areas for growth in industrial gases, including electronics, hydrogen for petroleum refining, health care, and Asia. International operations accounted for 53% of FY 08 (Sep.) sales.

The industrial gases businesses consists of nitrogen, oxygen, argon, hydrogen, helium, carbon monoxide, synthesis gas, and fluorine compounds for both merchant (44% of sales and 55% of profits in FY 09) and on-site tonnage (31%, 33%) customers. Sales of atmospheric gases (oxygen, nitrogen and argon) accounted for 18% of the total in FY 08. APD is the world's leading supplier of hydrogen (17% of total sales) and carbon monoxide products (HYCO) and helium. Beginning with the fourth quarter of FY 08, the European healthcare business (sales of $360 million in FY 07) has been reported as part of the merchant gases segment. APD is the market leader in Spain, Portugal, and the U.K. Beginning in FY 08, the polyurethane intermediates business was reported as part of the tonnage gases segment. The business had sales of $340 million in FY 07.

The electronics and performance materials segment (19%, 8%) supplies spe-

cialty gases (nitrogen trifluoride, silane, phosphine), tonnage gases, specialty and bulk chemicals, services and equipment to makers of silicone and semiconductors, displays and photovoltaic devices. Performance materials include epoxy and polyurethane additives, specialty amines, and surfactants for coatings, adhesives, personal care and cleaning products, and polyurethanes.

Equipment and energy (6%, 4%) includes cryogenic and process equipment for air separation, gas processing, natural gas liquefaction (LNG), and hydrogen purification. The segment also includes 50%-owned ventures in power cogeneration and flue gas desulfurization facilities.

In July 2008, APD decided to sell its U.S. healthcare business (sales of $240 million in FY 08; reported as discontinued operations beginning in FY 08). The business had a net loss of $268 million in FY 08 with after-tax charges totaling $246.2 million ($1.12 a share), primarily for goodwill. APD sold the remaining portions of the U.S. business in the FY 09 fourth quarter.

Company Financials Fiscal Year Ended Sep. 30

Per Share Data ($)	2009	2008	2007	2006	2005	2004	2003	2002	2001	2000
Tangible Book Value	NA	18.21	22.01	17.59	16.03	15.45	12.99	13.33	10.79	10.78
Cash Flow	NA	8.94	8.44	6.64	6.22	5.76	4.65	4.97	4.95	3.24
Earnings	3.00	4.98	4.67	3.29	3.08	2.64	1.79	2.36	2.12	0.57
S&P Core Earnings	NA	4.56	4.65	2.94	3.01	2.63	1.66	1.67	1.70	NA
Dividends	1.79	1.70	1.48	1.34	1.25	1.04	0.88	0.82	0.78	0.74
Payout Ratio	60%	34%	32%	41%	41%	39%	49%	35%	37%	130%
Prices:High	85.44	106.06	105.02	72.45	65.81	59.18	53.07	53.52	49.00	42.25
Prices:Low	43.44	41.46	68.58	58.01	53.00	46.71	36.97	40.00	32.25	23.00
P/E Ratio:High	28	21	22	22	21	22	30	23	23	74
P/E Ratio:Low	14	8	15	18	17	18	21	17	15	40

Income Statement Analysis (Million $)										
Revenue	8,256	10,415	10,038	8,850	8,144	7,411	6,297	5,401	5,717	5,496
Operating Income	NA	2,360	2,179	1,777	1,700	1,567	1,218	1,319	1,313	1,407
Depreciation	840	869	840	763	728	715	640	581	573	576
Interest Expense	NA	184	176	119	110	121	124	122	191	197
Pretax Income	837	1,479	1,376	1,049	998	851	565	784	737	118
Effective Tax Rate	22.2%	24.7%	21.9%	25.8%	26.4%	26.6%	26.0%	30.7%	29.7%	NM
Net Income	640	1,091	1,043	748	712	604	400	525	513	124
S&P Core Earnings	NA	1,001	1,038	670	695	601	369	369	370	NA

Balance Sheet & Other Financial Data (Million $)										
Cash	488	104	42.3	35.2	55.8	146	76.2	254	66.2	94.1
Current Assets	NA	2,848	2,858	2,613	2,415	2,417	2,068	1,909	1,685	1,805
Total Assets	13,080	12,490	12,660	11,181	10,409	10,040	9,432	8,495	8,084	8,271
Current Liabilities	NA	2,212	2,423	2,323	1,943	1,706	1,581	1,256	1,352	1,375
Long Term Debt	3,716	3,515	2,977	2,280	2,053	Nil	2,169	2,041	2,028	2,616
Common Equity	4,792	5,031	5,496	4,924	4,576	4,444	3,783	3,460	3,106	2,821
Total Capital	9,098	9,309	9,362	8,215	7,644	5,401	6,845	6,411	6,030	6,334
Capital Expenditures	1,179	1,085	1,055	1,261	930	706	613	628	708	768
Cash Flow	NA	1,960	1,883	1,511	1,440	1,319	1,040	1,106	1,086	700
Current Ratio	1.2	1.3	1.2	1.1	1.2	1.4	1.3	1.5	1.2	1.3
% Long Term Debt of Capitalization	40.8	37.8	31.8	27.8	26.9	Nil	31.7	31.8	33.6	41.3
% Net Income of Revenue	7.8	10.5	10.4	8.5	8.7	8.2	6.4	9.7	9.0	2.3
% Return on Assets	5.0	8.7	8.8	6.9	7.0	6.2	4.5	6.3	6.3	1.5
% Return on Equity	13.0	20.7	20.0	15.8	15.8	14.7	11.1	16.0	17.3	4.3

Data as orig reptd.; bef. results of disc opers/spec. items. Per share data adj. for stk. divs.; EPS diluted. E-Estimated. NA-Not Available. NM-Not Meaningful. NR-Not Ranked. UR-Under Review.

Office: 7201 Hamilton Boulevard, Allentown, PA 18195-1501.
Telephone: 610-481-4911.
Website: http://www.airproducts.com
Chrmn, Pres & CEO: J. McGlade

SVP & CFO: P.E. Huck
SVP & General Counsel: J. Stanley
CTO: M. Alger
Treas: G.G. Bitto

Investor Contact: N. Squires (610-481-7461)
Board Members: M. L. Baeza, W. L. Davis, III, M. J. Donahue, U. O. Fairbairn, W. D. Ford, E. E. Hagenlocker, E. Henkes, J. McGlade, M. G. McGlynn, C. H. Noski, L. S. Smith

Founded: 1940
Domicile: Delaware
Employees: 21,100

Akamai Technologies Inc

S&P Recommendation	HOLD ★★★★★	Price	12-Mo. Target Price	Investment Style
		$23.92 (as of Nov 27, 2009)	$25.00	Large-Cap Growth

GICS Sector Information Technology
Sub-Industry Internet Software & Services

Summary This company develops and deploys solutions designed to accelerate and improve the delivery of Internet content and applications.

Key Stock Statistics (Source S&P, Vickers, company reports)

52-Wk Range	$25.19– 11.03	S&P Oper. EPS 2009**E**	0.76	Market Capitalization(B)	$4.097	Beta		0.90
Trailing 12-Month EPS	$0.79	S&P Oper. EPS 2010**E**	0.84	Yield (%)	Nil	S&P 3-Yr. Proj. EPS CAGR(%)		8
Trailing 12-Month P/E	30.3	P/E on S&P Oper. EPS 2009**E**	31.5	Dividend Rate/Share	Nil	S&P Credit Rating		NR
$10K Invested 5 Yrs Ago	$17,985	Common Shares Outstg. (M)	171.3	Institutional Ownership (%)	84			

Price Performance

30-Week Mov. Avg. ··· 10-Week Mov. Avg. − − **GAAP Earnings vs. Previous Year** Volume Above Avg. STARS
12-Mo. Target Price — Relative Strength — ▲ Up ▼ Down ▶ No Change Below Avg. ★

Options: ASE, CBOE, P, Ph

Analysis prepared by **Scott H. Kessler** on November 02, 2009, when the stock traded at **$ 22.45**.

Highlights

► We project that revenues will rise 7% in 2009 and 8% in 2010, reflecting what we consider solid secular growth, driven by the increasing use and importance of the Internet to distribute content and applications, and improving volumes, offset somewhat by the challenging global economy and pricing pressures.

► We foresee annual gross, operating and net margins bottoming in 2009. We see scale and efficiency benefits, offset somewhat by pricing pressures and higher bandwidth costs.

► AKAM has made some $435 million of technology-focused acquisitions since late 2006, enhancing its capabilities regarding content and application transmission speeds, rich-media distribution, and peer-to-peer networks. In December 2006, it purchased Nine Systems for some $158 million in cash and stock. In March 2007, AKAM bought Netli for $162 million in stock. In April 2007, the company acquired Red Swoosh for $15 million in stock. In November 2008, it bought acerno for up to $100 million. As of September 2009, AKAM had roughly $773 million of net cash and equivalents. In April 2009, AKAM announced a $100 million stock buyback.

Investment Rationale/Risk

► AKAM was a pioneer in content and application distribution. We believe this area will continue to grow notably, reflecting increasing demand for online video offerings, but think AKAM faces challenges related to macroeconomic weakness and companies providing less sophisticated offerings. In conjunction with the financial results following the second quarter of 2009, AKAM indicated that it was making material price concessions to larger and more strategic customers.

► Risks to our recommendation and target price include continuing notable pricing issues, weaker demand for AKAM's solutions than we expect, more significant competition, and worse corporate execution than we foresee.

► Our DCF analysis, with assumptions including a WACC of 11.5%, free cash flow growth averaging 11% from 2009 to 2013, and a terminal growth rate of 3%, leads to an intrinsic value of $25, which is our 12-month target price. We think DCF considerations constitute the best way to value AKAM, because non-cash items, such as stock-based compensation, are very material to the company's GAAP results.

Qualitative Risk Assessment

LOW	MEDIUM	HIGH

Our risk assessment reflects what we view as rapidly evolving technologies, and notable and increasing competition.

Quantitative Evaluations

S&P Quality Ranking   B-

D	C	B-	B	B+	A-	A	A+

Relative Strength Rank   **STRONG**

88

LOWEST = 1   HIGHEST = 99

Revenue/Earnings Data

Revenue (Million $)

	1Q	2Q	3Q	4Q	Year
2009	210.4	204.6	206.5	--	--
2008	187.0	194.0	197.4	212.6	790.9
2007	139.3	152.7	161.2	183.2	636.4
2006	90.83	100.7	111.5	125.7	428.7
2005	60.10	64.65	75.71	82.66	283.1
2004	48.37	50.79	53.29	57.58	210.0

Earnings Per Share ($)

2009	0.20	0.19	0.17	E0.19	E0.76
2008	0.20	0.19	0.18	0.22	0.79
2007	0.11	0.12	0.13	0.20	0.56
2006	0.07	0.07	0.08	0.12	0.34
2005	0.10	0.11	1.71	0.16	2.11
2004	0.02	0.05	0.08	0.10	0.25

Fiscal year ended Dec. 31. Next earnings report expected: Early February. EPS Estimates based on S&P Operating Earnings; historical GAAP earnings are as reported.

Dividend Data

No cash dividends have been paid.

Akamai Technologies Inc

STANDARD &POOR'S

Business Summary November 02, 2009

CORPORATE OVERVIEW. The Internet plays a crucial role in the way entities conduct business; however, it was not originally intended to accommodate the volume or complexity of today's demands. As a result, online information is often delayed or lost.

Akamai Technologies has developed solutions to accelerate and improve the delivery of Internet content and applications. Its solutions are designed to help customers enhance their revenues and reduce costs by maximizing the performance of their online businesses. Advancing website performance and reliability enable AKAM's customers to improve end-user experiences and promote more effective operations. Specifically, AKAM seeks to address issues related to performance, scalability and security. The company offers solutions focused on digital media distribution and storage, content and application delivery, application performance, on-demand managed services, and website intelligence. Importantly, we believe the company's offerings help clients monetize traffic and save/conserve capital.

CORPORATE STRATEGY. AKAM believes it has deployed the world's largest globally distributed computing platform, which includes more than 56,000 servers around the world. The company employs its proprietary solutions and specialized technologies such as advanced routing, load balancing, and data collection and monitoring to deliver customer content and applications. We perceive this platform and the related intellectual property as a notable competitive advantage the company will continue to leverage.

Although competition in this area has increased over the past few years, AKAM's focus on both dynamic (i.e., back and forth) distribution and segments beyond media and entertainment help insulate the company from substantial pricing pressures, in our view. Nonetheless, we believe lower-end business is more at risk given additional players entering the market.

We believe recent acquisitions have bolstered the company's base and breadth of technologies related to streaming rich media, enhancing distribution speeds, peer-to-peer networks, and online advertising. We see these areas contributing to significant growth, and expect AKAM to continue pursuing transactions that are not transformational in nature. We note that value-added services have been growing as a percentage of the company's revenues.

Company Financials Fiscal Year Ended Dec. 31

Per Share Data ($)	2008	2007	2006	2005	2004	2003	2002	2001	2000	1999
Tangible Book Value	6.04	5.47	4.10	3.19	NM	NM	NM	NM	2.02	3.04
Cash Flow	1.30	0.93	0.58	2.25	0.37	0.17	-1.01	-20.40	-1.98	-1.75
Earnings	0.79	0.56	0.34	2.11	0.25	-0.25	-1.81	-23.59	-10.07	-1.87
S&P Core Earnings	0.79	0.56	0.34	1.93	-0.16	-0.64	-2.05	-12.47	NA	NA
Dividends	Nil	Nil	Nil	Nil	Nil	Nil	Nil	Nil	Nil	Nil
Payout Ratio	Nil	Nil	Nil	Nil	Nil	Nil	Nil	Nil	Nil	Nil
Prices:High	40.90	59.69	56.80	22.25	18.47	14.20	6.34	37.44	345.50	344.87
Prices:Low	9.25	27.75	19.57	10.64	10.74	1.18	0.56	2.52	18.06	26.00
P/E Ratio:High	52	NM	NM	11	74	NM	NM	NM	NM	NM
P/E Ratio:Low	12	NM	NM	5	43	NM	NM	NM	NM	NM

Income Statement Analysis (Million $)	2008	2007	2006	2005	2004	2003	2002	2001	2000	1999
Revenue	791	636	429	283	210	161	145	163	89.8	3.99
Operating Income	313	217	124	98.5	69.2	30.1	-46.3	-131	-187	-53.0
Depreciation	98.1	71.9	45.6	25.2	20.2	49.7	90.4	330	712	3.43
Interest Expense	2.83	3.09	3.17	5.33	10.2	18.3	18.4	18.9	8.93	2.15
Pretax Income	235	168	98.5	70.4	35.1	-28.7	-204	-2,434	-886	-54.2
Effective Tax Rate	38.1%	40.0%	41.7%	NM	2.20%	NM	NM	NM	NM	NM
Net Income	145	101	57.4	328	34.4	-29.3	-204	-2,436	-886	-54.2
S&P Core Earnings	145	101	57.2	300	-19.9	-75.6	-231	-1,286	NA	NA

Balance Sheet & Other Financial Data (Million $)	2008	2007	2006	2005	2004	2003	2002	2001	2000	1999
Cash	327	546	270	292	70.6	165	115	211	310	270
Current Assets	502	695	375	355	109	202	142	228	355	274
Total Assets	1,881	1,656	1,248	891	183	279	230	421	2,791	301
Current Liabilities	100	88.4	89.3	61.9	46.8	62.7	81.1	91.3	84.9	18.6
Long Term Debt	200	200	200	200	257	386	301	300	300	0.73
Common Equity	1,569	1,359	955	624	-126	-175	-168	17.2	2,404	281
Total Capital	1,769	1,559	1,155	824	131	211	133	317	2,705	285
Capital Expenditures	115	100	56.8	26.9	12.3	1.42	7.25	64.5	132	25.7
Cash Flow	243	173	103	353	54.6	20.5	-114	-2,106	-174	-53.0
Current Ratio	5.0	7.9	4.2	5.7	2.3	3.2	1.7	2.5	4.2	14.7
% Long Term Debt of Capitalization	11.3	12.8	17.3	24.3	196.4	183.2	226.5	94.6	11.1	0.3
% Net Income of Revenue	18.4	15.9	13.4	115.9	16.4	NM	NM	NM	NM	NM
% Return on Assets	8.2	7.0	5.4	61.1	14.9	NM	NM	NM	NM	NM
% Return on Equity	9.9	8.7	7.3	131.7	NM	NM	NM	NM	NM	NM

Data as orig reptd.; bef. results of disc opers/spec. items. Per share data adj. for stk. divs.; EPS diluted. E-Estimated. NA-Not Available. NM-Not Meaningful. NR-Not Ranked. UR-Under Review.

Office: 8 Cambridge Center, Cambridge, MA 02142-1413.
Telephone: 617-444-3000.
Email: ir@akamai.com
Website: http://www.akamai.com

Chrmn: G.H. Conrades
Pres & CEO: P.L. Sagan
COO: R. Blumofe
SVP & CTO: M.M. Afergan

SVP, Secy & General Counsel: M. Haratunian
Investor Contact: S. Smith (617-444-2804)
Board Members: G. H. Conrades, M. M. Coyne, II, C. K. Goodwin, R. L. Graham, J. A. Greenthal, D. Kenny, P. J. Kight, F. T. Leighton, G. A. Moore, P. L. Sagan, F. V. Salerno, N. Seligman

Founded: 1998
Domicile: Delaware
Employees: 1,500

The McGraw-Hill Companies

AK Steel Holding Corp

STANDARD
&POOR'S

S&P Recommendation	BUY ★★★★☆	Price	12-Mo. Target Price	Investment Style
		$19.55 (as of Nov 27, 2009)	$22.00	Large-Cap Blend

GICS Sector Materials
Sub-Industry Steel

Summary This company produces carbon flat-rolled steel for the automotive, appliance, construction and manufacturing markets.

Key Stock Statistics (Source S&P, Vickers, company reports)

52-Wk Range	$24.27– 5.39	S&P Oper. EPS 2009E	-0.83	Market Capitalization(B)	$2.138	Beta	3.33
Trailing 12-Month EPS	$-4.96	S&P Oper. EPS 2010E	1.63	Yield (%)	1.02	S&P 3-Yr. Proj. EPS CAGR(%)	-15
Trailing 12-Month P/E	NM	P/E on S&P Oper. EPS 2009E	NM	Dividend Rate/Share	$0.20	S&P Credit Rating	BB-
$10K Invested 5 Yrs Ago	$15,260	Common Shares Outstg. (M)	109.4	Institutional Ownership (%)	89		

Price Performance

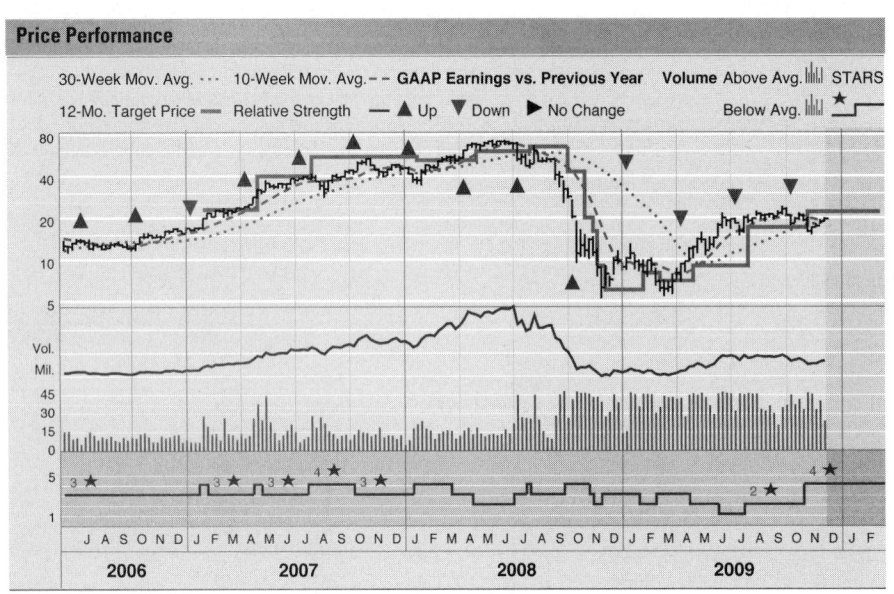

30-Week Mov. Avg. · · · 10-Week Mov. Avg. – – GAAP Earnings vs. Previous Year Volume Above Avg. STARS
12-Mo. Target Price — Relative Strength ▲ Up ▼ Down ► No Change Below Avg.

Options: ASE, CBOE, P, Ph

Analysis prepared by **Leo J. Larkin** on October 27, 2009, when the stock traded at **$ 17.25**.

Highlights

► Following a projected drop of 47% in 2009, we look for a 30% sales increase in 2010, reflecting our expectation for a recovery in shipment volume and higher revenue per ton. Our forecast rests on several assumptions. First, S&P forecasts GDP growth of 1.8% in 2010, versus a decline in GDP of 2.7% estimated for 2009. We see this resulting in rising demand for durable goods. Second, S&P Economics projects auto sales of 10.9 million units in 2010, up from 10.2 million units projected for 2009. Third, after cutting their inventories through most of 2009, we think that distributors will add to inventory in 2010. Finally, we expect that sales will be aided by a more lucrative product mix.

► Aided by higher volume and increased revenue per ton, we look for a sizable improvement in margins and a return to operating profit in 2010. After interest expense and taxes, we project EPS of $1.63 in 2010, versus an operating loss per share of $0.83 estimated for 2009, which excludes unusual expense of $0.05.

► Longer term, we think earnings will rise on a gradual decline in pension and health care costs, and greater internal sourcing of raw materials.

Investment Rationale/Risk

► For the long term, we view AKS as poised for a turnaround. AKS has cut costs and has reduced funded debt and underfunded pension and health care liabilities. It also has obtained concessions on health care and retiree costs on its labor contracts, eliminating a sizable cost disadvantage versus other domestic steel companies. Thus, we think AKS now has a lower, more competitive cost structure, which should help boost earnings as steel demand recovers. Moreover, we believe that long-term results will also benefit from rising demand for the company's stainless/electrical steel products. We think the shares are attractively valued, recently trading at 10.7X our 2010 EPS estimate.

► Risks to our recommendation and target price include a decline in the volume of shipments and the average realized price per ton in 2010 instead of the increases we currently expect.

► Applying a multiple of 13.5X to our 2010 EPS estimate, at the low end of the historical range, and a multiple of 7.1X to cash and cash equivalents per share at the end of 2009's third quarter, we arrive at our 12-month target price of $22.

Qualitative Risk Assessment

LOW	MEDIUM	HIGH

Our risk assessment reflects AKS's exposure to the auto industry and other cyclical markets, along with its high ratio of total liabilities to assets versus peers. Partially offsetting these factors are AKS's debt reduction and cost-cutting in recent years.

Quantitative Evaluations

S&P Quality Ranking B-

D	C	B-	B	B+	A-	A	A+

Relative Strength Rank STRONG

73

LOWEST = 1 HIGHEST = 99

Revenue/Earnings Data

Revenue (Million $)

	1Q	2Q	3Q	4Q	Year
2009	922.2	793.6	1,041	--	--
2008	1,791	2,237	2,158	1,459	7,644
2007	1,720	1,870	1,722	1,692	7,003
2006	1,436	1,497	1,554	1,582	6,069
2005	1,423	1,455	1,393	1,377	5,647
2004	1,134	1,312	1,337	1,434	5,217

Earnings Per Share ($)

	1Q	2Q	3Q	4Q	Year
2009	-0.67	-0.43	-0.06	E0.25	E-0.83
2008	0.90	1.29	1.67	-3.88	0.04
2007	0.56	0.98	0.97	0.95	3.46
2006	0.06	0.26	0.23	-0.45	0.11
2005	0.54	0.08	-0.26	0.37	0.01
2004	-0.15	0.18	1.09	-0.84	0.28

Fiscal year ended Dec. 31. Next earnings report expected: Late January. EPS Estimates based on S&P Operating Earnings; historical GAAP earnings are as reported.

Dividend Data (Dates: mm/dd Payment Date: mm/dd/yy)

Amount ($)	Date Decl.	Ex-Div. Date	Stk. of Record	Payment Date
0.050	01/27	02/11	02/13	03/10/09
0.050	04/21	05/13	05/15	06/10/09
0.050	07/21	08/12	08/14	09/10/09
0.050	10/27	11/10	11/13	12/10/09

Dividends have been paid since 2008. Source: Company reports.

Please read the Required Disclosures and Analyst Certification on the last page of this report.

The McGraw-Hill Companies

AK Steel Holding Corp

STANDARD
&POOR'S

Business Summary October 27, 2009

CORPORATE OVERVIEW. AK Steel Holding, the third largest integrated U.S. steelmaker in terms of production, sells premium quality coated, cold rolled, and hot rolled carbon steel to the automotive, appliance, and manufacturing markets, as well as to the construction industry and independent steel distributors and service centers.

Sales by market in 2008 were: automotive 32% (40% in 2007), appliance, industrial machinery, construction and manufacturing 29% (26%), and distribution and service centers 39% (34%).

Shipments in 2008 totaled 5,866,000 tons, versus 6,478,700 tons in 2007. There was an operating profit per ton of $124 in 2008, versus $103 in 2007.

CORPORATE STRATEGY. The company's goal to achieve sustained profitability by controlling costs and directing its marketing efforts toward those customers who require the highest quality flat-rolled steel with precise just-in-time delivery and technical support. AKS believes that its enhanced product quality and delivery capabilities, and its emphasis on customer technical support and product planning, are areas in which it excels in serving this market segment.

MARKET PROFILE. The primary factors affecting demand for steel products are economic growth in general and growth in demand for durable goods in particular. The two largest end markets for steel products in the U.S. are autos and construction. In 2008, these two markets accounted for 35% of shipments in the U.S. market. Other end markets include appliances, containers, machinery, and oil and gas. Distributors, also known as service centers, accounted for 25% of industry shipments in the U.S. market in 2008. Distributors are the largest single market for the steel industry in the U.S. Because distributors sell to a wide variety of OEMs, it is impossible to track the final destination of much of the industry's shipments. Consequently, demand for steel from the auto, construction and other industries may be higher than the shipment data would suggest. In terms of shipments, the size of the U.S. market was 97.8 million tons in 2008, and AKS's market share was 6.0%. In the U.S. market, consumption decreased at a compound annual growth rate (CAGR) of 1.8% from 1999 through 2008. Global steel production was 1.33 billion metric tons in 2008. Consumption grew at a CAGR of 6.4% from 1998 through 2007.

Company Financials Fiscal Year Ended Dec. 31

Per Share Data ($)	2008	2007	2006	2005	2004	2003	2002	2001	2000	1999
Tangible Book Value	8.43	7.51	3.44	1.30	0.92	NM	3.02	7.40	11.03	10.42
Cash Flow	1.84	5.22	1.95	1.86	2.29	-3.44	-2.32	1.41	3.45	2.53
Earnings	0.04	3.46	0.11	0.01	0.28	-5.48	-4.42	-0.87	1.20	0.62
S&P Core Earnings	2.41	3.43	1.00	0.84	2.70	-2.71	-1.06	-1.89	NA	NA
Dividends	0.20	Nil	Nil	Nil	Nil	Nil	Nil	0.13	0.50	0.50
Payout Ratio	500%	Nil	Nil	Nil	Nil	Nil	Nil	NM	42%	81%
Prices:High	73.07	53.97	17.31	18.23	16.00	8.90	14.85	15.00	20.13	29.63
Prices:Low	5.20	16.13	7.58	6.23	3.65	1.74	6.45	7.50	7.50	13.75
P/E Ratio:High	NM	16	NM	NM	57	NM	NM	NM	17	48
P/E Ratio:Low	NM	5	NM	NM	13	NM	NM	NM	6	22

Income Statement Analysis (Million $)										
Revenue	7,644	7,003	6,069	5,647	5,217	4,042	4,289	3,994	4,612	4,285
Operating Income	930	860	409	397	139	155	331	370	586	572
Depreciation	202	196	204	205	219	222	225	245	248	227
Interest Expense	50.9	68.3	89.1	86.8	110	118	128	133	136	124
Pretax Income	-6.90	591	-3.10	38.0	-193	-241	-803	-147	210	142
Effective Tax Rate	NM	34.4%	NM	NM	NM	NM	NM	NM	37.0%	45.0%
Net Income	4.00	388	12.0	-0.80	30.5	-594	-476	-92.4	132	71.3
S&P Core Earnings	269	385	110	92.4	295	-326	-125	-204	NA	NA

Balance Sheet & Other Financial Data (Million $)										
Cash	563	714	519	520	377	54.7	283	101	86.8	54.4
Current Assets	2,003	2,427	2,548	2,246	2,107	1,358	1,700	1,548	1,522	1,433
Total Assets	4,677	5,197	5,518	5,488	5,453	5,026	5,400	5,226	5,240	5,202
Current Liabilities	734	973	932	903	747	779	860	954	890	868
Long Term Debt	633	653	1,115	1,115	1,110	1,198	1,260	1,325	1,388	1,451
Common Equity	963	875	417	220	197	-52.8	529	1,021	1,307	1,263
Total Capital	1,596	1,527	1,532	1,335	1,307	1,145	1,789	2,358	2,707	2,929
Capital Expenditures	167	104	76.2	174	98.8	79.6	93.8	109	138	337
Cash Flow	206	584	216	204	250	-373	-250	152	379	278
Current Ratio	2.7	2.5	2.7	2.5	2.8	1.7	2.0	1.6	1.7	1.7
% Long Term Debt of Capitalization	39.6	42.7	72.8	83.5	84.9	104.6	70.4	56.2	51.3	53.1
% Net Income of Revenue	0.1	5.5	NM	NM	NM	NM	NM	NM	2.9	1.7
% Return on Assets	0.1	7.2	NM	NM	NM	NM	NM	NM	2.5	1.4
% Return on Equity	0.4	60.0	NM	NM	NM	NM	NM	NM	10.2	4.3

Data as orig reptd.; bef. results of disc opers/spec. items. Per share data adj. for stk. divs.; EPS diluted. E-Estimated. NA-Not Available. NM-Not Meaningful. NR-Not Ranked. UR-Under Review.

Office: 9227 Centre Pointe Dr, West Chester, OH 45069-4822.
Telephone: 513-425-5000.
Website: http://www.aksteel.com
Chrmn, Pres & CEO: J.L. Wainscott

COO: J.F. Kaloski
SVP, Secy & General Counsel: D.C. Horn
Investor Contact: A.E. Ferrara, Jr. (513-425-2888)
Chief Acctg Officer & Cntlr: R.K. Newport

Board Members: R. A. Abdoo, J. S. Brinzo, D. C. Cuneo, W. K. Gerber, B. Hill, R. H. Jenkins, R. S. Michael, III, S. D. Peterson, J. A. Thomson, J. L. Wainscott

Founded: 1900
Domicile: Delaware
Employees: 6,800

The McGraw-Hill Companies

Alcoa Inc.

STANDARD &POOR'S

S&P Recommendation	BUY ★★★★☆	Price	12-Mo. Target Price	Investment Style
		$12.66 (as of Nov 27, 2009)	$18.00	Large-Cap Value

GICS Sector Materials
Sub-Industry Aluminum

Summary Alcoa is one of the world's largest producers of aluminum and alumina.

Key Stock Statistics (Source S&P, Vickers, company reports)

52-Wk Range	$15.11– 4.97	S&P Oper. EPS 2009**E**	-0.78	Market Capitalization(B)	$12.336	Beta	2.07
Trailing 12-Month EPS	$-2.31	S&P Oper. EPS 2010**E**	0.88	Yield (%)	0.95	S&P 3-Yr. Proj. EPS CAGR(%)	5
Trailing 12-Month P/E	NM	P/E on S&P Oper. EPS 2009**E**	NM	Dividend Rate/Share	$0.12	S&P Credit Rating	BBB-
$10K Invested 5 Yrs Ago	$4,115	Common Shares Outstg. (M)	974.4	Institutional Ownership (%)	68		

Price Performance

30-Week Mov. Avg. ··· 10-Week Mov. Avg. - - **GAAP Earnings vs. Previous Year** Volume Above Avg. STARS
12-Mo. Target Price — Relative Strength ▲ Up ▼ Down ► No Change Below Avg. ★

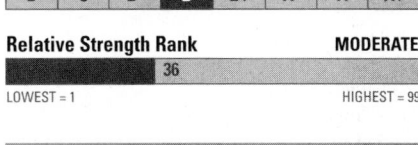

Options: ASE, CBOE, P, Ph

Analysis prepared by **Leo J. Larkin** on October 08, 2009, when the stock traded at **$ 14.33.**

Highlights

► Assuming U.S. real GDP of 1.6% for 2010, versus an estimated decline in GDP of 2.7% for 2009, and a recovery in the global economy, we look for a sales increase of 16% in 2010, versus a projected drop of 35% in 2009. In our view, a recovery in residential construction and a small gain in auto sales should boost volume in the downstream business units. S&P estimates a 10% rise in residential construction spending in 2010, versus a projected decline of 22.1% for such spending in 2009, and motor vehicle sales of 10.9 million units in 2010, versus 2009's estimated level of 10.3 million units. We look for a higher aluminum price in 2010 on increased world demand and gradually declining metal exchange inventories.

► We look for a return to operating profit from higher realized prices for aluminum, a recovery in volume, and cost cutting implemented in 2009. After interest expense and more shares outstanding, we estimate operating EPS of $0.88 in 2010, versus an estimated operating loss per share of $0.78 in 2009.

► Longer term, we think EPS will rise on improving aluminum industry fundamentals and a shift to lower-cost aluminum plants.

Investment Rationale/Risk

► We view AA as a special situation turnaround and a vehicle to benefit from an improvement in aluminum market fundamentals. In our opinion, AA's extensive cost-cutting together with increased production from new lower-cost facilities should result in a lower breakeven point. In turn, we believe that a lower cost structure will lead to a return to profitability and positive free cash flow. Our expectation for positive free cash flow assumes a large decline 2010's capital spending. Finally, we are cautiously optimistic that the production discipline demonstrated by China in 2009 will continue in the future and help boost the aluminum price. Market surpluses caused by the emergence of China as a net exporter in 2002 have been a drag on the aluminum price in recent years.

► Risks to our recommendation and target price include a decline in the price of aluminum in 2010 instead of the increase we project.

► Our 12-month target price of $18 is based on our view the stock will trade at 20.5X our 2010 estimate. On our target P/E, AA would trade at about the mid-point of its historical range of the past 10 years and at a sizable premium to its year end 2008 tangible book value.

Qualitative Risk Assessment

LOW	MEDIUM	HIGH

Our risk assessment reflects our view that AA's sales and earnings are exposed to cyclical markets, such as autos and the homebuilding sector of the construction market. We think this is offset by the company's large share in the markets it serves.

Quantitative Evaluations

S&P Quality Ranking   B

D	C	B-	B	B+	A-	A	A+

Relative Strength Rank   MODERATE

36

LOWEST = 1   HIGHEST = 99

Revenue/Earnings Data

Revenue (Million $)

	1Q	2Q	3Q	4Q	Year
2009	4,147	4,244	4,615	--	--
2008	6,998	7,245	6,970	5,688	26,901
2007	7,908	8,066	7,387	7,387	30,748
2006	7,244	7,959	7,631	7,840	30,379
2005	6,226	6,698	6,566	6,669	26,159
2004	5,588	5,971	5,878	6,041	23,478

Earnings Per Share ($)

2009	-0.59	-0.32	-0.07	E-0.04	E-0.78
2008	0.36	0.67	0.37	-1.16	0.28
2007	0.77	0.81	0.64	0.74	2.95
2006	0.70	0.86	0.62	0.29	2.47
2005	0.30	0.53	0.33	0.24	1.40
2004	0.41	0.46	0.34	0.39	1.60

Fiscal year ended Dec. 31. Next earnings report expected: Mid January. EPS Estimates based on S&P Operating Earnings; historical GAAP earnings are as reported.

Dividend Data (Dates: mm/dd Payment Date: mm/dd/yy)

Amount ($)	Date Decl.	Ex-Div. Date	Stk. of Record	Payment Date
0.170	01/23	02/04	02/06	02/25/09
0.030	03/16	05/06	05/08	05/25/09
0.030	07/24	08/05	08/07	08/25/09
0.030	09/25	11/04	11/06	11/25/09

Dividends have been paid since 1939. Source: Company reports.

Alcoa Inc.

STANDARD &POOR'S

Business Summary October 08, 2009

CORPORATE OVERVIEW. Alcoa is one of the world's largest producers of primary aluminum and is one of the world's largest supplier of alumina, an intermediate raw material used to make aluminum. In 2008, primary aluminum production totaled 4.0 million metric tons, versus 3.7 million tons in 2007; alumina production totaled 15.3 million metric tons, versus 15.1 million metric tons in 2007.

MARKET PROFILE. The primary factor affecting demand for aluminum products is economic growth, in general, and growth in demand for durable goods, in particular. The three largest end markets for aluminum in North America are transportation, containers/packaging, and construction. In 2007, these markets accounted for 64.5% of revenues in North America. In terms of primary production, the size of the world market was 25.7 million metric tons in 2008. Alcoa's market share was 15.6%. From 1999 through 2008, global consumption rose at a compound annual growth rate (CAGR) of 5.6%.

COMPETITIVE LANDSCAPE. Alcoa's direct competitors in the aluminum market are Aleris International, Inc., Aluminum Corp. of China, Century Aluminum, Kaiser Aluminum, Norsk Hydro, United Company RUSAL and Quanex. Indirect competitors include mining companies that have aluminum and alumina oper-

ations, such as Vale, BHP Billiton and Rio Tinto. Led mostly by Alcoa and Alcan (now a subsidiary of Rio Tinto), consolidation of the industry accelerated in the late 1990s and thereafter. However, the price of aluminum in the recent economic expansion lagged the gains in other base metals such as carbon steel, copper and nickel by a wide margin. In our view, the reason for the less buoyant aluminum price is that exports from China have kept the aluminum market in overall surplus.

Beginning in 2003, China became a net exporter of aluminum, and we believe that its production has become a drag on the aluminum price. Aluminum faces competition from such materials as plastics, steel, glass, and ceramics. Plastic, in the form of polyethylene terephthalate (PET), provides strong competition in the container market. Steel competes with aluminum in automotive applications. After gaining substantial share in auto applications in the 1970s and 1980s, aluminum's rate of gain in market share slowed in the 1990s and thereafter.

Company Financials Fiscal Year Ended Dec. 31

Per Share Data ($)	2008	2007	2006	2005	2004	2003	2002	2001	2000	1999
Tangible Book Value	7.61	12.75	8.53	6.96	6.72	5.36	3.27	4.96	6.19	6.62
Cash Flow	1.79	4.42	3.96	2.85	2.98	2.61	3.20	2.49	3.29	2.61
Earnings	0.28	2.95	2.47	1.40	1.60	1.20	0.58	1.05	1.81	1.41
S&P Core Earnings	-0.26	1.74	2.46	1.05	1.52	0.92	-0.17	0.17	NA	NA
Dividends	0.68	0.68	0.60	0.60	0.60	0.60	0.60	0.60	0.50	0.40
Payout Ratio	243%	23%	24%	43%	38%	50%	103%	57%	28%	29%
Prices:High	44.77	48.77	36.96	32.29	39.44	38.92	39.75	45.71	43.63	41.69
Prices:Low	6.80	28.09	26.39	22.28	28.51	18.45	17.62	27.36	23.13	17.97
P/E Ratio:High	NM	17	15	23	25	32	69	44	24	30
P/E Ratio:Low	NM	10	11	16	18	15	30	26	13	13

Income Statement Analysis (Million $)										
Revenue	26,901	30,748	30,379	26,159	23,478	21,504	20,263	22,859	22,936	16,323
Operating Income	3,505	4,779	5,410	3,398	3,397	2,885	2,663	3,523	4,304	2,821
Depreciation	1,234	1,268	1,280	1,267	1,212	1,202	2,224	1,253	1,219	901
Interest Expense	574	401	384	339	270	314	350	393	427	195
Pretax Income	792	4,491	3,432	1,933	2,204	1,669	925	1,641	2,812	1,849
Effective Tax Rate	43.2%	34.6%	24.3%	22.8%	25.3%	24.2%	31.6%	32.0%	33.5%	29.9%
Net Income	229	2,571	2,161	1,233	1,402	1,034	498	908	1,489	1,054
S&P Core Earnings	-210	1,511	2,154	924	1,334	777	-143	146	NA	NA

Balance Sheet & Other Financial Data (Million $)										
Cash	762	483	506	762	457	576	344	512	315	237
Current Assets	8,150	8,086	9,157	8,790	7,493	6,740	6,313	6,792	7,578	4,800
Total Assets	37,822	38,803	37,183	33,696	32,609	31,711	29,810	28,355	31,691	17,066
Current Liabilities	7,279	7,166	7,281	7,368	6,298	5,084	4,461	5,003	7,954	3,003
Long Term Debt	8,509	6,371	5,910	5,279	5,346	6,692	8,365	6,388	4,987	2,657
Common Equity	11,680	15,961	14,576	13,318	13,245	12,020	9,872	10,614	11,366	6,262
Total Capital	23,162	24,847	23,103	20,892	20,852	20,911	20,087	18,927	18,892	10,870
Capital Expenditures	3,438	3,636	3,201	2,124	1,142	863	1,263	1,177	1,121	920
Cash Flow	1,461	3,839	3,441	2,498	2,612	2,234	2,720	2,159	2,706	1,953
Current Ratio	1.1	1.1	1.3	1.2	1.2	1.3	1.4	1.4	1.0	1.6
% Long Term Debt of Capitalization	36.7	25.6	25.6	25.3	25.6	32.0	41.6	33.8	26.4	24.4
% Net Income of Revenue	0.9	8.3	7.1	4.7	6.0	4.8	2.5	4.0	6.5	6.5
% Return on Assets	0.6	6.7	6.1	3.7	4.4	3.4	1.7	3.0	6.1	6.1
% Return on Equity	1.7	10.2	15.5	9.3	11.1	9.4	4.9	8.2	16.9	17.2

Data as orig reptd.; bef. results of disc opers/spec. items. Per share data adj. for stk. divs.; EPS diluted. E-Estimated. NA-Not Available. NM-Not Meaningful. NR-Not Ranked. UR-Under Review.

Office: 390 Park Ave, New York, NY 10022-4608.
Telephone: 212-836-2674.
Email: investor.relations@alcoa.com
Website: http://www.alcoa.com

Chrmn, Pres & CEO: K. Kleinfeld
EVP & CFO: C.D. McLane, Jr.
EVP & CTO: M.A. Zaidi
EVP & General Counsel: N. DeRoma

Chief Acctg Officer & Cntlr: T.R. Thene
Board Members: A. J. Belda, K. S. Fuller, C. Ghosn, J. T. Gorman, J. M. Gueron, K. Kleinfeld, M. G. Morris, E. S. O'Neal, J. W. Owens, P. F. Russo, H. B. Schacht, R. N. Tata, F. A. Thomas, E. Zedillo

Founded: 1888
Domicile: Pennsylvania
Employees: 87,000

The McGraw-Hill Companies

Allegheny Energy Inc.

STANDARD &POOR'S

S&P Recommendation **BUY** ★★★★☆	Price $21.95 (as of Nov 27, 2009)	12-Mo. Target Price $28.00	Investment Style Large-Cap Blend

GICS Sector Utilities
Sub-Industry Electric Utilities

Summary This diversified energy company engages in electric generation, transmission and delivery, and invests in and develops telecommunications and energy-related projects.

Key Stock Statistics (Source S&P, Vickers, company reports)

52-Wk Range	$35.97–20.32	S&P Oper. EPS 2009**E**	2.21	Market Capitalization(B)	$3.722	Beta	0.90
Trailing 12-Month EPS	$1.76	S&P Oper. EPS 2010**E**	2.73	Yield (%)	2.73	S&P 3-Yr. Proj. EPS CAGR(%)	7
Trailing 12-Month P/E	12.5	P/E on S&P Oper. EPS 2009**E**	9.9	Dividend Rate/Share	$0.60	S&P Credit Rating	BBB-
$10K Invested 5 Yrs Ago	$11,757	Common Shares Outstg. (M)	169.6	Institutional Ownership (%)	83		

Price Performance

30-Week Mov. Avg. · · · 10-Week Mov. Avg. – – **GAAP Earnings vs. Previous Year** Volume Above Avg. STARS

12-Mo. Target Price — Relative Strength — ▲ Up ▼ Down ► No Change Below Avg.

Options: ASE, CBOE, P

Analysis prepared by **Christopher B. Muir** on November 04, 2009, when the stock traded at **$ 22.55**.

Highlights

► We see 2009 revenues falling 2.9% , hurt by unregulated operations. We expect regulated utility revenues to increase by 9.0%, benefiting from customer growth, a West Virginia rate increase and expiration of rate caps in Maryland. We look for unregulated revenues to fall due to lower realized power prices, partly offset by increased generation capacity factors, rate hikes for providers of last resort (POLR) service in Pennsylvania, and the transitioning of Virginia customers to market-based rates. In 2010, we see revenues rising 4.1%.

► We expect operating margins to rise to 25.5% in 2009 and 27.1% in 2010, from 23.7% in 2008, as a result of lower per-revenue fuel and non-fuel operating expenses. We expect pretax profit margins to widen to 18.5% in 2009 and 21.0% in 2010, from 17.5% in 2008, helped by lower interest expense, partly offset by relatively stable nonoperating income.

► We forecast 2009 operating EPS of $2.21, excluding $0.05 in net nonrecurring gains, down 3.5% from $2.29 in 2008, which excludes $0.42 in nonrecurring gains. Our 2010 EPS estimate is $2.73, a projected 24% increase.

Investment Rationale/Risk

► Operationally, we like AYE's focus on improving plant performance and controlling operational expenses. We also like the rate increases for POLR service in Pennsylvania, the ending of residential generation caps in Maryland in 2008 and the July 2008 rate increase to recover purchased power costs in Virginia. We view positively AYE's debt to total capitalization ratio of 59.6% as of September 30, 2009, versus 59.6%, 61.5%, and 63.3% at the end of 2008, 2007, and 2006, respectively.

► Risks to our recommendation and target price include lower-than-expected cash flows and a weaker-than-projected economy.

► The shares recently traded at 7.8X our 2010 EPS estimate, a 31% discount to electric utility peers. Our 12-month target price of $28 values the stock at a P/E multiple of 9.8X our 2009 EPS estimate, a 22% discount to our peer target. We see this as merited by what we view as AYE's lack of clarity surrounding its dividend policy and higher risk than peers, partly offset by a prospects for double-digit earnings growth and significant strengthening of its balance sheet.

Qualitative Risk Assessment

LOW	**MEDIUM**	HIGH

Our risk assessment reflects the company's mid-level capitalization and balanced sources of earnings, which include both low-risk regulated electric utility and higher-risk unregulated power generation operations.

Quantitative Evaluations

S&P Quality Ranking B

D	C	B-	**B**	B+	A-	A	A+

Relative Strength Rank WEAK

18

LOWEST = 1   HIGHEST = 99

Revenue/Earnings Data

Revenue (Million $)

	1Q	2Q	3Q	4Q	Year
2009	957.2	814.7	793.7	--	--
2008	875.0	953.5	849.6	707.8	3,386
2007	847.6	826.5	846.6	786.3	3,307
2006	845.6	722.2	816.6	737.0	3,121
2005	754.0	714.7	845.1	724.1	3,038
2004	735.4	608.9	723.3	688.5	2,756

Earnings Per Share ($)

2009	0.79	0.43	0.45	E0.54	E2.21
2008	0.80	0.91	0.52	0.10	2.33
2007	0.65	0.45	0.67	0.65	2.43
2006	0.68	0.19	0.65	0.37	1.89
2005	0.24	-0.04	0.26	0.02	0.47
2004	0.23	-0.26	0.37	0.53	0.99

Fiscal year ended Dec. 31. Next earnings report expected: Mid February. EPS Estimates based on S&P Operating Earnings; historical GAAP earnings are as reported.

Dividend Data (Dates: mm/dd Payment Date: mm/dd/yy)

Amount ($)	Date Decl.	Ex-Div. Date	Stk. of Record	Payment Date
0.150	02/27	03/05	03/09	03/23/09
0.150	05/21	06/04	06/08	06/22/09
0.150	07/09	09/10	09/14	09/28/09
0.150	10/15	12/10	12/14	12/28/09

Dividends have been paid since 2007. Source: Company reports.

Please read the Required Disclosures and Analyst Certification on the last page of this report.

The McGraw-Hill Companies

Allegheny Energy Inc.

STANDARD & POOR'S

Business Summary November 04, 2009

CORPORATE OVERVIEW. Allegheny Energy (AYE) is an integrated electric distribution and generation company operating in the Mid-Atlantic region. The company has two operating segments: Delivery and Services, which includes AYE's electric transmission and distribution (T&D) operations, and Generation and Marketing, which includes the company's generation and unregulated businesses.

AYE's three distribution businesses operate under the trade name Allegheny Power. West Penn operates a T&D system in southwestern, northern and south central Pennsylvania, serving approximately 713,000 customers as of December 31, 2008. Potomac Edison operates a T&D system in portions of West Virginia, Maryland and Virginia. Potomac Edison serves approximately 480,000 electric customers. Monongahela conducts a T&D business that serves roughly 381,000 electric customers in northern West Virginia. The Delivery Services segment also includes investments in transmission line projects (TrAIL and PATH) and Allegheny Ventures (includes unregulated energy-related businesses).

Allegheny Energy Supply (AE Supply), AYE's primary unregulated generating division, ended 2008 with 6,919 megawatts (MW) of capacity. The division's capacity grew from 1999 to 2001 through the transfer of regulated power

plants in Pennsylvania, Maryland, Virginia and Ohio from AYE's regulated utilities, acquisition of existing plants, and construction activities. AE Supply currently is contractually obligated to provide Potomac Edison and West Penn with the power that they need to meet a majority of their obligations, which represents a majority of AE Supply's operating capacity. In July 2005, Allegheny Energy Supply was awarded contracts to meet Allegheny Power's 2009 and 2010 generation supply needs in Pennsylvania.

Monongahela owns or controls about 2,811 MW of generating capacity, most of which is delivered to AYE's electric utilities. Additionally, AYE owns a 40% interest (or 1,084 MW) in the Bath County pumped-storage hydroelectric power station.

As of December 31, 2008, about 78.3% of AYE's 9,730 MW of owned and controlled capacity was coal-fired, 11.7% was gas-fired, 9.2% was hydroelectric, and 0.8% was oil-fired.

Company Financials Fiscal Year Ended Dec. 31

Per Share Data ($)	2008	2007	2006	2005	2004	2003	2002	2001	2000	1999
Tangible Book Value	14.66	12.97	10.36	7.98	6.94	9.05	12.05	16.48	13.80	14.97
Earnings	2.33	2.43	1.89	0.47	0.99	-2.64	-4.00	3.73	2.84	2.45
S&P Core Earnings	2.08	2.28	1.90	0.45	0.56	-2.60	-4.22	3.24	NA	NA
Dividends	0.60	0.15	Nil	Nil	Nil	Nil	1.29	1.72	1.72	1.72
Payout Ratio	26%	6%	Nil	Nil	Nil	Nil	NM	46%	61%	77%
Prices:High	64.75	65.48	46.25	32.32	20.20	13.09	43.86	55.09	48.75	35.19
Prices:Low	23.86	44.28	31.33	18.25	11.75	4.70	2.95	32.99	23.63	26.19
P/E Ratio:High	28	27	24	69	20	NM	NM	15	17	14
P/E Ratio:Low	10	18	16	39	12	NM	NM	9	8	11

Income Statement Analysis (Million $)	2008	2007	2006	2005	2004	2003	2002	2001	2000	1999
Revenue	3,386	3,307	3,121	3,038	2,756	2,472	2,988	10,379	4,012	2,808
Depreciation	274	277	273	308	299	327	309	302	248	257
Maintenance	NA	NA	NA	NA	NA	NA	NA	288	230	224
Fixed Charges Coverage	3.59	4.54	2.80	1.39	1.28	-0.35	-1.21	3.38	3.11	3.25
Construction Credits	NA	NA	NA	NA	NA	NA	13.0	11.5	7.28	6.91
Effective Tax Rate	34.0%	37.6%	35.0%	46.1%	NM	NM	NM	35.2%	37.1%	36.6%
Net Income	395	412	320	75.1	130	-334	-502	449	314	285
S&P Core Earnings	352	386	321	-72.0	61.8	-329	-530	391	NA	NA

Balance Sheet & Other Financial Data (Million $)	2008	2007	2006	2005	2004	2003	2002	2001	2000	1999
Gross Property	12,996	11,993	11,150	10,786	10,644	11,831	11,357	11,087	9,507	8,840
Capital Expenditures	994	848	447	306	266	254	403	463	402	467
Net Property	8,002	7,197	6,513	6,277	6,303	7,453	6,883	6,853	5,539	5,207
Capitalization:Long Term Debt	4,116	3,983	3,434	3,665	4,639	5,234	229	3,274	2,634	2,328
Capitalization:% Long Term Debt	59.1	61.1	62.3	58.8	77.4	77.5	10.6	54.7	60.2	57.9
Capitalization:Preferred	Nil	Nil	Nil	Nil	Nil	Nil	Nil	Nil	Nil	Nil
Capitalization:% Preferred	Nil	Nil	Nil	Nil	Nil	Nil	Nil	Nil	Nil	Nil
Capitalization:Common	2,851	2,535	2,080	1,695	1,354	1,516	1,932	2,710	1,741	1,695
Capitalization:% Common	40.9	38.9	37.7	98.6	22.6	22.5	89.4	45.3	39.8	42.1
Total Capital	8,314	7,877	6,462	6,228	6,733	7,713	3,358	7,090	5,372	5,062
% Operating Ratio	82.1	82.9	82.3	83.5	82.1	99.3	101.9	93.1	86.6	83.1
% Earned on Net Property	10.7	11.9	11.5	8.5	11.5	NM	NM	11.5	10.0	9.3
% Return on Revenue	11.7	12.5	10.2	2.5	4.7	NM	NM	4.3	7.8	10.2
% Return on Invested Capital	7.7	11.0	9.3	23.3	7.4	2.6	4.2	11.9	10.5	9.2
% Return on Common Equity	14.7	17.9	16.9	-4.9	9.0	NM	NM	20.2	18.3	15.3

Data as orig reptd.; bef. results of disc opers/spec. items. Per share data adj. for stk. divs.; EPS diluted. E-Estimated. NA-Not Available. NM-Not Meaningful. NR-Not Ranked. UR-Under Review.

Office: 800 Cabin Hill Dr, Greensburg, PA 15601-1689.
Telephone: 724-837-3000.
Email: investorinfo@alleghenypower.com
Website: http://www.alleghenyenergy.com

Chrmn, Pres & CEO: P.J. Evanson
SVP & CFO: K.R. Oliver
Chief Admin Officer: P.E. Slobodian
Chief Acctg Officer & Cntlr: W.F. Wahl, III

Treas: B.E. Pakenham
Investor Contact: M. Kuniansky (724-838-6895)
Board Members: H. F. Baldwin, E. Baum, P. J. Evanson, C. F. Freidheim, Jr., J. L. Johnson, T. J. Kleisner, C. D. Pappas, S. H. Rice, G. E. Sarsten, M. H. Sutton

Founded: 1925
Domicile: Maryland
Employees: 4,455

The McGraw-Hill Companies

Allegheny Technologies Inc

STANDARD
&POOR'S

S&P Recommendation **HOLD** ★★★☆☆	Price $34.19 (as of Nov 27, 2009)	12-Mo. Target Price $32.00	Investment Style Large-Cap Blend

GICS Sector Materials
Sub-Industry Steel

Summary This company is a leading producer of specialty metals for a wide variety of end markets.

Key Stock Statistics (Source S&P, Vickers, company reports)

52-Wk Range	$44.09– 16.92	S&P Oper. EPS 2009**E**	0.09	Market Capitalization(B)	$3.353	Beta	1.89
Trailing 12-Month EPS	$1.08	S&P Oper. EPS 2010**E**	1.59	Yield (%)	2.11	S&P 3-Yr. Proj. EPS CAGR(%)	-18
Trailing 12-Month P/E	31.7	P/E on S&P Oper. EPS 2009**E**	NM	Dividend Rate/Share	$0.72	S&P Credit Rating	BBB-
$10K Invested 5 Yrs Ago	$15,827	Common Shares Outstg. (M)	98.1	Institutional Ownership (%)	74		

Price Performance

30-Week Mov. Avg. · · · 10-Week Mov. Avg. — — **GAAP Earnings vs. Previous Year** Volume Above Avg. ⅠⅠⅠⅠ STARS

12-Mo. Target Price — Relative Strength ▲ Up ▼ Down ► No Change Below Avg. ⅠⅠⅠⅠ ★

Options: ASE, CBOE, P, Ph

Analysis prepared by **Leo J. Larkin** on October 29, 2009, when the stock traded at **$ 31.47**.

Highlights

▶ We project a 24% sales gain in 2010 following an estimated sales decrease of 44% in 2009. Our estimate reflects several assumptions. First, S&P estimates 1.8% U.S. GDP growth in 2010, versus an estimated decline in GDP of 2.7% in 2009. In our view, this will lead to a rebound in demand for durable goods and help boost shipments and prices for stainless steel. Second, after keeping their stainless inventories low in 2009, we think distributors will restock in 2010. Third, we think the impact on aerospace demand of the Boeing strike and the delay of the Boeing 787 will be less of a drag on sales of high performance metals than in 2009.

▶ We look for a rebound in operating profit on improved volume and firmer pricing along with lower pension and other post-retirement expenses. After interest expense and taxes, we project EPS of $1.59 in 2010, versus estimated operating EPS of $0.09 in 2009, which excludes unusual expense of $0.17 in the second quarter.

▶ We think that consolidation in the stainless steel industry, along with a recovery in aerospace and other capital goods markets, will boost ATI's long-term earnings.

Investment Rationale/Risk

▶ We see ATI's EPS rising on consolidation in the stainless steel industry. We believe the concentration of stainless steel production in fewer hands will lead to better industry pricing discipline and result in less volatile sales and profits over the business cycle. We note that despite one of the steepest declines in demand on record, ATI's stainless operations were profitable in 2009. Also, we see ATI's long-term EPS rising on a recovery and secular growth in the aerospace industry and other capital goods markets such as oil and gas, mining, and electrical power generation. However, with ATI recently trading with just modest upside potential to our target price, we would not add to positions.

▶ Risks to our recommendation and target price include the possibility that prices for stainless steel and high performance metals will decline in 2010 instead of increasing as we project.

▶ Applying a multiple of 20X to our 2010 EPS estimate, toward the high end of ATI's range of the past 10 years, our 12-month target price for these volatile shares is $32. On this projected multiple, ATI would trade at a discount to the P/E we apply to specialty metals peers.

Qualitative Risk Assessment

LOW	**MEDIUM**	HIGH

Our risk assessment reflects ATI's exposure to cyclical markets such as aerospace and chemical processing, along with volatile raw material costs. Offsetting these factors are the company's solid shares of the markets it serves and its moderate balance sheet leverage.

Quantitative Evaluations

S&P Quality Ranking   B

D	C	B	**B**	B+	A-	A	A+

Relative Strength Rank   MODERATE

64

LOWEST = 1   HIGHEST = 99

Revenue/Earnings Data

Revenue (Million $)

	1Q	2Q	3Q	4Q	Year
2009	831.6	710.0	697.6	--	--
2008	1,343	1,461	1,392	1,113	5,310
2007	1,373	1,471	1,335	1,274	5,453
2006	1,041	1,211	1,288	1,397	4,937
2005	879.6	904.2	861.7	894.4	3,540
2004	577.8	646.5	730.6	778.1	2,733

Earnings Per Share ($)

2009	0.06	-0.14	0.01	E-0.01	E0.09
2008	1.40	1.66	1.45	1.15	5.67
2007	1.92	2.00	1.88	1.45	7.26
2006	1.00	1.37	1.58	1.63	5.59
2005	0.61	0.91	0.87	1.19	3.59
2004	-0.63	0.31	0.09	0.35	0.22

Fiscal year ended Dec. 31. Next earnings report expected: Late January. EPS Estimates based on S&P Operating Earnings; historical GAAP earnings are as reported.

Dividend Data (Dates: mm/dd Payment Date: mm/dd/yy)

Amount ($)	Date Decl.	Ex-Div. Date	Stk. of Record	Payment Date
0.180	12/11	12/17	12/19	12/26/08
0.180	02/19	03/10	03/12	03/27/09
0.180	05/07	05/26	05/28	06/18/09
0.180	09/10	09/17	09/21	09/29/09

Dividends have been paid since 1996. Source: Company reports.

Allegheny Technologies Inc

Business Summary October 29, 2009

In November 1999, Allegheny Technologies spun off all of the common stock of Teledyne Technologies Inc. (NYSE: TDY) and Water Pik Technologies, Inc. to ATI stockholders, and changed its name from Allegheny Teledyne Inc.

Following the spin-offs, ATI operates in three segments: Flat-Rolled Products, High Performance Metals, and Engineered Products. Markets for the three units include aerospace, oil and gas, transportation, food, chemical processing, consumer products, medical, and power generation.

The Flat-Rolled Products segment (55% of 2008 sales; 40% of operating profits) consists of Allegheny Ludlum Corp., Rodney Metals, the Allegheny Rodney Strip division of Allegheny Ludlum, and the company's interest in a Chinese joint venture, Shanghai STAL Precision Stainless Steel Ltd. The companies in this segment produce, convert and distribute stainless steel sheet, strip and plate, precision rolled strip products, flat-rolled nickel-based alloys and titanium, silicon electrical steels and tool steels.

Shipments totaled 542,382 tons in 2008, versus 524,454 tons in 2007. The average realized price per ton was $5,364 in 2008, versus $5,629 in 2007. Operating profits totaled $377.4 million in 2008, versus $505.2 million in 2007.

Competitors in flat-rolled stainless include AK Steel Holding and North American Stainless.

The High Performance Metals segment (36%; 58%) consists of Allvac, Allvac Ltd., Oremet-Wah Chang, Titanium Industries, and Rome Metals. These companies produce, convert and distribute nickel- and cobalt-based alloys and superalloys, titanium and titanium-based alloys, zirconium and zirconium chemicals, hafnium and niobium, tantalum and other special metals, primarily in long-product form. The unit's titanium products are sold mostly to aircraft and jet engine manufacturers.

Shipments of titanium mill products totaled 32,530 lbs. in 2008, versus 30,689 lbs. in 2007; shipments of nickel-based alloys were 42,525 lbs. in 2008, versus 44,688 lbs. in 2007; shipments of exotic alloys totaled 5,473 lbs. in 2008, versus 5,169 lbs. in 2007. Operating profits totaled $539 million in 2008, versus $729.1 million in 2007.

Competitors in high performance and exotic metals include Titanium Metals Corp., RTI International Metals, Verkhnaya Salda Metallurgical Production Organization and UNITI and certain Japanese producers in the industrial and emerging markets.

Company Financials Fiscal Year Ended Dec. 31

Per Share Data ($)	2008	2007	2006	2005	2004	2003	2002	2001	2000	1999
Tangible Book Value	18.19	19.82	12.71	6.11	2.30	NM	3.15	9.42	10.51	11.02
Cash Flow	6.71	8.26	6.48	4.47	1.00	-2.96	0.30	0.91	2.80	2.15
Earnings	5.67	7.26	5.59	3.59	0.22	-3.87	-0.82	-0.31	1.60	1.16
S&P Core Earnings	4.42	7.12	5.92	3.76	0.26	-3.19	-2.17	-2.09	NA	NA
Dividends	0.72	0.57	0.43	0.28	0.24	0.24	0.66	0.80	0.80	1.28
Payout Ratio	13%	8%	8%	8%	109%	NM	NM	NM	50%	110%
Prices:High	87.32	119.70	98.72	36.66	23.48	14.00	19.10	21.07	26.81	48.37
Prices:Low	15.00	80.00	35.47	17.30	8.64	2.10	5.21	12.50	12.50	20.25
P/E Ratio:High	15	16	18	10	NM	NM	NM	NM	17	42
P/E Ratio:Low	3	11	6	5	NM	NM	NM	NM	8	17

Income Statement Analysis (Million $)	2008	2007	2006	2005	2004	2003	2002	2001	2000	1999
Revenue	5,310	5,453	4,937	3,540	2,733	1,937	1,908	2,128	2,460	2,296
Operating Income	973	1,256	970	452	87.7	-110	65.0	166	358	284
Depreciation	104	103	84.2	77.3	76.1	74.6	90.0	98.6	99.7	95.3
Interest Expense	38.3	4.80	23.3	38.6	35.5	27.7	34.3	29.3	34.4	25.9
Pretax Income	860	1,147	869	307	19.8	-280	-104	-36.4	209	174
Effective Tax Rate	34.2%	34.9%	34.2%	NM	NM	NM	NM	NM	36.5%	36.3%
Net Income	566	747	572	362	19.8	-313	-65.8	-25.2	133	111
S&P Core Earnings	441	733	605	378	23.3	-258	-176	-168	NA	NA

Balance Sheet & Other Financial Data (Million $)	2008	2007	2006	2005	2004	2003	2002	2001	2000	1999
Cash	470	623	502	363	251	79.6	59.4	33.7	26.2	50.7
Current Assets	1,929	2,249	1,988	1,484	1,160	743	812	926	1,023	1,034
Total Assets	4,170	4,096	3,282	2,732	2,316	1,885	2,093	2,643	2,776	2,751
Current Liabilities	694	704	646	561	493	395	342	333	414	540
Long Term Debt	495	507	530	547	553	504	509	573	491	200
Common Equity	1,961	2,224	1,493	800	426	175	449	945	1,039	1,200
Total Capital	2,524	2,731	2,023	1,347	979	679	958	1,671	1,689	1,401
Capital Expenditures	516	447	235	90.1	49.9	74.4	48.7	104	60.2	74.1
Cash Flow	670	850	656	439	95.9	-239	24.2	73.4	232	206
Current Ratio	2.8	3.2	3.1	2.6	2.4	1.9	2.4	2.8	2.5	1.9
% Long Term Debt of Capitalization	19.6	18.6	26.2	40.6	56.5	74.3	53.2	34.3	29.1	14.3
% Net Income of Revenue	10.7	13.7	11.6	10.2	0.7	NM	NM	NM	5.4	4.8
% Return on Assets	13.7	20.3	19.0	14.3	0.9	NM	NM	NM	4.8	3.9
% Return on Equity	27.1	40.2	49.9	59.0	6.6	NM	NM	NM	11.8	8.7

Data as orig reptd.; bef. results of disc opers/spec. items. Per share data adj. for stk. divs.; EPS diluted. E-Estimated. NA-Not Available. NM-Not Meaningful. NR-Not Ranked. UR-Under Review.

Office: 1000 Six PPG Pl, Pittsburgh, PA 15222-5479.
Telephone: 412-394-2800.
Website: http://www.alleghenytechnologies.com
Chrmn, Pres & CEO: L.P. Hassey

EVP & CFO: R.J. Harshman
EVP, Secy & General Counsel: J.D. Walton
Chief Acctg Officer, Treas & Cntlr: D.G. Reid
Investor Contact: D.L. Greenfield (412-394-3004)

Board Members: D. C. Creel, J. C. Diggs, J. B. Harvey, L. P. Hassey, B. S. Jeremiah, M. J. Joyce, J. E. Rohr, L. J. Thomas, J. D. Turner

Founded: 1960
Domicile: Delaware
Employees: 9,600

Allergan Inc.

**STANDARD
&POOR'S**

S&P Recommendation	HOLD ★★★☆☆	Price $58.29 (as of Nov 27, 2009)	12-Mo. Target Price $65.00	Investment Style Large-Cap Growth

GICS Sector Health Care
Sub-Industry Pharmaceuticals

Summary This technology-driven global health care company develops and commercializes products in the eye care, neuromodulator, skin care and other specialty markets.

Key Stock Statistics (Source S&P, Vickers, company reports)

52-Wk Range	$60.85– 32.17	S&P Oper. EPS 2009**E**	2.77	Market Capitalization(B)	$17.717	Beta	0.98
Trailing 12-Month EPS	$1.84	S&P Oper. EPS 2010**E**	3.20	Yield (%)	0.34	S&P 3-Yr. Proj. EPS CAGR(%)	11
Trailing 12-Month P/E	31.7	P/E on S&P Oper. EPS 2009**E**	21.0	Dividend Rate/Share	$0.20	S&P Credit Rating	A
$10K Invested 5 Yrs Ago	$15,048	Common Shares Outstg. (M)	303.9	Institutional Ownership (%)	91		

Price Performance

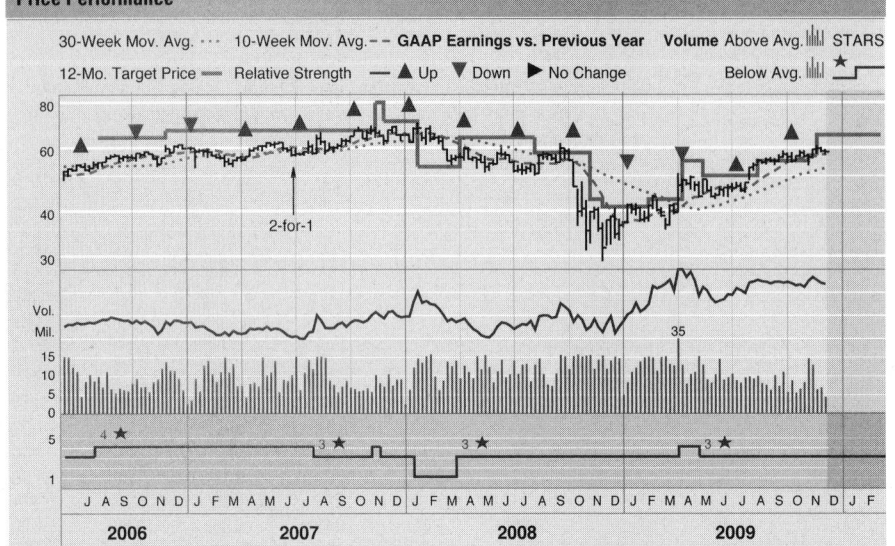

30-Week Mov. Avg. · · · 10-Week Mov. Avg. – – **GAAP Earnings vs. Previous Year** Volume Above Avg. STARS
12-Mo. Target Price — Relative Strength ▲ Up ▼ Down ► No Change Below Avg. ★

Options: ASE, CBOE, Ph

Analysis prepared by **Herman B. Saftlas** on November 11, 2009, when the stock traded at **$ 59.96**.

Highlights

► We see revenues rising 10% in 2010, from the $4.4 billion indicated for 2009, helped by improved volume and more favorable foreign exchange. Botox sales should climb about 15% on likely firmer trends in consumer spending, stepped up advertising, and new indications for migraine and spasticity (subject to FDA approval). We expect growth in eye care pharmaceuticals, with projected gains for Lumigan, Restasis and recently launched Ozurdex more than offsetting generic erosion in the Alphagan line. We also project growth for skin care and breast aesthetic products.

► We expect 2010 gross margins to be slightly higher than the 83.2% that we forecast for 2009, helped by higher volume and manufacturing efficiencies. We look for the SG&A cost ratio to decrease but for the R&D cost ratio to rise on increased spending on new products. Interest income, however, should be higher.

► After an estimated 2010 tax rate similar to the 28.5% that we see for 2009, we project operating EPS of $3.20 for 2010, up from $2.77 indicated for 2009, before goodwill amortization.

Investment Rationale/Risk

► We view Allergan as well positioned in ophthalmic drugs and aesthetics products markets. Although the soft economy is likely to continue to affect certain lines, we see growth accelerating in 2010, helped by projected firming economic trends and new products. Despite competition from Dysport, we project Botox sales rebounding to over $1.3 billion in 2010, lifted by the launch of Botox for cosmetic uses in Japan. AGN also plans new spasticity and migraine indications for Botox, subject to FDA approval. Other new products that we expect to drive growth include Ozurdex for macular edema and Latisse for eyelash thickening.

► Risks to our recommendation and target price include a prolonged economic slump, greater-than-expected competitive pressures, and pipeline setbacks.

► Our 12-month target price of $65 applies an above-peers P/E of 20.3X to our $3.20 EPS estimate for 2010. We believe this premium multiple is reasonable, given our view of above-average growth prospects for key aesthetic and eye care pharmaceutical franchises, and good cost management.

Qualitative Risk Assessment

LOW	MEDIUM	HIGH

Our risk assessment reflects AGN's increased diversification of aesthetic products and markets via the acquisition of Inamed, our view of its strong focus on R&D, its leading market position in several ophthalmic drugs, and continued strong demand for Botox. However, we view the eye care and aesthetics markets as competitive, with the latter affected by the economic environment. We also note that certain pipeline products may not be successful.

Quantitative Evaluations

S&P Quality Ranking B

D	C	B-	B	B+	A-	A	A+

Relative Strength Rank MODERATE

64

LOWEST = 1   HIGHEST = 99

Revenue/Earnings Data

Revenue (Million $)

	1Q	2Q	3Q	4Q	Year
2009	1,007	1,131	1,141	--	--
2008	1,077	1,172	1,098	1,057	4,403
2007	886.5	988.1	993.7	1,091	3,939
2006	625.7	801.7	806.8	829.1	3,063
2005	527.2	591.0	606.1	594.9	2,319
2004	472.4	506.2	510.8	556.2	2,046

Earnings Per Share ($)

2009	0.15	0.58	0.59	E0.77	E2.77
2008	0.36	0.48	0.55	0.50	2.57
2007	0.14	0.45	0.50	0.52	1.62
2006	-1.65	0.25	0.35	0.45	-0.44
2005	0.30	0.13	0.56	0.52	1.51
2004	0.31	0.35	0.35	0.43	1.41

Fiscal year ended Dec. 31. Next earnings report expected: Early February. EPS Estimates based on S&P Operating Earnings; historical GAAP earnings are as reported.

Dividend Data (Dates: mm/dd Payment Date: mm/dd/yy)

Amount ($)	Date Decl.	Ex-Div. Date	Stk. of Record	Payment Date
0.050	02/04	02/18	02/20	03/13/09
0.050	05/01	05/14	05/18	06/08/09
0.050	07/31	08/13	08/17	09/07/09
0.050	10/22	11/05	11/09	11/30/09

Dividends have been paid since 1989. Source: Company reports.

Please read the Required Disclosures and Analyst Certification on the last page of this report.

Allergan Inc.

STANDARD
&POOR'S

Business Summary November 11, 2009

CORPORATE OVERVIEW. Allergan is a leading producer of ophthalmic, neuro-muscular and skin care pharmaceuticals, and, with its March 2006 acquisition of Inamed Corp., aesthetic products. Eye care drugs accounted for 46.3% of 2008 sales from continuing operations, Botox/neuromodulators 30.2%, skin care treatments 2.6%, urologics 1.6%, breast implants 7.1%, devices for obesity treatment 6.8%, and dermal fillers 5.3%. Over 35% of 2008 sales were derived from foreign markets.

Eye care drugs include prescription and nonprescription products to treat eye diseases and disorders, including glaucoma, inflammation, infection, allergy, and dry eye. Important products are Alphagan, Alphagan P, and Combigan (sales of $398 million in 2008, versus $341 million in 2007), Lumigan ($426 million versus $392 million) treatments, which are used to lower eye pressure in patients with open-angle glaucoma or ocular hypertension, and Restasis ($444 million, versus $345 million), for dry eye disease. Other eye care products include Acular, Alocril and Elestat, for seasonal allergic conjunctivitis; and Zymar and Ocuflox, for bacterial conjunctivitis.

Originally used for ophthalmic movement disorders, AGN believes that Botox (botulinum toxin type A) is the widely accepted treatment for neuromuscular

disorders and related pain. More recently, Botox garnered a rapidly growing market as a facial cosmetic agent. In April 2002, the FDA approved the injectable drug for removing brow furrows and other facial wrinkles. About 52% of Botox sales in 2006 (57% in 2005) were for therapeutic indications, with cosmetic uses comprising the balance. Botox is being studied for treating excessive sweating, post-stroke spasticity, back spasms, and migraines.

Skin care products include Zorac/Tazorac receptor-selective retinoids for acne and psoriasis; Prevage for fine lines and wrinkles; and Avage for facial fine wrinkling and blotchy skin discoloration.

Aesthetic products include breast implants for aesthetic augmentation and reconstructive surgery following mastectomy, a range of dermal products to correct facial wrinkles, and the Lap-Band and Intragastric Balloon (BIB) systems for obesity treatment.

Company Financials Fiscal Year Ended Dec. 31

Per Share Data ($)	2008	2007	2006	2005	2004	2003	2002	2001	2000	1999
Tangible Book Value	1.48	0.72	0.88	5.34	3.99	2.47	3.02	3.24	2.82	1.87
Cash Flow	2.75	2.32	0.08	1.82	1.69	0.03	0.42	1.19	1.09	0.97
Earnings	2.57	1.62	-0.44	1.51	1.41	-0.20	0.25	0.85	0.81	0.70
S&P Core Earnings	1.85	1.64	-0.42	1.36	1.26	-0.33	0.45	0.70	NA	NA
Dividends	0.20	0.20	0.20	0.20	0.18	0.18	0.18	0.18	0.16	0.14
Payout Ratio	8%	12%	NM	13%	13%	NM	73%	21%	20%	20%
Prices:High	70.40	69.15	61.51	55.25	46.31	40.90	37.55	49.69	50.56	28.91
Prices:Low	28.95	52.50	46.29	34.51	33.39	35.83	24.53	29.50	22.25	15.84
P/E Ratio:High	27	43	NM	37	33	NM	NM	59	63	42
P/E Ratio:Low	11	32	NM	23	24	NM	NM	35	28	23

Income Statement Analysis (Million $)										
Revenue	4,403	3,939	3,063	2,319	2,046	1,771	1,425	1,746	1,626	1,452
Operating Income	1,170	1,060	854	694	603	39.1	349	404	372	326
Depreciation	264	215	152	78.9	68.3	59.6	45.0	85.5	77.7	73.8
Interest Expense	62.0	72.7	60.2	12.4	18.1	15.6	17.4	21.4	19.8	15.1
Pretax Income	1,080	688	-19.5	599	532	-29.5	89.8	336	304	269
Effective Tax Rate	27.0%	27.1%	NM	32.1%	28.9%	NM	28.0%	32.4%	29.0%	30.0%
Net Income	786	501	-127	404	377	-52.5	64.0	227	215	188
S&P Core Earnings	567	507	-123	363	339	-87.3	118	187	NA	NA

Balance Sheet & Other Financial Data (Million $)										
Cash	1,110	1,158	1,369	1,296	895	508	774	782	774	163
Current Assets	2,271	2,124	2,130	1,826	1,376	928	1,200	1,325	1,326	698
Total Assets	6,791	6,579	5,767	2,851	2,257	1,755	1,807	2,046	1,971	1,339
Current Liabilities	697	716	658	1,044	460	383	404	490	433	420
Long Term Debt	1,635	1,630	1,606	57.5	570	573	526	521	585	209
Common Equity	4,010	3,739	3,143	1,567	1,116	719	808	977	874	634
Total Capital	5,652	5,551	4,836	1,626	1,689	1,294	1,337	1,499	1,459	843
Capital Expenditures	190	142	131	78.5	96.4	110	78.8	89.9	66.9	63.3
Cash Flow	843	716	25.0	483	445	7.10	109	312	293	262
Current Ratio	3.3	3.0	3.2	1.7	3.0	2.4	3.0	2.7	3.1	1.7
% Long Term Debt of Capitalization	28.9	29.8	33.2	3.5	33.8	44.3	39.4	34.7	40.1	24.8
% Net Income of Revenue	17.9	12.7	NM	17.4	18.4	NM	4.5	13.0	13.2	13.0
% Return on Assets	11.8	8.1	NM	15.8	18.8	NM	3.3	11.3	13.0	14.1
% Return on Equity	20.3	14.6	NM	30.1	41.1	NM	7.2	24.5	28.5	28.3

Data as orig reptd.; bef. results of disc opers/spec. items. Per share data adj. for stk. divs.; EPS diluted. E-Estimated. NA-Not Available. NM-Not Meaningful. NR-Not Ranked. UR-Under Review.

Office: 2525 Dupont Drive, Irvine, CA 92612.
Telephone: 714-246-4500.
Email: corpinfo@allergan.com
Website: http://www.alergan.com

Chrmn & CEO: D.E. Pyott
Pres: M. Ball
Vice Chrmn: H.W. Boyer
EVP, Chief Admin Officer, Secy & General Counsel: D.S. Ingram

SVP, Chief Acctg Officer & Cntlr: J.F. Barlow
Investor Contact: J. Hindman (714-246-4636)
Board Members: H. W. Boyer, D. Dunsire, M. R. Gallagher, G. S. Herbert, D. Hudson, R. A. Ingram, T. M. Jones, L. J. Lavigne, Jr., D. E. Pyott, R. T. Ray, S. J. Ryan, L. D. Schaeffer

Founded: 1948
Domicile: Delaware
Employees: 8,740

Allstate Corp (The)

STANDARD &POOR'S

S&P Recommendation	HOLD ★★★☆☆	Price	12-Mo. Target Price	Investment Style
		$28.27 (as of Nov 27, 2009)	$30.00	Large-Cap Blend

GICS Sector Financials
Sub-Industry Property & Casualty Insurance

Summary Allstate, the second largest U.S. personal lines property-casualty insurer, also offers an array of life insurance and retirement savings products.

Key Stock Statistics (Source S&P, Vickers, company reports)

52-Wk Range	$33.50– 13.77	S&P Oper. EPS 2009E	3.29	Market Capitalization(B)	$15.166	Beta	1.70
Trailing 12-Month EPS	$-1.48	S&P Oper. EPS 2010E	4.35	Yield (%)	2.83	S&P 3-Yr. Proj. EPS CAGR(%)	2
Trailing 12-Month P/E	NM	P/E on S&P Oper. EPS 2009E	8.6	Dividend Rate/Share	$0.80	S&P Credit Rating	A-
$10K Invested 5 Yrs Ago	$6,446	Common Shares Outstg. (M)	536.5	Institutional Ownership (%)	71		

Price Performance

30-Week Mov. Avg. · · · 10-Week Mov. Avg. – – GAAP Earnings vs. Previous Year Volume Above Avg. STARS
12-Mo. Target Price — Relative Strength — ▲ Up ▼ Down ► No Change Below Avg.

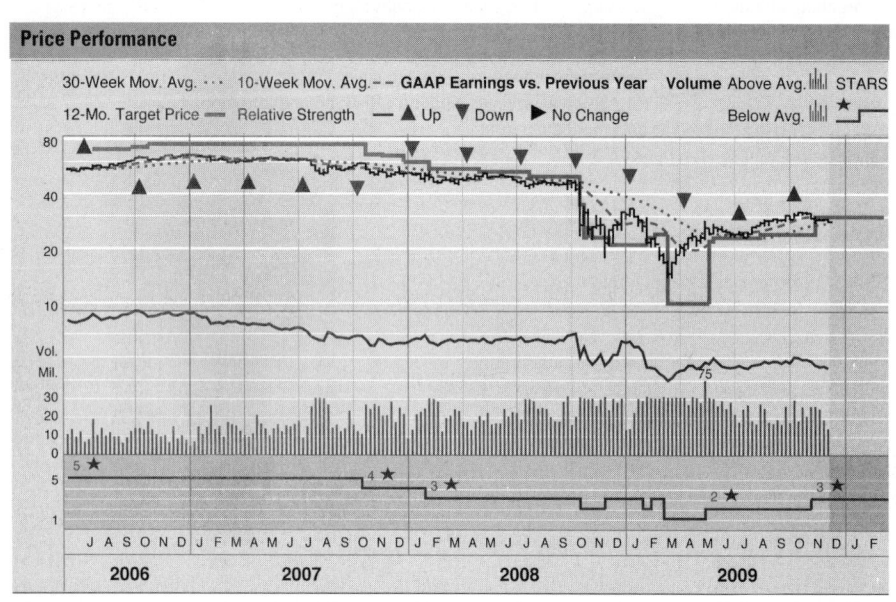

Options: ASE, CBOE, P, Ph

Analysis prepared by **Cathy A. Seifert** on November 11, 2009, when the stock traded at **$ 29.28**.

Qualitative Risk Assessment

LOW	MEDIUM	HIGH

Our risk assessment reflects our view of ALL's potential exposure to an outsized level of claims from catastrophes, partly offset by ALL's geographically diversified base of business. We also remain concerned about the level of illiquid assets in its investment portfolio.

Quantitative Evaluations

S&P Quality Ranking   B

D	C	B-	B	B+	A-	A	A+

Relative Strength Rank   MODERATE

33

LOWEST = 1   HIGHEST = 99

Revenue/Earnings Data

Revenue (Million $)

	1Q	2Q	3Q	4Q	Year
2009	7,883	8,490	7,582	--	--
2008	8,087	7,418	7,320	6,569	29,394
2007	9,331	9,455	8,992	8,991	36,769
2006	9,081	8,875	8,738	9,102	35,796
2005	8,705	8,791	8,942	8,945	35,383
2004	8,311	8,304	8,442	8,879	33,936

Earnings Per Share ($)

2009	-0.51	0.72	0.41	E0.91	E3.29
2008	0.62	0.05	-1.71	-2.11	-3.07
2007	2.41	2.30	1.70	1.36	7.77
2006	2.19	1.89	1.83	1.93	7.84
2005	1.64	1.71	-2.36	1.59	2.64
2004	1.59	1.47	0.09	1.64	4.79

Fiscal year ended Dec. 31. Next earnings report expected: Late January. EPS Estimates based on S&P Operating Earnings; historical GAAP earnings are as reported.

Highlights

► We expect operating revenues to decline 3% to 5% in 2009, reflecting our forecast of flat to lower property-casualty earned premiums, very little growth in financial services revenues, and a 15% to 17% decrease in net investment income. For 2010, we anticipate a modest 3% to 5% rise in operating revenues amid fractionally higher earned premiums and a recovery in investment income.

► We expect underwriting results to remain modestly profitable this year, although we see margins contracting amid an ongoing deterioration in claim trends in a number of core lines. Catastrophe losses of $1.7 billion in the first nine months of 2009, versus $3.1 billion in the 2008 interim, led to a combined ratio of 97.2%, versus 100.4%. The combined ratio excluding catastrophes was 88.4% in the 2009 interim, versus 85.2% in the 2008 period.

► We estimate operating EPS of $3.29 in 2009 and $4.35 in 2010, versus $3.22 in 2008. Our operating EPS estimates assume a "normal" level of catastrophe losses and no significant reserve increases or asset write-downs.

Investment Rationale/Risk

► Our hold recommendation reflects our view that the shares are fairly valued versus peers, based on a ratio of price-to-tangible capital, which excludes goodwill and deferred acquisition costs. Under this framework, the shares trade at more than 1.6X September 30, 2009 tangible capital, against an average of some 1.3X for most property-casualty peers. We also believe that ALL's invested asset mix is less liquid than many of its peers in our coverage universe. At September 30, 2009, 18.7% (or $17.8 billion) of ALL's $96.2 billion of invested assets were classified as "level 3" under FAS fair value accounting rule 157. Level 3 assets are deemed the be the least liquid of a company's assets.

► Risks to our opinion and target price include a greater than anticipated erosion in underwriting and investment results and a greater than expected deterioration in the credit quality and liquidity of ALL's investment portfolio.

► Our 12-month target price of $30 assumes that the shares will trade at about 9.1X our estimate of 2009 operating earnings per share and at about 6.9X estimated 2010 operating earnings per share. These multiples represent a discount to those of ALL's closest peers.

Dividend Data (Dates: mm/dd Payment Date: mm/dd/yy)

Amount ($)	Date Decl.	Ex-Div. Date	Stk. of Record	Payment Date
0.200	02/24	03/11	03/13	04/01/09
0.200	05/19	05/27	05/29	07/01/09
0.200	07/21	08/27	08/31	10/01/09
0.200	11/10	11/25	11/30	01/05/10

Dividends have been paid since 1993. Source: Company reports.

Allstate Corp (The)

STANDARD &POOR'S

Business Summary November 11, 2009

CORPORATE OVERVIEW. Established in 1931 by Sears, Roebuck & Co., Allstate is the second largest U.S. personal lines property-casualty insurer (based on earned premiums), and the 12th largest life insurer (based on life insurance in force). It writes business mainly through 14,900 exclusive agencies. ALL has also implemented a multi-access distribution model designed to allow customers to purchase company products through agents, over the Internet, via telephone, and through The Good Hands Network. ALL became an independent company in June 1995, when Sears, Roebuck & Co. spun off its 80% interest in the company.

The company's primary business is the sale of private passenger automobile and homeowners insurance, and it maintains national market shares of 11% to 12% in each of these lines. ALL is licensed to write policies in all 50 states, the District of Columbia, Puerto Rico, and Canada. In 2008, property-liability net written premiums equaled $26.6 billion, down from $27.2 billion in 2007. Earned premiums totaled just under $27 billion in 2008, down from $27.2 billion in 2007. Of the 2008 total, standard automobile policies accounted for 63%, non-standard automobile policies 4%, homeowners' coverage 23%, and other (which includes commercial lines and other personal lines) for the remaining

10%. Underwriting results in 2008 deteriorated from the unusually favorable (in our view) results in 2007, reflecting a higher level of catastrophe losses and an erosion in underlying claim trends. As a result, pretax underwriting profits plunged 94% in 2008, to $164 million, from $2.8 billion in 2007. The combined loss and expense ratio deteriorated to 99.4% in 2008, from 89.8% in 2007.

Allstate Financial (formerly Allstate Life) offers an array of life insurance, annuity, savings and investment and pension products through Allstate agents, financial institutions, independent agents and brokers, and direct marketing. Total premiums and deposits increased nearly 15% in 2008, to $11.0 billion, from $9.6 billion in 2007. Of the 2007 total (latest available), interest-sensitive life insurance products accounted for 15%, traditional and other life insurance for 8%, fixed deferred annuities 28%, indexed annuities 6%, fixed immediate annuities 6%, institutional products 31%, and bank deposits 6%.

Company Financials Fiscal Year Ended Dec. 31

Per Share Data ($)	2008	2007	2006	2005	2004	2003	2002	2001	2000	1999
Tangible Book Value	21.66	37.35	33.80	29.97	30.74	27.89	23.52	22.35	22.26	21.09
Operating Earnings	NA	NA	NA	NA	NA	3.77	2.94	2.06	2.68	2.59
Earnings	-3.07	7.77	7.84	2.64	4.79	3.85	1.13	1.61	2.95	3.38
S&P Core Earnings	2.78	6.56	7.91	2.21	4.33	3.82	2.64	1.66	NA	NA
Dividends	1.64	1.52	1.40	1.28	1.12	0.92	0.84	0.76	0.68	0.58
Relative Payout	NM	20%	18%	48%	23%	24%	74%	47%	23%	17%
Prices:High	52.90	65.85	66.14	63.22	51.99	43.27	41.95	45.90	44.75	41.00
Prices:Low	17.72	48.90	50.22	49.66	42.55	30.05	31.03	30.00	17.19	22.88
P/E Ratio:High	NM	8	8	24	11	11	37	29	15	12
P/E Ratio:Low	NM	6	6	19	9	8	27	19	6	7

Income Statement Analysis (Million $)										
Life Insurance in Force	NA	NA	NA	NA	NA	409,068	396,943	387,039	367,914	334,895
Premium Income:Life A & H	26,967	27,233	27,369	27,039	25,989	24,677	23,361	2,230	2,205	1,623
Premium Income:Casualty/Property.	1,895	1,866	1,964	2,049	2,072	2,304	2,293	22,197	21,871	20,112
Net Investment Income	5,622	6,435	6,177	5,746	5,284	4,972	4,854	4,796	4,633	4,112
Total Revenue	29,394	36,769	35,796	35,383	33,936	32,149	29,579	28,865	29,134	26,959
Pretax Income	-3,025	6,653	7,178	2,088	4,586	3,566	868	1,240	3,006	3,868
Net Operating Income	NA	NA	NA	NA	NA	2,662	2,075	1,492	2,004	2,082
Net Income	-1,679	4,636	4,993	1,765	3,356	2,720	803	1,167	2,211	2,720
S&P Core Earnings	1,514	3,915	5,040	1,487	3,028	2,692	1,879	1,201	NA	NA

Balance Sheet & Other Financial Data (Million $)										
Cash & Equivalent	1,299	6,113	4,935	1,387	1,428	1,434	1,408	1,146	1,164	1,066
Premiums Due	4,842	4,879	4,789	4,739	4,721	4,386	6,958	6,674	3,802	3,927
Investment Assets:Bonds	68,608	94,451	98,320	98,065	95,715	87,741	77,152	65,720	60,758	55,286
Investment Assets:Stocks	5,596	7,758	7,777	6,164	5,895	5,288	3,683	5,245	6,086	6,738
Investment Assets:Loans	10,229	10,830	9,467	8,748	7,856	6,539	6,092	5,710	4,599	4,068
Investment Assets:Total	95,998	118,980	119,757	118,297	115,530	103,081	90,650	79,876	74,483	69,645
Deferred Policy Costs	8,542	5,768	5,332	5,802	4,968	4,842	4,385	4,421	4,309	4,119
Total Assets	134,798	156,408	157,554	156,072	149,725	134,142	117,426	109,175	104,808	98,119
Debt	5,659	5,640	4,620	4,887	5,291	5,073	4,161	3,894	3,862	3,150
Common Equity	12,641	21,851	21,846	20,186	21,823	20,565	34,128	17,196	17,451	16,601
Combined Loss-Expense Ratio	99.4	89.6	83.6	102.4	93.0	94.6	98.9	102.9	99.2	97.4
% Return on Revenue	NM	12.6	13.9	5.0	9.9	8.5	2.7	4.0	7.6	10.1
% Return on Equity	NM	21.2	23.8	8.4	15.8	14.3	2.4	6.7	13.0	16.1
% Investment Yield	5.2	5.3	5.2	4.9	4.8	5.1	5.7	6.2	6.4	6.0

Data as orig reptd.; bef. results of disc opers/spec. items. Per share data adj. for stk. divs.; EPS diluted. E-Estimated. NA-Not Available. NM-Not Meaningful. NR-Not Ranked. UR-Under Review.

Office: 2775 Sanders Road, Northbrook, IL 60062-6127.
Telephone: 800-574-3553.
Website: http://www.allstate.com
Chrmn, Pres & CEO: T.J. Wilson, II

CFO: D. Civgin
Secy: M.J. McGinn
General Counsel: M.C. Mayes
Cntlr: S.H. Pilch

Board Members: F. D. Ackerman, R. D. Beyer, W. J. Farrell, J. M. Greenberg, R. T. LeMay, H. J. Riley, Jr., J. I. Smith, J. A. Sprieser, M. A. Taylor, T. J. Wilson, II

Founded: 1953
Domicile: Delaware
Employees: 38,900

The **McGraw·Hill** Companies

Altera Corp

STANDARD &POOR'S

S&P Recommendation	BUY ★★★★☆	Price $20.91 (as of Nov 27, 2009)	12-Mo. Target Price $25.00	Investment Style Large-Cap Growth

GICS Sector Information Technology
Sub-Industry Semiconductors

Summary This company is one of the largest makers of high-performance, high-density programmable logic devices (PLDs) and associated computer-aided engineering logic development tools.

Key Stock Statistics (Source S&P, Vickers, company reports)

52-Wk Range	$22.15– 12.99	S&P Oper. EPS 2009E	0.77	Market Capitalization(B)	$6.176	Beta	0.99
Trailing 12-Month EPS	$0.78	S&P Oper. EPS 2010E	1.23	Yield (%)	0.96	S&P 3-Yr. Proj. EPS CAGR(%)	6
Trailing 12-Month P/E	26.8	P/E on S&P Oper. EPS 2009E	27.2	Dividend Rate/Share	$0.20	S&P Credit Rating	NA
$10K Invested 5 Yrs Ago	$9,439	Common Shares Outstg. (M)	295.4	Institutional Ownership (%)	NM		

Price Performance

- 30-Week Mov. Avg. ···· 10-Week Mov. Avg. -- GAAP Earnings vs. Previous Year   Volume Above Avg. STARS
- 12-Mo. Target Price — Relative Strength   ▲ Up ▼ Down ▶ No Change   Below Avg.

Options: ASE, CBOE, P, Ph

Analysis prepared by **Clyde Montevirgen** on October 14, 2009, when the stock traded at **$ 21.82**.

Highlights

► We see sales advancing 20% in 2010, after a projected 16% drop in 2009, reflecting our view of increasing orders for computer, industrial and consumer chips as macroeconomic conditions improve. We also think sales will be supported by recent design wins for products that customers recently launched or will soon introduce. Furthermore, we view favorably ALTR's 40 nanometer (nm) offerings, and we think its relatively quick migration to the 40nm node will help it gain market share.

► We believe that the gross margin will widen to around 68% in 2010, from an estimated 66% in 2009. ALTR outsources its manufacturing, which we see helping to keep gross margins afloat during the downturn. We also see cost efficiencies and a more favorable sales mix supporting higher gross margins. Consequently, we think the adjusted operating margin will expand to around 31% in 2010, from an expected 24% in 2009, on our expectation that sales will increase faster than expenses.

► Our 2009 EPS estimate assumes a 15% effective tax rate and includes around $0.04 of stock-based compensation.

Investment Rationale/Risk

► Our buy recommendation reflects our view of relatively attractive fundamentals and valuations. We think ALTR's latest 40nm offerings will help offset potential weakness in its 65nm offerings, and we believe that ALTR can gain market share. With design wins materializing, we see above industry growth over the long term, and project margins and return on equity above industry averages. Although we are modeling weak 2009 results due to seasonal factors and challenging economic conditions, we see earnings power next year and modest multiple expansion supporting share price appreciation.

► Risks to our recommendation and target price include a prolonged recession, market share losses, and increases in foundry costs.

► Our 12-month target price of $25 is based on our discounted cash flow model, which includes a weighted cost of capital of around 10% and a terminal growth rate of 4%. This is supported by applying a price-to-sales multiple of 5.2X, near ALTR's historical average, to our forward 12-month sales per share estimate, also yielding a value of $25.

Qualitative Risk Assessment

LOW	MEDIUM	HIGH

Our risk assessment reflects our view that Altera is subject to the sales swings of the semiconductor industry and competition from a larger rival. This is offset by the company's participation in a high-growth niche market.

Quantitative Evaluations

S&P Quality Ranking   **B**

D	C	B-	B	B+	A-	A	A+

Relative Strength Rank   **MODERATE**

69

LOWEST = 1   HIGHEST = 99

Revenue/Earnings Data

Revenue (Million $)

	1Q	2Q	3Q	4Q	Year
2009	264.6	279.2	286.6	--	--
2008	336.1	359.9	356.8	314.5	1,367
2007	304.9	319.7	315.8	323.2	1,264
2006	292.8	334.1	341.2	317.4	1,286
2005	264.8	285.5	291.5	281.9	1,124
2004	242.9	269.0	264.6	239.9	1,016

Earnings Per Share ($)

2009	0.15	0.16	0.19	E0.25	E0.77
2008	0.27	0.32	0.31	0.28	1.18
2007	0.21	0.22	0.20	0.20	0.82
2006	0.16	0.21	0.24	0.27	0.88
2005	0.17	0.18	0.21	0.19	0.74
2004	0.15	0.20	0.22	0.15	0.72

Fiscal year ended Dec. 31. Next earnings report expected: Late January. EPS Estimates based on S&P Operating Earnings; historical GAAP earnings are as reported.

Dividend Data (Dates: mm/dd Payment Date: mm/dd/yy)

Amount ($)	Date Decl.	Ex-Div. Date	Stk. of Record	Payment Date
0.050	01/26	02/06	02/10	03/02/09
0.050	04/21	05/07	05/11	06/01/09
0.050	07/14	08/06	08/10	09/01/09
0.050	10/13	11/06	11/10	12/01/09

Dividends have been paid since 2007. Source: Company reports.

Please read the Required Disclosures and Analyst Certification on the last page of this report.

The McGraw·Hill Companies

Altera Corp

STANDARD
&POOR'S

Business Summary October 14, 2009

CORPORATE OVERVIEW. Altera Corp. is a worldwide supplier of program-mable logic devices (PLDs), HardCopy brand structured application specific integrated circuits (ASICs), pre-defined design building blocks known as intel-lectual property cores, and associated software for logic development. PLDs are a high-growth category of semiconductors that address many applica-tions in the communications, computer peripheral, consumer and industrial markets. PLDs offer high speed, high density, and low power characteristics.

The company's PLDs are standard products, shipped blank for user program-ming. They are programmed at the customer's PC or workstation, using AL-TR's proprietary software. Since the company's chips are programmed at a desktop and not at a foundry, product time to market is dramatically short-ened. In addition, because ALTR's integrated circuits are standard products, inventory risks are minimized for both the company and customers. The Hard-Copy product line assists customers who use PLDs for prototyping ASIC chips in converting the design for low cost production of non-programmable ASIC products.

Field Programmable Gate Arrays (FPGAs) include the Stratix lines, aimed at high performance applications, and the Cyclone product family, aimed at low-cost, high volume applications. General purpose Complex Programmable Log-ic Device (CPLD) product lines include the MAX family, which aims at low-

cost, high volume markets. Sales of FPGA, CPLD and other products in 2008 were 74%, 18% and 8%, respectively, of the total. By end market, sales were as follows: communications 43% (40% in 2007), industrial 35% (35%), con-sumer 15% (16%), and computer and storage 7% (9%).

Sales outside of the U.S. and Canada provided 77% of total sales in 2008, with Japan and China accounting for 19% of total revenues each. About 91% of 2008 sales were handled by independent distributors, with about 45% by Ar-row Electronics and 14% by Altima Corp., which serves the Japanese market. No single end customer accounted for over 10% of sales.

We believe competitive advantages offered to electronic system manufactur-ers by ALTR's products include enhanced design flexibility, shorter design cy-cles, lower up-front development costs, and the ability to get end-products to market faster, which can lead to significant cost savings for the customer. Drawbacks of PLDs compared to traditional ASICs include larger die size and higher cost per chip.

Company Financials Fiscal Year Ended Dec. 31

Per Share Data ($)	2008	2007	2006	2005	2004	2003	2002	2001	2000	1999
Tangible Book Value	2.73	2.74	4.46	3.52	3.42	2.93	2.95	2.89	3.21	2.82
Cash Flow	1.28	0.91	0.96	0.82	0.80	0.51	0.36	0.04	1.29	0.61
Earnings	1.18	0.82	0.88	0.74	0.72	0.40	0.23	-0.10	1.19	0.54
S&P Core Earnings	1.18	0.82	0.88	0.54	0.48	0.19	-0.02	-0.28	NA	NA
Dividends	NA	0.12	Nil	Nil	Nil	Nil	Nil	Nil	Nil	Nil
Payout Ratio	16%	15%	Nil	Nil	Nil	Nil	Nil	Nil	Nil	Nil
Prices:High	24.19	26.24	22.29	22.99	26.82	25.64	26.18	34.69	67.13	34.28
Prices:Low	12.99	18.00	15.54	15.96	17.50	10.30	8.32	14.66	19.63	11.97
P/E Ratio:High	21	32	25	31	37	64	NM	NM	56	63
P/E Ratio:Low	11	22	18	22	24	26	NM	NM	16	22

Income Statement Analysis (Million $)	2008	2007	2006	2005	2004	2003	2002	2001	2000	1999
Revenue	1,367	1,264	1,286	1,124	1,016	827	712	839	1,377	837
Operating Income	452	306	331	352	345	243	146	48.8	598	335
Depreciation	30.0	31.1	29.7	29.4	30.5	45.3	48.5	54.3	40.1	29.4
Interest Expense	15.5	Nil	Nil	Nil	Nil	Nil	Nil	Nil	Nil	Nil
Pretax Income	419	338	360	357	331	213	123	-13.0	744	335
Effective Tax Rate	14.2%	14.1%	10.1%	21.9%	16.8%	27.0%	26.0%	NM	33.2%	33.2%
Net Income	360	290	323	279	275	155	91.3	-39.8	497	224
S&P Core Earnings	360	290	323	204	182	70.7	-8.66	-106	NA	NA

Balance Sheet & Other Financial Data (Million $)	2008	2007	2006	2005	2004	2003	2002	2001	2000	1999
Cash	1,217	1,021	738	788	580	259	255	145	496	164
Current Assets	1,627	1,534	1,735	1,495	1,537	1,270	1,176	1,129	1,769	1,107
Total Assets	1,880	1,770	2,215	1,823	1,747	1,488	1,372	1,361	2,004	1,440
Current Liabilities	386	490	598	555	468	385	241	247	756	322
Long Term Debt	503	250	1.30	3.87	Nil	Nil	Nil	Nil	Nil	Nil
Common Equity	800	861	1,608	1,326	1,279	1,102	1,131	1,115	1,248	1,118
Total Capital	1,302	1,111	1,609	1,330	1,279	1,102	1,131	1,115	1,248	1,118
Capital Expenditures	40.3	31.2	36.5	25.9	24.7	13.9	9.87	65.8	87.5	29.8
Cash Flow	390	321	353	308	306	200	140	14.5	537	253
Current Ratio	4.2	3.1	2.9	2.7	3.3	3.3	4.9	4.6	2.3	3.4
% Long Term Debt of Capitalization	38.6	22.5	0.1	0.3	Nil	Nil	Nil	Nil	Nil	Nil
% Net Income of Revenue	26.3	23.0	25.1	24.8	27.1	18.8	12.8	NM	36.1	26.8
% Return on Assets	19.7	14.6	16.0	15.5	17.1	10.9	6.7	NM	28.9	17.7
% Return on Equity	43.3	23.5	22.5	21.0	23.1	13.9	8.1	NM	42.0	22.4

Data as orig reptd.; bef. results of disc opers/spec. items. Per share data adj. for stk. divs.; EPS diluted. E-Estimated. NA-Not Available. NM-Not Meaningful. NR-Not Ranked. UR-Under Review.

Office: 101 Innovation Drive, San Jose, CA 95134.
Telephone: 408-544-7000.
Email: inv_rel@altera.com
Website: http://www.altera.com

Chrmn, Pres & CEO: J.P. Daane
COO: W.Y. Hata
CFO & Cntlr: J.W. Callas
Secy & General Counsel: K.E. Schuelke

Investor Contact: S. Wylie (408-544-6996)
Board Members: J. P. Daane, R. J. Finocchio, Jr., K. McGarity, G. Myers, K. Prabhu, J. C. Shoemaker, S. Wang

Founded: 1983
Domicile: Delaware
Employees: 2,760

Altria Group Inc.

STANDARD
&POOR'S

S&P Recommendation **STRONG BUY** ★★★★★	Price	12-Mo. Target Price	Investment Style
	$19.00 (as of Nov 27, 2009)	$21.00	Large-Cap Blend

GICS Sector Consumer Staples
Sub-Industry Tobacco

Summary Altria Group (formerly Philip Morris Companies) is the largest U.S. cigarette producer. It spun off Kraft Foods in 2007 and its international cigarette operations in 2008.

Key Stock Statistics (Source S&P, Vickers, company reports)

52-Wk Range	$19.48– 14.42	S&P Oper. EPS 2009E	1.75	Market Capitalization(B)	$39.372	Beta	0.39
Trailing 12-Month EPS	$1.53	S&P Oper. EPS 2010E	1.82	Yield (%)	7.16	S&P 3-Yr. Proj. EPS CAGR(%)	6
Trailing 12-Month P/E	12.4	P/E on S&P Oper. EPS 2009E	10.9	Dividend Rate/Share	$1.36	S&P Credit Rating	BBB
$10K Invested 5 Yrs Ago	NA	Common Shares Outstg. (M)	2,072.2	Institutional Ownership (%)	66		

Price Performance

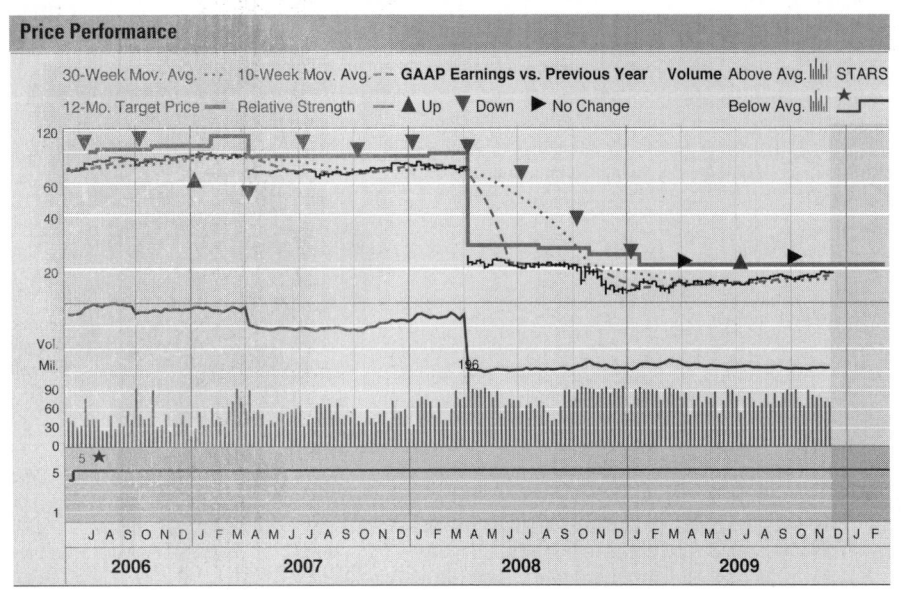

30-Week Mov. Avg. ···· 10-Week Mov. Avg. --- GAAP Earnings vs. Previous Year   Volume Above Avg. STARS
12-Mo. Target Price — Relative Strength   ▲ Up ▼ Down ▶ No Change   Below Avg.

Options: ASE, CBOE, P, Ph

Analysis prepared by **Esther Y. Kwon, CFA** on November 03, 2009, when the stock traded at **$ 18.30**.

Highlights

► In March 2008, Altria completed the spinoff of Philip Morris International to shareholders with a share distribution ratio of one for one. The board of directors set Altria's initial dividend at a payout ratio of 75% and announced a $7.5 billion share repurchase program.

► We believe sales volume will drop at a high single digit rate in 2009, with brand investments, acquisitions, line extensions and new product introductions somewhat offsetting declining consumption trends. We see revenues rising about 4% on higher pricing in both 2009 and 2010. Over the next several years, we expect MO's margins to widen on restructuring actions, including the closure of its Cabarrus facility, consolidation of all manufacturing in Richmond, VA, and $500 million of new SG&A expense reductions, up from $300 million estimated originally.

► On an effective tax rate of about 35.0%, versus 2008's 35.4%, we estimate 2009 operating EPS of $1.75; we see $1.82 in 2010 on a higher effective tax rate of around 37%. Due to capital market uncertainty, MO has suspended its repurchase program, with $1.2 billion completed; it expects to re-evaluate its plans in early 2010.

Investment Rationale/Risk

► On June 22, President Obama signed the Family Smoking Prevention and Tobacco Control Act, granting the U.S. Food and Drug Administration the authority to regulate tobacco products. While we see this as a negative for the industry, it was well anticipated, and we see the restrictions solidifying market share leader Atria's dominant position and handicapping its smaller competitors. Operationally, we think Altria is likely to benefit from several factors over the next several years, including the integration of its recent acquisition of smokeless tobacco company UST and benefits from recent restructuring actions.

► Risks to our recommendation and target price include possible pressures on trading multiples as investors remain cautious about court trials, and potential increases in excise taxes and smoking bans at the state and local level.

► Our 12-month target price of $21 is based on historical and peer forward P/Es. We apply a slightly below historical forward P/E of 11.5X to our 2010 EPS estimate to calculate our target price. Reflecting strong cash generation and the stock's indicated dividend yield of well over 7%, we continue to find MO compelling.

Qualitative Risk Assessment

LOW	MEDIUM	HIGH

MO is a large-cap company in an industry that is operationally very stable. However, the tobacco industry is beset by litigation. The company is subject to several ongoing legal actions, which could have a material impact on future cash flows.

Quantitative Evaluations

S&P Quality Ranking   A

D	C	B-	B	B+	A-	A	A+

Relative Strength Rank   MODERATE

70

LOWEST = 1   HIGHEST = 99

Revenue/Earnings Data

Revenue (Million $)

	1Q	2Q	3Q	4Q	Year
2009	3,812	6,719	6,300	--	--
2008	3,604	4,179	4,341	3,833	15,957
2007	17,556	18,809	19,207	18,229	38,051
2006	24,355	25,769	25,885	25,398	101,407
2005	23,618	24,784	24,962	24,490	97,854
2004	21,721	22,894	22,615	22,380	89,610

Earnings Per Share ($)

2009	0.29	0.49	0.42	E0.40	E1.75
2008	0.29	0.43	0.42	0.33	1.48
2007	1.01	1.05	1.24	1.03	4.33
2006	1.65	1.29	1.36	1.40	5.71
2005	1.24	1.40	1.38	1.09	5.10
2004	1.06	1.26	1.28	0.96	4.57

Fiscal year ended Dec. 31. Next earnings report expected: Late January. EPS Estimates based on S&P Operating Earnings; historical GAAP earnings are as reported.

Dividend Data (Dates: mm/dd Payment Date: mm/dd/yy)

Amount ($)	Date Decl.	Ex-Div. Date	Stk. of Record	Payment Date
0.320	12/10	12/22	12/24	01/09/09
0.320	02/26	03/12	03/16	04/10/09
0.320	05/20	06/11	06/15	07/10/09
0.340	08/27	09/11	09/15	10/09/09

Dividends have been paid since 1928. Source: Company reports.

Please read the Required Disclosures and Analyst Certification on the last page of this report.

The McGraw·Hill Companies

Altria Group Inc.

STANDARD
&POOR'S

Business Summary November 03, 2009

CORPORATE OVERVIEW. Altria Group (formerly Philip Morris Cos., Inc.) is a holding company for wholly owned and majority owned subsidiaries that make and market various consumer products, now primarily including cigarettes. Prior to the March 30, 2007, spinoff of Kraft Foods, Altria Group's reportable segments were domestic tobacco, international tobacco, North American food, international food and financial services. The spinoff of Philip Morris International was completed on March 28, 2008, at a one-for-one exchange rate.

Philip Morris U.S.A. (PM USA) is the largest U.S. tobacco company, with total U.S. cigarette shipments amounting to 169.4 billion units in 2008 (down 3.3% from 2007), accounting for 50.7% of total U.S. cigarette market shipments (up from 50.6% in 2007). Focus brands include Marlboro (the largest selling brand in the U.S.), Virginia Slims and Parliament in the premium category, and Basic in the discount category.

In January 2009, Altria completed the acquisition of UST Inc., the largest U.S. manufacturer and marketer of smokeless tobacco products, for $11.7 billion, which includes the assumption of about $1.3 billion of debt.

Kraft Foods, the largest packaged food company in North America and sec-

ond largest in the world, was spun off on March 30, 2007, to MO shareholders as a tax-free stock dividend. MO shareholders received approximately 0.68 of a KFT share per MO share owned as a stock dividend at the end of March 2007, and cash in lieu of fractional shares.

In July 2002, MO sold its Miller Brewing Co. subsidiary to South African Brewers, plc., receiving $3.38 billion worth of shares in the newly formed company, SABMiller. As of December 31, 2008, this stake represented a 28.5% economic and voting interest.

CORPORATE STRATEGY. After considering a number of restructuring alternatives, including the possibility of separating Altria Group, Inc. into two, or potentially three, independent entities, the company in June 2007 announced that cigarette production for international markets would be shifted from U.S. facilities to European plants. It subsequently decided to spin off its international tobacco operations, with an effective date of March 28, 2008.

Company Financials Fiscal Year Ended Dec. 31

Per Share Data ($)	2008	2007	2006	2005	2004	2003	2002	2001	2000	1999
Tangible Book Value	NM	3.97	NM	NM	NM	NM	NM	NM	NM	NM
Cash Flow	1.58	4.79	6.57	5.92	5.35	5.22	6.10	4.93	4.50	3.90
Earnings	1.48	4.33	5.71	5.10	4.57	4.52	5.21	3.88	3.75	3.19
S&P Core Earnings	1.29	4.33	5.62	5.14	4.54	4.49	4.03	3.62	NA	NA
Dividends	1.68	3.05	3.32	3.06	2.82	2.64	2.44	2.22	2.02	1.80
Payout Ratio	1%	70%	58%	60%	62%	58%	47%	57%	54%	56%
Prices:High	79.59	90.50	86.56	78.68	61.88	55.03	57.79	53.88	45.94	55.56
Prices:Low	14.34	63.13	68.36	60.40	44.50	27.70	35.40	38.75	18.69	21.25
P/E Ratio:High	54	21	15	15	14	12	11	14	12	17
P/E Ratio:Low	10	15	12	12	10	6	7	10	5	7

Income Statement Analysis (Million $)										
Revenue	15,957	38,051	70,324	68,920	63,963	60,704	62,182	72,944	63,276	61,751
Operating Income	5,229	14,892	19,705	19,004	17,929	17,663	18,476	18,039	16,396	15,192
Depreciation	215	980	1,804	1,675	1,607	1,440	1,331	2,337	1,717	1,702
Interest Expense	237	653	877	1,556	1,417	1,367	1,327	1,659	1,078	1,100
Pretax Income	4,789	13,257	16,536	15,435	14,004	14,760	18,098	14,284	13,960	12,695
Effective Tax Rate	35.5%	30.9%	26.3%	29.9%	32.4%	34.9%	35.5%	37.9%	39.0%	39.5%
Net Income	3,090	9,161	12,022	10,668	9,420	9,204	11,102	8,566	8,510	7,675
S&P Core Earnings	2,687	9,163	11,818	10,766	9,348	9,145	8,593	7,959	NA	NA

Balance Sheet & Other Financial Data (Million $)										
Cash	7,916	6,498	5,020	6,258	5,744	3,777	565	453	937	5,100
Current Assets	NA	NA	26,152	25,781	25,901	21,382	17,441	17,275	17,238	20,895
Total Assets	27,215	57,211	104,270	107,949	101,648	96,175	87,540	84,968	79,067	61,381
Current Liabilities	NA	NA	25,427	26,158	23,574	21,393	19,082	20,141	25,949	18,017
Long Term Debt	6,839	11,046	14,498	17,868	18,683	21,163	21,355	18,651	19,154	12,226
Common Equity	2,828	18,554	39,619	35,707	30,714	25,077	19,478	19,620	15,005	15,305
Total Capital	14,662	33,610	68,496	71,945	67,714	64,110	56,832	52,768	40,824	33,211
Capital Expenditures	241	1,458	2,454	2,206	1,913	1,974	2,009	1,922	1,682	1,749
Cash Flow	3,305	10,141	13,826	12,343	11,027	10,644	12,433	10,903	10,227	9,377
Current Ratio	2.2	1.5	1.0	1.0	1.1	1.0	0.9	0.9	0.7	1.2
% Long Term Debt of Capitalization	46.6	30.0	21.2	24.8	27.6	33.0	37.6	35.3	46.9	36.8
% Net Income of Revenue	19.4	24.1	17.1	15.5	14.7	15.2	17.9	11.7	13.4	12.4
% Return on Assets	7.3	11.4	11.3	10.2	9.5	10.0	12.9	10.4	12.1	12.7
% Return on Equity	28.9	31.5	31.9	32.1	33.8	41.3	56.8	49.5	56.2	48.7

Data as orig reptd.; bef. results of disc opers/spec. items. Per share data adj. for stk. divs.; EPS diluted. E-Estimated. NA-Not Available. NM-Not Meaningful. NR-Not Ranked. UR-Under Review.

Office: 6601 W Broad St, Richmond, VA 23230-1723.
Telephone: 804-274-2200.
Website: http://www.altria.com
Chrmn & CEO: M. Szymanczyk

EVP & CFO: D.R. Beran
EVP & Chief Admin Officer: M.J. Barrington
EVP & CTO: J.R. Nelson
EVP & General Counsel: D.F. Keane

Investor Contact: C.B. Fleet (804-484-8222)
Board Members: E. E. Bailey, G. L. Baliles, D. S. Devitre, T. F. Farrell, II, R. E. Huntley, T. W. Jones, G. Munoz, N. Y. Sakkab, M. Szymanczyk

Founded: 1919
Domicile: Virginia
Employees: 10,400

The McGraw-Hill Companies

Amazon.com Inc

STANDARD &POOR'S

S&P Recommendation	HOLD ★★★☆☆	Price $135.91 (as of Nov 30, 2009)	12-Mo. Target Price $110.00	Investment Style Large-Cap Growth

GICS Sector Consumer Discretionary
Sub-Industry Internet Retail

Summary This leading online retailer sells a broad range of items from books to consumer electronics to home and garden products.

Key Stock Statistics (Source S&P, Vickers, company reports)

52-Wk Range	$136.08– 38.82	S&P Oper. EPS 2009**E**	1.99	Market Capitalization(B)	$58.847	Beta	1.30
Trailing 12-Month EPS	$1.70	S&P Oper. EPS 2010**E**	2.56	Yield (%)	Nil	S&P 3-Yr. Proj. EPS CAGR(%)	25
Trailing 12-Month P/E	80.0	P/E on S&P Oper. EPS 2009**E**	68.3	Dividend Rate/Share	Nil	S&P Credit Rating	BBB
$10K Invested 5 Yrs Ago	$33,702	Common Shares Outstg. (M)	433.0	Institutional Ownership (%)	70		

Price Performance

30-Week Mov. Avg. · · · 10-Week Mov. Avg. – – GAAP Earnings vs. Previous Year — Volume Above Avg. ▌▌ STARS
12-Mo. Target Price — Relative Strength — ▲ Up ▼ Down ► No Change — Below Avg. ▌▌ ★

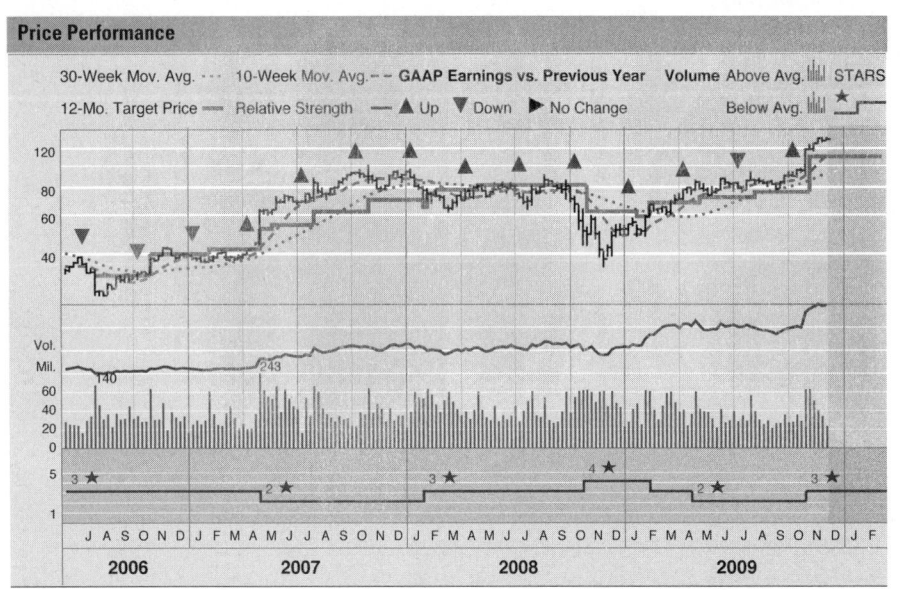

Options: ASE, CBOE, P, Ph

Analysis prepared by **Michael Souers** on October 26, 2009, when the stock traded at **$ 118.49**.

Qualitative Risk Assessment

LOW	MEDIUM	HIGH

Our risk assessment reflects AMZN's large market capitalization and leading position in the e-commerce industry, offset by increasing competition and the stock's high beta.

Quantitative Evaluations

S&P Quality Ranking   B-

D	C	B-	B	B+	A-	A	A+

Relative Strength Rank   **STRONG**

96

LOWEST = 1   HIGHEST = 99

Revenue/Earnings Data

Revenue (Million $)

	1Q	2Q	3Q	4Q	Year
2009	4,889	4,651	5,449	--	--
2008	4,135	4,063	4,264	6,704	19,166
2007	3,015	2,886	3,262	5,673	14,835
2006	2,279	2,139	2,307	3,986	10,711
2005	1,902	1,753	1,858	2,977	8,490
2004	1,530	1,387	1,462	2,541	6,921

Earnings Per Share ($)

2009	0.41	0.32	0.45	E0.72	E1.99
2008	0.34	0.37	0.27	0.52	1.49
2007	0.26	0.19	0.19	0.49	1.12
2006	0.12	0.05	0.05	0.23	0.45
2005	0.12	0.12	0.07	0.47	0.78
2004	0.26	0.18	0.13	0.82	1.39

Fiscal year ended Dec. 31. Next earnings report expected: Late January. EPS Estimates based on S&P Operating Earnings; historical GAAP earnings are as reported.

Dividend Data

No cash dividends have been paid.

Highlights

► We estimate net sales will rise 21% in 2010, following our projections of a 25% advance in 2009. We expect this rapid growth to be driven by international expansion, acquisitions and an increase in third-party sellers. The 2007 launch of Amazon Prime in the U.K., Germany, and Japan continues to drive increased sales results and build customer loyalty abroad. In our view, AMZN's relentless focus on providing value to consumers through selection and price bodes well for the company to gain notable market share during this economic downturn.

► For 2010, we expect gross margins will narrow slightly due to a shift in product mix and competitive pressures, partially offset by an increase in third-party product sales. Due to modestly lower projected G&A and technology and content expenses, we look for a 50 basis point increase in operating margins compared to 2009.

► After modestly higher net interest income and a tax rate of 28.0%, we project 2010 EPS of $2.56, a 29% increase from the $1.99 we project the company to earn in 2009, which excludes a $0.09 charge related to a litigation settlement.

Investment Rationale/Risk

► AMZN continues to demonstrate the strength and worldwide potential of its business model, in our view. Continued investments in long-term growth opportunities such as Amazon Prime, seller platforms and digital media stores should provide new sources of revenue over the next few years. Longer term, we expect AMZN's initiatives to result in continued strong sales results and significant margin expansion, as it leverages its leading brand name and position as an Internet retailer. We consider AMZN a best-in-class retailer that generates significant free cash flow. While valuation remains a concern to us, with the shares trading at about 46X our 2010 EPS estimate, we think AMZN's long-term growth potential offsets this.

► Risks to our opinion and target price include a double-dip recession, the potential for lower-than-projected revenues should growth initiatives fail to live up to their potential, and unfavorable currency impacts.

► Our 12-month target price of $110 is based on our discounted cash flow analysis, which assumes a weighted average cost of capital of 10.6% and a terminal growth rate of 4%.

Amazon.com Inc

STANDARD &POOR'S

Business Summary October 26, 2009

CORPORATE OVERVIEW. Since opening for business as "Earth's Biggest Bookstore" in July 1995, Amazon.com has expanded into a number of other product categories, including: apparel, shoes and jewelry; electronics and computers; movies, music and games; toys, kids and baby; sports and outdoors; home and garden; tools, auto and industrial; grocery; health and beauty; and digital downloads.

AMZN has virtually unlimited online shelf space, and can offer customers a vast selection of products through an efficient search and retrieval interface. The company personalizes shopping by recommending items which, based on previous purchases, are likely to interest a particular customer. Key Web site features also include editorial and customer reviews, manufacturer product information, secure payment systems, wedding and baby registries, customer wish lists, and the ability to view selected interior pages and search the entire contents of many books (Look Inside the Book and Search Inside the Book).

The company operates the following retail Web sites: www.amazon.com (U.S.), www.amazon.co.uk (U.K.), www.amazon.de (Germany), www.amazon.fr (France), www.amazon.co.jp (Japan), www.amazon.ca (Canada), www.amazon.cn (China), www.joyo.cn, www.shopbop.com, and

www.endless.com. Amazon also designs, manufactures and sells a wireless e-reading device, the Amazon Kindle. It focuses first and foremost on the customer experience by offering a wide selection of merchandise, low prices and convenience.

In addition to being the seller of record for a broad range of new products, AMZN allows other businesses and individuals to sell new, used and collectible products on its Web sites through its Merchant and Amazon Marketplace programs. The company earns fixed fees, sales commissions, and/or per-unit activity fees under these programs.

Starting in 2003, the company began reporting results for two core segments: North America (53% of 2008 net sales) and International (47%). In 2008, media products accounted for 58% of net sales, electronics and other general merchandise 39%, and other 3%.

Company Financials Fiscal Year Ended Dec. 31

Per Share Data ($)	2008	2007	2006	2005	2004	2003	2002	2001	2000	1999
Tangible Book Value	4.44	2.30	0.58	0.15	NM	NM	NM	NM	NM	NM
Cash Flow	2.28	1.76	0.93	1.07	1.56	0.27	-0.16	-0.80	-2.86	-3.26
Earnings	1.49	1.12	0.45	0.78	1.39	0.08	-0.40	-1.53	-4.02	-2.20
S&P Core Earnings	1.41	1.12	0.48	0.83	1.27	0.02	-0.64	-2.49	NA	NA
Dividends	Nil	Nil	Nil	Nil	Nil	Nil	Nil	Nil	Nil	Nil
Payout Ratio	Nil	Nil	Nil	Nil	Nil	Nil	Nil	Nil	Nil	Nil
Prices:High	97.43	101.09	48.58	50.00	57.82	61.15	25.00	22.38	91.50	113.00
Prices:Low	34.68	36.30	25.76	30.60	33.00	18.55	9.03	5.51	14.88	41.00
P/E Ratio:High	65	90	NM	64	42	NM	NM	NM	NM	NM
P/E Ratio:Low	23	32	NM	39	24	NM	NM	NM	NM	NM

Income Statement Analysis (Million $)										
Revenue	19,166	14,835	10,711	8,490	6,921	5,264	3,933	3,122	2,762	1,640
Operating Income	1,129	926	629	553	508	349	193	35.1	-257	-346
Depreciation	340	271	205	121	75.7	78.3	87.8	266	406	253
Interest Expense	71.0	77.0	78.0	92.0	107	130	143	139	131	84.6
Pretax Income	892	660	377	428	356	35.3	-150	-557	-1,411	-720
Effective Tax Rate	27.7%	27.9%	49.6%	22.2%	NM	NM	NM	NM	NM	NM
Net Income	645	476	190	333	588	35.3	-150	-557	-1,411	-720
S&P Core Earnings	609	476	203	354	539	10.3	-242	-910	NA	NA

Balance Sheet & Other Financial Data (Million $)										
Cash	3,727	3,112	2,019	2,000	1,779	1,395	1,301	997	1,101	706
Current Assets	6,157	5,164	3,373	2,929	2,539	1,821	1,616	1,208	1,361	1,012
Total Assets	8,314	6,485	4,363	3,696	3,249	2,162	1,990	1,638	2,135	2,472
Current Liabilities	4,746	3,714	2,532	1,929	1,620	1,253	1,066	921	975	739
Long Term Debt	533	1,282	1,247	1,521	1,855	1,945	2,277	2,156	2,127	1,466
Common Equity	2,672	1,197	431	246	-227	-1,036	-1,353	-1,440	-967	266
Total Capital	3,205	2,479	1,678	1,767	1,628	909	924	716	1,160	1,733
Capital Expenditures	333	224	216	204	89.1	46.0	39.2	50.3	135	287
Cash Flow	985	747	395	454	664	114	-62.2	-291	-1,005	-1,015
Current Ratio	1.3	1.4	1.3	1.5	1.6	1.5	1.5	1.3	1.4	1.4
% Long Term Debt of Capitalization	16.6	51.7	74.3	86.1	113.9	213.9	246.3	301.1	183.4	84.6
% Net Income of Revenue	3.4	3.2	1.8	3.9	8.5	0.7	NM	NM	NM	NM
% Return on Assets	8.7	8.8	4.7	9.6	21.8	1.7	NM	NM	NM	NM
% Return on Equity	33.3	58.5	56.1	NM	NM	NM	NM	NM	NM	NM

Data as orig reptd.; bef. results of disc opers/spec. items. Per share data adj. for stk. divs.; EPS diluted. E-Estimated. NA-Not Available. NM-Not Meaningful. NR-Not Ranked. UR-Under Review.

Office: 1200 12th Avenue South, Seattle, WA 98144-2734.
Telephone: 206-266-1000.
Email: ir@amazon.com
Website: http://www.amazon.com

Chrmn, Pres & CEO: J.P. Bezos
COO: M.A. Onetto
SVP & CFO: T.J. Szkutak
SVP, Secy & General Counsel: L.M. Wilson

Chief Acctg Officer & Cntlr: S.L. Reynolds
Investor Contact: R. Eldridge (206-266-2171)
Board Members: T. A. Alberg, J. P. Bezos, J. S. Brown, L. Doerr, III, W. B. Gordon, A. Monie, T. O. Ryder, P. Q. Stonesifer

Founded: 1994
Domicile: Delaware
Employees: 20,700

Ameren Corp

STANDARD &POOR'S

S&P Recommendation BUY ★★★★☆	Price	12-Mo. Target Price	Investment Style
	$25.58 (as of Nov 27, 2009)	$28.00	Large-Cap Value

GICS Sector Utilities
Sub-Industry Multi-Utilities

Summary Ameren is the holding company for the largest electric utility in the state of Missouri, and several utilities in Illinois.

Key Stock Statistics (Source S&P, Vickers, company reports)

52-Wk Range	**$35.35– 19.51**	S&P Oper. EPS 2009**E**	**2.75**	Market Capitalization(B)	**$6.060**	Beta	**0.72**
Trailing 12-Month EPS	**$2.76**	S&P Oper. EPS 2010**E**	**2.49**	Yield (%)	**6.02**	S&P 3-Yr. Proj. EPS CAGR(%)	**-1**
Trailing 12-Month P/E	**9.3**	P/E on S&P Oper. EPS 2009**E**	**9.3**	Dividend Rate/Share	**$1.54**	S&P Credit Rating	**BBB-**
$10K Invested 5 Yrs Ago	**$6,753**	Common Shares Outstg. (M)	**236.9**	Institutional Ownership (%)	**60**		

Price Performance

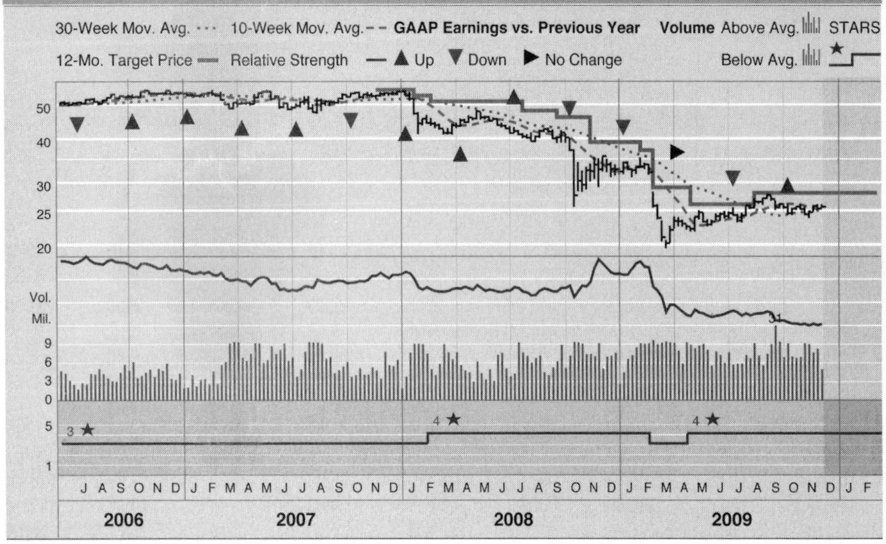
30-Week Mov. Avg.
10-Week Mov. Avg.
GAAP Earnings vs. Previous Year
Volume Above Avg.
STARS
12-Mo. Target Price
Relative Strength
Up
Down
No Change
Below Avg.
Vol.
Mil.
J A S O N D J F M A M J J A S O N D J F M A M J J A S O N D J F M A M J J A S O N D J F
2006
2007
2008
2009

Options: P, Ph

Analysis prepared by **Justin McCann** on November 05, 2009, when the stock traded at **$ 24.60**.

Highlights

- Excluding $0.02 in net one-time gains, we expect 2009 operating EPS to decline nearly 6% from 2008's $2.95, due to the weak economy and higher operating and financing costs. We believe EPS will benefit from rate increases in Illinois and Missouri, but we expect a decline at the generation business. We look for the Missouri utilities to earn about $1.06 a share (after $1.12 in 2008), the Illinois utilities $0.51 ($0.24), and the generating segment $1.18 ($1.59).
- For 2010, we expect operating EPS to decline about 9% from anticipated results in 2009, primarily reflecting reduced margins in the merchant generating segment due to a decrease in power prices. This should be partially offset by sharply reduced operating expenses due to the company's cost-cutting measures.
- On January 27, 2009, the Missouri Public Service Commission (MPSC) issued a final order authorizing Ameren's Union Electric Company subsidiary a rate increase of $162 million (7.8%). The increase was based upon a 10.76% return on equity, with equity at 52.009% of total capital. The MPSC also approved a fuel adjustment clause that would enable Union Electric to recover from customers a rise in its fuel costs.

Investment Rationale/Risk

- The stock has rebounded about 24% from its multi-year low reached in March, but is down about 27% year to date. With an above-peers yield from a dividend we now view as secure, we believe AEE is attractive for above-average total return potential. In February, AEE announced a 39% cut in its dividend and reduced its EPS outlook for 2009. With a weak economy and power market, and rising environmental expenses expected to result in lower earnings and higher financing costs, AEE considered the cut essential for its financial strength.
- Risks to our recommendation and target price include a sharp decline in power supply margins, and a sharp drop in the average P/E ratio of AEE's peer group as a whole.
- With the cut in its dividend, AEE reduced its dividend payout ratio from 92% of our operating EPS estimate for 2009, to 56%, which is below the recent peer average of about 62%. In addition, with the yield from the reduced dividend (recently 6.4%) still above the industry average (5.0%), we expect the stock to gradually recover a greater portion of its decline. Our 12-month target price is $28, reflecting a discount-to-peers P/E of 11.2X our EPS forecast for 2010.

Qualitative Risk Assessment

LOW	MEDIUM	HIGH

Our risk assessment reflects our expectation of steady cash flow from the company's regulated utilities, which have the benefit of fuel costs that are below the industry average. We believe that this, as well as the electric rate settlement agreement in Illinois, should help offset the impact of the current credit market environment and the economic slowdown.

Quantitative Evaluations

S&P Quality Ranking B+

D	C	B-	B	B+	A-	A	A+

Relative Strength Rank MODERATE

55

LOWEST = 1 HIGHEST = 99

Revenue/Earnings Data

Revenue (Million $)

	1Q	2Q	3Q	4Q	Year
2009	1,916	1,684	1,815	--	--
2008	2,079	1,788	2,060	1,908	7,839
2007	2,019	1,723	1,997	1,807	7,546
2006	1,800	1,550	1,910	1,620	6,880
2005	1,626	1,586	1,868	1,701	6,780
2004	1,216	1,152	1,317	1,475	5,160

Earnings Per Share ($)

2009	0.66	0.77	1.04	**E**0.30	**E**2.75
2008	0.66	0.98	0.97	0.27	2.88
2007	0.59	0.69	1.18	0.52	2.98
2006	0.34	0.60	1.42	0.30	2.66
2005	0.62	0.93	1.37	0.21	3.13
2004	0.55	0.65	1.20	0.42	2.84

Fiscal year ended Dec. 31. Next earnings report expected: Mid February. EPS Estimates based on S&P Operating Earnings; historical GAAP earnings are as reported.

Dividend Data (Dates: mm/dd Payment Date: mm/dd/yy)

Amount ($)	Date Decl.	Ex-Div. Date	Stk. of Record	Payment Date
0.385	02/13	03/09	03/11	03/31/09
0.385	04/28	06/08	06/10	06/30/09
0.385	08/14	09/08	09/10	09/30/09
0.385	10/09	12/07	12/09	12/31/09

Dividends have been paid since 1906. Source: Company reports.

Please read the Required Disclosures and Analyst Certification on the last page of this report.
Redistribution or reproduction is prohibited without written permission. Copyright ©2009 The McGraw-Hill Companies, Inc.

The McGraw·Hill Companies

Ameren Corp

STANDARD
&POOR'S

Business Summary November 05, 2009

CORPORATE OVERVIEW. Ameren Corporation (AEE) is a holding company that operates regulated electric and natural gas utilities and non-regulated operations, including energy marketing, trading and consulting services, in Missouri and Illinois. AEE's Utility Operations segment is comprised of its electric generation and electric and gas transmission and distribution operations. The company's subsidiaries include Union Electric Company (UE), Central Illinois Light Company (CILCO), Central Illinois Public Service Company (CIPS), Ameren Energy Generating Company (Genco), CILCORP Inc., and Illinois Power Company (IP). In 2008, the company's electric services contributed 81.2% of its consolidated operating revenues (83.1% in 2007) while its gas services contributed 18.8% (16.9%).

CORPORATE STRATEGY. Although AEE has attempted to keep its rates low through disciplined cost control and efficient operations, the costs of nearly

every aspect of its business have been rising at a rapid pace. Since new customer rates are usually established on historical costs after an approximate one-year regulatory review, by the time they have been implemented they are already inadequate to fully recover the current costs and to earn a fair return on the company's investment. AEE has determined that in order to deal with this problem more effectively (and to avoid customer shock at a sudden sharp increase in rates), it intends to seek smaller and more frequent rate increases. It also plans to seek automatic cost recovery mechanisms for its most expensive items, such as its fuel costs and environmental investments.

Company Financials Fiscal Year Ended Dec. 31

Per Share Data ($)	2008	2007	2006	2005	2004	2003	2002	2001	2000	1999
Tangible Book Value	28.10	27.48	26.80	25.08	24.92	23.19	24.95	24.26	23.34	22.55
Earnings	2.88	2.98	2.66	3.13	2.84	3.14	2.60	3.45	3.33	2.81
S&P Core Earnings	2.09	3.04	2.90	3.32	3.12	3.28	2.36	2.81	NA	NA
Dividends	2.54	2.54	2.54	2.54	2.54	2.54	2.54	2.54	2.54	2.54
Payout Ratio	88%	85%	95%	81%	89%	81%	98%	74%	76%	90%
Prices:High	54.29	55.00	55.24	56.77	50.36	46.50	45.25	46.00	46.94	42.94
Prices:Low	25.51	47.10	47.96	47.51	40.55	42.55	34.72	36.53	27.56	32.00
P/E Ratio:High	19	18	21	18	18	15	17	13	14	15
P/E Ratio:Low	9	16	18	15	14	14	13	11	8	11

Income Statement Analysis (Million $)	2008	2007	2006	2005	2004	2003	2002	2001	2000	1999
Revenue	7,839	7,546	6,880	6,780	5,160	4,593	3,841	4,506	3,856	3,524
Depreciation	742	681	661	632	557	519	431	406	382	351
Maintenance	NA	NA	NA	NA	NA	NA	NA	382	368	371
Fixed Charges Coverage	3.21	3.33	3.48	4.32	3.81	3.61	4.04	4.65	4.86	4.48
Construction Credits	NA	NA	NA	NA	NA	4.00	11.0	20.8	14.0	14.0
Effective Tax Rate	33.7%	33.5%	32.7%	35.6%	34.7%	37.3%	38.3%	38.7%	39.7%	40.2%
Net Income	605	629	558	628	530	506	382	475	457	385
S&P Core Earnings	440	632	597	666	582	530	347	387	NA	NA

Balance Sheet & Other Financial Data (Million $)	2008	2007	2006	2005	2004	2003	2002	2001	2000	1999
Gross Property	25,066	23,484	22,013	20,800	20,291	17,511	15,745	14,962	13,910	13,056
Capital Expenditures	1,896	1,381	992	947	806	682	787	1,103	929	571
Net Property	16,567	15,069	14,286	13,572	13,297	10,917	8,914	8,427	7,706	7,165
Capitalization:Long Term Debt	6,749	5,902	5,498	5,568	5,236	4,273	3,626	3,071	2,980	2,683
Capitalization:% Long Term Debt	49.2	46.7	45.5	46.7	47.4	49.5	48.6	47.8	48.3	46.5
Capitalization:Preferred	Nil	Nil	Nil	Nil	Nil	Nil	Nil	Nil	Nil	Nil
Capitalization:% Preferred	Nil	Nil	Nil	Nil	Nil	Nil	Nil	Nil	Nil	Nil
Capitalization:Common	6,963	6,752	6,583	6,364	5,800	4,354	3,842	3,349	3,196	3,089
Capitalization:% Common	50.8	53.3	54.5	53.3	52.6	50.5	51.4	52.2	51.7	53.5
Total Capital	15,964	14,722	14,241	14,047	13,075	10,653	9,339	8,144	7,884	7,441
% Operating Ratio	86.8	86.6	87.1	86.3	84.6	83.9	81.0	85.2	83.4	84.1
% Earned on Net Property	8.6	9.1	8.4	9.6	8.9	10.7	7.2	8.2	8.6	8.0
% Return on Revenue	7.7	8.4	8.0	9.3	10.3	11.0	9.9	10.6	11.9	10.9
% Return on Invested Capital	7.0	7.5	6.6	7.0	6.9	7.4	8.1	8.6	8.5	7.7
% Return on Common Equity	8.8	9.3	8.4	10.3	10.4	12.3	10.6	14.5	14.5	12.5

Data as orig reptd.; bef. results of disc opers/spec. items. Per share data adj. for stk. divs.; EPS diluted. E-Estimated. NA-Not Available. NM-Not Meaningful. NR-Not Ranked. UR-Under Review.

Office: 1901 Chouteau Avenue, St. Louis, MO 63103.
Telephone: 314-621-3222.
Email: invest@ameren.com
Website: http://www.ameren.com

Chrmn: G.L. Rainwater
Pres & CEO: T.R. Voss
SVP, CFO, Chief Acctg Officer & Cntlr: M.J. Lyons
SVP, Secy & General Counsel: S.R. Sullivan

Chief Admin Officer: D.F. Cole
Investor Contact: D. Fischer (314-554-4859)
Board Members: S. F. Brauer, S. S. Elliott, E. M. Fitzsimmons, W. J. Galvin, G. P. Jackson, J. C. Johnson, C. W. Mueller, D. R. Oberhelman, G. L. Rainwater, H. Saligman, P. T. Stokes, T. R. Voss, J. D. Woodard

Founded: 1881
Domicile: Missouri
Employees: 9,524

American Electric Power Co Inc

STANDARD &POOR'S

S&P Recommendation BUY ★★★★☆	Price $31.55 (as of Nov 27, 2009)	12-Mo. Target Price $35.00	Investment Style Large-Cap Value

GICS Sector Utilities
Sub-Industry Electric Utilities

Summary This electric utility holding company has subsidiaries operating in 11 states in the U.S.

Key Stock Statistics (Source S&P, Vickers, company reports)

52-Wk Range	$34.34– 24.00	S&P Oper. EPS 2009**E**	2.99	Market Capitalization(B)	$15.070	Beta	0.56
Trailing 12-Month EPS	$2.88	S&P Oper. EPS 2010**E**	3.05	Yield (%)	5.20	S&P 3-Yr. Proj. EPS CAGR(%)	1
Trailing 12-Month P/E	11.0	P/E on S&P Oper. EPS 2009**E**	10.6	Dividend Rate/Share	$1.64	S&P Credit Rating	BBB
$10K Invested 5 Yrs Ago	$11,062	Common Shares Outstg. (M)	477.7	Institutional Ownership (%)	69		

Price Performance

30-Week Mov. Avg. ···   10-Week Mov. Avg. - -   **GAAP Earnings vs. Previous Year**   Volume Above Avg. STARS
12-Mo. Target Price —   Relative Strength —   ▲ Up ▼ Down ▶ No Change   Below Avg. ★

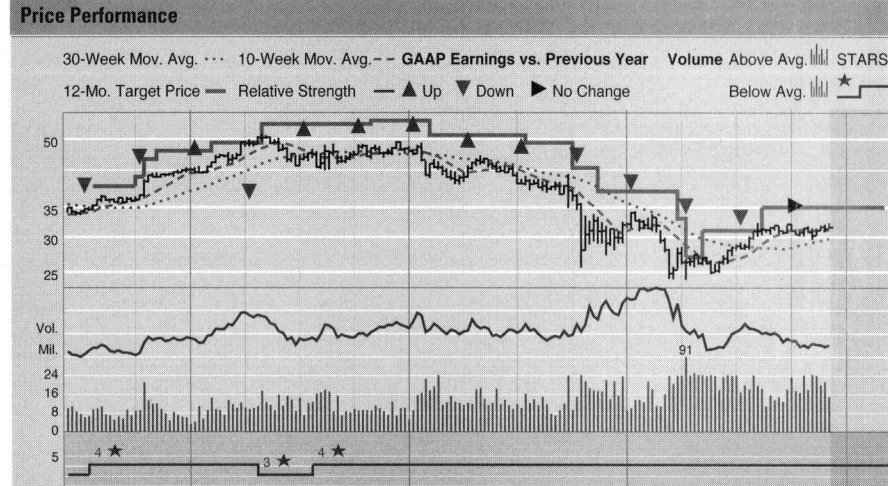

Options: ASE, CBOE, P, Ph

Analysis prepared by **Justin McCann** on October 27, 2009, when the stock traded at **$ 30.39**.

Highlights

▶ Excluding a net one-time charge of $0.01, we expect 2009 operating EPS to decline more than 10% from 2008 operating EPS of $3.24. In addition to more shares outstanding, we believe the projected EPS decline in 2009 will reflect the impact of the economic downturn and the milder weather resulting in a significant decrease in retail electricity demand and off-system sales, as well as a rise in interest expense, taxes, depreciation and amortization, and higher expenses at the holding company. However, we believe this will be partially offset by the benefit of rate increases and a sharp decline in operation and maintenance costs.

▶ For 2010, we project operating EPS to increase about 5% from anticipated results in 2009. In addition to expected rate increases in Arkansas, Ohio, Virginia and West Virginia, we look for earnings to reflect a return to more normal weather and a gradual improvement in the economy and off-system sales.

▶ We expect AEP's long-term annual EPS growth rate to range between 4% and 6%, with results driven by rate base investments in the company's generation and transmission operations.

Investment Rationale/Risk

▶ The shares have recovered more than 25% from their multi-year low reached at the end of March. We believe the stock had been hurt by the impact of the economic slowdown and the reduced earnings outlook for 2009. There have also been concerns over the potential impact of probable greenhouse gas legislation. However, we do not see a significant financial impact until after 2020, and we believe AEP's substantial environmental investments will smooth the transition. We expect the shares to realize an above-average total return.

▶ Risks to our recommendation and target price include the potential for weaker-than-anticipated results from wholesale operations and a sharp decline in the average P/E multiple of the group as a whole.

▶ Due to the crisis in the capital markets, AEP decided to maintain its dividend at the current level. Following the rebound in the shares, the recent yield from the dividend was 5.4%, which remains above the recent average for AEP's peers of 5.1%. Our 12-month target price is $35, which reflects an approximate peer P/E of 11.5X our EPS estimate for 2010.

Qualitative Risk Assessment

LOW	MEDIUM	HIGH

Our risk assessment reflects our view of the steady cash flow expected from the regulated utilities, with their low-cost fuel sources and generally supportive regulatory environments. The proceeds from the divestiture of most of AEP's high-risk unregulated energy businesses were used to enhance its balance sheet and financial strength.

Quantitative Evaluations

S&P Quality Ranking B

D	C	B-	B	B+	A-	A	A+

Relative Strength Rank MODERATE

61

LOWEST = 1   HIGHEST = 99

Revenue/Earnings Data

Revenue (Million $)

	1Q	2Q	3Q	4Q	Year
2009	3,458	3,202	3,547	--	--
2008	3,467	3,546	4,191	3,236	14,440
2007	3,169	3,146	3,789	3,276	13,380
2006	3,108	2,936	3,594	2,984	12,622
2005	3,065	2,819	3,328	2,899	12,111
2004	3,364	3,408	3,780	3,505	14,057

Earnings Per Share ($)

	1Q	2Q	3Q	4Q	Year
2009	0.81	0.68	0.93	E0.52	E2.99
2008	1.43	0.70	0.93	0.34	3.39
2007	0.68	0.64	1.02	0.52	2.86
2006	0.95	0.43	0.67	0.44	2.50
2005	0.90	0.57	0.94	0.23	2.63
2004	0.73	0.38	1.04	0.69	2.85

Fiscal year ended Dec. 31. Next earnings report expected: Late January. EPS Estimates based on S&P Operating Earnings; historical GAAP earnings are as reported.

Dividend Data (Dates: mm/dd Payment Date: mm/dd/yy)

Amount ($)	Date Decl.	Ex-Div. Date	Stk. of Record	Payment Date
0.410	01/28	02/06	02/10	03/10/09
0.410	04/28	05/06	05/08	06/10/09
0.410	07/29	08/06	08/10	09/10/09
0.410	10/27	11/06	11/10	12/10/09

Dividends have been paid since 1909. Source: Company reports.

Please read the Required Disclosures and Analyst Certification on the last page of this report.

American Electric Power Co Inc

STANDARD &POOR'S

Business Summary October 27, 2009

CORPORATE OVERVIEW. AEP is a holding company that primarily operates electric utility services through its regulated subsidiaries. The utility services include the generation, transmission and distribution of electricity for sale to retail and wholesale customers in the U.S. AEP's non-regulated operations include the MEMCO Barge Line subsidiary, which is engaged in the transportation of coal and dry bulk commodities, mainly on the Ohio, Illinois and lower Mississippi rivers. In 2008, the utility segment accounted for 92.3% of total revenues.

CORPORATE STRATEGY. AEP focuses on its core utility operations and seeks to deliver low-cost electric power to the communities it serves. The company plans to improve its efficiency and to maximize the power delivered from its generation facilities. In order to provide safe and reliable power, AEP will continue to make investments to upgrade its transmission and distribution infrastructure, as well as to be in compliance with the appropriate environmental standards. However, due to the conditions in the capital markets, these investments will be lower than previously projected, with AEP having lowered its 2009 capital investment budget by $750 million, a roughly 23% reduction, and 35% below its expenditures in 2008. While this plan will lessen its need to

access credit, AEP has noted that it must still address the critical problem of not allowing the recent decline in its cash flow to hurt its overall financial strength.

MARKET PROFILE. AEP provides electric utility services to over 5 million retail customers in 11 states over a total area of 197,500 square miles. The company derived 39.8% of its total utility operating revenues in 2008 from Ohio, while Virginia, Indiana and Oklahoma contributed 21.7, 16.3% and 12.4%, respectively. In 2008, the residential segment contributed 32.0% of utility retail revenues (41.5% in 2007), followed by commercial and industrial, which contributed 23.4% (30.2%) and 22.2% (27.8%), respectively. Wholesale sales accounted for 20.6% of total utility sales in 2008, up from 17.8% in 2007, while other sales accounted for the remainder. At the end of 2008, AEP had 100% ownership of 224,095 overhead circuit miles of transmission and distribution lines.

Company Financials Fiscal Year Ended Dec. 31

Per Share Data ($)	2008	2007	2006	2005	2004	2003	2002	2001	2000	1999
Tangible Book Value	26.09	25.17	24.88	22.87	21.31	19.74	19.67	20.92	20.72	25.80
Earnings	3.39	2.86	2.50	2.63	2.85	1.35	0.06	3.11	0.94	2.69
S&P Core Earnings	2.29	2.77	2.35	2.26	2.58	1.47	0.07	2.17	NA	NA
Dividends	1.64	1.58	1.50	1.42	1.40	1.65	2.40	2.40	2.40	2.40
Payout Ratio	48%	58%	60%	54%	49%	NM	NM	77%	255%	89%
Prices:High	49.11	51.24	43.13	40.80	35.53	31.51	48.80	51.20	48.94	48.19
Prices:Low	25.54	41.67	32.27	32.25	28.50	19.01	15.10	39.25	25.94	30.56
P/E Ratio:High	14	19	17	16	12	23	NM	16	52	18
P/E Ratio:Low	8	15	13	12	10	14	NM	13	28	11

Income Statement Analysis (Million $)										
Revenue	14,440	13,380	12,622	12,111	14,057	14,545	14,555	61,257	13,694	6,916
Depreciation	1,571	1,513	1,467	1,318	1,300	1,299	1,377	1,383	1,062	600
Maintenance	NA	NA	NA	NA	NA	NA	NA	NA	NA	NA
Fixed Charges Coverage	3.09	2.96	2.96	2.80	2.60	2.97	2.84	2.64	1.95	2.44
Construction Credits	45.0	33.0	30.0	21.0	NA	NA	NA	NA	NA	NA
Effective Tax Rate	31.9%	31.0%	32.7%	29.4%	33.7%	39.8%	79.3%	35.9%	66.4%	33.3%
Net Income	1,368	1,144	992	1,029	1,127	522	21.0	1,003	302	520
S&P Core Earnings	924	1,107	934	883	1,021	573	21.1	698	NA	NA

Balance Sheet & Other Financial Data (Million $)										
Gross Property	49,710	46,145	42,021	39,121	37,286	36,033	37,857	40,709	38,088	22,205
Capital Expenditures	3,960	3,556	3,528	2,404	1,693	1,358	1,722	1,832	1,773	867
Net Property	32,987	29,870	26,781	24,284	22,801	22,029	21,684	24,543	22,393	13,055
Capitalization:Long Term Debt	15,597	14,263	12,490	11,073	11,069	12,459	9,329	10,230	10,097	6,500
Capitalization:% Long Term Debt	59.3	58.6	57.0	54.9	56.5	61.3	56.9	55.4	55.6	56.5
Capitalization:Preferred	Nil	Nil	Nil	Nil	Nil	Nil	Nil	Nil	Nil	Nil
Capitalization:% Preferred	Nil	Nil	Nil	Nil	Nil	Nil	Nil	Nil	Nil	Nil
Capitalization:Common	10,693	10,079	9,412	9,088	8,515	7,874	7,064	8,229	8,054	5,006
Capitalization:% Common	40.7	41.4	43.0	45.1	43.5	38.7	43.1	44.6	44.4	43.5
Total Capital	31,418	29,072	26,802	25,032	24,403	24,290	21,523	24,523	23,554	14,577
% Operating Ratio	85.1	86.5	87.2	84.1	85.8	88.8	91.3	96.1	85.2	81.1
% Earned on Net Property	8.9	8.2	7.7	8.2	8.9	7.7	5.8	10.2	9.2	10.1
% Return on Revenue	9.5	8.6	7.9	8.5	8.0	3.6	0.1	1.6	2.2	7.5
% Return on Invested Capital	7.7	7.1	7.5	6.2	6.1	9.4	8.8	8.4	6.8	7.2
% Return on Common Equity	13.2	11.7	10.7	11.7	13.8	7.0	0.3	12.3	3.6	10.6

Data as orig reptd.; bef. results of disc opers/spec. items. Per share data adj. for stk. divs.; EPS diluted. E-Estimated. NA-Not Available. NM-Not Meaningful. NR-Not Ranked. UR-Under Review.

Office: 1 Riverside Plz, Columbus , OH 43215-2373.
Telephone: 614-716-1000.
Email: corpcomm@aep.com
Website: http://www.aep.com

Chrmn, Pres & CEO: M.G. Morris
COO: C.L. English
EVP & CFO: B.X. Tierney
EVP, Secy & General Counsel: J.B. Keane

SVP, Chief Acctg Officer & Cntlr: J.M. Buonaiuto
Investor Contact: B. Rozsa (614-716-2840)
Board Members: E. R. Brooks, D. M. Carlton, J. F. Cordes, R. D. Crosby, Jr., L. A. Goodspeed, T. E. Hoaglin, L. A. Hudson, Jr., M. G. Morris, L. L. Nowell, III, R. L. Sandor, K. D. Sullivan, S. M. Tucker, J. F. Turner

Founded: 1906
Domicile: New York
Employees: 21,912

The McGraw-Hill Companies

American Express Co

STANDARD
&POOR'S

S&P Recommendation HOLD ★★★☆☆	Price $40.84 (as of Nov 27, 2009)	12-Mo. Target Price $44.00	Investment Style Large-Cap Growth

GICS Sector Financials
Sub-Industry Consumer Finance

Summary American Express is a leading global payments and travel company.

Key Stock Statistics (Source S&P, Vickers, company reports)

52-Wk Range	$42.20– 9.71	S&P Oper. EPS 2009**E**	1.52	Market Capitalization(B)	$48.566	Beta	2.10
Trailing 12-Month EPS	$1.16	S&P Oper. EPS 2010**E**	2.45	Yield (%)	1.76	S&P 3-Yr. Proj. EPS CAGR(%)	2
Trailing 12-Month P/E	35.2	P/E on S&P Oper. EPS 2009**E**	26.9	Dividend Rate/Share	$0.72	S&P Credit Rating	BBB+
$10K Invested 5 Yrs Ago	NA	Common Shares Outstg. (M)	1,189.2	Institutional Ownership (%)	79		

Price Performance

30-Week Mov. Avg. ··· 10-Week Mov. Avg. – – GAAP Earnings vs. Previous Year Volume Above Avg. STARS
12-Mo. Target Price — Relative Strength — ▲ Up ▼ Down ► No Change Below Avg. ★

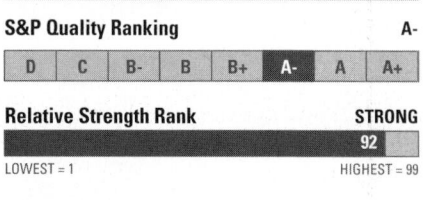

Options: ASE, CBOE, P, Ph

Analysis prepared by **Stuart Plesser** on November 19, 2009, when the stock traded at **$ 41.16**.

Highlights

► After a projected 14.5% decline in revenue in 2009, we expect 2010 revenue to increase roughly 6.0%, largely reflecting higher consumer spending assuming the economy improves, offset partially by AXP's cutback on outstanding credit lines. We see sales increasing in all of AXP's divisions, with its U.S. card division posting the most robust gains.

► We project a pickup in expenses in 2010, as we anticipate that marketing expenses will increase as AXP will likely attempt to reinforce its brand presence. In addition, higher interest rates will likely crimp margins. We see a decrease in the provision for losses of about 20% due largely to declining write-offs and delinquency rates, and our assumption that unemployment will peak in the first half of 2010. With reserves totaling 10.7% of owned loans at the end of the third quarter, versus 9.9% three months earlier, we think AXP remains conservative regarding a possible further downturn in the economy.

► Including the repayment of TARP funds and the repurchase of warrants, we see EPS of $1.52 in 2009. In 2010, we look for EPS of $2.45.

Investment Rationale/Risk

► We think chargeoffs in AXP's U.S. card business will stabilize as early delinquencies are slowing despite rising unemployment rates. We also think that revenue will trend higher as consumer spending seems to have stabilized. We think AXP's provisions will remain elevated in 2010 due to historically high chargeoff levels. Still, with early delinquencies slowing down, chargeoffs should decline on a sequential basis. Savings from lower chargeoffs will likely be used to invest in AXP's more profitable business lines. We note that AXP's business model has become more capital intensive and that return on equity should decline even after credit deterioration subsides.

► Risks to our recommendation and target price include a higher-than-expected slowdown in consumer and business spending, and a rise in unemployment above our expectations, exacerbating credit quality concerns.

► Our 12-month target price of $44 values the stock at 17.9X our 2010 EPS estimate of $2.45, slightly below its historical 12-month P/E multiple. We think this is an appropriate valuation multiple given higher capital requirements in AXP's business.

Qualitative Risk Assessment

LOW	MEDIUM	HIGH

Our risk assessment reflects what we see as solid business fundamentals and a strong customer base. We view AXP as able to withstand a major global or U.S. economic downturn. Although we look for AXP to remain profitable, the extent of write-downs is uncertain due to unprecedented national home price declines and rising unemployment rates.

Quantitative Evaluations

S&P Quality Ranking   A-

D	C	B-	B	B+	A-	A	A+

Relative Strength Rank   STRONG

92

LOWEST = 1   HIGHEST = 99

Revenue/Earnings Data

Revenue (Million $)

	1Q	2Q	3Q	4Q	Year
2009	8,073	8,656	6,559	--	--
2008	8,105	8,340	8,007	7,468	31,920
2007	7,631	8,199	7,953	7,364	31,557
2006	6,319	6,850	6,759	7,208	27,136
2005	5,672	6,090	6,068	6,437	24,267
2004	6,910	7,232	7,202	7,771	29,115

Earnings Per Share ($)

	1Q	2Q	3Q	4Q	Year
2009	0.32	0.09	0.54	E0.57	E1.52
2008	0.90	0.57	0.74	0.27	2.48
2007	0.88	0.88	0.90	0.71	3.39
2006	0.70	0.78	0.78	0.76	3.01
2005	0.59	0.69	0.69	0.60	2.56
2004	0.66	0.68	0.69	0.71	2.74

Fiscal year ended Dec. 31. Next earnings report expected: Late January. EPS Estimates based on S&P Operating Earnings; historical GAAP earnings are as reported.

Dividend Data (Dates: mm/dd Payment Date: mm/dd/yy)

Amount ($)	Date Decl.	Ex-Div. Date	Stk. of Record	Payment Date
0.180	11/17	01/07	01/09	02/10/09
0.180	03/23	04/01	04/03	05/08/09
0.180	05/18	06/30	07/02	08/10/09
0.180	09/21	09/30	10/02	11/10/09

Dividends have been paid since 1870. Source: Company reports.

American Express Co

STANDARD
&POOR'S

Business Summary November 19, 2009

CORPORATE OVERVIEW. American Express is a leading global payments and travel company. Its businesses are organized into two customer-focused groups -- global consumer and global business-to-business. Accordingly, U.S. card services and international card services are aligned within the global consumer group and global commercial services and global network & merchant services are alligned within the global business-to-business group.

U.S. Card Services includes the U.S. proprietary consumer card business, OPEN from American Express, the global Travelers Cheques and Prepaid Services business, and the American Express U.S. Consumer Travel Network.

International Card Services issues proprietary consumer and small business cards outside the U.S.

Global Commercial Services offers global corporate payment and travel-related products and services to large and midsized companies. It offers five primary products and services: Corporate Card, issued to individuals through a corporate account established by their employer and designed primarily for travel and entertainment spending; Corporate Purchasing Solutions, an account established by corporations to pay for everyday business expenses such as office and computer supplies; Buyer Initiated Payment, an electronic

solution for companies looking to streamline their payment processes; vPayment technology, which provides fast and efficient payment for large ticket purchases and permits the processing of large transactions with effective fraud; and American Express Business Travel, which helps businesses manage and optimize their travel expenses through a variety of travel-related products, services and solutions.

Global Network & Merchant Services consists of the merchant services businesses and global network services. Global Network Services develops and manages relationships with third parties that issue American Express branded cards. The Global Merchant Services businesses develop and manage relationships with merchants that accept American Express branded cards; authorize and record transactions; pay merchants; and provide a variety of value-added point of sale and back office services. In addition, in particular emerging markets, issuance of certain proprietary cards is managed within the Global Network Services business.

Company Financials Fiscal Year Ended Dec. 31

Per Share Data ($)	2008	2007	2006	2005	2004	2003	2002	2001	2000	1999
Tangible Book Value	7.61	8.22	7.52	8.50	12.83	11.93	10.62	9.04	8.81	7.53
Earnings	2.48	3.39	3.01	2.56	2.74	2.31	2.01	0.98	2.07	1.81
S&P Core Earnings	2.08	2.87	2.85	2.49	2.53	2.09	1.68	0.73	NA	NA
Dividends	0.72	0.60	0.54	0.48	0.32	0.38	0.32	0.32	0.32	0.30
Payout Ratio	29%	18%	18%	19%	12%	16%	16%	33%	15%	17%
Prices:High	52.63	65.89	62.50	59.50	57.05	49.11	44.91	57.06	63.00	56.29
Prices:Low	16.55	50.37	49.73	46.59	47.32	30.90	26.55	24.20	39.83	31.63
P/E Ratio:High	21	19	21	23	21	21	22	58	30	31
P/E Ratio:Low	7	15	17	18	17	13	13	25	19	18

Income Statement Analysis (Million $)	2008	2007	2006	2005	2004	2003	2002	2001	2000	1999
Cards in Force	92.4	86.4	78.0	71.0	65.4	60.5	57.3	55.2	51.7	46.0
Card Charge Volume	NA	NA	NA	484,400	416,100	352,200	311,400	298,000	296,700	254,100
Premium Income	Nil	Nil	Nil	Nil	1,525	1,366	802	674	575	517
Commissions	4,317	4,343	4,333	4,236	4,079	3,484	3,521	3,969	4,165	3,626
Interest & Dividends	7,201	6,145	4,535	3,635	3,118	3,063	2,991	3,049	4,277	4,679
Total Revenue	31,920	31,557	27,136	24,267	29,115	25,866	23,807	22,582	23,675	16,599
Net Before Taxes	3,473	5,566	5,328	4,248	4,951	4,247	3,727	1,596	3,908	3,438
Net Income	2,871	4,048	3,729	3,221	3,516	3,000	2,671	1,311	2,810	2,475
S&P Core Earnings	2,412	3,426	3,531	3,144	3,244	2,723	2,245	986	NA	NA

Balance Sheet & Other Financial Data (Million $)	2008	2007	2006	2005	2004	2003	2002	2001	2000	1999
Total Assets	126,000	149,830	127,853	113,960	192,638	175,001	157,253	151,100	154,423	148,517
Cash Items	21,000	14,036	11,270	7,126	9,907	5,726	10,288	7,222	8,487	7,471
Investment Assets:Bonds	Nil	Nil	Nil	Nil	Nil	Nil	Nil	Nil	Nil	Nil
Investment Assets:Stocks	Nil	Nil	Nil	Nil	Nil	Nil	Nil	Nil	Nil	Nil
Investment Assets:Loans	40,659	53,436	50,248	40,801	35,942	33,421	29,003	27,401	26,884	24,332
Investment Assets:Total	53,185	67,472	61,518	62,135	60,809	57,067	53,638	46,488	43,747	43,052
Accounts Receivable	36,571	95,441	89,099	35,497	34,650	31,269	29,087	29,498	30,543	26,467
Customer Deposits	15,486	15,397	24,656	24,579	21,091	21,250	18,317	14,557	13,870	12,197
Travel Cheques Outstanding	6,433	7,197	7,215	7,175	7,287	6,819	6,623	6,190	6,127	6,213
Debt	69,034	73,047	57,909	30,781	33,061	30,809	16,819	8,288	5,211	6,495
Common Equity	12,000	11,029	10,511	10,549	16,020	15,323	13,861	12,037	11,684	10,095
% Return on Assets	2.0	2.9	3.1	2.1	1.9	1.8	1.7	0.9	1.9	1.8
% Return on Equity	24.3	37.6	35.4	24.2	22.4	20.6	20.6	11.1	25.8	25.0

Data as orig reptd.; bef. results of disc opers/spec. items. Per share data adj. for stk. divs.; EPS diluted. E-Estimated. NA-Not Available. NM-Not Meaningful. NR-Not Ranked. UR-Under Review.

Office: World Financial Ctr, 200 Vesey Street, New York, NY 10285-4814.
Telephone: 212-640-2000.
Website: http://www.americanexpress.com
Chrmn & CEO: K.I. Chenault

Pres: A.F. Kelly, Jr.
EVP & CFO: D.T. Henry
EVP & General Counsel: L.M. Parent
EVP & Cntlr: J. Amble

Investor Contact: R. Stovall (212-640-5574)
Board Members: D. F. Akerson, C. Barshefsky, U. M. Burns, K. I. Chenault, P. Chernin, J. Leschly, R. C. Levin, R. A. McGinn, E. D. Miller, Jr., S. S. Reinemund, R. D. Walter, R. A. Williams

Founded: 1868
Domicile: New York
Employees: 66,000

American International Group Inc

STANDARD &POOR'S

S&P Recommendation HOLD ★★★☆☆

Price	12-Mo. Target Price
$33.30 (as of Nov 27, 2009)	$45.00

GICS Sector Financials
Sub-Industry Multi-line Insurance

Summary AIG provides property, casualty and life insurance, as well as other financial services, in 130 countries.

Key Stock Statistics (Source S&P, Vickers, company reports)

52-Wk Range	$55.90– 6.60	S&P Oper. EPS 2009**E**	3.51	Market Capitalization(B)	$4.482	Beta	4.02
Trailing 12-Month EPS	$-484.10	S&P Oper. EPS 2010**E**	4.00	Yield (%)	Nil	S&P 3-Yr. Proj. EPS CAGR(%)	NM
Trailing 12-Month P/E	NM	P/E on S&P Oper. EPS 2009**E**	9.5	Dividend Rate/Share	Nil	S&P Credit Rating	A-
$10K Invested 5 Yrs Ago	$275	Common Shares Outstg. (M)	134.6	Institutional Ownership (%)	26		

Price Performance

30-Week Mov. Avg. · · · ·   10-Week Mov. Avg. – –   **GAAP Earnings vs. Previous Year**   Volume Above Avg. ▮▮▮ STARS
12-Mo. Target Price —   Relative Strength —   ▲ Up ▼ Down ▶ No Change   Below Avg. ▮▮▮

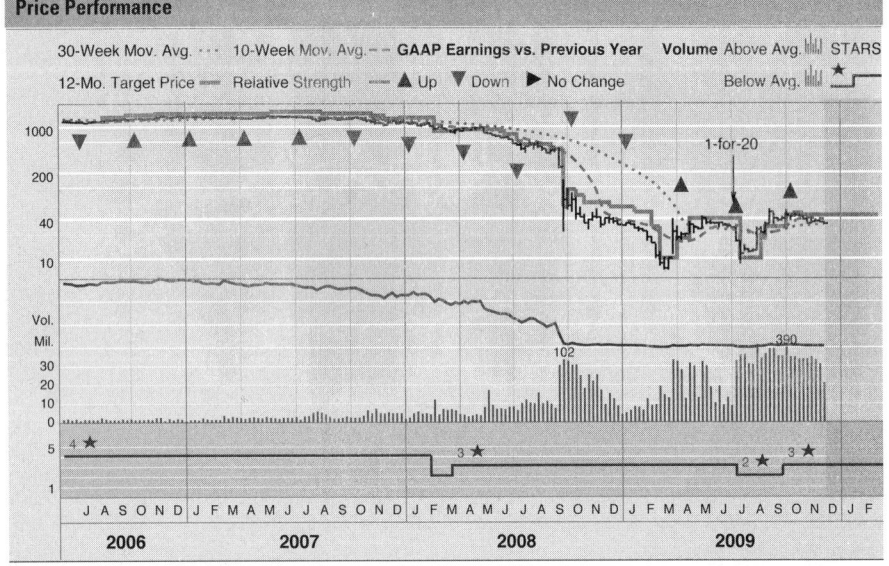

Options: ASE, CBOE, P, Ph

Analysis prepared by **Cathy A. Seifert** on October 22, 2009, when the stock traded at **$ 39.03**.

Highlights

▶ AIG entered into an $85 billion revolving credit facility with the Federal Reserve Bank of New York in September 2008, after its outsized exposure to mortgage and credit default swap losses threatened the firm. Initial terms of the two-year facility included an interest rate of 3-month LIBOR plus 8.5%, plus commitment fees. The credit facility is secured by a pledge of AIG's assets. Modifications to the loan in early November included a reduction in principal to $60 billion, an interest rate of LIBOR plus 3%, and a term of five years. AIG also sold $40 billion of a new issue of preferred stock to the Treasury, and entered a securities lending agreement with the Fed. In early 2009, AIG obtained an easing of certain terms and an additional $30 billion credit line.

▶ AIG was also required, under terms of the agreement, to issue a new series of preferred stock, convertible at any time into 77.9% of the common stock of the company. The preferred shares were issued on March 4, 2009, held in a trust for the benefit of the U.S. Treasury.

▶ We estimate an operating loss of $13.40 a share in 2009, versus the $37.84 a share net loss reported for 2008.

Investment Rationale/Risk

▶ Despite the recent rebound in the shares, we still view AIG's financial position as strained and its turnaround strategy fraught with execution risk. Stated shareholders' equity at June 30 was $58.0 billion, but we estimate tangible common shareholders' equity (excluding goodwill, deferred acquisition costs, and preferred shareholder interests) to be -$35.4 billion. The March 4, 2009, issuance of 100,000 shares of Series C convertible preferred stock to a trust established for the benefit of the U.S. Treasury effected a change of control of AIG, since the Series C preferred represents some 77.9% of the aggregate voting power of AIG common stock, assuming conversion of the preferred.

▶ Risks to our recommendation and target price include AIG's ability to sell enough assets and restructure its existing operations in a timely manner to repay the Federal Reserve loan.

▶ Our 12-month target price of $45 assumes the shares trade at a discount to peers on a price-to-book value basis. We believe this discount is warranted amid our view that book value is heavily weighted with intangible assets, the value of which we are not certain AIG will be able to maintain.

Qualitative Risk Assessment

LOW	MEDIUM	**HIGH**

AIG's outsized exposure (versus peers in the insurance industry) to the mortgage industry and to the credit default swap market led to an emergency bailout by the Federal Reserve in 2008 and additional capital infusions in early 2009. Going forward, we believe there remains a high degree of execution risk as AIG seeks to restructure. We cannot rule out the need for additional capital infusions or further government intervention.

Quantitative Evaluations

S&P Quality Ranking   B

D	C	B-	**B**	B+	A-	A	A+

Relative Strength Rank   WEAK

20

LOWEST = 1   HIGHEST = 99

Revenue/Earnings Data

Revenue (Million $)

	1Q	2Q	3Q	4Q	Year
2009	20,458	29,525	26,049	--	--
2008	14,031	19,933	898.0	-23,758	11,104
2007	30,645	31,150	29,836	18,433	110,064
2006	27,259	26,743	29,199	29,993	113,194
2005	27,202	27,903	26,408	27,392	108,905
2004	23,637	23,809	25,411	25,760	97,987

Earnings Per Share ($)

2009	-39.60	2.30	0.68	E2.00	E3.51
2008	-61.80	-41.20	-181.00	-459.00	-756.80
2007	31.60	32.80	23.80	-41.40	47.80
2006	24.20	24.20	32.20	26.20	107.00
2005	29.00	34.20	13.20	3.40	79.80
2004	21.60	21.80	19.00	23.00	75.00

Fiscal year ended Dec. 31. Next earnings report expected: Early March. EPS Estimates based on S&P Operating Earnings; historical GAAP earnings are as reported.

Dividend Data

No cash dividends have been paid on the common shares since September 2008.

American International Group Inc

STANDARD
&POOR'S

Business Summary October 22, 2009

American International Group provides an array of insurance and financial services in 130 countries and territories. Investigations several years ago by the New York Attorney General and the SEC into AIG's use of non-traditional insurance products and certain assumed reinsurance transactions culminated in a number of events, including a management shake-up that led to the resignation of AIG's long-time CEO Maurice Greenberg; a writedown against earnings from 2000-2004 of nearly $4 billion; and a writedown of shareholders' equity of $2.26 billion. During 2005, AIG also incurred after-tax charges totaling $1.15 billion to settle numerous regulatory issues and $1.19 billion to boost loss reserves. During 2007 and 2008, AIG was confronted with the downward spiral of the U.S. residential mortgage market and subsequent deterioration in broader credit market conditions. To help replenish its capital, AIG in May 2008 raised $20 billion of new capital that included the sale of 196,710,525 common shares for $7.47 billion.

These moves proved insufficient, and in late September 2008, AIG was forced to accept an emergency line of credit from the Federal Reserve. To repay the Federal Reserve loan, AIG is undergoing a planned sale of its assets, including the December 2008 sale of Hartford Steam Boiler (HSB) to Munich Re for $742

million in cash and the assumption of $76 million of debt (less than the $1.2 billion AIG paid for HSB in 2000), the January 2009 sale of AIG Life Insurance Co. of Canada to BMO Financial Group for about $308 million in cash, and the June 2009 sale of 29.9 million shares of Transatlantic Holdings, Inc. (TRH) for gross proceeds of $1.1 billion. Subsequent revisions and additions to the original terms have resulted in AIG receiving federal aid valued at approximately $173 billion and in trusts established for the benefit of the U.S. Treasury controlling approximately 77.9% of the voting power of AIG common stock.

Revenues totaled $11.1 billion in 2008, down nearly 90% from $110.1 billion in 2007, largely due to a 57% drop in investment income, $55.5 billion of pretax realized investment losses, and $28.6 billion of writedowns of the credit default swap portfolio. Following an 18.5% rise in benefits and expenses (including a surge in interest expense), the company reported a $99.3 billion net loss ($37.84 a share), versus a 2007 profit of $6.2 billion ($2.39 a share).

Company Financials Fiscal Year Ended Dec. 31

Per Share Data ($)	2008	2007	2006	2005	2004	2003	2002	2001	2000	1999
Tangible Book Value	347.20	683.00	759.20	602.60	554.60	487.80	406.40	398.80	339.60	286.67
Operating Earnings	NA	NA	NA	NA	NA	NA	NA	NA	49.00	42.60
Earnings	-756.80	47.80	107.00	79.80	75.00	70.60	42.00	41.40	48.20	43.07
S&P Core Earnings	-388.40	66.20	107.20	87.00	75.40	77.80	52.60	41.20	NA	NA
Dividends	12.40	14.60	12.60	11.00	5.60	4.40	3.56	3.16	2.81	2.53
Relative Payout	NM	31%	12%	14%	7%	6%	8%	8%	6%	6%
Prices:High	1188	1459	1459	1469	1547	1327	1600	1966	2075	1505
Prices:Low	25.00	1017	1150	998.20	1086	858.40	952.20	1320	1048	1020
P/E Ratio:High	NM	31	14	18	21	19	38	47	43	35
P/E Ratio:Low	NM	21	11	13	14	12	23	32	22	24

Income Statement Analysis (Million $)										
Life Insurance in Force	2,378,314	2,312,045	2,070,600	1,852,833	1,858,094	1,596,626	1,324,451	1,228,501	583,059	584,959
Premium Income:Life A & H	37,295	33,627	30,636	29,400	28,082	22,879	20,320	19,243	13,610	11,942
Premium Income:Casualty/Property.	46,222	45,682	43,451	41,872	40,607	31,734	24,269	19,365	17,407	15,544
Net Investment Income	12,222	28,619	25,292	22,165	18,434	16,662	15,034	14,628	9,824	8,723
Total Revenue	11,104	110,064	113,194	108,905	97,987	81,303	67,482	52,852	40,717	36,356
Pretax Income	-108,761	8,943	21,687	15,213	14,950	13,908	8,142	8,139	8,349	7,512
Net Operating Income	NA	NA	NA	105	NA	NA	NA	NA	5,737	4,999
Net Income	-99,289	6,200	14,014	10,477	9,875	9,265	5,519	5,499	5,636	5,055
S&P Core Earnings	-51,166	8,585	14,018	11,396	9,928	10,208	6,931	5,476	NA	NA

Balance Sheet & Other Financial Data (Million $)										
Cash & Equivalent	14,641	8,871	7,681	7,624	7,597	5,881	1,165	698	256	132
Premiums Due	17,330	18,395	17,789	15,333	15,137	14,166	13,088	11,647	11,832	12,737
Investment Assets:Bonds	404,134	428,935	417,865	385,680	365,677	309,254	243,366	200,616	102,010	90,144
Investment Assets:Stocks	21,143	41,646	30,222	23,588	17,851	9,584	7,066	7,937	7,181	6,714
Investment Assets:Loans	34,687	33,727	28,418	24,909	22,463	21,249	19,928	18,092	12,243	12,134
Investment Assets:Total	554,446	755,596	719,685	614,759	494,592	449,657	339,320	357,602	140,910	185,882
Deferred Policy Costs	45,782	43,150	37,235	33,248	29,736	26,398	22,256	17,443	10,189	9,624
Total Assets	860,418	1,060,505	979,414	853,370	798,660	678,346	561,229	492,982	306,577	268,238
Debt	155,904	162,935	186,866	78,625	66,850	57,877	50,076	34,503	5,801	23,795
Common Equity	52,690	95,801	101,677	86,317	80,607	71,253	59,103	52,150	39,619	33,306
Combined Loss-Expense Ratio	109.1	90.3	89.1	104.7	100.1	92.4	106.0	100.7	96.7	96.4
% Return on Revenue	NM	5.6	12.4	9.6	10.1	11.4	8.2	10.5	13.8	13.9
% Return on Equity	NM	6.3	14.9	12.6	13.1	14.2	9.9	11.0	15.5	15.9
% Investment Yield	2.0	3.9	3.8	3.7	3.9	4.1	4.8	4.5	7.4	4.9

Data as orig reptd.; bef. results of disc opers/spec. items. Per share data adj. for stk. divs.; EPS diluted. E-Estimated. NA-Not Available. NM-Not Meaningful. NR-Not Ranked. UR-Under Review.

Office: 70 Pine Street, New York, NY 10270-0094.
Telephone: 212-770-7000.
Website: http://www.aigcorporate.com
Chrmn: H. Golub

Pres & CEO: R.H. Benmosche
COO: G. Flood
EVP & CFO: D.L. Herzog
EVP & General Counsel: A.D. Kelly

Investor Contact: S.J. Bensinger
Board Members: R. H. Benmosche, D. D. Dammerman, H. Golub, S. N. Johnson, L. T. Koellner, C. S. Lynch, A. C. Martinez, G. L. Miles, Jr., R. S. Miller, M. W. Offit, J. J. Roberts, D. M. Steenland

Founded: 1967
Domicile: Delaware
Employees: 116,000

The McGraw-Hill Companies

American Tower Corp

STANDARD &POOR'S

S&P Recommendation **STRONG BUY** ★★★★★	Price $40.88 (as of Nov 27, 2009)	12-Mo. Target Price $49.00	Investment Style Large-Cap Blend

GICS Sector Telecommunication Services
Sub-Industry Wireless Telecommunication Services

Summary This company operates the largest independent portfolio of wireless communications and broadcast towers in North America.

Key Stock Statistics (Source S&P, Vickers, company reports)

52-Wk Range	$41.78–24.95	S&P Oper. EPS 2009**E**	0.65	Market Capitalization(B)	$16.411	Beta	0.90
Trailing 12-Month EPS	$0.67	S&P Oper. EPS 2010**E**	0.87	Yield (%)	Nil	S&P 3-Yr. Proj. EPS CAGR(%)	20
Trailing 12-Month P/E	61.0	P/E on S&P Oper. EPS 2009**E**	62.9	Dividend Rate/Share	Nil	S&P Credit Rating	BB+
$10K Invested 5 Yrs Ago	$22,838	Common Shares Outstg. (M)	401.5	Institutional Ownership (%)	94		

Price Performance

30-Week Mov. Avg. ··· 10-Week Mov. Avg. - - **GAAP Earnings vs. Previous Year** Volume Above Avg. STARS
12-Mo. Target Price — Relative Strength — ▲ Up ▼ Down ▶ No Change Below Avg.

Options: ASE, CBOE, P, Ph

Analysis prepared by **James Moorman, CFA** on November 05, 2009, when the stock traded at **$38.84**.

Highlights

▶ Following a 9.4% revenue increase in 2008, we forecast a rise of 8.1% for 2009 and 8.3% for 2010, reflecting higher lease activity per active tower and more new towers. We believe AMT will benefit from favorable tower industry trends such as wireless carriers' demands to improve their network quality and coverage both in the U.S. and internationally.

▶ We are positive on AMT's operating discipline, and we look for operating expenses as a percentage of sales to decline in 2009 and then tick up slightly in 2010. We expect EBITDA margins, driven by higher tower utilization, to widen by roughly 20 basis points to 67.7% in 2009 and then to 68.4% in 2010, from 67.5% in 2008, levels well above the peer average. We believe this efficiency will enable free cash flow to increase to $656 million in 2009 and $841 million in 2010, from $597 million in 2008.

▶ We estimate EPS of $0.65 for 2009 and $0.87 for 2010, following $0.58 in 2008, including projected stock option expense of $0.15 in 2009. The company repurchased 3.6 million of its shares in the third quarter of 2009 for roughly $117.6 million.

Investment Rationale/Risk

▶ AMT is the market leader in the wireless tower industry, and we think further tower purchases will enable it to continue to achieve greater economies of scale. In our view, the recent spectrum auction will provide an additional revenue boost over the next several years. AMT has an estimated 2009 net debt/EBITDA ratio of 3.3X, well below peers. We also expect AMT to continue to expand internationally in Mexico and Brazil, with additional expansion into India. We consider the shares highly attractive for purchase.

▶ Risks to our recommendation and target price include slower demand in the tower lease business if carriers begin to cut back on spending. Another risk we see is the company's $4.2 billion of debt obligations.

▶ Our 12-month target price of $49 is largely based on 24X our free cash flow estimate for 2010, above the peer mean. Our target price also represents an enterprise value of 18.9X our 2010 EBITDA estimate, slightly above the industry average.

Qualitative Risk Assessment

LOW	MEDIUM	**HIGH**

Our risk assessment reflects the company's high total debt to total capitalization ratio, partly offset by our view of its steady cash flow and sufficient cash and investments to meet its working capital, capital expenditure and debt requirements.

Quantitative Evaluations

S&P Quality Ranking   B

D	C	B-	**B**	B+	A-	A	A+

Relative Strength Rank   **STRONG**

85

LOWEST = 1   HIGHEST = 99

Revenue/Earnings Data

Revenue (Million $)

	1Q	2Q	3Q	4Q	Year
2009	408.7	423.4	444.1	--	--
2008	382.2	393.7	409.3	408.3	1,594
2007	352.5	358.4	367.6	378.1	1,457
2006	320.4	325.9	333.5	337.7	1,317
2005	184.4	188.1	264.8	307.6	944.8
2004	168.8	172.3	180.9	184.7	706.7

Earnings Per Share ($)

2009	0.14	0.13	0.17	E0.19	E0.65
2008	0.10	0.12	0.15	0.21	0.58
2007	0.05	0.03	0.14	-0.01	0.22
2006	-0.01	0.02	0.01	0.04	0.06
2005	-0.14	-0.14	-0.06	0.13	-0.44
2004	-0.19	-0.27	-0.25	-0.30	-1.07

Fiscal year ended Dec. 31. Next earnings report expected: Late February. EPS Estimates based on S&P Operating Earnings; historical GAAP earnings are as reported.

Dividend Data

No cash dividends have been paid.

American Tower Corp

STANDARD &POOR'S

Business Summary November 05, 2009

CORPORATE OVERVIEW. American Tower Corp. operates the largest independent portfolio of wireless communications and broadcast towers in North America, based on the number of towers and revenue. The company's primary business is leasing antenna space on multi-tenant communications towers to wireless service providers and radio and television broadcast companies. The tower portfolio provides AMT with a recurring base of leased revenues from its customers and growth potential to add more tenants and equipment to these towers from its unused capacity. AMT also continues to expand its operations in Mexico and Brazil, and has started a controlled buildout in India.

PRIMARY BUSINESS DYNAMICS. Rental and management of the antenna sites is AMT's principal business, and accounted for 97% of revenue in the third quarter of 2009. AMT operated a tower portfolio of about 26,374 multi-user sites in the U.S., Mexico, Brazil and India, as of September 30, 2009. The company signs service providers to long-term leases of usually five to 10 years that contain annual lease rate escalations of 3%-5%. Sprint Nextel, AT&T Wireless and Verizon Wireless accounted for roughly 55% of AMT's 2008 tower revenue, putting AMT in a prime position for further market expansion projects, in our view. AMT could also benefit from increased data usage that will require service providers to add capacity to their cell sites, as well as

from carriers that expand their networks. Carriers such as Leap Wireless, MetroPCS and Clearwire are currently building out new networks, and we believe this will increase growth. In addition, U.S. carriers spent close to $20 billion on 700MHz spectrum, and could begin to enhance their networks as early as 2009, potentially with 4G networks.

International growth should benefit AMT in 2009, by our analysis. AMT has about 2,300 wireless towers and approximately 200 broadcast towers in Mexico and about 1,100 wireless towers in Brazil. Mexico accounted for roughly 9.8% of revenue in 2008, Brazil 4.5% and India less than 1%. Mexico and Brazil have penetration rates of about 75%, versus 85% in the U.S., and we believe that service providers will continue to build out their networks as well as deploy 3G networks with recently acquired spectrum. We think these markets will continue to provide significant growth as we believe they are also seeing significant data growth, which could lead to additional capacity requirements.

Company Financials Fiscal Year Ended Dec. 31

Per Share Data ($)	2008	2007	2006	2005	2004	2003	2002	2001	2000	1999
Tangible Book Value	NM	2.41	0.88	0.74	NM	0.28	NM	1.94	2.06	13.78
Cash Flow	1.83	1.41	1.28	0.92	0.40	0.34	0.01	-0.05	0.55	0.53
Earnings	0.58	0.22	0.06	-0.44	-1.07	-1.17	-1.61	-2.35	-1.13	-0.33
S&P Core Earnings	0.58	0.20	0.05	-0.50	-1.17	-1.35	-1.60	-2.50	NA	NA
Dividends	Nil	Nil	Nil	Nil	Nil	Nil	Nil	Nil	Nil	Nil
Payout Ratio	Nil	Nil	Nil	Nil	Nil	Nil	Nil	Nil	Nil	Nil
Prices:High	46.10	46.53	38.74	28.33	18.75	12.00	10.40	41.50	55.50	33.25
Prices:Low	19.35	36.34	26.66	16.28	9.89	3.55	0.60	5.25	27.63	17.13
P/E Ratio:High	79	NM	NM	NM	NM	NM	NM	NM	NM	NM
P/E Ratio:Low	33	NM	NM	NM	NM	NM	NM	NM	NM	NM

Income Statement Analysis (Million $)										
Revenue	1,594	1,457	1,317	945	707	715	788	1,134	735	258
Operating Income	1,020	898	803	589	423	377	312	251	196	91.5
Depreciation	527	510	528	411	329	313	317	440	283	133
Interest Expense	254	240	217	224	264	280	257	309	186	27.5
Pretax Income	372	153	70.9	-130	-317	-305	-248	-567	-250	-49.0
Effective Tax Rate	36.4%	39.1%	58.9%	NM	NM	NM	NM	NM	NM	NM
Net Income	236	92.7	28.3	-134	-239	-242	-315	-450	-190	-49.4
S&P Core Earnings	236	85.6	24.6	-154	-261	-281	-313	-480	NA	NA

Balance Sheet & Other Financial Data (Million $)										
Cash	145	94.0	281	113	216	105	127	130	128	25.2
Current Assets	474	246	486	226	309	412	536	522	471	139
Total Assets	8,212	8,130	8,613	8,768	5,086	5,332	5,662	6,830	5,661	3,019
Current Liabilities	303	317	570	453	332	295	670	343	298	125
Long Term Debt	4,331	4,240	3,289	3,451	3,155	3,284	3,195	3,549	2,457	736
Common Equity	2,991	3,022	4,382	4,527	1,464	1,706	1,740	2,869	2,877	2,145
Total Capital	7,326	7,309	7,678	7,988	4,626	5,008	4,950	6,433	5,350	2,890
Capital Expenditures	243	154	127	88.6	42.2	61.6	180	568	549	294
Cash Flow	763	603	556	277	90.2	71.0	2.11	-9.72	93.1	83.2
Current Ratio	1.6	0.8	0.9	0.5	0.9	1.4	0.8	1.5	1.6	1.1
% Long Term Debt of Capitalization	59.1	58.6	42.9	43.2	68.2	65.6	64.5	55.2	45.9	25.5
% Net Income of Revenue	14.8	6.4	2.2	NM	NM	NM	NM	NM	NM	NM
% Return on Assets	2.9	1.1	0.3	NM	NM	NM	NM	NM	NM	NM
% Return on Equity	7.9	2.5	0.6	NM	NM	NM	NM	NM	NM	NM

Data as orig reptd.; bef. results of disc opers/spec. items. Per share data adj. for stk. divs.; EPS diluted. E-Estimated. NA-Not Available. NM-Not Meaningful. NR-Not Ranked. UR-Under Review.

Office: 116 Huntington Avenue, Boston, MA 02116.
Telephone: 617-375-7500.
Email: ir@americantower.com
Website: http://www.americantower.com

Chrmn, Pres & CEO: J.D. Taiclet, Jr.
Pres: D. Carey
COO: W.H. Hess
EVP & CFO: T.A. Bartlett

EVP, Chief Admin Officer, Secy & General Counsel: E. DiSanto
Investor Contact: M. Powell (617-375-7500)
Board Members: G. L. Cantu, R. P. Dolan, R. Dykes, C. F. Katz, J. A. Reed, P. D. Reeve, D. E. Sharbutt, J. D. Taiclet, Jr., S. L. Thompson

Founded: 1995
Domicile: Delaware
Employees: 1,198

Stock Report | November 28, 2009 | NYS Symbol: **AMP** | **AMP** is in the S&P 500

Ameriprise Financial Inc

STANDARD &POOR'S

S&P Recommendation	HOLD ★★★☆☆	Price $37.05 (as of Nov 27, 2009)	12-Mo. Target Price $39.00	Investment Style Large-Cap Growth

GICS Sector Financials
Sub-Industry Asset Management & Custody Banks

Summary This diversified financial services company, spun off from American Express in September 2005, provides insurance, investment and asset management services.

Key Stock Statistics (Source S&P, Vickers, company reports)

52-Wk Range	$40.00– 13.50	S&P Oper. EPS 2009E	2.82	Market Capitalization(B)	$9.448	Beta	2.12
Trailing 12-Month EPS	$0.50	S&P Oper. EPS 2010E	3.18	Yield (%)	1.84	S&P 3-Yr. Proj. EPS CAGR(%)	NM
Trailing 12-Month P/E	74.1	P/E on S&P Oper. EPS 2009E	13.1	Dividend Rate/Share	$0.68	S&P Credit Rating	A
$10K Invested 5 Yrs Ago	NA	Common Shares Outstg. (M)	255.0	Institutional Ownership (%)	87		

Price Performance

Options: ASE, CBOE, P, Ph

Analysis prepared by **Matthew Albrecht** on October 23, 2009, when the stock traded at **$ 38.24**.

Highlights

► Client assets have begun to rebound, helping wealth and asset management segment results. The company has also agreed to acquire Columbia Management from Bank of America (BAC 16, Strong Buy) in a cash deal in which it will gain at least $165 billion in client assets. Recent performance at RiversSource funds has also improved. Market gains have boosted variable annuity sales too, while fixed annuity sales have slowed. The Protection segment continues to perform well. And while losses have declined in the investment portfolio, exposure to commercial and residential loans remains, raising its risk profile. We see modest top line growth in both 2009 and 2010.

► We expect the pretax margin to turn positive this year. We see the distribution margin improving, and while interest credited to fixed accounts should rise with fixed annuity balances, cost-cutting measures should help G&A costs. We expect deferred acquisition cost reversals to also boost margins in 2009 after sharp market declines caused DAC to jump 69% in 2008.

► We estimate EPS of $2.82 in 2009 and $3.18 in 2010.

Investment Rationale/Risk

► We believe AMP's focus on insurance products merits a lower valuation than some other asset managers. In our view, lower average asset balances will continue to hamper results. We also remain cautious on its investment portfolio, which includes residential and commercial mortgage securities and corporate debt and other asset-backed security holdings. Still asset balances are recovering, clients are re-engaging, and the Columbia acquisition could prove favorable to revenues and margins.

► Risks to our recommendation and target price include potential market depreciation and greater regulatory concerns.

► AMP recently traded at about 13.6X our 2009 EPS estimate, a discount to its asset management peers. We expect the shares to trade at a discount to peers due to AMP's revenue mix, with more reliance on insurance and annuity products. Our 12-month target price of $39 is equal to about 12.5X our forward 12-month earnings estimate of $3.13, a discount to its asset management peers.

Qualitative Risk Assessment

LOW	MEDIUM	HIGH

Our risk assessment reflects our view of the company's significant franchise value, offset by our concerns that the loss of the widely recognized American Express name could negatively affect AMP's ability to raise and retain client assets.

Quantitative Evaluations

S&P Quality Ranking NR

D	C	B-	B	B+	A-	A	A+

Relative Strength Rank STRONG

78

LOWEST = 1   HIGHEST = 99

Revenue/Earnings Data

Revenue (Million $)

	1Q	2Q	3Q	4Q	Year
2009	1,761	1,877	1,983	--	--
2008	2,000	1,979	1,641	1,350	6,970
2007	2,096	2,204	2,227	2,319	8,909
2006	1,949	2,053	1,977	2,161	8,140
2005	1,847	1,895	1,873	1,869	7,484
2004	1,783	1,788	1,712	2,061	6,770

Earnings Per Share ($)

2009	0.58	0.41	1.00	E0.83	E2.82
2008	0.82	0.93	-0.32	-1.69	-0.17
2007	0.68	0.81	0.83	1.08	3.39
2006	0.57	0.57	0.71	0.69	2.54
2005	0.71	0.61	0.50	0.44	2.26
2004	--	--	0.76	1.08	2.80

Fiscal year ended Dec. 31. Next earnings report expected: Late January. EPS Estimates based on S&P Operating Earnings; historical GAAP earnings are as reported.

Dividend Data (Dates: mm/dd Payment Date: mm/dd/yy)

Amount ($)	Date Decl.	Ex-Div. Date	Stk. of Record	Payment Date
0.170	01/26	02/04	02/06	02/20/09
0.170	04/21	04/30	05/04	05/18/09
0.170	07/23	07/30	08/03	08/17/09
0.170	10/21	10/29	11/02	11/16/09

Dividends have been paid since 2005. Source: Company reports.

Please read the Required Disclosures and Analyst Certification on the last page of this report.

The McGraw-Hill Companies

Redistribution or reproduction is prohibited without written permission. Copyright ©2009 The McGraw-Hill Companies, Inc.

Ameriprise Financial Inc

STANDARD & POOR'S

Business Summary October 23, 2009

CORPORATE OVERVIEW. Ameriprise Financial completed its spinoff from American Express on September 30, 2005, and began trading on the New York Stock Exchange on October 3 under the symbol AMP. As of December 31, 2008, Ameriprise owned, managed and administered $372 billion in client assets and operated a network of more than 12,000 financial advisers. Ameriprise offers a broad assortment of products, including mutual funds, annuities and life insurance products. Ameriprise was originally named Investors Diversified Services before it was acquired by American Express in 1984. We think AMP will need to prove that it can grow and prosper without the benefits of its previous owner, American Express, which spun off the company in 2005. We believe the spinoff and new marketing campaign have raised AMP's visibility among prospective clients and may also help attract and retain financial advisers. In terms of corporate governance, we view favorably the high proportion of independent directors on the board, but would prefer that the company split the roles of chairman and CEO.

Ameriprise reorganized the company late in 2007, and now has five operating segments. Advice and Wealth Management accounted for about 45% of net revenues in 2008, but posted a pretax loss, and provides financial advice and full-service brokerage and banking services, primarily to retail clients, through its financial advisers. The Asset Management segment (18%, $77 million in

pretax earnings) provides investment advice and investment products to retail and institutional clients. Threadneedle Investments predominantly provides international investment products and services, and RiverSource Investments predominantly provides products and services in the U.S. for domestic customers. Its domestic products are primarily distributed through the Advice and Wealth Management segment and third parties, while international products are mostly distributed through third parties. The Annuities segment (23%, pretax loss) provides RiverSource Life variable and fixed annuity products to retail clients, primarily through the Advice and Wealth Management segment. The Protection segment (29%, $352 million in pretax earnings) offers a variety of protection products to address the identified protection and risk management needs of retail clients including life, disability income and property-casualty insurance. The Corporate and Other segment consists of net investment income on corporate level assets, including unallocated equity and other revenues from various investments as well as unallocated corporate expenses. This segment, including intersegment eliminations, reduced net revenues by over $1 billion and contributed a pretax loss in 2008.

Company Financials Fiscal Year Ended Dec. 31

Per Share Data ($)	2008	2007	2006	2005	2004	2003	2002	2001	2000	1999
Tangible Book Value	22.41	34.81	31.10	30.75	6.45	NA	NA	NA	NA	NA
Cash Flow	-0.74	4.11	3.21	2.26	NA	NA	NA	NA	NA	NA
Earnings	-0.17	3.39	2.54	2.26	2.80	3.00	NA	NA	NA	NA
S&P Core Earnings	1.98	3.26	2.41	2.37	3.02	2.46	NA	NA	NA	NA
Dividends	0.64	0.56	0.44	0.11	NA	NA	NA	NA	NA	NA
Payout Ratio	NM	17%	17%	5%	NA	NA	NA	NA	NA	NA
Prices:High	57.55	69.25	55.79	44.78	NA	NA	NA	NA	NA	NA
Prices:Low	11.74	51.31	40.30	32.00	NA	NA	NA	NA	NA	NA
P/E Ratio:High	NM	20	22	20	NA	NA	NA	NA	NA	NA
P/E Ratio:Low	NM	15	16	14	NA	NA	NA	NA	NA	NA

Income Statement Analysis (Million $)

	2008	2007	2006	2005	2004	2003	2002	2001	2000	1999
Income Interest	2,899	3,238	2,204	2,241	2,125	NA	NA	NA	NA	NA
Income Other	4,250	5,671	5,936	5,243	4,645	NA	NA	NA	NA	NA
Total Income	7,149	8,909	8,140	7,484	6,770	6,361	5,793	NA	NA	NA
General Expenses	7,028	7,353	7,343	6,739	5,756	NA	NA	NA	NA	NA
Interest Expense	288	367	116	73.0	78.0	NA	NA	NA	NA	NA
Depreciation	204	173	166	164	NA	NA	NA	NA	NA	NA
Net Income	-38.0	814	631	556	708	738	674	NA	NA	NA
S&P Core Earnings	440	784	599	588	762	622	NA	NA	NA	NA

Balance Sheet & Other Financial Data (Million $)

	2008	2007	2006	2005	2004	2003	2002	2001	2000	1999
Cash	6,729	7,037	4,775	2,474	3,319	1,869	NA	NA	NA	NA
Receivables	3,887	7,244	6,668	2,172	2,526	NA	NA	NA	NA	NA
Cost of Investments	27,522	30,625	35,553	39,100	40,157	NA	NA	NA	NA	NA
Total Assets	95,689	109,230	104,172	93,121	90,934	85,384	NA	NA	NA	NA
Loss Reserve	Nil	Nil	Nil	Nil	Nil	NA	NA	NA	NA	NA
Short Term Debt	Nil	Nil	Nil	Nil	Nil	NA	NA	NA	NA	NA
Capitalization:Debt	2,027	2,018	2,225	1,833	1,878	NA	NA	NA	NA	NA
Capitalization:Equity	6,191	7,810	7,925	7,687	8,058	7,288	NA	NA	NA	NA
Capitalization:Total	8,218	9,828	10,150	9,520	9,936	NA	NA	NA	NA	NA
Price Times Book Value:High	2.6	2.0	1.7	1.5	NA	NA	NA	NA	NA	NA
Price Times Book Value:Low	0.5	1.5	1.2	1.0	NA	NA	NA	NA	NA	NA
Cash Flow	166	987	759	556	NA	NA	NA	NA	NA	NA
% Expense/Operating Revenue	105.2	88.6	90.2	90.0	86.2	NA	NA	NA	NA	NA
% Earnings & Depreciation/Assets	0.2	0.9	0.1	0.1	NA	NA	NA	NA	NA	NA

Data as orig reptd.; bef. results of disc opers/spec. items. Per share data adj. for stk. divs.; EPS diluted. E-Estimated. NA-Not Available. NM-Not Meaningful. NR-Not Ranked. UR-Under Review.

Office: 55 Ameriprise Financial Ctr, Minneapolis, MN 55474-9900.
Telephone: 612-671-3131.
Website: http://www.ameriprise.com
Chrmn & CEO: J. Cracchiolo

EVP & CFO: W.S. Berman
EVP & General Counsel: J.C. Junek
SVP, Chief Acctg Officer & Cntlr: D.K. Stewart
SVP & Secy: T.R. Moore

Investor Contact: L. Gagnon (612-671-2080)
Board Members: J. Cracchiolo, W. D. Knowlton, W. W. Lewis, S. S. Marshall, J. Noddle, H. J. Sarles, R. F. Sharpe, Jr., W. H. Turner

Founded: 1983
Domicile: Delaware
Employees: 11,093

The McGraw-Hill Companies

AmerisourceBergen Corp

STANDARD &POOR'S

S&P Recommendation **BUY** ★★★★☆	Price $24.86 (as of Nov 27, 2009)	12-Mo. Target Price $27.00	Investment Style Large-Cap Blend

GICS Sector Health Care
Sub-Industry Health Care Distributors

Summary This distributor of pharmaceutical products and related health care services was formed via the August 2001 merger of Amerisource Health Corp. and Bergen Brunswig Corp.

Key Stock Statistics (Source S&P, Vickers, company reports)

52-Wk Range	$25.19–13.75	S&P Oper. EPS 2010**E**	1.92	Market Capitalization(B)	$7.390	Beta	0.71
Trailing 12-Month EPS	$1.66	S&P Oper. EPS 2011**E**	2.10	Yield (%)	1.29	S&P 3-Yr. Proj. EPS CAGR(%)	10
Trailing 12-Month P/E	15.0	P/E on S&P Oper. EPS 2010**E**	12.9	Dividend Rate/Share	$0.32	S&P Credit Rating	BBB+
$10K Invested 5 Yrs Ago	NA	Common Shares Outstg. (M)	297.3	Institutional Ownership (%)	91		

Price Performance

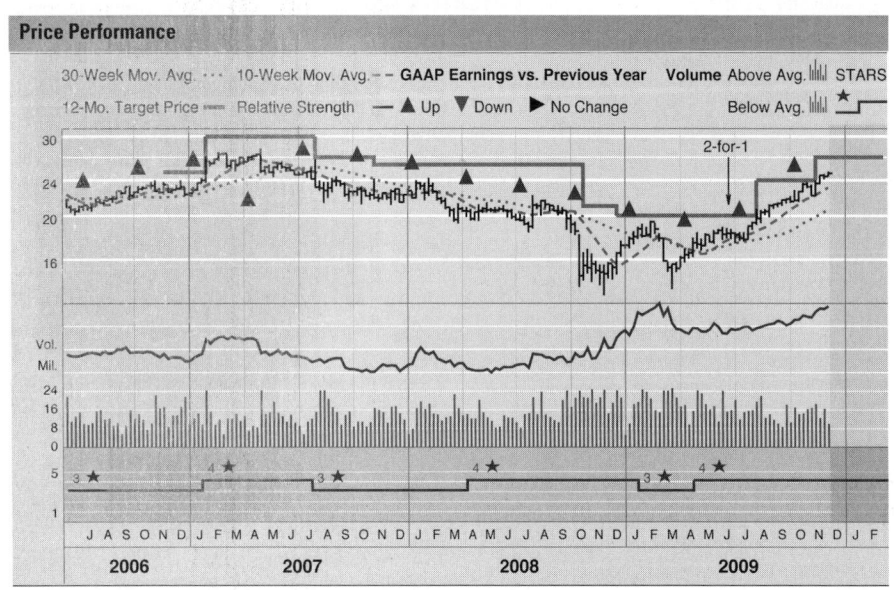

30-Week Mov. Avg. ···· 10-Week Mov. Avg. – – 12-Mo. Target Price — Relative Strength — GAAP Earnings vs. Previous Year ▲ Up ▼ Down ▶ No Change Volume Above Avg. Below Avg. STARS

Options: ASE, CBOE, P

Analysis prepared by **Phillip M. Seligman** on November 11, 2009, when the stock traded at **$24.34**.

Highlights

▶ We expect FY 10 (Sep.) revenues to increase 5.8%, to $75.9 billion. We expect overall market growth to remain in the low- to mid-single digits. We see ABC beating the market in the first half on new customer wins, primarily two large group purchasing organizations, that lap in March 2010, after which it should grow in line with the market. We also expect generic drug volumes, which carry above-average margins, to continue to rise faster than total volumes, but we expect increased penetration of generic drugs to dampen the top line's growth, given the lower average prices commanded by such products.

▶ We see operating margins widening slightly as the positive impacts from generic drug and specialty drug penetration and increased fees from brand-name drug makers outweigh ABC's incremental spending on its enterprise resource planning software implementation.

▶ We expect FY 10 EPS of $1.92, vs. FY 09's $1.72 (before one-time costs of $0.05), with EPS growth aided by share buybacks.

Investment Rationale/Risk

▶ We believe ABC has the resiliency to manage through this period of economic weakness. The company controls costs tightly, in our view, and we remain positive about its focus on generic drugs and oncology drugs and services (over 50% of the specialty group's business), which we view as among its fastest-growing and most profitable revenue drivers. ABC has no scheduled debt repayments for several years, and we expect its operating cash flow to remain healthy, providing financial flexibility. Indeed, ABC suggested that it is considering one or more acquisitions, including a large one, and that it has the financial wherewithal for such transactions. Looking ahead, we view key proposed health care reforms as having potential positive impacts on ABC's business.

▶ Risks to our opinion and target price include intensified competition and a major client loss.

▶ Our 12-month target price of $27 is based on our calendar 2010 EPS estimate of $1.94 and our above-peer P/E target multiple of 14X, also reflecting recent groupwide valuation expansion.

Qualitative Risk Assessment

LOW	MEDIUM	HIGH

Our risk assessment reflects what we view as ABC's improving financial performance, its ability to attract new accounts to more than compensate for account losses, and its healthy operating cash flow. However, we think the drug distribution arena is highly competitive, and that ABC is less diversified than many of its large health care distribution peers.

Quantitative Evaluations

S&P Quality Ranking   A-

D	C	B-	B	B+	A-	A	A+

Relative Strength Rank   STRONG

87

LOWEST = 1   HIGHEST = 99

Revenue/Earnings Data

Revenue (Million $)

	1Q	2Q	3Q	4Q	Year
2009	17,338	17,312	18,394	18,716	71,760
2008	17,279	17,756	17,997	17,158	70,190
2007	16,725	16,513	16,446	16,390	66,074
2006	14,653	15,221	15,686	15,643	61,203
2005	13,639	13,192	13,832	13,918	54,577
2004	13,355	13,364	13,072	13,389	53,179

Earnings Per Share ($)

2009	0.37	0.48	0.42	0.44	1.69
2008	0.33	0.41	0.35	0.37	1.45
2007	0.32	0.34	0.35	0.32	1.32
2006	0.24	0.31	0.29	0.31	1.13
2005	0.17	0.23	0.24	0.05	0.69
2004	0.24	0.31	0.27	0.20	1.02

Fiscal year ended Sep. 30. Next earnings report expected: Late January. EPS Estimates based on S&P Operating Earnings; historical GAAP earnings are as reported.

Dividend Data (Dates: mm/dd Payment Date: mm/dd/yy)

Amount ($)	Date Decl.	Ex-Div. Date	Stk. of Record	Payment Date
0.100	05/06	05/14	05/18	06/01/09
2-for-1	05/19	06/16	05/29	06/15/09
0.060	08/06	08/20	08/24	09/08/09
0.080	11/12	11/19	11/23	12/07/09

Dividends have been paid since 2001. Source: Company reports.

Please read the Required Disclosures and Analyst Certification on the last page of this report.

The McGraw-Hill Companies

AmerisourceBergen Corp

STANDARD
&POOR'S

Business Summary November 11, 2009

CORPORATE OVERVIEW. AmerisourceBergen Corp., one of the largest U.S. pharmaceutical distributors, began operation in August 2001, following the merger of Amerisource Health Corp. and Bergen Brunswig Corp. ABC accounted for the merger as an acquisition by Amerisource of Bergen.

The pharmaceutical distribution segment includes the AmerisourceBergen Drug Corporation (ABDC), AmerisourceBergen Specialty Group (ABSG) and the AmerisourceBergen Packaging Group (ABPG). ABDC distributes branded and generic pharmaceuticals, over-the-counter health care products, and home health care supplies and equipment to hospitals, pharmacies, mail order facilities, clinics, and alternate site facilities. ABSG ($14.6 billion of operating revenue in FY 08 (Sep.), versus $12.2 billion in FY 07) supplies goods and services to physicians and alternate care providers that specialize in disease states, such as oncology. ABPG repackages drugs from bulk to unit dose, unit of use, blister pack and standard bottle sizes.

National and retail drugstore chains, independent community drugstores, and pharmacy departments of supermarkets and mass merchandisers account for its retail market segment (32% of FY 08 total revenue), while the hospital/acute care, mail order and specialty pharmaceuticals markets together comprise its institutional market segment (68%). Revenues generated from sales to pharmacy benefit manager Medco Health Solutions (MHS) accounted for 17% of its total revenue in FY 08.

The "Other" segment is PharMerica's workers' compensation-related business, which provides pharmacy services to chronically and catastrophically ill patients under workers' comp programs, and provides pharmaceutical claims administration services for payors. On July 31, 2007, ABC spun off the PharMerica segment's long-term care business, a national dispenser of pharmaceutical products and services to patients in long-term care facilities. In October 2008, it sold the workers' comp business, which had total revenues and a loss before income taxes of about $404 million and $216 million, respectively in FY 08.

Company Financials Fiscal Year Ended Sep. 30

Per Share Data ($)	2009	2008	2007	2006	2005	2004	2003	2002	2001	2000
Tangible Book Value	NA	NM	0.03	3.96	3.69	4.31	3.61	2.61	0.90	1.20
Cash Flow	NA	1.70	1.59	1.36	0.87	1.18	1.10	0.90	0.58	0.55
Earnings	1.69	1.45	1.32	1.13	0.69	1.02	0.97	0.79	0.52	0.48
S&P Core Earnings	NA	1.40	1.23	1.04	0.62	0.78	0.93	0.76	0.42	NA
Dividends	0.21	0.15	0.10	0.05	0.03	0.03	0.03	0.03	Nil	Nil
Payout Ratio	12%	10%	8%	4%	4%	2%	3%	3%	Nil	Nil
Prices:High	25.19	24.30	28.28	24.48	21.09	16.00	18.36	20.71	18.00	13.42
Prices:Low	13.75	13.33	21.11	20.08	13.24	12.44	11.41	12.55	10.03	3.00
P/E Ratio:High	15	17	22	22	31	16	19	26	34	28
P/E Ratio:Low	8	9	16	18	19	12	12	16	19	6

Income Statement Analysis (Million $)										
Revenue	71,760	70,190	66,074	61,203	54,577	53,179	49,657	45,235	16,191	11,645
Operating Income	NA	919	912	814	723	978	963	804	302	217
Depreciation	78.9	82.1	104	96.9	81.2	87.1	71.0	61.2	21.6	16.1
Interest Expense	NA	75.1	32.0	12.5	57.2	113	145	141	45.7	41.9
Pretax Income	824	761	7.85	741	469	760	726	572	202	160
Effective Tax Rate	37.9%	38.4%	37.1%	36.8%	37.7%	38.4%	39.2%	39.7%	38.6%	38.0%
Net Income	512	469	494	468	292	468	441	345	124	99.0
S&P Core Earnings	NA	452	462	429	264	356	421	333	99.8	NA

Balance Sheet & Other Financial Data (Million $)										
Cash	1,009	878	640	1,261	1,316	871	800	663	298	121
Current Assets	NA	8,670	8,714	9,210	7,988	8,295	8,859	8,350	7,513	2,321
Total Assets	13,573	12,153	12,310	12,784	11,381	11,654	12,040	11,213	10,291	2,459
Current Liabilities	NA	8,168	7,857	7,459	6,052	6,104	6,256	6,100	5,532	1,751
Long Term Debt	1,177	1,187	1,227	1,094	951	1,157	1,723	1,756	1,872	413
Common Equity	2,716	2,710	3,100	4,141	4,280	4,339	4,005	3,316	5,677	565
Total Capital	3,894	3,899	4,327	5,235	5,232	5,496	5,728	5,073	7,549	978
Capital Expenditures	146	137	118	113	203	189	90.6	64.2	23.4	16.6
Cash Flow	NA	551	598	565	373	555	512	406	145	115
Current Ratio	1.1	1.1	1.1	1.2	1.3	1.4	1.4	1.4	1.4	1.3
% Long Term Debt of Capitalization	30.2	30.5	28.3	20.9	18.2	21.1	30.1	34.6	24.8	42.3
% Net Income of Revenue	0.7	0.7	0.7	0.8	0.5	0.9	0.9	0.8	0.8	0.9
% Return on Assets	4.0	3.8	3.9	3.9	2.5	4.0	3.8	3.2	1.9	4.4
% Return on Equity	18.9	16.2	13.6	11.1	6.8	11.2	12.1	11.2	4.0	22.1

Data as orig reptd.; bef. results of disc opers/spec. items. Per share data adj. for stk. divs.; EPS diluted. E-Estimated. NA-Not Available. NM-Not Meaningful. NR-Not Ranked. UR-Under Review.

Office: 1300 Morris Drive, Chesterbrook, PA 19087-5594.
Telephone: 610-727-7000.
Email: investorrelations@amerisourcebergen.com
Website: http://www.amerisourcebergen.com

Chrmn: R.C. Gozon
Pres & CEO: R.D. Yost
COO: D. Shane
EVP, CFO & Chief Acctg Officer: M.D. Dicandilo

SVP, Secy & General Counsel: J.G. Chou
Auditor: Ernst & Young LLP
Board Members: C. H. Cotros, M. A. Delaney, R. W. Gochnauer, R. C. Gozon, E. E. Hagenlocker, J. E. Henney, M. J. Long, H. W. McGee, R. D. Yost

Founded: 1985
Domicile: Delaware
Employees: 10,900

The McGraw·Hill Companies

Amgen Inc

S&P Recommendation	BUY ★★★★☆	Price	12-Mo. Target Price	Investment Style
		$56.50 (as of Nov 27, 2009)	$66.00	Large-Cap Growth

GICS Sector Health Care
Sub-Industry Biotechnology

Summary Amgen, among the world's leading biotech companies, has major treatments for anemia, neutropenia, rheumatoid arthritis, psoriatic arthritis, psoriasis and cancer.

Key Stock Statistics (Source S&P, Vickers, company reports)

52-Wk Range	$64.76– 44.96	S&P Oper. EPS 2009**E**	5.00	Market Capitalization(B)	$57.186	Beta	0.51
Trailing 12-Month EPS	$4.59	S&P Oper. EPS 2010**E**	5.00	Yield (%)	Nil	S&P 3-Yr. Proj. EPS CAGR(%)	12
Trailing 12-Month P/E	12.3	P/E on S&P Oper. EPS 2009**E**	11.3	Dividend Rate/Share	Nil	S&P Credit Rating	A+
$10K Invested 5 Yrs Ago	$9,384	Common Shares Outstg. (M)	1,012.1	Institutional Ownership (%)	80		

Price Performance

30-Week Mov. Avg. · · · · 10-Week Mov. Avg. - - **GAAP Earnings vs. Previous Year** Volume Above Avg. STARS
12-Mo. Target Price — Relative Strength — ▲ Up ▼ Down ► No Change Below Avg. ★

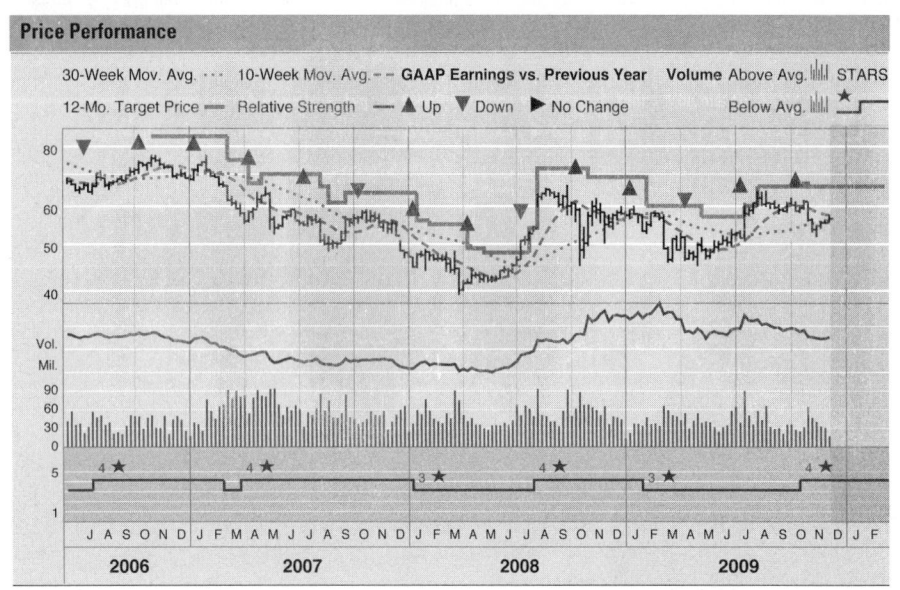

Options: ASE, CBOE, P, Ph

Analysis prepared by **Steven Silver** on October 26, 2009, when the stock traded at **$ 54.45.**

Highlights

► We forecast 2009 revenues of $14.6 billion, 3% lower than 2008's $15.0 billion, as we see AMGN navigating challenges to its core anemia franchise over regulatory restrictions related to safety, and to Enbrel due to recession-related pressures and increased competition. We project 6% higher 2010 revenues to $15.5 billion, driven by the expected launch of Prolia (denosumab) in the second half of the year. Longer term, we see potential for recent positive data to position cancer drug Vectibix for renewed sales growth.

► We project 2009 and 2010 adjusted operating margins near 42%, which would compare favorably with 2008's 41%. We see AMGN with considerable cost leverage to support EPS amid revenue instability, while using its robust cash flows to repurchase shares. We expect near-term adjusted R&D expenses of around 18% of product sales, similar to peers, and adjusted SG&A expenses of 24-25%, reflecting costs related to the expected launch of Prolia in 2010.

► We project 2009 and 2010 adjusted EPS of $5.00, with 2009 results boosted by several one-time tax benefits. Both periods exclude acquisition and restructuring expenses.

Investment Rationale/Risk

► We have a favorable outlook for approval and launch of Prolia for treatment of osteoporosis during 2010, despite the October 2009 FDA approval delay to review AMGN's risk mitigation program. We view Prolia as AMGN's key sales growth driver, as we see modest growth prospects beyond price leverage across AMGN's core product portfolio. Although we expect share price volatility following the FDA's request for additional studies, we see Prolia as likely to ultimately be approved for cancer-induced bone loss. We expect the drug to surpass $2 billion in sales and see its approval shifting investor focus to AMGN's long-term pipeline, which we view favorably.

► Risks to our recommendation and target price include failure to secure denosumab regulatory approval, further FDA and Medicare restrictions on anemia drug sales, negative clinical outcomes, and increased competition.

► Our 12-month target price of $66 applies a 13.2X multiple to our 2010 EPS estimate, 1.1X our projected three-year EPS growth rate of 12%, a slight premium to peers to reflect our view of robust cash flows and EPS stability.

Qualitative Risk Assessment

LOW	MEDIUM	HIGH

Our risk assessment reflects that the company's products are sold in highly competitive markets and are subject to government regulation. Changes to government reimbursement policies could significantly affect AMGN's revenues and profitability. Although adoption has been mild thus far, we believe that generic versions of several of AMGN's drugs pose a long-term threat in Europe.

Quantitative Evaluations

S&P Quality Ranking   B+

D	C	B-	B	B+	A-	A	A+

Relative Strength Rank   MODERATE

45

LOWEST = 1   HIGHEST = 99

Revenue/Earnings Data

Revenue (Million $)

	1Q	2Q	3Q	4Q	Year
2009	3,308	3,713	3,812	--	--
2008	3,613	3,764	3,875	3,751	15,003
2007	3,687	3,728	3,611	3,745	14,771
2006	3,217	3,491	3,503	3,737	14,268
2005	2,833	3,172	3,154	3,271	12,430
2004	2,343	2,585	2,713	2,909	10,550

Earnings Per Share ($)

2009	0.98	1.25	1.36	E1.20	E5.00
2008	1.04	0.87	1.09	0.91	3.90
2007	0.94	0.90	0.18	0.77	2.82
2006	0.82	0.01	0.94	0.71	2.48
2005	0.67	0.82	0.77	0.66	2.93
2004	0.52	0.57	0.18	0.53	1.81

Fiscal year ended Dec. 31. Next earnings report expected: Late January. EPS Estimates based on S&P Operating Earnings; historical GAAP earnings are as reported.

Dividend Data

No cash dividends have been paid.

Amgen Inc

STANDARD
&POOR'S

Business Summary October 26, 2009

CORPORATE OVERVIEW. Amgen, among the world's largest biotech companies, makes and markets five of the world's best-selling biotech drugs.

Epogen is a genetically engineered version of human erythropoietin (EPO), a hormone that stimulates red blood cell production in bone marrow. Its primary market is dialysis patients suffering from chronic anemia. Epogen sales were $2.46 billion in 2008 ($2.49 billion in 2007). Aranesp, a recombinant protein that stimulates the production of red blood cells in pre-dialysis and dialysis patients, is approved to treat anemia associated with chronic renal failure and cancer patients with chemotherapy-induced anemia (CIA).

Aranesp sales were $3.14 billion in 2008 ($3.61 billion in 2007). AMGN is developing AMG 114, a next-generation EPO drug. In 2007, Phase III trial data showed a higher rate of death when using Aranesp in treating anemia-of-cancer (AoC) not associated with chemotherapy, an off-label prescribed use. Medicare removed AoC as a reimbursable use for Aranesp. During 2007, several studies emerged suggesting that Aranesp may foster tumor growth in several cancers when dosed at or above the approved 12 g/dl dose, which

has led to Medicare and FDA restrictions over its use.

Neupogen stimulates neutrophils (white blood cells that defend against bacterial infection) production in cancer patients whose natural neutrophils were destroyed by chemotherapy. In 2002, the FDA approved Neulasta, a long-acting white blood cell stimulant protecting chemo patients from infection. Total Neupogen and Neulasta 2008 sales were $4.66 billion ($4.28 billion in 2007).

Enbrel, acquired through the purchase of Immunex, (co-marketed with Wyeth) had 2008 sales of $3.60 billion ($3.23 billion in 2007) and is approved to treat rheumatoid arthritis (RA), psoriatic arthritis, and adults with moderate to severe chronic plaque psoriasis.

Company Financials Fiscal Year Ended Dec. 31

Per Share Data ($)	2008	2007	2006	2005	2004	2003	2002	2001	2000	1999
Tangible Book Value	5.79	3.03	3.36	5.08	4.08	4.06	2.80	4.99	4.16	2.97
Cash Flow	4.90	3.89	3.29	3.59	2.35	2.19	-0.82	1.28	1.24	1.18
Earnings	3.90	2.82	2.48	2.93	1.81	1.69	-1.21	1.03	1.05	1.02
S&P Core Earnings	4.08	2.74	2.48	2.77	1.58	1.50	-1.46	0.87	NA	NA
Dividends	Nil	Nil	Nil	Nil	Nil	Nil	Nil	Nil	Nil	Nil
Payout Ratio	Nil	Nil	Nil	Nil	Nil	Nil	Nil	Nil	Nil	Nil
Prices:High	66.51	76.95	81.24	86.92	66.88	72.37	62.94	75.06	80.44	66.44
Prices:Low	39.16	46.21	63.52	56.19	52.00	48.09	30.57	45.44	50.00	25.69
P/E Ratio:High	17	27	33	30	37	43	NM	73	77	65
P/E Ratio:Low	10	16	26	19	29	28	NM	44	48	25

Income Statement Analysis (Million $)

	2008	2007	2006	2005	2004	2003	2002	2001	2000	1999
Revenue	15,003	14,771	14,268	12,430	10,550	8,356	5,523	4,016	3,629	3,340
Operating Income	6,726	6,631	6,022	5,689	4,636	3,758	2,501	2,003	1,761	1,638
Depreciation	1,073	1,202	963	841	734	686	447	266	212	177
Interest Expense	338	305	129	99.0	38.0	31.5	44.2	13.6	15.9	15.2
Pretax Income	5,250	3,961	4,020	4,868	3,395	3,173	-684	1,686	1,674	1,566
Effective Tax Rate	20.1%	20.1%	26.6%	24.5%	30.4%	28.8%	NM	33.6%	32.0%	30.0%
Net Income	4,196	3,166	2,950	3,674	2,363	2,260	-1,392	1,120	1,139	1,096
S&P Core Earnings	4,390	3,072	2,951	3,470	2,074	2,006	-1,683	936	NA	NA

Balance Sheet & Other Financial Data (Million $)

	2008	2007	2006	2005	2004	2003	2002	2001	2000	1999
Cash	9,552	7,151	6,277	5,255	5,808	5,123	4,664	2,662	2,028	1,333
Current Assets	15,221	13,041	11,712	9,235	9,170	7,402	6,404	3,859	2,937	2,065
Total Assets	36,443	34,639	33,788	29,297	29,221	26,177	24,456	6,443	5,400	4,078
Current Liabilities	4,886	6,179	7,022	3,595	4,157	2,246	1,529	1,003	862	831
Long Term Debt	9,176	11,177	7,134	3,957	3,937	3,080	3,048	223	223	223
Common Equity	20,386	17,869	18,964	20,451	19,705	19,389	18,286	5,217	4,315	3,024
Total Capital	29,792	27,526	26,465	25,571	24,936	23,930	22,927	5,440	4,538	3,247
Capital Expenditures	672	1,267	1,218	867	1,336	1,357	658	442	438	304
Cash Flow	5,269	4,368	3,913	4,515	3,097	2,946	-945	1,386	1,350	1,273
Current Ratio	3.1	2.1	1.7	2.6	2.2	3.3	4.2	3.8	3.4	2.5
% Long Term Debt of Capitalization	30.8	33.9	27.0	15.5	15.8	12.9	13.3	4.1	4.9	6.9
% Net Income of Revenue	28.0	21.4	20.7	29.6	22.4	27.0	NM	27.9	31.4	32.8
% Return on Assets	11.8	9.3	9.4	12.6	8.5	8.9	NM	18.9	24.0	28.3
% Return on Equity	21.9	17.2	15.0	18.3	12.1	12.0	NM	23.5	31.0	39.3

Data as orig reptd.; bef. results of disc opers/spec. items. Per share data adj. for stk. divs.; EPS diluted. E-Estimated. NA-Not Available. NM-Not Meaningful. NR-Not Ranked. UR-Under Review.

Office: One Amgen Center Drive, Thousand Oaks, CA 91320-1799.
Telephone: 805-447-1000.
Email: investor.relations@amgen.com
Website: http://www.amgen.com

Chrmn, Pres & CEO: K.W. Sharer
COO: F.J. Bonanni
EVP & CFO: R.A. Bradway
SVP, Secy & General Counsel: D.J. Scott

SVP & CIO: T.J. Flanagan
Investor Contact: A. Sood (805-447-1060)
Board Members: D. Baltimore, F. J. Biondi, Jr., J. D. Choate, V. D. Coffman, F. W. Gluck, R. M. Henderson, F. C. Herringer, G. S. Omenn, J. C. Pelham, J. P. Reason, L. D. Schaeffer, K. W. Sharer, F. de Carbonnel

Founded: 1980
Domicile: Delaware
Employees: 16,900

Amphenol Corp

STANDARD
&POOR'S

S&P Recommendation	BUY ★★★★☆	Price $41.35 (as of Nov 27, 2009)	12-Mo. Target Price $50.00	Investment Style Large-Cap Growth

GICS Sector Information Technology
Sub-Industry Electronic Components

Summary This company makes connectors, cable, and interconnect systems for electronics, cable TV, telecommunications, aerospace, transportation, and industrial applications.

Key Stock Statistics (Source S&P, Vickers, company reports)

52-Wk Range	$43.60– 19.97	S&P Oper. EPS 2009**E**	1.80	Market Capitalization(B)	$7.091	Beta	1.33
Trailing 12-Month EPS	$1.89	S&P Oper. EPS 2010**E**	2.10	Yield (%)	0.15	S&P 3-Yr. Proj. EPS CAGR(%)	2
Trailing 12-Month P/E	21.9	P/E on S&P Oper. EPS 2009**E**	23.0	Dividend Rate/Share	$0.06	S&P Credit Rating	BBB-
$10K Invested 5 Yrs Ago	$22,933	Common Shares Outstg. (M)	171.5	Institutional Ownership (%)	99		

Price Performance

30-Week Mov. Avg. ··· 10-Week Mov. Avg. - - **GAAP Earnings vs. Previous Year** Volume Above Avg. STARS
12-Mo. Target Price — Relative Strength — ▲ Up ▼ Down ► No Change Below Avg.

2-for-1

Options: ASE, P, Ph

Analysis prepared by **Michael W. Jaffe** on October 15, 2009, when the stock traded at **$ 40.80.**

Highlights

► We forecast a 6% increase in sales in 2010. Difficult economic trends in the U.S., Western Europe, and elsewhere have limited demand for APH's products since the second half of 2008. However, on what now appear to be stabilizing U.S. and global economies, we see a modest upturn in APH's revenue base in 2010. We also see APH's top line being assisted in coming periods by the weakening of the U.S. dollar against foreign currencies over the past few quarters.

► We see the better sales trends that we forecast aiding margins in 2010. We also see profitability being assisted by APH's ongoing focus on cost controls, including major workforce reductions that were taken as demand eroded for Amphenol's offerings.

► APH recorded a 17% year to year sales decline in 2009's third quarter, but strengthening demand from information and data communications, mobile devices and automotive markets enabled the company to record sequential rises of 5% in sales and 12% in orders. Amphenol also achieved a 1.04-to-1 book-to-bill ratio in the quarter, its first positive ratio in a year.

Investment Rationale/Risk

► We think that government stimulus packages have started to assist global economies, and that Amphenol's business is in the early stages of a revival. Moreover, we have a favorable outlook for APH's long-term prospects, on what we expect to be an ongoing expansion of the global communications infrastructure, increasing sophistication of military and space systems, and the use of more electronic devices in automobiles and other industrial products. Based on these factors and our relative P/E analysis, we view APH as undervalued.

► Risks to our recommendation and target price include a reversal of the recent stabilizing trends in the global economy and a resultant lack of demand for APH's products.

► The shares recently traded at about 20X our 2010 EPS estimate, in the middle of APH's range of the past decade. Based on our belief that more favorable economic conditions will enable APH's business to start a recovery over the coming year, we think a higher valuation is merited. We have set our 12-month target price at $50, almost 24X our 2010 estimate, and at the higher end of APH's historical valuation.

Qualitative Risk Assessment

LOW	MEDIUM	HIGH

Our risk assessment for APH reflects our view of the company's typically solid levels of cash flow and a strong business model, offset by the inherent cyclicality of APH's business.

Quantitative Evaluations

S&P Quality Ranking B+

D	C	B-	B	B+	A-	A	A+

Relative Strength Rank STRONG

73

LOWEST = 1   HIGHEST = 99

Revenue/Earnings Data

Revenue (Million $)

	1Q	2Q	3Q	4Q	Year
2009	660.0	685.2	716.6	--	--
2008	770.7	846.8	863.7	755.3	3,236
2007	651.1	688.8	733.9	777.3	2,851
2006	569.0	606.6	636.4	659.4	2,471
2005	409.4	443.6	447.0	508.1	1,808
2004	355.3	387.1	384.1	404.0	1,530

Earnings Per Share ($)

2009	0.43	0.43	0.47	E0.49	E1.80
2008	0.54	0.61	0.63	0.56	2.34
2007	0.43	0.46	0.50	0.55	1.94
2006	0.32	0.29	0.37	0.43	1.40
2005	0.26	0.29	0.29	0.31	1.14
2004	0.20	0.23	0.24	0.26	0.91

Fiscal year ended Dec. 31. Next earnings report expected: Mid January. EPS Estimates based on S&P Operating Earnings; historical GAAP earnings are as reported.

Dividend Data (Dates: mm/dd Payment Date: mm/dd/yy)

Amount ($)	Date Decl.	Ex-Div. Date	Stk. of Record	Payment Date
0.015	01/23	03/09	03/11	04/01/09
0.015	04/23	06/08	06/10	07/01/09
0.015	07/24	09/14	09/16	10/07/09
0.015	10/26	12/14	12/16	01/06/10

Dividends have been paid since 2005. Source: Company reports.

Please read the Required Disclosures and Analyst Certification on the last page of this report.

Amphenol Corp

STANDARD
&POOR'S

Business Summary October 15, 2009

CORPORATE OVERVIEW. Amphenol makes electrical, electronic and fiber optic connectors, interconnect systems, and coaxial and flat ribbon cable. In 2008, APH derived 62% of its revenues from information technology and communications markets, 19% from industrial/automotive, and 19% from commercial aerospace and military. It derived 40% of its sales in North America, 21% in Europe, and 39% in Asia and elsewhere.

APH makes a broad range of interconnect products and assemblies (91% of 2008 revenues) for voice, video and data communications systems, commercial aerospace and military systems, automotive and mass transportation applications, and industrial and factory automation equipment. Its connectors and interconnect systems are mostly used to conduct electrical and optical signals for sophisticated electronic applications.

In communications, the company supplies connector and cable assembly products used in base stations for wireless communication systems and Internet networking equipment; smart card acceptor devices used in mobile telephones, set top boxes and other applications to facilitate reading data from smart cards; fiber optic connectors used in fiber optic transmissions; backplane and input/output connectors for servers and data storage devices, and

for linking PCs and peripheral equipment; and sculptured flexible circuits for integrating circuit boards.

APH also makes radio frequency connector products and antennas used in telecommunications, computer and office equipment, instrumentation equipment, local area networks and automotive electronics. Radio frequency connectors are also used in base stations, mobile communications devices and other components of cellular and personal communication networks.

The company believes it is the largest supplier of high-performance, military-specification, circular environmental connectors, generally used in sophisticated aerospace, military, commercial and industrial equipment. APH also makes industrial interconnect products, used in applications such as factory automation equipment, mass transportation applications and automotive safety products.

Company Financials Fiscal Year Ended Dec. 31

Per Share Data ($)	2008	2007	2006	2005	2004	2003	2002	2001	2000	1999
Tangible Book Value	0.35	1.00	NM	NM	NM	NM	NM	NM	NM	NM
Cash Flow	2.86	2.38	1.79	1.42	1.13	0.80	0.66	0.76	0.88	0.49
Earnings	2.34	1.94	1.40	1.14	0.91	0.59	0.46	0.49	0.63	0.30
S&P Core Earnings	2.27	1.97	1.43	1.14	0.90	0.57	0.35	0.36	NA	NA
Dividends	0.06	0.08	0.06	0.06	Nil	Nil	Nil	Nil	Nil	Nil
Payout Ratio	3%	4%	4%	5%	Nil	Nil	Nil	Nil	Nil	Nil
Prices:High	52.28	47.24	35.25	23.10	18.76	16.03	12.94	14.50	17.59	8.94
Prices:Low	18.38	30.61	21.94	16.62	13.95	9.25	6.87	7.08	7.58	3.68
P/E Ratio:High	22	24	25	20	21	27	28	30	28	30
P/E Ratio:Low	8	16	16	15	15	16	15	15	12	12

Income Statement Analysis (Million $)										
Revenue	3,236	2,851	2,471	1,808	1,530	1,240	1,062	1,104	1,360	1,011
Operating Income	724	635	518	394	315	241	209	229	287	201
Depreciation	91.3	82.3	72.6	50.7	38.8	37.0	34.8	46.7	42.8	27.7
Interest Expense	39.6	36.9	38.8	24.1	22.5	29.5	45.9	56.1	61.7	79.3
Pretax Income	582	501	373	308	247	158	123	135	173	76.2
Effective Tax Rate	28.0%	29.5%	31.5%	33.0%	34.0%	34.0%	34.5%	38.2%	37.7%	41.8%
Net Income	419	353	256	206	163	104	80.3	83.7	108	44.3
S&P Core Earnings	408	359	261	206	161	99.8	60.0	62.0	NA	NA

Balance Sheet & Other Financial Data (Million $)										
Cash	215	184	74.1	38.7	30.2	23.5	20.7	28.0	24.6	12.9
Current Assets	1,336	1,224	935	710	529	451	389	370	413	335
Total Assets	2,994	2,676	2,195	1,933	1,307	1,181	1,079	1,027	1,004	836
Current Liabilities	635	520	448	336	278	218	236	203	243	146
Long Term Debt	786	722	677	766	432	532	566	661	700	746
Common Equity	1,349	1,265	903	689	482	323	167	104	29.2	-81.2
Total Capital	2,153	1,986	1,580	1,455	914	856	733	765	729	664
Capital Expenditures	107	104	82.4	57.1	44.3	30.2	18.8	38.6	53.1	23.5
Cash Flow	510	435	328	257	202	141	115	130	151	72.0
Current Ratio	2.1	2.4	2.1	2.1	1.9	2.1	1.6	1.8	1.7	2.3
% Long Term Debt of Capitalization	36.8	36.4	42.9	52.6	47.3	62.2	77.2	86.4	96.0	112.2
% Net Income of Revenue	13.0	12.4	10.3	11.4	10.7	8.4	7.6	7.6	7.9	4.4
% Return on Assets	14.8	14.5	12.4	12.7	13.1	9.2	7.6	8.2	11.7	5.4
% Return on Equity	32.1	32.6	32.1	35.2	40.6	42.4	59.3	125.7	NM	NM

Data as orig reptd.; bef. results of disc opers/spec. items. Per share data adj. for stk. divs.; EPS diluted. E-Estimated. NA-Not Available. NM-Not Meaningful. NR-Not Ranked. UR-Under Review.

Office: 358 Hall Avenue, Wallingford, CT 06492.
Telephone: 203-265-8900.
Email: aphinfo@amphenol.com
Website: http://www.amphenol.com

Chrmn: M.H. Loeffler
Pres: M.L. Schneider
Pres & CEO: R.A. Norwitt
SVP, CFO & Chief Acctg Officer: D.G. Reardon

Secy & General Counsel: E.C. Wetmore
Investor Contact: D. Reardon (203-265-8630)
Board Members: R. P. Badie, S. L. Clark, E. G. Jepsen, A. E. Lietz, M. H. Loeffler, J. R. Lord, R. A. Norwitt, D. H. Secord

Founded: 1932
Domicile: Delaware
Employees: 30,000

The McGraw-Hill Companies

Anadarko Petroleum Corp

S&P Recommendation	HOLD ★★★☆☆	Price	12-Mo. Target Price	Investment Style
		$60.67 (as of Nov 27, 2009)	$67.00	Large-Cap Blend

GICS Sector Energy
Sub-Industry Oil & Gas Exploration & Production

Summary One of the largest independent exploration and production companies in the world, this U.S. concern has associated businesses in marketing, trading and minerals.

Key Stock Statistics (Source S&P, Vickers, company reports)

52-Wk Range	$69.37– 30.88	S&P Oper. EPS 2009**E**	-2.62	Market Capitalization(B)	$29.820	Beta	1.11
Trailing 12-Month EPS	$0.95	S&P Oper. EPS 2010**E**	0.67	Yield (%)	0.59	S&P 3-Yr. Proj. EPS CAGR(%)	-43
Trailing 12-Month P/E	63.9	P/E on S&P Oper. EPS 2009**E**	NM	Dividend Rate/Share	$0.36	S&P Credit Rating	BBB-
$10K Invested 5 Yrs Ago	$17,982	Common Shares Outstg. (M)	491.5	Institutional Ownership (%)	85		

Price Performance

30-Week Mov. Avg. ···· 10-Week Mov. Avg. – – **GAAP Earnings vs. Previous Year** Volume Above Avg. STARS
12-Mo. Target Price — Relative Strength — ▲ Up ▼ Down ► No Change Below Avg. ★

Options: ASE, CBOE, P, Ph

Analysis prepared by **Michael Kay** on October 06, 2009, when the stock traded at **$ 65.18**.

Highlights

► Production fell 3% in 2008, reflecting asset sales, downtime at Independence Hub, and the impact of hurricanes. With lower oil and gas prices, drilling budgets and activity, we see 2009 volumes up 6%, followed by a 3% decline in 2010 on lower drilling activity. Onshore programs at Haynesville and Marcellus shales are showing encouraging results and exposure to low cost domestic natural gas plays. We also see significant exploration potential at 12 deepwater exploration wells planned for 2009, each targeting over 100 MMBOE.

► APC plans $4-$4.5 billion in 2009 capital spending, with $2 billion slated for maintenance and the remainder to be spent on high-impact long-term exploration projects. APC sees the cutback in rigs driving costs down in the second half of 2009.

► Operating earnings in 2008 of $7.24, including $1.49 non-cash derivative gain and $1.23 asset sale gain, were up from $3.60 in 2007, on higher realized crude oil and natural gas prices. With the sharp decline in prices, we see a 2009 per share loss of $2.58 (with a $0.96 non-cash derivative loss in the first half), followed by a loss of $0.20 in 2010 on lower production.

Investment Rationale/Risk

► While acquisitions have made APC larger with a focus shifted toward natural gas in the Rockies, the transformation originally weakened its balance sheet and led to increased costs. As a result, APC has raised cash through asset sales to repay debt from acquisitions. Recently, APC has taken steps to lower its debt levels below $12 billion and improve its cash position to over $3 billion. We see APC being selective with its international exploration efforts going forward, and we expect any additional tightening of credit and setbacks in the economy to result in further drilling capex cutbacks in 2009.

► Risks to our recommendation and target price include unfavorable changes to economic, industrial or operating conditions, such as rising costs or difficulty in replacing reserves.

► We see markets discounting probable reserves, and we value APC on proved reserve NAV estimates. We blend our NAV estimate of $69 with DCF ($63 intrinsic value assuming a WACC of 8.9% and terminal growth of 3%) and relative metrics, to arrive at our 12-month target price of $67. We apply premium relative valuations given our view of APC's portfolio of high-quality projects.

Qualitative Risk Assessment

LOW	MEDIUM	HIGH

Our risk assessment reflects our view of APC's aggressive financial profile, and a business profile limited by participation in the cyclical, competitive and capital-intensive exploration and production sector, and by U.S. and international oil and gas operations that carry heightened political and operational risk.

Quantitative Evaluations

S&P Quality Ranking   B+

D	C	B-	B	B+	A-	A	A+

Relative Strength Rank   MODERATE

43

LOWEST = 1   HIGHEST = 99

Revenue/Earnings Data

Revenue (Million $)

	1Q	2Q	3Q	4Q	Year
2009	1,595	1,745	2,740	--	--
2008	2,978	2,786	6,149	3,810	15,723
2007	2,683	3,313	3,030	3,062	11,232
2006	1,701	1,809	3,498	3,179	10,187
2005	1,526	1,592	1,737	2,245	7,100
2004	1,460	1,443	1,562	1,602	6,067

Earnings Per Share ($)

2009	-0.73	-0.47	-0.40	E0.01	E-2.62
2008	0.50	0.03	4.62	1.70	6.84
2007	0.17	1.38	1.10	0.35	8.05
2006	1.22	1.43	2.98	0.40	6.02
2005	1.03	1.06	1.26	1.87	5.20
2004	0.78	0.80	0.79	0.82	3.18

Fiscal year ended Dec. 31. Next earnings report expected: Early February. EPS Estimates based on S&P Operating Earnings; historical GAAP earnings are as reported.

Dividend Data (Dates: mm/dd Payment Date: mm/dd/yy)

Amount ($)	Date Decl.	Ex-Div. Date	Stk. of Record	Payment Date
0.090	02/10	03/09	03/11	03/25/09
0.090	05/19	06/08	06/10	06/24/09
0.090	08/10	09/04	09/09	09/23/09
0.090	11/11	12/07	12/09	12/23/09

Dividends have been paid since 1986. Source: Company reports.

Please read the Required Disclosures and Analyst Certification on the last page of this report.

Anadarko Petroleum Corp

**STANDARD
&POOR'S**

Business Summary October 06, 2009

CORPORATE OVERVIEW. One of the largest independent exploration and production companies in the world, Anadarko Petroleum (APC) is engaged in the
exploration, development, production, gathering, processing and marketing of
natural gas, crude oil, condensate and natural gas liquids (NGLs). The Company's major areas of operation are located onshore in the United States, the
deepwater of the Gulf of Mexico and Algeria. Anadarko also has production in
China and is executing strategic exploration programs in several other countries, including Ghana and Brazil.

Proved oil and gas reserves dropped 6%, to 2.277 billion barrel oil equivalent
(boe; 70% developed, 41% liquids, 90% located in the U.S.), in 2008, reflecting
divestitures of non-core properties and price-related revisions. APC estimates
a reduction of approximately 137 MMBOE associated with property divestitures and 102 million BOE as a result of price-related revisions, primarily associated with the year-over-year decline in prices for crude oil and NGLs. Reserve additions were primarily driven by development and infill activities in
the Rockies and appraisal drilling in the Gulf of Mexico. No reserves were
booked in 2008 in association with the world-class Jubilee field discovery off-

shore Ghana or the pre-salt Wahoo discovery in Brazil.

Oil and gas production declined 3%, to 206 MMBOE (39% liquids), in 2008. We
estimate APC's organic reserve replacement at 91%. We estimate APC's
three-year (2006-08) finding and development costs at $58.02 per boe, above
the peer average; its three-year reserve replacement costs at $27.42 per boe,
above the peer average; and its three-year reserve replacement at 249%, in
line with the peer average.

APC invests in Midstream (gathering and processing) facilities in order to
complement its oil and gas operations in regions where the company has natural gas production.

The company's Marketing segment manages the sales of APC's natural gas,
crude oil and NGLs.

Company Financials Fiscal Year Ended Dec. 31

Per Share Data ($)	2008	2007	2006	2005	2004	2003	2002	2001	2000	1999
Tangible Book Value	29.40	23.89	21.95	21.06	16.45	13.97	11.01	9.59	10.50	5.15
Cash Flow	14.13	14.23	10.28	8.04	6.05	5.01	3.74	2.09	3.64	1.00
Earnings	6.84	8.05	6.02	5.20	3.18	2.46	1.61	-0.37	2.13	0.13
S&P Core Earnings	5.13	1.65	6.09	5.22	3.27	2.47	1.53	-0.49	NA	NA
Dividends	0.36	0.36	0.36	0.36	0.28	0.22	0.16	0.11	0.10	0.10
Payout Ratio	5%	4%	6%	7%	9%	9%	10%	NM	5%	80%
Prices:High	81.36	68.00	56.98	50.71	35.78	25.86	29.28	36.99	37.97	21.38
Prices:Low	24.57	38.40	39.51	30.01	24.00	20.14	18.39	21.50	13.78	13.13
P/E Ratio:High	12	8	9	10	11	11	18	NM	18	NM
P/E Ratio:Low	4	5	7	6	8	8	11	NM	6	NM

Income Statement Analysis (Million $)										
Revenue	14,640	15,892	10,187	7,100	6,067	5,122	3,860	8,369	5,686	701
Operating Income	8,578	10,328	6,945	5,436	4,400	3,648	2,585	3,702	2,190	421
Depreciation, Depletion and Amortization	3,417	2,891	1,976	1,343	1,447	1,297	1,121	1,227	593	218
Interest Expense	742	1,214	655	201	352	253	203	92.0	Nil	74.1
Pretax Income	5,429	6,329	4,238	3,895	2,477	1,974	1,207	-390	1,426	105
Effective Tax Rate	40.0%	40.4%	34.0%	36.6%	35.2%	36.9%	31.2%	NM	42.2%	59.4%
Net Income	3,236	3,770	2,796	2,471	1,606	1,245	831	-176	824	42.6
S&P Core Earnings	2,400	773	2,826	2,478	1,646	1,248	785	-243	NA	NA

Balance Sheet & Other Financial Data (Million $)										
Cash	2,360	1,268	491	739	874	62.0	34.0	37.0	199	44.8
Current Assets	5,375	4,516	4,614	2,916	2,502	1,324	1,280	1,201	1,894	356
Total Assets	48,953	48,481	58,844	22,588	20,192	20,546	18,248	16,771	16,590	4,098
Current Liabilities	5,536	5,257	16,758	2,403	1,993	1,715	1,861	1,801	1,676	387
Long Term Debt	10,867	14,747	11,520	3,555	3,671	5,058	5,171	4,638	3,984	1,443
Common Equity	18,856	16,319	15,201	10,967	9,219	8,510	6,673	6,262	6,586	1,335
Total Capital	39,997	39,929	39,673	19,330	17,393	17,909	15,578	14,454	10,770	3,555
Capital Expenditures	4,801	4,246	1,086	3,408	3,064	2,772	2,388	3,316	1,708	680
Cash Flow	6,614	6,658	4,769	3,809	3,048	2,537	1,946	1,044	1,406	250
Current Ratio	1.0	0.9	0.3	1.2	1.3	0.8	0.7	0.7	1.1	0.9
% Long Term Debt of Capitalization	27.2	44.9	28.8	18.4	21.1	28.2	33.2	32.1	37.0	40.6
% Return on Assets	6.6	7.0	6.9	11.5	7.9	6.4	4.7	NM	8.0	1.1
% Return on Equity	18.4	24.2	21.3	24.4	17.9	16.1	12.8	NM	20.5	2.6

Data as orig reptd.; bef. results of disc opers/spec. items. Per share data adj. for stk. divs.; EPS diluted. E-Estimated. NA-Not Available. NM-Not Meaningful. NR-Not Ranked. UR-Under Review.

Office: 1201 Lake Robbins Drive, The Woodlands, TX
77380-1124.
Telephone: 832-636-1000.
Website: http://www.anadarko.com
Chrmn, Pres & CEO: J.T. Hackett

COO: R.A. Walker
SVP & CFO: R.G. Gwin
SVP, Chief Admin Officer & General Counsel: R.K.
Reeves
Chief Acctg Officer: M.C. Douglas

Investor Contact: J. Colglazier (832-636-2306)
Board Members: R. J. Allison, Jr., L. Barcus, J. R.
Butler, Jr., L. R. Corbett, H. P. Eberhart, P. J. Fluor, P. M.
Geren, III, J. R. Gordon, J. T. Hackett, L. M. Jones, J. W.
Poduska, P. R. Reynolds

Founded: 1985
Domicile: Delaware
Employees: 4,300

The **McGraw·Hill** Companies

Analog Devices Inc.

STANDARD
&POOR'S

S&P Recommendation	HOLD ★★★☆☆	Price $29.75 (as of Nov 27, 2009)	12-Mo. Target Price $31.00	Investment Style Large-Cap Growth

GICS Sector Information Technology
Sub-Industry Semiconductors

Summary This company manufactures high-performance integrated circuits (ICs) used in analog and digital signal processing applications.

Key Stock Statistics (Source S&P, Vickers, company reports)

52-Wk Range	$30.15– 15.29	S&P Oper. EPS 2010**E**	1.68	Market Capitalization(B)	$8.683	Beta	1.00
Trailing 12-Month EPS	$0.98	S&P Oper. EPS 2011**E**	NA	Yield (%)	2.69	S&P 3-Yr. Proj. EPS CAGR(%)	0
Trailing 12-Month P/E	30.4	P/E on S&P Oper. EPS 2010**E**	17.7	Dividend Rate/Share	$0.80	S&P Credit Rating	BBB+
$10K Invested 5 Yrs Ago	$8,562	Common Shares Outstg. (M)	291.9	Institutional Ownership (%)	87		

Price Performance

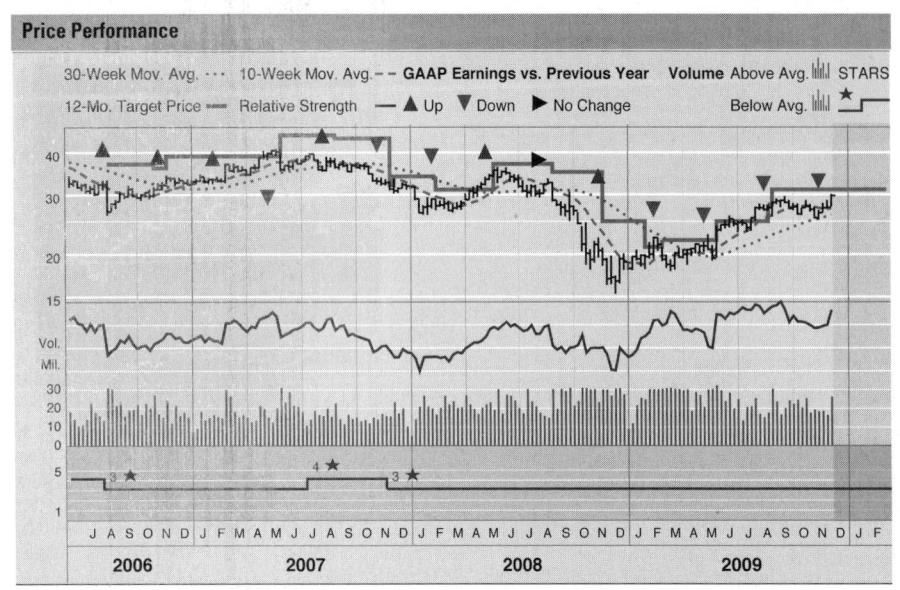

Options: ASE, CBOE, P, Ph

Analysis prepared by **Clyde Montevirgen** on November 13, 2009, when the stock traded at **$ 27.40**.

Highlights

► We expect sales to rise about 10% in FY 10 (Oct.), compared to a projected 24% fall in FY 09. Although we remain cautious of demand because of macroeconomic headwinds, we believe that sales will advance as orders slowly come back. With its relatively large exposure to industrial and consumer related end-markets, which are increasingly employing semiconductors in various applications, we believe ADI has notable long-term growth opportunities due to recent design wins, long product cycles, and its diversified customer base.

► We are modeling a gross margin of 58% for FY 10, above the anticipated 55% for FY 09. We believe that margins will widen as plant utilization improves and as the sales mix shifts to higher-margin products. ADI has divested less profitable product lines and consolidated manufacturing over the last couple of years, which should aid long-term profitability. Similarly, we see the non-GAAP operating margin widening to around 23% for FY 10, from an estimated 15% in FY 09, reflecting operating leverage benefits.

► Our EPS estimates assume an effective tax rate of around 20% and include stock based compensation.

Investment Rationale/Risk

► We believe ADI's analog portfolio is very competitive, and should drive stable revenue growth when economic conditions improve. We anticipate improving margins from capacity reductions and an improving sales mix, and expect even better operating leverage as orders return. ADI has what we view as a strong balance sheet with a substantial net cash position. Still, we think projected growth is largely reflected in valuations, which are already notably above the industry's.

► Risks to our recommendation and target price include steep market share declines, a worse than anticipated economic slowdown, and a less favorable sales mix.

► Our 12-month target price of $31 is based on a weighted blend of our discounted cash flow (DCF) model and relative metrics. Our DCF model assumes a WACC of about 10% and a terminal growth rate of 4%, implying an intrinsic value of $31. We apply a price-to-sales multiple of around 4.2X, above the industry average, to our forward 12-month sales per share estimate to derive a value of $31.

Qualitative Risk Assessment

LOW	MEDIUM	HIGH

Our risk assessment reflects that ADI is subject to the sales cycles of the semiconductor industry, offset by our view of relatively stable chip pricing owing to high proprietary design content, broad end-markets, a leading market share in key converter and amplifier product categories and what we consider a lack of debt.

Quantitative Evaluations

S&P Quality Ranking   B

D	C	B-	B	B+	A-	A	A+

Relative Strength Rank   STRONG

86

LOWEST = 1   HIGHEST = 99

Revenue/Earnings Data

Revenue (Million $)

	1Q	2Q	3Q	4Q	Year
2009	476.6	474.8	492.0	571.6	2,015
2008	613.9	649.3	659.0	660.7	2,583
2007	645.9	614.7	637.0	648.5	2,511
2006	621.3	643.9	663.7	644.3	2,573
2005	580.5	603.7	582.4	622.1	2,389
2004	605.4	678.5	717.8	632.1	2,634

Earnings Per Share ($)

2009	0.08	0.18	0.22	0.36	0.85
2008	0.40	0.44	0.44	0.49	1.77
2007	0.45	0.37	0.44	0.31	1.51
2006	0.32	0.39	0.39	0.39	1.48
2005	0.28	0.31	0.32	0.18	1.08
2004	0.30	0.39	0.43	0.34	1.45

Fiscal year ended Oct. 31. Next earnings report expected: Mid February. EPS Estimates based on S&P Operating Earnings; historical GAAP earnings are as reported.

Dividend Data (Dates: mm/dd Payment Date: mm/dd/yy)

Amount ($)	Date Decl.	Ex-Div. Date	Stk. of Record	Payment Date
0.200	02/17	03/04	03/06	03/25/09
0.200	05/19	05/27	05/29	06/17/09
0.200	08/18	08/25	08/27	09/16/09
0.200	11/19	12/02	12/04	12/23/09

Dividends have been paid since 2003. Source: Company reports.

Analog Devices Inc.

Business Summary November 13, 2009

CORPORATE OVERVIEW. Analog Devices designs, manufactures, and markets a broad line of high-performance analog, mixed-signal and digital signal processing (DSP) integrated circuits (ICs) that address a wide range of real-world signal processing applications. Real-world phenomena that these applications are designed for include temperature, pressure, sound, images, speed, acceleration, position and rotation. These phenomena are specifically analog in nature, consisting of continuously varying information.

The expansion of broadband and wireless communications applications helps drive demand for analog and DSP chips. ADI's products are built into wireless telephones, base station equipment, and remote access servers, among others. The company's analog products are typically general purpose in nature and are used in a wide variety of equipment and systems. The company's chips are increasingly sold to PC and digital entertainment markets, as consumer equipment to handle voice, video and images becomes increasingly complex and sells to a wider audience.

ADI's products are sold both to OEMs and to customers building their own equipment. Key markets are industrial, which accounted for approximately 49% of sales in FY 08, communications 25%, consumer 21%, and computers

5%. The customer base is fairly broad: the 20 largest customers, excluding distributors, accounted for about 32% of sales in FY 08, and the largest customer, excluding distributors, accounted for approximately 4%. About 53% of FY 08 sales were derived from sales made through distributors.

CORPORATE STRATEGY. Analog Devices is a leading provider of high-performance analog and mixed-signal, and DSP integrated circuits, two of the faster growing segments within the broader semiconductor industry. We believe that the higher-end analog space will continue to attract new entrants given its anticipated growth rate, relatively dispersed market share, stable pricing, higher-margin sales, and low capital expenditures. Lending to less risk, we think chipmakers in this segment generally post less variable operating results and more stable free cash flows than most semiconductor makers, which tend to experience volatile swings during various stages of the industry's business cycle.

Company Financials Fiscal Year Ended Oct. 31

Per Share Data ($)	2009	2008	2007	2006	2005	2004	2003	2002	2001	2000
Tangible Book Value	NA	7.46	6.71	9.17	9.61	9.66	8.42	7.50	7.20	5.90
Cash Flow	NA	2.28	1.97	1.95	1.49	1.84	1.22	0.90	1.48	2.00
Earnings	0.85	1.77	1.51	1.48	1.08	1.45	0.78	0.28	0.93	1.59
S&P Core Earnings	NA	1.74	1.45	1.46	0.29	0.91	0.20	-0.32	0.44	NA
Dividends	0.80	0.76	0.70	0.56	0.32	0.20	Nil	Nil	Nil	Nil
Payout Ratio	94%	43%	46%	38%	30%	14%	Nil	Nil	Nil	Nil
Prices:High	30.15	36.35	41.10	41.48	41.40	52.37	50.35	48.84	64.00	103.00
Prices:Low	17.82	15.29	30.19	26.07	31.71	31.36	22.58	17.88	29.00	41.31
P/E Ratio:High	35	21	27	28	38	36	65	NM	69	65
P/E Ratio:Low	21	9	20	18	29	22	29	NM	31	26

Income Statement Analysis (Million $)										
Revenue	2,015	2,583	2,546	2,573	2,389	2,634	2,047	1,708	2,277	2,578
Operating Income	NA	782	916	771	703	852	552	405	675	924
Depreciation	140	153	155	172	156	153	168	238	210	157
Interest Expense	NA	Nil	Nil	0.05	0.03	0.22	32.2	44.5	62.5	5.84
Pretax Income	297	666	659	664	588	733	382	140	507	866
Effective Tax Rate	16.8%	21.2%	24.0%	17.1%	29.4%	22.1%	21.9%	25.0%	29.7%	29.9%
Net Income	247	525	501	549	415	571	298	105	356	607
S&P Core Earnings	NA	517	481	542	113	364	74.2	-118	170	NA

Balance Sheet & Other Financial Data (Million $)										
Cash	1,816	1,310	425	344	628	519	518	1,614	1,365	1,736
Current Assets	NA	2,090	1,979	3,011	3,732	3,529	2,886	3,624	3,435	3,168
Total Assets	3,404	3,091	2,972	3,987	4,583	4,720	4,093	4,980	4,885	4,411
Current Liabilities	NA	569	548	491	819	567	463	484	528	650
Long Term Debt	489	Nil	Nil	Nil	Nil	Nil	Nil	1,274	1,206	1,213
Common Equity	2,529	2,420	2,338	3,436	3,692	3,800	3,288	2,900	2,843	2,304
Total Capital	3,018	2,435	2,348	3,439	3,692	3,810	3,305	4,197	4,100	3,568
Capital Expenditures	56.1	157	142	129	85.5	146	67.7	57.4	297	275
Cash Flow	NA	679	656	722	570	723	467	343	567	764
Current Ratio	6.4	3.7	3.6	6.1	4.6	6.2	6.2	7.5	6.5	4.9
% Long Term Debt of Capitalization	16.2	Nil	Nil	Nil	Nil	Nil	Nil	30.4	29.4	34.0
% Net Income of Revenue	12.3	20.3	19.6	21.4	17.4	21.7	14.6	6.2	15.7	23.6
% Return on Assets	7.6	17.3	14.3	12.8	8.9	13.0	6.6	2.1	7.7	18.3
% Return on Equity	10.0	22.1	17.3	15.4	11.1	16.1	9.6	3.7	13.8	31.0

Data as orig reptd.; bef. results of disc opers/spec. items. Per share data adj. for stk. divs.; EPS diluted. E-Estimated. NA-Not Available. NM-Not Meaningful. NR-Not Ranked. UR-Under Review.

Office: One Technology Way, Norwood, MA 02062-9106.
Telephone: 800-262-5643.
Email: investor.relations@analog.com
Website: http://www.analog.com

Chrmn: R. Stata
Pres & CEO: J.G. Fishman
CFO: D.A. Zinsner
CTO: S.H. Fuller

Chief Acctg Officer & Cntlr: S. Brennan
Investor Contact: M. Kohl (781-461-3759)
Board Members: J. Champy, J. L. Doyle, J. G. Fishman, J. C. Hodgson, Y. Istel, N. Novich, F. G. Saviers, P. J. Severino, K. J. Sicchitano, R. Stata

Founded: 1965
Domicile: Massachusetts
Employees: 9,000

Aon Corp.

S&P Recommendation BUY ★★★★☆	Price $38.39 (as of Nov 27, 2009)	12-Mo. Target Price $46.00	Investment Style Large-Cap Blend

GICS Sector Financials
Sub-Industry Insurance Brokers

Summary This global provider of insurance brokerage services also offers consulting services and risk and insurance advice.

Key Stock Statistics (Source S&P, Vickers, company reports)

52-Wk Range	$46.50–34.81	S&P Oper. EPS 2009**E**	3.10	Market Capitalization(B)	$10.516	Beta	0.58
Trailing 12-Month EPS	$1.88	S&P Oper. EPS 2010**E**	3.47	Yield (%)	1.56	S&P 3-Yr. Proj. EPS CAGR(%)	17
Trailing 12-Month P/E	20.4	P/E on S&P Oper. EPS 2009**E**	12.4	Dividend Rate/Share	$0.60	S&P Credit Rating	BBB+
$10K Invested 5 Yrs Ago	$19,872	Common Shares Outstg. (M)	273.9	Institutional Ownership (%)	80		

Price Performance

30-Week Mov. Avg. ··· 10-Week Mov. Avg. – – **GAAP Earnings vs. Previous Year** Volume Above Avg. ▮▮ STARS
12-Mo. Target Price — Relative Strength — ▲ Up ▼ Down ▶ No Change   Below Avg. ▮▮ ★

Options: ASE, CBOE, P, Ph

Analysis prepared by **Bret Howlett** on November 03, 2009, when the stock traded at **$ 38.54**.

Highlights

▶ We expect brokerage organic revenue growth to be up in the mid-single digits in 2010 as we see improved top-line gains in the Americas and in Europe, the Middle East and Africa (EMEA), strong growth in reinsurance, and higher investment income, partially offset by lower exposures. We anticipate that the Asia-Pacific region will experience solid new business growth in China, Korea and Indonesia, and expect organic revenue to be up 4%. We see the adjusted pretax margin for brokerage increasing to near 21%, helped by improved pricing and aggressive cost-cutting initiatives. We believe that the company's restructuring program will result in $467 million in annualized savings by 2010.

▶ We see revenues up slightly in the consulting segment as the global economy begins to recover. However, consulting contributes only a modest amount to AOC's total revenues. We believe AOC's recent acquisition of Benfield will increase its market share in reinsurance, and we think that business will benefit from a firming of rates into 2010.

▶ We estimate EPS from continuing operations at $3.10 in 2009 and $3.47 in 2010.

Investment Rationale/Risk

▶ Our buy recommendation reflects our belief that AOC possesses a business platform that can drive organic growth in an unfavorable environment and that the company is well positioned for margin expansion and our expectations for an improved pricing environment in 2010. AOC has been gaining new businesses both in the U.S. and abroad, while maintaining a solid retention rate. We expect AOC to face headwinds in brokerage in the U.S. as the slowing economy pressures margin expansion and volumes. However, we believe AOC's aggressive cost-cutting initiatives, a share buyback program, exposure to reinsurance, and earnings contributions from overseas will more than offset the impact from the difficult operating environment.

▶ Risks to our recommendation and target price include continuing organic revenue growth and margin pressure from a soft property and casualty market; currency risks; and potential additional contingent commission probes by international authorities.

▶ Our 12-month target price of $46 is about 13.3X our estimate of 2010 EPS from continuing operations, in line with historical multiples.

Qualitative Risk Assessment

LOW	MEDIUM	HIGH

Our risk assessment reflects what see as the company's well diversified operations and solid balance sheet, with low debt, offset by the impact of the loss of contingent commissions and business restructuring, soft insurance pricing environment, and the potential for increased amortization of intangible assets.

Quantitative Evaluations

S&P Quality Ranking   B+

D	C	B-	B	B+	A-	A	A+

Relative Strength Rank   MODERATE

31

LOWEST = 1   HIGHEST = 99

Revenue/Earnings Data

Revenue (Million $)

	1Q	2Q	3Q	4Q	Year
2009	1,854	1,885	1,808	--	--
2008	1,932	1,980	1,847	1,924	7,631
2007	1,798	1,866	1,775	2,032	7,471
2006	2,165	2,208	2,168	2,413	8,954
2005	2,464	2,456	2,387	2,530	9,837
2004	2,564	2,544	2,402	2,662	10,172

Earnings Per Share ($)

	1Q	2Q	3Q	4Q	Year
2009	0.80	0.51	0.40	E0.90	E3.10
2008	0.56	0.55	0.53	0.43	2.06
2007	0.51	0.57	0.42	0.11	2.10
2006	0.57	0.53	0.27	0.57	1.86
2005	0.58	0.54	0.35	0.42	1.89
2004	0.58	0.54	0.36	0.25	1.72

Fiscal year ended Dec. 31. Next earnings report expected: Early February. EPS Estimates based on S&P Operating Earnings; historical GAAP earnings are as reported.

Dividend Data (Dates: mm/dd Payment Date: mm/dd/yy)

Amount ($)	Date Decl.	Ex-Div. Date	Stk. of Record	Payment Date
0.150	01/13	01/29	02/02	02/16/09
0.150	04/17	04/29	05/01	05/15/09
0.150	07/17	07/30	08/03	08/17/09
0.150	10/12	10/29	11/02	11/16/09

Dividends have been paid since 1950. Source: Company reports.

Please read the Required Disclosures and Analyst Certification on the last page of this report.

Aon Corp.

**STANDARD
&POOR'S**

Business Summary November 03, 2009

CORPORATE OVERVIEW. Aon Corp. is a global provider of insurance broker-age services, insurance products, and risk and insurance advice, as well as other consulting services, conducting business in more than 120 countries and sovereignties. In 2008, Aon was ranked by Business Insurance as the world's largest insurance broker.

AOC classifies its businesses into two operating segments: risk and insurance brokerage, and consulting. The risk and insurance brokerage segment accounted for 82% of total revenue from continuing operations in 2008, and the consulting segment 18%.

CORPORATE STRATEGY. Aon employs a growth-through-acquisition strategy, which it believes has been vital in building its network of resources and capabilities. Over the past 21 years, Aon has completed more than 440 acquisitions. In 2008, AOC purchased a total of 31 companies, mostly related to its risk and insurance brokerage operations.

IMPACT OF MAJOR DEVELOPMENTS. In August 2008, AOC announced plans to acquire Benfield, a leading reinsurance intermediary, for $1.75 billion. The transaction closed in November 2008 for $1.43 billion, due to a strengthening

of the U.S. dollar versus the British pound. In connection with the transaction, AOC announced a global restructuring program. This program is expected to result in $185 million of charges over a three-year period and achieve $33-$41 million of savings in 2009. In 2010, the program is expected to save $84-$94 million, and $122 million of cumulative annualized savings by 2010.

In December 2007, the company signed separate definitive agreements to sell its Combined Insurance Company of America (CICA) and Sterling Life Insurance Company businesses. AOC agreed to sell its CICA business to ACE Limited for cash consideration of $2.56 billion, and its Sterling business to Munich Re Group for cash consideration of $352 million. AOC received a one-time cash dividend of $325 million from CICA prior to the close of the transaction. Total after-tax cash proceeds and dividends were $2.7 billion. The Sterling transaction was completed on April 1, 2008, and the CICA sale at the end of the second quarter of 2008.

Company Financials Fiscal Year Ended Dec. 31

Per Share Data ($)	2008	2007	2006	2005	2004	2003	2002	2001	2000	1999
Tangible Book Value	NM	4.37	2.14	2.48	0.76	NM	NM	NM	NM	NM
Cash Flow	2.74	2.67	NA	NA	NA	NA	NA	NA	NA	NA
Earnings	2.06	2.10	1.86	1.89	1.72	2.08	1.64	0.73	1.82	1.33
S&P Core Earnings	1.22	1.66	2.03	2.10	2.29	2.05	1.00	-0.06	NA	NA
Dividends	0.60	0.60	0.75	0.60	0.60	0.60	0.83	0.90	0.87	0.81
Payout Ratio	29%	29%	40%	32%	35%	29%	50%	123%	48%	61%
Prices:High	50.00	51.32	42.76	37.14	29.44	26.79	39.63	44.80	42.75	46.67
Prices:Low	32.83	34.30	31.01	20.64	18.15	17.41	13.30	29.75	20.69	26.06
P/E Ratio:High	24	24	23	20	17	13	24	61	23	35
P/E Ratio:Low	16	16	17	11	11	8	8	41	11	20
Income Statement Analysis (Million $)										
Revenue	7,631	7,471	8,954	9,837	10,172	9,810	8,822	7,676	7,375	7,070
Operating Income	1,536	1,437	1,426	NA	NA	NA	NA	NA	NA	NA
Depreciation	204	189	244	277	309	314	263	339	333	355
Interest Expense	126	138	129	NA	NA	NA	NA	NA	NA	NA
Pretax Income	863	1,024	920	965	880	1,110	793	399	854	635
Effective Tax Rate	28.0%	34.4%	32.0%	33.5%	34.4%	38.3%	38.6%	43.5%	40.9%	40.8%
Net Income	621	672	626	642	577	663	466	203	481	352
S&P Core Earnings	368	531	683	709	765	652	281	-19.4	NA	NA
Balance Sheet & Other Financial Data (Million $)										
Cash	1,236	4,915	4,726	476	570	540	506	439	1,118	837
Current Assets	14,526	17,973	NA	NA	NA	NA	NA	NA	NA	NA
Total Assets	23,172	24,948	24,318	27,818	28,329	27,027	25,334	22,386	22,251	21,132
Current Liabilities	12,803	14,553	NA	NA	NA	NA	NA	NA	NA	NA
Long Term Debt	1,872	2,145	1,588	2,105	1,523	1,787	2,064	2,363	2,586	1,804
Common Equity	5,314	6,221	5,218	5,303	5,103	4,498	3,895	3,521	3,388	3,051
Total Capital	7,287	8,223	6,806	7,408	7,268	6,643	6,318	6,065	6,036	4,912
Capital Expenditures	103	170	152	126	80.0	185	278	281	179	271
Cash Flow	825	861	863	NA	NA	NA	NA	NA	NA	NA
Current Ratio	1.1	1.2	1.1	1.0	1.0	1.0	0.9	0.9	1.0	0.9
% Long Term Debt of Capitalization	25.6	23.3	23.3	28.4	21.0	26.9	32.7	39.0	42.8	36.7
% Net Income of Revenue	8.1	9.0	7.0	6.5	5.7	6.8	5.3	2.6	6.5	5.0
% Return on Assets	2.6	2.7	2.4	2.3	2.1	2.5	2.0	0.9	2.2	1.7
% Return on Equity	10.8	11.8	11.9	12.3	12.0	15.8	12.6	5.9	14.9	11.6

Data as orig reptd.; bef. results of disc opers/spec. items. Per share data adj. for stk. divs.; EPS diluted. E-Estimated. NA-Not Available. NM-Not Meaningful. NR-Not Ranked. UR-Under Review.

Office: 200 E Randolph St Lowr, Chicago, IL 60601-6436.
Telephone: 312-381-1000.
Website: http://www.aon.com
Chrmn: P. Manduca

Pres & CEO: G.C. Case
EVP & CFO: C. Davies
EVP & Chief Admin Officer: G.J. Besio
EVP & General Counsel: P. Lieb

Investor Contact: S. Malchow (312-381-3983)
Board Members: G. C. Case, F. Conti, E. D. Jannotta, P. J. Kalff, L. B. Knight, III, J. M. Losh, P. Manduca, R. E. Martin, A. J. McKenna, R. S. Morrison, R. B. Myers, R. C. Notebaert, J. W. Rogers, Jr., G. Santona, C. Stoddart, C. Y. Woo

Founded: 1919
Domicile: Delaware
Employees: 37,700

The **McGraw-Hill** Companies

Apache Corp

S&P Recommendation	**STRONG BUY** ★★★★★	Price $95.75 (as of Nov 27, 2009)	12-Mo. Target Price $120.00	Investment Style Large-Cap Blend

GICS Sector Energy
Sub-Industry Oil & Gas Exploration & Production

Summary One of the largest independent exploration and production companies in the U.S., Apache explores for, develops and produces natural gas, crude oil and natural gas liquids.

Key Stock Statistics (Source S&P, Vickers, company reports)

52-Wk Range	$105.59– 51.03	S&P Oper. EPS 2009**E** 5.36	Market Capitalization(B) $32.189	Beta	1.21
Trailing 12-Month EPS	$-11.39	S&P Oper. EPS 2010**E** 7.89	Yield (%) 0.63	S&P 3-Yr. Proj. EPS CAGR(%)	0
Trailing 12-Month P/E	NM	P/E on S&P Oper. EPS 2009**E** 17.9	Dividend Rate/Share $0.60	S&P Credit Rating	A-
$10K Invested 5 Yrs Ago	$18,457	Common Shares Outstg. (M) 336.2	Institutional Ownership (%) 84		

Price Performance

30-Week Mov. Avg. · · · 10-Week Mov. Avg. – – **GAAP Earnings vs. Previous Year** Volume Above Avg. STARS
12-Mo. Target Price — Relative Strength ▲ Up ▼ Down ▶ No Change Below Avg. ★

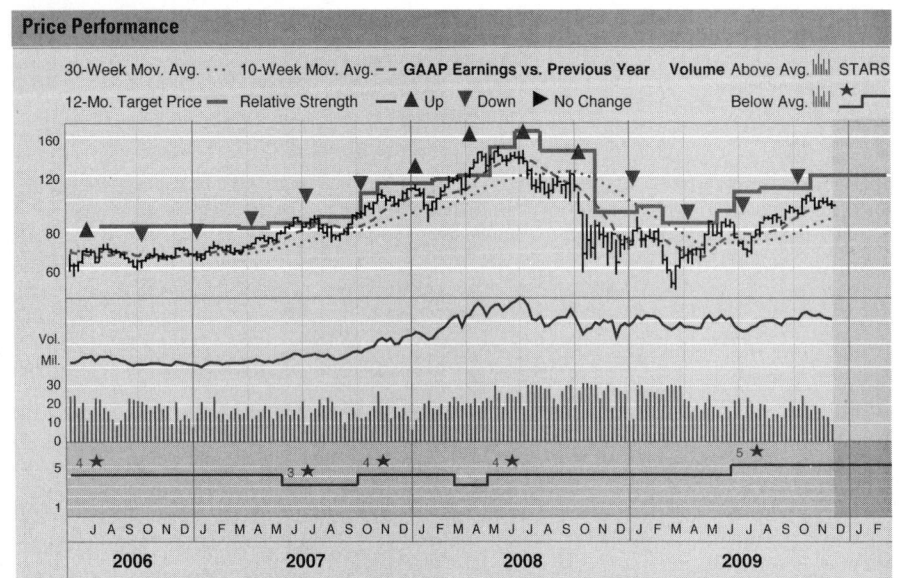

Options: ASE, CBOE, P, Ph

Analysis prepared by **Michael Kay** on October 27, 2009, when the stock traded at **$ 98.16**.

Highlights

► Production fell 5% in 2008, on a pipeline rupture in Australia, a strike in Scotland at the Forties Field and hurricane shut-ins hampered production. However, APA has a pipeline of seven projects scheduled to begin production between 2009 and 2012, which should contribute about 150,000 boe/d of net new oil and gas production. For 2009, APA sees volume growth of 6%-14%, and we forecast 10% growth, followed by 6% in 2010. Initial volumes in Egypt and the Gulf of Mexico have led to better-than-forecast production so far in 2009.

► For 2009, APA sees growth with the start-up of the Salam gas plant in Egypt, and restored production in Australia and Scotland. APA's 2009 capex budget is $3.5 billion-$4 billion, down 33%-42%, on lower activity. In April, APA acquired nine Permian Basin fields with production of 3,500 BOE/day, for $187 million.

► We see operating EPS (before impairments) of $5.36 in 2009, down from $11.28 in 2008, on lower prices, before rising to $7.63 in 2010 on production and price gains. APA ended the second quarter with a debt-to-capital ratio of 25% and maintains what we consider one of the strongest balance sheet among peers.

Investment Rationale/Risk

► APA continues to exploit mature North American reserves and focus growth capital on international development projects (Geauxpher in the Gulf of Mexico, the Van Gogh, Pyrenees, Julimar and Reindeer projects in Australia, and the Salam gas plant in Egypt), which should contribute to growth over the next three years. In addition, APA has added a new gas plant in Egypt, and we think the Ootla project in Canada has the potential to become another major development project. We expect APA to protect its balance sheet in 2009, and we see sufficient cash flow to fund its projects.

► Risks to our opinion and target price include unfavorable changes to economic, industrial and operating conditions, including increased costs, and difficulty replacing reserves.

► Our strong buy opinion reflects our view that large crude oil projects, especially internationally, provide solid production growth visibility. APA has a solid diversified position with one of the lowest cost structures and debt levels among E&P peers, in our view. We blend our NAV estimate ($116) with DCF ($121; WACC of 11%, terminal growth of 3%) and relative metrics to derive our 12-month target price of $120.

Qualitative Risk Assessment

LOW	MEDIUM	**HIGH**

Our risk assessment for APA reflects its participation in a highly capital-intensive industry that derives value based on commodity prices that can be highly volatile. APA is a super-large exploration and production company diversified across major producing regions, focused on exploiting North American reserves and growing capital internationally.

Quantitative Evaluations

S&P Quality Ranking A

D	C	B-	B	B+	A-	**A**	A+

Relative Strength Rank MODERATE

55

LOWEST = 1   HIGHEST = 99

Revenue/Earnings Data

Revenue (Million $)

	1Q	2Q	3Q	4Q	Year
2009	1,634	2,093	2,332	--	--
2008	3,188	3,900	3,365	1,937	12,390
2007	1,997	2,468	2,499	3,014	9,978
2006	1,999	2,062	2,261	1,967	8,289
2005	1,662	1,759	2,061	2,102	7,584
2004	1,150	1,241	1,407	1,535	5,333

Earnings Per Share ($)

	1Q	2Q	3Q	4Q	Year
2009	-5.25	1.31	1.30	E1.72	E5.36
2008	3.03	4.28	3.52	-8.80	2.10
2007	1.47	1.89	1.83	3.19	8.39
2006	1.97	2.17	1.94	1.56	7.64
2005	1.67	1.76	2.05	2.35	7.84
2004	1.05	1.16	1.30	1.53	5.04

Fiscal year ended Dec. 31. Next earnings report expected: Mid February. EPS Estimates based on S&P Operating Earnings; historical GAAP earnings are as reported.

Dividend Data (Dates: mm/dd Payment Date: mm/dd/yy)

Amount ($)	Date Decl.	Ex-Div. Date	Stk. of Record	Payment Date
0.150	12/11	01/20	01/22	02/23/09
0.150	02/26	04/20	04/22	05/22/09
0.150	05/14	07/20	07/22	08/22/09
0.150	08/17	10/20	10/22	11/23/09

Dividends have been paid since 1965. Source: Company reports.

Please read the Required Disclosures and Analyst Certification on the last page of this report.

The McGraw-Hill Companies

Apache Corp

STANDARD &POOR'S

Business Summary October 27, 2009

CORPORATE OVERVIEW. As one of the largest independent exploration and production (E&P) companies in the U.S., Apache Corp. (APA) explores for, develops and produces natural gas, crude oil and natural gas liquids (NGLs).

In North America, APA's interests are focused in the Gulf of Mexico, the Gulf Coast, East Texas, the Permian Basin, the Anadarko Basin, and the Western Sedimentary Basin of Canada. Outside of North America, APA has interests in Egypt, offshore Western Australia, offshore the U.K. in the North Sea, and onshore Argentina. In November 2007, APA was a high bidder on two exploration blocks on the Chilean side of the island of Tierra del Fuego.

Proved oil and gas reserves declined 2%, to 2.4 billion barrel oil equivalent (boe; 69% developed; 46% liquids), in 2008, due to a 2.6% negative reserve revision associated with low commodity prices at year-end. Oil and gas production declined 5%, to 534,500 boe per day (47% liquids). APA estimates 2008 organic reserve replacement at 118% and all-in reserve replacement at 122%. Using data from John S. Herold, we estimate APA's three-year (2005-2007) re-

serve replacement at 197%, below peers; three-year finding and development costs at $16.08 per boe, in line with peers; three-year proved acquisition costs at $13.81 per boe, above the peer average; and three-year reserve replacement costs at $14.85 per boe, in line with peers.

MARKET PROFILE. APA has a large, geographically diversified reserve base with what we view as a good history of organic reserve replacement at an attractive cost. Nonetheless, the company has a history of supplementing its organic growth with acquisitions consistent with a strategy that emphasizes development over exploration. We expect mid-single digit production growth from 2009-2012 on exploration and development projects in the company's ACE (Australia, Canada, Egypt) core growth areas.

Company Financials Fiscal Year Ended Dec. 31

Per Share Data ($)	2008	2007	2006	2005	2004	2003	2002	2001	2000	1999
Tangible Book Value	48.63	46.49	39.30	31.06	24.18	19.25	15.33	14.69	12.07	8.97
Cash Flow	25.68	15.41	13.19	12.22	8.81	6.67	4.55	5.30	4.46	2.51
Earnings	2.10	8.39	7.64	7.84	5.04	3.35	1.80	2.37	2.48	0.74
S&P Core Earnings	2.08	8.38	7.30	7.60	5.19	3.29	1.73	2.28	NA	NA
Dividends	0.70	0.60	0.60	0.34	0.32	0.21	0.19	0.12	0.09	0.12
Payout Ratio	33%	7%	8%	4%	6%	6%	11%	5%	4%	16%
Prices:High	149.23	109.32	76.25	78.15	55.16	41.68	28.88	31.55	32.12	21.62
Prices:Low	57.11	63.01	56.50	47.45	36.79	26.26	21.12	16.56	13.91	7.63
P/E Ratio:High	71	13	10	10	11	12	16	13	13	29
P/E Ratio:Low	27	8	7	6	7	8	12	7	6	10

Income Statement Analysis (Million $)										
Revenue	12,390	9,978	8,289	7,584	5,333	4,190	2,560	2,777	2,284	1,300
Operating Income	8,988	7,224	5,753	5,792	4,119	3,241	1,048	2,146	1,310	870
Depreciation, Depletion and Amortization	7,952	2,348	1,816	1,416	1,222	1,073	844	821	584	443
Interest Expense	166	312	158	122	120	127	133	132	109	84.6
Pretax Income	932	4,673	4,010	4,206	2,663	1,922	899	1,199	1,204	345
Effective Tax Rate	23.6%	39.8%	36.3%	37.6%	37.3%	43.0%	38.3%	39.7%	40.1%	41.7%
Net Income	712	2,812	2,552	2,624	1,670	1,095	554	723	721	201
S&P Core Earnings	701	2,805	2,434	2,539	1,713	1,069	524	681	NA	NA

Balance Sheet & Other Financial Data (Million $)										
Cash	1,973	126	141	229	111	33.5	51.9	35.6	37.2	13.2
Current Assets	4,451	2,752	2,490	2,162	1,349	899	767	698	630	343
Total Assets	29,186	28,635	24,308	19,272	15,502	12,416	9,460	8,934	7,482	5,503
Current Liabilities	2,615	2,665	3,812	2,187	1,283	820	532	522	553	337
Long Term Debt	4,809	4,227	2,020	2,192	2,588	2,327	2,159	2,244	2,193	1,880
Common Equity	16,509	15,280	13,093	10,443	8,106	6,434	4,826	4,112	3,448	2,361
Total Capital	24,484	23,315	18,830	12,733	10,793	8,860	7,083	7,655	5,948	4,549
Capital Expenditures	5,973	5,807	3,892	3,716	2,456	1,595	1,037	1,525	1,011	591
Cash Flow	8,658	5,154	4,363	4,034	2,887	2,163	1,387	1,525	1,284	629
Current Ratio	1.7	1.0	0.7	1.0	1.1	1.1	1.4	1.3	1.1	1.0
% Long Term Debt of Capitalization	19.6	20.7	13.3	17.2	24.0	26.3	30.5	29.3	36.9	41.3
% Return on Assets	2.5	10.6	11.7	15.1	12.0	10.0	6.0	8.8	11.1	4.2
% Return on Equity	4.5	19.8	21.6	28.2	22.9	19.4	12.2	18.6	24.1	9.2

Data as orig reptd.; bef. results of disc opers/spec. items. Per share data adj. for stk. divs.; EPS diluted. E-Estimated. NA-Not Available. NM-Not Meaningful. NR-Not Ranked. UR-Under Review.

Office: 2000 Post Oak Blvd Ste 100, Houston, TX 77056-4400.
Telephone: 713-296-6000.
Website: http://www.apachecorp.com
Chrmn & CEO: G.S. Farris

Pres & CFO: R.B. Plank
COO: R.J. Eichler
COO: J.A. Crum
EVP & General Counsel: P.A. Lannie

Investor Contact: T. Chambers (713-296-6685)
Board Members: F. M. Bohen, G. S. Farris, R. M. Ferlic, E. C. Fiedorek, A. Frazier, Jr., P. A. Graham, J. A. Kocur, G. D. Lawrence, Jr., F. H. Merelli, R. D. Patton, C. Pitman

Founded: 1954
Domicile: Delaware
Employees: 3,639

Apartment Investment and Management Co

STANDARD
&POOR'S

S&P Recommendation HOLD ★ ★ ★ ☆ ☆

Price	12-Mo. Target Price	Investment Style
$12.85 (as of Nov 27, 2009)	$13.00	Large-Cap Value

GICS Sector Financials
Sub-Industry Residential REITS

Summary This real estate investment trust is one of the largest U.S. owners and managers of multi-family apartment properties.

Key Stock Statistics (Source S&P, Vickers, company reports)

52-Wk Range	$16.05– 4.57	S&P FFO/Sh. 2009E	1.67	Market Capitalization(B)	$1.503	Beta	2.40
Trailing 12-Month FFO/Share	NA	S&P FFO/Sh. 2010E	1.45	Yield (%)	3.11	S&P 3-Yr. FFO/Sh. Proj. CAGR(%)	-2
Trailing 12-Month P/FFO	NA	P/FFO on S&P FFO/Sh. 2009E	7.7	Dividend Rate/Share	$0.40	S&P Credit Rating	BB+
$10K Invested 5 Yrs Ago	$6,795	Common Shares Outstg. (M)	117.0	Institutional Ownership (%)	90		

Price Performance

30-Week Mov. Avg. · · · · 10-Week Mov. Avg. - - **GAAP Earnings vs. Previous Year** Volume Above Avg. STARS
12-Mo. Target Price — Relative Strength — ▲ Up ▼ Down ▶ No Change Below Avg.

Options: CBOE, P, Ph

Analysis prepared by **Royal F. Shepard, CFA** on November 03, 2009, when the stock traded at **$ 12.41**.

Highlights

▶ AIV projects it will sell about $1.3 billion in assets in 2009, including over $500 million in the fourth quarter. We think proceeds will go toward the payment of outstanding debt. In our view, the transactions are serving to upgrade the quality of AIV's portfolio. AIV's active redevelopment program is also likely to make a positive contribution to revenues and earnings in 2009 and 2010. In our estimation, however, average rents at stabilized properties will decline about 2%-3% in 2009 and an additional 1% in 2009, due to job losses and a weak economy.

▶ Our FFO per share estimate of $1.67 for 2009, falling to $1.45 in 2010, reflects more shares outstanding, dilution from asset sales, and lower transaction related income. We also expect ongoing pressure on rents as leases renew, and inflationary increases in property level operating expenses.

▶ AIV recently reduced its 2009 quarterly cash dividend to $0.10, a cut of over 80% from 2008. We believe the payout is now at a level that approximates taxable income.

Investment Rationale/Risk

▶ AIV holds what we view as a large and diversified portfolio of conventional and affordable residential properties. We think challenging economic conditions will force apartment owners to lower rents on new leases through the first half of 2010, even at AIV's mostly middle-market properties. However, recurring management fees provide a degree of stability. Also, we think the trust can fund the refinancing of its balance sheet with proceeds from planned assets sales. Still, assets sales are likely to dilute earnings potential through 2010, and justify, in our view, a discounted valuation relative to peers.

▶ Risks to our opinion and target price include slower-than-expected employment growth in AIV's markets, higher borrowing rates on floating rate debt, and a significant increase in new construction that creates competitive supply.

▶ Our 12-month target price of $13 is based partly on a multiple of 9.0X our 2010 FFO estimate of $1.45, a discount to peers, reflecting our view of AIV's below-average financial position. We blend in our net asset value model, based on recent transactions and a one-year cash return of 6.75%, leading to intrinsic value of $12.

Qualitative Risk Assessment

LOW	MEDIUM	HIGH

Our risk assessment for AIV reflects its recent weak operating performance, further potential cuts in the common dividend, and dependence on asset sales.

Quantitative Evaluations

S&P Quality Ranking B-

D	C	B-	B	B+	A-	A	A+

Relative Strength Rank MODERATE

37

LOWEST = 1 HIGHEST = 99

Revenue/FFO Data

Revenue (Million $)

	1Q	2Q	3Q	4Q	Year
2009	349.3	334.8	319.4	--	--
2008	349.2	374.0	375.1	359.6	1,458
2007	413.1	426.4	426.7	455.0	1,721
2006	408.5	420.0	423.9	438.6	1,691
2005	361.6	372.3	386.8	400.9	1,522
2004	376.4	380.2	334.1	384.4	1,469

FFO Per Share ($)

	1Q	2Q	3Q	4Q	Year
2009	0.42	E0.45	E0.41	E0.39	E1.67
2008	0.79	0.83	0.82	-0.34	1.45
2007	0.74	0.88	0.83	0.83	3.17
2006	0.68	0.73	0.74	0.91	3.07
2005	0.63	0.67	0.58	0.60	2.48
2004	0.67	0.63	0.78	0.72	2.79

Fiscal year ended Dec. 31. Next earnings report expected: Early February. FFO Estimates based on S&P Funds From Operations Est..

Dividend Data (Dates: mm/dd Payment Date: mm/dd/yy)

Amount ($)	Date Decl.	Ex-Div. Date	Stk. of Record	Payment Date
2.08 Spl.	12/18	12/24	12/29	01/29/09
0.100	05/01	05/13	05/15	05/29/09
0.100	07/29	08/19	08/21	08/31/09
0.100	10/29	11/18	11/20	11/30/09

Dividends have been paid since 1994. Source: Company reports.

Please read the Required Disclosures and Analyst Certification on the last page of this report.

The McGraw·Hill Companies

Apartment Investment and Management Co

STANDARD
&POOR'S

Business Summary November 03, 2009

CORPORATE OVERVIEW. Apartment Investment and Management Co. is one of the largest U.S. multi-family residential REITs in terms of units. At December 31, 2008, it owned, held an equity interest in, or managed a geographically diversified portfolio of 992 properties, including about 162,807 apartment units, located in 44 states, the District of Columbia and Puerto Rico.

The trust conducts substantially all its business, and owns all its assets, through AIMCO Properties, L.P., of which AIV owns approximately a 91% interest. AIV operates in two segments: the ownership, operation and management of apartment properties; and the management of apartment properties for third parties and affiliates.

MARKET PROFILE. The U.S. housing market is highly fragmented, and is characterized broadly by two types of housing units -- multi-family and single-family. At the end of 2008, the U.S. Census Bureau estimated that there were 130.84 million housing units in the country, an increase of 1.7% from 2006. Partially due to the high fragmentation since residents have the option of either being owners or tenants (renters), the housing market can be highly competitive. Main demand drivers for apartments are household formation and em-

ployment growth. We estimate that 0.7 million new households were formed in 2008. Supply is created by new housing unit construction, which could consist of single-family homes, or multi-family apartment buildings or condominiums. The U.S. Department of Housing estimates that 0.90 million total housing units were started in 2008, down about 33% from 2007. Multi-family starts, for structures with more than five units, fell significantly less, declining approximately 4.5%.

With apartment tenants on relatively short leases compared to those of commercial and industrial properties, apartment REITs are generally more sensitive to changes in market conditions than REITs in other property categories. Results could be hurt by new construction that adds new space in excess of actual demand. Trends in home price affordability also affect both rent levels and the level of new construction, since the relative price attractiveness of owning versus renting is an important factor in consumer decision making.

Company Financials Fiscal Year Ended Dec. 31

Per Share Data ($)	2008	2007	2006	2005	2004	2003	2002	2001	2000	1999
Tangible Book Value	5.51	9.82	NA	NA	NA	NA	NA	18.90	23.33	24.27
Earnings	-1.51	-1.14	-1.29	-1.25	-0.39	-0.25	0.94	0.23	0.52	0.38
S&P Core Earnings	-1.51	-1.12	-1.29	-1.25	-0.39	-0.32	0.89	0.19	NA	NA
Dividends	1.20	2.40	NA	NA	NA	NA	NA	3.12	2.80	2.50
Payout Ratio	NM	NM	NM	NM	NM	NM	NM	NM	NM	NM
Prices:High	43.67	65.79	59.17	44.14	39.25	42.05	51.46	50.13	50.06	44.13
Prices:Low	7.01	33.97	37.76	34.17	26.45	33.00	33.90	39.25	36.31	34.06
P/E Ratio:High	1458	NM	NM	NM	NM	NM	55	NM	96	NM
P/E Ratio:Low	NM	NM	NM	NM	NM	NM	36	NM	70	NM

Income Statement Analysis (Million $)										
Rental Income	1,351	1,641	1,630	1,460	1,402	1,446	1,292	1,298	1,051	534
Mortgage Income	Nil	Nil	Nil	Nil	Nil	Nil	Nil	Nil	Nil	43.5
Total Income	1,458	1,721	1,691	1,522	1,469	1,516	1,506	1,464	1,101	577
General Expenses	795	886	874	816	768	729	664	652	485	406
Interest Expense	369	422	408	368	367	373	340	316	270	140
Provision for Losses	Nil	Nil	Nil	Nil	Nil	Nil	Nil	Nil	Nil	Nil
Depreciation	459	NA	471	412	369	328	289	364	330	151
Net Income	-129	-48.1	-42.7	-27.9	55.7	70.7	175	107	99.2	83.7
S&P Core Earnings	-183	-112	-124	-117	-35.5	-29.2	77.1	13.8	NA	NA

Balance Sheet & Other Financial Data (Million $)										
Cash	300	210	230	330	293	98.0	97.0	820	1,068	1,123
Total Assets	9,403	10,607	10,290	10,017	10,072	10,113	10,317	8,323	7,700	5,685
Real Estate Investment	10,885	12,384	11,982	10,990	10,800	10,601	10,227	8,416	7,012	4,509
Loss Reserve	Nil	Nil	Nil	Nil	Nil	Nil	Nil	Nil	Nil	Nil
Net Investment	8,102	9,349	9,081	8,752	8,785	8,753	8,616	6,796	6,099	4,092
Short Term Debt	Nil	Nil	Nil	Nil	Nil	Nil	Nil	214	329	630
Capitalization:Debt	6,777	7,532	6,873	6,284	5,734	6,198	5,529	4,670	4,031	2,525
Capitalization:Equity	722	1,026	1,516	1,706	1,967	2,005	2,218	1,592	1,664	1,622
Capitalization:Total	8,632	9,838	9,165	9,436	9,246	9,580	9,180	7,904	7,037	5,181
% Earnings & Depreciation/Assets	3.3	4.2	4.2	3.8	4.2	3.9	5.0	5.9	1.5	4.7
Price Times Book Value:High	7.9	6.7	4.0	2.5	1.9	2.0	2.3	2.7	2.1	1.8
Price Times Book Value:Low	1.3	3.5	2.5	1.9	1.3	1.6	1.5	2.1	1.6	1.4

Data as orig reptd.; bef. results of disc opers/spec. items. Per share data adj. for stk. divs.; EPS diluted. E-Estimated. NA-Not Available. NM-Not Meaningful. NR-Not Ranked. UR-Under Review.

Office: 4582 S Ulster St Pkwy Ste 1100, Denver, CO 80237-2662.
Telephone: 303-757-8101.
Email: investor@aimco.com
Website: http://www.aimco.com

Chrmn & CEO: T.T. Considine
Pres: D.R. Robertson
COO & Co-Pres: T.J. Beaudin
EVP & CFO: E.M. Freedman

EVP & Chief Admin Officer: M. Cortez
Investor Contact: J. Martin (303-691-4440)
Board Members: T. T. Considine, S. D. Cordes

Founded: 1994
Domicile: Maryland
Employees: 4,500

The McGraw·Hill Companies

Apollo Group Inc

STANDARD &POOR'S

S&P Recommendation	HOLD ★★★☆☆	Price $55.76 (as of Nov 27, 2009)	12-Mo. Target Price $65.00	Investment Style Large-Cap Growth

GICS Sector Consumer Discretionary
Sub-Industry Education Services

Summary This provider of higher education programs for working adults offers educational programs and services throughout the U.S. and in a small number of foreign markets.

Key Stock Statistics (Source S&P, Vickers, company reports)

52-Wk Range	$90.00–52.79	S&P Oper. EPS 2010**E**	4.85	Market Capitalization(B)	$8.607	Beta	-0.11
Trailing 12-Month EPS	$3.75	S&P Oper. EPS 2011**E**	5.30	Yield (%)	Nil	S&P 3-Yr. Proj. EPS CAGR(%)	12
Trailing 12-Month P/E	14.9	P/E on S&P Oper. EPS 2010**E**	11.5	Dividend Rate/Share	Nil	S&P Credit Rating	NA
$10K Invested 5 Yrs Ago	$7,144	Common Shares Outstg. (M)	154.8	Institutional Ownership (%)	87		

Price Performance

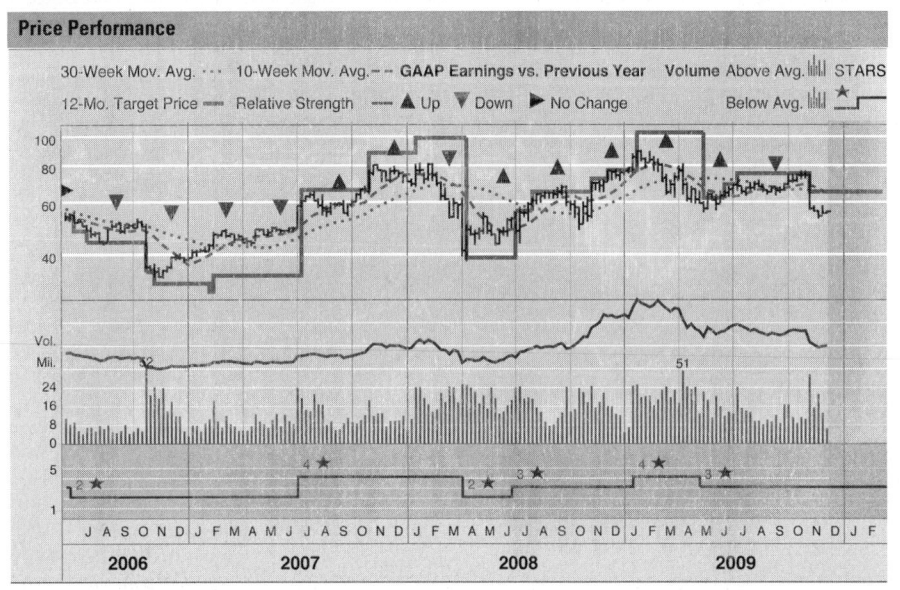

30-Week Mov. Avg. · · · 10-Week Mov. Avg. - - GAAP Earnings vs. Previous Year Volume Above Avg. STARS
12-Mo. Target Price — Relative Strength ▲ Up ▼ Down ► No Change Below Avg.

Options: ASE, CBOE, P, Ph

Qualitative Risk Assessment

LOW	MEDIUM	HIGH

Our risk assessment reflects a lack of consistent conditions in the for-profit education market, APOL's current transformation of its business model and recent executive changeover. In the corporate governance area, we have a negative view of the near 100% voting control held by insiders through separate voting shares. We believe these factors are offset by what we view as APOL's consistently solid levels of cash flow and a healthy balance sheet.

Quantitative Evaluations

S&P Quality Ranking   B+

D	C	B-	B	B+	A-	A	A+

Relative Strength Rank   WEAK

15

LOWEST = 1   HIGHEST = 99

Highlights

► The 12-month target price for APOL has recently been changed to $65.00 from $75.00. The Highlights section of this Stock Report will be updated accordingly.

Investment Rationale/Risk

► The Investment Rationale/Risk section of this Stock Report will be updated shortly. For the latest News story on APOL from MarketScope, see below.

► 10/28/09 10:23 am ET ... S&P MAINTAINS HOLD OPINION ON APOLLO GROUP SHARES (APOL 62.3***): Aug-Q adjusted EPS of $1.06 vs. $0.75 beats our view by $0.06. But the shares are down 15% today, as the SEC starts an informal inquiry into APOL's revenue recognition methods. We think APOL's business remains robust, as total and new students both rose 23% in Aug-Q. But we see valuation being limited by the inquiry and our belief that likely economic rebound will rein in values of companies seen as counter-cyclical. We still see $4.85 EPS in FY 10 (Aug.) and start FY 11 at $5.30. We cut target price by $10 to $65, 13X calendar '10 est, the bottom of historical range. /M.Jaffe

Revenue/Earnings Data

Revenue (Million $)

	1Q	2Q	3Q	4Q	Year
2009	971.0	876.1	1,051	1,076	3,974
2008	780.7	693.6	835.2	831.4	3,141
2007	667.8	608.7	733.4	713.9	2,724
2006	628.9	569.6	653.6	624.2	2,478
2005	534.9	505.7	619.0	591.8	2,251
2004	411.8	396.9	497.0	492.8	1,798

Earnings Per Share ($)

	1Q	2Q	3Q	4Q	Year
2009	1.12	0.77	1.26	0.59	3.75
2008	0.83	-0.19	0.85	1.43	2.87
2007	0.65	0.35	0.75	0.60	2.35
2006	0.73	0.46	0.77	0.54	2.35
2005	0.58	0.47	0.77	0.58	2.39
2004	0.44	0.35	0.56	-0.59	0.77

Fiscal year ended Aug. 31. Next earnings report expected: Early January. EPS Estimates based on S&P Operating Earnings; historical GAAP earnings are as reported.

Dividend Data

No cash dividends have been paid.

Please read the Required Disclosures and Analyst Certification on the last page of this report.

The McGraw-Hill Companies

Apollo Group Inc

**STANDARD
&POOR'S**

Business Summary September 28, 2009

CORPORATE OVERVIEW. Historically, Apollo Group derived most of its revenues through the provision of higher education programs for working adults. It has several school units, but the large majority of its students have taken education programs at its University of Phoenix (UOP) unit. UOP offers its education programs at campuses, as well as through online programs. They consist mostly of associates, bachelors and masters degree programs in business, education, information technology, criminal justice and nursing. As of May 31, 2009, APOL offered programs and services in 40 states, the District of Columbia, Puerto Rico, Canada, the Netherlands, Chile and Mexico. Enrollment at UOP (including the Axia associates degree program, which became part of UOP in mid-calendar 2006) and Western International University totaled 420,700 at May 31, 2009, up from 362,100 at FY 08 (Aug.) year end, and 313,700 at August 31, 2007.

CORPORATE STRATEGY. The level of Apollo's enrollment growth fell from 27.7% in FY 04's fourth quarter (under the old definition of enrollments), to 3.3% in FY 06's third quarter (under the new definition; it now reports only UOP and Western International University), with sequential growth levels declining in all but one quarter. However, growth has since revived, and stood at 21.8% in FY 09's third quarter. We attribute the initial downturn to changing demographic trends, greater competition and more regulatory scrutiny. Until recently, APOL focused almost entirely on students who were older than the tra-

ditional 18-to-22 year-old college student, particularly baby boomers. Yet, with the youngest baby boomers now over the age of 40, APOL has started to seek students in other demographic categories. As a result, it began to place much more concentration on associate degrees, targeting younger students. We believe early results of its shift in focus have been encouraging.

In October 2007, Apollo formed a $1 billion joint venture (Apollo Global) with the Carlyle Group, a private equity firm, to make a range of investments in the foreign education services sector. APOL committed up to $801 million, and was to own 80.1% of the venture (86.1% as of late July 2009). We view this as an important step for APOL in preparing to expand its global footprint. In July 2009, Apollo Global purchased U.K.-based BPP Holdings plc (revenues of $263 million and pretax profit of $31.2 million in calendar 2008), which provides education and training to legal and financial professionals, for $607 million, net of and including certain items. This followed Apollo Global's April 2008 acquisition of Universidad de Artes, Ciencias y Comunicacion, an accredited, private arts and communications university in Chile; and its August 2008 purchase of a 65% interest in Universidad Latinoamericana.

Company Financials Fiscal Year Ended Aug. 31

Per Share Data ($)	2009	2008	2007	2006	2005	2004	2003	2002	2001	2000
Tangible Book Value	2.79	4.56	3.62	3.40	3.73	4.89	5.23	3.60	2.47	1.39
Cash Flow	NA	3.35	2.77	2.74	2.68	1.79	1.62	1.12	0.81	0.57
Earnings	3.75	2.87	2.35	2.35	2.39	0.77	1.30	0.87	0.60	0.41
S&P Core Earnings	4.08	2.87	2.35	2.42	2.30	0.72	1.22	0.79	0.52	NA
Dividends	Nil	Nil	Nil	Nil	Nil	Nil	Nil	Nil	Nil	Nil
Payout Ratio	Nil	Nil	Nil	Nil	Nil	Nil	Nil	Nil	Nil	Nil
Prices:High	90.00	81.68	80.75	63.26	84.20	98.01	73.09	46.15	33.31	22.64
Prices:Low	52.79	37.92	39.02	33.33	57.40	62.55	40.72	28.13	19.33	8.17
P/E Ratio:High	24	28	34	25	35	NM	56	53	56	55
P/E Ratio:Low	14	13	17	13	24	NM	31	32	32	20

Income Statement Analysis (Million $)										
Revenue	3,974	3,141	2,724	2,478	2,251	1,798	1,340	1,009	769	610
Operating Income	NA	829	697	738	767	481	428	293	194	141
Depreciation	88.0	79.7	71.1	67.3	54.5	43.2	40.3	35.2	32.7	27.4
Interest Expense	NA	Nil	Nil	Nil	Nil	Nil	Nil	Nil	Nil	Nil
Pretax Income	1,040	783	657	668	730	456	402	266	175	120
Effective Tax Rate	42.9%	39.2%	37.8%	37.9%	39.1%	39.1%	38.5%	39.4%	38.4%	40.8%
Net Income	598	477	409	415	445	278	247	161	108	71.2
S&P Core Earnings	651	477	409	428	427	131	218	140	90.1	NA

Balance Sheet & Other Financial Data (Million $)										
Cash	968	486	370	355	595	677	800	610	375	154
Current Assets	NA	1,170	925	803	835	855	950	730	487	247
Total Assets	3,263	1,860	1,450	1,283	1,303	1,452	1,378	980	680	405
Current Liabilities	NA	866	744	596	518	465	335	264	182	131
Long Term Debt	128	Nil	Nil	Nil	Nil	Nil	Nil	15.5	14.8	9.97
Common Equity	1,158	834	634	604	707	957	1,027	699	482	261
Total Capital	1,352	849	634	604	707	957	1,027	715	497	272
Capital Expenditures	127	105	61.2	44.6	104	80.3	55.8	36.7	44.4	34.8
Cash Flow	NA	556	480	482	499	321	287	196	141	98.6
Current Ratio	1.1	1.4	1.2	1.3	1.6	1.8	2.8	2.8	2.7	1.9
% Long Term Debt of Capitalization	9.4	Nil	Nil	Nil	Nil	Nil	Nil	2.2	3.0	3.7
% Net Income of Revenue	15.1	15.2	15.0	16.7	19.8	15.4	18.4	16.0	14.0	11.7
% Return on Assets	23.4	28.8	29.9	32.4	31.8	19.6	20.9	19.4	19.9	18.9
% Return on Equity	60.1	64.9	66.0	67.0	53.5	28.0	28.6	29.3	29.0	28.9

Data as orig reptd.; bef. results of disc opers/spec. items. Per share data adj. for stk. divs.; EPS diluted. E-Estimated. NA-Not Available. NM-Not Meaningful. NR-Not Ranked. UR-Under Review.

Office: 4025 S. Riverpoint Pkwy, Phoenix, AZ 85040.
Telephone: 480-966-5394.
Website: http://www.apollogrp.edu
Chrmn: J. Sperling

Pres & COO: J.L. D'Amico
Vice Chrmn & SVP: P. Sperling
Co-CEO: G.W. Cappelli
Co-CEO: C.B. Edelstein

Investor Contact: J. Pasinski (800-990-2765)
Board Members: T. C. Bishop, G. W. Cappelli, D. J. Deconcini, C. B. Edelstein, S. J. Giusto, R. A. Herberger, Jr., A. Kirschner, K. S. Redman, J. R. Reis, M. F. Rivelo, J. Sperling, P. Sperling, G. Zimmer

Founded: 1981
Domicile: Arizona
Employees: 52,385

The McGraw-Hill Companies

Apple Inc

STANDARD &POOR'S

S&P Recommendation BUY ★★★★☆	Price $200.59 (as of Nov 27, 2009)	12-Mo. Target Price $220.00	Investment Style Large-Cap Growth

GICS Sector Information Technology
Sub-Industry Computer Hardware

Summary This company is a prominent provider of hardware and software, including the Macintosh (Mac) computer, the iPod digital media player, and the iPhone.

Key Stock Statistics (Source S&P, Vickers, company reports)

52-Wk Range	$208.71– 78.20	S&P Oper. EPS 2010E	7.14	Market Capitalization(B)	$180.667	Beta	1.62
Trailing 12-Month EPS	$6.29	S&P Oper. EPS 2011E	NA	Yield (%)	Nil	S&P 3-Yr. Proj. EPS CAGR(%)	21
Trailing 12-Month P/E	31.9	P/E on S&P Oper. EPS 2010E	28.1	Dividend Rate/Share	Nil	S&P Credit Rating	NR
$10K Invested 5 Yrs Ago	$62,150	Common Shares Outstg. (M)	900.7	Institutional Ownership (%)	71		

Price Performance

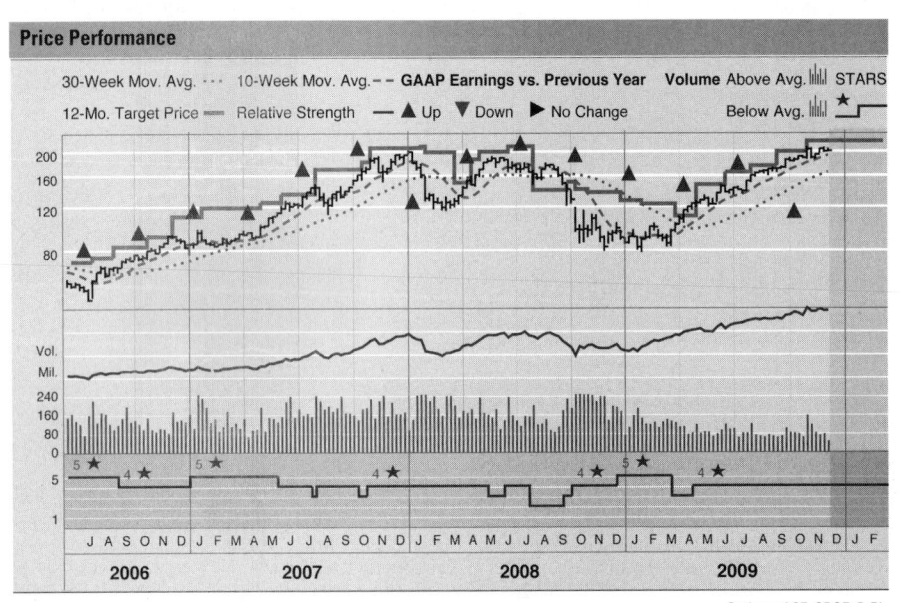

30-Week Mov. Avg. · · · 10-Week Mov. Avg. – – GAAP Earnings vs. Previous Year   Volume Above Avg. STARS
12-Mo. Target Price — Relative Strength   ▲ Up ▼ Down ▶ No Change   Below Avg. ★

Options: ASE, CBOE, P, Ph

Analysis prepared by **Clyde Montevirgen** on October 21, 2009, when the stock traded at **$ 198.76.**

Highlights

▶ We project sales growth of 13% for FY 10, a tick above FY 09 results. We believe the combination of AAPL's opportunistic management, brand recognition, and innovative, integrative and quality products will result in share gains in the computer, handset and MP3 player and related markets. We see iPhone, laptop, and iTunes sales largely offsetting slower desktop and iPod shipments. We also think the release of a tablet/ mobile Internet device would provide incremental sales opportunities.

▶ We expect the gross margin to remain around 36% as the positive impact from increasing iPhone sales, higher volumes, and product refreshes balance larger expenses for new product launches and transitions, and lower average selling prices for older products. We expect R&D expenses as a percentage of sales to rise modestly as AAPL invests in new platforms and product introductions. However, we expect SG&A expenses to moderate as volumes increase. All told, we believe the operating margin will remain in the low-20% range over the next couple of years.

▶ Our EPS projections assume an effective tax rate of 30%, and an essentially flat share count.

Investment Rationale/Risk

▶ Our buy opinion reflects our favorable view of AAPL's management, products and growth potential. Although we are concerned about soft demand for various consumer electronics products, and are wary about continuing pricing pressure, we think iPhone and iTunes sales growth, iPod and MacBook product refreshes, and new product launches will contribute to continuing earnings growth, a feat that we believe many technology companies cannot accomplish in the current economic environment. We view AAPL's balance sheet and cash generation as healthy, and valuations as attractive.

▶ Risks to our recommendation and target price include weaker end-market demand, pricing pressure, competitive threats to AAPL's digital media offerings and the iPhone, and the potential absence of visionary CEO Steve Jobs.

▶ Our 12-month target price of $220 is based on our discounted cash flow model, which assumes a terminal growth rate of 4% and a weighted average cost of capital of approximately 12%.

Qualitative Risk Assessment

LOW	MEDIUM	HIGH

Our risk assessment reflects our view of a seemingly ever-evolving market for consumer-oriented technology products, potential challenges associated with the company's growing size and offerings, and the critical importance to the company of founder and CEO Steve Jobs.

Quantitative Evaluations

S&P Quality Ranking   B

D	C	B-	B	B+	A-	A	A+

Relative Strength Rank   STRONG

80

LOWEST = 1   HIGHEST = 99

Revenue/Earnings Data

Revenue (Million $)

	1Q	2Q	3Q	4Q	Year
2009	10,167	8,163	8,337	9,870	36,537
2008	9,608	7,512	7,464	7,895	32,479
2007	7,115	5,264	5,410	6,217	24,006
2006	5,749	4,359	4,370	4,837	19,315
2005	3,490	3,243	3,520	3,678	13,931
2004	2,006	1,909	2,014	2,350	8,279

Earnings Per Share ($)

2009	1.78	1.33	1.35	1.82	6.29
2008	1.76	1.16	1.19	1.26	5.36
2007	1.14	0.87	0.92	1.01	3.93
2006	0.65	0.47	0.54	0.62	2.27
2005	0.35	0.34	0.37	0.50	1.56
2004	0.09	0.06	0.08	0.13	0.36

Fiscal year ended Sep. 30. Next earnings report expected: Late January. EPS Estimates based on S&P Operating Earnings; historical GAAP earnings are as reported.

Dividend Data

No cash dividends have been paid since 1996.

Please read the Required Disclosures and Analyst Certification on the last page of this report.

The McGraw-Hill Companies

Apple Inc

Business Summary October 21, 2009

CORPORATE OVERVIEW. Apple Inc. (AAPL) may have a relatively small share of the worldwide market for computers (about 3.3% in the third quarter of calendar 2008, according to market research firm IDC), but in the digital media player market, it has dominated with the success of the iPod. We believe the iPod has contributed to greater demand for AAPL computers. In fact, AAPL's share of the U.S. computer market climbed from about 3% a few years ago to 8% in the third quarter of calendar 2008. We anticipate further growth in brand awareness from wider adoption of the iPhone smart phone product, which experienced fast-paced sales in its first five quarters on the market: 13 million iPhone units were sold from its introduction in late June 2007 through September 2008. Thus, we view AAPL as offering a group of related consumer electronics products, with the success of one line having the potential to reinforce the success of others.

Personal computers, representing 44% of total sales, was the largest product category in FY 08 (Sep.). Portable PCs represented 27% of net sales (26% of FY 07 sales), desktop PCs 17% (17%), iPod 28% (35%), music 10% (10%), iPhone

6% (1%), peripherals and other hardware 5% (5%), and software, service and other 7% (6%).

The company has been ahead of an industry trend toward selling more laptop PC units than desktop models, with the crossover for AAPL occurring in FY 06, about a year earlier than for rival Dell.

The company sourced about 57% of revenues from inside the U.S. in FY 08. Viewed according to reporting segment, AAPL sourced 45% of net sales in FY 08 from the Americas (48% in FY 07), 23% (23%) from Europe, 5% (5%) from Japan, 19% (17%) from Retail, and 8% (7%) from other segments. The company distributes through various wholesalers and retailers, and no single customer accounted for more than 10% of sales in FY 08 or FY 07.

Company Financials Fiscal Year Ended Sep. 30

Per Share Data ($)	2009	2008	2007	2006	2005	2004	2003	2002	2001	2000
Tangible Book Value	30.31	23.04	16.27	11.47	8.83	6.36	5.61	5.54	5.59	6.00
Cash Flow	NA	5.88	4.29	2.52	1.77	0.55	0.50	0.25	0.09	1.21
Earnings	6.29	5.36	3.93	2.27	1.56	0.36	0.10	0.09	-0.06	1.09
S&P Core Earnings	6.29	5.36	3.93	2.27	1.47	0.22	-0.17	-0.19	-0.72	NA
Dividends	Nil	Nil	Nil	Nil	Nil	Nil	Nil	Nil	Nil	Nil
Payout Ratio	Nil	Nil	Nil	Nil	Nil	Nil	Nil	Nil	Nil	Nil
Prices:High	208.71	200.26	202.96	93.16	75.46	34.79	12.51	13.09	13.56	37.59
Prices:Low	78.20	79.14	81.90	50.16	31.30	10.59	6.36	6.68	7.22	6.81
P/E Ratio:High	33	37	52	41	48	98	NM	NM	NM	34
P/E Ratio:Low	12	15	21	22	20	30	NM	NM	NM	6

Income Statement Analysis (Million $)										
Revenue	36,537	32,479	24,006	19,315	13,931	8,279	6,207	5,742	5,363	7,983
Operating Income	NA	6,748	4,726	2,645	1,829	499	138	164	-231	704
Depreciation	703	473	317	225	179	150	113	118	102	84.0
Interest Expense	NA	Nil	Nil	Nil	Nil	3.00	8.00	11.0	16.0	21.0
Pretax Income	7,984	6,895	5,008	2,818	1,815	383	92.0	87.0	-52.0	1,092
Effective Tax Rate	28.6%	29.9%	30.2%	29.4%	26.4%	27.9%	26.1%	25.3%	NM	28.0%
Net Income	5,704	4,834	3,496	1,989	1,335	276	68.0	65.0	-37.0	786
S&P Core Earnings	5,704	4,834	3,496	1,989	1,259	164	-119	-137	-465	NA

Balance Sheet & Other Financial Data (Million $)										
Cash	23,464	24,490	9,352	6,392	3,491	2,969	3,396	2,252	2,310	1,191
Current Assets	NA	34,690	21,956	14,509	10,300	7,055	5,887	5,388	5,143	5,427
Total Assets	53,851	39,572	25,347	17,205	11,551	8,050	6,815	6,298	6,021	6,803
Current Liabilities	NA	14,092	9,299	6,471	3,484	2,680	2,357	1,658	1,518	1,933
Long Term Debt	NA	Nil	Nil	Nil	Nil	Nil	Nil	316	317	300
Common Equity	27,832	21,030	14,532	9,984	7,466	5,076	4,223	4,095	3,920	4,031
Total Capital	27,832	21,705	15,151	10,365	7,466	5,076	4,223	4,640	4,503	4,870
Capital Expenditures	1,144	1,091	735	657	260	176	164	174	735	107
Cash Flow	NA	5,307	3,813	2,214	1,514	426	181	183	65.0	870
Current Ratio	1.9	2.5	2.4	2.2	3.0	2.6	2.5	3.2	3.4	2.8
% Long Term Debt of Capitalization	Nil	Nil	Nil	Nil	Nil	Nil	Nil	6.8	7.0	6.2
% Net Income of Revenue	15.6	14.9	14.6	10.3	9.6	3.3	1.1	1.1	NM	9.8
% Return on Assets	12.2	14.9	16.4	13.9	13.6	3.7	1.0	1.1	NM	13.1
% Return on Equity	23.4	27.2	28.5	22.8	21.3	5.9	1.6	1.6	NM	22.5

Data as orig reptd.; bef. results of disc opers/spec. items. Per share data adj. for stk. divs.; EPS diluted. E-Estimated. NA-Not Available. NM-Not Meaningful. NR-Not Ranked. UR-Under Review.

Office: 1 Infinite Loop, Cupertino, CA 95014.
Telephone: 408-996-1010.
Email: investor_relations@apple.com
Website: http://www.apple.com

CEO: S.P. Jobs
COO: T.D. Cook
Investor Contact: P. Oppenheimer (408-974-3123)
SVP & CFO: P. Oppenheimer

SVP & General Counsel: B. Sewell
Board Members: W. V. Campbell, M. S. Drexler, A. A. Gore, Jr., S. P. Jobs, A. Jung, A. D. Levinson, J. B. York

Founded: 1977
Domicile: California
Employees: 36,800

Stock Report | November 28, 2009 | NNM Symbol: **AMAT** | **AMAT** is in the S&P 500

Applied Materials Inc

| S&P Recommendation **STRONG BUY** ★★★★★ | Price $12.29 (as of Nov 27, 2009) | 12-Mo. Target Price $17.00 | Investment Style Large-Cap Blend |

GICS Sector Information Technology
Sub-Industry Semiconductor Equipment

Summary This company is the world's largest manufacturer of wafer fabrication equipment for the semiconductor industry.

Key Stock Statistics (Source S&P, Vickers, company reports)

52-Wk Range	$14.19–8.19	S&P Oper. EPS 2010**E**	0.53	Market Capitalization(B)	$16.391	Beta	1.05
Trailing 12-Month EPS	$-0.23	S&P Oper. EPS 2011**E**	0.95	Yield (%)	1.95	S&P 3-Yr. Proj. EPS CAGR(%)	NM
Trailing 12-Month P/E	NM	P/E on S&P Oper. EPS 2010**E**	23.2	Dividend Rate/Share	$0.24	S&P Credit Rating	A-
$10K Invested 5 Yrs Ago	$7,703	Common Shares Outstg. (M)	1,333.7	Institutional Ownership (%)	84		

Price Performance

30-Week Mov. Avg. · · · 10-Week Mov. Avg. - - GAAP Earnings vs. Previous Year Volume Above Avg. STARS
12-Mo. Target Price — Relative Strength ▲ Up ▼ Down ▶ No Change Below Avg. ★

Options: ASE, CBOE, P, Ph

Analysis prepared by **Angelo Zino** on November 18, 2009, when the stock traded at **$ 12.91**.

Highlights

► Following a revenue decline of 38% in FY 09 (Oct.), we project sales to increase 35% in FY 10 and 44% in FY 11, as we see semiconductor customers investing in technology purchases as well as some capacity expansion. We expect semiconductor equipment sales to improve, as customer inventory levels appear lean and utilization rates rise. We think flat panel display spending is being driven by lower-priced televisions and stimulus spending in China. We view solar as a large growth driver and see customer capacity expansion next year, but remain concerned about the ability of customers to obtain financing.

► We project gross margins of 40% in FY 10 and 44% in FY 11, compared to 29% in FY 08. We expect AMAT to reduce its global work force by 10% to 12%, which we estimate will result in an additional $460 million in annualized savings. We think AMAT's solar-related business will be profitable on an operating basis in FY 10. We look for R&D expenses to comprise about 15% of sales in FY 10 and 14% in FY 11.

► We forecast operating EPS of $0.53 in FY 10, which excludes $0.06 of projected non-recurring charges, and $0.95 in FY 11.

Investment Rationale/Risk

► We have a favorable view of AMAT's valuation as well as its diversified end markets relative to peers, as we think both semiconductor and flat panel equipment spending are poised to experience strong year-over-year growth in 2010. We think AMAT's silicon systems group will benefit from higher memory orders and the transition to DDR3 technology. We project greater solar-related orders, as China-based manufacturers expand capacity, and we see the segment becoming profitable in FY 10. We believe AMAT's goal of 12% panel conversion efficiency at $0.70 cost/watt for its SunFab thin film modules by 2012 is attainable.

► Risks to our recommendation and target price include a greater-than-expected slowdown in the global economy, which could weaken demand for chips and increase pricing pressure.

► We derive our 12-month target price of $17 by applying a peer-premium price/sales (P/S) multiple of 3.3X to our calendar year 2010 sales per share forecast of $5.13, warranted, we believe, by AMAT's financial position and leading market share position. We believe large front-end semiconductor equipment peers recently traded at a P/S multiple of 2.8X our 2010 estimates.

Qualitative Risk Assessment

| LOW | MEDIUM | HIGH |

Our risk assessment reflects the historical cyclicality of the semiconductor equipment industry, a lack of visibility in the intermediate term, the dynamic nature of the change in semiconductor technology, and intense competition. This is offset by AMAT's market leadership, size, and what we consider its solid balance sheet.

Quantitative Evaluations

S&P Quality Ranking B-

| D | C | B- | B | B+ | A- | A | A+ |

Relative Strength Rank MODERATE

32

LOWEST = 1   HIGHEST = 99

Revenue/Earnings Data

Revenue (Million $)

	1Q	2Q	3Q	4Q	Year
2009	1,333	1,020	1,134	1,526	5,014
2008	2,087	2,150	1,848	2,044	8,129
2007	2,277	2,530	2,561	2,367	9,735
2006	1,858	2,248	2,543	2,518	9,167
2005	1,781	1,861	1,632	1,718	6,992
2004	1,555	2,018	2,236	2,203	8,013

Earnings Per Share ($)

2009	-0.10	-0.19	-0.04	0.10	-0.23
2008	0.19	0.22	0.12	0.17	0.70
2007	0.29	0.29	0.12	0.30	1.20
2006	0.09	0.26	0.33	0.30	0.97
2005	0.17	0.18	0.23	0.15	0.73
2004	0.05	0.22	0.26	0.27	0.78

Fiscal year ended Oct. 31. Next earnings report expected: Mid February. EPS Estimates based on S&P Operating Earnings; historical GAAP earnings are as reported.

Dividend Data (Dates: mm/dd Payment Date: mm/dd/yy)

Amount ($)	Date Decl.	Ex-Div. Date	Stk. of Record	Payment Date
0.060	12/09	02/10	02/12	03/05/09
0.060	03/10	05/12	05/14	06/04/09
0.060	06/09	08/11	08/13	09/03/09
0.060	09/16	11/09	11/12	12/03/09

Dividends have been paid since 2005. Source: Company reports.

Please read the Required Disclosures and Analyst Certification on the last page of this report.

Redistribution or reproduction is prohibited without written permission. Copyright ©2009 The McGraw-Hill Companies, Inc.

The McGraw·Hill Companies

Applied Materials Inc

STANDARD
&POOR'S

Business Summary November 18, 2009

CORPORATE OVERVIEW. At the end of FY 08 (Oct.), Applied Materials (AMAT) was the worldwide leader in the manufacturing of semiconductor capital equipment. AMAT divides its business into four segments. The Silicon segment, which accounted for 49% of FY 08 sales (67% in FY 07), is focused on developing and selling equipment for use in the front end of the semiconductor fabrication process. The Applied Global Services segment, which accounted for 29% (22%) of FY 08 sales, provides solutions to optimize and increase productivity at customers fabs (semiconductor fabrication facilities). The Display segment, which accounted for 12% (9%) of FY 08 sales, develops equipment for the fabrication of flat panel displays. The Energy and Environmental Solutions segment accounted for 10% (2%) of sales in FY 08, and involves products targeting the solar PV cell market and energy efficient glass. We expect significant growth in AMAT's solar business over the next several years.

AMAT's equipment in the silicon segment addresses most of the primary steps in chip fabrication. AMAT's deposition products are used to plant thin films of conductive or insulating material to form an integrated circuit (IC).

AMAT deposition equipment uses various technologies, including ALD (atomic layer deposition), CVD (chemical vapor deposition), PVD (physical vapor deposition), and ECP (Electrochemical plating). AMAT's etch products selectively remove thin films of three different types of materials: metal, silicon, and dielectric thin films. Chemical-mechanical polishing products are used to smooth the surface of a wafer following deposition in order to facilitate subsequent processing steps. Metrology and inspection tools are used to measure critical parameters and find and classify defects.

Sales by geographic region in FY 08 were as follows: Taiwan 23% (28% in FY 07), Korea 19% (19%), North America 16% (16%), Asia-Pacific 16% (12%), Japan 15% (15%), and Europe 12% (10%).

Company Financials Fiscal Year Ended Oct. 31

Per Share Data ($)	2009	2008	2007	2006	2005	2004	2003	2002	2001	2000
Tangible Book Value	NA	4.50	4.65	5.80	5.30	5.33	4.62	4.67	4.51	4.20
Cash Flow	NA	0.93	1.39	1.14	0.91	0.99	0.14	0.39	0.69	1.41
Earnings	-0.23	0.70	1.20	0.97	0.73	0.78	-0.09	0.16	0.46	1.20
S&P Core Earnings	NA	0.69	1.20	0.97	0.54	0.59	-0.33	-0.04	0.33	NA
Dividends	0.24	0.24	0.22	0.16	0.06	Nil	Nil	Nil	Nil	Nil
Payout Ratio	NM	34%	18%	16%	8%	Nil	Nil	Nil	Nil	Nil
Prices:High	14.19	21.75	23.00	21.06	19.47	24.75	25.94	27.95	29.55	57.50
Prices:Low	8.19	7.17	17.35	14.39	14.33	15.36	11.25	10.26	13.30	17.06
P/E Ratio:High	NM	31	19	22	27	32	NM	NM	65	48
P/E Ratio:Low	NM	10	14	15	20	20	NM	NM	29	14

Income Statement Analysis (Million $)										
Revenue	5,014	8,129	9,735	9,167	6,992	8,013	4,477	5,062	7,343	9,564
Operating Income	NA	1,695	2,665	2,517	1,748	2,313	440	683	1,538	3,149
Depreciation	291	320	268	270	300	356	382	388	387	362
Interest Expense	NA	20.5	38.6	36.1	37.8	52.9	46.9	49.4	47.6	51.4
Pretax Income	-486	1,409	2,440	2,167	1,582	1,829	-212	341	1,104	2,948
Effective Tax Rate	37.2%	31.8%	29.9%	30.0%	23.5%	26.1%	NM	21.0%	29.8%	30.0%
Net Income	-305	961	1,710	1,517	1,210	1,351	-149	269	775	2,064
S&P Core Earnings	NA	936	1,710	1,511	905	1,017	-562	-65.2	558	NA

Balance Sheet & Other Financial Data (Million $)										
Cash	2,215	2,101	1,203	861	990	2,282	1,365	1,285	1,356	1,648
Current Assets	NA	6,664	6,606	6,081	9,449	10,282	8,371	8,073	7,782	8,839
Total Assets	9,574	10,906	10,654	9,481	11,269	12,093	10,312	10,225	9,829	10,546
Current Liabilities	NA	2,946	2,373	2,436	1,765	2,288	1,641	1,501	1,533	2,760
Long Term Debt	201	202	202	205	407	410	456	574	565	573
Common Equity	7,095	7,449	7,821	6,651	8,929	9,262	8,068	8,020	7,607	7,104
Total Capital	7,297	7,808	8,023	6,856	9,336	9,672	8,524	8,594	8,172	7,677
Capital Expenditures	248	288	265	179	200	191	265	417	711	383
Cash Flow	NA	1,281	1,978	1,787	1,510	1,707	233	657	1,162	2,426
Current Ratio	2.9	2.3	2.8	2.5	5.4	4.5	5.1	5.4	5.1	3.2
% Long Term Debt of Capitalization	2.8	2.6	2.5	3.0	4.4	4.2	5.4	6.7	6.9	7.5
% Net Income of Revenue	NM	11.8	17.5	16.5	17.3	16.9	NM	5.3	10.5	21.6
% Return on Assets	NM	8.9	16.9	14.6	10.4	12.1	NM	2.7	7.6	23.5
% Return on Equity	NM	12.6	23.6	19.5	13.3	15.6	NM	3.4	10.5	35.3

Data as orig reptd.; bef. results of disc opers/spec. items. Per share data adj. for stk. divs.; EPS diluted. E-Estimated. NA-Not Available. NM-Not Meaningful. NR-Not Ranked. UR-Under Review.

Office: 3050 Bowers Avenue, Santa Clara, CA, United States 95054-3298.
Telephone: 408-727-5555.
Email: investor_relations@appliedmaterials.com
Website: http://www.appliedmaterials.com

Chrmn, Pres & CEO: M.R. Splinter
SVP & CFO: G.S. Davis
SVP & CTO: M. Pinto
SVP, Secy & General Counsel: J.J. Sweeney

Treas: R.M. Friess
Board Members: S. R. Forrest, P. V. Gerdine, T. J. Iannotti, A. A. Karsner, G. H. Parker, D. D. Powell, W. P. Roelandts, J. E. Rogers, M. R. Splinter, R. H. Swan, A. J. de Geus

Founded: 1967
Domicile: Delaware
Employees: 14,824

Archer-Daniels-Midland Co

STANDARD
&POOR'S

S&P Recommendation **HOLD** ★★★☆☆	Price $30.65 (as of Nov 27, 2009)	12-Mo. Target Price $34.00	Investment Style Large-Cap Blend

GICS Sector Consumer Staples
Sub-Industry Agricultural Products

Summary This company is one of the world's leading agribusiness companies, with major market positions in agricultural processing and merchandising.

Key Stock Statistics (Source S&P, Vickers, company reports)

52-Wk Range	$33.00– 23.13	S&P Oper. EPS 2010**E**	2.70	Market Capitalization(B)	$19.688	Beta	0.32
Trailing 12-Month EPS	$1.80	S&P Oper. EPS 2011**E**	2.90	Yield (%)	1.83	S&P 3-Yr. Proj. EPS CAGR(%)	4
Trailing 12-Month P/E	17.0	P/E on S&P Oper. EPS 2010**E**	11.4	Dividend Rate/Share	$0.56	S&P Credit Rating	A
$10K Invested 5 Yrs Ago	$15,576	Common Shares Outstg. (M)	642.4	Institutional Ownership (%)	70		

Price Performance

30-Week Mov. Avg. · · · 10-Week Mov. Avg. – – **GAAP Earnings vs. Previous Year** Volume Above Avg. STARS
12-Mo. Target Price — Relative Strength — ▲ Up ▼ Down ► No Change Below Avg.

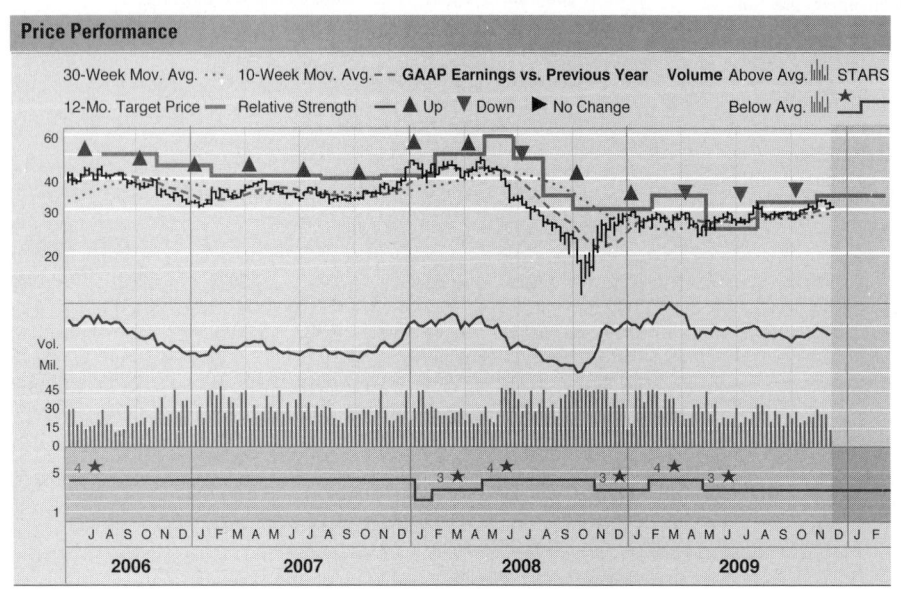

Options: ASE, CBOE, P, Ph

Analysis prepared by **Tom Graves, CFA** on November 09, 2009, when the stock traded at **$ 32.46**.

Highlights

► We look for net sales to decline moderately in FY 10 (Jun.) from the $69.2 billion reported for FY 09, partly due to lower selling prices. However, we expect global economies to improve in FY 10, contributing to some increased demand for products or services offered by ADM. Over time, we expect ADM's market position to benefit from investment in new plants and cargo capacity. In FY 10's first quarter, ADM's total purchases of property, plant and equipment amounted to almost $500 million.

► Near-term, we look for ADM to benefit from a relatively large U.S. harvest of some major crops. Also, in FY 10's first quarter, ADM's reported EPS of $0.77 included a $0.07 benefit from a change in LIFO inventory valuations. In the year-ago quarter, for which ADM had reported EPS of $1.62, there was a $0.44 LIFO-related benefit. Excluding any future LIFO adjustments, we estimate FY 10 EPS at $2.70, followed by $2.90 in FY 11.

► In November 2009, ADM said that it has started production at its first sugarcane ethanol plant in Brazil, and has begun production at a new Nebraska ethanol plant.

Investment Rationale/Risk

► As an internationally diversified agribusiness company, we think ADM is well positioned to outperform its peers based on scale and integration in the long term. While we think the global economic downturn has slowed demand for ADM's products, we believe the company is also well positioned to benefit from long-term global population growth and economic expansion.

► Risks to our recommendation and target price include adverse changes in plantings, government farm programs and policies, and in economic, operational and industry conditions, such as fluctuations in commodity prices.

► Our 12-month target price of $34 is based on our view that the stock should trade at about 12.7X our estimate of year-ahead EPS, which would be a discount to an average forward P/E that we see for the stock in much of the past decade. We think the discount is warranted by a relatively difficult economic environment. Also, the stock recently had an indicated dividend yield of 1.7%.

Qualitative Risk Assessment

LOW	**MEDIUM**	HIGH

Our risk assessment reflects the company's exposure to volatile commodity industry conditions, and moderately aggressive financial policies and leverage levels given the inherent cyclicality of the company's agricultural operations.

Quantitative Evaluations

S&P Quality Ranking   A

D	C	B-	B	B+	A-	**A**	A+

Relative Strength Rank   MODERATE

55

LOWEST = 1   HIGHEST = 99

Revenue/Earnings Data

Revenue (Million $)

	1Q	2Q	3Q	4Q	Year
2010	14,921	--	--	--	--
2009	21,160	16,673	14,842	16,532	69,207
2008	12,828	16,496	18,708	21,784	69,816
2007	9,447	10,976	11,381	12,214	44,018
2006	8,627	9,299	9,123	9,547	36,596
2005	8,972	9,064	8,484	9,424	35,944

Earnings Per Share ($)

2010	0.77	E0.70	E0.70	E0.53	E2.70
2009	1.63	0.91	0.01	0.10	2.65
2008	0.68	0.73	0.80	0.58	2.79
2007	0.61	0.67	0.56	1.47	3.30
2006	0.29	0.56	0.53	0.62	2.00
2005	0.41	0.48	0.41	0.30	1.59

Fiscal year ended Jun. 30. Next earnings report expected: Early February. EPS Estimates based on S&P Operating Earnings; historical GAAP earnings are as reported.

Dividend Data (Dates: mm/dd Payment Date: mm/dd/yy)

Amount ($)	Date Decl.	Ex-Div. Date	Stk. of Record	Payment Date
0.140	02/05	02/17	02/19	03/12/09
0.140	05/07	05/19	05/21	06/11/09
0.140	08/06	08/18	08/20	09/10/09
0.140	11/05	11/17	11/19	12/10/09

Dividends have been paid since 1927. Source: Company reports.

Please read the Required Disclosures and Analyst Certification on the last page of this report.

The McGraw·Hill Companies

Archer-Daniels-Midland Co

STANDARD
&POOR'S

Business Summary November 09, 2009

CORPORATE OVERVIEW. As successor to the Daniels Linseed Co., founded in 1902, Archer Daniels Midland (ADM) is one of the world's largest agricultural processors, with a global network of processing plants. The company operates in four business segments: Oilseeds Processing (35% of FY 09 (Jun.) sales to external customers; 52% of FY 09 segment operating profit), Corn Processing (11%; 8%), Agricultural Services (46%; 41%), and Other (8%; 0%).

The Oilseeds Processing segment includes activities related to the processing of oilseeds such as soybeans, cottonseed, sunflower seeds, canola, rapeseed, peanuts, and flaxseed into vegetable oils and protein meals, principally for the food and feed industries. Also, partially refined oil is sold for use in paints and other industrial products, and refined oil can be further processed for use in the production of biodiesel. Cottonseed flour is sold primarily to the pharmaceutical industry, and cotton cellulose pulp is sold to the chemical, paper and filter markets. Golden Peanut Co. LLC, a joint venture between ADM (50%) and Alimenta (U.S.A.) Inc., is a major supplier of peanuts to domestic and international markets. Also, in 2009, ADM had a 16% ownership interest in Wilmar International Ltd., a leading agribusiness group in Asia.

The Corn Processing segment includes activities related to the production of sweeteners, starches, glucose, dextrose, and syrups for the food and beverage industry as well as activities related to the production, by fermentation, of alcohol, amino acids, and other specialty food and feed ingredients. Ethyl al-

cohol may be produced for use as ethanol. ADM owns a 50% interest in Almidones Mexicanos S.A., which operates a wet corn milling plant in Mexico, and a 50% interest in Eaststarch C.V. (Netherlands), which owns interests in companies that operate wet corn milling plants in Bulgaria, Hungary, Romania, Slovakia, and Turkey.

The Agricultural Services segment utilizes the company's extensive grain elevator and transportation network to buy, store, clean, and transport agricultural commodities, such as oilseeds, corn, wheat, milo, oats, rice and barley, and resells these commodities primarily as feed ingredients and as raw materials for the agricultural processing industry. Agricultural Services includes activities of A.C. Toepfer International (ADM has an 80% interest), a global merchandiser of agricultural commodities and processed products. ADM also has a 45% interest in Kalama Export Co., a grain export elevator in Washington.

Other includes remaining operations, including milling, processing, and financial activities.

Company Financials Fiscal Year Ended Jun. 30

Per Share Data ($)	2009	2008	2007	2006	2005	2004	2003	2002	2001	2000
Tangible Book Value	20.20	20.16	17.01	14.47	12.47	11.31	10.43	10.39	9.56	9.21
Cash Flow	3.80	3.91	4.36	3.00	2.60	1.82	1.69	1.64	1.44	1.35
Earnings	2.65	2.79	3.30	2.00	1.59	0.76	0.70	0.78	0.58	0.46
S&P Core Earnings	2.50	2.64	2.31	2.02	1.53	1.14	0.61	0.55	0.58	NA
Dividends	0.54	0.49	0.43	0.37	0.32	0.27	0.24	0.20	0.19	0.14
Payout Ratio	20%	18%	13%	19%	20%	36%	34%	25%	32%	30%
Prices:High	33.00	48.95	47.33	46.71	25.55	22.55	15.24	14.85	15.80	14.46
Prices:Low	23.13	13.53	30.20	24.05	17.50	14.90	10.50	10.00	10.24	7.80
P/E Ratio:High	12	18	14	23	16	30	22	19	27	32
P/E Ratio:Low	9	5	9	12	11	20	15	13	18	17

Income Statement Analysis (Million $)										
Revenue	69,207	69,816	44,018	36,596	35,944	36,151	30,708	23,454	20,051	12,877
Operating Income	3,420	3,188	2,743	2,450	2,015	1,432	1,423	1,424	1,272	1,094
Depreciation	743	721	701	657	665	686	644	567	572	604
Interest Expense	430	529	Nil	365	Nil	Nil	Nil	356	397	377
Pretax Income	2,534	2,624	3,154	1,855	1,516	718	631	719	522	353
Effective Tax Rate	32.6%	31.3%	31.5%	29.3%	31.1%	31.1%	28.5%	28.9%	26.6%	14.7%
Net Income	1,707	1,802	2,162	1,312	1,044	495	451	511	383	301
S&P Core Earnings	1,615	1,706	1,508	1,322	1,001	739	397	363	382	NA

Balance Sheet & Other Financial Data (Million $)										
Cash	1,055	1,265	2,087	2,334	1,430	1,412	765	844	676	477
Current Assets	19,408	25,455	15,122	11,826	9,711	10,339	8,422	7,363	6,150	6,162
Total Assets	23,104	25,790	25,118	21,269	18,598	19,369	17,183	15,416	14,340	14,423
Current Liabilities	8,885	14,621	7,868	6,165	5,367	6,750	5,147	4,719	3,867	4,333
Long Term Debt	7,848	7,690	4,752	4,050	3,530	3,740	3,872	3,111	3,351	3,277
Common Equity	13,499	13,490	11,253	9,807	8,433	7,698	7,069	6,755	6,332	6,110
Total Capital	21,577	21,653	16,537	14,614	12,743	12,092	11,485	10,498	10,327	9,948
Capital Expenditures	1,898	1,779	1,198	762	624	509	420	350	273	429
Cash Flow	2,450	2,523	2,863	1,969	1,709	1,180	1,095	1,078	955	905
Current Ratio	30.7	1.7	1.9	1.9	1.8	1.5	1.6	1.6	1.6	1.4
% Long Term Debt of Capitalization	36.4	35.5	28.7	27.7	27.7	30.9	33.7	29.6	32.4	32.9
% Net Income of Revenue	2.5	2.6	4.9	3.6	2.9	1.4	1.5	2.2	1.9	2.3
% Return on Assets	5.7	7.1	9.3	6.6	5.5	2.7	2.8	3.4	2.7	2.1
% Return on Equity	12.7	14.6	20.5	14.4	12.9	6.7	6.5	7.8	6.2	4.9

Data as orig reptd.; bef. results of disc opers/spec. items. Per share data adj. for stk. divs.; EPS diluted. E-Estimated. NA-Not Available. NM-Not Meaningful. NR-Not Ranked. UR-Under Review.

Office: 4666 Faries Parkway, Decatur, IL 62525.
Telephone: 217-424-5200.
Website: http://www.admworld.com
Chrmn, Pres & CEO: P. Woertz

EVP & CFO: S.R. Mills
EVP, Secy & General Counsel: D.J. Smith
Treas: V. Luthar
Investor Contact: D. Grimestad (217-424-4586)

Board Members: G. W. Buckley, M. H. Carter, D. E. Felsinger, V. F. Haynes, P. J. Moore, B. R. Mulroney, A. M. Neto, T. F. O'Neill, K. R. Westbrook, P. Woertz

Founded: 1898
Domicile: Delaware
Employees: 28,200

The McGraw·Hill Companies

Assurant Inc.

S&P Recommendation BUY ★ ★ ★ ★ ☆	Price $30.26 (as of Nov 27, 2009)	12-Mo. Target Price $35.00	Investment Style Large-Cap Value

GICS Sector Financials
Sub-Industry Multi-line Insurance

Summary This company pursues a differentiated strategy of building leading positions in niche insurance markets.

Key Stock Statistics (Source S&P, Vickers, company reports)

52-Wk Range	$33.37– 16.34	S&P Oper. EPS 2009**E**	4.10	Market Capitalization(B)	$3.534	Beta	1.67
Trailing 12-Month EPS	$5.05	S&P Oper. EPS 2010**E**	4.65	Yield (%)	1.98	S&P 3-Yr. Proj. EPS CAGR(%)	-7
Trailing 12-Month P/E	6.0	P/E on S&P Oper. EPS 2009**E**	7.4	Dividend Rate/Share	$0.60	S&P Credit Rating	NA
$10K Invested 5 Yrs Ago	$10,943	Common Shares Outstg. (M)	116.8	Institutional Ownership (%)	92		

Price Performance

30-Week Mov. Avg. · · · 10-Week Mov. Avg. – – GAAP Earnings vs. Previous Year   Volume Above Avg. STARS
12-Mo. Target Price — Relative Strength ▲ Up ▼ Down ► No Change   Below Avg.

Options: ASE, CBOE, P, Ph

Analysis prepared by **Bret Howlett** on October 30, 2009, when the stock traded at **$ 30.89**.

Highlights

▶ In Solutions, we expect premiums in 2010 to increase 8% due to our expectations of a rebound in consumer spending. We forecast earnings to increase roughly 10% on an improvement in the combined ratio, the addition of new clients, and aggressive expense management. In Health, we believe losses will stabilize and think the segment will be profitable in the second half of the year. Health results have been hurt by a higher utilization rate, reflecting increased doctor visits as more customers fear losing health insurance. We see earnings in Benefits increasing slightly on an improved loss ratio as unemployment moderates.

▶ We expect Specialty Property revenues to be hurt by lower new loan volumes, reflecting consolidation in the lending space and a reduction in inventory of subprime loans, as well as a decrease in real estate owned business, partially offset by gains in creditor-placed homeowners insurance, higher average insured values, and acquisitions.

▶ We estimate operating EPS of $4.10 in 2009 and $4.65 in 2010. Our estimates exclude realized investment gains or losses.

Investment Rationale/Risk

▶ We forecast that operating earnings will increase roughly 10% in 2010 as AIZ's economically sensitive businesses benefit from a recovery in the global economy. In 2009, AIZ's operating fundamentals have deteriorated due to the weak economy and as a result, we believe the stock is attractively priced at current levels. Although AIZ is likely to face headwinds in some businesses over the near term, we believe the company is on track to achieve better returns in all of its businesses in 2010. We think AIZ's underwriting expertise in most areas is strong, and that it has a high level of expertise in the specialized lines it markets. In our view, AIZ's maintains a solid financial position, and we expect the company to redeploy $300-$400 million in excess capital toward a share repurchase program and/or increasing its dividend.

▶ Risks to our recommendation and target price include competitive pricing in the individual medical market, catastrophe risks, the possibility that demand for homeowners coverage will slow, and potential for investment losses.

▶ Our 12-month target price of $35 is 7.5X our 2009 operating EPS estimate, below AIZ's average historical multiple.

Qualitative Risk Assessment

LOW	MEDIUM	HIGH

Our risk assessment for Assurant reflects the difficult operating environment for insurers and the company's earnings sensitivity to the weakening global economy. However, AIZ has a solid track record of disciplined capital management, and we believe the company's balance sheet is more conservatively positioned versus peers due to less debt and more conservative investment holdings.

Quantitative Evaluations

S&P Quality Ranking NR

D	C	B-	B	B+	A-	A	A+

Relative Strength Rank MODERATE

48

LOWEST = 1   HIGHEST = 99

Revenue/Earnings Data

Revenue (Million $)

	1Q	2Q	3Q	4Q	Year
2009	2,088	2,274	2,157	--	--
2008	2,177	2,249	1,955	2,221	8,601
2007	2,057	2,065	2,148	2,183	8,454
2006	1,930	1,949	1,984	2,208	8,071
2005	1,862	1,874	1,879	1,882	7,498
2004	1,858	1,837	1,832	1,877	7,403

Earnings Per Share ($)

	1Q	2Q	3Q	4Q	Year
2009	0.68	1.63	1.22	E1.02	E4.10
2008	1.57	1.59	-0.95	1.55	3.77
2007	1.45	1.36	1.56	1.01	5.38
2006	1.22	1.16	1.18	2.01	5.56
2005	0.82	0.92	0.74	1.03	3.50
2004	0.73	0.67	0.53	0.61	2.53

Fiscal year ended Dec. 31. Next earnings report expected: Early February. EPS Estimates based on S&P Operating Earnings; historical GAAP earnings are as reported.

Dividend Data (Dates: mm/dd Payment Date: mm/dd/yy)

Amount ($)	Date Decl.	Ex-Div. Date	Stk. of Record	Payment Date
0.150	05/15	05/21	05/26	06/09/09
0.150	07/23	08/27	08/31	09/15/09
0.150	07/23	08/27	08/31	09/15/09
0.150	11/13	11/25	11/30	12/14/09

Dividends have been paid since 2004. Source: Company reports.

Please read the Required Disclosures and Analyst Certification on the last page of this report.

The McGraw-Hill Companies

Assurant Inc.

STANDARD &POOR'S

Business Summary October 30, 2009

CORPORATE OVERVIEW. Assurant Inc. provides specialized insurance products in North America and other selected markets. The company was indirectly wholly owned by Fortis N.V. until February 2004, when Fortis sold about 65% of its stake via an IPO. In January 2005, Fortis sold 27.2 million shares of AIZ in a secondary public offering at $30.60 per share. In conjunction with the offering, Fortis issued $774 million of 7.75% bonds that were mandatorily exchangeable for up to 23.0 million shares of AIZ, or the cash value thereof, by January 2008. Fortis distributed most of its remaining AIZ shares to the holders of these bonds in January 2008, leaving it with about a 3% interest in AIZ. In August 2008, AIZ purchased one million shares of its common shares from Fortis.

As of March 2009, AIZ believed it was a leader or was aligned with clients who were leaders in creditor-placed homeowners insurance (based on servicing volume), manufactured housing homeowners insurance (based on the number of homes built), debt protection administration (based on credit card balances outstanding), group dental plans sponsored by employers (based on

the number of subscribers and master contracts in force), and pre-funded funeral insurance (based on the face amount of new policies sold).

On April 1, 2006, the company separated its Assurant Solutions unit into two business segments: Assurant Solutions and Assurant Specialty Property. In addition, with the creation of the new Assurant Solutions and Assurant Specialty Property segments, the company realigned the PreNeed segment under the new Assurant Solutions segment. In total, AIZ operates through four decentralized business segments: Assurant Solutions (35% of net earned premiums and other consideration in 2008); Assurant Specialty Property (26%); Assurant Health (25%); and Assurant Employee Benefits (14%). AIZ also reports a fifth segment, Corporate and Other.

Company Financials Fiscal Year Ended Dec. 31

Per Share Data ($)	2008	2007	2006	2005	2004	2003	2002	2001	2000	1999
Tangible Book Value	19.06	NM	28.46	21.01	18.90	14.76	NA	NA	NA	NA
Operating Earnings	NA	NA	NA	NA	NA	NA	NA	NA	NA	NA
Earnings	3.77	5.38	5.56	3.50	2.53	1.70	31.29	11.81	10.93	NA
S&P Core Earnings	5.79	5.60	4.77	3.49	2.50	1.72	38.61	15.43	NA	NA
Dividends	0.54	0.46	0.38	0.31	0.21	NA	NA	NA	NA	NA
Relative Payout	14%	9%	7%	9%	8%	NA	NA	NA	NA	NA
Prices:High	71.31	69.77	56.78	44.68	31.29	NA	NA	NA	NA	NA
Prices:Low	12.52	45.27	42.72	29.70	22.00	NA	NA	NA	NA	NA
P/E Ratio:High	19	13	10	13	12	NA	NA	NA	NA	NA
P/E Ratio:Low	3	8	8	8	9	NA	NA	NA	NA	NA

Income Statement Analysis (Million $)

	2008	2007	2006	2005	2004	2003	2002	2001	2000	1999
Life Insurance in Force	85,013	94,087	99,645	111,186	166,452	169,787	192,984	203,660	NA	NA
Premium Income:Life A & H	3,828	4,061	4,203	4,595	4,789	4,565	4,385	4,215	NA	NA
Premium Income:Casualty/Property.	4,097	3,347	2,641	1,926	1,694	1,591	1,297	1,027	NA	NA
Net Investment Income	774	799	737	687	635	607	632	712	691	NA
Total Revenue	8,601	8,454	8,071	7,498	7,403	7,066	6,532	6,187	6,212	NA
Pretax Income	563	1,011	1,096	656	536	259	370	206	194	NA
Net Operating Income	NA	NA	NA	NA	NA	NA	NA	NA	NA	NA
Net Income	448	654	716	479	351	186	260	98.1	89.7	NA
S&P Core Earnings	689	680	613	477	345	187	320	128	NA	NA

Balance Sheet & Other Financial Data (Million $)

	2008	2007	2006	2005	2004	2003	2002	2001	2000	1999
Cash & Equivalent	1,185	954	1,125	NA	NA	NA	550	559	NA	NA
Premiums Due	513	580	612	455	435	368	NA	NA	NA	NA
Investment Assets:Bonds	8,591	10,126	9,118	8,962	9,178	8,729	NA	NA	NA	NA
Investment Assets:Stocks	475	636	742	693	527	456	NA	NA	NA	NA
Investment Assets:Loans	1,565	1,491	1,325	1,273	1,119	1,001	NA	NA	NA	NA
Investment Assets:Total	12,067	13,747	12,429	12,516	13,472	10,924	10,029	9,601	NA	NA
Deferred Policy Costs	2,651	2,895	2,398	2,022	1,648	1,394	NA	NA	NA	NA
Total Assets	24,515	26,750	25,165	25,365	24,504	23,728	22,924	24,450	NA	NA
Debt	972	972	972	972	972	1,946	975	NA	NA	NA
Common Equity	3,710	4,089	3,833	3,778	3,768	2,832	3,346	3,452	NA	NA
Combined Loss-Expense Ratio	76.4	92.0	91.4	90.8	92.4	93.3	NA	NA	NA	NA
% Return on Revenue	5.2	7.7	8.9	6.4	4.9	2.6	4.0	1.6	1.4	NA
% Return on Equity	11.5	16.5	18.7	12.8	10.6	6.7	NA	NA	NA	NA
% Investment Yield	1.2	6.1	5.7	5.2	5.2	5.8	6.4	14.8	NA	NA

Data as orig reptd.; bef. results of disc opers/spec. items. Per share data adj. for stk. divs.; EPS diluted. E-Estimated. NA-Not Available. NM-Not Meaningful. NR-Not Ranked. UR-Under Review.

Office: One Chase Manhattan Plaza, New York, NY 10005.
Telephone: 212-859-7000.
Website: http://www.assurant.com
Chrmn: J.M. Palms

Pres & CEO: R.B. Pollock
EVP & CFO: M.J. Peninger
EVP & Treas: C.J. Pagano
EVP, Secy & General Counsel: B.R. Schwartz

Investor Contact: M. Kivett (212-859-7029)
Board Members: R. J. Blendon, B. L. Bronner, H. L. Carver, J. N. Cento, A. R. Freedman, L. V. Jackson, D. B. Kelso, C. J. Koch, H. C. Mackin, J. M. Palms, R. B. Pollock, E. D. Rosen

Founded: 1969
Domicile: Delaware
Employees: 15,000

AT&T Inc

STANDARD &POOR'S

S&P Recommendation	STRONG BUY ★★★★★	Price $26.99 (as of Nov 27, 2009)	12-Mo. Target Price $31.00	Investment Style Large-Cap Value

GICS Sector Telecommunication Services
Sub-Industry Integrated Telecommunication Services

Summary AT&T Inc. (formerly SBC Communications) provides telephone and broadband service and holds full ownership of AT&T Mobility (formerly Cingular Wireless). AT&T Corp. was acquired in late 2005 and BellSouth in late 2006.

Key Stock Statistics (Source S&P, Vickers, company reports)

52-Wk Range	$30.65–21.44	S&P Oper. EPS 2009**E**	2.14	Market Capitalization(B)	$159.268	Beta	0.67
Trailing 12-Month EPS	$2.02	S&P Oper. EPS 2010**E**	2.26	Yield (%)	6.08	S&P 3-Yr. Proj. EPS CAGR(%)	6
Trailing 12-Month P/E	13.4	P/E on S&P Oper. EPS 2009**E**	12.6	Dividend Rate/Share	$1.64	S&P Credit Rating	A
$10K Invested 5 Yrs Ago	$13,604	Common Shares Outstg. (M)	5,901.0	Institutional Ownership (%)	56		

Price Performance

30-Week Mov. Avg. · · · 10-Week Mov. Avg. - - GAAP Earnings vs. Previous Year   Volume Above Avg. STARS
12-Mo. Target Price — Relative Strength — ▲ Up ▼ Down ► No Change   Below Avg.

Options: ASE, CBOE, P, Ph

Analysis prepared by **Todd Rosenbluth** on October 26, 2009, when the stock traded at **$ 25.35**.

Highlights

▶ Following what we expect to be flat revenues in 2009, we forecast 2% growth in 2010. We look for wireless revenue growth of 9% in 2010 on customer additions and wireless data service, and smaller revenue gains in broadband business, helping to outweigh competitive and economic pressures in consumer and business voice operations.

▶ We see operating margins widening to 18.5% in 2010, from a projected 18.0% in 2009, but still down from 23% in 2008. The decline from 2008 is largely due to the impact of accounting changes for pension expenses and inclusion of amortization expenses previously viewed as one-time items and for wireless handset subsidies. However, we believe wireless data and U-verse are generating improved profitability and we see further benefits from workforce reductions undertaken in 2009.

▶ We estimate EPS of $2.14 in 2009 and $2.26 in 2010, relative to $2.16 in GAAP EPS during 2008, and 2008 operating EPS of $2.83 that included goodwill amortization and other merger-related charges. We expect cash to be used for debt reduction and not share repurchases.

Investment Rationale/Risk

▶ We expect gains in consumer wireless and broadband to offset some wireline voice pressure and believe that AT&T's fundamentals will remain strong. We see cash accounting expenses pressuring earnings along with the delayed recovery in enterprise that is more dependent upon an improved labor market, in our opinion. Despite increased competition and regulatory oversight, we believe AT&T's strong brand loyalty and improved balance sheet are positives. We view its dividend as secure.

▶ Risks to our recommendation and target price include balance sheet weakness, increased pricing competition in wireline and wireless, and worse-than-projected wireless services execution.

▶ We view T as undervalued, trading at a forward P/E of about 11X our 2010 estimate, relative to the 6% EPS growth we forecast and with much of the near-term earnings pressure due to non-cash items. Our 12-month target price of $31 is based on our relative analysis, which assumes a P/E of 13.8X our EPS estimate, a slight premium to peers but a discount to the broader market. The dividend yield was recently 6.4%.

Qualitative Risk Assessment

LOW	MEDIUM	HIGH

Our risk assessment reflects our view of the company's strong balance sheet and its power over suppliers, offset by the competitive nature of the telecom business and the integration challenges of numerous acquisitions.

Quantitative Evaluations

S&P Quality Ranking   B+

D	C	B-	B	B+	A-	A	A+

Relative Strength Rank   MODERATE

70

LOWEST = 1   HIGHEST = 99

Revenue/Earnings Data

Revenue (Million $)

	1Q	2Q	3Q	4Q	Year
2009	30,571	30,734	30,855	--	--
2008	30,744	30,866	31,342	31,076	124,028
2007	28,969	29,478	30,132	30,349	118,928
2006	15,756	15,770	15,638	15,891	63,055
2005	10,248	10,328	10,320	12,966	43,862
2004	10,128	10,314	10,292	10,287	40,787

Earnings Per Share ($)

	1Q	2Q	3Q	4Q	Year
2009	0.53	0.54	0.54	E0.53	E2.14
2008	0.57	0.63	0.55	0.41	2.16
2007	0.45	0.47	0.50	0.52	1.94
2006	0.37	0.46	0.56	0.50	1.89
2005	0.27	0.30	0.38	0.46	1.42
2004	0.59	0.35	0.38	0.21	1.50

Fiscal year ended Dec. 31. Next earnings report expected: Late January. EPS Estimates based on S&P Operating Earnings; historical GAAP earnings are as reported.

Dividend Data (Dates: mm/dd Payment Date: mm/dd/yy)

Amount ($)	Date Decl.	Ex-Div. Date	Stk. of Record	Payment Date
0.410	12/12	01/07	01/09	02/02/09
0.410	03/27	04/07	04/09	05/01/09
0.410	06/26	07/08	07/10	08/03/09
0.410	09/25	10/07	10/09	11/02/09

Dividends have been paid since 1984. Source: Company reports.

Please read the Required Disclosures and Analyst Certification on the last page of this report.

The McGraw·Hill Companies

AT&T Inc

Business Summary October 26, 2009

CORPORATE OVERVIEW. AT&T Inc. (T) combined SBC Communications with the acquired assets of AT&T Corp. following a November 2005 acquisition. At the end of 2006, T closed on its acquisition of BellSouth (BLS) for $86 billion in stock. As of September 2009, the company had 28 million consumer voice connections (down 12% from a year earlier) and 13.5 million consumer broadband customers (up 6%). With the acquisition of BLS, T took full control of Cingular Wireless, the second largest U.S. carrier now with 81.6 million subscribers (up 9% from a year earlier), and expanded its wireline presence into the Southeastern U.S. In early 2007, Cingular was renamed AT&T.

IMPACT OF MAJOR DEVELOPMENTS. In June 2006, T launched its new fiber-based network, which offers video and faster-speed broadband services. As of September 2009, the service, called U-verse, had been rolled out in part of T's operating territory with 1.8 million customers, more than double from a year earlier. T has deployed the service to about 17 million households and aims to deploy it to 30 million households by 2011, a slight delay from prior expectations.

At the end of June 2007, T became the exclusive provider of the iPhone, and by that December, over 2 million customers had signed up for the service. In June 2008, the company announced an upgraded 3G version of the handset

that T has been subsidizing to drive customer demand and revenue per user. In the second half of 2008, T activated 4.3 million iPhones and more than 7 million in the first nine months of 2009, with the June launch of a newer, faster iPhone. Even with faster revenue growth and supporting customer loyalty in a competitive market, the iPhone has been earnings dilutive thus far in 2009 due to T's subsidies of the product. We believe T has a broad lineup of appealing 3G-enabled handsets.

In January 2009, T announced that it would be including intangible amortization expenses in its results and not refer to them as one-time items as it did in prior years. In our view, this will reduce T's net income.

COMPETITIVE LANDSCAPE. T faces competition from wireless and cable telephony (75% overlap with T's access line base) for consumer wireline and regional business operations. In addition, the weak U.S. economy caused customers to look to reduce costs including dropping wireline and broadband connections.

Company Financials Fiscal Year Ended Dec. 31

Per Share Data ($)	2008	2007	2006	2005	2004	2003	2002	2001	2000	1999
Tangible Book Value	NM	NM	NM	8.29	11.77	11.09	9.51	8.62	7.38	5.87
Cash Flow	5.50	5.43	2.77	3.68	3.80	4.16	4.79	2.25	5.16	4.37
Earnings	2.16	1.94	1.89	1.42	1.50	1.80	2.23	2.14	2.32	1.90
S&P Core Earnings	1.39	1.66	1.82	1.24	1.22	1.50	1.21	1.39	NA	NA
Dividends	1.60	1.42	1.33	1.29	1.25	1.37	1.07	1.02	1.01	0.97
Payout Ratio	74%	73%	70%	91%	83%	76%	48%	48%	43%	51%
Prices:High	41.94	42.97	36.21	25.98	27.73	31.65	40.99	53.06	59.00	59.94
Prices:Low	20.90	31.94	24.24	21.75	22.98	18.85	19.57	36.50	34.81	44.06
P/E Ratio:High	19	22	19	18	18	18	18	25	25	32
P/E Ratio:Low	10	16	13	15	15	10	9	17	15	23

Income Statement Analysis (Million $)										
Revenue	124,028	118,928	63,055	43,862	40,787	40,843	43,138	45,908	51,476	49,489
Depreciation	19,883	21,577	9,907	7,643	7,564	7,870	8,578	9,077	9,748	8,553
Maintenance	NA	NA	NA	NA	NA	NA	NA	NA	NA	NA
Construction Credits	NA	NA	NA	36.0	31.0	37.0	58.0	119	81.0	81.0
Effective Tax Rate	35.4%	34.0%	32.4%	16.3%	30.5%	32.9%	28.5%	36.1%	38.2%	39.4%
Net Income	12,867	11,951	7,356	4,786	4,979	5,971	7,473	7,260	7,967	6,573
S&P Core Earnings	8,235	10,225	7,080	4,189	4,031	5,000	4,048	4,717	NA	NA

Balance Sheet & Other Financial Data (Million $)										
Gross Property	218,579	210,518	202,149	149,238	136,177	133,923	131,755	127,524	119,753	116,332
Net Property	99,088	95,890	94,596	58,727	50,046	52,128	48,490	49,827	47,195	46,571
Capital Expenditures	20,335	17,717	8,320	5,576	5,099	5,219	6,808	11,189	13,124	10,304
Total Capital	176,415	197,561	193,009	96,727	77,544	69,607	62,705	58,476	54,079	50,411
Fixed Charges Coverage	6.6	6.0	5.8	4.4	6.9	7.0	6.9	6.6	8.0	7.5
Capitalization:Long Term Debt	60,872	57,255	50,063	26,115	21,231	16,060	18,536	17,133	16,492	18,415
Capitalization:Preferred	Nil	Nil	Nil	Nil	Nil	Nil	Nil	Nil	Nil	Nil
Capitalization:Common	96,347	115,367	115,540	54,690	40,504	38,248	33,199	32,491	30,463	26,726
% Return on Revenue	10.4	10.0	11.7	10.9	12.2	14.6	17.3	15.8	15.5	13.3
% Return on Invested Capital	8.3	7.6	4.9	6.5	7.0	9.0	11.4	12.9	16.6	15.0
% Return on Common Equity	12.2	10.4	8.6	10.1	12.6	16.7	22.6	23.1	27.9	26.6
% Earned on Net Property	23.7	21.4	13.4	11.3	11.6	12.9	17.5	22.4	22.9	25.6
% Long Term Debt of Capitalization	38.7	33.2	30.3	32.3	34.4	29.6	35.8	34.5	35.1	40.9
Capital % Preferred	Nil	Nil	Nil	Nil	Nil	Nil	Nil	Nil	Nil	Nil
Capitalization:% Common	61.3	66.8	67.8	67.7	65.6	70.4	64.2	65.5	64.9	59.1

Data as orig reptd.; bef. results of disc opers/spec. items. Per share data adj. for stk. divs.; EPS diluted. E-Estimated. NA-Not Available. NM-Not Meaningful. NR-Not Ranked. UR-Under Review.

Office: 2088 S Akard St, Dallas, TX 75202.
Telephone: 210-821-4105.
Website: http://www.att.com
Chrmn, Pres & CEO: R.L. Stephenson

EVP, CFO & Chief Acctg Officer: R.G. Lindner
EVP & General Counsel: D.W. Watts
SVP & Secy: A.E. Meuleman
SVP & Cntlr: J.J. Stephens

Investor Contact: D. Cessac (210-351-2058)
Board Members: W. F. Aldinger, III, G. F. Amelio, R. V. Anderson, J. H. Blanchard, A. A. Busch, III, J. A. Harris, J. P. Kelly, J. C. Madonna, L. M. Martin, J. B. McCoy, M. S. Metz, J. C. Pardo, J. M. Roche, R. L. Stephenson, L. D. Tyson, P. P. Upton

Founded: 1983
Domicile: Delaware
Employees: 302,660

Autodesk Inc

STANDARD &POOR'S

S&P Recommendation **SELL** ★★☆☆☆	Price $23.62 (as of Nov 27, 2009)	12-Mo. Target Price $24.00	Investment Style Large-Cap Growth

GICS Sector Information Technology
Sub-Industry Application Software

Summary This company develops, markets and supports computer-aided design and drafting (CAD) software for use on desktop computers and workstations.

Key Stock Statistics (Source S&P, Vickers, company reports)

52-Wk Range	$27.97– 11.70	S&P Oper. EPS 2010**E**	0.15	Market Capitalization(B)	$5.426	Beta		2.25
Trailing 12-Month EPS	$-0.43	S&P Oper. EPS 2011**E**	0.31	Yield (%)	Nil	S&P 3-Yr. Proj. EPS CAGR(%)		20
Trailing 12-Month P/E	NM	P/E on S&P Oper. EPS 2010**E**	NM	Dividend Rate/Share	Nil	S&P Credit Rating		NA
$10K Invested 5 Yrs Ago	$7,274	Common Shares Outstg. (M)	229.7	Institutional Ownership (%)	88			

Price Performance

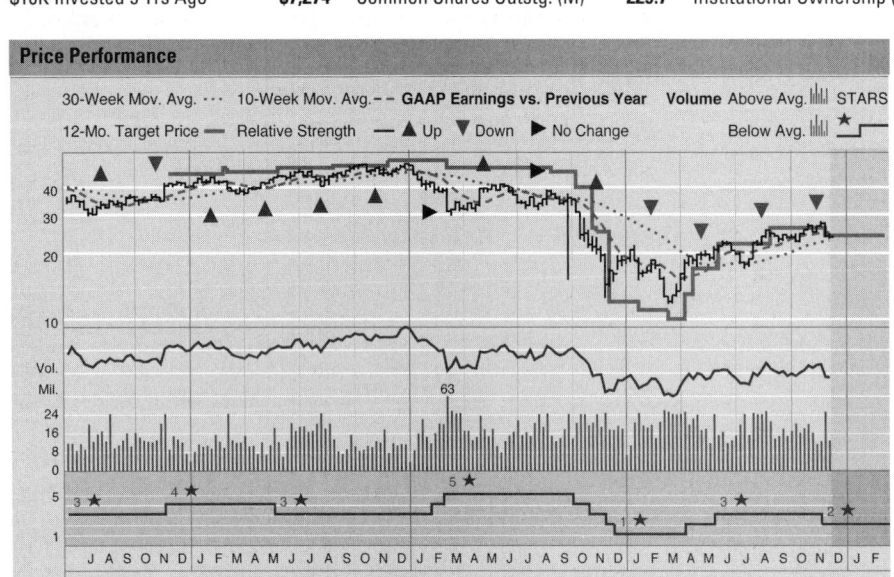

- 30-Week Mov. Avg. · · · 10-Week Mov. Avg. - - ▬ GAAP Earnings vs. Previous Year   Volume Above Avg. ▮▮ STARS
- 12-Mo. Target Price ▬ Relative Strength   ▲ Up ▼ Down ► No Change   Below Avg. ▮▮ ★

Options: ASE, CBOE, P, Ph

Analysis prepared by **Jim Yin** on November 19, 2009, when the stock traded at **$ 23.90**.

Highlights

► We estimate total revenue in FY 11 (Jan.) will rise 0.5%, following a 27% decline we see for FY 10. Our outlook is based on our view of a sluggish recovery in IT spending, particularly in the manufacturing industry given its low capacity utilization rate. Even though we expect customers to resume spending on new projects, we forecast a mere 1.5% rise in license revenue in FY 11 due to ADSK's long sales cycles. We expect maintenance revenue to decrease 0.8% in FY 11, reflecting weak license revenues and lower customer subscription renewal rates as some companies reduce their work forces.

► We see gross margins in FY 11 staying at 89%, the same as in FY 10. We look for total operating expenses to decrease as a percentage of revenue due to further staff and cost reductions. We estimate that operating margins will widen to 4.7% in FY 11, from 2.6% in FY 10.

► Our EPS estimates are $0.15 for FY 10 and $0.31 for FY 11. Even though we project flat revenues and $45 million in restructuring costs in FY 11, we believe earnings will increase on further cost reductions.

Investment Rationale/Risk

► We recently lowered our recommendation to sell, from hold, based on our view of a sluggish recovery in IT spending. Although the economy is improving, we believe companies will be cautious in their capital expenditures until they see further signs of an economic uptrend. We believe growth in ADSK's software license revenues will lag the overall economy, due to the company's long sales cycles. We also think ADSK is losing market share to low-cost providers in this difficult environment.

► Risks to our opinion and target price include a stronger-than-expected economic recovery, additional economic stimulus programs by countries to rebuild their infrastructure, and greater cost savings from restructuring.

► Our 12-month target price of $24 is based on a blend of our discounted cash flow (DCF) and enterprise value (EV)-to-sales valuations. Our DCF model assumes a 13% weighted average cost of capital and 3% terminal growth, yielding intrinsic value of $26. From our EV-to-sales analysis, we derive a value of $22, based on an EV-to-sales ratio of 2.4X, slightly below the industry's average of 2.5X, reflecting ADSK's low profitability.

Qualitative Risk Assessment

LOW	MEDIUM	**HIGH**

Our risk assessment reflects our view of a sluggish recovery in IT spending, the cyclical nature of ADSK's business, and intense competition in the computer-aided design market.

Quantitative Evaluations

S&P Quality Ranking   **B**

D	C	B-	**B**	B+	A-	A	A+

Relative Strength Rank   **MODERATE**

     31

LOWEST = 1   HIGHEST = 99

Revenue/Earnings Data

Revenue (Million $)

	1Q	2Q	3Q	4Q	Year
2010	425.8	414.9	416.9	--	--
2009	598.8	619.5	607.1	489.8	2,315
2008	508.5	525.9	538.4	599.1	2,172
2007	436.0	449.6	456.8	497.4	1,840
2006	355.1	373.0	378.3	416.8	1,523
2005	297.9	279.6	300.2	356.2	1,234

Earnings Per Share ($)

2010	-0.14	0.05	0.13	E0.12	E0.15
2009	0.41	0.39	0.45	-0.47	0.80
2008	0.34	0.39	0.35	0.40	1.47
2007	0.20	0.36	0.24	0.40	1.19
2006	0.31	0.30	0.38	0.33	1.33
2005	0.18	0.16	0.30	0.26	0.90

Fiscal year ended Jan. 31. Next earnings report expected: Late February. EPS Estimates based on S&P Operating Earnings; historical GAAP earnings are as reported.

Dividend Data

Quarterly cash dividends were discontinued after April 2005.

Autodesk Inc

Business Summary November 19, 2009

CORPORATE OVERVIEW. Autodesk (ADSK) develops software solutions that enable customers in the architectural, engineering, construction, manufacturing, infrastructure, media and entertainment markets to create, manage and share their data and designs digitally. ADSK's software helps its customers to improve their designs before they actually begin the building process, thus saving time and money. The company is organized into two reportable operating segments: the Design Solutions segment, which accounted for 89% of net revenue in FY 09 (Jan.), and the Media and Entertainment segment, which accounted for 11%.

The Design Solutions segment sells design software for professionals and consumers who design, build and manage building and other infrastructure projects for both public and private users. The segment is comprised of three divisions: Platform Technology and Other, which accounted for 44% of the segment's revenues in FY 09; Architecture, Engineering and Construction, 23%; and Manufacturing Solutions, 21%.

Principal products sold by the Design Solutions segment include AutoCAD, a general-purpose computer aided design (CAD) tool for design, modeling, drafting, mapping, rendering and facility management tasks, AutoCAD LT, a

low-cost CAD package with 2D and basic 3D drafting capabilities, and Autodesk Buzzsaw, an online collaboration service that allows users to store, manage and share project documents from any Internet connection. Other products include Autodesk Mechanical Desktop, Autodesk Civil 3D, and Autodesk Revit products. The Design Solutions segment also offers a range of services including consulting, support and training.

The Media and Entertainment segment develops digital systems and software for creating 3D animation, color grading, visual effects compositing, editing and finishing. Its products are used for PC and console game development, animation, film, television, and design visualization. Products include Autodesk 3ds Max, a 3D modeling and animation software package; Autodesk Flame, a digital system used by professionals to create and edit special visual effects in real-time; and Autodesk Inferno, which provides all the features of flame with film tools, and increased image resolution and color control for digital film work.

Company Financials Fiscal Year Ended Jan. 31

Per Share Data ($)	2009	2008	2007	2006	2005	2004	2003	2002	2001	2000
Tangible Book Value	2.89	3.14	3.07	2.06	2.07	2.07	1.84	2.20	1.85	2.22
Cash Flow	1.24	1.68	1.37	1.51	1.11	0.74	0.35	0.68	0.69	0.36
Earnings	0.80	1.47	1.19	1.33	0.90	0.52	0.14	0.40	0.40	0.04
S&P Core Earnings	1.18	1.49	1.19	1.05	0.67	0.33	-0.07	0.09	0.17	NA
Dividends	Nil	Nil	0.02	0.06	0.06	0.06	0.06	0.06	0.06	0.06
Payout Ratio	Nil	Nil	2%	5%	7%	12%	43%	15%	15%	150%
Calendar Year	2008	2007	2006	2005	2004	2003	2002	2001	2000	1999
Prices:High	49.71	51.32	44.75	48.27	38.98	12.45	11.84	10.55	14.02	12.36
Prices:Low	12.45	36.74	29.56	26.20	12.10	6.41	5.09	6.05	4.86	4.25
P/E Ratio:High	62	35	38	36	43	24	85	26	35	NM
P/E Ratio:Low	16	25	25	20	13	12	36	15	12	NM

Income Statement Analysis (Million $)										
Revenue	2,315	2,172	1,840	1,523	1,234	952	825	947	936	820
Operating Income	543	539	440	414	314	0.16	99.7	195	208	115
Depreciation	102	49.8	43.9	43.7	51.9	50.3	48.8	62.9	68.8	79.7
Interest Expense	Nil	Nil	2.10	Nil	Nil	Nil	Nil	Nil	Nil	Nil
Pretax Income	253	470	367	383	246	117	38.5	55.1	41.7	23.9
Effective Tax Rate	27.3%	24.2%	21.0%	14.1%	10.1%	NM	17.1%	NM	NM	59.0%
Net Income	184	356	290	329	222	120	31.9	90.3	93.2	9.81
S&P Core Earnings	271	362	292	258	161	74.4	-16.2	19.5	38.5	NA

Balance Sheet & Other Financial Data (Million $)										
Cash	981	949	778	369	533	364	247	505	423	359
Current Assets	1,388	1,482	1,190	739	782	597	450	564	491	545
Total Assets	2,421	2,209	1,798	1,361	1,142	1,017	884	902	808	907
Current Liabilities	800	746	574	507	477	385	310	371	334	299
Long Term Debt	Nil	Nil	Nil	Nil	Nil	Nil	Nil	Nil	Nil	Nil
Common Equity	1,311	1,231	1,115	791	648	622	569	529	460	602
Total Capital	1,333	1,231	1,115	791	648	629	571	529	473	607
Capital Expenditures	78.4	43.3	35.3	20.5	40.8	25.9	36.1	45.1	32.4	14.9
Cash Flow	286	406	334	373	273	171	80.7	153	162	89.6
Current Ratio	1.7	2.0	2.1	1.5	1.6	1.6	1.5	1.5	1.5	1.8
% Long Term Debt of Capitalization	Nil	Nil	Nil	Nil	Nil	Nil	Nil	Nil	Nil	Nil
% Net Income of Revenue	7.9	16.4	15.8	21.6	18.0	12.6	3.9	9.5	10.0	1.2
% Return on Assets	7.9	17.8	18.4	26.3	20.5	12.7	3.6	10.6	10.9	1.1
% Return on Equity	14.5	30.4	30.4	45.7	34.9	20.2	5.8	18.3	17.6	1.7

Data as orig reptd.; bef. results of disc opers/spec. items. Per share data adj. for stk. divs.; EPS diluted. E-Estimated. NA-Not Available. NM-Not Meaningful. NR-Not Ranked. UR-Under Review.

Office: 111 McInnis Parkway, San Rafael, CA 94903-2700.
Telephone: 415-507-5000.
Email: investor.relations@autodesk.com
Website: http://www.autodesk.com

Chrmn: C.W. Beveridge
Pres & CEO: C. Bass
COO & SVP: M. Chin
EVP, CFO & Chief Acctg Officer: M.J. Hawkins

SVP, Secy & General Counsel: P.W. Di Fronzo
Investor Contact: S. Pirri (415-507-6467)
Board Members: C. Bass, C. W. Beveridge, J. H. Dawson, P. Halvorsen, S. Maloney, E. Nelson, C. Robel, S. West

Founded: 1982
Domicile: Delaware
Employees: 7,800

Automatic Data Processing Inc.

STANDARD &POOR'S

S&P Recommendation HOLD ★★★☆☆

Price	**12-Mo. Target Price**	**Investment Style**
$43.53 (as of Nov 27, 2009)	$43.00	Large-Cap Growth

GICS Sector Information Technology
Sub-Industry Data Processing & Outsourced Services

Summary ADP, one of the world's largest independent computing services companies, provides a broad range of data processing services.

Key Stock Statistics (Source S&P, Vickers, company reports)

52-Wk Range	$44.37–32.03	S&P Oper. EPS 2010**E**	2.38	Market Capitalization(B)	$21.967	Beta	0.53
Trailing 12-Month EPS	$2.66	S&P Oper. EPS 2011**E**	2.50	Yield (%)	3.12	S&P 3-Yr. Proj. EPS CAGR(%)	5
Trailing 12-Month P/E	16.4	P/E on S&P Oper. EPS 2010**E**	18.3	Dividend Rate/Share	$1.36	S&P Credit Rating	AAA
$10K Invested 5 Yrs Ago	NA	Common Shares Outstg. (M)	504.6	Institutional Ownership (%)	76		

Price Performance

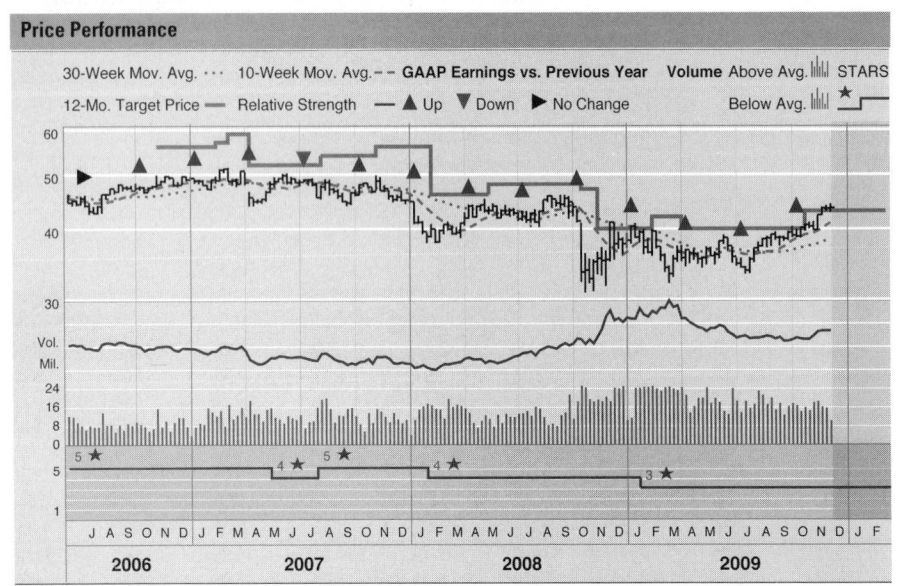

30-Week Mov. Avg. · · · 10-Week Mov. Avg. – – GAAP Earnings vs. Previous Year   Volume Above Avg. STARS
12-Mo. Target Price — Relative Strength   ▲ Up ▼ Down ► No Change   Below Avg.

Options: ASE, CBOE, P, Ph

Analysis prepared by **Dylan Cathers** on November 10, 2009, when the stock traded at **$ 43.16**.

Highlights

► We look for revenues to decline 1% in FY 10 (June), after a 1% increase in FY 09. Sales in the company's core payroll and tax-filing business remain under pressure, reflecting the employment picture. We think payroll data will continue to be weak, given the soft economy. Other issues include an increase in companies going out of business, decreased discretionary spending by clients, delayed new signings, and weakness in the Dealer Services unit. We see low prevailing interest rates reducing income from funds held for clients, although we believe ADP is doing a good job of mitigating these declines through portfolio management. Also, lower borrowing costs should aid results. We look for revenue growth of 5% in FY 11.

► We project a modest narrowing of operating margins in FY 10, despite cost containment measures as ADP deals with lower levels of revenue and reduced leverage, as well as pricing pressures.

► Our FY 10 EPS estimate is $2.38, assuming a modest level of share buybacks, down from operating EPS of $2.35 in FY 09, which excludes a tax benefit. We look for EPS of $2.50 in FY 11.

Investment Rationale/Risk

► Our hold opinion on the shares is based on valuation. We are seeing headwinds that will likely affect the company in the near term, namely slower employment growth, continued weak U.S. vehicle sales, and low interest rates. Over the longer term, we think the market for payroll outsourcing is relatively untapped, especially in the small and medium-sized business market and overseas, providing opportunities for future earnings growth. We view ADP's balance sheet as strong, even after it spent $550 million on share repurchases in FY 09.

► Risks to our recommendation and target price include competition in the business process outsourcing market, an area into which ADP is venturing, which could lead to downward pressure on pricing and profit margins; a decrease in payrolls due to a declining economy; and failure of ADP to expand further into small and mid-sized businesses and international markets.

► Our 12-month target price of $43 is based on our relative valuation analysis, applying a peer-average P/E of 17.7X to our calendar 2010 EPS estimate of $2.40.

Qualitative Risk Assessment

LOW	MEDIUM	HIGH

Our risk assessment reflects what we see as the company's strong balance sheet, steady cash inflow, and recurring revenue stream, offset by intense competition in payroll processing and the threat of new entrants into the marketplace.

Quantitative Evaluations

S&P Quality Ranking A+

D	C	B-	B	B+	A-	A	A+

Relative Strength Rank STRONG

81

LOWEST = 1   HIGHEST = 99

Revenue/Earnings Data

Revenue (Million $)

	1Q	2Q	3Q	4Q	Year
2010	2,103	--	--	--	--
2009	2,182	2,203	2,375	2,108	8,867
2008	1,992	2,150	2,427	2,207	8,777
2007	1,755	1,874	2,171	2,000	7,800
2006	1,922	2,047	2,439	2,474	8,882
2005	1,855	1,994	2,349	2,302	8,499

Earnings Per Share ($)

	1Q	2Q	3Q	4Q	Year
2010	0.56	E0.52	E0.81	E0.49	E2.38
2009	0.54	0.59	0.80	0.69	2.63
2008	0.45	0.53	0.77	0.44	2.20
2007	0.39	0.45	0.65	0.35	1.83
2006	0.36	0.44	0.61	0.44	1.85
2005	0.35	0.42	0.57	0.44	1.79

Fiscal year ended Jun. 30. Next earnings report expected: Early February. EPS Estimates based on S&P Operating Earnings; historical GAAP earnings are as reported.

Dividend Data (Dates: mm/dd Payment Date: mm/dd/yy)

Amount ($)	Date Decl.	Ex-Div. Date	Stk. of Record	Payment Date
0.330	02/10	03/11	03/13	04/01/09
0.330	04/30	06/10	06/12	07/01/09
0.330	08/13	09/09	09/11	10/01/09
0.340	11/10	12/09	12/11	01/01/10

Dividends have been paid since 1974. Source: Company reports.

Please read the Required Disclosures and Analyst Certification on the last page of this report.

The McGraw·Hill Companies

Automatic Data Processing Inc.

**STANDARD
&POOR'S**

Business Summary November 10, 2009

CORPORATE OVERVIEW. Automatic Data Processing (ADP) is the largest global provider of payroll outsourcing services based on revenue. The company also offers human resources outsourcing, tax filing, and benefits administration, with a broad range of data processing services in two business segments: employer and dealer.

Employer Services provides payroll, human resource, benefits administration, time and attendance, and tax filing and reporting services to more than 570,000 clients in North America, Europe, Australia, Asia and Brazil. Dealer Services provides transaction systems, data products and professional services to automobile and truck dealers and manufacturers worldwide.

MARKET PROFILE. The market for HR management services, which is the largest segment of ADP's Employer Services division, totaled $104.6 billion in worldwide in calendar 2008, according to market researcher IDC. Between 2008 and 2013, IDC expects this area to expand at a compound annual growth rate (CAGR) of 5.3%, with the market in the U.S. increasing 5.7%, from $50.4 billion in 2008. For the more narrow processing services market, where ADP is the dominant company, IDC sees a CAGR of 4.8% in the U.S. between 2008 and 2013. In contrast, in the market for business process outsourcing (BPO) services, an area in which we see ADP expanding further, IDC expects a CAGR of

6.8% over the same time frame.

IMPACT OF MAJOR DEVELOPMENTS. In April 2006, ADP completed the sale of its Claims Services business for $975 million in cash, netting $480 million after taxes. In August 2006, ADP announced its intention to spin off its Brokerage Services business. The new public company, Broadridge Financial Services, which began trading on April 2, 2007, had sales of about $2 billion in FY 07 (Jun.), a high level of recurring revenues, and a revenue growth rate in the mid-single digits. This growth rate is below what we think the remaining Employer Services and Dealer Services units are capable of, especially given what we believe are strong overseas prospects. Further, the disposition of the Brokerage business (as well as the Claims sale) allows management to better concentrate on its two remaining businesses, in our opinion. With the Brokerage business spin-off complete, the new company distributed $690 million to ADP, which it used primarily for share buybacks, acquiring 40 million shares at a cost of about $2 billion in FY 07.

Company Financials Fiscal Year Ended Jun. 30

Per Share Data ($)	2009	2008	2007	2006	2005	2004	2003	2002	2001	2000
Tangible Book Value	4.72	3.97	3.93	5.21	4.55	4.23	4.57	5.25	4.97	4.71
Cash Flow	3.24	2.40	2.35	5.35	2.30	2.07	2.13	2.19	1.93	1.74
Earnings	2.63	2.20	1.83	1.85	1.79	1.56	1.68	1.75	1.44	1.31
S&P Core Earnings	2.58	2.11	1.78	1.85	1.60	1.38	1.42	1.49	1.31	NA
Dividends	1.28	1.10	1.06	0.71	0.61	0.54	0.48	0.45	0.40	0.34
Payout Ratio	49%	50%	58%	38%	34%	35%	28%	26%	27%	26%
Prices:High	44.37	45.97	51.50	49.94	48.11	47.31	40.81	59.53	63.56	69.31
Prices:Low	32.03	30.83	43.89	42.50	40.37	38.60	27.24	31.15	41.00	40.00
P/E Ratio:High	17	21	28	27	27	30	24	34	44	53
P/E Ratio:Low	12	14	24	23	23	25	16	18	28	31

Income Statement Analysis (Million $)

	2009	2008	2007	2006	2005	2004	2003	2002	2001	2000
Revenue	8,867	8,777	7,800	8,882	8,499	7,755	7,147	7,004	7,018	6,288
Operating Income	2,138	1,832	1,795	1,967	1,948	1,745	1,793	1,952	1,938	1,904
Depreciation	308	106	289	289	304	307	275	279	321	284
Interest Expense	33.3	80.5	94.9	72.8	32.3	Nil	Nil	21.2	14.3	13.1
Pretax Income	1,905	1,812	1,624	3,486	1,678	1,495	1,645	1,787	1,525	1,290
Effective Tax Rate	30.3%	35.9%	37.1%	19.2%	37.1%	37.4%	38.1%	38.4%	39.4%	34.8%
Net Income	1,328	1,162	1,021	2,815	1,055	936	1,018	1,101	925	841
S&P Core Earnings	1,302	1,115	992	1,077	940	824	857	940	842	NA

Balance Sheet & Other Financial Data (Million $)

	2009	2008	2007	2006	2005	2004	2003	2002	2001	2000
Cash	2,296	1,584	1,817	2,269	1,671	1,129	2,344	2,750	1,791	1,824
Current Assets	20,704	18,809	3,364	4,760	4,441	2,762	3,676	2,817	3,083	3,064
Total Assets	25,352	23,734	26,649	27,490	27,615	21,121	19,834	18,277	17,889	16,851
Current Liabilities	18,756	17,342	1,791	2,593	2,801	1,768	1,999	1,411	1,336	1,297
Long Term Debt	42.7	52.1	43.5	74.3	75.8	76.2	84.7	90.6	110	132
Common Equity	5,323	5,087	5,148	6,012	5,784	5,418	5,371	5,114	4,701	4,583
Total Capital	5,620	5,309	5,319	6,210	6,150	5,778	5,777	5,442	5,019	4,866
Capital Expenditures	158	181	173	292	196	196	134	146	185	166
Cash Flow	1,636	1,268	1,310	3,104	1,360	1,242	1,293	1,380	1,246	1,125
Current Ratio	1.1	1.1	1.9	1.8	1.6	1.6	1.8	2.0	2.3	2.4
% Long Term Debt of Capitalization	0.7	1.0	0.8	1.2	1.2	1.3	1.5	1.7	2.2	2.7
% Net Income of Revenue	15.0	13.2	13.1	31.7	12.4	12.1	14.2	15.7	13.2	13.4
% Return on Assets	5.4	4.6	3.8	10.2	4.3	4.6	5.3	6.1	5.3	5.7
% Return on Equity	25.5	22.7	18.3	47.7	18.8	17.3	19.4	22.4	19.9	19.6

Data as orig reptd.; bef. results of disc opers/spec. items. Per share data adj. for stk. divs.; EPS diluted. E-Estimated. NA-Not Available. NM-Not Meaningful. NR-Not Ranked. UR-Under Review.

Office: 1 Adp Blvd, Roseland, NJ 07068-1728.
Telephone: 973-974-5000.
Website: http://www.adp.com
Chrmn: L.A. Brun

Pres & CEO: G.C. Butler
CFO: F. Anderson, Jr.
CFO: C.R. Reidy
Chief Acctg Officer & Cntlr: A. Sheiness

Board Members: G. D. Brenneman, L. A. Brun, G. C. Butler, L. G. Cooperman, E. C. Fast, L. R. Gooden, R. G. Hubbard, J. P. Jones, III, C. H. Noski, S. T. Rowlands, G. L. Summe

Founded: 1949
Domicile: Delaware
Employees: 45,000

The McGraw-Hill Companies

AutoNation Inc

STANDARD &POOR'S

S&P Recommendation **BUY** ★★★★☆	Price $17.44 (as of Nov 27, 2009)	12-Mo. Target Price $21.00	Investment Style Large-Cap Blend

GICS Sector Consumer Discretionary
Sub-Industry Automotive Retail

Summary AutoNation, the largest U.S. retail auto dealer, owns and operates about 245 new vehicle franchises in 15 states.

Key Stock Statistics (Source S&P, Vickers, company reports)

52-Wk Range	$21.60– 7.62	S&P Oper. EPS 2009**E**	1.11	Market Capitalization(B)	$3.043	Beta	1.35
Trailing 12-Month EPS	$1.14	S&P Oper. EPS 2010**E**	1.35	Yield (%)	Nil	S&P 3-Yr. Proj. EPS CAGR(%)	6
Trailing 12-Month P/E	15.3	P/E on S&P Oper. EPS 2009**E**	15.7	Dividend Rate/Share	Nil	S&P Credit Rating	BB+
$10K Invested 5 Yrs Ago	$9,397	Common Shares Outstg. (M)	174.5	Institutional Ownership (%)	NM		

Price Performance

30-Week Mov. Avg. · · · 10-Week Mov. Avg. – – GAAP Earnings vs. Previous Year   Volume Above Avg. STARS
12-Mo. Target Price — Relative Strength — ▲ Up ▼ Down ▶ No Change   Below Avg. ★

Options: ASE, CBOE, P, Ph

Analysis prepared by **Efraim Levy, CFA** on November 03, 2009, when the stock traded at **$ 18.03**.

Highlights

▶ New vehicle sales in 2009 have been hurt by the U.S. recession, weaker housing markets, and the impact of the credit crunch and lower stock market valuations. We see same-store new vehicle sales falling on sharply lower industry volume. In addition, several domestic branded AN dealerships were closed or received notices from automakers that they will be closed. We expect revenues to rise 10% in 2010, as the economy should improve and help consumer confidence.

▶ In 2010, we project that higher industry volume and macroeconomic factors will help new and used vehicle sales, although we see continued pressure on car prices and intense competition. We expect SG&A expenses to rise as demand rebounds. However, we see cost-cutting positioning the company for improved profitability as demand recovers.

▶ We see AutoNation's 2010 operating EPS rising on increased operating efficiencies, which should help profit comparisons. Although we see a resurgence of capital spending in 2010, we see cash flow supportive of expanding the business internally and via acquisitions and re-purchasing shares.

Investment Rationale/Risk

▶ The stock recently traded at P/E and price to free cash flow multiples above peer averages, based on our 2009 estimates. We believe the company warrants a premium given that AN's net margins are above the peer average. Based on S&P's Core Earnings methodology, we project AN's earnings quality for 2010 to be high, as the company does not offer its employees a pension plan.

▶ Risks to our recommendation and target price include lower multiples for automotive retailers, and less-than-expected vehicle demand and weaker pricing for new and used vehicles.

▶ Applying a P/E of 18X, reflecting peer and historical P/E comparisons, to our 2010 EPS estimate of $1.35 leads to a value of about $24. Our DCF model, which assumes a weighted average cost of capital of 11.6%, a compound annual growth rate of 2.8% over the next 15 years, and terminal growth of 3%, calculates intrinsic value of $13.50. Based on a weighted blend of these metrics, our 12-month target price is $21. We see cash flow remaining positive and sufficient to meet current needs.

Qualitative Risk Assessment

LOW	MEDIUM	HIGH

Our risk assessment reflects the cyclical nature of the automotive retailing industry, which is affected by interest rates, consumer confidence, and personal discretionary spending, offset by the company's highly variable cost structure.

Quantitative Evaluations

S&P Quality Ranking   B-

D	C	B-	B	B+	A-	A	A+

Relative Strength Rank   WEAK

28

LOWEST = 1   HIGHEST = 99

Revenue/Earnings Data

Revenue (Million $)

	1Q	2Q	3Q	4Q	Year
2009	2,473	2,610	2,916	--	--
2008	3,970	3,885	3,540	2,737	14,132
2007	4,395	4,559	4,602	4,214	17,692
2006	4,612	4,959	4,945	4,473	18,989
2005	4,561	5,019	5,188	4,485	19,253
2004	4,630	4,916	5,041	4,838	19,425

Earnings Per Share ($)

	1Q	2Q	3Q	4Q	Year
2009	0.27	0.31	0.36	E0.23	E1.11
2008	0.31	0.30	-7.95	0.40	-6.89
2007	0.39	0.38	0.39	0.27	1.44
2006	0.37	0.33	0.40	0.35	1.45
2005	0.33	0.40	0.45	0.30	1.48
2004	0.32	0.35	0.35	0.43	1.45

Fiscal year ended Dec. 31. Next earnings report expected: Late January. EPS Estimates based on S&P Operating Earnings; historical GAAP earnings are as reported.

Dividend Data

No cash dividends have been paid.

Please read the Required Disclosures and Analyst Certification on the last page of this report.

The McGraw-Hill Companies

AutoNation Inc

Business Summary November 03, 2009

CORPORATE OVERVIEW. AutoNation's vehicle retailing unit segment operates in saturated markets, in our view. Although the company is the largest U.S. auto retailer, it controls only about 2% of the $1 trillion U.S. new and used car market. About 75% of total U.S. vehicle sales are to replace existing autos. AN's new auto retailing operations (55% of 2008 revenues) consist of about 300 dealerships.

The sale of used vehicles accounted for nearly 24% of revenues in 2008. Fixed operations provided nearly 17% of sales, while finance and insurance and other accounted for the balance.

Investor Edward Lampert's ESL Investments Inc. owns about 45% of AutoNation's common shares. In January, the company's board of directors approved agreements with the certain automakers to permit ESL and certain affiliates to acquire 50% or more of the company. ESL has agreed to vote all shares above 50% in proportion to all non-ESL shares voted. Bill Gates controls about 12%

of AutoNation's common shares through the Bill & Melinda Gates Foundation Trust and through Cascade Investment LLC.

CORPORATE STRATEGY. The company plans to maximize the return on its investment by using cash flow to purchase dealerships and buy back common shares, although given the current economic environment we expect this activity to be below the level of recent years. It also plans to divest non-core stores. In addition, AN intends to increase its mix of higher volume import and premium luxury stores. In 2007 and 2008, 65% of new vehicle sales were generated by import and luxury franchises; domestic franchises accounted for 35%.

Company Financials Fiscal Year Ended Dec. 31

Per Share Data ($)	2008	2007	2006	2005	2004	2003	2002	2001	2000	1999
Tangible Book Value	4.93	2.37	2.66	6.53	4.53	3.91	3.14	2.99	2.64	4.72
Cash Flow	-6.38	1.90	1.81	1.78	1.78	2.01	1.40	1.18	1.28	0.07
Earnings	-6.89	1.44	1.45	1.48	1.45	1.76	1.19	0.73	0.91	-0.07
S&P Core Earnings	1.32	1.44	1.45	1.44	1.41	1.69	1.12	0.57	NA	NA
Dividends	Nil	Nil	Nil	Nil	Nil	Nil	Nil	Nil	Nil	Nil
Payout Ratio	Nil	Nil	Nil	Nil	Nil	Nil	Nil	Nil	Nil	Nil
Prices:High	19.59	23.19	22.94	22.84	19.33	19.19	18.73	13.07	10.75	18.38
Prices:Low	3.97	14.65	18.95	17.91	15.01	11.61	9.05	4.94	4.63	7.50
P/E Ratio:High	NM	16	16	15	13	11	16	18	12	NM
P/E Ratio:Low	NM	10	13	12	10	7	8	7	5	NM

Income Statement Analysis (Million $)	2008	2007	2006	2005	2004	2003	2002	2001	2000	1999
Revenue	14,132	17,692	18,989	19,253	19,425	19,381	19,479	19,989	20,610	20,112
Operating Income	566	798	879	888	861	805	786	667	855	461
Depreciation	90.8	91.7	82.9	80.7	89.7	71.0	69.7	152	134	60.0
Interest Expense	177	247	267	191	159	143	125	43.7	248	35.0
Pretax Income	-1,423	459	542	623	607	591	618	401	525	-27.0
Effective Tax Rate	NM	37.3%	38.9%	36.5%	34.7%	14.4%	38.3%	38.9%	37.5%	NM
Net Income	-1,225	288	331	396	396	506	382	245	328	-31.0
S&P Core Earnings	234	288	331	385	385	486	359	192	NA	NA

Balance Sheet & Other Financial Data (Million $)	2008	2007	2006	2005	2004	2003	2002	2001	2000	1999
Cash	111	32.8	52.2	244	107	171	176	128	82.2	369
Current Assets	2,554	3,238	3,386	3,880	3,678	3,990	3,629	3,153	4,176	4,301
Total Assets	6,014	8,480	8,607	8,825	8,699	8,823	8,585	8,065	8,830	9,613
Current Liabilities	2,456	2,902	3,031	3,412	3,411	3,810	2,981	2,578	3,141	3,165
Long Term Debt	1,226	3,917	1,558	484	798	808	643	647	850	836
Common Equity	2,198	3,474	3,713	4,670	4,263	3,950	3,910	3,828	3,843	4,601
Total Capital	3,424	5,446	5,496	5,340	5,218	4,935	5,500	5,329	5,570	6,241
Capital Expenditures	117	160	170	132	133	133	183	164	148	242
Cash Flow	-1,135	380	414	476	486	577	451	397	462	29.0
Current Ratio	1.0	1.1	1.1	1.1	1.1	1.0	1.2	1.2	1.3	1.4
% Long Term Debt of Capitalization	35.8	33.5	28.3	9.1	15.3	16.4	11.7	12.1	15.3	13.4
% Net Income of Revenue	NM	1.6	1.7	2.1	2.0	2.6	2.0	1.2	1.6	NM
% Return on Assets	NM	3.4	3.8	4.5	4.5	5.8	4.6	2.9	3.6	NM
% Return on Equity	NM	8.0	7.9	8.9	9.7	12.9	9.9	6.4	7.8	NM

Data as orig reptd.; bef. results of disc opers/spec. items. Per share data adj. for stk. divs.; EPS diluted. E-Estimated. NA-Not Available. NM-Not Meaningful. NR-Not Ranked. UR-Under Review.

Office: 110 SE 6th St, Ft. Lauderdale, FL 33301-5012.
Telephone: 954-769-7000.
Website: http://www.autonation.com
Chrmn & CEO: M.J. Jackson

Pres & COO: M.E. Maroone
EVP & CFO: M. Short
EVP, Secy & General Counsel: J.P. Ferrando
Chief Acctg Officer & Cntlr: M.J. Stephan

Board Members: R. L. Burdick, W. C. Crowley, D. B. Edelson, K. Goodman, R. R. Grusky, M. J. Jackson, M. E. Maroone, C. A. Migoya
Founded: 1991
Domicile: Delaware
Employees: 20,000

AutoZone Inc

STANDARD &POOR'S

S&P Recommendation **BUY** ★★★★☆	Price $150.05 (as of Nov 27, 2009)	12-Mo. Target Price $175.00	Investment Style Large-Cap Growth

GICS Sector Consumer Discretionary
Sub-Industry Automotive Retail

Summary This retailer of automotive parts and accessories operates over 4,000 AutoZone stores throughout most of the U.S. and in Mexico.

Key Stock Statistics (Source S&P, Vickers, company reports)

52-Wk Range	$169.99– 98.67	S&P Oper. EPS 2010**E**	13.04	Market Capitalization(B)	$7.483	Beta	0.51
Trailing 12-Month EPS	$11.74	S&P Oper. EPS 2011**E**	14.12	Yield (%)	Nil	S&P 3-Yr. Proj. EPS CAGR(%)	9
Trailing 12-Month P/E	12.8	P/E on S&P Oper. EPS 2010**E**	11.5	Dividend Rate/Share	Nil	S&P Credit Rating	BBB
$10K Invested 5 Yrs Ago	$17,267	Common Shares Outstg. (M)	49.9	Institutional Ownership (%)	99		

Price Performance

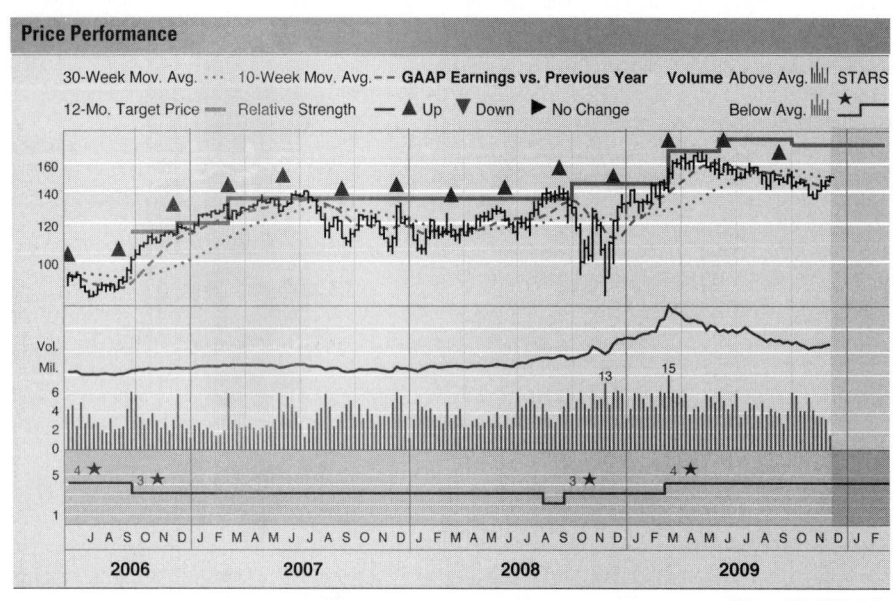

30-Week Mov. Avg. ···· 10-Week Mov. Avg. ‑ ‑ **GAAP Earnings vs. Previous Year** Volume Above Avg. STARS
12-Mo. Target Price — Relative Strength — ▲ Up ▼ Down ► No Change Below Avg.

Options: ASE, CBOE, P, Ph

Analysis prepared by **Michael Souers** on September 25, 2009, when the stock traded at **$ 143.54**.

Highlights

► We see sales growth of 4.5% in FY 10 (Aug.), following a 4.5% advance in FY 09. This reflects our projections of approximately 200 new stores in the U.S. and Mexico, along with same-store sales growth of 2%-3%. While macroeconomic pressures are putting a financial strain on consumers, likely inducing them to delay preventive maintenance on their vehicles, we continue to view industry-specific drivers favorably, including a pick-up in miles driven.

► We look for flat operating margins, as supply chain efficiencies and increased sales of private-label products are offset by a slight deleveraging of fixed costs due to a meager comp-store sales increase, along with an increased proportion of lower-margin commercial sales in the mix.

► After modestly higher interest expense, taxes at an effective rate of 36.6%, and about 8% fewer shares due to AZO's active share repurchase program, we forecast that FY 10 operating EPS will increase 11%, to $13.04, from the $11.73 the company earned in FY 09. We project FY 11 EPS of $14.12.

Investment Rationale/Risk

► AutoZone maintains an industry-leading sales-to-square foot ratio, and sports higher gross, operating and net margins than any of its peers. In addition, we think longer-term trends for the automotive aftermarket retail industry are extremely favorable, with an aging vehicle population and pent-up demand from recent maintenance deferrals. Near term, the year-over-year decline in gasoline prices should help fuel spending on vehicle maintenance somewhat, and AZO's comps in its past three quarters were impressive given the macro challenges, in our view. We expect a continued rational pricing environment to lead to stable gross margins in the near term.

► Risks to our recommendation and target price include a significant decline in consumer spending; a sharp hike in oil prices; a decrease in auto usage and miles driven; and declines in same-store-sales, which would cause expense deleverage.

► Our 12-month target price of $175, based on our DCF analysis, is equal to about 13X our FY 10 EPS estimate. Our DCF model assumes a weighted average cost of capital of 9.4% and a terminal growth rate of 3.0%.

Qualitative Risk Assessment

LOW	MEDIUM	HIGH

Our risk assessment for AutoZone reflects the cyclical and seasonal nature of the auto parts retailing industry, which is sensitive to various economic data points, offset by what we view as the company's strong financial metrics and margins.

Quantitative Evaluations

S&P Quality Ranking B+

D	C	B-	B	B+	A-	A	A+

Relative Strength Rank MODERATE

70

LOWEST = 1   HIGHEST = 99

Revenue/Earnings Data

Revenue (Million $)

	1Q	2Q	3Q	4Q	Year
2009	1,478	1,448	1,658	2,232	6,817
2008	1,456	1,339	1,517	2,211	6,523
2007	1,393	1,300	1,474	2,003	6,170
2006	1,338	1,254	1,417	1,939	5,948
2005	1,286	1,204	1,338	1,882	5,711
2004	1,282	1,159	1,360	1,836	5,637

Earnings Per Share ($)

2009	2.23	2.03	3.13	4.43	11.73
2008	2.02	1.67	2.49	3.88	10.04
2007	1.73	1.45	2.17	3.23	8.53
2006	1.48	1.25	1.89	2.92	7.50
2005	1.52	1.16	1.86	2.66	7.18
2004	1.35	1.04	1.68	2.53	6.56

Fiscal year ended Aug. 31. Next earnings report expected: Early December. EPS Estimates based on S&P Operating Earnings; historical GAAP earnings are as reported.

Dividend Data

No cash dividends have been paid.

Please read the Required Disclosures and Analyst Certification on the last page of this report.

The McGraw-Hill Companies

AutoZone Inc

STANDARD &POOR'S

Business Summary September 25, 2009

CORPORATE OVERVIEW. AutoZone is the nation's leading specialty retailer and a leading distributor of automotive replacement parts and accessories, focusing primarily on do-it-yourself (DIY) consumers. As of August 30, 2008, the company operated 4,092 U.S. AutoZone stores, in 48 states, the District of Columbia and Puerto Rico, and 148 stores in Mexico. AZO also sells automotive diagnostic equipment and repair software through ALLDATA, and diagnostic and repair information, along with and parts and accessories, online at www.autozone.com.

The company's 4,092 U.S. stores represented 26.2 million sq. ft., up from 3,933 stores and 25.1 million sq. ft. a year earlier. Each store's product line includes new and remanufactured automotive hard parts, such as alternators, starters, water pumps, brake shoes and pads, carburetors, clutches and engines; maintenance items, such as oil, antifreeze, transmission, brake and power steering fluids, engine additives, protectants and waxes; and accessories, such as car stereos and floor mats. Parts are carried for domestic and foreign cars, sport utility vehicles, vans, and light trucks.

Stores, generally in high-visibility locations, range in size from about 4,000 sq. ft. to 8,100 sq. ft., with new stores increasingly using a larger format. As of Au-

gust 30, 2008, AutoZone stores were principally in the following locations: 512 stores in Texas, 438 in California, 211 in Ohio, 197 in Illinois, 185 in Florida, 171 in Georgia, 157 in North Carolina, 150 in Tennessee, 140 in Michigan, 131 in Indiana, 116 in Arizona, 114 in New York, 107 in Pennsylvania and 105 in Louisiana, with the rest in other states.

CORPORATE STRATEGY. AZO offers everyday low prices, and attempts to be the price leader in hard parts. Stores generally carry about 21,000 stock-keeping units. In addition to targeting the DIY customer, the company has a commercial sales program in the U.S. (AZ Commercial), which provides commercial credit and delivery of parts and other products to local, regional and national repair garages, dealers and service stations. As of August 30, 2008, 2,236 stores had commercial sales programs. The hub stores provide fast replenishment of key merchandise to support the DIY and commercial sales businesses. AZO does not perform repairs or installations.

Company Financials Fiscal Year Ended Aug. 31

Per Share Data ($)	2009	2008	2007	2006	2005	2004	2003	2002	2001	2000
Tangible Book Value	NM	NM	1.52	2.35	1.15	NM	0.90	3.87	5.13	5.49
Cash Flow	NA	12.70	10.82	9.34	8.92	7.79	6.47	5.10	2.70	2.88
Earnings	11.73	10.04	8.53	7.50	7.18	6.56	5.34	4.00	1.54	2.00
S&P Core Earnings	11.58	9.91	8.53	7.50	7.03	6.40	5.09	3.87	1.45	NA
Dividends	Nil	Nil	Nil	Nil	Nil	Nil	Nil	Nil	Nil	Nil
Payout Ratio	Nil	Nil	Nil	Nil	Nil	Nil	Nil	Nil	Nil	Nil
Prices:High	169.99	143.80	140.29	120.37	103.94	92.35	103.53	89.34	80.00	32.50
Prices:Low	125.80	84.66	103.40	83.81	77.76	70.35	58.21	59.20	24.37	21.00
P/E Ratio:High	14	14	16	16	14	14	19	22	52	16
P/E Ratio:Low	11	8	12	11	11	11	11	15	16	10

Income Statement Analysis (Million $)	2009	2008	2007	2006	2005	2004	2003	2002	2001	2000
Revenue	6,817	6,523	6,170	5,948	5,711	5,637	5,457	5,326	4,818	4,483
Operating Income	NA	1,294	1,215	1,239	1,114	1,106	1,028	889	646	630
Depreciation	180	170	159	139	138	107	110	118	131	118
Interest Expense	NA	121	119	110	104	93.0	84.8	79.9	101	76.8
Pretax Income	1,034	1,007	936	902	873	906	833	691	287	435
Effective Tax Rate	36.4%	36.3%	36.4%	36.9%	34.6%	37.5%	37.9%	38.1%	38.8%	38.5%
Net Income	657	642	596	569	571	566	518	428	176	268
S&P Core Earnings	649	633	596	569	560	553	492	415	165	NA

Balance Sheet & Other Financial Data (Million $)	2009	2008	2007	2006	2005	2004	2003	2002	2001	2000
Cash	92.7	242	86.7	91.6	74.8	76.9	6.74	6.50	7.29	6.97
Current Assets	NA	2,586	2,270	2,119	1,929	1,756	1,585	1,450	1,329	1,187
Total Assets	5,318	5,257	4,805	4,526	4,245	3,913	3,680	3,478	3,433	3,333
Current Liabilities	NA	2,519	2,286	2,055	1,811	1,818	1,676	1,534	1,267	1,035
Long Term Debt	2,727	2,250	1,936	1,857	1,862	1,869	1,547	1,195	1,225	1,250
Common Equity	-433	230	403	470	391	171	374	1,378	866	997
Total Capital	2,294	2,480	2,339	2,327	2,253	2,046	1,921	2,573	2,092	2,247
Capital Expenditures	272	244	224	264	283	185	182	117	169	250
Cash Flow	NA	811	755	709	709	673	627	546	307	386
Current Ratio	1.0	1.0	1.0	1.0	1.1	1.0	0.9	0.9	1.0	1.1
% Long Term Debt of Capitalization	118.9	90.7	82.8	79.8	82.6	91.3	80.5	46.4	58.6	55.6
% Net Income of Revenue	9.6	9.8	9.7	9.6	10.0	10.0	9.5	8.0	3.6	6.0
% Return on Assets	12.4	12.8	12.8	13.0	14.0	14.7	14.5	12.4	5.2	8.1
% Return on Equity	NM	202.8	136.5	132.3	203.1	207.7	97.4	27.5	18.9	23.1

Data as orig reptd.; bef. results of disc opers/spec. items. Per share data adj. for stk. divs.; EPS diluted. E-Estimated. NA-Not Available. NM-Not Meaningful. NR-Not Ranked. UR-Under Review.

Office: 123 South Front Street, Memphis, TN 38103-3607.
Telephone: 901-495-6500.
Email: investor.relations@autozone.com
Website: http://www.autozone.com

Chrmn, Pres & CEO: W.C. Rhodes, III
EVP, CFO & Treas: W.T. Giles
EVP, Secy & General Counsel: H.L. Goldsmith
SVP, Chief Acctg Officer & Cntlr: C. Pleas, III

SVP & CIO: J.A. Bascom
Investor Contact: B. Campbell (901-495-7005)
Board Members: W. C. Crowley, S. E. Gove, E. B. Graves, Jr., R. R. Grusky, J. R. Hyde, III, W. A. McKenna, G. R. Mrkonic, Jr., L. P. Nieto, Jr., W. C. Rhodes, III, T. W. Ullyot

Founded: 1979
Domicile: Nevada
Employees: 60,000

AvalonBay Communities Inc.

STANDARD &POOR'S

S&P Recommendation **SELL** ★ ★ ☆ ☆ ☆	Price $69.12 (as of Nov 27, 2009)	12-Mo. Target Price $60.00	Investment Style Large-Cap Blend

GICS Sector Financials
Sub-Industry Residential REITS

Summary This real estate investment trust, formed via the 1998 merger of Bay Apartment Communities and Avalon Properties, specializes in upscale apartment communities.

Key Stock Statistics (Source S&P, Vickers, company reports)

52-Wk Range	$78.75–38.34	S&P FFO/Sh. 2009E	4.45	Market Capitalization(B)	$5.629	Beta		1.51
Trailing 12-Month FFO/Share	NA	S&P FFO/Sh. 2010E	4.25	Yield (%)	5.16	S&P 3-Yr. FFO/Sh. Proj. CAGR(%)		1
Trailing 12-Month P/FFO	NA	P/FFO on S&P FFO/Sh. 2009E	15.5	Dividend Rate/Share	$3.57	S&P Credit Rating		BBB+
$10K Invested 5 Yrs Ago	$12,185	Common Shares Outstg. (M)	81.4	Institutional Ownership (%)	NM			

Price Performance

30-Week Mov. Avg. ··· 10-Week Mov. Avg. - - **GAAP Earnings vs. Previous Year**   Volume Above Avg. ▮▮▮ STARS
12-Mo. Target Price — Relative Strength — ▲ Up ▼ Down ▶ No Change   Below Avg. ▮▮▮

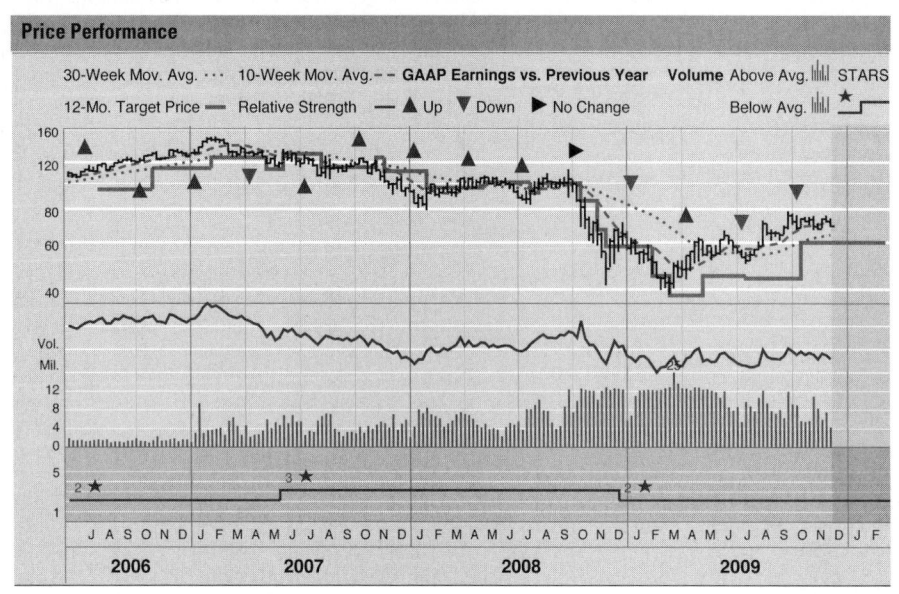

Options: ASE, CBOE, P

Analysis prepared by **Royal F. Shepard, CFA** on November 02, 2009, when the stock traded at **$ 68.29**.

Highlights

▶ We think AVB is experiencing significant pressure on rental rates to attract new leases, particularly due to job losses in west coast markets such as San Francisco and Los Angeles. In order to maintain occupancy close to 96.0%, we believe AVB has lowered rents on new leases close to 10% below those previously in place. In addition, excess housing inventories could push occupancy moderately lower in early 1010.

▶ In our view, demand for apartments could begin to improve with a brighter job outlook in the second half of 2010. Also, the supply of new apartment homes, as measured by multi-family housing starts, has slowed due to recession. As a result, we think AVB may consider revamping new development activities to meet future demand. At present, the trust has 9 communities under construction at a total cost of about $1.2 billion.

▶ Our 2010 FFO per share forecast of $4.25 is down from $4.45 seen in 2009, which excludes non-cash impairment charges of $0.28. We believe cash flow still adequately covers AVB's cash payout, which was maintained at $3.57 a share in 2009.

Investment Rationale/Risk

▶ We believe job losses will keep pressure on earnings from AVB's west coast properties through the first half of 2010. AVB's focus on upscale projects, in our view, may make it more vulnerable to excess inventories of single-family homes for rent. We consider the trust's large pipeline of new development projects to be a positive driver of long-term value, but not until the economic outlook brightens. We view the shares, recently selling 16.5X our 2010 FFO estimate, a 20% premium to peers, as overvalued.

▶ Risks to our recommendation and target price include the potential for faster-than-expected employment growth; decreased competition from unsold inventories of single-family homes; and more liquid credit markets that increase investor demand for real estate assets.

▶ Our 12-month target price of $60 is based on applying a multiple of 14.1X to our 2010 FFO per share estimate of $4.25, a modest premium to apartment REIT peers. Our valuation reflects AVB's relatively strong financial position, offset by its geographic exposure to what we view as price-sensitive markets.

Qualitative Risk Assessment

LOW	MEDIUM	HIGH

Our risk assessment reflects AVB's geographically diverse asset base and strong dividend coverage ratio.

Quantitative Evaluations

S&P Quality Ranking

D	C	B-	B	B+	A-	**A**	A+

A

Relative Strength Rank

42

MODERATE

LOWEST = 1   HIGHEST = 99

Revenue/FFO Data

Revenue (Million $)

	1Q	2Q	3Q	4Q	Year
2009	222.9	222.1	222.2	--	--
2008	204.2	211.2	218.5	220.4	854.2
2007	192.7	199.5	208.2	212.4	812.7
2006	175.2	180.7	187.7	193.8	737.3
2005	161.3	165.6	170.8	173.1	670.7
2004	154.8	160.0	165.2	168.4	648.5

FFO Per Share ($)

2009	1.27	0.90	E1.09	E0.97	E4.45
2008	1.24	1.26	1.28	0.30	4.07
2007	1.11	1.17	1.19	1.14	4.61
2006	1.15	1.03	1.11	1.09	4.38
2005	0.96	0.97	0.91	0.93	3.77
2004	0.79	0.83	0.86	0.88	3.36

Fiscal year ended Dec. 31. Next earnings report expected: Early February. FFO Estimates based on S&P Funds From Operations Est..

Dividend Data (Dates: mm/dd Payment Date: mm/dd/yy)

Amount ($)	Date Decl.	Ex-Div. Date	Stk. of Record	Payment Date
1.8075 Spl.	12/17	12/24	12/29	01/29/09
0.893	02/24	03/30	04/01	04/15/09
0.893	05/21	06/26	06/30	07/15/09
0.893	09/14	09/24	09/28	10/15/09

Dividends have been paid since 1994. Source: Company reports.

Please read the Required Disclosures and Analyst Certification on the last page of this report.

The McGraw·Hill Companies

AvalonBay Communities Inc.

STANDARD
&POOR'S

Business Summary November 02, 2009

CORPORATE OVERVIEW. AvalonBay Communities (AVB) is a real estate investment trust (REIT) specializing in the ownership of multi-family apartment communities. At December 31, 2008, AVB owned or held an interest in 178 apartment communities containing 50,292 apartment homes in 10 states and the District of Columbia, of which 14 communities were under construction and nine communities were under reconstruction. AVB also owned a direct or indirect ownership interest in rights to develop an additional 27 communities; if developed in the manner expected, these would contain an estimated 7,304 apartment homes.

MARKET PROFILE. The housing market is highly fragmented and is broadly characterized by two types of housing units, multi-family and single-family. At the end of 2008, the U.S. Census Bureau estimated that there were 130.84 million housing units in the country, an increase of 1.7% from 2007. Partially on high fragmentation and the fact that residents have the option of either being owners or tenants (renters), the housing market can be highly competitive. Main demand drivers for apartments are household formation and employment growth. We estimate that 0.7 million new households were formed in 2008. Supply is created by new housing unit construction, which could consist

of single-family homes, or multi-family apartment buildings or condominiums. The U.S. Department of Housing estimates that 900,000 housing units were started in 2008, down about 33% from 2007. Multi-family starts, for structures with more than five units, dropped significantly less, falling approximately 4.5%.

With apartment tenants on relatively short leases compared to those of commercial and industrial properties, we believe apartment REITs are generally more sensitive to changes in market conditions than REITs in other property categories. Results could be hurt by new construction that adds new space in excess of actual demand. Trends in home price affordability also affect both rent levels and the level of new construction, since the relative price attractiveness of owning versus renting is an important factor in consumer decision making.

Company Financials Fiscal Year Ended Dec. 31

Per Share Data ($)	2008	2007	2006	2005	2004	2003	2002	2001	2000	1999
Tangible Book Value	37.82	37.85	NA	NA	NA	NA	31.88	NA	29.31	36.04
Earnings	1.34	3.00	2.27	1.34	1.09	1.30	1.48	3.12	2.53	2.00
S&P Core Earnings	1.34	3.00	2.12	1.34	1.09	1.27	1.22	3.07	NA	NA
Dividends	5.38	3.33	NA	NA	NA	NA	NA	2.56	2.24	2.05
Payout Ratio	401%	111%	137%	NM	NM	NM	188%	82%	89%	102%
Prices:High	113.07	149.94	134.60	92.99	75.93	49.71	52.65	51.90	50.63	37.00
Prices:Low	41.43	88.94	88.95	64.98	46.72	35.24	36.38	42.45	32.63	30.81
P/E Ratio:High	84	50	59	69	65	38	35	17	20	18
P/E Ratio:Low	31	30	39	48	40	27	24	14	13	15

Income Statement Analysis (Million $)

	2008	2007	2006	2005	2004	2003	2002	2001	2000	1999
Rental Income	848	807	731	666	648	Nil	Nil	637	572	503
Mortgage Income	Nil	Nil	Nil	Nil	Nil	Nil	Nil	Nil	Nil	Nil
Total Income	854	813	737	671	648	610	639	642	573	505
General Expenses	436	346	236	376	368	192	247	229	203	186
Interest Expense	115	97.5	111	127	131	135	121	103	83.6	74.7
Provision for Losses	Nil	Nil	Nil	Nil	Nil	Nil	Nil	Nil	Nil	Nil
Depreciation	194	180	163	159	152	151	144	130	123	110
Net Income	114	248	180	108	86.3	100	121	249	211	172
S&P Core Earnings	104	239	159	98.9	76.7	87.6	85.7	213	NA	NA

Balance Sheet & Other Financial Data (Million $)

	2008	2007	2006	2005	2004	2003	2002	2001	2000	1999
Cash	259	210	146	48.0	4,921	4,744	4,813	4,479	4,286	4,068
Total Assets	7,173	6,736	5,813	5,165	5,068	4,910	4,952	4,664	4,397	4,155
Real Estate Investment	5,297	5,038	5,662	5,874	NA	5,431	5,369	4,838	4,875	4,259
Loss Reserve	Nil	Nil	Nil	Nil	NA	Nil	Nil	Nil	Nil	Nil
Net Investment	6,650	6,297	4,562	4,946	4,919	4,736	4,800	4,391	4,212	4,052
Short Term Debt	310	514	Nil	Nil	Nil	Nil	165	101	14.1	3.60
Capitalization:Debt	3,365	2,694	2,705	2,177	2,335	2,337	2,307	1,983	1,716	1,411
Capitalization:Equity	2,916	3,027	2,631	2,542	2,385	2,311	2,194	2,314	2,442	2,370
Capitalization:Total	6,290	5,534	5,194	4,738	4,741	2,336	4,579	4,353	4,208	3,817
% Earnings & Depreciation/Assets	8.7	6.8	6.2	5.2	NA	5.1	5.5	8.4	7.8	6.8
Price Times Book Value:High	3.0	4.0	4.0	2.8	NA	1.5	1.7	1.6	1.7	1.0
Price Times Book Value:Low	1.1	2.3	2.7	2.0	NA	1.1	1.1	1.3	1.1	0.9

Data as orig reptd.; bef. results of disc opers/spec. items. Per share data adj. for stk. divs.; EPS diluted. E-Estimated. NA-Not Available. NM-Not Meaningful. NR-Not Ranked. UR-Under Review.

Office: 2900 Eisenhower Avenue, Alexandria, VA 22314.
Telephone: 703-329-6300.
Email: investments@avalonbay.com
Website: http://www.avalonbay.com

Chrmn & CEO: B. Blair
Pres: T.J. Naughton
COO: L.S. Horey
EVP & CFO: T.J. Sargeant

SVP, Secy & General Counsel: E.M. Schulman
Board Members: B. Blair, B. A. Choate, J. J. Healy, Jr., G. M. Meyer, T. J. Naughton, L. R. Primis, P. S. Rummell, H. J. Sarles, W. E. Walter

Founded: 1978
Domicile: Maryland
Employees: 1,830

The McGraw·Hill Companies

Avery Dennison Corp

STANDARD &POOR'S

S&P Recommendation `HOLD` ★★★☆☆

Price	$37.69 (as of Nov 27, 2009)
12-Mo. Target Price	$40.00
Investment Style	Large-Cap Blend

GICS Sector Industrials
Sub-Industry Office Services & Supplies

Summary This company is a leading worldwide manufacturer of pressure-sensitive adhesives and materials, office products, labels, retail systems and specialty chemicals.

Key Stock Statistics (Source S&P, Vickers, company reports)

52-Wk Range	$40.14–17.02	S&P Oper. EPS 2009**E**	2.00	Market Capitalization(B)	$4.249	Beta	1.38
Trailing 12-Month EPS	$-7.40	S&P Oper. EPS 2010**E**	2.30	Yield (%)	2.12	S&P 3-Yr. Proj. EPS CAGR(%)	10
Trailing 12-Month P/E	NM	P/E on S&P Oper. EPS 2009**E**	18.8	Dividend Rate/Share	$0.80	S&P Credit Rating	BBB
$10K Invested 5 Yrs Ago	$7,621	Common Shares Outstg. (M)	112.7	Institutional Ownership (%)	89		

Price Performance

30-Week Mov. Avg. · · · 10-Week Mov. Avg. – – **GAAP Earnings vs. Previous Year** Volume Above Avg. STARS
12-Mo. Target Price — Relative Strength — ▲ Up ▼ Down ▶ No Change Below Avg. ★

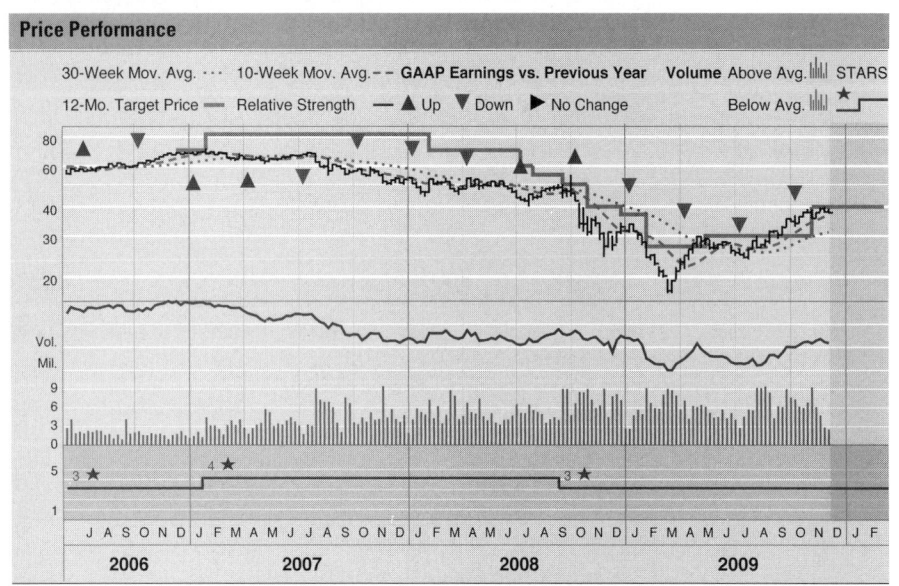

Options: CBOE, P, Ph

Analysis prepared by **Richard O'Reilly, CFA** on November 03, 2009, when the stock traded at **$ 36.07**.

Highlights

▶ After a 14% decline in organic sales in the first half of 2009, we expect smaller declines in the second half. We project a sales recovery of about 10% in 2010, assuming better consumer staple and retail apparel markets and favorable currency rates.

▶ The economically sensitive graphics and specialty tapes and films product lines would likely recovery on a healthier durable goods sector. Margins in 2010 should be helped by the better volumes and additional cost reductions, especially in retail information, although raw material costs will likely trend higher through early 2010. We project $85 million of additional restructuring savings in 2010 on top of the $115 million in 2009. AVY had realized by early 2009 almost all of the projected $120 million of annual merger cost savings from the acquisition of Paxar in 2007.

▶ For 2010, we expect higher pension expense and a higher effective tax rate of about 22%, versus 14% projected for 2009. Our EPS estimate for 2009 excludes restructuring and goodwill charges (including $9.33 in the first nine months.)

Investment Rationale/Risk

▶ The organic sales decline of 6% in the third quarter of 2009 was smaller than we had expected, and we project modest improvement for the rest of 2009. We were surprised that AVY reduced its dividend by 51% in July 2009, citing a focus on reducing debt along with increased future pension requirements. We believe long-term fundamentals remain sound, with growth driven by the increasing use of non-impact printing systems for computers and for product tracking and information needs. We see a proliferation of high-quality graphics spurring sales of pressure-sensitive labels.

▶ Risks to our recommendation and target price include the potentially adverse impact of remaining antitrust investigations and related civil suits involving AVY, and an inability to introduce new products or raise selling prices in response to changes in raw material costs.

▶ Our 12-month target price is $40. We value AVY shares using a P/E of about 17X our 2010 EPS projection, higher than the stock's historical premium to the S&P 500, reflecting what we view as a cyclical recovery in earnings. We believe that AVY will be able to maintain its reduced dividend.

Qualitative Risk Assessment

LOW	**MEDIUM**	HIGH

Our risk assessment reflects the company's leading market shares in pressure-sensitive adhesives and office products, and our view of above-average growth rates in key end markets and relatively strong cash flow, offset by current sluggish markets.

Quantitative Evaluations

S&P Quality Ranking B+

D	C	B-	B	**B+**	A-	A	A+

Relative Strength Rank STRONG

76

LOWEST = 1   HIGHEST = 99

Revenue/Earnings Data

Revenue (Million $)

	1Q	2Q	3Q	4Q	Year
2009	1,426	1,455	1,549	--	--
2008	1,645	1,829	1,725	1,512	6,710
2007	1,390	1,524	1,680	1,714	6,308
2006	1,337	1,410	1,418	1,411	5,576
2005	1,346	1,419	1,363	1,364	5,474
2004	1,247	1,324	1,336	1,434	5,341

Earnings Per Share ($)

2009	-8.99	0.38	0.59	E0.53	E2.00
2008	0.69	0.93	0.63	0.43	2.70
2007	0.80	0.87	0.59	0.81	3.07
2006	0.69	0.96	0.85	1.01	3.51
2005	0.58	0.89	0.86	0.57	2.90
2004	0.52	0.68	0.75	0.83	2.78

Fiscal year ended Dec. 31. Next earnings report expected: Late January. EPS Estimates based on S&P Operating Earnings; historical GAAP earnings are as reported.

Dividend Data (Dates: mm/dd Payment Date: mm/dd/yy)

Amount ($)	Date Decl.	Ex-Div. Date	Stk. of Record	Payment Date
0.410	01/22	03/02	03/04	03/18/09
0.410	04/23	06/01	06/03	06/17/09
0.200	07/30	08/31	09/02	09/16/09
0.200	10/22	11/30	12/02	12/16/09

Dividends have been paid since 1964. Source: Company reports.

Please read the Required Disclosures and Analyst Certification on the last page of this report.

The McGraw-Hill Companies

Avery Dennison Corp

STANDARD
&POOR'S

Business Summary November 03, 2009

CORPORATE OVERVIEW. Avery Dennison is the leading global manufacturer of pressure-sensitive technology and self-adhesive solutions for consumer products and label systems, including office products, product identification and control systems, and specialty tapes and chemicals.

Foreign operations accounted for 67% of sales in 2008.

The pressure-sensitive materials group (54% of sales and 61% of operating profits in 2008) includes Fasson- and JAC-brand pressure sensitive, self-adhesive coated papers, plastic films, metal foils, and fabrics in roll and sheet form; graphic and reflective decoration films and labels; and adhesives, protective coatings and electroconductive resins for industrial, automotive, aerospace, appliance, electronic, medical and consumer markets.

The office and consumer products group (14% and 35%) consists of consumer and office products such as pressure-sensitive labels; copier, laser and ink-jet printer labels and template software; presentation and organizing products (binders, sheet protectors, dividers); writing instruments and marking devices; security badge systems; and other products sold under the Avery, Marks-A-Lot, and Hi-Liter brands for office, home, and school uses.

Retail information services (23% and 2%) sell a variety of price marking and brand identification products for retailers, apparel manufacturers, distributors and industrial customers. Products include woven and printed labels; heat transfers; graphic and barcode tags; patches; integrated tags; price tickets; customer hard and soft good packaging; barcode printers; software; plastics fastening; and applications devices for use in identification, tracking and control applications.

Other businesses (9% and 2%) consists of specialty fastening, bonding and sealing tapes sold in roll form; industrial and automotive labels, decoration films and graphics sold primarily to original equipment manufacturers; self-adhesive postal stamps and on-battery testing labels; and the radio frequency identification (RFID) business (inlays and labels). The RFID business had a net loss of about $30 million in each of 2005 and 2006, but the loss declined in both 2007 and 2008 and we expected a further reduction in 2009.

Company Financials Fiscal Year Ended Dec. 31

Per Share Data ($)	2008	2007	2006	2005	2004	2003	2002	2001	2000	1999
Tangible Book Value	NM	NM	8.84	6.74	5.85	4.08	2.53	4.70	3.94	3.66
Cash Flow	5.10	5.13	5.50	4.95	4.66	4.22	4.12	4.05	4.41	3.61
Earnings	2.70	3.07	3.51	2.90	2.78	2.43	2.59	2.47	2.84	2.13
S&P Core Earnings	2.20	2.98	3.48	2.66	2.51	2.05	2.02	1.81	NA	NA
Dividends	1.65	1.61	1.57	1.53	1.49	1.45	1.35	1.23	1.11	0.99
Payout Ratio	61%	52%	45%	53%	54%	60%	52%	50%	39%	46%
Prices:High	55.00	71.35	69.31	63.58	66.60	63.75	69.70	60.50	78.50	73.00
Prices:Low	24.30	49.69	54.95	49.60	53.50	46.25	52.06	43.25	41.13	39.38
P/E Ratio:High	20	23	20	22	24	26	27	24	28	34
P/E Ratio:Low	9	16	16	17	19	19	20	18	14	18

Income Statement Analysis (Million $)										
Revenue	6,710	6,308	5,576	5,474	5,341	4,763	4,207	3,803	3,894	3,768
Operating Income	684	787	683	690	655	602	593	566	638	589
Depreciation	237	204	199	202	188	179	153	156	157	150
Interest Expense	122	111	55.5	57.9	58.5	57.7	43.7	50.2	54.6	43.4
Pretax Income	271	375	426	367	373	335	365	360	426	330
Effective Tax Rate	1.66%	19.1%	17.2%	20.4%	25.1%	27.5%	29.5%	32.4%	33.5%	34.8%
Net Income	266	304	353	292	280	243	257	243	284	215
S&P Core Earnings	217	294	348	269	251	205	201	179	NA	NA

Balance Sheet & Other Financial Data (Million $)										
Cash	106	71.5	58.5	98.5	84.8	29.5	22.8	19.1	11.4	6.90
Current Assets	1,930	2,058	1,655	1,558	1,542	1,441	1,216	982	982	956
Total Assets	6,036	6,245	4,294	4,204	4,399	4,105	3,652	2,819	2,699	2,593
Current Liabilities	2,058	2,478	1,699	1,526	1,387	1,496	1,296	951	801	850
Long Term Debt	1,545	1,145	502	723	1,007	888	837	627	773	701
Common Equity	1,750	1,989	1,681	1,512	1,549	1,319	1,056	929	828	810
Total Capital	3,295	3,376	2,261	2,235	2,647	2,274	1,968	1,647	1,695	1,610
Capital Expenditures	129	191	162	163	179	201	152	135	198	178
Cash Flow	504	508	552	493	468	422	410	399	440	366
Current Ratio	0.9	0.8	1.0	1.0	1.1	1.0	0.9	1.0	1.2	1.1
% Long Term Debt of Capitalization	46.9	33.9	22.2	32.4	38.1	39.0	42.5	38.0	45.6	43.5
% Net Income of Revenue	4.0	4.8	6.3	5.3	5.2	5.1	6.1	6.4	7.3	5.7
% Return on Assets	4.3	5.8	8.3	6.8	6.6	6.3	7.8	8.8	10.7	9.1
% Return on Equity	14.2	16.5	22.1	19.1	19.5	20.4	25.9	27.7	34.6	26.2

Data as orig reptd.; bef. results of disc opers/spec. items. Per share data adj. for stk. divs.; EPS diluted. E-Estimated. NA-Not Available. NM-Not Meaningful. NR-Not Ranked. UR-Under Review.

Office: 150 North Orange Grove Boulevard, Pasadena, CA 91103.
Telephone: 626-304-2000.
Email: investorcom@averydennison.com
Website: http://www.averydennison.com

Chrmn: K. Kresa
Pres & CEO: D.A. Scarborough
EVP & CFO: D.R. O'Bryant
SVP & Secy: S.C. Miller

SVP & CIO: R.W. Hoffman
Investor Contact: E.M. Leeds (626-304-2029)
Board Members: P. K. Barker, R. Borjesson, J. T. Cardis, R. M. Ferry, K. C. Hicks, K. Kresa, P. W. Mullin, D. E. Pyott, D. L. Reed, D. A. Scarborough, P. T. Siewert, J. A. Stewart

Founded: 1935
Domicile: Delaware
Employees: 35,700

Avon Products Inc.

STANDARD
&POOR'S

S&P Recommendation HOLD ★★★☆☆	Price $34.69 (as of Nov 27, 2009)	12-Mo. Target Price $37.00	Investment Style Large-Cap Growth

GICS Sector Consumer Staples
Sub-Industry Personal Products

Summary This company is the world's leading direct marketer of cosmetics, toiletries, fashion jewelry, and fragrances, with more than 5 million sales representatives worldwide.

Key Stock Statistics (Source S&P, Vickers, company reports)

52-Wk Range	$36.36– 14.40	S&P Oper. EPS 2009E	1.69	Market Capitalization(B)	$14.815	Beta	1.43
Trailing 12-Month EPS	$1.38	S&P Oper. EPS 2010E	2.07	Yield (%)	2.42	S&P 3-Yr. Proj. EPS CAGR(%)	7
Trailing 12-Month P/E	25.1	P/E on S&P Oper. EPS 2009E	20.5	Dividend Rate/Share	$0.84	S&P Credit Rating	NR
$10K Invested 5 Yrs Ago	$10,112	Common Shares Outstg. (M)	427.1	Institutional Ownership (%)	90		

Price Performance

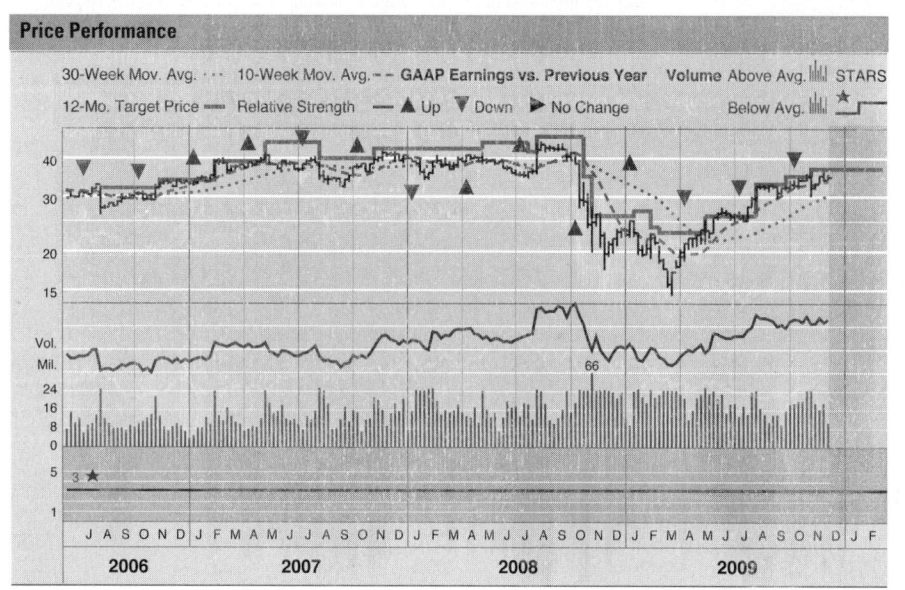

Options: ASE, CBOE, P, Ph

Analysis prepared by **Loran Braverman, CFA** on November 02, 2009, when the stock traded at **$ 32.05**.

Highlights

▶ In late 2005, AVP announced a multi-year restructuring plan in an effort to drive revenue and profit growth. Year-to-year sales comparisons started to pick up in mid-2006, but softened late in 2008's third quarter due to deteriorating economies in a number of major markets. However, significant cost savings were seen in 2008, and we expect more in 2009 and 2010.

▶ The foreign currency effect turned negative in the December 2008 quarter at -11% and continued negative through the September 2009 quarter. This impact plus weak consumer spending in the U.S. and many other major markets is the basis for our 4% sales decline forecast for 2009. However, our 2010 sales growth forecast is 7%, with foreign currency expected to have a positive effect.

▶ The operating margin improved about 270 basis points in 2008 (excluding restructuring and other charges in both years). We see a narrowing in 2009 as weak reported sales and foreign currency translation and foreign currency transaction effects offset productivity improvements. Our 2009 EPS estimate is $1.69, down from 2008's operating EPS of $2.04, with both periods excluding restructuring charges. For 2010, we see a partial recovery to $2.07.

Investment Rationale/Risk

▶ AVP's various restructuring and rationalization plans, including one announced in February, entail reorganizing and downsizing the organization, implementing global manufacturing, and increasing supply chain efficiencies. AVP plans to reinvest the savings from these plans in marketing and R&D, and incentivizing its sales force. However, the benefits in 2009 will likely be masked by foreign exchange issues and the difficult economic conditions in both developed and developing markets. Thus, we would not add to positions.

▶ Risks to our recommendation and target price include renewed weakness in the U.S. market, political and economic instability in international markets, competition from various sales channels, significant changes in foreign exchange rates, and unfavorable consumer reception of new products.

▶ Our 12-month target price of $37 is a blend of our historical and relative analyses. Our historical analysis applies a multiple of 18.9X, a discount to the 10-year historical average, to our 2010 EPS estimate, implying a value of $39. Our peer analysis applies a P/E multiple of 16.6X, close to the peer average, for a value of $34.

Qualitative Risk Assessment

LOW	MEDIUM	HIGH

Our risk assessment reflects that demand for personal care products is usually static and not generally affected by changes in the economy or geopolitical factors. However, certain product categories such as fragrances may be more susceptible to the aforementioned factors.

Quantitative Evaluations

S&P Quality Ranking   A

D	C	B-	B	B+	A-	A	A+

Relative Strength Rank   STRONG

75

LOWEST = 1   HIGHEST = 99

Revenue/Earnings Data

Revenue (Million $)

	1Q	2Q	3Q	4Q	Year
2009	2,180	2,470	2,551	--	--
2008	2,502	2,736	2,645	2,808	10,690
2007	2,185	2,329	2,349	3,076	9,939
2006	2,003	2,080	2,059	2,623	8,764
2005	1,881	1,984	1,886	2,398	8,150
2004	1,765	1,866	1,806	2,311	7,748

Earnings Per Share ($)

	1Q	2Q	3Q	4Q	Year
2009	0.27	0.19	0.36	E0.65	E1.69
2008	0.43	0.55	0.52	0.54	2.04
2007	0.34	0.26	0.32	0.30	1.22
2006	0.12	0.34	0.19	0.41	1.06
2005	0.36	0.69	0.35	0.40	1.81
2004	0.31	0.49	0.37	0.61	1.77

Fiscal year ended Dec. 31. Next earnings report expected: Early February. EPS Estimates based on S&P Operating Earnings; historical GAAP earnings are as reported.

Dividend Data (Dates: mm/dd Payment Date: mm/dd/yy)

Amount ($)	Date Decl.	Ex-Div. Date	Stk. of Record	Payment Date
0.210	02/03	02/12	02/17	03/02/09
0.210	05/07	05/19	05/21	06/01/09
0.210	08/03	08/13	08/17	09/01/09
0.210	11/04	11/18	11/20	12/01/09

Dividends have been paid since 1919. Source: Company reports.

Please read the Required Disclosures and Analyst Certification on the last page of this report.

Avon Products Inc.

STANDARD
&POOR'S

Business Summary November 02, 2009

CORPORATE OVERVIEW. Avon Products, which began operations in 1886, is a global manufacturer and marketer of beauty and related products. Beginning in the fourth quarter of 2008, AVP changed its product categories from Beauty, Beauty Plus and Beyond Beauty to Beauty, Fashion and Home & Other. Beauty consists of cosmetics, fragrances, skin care and toiletries and accounted for 71% of sales in 2008. Fashion (18%) consists of fashion jewelry, watches, apparel, footwear, and accessories. Home & Other (11%) consists of gift and decorative products, housewares, entertainment & leisure, kids and nutrition. The company has operations in 66 countries and territories, including the U.S., and its products are distributed in 44 more, for coverage in 110 markets. Geographically, 23% of 2008 sales were derived from North America, while Latin America accounted for 37%, Western Europe, the Middle East & Africa 13%, Central & Eastern Europe 16%, Asia-Pacific 8%, and China 3%. Operations outside North America accounted for 86% of operating profits in 2008. Sales are made to the ultimate customer mainly through a combination of direct selling and marketing by about 5.8 million independent Avon representatives, around 457,000 of whom are in the U.S.

For 2008, the number of active representatives rose, year to year, 2% in North America, 6% in Latin America, 4% in Western Europe, Middle East & Africa, 12% in Central & Eastern Europe, 4% in Asia-Pacific, 79% in China (from a very low base) and 7% overall.

CORPORATE STRATEGY. AVP embarked on a multi-year restructuring plan in November 2005 in an effort to drive revenue and profit growth. The plan entails reorganizing and downsizing the organization, implementing global manufacturing, and increasing supply chain efficiencies. AVP expects restructuring benefits to help fund an increase in consumer research, marketing, and product development, which, in turn, is expected to enhance sales and ultimately profits. In fact, we saw an improvement in the quarterly year-to-year sales growth rate starting in mid-2006, but savings from the plan were not large enough to offset increases in the expenses mentioned above until 2008. Also in 2005, Avon started to implement a global supply chain strategy, which includes the development of a new common systems platform, known as enterprise resource planning (ERP).

In February 2009, AVP announced a new restructuring program, with implementation expected to start in the second half of 2009 and full implementation by 2012 to 2013.

Company Financials Fiscal Year Ended Dec. 31

Per Share Data ($)	2008	2007	2006	2005	2004	2003	2002	2001	2000	1999
Tangible Book Value	0.76	1.66	1.79	1.68	2.02	0.79	NM	NM	NM	NM
Cash Flow	2.41	1.55	1.42	2.10	2.05	1.63	1.34	1.10	1.20	0.74
Earnings	2.04	1.22	1.06	1.81	1.77	1.39	1.11	0.90	1.01	0.58
S&P Core Earnings	1.94	1.25	1.16	1.80	1.80	1.37	0.95	0.77	NA	NA
Dividends	0.80	0.74	0.70	0.66	0.70	0.42	0.40	0.38	0.37	0.36
Payout Ratio	39%	61%	66%	36%	40%	30%	36%	42%	37%	62%
Prices:High	45.34	42.51	34.25	45.66	46.65	34.88	28.55	25.06	24.88	29.56
Prices:Low	17.45	31.95	26.16	24.33	30.81	24.47	21.75	17.78	12.63	11.66
P/E Ratio:High	22	35	32	25	26	25	26	28	25	51
P/E Ratio:Low	9	26	25	13	17	18	20	20	12	20

Income Statement Analysis (Million $)										
Revenue	10,690	9,939	8,764	8,150	7,748	6,876	6,228	5,995	5,715	5,289
Operating Income	1,558	1,176	1,146	1,289	1,361	1,162	1,029	951	886	762
Depreciation	158	145	160	140	135	124	125	109	97.1	83.0
Interest Expense	105	125	99.6	54.1	33.8	33.3	52.0	71.1	84.7	43.2
Pretax Income	1,238	796	704	1,124	1,188	994	836	666	691	507
Effective Tax Rate	29.3%	33.0%	31.8%	24.0%	27.8%	32.1%	35.0%	34.7%	29.2%	40.3%
Net Income	875	531	478	848	846	665	535	430	485	302
S&P Core Earnings	833	549	518	845	859	652	455	367	NA	NA

Balance Sheet & Other Financial Data (Million $)										
Cash	1,105	963	1,199	1,059	770	694	607	509	123	117
Current Assets	3,557	3,515	3,334	2,921	2,506	2,226	2,048	1,889	1,546	1,338
Total Assets	6,074	5,716	5,238	4,763	4,148	3,562	3,328	3,193	2,826	2,529
Current Liabilities	2,912	3,053	2,550	2,502	1,526	1,588	1,976	1,461	1,359	1,713
Long Term Debt	1,456	1,168	1,171	766	866	878	767	1,236	1,108	701
Common Equity	675	712	790	794	950	371	-128	-74.6	-216	-406
Total Capital	2,205	2,089	2,028	1,595	1,829	1,300	712	1,192	954	365
Capital Expenditures	381	279	175	207	250	163	127	155	194	203
Cash Flow	1,034	676	637	987	981	788	659	539	582	385
Current Ratio	1.2	1.2	1.3	1.2	1.6	1.4	1.0	1.3	1.1	0.8
% Long Term Debt of Capitalization	66.1	62.1	58.8	48.1	47.4	67.5	107.8	103.7	116.1	192.3
% Net Income of Revenue	8.2	5.3	5.4	10.4	10.9	9.7	8.6	7.2	8.5	5.7
% Return on Assets	14.9	9.7	9.6	19.0	21.9	19.3	16.4	14.3	18.1	12.2
% Return on Equity	126.3	70.7	60.3	97.2	128.0	545.8	NM	NM	NM	NM

Data as orig reptd.; bef. results of disc opers/spec. items. Per share data adj. for stk. divs.; EPS diluted. E-Estimated. NA-Not Available. NM-Not Meaningful. NR-Not Ranked. UR-Under Review.

Office: 1345 Avenue Of The Americas, New York, NY 10105-0196.
Telephone: 212-282-5000.
Email: individual.investor@avon.com
Website: http://www.avoninvestor.com

Chrmn & CEO: A. Jung
COO: A. Slater
SVP, Secy & General Counsel: K.K. Rucker
SVP & CIO: D. Herlihy

CFO: C.W. Cramb
Investor Contact: R. Johansen (212-282-5320)
Board Members: W. D. Cornwell, E. T. Fogarty, V. A. Hailey, F. Hassan, A. Jung, M. E. Lagomasino, A. S. Moore, P. S. Pressler, G. M. Rodkin, P. Stern, L. A. Weinbach

Founded: 1886
Domicile: New York
Employees: 42,000

The McGraw-Hill Companies

STANDARD &POOR'S

Baker Hughes Inc

S&P Recommendation	Price	12-Mo. Target Price	Investment Style
HOLD ★★★★★	$40.36 (as of Nov 27, 2009)	$47.00	Large-Cap Growth

GICS Sector Energy
Sub-Industry Oil & Gas Equipment & Services

Summary This company is one of the world's largest oilfield services companies, providing products and services to the energy industry.

Key Stock Statistics (Source S&P, Vickers, company reports)

52-Wk Range	**$48.19–24.40**	S&P Oper. EPS 2009**E**	**1.69**	Market Capitalization(B)	**$12.507**	Beta	**1.57**
Trailing 12-Month EPS	**$2.48**	S&P Oper. EPS 2010**E**	**2.15**	Yield (%)	**1.49**	S&P 3-Yr. Proj. EPS CAGR(%)	**-23**
Trailing 12-Month P/E	**16.3**	P/E on S&P Oper. EPS 2009**E**	**23.9**	Dividend Rate/Share	**$0.60**	S&P Credit Rating	**A**
$10K Invested 5 Yrs Ago	**$9,462**	Common Shares Outstg. (M)	**309.9**	Institutional Ownership (%)	**87**		

Price Performance

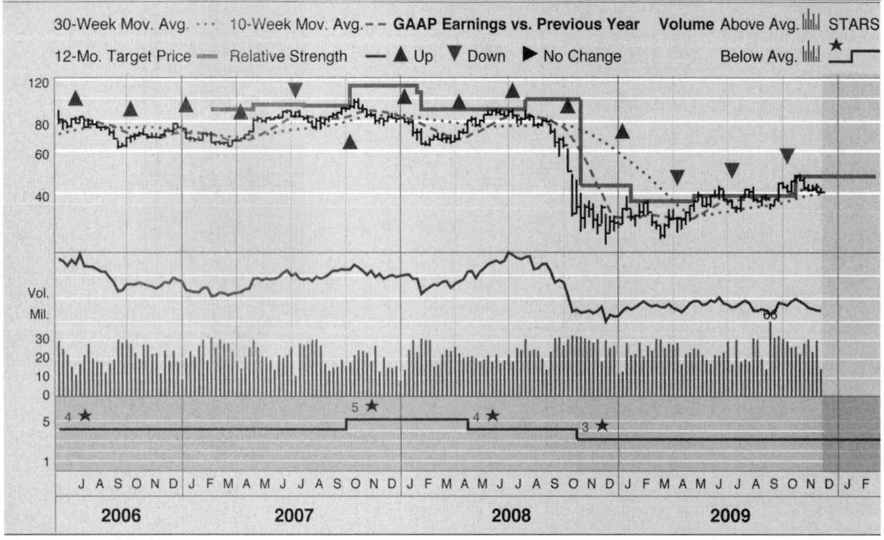

30-Week Mov. Avg. 10-Week Mov. Avg. GAAP Earnings vs. Previous Year Volume Above Avg. STARS
12-Mo. Target Price Relative Strength ▲ Up ▼ Down ▶ No Change Below Avg.
120
80
60
40
Vol.
Mil.
30
20
10
0
5
1
4★
5★
4★
3★
J A S O N D J F M A M J J A S O N D J F M A M J J A S O N D J F M A M J J A S O N D J F
2006
2007
2008
2009

Options: ASE, CBOE, P, Ph

Analysis prepared by **Stewart Glickman, CFA** on October 14, 2009, when the stock traded at **$ 46.21**.

Highlights

- On August 31, BHI announced an agreement to acquire BJ Services (BJS 21, hold) in a deal valued at $5.5 billion, a 16% premium to the BJS closing price on August 28. Subject to approvals, we like the deal for BHI, as it would provide a significant presence in the pressure pumping market, which we think may hold strategic value for BHI in terms of winning overseas projects. While we believe 16% is a low premium for obtaining control of another company, we think it reflects the relatively weak near-term expectations for pressure pumping demand, given persistent weakness in natural gas prices.

- Longer term, we see strong growth opportunities outside of North America and view this as a primary potential catalyst for BHI. With oil prices remaining fairly resilient as we enter the 2010 budgeting season for upstream operators, we expect capital spending growth in 2010, in contrast to the pullback in 2009, which should augur well for BHI's expansion plans.

- We see revenues dropping 24% in 2009, and EPS of $1.69, down 69% from 2008. For 2010, we see revenues 5% lower, but on higher expected margins, project EPS rebounding to $2.15.

Investment Rationale/Risk

- Looking out to 2010, we think BHI's growth prospects are improving. The uptick in oil prices should help build overseas enthusiasm by upstream customers, and we also note a modestly improving U.S. rig count (albeit mainly on the strength of oil-directed activity). We expect BHI to undertake a more aggressive push into international markets, and, should the BJS merger be approved, would view BHI as better positioned to win potential integrated project management tenders.

- Risks to our recommendation and target price include lower energy prices; reduced drilling activity in international markets; slower-than-planned infrastructure build; higher-than-expected cost inflation; and delays in completing the planned BJS acquisition.

- Our discounted cash flow model, which assumes terminal growth of 3%, and a WACC of 11.7%, shows intrinsic value of about $35. Using multiples of 10.5X projected 2010 EBITDA and 11.5X estimated 2010 cash flows (about in line with peers), and blending these results with our DCF model, our 12-month target price is $47.

Qualitative Risk Assessment

LOW | **MEDIUM** | HIGH

Our risk assessment reflects BHI's exposure to volatile crude oil and natural gas prices, capital spending decisions by its exploration and production customers, and political risk associated with operating in frontier regions. Offsetting these risks is BHI's strong position in drilling and completion products.

Quantitative Evaluations

S&P Quality Ranking **B+**

D | C | B- | B | **B+** | A- | A | A+

Relative Strength Rank **MODERATE**

34

LOWEST = 1 HIGHEST = 99

Revenue/Earnings Data

Revenue (Million $)

	1Q	2Q	3Q	4Q	Year
2009	2,668	2,336	2,232	--	--
2008	2,670	2,998	3,010	3,186	11,864
2007	2,473	2,538	2,678	2,740	10,428
2006	2,062	2,203	2,309	2,453	9,027
2005	1,643	1,768	1,785	1,989	7,186
2004	1,388	1,499	1,538	1,679	6,104

Earnings Per Share ($)

2009	0.63	0.28	0.18	**E**0.40	**E**1.69
2008	1.27	1.23	1.39	1.41	5.30
2007	1.17	1.09	1.22	1.26	4.73
2006	0.93	4.14	1.09	1.02	7.21
2005	0.53	0.64	0.64	0.76	2.56
2004	0.28	0.35	0.41	0.53	1.57

Fiscal year ended Dec. 31. Next earnings report expected: Late January. EPS Estimates based on S&P Operating Earnings; historical GAAP earnings are as reported.

Dividend Data (Dates: mm/dd Payment Date: mm/dd/yy)

Amount ($)	Date Decl.	Ex-Div. Date	Stk. of Record	Payment Date
0.150	01/22	01/29	02/02	02/13/09
0.150	04/23	04/30	05/04	05/15/09
0.150	07/23	07/30	08/03	08/14/09
0.150	10/22	10/29	11/02	11/13/09

Dividends have been paid since 1987. Source: Company reports.

Redistribution or reproduction is prohibited without written permission. Copyright ©2009 The McGraw-Hill Companies, Inc.

The McGraw-Hill Companies

Baker Hughes Inc

STANDARD
&POOR'S

Business Summary October 14, 2009

CORPORATE OVERVIEW. Baker Hughes was formed through the 1987 merger of Baker International Corp. and Hughes Tool Co. In 1998, it acquired seismic and wireline logging company Western Atlas, creating the third largest oilfield services company. BHI has operations in over 90 countries. North America accounted for 43% of total revenues in 2008, followed by the Europe, CIS and Africa region (28%) and the Middle East and Asia-Pacific region (18%). In 2005, the company reorganized its seven product-line focused divisions into three operating segments: Drilling & Evaluation; Completion & Production; and Western Geco (which provides reservoir imaging, monitoring and development services). In April 2006, however, BHI sold its 30% minority stake in seismic company Western Geco to the majority joint venture partner, Schlumberger. We like the deal for BHI, as we think it should enable BHI to focus on its core oilfield operations of drilling, completion and production.

The Drilling & Evaluation segment (51% of 2008 total oilfield revenues and 52% of total oilfield segment income) consists of four operating divisions: Baker Hughes Drilling Fluids, Hughes Christensen, INTEQ, and Baker Atlas. The products and services in this segment are typically used in the drilling of crude oil and natural gas wells.

Baker Hughes Drilling Fluids provides drilling and completion fluids, and fluid

environmental services. Fluids are used in order to control downhole pressure, clean the bottom of the well, and to cool and lubricate the drill bit and drill string. Hughes Christensen manufactures drill bit products, primarily Tricone roller cone drill bits and polycrystalline diamond compact (PDC) fixed cutter bits. INTEQ supplies directional and horizontal drilling services, coring services, subsurface surveying, logging-while-drilling, and measurement-while-drilling services.

Baker Atlas provides formation evaluation and perforating services for oil and natural gas wells. Formation evaluation involves measuring and analyzing specific physical properties of the rock in the vicinity of the wellbore to determine a reservoir's boundaries, hydrocarbon volume, and ability to produce fluids to the surface. Perforating services involve puncturing a well's steel casing and cement sheath with explosive charges; this creates a fracture in the formation, and provides a path for the hydrocarbons in the formation to enter the wellbore.

Company Financials Fiscal Year Ended Dec. 31

Per Share Data ($)	2008	2007	2006	2005	2004	2003	2002	2001	2000	1999
Tangible Book Value	16.89	15.14	11.58	9.42	7.35	5.87	6.05	5.69	4.64	4.17
Cash Flow	7.35	6.36	8.85	3.68	2.69	1.59	1.56	2.32	2.14	2.52
Earnings	5.30	4.73	7.21	2.56	1.57	0.40	0.66	1.31	0.31	0.16
S&P Core Earnings	5.33	4.70	4.24	2.47	1.50	0.62	0.55	1.17	NA	NA
Dividends	0.56	0.52	0.52	0.48	0.46	0.46	0.46	0.46	0.46	0.46
Payout Ratio	11%	11%	7%	19%	29%	115%	70%	35%	148%	NM
Prices:High	90.81	100.29	89.30	63.13	45.30	36.15	39.95	45.29	43.38	36.25
Prices:Low	24.40	62.26	60.60	40.73	31.56	26.90	22.60	25.76	19.63	15.00
P/E Ratio:High	17	21	12	25	29	90	61	35	NM	NM
P/E Ratio:Low	5	13	8	16	20	67	34	20	NM	NM

Income Statement Analysis (Million $)										
Revenue	11,864	10,428	9,027	7,186	6,104	5,293	5,020	5,382	5,234	4,547
Operating Income	3,075	2,799	2,417	1,616	1,195	957	856	1,077	1,076	992
Depreciation, Depletion and Amortization	637	521	434	382	374	349	302	345	612	778
Interest Expense	89.0	66.1	68.9	72.3	83.6	103	111	126	173	159
Pretax Income	2,319	2,257	3,737	1,279	780	328	380	662	236	85.0
Effective Tax Rate	29.5%	32.9%	35.8%	31.6%	32.3%	45.1%	41.2%	33.7%	56.7%	37.6%
Net Income	1,635	1,514	2,399	874	528	180	224	439	102	53.0
S&P Core Earnings	1,645	1,504	1,393	842	506	209	186	393	NA	NA

Balance Sheet & Other Financial Data (Million $)										
Cash	1,955	1,054	750	697	319	98.4	144	45.4	34.6	18.0
Current Assets	7,145	5,456	4,968	3,840	2,967	2,524	2,556	2,697	2,487	2,330
Total Assets	11,861	9,857	8,706	7,807	6,821	6,302	6,401	6,676	6,453	7,040
Current Liabilities	2,511	1,618	1,622	1,361	1,236	1,302	1,080	1,212	988	1,000
Long Term Debt	1,775	1,069	1,074	1,078	1,086	1,133	1,424	1,682	2,050	2,706
Common Equity	6,807	6,306	5,243	4,698	3,895	3,350	3,397	3,328	3,047	3,072
Total Capital	8,966	7,791	6,617	6,004	5,214	4,611	4,988	5,221	5,255	5,813
Capital Expenditures	1,303	1,127	922	478	348	405	317	319	599	634
Cash Flow	2,272	2,035	2,832	1,257	902	529	525	783	714	831
Current Ratio	2.9	3.4	3.1	2.8	2.4	1.9	2.4	2.2	2.5	2.3
% Long Term Debt of Capitalization	19.8	13.7	16.2	18.0	20.8	24.6	28.6	32.2	39.0	46.6
% Return on Assets	15.1	16.3	29.1	12.0	8.0	2.8	3.4	6.7	1.5	0.7
% Return on Equity	24.9	26.2	48.3	20.4	14.6	5.3	6.7	13.8	3.3	1.7

Data as orig reptd.; bef. results of disc opers/spec. items. Per share data adj. for stk. divs.; EPS diluted. E-Estimated. NA-Not Available. NM-Not Meaningful. NR-Not Ranked. UR-Under Review.

Office: 2929 Allen Pkwy Ste 2100, Houston, TX 77019-2118.
Telephone: 713-439-8600.
Website: http://www.bakerhughes.com
Chrmn, Pres & CEO: C.C. Deaton

COO & SVP: M. Craighead
SVP & CFO: P.A. Ragauss
SVP & General Counsel: A.R. Crain, Jr.
CTO: D. Mathieson

Board Members: L. D. Brady, II, C. P. Cazalot, Jr., C. C. Deaton, E. P. Djerejian, A. G. Fernandes, C. W. Gargalli, P. Jungels, I, J. A. Lash, J. L. Nichols, H. J. Riley, Jr., C. L. Watson

Founded: 1972
Domicile: Delaware
Employees: 39,800

Ball Corp

STANDARD &POOR'S

S&P Recommendation BUY ★★★★☆	**Price** $49.85 (as of Nov 27, 2009)	**12-Mo. Target Price** $57.00	**Investment Style** Large-Cap Blend

GICS Sector Materials
Sub-Industry Metal & Glass Containers

Summary Ball, one of the largest producers of metal beverage cans in the world, derives about 10% of its revenues from sales of hi-tech equipment to the aerospace industry.

Key Stock Statistics (Source S&P, Vickers, company reports)

52-Wk Range	$52.46–32.05	S&P Oper. EPS 2009E	4.05	Market Capitalization(B)	$4.691	Beta	0.66
Trailing 12-Month EPS	$3.59	S&P Oper. EPS 2010E	4.45	Yield (%)	0.80	S&P 3-Yr. Proj. EPS CAGR(%)	8
Trailing 12-Month P/E	13.9	P/E on S&P Oper. EPS 2009E	12.3	Dividend Rate/Share	$0.40	S&P Credit Rating	BB+
$10K Invested 5 Yrs Ago	$11,932	Common Shares Outstg. (M)	94.1	Institutional Ownership (%)	79		

Price Performance

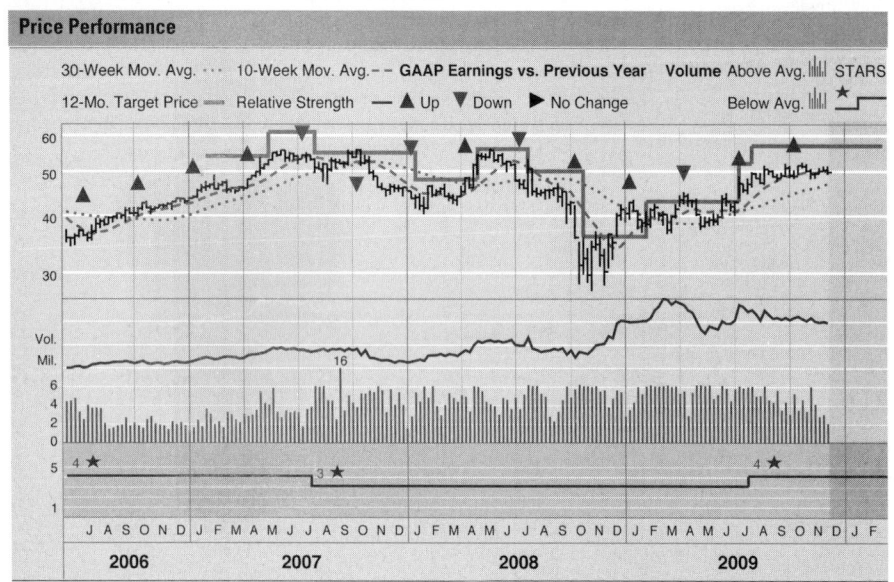

- 30-Week Mov. Avg. ···· 10-Week Mov. Avg. - - GAAP Earnings vs. Previous Year Volume Above Avg. STARS
- 12-Mo. Target Price — Relative Strength — ▲ Up ▼ Down ► No Change Below Avg. ★

Options: ASE, CBOE, P, Ph

Analysis prepared by **Stewart Scharf** on November 09, 2009, when the stock traded at **$ 50.86**.

Highlights

► We project a low single digit sales decline for 2009, primarily reflecting weak global demand for plastic and metal beverage containers. We expect sales growth to return in 2010 as market conditions improve in North America, Europe and Asia. In our view, strength will continue in the Metal Food & Household Packaging segment, while demand picks up for specialty plastic packaging for food and beverages.

► In our view, gross margins (before D&A) will near 18% in 2009, versus 16.1% in 2008, with further expansion likely in 2010, reflecting pricing and supply chain initiatives, a better mix and the elimination of higher-priced metal in inventories. We look for EBITDA margins to widen further in 2010 (we project over 13% in 2009), based on improved productivity via plant closings and synergies from plant acquisitions. Interest expense should decline due to lower rates and debt levels.

► We project a lower effective tax rate of 30% for 2009, and estimate operating EPS of $4.05 (before at net charges), advancing to $4.45 in 2010.

Investment Rationale/Risk

► Our Buy opinion is based on our valuation metrics, as well as our view of improving trends for beverage cans, a better cost structure and strong cash generation. We expect BLL to keep capacity in line with demand based on still challenging global economic conditions.

► Risks to our recommendation and target price include negative exchange rate fluctuations; a decline in sales of imported beer and, to some extent, domestic soft drinks; cost pressures in Europe and China; supply disruptions due to strikes at facilities; integration problems; and a sharp rebound in raw material costs.

► The stock's recent P/E of 11X our 2010 EPS estimate was at a modest discount to BLL's closest peers, and 25% below our projected P/E for the S&P 500 Index. Based on our relative metrics, including below-peer price-to-sales and PEG (P/E-to-growth) ratios, we value the stock at $54. Our DCF model, which assumes a 3% perpetual growth rate and a WACC of 7%, derives an intrinsic value of $60. Blending these valuations, our 12-month target price is $57.

Qualitative Risk Assessment

LOW	**MEDIUM**	HIGH

Our risk assessment reflects the seasonality inherent in the beverage can business, our view of BLL's high debt levels, our corporate governance concerns related to board and audit issues, and volatile raw material prices. These factors are offset by our expectations of lower interest expense due to debt refinancing and redemptions.

Quantitative Evaluations

S&P Quality Ranking B+

D	C	B-	B	**B+**	A-	A	A+

Relative Strength Rank MODERATE

50

LOWEST = 1 HIGHEST = 99

Revenue/Earnings Data

Revenue (Million $)

	1Q	2Q	3Q	4Q	Year
2009	1,586	1,926	1,969	--	--
2008	1,740	2,080	2,008	1,733	7,562
2007	1,694	2,033	1,992	1,756	7,475
2006	1,365	1,843	1,822	1,592	6,622
2005	1,324	1,552	1,584	1,291	5,751
2004	1,232	1,467	1,479	1,263	5,440

Earnings Per Share ($)

2009	0.73	1.40	1.09	E0.72	E4.05
2008	0.85	1.02	1.05	0.36	3.29
2007	0.78	1.03	0.59	0.33	2.74
2006	0.43	1.23	1.02	0.46	3.14
2005	0.51	0.71	0.73	0.42	2.38
2004	0.41	0.80	0.90	0.50	2.60

Fiscal year ended Dec. 31. Next earnings report expected: Late January. EPS Estimates based on S&P Operating Earnings; historical GAAP earnings are as reported.

Dividend Data (Dates: mm/dd Payment Date: mm/dd/yy)

Amount ($)	Date Decl.	Ex-Div. Date	Stk. of Record	Payment Date
0.100	01/28	02/26	03/02	03/16/09
0.100	04/22	05/28	06/01	06/15/09
0.100	07/22	08/28	09/01	09/15/09
0.100	10/28	11/27	12/01	12/14/09

Dividends have been paid since 1958. Source: Company reports.

Ball Corp

STANDARD &POOR'S

Business Summary November 09, 2009

CORPORATE OVERVIEW. Ball Corp. primarily manufactures rigid packaging products for beverages and foods. Two beverage companies account for a substantial part of its packaging sales: SABMiller plc and PepsiCo. BLL is comprised of five segments: Metal Beverage Packaging (Americas/Asia); Metal Beverage Packaging (Europe); Metal Food & Household Packaging (Americas); Plastic Packaging (Americas); and Aerospace and Technologies. The Aerospace and Technologies segment provides products and services to the defense and commercial markets, with U.S. government agencies accounting for 91% of the segment's sales in 2008. In the first quarter of 2008, BLL's China operations were merged into the metal beverage packaging (Americas) segments due to management reporting changes. BLL produced more than 30 billion recyclable beverage cans in the U.S. and Canada in 2008, about 30% of the total market. Aluminum and steel beverage cans accounted for 65% of the company's net sales and 75% of EBIT in 2008.

The company's packaging products include aluminum and steel two-piece beverage cans, and two- and three-piece steel food cans. Metal Beverage Packaging (Americas) segment net sales represented 40% of the total in 2008 ($284 million of pretax earnings); Metal Beverage Packaging (Europe/Asia) 25% ($231 million); Metal Food and Household Packaging (Americas) 16% ($68 million); Plastic Packaging (Americas) 9.7% ($8.3 million loss); and Aerospace and Technologies 10% ($76 million). BLL entered the plastics business in 1995, when it began to make polyethylene terephthalate (PET) bottles. Sales vol-

umes of metal food containers in North America tend to be highest from June through October due to seasonal vegetable and salmon packs. BLL believes this accounts for more than 30% of all North American metal beverage can shipments. In 2008, no customer accounted for more than 10% of sales; in 2007, sales to SABMiller plc and PepsiCo. accounted for 11% and 9% of net sales, respectively.

In the third quarter of 2009, BLL incurred a $0.06 per share charge for costs related to the purchase of four metal beverage can plants, and a $0.09 charge related to closing two plastic plants. In the second quarter of 2009, BLL recorded a $0.32 a share gain on the sale of its stake in DigitGlobe, and a $0.12 charge mainly for closing two plastic packaging plants and costs related to its pending acquisition of AB InBev's plants. In 2008, BLL incurred pretax charges of $0.38 a share for business consolidations and plant closures, including its aluminum beverage can manufacturing plant in Kent, WA. In the first quarter of 2008, it recorded a $0.05 a share gain on the sale of an aerospace engineering services business in Australia. In the fourth quarter of 2007, BLL recorded a $0.27 a share charge related to plant closures and equipment relocations.

Company Financials Fiscal Year Ended Dec. 31

Per Share Data ($)	2008	2007	2006	2005	2004	2003	2002	2001	2000	1999
Tangible Book Value	NM	NM	NM	NM	NM	NM	NM	1.27	1.81	1.27
Cash Flow	6.36	5.47	5.55	4.30	4.49	3.81	2.68	0.44	1.81	2.03
Earnings	3.29	2.74	3.14	2.38	2.60	2.01	1.38	-0.93	0.54	0.79
S&P Core Earnings	2.78	3.31	2.30	2.54	2.67	2.12	1.10	-0.88	NA	NA
Dividends	0.40	0.40	0.40	0.40	0.35	0.24	0.18	0.15	0.15	0.15
Payout Ratio	12%	15%	13%	17%	13%	12%	13%	NM	28%	19%
Prices:High	56.20	56.05	45.00	46.45	45.20	29.88	27.25	18.03	11.98	14.78
Prices:Low	27.37	43.51	34.16	35.06	28.26	21.15	16.30	9.52	6.50	8.84
P/E Ratio:High	17	20	14	20	17	15	20	NM	22	19
P/E Ratio:Low	8	16	11	15	11	11	12	NM	12	11

Income Statement Analysis (Million $)	2008	2007	2006	2005	2004	2003	2002	2001	2000	1999
Revenue	7,562	7,475	6,622	5,751	5,440	4,977	3,859	3,686	3,665	3,584
Operating Income	926	914	729	697	739	663	458	127	445	442
Depreciation	297	281	253	214	215	206	149	153	159	163
Interest Expense	145	156	134	116	104	126	75.6	88.3	95.2	108
Pretax Income	467	377	462	362	436	331	245	-110	110	171
Effective Tax Rate	31.5%	25.4%	28.5%	27.5%	31.9%	30.2%	34.3%	NM	38.9%	38.0%
Net Income	320	281	330	262	296	230	159	-99.2	68.2	104
S&P Core Earnings	270	340	242	280	304	242	127	-96.0	NA	NA

Balance Sheet & Other Financial Data (Million $)	2008	2007	2006	2005	2004	2003	2002	2001	2000	1999
Cash	127	152	152	61.0	199	36.5	259	83.1	25.6	35.8
Current Assets	2,165	1,843	1,761	1,226	1,246	924	1,225	794	969	896
Total Assets	6,369	6,021	5,841	4,343	4,478	4,070	4,132	2,314	2,650	2,732
Current Liabilities	1,862	1,513	1,454	1,176	996	861	1,069	575	659	670
Long Term Debt	2,107	2,182	2,270	1,473	1,538	1,579	1,854	949	1,012	1,093
Common Equity	1,086	1,343	1,165	835	1,087	808	493	504	640	635
Total Capital	3,342	3,525	3,437	2,314	2,631	2,393	2,353	1,463	1,709	1,803
Capital Expenditures	307	309	280	292	196	137	158	68.5	98.7	107
Cash Flow	617	562	582	475	511	435	309	51.3	225	264
Current Ratio	1.2	1.2	1.2	1.0	1.3	1.1	1.1	1.4	1.5	1.3
% Long Term Debt of Capitalization	63.0	61.9	66.1	63.7	58.5	66.0	78.8	64.9	59.2	60.6
% Net Income of Revenue	4.2	3.8	5.0	4.5	5.4	4.6	4.1	NM	1.9	2.9
% Return on Assets	5.2	4.7	6.5	5.9	6.9	5.6	4.9	NM	2.5	3.7
% Return on Equity	26.3	22.4	32.7	27.2	31.2	35.4	32.0	NM	10.1	16.9

Data as orig reptd.; bef. results of disc opers/spec. items. Per share data adj. for stk. divs.; EPS diluted. E-Estimated. NA-Not Available. NM-Not Meaningful. NR-Not Ranked. UR-Under Review.

Office: 10 Longs Peak Dr, Broomfield, CO 80021-2510.
Telephone: 303-469-3131.
Website: http://www.ball.com
Chrmn, Pres & CEO: R.D. Hoover

COO & EVP: J.A. Hayes
EVP, CFO & Chief Acctg Officer: R.J. Seabrook
EVP & Secy: D.A. Westerlund
Treas: S.C. Morrison

Investor Contact: A.T. Scott (303-460-3537)
Board Members: R. W. Alspaugh, H. C. Fiedler, R. D. Hoover, J. F. Lehman, G. R. Nelson, J. Nicholson, G. M. Smart, T. M. Solso, S. A. Taylor, II, E. H. Van Der Kaay

Founded: 1880
Domicile: Indiana
Employees: 14,500

The McGraw-Hill Companies

Bank of America Corp

STANDARD &POOR'S

S&P Recommendation	STRONG BUY ★★★★★	Price $15.47 (as of Nov 27, 2009)	12-Mo. Target Price $22.00	Investment Style Large-Cap Blend

GICS Sector Financials
Sub-Industry Other Diversified Financial Services

Summary This banking company, with offices in 32 states and the District of Columbia, also provides international corporate financial services.

Key Stock Statistics (Source S&P, Vickers, company reports)

52-Wk Range	$19.10–2.53	S&P Oper. EPS 2009E	0.42	Market Capitalization(B)	$133.827	Beta	2.42
Trailing 12-Month EPS	$0.09	S&P Oper. EPS 2010E	0.15	Yield (%)	0.26	S&P 3-Yr. Proj. EPS CAGR(%)	29
Trailing 12-Month P/E	NM	P/E on S&P Oper. EPS 2009E	36.8	Dividend Rate/Share	$0.04	S&P Credit Rating	A
$10K Invested 5 Yrs Ago	$4,163	Common Shares Outstg. (M)	8,650.8	Institutional Ownership (%)	65		

Price Performance

30-Week Mov. Avg. · · · 10-Week Mov. Avg. - - - **GAAP Earnings vs. Previous Year** Volume Above Avg. STARS
12-Mo. Target Price — Relative Strength — ▲ Up ▼ Down ► No Change Below Avg.

Options: ASE, CBOE, P, Ph

Analysis prepared by **Stuart Plesser** on October 19, 2009, when the stock traded at **$ 17.29**.

Qualitative Risk Assessment

LOW	MEDIUM	HIGH

Our risk assessment reflects deteriorating U.S. consumer trends, exposure to residential lending and credit cards, and a lower than historical tangible capital ratio, offset by what we see as a strong U.S. presence with a robust customer base.

Quantitative Evaluations

S&P Quality Ranking   B+

D	C	B-	B	B+	A-	A	A+

Relative Strength Rank   MODERATE

34

LOWEST = 1   HIGHEST = 99

Revenue/Earnings Data

Revenue (Million $)

	1Q	2Q	3Q	4Q	Year
2009	45,417	40,736	33,135	--	--
2008	28,871	29,721	30,175	24,176	113,106
2007	30,447	32,409	29,347	26,987	119,190
2006	27,026	28,895	30,739	30,357	117,017
2005	19,168	21,222	21,621	22,280	83,980
2004	12,282	16,471	16,409	18,162	63,324

Earnings Per Share ($)

2009	0.44	0.33	-0.26	E-0.09	E0.42
2008	0.23	0.72	0.15	-0.48	0.55
2007	1.16	1.28	0.82	0.05	3.30
2006	1.07	1.19	1.18	1.16	4.59
2005	1.07	1.17	0.95	0.88	4.04
2004	0.92	0.93	0.91	0.94	3.69

Fiscal year ended Dec. 31. Next earnings report expected: Mid January. EPS Estimates based on S&P Operating Earnings; historical GAAP earnings are as reported.

Highlights

► We forecast relatively flat revenue growth in 2010, largely due to the absence of asset sales in the first half of 2009. Assuming BAC puts to work some of the roughly $150 billion parked in short-term securities, we look for net interest margin to increase to roughly 2.70% in 2010, from a projected 2.65% in 2009. We expect continued growth in noninterest income, reflecting a high level of mortgage banking income, higher underwriting fees and strong trading revenue. BAC's average earning assets will likely decrease in the low single digits, as loan growth will likely continue to slow due to a weakened economy.

► We don't view possible additional losses from distressed securities as significant in 2010, as exposure has been reduced. Based on unemployment soon leveling off, we look for charge-offs to peak in the second quarter of 2010 and for provisions to decline in the second half of the year. We think expenses will remain under tight control.

► We estimate EPS of $0.42 in 2009. Including a reserve build to move $125 billion of assets onto BAC's balance sheet, we look for EPS of $0.15 in 2010.

Investment Rationale/Risk

► With a Tier 1 ratio of 12.46%, well above peers, we think capital levels are adequate. We think BAC will soon use some of its excess capital to pay back a portion of TARP funds, which should act as a catalyst for the stock. The Merrill Lynch acquisition is already adding to BAC's bottom line and should continue to do so. Chargeoffs are apt to remain high, particularly in commercial loans. We look favorably on a deceleration of sequential chargeoffs and nonperforming loans in the third quarter. Ultimate chargeoff levels will likely hinge on unemployment rates and success of loan modifications. We think BAC has enough capital to withstand an adverse downturn in these metrics.

► Risks to our recommendation and target price include worse-than-expected credit conditions, greater-than-expected securities writedowns, and more onerous regulations.

► Our 12-month target price of $22 equates to about 1.8X current tangible book value, a discount to historical levels that we think is warranted by uncertainty regarding loan default rates.

Dividend Data (Dates: mm/dd Payment Date: mm/dd/yy)

Amount ($)	Date Decl.	Ex-Div. Date	Stk. of Record	Payment Date
0.010	01/16	03/04	03/06	03/27/09
0.010	04/29	06/03	06/05	06/26/09
0.010	07/21	09/02	09/04	09/25/09
0.010	10/28	12/02	12/04	12/24/09

Dividends have been paid since 1903. Source: Company reports.

Please read the Required Disclosures and Analyst Certification on the last page of this report.

The McGraw·Hill Companies

Bank of America Corp

STANDARD &POOR'S

Business Summary October 19, 2009

CORPORATE OVERVIEW. Bank of America has operations in 32 states, the District of Columbia and 44 foreign countries. In the U.S., it has more than 6,100 retail banking centers and approximately 18,500 ATMs. BAC reports the results of its operations through three business segments: Global Consumer and Small Business Banking, Global Corporate and Investment Banking, and Global Wealth and Investment Management.

Global Consumer and Small Business Banking has about 59 million consumer and mass-market small business relationships and provides a diversified range of products and services to individuals and small businesses through multiple delivery channels. Global Corporate and Investment Banking provides comprehensive financial solutions. Services include: bank deposit and credit products; risk management, cash management and payment services; equity and debt capital raising; and advisory services. Global Wealth and Investment Management offers comprehensive banking and investment services to more than three million individual and institutional customers. Clients have access to services from three primary businesses: U.S. Trust, Bank of America Private Wealth Management; Columbia Management; and Premier Banking & Investments. Services include investment services, estate management, finan-

cial planning services, fiduciary management, credit and banking expertise, and diversified asset management products to institutional clients as well as high-net-worth individuals.

IMPACT OF MAJOR DEVELOPMENTS. On September 15, 2008, BAC agreed to acquire Merrill Lynch & Co., Inc. in a $50 billion all-stock transaction. The deal ultimately closed at a $29 billion purchase price due to the decline in BAC's stock. We think the deal is a good fit for BAC, particularly as it added 20,000 financial advisers and created cross-selling opportunities, but integration will likely be difficult.

On July 1, 2008, BAC acquired Countrywide Financial in a stock deal valued at $2.5 billion. Although the acquisition makes BAC a top U.S. mortgage originator, we believe it increases BAC's risk profile due to Countrywide's loan portfolio, which has a high proportion of Option Arm loans.

Company Financials Fiscal Year Ended Dec. 31

Per Share Data ($)	2008	2007	2006	2005	2004	2003	2002	2001	2000	1999
Tangible Book Value	7.14	11.54	12.18	13.18	12.41	12.34	12.59	11.65	10.66	9.06
Earnings	0.55	3.30	4.59	4.04	3.69	3.57	2.96	2.09	2.26	2.24
S&P Core Earnings	0.35	3.26	4.47	4.06	3.75	3.54	2.70	1.96	NA	NA
Dividends	2.24	2.40	2.12	1.90	1.70	1.44	1.22	1.14	1.03	0.93
Payout Ratio	407%	73%	46%	47%	46%	40%	41%	55%	46%	41%
Prices:High	45.08	54.21	55.08	47.44	47.47	42.45	38.54	32.77	30.50	38.19
Prices:Low	10.01	40.61	40.93	41.13	38.51	32.13	26.98	22.50	18.16	23.81
P/E Ratio:High	82	16	12	12	13	12	13	16	13	17
P/E Ratio:Low	18	12	9	10	10	9	9	11	8	11

Income Statement Analysis (Million $)

	2008	2007	2006	2005	2004	2003	2002	2001	2000	1999
Net Interest Income	45,360	34,433	34,591	30,737	28,797	21,464	20,923	20,290	18,442	18,237
Tax Equivalent Adjustment	1,194	1,749	1,224	832	716	643	588	343	322	215
Non Interest Income	27,422	31,706	38,432	26,438	20,097	16,422	13,571	14,348	14,489	14,069
Loan Loss Provision	26,825	8,385	5,010	4,014	2,769	2,839	3,697	4,287	2,535	182
% Expense/Operating Revenue	57.1%	56.0%	47.9%	50.4%	54.5%	52.2%	63.1%	59.8%	63.7%	56.9%
Pretax Income	4,428	20,924	31,973	24,480	21,221	15,861	12,991	10,117	11,788	12,215
Effective Tax Rate	9.48%	28.4%	33.9%	32.7%	33.4%	31.8%	28.8%	32.9%	36.2%	35.5%
Net Income	4,008	14,982	21,133	16,465	14,143	10,810	9,249	6,792	7,517	7,882
% Net Interest Margin	2.98	2.60	2.82	2.84	3.26	3.36	3.75	3.68	3.22	3.47
S&P Core Earnings	1,656	14,615	20,568	16,499	14,308	10,708	8,452	6,384	NA	NA

Balance Sheet & Other Financial Data (Million $)

	2008	2007	2006	2005	2004	2003	2002	2001	2000	1999
Money Market Assets	251,570	303,389	302,482	294,292	197,308	153,090	115,687	81,384	76,544	81,226
Investment Securities	277,589	214,056	192,846	221,603	195,073	68,240	69,148	85,499	65,838	83,069
Commercial Loans	342,767	325,143	240,785	218,334	193,930	131,304	145,170	163,898	203,542	195,779
Other Loans	588,679	551,201	465,705	355,457	327,907	240,159	197,585	165,255	188,651	174,883
Total Assets	1,817,943	1,715,746	1,459,737	1,291,803	1,110,457	736,445	660,458	621,764	642,191	632,574
Demand Deposits	277,998	192,227	184,808	186,736	169,899	121,530	124,359	113,934	100,645	95,469
Time Deposits	664,999	612,950	508,689	447,934	448,671	292,583	262,099	259,561	263,599	251,804
Long Term Debt	268,292	197,508	146,000	100,848	98,078	75,343	67,176	68,026	72,502	60,441
Common Equity	139,351	142,394	132,421	101,262	99,374	47,926	50,261	48,455	47,556	44,355
% Return on Assets	0.2	0.9	1.5	1.4	1.5	1.5	1.4	1.1	1.2	1.3
% Return on Equity	2.9	10.8	18.1	16.3	19.2	22.0	18.7	14.1	16.3	17.5
% Loan Loss Reserve	2.5	1.3	0.4	1.4	1.7	1.7	2.0	2.1	1.7	1.8
% Loans/Deposits	105.5	105.5	304.3	87.4	84.4	89.7	88.4	97.8	107.7	106.7
% Equity to Assets	8.0	8.7	8.5	8.4	8.0	7.0	7.7	7.6	7.2	7.2

Data as orig reptd.; bef. results of disc opers/spec. items. Per share data adj. for stk. divs.; EPS diluted. E-Estimated. NA-Not Available. NM-Not Meaningful. NR-Not Ranked. UR-Under Review.

Office: 100 N Tryon St, Charlotte, NC 28255.
Telephone: 704-386-8486.
Website: http://www.bankofamerica.com
Chrmn: W.E. Massey

Pres & CEO: K.D. Lewis
CFO: J.L. Price
Chief Admin Officer: J.S. Alphin
CTO: M. Alexander

Investor Contact: K. Stitt (704-386-5667)
Board Members: S. S. Bies, W. P. Boardman, F. P. Bramble, V. W. Colbert, C. K. Gifford, C. O. Holliday, Jr., D. P. Jones, K. D. Lewis, M. Lozano, W. E. Massey, T. J. May, D. E. Powell, C. O. Rossotti, T. M. Ryan, R. W. Scully, A. Spence

Founded: 1874
Domicile: Delaware
Employees: 302,000

Bank of New York Mellon Corp (The)

STANDARD &POOR'S

S&P Recommendation	BUY ★★★★☆	Price $26.30 (as of Nov 27, 2009)	12-Mo. Target Price $33.00	Investment Style Large-Cap Blend

GICS Sector Financials
Sub-Industry Asset Management & Custody Banks

Summary This company is a leader in securities processing, and also provides a complete range of banking, asset management and other financial services.

Key Stock Statistics (Source S&P, Vickers, company reports)

52-Wk Range	$33.62– 15.44	S&P Oper. EPS 2009E	-1.03	Market Capitalization(B)	$31.672	Beta	0.71
Trailing 12-Month EPS	$-1.65	S&P Oper. EPS 2010E	2.49	Yield (%)	1.37	S&P 3-Yr. Proj. EPS CAGR(%)	27
Trailing 12-Month P/E	NM	P/E on S&P Oper. EPS 2009E	NM	Dividend Rate/Share	$0.36	S&P Credit Rating	AA-
$10K Invested 5 Yrs Ago	$8,522	Common Shares Outstg. (M)	1,204.2	Institutional Ownership (%)	80		

Price Performance

30-Week Mov. Avg. · · · · 10-Week Mov. Avg. - - GAAP Earnings vs. Previous Year Volume Above Avg. STARS
12-Mo. Target Price — Relative Strength — ▲ Up ▼ Down ► No Change   Below Avg.

0.9434-for

Options: ASE, CBOE, P, Ph

Analysis prepared by **Stuart Plesser** on October 23, 2009, when the stock traded at **$ 29.31**.

Highlights

► Excluding realized securities losses, we expect total revenues for 2010 to increase 5.5% from projected 2009 levels of $12.9 billion, reflecting a wider net interest margin and higher fees. Our assumptions include a rate hike sometime in 2010 which should help improve the net interest margin. We forecast a net interest margin of roughly 1.88%. Fees from the asset management business should also be higher due to continued strength in the equity and fixed income markets. We see BK continuing to control non-merger-related expense growth. We expect much of the benefits of scale from the merger with Mellon Financial to help growth in international operations, which recently accounted for roughly 35% of revenue.

► We expect new business wins to continue as clients will likely seek more help from custody banks due to staff cuts. We see continued expense discipline and expansion through smaller acquisitions and international alliances. Impairment charges on BK's investments should be minimal in upcoming quarters as BK has taken losses on most of its troubled securities.

► We forecast an operating loss of $1.03 per share in 2009. In 2010, we look for EPS of $2.49.

Investment Rationale/Risk

► We believe BK has taken the right steps to become a major global player in custody banking and corporate trust. We see the net interest margin widening as 2010 progresses as BK will likely become more aggressive in terms of its investments. We view favorably BK's sale of troubled assets in its securities portfolio as it should result in less volatility in earnings going forward. We are encouraged by the strong performance of future growth drivers for BK, including new business wins, and expense savings. Rising equity markets should also have a positive effect on BK's bottom line. A $22.5 billion Russian lawsuit was recently settled and as a result, we believe a major overhang on the stock has been removed.

► Risks to our recommendation and target price include a significant decline in capital markets activity, credit losses that are greater than our expectations, execution risks, and the need to support client funds.

► Our 12-month target price of $33 equates to a P/E of 13.2X our 2010 estimate of $2.49, a slight discount to BK's historical forward multiple average to reflect a slowdown in revenue growth.

Qualitative Risk Assessment

LOW	MEDIUM	HIGH

Our risk assessment reflects what we view as solid fundamentals and diverse business lines. BK recently settled a $22.5 billion lawsuit by the Russian government alleging money laundering; it also significantly reduced the riskiest exposure of its securities portfolio. BK has provided stable earnings over the long term, and we believe it would be able to weather a prolonged economic downturn.

Quantitative Evaluations

S&P Quality Ranking   B+

D	C	B-	B	B+	A-	A	A+

Relative Strength Rank   WEAK

29

LOWEST = 1   HIGHEST = 99

Revenue/Earnings Data

Revenue (Million $)

	1Q	2Q	3Q	4Q	Year
2009	3,136	--	--	--	--
2008	3,745	4,078	4,262	3,367	16,339
2007	2,496	2,893	3,600	3,044	9,031
2006	2,074	2,276	2,219	2,493	9,062
2005	1,917	2,077	2,126	2,230	8,312
2004	1,671	1,767	1,739	1,968	7,144

Earnings Per Share ($)

2009	0.28	0.23	-2.04	E0.50	E-1.03
2008	0.65	0.26	0.27	0.05	1.22
2007	0.60	0.59	0.56	0.61	2.38
2006	0.50	0.55	0.41	0.59	2.05
2005	0.52	0.55	0.54	0.56	2.15
2004	0.50	0.51	0.49	0.48	1.96

Fiscal year ended Dec. 31. Next earnings report expected: Late January. EPS Estimates based on S&P Operating Earnings; historical GAAP earnings are as reported.

Dividend Data (Dates: mm/dd Payment Date: mm/dd/yy)

Amount ($)	Date Decl.	Ex-Div. Date	Stk. of Record	Payment Date
0.240	01/13	01/21	01/23	02/03/09
0.090	04/21	04/29	05/01	05/11/09
0.090	07/22	07/30	08/03	08/11/09
0.090	10/20	10/28	10/30	11/10/09

Dividends have been paid since 1785. Source: Company reports.

Please read the Required Disclosures and Analyst Certification on the last page of this report.

The McGraw-Hill Companies

Bank of New York Mellon Corp (The)

STANDARD
&POOR'S

Business Summary October 23, 2009

CORPORATE OVERVIEW. Bank of New York Mellon provides a comprehensive array of services that enable institutions and individuals to move and manage their financial assets in more than 100 markets worldwide. The company has several core competencies: institutional services, private banking, and asset management. Its global client base includes a broad range of leading financial institutions, corporations, government entities, endowments, and foundations.

Key products include advisory and asset management services to support the investment decision, trade execution, clearance and settlement capabilities, custody, securities lending, accounting, and administrative services for investment portfolios, sophisticated risk and performance measurement tools for analyzing portfolios, and services for issuers of both equity and debt securities.

CORPORATE STRATEGY. BK's strategy over the past decade has been to focus on scalable, fee-based securities servicing and fiduciary businesses, and it has achieved a top-three market share in most of its major product lines. The company attempts to distinguish itself competitively by offering products and services around the investment lifecycle.

By providing integrated solutions for clients' needs, BK strives to be the pre-ferred partner in helping its clients succeed in the world's rapidly evolving financial markets. The company's key objectives include achieving positive operating leverage on an annual basis, successful integration of acquisitions and increasing the percentage of revenue and income derived from outside the U.S.

To achieve its top objectives, BK has grown both through internal reinvestments as well as the execution of strategic acquisitions to expand product offerings and increase market share in its scale businesses. Internal reinvestment occurs mainly through increased technology spending, staffing levels, marketing/branding initiatives, quality programs, and product development. The company invests in technology to improve the breadth and quality of its product offerings, and to increase economies of scale. BK has acquired over 90 businesses over the past 10 years, almost exclusively in its securities servicing and asset management areas.

Company Financials Fiscal Year Ended Dec. 31

Per Share Data ($)	2008	2007	2006	2005	2004	2003	2002	2001	2000	1999
Tangible Book Value	3.06	5.83	11.50	7.48	6.84	5.93	6.00	6.14	8.80	7.37
Earnings	1.22	2.38	2.05	2.15	1.96	1.61	1.31	1.92	2.04	2.41
S&P Core Earnings	1.05	2.33	2.01	2.11	1.83	1.55	1.07	1.65	NA	NA
Dividends	0.96	0.95	0.91	0.87	0.84	0.81	0.81	0.76	0.70	0.61
Payout Ratio	79%	40%	45%	40%	43%	50%	61%	40%	34%	26%
Prices:High	49.90	50.26	42.98	35.71	36.94	35.50	49.29	61.61	62.94	47.90
Prices:Low	20.49	38.30	32.66	28.55	28.88	20.40	22.10	31.53	31.53	33.72
P/E Ratio:High	40	21	21	17	19	22	37	32	31	20
P/E Ratio:Low	17	16	16	13	15	13	17	16	15	14

Income Statement Analysis (Million $)	2008	2007	2006	2005	2004	2003	2002	2001	2000	1999
Net Interest Income	13,521	2,300	1,499	1,909	1,645	1,609	1,665	1,681	1,870	1,701
Tax Equivalent Adjustment	22.0	12.0	NA	29.0	30.0	35.0	49.0	60.0	54.0	44.0
Non Interest Income	10,701	9,232	5,337	4,888	4,613	3,971	3,261	3,386	2,959	3,294
Loan Loss Provision	131	-10.0	20.0	15.0	15.0	155	685	375	105	135
% Expense/Operating Revenue	37.8%	70.4%	68.6%	65.7%	65.6%	65.9%	55.3%	54.4%	51.4%	44.0%
Pretax Income	1,939	3,225	2,170	2,367	2,199	1,762	1,372	2,058	2,251	2,840
Effective Tax Rate	25.6%	31.0%	32.0%	33.6%	34.5%	34.3%	34.3%	34.7%	36.5%	38.8%
Net Income	1,442	2,227	1,476	1,571	1,440	1,157	902	1,343	1,429	1,739
% Net Interest Margin	1.92	2.08	2.01	2.36	2.07	2.22	2.62	2.57	2.96	3.11
S&P Core Earnings	1,217	2,179	1,452	1,536	1,350	1,097	728	1,159	NA	NA

Balance Sheet & Other Financial Data (Million $)	2008	2007	2006	2005	2004	2003	2002	2001	2000	1999
Money Market Assets	41,126	49,840	23,830	16,999	18,527	18,521	13,798	19,684	23,178	20,948
Investment Securities	39,435	48,698	21,106	27,326	23,802	22,903	18,300	12,862	7,401	6,899
Commercial Loans	7,205	4,766	5,925	13,252	12,624	13,646	20,335	19,034	21,327	17,851
Other Loans	35,774	43,465	31,868	27,474	23,157	21,637	11,004	16,713	14,934	21,251
Total Assets	237,009	197,656	103,370	102,074	94,529	92,397	77,564	81,025	77,114	74,756
Demand Deposits	55,816	32,372	19,554	18,236	17,442	14,789	13,301	12,635	13,255	12,162
Time Deposits	103,857	85,753	45,992	46,188	41,279	41,617	42,086	43,076	43,121	43,589
Long Term Debt	13,991	16,873	8,773	Nil	Nil	Nil	Nil	Nil	4,536	4,311
Common Equity	25,264	29,403	11,593	9,876	9,290	8,428	6,684	6,317	6,151	5,142
% Return on Assets	0.7	1.5	1.4	1.6	1.5	1.4	1.1	1.7	1.9	2.5
% Return on Equity	5.3	10.9	13.7	16.4	16.3	15.3	13.9	21.5	25.3	32.8
% Loan Loss Reserve	0.9	0.6	0.8	1.0	1.7	1.9	2.7	1.7	1.7	1.6
% Loans/Deposits	29.0	49.3	60.8	63.2	60.9	62.6	56.6	64.2	64.3	67.3
% Equity to Assets	12.6	13.6	10.5	9.7	9.5	8.9	8.2	7.9	7.4	7.7

Data as orig reptd.; bef. results of disc opers/spec. items. Per share data adj. for stk. divs.; EPS diluted. E-Estimated. NA-Not Available. NM-Not Meaningful. NR-Not Ranked. UR-Under Review.

Office: One Wall Street, New York, NY 10286.
Telephone: 212-495-1784.
Email: shareowner-svcs@bankofny.com
Website: http://www.bankofny.com

Chrmn & CEO: R.P. Kelly
Pres: G.L. Hassell
EVP & CFO: T.P. Gibbons
EVP & Treas: K. Peetz

EVP & General Counsel: C. Krasik
Board Members: R. E. Bruch, N. M. Donofrio, G. L. Hassell, E. F. Kelly, R. P. Kelly, R. J. Kogan, M. J. Kowalski, J. A. Luke, Jr., R. Mehrabian, M. A. Nordenberg, C. A. Rein, W. C. Richardson, S. C. Scott, III, J. Surma, Jr., W. W. von Schack

Founded: 1784
Domicile: Delaware
Employees: 42,900

The McGraw-Hill Companies

Bard (C.R.) Inc

STANDARD
&POOR'S

S&P Recommendation BUY ★★★★☆	Price $81.86 (as of Nov 27, 2009)	12-Mo. Target Price $89.00	Investment Style Large-Cap Growth

GICS Sector Health Care
Sub-Industry Health Care Equipment

Summary This diversified maker of therapeutic and diagnostic medical devices has exposure to the vascular, urology, oncology and specialty surgical markets.

Key Stock Statistics (Source S&P, Vickers, company reports)

52-Wk Range	$88.43– 68.94	S&P Oper. EPS 2009E	5.06	Market Capitalization(B)	$7.902	Beta	0.22
Trailing 12-Month EPS	$4.99	S&P Oper. EPS 2010E	5.70	Yield (%)	0.83	S&P 3-Yr. Proj. EPS CAGR(%)	13
Trailing 12-Month P/E	16.4	P/E on S&P Oper. EPS 2009E	16.2	Dividend Rate/Share	$0.68	S&P Credit Rating	A
$10K Invested 5 Yrs Ago	$14,160	Common Shares Outstg. (M)	96.5	Institutional Ownership (%)	88		

Price Performance

30-Week Mov. Avg. · · · 10-Week Mov. Avg. – – GAAP Earnings vs. Previous Year Volume Above Avg. ▮▮▮ STARS
12-Mo. Target Price — Relative Strength — ▲ Up ▼ Down ▶ No Change   Below Avg. ▮▮▮ ★

Options: ASE, CBOE, P, Ph

Analysis prepared by **Phillip M. Seligman** on October 27, 2009, when the stock traded at **$ 75.93**.

Qualitative Risk Assessment

LOW	MEDIUM	HIGH

Our risk assessment reflects the highly competitive environment in which BCR operates. In addition, hospital customers generate a large portion of revenues from Medicare, and are therefore subject to reimbursement risks that could reduce prices paid to suppliers. However, we believe BCR's product line is largely focused on areas that have not been subject to intense pricing pressure, and we think management has a solid track record in terms of identifying and integrating acquisitions.

Quantitative Evaluations

S&P Quality Ranking   A

D	C	B-	B	B+	A-	A	A+

Relative Strength Rank   STRONG

75

LOWEST = 1   HIGHEST = 99

Highlights

► We believe that net sales in 2009 will be up 3.1% (more than 6% in constant currency), to almost $2.53 billion. Drivers we see include growth of about 6% in the vascular category, aided by new products, 4% in oncology, reflecting a slowdown in hospital spending and the timing of BCR's launches, and 3%-4% in surgical specialties, and under 0.5% growth in urology sales, partly on slow procedure growth. In addition to unfavorable currency exchange, European sales are being hurt by a sales force restructuring. We look for 7.3% top-line growth in 2010, on new products and assuming that some of 2009's headwinds will have dissipated.

► We forecast that gross margins will expand to slightly over 62% by 2009, from 2008's 61.4%, and rise modestly in 2010, due to increased throughput at the Puerto Rico manufacturing facility and new products. We also forecast that SG&A costs will decline to below 27% of sales in 2009 and edge down some more in 2010, but we think R&D costs will absorb 6.5% or more of sales for the foreseeable future.

► Excluding restructuring charges, our 2009 EPS estimate is $5.06, versus 2008's $4.44, and we see $5.70 in 2010.

Investment Rationale/Risk

► We see long-term revenue growth of 8%-10% in constant currency, versus low double-digit growth in the past. Despite our view of promising new products, we see a sustained decline in elective procedure rates. While BCR is finding it difficult to sell its premium products, we are encouraged it views pricing as stable and it has not lost market share in most of its businesses. Meanwhile, we think BCR's SG&A cost control will help it realize at least 13% EPS growth for the next couple of years. To sustain such growth afterward, we think it must pick up the pace of new product offerings. In this regard, we like its plan to increase R&D spending, but we believe it will also boost M&A.

► Risks to our recommendation and target price include unfavorable patent litigation outcomes, reduced reimbursement, and failure to commercialize new products in a timely fashion.

► Our projected three-year EPS growth rate of 13% for BCR is modestly above peers and, hence, we believe a small premium valuation is appropriate. By applying a forward P/E to earnings growth ratio of 1.35X to our three-year projected growth rate and our 2009 EPS estimate, our 12-month target price is $89.

Revenue/Earnings Data

Revenue (Million $)

	1Q	2Q	3Q	4Q	Year
2009	596.4	624.6	637.0	--	--
2008	584.0	617.1	616.8	634.2	2,452
2007	528.2	545.7	544.8	583.3	2,202
2006	467.5	498.2	498.9	520.9	1,986
2005	428.6	447.4	443.3	452.0	1,771
2004	393.8	416.3	421.9	424.1	1,656

Earnings Per Share ($)

	1Q	2Q	3Q	4Q	Year
2009	1.10	1.11	1.31	E1.36	E5.06
2008	0.76	0.76	1.09	1.47	4.06
2007	0.95	0.91	0.96	1.01	3.84
2006	0.76	0.76	0.82	0.21	2.55
2005	0.75	0.79	0.83	0.75	3.12
2004	0.68	0.55	0.95	0.65	2.82

Fiscal year ended Dec. 31. Next earnings report expected: Late January. EPS Estimates based on S&P Operating Earnings; historical GAAP earnings are as reported.

Dividend Data (Dates: mm/dd Payment Date: mm/dd/yy)

Amount ($)	Date Decl.	Ex-Div. Date	Stk. of Record	Payment Date
0.160	12/10	01/22	01/26	02/06/09
0.160	04/15	04/23	04/27	05/08/09
0.170	06/10	07/16	07/20	07/31/09
0.170	10/14	10/22	10/26	11/06/09

Dividends have been paid since 1960. Source: Company reports.

Please read the Required Disclosures and Analyst Certification on the last page of this report.

The McGraw·Hill Companies

Bard (C.R.) Inc

Business Summary October 27, 2009

CORPORATE OVERVIEW. C.R. Bard offers a range of medical, surgical, diagnostic and patient care devices. Sales in 2008 came from urology (29%), vascular (26%), oncology (26%), surgical specialties (15%) and other (4%) products.

Bard's vascular products include percutaneous transluminal angioplasty catheters, guide wires, introducers and accessories, peripheral stents, vena cava filters and biopsy devices; electrophysiology products such as lab systems, and diagnostic therapeutic and temporary pacing electrode catheters; and fabrics, meshes and implantable vascular grafts.

Urological diagnosis and intervention products include Foley catheters, procedure kits and trays, and related urine monitoring and collection systems; urethral stents; and specialty devices for incontinence, endoscopic procedures, and stone removal. Newer products include the Infection Control Foley catheter that reduces the rate of urinary tract infections; a collagen implant and sling materials used to treat urinary incontinence; and brachytherapy services, devices, and radioactive seeds to treat prostate cancer.

Oncology products include specialty access catheters and ports; gastroenterological products (endoscopic accessories, percutaneous feeding devices and stents); biopsy devices; and a suturing system for gastroesophageal reflux disease.

Surgical specialties products include meshes for hernia and other soft tissue repairs; irrigation devices for orthopedic, laparoscopic and gynecological procedures; and topical hemostatic devices. In January 2003, Bard introduced the VentralexT hernia patch, a simplified intra-abdominal hernia repair technology characterized by minimal suturing, small incisions, and potentially shorter recovery times. In December 2007, Bard entered into a license agreement with Genzyme Corp. to manufacture and market the Sepramesh IP hernia repair product line and incorporate the related Sepra coating technology into the development of future hernia repair applications.

Company Financials Fiscal Year Ended Dec. 31

Per Share Data ($)	2008	2007	2006	2005	2004	2003	2002	2001	2000	1999
Tangible Book Value	11.62	10.73	9.46	10.39	7.26	5.35	4.84	3.97	2.53	2.34
Cash Flow	4.95	4.59	3.25	3.71	3.33	2.03	1.87	1.89	1.53	1.61
Earnings	4.06	3.84	2.55	3.12	2.82	1.60	1.47	1.38	1.04	1.14
S&P Core Earnings	3.96	3.86	2.96	2.86	2.29	1.73	1.27	1.21	NA	NA
Dividends	0.62	0.58	0.54	0.50	0.47	0.45	0.43	0.42	0.41	0.39
Payout Ratio	15%	15%	21%	16%	17%	28%	29%	31%	39%	34%
Prices:High	101.61	95.33	85.72	72.79	65.13	40.80	31.97	32.47	27.47	29.94
Prices:Low	70.00	76.61	59.89	60.82	40.09	27.02	22.05	20.43	17.50	20.84
P/E Ratio:High	25	25	34	23	23	25	22	24	26	26
P/E Ratio:Low	17	20	23	19	14	17	15	15	17	18

Income Statement Analysis (Million $)

	2008	2007	2006	2005	2004	2003	2002	2001	2000	1999
Revenue	2,452	2,202	1,986	1,771	1,656	1,433	1,274	1,181	1,099	1,037
Operating Income	735	638	550	503	418	333	295	266	244	239
Depreciation	90.9	79.8	74.9	63.8	54.7	44.7	42.3	53.2	49.6	49.1
Interest Expense	12.1	11.9	16.9	12.2	12.7	12.5	12.6	14.2	19.3	19.3
Pretax Income	550	577	348	450	414	223	211	205	154	173
Effective Tax Rate	24.3%	29.6%	21.7%	25.0%	26.9%	24.5%	26.5%	30.1%	30.6%	31.9%
Net Income	417	406	272	337	303	169	155	143	107	118
S&P Core Earnings	407	409	317	309	244	182	134	126	NA	NA

Balance Sheet & Other Financial Data (Million $)

	2008	2007	2006	2005	2004	2003	2002	2001	2000	1999
Cash	592	571	416	754	541	417	23.1	30.8	21.3	17.3
Current Assets	1,354	1,242	1,134	1,264	1,054	875	758	647	527	529
Total Assets	2,666	2,476	2,277	2,266	2,009	1,692	1,417	1,231	1,089	1,126
Current Liabilities	273	282	296	641	390	422	317	235	225	353
Long Term Debt	150	150	151	0.80	151	152	152	156	204	158
Common Equity	1,977	1,848	1,698	1,536	1,360	1,046	880	789	614	574
Total Capital	2,151	2,018	1,871	1,544	1,534	1,197	1,033	945	818	733
Capital Expenditures	50.6	50.7	70.4	97.2	74.0	72.1	41.0	27.4	19.4	26.1
Cash Flow	507	486	347	401	358	213	197	196	157	167
Current Ratio	5.0	4.4	3.8	2.0	2.7	2.1	2.4	2.8	2.3	1.5
% Long Term Debt of Capitalization	7.0	7.4	8.1	0.1	9.9	12.7	14.7	16.5	25.0	21.6
% Net Income of Revenue	17.0	18.5	13.7	19.0	18.3	11.8	12.2	12.1	9.7	11.4
% Return on Assets	16.2	17.1	12.0	15.8	16.4	10.8	11.5	12.3	9.6	10.7
% Return on Equity	21.8	22.9	16.8	23.3	25.2	17.5	18.6	20.4	18.0	20.7

Data as orig reptd.; bef. results of disc opers/spec. items. Per share data adj. for stk. divs.; EPS diluted. E-Estimated. NA-Not Available. NM-Not Meaningful. NR-Not Ranked. UR-Under Review.

Office: 730 Central Avenue, Murray Hill, NJ 07974.
Telephone: 908-277-8000.
Website: http://www.crbard.com
Chrmn & CEO: T.M. Ring

Pres & COO: J.H. Weiland
SVP & CFO: T.C. Schermerhorn
Chief Acctg Officer & Cntlr: F. Lupisella, Jr.
Treas: S.T. Lowry

Investor Contact: E.J. Shick (908-277-8413)
Board Members: D. M. Barrett, M. C. Breslawsky, P. G. Christian, T. K. Dunnigan, H. L. Henkel, T. E. Martin, G. K. Naughton, T. M. Ring, T. G. Thompson, J. H. Weiland, A. Welters, T. L. White

Founded: 1907
Domicile: New Jersey
Employees: 11,000

Baxter International Inc

STANDARD &POOR'S

S&P Recommendation	**BUY** ★★★★☆	Price	12-Mo. Target Price	Investment Style
		$54.83 (as of Nov 27, 2009)	$65.00	Large-Cap Growth

GICS Sector Health Care
Sub-Industry Health Care Equipment

Summary This global medical products and services company provides critical therapies for people with life-threatening conditions.

Key Stock Statistics (Source S&P, Vickers, company reports)

52-Wk Range	$60.99– 45.46	S&P Oper. EPS 2009**E**	3.80	Market Capitalization(B)	$33.055	Beta	0.41
Trailing 12-Month EPS	$3.56	S&P Oper. EPS 2010**E**	4.30	Yield (%)	2.12	S&P 3-Yr. Proj. EPS CAGR(%)	12
Trailing 12-Month P/E	15.4	P/E on S&P Oper. EPS 2009**E**	14.4	Dividend Rate/Share	$1.16	S&P Credit Rating	A+
$10K Invested 5 Yrs Ago	$18,565	Common Shares Outstg. (M)	602.9	Institutional Ownership (%)	84		

Price Performance

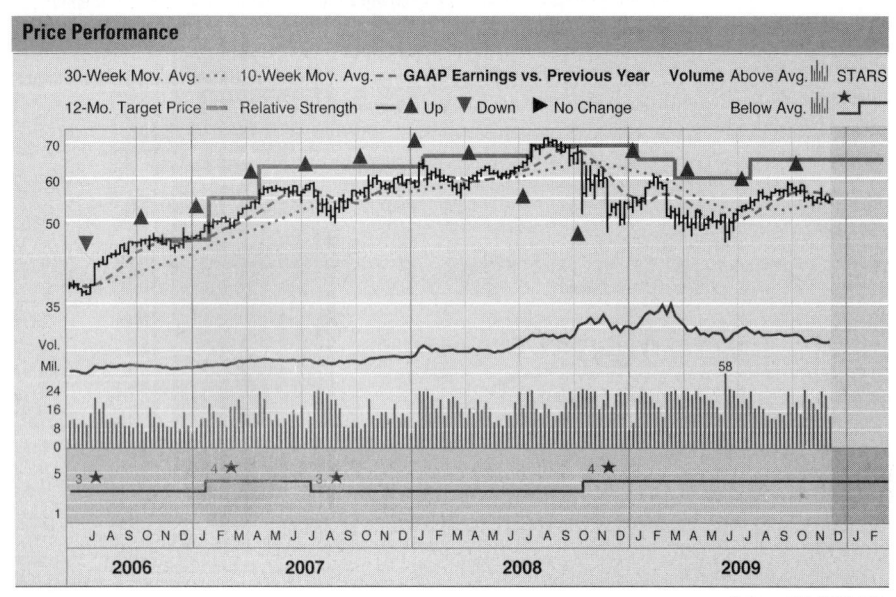

Options: ASE, CBOE, P, Ph

Analysis prepared by **Herman B. Saftlas** on October 05, 2009, when the stock traded at **$ 56.57**.

Qualitative Risk Assessment

LOW	MEDIUM	HIGH

Our risk assessment reflects BAX's operations in a highly competitive business characterized by rapid technological change and new market entrants. In addition, the business entails regulatory and reimbursement risks, as well as liability risk from malfunctioning products. This is offset by our belief that health care products are largely immune to economic cycles, and that long-term demand should benefit from demographic growth of the elderly and a greater penetration of developing global markets.

Quantitative Evaluations

S&P Quality Ranking A-

D	C	B-	B	B+	A-	A	A+

Relative Strength Rank MODERATE

44

LOWEST = 1   HIGHEST = 99

Highlights

► We see 2009 revenues rising modestly from 2008's $12.3 billion, with projected mid-single-digit constant currency growth offsetting negative foreign exchange (foreign business was 57% of first-half 2009 sales). Bolstered by increased demand for recombinants such as Advate factor VIII, plasma proteins, and antibody therapies, we expect BioScience unit sales to climb about 4%. However, we project flat Medication Delivery sales, with gains in anesthesia products to be roughly offset by declines in sales of infusion therapies. Renal Care sales are expected to drop, primarily due to lower volume in the older hemodialysis line.

► We see gross margins expanding to about 52.7% in 2009, from 2008's adjusted 50.7%, helped by a more profitable sales mix, firmer pricing, and ongoing productivity enhancements. We also expect good control over SG&A costs. However, R&D spending is likely to move higher to fund new products.

► After a projected tax rate of about 18.7%, up from 2008's 17.8%, we forecast 2009 operating EPS of $3.80, up from 2008's $3.38. We see further EPS growth to $4.30 in 2010.

Investment Rationale/Risk

► We credit management with improving BAX's profitability by focusing on high-margin recombinants, plasma proteins, and antibody therapies, divesting low-margin businesses, and closing excess manufacturing capacity. Despite the effects of tougher plasma pricing and negative foreign exchange, we expect BAX to benefit from positive momentum in its principal recession-resistant businesses, as well as benefits from acquisitions and ongoing gross margin expansion. We believe the recent acquisition of a hemofiltration product line from Edwards Lifesciences (EW 68, Strong Buy) will bolster BAX's sluggish Renal Care division.

► Risks to our recommendation and target price include lower-than-expected Advate sales, adverse adjustments to Medicare reimbursement rates, and an inability to further streamline operating costs.

► Our 12-month target price of $65 assumes a modest premium-to-peers multiple of 17X our 2009 EPS forecast. Our target price also matches our intrinsic value estimate for BAX, derived from our discounted cash flow model, which assumes a WACC of 8.4% and a terminal growth rate of 2%.

Revenue/Earnings Data

Revenue (Million $)

	1Q	2Q	3Q	4Q	Year
2009	2,824	3,123	3,145	--	--
2008	2,877	3,189	3,151	3,131	12,348
2007	2,675	2,829	2,750	3,009	11,263
2006	2,409	2,649	2,557	2,763	10,378
2005	2,383	2,577	2,398	2,491	9,849
2004	2,209	2,379	2,320	2,601	9,509

Earnings Per Share ($)

2009	0.83	0.96	0.87	E1.05	E3.80
2008	0.67	0.85	0.74	0.91	3.16
2007	0.61	0.65	0.61	0.74	2.61
2006	0.43	0.47	0.57	0.66	2.13
2005	0.36	0.51	0.18	0.46	1.52
2004	0.30	-0.28	0.42	0.17	0.62

Fiscal year ended Dec. 31. Next earnings report expected: Late January. EPS Estimates based on S&P Operating Earnings; historical GAAP earnings are as reported.

Dividend Data (Dates: mm/dd Payment Date: mm/dd/yy)

Amount ($)	Date Decl.	Ex-Div. Date	Stk. of Record	Payment Date
0.260	02/17	03/06	03/10	04/01/09
0.260	05/05	06/08	06/10	07/01/09
0.260	07/28	09/08	09/10	10/01/09
0.290	11/10	12/08	12/10	01/05/10

Dividends have been paid since 1934. Source: Company reports.

Baxter International Inc

STANDARD
&POOR'S

Business Summary October 05, 2009

CORPORATE OVERVIEW. Founded in 1931 as the first producer of commercially prepared intravenous (IV) solutions, Baxter International makes and distributes medical products and equipment, with a focus on the blood and circulatory system. In 2007, international sales accounted for 57% of the total. In March 2007, the company divested its Transfusion Therapies business.

The BioSciences unit (44% of 2008 sales) produces plasma-based and recombinant clotting factors for hemophilia, as well as biopharmaceuticals for immune deficiencies, cancer, and other disorders. It also offers biosurgery products for hemostasis, tissue sealing and tissue regeneration, vaccines, and blood processing and storage systems used by hospitals, blood banks and others. In addition, BAX sells a meningitis C vaccine, and is developing cell culture-derived vaccines for influenza, smallpox, Severe Acute Respiratory Syndrome and other diseases. Its most important Biosciences product is Advate, a recombinant blood-clotting agent produced without adding human or animal proteins in the cell culture, purification or final formulation process.

The Medication Delivery unit (37%) makes IV solutions and various specialty

products such as critical-care generic injectable drugs, anesthetic agents, and nutrition and oncology products. The products work with devices such as drug-reconstitution systems, IV infusion pumps, nutritional compounding equipment, and medication management systems to provide fluid replenishment, general anesthesia, parenteral nutrition, pain management, antibiotic therapy, and chemotherapy.

Renal Care products (19%) comprise dialysis equipment and other products and services provided for kidney failure patients. BAX sells products for peritoneal dialysis (PD), including solutions, container systems and automated machines that cleanse patients' blood overnight while they sleep. The company also makes dialyzers and instrumentation for hemodialysis (HD). Another renal care product is Extraneal (icodextrin) solution, which facilitates increased fluid removal from the bloodstream during dialysis.

Company Financials Fiscal Year Ended Dec. 31

Per Share Data ($)	2008	2007	2006	2005	2004	2003	2002	2001	2000	1999
Tangible Book Value	6.79	7.53	6.42	3.61	2.45	1.74	1.53	3.44	2.43	4.19
Cash Flow	4.11	3.46	3.01	2.45	1.59	2.42	2.38	1.81	1.91	1.95
Earnings	3.16	2.61	2.13	1.52	0.62	1.52	1.67	1.09	1.24	1.32
S&P Core Earnings	2.99	2.68	2.24	1.38	0.52	1.25	1.30	0.53	NA	NA
Dividends	0.91	0.72	0.58	0.58	0.58	0.58	0.58	0.58	0.15	0.58
Payout Ratio	29%	28%	27%	38%	94%	38%	35%	53%	12%	44%
Prices:High	71.53	61.09	48.54	41.07	34.84	31.32	59.90	55.90	45.13	38.00
Prices:Low	47.41	46.07	35.12	33.08	27.10	18.18	24.07	40.06	25.88	28.41
P/E Ratio:High	23	23	23	27	56	21	36	51	37	29
P/E Ratio:Low	15	18	16	22	44	12	14	37	21	22

Income Statement Analysis (Million $)	2008	2007	2006	2005	2004	2003	2002	2001	2000	1999
Revenue	12,348	11,263	10,378	9,849	9,509	8,916	8,110	7,663	6,896	6,380
Operating Income	3,333	2,913	2,479	2,110	2,039	2,161	2,168	1,934	1,673	1,522
Depreciation	606	558	575	580	601	545	439	441	405	372
Interest Expense	165	136	101	166	99.0	118	71.0	108	124	152
Pretax Income	2,451	2,114	1,746	1,444	430	1,150	1,397	964	946	1,052
Effective Tax Rate	17.8%	19.3%	19.9%	33.7%	10.9%	19.8%	26.1%	31.1%	22.0%	26.0%
Net Income	2,014	1,707	1,398	958	383	922	1,033	664	738	779
S&P Core Earnings	1,906	1,757	1,467	864	323	756	794	313	NA	NA

Balance Sheet & Other Financial Data (Million $)	2008	2007	2006	2005	2004	2003	2002	2001	2000	1999
Cash	2,131	2,539	2,485	841	1,109	927	1,169	582	579	606
Current Assets	7,148	7,555	6,970	5,116	6,019	5,437	5,160	3,977	3,651	3,819
Total Assets	15,405	15,294	14,686	12,727	14,147	13,779	12,478	10,343	8,733	9,644
Current Liabilities	3,635	3,812	3,610	4,165	4,286	3,819	3,851	3,294	3,372	2,700
Long Term Debt	3,362	2,664	2,567	2,414	3,933	4,421	4,398	2,486	1,726	2,601
Common Equity	6,229	6,916	6,272	4,299	3,705	3,323	2,939	3,757	2,659	3,348
Total Capital	9,597	9,580	8,839	6,713	7,638	7,744	7,366	6,461	4,545	6,260
Capital Expenditures	954	692	526	444	558	789	734	669	101	529
Cash Flow	2,620	2,265	1,973	1,538	984	1,467	1,472	1,105	1,143	1,151
Current Ratio	2.0	2.0	1.9	1.2	1.4	1.4	1.3	1.2	1.1	1.4
% Long Term Debt of Capitalization	35.1	27.8	29.0	36.0	51.5	57.1	59.7	38.5	38.0	41.5
% Net Income of Revenue	16.3	15.2	13.5	9.7	4.0	10.3	12.7	8.7	10.7	12.2
% Return on Assets	13.1	11.4	10.2	7.1	2.8	7.0	9.1	7.0	8.0	8.0
% Return on Equity	30.6	25.9	26.4	23.9	10.8	29.4	30.9	20.7	24.6	25.2

Data as orig reptd.; bef. results of disc opers/spec. items. Per share data adj. for stk. divs.; EPS diluted. E-Estimated. NA-Not Available. NM-Not Meaningful. NR-Not Ranked. UR-Under Review.

Office: One Baxter Parkway, Deerfield, IL 60015.
Telephone: 847-948-2000.
Website: http://www.baxter.com
Chrmn, Pres & CEO: R.L. Parkinson, Jr.

CFO: R.M. Davis
CSO: N.G. Riedel
Chief Acctg Officer & Cntlr: M.J. Baughman
Treas: R.J. Hombach

Investor Contact: M. Ladone (847-948-3371)
Board Members: W. E. Boomer, B. E. Devitt, P. C. Farrell, J. D. Forsyth, G. D. Fosler, J. R. Gavin, III, P. S. Hellman, W. T. Hockmeyer, J. B. Martin, R. L. Parkinson, Jr., C. J. Shapazian, T. T. Stallkamp, K. J. Storm, A. P. Stroucken

Founded: 1931
Domicile: Delaware
Employees: 48,500

BB&T Corp

STANDARD &POOR'S

| S&P Recommendation **BUY** ★★★★☆ | Price $24.26 (as of Nov 27, 2009) | 12-Mo. Target Price $31.00 | Investment Style Large-Cap Blend |

GICS Sector Financials
Sub-Industry Regional Banks

Summary This bank holding company has a large presence in its home state of North Carolina, as well as in Virginia, and has additional offices in Georgia, South Carolina, the District of Columbia, and seven other states.

Key Stock Statistics (Source S&P, Vickers, company reports)

52-Wk Range	$30.88– 12.90	S&P Oper. EPS 2009E	1.25	Market Capitalization(B)	$16.682	Beta	0.95
Trailing 12-Month EPS	$1.38	S&P Oper. EPS 2010E	2.06	Yield (%)	2.47	S&P 3-Yr. Proj. EPS CAGR(%)	3
Trailing 12-Month P/E	17.6	P/E on S&P Oper. EPS 2009E	19.4	Dividend Rate/Share	$0.60	S&P Credit Rating	A
$10K Invested 5 Yrs Ago	$7,261	Common Shares Outstg. (M)	687.6	Institutional Ownership (%)	50		

Price Performance

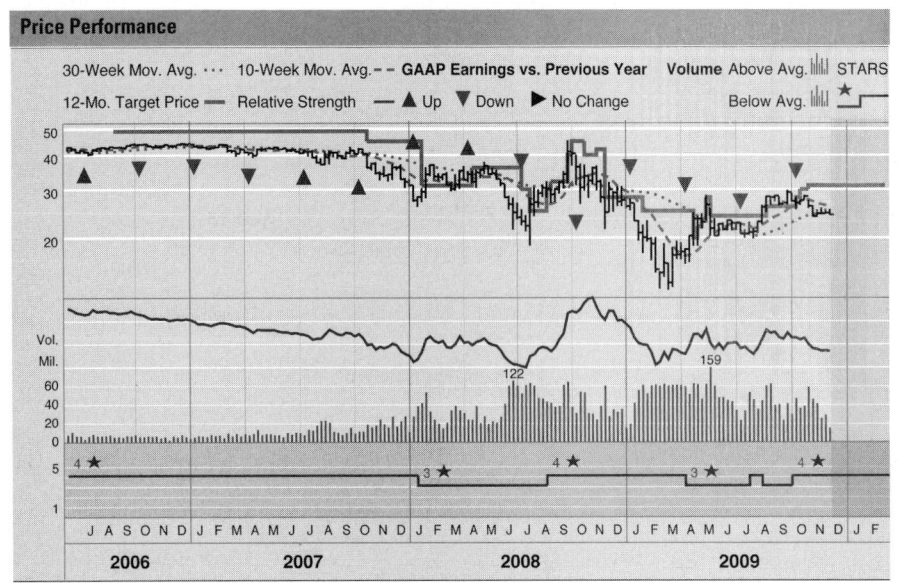

30-Week Mov. Avg. ···   10-Week Mov. Avg. --   **GAAP Earnings vs. Previous Year**   Volume Above Avg. STARS
12-Mo. Target Price —   Relative Strength —   ▲ Up   ▼ Down   ▶ No Change   Below Avg.

Options: ASE, CBOE, P, Ph

Analysis prepared by **Erik Oja** on October 26, 2009, when the stock traded at **$ 25.85**.

Highlights

► BBT's tax-equivalent net interest margin rose to 3.68% in the third quarter, from 3.56% in the second quarter and 3.57% in the first quarter, as loan and securities yields increased slightly, while interest-bearing liabilities declined. We expect full-year net interest margin of 3.65%, up from our previous forecast of 3.60%, and net interest income of about $4.6 billion, up 8.0% from 2008. We also forecast fee income, excluding gains and losses, of $3.5 billion in 2009, up 16.3% from 2008, due to strong year-to-date results in mortgage banking.

► We are modeling 2009 loan loss provisions of about $2.6 billion, up from about $1.45 billion in 2008, based on our forecast of 1.80% annualized net chargeoffs, or about $1.8 billion, versus $851 million in 2008. We also expect reserve building of $785 million, versus $594 million in 2008. For 2010, we expect chargeoffs to moderate to $1.5 billion, and we see loan loss provisions of $1.5 billion as well. In addition, we forecast a 53.0% non-interest expenses to revenues ratio in 2009, up slightly from the 52.7% of 2008.

► We see EPS of $1.23 in 2009 and $2.10 in 2010.

Investment Rationale/Risk

► Third quarter results were better than we expected for net interest income and mortgage banking, but were overshadowed by loan loss provisioning expenses of $709 million. During the third quarter, nonperforming loans increased 23.8% from the second quarter, led by home equity and commercial loans and leases, suggesting to us that an improvement in credit quality will likely take at least two more quarters. Also, noninterest expenses such as personnel, occupancy, and foreclosed property expense were all higher than in previous quarters, but some of this is attributable to the recent acquisition of the assets of Colonial Bank. However, we keep our positive view of BBT's core earnings power, capital levels, reserve levels, and lack of TARP-related constraints.

► Risks to our opinion and target price include a steeper than expected decline in credit quality, and a decline in net interest income.

► Our 12-month target price of $31 is a peer equivalent 16.3X our forward four-quarter EPS estimate of $1.90, equal to an above-peers 2.3X our December 31 tangible book value per share estimate of $13.48.

Qualitative Risk Assessment

| LOW | **MEDIUM** | HIGH |

Our risk assessment reflects the company's large-cap valuation, our view of the strong credit quality of its loan portfolio, and its history of profitability, offset by its exposure to the banking industry's current issues regarding funding and credit quality.

Quantitative Evaluations

S&P Quality Ranking   B+

| D | C | B- | B | **B+** | A- | A | A+ |

Relative Strength Rank   WEAK

| 29 |
LOWEST = 1   HIGHEST = 99

Revenue/Earnings Data

Revenue (Million $)

	1Q	2Q	3Q	4Q	Year
2009	2,740	2,633	2,685	--	--
2008	2,655	2,617	2,585	2,536	10,404
2007	2,543	2,690	2,719	2,747	10,668
2006	2,165	2,319	2,463	2,468	9,414
2005	1,760	1,918	2,036	2,118	7,831
2004	1,559	1,693	1,698	1,736	6,666

Earnings Per Share ($)

2009	0.48	0.20	0.23	E0.36	E1.25
2008	0.78	0.78	0.65	0.51	2.71
2007	0.77	0.83	0.80	0.75	3.14
2006	0.79	0.79	0.77	0.46	2.81
2005	0.71	0.70	0.80	0.78	3.00
2004	0.60	0.72	0.74	0.75	2.80

Fiscal year ended Dec. 31. Next earnings report expected: Late January. EPS Estimates based on S&P Operating Earnings; historical GAAP earnings are as reported.

Dividend Data (Dates: mm/dd Payment Date: mm/dd/yy)

Amount ($)	Date Decl.	Ex-Div. Date	Stk. of Record	Payment Date
0.470	12/16	01/07	01/09	02/02/09
0.470	02/24	04/07	04/10	05/01/09
0.150	05/11	07/08	07/10	08/03/09
0.150	08/25	10/14	10/16	11/02/09

Dividends have been paid since 1903. Source: Company reports.

Please read the Required Disclosures and Analyst Certification on the last page of this report.

The McGraw-Hill Companies

BB&T Corp

&POOR'S

Business Summary October 26, 2009

CORPORATE OVERVIEW. BBT has bank operations providing loan, deposit and financial products primarily in the Southeast. BBT has seven reportable business segments: Banking Network, Mortgage Banking, Trust Services, Insurance Services, Investment Banking and Brokerage, Specialized Lending, and Treasury.

MARKET PROFILE. As of June 30, 2008, which is the latest available FDIC branch-level data, BBT had 1,466 branches and $85.9 billion in deposits, with 56% of its deposits concentrated in North Carolina and Virginia, by our calculations. In North Carolina, BBT had 345 branches, $28.4 billion of deposits, and a deposit market share of about 12%, ranking second. In Virginia, BBT had 390 branches, $19.8 billion of deposits, and a deposit market share of about 7.9%, ranking fifth. In Georgia, BBT had 151 branches, $8.6 billion of deposits, and a

deposit market share of about 4.4%, ranking fifth. In South Carolina, BBT had 113 branches, $6.3 billion of deposits, and a deposit market share of about 8.6%, ranking third. In Maryland, BBT had 127 branches, $6.3 billion of deposits, and a deposit market share of about 5.7%, ranking seventh. In Florida, BBT had 106 branches, $3.7 billion of deposits, and a deposit market share of about 0.9%, ranking 18th. In addition, BBT had a number one market ranking in West Virginia, and was fourth in Kentucky, eighth in DC, and sixth in Tennessee. Finally, BBT had a small presence in Alabama and Indiana.

Company Financials Fiscal Year Ended Dec. 31

Per Share Data ($)	2008	2007	2006	2005	2004	2003	2002	2001	2000	1999
Tangible Book Value	11.86	12.73	11.04	11.76	12.26	11.66	12.04	13.50	11.91	9.66
Earnings	2.71	3.14	2.81	3.00	2.80	2.07	2.70	2.12	1.55	1.83
S&P Core Earnings	2.54	3.09	2.79	2.90	2.75	1.97	2.59	2.02	NA	NA
Dividends	1.86	1.76	1.60	1.46	1.34	1.22	1.10	0.98	0.86	0.75
Payout Ratio	67%	56%	57%	49%	48%	59%	41%	46%	55%	41%
Prices:High	45.31	44.30	44.74	43.92	43.25	39.69	39.47	38.84	38.25	40.63
Prices:Low	18.71	30.36	38.24	37.04	33.02	30.66	31.03	30.24	21.69	27.19
P/E Ratio:High	17	14	16	15	15	19	15	18	25	22
P/E Ratio:Low	7	10	14	12	12	15	11	14	14	15

Income Statement Analysis (Million $)	2008	2007	2006	2005	2004	2003	2002	2001	2000	1999
Net Interest Income	4,238	3,880	3,708	3,525	3,348	3,082	2,747	2,434	2,018	1,582
Tax Equivalent Adjustment	83.0	68.0	NA	82.7	NA	21.2	151	19.1	130	86.7
Non Interest Income	3,197	2,777	2,594	2,326	2,113	1,782	1,522	1,256	996	639
Loan Loss Provision	1,445	448	240	217	249	248	264	224	127	92.1
% Expense/Operating Revenue	54.4%	54.6%	55.8%	53.4%	57.6%	63.6%	54.0%	60.1%	56.0%	58.4%
Pretax Income	2,069	2,570	2,473	2,467	2,322	1,617	1,791	1,360	906	904
Effective Tax Rate	26.6%	32.5%	38.2%	33.0%	32.9%	34.1%	27.8%	28.4%	30.8%	32.2%
Net Income	1,519	1,734	1,528	1,654	1,558	1,065	1,293	974	626	613
% Net Interest Margin	3.63	3.52	3.74	3.89	4.04	4.06	4.25	4.17	3.56	4.27
S&P Core Earnings	1,406	1,707	1,514	1,608	1,529	1,012	1,241	927	NA	NA

Balance Sheet & Other Financial Data (Million $)	2008	2007	2006	2005	2004	2003	2002	2001	2000	1999
Money Market Assets	1,101	1,067	688	697	1,244	604	591	458	379	390
Investment Securities	33,219	23,428	22,868	20,489	19,173	16,317	17,655	16,662	13,851	10,579
Commercial Loans	50,480	44,870	41,300	37,655	34,321	12,429	7,061	6,551	5,894	4,593
Other Loans	48,189	46,037	41,611	36,739	33,228	49,151	44,079	38,985	33,561	24,320
Total Assets	152,015	132,618	121,351	109,170	100,509	90,467	80,217	70,870	59,340	43,481
Demand Deposits	16,225	14,260	14,726	13,477	12,246	11,098	7,864	6,940	5,064	3,908
Time Deposits	82,388	72,506	66,245	60,805	55,453	48,252	43,416	37,794	32,951	23,343
Long Term Debt	18,032	18,693	12,604	13,119	11,420	10,808	13,588	11,721	8,355	5,492
Common Equity	16,037	448	11,745	11,129	10,874	9,935	7,388	6,150	4,786	3,199
% Return on Assets	1.1	1.3	1.3	1.6	1.6	1.2	1.7	1.4	1.1	1.5
% Return on Equity	10.6	14.0	13.4	15.0	15.0	12.3	19.1	16.8	14.2	19.2
% Loan Loss Reserve	1.6	1.1	1.1	1.1	1.2	1.3	1.4	1.4	1.3	1.3
% Loans/Deposits	98.6	103.6	103.2	99.0	100.7	105.0	104.4	106.1	106.0	107.1
% Equity to Assets	9.0	9.6	9.9	10.5	10.9	10.1	9.0	8.4	7.9	7.7

Data as orig reptd.; bef. results of disc opers/spec. items. Per share data adj. for stk. divs.; EPS diluted. E-Estimated. NA-Not Available. NM-Not Meaningful. NR-Not Ranked. UR-Under Review.

Office: 200 West Second Street, Winston-Salem, NC 27101.
Telephone: 336-733-2000.
Website: http://www.bbandt.com
Chrmn: J.A. Allison, IV

Pres & CEO: K.S. King
COO: C.L. Henson
EVP & CFO: D.N. Bible
SVP, Chief Acctg Officer & Cntlr: C.B. Powell

Investor Contact: T. Gjesdal (336-733-3058)
Board Members: J. A. Allison, IV, J. S. Banner, K. D. Boyer, Jr., A. R. Cablik, N. R. Chilton, R. E. Deal, T. D. Efird, B. J. Fitzpatrick, J. L. Glover, Jr., L. V. Hackley, J. P. Helm, E. M. Holland, J. P. Howe, III, K. S. King, A. O. Maccauley, J. H. Maynard, A. O. McCauley, J. H. Morrison, N. R. Qubein, T. E. Skains, T. N. Thompson, S. T. Williams

Founded: 1968
Domicile: North Carolina
Employees: 29,600

Becton, Dickinson and Co

STANDARD &POOR'S

S&P Recommendation HOLD ★★★☆☆

Price	12-Mo. Target Price	Investment Style
$74.72 (as of Nov 27, 2009)	$76.00	Large-Cap Growth

GICS Sector Health Care
Sub-Industry Health Care Equipment

Summary This company provides a wide range of medical devices and diagnostic products used in hospitals, doctors' offices, research labs and other settings.

Key Stock Statistics (Source S&P, Vickers, company reports)

52-Wk Range	$77.11–60.40	S&P Oper. EPS 2010**E**	5.08	Market Capitalization(B)	$17.887	Beta	0.57
Trailing 12-Month EPS	$4.99	S&P Oper. EPS 2011**E**	5.55	Yield (%)	1.98	S&P 3-Yr. Proj. EPS CAGR(%)	8
Trailing 12-Month P/E	15.0	P/E on S&P Oper. EPS 2010**E**	14.7	Dividend Rate/Share	$1.48	S&P Credit Rating	AA-
$10K Invested 5 Yrs Ago	$14,859	Common Shares Outstg. (M)	239.4	Institutional Ownership (%)	84		

Price Performance

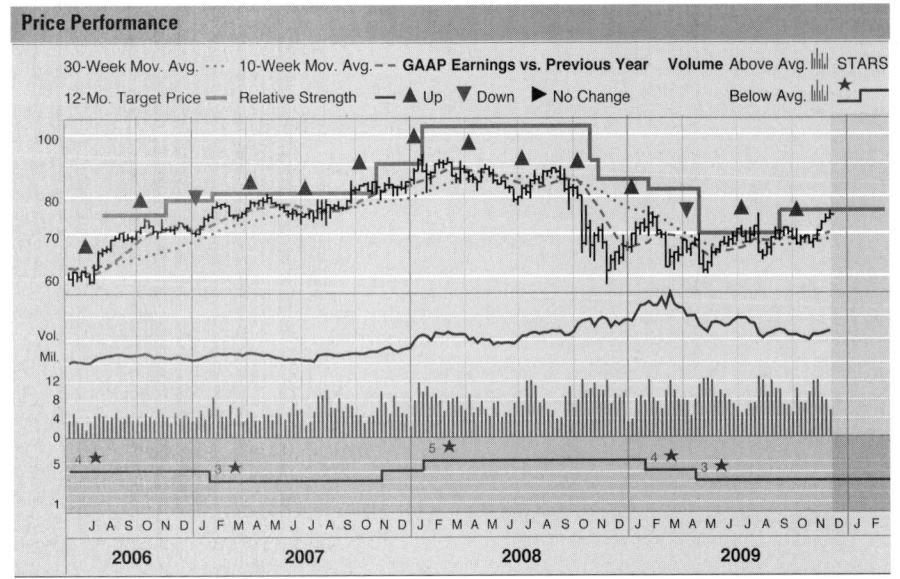

30-Week Mov. Avg. · · · 10-Week Mov. Avg. - - **GAAP Earnings vs. Previous Year** Volume Above Avg. STARS
12-Mo. Target Price — Relative Strength — ▲ Up ▼ Down ▶ No Change Below Avg.

Options: CBOE, P, Ph

Analysis prepared by **Phillip M. Seligman** on November 18, 2009, when the stock traded at **$73.47**.

Highlights

► We expect revenues to rise 6.1% in FY 10 (Sep.), as we see more favorable foreign exchange, and medical segment revenues growing 5.8% on worldwide demand for safety and diabetes care products, including pen needles, and a $52 million U.S. government order for H1N1 vaccination supplies. We also believe diagnostics revenues will rise 6.9% on worldwide demand for safety products and tests to detect C. difficile infections and cervical cancer, but we think biosciences revenues will grow 3.0% at best, aided by $20 million to $25 million of U.S. stimulus orders and modest improvements BDX sees in the U.S. academic market.

► We see gross margins narrowing in FY 10, as the lapping of one-time gains that benefited FY 09 EPS, start-up costs and incremental pension costs outweigh productivity and product mix gains. We see a stable R&D cost ratio, while the SG&A cost ratio declines on cost controls, despite incremental IT spending.

► Our FY 10 EPS estimate is $5.08, compared to FY 09's $4.95, which benefited from a $0.26 hedge gain and a $0.09 foreign currency holding gain. We forecast FY 11 EPS of $5.55.

Investment Rationale/Risk

► We think BDX has the product lines and pipeline to eventually achieve its long-term annual revenue growth target of 7% to 9% and 10% to 12% annual earnings growth. We believe such growth is also supported by its growing cash flow and cash position. Nonetheless, we think it will take time for BDX to realize its targets, assuming continued softness in U.S. hospital buying patterns and in Eastern European economies. While BDX expects to benefit over the long term from continued strong global demand for safety and diabetes care supplies, it sees total revenues from flu-related products in FY 10 at the same level as in FY 09, and modest recovery in the life sciences markets.

► Risks to our opinion and target price include a slower-than-expected recovery in key life science markets, continued cutbacks in spending by the company's hospital customers, adverse patent litigation, and greater-than-anticipated unfavorable foreign currency fluctuations.

► Our 12-month target price of $76 is determined by applying a multiple of 14.5X to our calendar 2010 EPS estimate of $5.17, below the stock's historical valuation levels.

Qualitative Risk Assessment

LOW	MEDIUM	HIGH

BDX's markets are competitive, and new product introductions by current and future competitors have the potential to significantly affect market dynamics. In addition, changes in domestic and foreign health care industry practices and regulations may result in increased pricing pressures and lower reimbursements for some of its products. However, we believe BDX's product line has more favorable demand and pricing characteristics than those in the medical equipment industry in general.

Quantitative Evaluations

S&P Quality Ranking A

D	C	B-	B	B+	A-	A	A+

Relative Strength Rank STRONG

80

LOWEST = 1 HIGHEST = 99

Revenue/Earnings Data

Revenue (Million $)

	1Q	2Q	3Q	4Q	Year
2009	1,734	1,741	1,820	1,898	7,161
2008	1,706	1,747	1,868	1,836	7,156
2007	1,502	1,576	1,631	1,651	6,360
2006	1,414	1,449	1,484	1,488	5,835
2005	1,288	1,366	1,381	1,379	5,415
2004	1,185	1,254	1,243	1,253	4,935

Earnings Per Share ($)

2009	1.26	1.06	1.38	1.25	4.92
2008	1.07	1.09	1.18	1.13	4.46
2007	0.51	0.92	0.95	0.98	3.36
2006	0.85	0.61	0.81	0.69	2.95
2005	0.74	0.71	0.73	0.47	2.66
2004	0.48	0.62	0.41	0.70	2.21

Fiscal year ended Sep. 30. Next earnings report expected: Late January. EPS Estimates based on S&P Operating Earnings; historical GAAP earnings are as reported.

Dividend Data (Dates: mm/dd Payment Date: mm/dd/yy)

Amount ($)	Date Decl.	Ex-Div. Date	Stk. of Record	Payment Date
0.330	02/03	03/06	03/10	03/31/09
0.330	05/20	06/05	06/09	06/30/09
0.330	07/28	09/04	09/09	09/30/09
0.370	11/24	12/10	12/14	01/04/10

Dividends have been paid since 1926. Source: Company reports.

Please read the Required Disclosures and Analyst Certification on the last page of this report.

The McGraw·Hill Companies

Becton, Dickinson and Co

STANDARD
&POOR'S

Business Summary November 18, 2009

Becton, Dickinson traces its roots to a concern started by Maxwell Becton and Fairleigh Dickinson in 1897. One of the first companies to sell U.S.-made glass syringes, BDX was also a pioneer in the production of hypodermic needles. The company now manufactures and sells medical supplies, devices, lab equipment and diagnostic products used by health care institutions, life science researchers, clinical laboratories, industry and the general public. In FY 09 (Sep.), 60% of the company's sales were generated from non-U.S. markets.

Major products in the core medical systems division (52% of FY 09 revenues) include hypodermic syringes and needles for injection, insulin syringes and pen needles for diabetes care, infusion therapy devices, prefillable drug delivery systems, and surgical blades and scalpels. The segment also markets specialty blades and cannulas for ophthalmic surgery procedures, anesthesia needles, critical care systems, elastic support products, and thermometers. The blood glucose monitoring and test strip business was sold in December 2006.

The diagnostics segment (31%) provides a range of products designed for the safe collection and transport of diagnostic specimens and instrumentation for analysis across a wide range of infectious disease testing, including health care-associated infections (HAIs). Its principal products and services include

integrated systems for specimen collection; an extensive line of safety-engineered blood collection products and systems; plated media; automated blood culturing systems; molecular testing systems for sexually transmitted diseases and HAIs; microorganism identification and drug susceptibility systems; liquid-based cytology systems for cervical cancer screening; and rapid diagnostic assays. The segment also includes consulting services and customized, automated bar-code systems for patient identification and point-of-care data capture.

The biosciences unit (17%) provides research tools and reagents to clinicians and medical researchers studying genes, proteins and cells in order to better understand disease, improve diagnosis and disease management, and facilitate the discovery and development of novel therapeutics. Products include instrument systems for cell sorting and analysis, monoclonal antibody reagents and kits for diagnostic and research use, tools to aid in drug discovery and vaccine development, molecular biology products, fluid handling, cell growth and screening products.

Company Financials Fiscal Year Ended Sep. 30

Per Share Data ($)	2009	2008	2007	2006	2005	2004	2003	2002	2001	2000
Tangible Book Value	NA	15.38	13.41	11.96	10.28	9.28	8.82	6.06	5.35	3.80
Cash Flow	NA	5.89	5.09	4.52	4.36	3.57	3.54	2.92	2.76	2.58
Earnings	4.92	4.46	3.36	2.95	2.66	2.21	2.07	1.79	1.63	1.49
S&P Core Earnings	NA	4.22	3.38	2.99	2.75	2.39	2.01	1.57	1.38	NA
Dividends	1.32	1.14	0.98	0.86	0.72	0.60	0.40	0.39	0.38	0.37
Payout Ratio	27%	26%	29%	29%	27%	27%	19%	22%	23%	25%
Prices:High	77.11	93.24	85.89	74.25	61.17	58.18	41.82	38.60	39.25	35.31
Prices:Low	60.40	58.14	69.30	58.08	49.71	40.90	28.82	24.70	29.96	23.75
P/E Ratio:High	16	21	26	25	23	26	20	22	24	24
P/E Ratio:Low	12	13	21	20	19	19	14	14	18	16

Income Statement Analysis (Million $)										
Revenue	7,161	7,156	6,360	5,835	5,415	4,935	4,528	4,033	3,754	3,618
Operating Income	NA	1,912	1,644	1,456	1,419	1,244	1,094	1,002	952	861
Depreciation	NA	360	441	405	387	357	344	305	306	288
Interest Expense	NA	66.2	46.0	66.0	55.7	29.6	73.1	33.3	47.1	78.3
Pretax Income	1,639	1,554	1,204	1,035	1,005	753	710	629	577	520
Effective Tax Rate	26.0%	27.4%	28.8%	27.0%	31.1%	22.6%	22.9%	23.6%	24.0%	24.4%
Net Income	1,213	1,128	856	756	692	583	547	480	438	393
S&P Core Earnings	NA	1,068	863	766	714	628	523	417	364	NA

Balance Sheet & Other Financial Data (Million $)										
Cash	NA	1,030	511	1,000	1,043	719	520	243	82.1	49.2
Current Assets	NA	3,615	3,131	3,185	2,975	2,641	2,339	1,929	1,763	1,661
Total Assets	NA	7,913	7,329	6,825	6,072	5,753	5,572	5,040	4,802	4,505
Current Liabilities	NA	1,417	1,479	1,576	1,299	1,050	1,043	1,252	1,265	1,354
Long Term Debt	NA	953	956	957	1,061	1,172	1,184	803	1,902	780
Common Equity	NA	4,936	4,362	3,836	3,284	3,037	2,863	2,450	2,288	1,912
Total Capital	NA	5,924	5,318	4,793	4,345	4,328	4,200	3,396	4,321	2,823
Capital Expenditures	NA	602	556	459	318	266	261	260	371	376
Cash Flow	NA	1,488	1,297	1,161	1,080	940	889	783	742	679
Current Ratio	NA	2.6	2.1	2.0	2.3	2.5	2.2	1.5	1.4	1.2
% Long Term Debt of Capitalization	Nil	16.1	17.9	20.0	24.4	27.1	28.2	23.6	44.0	27.6
% Net Income of Revenue	16.9	15.8	13.4	12.9	12.8	11.8	12.1	11.9	11.7	10.9
% Return on Assets	NA	14.8	12.0	11.7	11.7	10.3	10.3	9.8	9.4	8.8
% Return on Equity	NA	24.3	20.8	21.2	21.9	19.7	20.5	20.2	20.8	21.5

Data as orig reptd.; bef. results of disc opers/spec. items. Per share data adj. for stk. divs.; EPS diluted. E-Estimated. NA-Not Available. NM-Not Meaningful. NR-Not Ranked. UR-Under Review.

Office: One Becton Drive, Franklin Lakes, NJ 07417-1880.
Telephone: 201-847-6800.
Email: investor_relations@bdhq.bd.com
Website: http://www.bd.com

Chrmn & CEO: E.J. Ludwig
Pres: V.A. Forlenza
EVP & CFO: D.V. Elkins
SVP & CTO: S.P. Bruder

SVP & General Counsel: J.S. Sherman
Investor Contact: P.A. Spinella (201-847-5453)
Board Members: B. L. Anderson, H. P. Becton, Jr., E. F. DeGraan, C. M. Fraser-Liggett, M. O. Larsen, E. J. Ludwig, A. Mahmoud, G. A. Mecklenburg, C. Minehan, J. F. Orr, W. J. Overlock, Jr., B. L. Scott, A. Sommer

Founded: 1897
Domicile: New Jersey
Employees: 28,277

The McGraw-Hill Companies

Bed Bath & Beyond Inc

STANDARD
&POOR'S

S&P Recommendation **SELL** ★★☆☆☆	Price	12-Mo. Target Price	Investment Style
	$36.99 (as of Nov 27, 2009)	$34.00	Large-Cap Growth

GICS Sector Consumer Discretionary
Sub-Industry Homefurnishing Retail

Summary This company operates a nationwide chain of more than 900 Bed Bath & Beyond superstores selling better-quality domestics merchandise and home furnishings. It also has retail stores under the names Christmas Tree Shops, Harmon and buybuy BABY.

Key Stock Statistics (Source S&P, Vickers, company reports)

52-Wk Range	$40.23– 18.12	S&P Oper. EPS 2010**E**	1.82	Market Capitalization(B)	$9.717	Beta	1.17
Trailing 12-Month EPS	$1.75	S&P Oper. EPS 2011**E**	1.97	Yield (%)	Nil	S&P 3-Yr. Proj. EPS CAGR(%)	8
Trailing 12-Month P/E	21.1	P/E on S&P Oper. EPS 2010**E**	20.3	Dividend Rate/Share	Nil	S&P Credit Rating	BBB
$10K Invested 5 Yrs Ago	$8,954	Common Shares Outstg. (M)	262.7	Institutional Ownership (%)	98		

Price Performance

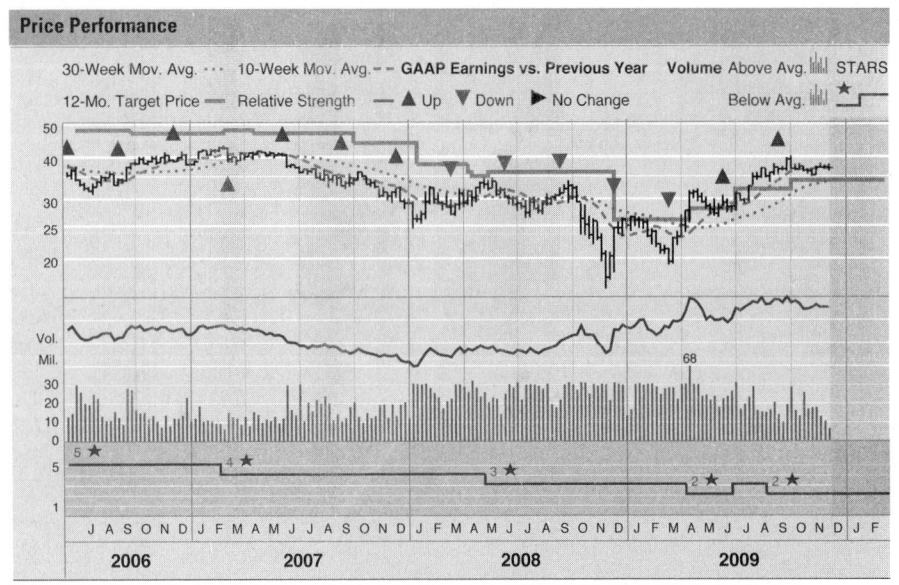

30-Week Mov. Avg. ···· 10-Week Mov. Avg. --- GAAP Earnings vs. Previous Year Volume Above Avg. STARS
12-Mo. Target Price — Relative Strength ▲ Up ▼ Down ▶ No Change Below Avg.

Options: ASE, CBOE, Ph

Analysis prepared by **Michael Souers** on September 28, 2009, when the stock traded at **$ 37.74**.

Highlights

► We expect sales to rise 4.3% in FY 10 (Feb.), following a 2.3% advance in FY 09. This reflects the projected addition of 35 new Bed Bath & Beyond stores and flat same-store sales results. We also anticipate the opening of six to eight new Christmas Tree Shops, as well as 12 buybuy BABY stores and four Harmon stores. We see same-store sales reflecting a slight decline in foot traffic, offset by a slight increase in average ticket.

► We expect gross margins to widen slightly, as the benefit from the liquidation of competitor Linens 'N Things is partially offset by higher occupancy costs. We forecast a 100 basis point increase in operating margins, driven by significant cost-cutting efforts in payroll and advertising, along with a reduction in new store openings.

► After slightly lower projected interest income, an anticipated effective tax rate of 38.9%, and a slight increase in the diluted share count, we estimate FY 10 EPS of $1.82, an 11% increase from the $1.64 the company earned in FY 09. We see EPS of $1.97 in FY 11.

Investment Rationale/Risk

► Despite the company's recent solid execution, our enthusiasm for the shares is tempered on valuation concerns, with BBBY at about 19X our FY 11 EPS estimate, a sizable premium to the S&P 500. In addition, while we think the home furnishings industry is near a cyclical bottom -- plagued by cash-strapped consumers and a weak housing market, we expect it will take years for a solid recovery to build. On a positive note, we expect BBBY will continue to gain market share in home furnishings, with better merchandising and execution than peers, and to benefit from the recent bankruptcy of privately held Linens 'n Things.

► Risks to our recommendation and target price include a recovery in consumer spending, an unanticipated shift in spending toward home-centric products, and market share gains from strong company execution.

► Our 12-month target price of $34, or about 17X our FY 11 EPS estimate, is based on our discounted cash flow analysis, which assumes a weighted average cost of capital of 10.3% and a terminal growth rate of 3.5%.

Qualitative Risk Assessment

LOW	MEDIUM	HIGH

Our risk assessment reflects the cyclical nature of the home furnishing retail industry, which relies heavily on consumer spending, and, to a lesser extent, housing turnover, offset by significant growth areas we see in major domestic metro markets and Canada.

Quantitative Evaluations

S&P Quality Ranking B+

D	C	B-	B	B+	A-	A	A+

Relative Strength Rank MODERATE

59

LOWEST = 1   HIGHEST = 99

Revenue/Earnings Data

Revenue (Million $)

	1Q	2Q	3Q	4Q	Year
2010	1,694	1,915	--	--	--
2009	1,648	1,854	1,783	1,923	7,208
2008	1,553	1,768	1,795	1,933	7,049
2007	1,396	1,607	1,619	1,995	6,617
2006	1,244	1,431	1,449	1,685	5,810
2005	1,101	1,274	1,305	1,468	5,148

Earnings Per Share ($)

2010	0.34	0.52	E0.40	E0.57	E1.82
2009	0.30	0.46	0.34	0.55	1.64
2008	0.38	0.55	0.52	0.66	2.10
2007	0.35	0.51	0.50	0.72	2.09
2006	0.33	0.47	0.45	0.67	1.92
2005	0.27	0.39	0.40	0.59	1.65

Fiscal year ended Feb. 28. Next earnings report expected: Early January. EPS Estimates based on S&P Operating Earnings; historical GAAP earnings are as reported.

Dividend Data

No cash dividends have been paid.

Bed Bath & Beyond Inc

STANDARD &POOR'S

Business Summary September 28, 2009

CORPORATE OVERVIEW. Bed Bath & Beyond operates one of the largest U.S. chains of superstores selling domestics merchandise and home furnishings. BBBY stores predominantly range in size from 20,000 sq. ft. to 50,000 sq. ft., with some encompassing 100,000 sq. ft. The company has grown rapidly, from 34 stores at the end of FY 93 (Feb.) to 930 Bed Bath & Beyond stores in 49 states, the District of Columbia, Puerto Rico and Canada at year-end FY 09. BBBY opened 49 Bed Bath & Beyond Stores stores in FY 09, after opening 66 stores in FY 08; it expects to open 35 new stores in FY 10. During FY 09, total square footage of Bed Bath & Beyond stores grew 6.3%, to 32.1 million sq. ft., from 30.2 million sq. ft. Company stores are principally located in suburban areas of medium- and large-sized cities. These stores are situated in strip and power strip shopping centers, as well as in major off-price and conventional malls, and freestanding buildings.

In March 2002, the company acquired Harmon Stores, Inc., a health and beau-

ty care retailer. The Harmon chain had 40 stores in three states at February 28, 2009, ranging in size from approximately 5,000 to 9,000 sq. ft. In June 2003, BBBY acquired Christmas Tree Shops, a retailer of home decor, giftware, housewares, food, paper goods and seasonal products, for approximately $194.4 million, net of cash acquired. The company operated 52 Christmas Tree Shops in 13 states at year-end FY 09, ranging in size between 30,000 and 50,000 sq. ft. In March 2007, BBBY acquired buybuy BABY, a retailer of infant and toddler merchandise, for approximately $67 million, net of cash acquired. The company operated 15 buybuy BABY stores at year-end FY 09, ranging in size from 28,000 to 60,000 square feet.

Company Financials Fiscal Year Ended Feb. 28

Per Share Data ($)	2009	2008	2007	2006	2005	2004	2003	2002	2001	2000
Tangible Book Value	10.67	11.34	9.56	8.05	6.99	6.14	4.93	3.75	2.84	1.99
Cash Flow	2.32	2.69	2.56	2.29	1.96	1.59	1.25	0.94	0.75	0.57
Earnings	1.64	2.10	2.09	1.92	1.65	1.31	1.00	0.74	0.59	0.46
S&P Core Earnings	1.64	2.10	2.09	1.87	1.55	1.23	0.92	0.67	0.53	NA
Dividends	Nil	Nil	Nil	Nil	Nil	Nil	Nil	Nil	Nil	Nil
Payout Ratio	Nil	Nil	Nil	Nil	Nil	Nil	Nil	Nil	Nil	Nil
Calendar Year	2008	2007	2006	2005	2004	2003	2002	2001	2000	1999
Prices:High	34.73	43.32	41.72	46.99	44.43	45.00	37.90	35.70	27.31	19.69
Prices:Low	16.23	27.96	30.92	35.50	33.88	30.18	26.70	18.70	11.00	12.75
P/E Ratio:High	21	21	20	24	27	34	38	48	46	43
P/E Ratio:Low	10	13	15	18	21	23	27	25	19	28

Income Statement Analysis (Million $)

	2009	2008	2007	2006	2005	2004	2003	2002	2001	2000
Revenue	7,208	7,049	6,617	5,810	5,148	4,478	3,665	2,928	2,397	1,878
Operating Income	850	996	1,026	990	890	724	555	409	319	241
Depreciation	176	158	136	111	97.5	84.6	74.8	62.5	46.7	31.6
Interest Expense	Nil	Nil	Nil	Nil	Nil	Nil	Nil	Nil	Nil	Nil
Pretax Income	683	865	933	915	811	650	491	357	282	215
Effective Tax Rate	37.8%	35.0%	36.3%	37.4%	37.8%	38.5%	38.5%	38.5%	39.0%	39.0%
Net Income	425	563	594	573	505	399	302	220	172	131
S&P Core Earnings	425	563	594	557	470	370	277	200	155	NA

Balance Sheet & Other Financial Data (Million $)

	2009	2008	2007	2006	2005	2004	2003	2002	2001	2000
Cash	670	224	988	652	851	867	617	429	239	144
Current Assets	2,563	2,080	2,699	2,072	2,097	1,969	1,594	1,227	886	647
Total Assets	4,269	3,844	3,959	3,382	3,200	2,865	2,189	1,648	1,196	866
Current Liabilities	953	1,014	1,145	990	874	770	680	511	353	287
Long Term Debt	Nil	Nil	Nil	Nil	Nil	Nil	Nil	Nil	Nil	Nil
Common Equity	3,000	2,562	2,649	2,262	2,204	1,991	1,452	1,094	817	559
Total Capital	3,000	2,562	2,649	2,262	2,204	1,991	1,452	1,094	817	559
Capital Expenditures	216	358	318	220	191	113	135	121	140	90.1
Cash Flow	601	721	731	684	602	484	377	282	219	163
Current Ratio	2.7	2.1	2.4	2.1	2.4	2.6	2.3	2.4	2.5	2.3
% Long Term Debt of Capitalization	Nil	Nil	Nil	Nil	Nil	Nil	Nil	Nil	Nil	Nil
% Net Income of Revenue	5.9	8.0	9.0	9.9	9.8	8.9	8.2	7.5	7.2	7.0
% Return on Assets	10.5	14.4	16.2	17.4	16.7	15.8	15.8	15.4	16.7	17.5
% Return on Equity	15.3	21.6	24.2	25.7	24.1	23.2	23.7	23.0	25.0	27.1

Data as orig reptd.; bef. results of disc opers/spec. items. Per share data adj. for stk. divs.; EPS diluted. E-Estimated. NA-Not Available. NM-Not Meaningful. NR-Not Ranked. UR-Under Review.

Office: 650 Liberty Ave, Union, NJ 07083-8135.
Telephone: 908-688-0888.
Website: http://www.bedbathandbeyond.com
Co-Chrmn: L. Feinstein

Co-Chrmn & Secy: W. Eisenberg
Pres: A. Stark
CEO: S.H. Temares
COO & CTO: K. Wanner

Investor Contact: R. Curwin (908-688-0888)
Board Members: D. S. Adler, S. F. Barshay, W. Eisenberg, K. Eppler, L. Feinstein, P. R. Gaston, J. Heller, V. A. Morrison, F. Stoller, S. H. Temares

Founded: 1971
Domicile: New York
Employees: 37,000

Bemis Co Inc

STANDARD &POOR'S

S&P Recommendation BUY ★★★★☆	Price $28.76 (as of Nov 27, 2009)	12-Mo. Target Price $32.00	Investment Style Large-Cap Blend

GICS Sector Materials
Sub-Industry Paper Packaging

Summary This company is a leading maker of a broad range of flexible packaging and pressure-sensitive materials.

Key Stock Statistics (Source S&P, Vickers, company reports)

52-Wk Range	$29.54– 16.85	S&P Oper. EPS 2009**E**	1.85	Market Capitalization(B)	$3.112	Beta	0.75
Trailing 12-Month EPS	$1.51	S&P Oper. EPS 2010**E**	2.05	Yield (%)	3.13	S&P 3-Yr. Proj. EPS CAGR(%)	6
Trailing 12-Month P/E	19.1	P/E on S&P Oper. EPS 2009**E**	15.5	Dividend Rate/Share	$0.90	S&P Credit Rating	A
$10K Invested 5 Yrs Ago	$12,081	Common Shares Outstg. (M)	108.2	Institutional Ownership (%)	70		

Price Performance

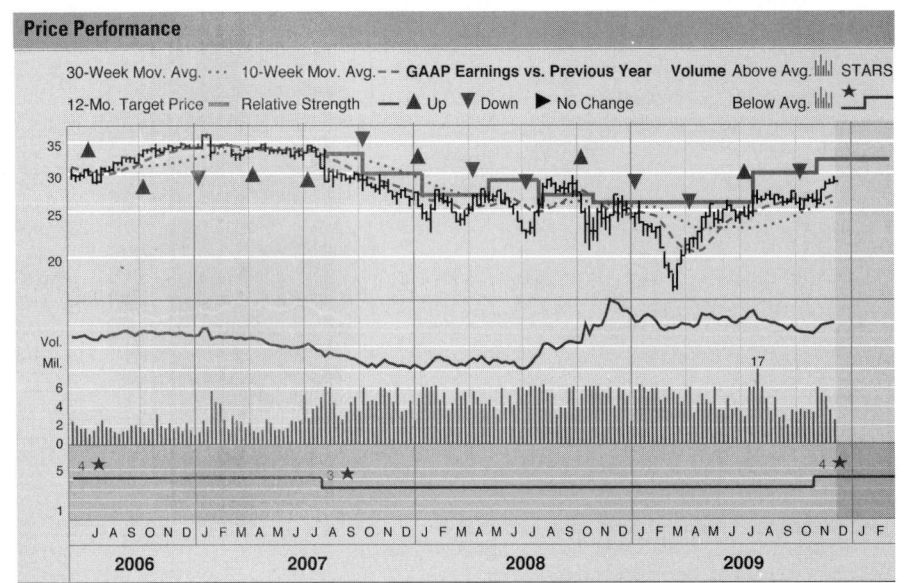

30-Week Mov. Avg. · · · 10-Week Mov. Avg. - - **GAAP Earnings vs. Previous Year** Volume Above Avg. STARS
12-Mo. Target Price — Relative Strength — ▲ Up ▼ Down ► No Change Below Avg.

2006 2007 2008 2009

Options: ASE, CBOE, P

Analysis prepared by **Stewart Scharf** on October 28, 2009, when the stock traded at **$ 26.90.**

Highlights

► We expect sales to decline about 8% in 2009, reflecting negative foreign exchange and weak global consumer demand for both flexible and pressure-sensitive materials packaging products. We see a gradual sequential rebound during 2010 as we think organic unit volume will pick up in key flexible markets, such as meat and cheese, and health and hygiene, while better pricing and mix should aid sales. Acquisitions and a weaker U.S. dollar should also contribute to total sales growth.

► We see gross margins expanding further in 2010, from our 20% projection for 2009 (17.2% in 2008), based on pricing initiatives, more stable resin and other raw material costs, and a better sales mix due to new higher-margin products. In our view, operating margins (EBITDA) will also widen from near 13.5% seen for 2009, reflecting improved productivity and cost controls.

► We project an effective tax rate for 2009 of 36.3%, in line with 2008's, and operating EPS of $1.85 (before at least $0.15 of net charges), advancing 11% in 2010, to $2.05. Results exclude the pending acquisition of Alcan Packaging Food Americas.

Investment Rationale/Risk

► We recently upgraded our recommendation to buy from hold, based on our valuation metrics, along with the company's cash flow and capital structure. Although BMS's debt ratio has risen due to financing related to its proposed Alcan Packaging acquisition, we believe the deal will be a good strategic fit and cash generation will be sufficient to pay down debt.

► Risks to our recommendation and target price include another surge in commodity prices, softer global demand, and negative foreign exchange rates. We have some corporate governance concerns based on the CEO being a party to one or more related-party transactions.

► With the stock's recent dividend yield of 3.3%, versus 2% for the S&P 500 Index, and BMS's solid earnings track record, we apply an above five-year historical forward P/E of 17.5X to our 2010 EPS estimate to derive a value of $36. Based on our DCF analysis, the stock has an intrinsic value of $28, assuming a 3% terminal growth rate and an 8.3% weighted average cost of capital. Blending these valuations, we arrive at our 12-month target price of $32.

Qualitative Risk Assessment

LOW	MEDIUM	HIGH

Our risk assessment reflects challenging global economic conditions, volatile raw material prices and possible difficulty in integrating acquisitions. However, BMS has an S&P Quality Ranking of A-, which indicates above-average long-term earnings and dividend growth.

Quantitative Evaluations

S&P Quality Ranking A-

D	C	B-	B	B+	A-	A	A+

Relative Strength Rank STRONG

80

LOWEST = 1 HIGHEST = 99

Revenue/Earnings Data

Revenue (Million $)

	1Q	2Q	3Q	4Q	Year
2009	843.4	866.4	898.9	--	--
2008	947.3	980.0	984.3	867.9	3,779
2007	909.1	921.8	905.7	912.7	3,649
2006	901.7	933.8	903.3	900.6	3,639
2005	831.9	879.9	870.1	892.1	3,474
2004	684.0	712.9	711.9	725.6	2,834

Earnings Per Share ($)

2009	0.36	0.47	0.33	E0.44	E1.85
2008	0.42	0.46	0.44	0.33	1.65
2007	0.45	0.47	0.40	0.42	1.74
2006	0.35	0.46	0.45	0.39	1.65
2005	0.30	0.38	0.41	0.42	1.51
2004	0.40	0.42	0.41	0.44	1.67

Fiscal year ended Dec. 31. Next earnings report expected: Late January. EPS Estimates based on S&P Operating Earnings; historical GAAP earnings are as reported.

Dividend Data (Dates: mm/dd Payment Date: mm/dd/yy)

Amount ($)	Date Decl.	Ex-Div. Date	Stk. of Record	Payment Date
0.225	01/29	02/11	02/13	03/02/09
0.225	05/07	05/19	05/21	06/01/09
0.225	07/30	08/14	08/18	09/01/09
0.225	10/29	11/12	11/16	12/01/09

Dividends have been paid since 1922. Source: Company reports.

Please read the Required Disclosures and Analyst Certification on the last page of this report.

The McGraw-Hill Companies

Bemis Co Inc

STANDARD &POOR'S

Business Summary October 28, 2009

CORPORATE OVERVIEW. Bemis Co., a leading North American producer of flexible packaging products, as well as pressure-sensitive materials, focuses primarily on the food industry (about 60% of sales). Markets also include the chemicals, agribusiness, pharmaceutical, personal care products, electronics, automotive and graphic industries. BMS has 50 manufacturing plants (five leased) in 13 U.S. states plus 10 countries.

Although BMS focuses on marketing its products in the U.S. (64% of 2008 net sales) and Europe (17%), it has broadened its reach to South America (15%), Southeast Asia and Mexico, due to strong demand for barrier films to extend the shelf life of perishable foods. Canada had sales of 0.3%, while 2.6% came from other regions.

The Flexible Packaging Products segment (84% of net sales in 2008; $316 million of operating profits) produces a wide range of consumer and industrial packaging products, including high barrier, polyethylene and paper products. High barrier products, which comprise more than 50% of net sales, include flexible polymer film structures and barrier laminates for food, medical and personal care products.

The Pressure Sensitive Materials segment (16%; $34 million in operating profits) produces printing products, decorative and sheet products, and technical products.

Flexible packaging competitors include Sealed Air, Sonoco Products, Smurfit-Stone Container and Hood Packaging. Pressure-sensitive materials competitors include Avery Dennison, Minnesota Mining and Manufacturing (3M), Ricoh, Flexcon and Spinnaker Industries.

In January 2005, the company acquired majority ownership of Brazil-based Dixie Toga, a leading South American packaging company, for $250 million in cash (less than 6X Dixie's 2004 EBITDA). Dixie had annual sales of over $450 million in 2005. BMS controls 85% of Dixie's preferred shares.

Company Financials Fiscal Year Ended Dec. 31

Per Share Data ($)	2008	2007	2006	2005	2004	2003	2002	2001	2000	1999
Tangible Book Value	6.72	9.70	7.31	6.29	7.48	5.81	4.11	4.39	4.76	5.52
Cash Flow	3.26	3.28	3.08	2.98	2.88	2.56	2.65	2.49	2.24	2.02
Earnings	1.65	1.74	1.65	1.51	1.67	1.37	1.54	1.32	1.22	1.09
S&P Core Earnings	1.40	1.67	1.64	1.48	1.65	1.32	1.28	1.02	NA	NA
Dividends	0.66	0.84	0.76	0.72	0.64	0.56	0.52	0.50	0.48	0.46
Payout Ratio	40%	48%	46%	48%	38%	41%	34%	38%	39%	42%
Prices:High	29.70	36.53	34.99	32.50	29.49	25.58	29.12	26.24	19.66	20.19
Prices:Low	20.62	25.53	27.86	23.20	23.24	19.67	19.70	14.34	11.47	15.09
P/E Ratio:High	18	21	21	22	18	19	19	20	16	19
P/E Ratio:Low	12	15	17	15	14	14	13	11	9	14

Income Statement Analysis (Million $)	2008	2007	2006	2005	2004	2003	2002	2001	2000	1999
Revenue	3,779	3,649	3,639	3,474	2,834	2,635	2,369	2,293	2,165	1,918
Operating Income	443	468	492	472	420	384	401	384	363	316
Depreciation	163	159	152	151	131	128	119	124	108	97.7
Interest Expense	42.0	54.5	49.3	38.7	15.5	12.6	15.4	30.3	31.6	21.2
Pretax Income	269	290	289	282	294	240	268	228	212	190
Effective Tax Rate	35.9%	36.0%	37.8%	40.3%	38.7%	38.4%	37.9%	38.2%	38.2%	37.4%
Net Income	166	182	176	163	180	147	166	140	131	115
S&P Core Earnings	142	174	176	160	179	142	137	108	NA	NA

Balance Sheet & Other Financial Data (Million $)	2008	2007	2006	2005	2004	2003	2002	2001	2000	1999
Cash	48.3	147	112	91.1	93.9	76.5	56.4	35.1	28.9	18.2
Current Assets	983	1,137	1,094	988	874	752	722	587	640	584
Total Assets	2,827	3,191	3,039	2,965	2,487	2,293	2,257	1,923	1,889	1,532
Current Liabilities	422	535	555	474	375	316	326	238	495	253
Long Term Debt	660	843	722	790	534	583	718	595	438	372
Common Equity	1,342	1,562	1,472	1,349	1,308	1,139	959	886	799	726
Total Capital	2,147	2,533	2,358	2,336	2,019	1,878	1,788	1,606	1,342	1,227
Capital Expenditures	121	179	159	187	135	106	91.0	117	100	137
Cash Flow	329	341	329	313	311	275	285	264	239	212
Current Ratio	2.3	2.1	2.0	2.1	2.3	2.4	2.2	2.5	1.3	2.3
% Long Term Debt of Capitalization	30.7	32.6	30.6	33.8	26.4	31.1	40.2	37.1	32.6	30.3
% Net Income of Revenue	4.4	5.0	4.8	4.7	6.3	5.6	7.0	6.1	6.0	6.0
% Return on Assets	5.5	5.8	5.9	6.0	7.5	6.5	7.9	7.4	7.6	7.6
% Return on Equity	11.5	12.0	12.5	12.2	14.7	14.0	17.9	16.7	17.1	16.2

Data as orig reptd.; bef. results of disc opers/spec. items. Per share data adj. for stk. divs.; EPS diluted. E-Estimated. NA-Not Available. NM-Not Meaningful. NR-Not Ranked. UR-Under Review.

Office: 1 Neenah Ctr 4th Fl, Neenah, WI 54957-0669.
Telephone: 920-727-4100.
Website: http://www.bemis.com
Chrmn: J.H. Curler

Pres & CEO: H.J. Theisen
COO: W.F. Austen
SVP & CFO: G.C. Wulf
CTO: R. Germonprez

Investor Contact: M.E. Miller (920-527-5045)
Board Members: W. J. Bolton, J. H. Curler, D. S. Haffner, B. L. Johnson, T. M. Manganello, R. D. O'Shaughnessy, P. S. Peercy, E. N. Perry, W. J. Scholle, H. J. Theisen, H. A. Van Deursen, P. G. Weaver, G. C. Wulf

Founded: 1858
Domicile: Missouri
Employees: 15,394

Best Buy Co. Inc.

STANDARD &POOR'S

| S&P Recommendation | HOLD ★★★☆☆ | Price $42.83 (as of Nov 27, 2009) | 12-Mo. Target Price $43.00 | Investment Style Large-Cap Growth |

GICS Sector Consumer Discretionary
Sub-Industry Computer & Electronics Retail

Summary This leading retailer of consumer electronics and entertainment software operates approximately 4,000 stores in the U.S., Canada, China and Europe.

Key Stock Statistics (Source S&P, Vickers, company reports)

52-Wk Range	$44.32– 18.49	S&P Oper. EPS 2010**E**	2.87	Market Capitalization(B)	$17.840	Beta	1.33
Trailing 12-Month EPS	$2.21	S&P Oper. EPS 2011**E**	2.98	Yield (%)	1.31	S&P 3-Yr. Proj. EPS CAGR(%)	9
Trailing 12-Month P/E	19.4	P/E on S&P Oper. EPS 2010**E**	14.9	Dividend Rate/Share	$0.56	S&P Credit Rating	BBB-
$10K Invested 5 Yrs Ago	$11,493	Common Shares Outstg. (M)	416.5	Institutional Ownership (%)	72		

Price Performance

30-Week Mov. Avg. · · · 10-Week Mov. Avg. - - **GAAP Earnings vs. Previous Year** Volume Above Avg. ⅢⅢ STARS
12-Mo. Target Price — Relative Strength — ▲ Up ▼ Down ▶ No Change Below Avg. ⅢⅢ ★

Options: ASE, CBOE, P, Ph

Analysis prepared by **Michael Souers** on October 27, 2009, when the stock traded at **$ 39.39**.

Highlights

► We view BBY as the best-of-class U.S. consumer electronics retailer, based on its digital product focus, knowledgeable sales staff, and effective marketing campaigns. We think BBY's focus on advanced TVs, notebook computers, video gaming devices, mobile phones and GPS devices will support solid revenue growth near term.

► We project an 8.1% increase in revenues for FY 10 (Feb.), following a 13% advance in FY 09. We expect this growth to be driven by the acquisition of Carphone Warehouse and approximately 65 net new stores worldwide, along with market share gains from Circuit City's liquidation. We believe these positive drivers will be partially offset by a 1%-2% decline in comparable-store sales, given our forecast of a modest decrease in consumer spending. We expect operating margins to narrow slightly, as a projected improvement in gross margins is offset by the deleveraging of SG&A expenses due to weak same-store sales results.

► Excluding a restructuring charge, we project FY 10 EPS of $2.87, a 0.3% decline from the $2.88 the company earned in FY 09, excluding one-time items. We see FY 11 EPS of $2.98.

Investment Rationale/Risk

► We favor BBY's recent decision to curb capital spending and its plan to slash SG&A expenses in the current challenging macroeconomic environment. We also expect continued market share gains given the recent bankruptcy of peer Circuit City. We think these steps, combined with BBY's customer focus, will enable the company to continue to differentiate itself in a competitive marketplace. However, we are concerned that the industry faces the potential saturation of flat-panel TVs in the near term, and think revolutionary "must-have" products may be several years away. Following a recent increase in the stock price, we think the shares are fairly valued at 13X our FY 11 EPS estimate, a modest discount to historical averages.

► Risks to our recommendation and target price include sharp deterioration in the economic climate and consumer confidence, and the risk that BBY will be unable to successfully execute its strategic objectives.

► Our 12-month target price of $43, about 14X our FY 11 EPS projection, is based on our DCF analysis, which assumes a weighted average cost of capital of 10.8% and a terminal growth rate of 3.5%.

Qualitative Risk Assessment

| LOW | MEDIUM | HIGH |

Our risk assessment reflects what we view as BBY's strong balance sheet, sizable market share, numerous suppliers and buyers, and a history of profitability, offset by a highly competitive environment for consumer electronics retailing, with numerous rivals and strong price competition.

Quantitative Evaluations

S&P Quality Ranking B+

| D | C | B- | B | B+ | A- | A | A+ |

Relative Strength Rank STRONG

83

LOWEST = 1 HIGHEST = 99

Revenue/Earnings Data

Revenue (Million $)

	1Q	2Q	3Q	4Q	Year
2010	10,095	11,022	--	--	--
2009	8,990	9,801	11,500	14,724	45,015
2008	7,927	8,750	9,928	13,418	40,023
2007	6,959	7,603	8,473	12,899	35,934
2006	6,118	6,702	7,335	10,693	30,848
2005	5,479	6,080	6,647	9,227	27,433

Earnings Per Share ($)

2010	0.36	0.37	E0.44	E1.63	E2.87
2009	0.43	0.48	0.13	1.35	2.39
2008	0.39	0.48	0.53	1.71	3.12
2007	0.47	0.47	0.31	1.55	2.79
2006	0.34	0.37	0.28	1.29	2.27
2005	0.23	0.30	0.29	1.03	1.86

Fiscal year ended Feb. 28. Next earnings report expected: NA. EPS Estimates based on S&P Operating Earnings; historical GAAP earnings are as reported.

Dividend Data (Dates: mm/dd Payment Date: mm/dd/yy)

Amount ($)	Date Decl.	Ex-Div. Date	Stk. of Record	Payment Date
0.140	12/17	01/02	01/06	01/27/09
0.140	03/27	04/14	04/16	05/07/09
0.140	06/17	07/02	07/07	07/28/09
0.140	09/16	10/02	10/06	10/27/09

Dividends have been paid since 2003. Source: Company reports.

Please read the Required Disclosures and Analyst Certification on the last page of this report.

The McGraw-Hill Companies

Best Buy Co. Inc.

STANDARD &POOR'S

Business Summary October 27, 2009

CORPORATE OVERVIEW. This leading consumer electronics retailer operated, as of February 28, 2009, 1,023 Best Buy stores, 38 Best Buy Mobile stand-alone stores, 34 Pacific Sales showrooms, six Magnolia Audio Video stores, nine Best Buy Mobile stand-alone stores, and six Geek Squad stand-alone stores in the U.S. Following the acquisition of Carphone Warehouse in Europe in June 2008, BBY operated 897 Carphone Warehouse and 1,568 The Phone House Stores in Europe as of February 28, 2009. Other international operations include 58 Canada Best Buy stores, 139 Future Shop stores in Canada, 164 Five Star stores in China, five Best Buy China stores and one Best Buy Mexico store at the end of BBY's 2009 fiscal year.

U.S. Best Buy stores average approximately 39,000 retail square feet, and offer products in six revenue categories: consumer electronics (36% of FY 09 (Feb.) revenues), home office (34%), entertainment software (17%), appliances (6%), services (7%), and other (0%). Best Buy's largest category, consumer electronics, includes products such as televisions, digital cameras and accessories, digital camcorders and accessories, DVD players, MP3 players and accessories, navigation products, home theater audio systems and components, and mobile electronics including car stereo and satellite radio products.

CORPORATE STRATEGY. BBY's business strategy centers on meeting individual consumer electronics needs with end-to-end solutions, which involves greater employee involvement and increased services. BBY is committed to scaling BBY customer-centricity across the organization, and completed the transition of all remaining stores to the customer-centric operating model in FY 08. In FY 10, BBY plans to open 40-50 new stores in the U.S., three Future Shop stores, four Best Buy Canada Stores, seven net new Five Star stores, one Best Buy China store, five Best Buy Mexico stores, and the company's first Best Buy Turkey store.

Company Financials Fiscal Year Ended Feb. 28

Per Share Data ($)	2009	2008	2007	2006	2005	2004	2003	2002	2001	2000
Tangible Book Value	4.70	7.99	10.82	9.60	7.91	5.97	4.70	3.65	3.07	2.44
Cash Flow	4.25	4.40	3.80	3.16	2.76	2.41	1.91	1.91	1.18	0.95
Earnings	2.39	3.12	2.79	2.27	1.86	1.63	1.27	1.18	0.83	0.72
S&P Core Earnings	2.77	3.12	2.76	2.27	1.77	1.45	1.11	1.08	0.76	NA
Dividends	0.46	0.46	0.36	0.31	0.50	0.27	Nil	Nil	Nil	Nil
Payout Ratio	19%	15%	13%	14%	38%	17%	Nil	Nil	Nil	Nil
Calendar Year	2008	2007	2006	2005	2004	2003	2002	2001	2000	1999
Prices:High	52.98	53.90	59.50	18.03	41.47	41.80	35.83	33.42	39.50	35.78
Prices:Low	16.42	41.85	43.32	14.84	29.25	15.77	11.33	12.36	9.33	13.72
P/E Ratio:High	22	17	21	14	22	26	28	28	48	49
P/E Ratio:Low	7	13	16	11	16	10	9	10	11	19

Income Statement Analysis (Million $)										
Revenue	45,015	40,023	35,934	30,848	27,433	24,547	20,946	19,597	15,327	12,494
Operating Income	2,807	2,746	2,508	2,100	1,901	1,699	1,320	1,246	772	649
Depreciation	793	585	509	456	459	385	310	309	167	110
Interest Expense	94.0	62.0	Nil	30.0	44.0	31.0	25.0	2.00	6.90	5.10
Pretax Income	1,707	2,225	2,130	1,721	1,443	1,296	1,014	936	642	563
Effective Tax Rate	39.5%	36.6%	35.3%	33.8%	35.3%	38.3%	38.7%	39.1%	38.3%	38.3%
Net Income	1,003	1,407	1,377	1,140	934	800	622	570	396	347
S&P Core Earnings	1,163	1,407	1,364	1,140	873	704	538	512	361	NA

Balance Sheet & Other Financial Data (Million $)										
Cash	498	1,438	1,205	681	470	2,600	1,914	1,855	747	751
Current Assets	8,192	7,342	9,081	7,985	6,903	5,724	4,867	4,611	2,929	2,238
Total Assets	15,826	12,758	13,570	11,864	10,294	8,652	7,663	7,375	4,840	2,995
Current Liabilities	8,435	6,769	6,301	6,056	4,959	4,501	3,793	3,730	2,715	1,785
Long Term Debt	1,126	627	590	178	528	482	828	813	181	14.9
Common Equity	4,643	4,484	6,201	5,257	4,449	3,422	2,730	2,521	1,822	1,096
Total Capital	6,071	5,151	6,826	5,435	4,977	3,904	3,558	3,334	2,003	1,111
Capital Expenditures	1,303	797	733	648	502	545	725	627	658	361
Cash Flow	1,796	1,992	1,886	1,596	1,393	1,185	932	925	563	457
Current Ratio	1.0	1.1	1.4	1.3	1.4	1.3	1.3	1.2	1.1	1.3
% Long Term Debt of Capitalization	17.8	12.2	8.6	3.3	10.6	12.3	23.3	24.4	9.0	1.4
% Net Income of Revenue	2.2	3.5	3.8	3.7	3.4	3.3	3.0	2.9	2.6	2.8
% Return on Assets	7.0	10.7	10.8	10.3	9.9	9.8	8.3	9.3	10.1	12.6
% Return on Equity	22.0	26.3	24.0	23.5	23.7	26.0	23.8	26.2	27.1	32.6

Data as orig reptd.; bef. results of disc opers/spec. items. Per share data adj. for stk. divs.; EPS diluted. E-Estimated. NA-Not Available. NM-Not Meaningful. NR-Not Ranked. UR-Under Review.

Office: 7601 Penn Avenue South, Richfield, MN 55423-3683.
Telephone: 612-291-1000.
Email: moneytalk@bestbuy.com
Website: http://www.bestbuy.com

Chrmn: R.M. Schulze
CEO: B.J. Dunn
EVP & CFO: J.L. Muehlbauer
SVP & Treas: R. Robinson

SVP & General Counsel: J.M. Joyce
Investor Contact: J. Driscoll (612-291-6110)
Board Members: B. H. Anderson, B. J. Dunn, K. J. Higgins, R. James, E. S. Kaplan, S. Khosla, A. U. Lenzmeier, G. L. Mikan, III, M. H. Paull, R. M. Rebolledo, R. M. Schulze, F. D. Trestman, H. Tyabji, G. R. Vittecoq

Founded: 1966
Domicile: Minnesota
Employees: 155,000

Big Lots Inc

STANDARD &POOR'S

S&P Recommendation **HOLD** ★★★☆☆	Price $24.01 (as of Nov 27, 2009)	12-Mo. Target Price $28.00	Investment Style Large-Cap Blend

GICS Sector Consumer Discretionary
Sub-Industry General Merchandise Stores

Summary This leading broadline closeout retailer has over 1,350 Big Lots stores in 47 states.

Key Stock Statistics (Source S&P, Vickers, company reports)

52-Wk Range	$28.50– 12.62	S&P Oper. EPS 2010**E**	2.03	Market Capitalization(B)	$1.984	Beta	1.14
Trailing 12-Month EPS	$1.89	S&P Oper. EPS 2011**E**	2.20	Yield (%)	Nil	S&P 3-Yr. Proj. EPS CAGR(%)	9
Trailing 12-Month P/E	12.7	P/E on S&P Oper. EPS 2010**E**	11.8	Dividend Rate/Share	Nil	S&P Credit Rating	BBB-
$10K Invested 5 Yrs Ago	$19,208	Common Shares Outstg. (M)	82.6	Institutional Ownership (%)	NM		

Price Performance

30-Week Mov. Avg. · · · ·   10-Week Mov. Avg. - - **GAAP Earnings vs. Previous Year**   Volume Above Avg. STARS
12-Mo. Target Price —   Relative Strength —   ▲ Up ▼ Down ▶ No Change   Below Avg. ★

Options: P, Ph

Analysis prepared by **Jason N. Asaeda** on November 25, 2009, when the stock traded at **$ 24.19**.

Highlights

▶ In FY 10 (Jan.) and FY 11, we anticipate an increased focus on traffic-driving brand-name closeouts and "treasure hunt" items, and improved product quality and in-stock levels, particularly on consumables. While we anticipate stability in BIG's consumables business, we are concerned that aggressive pricing by competitors could dampen sales of hardlines, seasonal goods, and furniture. Annually, we see same-store sales flat to down modestly and expect modest growth in selling square footage, with BIG limiting new store openings to its most successful trade areas in an effort to achieve high sales productivity. All told, we project net sales of $4.64 billion in FY 10 and $4.71 billion in FY 11.

▶ Operating margins are likely to widen annually on improving initial markups, supported by global sourcing and a favorable closeout deal environment; BIG's taking of markdowns more consistently in an effort to drive both sales growth and higher inventory turns; a reduction in depreciation expense on disciplined capital allocation; and cost saving initiatives.

▶ Assuming modest share dilution, we see EPS of $2.03 in FY 10 and $2.20 in FY 11.

Investment Rationale/Risk

▶ Our Hold recommendation is based on valuation. We look for BIG to weather a tough retail environment and to maintain strong cash flow in FY 10, supported by the company's efforts to raise sales productivity and lower its cost structure by better aligning products with customer preferences, moving to a new store layout that brings more merchandise to the selling floor and allocates more square footage to key categories, and accelerating the closure of underperforming units. Given what we see as its strong price-value proposition and attractive mix of basic necessities and more discretionary-purchase items, we also see potential for BIG to gain incremental business from higher-income consumers trading down from national drugstore and supermarket chains and mass merchandisers.

▶ Risks to our recommendation and target price include sales shortfalls due to problems with merchandise availability and increased promotional activity by competitors.

▶ Our 12-month target price of $28 reflects a peer-median EV/EBITDA multiple of 6.0X applied to our FY 11 EBITDA estimate of $377 million.

Qualitative Risk Assessment

LOW	**MEDIUM**	HIGH

Our risk assessment reflects our expectation of improving company fundamentals, supported by BIG's new merchandising and cost reduction initiatives, offset by what we see as a challenging retail environment that could hinder a turnaround.

Quantitative Evaluations

S&P Quality Ranking B-

D	C	**B-**	B	B+	A-	A	A+

Relative Strength Rank MODERATE

31

LOWEST = 1   HIGHEST = 99

Revenue/Earnings Data

Revenue (Million $)

	1Q	2Q	3Q	4Q	Year
2010	1,142	1,087	--	--	--
2009	1,152	1,105	1,022	1,367	4,645
2008	1,128	1,085	1,031	1,412	4,656
2007	1,092	1,057	1,050	1,545	4,743
2006	1,099	1,051	1,041	1,395	4,430
2005	1,019	995.0	980.0	1,381	4,375

Earnings Per Share ($)

2010	0.44	0.35	E0.20	E1.04	E2.03
2009	0.42	0.32	0.15	1.00	1.89
2008	0.26	0.32	0.14	0.97	1.47
2007	0.13	0.04	0.02	0.83	1.01
2006	0.07	-0.12	-0.17	0.33	0.14
2005	0.05	-0.07	-0.23	0.51	0.27

Fiscal year ended Jan. 31. Next earnings report expected: Early December. EPS Estimates based on S&P Operating Earnings; historical GAAP earnings are as reported.

Dividend Data

Proceeds from the sale of rights amounting to $0.01 a share were distributed in 2001.

Please read the Required Disclosures and Analyst Certification on the last page of this report.

The McGraw-Hill Companies

Big Lots Inc

Business Summary November 25, 2009

CORPORATE OVERVIEW. BIG's strategy is to position itself as a preferred shopping destination for middle-income consumers seeking savings on brand-name closeouts and other value-priced merchandise. The company's product offerings range from everyday essentials such as food and other consumables, to more discretionary-purchase items, including furniture, holiday assortments, electronics, apparel, and small appliances. In our view, FY 07 (Jan.) was a transitional year for BIG, as the company slowed chain expansion in order to better focus on implementing operational changes to reverse a two-year trend of declining operating profits. Since then, we have seen BIG apply successful new merchandising and marketing strategies to further strengthen its financial performance.

CORPORATE STRATEGY. BIG's primary growth driver is expansion. The company seeks to build on its leadership position in broadline closeout retailing by expanding its market presence in both existing and new markets. From FY 00 through FY 05, the company increased its selling square footage at a compound annual growth rate (CAGR) of about 6% as it expanded its store count from 1,230 to 1,502. In FY 06, BIG continued to expand its store base, adding 73 new stores. However, the company also accelerated the closure of underperforming locations as part of its What's Important Now (WIN) turnaround strat-

egy, which was announced in November 2005. BIG closed 174 stores in FY 06. As a result, the company ended the fiscal year with 1,401 stores in 47 states, reflecting a 3.5% decline in selling square footage.

WIN is aimed at improving BIG's financial performance via changes in the company's merchandising, cost structure, and real estate. As its first steps, BIG is attempting to raise productivity of its chain by closing low-volume stores located mainly in small, rural, or weaker performing markets, and by moving from an opportunistic real estate strategy to one focused on its most successful trade areas. These areas include California, Arizona, Washington, New York and New Jersey. The company closed a net of 26 stores in FY 07 and an additional 22 stores in FY 08. BIG remained committed to its market focused real estate strategy in FY 09, opening only 21 new stores and closing 35 locations. The company ended FY 09 with 1,339 stores. BIG plans to open 50 new stores and close 40 underperforming units in FY 10.

Company Financials Fiscal Year Ended Jan. 31

Per Share Data ($)	2009	2008	2007	2006	2005	2004	2003	2002	2001	2000
Tangible Book Value	9.61	13.34	11.10	9.47	9.54	9.51	8.83	8.11	8.28	11.71
Cash Flow	2.84	2.34	1.91	1.15	1.17	1.56	1.38	0.37	1.44	1.74
Earnings	1.89	1.47	1.01	0.14	0.27	0.77	0.65	-0.25	0.87	0.85
S&P Core Earnings	1.86	1.38	1.06	0.05	0.25	0.78	0.60	-0.32	0.83	NA
Dividends	Nil	Nil	Nil	Nil	Nil	Nil	Nil	Nil	Nil	Nil
Payout Ratio	Nil	Nil	Nil	Nil	Nil	Nil	Nil	Nil	Nil	Nil
Calendar Year	2008	2007	2006	2005	2004	2003	2002	2001	2000	1999
Prices:High	35.33	36.15	26.36	14.29	15.62	18.39	19.90	15.75	16.38	38.13
Prices:Low	12.40	15.35	11.83	10.06	11.05	9.92	9.75	7.15	8.25	13.69
P/E Ratio:High	19	25	26	NM	58	24	31	NM	19	45
P/E Ratio:Low	7	10	12	NM	41	13	15	NM	9	16

Income Statement Analysis (Million $)

	2009	2008	2007	2006	2005	2004	2003	2002	2001	2000
Revenue	4,645	4,656	4,743	4,430	4,375	4,174	3,869	3,433	3,277	4,700
Operating Income	334	315	276	141	172	222	231	43.4	249	271
Depreciation	78.6	88.5	101	115	104	93.7	85.7	72.0	64.5	100
Interest Expense	5.28	2.51	0.68	6.27	24.8	16.4	21.0	20.5	23.6	25.3
Pretax Income	250	239	170	20.9	43.3	113	125	-48.7	161	145
Effective Tax Rate	38.0%	36.8%	34.0%	24.8%	29.8%	20.6%	39.5%	NM	39.5%	39.5%
Net Income	155	151	113	15.7	30.4	89.9	75.7	-29.5	97.6	96.1
S&P Core Earnings	153	142	118	4.93	27.8	91.6	70.7	-36.7	92.6	NA

Balance Sheet & Other Financial Data (Million $)

	2009	2008	2007	2006	2005	2004	2003	2002	2001	2000
Cash	34.8	37.1	282	1.71	2.52	174	160	NA	NA	96.3
Current Assets	871	891	1,149	994	1,035	1,134	NA	NA	NA	1,420
Total Assets	1,432	1,444	1,721	1,625	1,734	1,801	1,656	1,470	1,528	2,187
Current Liabilities	515	500	474	437	413	416	NA	NA	NA	711
Long Term Debt	3.64	165	Nil	5.50	159	204	204	204	268	60.5
Common Equity	775	638	1,130	1,167	1,075	1,109	1,020	923	924	1,300
Total Capital	837	804	1,130	1,173	1,235	1,313	1,224	1,127	1,192	1,468
Capital Expenditures	88.7	60.4	35.9	68.5	135	170	110	NA	NA	147
Cash Flow	233	240	214	130	135	184	161	42.5	162	197
Current Ratio	1.7	1.8	2.4	2.3	2.5	2.7	NA	NA	NA	2.0
% Long Term Debt of Capitalization	0.4	20.6	Nil	0.5	12.9	15.5	16.7	18.1	22.5	4.1
% Net Income of Revenue	3.3	3.3	2.4	0.4	0.7	2.2	2.0	NM	3.0	2.0
% Return on Assets	10.8	9.6	6.7	0.9	1.7	5.2	4.8	NM	5.3	4.5
% Return on Equity	21.9	17.1	10.2	1.4	2.8	8.4	7.8	NM	8.8	7.7

Data as orig reptd.; bef. results of disc opers/spec. items. Per share data adj. for stk. divs.; EPS diluted. E-Estimated. NA-Not Available. NM-Not Meaningful. NR-Not Ranked. UR-Under Review.

Office: 300 Phillipi Road, Columbus, OH 43228-5311.
Telephone: 614-278-6822.
Website: http://www.biglots.com
Chrmn, Pres & CEO: S.S. Fishman

SVP, CFO, Chief Acctg Officer & Treas: J.R. Cooper
SVP, Secy & General Counsel: C.W. Haubiel, II
SVP & CIO: L.M. Bachmann
Investor Contact: T.A. Johnson (614-278-6622)

Board Members: J. Berger, S. S. Fishman, P. J. Hayes, D. T. Kollat, B. J. Lauderback, P. E. Mallott, R. Solt, J. R. Tener, D. B. Tishkoff

Founded: 1983
Domicile: Ohio
Employees: 37,000

Biogen Idec Inc

STANDARD &POOR'S

S&P Recommendation SELL ★ ★ ☆ ☆ ☆	Price $46.92 (as of Nov 27, 2009)	12-Mo. Target Price $42.00	Investment Style Large-Cap Growth

GICS Sector Health Care
Sub-Industry Biotechnology

Summary This major biopharmaceutical concern develops and markets targeted therapies for the treatment of multiple sclerosis, non-Hodgkin's lymphoma, and rheumatoid arthritis.

Key Stock Statistics (Source S&P, Vickers, company reports)

52-Wk Range	$55.34–39.01	S&P Oper. EPS 2009E	3.93	Market Capitalization(B)	$13.569	Beta	0.53
Trailing 12-Month EPS	$2.99	S&P Oper. EPS 2010E	4.24	Yield (%)	Nil	S&P 3-Yr. Proj. EPS CAGR(%)	10
Trailing 12-Month P/E	15.7	P/E on S&P Oper. EPS 2009E	11.9	Dividend Rate/Share	Nil	S&P Credit Rating	BBB+
$10K Invested 5 Yrs Ago	$8,030	Common Shares Outstg. (M)	289.2	Institutional Ownership (%)	89		

Price Performance

30-Week Mov. Avg. ···· 10-Week Mov. Avg. – – **GAAP Earnings vs. Previous Year** Volume Above Avg. STARS
12-Mo. Target Price — Relative Strength — ▲ Up ▼ Down ▶ No Change Below Avg. ★

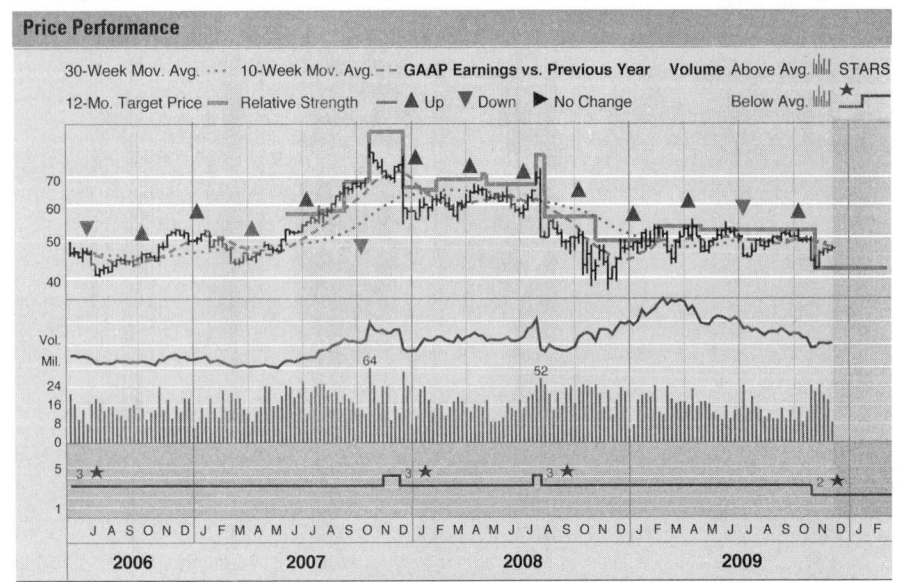

Options: ASE, CBOE, P, Ph

Analysis prepared by **Steven Silver** on October 26, 2009, when the stock traded at **$ 44.20**.

Highlights

► We see revenues of $4.37 billion in 2009, almost 7% higher than 2008's $4.1 billion, and we project 4% revenue growth in 2010, to about $4.53 billion. We expect Tysabri expansion to remain BIIB's key driver over the coming years, as we see Avonex sales moderating, as recent price hikes have offset slowing unit and share growth trends. We also expect lower Rituxan revenues as ex-U.S. royalty agreements expire. However, we see the 29% revenue growth in 2008 positioning BIIB to reach its 2007-2010 compound annual revenue growth goal of 15%.

► We expect operating expenses of 50% of total revenues in 2009 and 46% in 2010, compared to 48% in 2008, with the 2009 figure inflated by a $110 million payment to license MS drug Fampridene-SR. We expect BIIB to seek to deploy its $2.9 billion in cash and securities as of September 30, 2009, by repurchasing shares after newly authorizing a $1 billion plan and by seeking new pipeline assets to drive future growth.

► Our adjusted 2009 and 2010 EPS estimates of $3.93 and $4.24, respectively, exclude amortization of intangible assets and in-process R&D costs.

Investment Rationale/Risk

► We expect BIIB's valuation to be constrained by Tysabri safety concerns, as its label may be updated to reflect a higher risk for brain infection PML as therapy duration increases. We are concerned about the potential for further restrictions on its use, as the European Medicines Agency has started a review of its risk/benefit profile, citing 23 cases of PML, versus BIIB's last disclosure of 13 confirmed cases. As of September 30, 2009, BIIB cited 46,200 patients on Tysabri worldwide, up roughly 3,000 patients per quarter in 2009. We also project intensifying competition in the MS market, as several orally dosed candidates near the market. We do, however, see potential in BIIB's long-term cardiovascular pipeline.

► Risks to our recommendation and target price include easing of safety concerns or accelerated adoption of Tysabri use, decreased MS market competition, and successful advancement of BIIB's clinical pipeline.

► Our 12-month target price of $42 applies a multiple of 10X to our 2010 EPS estimate of $4.24, a discount to the large-cap peer average due to Tysabri safety concerns and competition in BIIB's core multiple sclerosis market.

Qualitative Risk Assessment

LOW	MEDIUM	HIGH

Our risk assessment reflects that Biogen Idec sells products in competitive markets, and its biggest near-term growth driver faces safety concerns, requiring a comprehensive risk minimization program. The company also is engaged in the development of new drugs in new markets, outside of its core multiple sclerosis area of expertise.

Quantitative Evaluations

S&P Quality Ranking B

D	C	B-	**B**	B+	A-	A	A+

Relative Strength Rank MODERATE

46

LOWEST = 1   HIGHEST = 99

Revenue/Earnings Data

Revenue (Million $)

	1Q	2Q	3Q	4Q	Year
2009	1,036	1,093	1,121	--	--
2008	942.2	993.4	1,093	1,069	4,098
2007	715.9	773.2	789.2	893.3	3,172
2006	611.2	660.0	703.5	708.3	2,683
2005	587.8	605.6	596.2	632.9	2,423
2004	541.7	538.8	543.3	587.8	2,212

Earnings Per Share ($)

2009	0.84	0.49	0.95	E1.07	E3.93
2008	0.54	0.70	0.70	0.70	2.65
2007	0.38	0.54	0.41	0.67	1.99
2006	0.35	-0.50	0.45	0.32	0.62
2005	0.12	0.10	0.08	0.16	0.47
2004	-0.12	Nil	0.10	0.08	0.07

Fiscal year ended Dec. 31. Next earnings report expected: Early February. EPS Estimates based on S&P Operating Earnings; historical GAAP earnings are as reported.

Dividend Data

No cash dividends have been paid.

The McGraw·Hill Companies

Biogen Idec Inc

STANDARD
&POOR'S

Business Summary October 26, 2009

CORPORATE OVERVIEW. Formed through the 2003 merger of IDEC Pharmaceuticals and Biogen, Biogen Idec researches, develops and markets therapeutics to treat cancer and autoimmune diseases.

BIIB's core franchise has been in autoimmune disorder multiple sclerosis, led by Avonex, which was approved by the FDA in 1996 to treat relapsing multiple sclerosis (MS), and in Europe in 1997. Avonex sales were $2.2 billion in 2008, up 18% from $1.87 billion in 2007. However, recent growth has been driven by price increases, as increased competition has slowed prescription growth. A new method of use patent for Avonex is expected to extend the franchise until 2026.

Rituxan is a treatment for relapsed or refractory low-grade or follicular B-cell non-Hodgkin's lymphomas (NHL). There are over 300,000 U.S. patients with various forms of this disease. Rituxan is marketed and sold in the U.S. under a co-promotion agreement with Roche; BIIB receives joint business revenues on a percentage of sales. Roche sells the drug under the name MabThera outside the U.S., with BIIB receiving royalties. U.S. Rituxan sales generated revenues of $1.1 million for BIIB in 2008, about 19% higher than 2007's $926 million. Rituxan is being explored for MS, but failed in a study for progressive MS and one for systemic lupus erythematous (SLE) during 2008.

Tysabri, developed with Elan Corp., was approved for treating relapsing MS in late 2004. However, three confirmed cases of progressive multifocal leukoencephalopathy (PML) -- a rare, fatal nervous system disorder -- in 2005, prompted the drug's removal from the market. Following safety evaluations and additional data analyses, Tysabri was approved for re-launch in both the U.S. and Europe in 2006, contingent upon a restricted distribution program. As of September 30, 2009, BIIB cited 46,200 patients on Tysabri worldwide, a 7% increase over the second quarter. As of September 2009, BIIB had confirmed 13 new cases of PML, but the European Medicines Agency started a review of Tysabri's risk/benefit profile in October 2009, citing 23 cases of PML since re-launch. BIIB recognized $588 million of Tysabri revenues in 2008.

Tysabri is also used for moderate-to-severe Crohn's disease, which afflicts nearly one million people worldwide, in the U.S., after FDA approved this use in early 2008. Use in this patient setting has been modest to date. The European Medicines Agency (EMEA) has issued a negative ruling that BIIB and Elan are appealing.

Company Financials Fiscal Year Ended Dec. 31

Per Share Data ($)	2008	2007	2006	2005	2004	2003	2002	2001	2000	1999
Tangible Book Value	8.70	6.44	9.60	8.38	7.08	6.85	7.25	6.22	4.63	1.11
Cash Flow	4.22	3.18	1.71	1.63	1.35	-4.57	0.88	0.62	0.39	0.31
Earnings	2.65	1.99	0.62	0.47	0.07	-4.92	0.85	0.59	0.36	0.29
S&P Core Earnings	2.76	2.01	0.69	0.16	-0.06	-5.13	0.54	0.34	NA	NA
Dividends	Nil	Nil	Nil	Nil	Nil	Nil	Nil	Nil	Nil	Nil
Payout Ratio	Nil	Nil	Nil	Nil	Nil	Nil	Nil	Nil	Nil	Nil
Prices:High	73.59	84.75	52.72	70.00	68.13	42.15	71.40	75.00	77.65	35.00
Prices:Low	37.21	42.86	40.24	33.18	36.60	27.80	20.76	32.63	18.54	6.60
P/E Ratio:High	28	43	85	NM	NM	NM	84	NM	NM	NM
P/E Ratio:Low	14	22	65	NM	NM	NM	24	NM	NM	NM

Income Statement Analysis (Million $)

	2008	2007	2006	2005	2004	2003	2002	2001	2000	1999
Revenue	4,098	3,172	2,683	2,423	2,212	679	404	273	155	118
Operating Income	1,832	1,260	1,117	756	483	14.6	285	137	60.6	45.8
Depreciation	462	380	376	402	439	61.3	10.2	6.31	4.74	4.37
Interest Expense	75.2	50.6	Nil	Nil	18.9	15.2	16.1	7.30	7.05	6.06
Pretax Income	1,149	852	492	256	64.1	-881	232	162	69.3	45.6
Effective Tax Rate	31.8%	32.0%	56.6%	37.3%	60.9%	NM	36.0%	37.1%	17.2%	5.37%
Net Income	783	638	214	161	25.1	-875	148	102	57.4	43.2
S&P Core Earnings	816	642	237	56.6	-21.6	-914	93.4	61.4	NA	NA

Balance Sheet & Other Financial Data (Million $)

	2008	2007	2006	2005	2004	2003	2002	2001	2000	1999
Cash	1,342	1,187	2,315	851	1,058	836	373	426	401	61.4
Current Assets	2,458	2,368	1,713	1,618	1,931	1,839	978	700	631	279
Total Assets	8,479	8,629	8,553	8,367	9,166	9,504	2,060	1,141	856	307
Current Liabilities	923	2,189	583	583	1,261	405	56.2	35.3	23.0	15.6
Long Term Debt	1,085	1,563	96.7	43.4	102	887	866	136	129	123
Common Equity	5,806	5,534	7,150	6,906	6,826	7,053	1,110	956	695	160
Total Capital	7,248	6,108	7,890	7,712	7,850	9,049	1,976	1,092	824	283
Capital Expenditures	276	284	198	318	361	301	166	0.07	31.4	4.29
Cash Flow	1,244	1,017	590	563	465	-814	158	108	62.1	47.5
Current Ratio	2.7	1.1	2.9	2.8	1.5	4.5	17.4	19.8	27.4	17.8
% Long Term Debt of Capitalization	15.0	0.9	1.2	0.6	1.3	9.8	43.8	12.4	15.7	43.4
% Net Income of Revenue	19.1	20.1	8.0	6.6	1.1	NM	36.6	37.3	37.1	36.6
% Return on Assets	9.2	7.4	2.5	1.8	0.3	NM	9.3	10.2	9.9	20.0
% Return on Equity	13.8	10.1	3.0	2.3	0.4	NM	14.3	12.3	13.4	32.4

Data as orig reptd.; bef. results of disc opers/spec. items. Per share data adj. for stk. divs.; EPS diluted. E-Estimated. NA-Not Available. NM-Not Meaningful. NR-Not Ranked. UR-Under Review.

Office: 14 Cambridge Center, Cambridge, MA 02142.
Telephone: 617-679-2000.
Website: http://www.biogenidec.com
Chrmn: B.R. Ross

Pres & CEO: J.C. Mullen
COO & EVP: R. Hamm
EVP & CFO: P.J. Clancy
EVP & Secy: S.H. Alexander

Investor Contact: R. Jacobson (617-679-3710)
Board Members: M. E. Dekkers, A. J. Denner, D. Gollerkeri, N. L. Leaming, J. C. Mullen, R. C. Mulligan, R. W. Pangia, S. Papadopoulos, B. S. Posner, B. R. Ross, L. Schenk, W. D. Young

Founded: 1985
Domicile: Delaware
Employees: 4,700

BJ Services Co

STANDARD &POOR'S

| S&P Recommendation | HOLD ★★★☆☆ | Price $18.55 (as of Nov 27, 2009) | 12-Mo. Target Price $18.00 | Investment Style Large-Cap Growth |

GICS Sector Energy
Sub-Industry Oil & Gas Equipment & Services

Summary This company provides pressure pumping and other oilfield services to the petroleum industry worldwide, and has agreed to be acquired.

Key Stock Statistics (Source S&P, Vickers, company reports)

52-Wk Range	$21.59– 8.34	S&P Oper. EPS 2010**E**	0.50	Market Capitalization(B)	$5.444	Beta	1.41
Trailing 12-Month EPS	$0.51	S&P Oper. EPS 2011**E**	NA	Yield (%)	1.08	S&P 3-Yr. Proj. EPS CAGR(%)	-42
Trailing 12-Month P/E	36.4	P/E on S&P Oper. EPS 2010**E**	37.1	Dividend Rate/Share	$0.20	S&P Credit Rating	BBB+
$10K Invested 5 Yrs Ago	$7,456	Common Shares Outstg. (M)	293.5	Institutional Ownership (%)	NM		

Price Performance

30-Week Mov. Avg. · · · 10-Week Mov. Avg. - - GAAP Earnings vs. Previous Year   Volume Above Avg. ▎▍▌ STARS
12-Mo. Target Price — Relative Strength — ▲ Up ▼ Down ▶ No Change   Below Avg. ▎▍▌ ★

Options: ASE, CBOE, P, Ph

Analysis prepared by **Stewart Glickman, CFA** on September 16, 2009, when the stock traded at **$ 17.75**.

Highlights

► In late August, BJS agreed to be acquired by oilfield services peer Baker Hughes (BHI 38, Hold) in a cash and stock deal valued at approximately $5.5 billion. Subject to approvals, the deal represented about a 16% premium to BJS shares on the day prior to the announcement, which we think is indicative of relatively weak prospects for the domestic pressure pumping industry. BJS's main growth driver continues to be the U.S. market, which is relatively sensitive to natural gas price expectations. Based on data from IHS Global Insight, we do not project natural gas prices averaging more than $4.00 per million BTU until 2011, which does not bode well for near-term domestic demand.

► June-quarter operating margins showed continued degradation in the U.S./Mexico pressure pumping segment. We believe industry capacity build helped weaken pricing, leading to the lower margins. Long-term, we expect margins to recover as smaller competitors should exit the marketplace and thus alleviate some of the supply-demand imbalance.

► Excluding the merger, we see EPS of $0.67 in FY 09 (Sep.), declining to $0.50 in FY 10.

Investment Rationale/Risk

► In the short term, we see U.S. operating margins constrained by swollen industry capacity additions, reduced pressure pumping demand due to the tight credit environment and high recent natural gas production. International demand should be relatively stronger, but even there we expect a pullback in near-term demand due to the weakening global economy and recent completion of overseas natural gas projects. While unconventional natural gas plays offer a long-term catalyst for BJS, we think the merger is a reasonable opportunity for shareholders, given significant near-term challenges.

► Risks to our recommendation and target price include lower demand for pressure pumping; higher-than-expected cost inflation; and lower-than-projected natural gas and oil prices.

► Our DCF model, which assumes free cash flow growth of about 11%, terminal growth of 3%, discounted at a WACC of 13%, shows intrinsic value of about $20. Applying peer-average multiples of 10.5X projected CY 2010 EBITDA, 12.0X estimated CY 2010 operating cash flows, and our DCF analysis, we arrive at our 12-month target price of $18.

Qualitative Risk Assessment

| LOW | MEDIUM | HIGH |

Our risk assessment reflects exposure to volatile hydrocarbon prices, particularly natural gas, the company's leverage to the North American market, and concerns over capacity additions for pressure pumping. We think the company's strong position in pressure pumping services partially offsets these risks.

Quantitative Evaluations

S&P Quality Ranking B+

| D | C | B- | B | B+ | A- | A | A+ |

Relative Strength Rank MODERATE

45

LOWEST = 1   HIGHEST = 99

Revenue/Earnings Data

Revenue (Million $)

	1Q	2Q	3Q	4Q	Year
2009	1,417	1,047	780.3	878.2	4,122
2008	1,285	1,283	1,328	1,530	5,426
2007	1,184	1,187	1,153	1,279	4,802
2006	956.2	1,079	1,117	1,216	4,368
2005	737.8	795.9	817.3	892.3	3,243
2004	600.8	647.1	658.7	694.5	2,601

Earnings Per Share ($)

2009	0.51	0.16	-0.10	-0.01	0.57
2008	0.58	0.43	0.48	0.57	2.06
2007	0.70	0.64	0.57	0.64	2.55
2006	0.48	0.62	0.67	0.76	2.52
2005	0.29	0.33	0.35	0.41	1.38
2004	0.19	0.23	0.40	0.29	1.11

Fiscal year ended Sep. 30. Next earnings report expected: Late January. EPS Estimates based on S&P Operating Earnings; historical GAAP earnings are as reported.

Dividend Data (Dates: mm/dd Payment Date: mm/dd/yy)

Amount ($)	Date Decl.	Ex-Div. Date	Stk. of Record	Payment Date
0.050	12/05	12/11	12/15	01/13/09
0.050	01/29	03/12	03/16	04/15/09
0.050	05/28	06/12	06/16	07/15/09
0.050	07/23	09/11	09/15	10/14/09

Dividends have been paid since 2004. Source: Company reports.

The **McGraw·Hill** Companies

BJ Services Co

STANDARD &POOR'S

Business Summary September 16, 2009

CORPORATE OVERVIEW. BJ Services is a leading provider of pressure pumping and other oilfield services to the petroleum industry worldwide. Demand for its services depends on the number of oil and natural gas wells being drilled, the depth and drilling conditions of the wells, the number of well completions, and the level of workover activity worldwide. BJS's principal customers consist of major and independent oil and natural gas producing companies. The company operates in 50 countries in the major international oil and natural gas producing areas of Canada, Latin America, Europe, Africa, Asia and the Middle East, including Russia and China. In FY 08 (Sep.), 51% of revenues were generated by U.S./Mexico pressure pumping; 8% by Canada pressure pumping; 23% by International pressure pumping; and 18% by oilfield services. Other than Canada, the international market tends to be less volatile than the U.S. due to the size and complexity of investment, and projects tend to be managed with a longer-term perspective with regard to commodity prices. In addition, the international market is dominated by major oil and national oil companies, which tend to have different objectives and more operating stability than typical independent U.S. producers.

Pressure pumping services (82% of FY 08 revenues and 81% of operating profits before corporate expenses) are used in the completion of oil and gas wells, both onshore and offshore. Customers are mainly served in the United States. Stimulation services (which accounted for 69% of this segment's revenues in FY 08) are designed to improve the flow of oil and natural gas from producing formations using fracturing, acidizing, sand control, nitrogen, coiled tubing and downhole tool services. Cementing (31% of segment revenues) is done between the casing pipe and the wellbore during the drilling and completion phase of a well. This is done to isolate fluids that could damage productivity, seal the casing from corrosive fluids, and provide structural support for the casing string. Cementing services are also used when recompleting wells from one producing zone to another, and when plugging and abandoning wells.

Company Financials Fiscal Year Ended Sep. 30

Per Share Data ($)	2009	2008	2007	2006	2005	2004	2003	2002	2001	2000
Tangible Book Value	NA	8.38	6.47	4.16	4.94	3.73	2.44	1.74	2.79	2.40
Cash Flow	NA	2.97	3.25	3.05	1.79	1.49	0.96	0.84	1.36	0.65
Earnings	0.57	2.06	2.55	2.52	1.38	1.11	0.59	0.52	1.04	0.35
S&P Core Earnings	NA	2.06	2.55	2.52	1.35	0.90	0.54	0.45	0.97	NA
Dividends	0.20	0.20	0.20	0.20	0.12	0.04	Nil	Nil	Nil	Nil
Payout Ratio	35%	10%	8%	8%	9%	4%	Nil	Nil	Nil	Nil
Prices:High	21.59	34.94	31.26	42.85	39.78	27.33	21.20	19.75	21.55	19.19
Prices:Low	8.72	8.34	23.12	27.43	21.13	17.42	14.63	11.50	7.28	9.53
P/E Ratio:High	38	17	12	17	29	25	36	38	21	53
P/E Ratio:Low	15	4	9	11	15	16	25	22	7	26

Income Statement Analysis (Million $)										
Revenue	4,122	5,426	4,802	4,368	3,243	2,601	2,143	1,866	2,234	1,555
Operating Income	NA	1,180	1,360	1,340	788	567	414	368	641	297
Depreciation, Depletion and Amortization	NA	269	209	167	137	126	120	105	105	102
Interest Expense	27.3	28.1	32.7	14.6	11.0	16.4	31.9	8.98	13.3	20.0
Pretax Income	194	868	1,113	1,172	653	521	276	253	529	175
Effective Tax Rate	14.5%	29.8%	32.3%	31.4%	30.7%	30.7%	31.7%	34.1%	34.0%	32.7%
Net Income	166	609	754	805	453	361	188	166	349	118
S&P Core Earnings	NA	610	754	805	447	295	174	142	324	NA

Balance Sheet & Other Financial Data (Million $)										
Cash	NA	150	58.2	92.4	357	425	278	84.7	84.1	6.47
Current Assets	NA	1,961	1,704	1,459	1,334	1,424	942	649	733	506
Total Assets	NA	5,322	4,715	3,862	3,396	3,331	2,786	2,442	1,985	1,785
Current Liabilities	NA	1,020	1,313	948	684	910	471	356	390	337
Long Term Debt	NA	502	250	500	Nil	78.9	494	489	79.4	142
Common Equity	NA	3,442	2,851	2,147	2,484	2,094	1,651	1,419	1,370	1,170
Total Capital	NA	4,098	3,197	2,713	2,548	2,262	2,152	1,917	1,460	1,320
Capital Expenditures	NA	607	752	460	324	201	167	179	183	80.5
Cash Flow	NA	878	963	971	590	487	308	271	454	220
Current Ratio	NA	1.9	1.3	1.5	2.0	1.6	2.0	1.8	1.9	1.5
% Long Term Debt of Capitalization	Nil	12.3	7.8	18.4	Nil	3.5	22.9	25.5	5.4	10.8
% Return on Assets	NA	12.1	17.6	22.1	13.5	11.8	7.2	7.5	18.5	6.5
% Return on Equity	NA	19.4	30.2	34.7	19.8	19.3	12.3	11.9	27.5	11.5

Data as orig reptd.; bef. results of disc opers/spec. items. Per share data adj. for stk. divs.; EPS diluted. E-Estimated. NA-Not Available. NM-Not Meaningful. NR-Not Ranked. UR-Under Review.

Office: 4601 Westway Park Blvd, Houston, TX 77041-2037.
Telephone: 713-462-4239.
Website: http://www.bjservices.com
Chrmn, Pres & CEO: J.W. Stewart

COO & EVP: D.D. Dunlap
Investor Contact: J.E. Smith ()
SVP & CFO: J.E. Smith
CTO: J. Hibbeler

Board Members: L. W. Heiligbrodt, J. R. Huff, D. D. Jordan, M. E. Patrick, J. L. Payne, J. W. Stewart, W. White

Founded: 1872
Domicile: Delaware
Employees: 18,000

Black & Decker Corp (The)

STANDARD &POOR'S

S&P Recommendation	HOLD ★★★☆☆		

Price	12-Mo. Target Price	Investment Style
$61.06 (as of Nov 27, 2009)	$52.00	Large-Cap Blend

GICS Sector Consumer Discretionary
Sub-Industry Household Appliances

Summary This company is a leading global producer of power tools, hardware and home improvement products, and fastening systems.

Key Stock Statistics (Source S&P, Vickers, company reports)

52-Wk Range	$63.63– 20.10	S&P Oper. EPS 2009E	2.65	Market Capitalization(B)	$3.678	Beta	1.63
Trailing 12-Month EPS	$2.41	S&P Oper. EPS 2010E	3.75	Yield (%)	0.79	S&P 3-Yr. Proj. EPS CAGR(%)	13
Trailing 12-Month P/E	25.3	P/E on S&P Oper. EPS 2009E	23.0	Dividend Rate/Share	$0.48	S&P Credit Rating	BBB
$10K Invested 5 Yrs Ago	$8,024	Common Shares Outstg. (M)	60.2	Institutional Ownership (%)	95		

Price Performance

30-Week Mov. Avg. · · ·   10-Week Mov. Avg. - - -   **GAAP Earnings vs. Previous Year**   Volume Above Avg. ▥▥ STARS
12-Mo. Target Price —   Relative Strength   — ▲ Up ▼ Down ▶ No Change   Below Avg. ▥▥ ★

Options: CBOE, P, Ph

Analysis prepared by **Kenneth M. Leon, CPA** on October 22, 2009, when the stock traded at **$ 49.31**.

Highlights

▶ Following an estimated revenue decline of 23% in 2009, we forecast growth of 5% in 2010 and 8% in 2011, as BDK's customer markets begin to recover from weak economies in Europe and North America. We believe all three business segments will show positive growth in 2010, while only the Fastening and Assembly Systems unit showed positive growth in the 2009 third quarter.

▶ We see gross margins of 32.8% in 2010 and 33% in 2011, compared to an estimated 32.2% margin in 2009. With well controlled SG&A expenses, we estimate operating margins of 7.5% in 2010 and 7.8% in 2011, versus an estimated 6.2% in 2009, and 7.5% in 2008. Margins were as high as 13.5% in the 2006 second quarter, which we view as the top of the cycle for BDK's customer markets.

▶ We expect the company to continue to reduce costs to achieve operating leverage when customer markets rebound. In our opinion, price stability for BDK's products with rising unit sales volumes can drive other higher profitability. Including a much lower effective tax rate of 18% to 20%, down from 35%, we estimate EPS of $2.65 in 2009, $3.75 in 2010 and $4.25 in 2011.

Investment Rationale/Risk

▶ We believe recent progress to improve operating margins through restructuring and productivity initiatives has been lessened by global recession and weakening customer markets. With only one-third of its total sales from non-U.S. markets, we believe BDK will be challenged to drive sales growth above single digits in the next 12 to 18 months. We expect market conditions to be challenging but improved in 2010 as power tools and home improvement markets begin to recover.

▶ Risks to our recommendation and target price include a prolonged recession in the company's major markets, even weaker demand from BDK's customers, lower market acceptance of new products, and unfavorable shifts in currency exchange rates or raw material prices that hurt operating earnings and cash flow.

▶ Our 12-month target price of $52 represents a target multiple just below 14X our 2010 EPS estimate, at the mid-point of BDK's historical range. We believe this valuation is appropriate, as BDK's addressable markets are only just beginning to recover from recession.

Qualitative Risk Assessment

LOW	MEDIUM	HIGH

Our risk assessment reflects our view of BDK's weakened residential and commercial markets, as well as lower cash flow reflecting lower sales volumes. Weak U.S. and European economies remain a drag on the company's sales, which are exhibiting modest growth in emerging markets.

Quantitative Evaluations

S&P Quality Ranking   B+

D	C	B-	B	B+	A-	A	A+

Relative Strength Rank   STRONG
                                            94
LOWEST = 1   HIGHEST = 99

Revenue/Earnings Data

Revenue (Million $)

	1Q	2Q	3Q	4Q	Year
2009	1,074	1,191	1,209	--	--
2008	1,496	1,642	1,571	1,378	6,086
2007	1,577	1,700	1,634	1,653	6,563
2006	1,529	1,697	1,610	1,611	6,447
2005	1,519	1,699	1,576	1,730	6,524
2004	1,093	1,298	1,283	1,725	5,398

Earnings Per Share ($)

2009	0.08	0.64	0.93	E0.87	E2.65
2008	1.09	1.58	1.42	0.73	4.91
2007	1.61	1.75	1.59	2.94	7.85
2006	1.45	1.98	1.74	1.38	6.55
2005	1.79	1.88	1.73	1.28	6.69
2004	0.93	1.50	1.35	1.60	5.40

Fiscal year ended Dec. 31. Next earnings report expected: Late January. EPS Estimates based on S&P Operating Earnings; historical GAAP earnings are as reported.

Dividend Data (Dates: mm/dd Payment Date: mm/dd/yy)

Amount ($)	Date Decl.	Ex-Div. Date	Stk. of Record	Payment Date
0.420	02/12	03/11	03/13	03/27/09
0.120	04/30	06/10	06/12	06/26/09
0.120	07/24	09/09	09/11	09/25/09
0.120	10/15	12/14	12/16	12/30/09

Dividends have been paid since 1937. Source: Company reports.

Please read the Required Disclosures and Analyst Certification on the last page of this report.

The McGraw-Hill Companies

Black & Decker Corp (The)

STANDARD
&POOR'S

Business Summary October 22, 2009

CORPORATE OVERVIEW. Black & Decker, incorporated in 1910, is a global manufacturer and marketer of power tools and accessories, hardware and home improvement products, and technology-based fastening systems. Its products are sold under a number of well known brand names in more than 100 countries. The company has 44 manufacturing facilities, including 24 located outside the U.S. in 10 foreign countries.

MARKET PROFILE. BDK is one of the world's leading producers of portable electric power tools and electric lawn and garden tools, as well as one of the largest suppliers of power tool accessories and specialized, engineered fastening and assembly systems in the markets it serves. Its plumbing products business is one of the largest North American faucet makers. Operations consist of three segments: Power Tools and Accessories (72% of 2008 sales), Hardware and Home Improvement (15%), and Fastening and Assembly Systems (11%). The U.S. accounted for two thirds of sales in 2008, Europe 20%, and other countries 15%.

The Power Tools and Accessories segment manufactures and sells consumer and professional power tools (such as drills, screwdrivers and saws) and accessories, outdoor products (electric lawn and garden tools), cleaning and

lighting products and product services. Products are sold mainly to retailers, wholesalers, jobbers, and distributors, although some discontinued or reconditioned products are sold through company-operated service centers and factory outlets directly to end users. Principal materials used to manufacture products in this segment include plastics, aluminum, copper, steel, certain electronic components, and batteries.

The Hardware and Home Improvement segment (formerly building products) makes and sells security hardware (locksets and deadbolts) and plumbing products (faucets, shower heads and bath accessories). Products are sold primarily to retailers, wholesalers, distributors, and jobbers. Certain security hardware products are sold to commercial, institutional, and industrial customers. The principal materials used in the manufacture of products in this segment are plastics, aluminum, steel, brass, zamak (zinc alloy), and ceramics.

Company Financials Fiscal Year Ended Dec. 31

Per Share Data ($)	2008	2007	2006	2005	2004	2003	2002	2001	2000	1999
Tangible Book Value	NM	3.91	NM	5.27	4.57	0.96	NM	NM	NM	0.66
Cash Flow	7.04	9.09	9.61	8.97	7.12	5.40	4.49	3.30	5.28	5.21
Earnings	4.91	7.85	6.55	6.69	5.40	3.68	2.84	1.33	3.34	3.40
S&P Core Earnings	3.80	8.08	6.79	6.22	4.93	3.23	1.56	0.11	NA	NA
Dividends	1.68	1.68	1.52	1.12	0.84	0.57	0.48	0.48	0.48	0.48
Payout Ratio	34%	21%	23%	17%	16%	15%	17%	36%	14%	14%
Prices:High	74.24	97.01	94.90	93.71	89.64	49.90	50.50	46.95	52.38	64.63
Prices:Low	32.31	69.15	66.04	75.70	48.07	33.20	35.00	28.26	27.56	41.00
P/E Ratio:High	15	12	14	14	17	14	18	35	16	19
P/E Ratio:Low	7	9	10	11	9	9	12	21	8	12

Income Statement Analysis (Million $)	2008	2007	2006	2005	2004	2003	2002	2001	2000	1999
Revenue	6,086	6,563	6,447	6,524	5,398	4,483	4,394	4,333	4,561	4,521
Operating Income	612	785	894	964	772	594	549	407	686	696
Depreciation	135	82.0	155	151	143	133	128	159	163	160
Interest Expense	101	102	103	81.9	57.9	60.7	84.3	84.3	104	126
Pretax Income	365	498	664	819	604	391	307	155	405	441
Effective Tax Rate	19.5%	NM	26.8%	33.6%	27.0%	26.5%	25.3%	30.5%	30.3%	32.0%
Net Income	294	518	486	544	441	287	230	108	282	300
S&P Core Earnings	231	533	505	506	401	251	126	9.48	NA	NA

Balance Sheet & Other Financial Data (Million $)	2008	2007	2006	2005	2004	2003	2002	2001	2000	1999
Cash	278	255	233	968	514	308	517	245	135	147
Current Assets	2,604	2,840	2,703	3,347	2,927	2,203	2,194	1,892	1,962	1,911
Total Assets	5,183	5,411	5,248	5,817	5,531	4,223	4,131	4,014	4,090	4,013
Current Liabilities	1,484	1,881	1,780	2,264	1,793	1,312	1,453	1,071	1,632	1,573
Long Term Debt	1,445	1,179	1,170	1,030	1,201	916	928	1,191	798	847
Common Equity	1,125	1,459	1,164	1,524	1,559	846	600	751	692	801
Total Capital	2,570	2,638	2,532	2,742	2,930	1,942	1,739	2,204	1,712	1,892
Capital Expenditures	98.8	116	105	111	118	103	96.6	135	200	171
Cash Flow	429	600	641	695	584	421	358	267	445	460
Current Ratio	1.8	1.5	1.5	1.5	1.6	1.7	1.5	1.8	1.2	1.2
% Long Term Debt of Capitalization	56.2	55.3	46.2	37.6	41.0	47.1	53.4	54.1	46.6	44.8
% Net Income of Revenue	4.8	7.8	7.5	8.3	8.2	6.4	5.2	2.5	6.2	6.6
% Return on Assets	5.5	9.7	8.8	9.6	9.0	6.9	5.6	2.7	7.0	7.6
% Return on Equity	22.7	39.4	35.7	35.3	36.7	39.7	34.0	15.0	37.8	43.7

Data as orig reptd.; bef. results of disc opers/spec. items. Per share data adj. for stk. divs.; EPS diluted. E-Estimated. NA-Not Available. NM-Not Meaningful. NR-Not Ranked. UR-Under Review.

Office: 701 East Joppa Road, Towson, MD 21286.
Telephone: 410-716-3900.
Email: investor.relations@bdk.com
Website: http://www.bdk.com

Chrmn, Pres & CEO: N.D. Archibald
SVP & CFO: S.F. Reeves
SVP & General Counsel: C.E. Fenton
Investor Contact: M.M. Rothleitner (410-716-3979)

Secy: N.A. Shields
Board Members: N. D. Archibald, N. R. Augustine, B. L. Bowles, G. W. Buckley, M. A. Burns, K. B. Clark, M. A. Fernandez, B. H. Griswold, IV, A. Luiso, R. L. Ryan, M. H. Willes

Founded: 1910
Domicile: Maryland
Employees: 22,100

The McGraw-Hill Companies

BMC Software Inc

STANDARD &POOR'S

S&P Recommendation HOLD ★★★☆☆	Price $38.49 (as of Nov 27, 2009)	12-Mo. Target Price $41.00	Investment Style Large-Cap Blend

GICS Sector Information Technology
Sub-Industry Systems Software

Summary This company provides systems management software that improves the availability, performance and recovery of applications and data.

Key Stock Statistics (Source S&P, Vickers, company reports)

52-Wk Range	$39.56– 22.03	S&P Oper. EPS 2010E	2.02	Market Capitalization(B)	$7.059	Beta	0.69
Trailing 12-Month EPS	$1.83	S&P Oper. EPS 2011E	2.23	Yield (%)	Nil	S&P 3-Yr. Proj. EPS CAGR(%)	10
Trailing 12-Month P/E	21.0	P/E on S&P Oper. EPS 2010E	19.1	Dividend Rate/Share	Nil	S&P Credit Rating	BBB
$10K Invested 5 Yrs Ago	$21,431	Common Shares Outstg. (M)	183.4	Institutional Ownership (%)	93		

Price Performance

30-Week Mov. Avg. · · · · 10-Week Mov. Avg. - - **GAAP Earnings vs. Previous Year**   **Volume** Above Avg. ▦ STARS
12-Mo. Target Price — Relative Strength — ▲ Up ▼ Down ► No Change   Below Avg. ▥

Options: ASE, CBOE, P, Ph

Analysis prepared by **Jim Yin** on October 30, 2009, when the stock traded at **$ 38.30**.

Highlights

► We expect revenues to increase 5.3% in FY 11 (Mar.), following a 0.9% advance we see for FY 10. Our forecast reflects our view of a modest economic recovery in 2010 with overall corporate IT spending rising 4%. We think BMC will grow faster than the industry's average due to a gain in market share. The company has been improving its products and services through internal development and acquisitions during the downturn. We project high single digit growth in the Enterprise Service Management business segment and flat revenues in the Mainframe Service Management segment in FY 11.

► We forecast FY 11 gross margins of 79%, the same as in FY 10. We expect operating expenses as a percentage of revenue to decline to 50% in FY 11, from 51% in FY 10, due to cost-saving initiatives and lower acquisition-related expenses. We believe operating margins in FY 11 will increase to 29%, from 28% in FY 10.

► Our EPS estimate for FY 11 is $2.23, up from $2.02 projected for FY 10, as a result of higher revenues, improved operating margins, lower acquisition-related charges, and fewer shares outstanding as a result of the company's share repurchase program.

Investment Rationale/Risk

► We recently lowered our recommendation to hold, from buy, on valuation. We are also concerned about a sluggish recovery in IT spending. Although the IT spending environment has improved recently, sales cycles on large contracts remained elongated, as customers negotiate for more favorable terms. However, we think BMC can gain market share. Additionally, we project expanding operating margins, as the company has been effectively controlling its operating expenses.

► Risks to our recommendation and target price include a weaker than expected recovery in the global economy, heightened competition from large platform vendors, a decline in corporate spending on information technology, and greater pricing pressures.

► Our 12-month target price of $41 is based on a blend of our discounted cash flow (DCF) and P/E analyses. Our DCF model assumes an 11% weighted average cost of capital and 3% terminal growth, and yields an intrinsic value of $42. From our P/E analysis, we derive a value of $40 based on an industry P/E-to-growth ratio of 1.8X, or 18X our FY 11 EPS estimate of $2.23.

Qualitative Risk Assessment

LOW	MEDIUM	HIGH

Our risk assessment for BMC Software reflects our concern about a sluggish recovery in IT spending and increased competition in its mainframe business from hardware vendors, offset by the company's cost-cutting measures.

Quantitative Evaluations

S&P Quality Ranking   C

D	C	B-	B	B+	A-	A	A+

Relative Strength Rank   MODERATE

67

LOWEST = 1   HIGHEST = 99

Revenue/Earnings Data

Revenue (Million $)

	1Q	2Q	3Q	4Q	Year
2010	450.0	461.8	--	--	--
2009	437.5	466.7	488.4	479.3	1,872
2008	385.0	420.7	459.0	466.9	1,732
2007	361.4	386.7	412.9	419.4	1,580
2006	348.3	361.8	380.3	407.9	1,498
2005	326.0	355.1	386.8	395.1	1,463

Earnings Per Share ($)

2010	0.44	0.50	E0.53	E0.55	E2.02
2009	0.01	0.36	0.45	0.45	1.25
2008	0.27	0.38	0.45	0.46	1.57
2007	0.15	0.28	0.30	0.30	1.03
2006	-0.19	0.19	0.22	0.31	0.47
2005	0.05	0.06	0.16	0.07	0.34

Fiscal year ended Mar. 31. Next earnings report expected: Early February. EPS Estimates based on S&P Operating Earnings; historical GAAP earnings are as reported.

Dividend Data

No cash dividends have been paid.

Stock Report | November 28, 2009 | NNM Symbol: **BMC**

BMC Software Inc

Business Summary October 30, 2009

CORPORATE OVERVIEW. BMC Software is a leading independent software vendor. The company's software, called Business Service Management (BSM), helps customers increase productivity and reduce costs by automating IT processes and improving IT responses to business decisions and challenges. BMC focuses on eight areas of BSM: Incident and Problem Management, Asset Management and Discovery, Identity Management, Service Impact and Event Management, Service Level Management, Capacity Management and Provisioning, Infrastructure and Application Management and Change and Configuration Management. These solutions are supported by a family of enabling technologies called BMC Atrium that provide a shared view of how IT supports business priorities.

BMC sells its software directly through its sales force and indirectly through resellers, distributors and systems integrators. The company also provides maintenance and support, which give customers the right to receive product upgrades. Product license and maintenance revenues accounted for 92% and 93% of total revenues in FY 09 (Mar.) and FY 08, respectively. BMC also provides professional services, which include implementation, integration and education services and contributed 8% and 7% of total revenues in FY 09 and FY 08, respectively.

In FY 07, BMC reorganized its software business into two segments. The Enterprise Service Management (ESM) business segment targets non-mainframe computing and addresses broad categories of IT management issues including Service Support, Service Assurance and Service Automation. ESM license revenue accounted for 61%, 54% and 58% of total license revenue in FY 09, FY 08 and FY 07, respectively.

The Mainframe Service Management (MSM) segment includes automated tools that enhance the performance and availability of database management systems on mainframe platforms. This segment includes BMC's mainframe performance monitoring and management product line, MAINVIEW. It also includes the management and recovery of IBM's DB2 and IMS databases. MSM license revenue accounted for 39%, 46% and 42% of total license revenue for FY 09, FY 08 and FY 07, respectively.

Company Financials Fiscal Year Ended Mar. 31

Per Share Data ($)	2009	2008	2007	2006	2005	2004	2003	2002	2001	2000
Tangible Book Value	NM	0.41	1.66	2.31	2.60	3.11	3.70	5.49	5.67	5.67
Cash Flow	1.89	2.01	1.79	1.40	1.33	1.03	1.25	0.78	1.42	1.89
Earnings	1.25	1.57	1.03	0.47	0.34	-0.12	0.20	-0.75	0.17	0.96
S&P Core Earnings	1.28	1.54	1.00	0.29	-0.03	-0.56	-0.01	-0.94	-0.19	NA
Dividends	Nil	Nil	Nil	Nil	Nil	Nil	Nil	Nil	Nil	Nil
Payout Ratio	Nil	Nil	Nil	Nil	Nil	Nil	Nil	Nil	Nil	Nil
Calendar Year	2008	2007	2006	2005	2004	2003	2002	2001	2000	1999
Prices:High	40.87	37.05	33.67	21.68	21.87	19.84	23.00	33.00	86.63	84.06
Prices:Low	20.58	24.77	19.90	14.44	13.70	13.18	10.85	11.50	13.00	30.00
P/E Ratio:High	33	24	33	41	64	NM	NM	NM	NM	88
P/E Ratio:Low	16	16	19	27	40	NM	NM	NM	NM	31

Income Statement Analysis (Million $)										
Revenue	1,872	1,732	1,580	1,498	1,463	1,419	1,327	1,289	1,504	1,719
Operating Income	573	464	413	334	264	162	349	400	336	656
Depreciation	121	88.2	161	205	222	259	248	376	315	236
Interest Expense	18.7	16.9	1.50	1.70	2.00	1.10	Nil	0.40	11.3	23.4
Pretax Income	364	434	301	204	98.2	-29.4	69.3	-231	60.4	311
Effective Tax Rate	34.6%	27.8%	28.2%	50.0%	23.3%	NM	30.7%	NM	29.8%	22.1%
Net Income	238	314	216	102	75.3	-26.8	48.0	-184	42.4	243
S&P Core Earnings	243	308	211	63.9	-5.94	-128	-3.42	-232	-46.6	NA

Balance Sheet & Other Financial Data (Million $)										
Cash	1,097	1,351	1,296	1,063	929	909	1,015	546	146	152
Current Assets	1,561	1,803	1,790	1,506	1,440	1,425	1,098	997	903	896
Total Assets	3,698	3,346	3,260	3,211	3,298	3,045	2,846	2,676	3,034	2,962
Current Liabilities	1,333	1,289	1,233	1,202	1,085	987	839	681	829	884
Long Term Debt	314	6.30	Nil	Nil	Nil	Nil	Nil	Nil	Nil	Nil
Common Equity	1,049	994	1,049	1,099	1,262	1,215	1,383	1,507	1,815	1,781
Total Capital	1,362	994	1,049	1,099	1,262	1,215	1,383	1,507	1,815	1,781
Capital Expenditures	28.0	38.4	33.7	24.1	57.7	50.4	23.6	64.3	183	148
Cash Flow	359	402	377	307	297	233	296	192	357	478
Current Ratio	1.2	1.4	1.5	1.3	1.3	1.4	1.3	1.5	1.1	1.0
% Long Term Debt of Capitalization	23.0	Nil	Nil	Nil	Nil	Nil	Nil	Nil	Nil	Nil
% Net Income of Revenue	12.7	18.1	13.7	6.8	5.1	NM	3.6	NM	2.8	14.1
% Return on Assets	6.8	9.5	6.7	3.1	2.4	NM	1.7	NM	1.4	9.2
% Return on Equity	23.3	30.7	20.1	8.6	6.1	NM	3.3	NM	2.4	15.6

Data as orig reptd.; bef. results of disc opers/spec. items. Per share data adj. for stk. divs.; EPS diluted. E-Estimated. NA-Not Available. NM-Not Meaningful. NR-Not Ranked. UR-Under Review.

Office: 2101 Citywest Boulevard, Houston, TX 77042-2827.
Telephone: 713-918-8800.
Email: investor@bmc.com
Website: http://www.bmc.com

Chrmn, Pres & CEO: R.E. Beauchamp
Investor Contact: S.B. Solcher
SVP & CFO: S.B. Solcher
SVP & Chief Admin Officer: H.S. Castro

SVP, Secy & General Counsel: D.M. Clolery
Board Members: J. E. Barfield, R. E. Beauchamp, G. L. Bloom, B. G. Cupp, M. K. Gafner, P. T. Jenkins, L. J. Lavigne, Jr., K. O'Neil, T. C. Tinsley

Founded: 1980
Domicile: Delaware
Employees: 5,800

Redistribution or reproduction is prohibited without written permission. Copyright ©2009 The McGraw-Hill Companies, Inc.

The McGraw-Hill Companies

Boeing Co (The)

STANDARD &POOR'S

S&P Recommendation	BUY ★★★★☆	Price $52.45 (as of Nov 27, 2009)	12-Mo. Target Price $60.00	Investment Style Large-Cap Growth

GICS Sector Industrials
Sub-Industry Aerospace & Defense

Summary This company is the world's second largest manufacturer of commercial jets and military weapons.

Key Stock Statistics (Source S&P, Vickers, company reports)

52-Wk Range	$55.48–29.05	S&P Oper. EPS 2009**E**	1.45	Market Capitalization(B)	$38.110	Beta	1.26
Trailing 12-Month EPS	$-0.06	S&P Oper. EPS 2010**E**	4.40	Yield (%)	3.20	S&P 3-Yr. Proj. EPS CAGR(%)	NM
Trailing 12-Month P/E	NM	P/E on S&P Oper. EPS 2009**E**	36.2	Dividend Rate/Share	$1.68	S&P Credit Rating	A
$10K Invested 5 Yrs Ago	$10,809	Common Shares Outstg. (M)	726.6	Institutional Ownership (%)	58		

Price Performance

30-Week Mov. Avg. ··· 10-Week Mov. Avg. – – **GAAP Earnings vs. Previous Year** Volume Above Avg. ▮▮▮ STARS
12-Mo. Target Price — Relative Strength — ▲ Up ▼ Down ► No Change Below Avg. ▮▮▮ ★

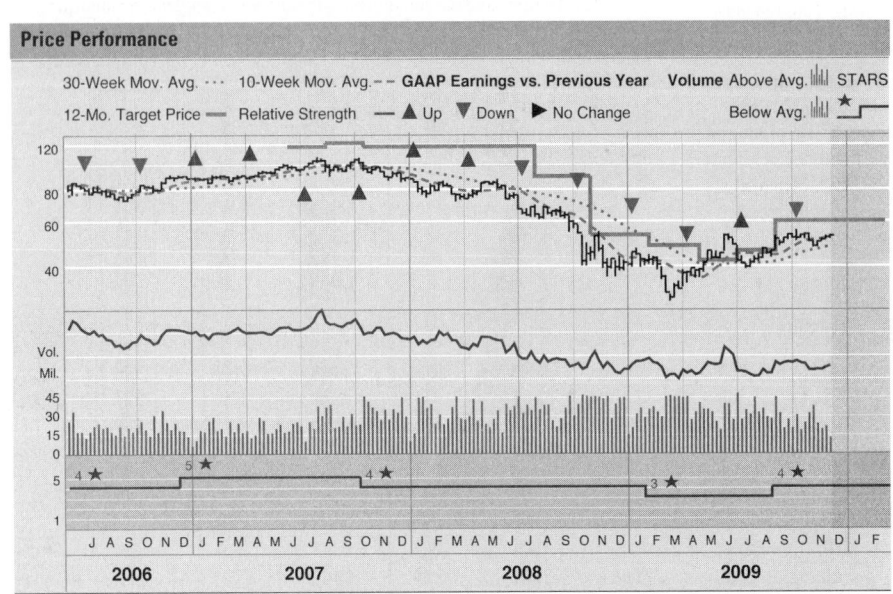

Options: ASE, CBOE, P, Ph

Analysis prepared by **Richard Tortoriello** on November 23, 2009, when the stock traded at **$ 52.97**.

Highlights

► We project a 10% sales rise in 2009, following an 8% decline in 2008, which was due to an extended machinists' union strike that was settled in October 2008. For 2010, we project an approximate 5% revenue decline as we expect slow growth (about 2%) in the defense segment to be offset by a 12% decline in Commercial Airplanes, as Boeing adjusts production to meet current demand from cash-strapped airlines.

► We look for operating margins to widen to 7.9% in 2009, from 6.5% in 2008. However, our 2009 margin estimate excludes $3.6 billion in one-time charges relating to delays on the 787 and 747-8, which were taken in the third quarter of 2009. We project operating margins of 7.6% in 2010, on a decline in Commercial Aerospace production volume.

► We project EPS of $1.45 in 2009, including the one-time charges mentioned above, and $4.45 in 2010. We forecast free cash flow per share of about $2.00 this year, as BA makes supplier payments and pays customer penalties for the delayed 787, but we expect improvement in 2010.

Investment Rationale/Risk

► We see the following factors supporting the shares: 1) we expect emerging economies in Asia and the Middle East to improve, which should sustain demand for narrow-body aircraft; 2) U.S. airlines continue to take deliveries to improve efficiency of aging fleets; 3) we believe the financing market for commercial aircraft is improving; 4) we expect the first flight of the 787 (scheduled for late 2009 and first delivery for late 2010) to act as a catalyst for shares, with 840 aircraft recently on order; 5) valuations are currently below commercial aerospace peers and below BA's historical averages on a number of measures.

► Risks to our opinion and target price include a worsening financing or economic environment, further delays on major programs, and manufacturing issues.

► Our 12-month target price of $60 is based on an enterprise value to EBITDA multiple of 7X our 2010 EBITDA estimate. This compares favorably with BA's 20-year historical average EV-to-EBITDA multiple of 11.5X, and is below current peer multiples of about 8X.

Qualitative Risk Assessment

LOW	MEDIUM	HIGH

Our risk assessment reflects BA's participation in highly cyclical, very competitive and capital-intensive businesses. This is offset by what we see as its solid cash position and strong free cash flow generation, along with a healthy and rising backlog of business.

Quantitative Evaluations

S&P Quality Ranking B+

D	C	B-	B	B+	A-	A	A+

Relative Strength Rank STRONG

75

LOWEST = 1   HIGHEST = 99

Revenue/Earnings Data

Revenue (Million $)

	1Q	2Q	3Q	4Q	Year
2009	16,502	14,296	16,688	--	--
2008	15,990	16,962	15,293	12,664	60,909
2007	15,365	17,028	16,517	17,477	66,387
2006	14,264	14,986	14,739	17,541	61,530
2005	12,987	15,025	12,629	14,204	54,845
2004	12,903	13,088	13,152	13,314	52,457

Earnings Per Share ($)

	1Q	2Q	3Q	4Q	Year
2009	0.87	1.41	-2.22	E1.37	E1.45
2008	1.61	1.16	0.94	-0.12	3.65
2007	1.12	1.35	1.43	1.35	5.26
2006	0.88	-0.21	0.89	1.28	2.84
2005	0.64	0.70	1.26	0.59	3.19
2004	0.76	0.72	0.54	0.23	2.24

Fiscal year ended Dec. 31. Next earnings report expected: Late January. EPS Estimates based on S&P Operating Earnings; historical GAAP earnings are as reported.

Dividend Data (Dates: mm/dd Payment Date. mm/dd/yy)

Amount ($)	Date Decl.	Ex-Div. Date	Stk. of Record	Payment Date
0.420	12/15	02/04	02/06	03/06/09
0.420	04/28	05/06	05/08	06/05/09
0.420	06/22	08/05	08/07	09/04/09
0.420	10/26	11/04	11/06	12/04/09

Dividends have been paid since 1942. Source: Company reports.

Boeing Co (The)

STANDARD &POOR'S

Business Summary November 23, 2009

CORPORATE OVERVIEW. This $61 billion in revenues global aerospace and defense giant conducts business through three operating segments. Boeing Commercial Airplanes (BCA; 46% of revenues and 26% of operating profits in 2008) and EADS's Airbus division are the world's only makers of 130-plus seat passenger jets. Integrated Defense Systems (IDS; 53%, 71%) is the world's second largest military contractor behind Lockheed Martin Corp. Boeing Capital Corp. (1%, 3%) primarily finances commercial aircraft for airlines.

BCA's commercial jet aircraft family includes the 737 Next-Generation narrow body model and the 747, 767, 777 and 787 wide body models. The 787 (Dreamliner) is Boeing's newest model, and is scheduled for first delivery, following a more than two-year delay, in the final quarter of 2010. BCA also offers aviation support, aircraft modifications, spare parts, training, maintenance documents, and technical advice. A new, larger 747 model is also under development, the 747-8 Intercontinental, as is a freighter version of the 747-8. Boeing had a commercial aircraft backlog at year-end 2008 of $279 billion. However, we expect BA to experience significant order cancellations and deferrals in 2009.

IDS designs, develops and supports military aircraft, including fighters, transports, tankers, intelligence surveillance and reconnaissance aircraft, and heli-

copters; unmanned systems; missiles; space systems; missile defense systems; satellites and satellite launch vehicles, and communication, information and battle management systems. IDS's primary customer is the U.S. Department of Defense (80% of 2008 sales), but it also sells to NASA, international defense customers, civilian markets, and commercial satellite markets. Major programs include the AH-64 Apache and CH-47 Chinook helicopters, the C-17 Globemaster military transport, F/A-18E/F Super Hornet and F-15 Eagle fighter jets, as well as commercial and military satellites.

MARKET PROFILE. Based on total unit orders of 130-plus seat jetliners in the three years through 2008, Boeing and Airbus each control about half of the large commercial aircraft market. Demand for jetliners is driven primarily by growth in international air travel. Since 2002, passenger air traffic has grown by an average of over 6% annually. However, Standard & Poor's estimates that passenger air traffic will decline about 6% in 2009, due to a global economic downturn.

Company Financials Fiscal Year Ended Dec. 31

Per Share Data ($)	2008	2007	2006	2005	2004	2003	2002	2001	2000	1999
Tangible Book Value	NM	3.78	NM	10.33	10.08	6.17	4.53	5.23	6.63	10.14
Cash Flow	5.26	7.18	4.76	5.08	4.00	2.68	2.46	5.52	4.14	4.27
Earnings	3.65	5.26	2.84	3.19	2.24	0.89	2.87	3.41	2.44	2.49
S&P Core Earnings	0.87	5.41	3.90	3.05	1.99	1.33	0.26	-0.06	NA	NA
Dividends	1.60	1.40	1.20	1.00	0.77	0.68	0.68	0.68	0.56	0.56
Payout Ratio	44%	27%	42%	31%	34%	76%	24%	20%	23%	22%
Prices:High	88.29	107.83	92.05	72.40	55.48	43.37	51.07	69.85	70.94	48.50
Prices:Low	36.17	84.60	65.90	49.52	38.04	24.73	28.53	27.60	32.00	32.56
P/E Ratio:High	24	20	32	23	25	49	18	20	29	19
P/E Ratio:Low	10	16	23	16	17	28	10	8	13	13

Income Statement Analysis (Million $)										
Revenue	60,909	66,387	61,530	54,845	52,457	50,485	54,069	58,198	51,321	57,993
Operating Income	5,107	7,090	5,176	3,707	3,405	3,198	5,447	6,467	4,996	4,724
Depreciation	1,179	1,486	1,545	1,503	1,509	1,450	1,497	1,750	1,479	1,645
Interest Expense	524	196	593	653	685	800	730	650	445	431
Pretax Income	4,033	6,118	1,218	2,819	1,960	550	1,353	3,565	2,999	3,324
Effective Tax Rate	33.5%	33.6%	NM	9.12%	7.14%	NM	63.6%	20.7%	29.0%	30.5%
Net Income	2,684	4,058	2,206	2,562	1,820	718	492	2,827	2,128	2,309
S&P Core Earnings	619	4,177	3,042	2,450	1,616	1,074	203	284	NA	NA

Balance Sheet & Other Financial Data (Million $)										
Cash	3,279	7,042	6,118	5,412	3,204	4,633	2,333	633	1,010	3,354
Current Assets	25,964	27,280	22,983	21,968	15,100	17,258	16,855	16,206	15,864	15,712
Total Assets	53,801	58,986	51,794	60,058	53,963	53,035	52,342	48,343	42,028	36,147
Current Liabilities	30,925	31,538	29,701	28,188	20,835	18,448	19,810	20,486	18,289	13,656
Long Term Debt	6,952	7,455	8,157	9,538	10,879	13,299	12,589	10,866	7,567	5,980
Common Equity	-1,264	9,004	4,739	11,059	11,286	8,139	7,696	10,825	11,020	11,462
Total Capital	5,658	17,649	12,896	22,664	23,255	21,438	20,285	21,868	18,587	17,614
Capital Expenditures	1,674	1,731	1,681	1,547	978	741	1,001	1,068	932	1,236
Cash Flow	3,833	5,544	3,751	4,065	3,329	2,168	1,989	4,577	3,607	3,954
Current Ratio	0.8	0.9	0.8	0.8	0.7	0.9	0.9	0.8	0.9	1.2
% Long Term Debt of Capitalization	122.9	42.2	63.3	42.1	46.8	62.0	62.1	49.7	40.7	34.0
% Net Income of Revenue	4.4	6.1	3.6	4.7	3.5	1.4	0.9	4.9	4.1	4.0
% Return on Assets	4.8	7.3	3.9	4.4	3.4	1.4	1.0	6.2	5.4	6.3
% Return on Equity	NM	59.0	27.9	22.9	18.7	9.1	5.3	25.9	18.9	19.4

Data as orig reptd.; bef. results of disc opers/spec. items. Per share data adj. for stk. divs.; EPS diluted. E-Estimated. NA-Not Available. NM-Not Meaningful. NR-Not Ranked. UR-Under Review.

Office: 100 N Riverside, Chicago, IL 60606-1596.
Telephone: 312-544-2000 .
Website: http://www.boeing.com
Chrmn, Pres & CEO: W.J. McNerney, Jr.

COO & CTO: J.J. Tracy
EVP & CFO: J.A. Bell
EVP & General Counsel: J.M. Luttig
Chief Admin Officer: R.D. Stephens

Investor Contact: R. Young (312-544-2140)
Board Members: J. H. Biggs, J. E. Bryson, D. L. Calhoun, A. D. Collins, Jr., L. Cook, W. M. Daley, K. M. Duberstein, E. Giambastiani, Jr., J. F. McDonnell, W. J. McNerney, Jr., M. Zafirovski

Founded: 1916
Domicile: Delaware
Employees: 162,200

The McGraw-Hill Companies

Boston Properties Inc

STANDARD &POOR'S

S&P Recommendation HOLD ★★★☆☆

Price	**12-Mo. Target Price**	**Investment Style**
$63.79 (as of Nov 27, 2009)	$64.00	Large-Cap Blend

GICS Sector Financials
Sub-Industry Office REITS

Summary This real estate investment trust primarily owns office buildings in the Boston, Washington, DC, New York City, San Francisco and Princeton markets.

Key Stock Statistics (Source S&P, Vickers, company reports)

52-Wk Range	$72.23–29.30	S&P FFO/Sh. 2009E	4.75	Market Capitalization(B)	$8.849	Beta	1.56
Trailing 12-Month FFO/Share	NA	S&P FFO/Sh. 2010E	4.10	Yield (%)	3.14	S&P 3-Yr. FFO/Sh. Proj. CAGR(%)	3
Trailing 12-Month P/FFO	NA	P/FFO on S&P FFO/Sh. 2009E	13.4	Dividend Rate/Share	$2.00	S&P Credit Rating	A-
$10K Invested 5 Yrs Ago	$14,659	Common Shares Outstg. (M)	138.7	Institutional Ownership (%)	NM		

Price Performance

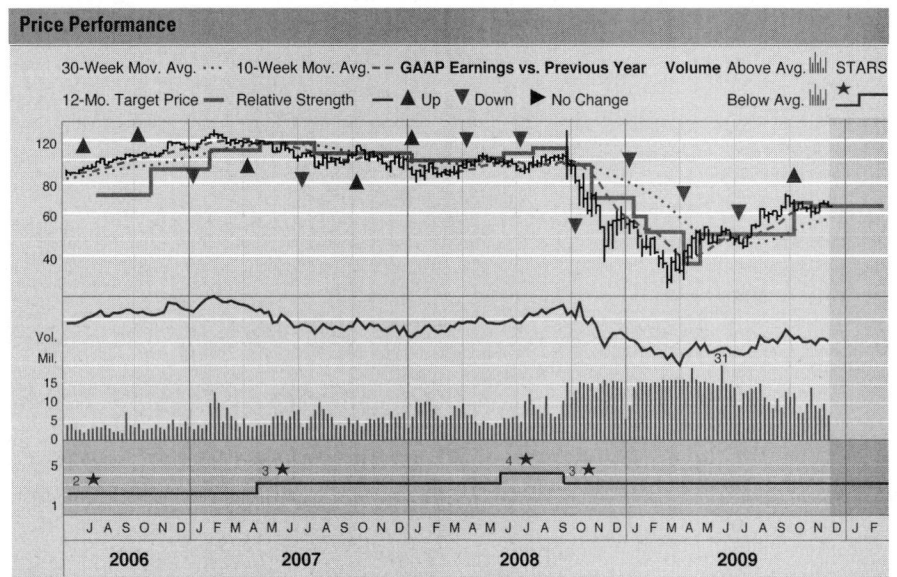

- 30-Week Mov. Avg. ··· 10-Week Mov. Avg. – – GAAP Earnings vs. Previous Year   Volume Above Avg. STARS
- 12-Mo. Target Price — Relative Strength — ▲ Up ▼ Down ► No Change   Below Avg.

Options: ASE, CBOE, P

Analysis prepared by **Royal F. Shepard, CFA** on October 29, 2009, when the stock traded at **$ 59.15**.

Highlights

► We expect downward pressure on market rents through 2010, due to recent job losses in BXP's urban markets. The trust has also lost certain tenants to bankruptcy, including Lehman Brothers and General Motors. We estimate 2009 year-end occupancy will be 91.5%, down from 94.5% at the end of 2008, before stabilizing in late 2010. Just over 20% of BXP's total space is subject to lease expiration by the end of 2011, a moderate level relative to peers.

► BXP is building a large cash cushion, in our view, to use for acquisitions once market conditions improve. In June, it completed a 17.25 million common share offering netting proceeds of about $842.0 million. More recently, in October, it offering $700 million in 5.875% unsecured notes due in 2019. The trust may use a portion of proceeds to address scheduled debt maturities of $355 million in late 2009 and 2010.

► Our 2009 and 2010 FFO per share estimates of $4.75 and $4.10, respectively, reflect pressure on occupancy and lower development fees, and near-term dilution from recent debt and equity financing. We exclude one-time charges of $0.24 a share in 2009.

Investment Rationale/Risk

► In view of low tenant turnover, we think BXP's high-quality portfolio will hold up reasonably well in challenging market conditions. We believe average rents will slowly decline as long-term leases renew at lower levels. The potential of future fees from new development projects, though, appears very limited until credit market conditions improve. Also, we expect BXP to hold off on new acquisition opportunities until leasing metrics stabilize. With the shares recently trading at 14.3X our 2009 FFO per share outlook, a premium to peers, we believe BXP's long-term growth potential is reflected in its price.

► Risks to our recommendation and target price include national employment growth lagging our expectations, and lower-than-anticipated regional economic strength in BXP's markets.

► Our 12-month target price of $64 is based primarily on applying a multiple of about 15.5X to our 2010 FFO per share estimate, a premium to office REITs serving less attractive suburban markets. We blend in our $66 estimate of net asset value (NAV), based on recent market transactions and a one-year cash yield of 6.5%.

Qualitative Risk Assessment

LOW	MEDIUM	HIGH

Our risk assessment reflects what we see as BXP's large and diverse asset portfolio, relatively unleveraged balance sheet, and consistent cash distribution.

Quantitative Evaluations

S&P Quality Ranking B+

D	C	B-	B	B+	A-	A	A+

Relative Strength Rank MODERATE

62

LOWEST = 1   HIGHEST = 99

Revenue/FFO Data

Revenue (Million $)

	1Q	2Q	3Q	4Q	Year
2009	381.7	388.7	377.3	--	--
2008	370.6	366.3	357.1	201.9	1,287
2007	360.7	372.2	368.6	380.8	1,482
2006	356.1	370.4	372.5	378.7	1,502
2005	356.2	360.6	361.8	366.3	1,438
2004	333.3	344.9	359.7	362.6	1,400

FFO Per Share ($)

	1Q	2Q	3Q	4Q	Year
2009	1.11	1.32	E1.13	E1.05	E4.75
2008	1.18	1.19	1.13	0.05	3.49
2007	0.42	0.32	0.32	1.22	4.64
2006	0.27	0.39	0.32	0.32	4.17
2005	0.23	0.16	0.16	0.24	4.31
2004	-1.16	0.11	0.22	0.22	4.16

Fiscal year ended Dec. 31. Next earnings report expected: Late January. FFO Estimates based on S&P Funds From Operations Est..

Dividend Data (Dates: mm/dd Payment Date: mm/dd/yy)

Amount ($)	Date Decl.	Ex-Div. Date	Stk. of Record	Payment Date
0.680	12/15	12/29	12/31	01/30/09
0.680	03/17	03/27	03/31	04/30/09
0.500	06/17	06/26	06/30	07/31/09
0.500	09/17	09/28	09/30	10/30/09

Dividends have been paid since 1997. Source: Company reports.

Please read the Required Disclosures and Analyst Certification on the last page of this report.

The McGraw-Hill Companies

Boston Properties Inc

**STANDARD
&POOR'S**

Business Summary October 29, 2009

CORPORATE OVERVIEW. Boston Properties, founded in 1970, is a real estate investment trust (REIT) that develops, acquires, manages, operates, and is one of the largest U.S. owners of, Class A office properties. BXP conducts substantially all of its business through its limited partnership, of which it is the sole general partner, and holds an 84% economic interest.

At December 31, 2008, the property portfolio consisted of 147 properties, totaling 49.8 million net rentable sq. ft. and structured parking facilities for vehicles containing approximately 9.9 million sq. ft. The properties included 136 in-service office buildings and one hotel in Cambridge, Massachusetts. In addition, BXP had 10 properties under construction totaling 3.8 million sq. ft.

MARKET PROFILE The market for office leases is inherently cyclical. Local economic conditions, particularly the employment level, play an important role in determining competitive dynamics. Standard & Poor's estimates that non-farm monthly payrolls will decline through 2009, with an increase in the unemployment rate to 10.0% in early 2010, from 7.2% as of December 2008.

The U.S. office market tends to track the overall economy on a lagged basis. At the end of December 2008, we believe the national vacancy rate was about 14.5%, an increase from a cyclical low of about 12.5% at the end of 2007. Going forward, we believe vacancy levels will continue to rise in 2009 due to a

recessionary economic environment. In our opinion, BXP's principal markets, including Washington, DC, Manhattan, Boston, and San Francisco, are among the nation's strongest due to limited new construction activity in recent years. However, potential layoffs in the financial services sector, particularly in New York City, may pressure rents in coming months. In total, as of December 31, 2008, BXP had an office vacancy rate at established properties of 4.8%, much better than the national averages. Leases will expire on only about 6.8% of existing office space in 2009, limiting the trust's exposure to declining market rents. These lease rollovers are concentrated primarily in the Boston and Washington, DC, metropolitan areas.

Competition for leasing real estate is high. In addition, we believe that competition for the acquisition of new properties is intensifying from other REITs, private real estate funds, financial institutions, insurance companies and others. As a result, we think BXP could have difficulty finding new assets at attractive prices.

Company Financials Fiscal Year Ended Dec. 31

Per Share Data ($)	2008	2007	2006	2005	2004	2003	2002	2001	2000	1999
Tangible Book Value	29.14	30.72	27.45	25.92	26.61	22.51	20.79	19.34	19.02	15.57
Earnings	1.03	9.06	7.46	3.46	2.35	2.94	4.40	2.26	2.01	1.71
S&P Core Earnings	1.03	9.06	7.46	3.46	2.34	2.88	4.37	2.20	NA	NA
Dividends	1.52	2.72	2.72	5.19	2.58	2.50	2.41	2.27	1.96	1.73
Payout Ratio	NM	30%	36%	150%	110%	85%	55%	100%	96%	101%
Prices:High	50.63	133.02	118.22	76.67	64.90	48.47	41.55	43.88	44.88	37.50
Prices:Low	19.69	87.78	72.98	56.66	42.99	34.80	32.95	34.00	29.00	27.25
P/E Ratio:High	60	15	16	22	28	16	9	19	22	22
P/E Ratio:Low	23	10	10	16	18	12	7	15	14	16
Income Statement Analysis (Million $)										
Rental Income	1,402	1,334	1,344	1,339	1,293	1,219	1,174	1,008	859	765
Mortgage Income	Nil	Nil	Nil	Nil	Nil	Nil	Nil	Nil	Nil	Nil
Total Income	1,488	1,482	1,502	1,438	1,400	1,310	1,235	1,033	879	787
General Expenses	588	554	557	545	528	498	464	351	300	279
Interest Expense	272	286	298	308	306	299	272	223	217	205
Provision for Losses	Nil	Nil	Nil	Nil	Nil	Nil	Nil	Nil	Nil	Nil
Depreciation	304	286	277	267	252	210	186	150	133	120
Net Income	125	1,098	874	393	255	290	420	215	153	120
S&P Core Earnings	125	1,094	874	393	254	284	413	203	NA	NA
Balance Sheet & Other Financial Data (Million $)										
Cash	242	1,716	752	377	345	133	199	201	378	88.7
Total Assets	10,912	11,193	9,695	8,902	9,063	8,551	8,427	7,254	6,226	5,435
Real Estate Investment	10,618	10,250	9,552	9,151	9,291	8,983	8,671	7,458	6,113	5,612
Loss Reserve	Nil	Nil	Nil	Nil	Nil	Nil	Nil	Nil	Nil	Nil
Net Investment	8,850	8,718	8,160	7,886	8,148	7,981	7,848	6,738	5,526	5,142
Short Term Debt	100	Nil	Nil	Nil	Nil	Nil	Nil	282	194	680
Capitalization:Debt	6,172	5,492	4,559	4,679	4,733	5,005	3,336	4,033	3,415	2,642
Capitalization:Equity	3,531	3,669	3,223	2,917	2,936	2,400	2,160	1,754	1,648	1,058
Capitalization:Total	10,302	9,216	8,406	8,335	8,455	8,235	6,340	6,732	6,040	4,582
% Earnings & Depreciation/Assets	3.9	13.3	12.3	7.3	5.8	5.9	7.7	5.4	4.9	4.5
Price Times Book Value:High	4.5	4.3	4.3	3.0	2.4	2.1	2.0	2.3	2.4	2.4
Price Times Book Value:Low	1.3	2.9	2.7	2.2	1.6	1.5	1.6	1.8	1.5	1.8

Data as orig reptd.; bef. results of disc opers/spec. items. Per share data adj. for stk. divs.; EPS diluted. E-Estimated. NA-Not Available. NM-Not Meaningful. NR-Not Ranked. UR-Under Review.

Office: 800 Boylston St Ste 1900, Boston, MA 02199-8103.
Telephone: 617-236-3300.
Email: investor_relations@bostonproperties.com
Website: http://www.bostonproperties.com

Chrmn: M.B. Zuckerman
Pres: D. Linde
CEO: E. Linde
COO & EVP: E.M. Norville

SVP, CFO & Treas: M.E. LaBelle
Investor Contact: M. Walsh (617-236-3300)
Board Members: L. S. Bacow, Z. Baird, C. B. Einiger, F. J. Iseman, E. Linde, A. J. Patricof, R. E. Salomon, M. Turchin, D. A. Twardock, M. B. Zuckerman

Founded: 1970
Domicile: Delaware
Employees: 700

Boston Scientific Corp

STANDARD &POOR'S

S&P Recommendation **BUY** ★★★★☆	Price	12-Mo. Target Price	Investment Style
	$8.50 (as of Nov 27, 2009)	$12.00	Large-Cap Growth

GICS Sector Health Care
Sub-Industry Health Care Equipment

Summary This manufacturer of minimally invasive medical devices acquired device rival Guidant Corp. in April 2006 for $27 billion in cash and stock.

Key Stock Statistics (Source S&P, Vickers, company reports)

52-Wk Range	$11.77– 5.80	S&P Oper. EPS 2009**E**	0.55	Market Capitalization(B)	$12.839	Beta	1.09
Trailing 12-Month EPS	$-1.56	S&P Oper. EPS 2010**E**	0.66	Yield (%)	Nil	S&P 3-Yr. Proj. EPS CAGR(%)	8
Trailing 12-Month P/E	NM	P/E on S&P Oper. EPS 2009**E**	15.5	Dividend Rate/Share	Nil	S&P Credit Rating	BB+
$10K Invested 5 Yrs Ago	$2,477	Common Shares Outstg. (M)	1,510.4	Institutional Ownership (%)	84		

Price Performance

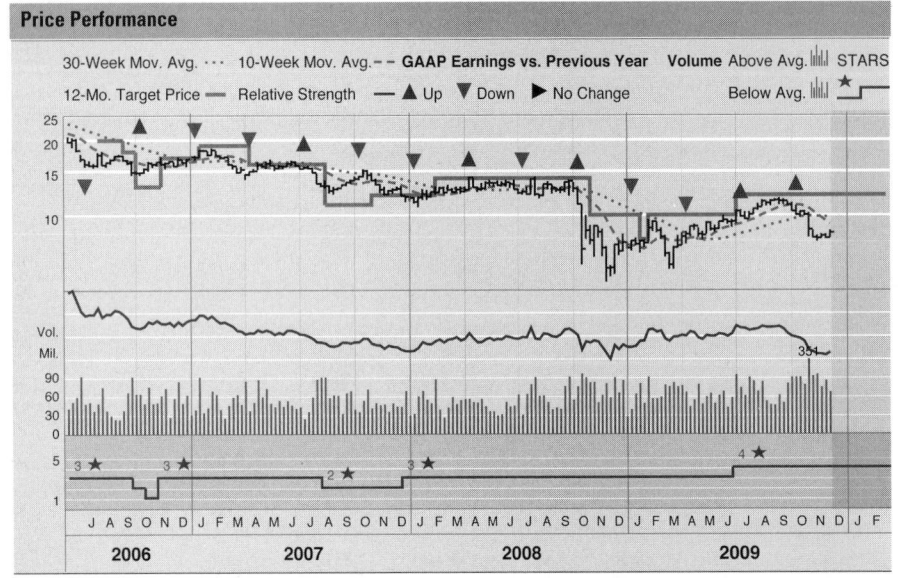

30-Week Mov. Avg. ···· 10-Week Mov. Avg. – – **GAAP Earnings vs. Previous Year**   Volume Above Avg. STARS
12-Mo. Target Price — Relative Strength — ▲ Up ▼ Down ► No Change   Below Avg.

Options: ASE, CBOE, P, Ph

Analysis prepared by **Jeffrey Englander, CFA** on November 11, 2009, when the stock traded at **$ 8.38**.

Highlights

► We see revenues increasing about 2% in 2009 and 5% in 2010. While we expect that somewhat challenging conditions will persist in the defibrillator and stent markets through 2009, we expect BSX to at least maintain share in the stent market and to pick up share in the ICD market and to potentially benefit from a move to higher priced ICD-CRT devices, following the full analysis of trial data later in 2009.

► We look for restructuring to reduce debt and realign operating costs, but we expect this to be offset by pricing pressure from customers. As a result, we look for gross margins to remain flat through 2010. We forecast that R&D will decline modestly in 2009 as BSX invests prudently, and we see SG&A expenses increasing as BSX works to maintain share. We look for R&D and SG&A expense declines to continue into 2010 relative to sales, as cost optimization efforts cut expenses.

► We see operating EPS of $0.55 in 2009 and $0.66 in 2010, including restructuring charges and two separate and unrelated charges for patent infringement, due to the recurring nature of such charges recorded by the company in recent years.

Investment Rationale/Risk

► We expect BSX to benefit from its licensing agreement with Abbott Laboratories (ABT 44, Buy) to market BSX's PROMUS version of ABT's successful XIENCE drug-eluting stent. Moreover, we think BSX's recent release of positive preliminary results of MADIT-CRT data should help propel growth in the ICD market. We also expect the recent appointment of former Zimmer Holdings CEO Ray Elliott as CEO to speed the pace of change, help BSX attain best-in-class compliance, and refocus the organization on profitable growth.

► Risks to our recommendation and target price include unfavorable litigation outcomes, intensified competition in key markets, and delays in commercializing key products in the pipeline.

► Our 12-month target price of $12 assumes BSX will trade at 18X our 2010 operating EPS estimate, a modest premium to peers. We think this is warranted as the company likely enters a period of accelerating growth, following several years of difficult results. We think valuation on forward P/E is most relevant given the recent appointment of a new CEO, the number of initiatives the company is undertaking, and the time required for these actions to produce results.

Qualitative Risk Assessment

LOW	MEDIUM	HIGH

Our risk assessment reflects the company's operations within intensely competitive areas of the health care industry, and its dependence for growth on the development and commercialization of new products. In addition, a large percentage of customers are reimbursed by the federal Medicare program, and we believe the government is likely to reduce the pace of expenditure growth by lowering reimbursement rates for expensive medical devices such as defibrillators and cardiac stents.

Quantitative Evaluations

S&P Quality Ranking   C

D	C	B-	B	B+	A-	A	A+

Relative Strength Rank   WEAK

22

LOWEST = 1   HIGHEST = 99

Revenue/Earnings Data

Revenue (Million $)

	1Q	2Q	3Q	4Q	Year
2009	2,010	2,074	2,025	--	--
2008	2,046	2,024	1,978	2,002	8,050
2007	2,086	2,071	2,048	2,152	8,357
2006	1,620	2,110	2,206	2,065	7,821
2005	1,615	1,617	1,511	1,540	6,283
2004	1,082	1,460	1,482	1,600	5,624

Earnings Per Share ($)

	1Q	2Q	3Q	4Q	Year
2009	-0.01	0.10	0.13	E0.17	E0.55
2008	0.22	0.07	-0.04	-1.62	-1.38
2007	0.08	0.08	-0.18	-0.31	-0.33
2006	0.40	-3.21	0.05	0.19	-2.81
2005	0.42	0.24	-0.33	0.40	0.75
2004	0.23	0.36	0.30	0.35	1.24

Fiscal year ended Dec. 31. Next earnings report expected: Late January. EPS Estimates based on S&P Operating Earnings; historical GAAP earnings are as reported.

Dividend Data

No cash dividends have been paid.

Please read the Required Disclosures and Analyst Certification on the last page of this report.

The McGraw·Hill Companies

Boston Scientific Corp

**STANDARD
&POOR'S**

Business Summary November 11, 2009

CORPORATE OVERVIEW. Boston Scientific develops and markets minimally invasive medical devices that are used in a broad range of interventional medical specialties, including interventional cardiology, cardiac rhythm management, peripheral intervention, electrophysiology, gynecology, oncology, urology and neuromodulation.

Within the cardiovascular market, the company sells products used to treat coronary vessel disease known as arteriosclerosis. The majority of BSX's cardiovascular products are used in percutaneous transluminal coronary angioplasty (PTCA) and percutaneous transluminal coronary rotational atherectomy. These products include PTCA balloon catheters, rotational atherectomy systems, guide wires, guide catheters, diagnostic catheters, and, more recently, a cutting balloon catheter. Other products include thrombectomy catheters, peripheral vascular stents, embolic protection filters, blood clot fil-

ter systems, and electrophysiology products.

BSX also sells balloon-expandable and self-expanding coronary stent systems. In early 2004, BSX launched Taxus, an Express stent coated with a polymer embedded with the anticancer compound paclitaxel. In January 2005, BSX launched its next-generation Taxus Liberte paclitaxel-eluting coronary stent in 18 Inter-Continental countries and in Europe. Taxus Liberte was launched in the U.S. in 2008. Through an agreement with Abbott Labs, BSX also sells the PROMUS everolimus-eluting stent system in the U.S. During 2008, drug-coated coronary stents accounted for 20% of total revenues.

Company Financials Fiscal Year Ended Dec. 31

Per Share Data ($)	2008	2007	2006	2005	2004	2003	2002	2001	2000	1999
Tangible Book Value	NM	NM	NM	0.67	0.82	0.49	0.12	NM	0.33	NM
Cash Flow	-0.78	0.30	-1.90	1.12	1.60	0.79	0.64	0.22	0.68	0.67
Earnings	-1.38	-0.33	-2.81	0.75	1.24	0.56	0.45	-0.07	0.46	0.45
S&P Core Earnings	-0.16	0.16	-2.75	1.39	1.27	0.50	0.33	-0.10	NA	NA
Dividends	Nil	Nil	Nil	Nil	Nil	Nil	Nil	Nil	Nil	Nil
Payout Ratio	Nil	Nil	Nil	Nil	Nil	Nil	Nil	Nil	Nil	Nil
Prices:High	14.22	18.69	26.56	35.50	46.10	36.85	22.15	13.95	14.59	23.53
Prices:Low	5.41	11.27	14.43	22.80	31.25	19.10	10.24	6.63	6.09	8.78
P/E Ratio:High	NM	NM	NM	47	37	66	49	NM	32	52
P/E Ratio:Low	NM	NM	NM	30	25	34	23	NM	13	20

Income Statement Analysis (Million $)

	2008	2007	2006	2005	2004	2003	2002	2001	2000	1999
Revenue	8,050	8,357	7,821	6,283	5,624	3,476	2,919	2,673	2,664	2,842
Operating Income	2,159	2,158	-2,383	2,338	1,989	945	757	614	819	857
Depreciation	864	939	781	314	275	196	161	232	181	178
Interest Expense	468	570	435	90.0	64.0	46.0	43.0	59.0	70.0	118
Pretax Income	-2,062	-569	-3,535	891	1,494	643	549	44.0	527	562
Effective Tax Rate	NM	NM	NM	29.5%	28.9%	26.6%	32.1%	NM	29.2%	34.0%
Net Income	-2,072	-495	-3,577	628	1,062	472	373	-54.0	373	371
S&P Core Earnings	-231	240	-3,498	1,162	1,082	423	269	-77.0	NA	NA

Balance Sheet & Other Financial Data (Million $)

	2008	2007	2006	2005	2004	2003	2002	2001	2000	1999
Cash	1,641	1,452	1,688	848	1,640	671	277	180	54.0	64.0
Current Assets	5,452	5,921	4,901	2,631	3,289	1,880	1,208	1,106	992	1,055
Total Assets	27,080	31,197	31,096	8,196	8,170	5,699	4,450	3,974	3,427	3,572
Current Liabilities	3,233	3,250	2,630	1,479	2,605	1,393	923	831	819	1,055
Long Term Debt	6,743	8,161	8,895	1,864	1,139	1,172	847	973	562	678
Common Equity	13,138	15,097	15,298	4,282	4,025	2,862	2,467	2,015	1,935	1,724
Total Capital	22,143	25,314	26,977	6,408	5,423	4,185	3,414	2,988	2,497	2,402
Capital Expenditures	362	363	341	341	274	188	112	121	76.0	80.0
Cash Flow	-1,172	444	-2,796	942	1,337	668	534	178	554	549
Current Ratio	1.7	1.8	1.9	1.8	1.3	1.3	1.3	1.3	1.2	1.0
% Long Term Debt of Capitalization	30.5	34.5	33.0	29.1	21.0	28.0	24.8	32.6	22.5	28.2
% Net Income of Revenue	NM	NM	NM	10.0	18.9	13.6	12.8	NM	14.0	13.1
% Return on Assets	NM	NM	NM	7.7	15.3	9.3	8.9	NM	10.7	9.9
% Return on Equity	NM	NM	NM	15.1	30.8	17.7	16.6	NM	20.4	29.2

Data as orig reptd.; bef. results of disc opers/spec. items. Per share data adj. for stk. divs.; EPS diluted. E-Estimated. NA-Not Available. NM-Not Meaningful. NR-Not Ranked. UR-Under Review.

Office: One Boston Scientific Pl, Natick, MA 01760-1537.
Telephone: 508-650-8000.
Email: investor_relations@bsci.com
Website: http://www.bostonscientific.com

Chrmn: P.M. Nicholas, Jr.
Pres & CEO: J.R. Elliott
COO: K.J. Pucel
EVP & CFO: S.R. Leno

EVP & CSO: D.S. Baim
Board Members: J. E. Abele, K. T. Bartlett, B. L. Byrnes, J. R. Elliott, M. A. Fox, R. J. Groves, E. Mario, N. J. Nicholas, Jr., P. M. Nicholas, Jr., J. Pepper, Jr., U. E. Reinhardt, W. B. Rudman, J. E. Sununu

Founded: 1979
Domicile: Delaware
Employees: 24,800

The McGraw-Hill Companies

Bristol-Myers Squibb Co

STANDARD &POOR'S

S&P Recommendation	HOLD ★★★☆☆	Price $25.38 (as of Nov 27, 2009)	12-Mo. Target Price $26.00	Investment Style Large-Cap Value

GICS Sector Health Care
Sub-Industry Pharmaceuticals

Summary Bristol-Myers Squibb is a leading global drugmaker, with strengths in cardiovascular, anti-infective and anticancer therapeutics.

Key Stock Statistics (Source S&P, Vickers, company reports)

52-Wk Range	$25.75– 17.23	S&P Oper. EPS 2009E	2.03	Market Capitalization(B)	$50.277	Beta	0.66
Trailing 12-Month EPS	$1.93	S&P Oper. EPS 2010E	2.25	Yield (%)	4.89	S&P 3-Yr. Proj. EPS CAGR(%)	13
Trailing 12-Month P/E	13.2	P/E on S&P Oper. EPS 2009E	12.5	Dividend Rate/Share	$1.24	S&P Credit Rating	A+
$10K Invested 5 Yrs Ago	$13,673	Common Shares Outstg. (M)	1,981.0	Institutional Ownership (%)	71		

Price Performance

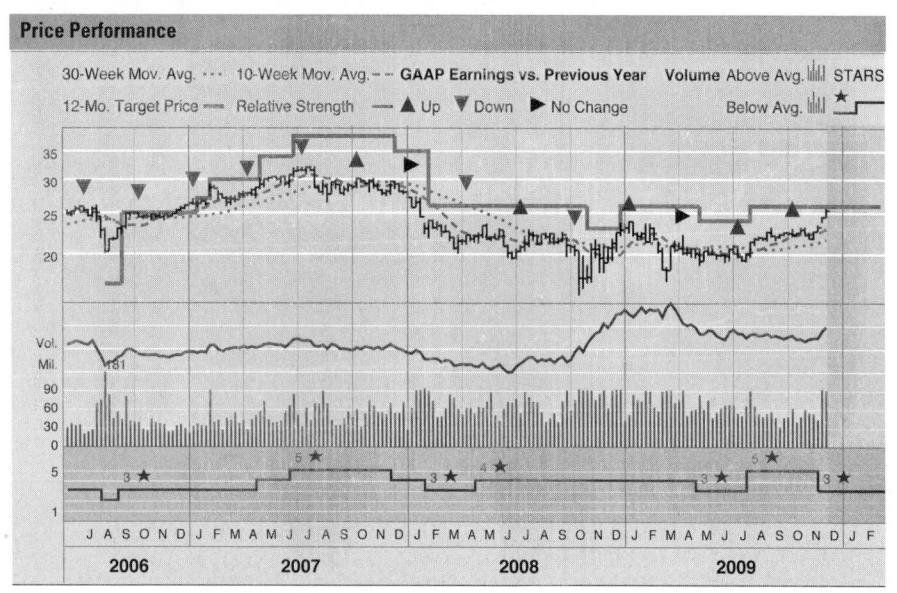

30-Week Mov. Avg. ··· 10-Week Mov. Avg. — GAAP Earnings vs. Previous Year   Volume Above Avg. STARS
12-Mo. Target Price — Relative Strength — ▲ Up ▼ Down ► No Change   Below Avg.

Options: ASE, CBOE, P, Ph

Analysis prepared by **Herman B. Saftlas** on November 19, 2009, when the stock traded at **$ 24.04**.

Qualitative Risk Assessment

LOW	MEDIUM	HIGH

In common with other large capitalization drugmakers, BMY is subject to generic challenges to its branded drugs, as well as risks associated with new drug development and regulatory approval. Although BMY faces the loss of patent protection on several key drugs over the 2011-2012 period, we believe these losses may be offset by new products and significant cost savings.

Quantitative Evaluations

S&P Quality Ranking   B+

D	C	B-	B	B+	A-	A	A+

Relative Strength Rank   STRONG   89

LOWEST = 1   HIGHEST = 99

Highlights

► We see sales from continuing operations rising 6% in 2010, from the $21.5 billion that we forecast for 2009 (excluding the planned sale of the Mead Johnson nutritional products business). In our opinion, top-line growth should reflect more favorable foreign exchange, and gains in key drug franchises. Sales of Plavix (BMY's most important product) should benefit from greater penetration of the peripheral arterial disease market. Volume should also be augmented by gains in Abilify and Sustiva, as well as from new products such as Orencia for rheumatoid arthritis, and Onglyza for type 2 diabetes.

► We see gross margins in 2010 holding steady with the 72.4% that we forecast for 2009. Although we expect tight control of SG&A expenses, we believe R&D expenses will rise on stepped-up spending on new drugs. Other income will likely decline.

► After an estimated 2010 tax rate near the 24.5% that we estimate for 2009, we forecast operating EPS of $2.25 for 2010, up from $2.03 that we estimate for 2009. We see dilution from the recent Medarex acquisition of $0.02 in 2009 and $0.08 in 2010.

Investment Rationale/Risk

► BMY recently announced plans to split off its 83% interest in Mead Johnson (MJN 44, NR) to BMY shareholders. Under terms of a planned exchange offer, BMY holders would receive about $1.11 in MJN shares for each $1.00 in BMY shares tendered, subject to limits. Some 14% of BMY's shares outstanding would be retired if the proposed exchange offer is fully subscribed. With a lower share base, and reduced cash dividend outlays, we expect the transaction to be accretive to 2010 EPS by $0.05-$0.10. However, we see the loss of MJN as a long-term negative as it removes a source of steady, albeit slow growing, cash flow. We also note that BMY faces the loss of patent protection on its key drug Plavix in 2011.

► Risks to our recommendation and target price include increased competitive pressures in key product lines, and possible pipeline setbacks.

► Our 12-month target price of $26 applies a near peer-parity multiple of 11.6X to our 2010 EPS estimate. Our DCF model, which assumes a WACC of 7.5% and terminal growth of 1%, also indicates intrinsic value of $26. The dividend recently yielded 5.2%.

Revenue/Earnings Data

Revenue (Million $)

	1Q	2Q	3Q	4Q	Year
2009	5,015	5,384	54,878	--	--
2008	4,891	5,203	5,254	5,249	20,597
2007	4,317	4,757	4,893	5,381	19,348
2006	4,676	4,871	4,154	4,213	17,914
2005	4,532	4,889	4,767	5,019	19,207
2004	4,626	4,819	4,778	5,157	19,380

Earnings Per Share ($)

2009	0.32	0.49	0.48	E0.47	E2.03
2008	0.32	0.36	0.30	0.61	1.59
2007	0.33	0.33	0.41	-0.07	0.99
2006	0.36	0.34	0.17	-0.07	0.81
2005	0.27	0.50	0.49	0.26	1.52
2004	0.49	0.27	0.38	0.07	1.21

Fiscal year ended Dec. 31. Next earnings report expected: Late January. EPS Estimates based on S&P Operating Earnings; historical GAAP earnings are as reported.

Dividend Data (Dates: mm/dd Payment Date: mm/dd/yy)

Amount ($)	Date Decl.	Ex-Div. Date	Stk. of Record	Payment Date
0.310	12/18	12/30	01/02	02/02/09
0.310	03/03	04/01	04/03	05/01/09
0.310	06/10	07/01	07/06	08/03/09
0.310	09/09	09/30	10/02	11/02/09

Dividends have been paid since 1900. Source: Company reports.

Please read the Required Disclosures and Analyst Certification on the last page of this report.

Bristol-Myers Squibb Co

STANDARD &POOR'S

Business Summary November 19, 2009

CORPORATE OVERVIEW. Bristol-Myers Squibb is a major global drugmaker, offering a wide range of prescription drugs. In recent years, BMY divested non-core beauty care, orthopedic devices, imaging products and cancer drug distribution businesses. Prescription drugs accounted for 86% of sales in 2008, with nutritionals representing the balance. Foreign sales accounted for 42% of total sales in 2008.

The company's largest selling drug is Plavix (sales of $5.6 billion in 2008), a platelet aggregation inhibitor for the prevention of stroke, heart attack and vascular disease. Plavix is produced through a joint venture with French drug-maker Sanofi-Aventis SA. Other cardiovasculars include Avapro/Avalide ($1.3 billion), an angiotensin II receptor blocker for hypertension; and Pravachol anticholesterol ($203 million). Principal anticancer drugs are Erbitux ($749 million), Taxol ($385 million) and Sprycel ($310 million).

The company's principal anti-infective drugs are HIV/AIDS treatments such as Reyataz ($1.3 billion), Sustiva ($1.1 billion), and Baraclude ($541 million). BMY also offers Cefzil, Tequin, Maxipime, and other antibiotics. Central nervous

system agents include Abilify, an antipsychotic ($2.2 billion); Orencia, a treatment for rheumatoid arthritis ($441 million); Sinemet for Parkinson's disease; and various other drugs.

The Mead Johnson division offers nutritionals, consisting of infant formulas such as Enfamil and ProSobee, as well as other related items. In February 2009, BMY sold a 17% interest in Mead Johnson (MJN 44, NR) through an IPO, raising close to $1 billion. In November 2009, BMY announced plans to divest its remaining 83% interest in MJN by exchanging its MJN shares for BMY shares, which would then be retired.

During 2008, BMY sold its ConvaTec ostomy and wound care and its Medical Imaging businesses for a combined total of $4.5 billion in cash.

Company Financials Fiscal Year Ended Dec. 31

Per Share Data ($)	2008	2007	2006	2005	2004	2003	2002	2001	2000	1999
Tangible Book Value	3.17	2.14	1.68	2.28	1.76	1.62	0.88	1.70	3.96	3.61
Cash Flow	1.94	1.39	1.28	1.98	1.66	1.99	1.43	1.68	2.42	2.39
Earnings	1.59	0.99	0.81	1.52	1.21	1.59	1.05	1.29	2.36	2.06
S&P Core Earnings	1.24	1.02	0.88	1.43	1.24	1.57	1.07	0.67	NA	NA
Dividends	1.24	1.12	1.12	1.12	1.12	1.12	1.12	1.10	0.98	0.86
Payout Ratio	27%	113%	138%	74%	93%	70%	107%	85%	42%	42%
Prices:High	27.37	32.35	26.41	26.60	31.30	29.21	51.95	73.50	74.88	79.25
Prices:Low	16.00	25.73	20.08	20.70	22.22	21.00	19.49	48.50	42.44	57.25
P/E Ratio:High	17	33	33	17	26	18	49	57	32	38
P/E Ratio:Low	10	26	25	14	18	13	19	38	18	28

Income Statement Analysis (Million $)										
Revenue	20,597	19,348	17,914	19,207	19,380	20,894	18,119	19,423	18,216	20,222
Operating Income	5,152	4,309	3,483	4,880	5,373	5,726	4,851	7,034	6,732	6,531
Depreciation	728	776	927	929	909	779	735	781	746	678
Interest Expense	333	457	498	349	310	277	410	182	108	130
Pretax Income	5,471	3,534	2,635	4,516	4,418	4,694	2,647	2,986	5,478	5,767
Effective Tax Rate	24.1%	22.7%	23.1%	20.6%	34.4%	25.9%	16.4%	15.4%	25.2%	27.7%
Net Income	3,155	1,968	1,585	2,992	2,378	3,106	2,034	2,527	4,096	4,167
S&P Core Earnings	2,465	2,024	1,727	2,808	2,448	3,043	2,076	1,321	NA	NA

Balance Sheet & Other Financial Data (Million $)										
Cash	8,265	2,225	4,013	5,799	7,474	5,457	3,989	5,654	3,385	2,957
Current Assets	14,763	10,348	10,302	12,283	14,801	11,918	9,975	12,349	9,824	9,267
Total Assets	29,552	26,172	25,575	28,138	30,435	27,471	24,874	27,057	17,578	17,114
Current Liabilities	6,710	8,644	6,496	6,890	9,843	7,530	8,220	8,826	5,632	5,537
Long Term Debt	6,585	4,381	7,248	8,364	8,463	8,522	6,261	6,237	1,336	1,342
Common Equity	12,241	10,562	9,991	11,208	10,202	19,572	8,967	10,736	9,180	8,645
Total Capital	18,885	14,943	17,307	19,572	18,665	28,094	15,228	16,973	10,516	9,987
Capital Expenditures	941	843	762	738	676	937	997	1,023	589	709
Cash Flow	3,883	2,744	2,512	3,921	3,287	3,885	2,769	3,308	4,842	4,845
Current Ratio	2.2	1.2	1.6	1.8	1.5	1.6	1.2	1.4	1.7	1.7
% Long Term Debt of Capitalization	34.9	29.3	42.0	42.7	45.3	30.3	41.1	36.7	12.7	13.4
% Net Income of Revenue	15.3	10.2	8.8	15.6	12.3	14.9	11.2	13.0	22.5	20.6
% Return on Assets	11.4	7.6	5.9	10.2	8.2	11.8	7.7	11.3	23.6	25.0
% Return on Equity	27.7	19.2	15.0	27.9	23.8	16.8	22.5	25.4	46.0	51.4

Data as orig reptd.; bef. results of disc opers/spec. items. Per share data adj. for stk. divs.; EPS diluted. E-Estimated. NA-Not Available. NM-Not Meaningful. NR-Not Ranked. UR-Under Review.

Office: 345 Park Ave , New York, NY 10154-0037.
Telephone: 212-546-4000.
Website: http://www.bms.com
Chrmn & CEO: J.M. Cornelius

Pres & COO: L. Andreotti
EVP & CFO: J. Huet
EVP & CSO: E. Sigal
SVP, Secy & General Counsel: S. Leung

Investor Contact: J. Elicker (212-546-3775)
Board Members: L. Andreotti, L. B. Campbell, J. M. Cornelius, L. J. Freeh, L. H. Glimcher, M. Grobstein, L. Johansson, A. J. Lacy, V. L. Sato, T. D. West, Jr., R. S. Williams

Founded: 1887
Domicile: Delaware
Employees: 35,000

Broadcom Corp

STANDARD &POOR'S

S&P Recommendation **BUY** ★★★★☆	Price $28.97 (as of Nov 27, 2009)	12-Mo. Target Price $32.00	Investment Style Large-Cap Blend

GICS Sector Information Technology
Sub-Industry Semiconductors

Summary This company provides semiconductors for broadband communications markets, including cable set-top boxes, cable modems, office networks, and home networking.

Key Stock Statistics (Source S&P, Vickers, company reports)

52-Wk Range	$31.20– 13.67	S&P Oper. EPS 2009**E**	0.20	Market Capitalization(B)	$12.645	Beta		1.48
Trailing 12-Month EPS	$-0.31	S&P Oper. EPS 2010**E**	0.87	Yield (%)	Nil	S&P 3-Yr. Proj. EPS CAGR(%)		3
Trailing 12-Month P/E	NM	P/E on S&P Oper. EPS 2009**E**	NM	Dividend Rate/Share	Nil	S&P Credit Rating		NA
$10K Invested 5 Yrs Ago	$13,635	Common Shares Outstg. (M)	495.1	Institutional Ownership (%)	89			

Price Performance

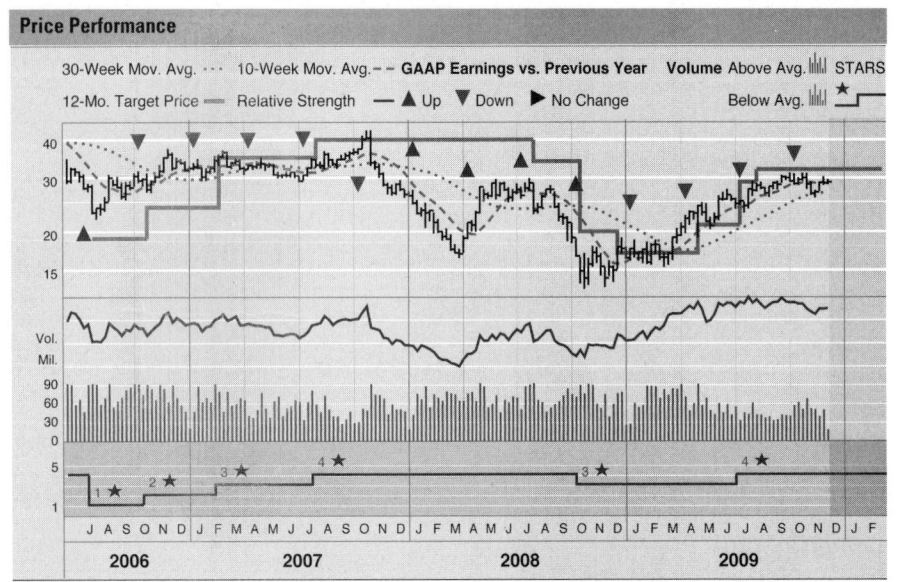

30-Week Mov. Avg. · · · 10-Week Mov. Avg. - - **GAAP Earnings vs. Previous Year** Volume Above Avg. ▌▌▌ STARS

12-Mo. Target Price — Relative Strength — ▲ Up ▼ Down ▶ No Change Below Avg. ▌▌▌ ★

Options: ASE, CBOE, P, Ph

Analysis prepared by **Clyde Montevirgen** on October 26, 2009, when the stock traded at **$ 28.50**.

Highlights

► We anticipate a 21% revenue increase in 2010, following a projected 5% decrease in 2009. Although we see soft orders over the near-term because of the economic environment, we believe BRCM has a well diversified and innovative product portfolio, which should lead to higher market share. We think that recent design wins for various DTV, Bluetooth, Wireless LAN, FM and mobile handset products will help boost sales when consumer demand recovers. Also, licensing revenues from a recent settlement should aid growth over the next few years.

► We see the gross margin widening to around 52% in 2010 from an expected 50% in 2009, as higher margin licensing revenues offset lower product margins from its other businesses. BRCM outsources its manufacturing, which should help to keep gross margins relatively stable. We see the operating margin expanding to 9% in 2010 from around 2% seen in 2009, reflecting benefits from operating leverage as sales increase.

► Our EPS estimates assume a low effective tax rate around 7% and include nearly $1.00 in stock based compensation.

Investment Rationale/Risk

► Our buy recommendation reflects our view of above industry growth, which should garner higher multiples and valuations. We like BRCM's focus on making integrated and multi-functional chips, and we think recent mobile and wireless product orders will contribute to above industry growth in coming quarters and years. Although we believe the company's cost structure has weighed on profitability at current sales levels, we see accelerating top-line growth providing operating leverage, leading to improving margins and earnings power.

► Risks to our recommendation and target price include lower-than-anticipated enterprise spending, slower-than-anticipated orders for handset chips, and rising operating expenses.

► Our 12-month target price of $32 is based on a weighted blend of our DCF and price-to-sales (P/S) analyses. Our DCF model assumes a WACC of around 11% and a terminal growth rate of 4%, implying a value of $31. We apply a P/S multiple of 3.2X, above the peer average to account for our view of BRCM's growth, to our forward 12-month sales per share estimate, suggesting a value of $33.

Qualitative Risk Assessment

LOW	MEDIUM	**HIGH**

Our risk assessment reflects Broadcom's exposure to the sales cycles of the semiconductor industry, dependence on foundry partners for production, and greater reliance than most companies on stock-based compensation. This is partially offset by our view of a lack of debt and a broadening base of end users.

Quantitative Evaluations

S&P Quality Ranking B-

D	C	**B-**	B	B+	A-	A	A+

Relative Strength Rank MODERATE

59

LOWEST = 1 HIGHEST = 99

Revenue/Earnings Data

Revenue (Million $)

	1Q	2Q	3Q	4Q	Year
2009	853.4	1,040	1,254	--	--
2008	1,032	1,201	1,298	1,127	4,658
2007	901.5	897.9	950.0	1,027	3,776
2006	900.7	941.1	902.6	923.5	3,668
2005	550.3	604.9	695.0	820.6	2,671
2004	573.4	641.3	646.5	539.4	2,401

Earnings Per Share ($)

2009	-0.19	0.03	0.16	E0.18	E0.20
2008	0.14	0.25	0.31	-0.32	0.41
2007	0.10	0.06	0.05	0.16	0.37
2006	0.20	0.18	0.19	0.08	0.64
2005	0.13	0.03	0.23	0.33	0.73
2004	0.08	0.12	0.09	0.13	0.42

Fiscal year ended Dec. 31. Next earnings report expected: Late January. EPS Estimates based on S&P Operating Earnings; historical GAAP earnings are as reported.

Dividend Data

No cash dividends have been paid.

Please read the Required Disclosures and Analyst Certification on the last page of this report.

The **McGraw·Hill** Companies

Broadcom Corp

STANDARD
&POOR'S

Business Summary October 26, 2009

CORPORATE OVERVIEW. Founded in 1991, Broadcom is a global provider of semiconductors for wired and wireless communications. The company's products enable the delivery of voice, video, data and multimedia to and throughout the home, the office and the mobile environment. Broadcom's diverse product portfolio includes solutions for digital cable, satellite and Internet Protocol (IP) set-top boxes and media servers; high definition television (HDTV); high definition DVD players and personal video recording (PVR) devices; cable and DSL modems and residential gateways; high-speed transmission and switching for local, metropolitan, wide area and storage networking; System I/O server solutions; broadband network and security processors; wireless and personal area networking; cellular communications; global positioning system (GPS) applications; mobile multimedia and applications processors; mobile power management; and Voice over Internet Protocol (VoIP) gateway and telephony systems.

The company has one reportable segment, but we believe that sales can be separated into three main target markets: Broadband Communications, Enterprise Networking, and Mobile and Wireless Networking. Broadband Commu-

nication products offer manufacturers a range of broadband communications and consumer electronics systems-on-a-chip (SoCs) that enable voice, video and data services over residential wired and wireless networks. Enterprise Networking enable a robust, scalable, secure and easy-to-manage network infrastructure for the carrier/service provider, data center, enterprise and small-to-medium-sized business, or SMB, markets. Its solutions aim to enable these networks to offer higher capacities and faster, more cost-efficient transport and management of voice, data and video traffic across wired and wireless networks. Mobile and Wireless Networking allow manufacturers to develop leading-edge mobile devices, enabling end-to-end wireless opportunities for the home, business and mobile markets. In 2008, net revenue by major target market was 37% broadband communications; 27% enterprise networking; and 36% mobile and wireless.

Company Financials Fiscal Year Ended Dec. 31

Per Share Data ($)	2008	2007	2006	2005	2004	2003	2002	2001	2000	1999
Tangible Book Value	4.63	4.86	5.43	3.79	2.59	1.43	0.94	2.19	3.31	1.59
Cash Flow	0.60	0.48	0.73	0.85	0.59	-1.98	-5.20	-4.87	-1.59	0.28
Earnings	0.41	0.37	0.64	0.73	0.42	-2.19	-5.57	-7.19	-2.09	0.24
S&P Core Earnings	0.62	0.37	0.64	-0.04	-0.70	-2.31	-5.07	-6.87	NA	NA
Dividends	Nil	Nil	Nil	Nil	Nil	Nil	Nil	Nil	Nil	Nil
Payout Ratio	Nil	Nil	Nil	Nil	Nil	Nil	Nil	Nil	Nil	Nil
Prices:High	29.91	43.07	50.00	33.28	31.37	25.10	35.57	93.00	183.17	96.33
Prices:Low	12.98	25.70	21.98	18.25	16.83	7.91	6.35	12.27	49.83	15.42
P/E Ratio:High	73	NM	78	46	75	NM	NM	NM	NM	NM
P/E Ratio:Low	32	NM	34	25	40	NM	NM	NM	NM	NM

Income Statement Analysis (Million $)										
Revenue	4,658	3,776	3,668	2,671	2,401	1,610	1,083	962	1,096	518
Operating Income	490	148	309	557	450	-30.4	-442	-573	-169	157
Depreciation	97.5	62.0	47.6	68.5	91.7	90.9	147	889	165	14.0
Interest Expense	Nil	Nil	Nil	Nil	Nil	Nil	3.60	5.00	0.33	0.55
Pretax Income	222	219	367	392	294	-935	-1,939	-2,799	-692	119
Effective Tax Rate	3.38%	2.70%	NM	NM	25.7%	NM	NM	NM	NM	30.2%
Net Income	215	213	379	412	219	-960	-2,237	-2,742	-688	83.3
S&P Core Earnings	319	215	379	-25.7	-330	-1,011	-2,039	-2,617	NA	NA

Balance Sheet & Other Financial Data (Million $)										
Cash	1,898	2,329	2,680	1,733	1,183	606	503	540	524	174
Current Assets	2,751	3,054	3,352	2,336	1,584	996	722	674	876	391
Total Assets	4,393	4,838	4,877	3,752	2,886	2,018	2,216	3,623	4,678	585
Current Liabilities	717	758	679	595	497	504	534	412	203	86.1
Long Term Debt	Nil	Nil	Nil	Nil	Nil	Nil	1.21	4.01	Nil	0.55
Common Equity	3,607	4,036	4,192	3,145	2,366	1,490	1,645	3,207	4,475	499
Total Capital	3,607	4,036	4,192	3,145	2,366	1,490	1,646	3,211	4,475	499
Capital Expenditures	82.8	160	92.5	41.8	49.9	47.9	75.2	71.4	80.7	29.2
Cash Flow	312	275	427	480	310	-869	-2,090	-1,853	-523	97.3
Current Ratio	3.8	4.0	4.9	3.9	3.2	2.0	1.4	1.6	4.3	4.5
% Long Term Debt of Capitalization	Nil	Nil	Nil	Nil	Nil	Nil	0.1	0.1	Nil	0.1
% Net Income of Revenue	4.6	5.6	10.3	15.4	9.1	NM	NM	NM	NM	16.1
% Return on Assets	4.7	4.3	8.8	12.4	8.9	NM	NM	NM	NM	19.7
% Return on Equity	5.6	5.1	10.3	14.9	11.3	NM	NM	NM	NM	23.3

Data as orig reptd.; bef. results of disc opers/spec. items. Per share data adj. for stk. divs.; EPS diluted. E-Estimated. NA-Not Available. NM-Not Meaningful. NR-Not Ranked. UR-Under Review.

Office: 5300 California Ave, Irvine, CA 92617-3038.
Telephone: 949-926-5000.
Email: investorinfo@broadcom.com
Website: http://www.broadcom.com

Chrmn: J.E. Major
Pres & CEO: S.A. McGregor
SVP & CFO: E.K. Brandt
SVP, Secy & General Counsel: A. Chong

SVP & CIO: K. Venner
Investor Contact: T.P. Andrew (949-926-5663)
Board Members: J. Amble, G. L. Farinsky, N. H. Handel, E. W. Hartenstein, J. E. Major, S. A. McGregor, W. T. Morrow, R. E. Switz

Founded: 1991
Domicile: California
Employees: 7,402

The *McGraw-Hill* Companies

Brown-Forman Corp

STANDARD &POOR'S

S&P Recommendation	HOLD ★★★★★	Price $50.39 (as of Nov 27, 2009)	12-Mo. Target Price $53.00	Investment Style Large-Cap Growth

GICS Sector Consumer Staples
Sub-Industry Distillers & Vintners

Summary This leading distiller and importer of alcoholic beverages, markets Jack Daniel's, Southern Comfort, Finlandia, Korbel and Bolla brands.

Key Stock Statistics (Source S&P, Vickers, company reports)

52-Wk Range	$53.78– 34.97	S&P Oper. EPS 2010**E**	2.96	Market Capitalization(B)	$4.630	Beta	0.72
Trailing 12-Month EPS	$3.10	S&P Oper. EPS 2011**E**	3.20	Yield (%)	2.38	S&P 3-Yr. Proj. EPS CAGR(%)	8
Trailing 12-Month P/E	16.3	P/E on S&P Oper. EPS 2010**E**	17.0	Dividend Rate/Share	$1.20	S&P Credit Rating	A
$10K Invested 5 Yrs Ago	$15,015	Common Shares Outstg. (M)	148.5	Institutional Ownership (%)	61		

Price Performance

30-Week Mov. Avg. · · · · 10-Week Mov. Avg. - - - GAAP Earnings vs. Previous Year Volume Above Avg. STARS
12-Mo. Target Price — Relative Strength — ▲ Up ▼ Down ► No Change Below Avg.

Analysis prepared by **Esther Y. Kwon, CFA** on November 17, 2009, when the stock traded at **$ 51.45**.

Highlights

► We forecast about a 2% wine and spirits sales decline in FY 10 (Apr.) on negative foreign currency and inventory draw down at distributors in the first half, following an approximately 3% sales drop in FY 09. In constant currency, we see Jack Daniel's branded product sales rising, but expect a decline in Southern Comfort while Finlandia should continue to rise despite a negative foreign exchange impact. Long term, with 52% of FY 09 net sales from outside the U.S., we see Finlandia and, secondarily, Jack Daniel's driving more than 50% of net sales growth. In FY 11, we project an approximately 3% increase in revenue.

► We look for gross margins to contract on higher raw material costs in the first half on negative foreign exchange, lower margin product and geographic mix and a continued high level of value added pack promotions. We forecast good operating expense controls as BF benefits from workforce reductions taken in FY 09.

► On a roughly 1% increase in diluted shares outstanding, we estimate FY 10 EPS of $2.96, with about a $0.12 hit from foreign currency based on spot rates at the beginning of June. BF has forecast FY 10 EPS of $2.60 to $3.00.

Investment Rationale/Risk

► Long term, we look for continued strength in the global market, and think that spirits will continue to make successful inroads in the 21 to 27-year old demographic. BF should continue to capitalize on what we see as positive industry trends with its strong portfolio of spirits and international reach, particularly with its Jack Daniel's brand. In the near term, however, we see spirits losing marketshare in the alcoholic beverage category as consumers continue to trade down to wine and beer and consumption shifts more rapidly to off-premise from on-premise on global economic weakness.

► Risks to our recommendation and target price include an unexpected slowdown in the growth of top-performing brands. Also, BF's dual-class structure and the majority representation of insiders on its board of directors pose corporate governance concerns to us.

► Our 12-month target price of $53 is supported by our P/E analysis, which applies a P/E of 16.5X, a discount to the stock's historical average in the low 20s but still a premium to peers, to our FY 11 EPS estimate of $3.20. The shares had a recent dividend yield of about 2.3%.

Qualitative Risk Assessment

LOW	MEDIUM	HIGH

Brown-Forman is a large-cap competitor in an industry that has historically demonstrated relative stability. However, we believe the company's dual-class structure and the majority representation of insiders on its board of directors pose corporate governance concerns.

Quantitative Evaluations

S&P Quality Ranking A

D	C	B-	B	B+	A-	A	A+

Relative Strength Rank MODERATE

70

LOWEST = 1   HIGHEST = 99

Revenue/Earnings Data

Revenue (Million $)

	1Q	2Q	3Q	4Q	Year
2010	570.8	--	--	--	--
2009	790.0	935.0	784.0	683.0	3,192
2008	739.0	893.0	877.0	772.0	3,282
2007	633.0	727.0	754.8	690.8	2,218
2006	547.0	666.0	637.0	594.0	2,444
2005	578.0	780.0	758.0	613.0	2,729

Earnings Per Share ($)

2010	0.81	E0.85	E0.72	E0.58	E2.96
2009	0.58	0.94	0.81	0.53	2.87
2008	0.58	0.83	0.74	0.65	2.85
2007	0.61	0.80	0.72	0.45	2.58
2006	0.57	0.73	0.78	0.49	2.56
2005	0.34	0.66	0.62	0.39	2.02

Fiscal year ended Apr. 30. Next earnings report expected: Early December. EPS Estimates based on S&P Operating Earnings; historical GAAP earnings are as reported.

Dividend Data (Dates: mm/dd Payment Date: mm/dd/yy)

Amount ($)	Date Decl.	Ex-Div. Date	Stk. of Record	Payment Date
0.288	01/22	03/04	03/06	04/01/09
0.288	05/28	06/04	06/08	07/01/09
0.288	07/23	09/03	09/08	10/01/09
0.300	11/16	12/03	12/07	01/04/10

Dividends have been paid since 1960. Source: Company reports.

Brown-Forman Corp

STANDARD
&POOR'S

Business Summary November 17, 2009

CORPORATE OVERVIEW. Brown-Forman Corp.'s origins date back to 1870. It is the world's fourth largest producer of distilled spirits. With a portfolio of well known brands, the company is best known for its popular Jack Daniel's Tennessee Whiskey, which continues to be its largest sales and profit producer.

Although many alcoholic beverage companies have moved in recent years to reduce their dependence on the highly mature brown spirits market, BF has remained whiskey-oriented. Its product line is stocked with well known whiskies, bourbons, vodkas, tequilas, rums, and liqueurs. Brands include Jack Daniel's, Southern Comfort, Tequila Herradura, el Jimador Tequila, and Canadian Mist. Global depletions of Jack Daniel's in FY 09 (Apr.) increased less than 1%, compared to 4% in FY 08. Statistics based on case sales rank Jack Daniel's as the largest selling American whiskey in the world, Canadian Mist as the second largest selling Canadian whiskey in the U.S. and the third largest in the world, and Southern Comfort as the largest selling domestic proprietary liqueur in the U.S. Other major alcoholic beverage lines include Fetzer and Bolla wines, Finlandia vodka, Chambord liqueur, and Korbel Champagnes.

International sales, consisting principally of exports of wines and spirits, in-

creased to over $1.7 billion in FY 09, accounting for 52% of total net revenues. Beverage growth in recent years has come primarily from international markets for the company's spirits brands. The key export markets for brands include the U.K., Australia, Poland, Germany, Mexico, South Africa, Spain, France, Canada and Japan.

Until year-end FY 05, the consumer durables segment consisted of the Lenox Inc. subsidiary, which produced and marketed china, crystal and giftware under the Lenox and Gorham trademarks. The segment also included Dansk, a producer of tableware and giftware, Gorham, Kirk Steiff, and Hartmann Luggage. In July 2005, following a strategic review, the company agreed to sell Lenox. On September 1, 2005, BF consummated the sale of substantially all of Lenox to Department 56 for $196 million. Consumer durables was eliminated as a segment, and in May 2007, the sale of substantially all of the assets of Hartmann to Clarion Capital Partners was completed.

Company Financials Fiscal Year Ended Apr. 30

Per Share Data ($)	2009	2008	2007	2006	2005	2004	2003	2002	2001	2000
Tangible Book Value	3.03	2.24	1.42	6.79	4.55	3.43	1.93	6.17	5.40	4.54
Cash Flow	3.23	3.18	2.89	2.88	2.38	1.83	1.76	1.64	1.72	1.62
Earnings	2.87	2.85	2.58	2.56	2.02	1.69	1.45	1.33	1.36	1.27
S&P Core Earnings	2.62	2.82	2.54	2.52	1.90	1.66	1.24	1.11	1.22	NA
Dividends	0.81	2.25	0.62	0.73	0.64	0.58	0.58	0.54	0.51	0.48
Payout Ratio	28%	79%	24%	29%	32%	34%	40%	41%	38%	38%
Calendar Year	2008	2007	2006	2005	2004	2003	2002	2001	2000	1999
Prices:High	63.02	63.90	66.04	57.92	40.07	38.05	32.22	28.80	27.70	30.90
Prices:Low	40.46	50.54	52.22	37.30	34.24	24.10	23.48	23.06	16.75	21.97
P/E Ratio:High	22	22	26	23	20	23	22	22	20	24
P/E Ratio:Low	14	18	20	15	17	14	16	17	12	17

Income Statement Analysis (Million $)										
Revenue	2,481	3,282	2,806	2,444	2,729	2,577	2,378	1,958	1,924	1,877
Operating Income	730	735	627	560	513	473	429	408	438	410
Depreciation	55.0	52.0	44.0	44.0	58.0	56.0	55.0	55.0	64.0	62.0
Interest Expense	37.0	49.0	34.0	18.0	21.0	21.0	8.00	8.00	16.0	15.0
Pretax Income	630	644	586	559	476	388	373	348	366	343
Effective Tax Rate	31.1%	31.7%	31.7%	29.3%	35.3%	33.5%	34.3%	34.5%	36.3%	36.4%
Net Income	434	440	400	395	308	258	245	228	233	218
S&P Core Earnings	397	438	393	389	289	252	209	190	208	NA

Balance Sheet & Other Financial Data (Million $)										
Cash	340	119	283	475	295	68.0	72.0	116	86.0	180
Current Assets	1,574	1,456	1,635	1,610	1,317	1,083	1,068	1,029	994	1,020
Total Assets	3,475	3,405	3,551	2,728	2,624	2,376	2,264	2,016	1,939	1,802
Current Liabilities	836	984	1,347	569	638	369	548	495	538	522
Long Term Debt	509	417	422	351	352	630	629	40.0	40.0	41.0
Common Equity	1,816	1,725	1,672	1,563	1,310	1,085	840	1,311	1,187	1,048
Total Capital	2,405	2,231	2,150	2,047	1,794	1,837	1,547	1,409	1,289	1,184
Capital Expenditures	49.0	41.0	58.0	52.0	49.0	56.0	119	71.0	96.0	78.0
Cash Flow	490	492	444	439	366	314	300	283	297	280
Current Ratio	1.9	1.5	1.2	2.8	2.1	2.9	1.9	2.1	1.8	2.0
% Long Term Debt of Capitalization	21.2	18.7	19.6	17.1	19.6	34.3	40.7	2.8	3.1	3.5
% Net Income of Revenue	17.5	13.4	14.3	16.2	11.3	10.0	10.3	11.6	12.1	11.6
% Return on Assets	12.6	12.7	12.7	14.7	12.3	11.1	11.4	11.5	12.5	12.3
% Return on Equity	24.5	26.7	24.7	27.5	25.6	26.8	22.8	18.3	20.9	22.2

Data as orig reptd.; bef. results of disc opers/spec. items. Per share data adj. for stk. divs.; EPS diluted. E-Estimated. NA-Not Available. NM-Not Meaningful. NR-Not Ranked. UR-Under Review.

Office: 850 Dixie Highway, Louisville, KY 40210-1038.
Telephone: 502-585-1100.
Website: http://www.brown-forman.com
Co-Chrmn: G.G. Brown, IV

Co-Chrmn & CEO: P.C. Varga
Vice Chrmn: J.S. Welch, Jr.
COO & EVP: M.I. McCallum
EVP & CFO: D.C. Berg

Investor Contact: T. Graven (502-774-7442)
Board Members: P. Bousquet-Chavanne, G. G. Brown, IV, M. S. Brown, Jr., J. D. Cook, S. A. Frazier, R. P. Mayer, W. E. Mitchell, W. M. Street, D. B. Stubbs, P. C. Varga, J. S. Welch, Jr.

Founded: 1870
Domicile: Delaware
Employees: 4,100

Burlington Northern Santa Fe Corp

STANDARD &POOR'S

S&P Recommendation HOLD ★★★☆☆	**Price** $98.26 (as of Nov 27, 2009)	**12-Mo. Target Price** $100.00	**Investment Style** Large-Cap Growth

GICS Sector Industrials
Sub-Industry Railroads

Summary Through BNSF Railway Co., BNI owns one of the largest railroad networks in the U.S., operating over a network spanning approximately 32,000 miles.

Key Stock Statistics (Source S&P, Vickers, company reports)

52-Wk Range	$98.43– 50.86	S&P Oper. EPS 2009**E**	4.74	Market Capitalization(B)	$33.451	Beta	0.99
Trailing 12-Month EPS	$5.26	S&P Oper. EPS 2010**E**	5.48	Yield (%)	1.63	S&P 3-Yr. Proj. EPS CAGR(%)	10
Trailing 12-Month P/E	18.7	P/E on S&P Oper. EPS 2009**E**	20.7	Dividend Rate/Share	$1.60	S&P Credit Rating	BBB
$10K Invested 5 Yrs Ago	$23,578	Common Shares Outstg. (M)	340.4	Institutional Ownership (%)	78		

Price Performance

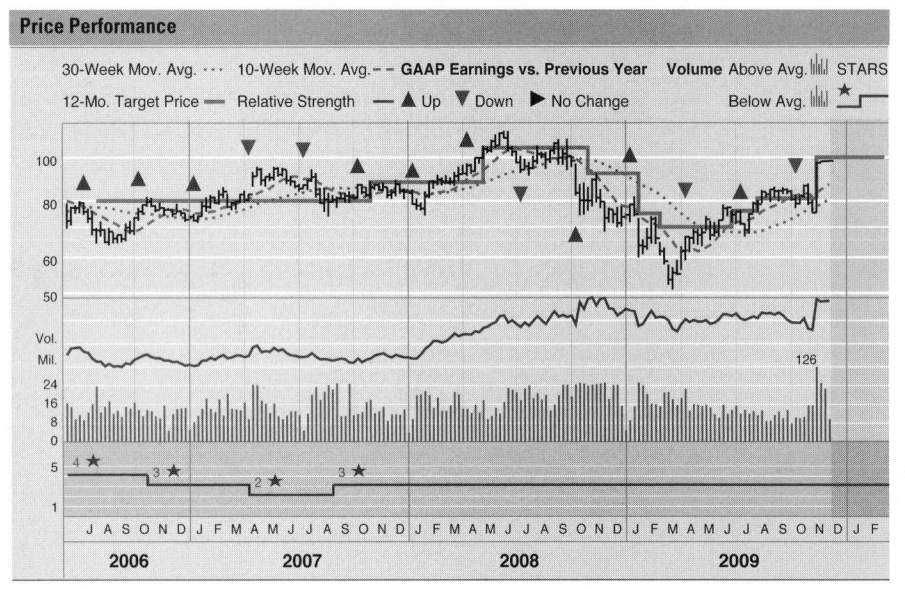

Options: ASE, CBOE, P

Analysis prepared by **Kevin Kirkeby** on November 09, 2009, when the stock traded at **$ 97.35**.

Highlights

▶ On November 3, 2009, Berkshire Hathaway (BRK.A 102,400, Hold) announced an agreement to acquire the remaining 77.4% of BNI that it did not already own. The transaction, using a mix of cash and stock, values BNI at nearly $100 per share. The proposed purchase, which targets a first-quarter 2010 closing, is subject to regulatory and shareholder approval.

▶ Following an expected 22% decline in 2009, we forecast revenues to increase 7% in 2010. Volumes appear to have bottomed in the second quarter of 2009, though BNI's two largest shipment categories, coal and intermodal, remain weak. Based on a general improvement, albeit gradual, in the economy, our revenue forecast for 2010 anticipates a 3.6% rise in carloadings and 2.9% improvement in yield.

▶ Whereas margins are expected to end 2009 relatively unchanged from the prior year, we see them widening in 2010 as volumes come back into the network. Still, we think costs will have an upward bias during the year as a greater proportion of expenses than in the past vary with volumes. Our EPS estimate for 2009 of $4.74 excludes $0.10 in net special charges.

Investment Rationale/Risk

▶ Longer term, we think BNI will generate above-average revenue growth, driven by its exposure to the intermodal transport, long-haul coal and grain markets. For the 2009-2012 period, we see a compound annual growth rate in revenue of 7%, down from 12% over the prior three years. Despite the near-term challenges facing coal volumes, given high customer inventories, we think the share price will gravitate towards the $100 purchase price embedded in the proposed Berkshire Hathaway transaction.

▶ Risks to our recommendation and target price include failure to receive the necessary regulatory or shareholder approvals needed to complete the acquisition, a greater role by regulators in setting rates, and a rerouting of containership cargoes away from West Coast ports due to high fees.

▶ Our target price of $100 approximates the value of the proposed acquisition by Berkshire Hathaway. This price represents a multiple of enterprise value to our four-quarter forward EBITDA estimate of 8.5X, which is near the top of the 10-year range. At a ratio of price-to-invested capital of 1.5X, the price is also in the upper quartile of the historical range.

Qualitative Risk Assessment

LOW	MEDIUM	HIGH

Our risk assessment reflects what we believe is BNI's strong profitability, cash flow generation, and balance sheet, as well as a diverse customer base, offset somewhat by its exposure to economic cycles, freight demand, and regulations.

Quantitative Evaluations

S&P Quality Ranking **A**

D	C	B-	B	B+	A-	A	A+

Relative Strength Rank **STRONG**

90

LOWEST = 1   HIGHEST = 99

Revenue/Earnings Data

Revenue (Million $)

	1Q	2Q	3Q	4Q	Year
2009	3,424	3,316	3,595	--	--
2008	4,261	4,478	4,906	4,373	18,018
2007	3,645	3,843	4,069	4,245	15,802
2006	3,463	3,701	3,939	3,882	14,985
2005	2,982	3,138	3,317	3,550	12,987
2004	2,490	2,685	2,793	2,978	10,946

Earnings Per Share ($)

2009	0.86	1.18	1.42	E1.18	E4.74
2008	1.30	1.00	2.00	1.79	6.08
2007	0.96	1.20	1.48	1.46	5.10
2006	1.09	1.27	1.33	1.42	5.10
2005	0.83	0.96	1.09	1.13	4.01
2004	0.52	0.67	0.01	0.91	2.10

Fiscal year ended Dec. 31. Next earnings report expected: Late January. EPS Estimates based on S&P Operating Earnings; historical GAAP earnings are as reported.

Dividend Data (Dates: mm/dd Payment Date: mm/dd/yy)

Amount ($)	Date Decl.	Ex-Div. Date	Stk. of Record	Payment Date
0.400	02/13	03/09	03/11	04/01/09
0.400	04/23	06/08	06/10	07/01/09
0.400	07/23	09/08	09/10	10/01/09
0.400	10/22	12/10	12/14	01/04/10

Dividends have been paid since 1940. Source: Company reports.

Please read the Required Disclosures and Analyst Certification on the last page of this report.

The McGraw-Hill Companies

Burlington Northern Santa Fe Corp

STANDARD &POOR'S

Business Summary November 09, 2009

CORPORATE OVERVIEW. Burlington Northern Santa Fe Corp., through its BNSF Railway Co. subsidiary, operates the second largest U.S. rail system, delivering about 49% of rail traffic in the West, and about 26% of U.S. rail traffic. BNSF operates a rail system of about 32,000 miles (23,000 owned, 9,000 trackage rights) that spans 28 western and midwestern states and two Canadian provinces.

MARKET PROFILE. We believe BNI's consumer/intermodal business, sensitive to U.S. import and consumption trends, is the industry volume leader, and is at the heart of its competitive strategy. Consumer freight provided 34% of freight revenues in 2008 and consisted primarily of intermodal service: international container traffic, services to United Parcel Service, less-than-truckload and truckload carriers, and automotive traffic. Industrial products, sensitive to U.S. GDP and manufacturing trends, provided 23% of freight revenues in 2008, and was comprised of construction and building products, chemicals, and petroleum. Coal accounted for 23% of 2008 freight revenues. A major transporter of low-sulfur coal, over 90% of BNI's coal traffic originates in the Powder River Basin of Wyoming and Montana, primarily delivered to power utilities. Agri-

cultural products, sensitive to annual crop volumes and global grain trade patterns, accounted for 20% of 2008 freight revenues, including deliveries of grains, ethanol and fertilizer.

COMPETITIVE LANDSCAPE. The U.S. rail industry has an oligopoly-like structure, with over 80% of revenues generated by the four largest railroads: BNI and Union Pacific Corp. operating on the West Coast, and CSX Corp. and Norfolk Southern Corp. operating on the East Coast. Railroads simultaneously compete for customers while cooperating by sharing assets, interfacing systems, and cooperatively fulfilling customer transports. Railroads also compete with other modes of transportation, namely trucking, shipping, and pipelines. Interestingly, BNI has also said that its three largest customers are trucking companies. Railroads transport about 40% of U.S. intercity freight ton-miles, but receive less than 10% of intercity revenue.

Company Financials Fiscal Year Ended Dec. 31

Per Share Data ($)	2008	2007	2006	2005	2004	2003	2002	2001	2000	1999
Tangible Book Value	32.83	70.50	29.04	25.57	24.71	22.84	21.10	20.33	19.08	17.96
Cash Flow	10.10	8.70	8.16	6.83	4.79	4.53	4.44	4.21	4.52	4.36
Earnings	6.08	5.10	5.10	4.01	2.10	2.09	2.00	1.89	2.36	2.45
S&P Core Earnings	6.20	5.15	5.13	4.10	2.03	2.01	1.75	1.73	NA	NA
Dividends	1.44	1.14	0.90	0.74	0.64	0.54	0.48	0.49	0.48	0.48
Payout Ratio	24%	22%	18%	18%	30%	26%	24%	26%	20%	20%
Prices:High	114.58	95.47	87.99	72.00	49.25	32.50	31.75	34.00	29.56	37.94
Prices:Low	68.31	71.51	63.80	44.58	29.52	23.29	23.18	22.40	19.06	22.88
P/E Ratio:High	19	19	17	18	23	16	16	18	13	15
P/E Ratio:Low	11	14	13	11	14	11	12	12	8	9

Income Statement Analysis (Million $)										
Revenue	18,018	15,802	14,985	12,987	10,946	9,413	8,979	9,208	9,205	9,100
Operating Income	5,484	4,860	4,625	3,997	2,698	2,575	2,587	2,664	3,003	3,096
Depreciation	1,397	1,293	1,130	1,075	1,012	910	931	909	895	897
Interest Expense	550	528	485	437	409	420	428	463	453	387
Pretax Income	3,368	2,957	2,992	2,448	1,273	1,231	1,216	1,182	1,585	1,819
Effective Tax Rate	37.2%	38.2%	36.9%	37.5%	37.9%	36.9%	37.5%	37.6%	38.2%	37.5%
Net Income	2,115	1,829	1,887	1,531	791	777	760	737	980	1,137
S&P Core Earnings	2,158	1,845	1,898	1,563	767	743	667	676	NA	NA

Balance Sheet & Other Financial Data (Million $)										
Cash	633	330	375	75.0	322	18.0	28.0	26.0	11.0	22.0
Current Assets	2,665	2,181	2,181	1,880	1,615	862	791	723	976	1,066
Total Assets	36,403	33,583	31,643	30,304	28,925	26,939	25,767	24,721	24,375	23,700
Current Liabilities	3,646	3,235	3,326	3,229	2,716	2,346	2,091	2,161	2,186	2,075
Long Term Debt	9,099	7,735	6,912	6,698	6,051	6,440	6,641	6,363	6,614	5,655
Common Equity	11,131	11,144	10,396	9,925	9,311	8,495	7,932	7,849	7,480	8,172
Total Capital	28,820	27,363	25,524	24,539	23,182	22,416	21,548	20,943	20,516	19,924
Capital Expenditures	2,832	2,248	2,014	1,750	1,527	1,726	1,358	1,459	1,399	1,788
Cash Flow	3,512	3,122	3,017	2,606	1,803	1,687	1,691	1,646	1,875	2,034
Current Ratio	0.7	0.7	0.7	0.6	0.6	0.4	0.4	0.3	0.4	0.5
% Long Term Debt of Capitalization	31.6	28.3	27.1	27.3	26.1	28.7	30.8	30.4	32.2	28.4
% Net Income of Revenue	11.7	11.6	12.6	11.8	7.2	8.3	8.5	8.0	10.6	12.5
% Return on Assets	6.0	5.6	6.1	5.2	2.8	2.9	3.0	3.0	4.1	4.9
% Return on Equity	19.0	17.0	18.9	15.6	8.9	9.5	9.6	9.6	12.5	14.3

Data as orig reptd.; bef. results of disc opers/spec. items. Per share data adj. for stk. divs.; EPS diluted. E-Estimated. NA-Not Available. NM-Not Meaningful. NR-Not Ranked. UR-Under Review.

Office: 2650 Lou Menk Dr, Fort Worth, TX 76131-2830.
Telephone: 800-795-2673.
Email: investor.relations@bnsf.com
Website: http://www.bnsf.com

Chrmn, Pres & CEO: M.K. Rose
COO & EVP: C.R. Ice
EVP & CFO: T.N. Hund
EVP & Secy: R. Nober

CTO & CIO: J. Olsovsky
Investor Contact: M. Bracker (817-352-4813)
Board Members: A. L. Boeckmann, D. G. Cook, M. Racicot, R. S. Roberts, M. K. Rose, M. J. Shapiro, C. A. Telles, J. C. Watts, Jr., R. H. West, J. S. Whisler, E. E. Whitacre, Jr.

Founded: 1994
Domicile: Delaware
Employees: 40,000

The McGraw-Hill Companies

Cabot Oil & Gas Corp

STANDARD &POOR'S

S&P Recommendation **BUY** ★★★★☆	Price $38.18 (as of Nov 27, 2009)	12-Mo. Target Price $49.00	Investment Style Large-Cap Growth

GICS Sector Energy
Sub-Industry Oil & Gas Exploration & Production

Summary This company explores for, produces, purchases and markets natural gas, and, to a lesser extent, produces and sells crude oil.

Key Stock Statistics (Source S&P, Vickers, company reports)

52-Wk Range	$42.80–17.84	S&P Oper. EPS 2009**E**	1.62	Market Capitalization(B)	$3.958	Beta	1.34
Trailing 12-Month EPS	$1.49	S&P Oper. EPS 2010**E**	1.55	Yield (%)	0.31	S&P 3-Yr. Proj. EPS CAGR(%)	-4
Trailing 12-Month P/E	25.6	P/E on S&P Oper. EPS 2009**E**	23.6	Dividend Rate/Share	$0.12	S&P Credit Rating	NA
$10K Invested 5 Yrs Ago	$24,364	Common Shares Outstg. (M)	103.7	Institutional Ownership (%)	92		

Price Performance

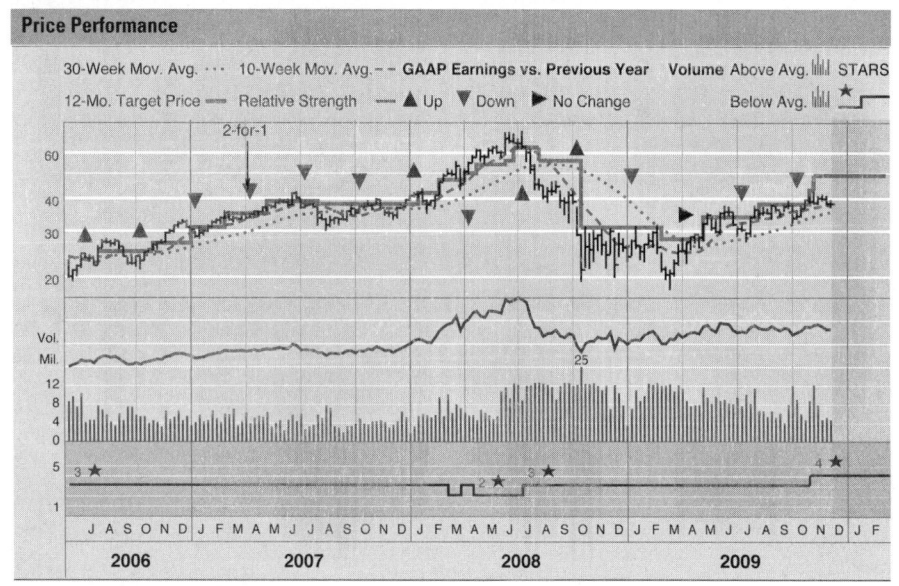

- 30-Week Mov. Avg. ···· 10-Week Mov. Avg. - - GAAP Earnings vs. Previous Year   Volume Above Avg. STARS
- 12-Mo. Target Price — Relative Strength — ▲ Up ▼ Down ▶ No Change   Below Avg.

Options: ASE, CBOE, P, Ph

Analysis prepared by **Michael Kay** on October 27, 2009, when the stock traded at **$ 42.39**.

Highlights

► Production increased 11%, to 95 Bcfe, in 2008, on success at the Marcellus Shale, where production is over 50 Mmcf/d. Furthermore, continued drilling success, especially in the Gulf Coast at the County Line and Minden fields, as well as increases in Appalachia, has led to growth. COG plans to complete one well per week at Marcellus for the remainder of 2009, and we forecast 17% production growth, above previous estimates. COG expects Marcellus production to reach 140-150 Mmcf/d by year-end 2010 and plans to drill 80 wells for the year.

► In our view, asset sales have lowered the risk on COG's portfolio and improved drilling success. COG maintains a below-average cost profile, and we see a 4% decline in lease operating expense per unit in 2009.

► EBITDA rose 36% and EPS 39% in 2008, on higher production and natural gas prices. On lower prices and 17% production growth, we see 2009 EBITDA up 4%. After higher exploration and DD&A charges, we think EPS will be down 30%. COG's exploration and development spending is expected to be $500 million in 2009 and $585 million in 2010, with most allocated to the Marcellus Shale and East Texas.

Investment Rationale/Risk

► We believe COG's core operating areas are performing well, with horizontal drilling programs in the Marcellus Shale and the County Line project in East Texas moving ahead nicely. We see strong potential for its large undeveloped acreage, especially at Marcellus and Haynesville. COG plans five rigs to be redirected to the Marcellus Shale in 2009. It recently provided what we view as promising data on Marcellus Shale wells. An order from the Pennsylvania Department of Environmental Protection (DEP) to halt fracturing at the Marcellus Shale was recently lifted, and we see only a minimal impact in well completion delays, with COG working with the DEP going forward.

► Risks to our recommendation and target price include declining oil and gas prices, difficulty replacing reserves, and production declines.

► We discount probable reserves and value companies on proven reserve NAV estimates, which discount significant potential from Haynesville and Marcellus Shales. We blend our proven reserve NAV estimate of $49 with a target enterprise value to 2010 EBITDA of 7.5X and our DCF analysis ($49; WACC 9%; terminal growth 3%), for a 12-month target price of $49.

Qualitative Risk Assessment

LOW	MEDIUM	**HIGH**

Our risk assessment reflects that COG operates in a very capital-intensive industry that is cyclical and derives value from producing a commodity whose price is extremely volatile. In addition, we think the company struggles under a relatively uncompetitive cost structure. Partially offsetting this is its moderate use of debt and the primarily internal funding of its capital expenditures.

Quantitative Evaluations

S&P Quality Ranking   **B+**

D	C	B-	B	**B+**	A-	A	A+

Relative Strength Rank   **MODERATE**

50

LOWEST = 1   HIGHEST = 99

Revenue/Earnings Data

Revenue (Million $)

	1Q	2Q	3Q	4Q	Year
2009	233.9	204.8	207.0	--	--
2008	219.7	248.9	244.8	232.5	945.8
2007	191.6	175.8	170.9	193.9	732.2
2006	214.8	190.8	184.7	171.7	762.0
2005	144.1	151.9	161.8	225.1	682.8
2004	136.6	119.7	119.4	154.6	530.4

Earnings Per Share ($)

2009	0.46	0.24	0.37	E0.47	E1.62
2008	0.46	0.55	0.64	0.42	2.10
2007	0.50	0.42	0.36	0.43	1.71
2006	0.55	0.47	1.92	0.33	3.32
2005	0.21	0.36	0.34	0.59	1.50
2004	0.19	0.20	0.18	0.33	0.90

Fiscal year ended Dec. 31. Next earnings report expected: Mid February. EPS Estimates based on S&P Operating Earnings; historical GAAP earnings are as reported.

Dividend Data (Dates: mm/dd Payment Date: mm/dd/yy)

Amount ($)	Date Decl.	Ex-Div. Date	Stk. of Record	Payment Date
0.030	01/26	02/03	02/05	02/19/09
0.030	04/28	05/08	05/12	05/26/09
0.030	07/23	08/04	08/06	08/20/09
0.030	10/26	11/06	11/11	11/25/09

Dividends have been paid since 1990. Source: Company reports.

Please read the Required Disclosures and Analyst Certification on the last page of this report.

The McGraw-Hill Companies

Cabot Oil & Gas Corp

STANDARD &POOR'S

Business Summary October 27, 2009

CORPORATE OVERVIEW. Cabot Oil & Gas Corp. is an independent oil and gas company engaged in exploration, development, acquisition and exploitation of oil and gas properties located in five principal areas, including the Appalachian Basin, the Rocky Mountains, the Anadarko Basin, onshore and offshore the Texas and Louisiana Gulf Coast, and the gas basin of western Canada.

Preliminary year-end 2008 reserve data indicates a 20% rise in proved reserves. COG drilled about 432 gross wells in 2008 with a 97% success rate. Year-end 2008 proved reserves increased to 1,942 Bcfe as a result of a 443% reserve replacement ratio, which compares to a 3-year average of about 300%. We estimate 2008 capital spending at $750 million, up from $564 million in 2007.

In 2007, COG drilled 461 gross wells, with a success rate of 96%, compared to 387 gross wells, with a success rate of 96% in 2006. COG's proved reserves totaled 1,616 Bcfe at December 31, 2007, of which 97% was natural gas. In 2007, capital and exploration spending was $564.4 million, compared to $456.3 million of total capital and exploration spending in 2006. At the end of 2007, 73% of total proved reserves were developed and we estimate COG's reserve life to be 18.9 years, compared to 16.1 years at the end of 2006.

COG remains focused on its strategies of balancing its capital investments between acceptable risk and the strongest economics, along with balancing longer life investments that affect exploration opportunities. COG continues to use a portion of the cash flow from its long-lived natural gas reserves in the East and the Mid-Continent to fund exploration and development efforts in the Gulf Coast and Rocky Mountains areas.

MARKET PROFILE. COG's addressable market is the North American continent. As a relatively small onshore natural gas producer, COG competes in a fragmented market that is beginning to rationalize, in our view, with several large onshore players such as Devon Energy (DVN) and Chesapeake Energy (CHK) being the major agents of consolidation. We believe North America is a relatively mature supply source for hydrocarbons, and natural gas production has been relatively flat over the past seven years. We think that COG is beginning to create value in both the East and West regions employing so-called unconventional resource recovery techniques.

Company Financials Fiscal Year Ended Dec. 31

Per Share Data ($)	2008	2007	2006	2005	2004	2003	2002	2001	2000	1999
Tangible Book Value	NA	11.60	9.83	6.18	4.69	3.78	3.67	3.66	2.77	2.51
Cash Flow	4.31	3.36	4.57	2.58	1.94	1.27	1.18	1.41	0.93	0.79
Earnings	2.10	1.71	3.32	1.50	0.90	0.29	0.17	0.51	0.36	0.07
S&P Core Earnings	1.76	1.63	1.74	1.49	0.88	0.20	0.15	0.49	NA	NA
Dividends	0.12	0.11	0.08	0.07	0.05	0.05	0.05	0.05	0.05	0.05
Payout Ratio	6%	6%	2%	5%	6%	18%	32%	10%	15%	76%
Prices:High	72.92	42.50	33.26	26.75	16.30	10.17	8.85	11.45	10.67	6.67
Prices:Low	19.18	27.87	19.13	13.72	9.57	7.50	5.92	5.42	4.69	3.58
P/E Ratio:High	35	25	10	18	18	35	53	22	30	95
P/E Ratio:Low	9	16	6	9	11	26	36	11	13	51

Income Statement Analysis (Million $)										
Revenue	946	732	762	683	530	509	354	447	369	182
Operating Income	550	423	436	380	278	252	182	191	132	35.5
Depreciation, Depletion and Amortization	227	162	129	108	103	94.9	96.5	80.6	53.4	53.4
Interest Expense	36.4	17.2	18.4	22.5	22.0	23.5	25.3	20.8	22.9	25.8
Pretax Income	336	258	511	236	139	43.0	23.8	74.5	41.9	13.7
Effective Tax Rate	37.1%	35.0%	37.1%	37.2%	36.2%	35.0%	32.3%	36.8%	39.3%	37.7%
Net Income	211	167	321	148	88.4	28.0	16.1	47.1	25.5	8.52
S&P Core Earnings	178	159	172	148	87.2	19.1	14.4	45.1	NA	NA

Balance Sheet & Other Financial Data (Million $)										
Cash	28.1	30.1	41.9	10.6	10.0	0.72	2.56	5.71	7.57	1.68
Current Assets	461	221	316	230	195	121	93.1	85.0	110	66.6
Total Assets	3,702	2,209	1,834	1,495	1,211	1,024	1,055	1,069	736	659
Current Liabilities	379	252	251	219	197	155	123	110	118	89.9
Long Term Debt	831	350	220	320	250	270	365	393	253	277
Common Equity	1,791	1,070	945	600	456	365	351	347	243	186
Total Capital	3,221	1,882	1,513	1,210	953	815	916	940	604	559
Capital Expenditures	1,454	557	467	351	207	122	103	127	99.4	82.2
Cash Flow	438	329	450	257	192	123	113	128	76.7	58.5
Current Ratio	1.2	0.9	1.3	1.1	1.0	0.8	0.8	0.8	0.9	0.7
% Long Term Debt of Capitalization	25.8	23.6	14.5	26.5	26.2	33.1	39.9	41.8	41.9	49.6
% Return on Assets	NA	8.3	19.3	11.0	7.8	2.7	1.5	5.2	3.7	1.2
% Return on Equity	14.8	16.6	41.6	28.1	21.5	7.8	4.6	16.0	10.9	2.8

Data as orig reptd.; bef. results of disc opers/spec. items. Per share data adj. for stk. divs.; EPS diluted. E-Estimated. NA-Not Available. NM-Not Meaningful. NR-Not Ranked. UR-Under Review.

Office: 1200 Enclave Parkway, Houston, TX 77077-1607.
Telephone: 281-589-4600.
Website: http://www.cabotog.com
Chrmn, Pres & CEO: D.O. Dinges

COO & SVP: M.B. Walen
Investor Contact: S.C. Schroeder (281-589-4993)
Chief Acctg Officer, Treas & Cntlr: H.C. Smyth
Secy: L.A. Machesney

Board Members: R. J. Best, D. M. Carmichael, D. O. Dinges, R. L. Keiser, R. Kelley, P. D. Peacock, W. P. Vititoe

Founded: 1989
Domicile: Delaware
Employees: 560

The McGraw-Hill Companies

Cameron International Corp

STANDARD &POOR'S

S&P Recommendation **BUY** ★★★★☆	Price $37.24 (as of Nov 27, 2009)	12-Mo. Target Price $49.00	Investment Style Large-Cap Growth

GICS Sector Energy
Sub-Industry Oil & Gas Equipment & Services

Summary This company is a leading international manufacturer of oil and gas blowout preventers, flow control valves, surface and subsea production systems, and related oilfield services products.

Key Stock Statistics (Source S&P, Vickers, company reports)

52-Wk Range	$42.39– 16.15	S&P Oper. EPS 2009**E**	2.21	Market Capitalization(B)	$9.102	Beta		1.56
Trailing 12-Month EPS	$2.43	S&P Oper. EPS 2010**E**	2.41	Yield (%)	Nil	S&P 3-Yr. Proj. EPS CAGR(%)		11
Trailing 12-Month P/E	15.3	P/E on S&P Oper. EPS 2009**E**	16.9	Dividend Rate/Share	Nil	S&P Credit Rating		BBB+
$10K Invested 5 Yrs Ago	$28,260	Common Shares Outstg. (M)	244.4	Institutional Ownership (%)	94			

Price Performance

30-Week Mov. Avg. · · · 10-Week Mov. Avg. - - GAAP Earnings vs. Previous Year   Volume Above Avg. STARS
12-Mo. Target Price — Relative Strength   ▲ Up ▼ Down ► No Change   Below Avg. ★

Options: ASE, CBOE, P, Ph

Analysis prepared by **Stewart Glickman, CFA** on November 19, 2009, when the stock traded at **$ 38.90**.

Highlights

► In November, CAM completed its previously announced acquisition of Natco Group (NTG), a manufacturer of energy capital equipment and separation systems. Strategically, we like the deal and expect CAM to leverage this technology across its broader international footprint. We expect CAM to improve its international positioning over time, dovetailing with recent efforts to expand manufacturing capabilities in Asia and in Eastern Europe.

► Based on the agreed-upon exchange ratio of 1.185 CAM shares per NTG share, we expect CAM's diluted share count to rise approximately 11%. Nonetheless, from a financial perspective, we see a modest accretive impact from the deal on 2010 earnings. We see 2010 revenue growth of about 20% (pre-NTG, we project a 6.5% gain), albeit with narrower operating margins, owing to slightly weaker margins on the NTG side. NTG has backlog of about $314 million, or 6% of CAM's backlog of $5.0 billion at the end of the third quarter.

► Overall, we see EPS of $2.21 in 2009 (a drop of 15% from 2008), rising to $2.41 in 2010.

Investment Rationale/Risk

► Fundamentally, we view CAM as a play on expected growth in demand for oilfield capital equipment, where we see robust prospects in the long term, albeit with some short-term concern over North American natural gas capital equipment demand. As a major provider in the subsea completion market, CAM should benefit from expected gains in deepwater drilling. Longer term, we think that North American demand for surface equipment, distributed valves and engineered valves will improve as a result of growing interest in unconventional natural gas plays.

► Risks to our recommendation and target price include lower than expected oil and natural gas prices; delays in manufacturing facility expansions; and unexpected contract cancellations.

► Our DCF model, assuming terminal growth of 3% and a weighted average cost of capital of 12.9%, indicates intrinsic value of about $53. Using a 12X multiple of projected 2010 EBITDA and a 14X multiple of estimated 2010 operating cash flow (slightly above peers, merited by above-average ROIC), and blending with our DCF model, our 12-month target price is $49.

Qualitative Risk Assessment

LOW	MEDIUM	HIGH

Our risk assessment reflects CAM's exposure to volatile crude oil and natural gas prices, capital spending decisions made by its oil and gas producing customers, and political risk associated with operating in frontier regions. Offsetting these risks is CAM's strength in deepwater-related applications.

Quantitative Evaluations

S&P Quality Ranking   B+

D	C	B-	B	B+	A-	A	A+

Relative Strength Rank   MODERATE

38

LOWEST = 1   HIGHEST = 99

Revenue/Earnings Data

Revenue (Million $)

	1Q	2Q	3Q	4Q	Year
2009	1,257	1,270	1,232	--	--
2008	1,339	1,481	1,505	1,524	5,849
2007	997.0	1,139	1,186	1,344	4,666
2006	829.7	857.8	978.8	1,077	3,743
2005	547.9	594.8	636.6	738.6	2,518
2004	462.5	544.6	538.5	547.3	2,093

Earnings Per Share ($)

	1Q	2Q	3Q	4Q	Year
2009	0.52	0.63	0.56	E0.50	E2.21
2008	0.55	0.65	0.73	0.67	2.60
2007	0.44	0.54	0.66	0.54	2.17
2006	0.24	0.32	0.39	0.42	1.36
2005	0.13	0.18	0.22	0.24	0.76
2004	0.08	0.09	0.14	0.14	0.44

Fiscal year ended Dec. 31. Next earnings report expected: Early February. EPS Estimates based on S&P Operating Earnings; historical GAAP earnings are as reported.

Dividend Data

No cash dividends have been paid.

Please read the Required Disclosures and Analyst Certification on the last page of this report.

The McGraw·Hill Companies

Cameron International Corp

STANDARD
&POOR'S

Business Summary November 19, 2009

CORPORATE OVERVIEW. Cameron International, an international provider of oil and gas pressure control equipment, is organized into three business segments: Drilling & Production Systems (DPS), Valves & Measurement (V&M), and Compression. Primary customers of DPS, V&M and Compression are major and independent oil and gas exploration companies, foreign national oil and gas companies, drilling contractors, pipeline companies, refiners, and other industrial and petrochemical processing companies. The company serves customers in North America (35% of 2008 revenues), Europe (22%), Asia/Middle East (19%), Africa (12%), South America (7%) and Other (5%).

Drilling & Production Systems (DPS; 64% of 2008 revenues and 61% of 2008 segment pretax income) manufactures pressure control equipment used at the wellhead in drilling, production and transmission of oil and gas, both onshore and offshore. Primary products include wellheads, drilling valves, blowout preventers, and control systems, marketed under the brand names Cameron, W-K-M, McEvoy, Willis, and Ingram Cactus. The segment also makes subsea production systems, which tend to be highly sophisticated technically. The company believes subsea capacity additions at manufactur-

ing plants in England, Brazil and Germany provide support for increased completions of subsea trees and associated manifolds, production controls and other equipment in the future.

Valves & Measurement (VMS; 25%, 29%), split out from the DPS division as a separately managed business in 1995, provides a full range of ball valves, gate valves, butterfly valves, and accessories used primarily to control pressures and direct oil and gas as they are moved from individual wellheads through transmission systems to refineries, petrochemical plants, and other processing centers. In September 2005, CAM announced an agreement to acquire substantially all of the flow control businesses of Dresser Inc.; the acquisition was completed in January 2006. The acquisition, which expanded the company's valve product line, totaled $217.5 million in cash and assumed debt. The acquired businesses were added to the company's V&M segment.

Company Financials Fiscal Year Ended Dec. 31

Per Share Data ($)	2008	2007	2006	2005	2004	2003	2002	2001	2000	1999
Tangible Book Value	6.88	6.67	5.11	4.40	3.83	3.81	3.39	2.92	2.69	2.14
Cash Flow	3.03	2.52	1.79	1.11	0.83	0.59	0.58	0.78	0.47	0.58
Earnings	2.60	2.17	1.36	0.76	0.44	0.26	0.28	0.44	0.13	0.20
S&P Core Earnings	2.63	2.27	1.43	0.73	0.34	0.17	0.12	0.21	NA	NA
Dividends	Nil	Nil	Nil	Nil	Nil	Nil	Nil	Nil	Nil	Nil
Payout Ratio	Nil	Nil	Nil	Nil	Nil	Nil	Nil	Nil	Nil	Nil
Prices:High	58.53	53.83	28.91	21.55	14.19	13.90	14.90	18.25	20.97	12.50
Prices:Low	16.15	24.30	19.04	12.76	10.01	10.25	8.98	7.21	10.59	5.56
P/E Ratio:High	23	25	21	28	32	53	54	42	NM	64
P/E Ratio:Low	6	11	14	17	23	39	33	16	NM	29

Income Statement Analysis (Million $)										
Revenue	5,849	4,666	3,743	2,518	2,093	1,634	1,538	1,564	1,387	1,465
Operating Income	1,023	814	605	340	232	164	196	251	215	193
Depreciation, Depletion and Amortization	98.7	81.5	101	78.4	82.8	83.6	77.9	83.1	75.3	83.7
Interest Expense	49.7	23.3	20.7	12.0	17.8	8.16	7.98	5.62	18.0	27.8
Pretax Income	872	708	489	263	133	77.6	85.1	143	43.8	70.9
Effective Tax Rate	31.9%	29.3%	35.0%	34.9%	29.0%	26.2%	29.0%	31.0%	36.8%	39.4%
Net Income	594	501	318	171	94.4	57.2	60.5	98.3	27.7	43.0
S&P Core Earnings	601	527	333	167	73.1	37.5	23.3	44.0	NA	NA

Balance Sheet & Other Financial Data (Million $)										
Cash	1,621	740	1,034	362	227	292	274	112	16.6	8.22
Current Assets	4,056	3,072	2,908	1,728	1,205	1,148	1,018	965	688	705
Total Assets	5,902	4,731	4,351	3,099	2,356	2,141	1,998	1,875	1,494	1,471
Current Liabilities	2,112	1,693	1,628	922	528	680	375	378	346	422
Long Term Debt	1,256	742	745	444	458	204	463	459	188	196
Common Equity	2,320	2,095	1,741	1,595	1,228	1,137	1,041	976	842	714
Total Capital	3,662	2,909	2,577	2,078	1,727	1,387	1,550	1,477	1,069	949
Capital Expenditures	272	246	185	77.5	53.5	64.7	82.1	125	66.6	55.7
Cash Flow	692	582	419	250	177	141	138	181	103	127
Current Ratio	1.9	1.8	1.8	1.9	2.3	1.7	2.7	2.6	2.0	1.7
% Long Term Debt of Capitalization	34.3	26.2	28.9	21.4	26.5	14.7	29.9	31.1	17.6	20.6
% Return on Assets	11.2	11.0	8.5	6.3	4.2	2.8	3.1	5.8	1.9	2.6
% Return on Equity	26.9	26.1	19.1	12.1	8.0	5.3	6.2	10.6	3.6	5.8

Data as orig reptd.; bef. results of disc opers/spec. items. Per share data adj. for stk. divs.; EPS diluted. E-Estimated. NA-Not Available. NM-Not Meaningful. NR-Not Ranked. UR-Under Review.

Office: 1333 W Loop S Ste 1700, Houston, TX 77027-9118.
Telephone: 713-513-3300.
Website: http://www.c-a-m.com
Chrmn: S.R. Erikson

Pres & CEO: J.B. Moore
SVP & CFO: C.M. Sledge
SVP & General Counsel: W.C. Lemmer
CTO: J.C. Bartos

Investor Contact: R.S. Amann (713-513-3344)
Board Members: C. B. Cunningham, S. R. Erikson, P. J. Fluor, D. L. Foshee, J. B. Moore, M. E. Patrick, J. E. Reinhardsen, D. W. Ross, III, B. W. Wilkinson

Founded: 1994
Domicile: Delaware
Employees: 17,100

Campbell Soup Co

STANDARD &POOR'S

S&P Recommendation HOLD ★★★☆☆	**Price** $35.16 (as of Nov 27, 2009)	**12-Mo. Target Price** $36.00	**Investment Style** Large-Cap Growth

GICS Sector Consumer Staples
Sub-Industry Packaged Foods & Meats

Summary This company is a major producer of branded soups and other grocery food products.

Key Stock Statistics (Source S&P, Vickers, company reports)

52-Wk Range	$35.61–24.63	S&P Oper. EPS 2010E	2.45	Market Capitalization(B)	$12.141	Beta	0.32
Trailing 12-Month EPS	$2.20	S&P Oper. EPS 2011E	2.62	Yield (%)	3.13	S&P 3-Yr. Proj. EPS CAGR(%)	8
Trailing 12-Month P/E	16.0	P/E on S&P Oper. EPS 2010E	14.4	Dividend Rate/Share	$1.10	S&P Credit Rating	A
$10K Invested 5 Yrs Ago	$13,987	Common Shares Outstg. (M)	345.3	Institutional Ownership (%)	49		

Price Performance

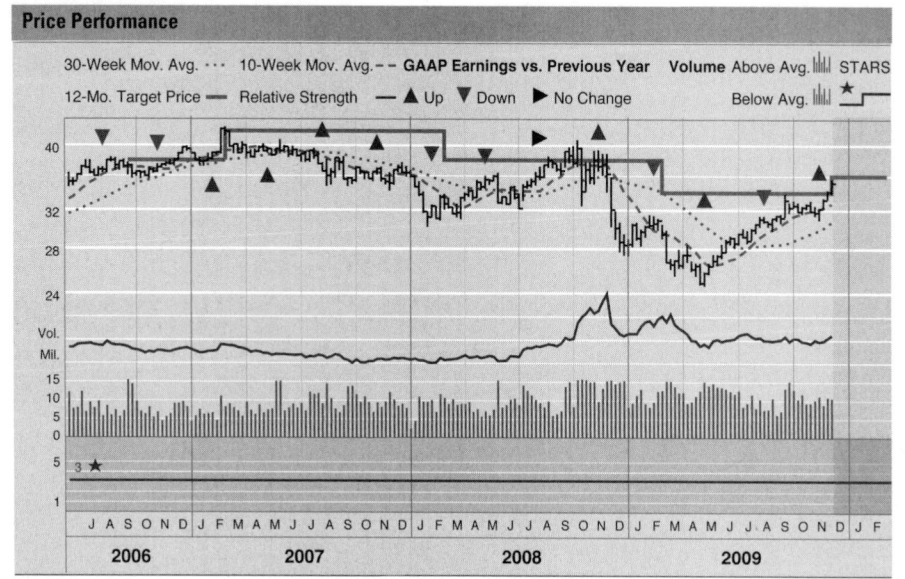

30-Week Mov. Avg. · · · · 10-Week Mov. Avg. – – **GAAP Earnings vs. Previous Year** Volume Above Avg. STARS
12-Mo. Target Price — Relative Strength — ▲ Up ▼ Down ▶ No Change Below Avg. ★

Options: ASE, CBOE, P, Ph

Qualitative Risk Assessment

LOW	MEDIUM	HIGH

Our risk assessment for Campbell Soup reflects the relatively stable nature of the company's end markets, our view that the company has strong cash flow, and corporate governance practices that we see as favorable relative to peers.

Quantitative Evaluations

S&P Quality Ranking B+

D	C	B-	B	B+	A-	A	A+

Relative Strength Rank STRONG

85

LOWEST = 1   HIGHEST = 99

Highlights

► The 12-month target price for CPB has recently been changed to $36.00 from $34.00. The Highlights section of this Stock Report will be updated accordingly.

Investment Rationale/Risk

► The Investment Rationale/Risk section of this Stock Report will be updated shortly. For the latest News story on CPB from MarketScope, see below.

► 11/23/09 01:40 pm ET ... S&P REITERATES HOLD OPINION ON SHARES OF CAMPBELL SOUP (CPB 34.35***): Before year-ago special items, Oct-Q EPS of $0.87 vs. $0.76 exceeds our view by $0.06. Sales were weaker than we expected, but included tough comparison in U.S. soup business, where year-ago sales rose 12%, with contributions from product launches and increased marketing support. We are pleased by CPB profit margin expansion in Oct-Q. We are raising our FY 10 (Jul) EPS estimate to $2.45 from $2.37, and initiate FY 11's estimate of $2.62. On an improved EPS outlook, we raise our 12-month target price to $36 from $34. Indicated dividend yield is 3.2%. /TGraves-CFA

Revenue/Earnings Data

Revenue (Million $)

	1Q	2Q	3Q	4Q	Year
2010	2,203	--	--	--	--
2009	2,250	2,122	1,686	1,528	7,586
2008	2,185	2,218	1,880	1,715	7,998
2007	2,153	2,252	1,868	1,594	7,867
2006	2,002	2,159	1,728	1,454	7,343
2005	2,091	2,223	1,736	1,498	7,548

Earnings Per Share ($)

2010	0.88	E0.72	E0.53	E0.33	E2.45
2009	0.71	0.63	0.49	0.20	2.04
2008	0.69	0.67	0.14	0.24	1.76
2007	0.66	0.72	0.55	0.24	2.08
2006	0.69	0.58	0.35	0.20	1.82
2005	0.56	0.57	0.35	0.23	1.71

Fiscal year ended Jul. 31. Next earnings report expected: Late February. EPS Estimates based on S&P Operating Earnings; historical GAAP earnings are as reported.

Dividend Data (Dates: mm/dd Payment Date: mm/dd/yy)

Amount ($)	Date Decl.	Ex-Div. Date	Stk. of Record	Payment Date
0.250	03/26	04/02	04/06	05/04/09
0.250	06/25	07/01	07/06	08/03/09
0.250	09/24	10/01	10/05	11/02/09
0.275	11/18	12/28	12/30	02/01/10

Dividends have been paid since 1902. Source: Company reports.

Campbell Soup Co

STANDARD &POOR'S

Business Summary November 19, 2009

CORPORATE OVERVIEW. Probably known best for its ubiquitous red and white soup cans (elevated to icon status by Andy Warhol), Campbell Soup Co. is a major force in the U.S. packaged foods industry. The company, which traces its origins in the food business back to 1869, manufactures and markets a wide array of branded, prepared convenience food products worldwide.

In FY 09 (Jul.), operations outside the U.S. accounted for 27% of net sales and 13% of segment operating profits (before corporate expense). However, if $89 million of costs related to restructuring and an impairment charge are excluded, international profit would represent 18% of the total. CPB's largest customer, Wal-Mart Stores, Inc., and its affiliates accounted for about 18% of CPB's net sales in FY 09, up from 16% in FY 08.

The company reports results based on the following segments: U.S. Soup, Sauces and Beverages (50% of FY 09 sales, 72% of segment profits); Baking and Snacking (24%, 20%), International Soup, Sauces and Beverages (18%, 5%); and North America Foodservice (8%, 3%). Excluding costs related to restructuring and an impairment charge, the segment profit contributions would have been 67%, 19%, 10% and 4%, respectively.

Campbell's U.S. Soup, Sauces and Beverages segment includes Campbell's

condensed and ready-to-serve soups; Swanson broth, stocks and canned poultry; Prego pasta sauce; Pace Mexican sauce; Campbell's Chunky chili; Campbell's canned pasta, gravies and beans; V8 juice and juice drinks; Campbell's tomato juice; and Wolfgang Puck soups, stocks and broth.

The company's Baking and Snacking division includes Pepperidge Farm cookies, crackers, bakery and frozen products in the U.S.; Arnotts biscuits in Australia and Asia Pacific; and Arnotts salty snacks in Australia. The International Soup, Sauces and Beverages segment includes soup, sauce and beverage businesses outside of the United States, including Europe, Latin America, the Asia Pacific region, the emerging markets of Russia and China, and the retail business in Canada.

The North America Food Service segment includes CPB's Away From Home operations, which represent the distribution of products such as soup, specialty entrees, beverage products, other prepared foods and Pepperidge Farm products through various foodservice channels in the U.S. and Canada.

Company Financials Fiscal Year Ended Jul. 31

Per Share Data ($)	2009	2008	2007	2006	2005	2004	2003	2002	2001	2000
Tangible Book Value	NM	NM	NM	NM	NM	NM	NM	NM	NM	NM
Cash Flow	NA	2.47	2.79	2.52	2.39	2.20	2.11	2.05	2.19	2.23
Earnings	2.04	1.76	2.08	1.82	1.71	1.57	1.52	1.28	1.55	1.65
S&P Core Earnings	1.78	1.52	1.95	1.81	1.63	1.47	1.46	1.00	1.28	NA
Dividends	1.00	0.88	0.80	0.72	0.68	0.63	0.63	0.63	0.90	0.68
Payout Ratio	49%	50%	38%	40%	40%	40%	41%	49%	58%	41%
Prices:High	35.61	40.85	42.65	39.98	31.60	30.52	27.90	30.00	35.44	39.63
Prices:Low	24.63	27.35	34.17	28.88	27.35	25.03	19.95	19.65	25.52	23.75
P/E Ratio:High	17	23	21	22	18	19	18	23	23	24
P/E Ratio:Low	12	16	16	16	16	16	13	15	16	14

Income Statement Analysis (Million $)										
Revenue	7,586	7,998	7,867	7,343	7,548	7,109	6,678	6,133	6,664	6,267
Operating Income	NA	1,564	1,541	1,445	1,483	1,394	1,376	1,442	1,470	1,516
Depreciation	264	271	23.0	289	279	260	243	319	266	251
Interest Expense	NA	171	163	165	184	174	186	190	216	192
Pretax Income	1,079	939	1,149	1,001	1,030	947	924	798	987	1,077
Effective Tax Rate	32.2%	28.5%	28.4%	24.6%	31.4%	31.7%	32.3%	34.2%	34.2%	33.7%
Net Income	732	671	823	755	707	647	626	525	649	714
S&P Core Earnings	640	579	772	751	675	603	604	413	536	NA

Balance Sheet & Other Financial Data (Million $)										
Cash	51.0	81.0	71.0	657	40.0	32.0	32.0	21.0	24.0	27.0
Current Assets	NA	1,693	1,578	2,112	1,512	1,481	1,290	1,199	1,221	1,168
Total Assets	6,056	6,474	6,445	7,870	6,776	6,675	6,205	5,721	5,927	5,196
Current Liabilities	NA	2,403	2,030	2,962	2,002	2,339	2,783	2,678	3,120	3,032
Long Term Debt	2,246	1,633	2,074	2,116	2,542	2,543	2,249	2,449	2,243	1,218
Common Equity	728	1,318	1,295	1,768	1,270	874	387	-114	-247	137
Total Capital	2,974	3,251	3,369	3,884	3,812	3,417	2,636	2,335	1,996	1,355
Capital Expenditures	345	298	334	309	332	288	283	269	200	200
Cash Flow	NA	942	1,106	1,044	986	907	869	844	915	965
Current Ratio	1.0	0.7	0.8	0.7	0.8	0.6	0.5	0.4	0.4	0.4
% Long Term Debt of Capitalization	75.5	49.4	61.6	54.5	66.7	74.4	85.3	104.9	112.4	89.9
% Net Income of Revenue	9.7	8.4	10.5	10.3	9.4	9.1	9.4	8.6	9.7	11.4
% Return on Assets	11.7	10.4	11.5	10.3	10.5	10.0	10.5	9.0	11.7	13.3
% Return on Equity	71.6	51.4	53.7	49.7	66.0	102.6	458.6	NM	NM	383.9

Data as orig reptd.; bef. results of disc opers/spec. items. Per share data adj. for stk. divs.; EPS diluted. E-Estimated. NA-Not Available. NM-Not Meaningful. NR-Not Ranked. UR-Under Review.

Office: 1 Campbell Pl, Camden, NJ 08103-1799.
Telephone: 856-342-4800.
Website: http://www.campbellsoupcompany.com
Chrmn: P.R. Charron

Pres & CEO: D.R. Conant
SVP, CFO & Chief Admin Officer: B.C. Owens
SVP & CIO: J.C. Spagnoletti
Treas: A. Madhavan

Investor Contact: L.F. Griehs (856-342-6427)
Board Members: E. M. Carpenter, P. R. Charron, D. R. Conant, B. Dorrance, H. Golub, L. C. Karlson, R. W. Larrimore, M. A. Malone, S. Mathew, W. D. Perez, C. R. Perrin, A. B. Rand, N. Shreiber, L. C. Vinney, C. C. Weber, A. D. van Beuren

Founded: 1869
Domicile: New Jersey
Employees: 18,700

The McGraw-Hill Companies

CA Inc

STANDARD &POOR'S

S&P Recommendation **HOLD** ★★★☆☆	Price $22.00 (as of Nov 27, 2009)	12-Mo. Target Price $22.00	Investment Style Large-Cap Blend

GICS Sector Information Technology
Sub-Industry Systems Software

Summary This company (formerly Computer Associates International) develops systems software, database management systems and applications software.

Key Stock Statistics (Source S&P, Vickers, company reports)

52-Wk Range	$24.15–14.59	S&P Oper. EPS 2010E	1.52	Market Capitalization(B)	$11.478	Beta	0.85
Trailing 12-Month EPS	$1.32	S&P Oper. EPS 2011E	1.60	Yield (%)	0.73	S&P 3-Yr. Proj. EPS CAGR(%)	8
Trailing 12-Month P/E	16.7	P/E on S&P Oper. EPS 2010E	14.5	Dividend Rate/Share	$0.16	S&P Credit Rating	BBB
$10K Invested 5 Yrs Ago	$7,396	Common Shares Outstg. (M)	521.7	Institutional Ownership (%)	68		

Price Performance

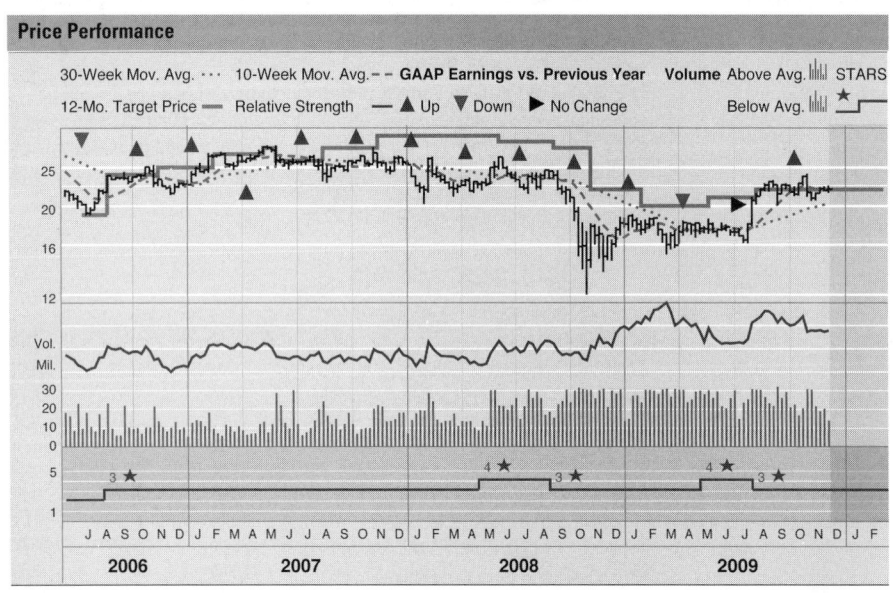

30-Week Mov. Avg. · · · 10-Week Mov. Avg. - - GAAP Earnings vs. Previous Year Volume Above Avg. STARS
12-Mo. Target Price — Relative Strength — ▲ Up ▼ Down ▶ No Change Below Avg. ★

Options: ASE, CBOE, P, Ph

Analysis prepared by **Jim Yin** on October 27, 2009, when the stock traded at **$21.36**.

Highlights

▶ We estimate total revenues will increase 3.7% in FY 11 (Mar.), following 0.9% growth seen for FY 10. Our forecast for modest revenue growth reflects our view of a 4% rise in overall IT spending in 2010. We believe CA's revenues will grow slower than other IT companies due in part to its ratable subscription revenue and the maturity of the mainframe business. However, we expect the company to gain market share through new product offerings.

▶ We expect gross margins in FY 11 of 83%, the same percentage as we project for FY 10, as a larger revenue contribution from subscription revenue offsets higher amortization of capitalized software costs. We see operating expenses decreasing as a percentage of revenues to 48% in FY 11, from 49% in FY 10, on further cost savings. We forecast that operating margins in FY 10 will rise to 31.4%, from an expected 30.9% in FY 10.

▶ Our EPS estimates are $1.52 and $1.60 for FY 10 and FY 11, respectively, compared to $1.29 in FY 09. The projected rise in earnings reflects our forecast for slight increases in revenues and wider operating margins.

Investment Rationale/Risk

▶ We are concerned about a sluggish recovery in IT spending in 2010. We believe software license revenues tend to lag the overall economy. We also think CA will recover slower than other software companies because it derives a larger percentage of its revenues from long-term contracts. On the positive side, CA has reduced its operating expenses by streamlining operations and cutting its workforce, and we see operating margins expanding in FY 10 and FY 11.

▶ Risks to our opinion and target price include significant declines in corporate spending on enterprise software from current levels, pricing pressure from increased competition, and further weakness in the global economy.

▶ Our 12-month target price of $22 is based on a blend of our discounted cash flow (DCF) and P/E analyses. Our DCF model assumes a 12.7% weighted average cost of capital and 3% terminal growth, yielding an intrinsic value of $24. From our P/E analysis, we derive a value of $21 based on an industry average P/E-to-growth ratio of 1.7X, or 14X our FY 10 EPS estimate.

Qualitative Risk Assessment

LOW	MEDIUM	HIGH

Our risk assessment for the company reflects our concerns regarding what we consider to be inconsistent financial results, modest underlying growth and a slowing global economy.

Quantitative Evaluations

S&P Quality Ranking B-

D	C	B-	B	B+	A-	A	A+

Relative Strength Rank MODERATE

56

LOWEST = 1   HIGHEST = 99

Revenue/Earnings Data

Revenue (Million $)

	1Q	2Q	3Q	4Q	Year
2010	1,050	1,072	--	--	--
2009	1,087	110.7	1,042	1,035	4,271
2008	1,025	1,067	1,100	1,085	4,277
2007	949.0	987.0	1,002	1,005	3,943
2006	927.0	950.0	971.0	948.0	3,796
2005	850.0	858.0	910.0	912.0	3,530

Earnings Per Share ($)

2010	0.37	0.41	E0.38	E0.38	E1.52
2009	0.37	0.39	0.40	0.13	1.29
2008	0.24	0.26	0.31	0.14	0.93
2007	0.06	0.09	0.10	-0.04	0.22
2006	0.16	0.08	0.09	-0.07	0.26
2005	0.08	-0.16	0.06	0.04	0.02

Fiscal year ended Mar. 31. Next earnings report expected: Early December. EPS Estimates based on S&P Operating Earnings; historical GAAP earnings are as reported.

Dividend Data (Dates: mm/dd Payment Date: mm/dd/yy)

Amount ($)	Date Decl.	Ex-Div. Date	Stk. of Record	Payment Date
0.040	02/05	02/12	02/17	03/13/09
0.040	05/20	05/27	05/31	06/16/09
0.040	07/29	08/06	08/10	08/19/09
0.040	11/05	11/13	11/17	11/30/09

Dividends have been paid since 1990. Source: Company reports.

Please read the Required Disclosures and Analyst Certification on the last page of this report.

CA Inc

STANDARD &POOR'S

Business Summary October 27, 2009

CORPORATE OVERVIEW. CA provides information technology (IT) management software, which helps customers better manage their IT infrastructure. The company has a broad portfolio of software products and services that span the areas of infrastructure management, IT security management, storage management, application performance management and business service optimization.

CORPORATE STRATEGY. In April 2007, CA announced a new strategy, Enterprise IT Management (EITM), for transforming the way companies manage their IT. The goal of EITM is to unify disparate elements of IT, including hardware, processes and people, so customers can have better control and manage these resources rather than replace existing IT investments. For example, CA's Unicenter Advanced Systems Management provides centralized management for virtualized and clustered server environments, enabling customers to assess and optimize network resources.

Key parts of CA's EITM strategy include:

Internal Product Development - CA plans to ship new versions of every major product, including those products obtained through acquisitions. The company has added headcount in India and Czech Republic research centers.

Strengthening Partner Relationships - CA intends to strengthen its global distribution by recruiting and educating channel partners on CA products and services. The company formed a Mid-Market and Storage organization that targets enterprises with 500-5,000 employees.

International Expansion - CA will invest in regions outside the U.S., especially in emerging markets such as China and India to increase the volume of enterprise sales. The company has also pursued small- and medium-sized customers in the Europe, Middle East and Africa (EMEA) region. International revenue comprised nearly 46% of total sales in FY 09 (Mar.), down from 48% in FY 08.

Strategic Acquisitions - CA has made several small acquisitions that the company considers strategic and complementary to its systems and security management offerings. In FY 07, the company completed the acquisitions of Cendura Corporation, XOsoft, Inc., MDY Group International, Inc. and Cybermation, Inc.

Company Financials Fiscal Year Ended Mar. 31

Per Share Data ($)	2009	2008	2007	2006	2005	2004	2003	2002	2001	2000
Tangible Book Value	NM	NM	NM	NM	0.50	8.09	NM	NM	0.66	1.71
Cash Flow	1.56	1.21	0.47	1.22	0.24	0.17	0.60	-0.01	0.89	2.32
Earnings	1.29	0.93	0.22	0.26	0.02	-0.06	-0.46	-1.91	-1.02	1.25
S&P Core Earnings	1.31	0.97	0.23	0.26	0.22	0.02	-0.53	-2.05	-1.18	NA
Dividends	0.16	0.16	0.16	0.08	0.08	0.08	0.08	0.08	0.08	0.08
Payout Ratio	12%	17%	73%	31%	NM	NM	NM	NM	NM	6%
Calendar Year	2008	2007	2006	2005	2004	2003	2002	2001	2000	1999
Prices:High	26.68	28.46	29.50	31.35	31.71	29.29	38.74	39.03	79.44	70.63
Prices:Low	12.00	22.86	18.97	26.04	22.37	12.39	7.47	18.31	18.13	32.13
P/E Ratio:High	21	31	NM	NM	NM	NM	NM	NM	NM	56
P/E Ratio:Low	9	25	NM	NM	NM	NM	NM	NM	NM	26

Income Statement Analysis (Million $)										
Revenue	4,271	4,277	3,943	3,796	3,530	3,276	3,116	2,964	4,198	6,766
Operating Income	1,377	1,137	560	836	504	417	421	-62.0	604	3,318
Depreciation	149	156	148	583	130	134	612	1,096	1,110	594
Interest Expense	95.0	370	126	41.0	106	Nil	172	227	344	339
Pretax Income	1,102	808	154	121	11.0	-54.0	-363	-1,385	-666	1,590
Effective Tax Rate	37.0%	38.1%	21.4%	NM	NM	NM	NM	NM	NM	56.2%
Net Income	694	500	121	156	13.0	-36.0	-267	-1,102	-591	696
S&P Core Earnings	704	522	122	155	136	7.10	-301	-1,185	-688	NA

Balance Sheet & Other Financial Data (Million $)										
Cash	2,713	2,796	2,280	1,865	3,125	1,902	1,512	1,180	850	1,387
Current Assets	4,180	4,468	3,101	2,648	3,954	3,358	3,565	3,061	2,643	3,992
Total Assets	11,252	11,756	10,585	10,438	11,082	10,679	11,054	12,226	14,143	17,493
Current Liabilities	4,078	4,278	3,714	3,377	3,664	2,455	2,974	2,321	2,286	3,004
Long Term Debt	1,287	2,221	2,572	1,810	1,810	2,298	2,298	3,334	3,639	4,527
Common Equity	4,344	3,709	3,690	4,680	4,840	4,718	4,363	4,617	5,780	7,037
Total Capital	5,767	6,291	6,282	6,536	6,822	7,634	7,525	9,218	11,319	13,929
Capital Expenditures	83.0	117	150	143	69.0	30.0	30.0	25.0	89.0	198
Cash Flow	843	656	269	739	143	98.0	345	-6.00	519	1,290
Current Ratio	1.0	1.0	0.8	0.8	1.1	1.4	1.2	1.3	1.2	1.3
% Long Term Debt of Capitalization	22.3	36.2	41.1	27.7	26.5	30.1	30.5	36.2	32.1	32.5
% Net Income of Revenue	16.3	11.7	3.1	4.1	0.4	NM	NM	NM	NM	10.2
% Return on Assets	6.0	4.5	1.2	1.4	0.1	NM	NM	NM	NM	5.4
% Return on Equity	17.2	13.5	2.9	3.2	0.3	NM	NM	NM	NM	14.3

Data as orig reptd.; bef. results of disc opers/spec. items. Per share data adj. for stk. divs.; EPS diluted. E-Estimated. NA-Not Available. NM-Not Meaningful. NR-Not Ranked. UR-Under Review.

Office: 1 Computer Associates Plz, Islandia, NY 11749-7000.
Telephone: 631-342-6000.
Email: cainvestor@ca.com
Website: http://www.ca.com

Chrmn: W.E. McCracken
Pres & COO: M.J. Christenson
CEO: J.A. Swainson
EVP & CFO: N.E. Cooper

EVP & Chief Admin Officer: J.E. Bryant
Investor Contact: R.G. Cirabisi (631-342-6000)
Board Members: R. Bromark, G. J. Fernandes, K. Koplovitz, C. B. Lofgren, W. E. McCracken, R. Sulpizio, J. A. Swainson, L. Unger, A. F. Weinbach, R. Zambonini

Founded: 1974
Domicile: Delaware
Employees: 13,200

Capital One Financial Corp.

STANDARD &POOR'S

S&P Recommendation	BUY ★★★★☆	Price $37.24 (as of Nov 27, 2009)	12-Mo. Target Price $48.00	Investment Style Large-Cap Blend

GICS Sector Financials
Sub-Industry Consumer Finance

Summary This diversified consumer finance company is one of the largest issuers of Visa and MasterCard credit cards in the world.

Key Stock Statistics (Source S&P, Vickers, company reports)

52-Wk Range	$42.90– 7.80	S&P Oper. EPS 2009**E**	0.45	Market Capitalization(B)	$16.755	Beta	1.95
Trailing 12-Month EPS	$-3.58	S&P Oper. EPS 2010**E**	1.77	Yield (%)	0.54	S&P 3-Yr. Proj. EPS CAGR(%)	-5
Trailing 12-Month P/E	NM	P/E on S&P Oper. EPS 2009**E**	82.8	Dividend Rate/Share	$0.20	S&P Credit Rating	BBB
$10K Invested 5 Yrs Ago	$4,986	Common Shares Outstg. (M)	449.9	Institutional Ownership (%)	91		

Price Performance

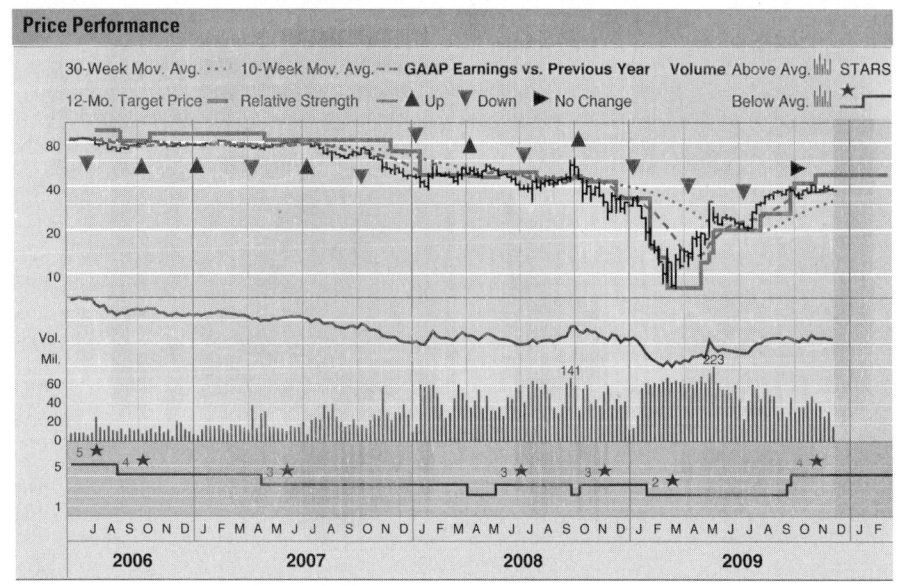

30-Week Mov. Avg. · · · · 10-Week Mov. Avg. — **GAAP Earnings vs. Previous Year** Volume Above Avg. ‖‖ STARS
12-Mo. Target Price — Relative Strength — ▲ Up ▼ Down ▶ No Change   Below Avg. ‖‖ ★

Options: ASE, CBOE, P, Ph

Analysis prepared by **Stuart Plesser** on November 04, 2009, when the stock traded at **$ 37.84**.

Highlights

► We expect revenues in 2010 to decline modestly from 2009 projected levels, reflecting a weak economy and slowing consumer spending. Management has tightened lending standards, and we expect to see a continued slowdown in loan growth. Although we forecast a continued rise in delinquencies and loan-loss provisions in all of COF's business lines in the first half of 2010, we think chargeoffs will peak after the second quarter of 2010.

► Besides projected credit improvement next year, assuming unemployment levels peak in the second quarter of 2010, COF's total charge-offs should stablize due to a decline in average balances outstanding. Although regulation in COF's U.S. card business will likely hurt revenue due to a mandated change in minimum payment policies, we think COF will come up with alternative means to make up for some of the lost revenue. While we anticipate the continuation of solid expense management, we do not expect significant further reductions as the marketing budget will likely rise.

► We estimate a gain of $0.45 per share for 2009. In 2010, assuming an economic recovery by the beginning of the year, we look for EPS of $1.77.

Investment Rationale/Risk

► Although we see higher chargeoffs, particularly as they relate to COF's prime, home equity, and credit card loans, we are encouraged by a stabilization of early delinquency rates. We remain concerned about higher unemployment rates in the U.S. and U.K., but think peak levels will be lower than we previously expected. Capital levels seem adequate to us, further confirmed by the company's action to pay back TARP. Uncertainty remains regarding the impact of recent credit card regulation, as fee income will likely come under pressure. But COF will likely attempt to recoup lost fee revenue from other facets of its business.

► Risks to our recommendation and target price include a decrease in consumer confidence; higher-than-expected deterioration in COF's mortgage portfolio; and, higher-than-expected unemployment rates that would hurt credit quality.

► Our 12-month target price of $48 is equal to 1.77X current tangible book value of $27.02. This valuation multiple is a discount to COF's historical averages but is warranted, in our opinion, by ongoing credit risks.

Qualitative Risk Assessment

LOW	MEDIUM	HIGH

Our risk assessment reflects what we perceive as the risk of higher chargeoff and unemployment levels, offset by strong capital levels and favorable early delinquency trends.

Quantitative Evaluations

S&P Quality Ranking   A-

D	C	B-	B	B+	A-	A	A+

Relative Strength Rank   MODERATE

58

LOWEST = 1   HIGHEST = 99

Revenue/Earnings Data

Revenue (Million $)

	1Q	2Q	3Q	4Q	Year
2009	3,739	3,946	4,300	--	--
2008	4,936	4,269	4,463	4,137	17,856
2007	4,598	4,719	4,910	5,119	19,132
2006	3,737	3,607	2,826	4,021	15,191
2005	2,852	2,934	2,999	3,300	12,085
2004	2,608	2,548	2,768	2,771	10,695

Earnings Per Share ($)

	1Q	2Q	3Q	4Q	Year
2009	-0.39	-0.64	1.03	E0.45	E0.45
2008	1.70	1.24	1.03	-3.67	0.14
2007	1.62	1.89	-2.09	0.85	6.55
2006	2.86	1.78	1.89	1.14	7.62
2005	1.99	2.03	1.81	0.97	6.73
2004	1.84	1.65	1.97	0.77	6.21

Fiscal year ended Dec. 31. Next earnings report expected: Late January. EPS Estimates based on S&P Operating Earnings; historical GAAP earnings are as reported.

Dividend Data (Dates: mm/dd Payment Date: mm/dd/yy)

Amount ($)	Date Decl.	Ex-Div. Date	Stk. of Record	Payment Date
0.375	01/29	02/06	02/10	02/20/09
0.050	04/23	05/07	05/11	05/20/09
0.050	07/30	08/07	08/11	08/20/09
0.050	10/29	11/06	11/11	11/20/09

Dividends have been paid since 1995. Source: Company reports.

Please read the Required Disclosures and Analyst Certification on the last page of this report.

Capital One Financial Corp.

STANDARD
&POOR'S

Business Summary November 04, 2009

CORPORATE OVERVIEW. Capital One Financial (COF) is one of the largest banks in the United States. It is a diversified banking corporation focused primarily on consumer and commercial lending and deposit origination. The company's principal business segments are national lending and local banking. The national lending segment consists of two sub-segments: U.S. Card, and Other National Lending. The Other National Lending sub-segment includes the Auto Finance sub-segment and International sub-segment.

The U.S. Card segment consists of domestic consumer credit card lending, national small business lending, installment loans and other unsecured consumer financial service activities. COF offers a wide variety of credit card and small business products, in addition to unsecured closed-end loans throughout the U.S., which it customizes to appeal to different consumer preferences and needs. Its product offerings are supported by extensive brand advertising. It routinely tests new products to develop products that appeal to different and changing consumer preferences. Its customized products include products offered to a wide range of consumer credit risk profiles, as well as products aimed at special consumer interests.

The Auto Finance segment consists of automobile and other motor vehicle financing activities. COF purchases retail installment contracts, secured by new and used automobiles or other motor vehicles, through dealer networks throughout the U.S. Additionally, it utilizes direct marketing, including the Internet, to offer automobile financing directly to consumers for the purchase of new and used vehicles, as well as refinancing of existing motor vehicle loans. As of December 31, 2008, COF was the fourth largest non-captive provider of auto financing in the U.S. In January 2005, it acquired Onyx Acceptance Corporation, an auto finance company that provides financing to franchised and select independent dealerships throughout the U.S. The company also completed the acquisition of Key Bank's non-prime auto loan portfolio in 2005. Similar to its credit card strategy, COF customizes product features, such as interest rate, loan amount and loan terms, enabling it to lend to customers with a wide range of credit profiles.

Company Financials Fiscal Year Ended Dec. 31

Per Share Data ($)	2008	2007	2006	2005	2004	2003	2002	2001	2000	1999
Tangible Book Value	NA	31.86	25.37	33.99	33.98	25.75	20.44	15.33	9.94	7.69
Earnings	0.14	6.55	7.62	6.73	6.21	4.92	3.93	2.91	2.24	1.72
S&P Core Earnings	1.83	6.55	7.61	6.61	5.72	4.41	3.37	2.55	NA	NA
Dividends	NA	0.11	0.11	0.11	0.11	0.11	0.11	0.11	0.11	0.11
Payout Ratio	NA	2%	1%	2%	2%	2%	3%	4%	5%	6%
Prices:High	NA	83.84	90.04	88.56	84.45	64.25	66.50	72.58	73.25	60.25
Prices:Low	NA	44.40	69.30	69.09	60.04	24.91	24.05	36.40	32.06	35.81
P/E Ratio:High	NA	13	12	13	14	13	17	25	33	35
P/E Ratio:Low	NA	7	9	10	10	5	6	13	14	21

Income Statement Analysis (Million $)										
Net Interest Income	NA	6,530	5,100	3,680	3,003	2,785	2,719	1,663	1,589	1,053
Non Interest Income	6,692	8,054	6,997	6,358	5,900	5,416	5,467	4,420	3,034	2,372
Loan Loss Provision	NA	2,637	1,476	1,491	1,221	1,517	2,149	990	718	383
Non Interest Expenses	NA	8,078	6,967	5,718	5,322	4,857	4,586	4,058	3,148	2,465
% Expense/Operating Revenue	NA	55.4%	57.6%	57.0%	59.8%	59.2%	56.0%	66.7%	68.1%	72.0%
Pretax Income	582	3,870	3,653	2,829	2,360	1,827	1,451	1,035	757	577
Effective Tax Rate	85.5%	33.0%	33.9%	36.1%	34.6%	37.0%	38.0%	38.0%	38.0%	37.1%
Net Income	84.5	2,592	2,414	1,809	1,543	1,151	900	642	470	363
% Net Interest Margin	5.38	6.46	6.03	6.63	6.44	7.45	8.73	8.03	12.0	10.8
S&P Core Earnings	691	2,591	2,412	1,792	1,431	1,012	742	545	NA	NA

Balance Sheet & Other Financial Data (Million $)										
Money Market Assets	NA	2,444	1,843	2,049	1,084	1,598	641	352	162	112
Investment Securities	NA	19,782	15,452	14,350	9,300	5,867	4,424	3,116	1,697	1,856
Earning Assets:Total Loans	101,342	98,842	106,947	59,848	38,216	32,850	27,854	20,921	14,059	9,914
Total Assets	165,981	150,590	149,739	88,701	53,747	46,284	37,382	28,184	18,889	13,336
Demand Deposits	11,294	11,047	11,648	4,841	NA	Nil	Nil	Nil	Nil	Nil
Time Deposits	NA	71,944	74,123	43,092	NA	22,416	17,326	12,839	8,379	3,784
Long Term Debt	16,736	20,237	20,217	14,863	Nil	14,813	8,124	Nil	4,051	4,181
Common Equity	23,516	24,294	25,235	14,129	8,388	6,052	4,623	3,324	1,963	1,518
% Return on Assets	0.1	1.7	2.0	2.5	3.1	2.8	2.7	2.7	2.9	3.2
% Return on Equity	0.4	10.5	12.3	16.1	21.4	21.6	22.6	24.3	27.0	26.0
% Loan Loss Reserve	4.5	2.9	2.0	3.0	3.9	4.9	6.2	4.0	3.7	3.5
% Loans/Deposits	93.0	114.5	124.7	124.8	149.1	146.5	160.8	162.9	167.8	262.0
% Loans/Assets	NA	64.2	70.0	68.8	71.0	71.9	74.4	74.3	72.3	70.6
% Equity to Assets	15.1	16.5	16.5	15.8	14.4	12.8	12.1	11.2	10.8	12.3

Data as orig reptd.; bef. results of disc opers/spec. items. Per share data adj. for stk. divs.; EPS diluted. E-Estimated. NA-Not Available. NM-Not Meaningful. NR-Not Ranked. UR-Under Review.

Office: 1680 Capital One Drive, McLean, VA 22102-3407.
Telephone: 703-720-1000.
Email: investor.relations@capitalone.com
Website: http://www.capitalone.com

Chrmn, Pres & CEO: R.D. Fairbank
Pres: S. Yajnik
EVP, CFO & Chief Acctg Officer: G.L. Perlin
SVP & Chief Acctg Officer: F.A. Thacker

SVP & Treas: S. Linehan
Investor Contact: M. Rowen (703-720-2455)
Board Members: E. R. Campbell, W. R. Dietz, R. D. Fairbank, P. W. Gross, A. F. Hackett, L. Hay, III, P. Leroy, M. A. Shattuck, III, B. H. Warner, S. I. Westreich

Founded: 1993
Domicile: Delaware
Employees: 25,800

The McGraw-Hill Companies

Cardinal Health Inc

STANDARD
&POOR'S

S&P Recommendation **HOLD** ★★★☆☆	Price $32.03 (as of Nov 27, 2009)	12-Mo. Target Price $33.00	Investment Style Large-Cap Blend

GICS Sector Health Care
Sub-Industry Health Care Distributors

Summary This company is one of the leading wholesale distributors of pharmaceuticals, medical/surgical supplies, and related products to a broad range of health care customers.

Key Stock Statistics (Source S&P, Vickers, company reports)

52-Wk Range	$39.87–24.87	S&P Oper. EPS 2010**E**	2.00	Market Capitalization(B)	$11.617	Beta	0.84
Trailing 12-Month EPS	$2.39	S&P Oper. EPS 2011**E**	2.20	Yield (%)	2.19	S&P 3-Yr. Proj. EPS CAGR(%)	1
Trailing 12-Month P/E	13.4	P/E on S&P Oper. EPS 2010**E**	16.0	Dividend Rate/Share	$0.70	S&P Credit Rating	BBB+
$10K Invested 5 Yrs Ago	NA	Common Shares Outstg. (M)	362.7	Institutional Ownership (%)	78		

Price Performance

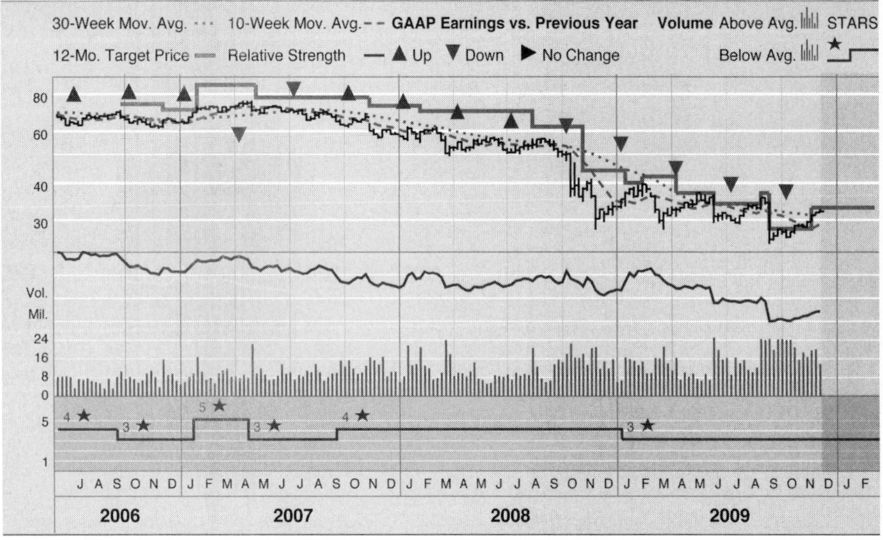

30-Week Mov. Avg. · · · · 10-Week Mov. Avg. — **GAAP Earnings vs. Previous Year** Volume Above Avg. ▏▍▎▎ STARS
12-Mo. Target Price — Relative Strength — ▲ Up ▼ Down ► No Change Below Avg. ▏▍▎▎ ★

[Price performance chart with years 2006, 2007, 2008, 2009 shown across the bottom]

Options: ASE, CBOE, P, Ph

Analysis prepared by **Phillip M. Seligman** on November 17, 2009, when the stock traded at **$31.46**.

Highlights

► Following CAH's August 31, 2009, spinoff of 81% of its Clinical and Medical Products segment, now called CareFusion Corp. (CFN 26, Buy), we look for the company's revenue to rise by 3.4% in FY 10 (Jun.) to $99.2 billion, from its pro-forma FY 09 revenue of $96.0 billion. Drivers we see include branded drug price inflation and modestly improved prescription trends, partly offset by sell-side pricing pressures, customer losses and increased penetration of generic drugs, which carry lower prices than branded drugs, but also higher margins.

► We project that gross and operating margins will narrow in FY 10, on contract renewals, internal investments, generic drug price deflation and unfavorable timing of the generic drug launches and the new Pfizer fee-for-service agreement.

► Our FY 10 EPS estimate is $2.00 before $0.71 of one time costs, versus FY 09's $2.26 (pro forma) before $0.14 of one-time costs. We project EPS of $2.20 in FY 11, assuming easier comparisons and more favorable generic drug launch timing.

Investment Rationale/Risk

► Following September-quarter earnings that were well above our and Street expectations, we note that CAH benefited from timing or one-time events, including accelerated revenue recognition tied to the CFN spinoff, earlier-than-expected brand price increases, and a deferred state tax accrual. Given the headwinds we see, including unfavorable timing of generic drug launches and customer contract repricings, we look for FY 10 EPS to be at the high end of its prior guidance of $1.90-$2.00. Looking ahead, however, we forecast a return to EPS growth in FY 11, assuming some of the headwinds dissipate. Meanwhile, we like CAH's improved nuclear pharmacy performance and cash flow, and are encouraged by its operating improvement initiatives, although we expect benefits from these initiatives to be more visible after FY 10.

► Risks to our recommendation and target price include intensified competition, the loss of major accounts, and unfavorable changes in contracts with drugmakers or retailers.

► Our 12-month target price of $33 is based on a peer-level forward P/E of 16X applied to our calendar 2010 EPS estimate of $2.05.

Qualitative Risk Assessment

LOW	**MEDIUM**	HIGH

Our risk assessment reflects CAH's diversified products and services and what we believe are good growth prospects for its contract drugmaking and its drug dispensing systems. However, we also see intense competition in the drug distribution market, and we believe that future drugmaker-distributor contract negotiations could be less favorable to distributors.

Quantitative Evaluations

S&P Quality Ranking   A-

D	C	B-	B	B+	**A-**	A	A+

Relative Strength Rank   STRONG

        83

LOWEST = 1   HIGHEST = 99

Revenue/Earnings Data

Revenue (Million $)

	1Q	2Q	3Q	4Q	Year
2010	24,781	--	--	--	--
2009	24,321	25,075	24,918	25,199	99,512
2008	21,973	23,283	22,910	22,926	91,091
2007	20,938	21,785	21,867	22,263	86,852
2006	19,237	19,781	20,638	21,708	81,364
2005	17,796	18,555	19,103	19,457	74,911

Earnings Per Share ($)

2010	-0.17	E0.46	E0.53	E0.47	E2.00
2009	0.68	0.88	0.87	0.74	3.16
2008	0.82	0.89	1.02	0.89	3.62
2007	0.71	0.77	-0.01	0.61	2.08
2006	0.55	0.72	0.83	0.80	2.90
2005	0.50	0.47	0.84	0.59	2.40

Fiscal year ended Jun. 30. Next earnings report expected: Early February. EPS Estimates based on S&P Operating Earnings; historical GAAP earnings are as reported.

Dividend Data (Dates: mm/dd Payment Date: mm/dd/yy)

Amount ($)	Date Decl.	Ex-Div. Date	Stk. of Record	Payment Date
0.175	05/06	06/29	07/01	07/15/09
Stk.	07/13	09/01	08/25	08/31/09
0.175	08/05	09/29	10/01	10/15/09
0.175	11/04	12/29	01/01	01/15/10

Dividends have been paid since 1983. Source: Company reports.

Please read the Required Disclosures and Analyst Certification on the last page of this report.

The **McGraw·Hill** Companies

Cardinal Health Inc

STANDARD
&POOR'S

Business Summary November 17, 2009

CORPORATE OVERVIEW. Until September 1, Cardinal Health's reportable segments were aligned into two main segments: Healthcare Supply Chain Services, comprising two sub-segments; and Clinical and Medical Products, which was spun off as CareFusion Corp. on August 31, 2009:

Healthcare Supply Chain Services - Pharmaceutical (HSCS-Pharma: 86.5% of FY 09 operating revenue) distributes pharmaceutical and related health care products to independent and chain drug stores, hospitals, alternate care centers, and supermarket and mass merchandiser pharmacies. PDS operates a pharmaceutical repackaging and distribution program for retail and mail order customers.

Healthcare Supply Chain Services - Medical (HSCS-Medical; 8.0%) -- provides non-pharmaceutical health care products for hospitals and other health care providers.

Clinical and Medical Products (CMP; 4.5%) - Develops, manufactures and markets automation and information products and services, as well as sterile and non-sterile procedure kits, single-use surgical drapes, gowns and apparel, exam and surgical gloves, fluid suction and collection systems, respiratory therapy products, surgical instruments, special procedure products and other products. This segment was spun off after the close of trading on August 31, 2009.

As of September 1, Cardinal Health consists only of HSCS and the remaining businesses within the third reporting segment (1.0%), which originally comprised of Medicine Shoppe International, Pharmacy services, Tecomet (orthopedic implants and instruments), and MedSystems (enteral devices and surgical protection products). Tecomet and Medsystems were sold in the first quarter of FY 09.

Company Financials Fiscal Year Ended Jun. 30

Per Share Data ($)	2009	2008	2007	2006	2005	2004	2003	2002	2001	2000
Tangible Book Value	7.30	4.26	4.12	8.52	8.20	7.05	12.10	11.50	9.50	7.28
Cash Flow	4.27	4.65	2.87	3.82	3.34	4.15	3.70	2.98	2.50	2.17
Earnings	3.16	3.62	2.07	2.90	2.40	3.47	3.12	2.45	1.88	1.59
S&P Core Earnings	3.16	3.64	3.08	2.88	2.16	3.14	2.78	2.26	1.69	NA
Dividends	0.60	0.50	0.39	0.27	0.15	0.12	0.11	0.10	0.09	0.05
Payout Ratio	19%	14%	19%	9%	6%	3%	4%	4%	5%	3%
Prices:High	39.87	62.25	76.15	75.74	69.64	76.54	67.96	73.70	77.32	69.96
Prices:Low	24.87	27.79	56.41	61.15	52.85	36.08	50.00	46.60	56.67	24.67
P/E Ratio:High	13	17	37	26	29	22	22	30	41	44
P/E Ratio:Low	8	8	27	21	22	10	16	19	30	15

Income Statement Analysis (Million $)

	2009	2008	2007	2006	2005	2004	2003	2002	2001	2000
Revenue	99,512	91,091	86,852	81,364	74,911	65,054	50,467	44,394	47,948	29,871
Operating Income	2,488	2,594	2,485	2,474	2,555	2,694	3,723	2,216	1,893	1,377
Depreciation	399	375	322	393	410	299	266	244	281	246
Interest Expense	219	171	121	132	134	98.9	115	133	155	117
Pretax Income	1,667	1,957	1,252	1,835	1,629	2,238	2,127	1,701	1,332	1,078
Effective Tax Rate	31.5%	32.3%	32.9%	32.2%	35.8%	31.9%	33.6%	33.8%	35.6%	36.9%
Net Income	1,143	1,325	840	1,245	1,047	1,525	1,412	1,126	857	680
S&P Core Earnings	1,142	1,326	1,247	1,236	936	1,369	1,266	1,045	771	NA

Balance Sheet & Other Financial Data (Million $)

	2009	2008	2007	2006	2005	2004	2003	2002	2001	2000
Cash	1,848	1,291	1,309	1,321	1,412	1,096	1,724	1,382	934	505
Current Assets	15,799	14,184	14,545	14,777	13,443	13,058	13,250	11,907	10,716	6,871
Total Assets	25,119	23,448	23,154	23,374	22,059	21,369	18,521	16,438	14,642	10,265
Current Liabilities	11,400	10,376	11,460	11,373	10,105	9,369	7,314	6,810	6,575	4,262
Long Term Debt	3,280	3,687	3,457	2,600	2,320	2,835	2,472	2,207	1,871	1,486
Common Equity	8,725	7,756	7,377	8,491	8,593	7,976	7,758	6,393	5,437	3,981
Total Capital	12,005	11,444	10,834	11,090	10,913	12,000	11,207	8,600	7,308	5,467
Capital Expenditures	533	376	1,630	443	572	410	423	285	341	308
Cash Flow	1,542	1,691	1,162	1,637	1,456	1,824	1,678	1,370	1,138	926
Current Ratio	1.4	1.4	1.3	1.3	1.3	1.4	1.8	1.7	1.6	1.6
% Long Term Debt of Capitalization	27.3	32.2	31.9	23.4	21.3	23.6	22.1	25.7	25.6	27.2
% Net Income of Revenue	1.2	1.5	1.0	1.5	1.4	2.3	2.8	2.5	1.8	2.3
% Return on Assets	4.7	5.7	3.6	5.5	4.8	7.7	8.1	7.2	6.4	7.3
% Return on Equity	13.9	17.5	10.6	14.6	12.6	19.5	20.0	19.0	17.4	18.0

Data as orig reptd.; bef. results of disc opers/spec. items. Per share data adj. for stk. divs.; EPS diluted. E-Estimated. NA-Not Available. NM-Not Meaningful. NR-Not Ranked. UR-Under Review.

Office: 7000 Cardinal Place, Dublin, OH 43017.
Telephone: 614-757-5000.
Website: http://www.cardinal.com
Chrmn & CEO: G.S. Barrett

EVP & Secy: S.T. Falk
CFO: J.W. Henderson
General Counsel: C.S. Morford
CIO: P. Morrison

Board Members: C. F. Arnold, G. S. Barrett, G. A. Britt, C. Darden, B. L. Downey, J. F. Finn, G. B. Kenny, R. C. Notebaert, D. W. Raisbeck, J. G. Spaulding

Founded: 1979
Domicile: Ohio
Employees: 46,500

The McGraw-Hill Companies

CareFusion Corp

STANDARD
&POOR'S

S&P Recommendation **BUY** ★★★★☆	Price $25.79 (as of Nov 27, 2009)	12-Mo. Target Price $28.00	Investment Style Large-Cap Growth

GICS Sector Health Care
Sub-Industry Health Care Equipment

Summary This leading maker of infusion pumps, dispensing systems, and respiratory and infection prevention products was spun off from Cardinal Health on August 31, 2009.

Key Stock Statistics (Source S&P, Vickers, company reports)

52-Wk Range	$26.99– 17.25	S&P Oper. EPS 2010E	1.45	Market Capitalization(B)	$5.709	Beta	NA
Trailing 12-Month EPS	$2.42	S&P Oper. EPS 2011E	1.60	Yield (%)	Nil	S&P 3-Yr. Proj. EPS CAGR(%)	NM
Trailing 12-Month P/E	10.7	P/E on S&P Oper. EPS 2010E	17.8	Dividend Rate/Share	Nil	S&P Credit Rating	BBB-
$10K Invested 5 Yrs Ago	NA	Common Shares Outstg. (M)	221.4	Institutional Ownership (%)	31		

Price Performance

30-Week Mov. Avg. · · ·   10-Week Mov. Avg. – –   **GAAP Earnings vs. Previous Year**   Volume Above Avg. STARS
12-Mo. Target Price —   Relative Strength —   ▲ Up ▼ Down ► No Change   Below Avg.

Analysis prepared by **Phillip M. Seligman** on November 17, 2009, when the stock traded at **$ 25.55**.

Highlights

► We look for CFN's revenue in FY 10 (Jun.) to grow by 8.7%, to $3.9 billion, from the pro forma $3.6 billion in FY 09. Revenue growth drivers we see include the resumption of shipping of Alaris infusion pumps, with all of the backlog fulfilled in the first half, the CDC's order of 4,500 ventilators for H1N1 flu preparations, the launch of the EnVe ventilator, and CFN's plans to launch 40 new products through December 2011. We also see continued strength in international sales and strong demand for respiratory and infection protection products. However, we view the potential FY 10 benefit from the HCA order for Pyxis products as modest, since shipments will occur over a five-year period.

► We forecast modestly narrower gross margins in FY 10 on product and geographic mix shifts. We also expect operating expenses to expand to 30.3% of revenue, on incremental operating costs related to CFN's first year as a public company and its IT investments.

► We look for FY 10 EPS of $1.45 and FY 11 EPS of $1.60. CFN expects to have operating cash flow of $400 million to $450 million in FY 10, which we view as providing financial flexibility.

Investment Rationale/Risk

► We recently upgraded our opinion on the shares to buy, from hold. We do not expect U.S. hospitals to return to the levels of capital spending prior to the recession, but we believe the cutbacks have stabilized, and CFN noted seeing as early as April a modest uptick in customer orders for its capital equipment. Indeed, we expect CFN to benefit strongly from hospitals seeking to reduce medication errors and hospital-acquired infections. We are also encouraged by its intention to step up R&D spending from 4% of FY 10 revenues to 6% to 7% over the next three to five years, as it seeks to expand revenues from products launched in the prior 36 months from the 20% it sees in FY 10 to 30% in FY 12.

► Risks to our recommendation and target price include further declines in hospital capital spending, intensified competition, product pricing pressures, product recalls, and increased health care regulation.

► Our 12-month target price of $28 represents a forward multiple of 18.5X our calendar 2010 EPS estimate of $1.52. This multiple is above those of medical device peers to reflect our view of the company's superior growth prospects.

Qualitative Risk Assessment

LOW	MEDIUM	HIGH

Our risk assessment reflects our belief that U.S. hospital capital spending will remain under pressure over the long term, limiting the sales growth of CFN's capital equipment, which represents about 40% of its overall business. Still, we expect these and CFN's disposables products to benefit from hospitals seeking to improve patient safety.

Quantitative Evaluations

S&P Quality Ranking NR

D	C	B-	B	B+	A-	A	A+

Relative Strength Rank **STRONG**
92
LOWEST = 1   HIGHEST = 99

Revenue/Earnings Data

Revenue (Million $)

	1Q	2Q	3Q	4Q	Year
2010	923.0	--	--	--	--
2009	1,167	1,167	1,076	1,091	4,501
2008	1,060	1,060	1,150	1,248	4,518
2007	--	--	--	--	3,478
2006	--	--	--	--	3,052
2005	--	--	--	--	--

Earnings Per Share ($)

	1Q	2Q	3Q	4Q	Year
2010	0.25	E0.36	E0.34	E0.37	E1.45
2009	0.14	--	--	0.44	2.57
2008	--	--	--	--	--
2007	--	--	--	--	--
2006	--	--	--	--	--
2005	--	--	--	--	--

Fiscal year ended Jun. 30. Next earnings report expected: NA. EPS Estimates based on S&P Operating Earnings; historical GAAP earnings are as reported.

Dividend Data

No cash dividends have been paid.

CareFusion Corp

STANDARD &POOR'S

Business Summary November 17, 2009

CORPORATE OVERVIEW. CareFusion Corp. is a global medical technology company with leading products and services designed to improve the safety and quality of health care. In 2008, Cardinal Health reorganized and consolidated the businesses comprising the majority of CareFusion into Cardinal Health's Clinical and Medical Products segment. CareFusion was incorporated in Delaware on January 14, 2009, for the purpose of holding the segment in connection with its planned spinoff, and transferred the equity interests of the entities that hold the assets and liabilities of the clinical and medical products businesses to CareFusion. Approximately 81% of the equity of CareFusion was spun off to Cardinal Health shareholders after the close of trading on August 31, 2009, and Cardinal plans to divest the remaining amount over time.

CFN consists of two segments: Critical Care Technologies and Medical Technologies and Services. Critical Care Technologies includes intravenous, or IV, infusion, medication and supply dispensing and respiratory care businesses that develop, manufacture and sell capital equipment and related dedicated and non-dedicated disposables. Medical Technologies and Services includes infection prevention and medical specialties products and services businesses that develop, manufacture and sell primarily single-use, disposable prod-

ucts and reusable surgical instruments. Its primary customers include hospitals, ambulatory surgical centers, clinics, long-term care facilities and physician offices in the U.S., and hospitals in 120 countries worldwide.

Primary product brands include: (1) Alaris IV infusion systems that feature proprietary software, Guardrails, an application that alerts the clinician when a parameter is outside the institution's pre-established limitations for that medication, thereby helping to reduce IV medication errors; (2) Pyxis automated medication dispensing systems that provide medication management and Pyxis automated medical supply dispensing systems; (3) AVEA and Pulmonetic Systems ventilation and respiratory products, and Jaeger and SensorMedics pulmonary products; (4) ChloraPrep products that help prevent vascular and surgical-site infections and MedMined software and services that help target and reduce hospital-acquired infections (HAIs); and (5) V. Mueller surgical instruments and related products and services.

Company Financials Fiscal Year Ended Jun. 30

Per Share Data ($)	2009	2008	2007	2006	2005	2004	2003	2002	2001	2000
Tangible Book Value	4.73	NA	NA	NA	NA	NA	NA	NA	NA	NA
Cash Flow	3.45	NA	NA	NA	NA	NA	NA	NA	NA	NA
Earnings	2.57	NA	NA	NA	NA	NA	NA	NA	NA	NA
S&P Core Earnings	2.51	2.93	2.23	NA	NA	NA	NA	NA	NA	NA
Dividends	Nil	NA	NA	NA	NA	NA	NA	NA	NA	NA
Payout Ratio	Nil	NA	NA	NA	NA	NA	NA	NA	NA	NA
Prices:High	26.99	NA	NA	NA	NA	NA	NA	NA	NA	NA
Prices:Low	17.25	NA	NA	NA	NA	NA	NA	NA	NA	NA
P/E Ratio:High	11	NA	NA	NA	NA	NA	NA	NA	NA	NA
P/E Ratio:Low	7	NA	NA	NA	NA	NA	NA	NA	NA	NA

Income Statement Analysis (Million $)	2009	2008	2007	2006	2005	2004	2003	2002	2001	2000
Revenue	4,501	4,518	3,478	3,052	NA	NA	NA	NA	NA	NA
Operating Income	856	945	691	NA	NA	NA	NA	NA	NA	NA
Depreciation	194	165	117	109	NA	NA	NA	NA	NA	NA
Interest Expense	NA	NA	NA	NA	NA	NA	NA	NA	NA	NA
Pretax Income	719	847	619	567	NA	NA	NA	NA	NA	NA
Effective Tax Rate	21.0%	21.8%	18.8%	18.8%	NA	NA	NA	NA	NA	NA
Net Income	568	663	502	460	NA	NA	NA	NA	NA	NA
S&P Core Earnings	568	663	502	NA	NA	NA	NA	NA	NA	NA

Balance Sheet & Other Financial Data (Million $)	2009	2008	2007	2006	2005	2004	2003	2002	2001	2000
Cash	783	607	677	NA	NA	NA	NA	NA	NA	NA
Current Assets	2,390	2,322	NA	NA	NA	NA	NA	NA	NA	NA
Total Assets	8,349	8,329	7,876	NA	NA	NA	NA	NA	NA	NA
Current Liabilities	762	762	NA	NA	NA	NA	NA	NA	NA	NA
Long Term Debt	1,159	1,539	1,268	NA	NA	NA	NA	NA	NA	NA
Common Equity	5,451	5,048	4,887	NA	NA	NA	NA	NA	NA	NA
Total Capital	6,740	6,657	6,167	NA	NA	NA	NA	NA	NA	NA
Capital Expenditures	129	188	115	105	NA	NA	NA	NA	NA	NA
Cash Flow	762	828	620	NA	NA	NA	NA	NA	NA	NA
Current Ratio	3.1	2.9	3.2	NA	NA	NA	NA	NA	NA	NA
% Long Term Debt of Capitalization	17.2	23.1	20.6	Nil	NA	NA	NA	NA	NA	NA
% Net Income of Revenue	12.6	14.7	14.5	15.1	NA	NA	NA	NA	NA	NA
% Return on Assets	6.8	8.2	NA	NA	NA	NA	NA	NA	NA	NA
% Return on Equity	10.8	13.3	NA	NA	NA	NA	NA	NA	NA	NA

Data as orig reptd.; bef. results of disc opers/spec. items. Per share data adj. for stk. divs.; EPS diluted. E-Estimated. NA-Not Available. NM-Not Meaningful. NR-Not Ranked. UR-Under Review.

Office: 3750 Torrey View Court, San Diego, CA 92130.
Telephone: 858-617-2000.
Website: http://www.carefusion.com
Chrmn & CEO: D. Schlotterbeck

COO: D. Winstead
EVP, Secy & General Counsel: J. Stafslien
CFO: E. Borkowski
Chief Acctg Officer: J. Maschal

Investor Contact: C. Cox (858-617-2020)
Board Members: P. Francis, R. Friel, J. Kosecoff, J. M. Losh, G. T. Lucier, E. Miller, M. O'Halleran, D. Schlotterbeck, R. Wayman

Auditor: Ernst & Young
Employees: 16,000

Carnival Corp

STANDARD &POOR'S

S&P Recommendation	HOLD ★★★☆☆	Price $32.02 (as of Nov 27, 2009)	12-Mo. Target Price $35.00	Investment Style Large-Cap Blend

GICS Sector Consumer Discretionary
Sub-Industry Hotels, Resorts & Cruise Lines

Summary Carnival Corp. and Carnival plc own businesses that operate more than 80 cruise ships, as well as tour companies in Alaska and Canada.

Key Stock Statistics (Source S&P, Vickers, company reports)

52-Wk Range	$34.95– 16.80	S&P Oper. EPS 2009E	2.17	Market Capitalization(B)	$26.822	Beta	1.39
Trailing 12-Month EPS	$2.46	S&P Oper. EPS 2010E	2.53	Yield (%)	Nil	S&P 3-Yr. Proj. EPS CAGR(%)	-4
Trailing 12-Month P/E	13.0	P/E on S&P Oper. EPS 2009E	14.8	Dividend Rate/Share	Nil	S&P Credit Rating	BBB+
$10K Invested 5 Yrs Ago	$6,849	Common Shares Outstg. (M)	837.7	Institutional Ownership (%)	53		

Price Performance

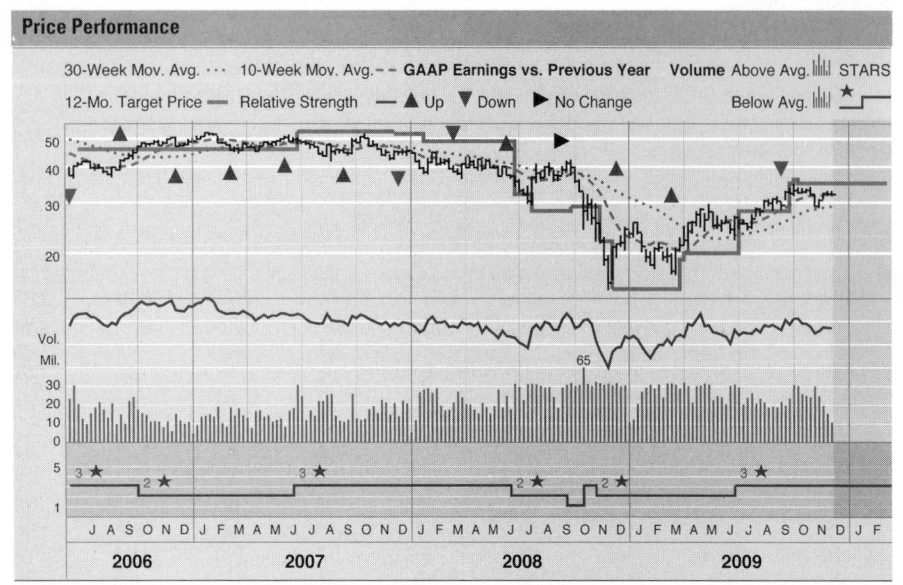

30-Week Mov. Avg. ···· 10-Week Mov. Avg. -- **GAAP Earnings vs. Previous Year** Volume Above Avg. ▍▋▍ STARS
12-Mo. Target Price — Relative Strength — ▲ Up ▼ Down ▶ No Change Below Avg. ▍▍▍ ★

Options: ASE, CBOE, P, Ph

Analysis prepared by **Preeti Rambhiya** on September 29, 2009, when the stock traded at **$ 33.31**.

Highlights

► In our view, positive economic data, recovering consumer confidence in the U.S., a likely bottoming out in pricing trends, and a weaker U.S. dollar are favorable for Carnival, which we think is still struggling to fill ships amid a highly promotional business environment.

► While pricing remains weak, we believe investors should focus on prospective improvement in 2010. That said, we think that capacity growth will create a headwind and limit pricing gains. Also, our outlook for FY 10 (Nov.) onboard spending is improving amid stabilizing consumer confidence. In FY 10, we look for Carnival's overall revenue to increase 10% from the $12.9 billion projected for FY 09. Also, we believe that Carnival has done a good job in cost management, and we expect efficiency savings to continue.

► We think that Carnival's booking windows are lengthening, which we view as a positive. For FY 10, we estimate EPS of $2.53, up from the $2.17 that we project for FY 09.

Investment Rationale/Risk

► Our recommendation on the stock is hold. This reflects our expectation that the market will shrug off economic gloom and increasingly focus on prospects for recovery in 2010. We expect a bottoming out and an upturn in cruise pricing over the next few quarters.

► Downside risks to our target price and recommendation include a prolonged impact from the H1N1 flu virus, continued increases in fuel costs, material disappointment on pricing and advance bookings, significant deterioration in consumer confidence, and terrorism fears.

► Our 12-month target price of $35 is derived from an equal weighted blend of EV/EBITDA and P/E analyses and DCF valuation. Based on our FY 10 EBITDA estimate of $3.80 billion, we apply a multiple of 9.9X, in line with the five-year historical average, producing a value of about $34. Our DCF analysis (WACC 8.9%, terminal rate 2.5%) indicates an intrinsic value of about $34, and our P/E approach implies a value of about $36.

Qualitative Risk Assessment

LOW	MEDIUM	HIGH

Our risk assessment reflects the capital intensity of the cruise sector and its sensitivity to economic cycles. This is offset by our view of Carnival's premier position in a consolidated industry with high barriers to entry, economies of scale, and Carnival's strong operating profile.

Quantitative Evaluations

S&P Quality Ranking NR

D	C	B-	B	B+	A-	A	A+

Relative Strength Rank MODERATE

64

LOWEST = 1   HIGHEST = 99

Revenue/Earnings Data

Revenue (Million $)

	1Q	2Q	3Q	4Q	Year
2009	2,864	2,948	4,139	--	--
2008	3,152	3,378	4,814	3,302	14,646
2007	2,688	2,900	4,321	3,124	13,033
2006	2,463	2,662	3,905	2,809	11,839
2005	2,396	2,519	3,605	2,567	11,087
2004	1,980	2,256	3,245	2,243	9,727

Earnings Per Share ($)

2009	0.32	E0.30	1.33	E0.14	E2.17
2008	0.30	0.49	1.64	0.46	2.86
2007	0.35	0.48	1.64	0.44	2.95
2006	0.31	0.46	1.49	0.51	2.77
2005	0.42	0.49	1.36	0.43	2.70
2004	0.25	0.41	1.23	0.36	2.24

Fiscal year ended Nov. 30. Next earnings report expected: Mid December. EPS Estimates based on S&P Operating Earnings; historical GAAP earnings are as reported.

Dividend Data (Dates: mm/dd Payment Date: mm/dd/yy)

Amount ($)	Date Decl.	Ex-Div. Date	Stk. of Record	Payment Date
0.400	10/31	11/19	11/21	12/12/08

Dividends have been paid since 1988. Source: Company reports.

Please read the Required Disclosures and Analyst Certification on the last page of this report.

The McGraw-Hill Companies

Carnival Corp

Business Summary September 29, 2009

CORPORATE OVERVIEW. Carnival Corp. is part of the world's largest cruise ship business, and has grown significantly through acquisitions and the addition of new ships. In 2003, Carnival merged with P&O Princess Cruises plc, which was renamed Carnival plc (CUK 34, Hold). As of January 2009, the combined Carnival operated 88 cruise ships with capacity for more than 169,000 passengers (based on two passengers per cabin, even though some cabins could accommodate more passengers). Also, Carnival has tour operations in Alaska and the Canadian Yukon.

With Carnival's dual listing company (DLC) format, there are separate stocks trading under the Carnival Corp. and Carnival plc names. Each company has retained its separate legal identity, but the two share a single senior executive management team, have identical boards of directors, and are run as if they were a single economic enterprise. In valuing the shares, we look at the combined financial results and equity base of the Carnival entities.

MARKET PROFILE. Looking ahead, we expect demand for cruise ship vacations to grow. In the U.S., we believe that most people have never taken a multi-night cruise ship vacation, and we expect that an aging U.S. population will lead to more interest in cruises. Also, we believe that a continued industry emphasis on providing ships with more features and the addition of more local ports will bolster passenger demand.

COMPETITIVE LANDSCAPE. We see Carnival enhancing its competitive position through the addition of new ships, which should encourage both returning and new customers. As of January 2009, there were 17 Carnival ships under contract for construction. These ships were expected to enter service between March 2009 and June 2012. However, one or more other ships could leave Carnival's fleet during this period.

In terms of capacity, Carnival was recently more than twice the size of its biggest competitor -- Royal Caribbean Cruises Ltd. (RCL 24, Buy).

Company Financials Fiscal Year Ended Nov. 30

Per Share Data ($)	2008	2007	2006	2005	2004	2003	2002	2001	2000	1999
Tangible Book Value	18.52	19.01	17.10	15.47	13.96	11.83	11.48	10.13	8.84	8.86
Cash Flow	4.39	4.24	3.89	3.91	3.13	2.46	2.38	2.21	2.08	2.06
Earnings	2.86	2.95	2.77	2.77	2.70	2.24	1.66	1.73	1.58	1.60	1.66
Dividends	1.60	1.38	1.03	0.80	0.52	0.44	0.42	0.42	0.42	0.38
Payout Ratio	56%	47%	37%	30%	23%	27%	24%	27%	26%	23%
Prices:High	45.22	52.73	56.14	58.98	58.75	39.84	34.64	34.94	51.25	53.50
Prices:Low	14.85	41.70	36.40	45.78	39.75	20.34	22.07	16.95	18.31	38.13
P/E Ratio:High	6	18	20	22	26	24	20	22	32	32
P/E Ratio:Low	2	14	13	17	18	12	13	11	11	23

Income Statement Analysis (Million $)	2008	2007	2006	2005	2004	2003	2002	2001	2000	1999
Revenue	14,646	13,033	11,839	11,087	9,727	6,718	4,368	4,536	3,779	3,497
Operating Income	3,921	3,826	3,601	3,541	2,985	1,968	1,444	1,448	1,233	1,188
Depreciation	1,249	1,101	988	902	812	585	382	372	288	244
Interest Expense	466	367	312	330	284	195	111	121	41.4	47.0
Pretax Income	2,377	2,424	2,240	2,184	1,901	1,223	959	948	967	1,044
Effective Tax Rate	1.98%	0.10%	NM	NM	2.47%	2.37%	NM	2.34%	0.11%	0.27%
Net Income	2,330	2,408	2,279	2,257	1,854	1,194	1,016	926	965	1,027

Balance Sheet & Other Financial Data (Million $)	2008	2007	2006	2005	2004	2003	2002	2001	2000	1999
Cash	650	943	1,163	1,178	643	1,070	667	1,421	189	522
Current Assets	1,650	1,976	1,995	2,215	1,728	2,132	1,132	1,959	549	792
Total Assets	33,400	34,181	30,552	28,432	27,636	24,491	12,335	11,564	9,831	8,286
Current Liabilities	5,781	7,260	5,415	5,192	5,034	3,315	1,620	1,480	1,715	1,405
Long Term Debt	7,735	6,313	6,355	5,727	6,291	6,918	3,012	2,955	2,099	868
Common Equity	19,098	19,963	18,210	16,972	15,760	13,793	7,418	6,591	5,871	5,931
Total Capital	27,914	26,276	24,565	22,699	22,051	20,711	10,430	9,546	7,970	6,799
Capital Expenditures	3,353	3,312	2,480	1,977	3,586	2,516	1,986	827	1,003	873
Cash Flow	3,579	3,509	3,267	3,159	2,666	1,779	1,398	1,298	1,253	1,271
Current Ratio	0.3	0.3	0.4	0.4	0.3	0.6	0.7	1.3	0.3	0.6
% Long Term Debt of Capitalization	27.7	24.0	25.9	25.2	28.5	33.4	28.9	31.0	26.3	12.8
% Net Income of Revenue	15.9	18.4	19.2	20.4	19.1	17.8	23.3	20.4	25.6	29.4
% Return on Assets	6.9	7.4	7.7	8.1	7.1	6.5	8.5	8.7	10.7	13.3
% Return on Equity	11.9	12.6	13.0	13.8	12.5	11.3	14.5	14.9	16.4	20.1

Data as orig reptd.; bef. results of disc opers/spec. items. Per share data adj. for stk. divs.; EPS diluted. E-Estimated. NA-Not Available. NM-Not Meaningful. NR-Not Ranked. UR-Under Review.

Office: 3655 NW 87th Avenue, Doral, FL 33178-2428.
Telephone: 305-599-2600.
Website: http://www.carnivalcorp.com
Chrmn & CEO: M. Arison

Vice Chrmn & COO: H.S. Frank
SVP & CFO: D. Bernstein
SVP, Secy & General Counsel: A. Perez
Chief Acctg Officer & Cntlr: L. Freedman

Investor Contact: B. Roberts (305-406-4832)
Board Members: M. Arison, R. G. Capen, Jr., R. H. Dickinson, A. W. Donald, P. L. Foschi, H. S. Frank, R. J. Glasier, M. A. Maidique, J. Parker, P. G. Ratcliffe, S. Subotnick, L. A. Weil, R. J. Weisenburger, U. Zucker

Founded: 1974
Domicile: Panama
Employees: 85,900

Caterpillar Inc

STANDARD &POOR'S

S&P Recommendation	BUY ★★★★☆	Price $57.45 (as of Nov 27, 2009)	12-Mo. Target Price $78.00	Investment Style Large-Cap Blend

GICS Sector Industrials
Sub-Industry Construction & Farm Machinery & Heavy Trucks

Summary CAT, the world's largest producer of earthmoving equipment, is also a big maker of electric power generators and engines used in petroleum markets.

Key Stock Statistics (Source S&P, Vickers, company reports)

52-Wk Range	$61.28–21.71	S&P Oper. EPS 2009E	2.25	Market Capitalization(B)	$35.776	Beta	1.86
Trailing 12-Month EPS	$2.14	S&P Oper. EPS 2010E	3.00	Yield (%)	2.92	S&P 3-Yr. Proj. EPS CAGR(%)	-9
Trailing 12-Month P/E	26.9	P/E on S&P Oper. EPS 2009E	25.5	Dividend Rate/Share	$1.68	S&P Credit Rating	A
$10K Invested 5 Yrs Ago	$13,975	Common Shares Outstg. (M)	622.7	Institutional Ownership (%)	64		

Price Performance

30-Week Mov. Avg. · · · 10-Week Mov. Avg. – – GAAP Earnings vs. Previous Year Volume Above Avg. STARS
12-Mo. Target Price — Relative Strength — ▲ Up ▼ Down ► No Change Below Avg. ★

Options: ASE, CBOE, P, Ph

Analysis prepared by **Michael W. Jaffe** on November 24, 2009, when the stock traded at **$ 58.14.**

Highlights

▶ We expect revenues to increase by 10% in 2010. Weak global economies, tight credit markets and the resultant slowdowns in residential and commercial construction have brought large sales declines in recent quarters, particularly for CAT's machinery products. We anticipate challenging conditions for a while longer, but see CAT's business starting a recovery in the near term, on government stimulus packages and the seeming start of a modest global economic recovery. We also see CAT's top line being aided by improved foreign exchange, as the dollar has weakened over the past year.

▶ We look for margins to widen in 2010, reflecting our outlook for improved sales trends. We also see margins being aided to an extent by incremental benefits from CAT's aggressive cost cuts of the past year, which have included major work force reductions, suspension of salary increases for most support and management employees, and large reductions in total compensation for executives and senior managers.

▶ Our 2009 EPS forecast excludes $0.75 a share of expected severance-related charges, including $0.70 a share recorded in the first nine months.

Investment Rationale/Risk

▶ Depressed economic conditions have greatly impacted CAT's client markets in recent quarters. However, in light of aggressive stimulus packages being put in place by governments throughout the world, we believe its business is already in the process of bottoming, and that it has also done a solid job of controlling costs. Based on these factors and our valuation model, we believe CAT's shares are undervalued.

▶ Risks to our opinion and target price include less robust than expected results from global stimulus packages, and an even longer than expected freeze in global credit markets.

▶ The shares recently traded at about 19X our 2010 EPS forecast, which is in the middle of CAT's typical valuation range as it emerged from business downturns. We see the stock as undervalued, based on our belief that government stimulus packages and improving credit conditions will allow its business to bounce back over the next few years, with CAT's recent aggressive streamlining actions likely to lead to robust earnings growth. We set our 12-month target price at $78, or 26X our 2010 EPS forecast, at the high end of its typical early cycle valuation.

Qualitative Risk Assessment

LOW	MEDIUM	HIGH

Our risk assessment for Caterpillar reflects its leading position in many of the end markets it serves, offset by the highly cyclical nature of the construction equipment, agricultural equipment and engine businesses.

Quantitative Evaluations

S&P Quality Ranking A+

D	C	B-	B	B+	A-	A	A+

Relative Strength Rank STRONG

81

LOWEST = 1   HIGHEST = 99

Revenue/Earnings Data

Revenue (Million $)

	1Q	2Q	3Q	4Q	Year
2009	9,225	7,975	7,298	--	--
2008	11,796	13,624	12,981	12,923	51,324
2007	10,016	11,356	11,442	12,144	44,958
2006	9,392	10,605	10,517	11,003	41,517
2005	8,339	9,360	8,977	9,663	36,339
2004	6,467	7,564	7,649	8,571	30,251

Earnings Per Share ($)

2009	-0.19	0.60	0.64	E0.50	E2.25
2008	1.45	1.74	1.39	1.08	5.66
2007	1.23	1.24	1.40	1.50	5.37
2006	1.20	1.52	1.14	1.32	5.17
2005	0.81	1.08	0.94	1.20	4.04
2004	0.60	0.80	0.71	0.78	2.88

Fiscal year ended Dec. 31. Next earnings report expected: Late January. EPS Estimates based on S&P Operating Earnings; historical GAAP earnings are as reported.

Dividend Data (Dates: mm/dd Payment Date: mm/dd/yy)

Amount ($)	Date Decl.	Ex-Div. Date	Stk. of Record	Payment Date
0.420	12/10	01/15	01/20	02/20/09
0.420	04/08	04/16	04/20	05/20/09
0.420	06/10	07/16	07/20	08/20/09
0.420	10/14	10/22	10/26	11/20/09

Dividends have been paid since 1914. Source: Company reports.

Caterpillar Inc

**STANDARD
&POOR'S**

Business Summary November 24, 2009

CORPORATE OVERVIEW. Caterpillar's distinctive yellow machines are in service in nearly every country in the world, with 67% of the company's revenues derived from foreign markets in 2008 (63% in 2007). As of year-end 2008, 71% of CAT's independent dealers were located outside of the U.S. CAT operates in three principal lines of business: Machinery, Engines and Financial Products.

CAT's largest operating segment, the Machinery unit (62% of revenues in 2008 and 39% of operating profits), makes earthmoving equipment. Operations include the design, manufacture, marketing and sale of construction, mining and forestry machinery including track and wheel tractors, track and wheel loaders, pipelayers, motor graders, wheel tractor-scrapers, track and wheel excavators, backhoe loaders, log skidders, log loaders, off-highway trucks, articulated trucks, paving products, skid steer loaders and related parts. This segment also includes logistics services for other companies and the design, manufacture, remanufacture, maintenance and servicing of rail-related products. The division's products are used predominantly in heavy construction

(including infrastructure), general construction, mining, and quarry/aggregates markets. These end markets are very cyclical and competitive.

The engine segment (32% and 49%) makes diesel, heavy fuel and natural gas reciprocating engines for both CAT's own earthmoving equipment and third party customers. Operations includes the design, manufacture, marketing and sale of engines for Caterpillar machinery; electric power generation systems; on-highway vehicles and locomotives; marine, petroleum, construction, industrial, agricultural and other applications; and related parts. This area also includes remanufacturing of Caterpillar engines and a variety of Caterpillar machine and engine components and remanufacturing services for other companies. The division's major end markets are petroleum, electric power generation, industrial, marine and on-highway vehicles.

Company Financials Fiscal Year Ended Dec. 31

Per Share Data ($)	2008	2007	2006	2005	2004	2003	2002	2001	2000	1999
Tangible Book Value	5.51	14.88	7.07	9.77	8.34	6.48	5.51	5.75	5.97	5.56
Cash Flow	8.80	8.09	7.52	6.14	4.85	3.48	2.91	2.85	2.97	2.63
Earnings	5.66	5.37	5.17	4.04	2.88	1.57	1.15	1.16	1.51	1.32
S&P Core Earnings	4.56	5.46	5.48	4.05	2.76	1.50	0.20	0.16	NA	NA
Dividends	1.68	1.32	1.10	0.91	0.78	0.71	0.70	0.69	0.67	0.63
Payout Ratio	30%	25%	21%	23%	27%	45%	61%	59%	44%	48%
Prices:High	85.96	87.00	82.03	59.88	49.36	42.48	30.00	28.42	27.56	33.22
Prices:Low	31.95	57.98	57.05	41.31	34.25	20.62	16.88	19.88	14.78	21.00
P/E Ratio:High	15	16	16	15	17	27	26	24	18	25
P/E Ratio:Low	6	11	11	10	12	13	15	17	10	16

Income Statement Analysis (Million $)										
Revenue	51,324	44,958	41,517	36,339	30,251	22,763	20,152	20,450	20,175	19,702
Operating Income	7,569	7,850	7,634	6,029	4,650	3,505	3,060	3,137	3,447	2,999
Depreciation	1,968	1,797	1,602	1,477	1,397	1,347	1,220	1,169	1,022	945
Interest Expense	1,427	1,420	1,297	1,028	750	716	800	942	980	829
Pretax Income	4,510	5,026	4,942	3,974	2,766	1,497	1,110	1,172	1,500	1,401
Effective Tax Rate	21.1%	29.6%	28.4%	28.2%	26.4%	26.6%	28.1%	31.3%	29.8%	32.5%
Net Income	3,557	3,541	3,537	2,854	2,035	1,099	798	805	1,053	946
S&P Core Earnings	2,867	3,604	3,748	2,860	1,951	1,052	133	98.7	NA	NA

Balance Sheet & Other Financial Data (Million $)										
Cash	1,517	1,122	530	1,108	445	342	309	400	334	548
Current Assets	31,633	25,477	23,093	22,790	20,856	16,791	14,628	13,400	12,521	11,734
Total Assets	67,782	56,132	50,879	47,069	43,091	36,465	32,851	30,657	28,464	26,635
Current Liabilities	26,069	22,245	19,252	19,092	16,210	12,621	11,344	10,276	8,568	8,178
Long Term Debt	22,834	17,829	17,680	15,677	15,837	14,078	11,596	11,291	11,334	9,928
Common Equity	6,087	8,883	6,859	8,432	7,467	6,078	5,472	5,611	5,600	5,465
Total Capital	29,575	26,712	24,539	24,109	23,304	20,156	17,068	16,902	16,934	15,393
Capital Expenditures	4,011	3,040	2,675	2,415	2,114	1,765	1,773	1,968	1,388	1,280
Cash Flow	5,525	5,338	5,139	4,331	3,432	2,446	2,018	1,974	2,075	1,891
Current Ratio	1.2	1.2	1.2	1.2	1.3	1.3	1.3	1.3	1.5	1.4
% Long Term Debt of Capitalization	77.2	66.7	72.0	65.0	68.0	69.8	67.9	66.8	66.9	64.5
% Net Income of Revenue	6.9	7.9	8.5	7.9	6.7	4.8	4.0	3.9	5.2	4.8
% Return on Assets	5.7	6.6	7.2	6.3	5.1	3.2	2.5	2.7	3.8	3.7
% Return on Equity	47.5	45.0	46.3	35.9	30.0	19.0	14.4	14.4	19.0	17.9

Data as orig reptd.; bef. results of disc opers/spec. items. Per share data adj. for stk. divs.; EPS diluted. E-Estimated. NA-Not Available. NM-Not Meaningful. NR-Not Ranked. UR-Under Review.

Office: 100 N.E. Adams Street, Peoria, IL 61629.
Telephone: 309-675-1000.
Email: catir@cat.com
Website: http://www.cat.com

Chrmn & CEO: J.W. Owens
Pres: L.C. Calil
Investor Contact: D. Burritt
CTO: T.L. Utley

Chief Acctg Officer: J.A. Copeland
Board Members: W. Blount, J. R. Brazil, D. M. Dickinson, J. T. Dillon, E. V. Fife, G. D. Fosler, J. Gallardo, D. Goode, P. Magowan, W. A. Osborn, J. W. Owens, C. D. Powell, E. B. Rust, Jr., S. C. Schwab, J. I. Smith

Founded: 1925
Domicile: Delaware
Employees: 112,887

CB Richard Ellis Group Inc

STANDARD &POOR'S

S&P Recommendation [HOLD] ★★★☆☆

Price	12-Mo. Target Price	Investment Style
$10.82 (as of Nov 27, 2009)	$13.00	Large-Cap Growth

GICS Sector Financials
Sub-Industry Real Estate Services

Summary CB Richard Ellis Group is a global commercial real estate services company.

Key Stock Statistics (Source S&P, Vickers, company reports)

52-Wk Range	$13.77–2.34	S&P Oper. EPS 2009**E**	0.30	Market Capitalization(B)	$3.168	Beta	2.66
Trailing 12-Month EPS	$-4.30	S&P Oper. EPS 2010**E**	0.70	Yield (%)	Nil	S&P 3-Yr. Proj. EPS CAGR(%)	-20
Trailing 12-Month P/E	NM	P/E on S&P Oper. EPS 2009**E**	36.1	Dividend Rate/Share	Nil	S&P Credit Rating	NA
$10K Invested 5 Yrs Ago	$12,067	Common Shares Outstg. (M)	292.8	Institutional Ownership (%)	NM		

Price Performance

30-Week Mov. Avg. · · · · 10-Week Mov. Avg. – – **GAAP Earnings vs. Previous Year** Volume Above Avg. STARS
12-Mo. Target Price — Relative Strength — ▲ Up ▼ Down ▶ No Change Below Avg.

J A S O N D | J F M A M J J A S O N D | J F M A M J J A S O N D | J F M A M J J A S O N D | J F
2006 | 2007 | 2008 | 2009

Options: ASE, CBOE, P, Ph

Analysis prepared by **Robert McMillan** on October 30, 2009, when the stock traded at **$ 10.47**.

Highlights

► After a 15% decline in 2008, we expect revenues to drop about 23% in 2009, reflecting lower sales activity due to continued weakness in the global credit markets, before rising 30% in 2010 on an expected rebound in commercial real estate transactions. We look for CBG's property management and investment management businesses to recover before its sales and leasing business. We think a gradual thawing of the credit markets and more prudent underwriting will contribute to an eventual and sustained pickup in the property sales business, while a rebound in the economy should help the leasing business.

► During the third quarter, operating income fell 47% (an improvement from the 56% decline in the second quarter) on declines in the Americas and Europe and investment management businesses; operating income in the Asia-Pacific region rose. We think the company's restructuring business could benefit in the near term from the rush to sell distressed properties. We think aggressive expense reductions should improve CBG's operating leverage.

► We see EPS of $0.30 in 2009 and $0.70 in 2010.

Investment Rationale/Risk

► We see CBG suffering from a sharp downturn in commercial real estate activity and turmoil in the credit markets. Longer term, however, we expect the company to benefit from its large size and broad array of products and services relative to peers. We think the global reach of CBG's operations helps generate economies of scale that few other real estate firms can match, helping create sustainable barriers to entry. Nevertheless, we see the shares remaining volatile until the turmoil in the financial markets abates.

► Risks to our recommendation and target price include lower-than-expected demand for office and industrial space, greater competition, and a further decline in financing activity for commercial real estate transactions.

► The stock recently traded at a P/E of 15.8X our 2010 EPS estimate. Our 12-month target price of $13 reflects a P/E multiple of about 19X our 2010 forecast, on our assumption that the multiple will gradually expand as concerns about tight credit conditions abate and CBG's operating prospects improve. We believe CBG's recent equity and debt offerings have helped ease concerns about its liquidity.

Qualitative Risk Assessment

LOW	MEDIUM	HIGH

Our risk assessment reflects ongoing turmoil in the capital markets and continuing near-term declines in commercial real estate transactions, which we think outweigh the company's position as one of the world's largest commercial real estate firms.

Quantitative Evaluations

S&P Quality Ranking NR

D	C	B-	B	B+	A-	A	A+

Relative Strength Rank MODERATE

31

LOWEST = 1   HIGHEST = 99

Revenue/Earnings Data

Revenue (Million $)

	1Q	2Q	3Q	4Q	Year
2009	890.5	955.7	--	--	--
2008	1,231	1,315	1,300	1,283	5,129
2007	1,214	1,490	1,493	1,837	6,034
2006	903.5	751.3	967.9	1,409	4,032
2005	538.3	672.2	744.2	956.0	2,911
2004	441.0	550.9	575.0	798.2	2,365

Earnings Per Share ($)

2009	-0.14	-0.02	0.04	E0.26	E0.30
2008	0.10	0.08	0.15	0.03	0.34
2007	0.05	0.59	0.48	0.53	1.65
2006	0.16	0.27	0.39	0.53	1.35
2005	0.06	0.22	0.25	0.41	0.95
2004	-0.09	0.01	0.05	0.29	0.30

Fiscal year ended Dec. 31. Next earnings report expected: Mid February. EPS Estimates based on S&P Operating Earnings; historical GAAP earnings are as reported.

Dividend Data

No cash dividends have been paid.

Please read the Required Disclosures and Analyst Certification on the last page of this report.

The McGraw-Hill Companies

CB Richard Ellis Group Inc

STANDARD &POOR'S

Business Summary October 30, 2009

CB Richard Ellis Group, Inc. is one of the largest global commercial real estate services companies in the world. The company's business is focused on several service competencies, including strategic advice and execution assistance for property leasing and sales, forecasting, valuations, origination and servicing of commercial mortgage loans, facilities and project management, and real estate investment management. The company generates revenues both on a per project or transaction basis and from annual management fees.

The company's primary business objective is to leverage its integrated global platform to garner an increasing share of industry revenues relative to competitors. CBG believes this will enable the company to maximize and sustain its long-term cash flow and increase long-term stockholder value. Management's strategy to achieve these business objectives consists of several elements: increasing revenues from large clients; capitalizing on cross-selling opportunities; continuing to grow the investment management business; expanding through fill-in acquisitions; and focusing on improving operating efficiency.

CBG's Real Estate Services business offers a broad spectrum of services to occupiers/tenants and investors/owners. Real estate services include offering strategic advice and execution to owners, investors and occupiers of real estate in connection with the leasing, disposition and acquisition of property. During 2008, the company advised on over 29,000 lease transactions (compared with 31,000 in 2007) involving aggregate rents of approximately $43.2 billion (down from $48.3 billion in 2007) and over 4,600 real estate sales transactions (compared with 7,000 in 2007) with an aggregate value of approximately $39.3 billion (versus $87.8 billion in 2007). Given continued turmoil in the economy as well as more stringent lending and credit conditions, which have hampered buying activity, we expect activity in this business to remain very weak in 2009. This segment also provides investment sales property and valuation advice.

Company Financials Fiscal Year Ended Dec. 31

Per Share Data ($)	2008	2007	2006	2005	2004	2003	2002	2001	2000	1999
Tangible Book Value	NM	NM	NM	NM	NM	NM	NA	NA	NA	NA
Cash Flow	0.84	2.09	1.64	1.14	0.56	0.38	NA	NA	NA	NA
Earnings	0.34	1.65	1.35	0.95	0.30	-0.11	0.15	0.32	NA	NA
S&P Core Earnings	-1.30	1.71	1.33	0.94	0.30	NA	NA	NA	NA	NA
Dividends	Nil	Nil	Nil	Nil	Nil	Nil	NA	NA	NA	NA
Payout Ratio	Nil	Nil	Nil	Nil	Nil	Nil	NA	NA	NA	NA
Prices:High	24.50	42.74	34.26	19.92	11.36	NA	NA	NA	NA	NA
Prices:Low	3.00	17.49	19.46	10.40	6.03	NA	NA	NA	NA	NA
P/E Ratio:High	72	26	25	21	37	NA	NA	NA	NA	NA
P/E Ratio:Low	9	11	14	11	20	NA	NA	NA	NA	NA

Income Statement Analysis (Million $)	2008	2007	2006	2005	2004	2003	2002	2001	2000	1999
Commissions	Nil	Nil	Nil	Nil	Nil	Nil	NA	NA	NA	NA
Interest Income	18.0	29.0	9.80	9.30	4.30	6.00	NA	NA	NA	NA
Total Revenue	5,129	6,034	4,032	2,911	2,365	1,949	1,170	675	NA	NA
Interest Expense	167	163	45.0	54.3	65.4	71.3	NA	NA	NA	NA
Pretax Income	134	592	523	358	108	-41.0	48.8	42.5	NA	NA
Effective Tax Rate	85.4%	32.5%	37.9%	38.8%	40.2%	NM	61.7%	50.8%	NA	NA
Net Income	73.7	388	319	217	64.7	-34.7	18.7	20.9	NA	NA
S&P Core Earnings	-272	403	314	216	64.0	NA	NA	NA	NA	NA

Balance Sheet & Other Financial Data (Million $)	2008	2007	2006	2005	2004	2003	2002	2001	2000	1999
Total Assets	5,818	6,243	5,945	2,816	2,272	2,213	1,325	1,359	NA	NA
Cash Items	159	392	244	449	257	164	79.7	57.5	NA	NA
Receivables	962	1,337	985	739	532	553	NA	NA	NA	NA
Securities Owned	Nil	Nil	Nil	Nil	Nil	Nil	NA	NA	NA	NA
Securities Borrowed	Nil	Nil	Nil	Nil	Nil	Nil	NA	NA	NA	NA
Due Brokers & Customers	Nil	Nil	Nil	Nil	Nil	Nil	NA	NA	NA	NA
Other Liabilities	1,937	2,428	1,906	1,138	809	833	NA	NA	NA	NA
Capitalization:Debt	2,254	1,992	2,193	821	761	1,061	NA	NA	NA	NA
Capitalization:Equity	1,211	989	1,182	794	560	333	251	257	NA	NA
Capitalization:Total	3,465	3,244	3,573	1,622	1,321	1,394	779	794	NA	NA
% Return on Revenue	1.4	6.4	7.8	7.4	2.7	NM	1.6	3.1	NA	NA
% Return on Assets	1.2	6.4	7.2	8.5	2.8	NM	1.4	NA	NA	NA
% Return on Equity	6.7	35.8	32.2	32.0	14.4	NM	7.4	NA	NA	NA

Data as orig reptd.; bef. results of disc opers/spec. items. Per share data adj. for stk. divs.; EPS diluted. E-Estimated. NA-Not Available. NM-Not Meaningful. NR-Not Ranked. UR-Under Review.

Office: 11150 Santa Monica Blvd Ste 1600, Los Angeles, CA 90025-3385.
Telephone: 310-405-8900.
Website: http://www.cbre.com
Chrmn: R.C. Blum

Pres & CEO: W.B. White
Vice Chrmn: R.E. Wirta
COO & EVP: C.W. Frese, Jr.
EVP & Chief Acctg Officer: G. Borok

Investor Contact: N. Kormeluk (949-809-4308)
Board Members: R. C. Blum, P. M. Daniels, C. F. Feeny, B. M. Freeman, M. Kantor, F. V. Malek, J. J. Su, B. White, G. L. Wilson, R. Wirta

Founded: 2001
Domicile: Delaware
Employees: 30,000

The McGraw-Hill Companies

CBS Corp

STANDARD &POOR'S

S&P Recommendation SELL ★★☆☆☆

Price $13.17 (as of Nov 27, 2009)	**12-Mo. Target Price** $10.00	**Investment Style** Large-Cap Value

GICS Sector Consumer Discretionary
Sub-Industry Broadcasting & Cable TV

Summary This major operator of TV, radio, and outdoor advertising properties is one of the two companies created after the 2006 separation of the "old" Viacom into two public entities.

Key Stock Statistics (Source S&P, Vickers, company reports)

52-Wk Range	$14.04–3.06	S&P Oper. EPS 2009**E**	0.51	Market Capitalization(B)	$8.236	Beta	2.09
Trailing 12-Month EPS	$0.45	S&P Oper. EPS 2010**E**	0.89	Yield (%)	1.52	S&P 3-Yr. Proj. EPS CAGR(%)	6
Trailing 12-Month P/E	29.3	P/E on S&P Oper. EPS 2009**E**	25.8	Dividend Rate/Share	$0.20	S&P Credit Rating	BBB-
$10K Invested 5 Yrs Ago	NA	Common Shares Outstg. (M)	677.2	Institutional Ownership (%)	79		

Price Performance

30-Week Mov. Avg. · · · 10-Week Mov. Avg. - - **GAAP Earnings vs. Previous Year** Volume Above Avg. STARS
12-Mo. Target Price — Relative Strength — ▲ Up ▼ Down ▶ No Change Below Avg.

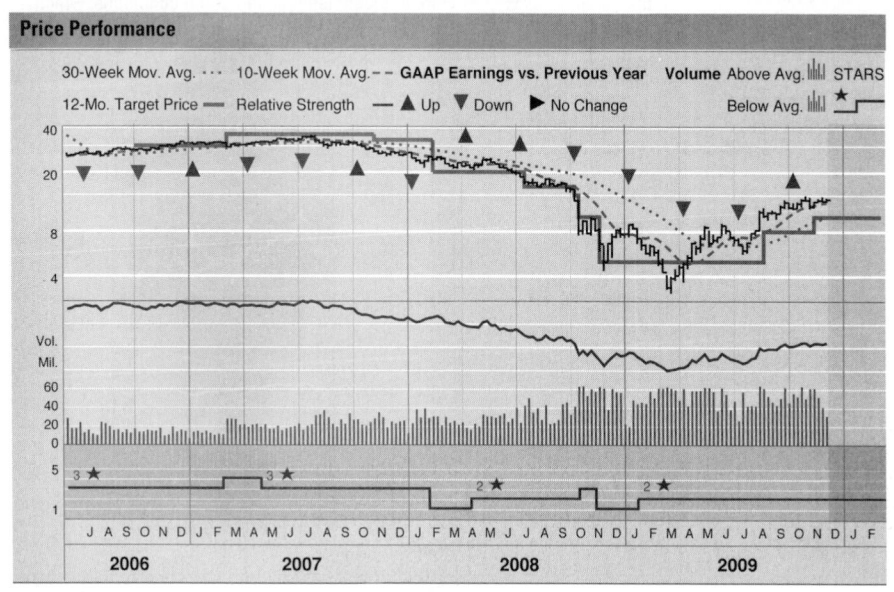

Options: ASE, CBOE, P

Analysis prepared by **Tuna N. Amobi, CFA, CPA** on November 17, 2009, when the stock traded at **$13.67**.

Highlights

▶ After an expected 2009 consolidated revenue decline of 8% (on sharp drops in all of the core local advertising businesses), we expect a modest recovery of more than 3% growth in 2010, to about $13.2 billion. This should mainly reflect improvements in the TV and outdoor divisions, and relatively modest gains for the publishing and interactive businesses, partly offset by some further contraction in the radio division. Starting in the 2009 fourth quarter, management realigned its segment presentation into entertainment, cable networks, publishing, local broadcasting, and outdoor divisions.

▶ We project 2009 total EBITDA to decline about 30% to $1.84 billion -- near the mid-point of management's guidance range of $1.725 billion to $1.925 billion. However, with improved operating leverage reflecting restructuring-related cost savings, we expect 2010 total EBITDA to sharply advance to more than $2.1 billion.

▶ After D&A, interest expense, and taxes, we forecast 2009 and 2010 operating EPS of $0.51 and $0.89, respectively. Our estimates reflect the company as presently constituted (no major acquisitions or divestitures), and we also assume no sizable share buybacks.

Investment Rationale/Risk

▶ After a string of lackluster results through the 2009 first half, we think CBS's third quarter results showed signs of a meaningful advertising rebound, particularly in its TV businesses. Looking ahead to the fourth quarter and 2010, however, much of this sentiment seems already reflected in the shares, which have risen sharply in recent months. We see a potentially more arduous recovery in radio advertising, amid lingering structural challenges. Also, we think CBS's realignment of its interactive businesses (including CNET) into a new Entertainment segment appears somewhat consistent with an incongruous digital strategy. We also have some corporate governance concerns related to voting control and board independence.

▶ Risks to our opinion and target price include a stronger-than-expected ad rebound; potential upside on CBS network's ratings; a relatively strong balance sheet; and, currency translation.

▶ Based on P/E-to-growth (PEG) analysis using our 2010 estimates, our 12-month target price of $10, suggests potential downside from current levels. The stock recently offered a 1.5% yield. We also note CBS's recent net operating loss carryforwards of more than $1 billion.

Qualitative Risk Assessment

LOW	MEDIUM	HIGH

Our risk assessment reflects what we view as steady free cash flow-generating businesses and ownership of some relatively well-established traditional media brands versus a relatively high exposure to cyclical ad-dependent businesses as well as potential structural challenges.

Quantitative Evaluations

S&P Quality Ranking B-

D	C	B-	B	B+	A-	A	A+

Relative Strength Rank STRONG

86

LOWEST = 1 HIGHEST = 99

Revenue/Earnings Data

Revenue (Million $)

	1Q	2Q	3Q	4Q	Year
2009	3,160	3,006	3,350	--	--
2008	3,654	3,394	3,376	3,527	13,950
2007	3,658	3,375	3,281	3,759	14,073
2006	3,575	3,483	3,379	3,883	14,320
2005	5,577	5,876	5,943	3,828	14,536
2004	6,772	6,842	5,485	6,296	22,526

Earnings Per Share ($)

2009	-0.08	0.02	0.30	E0.28	E0.51
2008	0.36	0.61	-18.53	0.20	-17.43
2007	0.28	0.55	0.48	0.40	1.70
2006	0.31	0.64	0.42	0.43	1.79
2005	0.72	0.94	0.94	-6.07	-5.27
2004	0.82	0.86	0.84	-20.42	-17.56

Fiscal year ended Dec. 31. Next earnings report expected: Mid February. EPS Estimates based on S&P Operating Earnings; historical GAAP earnings are as reported.

Dividend Data (Dates: mm/dd Payment Date: mm/dd/yy)

Amount ($)	Date Decl.	Ex-Div. Date	Stk. of Record	Payment Date
0.050	02/18	03/09	03/11	04/01/09
0.050	04/07	06/08	06/10	07/01/09
0.050	07/29	09/08	09/10	10/01/09
0.050	11/16	12/09	12/11	01/01/10

Dividends have been paid since 2003. Source: Company reports.

CBS Corp

STANDARD &POOR'S

Business Summary November 17, 2009

CORPORATE OVERVIEW. In its current form, the company is one of the two in-dependent public entities created after the early 2006 separation of the "old" Viacom (which was renamed CBS Corp., while the other entity adopted the "Vi-acom" name). Pursuant to the separation, each Class A and B shareholder of the "old" Viacom received 0.5 of a share of corresponding A or B stock of each of the new entities. We believe that CBS Corp. was the lower-growth entity resulting from the separation, and that it was targeted to value-oriented in-vestors. Nearly 70% of its revenues are generated from advertising-related businesses.

The television segment includes the CBS networks, CW network (a new joint venture with Time Warner's WB), 39 owned and operated (O&O) TV stations, Showtime cable networks and Paramount/King World TV production and syn-dication. The radio division, CBS Radio, operates 137 radio stations in 29 U.S. markets (it also has a programming agreement with, and minority stake in Westwood One). The outdoor unit, CBS Outdoor, operates billboards and out-of-home displays in the U.S. and abroad. The publishing segment mainly in-cludes book publishers Simon & Schuster. In 2006, CBS sold its Paramount Parks for $1.24 billion in cash. It also owns a start-up movie studio to help pro-vide some content to Showtime. (The company recently realigned its segment presentation into the entertainment, cable networks, pubnlishing, local broad-casting, and outdoor divisions).

CORPORATE STRATEGY. In June 2008, aiming to bulk up its online businesses, CBS acquired CNET Networks for about $1.8 billion in cash. CNET became part of a new interactive segment (including its online audience network), aligned into five new verticals: Technology, Entertainment, Sports, News and Business. CBS's online video syndication network has several distribution partners such as AOL, Microsoft, Comcast, Joost, Bebo, Brightcove, Netvibes, Sling Media, and Veoh. In recent years, the company has divested several dozen radio stations (and some TV stations) in smaller markets. In May 2007, CBS acquired Last.fm, a music-based social network with nearly 20 million users in more than 200 countries, for $280 million in cash. In January 2006, CBS acquired College Sports Network cable channel for about $325 million in stock.

Company Financials Fiscal Year Ended Dec. 31

Per Share Data ($)	2008	2007	2006	2005	2004	2003	2002	2001	2000	1999
Tangible Book Value	NM	NM	NM	NM	NM	NM	NM	NM	NM	NM
Cash Flow	-16.64	2.34	2.36	-9.91	-16.62	2.77	3.55	3.31	3.04	3.43
Earnings	-17.43	1.70	1.79	-5.27	-17.56	1.62	2.48	-0.26	-0.60	1.02
S&P Core Earnings	-7.03	1.72	1.90	1.10	2.92	2.40	2.08	-0.76	NA	NA
Dividends	1.06	0.94	0.68	0.56	0.50	0.24	Nil	Nil	Nil	Nil
Payout Ratio	NM	55%	NM	NM	NM	15%	Nil	Nil	Nil	Nil
Prices:High	27.18	35.75	32.04	77.98	90.10	99.50	103.78	119.00	151.75	120.87
Prices:Low	4.36	25.57	23.85	59.86	60.18	66.22	59.50	56.50	88.63	70.75
P/E Ratio:High	NM	21	18	NM	NM	61	42	NM	NM	NM
P/E Ratio:Low	NM	15	13	NM	NM	41	24	NM	NM	NM

Income Statement Analysis (Million $)										
Revenue	13,950	14,073	14,320	14,536	22,526	26,585	24,606	23,223	20,044	12,859
Operating Income	2,691	3,078	3,135	3,165	5,838	5,957	5,542	4,667	4,243	2,162
Depreciation	532	456	440	499	810	1,000	946	3,087	2,224	845
Interest Expense	547	571	566	720	719	776	848	963	822	449
Pretax Income	-12,593	2,052	2,036	-7,513	-13,676	2,861	3,695	656	436	783
Effective Tax Rate	NM	40.0%	32.0%	NM	NM	55.9%	39.2%	NM	NM	52.5%
Net Income	-11,673	1,231	1,383	-8,322	-15,060	1,435	2,207	-220	-364	372
S&P Core Earnings	-4,713	1,247	1,468	871	2,497	2,087	1,845	-656	NA	NA

Balance Sheet & Other Financial Data (Million $)										
Cash	420	1,347	3,075	1,655	928	851	631	727	934	681
Current Assets	5,193	6,031	8,144	6,796	7,494	7,736	7,167	7,206	7,832	5,198
Total Assets	26,889	40,430	43,509	43,030	68,002	89,849	89,754	90,810	82,646	24,486
Current Liabilities	4,801	4,405	4,400	5,379	6,880	7,585	7,341	7,562	7,758	4,400
Long Term Debt	6,975	6,979	7,027	7,153	9,649	9,683	10,205	10,824	12,474	Nil
Common Equity	8,597	21,472	24,153	21,737	59,862	63,205	62,488	62,717	47,967	11,132
Total Capital	15,593	30,490	32,862	31,007	70,879	73,812	74,337	75,884	67,481	12,379
Capital Expenditures	474	469	394	376	415	534	537	515	659	706
Cash Flow	-11,142	1,687	1,822	-7,823	-14,250	2,435	3,152	2,867	1,860	1,216
Current Ratio	1.1	1.4	1.9	1.3	1.1	1.0	1.0	1.0	1.0	1.2
% Long Term Debt of Capitalization	44.7	24.8	21.0	23.1	13.6	13.1	13.7	14.3	18.5	Nil
% Net Income of Revenue	NM	8.8	9.7	NM	NM	5.4	9.0	NM	NM	2.9
% Return on Assets	NM	2.9	3.2	NM	NM	1.6	2.4	NM	NM	1.5
% Return on Equity	NM	5.5	5.9	NM	NM	2.3	3.5	NM	NM	3.3

Data as orig reptd.; bef. results of disc opers/spec. items. Per share data adj. for stk. divs.; EPS diluted. Data as orig. reptd., for "old" Viacom through third qtr. 2005. E-Estimated. NA-Not Available. NM-Not Meaningful. NR-Not Ranked. UR-Under Review.

Office: 51 W 52nd St, New York, NY 10019-6188.
Telephone: 212-975-4321.
Website: http://www.cbscorporation.com
Chrmn: S.M. Redstone

Pres & CEO: L. Moonves
Vice Chrmn: S.E. Redstone
EVP & CFO: J.R. Ianniello
EVP & General Counsel: L.J. Briskman

Board Members: D. R. Andelman, J. A. Califano, Jr., W. S. Cohen, G. L. Countryman, C. K. Gifford, L. Goldberg, B. S. Gordon, L. M. Griego, A. Kopelson, L. Moonves, D. P. Morris, S. E. Redstone, S. M. Redstone, F. V. Salerno

Founded: 1986
Domicile: Delaware
Employees: 25,920

The McGraw-Hill Companies

Celgene Corp

STANDARD
&POOR'S

S&P Recommendation	STRONG BUY ★★★★★	Price $54.97 (as of Nov 27, 2009)	12-Mo. Target Price $69.00	Investment Style Large-Cap Growth

GICS Sector Health Care
Sub-Industry Biotechnology

Summary This company primarily develops and commercializes small molecule drugs for the treatment of bloodborne and solid tumor cancers and inflammatory disease.

Key Stock Statistics (Source S&P, Vickers, company reports)

52-Wk Range	$58.31– 36.90	S&P Oper. EPS 2009**E**	1.86	Market Capitalization(B)	$25.264	Beta	0.44
Trailing 12-Month EPS	$0.80	S&P Oper. EPS 2010**E**	2.41	Yield (%)	Nil	S&P 3-Yr. Proj. EPS CAGR(%)	26
Trailing 12-Month P/E	68.7	P/E on S&P Oper. EPS 2009**E**	29.6	Dividend Rate/Share	Nil	S&P Credit Rating	NR
$10K Invested 5 Yrs Ago	$40,139	Common Shares Outstg. (M)	459.6	Institutional Ownership (%)	83		

Price Performance

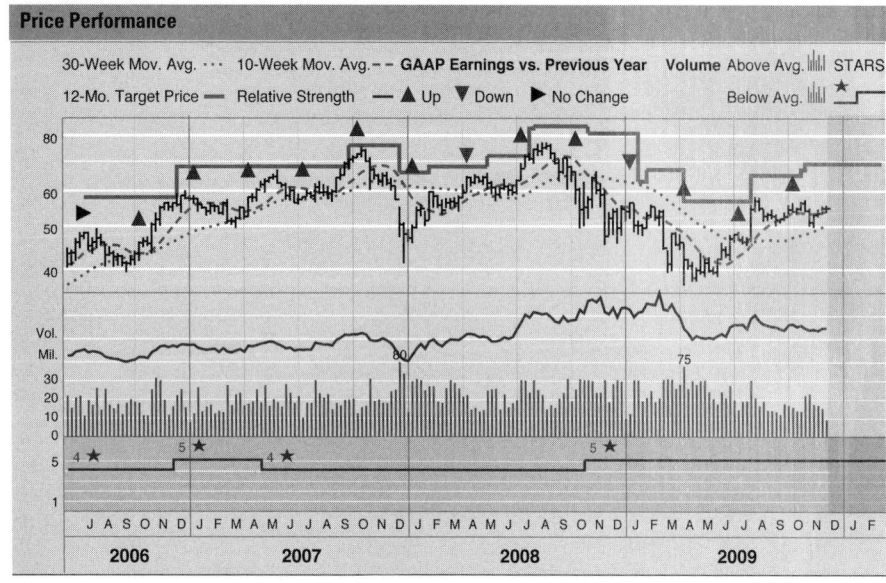

30-Week Mov. Avg. · · · 10-Week Mov. Avg. ‑ ‑ **GAAP Earnings vs. Previous Year** Volume Above Avg. STARS
12-Mo. Target Price — Relative Strength — ▲ Up ▼ Down ► No Change Below Avg. ★

Options: ASE, CBOE, P, Ph

Analysis prepared by **Steven Silver** on October 26, 2009, when the stock traded at **$ 54.19.**

Qualitative Risk Assessment

LOW	MEDIUM	**HIGH**

Our risk assessment reflects the strong competition we see in the blood cancer treatment markets, particularly from Velcade in multiple myeloma. Further, in Thalomid and Revlimid, the company currently depends on two products in the same markets for the majority of its revenues. We also see inherent risk in CELG's drugs maintaining a competitive safety profile versus peers.

Quantitative Evaluations

S&P Quality Ranking   C

D	**C**	B-	B	B+	A-	A	A+

Relative Strength Rank   MODERATE

68

LOWEST = 1   HIGHEST = 99

Highlights

► We project 2009 revenues of $2.66 billion, 19% higher than 2008, with 27% growth in Revlimid sales to $1.69 billion, representing nearly 64% of the total. We continue to see significant long-term growth for Revlimid, with new uses being explored in multiple blood cancers, and with its global expansion still in early stages. Further, we expect Vidaza, recently approved in Europe and re-launched with an enhanced U.S. label, to provide revenue diversification.

► We forecast a 2009 gross margin of around 92%, as CELG improves manufacturing efficiencies and discontinued sales of low-margin Alkeran early in 2009. We expect 2009 operating margin expansion to 36%, from 2008's 33%, and further to 40% in 2010, on leverage from a global infrastructure after the purchase of Pharmion. We also view R&D progress favorably, as pipeline candidates in psoriasis and small cell lung cancer near late-stage study.

► We project adjusted 2009 and 2010 EPS of $1.86 and $2.41, excluding amortized intangible assets. We expect CELG to reduce its effective tax rate to 23% for 2009, from 2008's 24%, and further over time, on higher sales in lower tax jurisdictions.

Investment Rationale/Risk

► In our view, CELG possesses the brightest growth prospects among large-cap biotech peers. Further, we view CELG's financial position as strong, with $2.76 billion in cash and no debt at September 30, 2009, enabling it to aggressively repurchase shares and to acquire additional growth assets. We expect Revlimid and Vidaza to drive revenue growth, and we see Revlimid's prospects bolstered by a positive efficacy result in a key study in newly diagnosed multiple myeloma patients. We also look for the drug to benefit from its oral formulation and superior safety profile. Further, we have a favorable view of CELG's emerging robust pipeline, which we believe is underappreciated and is poised to bolster its long-term growth profile.

► Risks to our opinion and target price include slower-than-expected Revlimid sales growth, reimbursement issues for the drug, and clinical failure of CELG's other pipeline candidates.

► Our 12-month target price of $69 applies a 28.6X multiple to our 2010 adjusted EPS estimate of $2.41, 1.1X its long-term growth rate, a premium to large cap peers, given our view of CELG's superior growth prospects.

Revenue/Earnings Data

Revenue (Million $)

	1Q	2Q	3Q	4Q	Year
2009	605.1	628.7	695.1	--	--
2008	462.6	571.5	592.5	628.3	2,255
2007	293.4	347.9	349.9	414.6	1,406
2006	181.8	197.2	244.8	275.0	898.9
2005	112.4	145.7	129.5	149.3	536.9
2004	82.87	87.75	101.5	105.4	377.5

Earnings Per Share ($)

2009	0.35	0.31	0.46	E0.57	E1.86
2008	-3.98	0.26	0.29	-0.33	-3.46
2007	0.14	0.13	0.09	0.18	0.54
2006	0.04	0.03	0.05	0.06	0.18
2005	0.13	0.03	Nil	0.01	0.18
2004	0.03	0.01	0.06	0.07	0.16

Fiscal year ended Dec. 31. Next earnings report expected: Late January. EPS Estimates based on S&P Operating Earnings; historical GAAP earnings are as reported.

Dividend Data

No cash dividends have been paid.

Celgene Corp

Business Summary October 26, 2009

CORPORATE OVERVIEW. Celgene develops and markets pharmaceuticals to treat cancer, immunological disorders, and other diseases. Its research focuses on small molecule compounds that inhibit Tumor Necrosis Factor alpha (TNFa) production or aberrant estrogen production, or may regulate kinases and ligases (enzymes involved in gene function that may contribute to disease when their proper function is altered).

The company is using its small molecule technology to develop Immunomodulatory Drugs (IMiDs) and Selective Cytokine Inhibitory Drugs (SelCIDs), an array of potent, orally available agents to fight acute and chronic diseases. The company's primary focus to date has been treating multiple myeloma (MM), the second most commonly diagnosed blood cancer. According to the International Myeloma Foundation, there are an estimated 750,000 people with MM worldwide. At any one time, there are more than 85,000 men and women in Europe undergoing treatment for multiple myeloma, and it is estimated that 25,000 people died from this blood cancer in 2007.

To date, Celgene's primary marketed products have been Thalomid and Revlimid. Thalomid is CELG's version of thalidomide, an antiangiogenic agent capable of inhibiting blood vessel growth and down-regulating TNFa. In 1998, Thalomid was approved by the FDA to treat leprosy-related conditions. FDA

approved Thalomid to treat multiple myeloma in May 2006. European rights to Thalomid were re-acquired in the March 2008 acquisition of Pharmion, and the drug was approved in Europe for front-line multiple myeloma in April 2008.

In December 28, 2005, FDA approved Revlimid (the company's primary IMiD) to treat MDS patients with a rare chromosomal deletion (5q minus). Revlimid has been approved by the FDA in combination with dexamethasone for the treatment of relapsed or refractory MM and, in June 2007, was approved in Europe for the same indications. The drug is also being tested in a number of earlier-stage trials including multiple myeloma in a first-line setting, amyloidosis, non-Hodgkin's lymphoma, and various solid tumor cancers. In July 2009, a pivotal Phase III study, MM-015, was stopped at the first interim analysis after an independent data monitoring committee determined that Revlimid plus melphalan and prednisone surpassed its progression-free survival endpoint in newly diagnosed multiple myeloma patients. We expect CELG to file the drug for front-line MM in the U.S. and Europe during 2010.

Company Financials Fiscal Year Ended Dec. 31

Per Share Data ($)	2008	2007	2006	2005	2004	2003	2002	2001	2000	1999
Tangible Book Value	5.37	6.80	4.83	1.48	1.06	0.93	0.85	1.03	1.00	NM
Cash Flow	-3.13	0.60	0.23	0.23	0.18	0.06	-0.31	0.01	-0.05	-0.31
Earnings	-3.46	0.54	0.18	0.18	0.16	0.04	-0.33	-0.01	-0.06	-0.11
S&P Core Earnings	-3.45	0.55	0.19	0.05	0.08	-0.04	-0.33	-0.09	NA	NA
Dividends	Nil	Nil	Nil	Nil	Nil	Nil	Nil	Nil	Nil	Nil
Payout Ratio	Nil	Nil	Nil	Nil	Nil	Nil	Nil	Nil	Nil	Nil
Prices:High	77.39	75.44	60.12	32.68	16.29	12.22	8.05	9.72	19.00	6.05
Prices:Low	45.44	41.26	31.51	12.35	9.37	5.04	2.83	3.60	4.58	0.94
P/E Ratio:High	NM	NM	NM	NM	NM	NM	NM	NM	NM	NM
P/E Ratio:Low	NM	NM	NM	NM	NM	NM	NM	NM	NM	NM

Income Statement Analysis (Million $)

	2008	2007	2006	2005	2004	2003	2002	2001	2000	1999
Revenue	2,255	1,406	899	537	378	271	136	114	84.2	26.2
Operating Income	742	457	200	97.9	52.4	5.38	-31.0	-19.9	-23.9	-21.7
Depreciation	149	31.5	25.7	14.3	9.69	8.03	5.18	5.09	3.72	0.99
Interest Expense	4.44	11.1	9.42	9.50	9.55	5.67	0.03	0.08	2.08	2.84
Pretax Income	-1,369	517	203	84.2	63.2	12.0	-101	-4.14	-18.8	-24.8
Effective Tax Rate	NM	56.2%	66.0%	24.4%	16.5%	NM	NM	NM	NM	NM
Net Income	-1,534	226	69.0	63.7	52.8	12.8	-101	-2.90	-17.0	-21.8
S&P Core Earnings	-1,528	230	71.5	10.8	25.0	-13.0	-88.6	-26.5	NA	NA

Balance Sheet & Other Financial Data (Million $)

	2008	2007	2006	2005	2004	2003	2002	2001	2000	1999
Cash	2,222	2,739	1,982	724	749	667	261	310	161	15.3
Current Assets	2,841	3,084	2,311	973	850	730	296	336	332	27.8
Total Assets	4,445	3,611	2,736	1,247	1,107	791	327	354	347	32.3
Current Liabilities	527	433	240	136	141	71.8	44.3	30.0	33.8	9.30
Long Term Debt	22.2	22.6	400	400	400	400	0.04	11.8	12.3	38.5
Common Equity	3,491	2,844	1,976	636	477	310	277	310	296	-15.7
Total Capital	3,514	2,877	2,376	1,036	877	710	277	322	308	22.8
Capital Expenditures	77.4	64.4	46.1	35.9	36.0	11.2	11.1	7.87	9.64	1.78
Cash Flow	-1,385	258	94.7	77.9	62.4	20.8	-95.8	2.18	-13.3	-20.8
Current Ratio	5.4	7.1	9.6	7.2	6.0	10.2	6.7	11.2	9.8	3.0
% Long Term Debt of Capitalization	0.6	0.8	16.8	38.6	45.6	56.3	0.0	3.7	4.0	168.9
% Net Income of Revenue	NM	16.1	7.7	11.9	14.0	4.7	NM	NM	NM	NM
% Return on Assets	NM	7.1	3.5	5.4	5.5	2.3	NM	NM	NM	NM
% Return on Equity	NM	9.4	5.3	11.4	13.0	4.3	NM	NM	NM	NM

Data as orig reptd.; bef. results of disc opers/spec. items. Per share data adj. for stk. divs.; EPS diluted. E-Estimated. NA-Not Available. NM-Not Meaningful. NR-Not Ranked. UR-Under Review.

Office: 86 Morris Ave, Summit, NJ 07901-3915.
Telephone: 908-673-9000.
Email: info@celgene.com
Website: http://www.celgene.com

Chrmn & CEO: S.J. Barer
Pres, COO & Secy: R.J. Hugin
SVP & CFO: D.W. Gryska
Chief Acctg Officer & Cntlr: A. Van Hoek

Treas: C.B. Elflein
Investor Contact: B.P. Gill (908-673-9530)
Board Members: S. J. Barer, M. D. Casey, R. L. Drake, A. H. Hayes, Jr., R. J. Hugin, G. Kaplan, J. J. Loughlin, E. Mario, W. L. Robb

Founded: 1986
Domicile: Delaware
Employees: 2,441

CenterPoint Energy Inc.

STANDARD &POOR'S

S&P Recommendation	HOLD ★★★☆☆	Price $12.96 (as of Nov 27, 2009)	12-Mo. Target Price $12.00	Investment Style Large-Cap Value

GICS Sector Utilities
Sub-Industry Multi-Utilities

Summary This Houston-based energy company (formerly Reliant Energy) is one of the largest electric and natural gas delivery companies in the U.S.

Key Stock Statistics (Source S&P, Vickers, company reports)

52-Wk Range	$14.53–8.66	S&P Oper. EPS 2009**E**	1.09	Market Capitalization(B)	$5.059	Beta	0.74
Trailing 12-Month EPS	$1.00	S&P Oper. EPS 2010**E**	1.20	Yield (%)	5.86	S&P 3-Yr. Proj. EPS CAGR(%)	1
Trailing 12-Month P/E	13.0	P/E on S&P Oper. EPS 2009**E**	11.9	Dividend Rate/Share	$0.76	S&P Credit Rating	BBB
$10K Invested 5 Yrs Ago	$14,343	Common Shares Outstg. (M)	390.4	Institutional Ownership (%)	67		

Price Performance

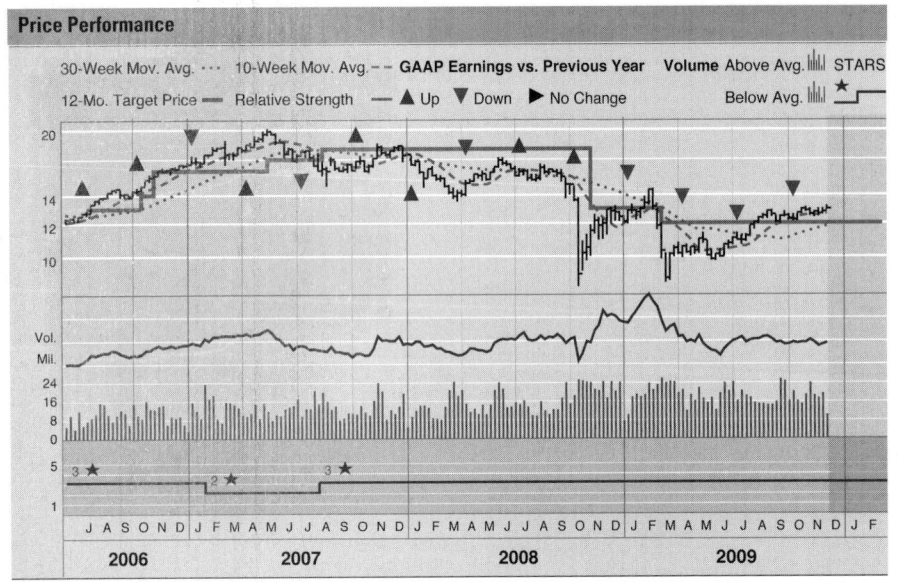

30-Week Mov. Avg. ··· 10-Week Mov. Avg. – – **GAAP Earnings vs. Previous Year** Volume Above Avg. STARS
12-Mo. Target Price — Relative Strength — ▲ Up ▼ Down ▶ No Change Below Avg. ★

Options: ASE, CBOE, P, Ph

Analysis prepared by **Justin McCann** on November 05, 2009, when the stock traded at **$12.74**.

Highlights

► We expect operating EPS in 2009 to decline about 16% from 2008's $1.30. While operating earnings in 2009 will reflect the restoration of the electric revenues lost due to Hurricane Ike and rate increases in the natural gas distribution business, we believe this will be more than offset by a reduced level of earnings at the interstate pipelines and field services operations, reflecting the impact of the weak economy, sharply lower commodity prices, and higher operating and pension expenses.

► For 2010, we expect operating EPS to increase about 10% from anticipated results in 2009. We believe the increase will be driven by reduced operating expenses and a gradual recovery in both the economy and the energy markets.

► As a result of legislation enacted by the Texas Legislature in April 2009, CenterPoint Energy Houston recorded a regulatory asset of $41 million for carrying costs incurred through June 30, 2009, on its expenditures for the Hurricane Ike storm restoration. Of that amount, $14 million was reflected in second-quarter earnings, and the remainder will be recognized over the life of the storm cost recovery bonds the Texas utility commission approved in August 2009.

Investment Rationale/Risk

► The stock has rebounded more than 45% from its 2009 low and is up approximately 2% year to date. The stock had dropped more than 11% on February 25, the day CNP announced a sharp reduction in its 2009 earnings outlook due to an increase in its projected pension expense. While we expect the shares to be restricted by the impact of the economic downturn and the continuing situation in the credit markets, we believe they will be partially supported by a well-above peers dividend yield and the company's improved financial strength.

► Risks to our investment recommendation and target price include a potential weakening of the company's financial strength, including a decreased ability to access capital markets on reasonable terms, as well as a sharp drop in the average P/E of the stock's industry peers.

► Despite the strong rebound in the shares, the dividend yield (recently at 6.0%) was still well above the recent peer average of 5.0%. Given the estimated 63% payout ratio on our EPS estimate for 2010, we believe the dividend is secure. However, we expect the stock to trade at a discount-to-peers P/E of about 10X our EPS estimate. Our 12-month target price is $12.

Qualitative Risk Assessment

LOW	MEDIUM	HIGH

Our risk assessment reflects the strong and steady cash flow we expect from the Houston electric operations, which have a growing service territory; a low commodity risk profile; a generally supportive regulatory environment; and, the gas purchase adjustment clauses that reduce the commodity risks related to the company's more diversified gas distribution operations.

Quantitative Evaluations

S&P Quality Ranking   B

D	C	B-	**B**	B+	A-	A	A+

Relative Strength Rank   MODERATE

69

LOWEST = 1   HIGHEST = 99

Revenue/Earnings Data

Revenue (Million $)

	1Q	2Q	3Q	4Q	Year
2009	2,766	1,640	1,576	--	--
2008	3,363	2,670	2,515	2,774	11,322
2007	3,106	2,033	1,882	2,602	9,623
2006	3,077	1,843	1,935	2,464	9,319
2005	2,762	1,932	2,073	3,212	9,722
2004	2,959	2,241	1,667	2,618	8,510

Earnings Per Share ($)

2009	0.19	0.24	0.31	E0.33	E1.09
2008	0.36	0.30	0.39	0.25	1.30
2007	0.38	0.20	0.27	0.32	1.17
2006	0.28	0.61	0.26	0.20	1.33
2005	0.20	0.09	0.15	0.25	0.67
2004	0.24	0.19	0.05	0.46	0.61

Fiscal year ended Dec. 31. Next earnings report expected: Late February. EPS Estimates based on S&P Operating Earnings; historical GAAP earnings are as reported.

Dividend Data (Dates: mm/dd Payment Date: mm/dd/yy)

Amount ($)	Date Decl.	Ex-Div. Date	Stk. of Record	Payment Date
0.190	01/22	02/11	02/16	03/10/09
0.190	04/23	05/13	05/15	06/10/09
0.190	07/23	08/12	08/14	09/10/09
0.190	10/22	11/12	11/16	12/10/09

Dividends have been paid since 1922. Source: Company reports.

Please read the **Required Disclosures and Analyst Certification** on the last page of this report.

The **McGraw·Hill** Companies

CenterPoint Energy Inc.

STANDARD &POOR'S

Business Summary November 05, 2009

CORPORATE OVERVIEW. CenterPoint Energy (formerly Reliant Energy) is a Houston-based energy delivery company with operations that include electric transmission and distribution (42.8% of operating income in 2008), interstate pipelines (23.0%), natural gas distribution (16.9%), field services (11.5%), and competitive natural gas sales and services (4.9%).

MARKET PROFILE. The CenterPoint Energy Houston Electric (CEHE) utility serves more than 2 million customers in a 5,000 square mile territory that includes the cities of Houston and Galveston, TX, and (with the exception of Texas City), nearly all of the Houston/Galveston metropolitan area. Following the deregulation of the industry in Texas, wholesale and retail suppliers pay the company to deliver the electricity over its transmission lines. The natural gas subsidiary, CenterPoint Energy Resources Corp. (CERC), serves about 3.2 million residential, commercial and industrial customers in Arkansas, Louisiana, Minnesota, Mississippi, Oklahoma and Texas. In 2007, approximately 43% of total demand was accounted for by residential customers, and about 57% was from commercial and industrial customers.

CERC's interstate pipeline business owns and operates approximately 8,000 miles of gas transmission lines primarily located in Arkansas, Illinois, Louisiana, Missouri, Oklahoma and Texas. It also owns and operates six natural gas storage fields with a combined daily volume of about 1.2 billion cubic feet per day. CERC's field services business owns and operates around 3,500 miles of gathering pipelines and processing plants, and around 150 natural gas gathering systems in Arkansas, Oklahoma, Louisiana, and Texas. On January 31, 2007, CNP agreed to discontinue the development of its proposed pipeline with Spectra Energy (the spun-off gas transmission unit of Duke Energy) due to market conditions. The proposed pipeline (announced on June 1, 2006) would have stretched from Texas to Pennsylvania.

Company Financials Fiscal Year Ended Dec. 31

Per Share Data ($)	2008	2007	2006	2005	2004	2003	2002	2001	2000	1999
Tangible Book Value	0.99	NM	NM	NM	NM	NM	NM	13.05	8.11	7.69
Earnings	1.30	1.17	1.33	0.67	0.61	1.37	1.29	3.14	2.68	5.82
S&P Core Earnings	1.31	1.31	1.18	0.75	0.65	1.28	2.17	3.00	NA	NA
Dividends	0.73	0.68	0.60	0.40	0.40	0.40	1.07	1.50	1.50	1.50
Payout Ratio	56%	58%	45%	60%	66%	29%	83%	48%	56%	26%
Prices:High	17.35	20.20	16.87	15.14	12.32	10.49	27.10	50.45	49.00	32.50
Prices:Low	8.48	14.70	11.62	10.55	9.66	4.35	4.24	23.27	19.75	22.75
P/E Ratio:High	13	17	13	23	20	8	21	16	18	6
P/E Ratio:Low	7	13	9	16	16	3	3	7	7	4

Income Statement Analysis (Million $)	2008	2007	2006	2005	2004	2003	2002	2001	2000	1999
Revenue	11,322	9,623	9,319	9,722	8,510	9,760	7,923	46,226	29,339	15,303
Depreciation	708	631	599	541	490	625	616	911	906	911
Maintenance	NA	NA	NA	NA	NA	NA	NA	NA	NA	NA
Fixed Charges Coverage	2.11	1.95	1.80	1.35	1.15	1.37	1.80	3.33	2.60	2.32
Construction Credits	NA	NA	NA	NA	NA	NA	NA	NA	NA	Nil
Effective Tax Rate	38.3%	32.8%	12.6%	40.5%	NM	35.6%	35.0%	33.3%	32.9%	35.0%
Net Income	447	399	432	225	206	420	386	919	771	1,666
S&P Core Earnings	451	444	384	254	224	390	642	868	NA	NA

Balance Sheet & Other Financial Data (Million $)	2008	2007	2006	2005	2004	2003	2002	2001	2000	1999
Gross Property	14,006	13,250	12,567	11,558	10,963	11,812	11,409	24,214	15,260	20,133
Capital Expenditures	1,020	1,114	1,007	693	530	648	854	2,053	1,842	1,179
Net Property	10,296	9,740	9,204	8,492	8,186	11,812	11,409	15,857	15,260	13,267
Capitalization:Long Term Debt	10,181	8,364	7,802	8,568	7,193	10,783	9,194	6,448	5,701	5,666
Capitalization:% Long Term Debt	81.1	82.2	83.4	86.9	86.7	86.0	71.0	48.4	51.0	51.6
Capitalization:Preferred	Nil	Nil	Nil	Nil	Nil	Nil	Nil	Nil	10.0	10.0
Capitalization:% Preferred	Nil	Nil	Nil	Nil	Nil	Nil	Nil	Nil	0.09	0.09
Capitalization:Common	2,037	1,810	1,556	1,296	1,106	1,761	3,756	6,881	5,472	5,296
Capitalization:% Common	13.7	17.8	16.6	13.1	13.3	14.0	29.0	51.6	48.9	48.3
Total Capital	14,851	12,440	12,036	12,769	10,767	12,934	13,180	16,970	13,998	13,694
% Operating Ratio	87.9	87.7	88.8	90.3	88.2	85.8	85.8	96.6	94.9	97.8
% Earned on Net Property	12.7	12.5	11.8	11.3	10.6	21.8	17.2	12.8	13.2	10.0
% Return on Revenue	4.0	4.1	2.8	1.4	2.4	4.3	4.9	2.0	2.6	10.9
% Return on Invested Capital	7.3	8.5	8.3	7.9	7.6	11.1	14.7	11.2	10.3	20.5
% Return on Common Equity	23.2	23.7	30.3	18.7	14.4	26.4	10.3	14.8	14.3	34.7

Data as orig reptd.; bef. results of disc opers/spec. items. Per share data adj. for stk. divs.; EPS diluted. E-Estimated. NA-Not Available. NM-Not Meaningful. NR-Not Ranked. UR-Under Review.

Office: 1111 Louisiana Street, Houston, TX 77002-5230.
Telephone: 713-207-1111.
Email: info@reliantenergy.nl
Website: http://www.centerpointenergy.com

Chrmn: M. Carroll
Pres & CEO: D.M. McClanahan
EVP & CFO: G.L. Whitlock
EVP, Secy & General Counsel: S.E. Rozzell

Investor Contact: M. Paulsen (713-207-6500)
Board Members: D. R. Campbell, M. Carroll, D. Cody, O. H. Crosswell, M. P. Johnson, J. M. Longoria, T. F. Madison, D. M. McClanahan, R. T. O'Connell, S. O. Rheney, M. E. Shannon, P. S. Wareing, S. M. Wolff

Founded: 1882
Domicile: Texas
Employees: 8,801

CenturyTel Inc.

STANDARD &POOR'S

S&P Recommendation **BUY** ★★★★☆	Price $36.31 (as of Nov 27, 2009)	12-Mo. Target Price $38.00	Investment Style Large-Cap Blend

GICS Sector Telecommunication Services
Sub-Industry Integrated Telecommunication Services

Summary CTL acquired larger telecom peer Embarq in a stock deal in July 2009. Combined, the company provides voice service to 7 million customers and Internet service to 2 million customers in both rural towns and larger cities, like Las Vegas.

Key Stock Statistics (Source S&P, Vickers, company reports)

52-Wk Range	$36.59– 23.27	S&P Oper. EPS 2009**E**	3.40	Market Capitalization(B)	$10.803	Beta	0.79
Trailing 12-Month EPS	$3.46	S&P Oper. EPS 2010**E**	3.39	Yield (%)	7.71	S&P 3-Yr. Proj. EPS CAGR(%)	5
Trailing 12-Month P/E	10.5	P/E on S&P Oper. EPS 2009**E**	10.7	Dividend Rate/Share	$2.80	S&P Credit Rating	BBB-
$10K Invested 5 Yrs Ago	$12,824	Common Shares Outstg. (M)	297.5	Institutional Ownership (%)	68		

Price Performance

30-Week Mov. Avg. ···· 10-Week Mov. Avg. - - **GAAP Earnings vs. Previous Year**   **Volume** Above Avg. ▦ STARS
12-Mo. Target Price — Relative Strength — ▲ Up ▼ Down ► No Change   Below Avg. ▦ ★

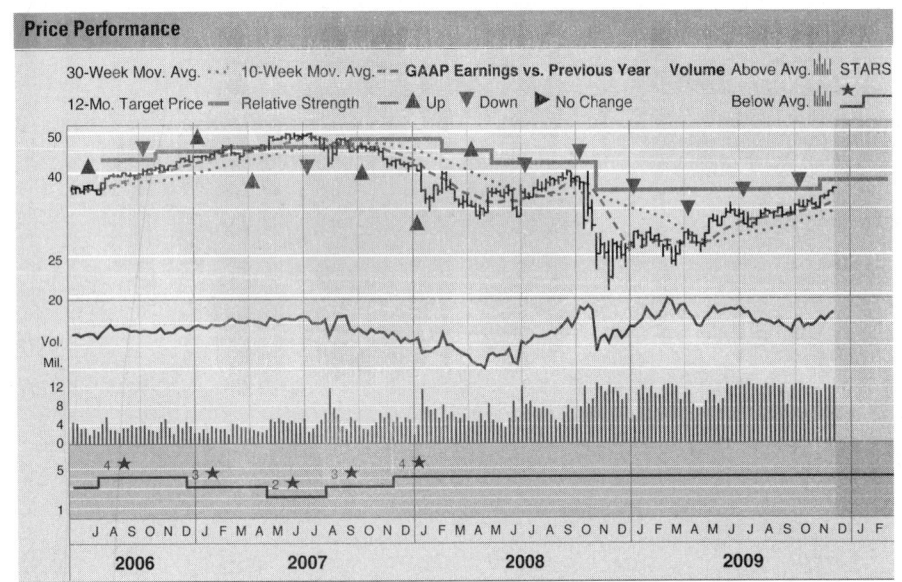

Options: Cycle P, Ph

Analysis prepared by **Todd Rosenbluth** on November 16, 2009, when the stock traded at **$ 34.96**.

Highlights

▶ We see revenues of $7.4 billion in 2010, up from a projected $5.0 billion in 2009 that only partially reflected the acquisition of Embarq in the second half of 2009. We expect approximately two-thirds of CTL's revenues in 2010 to be derived from these new assets. We foresee growth in DSL services being offset by the impact of weakness in voice services on fewer access lines and lower universal service revenues. But as the macroeconomy improves in 2010, we expect CTL to be able to partially stem access line losses.

▶ We look for EBITDA margins of 49% in 2009 and 2010, as benefits from lower personnel costs due to merger synergies are counterbalanced by increased selling and marketing costs and as demand for higher-margin services declines. We look for depreciation costs to decline on a pro-forma basis in 2010.

▶ CTL reduced its share count by 10% in 2008, helping boost EPS. With the completion of the Embarq acquisition and a focus on integration, we expect no additional repurchases. We estimate EPS of $3.40 in 2009 and $3.39 in 2010.

Investment Rationale/Risk

▶ We view the stock-based acquisition of Embarq as positive. We believe CTL received a discounted price for assets that, despite strong competitive pressure, offer sizable operating cost synergies. We think the combined company has credit access and believe its cash flow provides ample dividend support. In addition to cost savings, we see some gains through broadband but also revenue pressure from competitive and economic pressures. We believe CTL's above-average dividend yield adds to its investment appeal.

▶ Risks to our recommendation and target price include adjustments to the universal service fund or access charges, from which CTL receives revenues; operating risk from its recent acquisition; and, an increase in customer migration or line losses.

▶ Supported by a dividend yield of 8%, we think the shares are attractive. Our 12-month target price of $38 is based on an 11X P/E applied to our 2010 EPS estimate, a slight discount to multiples we expect for peers. At our target price, CTL would also trade at a discount on enterprise value/EBITDA basis.

Qualitative Risk Assessment

LOW	MEDIUM	HIGH

Our risk assessment reflects what we see as CTL's relatively strong balance sheet and cash flow generation offset by the competitive nature of its markets and integration of a large acquisition.

Quantitative Evaluations

S&P Quality Ranking   A-

D	C	B-	B	B+	A-	A	A+

Relative Strength Rank   STRONG

86

LOWEST = 1   HIGHEST = 99

Revenue/Earnings Data

Revenue (Million $)

	1Q	2Q	3Q	4Q	Year
2009	636.4	634.5	1,874	--	--
2008	648.6	658.1	650.1	643.0	2,600
2007	600.9	690.0	708.8	656.6	2,656
2006	611.3	608.9	619.8	607.7	2,448
2005	595.3	606.4	657.1	620.5	2,479
2004	593.7	603.6	603.9	606.2	2,407

Earnings Per Share ($)

2009	0.67	0.69	0.50	E0.85	E3.40
2008	0.83	0.88	0.84	1.01	3.56
2007	0.68	1.00	1.01	1.05	3.72
2006	0.55	1.26	0.64	0.62	3.07
2005	0.59	0.64	0.68	0.59	2.49
2004	0.58	0.60	0.63	0.62	2.41

Fiscal year ended Dec. 31. Next earnings report expected: Mid February. EPS Estimates based on S&P Operating Earnings; historical GAAP earnings are as reported.

Dividend Data (Dates: mm/dd Payment Date: mm/dd/yy)

Amount ($)	Date Decl.	Ex-Div. Date	Stk. of Record	Payment Date
0.700	02/26	03/13	03/17	03/31/09
0.700	05/28	06/12	06/16	06/30/09
0.700	08/24	09/03	09/08	09/21/09
0.700	11/18	11/30	12/02	12/15/09

Dividends have been paid since 1974. Source: Company reports.

Please read the Required Disclosures and Analyst Certification on the last page of this report.

The McGraw-Hill Companies

CenturyTel Inc.

STANDARD
&POOR'S

Business Summary November 16, 2009

CORPORATE OVERVIEW. As of September 2009, CenturyTel Inc. operated 7.2 million telephone access lines, following the acquisition of Embarq in July 2009. The company also provided DSL broadband to 2.1 million customers (39% penetration of residential customer base), and has partnered with EchoStar Communications to offer wholesale satellite services to more than 500,000 customers (11% penetration of primary residential lines) through CTL's product bundles. In the third quarter of 2009, 63% of revenues were from voice and network access services, with the remainder from data and fiber transport services.

In early July, 2009, CTL completed its planned acquisition of its larger, fellow telco Embarq Corp (EQ). The deal involved a swap of 1.37 CTL shares per EQ share and the assumption of $6 billion in debt. On a pro-forma basis, the new company had 7.3 million access lines and 2.15 million DSL customers at the end of June 2009. Revenues would have been $1.96 billion during the second quarter of 2009 and EBITDA of $968 as a combined company, before any synergies. The new company plans to operate under the name CenturyLink and a formal name change is likely in 2010.

COMPETITIVE LANDSCAPE. We believe CTL faces challenges from technology substitution to cable telephony and to wireless. The penetration of the nec-

essary broadband connection is smaller in the Tier II and Tier III markets in which CTL previously operated; as of late 2009, more than 65% of its access line customers had the option of cable broadband from companies such as Comcast. However, Embarq's operations included larger cities in Florida and Nevada that faced greater competition and were hurt by weakness in the housing market. In the third quarter of 2009, CTL highlighted that primary residential access lines declined 10.3% from a year earlier, which is narrower than the 11.2% line loss on a pro-forma basis in the second quarter. But in our view, this line loss remains higher than peers.

CORPORATE STRATEGY. In November 2009, CTL said that it expects to realize approximately $375 million in synergies from the combination with Embarq with the first milestone being an expected conversion onto one billing system in late 2009. We believe CTL's management has a strong track record of wringing cost savings from its operations. In addition to cost savings, we expect CTL to focus on growing the DSL customer base in the new markets to stem the line losses.

Company Financials Fiscal Year Ended Dec. 31

Per Share Data ($)	2008	2007	2006	2005	2004	2003	2002	2001	2000	1999
Tangible Book Value	NM	NM	NM	1.41	NM	0.37	NM	NM	NM	1.39
Cash Flow	8.64	8.44	7.31	6.37	5.90	5.63	4.21	5.73	4.36	4.16
Earnings	3.56	3.72	3.07	2.49	2.41	2.38	1.33	2.41	1.63	1.70
S&P Core Earnings	3.33	3.37	2.52	2.30	2.36	2.35	1.08	1.21	NA	NA
Dividends	1.61	0.26	0.25	0.24	0.23	0.22	0.21	0.20	0.19	0.18
Payout Ratio	45%	7%	8%	10%	10%	9%	16%	8%	12%	5%
Prices:High	42.00	49.94	44.11	36.50	35.54	36.76	35.50	39.88	47.31	49.00
Prices:Low	20.45	39.91	32.54	29.55	26.20	25.25	21.13	25.45	24.44	35.19
P/E Ratio:High	12	13	14	15	15	15	27	17	29	29
P/E Ratio:Low	6	11	11	12	11	11	16	11	15	21

Income Statement Analysis (Million $)

	2008	2007	2006	2005	2004	2003	2002	2001	2000	1999
Revenue	2,600	2,656	2,448	2,479	2,407	2,381	1,972	2,117	1,846	1,677
Depreciation	524	536	524	532	501	471	412	473	388	349
Maintenance	NA	NA	NA	NA	NA	NA	NA	NA	NA	NA
Construction Credits	NA	NA	NA	NA	NA	NA	NA	NA	NA	NA
Effective Tax Rate	34.7%	32.4%	37.4%	37.8%	38.4%	35.2%	35.3%	37.2%	39.0%	41.5%
Net Income	3,294	418	370	334	337	345	190	343	231	240
S&P Core Earnings	342	377	302	307	330	339	153	171	NA	NA

Balance Sheet & Other Financial Data (Million $)

	2008	2007	2006	2005	2004	2003	2002	2001	2000	1999
Gross Property	8,869	8,666	7,894	7,801	7,431	3,455	6,668	5,839	5,915	4,194
Net Property	2,896	3,108	3,109	3,304	3,341	3,455	3,532	3,000	2,959	2,256
Capital Expenditures	287	326	314	415	385	378	386	507	450	390
Total Capital	7,311	6,962	5,604	5,993	6,172	6,588	6,666	4,425	5,082	3,926
Fixed Charges Coverage	3.6	3.9	4.4	3.6	3.6	3.4	2.3	3.4	3.2	3.4
Capitalization:Long Term Debt	NA	2,734	2,413	2,376	2,762	3,109	3,578	2,088	3,050	2,078
Capitalization:Preferred	NA	Nil	Nil	Nil	Nil	7.98	7.98	7.98	7.98	7.98
Capitalization:Common	3,163	3,409	3,191	3,617	3,410	3,471	3,080	2,329	2,024	1,840
% Return on Revenue	14.1	15.8	15.1	13.5	14.0	14.5	9.6	16.2	12.5	14.3
% Return on Invested Capital	7.5	9.5	9.8	8.8	8.6	8.6	7.4	12.2	9.4	10.4
% Return on Common Equity	11.1	12.7	10.9	9.5	9.8	10.5	7.0	15.7	12.0	14.2
% Earned on Net Property	24.2	25.5	20.8	38.2	36.9	35.0	31.5	34.6	35.0	37.2
% Long Term Debt of Capitalization	50.9	44.5	43.1	39.6	44.8	47.2	53.7	47.2	60.0	52.9
Capital % Preferred	Nil	Nil	Nil	Nil	Nil	0.1	0.1	0.2	0.2	0.2
Capitalization:% Common	43.3	55.5	56.9	60.4	55.2	52.7	46.2	52.6	39.8	46.9

Data as orig reptd.; bef. results of disc opers/spec. items. Per share data adj. for stk. divs.; EPS diluted. E-Estimated. NA-Not Available. NM-Not Meaningful. NR-Not Ranked. UR-Under Review.

Office: 100 CenturyTel Dr, Monroe, LA 71203.
Telephone: 318-388-9000.
Website: http://www.centurytel.com
Chrmn: W.A. Owens

Pres & CEO: G.F. Post, III
Vice Chrmn: H.P. Perry
Vice Chrmn: T.A. Gerke
COO & EVP: K.A. Puckett

Investor Contact: T. Davis (800-833-1188)
Board Members: V. Boulet, P. C. Brown, R. A. Gephardt, T. A. Gerke, W. B. Hanks, G. J. McCray, III, C. G. Melville, Jr., F. R. Nichols, W. A. Owens, H. P. Perry, G. F. Post, III, S. M. Shern, L. A. Siegel, J. R. Zimmel

Founded: 1968
Domicile: Louisiana
Employees: 6,500

Cephalon Inc

STANDARD
&POOR'S

S&P Recommendation	BUY ★★★★☆	Price $55.23 (as of Nov 27, 2009)	12-Mo. Target Price $72.00	Investment Style Large-Cap Growth

GICS Sector Health Care
Sub-Industry Biotechnology

Summary This biopharmaceutical company markets and develops human therapeutics for the treatment of neurological disorders, pain indications and, most recently, oncology.

Key Stock Statistics (Source S&P, Vickers, company reports)

52-Wk Range	$81.35– 52.55	S&P Oper. EPS 2009**E**	5.86	Market Capitalization(B)	$4.123	Beta	0.47
Trailing 12-Month EPS	$3.62	S&P Oper. EPS 2010**E**	6.20	Yield (%)	Nil	S&P 3-Yr. Proj. EPS CAGR(%)	13
Trailing 12-Month P/E	15.3	P/E on S&P Oper. EPS 2009**E**	9.4	Dividend Rate/Share	Nil	S&P Credit Rating	NA
$10K Invested 5 Yrs Ago	$11,714	Common Shares Outstg. (M)	74.7	Institutional Ownership (%)	NM		

Price Performance

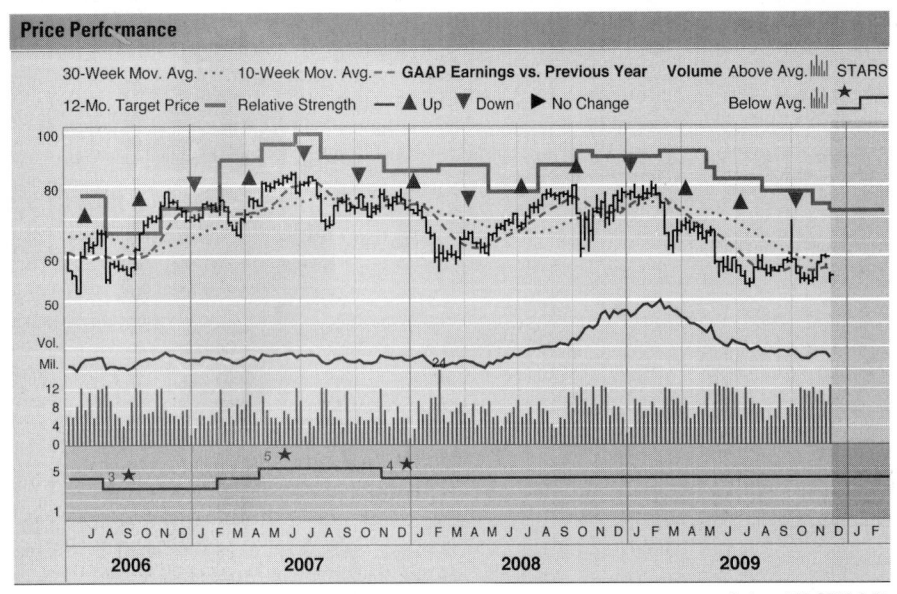

30-Week Mov. Avg. · · · · 10-Week Mov. Avg. – – **GAAP Earnings vs. Previous Year**   Volume Above Avg. ▮▮▮ STARS
12-Mo. Target Price — Relative Strength — ▲ Up ▼ Down ▶ No Change   Below Avg. ▮▮▮ ★

Options: ASE, CBOE, P, Ph

Analysis prepared by **Steven Silver** on November 24, 2009, when the stock traded at **$ 54.97**.

Highlights

▶ We estimate 2009 sales of $2.17 billion, which represents a 10% advance from 2008, and forecast 7% sales growth in 2010, to $2.31 billion. We expect CEPH's near-term sales growth to be driven by new approved uses for Nuvigil beginning as early as mid-2010, as well as adoption of Treanda and Amrix, helping to offset slowing trends of its pain franchise due to Actiq sales eroded by generic competition and Fentora label expansion hampered by patient misuse concerns.

▶ We see an operating margin of 31% in 2009 and 2010, up from 28% in 2008, fueled by operating leverage from new product launches within an existing infrastructure, as in the current launch of Amrix within the Provigil-led central nervous system unit. We expect CEPH to incur higher rollout costs related to its newer products and higher R&D spending on its growing pipeline, but see solid cash flows supporting these investments.

▶ Our 2009 and 2010 adjusted EPS estimates of $5.86 and $6.20 per share, respectively, exclude amortized intangible assets and acquisition-related charges.

Investment Rationale/Risk

▶ We view favorably CEPH's investments in building a biologics-focused pipeline, aggressively shifting from its current drug portfolio, which we expect to face increased generics exposure in the coming years. Among current products, we see potential for renewed Treanda sales growth in non-Hodgkin's lymphoma and new uses of Nuvigil, after recently being granted FDA priority review for jet lag, and producing positive study results in bipolar depression. However, we see CEPH's valuation being constrained by looming expiration for Provigil's patents in 2012, increased competition and generic entrants in its pain markets.

▶ Risks to our recommendation and target price include failure to expand Nuvigil's product label, clinical failure of late-stage pipeline candidates, failure to expand the market for Fentora to offset erosion from generic Actiq, and further regulatory issues over product marketing.

▶ Our 12-month target price of $72 applies an 11.6X multiple to our 2010 adjusted EPS estimate, about 0.9X our projected long-term growth rate, a discount to profitable peers, on our view of CEPH's generic drugs exposure and reliance on advancing its long-term pipeline.

Qualitative Risk Assessment

LOW	MEDIUM	HIGH

Cephalon faces generic pressures in its pain franchise and in its wakefulness franchise early next decade, and has been subject to regulatory oversight of its marketing practices and drug safety. Also, the company is developing new drugs for competitive markets, which we view as a highly risky endeavor.

Quantitative Evaluations

S&P Quality Ranking   B-

D	C	B-	B	B+	A-	A	A+

Relative Strength Rank   MODERATE

35

LOWEST = 1   HIGHEST = 99

Revenue/Earnings Data

Revenue (Million $)

	1Q	2Q	3Q	4Q	Year
2009	520.0	547.8	549.4	--	--
2008	433.9	485.0	489.7	534.9	1,975
2007	437.0	447.2	438.4	450.0	1,773
2006	356.9	440.1	482.3	484.7	1,764
2005	280.0	286.0	309.5	336.4	1,212
2004	215.0	239.5	262.0	299.0	1,015

Earnings Per Share ($)

2009	0.75	1.11	1.31	E1.50	E5.86
2008	0.52	0.80	1.42	0.15	2.92
2007	0.99	-0.06	-4.58	0.56	-2.88
2006	0.05	0.76	1.43	-0.08	2.08
2005	0.44	-4.29	0.50	0.30	-3.01
2004	0.37	-0.15	-2.94	1.23	-1.31

Fiscal year ended Dec. 31. Next earnings report expected: Mid February. EPS Estimates based on S&P Operating Earnings; historical GAAP earnings are as reported.

Dividend Data

No cash dividends have been paid.

Please read the Required Disclosures and Analyst Certification on the last page of this report.

The *McGraw-Hill* Companies

Cephalon Inc

**STANDARD
&POOR'S**

Business Summary November 24, 2009

CORPORATE OVERVIEW. Cephalon develops, manufactures and markets therapeutics for the treatment of sleep disorders, neurodegenerative conditions and cancer.

CEPH's Provigil (modafinil), is approved for excessive daytime sleepiness (EDS) due to narcolepsy (a chronic, lifelong sleep disorder), obstructive sleep apnea/hypopnea syndrome and shift work sleep disorder. Provigil has patent protection until 2012. CEPH has developed Nuvigil, a single-isomer version of Provigil, with a longer duration of action and an improved side effect profile, which it launched in June 2009, and is transitioning Provigil users to Nuvigil. In October 2009, Teva Pharmaceuticals filed to produce a generic version of Nuvigil, which we expect CEPH will challenge. Provigil sales rose 16%, to $988 million, in 2008, representing about half of CEPH's 2008 product sales.

CEPH's Actiq (oral fontanel citrate) for breakthrough cancer pain control, saw sales decline by 26% in 2008 (after a 41% fall in 2007), upon entry of generic competitors. CEPH receives royalties on net profits from generic U.S. sales by Barr Labs. In 2006 and 2008, CEPH launched Fentora for the same indication in

the U.S. and Europe, respectively. In September 2007, several deaths resulting from inappropriate Fentora prescribing and dosing were reported. Citing concern over mis-use, in September 2008, FDA delayed approving Fentora's use in non-cancer pain indications, pending an approved risk minimization program. In June 2008, Watson Labs announced plans to seek a generic version of Fentora. CEPH filed to defend its patents.

In 2008, CEPH received FDA approval for Treanda for treatment of chronic lymphocytic leukemia (CLL), the most common leukemia and for relapsed indolent non-Hodgkin's lymphoma (NHL). To date, the majority of Treanda sales have come from CLL, but CEPH expects NHL sales to expand upon publication of key Treanda data in late 2009. Treanda's patents expire in 2014. Treanda sales were $75 million in 2008.

Company Financials Fiscal Year Ended Dec. 31

Per Share Data ($)	2008	2007	2006	2005	2004	2003	2002	2001	2000	1999
Tangible Book Value	6.55	0.11	5.93	NM	NM	1.98	NM	NM	NM	4.86
Cash Flow	4.96	-1.02	3.75	-1.56	-0.37	2.01	3.12	-1.03	-2.42	-1.75
Earnings	2.92	-2.88	2.08	-3.01	-1.31	1.44	2.84	-1.33	-2.51	-2.10
S&P Core Earnings	3.13	3.44	2.14	-3.30	-1.43	0.90	2.08	-1.86	NA	NA
Dividends	Nil	Nil	Nil	Nil	Nil	Nil	Nil	Nil	Nil	Nil
Payout Ratio	Nil	Nil	Nil	Nil	Nil	Nil	Nil	Nil	Nil	Nil
Prices:High	80.39	84.83	82.92	66.92	60.98	54.95	78.88	78.40	83.63	37.13
Prices:Low	56.20	64.65	51.58	37.35	41.58	36.92	35.82	36.38	29.88	7.25
P/E Ratio:High	28	NM	40	NM	NM	38	28	NM	NM	NM
P/E Ratio:Low	19	NM	25	NM	NM	26	13	NM	NM	NM

Income Statement Analysis (Million $)										
Revenue	1,975	1,773	1,764	1,212	1,015	715	507	267	112	44.9
Operating Income	533	450	428	249	282	201	132	37.8	-57.8	-45.5
Depreciation	155	124	117	84.3	52.8	45.1	35.5	14.4	3.95	10.3
Interest Expense	28.5	19.8	67.0	25.2	50.4	28.9	38.2	73.1	Nil	8.25
Pretax Income	181	-68.4	238	-245	-28.2	130	62.4	-58.5	-93.7	-58.8
Effective Tax Rate	NM	NM	39.2%	NM	NM	35.6%	NM	NM	NM	NM
Net Income	223	-192	145	-175	-73.8	83.9	175	-58.5	-93.7	-58.8
S&P Core Earnings	239	230	149	-191	-80.6	51.1	140	-89.9	NA	NA

Balance Sheet & Other Financial Data (Million $)										
Cash	524	826	497	205	574	1,116	486	549	36.6	13.2
Current Assets	1,330	1,422	1,198	1,049	1,180	1,370	786	734	141	212
Total Assets	3,169	3,506	3,045	2,819	2,440	2,382	1,689	1,389	308	234
Current Liabilities	1,422	2,006	1,377	1,279	216	138	120	107	80.8	57.5
Long Term Debt	3.69	3.79	225	763	1,284	1,409	861	867	55.1	14.0
Common Equity	1,503	1,302	1,309	612	830	770	643	399	165	317
Total Capital	1,585	1,362	1,607	1,486	2,209	2,225	1,556	1,265	220	331
Capital Expenditures	75.9	96.9	160	118	50.2	40.5	27.3	12.5	7.46	0.38
Cash Flow	378	-67.9	261	-90.6	-21.0	129	211	-49.7	-98.9	-51.9
Current Ratio	0.9	0.7	0.9	0.8	5.5	9.9	6.6	6.9	1.7	3.7
% Long Term Debt of Capitalization	0.2	0.3	14.0	51.4	58.2	63.3	55.3	68.5	25.0	4.2
% Net Income of Revenue	11.3	NM	8.2	NM	NM	11.7	34.5	NM	NM	NM
% Return on Assets	6.7	NM	4.9	NM	NM	4.1	11.2	NM	NM	NM
% Return on Equity	15.9	NM	15.1	NM	NM	11.9	33.6	NM	NM	NM

Data as orig reptd.; bef. results of disc opers/spec. items. Per share data adj. for stk. divs.; EPS diluted. E-Estimated. NA-Not Available. NM-Not Meaningful. NR-Not Ranked. UR-Under Review.

Office: 41 Moores Rd, Frazer, PA 19355-1113.
Telephone: 610-344-0200.
Email: investorrelations@cephalon.com
Website: http://www.cephalon.com

Chrmn, Pres & CEO: F. Baldino, Jr.
COO: B. Repella
EVP, CFO & Chief Acctg Officer: K. Buchi
EVP & Chief Admin Officer: C.A. Savini

EVP & CSO: J. Vaught
Investor Contact: C. Merritt (610-738-6376)
Board Members: F. Baldino, Jr., W. P. Egan, M. D.
Greenacre, V. M. Kailian, K. E. Moley, C. A. Sanders, G.
Wilensky, D. L. Winger

Founded: 1987
Domicile: Delaware
Employees: 2,780

CF Industries Holdings Inc

STANDARD &POOR'S

S&P Recommendation	HOLD ★★★☆☆	Price $83.94 (as of Nov 27, 2009)	12-Mo. Target Price $89.00	Investment Style Large-Cap Value

GICS Sector Materials
Sub-Industry Fertilizers & Agricultural Chemicals

Summary This company is a major manufacturer and distributor of nitrogen and phosphate fertilizer products in North America.

Key Stock Statistics (Source S&P, Vickers, company reports)

52-Wk Range	$95.13– 41.51	S&P Oper. EPS 2009**E**	6.84	Market Capitalization(B)	$4.076	Beta	0.96
Trailing 12-Month EPS	$10.07	S&P Oper. EPS 2010**E**	7.01	Yield (%)	0.48	S&P 3-Yr. Proj. EPS CAGR(%)	9
Trailing 12-Month P/E	8.3	P/E on S&P Oper. EPS 2009**E**	12.3	Dividend Rate/Share	$0.40	S&P Credit Rating	NA
$10K Invested 5 Yrs Ago	NA	Common Shares Outstg. (M)	48.6	Institutional Ownership (%)	92		

Price Performance

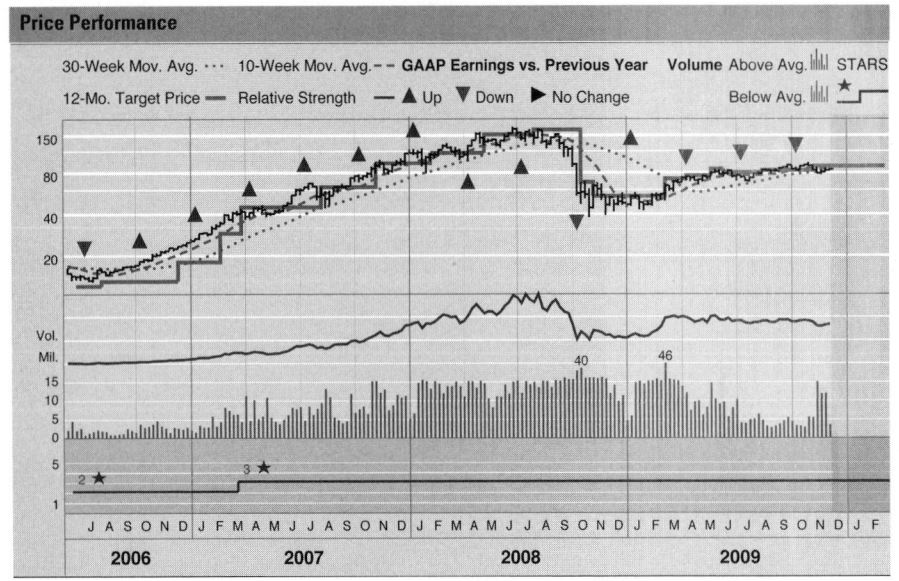

30-Week Mov. Avg. ···· 10-Week Mov. Avg. - - **GAAP Earnings vs. Previous Year** Volume Above Avg. STARS
12-Mo. Target Price — Relative Strength — ▲ Up ▼ Down ▶ No Change Below Avg.

Options: ASE, CBOE, Ph

Analysis prepared by **Kevin Kirkeby** on November 05, 2009, when the stock traded at **$ 79.28**.

Highlights

▶ After making an offer to acquire Terra Industries (TRA 36, NR) in January 2009, CF found itself the target of an unsolicited bid from Canada's Agrium (AGU 50, NR) a month later. As of early November 2009, following three upward revisions to its bid, CF's offer values TRA at nearly $4.1 billion. AGU's most recent bid values CF at approximately $4.6 billion, equal to about $93 per CF share. CF believes it has the necessary regulatory approvals to proceed with its proposed transaction, while AGU has signed a consent agreement with regulatory authorities in Canada.

▶ Our forecast for a 32% decline in revenues in 2009 reflects sharply lower selling prices and a 4% rise in volumes. Absent forward purchase orders struck at higher prices that benefited 2009 results, we expect CF's revenues to decline 13% in 2010. Still, we think its Keytrade AG operations will continue to boost volume sales as it did in 2009 by finding additional opportunities for export, contributing to a 4% increase in volumes for 2010.

▶ Our EPS estimate for 2009 excludes unrealized mark-to-market gains on CF's natural gas derivatives.

Investment Rationale/Risk

▶ CF Industries has a smaller geographic reach than most of its peers, and we consider it to be concentrated in more volatile market segments. However, CF has a significant net cash position, which we see it using to reduce dependence on high-cost feedstock sources and to broaden its geographic coverage. We think its proposed acquisition of Terra Industries is an example of this, as is a plan to build a new facility in Peru. We note that AGU's proposal is dependent upon CF not buying Terra Industries.

▶ Risks to our recommendation and target price include CF raising the bid in its proposed takeover of Terra Industries, Agrium abandoning its attempted purchase of CF in light of CF's anti-takeover measures, and increases in natural gas costs.

▶ We think CF would benefit more from a combination with Agrium than with Terra, as it would result in greater overall market share. Our 12-month target price of $89 balances the value of AGU's bid, which approximates $93 per one CF share, with the risk that the deal does not proceed. At $89, the shares would trade near 12.7X our four-quarter forward EPS estimate, above the historical average.

Qualitative Risk Assessment

LOW	MEDIUM	HIGH

Our risk assessment reflects the cyclical and seasonal nature of the agriculture industry and the company's reliance on the volatile natural gas industry for much of its raw materials, partly offset by the competitive advantage of many overseas suppliers.

Quantitative Evaluations

S&P Quality Ranking   NR

D	C	B-	B	B+	A-	A	A+

Relative Strength Rank   MODERATE

48

LOWEST = 1   HIGHEST = 99

Revenue/Earnings Data

Revenue (Million $)

	1Q	2Q	3Q	4Q	Year
2009	680.6	991.0	430.1	--	--
2008	667.3	1,161	1,021	1,072	3,921
2007	447.7	848.9	582.9	852.5	2,757
2006	400.5	664.8	378.0	506.2	1,950
2005	459.3	626.7	359.4	463.0	1,908
2004	324.7	520.7	326.7	478.6	1,651

Earnings Per Share ($)

2009	1.28	4.33	0.78	E1.48	E6.84
2008	2.77	5.02	0.82	3.59	12.14
2007	1.02	1.65	1.52	2.38	6.57
2006	-0.45	0.77	0.13	0.14	0.60
2005	0.41	0.78	-1.81	-0.18	-0.66
2004	--	--	--	--	1.23

Fiscal year ended Dec. 31. Next earnings report expected: Mid February. EPS Estimates based on S&P Operating Earnings; historical GAAP earnings are as reported.

Dividend Data (Dates: mm/dd Payment Date: mm/dd/yy)

Amount ($)	Date Decl.	Ex-Div. Date	Stk. of Record	Payment Date
0.100	02/02	02/12	02/17	03/02/09
0.100	04/21	05/12	05/14	06/01/09
0.100	07/22	08/12	08/14	08/31/09
0.100	10/22	11/12	11/16	11/30/09

Dividends have been paid since 2005. Source: Company reports.

Please read the Required Disclosures and Analyst Certification on the last page of this report.

The McGraw·Hill Companies

CF Industries Holdings Inc

STANDARD &POOR'S

Business Summary November 05, 2009

CORPORATE OVERVIEW. CF Industries is a major manufacturer and distributor of nitrogen and phosphate fertilizer products in North America. The company's principal products are ammonia, urea, urea ammonium nitrate solution (UAN), diammonium phosphate (DAP), and monoammonium phosphate (MAP). Its market share for the nitrogen segment is about 22%, and for phosphates, it is about 14% for agricultural fertilizer applications in the U.S. Core markets and distribution facilities for the company are concentrated in the midwestern U.S. grain-producing states.

PRIMARY BUSINESS DYNAMICS. Nitrogen, phosphates, along with potash are the three primary plant nutrients that are essential for proper crop nutrition and maximum yields. There are no substitutes for them and they are generally not substitutable for each other. Each of these fertilizers are actively traded in the global marketplace, with price being the primary means of differentiation. The U.S. is a net exporter of phosphate fertilizers, while it tends to import a significant amount of nitrogen-based product. Producers typically build their inventories ahead of the spring planting season when demand is the highest, and over the summer in advance of post-harvest fertilizer applica-

tions. The company's primary competitors are Potash Corp., Agrium Inc., Terra Industries, The Mosaic Company, and Koch Nitrogen.

In 2008, natural gas purchases accounted for about 56% of CF's total cost of sales of nitrogen fertilizers and a substantially higher percentage of cash costs. The company uses a combination of spot and term purchases of varied duration from a number of suppliers to maintain a reliable, competitively priced natural gas supply, and it also uses certain financial instruments to hedge natural gas prices. It has developed a forward pricing program under which it sells about half of its nitrogen fertilizer, and this system provides some margin certainty. However, many of CF's competitors benefit from access to lower-priced natural gas through manufacturing facilities or interests in manufacturing facilities located in regions with abundant supplies of natural gas, in our view.

Company Financials Fiscal Year Ended Dec. 31

Per Share Data ($)	2008	2007	2006	2005	2004	2003	2002	2001	2000	1999
Tangible Book Value	27.72	21.09	13.88	13.73	12.96	NA	NA	NA	NA	NA
Cash Flow	13.93	8.06	2.32	1.11	3.21	1.57	2.14	0.77	1.57	NA
Earnings	12.14	6.57	0.60	-0.66	1.23	-0.33	-0.51	-1.35	-0.47	NA
S&P Core Earnings	11.91	6.56	0.63	-0.68	1.22	-0.35	NA	NA	NA	NA
Dividends	0.40	0.08	0.08	0.02	NA	NA	NA	NA	NA	NA
Payout Ratio	3%	1%	13%	NM	NA	NA	NA	NA	NA	NA
Prices:High	172.99	118.88	26.60	18.00	NA	NA	NA	NA	NA	NA
Prices:Low	37.71	25.70	12.91	11.19	NA	NA	NA	NA	NA	NA
P/E Ratio:High	14	18	44	NM	NA	NA	NA	NA	NA	NA
P/E Ratio:Low	3	4	22	NM	NA	NA	NA	NA	NA	NA

Income Statement Analysis (Million $)										
Revenue	3,921	2,757	1,950	1,908	1,651	1,370	1,014	1,160	1,160	NA
Operating Income	1,313	686	166	236	258	99.4	89.6	-32.1	97.6	NA
Depreciation	101	84.5	94.6	97.5	109	105	108	102	112	NA
Interest Expense	1.60	1.70	2.90	14.0	22.7	23.9	23.6	31.8	21.1	NA
Pretax Income	1,180	627	81.8	110	132	-25.0	-38.3	-151	-40.1	NA
Effective Tax Rate	32.1%	31.8%	24.1%	NM	31.3%	NM	NM	NM	NM	NA
Net Income	685	373	33.3	-36.2	67.7	-18.4	-28.1	-59.7	-25.8	NA
S&P Core Earnings	671	372	34.9	-37.1	67.5	-19.7	NA	NA	NA	NA

Balance Sheet & Other Financial Data (Million $)										
Cash	625	861	25.4	37.4	72.8	169	NA	NA	NA	NA
Current Assets	1,433	1,279	633	576	NA	NA	NA	NA	NA	NA
Total Assets	2,388	2,013	1,290	1,228	1,149	1,405	NA	NA	NA	NA
Current Liabilities	818	629	353	341	NA	NA	NA	NA	NA	NA
Long Term Debt	Nil	4.90	4.20	4.20	4.01	255	NA	NA	NA	NA
Common Equity	1,338	1,187	767	756	720	-0.79	NA	NA	NA	NA
Total Capital	1,357	1,241	785	782	724	1,038	NA	NA	NA	NA
Capital Expenditures	142	105	59.3	69.4	33.7	28.7	26.3	41.7	52.3	NA
Cash Flow	785	457	128	61.3	176	86.6	118	42.3	86.2	NA
Current Ratio	1.8	2.0	1.8	1.7	NA	1.5	NA	NA	NA	NA
% Long Term Debt of Capitalization	Nil	0.4	0.5	0.5	0.6	24.6	Nil	NA	NA	NA
% Net Income of Revenue	17.5	13.5	1.7	NM	4.1	NM	NM	NM	NM	NA
% Return on Assets	31.1	22.6	2.6	NM	NM	NA	NA	NA	NA	NA
% Return on Equity	54.2	38.2	4.4	NM	NA	NA	NA	NA	NA	NA

Data as orig reptd.; bef. results of disc opers/spec. items. Per share data adj. for stk. divs.; EPS diluted. 2004 pro forma as adjusted bal. sheet and book val. as of Jun. 30, 2005. Prior to 2005, per sh. data based on pro forma shs. E-Estimated. NA-Not Available. NM-Not Meaningful. NR-Not Ranked. UR-Under Review.

Office: 4 Parkway N Ste 400, Deerfield, IL 60015-2590.
Telephone: 847-405-2400.
Website: http://www.cfindustries.com
Chrmn, Pres & CEO: S.R. Wilson
SVP & CFO: T. Nocchiero
Chief Acctg Officer & Cntlr: R.A. Hoker
Treas: R.W. Selgrad
Secy & General Counsel: D.C. Barnard
Investor Contact: C. Nekvasil (847-307-2515)
Board Members: R. C. Arzbaecher, W. W. Creek, W. Davisson, S. A. Furbacher, D. R. Harvey, J. D. Johnson, E. A. Schmitt, S. R. Wilson
Founded: 1946
Domicile: Delaware
Employees: 1,600

The McGraw-Hill Companies

Chesapeake Energy Corp

STANDARD &POOR'S

S&P Recommendation BUY ★★★★☆

Price	12-Mo. Target Price	Investment Style
$24.17 (as of Nov 27, 2009)	$31.00	Large-Cap Blend

GICS Sector Energy
Sub-Industry Oil & Gas Exploration & Production

Summary One of the largest independent exploration and production companies in the U.S., CHK focuses on U.S. onshore natural gas production east of the Rocky Mountains.

Key Stock Statistics (Source S&P, Vickers, company reports)

52-Wk Range	$30.00– 9.84	S&P Oper. EPS 2009**E**	2.02	Market Capitalization(B)	$15.655	Beta	1.36
Trailing 12-Month EPS	$-10.42	S&P Oper. EPS 2010**E**	2.42	Yield (%)	1.24	S&P 3-Yr. Proj. EPS CAGR(%)	-4
Trailing 12-Month P/E	NM	P/E on S&P Oper. EPS 2009**E**	12.0	Dividend Rate/Share	$0.30	S&P Credit Rating	BB
$10K Invested 5 Yrs Ago	$13,953	Common Shares Outstg. (M)	647.7	Institutional Ownership (%)	74		

Price Performance

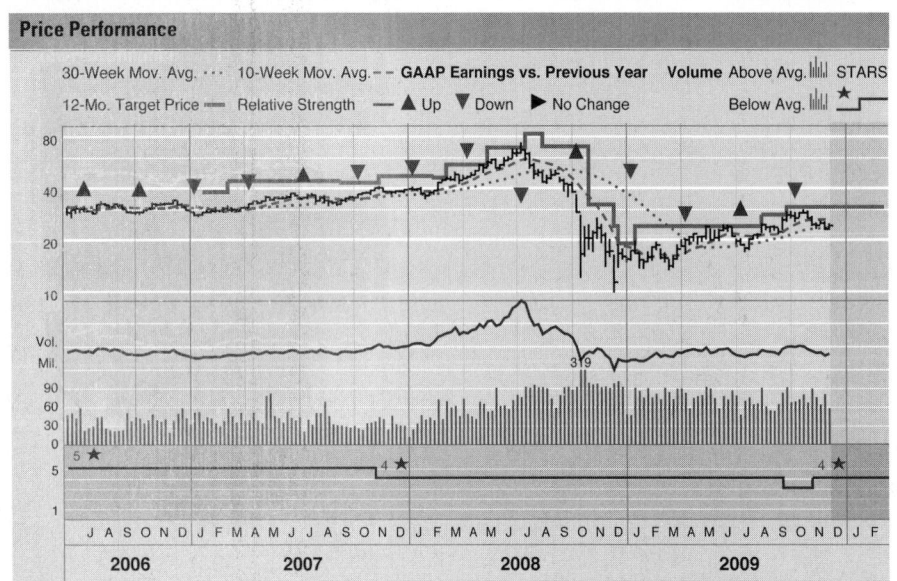

30-Week Mov. Avg. · · · · 10-Week Mov. Avg. – – GAAP Earnings vs. Previous Year Volume Above Avg. STARS
12-Mo. Target Price — Relative Strength — ▲ Up ▼ Down ► No Change Below Avg. ★

Options: ASE, CBOE, P, Ph

Analysis prepared by **Michael Kay** on November 20, 2009, when the stock traded at **$ 22.89**.

Highlights

► Production rose 18% in 2008, but in 2009 CHK has reduced its rig count to around 95, from a peak of 158 in August 2008. We see production growth of 6% in 2009 followed by 8% in 2010 on volume growth from its four large shale plays. We believe recent joint ventures (JVs) with Plains E&P, BP plc and StatoilHydro will accelerate Haynesville, Fayetteville and Marcellus shale development. CHK is running 20 rigs in the Marcellus and sees 28 in 2010. At Haynesville, CHK is running 35 rigs with production of 330 MMcfe/d, and expects a boost to 40 rigs in 2010 with growth of 35%.

► CHK has closed on three JV asset montetizations, which we believe have increased shareholder value at Haynesville, Fayetteville, and Marcellus. We believe CHK is looking for a fourth partner to monetize its substantive Barnett Shale assets.

► After 2008 EPS of $3.88 (with $0.27 non-cash derivative gain), we see $2.02 (with a $0.26 non-cash loss) in 2009 on lower prices, and $2.42 in 2010 on volume and price gains. CHK has 53% of forecasted 2009 natural gas production hedged at 6.85/Mcf, and about 15% of 2010 production at $9.53/Mcf.

Investment Rationale/Risk

► CHK's aggressive acquisition strategy has seen it spend over $14 billion over the past 10 years, focused on unconventional natural gas plays. With recent turmoil in credit markets, and a highly leveraged balance sheet, CHK has monetized assets through JVs, is planning to sell certain non-Haynesville Shale producing assets in Louisiana for $225-$250 million, and is in talks on the possible formation of a JV in the Barnett Shale. With asset sales and lower drilling capex, CHK anticipates excess cash of $2 billion in each of 2009 and 2010 for debt reduction.

► Risks to our recommendation and target price include weaker economic and operating conditions, a sustained decline in natural gas prices, and difficulty in replacing reserves.

► We think recent cuts in spending and production forecasts for 2009 and 2010 will lead to lower activity, but improved financial and liquidity positions. Given uncertain debt and equity markets, we expect markets to discount unproven resource potential, and we value CHK on our proved reserve NAV estimates. Our 12-month target price of $31 blends our proved NAV ($30) with our DCF ($30; 8.1% WACC; 3% terminal growth) and relative metrics ($33).

Qualitative Risk Assessment

LOW	MEDIUM	HIGH

Our risk assessment reflects CHK's business profile in a volatile, cyclical and capital-intensive segment of the energy industry. We believe CHK's financial strategy is aggressive, as the company has been one of the most active acquirers in exploration and production, and one of the most active users of commodity hedges. This is partly offset by what we see as strong volume growth and good drilling prospects.

Quantitative Evaluations

S&P Quality Ranking B

D	C	B-	B	B+	A-	A	A+

Relative Strength Rank MODERATE

32

LOWEST = 1   HIGHEST = 99

Revenue/Earnings Data

Revenue (Million $)

	1Q	2Q	3Q	4Q	Year
2009	1,995	1,673	1,811	--	--
2008	1,611	3,372	7,491	2,981	11,629
2007	1,580	2,105	2,027	2,089	7,800
2006	1,945	1,584	1,929	1,868	7,326
2005	783.5	1,048	1,083	1,751	4,665
2004	563.1	574.3	629.8	942.1	2,709

Earnings Per Share ($)

2009	-9.63	0.39	0.30	E0.68	E2.02
2008	-0.29	-3.16	5.61	-1.51	1.14
2007	0.50	1.01	0.72	0.27	2.62
2006	1.44	0.82	1.13	0.96	4.35
2005	0.36	0.52	0.43	1.11	2.51
2004	0.38	0.30	0.29	0.52	1.53

Fiscal year ended Dec. 31. Next earnings report expected: Late January. EPS Estimates based on S&P Operating Earnings; historical GAAP earnings are as reported.

Dividend Data (Dates: mm/dd Payment Date: mm/dd/yy)

Amount ($)	Date Decl.	Ex-Div. Date	Stk. of Record	Payment Date
0.075	12/15	12/30	01/02	01/15/09
0.075	03/17	03/30	04/01	04/15/09
0.075	06/15	06/29	07/01	07/15/09
0.075	09/24	09/29	10/01	10/15/09

Dividends have been paid since 2002. Source: Company reports.

Please read the Required Disclosures and Analyst Certification on the last page of this report.

The McGraw-Hill Companies

Chesapeake Energy Corp

STANDARD &POOR'S

Business Summary November 20, 2009

CORPORATE OVERVIEW. As the largest producer of natural gas in the U.S. as of year-end 2008, Chesapeake Energy Corp. (CHK) is focused on discovering, acquiring and developing conventional and unconventional natural gas reserves onshore in the U.S., east of the Rocky Mountains, primarily in the "Big 4" natural gas shale plays -- the Barnett Shale in the Fort Worth Basin, the Haynesville Shale in Louisiana, the Fayetteville Shale in the Arkoma Basin, and the Marcellus Shale in the Appalachian Basin.

CHK operations are concentrated in six U.S. operating areas: Mid-Continent, Barnett Shale, Appalachian Basin, Permian and Delaware Basin, Ark-La-Tex, and South Texas and Texas Gulf Coast. Proved oil and gas reserves rose 11%, to 12.05 trillion cubic feet equivalent (Tcfe; 94% natural gas, 67% developed) in 2008. Oil and gas production rose 18%, to 842.8 billion cubic feet equivalent (92% natural gas), in 2008. We estimate CHK's 2008 organic reserve replacement at 302%. We estimate CHK's three-year (2006-08) finding and development costs at $27.30 per boe, above the peer average, its three-year reserve replacement costs at $24.66 per boe, above the peer average, and its three-year reserve replacement at 451%, above the peer average.

As of year-end 2008, CHK owned interests in about 41,200 producing oil and gas wells. During 2008, CHK drilled 1,819 gross (1,491 net) operated wells and participated in 1,857 gross (242 net) wells operated by other companies. The company's drilling success rate was 99% for company-operated wells.

MARKET PROFILE. From 1998 to the present, CHK has integrated an aggressive and technologically advanced drilling program with an active property consolidation program focused on small to medium-sized corporate and property acquisitions. Beginning in 2006, CHK shifted its strategy from drilling inventory capture to drilling inventory conversion. In doing so, CHK has de-emphasized its acquisitions of proved properties while further emphasizing its drilling program and converting its substantial backlog of drilling opportunities into proved developed producing reserves.

CHK believes one of its most distinctive characteristics is its ability to increase its reserves and production organically. In 2008, CHK averaged 145 operated drilling rigs and 110 non-operated drilling rigs to conduct the most active drilling program in the U.S. CHK is active in most unconventional plays in the U.S. east of the Rockies, where the company drills more horizontal wells than any other company in the industry.

Company Financials Fiscal Year Ended Dec. 31

Per Share Data ($)	2008	2007	2006	2005	2004	2003	2002	2001	2000	1999
Tangible Book Value	26.00	21.87	20.32	12.42	8.57	5.45	3.99	3.75	2.05	NM
Cash Flow	5.21	6.87	7.36	5.05	3.56	2.61	1.54	2.52	3.67	1.30
Earnings	1.14	2.62	4.35	2.51	1.53	1.20	0.17	1.51	3.01	0.16
S&P Core Earnings	1.35	2.51	4.19	2.48	1.50	1.19	0.17	1.36	NA	NA
Dividends	0.29	0.26	0.23	0.20	0.17	0.14	0.06	Nil	Nil	Nil
Payout Ratio	26%	10%	5%	8%	11%	11%	35%	Nil	Nil	Nil
Prices:High	74.00	41.19	35.57	40.20	18.31	14.00	8.55	11.06	10.50	4.13
Prices:Low	9.84	27.27	26.81	15.06	11.70	7.27	4.50	4.50	1.94	0.63
P/E Ratio:High	65	16	8	16	12	12	50	7	3	26
P/E Ratio:Low	9	10	6	6	8	6	26	3	1	4

Income Statement Analysis (Million $)	2008	2007	2006	2005	2004	2003	2002	2001	2000	1999
Revenue	11,629	7,800	7,326	4,665	2,709	1,717	738	969	628	355
Operating Income	3,631	4,638	3,413	1,773	992	675	191	597	384	207
Depreciation, Depletion and Amortization	2,147	1,989	1,463	945	611	386	235	178	105	99.5
Interest Expense	314	675	301	220	167	154	111	98.3	86.3	81.1
Pretax Income	1,186	2,341	3,255	1,493	805	501	67.1	438	196	35.0
Effective Tax Rate	39.0%	38.0%	38.5%	36.5%	36.0%	38.0%	40.0%	39.9%	NM	5.04%
Net Income	723	1,451	2,003	948	515	311	40.3	263	456	33.3
S&P Core Earnings	737	1,178	1,831	871	431	283	29.9	235	NA	NA

Balance Sheet & Other Financial Data (Million $)	2008	2007	2006	2005	2004	2003	2002	2001	2000	1999
Cash	1,749	1.00	2.52	60.0	6.90	40.6	248	125	3.50	38.9
Current Assets	4,292	1,396	1,154	1,183	568	342	435	361	167	97.5
Total Assets	38,444	30,734	24,417	16,118	8,245	4,572	2,876	2,287	1,440	851
Current Liabilities	3,621	2,761	1,890	1,964	964	513	266	173	163	88.2
Long Term Debt	14,184	10,950	7,376	5,490	3,075	2,058	1,651	1,329	945	964
Common Equity	16,297	11,170	9,293	4,598	2,672	1,180	758	617	282	-447
Total Capital	34,244	27,046	21,944	13,469	7,172	3,982	2,559	2,097	1,270	753
Capital Expenditures	9,177	9,705	986	484	127	71.5	33.6	24.9	78.9	49.9
Cash Flow	2,837	3,346	3,377	1,851	1,087	674	265	439	556	133
Current Ratio	1.2	0.5	0.6	0.6	0.6	0.7	1.6	2.1	1.0	1.1
% Long Term Debt of Capitalization	41.4	47.4	33.6	40.8	42.9	51.7	64.5	63.4	74.4	128.0
% Return on Assets	4.5	4.9	9.9	7.8	8.0	8.3	1.6	14.1	39.8	4.0
% Return on Equity	5.3	13.3	27.6	24.9	24.7	29.7	4.4	58.1	NM	NM

Data as orig reptd.; bef. results of disc opers/spec. items. Per share data adj. for stk. divs.; EPS diluted. E-Estimated. NA-Not Available. NM-Not Meaningful. NR-Not Ranked. UR-Under Review.

Office: 6100 North Western Avenue, Oklahoma City, OK 73118.
Telephone: 405-848-8000.
Website: http://www.chk.com
Chrmn & CEO: A.K. McClendon

Pres: J.M. Stice
COO & EVP: S.C. Dixon
EVP & CFO: M.C. Rowland
SVP, Chief Acctg Officer & Cntlr: M.A. Johnson

Investor Contact: J.L. Mobley (405-767-4763)
Board Members: R. K. Davidson, V. B. Hargis, F. Keating, C. T. Maxwell, A. K. McClendon, M. A. Miller, Jr., D. L. Nickles, F. B. Whittemore

Founded: 1989
Domicile: Oklahoma
Employees: 7,600

Chevron Corp

STANDARD &POOR'S

S&P Recommendation **STRONG BUY** ★★★★★	Price $78.17 (as of Nov 27, 2009)	12-Mo. Target Price $90.00	Investment Style Large-Cap Blend

GICS Sector Energy
Sub-Industry Integrated Oil & Gas

Summary This global integrated oil company (formerly ChevronTexaco) has interests in exploration, production, refining and marketing, and petrochemicals.

Key Stock Statistics (Source S&P, Vickers, company reports)

52-Wk Range	$81.92– 56.12	S&P Oper. EPS 2009**E**	5.13	Market Capitalization(B)	$156.830	Beta		0.65
Trailing 12-Month EPS	$6.15	S&P Oper. EPS 2010**E**	8.20	Yield (%)	3.48	S&P 3-Yr. Proj. EPS CAGR(%)		-6
Trailing 12-Month P/E	12.7	P/E on S&P Oper. EPS 2009**E**	15.2	Dividend Rate/Share	$2.72	S&P Credit Rating		AA
$10K Invested 5 Yrs Ago	$16,716	Common Shares Outstg. (M)	2,006.3	Institutional Ownership (%)	62			

Price Performance

30-Week Mov. Avg. · · · · 10-Week Mov. Avg. — **GAAP Earnings vs. Previous Year** Volume Above Avg. ▐▌▌ STARS
12-Mo. Target Price — Relative Strength — ▲ Up ▼ Down ▶ No Change Below Avg. ▐▌ ★

Options: ASE, CBOE, P, Ph

Analysis prepared by **Tina J. Vital** on November 02, 2009, when the stock traded at **$ 76.54**.

Highlights

▶ Deepwater start-ups slated for 2009 include Tahiti (58% CVX-owned; commenced May 2009) in the U.S. Gulf of Mexico, Tombua-Landana (31%) and Mafumeira Norte (39.2%; July 2009) in Angola, and Frade (52%; June 2009) in Brazil. We expect oil and gas production to rise over 6% in 2009 as projects ramp-up, to about 2.68 million boe per day; we look for annual growth of about 4% between 2008-2013.

▶ Demand for petroleum products fell amid the global economic slowdown, and refining margins narrowed. We expect this trend to continue over the next 12-months. In response, CVX has focused on cost management efforts; as of the third quarter the company said it was ahead of its targeted $2.5 billion reduction in operating, selling, general & administrative expenses for 2009. Overall, we look for U.S. Gulf Coast 3-2-1 crack spreads to narrow about 16% in 2009 before widening about 7% in 2010.

▶ Operating EPS excluded special charges of $0.20 related to asset sales and taxes during the 2009 first nine months. We look for reduced pricing to lead after-tax operating earnings down by 57% in 2009, before a 60% rebound in 2010 on an improved economic outlook.

Investment Rationale/Risk

▶ We have a positive outlook for CVX's upstream business, given its 2005 acquisition of Unocal and its ongoing international "Big Five" up-stream development projects. We consider CVX's three-year reserve replacement rate as solid but below the peer average, and its three-year finding and development costs, proved acquisition costs and reserve replacement costs as above peer averages.

▶ Risks to our recommendation and target price include declines in economic, industry and operating conditions. A pending 2003 lawsuit in Ecuador alleges environmental damages related to Texaco's prior operations, but we see little near-term financial impact since CVX has no operations there. (Texaco spent $40 million on a clean-up in Ecuador before leaving in 1997, at which time Ecuador released it from responsibility from its operations.)

▶ Blending our discounted cash flow ($89 intrinsic value, assuming a WACC of 7.8% and terminal growth of 3%) and relative market valuations, our 12-month target is $90. This represents an expected enterprise value of about 5.4X our 2010 EBITDA estimate, a discount to peers.

Qualitative Risk Assessment

LOW	MEDIUM	HIGH

Our risk assessment reflects Chevron's diversified and strong business profile in volatile, cyclical and capital-intensive segments of the energy industry. With improved returns since the Texaco merger in 2001, we view its corporate governance practices as generally sound and its earnings stability as favorable.

Quantitative Evaluations

S&P Quality Ranking A-

D	C	B-	B	B+	A-	A	A+

Relative Strength Rank STRONG

75

LOWEST = 1 HIGHEST = 99

Revenue/Earnings Data

Revenue (Million $)

	1Q	2Q	3Q	4Q	Year
2009	36,130	40,205	45,180	--	--
2008	65,903	78,310	73,615	43,145	264,958
2007	46,302	54,344	53,545	59,900	203,970
2006	54,624	53,536	54,212	47,746	210,118
2005	41,607	48,343	54,456	53,794	198,200
2004	33,063	36,579	39,611	41,612	155,300

Earnings Per Share ($)

2009	0.92	0.87	1.92	E1.62	E5.13
2008	2.48	2.89	3.86	2.43	11.67
2007	2.18	2.52	1.75	2.32	8.77
2006	1.80	1.97	2.29	1.74	7.80
2005	1.28	1.76	1.64	1.86	6.54
2004	1.20	1.93	1.38	1.63	6.14

Fiscal year ended Dec. 31. Next earnings report expected: Early February. EPS Estimates based on S&P Operating Earnings; historical GAAP earnings are as reported.

Dividend Data (Dates: mm/dd Payment Date: mm/dd/yy)

Amount ($)	Date Decl.	Ex-Div. Date	Stk. of Record	Payment Date
0.650	01/28	02/12	02/17	03/10/09
0.650	04/29	05/15	05/19	06/10/09
0.680	07/29	08/17	08/19	09/10/09
0.680	10/28	11/16	11/18	12/10/09

Dividends have been paid since 1912. Source: Company reports.

Please read the Required Disclosures and Analyst Certification on the last page of this report.

The **McGraw·Hill** Companies

Chevron Corp

STANDARD
&POOR'S

Business Summary November 02, 2009

CORPORATE OVERVIEW. In October 2001, Chevron Corp. (CHV) and Texaco Inc. (TX) merged, creating the second largest U.S.-based oil company at the time, ChevronTexaco Corp. (CVX). In May 2005, the company changed its name to Chevron Corp.

CVX separately manages its exploration and production (27% of 2008 revenues; 86% of 2008 segment income); refining, marketing and transportation (72%; 13%); chemicals (1%; 1%); and other businesses, which includes its mining operations of coal and other minerals, power generation, insurance and real estate operations, and technical companies.

Net production of crude oil, natural gas liquids (NGLs) and natural gas declined 3.4%, to 2.530 million barrel oil equivalent (boe) per day (66% liquids), including Athabasca oil sands and equity share in affiliates, in 2008. Net proved oil and gas reserves, including equity share in affiliates, rose 3.9%, to 11.20 billion boe (65% liquids, 65% developed). Using data from John S. Herold, we estimate CVX's three-year (2005-2007) reserve replacement rate at 105%,

below the peer average; three-year finding and development costs at $48.45 per boe, above the peer average; three-year proved acquisition costs at $6.91 per boe, above the peer average; and reserve replacement costs at $19.00 per boe, above the peer average. Excluding affiliated companies, we estimate CVX's 2008 organic reserve replacement rate at 99%.

As of December 31, 2008, CVX owned 7 refineries and one asphalt plants, and had interests in ten international refineries, for a total operable capacity of 2.139 million b/d (50% North America). CVX processes imported (88% of 2008 refinery inputs) and domestic (12%) crude oil in its U.S. refining operations. As of year-end 2008, it had a network of about 25,000 (39% U.S.) branded retail sites worldwide.

Company Financials Fiscal Year Ended Dec. 31

Per Share Data ($)	2008	2007	2006	2005	2004	2003	2002	2001	2000	1999
Tangible Book Value	40.93	34.66	29.71	25.99	21.47	16.98	14.80	15.92	15.54	13.53
Cash Flow	16.32	12.67	11.38	8.96	8.53	5.99	2.98	5.17	6.17	3.74
Earnings	11.67	8.77	7.80	6.54	6.14	3.57	0.54	1.85	3.99	1.57
S&P Core Earnings	10.90	8.34	7.88	6.62	5.88	3.50	1.22	1.66	NA	NA
Dividends	2.53	2.26	2.01	1.75	1.53	1.43	1.40	1.33	1.30	1.24
Payout Ratio	22%	26%	26%	27%	25%	40%	NM	72%	33%	79%
Prices:High	104.63	95.50	76.20	65.98	56.07	43.50	45.80	49.25	47.44	52.47
Prices:Low	55.50	64.99	53.76	49.81	42.00	30.66	32.71	39.22	34.97	36.56
P/E Ratio:High	9	11	10	10	9	12	86	27	12	33
P/E Ratio:Low	5	7	7	8	7	9	61	21	9	23

Income Statement Analysis (Million $)										
Revenue	264,958	214,091	204,892	193,641	150,865	120,032	98,691	104,409	50,592	35,448
Operating Income	45,238	33,936	35,748	27,129	21,542	49,336	28,848	16,031	15,834	5,848
Depreciation, Depletion and Amortization	9,528	8,309	7,506	5,913	4,935	5,384	5,231	7,059	2,848	2,866
Interest Expense	2.00	468	451	482	406	474	565	833	460	463
Pretax Income	43,057	32,274	32,046	25,293	20,636	12,850	4,213	8,412	9,270	3,648
Effective Tax Rate	44.2%	41.8%	46.3%	43.9%	36.4%	41.6%	71.8%	51.8%	44.1%	43.3%
Net Income	23,931	18,688	17,138	14,099	13,034	7,426	1,132	3,931	5,185	2,070
S&P Core Earnings	22,346	17,772	17,310	14,277	12,471	7,454	2,590	3,518	NA	NA

Balance Sheet & Other Financial Data (Million $)										
Cash	9,560	8,094	11,446	11,144	10,742	5,267	3,781	3,150	2,630	2,032
Current Assets	36,470	39,377	36,304	34,336	28,503	19,426	17,776	18,327	8,213	8,297
Total Assets	161,165	148,786	132,628	125,833	93,208	81,470	77,359	77,572	41,264	40,668
Current Liabilities	32,023	33,798	28,409	25,011	18,795	16,111	19,876	20,654	7,674	8,889
Long Term Debt	6,083	6,753	7,679	12,131	10,456	10,894	10,911	8,989	5,153	5,485
Common Equity	86,648	77,088	73,684	66,722	48,575	40,022	36,176	37,120	21,761	17,749
Total Capital	104,739	95,532	93,219	90,315	66,471	57,601	53,009	52,524	31,822	28,244
Capital Expenditures	19,666	16,678	13,813	8,701	6,310	5,625	7,597	9,713	3,657	4,366
Cash Flow	33,459	26,997	24,644	20,012	17,969	12,810	6,363	10,990	8,033	4,936
Current Ratio	1.1	1.2	1.3	1.4	1.5	1.2	0.9	0.9	1.1	0.9
% Long Term Debt of Capitalization	5.8	7.3	8.2	13.4	15.7	18.9	20.6	17.1	16.2	19.4
% Return on Assets	15.4	13.3	13.3	12.9	14.9	9.4	1.5	5.1	12.7	5.4
% Return on Equity	29.2	25.6	24.4	24.5	29.4	19.5	3.1	10.7	25.1	11.9

Data as orig reptd.; bef. results of disc opers/spec. items. Per share data adj. for stk. divs.; EPS diluted. Quarterly revs. incl. other inc. E-Estimated. NA-Not Available. NM-Not Meaningful. NR-Not Ranked. UR-Under Review.

Office: 6001 Bollinger Canyon Road, San Ramon, CA 94583-2324.
Telephone: 925-842-1000.
Email: invest@chevrontexaco.com
Website: http://www.chevrontexaco.com

Chrmn & CEO: D. O'Reilly
Vice Chrmn: J.S. Watson
CFO: P.E. Yarrington
CTO: J.W. McDonald

Chief Acctg Officer & Cntlr: M.A. Humphrey
Board Members: S. H. Armacost, L. F. Deily, R. E. Denham, R. J. Eaton, E. Hernandez, Jr., F. G. Jenifer, S. A. Nunn, D. O'Reilly, D. B. Rice, K. W. Sharer, C. R. Shoemate, R. D. Sugar, C. Ware, J. S. Watson

Founded: 1901
Domicile: Delaware
Employees: 67,000

C.H. Robinson Worldwide Inc

STANDARD &POOR'S

S&P Recommendation **STRONG BUY** ★★★★★	Price $55.83 (as of Nov 27, 2009)	12-Mo. Target Price $80.00	Investment Style Large-Cap Growth

GICS Sector Industrials
Sub-Industry Air Freight & Logistics

Summary This global provider of multimodal transportation services and logistics solutions has a network of over 200 offices in North America, South America, Europe, and Asia.

Key Stock Statistics (Source S&P, Vickers, company reports)

52-Wk Range	$61.69–37.36	S&P Oper. EPS 2009**E**	2.16	Market Capitalization(B)	$9.365	Beta	0.85
Trailing 12-Month EPS	$2.13	S&P Oper. EPS 2010**E**	2.46	Yield (%)	1.79	S&P 3-Yr. Proj. EPS CAGR(%)	13
Trailing 12-Month P/E	26.2	P/E on S&P Oper. EPS 2009**E**	25.8	Dividend Rate/Share	$1.00	S&P Credit Rating	NA
$10K Invested 5 Yrs Ago	$22,752	Common Shares Outstg. (M)	167.7	Institutional Ownership (%)	80		

Price Performance

30-Week Mov. Avg. · · · · 10-Week Mov. Avg. – – **GAAP Earnings vs. Previous Year** Volume Above Avg. STARS
12-Mo. Target Price — Relative Strength — ▲ Up ▼ Down ▶ No Change Below Avg.

Options: ASE, CBOE, P, Ph

Analysis prepared by **Jim Corridore** on October 22, 2009, when the stock traded at **$ 58.61.**

Qualitative Risk Assessment

LOW	MEDIUM	HIGH

Our risk assessment reflects CHRW's lack of long-term debt and our favorable view of a high quality of earnings and a non-asset-based structure. This is only partially offset, in our view, by exposure to cyclical economic slowdowns and volatile transportation costs.

Quantitative Evaluations

S&P Quality Ranking A+

D	C	B-	B	B+	A-	A	A+

Relative Strength Rank MODERATE

39

LOWEST = 1   HIGHEST = 99

Highlights

► We forecast a 2009 gross revenue decline of 15%, versus the 17% growth CHRW experienced in 2008, reflecting decreased volume and pricing for truck, intermodal, ocean, and air shipping services. We expect declining volumes to be partly offset by market share gains as CHRW increases penetration into existing accounts and adds new accounts. For 2010, we see gross revenues rising about 7% on improving demand related to a strengthening U.S. economy.

► We expect operating margins to widen sharply in 2009 and 2010, reflecting lower purchased transportation costs driven by excess capacity and reduced fuel costs. Partly offsetting this, we see a higher percentage of business from slightly less profitable large customers and expect SG&A to rise modestly as a percentage of revenues. We see operating margins of 8.0% in 2009, and 8.6% in 2010, versus 6.7% in 2008.

► Our 2009 EPS estimate is $2.15, up 3.4% from 2008 EPS of $2.08. For 2010, we see EPS rising 14% to $2.46. We believe the quality of CHRW's earnings is high relative to most other transportation companies we cover.

Investment Rationale/Risk

► We are positive on CHRW's history of strong returns on assets and equity relative to most other transportation companies. Also, CHRW has no long-term debt and has been a generator of cash over the past few years, and we think the quality of its reported earnings has been high relative to peers, as it has no defined benefit pension plan. We also think the company has shown an ability to leverage its non-asset model to generate profits during periods of declining demand, which we think will allow the company to financially outperform most peers during the current difficult economic climate.

► Risks to our recommendation and target price include the possibility of investor rotation out of transportation stocks, a potential further weakening of transport volumes, and sharply lower pricing related to excess industry transportation capacity.

► Our 12-month target price of $80 values the stock at 32.5X our 2010 EPS estimate of $2.46. Our valuation is above peer levels, and within CHRW's historical P/E range over the past five years of 17.5X-36.1X earnings.

Revenue/Earnings Data

Revenue (Million $)

	1Q	2Q	3Q	4Q	Year
2009	1,688	1,926	1,955	--	--
2008	1,985	2,322	2,317	1,955	8,579
2007	1,619	1,880	1,865	1,952	7,316
2006	1,499	1,701	1,713	1,643	6,556
2005	1,215	1,405	1,485	1,584	5,689
2004	946.6	1,077	1,124	1,194	4,342

Earnings Per Share ($)

2009	0.50	0.54	0.57	E0.55	E2.16
2008	0.50	0.52	0.54	0.52	2.08
2007	0.42	0.47	0.48	0.49	1.86
2006	0.33	0.38	0.40	0.42	1.53
2005	0.24	0.29	0.31	0.33	1.16
2004	0.17	0.19	0.22	0.22	0.80

Fiscal year ended Dec. 31. Next earnings report expected: Late January. EPS Estimates based on S&P Operating Earnings; historical GAAP earnings are as reported.

Dividend Data (Dates: mm/dd Payment Date: mm/dd/yy)

Amount ($)	Date Decl.	Ex-Div. Date	Stk. of Record	Payment Date
0.250	02/12	12/02	12/04	01/04/10

Dividends have been paid since 1997. Source: Company reports.

Please read the Required Disclosures and Analyst Certification on the last page of this report.

The McGraw-Hill Companies

C.H. Robinson Worldwide Inc

STANDARD
&POOR'S

Business Summary October 22, 2009

CORPORATE OVERVIEW. With 2008 gross revenues of about $8.6 billion, C.H. Robinson Worldwide is one of the largest third-party logistics companies in North America. At December 31, 2008, the company provided multimodal transportation services and logistics solutions through a network of 228 offices in North America, South America, Europe and Asia. In 2008, gross profits were divided as follows: 89% from transportation, 8% from sourcing, and 3% from information services. Within the transportation segment, CHRW offers several modes of service, including trucks (84% of gross profits in the transportation segment in 2008), intermodal (4%), ocean (6%), air (3%), and miscellaneous (3%).

Through contracts with about 50,000 transportation companies, including motor carriers, railroads, and air freight and ocean carriers, the company maintains the largest network of motor carrier capacity in North America. One of the largest third-party providers of intermodal services in the U.S., it also provides air, ocean and customs services. In addition, CHRW operates value-added logistics services, including fresh produce sourcing, freight consolidation and cross-docking. In 2008, the company handled more than 7.3 million shipments for more than 32,000 customers.

CORPORATE STRATEGY. CHRW has historically grown through internal growth, by expanding current offices, opening new branch offices and hiring additional sales people. Growth has also been augmented through selective acquisitions. In February 2005, the company acquired three produce sourcing and marketing companies: FoodSource Inc., FoodSource Procurement, LLC, and Epic Roots, Inc. The three companies had about $270 million in gross revenues in 2004. In the third quarter of 2005, CHRW purchased two freight forwarding businesses: Hirdes Group Worldwide and Bussini Transport S.r.l., with combined gross revenues of about $52 million in 2004. In May 2006, CHRW acquired certain assets of Paine Lynch and Associates, a third-party logistics company, for $30 million. In July 2007, CHRW purchased LXSI Services, a third-party domestic air and expedited services provider with gross revenues of about $25 million.

Company Financials Fiscal Year Ended Dec. 31

Per Share Data ($)	2008	2007	2006	2005	2004	2003	2002	2001	2000	1999
Tangible Book Value	4.46	4.47	3.86	3.11	2.60	2.09	1.59	1.23	0.85	0.55
Cash Flow	2.24	2.00	1.66	1.27	0.86	0.73	0.64	0.60	0.52	0.38
Earnings	2.08	1.86	1.53	1.16	0.80	0.67	0.56	0.49	0.42	0.32
S&P Core Earnings	2.08	1.86	1.53	1.16	0.79	0.63	0.56	0.47	NA	NA
Dividends	0.90	0.75	0.57	0.36	0.26	0.18	0.13	0.11	0.08	0.07
Payout Ratio	43%	0%	37%	31%	32%	27%	23%	21%	19%	22%
Prices:High	67.36	58.19	55.18	41.70	28.20	21.50	17.70	16.13	16.44	10.52
Prices:Low	36.50	42.11	35.55	23.60	18.30	13.50	12.92	11.41	8.58	6.00
P/E Ratio:High	32	31	36	36	35	32	32	33	40	33
P/E Ratio:Low	18	23	23	20	23	20	23	23	21	19

Income Statement Analysis (Million $)	2008	2007	2006	2005	2004	2003	2002	2001	2000	1999
Revenue	8,579	7,316	6,556	5,689	4,342	3,614	3,294	3,090	2,882	2,261
Operating Income	598	534	439	345	235	195	171	153	134	94.0
Depreciation	26.9	24.1	23.9	18.5	11.8	11.0	14.0	19.1	17.3	10.1
Interest Expense	Nil	Nil	Nil	Nil	Nil	Nil	Nil	Nil	Nil	Nil
Pretax Income	578	524	430	333	226	186	158	138	118	88.5
Effective Tax Rate	37.9%	38.1%	37.9%	38.9%	39.3%	38.7%	39.0%	39.3%	39.5%	39.7%
Net Income	359	324	267	203	137	114	96.3	84.0	71.2	53.3
S&P Core Earnings	359	324	267	203	136	107	94.9	79.8	NA	NA

Balance Sheet & Other Financial Data (Million $)	2008	2007	2006	2005	2004	2003	2002	2001	2000	1999
Cash	497	455	349	231	166	199	133	116	79.9	49.6
Current Assets	1,348	1,389	1,256	1,085	846	717	589	503	460	343
Total Assets	1,816	1,811	1,632	1,395	1,081	908	778	683	644	523
Current Liabilities	698	758	687	612	453	381	343	324	346	276
Long Term Debt	Nil	Nil	Nil	Nil	Nil	Nil	Nil	Nil	Nil	Nil
Common Equity	1,107	1,042	944	780	621	517	426	356	297	247
Total Capital	1,107	1,042	944	782	621	524	432	359	298	247
Capital Expenditures	23.8	43.7	43.2	21.8	34.7	8.57	17.3	17.1	15.5	9.43
Cash Flow	386	348	291	222	149	125	110	103	88.6	63.5
Current Ratio	1.9	1.8	1.8	1.8	1.9	1.9	1.7	1.6	1.3	1.2
% Long Term Debt of Capitalization	Nil	Nil	Nil	Nil	Nil	Nil	Nil	Nil	Nil	Nil
% Net Income of Revenue	4.2	4.4	4.1	3.6	3.2	3.2	2.9	2.7	2.5	2.4
% Return on Assets	19.8	18.8	17.6	16.4	13.8	13.5	13.2	12.7	12.2	11.5
% Return on Equity	33.4	32.7	31.0	29.0	24.1	24.2	24.6	25.7	26.2	25.6

Data as orig reptd.; bef. results of disc opers/spec. items. Per share data adj. for stk. divs.; EPS diluted. E-Estimated. NA-Not Available. NM-Not Meaningful. NR-Not Ranked. UR-Under Review.

Office: 14701 Charlson Rd, Eden Prairie, MN 55347-5076.
Telephone: 952-937-8500.
Website: http://www.chrobinson.com
Chrmn, Pres & CEO: J.P. Wiehoff

SVP, CFO & Chief Acctg Officer: C.M. Lindbloom
Treas: T.A. Renner
Secy & General Counsel: B.G. Campbell
Investor Contact: A. Freeman (952-937-7847)

Board Members: R. Ezrilov, W. M. Fortun, S. L. Polacek, R. K. Roloff, B. Short, J. B. Stake, M. Wickham, J. P. Wiehoff

Founded: 1905
Domicile: Delaware
Employees: 7,961

Chubb Corp (The)

STANDARD &POOR'S

S&P Recommendation **BUY** ★★★★☆	Price $49.54 (as of Nov 27, 2009)	12-Mo. Target Price $58.00	Investment Style Large-Cap Blend

GICS Sector Financials
Sub-Industry Property & Casualty Insurance

Summary One of the largest U.S. property-casualty insurers, Chubb has carved out a number of niches, including high-end personal lines and specialty liability lines coverage.

Key Stock Statistics (Source S&P, Vickers, company reports)

52-Wk Range	$53.79– 34.44	S&P Oper. EPS 2009**E**	5.95	Market Capitalization(B)	$16.921	Beta		0.53
Trailing 12-Month EPS	$5.31	S&P Oper. EPS 2010**E**	5.55	Yield (%)	2.83	S&P 3-Yr. Proj. EPS CAGR(%)		2
Trailing 12-Month P/E	9.3	P/E on S&P Oper. EPS 2009**E**	8.3	Dividend Rate/Share	$1.40	S&P Credit Rating		A+
$10K Invested 5 Yrs Ago	$14,642	Common Shares Outstg. (M)	341.6	Institutional Ownership (%)	86			

Price Performance

- 30-Week Mov. Avg. ··· 10-Week Mov. Avg. -- **GAAP Earnings vs. Previous Year** Volume Above Avg. STARS
- 12-Mo. Target Price — Relative Strength — ▲ Up ▼ Down ▶ No Change Below Avg.

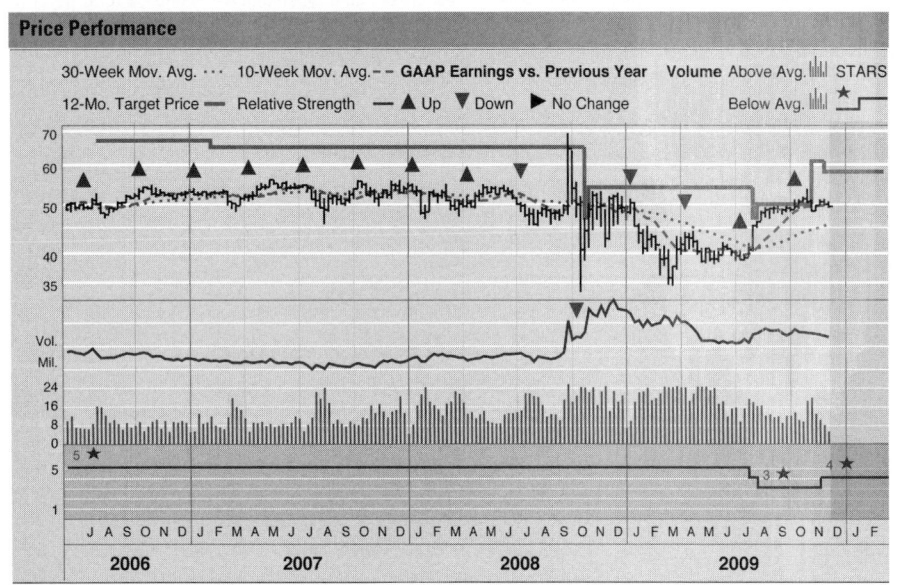

Options: ASE, CBOE, P, Ph

Analysis prepared by **Cathy A. Seifert** on November 16, 2009, when the stock traded at **$ 50.97**.

Highlights

▶ We expect earned premiums from ongoing operations to decline fractionally in 2009, reflecting a weak economy and the legacy impact of soft pricing on business already booked. Earned premiums declined fractionally in 2008, in line with our forecast. We expect CB to leverage its financial strength and gain market share as some of its competitors experience financial stress. Pricing across many lines of business is also beginning to firm. These two factors should aid premium growth in 2010, by our analysis.

▶ We see investment income declining approximately 5% in 2009, as still relatively low investment yields are being offset by relatively favorable cash flow trends. EPS results will likely be aided by share buybacks, such as the 26.3 million shares repurchased during 2008 at a cost of $1.3 billion.

▶ Our operating EPS estimates of $5.95 for 2009 and $5.55 for 2010 (versus the $5.58 reported for 2008 and the $6.41 reported for 2007) reflect our view that underwriting margins will narrow amid a return to "normal" levels of catastrophe claims in 2010, but that CB will not incur any large one-time reserve boosts.

Investment Rationale/Risk

▶ We recently upgraded our recommendation on the shares to Buy, from Hold. We believe concerns over the adequacy of loss reserves in the professional liability unit may be eased by $545 million of favorable (year to date through 9/30/09) prior-year loss development trends that CB said included its professional liability lines. We also think CB has a superior personal lines franchise; and a wider margin mix of business and higher quality balance sheet than many of its peers. However, our outlook is tempered by our concern that a weak economy will continue to dampen CB's top-line results.

▶ Risks to our recommendation and target price include deterioration in claim trends and loss reserves, and greater-than-expected deterioration in the company's investment portfolio. There is also a risk that competitive pricing pressures may not ease as much as expected.

▶ Our 12-month target price of $58 assumes that the stock's forward P/E will increase to about 10.5X our operating EPS estimate for 2010. This multiple is about in the line with CB's closest peers, and is approximately the midpoint of its historical range.

Qualitative Risk Assessment

LOW	MEDIUM	HIGH

Our risk assessment reflects our view that CB is a superior underwriter with sound capital and risk management practices and an attractive mix of business. This is offset by our concerns about the impact a prolonged economic slowdown could have on CB's business, and by its exposure to catastrophe and professional liability claims.

Quantitative Evaluations

S&P Quality Ranking A-

D	C	B-	B	B+	A-	A	A+

Relative Strength Rank MODERATE

51

LOWEST = 1   HIGHEST = 99

Revenue/Earnings Data

Revenue (Million $)

	1Q	2Q	3Q	4Q	Year
2009	2,965	3,266	3,320	--	--
2008	3,489	3,354	3,303	3,075	13,221
2007	3,519	3,521	3,549	3,518	14,107
2006	3,506	3,445	3,451	3,601	14,003
2005	3,449	3,451	3,479	3,703	14,082
2004	3,178	3,206	3,345	3,448	13,177

Earnings Per Share ($)

2009	0.95	1.54	1.69	E1.46	E5.95
2008	1.77	1.27	0.73	1.13	4.92
2007	1.71	1.75	1.87	1.68	7.01
2006	1.58	1.41	1.43	1.56	5.98
2005	1.18	1.23	0.60	1.46	4.47
2004	0.94	0.93	0.94	1.20	4.01

Fiscal year ended Dec. 31. Next earnings report expected: Late January. EPS Estimates based on S&P Operating Earnings; historical GAAP earnings are as reported.

Dividend Data (Dates: mm/dd Payment Date: mm/dd/yy)

Amount ($)	Date Decl.	Ex-Div. Date	Stk. of Record	Payment Date
0.330	12/04	12/17	12/19	01/13/09
0.350	02/26	03/18	03/20	04/07/09
0.350	06/11	06/24	06/26	07/14/09
0.350	09/03	09/16	09/18	10/06/09

Dividends have been paid since 1902. Source: Company reports.

Please read the Required Disclosures and Analyst Certification on the last page of this report.

The McGraw-Hill Companies

Chubb Corp (The)

STANDARD
&POOR'S

Business Summary November 16, 2009

CORPORATE OVERVIEW. Chubb Corp.'s property-casualty operations are divided into three strategic business units: Personal Lines (33% of net written insurance premiums in 2008); Commercial Insurance (42%); and Specialty Insurance (25%). Net written premiums totaled $11.78 billion in 2008, down less than 1% from net written premiums of $11.87 billion recorded in 2007. During 2008, 76% of CB's written premiums originated in the United States, while 24% was derived from overseas.

The Personal Insurance division offers primarily automobile and homeowners' insurance coverage. The company's products are typically targeted to individuals with upscale homes and automobiles, requiring more coverage choices and higher policy limits than are offered under standard insurance policies. Net written premiums totaled $3.8 billion in 2008 (up 2.7% from $3.7 billion in 2007), and were divided as follows: homeowners' 64%, automobile 16%, and other (mainly personal article coverage) 20%.

Chubb Commercial Insurance underwrites an array of commercial insurance

policies, including those for multiple peril, casualty, workers' compensation, and property and marine coverage. Net written premiums totaled $4.99 billion in 2008 (down 1.8% from $5.08 billion in 2007) and were divided as follows: commercial casualty 33%, commercial multi-peril 24%, property and marine 26%, and workers' compensation 17%.

Chubb Specialty Insurance offers a variety of specialized executive protection and professional liability products for privately and publicly owned companies, financial institutions, professional firms, and health care organizations. Net written premiums totaled $2.9 billion in 2008 (down fractionally from $2.94 billion in 2007), and were divided as follows: professional liability 88% and surety 12%. Reinsurance assumed totaled $64 million in 2008, down from $136 million in 2007.

Company Financials Fiscal Year Ended Dec. 31

Per Share Data ($)	2008	2007	2006	2005	2004	2003	2002	2001	2000	1999
Tangible Book Value	36.63	37.31	32.57	28.56	25.06	21.50	18.67	17.81	18.58	16.42
Operating Earnings	NA	NA	NA	NA	NA	NA	0.58	0.31	1.91	1.67
Earnings	4.92	7.01	5.98	4.47	4.01	2.23	0.65	0.32	2.01	1.83
S&P Core Earnings	5.58	6.41	5.63	3.87	3.63	2.08	0.42	0.19	NA	NA
Dividends	1.32	1.45	1.00	1.08	0.78	0.72	0.70	0.68	0.66	0.64
Payout Ratio	27%	21%	17%	24%	19%	32%	109%	NM	33%	35%
Prices:High	69.39	55.99	54.73	49.73	38.73	34.65	39.32	43.31	45.13	38.19
Prices:Low	33.47	45.65	46.61	36.51	31.50	20.89	25.96	27.77	21.63	22.00
P/E Ratio:High	14	8	9	11	10	16	61	NM	23	21
P/E Ratio:Low	7	7	8	8	8	9	40	NM	11	12

Income Statement Analysis (Million $)										
Premium Income	11,828	11,946	11,958	12,176	11,636	10,183	8,035	6,656	6,146	5,652
Net Investment Income	1,732	1,738	1,580	1,408	1,256	1,118	997	983	957	893
Other Revenue	-339	423	465	12,675	286	93.2	57.7	115	6,294	184
Total Revenue	13,221	14,107	14,003	14,082	13,177	11,394	9,140	7,754	7,252	6,730
Pretax Income	2,537	3,937	3,525	2,447	2,068	934	168	-66.0	851	710
Net Operating Income	NA	NA	NA	NA	NA	NA	201	111	681	565
Net Income	1,804	2,807	2,528	1,826	1,548	809	223	112	715	621
S&P Core Earnings	2,045	2,564	2,378	1,578	1,402	754	146	65.2	NA	NA

Balance Sheet & Other Financial Data (Million $)										
Cash & Equivalent	491	489	449	427	392	1,044	1,644	691	720	735
Premiums Due	2,201	2,227	2,314	2,319	2,336	2,188	6,112	6,198	3,263	1,235
Investment Assets:Bonds	32,755	33,871	31,966	30,523	28,009	22,412	18,263	16,117	15,564	14,519
Investment Assets:Stocks	1,479	2,320	1,957	2,212	1,841	1,514	795	710	831	769
Investment Assets:Loans	Nil	Nil	Nil	Nil	Nil	Nil	Nil	Nil	Nil	Nil
Investment Assets:Total	38,738	40,081	37,693	34,893	31,504	26,934	21,279	17,784	17,001	16,019
Deferred Policy Costs	1,532	1,556	1,480	1,445	1,435	1,343	1,150	929	842	780
Total Assets	48,429	50,574	50,277	48,061	44,260	38,361	34,114	29,449	25,027	23,537
Debt	3,975	3,460	1,791	2,467	2,814	2,814	1,959	2,901	754	759
Common Equity	13,432	14,445	13,863	12,407	10,126	8,522	6,859	6,525	6,982	6,272
Property & Casualty:Loss Ratio	58.5	52.8	55.2	64.3	63.1	67.6	75.4	80.8	67.5	70.3
Property & Casualty:Expense Ratio	30.2	30.1	29.0	28.0	29.2	30.4	31.3	32.6	32.9	32.5
Property & Casualty Combined Ratio	88.7	82.9	84.2	92.3	92.3	98.0	106.7	113.4	100.4	102.8
% Return on Revenue	13.6	19.8	18.1	13.0	11.8	7.1	2.4	1.4	9.9	9.2
% Return on Equity	12.9	19.8	19.2	16.2	16.6	10.5	3.3	1.7	10.8	10.4

Data as orig reptd.; bef. results of disc opers/spec. items. Per share data adj. for stk. divs.; EPS diluted. E-Estimated. NA-Not Available. NM-Not Meaningful. NR-Not Ranked. UR-Under Review.

Office: 15 Mountain View Road, Warren, NJ 07061-1615.
Telephone: 908-903-2000.
Email: info@chubb.com
Website: http://www.chubb.com

Chrmn, Pres & CEO: J.D. Finnegan
Vice Chrmn & COO: J.J. Degnan
EVP & CFO: R.G. Spiro
EVP & Chief Admin Officer: D.E. Robusto

EVP & General Counsel: M.A. Brundage
Investor Contact: G.A. Montgomery (908-903-2365)
Board Members: Z. Baird, S. P. Burke, J. I. Cash, Jr., J. J. Cohen, J. J. Degnan, J. D. Finnegan, K. J. Mangold, M. G. McGuinn, S. R. Pozzi, L. M. Small, J. Soderberg, D. E. Somers, K. H. Williams, J. M. Zimmerman, A. W. Zollar

Founded: 1967
Domicile: New Jersey
Employees: 10,400

CIENA Corp

STANDARD &POOR'S

S&P Recommendation HOLD ★★★☆☆

Price
$12.15 (as of Nov 27, 2009)

12-Mo. Target Price
$13.00

Investment Style
Large-Cap Blend

GICS Sector Information Technology
Sub-Industry Communications Equipment

Summary This company manufactures telecommunications equipment used to increase the capacity of fiber optic networks.

Key Stock Statistics (Source S&P, Vickers, company reports)

52-Wk Range	$16.64–4.98	S&P Oper. EPS 2009**E**	-0.86	Market Capitalization(B)	$1.112	Beta	2.15
Trailing 12-Month EPS	$-6.37	S&P Oper. EPS 2010**E**	-0.15	Yield (%)	Nil	S&P 3-Yr. Proj. EPS CAGR(%)	13
Trailing 12-Month P/E	NM	P/E on S&P Oper. EPS 2009**E**	NM	Dividend Rate/Share	Nil	S&P Credit Rating	B
$10K Invested 5 Yrs Ago	$7,053	Common Shares Outstg. (M)	91.5	Institutional Ownership (%)	100		

Price Performance

30-Week Mov. Avg. · · · 10-Week Mov. Avg. - - **GAAP Earnings vs. Previous Year** Volume Above Avg. ▨▨ STARS
12-Mo. Target Price — Relative Strength — ▲ Up ▼ Down ▶ No Change Below Avg. ▨▨ ★

Options: ASE, CBOE, P, Ph

Analysis prepared by **Ari Bensinger** on October 29, 2009, when the stock traded at **$11.76**.

Highlights

▸ Following an estimated 29% sales decline in FY 09 (Oct.), we forecast sales to advance 11% in FY 10, reflecting a rebound in demand for optical transport and switching products as the macroeconomic environment begins to improve. We look for CIEN to benefit from new product introductions during FY 10. The company has particular sales exposure to AT&T, which accounts for approximately 25% of its revenue.

▸ We see FY 10 gross margins widening roughly 300 basis points, to 47%, from expected FY 09 levels, on higher sales volume and manufacturing efficiencies. We look for FY 10 operating expenses as a percentage of sales to decline from projected FY 09 levels on cost management programs, despite increased investment in R&D to support higher prototype costs.

▸ After lower interest income and minimal taxes expected (due to loss carryovers), we project a FY 10 operating loss of $0.15 per share, compared to the $0.86 loss we forecast for FY 09. Estimates for both periods include projected stock option expense of $0.36.

Investment Rationale/Risk

▸ Despite a challenging near-term economic climate, we are positive on CIEN's long-term prospects given our forecast for a material increase in bandwidth demand. We see the pending acquisition of Nortel Networks' Metro Ethernet Networking business improving CIEN's optical transport standing, particularly in the emerging 40G arena, and diversifying its concentrated customer base. However, we note that the $521 million purchase price, which includes $390 million cash, will put the company in a net debt position.

▸ Risks to our recommendation and target price include a prolonged downturn in telecom spending, slower-than-expected sales generation from new products, and integration risks related to the pending Nortel asset acquisition.

▸ Our 12-month target price of $13 equals 2.4X book value and 1.7X our FY 10 sales per share estimate, in line with peers. These multiples, however, are toward the low end of CIEN's historical valuation ranges, warranted, in our view, by the company's poor sales visibility, continued operating losses, and customer concentration risk.

Qualitative Risk Assessment

LOW	MEDIUM	HIGH

Our risk assessment reflects the intense competitive environment in which the company operates and the increased buying power of customers. Given that CIEN competes against larger equipment companies with broader product offerings and larger service teams to meet customer needs, we think profitability runs the risk of being pressured.

Quantitative Evaluations

S&P Quality Ranking B

D	C	B-	B	B+	A-	A	A+

Relative Strength Rank WEAK

25

LOWEST = 1   HIGHEST = 99

Revenue/Earnings Data

Revenue (Million $)

	1Q	2Q	3Q	4Q	Year
2009	167.4	144.2	164.8	--	--
2008	227.4	242.2	253.2	179.7	902.5
2007	165.1	193.5	205.0	216.2	779.8
2006	120.4	131.2	152.5	160.0	564.1
2005	94.75	103.9	110.5	118.2	427.3
2004	66.41	74.70	75.59	82.01	298.7

Earnings Per Share ($)

2009	-0.27	-5.53	-0.29	E-0.18	E-0.86
2008	0.28	0.23	0.12	-0.28	0.42
2007	0.12	0.14	0.12	0.30	0.87
2006	-0.08	-0.02	-0.05	0.14	0.01
2005	-0.70	-0.91	-0.63	-3.08	-5.32
2004	-1.12	-1.12	-1.75	-6.09	-10.57

Fiscal year ended Oct. 31. Next earnings report expected: Mid December. EPS Estimates based on S&P Operating Earnings; historical GAAP earnings are as reported.

Dividend Data

No cash dividends have been paid.

The **McGraw-Hill** Companies

CIENA Corp

Business Summary October 29, 2009

CORPORATE OVERVIEW. CIENA Corp. supplies communications networking equipment, software and services to communications service providers, cable operators, governments and enterprises. The company specializes in transitioning legacy communications networks to converged, next-generation architectures, capable of efficiently delivering a broader mix of high-bandwidth services. Customers AT&T and British Telecom accounted for 25% and 13% of FY 08 (Oct.) sales, respectively. International sales represented 35% of FY 08 sales, up from 29% in the prior period. Product revenue is categorized in two primary business segments: optical service delivery and carrier Ethernet service delivery.

PRIMARY BUSINESS DYNAMICS. Optical service delivery products account for the majority of company revenue (81% of FY 08 sales) and consist of metro and core transport and switching products, multiservice optical access solutions, and legacy data networking products. These products enable service providers to increase the efficiency and bandwidth of their communications networks, allowing them to service more customers, more cost effectively. Flagship offerings include the CoreDirector optical switch and the CN 4200

FlexSelect advanced services platform.

Carrier Ethernet service delivery products (6%) include service delivery switching and aggregation platforms acquired from the March 2008 acquisition of World Wide Packet, broadband access products for residential services and Ethernet access products for enterprise broadband. These products allow telecommunications service providers to transition their legacy voice networks to support next-generation services such as Internet-based (IP) telephony, video services and DSL. These products also facilitate broader service offerings to compete with cable operators.

The company also offers its customers a wide variety of services support, including installation, deployment, maintenance and training activities under the global network services segment (12%).

Company Financials Fiscal Year Ended Oct. 31

Per Share Data ($)	2008	2007	2006	2005	2004	2003	2002	2001	2000	1999
Tangible Book Value	4.99	6.37	5.19	0.66	6.58	13.10	20.24	40.62	19.54	26.19
Cash Flow	0.86	1.25	0.54	-4.41	-9.17	-4.59	-28.08	-33.96	3.39	2.44
Earnings	0.42	0.87	0.01	-5.32	-10.57	-6.09	-30.60	-40.27	1.89	-0.11
S&P Core Earnings	0.50	0.92	-0.05	-4.48	-7.70	-6.09	-23.52	-22.47	NA	NA
Dividends	Nil	Nil	Nil	Nil	Nil	Nil	Nil	Nil	Nil	Nil
Payout Ratio	Nil	Nil	Nil	Nil	Nil	Nil	Nil	Nil	Nil	Nil
Prices:High	35.82	49.55	39.36	24.02	57.00	54.20	121.15	756.30	1057	261.07
Prices:Low	5.07	24.75	20.38	11.51	11.69	29.35	16.88	64.43	158.88	47.71
P/E Ratio:High	85	57	NM	NM	NM	NM	NM	NM	NM	NM
P/E Ratio:Low	12	28	NM	NM	NM	NM	NM	NM	NM	NM

Income Statement Analysis (Million $)										
Revenue	902	780	564	427	299	283	361	1,603	859	482
Operating Income	87.2	83.0	15.1	-115	-185	-209	-569	324	163	43.5
Depreciation	56.6	42.0	45.5	76.0	107	93.7	131	283	63.6	50.4
Interest Expense	12.9	27.0	24.2	25.4	26.8	36.3	45.3	30.6	0.34	0.50
Pretax Income	41.5	85.7	1.98	-434	-788	-385	-1,487	-1,707	121	-5.99
Effective Tax Rate	6.37%	3.40%	69.9%	NM	NM	NM	NM	NM	32.5%	NM
Net Income	38.9	82.8	0.60	-436	-789	-387	-1,597	-1,794	81.4	-3.92
S&P Core Earnings	47.2	87.6	-3.97	-367	-573	-386	-1,225	-1,001	NA	NA

Balance Sheet & Other Financial Data (Million $)										
Cash	917	892	220	373	203	310	377	398	238	262
Current Assets	1,185	1,969	1,098	1,102	1,079	1,229	1,638	2,191	813	533
Total Assets	2,025	2,416	1,840	1,675	2,137	2,378	2,751	3,317	1,027	678
Current Liabilities	179	730	162	178	159	186	224	254	173	106
Long Term Debt	798	802	844	650	692	794	919	870	Nil	Nil
Common Equity	999	850	754	735	1,154	1,331	1,527	2,129	810	530
Total Capital	1,797	1,652	1,598	1,385	1,846	2,125	2,246	3,063	849	567
Capital Expenditures	30.0	32.0	33.0	11.3	33.0	29.5	66.3	239	124	46.8
Cash Flow	95.5	125	46.0	-360	-682	-293	-1,466	-1,511	145	46.5
Current Ratio	6.6	2.7	6.8	6.2	6.8	6.6	7.3	8.6	4.7	5.1
% Long Term Debt of Capitalization	44.4	48.5	52.8	46.9	37.5	37.4	37.6	28.4	Nil	Nil
% Net Income of Revenue	4.3	10.6	0.1	NM	NM	NM	NM	NM	9.5	NM
% Return on Assets	1.8	3.8	0.0	NM	NM	NM	NM	NM	9.5	NM
% Return on Equity	4.2	10.3	0.1	NM	NM	NM	NM	NM	12.1	NM

Data as orig reptd.; bef. results of disc opers/spec. items. Per share data adj. for stk. divs.; EPS diluted. E-Estimated. NA-Not Available. NM-Not Meaningful. NR-Not Ranked. UR-Under Review.

Office: 1201 Winterson Road, Linthicum, MD 21090-2205.
Telephone: 410-865-8500.
Email: ir@ciena.com
Website: http://www.ciena.com

Chrmn: P.H. Nettles
Chrmn: J.W. Bayless
Pres & CEO: G.B. Smith
COO & SVP: A.D. Smith

SVP & CFO: J.E. Moylan, Jr.
Board Members: J. W. Bayless, S. P. Bradley, H. B. Cash, B. L. Claflin, L. W. Fitt, P. T. Gallagher, P. H. Nettles, J. M. O'Brien, M. J. Rowny, G. B. Smith

Founded: 1992
Domicile: Delaware
Employees: 2,203

CIGNA Corp.

STANDARD &POOR'S

S&P Recommendation HOLD ★★★★★	Price $32.64 (as of Nov 27, 2009)	12-Mo. Target Price $34.00	Investment Style Large-Cap Growth

GICS Sector Health Care
Sub-Industry Managed Health Care

Summary CIGNA is one of the largest investor-owned employee benefits organizations in the U.S. Its subsidiaries are major providers of employee benefits offered through the workplace.

Key Stock Statistics (Source S&P, Vickers, company reports)

52-Wk Range	$33.25–11.01	S&P Oper. EPS 2009E	3.90	Market Capitalization(B)	$8.925	Beta		1.82
Trailing 12-Month EPS	$2.80	S&P Oper. EPS 2010E	4.00	Yield (%)	0.12	S&P 3-Yr. Proj. EPS CAGR(%)		8
Trailing 12-Month P/E	11.7	P/E on S&P Oper. EPS 2009E	8.4	Dividend Rate/Share	$0.04	S&P Credit Rating		BBB
$10K Invested 5 Yrs Ago	$14,024	Common Shares Outstg. (M)	273.4	Institutional Ownership (%)	81			

Price Performance

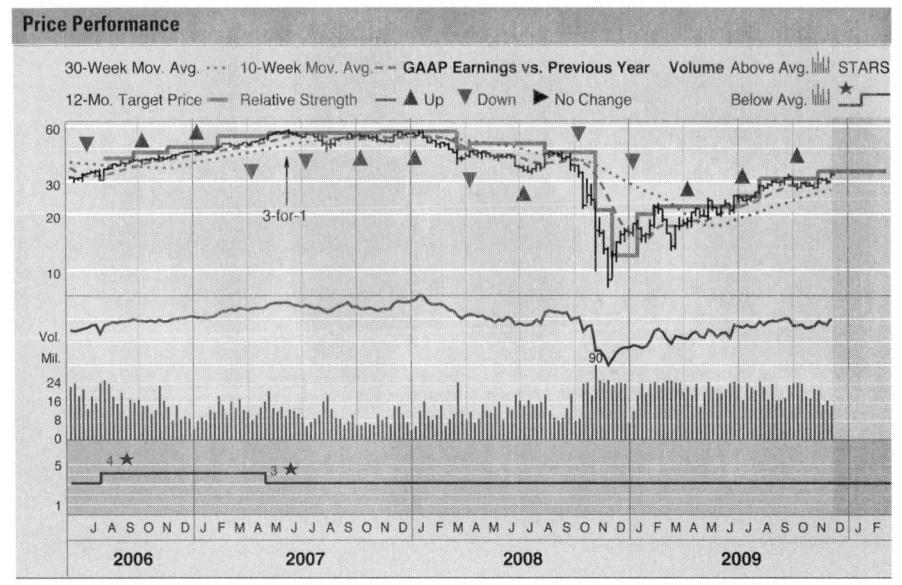

30-Week Mov. Avg. · · · 10-Week Mov. Avg. - - - GAAP Earnings vs. Previous Year   Volume Above Avg. STARS
12-Mo. Target Price — Relative Strength — ▲ Up ▼ Down ► No Change   Below Avg.

3-for-1

Options: ASE, CBOE, P, Ph

Analysis prepared by **Phillip M. Seligman** on November 18, 2009, when the stock traded at **$ 30.34**.

Highlights

► We look for health care segment operating revenue to grow by less than 1% in 2010, assuming medical enrollment stabilizes, following an almost 3% revenue decline amid a 5%-5.5% drop in members we see in 2009.

► CI has been realizing medical cost trends near the upper end of the 7%-8% range (up 50 basis points, or bps, from 2008) it previously targeted, driven by the impact of H1N1, which, along with unfavorable reserve development, pressured health care segment earnings. Looking ahead, we expect 2010 segment earnings to continue to be pressured by H1N1 costs, but to benefit from operating cost initiatives under way in 2009. Elsewhere, we look for the group disability and life and international segments to continue to expand, but also to realize unfavorable claims experience.

► We estimate operating EPS of $3.90 in 2009, before $0.58 of net one-time gains, versus $3.42 in 2008, after $1.58 of variable annuity death benefits reserve charges in the run-off reinsurance unit and $0.40 of other one-time charges. We look for $4.00 in 2010.

Investment Rationale/Risk

► CI appears to be losing a greater percentage of commercial members than its peers amid intensified competition and the soft economy. While we are taking a wait-and-see attitude regarding whether new individual and small-group products will help stem the enrollment decline, we are cautiously optimistic. Meanwhile, we think CI has made gains in improving its health care segment's operating cost structure, but has more to go to attain optimal cost levels for its lower medical membership. On the upside, we also view CI as well capitalized and its investment portfolio as healthy, despite investment losses. We do not see a change in CI's strategies with the planned retirement of its chairman and CEO. We think CI would realize improved financial flexibility should it decide to sell its pharmacy benefit management unit (PBM), as WellPoint (WLP 53, Buy) has agreed to do.

► Risks to our recommendation and target price include intensified competition and higher-than-expected medical costs.

► Our 12-month target price of $34 assumes a below-peer multiple of 8.5X our 2010 EPS estimate.

Qualitative Risk Assessment

LOW	MEDIUM	HIGH

Our risk assessment reflects our view of CI's improving cost structure, strong cash flow, diversity, and wide range of products. However, competition is intensifying in the managed care market, and CI's focus on maintaining pricing discipline amid a weak economy is contributing to declines in enrollment.

Quantitative Evaluations

S&P Quality Ranking   B

D	C	B-	B	B+	A-	A	A+

Relative Strength Rank   STRONG
89
LOWEST = 1   HIGHEST = 99

Revenue/Earnings Data

Revenue (Million $)

	1Q	2Q	3Q	4Q	Year
2009	4,773	4,488	4,517	--	--
2008	4,569	4,863	4,852	4,817	19,101
2007	4,374	4,381	4,413	4,455	17,623
2006	4,107	4,098	4,137	4,205	16,547
2005	4,345	4,107	4,022	4,210	16,684
2004	4,722	4,633	4,479	4,342	18,176

Earnings Per Share ($)

2009	0.76	1.58	1.19	E0.93	E3.90
2008	0.20	0.98	0.62	-0.78	1.04
2007	0.93	0.75	1.28	0.93	3.88
2006	0.96	0.78	0.93	0.76	3.44
2005	1.09	0.94	0.67	0.59	3.28
2004	0.49	1.20	0.75	1.39	3.81

Fiscal year ended Dec. 31. Next earnings report expected: Early February. EPS Estimates based on S&P Operating Earnings; historical GAAP earnings are as reported.

Dividend Data (Dates: mm/dd Payment Date: mm/dd/yy)

Amount ($)	Date Decl.	Ex-Div. Date	Stk. of Record	Payment Date
0.040	02/25	03/09	03/11	04/10/09

Dividends have been paid since 1867. Source: Company reports.

Please read the Required Disclosures and Analyst Certification on the last page of this report.

The McGraw·Hill Companies

CIGNA Corp.

STANDARD &POOR'S

Business Summary November 18, 2009

CORPORATE OVERVIEW. CIGNA Corp., one of the largest U.S. employee benefits organizations, provides health care products and services and group life, accident and disability insurance.

Health Care offers group medical, dental, behavioral health and pharmacy services products. Medical products include consumer directed health plans (CDHPs), HMOs, network only, point-of-service (POS) plans, preferred provider organizations (PPOs), and traditional indemnity coverage. The health care products and services are offered through guaranteed cost, retrospectively experience-rated, administrative services only (ASO) and minimum premium funding arrangements. Under ASO, the employer or other plan sponsor self-funds all of its claims and assumes the risk for claim costs incurred. CI's CDHPs offer a modular product portfolio that provides a choice of benefits network and various funding, medical management, consumerism and health advocacy options for employers and consumers.

Medical covered lives at September 30, 2009, totaled 11,104,000 (versus 11,679,000 as of December 31, 2008): 1,033,000 (1,127,000) guaranteed cost (commercial HMO, Medicare, and voluntary/limited benefits); 764,000 (864,000) experience-related indemnity; and 9,307,000 (9,688,000) ASO.

Disability and Life, which provides employer-paid and voluntary life, accident and disability products, held group life insurance policies covering 6.2 million lives at year-end 2008, up from 6.0 million at year-end 2007. International operates in selected markets outside the U.S., providing individual and group life, accident and health, health care and pension products. CI's invested assets under management at year-end 2008 totaled $18.0 billion, versus $17.5 billion at year-end 2007.

Company Financials Fiscal Year Ended Dec. 31

Per Share Data ($)	2008	2007	2006	2005	2004	2003	2002	2001	2000	1999
Tangible Book Value	0.21	13.93	8.73	10.30	9.05	6.85	2.74	7.62	7.75	8.22
Operating Earnings	NA	NA	NA	NA	NA	NA	NA	2.45	2.02	1.17
Earnings	1.04	3.88	3.44	3.28	3.81	1.47	-0.94	2.20	2.03	1.18
S&P Core Earnings	1.21	4.10	3.34	2.80	2.62	1.21	-0.24	1.77	NA	NA
Dividends	NA	0.04	0.03	0.03	0.14	0.44	0.44	0.43	0.41	0.40
Relative Payout	NA	1%	1%	1%	4%	30%	NM	19%	20%	34%
Prices:High	NA	57.61	44.59	39.94	27.76	19.53	37.00	44.98	45.58	32.88
Prices:Low	NA	42.33	29.35	26.04	17.63	13.03	11.38	23.29	20.25	21.15
P/E Ratio:High	NA	15	13	12	7	13	NM	20	22	28
P/E Ratio:Low	NA	11	9	8	5	9	NM	11	10	18

Income Statement Analysis (Million $)										
Life Insurance in Force	NA	NA	NA	NA	NA	459,995	516,661	609,970	647,464	662,693
Premium Income:Life A & H	NA	15,008	13,641	13,695	14,236	15,441	15,737	15,367	16,328	15,079
Premium Income:Casualty/Property.	NA	NA	NA	Nil	Nil	Nil	Nil	Nil	Nil	Nil
Net Investment Income	NA	1,114	1,195	1,359	1,643	2,594	2,716	2,843	2,942	2,959
Total Revenue	19,101	17,623	16,547	16,684	18,176	18,808	19,348	19,115	19,994	18,781
Pretax Income	288	1,631	1,731	1,793	2,375	903	-569	1,497	1,497	1,219
Net Operating Income	NA	NA	NA	NA	NA	NA	NA	1,101	983	695
Net Income	288	1,120	1,159	1,276	1,577	620	-397	989	987	699
S&P Core Earnings	335	1,180	1,127	1,090	1,082	509	-99.2	794	NA	NA

Balance Sheet & Other Financial Data (Million $)										
Cash & Equivalent	1,439	2,203	1,647	1,991	2,804	1,860	2,079	2,455	2,739	2,732
Premiums Due	NA	8,736	9,501	8,616	16,223	9,421	9,981	2,832	2,814	2,475
Investment Assets:Bonds	NA	12,081	12,155	14,947	16,136	17,121	27,803	23,401	24,776	22,944
Investment Assets:Stocks	NA	132	131	135	33.0	11,300	295	404	569	585
Investment Assets:Loans	NA	4,727	5,393	5,271	5,123	10,227	11,134	12,694	12,755	12,816
Investment Assets:Total	17,921	17,530	18,303	21,376	21,919	39,658	40,362	38,261	41,516	38,295
Deferred Policy Costs	NA	816	707	618	544	580	494	448	1,052	927
Total Assets	41,406	40,065	42,399	44,863	81,059	90,953	88,950	91,589	95,088	95,333
Debt	NA	1,790	1,294	1,338	1,438	1,500	1,500	1,627	1,163	1,359
Common Equity	3,592	4,748	4,330	5,360	5,203	4,465	3,665	5,055	5,634	6,149
Combined Loss-Expense Ratio	NA	NA	NA	NA	NA	NA	NA	NA	NA	NA
% Return on Revenue	1.5	6.4	7.0	7.6	8.7	3.3	NM	5.2	4.9	3.7
% Return on Equity	NA	24.7	23.9	24.2	32.2	15.3	NM	18.9	16.5	9.1
% Investment Yield	6.0	6.3	6.0	6.3	5.3	6.5	6.9	7.3	7.1	7.4

Data as orig reptd.; bef. results of disc opers/spec. items. Per share data adj. for stk. divs.; EPS diluted. E-Estimated. NA-Not Available. NM-Not Meaningful. NR-Not Ranked. UR-Under Review.

Office: 2 Liberty Pl 1601 Chestnut St, Philadelphia, PA 19192-0001.
Telephone: 215-761-1000.
Website: http://www.cigna.com
Chrmn & CEO: H.E. Hanway

Pres & COO: D.M. Cordani
Vice Chrmn: I. Harris, Jr.
EVP & CFO: A.T. Hagan
EVP & General Counsel: C.A. Petren

Investor Contact: T. Detrick (215-761-1414)
Board Members: R. H. Campbell, D. M. Cordani, H. E. Hanway, I. Harris, Jr., J. E. Henney, P. Larson, R. Martinez, IV, J. M. Partridge, J. E. Rogers, C. C. Wait, E. C. Wiseman, D. F. Zarcone, W. D. Zollars

Founded: 1792
Domicile: Delaware
Employees: 30,300

The McGraw·Hill Companies

Cincinnati Financial Corp

STANDARD &POOR'S

S&P Recommendation SELL ★★☆☆☆

Price	12-Mo. Target Price	Investment Style
$25.20 (as of Nov 27, 2009)	$23.00	Large-Cap Blend

GICS Sector Financials
Sub-Industry Property & Casualty Insurance

Summary This insurance holding company markets primarily property and casualty coverage; it also conducts life insurance and asset management operations.

Key Stock Statistics (Source S&P, Vickers, company reports)

52-Wk Range	$31.85–17.84	S&P Oper. EPS 2009**E**	1.12	Market Capitalization(B)	$4.100	Beta	0.72
Trailing 12-Month EPS	$2.14	S&P Oper. EPS 2010**E**	1.92	Yield (%)	6.27	S&P 3-Yr. Proj. EPS CAGR(%)	1
Trailing 12-Month P/E	11.8	P/E on S&P Oper. EPS 2009**E**	22.5	Dividend Rate/Share	$1.58	S&P Credit Rating	BBB+
$10K Invested 5 Yrs Ago	$7,214	Common Shares Outstg. (M)	162.7	Institutional Ownership (%)	59		

Price Performance

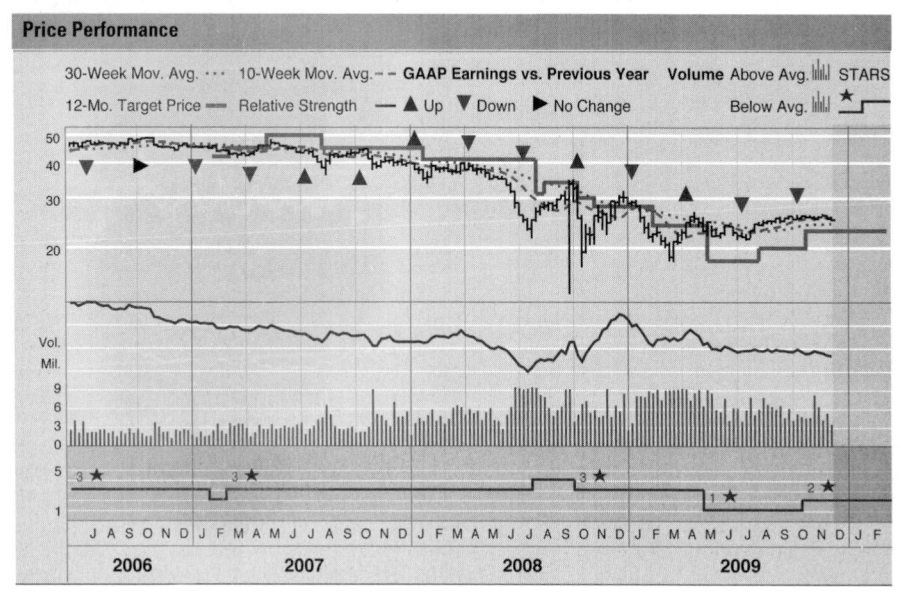

Options: CBOE, P

Analysis prepared by **Cathy A. Seifert** on October 12, 2009, when the stock traded at **$25.95**.

Highlights

► We expect property-casualty earned premiums to decrease 2% to 4% in 2009, following the 3.5% decline in 2008. We see the effects of CINF's expansion being offset by price competition, although we expect competitive pressures to ease somewhat. Competition in many non-coastal regions (such as those where CINF operates) is expected to remain intense. Underwriting margins are likely to remain under pressure amid higher weather-related losses and some cost inflation.

► We estimate that net investment income will decline by more than 10% in 2009, versus the 12% decrease in 2008. This projected decline is worse than the results forecasted for many of CINF's peers, partly reflecting a different asset mix. As of December 31, 2008, nearly 33% of CINF's invested assets were in equity securities, versus an industry average that we estimate at less than 15%. We expect this asset mix to shift away from equities in 2009 as CINF repositions its investment portfolio.

► We see challenging investment and underwriting climates producing operating EPS of $0.68 in 2009 and $1.92 in 2010, versus operating EPS of $2.10 in 2008 and $3.54 in 2007.

Investment Rationale/Risk

► CINF's first-half 2009 results were disappointing, in our view. Our outlook still reflects what we see as the dual challenges of heightened price competition in many of CINF's core lines of business and a more challenging investment environment. We believe CINF's results on both of those fronts lag those of many of its peers. We also believe there exists a high degree of execution risk in a number of the company's expansion strategies. At recent levels, we view the shares as overvalued, particularly on a price-to-earnings basis.

► Risks to our opinion and target price include a significant rebound in underwriting results (including an upturn in earned premiums and a significant widening of underwriting margins); and an improvement in investment results.

► Our 12-month target price of $23 assumes the shares will trade at approximately 12X our 2010 operating EPS estimate, a premium of about 15% to 20% to most of the company's peers, but at the lower end of CINF's historical range.

Qualitative Risk Assessment

LOW | **MEDIUM** | HIGH

Our risk assessment reflects our view of the company as a fairly conservative underwriter with sound risk and capital management policies. However, CINF's investment allocation is more heavily weighted toward equity holdings than that of its peers, although the company has taken steps to re-balance its investments.

Quantitative Evaluations

S&P Quality Ranking A

D | C | B- | B | B+ | A- | **A** | A+

Relative Strength Rank MODERATE
43
LOWEST = 1   HIGHEST = 99

Revenue/Earnings Data

Revenue (Million $)

	1Q	2Q	3Q	4Q	Year
2009	890.0	874.0	1,007	--	--
2008	704.0	917.0	1,186	1,018	3,824
2007	1,031	1,270	982.0	983.0	4,259
2006	1,607	981.0	967.0	995.0	4,550
2005	916.0	940.0	944.0	967.0	3,767
2004	870.0	923.0	879.0	942.0	3,614

Earnings Per Share ($)

2009	0.22	-0.12	1.05	E0.33	E1.12
2008	-0.25	0.38	1.50	0.99	2.63
2007	1.11	2.02	0.72	1.11	4.97
2006	3.13	0.76	0.66	0.75	5.30
2005	0.81	0.89	0.66	1.03	3.40
2004	0.82	0.87	0.50	1.09	3.28

Fiscal year ended Dec. 31. Next earnings report expected: Early February. EPS Estimates based on S&P Operating Earnings; historical GAAP earnings are as reported.

Dividend Data (Dates: mm/dd Payment Date: mm/dd/yy)

Amount ($)	Date Decl.	Ex-Div. Date	Stk. of Record	Payment Date
0.390	02/02	03/18	03/20	04/15/09
0.390	05/22	06/17	06/19	07/15/09
0.395	08/17	09/16	09/18	10/15/09
0.395	11/20	12/21	12/23	01/15/10

Dividends have been paid since 1954. Source: Company reports.

Cincinnati Financial Corp

STANDARD
&POOR'S

Business Summary October 12, 2009

CORPORATE OVERVIEW. Cincinnati Financial Corp. (CINF) underwrites and sells property-casualty insurance primarily in the Midwest and Southeast, through a network of independent agents. Operations as of year-end 2008 were conducted in 35 states, through a network of 1,403 independent insurance agencies, many of which own stock in the company. The company is licensed in all 50 states, the District of Columbia, and Puerto Rico. An ongoing geographical expansion plan is being implemented. Ten states accounted for about 69% of earned premium volume in 2007 (latest available): Ohio (21%), Illinois (9%), Indiana (7%), Pennsylvania (6%), North Carolina (5%), Georgia (5%), Michigan (5%), Virginia (5%), Wisconsin (4%), and Tennessee (3%).

Property-casualty net earned premiums totaled $3.0 billion in 2008, with commercial lines accounting for 77% and personal lines for 23%. During 2007 (latest available), commercial casualty lines of coverage accounted for 34% of commercial lines earned premiums, while commercial property lines coverage accounted for 21%, commercial auto for 18%, workers' compensation for 15%, special package coverages for 6%, surety and executive risk for 4%, and other for 1%. Personal auto accounted for 48% of personal lines earned premiums in 2007, homeowners' coverage for 40%, and other personal lines for 12%.

Underwriting results deteriorated in 2008, largely due to a higher level of catastrophe losses. The loss ratio in 2008 equaled 68.3% (including 6.8 points of catastrophe losses), versus 58.6% (including 0.8 points of catastrophe losses). The expense ratio inched upward, to 32.3%, from 31.7%. Taken together, the combined ratio (before policyholder dividends) equaled 100.6% in 2008, a deterioration from 2007's combined ratio of 90.3%. (A combined ratio of under 100% indicates an underwriting profit, while one in excess of 100% signals an underwriting loss.)

Life, accident and health insurance is marketed through property-casualty agents and independent life insurance agents. This unit has been expanding its work site marketing activities, introducing a new product line and exploring expansion opportunities. Term life insurance represents this unit's largest product line. Life insurance earned premiums totaled $126 million in 2008, up fractionally from earned premiums of $125 million in 2007.

Company Financials Fiscal Year Ended Dec. 31

Per Share Data ($)	2008	2007	2006	2005	2004	2003	2002	2001	2000	1999
Tangible Book Value	25.79	43.60	39.38	34.88	35.60	35.10	31.42	33.62	33.80	30.35
Operating Earnings	NA	NA	2.82	3.02	2.93	NA	1.67	1.17	0.82	1.38
Earnings	2.63	4.97	5.30	3.40	3.28	2.10	1.32	1.08	0.66	1.38
S&P Core Earnings	2.16	3.49	2.78	3.10	2.87	2.09	1.55	1.06	NA	NA
Dividends	1.56	1.42	1.34	1.21	1.04	0.91	0.81	0.76	0.69	0.60
Relative Payout	59%	29%	25%	35%	32%	43%	61%	71%	104%	44%
Prices:High	40.24	48.45	49.19	45.95	43.52	38.01	42.90	38.94	39.29	38.55
Prices:Low	13.68	36.00	41.21	38.38	36.57	30.00	29.42	30.84	23.75	27.32
P/E Ratio:High	15	10	9	14	13	18	32	36	59	28
P/E Ratio:Low	5	7	8	11	11	14	22	29	36	20

Income Statement Analysis (Million $)	2008	2007	2006	2005	2004	2003	2002	2001	2000	1999
Life Insurance in Force	65,887	61,873	56,971	51,493	44,921	48,492	32,486	27,534	23,525	17,890
Premium Income:Life A & H	126	125	115	106	101	95.0	87.0	81.0	79.3	75.0
Premium Income:Casualty/Property.	3,010	3,125	3,163	3,058	2,919	2,653	2,391	2,071	1,828	1,657
Net Investment Income	537	608	570	526	492	465	445	421	415	387
Total Revenue	3,824	4,259	4,550	3,767	3,614	3,181	2,843	2,561	2,331	2,128
Pretax Income	540	1,192	1,329	823	800	480	279	221	109	322
Net Operating Income	NA	NA	496	562	524	286	300	210	120	255
Net Income	429	855	930	602	584	374	238	193	118	255
S&P Core Earnings	354	602	487	549	512	372	279	189	NA	NA

Balance Sheet & Other Financial Data (Million $)	2008	2007	2006	2005	2004	2003	2002	2001	2000	1999
Cash & Equivalent	1,009	226	202	119	306	91.0	112	93.0	60.3	420
Premiums Due	1,818	1,861	1,811	1,797	1,799	1,677	1,483	732	652	192
Investment Assets:Bonds	5,827	5,848	5,805	5,476	5,141	3,925	3,305	3,010	2,721	2,617
Investment Assets:Stocks	2,896	6,249	7,799	7,106	7,498	8,524	7,884	8,495	8,526	7,511
Investment Assets:Loans	Nil	Nil	Nil	Nil	Nil	Nil	Nil	Nil	Nil	Nil
Investment Assets:Total	8,890	12,261	13,759	12,702	12,677	12,527	11,257	11,571	11,316	10,194
Deferred Policy Costs	509	461	453	429	400	372	343	286	259	154
Total Assets	13,369	16,637	17,222	16,003	16,107	15,509	14,059	13,959	13,287	11,380
Debt	840	860	840	791	791	603	420	609	449	457
Common Equity	4,182	5,929	6,808	4,145	6,249	6,204	5,998	5,998	5,995	5,420
Combined Loss-Expense Ratio	100.6	90.3	94.3	89.2	89.8	94.7	98.4	104.9	112.5	100.0
% Return on Revenue	11.2	20.1	23.4	16.0	16.2	11.8	8.4	7.5	5.1	12.0
% Return on Equity	8.5	13.4	14.4	15.4	8.0	5.4	3.6	3.2	1.0	4.6
% Investment Yield	5.3	4.7	4.3	4.1	3.9	3.9	3.9	3.7	3.9	3.8

Data as orig reptd.; bef. results of disc opers/spec. items. Per share data adj. for stk. divs.; EPS diluted. E-Estimated. NA-Not Available. NM-Not Meaningful. NR-Not Ranked. UR-Under Review.

Office: 6200 South Gilmore Road, Fairfield, OH 45014-5141.
Telephone: 513-870-2000.
Email: investor_inquiries@cinfin.com
Website: http://www.cinfin.com

Chrmn: J.J. Schiff, Jr.
Pres & CEO: K.W. Stecher
Vice Chrmn: J.E. Benoski
SVP & Chief Acctg Officer: E.N. Mathews

CFO, Treas & Secy: S.J. Johnston
Investor Contact: H.J. Wietzel (513-870-2768)
Board Members: W. F. Bahl, J. E. Benoski, G. T. Bier, K. C. Lichtendahl, W. R. McMullen, G. W. Price, T. R. Schiff, J. J. Schiff, Jr., D. S. Skidmore, K. W. Stecher, J. F. Steele, Jr., L. R. Webb, E. A. Woods

Founded: 1950
Domicile: Ohio
Employees: 4,179

Cintas Corp

STANDARD &POOR'S

S&P Recommendation HOLD ★★★☆☆	Price $28.33 (as of Nov 27, 2009)	12-Mo. Target Price $31.00	Investment Style Large-Cap Growth

GICS Sector Industrials
Sub-Industry Diversified Support Services

Summary A leader in the corporate identity uniform business, Cintas also provides entrance mats, sanitation supplies, and first aid and safety products.

Key Stock Statistics (Source S&P, Vickers, company reports)

52-Wk Range	$30.85– 18.09	S&P Oper. EPS 2010E	1.90	Market Capitalization(B)	$4.331	Beta	1.00
Trailing 12-Month EPS	$1.32	S&P Oper. EPS 2011E	2.00	Yield (%)	1.66	S&P 3-Yr. Proj. EPS CAGR(%)	4
Trailing 12-Month P/E	21.5	P/E on S&P Oper. EPS 2010E	14.9	Dividend Rate/Share	$0.47	S&P Credit Rating	A-
$10K Invested 5 Yrs Ago	$6,693	Common Shares Outstg. (M)	152.9	Institutional Ownership (%)	72		

Price Performance

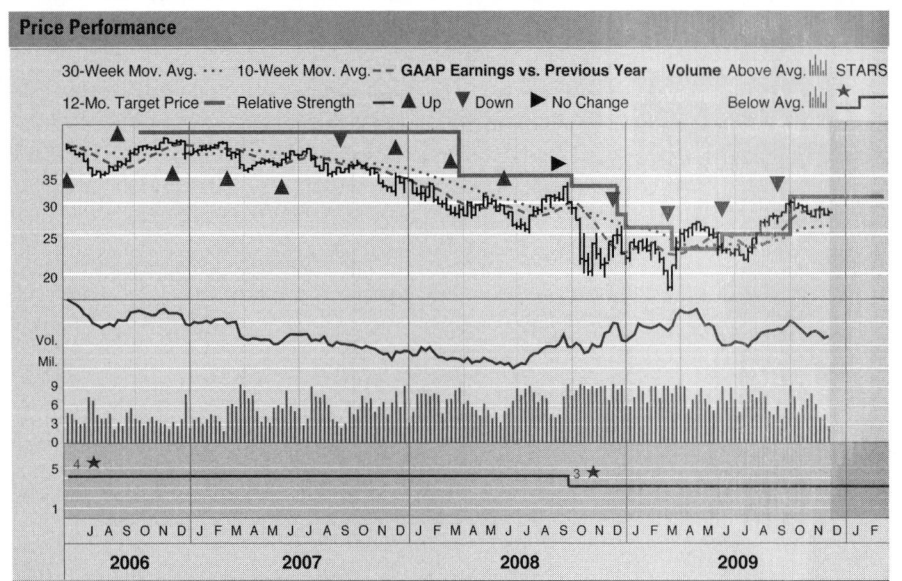

30-Week Mov. Avg. · · · 10-Week Mov. Avg. – – GAAP Earnings vs. Previous Year Volume Above Avg. STARS
12-Mo. Target Price — Relative Strength — ▲ Up ▼ Down ▶ No Change Below Avg.

Options: ASE, CBOE, P, Ph

Analysis prepared by **Kevin Kirkeby** on September 28, 2009, when the stock traded at **$ 30.65**.

Highlights

► We forecast revenues will decline about 3.0% in FY 10 (May), due mostly to ongoing weakness in the uniform segment. Rising unemployment is contributing to fewer uniform rentals and a reduction in laundry services. Auto dealership closures are expected to negatively affect this segment in FY 10. We also expect CTAS's other services, including document management and first aid, to decline due to reduced business activity. However, we anticipate that manufacturing and auto production will show further signs of stabilization in coming months.

► We see margins widening modestly in FY 10, following the late FY 09 facility closures and route consolidation efforts. We also believe that investments in the sales force are taking hold, and helping to improve the add-stop ratio. Still, margin expansion is likely to be muted until there is a turnaround in volumes, given CTAS's operating cost structure, which we consider to have a high fixed component.

► We forecast EPS of $1.90 in FY 10, up from $1.83, excluding restructuring charges, in FY 09. Our estimate does not factor in any additional stock buybacks, as we believe acquisitions will take priority.

Investment Rationale/Risk

► Valuations have steadily compressed during the past four years and are now in line with the S&P 500. We think this is partly due to slowing revenue growth as CTAS's traditional customer base in manufacturing has generally been reducing head count. At the same time, CTAS has been investing heavily to achieve sufficient scale in its non-uniform service offerings. Until these businesses mature and the economy begins to improve, pulling employment higher with it, we see muted net income growth.

► Risks to our recommendation and target price include renewed economic weakness, another rise in fuel prices, further declines in the prices CTAS receives for recycled paper, and regulatory changes that raise labor costs.

► Applying a 16.5X multiple, modestly ahead of the S&P 500 but still below the historical average, to our calendarized 2010 EPS estimate, we calculate a value of $33. Our DCF model yields an intrinsic value of $29, assuming a 9.0% weighted average cost of capital, 5% annual net income growth over the next five years, and 3% growth in perpetuity. Using a weighted blend of these two valuation models results in our 12-month target price of $31.

Qualitative Risk Assessment

LOW	MEDIUM	HIGH

Our risk assessment reflects the company's leading position in its core business, other related services that we believe are showing good growth, and what we view as a relatively strong balance sheet and cash flow.

Quantitative Evaluations

S&P Quality Ranking   **A**

D	C	B-	B	B+	A-	A	A+

Relative Strength Rank   **MODERATE**

51

LOWEST = 1   HIGHEST = 99

Revenue/Earnings Data

Revenue (Million $)

	1Q	2Q	3Q	4Q	Year
2010	891.6	--	--	--	--
2009	1,002	985.2	908.6	878.7	3,775
2008	969.1	983.9	976.0	1,009	3,938
2007	914.2	923.3	905.4	964.1	3,707
2006	823.5	835.8	836.4	907.9	3,404
2005	746.0	756.8	755.2	809.3	3,067

Earnings Per Share ($)

2010	0.35	E0.47	E0.49	E0.51	E1.90
2009	0.51	0.47	0.47	0.03	1.48
2008	0.51	0.53	0.53	0.58	2.15
2007	0.53	0.51	0.48	0.57	2.09
2006	0.47	0.46	0.46	0.55	1.94
2005	0.42	0.43	0.41	0.48	1.74

Fiscal year ended May 31. Next earnings report expected: Late December. EPS Estimates based on S&P Operating Earnings; historical GAAP earnings are as reported.

Dividend Data (Dates: mm/dd Payment Date: mm/dd/yy)

Amount ($)	Date Decl.	Ex-Div. Date	Stk. of Record	Payment Date
0.470	01/13	02/02	02/04	03/11/09

Dividends have been paid since 1984. Source: Company reports.

Please read the Required Disclosures and Analyst Certification on the last page of this report.

The McGraw-Hill Companies

Cintas Corp

Business Summary September 28, 2009

CORPORATE OVERVIEW. Cintas Corp. is North America's leading supplier of corporate uniforms, as well as a significant provider of related services. In FY 09 (May), for the first time in 40 years, the company was unable to deliver an increase in revenues and net profits, reflecting the economic downturn. The company reports financial results using four segments: Rental Uniforms and Ancillary Services, Uniform Direct Sales, Document Management, and First Aid, Safety & Fire Protection.

The Rental operating segment (73% of total revenues in FY 09 and 77% of gross profits, with a 43.3% margin) designs and manufactures corporate uniforms that it rents to its customers. Services provided to the rental markets by the company also include the cleaning of uniforms, as well as the provision of ongoing replacements as required by each customer. The company also offers ancillary products, including the rental or sale of entrance and special purpose mats, towels, mops, and linen products, as well as sanitation supplies and services and cleanroom supplies. It operates through about 7,900 local delivery routes (down from about 8,400 at the end FY 08 following a route re-structuring initiative).

The Uniform Direct Sales segment (11%, 7%, and 24.8% margin) includes the

design, manufacture and direct sale of uniforms to CTAS's national account customers. In recent years, there has been an effort to offer more branded items in its catalogs alongside the traditional propriety uniform and apparel lines. This segment generally has less recurring business than the rental operations.

The First Aid, Safety and Fire Protection segment (10%, 9%, and 38.1% margin) provides first aid equipment, inspection, repair and recharging of portable fire extinguishers, fire suppression systems, and emergency and exit lights. In a short period of time, CTAS believes it has become the second-largest fire protection services company in the U.S., with capabilities in at least 23 of the top 50 cities. Although the company estimated the market for first aid and fire protection services to be about $4.5 billion a year, the recession and an expected decline in non-residential construction over the next year, has prompted the company to re-evaluate its goals for this segment. We expect CTAS to cease providing fire protection services in certain smaller markets.

Company Financials Fiscal Year Ended May 31

Per Share Data ($)	2009	2008	2007	2006	2005	2004	2003	2002	2001	2000
Tangible Book Value	5.83	4.92	4.73	4.73	6.15	6.32	5.42	4.39	6.42	5.42
Cash Flow	2.50	3.10	2.96	2.78	2.43	2.26	2.12	1.95	1.82	1.60
Earnings	1.48	2.15	2.09	1.94	1.74	1.58	1.45	1.36	1.30	1.14
S&P Core Earnings	1.48	2.15	2.09	1.92	1.69	1.54	1.43	1.33	1.27	NA
Dividends	0.46	0.39	0.35	0.32	0.32	0.29	0.27	0.25	0.22	0.19
Payout Ratio	31%	18%	17%	16%	18%	18%	19%	18%	17%	17%
Calendar Year	2008	2007	2006	2005	2004	2003	2002	2001	2000	1999
Prices:High	33.89	42.89	44.30	45.50	50.35	50.68	56.62	53.25	54.00	52.25
Prices:Low	19.51	31.14	34.57	37.51	39.51	30.60	39.15	33.75	23.17	26.00
P/E Ratio:High	23	20	21	23	29	32	42	39	42	46
P/E Ratio:Low	13	14	17	19	23	19	29	25	18	23

Income Statement Analysis (Million $)										
Revenue	3,775	3,938	3,707	3,404	3,067	2,814	2,687	2,271	2,161	1,902
Operating Income	653	726	713	674	614	602	539	478	459	423
Depreciation	158	149	135	127	120	117	115	101	90.2	78.5
Interest Expense	52.5	16.6	50.3	31.8	24.4	25.1	30.9	11.0	15.1	15.9
Pretax Income	362	531	534	522	477	432	396	372	356	312
Effective Tax Rate	37.4%	36.8%	37.3%	37.3%	37.0%	37.0%	37.0%	37.0%	37.6%	38.0%
Net Income	226	335	335	327	301	272	249	234	222	193
S&P Core Earnings	226	335	335	324	293	265	245	229	219	NA

Balance Sheet & Other Financial Data (Million $)										
Cash	250	192	155	241	309	254	57.7	85.1	110	110
Current Assets	1,270	1,282	1,157	1,178	1,167	1,034	878	853	820	721
Total Assets	3,695	3,809	3,570	3,425	3,060	2,810	2,583	2,519	1,752	1,581
Current Liabilities	317	367	403	412	356	326	305	313	251	235
Long Term Debt	786	943	877	794	465	474	535	703	221	254
Common Equity	2,367	2,254	2,168	2,088	2,104	1,888	1,646	1,424	1,231	1,043
Total Capital	3,154	3,198	3,167	3,013	2,703	2,485	2,278	2,207	1,501	1,346
Capital Expenditures	160	190	181	157	141	113	115	170	147	161
Cash Flow	384	484	470	454	420	389	365	335	313	272
Current Ratio	4.0	3.5	2.9	2.9	3.3	3.2	2.9	2.7	3.3	3.1
% Long Term Debt of Capitalization	24.9	28.4	27.7	26.4	17.2	19.1	23.5	31.9	14.7	18.9
% Net Income of Revenue	6.0	8.5	9.0	9.6	9.8	44.4	9.3	10.3	10.3	10.3
% Return on Assets	6.0	9.1	9.6	10.1	10.2	10.1	9.8	11.0	13.3	12.9
% Return on Equity	9.8	15.2	15.7	15.6	15.1	15.4	16.2	17.6	19.6	20.2

Data as orig reptd.; bef. results of disc opers/spec. items. Per share data adj. for stk. divs.; EPS diluted. E-Estimated. NA-Not Available. NM-Not Meaningful. NR-Not Ranked. UR-Under Review.

Office: 6800 Cintas Boulevard, Cincinnati, OH 45262-5737.
Telephone: 513-459-1200.
Website: http://www.cintas.com
Chrmn: R.J. Kohlhepp

Pres & COO: J.P. Holloman
CEO: S.D. Farmer
Investor Contact: W.C. Gale (513-459-1200)
SVP, CFO & Chief Acctg Officer: W.C. Gale

Board Members: G. S. Adolph, G. V. Dirvin, J. Dirvin, R. T. Farmer, S. D. Farmer, J. Hergenhan, J. J. Johnson, R. J. Kohlhepp, D. C. Phillips, R. W. Tysoe
Founded: 1968
Domicile: Washington
Employees: 31,000

Cisco Systems Inc

STANDARD &POOR'S

S&P Recommendation BUY ★★★★☆

Price	**12-Mo. Target Price**	**Investment Style**
$23.38 (as of Nov 27, 2009)	$28.00	Large-Cap Growth

GICS Sector Information Technology
Sub-Industry Communications Equipment

Summary This company offers a complete line of routers and switching products that connect and manage communications among local and wide area computer networks employing a variety of protocols.

Key Stock Statistics (Source S&P, Vickers, company reports)

52-Wk Range	$24.83– 13.61	S&P Oper. EPS 2010**E**	1.30	Market Capitalization(B)	$134.495	Beta	1.21
Trailing 12-Month EPS	$0.98	S&P Oper. EPS 2011**E**	1.45	Yield (%)	Nil	S&P 3-Yr. Proj. EPS CAGR(%)	12
Trailing 12-Month P/E	23.9	P/E on S&P Oper. EPS 2010**E**	18.0	Dividend Rate/Share	Nil	S&P Credit Rating	A+
$10K Invested 5 Yrs Ago	$12,158	Common Shares Outstg. (M)	5,752.6	Institutional Ownership (%)	71		

Price Performance

30-Week Mov. Avg. ···   10-Week Mov. Avg. - - -   **GAAP Earnings vs. Previous Year**   Volume Above Avg. STARS
12-Mo. Target Price —   Relative Strength —   ▲ Up   ▼ Down   ▶ No Change   Below Avg.

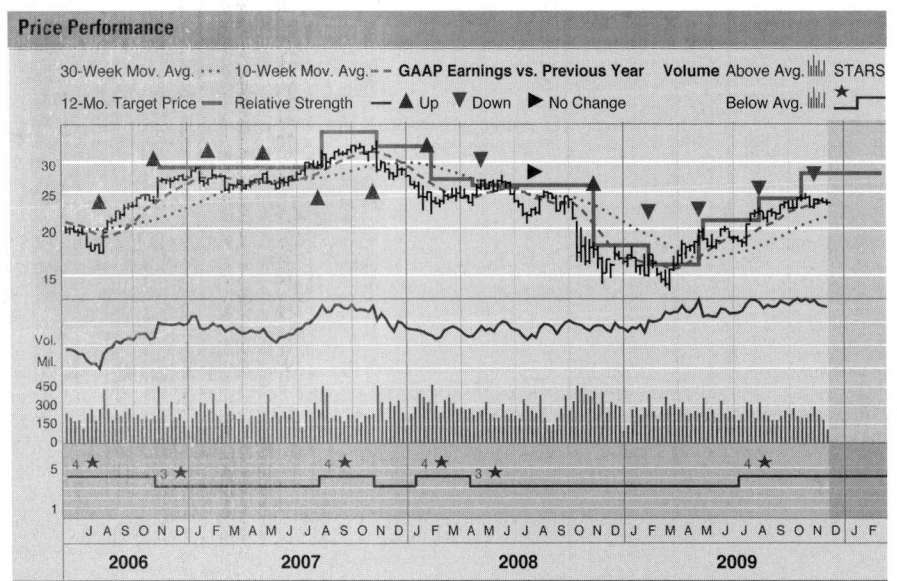

Options: ASE, CBOE, P, Ph

Analysis prepared by **Ari Bensinger** on November 05, 2009, when the stock traded at **$ 23.92**.

Highlights

► Following a 9% decline in FY 09 (Jul.), we see sales increasing 6% in FY 10, on higher networking product demand as the macroeconomic environment begins to improve. With its dominant market share in the large routing and switching sectors and successful positioning in several advanced technology areas, including telepresence, cloud computing, and smart grid, we see CSCO as well positioned for sustained low double-digit sales growth.

► We look for gross margins to remain flat in FY 10, at 65%, as the benefits from higher sales volume and cost savings are offset by a less favorable product mix. We believe CSCO will manage FY 10 costs prudently, and see operating expenses rising at a slower rate than sales. We estimate FY 10 operating margins at 28%.

► After a 22% effective tax rate and continued share repurchases, we project FY 10 operating EPS of $1.30, up from the $1.20 operating EPS posted in FY 09, which excludes $0.15 of non-recurring items, largely consisting of intangible asset amortization expense. We see FY 11 EPS at $1.45.

Investment Rationale/Risk

► We think an industry rebound is underway and view CSCO as well positioned to capture customer spending opportunities that were postponed during the downturn. We like CSCO's more aggressive approach in targeting new market adjacencies, with new product announcements like unified computing (servers), and recent pending acquisitions, such as Tandberg (video conferencing) and Starent (wireless data). We see the continued rapid rise in network traffic usage acting as a strong underlying growth driver for the company.

► Risks to our recommendation and target price include a slower-than-expected recovery in enterprise and telecom spending, increased competition, and intensifying pricing pressures.

► Our 12-month target price of $28 equals 21.5X our FY 10 EPS estimate and 4.3X our FY 10 sales forecast, slightly above the industry mean, justified by our view of CSCO's market leadership position and strong financials. Our discounted cash flow model, assuming a weighted average cost of capital of 11.2% and terminal growth of 3%, indicates an intrinsic value of about $29.

Qualitative Risk Assessment

LOW	**MEDIUM**	HIGH

Our risk assessment for CSCO reflects the highly competitive nature of the industry in which it operates, balanced by our view of its strong financials, including $35 billion in cash and investments, and a dominant market position.

Quantitative Evaluations

S&P Quality Ranking   B+

D	C	B-	B	**B+**	A-	A	A+

Relative Strength Rank   MODERATE

57

LOWEST = 1   HIGHEST = 99

Revenue/Earnings Data

Revenue (Million $)

	1Q	2Q	3Q	4Q	Year
2010	9,021	--	--	--	--
2009	10,331	9,089	8,162	8,535	36,117
2008	9,554	9,831	9,791	10,364	39,540
2007	8,184	8,439	8,866	9,433	34,922
2006	6,550	6,628	7,322	7,984	28,484
2005	5,971	6,062	6,187	6,581	24,801

Earnings Per Share ($)

2010	0.30	E0.32	E0.33	E0.33	E1.30
2009	0.37	0.26	0.23	0.19	1.05
2008	0.35	0.33	0.29	0.33	1.31
2007	0.26	0.31	0.30	0.33	1.17
2006	0.20	0.22	0.22	0.25	0.89
2005	0.21	0.21	0.21	0.24	0.87

Fiscal year ended Jul. 31. Next earnings report expected: Early February. EPS Estimates based on S&P Operating Earnings; historical GAAP earnings are as reported.

Dividend Data

No cash dividends have been paid.

Please read the Required Disclosures and Analyst Certification on the last page of this report.

Cisco Systems Inc

STANDARD
&POOR'S

Business Summary November 05, 2009

CORPORATE OVERVIEW. Cisco Systems, which supplies the majority of Internet Protocol (IP)networking gear used for the Internet, is the world's largest supplier of high-performance computer internetworking systems. The company's sales strategy is primarily based on distribution channel partners, with over 40,000 reseller partner sales representatives around the world. Geographically, FY 08 (Jul.) sales were distributed to the following regions: United States and Canada (54%), Europe (21%), the Emerging Markets (11%), Asia Pacific (11%), and Japan (3%).

Product families are categorized into four segments: switches (40% of total FY 08 product sales), routers (24%), advanced technologies (29%), and other. There are currently seven primary advanced technology segments: home networking, unified communications, security, storage area networking, wireless technology, application networking services, and video systems. The company also has a broad range of service offerings, including technical support services and advanced services.

In our view, the primary driver of company sales growth will be the advanced technologies segment. CSCO distinguishes its advanced technology sub-

segments as industry segments with the potential to become billion dollar businesses. We see the company continuing to identify additional advanced technology sub-segments in markets that build upon its networking expertise. The company is also actively developing a new wave of technologies, referred to as emerging technologies, including such products as TelePresence systems, physical security, and digital media.

MARKET PROFILE. With a dominant market share of approximately 70% of the overall Ethernet switching market, we believe CSCO has become the de facto choice for Ethernet switches. We view the company's large installed base as a significant competitive advantage over peers, especially in cases of modular switching solutions, where it is very difficult for competitors to displace the large modular chassis equipment. In the beginning of 2008, the company introduced its new Nexus series of switches that aims to unify storage and computing in data centers.

Company Financials Fiscal Year Ended Jul. 31

Per Share Data ($)	2009	2008	2007	2006	2005	2004	2003	2002	2001	2000
Tangible Book Value	4.15	3.37	2.76	2.07	2.74	3.16	3.35	3.33	3.07	3.14
Cash Flow	NA	1.59	1.40	1.10	1.02	0.91	0.72	0.52	0.17	0.47
Earnings	1.05	1.31	1.17	0.89	0.87	0.70	0.50	0.25	-0.14	0.36
S&P Core Earnings	1.06	1.30	1.15	0.88	0.70	0.52	0.28	0.12	-0.37	NA
Dividends	Nil	Nil	Nil	Nil	Nil	Nil	Nil	Nil	Nil	Nil
Payout Ratio	Nil	Nil	Nil	Nil	Nil	Nil	Nil	Nil	Nil	Nil
Prices:High	24.83	27.72	34.24	27.96	20.25	29.39	24.60	21.84	44.50	82.00
Prices:Low	13.61	14.20	24.82	17.10	16.83	17.53	12.33	12.24	11.04	35.16
P/E Ratio:High	24	21	29	31	23	42	49	87	NM	NM
P/E Ratio:Low	13	11	21	19	19	25	25	49	NM	98

Income Statement Analysis (Million $)										
Revenue	36,117	39,540	34,922	28,484	24,801	22,045	18,878	18,915	22,293	18,928
Operating Income	NA	11,189	10,034	8,380	8,451	7,738	6,477	4,941	2,257	4,098
Depreciation	1,768	1,744	1,413	1,293	1,009	1,443	1,591	1,957	2,236	863
Interest Expense	NA	319	Nil	Nil	Nil	Nil	Nil	Nil	Nil	Nil
Pretax Income	7,693	10,255	9,461	7,633	8,036	6,992	5,013	2,710	-874	4,343
Effective Tax Rate	20.3%	21.5%	22.5%	26.9%	28.6%	28.9%	28.6%	30.1%	NM	38.6%
Net Income	6,134	8,052	7,333	5,580	5,741	4,968	3,578	1,893	-1,014	2,668
S&P Core Earnings	6,186	7,985	7,197	5,499	4,645	3,652	2,051	931	-2,641	NA

Balance Sheet & Other Financial Data (Million $)										
Cash	35,001	26,235	3,728	3,297	4,742	3,722	3,925	9,484	4,873	4,234
Current Assets	NA	35,699	31,574	25,676	13,031	14,343	13,415	17,433	12,835	11,110
Total Assets	68,128	58,734	53,340	43,315	33,883	35,594	37,107	37,795	35,238	32,870
Current Liabilities	NA	13,858	13,358	11,313	9,511	8,703	8,294	8,375	8,096	5,196
Long Term Debt	10,295	6,393	6,408	6,332	Nil	Nil	Nil	Nil	Nil	Nil
Common Equity	38,647	34,353	31,480	23,912	23,174	25,826	28,029	28,656	27,120	26,497
Total Capital	48,972	40,875	37,898	30,250	23,184	25,916	28,039	28,671	27,142	27,674
Capital Expenditures	1,005	1,268	1,251	772	692	613	717	2,641	2,271	1,086
Cash Flow	NA	9,796	8,746	6,873	6,750	6,411	5,169	3,850	1,222	3,531
Current Ratio	3.2	2.6	2.4	2.3	1.4	1.6	1.6	2.1	1.6	2.1
% Long Term Debt of Capitalization	21.0	15.6	16.9	20.9	Nil	Nil	Nil	Nil	Nil	Nil
% Net Income of Revenue	17.0	20.4	21.0	19.6	23.1	22.5	19.0	10.0	NM	14.1
% Return on Assets	9.7	14.4	15.2	14.5	16.5	13.7	9.6	5.2	NM	11.2
% Return on Equity	16.8	24.5	26.5	23.7	23.4	18.4	12.6	6.8	NM	13.9

Data as orig reptd.; bef. results of disc opers/spec. items. Per share data adj. for stk. divs.; EPS diluted. E-Estimated. NA-Not Available. NM-Not Meaningful. NR-Not Ranked. UR-Under Review.

Office: 170 West Tasman Drive, San Jose, CA 95134-1706.
Telephone: 408-526-4000.
Email: investor-relations@cisco.com
Website: http://www.cisco.com

Chrmn, Pres & CEO: J.T. Chambers
COO: R.W. Lloyd
EVP & CFO: F.A. Calderoni
SVP & Treas: D.K. Holland

SVP, Secy & General Counsel: M. Chandler
Investor Contact: L. Graves (408-526-6521)
Board Members: C. A. Bartz, M. M. Burns, M. D. Capellas, L. R. Carter, J. T. Chambers, M. A. Cirillo, B. L. Halla, J. L. Hennessy, R. M. Kovacevich, R. C. McGeary, M. K. Powell, A. S. Rachleff, A. Sarin, S. West, J. Yang

Founded: 1984
Domicile: California
Employees: 65,550

Citigroup Inc.

STANDARD &POOR'S

S&P Recommendation HOLD ★★★☆☆	Price $4.06 (as of Nov 27, 2009)	12-Mo. Target Price $5.50	Investment Style Large-Cap Blend

GICS Sector Financials
Sub-Industry Other Diversified Financial Services

Summary This diversified financial services company provides a wide range of financial services to consumers and corporate customers in more than 100 countries and territories.

Key Stock Statistics (Source S&P, Vickers, company reports)

52-Wk Range	$9.00– 0.97	S&P Oper. EPS 2009**E**	0.01	Market Capitalization(B)	$92.828	Beta	2.80
Trailing 12-Month EPS	$-2.78	S&P Oper. EPS 2010**E**	-0.14	Yield (%)	Nil	S&P 3-Yr. Proj. EPS CAGR(%)	NM
Trailing 12-Month P/E	NM	P/E on S&P Oper. EPS 2009**E**	NM	Dividend Rate/Share	Nil	S&P Credit Rating	BBB+
$10K Invested 5 Yrs Ago	$1,069	Common Shares Outstg. (M)	22,863.9	Institutional Ownership (%)	17		

Price Performance

30-Week Mov. Avg. ···   10-Week Mov. Avg. − −   **GAAP Earnings vs. Previous Year**   Volume Above Avg. STARS
12-Mo. Target Price —   Relative Strength —   ▲ Up   ▼ Down   ► No Change   Below Avg.

Options: ASE, CBOE, P, Ph

Analysis prepared by **Stuart Plesser** on November 03, 2009, when the stock traded at **$ 4.04**.

Qualitative Risk Assessment

LOW	MEDIUM	HIGH

Our risk assessment reflects our view of C's exposure to risky assets on its balance sheet and its exposure to deteriorating credit in both domestic and international markets. It also reflects the possibility of attrition of C's customers and trading partners.

Quantitative Evaluations

S&P Quality Ranking   B+

D	C	B-	B	B+	A-	A	A+

Relative Strength Rank   MODERATE

32

LOWEST = 1   HIGHEST = 99

Revenue/Earnings Data

Revenue (Million $)

	1Q	2Q	3Q	4Q	Year
2009	32,500	36,811	27,070	--	--
2008	29,696	32,392	29,456	16,253	105,782
2007	43,021	45,802	43,197	27,209	159,229
2006	34,290	35,899	36,323	40,046	146,558
2005	28,620	28,837	31,147	31,714	120,318
2004	25,976	27,287	26,408	28,605	108,276

Earnings Per Share ($)

2009	-0.17	0.53	-0.23	E-0.06	E0.01
2008	-1.04	-0.51	-0.71	-4.12	-4.72
2007	1.01	1.24	0.44	-1.99	0.72
2006	1.11	1.05	1.06	1.03	4.25
2005	0.98	0.91	0.97	0.98	3.82
2004	1.01	0.22	1.02	1.02	3.26

Fiscal year ended Dec. 31. Next earnings report expected: Mid January. EPS Estimates based on S&P Operating Earnings; historical GAAP earnings are as reported.

Highlights

► We look for C's revenue to decline 11.0% in 2010, largely due to a planned reduction in the size of the company. We acknowledge that year-over-year comparisons are difficult, as C's 2009 results include several one-time items, including the sale of business units and marks on its securities. C has split itself into two separate entities and is attempting to shed additional assets, which should lead to a more stable earnings stream as it puts more of a focus on international core markets.

► We look for net interest income to decrease in 2010 due to a lower asset base. We see continued rising credit losses in the U.S. and international consumer segments resulting in elevated provisions in 2009 and 2010. After significant cost-cutting in 2009, expenses will likely tick modestly higher in 2010. With spreads narrowing and C adding troubled securities to its held-for-investment portfolio, securities write-downs have stabilized.

► Acknowledging limited earnings visibility, we see a per-share profit of $0.01 in 2009, which includes a gain from the sale of a portion of C's ownership of Smith Barney, and estimate a loss of $0.14 per share in 2010.

Investment Rationale/Risk

► C has restructured its business into Citicorp and Citi Holdings, with Citi Holdings carrying mostly non-core and distressed assets. The plan is ultimately to unwind Citi Holdings, which should lead to a more stable revenue stream. With the government and public and private investors converting their preferred shares into common equity, tangible capital levels now seem adequate to us. Credit losses on loans held will likely remain elevated through most of 2010. The success of C's loan modifications will likely determine whether chargeoffs escalate from current levels. We think that due to dilution and asset shrinkage, C probably will not regain the earnings power it once had. After a recent run-up in the stock price, we now view the shares as fairly valued.

► Risks to our recommendation and target price include a greater-than-expected downturn in global economic conditions, greater-than-expected credit losses, and an inability to execute C's business plan.

► Our 12-month target price of $5.50 is equal to roughly 1.2X current tangible book value of $4.47, below C's historical average, reflecting uncertainty we see about future write-downs.

Dividend Data (Dates: mm/dd Payment Date: mm/dd/yy)

Amount ($)	Date Decl.	Ex-Div. Date	Stk. of Record	Payment Date
0.160	10/20	10/30	11/03	11/26/08
0.010	01/20	01/29	02/02	02/27/09

Source: Company reports.

Please read the Required Disclosures and Analyst Certification on the last page of this report.

The **McGraw·Hill** Companies

Citigroup Inc.

STANDARD
&POOR'S

Business Summary November 03, 2009

CORPORATE OVERVIEW. Citigroup's activities were recently conducted through the Global Cards, Consumer Banking, Institutional Clients Group (ICG), Global Wealth Management (GWM) and Corporate/Other business segments. The Global Cards segment is a global issuer of credit cards through the MasterCard, Visa, Diners Club, Private Label and American Express platforms. The Consumer Banking segment includes a global, full-service consumer franchise delivering a wide array of banking, lending, insurance and investment services through a network of local branches, offices and electronic delivery systems. The Institutional Clients Group operates in about 100 countries and advises companies, governments and institutional investors on the best ways to realize their strategic objectives. The Global Wealth Management comprises of The Citigroup Private Bank, which provides personalized wealth management services for high-net-worth clients and Smith Barney Private Client businesses, which provides investment advice, financial planning and brokerage services to affluent individuals, companies and non-profits.

The company has since restructured its business into Citicorp and Citi Holdings, with Citi Holdings carrying mostly non-core and distressed assets.

CORPORATE STRATEGY. Citigroup has seven goals for 2009: returning to profitability, risk reduction and mitigation, implementation and management of TARP and TARP funds, expense reduction, head count reduction, asset reduction, and implementing organizational changes/management realignment.

UPCOMING CATALYSTS. A key catalyst for C, in our opinion, will be its ability to sell non-core assets and, in turn, improve capital levels. In 2008, C embarked on the 2008 Re-engineering Projects and Restructuring Initiatives, whose primary goals were: eliminate layers of management/improve workforce management; consolidate certain back-office, middle-office and corporate functions; increase the use of shared services; expand centralized procurement; and continue to rationalize operational spending on technology. This initiative is expected to generate head count reductions of approximately 20,600.

Company Financials Fiscal Year Ended Dec. 31

Per Share Data ($)	2008	2007	2006	2005	2004	2003	2002	2001	2000	1999
Tangible Book Value	4.41	9.95	14.14	12.76	11.72	10.75	9.70	15.49	12.84	10.64
Earnings	-4.72	0.72	4.25	3.82	3.26	3.42	2.59	2.75	2.62	2.12
S&P Core Earnings	-4.97	0.43	4.09	3.69	4.02	3.35	2.33	2.51	NA	NA
Dividends	1.12	2.16	1.96	1.76	1.60	1.10	0.70	0.60	0.52	0.41
Payout Ratio	NM	NM	46%	46%	49%	32%	27%	22%	20%	19%
Prices:High	29.89	56.28	57.00	49.99	52.88	49.15	52.20	57.38	59.13	43.69
Prices:Low	3.05	28.80	44.81	42.91	42.10	30.25	24.48	34.51	35.34	24.50
P/E Ratio:High	NM	78	13	13	16	14	20	21	23	21
P/E Ratio:Low	NM	40	11	11	13	9	9	13	13	12

Income Statement Analysis (Million $)	2008	2007	2006	2005	2004	2003	2002	2001	2000	1999
Premium Income	3,221	3,132	3,202	3,132	3,993	3,749	3,410	13,460	12,429	10,441
Investment Income	NA	29,705	34,177	28,833	22,728	18,937	21,036	26,949	27,562	21,728
Other Revenue	NA	126,392	109,179	88,353	81,555	72,027	68,110	71,613	71,835	49,836
Total Revenue	105,782	159,229	146,558	120,318	108,276	94,713	92,556	112,022	111,826	82,005
Interest Expense	52,963	48,790	56,943	36,676	22,086	17,271	21,248	31,965	36,638	24,768
% Expense/Operating Revenue	117.3%	87.3%	74.3%	75.5%	77.6%	72.2%	77.8%	80.5%	81.1%	80.6%
Pretax Income	-43,113	1,701	29,639	29,433	24,182	26,333	20,537	21,897	21,143	15,948
Effective Tax Rate	45.6%	NM	27.3%	30.8%	28.6%	31.1%	34.1%	34.4%	35.6%	35.8%
Net Income	-23,125	3,617	21,249	19,806	17,046	17,853	13,448	14,284	13,519	9,994
S&P Core Earnings	-26,217	2,154	20,311	19,114	20,934	17,424	12,000	12,943	NA	NA

Balance Sheet & Other Financial Data (Million $)	2008	2007	2006	2005	2004	2003	2002	2001	2000	1999
Receivables	44,278	57,359	44,445	42,823	44,056	31,053	29,714	47,528	36,237	32,677
Cash & Investment	763,760	242,663	300,105	208,970	236,799	204,041	186,839	179,352	134,743	127,284
Loans	694,216	777,993	679,192	583,503	548,829	478,006	447,805	391,933	367,022	244,206
Total Assets	1,945,263	2,187,631	1,884,318	1,494,037	1,484,101	1,264,032	1,097,190	1,051,450	902,210	716,937
Capitalization:Debt	359,593	427,112	288,494	217,499	207,910	168,759	133,079	128,756	116,698	52,012
Capitalization:Equity	80,110	113,598	118,783	111,412	108,166	96,889	85,318	79,722	64,461	47,761
Capitalization:Total	501,223	540,710	408,277	330,036	317,201	284,251	219,797	210,003	182,904	101,698
Price Times Book Value:High	6.8	5.7	4.0	3.9	4.5	4.6	5.4	3.7	4.6	4.1
Price Times Book Value:Low	0.7	2.9	3.2	3.4	3.5	2.8	2.5	2.2	2.7	2.3
% Return on Revenue	NM	2.3	22.0	16.5	15.7	18.8	14.5	12.8	12.9	12.2
% Return on Assets	NM	0.2	1.3	1.3	1.2	1.5	1.3	1.5	1.6	1.4
% Return on Equity	NM	3.1	18.5	18.0	16.6	19.5	11.6	19.7	22.2	22.3
Loans/Equity	8.0	6.3	5.5	5.2	5.1	5.1	3.6	5.3	5.6	5.3

Data as orig reptd.; bef. results of disc opers/spec. items. Per share data adj. for stk. divs.; EPS diluted. E-Estimated. NA-Not Available. NM-Not Meaningful. NR-Not Ranked. UR-Under Review.

Office: 399 Park Avenue, New York, NY, USA 10043.
Telephone: 212-559-1000.
Website: http://www.citigroup.com
Chrmn: R.D. Parsons

Pres: W. McNamee
Vice Chrmn: J.B. Lane
CEO: V.S. Pandit
COO & CTO: K. Kessinger

Board Members: C. M. Armstrong, A. J. Belda, T. Browne, T. C. Collins, J. M. Deutch, J. A. Grundhofer, L. Joss, A. N. Liveris, A. M. Mulcahy, M. E. O'Neill, V. S. Pandit, R. D. Parsons, L. R. Ricciardi, J. H. Rodin, R. L. Ryan, A. M. Santomero, D. L. Taylor, W. S. Thompson, Jr.

Founded: 1901
Domicile: Delaware
Employees: 326,900

Citrix Systems Inc

STANDARD &POOR'S

S&P Recommendation	SELL ★ ★ ★ ★ ★	Price $37.88 (as of Nov 27, 2009)	12-Mo. Target Price $32.00	Investment Style Large-Cap Growth

GICS Sector Information Technology
Sub-Industry Application Software

Summary This company is a leading developer and supplier of access infrastructure software and services.

Key Stock Statistics (Source S&P, Vickers, company reports)

52-Wk Range	$43.78– 20.00	S&P Oper. EPS 2009E	0.87	Market Capitalization(B)	$6.931	Beta	1.02
Trailing 12-Month EPS	$0.89	S&P Oper. EPS 2010E	1.24	Yield (%)	Nil	S&P 3-Yr. Proj. EPS CAGR(%)	18
Trailing 12-Month P/E	42.6	P/E on S&P Oper. EPS 2009E	43.5	Dividend Rate/Share	Nil	S&P Credit Rating	NR
$10K Invested 5 Yrs Ago	$16,299	Common Shares Outstg. (M)	183.0	Institutional Ownership (%)	88		

Price Performance

30-Week Mov. Avg. ···· 10-Week Mov. Avg. – – GAAP Earnings vs. Previous Year Volume Above Avg. STARS
12-Mo. Target Price — Relative Strength — ▲ Up ▼ Down ▶ No Change Below Avg.

Options: ASE, CBOE, P, Ph

Analysis prepared by **Jim Yin** on October 26, 2009, when the stock traded at **$ 39.03**.

Highlights

► We estimate that total revenue will rise 6.9% in 2010, following 0.6% growth seen in 2009. Our forecast is based on our view of a 4% rebound in overall IT spending in 2010. We see product license revenue increasing 4.8% in 2010, following a 17% decline in 2009, as customers cautiously resume spending on new projects. We expect stronger growth in license updates and services, with growth rates of 6.8% and 7.0%, respectively. We forecast 10.0% growth in on-line services, on greater adoption of CTXS's real-time collaboration services.

► We believe the gross margin in 2010 will be 89%, the same percentage as expected in 2009. We project that operating expenses will decrease to 72% of revenue, from 77% seen in 2009, due to cost savings as a result of workforce reduction. We expect operating margins in 2010 to rise to 17%, from 11% seen in 2009.

► We see EPS of $0.87 and $1.24 for 2009 and 2010, respectively. The expected increase in 2010 reflects our projection of higher revenues and operating margins resulting from an economic recovery and better IT spending.

Investment Rationale/Risk

► Our sell recommendation is based mostly on valuation, following significant price appreciation. We think the recovery in IT spending could be sluggish, rising just 4% in 2010 following a sharper decline in 2009, and that new software license revenues will remain weak. We are also concerned about increased operating expenses as a result of the XenSource acquisition. We think the acquisition poses execution risks, because CTXS will enter a new market and trails the market leader, VMWare (VMW 45, Sell).

► Risks to our recommendation and target price include a stronger-than-expected economic recovery, gains in market share for server virtualization products, and greater revenue contributions from recent acquisitions.

► Our 12-month target price of $32 is based on a blend of our discounted cash flow (DCF) and P/E analyses. Our DCF model assumes a 12% weighted average cost of capital and 3% terminal growth, yielding an intrinsic value of $26. From our P/E analysis, we derive a value of $38, based on an industry average P/E-to-growth ratio of 1.7X, or 31X our 2010 EPS estimate of $1.24.

Qualitative Risk Assessment

LOW	MEDIUM	HIGH

Our risk assessment reflects rapidly changing technology and the competitive nature of the enterprise software market.

Quantitative Evaluations

S&P Quality Ranking B+

D	C	B-	B	B+	A-	A	A+

Relative Strength Rank MODERATE

46

LOWEST = 1   HIGHEST = 99

Revenue/Earnings Data

Revenue (Million $)

	1Q	2Q	3Q	4Q	Year
2009	369.1	392.8	401.0	--	--
2008	377.0	391.7	398.9	415.7	1,583
2007	308.1	334.4	349.9	399.6	1,392
2006	260.0	275.5	277.9	321.0	1,134
2005	201.9	211.2	227.0	268.7	908.7
2004	161.3	178.3	187.6	214.0	741.2

Earnings Per Share ($)

2009	0.04	0.23	0.29	E0.31	E0.87
2008	0.18	0.18	0.26	0.33	0.96
2007	0.20	0.29	0.33	0.33	1.14
2006	0.22	0.23	0.23	0.29	0.97
2005	0.22	0.16	0.23	0.32	0.93
2004	0.05	0.18	0.22	0.30	0.75

Fiscal year ended Dec. 31. Next earnings report expected: Late January. EPS Estimates based on S&P Operating Earnings; historical GAAP earnings are as reported.

Dividend Data

No cash dividends have been paid.

The McGraw-Hill Companies

Citrix Systems Inc

STANDARD &POOR'S

Business Summary October 26, 2009

CORPORATE OVERVIEW. Citrix Systems (CTXS) designs, develops and markets server and desktop virtualization software solutions that enable users to access and share applications and files on-demand with a higher performance and level of security. CTXS's solutions help people conduct business in remote and mobile locations as they move from location to location, use multiple devices, and connect with a wide range of heterogeneous applications over wired, wireless and Internet networks.

CTXS organizes its products into three groups: Citrix Delivery Center, Online Services and Technical Services.

Citrix Delivery Center is focused on application virtualization, application networking and desktop virtualization. It includes Server Virtualization products, which allow servers to run multiple operating systems, thus enabling them to process multiple business applications. As a result, enterprises can reduce infrastructure costs by aggregating servers and data storage into pools of shared resources. The key product is Citrix XenServer, which was obtained through the acquisition of XenSource. CTXS and Microsoft entered into patent cross license and source code licensing agreements related to Microsoft's operating systems. The technology collaboration agreement expires in December 2009.

Another key application in Citrix Delivery Center is Citrix XenApp, previously

called Citrix Presentation Server, which runs the business logic of applications on a central server and displays the video on the users' computers. By keeping applications under a centralized control, it improves data security and reduces the costs of managing many different applications on every user's desktop. Other products include Citrix NetScaler and Citrix Repeater, which optimize the performance of a network by balancing the load and providing firewall protection.

Online Services are Web-based access and collaboration software and services. GoToMyPC allows users to remotely access PCs via the Internet. GoToMeeting enables online meetings, training sessions and collaborative gatherings. GoToAssist is an online solution that enables businesses to provide customer support over the Internet. GoToWebinar helps organizations conduct online events, such as large marketing events.

Technical Services include consulting, support, and training to help ensure that customers are achieving the maximum value of CTXS's products and services.

Company Financials Fiscal Year Ended Dec. 31

Per Share Data ($)	2008	2007	2006	2005	2004	2003	2002	2001	2000	1999
Tangible Book Value	4.13	3.59	3.92	2.68	2.80	3.24	2.57	2.48	2.94	2.59
Cash Flow	1.62	1.60	1.32	1.06	0.95	0.94	0.75	0.95	0.72	0.75
Earnings	0.96	1.14	0.97	0.93	0.75	0.74	0.52	0.54	0.47	0.61
S&P Core Earnings	0.99	1.14	0.97	0.74	0.48	0.23	-0.34	-0.19	NA	NA
Dividends	Nil	Nil	Nil	Nil	Nil	Nil	Nil	Nil	Nil	Nil
Payout Ratio	Nil	Nil	Nil	Nil	Nil	Nil	Nil	Nil	Nil	Nil
Prices:High	38.95	43.90	45.50	29.46	26.00	27.86	24.70	37.19	122.31	65.00
Prices:Low	19.00	26.10	26.62	20.70	15.02	10.48	4.70	16.88	14.25	13.25
P/E Ratio:High	41	39	47	32	35	38	47	69	NM	NM
P/E Ratio:Low	20	23	27	22	20	14	9	31	NM	NM

Income Statement Analysis (Million $)	2008	2007	2006	2005	2004	2003	2002	2001	2000	1999
Revenue	1,583	1,392	1,134	909	741	589	527	592	471	403
Operating Income	295	297	267	233	212	189	145	216	172	201
Depreciation	124	85.2	63.6	22.0	33.6	34.3	41.4	79.6	50.2	27.6
Interest Expense	0.44	0.74	0.93	2.23	4.37	18.3	18.2	20.6	17.0	12.6
Pretax Income	197	251	243	226	164	161	113	153	135	183
Effective Tax Rate	9.47%	14.5%	24.7%	26.2%	20.0%	21.0%	17.0%	31.0%	30.0%	36.0%
Net Income	178	214	183	166	132	127	93.9	105	94.5	117
S&P Core Earnings	184	214	183	131	83.5	39.3	-60.5	-36.2	NA	NA

Balance Sheet & Other Financial Data (Million $)	2008	2007	2006	2005	2004	2003	2002	2001	2000	1999
Cash	575	580	349	484	73.5	359	143	140	375	216
Current Assets	940	934	812	726	427	809	375	346	587	570
Total Assets	2,694	2,535	2,024	1,682	1,286	1,345	1,162	1,208	1,113	1,038
Current Liabilities	731	654	536	426	342	626	189	193	159	137
Long Term Debt	Nil	Nil	Nil	31.0	Nil	Nil	334	346	330	314
Common Equity	1,918	1,838	1,464	1,203	925	707	622	647	593	533
Total Capital	1,918	1,838	1,464	1,234	925	707	955	994	923	847
Capital Expenditures	181	85.9	52.1	26.4	24.4	11.1	19.1	60.6	43.5	26.3
Cash Flow	302	300	247	188	165	161	135	185	145	145
Current Ratio	1.3	1.4	1.5	1.7	1.2	1.3	2.0	1.8	3.7	4.2
% Long Term Debt of Capitalization	Nil	Nil	Nil	2.5	Nil	Nil	34.9	34.8	35.8	37.1
% Net Income of Revenue	11.3	15.4	16.1	18.3	17.7	21.6	17.8	17.8	10.0	29.0
% Return on Assets	6.8	9.4	9.8	11.2	10.0	10.1	7.9	9.1	8.8	15.9
% Return on Equity	9.5	13.0	13.7	15.6	16.1	19.1	14.6	17.0	16.8	28.2

Data as orig reptd.; bef. results of disc opers/spec. items. Per share data adj. for stk. divs.; EPS diluted. E-Estimated. NA-Not Available. NM-Not Meaningful. NR-Not Ranked. UR-Under Review.

Office: 851 West Cypress Creek Road, Fort Lauderdale, FL 33309.
Telephone: 954-267-3000.
Email: investor@citrix.com
Website: http://www.citrix.com

Chrmn: T.F. Bogan
Pres & CEO: M.B. Templeton
SVP, CFO & Chief Acctg Officer: D.J. Henshall
Treas: K. Leopardi

Secy: A.G. Gomes
Investor Contact: E. Fleites (954-267-3000)
Board Members: T. F. Bogan, N. E. Caldwell, M. J. Demo, S. M. Dow, A. Hirji, G. E. Morin, G. Sullivan, M. B. Templeton

Founded: 1989
Domicile: Delaware
Employees: 5,040

The McGraw-Hill Companies

Clorox Co (The)

STANDARD &POOR'S

S&P Recommendation	HOLD ★★★☆☆	Price $60.05 (as of Nov 27, 2009)	12-Mo. Target Price $67.00	Investment Style Large-Cap Growth

GICS Sector Consumer Staples
Sub-Industry Household Products

Summary This diversified producer of household cleaning, grocery and specialty food products is also a leading producer of natural personal care products.

Key Stock Statistics (Source S&P, Vickers, company reports)

52-Wk Range	$61.64– 45.67	S&P Oper. EPS 2010**E**	4.24	Market Capitalization(B)	$8.395	Beta	0.38
Trailing 12-Month EPS	$4.01	S&P Oper. EPS 2011**E**	NA	Yield (%)	3.33	S&P 3-Yr. Proj. EPS CAGR(%)	8
Trailing 12-Month P/E	15.0	P/E on S&P Oper. EPS 2010**E**	14.2	Dividend Rate/Share	$2.00	S&P Credit Rating	BBB+
$10K Invested 5 Yrs Ago	$12,426	Common Shares Outstg. (M)	139.8	Institutional Ownership (%)	73		

Price Performance

30-Week Mov. Avg. · · · 10-Week Mov. Avg. - - **GAAP Earnings vs. Previous Year**   Volume Above Avg. ▍▎▍ STARS
12-Mo. Target Price — Relative Strength — ▲ Up ▼ Down ▶ No Change   Below Avg. ▍▎▍ ★

Options: ASE, CBOE, P, Ph

Analysis prepared by **Loran Braverman, CFA** on November 02, 2009, when the stock traded at **$ 59.36**.

Highlights

► In FY 09 (Jun.), CLX reported sales growth of 3.3%, including 1.5% from an extra five months of Burt's Bees (a natural personal care products company acquired December 1, 2007), a -2% foreign currency impact, and -0.6% from exiting the private label food bags business. Base sales grew 4.4%. For FY 10, we see sales growth of 1.5%, with limited foreign currency impact. While the recession has dampened demand for items in the natural home/personal care products categories, we view these as additive to CLX's growth for the long term.

► CLX was able to widen its operating margin (excluding restructuring costs) by 190 basis points in FY 09, helped by pricing, cost savings and moderating commodity cost pressures in the second half of the year. For FY 10, we look for additional margin widening of about 120 bps from moderating commodity costs and leveraging of corporate expenses, partially offset by higher advertising and promotional expense for the introduction of new and improved products and competitive pressures in laundry additives and trash bags.

► Our FY 10 EPS estimate is $4.24. Including restructuring charges, CLX earned $3.81 in FY 09.

Investment Rationale/Risk

► In recent years, CLX's performance has been positive but erratic, in our view, due to the seasonal nature of some businesses, the diverse categories in which it operates, and the timing of new product introductions. However, we think its level of product innovation is respectable and bolsters the company's pricing power and competitive stance. We view positively CLX's increased presence in the natural home/personal care products arena through Burt's Bees and Green Works.

► Risks to our recommendation and target price include increased competition and promotional activity that would affect profitability, poor consumer acceptance of new products, unfavorable foreign exchange, and potential challenges in the implementation of new enterprise resource planning system software.

► Our 12-month target price of $67 reflects a blend of our historical and relative analyses. Our historical analysis applies a P/E below the 10-year historical average to our pre-restructuring charge calendar 2010 EPS estimate of $4.53, implying a $72 value. Our relative analysis applies a slight discount to the average peer P/E multiple, for a value of $61.

Qualitative Risk Assessment

LOW	MEDIUM	HIGH

Our risk assessment reflects our view of stable demand for household and personal care products, which is generally not affected by changes in the economy or by geopolitical factors.

Quantitative Evaluations

S&P Quality Ranking A

D	C	B-	B	B+	A-	A	A+

Relative Strength Rank MODERATE

62

LOWEST = 1   HIGHEST = 99

Revenue/Earnings Data

Revenue (Million $)

	1Q	2Q	3Q	4Q	Year
2010	1,372	--	--	--	--
2009	1,384	1,216	1,350	1,500	5,450
2008	1,239	1,186	1,353	1,495	5,273
2007	1,161	1,101	1,241	1,344	4,847
2006	1,104	1,064	1,157	1,319	4,644
2005	1,048	1,000	1,086	1,254	4,388

Earnings Per Share ($)

	1Q	2Q	3Q	4Q	Year
2010	1.11	E0.73	E1.13	E1.27	E4.24
2009	0.91	1.08	1.09	1.20	3.81
2008	0.76	0.65	0.71	1.13	3.25
2007	0.73	0.59	0.84	1.07	3.22
2006	0.70	0.55	0.72	0.92	2.89
2005	0.50	0.72	0.75	1.00	2.88

Fiscal year ended Jun. 30. Next earnings report expected: Early February. EPS Estimates based on S&P Operating Earnings; historical GAAP earnings are as reported.

Dividend Data (Dates: mm/dd Payment Date: mm/dd/yy)

Amount ($)	Date Decl.	Ex-Div. Date	Stk. of Record	Payment Date
0.460	02/12	04/23	04/27	05/15/09
0.500	06/11	07/23	07/27	08/14/09
0.500	09/15	10/26	10/28	11/13/09
0.500	11/19	01/26	01/28	02/12/10

Dividends have been paid since 1968. Source: Company reports.

Please read the Required Disclosures and Analyst Certification on the last page of this report.

The McGraw-Hill Companies

Clorox Co (The)

STANDARD & POOR'S

Business Summary November 02, 2009

CORPORATE OVERVIEW. From its divestiture from The Procter & Gamble Company in 1969 through its January 1999 acquisition of First Brands and beyond, Clorox has expanded into a company with approximately $5.3 billion in annual sales, by focusing on building big-share brands in mid-sized categories. In November 2004, CLX completed the exchange of its ownership interest in a subsidiary for approximately 61.4 million of its shares held by Henkel KGaA, which represented about 29% of CLX's outstanding common stock prior to the exchange. The subsidiary transferred to Henkel contained CLX's existing insecticides and Soft Scrub cleaner businesses, its 20% interest in the Henkel Iberica, S.A. joint venture, and approximately $2.1 billion in cash.

As of FY 10 (Jun.), Clorox has four segments for reporting purposes: North America-Cleaning (34% of FY 09 sales and 37% of segmental profits); North America-Household (31% and 26%); North America-Lifestyle (15% and 24%); and International, which now includes Canada (20% and 13%). In FY 09, Wal-Mart Stores and its affiliated companies accounted for 27% of consolidated net sales.

Clorox's products include: laundry additives, including bleaches, under the Clorox, Clorox 2 and Javex brands; cleaning products, primarily under the Clorox, Formula 409, Liquid-Plumr, Pine-Sol, S.O.S., and Tilex brands; natural cleaning products under the Green Works brand (introduced in January 2008); water-filtration systems and filters under the Brita brand; professional cleaning products for institutional, janitorial, health care and food service markets; auto care products, primarily under the Armor All and STP brands; plastic bags, wraps and containers, under the Glad brand; cat litter products, primarily under the Fresh Step and Scoop Away brands; food products, primarily under the Hidden Valley and KC Masterpiece brands; charcoal products under the Kingsford and Match Light brands; and natural personal care products under the Burt's Bees brand. In FY 09, liquid bleach represented 13% of sales, trash bags 13%, and charcoal 10%.

CLX owns or leases and operates 23 manufacturing facilities in North America. The company also owns and operates 17 manufacturing facilities outside North America. CLX leases seven distribution centers located in North America and several other warehouse facilities.

Company Financials Fiscal Year Ended Jun. 30

Per Share Data ($)	2009	2008	2007	2006	2005	2004	2003	2002	2001	2000
Tangible Book Value	NM	NM	NM	NM	NM	0.77	NM	0.24	1.38	1.10
Cash Flow	5.16	4.61	4.47	4.12	3.95	3.47	3.19	2.18	2.30	2.48
Earnings	3.81	3.25	3.22	2.89	2.88	2.55	2.33	1.37	1.36	1.64
S&P Core Earnings	3.70	3.15	3.26	2.94	2.73	2.43	2.26	1.63	1.11	NA
Dividends	1.84	1.60	1.20	1.14	1.10	1.08	0.88	0.84	0.84	0.61
Payout Ratio	48%	49%	37%	39%	38%	42%	38%	61%	62%	37%
Prices:High	61.64	65.25	69.36	66.00	66.04	59.45	49.16	47.95	40.85	56.38
Prices:Low	45.67	47.48	56.22	56.17	52.50	46.50	37.40	31.92	29.95	28.38
P/E Ratio:High	16	20	22	23	23	23	21	35	30	34
P/E Ratio:Low	12	15	17	19	18	18	16	23	22	17

Income Statement Analysis (Million $)	2009	2008	2007	2006	2005	2004	2003	2002	2001	2000
Revenue	5,450	5,273	4,847	4,644	4,388	4,324	4,144	4,061	3,903	4,083
Operating Income	1,208	1,116	1,059	967	1,011	1,069	1,046	942	895	981
Depreciation	190	193	192	188	190	197	191	190	225	201
Interest Expense	161	168	113	127	79.0	30.0	28.0	39.0	88.0	98.0
Pretax Income	811	693	743	653	731	840	802	498	487	622
Effective Tax Rate	33.8%	33.5%	33.2%	32.2%	29.3%	35.0%	35.9%	35.3%	33.3%	36.7%
Net Income	537	461	496	443	517	546	514	322	325	394
S&P Core Earnings	521	448	501	450	489	521	496	383	266	NA

Balance Sheet & Other Financial Data (Million $)	2009	2008	2007	2006	2005	2004	2003	2002	2001	2000
Cash	206	214	182	192	293	232	172	177	251	245
Current Assets	1,180	1,249	1,032	1,007	1,090	1,043	951	1,002	1,103	1,454
Total Assets	4,576	4,708	3,666	3,616	3,617	3,834	3,652	3,630	3,995	4,353
Current Liabilities	1,937	1,661	1,427	1,130	1,348	1,268	1,451	1,225	1,069	1,541
Long Term Debt	2,151	2,720	1,462	1,966	2,122	475	495	678	685	590
Common Equity	-175	-370	171	-156	-553	1,540	1,215	1,354	1,900	1,794
Total Capital	1,999	2,447	1,723	1,939	1,651	2,189	1,825	2,174	2,732	2,608
Capital Expenditures	197	170	147	180	151	172	205	177	192	158
Cash Flow	727	654	688	631	707	743	705	512	550	595
Current Ratio	0.6	0.8	0.7	0.9	0.8	0.8	0.7	0.8	1.0	0.9
% Long Term Debt of Capitalization	107.6	111.2	84.9	101.4	128.5	21.7	27.1	31.2	25.1	22.6
% Net Income of Revenue	9.9	8.7	10.2	9.5	11.8	12.6	12.4	7.9	8.3	9.6
% Return on Assets	11.6	11.0	13.6	12.2	13.9	14.6	14.3	8.4	7.8	9.3
% Return on Equity	NM	NM	6613.3	NM	104.8	39.6	39.8	19.8	17.6	23.4

Data as orig reptd.; bef. results of disc opers/spec. items. Per share data adj. for stk. divs.; EPS diluted. E-Estimated. NA-Not Available. NM-Not Meaningful. NR-Not Ranked. UR-Under Review.

Office: 1221 Broadway, Oakland, CA, USA 94612-1888.
Telephone: 510-271-7000.
Email: investor_relations@clorox.com
Website: http://www.thecloroxcompany.com

Chrmn & CEO: D.R. Knauss
SVP & CFO: D.J. Heinrich
SVP & General Counsel: L. Stein
Secy: A.C. Hilt

Investor Contact: S. Austenfeld
Board Members: D. Boggan, Jr., R. H. Carmona, T. M. Friedman, G. J. Harad, D. R. Knauss, R. W. Matschullat, G. G. Michael, E. A. Mueller, J. L. Murley, P. Thomas-Graham, C. M. Ticknor

Founded: 1913
Domicile: Delaware
Employees: 8,300

CME Group Inc

STANDARD &POOR'S

S&P Recommendation	HOLD ★★★☆☆	Price $322.65 (as of Nov 27, 2009)	12-Mo. Target Price $310.00	Investment Style Large-Cap Growth

GICS Sector Financials
Sub-Industry Specialized Finance

Summary The CME Group, a combination of the Chicago Mercantile Exchange and CBOT Holdings, is the world's largest futures exchange.

Key Stock Statistics (Source S&P, Vickers, company reports)

52-Wk Range	$346.24– 155.06	S&P Oper. EPS 2009**E**	13.02	Market Capitalization(B)	$21.462	Beta	1.18
Trailing 12-Month EPS	$10.29	S&P Oper. EPS 2010**E**	15.21	Yield (%)	1.43	S&P 3-Yr. Proj. EPS CAGR(%)	11
Trailing 12-Month P/E	31.4	P/E on S&P Oper. EPS 2009**E**	24.8	Dividend Rate/Share	$4.60	S&P Credit Rating	AA
$10K Invested 5 Yrs Ago	$17,039	Common Shares Outstg. (M)	66.5	Institutional Ownership (%)	72		

Price Performance

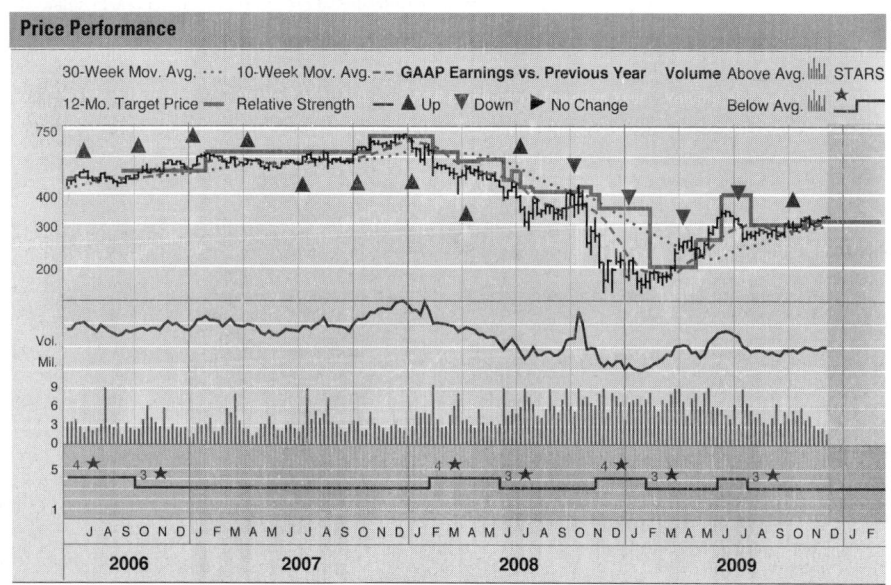

30-Week Mov. Avg. ··· 10-Week Mov. Avg. - - **GAAP Earnings vs. Previous Year** Volume Above Avg. STARS
12-Mo. Target Price — Relative Strength — ▲ Up ▼ Down ► No Change Below Avg.

Options: ASE, CBOE, P, Ph

Analysis prepared by **Rafay Khalid, CFA** on October 30, 2009, when the stock traded at **$ 310.06**.

Highlights

► We think trading volumes in 2009 will be low relative to historical levels due to de-leveraging, low interest rates, and general risk aversion. Uncertainty about the direction of interest rates and the price of oil and gas has increased, which will lead to a pick-up in hedging and speculative activity during the rest of 2009, in our view. In 2010, we believe CME's trading volume will generate positive growth, supported by our view of strength in domestic products and expansion into new international markets.

► We forecast a pro forma (to include 2008 full-year CBOT and NYMEX results) 4% increase in revenues for 2009 based on our estimate of a 16% rise in average rate per contract, but partially offset by our forecast for a 21% decrease in average daily volumes. We believe expenses as a percentage of sales will remain flat at 38% in 2009, as the company maintains tight control. As a result, we see operating margins rising to 62% in 2009 and remaining at a similar level in 2010, from 60% in 2008.

► We forecast EPS of $13.02 in 2009 and $15.21 in 2010.

Investment Rationale/Risk

► We believe CME has broad product exposure, highly defensible positioning, and a low variable cost model. We expect CME to benefit from an ongoing migration of derivative products to a centrally cleared exchange model from OTC markets in the aftermath of the current economic crisis. However, the Commodity Futures Trading Commission hearings concerning position limits did little to lessen uncertainty about hedge exemptions and the role of speculative trading. Should hedge exemptions become more restrictive, we believe there could be a significant reduction in exchange-based commodities trading.

► Risks to our recommendation and target price include increased price competition from competitors, increased regulation that curbs speculative trading, and a slower-than-anticipated transition of OTC products to exchanges.

► Our 12-month target price of $310 is based on a two-year historical average P/E ratio of 20.4X our 2010 EPS forecast.

Qualitative Risk Assessment

LOW	MEDIUM	HIGH

Our risk assessment reflects potential volatility in results due to changes in futures trading volumes, recent acquisition activity in the sector, and a changing regulatory environment.

Quantitative Evaluations

S&P Quality Ranking NR

D	C	B-	B	B+	A-	A	A+

Relative Strength Rank STRONG

79

LOWEST = 1   HIGHEST = 99

Revenue/Earnings Data

Revenue (Million $)

	1Q	2Q	3Q	4Q	Year
2009	647.1	647.8	650.4	--	--
2008	625.1	563.2	681.0	691.8	2,561
2007	332.3	329.0	565.2	529.5	1,756
2006	251.7	282.2	274.7	281.3	1,090
2005	223.9	252.2	249.6	251.6	977.3
2004	169.6	190.5	192.4	196.0	752.8

Earnings Per Share ($)

2009	3.00	3.33	3.04	E3.64	E13.02
2008	5.25	3.67	2.81	0.93	12.13
2007	3.69	3.57	3.87	3.75	14.93
2006	2.61	3.12	2.95	2.91	11.60
2005	2.04	2.36	2.22	2.18	8.81
2004	1.35	1.66	1.72	1.64	6.38

Fiscal year ended Dec. 31. Next earnings report expected: Early February. EPS Estimates based on S&P Operating Earnings; historical GAAP earnings are as reported.

Dividend Data (Dates: mm/dd Payment Date: mm/dd/yy)

Amount ($)	Date Decl.	Ex-Div. Date	Stk. of Record	Payment Date
1.150	02/04	03/06	03/10	03/25/09
1.150	05/14	06/08	06/10	06/25/09
1.150	08/06	09/08	09/10	09/25/09
1.150	11/10	12/08	12/10	12/28/09

Dividends have been paid since 2003. Source: Company reports.

The **McGraw·Hill** Companies

CME Group Inc

STANDARD &POOR'S

Business Summary October 30, 2009

CORPORATE OVERVIEW. The largest futures exchange in the world, CME Group was formed in July 2007 from the merger of the Chicago Mercantile Exchange and CBOT Holdings. CME serves the risk management needs of clients worldwide through a diverse range of futures and options-on-futures products on its CME Globex electronic trading platform and on its trading floors. CME offers futures and options on futures primarily in four product areas: interest rates, stock indexes, foreign exchange, and commodities. CME is the leading exchange for trading Eurodollar futures, the world's most actively traded futures contract and a benchmark for measuring the relative value of U.S. dollar-denominated short-term fixed income securities.

CME operates its own clearing house, which clears, settles and guarantees every contract traded through its exchange. We view CME's internal clearing capabilities as a key competitive advantage as CME is able to capture the revenue associated with both the trading and clearing of its products. We expect CME to expand its clearing business by partnering with other exchanges, both domestically and abroad, and clearing over-the-counter (OTC) transactions.

In 2008, CME derived 83% of its revenue from fees associated with trading and clearing its products. These fees include per contract charges for trade execution, clearing and CME Globex fees. Within trading and clearing, interest rate products contributed 38% of fees, while equity products contributed 31%, foreign exchange products 7%, and commodities 23%. CME Globex is the company's electronic platform through which it conducts more than 75% of CME's trading volume. Fees are charged at various rates based on the product traded, the method of trade, and the exchange trading privileges of the customer making the trade. Generally, members are charged lower fees than non-members. Certain customers benefit from volume discounts and limits on fees to encourage increased liquidity.

Company Financials Fiscal Year Ended Dec. 31

Per Share Data ($)	2008	2007	2006	2005	2004	2003	2002	2001	2000	1999
Tangible Book Value	NM	NM	42.91	32.38	23.83	17.10	13.71	12.39	NA	NA
Cash Flow	16.08	18.00	13.67	10.71	7.93	5.16	4.76	3.61	NA	NA
Earnings	12.13	14.93	11.60	8.81	6.38	3.60	3.13	2.33	-0.21	0.10
S&P Core Earnings	15.26	14.96	11.59	8.80	6.37	3.61	3.23	NA	NA	NA
Dividends	9.60	3.44	2.52	1.84	1.04	0.63	Nil	NA	NA	NA
Payout Ratio	79%	23%	22%	21%	16%	18%	Nil	NA	NA	NA
Prices:High	686.43	714.48	557.97	396.90	229.80	79.30	45.50	NA	NA	NA
Prices:Low	155.49	497.00	354.50	163.80	72.50	41.35	35.00	NA	NA	NA
P/E Ratio:High	57	48	48	45	36	22	15	NA	NA	NA
P/E Ratio:Low	13	33	31	19	11	11	11	NA	NA	NA

Income Statement Analysis (Million $)

	2008	2007	2006	2005	2004	2003	2002	2001	2000	1999
Revenue	2,561	1,756	1,090	977	753	545	469	397	227	211
Operating Income	1,946	1,258	694	631	464	290	NA	NA	NA	NA
Depreciation	233	136	72.8	66.0	53.0	53.0	48.5	37.6	33.5	25.3
Interest Expense	56.5	115	92.1	57.0	19.0	8.74	15.9	9.48	NA	NA
Pretax Income	1,248	1,096	672	508	368	206	154	114	-8.08	6.64
Effective Tax Rate	42.7%	39.9%	39.4%	39.6%	40.2%	40.7%	39.0%	40.3%	41.3%	27.9%
Net Income	715	659	407	307	220	122	94.1	68.3	-5.91	2.66
S&P Core Earnings	900	660	407	307	219	123	97.2	NA	NA	NA

Balance Sheet & Other Financial Data (Million $)

	2008	2007	2006	2005	2004	2003	2002	2001	2000	1999
Cash	608	4,744	3,872	904	660	442	339	292	75.0	74.4
Current Assets	19,112	4,987	4,030	3,783	2,695	4,723	3,215	2,818	NA	NA
Total Assets	48,133	20,306	4,307	3,969	2,857	4,873	3,355	2,958	381	303
Current Liabilities	18,643	4,076	2,755	2,830	2,026	4,288	2,889	2,544	NA	NA
Long Term Debt	2,966	Nil	Nil	Nil	Nil	Nil	2.33	8.22	NA	NA
Common Equity	18,689	12,306	1,519	1,119	813	563	446	394	164	169
Total Capital	29,383	16,154	1,519	1,119	813	563	448	402	164	169
Capital Expenditures	200	164	87.8	85.6	67.0	63.0	56.3	16.3	11.2	37.5
Cash Flow	948	794	480	373	273	175	143	106	NA	NA
Current Ratio	1.0	1.2	1.5	1.3	1.3	1.1	1.1	1.1	1.4	1.6
% Long Term Debt of Capitalization	10.1	Nil	Nil	Nil	Nil	Nil	0.5	2.0	Nil	Nil
% Net Income of Revenue	27.9	37.5	37.4	31.4	29.2	22.5	20.1	17.2	NM	1.3
% Return on Assets	2.1	5.4	9.8	8.9	5.6	3.0	3.5	5.6	NM	NA
% Return on Equity	4.6	9.5	30.9	31.7	31.9	24.2	27.1	33.0	NM	NA

Data as orig reptd.; bef. results of disc opers/spec. items. Per share data adj. for stk. divs.; EPS diluted. E-Estimated. NA-Not Available. NM-Not Meaningful. NR-Not Ranked. UR-Under Review.

Office: 20 S Wacker Dr, Chicago, IL 60606-7408.
Telephone: 312-930-1000.
Email: info@cme.com
Website: http://www.cme.com

Chrmn: L. Rosenberg
Chrmn: T.A. Duffy
Pres: P.S. Gill
Vice Chrmn: C.P. Carey

CEO: C.S. Donohue
Investor Contact: J. Peschier (312-930-8491)
Board Members: J. M. Bernacchi, T. S. Bitsberger, C. P. Carey, M. Cermak, D. H. Chookaszian, J. Clegg, R. F. Corvino, J. A. Donaldson, C. S. Donohue, T. A. Duffy, M. J. Gepsman, L. G. Gerdes, D. R. Glickman, J. D. Hastert, B. F. Johnson, G. M. Katler, P. B. Lynch, L. Melamed, W. Miller, II, J. E. Newsome, J. Niciforo, C. C. Odom, II, J. Oliff, J. L. Pietrzak, A. J. Pollock, D. Puth, L. Rosenberg, J. F. Sandner, T. L. Savage, W. R. Shepard, H. J. Siegel, C. Stewart, D. A. Suskind, D. J. Wescott

Founded: 1898
Domicile: Delaware
Employees: 2,300

The McGraw-Hill Companies

CMS Energy Corp

STANDARD &POOR'S

S&P Recommendation **HOLD** ★★★☆☆	Price $14.14 (as of Nov 27, 2009)	12-Mo. Target Price $15.00	Investment Style Large-Cap Value

GICS Sector Utilities
Sub-Industry Multi-Utilities

Summary This energy holding company's principal subsidiary is Consumers Energy, the largest utility in Michigan and the sixth largest gas and 13th largest electric utility in the U.S.

Key Stock Statistics (Source S&P, Vickers, company reports)

52-Wk Range	$15.14–9.12	S&P Oper. EPS 2009**E**	1.24	Market Capitalization(B)	$3.247	Beta	0.61
Trailing 12-Month EPS	$1.21	S&P Oper. EPS 2010**E**	1.33	Yield (%)	3.54	S&P 3-Yr. Proj. EPS CAGR(%)	4
Trailing 12-Month P/E	11.7	P/E on S&P Oper. EPS 2009**E**	11.4	Dividend Rate/Share	$0.50	S&P Credit Rating	BBB-
$10K Invested 5 Yrs Ago	$14,830	Common Shares Outstg. (M)	229.6	Institutional Ownership (%)	NM		

Price Performance

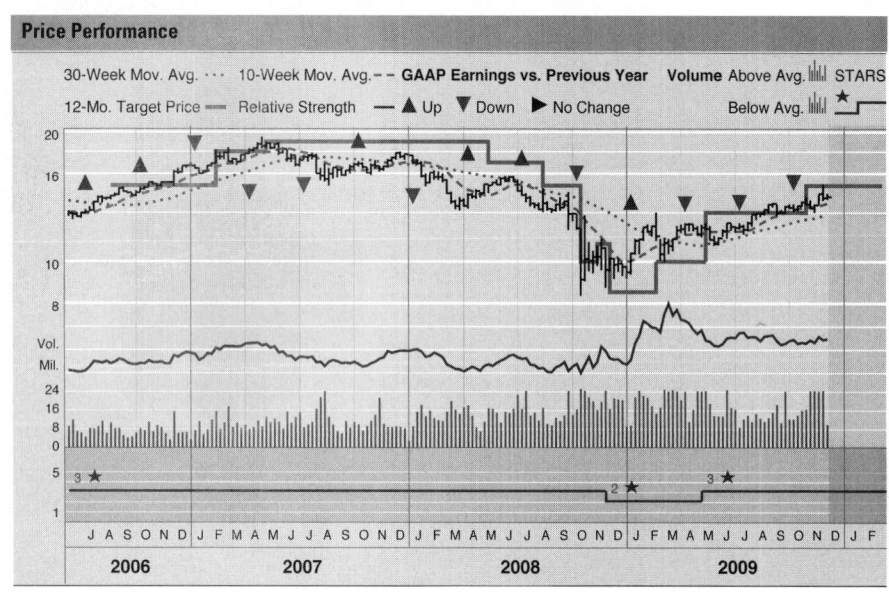

30-Week Mov. Avg. ··· 10-Week Mov. Avg. - - **GAAP Earnings vs. Previous Year** Volume Above Avg. ▪▪▪ STARS
12-Mo. Target Price — Relative Strength — ▲ Up ▼ Down ▶ No Change Below Avg. ▪▪▪ ★

Options: ASE, CBOE, P, Ph

Analysis prepared by **Justin McCann** on October 21, 2009, when the stock traded at **$13.92**.

Highlights

► Excluding net one-time gains of $0.05, we expect operating EPS for 2009 to be essentially flat with 2008 operating EPS of $1.25. While operating earnings in 2009 are expected to benefit from the company's rate base investments, we believe this will be offset by the decline in industrial sales due to the weakening Michigan economy and the problems in the auto sector, as well as the milder-than-normal weather.

► We expect 2010 operating EPS to grow about 6% from projected results in 2009. This would reflect a full year of annual surcharges of $91 million (implemented in June 2009) and $79 (starting in September 2009) for CMS's respective Energy Optimization and Renewable Energy plans, as well as an electric rate increase to be determined in November, for which CMS self-implemented (subject to refund) $179 million in May 2009, and a requested gas rate increase of $114 million, with self-implementation (subject to refund) planned for November.

► In October 2008, the governor of Michigan signed a favorable energy reform package that would modify the state's electric choice program and establish a 12-month deadline for the regulatory resolution of utility rate cases.

Investment Rationale/Risk

► We believe the 39% year to date increase in the stock, after a 42% decline in 2008, reflects a more positive outlook for CMS's long-term earnings growth. It plans to invest more than $6 billion in its utility over the next five years, which should significantly add to its rate base and enable it to grow earnings at an average annual rate of 6% to 8%. With CMS expected to contribute about $160 million to its underfunded pension plan in 2009, it has deferred about $180 million of planned capital expenditures.

► Risks to our recommendation and target price include a slower-than-expected recovery in both the financial markets and the Michigan economy, as well as a decrease in the average P/E multiple of the group as a whole.

► Following the 39% increase in the dividend (effective with the February 27 payment) and the sharp year-to-date advance in the shares, the recent yield was around 3.6%. However, with CMS stock having outperformed the company's electric and gas utility peers in 2009, the discount to the average peer yield (4.9%) has widened. Our 12-month target price is $15, a discount-to-peers multiple of approximately 11.3X our EPS estimate for 2010.

Qualitative Risk Assessment

LOW	MEDIUM	HIGH

Our risk assessment reflects the steady cash flow from the regulated electric and gas utility businesses, which operate within a generally supportive regulatory environment, and our view of a substantially improved financial risk profile. The company had used proceeds from recent asset sales to reduce its debt by about $650 million.

Quantitative Evaluations

S&P Quality Ranking   B

D	C	B-	**B**	B+	A-	A	A+

Relative Strength Rank   STRONG

73

LOWEST = 1   HIGHEST = 99

Revenue/Earnings Data

Revenue (Million $)

	1Q	2Q	3Q	4Q	Year
2009	2,106	1,228	1,274	--	--
2008	2,184	1,365	1,428	1,844	6,821
2007	2,237	1,319	1,282	1,674	6,464
2006	2,032	1,396	1,462	1,920	6,810
2005	1,845	1,230	1,307	1,906	6,288
2004	1,754	1,093	1,063	1,562	5,472

Earnings Per Share ($)

	1Q	2Q	3Q	4Q	Year
2009	0.30	0.19	0.31	E0.36	E1.24
2008	0.44	0.20	0.33	0.27	1.23
2007	-0.16	-0.26	0.34	-0.56	-0.62
2006	-0.13	0.30	-0.47	-0.16	-0.44
2005	0.74	0.12	-1.21	-0.09	-0.51
2004	-0.06	0.10	0.29	0.29	0.67

Fiscal year ended Dec. 31. Next earnings report expected: Late February. EPS Estimates based on S&P Operating Earnings; historical GAAP earnings are as reported.

Dividend Data (Dates: mm/dd Payment Date: mm/dd/yy)

Amount ($)	Date Decl.	Ex-Div. Date	Stk. of Record	Payment Date
0.125	01/23	02/04	02/06	02/27/09
0.125	04/20	05/06	05/08	05/29/09
0.125	07/21	08/06	08/10	08/31/09
0.125	10/23	11/04	11/06	11/30/09

Dividends have been paid since 2007. Source: Company reports.

Please read the Required Disclosures and Analyst Certification on the last page of this report.

The McGraw·Hill Companies

CMS Energy Corp

Business Summary October 21, 2009

CORPORATE OVERVIEW. CMS Energy (CMS) is the energy holding company for Consumers Energy (formerly Consumers Power Co.), a regulated electric and gas utility serving Michigan's Lower Peninsula, and CMS Enterprises, which is engaged in U.S. and international energy-related businesses. CMS operates in three business segments: electric utility, gas utility, and enterprises. CMS's electric utility operations include generation, purchase, distribution and sale of electricity. CMS's gas utility purchases, transports, stores, distributes and sells natural gas. The Enterprises segment, through its various subsidiaries and equity investments, is engaged in diversified energy businesses, including independent power production, electric distribution, and natural gas transmission, storage and processing.

MARKET PROFILE. CMS's electric utility provides electricity to approximately 1.8 million customers in 61 of the 68 counties in the lower peninsula of Michigan. In 2008, the electric utility had total electric deliveries of 39 billion kWh. Consumers' electric utility customer base includes a mix of residential, com-

mercial and diversified industrial customers, the largest segment of which is the automotive industry, which accounted for about 4% of total electric revenues in 2008. In April 2007, CMS completed the sale of the Palisades 798-megawatt nuclear power plant to Entergy (ETR) for $363 million. The transaction included a 15-year power purchase agreement with ETR. The company's gas utility serves some 1.7 million customers in 46 of the 68 counties in Michigan's lower peninsula. The gas utility also owned 1,671 miles of transmission lines at the end of 2008, and 15 gas storage fields in Michigan, with a storage capacity of 307 bcf. The electric utility segment accounted for 52.7% of consolidated revenues in 2008 (53.3% in 2007); the gas utility segment 41.4% (40.5%); Enterprises 5.6% (5.9%), and other 0.3% (0.3%).

Company Financials Fiscal Year Ended Dec. 31

Per Share Data ($)	2008	2007	2006	2005	2004	2003	2002	2001	2000	1999
Tangible Book Value	10.88	9.46	9.90	10.53	10.51	9.69	7.47	8.11	12.15	13.23
Earnings	1.23	-0.62	-0.44	-0.51	0.67	-0.30	-2.99	-2.53	0.36	2.17
S&P Core Earnings	1.01	-0.65	-0.16	-0.44	0.36	0.25	-3.75	-3.29	NA	NA
Dividends	0.36	0.20	Nil	Nil	Nil	Nil	1.09	1.46	1.46	1.39
Payout Ratio	29%	NM	Nil	Nil	Nil	Nil	NM	NM	NM	64%
Prices:High	17.47	19.55	17.00	16.80	10.65	10.74	24.80	31.80	32.25	48.44
Prices:Low	8.33	14.98	12.09	9.70	7.81	3.41	5.45	19.49	16.06	30.31
P/E Ratio:High	14	NM	NM	NM	16	NM	NM	NM	NM	22
P/E Ratio:Low	7	NM	NM	NM	12	NM	NM	NM	NM	14

Income Statement Analysis (Million $)										
Revenue	6,821	6,464	6,810	6,288	5,472	5,513	8,687	9,597	8,998	6,103
Depreciation	629	540	576	525	431	428	403	530	637	595
Maintenance	193	201	326	249	256	226	211	263	298	216
Fixed Charges Coverage	2.15	3.38	1.18	-0.56	1.01	1.23	0.12	1.26	1.63	1.73
Construction Credits	NA	NA	NA	NA	NA	NA	NA	NA	NA	Nil
Effective Tax Rate	31.6%	63.3%	NM	NM	NM	NM	NM	NM	57.7%	18.8%
Net Income	300	-126	-85.0	-98.0	127	-43.0	-416	-331	41.0	277
S&P Core Earnings	238	-145	-31.0	-93.1	63.4	40.6	-522	-431	NA	NA

Balance Sheet & Other Financial Data (Million $)										
Gross Property	13,618	12,894	13,293	12,448	14,751	11,790	11,344	15,195	14,087	14,278
Capital Expenditures	792	1,263	670	593	525	535	747	1,262	1,032	1,124
Net Property	9,190	8,728	7,976	7,325	8,636	6,944	5,234	8,362	7,835	8,121
Capitalization:Long Term Debt	6,287	5,832	6,466	7,286	7,307	8,652	6,399	6,983	7,913	7,075
Capitalization:% Long Term Debt	69.9	71.0	72.2	73.8	75.8	84.5	85.0	78.7	77.0	74.2
Capitalization:Preferred	243	250	261	261	261	Nil	Nil	Nil	Nil	Nil
Capitalization:% Preferred	2.70	3.00	2.91	2.64	2.71	Nil	Nil	Nil	Nil	Nil
Capitalization:Common	2,463	2,130	2,234	2,322	2,072	1,585	1,133	1,890	2,361	2,456
Capitalization:% Common	27.4	25.9	24.9	23.5	21.5	15.5	15.0	21.3	23.0	25.8
Total Capital	9,145	8,323	9,234	10,566	11,123	11,010	8,058	9,834	11,221	10,359
% Operating Ratio	90.6	100.4	92.8	84.8	88.2	91.5	92.1	89.6	88.9	84.7
% Earned on Net Property	8.9	8.8	NM	NM	7.6	8.1	1.8	3.7	9.1	12.9
% Return on Revenue	4.4	NM	NM	NM	2.3	NM	NM	NM	0.5	4.5
% Return on Invested Capital	8.0	4.4	8.1	11.0	9.5	6.7	7.9	9.4	9.5	10.0
% Return on Common Equity	13.1	NM	NM	NM	6.3	NM	NM	NM	1.7	11.9

Data as orig reptd.; bef. results of disc opers/spec. items. Per share data adj. for stk. divs.; EPS diluted. E-Estimated. NA-Not Available. NM-Not Meaningful. NR-Not Ranked. UR-Under Review.

Office: One Energy Plaza, Jackson, MI 49201-2357.
Telephone: 517-788-0550.
Email: invest@cmsenergy.com
Website: http://www.cmsenergy.com

Chrmn: K. Whipple, Jr.
Pres & CEO: D.W. Joos
EVP & CFO: T.J. Webb
SVP & Chief Admin Officer: J.M. Butler

SVP & General Counsel: J.E. Brunner
Investor Contact: L.L. Mountcastle (517-788-2590)
Board Members: M. S. Ayres, J. E. Barfield, S. E. Ewing, R. M. Gabrys, D. W. Joos, P. R. Lochner, Jr., M. T. Monahan, J. F. Paquette, Jr., P. Pierre, K. L. Way, K. Whipple, Jr., J. B. Yasinsky

Founded: 1987
Domicile: Michigan
Employees: 7,970

Coach Inc.

STANDARD
&POOR'S

S&P Recommendation	STRONG BUY ★★★★★	Price $35.29 (as of Nov 27, 2009)	12-Mo. Target Price $42.00	Investment Style Large-Cap Growth

GICS Sector Consumer Discretionary
Sub-Industry Apparel, Accessories & Luxury Goods

Summary COH designs, makes and markets fine accessories for women and men, including handbags, weekend and travel accessories, outerwear, footwear, and business cases.

Key Stock Statistics (Source S&P, Vickers, company reports)

52-Wk Range	$37.10– 11.41	S&P Oper. EPS 2010E	2.18	Market Capitalization(B)	$11.255	Beta	1.77
Trailing 12-Month EPS	$1.92	S&P Oper. EPS 2011E	2.44	Yield (%)	0.85	S&P 3-Yr. Proj. EPS CAGR(%)	15
Trailing 12-Month P/E	18.4	P/E on S&P Oper. EPS 2010E	16.2	Dividend Rate/Share	$0.30	S&P Credit Rating	NA
$10K Invested 5 Yrs Ago	$14,266	Common Shares Outstg. (M)	318.9	Institutional Ownership (%)	89		

Price Performance

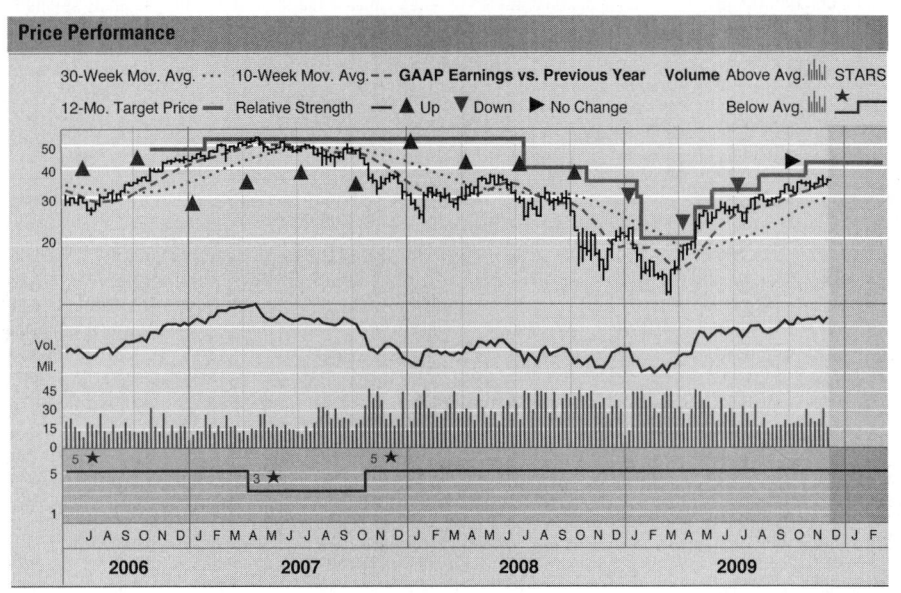

30-Week Mov. Avg. ···   10-Week Mov. Avg. - -   **GAAP Earnings vs. Previous Year**   Volume Above Avg. ▮▮▮ STARS
12-Mo. Target Price —   Relative Strength   — ▲ Up ▼ Down ► No Change   Below Avg. ▮▮▮ ★

Options: ASE, CBOE, P, Ph

Analysis prepared by **Marie Driscoll, CFA** on October 21, 2009, when the stock traded at **$ 33.83**.

Highlights

► We see COH's unique 'accessible luxury' positioning as a winning strategy with discriminating and value-focused U.S. shoppers. In the September quarter, handbag penetration in the direct channel rose 10%, to 57%, on heightened newness at accessible prices (about 50% of handbags are under $300). We see international expansion in Japan and China supporting global market share gains through 2015.

► We recently raised our FY 10 (Jun.) sales growth estimate to 6%, from 4%, on September quarter strength (+10%) in the direct channel. With a steady stream of new handbags expected this holiday season, we see North American comps turning positive in the December quarter, for a low single digit comp gain in FY 10. A 9% store expansion concentrating on new markets will boost sales as well, but we see a 14% contraction in the indirect channel reflecting reduced shipments to U.S. department stores.

► We look for gross margin expansion of 50 basis points (bps), to 72.4% of sales, in FY 10, along with 150 bps SG&A expense leverage on improved sales trends. Investments in the Reed Krakoff brand and China are projected to reduce EPS by $0.05.

Investment Rationale/Risk

► We see favorable long-term sales and earnings prospects for COH, based as much on management's acumen as brand potential both domestically and abroad. In our view, COH has adeptly navigated the consumer pullback by lowering price points, increasing the value equation and developing new marketing strategies to appeal to a younger audience. We believe COH is in solid financial shape with $995 million in cash at September 30, and inventories down 16% from a year earlier, positioning the company for growth opportunities. COH's productivity and profitability metrics are double those of its specialty apparel peers, at an estimated $2,045 trailing 12-month sales per square foot and a 30% EBIT margin.

► Risks to our recommendation and target price include a sharp decline in consumer spending patterns, and risks associated with sourcing, fashion and inventory.

► COH recently traded at about 15X our calendar 2010 EPS estimate of $2.31, a 20% discount to specialty apparel retail peers. Our 12-month target price of $42 is 18X our calendar 10 EPS estimate and in line with peers.

Qualitative Risk Assessment

LOW	MEDIUM	HIGH

Our risk assessment reflects our view of COH's strong brand equity and rising cash flow, offset by a highly competitive market amid retail consolidation.

Quantitative Evaluations

S&P Quality Ranking   B+

D	C	B-	B	B+	A-	A	A+

Relative Strength Rank   STRONG

83

LOWEST = 1   HIGHEST = 99

Revenue/Earnings Data

Revenue (Million $)

	1Q	2Q	3Q	4Q	Year
2010	761.4	--	--	--	--
2009	752.5	960.3	739.9	777.7	3,230
2008	676.7	978.0	744.5	781.5	3,181
2007	529.4	805.6	625.3	652.1	2,612
2006	449.0	650.3	497.9	514.4	2,112
2005	344.1	531.8	415.9	418.7	1,710

Earnings Per Share ($)

2010	0.44	E0.75	E0.49	E0.50	E2.18
2009	0.44	0.67	0.36	0.46	1.91
2008	0.41	0.69	0.46	0.62	2.17
2007	0.31	0.57	0.39	0.42	1.69
2006	0.24	0.45	0.28	0.31	1.27
2005	0.17	0.34	0.23	0.25	1.00

Fiscal year ended Jun. 30. Next earnings report expected: Late January. EPS Estimates based on S&P Operating Earnings; historical GAAP earnings are as reported.

Dividend Data (Dates: mm/dd Payment Date: mm/dd/yy)

Amount ($)	Date Decl.	Ex-Div. Date	Stk. of Record	Payment Date
0.075	04/21	06/04	06/08	06/29/09
0.075	08/18	09/03	09/08	09/28/09
0.075	11/19	12/03	12/07	12/28/09

Dividends have been paid since 2009. Source: Company reports.

Coach Inc.

STANDARD &POOR'S

Business Summary October 21, 2009

CORPORATE OVERVIEW. Coach is a leading U.S. designer and marketer of high-quality accessories. Founded in 1941, COH has over the past several years transformed the Coach brand, building on its popular core categories by introducing new products in a broader array of materials, styles and categories. The company has also implemented a flexible sourcing and manufacturing model, which it believes enables it to bring a broader range of products to market more rapidly and efficiently.

MARKET PROFILE. Coach is the number one luxury accessories brand in the U.S., with an estimated 20% share of this estimated $8.7 billion market ($100+ handbags). This sub-segment of the handbag/accessories market grew at an estimated 20% pace in 2007 and 2006, 17% in 2005, 30% in 2004, and 23% in 2003. While we estimate 2008 sales were flat, it remains one of the best-performing categories at retail. Moreover, COH has been able to outpace industry growth and add an estimated six market share points in the 2002-2007 period, as it executed its multi-channel growth strategy and continued to do so in 2008, with sales growth of 18%. The Japanese consumer makes up about 40% of the global luxury handbag market. COH estimates that it currently has 13% of the domestic Japanese market, and aims to increase its share to 15%

over the next five years by expansion and opening new stores. Developing markets represent the next leg of growth, supporting a global market projected at $25 billion in 2010. With a total of 33 locations in Greater China, COH currently holds an estimated 4% share of the market.

PRIMARY BUSINESS DYNAMICS. COH sells its products through direct to consumer and indirect channels, with the former accounting for 84% of total sales in FY 09 (Jun.) up from 80% in FY 08 and FY 07, 76% in FY 06 and 55% in FY 05 and FY 04. As of June 27, 2009, direct to consumer channels included the Internet, direct mail catalogs, 330 North American retail stores, 111 North American factory stores, and 160 department store shop-in-shops, retail stores and factory stores in Japan. Indirect channels include an estimated 900 U.S. department store locations and 140 international department store, retail store and duty free shop locations in 18 countries. COH opened 39 retail stores in FY 09, which generated about $1.6 million sales per location.

Company Financials Fiscal Year Ended Jun. 30

Per Share Data ($)	2009	2008	2007	2006	2005	2004	2003	2002	2001	2000
Tangible Book Value	4.41	3.73	4.52	2.57	2.07	2.00	1.11	0.67	0.43	0.15
Cash Flow	2.29	2.45	1.90	1.44	1.14	0.79	0.48	0.31	0.24	0.17
Earnings	1.91	2.17	1.69	1.27	1.00	0.68	0.40	0.24	0.19	0.10
S&P Core Earnings	1.91	2.17	1.69	1.26	0.91	0.61	0.35	0.21	0.17	NA
Dividends	0.08	Nil	Nil	Nil	Nil	Nil	Nil	Nil	Nil	NA
Payout Ratio	4%	Nil	Nil	Nil	Nil	Nil	Nil	Nil	Nil	NA
Prices:High	37.10	37.64	54.00	44.99	36.84	28.85	20.42	8.93	5.34	3.67
Prices:Low	11.41	13.19	29.22	25.18	24.51	16.88	7.26	4.30	2.50	2.00
P/E Ratio:High	19	17	32	35	37	42	52	38	28	NM
P/E Ratio:Low	6	6	17	20	25	25	18	18	13	NM

Income Statement Analysis (Million $)	2009	2008	2007	2006	2005	2004	2003	2002	2001	2000
Revenue	3,230	3,181	2,612	2,112	1,710	1,321	953	719	616	549
Operating Income	1,095	1,280	1,074	830	679	487	274	163	130	78.5
Depreciation	123	101	80.9	65.1	57.0	42.9	30.2	25.5	24.1	22.6
Interest Expense	NA	NA	Nil	Nil	1.22	0.81	0.70	1.12	2.26	6.60
Pretax Income	977	1,195	1,035	797	638	448	245	133	99.4	51.1
Effective Tax Rate	36.2%	34.5%	38.5%	38.0%	36.9%	37.5%	37.0%	35.5%	35.6%	30.6%
Net Income	623	783	637	494	389	262	147	85.8	64.0	35.4
S&P Core Earnings	625	783	637	492	356	236	129	74.9	58.3	NA

Balance Sheet & Other Financial Data (Million $)	2009	2008	2007	2006	2005	2004	2003	2002	2001	2000
Cash	800	699	557	143	155	263	229	94.0	3.69	NA
Current Assets	1,396	1,386	1,740	974	709	706	449	288	152	134
Total Assets	2,564	2,274	2,450	1,627	1,347	1,029	618	441	259	233
Current Liabilities	460	451	408	342	266	182	161	159	104	79.6
Long Term Debt	25.1	2.58	2.87	3.10	3.27	3.42	3.54	3.62	3.69	87.8
Common Equity	1,696	1,516	1,910	1,189	1,033	782	427	260	148	65.0
Total Capital	1,721	1,545	1,950	1,223	1,041	842	453	279	152	153
Capital Expenditures	240	175	141	134	94.6	67.7	57.1	42.8	31.9	26.1
Cash Flow	746	884	717	559	446	305	177	111	88.2	58.0
Current Ratio	3.0	3.1	4.3	2.9	2.7	3.9	2.8	1.8	1.5	1.7
% Long Term Debt of Capitalization	1.5	0.2	0.1	0.3	0.3	0.4	0.8	1.3	2.4	57.4
% Net Income of Revenue	19.3	24.6	24.4	23.4	22.7	19.8	15.4	11.9	10.4	6.4
% Return on Assets	25.8	33.2	31.2	33.0	32.5	31.8	27.7	24.5	23.1	13.3
% Return on Equity	38.8	45.7	41.1	44.0	42.8	43.3	42.7	42.0	35.5	18.6

Data as orig reptd.; bef. results of disc opers/spec. items. Per share data adj. for stk. divs.; EPS diluted. E-Estimated. NA-Not Available. NM-Not Meaningful. NR-Not Ranked. UR-Under Review.

Office: 516 W 34th St, New York, NY 10001-1394.
Telephone: 212-594-1850.
Email: info@coach.com
Website: http://www.coach.com

Chrmn & CEO: L. Frankfort
COO & Co-Pres: J. Stritzke
EVP, CFO & Chief Acctg Officer: M.F. Devine, III
SVP, Secy & General Counsel: T. Kahn

Treas: N. Walsh
Investor Contact: M. Devine (212-594-1850)
Board Members: L. Frankfort, S. J. Kropf, G. W. Loveman, I. M. Menezes, I. R. Miller, M. Murphy, J. J. Zeitlin

Founded: 1941
Domicile: Maryland
Employees: 12,000

Coca-Cola Co (The)

STANDARD
&POOR'S

S&P Recommendation **STRONG BUY** ★★★★★	Price $57.18 (as of Nov 27, 2009)	12-Mo. Target Price $62.00	Investment Style Large-Cap Growth

GICS Sector Consumer Staples
Sub-Industry Soft Drinks

Summary The world's largest soft drink company, KO also has a sizable fruit juice business. Its bottling interests include a 35% stake in NYSE-listed Coca-Cola Enterprises (CCE).

Key Stock Statistics (Source S&P, Vickers, company reports)

52-Wk Range	$58.43– 37.44	S&P Oper. EPS 2009**E**	3.06	Market Capitalization(B)	$132.496	Beta	0.58
Trailing 12-Month EPS	$2.70	S&P Oper. EPS 2010**E**	3.38	Yield (%)	2.87	S&P 3-Yr. Proj. EPS CAGR(%)	8
Trailing 12-Month P/E	21.2	P/E on S&P Oper. EPS 2009**E**	18.7	Dividend Rate/Share	$1.64	S&P Credit Rating	A+
$10K Invested 5 Yrs Ago	$16,626	Common Shares Outstg. (M)	2,317.2	Institutional Ownership (%)	64		

Price Performance

30-Week Mov. Avg. · · · · 10-Week Mov. Avg. – – **GAAP Earnings vs. Previous Year** Volume Above Avg. STARS
12-Mo. Target Price — Relative Strength — ▲ Up ▼ Down ▶ No Change Below Avg. ★

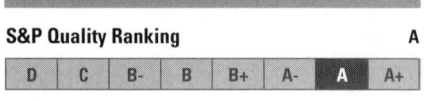

Options: ASE, CBOE, P, Ph

Analysis prepared by **Esther Y. Kwon, CFA** on November 02, 2009, when the stock traded at **$ 53.66**.

Highlights

▶ In 2007, KO acquired Energy Brands, maker of vitaminwater, for $4.1 billion. This deal accelerated growth of KO's non-carb beverage business in 2008, and we think it will again in 2009, in an area that has lagged chief competitor PepsiCo (PEP 61, Hold). KO's long-term financial objectives include 3% to 4% annual volume growth, 6% to 8% operating income growth, and EPS growth in the high single digits.

▶ For 2009, we see sales declining about 4%, as higher prices and international volume growth are more than offset by negative foreign exchange. We look for mid-single digit growth in volumes, with carbonated volumes increasing at a low single digit rate and non-carbonated volumes rising at a high single digit rate. We expect operating profits to be down slightly, as lean initiatives are offset by unfavorable mix, deleveraging and higher commodity costs, which we see abating in the second half. In 2010, we estimate sales growth of about 6%.

▶ Assuming a higher effective tax rate of 23.0%, we estimate EPS of $3.06 in 2009, down from operating EPS of $3.15 in 2008, which excludes asset impairment and restructuring charges. We see EPS of $3.38 in 2010.

Investment Rationale/Risk

▶ We look for volumes in KO's non-carb portfolio to continue to be healthy, as the company widens distribution and as premium pricing has held. We view KO's long-term growth targets as reasonable, particularly in light of its high exposure to international markets, which should offset low single digit volume declines at the Coke brand in the U.S. On increasing trial and awareness, we see Coca-Cola Zero driving trademark Coca-Cola volumes worldwide. We think a weakening of the dollar could provide a further boost to profits.

▶ Risks to our recommendation and target price include inability to meet growth targets, adverse foreign currency movements, and unfavorable weather conditions in the company's markets.

▶ Our 12-month target price of $62 is based on an analysis of historical and comparative peer P/E multiples. KO's forward P/E has ranged between 16X and 28X over the past few years, while PepsiCo's has been slightly lower. Given a more challenging economic environment, we think a multiple at the low end of that range and a premium to PepsiCo's is appropriate.

Qualitative Risk Assessment

LOW	MEDIUM	HIGH

Our risk assessment for the Coca-Cola Company reflects the relatively stable nature of the company's end markets, its dominant market share positions around the world, and our view of its strong balance sheet and cash flow.

Quantitative Evaluations

S&P Quality Ranking   A

D	C	B-	B	B+	A-	**A**	A+

Relative Strength Rank   **STRONG**

79

LOWEST = 1   HIGHEST = 99

Revenue/Earnings Data

Revenue (Million $)

	1Q	2Q	3Q	4Q	Year
2009	7,169	8,267	8,044	--	--
2008	7,379	9,046	8,393	7,126	31,944
2007	6,103	7,733	7,690	7,331	28,857
2006	5,226	6,476	6,454	5,932	24,088
2005	5,206	6,310	6,037	5,551	23,104
2004	5,078	5,965	5,662	5,257	21,962

Earnings Per Share ($)

2009	0.58	0.88	0.81	E0.64	E3.06
2008	0.64	0.61	0.81	0.43	2.49
2007	0.54	0.80	0.71	0.52	2.57
2006	0.47	0.78	0.62	0.29	2.16
2005	0.42	0.72	0.54	0.36	2.04
2004	0.46	0.65	0.39	0.50	2.00

Fiscal year ended Dec. 31. Next earnings report expected: Mid February. EPS Estimates based on S&P Operating Earnings; historical GAAP earnings are as reported.

Dividend Data (Dates: mm/dd Payment Date: mm/dd/yy)

Amount ($)	Date Decl.	Ex-Div. Date	Stk. of Record	Payment Date
0.410	02/19	03/11	03/15	04/01/09
0.410	04/23	06/11	06/15	07/01/09
0.410	07/23	09/11	09/15	10/01/09
0.410	10/22	11/27	12/01	12/15/09

Dividends have been paid since 1893. Source: Company reports.

Please read the Required Disclosures and Analyst Certification on the last page of this report.

Coca-Cola Co (The)

STANDARD &POOR'S

Business Summary November 02, 2009

CORPORATE OVERVIEW. The Coca-Cola Company is the world's largest producer of soft drink concentrates and syrups, as well as the world's biggest producer of juice and juice-related products. Finished soft drink products bearing the company's trademarks have been sold in the U.S. since 1886, and are now sold in more than 200 countries. It owns or licenses almost 500 brands. Sales by operating segment in 2008 were derived as follows: North America (25.7% of revenues); Bottling Investments (27.3%); European Union (15.0%); Pacific (13.7%); Latin America (11.3%); Eurasia and Africa (6.7%); and Corporate (0.3%)

The company's business encompasses the production and sale of soft drink and non-carbonated beverage concentrates and syrups. These products are sold to the company's authorized independent and company-owned bottling/canning operations, and fountain wholesalers. These customers then either combine the syrup with carbonated water, or combine the concentrate with sweetener, water and carbonated water to produce finished soft drinks. The finished soft drinks are packaged in containers bearing the company's well-known trademarks, which include Coca-Cola Classic (the best-selling soft drink in the world), caffeine free Coca-Cola, diet Coke (sold as Coke light in many markets outside the U.S.), Cherry Coke, Vanilla Coke, Coke Zero, Fanta, Full Throttle, Sprite, diet Sprite/Sprite Zero, Barq's, Pibb Xtra, Mello Yello, TAB, Fresca, Powerade, Aquarius, and other products developed for specific

markets. The company also markets the Schweppes and Canada Dry mixer (such as tonic water, club soda and ginger ale), Crush and Dr. Pepper brands outside of the U.S. In 2008, concentrates and syrups for beverages bearing the trademark "Coca-Cola" or including the trademark "Coke" accounted for approximately 52% of the company's total concentrate sales.

In 2008, concentrate sales in the U.S. represented approximately 23% of KO's worldwide sales. About 56% of concentrate sales were beverage concentrates and syrups to 74 authorized bottlers in 393 licensed territories, 32% were fountain syrups sold to fountain retailers and 470 fountain wholesalers, and the remaining 12% were sales by the company of finished products.

KO has equity positions in approximately 43 unconsolidated bottling, canning and distribution operations for its products worldwide, including bottlers that accounted for approximately 54% of the company's worldwide unit case volume in 2008. Coca-Cola Enterprises (CCE) accounted for approximately 42% of the company's U.S. concentrate sales. KO holds a 35% equity interest in CCE.

Company Financials Fiscal Year Ended Dec. 31

Per Share Data ($)	2008	2007	2006	2005	2004	2003	2002	2001	2000	1999
Tangible Book Value	3.45	8.53	5.08	5.29	5.02	4.14	3.34	3.53	2.98	3.06
Cash Flow	2.94	3.00	2.56	2.43	2.36	2.11	1.93	1.92	1.19	1.30
Earnings	2.49	2.57	2.16	2.04	2.00	1.77	1.60	1.60	0.88	0.98
S&P Core Earnings	2.40	2.51	2.04	2.03	2.08	1.77	1.62	1.46	NA	NA
Dividends	1.52	1.36	1.24	1.12	1.00	0.88	0.80	0.72	0.68	0.64
Payout Ratio	61%	53%	57%	55%	50%	50%	50%	45%	77%	65%
Prices:High	65.59	64.32	49.35	45.26	53.50	50.90	57.91	62.19	66.88	70.88
Prices:Low	40.29	45.56	39.36	40.31	38.30	37.01	42.90	42.37	42.88	47.31
P/E Ratio:High	26	25	23	22	27	29	36	39	76	72
P/E Ratio:Low	16	18	18	20	19	21	27	26	49	48

Income Statement Analysis (Million $)										
Revenue	31,944	28,857	24,088	23,104	21,962	21,044	19,564	20,092	20,458	19,805
Operating Income	9,862	8,532	7,246	7,017	6,591	6,071	6,264	6,155	4,464	4,774
Depreciation	1,066	1,012	938	932	893	850	806	803	773	792
Interest Expense	438	456	220	240	196	178	199	289	447	337
Pretax Income	7,439	7,873	6,578	6,690	6,222	5,495	5,499	5,670	3,399	3,819
Effective Tax Rate	21.9%	24.0%	22.8%	27.2%	22.1%	20.9%	27.7%	29.8%	36.0%	36.3%
Net Income	5,807	5,981	5,080	4,872	4,847	4,347	3,976	3,979	2,177	2,431
S&P Core Earnings	5,595	5,827	4,797	4,854	5,063	4,350	4,021	3,654	NA	NA

Balance Sheet & Other Financial Data (Million $)										
Cash	4,979	4,308	2,590	4,767	6,768	3,482	2,345	1,934	1,892	1,812
Current Assets	12,176	12,105	8,441	10,250	12,094	8,396	7,352	7,171	6,620	6,480
Total Assets	40,519	43,269	29,963	29,427	31,327	27,342	24,501	22,417	20,834	21,623
Current Liabilities	12,988	13,225	8,890	9,836	10,971	7,886	7,341	8,429	9,321	9,856
Long Term Debt	2,781	9,329	1,314	1,154	1,157	2,517	2,701	1,219	835	854
Common Equity	20,472	21,744	16,920	16,355	15,935	14,090	11,800	11,366	9,316	9,513
Total Capital	24,130	27,269	18,842	17,861	17,542	16,944	14,900	13,027	10,509	10,865
Capital Expenditures	1,968	1,648	1,407	899	755	812	851	769	733	1,069
Cash Flow	6,873	6,993	6,018	5,804	5,740	5,197	4,782	4,782	2,950	3,223
Current Ratio	0.9	0.9	0.9	1.0	1.1	1.1	1.0	0.9	0.7	0.7
% Long Term Debt of Capitalization	11.5	12.9	7.0	6.5	6.6	14.9	18.1	9.4	7.9	7.9
% Net Income of Revenue	18.2	20.7	21.1	21.1	22.1	20.7	20.3	19.8	10.6	12.3
% Return on Assets	13.9	16.3	17.1	16.0	16.5	16.8	16.9	18.4	10.3	11.9
% Return on Equity	27.5	30.9	30.5	30.2	32.3	33.6	34.3	38.5	23.1	27.1

Data as orig reptd.; bef. results of disc opers/spec. items. Per share data adj. for stk. divs.; EPS diluted. E-Estimated. NA-Not Available. NM-Not Meaningful. NR-Not Ranked. UR-Under Review.

Office: 1 Coca Cola Plz NW, Atlanta, GA 30313-2499.
Telephone: 404-676-2121.
Website: http://www.coca-cola.com
Chrmn: Z.W. Khouri

Chrmn, Pres & CEO: M. Kent
Investor Contact: G.P. Fayard
EVP & CFO: G.P. Fayard
EVP & Chief Admin Officer: A.B. Cummings, Jr.

Board Members: H. A. Allen, R. W. Allen, C. P. Black, B. Diller, A. Herman, M. Kent, D. R. Keough, Z. W. Khouri, M. E. Lagomasino, D. McHenry, S. A. Nunn, J. D. Robinson, III, P. V. Ueberroth, J. Wallenberg, J. B. Williams

Founded: 1886
Domicile: Delaware
Employees: 92,400

The McGraw-Hill Companies

Coca-Cola Enterprises Inc.

STANDARD &POOR'S

S&P Recommendation **BUY** ★★★★☆	Price $19.93 (as of Nov 27, 2009)	12-Mo. Target Price $24.00	Investment Style Large-Cap Blend

GICS Sector Consumer Staples
Sub-Industry Soft Drinks

Summary This company is the world's largest bottler of Coca-Cola beverage products, distributing to about 78% of the North American market. Coca-Cola Co. holds about 35% of CCE's common stock.

Key Stock Statistics (Source S&P, Vickers, company reports)

52-Wk Range	$21.44– 8.43	S&P Oper. EPS 2009**E**	1.59	Market Capitalization(B)	$9.744	Beta	1.30
Trailing 12-Month EPS	$-1.70	S&P Oper. EPS 2010**E**	1.71	Yield (%)	1.61	S&P 3-Yr. Proj. EPS CAGR(%)	10
Trailing 12-Month P/E	NM	P/E on S&P Oper. EPS 2009**E**	12.5	Dividend Rate/Share	$0.32	S&P Credit Rating	A
$10K Invested 5 Yrs Ago	$10,305	Common Shares Outstg. (M)	488.9	Institutional Ownership (%)	54		

Price Performance

30-Week Mov. Avg. · · · 10-Week Mov. Avg. – – GAAP Earnings vs. Previous Year   Volume Above Avg. STARS
12-Mo. Target Price — Relative Strength — ▲ Up ▼ Down ► No Change   Below Avg.

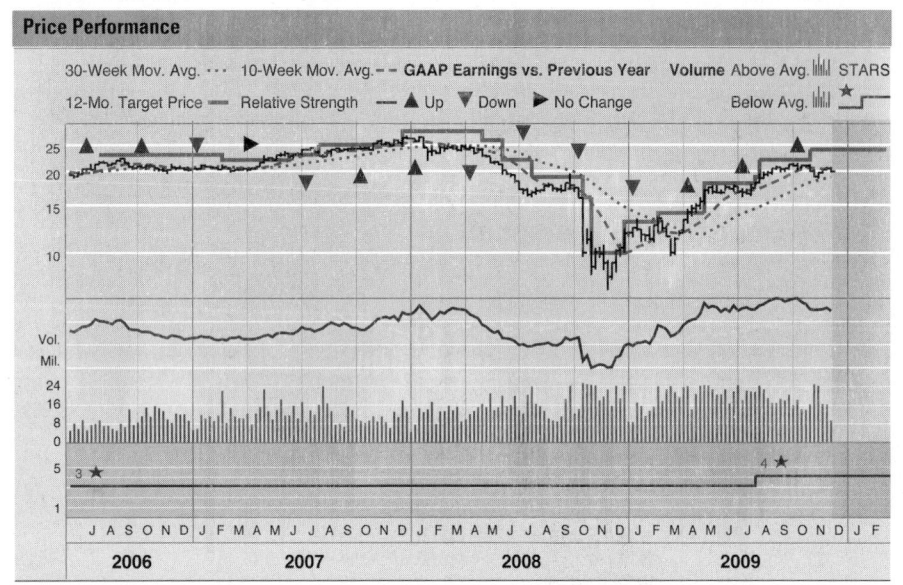

Options: ASE, CBOE, P, Ph

Analysis prepared by **Esther Y. Kwon, CFA** on October 21, 2009, when the stock traded at **$ 20.54**.

Highlights

► In 2009, we expect net revenues to be about flat with 2008 levels, as an increase of 4% to 6% in net revenues per case on higher pricing and mix benefits from recently acquired products is offset by a negative foreign currency impact. We project that North American volumes will decline due to higher pricing and weakness in carbonated soft drinks (CSDs) but see some improvement in the economically sensitive take home single-serve category. In 2010, we forecast revenue growth of approximately 4%.

► We see gross margins under pressure, as higher pricing is offset by rising sweetener, energy, and packaging costs and a mix shift away from higher-margin single-serve sales toward lower-margin glaceau products, but we forecast improvement later in the year as recent commodity price declines are realized. We estimate SG&A expenses will remain flat as a percentage of sales as CCE implements restructuring measures and cost cuts.

► On a higher tax rate, we project 2009 operating EPS of $1.50, up from 2008's $1.32, which excludes restructuring and license charges. In 2010, we see EPS of $1.69.

Investment Rationale/Risk

► Our buy recommendation reflects a more sanguine outlook for the Coca-Cola system's carbonated beverage brands and an improving outlook for material and fuel cost inflation. We see results lifted by pricing gains and think CCE benefits from the addition of the Monster energy drink portfolio as well as from less reliance on commodity bottled water. We are encouraged that significant price increases in CSDs has hurt volume less than we had expected in the U.S., and we see European volumes rising at a low to mid-single digit rate in 2009.

► Risks to our recommendation and target price include more rapid commodity cost inflation than we expect, potential consumer reluctance to accept new products, and CCE's ability to achieve sales and earnings growth forecasts. In terms of corporate governance, the board is controlled by a majority of insiders and affiliated outsiders, which we view unfavorably.

► Our 12-month target price of $24 is in line with peer multiples but is a discount to historical P/E and enterprise value-to-EBITDA multiples, on our view of lower relative international exposure and a relatively high-cost environment.

Qualitative Risk Assessment

LOW	MEDIUM	HIGH

Our risk assessment for Coca-Cola Enterprises reflects our view of the relatively stable nature of the company's end markets, its strong cash flow, and its relationship with corporate partner Coca-Cola Company.

Quantitative Evaluations

S&P Quality Ranking B-

D	C	B-	B	B+	A-	A	A+

Relative Strength Rank MODERATE

46

LOWEST = 1   HIGHEST = 99

Revenue/Earnings Data

Revenue (Million $)

	1Q	2Q	3Q	4Q	Year
2009	5,050	5,909	5,569	--	--
2008	4,892	5,935	5,743	5,237	21,807
2007	4,567	5,665	5,405	5,299	20,936
2006	4,333	5,467	5,218	4,786	19,804
2005	4,196	5,128	4,895	4,487	18,706
2004	4,240	4,844	4,670	4,404	18,158

Earnings Per Share ($)

2009	0.13	0.64	0.50	E0.21	E1.59
2008	0.02	-6.52	0.44	-2.99	-9.05
2007	0.03	0.56	0.55	0.32	1.46
2006	0.03	0.71	0.44	-3.59	-2.41
2005	0.10	0.70	0.40	-0.12	1.08
2004	0.22	0.43	0.44	0.17	1.26

Fiscal year ended Dec. 31. Next earnings report expected: Mid February. EPS Estimates based on S&P Operating Earnings; historical GAAP earnings are as reported.

Dividend Data (Dates: mm/dd Payment Date: mm/dd/yy)

Amount ($)	Date Decl.	Ex-Div. Date	Stk. of Record	Payment Date
0.070	02/10	03/11	03/13	03/26/09
0.070	04/21	06/10	06/12	06/25/09
0.080	07/29	09/09	09/11	09/24/09
0.080	10/27	11/24	11/27	12/10/09

Dividends have been paid since 1986. Source: Company reports.

Please read the Required Disclosures and Analyst Certification on the last page of this report.

Coca-Cola Enterprises Inc.

STANDARD &POOR'S

Business Summary October 21, 2009

CORPORATE OVERVIEW. Coca-Cola Enterprises is the world's largest bottler of Coca-Cola beverage products. The Coca-Cola Company (KO 49, strong buy) owns about 35% of the company's common stock. CCE's product line also includes other nonalcoholic beverages, such as still and sparkling waters, juices, isotonics and teas. In 2008, the company sold approximately 42 billion bottles and cans throughout its territories, representing about 16% of KO's worldwide volume. About 93% of this volume consisted of beverages produced and sold under licenses from KO. CCE also distributes Dr Pepper and several other beverage brands.

Based on net operating revenues in 2008, North America accounted for 70%, unchanged from 2007, and Europe for 30%. CCE operates in parts of 46 states in the U.S., the District of Columbia, the U.S. Virgin Islands, all 10 Canadian provinces, and portions of Europe that include Belgium, France, the U.K., Luxembourg, Monaco, and The Netherlands. At December 31, 2008, CCE's bottling territories encompassed an aggregate population of 419 million people. The company's five leading brands in North America in 2008 were Coca-Cola classic, Diet Coke, Sprite, Dasani, and POWERade, while the five leading brands in Europe were Coca-Cola, Diet Coke/Coke-Cola light, Fanta, Coca-Cola Zero and

Capri-Sun.

During 2008, the company's package mix (based on wholesale physical case volume) in North America was as follows: 57.5% cans, 41.0% PET plastic and 1.5% glass and other. In Europe, the package mix was as follows: 38.0% cans, 46.0% PET plastic and 16.0% glass and other.

In addition to concentrates, sweeteners, juices, and finished product, CCE purchases carbon dioxide, PET preforms, glass and plastic bottles, cans, closures, packaging such as plastic bags in cardboard boxes, and other packaging materials. The beverage agreements with The Coca-Cola Company provide that all authorized containers, closures, cases, cartons and other packages, and labels for the products of The Coca-Cola Company must be purchased from manufacturers approved by The Coca-Cola Company.

Company Financials Fiscal Year Ended Dec. 31

Per Share Data ($)	2008	2007	2006	2005	2004	2003	2002	2001	2000	1999
Tangible Book Value	NM	NM	NM	NM	NM	NM	NM	6.25	6.67	6.83
Cash Flow	-6.90	3.64	-0.28	3.27	3.52	3.88	3.35	3.08	3.48	3.22
Earnings	-9.05	1.46	-2.41	1.08	1.26	1.48	1.07	-0.05	0.54	0.13
S&P Core Earnings	0.83	1.45	-2.34	1.01	1.19	1.22	0.78	-0.34	NA	NA
Dividends	0.28	0.24	0.24	0.16	0.16	0.16	0.16	0.12	0.16	0.16
Payout Ratio	NM	16%	NM	15%	13%	11%	15%	NM	30%	123%
Prices:High	26.99	27.09	22.49	23.92	29.34	23.30	24.50	23.90	30.25	37.50
Prices:Low	7.25	19.78	18.83	18.52	18.45	16.85	15.94	13.46	14.00	16.81
P/E Ratio:High	NM	19	NM	22	23	16	23	NM	56	NM
P/E Ratio:Low	NM	14	NM	17	15	11	15	NM	26	NM

Income Statement Analysis (Million $)										
Revenue	21,807	20,936	19,804	18,706	18,158	17,330	16,889	15,700	14,750	14,406
Operating Income	2,510	2,537	2,439	2,475	2,504	2,674	2,409	1,954	2,387	2,187
Depreciation	1,050	1,067	1,012	1,044	1,068	1,097	1,045	1,353	1,261	1,348
Interest Expense	587	629	633	633	619	607	662	753	791	751
Pretax Income	-6,901	841	-2,118	790	818	972	705	-150	333	88.0
Effective Tax Rate	NM	15.4%	NM	34.9%	27.1%	30.5%	29.9%	NM	29.1%	33.0%
Net Income	-4,394	711	-1,143	514	596	676	494	-19.0	236	59.0
S&P Core Earnings	405	708	-1,110	478	563	563	356	-147	NA	NA

Balance Sheet & Other Financial Data (Million $)										
Cash	722	170	184	107	155	80.0	68.0	284	294	141
Current Assets	4,583	4,092	3,691	3,395	3,264	3,000	2,844	2,876	2,631	2,581
Total Assets	15,589	24,046	23,225	25,357	26,354	25,700	24,375	23,719	22,162	22,730
Current Liabilities	5,074	5,343	3,818	3,846	3,431	3,941	3,455	4,522	3,094	3,614
Long Term Debt	7,247	7,391	9,218	9,165	10,523	10,552	11,236	10,365	10,348	10,153
Common Equity	-31.0	5,689	4,526	5,643	5,378	4,365	3,310	2,783	2,790	2,877
Total Capital	8,324	19,048	17,801	19,914	21,139	19,882	19,122	17,521	17,956	18,028
Capital Expenditures	981	938	882	914	946	1,099	1,029	972	1,181	1,480
Cash Flow	-3,344	1,178	-131	1,558	1,664	1,771	1,536	1,331	1,494	1,404
Current Ratio	0.9	0.8	1.0	0.9	1.0	0.8	0.8	0.6	0.9	0.7
% Long Term Debt of Capitalization	87.1	38.8	51.8	46.0	49.8	53.1	58.8	59.2	57.6	56.3
% Net Income of Revenue	NM	3.3	NM	2.7	3.3	3.9	2.9	NM	1.6	0.4
% Return on Assets	NM	3.0	NM	2.0	2.3	2.7	2.1	NM	1.1	0.3
% Return on Equity	NM	13.9	NM	9.3	12.2	17.6	16.1	NM	8.2	2.1

Data as orig reptd.; bef. results of disc opers/spec. items. Per share data adj. for stk. divs.; EPS diluted. E-Estimated. NA-Not Available. NM-Not Meaningful. NR-Not Ranked. UR-Under Review.

Office: 2500 Windy Ridge Pkwy SE, Atlanta, GA 30339.
Telephone: 770-989-3000.
Website: http://www.cokecce.com
Chrmn & CEO: J.F. Brock, III

EVP & CFO: W.W. Douglas, III
SVP & General Counsel: J.R. Parker, Jr.
SVP & CIO: E. Sezer
Chief Acctg Officer & Cntlr: S.D. Patterson

Investor Contact: T. Erickson (770-989-3110)
Board Members: F. Aguirre, J. F. Brock, III, C. Darden, I. Finan, M. J. Herb, L. P. Humann, J. Hunter, O. H. Ingram, II, D. A. James, T. H. Johnson, S. Labarge, C. R. Welling
Founded: 1944
Domicile: Delaware
Employees: 72,000

Cognizant Technology Solutions Corp

STANDARD &POOR'S

S&P Recommendation BUY ★★★★☆

Price	$43.49 (as of Nov 27, 2009)
12-Mo. Target Price	$50.00
Investment Style	Large-Cap Growth

GICS Sector Information Technology
Sub-Industry IT Consulting & Other Services

Summary This company offers full life-cycle solutions to complex software development and maintenance problems.

Key Stock Statistics (Source S&P, Vickers, company reports)

52-Wk Range	$45.75– 15.39	S&P Oper. EPS 2009**E**	1.77	Market Capitalization(B)	$12.817	Beta	1.30
Trailing 12-Month EPS	$1.68	S&P Oper. EPS 2010**E**	1.95	Yield (%)	Nil	S&P 3-Yr. Proj. EPS CAGR(%)	14
Trailing 12-Month P/E	25.9	P/E on S&P Oper. EPS 2009**E**	24.6	Dividend Rate/Share	Nil	S&P Credit Rating	NA
$10K Invested 5 Yrs Ago	$22,194	Common Shares Outstg. (M)	294.7	Institutional Ownership (%)	96		

Price Performance

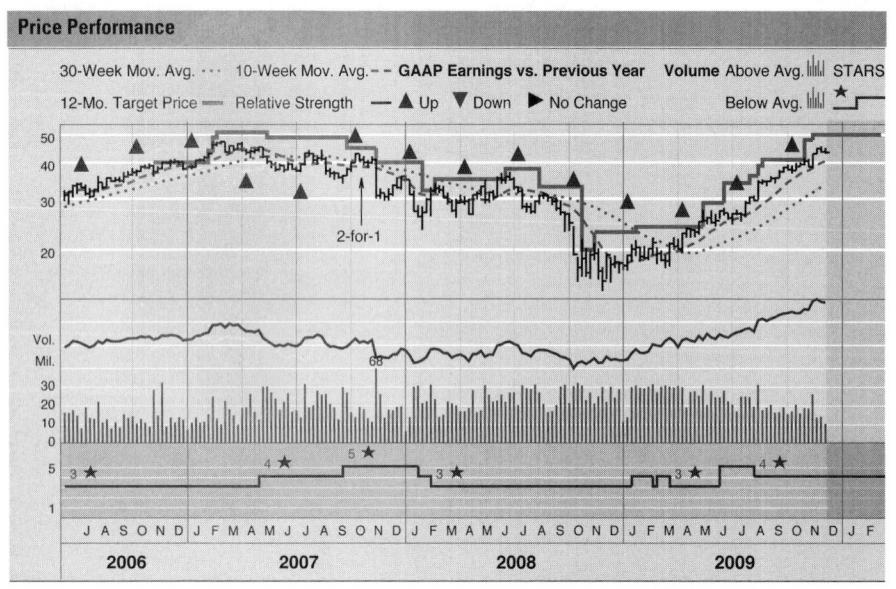

30-Week Mov. Avg. · · · 10-Week Mov. Avg. - - GAAP Earnings vs. Previous Year   Volume Above Avg. STARS
12-Mo. Target Price — Relative Strength   ▲ Up ▼ Down ► No Change   Below Avg.

2-for-1

2006 2007 2008 2009

Options: ASE, CBOE, P, Ph

Analysis prepared by **Dylan Cathers** on November 05, 2009, when the stock traded at **$ 42.25**.

Highlights

► We look for revenue growth of 16% in 2009 and 14% in 2010. We believe CTSH is continuing to see strong demand across all of its industry verticals, with notable gains coming from the healthcare, life sciences, and retail areas. Additionally, we believe that the financial services segment is improving, particularly within banking and insurance. In general, we think IT spending on outsourcing has bottomed out. Still, visibility will remain cloudy, in our opinion, until companies start setting IT spending budgets in early 2010.

► We expect operating margins to widen in 2009, including projected stock option expense. The gain we anticipate stems largely from increasing revenues, a high utilization rate, falling employee attrition, cost controls, and an improved mix of offshore/onsite workers. We think CTSH's investments in the business and in new geographies, as well as an expected higher level of variable salary costs in the form of bonuses, will partially offset these positives in 2010.

► We estimate EPS of $1.77 in 2009, rising to $1.95 in 2010.

Investment Rationale/Risk

► We continue to view CTSH shares favorably, given the company's strong balance sheet, with over $4.00 per share in cash and short-term investments and no debt, and its U.S. incorporation. Although we have some concerns about prospects for the financial services sector, those are lessening. Also, we think CTSH's revenue growth will be faster than that of many peers and believe the company has done a good job moving into high-growth verticals.

► Risks to our recommendation and target price include increasing competition in offshore outsourcing, with consequent margin pressures; rising wages of Indian employees; appreciation of the rupee; and immigration restrictions that could affect personnel. Our corporate governance concerns center around a classified board of directors and a "poison pill" that is in place.

► We apply a peer-premium P/E of 25.6X to our 2010 EPS estimate to arrive at our 12-month target price of $50. At that level, the stock's P/E-to-growth ratio would be about 1.8X, assuming an expected three-year growth rate of 14%.

Qualitative Risk Assessment

LOW	MEDIUM	HIGH

Our risk assessment reflects what we see as CTSH's strong balance sheet, steady cash inflows, and rapid revenue growth, offset by intense competition in the IT services peer group from both companies domiciled in India as well as multinationals.

Quantitative Evaluations

S&P Quality Ranking B+

D	C	B-	B	B+	A-	A	A+

Relative Strength Rank STRONG

86

LOWEST = 1   HIGHEST = 99

Revenue/Earnings Data

Revenue (Million $)

	1Q	2Q	3Q	4Q	Year
2009	745.9	776.6	853.5	--	--
2008	643.1	685.4	734.7	753.0	2,816
2007	460.3	516.5	558.8	600.0	2,136
2006	285.5	336.8	377.5	424.4	1,424
2005	181.7	211.7	235.5	256.9	885.8
2004	119.7	138.7	155.4	172.8	586.7

Earnings Per Share ($)

2009	0.38	0.47	0.45	E0.47	E1.77
2008	0.34	0.35	0.38	0.38	1.44
2007	0.25	0.27	0.32	0.32	1.15
2006	0.16	0.19	0.20	0.23	0.78
2005	0.11	0.13	0.14	0.20	0.57
2004	0.07	0.09	0.09	0.11	0.35

Fiscal year ended Dec. 31. Next earnings report expected: Mid February. EPS Estimates based on S&P Operating Earnings; historical GAAP earnings are as reported.

Dividend Data

No cash dividends have been paid.

The McGraw-Hill Companies

Cognizant Technology Solutions Corp

STANDARD
&POOR'S

Business Summary November 05, 2009

CORPORATE OVERVIEW. Cognizant Technology Solutions began operations in 1994 as an in-house technology development center for Dun & Bradstreet Corp. and its operating units. In its June 1998 IPO, 2,917,000 common shares were sold at $10 each.

The company's objective is to be a leading provider of full life-cycle e-business and application development projects, take full responsibility for ongoing management of a client's software systems, and help clients move legacy transformation projects through to completion. The company's solutions include application development and integration, application management, and re-engineering services.

Applications development services are provided using a full life-cycle application development approach in which the company assumes total start to finish responsibility and accountability for analysis, design, implementation, testing and integration of systems, or through cooperative development, in which CTSH employees work with the customer's in-house IT personnel. In either case, the company's on-site team members work closely with end users

of the application to develop specifications and define requirements.

CTSH applications management services seeks to ensure that a customer's core operational systems are free of defects and responsive to end-users' changing needs. The company is often able to introduce product and process enhancements and improve service levels.

Through its re-engineering services, the company works with customers to migrate systems based on legacy computing environments to newer, open systems-based platforms and client/server architectures, often in response to the more stringent demands of e-business. CTSH's re-engineering tools automate many processes required to implement advanced client/server technologies.

Company Financials Fiscal Year Ended Dec. 31

Per Share Data ($)	2008	2007	2006	2005	2004	2003	2002	2001	2000	1999
Tangible Book Value	6.05	4.42	3.60	2.44	1.61	0.98	0.62	0.42	0.29	0.20
Cash Flow	1.69	1.33	0.89	0.64	0.41	0.26	0.17	0.12	0.07	0.12
Earnings	1.44	1.15	0.78	0.57	0.35	0.21	0.14	0.09	0.07	0.05
S&P Core Earnings	1.44	1.15	0.78	0.51	0.30	0.16	0.09	0.07	NA	NA
Dividends	Nil	Nil	Nil	Nil	Nil	Nil	Nil	Nil	Nil	Nil
Payout Ratio	Nil	Nil	Nil	Nil	Nil	Nil	Nil	Nil	Nil	Nil
Prices:High	37.10	47.78	41.25	26.24	21.47	12.40	6.38	4.48	6.01	5.04
Prices:Low	14.38	29.44	24.26	17.79	9.80	4.28	2.70	1.48	2.02	0.80
P/E Ratio:High	26	42	53	46	61	59	47	49	83	NM
P/E Ratio:Low	10	26	31	31	28	20	20	16	28	NM

Income Statement Analysis (Million $)	2008	2007	2006	2005	2004	2003	2002	2001	2000	1999
Revenue	2,816	2,136	1,424	886	587	368	229	178	137	88.9
Operating Income	591	435	293	199	134	84.2	106	42.0	30.6	19.7
Depreciation	74.8	53.9	34.2	21.4	16.4	11.9	7.84	6.37	4.51	3.04
Interest Expense	Nil	Nil	Nil	Nil	Nil	Nil	Nil	Nil	Nil	Nil
Pretax Income	515	414	278	185	122	72.2	45.1	35.4	28.2	17.9
Effective Tax Rate	16.4%	15.5%	16.2%	10.3%	17.9%	20.6%	23.4%	37.4%	37.4%	37.4%
Net Income	431	350	233	166	100	57.4	34.6	22.2	17.7	11.2
S&P Core Earnings	431	350	233	148	85.1	42.4	23.0	16.3	NA	NA

Balance Sheet & Other Financial Data (Million $)	2008	2007	2006	2005	2004	2003	2002	2001	2000	1999
Cash	763	670	266	197	293	194	126	85.0	62.0	42.6
Current Assets	1,468	1,242	1,040	663	454	278	176	117	88.2	56.7
Total Assets	2,375	1,838	1,326	870	573	361	231	145	110	69.0
Current Liabilities	388	341	250	156	115	62.6	41.5	21.7	26.7	13.2
Long Term Debt	Nil	Nil	Nil	Nil	Nil	Nil	Nil	Nil	Nil	Nil
Common Equity	1,966	1,468	1,073	714	454	274	165	98.8	66.1	45.5
Total Capital	1,973	1,483	1,073	714	458	298	190	123	82.8	55.8
Capital Expenditures	169	182	105	71.8	46.6	30.0	22.3	15.0	10.7	5.92
Cash Flow	506	404	267	188	117	69.3	42.4	28.5	17.7	14.3
Current Ratio	3.8	3.7	4.2	4.3	3.9	4.4	4.2	5.4	3.3	4.3
% Long Term Debt of Capitalization	Nil	Nil	Nil	Nil	Nil	Nil	Nil	Nil	Nil	Nil
% Net Income of Revenue	15.3	16.4	16.3	18.8	17.1	15.6	15.1	12.5	12.9	12.6
% Return on Assets	20.5	22.1	21.2	23.1	21.4	19.4	18.4	17.4	19.8	18.6
% Return on Equity	25.1	27.6	26.0	28.5	27.6	26.1	26.2	26.9	31.7	28.8

Data as orig reptd.; bef. results of disc opers/spec. items. Per share data adj. for stk. divs.; EPS diluted. E-Estimated. NA-Not Available. NM-Not Meaningful. NR-Not Ranked. UR-Under Review.

Office: 500 Glenpointe Ctr W Ste, Teaneck, NJ 07666-6821.
Telephone: 201-801-0233.
Website: http://www.cognizant.com
Chrmn: J.E. Klein

Pres & CEO: F. D'Souza
Vice Chrmn: L. Narayanan
COO & CFO: G.J. Coburn
SVP, Secy & General Counsel: S.E. Schwartz

Investor Contact: G. Coburn (201-678-2712)
Board Members: M. Breakiron-Evans, F. D'Souza, J. N. Fox, Jr., R. W. Howe, J. E. Klein, L. Narayanan, R. E. Weissman, T. M. Wendel

Founded: 1988
Domicile: Delaware
Employees: 61,700

Colgate-Palmolive Co

STANDARD &POOR'S

S&P Recommendation	STRONG BUY ★ ★ ★ ★ ★	Price $83.63 (as of Nov 27, 2009)	12-Mo. Target Price $90.00	Investment Style Large-Cap Growth

GICS Sector Consumer Staples
Sub-Industry Household Products

Summary This major consumer products company markets oral, personal and household care, and pet nutrition products in more than 200 countries and territories.

Key Stock Statistics (Source S&P, Vickers, company reports)

52-Wk Range	$87.39– 54.51	S&P Oper. EPS 2009E	4.32	Market Capitalization(B)	$41.580	Beta	0.51
Trailing 12-Month EPS	$4.10	S&P Oper. EPS 2010E	4.82	Yield (%)	2.10	S&P 3-Yr. Proj. EPS CAGR(%)	10
Trailing 12-Month P/E	20.4	P/E on S&P Oper. EPS 2009E	19.4	Dividend Rate/Share	$1.76	S&P Credit Rating	AA-
$10K Invested 5 Yrs Ago	$20,357	Common Shares Outstg. (M)	497.2	Institutional Ownership (%)	71		

Price Performance

30-Week Mov. Avg. · · · 10-Week Mov. Avg. - - GAAP Earnings vs. Previous Year Volume Above Avg. STARS
12-Mo. Target Price — Relative Strength — ▲ Up ▼ Down ► No Change Below Avg. ★

Options: ASE, CBOE, P

Analysis prepared by **Loran Braverman, CFA** on October 29, 2009, when the stock traded at **$ 79.00**.

Highlights

► In December 2004, CL embarked on a four-year restructuring program that involved a 12% work force reduction, the closing of a third of its factories, an increased focus on faster-growing markets, new product innovation, and more efficient spending on marketing. We believe the benefits CL derives from the program are helping it maintain a more consistent earnings growth rate than its competitors enjoy.

► For 2009, we project a 0.6% sales drop (assuming about a 7% negative foreign exchange effect). Excluding one-time and restructuring charges, we expect the operating margin to widen about 230 basis points. We see the benefits from price increases, savings from various restructuring and other programs, and moderating commodity price pressures offsetting a negative currency effect and a lack of sales leverage. For 2010, we forecast sales rising 6.6%.

► We expect EPS in 2009 to increase to $4.32, from operating EPS of $3.87 in 2008, on close to a 2% reduction in average shares outstanding. The 2008 EPS excludes restructuring charges. Our 2010 EPS estimate is $4.82.

Investment Rationale/Risk

► Our strong buy opinion reflects our view that CL's restructuring program is likely to help drive EPS growth near 10% from 2008 onward for at least several years. We expect the company to continue to invest in R&D and marketing, with more resources to be allocated to faster-growing markets. In addition, we have seen a smooth CEO transition, from Reuben Mark, CEO since 1984, to Ian Cook, formerly COO and himself a long-time CL employee, who became CEO on July 1, 2007.

► Risks to our recommendation and target price include intensified competition in the global oral care market, unfavorable currency translation, and low consumer acceptance of new products.

► Our 12-month target price of $90 is a blend of our three valuation models. Our DCF model assumes a terminal WACC of 9.3% and a terminal growth rate of 3% to arrive at a value of $90. We believe the shares should trade at a premium to peers, and we apply a 17.0X P/E to our 2010 EPS estimate, for a value of $82. Our historical analysis uses a P/E of 20.3X, below the 10-year average, to value the stock at $98.

Qualitative Risk Assessment

LOW	MEDIUM	HIGH

Our risk assessment reflects that demand for household and personal care products is generally static, and not affected by changes in the economy or geopolitical factors. This is partially offset by the mature and competitive nature of these industries.

Quantitative Evaluations

S&P Quality Ranking A+

D	C	B-	B	B+	A-	A	A+

Relative Strength Rank STRONG

81

LOWEST = 1   HIGHEST = 99

Revenue/Earnings Data

Revenue (Million $)

	1Q	2Q	3Q	4Q	Year
2009	3,503	3,745	3,998	--	--
2008	3,713	3,965	3,988	3,664	15,330
2007	3,214	3,405	3,528	3,642	13,790
2006	2,871	3,014	3,144	3,209	12,238
2005	2,743	2,838	2,912	2,905	11,397
2004	2,514	2,572	2,696	2,803	10,584

Earnings Per Share ($)

2009	0.97	1.07	1.12	E1.16	E4.32
2008	0.87	0.92	0.94	0.94	3.66
2007	0.89	0.76	0.77	0.77	3.20
2006	0.59	0.51	0.63	0.73	2.46
2005	0.53	0.62	0.63	0.65	2.43
2004	0.59	0.66	0.58	0.50	2.33

Fiscal year ended Dec. 31. Next earnings report expected: Late January. EPS Estimates based on S&P Operating Earnings; historical GAAP earnings are as reported.

Dividend Data (Dates: mm/dd Payment Date: mm/dd/yy)

Amount ($)	Date Decl.	Ex-Div. Date	Stk. of Record	Payment Date
0.400	01/08	01/22	01/26	02/13/09
0.440	02/26	04/22	04/24	05/15/09
0.440	07/09	07/22	07/24	08/14/09
0.440	10/08	10/22	10/26	11/13/09

Dividends have been paid since 1895. Source: Company reports.

Please read the Required Disclosures and Analyst Certification on the last page of this report.

The McGraw-Hill Companies

Colgate-Palmolive Co

Business Summary October 29, 2009

CORPORATE OVERVIEW. Colgate-Palmolive Co. is a leading global consumer products company that operates in the oral, personal, and household care, and pet food markets. Its products are marketed in more than 200 countries and territories worldwide. Sales of oral, personal, and home care products accounted for 86% of total worldwide sales in 2008. The balance of revenues was derived from the sale of pet foods. The company's oral care products include toothbrushes, toothpaste and pharmaceutical products for oral health professionals. CL's personal care products include bar and liquid soaps, shampoos, conditioners, deodorants, antiperspirants, and shave products. The home care division produces major brands such as Palmolive and Ajax soaps. Oral, personal and home care sales outside of North America accounted for 67% of total sales in 2008. Sales in Latin America, Europe/South Pacific and Greater Asia/Africa accounted for 31%, 27% and 20% of total oral, personal and home care sales segment sales, respectively.

CORPORATE STRATEGY. CL follows a closely defined business strategy to develop and increase market leadership in key product categories. These categories are prioritized based on their capacity to maximize the use of the organization's core competencies and strong global equities and to deliver sustainable long-term growth. Operationally, CL is organized along geographic lines, with specific regional management teams having responsibility for the financial results in each region. On an ongoing basis, management focuses on a variety of key indicators to monitor business health and performance, including: market share; sales (including volume, pricing and foreign exchange components); gross profit margins; operating profits, net income; and EPS. CL also focuses on measures to optimize the management of working capital, capital expenditures, cash flow, and return on capital.

To enhance its global leadership position in its core businesses, in December 2004, CL commenced a four-year restructuring and business-building program. It involved: a 12% workforce reduction, the closing of a third of CL's factories, an increased focus on faster growing markets and new product innovations, and more efficient spending on marketing. The program cost $775.5 million after taxes through 2008, and the company estimates that it will generate annual savings of $350 million to $375 million.

Company Financials Fiscal Year Ended Dec. 31

Per Share Data ($)	2008	2007	2006	2005	2004	2003	2002	2001	2000	1999
Tangible Book Value	NM	NM	NM	NM	NM	NM	NM	NM	NM	NM
Cash Flow	4.26	3.76	3.06	2.97	2.86	3.15	2.65	2.40	2.32	1.96
Earnings	3.66	3.20	2.46	2.43	2.33	2.46	2.19	1.89	1.70	1.47
S&P Core Earnings	3.51	3.22	2.42	2.21	2.26	2.31	2.00	1.71	NA	NA
Dividends	1.56	1.40	1.25	1.11	0.96	0.90	0.72	0.68	0.63	0.59
Payout Ratio	43%	44%	51%	46%	41%	37%	33%	36%	37%	40%
Prices:High	81.98	81.27	67.08	57.15	59.04	60.99	58.86	64.75	66.75	65.00
Prices:Low	54.36	63.75	53.41	48.25	42.89	48.56	44.05	48.50	40.50	36.56
P/E Ratio:High	22	25	27	24	25	25	27	34	39	44
P/E Ratio:Low	15	20	22	20	18	20	20	26	24	25

Income Statement Analysis (Million $)										
Revenue	15,330	13,790	12,238	11,397	10,584	9,903	9,294	9,428	9,358	9,118
Operating Income	3,673	3,108	2,674	2,613	2,540	2,467	2,333	2,198	2,132	1,904
Depreciation	348	334	329	329	328	316	297	336	410	340
Interest Expense	115	173	159	143	124	124	151	192	200	212
Pretax Income	2,925	2,564	2,002	2,134	2,050	2,042	1,870	1,709	1,600	1,425
Effective Tax Rate	33.1%	29.6%	32.4%	34.1%	32.9%	30.4%	31.1%	30.6%	31.4%	32.1%
Net Income	1,957	1,737	1,353	1,351	1,327	1,421	1,288	1,147	1,064	937
S&P Core Earnings	1,848	1,718	1,306	1,207	1,262	1,309	1,152	1,011	NA	NA

Balance Sheet & Other Financial Data (Million $)										
Cash	567	451	490	341	320	265	168	173	213	235
Current Assets	3,710	3,619	3,301	2,757	2,740	2,497	2,228	2,203	2,347	2,355
Total Assets	9,979	10,112	9,138	8,507	8,673	7,479	7,087	6,985	7,252	7,423
Current Liabilities	2,953	3,163	3,469	2,743	2,731	2,445	2,149	2,124	2,244	2,274
Long Term Debt	3,585	3,508	2,720	2,918	3,090	2,685	3,211	2,812	2,537	2,243
Common Equity	1,922	2,308	1,188	1,380	971	594	27.3	505	1,115	1,467
Total Capital	5,711	5,882	4,441	5,106	4,845	4,028	4,050	4,139	4,453	4,701
Capital Expenditures	684	583	476	389	348	302	344	340	367	373
Cash Flow	2,276	2,043	1,682	1,653	1,629	1,736	1,563	1,461	1,453	1,255
Current Ratio	1.3	1.1	1.0	1.0	1.0	1.0	1.0	1.0	1.0	1.0
% Long Term Debt of Capitalization	62.8	57.4	61.3	57.1	63.8	66.7	79.3	67.9	57.0	47.7
% Net Income of Revenue	12.8	12.6	11.1	11.9	12.5	14.4	13.9	12.2	11.4	10.3
% Return on Assets	19.5	17.8	15.3	15.7	16.4	19.5	18.3	16.1	14.5	12.4
% Return on Equity	97.6	91.2	118.5	99.5	166.2	457.2	475.7	139.0	80.8	57.6

Data as orig reptd.; bef. results of disc opers/spec. items. Per share data adj. for stk. divs.; EPS diluted. E-Estimated. NA-Not Available. NM-Not Meaningful. NR-Not Ranked. UR-Under Review.

Office: 300 Park Avenue, New York, NY 10022.
Telephone: 212-310-2000.
Email: investor_relations@colpal.com
Website: http://www.colgate.com

Chrmn, Pres & CEO: I.M. Cook
SVP, Secy & General Counsel: A.D. Hendry
CFO: S.C. Patrick
Chief Acctg Officer & Cntlr: D.J. Hickey

Treas: E.J. Filusch
Investor Contact: B. Thompson (212-310-3072)
Board Members: J. T. Cahill, J. K. Conway, I. M. Cook, E. M. Hancock, D. W. Johnson, R. J. Kogan, D. Lewis, J. P. Reinhard, S. I. Sadove

Founded: 1806
Domicile: Delaware
Employees: 36,600

Comcast Corp

STANDARD &POOR'S

S&P Recommendation	**STRONG SELL** ★ ☆ ☆ ☆ ☆	Price $14.88 (as of Nov 27, 2009)	12-Mo. Target Price $12.00	Investment Style Large-Cap Blend

GICS Sector Consumer Discretionary
Sub-Industry Cable & Satellite

Summary With about 24 million subscribers, this company is the largest U.S. cable multiple system operator (MSO), as well as a provider of cable programming content.

Key Stock Statistics (Source S&P, Vickers, company reports)

52-Wk Range	$18.10– 11.10	S&P Oper. EPS 2009E	1.08	Market Capitalization(B)	$30.684	Beta	0.84
Trailing 12-Month EPS	$1.07	S&P Oper. EPS 2010E	1.09	Yield (%)	1.81	S&P 3-Yr. Proj. EPS CAGR(%)	8
Trailing 12-Month P/E	13.9	P/E on S&P Oper. EPS 2009E	13.8	Dividend Rate/Share	$0.27	S&P Credit Rating	BBB
$10K Invested 5 Yrs Ago	$7,511	Common Shares Outstg. (M)	2,854.7	Institutional Ownership (%)	80		

Price Performance

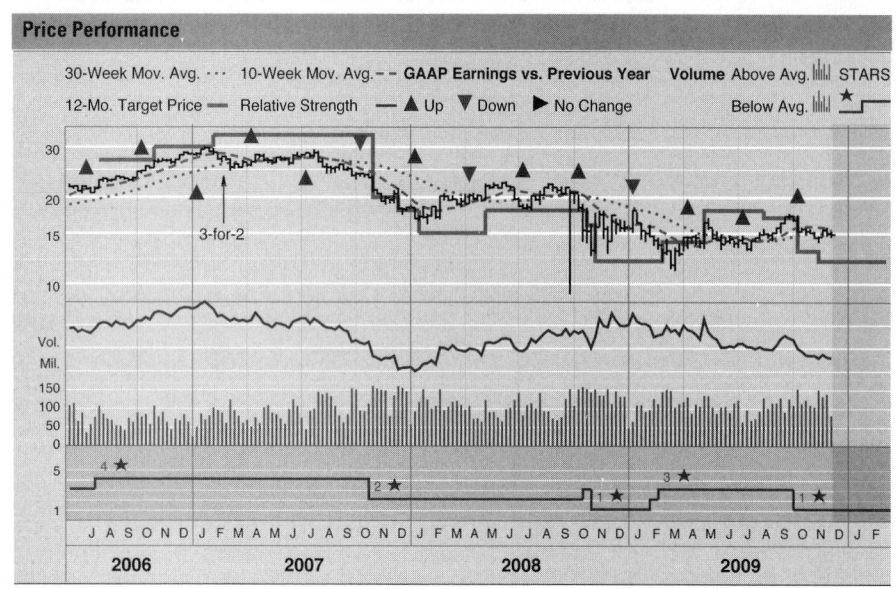

30-Week Mov. Avg. · · · · 10-Week Mov. Avg. - - **GAAP Earnings vs. Previous Year** Volume Above Avg. STARS
12-Mo. Target Price — Relative Strength — ▲ Up ▼ Down ► No Change Below Avg. ★

3-for-2

Analysis prepared by **Tuna N. Amobi, CFA, CPA** on November 04, 2009, when the stock traded at **$ 14.28**.

Options: ASE, CBOE, P, Ph

Highlights

► After projected 3% growth in 2009, we expect consolidated revenues to grow 5.0% in 2010, reaching about $36.8 billion. We expect further penetration of advanced video services, a growing base of commercial data and phone customers, plus improved contributions in 2010 from the regional and news networks, offset by some deceleration of revenue-generating unit (RGU) growth -- including some basic subscriber losses -- as well as increased promotional pricing for residential high-speed data and phone services, and stagnant local ad revenues. We assume mid- to high single digit growth for the programming unit.

► We see relatively limited margin expansion, as further declines in direct operating costs (phone and data), and moderating investments in content, technology and wireless initiatives, are partly offset by higher programming, marketing and customer service expenses.

► We estimate annual consolidated EBITDA growth of 5.0%, to about $13.8 billion and $14.8 billion in 2009 and 2010, respectively. After higher D&A charges, we project operating EPS of $1.08 and $1.09 in the respective years, with reduced share buybacks under a $7 billion plan.

Investment Rationale/Risk

► While a meaningful 2009 third quarter rebound in subscriber growth provided some reason for cautious optimism, we remain concerned about increased competition and maturation of some key product lines. Also, we note some merger execution risk on potential talks for a controlling stake in GE's (GE 14, Hold) NBC Universal -- a potentially dilutive deal that we think further underscores potential concerns with capital allocation, and conceivably could jeopardize current share buybacks and dividends. We see some governance issues on voting control by the Roberts family, and regulatory risk factors (net neutrality, etc.).

► Risks to our recommendation and target price include stronger-than-expected RGU growth; and potential upside from a growing base of commercial customers as well as other initiatives related to "DOCSIS 3.0" rollout, wireless broadband launch and ongoing Web TV trials.

► Based on 2010 estimates, our 12-month target price of $12 implies cable-only enterprise value near $2,300 per subscriber, or a 4.6X total EV/ EBITDA, with added risk premium versus peers. The stock recently had an implied 1.9% yield on the dividend, which was raised 8% in February.

Qualitative Risk Assessment

LOW	**MEDIUM**	HIGH

Our risk assessment mainly reflects our view of merger execution risk, amid an intensifying competition in relatively saturated and highly concentrated markets and businesses, offset by economies of scale and what we see as the company's relatively sound financial condition.

Quantitative Evaluations

S&P Quality Ranking   B

D	C	B-	**B**	B+	A-	A	A+

Relative Strength Rank   MODERATE

37

LOWEST = 1   HIGHEST = 99

Revenue/Earnings Data

Revenue (Million $)

	1Q	2Q	3Q	4Q	Year
2009	8,835	8,938	8,802	--	--
2008	8,389	8,553	8,549	8,765	34,256
2007	7,388	7,712	7,781	8,014	30,895
2006	5,595	5,908	6,432	7,031	24,966
2005	5,363	5,598	5,578	5,716	22,255
2004	4,908	5,066	5,098	5,235	20,307

Earnings Per Share ($)

2009	0.27	0.33	0.33	E0.24	E1.08
2008	0.24	0.21	0.26	0.14	0.86
2007	0.26	0.19	0.18	0.20	0.83
2006	0.15	0.13	0.31	0.14	0.70
2005	0.04	0.13	0.07	0.04	0.28
2004	0.02	0.08	0.07	0.13	0.29

Fiscal year ended Dec. 31. Next earnings report expected: Mid February. EPS Estimates based on S&P Operating Earnings; historical GAAP earnings are as reported.

Dividend Data (Dates: mm/dd Payment Date: mm/dd/yy)

Amount ($)	Date Decl.	Ex-Div. Date	Stk. of Record	Payment Date
0.068	02/18	04/06	04/08	04/29/09
0.068	05/13	07/06	07/08	07/29/09
0.068	08/06	10/05	10/07	10/28/09
0.068	11/04	01/04	01/06	01/27/10

Dividends have been paid since 2008. Source: Company reports.

Please read the Required Disclosures and Analyst Certification on the last page of this report.

Comcast Corp

Business Summary November 04, 2009

CORPORATE OVERVIEW. Comcast Corp. became the largest U.S. cable multiple system operator (MSO) after its acquisition of the former AT&T Broadband (ATTB) in November 2002. As of September 30, 2009, the company had nearly 23.8 million video subscribers (including over 18 million for digital video -- with advanced services such as HD and DVR), nearly 15.7 million for high-speed Internet service, and 7.4 million for digital phone.

The primary Cable segment (about 95% of total revenues) also includes the regional sports and news networks -- Comcast SportsNet: Philadelphia, Mid-Atlantic (Baltimore/Washington), Chicago, Sacramento, New England (Boston) and Northwest; Bay Area SportsNet (San Francisco); Cable Sports Southeast; CN8 -- The Comcast Network; and MountainWest Sports Network. The Programming segment include cable networks E! Entertainment Television, The Golf Channel, Versus, G4 and Style.

Other business interests include Comcast Spectacor (which owns the Philadelphia Flyers, the Philadelphia 76ers and two large, multipurpose arenas in Philadelphia and manages other venues); and Comcast Interactive Media

(comprising Internet assets such as Comcast.net, Fancast, thePlatform and Fandango).

COMPETITIVE LANDSCAPE. In a typical market, Comcast faces competition from satellite TV companies DirecTV Group and DISH Network -- which have recently launched new satellites to facilitate their core offerings of advanced video services. In recent years, incumbent telcos such as Verizon Communications and AT&T (which acquired the former BellSouth), which have long offered deeply discounted DSL data services, also began to deploy fiber-based video and broadband services in head-to-head competition with cable's triple-play bundle, while also partnering with DirecTV in several other markets. In a number of other markets, cable providers also compete with rural telcos as well as facilities-based overbuilders that provide video, voice and data services to residential, and in some cases, enterprise customers.

Company Financials Fiscal Year Ended Dec. 31

Per Share Data ($)	2008	2007	2006	2005	2004	2003	2002	2001	2000	1999
Tangible Book Value	NM	NM	NM	NM	NM	NM	NM	NM	NM	NM
Cash Flow	2.71	2.46	2.22	1.79	1.69	0.24	1.05	0.99	3.27	1.60
Earnings	0.86	0.83	0.70	0.28	0.29	-0.07	-0.17	-0.89	1.44	0.63
S&P Core Earnings	0.84	0.74	0.48	0.33	0.14	-0.30	0.47	-1.03	NA	NA
Dividends	0.19	Nil	Nil	Nil	Nil	Nil	Nil	Nil	Nil	0.01
Payout Ratio	22%	Nil	Nil	Nil	Nil	Nil	Nil	Nil	Nil	1%
Prices:High	22.86	30.18	28.94	23.00	24.33	23.23	25.03	30.54	34.91	36.42
Prices:Low	NA	17.37	16.90	17.20	17.50	15.61	11.37	21.23	18.62	18.71
P/E Ratio:High	27	36	41	82	85	NM	NM	NM	24	57
P/E Ratio:Low	NA	21	24	61	61	NM	NM	NM	13	30

Income Statement Analysis (Million $)										
Revenue	34,256	30,895	24,966	22,255	20,307	18,348	12,460	19,697	8,219	6,209
Operating Income	12,354	10,725	9,442	8,493	7,531	6,392	3,691	1,576	2,470	1,880
Depreciation	5,457	5,107	4,823	4,803	4,623	4,438	2,032	6,345	2,631	1,216
Interest Expense	2,439	2,289	2,064	1,796	1,876	2,018	884	2,341	691	538
Pretax Income	4,058	4,349	3,594	1,880	1,810	-137	70.0	-5,927	3,602	1,500
Effective Tax Rate	37.8%	41.4%	37.5%	49.6%	45.6%	NM	NM	NM	40.0%	48.2%
Net Income	2,547	2,587	2,235	928	970	-218	-276	-3,021	2,045	781
S&P Core Earnings	2,484	2,313	1,541	1,090	465	-979	792	-1,482	NA	NA

Balance Sheet & Other Financial Data (Million $)										
Cash	1,254	1,061	1,239	693	452	1,550	781	558	652	922
Current Assets	3,716	3,667	5,202	2,594	3,535	5,403	7,076	4,944	5,144	9,759
Total Assets	113,017	113,417	110,405	103,146	104,694	109,159	113,105	109,319	35,745	28,686
Current Liabilities	8,939	7,952	7,440	6,269	8,635	9,654	15,383	12,489	4,042	5,527
Long Term Debt	30,178	29,828	27,992	21,682	20,093	23,835	27,957	27,528	10,517	8,707
Common Equity	40,450	41,340	41,167	40,219	41,422	41,662	38,329	38,451	28,113	9,772
Total Capital	97,907	98,298	96,489	89,928	88,798	91,689	92,070	94,758	45,734	23,159
Capital Expenditures	5,750	6,158	4,395	3,621	3,660	4,161	1,975	NA	1,637	894
Cash Flow	8,004	7,694	7,058	5,731	5,593	4,220	1,756	3,324	4,653	1,967
Current Ratio	0.4	0.5	0.7	0.4	0.4	0.6	0.5	0.4	1.3	1.8
% Long Term Debt of Capitalization	30.8	30.3	29.0	24.1	22.6	26.0	30.4	29.1	23.0	37.6
% Net Income of Revenue	7.4	8.4	9.0	4.2	4.8	NM	NM	NM	24.9	12.6
% Return on Assets	2.3	2.3	2.1	0.9	0.9	NM	NM	NM	6.3	3.6
% Return on Equity	6.2	6.3	5.5	2.3	2.3	NM	NM	NM	8.4	11.5

Data as orig reptd.; bef. results of disc opers/spec. items. Per share data adj. for stk. divs.; EPS diluted. E-Estimated. NA-Not Available. NM-Not Meaningful. NR-Not Ranked. UR-Under Review.

Office: 1 Comcast Ctr, Philadelphia, PA 19103-2833.
Telephone: 215-286-1700.
Website: http://www.comcast.com
Chrmn, Pres & CEO: B.L. Roberts

Vice Chrmn: J.A. Brodsky
COO & EVP: S.B. Burke
EVP & CFO: M.J. Angelakis
SVP, Chief Acctg Officer & Cntlr: L.J. Salva

Investor Contact: M. Dooner (866-281-2100)
Board Members: S. D. Anstrom, K. J. Bacon, S. M. Bonovitz, E. D. Breen, J. A. Brodsky, J. J. Collins, J. M. Cook, G. L. Hassell, J. A. Honickman, B. L. Roberts, R. J. Roberts, J. H. Rodin, F. G. Rohatyn, M. I. Sovern, B. C. Watson, I. A. Wechsler

Founded: 1969
Domicile: Pennsylvania
Employees: 100,000

Comerica Inc

STANDARD &POOR'S

S&P Recommendation **BUY** ★★★★☆	Price $27.80 (as of Nov 27, 2009)	12-Mo. Target Price $34.00	Investment Style Large-Cap Value

GICS Sector Financials
Sub-Industry Diversified Banks

Summary This bank holding company operates banking affiliates mainly in Michigan, Texas, California, Arizona and Florida.

Key Stock Statistics (Source S&P, Vickers, company reports)

52-Wk Range	$32.30– 11.72	S&P Oper. EPS 2009**E**	-0.78	Market Capitalization(B)	$4.201	Beta	1.12
Trailing 12-Month EPS	$-0.35	S&P Oper. EPS 2010**E**	-0.30	Yield (%)	0.72	S&P 3-Yr. Proj. EPS CAGR(%)	NA
Trailing 12-Month P/E	NM	P/E on S&P Oper. EPS 2009**E**	NM	Dividend Rate/Share	$0.20	S&P Credit Rating	A-
$10K Invested 5 Yrs Ago	$5,552	Common Shares Outstg. (M)	151.1	Institutional Ownership (%)	76		

Price Performance

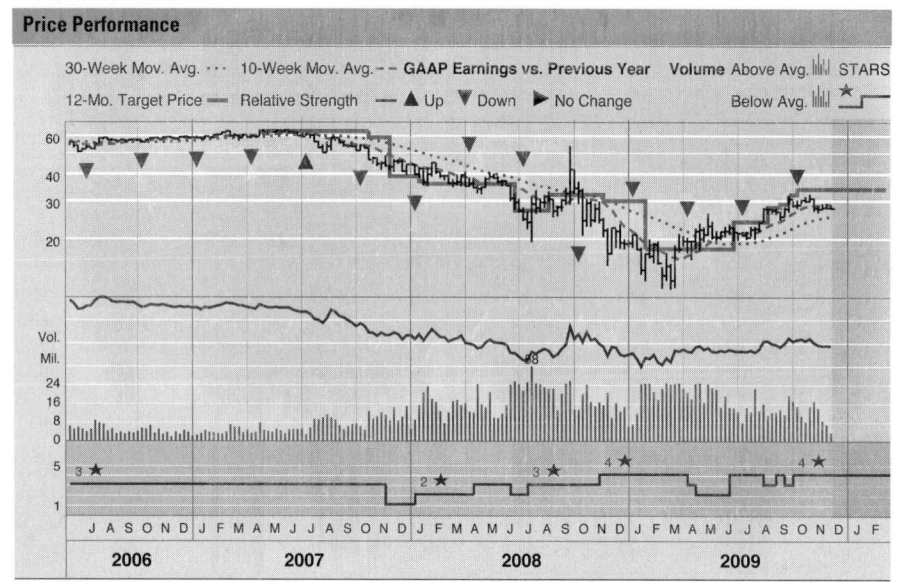

30-Week Mov. Avg. ···· 10-Week Mov. Avg. - - **GAAP Earnings vs. Previous Year** Volume Above Avg. STARS
12-Mo. Target Price — Relative Strength — ▲ Up ▼ Down ▶ No Change Below Avg.

Options: ASE, CBOE, P, Ph

Analysis prepared by **Erik Oja** on November 24, 2009, when the stock traded at **$ 28.57.**

Highlights

▶ We expect fee income, ex-gains and losses, of $205 million-$210 million per quarter in 2009, totaling $817 million, slightly below the 2008 level, on a drop in fiduciary income. In 2008, the net interest margin was a relatively low 3.02%, down sharply from 3.66% in 2007, as loan yields fell faster than deposit rates. For 2009, we see less downward pressure on deposit rates and loan yields, a net interest margin of 3.00%, and net interest income of $1.61 billion, down 12%, due to soft loan demand. We expect loan demand to fall for at least two more quarters, as a consequence of the economic slowdown.

▶ We expect increasing economic strength in California and Florida, offsetting our expectations of continuing weakness in Michigan. On this, we estimate net chargeoffs of $205 million for the fourth quarter, $625 million in 2010 and $460 million in 2011. We project loan loss provisions of about $1.08 billion for 2009, which includes our forecast of reserve building of $233 million. For 2010, we expect loan loss provisions of $625 million, with no further reserve building.

▶ We forecast losses per share of $0.78 in 2009 and $0.30 in 2010, and EPS of $1.25 in 2011.

Investment Rationale/Risk

▶ We consider CMA's capital levels, as measured by $7.04 billion of tangible equity, $4.9 billion of tangible common equity, and a tangible common equity to tangible assets ratio of 7.96%, to be well above most regional banks and capable of absorbing the $830 million of net chargeoffs we expect in the next five quarters. In addition, it is likely, in our view, that housing markets in CMA's Midwest and California lending territories are bottoming out. The shares recently traded at 0.92X tangible book value per share of $32.42, a valuation we see as below other banks with similar credit quality characteristics. We expect net profit growth to accelerate in 2011, but we see many large regional banking peers facing a similar length of time to earnings growth recovery.

▶ Risks to our recommendation and target price include a slower-than-expected economic recovery, or a relapse into recession.

▶ Our 12-month target price of $34 equals a discount-to-peers 1.05X CMA's tangible book value per share of $32.42, and 27.2X our 2011 EPS estimate, above CMA's historical range, reflecting our expectation of depressed earnings until 2012.

Qualitative Risk Assessment

LOW	**MEDIUM**	HIGH

Our risk assessment reflects CMA's long history of profitability and relatively high capital ratios, tempered by its exposure to the Michigan and California residential real estate markets.

Quantitative Evaluations

S&P Quality Ranking B+

D	C	B-	B	**B+**	A-	A	A+

Relative Strength Rank MODERATE
43
LOWEST = 1 HIGHEST = 99

Revenue/Earnings Data

Revenue (Million $)

	1Q	2Q	3Q	4Q	Year
2009	762.0	866.0	819.0	--	--
2008	1,100	979.0	975.0	890.0	3,944
2007	1,104	1,158	1,182	1,174	4,618
2006	967.0	1,048	1,088	1,174	4,277
2005	817.0	874.0	951.0	1,026	3,668
2004	763.0	773.0	764.0	794.0	3,094

Earnings Per Share ($)

2009	-0.16	-0.11	-0.10	E-0.42	E-0.78
2008	0.73	0.37	0.18	0.01	1.29
2007	1.19	1.25	1.17	0.77	4.40
2006	1.26	1.19	1.20	1.16	4.81
2005	1.16	1.28	1.41	1.25	5.11
2004	0.92	1.10	1.13	1.21	4.36

Fiscal year ended Dec. 31. Next earnings report expected: Late January. EPS Estimates based on S&P Operating Earnings; historical GAAP earnings are as reported.

Dividend Data (Dates: mm/dd Payment Date: mm/dd/yy)

Amount ($)	Date Decl.	Ex-Div. Date	Stk. of Record	Payment Date
0.050	01/27	03/11	03/15	04/01/09
0.050	05/19	06/11	06/15	07/01/09
0.050	07/28	09/11	09/15	10/01/09
0.050	11/17	12/11	12/15	01/01/10

Dividends have been paid since 1936. Source: Company reports.

Please read the Required Disclosures and Analyst Certification on the last page of this report.

The McGraw-Hill Companies

Comerica Inc

Business Summary November 24, 2009

CORPORATE OVERVIEW. One of Michigan's oldest banks, Comerica is now a Dallas-headquartered bank holding company that operates banking units in Michigan, California, Texas, Arizona and Florida. It also has international banking subsidiaries in Canada and Mexico.

In early 2007, CMA announced plans to relocate its corporate headquarters to Dallas, Texas. The relocation to Texas was partly done, in our view, to lessen investors' notion that CMA is purely a Midwestern bank. Comerica will maintain its significant presence in Detroit, and remain one of southeast Michigan's largest employers following the relocation to the new Dallas headquarters office.

Operations are divided into three major lines of business: the Business Bank, the Retail Bank (formerly known as Small Business and Personal Financial Services), and Wealth & Institutional Management. The Business Bank is primarily comprised of middle market, commercial real estate, national dealer services, global finance, large corporate, leasing, financial services, and technology and life sciences. This business segment offers various products and services, including commercial loans and lines of credit, deposits, cash management, capital market products, international trade finance, letters of credit, foreign exchange management services and loan syndication services.

The Retail Bank includes small business banking (entities with annual sales under $10 million) and personal financial services, consisting of consumer lending, consumer deposit gathering and mortgage loan origination. In addition to a full range of financial services provided to small businesses and their owners, this business segment offers a variety of consumer products, including deposit accounts, installment loans, credit and debit cards, student loans, home equity loans and lines of credit, and residential mortgage loans.

Wealth & Institutional Management offers products and services consisting of personal trust, which is designed to meet the personal financial needs of the affluent, private banking, institutional trust, retirement services, investment management and advisory services, investment banking, and discount securities brokerage services. This business segment also offers the sale of mutual funds and annuity products, as well as life, disability and long-term care insurance products.

Company Financials Fiscal Year Ended Dec. 31

Per Share Data ($)	2008	2007	2006	2005	2004	2003	2002	2001	2000	1999
Tangible Book Value	32.57	34.12	32.82	33.01	29.85	29.20	28.31	27.15	23.94	20.60
Earnings	1.29	4.40	4.81	5.11	4.36	3.75	3.40	3.88	4.63	4.14
S&P Core Earnings	0.86	4.48	4.71	4.90	4.27	3.72	3.30	3.27	NA	NA
Dividends	0.20	2.56	2.36	2.20	2.08	2.00	1.92	1.76	1.60	1.40
Payout Ratio	16%	58%	49%	43%	48%	53%	56%	45%	35%	34%
Prices:High	54.00	63.89	60.10	63.38	63.80	56.34	66.09	65.15	61.13	70.00
Prices:Low	15.05	39.62	50.12	53.17	50.45	37.10	35.20	44.02	32.94	44.00
P/E Ratio:High	42	15	12	12	15	15	19	17	13	17
P/E Ratio:Low	12	9	10	10	12	10	10	11	7	11

Income Statement Analysis (Million $)										
Net Interest Income	1,815	2,003	1,983	1,956	1,810	1,926	2,132	2,102	1,659	1,547
Tax Equivalent Adjustment	6.00	3.00	NA	4.00	3.00	3.00	4.00	4.00	4.00	5.00
Non Interest Income	893	881	855	942	857	837	819	784	827	711
Loan Loss Provision	686	212	37.0	-47.0	64.0	377	635	236	145	114
% Expense/Operating Revenue	66.2%	58.6%	59.0%	57.4%	55.9%	53.6%	51.3%	53.9%	53.6%	49.3%
Pretax Income	271	988	1,127	1,279	1,110	953	882	1,111	1,151	1,033
Effective Tax Rate	21.8%	31.0%	30.6%	32.7%	31.8%	30.6%	31.9%	36.1%	34.9%	34.9%
Net Income	212	682	782	861	757	661	601	710	749	673
% Net Interest Margin	3.02	3.66	3.79	4.06	3.86	3.95	4.55	4.61	4.54	4.55
S&P Core Earnings	131	694	766	826	744	657	584	587	NA	NA

Balance Sheet & Other Financial Data (Million $)										
Money Market Assets	202	36.0	2,632	1,159	3,230	4,013	2,446	1,079	165	613
Investment Securities	9,201	6,296	3,989	5,399	7,173	8,502	5,499	5,370	2,843	2,739
Commercial Loans	38,488	38,271	35,924	33,707	31,540	32,153	33,732	32,660	28,001	25,429
Other Loans	11,247	12,472	11,507	9,540	9,303	7,274	8,549	8,536	8,060	7,265
Total Assets	67,548	62,331	58,001	53,013	51,766	52,592	53,301	50,732	41,985	38,653
Demand Deposits	11,701	27,181	29,151	15,666	15,164	14,104	16,335	12,596	6,815	6,136
Time Deposits	17,817	17,097	15,776	26,765	25,772	27,359	25,440	24,974	20,353	17,155
Long Term Debt	15,053	8,821	5,949	3,961	4,286	4,801	5,216	5,503	8,089	8,580
Common Equity	5,023	5,126	5,153	5,068	5,105	5,110	4,947	4,807	3,757	3,225
% Return on Assets	0.3	1.1	1.4	1.6	1.5	1.2	1.2	1.4	1.9	1.8
% Return on Equity	4.2	13.3	15.3	16.9	14.8	13.1	12.3	15.4	21.0	21.8
% Loan Loss Reserve	1.5	1.1	1.0	1.2	-1.6	2.0	1.9	-1.6	1.5	1.5
% Loans/Deposits	120.4	110.1	105.6	101.9	99.8	99.3	101.2	109.7	132.7	140.4
% Equity to Assets	7.8	8.5	9.2	9.7	9.8	9.5	9.4	9.0	8.7	8.0

Data as orig reptd.; bef. results of disc opers/spec. items. Per share data adj. for stk. divs.; EPS diluted. E-Estimated. NA-Not Available. NM-Not Meaningful. NR-Not Ranked. UR-Under Review.

Office: 1717 Main St, Dallas, TX 75201-4612.
Telephone: 214-969-6476.
Website: http://www.comerica.com
Chrmn, Pres & CEO: R.W. Babb, Jr.

Vice Chrmn: J.J. Buttigieg, III
EVP & CFO: B. Acton
EVP, Secy & General Counsel: J.W. Bilstrom
EVP & CIO: J.R. Beran

Investor Contact: D.P. Persons (313-222-2840)
Board Members: R. W. Babb, Jr., L. Bauder, J. J. Buttigieg, III, J. F. Cordes, R. A. Cregg, T. K. DeNicola, X. G. Humrichouse, J. P. Kane, R. G. Lindner, A. A. Piergallini, R. S. Taubman, R. M. Turner, Jr., N. G. Vaca, K. L. Way

Founded: 1849
Domicile: Delaware
Employees: 10,186

Computer Sciences Corp

STANDARD &POOR'S

S&P Recommendation **STRONG BUY** ★★★★★	Price $54.26 (as of Nov 27, 2009)	12-Mo. Target Price $66.00	Investment Style Large-Cap Blend

GICS Sector Information Technology
Sub-Industry Data Processing & Outsourced Services

Summary This leading computer services company provides consulting, systems integration and outsourcing services.

Key Stock Statistics (Source S&P, Vickers, company reports)

52-Wk Range	$55.61– 25.48	S&P Oper. EPS 2010E	4.99	Market Capitalization(B)	$8.270	Beta	1.01
Trailing 12-Month EPS	$5.82	S&P Oper. EPS 2011E	5.14	Yield (%)	Nil	S&P 3-Yr. Proj. EPS CAGR(%)	9
Trailing 12-Month P/E	9.3	P/E on S&P Oper. EPS 2010E	10.9	Dividend Rate/Share	Nil	S&P Credit Rating	A-
$10K Invested 5 Yrs Ago	$10,150	Common Shares Outstg. (M)	152.4	Institutional Ownership (%)	89		

Price Performance

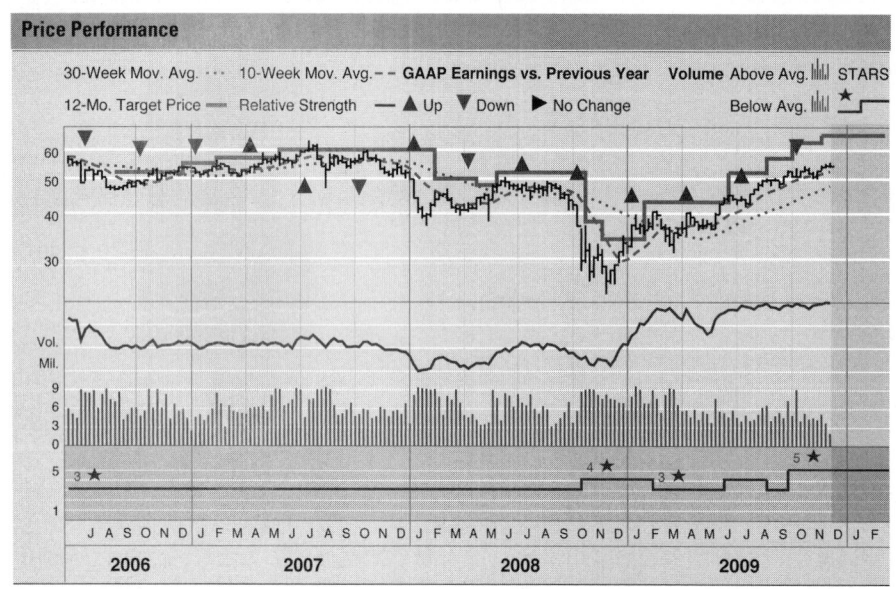

30-Week Mov. Avg. · · · 10-Week Mov. Avg. - - GAAP Earnings vs. Previous Year   Volume Above Avg. STARS
12-Mo. Target Price — Relative Strength — ▲ Up ▼ Down ► No Change   Below Avg.

Options: ASE, CBOE, P, Ph

Analysis prepared by **Dylan Cathers** on November 16, 2009, when the stock traded at **$ 54.58**.

Highlights

► We see revenues decreasing 3.5% in FY 10 (Mar.), before rebounding 5.5% in FY 11. We think that the Commercial segment will remain sluggish over the next couple of quarters, as clients look towards 2010 and begin to set their IT spending budgets. Further, we have some concerns about the pace of discretionary projects, but we think the worst is behind the company. Within the North American Public Sector segment, we think sales to the Department of Defense and related agencies will remain robust. We also see the potential for gains from the energy vertical, aided by the recent acquisition of BearingPoint's Brazil operations.

► We look for a slight widening of operating margins in FY 10, as a lower cost base after numerous restructurings and an improving sales mix are partially offset by increased bid activity, expenses for early-stage contracts, and investments in the business.

► We estimate FY 10 EPS of $4.99, aided by a reduction in the tax rate, versus operating EPS of $4.09 in FY 09, which excludes tax-related benefits and charges. We forecast EPS of $5.14 in FY 11.

Investment Rationale/Risk

► Our Strong Buy recommendation on the shares is based on valuation, as they recently traded at a notable discount to peers. We believe CSC is well positioned to take advantage of certain of the Obama administration's areas of emphasis, including health care, transportation, infrastructure, and cyber security. Nonetheless, we have some concerns about the company's pension obligations, as well as weakness in the Commercial segment.

► Risks to our recommendation and target price include increased competition for large long-term contracts in the IT infrastructure and outsourcing arena, further terminations of contracts in the commercial segment, and ongoing shareholder litigation against CSC. We also have concerns regarding corporate governance, including the combination of the chairman, president and CEO roles.

► Our 12-month target price of $66 is based on a slight peer-discount P/E of 13.1X using our calendar 2010 EPS estimate of $5.02. Our peer group is comprised of other U.S.-based multinational IT outsourcing companies that regularly compete with CSC.

Qualitative Risk Assessment

LOW	**MEDIUM**	HIGH

Our risk assessment reflects the highly competitive nature of the IT consulting and outsourcing market, offset by our view of CSC's strong balance sheet and the stability afforded the company by the numerous long-term contracts that it has signed with customers.

Quantitative Evaluations

S&P Quality Ranking   B+

D	C	B-	B	**B+**	A-	A	A+

Relative Strength Rank   STRONG

74

LOWEST = 1   HIGHEST = 99

Revenue/Earnings Data

Revenue (Million $)

	1Q	2Q	3Q	4Q	Year
2010	3,898	4,041	--	--	--
2009	4,437	4,239	3,952	4,112	16,740
2008	3,838	4,017	4,160	4,484	16,500
2007	3,561	3,609	3,641	4,046	14,857
2006	3,583	3,573	3,577	3,884	14,616
2005	3,736	3,935	3,517	3,879	14,059

Earnings Per Share ($)

2010	0.86	1.40	E1.20	E1.50	E4.99
2009	0.79	2.95	1.06	2.51	7.31
2008	0.61	0.43	1.05	1.15	3.20
2007	-0.31	0.51	0.62	1.42	2.16
2006	0.58	0.53	0.88	1.08	3.07
2005	0.58	0.68	0.69	0.86	2.59

Fiscal year ended Mar. 31. Next earnings report expected: Mid February. EPS Estimates based on S&P Operating Earnings; historical GAAP earnings are as reported.

Dividend Data

No cash dividends have been paid since 1998.

Please read the Required Disclosures and Analyst Certification on the last page of this report.

The McGraw·Hill Companies

Computer Sciences Corp

**STANDARD
&POOR'S**

Business Summary November 16, 2009

CORPORATE OVERVIEW. Computer Sciences offers what it believes is a broad array of services to clients in the global commercial and government markets. The company specializes in the application of complex information technology (IT) to achieve the strategic objectives of its customers. Offerings include IT and business process outsourcing, and IT and professional services.

Outsourcing involves operating all or a portion of a customer's technology infrastructure, including systems analysis, applications development, network operations, desktop computing, and data center management. CSC also provides business process outsourcing, which involves managing key functions for clients such as claims processing, credit checking, logistics, and customer call centers.

IT and professional services includes systems integration, consulting, and professional services. Systems integration encompasses designing, developing, implementing, and integrating complete information systems. Consulting

and professional services includes advising clients on the strategic acquisition and utilization of IT, and on business strategy, security, modeling, engineering, and business process re-engineering. CSC also licenses sophisticated software systems for health care and financial services markets, and provides a broad array of end-to-end e-business solutions to meet the needs of large commercial and government clients.

The company provides services to clients in global commercial industries and to the U.S. federal government. In the global commercial segment, offerings are marketed to clients in a wide variety of industries. In the U.S. federal government market, CSC provides traditional systems integration and outsourcing for complex project management and technical services.

Company Financials Fiscal Year Ended Mar. 31

Per Share Data ($)	2009	2008	2007	2006	2005	2004	2003	2002	2001	2000
Tangible Book Value	8.25	6.35	19.51	23.85	21.71	15.44	11.78	11.58	9.26	12.78
Cash Flow	15.08	9.26	8.95	9.42	8.56	8.29	6.95	7.02	5.17	5.59
Earnings	7.31	3.20	2.16	3.07	2.59	2.75	2.54	2.01	1.37	2.37
S&P Core Earnings	6.24	2.95	2.14	3.00	2.59	2.68	1.84	1.48	0.80	NA
Dividends	Nil	Nil	Nil	Nil	Nil	Nil	Nil	Nil	Nil	Nil
Payout Ratio	Nil	Nil	Nil	Nil	Nil	Nil	Nil	Nil	Nil	Nil
Calendar Year	2008	2007	2006	2005	2004	2003	2002	2001	2000	1999
Prices:High	50.52	63.76	60.39	59.90	58.00	44.99	53.47	66.71	99.88	94.63
Prices:Low	23.93	46.95	46.23	42.31	38.07	26.52	24.30	28.99	58.25	52.38
P/E Ratio:High	7	20	28	20	22	16	21	33	73	40
P/E Ratio:Low	3	15	21	14	15	10	10	14	43	22

Income Statement Analysis (Million $)	2009	2008	2007	2006	2005	2004	2003	2002	2001	2000
Revenue	16,740	16,500	14,857	14,616	14,059	14,768	11,347	11,426	10,524	9,371
Operating Income	2,396	2,205	2,211	2,149	1,845	1,968	1,609	1,497	1,302	1,239
Depreciation	1,186	1,032	1,162	1,188	1,146	1,038	858	858	649	546
Interest Expense	261	106	175	104	157	170	143	155	106	58.1
Pretax Income	949	918	607	821	715	747	612	497	330	611
Effective Tax Rate	NM	40.7%	35.9%	29.7%	30.6%	30.5%	28.0%	30.7%	29.4%	34.1%
Net Income	1,115	545	389	577	496	519	440	344	233	403
S&P Core Earnings	954	502	385	565	495	507	319	254	137	NA

Balance Sheet & Other Financial Data (Million $)	2009	2008	2007	2006	2005	2004	2003	2002	2001	2000
Cash	2,297	699	1,050	1,291	1,010	610	300	149	185	260
Current Assets	7,707	6,923	6,706	6,306	5,690	4,867	4,088	3,304	3,204	2,766
Total Assets	15,619	15,775	13,731	12,943	12,634	11,804	10,433	8,611	8,175	5,874
Current Liabilities	4,016	5,590	5,260	4,141	3,878	3,253	2,987	2,708	3,589	1,984
Long Term Debt	4,173	2,506	1,412	1,377	1,303	2,306	2,205	1,873	1,029	652
Common Equity	5,510	5,462	5,886	6,772	6,495	5,504	4,606	3,624	3,215	3,044
Total Capital	9,683	7,968	7,298	8,149	7,798	7,810	6,811	5,497	4,245	3,780
Capital Expenditures	699	877	686	827	855	725	638	672	897	586
Cash Flow	2,301	1,576	1,551	1,765	1,642	1,558	1,298	1,202	882	949
Current Ratio	1.9	1.2	1.3	1.5	1.5	1.5	1.4	1.2	0.9	1.4
% Long Term Debt of Capitalization	43.1	31.5	19.4	16.9	16.7	29.5	32.4	34.1	24.3	17.3
% Net Income of Revenue	6.7	3.3	2.6	3.9	3.5	3.5	3.9	3.0	2.2	4.3
% Return on Assets	7.1	3.7	2.9	4.5	4.1	4.7	4.6	4.1	3.3	7.2
% Return on Equity	20.3	9.6	6.3	8.7	8.3	10.3	10.7	10.1	7.5	14.3

Data as orig reptd.; bef. results of disc opers/spec. items. Per share data adj. for stk. divs.; EPS diluted. E-Estimated. NA-Not Available. NM-Not Meaningful. NR-Not Ranked. UR-Under Review.

Office: 3170 Fairview Park Dr, Falls Church, VA 22042-4516.
Telephone: 703-876-1000.
Email: investorrelations@csc.com
Website: http://www.csc.com

Chrmn, Pres & CEO: M.W. Laphen
CFO: M.J. Mancuso
Chief Acctg Officer & Cntlr: D.G. DeBuck
Secy & General Counsel: W.L. Deckelman, Jr.

Investor Contact: B. Lackey (310-615-1700)
Board Members: I. W. Bailey, II, D. J. Barram, S. L. Baum, R. F. Chase, J. R. Haberkorn, M. W. Laphen, F. W. McFarlan, C. S. Park, T. H. Patrick

Auditor: Deloitte & Touche LLP
Founded: 1959
Domicile: Nevada
Employees: 92,000

The McGraw-Hill Companies

Compuware Corp

STANDARD
&POOR'S

S&P Recommendation HOLD ★★★☆☆	Price $7.15 (as of Nov 27, 2009)	12-Mo. Target Price $8.50	Investment Style Large-Cap Blend

GICS Sector Information Technology
Sub-Industry Application Software

Summary This company provides software products and professional services designed to increase the productivity of information systems departments.

Key Stock Statistics (Source S&P, Vickers, company reports)

52-Wk Range	$8.95– 5.18	S&P Oper. EPS 2010E	0.59	Market Capitalization(B)	$1.648	Beta	1.41
Trailing 12-Month EPS	$0.67	S&P Oper. EPS 2011E	0.53	Yield (%)	Nil	S&P 3-Yr. Proj. EPS CAGR(%)	7
Trailing 12-Month P/E	10.7	P/E on S&P Oper. EPS 2010E	12.1	Dividend Rate/Share	Nil	S&P Credit Rating	NR
$10K Invested 5 Yrs Ago	$12,349	Common Shares Outstg. (M)	230.5	Institutional Ownership (%)	80		

Price Performance

30-Week Mov. Avg. · · · · 10-Week Mov. Avg. - - - GAAP Earnings vs. Previous Year Volume Above Avg. STARS
12-Mo. Target Price — Relative Strength — ▲ Up ▼ Down ► No Change Below Avg. ★

Options: CBOE, P

Analysis prepared by **Jim Yin** on October 26, 2009, when the stock traded at **$ 7.59**.

Highlights

► We estimate that total revenues will rise 2.7% in FY 11 (Mar.), following a 19% decline seen for FY 10. Our forecast reflects our view of a sluggish recovery in IT spending in 2010. We also think revenue growth will be hurt by the company's divestiture of Quality Solutions. We expect software license revenues to rise 5% in FY 11, as customers resume spending on new projects. We forecast flat professional service revenues in FY 11, as CPWR alters its business model, and we see a low single digit increase for maintenance revenues, reflecting modest software license revenue growth.

► We forecast that gross margins will increase to 71% in FY 11, from 70% in FY 10. We anticipate that non-GAAP operating margins, excluding one-time gains and restructuring charges, will rise to 19% in FY 11, from 18% in FY 10, as a result of discontinuation of less profitable businesses and further cost-saving measures.

► Our FY 11 EPS estimate is $0.53, down from $0.59 projected for FY 10, which included a one-time gain of $52 million related to divestiture of Quality Solutions. Excluding the gain, we expect earnings to improve along with the global economy.

Investment Rationale/Risk

► Our hold recommendation reflects our view of a modest improvement in IT spending. We expect overall IT spending to rise 4% in 2010, after declining about 6% in 2009. We view CPWR's core business as mature and think the company will recover more slowly than many other software companies due to its heavy reliance on the auto industry. We also believe the company has not kept pace with its competitors in enhancing its service offerings, and could be losing market share. However, we believe these adverse factors will be offset by the company's aggressive cost-saving measures.

► Risks to our opinion and target price include weaker-than-expected recovery in the global economy, increased competition, and pricing pressures from large platform vendors.

► Our 12-month target price of $8.50 is based on a blend of our discounted cash flow (DCF) and P/E analyses. Our DCF model assumes a weighted average cost of capital (WACC) of 11.1% and a terminal growth rate of 3%, yielding an intrinsic value of $9.50. From our P/E analysis, we derive a value of $7.50, based on an industry P/E-to-growth ratio of 1.8X, or 13X our FY 10 EPS estimate of $0.59.

Qualitative Risk Assessment

LOW	MEDIUM	HIGH

Our risk assessment reflects our concern about the maturity of CPWR's core businesses. Its newer initiatives have been slow to bear fruit, in our opinion. Absent a meaningful pickup in revenue growth, we expect future earnings growth to be driven by ongoing cost reductions and share repurchases.

Quantitative Evaluations

S&P Quality Ranking NR

D	C	B-	B	B+	A-	A	A+

Relative Strength Rank MODERATE

37

LOWEST = 1   HIGHEST = 99

Revenue/Earnings Data

Revenue (Million $)

	1Q	2Q	3Q	4Q	Year
2010	214.4	217.9	--	--	--
2009	298.6	269.9	268.7	253.4	1,090
2008	279.4	302.0	309.3	338.9	1,230
2007	296.3	288.5	315.2	313.0	1,213
2006	297.3	292.7	305.9	309.5	1,205
2005	287.1	295.5	330.5	318.8	1,232

Earnings Per Share ($)

	1Q	2Q	3Q	4Q	Year
2010	0.21	0.12	E0.13	E0.13	E0.59
2009	0.13	0.08	0.14	0.20	0.55
2008	Nil	0.13	0.13	0.23	0.47
2007	0.08	0.07	0.11	0.21	0.45
2006	0.06	0.06	0.10	0.15	0.37
2005	Nil	0.02	0.11	0.07	0.20

Fiscal year ended Mar. 31. Next earnings report expected: Late January. EPS Estimates based on S&P Operating Earnings; historical GAAP earnings are as reported.

Dividend Data

No cash dividends have been paid.

Please read the Required Disclosures and Analyst Certification on the last page of this report.

The McGraw-Hill Companies

Compuware Corp

STANDARD &POOR'S

Business Summary October 26, 2009

CORPORATE OVERVIEW. Originally founded as a professional services company, Compuware provides software, maintenance and professional services intended to increase the productivity of the information technology (IT) departments of businesses. The company has two main product lines: mainframe products and distributed products. CPWR's mainframe software products help customers maintain their IBM OS/390 and z/Series IT infrastructure. Keys mainframe products include File-AID, Xpeditor, Hiperstation, Abend-AID and Strobe. These products facilitate application analysis, testing, defect detection and remediation, fault management, file and data management. Mainframe product revenue accounted for 41% of total revenue in FY 09 (Mar.). We estimate CPWR derived an additional 20% of its total revenue from mainframe-related professional services.

CPWR's distributed software products help customers maximize the performance of their corporate IT infrastructure, which include multiple hardware, software and network platforms. The company's distributed products support requirements management (Changepoint), application development (Uniface and DevPartner), testing (Quality), and application performance analysis

(Vantage). Distributed product revenue accounted for 23% of total revenue in FY 09.

CPWR also provides applications services, which are marketed under the brand name "Covisint." Covisint provides a secure, collaborative platform that enables trading partners, customers, and vendors share vital business information and process transactions across disparate systems. Application services revenue accounted for about 3.2% of total revenue in FY 09.

The company derived 51% of its product revenue in the U.S. in FY 09, the same percentage as in FY 08. Meanwhile, revenue from Europe and Africa was 33% of total revenue. Other international operations comprised 16% of total product revenues in both FY 08 and FY 09.

Company Financials Fiscal Year Ended Mar. 31

Per Share Data ($)	2009	2008	2007	2006	2005	2004	2003	2002	2001	2000
Tangible Book Value	2.09	1.95	2.57	3.33	3.15	3.11	2.93	2.60	2.02	1.51
Cash Flow	0.67	0.58	0.70	0.51	0.34	0.27	0.41	-0.40	0.60	1.10
Earnings	0.55	0.47	0.45	0.37	0.20	0.13	0.27	-0.66	0.32	0.91
S&P Core Earnings	0.49	0.43	0.41	0.33	0.12	0.03	0.14	-0.15	0.17	NA
Dividends	Nil	Nil	Nil	Nil	Nil	Nil	Nil	Nil	Nil	Nil
Payout Ratio	Nil	Nil	Nil	Nil	Nil	Nil	Nil	Nil	Nil	Nil
Calendar Year	2008	2007	2006	2005	2004	2003	2002	2001	2000	1999
Prices:High	11.91	12.56	9.55	9.99	8.95	6.52	14.00	14.50	37.81	40.00
Prices:Low	5.08	7.32	6.02	5.51	4.35	3.22	2.35	6.25	5.63	16.38
P/E Ratio:High	22	27	NM	27	45	50	52	NM	NM	44
P/E Ratio:Low	9	16	NM	15	22	25	9	NM	NM	18

Income Statement Analysis (Million $)										
Revenue	1,090	1,230	1,213	1,205	1,232	1,265	1,375	1,729	2,010	2,231
Operating Income	220	224	188	198	143	90.5	188	264	296	641
Depreciation	30.4	32.8	55.0	50.2	56.4	55.2	53.8	98.2	104	71.5
Interest Expense	NA	31.3	Nil	Nil	Nil	Nil	6.10	7.43	31.3	24.5
Pretax Income	213	180	193	191	106	56.0	156	-245	192	562
Effective Tax Rate	34.4%	25.5%	18.1%	25.3%	28.0%	11.0%	34.0%	NM	38.0%	37.3%
Net Income	140	134	158	143	76.5	49.8	103	-245	119	352
S&P Core Earnings	124	124	143	126	46.1	9.72	51.2	-55.3	62.2	NA

Balance Sheet & Other Financial Data (Million $)										
Cash	278	286	261	612	498	455	319	233	53.3	30.5
Current Assets	859	919	921	1,445	1,358	1,143	1,050	1,063	1,004	988
Total Assets	1,875	2,019	2,029	2,511	2,478	2,234	2,123	1,994	2,279	2,416
Current Liabilities	562	645	529	545	578	493	469	556	569	596
Long Term Debt	Nil	Nil	Nil	Nil	Nil	Nil	Nil	Nil	140	450
Common Equity	881	927	1,132	1,579	1,516	1,414	1,332	1,170	1,377	1,204
Total Capital	905	955	1,167	1,605	1,516	1,418	1,332	1,170	1,538	1,667
Capital Expenditures	17.9	10.5	18.6	14.5	134	74.6	225	90.4	39.8	34.9
Cash Flow	170	167	213	193	133	105	157	-147	223	423
Current Ratio	1.5	1.4	1.7	2.6	2.3	2.3	2.2	1.9	1.8	1.7
% Long Term Debt of Capitalization	Nil	Nil	Nil	Nil	Nil	Nil	Nil	Nil	9.1	27.0
% Net Income of Revenue	12.8	10.9	13.0	11.9	6.2	3.9	7.5	NM	5.9	15.8
% Return on Assets	7.2	6.6	7.0	5.7	3.2	2.3	5.0	NM	5.1	17.2
% Return on Equity	15.5	13.1	11.7	9.2	5.2	3.6	8.2	NM	9.2	30.8

Data as orig reptd.; bef. results of disc opers/spec. items. Per share data adj. for stk. divs.; EPS diluted. E-Estimated. NA-Not Available. NM-Not Meaningful. NR-Not Ranked. UR-Under Review.

Office: 1 Campus Martius, Detroit, MI 48226-5099.
Telephone: 313-227-7300.
Email: investor.relations@compuware.com
Website: http://www.compuware.com

Chrmn & CEO: P. Karmanos, Jr.
Pres & COO: R.C. Paul
EVP, CFO, Chief Acctg Officer & Treas: L.L. Fournier
EVP & Chief Admin Officer: D.A. Knobblock

CTO: P.A. Czarnik
Investor Contact: L. Elkin (248-737-7345)
Board Members: D. W. Archer, G. S. Bedi, W. O. Grabe, W. R. Halling, P. Karmanos, Jr., F. A. Nelson, G. Price, W. J. Prowse, G. S. Romney, R. Szyganda, T. Thewes

Founded: 1973
Domicile: Michigan
Employees: 5,006

The McGraw-Hill Companies

ConAgra Foods Inc.

STANDARD &POOR'S

S&P Recommendation **HOLD** ★★★☆☆	Price $22.18 (as of Nov 27, 2009)	12-Mo. Target Price $24.00	Investment Style Large-Cap Value

GICS Sector Consumer Staples
Sub-Industry Packaged Foods & Meats

Summary This company is one of the largest U.S. packaged food processors.

Key Stock Statistics (Source S&P, Vickers, company reports)

52-Wk Range	$22.84–13.52	S&P Oper. EPS 2010E	1.70	Market Capitalization(B)	$9.824	Beta	0.76
Trailing 12-Month EPS	$1.56	S&P Oper. EPS 2011E	1.82	Yield (%)	3.61	S&P 3-Yr. Proj. EPS CAGR(%)	7
Trailing 12-Month P/E	14.2	P/E on S&P Oper. EPS 2010E	13.0	Dividend Rate/Share	$0.80	S&P Credit Rating	BBB
$10K Invested 5 Yrs Ago	$9,816	Common Shares Outstg. (M)	442.9	Institutional Ownership (%)	70		

Price Performance

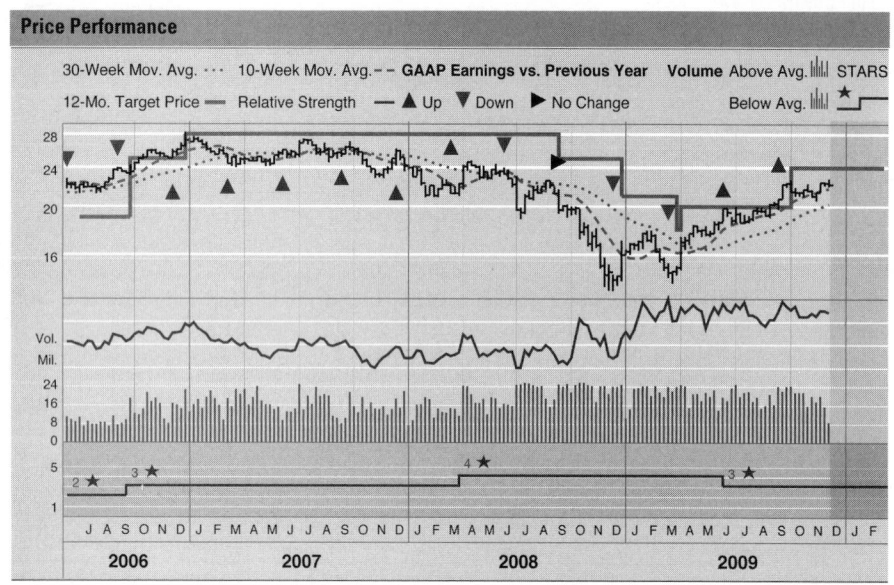

30-Week Mov. Avg. · · · · 10-Week Mov. Avg. – – **GAAP Earnings vs. Previous Year** Volume Above Avg. STARS
12-Mo. Target Price — Relative Strength — ▲ Up ▼ Down ▶ No Change Below Avg.

Options: ASE, CBOE, P

Analysis prepared by **Tom Graves, CFA** on September 24, 2009, when the stock traded at **$ 21.73**.

Highlights

► In FY 10 (May), we look for revenue from continuing operations to decline modestly from the $12.7 billion reported for FY 09, which had 53 weeks. Also, in FY 10, we expect that the absence of earnings from CAG's commodity trading and merchandising business, which was sold in June 2008, will be at least partly offset by the impact of stock repurchases, debt repayment and interest income related to proceeds from the sale of that business. We look for profit margins to be bolstered by cost reduction efforts and less input cost pressure.

► Before some possible special items, we estimate FY 10 EPS of $1.70, up from about $1.51 in FY 09, which excludes a net negative impact of about $0.09 a share from special items. In FY 11, we look for EPS of $1.82.

► In June 2009, there was an explosion at a CAG Slim Jim plant in Garner, NC. We believe that the financial impact will be eased by insurance proceeds. Also, CAG's diversified product line should limit the impact on overall results from any shortfall in Slim Jim inventory.

Investment Rationale/Risk

► Asset sales by ConAgra since 2003 have generated total pretax proceeds of more than $4 billion. Also, CAG's reported earnings have included a variety of special items, including asset sale gains, restructuring charges, and impairment charges.

► Risks to our recommendation and target price include competitive pressures in CAG's businesses, the potential for increased commodity cost inflation, and the company's ability to generate interest income and to achieve cost savings and efficiency targets.

► With the divestiture of the commodity trading and merchandising business, we anticipate increased profit stability and visibility from a reshaped ConAgra, and we expect the stock to be accorded a higher P/E valuation than it would have otherwise. Our 12-month target price of $24 reflects our view that the stock should receive a moderate P/E discount to what we have targeted, on average, for other packaged food stocks. CAG shares recently had an indicated dividend yield of about 3.5%.

Qualitative Risk Assessment

LOW	MEDIUM	HIGH

Our risk assessment reflects the relatively stable nature of the company's end markets, and what we view as relatively strong expected cash flows.

Quantitative Evaluations

S&P Quality Ranking   A-

D	C	B-	B	B+	A-	A	A+

Relative Strength Rank   MODERATE

70

LOWEST = 1   HIGHEST = 99

Revenue/Earnings Data

Revenue (Million $)

	1Q	2Q	3Q	4Q	Year
2010	2,961	--	--	--	--
2009	3,066	3,252	3,125	3,298	12,731
2008	2,956	3,511	3,528	3,078	11,606
2007	2,689	3,089	2,918	3,333	12,028
2006	2,700	3,026	2,879	2,975	11,579
2005	3,496	4,116	3,570	3,706	14,567

Earnings Per Share ($)

	1Q	2Q	3Q	4Q	Year
2010	0.37	E0.46	E0.44	E0.43	E1.70
2009	0.23	0.38	0.43	0.39	1.42
2008	0.23	0.50	0.63	-0.43	1.06
2007	0.21	0.39	0.37	0.38	1.35
2006	0.63	0.24	0.18	0.10	1.15
2005	0.26	0.47	0.32	0.20	1.27

Fiscal year ended May 31. Next earnings report expected: Mid December. EPS Estimates based on S&P Operating Earnings; historical GAAP earnings are as reported.

Dividend Data (Dates: mm/dd Payment Date: mm/dd/yy)

Amount ($)	Date Decl.	Ex-Div. Date	Stk. of Record	Payment Date
0.190	12/18	01/28	01/30	03/02/09
0.190	04/02	04/29	05/01	06/01/09
0.190	07/16	07/29	07/31	09/01/09
0.200	09/25	10/28	10/30	12/01/09

Dividends have been paid since 1976. Source: Company reports.

The McGraw-Hill Companies

ConAgra Foods Inc.

STANDARD &POOR'S

Business Summary September 24, 2009

CORPORATE OVERVIEW. ConAgra Foods is one of the largest food companies in North America. The company's continuing operations businesses are now being presented in two reporting segments: consumer foods, which provided 63% of total sales in FY 09 (May); and commercial foods (37%). In June 2008, CAG sold its trading and merchandising segment (12% of FY 07 sales), which was treated as a discontinued operation for FY 08 and FY 09.

The consumer foods segment included branded, private label and customized food products. CAG's brands include Hunt's, Healthy Choice, Chef Boyardee, Peter Pan, Wesson, Orville Redenbacher's, Slim Jim, PAM, Swiss Miss, Banquet, Marie Callender's, Kid Cuisine, Hebrew National, Egg Beaters, and Reddi-wip. In FY 09, within the consumer foods segment, CAG's North America grocery foods category had $2.9 billion of net sales. Other categories included frozen foods ($1.9 billion); snacks and store brands ($1.5 billion); and what GIS calls enabler brands ($1.6 billion), such as Blue Bonnet, La Choy, Libby's, The Max, Van Camp's, and Wesson.

CAG's commercial foods segment includes branded foods and ingredients, which are sold principally to foodservice, food manufacturing, and industrial customers. This segment's primary products include specialty potato products, milled grain ingredients, a variety of vegetable products, seasonings, blends, and flavors. Products are sold under brands such as Lamb Weston, ConAgra Mills, Gilroy Foods & Flavors, and Spicetec.

In FY 09, CAG's largest customer, Wal-Mart Stores, Inc., and its affiliates, accounted for about 16% of consolidated net sales.

CORPORATE STRATEGY. In recent years, CAG has been pursuing an acquisition and divestiture strategy to shift its focus toward its core branded and value-added food products, while exiting commodity-related businesses.

Company Financials Fiscal Year Ended May 31

Per Share Data ($)	2009	2008	2007	2006	2005	2004	2003	2002	2001	2000
Tangible Book Value	0.89	2.14	0.73	0.79	0.47	0.41	NM	NM	NM	1.22
Cash Flow	2.12	1.66	2.10	1.74	1.95	2.16	2.30	2.39	2.30	1.98
Earnings	1.42	1.06	1.35	1.15	1.27	1.50	1.58	1.47	1.33	0.86
S&P Core Earnings	1.20	1.05	1.29	0.91	1.14	1.39	1.42	1.27	1.20	NA
Dividends	0.75	0.72	0.72	1.08	1.03	0.98	NA	0.88	0.79	0.74
Payout Ratio	53%	68%	53%	94%	81%	65%	NA	60%	59%	86%
Calendar Year	2008	2007	2006	2005	2004	2003	2002	2001	2000	1999
Prices:High	24.87	27.73	28.35	30.24	29.65	26.41	27.65	26.00	26.19	34.38
Prices:Low	13.52	22.81	18.85	19.99	25.38	17.75	20.90	17.50	15.06	20.63
P/E Ratio:High	18	26	21	26	23	18	18	18	20	40
P/E Ratio:Low	10	22	14	17	20	12	14	12	11	24

Income Statement Analysis (Million $)										
Revenue	12,731	11,606	12,028	11,579	14,567	14,522	19,839	27,630	27,194	25,386
Operating Income	1,519	1,317	1,577	1,184	1,618	1,735	1,123	2,144	2,026	1,828
Depreciation	319	297	346	311	351	352	392	474	499	537
Interest Expense	268	467	226	307	341	275	276	402	423	303
Pretax Income	984	746	1,050	906	1,133	1,151	1,276	1,268	1,104	666
Effective Tax Rate	34.3%	30.5%	34.8%	34.2%	41.5%	30.9%	34.2%	38.1%	38.2%	38.0%
Net Income	646	519	684	596	663	796	840	785	682	413
S&P Core Earnings	547	512	657	470	589	740	750	668	612	NA

Balance Sheet & Other Financial Data (Million $)										
Cash	243	141	735	332	208	589	629	158	198	158
Current Assets	3,337	6,082	5,006	4,790	4,524	5,145	6,060	6,434	7,363	5,967
Total Assets	11,073	13,683	11,836	11,970	12,792	14,230	15,071	15,496	16,481	12,296
Current Liabilities	1,575	3,651	2,681	2,965	2,389	3,002	3,803	4,313	6,936	5,489
Long Term Debt	3,461	3,387	3,420	3,155	4,349	5,281	5,570	5,919	4,635	3,092
Common Equity	4,721	5,337	4,583	4,650	4,859	4,840	4,622	4,308	3,983	2,964
Total Capital	8,234	8,739	8,003	7,805	9,209	10,120	10,192	10,227	8,618	6,056
Capital Expenditures	442	490	425	263	453	352	390	531	560	539
Cash Flow	965	815	1,030	907	1,014	1,148	1,232	1,259	1,181	950
Current Ratio	2.1	1.7	1.9	1.6	1.9	1.7	1.6	1.5	1.1	1.1
% Long Term Debt of Capitalization	42.2	38.7	42.7	40.4	47.2	52.2	54.7	57.9	53.8	51.1
% Net Income of Revenue	5.1	4.5	5.7	5.1	4.6	5.5	4.2	2.8	2.5	1.6
% Return on Assets	5.2	4.1	5.7	4.8	4.9	5.4	5.5	4.9	4.8	3.4
% Return on Equity	12.9	10.5	14.8	12.5	13.7	16.8	18.8	18.9	19.9	14.1

Data as orig reptd.; bef. results of disc opers/spec. items. Per share data adj. for stk. divs.; EPS diluted. E-Estimated. NA-Not Available. NM-Not Meaningful. NR-Not Ranked. UR-Under Review.

Office: One Conagra Dr, Omaha, NE 68102-5001.
Telephone: 402-595-4000.
Website: http://www.conagra.com
Chrmn: S.F. Goldstone

Pres & CEO: G.M. Rodkin
EVP & CFO: J.F. Gehring
SVP & Treas: S.E. Messel
SVP, Secy & General Counsel: C.R. Batcheler

Investor Contact: C.W. Klinefelter (402-595-4154)
Board Members: M. C. Bay, K. A. Bousquette, S. G. Butler, S. F. Goldstone, J. A. Gregor, R. Johri, W. G. Jurgensen, R. H. Lenny, R. A. Marshall, S. Martin, G. M. Rodkin, A. J. Schindler, K. E. Stinson

Founded: 1919
Domicile: Delaware
Employees: 25,600

The McGraw-Hill Companies

ConocoPhillips

S&P Recommendation STRONG BUY ★ ★ ★ ★ ★	**Price** $51.92 (as of Nov 27, 2009)	**12-Mo. Target Price** $60.00	**Investment Style** Large-Cap Blend

GICS Sector Energy
Sub-Industry Integrated Oil & Gas

Summary This integrated oil and gas company (formerly Phillips Petroleum), the fourth largest integrated oil company in the world, acquired Tosco Corp. in 2001, and merged with Conoco Inc. in 2002.

Key Stock Statistics (Source S&P, Vickers, company reports)

52-Wk Range	$57.44– 34.12	S&P Oper. EPS 2009E	3.56	Market Capitalization(B)	$77.033	Beta	1.12
Trailing 12-Month EPS	$-18.92	S&P Oper. EPS 2010E	5.77	Yield (%)	3.85	S&P 3-Yr. Proj. EPS CAGR(%)	-12
Trailing 12-Month P/E	NM	P/E on S&P Oper. EPS 2009E	14.6	Dividend Rate/Share	$2.00	S&P Credit Rating	A
$10K Invested 5 Yrs Ago	$13,147	Common Shares Outstg. (M)	1,483.7	Institutional Ownership (%)	74		

Price Performance

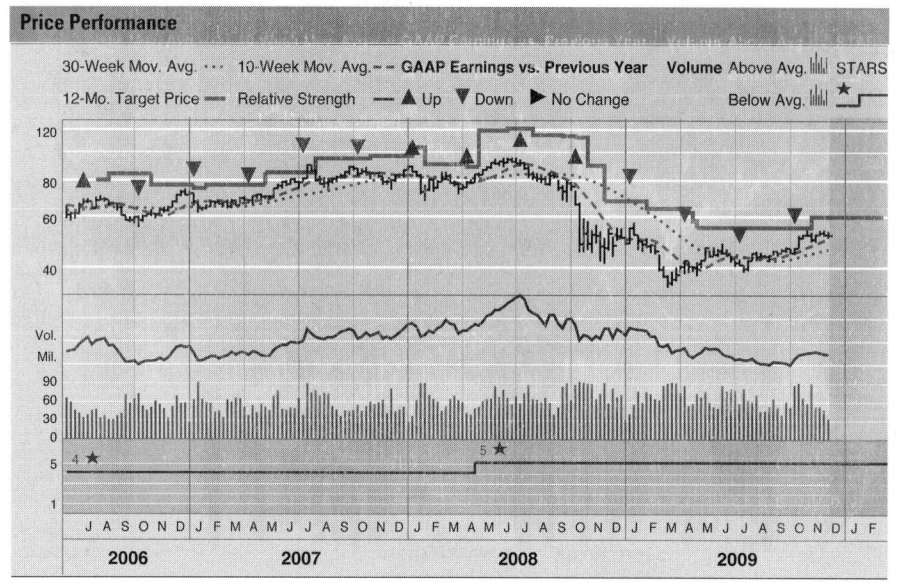

30-Week Mov. Avg. ··· 10-Week Mov. Avg. - - GAAP Earnings vs. Previous Year Volume Above Avg. STARS
12-Mo. Target Price — Relative Strength — ▲ Up ▼ Down ▶ No Change Below Avg.

Options: ASE, CBOE, P, Ph

Analysis prepared by **Tina J. Vital** on October 29, 2009, when the stock traded at **$ 50.17**.

Highlights

► We look for COP's oil and gas production (including Syncrude and Lukoil) to increase slightly in 2009, averaging 2.28 million boe per day, on reduced demand. However, we expect compound annual production growth of about 2% between 2008 and 2013, reflecting new developments in North America, Western and Eastern Europe, Asia-Pacific, and the Middle East.

► On the downstream, product demand has fallen and refining margins have narrowed; as a result, refiners have trimmed throughputs and initiated cost reductions. We look for U.S. Gulf Coast 3-2-1 crack spreads to narrow about 16% in 2009 before widening about 7% in 2010. Third quarter utilization rates averaged 90%, and we look for rates near these levels in the fourth quarter.

► First half 2009 operating EPS excluded $0.06 of net special gains. We look for after-tax operating earnings to fall about 69% in 2009 on reduced demand, before rebounding about 62% in 2010 on an improved economic outlook and cost initiatives.

Investment Rationale/Risk

► COP has been reshaping its upstream portfolio to focus on higher-growth assets. Reflecting weak markets, COP recorded asset impairments of $34.1 billion in the 2008 fourth quarter, including writedowns in its Lukoil investment. While COP had reduced its balance sheet debt, debt-to-capital ratios rose to 34% in the 2009 first half, reflecting the Origin Energy acquisition. In response, in October 2009, COP said it would sell about $10 billion of assets over the next two years and use proceeds to pay down debt.

► Risks to our recommendation and target price include unfavorable changes in economic, industrial and operating conditions, including COP's ability to replace its reserves; geopolitical risk; and operational risk.

► Blending our discounted cash flow ($61 per share, assuming a weighted average cost of capital of 5.0% and a terminal growth rate of 3%) and relative market valuations, our 12-month target price is $60, which represents an expected enterprise value of about 5.1X our 2010 EBITDA estimate, a peer discount.

Qualitative Risk Assessment

LOW	MEDIUM	HIGH

Our risk assessment reflects our view of the company's diversified and strong business profile in volatile, cyclical and capital-intensive segments of the energy industry. While COP has a history of aggressive acquisition activity, we believe its earnings stability is good and its corporate governance practices are sound.

Quantitative Evaluations

S&P Quality Ranking   B

D	C	B-	B	B+	A-	A	A+

Relative Strength Rank   STRONG

74

LOWEST = 1   HIGHEST = 99

Revenue/Earnings Data

Revenue (Million $)

	1Q	2Q	3Q	4Q	Year
2009	31,280	36,630	41,305	--	--
2008	54,883	71,411	70,044	44,504	246,182
2007	41,320	47,370	46,062	52,685	187,437
2006	46,906	47,149	48,076	41,519	183,650
2005	37,631	41,808	48,745	51,258	179,442
2004	29,813	31,528	34,350	39,385	135,076

Earnings Per Share ($)

	1Q	2Q	3Q	4Q	Year
2009	0.56	0.87	1.00	E1.19	E3.56
2008	2.62	3.50	3.39	-21.37	-11.16
2007	2.12	0.18	2.23	2.71	7.22
2006	2.34	3.09	2.31	1.91	9.66
2005	2.06	2.21	2.68	2.69	9.63
2004	1.16	1.44	1.44	1.76	5.79

Fiscal year ended Dec. 31. Next earnings report expected: Late January. EPS Estimates based on S&P Operating Earnings; historical GAAP earnings are as reported.

Dividend Data (Dates: mm/dd Payment Date: mm/dd/yy)

Amount ($)	Date Decl.	Ex-Div. Date	Stk. of Record	Payment Date
0.470	02/13	02/19	02/23	03/02/09
0.470	05/13	05/21	05/26	06/01/09
0.470	07/15	07/29	07/31	09/01/09
0.500	10/07	10/28	10/30	12/01/09

Dividends have been paid since 1934. Source: Company reports.

Please read the Required Disclosures and Analyst Certification on the last page of this report.

ConocoPhillips

STANDARD &POOR'S

Business Summary October 29, 2009

CORPORATE OVERVIEW. On August 30, 2002, Phillips Petroleum and Conoco merged, creating ConocoPhillips (COP). Today, we estimate COP is the second largest publicly integrated oil company in the U.S., based on a blend of its oil and gas reserves and production capacity. COP operates in six segments: exploration and production (E&P; 29% of 2008 sales, 2008 net loss of $13.48 billion); refining and marketing (R&M; 68%, net earnings of $2.32 billion); midstream (3%, net earnings of $0.54 billion); Lukoil investment; chemicals; and emerging businesses. At year-end 2008, COP owned a 20% stake in the Russian oil company Lukoil.

Including the Lukoil investment segment, Canadian Syncrude, and COP's share from equity affiliates, net oil and gas production declined 3.9% in 2008, to 2.23 million barrels of oil equivalent per day (boe/d), reflecting field declines and the expropriation of the company's Venezuelan oil interests. Net oil and gas production from COP's investment in Lukoil rose 0.2%, to 445,000 boe/d, in 2008. Syncrude production decreased 4.3%, to 22,000 b/d in 2008. Proved oil and gas reserves (including equity affiliates) declined 6%, to 9.98 billion barrels (58% liquids, 71% developed) in 2008.

Using data from John S. Herold, we estimate COP's three-year (2005-07) finding and development costs at $17.88 per boe, above the peer average; three-year proved acquisition costs at $9.12 per boe, above the peer average; three-year reserve replacement costs at $12.04 per boe, in line with peers; and its three-year reserve replacement at 234%, above the peer average.

As of December 31, 2008, COP owned or had interests in 12 U.S. refineries (net crude throughput capacity of 2.00 million barrels per day, b/d), four European refineries (610,000 b/d), and one refinery in Malaysia (60,000 b/d). At year-end 2008, gasoline and distillates were sold through wholesale and retail operations in the U.S. (under Phillips 66, Conoco, and 76 brands) and Europe (under the JET and Coop brand).

Company Financials Fiscal Year Ended Dec. 31

Per Share Data ($)	2008	2007	2006	2005	2004	2003	2002	2001	2000	1999
Tangible Book Value	34.15	36.40	29.69	25.49	18.53	12.85	9.91	14.07	10.77	8.06
Cash Flow	-3.86	12.54	14.19	12.63	8.49	5.90	5.31	5.14	5.94	2.97
Earnings	-11.16	7.22	9.66	9.63	5.79	3.53	0.74	2.79	3.63	1.20
S&P Core Earnings	4.96	7.49	9.59	9.72	5.88	3.43	0.64	2.60	NA	NA
Dividends	1.88	1.64	1.44	1.18	0.90	0.82	0.74	0.70	0.68	0.68
Payout Ratio	NM	23%	15%	12%	15%	23%	101%	25%	19%	57%
Prices:High	95.96	90.84	74.89	71.48	45.61	33.02	32.05	34.00	35.00	28.63
Prices:Low	41.27	61.59	54.90	41.40	32.15	26.80	22.02	25.00	17.97	18.84
P/E Ratio:High	NM	13	8	7	8	9	44	12	10	24
P/E Ratio:Low	NM	9	6	4	6	8	30	9	5	16

Income Statement Analysis (Million $)	2008	2007	2006	2005	2004	2003	2002	2001	2000	1999
Revenue	240,842	187,437	183,650	179,442	135,076	104,196	56,748	26,868	21,113	13,751
Operating Income	36,158	31,164	37,433	24,691	17,033	11,866	4,571	8,393	5,528	2,452
Depreciation, Depletion and Amortization	11,116	8,740	7,284	4,253	3,798	3,485	4,446	1,391	1,179	902
Interest Expense	935	1,801	1,087	497	546	864	614	391	422	332
Pretax Income	-3,523	23,359	28,409	23,580	14,401	8,337	2,164	3,302	3,769	1,185
Effective Tax Rate	NM	48.7%	45.0%	42.0%	43.5%	44.9%	67.0%	50.2%	50.6%	48.6%
Net Income	-16,998	11,891	15,550	13,640	8,107	4,593	714	1,643	1,862	609
S&P Core Earnings	7,569	12,317	15,442	13,753	8,241	4,697	618	1,533	NA	NA

Balance Sheet & Other Financial Data (Million $)	2008	2007	2006	2005	2004	2003	2002	2001	2000	1999
Cash	755	1,456	817	2,214	1,387	490	307	142	149	138
Current Assets	20,843	24,735	25,066	19,612	15,021	11,192	10,903	4,363	2,606	2,773
Total Assets	142,865	177,757	164,781	106,999	92,861	82,455	76,836	35,217	20,509	15,201
Current Liabilities	21,780	26,882	26,431	21,359	15,586	14,011	12,816	4,542	3,492	2,520
Long Term Debt	32,754	26,583	23,091	10,758	14,370	16,340	19,267	9,295	7,272	4,921
Common Equity	55,165	88,983	82,646	52,731	42,723	34,366	29,517	14,340	6,093	4,549
Total Capital	107,186	137,757	106,939	76,137	68,583	60,113	57,796	27,650	15,259	10,950
Capital Expenditures	19,099	11,791	15,596	11,620	9,496	6,169	4,388	3,085	2,022	1,690
Cash Flow	-5,882	20,631	22,834	17,893	11,905	8,078	5,160	3,034	3,041	1,511
Current Ratio	1.0	0.9	0.9	0.9	1.0	0.8	0.9	1.0	0.7	1.1
% Long Term Debt of Capitalization	30.6	19.3	21.6	14.1	21.0	27.2	33.3	33.6	47.7	44.9
% Return on Assets	NM	6.9	11.4	13.6	9.2	5.8	1.3	5.9	10.4	4.1
% Return on Equity	NM	13.9	23.0	28.6	21.0	14.4	3.3	16.1	35.0	13.9

Data as orig reptd.; bef. results of disc opers/spec. items. Per share data adj. for stk. divs.; EPS diluted. E-Estimated. NA-Not Available. NM-Not Meaningful. NR-Not Ranked. UR-Under Review.

Office: 600 N Dairy Ashford St, Houston, TX 77079-1175.
Telephone: 281-293-1000.
Website: http://www.conocophillips.com
Chrmn & CEO: J.J. Mulva

Pres & COO: J.A. Carrig
SVP & CFO: S.L. Cornelius
SVP & Chief Admin Officer: G.L. Batchelder
SVP & Chief Acctg Officer: R.C. Berney

Investor Contact: G. Russell (212-207-1996)
Board Members: R. L. Armitage, R. H. Auchinleck, J. Copeland, Jr., K. M. Duberstein, R. R. Harkin, H. McGraw, III, J. J. Mulva, H. Norvik, W. K. Reilly, B. Shackouls, V. J. Tschinkel, K. C. Turner, W. E. Wade, Jr.

Founded: 1917
Domicile: Delaware
Employees: 33,800

The **McGraw-Hill** Companies

Consolidated Edison Inc.

STANDARD &POOR'S

S&P Recommendation HOLD ★★★☆☆	Price $42.44 (as of Nov 27, 2009)	12-Mo. Target Price $41.00	Investment Style Large-Cap Value

GICS Sector Utilities
Sub-Industry Multi-Utilities

Summary This electric and gas utility holding company serves parts of New York, New Jersey, and Pennsylvania.

Key Stock Statistics (Source S&P, Vickers, company reports)

52-Wk Range	$42.99– 32.56	S&P Oper. EPS 2009**E**	3.16	Market Capitalization(B)	$11.692	Beta	0.27
Trailing 12-Month EPS	$3.00	S&P Oper. EPS 2010**E**	3.30	Yield (%)	5.56	S&P 3-Yr. Proj. EPS CAGR(%)	4
Trailing 12-Month P/E	14.2	P/E on S&P Oper. EPS 2009**E**	13.4	Dividend Rate/Share	$2.36	S&P Credit Rating	A-
$10K Invested 5 Yrs Ago	$12,174	Common Shares Outstg. (M)	275.5	Institutional Ownership (%)	42		

Price Performance

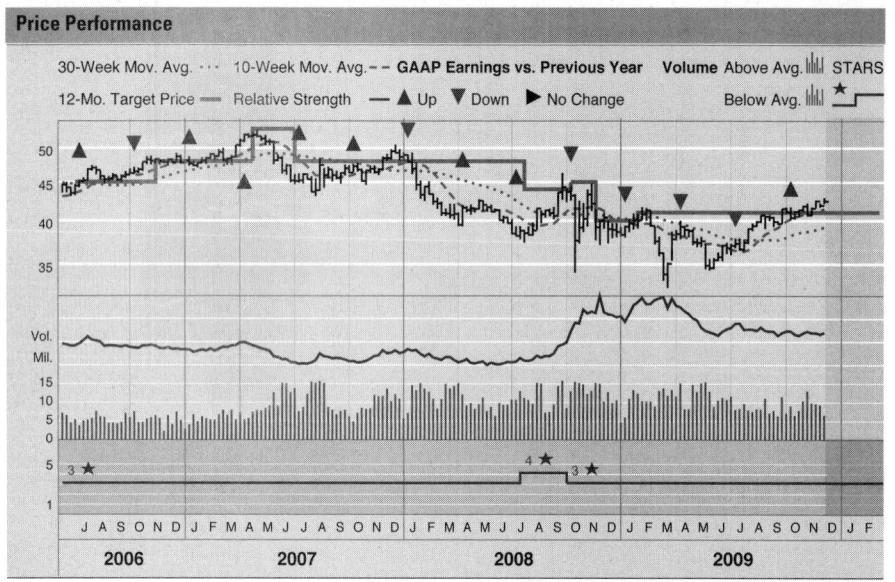

30-Week Mov. Avg. · · · 10-Week Mov. Avg. - - **GAAP Earnings vs. Previous Year**   Volume Above Avg. |ılıl STARS
12-Mo. Target Price — Relative Strength — ▲ Up ▼ Down ▶ No Change   Below Avg. ılıl ★

Options: ASE, CBOE, P, Ph

Analysis prepared by **Justin McCann** on November 20, 2009, when the stock traded at **$ 41.80**.

Highlights

► We expect operating EPS in 2009 to grow about 5% from 2008's $3.00, reflecting the benefit of new rate increases, partially offset by new issuances of common stock and long-term debt, higher interest, depreciation and operating expenses, and the slowdown in the New York City economy. In April 2009, the New York Public Service Commission (NYPSC) authorized Con Edison of New York an electric rate increase of $523 million, which became effective April 6.

► For 2010, we expect operating EPS to increase about 4% from anticipated results for 2009, reflecting an expected additional rate increase. In May 2009, Con Edison on New York filed with the NYPSC for a three-year plan of annual electric rate increases of $695 million effective April 2010, 2011, and 2012, or alternatively, a single-year increase of $854 million effective April 2010. A decision is expected in March 2010.

► On October 27, 2009, ED announced that the U.S. Department of Energy had awarded it $136 million in federal stimulus funding to help support the company's "smart grid" investments, which are being targeted for the technological upgrading of its electric grid system.

Investment Rationale/Risk

► The stock has rebounded approximately 28% from its multi-year low reached in March, and was up more than 7% year date. In addition to the impacts of the financial crisis, the slowdown in the economy, and the sharp drop in the stock market, we believe the stock had been hurt by the expected dilutive effect of new equity issuances, as well as the lingering negative political and regulatory environment that resulted from an extended power outage two summers ago. We believe the recent recovery reflects the expectation of additional rate increases, the appeal of the above-peer dividend yield, and the recovery in the broader market.

► Risks to our recommendation and target price include a significant weakening of the economy in the utility's service territory, unfavorable regulatory rulings, and a sharp decline in the average P/E multiple of the peer group as a whole.

► We believe the shares will be supported by a dividend yield (recently 5.6%) that is well above the industry average (around 4.8%). We expect the dividend to continue to be increased at an annual rate of approximately 1%. Our 12-month target price is $41, a premium-to-peers P/E multiple of 12.4X our EPS estimate for 2010.

Qualitative Risk Assessment

LOW	MEDIUM	HIGH

Our risk assessment reflects our view of the company's strong and steady cash flows from regulated electric and gas utility operations, its solid balance sheet and A- credit rating, a healthy economy in its service territory, and a supportive regulatory environment historically.

Quantitative Evaluations

S&P Quality Ranking   B+

D	C	B-	B	B+	A-	A	A+

Relative Strength Rank   MODERATE

69

LOWEST = 1   HIGHEST = 99

Revenue/Earnings Data

Revenue (Million $)

	1Q	2Q	3Q	4Q	Year
2009	3,423	2,845	3,489	--	--
2008	3,577	3,149	3,858	2,999	13,583
2007	3,357	2,956	3,579	3,228	13,120
2006	3,317	2,555	3,441	2,824	12,137
2005	2,801	2,406	3,375	3,108	11,690
2004	2,679	2,164	2,734	2,182	9,758

Earnings Per Share ($)

2009	0.66	0.55	1.22	E0.74	E3.16
2008	1.10	1.02	0.66	0.58	3.36
2007	0.99	0.58	1.15	0.76	3.46
2006	0.74	0.51	0.92	0.78	2.95
2005	0.75	0.48	1.17	0.59	2.99
2004	0.69	0.38	1.03	0.22	2.32

Fiscal year ended Dec. 31. Next earnings report expected: Late January. EPS Estimates based on S&P Operating Earnings; historical GAAP earnings are as reported.

Dividend Data (Dates: mm/dd Payment Date: mm/dd/yy)

Amount ($)	Date Decl.	Ex-Div. Date	Stk. of Record	Payment Date
0.590	01/22	02/13	02/18	03/15/09
0.590	04/16	05/11	05/13	06/15/09
0.590	07/16	08/17	08/19	09/15/09
0.590	10/15	11/16	11/18	12/15/09

Dividends have been paid since 1885. Source: Company reports.

Please read the Required Disclosures and Analyst Certification on the last page of this report.

The McGraw-Hill Companies

Consolidated Edison Inc.

STANDARD
&POOR'S

Business Summary November 20, 2009

CORPORATE OVERVIEW. Consolidated Edison is a holding company with electric and gas utilities serving a territory that includes New York City (except part of Queens), most of Westchester County, southeastern New York state, northern New Jersey, and northeastern Pennsylvania. Although the company also has some competitive subsidiaries that participate in energy-related businesses, we expect the two regulated utilities to provide substantially all of ED's earnings over the next few years.

MARKET PROFILE. The company's principal business operations are Con Edison of New York's regulated electric, gas and steam utility operations, and Orange and Rockland Utilities' (O&R) regulated electric and gas utility operations. In 2008, electric revenues accounted for 63.4% of consolidated sales (61.8% in 2007); gas revenues 15.4% (15.4%); non-utility revenues 16.0% (17.5%); and steam revenues 5.2% (5.2%). At December 31, 2008, the distribution system of Consolidated Edison Company of New York had about 36,648 miles of overhead distribution lines and around 94,929 miles of underground distribution lines. The distribution system of O&R had about 3,675 miles of overhead distribution lines, and 1,634 miles of underground distribution lines.

The company's Con Edison of New York (CENY) unit provides electric service

(75.6% of CENY's operating revenues in 2008) to about 3.3 million customers and gas service (17.6%) to around 1.1 million customers in New York City and Westchester County. It also provides steam service (6.8%) in parts of Manhattan to around 2,000 customers (mostly large office buildings, apartment houses and hospitals). Most of the electricity sold by CENY in 2008 was purchased under firm power contracts (primarily with non-utility generators) or through the wholesale electricity market administered by the New York Independent System Operator (NYISO). We expect this to continue for the foreseeable future.

The company's O&R unit provides electric and gas service in southeastern New York and adjacent areas of eastern Pennsylvania, and electric service in areas of New Jersey adjacent to its New York service territory. In 2008, electric sales accounted for 74.0% of its operating revenues and gas sales for 26.0%.

Company Financials Fiscal Year Ended Dec. 31

Per Share Data ($)	2008	2007	2006	2005	2004	2003	2002	2001	2000	1999
Tangible Book Value	37.05	34.83	32.13	30.69	29.86	29.09	25.40	24.23	23.50	22.41
Earnings	3.36	3.46	2.95	2.99	2.32	2.36	3.13	3.21	2.74	3.13
S&P Core Earnings	1.19	2.99	2.54	2.54	1.78	1.66	0.50	0.66	NA	NA
Dividends	2.34	2.32	2.30	2.28	2.26	2.24	2.22	2.20	2.18	2.14
Payout Ratio	70%	67%	78%	76%	97%	95%	71%	69%	80%	68%
Prices:High	49.30	52.90	49.28	49.29	45.59	46.02	45.40	43.37	39.50	53.44
Prices:Low	34.11	43.10	41.17	41.10	37.23	36.55	32.65	31.44	26.19	33.56
P/E Ratio:High	15	15	17	16	20	20	15	14	14	17
P/E Ratio:Low	10	12	14	14	16	15	10	10	10	11

Income Statement Analysis (Million $)										
Revenue	13,583	13,120	12,137	11,690	9,758	9,827	8,482	9,634	9,431	7,491
Depreciation	717	645	621	584	551	529	495	526	586	526
Maintenance	NA	NA	NA	NA	NA	353	387	430	458	438
Fixed Charges Coverage	3.09	3.49	2.97	3.19	2.64	3.13	3.25	3.46	3.06	4.03
Construction Credits	14.0	18.0	12.0	16.0	43.0	27.0	14.0	9.00	8.00	6.00
Effective Tax Rate	36.2%	31.8%	34.6%	34.6%	33.1%	37.5%	35.6%	38.9%	34.0%	34.3%
Net Income	922	925	738	732	549	525	680	696	596	715
S&P Core Earnings	329	800	635	621	421	370	106	141	NA	NA

Balance Sheet & Other Financial Data (Million $)										
Gross Property	25,993	24,698	23,028	21,467	20,394	19,294	18,000	16,630	17,021	16,088
Capital Expenditures	2,318	1,928	1,847	1,617	1,359	1,292	1,216	1,104	986	695
Net Property	20,874	19,914	18,445	17,112	16,106	15,225	13,330	12,136	11,786	11,354
Capitalization:Long Term Debt	9,445	7,824	8,511	7,641	6,807	6,769	6,206	5,542	5,447	4,560
Capitalization:% Long Term Debt	49.3	46.3	51.1	50.5	48.5	51.3	50.3	48.3	48.8	44.5
Capitalization:Preferred	Nil	Nil	Nil	Nil	Nil	Nil	Nil	250	250	250
Capitalization:% Preferred	Nil	Nil	Nil	Nil	Nil	Nil	Nil	2.18	2.24	2.44
Capitalization:Common	9,698	9,076	8,159	7,477	7,234	6,423	5,921	5,690	5,471	5,448
Capitalization:% Common	50.7	53.7	48.9	49.5	51.5	48.7	48.0	49.6	49.0	53.1
Total Capital	24,142	21,408	20,806	18,804	17,806	16,406	15,037	13,835	13,602	12,666
% Operating Ratio	87.8	89.4	89.5	90.3	90.3	88.8	74.1	88.1	117.8	86.0
% Earned on Net Property	8.1	9.6	7.1	7.0	5.9	6.4	8.3	9.4	8.8	9.0
% Return on Revenue	6.8	7.1	6.1	6.3	5.6	5.3	8.0	7.2	6.3	9.5
% Return on Invested Capital	5.3	6.8	6.7	6.7	5.9	7.3	7.8	8.3	7.7	8.2
% Return on Common Equity	9.8	11.0	9.4	10.0	7.9	8.5	11.5	12.2	10.7	12.2

Data as orig reptd.; bef. results of disc opers/spec. items. Per share data adj. for stk. divs.; EPS diluted. E-Estimated. NA-Not Available. NM-Not Meaningful. NR-Not Ranked. UR-Under Review.

Office: 4 Irving Place, New York, NY 10003-3502.
Telephone: 212-460-4600.
Email: corpcom@coned.com
Website: http://www.coned.com

Chrmn, Pres & CEO: K. Burke
SVP & CFO: R.N. Hoglund
Chief Acctg Officer & Cntlr: R. Muccilo
Treas: J.P. O'Brien

Secy: C. Sobin
Board Members: K. Burke, V. A. Calarco, G. Campbell, Jr., G. J. Davis, M. J. Del Giudice, E. Futter, J. F. Hennessy, III, S. Hernandez-Pinero, J. F. Killian, E. R. McGrath, M. W. Ranger, L. F. Sutherland

Founded: 1884
Domicile: New York
Employees: 15,628

CONSOL Energy Inc.

S&P Recommendation	HOLD ★★★☆☆	Price $45.89 (as of Nov 27, 2009)	12-Mo. Target Price $50.00	Investment Style Large-Cap Blend

GICS Sector Energy
Sub-Industry Coal & Consumable Fuels

Summary This company is a major producer of high-bituminous coal and coalbed methane gas. We estimate CNX is the second largest U.S. coal producer based on annual production, and has coal reserves of 4.5 billion tons.

Key Stock Statistics (Source S&P, Vickers, company reports)

52-Wk Range	$53.04–20.67	S&P Oper. EPS 2009**E**	2.94	Market Capitalization(B)	$8.298	Beta	1.47
Trailing 12-Month EPS	$3.14	S&P Oper. EPS 2010**E**	3.18	Yield (%)	0.87	S&P 3-Yr. Proj. EPS CAGR(%)	13
Trailing 12-Month P/E	14.6	P/E on S&P Oper. EPS 2009**E**	15.6	Dividend Rate/Share	$0.40	S&P Credit Rating	BB+
$10K Invested 5 Yrs Ago	$22,330	Common Shares Outstg. (M)	180.8	Institutional Ownership (%)	88		

Price Performance

- 30-Week Mov. Avg. · · · 10-Week Mov. Avg. – – **GAAP Earnings vs. Previous Year** Volume Above Avg. STARS
- 12-Mo. Target Price — Relative Strength — ▲ Up ▼ Down ▶ No Change Below Avg. ★

Options: ASE, CBOE, P, Ph

Analysis prepared by **Mathew Christy, CFA** on October 28, 2009, when the stock traded at **$ 44.73**.

Qualitative Risk Assessment

LOW	MEDIUM	**HIGH**

Our risk assessment reflects the cyclical nature of the coal market, our view of unfavorable corporate governance practices concerning takeover defenses, and the heavily regulated nature of the industry and its utilities end market, notwithstanding expected benefits from the pricing cycle and a rising market share.

Quantitative Evaluations

S&P Quality Ranking NR

D	C	B-	B	B+	A-	A	A+

Relative Strength Rank MODERATE

59

LOWEST = 1 HIGHEST = 99

Highlights

► We expect 2009 revenues to decline marginally from 2008 results, but forecast an increase of about 3.6% for 2010. Our 2009 estimate is based on a nearly 13% decrease in coal volumes, partially offset by a continued rise in the average price realization per ton, which we believe will advance to over $58, representing about a 20% increase from 2008 levels. In 2010, we look for revenue increases to be led by a nearly 2% projected gain in coal volumes and somewhat better pricing.

► We think 2009 EBIT (earnings before interest and taxes) margins will remain relatively flat as compared 2008 results, as a result of higher productivity, cost reduction efforts, and operating leverage from higher coal pricing. This is despite our expectation that the average cash cost per ton will increase almost 10% in 2009. In 2010, we see somewhat lower operating margins and think average production costs will increase about 4.7%.

► Assuming steady interest expense, tax rates and shares outstanding, we estimate EPS of $2.94 in 2009 and $3.18 in 2010.

Investment Rationale/Risk

► We continue to expect reduced coal demand due to the effects of a weak economy, high coal inventories, low natural gas prices, and utilities switching fuel sources in 2009. However, we believe CNX will benefit from improving pricing for coal from Appalachia through its long-term supply contracts, which began to display premiums in 2008. In addition, we view positively CNX's balance sheet due to its 31% total debt-to-capital ratio as of September 2009.

► Risks to our recommendation and target price include lower-than-expected prices for steam and metallurgical grade coal, reduced productivity, increased supply costs, greater fuel switching, and slower-than-forecast U.S. economic activity.

► Our 12-month target price of $50 is based on relative valuation analysis. We apply an EV/EBITDA multiple of about 7.4X to our 2010 EBITDA estimate. This multiple is ahead of peers to reflect our view of CNX's size and low-cost production.

Revenue/Earnings Data

Revenue (Million $)

	1Q	2Q	3Q	4Q	Year
2009	1,219	1,071	1,095	--	--
2008	951.1	1,200	1,137	1,198	4,652
2007	915.2	1,060	868.4	918.6	3,762
2006	985.9	932.3	843.4	953.7	3,715
2005	817.0	817.2	879.9	969.1	3,483
2004	650.9	674.6	659.9	791.4	2,777

Earnings Per Share ($)

	1Q	2Q	3Q	4Q	Year
2009	1.08	0.62	0.48	E0.77	E2.94
2008	0.41	0.54	0.49	0.97	2.40
2007	0.61	0.83	-0.03	0.04	1.45
2006	0.67	0.57	0.27	0.69	2.20
2005	0.41	0.22	2.02	0.47	3.13
2004	0.18	0.15	-0.07	0.37	0.64

Fiscal year ended Dec. 31. Next earnings report expected: Late January. EPS Estimates based on S&P Operating Earnings; historical GAAP earnings are as reported.

Dividend Data (Dates: mm/dd Payment Date: mm/dd/yy)

Amount ($)	Date Decl.	Ex-Div. Date	Stk. of Record	Payment Date
0.100	01/30	02/05	02/09	02/20/09
0.100	04/24	05/01	05/05	05/22/09
0.100	07/31	08/04	08/06	08/24/09
0.100	10/23	11/02	11/04	11/20/09

Dividends have been paid since 1999. Source: Company reports.

Please read the Required Disclosures and Analyst Certification on the last page of this report.

CONSOL Energy Inc.

Business Summary October 28, 2009

CORPORATE OVERVIEW. Through expansion and acquisitions, CONSOL Energy has grown from a single fuel mining company formed in 1860 into a multi-energy producer of coal and gas. CNX produces high Btu coal and gas, two fuels that collectively generate two-thirds of all U.S. electric power, from reserves located mainly east of the Mississippi River.

The coal segment (CNX Coal) has 17 mining complexes in the U.S., and sells steam coal to power generators and metallurgical coal to metal and coke producers. The company had an estimated 4.5 billion tons of proven and probable coal reserves at the end of 2008, nearly all of which was located in underground mines. About 63% of CNX's reserves are found in northern Appalachia, with 18% in the Midwest, 13% in Central Appalachia, 4% in the western U.S., and 2% in western Canada. The company is a major fuel supplier to the electric power industry in the northeast quadrant of the U.S. Coal produced at CNX's mines is transported to customers via railroad cars, barges, trucks and conveyor belts, or by a combination of such methods. In 2008, the company sold 66.1 million produced tons of coal, up from 65.3 million tons in 2007. Ap-

proximately 90% of coal produced in 2008 was sold under contracts with terms of one year or more. The average sales price per produced ton sold in 2008 was $48.76, versus $40.60 in 2007 while no customer accounted for more than 10% of revenue in 2008.

CONSOL Energy owns 83.3% of CNX Gas Corporation, which is one of the largest U.S. producers of coalbed methane (CBM), with daily gas production of 209 MMcf. CBM produces pipeline quality gas that is found in coal seams, usually in formations at depths of less than 2,500 feet versus conventional natural gas fields with depths of up to 15,000 feet. At the end of 2008, CNX Gas had 1.4 Tcf of proved CBM reserves, of which approximately 55% was developed. In 2008, the company sold 76.6 Bcf of gas at an average price of $8.99, versus 57.9 Bcf at $7.20 in 2007.

Company Financials Fiscal Year Ended Dec. 31

Per Share Data ($)	2008	2007	2006	2005	2004	2003	2002	2001	2000	1999
Tangible Book Value	8.10	6.77	5.84	5.54	2.59	NM	1.03	2.23	1.62	1.59
Cash Flow	4.53	3.24	3.80	4.54	2.17	1.40	1.74	2.71	2.24	1.24
Earnings	2.40	1.45	2.20	3.13	0.64	-0.05	0.08	1.17	0.68	0.31
S&P Core Earnings	2.13	1.02	1.88	2.05	0.69	0.04	0.03	0.98	NA	NA
Dividends	0.40	0.31	0.28	0.28	0.28	0.28	0.42	0.56	0.56	Nil
Payout Ratio	17%	21%	13%	9%	44%	NM	NM	48%	83%	Nil
Prices:High	119.10	74.18	49.09	39.91	21.95	13.40	14.16	21.24	14.00	8.00
Prices:Low	18.50	29.15	28.07	18.58	10.12	7.28	4.90	9.15	4.97	4.81
P/E Ratio:High	50	51	22	13	35	NM	NM	18	21	NM
P/E Ratio:Low	8	20	13	6	16	NM	NM	8	7	NM

Income Statement Analysis (Million $)										
Revenue	4,542	3,762	3,715	3,483	2,777	2,222	2,184	2,368	2,159	1,110
Operating Income	1,067	829	701	617	308	246	268	418	599	409
Depreciation	394	329	296	262	280	242	263	243	250	121
Interest Expense	36.2	45.4	25.1	27.3	31.4	34.5	46.2	57.6	55.0	30.5
Pretax Income	726	429	551	655	82.6	-33.5	-40.4	240	107	40.2
Effective Tax Rate	33.1%	31.7%	20.4%	9.83%	NM	NM	NM	23.6%	NM	0.30%
Net Income	442	268	409	581	115	-12.6	11.7	184	107	40.0
S&P Core Earnings	391	190	349	381	125	6.95	3.70	154	NA	NA

Balance Sheet & Other Financial Data (Million $)										
Cash	139	41.7	224	341	6.42	6.51	11.5	16.6	8.20	23.6
Current Assets	984	683	914	998	470	471	623	566	578	623
Total Assets	7,370	6,208	5,663	5,088	4,196	4,319	4,293	3,895	3,866	3,875
Current Liabilities	1,512	1,016	740	804	705	825	814	934	953	884
Long Term Debt	468	489	493	438	426	442	488	231	301	313
Common Equity	1,462	1,214	984	1,025	469	291	162	352	254	255
Total Capital	2,143	1,866	1,612	1,557	895	733	650	583	555	567
Capital Expenditures	1,062	743	659	523	411	291	295	214	143	105
Cash Flow	837	597	705	843	396	230	275	427	357	161
Current Ratio	0.7	0.7	1.2	1.2	0.7	0.6	0.8	0.6	0.6	0.7
% Long Term Debt of Capitalization	21.9	26.2	30.6	28.2	47.6	60.3	75.1	39.6	54.1	55.1
% Net Income of Revenue	9.7	7.1	11.5	17.2	4.1	NM	NM	7.8	4.9	3.6
% Return on Assets	6.5	4.5	7.6	12.5	2.7	NM	NM	4.7	2.7	NM
% Return on Equity	33.1	23.5	40.7	77.7	30.3	NM	NM	60.6	42.0	NM

Data as orig reptd.; bef. results of disc opers/spec. items. Per share data adj. for stk. divs.; EPS diluted. E-Estimated. NA-Not Available. NM-Not Meaningful. NR-Not Ranked. UR-Under Review.

Office: 1000 Consol Energy Dr, Canonsburg, PA 15317-6506.
Telephone: 724-485-4000.
Website: http://www.consolenergy.com
Chrmn: J.L. Whitmire, III

Pres & CEO: J.B. Harvey
COO & EVP: N.J. Deluliis
Investor Contact: W.J. Lyons
EVP, CFO & Chief Acctg Officer: W.J. Lyons

Board Members: J. E. Altmeyer, P. W. Baxter, W. E. Davis, R. K. Gupta, P. A. Hammick, D. C. Hardesty, Jr., J. B. Harvey, J. T. Mills, W. P. Powell, J. L. Whitmire, III, J. T. Williams

Founded: 1991
Domicile: Delaware
Employees: 8,176

Constellation Brands Inc.

STANDARD
&POOR'S

S&P Recommendation **BUY** ★★★★☆	Price $16.99 (as of Nov 27, 2009)	12-Mo. Target Price $19.00	Investment Style Large-Cap Growth

GICS Sector Consumer Staples
Sub-Industry Distillers & Vintners

Summary This leading international producer and marketer of alcoholic beverages has a broad portfolio of wine, imported beer and distilled spirits brands.

Key Stock Statistics (Source S&P, Vickers, company reports)

52-Wk Range	$17.56– 10.72	S&P Oper. EPS 2010E	1.65	Market Capitalization(B)	$3.361	Beta	0.99
Trailing 12-Month EPS	$-1.00	S&P Oper. EPS 2011E	1.79	Yield (%)	Nil	S&P 3-Yr. Proj. EPS CAGR(%)	5
Trailing 12-Month P/E	NM	P/E on S&P Oper. EPS 2010E	10.3	Dividend Rate/Share	Nil	S&P Credit Rating	BB
$10K Invested 5 Yrs Ago	$7,607	Common Shares Outstg. (M)	221.6	Institutional Ownership (%)	85		

Price Performance

30-Week Mov. Avg. · · · 10-Week Mov. Avg. − − **GAAP Earnings vs. Previous Year** Volume Above Avg. STARS

12-Mo. Target Price — Relative Strength — ▲ Up ▼ Down ► No Change Below Avg.

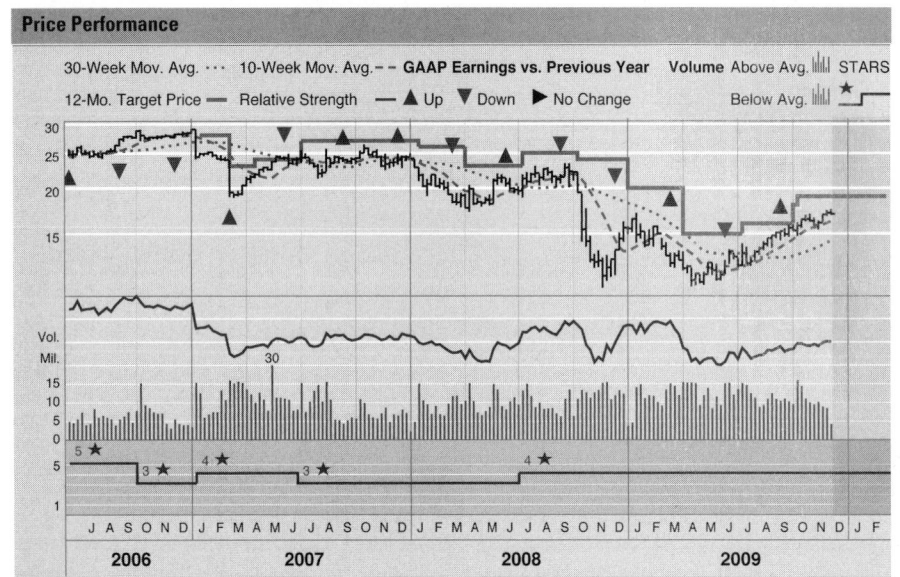

Analysis prepared by **Esther Y. Kwon, CFA** on October 02, 2009, when the stock traded at **$ 15.73**.

Options: ASE, CBOE, P, Ph

Highlights

► Following a 3% sales decline in FY 09 (Feb.) on negative foreign currency translation, divestitures and unit weakness in international markets, we see FY 10 net revenues down about 9%, on a continued negative foreign currency impact, divestiture of low-margin wine and spirits brands and demand weakness in the U.K. and Australia. However, we forecast organic net sales growth in North America. We estimate about 200 basis points of operating margin expansion in FY 10 on the restructuring of North American and U.K. facilities and the Australian wine business, consolidation of distributors, divestiture of lower-margin brands, and work force reductions.

► We expect STZ's 50/50 joint venture with Grupo Modelo to import and distribute beers, primarily top import brand Corona, to continue to face softness on market share losses, with equity earnings dropping over 12% in FY 10.

► With a reduction in interest expense, and an effective tax rate of 38% compared to just over 36% in FY 09, we estimate FY 10 operating EPS of $1.65, excluding restructuring charges and integration costs. For FY 10, we forecast operating EPS of $1.79.

Investment Rationale/Risk

► We view favorably STZ's moves into higher-growth segments, divestitures of value-priced, popular brands, and debt reduction. In December 2007, STZ completed the purchase of Fortune Brands' U.S. wine business, providing a stronger presence in the faster-growing super-premium and above segment. We look for healthy global demand for premium wines to continue over the longer term. With STZ's move away from acquisitions and a focus on debt reduction, we see healthy cash flow growth potential.

► Risks to our recommendation and target price include continued pricing pressures in the U.K. and Australian wine markets, resistance to further price increases, and foreign currency risk.

► Our 12-month target price of $19 is based on a multiple of 11.5X our FY 10 EPS estimate of $1.65. We think a discount to the recent historical average of 16X is appropriate amid a backdrop of slowing economic conditions and higher relative debt levels.

Qualitative Risk Assessment

LOW	MEDIUM	HIGH

STZ operates in an industry that we believe has demonstrated stable revenue streams. This is offset by our corporate governance concerns relating to STZ's dual class stock structure with unequal voting rights.

Quantitative Evaluations

S&P Quality Ranking B-

D	C	B-	B	B+	A-	A	A+

Relative Strength Rank STRONG

80

LOWEST = 1 HIGHEST = 99

Revenue/Earnings Data

Revenue (Million $)

	1Q	2Q	3Q	4Q	Year
2010	791.6	876.8	--	--	--
2009	931.8	956.5	1,031	735.1	3,655
2008	901.2	1,168	1,406	884.4	3,773
2007	1,156	1,418	1,501	1,142	5,216
2006	1,097	1,192	1,267	1,048	4,603
2005	927.3	1,037	1,086	1,038	4,088

Earnings Per Share ($)

	1Q	2Q	3Q	4Q	Year
2010	0.03	0.45	E0.53	E0.24	E1.65
2009	0.20	-0.11	0.38	-1.88	-1.40
2008	0.13	0.34	0.55	-3.92	-2.83
2007	0.36	0.28	0.45	0.29	1.38
2006	0.32	0.34	0.46	0.24	1.36
2005	0.23	0.35	0.42	0.20	1.19

Fiscal year ended Feb. 28. Next earnings report expected: Early January. EPS Estimates based on S&P Operating Earnings; historical GAAP earnings are as reported.

Dividend Data

No cash dividends have been paid.

Please read the Required Disclosures and Analyst Certification on the last page of this report.

Constellation Brands Inc.

STANDARD
&POOR'S

Business Summary October 02, 2009

CORPORATE OVERVIEW. Through an aggressive acquisition program over the past few years, Constellation Brands (formerly Canandaigua Brands) has become a leading international producer and marketer of alcoholic beverages in North America, Europe and Australia. STZ recently restructured into three divisions -- Constellation Wines, Constellation Spirits, and Crown Imports.

Constellation Wines produces and markets table wines, dessert wines and sparkling wines. It is a leading producer and marketer of wine in the U.S., Canada, Australia, and New Zealand and the largest marketer of wine in the U.K. The company sells wines in the popular, premium, super-premium and ultra-premium categories. The higher category wines are supported by vineyard holdings in California, Canada, Australia, New Zealand and Chile. At the end of FY 09 (Feb.), the company operated 19 wineries in the U.S., 11 in Australia, 10 in Canada, four in New Zealand, and one in South Africa.

STZ has developed a premium wine portfolio through acquisitions, selling 18 of the top 100 U.S. table wines in FY 09. Leading wine brands include Arbor Mist, Vendange, Robert Mondavi, Inniskillin, Kim Crawford, Hardys, Nobilo, Al-

ice White, Ruffino, Blackstone, Ravenswood, Estancia, Franciscan Oakville Estate, Simi, Clos du Bois, and Toasted Head.

The former Constellation Beers has been contributed to the Crown Imports joint venture. It imports and markets a diversified line of beer. The company is the largest marketer of imported beer in 25 mostly western states. It distributes six of the top 25 imported beer brands in the U.S.: Corona Extra, the best selling imported beer, Modelo Especial, Corona Light, Pacifico, St. Pauli Girl, and Negra Modelo. It also imports the top-selling Chinese beer, Tsingtao.

Constellation Spirits operates three facilities where it produces and bottles, imports and markets distilled spirits, wine and cider. Principal brands include Black Velvet, Barton, Skol, Fleischmann's Canadian LTD, Montezuma, Ten High, Chi-Chi's prepared cocktails, Mr. Boston, and Inver House.

Company Financials Fiscal Year Ended Feb. 28

Per Share Data ($)	2009	2008	2007	2006	2005	2004	2003	2002	2001	2000
Tangible Book Value	NM	NM	NM	NM	NM	NM	0.39	NM	NM	NM
Cash Flow	-0.69	-2.07	1.95	1.86	1.59	1.39	1.42	1.08	0.95	0.80
Earnings	-1.40	-2.83	-1.38	1.36	1.19	1.03	1.10	0.79	0.65	0.52
S&P Core Earnings	-0.04	1.13	1.41	1.24	1.02	0.96	0.97	0.66	0.54	NA
Dividends	Nil	Nil	Nil	Nil	Nil	Nil	Nil	Nil	Nil	Nil
Payout Ratio	Nil	Nil	Nil	Nil	Nil	Nil	Nil	Nil	Nil	Nil
Calendar Year	2008	2007	2006	2005	2004	2003	2002	2001	2000	1999
Prices:High	23.81	29.17	29.14	31.60	23.91	17.33	16.00	11.63	7.38	7.69
Prices:Low	10.66	18.83	23.32	21.15	14.65	10.95	10.53	6.63	5.05	5.36
P/E Ratio:High	NM	NM	22	23	20	17	15	15	11	15
P/E Ratio:Low	NM	NM	18	16	12	11	10	8	8	10

Income Statement Analysis (Million $)

	2009	2008	2007	2006	2005	2004	2003	2002	2001	2000
Revenue	3,655	3,773	5,216	4,603	4,088	3,552	2,732	2,821	2,397	2,340
Operating Income	711	704	895	840	689	601	470	394	315	281
Depreciation	150	160	140	128	104	82.0	60.1	51.9	44.6	40.9
Interest Expense	316	342	269	190	138	145	105	114	109	106
Pretax Income	-107	-441	535	477	432	344	335	230	162	129
Effective Tax Rate	NM	NM	38.0%	31.8%	36.0%	36.0%	39.3%	40.0%	40.0%	40.0%
Net Income	-301	-613	332	325	276	220	203	138	97.3	77.4
S&P Core Earnings	-10.7	243	334	288	230	199	181	115	80.7	NA

Balance Sheet & Other Financial Data (Million $)

	2009	2008	2007	2006	2005	2004	2003	2002	2001	2000
Cash	13.1	20.5	33.5	10.9	17.6	37.1	13.8	8.96	146	34.3
Current Assets	2,535	3,199	3,023	2,701	2,734	2,071	1,330	1,231	1,191	996
Total Assets	8,037	10,053	9,438	7,401	7,804	5,559	3,196	3,069	2,512	2,349
Current Liabilities	1,326	1,718	1,591	1,298	1,138	1,030	585	595	427	438
Long Term Debt	3,971	4,649	3,715	2,516	3,205	1,779	1,192	1,293	1,307	1,237
Common Equity	1,908	2,766	3,418	2,975	2,780	2,378	1,207	956	616	521
Total Capital	6,423	7,950	7,607	5,862	6,375	4,344	2,544	2,412	2,056	1,874
Capital Expenditures	129	144	192	132	120	105	71.6	71.1	68.2	57.7
Cash Flow	-151	-454	467	444	370	297	263	190	142	118
Current Ratio	1.9	1.9	1.9	2.1	2.4	2.0	2.3	2.1	2.8	2.3
% Long Term Debt of Capitalization	61.8	58.5	48.8	42.9	50.3	41.0	46.8	53.6	63.6	66.0
% Net Income of Revenue	NM	NM	6.4	7.1	6.8	6.2	7.4	4.9	4.1	3.3
% Return on Assets	NM	NM	3.9	4.3	4.1	5.0	6.5	4.9	4.0	3.7
% Return on Equity	NM	NM	10.2	11.0	10.3	12.1	18.5	17.5	17.1	16.2

Data as orig reptd.; bef. results of disc opers/spec. items. Per share data adj. for stk. divs.; EPS diluted. E-Estimated. NA-Not Available. NM-Not Meaningful. NR-Not Ranked. UR-Under Review.

Office: 207 High Point Dr Bldg 100, Victor, NY 14564-1061.
Telephone: 585-678-7100.
Website: http://www.cbrands.com
Chrmn: R. Sands

Pres & CEO: R. Sands
EVP, CFO & Chief Acctg Officer: R.P. Ryder
EVP & Chief Admin Officer: W.K. Wilson
EVP & General Counsel: T.J. Mullin

Investor Contact: P. Yahn-Urlaub (585-218-3838)
Board Members: B. A. Fromberg, J. K. Hauswald, J. A. Locke, III, P. M. Perez, R. Sands, R. Sands, P. L. Smith, P. H. Soderberg, M. Zupan

Founded: 1972
Domicile: Delaware
Employees: 6,600

The McGraw-Hill Companies

Constellation Energy Group Inc.

STANDARD
&POOR'S

S&P Recommendation	HOLD ★★★☆☆	Price $32.08 (as of Nov 27, 2009)	12-Mo. Target Price $33.00	Investment Style Large-Cap Blend

GICS Sector Utilities
Sub-Industry Independent Power Producers & Energy Traders

Summary This company, the largest wholesale power supplier in the U.S. and the parent of Baltimore Gas and Electric, has agreed to a major asset sale and partnership with Electricite de France.

Key Stock Statistics (Source S&P, Vickers, company reports)

52-Wk Range	$33.87– 15.05	S&P Oper. EPS 2009**E**	3.30	Market Capitalization(B)	$6.445	Beta		1.09
Trailing 12-Month EPS	$-7.11	S&P Oper. EPS 2010**E**	3.20	Yield (%)	2.99	S&P 3-Yr. Proj. EPS CAGR(%)		-1
Trailing 12-Month P/E	NM	P/E on S&P Oper. EPS 2009**E**	9.7	Dividend Rate/Share	$0.96	S&P Credit Rating		BBB-
$10K Invested 5 Yrs Ago	$8,276	Common Shares Outstg. (M)	200.9	Institutional Ownership (%)	67			

Price Performance

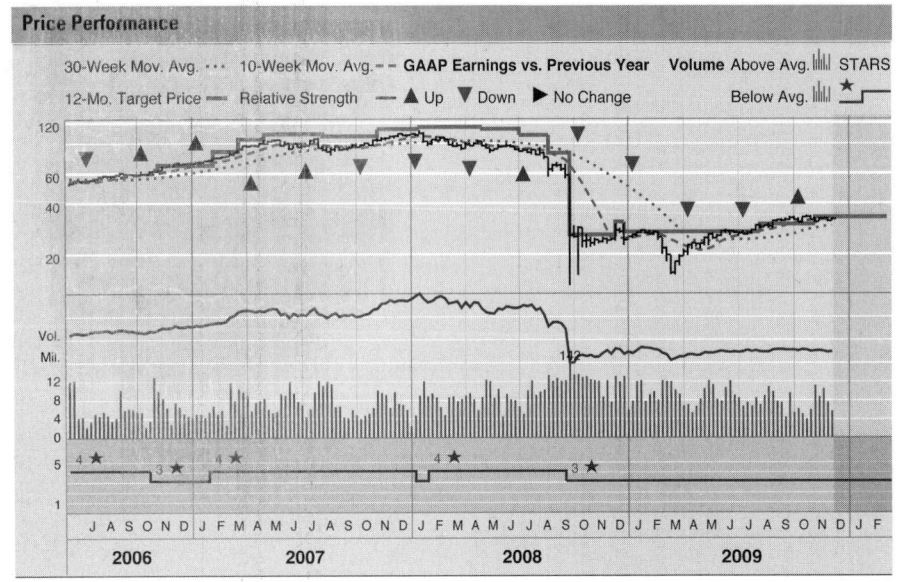

30-Week Mov. Avg. · · · 10-Week Mov. Avg. – – **GAAP Earnings vs. Previous Year** Volume Above Avg. ▌▐▐ STARS
12-Mo. Target Price — Relative Strength — ▲ Up ▼ Down ▶ No Change   Below Avg. ▐▐▐ ★

Options: ASE, CBOE, P, Ph

Analysis prepared by **Justin McCann** on October 27, 2009, when the stock traded at **$ 31.90**.

Highlights

► We expect the $6.5 billion investment agreement with Electricite de France to close, pending required approvals, in the fourth quarter of 2009. We believe the partnership with EDF has long-term strategic value given the expected expansion of nuclear facilities in the U.S. For the near term, we believe the transaction will strengthen CEG's liquidity position as it works through difficult market conditions.

► Excluding $2.41 of one-time charges (related to divestitures, impairments and merger costs), we expect operating EPS in 2009 to decline about 13% from 2008 operating EPS of $3.57, primarily reflecting the absence of earnings from divested assets, more shares outstanding, and reduced trading activities, partially offset by higher-margin power contract renewals.

► For 2010, we project an approximate 3% increase from anticipated operating EPS in 2009, reflecting our expectation of a gradual improvement in the economy and power markets. However, strong cash flow in the first half of 2009 increased CEG's cash balances by about $800 million, and its net available liquidity had doubled to around $5.0 billion as of June 30, 2009.

Investment Rationale/Risk

► While the transaction with Electricite de France values CEG's assets at nearly twice the $4.7 billion ($26.50 a share) that was offered in the terminated acquisition with MidAmerican Energy, the transaction is an asset sale and not a purchase of CEG shares. CEG initially had sought to be acquired, given a severe liquidity crisis brought about by the adverse effects that sharply higher commodity prices had on its derivative assets and liabilities, collateral requirements, and counterparty credit exposures.

► Risks to our recommendation and target price include the possibility that the Electicite de France transaction does not receive the required regulatory approvals, or that CEG's liquidity position substantially deteriorates.

► The stock has recovered more than 45% since the 8% decline that occurred on February 18, the day CEG declared a nearly 50% cut in its dividend. With the cut, which should result in annual savings of $190 million, the dividend payout ratio was reduced from nearly 60% of our current EPS estimate for 2009 to 31%. Our 12-month target price is $33, a discount-to-peers P/E of 10.3X our EPS forecast for 2010.

Qualitative Risk Assessment

LOW	MEDIUM	**HIGH**

Our risk assessment reflects our view that the stability of earnings provided by CEG's regulated electric and gas utility operations is more than offset by the cyclical and volatile earnings of the unregulated merchant energy business, including power generation, energy, and energy-related marketing and trading.

Quantitative Evaluations

S&P Quality Ranking B

D	C	B-	**B**	B+	A-	A	A+

Relative Strength Rank MODERATE

59

LOWEST = 1   HIGHEST = 99

Revenue/Earnings Data

Revenue (Million $)

	1Q	2Q	3Q	4Q	Year
2009	4,303	3,864	4,028	--	--
2008	4,827	5,077	5,324	4,926	19,818
2007	5,111	4,876	5,856	5,349	21,193
2006	4,859	4,379	5,393	4,644	19,285
2005	3,630	3,549	4,922	5,159	17,132
2004	3,037	2,793	3,435	3,286	12,550

Earnings Per Share ($)

2009	-0.62	0.04	0.69	E0.26	E3.30
2008	0.81	0.95	-1.26	-7.75	-7.34
2007	1.08	0.64	1.37	1.42	4.51
2006	0.56	0.41	1.69	1.46	4.12
2005	0.67	0.66	1.02	1.04	3.38
2004	0.66	0.77	1.19	0.76	3.40

Fiscal year ended Dec. 31. Next earnings report expected: Mid February. EPS Estimates based on S&P Operating Earnings; historical GAAP earnings are as reported.

Dividend Data (Dates: mm/dd Payment Date: mm/dd/yy)

Amount ($)	Date Decl.	Ex-Div. Date	Stk. of Record	Payment Date
0.240	02/18	03/06	03/10	04/01/09
0.240	05/29	06/08	06/10	07/01/09
0.240	07/24	09/08	09/10	10/01/09
0.240	10/23	12/08	12/10	01/04/10

Dividends have been paid since 1910. Source: Company reports.

Please read the Required Disclosures and Analyst Certification on the last page of this report.

The McGraw-Hill Companies

Constellation Energy Group Inc.

STANDARD &POOR'S

Business Summary October 27, 2009

CORPORATE OVERVIEW. Constellation Energy is the largest U.S. wholesale power seller and biggest competitive supplier of electricity to large commercial and industrial customers. It is also the holding company for Baltimore Gas & Electric Company, a regulated utility.

IMPACT OF MAJOR DEVELOPMENTS. On December 17, 2008, Constellation Energy reached a definitive agreement with EDF Development, Inc., a wholly owned subsidiary of Electricite de France, which has the largest and most modern nuclear capacity in the world, under which EDF would acquire a 49.99% interest in CEG's nuclear business for $4.5 billion. The agreement was announced on the same day that CEG and MidAmerican Energy Holdings, which is a privately held subsidiary of Berkshire Hathaway, announced that they had jointly agreed to terminate their merger agreement of September 19, 2008. The agreement with EDF (which is 84%-owned by the French state and already owns about 9.5% of CEG) included an immediate $1 billion cash investment in the form of nonconvertible preferred stock, which will be surrendered to CEG upon the completion of the transaction and credited against the $4.5 billion purchase price. EDF also provided CEG with a two-year asset put option to sell to EDF non-nuclear generation assets with a value of up to $2 billion, and a $600 million interim backstop liquidity facility that would remain available until either six months after the investment agreement or, if earlier, receipt of all the regulatory approvals related to the transfer of the non-nuclear generation assets. While the asset sale transaction will require feder-

al approvals, it will not require approval by shareholders or, since CEG's utility operations are not affected, state regulators. The transaction is expected to be completed, subject to required approvals, during the third quarter of 2009.

Under the terms of the September 19, 2008, merger agreement that was terminated on December 17, 2008, MidAmerican had agreed to purchase all of the outstanding shares of CEG for $4.7 billion in cash, or $26.50 a share. The announcement of that agreement followed several days of unprecedented volatility in CEG shares, which reflected, we believe, investor fears that the company would risk bankruptcy if it were unable to access the liquidity it needed for its commodities-trading business. Upon the signing of that agreement, CEG received $1 billion from MidAmerican in the form of preferred equity yielding 8.0%. Under the provisions of the termination agreement, these preferred shares were converted into a $1 billion note at 14% interest, that would mature on December 31, 2009. MidAmerican would also receive about 20 million shares of CEG common stock (about 9.9%), as well as a termination fee of $175 million and an additional $418 million for common stock that could not be issued due to regulatory limits.

Company Financials Fiscal Year Ended Dec. 31

Per Share Data ($)	2008	2007	2006	2005	2004	2003	2002	2001	2000	1999
Tangible Book Value	15.08	27.46	24.66	26.76	25.99	23.81	22.71	23.44	20.88	19.95
Earnings	-7.34	4.51	4.12	3.38	3.40	2.85	3.20	0.52	2.30	2.18
S&P Core Earnings	-7.77	4.26	3.93	3.31	3.33	2.66	1.75	0.34	NA	NA
Dividends	1.91	1.74	1.51	1.34	1.14	1.04	0.96	0.48	1.68	1.68
Payout Ratio	NM	39%	37%	40%	34%	36%	30%	92%	73%	77%
Prices:High	107.97	104.29	70.20	62.60	44.90	39.61	32.38	50.14	52.06	31.50
Prices:Low	13.00	68.78	50.55	43.01	35.89	25.17	19.30	20.90	27.06	24.69
P/E Ratio:High	NM	23	17	19	13	14	10	96	23	14
P/E Ratio:Low	NM	15	12	13	11	9	6	40	12	11

Income Statement Analysis (Million $)										
Revenue	19,818	21,193	19,285	17,132	12,550	9,703	4,703	3,928	3,879	3,787
Depreciation	560	558	524	542	526	479	481	419	470	450
Maintenance	NA	NA	NA	NA	NA	NA	NA	NA	NA	186
Fixed Charges Coverage	0.41	5.09	4.01	3.50	3.40	3.12	2.90	3.01	3.12	2.98
Construction Credits	NA	NA	NA	NA	NA	NA	NA	NA	NA	NA
Effective Tax Rate	NM	33.9%	31.9%	25.2%	22.6%	36.2%	37.1%	31.5%	40.0%	36.3%
Net Income	-1,314	822	749	607	589	476	526	82.4	345	326
S&P Core Earnings	-1,391	777	714	594	578	444	290	54.9	NA	NA

Balance Sheet & Other Financial Data (Million $)										
Gross Property	15,729	14,513	13,680	14,403	14,315	13,580	12,354	11,862	10,442	8,989
Capital Expenditures	1,934	1,296	963	760	704	658	850	1,318	1,079	436
Net Property	10,717	9,767	9,222	10,067	10,087	9,602	7,957	7,700	6,644	5,523
Capitalization:Long Term Debt	5,289	4,851	4,222	4,559	5,003	5,229	4,804	2,903	3,349	2,765
Capitalization:% Long Term Debt	62.4	47.6	47.8	48.1	51.4	55.8	55.4	43.0	51.5	48.0
Capitalization:Preferred	Nil	Nil	Nil	Nil	Nil	Nil	Nil	Nil	Nil	Nil
Capitalization:% Preferred	Nil	Nil	Nil	Nil	Nil	Nil	Nil	Nil	Nil	Nil
Capitalization:Common	3,181	5,340	4,609	4,916	4,727	4,141	3,862	3,844	3,153	2,993
Capitalization:% Common	37.6	52.4	52.2	51.9	48.6	44.2	44.6	57.0	48.5	52.0
Total Capital	9,211	11,849	10,419	10,720	11,105	10,833	10,083	8,271	7,943	7,157
% Operating Ratio	94.8	95.3	94.7	94.5	92.2	91.6	87.2	78.3	84.3	84.8
% Earned on Net Property	9.4	15.0	13.1	10.5	17.0	17.1	17.8	5.0	13.3	13.6
% Return on Revenue	NM	3.9	3.9	3.5	4.7	4.9	11.2	2.1	8.9	8.6
% Return on Invested Capital	2.7	10.1	11.4	9.2	9.0	8.2	9.8	10.5	8.2	7.8
% Return on Common Equity	NM	16.5	15.7	12.6	13.3	11.9	13.6	2.3	11.2	10.9

Data as orig reptd.; bef. results of disc opers/spec. items. Per share data adj. for stk. divs.; EPS diluted. E-Estimated. NA-Not Available. NM-Not Meaningful. NR-Not Ranked. UR-Under Review.

Office: 100 Constellation Way, Baltimore, MD 21202-3142.
Telephone: 410-783-2800.
Website: http://www.constellation.com
Chrmn, Pres & CEO: M.A. Shattuck, III

Vice Chrmn, COO & EVP: M.J. Wallace
SVP, Secy & General Counsel: C.A. Berardesco
CFO: J.W. Thayer
Chief Acctg Officer & Treas: R.K. Feuerman

Investor Contact: K. Hadlock (410-864-6440)
Board Members: A. C. Berzin, J. T. Brady, J. R. Curtiss, F. A. Hrabowski, III, N. Lampton, R. J. Lawless, L. M. Martin, M. A. Shattuck, III, J. L. Skolds, M. D. Sullivan, M. J. Wallace, Y. C. de Balmann

Founded: 1906
Domicile: Maryland
Employees: 10,200

The McGraw-Hill Companies

Convergys Corp

STANDARD
&POOR'S

S&P Recommendation	HOLD ★★★☆☆	Price $11.12 (as of Nov 27, 2009)	12-Mo. Target Price $12.00	Investment Style Large-Cap Growth

GICS Sector Information Technology
Sub-Industry Data Processing & Outsourced Services

Summary This company is a provider of outsourced billing and customer management solutions for communications companies and state governments.

Key Stock Statistics (Source S&P, Vickers, company reports)

52-Wk Range	$11.97–5.30	S&P Oper. EPS 2009**E**	1.11	Market Capitalization(B)	$1.367	Beta	1.59
Trailing 12-Month EPS	$-1.21	S&P Oper. EPS 2010**E**	1.16	Yield (%)	Nil	S&P 3-Yr. Proj. EPS CAGR(%)	7
Trailing 12-Month P/E	NM	P/E on S&P Oper. EPS 2009**E**	10.0	Dividend Rate/Share	Nil	S&P Credit Rating	BB+
$10K Invested 5 Yrs Ago	$7,345	Common Shares Outstg. (M)	123.0	Institutional Ownership (%)	86		

Price Performance

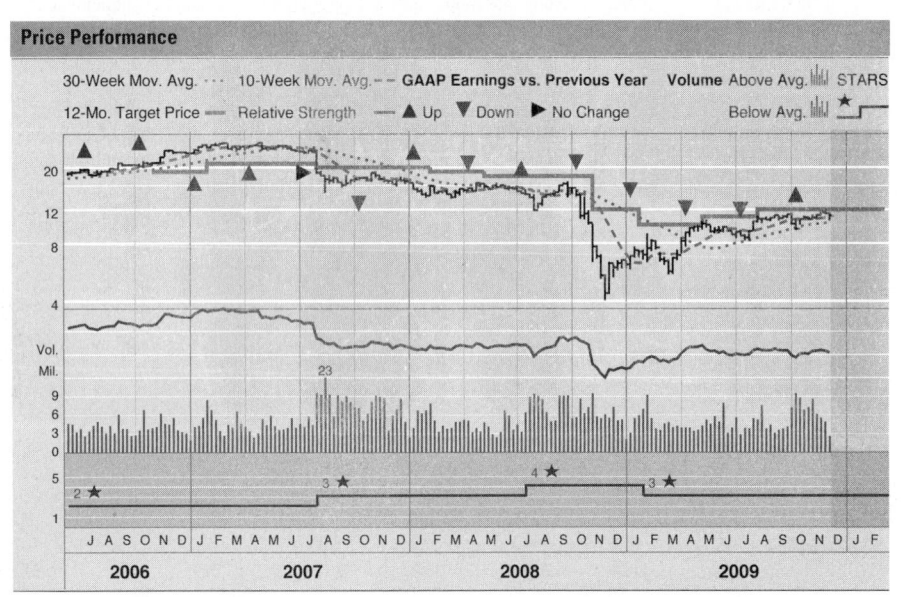

30-Week Mov. Avg. · · · · 10-Week Mov. Avg. - - **GAAP Earnings vs. Previous Year** Volume Above Avg. ▮▮▮ STARS
12-Mo. Target Price — Relative Strength — ▲ Up ▼ Down ► No Change Below Avg. ▮▮▮ ★

Options: CBOE, P, Ph

Analysis prepared by **James Moorman, CFA** on November 02, 2009, when the stock traded at **$ 10.70**.

Highlights

► Following a revenue decline of 2.1% in 2008, we expect a decline of 3.0% in 2009 and an increase of 2.6% in 2010, as we think gains at the larger customer management group (CMG) and in HR management will be largely offset by declines in the information management group (IMG). Growth at CMG started to pick up in late 2008, but has largely stalled in 2009. We think the company has a healthy pipeline that should provide low growth in 2010.

► We expect operating margins to contract slightly in 2009 to 5.9% but then expect an increase to 6.8% in 2010, from 6.5% in 2008. We believe the company remains diligent in reducing costs, and we expect significant cash flow improvement in the HR management group. In addition, we look for slight margin improvement at CMG.

► Following EPS of $1.22 in 2008, we expect $1.11 for 2009 and forecast $1.16 for 2010. The company repurchased 7.7 million shares in 2008, but we do not expect significant share repurchases over the near term as we believe management is focused on reducing debt.

Investment Rationale/Risk

► We believe recent restructuring efforts and buildout of the small HR management segment are intended to offset the sizable challenges we see related to customer migration and competition. We think HR management could become the growth engine, as we expect only slight growth from CMG in 2009 and expect a decline IMG in 2009. We believe the shares are fairly valued at current levels.

► Risks to our recommendation and target price include reduced business with large customers, below-average growth in demand from non-communications companies, ongoing operating losses in employee care, the integration of the Intervoice acquisition, and currency losses from international operations.

► We believe CVG deserves a P/E-to-growth roughly in line with peers. Our 12-month target price of $12 is based on a P/E-to-growth ratio of 1.4X, or a P/E of 10X applied to our 2010 EPS estimate. We believe CVG's cash balance provides some support for the shares.

Qualitative Risk Assessment

LOW	MEDIUM	HIGH

Our risk assessment for Convergys reflects the competitiveness of serving the communications industry, and concentration of its customer base with approximately 33% of revenues coming from three companies. This is offset by the company's use of long-term contracts.

Quantitative Evaluations

S&P Quality Ranking   B-

D	C	B-	B	B+	A-	A	A+

Relative Strength Rank   MODERATE

58

LOWEST = 1   HIGHEST = 99

Revenue/Earnings Data

Revenue (Million $)

	1Q	2Q	3Q	4Q	Year
2009	694.7	682.7	765.4	--	--
2008	716.4	689.5	676.2	703.7	2,786
2007	719.9	707.0	703.7	713.8	2,844
2006	675.3	691.8	702.7	720.0	2,790
2005	637.3	630.4	644.8	669.6	2,582
2004	573.9	601.7	639.9	672.2	2,488

Earnings Per Share ($)

2009	0.23	-0.50	-0.70	E0.32	E1.11
2008	0.28	0.32	-1.15	-0.24	-0.75
2007	0.31	0.28	0.30	0.34	1.23
2006	0.26	0.28	0.32	0.32	1.17
2005	0.22	0.18	0.30	0.16	0.86
2004	0.22	0.20	0.21	0.14	0.77

Fiscal year ended Dec. 31. Next earnings report expected: Late January. EPS Estimates based on S&P Operating Earnings; historical GAAP earnings are as reported.

Dividend Data

No cash dividends have been paid.

Convergys Corp

STANDARD
&POOR'S

Business Summary November 02, 2009

CORPORATE OVERVIEW. Convergys Corp. is a provider of outsourced, integrated billing, and employee, and customer care software and services. The information management group, known as IMG (13% of revenues and 3% operating margin in the third quarter of 2009), serves clients principally by providing and managing complex billing and information software that addresses all segments of the communications industry.

The customer management group, known as CMG (64% and 7%), provides outsourced customer management services for clients, utilizing its advanced information systems capabilities and industry experience through call centers and Web-based assistance programs. Communications customers contributed 58% of CMG revenues in 2007. Non-communications clients include technology companies and a number of financial institutions.

The HR management segment (23% due to accelerated revenue recognition, and operating losses) helps clients with administration of benefits, and human resources, recruiting and payroll services using a single point of contact system.

The company also has a 45% limited partnership interest in the Cellular Partnership, which operates a cellular telecommunications business in central and southwestern Ohio and northern Kentucky.

COMPETITIVE LANDSCAPE. Convergys's chief competitor for communications business is Amdocs, which serves the customer care and billing needs of telecom providers such as Sprint Nextel and wireline and wireless operations at AT&T Inc., as well as a number of cable providers. We expect DOX to compete aggressively to capture additional customers given the rollout of triple-play packages of voice, video and data services by telecom and cable providers. In January 2006, Sprint Nextel announced an eight-year agreement with Amdocs to provide a single billing and customer care platform, allowing the wireless phone company to migrate off of Convergys's system. This led to an accelerated decline in billing revenue from Sprint in the second half of 2007. The customer loss followed the migration of Cingular customers off of CVG's billing system, which was largely completed in the first quarter of 2007. The HR management and non-communications customer care businesses compete with companies such as Accenture, Automatic Data Processing and Hewitt Associates.

Company Financials Fiscal Year Ended Dec. 31

Per Share Data ($)	2008	2007	2006	2005	2004	2003	2002	2001	2000	1999
Tangible Book Value	0.38	4.56	3.85	3.13	2.62	2.60	2.54	3.08	2.41	1.13
Cash Flow	0.32	2.13	2.18	1.89	1.74	1.99	1.70	1.81	2.25	1.73
Earnings	-0.75	1.23	1.17	0.86	0.77	1.15	0.88	0.80	1.23	0.89
S&P Core Earnings	-0.44	1.23	1.12	0.81	0.60	0.91	0.54	0.51	NA	NA
Dividends	Nil	Nil	Nil	Nil	Nil	Nil	Nil	Nil	Nil	Nil
Payout Ratio	Nil	Nil	Nil	Nil	Nil	Nil	Nil	Nil	Nil	Nil
Prices:High	16.99	27.26	24.93	17.90	19.96	20.80	37.98	50.25	55.44	31.75
Prices:Low	4.02	14.67	15.43	12.57	12.30	11.30	12.50	24.46	26.63	14.50
P/E Ratio:High	NM	22	21	21	26	18	43	63	45	36
P/E Ratio:Low	NM	12	13	15	16	10	14	31	22	16

Income Statement Analysis (Million $)										
Revenue	2,786	2,844	2,790	2,582	2,488	2,289	2,286	2,321	2,163	1,763
Operating Income	310	378	408	392	327	415	498	543	489	388
Depreciation	133	124	143	147	141	124	137	176	161	130
Interest Expense	22.6	17.5	22.8	21.2	10.3	6.90	11.0	20.0	32.9	32.5
Pretax Income	-164	246	245	213	173	272	244	255	317	223
Effective Tax Rate	NM	31.0%	32.1%	42.5%	35.7%	36.8%	40.3%	45.5%	38.6%	38.4%
Net Income	-92.9	170	166	123	112	172	146	139	195	137
S&P Core Earnings	-53.6	169	160	117	87.6	133	88.9	91.3	NA	NA

Balance Sheet & Other Financial Data (Million $)										
Cash	240	120	236	196	58.4	37.2	12.2	41.1	28.2	30.8
Current Assets	978	862	930	849	593	420	418	523	481	298
Total Assets	2,841	2,564	2,540	2,411	2,208	1,810	1,620	1,743	1,780	1,580
Current Liabilities	798	427	596	618	577	543	462	492	359	387
Long Term Debt	406	259	260	298	302	58.8	4.60	3.60	291	250
Common Equity	1,150	1,522	1,455	1,355	1,285	1,144	1,126	1,227	1,113	927
Total Capital	1,816	1,862	1,759	1,697	1,588	1,202	1,131	1,230	1,403	1,178
Capital Expenditures	92.1	102	105	131	156	174	90.8	114	175	155
Cash Flow	39.6	294	309	270	253	296	283	315	356	267
Current Ratio	1.2	2.0	1.6	1.4	1.0	0.8	0.9	1.1	1.3	0.8
% Long Term Debt of Capitalization	22.3	14.6	14.8	17.5	19.0	4.9	0.4	0.3	20.7	21.3
% Net Income of Revenue	NM	6.0	6.0	4.7	4.5	7.5	6.4	6.0	9.0	7.8
% Return on Assets	NM	6.6	6.7	5.3	5.5	10.0	8.7	7.8	11.6	9.0
% Return on Equity	NM	11.4	11.8	9.3	9.2	15.1	12.4	11.8	19.1	16.5

Data as orig reptd.; bef. results of disc opers/spec. items. Per share data adj. for stk. divs.; EPS diluted. E-Estimated. NA-Not Available. NM-Not Meaningful. NR-Not Ranked. UR-Under Review.

Office: 201 E 4th St, Cincinnati, OH 45202-4206.
Telephone: 513-723-7000.
Email: investor@convergys.com
Website: http://www.convergys.com

Chrmn: P.A. Odeen
Pres & CEO: D.F. Dougherty
SVP, Chief Acctg Officer, Treas & Cntlr: T.M. Wesolowski
SVP, Secy & General Counsel: K.R. Bowman

CFO: E.C. Shanks
Board Members: Z. Baird, J. F. Barrett, W. W. Brittain, Jr., R. R. Devenuti, D. B. Dillon, D. F. Dougherty, J. H. Fox, J. E. Gibbs, T. L. Monahan, III, R. L. Nelson, P. A. Odeen, B. S. Rosenstein, R. F. Wallman, D. R. Whitwam

Founded: 1998
Domicile: Ohio
Employees: 75,000

Corning Inc

STANDARD
&POOR'S

S&P Recommendation **BUY** ★★★★☆		Price $16.58 (as of Nov 27, 2009)	12-Mo. Target Price $19.00	Investment Style Large-Cap Blend

GICS Sector Information Technology
Sub-Industry Electronic Components

Summary GLW, once an old-line housewares company, is now a leading maker of glass substrates used by the electronics industry and fiber optic equipment used by the telecommunications industry.

Key Stock Statistics (Source S&P, Vickers, company reports)

52-Wk Range	$17.22– 7.90	S&P Oper. EPS 2009**E**	1.30	Market Capitalization(B)	$25.800	Beta		1.28
Trailing 12-Month EPS	$0.97	S&P Oper. EPS 2010**E**	1.60	Yield (%)	1.21	S&P 3-Yr. Proj. EPS CAGR(%)		10
Trailing 12-Month P/E	17.1	P/E on S&P Oper. EPS 2009**E**	12.8	Dividend Rate/Share	$0.20	S&P Credit Rating		BBB+
$10K Invested 5 Yrs Ago	$13,671	Common Shares Outstg. (M)	1,556.1	Institutional Ownership (%)	79			

Price Performance

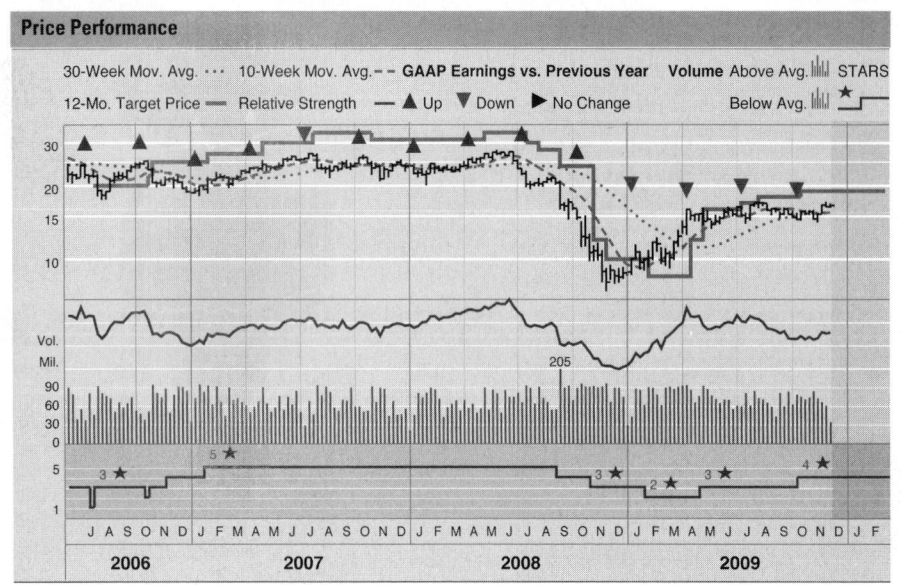

30-Week Mov. Avg. ··· 10-Week Mov. Avg. --- GAAP Earnings vs. Previous Year   Volume Above Avg. STARS
12-Mo. Target Price — Relative Strength ▲ Up ▼ Down ► No Change   Below Avg.

Options: ASE, CBOE, P, Ph

Analysis prepared by **Todd Rosenbluth** on October 27, 2009, when the stock traded at **$ 15.55.**

Highlights

► After a projected decline of 10% in sales during 2009, we see GLW's sales rebounding 10% in 2010. Following pressure in late 2008, we believe improved consumer spending and a more normalized supply chain in 2009 has led to a recovery in the previously hard-hit display segment, and we see this continuing as global economies improve. Due to increased broadband spending by customers, we see gains in the telecom unit during 2010, but with the U.S. automotive industry still weak, we expect the environmental segment to struggle.

► We believe gross margins bottomed at 27% in the first quarter of 2009. We forecast an average of 42% in 2010, up from a projected 38% in 2009. We expect the high-margin display segment to improve, as glass volumes climbed in the third quarter of 2009, even as investment in next-generation technology increases. With increased demand, we expect capacity utilization to stay at more normal levels in late 2009 and in 2010.

► We expect equity earnings and a minuscule tax rate to support net income. Our EPS estimates are $1.30 for 2009 and $1.60 for 2010.

Investment Rationale/Risk

► Upon reporting stronger-than-expected third-quarter 2009 results, GLW indicated that supply chain contraction that had plagued the supplier had improved significantly, supporting sales growth. We believe continued stability and improvement in display volume as global economies recover will result in margin expansion in 2010. We believe recent cost reductions and a sound balance sheet, even following a recent acquisition, provide additional investment merits for the company. We view the stock as undervalued at recent levels.

► Risks to our recommendation and target price include weaker-than-expected demand for flat panel displays, worsening pricing on display technologies products, and lackluster demand for products at the telecom unit.

► Our 12-month target price of $19 is based on a multiple of 12X our 2010 EPS estimate, a slight discount to peers that we believe have stronger growth prospects. At a recent P/E multiple of under 10X, we view GLW as attractive. GLW also has a dividend yield of approximately 1%.

Qualitative Risk Assessment

LOW	**MEDIUM**	HIGH

Our risk assessment reflects Corning's exposure to intense competition in its major businesses, offset by its market leadership and positive cash flow, and our view of its strong balance sheet.

Quantitative Evaluations

S&P Quality Ranking B

D	C	B-	**B**	B+	A-	A	A+

Relative Strength Rank STRONG

77

LOWEST = 1   HIGHEST = 99

Revenue/Earnings Data

Revenue (Million $)

	1Q	2Q	3Q	4Q	Year
2009	989.0	1,395	1,479	--	--
2008	1,617	1,692	1,555	1,084	5,948
2007	1,307	1,418	1,553	1,582	5,860
2006	1,262	1,261	1,282	1,369	5,174
2005	1,050	1,141	1,188	1,200	4,579
2004	844.0	971.0	1,006	1,033	3,854

Earnings Per Share ($)

2009	0.01	0.39	0.41	E0.39	E1.30
2008	0.64	2.01	0.49	0.16	3.32
2007	0.20	0.30	0.38	0.45	1.34
2006	0.16	0.32	0.27	0.41	1.16
2005	0.17	0.11	0.13	-0.02	0.38
2004	0.04	0.07	-1.79	0.11	-1.57

Fiscal year ended Dec. 31. Next earnings report expected: Late January. EPS Estimates based on S&P Operating Earnings; historical GAAP earnings are as reported.

Dividend Data (Dates: mm/dd Payment Date: mm/dd/yy)

Amount ($)	Date Decl.	Ex-Div. Date	Stk. of Record	Payment Date
0.050	02/04	02/26	03/02	03/31/09
0.050	04/30	05/28	06/01	06/30/09
0.050	07/15	08/27	08/31	09/30/09
0.050	10/07	11/12	11/16	12/18/09

Dividends have been paid since 2007. Source: Company reports.

Corning Inc

Business Summary October 27, 2009

CORPORATE OVERVIEW. Corning (GLW) is a maker of high-technology fiber optics for the global telecom industry and high-performance glass components for the personal computer and television manufacturing industries. Results are reported in the following primary business segments: display technologies (44% of sales in the first nine months of 2009), telecommunications (33%), environmental technologies (11%), life sciences (6%), and specialty materials and other (6%). In 2008, 55% of total sales were in Asia.

PRIMARY BUSINESS DYNAMICS. The display technologies segment manufactures glass substrates for active matrix liquid crystal displays (LCDs), which are used primarily in notebook computers, flat panel desktop monitors, and LCD televisions. Large substrates (Generation 5 and higher) allow LCD manufacturers to produce larger and a greater number of panels from each substrate. The larger size leads to economies of scale for LCD manufacturers and has enabled lower display prices for consumers, which may continue in the future. At the end of 2008, approximately 92% of Corning's and Samsung Corning Precision's volume of LCD glass was Generation 5 and higher. Due to weaker retail demand for end products and an inventory build at set assembly customers, glass volume in the fourth quarter of 2008 declined from the level

achieved in the third quarter. However, first half 2009 volume was stronger due to TV sales growth in China, Japan and North America, and improvement in the supply chain. Volume more than doubled sequentially in the second quarter of 2009, but was up only 4% in the third quarter. Nonetheless, improved demand has helped support GLW's gross margin expansion thus far in 2009, and we see room for expansion in 2010.

The telecom segment produces optical fiber and cable, and hardware and equipment products including cable assemblies, fiber optic hardware and components. We believe demand for fiber-to-the-premise (FTTP) products, which had 7% sequential sales growth in the third quarter of 2009, is being driven by demand from China. In early 2008, Corning initially announced that some existing customers would order its new product Clear Curve, and during its third quarter 2009 earnings call said it saw strong demand for the product, which allows equipment to bend around corners with almost no signal loss.

Company Financials Fiscal Year Ended Dec. 31

Per Share Data ($)	2008	2007	2006	2005	2004	2003	2002	2001	2000	1999
Tangible Book Value	8.49	5.97	4.43	3.43	2.38	2.65	2.14	3.39	3.56	2.60
Cash Flow	3.76	1.72	1.56	0.71	-1.20	0.23	-1.04	-4.74	1.34	1.15
Earnings	3.32	1.34	1.16	0.38	-1.57	-0.18	-1.85	-5.89	0.46	0.65
S&P Core Earnings	3.29	1.33	1.17	0.34	-1.03	-0.37	-1.89	-3.11	NA	NA
Dividends	0.20	0.10	Nil	Nil	Nil	Nil	Nil	0.12	0.24	0.24
Payout Ratio	6%	7%	Nil	Nil	Nil	Nil	Nil	NM	52%	37%
Prices:High	28.07	27.25	29.61	21.95	13.89	12.34	11.15	72.19	113.29	43.02
Prices:Low	7.36	18.12	17.50	10.61	9.29	3.34	1.10	6.92	34.33	14.92
P/E Ratio:High	8	20	26	58	NM	NM	NM	NM	NM	66
P/E Ratio:Low	2	14	15	28	NM	NM	NM	NM	NM	23

Income Statement Analysis (Million $)	2008	2007	2006	2005	2004	2003	2002	2001	2000	1999
Revenue	5,948	5,860	5,174	4,579	3,854	3,090	3,164	6,272	7,127	4,297
Operating Income	1,894	1,869	1,489	1,284	892	386	21.0	805	1,929	1,053
Depreciation	695	607	591	512	523	517	661	1,080	765	381
Interest Expense	90.0	101	76.0	116	141	154	179	153	107	79.9
Pretax Income	2,851	2,233	2,421	1,170	-1,137	-550	-2,604	-5,963	840	735
Effective Tax Rate	NM	3.58%	22.9%	49.4%	NM	NM	NM	NM	48.4%	25.7%
Net Income	5,257	2,150	1,855	585	-2,185	-223	-1,780	-5,498	410	477
S&P Core Earnings	5,200	2,134	1,865	520	-1,442	-463	-1,947	-2,908	NA	NA

Balance Sheet & Other Financial Data (Million $)	2008	2007	2006	2005	2004	2003	2002	2001	2000	1999
Cash	2,816	3,516	1,157	1,342	1,009	833	1,471	1,037	138	116
Current Assets	4,619	5,294	4,798	3,860	3,281	2,694	3,825	4,107	4,634	1,783
Total Assets	19,256	15,215	13,065	11,175	9,710	10,752	11,548	12,793	17,526	6,012
Current Liabilities	2,052	2,512	2,319	2,216	2,336	1,553	1,680	1,994	1,949	1,488
Long Term Debt	1,527	1,514	1,696	1,789	2,214	2,668	3,963	4,461	3,966	1,289
Common Equity	13,443	9,496	7,246	5,609	3,752	5,379	4,536	5,414	10,633	2,227
Total Capital	15,034	11,077	8,987	7,441	6,059	8,168	8,713	10,001	14,808	3,814
Capital Expenditures	1,921	1,262	1,182	1,553	857	366	357	1,800	1,525	733
Cash Flow	5,952	2,757	2,446	1,097	-1,662	294	-1,247	-4,418	1,175	858
Current Ratio	2.3	2.1	2.1	1.7	1.4	1.7	2.3	2.1	2.4	1.2
% Long Term Debt of Capitalization	10.2	13.7	18.9	24.0	36.5	32.7	45.5	44.6	26.8	33.8
% Net Income of Revenue	88.4	36.7	35.9	12.8	NM	NM	NM	NM	5.7	11.1
% Return on Assets	30.5	15.2	15.3	5.6	NM	NM	NM	NM	3.4	8.7
% Return on Equity	45.8	25.7	29.1	12.5	NM	NM	NM	NM	6.2	25.5

Data as orig reptd.; bef. results of disc opers/spec. items. Per share data adj. for stk. divs.; EPS diluted. E-Estimated. NA-Not Available. NM-Not Meaningful. NR-Not Ranked. UR-Under Review.

Office: One Riverfront Plaza, Corning, NY 14831-0001.
Telephone: 607-974-9000.
Email: info@corning.com
Website: http://www.corning.com

Chrmn & CEO: W.P. Weeks
Pres & COO: P.F. Volanakis
Vice Chrmn & CFO: J.B. Flaws
EVP & Chief Admin Officer: K.P. Gregg

EVP & CTO: J.A. Miller, Jr.
Board Members: J. S. Brown, R. F. Cummings, Jr., J. B. Flaws, G. Gund, C. M. Gutierrez, J. R. Houghton, K. M. Landgraf, J. J. O'Connor, D. D. Rieman, H. O. Ruding, W. D. Smithburg, H. E. Tookes, II, P. F. Volanakis, W. P. Weeks, M. S. Wrighton

Founded: 1851
Domicile: New York
Employees: 27,000

Costco Wholesale Corp

STANDARD
&POOR'S

S&P Recommendation	HOLD ★★★★★	Price	12-Mo. Target Price	Investment Style
		$60.03 (as of Nov 27, 2009)	$61.00	Large-Cap Blend

GICS Sector Consumer Staples
Sub-Industry Hypermarkets & Super Centers

Summary This company operates about 550 membership warehouses in the U.S., Puerto Rico, Canada, the U.K., Taiwan, Japan, Korea, and Mexico.

Key Stock Statistics (Source S&P, Vickers, company reports)

52-Wk Range	$61.25–38.17	S&P Oper. EPS 2010**E**	2.90	Market Capitalization(B)	$26.172	Beta	0.78
Trailing 12-Month EPS	$2.47	S&P Oper. EPS 2011**E**	NA	Yield (%)	1.20	S&P 3-Yr. Proj. EPS CAGR(%)	16
Trailing 12-Month P/E	24.3	P/E on S&P Oper. EPS 2010**E**	20.7	Dividend Rate/Share	$0.72	S&P Credit Rating	A
$10K Invested 5 Yrs Ago	$12,756	Common Shares Outstg. (M)	436.0	Institutional Ownership (%)	80		

Price Performance

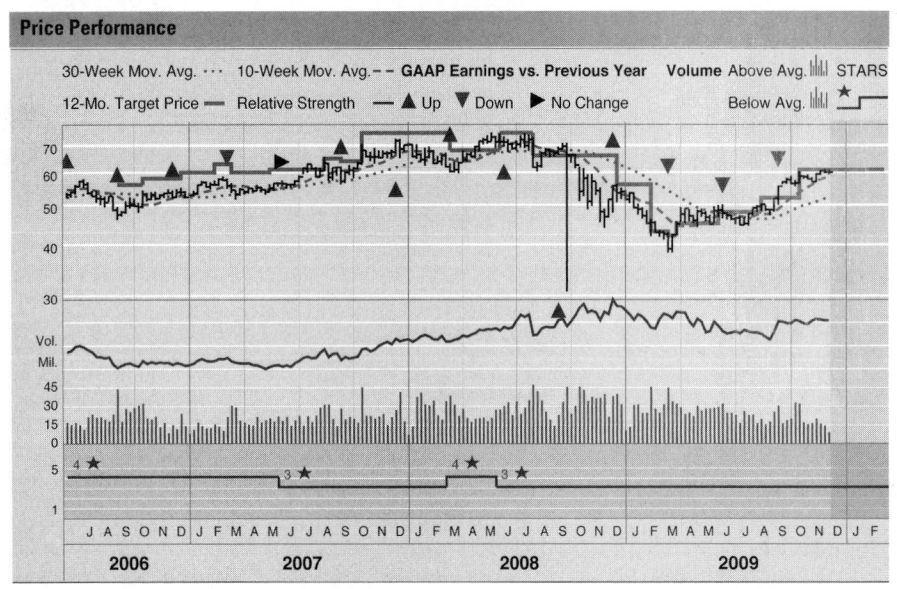

30-Week Mov. Avg. · · · 10-Week Mov. Avg. - - **GAAP Earnings vs. Previous Year** Volume Above Avg. STARS
12-Mo. Target Price — Relative Strength — ▲ Up ▼ Down ▶ No Change Below Avg.

Options: ASE, CBOE, P, Ph

Analysis prepared by **Joseph Agnese** on October 12, 2009, when the stock traded at **$58.51**.

Highlights

► We see net revenues increasing to $72.6 billion in FY 10 (Aug.) from $71.4 billion in FY 09, reflecting a same-store sales rise of 1%, excluding fuel and foreign exchange rates, and about 4% square footage growth. We expect increased traffic to offset lower average basket sizes caused by deflation in produce and electronics. We believe sales should benefit from easier comparisons despite negative impacts from lower gasoline prices and unfavorable foreign currency rates we see in the first quarter of the year.

► We project that margins will widen, reflecting increased demand for discretionary goods and declining product costs, despite rising employee health care costs and aggressive pricing to support traffic trends. We see increased pre-opening expenses, on a rise in new club openings, and higher net interest income due to increased investment income.

► After an expected modest reduction in the share count due to an active share repurchase program, we estimate that FY 10 EPS will increase 15%, to $2.90, from operating EPS of $2.52, excluding one-time charges, in FY 09.

Investment Rationale/Risk

► We expect COST to increase its market share, as we see it pricing aggressively as it maintains a strong value proposition and a relatively upscale product mix that appeals to a more affluent customer base. We see strength in fresh foods and expansion of ancillary businesses offsetting weaker demand for discretionary goods in an adverse economic environment. We think it is well positioned to generate future earnings growth due to new store expansion and what we view as a strong balance sheet.

► Risks to our recommendation and target price include a slowdown in sales due to weakness in the economy, more difficult foreign currency comparisons, and increased cannibalization from new store expansion.

► We believe the stock's valuation will be supported by market share gains stemming from COST's competitively priced offerings and by its strong balance sheet. We apply a P/E of 21X to our FY 10 EPS estimate of $2.90, in line with its five-year median P/E, but a 39% premium compared to the S&P 500, versus a 27% five-year median premium to the S&P 500, to arrive at our 12-month target price of $61.

Qualitative Risk Assessment

LOW	MEDIUM	HIGH

Our risk assessment for Costco Wholesale incorporates our view of its strong balance sheet, its market leadership position, and our expectation that consistent earnings and dividend growth will continue.

Quantitative Evaluations

S&P Quality Ranking A-

D	C	B-	B	B+	A-	A	A+

Relative Strength Rank STRONG

76

LOWEST = 1 HIGHEST = 99

Revenue/Earnings Data

Revenue (Million $)

	1Q	2Q	3Q	4Q	Year
2009	16,395	16,843	15,806	22,378	71,422
2008	15,810	16,960	16,614	23,100	72,483
2007	14,152	15,112	14,659	20,477	64,400
2006	12,933	14,059	13,284	19,875	60,151
2005	11,578	12,658	11,997	16,702	52,935
2004	10,521	11,549	10,897	15,139	48,107

Earnings Per Share ($)

2009	0.60	0.55	0.48	0.85	2.47
2008	0.59	0.74	0.67	0.90	2.89
2007	0.51	0.54	0.49	0.83	2.37
2006	0.45	0.62	0.49	0.75	2.30
2005	0.40	0.62	0.43	0.73	2.18
2004	0.34	0.48	0.42	0.62	1.85

Fiscal year ended Aug. 31. Next earnings report expected: Mid December. EPS Estimates based on S&P Operating Earnings; historical GAAP earnings are as reported.

Dividend Data (Dates: mm/dd Payment Date: mm/dd/yy)

Amount ($)	Date Decl.	Ex-Div. Date	Stk. of Record	Payment Date
0.160	01/28	02/11	02/13	02/27/09
0.180	04/28	05/13	05/15	05/29/09
0.180	07/27	08/12	08/14	08/28/09
0.180	10/08	10/21	10/23	11/06/09

Dividends have been paid since 2004. Source: Company reports.

Please read the Required Disclosures and Analyst Certification on the last page of this report.

Costco Wholesale Corp

**STANDARD
&POOR'S**

Business Summary October 12, 2009

CORPORATE OVERVIEW. Costco Wholesale (formerly Costco Companies, Inc., and prior to that, Price/Costco, Inc.) began the pioneering "I can get it for you wholesale" membership warehouse concept in 1976, in San Diego, CA. The company operated 550 warehouses worldwide as of November 2008, mainly in the U.S. and Canada (including 31 stores operated through a joint venture in Mexico). COST also operates an e-commerce Web site, costco.com.

A typical warehouse format averages about 142,000 sq. ft. Floor plans are designed for economy and efficiency in the use of selling space, in the handling of merchandise, and in the control of inventory. Merchandise is generally stored on racks above the sales floor, and is displayed on pallets containing large quantities of each item, reducing the labor required for handling and stocking. Specific items in each product line are limited to fast-selling models, sizes and colors. COST carries an average of about 4,000 stockkeeping units (SKUs) per warehouse, well below the 40,000 to 60,000 SKUs of a typical discount store or supermarket. By using a membership format, and strictly controlling entrances and exits, the company limited inventory losses (shrinkage) to less than 0.2% of net sales in the past several fiscal years, well below the average of discount competitors.

COST has two primary types of memberships: Gold Star (individual) and Busi-

ness members. Individual memberships are available to employees of federal, state and local governments; financial institutions; corporations; utility and transportation companies; public and private educational institutions; and other organizations. Gold Star membership is $50 annually. There were 20.2 million Gold Star memberships as of September 2008, up from 18.6 million as of September 2007.

Businesses, including individuals with retail sales or business licenses, may become Business members by paying an annual $50 fee, with add-on membership cards available for an annual fee of $40. As of September 2008, there were 5.6 million Business memberships, compared to 5.4 million in September 2007. Executive memberships, available for a $100 annual fee, offer business and individual members savings on services such as merchant credit card processing and small business loans, as well as a 2% annual reward, up to a maximum of $500 annually, on qualified purchases. Executive members made up approximately 26% of the primary membership base in FY 08 (Aug.), up from 23% and 20% in FY 07 and FY 06, respectively.

Company Financials Fiscal Year Ended Aug. 31

Per Share Data ($)	2009	2008	2007	2006	2005	2004	2003	2002	2001	2000
Tangible Book Value	23.27	21.08	19.73	19.78	18.80	16.48	14.33	12.51	10.71	9.37
Cash Flow	NA	4.36	3.60	3.37	3.13	2.74	2.32	2.17	1.90	1.86
Earnings	2.47	2.89	2.37	2.30	2.18	1.85	1.53	1.48	1.29	1.35
S&P Core Earnings	2.53	2.89	2.37	2.30	2.12	1.76	1.40	1.32	1.12	NA
Dividends	0.84	0.61	0.55	0.49	0.43	0.20	Nil	Nil	Nil	Nil
Payout Ratio	34%	21%	23%	21%	20%	11%	Nil	Nil	Nil	Nil
Prices:High	61.25	75.23	72.68	57.94	51.21	50.46	39.02	46.90	46.38	60.50
Prices:Low	38.17	30.70	51.52	46.00	39.48	35.05	27.00	27.09	29.83	25.94
P/E Ratio:High	25	26	31	25	23	27	26	32	36	45
P/E Ratio:Low	15	11	22	20	18	19	18	18	23	19

Income Statement Analysis (Million $)										
Revenue	71,422	72,483	64,400	60,151	52,935	48,107	42,546	38,763	34,797	32,164
Operating Income	NA	2,622	2,189	2,146	1,969	1,827	1,567	1,494	1,312	1,299
Depreciation	728	653	566	515	478	441	391	342	301	254
Interest Expense	NA	103	64.1	12.6	34.4	36.7	36.9	29.1	32.0	39.3
Pretax Income	1,714	1,999	1,710	1,751	1,549	1,401	1,158	1,138	1,003	1,052
Effective Tax Rate	36.6%	35.8%	36.7%	37.0%	31.4%	37.0%	37.8%	38.5%	40.0%	40.0%
Net Income	1,086	1,283	1,083	1,103	1,063	882	721	700	602	631
S&P Core Earnings	1,114	1,283	1,082	1,104	1,044	837	660	624	525	NA

Balance Sheet & Other Financial Data (Million $)										
Cash	3,727	3,275	2,780	1,511	2,063	2,823	1,545	806	603	525
Current Assets	NA	9,462	9,324	8,232	8,086	7,269	5,712	4,631	3,882	3,470
Total Assets	21,979	20,682	19,607	17,495	16,514	15,093	13,192	11,620	10,090	8,634
Current Liabilities	NA	8,874	8,582	7,819	6,609	6,171	5,011	4,450	4,112	3,404
Long Term Debt	2,135	2,206	2,108	215	711	994	1,290	1,211	859	790
Common Equity	10,018	9,192	8,623	9,143	8,881	7,625	6,555	5,694	4,883	4,240
Total Capital	12,319	11,480	10,801	9,422	9,650	8,922	8,181	7,025	5,858	5,139
Capital Expenditures	1,250	1,599	1,386	1,213	995	706	811	1,039	1,448	1,228
Cash Flow	NA	1,936	1,649	1,619	1,541	1,323	1,112	1,042	903	886
Current Ratio	1.1	1.1	1.1	1.1	1.2	1.2	1.1	1.0	0.9	1.0
% Long Term Debt of Capitalization	Nil	19.2	19.5	2.3	7.4	11.1	15.8	17.2	14.7	15.4
% Net Income of Revenue	1.5	1.8	1.7	1.8	2.0	1.8	1.7	1.8	1.7	2.0
% Return on Assets	NA	6.4	5.8	6.5	6.7	6.2	5.8	6.4	6.4	7.8
% Return on Equity	NA	14.4	12.2	12.2	12.9	12.4	11.8	13.2	13.2	16.2

Data as orig reptd.; bef. results of disc opers/spec. items. Per share data adj. for stk. divs.; EPS diluted. E-Estimated. NA-Not Available. NM-Not Meaningful. NR-Not Ranked. UR-Under Review.

Office: 999 Lake Dr Ste, Issaquah, WA 98027.
Telephone: 425-313-8100.
Email: investor@costco.com
Website: http://www.costco.com

Chrmn: J.H. Brotman
Pres & CEO: J.D. Sinegal
COO & EVP: R.D. DiCerchio
Investor Contact: R.A. Galanti (425-313-8203)

EVP & CFO: R.A. Galanti
Board Members: J. H. Brotman, B. S. Carson, S. Decker, R. D. DiCerchio, D. J. Evans, R. A. Galanti, W. H. Gates, J. Heisenbach, H. E. James, R. M. Libenson, J. W. Meisenbach, C. Munger, J. S. Raikes, J. S. Ruckelshaus, J. D. Sinegal

Founded: 1976
Domicile: Washington
Employees: 137,000

The McGraw·Hill Companies

Coventry Health Care Inc.

STANDARD &POOR'S

S&P Recommendation	BUY ★★★★☆	Price $22.85 (as of Nov 27, 2009)	12-Mo. Target Price $25.00	Investment Style Large-Cap Growth

GICS Sector Health Care
Sub-Industry Managed Health Care

Summary This national managed health care company operates health plans, insurance companies, network rental/managed care services companies, and workers' compensation services companies.

Key Stock Statistics (Source S&P, Vickers, company reports)

52-Wk Range	$24.84– 7.97	S&P Oper. EPS 2009E	2.03	Market Capitalization(B)	$3.381	Beta	1.93
Trailing 12-Month EPS	$1.50	S&P Oper. EPS 2010E	2.25	Yield (%)	Nil	S&P 3-Yr. Proj. EPS CAGR(%)	-3
Trailing 12-Month P/E	15.2	P/E on S&P Oper. EPS 2009E	11.3	Dividend Rate/Share	Nil	S&P Credit Rating	BBB-
$10K Invested 5 Yrs Ago	$7,082	Common Shares Outstg. (M)	148.0	Institutional Ownership (%)	98		

Price Performance

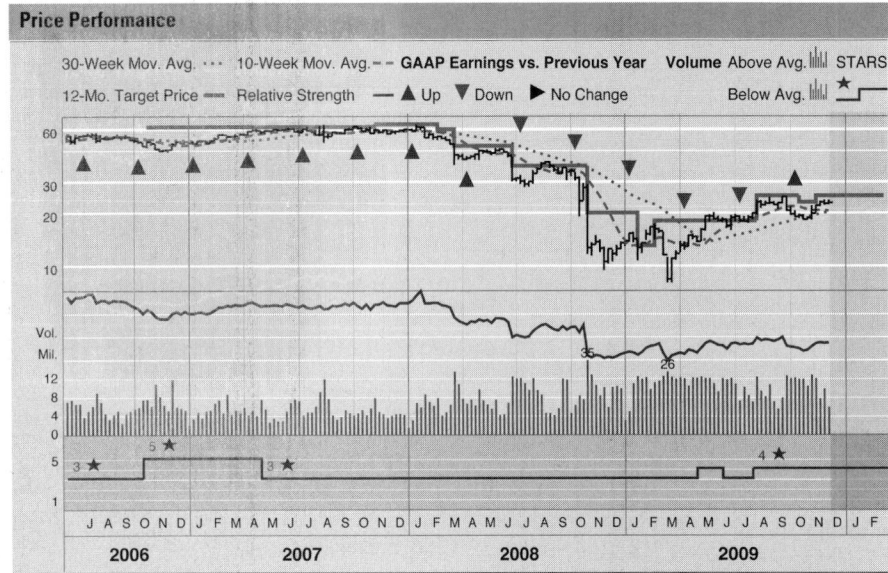

30-Week Mov. Avg. · · · · 10-Week Mov. Avg. – – **GAAP Earnings vs. Previous Year** Volume Above Avg. STARS
12-Mo. Target Price — Relative Strength — ▲ Up ▼ Down ► No Change Below Avg.

Options: ASE, CBOE, P, Ph

Analysis prepared by **Phillip M. Seligman** on November 12, 2009, when the stock traded at **$ 22.84**.

Highlights

► We expect revenues to rise almost 18% in 2009, to slightly more than $14.0 billion. Drivers include 145,000 more Medicare Advantage (MA), 710,000 more Medicare Part D (drug plan) and 22,000 more Medicaid members, offset by 220,000 fewer commercial risk and 90,000 fewer ASO members amid the soft economy. We look for revenues to decline by almost 20% in 2010, mainly on the planned exit from the MA PFFS product and the pending MA premium rate cut.

► We project the consolidated medical loss ratio (MLR) will rise by 180 basis points (bps), on a higher percentage of Medicare, Medicaid and COBRA revenue in the mix, the underpricing of PFFS plans and H1N1 flu costs. However, we expect it to decline by 230 bps in 2010, on intensified medical cost management, higher prices in the commercial book, and the exit from the PFFS program. We forecast that the SG&A cost ratio will decline by 180 bps on cost control, before rising by 200 bps in 2010 mainly on PFFS-related costs the company plans to eliminate.

► We estimate EPS of $2.03 in 2009 before $0.08 of one-time costs, versus 2008's $2.69 before $0.15 of one-time costs, and we see $2.25 in 2010.

Investment Rationale/Risk

► We think CVH's renewed emphasis on cost control and performance and focus on those businesses it views as the foundation for the future makes sense. On the commercial front, CVH raised prices and is focusing on small-group and individual accounts, which carry wider margins than large groups. It plans to exit its underperforming MA PFFS business in 2010, but will continue to support its MA coordinated-care and Part D businesses. It plans to expand its highly profitable workers' comp business and to seek more state Medicaid accounts. Finally, we view its cash flow as healthy, providing financial flexibility, and we see CVH making selected acquisitions. While CVH warned that cash flow in 2010 would be weaker due to the run-off of PFFS claims, it said the funds are already in a regulated subsidiary, and CVH's ability to generate free cash is not impeded.

► Risks to our recommendation and target price include intensified competition, sharply higher medical costs, and a weak economy.

► Our 12-month target price of $25 is based on an above-peer forward P/E of 11X applied to our 2010 EPS estimate, on CVH's turnaround efforts.

Qualitative Risk Assessment

LOW	MEDIUM	HIGH

Our risk assessment reflects CVH's increasingly diversified operations and its January 2005 acquisition of First Health, which we think provided good growth prospects. Even so, we think competition amid the soft economy and our view of rising unemployment will take a toll on commercial enrollment, although we see gains in Medicare and Medicaid enrollment.

Quantitative Evaluations

S&P Quality Ranking B+

D	C	B-	B	B+	A-	A	A+

Relative Strength Rank STRONG

84

LOWEST = 1 HIGHEST = 99

Revenue/Earnings Data

Revenue (Million $)

	1Q	2Q	3Q	4Q	Year
2009	3,574	3,537	3,444	--	--
2008	2,941	2,978	2,975	3,020	11,914
2007	2,237	2,332	2,523	2,788	9,880
2006	1,939	1,945	1,909	1,941	7,734
2005	1,565	1,653	1,674	1,719	6,611
2004	1,288	1,310	1,330	1,384	5,312

Earnings Per Share ($)

2009	0.30	0.13	0.68	E0.55	E2.03
2008	0.81	0.55	0.58	0.60	2.54
2007	0.76	0.96	1.08	1.18	3.98
2006	0.74	0.84	0.92	0.97	3.47
2005	0.73	0.79	0.81	0.77	3.10
2004	0.55	0.62	0.64	0.67	2.48

Fiscal year ended Dec. 31. Next earnings report expected: Mid February. EPS Estimates based on S&P Operating Earnings; historical GAAP earnings are as reported.

Dividend Data

No cash dividends have been paid.

Please read the Required Disclosures and Analyst Certification on the last page of this report.

The McGraw-Hill Companies

Coventry Health Care Inc.

STANDARD
&POOR'S

Business Summary November 12, 2009

CORPORATE OVERVIEW. Coventry Health Care is a diversified national managed care company. It traditionally offered individual and employer groups a full range of commercial risk products, including health maintenance organization (HMO), preferred provider organization (PPO) and point-of service (POS) products. Through its January 2005 acquisition of First Health Group (FH), it gained a nationwide provider network and high-margin, fee-based service businesses, such as network rental, clinical programs, workers' compensation administration, Medicaid health care management services, and pharmacy benefit management. CVH also gained additional PPO members, including the Federal Employee Health Benefit program, the largest employer-sponsored group health program in the U.S., and an administrative services only (ASO, or non-risk) product for large employers with locations in several states that self-insure. Starting in 2007, CVH combined the enrollment of its existing business with that of FH.

As of September 30, 2009, the company had a total of 3,604,000 members (versus 3,697,000 at December 31, 2008), excluding standalone Medicare prescription drug program members, divided into two operating segments -- the Commercial division and the Individual/Government division.

The Health Plan division is comprised of Health Plan Commercial Risk members (1,431,000, versus 1,575,000), Health Plan ASO (689,000, versus 714,000), Medicare Advantage Coordinated Care Plans (185,000, versus 137,000), and Medicaid Risk (391,000, versus 371,000). Health Plan Commercial Risk membership includes the Individual business (under 65 years of age).

Other medical membership consists of Medicare Advantage PFFS (Private Fee-For-Service; 336,000, versus 243,000), other National Risk (5,000, versus 24,000) and other National ASO (567,000, versus 633,000). In the ASO businesses, CVH offers management services and access to its provider networks to employers that self-insure their employee health benefits. The Other National ASO membership includes active National Accounts and Federal Employees Health Benefits Plan (FEHBP) administrative services business. Medicare Part D (Prescription Drug Program) had 1,636,000 members (versus 931,000).

Company Financials Fiscal Year Ended Dec. 31

Per Share Data ($)	2008	2007	2006	2005	2004	2003	2002	2001	2000	1999
Tangible Book Value	1.28	1.15	5.92	3.21	6.60	4.57	2.85	2.89	2.31	1.60
Cash Flow	3.54	4.89	4.17	3.63	2.61	1.97	1.24	0.72	0.60	0.50
Earnings	2.54	3.98	3.47	3.10	2.48	1.83	1.06	0.55	0.41	0.31
S&P Core Earnings	2.69	3.98	3.47	3.01	2.41	1.80	1.03	0.52	NA	NA
Dividends	Nil	Nil	Nil	Nil	Nil	Nil	Nil	Nil	Nil	Nil
Payout Ratio	Nil	Nil	Nil	Nil	Nil	Nil	Nil	Nil	Nil	Nil
Prices:High	63.89	64.00	61.88	60.31	36.20	29.46	16.89	12.22	13.31	6.81
Prices:Low	9.44	48.78	44.33	34.21	24.66	10.80	8.67	5.78	3.06	2.22
P/E Ratio:High	25	16	18	19	15	16	16	22	32	22
P/E Ratio:Low	4	12	13	11	10	6	8	11	7	7

Income Statement Analysis (Million $)										
Revenue	11,914	9,880	7,734	6,611	5,312	4,535	3,577	3,147	2,605	2,162
Operating Income	770	1,075	954	878	514	384	220	117	81.1	71.8
Depreciation	150	143	113	86.2	17.6	18.2	18.9	25.9	27.0	28.2
Interest Expense	96.4	73.1	52.4	58.4	14.3	15.1	13.4	Nil	Nil	Nil
Pretax Income	606	995	896	799	527	393	226	135	102	76.0
Effective Tax Rate	37.0%	37.1%	37.5%	37.3%	36.0%	36.4%	35.5%	38.0%	39.9%	42.8%
Net Income	382	626	560	502	337	250	146	83.5	61.3	43.4
S&P Core Earnings	404	627	560	485	328	245	143	78.5	NA	NA

Balance Sheet & Other Financial Data (Million $)										
Cash	1,123	1,101	1,371	392	418	253	187	312	256	240
Current Assets	2,410	1,847	2,134	1,326	973	534	424	579	507	483
Total Assets	7,727	7,159	5,665	4,895	2,341	1,982	1,643	1,451	1,239	1,082
Current Liabilities	2,026	1,750	1,652	1,270	932	855	801	752	632	523
Long Term Debt	1,902	1,662	750	760	171	171	175	Nil	Nil	Nil
Common Equity	3,431	3,301	2,953	2,555	1,212	929	646	689	662	480
Total Capital	5,551	5,193	3,704	3,315	1,383	1,099	821	689	662	527
Capital Expenditures	69.4	61.3	72.6	71.4	15.0	13.4	13.0	11.9	16.0	14.7
Cash Flow	532	769	673	588	355	268	164	109	88.4	71.6
Current Ratio	1.2	1.1	1.3	1.0	1.0	0.6	0.5	0.8	0.8	0.9
% Long Term Debt of Capitalization	34.3	33.5	20.3	22.9	12.3	15.5	21.3	Nil	Nil	Nil
% Net Income of Revenue	3.2	6.3	7.2	7.6	6.3	5.5	4.1	2.7	2.4	2.0
% Return on Assets	5.1	9.8	10.6	13.9	15.6	13.8	9.4	6.2	5.3	4.0
% Return on Equity	11.4	20.0	20.3	26.6	31.5	31.8	21.8	13.0	10.7	9.5

Data as orig reptd.; bef. results of disc opers/spec. items. Per share data adj. for stk. divs.; EPS diluted. E-Estimated. NA-Not Available. NM-Not Meaningful. NR-Not Ranked. UR-Under Review.

Office: 6705 Rockledge Drive, Bethesda, MD 20817.
Telephone: 301-581-0600.
Email: investor-relations@cvty.com
Website: http://www.coventryhealth.com

Chrmn & CEO: A.F. Wise
CEO: R.L. Dawson
EVP, CFO & Treas: S.M. Guertin
EVP & General Counsel: T.C. Zielinski

SVP & Cntlr: J.J. Ruhlmann
Board Members: J. Ackerman, L. D. Crandall, L. N. Kugelman, D. Mendelson, R. W. Moorhead, III, M. Stocker, E. E. Tallett, E. E. Tollett, T. T. Weglicki, A. F. Wise

Founded: 1986
Domicile: Delaware
Employees: 15,800

CSX Corp

STANDARD &POOR'S

S&P Recommendation	BUY ★★★★☆	Price $47.53 (as of Nov 27, 2009)	12-Mo. Target Price $53.00	Investment Style Large-Cap Value

GICS Sector Industrials
Sub-Industry Railroads

Summary CSX operates a major U.S. rail network, transporting bulk commodities, industrial products and intermodal containers over its network of approximately 21,000 route miles.

Key Stock Statistics (Source S&P, Vickers, company reports)

52-Wk Range	$50.15– 20.70	S&P Oper. EPS 2009E	2.75	Market Capitalization(B)	$18.658	Beta	1.18
Trailing 12-Month EPS	$2.77	S&P Oper. EPS 2010E	3.30	Yield (%)	1.85	S&P 3-Yr. Proj. EPS CAGR(%)	10
Trailing 12-Month P/E	17.2	P/E on S&P Oper. EPS 2009E	17.3	Dividend Rate/Share	$0.88	S&P Credit Rating	BBB-
$10K Invested 5 Yrs Ago	$26,941	Common Shares Outstg. (M)	392.6	Institutional Ownership (%)	69		

Price Performance

30-Week Mov. Avg. · · · · 10-Week Mov. Avg. - - - GAAP Earnings vs. Previous Year   Volume Above Avg. ▐▐▐ STARS
12-Mo. Target Price —— Relative Strength — ▲ Up ▼ Down ► No Change   Below Avg. ▐▐▐ ★

Options: ASE, CBOE, P, Ph

Analysis prepared by **Kevin Kirkeby** on October 14, 2009, when the stock traded at **$ 46.86.**

Highlights

► After an expected 19% decline in 2009, we are forecasting revenues will be up 5.6% next year. This is based on a 4% increase in volumes, with the remainder from price and mix. We think inventory realignments taken across the manufacturing and materials segments of the economy are largely completed, and that carloadings will show improvement through 2010. Serving as a partial offset will likely be coal shipments, where inventories at its utility customers are well above the historical average. Absent a very cold winter, this will dampen CSX's coal shipments during much of 2010, in our view.

► Cost cutting initiatives have taken hold in the second half of 2009, after lagging volume declines earlier in the year, reflecting the high fixed cost nature of CSX's operations. We think the company is on track to realize the $260 million in cost savings it has targeted by the end of 2010. In addition, lease expenses are expected to decline further as a portion of contracts tied to unused cars are allowed to lapse, and this should also contribute to improving profitability in 2010.

► Our EPS estimate for 2009 excludes net gains of $0.14 related mostly to a reserve reversal.

Investment Rationale/Risk

► We believe CSX will benefit from an eventual economic recovery in the U.S. given its role in transporting many of the basic materials required in manufacturing and construction, including coal and scrap used by steel mills. We also think the recession has forced a more intense focus on operating efficiencies, which will support wider margins during a period of rising volumes. In our view, a valuation above the historical average is warranted as we weigh CSX's solid cash flow generation and signs that volumes are bottoming against increased regulatory risk.

► Risks to our opinion and target price include greater-than-expected regulatory oversight, renewed softness in export coal shipments, and larger contributions (forecast to approach $250 million) to an underfunded pension plan.

► Our discounted cash flow model, using an 11.0% cost of equity and a 3.5% terminal growth rate, derives an intrinsic value near $47. Applying an enterprise value to EBITDA multiple of 8.7X, which is in the top half of the historical range, to our 2010 EBITDA forecast, we derive a value of $59. Blending these models, we arrive at our 12-month target price of $53.

Qualitative Risk Assessment

LOW	MEDIUM	HIGH

Our risk assessment reflects what we believe is CSX's exposure to economic cycles, freight demand and pricing, offset by its consistently positive cash flow generation and diverse customer base.

Quantitative Evaluations

S&P Quality Ranking B+

D	C	B-	B	B+	A-	A	A+

Relative Strength Rank STRONG

77

LOWEST = 1   HIGHEST = 99

Revenue/Earnings Data

Revenue (Million $)

	1Q	2Q	3Q	4Q	Year
2009	2,247	2,185	2,289	--	--
2008	2,713	2,907	2,961	2,674	11,255
2007	2,422	2,530	2,501	2,577	10,030
2006	2,331	2,421	2,418	2,396	9,566
2005	2,108	2,166	2,125	2,219	8,618
2004	1,915	1,995	1,938	2,172	8,020

Earnings Per Share ($)

	1Q	2Q	3Q	4Q	Year
2009	0.62	0.72	0.74	E0.78	E2.75
2008	0.85	0.93	0.94	0.63	3.34
2007	0.52	0.71	0.67	0.86	2.74
2006	0.53	0.83	0.71	0.75	2.82
2005	0.34	0.37	0.36	0.52	1.59
2004	0.06	0.26	0.26	0.36	0.94

Fiscal year ended Dec. 31. Next earnings report expected: Mid January. EPS Estimates based on S&P Operating Earnings; historical GAAP earnings are as reported.

Dividend Data (Dates: mm/dd Payment Date: mm/dd/yy)

Amount ($)	Date Decl.	Ex-Div. Date	Stk. of Record	Payment Date
0.220	02/11	02/25	02/27	03/13/09
0.220	05/06	05/27	05/29	06/15/09
0.220	07/15	08/27	08/31	09/15/09
0.220	09/09	11/25	11/30	12/15/09

Dividends have been paid since 1922. Source: Company reports.

Please read the Required Disclosures and Analyst Certification on the last page of this report.

The McGraw-Hill Companies

CSX Corp

STANDARD &POOR'S

Business Summary October 14, 2009

CORPORATE OVERVIEW. CSX operates the largest rail network in the eastern U.S., with a 21,000-mile rail network linking commercial markets in 23 states and two Canadian provinces, and owns companies providing intermodal and rail-to-truck transload services. In 1997, the company purchased a 42% stake in Conrail, bringing CSX's system into New York City, Boston, Philadelphia and Buffalo; in 2004, CSX gained direct ownership and control of Conrail's New York Central Lines. With these routes, the company was able to offer shippers broader geographic coverage, access more ports, and expand its share of north-south traffic.

MARKET PROFILE. We consider railroads to be a mature industry, and expect 2.0% annualized U.S. rail tonnage growth between 2008 and 2020. We believe CSX's growth opportunities are slightly ahead of the industry average, as we see above-average future growth in intermodal traffic, but average prospects in coal and chemicals shipments. We believe growth in CSX's intermodal business, representing 13% of 2008 revenue, will be above the peer average. This, in our view, will be driven by the overall level of economic activity and population density in the Eastern markets it serves. Its initiatives, like the National Gateway project, are designed to capitalize on highway congestion along a key East Coast freight corridors, by converting truck traffic over to rail

containers. CSX's service quality has generally lagged its primary competitor, but is an area that management has been working to address.

Coal accounted for 29% of 2008 revenues. Most of this traffic originates from the Appalachian coal fields and is primarily delivered to power utilities. We expect CSX's domestic coal tonnage to experience average growth as its customers balance the high sulfur content of coal against using more costly fuel alternatives. Coal shipments directed to export markets is expected to be more volatile than the domestic business, and be somewhat correlated to exchange rate fluctuations. CSX's merchandise freight provided 49% of freight revenues in 2008, and includes chemical, forest products, metals, and agricultural products. We believe this business is sensitive to U.S. GDP trends, and faces average long-term volume growth prospects. We think automotive freight, at 7% of revenues in 2008, has a weak volume growth outlook, due to poor consumer credit trends.

Company Financials Fiscal Year Ended Dec. 31

Per Share Data ($)	2008	2007	2006	2005	2004	2003	2002	2001	2000	1999
Tangible Book Value	20.44	21.14	20.42	18.25	15.77	15.01	14.52	14.32	14.13	13.20
Cash Flow	5.55	4.71	4.67	3.41	2.55	1.94	2.62	2.16	2.76	1.46
Earnings	3.34	2.74	2.82	1.59	0.94	0.44	1.10	0.69	0.44	0.12
S&P Core Earnings	3.41	2.74	2.57	1.60	0.90	0.66	0.85	0.59	NA	NA
Dividends	0.77	0.54	0.63	0.22	0.20	0.20	0.20	0.40	0.60	0.60
Payout Ratio	23%	20%	22%	14%	21%	45%	18%	58%	136%	NM
Prices:High	70.70	51.88	38.30	25.80	20.23	18.15	20.70	20.65	16.72	26.97
Prices:Low	30.01	33.50	24.29	18.45	14.40	12.75	12.55	12.41	9.75	14.41
P/E Ratio:High	21	19	14	16	22	41	19	30	38	NM
P/E Ratio:Low	9	12	9	12	15	29	11	18	22	NM

Income Statement Analysis (Million $)										
Revenue	11,255	10,030	9,566	8,618	8,020	7,793	8,152	8,110	8,191	10,811
Operating Income	3,667	3,112	2,837	2,345	1,730	1,269	1,776	1,579	1,405	1,685
Depreciation	904	883	867	833	730	643	649	622	600	621
Interest Expense	519	417	392	423	435	418	445	518	543	521
Pretax Income	2,146	1,932	1,841	1,036	637	265	723	448	656	130
Effective Tax Rate	36.4%	36.5%	28.8%	30.5%	34.4%	28.7%	35.4%	34.6%	13.9%	67.7%
Net Income	1,365	1,226	1,310	720	418	189	467	293	565	51.0
S&P Core Earnings	1,392	1,228	1,194	729	405	280	363	249	NA	NA

Balance Sheet & Other Financial Data (Million $)										
Cash	745	714	461	309	859	368	264	618	684	974
Current Assets	2,391	2,491	2,672	2,372	2,987	1,903	1,789	2,074	2,046	2,563
Total Assets	26,288	25,534	25,129	24,232	24,581	21,760	20,951	20,801	20,491	20,720
Current Liabilities	2,404	2,671	2,522	2,979	3,317	2,210	2,454	3,303	3,280	3,473
Long Term Debt	7,512	6,470	5,362	5,093	6,234	6,886	6,519	5,839	5,810	6,196
Common Equity	8,048	8,685	9,863	8,918	7,858	7,569	7,091	7,060	6,017	5,756
Total Capital	21,816	21,272	21,335	20,093	20,071	18,207	17,177	16,520	15,211	15,179
Capital Expenditures	1,740	1,773	1,639	1,136	1,030	1,059	1,080	930	913	1,517
Cash Flow	2,269	2,109	2,177	1,553	1,148	832	1,116	915	1,165	623
Current Ratio	1.0	0.9	1.1	0.8	0.9	0.9	0.7	0.6	0.6	0.7
% Long Term Debt of Capitalization	34.4	30.4	25.1	25.3	31.1	37.8	38.0	35.3	38.2	40.8
% Net Income of Revenue	12.1	12.2	13.7	8.4	5.2	2.4	5.7	3.6	6.9	0.5
% Return on Assets	5.3	4.8	5.3	2.9	1.8	0.9	2.2	1.4	2.7	0.2
% Return on Equity	16.3	13.9	14.0	8.6	5.4	2.6	6.6	4.2	9.6	0.9

Data as orig reptd.; bef. results of disc opers/spec. items. Per share data adj. for stk. divs.; EPS diluted. E-Estimated. NA-Not Available. NM-Not Meaningful. NR-Not Ranked. UR-Under Review.

Office: 500 Water Street , Jacksonville , FL 32202.
Telephone: 904-359-3200.
Website: http://www.csx.com
Chrmn, Pres & CEO: M.J. Ward

EVP & CFO: O. Munoz
SVP, Secy & General Counsel: E.M. Fitzsimmons
Chief Acctg Officer & Cntlr: C.T. Sizemore
Treas: D.A. Boor

Investor Contact: D. Baggs (904-359-4812)
Board Members: D. M. Alvarado, A. Behring, J. B. Breaux, S. T. Halverson, E. J. Kelly, III, G. H. Lamphere, J. D. McPherson, T. O'Toole, D. M. Ratcliffe, D. J. Shepard, M. J. Ward

Founded: 1978
Domicile: Virginia
Employees: 34,363

The McGraw-Hill Companies

Cummins Inc.

STANDARD &POOR'S

S&P Recommendation	HOLD ★★★☆☆	Price $45.34 (as of Nov 27, 2009)	12-Mo. Target Price $54.00	Investment Style Large-Cap Value

GICS Sector Industrials
Sub-Industry Construction & Farm Machinery & Heavy Trucks

Summary This leading manufacturer of truck engines also makes stand-by power equipment and industrial filters.

Key Stock Statistics (Source S&P, Vickers, company reports)

52-Wk Range	$51.65 – 18.34	S&P Oper. EPS 2009**E**	1.36	Market Capitalization(B)	$8.991	Beta	2.04
Trailing 12-Month EPS	$1.02	S&P Oper. EPS 2010**E**	2.20	Yield (%)	1.54	S&P 3-Yr. Proj. EPS CAGR(%)	6
Trailing 12-Month P/E	44.5	P/E on S&P Oper. EPS 2009**E**	33.3	Dividend Rate/Share	$0.70	S&P Credit Rating	BBB
$10K Invested 5 Yrs Ago	$24,482	Common Shares Outstg. (M)	198.3	Institutional Ownership (%)	88		

Price Performance

30-Week Mov. Avg. ··· 10-Week Mov. Avg. -- **GAAP Earnings vs. Previous Year** Volume Above Avg. STARS
12-Mo. Target Price — Relative Strength ▲ Up ▼ Down ▶ No Change Below Avg.

Options: ASE, CBOE, P, Ph

Analysis prepared by **Jim Corridore** on November 03, 2009, when the stock traded at **$ 44.80.**

Highlights

► We expect revenues to fall 32% in 2009, with engines sales down about 30%, power generation off 15%, components declining 35%, and distribution down 15%, as CMI's end markets are likely to continue to struggle with the global recession. CMI recently said it does not expect its markets to improve for the rest of 2009. We expect the infrastructure power generation segment to perform better relative to the rest of CMI's segments, but still to fall from 2008 levels. We see modest revenue growth in 2010 in most of CMI's segments, with the second half likely to be stronger than the first.

► We anticipate that operating margins will narrow sharply in 2009, reflecting the effect of leveraging fixed costs over the sharply smaller revenue base that we are forecasting. This is likely to more than offset benefits from cost reduction actions and the recent pullback in raw material and energy costs. However, we look for improving margins in 2010 on higher volumes and cost cuts.

► We estimate that EPS will decrease to $1.36 in 2009, from $4.08 in 2008. For 2010, we see EPS rebounding to $2.20.

Investment Rationale/Risk

► Over the long term, with over 50% of sales derived from outside North America, we see CMI benefiting from its leading edge technology in truck engines gaining market share in emerging market countries and infrastructure-related power generation equipment. We think CMI will continue to use technology and its strong balance sheet to increase market share amid a rapidly slowing global economy. However, given the risks of the current economic slowdown and a P/E multiple near the high end of its historical range, we would not add to positions.

► Risks to our recommendation and target price include weaker-than-projected demand in the truck manufacturing and/or power generation markets; slower-than-anticipated economic growth and/or industrial production; adverse forex volatility; and lower-than-estimated savings from expense reduction initiatives.

► Our 12-month target price of $54 values the shares at 24.5X our 2010 EPS estimate of $2.20, above CMI's five-year historical P/E range of 4.3X-19.4X EPS, reflecting our view that earnings are near trough levels for this highly cyclical company.

Qualitative Risk Assessment

LOW	MEDIUM	HIGH

Our risk assessment reflects the highly cyclical nature of the North America medium (class 5-7) and heavy-duty (class 8) truck markets and significant pension and post-retirement benefit obligations, offset by a geographically diverse mix of business and low leverage of CMI's balance sheet.

Quantitative Evaluations

S&P Quality Ranking B+

D	C	B-	B	B+	A-	A	A+

Relative Strength Rank MODERATE

44

LOWEST = 1   HIGHEST = 99

Revenue/Earnings Data

Revenue (Million $)

	1Q	2Q	3Q	4Q	Year
2009	2,439	2,431	2,530	--	--
2008	3,474	3,887	3,693	3,288	14,342
2007	2,817	3,343	3,372	3,516	13,048
2006	2,678	2,842	2,809	3,033	11,362
2005	2,208	2,490	2,467	2,753	9,918
2004	1,771	2,124	2,194	2,349	8,438

Earnings Per Share ($)

	1Q	2Q	3Q	4Q	Year
2009	0.04	0.28	0.48	E0.48	E1.36
2008	0.97	1.49	1.17	0.45	4.08
2007	0.71	1.06	0.92	1.00	3.70
2006	0.68	1.10	0.84	0.94	3.55
2005	0.49	0.71	0.73	0.83	2.75
2004	0.19	0.44	0.60	0.60	1.85

Fiscal year ended Dec. 31. Next earnings report expected: Early February. EPS Estimates based on S&P Operating Earnings; historical GAAP earnings are as reported.

Dividend Data (Dates: mm/dd Payment Date: mm/dd/yy)

Amount ($)	Date Decl.	Ex-Div. Date	Stk. of Record	Payment Date
0.175	02/10	02/18	02/20	03/02/09
0.175	05/13	05/20	05/22	06/01/09
0.175	07/14	08/19	08/21	09/01/09
0.175	10/20	11/18	11/20	12/01/09

Dividends have been paid since 1948. Source: Company reports.

Please read the Required Disclosures and Analyst Certification on the last page of this report.

The McGraw-Hill Companies

Cummins Inc.

STANDARD &POOR'S

Business Summary November 03, 2009

CORPORATE OVERVIEW. This global equipment company makes and services diesel and natural gas engines, electric power generation systems and engine-related component products.

Cummins (CMI), founded in 1919, has long-standing relationships with many of the customers it serves, including Chrysler LLC, Daimler AG, Volvo AB, PACCAR Inc., International Truck and Engine Corp. (a unit of Navistar), CNH Global N.V., Komatsu, Scania AB, Ford Motor Corp., and Volkswagen. CMI has over 500 company-owned and independent distributor locations and about 5,200 dealer locations in over 190 countries and territories. CMI's key markets are the on-highway, construction, and general industrial markets.

CMI believes that its competitive strengths include a group of leading brand names, alliances it has established with customers and partners, its global presence (international sales accounted for 59% of total sales in 2008), and its leading technology. In particular, Cummins' technology addresses the reduction of diesel engine emissions. CMI's engines met the EPA's heavy-duty on-

highway emission standards that went into effect in January 2007. In addition, its Dodge Ram 6.7-liter Turbo Diesel engine met the EPA's 2010 emission standards ahead of the required date.

The engine segment (50% of sales in 2008) manufactures and markets a broad range of diesel and natural-gas powered engines under the Cummins brand name for the heavy- and medium-duty truck, bus, recreational vehicle (RV), light-duty automotive, agricultural, construction, mining, marine, oil and gas, rail and governmental equipment markets. CMI manufactures engines with displacements from 1.4 to 91 liters and horsepower ranging from 31 to 3,500. In addition, it provides new parts and service, as well as remanufactured parts and engines, through its extensive distribution network.

Company Financials Fiscal Year Ended Dec. 31

Per Share Data ($)	2008	2007	2006	2005	2004	2003	2002	2001	2000	1999
Tangible Book Value	13.48	14.20	11.12	7.56	5.18	2.79	2.42	4.06	5.05	6.42
Cash Flow	5.44	5.15	4.96	4.54	3.38	1.75	1.79	0.85	1.62	2.52
Earnings	4.08	3.70	3.55	2.75	1.85	0.34	0.52	-0.67	-0.05	1.03
S&P Core Earnings	3.20	3.73	3.62	2.85	2.00	0.40	-0.39	-1.44	NA	NA
Dividends	0.60	0.43	0.33	0.30	0.30	0.30	0.30	0.30	0.30	0.28
Payout Ratio	15%	12%	9%	11%	16%	88%	58%	NM	NM	27%
Prices:High	75.98	71.73	34.80	23.47	21.17	13.08	12.57	11.38	12.50	16.42
Prices:Low	17.70	28.16	22.17	15.90	12.03	5.43	4.90	7.00	6.77	8.64
P/E Ratio:High	19	19	10	9	11	38	24	NM	NM	16
P/E Ratio:Low	4	8	6	6	7	16	10	NM	NM	8

Income Statement Analysis (Million $)										
Revenue	14,342	13,048	11,362	9,918	8,438	6,296	5,853	5,681	6,597	6,639
Operating Income	1,382	1,221	1,287	1,058	696	316	327	304	479	625
Depreciation	314	290	296	295	272	223	219	231	240	233
Interest Expense	60.0	59.0	96.0	109	113	101	82.0	87.0	86.0	75.0
Pretax Income	1,251	1,169	1,083	798	432	80.0	57.0	-129	3.00	221
Effective Tax Rate	30.9%	32.6%	29.9%	27.1%	13.0%	15.0%	NM	NM	NM	24.9%
Net Income	801	739	715	550	350	54.0	79.0	-102	8.00	160
S&P Core Earnings	631	744	729	570	380	62.8	-61.4	-221	NA	NA

Balance Sheet & Other Financial Data (Million $)										
Cash	503	697	935	840	690	195	298	92.0	62.0	74.0
Current Assets	4,713	4,815	4,488	3,916	3,273	2,130	1,982	1,635	1,830	2,180
Total Assets	8,491	8,195	7,465	6,885	6,527	5,126	4,837	4,335	4,500	4,697
Current Liabilities	2,639	2,711	2,399	2,218	2,197	1,391	1,329	970	1,223	1,314
Long Term Debt	629	555	647	1,213	1,299	1,380	1,290	1,206	1,032	1,092
Common Equity	3,277	3,409	2,802	1,864	2,802	949	841	1,025	1,336	1,429
Total Capital	4,139	4,257	3,703	3,302	4,309	2,452	2,223	2,314	2,440	2,595
Capital Expenditures	543	353	249	186	151	111	90.0	206	228	215
Cash Flow	1,069	1,029	1,011	845	622	277	298	129	248	393
Current Ratio	1.8	1.8	1.9	1.8	1.5	1.5	1.5	1.7	1.5	1.7
% Long Term Debt of Capitalization	15.1	13.0	17.5	36.7	30.1	56.3	58.0	52.1	42.3	42.1
% Net Income of Revenue	5.6	5.7	6.3	5.5	4.1	0.9	1.3	NM	0.1	2.4
% Return on Assets	9.6	9.4	10.0	8.2	6.0	1.1	1.7	NM	0.2	3.5
% Return on Equity	24.0	23.8	30.6	33.7	14.9	6.0	8.7	NM	0.6	11.8

Data as orig reptd.; bef. results of disc opers/spec. items. Per share data adj. for stk. divs.; EPS diluted. E-Estimated. NA-Not Available. NM-Not Meaningful. NR-Not Ranked. UR-Under Review.

Office: 500 Jackson Street, Columbus, IN 47202-3005.
Telephone: 812-377-3121.
Email: investor_relations@cummins.com
Website: http://www.cummins.com

Chrmn & CEO: T.M. Solso
Pres & COO: N.T. Linebarger
CFO: P.J. Ward
CTO: J. Wall

Chief Acctg Officer & Cntlr: M.L. Hunt
Investor Contact: D.A. Cantrell (812-377-3121)
Board Members: R. J. Bernhard, R. J. Darnall, R. K. Herdman, A. Herman, N. T. Linebarger, W. I. Miller, G. R. Nelson, T. M. Solso, C. Ware

Founded: 1919
Domicile: Indiana
Employees: 39,800

CVS Caremark Corp

STANDARD &POOR'S

S&P Recommendation **BUY** ★★★★☆	Price $31.20 (as of Nov 27, 2009)	12-Mo. Target Price $33.00	Investment Style Large-Cap Blend

GICS Sector Consumer Staples
Sub-Industry Drug Retail

Summary This company is a leading operator of both retail drug stores and pharmacy benefit management services in the U.S.

Key Stock Statistics (Source S&P, Vickers, company reports)

52-Wk Range	$38.27– 23.74	S&P Oper. EPS 2009**E**	2.62	Market Capitalization(B)	$44.009	Beta	0.79
Trailing 12-Month EPS	$2.46	S&P Oper. EPS 2010**E**	2.67	Yield (%)	0.98	S&P 3-Yr. Proj. EPS CAGR(%)	2
Trailing 12-Month P/E	12.7	P/E on S&P Oper. EPS 2009**E**	11.9	Dividend Rate/Share	$0.31	S&P Credit Rating	BBB+
$10K Invested 5 Yrs Ago	$14,122	Common Shares Outstg. (M)	1,410.5	Institutional Ownership (%)	88		

Price Performance

30-Week Mov. Avg. ··· 10-Week Mov. Avg. - - GAAP Earnings vs. Previous Year Volume Above Avg. ▮▮▮ STARS
12-Mo. Target Price — Relative Strength — ▲ Up ▼ Down ► No Change Below Avg. ▮▮▮ ★

Options: ASE, CBOE, P, Ph

Analysis prepared by **Joseph Agnese** on November 09, 2009, when the stock traded at **$ 30.59**.

Highlights

► We expect total sales in 2010 to increase about 5.3%, to $105.0 billion, up from our estimate of $99.8 billion in 2009, reflecting strong retail drugstore market share gains and about 3.0% net new square footage growth, partially offset by significant client losses in the pharmacy benefit management (PBM) business segment. Our estimates assume retail drugstore same-store sales growth of approximately 5% in 2010.

► We see margins contracting in 2010, reflecting negative sales leverage in the PBM segment due to significant client losses and with the renegotiation of a large federal employee contract entering a less profitable contract year. We see margin pressure from the PBM business partially offset by wider margins in the retail drugstore business reflecting approximately $0.04 to $0.05 in accretion from the turnaround of acquired drug stores versus our estimate of $0.04 to $0.05 of dilution in 2009, and reduced investment costs for instore health clinics.

► With strength in the retail drugstore business partially offset by weaker PBM business, we estimate 2010 EPS will rise only 1.9% to $2.67, up from our estimate of $2.62 in 2009.

Investment Rationale/Risk

► CVS is an experienced consolidator, and we have confidence in its ability to realize significant long-term synergies from recent drugstore acquisitions. However, we expect earnings growth in 2010 to be pressured by the loss of PBM business in 2009. We expect comparisons to ease in 2011, resulting in an acceleration in EPS growth in the longer term.

► Risks to our recommendation and target price include potential margin pressures resulting from decreased drug reimbursement from federal and state governments, as well as risk from exposure to weaker consumer spending in an adverse economic environment.

► Due to our expectation for weak earnings growth in 2010 as lower PBM profits offset strong earnings generation from the retail drugstore business, we believe the shares should near the low point of their five-year historical P/E range of 10.5X to 20.3X, and in line with their three-year median P/E ratio discount when compared to the S&P 500. Assuming that the shares trade at 12.2X, a 21% discount to the forward 12-month P/E estimate for the S&P 500, applied to our 2010 EPS estimate of $2.67, we arrive at our 12-month target price of $33.

Qualitative Risk Assessment

LOW	MEDIUM	HIGH

Our risk assessment reflects our view of the company's leadership position and strong market share position in a relatively stable U.S. retail drug industry, offset by the potential for acquisition integration risk and growth of non-traditional competitors.

Quantitative Evaluations

S&P Quality Ranking A+

D	C	B-	B	B+	A-	A	A+

Relative Strength Rank WEAK

23

LOWEST = 1   HIGHEST = 99

Revenue/Earnings Data

Revenue (Million $)

	1Q	2Q	3Q	4Q	Year
2009	23,394	24,871	24,642	--	--
2008	21,326	21,140	20,863	24,142	87,472
2007	13,189	20,703	20,495	21,942	76,330
2006	9,979	10,561	11,207	12,066	43,814
2005	9,182	9,122	8,970	9,732	37,006
2004	6,819	6,943	7,909	8,923	30,594

Earnings Per Share ($)

2009	0.51	0.60	0.71	E0.77	E2.62
2008	0.51	0.56	0.56	0.65	2.27
2007	0.43	0.47	0.45	0.55	1.92
2006	0.39	0.40	0.33	0.49	1.60
2005	0.35	0.33	0.30	0.48	1.45
2004	0.29	0.28	0.22	0.31	1.10

Fiscal year ended Dec. 31. Next earnings report expected: Mid February. EPS Estimates based on S&P Operating Earnings; historical GAAP earnings are as reported.

Dividend Data (Dates: mm/dd Payment Date: mm/dd/yy)

Amount ($)	Date Decl.	Ex-Div. Date	Stk. of Record	Payment Date
0.076	01/13	01/21	01/23	02/03/09
0.076	03/04	04/20	04/22	05/04/09
0.076	07/08	07/21	07/23	08/03/09
0.076	09/18	10/20	10/22	11/03/09

Dividends have been paid since 1916. Source: Company reports.

Please read the Required Disclosures and Analyst Certification on the last page of this report.

The McGraw·Hill Companies

CVS Caremark Corp

**STANDARD
&POOR'S**

Business Summary November 09, 2009

CORPORATE OVERVIEW. CVS Caremark Corporation is the largest provider of prescriptions in the U.S., dispensing 729 million prescriptions in 2008. The company operates one of the largest drug store chains and pharmacy benefit managers in the U.S., based on revenues, net income and store count. Drugstores offer prescription drugs and a wide assortment of general merchandise, including OTC drugs, beauty products and cosmetics, film and photo finishing services, seasonal merchandise, greeting cards and convenience foods. Pharmacy benefit management offerings include mail order pharmacy service, specialty pharmacy services, plan design and administration, formulary management and claims processing.

MARKET PROFILE. CVS is the largest U.S. drug store chain, based on store count, with about 6,900 stores as of December 2008, in 44 states and the District of Columbia. As of December 2008, the company has stores in 89 of the top 100 U.S. drug store markets, holding the number one or number two market share in 60 of these markets, and 67% of all markets in which it operates. It filled more than 559 million prescriptions in 2008, accounting for about 17% of the U.S. retail pharmacy market. Pharmacy operations are critical to CVS's success, in our view, accounting for 68% of retail store sales in 2008. Payments by third-party managed care providers under prescription drug plans

accounted for 96% of pharmacy sales in 2008. CVS's pharmacy benefit management (PBM) business generated $43.8 billion in sales in 2008, or 47% of total company sales. The company's specialty pharmacy operations, which operates 58 retail specialty pharmacy stores and 19 specialty pharmacy mail order pharmacies, generated over $10 billion in revenues in 2008.

CORPORATE STRATEGY. Through its retail and PBM services, the company plans to benefit from favorable industry trends which include an aging U.S. population, increased generic drug utilization, the discovery of new drugs, growth of specialty pharmacy services, and health care reform. CVS's long-term strategy focuses on expanding its retail drug store business in high-growth markets and increasing the size and product offerings of its PBM business. Historically, the company has grown, in large part, through acquisitions. In June 2006, the company acquired 700 stand-alone drugstores from Albertson's and in July 2004, CVS bought 1,268 Eckerd drug stores, as well as Eckerd's mail order, specialty pharmacy and PBM businesses, from J.C. Penney.

Company Financials Fiscal Year Ended Dec. 31

Per Share Data ($)	2008	2007	2006	2005	2004	2003	2002	2001	2000	1999
Tangible Book Value	NM	NM	6.29	6.77	4.98	5.98	5.05	4.45	4.11	3.44
Cash Flow	3.13	2.71	2.45	2.14	1.69	1.46	1.25	0.88	1.26	1.10
Earnings	2.27	1.92	1.60	1.45	1.10	1.03	0.88	0.50	0.92	0.78
S&P Core Earnings	2.27	1.92	1.61	1.41	1.06	0.98	0.80	0.41	NA	NA
Dividends	0.26	0.23	0.16	0.15	0.13	0.12	0.12	0.12	0.12	0.12
Payout Ratio	11%	12%	10%	10%	12%	11%	13%	23%	13%	15%
Prices:High	44.29	42.60	36.14	31.60	23.67	18.78	17.85	31.88	30.22	29.19
Prices:Low	23.19	30.45	26.06	22.02	16.87	10.92	11.52	11.45	13.88	15.00
P/E Ratio:High	20	22	23	22	22	18	20	64	33	38
P/E Ratio:Low	10	16	16	15	15	11	13	23	15	19

Income Statement Analysis (Million $)										
Revenue	87,472	76,330	43,814	37,006	30,594	26,588	24,182	22,241	20,088	18,098
Operating Income	7,343	5,970	3,175	2,609	1,952	1,765	1,517	1,091	1,619	1,413
Depreciation	1,274	1,095	733	589	497	342	310	321	297	278
Interest Expense	558	492	216	111	58.3	48.0	50.4	61.0	79.3	59.1
Pretax Income	5,537	4,359	2,226	1,909	1,396	1,376	1,156	710	1,243	1,076
Effective Tax Rate	39.6%	39.5%	38.5%	35.8%	34.2%	38.4%	38.0%	41.8%	40.0%	41.0%
Net Income	3,344	2,637	1,369	1,225	919	847	717	413	746	635
S&P Core Earnings	3,330	2,623	1,365	1,171	869	785	635	323	NA	NA

Balance Sheet & Other Financial Data (Million $)										
Cash	1,352	1,084	531	513	392	843	700	236	337	230
Current Assets	16,526	14,149	10,392	8,393	7,920	6,497	5,982	5,454	4,937	4,608
Total Assets	60,960	54,722	20,570	15,283	14,547	10,543	9,645	8,628	7,950	7,275
Current Liabilities	13,490	10,766	7,001	4,584	4,859	3,489	3,106	3,066	2,964	2,890
Long Term Debt	8,057	8,350	2,870	1,594	1,926	753	1,076	810	537	558
Common Equity	34,383	31,163	9,704	8,109	6,759	6,022	4,991	4,306	4,037	3,404
Total Capital	46,333	43,048	12,788	9,925	8,913	6,817	6,318	12,706	4,869	4,265
Capital Expenditures	2,180	1,805	1,769	1,495	1,348	1,122	1,109	714	695	494
Cash Flow	4,604	3,717	2,088	1,800	1,401	1,189	1,012	719	1,028	898
Current Ratio	1.2	1.3	1.5	1.8	1.6	1.9	1.9	1.8	1.7	1.6
% Long Term Debt of Capitalization	17.4	19.4	22.4	16.1	21.6	11.0	17.0	63.8	11.0	13.1
% Net Income of Revenue	3.8	3.5	3.1	3.3	3.0	3.2	3.0	1.9	3.7	3.5
% Return on Assets	5.8	7.0	7.6	8.2	7.3	8.4	7.8	5.0	9.8	9.1
% Return on Equity	10.2	12.8	15.2	16.3	14.4	15.4	15.1	9.6	19.7	19.9

Data as orig reptd.; bef. results of disc opers/spec. items. Per share data adj. for stk. divs.; EPS diluted. E-Estimated. NA-Not Available. NM-Not Meaningful. NR-Not Ranked. UR-Under Review.

Office: One CVS Drive, Woonsocket, RI 02895-6184.
Telephone: 401-765-1500.
Email: investorinfo@cvs.com
Website: http://www.cvs.com

Chrmn, Pres & CEO: T.M. Ryan
EVP, CFO & Chief Admin Officer: D.B. Rickard
EVP & General Counsel: D.A. Sgarro
SVP, Chief Acctg Officer & Cntlr: D.M. Denton

SVP & CIO: S. McGuigan
Investor Contact: N.R. Christal (914-722-4704)
Board Members: E. M. Banks, C. D. Brown, II, D. W. Dorman, M. L. Heard, W. H. Joyce, J. Millon, T. Murray, C. L. Piccolo, S. Z. Rosenberg, T. M. Ryan, R. J. Swift, K. E. Williams

Founded: 1892
Domicile: Delaware
Employees: 305,000

Danaher Corp

STANDARD
&POOR'S

| S&P Recommendation | BUY ★★★★☆ | Price $71.17 (as of Nov 27, 2009) | 12-Mo. Target Price $81.00 | Investment Style Large-Cap Growth |

GICS Sector Industrials
Sub-Industry Industrial Machinery

Summary This company is a leading maker of tools, including Sears Craftsman hand tools, and process/environmental controls and telecommunications equipment.

Key Stock Statistics (Source S&P, Vickers, company reports)

52-Wk Range	$73.81– 47.20	S&P Oper. EPS 2009E	3.43	Market Capitalization(B)	$22.862	Beta	0.83
Trailing 12-Month EPS	$3.59	S&P Oper. EPS 2010E	3.75	Yield (%)	0.17	S&P 3-Yr. Proj. EPS CAGR(%)	12
Trailing 12-Month P/E	19.8	P/E on S&P Oper. EPS 2009E	20.7	Dividend Rate/Share	$0.12	S&P Credit Rating	A+
$10K Invested 5 Yrs Ago	$12,383	Common Shares Outstg. (M)	321.2	Institutional Ownership (%)	75		

Price Performance

30-Week Mov. Avg. ··· 10-Week Mov. Avg. — — **GAAP Earnings vs. Previous Year** Volume Above Avg.▐▐ STARS
12-Mo. Target Price — Relative Strength — ▲ Up ▼ Down ▶ No Change Below Avg. ▐▐

Options: ASE, CBOE, P, Ph

Analysis prepared by **Efraim Levy, CFA** on October 23, 2009, when the stock traded at **$ 70.44.**

Highlights

► We expect revenue to decline 13% in 2009, assuming acquisitions cannot offset lower organic sales in a weakening U.S. and global economy and unfavorable currency exchange rate trends. We expect most regions to show declining organic sales, especially the U.S and Europe. Excluding not yet announced acquisitions, revenues in 2010 should rise in the low double digits, on resumed global economic growth.

► We see streamlining activities aiding margins, partly offset by narrower margins at some acquired businesses, and weakening global economies. Our 2009 EPS estimate includes most restructuring charges as part of ongoing operations.

► For the longer term, we look for sales increases to be driven by internal growth, supplemented by acquisitions. We anticipate that a steady flow of new and enhanced products, as well as greater sales of traditional tool lines, will aid comparisons. We expect margins to widen over time, as DHR consolidates acquisitions and likely benefits from higher capacity utilization, productivity gains and cost-cutting efforts. DHR has authorized a 10 million share buyback program that we view positively.

Investment Rationale/Risk

► Our buy opinion is based on our forecast of improving global economic activity. In addition, we view the company's balance sheet as strong. Based on several valuation measures, the stock is at a premium to some peers, which we believe reflects DHR's wider net margins and faster growth. Its earnings quality appears high to us, as we expect free cash flow in 2010 to exceed net income.

► Risks to our recommendation and target price include slowing demand for DHR's products, and unfavorable changes in foreign exchange rates. Also, we are concerned about some of Danaher's corporate governance practices, particularly its classified board of directors with staggered terms, which may allow certain policies to be entrenched longer despite shareholders' possible desire to change them.

► Given what we see as its sound balance sheet and strong cash flow growth, we think the company could raise its $0.12 annual cash dividend. Our 12-month target price of $81 is derived by applying a P/E of 21.6X to our 2010 EPS estimate of $3.75, reflecting relative historical P/E and rising peer multiples and brighter prospects for global GDP.

Qualitative Risk Assessment

| LOW | MEDIUM | HIGH |

Our risk assessment reflects our view of favorable growth prospects in most of the company's markets, good corporate leadership, and a solid balance sheet, offset by corporate governance issues.

Quantitative Evaluations

S&P Quality Ranking A+

| D | C | B- | B | B+ | A- | A | A+ |

Relative Strength Rank STRONG

71

LOWEST = 1   HIGHEST = 99

Revenue/Earnings Data

Revenue (Million $)

	1Q	2Q	3Q	4Q	Year
2009	2,628	2,674	2,751	--	--
2008	3,029	3,284	3,208	3,177	12,697
2007	2,556	2,671	2,731	3,141	11,026
2006	2,144	2,350	2,443	2,660	9,596
2005	1,826	1,929	1,966	2,264	7,985
2004	1,543	1,621	1,745	1,980	6,889

Earnings Per Share ($)

2009	0.72	0.89	1.05	E1.04	E3.43
2008	0.83	1.09	1.11	0.92	3.92
2007	0.78	0.96	1.03	0.97	3.72
2006	0.67	0.98	0.83	1.00	3.48
2005	0.58	0.70	0.70	0.78	2.76
2004	0.45	0.56	0.62	0.67	2.30

Fiscal year ended Dec. 31. Next earnings report expected: Late January. EPS Estimates based on S&P Operating Earnings; historical GAAP earnings are as reported.

Dividend Data (Dates: mm/dd Payment Date: mm/dd/yy)

Amount ($)	Date Decl.	Ex-Div. Date	Stk. of Record	Payment Date
0.030	12/12	12/23	12/26	01/30/09
0.030	02/25	03/25	03/27	04/24/09
0.030	05/07	06/24	06/26	07/31/09
0.030	09/18	09/23	09/25	10/30/09

Dividends have been paid since 1993. Source: Company reports.

Please read the Required Disclosures and Analyst Certification on the last page of this report.

The McGraw-Hill Companies

Danaher Corp

STANDARD
&POOR'S

Business Summary October 23, 2009

CORPORATE OVERVIEW. Danaher Corp. is a leading maker of hand tools and process and environmental controls. The company has four reporting segments: professional instrumentation (38% of 2008 sales), industrial technologies (26%), tools and components (10%), and medical technologies, formerly included in professional instrumentation (26%).

The professional instrumentation segment offers professional and technical customers various products and services that are used in connection with the performance of their work.

The industrial technologies segment manufactures products and sub-systems that are typically incorporated by original equipment manufacturers (OEMs) into various end-products and systems, as well as by customers and systems integrators into production and packaging lines.

The tools and components segment encompasses one strategic line of business -- mechanics' hand tools, and four focused niche businesses -- Delta Consolidated Industries, Hennessy Industries, Jacobs Chuck Manufacturing Company, and Jacobs Vehicle Systems.

Sales in 2008 by geographic destination were: U.S. 47%, Europe 31%, Asia 14%, and other regions 8%.

CORPORATE STRATEGY. The company's strategy is to expand revenues through a combination of internal growth and acquisitions. We expect the company to continue its tradition of successful acquisition integrations. During 2008, the company bought 17 businesses for an aggregate purchase price of about $423 million, versus 12 businesses for $3.6 billion in 2007 and 11 businesses in 2006 for approximately $2.7 billion.

In November 2007, as part of its acquisition strategy, the company purchased Tektronix Inc. for $38 per share, or about $2.8 billion including debt. Tektronix is a supplier of test, measurement and monitoring products, with about $1.1 billion in annual sales.

In May 2006, the company purchased Sybron Dental Specialties Inc. for $47 per share. The total transaction, including the assumption of debt, was valued at about $2 billion. Sybron manufactures a broad range of equipment for the dental industry and had about $650 million in revenues in its fiscal year ended September 30, 2005.

Company Financials Fiscal Year Ended Dec. 31

Per Share Data ($)	2008	2007	2006	2005	2004	2003	2002	2001	2000	1999
Tangible Book Value	NM	NM	NM	NM	NM	0.99	0.01	NM	0.28	1.46
Cash Flow	4.93	4.50	4.12	3.28	2.75	2.07	1.87	1.57	1.63	1.33
Earnings	3.92	3.72	3.48	2.76	2.30	1.69	1.49	1.01	1.12	0.90
S&P Core Earnings	3.73	3.72	3.47	2.70	2.20	1.55	1.20	0.85	NA	NA
Dividends	0.12	0.11	0.08	0.06	0.06	0.06	0.05	0.04	0.04	0.03
Payout Ratio	3%	3%	2%	2%	2%	4%	3%	4%	3%	3%
Prices:High	88.20	89.22	75.28	58.40	58.90	46.18	37.73	34.34	34.91	34.50
Prices:Low	47.20	69.11	54.04	48.32	43.83	29.78	26.30	21.95	18.22	21.38
P/E Ratio:High	23	24	22	21	26	27	25	34	31	39
P/E Ratio:Low	12	19	16	18	19	18	18	22	16	24

Income Statement Analysis (Million $)										
Revenue	12,697	11,026	9,596	7,985	6,889	5,294	4,577	3,782	3,778	3,197
Operating Income	2,350	2,055	1,719	1,446	1,253	957	824	750	702	584
Depreciation	339	268	217	177	156	133	130	178	150	126
Interest Expense	130	110	79.8	44.9	55.0	59.0	43.7	25.7	29.2	16.7
Pretax Income	1,749	1,637	1,446	1,234	1,058	797	657	476	523	430
Effective Tax Rate	24.7%	25.9%	22.4%	27.3%	29.5%	32.6%	29.4%	37.5%	38.0%	39.1%
Net Income	1,318	1,214	1,122	898	746	537	464	298	324	262
S&P Core Earnings	1,243	1,215	1,121	876	715	491	373	249	NA	NA

Balance Sheet & Other Financial Data (Million $)										
Cash	393	239	318	316	609	1,230	810	707	177	260
Current Assets	4,187	4,050	3,395	2,945	2,919	2,942	2,387	1,875	1,474	1,202
Total Assets	17,458	17,472	12,864	9,163	8,494	6,890	6,029	4,820	4,032	3,047
Current Liabilities	2,745	2,900	2,460	2,269	2,202	1,380	1,265	1,017	1,019	709
Long Term Debt	2,553	3,396	2,423	858	926	1,284	1,197	1,119	714	341
Common Equity	9,809	9,086	6,645	5,080	4,620	3,647	3,010	2,229	1,942	1,709
Total Capital	12,428	12,481	9,068	5,938	5,545	4,931	4,207	3,348	2,656	2,050
Capital Expenditures	194	162	138	121	116	80.3	65.4	80.6	88.5	88.9
Cash Flow	1,657	1,482	1,339	1,075	902	670	594	476	474	388
Current Ratio	1.5	1.4	1.4	1.3	1.3	2.1	1.9	1.8	1.4	1.7
% Long Term Debt of Capitalization	20.5	27.2	26.7	14.4	16.7	26.0	28.5	33.4	26.9	16.6
% Net Income of Revenue	10.4	11.0	11.7	11.2	10.8	10.1	10.1	7.9	8.6	8.2
% Return on Assets	7.5	8.0	10.2	10.2	9.7	8.3	8.6	6.7	9.2	8.9
% Return on Equity	14.0	15.4	19.1	18.5	18.0	16.1	17.7	14.3	17.8	16.8

Data as orig reptd.; bef. results of disc opers/spec. items. Per share data adj. for stk. divs.; EPS diluted. E-Estimated. NA-Not Available. NM-Not Meaningful. NR-Not Ranked. UR-Under Review.

Office: 2099 Pennsylvania Ave NW Fl 12, Washington, DC 20006-6807.
Telephone: 202-828-0850.
Email: ir@danaher.com
Website: http://www.danaher.com

Chrmn: S.M. Rales
Pres & CEO: H.L. Culp, Jr.
EVP & CFO: D.L. Comas
SVP & General Counsel: J.P. Graham

Chief Acctg Officer: R.S. Lutz
Board Members: M. M. Caplin, H. L. Culp, Jr., D. J. Ehrlich, L. Hefner, W. G. Lohr, Jr., M. P. Rales, S. M. Rales, J. T. Schwieters, A. G. Spoon

Founded: 1969
Domicile: Delaware
Employees: 50,300

The McGraw-Hill Companies

Darden Restaurants Inc.

STANDARD &POOR'S

S&P Recommendation **SELL** ★★★★★	Price $31.15 (as of Nov 27, 2009)	12-Mo. Target Price $30.00	Investment Style Large-Cap Growth

GICS Sector Consumer Discretionary
Sub-Industry Restaurants

Summary This restaurant company operates the Red Lobster, Olive Garden, Bahama Breeze and Seasons 52 chains, as well as the LongHorn Steakhouse and Capital Grille chains, which it acquired in October 2007.

Key Stock Statistics (Source S&P, Vickers, company reports)

52-Wk Range	$41.21– 15.77	S&P Oper. EPS 2010**E**	2.65	Market Capitalization(B)	$4.349	Beta	0.95
Trailing 12-Month EPS	$2.75	S&P Oper. EPS 2011**E**	2.75	Yield (%)	3.21	S&P 3-Yr. Proj. EPS CAGR(%)	3
Trailing 12-Month P/E	11.3	P/E on S&P Oper. EPS 2010**E**	11.8	Dividend Rate/Share	$1.00	S&P Credit Rating	BBB
$10K Invested 5 Yrs Ago	$12,400	Common Shares Outstg. (M)	139.6	Institutional Ownership (%)	83		

Price Performance

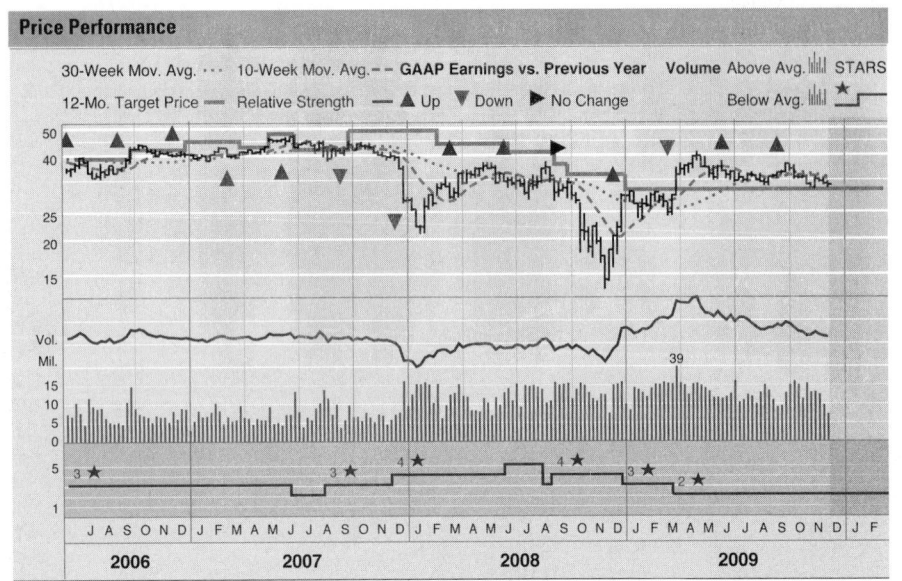

Analysis prepared by **Mark S. Basham** on September 15, 2009, when the stock traded at **$ 34.90**.

Options: ASE, CBOE, P, Ph

Highlights

▶ In FY 10 (May), we expect DRI to maintain a cautious approach to expansion, increasing its store base by about 3%. We think DRI likely will not implement material menu price increases, and with traffic likely to be down modestly in a sluggish economy, we see comparable sales declining about 1%. We see total sales increasing only slightly vs. FY 09, when a 53rd week provided a 2% boost to sales, according to company estimates.

▶ We look for some relief on food costs but see labor cost pressures in FY 10. We further expect DRI to keep discretionary spending under tight control, helping margins expand by about 5 to 15 basis points. Interest expense should decline slightly as DRI has adopted a more conservative cash flow policy whereby more cash flow is directed to debt reduction and dividends rather than more aggressive expansion or stock repurchases.

▶ We estimate EPS will be about flat with operating EPS of $2.75 in FY 09, which excludes $0.10 of integration costs associated with the 2007 acquisition of RARE Hospitality.

Investment Rationale/Risk

▶ Our sell recommendation is based on valuation, as the stock market rally has lifted the shares above our target price. We think the rise partly reflects several quarterly earnings reports that exceeded what we view as the company's conservative guidance, but more likely it has been in conjunction with the market rally on speculation of a robust economic recovery.

▶ Risks to our recommendation and target price include an unexpected further deceleration in food cost inflation. Also, consumers may be more resilient than we expect, suggesting traffic may hold up better than we anticipate, despite rising unemployment and ongoing economic uncertainty.

▶ Our 12-month target price of $30 is based on our discounted cash flow model, which assumes about 5% average annual free cash flow growth through FY 19, a weighted average cost of capital of 9.8% and a terminal growth rate of 3%. At $30, the shares would trade at approximately 10.5X our calendar 2010 EPS estimate of $2.85, a multiple that is at the low end of the range for DRI's peer group.

Qualitative Risk Assessment

LOW	**MEDIUM**	HIGH

DRI competes in the stable casual dining industry, and we believe that its Red Lobster and Olive Garden concepts have among the strongest brand name recognition in the industry. However, the casual dining segment over-expanded in recent years, in our opinion, and has begun a consolidation, a part of which includes DRI's disposal of its Smokey Bones Barbeque & Grill chain.

Quantitative Evaluations

S&P Quality Ranking   **A**

D	C	B-	B	B+	A-	**A**	A+

Relative Strength Rank   **MODERATE**

30

LOWEST = 1   HIGHEST = 99

Revenue/Earnings Data

Revenue (Million $)

	1Q	2Q	3Q	4Q	Year
2010	1,734	--	--	--	--
2009	1,774	1,669	1,799	1,976	7,218
2008	1,468	1,522	1,811	1,826	6,627
2007	1,360	1,298	1,450	1,460	5,567
2006	1,409	1,325	1,474	1,414	5,721
2005	1,279	1,229	1,376	1,394	5,278

Earnings Per Share ($)

	1Q	2Q	3Q	4Q	Year
2010	0.67	E0.50	E0.82	E0.66	E2.65
2009	0.58	0.42	0.78	0.87	2.65
2008	0.58	0.30	0.80	0.72	2.55
2007	0.62	0.45	0.79	0.67	2.53
2006	0.53	0.35	0.67	0.62	2.16
2005	0.44	0.26	0.56	0.52	1.78

Fiscal year ended May 31. Next earnings report expected: Mid December. EPS Estimates based on S&P Operating Earnings; historical GAAP earnings are as reported.

Dividend Data (Dates: mm/dd Payment Date: mm/dd/yy)

Amount ($)	Date Decl.	Ex-Div. Date	Stk. of Record	Payment Date
0.200	12/18	01/07	01/09	02/02/09
0.200	03/17	04/07	04/10	05/01/09
0.250	06/23	07/08	07/10	08/03/09
0.250	09/29	10/07	10/09	11/02/09

Dividends have been paid since 1995. Source: Company reports.

Please read the Required Disclosures and Analyst Certification on the last page of this report.

The McGraw-Hill Companies

Darden Restaurants Inc.

STANDARD
&POOR'S

Business Summary September 15, 2009

CORPORATE OVERVIEW. With systemwide sales from continuing operations of more than $7.2 billion in FY 09 (May), Darden Restaurants is the world's largest publicly held casual dining restaurant company. As of May 31, 2009, it operated approximately 1,775 restaurants in the U.S. and Canada, including 690 Red Lobster units, 691 Olive Garden units, 321 LongHorn Steakhouse locations, and about 75 restaurants divided among The Capital Grille, Bahama Breeze, and Seasons 52 chains.

Olive Garden is the U.S. market share leader among casual dining Italian food restaurants. FY 09 systemwide sales grew 7.9%, to $3.3 billion (including a 53rd week). Same-restaurant sales increased 0.3%, compared to 4.9% in FY 08. Average restaurant sales were $4.8 million. The average check per person was $15.50 to $16.00 in FY 09.

Red Lobster, founded by William Darden in 1968, is the largest U.S. casual dining seafood-specialty restaurant operator. Systemwide sales totaled $2.62 billion in FY 09, down 0.2% from FY 08. Average restaurant sales were $3.8 million in FY 09, down from $3.9 million in FY 08. Same-store sales fell 2.2% in FY 09,

following a 1.1% increase in FY 08. The average check per person was $19.00 to $19.50.

On October 1, 2007, DRI acquired RARE Hospitality International, Inc., in a cash tender offer for all RARE common shares at $38.15 per share, or total consideration of $1.41 billion in cash. Financing was obtained under a $1.2 billion senior interim credit facility and a $700 million senior revolver. Most members of RARE management agreed to join DRI in roles generally similar to those they had at RARE.

RARE operations included the LongHorn Steakhouse chain. Total sales increased 3.6% in FY 09. Annual sales per restaurant in FY 09 dipped slightly to $2.8 million from $2.9 million in FY 08. Same-store sales decreased 5.6%, following on a 1.1% decline in FY 08.

Company Financials Fiscal Year Ended May 31

Per Share Data ($)	2009	2008	2007	2006	2005	2004	2003	2002	2001	2000
Tangible Book Value	3.89	2.45	7.57	8.20	8.25	7.86	7.03	6.56	5.66	5.09
Cash Flow	4.61	4.19	3.88	3.57	3.08	2.60	2.43	2.20	1.85	1.55
Earnings	2.65	2.55	2.53	2.16	1.78	1.36	1.31	1.30	1.06	0.89
S&P Core Earnings	2.56	2.54	2.53	2.10	1.68	1.27	1.18	1.16	0.97	NA
Dividends	0.72	0.46	0.40	0.08	0.08	0.08	0.05	0.05	0.05	0.05
Payout Ratio	27%	18%	16%	4%	4%	6%	4%	4%	5%	6%
Calendar Year	2008	2007	2006	2005	2004	2003	2002	2001	2000	1999
Prices:High	37.83	47.60	44.43	39.53	28.54	23.01	29.76	24.98	18.00	15.58
Prices:Low	13.21	26.90	32.91	25.78	18.48	16.50	18.00	12.67	8.29	10.42
P/E Ratio:High	14	19	18	18	16	17	23	19	17	17
P/E Ratio:Low	5	11	13	12	10	12	14	10	8	12

Income Statement Analysis (Million $)										
Revenue	7,218	6,627	5,567	5,721	5,278	5,003	4,655	4,369	4,021	3,701
Operating Income	895	878	774	757	685	636	588	563	479	421
Depreciation	275	238	200	221	213	210	198	166	147	130
Interest Expense	118	35.2	40.7	43.1	43.1	43.7	44.1	37.8	31.5	23.1
Pretax Income	513	515	531	483	424	340	348	363	301	274
Effective Tax Rate	27.5%	28.2%	29.0%	29.9%	31.4%	31.9%	33.2%	34.5%	34.6%	35.5%
Net Income	372	370	377	338	291	231	232	238	197	177
S&P Core Earnings	360	367	378	330	274	214	208	212	181	NA

Balance Sheet & Other Financial Data (Million $)										
Cash	62.9	43.2	30.2	42.3	42.8	36.7	48.6	153	61.8	26.1
Current Assets	555	468	545	378	407	346	326	450	328	290
Total Assets	5,025	4,731	2,881	3,010	2,938	2,780	2,665	2,530	2,218	1,971
Current Liabilities	1,096	1,136	1,074	1,026	1,045	683	640	601	554	607
Long Term Debt	1,632	1,634	492	495	350	653	658	663	518	304
Common Equity	1,606	1,409	1,115	1,230	1,273	1,246	1,196	1,129	1,035	960
Total Capital	3,238	3,043	1,633	1,815	1,738	2,075	2,005	1,909	1,644	1,344
Capital Expenditures	535	429	345	338	329	354	423	318	355	269
Cash Flow	646	608	578	560	504	441	430	404	344	307
Current Ratio	0.5	0.4	0.5	0.4	0.4	0.5	0.5	0.7	0.6	0.5
% Long Term Debt of Capitalization	50.4	53.6	30.1	27.3	20.2	31.5	32.8	34.7	31.5	22.6
% Net Income of Revenue	5.2	5.6	6.8	5.9	5.5	4.6	5.0	5.4	4.9	4.8
% Return on Assets	7.6	9.7	12.8	11.4	10.2	8.5	8.9	10.0	9.4	9.2
% Return on Equity	24.7	29.5	31.6	27.0	23.7	19.0	20.0	22.0	19.7	18.4

Data as orig reptd.; bef. results of disc opers/spec. items. Per share data adj. for stk. divs.; EPS diluted. E-Estimated. NA-Not Available. NM-Not Meaningful. NR-Not Ranked. UR-Under Review.

Office: 5900 Lake Ellenor Drive, Orlando, FL 32809-4634.
Telephone: 407-245-4000.
Email: irinfo@darden.com
Website: http://www.darden.com

Chrmn & CEO: C. Otis, Jr.
Pres & COO: A.H. Madsen
Investor Contact: C.B. Richmond (407-245-4000)
SVP, CFO & Chief Acctg Officer: C.B. Richmond

SVP, Secy & General Counsel: P.J. Shives
Board Members: L. L. Berry, J. P. Birkelund, O. C. Donald, C. J. Fraleigh, V. D. Harker, D. H. Hughes, C. A. Ledsinger, Jr., W. M. Lewis, Jr., C. Mack, III, A. H. Madsen, C. Mcgillicudy, III, C. Otis, Jr., M. D. Rose, M. A. Sastre

Founded: 1968
Domicile: Florida
Employees: 178,692

DaVita Inc

STANDARD & POOR'S

S&P Recommendation	BUY ★★★★☆	Price $59.33 (as of Nov 27, 2009)	12-Mo. Target Price $64.00	Investment Style Large-Cap Growth

GICS Sector Health Care
Sub-Industry Health Care Services

Summary This company is one of the largest worldwide providers of integrated dialysis services for patients suffering from chronic kidney failure.

Key Stock Statistics (Source S&P, Vickers, company reports)

52-Wk Range	$60.49–41.21	S&P Oper. EPS 2009**E**	4.04	Market Capitalization(B)	$6.064	Beta	0.47
Trailing 12-Month EPS	$3.94	S&P Oper. EPS 2010**E**	4.34	Yield (%)	Nil	S&P 3-Yr. Proj. EPS CAGR(%)	5
Trailing 12-Month P/E	15.1	P/E on S&P Oper. EPS 2009**E**	14.7	Dividend Rate/Share	Nil	S&P Credit Rating	BB-
$10K Invested 5 Yrs Ago	$18,111	Common Shares Outstg. (M)	102.2	Institutional Ownership (%)	94		

Price Performance

30-Week Mov. Avg. · · · 10-Week Mov. Avg. – – – **GAAP Earnings vs. Previous Year** Volume Above Avg. ▥▥▥ STARS
12-Mo. Target Price — Relative Strength — ▲ Up ▼ Down ▶ No Change Below Avg. ▥▥▥ ★

Options: CBOE, P, Ph

Analysis prepared by **Jeffrey Englander, CFA** on November 10, 2009, when the stock traded at **$ 58.74**.

Highlights

► We see sales rising 8% in 2009 and 7% in 2010, reflecting an aging U.S. population, stable demand for dialysis services, and increased roll-out of additional services. We see revenues being driven by improving revenue per treatment growth and stabilizing erythropoietin (EPO) utilization, partially offset by managed care (private payor) reimbursement cuts and changes in payor mix due to rising unemployment.

► We forecast a decline in gross margins in 2009 on increases in center operating and Heparin costs as well as more gradual growth in revenue per treatment. We see a modest decline in G&A expenses as a percentage of sales leading to a lesser decline in EBITDA margins. For 2010, we look for flat gross margins, as patient care costs remain stable as a percentage of sales. We look for a modest rise in G&A expenses to be offset by a modest decline in bad debt expenses, all relative to sales. As a result, we look for steady gross margins in 2010.

► We estimate operating EPS of $4.04 in 2009 and $4.34 in 2010. We assume 104 million shares outstanding in 2009 and 103 million in 2010.

Investment Rationale/Risk

► We view dialysis provider fundamentals, including the rising senior population in the U.S., a higher incidence of diabetes and recurring demand, as favorable, and expect DVA's organic treatment volumes to continue to grow 3% to 5% annually. Meanwhile, we see DVA increasingly dependent on commercial pricing, which is sharply above Medicare rates, for its profits. DVA continues to experience pricing pressure from private payors, and its long-term performance will likely reflect the success of contract negotiations with the private payors. While we see early signs that EPO utilization has begun to stabilize, which should bolster results going forward, we view increased Heparin costs as a challenge. We believe Medicare's recently released bundled reimbursement rates are less onerous than feared.

► Risks to our recommendation and target price include headline risk over EPO utilization, unfavorable Medicare rule changes, heightened competition, and reduced reimbursement.

► Our 12-month target price of $64 assumes an 8.0X EV/EBITDA multiple of our 2010 EBITDA estimate, a slight discount to the historical average, and a P/E of 15X our 2010 EPS estimate.

Qualitative Risk Assessment

LOW	MEDIUM	HIGH

Our risk assessment reflects our view of stable demand for dialysis services, driven by a rising senior population in the U.S., offset by DVA's dependence on third-party payments, including Medicare and Medicaid.

Quantitative Evaluations

S&P Quality Ranking B

D	C	B-	B	B+	A-	A	A+

Relative Strength Rank STRONG

80

LOWEST = 1 HIGHEST = 99

Revenue/Earnings Data

Revenue (Million $)

	1Q	2Q	3Q	4Q	Year
2009	1,448	1,519	1,574	--	--
2008	1,345	1,407	1,447	1,461	5,660
2007	1,278	1,313	1,318	1,355	5,264
2006	1,163	1,208	1,237	1,273	4,881
2005	578.6	617.1	644.9	1,133	2,974
2004	535.4	551.6	595.5	616.0	2,299

Earnings Per Share ($)

2009	0.92	1.02	1.06	E1.05	E4.04
2008	0.80	0.90	0.89	0.94	3.53
2007	0.72	1.17	0.88	0.79	3.55
2006	0.55	0.61	0.88	0.70	2.73
2005	0.50	0.49	0.49	0.54	1.99
2004	0.51	0.50	0.59	0.56	2.16

Fiscal year ended Dec. 31. Next earnings report expected: Mid February. EPS Estimates based on S&P Operating Earnings; historical GAAP earnings are as reported.

Dividend Data

No cash dividends have been paid.

DaVita Inc

STANDARD
&POOR'S

Business Summary November 10, 2009

CORPORATE OVERVIEW. DaVita is a leading U.S. provider of dialysis and related services for patients suffering from chronic kidney failure, also known as end stage renal disease (ESRD). As of December 31, 2008, DVA provided dialysis and ancillary services to about 112,000 patients through a network of 1,449 outpatient dialysis facilities in 43 states. In addition, the company provided acute inpatient dialysis services at over 700 hospitals.

As a result of DVA's growth through acquisitions, it became highly leveraged, in our opinion. Since a management overhaul in 1999, the company has implemented a new strategy focusing on improving operations and restructuring the balance sheet. In 2005, DVA acquired 492 centers through the Gambro acquisition, as well as 12 independent centers. The company also opened 13 new centers.

In 2008, the company acquired 20 centers, opened 87 new centers, and closed nine. As of year end, it owned 1,426 centers outright, and provided administrative services to 23 third-party owned centers. Average revenue per treatment in 2008 was $333.52, up 1.6% from 2007.

Hemodialysis uses an artificial kidney, called a dialyzer, to remove certain toxins, fluids and salt from the patient's blood, together with a machine to control external blood flow and to monitor certain vital signs of the patient. Peritoneal dialysis uses the patient's peritoneal (abdominal) cavity to eliminate fluid and toxins. In 2008, outpatient hemodialysis, peritoneal dialysis and hospital inpatient dialysis accounted for 82%, 10% and 5% of total treatments, respectively.

Company Financials Fiscal Year Ended Dec. 31

Per Share Data ($)	2008	2007	2006	2005	2004	2003	2002	2001	2000	1999
Tangible Book Value	NM	NM	NM	NM	NM	NM	NM	NM	NM	NM
Cash Flow	5.43	5.36	4.37	3.14	3.00	2.20	1.85	1.56	1.03	-0.29
Earnings	3.53	3.55	2.73	1.99	2.16	1.66	1.52	1.01	0.13	-1.21
S&P Core Earnings	3.53	3.48	2.73	1.89	2.07	1.59	1.41	0.89	NA	NA
Dividends	Nil	Nil	Nil	Nil	Nil	Nil	Nil	Nil	Nil	Nil
Payout Ratio	Nil	Nil	Nil	Nil	Nil	Nil	Nil	Nil	Nil	Nil
Prices:High	60.23	67.44	60.70	53.90	41.10	26.94	17.63	16.33	11.88	19.75
Prices:Low	40.96	50.75	46.70	38.87	25.23	12.77	12.67	9.33	1.38	3.79
P/E Ratio:High	17	19	22	27	19	16	12	16	85	NM
P/E Ratio:Low	12	14	17	20	12	8	8	9	10	NM

Income Statement Analysis (Million $)	2008	2007	2006	2005	2004	2003	2002	2001	2000	1999
Revenue	5,660	5,264	4,881	2,974	2,299	2,016	1,855	1,651	1,486	1,445
Operating Income	1,069	1,046	911	607	510	461	456	423	291	188
Depreciation	201	193	173	120	86.7	74.7	64.7	105	112	112
Interest Expense	229	257	277	140	52.4	66.8	71.6	71.7	117	111
Pretax Income	656	628	512	353	376	296	325	250	45.0	-182
Effective Tax Rate	35.9%	39.2%	36.4%	35.0%	37.2%	38.1%	39.8%	41.8%	62.2%	NM
Net Income	374	382	289	207	222	176	187	136	16.9	-147
S&P Core Earnings	374	374	289	197	213	167	175	118	NA	NA

Balance Sheet & Other Financial Data (Million $)	2008	2007	2006	2005	2004	2003	2002	2001	2000	1999
Cash	446	487	310	432	252	61.7	96.5	36.7	31.2	108
Current Assets	2,128	1,976	1,709	1,654	869	605	545	475	398	655
Total Assets	7,286	6,944	6,492	6,280	2,512	1,946	1,776	1,663	1,597	2,057
Current Liabilities	1,163	1,087	1,112	990	442	363	293	299	250	1,699
Long Term Debt	3,618	3,684	3,730	4,085	1,322	1,117	1,311	811	974	6.00
Common Equity	1,952	1,732	1,246	851	523	307	70.3	504	349	326
Total Capital	5,808	5,733	5,224	5,100	2,048	1,563	1,474	1,359	1,342	355
Capital Expenditures	318	272	263	161	128	100	103	51.2	41.1	107
Cash Flow	575	575	463	327	309	250	251	242	129	-35.0
Current Ratio	1.8	1.8	1.5	1.7	2.0	1.7	1.9	1.6	1.6	0.4
% Long Term Debt of Capitalization	60.5	66.2	71.4	80.1	64.6	71.4	89.0	59.7	72.5	1.7
% Net Income of Revenue	6.6	7.3	5.9	7.0	9.7	8.7	10.1	8.3	1.1	NM
% Return on Assets	5.3	5.7	4.5	4.7	10.0	9.4	10.9	8.4	0.1	NM
% Return on Equity	20.3	25.6	27.6	30.2	53.6	93.2	65.1	32.0	5.0	NM

Data as orig reptd.; bef. results of disc opers/spec. items. Per share data adj. for stk. divs.; EPS diluted. E-Estimated. NA-Not Available. NM-Not Meaningful. NR-Not Ranked. UR-Under Review.

Office: 1627 Cole Blvd, Lakewood, CO 80401.
Telephone: 303-626-6000.
Email: ir@davita.com
Website: http://www.davita.com

Chrmn & CEO: K.J. Thiry
COO: D. Kogod
CFO: R.K. Whitney
Chief Acctg Officer & Cntlr: J.K. Hilger

Secy & General Counsel: K. Rivera
Investor Contact: L. Zumwalt (800-310-4872)
Board Members: P. M. Arway, C. G. Berg, W. W. Brittain, Jr., P. J. Diaz, P. T. Grauer, J. M. Nehra, W. Roper, K. J. Thiry, R. J. Valine, R. C. Vaughan

Founded: 1994
Domicile: Delaware
Employees: 32,500

Dean Foods Co

STANDARD &POOR'S

S&P Recommendation **HOLD** ★★★☆☆	Price $16.07 (as of Nov 27, 2009)	12-Mo. Target Price $22.00	Investment Style Large-Cap Blend

GICS Sector Consumer Staples
Sub-Industry Packaged Foods & Meats

Summary This leading U.S. dairy processor and distributor was formed in December 2001 when Suiza Foods, the largest U.S. dairy, acquired Dean Foods and adopted the Dean Foods name.

Key Stock Statistics (Source S&P, Vickers, company reports)

52-Wk Range	$22.09–13.24	S&P Oper. EPS 2009**E**	1.67	Market Capitalization(B)	$2.901	Beta	0.50
Trailing 12-Month EPS	$1.54	S&P Oper. EPS 2010**E**	1.73	Yield (%)	Nil	S&P 3-Yr. Proj. EPS CAGR(%)	10
Trailing 12-Month P/E	10.4	P/E on S&P Oper. EPS 2009**E**	9.6	Dividend Rate/Share	Nil	S&P Credit Rating	BB-
$10K Invested 5 Yrs Ago	NA	Common Shares Outstg. (M)	180.5	Institutional Ownership (%)	87		

Price Performance

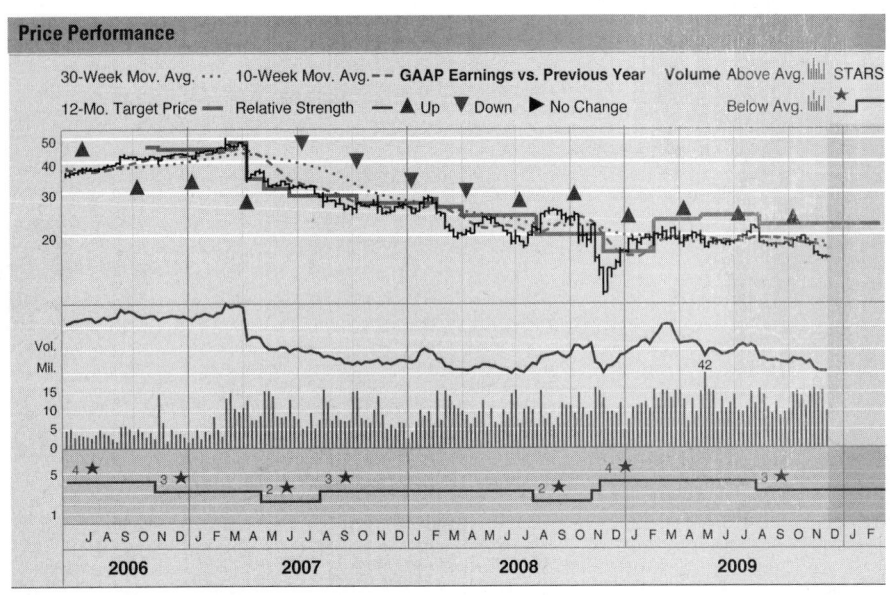

30-Week Mov. Avg. · · · 10-Week Mov. Avg. - - GAAP Earnings vs. Previous Year Volume Above Avg.▮▮▮ STARS
12-Mo. Target Price — Relative Strength — ▲ Up ▼ Down ► No Change Below Avg.▮▮▮ ★

Options: CBOE, P, Ph

Analysis prepared by **Tom Graves, CFA** on August 28, 2009, when the stock traded at **$ 18.18**.

Highlights

▶ In 2009, we look for net sales to decline from the $12.5 billion reported for 2008, largely due to lower prices, especially for conventional milk. In our view, while the overall cost outlook for 2009 is relatively good, we anticipate some future increases in dairy prices. Also, we expect some pricing pressure from competitors, and some consumer tradedown to less expensive dairy products.

▶ Before some special items, but including expected dilution related to a new joint venture, we estimate 2009 EPS of $1.62, with about 14% more shares outstanding. For 2010, with about 6% more shares, we estimate EPS of $1.70. In 2009's first six months, DF's reported EPS of $0.85 included a net negative impact of about $0.09 from special items.

▶ In May 2009, DF received net proceeds of about $445 million in connection with the public sale of some 25.4 million common shares. Proceeds were earmarked to repay some senior notes and to repay indebtedness under a receivables-backed facility.

Investment Rationale/Risk

▶ In the future, we expect that Dean Foods will aim for clear cost leadership in the fluid milk industry, through a focus on such areas as product standardization and sourcing, facility network optimization, improved productivity, and lower distribution costs. We expect that there will be some related investment costs. In July 2009, DF said it had completed the acquisition of a European provider of soy-based beverage and food products for about EUR325 million.

▶ Risks to our recommendation and target price include the possibility that consumer spending on dairy products, commodity costs, and milk prices will be less favorable than we expect, and that competitive conditions will be more difficult than anticipated.

▶ Our 12-month target price of $22 represents a 14% P/E discount to what we expect from a group of other food stocks, reflecting our view that DF is more of a commodity business. Also, DF does not pay a quarterly dividend to common shareholders.

Qualitative Risk Assessment

LOW	MEDIUM	HIGH

Our risk assessment reflects our view of DF's leading position in the U.S. milk market, and our expectation of future free cash flow. However, milk prices can be volatile, and some products are likely to enjoy stronger demand and growth than others.

Quantitative Evaluations

S&P Quality Ranking B

D	C	B-	B	B+	A-	A	A+

Relative Strength Rank WEAK

20

LOWEST = 1   HIGHEST = 99

Revenue/Earnings Data

Revenue (Million $)

	1Q	2Q	3Q	4Q	Year
2009	2,703	2,681	2,774	--	--
2008	3,077	3,103	3,195	3,080	12,455
2007	2,630	2,844	3,117	3,232	11,822
2006	2,509	2,478	2,518	2,594	10,099
2005	2,562	2,603	2,647	2,695	10,506
2004	2,452	2,807	2,773	2,791	10,822

Earnings Per Share ($)

2009	0.48	0.38	0.27	E0.38	E1.67
2008	0.21	0.31	0.24	0.43	1.21
2007	0.47	0.21	0.05	0.24	0.95
2006	0.37	0.53	0.54	0.56	2.01
2005	0.43	0.52	0.43	0.49	1.78
2004	0.43	0.47	0.25	0.64	1.78

Fiscal year ended Dec. 31. Next earnings report expected: Mid February. EPS Estimates based on S&P Operating Earnings; historical GAAP earnings are as reported.

Dividend Data

A special cash dividend of $15 a share was paid in April 2007.

Please read the Required Disclosures and Analyst Certification on the last page of this report.

The McGraw-Hill Companies

Dean Foods Co

STANDARD &POOR'S

Business Summary August 28, 2009

CORPORATE OVERVIEW. Dean Foods Co. is a leading U.S. processor and distributor of milk and other dairy products. In December 2001, Suiza Foods Corp., the largest U.S. dairy, acquired Dean Foods Co. Suiza subsequently changed its name to Dean Foods Co. The company has grown partly through an acquisition strategy and by realizing regional economies of scale and operating efficiencies by consolidating manufacturing and distribution operations. Some of DF's products are sold under licensed brand names.

The company's renamed Fresh Dairy Direct segment (previously known as DSD Dairy) manufactures, markets and distributes more than 50 regional branded and private-label dairy case products, including milk, creamers, ice cream, juices and teas, to retailers and various other customers. In 2008, the DSD Dairy segment had net sales of $9.8 billion, or 79% of DF's total. Fresh milk represented 71% of DSD's sales in 2008. Also, 52% of DSD sales were of products carrying DF brands, while 48% were of private label products. DSD's largest customer was Wal-Mart, which including its subsidiaries, accounted

for about 20% of DSD Dairy's net sales in 2008.

The WhiteWave-Morningstar segment (21% of sales) includes the WhiteWave business, which manufactures and sells a variety of nationally branded soy, dairy and dairy-related products, including Silk soymilk, Horizon Organic dairy products, International Delight coffee creamers, LAND O'LAKES creamers and fluid dairy products, and Rachel's Organic dairy products. The company's Morningstar business manufactures private label cultured and extended shelf life dairy products such as ice cream mix, sour and whipped cream, and cottage cheese. Wal-Mart and subsidiaries accounted for 14% of WhiteWave-Morningstar sales in 2008.

Company Financials Fiscal Year Ended Dec. 31

Per Share Data ($)	2008	2007	2006	2005	2004	2003	2002	2001	2000	1999
Tangible Book Value	NM	NM	NM	NM	NM	NM	NM	NM	NM	NM
Cash Flow	2.74	2.64	3.63	3.22	1.58	3.41	2.71	2.44	2.35	2.05
Earnings	1.21	0.95	2.01	1.78	1.78	2.27	1.77	1.23	1.27	1.04
S&P Core Earnings	1.15	0.92	2.00	1.66	1.58	1.85	1.57	0.91	NA	NA
Dividends	Nil	Nil	Nil	Nil	Nil	Nil	Nil	Nil	Nil	Nil
Payout Ratio	Nil	Nil	Nil	Nil	Nil	Nil	Nil	Nil	Nil	Nil
Prices:High	29.23	50.50	43.55	42.10	38.00	33.75	27.03	24.16	17.48	16.75
Prices:Low	11.20	24.11	34.66	31.60	28.25	24.60	18.05	14.00	12.00	9.88
P/E Ratio:High	24	53	22	24	21	15	15	20	14	16
P/E Ratio:Low	9	25	17	18	16	11	10	11	9	10

Income Statement Analysis (Million $)										
Revenue	12,455	11,822	10,099	10,506	10,822	9,185	8,991	6,230	5,756	4,482
Operating Income	869	810	903	867	919	889	856	542	524	406
Depreciation	236	232	228	221	224	192	174	155	145	155
Interest Expense	310	322	195	169	205	195	231	135	147	87.8
Pretax Income	300	214	456	439	462	574	421	231	234	193
Effective Tax Rate	38.3%	39.2%	38.5%	37.9%	38.3%	38.0%	36.4%	36.3%	38.4%	39.1%
Net Income	185	130	280	272	285	356	268	116	114	109
S&P Core Earnings	175	126	278	254	253	288	236	79.2	NA	NA

Balance Sheet & Other Financial Data (Million $)										
Cash	36.0	32.6	31.1	25.1	27.6	47.1	45.9	78.3	31.0	25.2
Current Assets	1,481	1,532	1,379	1,477	1,596	1,401	1,311	1,482	818	639
Total Assets	7,040	7,033	6,770	7,051	7,756	6,993	6,582	6,732	3,780	2,659
Current Liabilities	1,427	933	1,337	1,137	1,106	1,170	1,268	1,175	700	479
Long Term Debt	4,174	5,271	2,872	3,329	3,116	2,611	3,140	3,556	1,809	1,373
Common Equity	558	51.3	1,809	1,872	2,661	2,543	1,643	1,476	599	584
Total Capital	5,201	5,781	5,186	5,688	6,308	5,542	5,077	5,313	3,047	2,145
Capital Expenditures	257	241	237	307	356	292	242	137	137	188
Cash Flow	421	362	508	494	509	548	442	270	259	264
Current Ratio	1.0	1.6	1.0	1.3	1.4	1.2	1.0	1.3	1.2	1.3
% Long Term Debt of Capitalization	80.3	99.0	55.4	58.5	49.4	47.1	61.8	66.9	59.3	64.0
% Net Income of Revenue	1.5	1.1	2.8	2.6	2.6	3.9	3.0	1.9	1.9	2.4
% Return on Assets	2.6	1.9	4.1	3.7	3.9	5.2	4.0	2.2	3.5	3.8
% Return on Equity	60.7	14.0	15.1	12.0	11.0	17.0	17.2	11.1	19.2	17.6

Data as orig reptd.; bef. results of disc opers/spec. items. Per share data adj. for stk. divs.; EPS diluted. E-Estimated. NA-Not Available. NM-Not Meaningful. NR-Not Ranked. UR-Under Review.

Office: 2515 McKinney Avenue, Dallas, TX 75201.
Telephone: 214-303-3400.
Website: http://www.deanfoods.com
Chrmn & CEO: G.L. Engles

COO: J. Scalzo
EVP & CFO: J.F. Callahan, Jr.
EVP, Secy & General Counsel: S.J. Kemps
SVP & Chief Acctg Officer: R.L. McCrummen

Investor Contact: B. Sievert (214-303-3437)
Board Members: T. C. Davis, G. L. Engles, S. L. Green, J. S. Hardin, Jr., J. Hill, W. Mailloux, J. R. Muse, H. M. Nevares-La Costa, J. L. Turner, D. Wright

Founded: 1925
Domicile: Delaware
Employees: 25,820

The McGraw·Hill Companies

Deere & Co

STANDARD &POOR'S

S&P Recommendation	BUY ★★★★☆	Price $52.36 (as of Nov 27, 2009)	12-Mo. Target Price $65.00	Investment Style Large-Cap Blend

GICS Sector Industrials
Sub-Industry Construction & Farm Machinery & Heavy Trucks

Summary Deere is the world's biggest producer of farm equipment and is also a large maker of construction machinery and lawn and garden equipment.

Key Stock Statistics (Source S&P, Vickers, company reports)

52-Wk Range	$54.15– 24.51	S&P Oper. EPS 2009E	2.80	Market Capitalization(B)	$22.146	Beta	1.65
Trailing 12-Month EPS	$3.39	S&P Oper. EPS 2010E	3.20	Yield (%)	2.14	S&P 3-Yr. Proj. EPS CAGR(%)	16
Trailing 12-Month P/E	15.5	P/E on S&P Oper. EPS 2009E	18.7	Dividend Rate/Share	$1.12	S&P Credit Rating	BB
$10K Invested 5 Yrs Ago	$15,784	Common Shares Outstg. (M)	422.9	Institutional Ownership (%)	72		

Price Performance

30-Week Mov. Avg. ···· 10-Week Mov. Avg. - - GAAP Earnings vs. Previous Year Volume Above Avg. STARS
12-Mo. Target Price — Relative Strength — ▲ Up ▼ Down ▶ No Change Below Avg.

Options: ASE, CBOE, Ph

Analysis prepared by **Michael W. Jaffe** on November 19, 2009, when the stock traded at **$ 50.61**.

Highlights

▶ We expect a mid-single-digit revenue gain in FY 10 (Oct.). We see near-term demand for DE's products, especially those dependent on construction activity and consumer spending, being hurt by the weak global economy. We look for a smaller downturn in demand for agricultural equipment. Still, we see improvement as FY 10 progresses, as we think the global economy is in the early stages of a recovery, and that government stimulus will assist demand for construction equipment. We also anticipate a modest upturn in U.S. farm cash receipts in FY 10, on our outlook for better economic conditions, and some recent gains in crop prices after a major downturn since mid-2008.

▶ We project wider margins in FY 10, on our outlook for firming business trends. We also see Deere's bottom line being assisted by its ongoing cost reduction efforts, which have included selective workforce reductions and aggressive factory schedule adjustments.

▶ Our FY 09 operating EPS estimate excludes $144 million of expected pretax costs from a voluntary separation program for 800 workers, and the closure of a Canadian facility, with $16 million recorded in the third quarter.

Investment Rationale/Risk

▶ We see global economic challenges limiting DE's operating performance in the near term, but we expect certain end markets to bottom in the coming year, in light of government stimulus actions. We see agricultural equipment weathering the downturn better than the company's other markets. Based on these factors and our valuation model, we believe the stock is undervalued at current levels.

▶ Risks to our recommendation and target price include an ongoing global economic downturn, the resumption of a decline in crop prices and the likely resultant negative effect on farm equipment spending, and larger-than-expected loan provisions in the credit segment.

▶ The stock recently traded at a little under 16X our calendar 2010 EPS forecast of $3.25. We believe it is undervalued, as this falls well below DE's typical valuation during periods when its business is in the early stages of a recovery, which we believe will be taking place over the coming year. Based on these views, our 12-month target price is $65, or 20X our calendar 2010 forecast, which is closer to DE's typical valuation at this stage of its business cycle.

Qualitative Risk Assessment

LOW	MEDIUM	HIGH

Our risk assessment reflects Deere's leading position in many of the markets it serves, and a balance sheet that typically carries large cash balances. On the other hand, the company's businesses are highly cyclical.

Quantitative Evaluations

S&P Quality Ranking A-

D	C	B-	B	B+	A-	A	A+

Relative Strength Rank STRONG

91

LOWEST = 1   HIGHEST = 99

Revenue/Earnings Data

Revenue (Million $)

	1Q	2Q	3Q	4Q	Year
2009	5,146	6,748	5,885	--	--
2008	5,201	8,097	7,739	7,401	28,438
2007	4,425	6,883	6,634	6,141	24,082
2006	4,202	6,562	6,267	5,118	22,148
2005	4,127	6,621	6,005	5,177	21,931
2004	2,912	5,877	5,418	5,207	19,986

Earnings Per Share ($)

2009	0.48	1.11	0.99	E0.19	E2.80
2008	0.83	1.74	1.32	0.81	4.70
2007	0.52	1.36	1.32	0.94	4.00
2006	0.47	1.09	0.93	0.60	3.08
2005	0.45	1.22	0.79	0.48	2.94
2004	0.34	0.94	0.79	0.71	2.78

Fiscal year ended Oct. 31. Next earnings report expected: Early December. EPS Estimates based on S&P Operating Earnings; historical GAAP earnings are as reported.

Dividend Data (Dates: mm/dd Payment Date: mm/dd/yy)

Amount ($)	Date Decl.	Ex-Div. Date	Stk. of Record	Payment Date
0.280	12/10	12/29	12/31	02/02/09
0.280	02/25	03/27	03/31	05/01/09
0.280	05/27	06/26	06/30	08/03/09
0.280	08/26	09/28	09/30	11/02/09

Dividends have been paid since 1937. Source: Company reports.

Deere & Co

Business Summary November 19, 2009

CORPORATE OVERVIEW. Deere & Co. is the world's largest maker of farm tractors and combines, and a leading producer of construction equipment.

The agricultural equipment segment (58% of FY 08 (Oct.) revenues; 13% operating margin) primarily makes tractors; combine, cotton and sugar cane harvesters; tillage, seeding and soil preparation machinery; hay and forage equipment; material handling equipment; and integrated agricultural management systems technology for the global farming industry. Over the past five years, segment margins averaged about 9%.

The commercial and consumer equipment segment (C&CE; 16%; 7.0%) manufactures and distributes equipment and service parts for commercial and residential uses. Products include small tractors for lawn, garden, commercial and utility purposes; lawn mowers; golf course equipment; utility vehicles; landscape and irrigation equipment; and other outdoor products. Additionally, this division includes John Deere Landscapes, Inc., a distributor of irrigation equipment, nursery products and landscape products. The company expanded its C&CE division in 2007, through the acquisition of LESCO, which supplies consumable lawn care, landscape, golf course and pest control products.

Over the past five years, C&CE segment margins averaged 6%.

Effective May 1, 2009, DE combined its agricultural equipment and commercial and consumer equipment segments to form the ag and turf division. This streamlining action was put in place in an attempt by Deere to act on global market opportunities, leverage its global scale, optimize global product line results, standardize processes, share resources and reduce costs.

The construction and forestry segment (17%; 14%) manufactures and distributes a broad range of machines and service parts used in construction, earthmoving, material handling and timber harvesting. Products include backhoe loaders; crawler dozers and loaders; four-wheel-drive loaders; excavators; motor graders; articulated dump trucks; landscape loaders; skid-steer loaders; and log skidders, feller bunchers, harvesters and related attachments. Over the past five years, margins for this segment averaged 12%.

Company Financials Fiscal Year Ended Oct. 31

Per Share Data ($)	2008	2007	2006	2005	2004	2003	2002	2001	2000	1999
Tangible Book Value	12.19	13.17	13.92	12.13	10.93	5.91	4.75	6.57	7.78	8.12
Cash Flow	6.61	5.64	4.55	4.23	4.00	2.62	2.17	1.39	2.40	1.61
Earnings	4.70	4.00	3.08	2.94	2.78	1.32	0.67	-0.14	1.03	0.51
S&P Core Earnings	3.55	4.22	3.25	3.02	2.84	1.54	-0.19	-0.82	NA	NA
Dividends	1.06	0.91	0.78	0.61	0.53	0.44	0.44	0.44	0.44	0.44
Payout Ratio	23%	23%	22%	21%	19%	33%	66%	NM	43%	86%
Prices:High	94.89	93.74	50.70	37.21	37.47	33.71	25.80	23.06	24.81	22.97
Prices:Low	28.50	45.12	33.45	28.50	28.36	18.78	18.75	16.75	15.16	15.78
P/E Ratio:High	20	23	14	13	13	26	39	NM	24	45
P/E Ratio:Low	6	11	9	10	10	14	28	NM	15	31

Income Statement Analysis (Million $)										
Revenue	28,438	24,082	22,148	21,931	19,986	15,535	13,947	13,293	13,137	11,751
Operating Income	4,774	4,571	3,883	3,553	2,976	2,231	1,696	1,274	2,102	1,435
Depreciation	829	744	691	636	621	631	725	718	648	513
Interest Expense	1,163	1,151	1,018	761	592	1,257	637	766	676	557
Pretax Income	3,164	2,676	2,195	2,162	2,115	980	578	-46.3	779	374
Effective Tax Rate	35.1%	33.0%	33.8%	33.1%	33.5%	34.4%	44.7%	NM	37.7%	36.1%
Net Income	2,053	1,822	1,453	1,447	1,406	643	319	-64.0	486	239
S&P Core Earnings	1,556	1,917	1,534	1,483	1,430	743	-94.8	-385	NA	NA

Balance Sheet & Other Financial Data (Million $)										
Cash	1,834	3,902	3,504	4,708	3,428	4,616	3,004	1,206	419	612
Current Assets	NA	NA	NA	NA	NA	NA	NA	NA	NA	NA
Total Assets	38,735	38,576	34,720	33,637	28,754	26,258	23,768	22,663	20,469	17,578
Current Liabilities	NA	NA	NA	NA	NA	NA	NA	NA	NA	NA
Long Term Debt	13,899	11,798	11,584	11,739	11,090	10,404	8,950	6,561	4,764	3,806
Common Equity	6,533	7,156	7,565	6,825	6,350	2,834	1,797	3,992	4,302	4,094
Total Capital	20,603	19,137	19,214	18,564	17,441	13,238	10,772	10,566	9,141	7,963
Capital Expenditures	1,608	1,023	766	513	364	310	359	491	427	316
Cash Flow	2,882	2,566	2,145	2,083	2,027	1,275	1,045	654	1,133	752
Current Ratio	1.9	NA	2.2	2.4	3.0	2.5	2.2	1.7	1.7	1.8
% Long Term Debt of Capitalization	67.5	61.6	60.3	63.2	63.6	78.6	83.1	62.1	52.1	47.8
% Net Income of Revenue	7.2	7.5	6.6	6.6	7.0	4.2	2.4	NM	3.8	2.0
% Return on Assets	5.3	4.9	4.3	4.6	5.1	2.6	1.4	NM	2.6	1.3
% Return on Equity	30.0	24.7	20.2	22.0	30.6	27.8	11.8	NM	11.6	5.8

Data as orig reptd.; bef. results of disc opers/spec. items. Per share data adj. for stk. divs.; EPS diluted. E-Estimated. NA-Not Available. NM-Not Meaningful. NR-Not Ranked. UR-Under Review.

Office: One John Deere Place, Moline, IL 61265.
Telephone: 309-765-8000.
Email: stockholder@deere.com
Website: http://www.deere.com

Chrmn: R.W. Lane
Pres & CEO: S.R. Allen
SVP & CFO: J.M. Field
SVP & General Counsel: J.R. Jenkins

Treas: J.A. Davlin
Investor Contact: M. Ziegler (309-765-4491)
Board Members: S. R. Allen, C. C. Bowles, V. D. Coffman, C. O. Holliday, Jr., D. Jain, C. M. Jones, R. W. Lane, J. Milberg, R. B. Myers, T. H. Patrick, A. L. Peters, D. B. Speer

Founded: 1837
Domicile: Delaware
Employees: 56,653

STANDARD &POOR'S

Dell Inc

| S&P Recommendation | **HOLD** ★★★☆☆ | Price $14.12 (as of Nov 30, 2009) | 12-Mo. Target Price $17.00 | Investment Style Large-Cap Growth |

GICS Sector Information Technology
Sub-Industry Computer Hardware

Summary This company is the leading direct marketer and one of the world's 10 leading manufacturers of PCs compatible with industry standards established by IBM.

Key Stock Statistics (Source S&P, Vickers, company reports)

52-Wk Range	$17.26– 7.84	S&P Oper. EPS 2010**E**	1.00	Market Capitalization(B)	$27.613	Beta	1.35
Trailing 12-Month EPS	$0.74	S&P Oper. EPS 2011**E**	1.25	Yield (%)	Nil	S&P 3-Yr. Proj. EPS CAGR(%)	5
Trailing 12-Month P/E	19.1	P/E on S&P Oper. EPS 2010**E**	14.1	Dividend Rate/Share	Nil	S&P Credit Rating	A-
$10K Invested 5 Yrs Ago	$3,484	Common Shares Outstg. (M)	1,955.6	Institutional Ownership (%)	72		

Price Performance

30-Week Mov. Avg. ···· 10-Week Mov. Avg. ─ ─ **GAAP Earnings vs. Previous Year** Volume Above Avg. STARS
12-Mo. Target Price ── Relative Strength ▲ Up ▼ Down ▶ No Change Below Avg. ★

Options: ASE, CBOE, P, Ph

Analysis prepared by **Thomas W. Smith, CFA** on November 30, 2009, when the stock traded at **$ 14.03**.

Highlights

► We project that revenues will decrease about 16% in FY 10 (Jan.) before increasing 11% in FY 11, reflecting a global slowdown and an eventual rebound in demand for information technology goods, plus acquisitions. On November 3, 2009, the company completed its acquisition of Perot Systems for about $3.9 billion in cash. The combination should initially beef up DELL's IT services operations by about $2.6 billion in annual revenue, in our view.

► We see potential for margin improvements in FY 10 and FY 11, as higher volumes, the addition of Perot Systems operations, and potential savings we project from improved supply chain management outweigh rising component costs and pressure on average selling prices for PCs.

► We estimate FY 10 operating EPS of $1.00, excluding restructuring expenses of about $0.15 a share through the first nine months of FY 10 and acquisition costs from the recently completed Perot Systems transaction. For FY 11, we estimate operating EPS of $1.25.

Investment Rationale/Risk

► We believe that DELL's multi-year effort to move into new territories and offer more variety in products and services is taking effect slowly. We foresee PC industry unit demand moving higher in a cyclical rebound in calendar 2010, but we expect pricing pressure to continue. We see some potential for near-term margin improvement, as various reorganization efforts unfold and the Perot Systems operations are integrated.

► Risks to our recommendation and target price include the potential for market share losses and a slower recovery than we project for information technology spending. The company's shift to an international distribution system involving more partners and higher inventory levels might proceed less smoothly than we expect.

► Applying a target multiple of 14X, a discount to Information Technology Sector peers in the S&P 500 Index and below the mid-point of DELL's five-year historical range, to our 12-month forward EPS estimate of $1.19, we arrive at our 12-month target price of $17.

Qualitative Risk Assessment

| LOW | **MEDIUM** | HIGH |

Our risk assessment reflects our view of Dell's economies of scale and strong execution in asset management, offset by what we see as competitive pressures on product design and pricing, industry cyclicality, and a shift to greater reliance on retail partners around the world.

Quantitative Evaluations

S&P Quality Ranking B+

| D | C | B- | B | **B+** | A- | A | A+ |

Relative Strength Rank WEAK

28

LOWEST = 1   HIGHEST = 99

Revenue/Earnings Data

Revenue (Million $)

	1Q	2Q	3Q	4Q	Year
2010	12,342	12,764	12,896	--	--
2009	16,077	16,434	15,162	13,428	61,101
2008	14,722	14,776	15,646	15,989	61,133
2007	14,320	14,211	14,419	14,470	57,420
2006	13,386	13,428	13,911	15,183	55,908
2005	11,540	11,706	12,502	13,457	49,205

Earnings Per Share ($)

2010	0.15	0.24	0.17	E0.29	E1.00
2009	0.38	0.31	0.37	0.18	1.25
2008	0.34	0.31	0.34	0.31	1.31
2007	0.34	0.21	0.27	0.32	1.14
2006	0.37	0.41	0.25	0.43	1.46
2005	0.28	0.31	0.33	0.26	1.18

Fiscal year ended Jan. 31. Next earnings report expected: Late February. EPS Estimates based on S&P Operating Earnings; historical GAAP earnings are as reported.

Dividend Data

No cash dividends have been paid.

The McGraw-Hill Companies

Dell Inc

STANDARD
&POOR'S

Business Summary November 30, 2009

CORPORATE OVERVIEW. Headquartered in Round Rock, Texas, Dell Inc. (DELL) is a key player in the personal computer markets. DELL is number two in global PC unit shipments, with a 15.0% market share in calendar 2008 according to IDC, well up from 10.5% earlier in the decade, but below 2005's 18.2%. In 2008, DELL was number one by unit shipments in the U.S. market, where it sells almost half of its PCs.

The majority of DELL's sales are from PCs (60% of FY 09 (Jan.) total revenue), stemming from Desktop PCs (29%) and Mobility (31%). Other categories include Software and Peripherals (17%), Servers and Networking (10%), Services (9%), and Storage (4%). Within the PC category, sales of Mobility (mainly notebook PCs) are rising faster than sales of Desktop PCs. Revenue from notebooks pulled approximately even with desktop revenue for the first time in the FY 08 third quarter, and we expect notebooks to lead in the future.

The customer base is broad, with no single customer accounting for 10% of sales in FY 09 or the prior two fiscal years. The company is expanding in rapid-growth emerging markets including Brazil, Russia, India and China, and DELL's revenue from the BRIC countries rose 20% in FY 09. Revenues derived from outside the U.S. increased to 48% of total revenue in FY 09, from 47% in FY 08 and 44% in FY 07. Sales in FY 09 (FY 08) were derived 47% (49%) from the Americas Commercial segment, 22% (22%) from EMEA (Europe, Middle-East, Africa) Commercial, 12% (12%) from APJ (Asia, Pacific, Japan) Commercial, and 19% (17%) from Global Consumer.

IMPACT OF MAJOR DEVELOPMENTS. In January 2007, Michael Dell reassumed his role as CEO, while retaining his duties as chairman of the board. We are encouraged by this development, as we think it will reinvigorate the corporate culture and streamline the decision-making process.

Company Financials Fiscal Year Ended Jan. 31

Per Share Data ($)	2009	2008	2007	2006	2005	2004	2003	2002	2001	2000
Tangible Book Value	0.95	1.03	1.60	1.77	2.61	2.46	1.89	1.80	2.16	2.06
Cash Flow	1.64	1.58	1.34	1.62	1.32	1.11	0.88	0.54	0.90	0.67
Earnings	1.25	1.31	1.14	1.46	1.18	1.01	0.80	0.46	0.81	0.61
S&P Core Earnings	1.23	1.28	1.13	1.03	0.88	0.68	0.49	0.28	0.58	NA
Dividends	Nil	Nil	Nil	Nil	Nil	Nil	Nil	Nil	Nil	Nil
Payout Ratio	Nil	Nil	Nil	Nil	Nil	Nil	Nil	Nil	Nil	Nil
Calendar Year	2008	2007	2006	2005	2004	2003	2002	2001	2000	1999
Prices:High	26.04	30.77	30.77	42.30	42.57	37.18	31.06	31.32	59.69	55.00
Prices:Low	8.72	21.61	21.61	28.62	31.14	22.59	21.90	16.01	16.25	31.37
P/E Ratio:High	21	23	27	29	36	37	39	68	74	90
P/E Ratio:Low	7	16	19	20	26	22	27	35	20	51

Income Statement Analysis (Million $)

	2009	2008	2007	2006	2005	2004	2003	2002	2001	2000
Revenue	61,101	61,133	57,420	55,908	49,205	41,444	35,404	31,168	31,888	25,265
Operating Income	4,193	4,344	3,541	4,740	4,588	3,807	3,055	2,510	3,008	2,613
Depreciation	769	599	471	393	334	263	211	239	240	156
Interest Expense	93.0	45.0	45.0	28.0	16.0	14.0	17.0	29.0	47.0	34.0
Pretax Income	3,324	3,856	3,345	4,574	4,445	3,724	3,027	1,731	3,194	2,451
Effective Tax Rate	25.5%	22.8%	22.8%	21.9%	31.5%	29.0%	29.9%	28.0%	30.0%	32.0%
Net Income	2,478	2,947	2,583	3,572	3,043	2,645	2,122	1,246	2,236	1,666
S&P Core Earnings	2,445	2,871	2,563	2,494	2,227	1,806	1,356	781	1,602	NA

Balance Sheet & Other Financial Data (Million $)

	2009	2008	2007	2006	2005	2004	2003	2002	2001	2000
Cash	9,092	7,972	9,546	7,042	4,747	4,317	4,232	3,641	4,910	3,809
Current Assets	20,151	19,880	19,939	17,706	16,897	10,633	8,924	7,877	9,491	7,681
Total Assets	26,500	27,561	25,635	23,109	23,215	19,311	15,470	13,535	13,435	11,471
Current Liabilities	14,859	18,526	17,791	15,927	14,136	10,896	8,933	7,519	6,543	5,192
Long Term Debt	1,898	362	569	504	505	505	506	520	509	508
Common Equity	4,271	3,735	4,328	4,129	6,485	6,280	4,873	4,694	5,622	5,308
Total Capital	6,169	4,191	5,008	4,633	6,990	6,785	5,379	5,214	6,131	5,816
Capital Expenditures	440	831	896	728	525	329	305	303	482	397
Cash Flow	3,247	3,546	3,054	3,965	3,377	2,908	2,333	1,485	2,476	1,822
Current Ratio	1.4	1.1	1.1	1.1	1.2	1.0	1.0	1.0	1.5	1.5
% Long Term Debt of Capitalization	30.8	8.6	11.4	10.9	7.2	7.4	9.4	10.0	8.3	8.7
% Net Income of Revenue	4.1	4.8	4.5	6.4	6.2	6.4	6.0	4.0	7.0	6.6
% Return on Assets	9.2	11.1	10.6	15.4	14.3	15.2	14.6	9.2	18.0	18.2
% Return on Equity	61.9	73.1	61.1	67.3	47.7	47.4	44.4	24.2	40.9	43.7

Data as orig reptd.; bef. results of disc opers/spec. items. Per share data adj. for stk. divs.; EPS diluted. E-Estimated. NA-Not Available. NM-Not Meaningful. NR-Not Ranked. UR-Under Review.

Office: One Dell Way, Round Rock, TX 78682.
Telephone: 512-338-4400.
Email: investor_relations_fulfillment@dell.com
Website: http://www.dell.com

Chrmn & CEO: M.S. Dell
COO & CTO: J.R. Clarke
SVP & CFO: B.T. Gladden
SVP, Secy & General Counsel: L.P. Tu

Chief Acctg Officer: T.W. Sweet
Investor Contact: L.A. Tyson (512-723-1130)
Board Members: J. W. Breyer, D. J. Carty, M. S. Dell, W. H. Gray, III, J. C. Lewent, T. W. Luce, III, K. S. Luft, A. J. Mandl, S. Narayen, S. A. Nunn

Founded: 1984
Domicile: Delaware
Employees: 78,900

Denbury Resources Inc.

STANDARD & POOR'S

S&P Recommendation HOLD ★★★☆☆		**Price** $13.39 (as of Nov 27, 2009)	**12-Mo. Target Price** $15.00	**Investment Style** Large-Cap Growth

GICS Sector Energy
Sub-Industry Oil & Gas Exploration & Production

Summary This independent oil and gas company acquires, develops, exploits and produces oil and gas in the U.S., primarily in Mississippi and the Barnett Shale in Texas. DNR owns the largest reserves of CO2 used for tertiary oil recovery east of the Mississippi River.

Key Stock Statistics (Source S&P, Vickers, company reports)

52-Wk Range	$18.84– 7.07	S&P Oper. EPS 2009**E**	-0.11	Market Capitalization(B)	$3.345	Beta	1.21
Trailing 12-Month EPS	$-0.14	S&P Oper. EPS 2010**E**	0.79	Yield (%)	Nil	S&P 3-Yr. Proj. EPS CAGR(%)	-8
Trailing 12-Month P/E	NM	P/E on S&P Oper. EPS 2009**E**	NM	Dividend Rate/Share	Nil	S&P Credit Rating	BB
$10K Invested 5 Yrs Ago	$18,740	Common Shares Outstg. (M)	249.8	Institutional Ownership (%)	93		

Price Performance

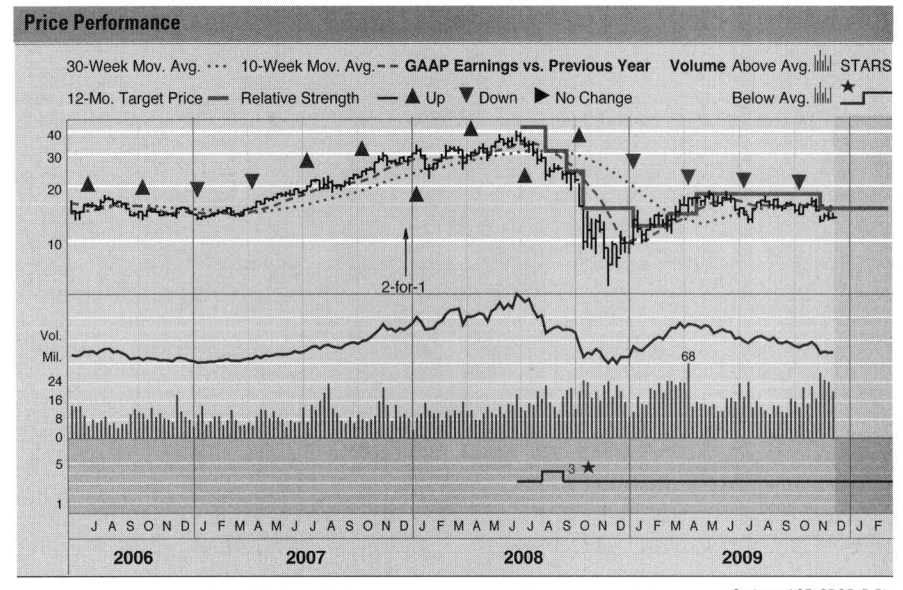

30-Week Mov. Avg. · · · 10-Week Mov. Avg. - - GAAP Earnings vs. Previous Year   Volume Above Avg. STARS
12-Mo. Target Price — Relative Strength — ▲ Up ▼ Down ► No Change   Below Avg.

2-for-1

Options: ASE, CBOE, P, Ph

Analysis prepared by **Michael Kay** on November 13, 2009, when the stock traded at **$13.45**.

Highlights

► In 2008, production rose 5% on the ramp-up of Phase II tertiary oil production in Mississippi at Martinville, Soso and Eucutta. In the past year, DNR has experienced hurricane shut-ins and equipment delays at projects at Brookhaven and McComb. We see more moderate 2009 production growth than previously, up 2%, on the Phase II ramp-up and Phase III oil recovery at Tinsley and Heidelburg, and a 6% decline in 2010 on a slowdown in activity. DNR closed on the sale of 60% of its Barnett Shale natural gas assets for $270 million in mid-2009.

► The disposal of assets in Louisiana placed upward pressure on 2008 lease operating expense (LOE), up 27%. We see industry costs subsiding in 2009 and expect LOE to fall about 4%.

► Operating EPS in 2008 was $2.15 (with $0.62 of non-cash derivative gains), and we see a 2009 loss per share of $0.11 (with an $0.80 non-cash derivative loss) on declining prices, partly offset by production gains, and we see 2010 EPS of $0.79. DNR's 2009 capital budget is $750 million, down from $950 million in 2008.

Investment Rationale/Risk

► In November, DNR announced a definitive agreement to acquire Encore Acquisition Company (EAC) for $4.5 billion, with closing, subject to approvals, expected in early 2010. EAC's enhanced recovery program in the Rockies should complement DNR's Gulf Coast tertiary operations, and we view as positive its entry into the Bakken oil shale. We expect DNR to continue dropping assets into Genesis Energy LP (GEL), of which it is the general partner. The Tinsley Field (Phase III) is showing positive results, and Cranfield (Phase IV) and Delhi (Phase V) are expected to commence in 2009.

► Risks to our opinion and target price include a sustained decline in oil and gas prices, and inability to replace reserves at a reasonable cost.

► Our 12-month target price of $15 blends an enterprise value multiple of 8X our 2010 EBITDA estimate with our DCF analysis ($16; WACC 19%, terminal growth 3%) and our proved NAV estimate of $16. We use peer-average valuation metrics to reflect a 29% increase in reserves, but given high debt levels and our view that capex will surpass cash flow in 2009, we view the shares as fairly valued.

Qualitative Risk Assessment

LOW	MEDIUM	HIGH

Our risk assessment reflects the company's operations in a capital-intensive industry that derives value from producing commodities whose price is very volatile.

Quantitative Evaluations

S&P Quality Ranking B

D	C	B-	B	B+	A-	A	A+

Relative Strength Rank WEAK

21

LOWEST = 1   HIGHEST = 99

Revenue/Earnings Data

Revenue (Million $)

	1Q	2Q	3Q	4Q	Year
2009	171.2	214.4	225.0	--	--
2008	317.3	416.6	405.6	222.6	1,361
2007	174.2	222.5	253.5	321.8	972.0
2006	178.9	193.3	192.0	167.3	731.5
2005	113.4	128.0	141.9	177.2	560.4
2004	97.75	106.2	88.03	90.98	383.0

Earnings Per Share ($)

2009	-0.07	-0.35	0.11	E0.18	E-0.11
2008	0.29	0.45	0.63	0.18	1.54
2007	0.07	0.25	0.27	0.42	1.00
2006	0.19	0.18	0.24	0.23	0.82
2005	0.13	0.17	0.16	0.24	0.70
2004	0.10	0.09	0.08	0.10	0.36

Fiscal year ended Dec. 31. Next earnings report expected: Late February. EPS Estimates based on S&P Operating Earnings; historical GAAP earnings are as reported.

Dividend Data

No cash dividends have been paid.

Please read the Required Disclosures and Analyst Certification on the last page of this report.

The McGraw·Hill Companies

Denbury Resources Inc.

STANDARD
&POOR'S

Business Summary November 13, 2009

CORPORATE OVERVIEW. Denbury Resources, Inc. (DNR) engages in the acquisition, development, operation and exploitation of oil and natural gas properties in the Gulf Coast region of the U.S., primarily in Louisiana, Mississippi, Alabama and Texas. DNR is the largest oil and natural gas operator in Mississippi and also owns the rights to a natural source of carbon dioxide (CO_2) reserves that it uses for injection in its tertiary oil recovery operations. DNR is the general partner of Genesis Energy, L.P., a pipeline master limited partnership.

As of December 31, 2008, DNR had estimated proved reserves (including tertiary-related reserves) of 250.5 MMBOE, of which 71% consisted of crude oil and 58% was proved developed. This compares to estimated proved reserves of 194.8 MMBOE, of which 69% consisted of crude oil and 69% was proved developed, at year-end 2007. As of December 31, 2008, DNR had total tertiary-related proved oil reserves of approximately 125.8 MMBbls, versus 69.5 MMbbls at the end of 2007. We estimate DNR's 2008 reserve life to be 14.9 years, compared to 12.3 years at the end of 2007.

DNR added 89.0 MMBOE of proved reserves during 2008, replacing approximately 525% of its 2008 production, virtually all from internal organic growth.

We estimate that DNR replaced 250% of production in 2007 (261% in 2006), mainly organically. We estimate 2007 finding and development costs (excluding acquisitions) of $14.18 per BOE, versus a three-year average of $15.05 per BOE and a reserve replacement cost (including acquisitions) of $14.18 per BOE, versus a three-year average of $14.21 per BOE.

CORPORATE STRATEGY. During 2008 and 2009, DNR plans to invest almost $2 billion to expand its CO_2 pipeline network from Louisiana to Texas and to implement and expand additional tertiary floods, as part of its strategic plan. If oil prices remain at their current levels, DNR believes most of this can be funded with internally generated cash flow, but if needed, can tap into other resources. DNR's biggest project during this period will be the construction of the $700 million Green Pipeline, a CO_2 pipeline that is expected to be completed around year-end 2009. DNR believes this project will create the backbone for a CO_2 gathering and distribution system in the southern Gulf Coast region.

Company Financials Fiscal Year Ended Dec. 31

Per Share Data ($)	2008	2007	2006	2005	2004	2003	2002	2001	2000	1999
Tangible Book Value	7.50	5.75	4.61	3.20	2.40	1.94	1.71	1.65	1.17	0.40
Cash Flow	2.42	1.77	1.42	1.11	0.79	0.67	0.65	0.63	0.96	0.19
Earnings	1.54	1.00	0.82	0.70	0.36	0.24	0.22	0.28	0.77	0.03
S&P Core Earnings	1.54	1.00	0.82	0.68	0.35	0.23	0.21	0.27	NA	NA
Dividends	Nil	Nil	Nil	Nil	Nil	Nil	Nil	Nil	Nil	Nil
Payout Ratio	Nil	Nil	Nil	Nil	Nil	Nil	Nil	Nil	Nil	Nil
Prices:High	40.32	30.56	18.30	12.86	7.33	3.56	2.99	3.08	2.88	1.67
Prices:Low	5.59	12.98	11.79	6.18	3.32	2.55	1.55	1.46	0.91	0.84
P/E Ratio:High	26	31	22	18	20	15	14	11	4	56
P/E Ratio:Low	4	13	14	9	9	10	7	5	1	28

Income Statement Analysis (Million $)										
Revenue	1,361	972	732	560	383	333	285	266	179	81.6
Operating Income	699	636	482	393	254	276	190	156	124	44.5
Depreciation, Depletion and Amortization	222	193	149	98.8	97.5	94.7	94.2	71.3	36.2	25.5
Interest Expense	32.6	51.2	23.6	18.0	19.5	23.2	26.8	22.3	15.3	15.8
Pretax Income	624	393	330	248	122	80.2	70.3	81.4	74.9	4.61
Effective Tax Rate	37.8%	35.7%	38.6%	32.9%	32.3%	32.7%	33.4%	30.5%	NM	NM
Net Income	388	253	202	166	82.4	53.9	46.8	56.6	142	4.61
S&P Core Earnings	388	253	202	161	79.7	49.8	43.9	53.8	NA	NA

Balance Sheet & Other Financial Data (Million $)										
Cash	17.1	60.1	53.9	165	33.0	24.2	23.9	23.5	22.3	11.8
Current Assets	415	240	183	299	173	108	128	103	98.0	30.5
Total Assets	3,590	2,771	2,140	1,505	993	983	895	790	457	253
Current Liabilities	386	265	200	154	82.9	127	95.9	79.9	38.8	25.2
Long Term Debt	853	675	514	379	0.23	298	345	335	199	153
Common Equity	1,840	1,404	1,106	734	542	421	374	353	216	72.4
Total Capital	3,126	2,432	1,856	1,284	639	788	790	707	415	225
Capital Expenditures	1,086	834	826	379	178	147	156	172	75.4	55.0
Cash Flow	610	446	352	265	180	149	141	128	178	30.1
Current Ratio	1.1	0.9	0.9	1.9	2.1	0.9	1.3	1.3	2.5	1.2
% Long Term Debt of Capitalization	27.3	32.6	27.7	29.6	0.0	37.8	43.6	47.4	47.9	67.8
% Return on Assets	12.2	10.3	11.1	13.3	8.3	5.7	5.6	9.1	40.1	2.0
% Return on Equity	23.9	20.2	22.0	26.1	17.1	13.7	12.9	19.8	98.6	23.0

Data as orig reptd.; bef. results of disc opers/spec. items. Per share data adj. for stk. divs.; EPS diluted. E-Estimated. NA-Not Available. NM-Not Meaningful. NR-Not Ranked. UR-Under Review.

Office: 5100 Tennyson Pkwy Ste 1200, Plano, TX 75024-7164.
Telephone: 972-673-2000.
Website: http://www.denbury.com
Co-Chrmn: W.F. Wettstein

Co-Chrmn: G. Roberts
Pres & COO: R.T. Evans
CEO: P. Rykhoek
SVP & CFO: M.C. Allen

Investor Contact: L. Burkes (972-673-2166)
Board Members: M. L. Beatty, M. B. Decker, R. G. Greene, D. I. Heather, G. L. McMichael, G. Roberts, R. Stein, W. F. Wettstein

Founded: 1951
Domicile: Delaware
Employees: 797

The McGraw-Hill Companies

DENTSPLY International Inc

STANDARD &POOR'S

S&P Recommendation **HOLD** ★★★☆☆	Price $33.30 (as of Nov 27, 2009)	12-Mo. Target Price $38.00	Investment Style Large-Cap Growth

GICS Sector Health Care
Sub-Industry Health Care Supplies

Summary This company is a designer, developer, manufacturer and marketer of a broad range of products for the dental market.

Key Stock Statistics (Source S&P, Vickers, company reports)

52-Wk Range	$36.80– 21.80	S&P Oper. EPS 2009**E**	1.84	Market Capitalization(B)	$5.063	Beta	0.97
Trailing 12-Month EPS	$1.80	S&P Oper. EPS 2010**E**	2.05	Yield (%)	0.60	S&P 3-Yr. Proj. EPS CAGR(%)	6
Trailing 12-Month P/E	18.5	P/E on S&P Oper. EPS 2009**E**	18.1	Dividend Rate/Share	$0.20	S&P Credit Rating	NA
$10K Invested 5 Yrs Ago	$13,105	Common Shares Outstg. (M)	152.0	Institutional Ownership (%)	90		

Price Performance

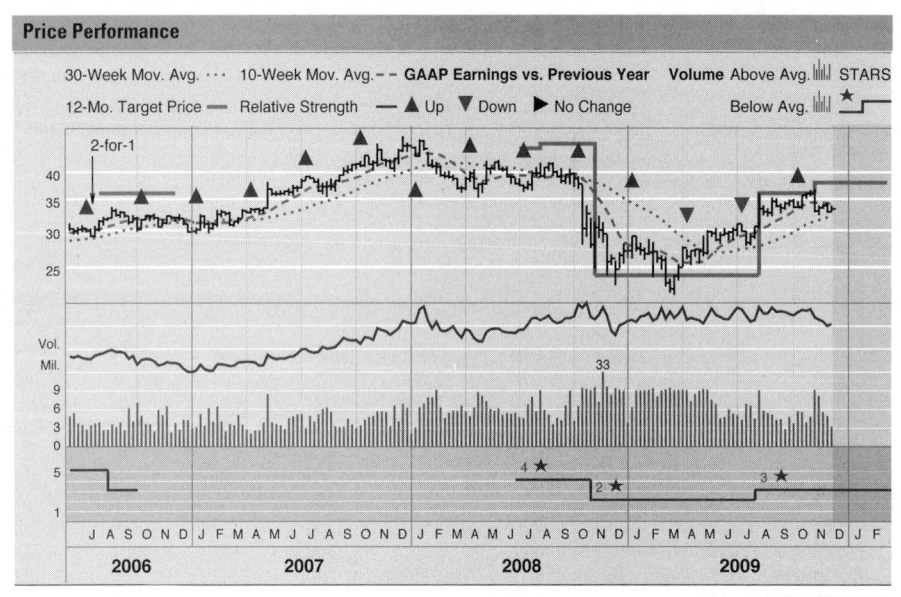

- 30-Week Mov. Avg. ··· 10-Week Mov. Avg. - - **GAAP Earnings vs. Previous Year** **Volume** Above Avg. STARS
- 12-Mo. Target Price — Relative Strength ▲ Up ▼ Down ► No Change Below Avg.

Options: CBOE, P, Ph

Analysis prepared by **Phillip M. Seligman** on November 11, 2009, when the stock traded at **$ 33.77**.

Highlights

► We expect 2009's net sales, excluding precious metal content, to be 1.3% below 2008's $2.0 billion. Drivers we see for 2009 include price increases in the consumable lines, recent acquisitions, and new products, mostly offset by the impacts from U.S. economic softness, channel destocking, softer European dental markets and a stronger U.S. dollar. We project net sales to rise by 7.8% in 2010, mainly on easy comparisons, recent acquisitions, and a weaker U.S. dollar.

► We expect gross margins to decline by 110 basis points (bps) in 2009, on lower production volumes, which affected the absorption of overhead, a less favorable product mix and unfavorable foreign exchange, but to widen by 70 bps in 2010, assuming lower fixed costs, easy comparisons, and an improved product mix. Meanwhile, we look for the SG&A cost ratio to decline by 40 bps, on cost containment, and to be flat in 2010, despite higher sales and marketing investments.

► We estimate operating EPS of $1.84 before $0.04 of net one-time costs in 2009, versus 2008's $1.88 before $0.01 of net one-time costs. We project $2.05 in 2010.

Investment Rationale/Risk

► We are encouraged by XRAY's view that the overall global dental market appears to be stabilizing, and that it has begun to see signs of improvements in certain geographic markets and in certain areas of dentistry in 2009's third quarter, including orthodontics and endodontics, while implant sales have been flat. But it also cited some areas of continued weakness, such as the lab market and the Eastern European market. Despite current market conditions, long-term fundamentals of the dental products business look favorable to us. These include an aging population in developed countries and rising standards of living in developing countries. Meanwhile, we view cash flow as healthy, providing financial flexibility, including enabling XRAY to remain a consolidator in the fragmented dental supply market.

► Risks to our recommendation and target price include intensified competition and a sharp decline in dental care in the U.S. and Europe.

► Applying a multiple of 18.5X, near XRAY's historical mid-point, to our 2010 EPS estimate, we derive our 12-month target price of $38.

Qualitative Risk Assessment

LOW	MEDIUM	HIGH

Our risk assessment reflects XRAY's long-term trend of relative stability and its broad product and geographic diversification, which we believe limits the impact of competition. We also believe XRAY's relatively low long-term debt to capitalization ratio provides some degree of protection from financial difficulties.

Quantitative Evaluations

S&P Quality Ranking A-

D	C	B-	B	B+	A-	A	A+

Relative Strength Rank MODERATE

42

LOWEST = 1   HIGHEST = 99

Revenue/Earnings Data

Revenue (Million $)

	1Q	2Q	3Q	4Q	Year
2009	507.0	553.2	531.0	--	--
2008	560.8	594.9	530.0	508.1	2,194
2007	472.9	507.4	488.1	541.5	2,010
2006	431.0	472.4	435.7	471.3	1,811
2005	407.0	444.8	416.0	447.4	1,715
2004	414.4	424.4	390.0	465.5	1,694

Earnings Per Share ($)

2009	0.41	0.47	0.45	E0.49	E1.84
2008	0.45	0.52	0.44	0.47	1.87
2007	0.38	0.42	0.42	0.45	1.68
2006	0.31	0.37	0.31	0.42	1.41
2005	0.30	0.36	-0.39	Nil	0.28
2004	0.28	0.30	0.29	0.42	1.28

Fiscal year ended Dec. 31. Next earnings report expected: Early February. EPS Estimates based on S&P Operating Earnings; historical GAAP earnings are as reported.

Dividend Data (Dates: mm/dd Payment Date: mm/dd/yy)

Amount ($)	Date Decl.	Ex-Div. Date	Stk. of Record	Payment Date
0.050	02/12	03/24	03/26	04/08/09
0.050	05/12	06/24	06/26	07/07/09
0.050	07/29	09/23	09/25	10/06/09
0.050	09/29	12/24	12/29	01/09/10

Dividends have been paid since 1994. Source: Company reports.

Please read the Required Disclosures and Analyst Certification on the last page of this report.

The McGraw-Hill Companies

DENTSPLY International Inc

Business Summary November 11, 2009

CORPORATE OVERVIEW. Dentsply International, Inc. (XRAY) was created by a merger of a predecessor Dentsply International Inc. and Gendex Corp. in 1993. The predecessor Dentsply, founded in 1899, manufactured and distributed artificial teeth, dental equipment and dental consumable products. Gendex, founded in 1983, manufactured dental x-ray equipment and handpieces. In early 2004, the company divested the dental x-ray equipment business. Dentsply believes it is the world's largest developer and manufacturer of a broad range of products for the dental market.

Dental consumables (35% of net sales in 2007 and 40% in 2006, excluding precious metal content) include dental sundries, such as dental anesthetics, prophylaxis paste, dental sealants, impression materials, restorative materials, bone grafting materials, tooth whiteners, and topical fluoride; and small equipment products, such as high and low speed handpieces, intraoral curing light systems, dental diagnostic systems, and ultrasonic scalers and polishers.

Dental laboratory products (19%;19%) are used in dental laboratories in the preparation of dental appliances. Products include dental prosthetics, including artificial teeth, precious metal dental alloys, dental ceramics, crown and bridge materials, computer aided machining (CAM) ceramics systems, and porcelain furnaces.

Dental specialty products (43%; 38%) include specialized treatment products, such as endodontic (root canal) instruments and materials, implants and related products, bone grafting materials, and orthodontic appliances and accessories.

In addition to the U.S., Dentsply conducts its business in over 120 foreign countries, principally through its foreign subsidiaries. For 2007 and 2006, net sales, excluding precious metal content, to customers outside the U.S., including export sales, accounted for approximately 59% and 58%, respectively, of net sales.

During 2007 and 2006, one customer, Henry Schein Incorporated, a dental distributor, accounted for 11.6% and 10.9%, respectively, of the company's net sales.

Company Financials Fiscal Year Ended Dec. 31

Per Share Data ($)	2008	2007	2006	2005	2004	2003	2002	2001	2000	1999
Tangible Book Value	1.39	2.07	1.39	1.52	1.17	NM	NM	NM	1.13	0.75
Cash Flow	2.25	2.00	1.71	0.59	1.58	1.34	1.20	1.11	0.91	0.82
Earnings	1.87	1.67	1.41	0.28	1.28	1.05	0.93	0.77	0.64	0.57
S&P Core Earnings	1.92	1.72	1.41	0.20	1.21	0.95	0.84	0.60	NA	NA
Dividends	0.19	0.17	0.15	0.13	0.11	0.10	0.09	0.09	0.09	0.08
Payout Ratio	10%	10%	10%	45%	8%	9%	10%	12%	13%	13%
Prices:High	47.06	47.84	33.76	29.22	28.42	23.70	21.75	17.34	14.46	9.77
Prices:Low	22.85	29.44	26.07	25.37	20.88	16.05	15.63	10.83	7.71	6.83
P/E Ratio:High	25	29	24	NM	22	22	24	23	22	17
P/E Ratio:Low	12	18	18	NM	16	15	17	14	12	12

Income Statement Analysis (Million $)	2008	2007	2006	2005	2004	2003	2002	2001	2000	1999
Revenue	2,194	2,010	1,810	1,715	1,694	1,571	1,514	1,129	890	831
Operating Income	469	416	370	356	352	317	298	238	205	189
Depreciation	56.6	50.3	47.4	50.6	49.3	45.7	43.9	54.3	41.4	39.6
Interest Expense	32.5	23.8	10.8	17.8	25.1	26.1	29.2	21.7	10.2	15.8
Pretax Income	355	358	315	71.0	274	251	221	185	152	138
Effective Tax Rate	20.1%	27.5%	28.9%	36.1%	23.3%	32.4%	33.0%	34.4%	33.5%	34.9%
Net Income	284	260	224	45.4	210	170	148	121	101	89.9
S&P Core Earnings	292	265	223	32.0	198	153	134	94.6	NA	NA

Balance Sheet & Other Financial Data (Million $)	2008	2007	2006	2005	2004	2003	2002	2001	2000	1999
Cash	204	169	65.1	435	506	164	25.7	33.7	15.4	7.28
Current Assets	950	982	718	1,030	1,056	727	541	484	325	315
Total Assets	2,830	2,676	2,181	2,407	2,798	2,446	2,087	1,798	867	860
Current Liabilities	360	312	311	741	405	338	366	359	168	176
Long Term Debt	424	482	367	270	780	790	770	724	110	145
Common Equity	1,588	1,516	1,274	1,242	1,444	1,122	836	610	520	469
Total Capital	2,152	2,060	1,694	1,555	2,283	1,964	1,634	1,366	651	637
Capital Expenditures	76.4	64.2	50.6	45.3	56.3	76.6	3.31	49.3	28.4	33.4
Cash Flow	340	310	271	96.0	260	216	192	176	142	129
Current Ratio	2.6	3.1	2.3	1.4	2.6	2.2	1.5	1.4	1.9	1.8
% Long Term Debt of Capitalization	19.7	23.4	21.7	17.4	34.2	40.2	47.1	53.0	16.8	22.8
% Net Income of Revenue	12.9	12.9	12.4	2.6	12.4	10.8	9.8	10.8	11.4	10.8
% Return on Assets	10.3	10.7	9.7	1.7	8.0	7.5	7.6	9.1	11.7	10.2
% Return on Equity	18.3	18.6	17.8	3.4	16.4	17.3	20.5	21.5	20.4	20.4

Data as orig reptd.; bef. results of disc opers/spec. items. Per share data adj. for stk. divs.; EPS diluted. E-Estimated. NA-Not Available. NM-Not Meaningful. NR-Not Ranked. UR-Under Review.

Office: 221 W Philadelphia St, York, PA, USA 17405-0872.
Telephone: 717-845-7511.
Email: investor@dentsply.com
Website: http://www.dentsply.com

Chrmn & CEO: B.W. Wise
Pres & COO: C.T. Clark
Investor Contact: W.R. Jellison (717-849-4243)
SVP, CFO & Chief Acctg Officer: W.R. Jellison

CTO: S.R. Jeffries
Board Members: M. C. Alfano, E. K. Brandt, P. H. Cholmondeley, M. Coleman, W. L. Dixon, W. F. Hecht, L. A. Jones, F. J. Lunger, J. C. Miles, II, W. K. Smith, B. W. Wise

Founded: 1983
Domicile: Delaware
Employees: 9,400

Devon Energy Corp

STANDARD &POOR'S

S&P Recommendation	BUY ★★★★☆	Price $67.48 (as of Nov 27, 2009)	12-Mo. Target Price $83.00	Investment Style Large-Cap Blend

GICS Sector Energy
Sub-Industry Oil & Gas Exploration & Production

Summary As one of the largest independent oil and gas exploration and production companies in the U.S., the firm has grown through acquisitions of Ocean Energy, Mitchell Energy, Anderson Exploration and Chief Holdings.

Key Stock Statistics (Source S&P, Vickers, company reports)

52-Wk Range	$75.30– 38.55	S&P Oper. EPS 2009**E**	3.39	Market Capitalization(B)	$29.968	Beta	1.18
Trailing 12-Month EPS	$-22.32	S&P Oper. EPS 2010**E**	6.13	Yield (%)	0.95	S&P 3-Yr. Proj. EPS CAGR(%)	-1
Trailing 12-Month P/E	NM	P/E on S&P Oper. EPS 2009**E**	19.9	Dividend Rate/Share	$0.64	S&P Credit Rating	BBB+
$10K Invested 5 Yrs Ago	$16,963	Common Shares Outstg. (M)	444.1	Institutional Ownership (%)	79		

Price Performance

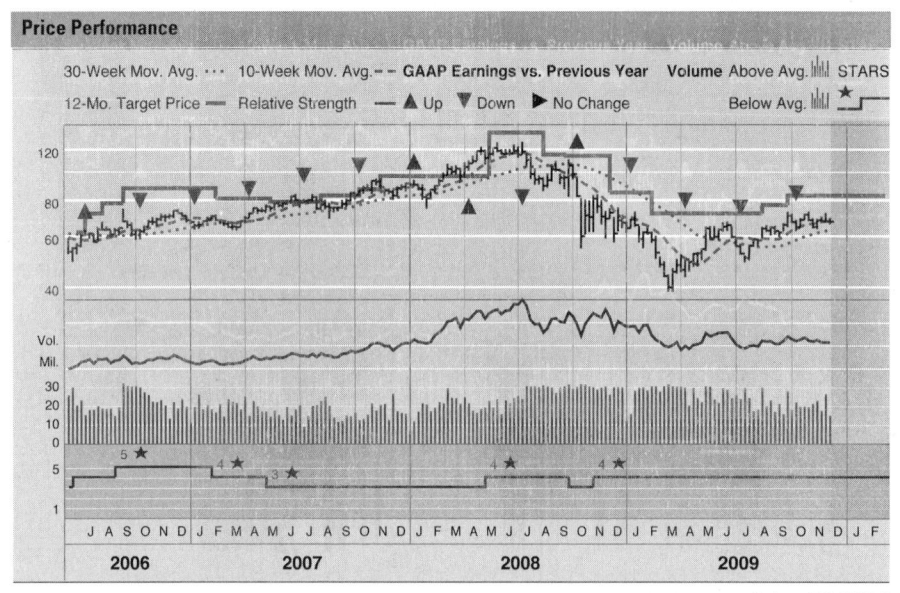

30-Week Mov. Avg. ··· 10-Week Mov. Avg. – – GAAP Earnings vs. Previous Year   Volume Above Avg. STARS
12-Mo. Target Price — Relative Strength — ▲ Up ▼ Down ► No Change   Below Avg.

Options: ASE, CBOE, P

Analysis prepared by **Michael Kay** on October 13, 2009, when the stock traded at **$ 69.95**.

Highlights

▶ Production grew 10% in 2008 on growth at Barnett Shale properties, where DVN is the largest producer, and the start-up of production at the Jackfish Canadian oil sands. DVN has increased acreage at Haynesville Shale and boosted production at Woodford Shale. We see drilling capex down 55% in 2009. We see declines in natural gas, however; ramp-ups at Brazil and Jackfish boosted first half oil volumes 6% and we see a 4% rise in the second half. We recently cut our production growth forecasts to 3% for 2009 and flat for 2010.

▶ DVN is selling international assets with lower growth to focus on higher-growth areas in the Barnett, Haynesville and Horn River shale plays. It has completed the divestiture in Africa for proceeds of $3 billion, closing on the sale of Equatorial Guinea assets for $2.2 billion.

▶ After a 57% rise in operating income in 2008, we see a 70% drop in 2009 on lower oil and gas prices. We see 2009 EPS of $3.01 (with a $0.09 derivative loss) vs. $10.03 (with a $0.13 derivative gain) in 2008. On higher prices and production, we forecast 2010 EPS of $5.09. DVN's 2009 capital budget is $3.5 billion-$4.1 billion.

Investment Rationale/Risk

▶ We believe recent discoveries have shifted focus to organic growth from restructuring acquisitions. Successful results in the Gulf of Mexico's Lower Tertiary Trend, and a strong portfolio of deepwater prospects, have raised production growth prospects, while increasing exposure in unconventional resources. We see DVN expanding its lease position in the Barnett and Haynesville shales and the Horn River play and growing its oil sands production from the Jackfish project. Much of DVN's 2009 budget will likely be spent on long-term projects.

▶ Risks to our opinion and target price include unfavorable changes in economic, industry and operating conditions, such as rising costs, and difficulty in organically replacing reserves.

▶ After a $10.4 billion ceiling-test writedown in 2008 and with a moderating growth outlook, the shares have struggled. DVN trades at a discount to our $84 proven-reserve NAV estimate, and with limited debt and no liquidity concerns, we see upside at current levels. Our 12-month target price of $83 blends our DCF value ($79 assuming WACC of 9.2%, terminal growth 3%), relative metrics, and NAV estimate.

Qualitative Risk Assessment

LOW	MEDIUM	HIGH

Our risk assessment for DVN reflects our view of its position as a large independent exploration and production company in a highly capital-intensive industry that derives value from producing crude oil and natural gas - commodities with very volatile prices.

Quantitative Evaluations

S&P Quality Ranking   B+

D	C	B-	B	B+	A-	A	A+

Relative Strength Rank   MODERATE

54

LOWEST = 1   HIGHEST = 99

Revenue/Earnings Data

Revenue (Million $)

	1Q	2Q	3Q	4Q	Year
2009	2,028	2,077	2,098	--	--
2008	3,763	4,763	4,386	2,453	15,365
2007	2,473	2,929	2,763	3,197	11,362
2006	2,684	2,589	2,696	2,609	10,578
2005	2,351	2,468	2,704	3,218	10,741
2004	2,238	2,219	2,267	2,465	9,189

Earnings Per Share ($)

	1Q	2Q	3Q	4Q	Year
2009	-8.92	0.66	1.12	E1.18	E3.39
2008	1.45	1.31	5.63	-15.46	-6.95
2007	1.27	1.82	1.43	2.45	6.97
2006	1.56	1.92	1.57	1.26	6.29
2005	1.14	1.38	1.63	2.14	6.26
2004	1.00	1.01	1.04	1.35	4.38

Fiscal year ended Dec. 31. Next earnings report expected: Early February. EPS Estimates based on S&P Operating Earnings; historical GAAP earnings are as reported.

Dividend Data (Dates: mm/dd Payment Date: mm/dd/yy)

Amount ($)	Date Decl.	Ex-Div. Date	Stk. of Record	Payment Date
0.160	03/02	03/12	03/16	03/31/09
0.160	06/01	06/11	06/15	06/30/09
0.160	09/01	09/11	09/15	09/30/09
0.160	09/16	12/11	12/15	12/31/09

Dividends have been paid since 1993. Source: Company reports.

Please read the Required Disclosures and Analyst Certification on the last page of this report.

Devon Energy Corp

STANDARD
&POOR'S

Business Summary October 13, 2009

CORPORATE OVERVIEW. Devon Energy Corp. (DVN) is an independent exploration and production company primarily engaged in the exploration, development and production of oil and natural gas; the acquisition of producing properties; the transportation of oil, natural gas and natural gas liquids (NGLs); and the processing of natural gas. The company began operations as a private company in 1971, and its common stock began trading publicly in 1988.

DVN's operations are focused in the U.S. (66% of 2007 revenues; 49% of 2007 earnings), Canada (22%; 20%), and internationally (12%; 31%). U.S. activities are concentrated in four regions: the Mid-Continent (mainly north and east Texas and Oklahoma), the Permian Basin (within Texas and New Mexico), the Rocky Mountains (from the Canadian border into northern New Mexico), offshore areas of the Gulf of Mexico, and onshore areas of the Gulf Coast (mainly in south Texas and south Louisiana). Canadian operations are located in the provinces of Alberta, British Columbia and Saskatchewan. Operations outside North America include Azerbaijan, Brazil and China. In January 2007, DVN announced plans to divest its assets and operations in West Africa.

DVN also has marketing and midstream operations that perform various activities to support its oil and gas operations.

Oil and gas production rose 10% to 239 million barrel oil equivalent (boe; 26% liquids) in 2008. Proved oil and gas reserves declined 3%, to 2.428 billion boe (79% developed, 32% liquids) in 2008.

We estimate its 2007 organic reserve replacement at 194%. Using data from John S. Herold, an industry research firm, we estimate DVN's three-year finding and development costs at $12.78 per boe, in line with peers; its three-year proved acquisition costs at $10.63 per boe, below the peer average; its three-year reserve replacement costs at $12.57 per boe, in line with peers; and its three-year average reserve replacement at 170%, strong but below the peer average.

Company Financials Fiscal Year Ended Dec. 31

Per Share Data ($)	2008	2007	2006	2005	2004	2003	2002	2001	2000	1999
Tangible Book Value	NA	35.31	26.09	20.31	16.30	11.50	3.20	4.32	11.03	16.03
Cash Flow	1.15	13.32	11.73	10.87	8.95	8.10	4.04	3.54	5.37	2.65
Earnings	-6.95	6.97	6.29	6.26	4.38	4.00	0.16	0.17	2.75	0.73
S&P Core Earnings	-7.24	6.99	6.29	6.01	4.30	3.99	0.47	0.09	NA	NA
Dividends	NA	0.56	0.45	0.30	0.20	0.10	0.10	0.10	0.10	0.10
Payout Ratio	NA	8%	7%	5%	5%	3%	63%	59%	4%	14%
Prices:High	NA	94.75	74.75	70.35	41.64	29.40	26.55	33.38	32.37	22.47
Prices:Low	NA	62.80	48.94	36.48	25.90	21.23	16.94	15.28	15.69	10.06
P/E Ratio:High	NA	14	12	11	10	7	NM	NM	12	31
P/E Ratio:Low	NA	9	8	6	6	5	NM	NM	6	14

Income Statement Analysis (Million $)										
Revenue	15,365	11,362	10,578	10,741	9,189	7,352	4,316	3,075	2,784	734
Operating Income	-153	7,380	6,938	7,290	6,038	4,589	2,403	2,350	2,094	491
Depreciation, Depletion and Amortization	3,595	2,858	2,442	2,191	2,290	1,793	1,211	876	693	254
Interest Expense	329	532	421	533	475	504	533	220	154	66.9
Pretax Income	-4,033	4,224	4,012	4,552	3,293	2,245	-134	84.0	1,142	160
Effective Tax Rate	23.7%	25.5%	29.6%	35.6%	33.6%	22.9%	NM	35.7%	36.0%	40.8%
Net Income	-3,079	3,146	2,823	2,930	2,186	1,731	59.0	54.0	730	94.6
S&P Core Earnings	-3,210	3,144	2,815	2,801	2,136	1,715	147	22.9	NA	NA

Balance Sheet & Other Financial Data (Million $)										
Cash	379	1,736	739	1,606	2,119	1,273	292	193	228	167
Current Assets	2,684	3,914	3,212	4,206	3,583	2,364	1,064	1,081	934	417
Total Assets	31,908	41,456	35,063	30,273	29,736	27,162	16,225	13,184	6,860	4,623
Current Liabilities	3,135	3,657	4,645	2,934	3,100	2,071	1,042	919	629	227
Long Term Debt	5,661	7,928	5,568	5,957	7,031	8,635	7,562	6,589	2,049	1,787
Common Equity	17,060	22,005	17,441	14,999	13,673	11,055	4,652	3,258	3,276	2,024
Total Capital	26,400	34,972	28,660	26,362	25,505	24,061	14,842	11,990	5,953	4,204
Capital Expenditures	9,375	6,158	7,551	4,090	3,103	2,587	3,426	5,326	1,280	315
Cash Flow	511	5,994	5,255	5,111	4,466	3,514	1,260	920	1,414	345
Current Ratio	0.9	1.1	0.7	1.4	1.2	1.1	1.0	1.2	1.5	1.8
% Long Term Debt of Capitalization	21.4	23.9	19.4	22.6	27.6	35.9	51.0	55.0	34.4	42.5
% Return on Assets	NA	8.2	8.6	9.7	7.7	8.0	NM	0.5	11.3	3.2
% Return on Equity	NM	15.9	17.4	20.3	17.6	21.9	NM	1.3	24.9	7.1

Data as orig reptd.; bef. results of disc opers/spec. items. Per share data adj. for stk. divs.; EPS diluted. E-Estimated. NA-Not Available. NM-Not Meaningful. NR-Not Ranked. UR-Under Review.

Office: 20 N Broadway, Oklahoma City, OK 73102-8260.
Telephone: 405-235-3611.
Website: http://www.devonenergy.com
Chrmn & CEO: J.L. Nichols

Pres: J. Richels
EVP & General Counsel: L.C. Taylor
SVP, CFO & Chief Acctg Officer: D.J. Heatly
Chief Admin Officer: R.A. Marcum

Investor Contact: V. White (405-552-4526)
Board Members: T. F. Ferguson, J. A. Hill, R. L. Howard, M. Kanovsky, J. T. Mitchell, R. A. Mosbacher, Jr., J. L. Nichols, M. P. Ricciardello, J. Richels

Founded: 1988
Domicile: Delaware
Employees: 5,500

The McGraw-Hill Companies

DeVry Inc

STANDARD &POOR'S

S&P Recommendation **HOLD** ★★★☆☆	Price $54.44 (as of Nov 27, 2009)	12-Mo. Target Price $60.00	Investment Style Large-Cap Growth

GICS Sector Consumer Discretionary
Sub-Industry Education Services

Summary DeVry offers career-oriented degree programs, preparatory coursework for the CPA and CFA exams, and medical, veterinary and nursing education.

Key Stock Statistics (Source S&P, Vickers, company reports)

52-Wk Range	$64.69 – 38.19	S&P Oper. EPS 2010**E**	3.00	Market Capitalization(B)	$3.867	Beta	0.18
Trailing 12-Month EPS	$2.56	S&P Oper. EPS 2011**E**	3.40	Yield (%)	0.37	S&P 3-Yr. Proj. EPS CAGR(%)	18
Trailing 12-Month P/E	21.3	P/E on S&P Oper. EPS 2010**E**	18.1	Dividend Rate/Share	$0.20	S&P Credit Rating	NA
$10K Invested 5 Yrs Ago	$32,221	Common Shares Outstg. (M)	71.0	Institutional Ownership (%)	84		

Price Performance

30-Week Mov. Avg. · · · · 10-Week Mov. Avg. – – **GAAP Earnings vs. Previous Year** Volume Above Avg. STARS

12-Mo. Target Price — Relative Strength — ▲ Up ▼ Down ▶ No Change Below Avg.

Options: CBOE, P, Ph

Analysis prepared by **Michael W. Jaffe** on November 19, 2009, when the stock traded at **$ 53.51**.

Highlights

▶ We think revenues will rise 22% in FY 10 (Jun.), on the full-year inclusion of U.S. Education (acquired in September 2008), growth in demand for DV's programs (particularly in the Business, Technology and Management segment), more campus openings, and tuition increases. We see these factors outweighing projected lower average tuition per student, on a likely higher proportion of part-time students and students taking fewer courses per semester. We also see demand remaining soft for DV's Professional Education programs.

▶ We expect slightly wider net margins in FY 10. We see leverage from the greater demand we forecast for DV's programs, together with recent cost cuts, being partly offset by the cost of investments in technology infrastructure and corporate growth. Our FY 10 EPS forecast of $3.00 compares with operating EPS of $2.36 in FY 09.

▶ We think DV will benefit from its five-year strategic plan, where it will seek to achieve the full potential of DeVry University; grow in adjacent vertical curriculum markets; put more focus on pre-baccalaureate and career college programs; and move into new geographies.

Investment Rationale/Risk

▶ In recent years, DeVry has seen better overall demand for its programs and benefits from cost-cutting actions. We are also positive on the September 2008 purchase of U.S. Education, as we like DV's recent plan of moving away from its previous dominant focus on technology programs. However, in light of what we view as a likely shift in investor psychology toward growth-oriented cyclical companies, we find DV shares near a fair valuation.

▶ Risks to our recommendation and target price include a greater-than-expected impact from currently tight U.S. lending markets and weaker trends in DV's primary areas of education.

▶ The stock recently traded at 17X our calendar 2010 EPS forecast of $3.20, which we believe is a deserved premium to DV's peer group. Although we are positive on DV's operating prospects, and we think it will record more consistent earnings gains than its peers, we think recent signs of economic stabilization might rein in valuations for firms viewed as countercyclical (although DV does not characterize itself in that manner). Applying a multiple of 18.8X to our calendar 2010 EPS estimate produces a value of $60, which is our 12-month target price.

Qualitative Risk Assessment

LOW	**MEDIUM**	HIGH

Our risk assessment reflects DV's operating struggles for a few years in the middle part of the decade and high levels of regulatory scrutiny being given to for-profit educators, offset by what we consider positive turnaround initiatives.

Quantitative Evaluations

S&P Quality Ranking B

D	C	B-	**B**	B+	A-	A	A+

Relative Strength Rank MODERATE

58

LOWEST = 1 HIGHEST = 99

Revenue/Earnings Data

Revenue (Million $)

	1Q	2Q	3Q	4Q	Year
2010	431.1	--	--	--	--
2009	303.7	369.6	391.9	396.2	1,461
2008	250.3	273.7	291.0	276.8	1,092
2007	219.2	235.6	245.8	232.8	933.5
2006	196.8	209.9	220.2	216.4	843.3
2005	188.4	194.5	201.9	196.5	781.3

Earnings Per Share ($)

2010	0.76	E0.75	E0.85	E0.64	E3.00
2009	0.48	0.59	0.70	0.51	2.28
2008	0.37	0.49	0.53	0.34	1.73
2007	0.29	0.23	0.32	0.22	1.07
2006	0.07	0.15	0.22	0.17	0.61
2005	0.04	0.08	0.17	0.09	0.38

Fiscal year ended Jun. 30. Next earnings report expected: Late January. EPS Estimates based on S&P Operating Earnings; historical GAAP earnings are as reported.

Dividend Data (Dates: mm/dd Payment Date: mm/dd/yy)

Amount ($)	Date Decl.	Ex-Div. Date	Stk. of Record	Payment Date
0.080	11/13	12/10	12/12	01/09/09
0.080	05/13	06/12	06/16	07/09/09
0.100	11/11	12/09	12/11	01/07/10

Dividends have been paid since 2007. Source: Company reports.

Please read the Required Disclosures and Analyst Certification on the last page of this report.

The **McGraw·Hill** Companies

DeVry Inc

Business Summary November 19, 2009

CORPORATE OVERVIEW. DeVry offers associate, undergraduate and graduate degree programs through its DeVry University institute. It also operates Becker Professional Education, which provides preparatory coursework for certification exams in accounting and finance; Ross University, which offers medical and veterinary education; Chamberlain College of Nursing, which offers nursing programs; U.S. Education (purchased in September 2008, for $290 million in cash), which operates Apollo College and Western Career College in the western U.S., offering certificate and associate degree programs in health care; Fanor (82% stake purchased on April 1, 2009, for $40.4 million in cash), a post-secondary education provider in Brazil; and Advanced Academics, which provides online secondary education to school districts throughout the U.S.

In August 2009, DV reported that it had reorganized its operating structure into four segments: Business, Technology and Management (comprised of DeVry University), Medical and Healthcare (Ross University, Chamberlain College of Nursing, and U.S. Education), Professional Education (Becker Professional Education), and Other Educational Services (Advanced Academics and Fanor). In FY 09 (Jun.), the Business, Technology and Management segment accounted for 68% of DV's revenues and 51% of operating profits; Medical and Healthcare schools accounted for 25% of revenues and 37% of operating profits; and the Professional Education segment contributed 6% and 12%, re-spectively. The remaining 2% and a small loss were derived from the Other Educational segment.

CORPORATE STRATEGY. In an effort to boost its appeal, DV offers weekend classes, compressed and accelerated course schedules, technology-assisted delivery options for classroom-based courses, and online programs. In FY 01, DV began to operate DeVry University Centers, which are smaller than its campus facilities and more conveniently located for working adults.

With operating results softening for a few years, DeVry initiated a turnaround plan in FY 05's second quarter, which focused largely on steps to reduce salary costs and revive demand. These actions led to a workforce reduction of about 230 employees, which DV saw cutting annual salary and benefit costs by at least $16.5 million. The company implemented additional workforce reduction programs in March and April 2007. A total of 70 workers accepted a voluntary offer, while DV reduced its staff by another 150 through a subsequent involuntary plan. The company sees annual savings of $10 million from the latest staff cuts.

Company Financials Fiscal Year Ended Jun. 30

Per Share Data ($)	2009	2008	2007	2006	2005	2004	2003	2002	2001	2000
Tangible Book Value	2.96	5.40	4.13	2.96	2.06	1.53	0.45	3.94	2.95	2.17
Cash Flow	2.98	2.28	1.69	1.29	1.19	1.62	1.45	1.42	1.27	1.04
Earnings	2.28	1.73	1.07	0.61	0.38	0.82	0.87	0.95	0.82	0.68
S&P Core Earnings	2.34	1.76	0.89	0.61	0.29	0.77	0.83	0.91	0.79	NA
Dividends	0.16	0.12	0.10	Nil	Nil	Nil	Nil	Nil	Nil	Nil
Payout Ratio	7%	7%	9%	Nil	Nil	Nil	Nil	Nil	Nil	Nil
Prices:High	64.69	61.57	59.97	28.75	24.84	32.38	30.15	34.76	40.25	41.50
Prices:Low	38.19	39.25	26.10	18.50	15.45	13.00	15.90	12.10	22.75	16.06
P/E Ratio:High	28	36	56	47	65	39	35	37	49	61
P/E Ratio:Low	17	23	24	30	41	16	18	13	28	24

Income Statement Analysis (Million $)	2009	2008	2007	2006	2005	2004	2003	2002	2001	2000
Revenue	1,461	1,092	933	843	781	785	680	648	568	507
Operating Income	2,994	206	132	116	101	139	128	144	128	105
Depreciation	50.5	39.7	44.0	48.1	57.6	55.6	40.3	33.5	32.0	25.3
Interest Expense	2.78	0.52	4.78	10.2	9.05	7.80	1.28	0.81	0.40	1.41
Pretax Income	237	172	105	57.5	34.7	81.4	86.5	111	95.9	78.1
Effective Tax Rate	30.2%	27.1%	27.4%	25.1%	23.1%	28.6%	29.3%	39.4%	39.8%	38.8%
Net Income	166	126	76.2	43.1	26.7	58.1	61.1	67.1	57.8	47.8
S&P Core Earnings	170	128	63.5	42.8	20.2	54.6	58.4	64.4	55.8	NA

Balance Sheet & Other Financial Data (Million $)	2009	2008	2007	2006	2005	2004	2003	2002	2001	2000
Cash	225	220	129	131	162	160	123	78.9	49.7	45.2
Current Assets	385	326	219	228	242	209	170	118	88.6	82.0
Total Assets	1,434	1,018	844	872	910	884	857	468	392	327
Current Liabilities	392	211	166	211	187	156	139	104	94.4	89.2
Long Term Debt	20.0	Nil	0.01	65.0	175	215	275	Nil	Nil	Nil
Common Equity	927	756	642	565	508	478	416	354	285	225
Total Capital	999	778	660	642	704	711	704	354	285	225
Capital Expenditures	74.0	62.8	38.6	25.3	42.9	42.8	43.8	85.9	74.6	40.8
Cash Flow	216	165	120	91.2	84.3	114	101	101	89.8	73.0
Current Ratio	1.0	1.6	1.3	1.1	1.3	1.3	1.2	1.1	0.9	0.9
% Long Term Debt of Capitalization	2.0	Nil	0.0	10.1	24.8	30.2	39.1	Nil	Nil	Nil
% Net Income of Revenue	11.3	11.5	8.2	5.1	3.4	7.4	9.0	10.4	10.2	9.4
% Return on Assets	13.5	13.5	8.9	4.8	3.0	6.7	9.2	15.6	16.1	16.3
% Return on Equity	19.7	18.0	12.6	8.0	5.4	13.0	15.9	21.0	22.7	23.9

Data as orig reptd.; bef. results of disc opers/spec. items. Per share data adj. for stk. divs.; EPS diluted. E-Estimated. NA-Not Available. NM-Not Meaningful. NR-Not Ranked. UR-Under Review.

Office: 1 Tower Ln Ste 1000, Oakbrook Terrace, IL 60181-4624.
Telephone: 630-571-7700.
Website: http://www.devryinc.com
Chrmn: H.T. Shapiro

Pres & CEO: D.M. Hamburger
SVP, CFO, Chief Acctg Officer & Treas: R.M. Gunst
SVP, Secy & General Counsel: G.S. Davis
SVP & CIO: E.P. Dirst

Investor Contact: J. Bates (630-574-1949)
Board Members: D. S. Brown, C. Curran, D. M. Hamburger, D. R. Huston, W. T. Keevan, L. Logan, J. A. McGee, L. W. Pickrum, F. Ruiz, H. T. Shapiro, R. L. Taylor

Founded: 1931
Domicile: Delaware
Employees: 10,200

Diamond Offshore Drilling Inc.

STANDARD &POOR'S

S&P Recommendation	BUY ★★★★☆	Price $99.46 (as of Nov 27, 2009)	12-Mo. Target Price $119.00	Investment Style Large-Cap Blend

GICS Sector Energy
Sub-Industry Oil & Gas Drilling

Summary This company provides offshore contract drilling services to the oil and gas industry, and owns one of the world's largest fleets of semisubmersible rigs.

Key Stock Statistics (Source S&P, Vickers, company reports)

52-Wk Range	$108.78– 53.30	S&P Oper. EPS 2009E	10.42	Market Capitalization(B)	$13.826	Beta	0.90
Trailing 12-Month EPS	$10.02	S&P Oper. EPS 2010E	9.92	Yield (%)	0.50	S&P 3-Yr. Proj. EPS CAGR(%)	15
Trailing 12-Month P/E	9.9	P/E on S&P Oper. EPS 2009E	9.5	Dividend Rate/Share	$0.50	S&P Credit Rating	A-
$10K Invested 5 Yrs Ago	$33,818	Common Shares Outstg. (M)	139.0	Institutional Ownership (%)	NM		

Price Performance

30-Week Mov. Avg. ··· 10-Week Mov. Avg. – – **GAAP Earnings vs. Previous Year** Volume Above Avg. |ıllıl STARS
12-Mo. Target Price — Relative Strength — ▲ Up ▼ Down ▶ No Change Below Avg. |ılıl

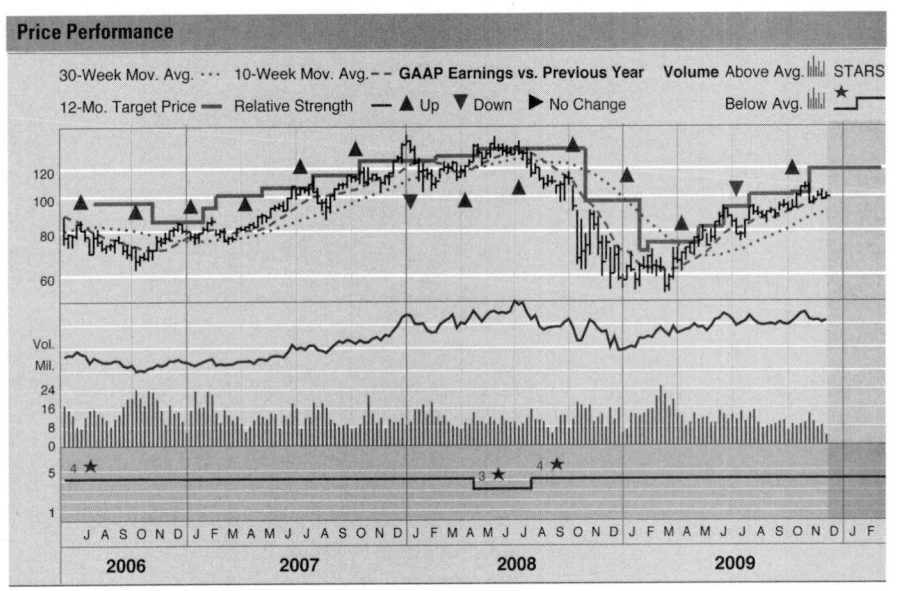

Options: ASE, CBOE, P

Analysis prepared by **Stewart Glickman, CFA** on October 23, 2009, when the stock traded at **$ 105.80.**

Highlights

► In the third quarter, DO acquired two newbuild semisubmersibles for a combined $950 million, renaming the rigs the Ocean Courage and the Ocean Valor. The Courage has already commenced operations in the U.S. Gulf of Mexico at a dayrate of $412,000 per day, while the Valor is being actively marketed and will be available in the first quarter of 2010. We view these investments positively, given DO's solid free cash flow, and DO's ability to grow the fleet quickly without the shipyard risk (nor the lag time) of undertaking brand new rig construction.

► With the Ocean Star moving to Brazil on a one-year deal, DO's floater exposure to the U.S. Gulf of Mexico will drop to just one rig by mid-2010. While DO also has three mat-supported jackup rigs in the Gulf, these rigs have been cold-stacked due to low expectations for future work.

► We estimate revenue growth of 2% in 2009, but see a 3% decline in 2010. We look for EPS of $10.42 this year (a 10% improvement over 2008), dropping to $9.92 in 2010 on modest weakness in projected midwater floater dayrates and for jackups.

Investment Rationale/Risk

► We view DO as among the better positioned offshore drillers for 2009, given a strong backlog of existing contracts, relatively few planned days in shipyard, and low capital spending needs. We estimate operating cash flow in 2010 to dwarf our projection of DO's maintenance capital needs, and as a result, we project substantial free cash flow that could be used either for enhancement of special dividends and/or to buy additional newbuilds to expand the active fleet.

► Risks to our recommendation and target price include reduced deepwater drilling activity; lower oil and natural gas prices; weaker than expected dayrates on international midwater floaters; and inability to contract the recently acquired Ocean Valor.

► Applying an 8X multiple to our 2010 estimated EBITDA, a 9X multiple on 2010 projected operating cash flows (both above peers, merited in our view by above-average ROIC), and blending these results with our net asset value model, our 12-month target price is $119. Through October, DO had declared $0.50 per share of regular dividends and $7.50 per share of special dividends, for an overall dividend yield of 7.5%.

Qualitative Risk Assessment

LOW	MEDIUM	HIGH

Our risk assessment reflects DO's exposure to volatile crude oil and natural gas prices, capital spending decisions made by its oil and gas producing customers, and risks associated with operating in frontier regions. Offsetting these risks, in our opinion, is DO's strong fleet of floater rigs.

Quantitative Evaluations

S&P Quality Ranking   B

D	C	B-	B	B+	A-	A	A+

Relative Strength Rank   MODERATE

62

LOWEST = 1   HIGHEST = 99

Revenue/Earnings Data

Revenue (Million $)

	1Q	2Q	3Q	4Q	Year
2009	885.7	946.4	908.4	--	--
2008	786.1	954.4	900.4	903.2	3,544
2007	608.2	648.9	644.0	666.7	2,568
2006	447.7	512.2	514.5	578.2	2,053
2005	258.8	283.4	310.5	368.3	1,221
2004	184.2	185.0	208.2	237.3	814.7

Earnings Per Share ($)

	1Q	2Q	3Q	4Q	Year
2009	2.51	2.79	2.62	E2.51	E10.42
2008	2.09	2.99	2.23	2.11	9.43
2007	1.64	1.81	1.48	1.19	6.12
2006	1.06	1.27	1.19	1.60	5.12
2005	0.23	0.31	0.60	0.78	1.91
2004	-0.08	-0.08	0.02	0.09	-0.06

Fiscal year ended Dec. 31. Next earnings report expected: Early February. EPS Estimates based on S&P Operating Earnings; historical GAAP earnings are as reported.

Dividend Data (Dates: mm/dd Payment Date: mm/dd/yy)

Amount ($)	Date Decl.	Ex-Div. Date	Stk. of Record	Payment Date
1.875 Spl.	04/23	04/29	05/01	06/01/09
0.125	07/23	07/30	08/30	09/01/09
1.875 Spl.	10/22	10/29	11/02	12/01/09
0.125	10/22	10/29	11/02	12/01/09

Dividends have been paid since 1997. Source: Company reports.

Please read the Required Disclosures and Analyst Certification on the last page of this report.

Diamond Offshore Drilling Inc.

STANDARD &POOR'S

Business Summary October 23, 2009

CORPORATE OVERVIEW. Diamond Offshore Drilling is engaged in contract drilling of offshore oil and gas wells, with a focus on deepwater drilling. As of January 2009, the company owned 46 mobile offshore drilling rigs: 30 semi-submersible rigs, 15 jackup rigs, and one drillship. The rigs operated in the Gulf of Mexico (GOM), the U.K. North Sea, South America, Africa, Australia and Southeast Asia. About 59% of 2008 revenues came from outside the United States. DO served 49 customers in 2008, with Petrobras accounting for 13% of total revenues.

Semisubmersible rigs, or floaters (83% of 2008 contract drilling revenues, and 85% of 2008 segment operating income), operate in a semisubmerged position, afloat off the bottom, with the lower hull 55 ft. to 90 ft. below the water line, and the upper deck well above the surface. Floaters are typically anchored in position, but three company floaters are held in position by computer-controlled thrusters (dynamically positioned, or DP). Of DO's 31 floaters, 12 are high specification rigs (39%, 43%), capable of working in harsh environ-

ments and water depths of up to 7,500 ft. The other 19 semisubmersibles (44%, 42%) operate in maximum water depths of 4,000 ft.

Jackup rigs (17%, 15%) are mobile, self-elevating drilling platforms equipped with legs that are lowered to the ocean floor until a foundation is established to support the rig. DO's 13 jackup rigs are used extensively for drilling in water depths from 20 ft. to 350 ft. The principal market for the jackups is the GOM, where 11 of them are located.

Drillships, typically self-propelled, are positioned over a drillsite through the use of either an anchoring or DP system. The company owns one drillship, the Ocean Clipper, operating offshore Brazil.

Company Financials Fiscal Year Ended Dec. 31

Per Share Data ($)	2008	2007	2006	2005	2004	2003	2002	2001	2000	1999
Tangible Book Value	24.09	20.72	17.95	14.38	12.64	12.91	13.68	13.74	12.86	13.02
Cash Flow	11.49	7.79	6.54	3.14	1.33	0.98	1.71	2.35	1.50	2.05
Earnings	9.43	6.12	5.12	1.91	-0.06	-0.37	0.47	1.31	0.53	1.11
S&P Core Earnings	9.41	6.07	5.13	1.84	-0.07	-0.35	0.30	1.15	NA	NA
Dividends	4.13	0.50	0.50	0.38	0.25	0.44	0.50	0.50	0.50	0.50
Payout Ratio	44%	8%	10%	20%	NM	NM	106%	38%	94%	45%
Prices:High	147.77	149.30	97.90	71.97	40.47	23.80	34.99	45.65	47.94	41.00
Prices:Low	54.52	73.50	62.26	37.91	20.00	17.06	17.30	22.83	26.50	20.25
P/E Ratio:High	16	24	19	38	NM	NM	74	35	90	37
P/E Ratio:Low	6	12	12	20	NM	NM	37	17	50	18

Income Statement Analysis (Million $)										
Revenue	3,544	2,568	2,053	1,221	815	681	753	885	659	821
Operating Income	2,233	1,454	1,141	510	213	138	229	395	203	367
Depreciation, Depletion and Amortization	287	235	201	184	179	176	177	170	146	143
Interest Expense	10.1	28.5	24.1	41.8	30.3	23.9	23.6	26.2	10.3	9.21
Pretax Income	1,848	1,247	966	356	-3.53	-54.2	96.2	272	111	240
Effective Tax Rate	29.0%	32.1%	26.9%	27.0%	NM	NM	35.0%	33.3%	34.8%	35.1%
Net Income	1,311	847	707	260	-7.24	-48.4	62.5	182	72.3	156
S&P Core Earnings	1,308	841	707	250	-10.5	-45.5	36.9	157	NA	NA

Balance Sheet & Other Financial Data (Million $)										
Cash	737	639	826	843	266	610	813	1,147	862	641
Current Assets	1,467	1,265	1,482	1,282	1,196	835	1,034	1,427	1,101	860
Total Assets	4,939	4,341	4,133	3,607	3,379	3,135	3,259	3,503	3,080	2,681
Current Liabilities	509	453	334	269	614	100	118	335	123	135
Long Term Debt	503	507	964	978	709	928	924	921	857	400
Common Equity	3,349	2,877	2,320	1,853	1,626	1,680	1,808	1,853	1,768	1,842
Total Capital	4,311	3,778	3,284	3,276	2,705	2,993	3,107	3,150	2,941	2,533
Capital Expenditures	667	647	551	294	89.2	209	274	269	324	324
Cash Flow	1,598	1,082	907	444	172	127	240	352	218	299
Current Ratio	2.9	2.8	4.4	4.8	1.9	8.4	8.7	4.3	8.9	6.4
% Long Term Debt of Capitalization	11.7	14.9	29.4	29.8	26.2	31.0	29.8	29.2	29.1	15.8
% Return on Assets	28.3	20.0	18.3	7.5	NM	NM	1.8	5.5	2.5	5.9
% Return on Equity	42.1	32.6	33.9	15.0	NM	NM	3.4	10.0	4.0	8.7

Data as orig reptd.; bef. results of disc opers/spec. items. Per share data adj. for stk. divs.; EPS diluted. E-Estimated. NA-Not Available. NM-Not Meaningful. NR-Not Ranked. UR-Under Review.

Office: 15415 Katy Freeway, Houston, TX 77094-1803.
Telephone: 281-492-5300.
Website: http://www.diamondoffshore.com
Chrmn: J.S. Tisch

Pres & CEO: L.R. Dickerson
COO & Chief Admin Officer: M.F. Baudoin
SVP & CFO: G.T. Krenek
SVP, Secy & General Counsel: W.C. Long

Investor Contact: L. Van Dyke (281-492-5370)
Board Members: J. R. Bolton, L. R. Dickerson, C. L. Fabrikant, P. G. Gaffney, II, E. Grebow, H. C. Hofmann, A. L. Rebell, J. S. Tisch, R. Troubh

Founded: 1989
Domicile: Delaware
Employees: 5,700

The McGraw-Hill Companies

DIRECTV

STANDARD &POOR'S

S&P Recommendation HOLD ★★★☆☆

Price $31.60 (as of Nov 27, 2009)	**12-Mo. Target Price** $35.00

Investment Style Large-Cap Blend

GICS Sector Consumer Discretionary
Sub-Industry Cable & Satellite

Summary This company is the larger of the two major U.S. providers of direct broadcast satellite (DBS) television service, with more than 18.4 million subscribers across the U.S., and 4.3 million in Latin America.

Key Stock Statistics (Source S&P, Vickers, company reports)

52-Wk Range	$32.30– 18.81	S&P Oper. EPS 2009E	1.34	Market Capitalization(B)	$30.237	Beta	0.76
Trailing 12-Month EPS	$1.29	S&P Oper. EPS 2010E	1.84	Yield (%)	Nil	S&P 3-Yr. Proj. EPS CAGR(%)	12
Trailing 12-Month P/E	24.5	P/E on S&P Oper. EPS 2009E	23.6	Dividend Rate/Share	Nil	S&P Credit Rating	BBB-
$10K Invested 5 Yrs Ago	$19,652	Common Shares Outstg. (M)	956.9	Institutional Ownership (%)	52		

Price Performance

30-Week Mov. Avg. · · · · 10-Week Mov. Avg. - - GAAP Earnings vs. Previous Year   Volume Above Avg. ▌▍▏ STARS
12-Mo. Target Price — Relative Strength — ▲ Up ▼ Down ▶ No Change   Below Avg. ▌▍▏

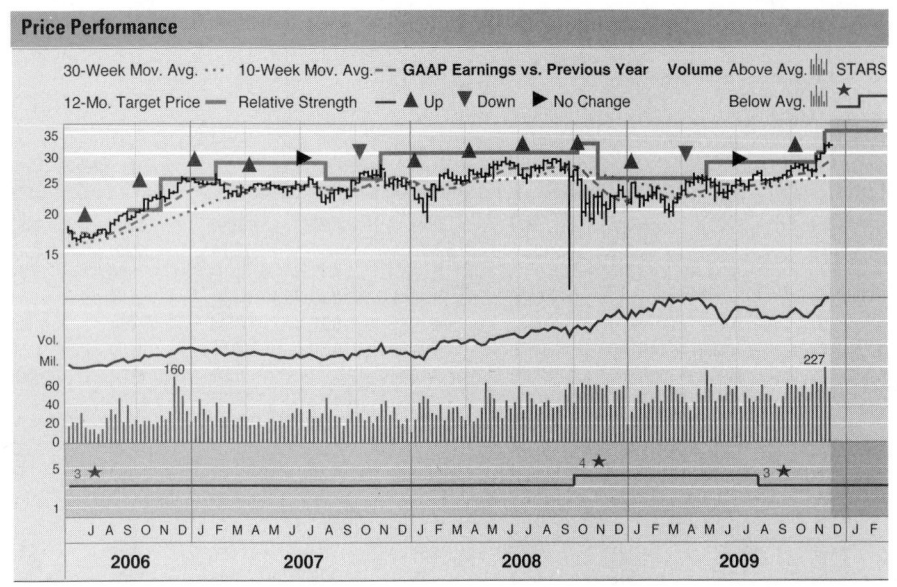

Options: ASE, CBOE, P, Ph

Analysis prepared by **Tuna N. Amobi, CFA, CPA** on November 18, 2009, when the stock traded at **$ 31.08**.

Highlights

▶ We see DTV U.S. projected 2009 gross adds slightly improving to 4.5 million in 2010, mainly on the direct sales and independent retail channels, and greater telco contributions spurred by the AT&T (T 26, Strong Buy) pact. Assuming relatively stable monthly churn of 1.5% to 1.6%, we see about 1.0 million net adds per year, reaching nearly 19.7 million U.S. subscribers by the end of 2010. Helped by advanced services, we see essentially flat 2009 ARPU also improving to low single-digit in 2010.

▶ With relatively stronger growth at DTV Latin America, and modest ad revenues, we expect 9% and 8% consolidated revenue growth in 2009 and 2010, respectively, to $23.2 billion for next year. We see 2009 results reflecting higher programming costs, as well as SAC and retention/upgrade expenses.

▶ However, with operating leverage benefiting from cost control, we project 2010 consolidated EBITDA will advance 16% to $6.1 billion. After higher satellite D&A, we forecast 2009 and 2010 EPS of $1.40 and $1.95, respectively, with share buybacks under a $2 billion repurchase plan.

Investment Rationale/Risk

▶ We expect DTV's November 2009 merger with Liberty Media's (LMDIA 36) Liberty Entertainment (LEI), upon which LEI holds a 57% stake in DTV (on Chairman John Malone's super-voting control), to somewhat complicate its governance structure. Still, continuing financial flexibility should allow the new entity to resume its share repurchases, and perhaps contemplate selective acquisitions. We are encouraged by DTV's 2009 results through September -- reinforcing the telco channel as a likely potent source of subscriber growth. In November, DTV named Michael White, a PepsiCo executive, as its new CEO effective January 1, 2010.

▶ Risks to our recommendation and target price include near-term potential strategic uncertainty (and governance concerns on new dual class shares) arising from the merger; a slower-than-expected economic recovery; and, increased competition from cable's bundle.

▶ Our 12-month target price is $35, on 6.0X 2010 EV/EBITDA, or $1,900 per subscriber, seen as ample relative to DISH Network (DISH 20, Strong Sell). DTV recently had about $1.7 billion of foreign net operating loss carryforwards.

Qualitative Risk Assessment

LOW	**MEDIUM**	HIGH

Our risk assessment reflects what we view as ample financial flexibility, and a projected acceleration of free cash flow, offset by increased competition from cable operators' bundled offerings.

Quantitative Evaluations

S&P Quality Ranking   B-

D	C	**B-**	B	B+	A-	A	A+

Relative Strength Rank   **STRONG**

92

LOWEST = 1   HIGHEST = 99

Revenue/Earnings Data

Revenue (Million $)

	1Q	2Q	3Q	4Q	Year
2009	4,901	--	--	--	--
2008	4,591	4,807	4,981	5,314	19,693
2007	3,908	4,135	4,327	4,876	17,246
2006	3,386	3,520	3,667	4,183	14,756
2005	3,148	3,188	3,233	3,596	13,165
2004	2,493	2,643	2,862	3,362	11,360

Earnings Per Share ($)

2009	0.20	0.40	0.38	E0.38	E1.34
2008	0.32	0.40	0.33	0.31	1.36
2007	0.27	0.36	0.27	0.30	1.19
2006	0.17	0.36	0.30	0.29	1.12
2005	-0.03	0.10	0.07	0.09	0.22
2004	0.13	-0.01	-0.67	-0.20	-0.77

Fiscal year ended Dec. 31. Next earnings report expected: Mid February. EPS Estimates based on S&P Operating Earnings; historical GAAP earnings are as reported.

Dividend Data

No cash dividends have been paid since 1997.

Please read the Required Disclosures and Analyst Certification on the last page of this report.

The McGraw-Hill Companies

DIRECTV

STANDARD
&POOR'S

Business Summary November 18, 2009

CORPORATE OVERVIEW. The DIRECTV Group (formerly Hughes Electronics) is a leading provider of direct broadcast satellite (DBS) television service, providing hundreds of digital video and audio channels to more than 18 million monthly subscribers in the U.S., and a selection of local and international programming to over 4.0 million subscribers in Latin America (mostly in Brazil, Argentina, Venezuela and Puerto Rico). DTV distributes its services mainly through direct sales and retail channels, and through co-branding partnerships with three of the four RBOCs.

In November 2009, DTV expected to merge with Liberty Entertainment (LEI), a proposed split-off from Liberty Entertainment (LMDIA, $36), and named Michael White, a retiring CEO of PepsiCo International, as its CEO effective January 1, 2010.

CORPORATE STRATEGY. We see several key strategic initiatives to launch enhanced features and services such as advanced high-definition (HD) and DVR offerings, amid a transition from MPEG-2 to MPEG-4 platform. After the launch of DIRECTV 11 in 2008, DTV recently offered more than 130 national HD channels, and local HD covering about 87% of U.S. TV homes. Other initiatives include a new video-on-demand (VOD) offering, broadband video, games, en-

hanced program guides, home networked DVRs, and portable devices. With NFL Sunday Ticket at the centerpiece of its sports programming offerings, DTV's contract with the pro football league extends through the 2014 season.

In September 2008, DTV entered into a deal under which telco AT&T (T 26, Strong Buy) began offering DTV as a co-branded satellite TV service since February 1, 2009. In July 2008, DTV acquired 180 Connect Inc., a major installation service provider, which it estimates fulfills 15%-20% of its work orders. In June 2007, DTV and DISH Network (DISH 18, Strong Sell) unveiled distribution pacts to offer Imax-based wireless high-speed broadband service from Clearwire (CLWR 8), which in turn will offer their DBS video services, with both DBS companies offering data, video and voice services in CLWR's markets starting in 2007. Earlier, in 2004, DTV divested assets such as Hughes Networks Systems and PanAmSat, and DTV Latin America emerged from a bankruptcy reorganization.

Company Financials Fiscal Year Ended Dec. 31

Per Share Data ($)	2008	2007	2006	2005	2004	2003	2002	2001	2000	1999
Tangible Book Value	NM	0.92	1.10	2.17	1.61	4.36	2.76	NM	4.20	6.78
Cash Flow	3.44	2.59	1.93	0.83	-0.16	0.27	0.88	0.50	0.73	0.55
Earnings	1.36	1.19	1.12	0.22	-0.77	-0.27	-0.21	-0.55	-0.34	-0.35
S&P Core Earnings	1.35	1.18	1.05	0.20	-0.96	-0.32	-0.78	-0.86	NA	NA
Dividends	Nil	Nil	Nil	Nil	Nil	Nil	Nil	Nil	Nil	Nil
Payout Ratio	Nil	Nil	Nil	Nil	Nil	Nil	Nil	Nil	Nil	Nil
Prices:High	29.10	27.73	25.57	17.01	18.81	16.91	17.55	28.00	46.67	32.54
Prices:Low	19.40	20.73	13.28	13.17	14.70	9.40	8.00	11.50	21.33	12.83
P/E Ratio:High	21	23	23	77	NM	NM	NM	NM	NM	NM
P/E Ratio:Low	14	17	12	60	NM	NM	NM	NM	NM	NM

Income Statement Analysis (Million $)

	2008	2007	2006	2005	2004	2003	2002	2001	2000	1999
Revenue	19,693	17,246	14,756	13,165	11,360	9,372	8,935	8,262	7,288	5,560
Operating Income	5,029	4,145	3,274	1,441	-1,281	617	668	390	594	219
Depreciation	2,320	1,684	1,034	853	838	755	1,067	1,148	948	647
Interest Expense	360	286	246	238	132	156	336	196	218	123
Pretax Income	2,471	2,388	542	480	-1,734	-478	-140	-990	-816	-660
Effective Tax Rate	35.0%	39.5%	NM	36.1%	NM	NM	NM	NM	NM	NM
Net Income	1,515	1,434	1,420	305	-1,056	-375	-213	-614	-355	-391
S&P Core Earnings	1,498	1,410	1,336	279	-1,312	-439	-862	-923	NA	NA

Balance Sheet & Other Financial Data (Million $)

	2008	2007	2006	2005	2004	2003	2002	2001	2000	1999
Cash	2,005	1,098	2,499	3,701	2,830	1,720	1,129	700	1,508	238
Current Assets	4,044	3,146	4,556	6,096	4,771	10,356	3,656	3,341	4,154	3,858
Total Assets	16,539	15,063	15,141	15,630	14,324	18,978	17,885	19,210	19,279	18,597
Current Liabilities	3,585	3,434	3,323	2,828	2,695	5,840	3,203	4,407	2,691	2,642
Long Term Debt	6,267	3,347	3,395	3,405	2,410	2,435	2,390	989	1,292	1,586
Common Equity	4,853	6,302	6,681	7,940	7,507	9,631	9,063	9,574	10,830	10,194
Total Capital	11,205	10,227	10,138	11,395	9,965	12,305	12,590	13,339	14,941	14,501
Capital Expenditures	2,229	2,692	1,754	889	1,023	444	566	799	939	472
Cash Flow	3,835	3,118	2,455	1,158	-218	380	808	438	496	205
Current Ratio	1.1	0.9	1.4	2.2	1.8	1.8	1.1	0.8	1.5	1.5
% Long Term Debt of Capitalization	55.9	32.7	33.5	29.9	24.2	19.8	19.0	7.4	8.6	10.9
% Net Income of Revenue	7.7	8.3	9.6	2.3	NM	NM	NM	NM	NM	NM
% Return on Assets	9.6	9.5	9.2	2.0	NM	NM	NM	NM	NM	NM
% Return on Equity	27.2	22.1	19.4	3.9	NM	NM	NM	NM	NM	NM

Data as orig reptd.; bef. results of disc opers/spec. items. Per share data adj. for stk. divs.; EPS diluted. E-Estimated. NA-Not Available. NM-Not Meaningful. NR-Not Ranked. UR-Under Review.

Office: 2230 E Imperial Hwy, El Segundo, CA 90245-3531.
Telephone: 310-964-5000.
Website: http://www.directv.com
Chrmn: J.C. Malone

CEO, Chief Admin Officer & General Counsel: L.D. Hunter
COO: M.W. Palkovic
EVP & CFO: P.T. Doyle
EVP & CTO: R.C. Pontual

Investor Contact: J. Rubin (212-462-5200)
Board Members: N. R. Austrian, R. F. Boyd, Jr., C. Carey, P. A. Gould, C. R. Lee, P. A. Lund, G. B. Maffei, J. C. Malone, N. S. Newcomb, H. Saban, J. F. Smith, Jr.

Founded: 1977
Domicile: Delaware
Employees: 19,600

Discover Financial Services Inc

STANDARD &POOR'S

S&P Recommendation	**STRONG BUY** ★★★★★	Price $15.13 (as of Nov 27, 2009)	12-Mo. Target Price $20.00	Investment Style Large-Cap Growth

GICS Sector Financials
Sub-Industry Consumer Finance

Summary This leading U.S. credit card issuer and payment services company offers credit and prepaid cards and provides payment processing services to merchants and financial institutions.

Key Stock Statistics (Source S&P, Vickers, company reports)

52-Wk Range	$17.36– 4.73	S&P Oper. EPS 2009**E**	2.41	Market Capitalization(B)	$8.213	Beta	1.72
Trailing 12-Month EPS	$2.68	S&P Oper. EPS 2010**E**	-1.51	Yield (%)	0.53	S&P 3-Yr. Proj. EPS CAGR(%)	-4
Trailing 12-Month P/E	5.7	P/E on S&P Oper. EPS 2009**E**	6.3	Dividend Rate/Share	$0.08	S&P Credit Rating	BBB-
$10K Invested 5 Yrs Ago	NA	Common Shares Outstg. (M)	542.8	Institutional Ownership (%)	81		

Price Performance

30-Week Mov. Avg. ··· 10-Week Mov. Avg. — — GAAP Earnings vs. Previous Year Volume Above Avg. STARS
12-Mo. Target Price — Relative Strength — ▲ Up ▼ Down ▶ No Change Below Avg. ↗

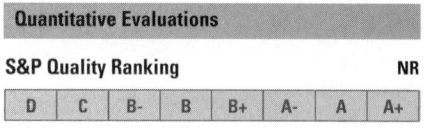

Options: ASE, CBOE, P

Analysis prepared by **Stuart Plesser** on September 18, 2009, when the stock traded at **$ 15.97**.

Highlights

► We expect average managed credit card loans to increase around 5.0% in FY 09 (Nov.) and FY 10, as we see a decline in spending and balance transfers offset by a slowdown in payments. By our analysis, net interest income should rise roughly 17% in FY 09 and 7% in FY 10, due largely to lower promotional pricing. We look for a net interest margin of 9.8% in FY 10, versus a projected 9.6% margin in FY 09. We expect managed revenue to be down 16% in FY 10, largely due to the absence of proceeds from an antitrust settlement.

► We think that managed chargeoffs will continue to rise through the first half of FY 10, due to the increasing strain on consumers from rising unemployment. We forecast that chargeoffs will peak at around 9.5%, and we see provisions up significantly largely due to a change in accounting requiring off-balance sheet consolidation of assets. We expect marketing costs to increase in FY 10, with expenses at around 31% of revenue.

► Including antitrust settlement proceeds, we estimate EPS of $2.41 in FY 09 and a loss of $1.51 in FY 10.

Investment Rationale/Risk

► Managed receivables growth will likely increase in FY 09, due to the addition of Diners Club, higher merchant acceptance and a slowdown in customer payments. Although we see chargeoffs picking up due to higher unemployment levels, we think DFS's should be lower than most of its peers given its more conservative customer base and lower market share in areas in which housing prices are under great pressure. An accounting change, which has no economic impact on the company, will likely result in a roughly $1.5 billion provision build in FY 10, and is reflected in our loss estimate. Based on a slowdown in chargeoff growth, we think the stock will eventually trade near its historical 1.8X multiple of tangible book value (TBV).

► Risks to our recommendation and target price include worse-than-expected deterioration of consumer spending and unemployment levels.

► Our 12-month target price of $20 values the stock at 1.60X current tangible book value, a discount to peers and still below DFS's historical range.

Qualitative Risk Assessment

LOW	**MEDIUM**	HIGH

Our risk assessment reflects what we see as solid business fundamentals and an increasing merchant base, tempered by DFS's exposure to consumer spending habits and the U.S. economy.

Quantitative Evaluations

S&P Quality Ranking NR

D	C	B-	B	B+	A-	A	A+

Relative Strength Rank MODERATE

64

LOWEST = 1   HIGHEST = 99

Revenue/Earnings Data

Revenue (Million $)

	1Q	2Q	3Q	4Q	Year
2009	2,006	1,939	2,149	--	--
2008	1,638	1,457	1,557	2,305	6,957
2007	1,506	1,575	1,601	1,752	6,434
2006	--	--	--	--	6,211
2005	--	--	--	--	--
2004	--	--	--	--	--

Earnings Per Share ($)

2009	0.25	0.43	1.07	E0.66	E2.41
2008	0.50	0.42	0.37	0.92	2.20
2007	0.55	0.44	0.42	-0.18	1.23
2006	--	0.72	0.51	0.39	1.89
2005	--	--	--	--	--
2004	--	--	--	--	--

Fiscal year ended Nov. 30. Next earnings report expected: Mid December. EPS Estimates based on S&P Operating Earnings; historical GAAP earnings are as reported.

Dividend Data (Dates: mm/dd Payment Date: mm/dd/yy)

Amount ($)	Date Decl.	Ex-Div. Date	Stk. of Record	Payment Date
0.060	12/18	12/30	01/02	01/22/09
0.020	03/19	03/30	04/01	04/22/09
0.020	06/18	06/29	07/01	07/22/09
0.020	09/16	09/29	10/01	10/22/09

Dividends have been paid since 2007. Source: Company reports.

Please read the Required Disclosures and Analyst Certification on the last page of this report.

The **McGraw-Hill** Companies

Discover Financial Services Inc

STANDARD &POOR'S

Business Summary September 18, 2009

CORPORATE OVERVIEW. Discover Financial Services (DFS), formerly a business segment of Morgan Stanley, is a credit card issuer and electronic payment services company. DFS offers credit and prepaid cards and other financial products and services to qualified customers in the United States, and provides payment processing and related services to merchants and financial institutions in the United States. DFS manages its operations through two business segments: U.S. Card and Third-Party Payments. The U.S. Card segment is the major contributor to the company, in terms of income before income taxes. The Third-Party Payments segment is modestly profitable but continues to comprise a growing portion of DFS's income stream.

The U.S. Card segment offers Discover Card-branded credit cards issued to more than 50 million individuals and small businesses over the Discover Network, which is the company's proprietary credit card network in the United States. The segment also includes DFS's other consumer products and ser-

vices businesses, including prepaid and other consumer lending and deposit products offered primarily through the company's Discover Bank subsidiary. The company entered the debit card business in 2006, allowing banks to offer Discover-branded debit cards.

In addition to credit cards, DFS offers installment loan products, including personal loans and student loans. It offers installment loan products to existing cardmembers as well as to new customers. DFS accepts applications for installment loans online, by phone or by mail. The company has grown its installment loan products significantly to $1.3 billion at November 30, 2008, from $0.2 billion at November 30, 2007.

Company Financials Fiscal Year Ended Nov. 30

Per Share Data ($)	2008	2007	2006	2005	2004	2003	2002	2001	2000	1999
Tangible Book Value	11.37	10.98	NA	NA	NA	NA	NA	NA	NA	NA
Earnings	2.20	1.23	1.89	NA	NA	NA	NA	NA	NA	NA
S&P Core Earnings	1.00	1.23	2.26	1.21	NA	NA	NA	NA	NA	NA
Dividends	0.24	0.06	Nil	NA	NA	NA	NA	NA	NA	NA
Payout Ratio	11%	5%	NA	NA	NA	NA	NA	NA	NA	NA
Prices:High	19.87	32.17	NA	NA	NA	NA	NA	NA	NA	NA
Prices:Low	6.59	14.81	NA	NA	NA	NA	NA	NA	NA	NA
P/E Ratio:High	9	26	NA	NA	NA	NA	NA	NA	NA	NA
P/E Ratio:Low	3	12	NA	NA	NA	NA	NA	NA	NA	NA
Income Statement Analysis (Million $)										
Net Interest Income	1,405	1,506	1,459	NA	NA	NA	NA	NA	NA	NA
Tax Equivalent Adjustment	NA	NA	NA	NA	NA	NA	NA	NA	NA	NA
Non Interest Income	4,264	3,546	3,539	NA	NA	NA	NA	NA	NA	NA
Loan Loss Provision	1,596	950	756	NA	NA	NA	NA	NA	NA	NA
% Expense/Operating Revenue	NA	49.0%	55.5%	NA	NA	NA	NA	NA	NA	NA
Pretax Income	1,658	945	1,467	924	1,219	NA	NA	NA	NA	NA
Effective Tax Rate	35.9%	37.7%	31.8%	37.5%	36.3%	NA	NA	NA	NA	NA
Net Income	1,063	589	1,001	578	776	NA	NA	NA	NA	NA
% Net Interest Margin	NA	NA	NA	NA	NA	NA	NA	NA	NA	NA
S&P Core Earnings	485	587	1,078	578	NA	NA	NA	NA	NA	NA
Balance Sheet & Other Financial Data (Million $)										
Money Market Assets	9,378	8,416	Nil	NA	NA	NA	NA	NA	NA	NA
Investment Securities	1,228	526	86.0	NA	NA	NA	NA	NA	NA	NA
Commercial Loans	Nil	234	111	NA	NA	NA	NA	NA	NA	NA
Other Loans	25,217	23,720	21,707	NA	NA	NA	NA	NA	NA	NA
Total Assets	39,892	37,376	32,403	26,944	NA	NA	NA	NA	NA	NA
Demand Deposits	78.4	82.0	86.0	NA	NA	NA	NA	NA	NA	NA
Time Deposits	28,452	24,644	21,042	NA	NA	NA	NA	NA	NA	NA
Long Term Debt	1,330	2,134	1,706	NA	NA	NA	NA	NA	NA	NA
Common Equity	5,916	5,599	5,425	4,600	NA	NA	NA	NA	NA	NA
% Return on Assets	86.5	1.8	NM	NA	NA	NA	NA	NA	NA	NA
% Return on Equity	18.5	10.4	NM	NA	NA	NA	NA	NA	NA	NA
% Loan Loss Reserve	NA	3.8	3.5	NA	NA	NA	NA	NA	NA	NA
% Loans/Deposits	NA	96.8	NM	NA	NA	NA	NA	NA	NA	NA
% Equity to Assets	14.9	17.1	NM	NA	NA	NA	NA	NA	NA	NA

Data as orig reptd.; bef. results of disc opers/spec. items. Per share data adj. for stk. divs.; EPS diluted. 2006 data pro forma; bal. sheet as of Feb. 28 '07. E-Estimated. NA-Not Available. NM-Not Meaningful. NR-Not Ranked. UR-Under Review.

Office: 2500 Lake Cook Road, Riverwoods, IL 60015.
Telephone: 224-405-0900.
Website: http://www.discover.com
Chrmn & CEO: D.W. Nelms

Pres & COO: R.C. Hochschild
EVP & CFO: R.A. Guthrie
EVP, Secy & General Counsel: K.M. Corley
SVP & Chief Acctg Officer: M.A. Zaeske

Board Members: J. S. Aronin, M. K. Bush, G. C. Case, R. M. Devlin, C. A. Glassman, R. H. Lenny, T. G. Maheras, M. H. Moskow, D. W. Nelms, E. F. Smith, L. A. Weinbach
Founded: 1960
Domicile: Delaware
Employees: 11,900

The McGraw-Hill Companies

Walt Disney Co (The)

STANDARD &POOR'S

S&P Recommendation **BUY** ★★★★☆	Price $30.35 (as of Nov 27, 2009)	12-Mo. Target Price $35.00	Investment Style Large-Cap Growth

GICS Sector Consumer Discretionary
Sub-Industry Movies & Entertainment

Summary This media and entertainment conglomerate has diversified global operations in theme parks, filmed entertainment, television broadcasting and merchandise licensing.

Key Stock Statistics (Source S&P, Vickers, company reports)

52-Wk Range	$30.93– 15.14	S&P Oper. EPS 2010**E**	1.96	Market Capitalization(B)	$56.407	Beta		1.10
Trailing 12-Month EPS	$1.76	S&P Oper. EPS 2011**E**	2.21	Yield (%)	1.15	S&P 3-Yr. Proj. EPS CAGR(%)		8
Trailing 12-Month P/E	17.2	P/E on S&P Oper. EPS 2010**E**	15.5	Dividend Rate/Share	$0.35	S&P Credit Rating		A
$10K Invested 5 Yrs Ago	**NA**	Common Shares Outstg. (M)	1,858.6	Institutional Ownership (%)	66			

Price Performance

30-Week Mov. Avg. · · · 10-Week Mov. Avg. – – **GAAP Earnings vs. Previous Year**   Volume Above Avg. STARS
12-Mo. Target Price — Relative Strength — ▲ Up ▼ Down ▶ No Change   Below Avg. ★

Options: ASE, CBOE, P, Ph

Analysis prepared by **Tuna N. Amobi, CFA, CPA** on November 20, 2009, when the stock traded at **$ 30.00**.

Highlights

▶ With the deal for Marvel Entertainment (MVL 52, Hold) expected to close in 2009, we see consolidated revenues up about 7% in FY 10 (Sep.) and 6% in FY 11, to nearly $40.9 billion, led by cable networks advertising and affiliate revenues (ESPN, Disney Channel, ABC Family). Also, we see gradual improvement in the domestic theme parks (Disney World, Disneyland) and broadcasting businesses (ABC network and stations), as well as the film division (Disney, Pixar, Marvel) and consumer products/licensing businesses (including the Disney retail stores).

▶ With the benefit of broad-based restructuring initiatives implemented during a very challenging FY 09 environment, we expect meaningful margin expansion over the next two years, partly offset by extended theme parks discounts, higher TV programming costs, and further investments in video games development.

▶ The MVL deal is expected to result in some relatively modest dilution through FY 11 (factoring in DIS's plans to repurchase nearly 60 million shares issued therewith). After interest expense and taxes, we forecast EPS of $1.96 and $2.21 for FY 10 and FY 11, respectively.

Investment Rationale/Risk

▶ Despite Marvel's ample $4 billion deal valuation, its library of over 5,000 comic book characters could ultimately deliver potentially compelling cross-platform revenue synergies (including incremental licensing and international opportunities). Meanwhile, we noted sequential improvement in DIS's September quarter and FY 09 results, with December quarter U.S. park bookings down a relatively encouraging 5%, and ABC scatter pricing up 20% (versus upfront). An enhanced film slate (Princess and the Frog, Alice in Wonderland, Prince of Persia, Toy Story 3, Sorcerer's Apprentice) and higher retransmission fees (TV stations) could add to near-term catalysts. We think DIS's strong balance sheet offers ample financial flexibility.

▶ Risks to our recommendation and target price include a slower-than-expected economic recovery and consumer spending rebound; heightened geopolitical uncertainties; and inherent volatility of film results.

▶ Our 12-month target price of $35 is derived from our sum-of-the-parts valuation analysis, reflecting relative enterprise values for the various business segments. The dividend recently offered a yield of about 1.2%.

Qualitative Risk Assessment

LOW	**MEDIUM**	HIGH

Our risk assessment reflects the strength of the company's content-oriented media and entertainment brands, counterbalanced by relatively high exposure to cyclical advertising-related and theme park businesses.

Quantitative Evaluations

S&P Quality Ranking A

D	C	B-	B	B+	A-	**A**	A+

Relative Strength Rank **STRONG**

82

LOWEST = 1 HIGHEST = 99

Revenue/Earnings Data

Revenue (Million $)

	1Q	2Q	3Q	4Q	Year
2009	9,599	8,087	8,956	9,867	36,149
2008	10,452	8,710	9,236	9,445	37,843
2007	9,581	7,954	9,045	8,930	35,510
2006	8,854	8,027	8,620	8,784	34,285
2005	8,666	7,829	7,715	7,734	31,944
2004	8,549	7,189	7,471	7,543	30,752

Earnings Per Share ($)

2009	0.45	0.33	0.51	0.48	1.76
2008	0.63	0.58	0.66	0.40	2.28
2007	0.79	0.43	0.58	0.44	2.24
2006	0.37	0.37	0.53	0.36	1.64
2005	0.33	0.31	0.39	0.20	1.24
2004	0.33	0.26	0.29	0.25	1.12

Fiscal year ended Sep. 30. Next earnings report expected: Early January. EPS Estimates based on S&P Operating Earnings; historical GAAP earnings are as reported.

Dividend Data (Dates: mm/dd Payment Date: mm/dd/yy)

Amount ($)	Date Decl.	Ex-Div. Date	Stk. of Record	Payment Date
0.350	12/03	12/11	12/15	01/20/09

Dividends have been paid since 1957. Source: Company reports.

Please read the Required Disclosures and Analyst Certification on the last page of this report.

The **McGraw·Hill** Companies

Walt Disney Co (The)

**STANDARD
&POOR'S**

Business Summary November 20, 2009

CORPORATE OVERVIEW. The Walt Disney Co. is a leading media conglomerate with key operations in theme parks, television, filmed entertainment and merchandise licensing. Theme Parks and Resorts (30% of FY 08 (Sep.) revenues) includes the company's best-known assets: Disney World and Disneyland parks in Orlando, FL, and Anaheim, CA, respectively; the Disney Cruise Line; Euro Disney, Paris (39%-owned); and Hong Kong Disneyland (43%-owned).

Media Networks (43% of revenues) includes the ABC broadcast network; 10 television stations; and cable networks ESPN (80%-owned), The Disney Channel, ABC Family and Lifetime (50%). In November 2006, DIS sold its 39.5% stake in the E! cable network to Comcast for $1.23 billion. Studio entertainment (19% of revenues) includes the film, television and home video businesses under the Walt Disney, Touchstone and Miramax brands. Consumer products (8% of revenues) includes merchandise licensing, children's book publishing, video game development, as well as nearly 225 retail stores in North America, and about 104 other stores mainly in Europe.

CORPORATE STRATEGY. As a content-oriented company, DIS's top strategic

priorities include creativity and innovation, international expansion, and leveraging new technology applications. Under CEO Robert Iger, we see senior management aggressively exploring new avenues to offer its branded content, characters and entertainment franchises across emerging digital platforms such as broadband, wireless and video games: e.g., content from its ABC networks and the film studios offered via Apple's video iPod, the launch of Disney Mobile cellular phone service, and an ad-supported streaming of ABC's shows.

In April 2008, DIS unveiled a slate of 10 new animated films (from Disney and Pixar) to be released through 2012. Earlier, in July 2006, the company restructured its studio and sharply reduced its annual film output (to 10 live-action/animation films plus two to three Touchstone titles), with a focus on Disney-branded films. It has aggressively expanded its Disney Channel in the past few years, and in September 2005, opened Hong Kong Disneyland.

Company Financials Fiscal Year Ended Sep. 30

Per Share Data ($)	2009	2008	2007	2006	2005	2004	2003	2002	2001	2000
Tangible Book Value	NA	4.18	3.15	3.10	3.24	3.15	2.01	1.78	3.99	2.24
Cash Flow	NA	3.09	3.08	2.40	1.93	1.69	1.17	1.11	0.89	1.48
Earnings	1.76	2.28	2.24	1.64	1.24	1.12	0.65	0.60	0.11	0.57
S&P Core Earnings	NA	2.15	1.96	1.69	1.27	1.04	0.49	0.29	0.21	NA
Dividends	0.35	0.35	0.31	0.27	0.24	0.21	0.21	0.21	0.21	0.21
Payout Ratio	20%	15%	14%	16%	19%	19%	32%	35%	191%	37%
Prices:High	30.93	35.02	36.79	34.89	29.99	28.41	23.80	25.17	34.80	43.88
Prices:Low	15.14	18.60	30.68	23.77	22.89	20.88	14.84	13.48	15.50	26.00
P/E Ratio:High	18	15	16	21	24	25	37	42	NM	77
P/E Ratio:Low	9	8	14	14	18	19	23	22	NM	46

Income Statement Analysis (Million $)										
Revenue	36,149	37,843	35,510	34,285	31,944	30,752	27,061	25,329	25,269	25,402
Operating Income	NA	8,986	8,272	6,914	5,446	5,258	3,790	3,426	4,586	5,043
Depreciation	1,631	1,582	1,491	1,436	1,339	1,210	1,077	1,042	1,754	2,195
Interest Expense	NA	774	593	592	605	629	666	453	417	558
Pretax Income	5,658	7,402	7,725	5,447	3,987	3,739	2,254	2,190	1,283	2,633
Effective Tax Rate	36.2%	36.1%	37.2%	34.7%	31.1%	32.0%	35.0%	38.9%	82.5%	61.0%
Net Income	3,307	4,427	4,674	3,374	2,569	2,345	1,338	1,236	120	920
S&P Core Earnings	NA	4,184	4,074	3,479	2,635	2,201	1,006	606	458	NA

Balance Sheet & Other Financial Data (Million $)										
Cash	3,417	3,001	3,670	2,411	1,723	2,042	1,583	1,239	618	842
Current Assets	NA	11,666	11,314	9,562	8,845	9,369	8,314	7,849	7,029	10,007
Total Assets	63,117	62,497	60,928	59,998	53,158	53,902	49,988	50,045	43,699	45,027
Current Liabilities	NA	11,591	11,391	10,210	9,168	11,059	8,669	7,819	6,219	8,402
Long Term Debt	11,495	11,351	11,892	10,843	10,157	9,395	10,643	12,467	8,940	6,959
Common Equity	33,734	32,323	30,753	31,820	26,210	26,081	23,791	23,445	22,672	24,100
Total Capital	48,126	47,368	45,218	46,657	40,045	39,224	37,574	38,943	34,724	34,248
Capital Expenditures	1,753	1,586	1,566	1,299	1,823	1,427	1,049	1,086	1,795	2,013
Cash Flow	NA	6,009	6,165	4,810	3,908	3,555	2,415	2,278	1,874	3,115
Current Ratio	1.3	1.0	1.0	0.9	1.0	0.8	1.0	1.0	1.1	1.2
% Long Term Debt of Capitalization	23.9	24.0	26.2	23.2	25.4	24.0	28.3	32.0	25.7	20.3
% Net Income of Revenue	9.2	11.7	13.1	9.8	8.0	7.6	4.9	4.9	0.5	3.6
% Return on Assets	5.3	7.2	7.7	6.0	4.8	4.5	2.7	2.6	0.3	2.1
% Return on Equity	10.0	14.0	14.9	11.6	9.8	9.4	5.7	5.4	0.5	4.1

Data as orig reptd.; bef. results of disc opers/spec. items. Per share data adj. for stk. divs.; EPS diluted. E-Estimated. NA-Not Available. NM-Not Meaningful. NR-Not Ranked. UR-Under Review.

Office: 500 South Buena Vista Street, Burbank, CA 91521.
Telephone: 818-560-1000.
Website: http://www.disney.com
Chrmn: J. Pepper, Jr.

Pres & CEO: R.A. Iger
EVP, CFO & Chief Acctg Officer: T. Staggs
EVP & Treas: C.M. McCarthy
EVP, Secy & General Counsel: A.N. Braverman

Investor Contact: L. Singer (818-560-6601)
Board Members: S. E. Arnold, J. E. Bryson, J. S. Chen, J. L. Estrin, R. A. Iger, S. P. Jobs, F. H. Langhammer, A. B. Lewis, M. Lozano, R. W. Matschullat, J. Pepper, Jr., O. Smith

Founded: 1936
Domicile: Delaware
Employees: 150,000

Dominion Resources Inc.

STANDARD &POOR'S

S&P Recommendation **STRONG BUY** ★★★★★	Price $36.14 (as of Nov 27, 2009)	12-Mo. Target Price $42.00	Investment Style Large-Cap Blend

GICS Sector Utilities
Sub-Industry Multi-Utilities

Summary This energy holding company's principal subsidiaries are Virginia Electric & Power Co. and Consolidated Natural Gas.

Key Stock Statistics (Source S&P, Vickers, company reports)

52-Wk Range	$37.30– 27.15	S&P Oper. EPS 2009E	3.30	Market Capitalization(B)	$21.584	Beta	0.50
Trailing 12-Month EPS	$2.79	S&P Oper. EPS 2010E	3.45	Yield (%)	4.84	S&P 3-Yr. Proj. EPS CAGR(%)	8
Trailing 12-Month P/E	13.0	P/E on S&P Oper. EPS 2009E	11.0	Dividend Rate/Share	$1.75	S&P Credit Rating	A-
$10K Invested 5 Yrs Ago	$13,191	Common Shares Outstg. (M)	597.2	Institutional Ownership (%)	57		

Price Performance

30-Week Mov. Avg. · · ·   10-Week Mov. Avg. – –   **GAAP Earnings vs. Previous Year**   Volume Above Avg. STARS
12-Mo. Target Price —   Relative Strength —   ▲ Up ▼ Down ▶ No Change   Below Avg.

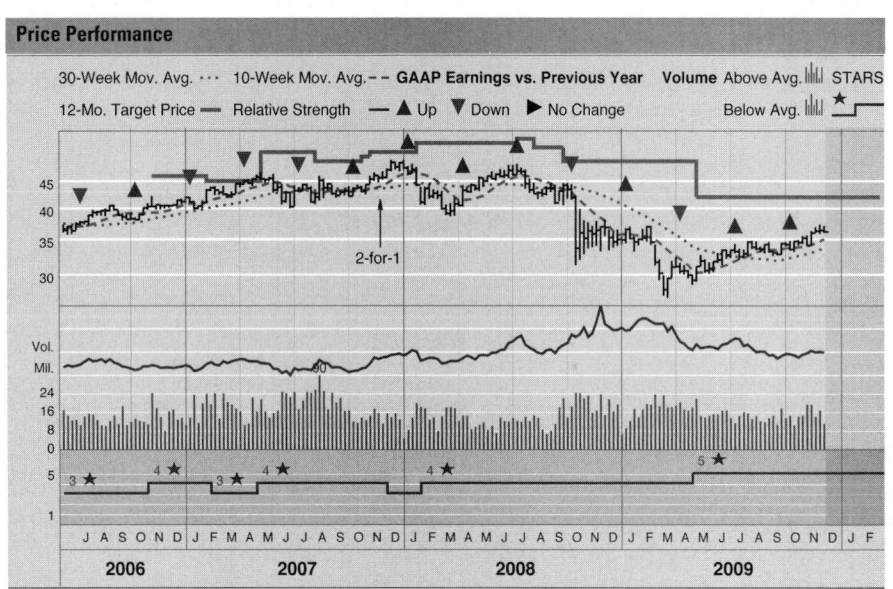

Options: ASE, CBOE, P, Ph

Analysis prepared by **Christopher B. Muir** on November 18, 2009, when the stock traded at **$ 37.01**.

Highlights

► We think revenues will fall 2.1% in 2009, mainly due to lower gas revenues, partly offset by the completion of the Cove Point LNG expansion project and higher regulated and unregulated electric revenues. Gas revenues should be lower due to lower commodity prices. We see utility revenues increasing 2.7% and nonutility revenues falling by 6.9%. In 2010, we expect revenues to rise 2.9%.

► We expect operating margins for 2009 and 2010 to widen to 24.4% and 25.3%, respectively, from 21.6% in 2008, on lower per-revenue fuel costs and operations & maintenance expense, partly offset by higher per-revenue depreciation expense. We look for per-revenue interest costs to rise in 2009 and fall in 2010, but we see lower non-operating income in both years. As a result, we project less of an improvement in pre-tax profit margins to 19.5% in 2009 and 20.5% in 2010, from 18.1% in 2008.

► Our 2009 recurring EPS estimate, which excludes $0.46 in net nonrecurring charges, is $3.30, up 4.4% from 2008's $3.16. Our 2010 EPS forecast is $3.45, an increase of 4.5%.

Investment Rationale/Risk

► We like D's continued focus on its core businesses. We also view the agreed-to sale, pending approvals, of its Pennsylvania and West Virginia utility businesses positively, as we see proceeds being used to reduce debt. We think D's announced target of a 55% payout ratio by 2010 will support a high single-digit dividend increase in 2010. We also like the company's planned expansion of its wind generation, as well as its various other expansion and growth projects.

► Risks to our recommendation and target price include sharply lower electric prices, sharply higher interest rates, an inability to complete the sale of its Hope and Peoples gas utilities, and a weaker economy.

► The stock recently traded at 10.7X our 2010 EPS estimate, an 11% discount to its multi-utility peers. Our 12-month target price of $42 is 12.2X our 2010 EPS estimate, a slight premium to our peer target. Our valuation considers D's above-peer-average dividend growth, average EPS growth, and somewhat levered balance sheet relative to its peers.

Qualitative Risk Assessment

LOW	**MEDIUM**	HIGH

Our risk assessment reflects our view of Dominion's relatively large capitalization and balanced sources of earnings, which include low-risk regulated electric and gas distribution and pipeline operations, offset by higher-risk exploration and production and energy marketing businesses.

Quantitative Evaluations

S&P Quality Ranking   B+

D	C	B-	B	**B+**	A-	A	A+

Relative Strength Rank   MODERATE

68

LOWEST = 1   HIGHEST = 99

Revenue/Earnings Data

Revenue (Million $)

	1Q	2Q	3Q	4Q	Year
2009	4,778	3,450	3,648	--	--
2008	4,389	3,452	4,231	4,173	16,290
2007	4,661	3,730	3,589	3,694	15,674
2006	4,951	3,548	4,016	3,967	16,482
2005	4,736	3,646	4,564	5,095	18,041
2004	3,879	3,040	3,292	3,761	13,972

Earnings Per Share ($)

2009	0.42	0.76	1.00	E0.70	E3.30
2008	1.18	0.52	0.87	0.60	3.16
2007	0.68	-0.56	3.63	0.52	4.13
2006	0.78	0.24	0.93	0.28	2.23
2005	0.63	0.49	0.02	0.38	1.50
2004	0.68	0.40	0.51	0.34	1.91

Fiscal year ended Dec. 31. Next earnings report expected: Late January. EPS Estimates based on S&P Operating Earnings; historical GAAP earnings are as reported.

Dividend Data (Dates: mm/dd Payment Date: mm/dd/yy)

Amount ($)	Date Decl.	Ex-Div. Date	Stk. of Record	Payment Date
0.438	12/17	02/25	02/27	03/20/09
0.438	05/05	05/27	05/29	06/20/09
0.438	08/06	08/26	08/28	09/20/09
0.438	10/16	11/25	11/30	12/30/09

Dividends have been paid since 1925. Source: Company reports.

Please read the Required Disclosures and Analyst Certification on the last page of this report.

The McGraw-Hill Companies

Dominion Resources Inc.

STANDARD &POOR'S

Business Summary November 18, 2009

CORPORATE OVERVIEW. Dominion Resources is a fully integrated gas and electric holding company. The company operates in three primary segments: Virginia Power, Energy, and Generation. The Virginia Power segment (20.7% of 2008 operating segment revenue) operates regulated electric transmission and distribution business in Virginia and northeastern North Carolina. The Energy segment (28.8%) operates a regulated natural gas distribution company in Ohio, regulated gas transmission pipeline and storage operations, regulated LNG operations, and the natural gas E&P business, which supports the company's gas distribution business. The Energy segment also includes a producer services business, which aggregates gas supply, provides gas transportation and storage market-based services and engages in associated gas trading and marketing. The Generation segment (52.8%) is involved in generation for the electric utility and merchant power along with energy marketing and risk management activities.

CORPORATE STRATEGY. D focuses its efforts mainly on the Northeast, Mid-Atlantic and Midwest regions of the U.S. As part of a strategy to concentrate on expanding its core businesses in the above-mentioned markets, D is committed to divesting all of its energy-related operations outside the U.S. D believes that focusing on its core businesses will reduce earnings volatility and help to grow EPS at rates above 6% annually after 2010. It has a proactive risk management strategy, and has entered into commodity derivative agreements to hedge against commodity price risks.

MARKET PROFILE. As of December 31, 2008, D had total power generation capacity of 27,090 MW, with 16,210 MW of utility generation, 1,860 MW of utility power purchase agreements, and 9,020 MW of merchant generation. Baseload generation accounted for 85% of its production. The Virginia Power segment served a total of 2.39 million regulated electric customers. Additionally, it had 1.6 million unregulated customer accounts (38% electricity, 21% natural gas and 40% products and services). The Energy segment serves about 368,400 gas sales and 827,400 gas transportation customers in Ohio and has about 14,000 miles of interstate natural gas transmission, gathering storage pipelines, 975 Bcf of storage capacity, and 1.2 trillion cubic feet equivalent of proved gas and oil reserves. This division also operates a liquefied natural gas (LNG) terminal at Cove Point, MD, which was recently expanded to a sendout capacity of 1.8 Bcfd with a storage capacity of 14.6 Bcf.

Company Financials Fiscal Year Ended Dec. 31

Per Share Data ($)	2008	2007	2006	2005	2004	2003	2002	2001	2000	1999
Tangible Book Value	10.05	9.21	11.45	8.79	16.37	9.60	9.09	7.85	7.10	12.40
Earnings	3.16	4.13	2.22	1.50	1.91	1.49	2.41	1.08	0.88	1.41
S&P Core Earnings	2.97	0.46	2.21	1.47	1.90	1.58	1.92	0.66	NA	NA
Dividends	1.58	2.25	0.35	1.34	1.30	1.29	1.29	1.29	1.29	1.29
Payout Ratio	50%	54%	16%	89%	68%	87%	54%	120%	147%	92%
Prices:High	48.50	49.38	42.22	43.49	34.43	32.97	33.53	35.00	33.97	24.69
Prices:Low	31.26	39.84	34.36	33.26	30.39	25.87	17.70	27.57	17.41	18.28
P/E Ratio:High	15	12	19	29	18	22	14	33	39	18
P/E Ratio:Low	10	10	15	22	16	17	7	26	20	13

Income Statement Analysis (Million $)	2008	2007	2006	2005	2004	2003	2002	2001	2000	1999
Revenue	16,290	15,674	16,482	18,041	13,972	12,078	10,218	10,558	9,260	5,520
Depreciation	1,191	1,368	1,606	1,412	1,305	1,216	1,258	1,245	1,176	716
Maintenance	NA	NA	NA	NA	NA	NA	NA	NA	NA	NA
Fixed Charges Coverage	4.23	4.82	3.42	2.63	3.09	2.63	3.15	2.02	1.99	2.44
Construction Credits	NA	Nil	Nil	Nil	Nil	Nil	Nil	Nil	Nil	Nil
Effective Tax Rate	32.4%	39.5%	37.0%	36.0%	35.6%	38.6%	33.3%	40.5%	30.5%	31.3%
Net Income	1,836	2,705	1,563	1,034	1,264	949	1,362	544	415	551
S&P Core Earnings	1,729	295	1,555	1,010	1,254	1,004	1,088	331	NA	NA

Balance Sheet & Other Financial Data (Million $)	2008	2007	2006	2005	2004	2003	2002	2001	2000	1999
Gross Property	35,448	33,331	43,575	42,063	38,663	37,107	32,631	33,105	31,011	18,646
Capital Expenditures	3,519	3,972	4,052	1,683	1,451	2,138	2,828	1,224	1,385	737
Net Property	23,274	21,352	29,382	28,940	26,716	25,850	20,257	18,681	14,849	10,764
Capitalization:Long Term Debt	15,213	13,492	15,048	14,910	15,764	16,033	13,714	12,119	10,486	7,321
Capitalization:% Long Term Debt	60.2	58.9	53.8	58.9	58.0	60.3	57.3	58.1	58.3	58.2
Capitalization:Preferred	Nil	Nil	Nil	Nil	Nil	Nil	Nil	Nil	509	509
Capitalization:% Preferred	Nil	Nil	Nil	Nil	Nil	Nil	Nil	Nil	2.83	4.05
Capitalization:Common	10,077	9,406	12,913	10,397	11,426	10,538	10,213	8,368	6,992	4,752
Capitalization:% Common	39.8	41.1	46.2	41.1	42.0	39.7	42.7	40.1	38.9	37.8
Total Capital	29,427	27,179	33,842	30,291	32,689	31,134	28,136	24,811	20,955	14,427
% Operating Ratio	82.9	75.9	85.3	89.7	85.6	83.7	78.5	85.6	80.5	80.9
% Earned on Net Property	16.4	21.9	11.5	8.8	10.3	10.6	21.4	10.6	11.9	10.6
% Return on Revenue	11.3	17.3	9.5	5.7	9.0	7.9	13.3	5.2	4.5	10.0
% Return on Invested Capital	9.5	12.7	8.1	6.4	6.5	6.5	8.5	7.2	10.7	7.9
% Return on Common Equity	18.2	24.2	13.4	9.5	11.5	9.1	14.7	7.1	7.1	10.9

Data as orig reptd.; bef. results of disc opers/spec. items. Per share data adj. for stk. divs.; EPS diluted. E-Estimated. NA-Not Available. NM-Not Meaningful. NR-Not Ranked. UR-Under Review.

Office: 120 Tredegar Street, Richmond, VA 23219.
Telephone: 804-819-2000.
Email: investor_relations@domres.com
Website: http://www.dom.com

Chrmn, Pres & CEO: T.F. Farrell, II
EVP & CFO: M.F. McGettrick
SVP & Chief Admin Officer: S.A. Rogers
SVP & Chief Acctg Officer: T.P. Wohlfarth

SVP & Treas: G.S. Hetzer
Investor Contact: J. O'Hare (804-819-2156)
Board Members: P. W. Brown, G. A. Davidson, Jr., T. F. Farrell, II, J. Harris, R. S. Jepson, Jr., M. J. Kington, B. J. Lambert, III, M. A. McKenna, F. S. Royal, D. A. Wollard

Founded: 1909
Domicile: Virginia
Employees: 18,000

R.R. Donnelley & Sons Co

STANDARD &POOR'S

S&P Recommendation	HOLD ★★★☆☆	Price	12-Mo. Target Price	Investment Style
		$20.67 (as of Nov 27, 2009)	$24.00	Large-Cap Value

GICS Sector Industrials
Sub-Industry Commercial Printing

Summary R.R. Donnelley, the largest U.S. commercial printer, specializes in the production of catalogs, inserts, magazines, books, directories, and financial and computer documentation.

Key Stock Statistics (Source S&P, Vickers, company reports)

52-Wk Range	$22.25– 5.54	S&P Oper. EPS 2009**E**	1.44	Market Capitalization(B)	$4.244	Beta		2.10
Trailing 12-Month EPS	$-3.09	S&P Oper. EPS 2010**E**	1.70	Yield (%)	5.03	S&P 3-Yr. Proj. EPS CAGR(%)		5
Trailing 12-Month P/E	NM	P/E on S&P Oper. EPS 2009**E**	14.4	Dividend Rate/Share	$1.04	S&P Credit Rating		BBB
$10K Invested 5 Yrs Ago	$7,353	Common Shares Outstg. (M)	205.3	Institutional Ownership (%)	94			

Price Performance

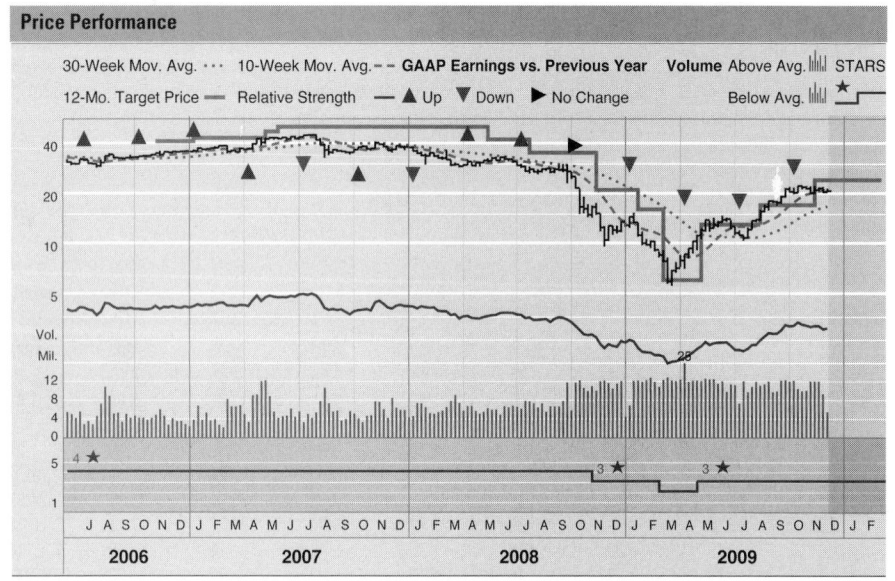

30-Week Mov. Avg. ··· 10-Week Mov. Avg. -- **GAAP Earnings vs. Previous Year** **Volume** Above Avg. ᴵᴵᴵ STARS
12-Mo. Target Price — Relative Strength ▲ Up ▼ Down ▶ No Change Below Avg. ᴵᴵᴵ ★

Options: CBOE, P, Ph

Analysis prepared by **Jim Corridore** on November 11, 2009, when the stock traded at **$ 21.02.**

Highlights

▶ We forecast that revenue will decline about 16% in 2009, reflecting the recessionary economies of the U.S. (77% of 2008 revenues) and Europe (12%), RRD's main end-markets. However, we see some improvement in both of those markets in 2010 driving 5% revenue growth, with most of the growth coming in the second half of the year. We expect meaningful growth in Europe to lag that of the U.S. by about six months. We see RRD focusing on improving working capital. RRD expects to generate over $700 million in free cash flow in 2009

▶ We expect operating margins to narrow in 2009, as the effect of leveraging fixed costs over a smaller revenue base is likely to more than off-set the benefits from restructuring actions, pro-ductivity increases and cost synergies from re-cent acquisitions. We expect improving rev-enues along with the benefits of restructurings to aid operating margins in 2010.

▶ We see 2009 operating EPS of $1.44, versus $2.96 in 2008, before one-time items. For 2010, we expect EPS of $1.70.

Investment Rationale/Risk

▶ We expect RRD to continue to gain market share by leveraging its geographic and product breadth, but also think its business model is un-dergoing a long-term secular shift as electronic media reduce the demand for financial and oth-er printing. We also see headwinds from a highly leveraged balance sheet and ongoing di-gestion of recent acquisitions. However, we think improving investor sentiment on the over-all U.S. economy is likely to lend support to the shares.

▶ Risks to our recommendation and target price include substantially higher raw material costs, negative forex translation charges, further sharp deterioration in the company's end-markets, and a greater-than-expected increase in the amount of information disseminated elec-tronically, which would lead to lower publishing demand.

▶ Our 12-month target price of $24 values the shares at 14X our 2010 EPS estimate of $1.70, toward the low end of RRD's five-year historical P/E range to reflect our concerns about the maturation of RRD's business segments and high balance sheet risk.

Qualitative Risk Assessment

LOW	MEDIUM	HIGH

Our risk assessment reflects economies of scale that the company realizes as the largest U.S. commercial printer in a fragmented print industry, offset by industry pricing pressure and the increasingly electronic nature of communication.

Quantitative Evaluations

S&P Quality Ranking   B-

D	C	B-	B	B+	A-	A	A+

Relative Strength Rank   MODERATE

67

LOWEST = 1   HIGHEST = 99

Revenue/Earnings Data

Revenue (Million $)

	1Q	2Q	3Q	4Q	Year
2009	2,456	2,356	2,463	--	--
2008	2,997	2,924	2,865	2,796	11,582
2007	2,793	2,796	2,910	3,088	11,587
2006	2,267	2,274	2,309	2,467	9,317
2005	1,927	1,932	2,184	2,388	8,430
2004	1,289	1,843	1,913	2,112	7,156

Earnings Per Share ($)

2009	0.07	0.12	0.06	E0.46	E1.44
2008	0.85	0.68	0.80	-3.35	-0.91
2007	0.63	-0.32	0.80	-1.37	-0.22
2006	0.52	0.57	0.75	-0.01	1.84
2005	0.50	0.44	0.59	-1.09	0.44
2004	-0.35	-0.06	0.52	0.61	0.88

Fiscal year ended Dec. 31. Next earnings report expected: Late February. EPS Estimates based on S&P Operating Earnings; historical GAAP earnings are as reported.

Dividend Data (Dates: mm/dd Payment Date: mm/dd/yy)

Amount ($)	Date Decl.	Ex-Div. Date	Stk. of Record	Payment Date
0.260	01/09	01/21	01/23	03/02/09
0.260	04/01	04/14	04/16	06/01/09
0.260	07/22	08/04	08/06	09/01/09
0.260	10/28	11/09	11/12	12/01/09

Dividends have been paid since 1911. Source: Company reports.

Please read the Required Disclosures and Analyst Certification on the last page of this report.

The McGraw-Hill Companies

R.R. Donnelley & Sons Co

STANDARD &POOR'S

Business Summary November 11, 2009

CORPORATE OVERVIEW. R.R. Donnelly & Sons (RRD) is the largest printing company in North America, serving customers in the publishing, health care, advertising, retail, telecommunications, technology, financial services and other industries. The company provides solutions in long- and short-run commercial printing, direct mail, financial printing, print fulfillment, forms and labels, logistics, digital printing, call centers, transactional print-and-mail, print management, online services, digital photography, color services, and content and database management. Geographically, the company derives the majority of its revenues from the U.S. (77% of 2008 revenues), with international accounting for about 23%.

The company has two reportable segments: U.S. Print and Related Services, and International. R.R. Donnelley management changed its reportable segments in the third quarter of 2007 to reflect changes in management reporting structure and the manner in which management assesses information for decision-making purposes.

The U.S. Print and Related Services segment (75% of revenues in 2008; 74% in

2007) consists of the following U.S. businesses: magazine, catalog and retail, which includes print services to consumer magazine and catalog publishers as well as retailers; book, which serves the consumer, religious, educational and specialty book and telecommunications sectors; directories, which serves the printing needs of yellow and white pages directory publishers; logistics, which delivers company and third-party printed products and distributes time-sensitive and secure material, and performs warehousing and fulfillment services; direct mail, which offers content creation, database management, printing, personalization finishing and distribution services to direct marketing companies; financial print; direct mail; and short-run commercial print, which provides print and print related services to a diversified customer base.

Company Financials Fiscal Year Ended Dec. 31

Per Share Data ($)	2008	2007	2006	2005	2004	2003	2002	2001	2000	1999
Tangible Book Value	NM	NM	0.54	NM	3.81	5.14	4.51	3.92	5.89	6.01
Cash Flow	2.02	2.52	3.96	2.40	5.07	4.43	4.32	3.41	5.34	5.29
Earnings	-0.91	-0.22	1.84	0.44	0.88	1.54	1.24	0.21	2.17	2.40
S&P Core Earnings	0.61	1.48	1.97	1.27	1.20	1.18	0.18	-0.65	NA	NA
Dividends	1.04	1.04	1.04	1.04	1.04	1.02	0.98	0.94	0.90	0.86
Payout Ratio	NM	NM	57%	NM	118%	66%	79%	NM	41%	36%
Prices:High	38.19	45.25	36.00	38.27	35.37	30.15	32.10	31.90	27.50	44.75
Prices:Low	9.53	32.59	28.50	29.54	27.62	16.94	18.50	24.30	19.00	21.50
P/E Ratio:High	NM	NM	20	87	40	20	26	NM	13	19
P/E Ratio:Low	NM	NM	15	67	31	11	15	NM	9	9

Income Statement Analysis (Million $)										
Revenue	11,582	11,587	9,317	8,430	7,156	4,787	4,755	5,298	5,764	5,183
Operating Income	1,761	1,752	1,420	1,295	952	617	686	722	891	905
Depreciation	617	598	463	425	771	329	352	379	390	374
Interest Expense	241	231	139	111	85.9	50.4	62.8	71.2	89.6	88.2
Pretax Income	-269	91.4	601	332	357	208	176	74.9	434	507
Effective Tax Rate	NM	NM	32.6%	71.5%	26.0%	15.3%	19.1%	66.6%	38.5%	38.5%
Net Income	-192	-48.4	403	95.6	265	177	142	25.0	267	312
S&P Core Earnings	129	322	430	275	243	136	21.3	-78.3	NA	NA

Balance Sheet & Other Financial Data (Million $)										
Cash	324	443	211	367	642	60.8	60.5	48.6	60.9	41.9
Current Assets	3,281	3,521	2,517	2,622	2,601	1,000	866	940	1,206	1,230
Total Assets	9,494	12,087	9,636	9,374	8,554	3,189	3,152	3,400	3,914	3,853
Current Liabilities	2,487	2,765	1,612	1,814	1,487	884	955	984	1,191	1,203
Long Term Debt	3,203	3,602	2,359	2,365	1,581	752	753	881	739	748
Common Equity	2,319	3,907	4,125	3,724	3,987	983	915	888	1,233	1,138
Total Capital	5,783	8,382	7,087	6,686	6,144	1,970	1,882	1,982	2,205	2,140
Capital Expenditures	323	482	374	471	265	203	242	273	237	276
Cash Flow	425	550	866	521	1,036	506	495	404	657	686
Current Ratio	1.3	1.3	1.6	1.4	1.7	1.1	0.9	1.0	1.0	1.0
% Long Term Debt of Capitalization	55.4	43.0	33.3	35.4	25.7	38.2	40.0	44.5	33.5	35.0
% Net Income of Revenue	NM	NM	4.3	1.1	3.7	3.7	3.0	0.5	4.6	6.0
% Return on Assets	NM	NM	4.2	1.1	4.5	5.5	4.4	0.7	6.9	8.1
% Return on Equity	NM	NM	10.3	2.5	10.7	18.6	15.8	2.4	22.5	25.5

Data as orig reptd.; bef. results of disc opers/spec. items. Per share data adj. for stk. divs.; EPS diluted. E-Estimated. NA-Not Available. NM-Not Meaningful. NR-Not Ranked. UR-Under Review.

Office: 111 S Wacker Dr, Chicago, IL 60606-4302.
Telephone: 312-326-8000.
Email: investor.info@rrd.com
Website: http://www.rrdonnelley.com

Chrmn: S. Wolf
Pres & CEO: T.J. Quinlan, III
COO: J. Paloian
EVP & CFO: M.W. McHugh

EVP, Secy & General Counsel: S.S. Bettman
Investor Contact: D. Leib (312-326-7710)
Board Members: L. A. Chaden, E. V. Goings, J. Hamilton, S. M. Ivey, T. S. Johnson, J. C. Pope, T. J. Quinlan, III, M. T. Riordan, O. R. Sockwell, Jr., S. Wolf

Founded: 1864
Domicile: Delaware
Employees: 62,000

Dover Corp

STANDARD
&POOR'S

S&P Recommendation	HOLD ★★★☆☆	Price	12-Mo. Target Price	Investment Style
		$40.58 (as of Nov 27, 2009)	$44.00	Large-Cap Growth

GICS Sector Industrials
Sub-Industry Industrial Machinery

Summary This company manufactures a broad range of specialized industrial products and sophisticated manufacturing equipment.

Key Stock Statistics (Source S&P, Vickers, company reports)

52-Wk Range	$43.10– 21.79	S&P Oper. EPS 2009**E**	1.99	Market Capitalization(B)	$7.555	Beta		1.26
Trailing 12-Month EPS	$2.03	S&P Oper. EPS 2010**E**	2.39	Yield (%)	2.56	S&P 3-Yr. Proj. EPS CAGR(%)		11
Trailing 12-Month P/E	20.0	P/E on S&P Oper. EPS 2009**E**	20.4	Dividend Rate/Share	$1.04	S&P Credit Rating		A
$10K Invested 5 Yrs Ago	$11,025	Common Shares Outstg. (M)	186.2	Institutional Ownership (%)	86			

Price Performance

30-Week Mov. Avg. · · · · 10-Week Mov. Avg. – – **GAAP Earnings vs. Previous Year**   Volume Above Avg. ▌▊▐ STARS
12-Mo. Target Price ▬ Relative Strength — ▲ Up ▼ Down ► No Change   Below Avg. ▖▌▖ ★

Options: CBOE, P, Ph

Analysis prepared by **Mathew Christy, CFA** on November 23, 2009, when the stock traded at **$ 42.27.**

Highlights

► We believe 2009 revenues will decline about 24.5%, as the global recession will negatively impact order rates across DOV's business units. In addition, our forecast is based on the negative effects of currency translation that more than offsets positive growth associated with acquisitions. However, we anticipate some gradual improvement in results, as we expect the economy to improve and as we believe revenues will return to more normal patterns in 2010, where we project a rise of nearly 6%.

► In our opinion, lower operating leverage and negative product mix will lead to a decline in overall gross margins in 2009. In addition, we believe that lower operating leverage will lead to significantly reduced operating margins in 2009, as we see SG&A expenses rising nearly 4 percentage points as a percent of sales. However, we expect improved gross and operating margins for 2010, on better operating leverage and cost savings expected from the DOV's procurement initiatives.

► With similar effective tax rates expected in 2009 and 2010, and excluding restructuring charges, we project operating EPS of $1.99 and $2.39 in the respective years.

Investment Rationale/Risk

► As a result of exiting 20 low-margin, capital-intensive businesses over the past two years, and replacing them with what we see as 17 new, steady-growth, high-margin units, we expect that DOV to drive both top- and bottom-line growth over the long term and produce steady free cash flow and dividend payments. We believe DOV continues to improve its ability to generate free cash flow as it enhances the quality of its business portfolio. However, we believe the shares are appropriately valued at about 9.5X our '10 EBITDA estimate.

► Risks to our recommendation and target price include weaker-than-expected economic growth, softer-than-expected industrial activity, potential value-diminishing acquisitions, and DOV's strategic change that is more focused on top-down initiatives.

► Our 12-month target price of $44 is a blend of valuation metrics. Our discounted cash flow model, which assumes 3% perpetual growth and 10% discount rates, indicates intrinsic value of $44. For our relative valuation, we apply an EV/EBITDA multiple of 10X, in line with the peer average, to our 2010 EBITDA estimates, also implying a value of $44.

Qualitative Risk Assessment

LOW	MEDIUM	HIGH

Our risk assessment reflects the company's acquisition strategy, its model of operating numerous different businesses as stand-alone entities, the company's strategic change to manage numerous aspects of the business using a more top-down approach, and exposure to several cyclical end markets.

Quantitative Evaluations

S&P Quality Ranking   A-

D	C	B-	B	B+	A-	A	A+

Relative Strength Rank   STRONG

73

LOWEST = 1   HIGHEST = 99

Revenue/Earnings Data

Revenue (Million $)

	1Q	2Q	3Q	4Q	Year
2009	1,379	1,390	1,500	--	--
2008	1,865	2,011	1,966	1,727	7,569
2007	1,780	1,859	1,844	1,860	7,226
2006	1,500	1,650	1,647	1,715	6,512
2005	1,383	1,525	1,556	1,614	6,078
2004	1,242	1,380	1,444	1,421	5,488

Earnings Per Share ($)

2009	0.33	0.54	0.58	E0.42	E1.99
2008	0.77	0.98	1.01	0.91	3.67
2007	0.67	0.85	0.88	0.86	3.22
2006	0.64	0.77	0.77	0.76	2.94
2005	0.47	0.59	0.65	0.61	2.32
2004	0.41	0.53	0.58	0.48	2.00

Fiscal year ended Dec. 31. Next earnings report expected: Late January. EPS Estimates based on S&P Operating Earnings; historical GAAP earnings are as reported.

Dividend Data (Dates: mm/dd Payment Date: mm/dd/yy)

Amount ($)	Date Decl.	Ex-Div. Date	Stk. of Record	Payment Date
0.250	02/12	02/25	02/28	03/15/09
0.250	05/08	05/27	05/31	06/15/09
0.260	08/06	08/27	08/31	09/15/09
0.260	11/05	11/25	11/30	12/15/09

Dividends have been paid since 1947. Source: Company reports.

The **McGraw·Hill** Companies

Dover Corp

STANDARD
&POOR'S

Business Summary November 23, 2009

CORPORATE OVERVIEW. Dover Corporation (DOV) is a diversified manufacturer of a broad range of specialized industrial products and manufacturing equipment. The company has evolved largely through acquisitions, with 79 acquisitions costing approximately $4.1 billion completed between January 2000 and December 2008. There are four operating segments: Industrial Products, Engineered Systems, Fluid Management and Electronic Technologies.

Industrial Products (33% of 2008 sales, with 10.3% operating margin) manufactures a diverse mix of equipment and components for use in the waste handling, bulk transport and automotive service industries. Its two sub-units are Material Handling and Mobile Equipment. Major units include Paladin, PDQ Manufacturing, Heil Environmental, Rotary Lift, Heil Trailer International, Chief Automotive, and Marathon Equipment.

Engineered Systems (26%, 11.9%) manufactures food equipment (refrigeration systems, display cases, walk-in coolers, etc.) and packaging machinery. It is composed of two primary sub-groups -- Product Identification and Engineered Products. The food equipment businesses (Hill Phoenix and Unified Brands)

sell to the institutional and commercial foodservice markets. The packaging machinery businesses sell to the beverage and food processing industries.

Fluid Management (24%, 24%) manufactures products primarily for the oil and gas, automotive fueling, fluid handling, engineered components, material handling and chemical equipment industries. This segment consists of two primary sub-units -- Energy and Fluid Solutions.

Electronic Technologies (17%, 17.4%) manufactures an array of specialized electronic, electromechanical and plastic components for OEMs in multiple end markets, including hearing aids, telecom, defense and aerospace electronics, and life sciences. It also supplies ATM hardware and software for retail applications and financial institutions, and chemical proportioning and dispensing systems for janitorial/sanitation applications.

Company Financials Fiscal Year Ended Dec. 31

Per Share Data ($)	2008	2007	2006	2005	2004	2003	2002	2001	2000	1999
Tangible Book Value	NM	NM	NM	NM	2.16	2.71	2.66	1.97	1.79	1.08
Cash Flow	5.05	4.43	3.92	3.18	2.78	2.14	1.83	1.89	3.60	2.79
Earnings	3.67	3.22	2.94	2.32	2.00	1.40	1.04	0.82	2.61	1.92
S&P Core Earnings	3.55	3.28	2.98	2.25	1.92	1.31	0.90	0.68	NA	NA
Dividends	0.90	0.77	0.71	0.66	0.62	0.57	0.54	0.52	0.48	0.44
Payout Ratio	25%	24%	24%	28%	31%	41%	52%	63%	18%	23%
Prices:High	54.57	54.59	51.92	42.11	44.13	40.45	43.55	43.55	54.38	47.94
Prices:Low	23.39	44.34	40.30	34.11	35.12	22.85	23.54	26.40	34.13	29.31
P/E Ratio:High	15	17	18	18	22	29	42	53	21	25
P/E Ratio:Low	6	14	14	15	18	16	23	32	13	15

Income Statement Analysis (Million $)										
Revenue	7,569	7,226	6,512	6,078	5,488	4,413	4,184	4,460	5,401	4,446
Operating Income	1,311	1,220	1,113	876	773	595	503	518	1,047	819
Depreciation	261	245	202	176	161	151	161	219	203	183
Interest Expense	96.0	89.0	77.0	72.2	61.3	62.2	70.0	91.2	97.5	53.4
Pretax Income	946	888	823	644	552	372	270	238	772	615
Effective Tax Rate	26.6%	26.4%	26.7%	26.3%	25.9%	23.3%	21.7%	30.0%	31.0%	34.1%
Net Income	695	653	603	474	409	285	211	167	533	405
S&P Core Earnings	672	667	613	460	392	267	182	138	NA	NA

Balance Sheet & Other Financial Data (Million $)										
Cash	827	602	374	191	358	370	295	177	187	138
Current Assets	2,614	2,544	2,272	1,976	2,150	1,850	1,658	1,655	1,975	1,612
Total Assets	7,867	8,070	7,627	6,573	5,792	5,134	4,437	4,602	4,892	4,132
Current Liabilities	1,238	1,681	1,434	1,207	1,356	911	697	819	1,605	1,345
Long Term Debt	1,861	1,452	1,480	1,344	753	1,004	1,030	1,033	632	608
Common Equity	3,793	3,946	3,811	3,330	3,119	2,743	2,395	2,520	2,442	2,039
Total Capital	5,968	5,714	5,656	5,046	4,168	3,980	3,561	3,656	3,141	2,689
Capital Expenditures	176	174	195	152	107	96.4	102	167	198	130
Cash Flow	956	898	805	650	570	437	372	386	737	588
Current Ratio	2.1	1.5	1.6	1.6	1.6	2.0	2.4	2.0	1.2	1.2
% Long Term Debt of Capitalization	31.2	25.4	26.2	26.6	18.1	25.2	28.9	28.3	20.1	22.6
% Net Income of Revenue	9.2	9.0	9.3	7.8	7.5	6.5	5.0	3.7	9.9	9.1
% Return on Assets	8.7	8.3	8.5	7.7	7.5	6.0	4.7	3.5	11.8	10.4
% Return on Equity	18.0	16.8	16.9	14.7	14.0	11.1	8.6	6.7	23.8	20.5

Data as orig reptd.; bef. results of disc opers/spec. items. Per share data adj. for stk. divs.; EPS diluted. E-Estimated. NA-Not Available. NM-Not Meaningful. NR-Not Ranked. UR-Under Review.

Office: 280 Park Ave Rm, New York, NY 10017-1215.
Telephone: 212-922-1640.
Website: http://www.dovercorporation.com
Chrmn: R.W. Cremin

Pres & CEO: R.A. Livingston
CFO: B.M. Cerepak
Chief Acctg Officer & Cntlr: R.T. McKay, Jr.
Investor Contact: P.E. Goldberg (212-922-1640)

Board Members: D. H. Benson, R. W. Cremin, T. J. Derosa, J. M. Ergas, P. T. Francis, K. C. Graham, J. L. Koley, R. A. Livingston, R. K. Lochridge, B. G. Rethore, M. B. Stubbs, M. A. Winston

Founded: 1947
Domicile: Delaware
Employees: 32,300

The McGraw-Hill Companies

Dow Chemical Co (The)

STANDARD
&POOR'S

S&P Recommendation	HOLD ★★★☆☆	Price $27.56 (as of Nov 27, 2009)	12-Mo. Target Price $30.00	Investment Style Large-Cap Blend

GICS Sector Materials
Sub-Industry Diversified Chemicals

Summary Dow Chemical, the largest U.S. chemical company, provides chemical, plastic and agricultural products and services to many consumer markets.

Key Stock Statistics (Source S&P, Vickers, company reports)

52-Wk Range	$29.50– 5.89	S&P Oper. EPS 2009**E**	0.50	Market Capitalization(B)	$31.521	Beta	2.31
Trailing 12-Month EPS	$-1.31	S&P Oper. EPS 2010**E**	1.50	Yield (%)	2.18	S&P 3-Yr. Proj. EPS CAGR(%)	20
Trailing 12-Month P/E	NM	P/E on S&P Oper. EPS 2009**E**	55.1	Dividend Rate/Share	$0.60	S&P Credit Rating	BBB-
$10K Invested 5 Yrs Ago	$6,715	Common Shares Outstg. (M)	1,143.7	Institutional Ownership (%)	63		

Price Performance

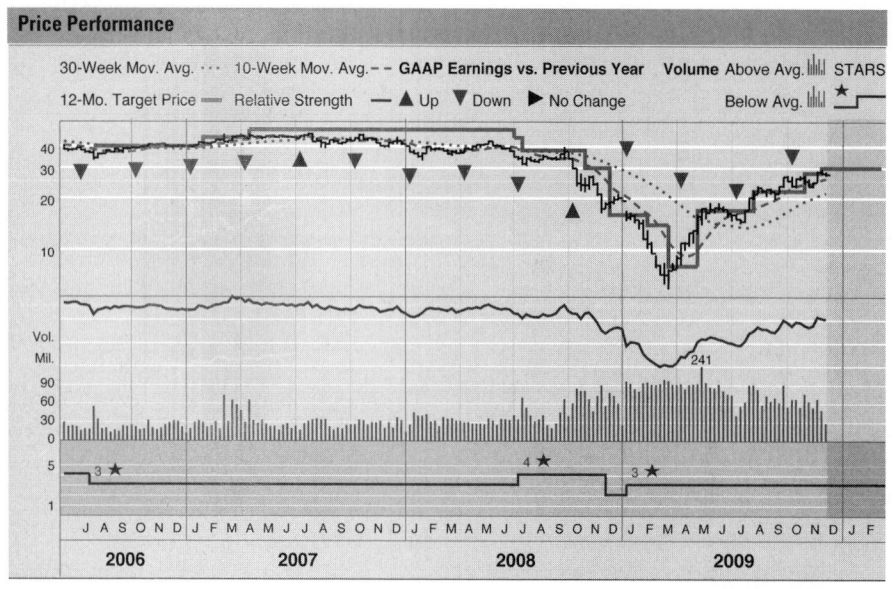

30-Week Mov. Avg. · · · 10-Week Mov. Avg. – – GAAP Earnings vs. Previous Year Volume Above Avg. STARS
12-Mo. Target Price — Relative Strength — ▲ Up ▼ Down ▶ No Change Below Avg. ★

Options: ASE, CBOE, P, Ph

Analysis prepared by **Richard O'Reilly, CFA** on November 17, 2009, when the stock traded at **$ 29.24**.

Highlights

▶ Reported sales for the last nine months of 2009 will include Rohm & Haas Co. (ROH), which was acquired on April 1. While sales on a pro forma basis in the first nine months declined 37% on lower volumes and prices, sales in the third quarter rose 6% from the second period. We expect business conditions to strengthen in late 2009 and into 2010, led by growth in emerging markets and signs of recovery in the U.S., resulting in favorable sales comparisons against weak year-earlier levels.

▶ Industry commodity plastic prices in 2009 have recovered some of the sharp drop that occurred in late 2008, but caustic soda prices have declined sharply since early 2009. For the near term, feedstock costs should be relatively stable and remain below the historical highs of 2008 due to lower natural gas costs.

▶ We expect restructuring actions to reduce annual costs by over $1 billion by 2010, while synergies from ROH are projected to reach a $1.3 billion rate in 2010. We expect modest earnings in 2009, including much greater interest expense, excluding restructuring and merger-related charges.

Investment Rationale/Risk

▶ On April 1, the company completed the delayed $16.2 billion purchase of Rohm & Haas, and on more favorable financial terms for itself. We view the purchase as positive for DOW for the long term, as less cyclical specialty products now account for about 60% of annual revenues, up from 51% in 2008. We also note that less cyclical products will now represent a larger percentage of profit.

▶ Risks to our recommendation and target price include worse-than-expected U.S. and global economies, rising energy costs, and unplanned production outages, and inability to achieve integration savings. We note that while the purchase of Rohm & Haas greatly increased debt and leverage, DOW has been successful in repaying and refinancing much of the merger debt.

▶ To reflect higher balance sheet risk, we base our 12-month target price of $30 on a historical bottom of cycle P/E of about 20X, applied to an annualized earnings rate of $1.50 that we believe DOW, as currently constituted, will achieve in 2010.

Qualitative Risk Assessment

LOW	MEDIUM	HIGH

Our risk assessment reflects the highly leveraged post-merger balance sheet and integration risks and the cyclical nature of the commodity chemical industry, partly offset by Dow's diverse business and geographic sales mix and manufacturing integration.

Quantitative Evaluations

S&P Quality Ranking   **B**

D	C	B-	**B**	B+	A-	A	A+

Relative Strength Rank   **STRONG**

87

LOWEST = 1   HIGHEST = 99

Revenue/Earnings Data

Revenue (Million $)

	1Q	2Q	3Q	4Q	Year
2009	9,087	11,322	12,046	--	--
2008	14,824	16,380	15,411	10,899	57,514
2007	12,432	13,265	13,589	14,227	53,513
2006	12,020	12,509	12,359	12,236	49,124
2005	11,679	11,450	11,261	11,917	46,307
2004	9,309	9,844	10,072	10,936	40,161

Earnings Per Share ($)

2009	0.03	-0.57	-0.64	E0.10	E0.50
2008	0.99	0.81	0.46	-1.68	0.62
2007	1.00	1.07	0.24	0.49	2.99
2006	1.24	1.05	0.53	1.00	3.82
2005	1.39	1.30	0.82	1.14	4.64
2004	0.50	0.72	0.65	1.06	2.93

Fiscal year ended Dec. 31. Next earnings report expected: Late January. EPS Estimates based on S&P Operating Earnings; historical GAAP earnings are as reported.

Dividend Data (Dates: mm/dd Payment Date: mm/dd/yy)

Amount ($)	Date Decl.	Ex-Div. Date	Stk. of Record	Payment Date
0.420	12/11	12/29	12/31	01/30/09
0.150	02/12	03/27	03/31	04/30/09
0.150	05/14	06/26	06/30	07/30/09
0.150	09/10	09/28	09/30	10/30/09

Dividends have been paid since 1911. Source: Company reports.

Please read the Required Disclosures and Analyst Certification on the last page of this report.

The **McGraw·Hill** Companies

Dow Chemical Co (The)

STANDARD &POOR'S

Business Summary November 17, 2009

CORPORATE OVERVIEW. Dow is the largest U.S. chemical company. Foreign operations accounted for 68% of 2008 sales.

Chemicals (10% of sales and no profits in 2008) include inorganics (chlorine, caustic soda, chlorinated solvents, calcium chlorides, ethylene dichloride and vinyl chloride), ethylene oxide/glycol, and vinyl acetate monomer, used primarily as raw materials in the manufacture of customer products. Performance chemicals (16%, 34%) consist of latex (including styrene-butadiene) coatings and binders, acrylics, water-based emulsions (acrylic latexes), water soluble polymers, cellulose ethers and resins, water solutions (ion exchange resins, membranes), biocides, and specialty chemicals (custom manufacturing, fine chemicals, glycols, amines, surfactants, heat transfer and deicing fluids, coolants, chelating agents, and lubricants and solvents). The segment also includes results of the Dow Corning joint venture.

Dow AgroSciences (8%, 26%) is a leading global maker of herbicides (Clincher, Starane), insecticides (Lorsban, Sentricon termite colony elimination system, Tracer) and fungicides for crop protection and industrial/commercial pest control. It is also building a plant genetics and biotechnology business in crop seeds (Mycogen, Nexera), traits (Herculex) and value-added grains.

The company, a major producer of plastics (23%, 33%), is the world's largest producer of polyethylene and polystyrene resins, which are used in a broad variety of applications. It also makes polypropylene and has a joint venture for PET polyester plastics. Performance plastics (27%, 9%) consist of engineering plastics (polycarbonates, ABS), elastomers, synthetic rubbers, adhesives and sealants, polyolefins for wire and cable insulation, SARAN resins and films, specialty films, polyurethanes (systems, sealants and adhesives, polyols, isocyanates, propylene oxide/glycol), epoxy resins and intermediates (phenol and acetone), building products (STYROFOAM insulation products, weather barrier products, foams, films, and adhesives), and technology licensing (UNIPOL for polyethylene and polypropylene, Meteor for ethylene oxide/glycol). The hydrocarbons and energy business (16%, -2%) procures fuels and raw materials and produces ethylene, propylene, aromatics, styrene, and power and steam.

Company Financials Fiscal Year Ended Dec. 31

Per Share Data ($)	2008	2007	2006	2005	2004	2003	2002	2001	2000	1999
Tangible Book Value	10.05	17.00	14.50	12.14	9.01	5.79	4.19	7.59	10.78	9.59
Cash Flow	2.86	5.09	5.83	6.83	5.12	3.93	4.57	1.55	4.14	3.91
Earnings	0.62	2.99	3.82	4.64	2.93	1.88	-0.44	-0.46	2.22	1.98
S&P Core Earnings	0.05	2.82	3.73	4.04	2.34	1.58	-1.41	-1.43	NA	NA
Dividends	1.68	1.64	1.50	1.34	1.34	1.34	1.34	1.30	1.16	1.16
Payout Ratio	271%	55%	39%	29%	46%	71%	NM	NM	52%	59%
Prices:High	43.42	47.96	45.15	56.75	51.34	42.00	37.00	39.67	47.17	46.00
Prices:Low	14.93	38.89	33.00	40.18	36.35	24.83	23.66	25.06	23.00	28.50
P/E Ratio:High	70	16	12	12	18	22	NM	NM	21	23
P/E Ratio:Low	24	13	9	9	12	13	NM	NM	10	14

Income Statement Analysis (Million $)										
Revenue	57,514	53,513	49,124	46,307	40,161	32,632	27,609	27,805	23,008	18,929
Operating Income	4,482	5,903	6,675	7,437	5,466	3,922	2,925	2,953	3,462	3,407
Depreciation	2,108	2,031	1,954	2,134	2,088	1,903	1,825	1,815	1,315	1,301
Interest Expense	745	669	689	702	747	828	774	733	460	431
Pretax Income	1,321	4,229	4,972	6,399	3,796	1,751	-622	-613	2,401	2,166
Effective Tax Rate	50.5%	29.4%	23.2%	27.8%	23.1%	NM	NM	NM	34.3%	35.4%
Net Income	579	2,887	3,724	4,535	2,797	1,739	-405	-417	1,513	1,331
S&P Core Earnings	29.0	2,734	3,638	3,956	2,236	1,462	-1,295	-1,303	NA	NA

Balance Sheet & Other Financial Data (Million $)										
Cash	2,800	1,737	2,910	3,838	3,192	2,434	1,573	264	304	1,212
Current Assets	16,060	18,654	17,209	17,404	15,890	13,002	11,681	10,308	9,260	8,847
Total Assets	45,474	48,801	45,581	45,934	45,885	41,891	39,562	35,515	27,645	25,499
Current Liabilities	13,108	12,445	10,601	10,663	10,506	9,534	8,856	8,125	7,873	6,295
Long Term Debt	8,042	7,581	8,036	10,186	12,629	12,763	12,659	10,266	5,365	5,022
Common Equity	13,511	19,389	17,065	15,324	12,270	9,175	7,626	9,993	9,186	8,323
Total Capital	22,868	29,238	27,465	27,241	26,649	23,438	21,645	21,376	15,848	14,642
Capital Expenditures	2,339	2,075	1,775	1,597	1,333	1,100	1,623	1,587	1,349	1,412
Cash Flow	2,687	4,918	5,678	6,669	4,885	3,642	1,420	1,398	2,828	2,627
Current Ratio	1.2	1.5	1.6	1.6	1.5	1.4	1.3	1.3	1.2	1.4
% Long Term Debt of Capitalization	35.2	25.9	30.4	37.4	47.4	54.5	58.5	48.0	33.9	34.3
% Net Income of Revenue	1.0	5.4	7.6	9.8	7.0	5.3	NM	NM	6.6	7.0
% Return on Assets	1.2	6.1	8.1	9.9	6.4	4.3	NM	NM	5.7	5.4
% Return on Equity	3.5	15.8	23.0	32.9	26.1	20.7	NM	NM	17.3	16.8

Data as orig reptd.; bef. results of disc opers/spec. items. Per share data adj. for stk. divs.; EPS diluted. E-Estimated. NA-Not Available. NM-Not Meaningful. NR-Not Ranked. UR-Under Review.

Office: 2030 Dow Center, Midland, MI 48674-0001.
Telephone: 989-636-1000.
Website: http://www.dow.com
Chrmn, Pres & CEO: A.N. Liveris

EVP & CTO: W.F. Banholzer
EVP, Secy & General Counsel: C.J. Kalil
EVP & CIO: D.E. Kepler, II
CFO & Cntlr: W.H. Weideman

Investor Contact: H. Ungerleider (989-636-1463)
Board Members: A. A. Allemang, J. K. Barton, J. A. Bell, J. M. Fettig, B. H. Franklin, J. B. Hess, A. N. Liveris, D. H. Reilley, J. M. Ringler, R. G. Shaw, P. G. Stern

Founded: 1897
Domicile: Delaware
Employees: 46,102

The McGraw-Hill Companies

D.R. Horton Inc.

STANDARD
&POOR'S

S&P Recommendation	BUY ★★★★☆	Price $10.54 (as of Nov 27, 2009)	12-Mo. Target Price $14.00	Investment Style Large-Cap Blend

GICS Sector Consumer Discretionary
Sub-Industry Homebuilding

Summary This company is one of the largest homebuilders in the U.S., based on number of homes sold and its nationwide presence.

Key Stock Statistics (Source S&P, Vickers, company reports)

52-Wk Range	$13.90– 5.72	S&P Oper. EPS 2010**E**	0.05	Market Capitalization(B)	$3.348	Beta	1.06
Trailing 12-Month EPS	$-1.72	S&P Oper. EPS 2011**E**	0.45	Yield (%)	1.42	S&P 3-Yr. Proj. EPS CAGR(%)	NM
Trailing 12-Month P/E	NM	P/E on S&P Oper. EPS 2010**E**	NM	Dividend Rate/Share	$0.15	S&P Credit Rating	BB-
$10K Invested 5 Yrs Ago	$4,308	Common Shares Outstg. (M)	317.7	Institutional Ownership (%)	85		

Price Performance

30-Week Mov. Avg. · · · ·   10-Week Mov. Avg. – – –   **GAAP Earnings vs. Previous Year**   **Volume** Above Avg. ⦙⦙⦙ STARS

12-Mo. Target Price —   Relative Strength —   ▲ Up ▼ Down ► No Change   Below Avg. ⦙⦙⦙

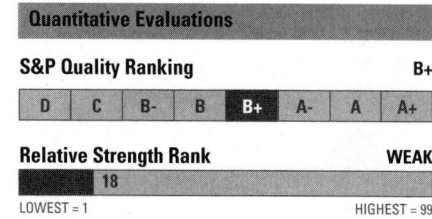

Options: ASE, CBOE, P, Ph

Analysis prepared by **Kenneth M. Leon, CPA** on November 23, 2009, when the stock traded at **$ 10.61**.

Highlights

► Following a 45% sales decline in FY 09 (Sep.), we forecast a 4.5% increase in FY 10 and 11% growth in FY 11, as the housing market recovers. At September 30, 2009, DHI realized an increase in backlog to $1.1 billion, which we view as a sign that the housing market is beginning to rebound. We believe the near-term outlook for DHI new contracts will benefit from a federal tax credit that was extended to April 2010.

► We estimate that DHI's homebuilding gross margin will improve to 16% in FY 10 and 18% in FY 11, from 13% in FY 09. DHI realized peak gross margin of 24% in FY 06. Asset impairment charges were $2.5 billion in FY 08, and eased to $345 million in FY 09. We believe these write-offs will ease further in FY 10.

► With wider gross margins, we believe DHI will maintain SG&A costs as a percentage of total revenues at the 14% to 15% level in FY 10 and FY 11, comparable to FY 08. We forecast operating EPS of $0.05 in FY 10 and $0.45 in FY 11, excluding any future impairment charges.

Investment Rationale/Risk

► DHI is one of the largest U.S. homebuilders, and we see reduced interest rates raising affordability in its target markets. Despite the company booking over $4.9 billion of asset impairments since the beginning of 2006, we still view DHI as one of the leading large homebuilders, with a strong balance sheet. We believe a rebound in the housing market would benefit DHI with a return to more stable home prices and improved sales for its communities as it gains market share.

► Risks to our recommendation and target price include the possibility of a worsening housing recession and deteriorating employment data. We see the potential for further writedowns of inventory and joint venture investments above our target, which would be detrimental to our EPS estimates and book value.

► Our 12-month target price of $14 reflects a target price-to-book multiple of just above 1.9X applied to our forward book value estimate of $7.15, near the high end of the historical range for DHI and just above peers, reflecting its strong cash position, operating scale advantages, and ability to generate free cash flow.

Qualitative Risk Assessment

LOW	MEDIUM	HIGH

Our risk assessment reflects DHI's exposure to an extended downturn in the housing market, partly offset by its focus on reducing debt with free cash flow from operations. As the largest U.S. homebuilder, DHI has scale advantages to reduce labor costs and material costs, but severe weakness in the housing market may delay profitability.

Quantitative Evaluations

S&P Quality Ranking B+

D	C	B-	B	B+	A-	A	A+

Relative Strength Rank WEAK

18

LOWEST = 1   HIGHEST = 99

Revenue/Earnings Data

Revenue (Million $)

	1Q	2Q	3Q	4Q	Year
2009	918.0	778.0	932.9	1,029	3,658
2008	1,708	1,624	1,464	1,782	6,646
2007	3,172	2,598	2,658	2,868	11,297
2006	2,903	3,598	3,668	4,883	15,051
2005	2,520	2,877	3,370	5,097	13,864
2004	2,205	2,335	2,790	3,511	10,841

Earnings Per Share ($)

2009	-0.20	-0.34	-0.45	-0.73	-1.72
2008	-0.41	-4.14	-1.26	-2.53	-8.34
2007	0.35	0.16	-2.62	-0.16	-2.27
2006	0.98	1.11	0.93	0.88	3.90
2005	0.76	0.92	1.17	1.77	4.62
2004	0.58	0.60	0.80	1.10	3.08

Fiscal year ended Sep. 30. Next earnings report expected: Early February. EPS Estimates based on S&P Operating Earnings; historical GAAP earnings are as reported.

Dividend Data (Dates: mm/dd Payment Date: mm/dd/yy)

Amount ($)	Date Decl.	Ex-Div. Date	Stk. of Record	Payment Date
0.038	02/03	02/11	02/16	02/26/09
0.038	05/04	05/15	05/19	05/27/09
0.038	08/04	08/17	08/19	08/28/09
0.038	11/20	12/02	12/04	12/15/09

Dividends have been paid since 1997. Source: Company reports.

Please read the Required Disclosures and Analyst Certification on the last page of this report.

The McGraw-Hill Companies

D.R. Horton Inc.

**STANDARD
&POOR'S**

Business Summary November 23, 2009

CORPORATE OVERVIEW. D.R. Horton was founded in 1978 by Donald Horton, now chairman. In 1992, it went public to gain broader access to capital markets, which has helped fuel its subsequent growth beyond its base in the Dallas/Fort Worth area. With operating divisions in 27 states and 76 markets, D.R. Horton is the largest domestic homebuilder by number of homes closed in FY 08 (Sep.), and the most geographically diversified.

The company was the first U.S. builder to sell 50,000 homes in a single year (FY 05), and it aims to be the first to eclipse the 100,000 unit mark, although market conditions may have pushed back that target into 2011 or 2012. By emphasizing entry level and first-time move-up buyers, it targets the broadest segments of the population. In FY 08, DHI closed on 26,396 homes with an average closing sales price of approximately $233,500, compared to $253,000 in FY 07 and $273,900 in FY 06. DHI's homes are among the most affordable of all public builders. Detached homes accounted for 77% (81%) of home sales revenue in FY 08 (FY 07).

CORPORATE STRATEGY. Most of D.R. Horton's growth in the past 15 to 20 years has been the result of organic initiatives, in our opinion. Generally, the

company has established satellite operations in new markets located in relatively close proximity to existing markets. We think the company has been successful at quickly ramping up volumes in these satellite operations -- often at the expense of smaller competitors -- aided by materials purchasing agreements struck at the regional level and relatively favorable access to capital markets.

Complementing this organic growth has been an aggressive takeover program, with close to 20 acquisitions since DHI went public. Most of these deals have occurred in new markets in an effort to either create a platform for future growth in a locale or to expand an existing satellite operation there. The majority of these acquisitions have been focused on a single market and have been asset-based transactions, rather than purchases of companies. However, in 2002, DHI bought Schuler Homes for about $1.8 billion, in a deal that increased its revenue base about 25%.

Company Financials Fiscal Year Ended Sep. 30

Per Share Data ($)	2009	2008	2007	2006	2005	2004	2003	2002	2001	2000
Tangible Book Value	7.07	8.90	17.64	18.75	15.28	10.87	7.93	5.77	4.83	3.81
Cash Flow	NA	-8.17	-2.06	4.10	4.87	3.24	2.16	1.54	1.24	0.94
Earnings	-1.72	-8.34	-2.27	3.90	4.62	3.08	2.05	1.44	1.10	0.84
S&P Core Earnings	NA	-8.18	-1.29	3.90	4.61	3.07	2.04	1.44	1.16	NA
Dividends	0.15	0.33	0.60	0.44	0.31	0.22	0.14	0.10	0.06	0.05
Payout Ratio	NM	NM	NM	11%	7%	7%	7%	7%	5%	5%
Prices:High	13.90	17.95	31.13	41.66	42.82	31.41	22.69	14.58	11.17	7.81
Prices:Low	5.72	3.79	10.15	19.52	26.83	18.47	8.48	8.02	5.83	3.00
P/E Ratio:High	NM	NM	NM	11	9	10	11	10	10	9
P/E Ratio:Low	NM	NM	NM	5	6	6	4	6	5	4

Income Statement Analysis (Million $)										
Revenue	3,658	6,646	11,297	15,051	13,864	10,841	8,728	6,739	4,456	3,654
Operating Income	NA	-2,474	-420	2,036	2,402	1,430	1,049	693	480	339
Depreciation	25.7	53.2	64.4	61.7	52.8	49.6	41.8	32.8	31.2	22.0
Interest Expense	NA	240	328	55.0	21.2	9.30	12.6	11.5	14.1	15.8
Pretax Income	-552	-2,632	-951	1,987	2,379	1,583	1,008	648	408	309
Effective Tax Rate	1.27%	NM	25.1%	37.9%	38.2%	38.4%	37.9%	37.5%	37.5%	38.0%
Net Income	-545	-2,634	-712	1,233	1,471	975	626	405	255	192
S&P Core Earnings	NA	-2,582	-404	1,233	1,463	969	622	406	267	NA

Balance Sheet & Other Financial Data (Million $)										
Cash	1,923	1,356	275	588	1,150	518	583	104	239	72.5
Current Assets	NA	NA	NA	NA	NA	NA	NA	NA	NA	NA
Total Assets	6,757	7,710	11,556	14,821	12,515	8,985	7,279	6,018	3,652	2,695
Current Liabilities	NA	NA	NA	NA	NA	NA	NA	NA	NA	NA
Long Term Debt	2,969	2,968	3,746	4,861	3,660	3,032	2,665	2,636	1,884	1,344
Common Equity	2,260	2,834	5,587	6,453	5,360	3,961	3,031	2,270	1,250	970
Total Capital	5,477	6,410	9,644	11,419	9,224	7,159	5,832	4,927	3,143	2,319
Capital Expenditures	6.20	6.60	39.8	83.3	68.2	55.2	48.7	39.8	33.4	19.6
Cash Flow	NA	-2,580	-648	1,295	1,523	1,025	668	437	286	214
Current Ratio	7.9	4.7	4.8	3.7	3.3	4.7	4.7	4.5	4.7	5.0
% Long Term Debt of Capitalization	54.2	46.3	39.1	42.6	39.7	42.4	45.7	53.5	59.9	58.0
% Net Income of Revenue	NM	NM	NM	8.2	10.6	8.9	7.2	6.0	5.7	5.2
% Return on Assets	NM	NM	NM	9.0	13.7	12.0	9.4	8.4	8.0	7.6
% Return on Equity	NM	NM	NM	20.9	31.5	27.9	23.6	23.0	23.0	21.7

Data as orig reptd.; bef. results of disc opers/spec. items. Per share data adj. for stk. divs.; EPS diluted. E-Estimated. NA-Not Available. NM-Not Meaningful. NR-Not Ranked. UR-Under Review.

Office: 301 Commerce St Ste 500, Fort Worth, TX 76102-4178.
Telephone: 817-390-8200.
Website: http://www.drhorton.com
Chrmn: D.R. Horton

Pres, Vice Chrmn & CEO: D.J. Tomnitz
EVP, CFO & Chief Acctg Officer: B.W. Wheat
Investor Contact: S.H. Dwyer (817-390-8200)
EVP & Treas: S.H. Dwyer

Board Members: B. S. Anderson, M. R. Buchanan, M. W. Hewatt, D. R. Horton, B. G. Scott, D. J. Tomnitz, B. W. Wheat

Founded: 1978
Domicile: Delaware
Employees: 3,800

The McGraw-Hill Companies

Dr Pepper Snapple Group Inc

STANDARD &POOR'S

S&P Recommendation	HOLD ★★★☆☆	Price	12-Mo. Target Price	Investment Style
		$26.27 (as of Nov 27, 2009)	$28.00	Large-Cap Growth

GICS Sector Consumer Staples
Sub-Industry Soft Drinks

Summary Spun off from Cadbury Schweppes in May 2008, DPS is the third largest marketer, bottler and distributor of non-alcoholic beverages in North America. Key brands include Dr Pepper, Snapple, 7UP, Mott's, Canada Dry and Schweppes.

Key Stock Statistics (Source S&P, Vickers, company reports)

52-Wk Range	$30.65– 11.83	S&P Oper. EPS 2009E	2.03	Market Capitalization(B)	$6.674	Beta	NA
Trailing 12-Month EPS	$-0.71	S&P Oper. EPS 2010E	2.13	Yield (%)	2.28	S&P 3-Yr. Proj. EPS CAGR(%)	8
Trailing 12-Month P/E	NM	P/E on S&P Oper. EPS 2009E	12.9	Dividend Rate/Share	$0.60	S&P Credit Rating	BBB-
$10K Invested 5 Yrs Ago	NA	Common Shares Outstg. (M)	254.1	Institutional Ownership (%)	90		

Price Performance

30-Week Mov. Avg. · · · 10-Week Mov. Avg. – – GAAP Earnings vs. Previous Year Volume Above Avg. STARS
12-Mo. Target Price — Relative Strength — ▲ Up ▼ Down ▶ No Change Below Avg.

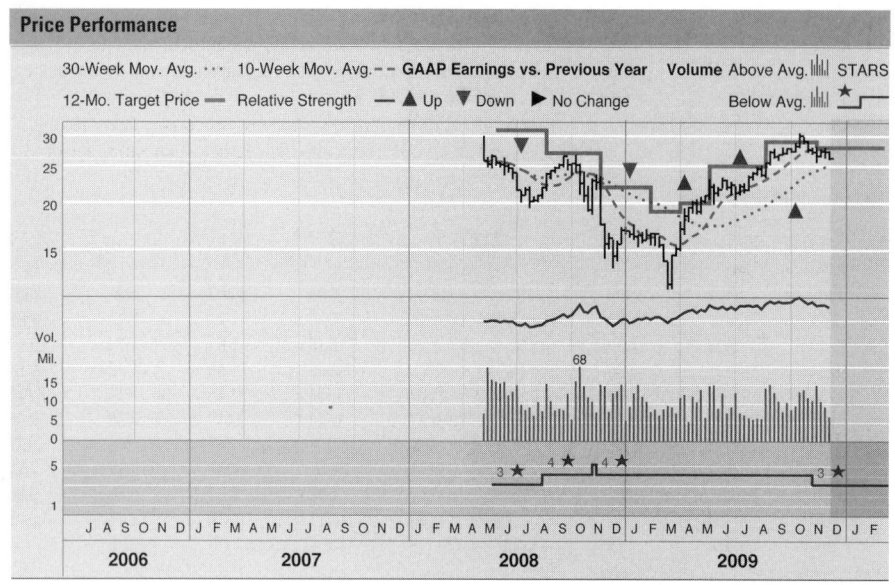

Options: CBOE, P, Ph

Analysis prepared by **Esther Y. Kwon, CFA** on November 06, 2009, when the stock traded at **$ 26.48**.

Highlights

► In 2009, we estimate revenue of $5.5 billion, down from 2008's $5.7 billion, as we project volume to be hurt by the loss of Hansen product distribution and negative foreign exchange, offset by price increases and gains in carbonated drink volume. Through increased distribution, the addition of Crush, and its focus on flavored colas, we expect DPS to outperform the carbonated drink category in volume, which we estimate will decline at a mid-single digit rate in 2009. In 2010, we project 2% revenue growth.

► We look for operating margin expansion this year as raw material cost pressures subside with contracts reflecting higher prices rolling off in the second half of the year, offset somewhat by increased advertising and marketing expenses in the second half to support new product introductions. In 2010, we look for raw materials costs to be up slightly.

► On lower interest expense, we estimate 2009 operating EPS of $2.03, excluding one-time gains. In 2010, we project EPS of $2.13. We do not anticipate dividends in the near term as DPS repays part of its $3.0 billion of debt.

Investment Rationale/Risk

► We think DPS will have more difficulty in expanding margins in the near term as favorable commodity cost benefits are lapped, manufacturing margins are negatively impacted by initial ramp up costs at its new Victorville, CA, production and distribution center, and higher oil prices likely squeeze bottling operation profits. In addition, while we still expect DPS's flavored carbonated brands to outperform the industry, we see tough comparisons on the annualization of the addition of Crush volumes.

► Risks to our recommendation and target price include more rapid commodity cost inflation than expected, potential consumer reluctance to accept new products, and unfavorable weather conditions in the company's markets.

► Our 12-month target price of $28 is derived from our peer multiple analysis. Given DPS's limited history as an independent company and limited exposure to the faster-growing non-carbonated beverage category, we apply about a 13X multiple to our 2010 EPS estimate of $2.13, a discount to the multiple we use for bottling peers and a discount to concentrate companies.

Qualitative Risk Assessment

LOW	MEDIUM	HIGH

Our risk assessment for Dr Pepper Snapple Group reflects our view of the relatively stable nature of the company's end markets and its strong cash flow generation ability.

Quantitative Evaluations

S&P Quality Ranking   NR

D	C	B-	B	B+	A-	A	A+

Relative Strength Rank   MODERATE

35

LOWEST = 1   HIGHEST = 99

Revenue/Earnings Data

Revenue (Million $)

	1Q	2Q	3Q	4Q	Year
2009	1,260	1,481	1,434	--	--
2008	1,295	1,545	1,494	1,376	5,710
2007	1,269	1,543	1,535	1,401	5,748
2006	990.0	990.0	1,378	1,378	4,735
2005	--	--	--	--	3,205
2004	--	--	--	--	3,065

Earnings Per Share ($)

2009	0.52	0.62	0.59	E0.50	E2.03
2008	0.38	0.42	0.41	-2.44	-1.23
2007	--	0.54	--	0.54	1.79
2006	--	--	--	--	--
2005	--	--	--	--	--
2004	--	--	--	--	--

Fiscal year ended Dec. 31. Next earnings report expected: Early March. EPS Estimates based on S&P Operating Earnings; historical GAAP earnings are as reported.

Dividend Data (Dates: mm/dd Payment Date: mm/dd/yy)

Amount ($)	Date Decl.	Ex-Div. Date	Stk. of Record	Payment Date
0.150	11/20	12/17	12/21	01/08/10

Dividends have been paid since 2010. Source: Company reports.

Dr Pepper Snapple Group Inc

STANDARD
&POOR'S

Business Summary November 06, 2009

CORPORATE OVERVIEW. Dr Pepper Snapple Group is the third largest marketer, bottler and distributor of non-alcoholic beverages in North America and the leading flavored carbonated soft drink (CSD) company in the United States. Its CSD brands include Dr Pepper, 7UP, Sunkist, A&W, Canada Dry, Schweppes, and Squirt. Its non-CSD brands include Snapple, Mott's, Hawaiian Punch and Clamato. The company also distributes FIJI mineral water and Arizona tea. A small portion of bottling group sales comes from fees paid by private label owners and others for bottling beverages and other products. Approximately one-third of the company's volume is generated by the Dr Pepper brand while 88% of manufactured volumes are related to company brands and 12% to third-party and private-label products.

The company has three main operating segments: beverage concentrates (23.7% of 2008 sales, with an operating profit margin of 57.5%), finished goods (28.4% of sales, with a 15.1% operating margin), and bottling (54.4%, with a $36 million loss). The Mexican and Caribbean segment accounted for the remaining sales, and had a 20.1% margin.

In 2008, DPS generated 89% of its sales in the United States, 4% in Canada, and the remainder in Mexico and the Caribbean.

CORPORATE STRATEGY. DPS's growth strategies include leveraging key brands through line extensions, such as launching Snapple super premium

teas and antioxidant waters with functional benefits through its Snapple line. DPS is also targeting opportunities in high growth and high margin categories, including ready to drink teas, energy drinks and other functional beverages, and plans to increase its presence in higher margin channels and packages. These channels include convenience stores, vending machines and small independent retail outlets, most often offering higher margin single-serve packages. With a slowing economy, however, Standard & Poor's remains cautious on this segment, which is particularly sensitive to changes in discretionary income. The company may also selectively enter into distribution agreements for high growth, third-party brands that can use DPS's bottling and distribution network.

In addition, DPS plans to continue to acquire regional bottling companies to broaden geographic coverage. Management believes the integrated model of brand ownership with bottling capabilities best aligns the economic interests of all parties involved. Finally, the company is targeting improvements in operating efficiencies as it integrates recent bottling acquisitions and reduces distribution costs.

Company Financials Fiscal Year Ended Dec. 31

Per Share Data ($)	2008	2007	2006	2005	2004	2003	2002	2001	2000	1999
Tangible Book Value	NM	NM	NA	NA	NA	NA	NA	NA	NA	NA
Cash Flow	-0.56	2.19	NA	NA	NA	NA	NA	NA	NA	NA
Earnings	-1.23	1.79	NA	NA	NA	NA	NA	NA	NA	NA
S&P Core Earnings	1.51	1.76	1.92	NA	NA	NA	NA	NA	NA	NA
Dividends	Nil	NA	NA	NA	NA	NA	NA	NA	NA	NA
Payout Ratio	Nil	NA	NA	NA	NA	NA	NA	NA	NA	NA
Prices:High	30.00	NA	NA	NA	NA	NA	NA	NA	NA	NA
Prices:Low	13.45	NA	NA	NA	NA	NA	NA	NA	NA	NA
P/E Ratio:High	NM	NA	NA	NA	NA	NA	NA	NA	NA	NA
P/E Ratio:Low	NM	NA	NA	NA	NA	NA	NA	NA	NA	NA

Income Statement Analysis (Million $)										
Revenue	5,710	5,748	4,735	3,205	3,065	NA	NA	NA	NA	NA
Operating Income	1,134	1,113	NA	NA	NA	NA	NA	NA	NA	NA
Depreciation	169	100	139	79.0	84.0	NA	NA	NA	NA	NA
Interest Expense	241	250	NA	NA	NA	NA	NA	NA	NA	NA
Pretax Income	-373	774	808	808	716	NA	NA	NA	NA	NA
Effective Tax Rate	NM	41.2%	36.9%	39.7%	37.7%	NA	NA	NA	NA	NA
Net Income	-312	455	510	487	446	NA	NA	NA	NA	NA
S&P Core Earnings	385	446	487	NA	NA	NA	NA	NA	NA	NA

Balance Sheet & Other Financial Data (Million $)										
Cash	214	100	35.0	28.0	NA	NA	NA	NA	NA	NA
Current Assets	1,237	1,179	NA	NA	NA	NA	NA	NA	NA	NA
Total Assets	8,638	9,598	9,346	7,433	NA	NA	NA	NA	NA	NA
Current Liabilities	801	2,764	NA	NA	NA	NA	NA	NA	NA	NA
Long Term Debt	3,505	1,999	3,084	2,858	NA	NA	NA	NA	NA	NA
Common Equity	2,607	2,922	3,250	2,426	NA	NA	NA	NA	NA	NA
Total Capital	6,112	6,245	7,042	5,688	NA	NA	NA	NA	NA	NA
Capital Expenditures	304	230	158	44.0	71.0	NA	NA	NA	NA	NA
Cash Flow	-143	555	NA	NA	NA	NA	NA	NA	NA	NA
Current Ratio	1.5	0.4	1.0	1.2	NA	NA	NA	NA	NA	NA
% Long Term Debt of Capitalization	57.3	32.0	43.8	50.3	Nil	NA	NA	NA	NA	NA
% Net Income of Revenue	NM	7.9	10.8	15.2	14.6	NA	NA	NA	NA	NA
% Return on Assets	NM	NA	6.1	NA	NA	NA	NA	NA	NA	NA
% Return on Equity	NM	NA	18.0	NA	NA	NA	NA	NA	NA	NA

Data as orig reptd.; bef. results of disc opers/spec. items. Per share data adj. for stk. divs.; EPS diluted. Pro forma data in 2007. E-Estimated. NA-Not Available. NM-Not Meaningful. NR-Not Ranked. UR-Under Review.

Office: 5301 Legacy Drive, Plano, TX 75024.
Telephone: 972-673-7000.
Website: http://www.drpeppersnapplegroup.com
Chrmn: W.R. Sanders

Pres & CEO: L.D. Young
EVP & CFO: J.O. Stewart
EVP, Secy & General Counsel: J.L. Baldwin, Jr.
SVP, Chief Acctg Officer & Cntlr: A.A. Stephens

Investor Contact: A. Noormohamed (972-673-6050)
Board Members: J. L. Adams, T. D. Martin, P. H. Patsley, R. G. Rogers, W. R. Sanders, J. L. Stahl, A. Szostak, M. F. Weinstein, L. D. Young

Founded: 2007
Domicile: Delaware
Employees: 20,000

The McGraw-Hill Companies

DTE Energy Co

STANDARD &POOR'S

S&P Recommendation	HOLD ★★★☆☆	Price	12-Mo. Target Price
		$39.83 (as of Nov 27, 2009)	$39.00

GICS Sector Utilities
Sub-Industry Multi-Utilities

Summary This diversified energy company is involved in the development and management of energy-related businesses and services nationwide.

Key Stock Statistics (Source S&P, Vickers, company reports)

52-Wk Range	$40.73– 23.32	S&P Oper. EPS 2009**E**	3.27	Market Capitalization(B)	$6.569	Beta	0.72
Trailing 12-Month EPS	$3.35	S&P Oper. EPS 2010**E**	3.30	Yield (%)	5.32	S&P 3-Yr. Proj. EPS CAGR(%)	5
Trailing 12-Month P/E	11.9	P/E on S&P Oper. EPS 2009**E**	12.2	Dividend Rate/Share	$2.12	S&P Credit Rating	BBB
$10K Invested 5 Yrs Ago	$11,326	Common Shares Outstg. (M)	164.9	Institutional Ownership (%)	55		

Price Performance

30-Week Mov. Avg. · · · 10-Week Mov. Avg. - - GAAP Earnings vs. Previous Year   Volume Above Avg. STARS
12-Mo. Target Price — Relative Strength — ▲ Up ▼ Down ▶ No Change   Below Avg.

Options: ASE, Ph

Analysis prepared by **Justin McCann** on October 27, 2009, when the stock traded at **$ 37.55**.

Qualitative Risk Assessment

LOW	MEDIUM	HIGH

Our risk assessment reflects a balance between the steady cash flow that we expect from the regulated utilities, which operate within a generally supportive regulatory environment, and most of the unregulated operations, which continue to contribute a significant portion of DTE's consolidated cash flow. While we expect DTE to benefit from the modification of Michigan's Electric Choice program, we remain concerned about the weak outlook for the state's economy .

Quantitative Evaluations

S&P Quality Ranking B

D	C	B-	B	B+	A-	A	A+

Relative Strength Rank STRONG

82

LOWEST = 1   HIGHEST = 99

Highlights

▶ Excluding $0.06 of net one-time charges, we expect operating EPS in 2009 to grow about 11% from 2008's $2.90. The growth should reflect an electric rate increase, lower operating, fuel and purchased power costs, tax credits, and strong results from the non-utility operations, partially offset by a decline in electric demand and higher pension and depreciation charges. In December 2008, the Michigan Public Service Commission (MPSC) authorized Detroit Edison an electric rate increase of $83.6 million. The MPSC order maintained the allowed return on equity at 11%, which was below the utility's request of 11.25%, but above the 10.50% recommended by the MPSC staff.

▶ For 2010, we expect operating EPS to increase only slightly from anticipated results in 2009, aided by a rate increase at the MichCon gas utility. Longer term, we expect EPS growth to reflect an expanded rate base resulting from the company's capital investment program.

▶ Under the energy reform package that the governor of Michigan signed into law in October 2008, the state's electric choice program was modified and a 12-month deadline for the resolution of utility rate cases was established.

Investment Rationale/Risk

▶ Afer a strong rebound from its sharp drop in the first nine weeks of 2009, the stock was up about 5% year to date and we expect it to stabilize at around its current level. While the shares had been hurt by the weakness of the state's economy, which was exacerbated by the crisis in the financial markets, we see clear long-term benefits from the energy legislation that modified Michigan's electric choice program and assured a more efficient rate case process.

▶ Risks to our recommendation and target price include a slower-than-expected recovery in both the financial markets and the Michigan economy, as well as a sharp decrease in the average P/E of the peer group as a whole.

▶ The dividend recently yielded about 5.7% on what we consider a secure payout, well above the recent peer average of 5.0%. The stock is likely to remain volatile in the current market, but we believe the dividend should provide some support for the shares. With a payout ratio of 66% of our operating EPS estimate for 2009, we expect the company to maintain the dividend at its current level. Our 12-month target price is $39, a discount-to-peers P/E of about 12.0X our EPS estimate for 2010.

Revenue/Earnings Data

Revenue (Million $)

	1Q	2Q	3Q	4Q	Year
2009	2,255	1,688	1,961	--	--
2008	2,570	2,251	2,338	2,170	9,329
2007	2,463	1,692	2,140	2,211	8,506
2006	2,635	1,895	2,196	2,296	9,022
2005	2,309	1,941	2,060	2,712	9,022
2004	2,093	1,501	1,594	1,926	7,114

Earnings Per Share ($)

2009	1.09	0.51	0.96	E0.66	E3.27
2008	1.23	0.17	1.03	0.80	3.23
2007	0.54	1.99	0.92	1.17	4.62
2006	0.76	-0.18	1.07	0.81	2.45
2005	0.72	0.19	0.17	2.18	3.27
2004	1.15	0.20	0.54	0.68	2.55

Fiscal year ended Dec. 31. Next earnings report expected: Late February. EPS Estimates based on S&P Operating Earnings; historical GAAP earnings are as reported.

Dividend Data (Dates: mm/dd Payment Date: mm/dd/yy)

Amount ($)	Date Decl.	Ex-Div. Date	Stk. of Record	Payment Date
0.530	12/05	12/11	12/15	01/15/09
0.530	03/06	03/12	03/16	04/15/09
0.530	06/08	06/11	06/15	07/15/09
0.530	09/03	09/17	09/21	10/15/09

Dividends have been paid since 1909. Source: Company reports.

Please read the Required Disclosures and Analyst Certification on the last page of this report.

The McGraw-Hill Companies

DTE Energy Co

**STANDARD
&POOR'S**

Business Summary October 27, 2009

CORPORATE OVERVIEW. DTE Energy, formed on January 1, 1996, is the holding company for The Detroit Edison Company and Michigan Consolidated Gas (MichCon), regulated electric and gas utilities serving customers within the state of Michigan, and three non-utility operations engaged in a variety of energy-related businesses in various portions of the United States. The electric utility business accounted for 51.2% of consolidated revenues in 2008; the gas utility business 22.6%; and the non-utility operations 26.2%.

MARKET PROFILE. Detroit Edison is a regulated electric utility serving approximately 2.2 million customers in southeastern Michigan. In 2008, residential customers accounted for 37.0% of the utility's revenues; commercial customers 37.6%; industrial customers 19.2%; other 3.6%; and wholesale 2.6%. With its high percentage of commercial and industrial customers, the utility had been hurt by the state's Customer Choice program, losing about 3% of retail sales in 2008, 4% in 2007, 6% in 2006, 12% in 2005, and 18% in 2004. Recent energy legislation in Michigan and orders by the Michigan Public Service Commission (MPSC) have placed a 10% cap on the total potential migration. When market conditions are favorable, Detroit Edison will sell excess power into the wholesale market. The utility's generating capability is heavily dependent on the availability of coal, and the majority of its coal needs are obtained through long-term contracts, with the remainder purchased through short-term agreements or purchases in the spot market.

MichCon is a regulated natural gas utility serving about 1.3 million residential, commercial and industrial customers in the state of Michigan. It also has subsidiaries involved in the gathering and transmission of natural gas in northern Michigan, and operates one of the largest natural gas distribution and transmission systems in the U.S., with connections to interstate pipelines providing access to most of the major natural gas producing regions in the Gulf Coast, Mid-Continent and Canadian regions. The company purchases its natural gas supplies on the open market through a diversified portfolio of supply contracts, and, given its storage capacity, should be able to meet its supply requirements.

Company Financials Fiscal Year Ended Dec. 31

Per Share Data ($)	2008	2007	2006	2005	2004	2003	2002	2001	2000	1999
Tangible Book Value	23.99	23.22	21.02	20.88	20.01	19.05	14.61	16.06	28.15	26.96
Earnings	3.23	4.62	2.45	3.27	2.55	2.85	3.83	2.14	3.27	3.33
S&P Core Earnings	1.69	1.55	2.88	2.13	1.97	3.22	2.80	2.09	NA	NA
Dividends	2.12	2.12	2.08	2.06	2.06	2.06	2.06	2.06	2.06	2.06
Payout Ratio	66%	46%	85%	63%	81%	72%	54%	96%	63%	62%
Prices:High	45.34	54.74	49.24	48.31	45.49	49.50	47.70	47.13	41.31	44.69
Prices:Low	27.82	43.96	38.77	41.39	37.88	34.00	33.05	33.13	28.44	31.06
P/E Ratio:High	14	12	20	15	18	17	12	22	13	13
P/E Ratio:Low	9	10	16	13	15	12	9	15	9	9

Income Statement Analysis (Million $)	2008	2007	2006	2005	2004	2003	2002	2001	2000	1999
Revenue	9,329	8,506	9,022	9,022	7,114	7,041	6,749	7,849	5,597	4,728
Depreciation	899	932	1,014	869	744	687	759	795	758	735
Maintenance	NA	NA	NA	NA	NA	NA	NA	NA	NA	NA
Fixed Charges Coverage	2.63	1.55	1.82	1.21	1.35	1.49	2.00	2.04	2.42	2.60
Construction Credits	NA	NA	NA	NA	NA	NA	NA	NA	NA	NA
Effective Tax Rate	35.2%	31.5%	NM	NM	NM	24.0%	NM	NM	1.89%	11.0%
Net Income	526	787	437	576	443	480	632	329	468	483
S&P Core Earnings	275	266	512	374	344	542	463	322	NA	NA

Balance Sheet & Other Financial Data (Million $)	2008	2007	2006	2005	2004	2003	2002	2001	2000	1999
Gross Property	20,065	18,809	19,224	18,660	18,011	17,679	17,862	17,067	13,162	12,746
Capital Expenditures	1,373	1,299	1,403	1,065	904	751	984	1,096	749	739
Net Property	12,231	11,408	11,451	10,830	10,491	10,324	9,813	9,543	7,387	7,148
Capitalization:Long Term Debt	7,741	6,971	7,474	7,080	7,606	7,669	7,785	7,928	4,062	4,052
Capitalization:% Long Term Debt	56.4	54.4	56.1	55.1	57.8	59.2	63.0	63.0	50.3	50.9
Capitalization:Preferred	Nil	Nil	Nil	Nil	Nil	Nil	Nil	Nil	Nil	Nil
Capitalization:% Preferred	Nil	Nil	Nil	Nil	Nil	Nil	Nil	Nil	Nil	Nil
Capitalization:Common	5,995	5,853	5,849	5,769	5,548	5,287	4,565	4,657	4,015	3,909
Capitalization:% Common	43.6	45.6	43.9	44.9	42.2	40.8	37.0	37.0	49.7	49.1
Total Capital	15,833	14,804	14,950	14,468	13,429	14,256	13,434	14,063	9,878	9,886
% Operating Ratio	91.0	95.2	91.2	96.1	93.4	91.1	82.8	86.3	85.3	82.2
% Earned on Net Property	9.5	6.8	7.4	8.9	8.1	7.2	11.4	8.2	11.4	12.8
% Return on Revenue	5.6	9.3	4.8	6.4	6.2	6.8	9.4	4.2	8.4	10.2
% Return on Invested Capital	3.5	3.1	5.4	6.0	6.1	7.5	9.1	8.9	8.1	8.3
% Return on Common Equity	8.9	13.5	7.5	10.2	8.2	9.7	13.8	7.6	11.8	12.7

Data as orig reptd.; bef. results of disc opers/spec. items. Per share data adj. for stk. divs.; EPS diluted. E-Estimated. NA-Not Available. NM-Not Meaningful. NR-Not Ranked. UR-Under Review.

Office: One Energy Plaza, Detroit, MI 48226-1279.
Telephone: 313-235-4000.
Email: shareholdersvcs@dteenergy.com
Website: http://www.dteenergy.com

Chrmn & CEO: A.F. Earley, Jr.
Pres & COO: G.M. Anderson
EVP & CFO: D.E. Meador
SVP & General Counsel: B.D. Peterson

SVP & CIO: L. Ellyn
Investor Contact: L. Muschong (313-235-8505)
Board Members: G. M. Anderson, L. Bauder, A. F. Earley, Jr., W. F. Fountain, A. D. Gilmour, F. M. Hennessey, R. Inatome, J. E. Lobbia, G. J. McGovern, E. A. Miller, M. A. Murray, C. W. Pryor, Jr., J. Robles, Jr., R. G. Shaw, J. H. Vandenberghe

Founded: 1995
Domicile: Michigan
Employees: 10,471

Duke Energy Corp

STANDARD &POOR'S

| S&P Recommendation | HOLD ★★★☆☆ | Price $16.69 (as of Nov 27, 2009) | 12-Mo. Target Price $16.00 | Investment Style Large-Cap Value |

GICS Sector Utilities
Sub-Industry Electric Utilities

Summary DUK provides service to 3.9 million electric customers in North Carolina, South Carolina, Indiana, Ohio and Kentucky, and 500,000 gas customers in Kentucky and Ohio.

Key Stock Statistics (Source S&P, Vickers, company reports)

52-Wk Range	$16.83– 11.72	S&P Oper. EPS 2009E	1.20	Market Capitalization(B)	$21.774	Beta	0.37
Trailing 12-Month EPS	$0.82	S&P Oper. EPS 2010E	1.28	Yield (%)	5.75	S&P 3-Yr. Proj. EPS CAGR(%)	NA
Trailing 12-Month P/E	20.4	P/E on S&P Oper. EPS 2009E	13.9	Dividend Rate/Share	$0.96	S&P Credit Rating	A-
$10K Invested 5 Yrs Ago	NA	Common Shares Outstg. (M)	1,304.6	Institutional Ownership (%)	51		

Price Performance

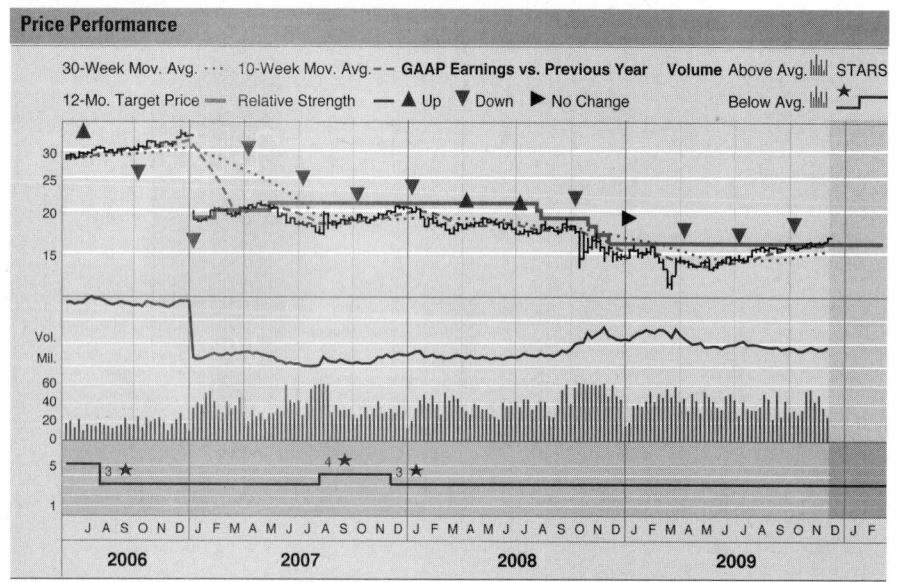

2006 2007 2008 2009

Options: ASE, CBOE, P, Ph

Analysis prepared by **Christopher B. Muir** on October 06, 2009, when the stock traded at **$ 15.59.**

Highlights

▶ We expect revenues to fall 4.5% in 2009, hurt by lower industrial volumes and the weak economy. At the unregulated power unit, we see lower prices, offset by increased availability. In 2010, we expect rate hikes in multiple jurisdictions at the utility to help boost revenues, which we believe will help to generate 2010 revenue growth of 3.5%.

▶ We forecast operating margins of 21.6% in 2009, up from 20.3% in 2008, as lower per-revenue fuel-related operating costs are partly offset by higher per-revenue operations & maintenance costs and depreciation expenses. We see operating margins widening to 22.4% in 2010. We project pretax margins of 18.7% in 2009 versus 17.4% in 2008, as we see higher interest expense more than offset by higher non-operating income. For 2010, we forecast pretax margins of 20.0%.

▶ Assuming an effective tax rate of 36.5%, we estimate 2009 recurring EPS of $1.20 up 2.6% from 2008 operating EPS of $1.17. EPS in 2009 excludes $0.02 in net non-recurring charges, while EPS in 2008 excludes $0.16. We see 2010 EPS rising 6.7%, to $1.28.

Investment Rationale/Risk

▶ We believe DUK's investments in its regulated business will allow its rate base to grow faster than depreciation, providing it with opportunities to raise rates. DUK's planned investments in its commercial renewable portfolio should complement its existing generating assets. We also like DUK's higher-growth Carolina service territories. While we view positively recent developments at the company, we believe the shares are fairly valued at recent levels.

▶ Risks to our recommendation and target price include lower electric margins, a higher-than-expected rise in interest rates, and unfavorable commodity price trends.

▶ DUK recently traded at 12.2X our 2010 EPS estimate, a 5% premium to its electric utility peers. Our 12-month target price of $16 is 12.5X our 2009 EPS projection, about even with our peer target. In our view, this valuation is warranted by what we see as earnings growth that is slower than peers, but a stronger than peers balance sheet. We also believe that DUK's relatively high dividend payout ratio will limit its ability to grow dividends faster than peers.

Qualitative Risk Assessment

| LOW | MEDIUM | HIGH |

Our risk assessment reflects DUK's large market capitalization and a balanced portfolio of businesses that include lower-risk regulated electric and gas utility services, partly offset by higher-risk unregulated businesses, although they make up less than 25% of the company's earnings.

Quantitative Evaluations

S&P Quality Ranking B

| D | C | B- | B | B+ | A- | A | A+ |

Relative Strength Rank STRONG

78

LOWEST = 1   HIGHEST = 99

Revenue/Earnings Data

Revenue (Million $)

	1Q	2Q	3Q	4Q	Year
2009	3,312	2,913	3,396	--	--
2008	3,337	3,229	3,508	3,133	13,207
2007	3,035	2,966	3,688	3,031	12,443
2006	3,106	3,865	4,143	4,070	15,184
2005	5,328	5,274	3,028	3,116	16,746
2004	5,635	5,318	5,504	6,046	22,503

Earnings Per Share ($)

	1Q	2Q	3Q	4Q	Year
2009	0.27	0.22	0.09	E0.30	E1.20
2008	0.37	0.27	0.17	0.21	1.01
2007	0.27	0.24	0.48	0.21	1.20
2006	0.50	0.34	0.60	0.31	1.70
2005	0.88	0.32	0.96	0.43	2.61
2004	0.07	0.43	0.42	0.36	1.27

Fiscal year ended Dec. 31. Next earnings report expected: Early February. EPS Estimates based on S&P Operating Earnings; historical GAAP earnings are as reported.

Dividend Data (Dates: mm/dd Payment Date: mm/dd/yy)

Amount ($)	Date Decl.	Ex-Div. Date	Stk. of Record	Payment Date
0.230	01/06	02/11	02/13	03/16/09
0.230	05/07	05/14	05/18	06/16/09
0.240	06/23	08/12	08/14	09/16/09
0.240	10/20	11/10	11/13	12/16/09

Dividends have been paid since 1926. Source: Company reports.

Please read the Required Disclosures and Analyst Certification on the last page of this report.

The McGraw-Hill Companies

Duke Energy Corp

STANDARD &POOR'S

Business Summary October 06, 2009

CORPORATE OVERVIEW. Duke provides electric and gas utility services, sells wholesale power, has investments in various South American generation plants, and owns 50% of a real estate joint venture. Operating segments include Franchised Electric and Gas, Commercial Power, Duke Energy International (DEI), and Crescent Resources.

MARKET PROFILE. Franchised Electric and Gas serves about 4 million electric customers over 47,000 square miles in North Carolina, South Carolina, Indiana, Ohio and Kentucky and about 500,000 gas customers in Kentucky and Ohio, and owns generating assets totaling 27,438 MW (49% coal; 20% natural gas, oil or other; 19% nuclear; and 12% hydro) as of December 2008. Electric sales in 2008 were 32% residential, 32% commercial, 26% industrial and 10% other.

The Commercial Power segment consists of 7,641 MW, mostly supporting regulated operations in Ohio. There are 5,813 MW located in Ohio, 640 MW in Illinois, 620 MW in Pennsylvania, 480 MW in Indiana, 59 MW in Texas and 29 MW in Wyoming. Commercial Power's fuel mix includes 49% natural gas, 46%

coal, 4% fuel oil, and 1% wind. DEI primarily consists of power generation (4,018 MW) in Central and South America. Crescent Resources develops and manages commercial, residential and multi-family real estate projects.

CORPORATE STRATEGY. We believe DUK has become an electric company focused on regulated operations and electric sales to regulated businesses. In September 2005, Duke began disposing a portion of its former wholesale power generation and marketing unit assets (9,860 net MW of generation capacity at 2004 year end) and contracts outside the Midwest. In March 2006, DUK purchased a Cincinnati-based electric distribution company; in September 2006, DUK sold 51% of Crescent Resources to Morgan Stanley; and in January 2007, the company spun-off its natural gas businesses to shareholders.

Company Financials Fiscal Year Ended Dec. 31

Per Share Data ($)	2008	2007	2006	2005	2004	2003	2002	2001	2000	1999
Tangible Book Value	12.25	12.55	13.54	13.65	12.54	10.74	12.51	14.11	11.21	10.69
Earnings	1.01	1.20	1.70	2.61	1.27	-1.13	1.22	2.56	2.38	1.13
S&P Core Earnings	0.82	1.22	1.80	1.29	1.24	-1.10	1.01	2.29	NA	NA
Dividends	0.90	0.86	0.95	1.17	1.10	1.10	1.10	1.10	1.10	1.10
Payout Ratio	89%	70%	56%	45%	87%	NM	90%	43%	46%	98%
Prices:High	20.60	21.30	34.50	30.55	26.16	21.57	40.00	47.74	45.22	32.66
Prices:Low	13.50	16.91	26.94	24.37	18.85	12.21	16.42	32.22	22.88	23.38
P/E Ratio:High	20	17	20	12	21	NM	33	19	19	29
P/E Ratio:Low	13	14	16	9	15	NM	13	13	10	21

Income Statement Analysis (Million $)	2008	2007	2006	2005	2004	2003	2002	2001	2000	1999
Revenue	13,207	12,720	15,184	16,746	22,503	22,529	15,663	59,503	49,318	21,742
Depreciation	1,670	1,746	2,049	1,728	1,851	1,803	1,571	1,336	1,167	968
Maintenance	NA	NA	NA	NA	NA	NA	NA	NA	NA	NA
Fixed Charges Coverage	3.61	4.03	2.77	2.91	2.40	1.96	2.46	5.33	4.25	3.16
Construction Credits	NA	NA	NA	NA	NA	NA	NA	53.0	63.0	82.0
Effective Tax Rate	32.6%	31.8%	28.8%	29.5%	27.5%	NM	35.1%	33.1%	32.9%	31.4%
Net Income	1,279	1,522	2,019	2,533	1,232	-1,005	1,034	1,994	1,776	847
S&P Core Earnings	1,041	1,551	2,131	1,249	1,199	-994	908	1,777	NA	NA

Balance Sheet & Other Financial Data (Million $)	2008	2007	2006	2005	2004	2003	2002	2001	2000	1999
Gross Property	50,304	46,056	58,330	40,574	46,806	47,157	48,677	39,464	34,615	30,436
Capital Expenditures	4,922	3,125	3,381	2,309	2,055	2,470	4,924	5,930	5,634	5,936
Net Property	34,036	31,110	41,447	29,200	33,506	34,986	36,219	28,415	24,469	20,995
Capitalization:Long Term Debt	13,250	9,498	18,118	14,547	16,932	20,622	21,629	13,728	12,425	10,087
Capitalization:% Long Term Debt	38.7	30.9	41.0	46.9	50.5	59.8	58.9	51.5	54.7	52.0
Capitalization:Preferred	Nil	Nil	Nil	Nil	134	134	157	234	247	313
Capitalization:% Preferred	Nil	Nil	Nil	Nil	0.40	0.39	0.43	0.88	1.09	1.61
Capitalization:Common	20,988	21,199	26,102	16,439	16,441	13,748	14,944	12,689	10,056	8,998
Capitalization:% Common	61.3	69.1	59.0	53.1	49.1	39.8	40.7	47.6	44.2	46.4
Total Capital	39,666	35,790	52,203	36,988	40,375	40,490	43,644	33,393	29,225	24,225
% Operating Ratio	85.7	86.0	87.6	89.6	88.6	85.4	87.1	95.0	94.3	93.8
% Earned on Net Property	7.8	6.9	9.0	11.5	8.9	NM	7.6	15.5	16.8	9.5
% Return on Revenue	9.7	12.0	13.3	15.1	5.5	NM	6.6	3.4	3.6	3.9
% Return on Invested Capital	5.5	4.7	7.5	11.1	7.0	8.7	6.3	10.5	11.2	7.6
% Return on Common Equity	6.1	6.4	9.5	15.3	8.1	NM	7.4	17.4	18.4	9.6

Data as orig reptd.; bef. results of disc opers/spec. items. Per share data adj. for stk. divs.; EPS diluted. E-Estimated. NA-Not Available. NM-Not Meaningful. NR-Not Ranked. UR-Under Review.

Office: 526 South Church Street, Charlotte, NC 28202-1904.
Telephone: 704-594-6200.
Website: http://www.duke-energy.com
Chrmn, Pres & CEO: J.E. Rogers

EVP & CIO: A.R. Mullinax
Investor Contact: S.G. De May ()
SVP & Treas: S.G. De May
SVP & Cntlr: S.K. Young

Board Members: W. Barnet, III, G. A. Bernhardt, M. G. Browning, D. R. DiMicco, J. H. Forsgren, Jr., A. M. Gray, J. H. Hance, Jr., E. J. Reinsch, J. T. Rhodes, J. E. Rogers, P. R. Sharp, D. S. Taft

Founded: 1917
Domicile: Delaware
Employees: 18,250

Dun & Bradstreet Corp (The)

STANDARD &POOR'S

S&P Recommendation **HOLD** ★★★☆☆	Price $78.67 (as of Nov 27, 2009)	12-Mo. Target Price $80.00	Investment Style Large-Cap Growth

GICS Sector Industrials
Sub-Industry Research & Consulting Services

Summary This company is a worldwide provider of business information and related decision support services and commercial receivables management services.

Key Stock Statistics (Source S&P, Vickers, company reports)

52-Wk Range	$84.76–68.13	S&P Oper. EPS 2009**E**	5.15	Market Capitalization(B)	$4.089	Beta	0.49
Trailing 12-Month EPS	$6.26	S&P Oper. EPS 2010**E**	6.20	Yield (%)	1.73	S&P 3-Yr. Proj. EPS CAGR(%)	8
Trailing 12-Month P/E	12.6	P/E on S&P Oper. EPS 2009**E**	15.3	Dividend Rate/Share	$1.36	S&P Credit Rating	A-
$10K Invested 5 Yrs Ago	$13,692	Common Shares Outstg. (M)	52.0	Institutional Ownership (%)	85		

Price Performance

- 30-Week Mov. Avg. · · · 10-Week Mov. Avg. – – GAAP Earnings vs. Previous Year Volume Above Avg. STARS
- 12-Mo. Target Price — Relative Strength ▲ Up ▼ Down ► No Change Below Avg.

Options: Ph

Analysis prepared by **Richard Tortoriello** on November 04, 2009, when the stock traded at **$ 77.88**.

Highlights

- We expect sales to fall 3% in 2009 to $1.7 billion, on a 1% decrease in revenue in North America and a 9% decline in the International segment. We believe that business conditions will remain difficult for the rest of 2009, as corporate and small-business budgets remain very tight. However, we project a 2% revenue increase in 2010, on our expectation of growth in both North America and Internationally.

- We look for operating margins to narrow in 2009, to 26.0% from 27.2% in 2008, as a decline in volume offsets significant business efficiency improvements. We believe that operating margin improvement has been a bright spot at DNB, with steady margin improvement over the past four years. We project an operating margin of over 27% in 2010.

- Excluding restructuring charges and one-time gains, we see 2009 EPS of $5.15, down from 2008's $5.32. We project EPS of $6.20 in 2010.

Investment Rationale/Risk

- We believe DNB's North American business will remain weak into 2010, as we project employment and corporate profits to recover only slowly in the U.S. and therefore expect DNB's customers to maintain tight budgets. We also see continued weakness among small businesses. We see DNB continuing to increase its presence internationally through investments, joint ventures and partnerships. We also expect the company to continue deploying free cash flow toward acquisitions, stock repurchases and dividends.

- Risks to our recommendation and target price include a stronger U.S. dollar depressing overseas profits, a deteriorating outlook for DNB's U.K. operations, and an inability by DNB to realize operating efficiencies from the company's business rationalization program.

- Our 12-month target price of $80 is based on an enterprise value to estimated 2010 EBITDA multiple of 9X, in line with DNB's 20-year historical average. We believe an average multiple is appropriate for the shares, given our view of good execution offset by weak end markets.

Qualitative Risk Assessment

LOW	MEDIUM	HIGH

Our risk assessment reflects DNB's global business database and proprietary identification system, which we think provides a competitive advantage, and DNB's notable record of continuous EPS growth, notwithstanding a slightly uncertain regulatory outlook for the ability to collect and use data.

Quantitative Evaluations

S&P Quality Ranking B+

D	C	B-	B	B+	A-	A	A+

Relative Strength Rank MODERATE

56

LOWEST = 1   HIGHEST = 99

Revenue/Earnings Data

Revenue (Million $)

	1Q	2Q	3Q	4Q	Year
2009	407.4	416.9	399.0	--	--
2008	414.7	427.7	409.2	474.7	1,726
2007	379.0	380.8	374.7	464.7	1,599
2006	367.2	367.4	359.2	437.5	1,531
2005	341.3	351.7	341.6	409.0	1,444
2004	343.4	349.9	333.2	387.5	1,414

Earnings Per Share ($)

2009	1.94	1.43	1.02	E1.48	E5.15
2008	1.05	1.51	1.18	1.85	5.58
2007	0.86	1.44	0.93	1.68	4.90
2006	0.75	0.79	0.72	1.46	3.70
2005	0.73	0.67	0.46	1.32	3.19
2004	0.66	0.54	0.65	1.04	2.90

Fiscal year ended Dec. 31. Next earnings report expected: Late January. EPS Estimates based on S&P Operating Earnings; historical GAAP earnings are as reported.

Dividend Data (Dates: mm/dd Payment Date: mm/dd/yy)

Amount ($)	Date Decl.	Ex-Div. Date	Stk. of Record	Payment Date
0.340	01/28	03/04	03/06	03/20/09
0.340	05/06	05/27	05/29	06/15/09
0.340	08/06	08/27	08/31	09/14/09
0.340	11/10	11/24	11/27	12/11/09

Dividends have been paid since 2007. Source: Company reports.

Please read the Required Disclosures and Analyst Certification on the last page of this report.

Dun & Bradstreet Corp (The)

**STANDARD
&POOR'S**

Business Summary November 04, 2009

CORPORATE OVERVIEW. Dun & Bradstreet (DNB) is a leading worldwide provider of business information and related decision support services. DNB believes it has the world's largest global business database, with over 140 million business records.

DNB operates its business through four customer solution sets: Risk Management Solutions (64% of 2008, 64% of 2007 revenues) (Risk Management includes Supply Management as of January 1, 2008), Sales and Marketing Solutions (29%, 29%), and Internet Solutions (7%, 7%). Sales in North America accounted for 77% of 2008 revenues and 78% of 2007 revenues, while the remaining 23% in 2008 and 22% in 2007 came from DNB's overseas presence, including strategic partner relationships and minority equity investments.

Risk Management Solutions helps clients extend commercial credit, set credit limits, and determine total credit risk exposure. It aims to help clients increase cash flow and profitability while minimizing operational, credit, and regulatory risk. Within this customer solution set, DNB offers traditional and what it considers value-added products. Traditional products (75% of segment revenue in 2008) consist of reports from DNB's database used primarily for making decisions about new credit applications. Value-added products generally support automated decision making and portfolio management through the use of scoring and integrated software solutions.

The Supply Management Solutions set helps customers understand their supplier base, rationalize their supplier rosters, leverage buying power, minimize supply-related risks, and identify and evaluate new sources of supply. Starting in January 2008, DNB started managing its Supply Management business as part of its Risk Management Solutions business.

Sales and Marketing Solutions helps customers conduct market segmentation, maintain updated customer relationship management systems, and offers client profiling, prospect selection and marketing list development. Traditional products (40% of segment revenue in 2008) generally consist of marketing lists, labels and customized data files used by DNB's customers in their direct mail and marketing activities. Value-added products primarily include decision making and customer information management solutions.

Internet Solutions represents the results of Hoover's, Inc., which DNB acquired in 2003, and AllBusiness.com. Hoover's provides information on public and private companies, primarily to senior executives and sales professionals, using a proprietary database.

Company Financials Fiscal Year Ended Dec. 31

Per Share Data ($)	2008	2007	2006	2005	2004	2003	2002	2001	2000	1999
Tangible Book Value	NM	NM	NM	NM	NM	NM	NM	NM	NM	NA
Cash Flow	5.93	5.19	4.21	3.71	3.54	3.15	2.96	3.02	2.25	1.33
Earnings	5.58	4.90	3.70	3.19	2.90	2.30	1.87	1.88	0.90	0.55
S&P Core Earnings	4.28	4.66	3.69	2.83	2.14	1.97	0.63	0.07	NA	NA
Dividends	1.20	1.00	Nil	Nil	Nil	Nil	Nil	Nil	Nil	NA
Payout Ratio	22%	20%	Nil	Nil	Nil	Nil	Nil	Nil	Nil	NA
Prices:High	98.90	108.45	84.98	68.00	60.80	50.81	43.40	36.90	27.00	NA
Prices:Low	64.00	81.50	65.03	54.90	47.85	32.31	28.26	20.99	13.00	NA
P/E Ratio:High	18	22	23	21	21	22	23	20	30	NA
P/E Ratio:Low	11	17	18	17	16	14	15	11	14	NA

Income Statement Analysis (Million $)										
Revenue	1,726	1,599	1,531	1,444	1,414	1,386	1,276	1,309	1,418	1,408
Operating Income	521	469	461	431	398	373	371	344	355	330
Depreciation	19.6	17.9	33.3	36.1	47.3	64.0	84.2	94.5	111	128
Interest Expense	47.4	28.3	20.3	21.1	18.9	18.6	19.5	16.4	8.60	Nil
Pretax Income	440	428	389	355	341	281	238	260	174	159
Effective Tax Rate	29.1%	31.8%	37.7%	37.7%	37.9%	37.8%	39.6%	38.9%	44.9%	43.7%
Net Income	310	293	241	221	212	175	143	153	73.6	89.5
S&P Core Earnings	238	278	240	197	156	151	48.5	6.51	NA	NA

Balance Sheet & Other Financial Data (Million $)										
Cash	164	176	138	305	336	239	192	145	70.1	54.8
Current Assets	696	718	645	759	762	731	614	580	539	496
Total Assets	1,586	1,659	1,360	1,613	1,636	1,625	1,528	1,431	1,424	1,428
Current Liabilities	908	910	806	1,029	714	736	718	663	743	697
Long Term Debt	904	725	459	0.10	300	300	300	300	Nil	Nil
Common Equity	-856	-440	-399	77.6	54.2	48.4	-18.8	-20.9	-51.0	9.10
Total Capital	53.7	288	62.4	77.7	354	348	281	280	251	312
Capital Expenditures	11.8	13.7	11.6	5.70	12.1	11.0	15.8	16.2	24.1	NA
Cash Flow	329	311	274	257	259	239	228	248	185	218
Current Ratio	0.8	0.8	0.8	0.7	1.1	1.0	0.9	0.9	0.7	0.7
% Long Term Debt of Capitalization	NM	251.4	NM	0.1	84.7	86.1	106.7	107.0	Nil	Nil
% Net Income of Revenue	17.9	18.3	15.7	15.3	15.0	12.6	11.2	11.7	5.2	6.4
% Return on Assets	19.1	19.4	16.2	13.6	13.0	11.1	9.6	10.7	4.9	NA
% Return on Equity	NM	NM	NM	335.7	412.9	1179.1	NM	NM	NM	NM

Data as orig reptd.; bef. results of disc opers/spec. items. Per share data adj. for stk. divs.; EPS diluted. E-Estimated. NA-Not Available. NM-Not Meaningful. NR-Not Ranked. UR-Under Review.

Office: 103 J F K Pkwy, Short Hills, NJ 07078-2708.
Telephone: 973-921-5500.
Website: http://www.dnb.com
Chrmn & CEO: S.W. Alesio

Pres & COO: S. Mathew
SVP & CFO: A.G. Konidaris
SVP, Secy & General Counsel: J.S. Hurwitz
CTO & CIO: W.S. Hauck, III

Investor Contact: R. Veldran (973-921-5863)
Board Members: A. A. Adams, A. Al Mazrui, J. W. Alden, S. W. Alesio, C. J. Coughlin, J. N. Fernandez, J. Judge, S. Mathew, V. A. Pelson, S. E. Peterson, M. R. Quinlan, N. Seligman, M. J. Winkler

Founded: 2000
Domicile: Delaware
Employees: 4,900

The McGraw-Hill Companies

STANDARD &POOR'S

E. I. du Pont de Nemours and Co

S&P Recommendation SELL ★★☆☆☆	Price $34.40 (as of Nov 27, 2009)	12-Mo. Target Price $20.00	Investment Style Large-Cap Value

GICS Sector Materials
Sub-Industry Diversified Chemicals

Summary This broadly diversified company is the second largest U.S. chemicals manufacturer.

Key Stock Statistics (Source S&P, Vickers, company reports)

52-Wk Range	$35.35–16.05	S&P Oper. EPS 2009**E**	2.00	Market Capitalization(B)	$31.088	Beta	1.41
Trailing 12-Month EPS	$0.74	S&P Oper. EPS 2010**E**	2.20	Yield (%)	4.77	S&P 3-Yr. Proj. EPS CAGR(%)	8
Trailing 12-Month P/E	46.5	P/E on S&P Oper. EPS 2009**E**	17.2	Dividend Rate/Share	$1.64	S&P Credit Rating	A
$10K Invested 5 Yrs Ago	$9,208	Common Shares Outstg. (M)	903.7	Institutional Ownership (%)	64		

Price Performance

30-Week Mov. Avg. · · · 10-Week Mov. Avg. - - **GAAP Earnings vs. Previous Year** Volume Above Avg. STARS
12-Mo. Target Price — Relative Strength — ▲ Up ▼ Down ► No Change Below Avg.

Options: ASE, CBOE, P, Ph

Analysis prepared by **Richard O'Reilly, CFA** on October 21, 2009, when the stock traded at **$ 33.87**.

Highlights

► We expect sales in late 2009 and early 2010 to be higher after sharp declines in the respective year-earlier periods, reflecting recovering global demand in DD's chemicals segments and favorable currency exchange rates. In our view, selling prices will be relatively stable in the near term, excluding pass-throughs of changes in metal and commodity prices. We expect raw material and energy costs to have bottomed in the third quarter of 2009 but to stay below 2008's high levels.

► We think the agriculture segment's sales and profits will continue to grow in 2010. Pharmaceutical profits are expected to be modestly higher in 2009 before declining in 2010 following the scheduled expiration of U.S. patents for Cozaar/Hyzaar.

► In 2009, we expect DD's expanded cost reduction program initiated in late 2008 to achieve $1 billion in savings, partly offset by about $0.40 a share of greater pension expense and a $0.36 adverse impact from currency. Currency impacts should be favorable in the fourth quarter. Our 2009 EPS estimate excludes a second-quarter $0.15 net restructuring charge.

Investment Rationale/Risk

► We have a sell opinion on the shares based on valuation. While DD reported better-than-expected EPS for the third quarter of 2009, aided by cost reductions, we expect it to continue to face headwinds from downturns in the global industrial, construction and auto markets, and lower pharmaceutical profits in 2010.

► Risks to our opinion and target price include better-than-expected global industrial activity, lower raw material costs than we assume, a greater increase in marketshare for corn seeds, and an ability to more quickly and successfully develop and launch new products.

► The stock recently traded at a P/E ratio of 15.4X our 2010 EPS estimate of $2.20, just below the P/E of a group of peer diversified chemical companies. Based on our 2010 EPS estimate and assuming a 14X P/E multiple, 12% below peers due to the challenging outlook we foresee including lower pharmaceutical profits beginning in 2010, our 12-month target price is $30.

Qualitative Risk Assessment

LOW	MEDIUM	HIGH

Our risk assessment reflects the company's diverse business and geographic sales mix and its leadership positions in key products, offset by the cyclical nature of the chemical industry and the volatility of raw material costs.

Quantitative Evaluations

S&P Quality Ranking B

D	C	B-	B	B+	A-	A	A+

Relative Strength Rank STRONG

74

LOWEST = 1   HIGHEST = 99

Revenue/Earnings Data

Revenue (Million $)

	1Q	2Q	3Q	4Q	Year
2009	7,270	7,088	6,156	--	--
2008	8,575	8,837	7,297	5,820	31,836
2007	7,845	7,875	6,675	6,983	29,378
2006	7,394	7,442	6,309	6,276	27,421
2005	7,431	7,511	5,870	5,827	26,639
2004	8,073	7,527	5,740	6,000	27,340

Earnings Per Share ($)

2009	0.54	0.46	0.45	E0.40	E2.00
2008	1.31	1.18	0.40	-0.70	2.20
2007	1.01	1.04	0.56	0.60	3.22
2006	0.88	1.04	0.52	0.94	3.38
2005	0.96	1.01	-0.09	0.16	2.07
2004	0.66	0.50	0.33	0.28	1.77

Fiscal year ended Dec. 31. Next earnings report expected: Late January. EPS Estimates based on S&P Operating Earnings; historical GAAP earnings are as reported.

Dividend Data (Dates: mm/dd Payment Date: mm/dd/yy)

Amount ($)	Date Decl.	Ex-Div. Date	Stk. of Record	Payment Date
0.410	01/21	02/11	02/13	03/13/09
0.410	04/21	05/13	05/15	06/12/09
0.410	07/28	08/12	08/14	09/11/09
0.410	10/21	11/10	11/13	12/14/09

Dividends have been paid since 1904. Source: Company reports.

Please read the Required Disclosures and Analyst Certification on the last page of this report.

The **McGraw-Hill** Companies

E. I. du Pont de Nemours and Co

STANDARD &POOR'S

Business Summary October 21, 2009

E.I. du Pont de Nemours and Company, the second largest domestic chemicals producer, has made several major changes in recent years, including expanding its life sciences businesses (now crop pesticides and nutrition). Foreign sales accounted for 64% of the total in 2008.

The Agricultural and Nutrition segment (26% of sales in 2008, and 30% of pretax operating income) consists of Pioneer Hi-Bred (50% of segment sales in 2008), the world's largest seed company, including corn (70% of sales) and soybeans; DuPont is also a major global supplier of crop protection chemicals (33%). The segment also includes nutrition and health (including the Solae soy business and food packaging products) and microbial diagnostic testing products. Segment sales rose 16% in 2008 and profits climbed 22%, reflecting gains in both seeds and crop protection products.

The Coatings and Color Technologies unit (21%, 9%) is one of the largest global auto paint suppliers (including OEM and refinish markets) and the largest maker of titanium dioxide pigments (34% of segment sales). The segment also includes industrial and powder coatings, and inks for digital printing. Segment

volume declined 8% in 2008 due to lower sales to automotive OEMs in North America and Europe and lower demand for titanium dioxide, partially offset by strong sales in emerging markets.

The Electronic and Communication Technologies segment (13%, 12%) includes electronic and advanced display materials and products (photoresins, slurries, films, laminants), and flexographic printing and proofing systems. DD is the world's largest maker of fluorochemicals (refrigerants, blowing agents, aerosols) and fluoropolymers (Teflon resins and coatings).

Performance Materials (21%, 3%) includes engineering polymers for auto, electrical, consumer and industrial uses; packaging and industrial polymers; polyester films; and elastomers.

Company Financials Fiscal Year Ended Dec. 31

Per Share Data ($)	2008	2007	2006	2005	2004	2003	2002	2001	2000	1999
Tangible Book Value	2.26	6.64	4.56	4.24	6.25	4.63	4.54	7.30	4.50	3.72
Cash Flow	3.79	4.70	4.49	3.45	3.11	2.58	3.35	5.83	3.96	1.73
Earnings	2.20	3.22	3.38	2.07	1.77	0.99	1.84	4.15	2.19	0.19
S&P Core Earnings	0.74	2.93	2.98	1.98	2.00	1.14	0.40	-1.04	NA	NA
Dividends	1.64	1.52	1.48	1.46	1.40	1.40	1.40	1.40	1.40	1.40
Payout Ratio	75%	47%	44%	71%	79%	141%	76%	34%	64%	NM
Prices:High	52.49	53.90	49.68	54.90	49.39	46.00	49.80	49.88	74.00	75.19
Prices:Low	21.32	42.25	38.52	37.60	39.88	38.60	35.02	32.64	38.19	50.06
P/E Ratio:High	24	17	15	27	28	46	27	12	34	NM
P/E Ratio:Low	10	13	11	18	23	39	19	8	17	NM

Income Statement Analysis (Million $)	2008	2007	2006	2005	2004	2003	2002	2001	2000	1999
Revenue	31,836	29,378	27,421	26,639	27,340	26,996	24,006	24,726	28,268	26,918
Operating Income	4,796	4,269	3,612	3,507	3,574	3,176	4,263	4,130	5,244	5,469
Depreciation	1,444	1,371	1,384	1,358	1,347	1,584	1,515	1,754	1,860	1,690
Interest Expense	425	430	460	518	362	347	359	590	810	535
Pretax Income	2,391	3,743	3,329	3,558	1,442	143	2,124	6,844	3,447	1,690
Effective Tax Rate	15.9%	20.0%	5.89%	41.3%	NM	NM	8.71%	36.0%	31.1%	83.4%
Net Income	2,007	2,988	3,148	2,053	1,780	1,002	1,841	4,328	2,314	219
S&P Core Earnings	677	2,713	2,768	1,965	2,008	1,132	398	-1,087	NA	NA

Balance Sheet & Other Financial Data (Million $)	2008	2007	2006	2005	2004	2003	2002	2001	2000	1999
Cash	3,704	1,436	1,893	1,851	3,536	3,298	4,143	5,848	1,617	1,582
Current Assets	15,311	13,160	12,870	12,422	15,211	18,462	13,459	14,801	11,656	12,653
Total Assets	36,209	34,131	31,777	33,250	35,632	37,039	34,621	40,319	39,426	40,777
Current Liabilities	9,710	8,541	7,940	7,463	7,939	13,043	7,096	8,067	9,255	11,228
Long Term Debt	7,638	5,955	6,013	6,783	5,548	4,301	5,647	5,350	6,658	6,625
Common Equity	6,888	10,899	9,185	8,670	11,140	9,544	8,826	14,215	13,062	12,638
Total Capital	15,330	18,335	16,145	17,346	19,001	15,087	18,755	24,916	22,442	21,677
Capital Expenditures	1,978	1,585	1,532	1,340	1,232	1,713	1,280	1,494	1,925	2,055
Cash Flow	3,441	4,349	4,532	3,411	3,117	2,576	3,346	6,072	4,164	1,899
Current Ratio	1.6	1.5	1.6	1.7	1.9	1.4	1.9	1.8	1.3	1.1
% Long Term Debt of Capitalization	49.8	32.5	37.2	39.1	29.2	28.5	30.1	21.5	29.7	30.6
% Net Income of Revenue	6.3	10.2	11.5	7.7	6.5	3.7	7.7	17.5	8.2	0.8
% Return on Assets	5.7	9.1	9.7	6.0	4.9	2.8	4.9	10.9	5.8	0.6
% Return on Equity	22.6	29.7	35.2	20.6	17.1	10.8	15.9	31.7	17.9	1.6

Data as orig reptd.; bef. results of disc opers/spec. items. Per share data adj. for stk. divs.; EPS diluted. Beginning in 2008 revenues include other income. E-Estimated. NA-Not Available. NM-Not Meaningful. NR-Not Ranked. UR-Under Review.

Office: 1007 Market Street, Wilmington, DE 19898.
Telephone: 302-774-1000.
Email: info@dupont.com
Website: http://www.dupont.com

Chrmn: C.O. Holliday, Jr.
Pres & CEO: E.J. Kullman
SVP & CFO: N.C. Fanandakis
SVP, CSO & CTO: U. Chowdhry

SVP & General Counsel: T.L. Sager
Investor Contact: K. Fletcher (800-441-7515)
Board Members: S. W. Bodman, III, R. H. Brown, R. A. Brown, B. P. Collomb, C. J. Crawford, A. M. Cutler, J. T. Dillon, M. A. Hewson, C. O. Holliday, Jr., L. D. Juliber, E. J. Kullman, T. D. Pont, II, W. K. Reilly, E. I. du Pont, II

Founded: 1802
Domicile: Delaware
Employees: 60,000

Dynegy Inc.

STANDARD &POOR'S

S&P Recommendation BUY ★★★★☆	Price $1.82 (as of Nov 27, 2009)	12-Mo. Target Price $3.00	Investment Style Large-Cap Value

GICS Sector Utilities
Sub-Industry Independent Power Producers & Energy Traders

Summary This company generates and sells wholesale power from plants located primarily in the U.S. Midwest, Northeast, and South.

Key Stock Statistics (Source S&P, Vickers, company reports)

52-Wk Range	$2.80– 1.00	S&P Oper. EPS 2009**E**	-0.23	Market Capitalization(B)	$0.920	Beta	1.59
Trailing 12-Month EPS	$-1.07	S&P Oper. EPS 2010**E**	0.06	Yield (%)	Nil	S&P 3-Yr. Proj. EPS CAGR(%)	5
Trailing 12-Month P/E	NM	P/E on S&P Oper. EPS 2009**E**	NM	Dividend Rate/Share	Nil	S&P Credit Rating	NA
$10K Invested 5 Yrs Ago	$3,106	Common Shares Outstg. (M)	845.6	Institutional Ownership (%)	72		

Price Performance

30-Week Mov. Avg. ··· 10-Week Mov. Avg. – – **GAAP Earnings vs. Previous Year** Volume Above Avg. STARS
12-Mo. Target Price — Relative Strength — ▲ Up ▼ Down ▶ No Change Below Avg. ★

Options: ASE, CBOE, P, Ph

Analysis prepared by **Christopher B. Muir** on October 08, 2009, when the stock traded at **$ 2.45**.

Highlights

▶ DYN's agreement to sell power plants to LS Power for $615 million in cash and 245 million class B DYN shares should help DYN increase liquidity to $3.0 billion, including $1.9 billion in cash; in our view, more than adequate to cover upcoming debt maturities and cash flow needs. We also expect Dynegy to remain in compliance with debt covenants. We see revenues falling 17% in 2009 and 4.6% in 2010.

▶ We look for operating margins of 10.3% in 2009, down from 11.7% in 2008, as we expect higher per-revenue operations & maintenance costs and depreciation & amortization expense, partly offset by lower per-revenue fuel costs. We see pretax margins of -2.7% in 2009, versus 0.7% in 2008, helped by declining interest expense. We see operating margins of 13.1% and pretax margins of 0.9% in 2010.

▶ We project a 2009 recurring loss per share of $0.16, which excludes $1.07 in nonrecurring charges, compared to recurring EPS of $0.23 in 2008, which excludes $0.02 in nonrecurring charges. Our 2010 EPS estimate is $0.14. Excluding mark-to-market, we expect a loss per share of $0.13 in 2009 and EPS $0.04 in 2010, versus EPS of $0.04 in 2008.

Investment Rationale/Risk

▶ We like DYN's predominantly gas fired power plant portfolio, which is weighted toward baseload and intermediate load generation. We see debt reduction efforts as temporarily stalled, as DYN aims to maintain its liquidity during the economic weakness. Due to the large amount of hedges that do not qualify for hedge accounting, we see a very volatile earnings stream due to mark-to-market accounting, but note that it has hedged 90% of its generation volumes through 2010. We also like DYN's new cost cutting efforts.

▶ Risks to our recommendation and target price include lower electricity demand. Also, the variability of sales volumes, fuel, and commodity prices and operational activities leads to less earnings visibility, in our opinion.

▶ The shares recently traded at 18.1X our 2010 EPS estimate, a large premium to peers. Our 12-month target price of $3.00 is 21.9X our 2010 EPS forecast, also a large premium to our peer target. We believe this valuation is warranted based on our view of faster than peers EPS growth beyond the current economic slowdown.

Qualitative Risk Assessment

LOW	MEDIUM	HIGH

Our risk assessment is based on Dynegy's significant exposure to cyclical power markets and volatile commodity markets for fuels that it uses to generate power.

Quantitative Evaluations

S&P Quality Ranking B-

D	C	B-	B	B+	A-	A	A+

Relative Strength Rank WEAK

14

LOWEST = 1   HIGHEST = 99

Revenue/Earnings Data

Revenue (Million $)

	1Q	2Q	3Q	4Q	Year
2009	904.0	493.0	673.0	--	--
2008	545.0	323.0	1,886	795.0	3,549
2007	505.0	828.0	1,046	724.0	3,103
2006	600.0	439.0	581.0	397.0	2,017
2005	462.0	459.0	770.0	622.0	2,313
2004	1,657	1,440	1,650	1,406	6,153

Earnings Per Share ($)

2009	-0.40	-0.42	-0.10	E-0.13	E-0.23
2008	-0.18	-0.32	0.72	0.01	0.20
2007	0.03	Nil	0.11	-0.07	0.15
2006	-0.01	-0.48	-0.14	-0.12	-0.80
2005	-0.71	-0.30	-0.05	-0.98	-2.13
2004	0.14	Nil	0.16	-0.47	-0.09

Fiscal year ended Dec. 31. Next earnings report expected: Late February. EPS Estimates based on S&P Operating Earnings; historical GAAP earnings are as reported.

Dividend Data

No cash dividends have been paid since 2002.

Please read the Required Disclosures and Analyst Certification on the last page of this report.

The McGraw·Hill Companies

Dynegy Inc.

STANDARD
&POOR'S

Business Summary October 08, 2009

CORPORATE OVERVIEW. At the end of 2008, DYN owned or leased 17,849 net megawatts (MW) of generating capacity. The company provides energy, capacity and ancillary services primarily through bilateral negotiated contracts with third parties and into regional central markets. The power generation business consists of three segments -- the Midwest (8,265 MW), the West (5,775 MW), and the Northeast (3,809 MW). About 78% of DYN's generation capacity is gas-fired, 20% is coal-fired, and 2% is oil-fired. About 14% of its capacity can be switched to alternate fuels, including gas or oil. In terms of dispatch type, about 20% is base load generation, 34% is intermediate, and 46% is peaking.

By 2006, DYN had completed the fuel conversion of all its Midwest coal generation facilities to exclusively burn Powder River Basin (PRB) coal. PRB coal is a cleaner-burning coal with lower sulfur content, making it more economic to burn while emitting lower amounts of sulfur dioxide. DYN believes the conversion to PRB coal and attendant upgrades to new equipment and technologies will allow its units to improve operating margins and reliability.

CORPORATE STRATEGY. Dynegy has sought to strengthen its balance sheet in the wake of credit, accounting, regulatory and operating difficulties that negatively affected the energy merchant industry in 2002 and 2003. The company

raised $389 million in cash from the sale or exchange of businesses and investments in 2006, versus $2.4 billion in 2005, $246 million in 2004, $72 million in 2003, and $1.58 billion in 2002. In recent years, however, the company gained the financial flexibility to make acquisitions, including Sithe Energies in 2005 and the mostly stock acquisition of LS Power's generation portfolio. But, we do not believe DYN can make any acquisitions in the current economic environment. Operationally, DYN aims to focus on operational excellence.

IMPACT OF MAJOR DEVELOPMENTS. In January 2005, DYN completed the acquisition of Sithe Energies for $135 million in cash and the assumption of $919 million of project debt. The acquisition included the 1,021 MW Independence power generation facility located near Scriba, NY, four natural gas-fired merchant facilities in New York, and four hydroelectric generation facilities in Pennsylvania. In addition, Dynegy acquired a 750 MW firm capacity sales agreement with Con Edison, which runs through 2014, and provides annual cash receipts of $100 million.

Company Financials Fiscal Year Ended Dec. 31

Per Share Data ($)	2008	2007	2006	2005	2004	2003	2002	2001	2000	1999
Tangible Book Value	4.32	4.26	3.86	5.58	4.87	5.04	4.57	8.85	6.49	4.03
Cash Flow	-0.01	0.59	-0.20	-1.06	0.64	-0.05	-4.00	3.23	2.71	1.22
Earnings	0.20	0.15	-0.80	-2.13	-0.09	1.30	-6.24	1.89	1.48	0.65
S&P Core Earnings	0.13	0.13	-0.68	-0.71	0.06	1.76	-1.96	0.73	NA	NA
Dividends	Nil	Nil	Nil	Nil	Nil	Nil	0.15	0.30	0.32	0.04
Payout Ratio	Nil	Nil	Nil	Nil	Nil	Nil	NM	16%	22%	5%
Prices:High	9.92	10.95	7.32	5.70	6.09	5.43	32.19	59.00	59.88	17.93
Prices:Low	1.50	6.47	4.50	3.21	3.40	1.13	0.49	20.00	17.12	7.34
P/E Ratio:High	50	73	NM	NM	NM	4	NM	31	40	27
P/E Ratio:Low	7	43	NM	NM	NM	1	NM	11	12	11

Income Statement Analysis (Million $)										
Revenue	3,549	3,103	2,017	2,313	6,153	5,787	5,553	42,242	29,445	15,430
Operating Income	-0.97	917	469	507	620	367	327	1,424	1,130	343
Depreciation	371	325	265	284	356	454	613	454	389	129
Interest Expense	0.34	399	382	389	480	509	374	259	251	78.2
Pretax Income	243	274	-526	-1,199	-74.0	-675	-2,546	977	791	243
Effective Tax Rate	NM	55.1%	NM	NM	NM	NM	NM	27.5%	33.0%	30.7%
Net Income	171	116	-358	-804	-10.0	-474	-1,955	646	501	152
S&P Core Earnings	112	106	-310	-274	27.6	734	-711	246	NA	NA

Balance Sheet & Other Financial Data (Million $)										
Cash	718	432	371	1,549	628	496	774	218	86.0	45.2
Current Assets	5.10	1,663	2,082	3,706	2,752	3,030	7,586	9,507	10,150	2,805
Total Assets	14,213	13,221	7,630	10,126	9,852	13,293	20,030	24,874	21,406	6,525
Current Liabilities	6.50	999	1,259	2,116	1,802	2,576	6,748	8,555	9,405	2,539
Long Term Debt	6,072	5,939	3,190	4,228	4,332	5,893	5,666	3,854	3,174	1,499
Common Equity	4,515	4,506	2,267	2,153	1,867	2,045	2,087	4,719	3,613	1,234
Total Capital	11,723	11,718	5,926	7,326	7,302	9,221	10,062	12,694	8,214	3,144
Capital Expenditures	611	379	155	195	311	333	947	1,845	769	365
Cash Flow	-1.20	441	-102	-542	324	-20.0	-1,672	1,097	855	281
Current Ratio	1.7	1.7	1.7	1.8	1.5	1.2	1.1	1.1	1.1	1.1
% Long Term Debt of Capitalization	51.8	56.7	53.8	57.7	59.3	63.9	56.3	30.4	38.6	47.7
% Net Income of Revenue	NM	3.7	NM	NM	NM	NM	NM	1.5	1.7	1.0
% Return on Assets	1.3	1.1	NM	NM	NM	NM	NM	2.8	3.6	2.6
% Return on Equity	3.8	3.4	NM	NM	NM	NM	NM	15.5	19.2	13.2

Data as orig reptd.; bef. results of disc opers/spec. items. Per share data adj. for stk. divs.; EPS diluted. E-Estimated. NA-Not Available. NM-Not Meaningful. NR-Not Ranked. UR-Under Review.

Office: 1000 Louisiana Street, Houston, TX 77002-5050.
Telephone: 713-507-6400.
Email: ir@dynegy.com
Website: http://www.dynegy.com

Chrmn, Pres & CEO: B.A. Williamson
COO: L.A. Lednicky
EVP & CFO: H.C. Nichols
SVP, Chief Acctg Officer & Treas: C.J. Stone

SVP & Cntlr: T.A. McLauchlin
Investor Contact: N. Grossman (713-507-6466)
Board Members: J. Bartlett, D. W. Biegler, T. D. Clark, Jr., V. Grijalva, P. A. Hammick, F. E. Hardenbergh, G. L. Mazanec, M. Segal, H. B. Sheppard, W. L. Trubeck, B. A. Williamson

Founded: 1985
Domicile: Delaware
Employees: 2,000

The McGraw-Hill Companies

Eastman Chemical Co

STANDARD &POOR'S

S&P Recommendation	BUY ★★★★☆	Price $59.49 (as of Nov 27, 2009)	12-Mo. Target Price $70.00	Investment Style Large-Cap Value

GICS Sector Materials
Sub-Industry Diversified Chemicals

Summary This global company manufactures and markets chemicals, fibers and polyester plastics products used in consumer and industrial products.

Key Stock Statistics (Source S&P, Vickers, company reports)

52-Wk Range	$61.53– 17.76	S&P Oper. EPS 2009**E**	3.50	Market Capitalization(B)	$4.325	Beta	1.91
Trailing 12-Month EPS	$2.27	S&P Oper. EPS 2010**E**	4.00	Yield (%)	2.96	S&P 3-Yr. Proj. EPS CAGR(%)	10
Trailing 12-Month P/E	26.2	P/E on S&P Oper. EPS 2009**E**	17.0	Dividend Rate/Share	$1.76	S&P Credit Rating	BBB
$10K Invested 5 Yrs Ago	$13,151	Common Shares Outstg. (M)	72.7	Institutional Ownership (%)	82		

Price Performance

30-Week Mov. Avg. ···· 10-Week Mov. Avg. -- GAAP Earnings vs. Previous Year Volume Above Avg. STARS
12-Mo. Target Price — Relative Strength ▲ Up ▼ Down ► No Change Below Avg.

Options: ASE, CBOE, P, Ph

Analysis prepared by **Richard O'Reilly, CFA** on November 18, 2009, when the stock traded at **$ 59.44**.

Highlights

► We expect sales in 2009 to fall about 25%, primarily due to the economic slowdown and inventory reductions by customers early in the year. We expect sales and profits for most segments to improve in 2010 with the end of destocking. We expect EMN to retain more than half of the $200 million in cost savings achieved in 2009, but overall raw material and energy costs should be volatile after a sizable decrease in 2009.

► We expect the polyester resin business to have a large loss in the seasonally slower 2009 fourth quarter, in part due to a planned shutdown to solve operating issues at the new U.S. plant that was expanded by 50% in late 2008. We see the business turning profitable in 2010. We believe fiber profits in 2010 will remain at 2009's record level, despite start-up costs for a pending new tow plant in Asia.

► EMN will likely incur lower development costs in 2009 related to a coal gasification project. We expect the effective tax rate in 2010 to be about 35%, down from about 38% for 2009, which includes a reversal of a tax credit. Our EPS estimate for 2009 excludes a first quarter charge of $0.22.

Investment Rationale/Risk

► Our buy opinion reflects the favorable business outlook we see. EMN recently reported results for the third quarter that were better than it originally anticipated. We expect the coatings, specialty plastics and fibers segments (over 80% of annual profits) to grow over the long term, and we think the challenging domestic polyester resin business will turn profitable in 2010 as a result of expansion of the new plant technology.

► Risks to our recommendation and target price include the cyclical character of polyester resins, unplanned production outages and interruptions, possible greater-than-estimated asbestos liabilities, and higher-than-expected raw material costs.

► We expect EMN to generate more than $300 million of free cash flow in 2009, versus a deficit in 2008, and we believe the dividend, which recently provided an above-average yield of 3.0%, is secure. Applying a premium-to-peers multiple of 17.5X to our 2010 EPS estimate of $4.00 results in our 12-month target price of $70.

Qualitative Risk Assessment

LOW	MEDIUM	HIGH

Our risk assessment reflects the diverse business and geographic sales mix of the company, offset by the cyclical nature of the chemicals industry and the volatility of raw material costs.

Quantitative Evaluations

S&P Quality Ranking   **B**

D	C	B-	B	B+	A-	A	A+

Relative Strength Rank   **STRONG**

85

LOWEST = 1   HIGHEST = 99

Revenue/Earnings Data

Revenue (Million $)

	1Q	2Q	3Q	4Q	Year
2009	1,129	1,253	1,337	--	--
2008	1,727	1,834	1,819	1,346	6,726
2007	1,795	1,895	1,813	1,737	6,830
2006	1,803	1,929	1,966	1,752	7,450
2005	1,762	1,752	1,816	1,729	7,059
2004	1,597	1,676	1,649	1,658	6,580

Earnings Per Share ($)

2009	0.03	0.89	1.38	E1.00	E3.50
2008	1.45	1.49	1.33	-0.03	4.32
2007	0.91	1.22	0.24	1.25	3.83
2006	1.27	1.37	1.15	1.12	4.91
2005	2.00	2.51	1.50	0.81	6.81
2004	-0.07	1.07	0.49	0.68	2.18

Fiscal year ended Dec. 31. Next earnings report expected: Late January. EPS Estimates based on S&P Operating Earnings; historical GAAP earnings are as reported.

Dividend Data (Dates: mm/dd Payment Date: mm/dd/yy)

Amount ($)	Date Decl.	Ex-Div. Date	Stk. of Record	Payment Date
0.440	12/04	12/11	12/15	01/02/09
0.440	02/19	03/12	03/16	04/01/09
0.440	05/07	06/11	06/15	07/01/09
0.440	08/06	09/10	09/14	10/01/09

Dividends have been paid since 1994. Source: Company reports.

Please read the Required Disclosures and Analyst Certification on the last page of this report.

The McGraw·Hill Companies

Eastman Chemical Co

STANDARD &POOR'S

Business Summary November 18, 2009

CORPORATE OVERVIEW. Eastman Chemical Co. is a large global maker of a broad range of chemicals, plastics and fibers. International operations accounted for 41% of sales in 2008. It reports results in five segments.

The coatings, adhesive, specialty polymers and inks segment (23% of 2008 sales, operating profits of $202 million) is a leading supplier of alcohols and solvents used in coatings (60% of segment sales) and resins, dispersions and specialty polymers used in adhesives (40%).

Performance chemicals and intermediates (32%, $153 million) includes oxo chemicals, acetyls, plasticizers and glycols used for polymers, photographic and home care products, agricultural chemicals and pharmaceutical intermediates; and additives for food and beverage ingredients. The segment also included contract ethylene sales of $314 million under a supply agreement related to a former polyethylene business. About 75% of annual segment sales is generated in North America.

In the fibers business (15%, $238 million), EMN is one of the world's two largest suppliers of acetate cigarette filter tow and the leader in acetate yarn. The company projects global growth in demand for filter tow of 1%-2% annually through 2012, with Asia and Eastern Europe having the fastest growth rates. The business also includes acetyl chemicals (acetate flake, acetic anhydride).

The Performance polymers segment (16%, loss of $57 million) consists of polyethylene terephthalate (PET) resins and various intermediates. EMN in 2006 was the world's largest producer of polyester plastics, consisting of polyethylene terephthalate (PET), used for packaging applications and beverage containers such as soft-drink bottles, with annual PET capacity of 3.3 billion lbs. at year-end 2006. In 2007, EMN decided to close or sell its unprofitable polyester production sites outside the U.S.; in December 2007, it sold its two facilities in Latin America (sales of $413 million in 2007 and a loss of $127 million, including a restructuring charge of $115 million). EMN in late March 2008 sold its remaining two European plants (sales of $542 million in 2007, including from a plant in Spain sold in April 2007; reported as discontinued operations beginning in late 2007). Eastman's domestic operations had sales of $936 million in 2008 and a loss of $54 million. In early 2007, EMN completed the start-up of a new U.S. plant with annual capacity of 770 million lbs. using new IntegRex technology. EMN has closed 880 million lbs. of higher-cost domestic capacity and in late 2008 expanded the new plant by 50%. IntegRex now accounts for about 65% of EMN's U.S. PET capacity of 1.7 billion lbs.

Company Financials Fiscal Year Ended Dec. 31

Per Share Data ($)	2008	2007	2006	2005	2004	2003	2002	2001	2000	1999
Tangible Book Value	15.52	26.63	20.42	15.85	10.70	9.00	9.06	9.92	15.64	16.81
Cash Flow	7.68	6.97	8.64	10.50	6.23	1.22	6.18	3.33	9.36	5.46
Earnings	4.32	3.83	4.91	6.81	2.18	-3.54	1.02	-2.33	3.94	0.61
S&P Core Earnings	3.30	3.79	4.42	5.63	2.23	-3.45	0.26	-3.06	NA	NA
Dividends	1.76	1.76	1.76	1.76	1.76	1.76	1.76	1.76	1.76	1.76
Payout Ratio	41%	46%	36%	26%	81%	NM	173%	NM	45%	NM
Prices:High	78.29	72.44	61.29	61.80	58.17	39.57	49.55	55.65	54.75	60.31
Prices:Low	25.87	57.54	47.30	44.10	38.00	27.56	34.53	29.03	33.63	36.00
P/E Ratio:High	18	19	12	9	27	NM	49	NM	14	99
P/E Ratio:Low	6	15	10	6	17	NM	34	NM	9	59

Income Statement Analysis (Million $)	2008	2007	2006	2005	2004	2003	2002	2001	2000	1999
Revenue	6,726	6,830	7,450	7,059	6,580	5,800	5,320	5,384	5,292	4,590
Operating Income	805	929	981	1,092	696	590	610	755	989	663
Depreciation	256	264	308	304	322	367	397	435	418	383
Interest Expense	106	113	80.0	100	115	124	128	140	135	126
Pretax Income	429	470	576	783	64.0	-381	84.0	-297	452	72.0
Effective Tax Rate	23.5%	31.7%	29.0%	28.9%	NM	NM	5.95%	NM	33.0%	33.3%
Net Income	328	321	409	557	170	-273	79.0	-179	303	48.0
S&P Core Earnings	252	316	368	459	173	-266	20.4	-236	NA	NA

Balance Sheet & Other Financial Data (Million $)	2008	2007	2006	2005	2004	2003	2002	2001	2000	1999
Cash	387	888	939	524	325	558	77.0	66.0	101	186
Current Assets	1,423	2,293	2,422	1,924	1,768	2,010	1,529	1,458	1,523	1,489
Total Assets	5,281	6,009	6,173	5,773	5,872	6,230	6,273	6,086	6,550	6,303
Current Liabilities	832	1,122	1,059	1,051	1,099	1,477	1,224	958	1,258	1,608
Long Term Debt	1,442	1,613	1,589	1,621	2,061	2,089	2,054	2,143	1,914	1,506
Common Equity	1,553	2,082	2,029	1,612	1,184	1,913	1,271	1,378	1,812	2,521
Total Capital	3,008	3,917	3,618	3,550	3,455	4,318	3,809	3,973	4,333	4,512
Capital Expenditures	634	518	389	343	248	230	427	234	226	292
Cash Flow	584	585	717	861	492	94.0	476	256	721	431
Current Ratio	1.7	2.0	2.3	1.8	1.6	1.4	1.2	1.5	1.2	0.9
% Long Term Debt of Capitalization	47.9	42.4	43.9	45.7	59.7	48.4	53.9	53.9	44.2	33.4
% Net Income of Revenue	4.9	4.7	5.5	7.9	2.6	NM	1.5	NM	5.7	1.0
% Return on Assets	5.8	5.3	6.8	9.6	2.8	NM	1.3	NM	4.7	0.8
% Return on Equity	18.1	15.6	22.5	39.8	15.3	NM	6.0	NM	17.0	1.9

Data as orig reptd.; bef. results of disc opers/spec. items. Per share data adj. for stk. divs.; EPS diluted. E-Estimated. NA-Not Available. NM-Not Meaningful. NR-Not Ranked. UR-Under Review.

Office: 200 S Wilcox Dr, Kingsport, TN, USA 37660-5147.
Telephone: 423-229-2000.
Website: http://www.eastman.com
Chrmn: J.B. Ferguson

Pres & CEO: J.P. Rogers
SVP & CFO: C.E. Espeland
SVP & Chief Admin Officer: N.P. Sneed
SVP & CTO: G.W. Nelson

Investor Contact: G. Riddle (212-835-1620)
Board Members: G. E. Anderson, M. P. Connors, S. R. Demeritt, J. B. Ferguson, R. M. Hernandez, R. Hornbaker, L. M. Kling, H. L. Lance, T. H. McLain, D. W. Raisbeck, J. P. Rogers, P. M. Wood

Founded: 1920
Domicile: Delaware
Employees: 10,500

Eastman Kodak Co

STANDARD &POOR'S

S&P Recommendation BUY ★★★★☆	Price $4.08 (as of Nov 27, 2009)	12-Mo. Target Price $6.50	Investment Style Large-Cap Value

GICS Sector Consumer Discretionary
Sub-Industry Photographic Products

Summary This multinational company has a large presence in consumer, professional, and health imaging.

Key Stock Statistics (Source S&P, Vickers, company reports)

52-Wk Range	$7.71– 2.01	S&P Oper. EPS 2009**E**	-2.43	Market Capitalization(B)	$1.094	Beta	1.71
Trailing 12-Month EPS	$-5.85	S&P Oper. EPS 2010**E**	-0.40	Yield (%)	Nil	S&P 3-Yr. Proj. EPS CAGR(%)	NM
Trailing 12-Month P/E	NM	P/E on S&P Oper. EPS 2009**E**	NM	Dividend Rate/Share	Nil	S&P Credit Rating	B-
$10K Invested 5 Yrs Ago	$1,402	Common Shares Outstg. (M)	268.2	Institutional Ownership (%)	89		

Price Performance

30-Week Mov. Avg. · · · · 10-Week Mov. Avg. - - - **GAAP Earnings vs. Previous Year**   Volume Above Avg. |||| STARS
12-Mo. Target Price —— Relative Strength — ▲ Up ▼ Down ► No Change   Below Avg. |||| ★⌐

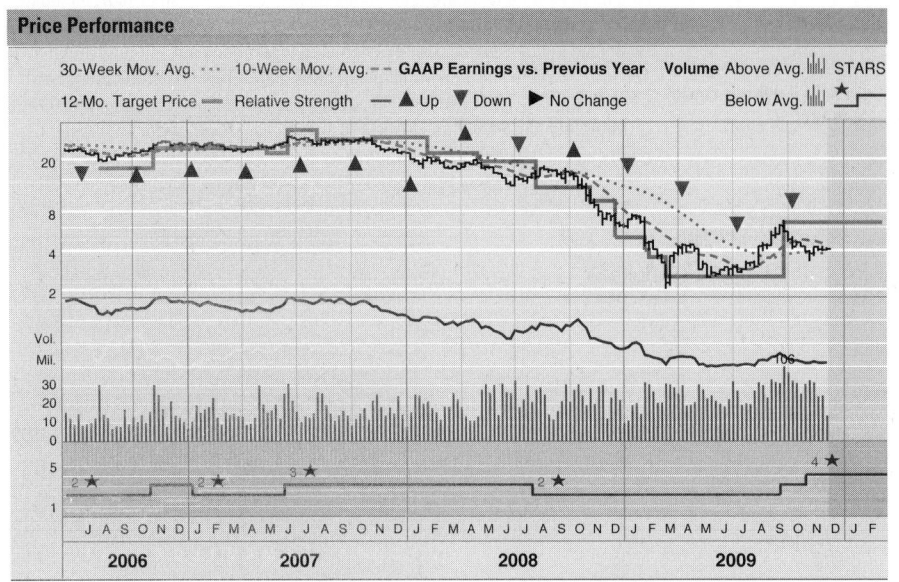

Options: ASE, CBOE, P, Ph

Analysis prepared by **Erik Kolb** on November 03, 2009, when the stock traded at **$ 3.73.**

Highlights

► We estimate revenue of $6.86 billion in 2009, down about 27% from 2008, and see a further 10% decline in 2010, as we project a sizable decrease in EK's traditional film market and a double-digit decline at the consumer digital imaging group on sharply lower global consumer demand. Although we believe revenues for the recently launched inkjet printer product line should ramp up, at this point, we are skeptical of management's near-term goals for the unit. We see a sizable decrease in graphic communications, as EK's digital plates and NEXPRESS commercial printing presses suffer from lower volumes.

► We see further challenges in EK's consumer digital imaging business in 2009. EK plans to cut 3,500-4,000 (14%-18%) positions in 2009, but we are skeptical whether this will be enough to offset top-line declines, and we see slightly lower EBITDA margins in 2009. In 2010, we see higher EBITDA margins as cost-cutting efforts take hold and the pace of revenue declines moderate.

► We estimate a $2.43 per share loss in 2009, compared to EPS of $0.19 in 2008. For 2010, we forecast a loss of $0.40 per share.

Investment Rationale/Risk

► We are encouraged by EK's comments that sales trends are rebounding from their worst levels. We believe EK has made modest progress in its shift toward a more digitally focused product line after completing a four-year, $3.4 billion, restructuring program, but we think the ultimate outcome remains in question. Looking ahead, we expect EK to have a narrower focus, including a greater profit dependence on consumer digital imaging and graphic communications, including new product lines such as ink-jet printers, areas we see having only modest margin growth potential.

► Risks to our recommendation and target price include a faster-than-anticipated decline in demand for traditional film product offerings, higher-than-forecast pricing pressure for digital products, failure of new product launches, and decreases in market share.

► Our 12-month target price of $6.50 reflects a 6.8X enterprise value-to-EBITDA multiple applied to a blend of our 2009 and 2010 estimates. This multiple is below EK's historical average, but we think it appropriately reflects our view of EK's shrinking profits and uncertain outlook.

Qualitative Risk Assessment

LOW	MEDIUM	HIGH

Our risk assessment is based on the company's ongoing shift toward digital photography. While we think EK has made progress in this endeavor, we are concerned about competitive threats and margin declines in this space.

Quantitative Evaluations

S&P Quality Ranking B-

D	C	B-	B	B+	A-	A	A+

Relative Strength Rank MODERATE

33

LOWEST = 1   HIGHEST = 99

Revenue/Earnings Data

Revenue (Million $)

	1Q	2Q	3Q	4Q	Year
2009	1,477	1,766	1,781	--	--
2008	2,093	2,485	2,405	2,433	9,416
2007	2,080	2,468	2,533	3,220	10,301
2006	2,889	3,360	3,204	3,821	13,274
2005	2,832	3,686	3,553	4,197	14,268
2004	2,919	3,469	3,364	3,765	13,517

Earnings Per Share ($)

2009	-1.34	-0.71	-0.41	E0.02	E-2.43
2008	-0.40	-0.67	0.35	-0.49	0.19
2007	-0.61	-0.53	0.11	0.28	-0.71
2006	-1.04	-0.98	-0.13	0.06	-2.09
2005	-0.49	-0.49	-3.62	-0.47	-5.05
2004	0.06	0.50	0.16	-0.06	0.28

Fiscal year ended Dec. 31. Next earnings report expected: Late January. EPS Estimates based on S&P Operating Earnings; historical GAAP earnings are as reported.

Dividend Data (Dates: mm/dd Payment Date: mm/dd/yy)

Amount ($)	Date Decl.	Ex-Div. Date	Stk. of Record	Payment Date
0.250	10/15	10/30	11/03	12/12/08
Div Suspended	04/30	04/30	--	04/30/09

Source: Company reports.

Please read the Required Disclosures and Analyst Certification on the last page of this report.

The McGraw-Hill Companies

Eastman Kodak Co

**STANDARD
&POOR'S**

Business Summary November 03, 2009

CORPORATE OVERVIEW. Eastman Kodak provides imaging technology products and services to the photographic and graphic communications markets. In 2008, the film products group accounted for 31.7% of net sales from continuing operations, compared to 35.3% in 2007, while consumer digital imaging represented 32.8% (31.5%), graphic communications 35.4% (33.1%), and other activities 0.1% (0.1%).

The consumer digital imaging group is a global provider of digital photography products and services for consumer markets. Offerings include digital products such as digital cameras and digital picture frames, retail printing, online imaging services, imaging sensors, and all-in-one printers. Kodak holds top three market shares in categories such as digital still cameras, retail printing, and digital picture frames. EK's strategy in this segment is to extend picture taking, picture search/organizing, creativity, sharing and printing to bring innovative new experiences to consumers.

The film products group is composed of traditional photographic products and services used to create motion pictures, and for consumer, professional and industrial imaging applications. The company manufactures and markets films

and one-time-use and re-loadable film cameras.

The graphic communications group serves a variety of customers in the creative, in-plant, data center, commercial printing, packaging, newspaper, and digital service bureau market segments with a range of software, media, and hardware products that provide customers with a variety of solutions for prepress equipment, workflow software, digital and traditional printing, document scanning, and multi-vendor IT services.

Through the years, EK has engaged in extensive and productive efforts in research and development. R&D expenses totaled $501 million (5.3% of sales) in 2008, compared to $535 million (5.2% of sales) in 2007, $578 million (5.5%) in 2006 and $739 million (6.5%) in 2005. The company also holds a portfolio of patents in several areas important to its business.

Company Financials Fiscal Year Ended Dec. 31

Per Share Data ($)	2008	2007	2006	2005	2004	2003	2002	2001	2000	1999
Tangible Book Value	NM	4.77	NM	NM	6.57	5.53	6.27	6.71	8.56	9.45
Cash Flow	-0.83	2.02	2.55	-0.18	3.88	3.72	5.52	3.42	7.48	7.19
Earnings	0.19	-0.71	-2.09	-5.05	0.28	0.83	2.72	0.26	4.59	4.33
S&P Core Earnings	-2.30	-1.58	-2.65	-4.93	-0.42	0.53	0.44	-1.86	NA	NA
Dividends	0.50	0.50	0.50	0.50	0.50	1.15	1.80	1.77	1.76	1.76
Payout Ratio	263%	NM	NM	NM	179%	139%	68%	NM	38%	41%
Prices:High	22.03	30.20	30.91	35.19	34.74	41.08	38.48	49.95	67.50	80.38
Prices:Low	5.93	21.42	18.93	20.77	24.25	20.39	25.58	24.40	35.31	56.63
P/E Ratio:High	NM	NM	NM	NM	NM	49	15	19	15	19
P/E Ratio:Low	NM	NM	NM	NM	NM	25	10	9	8	13

Income Statement Analysis (Million $)	2008	2007	2006	2005	2004	2003	2002	2001	2000	1999
Revenue	9,416	10,301	13,274	14,268	13,517	13,317	12,835	13,234	13,994	14,089
Operating Income	537	1,002	1,600	1,493	1,638	1,685	2,898	1,923	3,103	2,908
Depreciation	494	785	1,331	1,402	1,030	830	818	919	889	918
Interest Expense	108	113	262	211	168	148	173	219	178	142
Pretax Income	-89.0	-256	-346	-762	-92.0	196	946	97.0	2,132	2,109
Effective Tax Rate	NM	NM	NM	NM	NM	NM	16.1%	33.0%	34.0%	34.0%
Net Income	54.0	-205	-600	-1,455	81.0	238	793	76.0	1,407	1,392
S&P Core Earnings	-647	-453	-757	-1,419	-119	149	127	-541	NA	NA

Balance Sheet & Other Financial Data (Million $)	2008	2007	2006	2005	2004	2003	2002	2001	2000	1999
Cash	2,145	2,976	1,469	1,665	1,255	1,250	569	448	251	393
Current Assets	5,004	6,053	5,557	5,781	5,648	5,455	4,534	4,683	5,491	5,444
Total Assets	9,960	13,659	14,320	14,921	14,737	14,818	13,369	13,362	14,212	14,370
Current Liabilities	3,462	4,446	4,971	5,489	4,990	5,307	5,377	5,354	6,215	5,769
Long Term Debt	1,252	1,289	2,714	2,764	1,852	2,302	1,164	1,666	1,166	Nil
Common Equity	1,742	3,029	1,388	1,967	3,811	3,264	2,777	2,894	3,428	3,912
Total Capital	2,263	4,318	4,102	4,731	5,663	5,566	3,941	4,560	4,655	3,971
Capital Expenditures	254	259	379	472	460	506	577	743	945	1,127
Cash Flow	-233	580	731	-53.0	1,111	1,068	1,611	995	2,296	2,310
Current Ratio	1.5	1.4	1.1	1.1	1.1	1.0	0.8	0.9	0.9	0.9
% Long Term Debt of Capitalization	55.6	29.9	66.2	58.4	32.7	41.4	29.5	36.5	25.0	Nil
% Net Income of Revenue	0.6	NM	NM	NM	NM	1.8	6.2	0.6	10.1	9.9
% Return on Assets	0.5	NM	NM	NM	NM	1.7	5.9	0.6	9.8	9.6
% Return on Equity	2.3	NM	NM	NM	NM	7.9	27.9	2.4	38.3	35.2

Data as orig reptd.; bef. results of disc opers/spec. items. Per share data adj. for stk. divs.; EPS diluted. E-Estimated. NA-Not Available. NM-Not Meaningful. NR-Not Ranked. UR-Under Review.

Office: 343 State Street, Rochester, NY 14650.
Telephone: 585-724-4000.
Website: http://www.kodak.com
Chrmn & CEO: A.M. Perez

Pres & COO: P.J. Faraci
EVP & CFO: F.S. Sklarsky
SVP & General Counsel: J.P. Haag
CTO: T.R. Taber

Investor Contact: A.P. McCorvey
Board Members: R. Braddock, H. Y. Chen, A. H. Clammer, T. M. Donahue, M. Hawley, W. H. Hernandez, D. R. Lebda, D. L. Lee, D. Lewis, W. G. Parrett, A. M. Perez, J. Seligman, D. F. Strigl, L. D. Tyson

Founded: 1880
Domicile: New Jersey
Employees: 24,400

The McGraw-Hill Companies

Eaton Corp

STANDARD &POOR'S

S&P Recommendation BUY ★★★★☆	**Price** $64.27 (as of Nov 27, 2009)	**12-Mo. Target Price** $74.00	**Investment Style** Large-Cap Blend

GICS Sector Industrials
Sub-Industry Industrial Machinery

Summary This diversified industrial manufacturer's products include electrical systems and components for power management, truck transmissions and fluid power systems, and services for industrial, mobile and aircraft equipment.

Key Stock Statistics (Source S&P, Vickers, company reports)

52-Wk Range	$67.06– 30.02	S&P Oper. EPS 2009**E**	2.42	Market Capitalization(B)	$10.656	Beta	1.37
Trailing 12-Month EPS	$2.00	S&P Oper. EPS 2010**E**	3.92	Yield (%)	3.11	S&P 3-Yr. Proj. EPS CAGR(%)	9
Trailing 12-Month P/E	32.1	P/E on S&P Oper. EPS 2009**E**	26.6	Dividend Rate/Share	$2.00	S&P Credit Rating	A-
$10K Invested 5 Yrs Ago	$10,821	Common Shares Outstg. (M)	165.8	Institutional Ownership (%)	82		

Price Performance

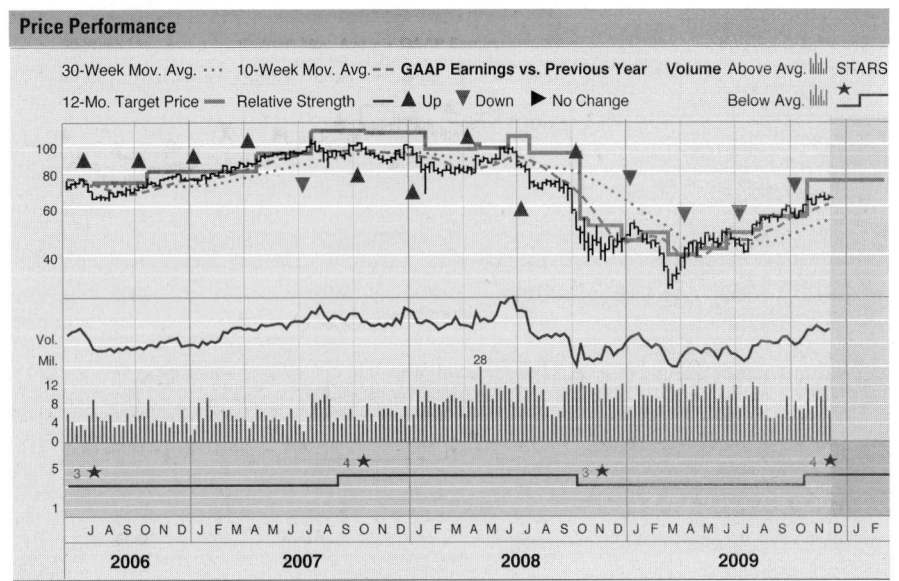

- 30-Week Mov. Avg. · · · ·
- 10-Week Mov. Avg. - -
- **GAAP Earnings vs. Previous Year**
- Volume Above Avg. | STARS
- 12-Mo. Target Price —
- Relative Strength —
- ▲ Up ▼ Down ► No Change
- Below Avg. |
- ★

Options: ASE, CBOE, P, Ph

Analysis prepared by **Mathew Christy, CFA** on October 19, 2009, when the stock traded at **$ 64.42**.

Highlights

- ► We expect 2009 sales to decrease nearly 23%, reflecting organic revenue declines across all of ETN's business units from the weak economy and negative effects of currency. This should only be partially offset by additional acquisition-related growth. Also, our forecast calls for 2009 NAFTA Class 8 truck volume to decline significantly from 2008 levels, and we see much lower car production negatively affecting results. In 2010, we project revenue to rise about 4.7%, and expect somewhat higher sales across ETN's segments.

- ► We look for operating margins to narrow significantly in 2009, as the benefits from ongoing expense reduction efforts are only partially offset by much lower operating leverage in the first half of 2009. Some of this decline should be offset by better third-quarter results and our forecast for better fourth-quarter operating rates. In 2010, we see better operating margins, due mainly to improved operating leverage.

- ► We project operating EPS of $2.42 for 2009 (excluding restructuring charges) and $3.92 in 2010, on higher interest and effective tax rates.

Investment Rationale/Risk

- ► We think ETN will post lower results in 2009 on weak world-wide economic growth and industrial activity. However, we are positive about ETN's efforts to obtain a better-balanced business portfolio that is less cyclical and capital-intensive and generates strong returns and cash flows. Also, we view positively ETN's ability to manage costs amid the decline in sales, and see it benefiting from an economic recovery that we believe began in the second half of 2009. We view the stock as attractively valued trading at about 16.5X our 2010 EPS estimate.

- ► Risks to our recommendation and target price include weaker economic growth, an inability to integrate recent acquisitions, and an adverse penalty ruling against ETN in ongoing antitrust litigation.

- ► Our 12-month target price of $74 blends two valuation metrics. Our discounted cash flow model, which assumes 3% perpetuity growth and a 10.6% discount rate, indicates an intrinsic value of $69. Regarding relative peer valuations, we apply a multiple of 20X, somewhat above the peer average, to our 2010 EPS estimate, implying a $79 valuation.

Qualitative Risk Assessment

LOW	MEDIUM	HIGH

Our risk assessment reflects our view that ETN has good geographic and product diversification, offset by the highly cyclical nature of the company's various end markets, and significant pension and other post-retirement benefit obligations.

Quantitative Evaluations

S&P Quality Ranking A-

D	C	B-	B	B+	A-	A	A+

Relative Strength Rank STRONG

82

LOWEST = 1   HIGHEST = 99

Revenue/Earnings Data

Revenue (Million $)

	1Q	2Q	3Q	4Q	Year
2009	2,813	2,901	3,028	--	--
2008	3,496	4,279	4,114	3,487	15,376
2007	3,153	3,248	3,298	3,374	13,033
2006	2,991	3,162	3,115	3,102	12,370
2005	2,654	2,834	2,789	2,838	11,115
2004	2,238	2,403	2,543	2,633	9,817

Earnings Per Share ($)

2009	-0.30	0.17	1.14	E1.19	E2.42
2008	1.62	2.04	1.87	0.98	6.50
2007	1.53	1.60	1.59	1.67	6.38
2006	1.35	1.63	1.39	1.59	5.97
2005	1.19	1.37	1.30	1.38	5.23
2004	0.85	1.03	1.09	1.16	4.13

Fiscal year ended Dec. 31. Next earnings report expected: Late January. EPS Estimates based on S&P Operating Earnings; historical GAAP earnings are as reported.

Dividend Data (Dates: mm/dd Payment Date: mm/dd/yy)

Amount ($)	Date Decl.	Ex-Div. Date	Stk. of Record	Payment Date
0.500	01/28	02/05	02/09	02/27/09
0.500	04/22	04/30	05/04	05/22/09
0.500	07/20	07/30	08/03	08/21/09
0.500	10/28	11/05	11/09	11/27/09

Dividends have been paid since 1923. Source: Company reports.

Eaton Corp

STANDARD &POOR'S

Business Summary October 19, 2009

CORPORATE OVERVIEW. Eaton Corp., a diversified industrial equipment and parts manufacturer with $15 billion in revenues in 2008, conducts business through five business segments.

ETN's Electrical segment (45% of 2008 revenues with 12.5% operating margins excluding one-time items) makes a wide range of power distribution and control equipment, such as switchboards, circuit boards, circuit breakers, starters, AC and DC Uninterruptible Power Systems (UPS) and power management software. The segment also produces electronic sensors that control industrial machinery, as well as electricity quality-monitoring systems. The unit's primary competitors include GE, Germany-based Siemens and Schneider Electric. Demand for ETN's electrical equipment and components mainly reflects the health of the non-residential, power quality, industrial, residential construction, and telecom industries.

The Hydraulics segment (16%; 11.3%) makes products including pumps, motors, valves cylinders, hydraulic power units, control and sensing products, fluid conveyance products, hoses and assemblies. The principal markets for the segment's products include various energy industries, marine, agriculture, construction, mining, forestry, utilities, material handling, automotive, machine tool, metals, and the entertainment industry. The segment also sells hydraulic and electromechanical equipment such as actuators, pumps, steering systems cockpit controls and pneumatic systems.

The Aerospace segment (12%; 15.6%) is a global provider of pumps, motors, hydraulic power units and other equipment, valves, cylinders, hoses and fittings, control and sensing products, fluid conveyance products, sensors, actuators and other products used in the aviation industry. The segments products are sold to both after-market customers and to manufactures of commercial and military aviation products.

With about 85% of the global truck transmission market (such as drive trains, clutches, gearboxes and shafts), ETN's Truck Component unit (15%; 14%) is the world's largest maker of medium and heavy duty truck transmissions. The segment's primary competitor is Germany-based ZedF. ETN is also a major manufacturer of brake clutches. The segment's primary competitor in this segment is Wabco. Other truck transmission and clutch makers include European truck manufacturers, which primarily make transmissions and clutches for their own trucks. Demand for ETN's truck components is mainly driven by the health of the medium and heavy duty truck market, which is expected to decline in 2009.

Company Financials Fiscal Year Ended Dec. 31

Per Share Data ($)	2008	2007	2006	2005	2004	2003	2002	2001	2000	1999
Tangible Book Value	NM	NM	2.30	0.09	3.46	3.14	NM	0.29	NM	0.64
Cash Flow	10.15	9.50	8.80	8.08	6.67	5.18	4.49	3.78	5.05	7.25
Earnings	6.50	6.38	5.97	5.23	4.13	2.56	1.96	1.20	2.50	4.18
S&P Core Earnings	6.09	6.86	6.45	5.40	4.15	2.43	0.99	-0.18	NA	NA
Dividends	2.00	1.72	1.48	1.24	1.08	0.92	0.88	0.88	0.88	0.88
Payout Ratio	31%	27%	24%	24%	26%	36%	45%	74%	35%	21%
Prices:High	98.14	104.12	79.98	72.69	72.64	54.70	44.34	40.72	43.28	51.75
Prices:Low	37.69	71.91	62.37	56.65	52.74	33.01	29.55	27.56	28.75	31.00
P/E Ratio:High	15	16	13	14	18	21	23	34	17	12
P/E Ratio:Low	6	11	10	11	13	13	15	23	11	7

Income Statement Analysis (Million $)	2008	2007	2006	2005	2004	2003	2002	2001	2000	1999
Revenue	15,376	13,033	12,370	11,115	9,817	8,061	7,209	7,299	8,309	8,402
Operating Income	1,847	1,646	1,487	1,468	1,287	984	870	703	1,013	1,170
Depreciation	592	469	434	409	400	394	353	355	364	441
Interest Expense	157	147	104	90.0	78.0	87.0	104	142	177	152
Pretax Income	1,128	1,041	989	996	781	508	399	278	552	963
Effective Tax Rate	6.47%	7.88%	7.79%	19.2%	17.0%	24.0%	29.6%	39.2%	34.2%	35.9%
Net Income	1,055	959	912	805	648	386	281	169	363	617
S&P Core Earnings	989	1,031	985	832	651	367	141	-25.0	NA	NA

Balance Sheet & Other Financial Data (Million $)	2008	2007	2006	2005	2004	2003	2002	2001	2000	1999
Cash	530	646	114	110	85.0	61.0	75.0	112	82.0	81.0
Current Assets	4,795	4,767	4,408	3,578	3,182	3,093	2,457	2,387	2,571	2,782
Total Assets	16,655	13,430	11,417	10,218	9,075	8,223	7,138	7,646	8,180	8,437
Current Liabilities	3,745	3,659	3,407	2,968	2,262	2,126	1,734	1,669	2,107	2,649
Long Term Debt	3,190	3,417	1,774	1,830	Nil	1,651	1,887	2,252	2,447	1,915
Common Equity	6,317	5,172	4,106	3,778	3,606	3,117	2,302	2,475	2,410	2,624
Total Capital	9,776	7,604	5,880	5,608	3,606	4,768	4,752	5,307	4,857	4,539
Capital Expenditures	448	354	360	363	330	2,733	228	295	386	496
Cash Flow	1,647	1,428	1,346	1,214	1,048	780	634	524	727	1,058
Current Ratio	1.3	1.3	1.3	1.2	1.4	1.5	1.4	1.4	1.2	1.1
% Long Term Debt of Capitalization	31.7	32.0	30.2	32.6	Nil	34.6	39.7	42.4	50.4	42.2
% Net Income of Revenue	6.9	7.4	7.4	7.2	6.6	4.8	3.9	2.3	4.4	7.3
% Return on Assets	7.0	7.7	8.4	8.3	7.5	5.0	3.8	2.1	4.4	8.8
% Return on Equity	18.4	20.7	23.1	21.8	19.3	14.2	11.8	6.9	14.4	26.4

Data as orig reptd.; bef. results of disc opers/spec. items. Per share data adj. for stk. divs.; EPS diluted. E-Estimated. NA-Not Available. NM-Not Meaningful. NR-Not Ranked. UR-Under Review.

Office: Eaton Center 1111 Superior Ave, Cleveland, OH 44114-2584.
Telephone: 216-523-5000.
Website: http://www.eaton.com
Chrmn, Pres & CEO: A.M. Cutler

EVP, CFO & General Counsel: R.H. Fearon
SVP & CTO: Y.P. Tsavalas
SVP, Chief Acctg Officer & Cntlr: B.K. Rawot
SVP & Secy: T.E. Moran

Investor Contact: B. Hartman (216-523-4501)
Board Members: C. M. Connor, M. J. Critelli, A. M. Cutler, C. E. Golden, E. Green, A. E. Johnson, N. C. Lautenbach, D. L. McCoy, J. R. Miller, G. Page, V. A. Pelson, G. L. Tooker

Founded: 1916
Domicile: Ohio
Employees: 75,000

eBay Inc

STANDARD &POOR'S

S&P Recommendation **BUY** ★★★★☆	Price $24.47 (as of Nov 30, 2009)	12-Mo. Target Price $26.00	Investment Style Large-Cap Growth

GICS Sector Information Technology
Sub-Industry Internet Software & Services

Summary EBAY owns one of the world's most popular e-commerce destinations, which bears its name, as well as PayPal, an online payments company, and 30% of Skype, an Internet communications business.

Key Stock Statistics (Source S&P, Vickers, company reports)

52-Wk Range	$25.80– 9.91	S&P Oper. EPS 2009**E**	1.06	Market Capitalization(B)	$31.639	Beta	1.95
Trailing 12-Month EPS	$1.08	S&P Oper. EPS 2010**E**	1.66	Yield (%)	Nil	S&P 3-Yr. Proj. EPS CAGR(%)	19
Trailing 12-Month P/E	22.7	P/E on S&P Oper. EPS 2009**E**	23.1	Dividend Rate/Share	Nil	S&P Credit Rating	NA
$10K Invested 5 Yrs Ago	$4,165	Common Shares Outstg. (M)	1,293.0	Institutional Ownership (%)	73		

Price Performance

30-Week Mov. Avg. · · · 10-Week Mov. Avg. - - GAAP Earnings vs. Previous Year   Volume Above Avg. ▐▍▌▏ STARS
12-Mo. Target Price — Relative Strength — ▲ Up ▼ Down ▶ No Change   Below Avg. ▐▍▌▏ ★

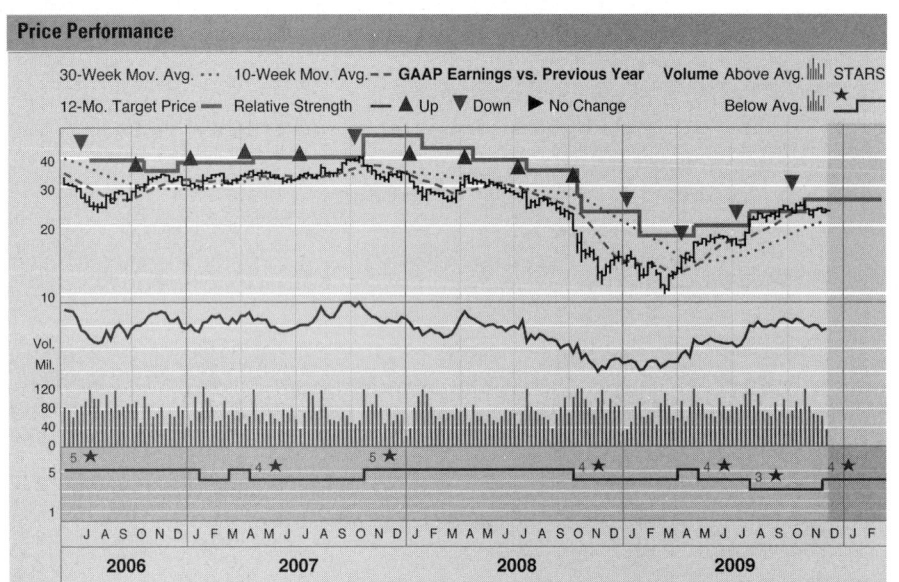

Options: ASE, CBOE, P, Ph

Analysis prepared by **Scott H. Kessler** on November 25, 2009, when the stock traded at **$ 23.55**.

Highlights

▶ Reflecting a challenging global economic backdrop that has started to show improvement, we project that net revenues will be flat in 2009 after declines in the first half, and increase 2% in 2010, reflecting the late 2009 sale of 70% of Skype. We believe EBAY will report a 6% decline at marketplaces (including eBay.com and the mid-2009-acquired Gmarket) in 2009 and growth of 8% in 2010, and revenue increases of 13% in payments (PayPal) in 2009 and 14% in 2010.

▶ We expect EBAY's annual non-GAAP operating margins to bottom in 2009, reflecting economic difficulties, notable retooling of and investment in the core marketplaces businesses around the world, and a less favorable revenue mix. We foresee improvement in 2010 and 2011.

▶ In November 2009, EBAY sold a 70% stake in Skype for $1.9 billion and a $125 million note. In June 2009, EBAY purchased South Korea's Gmarket for some $1.2 billion. In November 2008, EBAY purchased online consumer finance company Bill Me Later for some $945 million in cash and options.

Investment Rationale/Risk

▶ We see EBAY as the clear leader in online auctions, a mainstream Internet retail destination, a major facilitator of large transactions involving cars and real estate, a growing international presence, and the owner of the world's leading purely online payment platform. We are relatively optimistic about its international and payment segments, and believe a relatively new management team can eventually re-ignite growth at the marketplaces unit. We view the shares as attractively valued.

▶ Risks to our recommendation and target price include a further sharp weakening of consumer sentiment/spending, significant and increasing international competition, and potential issues related to a recent adverse French court decision related to the sale of counterfeit items on EBAY's platforms.

▶ Our DCF model, with assumptions that include a WACC of 10.4%, average annual free cash flow of 9% from 2009 to 2013, and a terminal growth rate of 3%, yields an intrinsic value of $26, which is our 12-month target price.

Qualitative Risk Assessment

LOW	MEDIUM	**HIGH**

Our risk assessment reflects our view that the company operates in fast-changing areas and faces notable competition. Over the past few years, we have viewed EBAY's quarterly results, financial outlook, strategic decisions and management changes as disappointing at times. This is only partially offset by our view of EBAY as a well-established leader in the Internet segment, with a business model that we see as attractive, and a strong balance sheet.

Quantitative Evaluations

S&P Quality Ranking   B

D	C	B-	**B**	B+	A-	A	A+

Relative Strength Rank   **STRONG**

82

LOWEST = 1   HIGHEST = 99

Revenue/Earnings Data

Revenue (Million $)

	1Q	2Q	3Q	4Q	Year
2009	2,021	2,098	2,238	--	--
2008	2,192	2,196	2,118	2,036	8,541
2007	1,768	1,418	1,889	2,181	7,672
2006	1,390	1,411	1,449	1,720	5,970
2005	1,032	1,086	1,106	1,329	4,552
2004	756.2	773.4	805.9	935.8	3,271

Earnings Per Share ($)

2009	0.28	0.25	0.27	E0.27	E1.06
2008	0.34	0.35	0.38	0.29	1.36
2007	0.27	0.27	-0.69	0.39	0.25
2006	0.17	0.17	0.20	0.25	0.79
2005	0.19	0.21	0.18	0.20	0.78
2004	0.15	0.14	0.13	0.15	0.57

Fiscal year ended Dec. 31. Next earnings report expected: Late January. EPS Estimates based on S&P Operating Earnings; historical GAAP earnings are as reported.

Dividend Data

No cash dividends have been paid.

eBay Inc

Business Summary November 25, 2009

CORPORATE OVERVIEW. eBay operates the world's largest online trading community. As of September 2009, the marketplaces segment had 89.2 million active users (compared with 87.2 million a year earlier) and in the third quarter of 2009 they accounted for total gross merchandise volume (including vehicles) of $14.6 billion ($14.2 billion). Following acquisitions in recent years, the company also owns Bill Me Later (online payments), PayPal (online payments), Rent.com (apartment and home rentals), Shopping.com (comparison shopping), 30% of Skype (Internet communications), and StubHub (online ticket sales). As of September 2009, PayPal had 78.0 million active registered accounts (65.3 million) and Skype had 520.8 million registered users (370.2 million). In November 2009, EBAY sold 70% of Skype to a group of investors in a transaction valuing the business at $2.75 billion.

EBAY and its affiliates have websites directed toward the following geographies: Argentina, Australia, Austria, Belgium, Brazil, Canada, China, France, Germany, Hong Kong, India, Ireland, Italy, Malaysia, Mexico, the Netherlands, New Zealand, the Philippines, Poland, Singapore, South Korea, Spain, Sweden, Switzerland, Taiwan, Thailand, Turkey, the U.K. and Vietnam. In December 2006, EBAY announced it would contribute its China operations to a joint

venture with Internet portal and wireless services company TOM Online. EBAY owns a 49% stake in the venture, which was created in February 2007.

CORPORATE STRATEGY. EBAY's stated goal is to become the world's most efficient and abundant marketplace by expanding its community of users, delivering value to buyers and sellers, creating a global marketplace, and providing a faster, easier and safer trading experience. EBAY has increasingly employed acquisitions to fulfill the aforementioned goal, with a focus on international expansion and offering more choices and services to its buyers and sellers. In our view, PayPal was an extremely successful acquisition because it dramatically enhanced the user experience. Moreover, the combination accelerated the benefits the companies already derived from the Network Effect (whereby a product/service becomes more valuable to its users as its number of users increases), in our opinion.

Company Financials Fiscal Year Ended Dec. 31

Per Share Data ($)	2008	2007	2006	2005	2004	2003	2002	2001	2000	1999
Tangible Book Value	2.59	3.90	2.69	2.21	2.73	2.23	1.46	1.11	0.93	0.81
Cash Flow	1.90	0.69	1.17	1.05	0.75	0.46	0.28	0.16	0.08	0.03
Earnings	1.36	0.25	0.79	0.78	0.57	0.34	0.21	0.08	0.04	0.01
S&P Core Earnings	1.36	1.26	0.79	0.61	0.43	0.21	0.04	-0.00	NA	NA
Dividends	Nil	Nil	Nil	Nil	Nil	Nil	Nil	Nil	Nil	Nil
Payout Ratio	Nil	Nil	Nil	Nil	Nil	Nil	Nil	Nil	NM	Nil
Prices:High	33.53	40.73	47.86	58.89	59.21	32.40	17.71	18.19	31.88	29.25
Prices:Low	10.91	28.60	22.83	30.78	31.30	16.88	12.21	7.11	6.69	6.92
P/E Ratio:High	25	NM	61	75	NM	95	83	NM	NM	NM
P/E Ratio:Low	8	NM	29	39	NM	50	57	NM	NM	NM

Income Statement Analysis (Million $)										
Revenue	8,541	7,672	5,970	4,552	3,271	2,165	1,214	749	431	225
Operating Income	2,845	2,606	1,968	1,820	1,313	828	431	227	74.6	23.8
Depreciation	711	602	545	378	254	159	76.6	86.6	38.1	20.7
Interest Expense	8.04	16.6	5.92	3.48	8.88	4.31	1.49	2.85	3.37	1.94
Pretax Income	2,184	751	1,547	1,549	1,128	662	398	163	78.0	20.5
Effective Tax Rate	18.5%	53.6%	27.2%	30.2%	30.5%	31.3%	36.7%	49.1%	42.0%	45.8%
Net Income	1,779	348	1,126	1,082	778	447	250	90.4	48.3	10.8
S&P Core Earnings	1,779	1,739	1,126	853	589	270	52.2	-4.04	NA	NA

Balance Sheet & Other Financial Data (Million $)										
Cash	3,353	5,984	2,663	1,314	1,330	1,382	1,109	524	202	220
Current Assets	6,287	7,123	4,971	3,183	2,911	2,146	1,468	884	675	460
Total Assets	15,592	15,366	13,494	11,789	7,991	5,820	4,124	1,679	1,182	964
Current Liabilities	3,705	3,100	2,518	1,485	1,085	647	386	180	137	88.8
Long Term Debt	Nil	Nil	Nil	Nil	0.08	124	13.8	12.0	11.4	15.0
Common Equity	11,084	11,705	10,905	10,048	6,728	4,896	3,556	1,429	1,014	852
Total Capital	11,084	11,705	10,905	10,264	6,868	5,139	3,715	1,479	1,038	867
Capital Expenditures	566	454	515	338	293	365	139	57.4	49.8	141
Cash Flow	2,490	950	1,670	1,460	1,032	606	326	177	86.3	31.5
Current Ratio	1.7	2.3	2.0	2.1	2.7	3.3	3.8	4.9	4.9	5.2
% Long Term Debt of Capitalization	Nil	Nil	Nil	Nil	NM	2.4	0.4	0.8	1.1	1.7
% Net Income of Revenue	20.8	4.5	18.9	23.8	23.8	20.7	20.6	12.1	11.2	4.8
% Return on Assets	11.5	2.4	8.9	10.9	11.3	9.1	8.6	6.3	4.5	1.9
% Return on Equity	15.6	3.1	10.7	12.9	13.4	10.6	10.0	7.4	5.2	2.3

Data as orig reptd.; bef. results of disc opers/spec. items. Per share data adj. for stk. divs.; EPS diluted. E-Estimated. NA-Not Available. NM-Not Meaningful. NR-Not Ranked. UR-Under Review.

Office: 2145 Hamilton Ave, San Jose, CA 95125-5905.
Telephone: 408-376-7400.
Email: investor_relations@ebay.com
Website: http://www.ebay.com

Chrmn: P.M. Omidyar
Pres & CEO: J.J. Donahoe
SVP & CFO: R.H. Swan
SVP, Secy & General Counsel: M.R. Jacobson

CTO: M.T. Carges
Investor Contact: T. Ford (408-376-7205)
Board Members: F. D. Anderson, M. L. Andreessen, E. W. Barnholt, P. Bourguignon, S. D. Cook, J. J. Donahoe, W. C. Ford, Jr., D. G. Lepore, D. M. Moffett, P. M. Omidyar, R. T. Schlosberg, III, H. D. Schultz, T. J. Tierney

Founded: 1995
Domicile: Delaware
Employees: 16,200

STANDARD
&POOR'S

Ecolab Inc.

S&P Recommendation	BUY ★★★★☆	Price $44.45 (as of Nov 27, 2009)	12-Mo. Target Price $50.00	Investment Style Large-Cap Growth

GICS Sector Materials
Sub-Industry Specialty Chemicals

Summary This company is the leading worldwide marketer of cleaning, sanitizing and maintenance products and services for the hospitality, institutional and industrial markets.

Key Stock Statistics (Source S&P, Vickers, company reports)

52-Wk Range	$47.88– 29.27	S&P Oper. EPS 2009**E**	2.00	Market Capitalization(B)	$10.559	Beta	0.68
Trailing 12-Month EPS	$1.59	S&P Oper. EPS 2010**E**	2.20	Yield (%)	1.26	S&P 3-Yr. Proj. EPS CAGR(%)	10
Trailing 12-Month P/E	28.0	P/E on S&P Oper. EPS 2009**E**	22.2	Dividend Rate/Share	$0.56	S&P Credit Rating	A
$10K Invested 5 Yrs Ago	$13,444	Common Shares Outstg. (M)	237.6	Institutional Ownership (%)	80		

Price Performance

30-Week Mov. Avg. · · · 10-Week Mov. Avg. – – GAAP Earnings vs. Previous Year   Volume Above Avg. STARS
12-Mo. Target Price — Relative Strength — ▲ Up ▼ Down ► No Change   Below Avg. ★

Options: CBOE, P, Ph

Analysis prepared by **Richard O'Reilly, CFA** on October 02, 2009, when the stock traded at **$ 45.35**.

Highlights

► We expect sales in 2009 to be 5% lower, hurt by unfavorable currency exchange rates. After a flat first half of 2009, we see modest organic sales growth for the second half and 2010, despite challenging end markets, aided by benefits from new products and customers, an continuing expansion of the sales force, and forecasted price increases of 2%.

► We look for the domestic Kay, food & beverage, and health care units to continue to expand despite slowdowns in the institutional division's full-service restaurant and lodging markets. A recent change in a promotional program in the institutional division will likely help sales late in 2009. We believe international sales will increase again in 2009, led by Canada and Latin America. We project that operating margins will widen in the second half based on an expected sales gain, new cost savings, and lower raw material costs.

► We assume an effective tax rate of 31%, down slightly from 2008. Our EPS estimate for 2009 includes a $0.14 impact from adverse exchange rate fluctuations, but excludes expected restructuring charges of up to $0.23, including $0.17 in the first half.

Investment Rationale/Risk

► We expect ECL to begin to post renewed sales growth and achieve continued EPS gains in coming periods, despite challenging business conditions in the global industries it serves. We believe that the repurchase in November 2008 of 4.6% of its outstanding shares will be accretive to EPS.

► Risks to our recommendation and target price include unexpected slowdowns in the hospitality, travel and foodservice industries, an inability to continue to successfully introduce new products and services, and higher-than-projected raw material costs (equal to 20% of sales).

► The shares recently traded at about 22.6X our 2009 EPS forecast, a 17% premium to the S&P 500, which is at the low end of ECL's historical annual P/E premium range. We believe that a steady grower such as ECL will be sought by investors as economic growth resume, and we think the shares offer solid upside potential. Our 12-month target price of $50 is 22.7X our 2010 EPS forecast of $2.20 reflects a P/E-to-growth (PEG) multiple of 2.27X applied to the 10% EPS gains we see for the next few years. The dividend has been raised for 17 consecutive years.

Qualitative Risk Assessment

LOW	MEDIUM	HIGH

Our risk assessment reflects the company's leading share positions in its core businesses, the stable nature of its end markets and customers, and our view of its strong balance sheet and cash generation. The stock's S&P Quality Ranking is A+, the highest possible, indicating a superior 10-year historical record of earnings and dividend growth.

Quantitative Evaluations

S&P Quality Ranking   A+

D	C	B-	B	B+	A-	A	A+

Relative Strength Rank   MODERATE

45

LOWEST = 1   HIGHEST = 99

Revenue/Earnings Data

Revenue (Million $)

	1Q	2Q	3Q	4Q	Year
2009	1,348	1,442	1,546	--	--
2008	1,458	1,570	1,626	1,483	6,138
2007	1,254	1,362	1,413	1,440	5,470
2006	1,120	1,226	1,279	1,271	4,896
2005	1,070	1,159	1,165	1,142	4,535
2004	979.4	1,043	1,090	1,073	4,185

Earnings Per Share ($)

2009	0.24	0.41	0.60	E0.56	E2.00
2008	0.41	0.55	0.50	0.33	1.80
2007	0.35	0.44	0.46	0.45	1.70
2006	0.30	0.36	0.43	0.34	1.43
2005	0.27	0.31	0.38	0.27	1.23
2004	0.25	0.30	0.36	0.27	1.19

Fiscal year ended Dec. 31. Next earnings report expected: Mid February. EPS Estimates based on S&P Operating Earnings; historical GAAP earnings are as reported.

Dividend Data (Dates: mm/dd Payment Date: mm/dd/yy)

Amount ($)	Date Decl.	Ex-Div. Date	Stk. of Record	Payment Date
0.140	12/04	12/12	12/16	01/15/09
0.140	02/27	03/06	03/10	04/15/09
0.140	05/08	06/12	06/16	07/15/09
0.140	08/07	09/11	09/15	10/15/09

Dividends have been paid since 1936. Source: Company reports.

The McGraw·Hill Companies

Ecolab Inc.

STANDARD &POOR'S

Business Summary October 02, 2009

CORPORATE OVERVIEW. Ecolab is a global supplier of cleaning, sanitizing, and maintenance products and services for hospitality, institutional, and industrial markets. In the U.S. cleaning and sanitizing business (44% of 2008 sales, 56% of profits), the institutional division (25% of 2008 total sales) is the leading provider of cleaners and sanitizers for warewashing, on-premise laundry, kitchen cleaning and general housekeeping, product dispensing equipment and dishwashing racks and related kitchen sundries to the food-service, lodging and health care industries. It also provides pool and spa treatment products. In addition, the division includes professional janitorial products (detergents, floor care, disinfectants, odor control) sold under the Airkem brand name.

The Kay division (5%) is the largest supplier of cleaning and sanitizing products (surface cleaners, degreasers, sanitizers and hand care products) for the quick-service restaurant, convenience store and food retail markets. The Food and Beverage division (9%) offers cleaning and sanitizing products and services to farms, dairy plants, food and beverage processors, and pharmaceutical plants; and water treatment products to institutional, laundry and food and beverage, and processing markets for boilers, cooling and waste treatment systems.

ECL also sells health care products (skin care, disinfectants and sterilants; 3%) under the Ecolab and Microtek names; textile care products (1%) for large institutional and commercial laundries; and vehicle care products (soaps, polishes, wheel treatments) for rental, fleet and retail car washes (1%).

Other U.S. services (7%, 7%) include institutional and commercial pest elimination and prevention services (5%) and GCS Services, a provider of commercial kitchen equipment repair and maintenance services (3%). ECL bought GCS Service in 1998, and has added to this business through small acquisitions; this business had operating losses for the six years through 2008.

The International business (49%, 37%) provides services similar to those offered in the U.S. to Canada (3%) and about 70 countries in Europe (34%), Latin America (4%), and the Asia/Pacific region (8%). The institutional and food & beverage businesses constitute a larger portion of the international business compared to the U.S.

Company Financials Fiscal Year Ended Dec. 31

Per Share Data ($)	2008	2007	2006	2005	2004	2003	2002	2001	2000	1999
Tangible Book Value	NM	1.33	1.67	2.00	1.33	1.14	0.83	0.41	1.77	1.98
Cash Flow	3.14	2.85	2.48	2.22	2.13	1.93	1.67	1.35	1.35	1.15
Earnings	1.80	1.70	1.43	1.23	1.19	1.06	0.81	0.73	0.79	0.66
S&P Core Earnings	1.52	1.69	1.46	1.24	1.10	0.98	0.64	0.61	NA	NA
Dividends	0.53	0.48	0.42	0.36	0.33	0.30	0.28	0.26	0.25	0.21
Payout Ratio	29%	28%	29%	29%	28%	28%	34%	36%	31%	32%
Prices:High	52.35	52.78	46.40	37.15	35.59	27.92	25.20	22.09	22.84	22.22
Prices:Low	29.56	37.01	33.64	30.68	26.12	23.08	18.27	14.25	14.00	15.84
P/E Ratio:High	29	31	32	30	30	26	31	30	29	34
P/E Ratio:Low	16	22	24	25	22	22	23	20	18	24

Income Statement Analysis (Million $)										
Revenue	6,138	5,470	4,896	4,535	4,185	3,762	3,404	2,355	2,264	2,080
Operating Income	1,073	978	880	799	786	713	656	482	471	714
Depreciation	335	291	269	257	247	230	223	163	148	135
Interest Expense	70.8	58.9	51.3	49.8	45.3	45.3	43.9	28.4	24.6	22.7
Pretax Income	651	616	567	498	489	448	354	306	338	286
Effective Tax Rate	31.2%	30.7%	35.0%	35.9%	36.5%	38.1%	39.6%	38.4%	38.3%	38.4%
Net Income	448	427	369	319	310	277	214	188	209	176
S&P Core Earnings	378	424	376	322	283	260	167	157	NA	NA

Balance Sheet & Other Financial Data (Million $)										
Cash	66.7	137	484	104	71.2	85.6	49.2	41.8	44.0	47.7
Current Assets	1,691	1,717	1,854	1,422	1,279	1,150	1,016	930	601	577
Total Assets	4,757	4,723	4,419	3,797	3,716	3,229	2,878	2,525	1,714	1,586
Current Liabilities	1,442	1,518	1,503	1,119	940	851	866	828	532	471
Long Term Debt	799	600	557	519	Nil	604	540	512	234	169
Common Equity	1,572	1,936	1,680	1,649	1,563	1,295	1,100	880	757	929
Total Capital	2,376	2,536	2,237	2,169	1,563	1,900	1,639	1,393	991	1,098
Capital Expenditures	327	362	288	269	276	212	213	158	150	146
Cash Flow	783	718	637	576	558	507	437	351	357	310
Current Ratio	1.2	1.1	1.2	1.3	1.4	1.4	1.2	1.1	1.1	1.2
% Long Term Debt of Capitalization	33.7	23.7	24.9	23.9	Nil	31.8	32.9	36.8	23.6	15.4
% Net Income of Revenue	7.3	7.8	7.5	7.0	7.4	7.4	6.3	8.0	9.2	8.5
% Return on Assets	9.5	9.3	9.0	8.5	8.9	9.1	7.9	8.9	12.6	11.5
% Return on Equity	25.6	23.6	22.1	19.7	21.7	23.2	21.6	23.0	27.5	18.9

Data as orig reptd.; bef. results of disc opers/spec. items. Per share data adj. for stk. divs.; EPS diluted. E-Estimated. NA-Not Available. NM-Not Meaningful. NR-Not Ranked. UR-Under Review.

Office: 370 North Wabasha Street, Saint Paul, MN 55102-1390.
Telephone: 651-292-2233.
Email: investor.info@ecolab.com
Website: http://www.ecolab.com

Chrmn, Pres & CEO: D.M. Baker, Jr.
Pres: J. Trotter
SVP & CTO: L.L. Berger
CFO: S.L. Fritze

Secy & General Counsel: L.T. Bell
Investor Contact: M.J. Monahan (651-293-2809)
Board Members: D. M. Baker, Jr., B. Beck, L. S. Biller, R. U. De Schutter, J. A. Grundhofer, J. W. Johnson, J. W. Levin, R. L. Lumpkins, C. S. O'Hara, B. M. Pritchard, V. J. Reich, J. Zillmer

Founded: 1924
Domicile: Delaware
Employees: 26,568

The McGraw-Hill Companies

Edison International

STANDARD &POOR'S

S&P Recommendation	BUY ★★★★☆	Price	12-Mo. Target Price	Investment Style
		$33.81 (as of Nov 27, 2009)	$37.00	Large-Cap Blend

GICS Sector Utilities
Sub-Industry Electric Utilities

Summary EIX is the holding company for Southern California Edison. Other businesses include electric power generation, financial investments, and real estate development.

Key Stock Statistics (Source S&P, Vickers, company reports)

52-Wk Range	$35.20– 23.09	S&P Oper. EPS 2009**E**	3.07	Market Capitalization(B)	$11.016	Beta		0.71
Trailing 12-Month EPS	$2.59	S&P Oper. EPS 2010**E**	3.50	Yield (%)	3.67	S&P 3-Yr. Proj. EPS CAGR(%)		-0
Trailing 12-Month P/E	13.1	P/E on S&P Oper. EPS 2009**E**	11.0	Dividend Rate/Share	$1.24	S&P Credit Rating		BBB-
$10K Invested 5 Yrs Ago	$12,050	Common Shares Outstg. (M)	325.8	Institutional Ownership (%)	73			

Price Performance

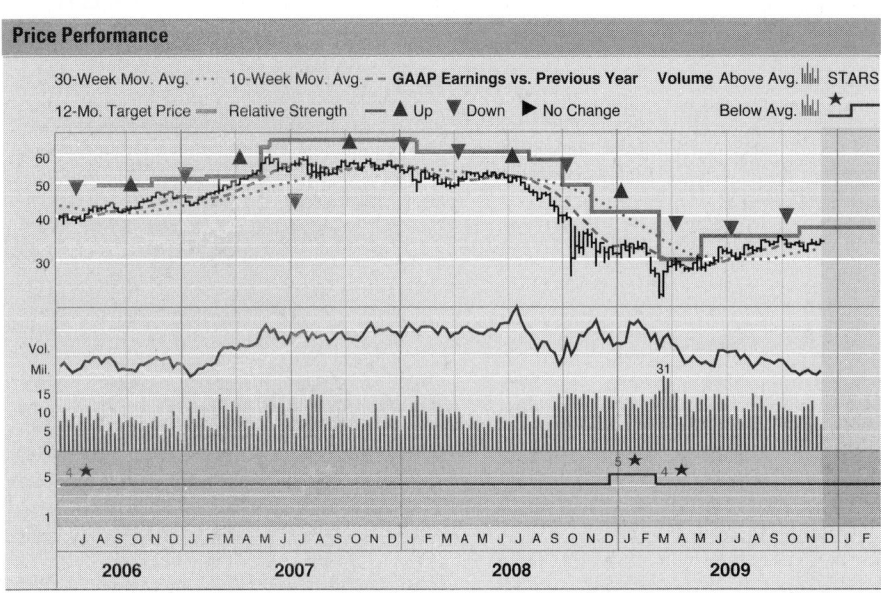

30-Week Mov. Avg. · · · 10-Week Mov. Avg. – – GAAP Earnings vs. Previous Year   Volume Above Avg. ⊪⊪⊪ STARS
12-Mo. Target Price — Relative Strength — ▲ Up ▼ Down ► No Change   Below Avg. ⊪⊪⊪ ★⌐

Options: ASE, CBOE, P

Analysis prepared by **Justin McCann** on October 22, 2009, when the stock traded at **$ 33.19**.

Highlights

► We expect operating EPS in 2009, which would exclude projected net one-time charges between $0.55 and $0.85, to decline more than 20% from 2008 operating EPS of $3.84. We believe operating results in 2009 will be hurt by sharply lower earnings at EMG, due to the decline in power prices, reduced demand, and lower trading income. We expect this to be partially offset by higher earnings at SCE, reflecting rate increases related to the three-year program approved in the 2009 General Rate Case.

► For 2010, we expect operating EPS to increase about 15% over anticipated results in 2009. We believe the increase will reflect a rate increase at SCE and an improved earnings outlook at EMG. Over the next few years, we see SCE's EPS growth being driven by its five-year, $20 billion infrastructure development plan, which is expected to result in annual rate base growth of 10% to 13% through 2013.

► EIX reported a charge of $0.81 in the second quarter of 2009. The charge is related to the tax settlement reached with the IRS and the related termination of cross-border leveraged leases, which is expected to have a positive cash flow impact of about $380 million.

Investment Rationale/Risk

► The stock has rebounded more than 40% from its multi-year low reached in March. We think the price had been hurt by a projected sharp earnings drop for EMG, due to the weak economy and power markets, with the rebound driven by the approval of rate increases for SCE, a favorable settlement with the IRS regarding a disputed tax issue, and the recovery of the broader market. We think the stock is still undervalued at a recent discount-to-peers P/E of about 9.5X our EPS estimate for 2010, and see the potential for above-average total return once the economy and power markets begin to recover.

► Risks to our recommendation and target price include the potential for unfavorable regulatory or legislative acts, a sharp decline in the gas/coal price spread, and a significant drop in the P/E of the electric utility group as a whole.

► Given the rebound in the shares, the recent yield from the dividend was about 3.7%. While this is still below the level of peers (recently about 5.0%), we believe it provides a base for an attractive total return over the next 12 months. Our 12-month target price is $37, reflecting a discount-to-peers P/E of about 10.6X our 2010 EPS estimate.

Qualitative Risk Assessment

LOW	MEDIUM	HIGH

Our risk assessment reflects our view that the strong and steady earnings and cash flow we expect from the regulated Southern California Edison utility, with its large and expanding service territory and generally supportive regulatory environment, is partially offset by the cyclical and volatile earnings of the unregulated independent power operations of Edison Mission Group.

Quantitative Evaluations

S&P Quality Ranking   **B**

D	C	B-	B	B+	A-	A	A+

Relative Strength Rank   **MODERATE**

65

LOWEST = 1   HIGHEST = 99

Revenue/Earnings Data

Revenue (Million $)

	1Q	2Q	3Q	4Q	Year
2009	2,812	2,834	3,664	--	--
2008	3,113	3,477	4,295	3,228	14,112
2007	2,912	3,047	3,942	3,211	13,113
2006	2,751	3,001	3,802	3,067	12,622
2005	2,446	2,649	3,783	2,975	11,852
2004	2,116	2,565	3,188	2,327	10,199

Earnings Per Share ($)

2009	0.75	-0.03	1.22	E0.42	E3.07
2008	0.92	0.79	1.31	0.66	3.68
2007	1.00	0.28	1.40	0.65	3.32
2006	0.56	0.53	1.39	0.80	3.28
2005	0.59	0.55	1.31	0.90	3.34
2004	0.16	-1.21	0.95	0.78	0.68

Fiscal year ended Dec. 31. Next earnings report expected: Early March. EPS Estimates based on S&P Operating Earnings; historical GAAP earnings are as reported.

Dividend Data (Dates: mm/dd Payment Date: mm/dd/yy)

Amount ($)	Date Decl.	Ex-Div. Date	Stk. of Record	Payment Date
0.310	12/11	12/29	12/31	01/31/09
0.310	02/26	03/27	03/31	04/30/09
0.310	06/18	06/26	06/30	07/31/09
0.310	09/03	09/28	09/30	10/31/09

Dividends have been paid since 2004. Source: Company reports.

Please read the Required Disclosures and Analyst Certification on the last page of this report.

Edison International

Business Summary October 22, 2009

CORPORATE OVERVIEW. Edison International (EIX) is the holding company of the regulated Southern California Edison (SCE) utility and several non-regulated subsidiaries. The principal non-utility companies are Edison Mission Energy (EME), an independent power producer that also conducts price risk management and energy trading activities, and Edison Capital, which holds equity investments in energy and infrastructure projects. In 2008, SCE accounted for 79.7% of EIX's consolidated revenues, the non-utility power generation business 19.9%, and financial services and other operations 0.4%. The utility's retail operations are regulated by the purview of the California Public Utilities Commission (CPUC), while its wholesale operations fall under the oversight of the Federal Energy Regulatory Commission (FERC).

CORPORATE STRATEGY. The company seeks to establish a balanced approach for growth, dividends, and balance sheet strength. It is working to re-

duce administration expenses in the non-utility companies and to establish a multi-year productivity effort at the utility. EIX has taken steps to rebalance its capital structure and to further reduce its debt. It has also worked to enhance its liquidity through strong cash flow generation. SCE is working on new projects that should expand its transmission and distribution systems, and intends to implement a comprehensive software system to support the majority of its critical business processes. We also expect to see EIX further strengthen the independent power business, expand investment in renewable energy, and evaluate prospects for growth in the non-utility sector.

Company Financials Fiscal Year Ended Dec. 31

Per Share Data ($)	2008	2007	2006	2005	2004	2003	2002	2001	2000	1999
Tangible Book Value	28.99	25.92	23.65	20.30	18.56	13.86	11.59	8.10	7.43	14.03
Earnings	3.68	3.32	3.28	3.34	0.68	2.37	3.46	7.36	-5.84	1.79
S&P Core Earnings	2.93	3.26	3.28	3.35	0.60	2.45	2.81	6.78	NA	NA
Dividends	1.23	1.17	1.10	1.02	1.05	Nil	Nil	Nil	1.11	1.07
Payout Ratio	33%	35%	34%	31%	154%	Nil	Nil	Nil	NM	60%
Prices:High	55.70	60.26	47.15	49.16	32.52	22.07	19.60	16.12	30.00	29.63
Prices:Low	26.73	42.76	37.90	30.43	21.24	10.57	7.80	6.25	14.13	21.63
P/E Ratio:High	15	18	14	15	48	9	6	2	NM	17
P/E Ratio:Low	7	13	12	9	31	4	2	1	NM	12

Income Statement Analysis (Million $)										
Revenue	14,112	13,113	12,622	11,852	10,199	12,135	11,488	11,436	11,717	9,670
Depreciation	1,419	1,264	1,181	1,061	1,022	1,184	1,030	973	1,933	1,794
Maintenance	NA	NA	NA	NA	NA	NA	NA	NA	NA	NA
Fixed Charges Coverage	3.34	3.38	3.18	3.28	2.20	1.73	1.91	3.38	-0.98	1.96
Construction Credits	NA	NA	NA	NA	NA	NA	NA	NA	NA	Nil
Effective Tax Rate	31.5%	27.4%	32.3%	26.4%	NM	21.5%	25.6%	40.7%	NM	32.0%
Net Income	1,215	1,100	1,083	1,108	226	779	1,135	2,402	-1,943	623
S&P Core Earnings	955	1,065	1,082	1,111	199	808	921	2,211	NA	NA

Balance Sheet & Other Financial Data (Million $)										
Gross Property	31,932	29,248	25,090	24,775	23,214	24,674	23,264	22,396	25,737	27,203
Capital Expenditures	2,824	2,826	2,536	1,868	1,733	1,288	1,590	933	1,488	1,231
Net Property	24,343	22,309	20,269	18,588	17,397	20,288	15,170	14,427	17,903	19,683
Capitalization:Long Term Debt	11,857	9,931	10,016	9,552	9,807	12,221	12,915	14,007	13,660	15,050
Capitalization:% Long Term Debt	55.5	54.0	56.5	59.1	61.3	69.4	74.4	81.1	85.0	74.3
Capitalization:Preferred	Nil	Nil	Nil	Nil	Nil	9.00	Nil	Nil	Nil	Nil
Capitalization:% Preferred	Nil	Nil	Nil	Nil	Nil	0.05	Nil	Nil	Nil	Nil
Capitalization:Common	9,517	8,444	7,709	6,615	6,049	5,383	4,437	3,272	2,420	5,211
Capitalization:% Common	44.5	46.0	43.5	40.9	37.8	30.6	25.6	18.9	15.0	25.7
Total Capital	27,485	23,980	23,415	21,854	21,688	24,246	23,786	24,163	21,609	26,252
% Operating Ratio	86.1	84.6	84.7	80.7	80.6	75.2	82.8	93.2	86.4	92.9
% Earned on Net Property	11.0	13.1	12.8	6.9	6.6	9.1	16.0	36.9	NM	11.6
% Return on Revenue	8.6	8.8	8.6	9.3	2.2	6.4	9.9	21.0	NM	6.4
% Return on Invested Capital	7.8	9.4	10.2	12.2	10.4	14.9	10.9	4.8	7.8	3.6
% Return on Common Equity	13.5	13.6	15.1	17.1	3.8	15.9	29.4	84.4	NM	12.1

Data as orig reptd.; bef. results of disc opers/spec. items. Per share data adj. for stk. divs.; EPS diluted. E-Estimated. NA-Not Available. NM-Not Meaningful. NR-Not Ranked. UR-Under Review.

Office: 2244 Walnut Grove Avenue, Rosemead, CA 91770-3714.
Telephone: 877-379-9515.
Website: http://www.edison.com
Chrmn, Pres & CEO: T.F. Craver, Jr.

EVP, CFO & Treas: W.J. Scilacci, Jr.
EVP & General Counsel: R.L. Adler
SVP, CFO, Chief Acctg Officer & Cntlr: L.G. Sullivan
Secy: B.E. Mathews

Investor Contact: S. Cunningham (877-379-9515)
Board Members: V. Chang, F. A. Cordova, T. F. Craver, Jr., C. B. Curtis, B. M. Freeman, L. G. Nogales, R. L. Olson, J. M. Rosser, R. T. Schlosberg, III, T. C. Sutton, W. B. White

Founded: 1886
Domicile: California
Employees: 18,291

Electronic Arts Inc

STANDARD &POOR'S

S&P Recommendation **SELL** ★ ★ ☆ ☆ ☆	Price $17.01 (as of Nov 27, 2009)	12-Mo. Target Price $14.00	Investment Style Large-Cap Growth

GICS Sector Information Technology
Sub-Industry Home Entertainment Software

Summary This company produces entertainment software for PCs, home video game consoles, and mobile gaming devices.

Key Stock Statistics (Source S&P, Vickers, company reports)

52-Wk Range	$23.76– 14.24	S&P Oper. EPS 2010E	-1.59	Market Capitalization(B)	$5.536	Beta	1.40
Trailing 12-Month EPS	$-4.06	S&P Oper. EPS 2011E	-0.33	Yield (%)	Nil	S&P 3-Yr. Proj. EPS CAGR(%)	NM
Trailing 12-Month P/E	NM	P/E on S&P Oper. EPS 2010E	NM	Dividend Rate/Share	Nil	S&P Credit Rating	NA
$10K Invested 5 Yrs Ago	$3,562	Common Shares Outstg. (M)	325.5	Institutional Ownership (%)	97		

Price Performance

30-Week Mov. Avg. · · · 10-Week Mov. Avg. — GAAP Earnings vs. Previous Year   Volume Above Avg. STARS
12-Mo. Target Price — Relative Strength — ▲ Up ▼ Down ▶ No Change   Below Avg. ★

Options: ASE, CBOE, P, Ph

Analysis prepared by **Jim Yin** on November 12, 2009, when the stock traded at **$ 18.29**.

Highlights

▶ We see revenue rising 3.8% in FY 11 (Mar.), following 12% decline we see for FY 10. Our forecast reflects our view of weak consumer spending even though we expect the economy to rebound in 2010. We believe rising unemployment and energy prices will adversely impact consumers' purchasing power. As a result, they are focusing their purchases on top-selling titles. We think sales will be hurt by the maturity of some of ERTS's game titles and lack of new hit titles. We also think the company will lose market share due to stronger growth in Asia and online games, in which ERTS has smaller market shares.

▶ We forecast a gross margin of 52% in FY 11, up from 48% projected for FY 10. We see operating expenses declining as a percentage of revenues, as ERTS plans to cut another 1,500 employees in FY 10. We project that FY 11 operating margins will improve to -5.1%, from -14% in FY 10, reflecting further cost reductions.

▶ We estimate losses per share of $1.59 and $0.33 in FY 10 and FY 11, respectively. We believe losses will diminish in FY 11, as the company reduces its operating expenses and curbs development on non-profitable games.

Investment Rationale/Risk

▶ Our sell recommendation reflects our view of weak consumer demand. We believe economic uncertainty including weak employment and rising energy prices will hurt sales of video games. We think consumers will continue to buy top-selling games, but fewer catalog titles, and believe the company's key franchises, including Madden NFL and NCAA Football, have been losing their appeal. We are concerned about ERTS's lack of new major game titles to offset this trend. We also think consumers may delay purchases in anticipation of the next generation of consoles.

▶ Risks to our recommendation and target price include a stronger-than-expected economic recovery and further cost reductions.

▶ Our 12-month target price of $14 is based on a blend of our discounted cash flow (DCF) and enterprise value (EV) to sales analyses. Our DCF model assumes a 12.5% weighted average cost of capital and 3% terminal growth, yielding an intrinsic value of $14. We derive a value of $15 based on an EV/sales multiple of 0.7X our FY 11 revenue estimate, a discount to the industry average of 2.5X, due to ERTS's inconsistent profitability.

Qualitative Risk Assessment

LOW	MEDIUM	**HIGH**

Our risk assessment takes into account weak consumer spending, the volatile nature of the home entertainment software industry, and our projection of ERTS's further loss in market share.

Quantitative Evaluations

S&P Quality Ranking B+

D	C	B-	B	**B+**	A-	A	A+

Relative Strength Rank WEAK

19

LOWEST = 1   HIGHEST = 99

Revenue/Earnings Data

Revenue (Million $)

	1Q	2Q	3Q	4Q	Year
2010	644.0	788.0	--	--	--
2009	804.0	894.0	1,654	860.0	4,212
2008	395.0	640.0	1,503	1,127	3,665
2007	413.0	784.0	1,281	613.0	3,091
2006	365.0	675.0	1,270	641.0	2,951
2005	431.6	715.7	1,428	553.0	3,129

Earnings Per Share ($)

2010	-0.72	-1.21	E0.54	E-0.20	E-1.59
2009	-0.52	-0.97	-2.00	-0.13	-3.40
2008	-0.42	-0.62	-0.10	-0.29	-1.45
2007	-0.26	0.07	0.50	-0.08	0.24
2006	-0.19	0.16	0.83	-0.05	0.75
2005	0.08	0.31	1.18	0.02	1.59

Fiscal year ended Mar. 31. Next earnings report expected: Early February. EPS Estimates based on S&P Operating Earnings; historical GAAP earnings are as reported.

Dividend Data

No cash dividends have been paid.

Please read the Required Disclosures and Analyst Certification on the last page of this report.

The McGraw-Hill Companies

Electronic Arts Inc

STANDARD
&POOR'S

Business Summary November 12, 2009

CORPORATE OVERVIEW. ERTS is one of the largest third-party developers of video games, which can be played on a variety of platforms including Sony PlayStation, Microsoft Xbox 360, Nintendo Wii, personal computers, and mobile devices. ERTS owns many of today's most popular video game franchises, including Madden NFL, The Sims, and Need for Speed. The company organizes its business into four labels: EA SPORTS, EA Games, EA Casual Entertainment and The Sims. Each label operates with dedicated studio and marketing teams.

ERTS publish titles across all major platforms, including consoles, PCs, and handheld gaming devices. The company has a diversified video game portfolio. In FY 09, the company produced 24 titles for Xbox 360, 22 for PlayStation 3, 22 for PCs, and 20 for Nintendo Wii. No title accounted for more than 10% of its total revenue in FY 09.

ERTS publishes and distributes games in over 35 countries throughout the world. Sales in North America were $2.4 billion, or 57% of total revenue, in FY 09. International revenue accounted for $1.8 billion, or 43% of total revenue, in FY 09.

CORPORATE STRATEGY. One of the company's strategic goals is to increase resources toward developing new titles for the next-generation of game consoles, which includes Microsoft Xbox 360, Nintendo Wii and Sony PlayStation 3. The installed base of these game consoles is expected to increase significantly in 2008 as consumers upgrade their video game systems. ERTS plans to release a limited number of titles for prior-generation consoles as product sales for these systems are expected to decline.

ERTS has completed several acquisitions to broaden its product portfolio, in particular internally developed video games, which provide higher operating margins than licensed intellectual properties. In January 2008, the company acquired BioWare Corp. and Pandemic Studios, two privately owned video game studios, for about $860 million in cash and stock. The two game studios are known for creating role-playing action/adventure games and have 10 franchises under development.

Company Financials Fiscal Year Ended Mar. 31

Per Share Data ($)	2009	2008	2007	2006	2005	2004	2003	2002	2001	2000
Tangible Book Value	6.52	9.19	9.93	8.29	10.66	8.52	11.62	3.92	3.33	2.86
Cash Flow	-2.81	-0.85	0.70	1.05	1.82	2.12	2.79	0.74	0.22	0.62
Earnings	-3.40	-1.45	0.24	0.75	1.59	1.87	1.09	0.36	-0.04	0.44
S&P Core Earnings	-2.51	-1.22	0.24	0.49	1.35	1.59	0.82	0.10	-0.25	NA
Dividends	Nil	Nil	Nil	Nil	Nil	Nil	Nil	Nil	Nil	Nil
Payout Ratio	Nil	Nil	Nil	Nil	Nil	Nil	Nil	Nil	Nil	Nil
Calendar Year	2008	2007	2006	2005	2004	2003	2002	2001	2000	1999
Prices:High	58.35	61.62	59.85	71.16	63.71	52.89	36.22	33.46	28.97	31.11
Prices:Low	14.79	46.27	39.99	47.45	43.38	23.76	24.74	17.25	12.25	9.50
P/E Ratio:High	NM	NM	NM	95	40	28	33	94	NM	71
P/E Ratio:Low	NM	NM	NM	63	27	13	23	49	NM	22

Income Statement Analysis (Million $)

	2009	2008	2007	2006	2005	2004	2003	2002	2001	2000
Revenue	4,212	3,665	3,091	2,951	3,129	2,957	2,482	1,725	1,322	1,420
Operating Income	-128	-60.0	204	454	759	863	629	267	42.1	207
Depreciation	189	186	147	95.0	75.0	77.5	91.6	111	69.7	46.7
Interest Expense	Nil	Nil	Nil	Nil	Nil	Nil	Nil	Nil	Nil	Nil
Pretax Income	-855	-507	138	389	725	797	461	148	-13.4	170
Effective Tax Rate	NM	NM	47.8%	37.8%	30.5%	27.5%	30.9%	31.0%	NM	30.9%
Net Income	-1,088	-454	76.0	236	504	577	317	102	-11.1	117
S&P Core Earnings	-805	-382	76.0	153	425	482	239	28.0	-68.2	NA

Balance Sheet & Other Financial Data (Million $)

	2009	2008	2007	2006	2005	2004	2003	2002	2001	2000
Cash	2,520	3,016	1,712	1,402	1,410	2,151	951	804	477	340
Current Assets	3,120	3,925	3,597	3,012	3,706	2,911	1,911	1,153	819	705
Total Assets	4,678	6,059	5,146	4,386	4,370	3,401	2,360	1,699	1,379	1,192
Current Liabilities	1,136	1,299	1,026	869	828	722	571	453	340	265
Long Term Debt	Nil	Nil	Nil	Nil	Nil	Nil	Nil	Nil	Nil	Nil
Common Equity	3,134	4,339	4,032	3,408	3,498	2,678	1,785	1,243	1,034	923
Total Capital	3,176	4,339	4,040	3,449	3,509	2,678	1,789	1,246	1,039	927
Capital Expenditures	115	84.0	178	123	126	89.6	59.1	51.5	120	135
Cash Flow	-899	-268	223	331	579	655	409	212	58.6	163
Current Ratio	2.8	3.0	3.5	3.5	4.5	4.0	3.3	2.5	2.4	2.7
% Long Term Debt of Capitalization	Nil	Nil	Nil	Nil	Nil	Nil	Nil	Nil	Nil	Nil
% Net Income of Revenue	NM	NM	2.5	8.0	16.1	19.5	12.8	5.9	NM	8.2
% Return on Assets	NM	NM	1.6	5.4	12.9	20.0	15.6	6.6	NM	11.2
% Return on Equity	NM	NM	2.0	6.8	16.3	25.9	20.9	8.9	NM	14.7

Data as orig reptd.; bef. results of disc opers/spec. items. Per share data adj. for stk. divs.; EPS diluted. E-Estimated. NA-Not Available. NM-Not Meaningful. NR-Not Ranked. UR-Under Review.

Office: 209 Redwood Shores Parkway, Redwood City, CA 94065-1175.
Telephone: 650-628-1500.
Email: investorrelations@ea.com
Website: http://www.ea.com

Chrmn: L.F. Probst, III
CEO: J. Riccitiello
COO: J. Schappert
EVP & CFO: E.F. Brown

SVP & Chief Acctg Officer: K.A. Barker
Investor Contact: J. Brown (650-628-7922)
Board Members: R. Asher, L. S. Coleman, Jr., J. T. Huber, G. M. Kusin, G. B. Laybourne, G. B. Maffei, V. Paul, L. F. Probst, III, J. Riccitiello, R. Simonson, L. J. Srere

Founded: 1982
Domicile: Delaware
Employees: 9,100

El Paso Corp

STANDARD &POOR'S

S&P Recommendation	HOLD ★★★☆☆	Price	12-Mo. Target Price	Investment Style
		$9.50 (as of Nov 27, 2009)	$11.00	Large-Cap Value

GICS Sector Energy
Sub-Industry Oil & Gas Storage & Transportation

Summary This provider of natural gas and related energy products owns North America's largest natural gas pipeline system and is a leading independent natural gas producer.

Key Stock Statistics (Source S&P, Vickers, company reports)

52-Wk Range	$11.37– 5.22	S&P Oper. EPS 2009**E**	1.09	Market Capitalization(B)	$6.662	Beta		1.21
Trailing 12-Month EPS	$-3.69	S&P Oper. EPS 2010**E**	0.85	Yield (%)	0.42	S&P 3-Yr. Proj. EPS CAGR(%)		-4
Trailing 12-Month P/E	NM	P/E on S&P Oper. EPS 2009**E**	8.7	Dividend Rate/Share	$0.04	S&P Credit Rating		BB
$10K Invested 5 Yrs Ago	$8,860	Common Shares Outstg. (M)	701.3	Institutional Ownership (%)	79			

Price Performance

30-Week Mov. Avg. ···   10-Week Mov. Avg.--   **GAAP Earnings vs. Previous Year**   Volume Above Avg.▥▥ STARS
12-Mo. Target Price —   Relative Strength —   ▲ Up ▼ Down ► No Change   Below Avg.▥▥ ★

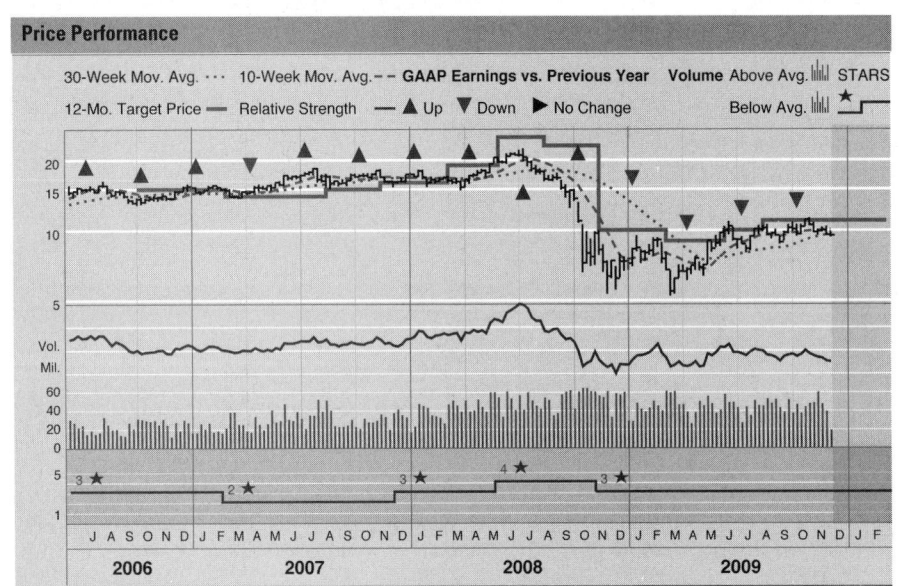

Options: ASE, CBOE, P

Analysis prepared by **Michael Kay** on November 23, 2009, when the stock traded at **$ 9.70**.

Highlights

► EP's pipeline segment is benefiting from several expansion projects placed into service, including the Medicine Bow expansion, the High Plains Pipeline, the Carthage expansion and the Totem Gas Storage project. EP has earmarked $8 billion for pipeline growth projects, with $1 billion in projects expected to be in service by year-end 2010, on time and on budget. In E&P, we see spending at low-risk onshore plays in the Haynesville Shale, Cotton Valley and the Eagle Ford Shale. EP is ramping up to five rigs at Haynesville, where production is expected to reach 130 MMcfe/d by year end.

► EP expects to sell $300-$500 million of assets in 2010. Also, E&P capex of $1 billion in 2009 is expected to remain flat in 2010, with 50% earmarked for the development of the Haynesville and Eagle Ford shales.

► We see a 9% EBITDA decline and a 15% drop in EPS in 2009, to $1.09. We project EPS of $0.85 in 2010 on lower realized prices. We think liquidity fears have eased on asset sales, debt offerings, and a new revolver. In November, EP cut its quarterly dividend to $0.01, from $0.05, which is expected to save $112 million in cash.

Investment Rationale/Risk

► We think EP's risk profile has risen but growth prospects have expanded with a greater E&P focus. EP will focus on high-return plays in 2009 and 2010, including at Haynesville, and on exploration in Brazil and Egypt. We expect a difficult near-term E&P environment, but we see lower costs and project start-ups boosting pipeline results. EP is partnering with Global Infrastructure Partners on the Ruby Pipeline, removing funding worries hanging over the project. We believe the success of Ruby is based on EP's ability to build it on time and on budget, and to secure financing and contract capacity at favorable rates. EP has formed a new Midstream business, focused on Haynesville Shale.

► Risks to our recommendation and target price include a major decline in natural gas prices, difficulty integrating acquisitions, and weaker-than-expected economic conditions.

► We are positive on EP's premier pipeline franchise and see improving E&P prospects given its entry into attractive plays. Our 12-month target price of $11 is based on a blend of an EV-to-estimated 2010 EBITDA ratio of 7X and a projected P/E of 11X our 2010 EPS estimate.

Qualitative Risk Assessment

LOW	MEDIUM	HIGH

Our risk assessment is based on our view of the struggling exploration and production (E&P) segment, which has proven to be very volatile. EP's balance sheet is highly leveraged, in our opinion, given the capital intensity of operations. Partly offsetting these risks is EP's involvement in several different business lines, including regulated pipelines.

Quantitative Evaluations

S&P Quality Ranking   B-

D	C	B-	B	B+	A-	A	A+

Relative Strength Rank   WEAK

29

LOWEST = 1   HIGHEST = 99

Revenue/Earnings Data

Revenue (Million $)

	1Q	2Q	3Q	4Q	Year
2009	1,484	973.0	981.0	--	--
2008	1,269	1,153	1,598	1,343	5,363
2007	1,022	1,198	1,166	1,262	4,648
2006	1,337	1,089	942.0	913.0	4,281
2005	1,108	1,184	768.0	957.0	4,017
2004	1,557	1,524	1,429	1,364	5,874

Earnings Per Share ($)

2009	-1.41	0.11	0.08	E0.27	E1.09
2008	0.33	0.25	0.58	-2.43	-1.24
2007	-0.08	0.22	0.20	0.20	0.57
2006	0.42	0.19	0.15	-0.30	0.72
2005	0.18	-0.34	-0.51	-0.45	-1.13
2004	-0.15	0.07	-0.31	-0.86	-1.25

Fiscal year ended Dec. 31. Next earnings report expected: Late February. EPS Estimates based on S&P Operating Earnings; historical GAAP earnings are as reported.

Dividend Data (Dates: mm/dd Payment Date: mm/dd/yy)

Amount ($)	Date Decl.	Ex-Div. Date	Stk. of Record	Payment Date
0.050	02/10	03/04	03/06	04/01/09
0.050	04/01	06/03	06/05	07/01/09
0.050	08/21	09/02	09/04	10/01/09
0.010	11/03	12/02	12/04	01/04/10

Dividends have been paid since 1992. Source: Company reports.

Please read the Required Disclosures and Analyst Certification on the last page of this report.

The McGraw·Hill Companies

El Paso Corp

STANDARD & POOR'S

Business Summary November 23, 2009

CORPORATE OVERVIEW. Founded in 1928, El Paso originally served as a regional natural gas pipeline company that ultimately expanded geographically and into complimentary business lines. By 2001, its total assets exceeded $44 billion and included natural gas production, power generation, trading operations and its traditional natural gas pipeline businesses. In late 2001 through 2003, various industry and company-specific events led to a substantial decline in EP's fundamentals. In late 2003, EP announced a long-term business strategy principally focused on core pipeline and production businesses. During the past several years, EP has sold off non-core assets to reduce debt and improve liquidity.

Operations are conducted through three primary segments: Pipelines, Exploration and Production, and Marketing. EP also has a Power segment that holds its remaining interests in international power plants in Brazil, Asia and Central America.

PRIMARY BUSINESS DYNAMICS. The Pipelines segment is the largest U.S. owner of interstate natural gas pipelines and owns or has interests in 42,000 miles of pipeline. The division also has 230 billion cubic feet (Bcf) of natural gas storage capacity, and a liquefied natural gas terminal at Elba Island, GA

with 806 million cubic feet (Mmcf) of daily base load sendout capacity. Each pipeline system and storage facility operates under Federal Energy Regulatory Commission (FERC) approved tariffs that establish rates, cost recovery mechanisms, and service terms and conditions. The established rates are a function of EP's costs of providing services, including a "reasonable" return on invested capital.

In February 2007, EP sold ANR Pipeline Company (ANR), its Michigan storage assets, and its 50% interest in Great Lakes Gas Transmission, which comprised approximately 12,600 miles of pipeline and 236 Bcf of storage capacity.

EP's strategy to create value in this segment is to expand systems into new markets while leveraging existing assets; recontract or contract available or expiring capacity and resolve open rate cases; leverage its coast-to-coast scale economies; and invest in maintenance and pipeline integrity projects to maintain the value and ensure the safety of its pipeline systems and assets.

Company Financials Fiscal Year Ended Dec. 31

Per Share Data ($)	2008	2007	2006	2005	2004	2003	2002	2001	2000	1999
Tangible Book Value	4.70	6.47	6.00	3.38	4.68	5.36	11.70	17.65	15.25	10.47
Cash Flow	0.50	2.25	2.09	0.61	0.45	0.99	0.21	2.76	4.82	1.61
Earnings	-1.24	0.57	0.72	-1.13	-1.25	-1.03	-2.30	0.13	2.44	-1.06
S&P Core Earnings	-1.46	0.54	0.69	-1.07	-0.84	-0.68	-1.95	-0.37	NA	NA
Dividends	0.18	0.16	0.16	0.16	0.16	0.16	0.87	0.85	0.82	0.79
Payout Ratio	NM	28%	22%	NM	NM	NM	NM	NM	34%	NM
Prices:High	22.47	18.56	16.39	14.16	11.85	10.30	46.89	75.30	74.25	43.44
Prices:Low	5.32	13.71	11.80	9.30	6.57	3.33	4.39	36.00	30.31	30.69
P/E Ratio:High	NM	33	23	NM	NM	NM	NM	NM	30	NM
P/E Ratio:Low	NM	24	16	NM	NM	NM	NM	NM	12	NM
Income Statement Analysis (Million $)										
Revenue	5,363	4,648	4,281	4,017	5,874	6,711	12,194	57,475	21,950	10,581
Operating Income	3,579	2,904	1,427	934	2,386	2,907	2,872	4,391	2,155	1,482
Depreciation	1,205	1,176	1,047	1,121	1,088	1,207	1,405	1,359	589	609
Interest Expense	914	1,044	1,228	1,389	1,632	1,839	1,400	1,155	538	453
Pretax Income	-1,034	664	523	-991	-777	-1,200	-1,567	466	1,012	-287
Effective Tax Rate	NM	33.4%	NM	NM	NM	NM	NM	39.1%	28.3%	NM
Net Income	-823	436	531	-702	-802	-616	-1,289	67.0	582	-242
S&P Core Earnings	-1,021	375	471	-696	-531	-401	-1,096	-194	NA	NA
Balance Sheet & Other Financial Data (Million $)										
Cash	1,024	285	537	2,132	2,117	1,429	1,591	1,139	688	545
Current Assets	3,051	1,712	7,167	6,185	5,632	8,922	11,924	12,659	10,076	2,911
Total Assets	23,668	24,579	27,261	31,838	31,383	37,084	46,224	48,171	27,445	16,657
Current Liabilities	3,243	2,413	6,151	5,712	4,572	7,074	10,350	13,565	10,467	3,702
Long Term Debt	12,818	12,483	13,260	17,054	18,608	20,722	19,727	14,109	6,574	5,548
Common Equity	3,285	4,530	3,436	2,639	3,439	4,474	8,377	9,356	3,569	2,947
Total Capital	17,979	19,485	18,396	21,850	23,358	25,196	31,680	31,012	14,623	11,601
Capital Expenditures	2,757	2,495	2,164	1,718	1,782	2,452	3,716	4,079	1,336	1,086
Cash Flow	345	1,575	1,541	392	286	591	116	1,426	1,171	367
Current Ratio	0.9	0.7	1.2	1.1	1.2	1.3	1.2	0.9	1.0	0.8
% Long Term Debt of Capitalization	71.3	64.1	72.1	78.1	79.7	82.2	62.3	45.5	45.0	47.8
% Net Income of Revenue	NM	9.4	12.4	NM	NM	NM	NM	0.1	2.7	NM
% Return on Assets	NM	1.7	1.8	NM	NM	NM	NM	0.1	2.6	NM
% Return on Equity	NM	10.0	16.3	NM	NM	NM	NM	0.8	17.9	NM

Data as orig reptd.; bef. results of disc opers/spec. items. Per share data adj. for stk. divs.; EPS diluted. E-Estimated. NA-Not Available. NM-Not Meaningful. NR-Not Ranked. UR-Under Review.

Office: El Paso Energy Building, Houston, TX 77002-5089.
Telephone: 713-420-2600.
Email: investorrelations@epenergy.com
Website: http://www.elpaso.com

Chrmn, Pres & CEO: D.L. Foshee
CEO: P.W. Hobby
EVP & General Counsel: R.W. Baker
SVP, CFO, Chief Acctg Officer & Cntlr: J.R. Sult

SVP & Chief Admin Officer: S.B. Ortenstone
Investor Contact: B. Connery (713-420-5855)
Board Members: J. C. Braniff, J. L. Dunlap, D. L. Foshee, R. W. Goldman, A. W. Hall, Jr., T. R. Hix, R. L. Kuehn, Jr., F. P. McClean, S. J. Shapiro, J. M. Talbert, R. F. Vagt, J. L. Whitmire, III

Founded: 1928
Domicile: Delaware
Employees: 5,344

The McGraw-Hill Companies

EMC Corp

STANDARD &POOR'S

S&P Recommendation	HOLD ★★★☆☆	Price $16.75 (as of Nov 27, 2009)	12-Mo. Target Price $19.00	Investment Style Large-Cap Blend

GICS Sector Information Technology
Sub-Industry Computer Storage & Peripherals

Summary This company is one of the world's largest suppliers of enterprise storage systems, software and services.

Key Stock Statistics (Source S&P, Vickers, company reports)

52-Wk Range	$18.44–9.61	S&P Oper. EPS 2009**E**	0.67	Market Capitalization(B)	$34.167	Beta	1.02
Trailing 12-Month EPS	$0.51	S&P Oper. EPS 2010**E**	0.87	Yield (%)	Nil	S&P 3-Yr. Proj. EPS CAGR(%)	8
Trailing 12-Month P/E	32.8	P/E on S&P Oper. EPS 2009**E**	25.0	Dividend Rate/Share	Nil	S&P Credit Rating	A-
$10K Invested 5 Yrs Ago	$12,603	Common Shares Outstg. (M)	2,039.8	Institutional Ownership (%)	80		

Price Performance

30-Week Mov. Avg. · · · 10-Week Mov. Avg. - - - GAAP Earnings vs. Previous Year   Volume Above Avg. ▍▍▍ STARS
12-Mo. Target Price — Relative Strength — ▲ Up ▼ Down ▶ No Change   Below Avg. ▍▍▍ ★

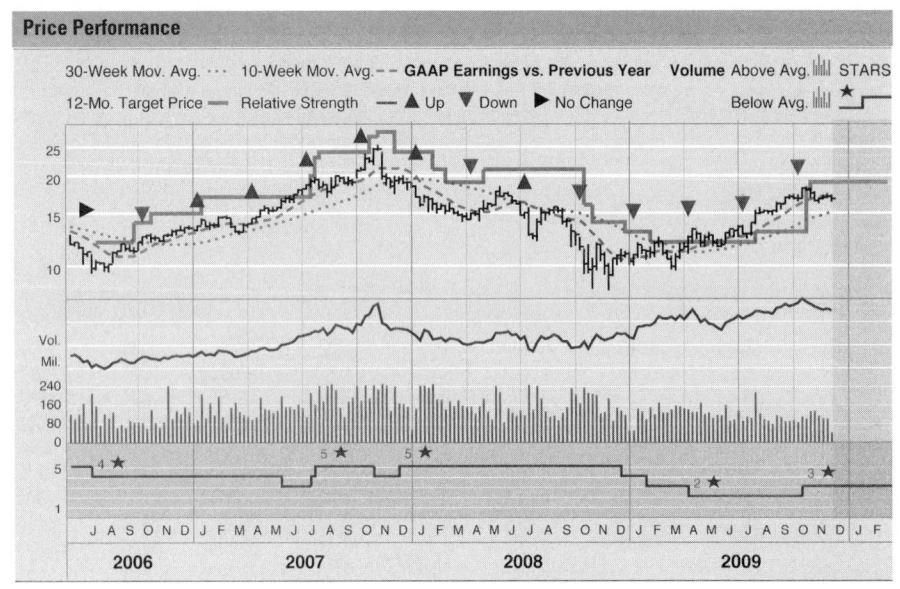

Analysis prepared by **Jim Yin** on October 27, 2009, when the stock traded at **$ 17.28**.

Options: ASE, CBOE, P, Ph

Highlights

► We expect revenues to increase 8.0% in 2010, following a 6.2% decline seen for 2009, reflecting our outlook for an improving global economy. We see overall corporate IT spending rising 4% in 2010 and think the data storage market will increase at a faster rate given its cyclical nature. We believe growth will be led by the server virtualization market, which we project to have a 20% compound annual growth rate for the next three years.

► We look for overall gross margins of 56% in 2010, up from 54% seen for 2009, due to faster growth in the virtual infrastructure business unit, which has higher gross margins. We believe expenses will decrease as a percentage of revenues in 2010 due to better economies of scale and effective cost controls. We project that non-GAAP operating margins will widen to 16.8% in 2010, from 13.9% in 2009.

► We forecast operating EPS of $0.87 in 2010, compared to $0.67 projected for 2009. Our estimates exclude $0.11 and $0.09 related to amortization of intangibles and other one-time charges in 2009 and 2010, respectively. The earnings increase reflects our outlook for an economic recovery next year.

Investment Rationale/Risk

► We expect improving end-user demand, as the world economy recovers from recession. We also think demand will rise from increased usage of video and electronic record keeping, particularly in the health care industry. We are positive on the company's recent restructuring, and we see operating margins expanding in 2010. We believe EMC is financially well positioned, with nearly $7 billion in net cash as of June 30, 2009, and we expect it to make additional acquisitions to strengthen its product offerings.

► Risks to our recommendation and target price include a weaker-than-expected economic recovery, lower corporate IT spending, and a significant loss in market share.

► Our 12-month target price of $19 is based on our DCF analysis. Our DCF model assumes an 11% weighted average cost of capital, 14% operating margin, 8.0% revenue growth rate for the next 10 years, and 3% terminal growth. Our analysis accounts for EMC's 84% stake in VMware (VMW 44, Sell).

Qualitative Risk Assessment

LOW	MEDIUM	HIGH

Our risk assessment reflects our view that EMC is a market leader, generates consistent free cash flow, and has a strong balance sheet. However, we see the storage segment as somewhat cyclical, highly competitive, and often typified by pricing pressure.

Quantitative Evaluations

S&P Quality Ranking B

D	C	B-	B	B+	A-	A	A+

Relative Strength Rank MODERATE

52

LOWEST = 1   HIGHEST = 99

Revenue/Earnings Data

Revenue (Million $)

	1Q	2Q	3Q	4Q	Year
2009	3,151	3,257	3,518	--	--
2008	3,470	3,674	3,716	4,017	14,876
2007	2,975	3,125	3,300	3,831	13,230
2006	2,551	2,575	2,815	3,215	11,155
2005	2,243	2,345	2,366	2,710	9,664
2004	1,872	1,971	2,029	2,358	8,229

Earnings Per Share ($)

2009	0.10	0.10	0.14	E0.24	E0.67
2008	0.13	0.18	0.20	0.14	0.65
2007	0.15	0.16	0.23	0.24	0.77
2006	0.12	0.12	0.13	0.18	0.54
2005	0.11	0.12	0.17	0.06	0.47
2004	0.06	0.08	0.09	0.13	0.36

Fiscal year ended Dec. 31. Next earnings report expected: Late January. EPS Estimates based on S&P Operating Earnings; historical GAAP earnings are as reported.

Dividend Data

No cash dividends have been paid.

EMC Corp

STANDARD &POOR'S

Business Summary October 27, 2009

CORPORATE OVERVIEW. EMC offers a wide range of storage systems, software and services designed to fulfill customers' needs in terms of performance, functionality, scalability, data availability, and cost. EMC's clients are located around the world and represent a cross-section of economic sectors and government entities. The company's products and services are used in conjunction with a variety of computing platforms that support key business processes, including transaction processing, data warehousing, electronic commerce, and content management.

The company reports revenues in four business segments -- Information Storage, Content Management and Archiving, RSA Information Security, and VMware Virtual Infrastructure. Information Storage accounted for 78% of sales in 2008, down from 80% in 2007. Information Storage sales rose 10% in 2007 and another 10% in 2008.

Revenues outside the U.S. accounted for 46% of EMC's total in 2008, up from 45% in 2007. Moreover, all of EMC's markets except the U.S. expanded at a double-digit rate during the year, with Latin America growing the fastest at 22%.

CORPORATE STRATEGY. EMC's strategy focuses on the concept of informa-

tion lifecycle management (ILM). This idea centers on the management of information across its entire "life," from creation, to usage, to archiving, to disposal. Via its utilization, ILM simultaneously lowers the cost and the risk of managing data, in our view, regardless of its format (documents, images, e-mal, etc.). ILM also provides for cost-effective business continuity and more efficient compliance with regulations.

As part of this plan, EMC has engaged in a number of acquisitions over the past few years. One of its more successful deals, in our opinion, was the purchase of VMware, Inc., a virtual infrastructure software company, which is operated as an independent subsidiary. VMW's software is designed to enable customers to achieve much higher utilization of the server, storage and network resources deployed within their operations, while dramatically simplifying how the workloads running on those systems are operated and managed.

Company Financials Fiscal Year Ended Dec. 31

Per Share Data ($)	2008	2007	2006	2005	2004	2003	2002	2001	2000	1999
Tangible Book Value	2.37	2.42	4.39	3.20	3.22	3.19	3.05	3.31	3.72	2.38
Cash Flow	0.92	1.02	0.87	0.73	0.61	0.45	0.24	0.07	1.02	0.66
Earnings	0.65	0.77	0.54	0.47	0.36	0.22	-0.05	-0.23	0.79	0.46
S&P Core Earnings	0.63	0.73	0.55	0.35	0.21	0.04	-0.23	-0.33	NA	NA
Dividends	Nil	Nil	Nil	Nil	Nil	Nil	Nil	Nil	Nil	Nil
Payout Ratio	Nil	Nil	Nil	Nil	Nil	Nil	Nil	Nil	Nil	Nil
Prices:High	18.60	25.47	14.75	15.09	15.80	14.66	17.97	82.00	104.94	55.50
Prices:Low	8.25	12.74	9.44	11.10	9.24	5.98	3.67	10.01	47.50	21.00
P/E Ratio:High	29	33	27	32	44	67	NM	NM	NM	NM
P/E Ratio:Low	13	17	17	24	26	27	NM	NM	NM	NM

Income Statement Analysis (Million $)	2008	2007	2006	2005	2004	2003	2002	2001	2000	1999
Revenue	14,876	13,230	11,155	9,664	8,229	6,237	5,438	7,091	8,873	6,716
Operating Income	2,459	2,302	2,170	2,222	1,716	988	310	355	2,774	1,897
Depreciation	561	530	764	640	616	521	654	655	517	447
Interest Expense	73.8	72.9	34.1	7.99	7.52	3.03	11.4	11.3	14.6	33.5
Pretax Income	1,703	2,060	1,390	1,652	1,185	571	-296	-577	2,441	1,357
Effective Tax Rate	18.4%	18.4%	11.7%	31.4%	26.5%	13.1%	NM	NM	27.0%	25.5%
Net Income	1,346	1,666	1,227	1,133	871	496	-119	-508	1,782	1,011
S&P Core Earnings	1,312	1,569	1,241	839	504	84.2	-477	-720	NA	NA

Balance Sheet & Other Financial Data (Million $)	2008	2007	2006	2005	2004	2003	2002	2001	2000	1999
Cash	6,807	6,127	1,828	2,322	1,477	1,869	1,687	2,129	1,983	1,109
Current Assets	10,665	10,053	6,521	6,574	4,831	4,687	4,217	4,923	6,100	4,320
Total Assets	23,875	22,285	18,566	16,790	15,423	14,093	9,590	9,890	10,628	7,173
Current Liabilities	5,218	4,408	3,881	3,674	2,949	2,547	2,042	2,179	2,114	1,398
Long Term Debt	3,450	3,450	3,450	127	128	130	Nil	Nil	14.5	687
Common Equity	13,042	12,521	10,326	12,065	11,523	10,885	7,226	7,601	8,177	4,952
Total Capital	17,038	16,448	13,776	12,368	11,793	11,015	7,226	7,601	8,494	5,764
Capital Expenditures	696	699	718	601	371	369	391	889	858	524
Cash Flow	1,907	2,196	1,992	1,773	1,488	1,017	535	147	2,299	1,458
Current Ratio	2.0	2.3	1.7	1.8	1.6	1.8	2.1	2.3	2.9	3.1
% Long Term Debt of Capitalization	20.3	21.4	25.0	1.0	1.1	1.2	Nil	Nil	0.2	11.9
% Net Income of Revenue	9.1	12.6	11.0	11.7	10.6	8.0	NM	NM	20.1	15.0
% Return on Assets	5.8	8.2	6.9	7.0	5.9	4.2	NM	NM	20.0	15.8
% Return on Equity	10.5	14.6	11.0	9.6	7.8	5.5	NM	NM	27.1	34.4

Data as orig reptd.; bef. results of disc opers/spec. items. Per share data adj. for stk. divs.; EPS diluted. E-Estimated. NA-Not Available. NM-Not Meaningful. NR-Not Ranked. UR-Under Review.

Office: 176 South Street, Hopkinton, MA 01748-2230.
Telephone: 508-435-1000.
Email: emc_ir@emc.com
Website: http://www.emc.com

Chrmn & CEO: J.M. Tucci
Pres: P.P. Gelsinger
EVP & CFO: D.I. Goulden
EVP & General Counsel: P.T. Dacier

SVP & CTO: J.M. Nick
Board Members: M. W. Brown, R. L. Cowen, M. J. Cronin, G. Deegan, J. R. Egan, W. P. Fitzgerald, E. F. Kelly, W. B. Priem, P. L. Sagan, D. N. Strohm, J. M. Tucci

Founded: 1979
Domicile: Massachusetts
Employees: 42,100

The McGraw-Hill Companies

Emerson Electric Co.

STANDARD &POOR'S

S&P Recommendation	HOLD ★★★☆☆	Price $41.50 (as of Nov 27, 2009)	12-Mo. Target Price $43.00	Investment Style Large-Cap Blend

GICS Sector Industrials
Sub-Industry Electrical Components & Equipment

Summary This company is a diversified designer, supplier, and service provider of electrical, automation, motors, appliances, and tools used in industrial, commercial, and consumer markets.

Key Stock Statistics (Source S&P, Vickers, company reports)

52-Wk Range	$42.93– 24.39	S&P Oper. EPS 2010**E**	2.18	Market Capitalization(B)	$31.214	Beta	1.16
Trailing 12-Month EPS	$2.27	S&P Oper. EPS 2011**E**	2.50	Yield (%)	3.23	S&P 3-Yr. Proj. EPS CAGR(%)	9
Trailing 12-Month P/E	18.3	P/E on S&P Oper. EPS 2010**E**	19.0	Dividend Rate/Share	$1.34	S&P Credit Rating	A
$10K Invested 5 Yrs Ago	$14,079	Common Shares Outstg. (M)	752.1	Institutional Ownership (%)	70		

Price Performance

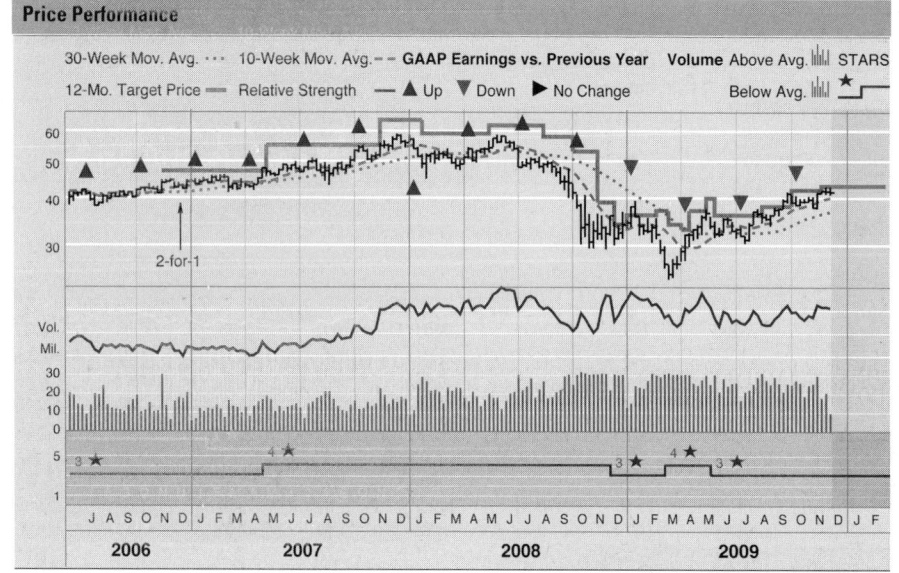

30-Week Mov. Avg. ··· 10-Week Mov. Avg. - - **GAAP Earnings vs. Previous Year** Volume Above Avg. |||| STARS
12-Mo. Target Price — Relative Strength ▲ Up ▼ Down ► No Change Below Avg. |||| ★

2-for-1

Options: ASE, CBOE, P, Ph

Analysis prepared by **Mathew Christy, CFA** on November 13, 2009, when the stock traded at **$ 41.89**.

Highlights

► After falling 16% in FY 09 (Sep), we expect sales to decline about 6% in FY 10, mainly on lower expected revenue results at EMR's Process Management and Industrial Automation units. In addition, our forecast also assumes reduced orders and declining backlogs in EMR's later-cycle businesses that outweigh the positive impact of improved economic conditions and the end of the inventory destocking on EMR's shorter-cycle businesses. For FY 11, we see revenue increasing 6% on better results across EMR's business units.

► We think operating margins will narrow in FY 10. This projection is based mainly on lower operating leverage and some raw material cost inflation despite, what we see, as the company's early efforts to realign costs to address the decline in demand and lower production rates across EMR's businesses. For FY 11, we project that operating margin will rise as sales and production rates improve.

► On projected tax rates of 31.5%, we project EPS of $2.18 in FY 10 and $2.50 in FY 11, representing a decline of about 4% and a gain of nearly 15% in the respective years.

Investment Rationale/Risk

► We forecast that EMR will experience soft end-market demand and lower overall revenue through most of FY 09 on slowing economic growth, reduced organic order growth, and declining order backlogs. However, we remain positive on the company for the longer term, as we see EMR's globally valued brand platforms, new product introductions in key business segments, strong balance sheet, and free cash flow as positives. We also think the company will be able to make acquisitions and will continue share repurchases.

► Risks to our recommendation and target price include weaker-than-expected global economic growth; softer industrial, energy and electronics markets; and, potential value-diminishing acquisitions.

► Our 12-month target price of $43 represents a blend of two valuation metrics. Our discounted cash flow model, which assumes a 3% perpetuity growth rate and a 10% discount rate, indicates an intrinsic value of $40. Our relative valuation applies a 21X P/E multiple, equal to the peer average, to our FY 10 EPS estimate, indicating a $46 value.

Qualitative Risk Assessment

LOW	**MEDIUM**	HIGH

Our risk assessment reflects the cyclical nature of several of the company's major end markets, its acquisition strategy, and corporate governance practices that we view as unfavorable versus peers. This is offset by our view of its strong competitive position in major product categories.

Quantitative Evaluations

S&P Quality Ranking A

D	C	B-	B	B+	A-	**A**	A+

Relative Strength Rank STRONG

76

LOWEST = 1   HIGHEST = 99

Revenue/Earnings Data

Revenue (Million $)

	1Q	2Q	3Q	4Q	Year
2009	5,415	5,087	5,091	5,322	20,915
2008	5,520	6,023	6,568	6,696	24,807
2007	5,051	5,513	5,874	6,134	22,572
2006	4,548	4,852	5,217	5,516	20,133
2005	3,970	4,227	4,465	4,643	17,305
2004	3,600	3,859	4,036	4,120	15,615

Earnings Per Share ($)

2009	0.60	0.49	0.51	0.67	2.27
2008	0.65	0.75	0.82	0.88	3.11
2007	0.55	0.61	0.72	0.78	2.66
2006	0.48	0.52	0.59	0.65	2.24
2005	0.35	0.42	0.43	0.51	1.70
2004	0.29	0.38	0.41	0.42	1.49

Fiscal year ended Sep. 30. Next earnings report expected: Early February. EPS Estimates based on S&P Operating Earnings; historical GAAP earnings are as reported.

Dividend Data (Dates: mm/dd Payment Date: mm/dd/yy)

Amount ($)	Date Decl.	Ex-Div. Date	Stk. of Record	Payment Date
0.330	02/03	02/11	02/13	03/10/09
0.330	05/05	05/13	05/15	06/10/09
0.330	08/04	08/12	08/14	09/10/09
0.335	11/03	11/10	11/13	12/10/09

Dividends have been paid since 1947. Source: Company reports.

Please read the Required Disclosures and Analyst Certification on the last page of this report.

The McGraw-Hill Companies

Emerson Electric Co.

**STANDARD
&POOR'S**

Business Summary November 13, 2009

CORPORATE OVERVIEW. Emerson Electric is an industrial conglomerate operating more than 60 diverse businesses in five primary business segments: Process Management, Industrial Automation, Network Power, Climate Technologies, and Appliance and Tools.

The company's Process Management segment, which accounted for 26.8% of FY 08 (Sep.) total revenues and 33.4% of operating profits, and had 19.6% operating margins, produces process management software and systems, analytical instrumentation, valves, control systems for measurement and control of fluid flow, and integrated solutions for process and industrial applications. Customers served by this segment include energy service companies; food and beverage firms; the pulp and paper industry; pharmaceutical manufacturers; and municipal water suppliers. In FY 08, 32% of segment sales were made within the U.S., 24% in Europe, 21% in Asia, and 23% elsewhere.

The Industrial Automation segment (19.4%, 18.6%, 15%) primarily makes industrial motors and drives, transmissions, alternators, controls and equipment for automated equipment. Products in this segment are sold predominantly to manufacturing firms. Geographic distribution of segment sales: 39% U.S., 42% Europe, 11% Asia, and 8% other regions.

The Network Power segment (25.4%, 20.3%, 12.6%) mainly makes power systems and precision cooling products used in computer, telecommunications and Internet infrastructure sold mainly to utility companies. In 2008, 41% of segment sales were generated in the U.S., 20% in Europe, 28% in Asia, and 11% elsewhere.

The Climate Technologies segment (15.2%, 14%, 14.6%) makes home and building thermostats and compressors (cooling components used in air conditioning units and refrigerators). Geographic distribution of 2008 segment sales: 55% U.S., 16% Europe, 18% Asia, and 11% other regions.

The Appliance and Tools segment (13.2%, 13.5%, 16.1%) mainly makes various household appliances, electric motors and controls for appliances, hand-held tools, and storage solutions used in various industries. Most (82%) of the segment's sales were generated in the U.S., with 5% in Europe, 3% in Asia, and 10% elsewhere.

Total sales in FY 08 came from the U.S. (46%), Europe (23%), Asia (18%), Latin America (5%), and other regions (8%).

Company Financials Fiscal Year Ended Sep. 30

Per Share Data ($)	2009	2008	2007	2006	2005	2004	2003	2002	2001	2000
Tangible Book Value	NA	2.25	2.99	2.67	2.34	2.36	1.81	0.99	1.11	1.27
Cash Flow	NA	3.92	3.47	3.04	2.41	4.37	1.84	1.90	2.07	2.44
Earnings	2.27	3.11	2.66	2.24	1.70	1.49	1.21	1.26	1.20	1.65
S&P Core Earnings	NA	2.94	2.67	2.24	1.70	1.49	1.13	0.94	0.88	NA
Dividends	1.32	1.20	1.05	0.89	0.83	0.80	0.79	0.78	0.77	0.72
Payout Ratio	58%	39%	39%	40%	49%	54%	65%	62%	64%	44%
Prices:High	42.93	58.72	59.05	45.21	38.92	35.44	32.50	33.04	39.63	39.88
Prices:Low	24.39	29.26	41.26	36.78	30.35	28.11	21.89	20.87	22.02	20.25
P/E Ratio:High	19	19	22	20	23	24	27	26	33	24
P/E Ratio:Low	11	9	16	16	18	19	18	17	18	12

Income Statement Analysis (Million $)										
Revenue	20,915	24,807	22,572	20,133	17,305	15,615	13,958	13,824	15,480	15,545
Operating Income	NA	4,639	4,174	3,676	3,150	2,842	2,497	2,443	2,988	3,219
Depreciation	727	638	656	607	562	557	534	541	708	678
Interest Expense	NA	244	261	225	243	234	246	250	304	288
Pretax Income	2,417	3,591	3,107	2,684	2,149	3,704	1,414	1,565	1,589	2,178
Effective Tax Rate	28.7%	31.7%	31.3%	31.3%	33.8%	16.1%	28.4%	32.3%	35.0%	34.7%
Net Income	1,724	2,454	2,136	1,845	1,422	3,109	1,013	1,060	1,032	1,422
S&P Core Earnings	NA	2,321	2,145	1,846	1,424	1,250	951	784	753	NA

Balance Sheet & Other Financial Data (Million $)										
Cash	1,560	1,777	1,008	810	1,233	1,346	696	381	356	281
Current Assets	NA	9,331	8,065	7,330	6,837	6,416	5,500	4,961	5,320	5,483
Total Assets	19,763	21,040	19,680	18,672	17,227	16,361	15,194	14,545	15,046	15,164
Current Liabilities	NA	6,573	5,546	5,374	4,931	4,339	3,417	4,400	5,379	5,219
Long Term Debt	3,998	3,297	3,372	3,128	3,128	3,136	3,733	2,990	2,256	2,248
Common Equity	8,555	9,113	8,772	7,848	7,400	12,266	6,460	5,741	6,114	10,248
Total Capital	12,553	13,131	12,144	10,976	10,528	15,402	10,193	8,731	8,370	12,496
Capital Expenditures	531	714	681	601	518	400	337	384	554	692
Cash Flow	NA	3,092	2,792	2,452	1,984	3,666	1,547	1,601	1,740	2,101
Current Ratio	1.5	1.4	1.5	1.4	1.4	1.5	1.6	1.1	1.0	1.1
% Long Term Debt of Capitalization	31.9	25.1	27.8	28.5	29.7	20.4	36.6	34.2	26.9	18.0
% Net Income of Revenue	8.2	9.9	9.5	9.2	8.2	19.9	7.3	7.7	6.7	9.2
% Return on Assets	8.5	12.1	11.1	10.3	8.5	19.7	6.8	7.2	6.8	9.9
% Return on Equity	19.5	27.4	25.7	24.1	19.4	26.1	16.6	17.9	16.5	14.5

Data as orig reptd.; bef. results of disc opers/spec. items. Per share data adj. for stk. divs.; EPS diluted. E-Estimated. NA-Not Available. NM-Not Meaningful. NR-Not Ranked. UR-Under Review.

Office: 8000 W Florissant Ave, Saint Louis, MO 63136.
Telephone: 314-553-2000.
Website: http://www.gotoemerson.com
Chrmn, Pres & CEO: D.N. Farr

Vice Chrmn & CFO: W.J. Galvin
COO: E.L. Monser
SVP, Secy & General Counsel: F.L. Steeves
SVP & Cntlr: F.J. Dellaquila

Investor Contact: C. Tucker (314-553-2197)
Board Members: C. A. Boersig, A. A. Busch, III, D. N. Farr, C. G. Fernandez, W. J. Galvin, A. F. Golden, H. Green, R. Horton, W. R. Johnson, V. R. Loucks, Jr., J. B. Menzer, C. A. Peters, J. W. Prueher, R. Ridgway, R. L. Stephenson

Founded: 1890
Domicile: Missouri
Employees: 140,700

The McGraw-Hill Companies

ENSCO International Inc.

STANDARD &POOR'S

S&P Recommendation **SELL** ★★☆☆☆	Price $44.00 (as of Nov 30, 2009)	12-Mo. Target Price $36.00	Investment Style Large-Cap Growth

GICS Sector Energy
Sub-Industry Oil & Gas Drilling

Summary This company provides offshore contract drilling services to the oil and gas industry worldwide.

Key Stock Statistics (Source S&P, Vickers, company reports)

52-Wk Range	$51.30– 22.04	S&P Oper. EPS 2009**E**	5.28	Market Capitalization(B)	$6.270	Beta		1.31
Trailing 12-Month EPS	$6.22	S&P Oper. EPS 2010**E**	4.07	Yield (%)	0.23	S&P 3-Yr. Proj. EPS CAGR(%)		-16
Trailing 12-Month P/E	7.1	P/E on S&P Oper. EPS 2009**E**	8.3	Dividend Rate/Share	$0.10	S&P Credit Rating		BBB+
$10K Invested 5 Yrs Ago	$14,270	Common Shares Outstg. (M)	142.5	Institutional Ownership (%)	91			

Price Performance

30-Week Mov. Avg. · · · 10-Week Mov. Avg. – – **GAAP Earnings vs. Previous Year**   Volume Above Avg. ▌▌▌ STARS
12-Mo. Target Price — Relative Strength — ▲ Up ▼ Down ▶ No Change   Below Avg. ▌▌▌ ★

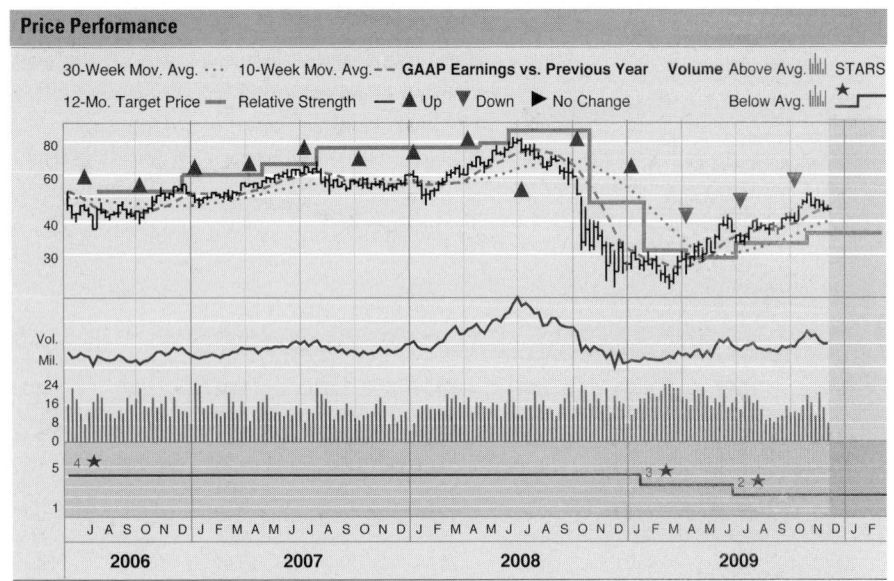

Options: ASE, CBOE, P

Analysis prepared by **Stewart Glickman, CFA** on November 30, 2009, when the stock traded at **$ 44.59**.

Qualitative Risk Assessment

LOW	MEDIUM	**HIGH**

Our risk assessment reflects ESV's exposure to volatile crude oil and natural gas prices, capital spending decisions made by its oil and gas producing customers, and its plans to construct seven new floaters through 2012, some of which are not yet under contract.

Quantitative Evaluations

S&P Quality Ranking   B+

D	C	B-	B	**B+**	A-	A	A+

Relative Strength Rank   MODERATE

46

LOWEST = 1   HIGHEST = 99

Revenue/Earnings Data

Revenue (Million $)

	1Q	2Q	3Q	4Q	Year
2009	514.1	511.6	425.4	--	--
2008	568.5	624.0	635.8	622.1	2,450
2007	514.1	548.6	551.9	529.2	2,144
2006	381.6	475.2	486.1	470.6	1,814
2005	210.6	246.3	275.1	314.9	1,047
2004	186.5	181.4	190.9	209.2	768.0

Earnings Per Share ($)

2009	1.56	1.59	1.05	E1.24	E5.28
2008	1.86	2.03	2.13	2.14	8.17
2007	1.54	1.72	1.82	1.66	6.74
2006	0.94	1.26	1.40	1.36	4.96
2005	0.27	0.39	0.52	0.67	1.86
2004	0.14	0.12	0.17	0.26	0.69

Fiscal year ended Dec. 31. Next earnings report expected: Late February. EPS Estimates based on S&P Operating Earnings; historical GAAP earnings are as reported.

Highlights

▶ We see ESV jackup utilization at about 70% in 2010, flat with estimated 2009 levels, and average dayrates in the low $120,000 range, down from the high $150,000 range in 2009. As of late November, according to ODS Petrodata, there are 66 newbuild jackups to come, only 10 of which (15%) have been contracted. Given that ESV has seven idle units (five available, and two cold-stacked), and another eight units currently working but without follow-on work beyond the first quarter of 2010, we think ESV faces above-average exposure to either zero-rate days and/or declining dayrates in 2010 for a material portion of its 42-unit jackup fleet.

▶ Notwithstanding these challenges, we see the start of a recovery in late 2010, and a marked uptick in utilization in 2011. We also note that ESV should benefit from a full year of activity for the Ensco 8500 and Ensco 8501 in 2010. The Ensco 8500, the second of seven deepwater newbuilds, commenced operations in June, and the Ensco 8501 began operations in October.

▶ We project EPS from continuing operations of $5.28 in 2009 (a 37% drop from 2008), falling another 23% in 2010 to $4.07.

Investment Rationale/Risk

▶ ESV is in the midst of a transformation to a company that is more balanced between shallow-water and deepwater drilling activity, which we view favorably given our expectations that deepwater fields represent the best growth opportunities for upstream players (and thus for rig contractors such as ESV). By 2012, we expect ESV's deepwater exposure to account for 41% of total revenues. Nonetheless, we remain concerned about near-term prospects given expected weakness in jackup dayrates and utilization. We project that ESV will generate only about 11% of contract drilling revenues from floaters in 2009, and only 28% in 2010, below its major peers.

▶ Risks to our recommendation and target price include rising dayrates and utilization; higher crude oil and natural gas prices; and lack of delays in newbuild deliveries.

▶ We see ROIC slightly below peers in 2010, and think this merits a modest peer discount. Assuming a 6X multiple applied to our 2010 EBITDA estimate and a 7X multiple applied to our 2010 cash flow forecast (both discounts to peers), and blending with our NAV model, our 12-month target price is $36.

Dividend Data (Dates: mm/dd Payment Date: mm/dd/yy)

Amount ($)	Date Decl.	Ex-Div. Date	Stk. of Record	Payment Date
0.025	02/19	03/05	03/09	03/20/09
0.025	05/28	06/04	06/08	06/19/09
0.025	08/04	09/02	09/07	09/18/09
0.025	11/03	12/03	12/07	12/18/09

Dividends have been paid since 1997. Source: Company reports.

Please read the Required Disclosures and Analyst Certification on the last page of this report.

The McGraw-Hill Companies

ENSCO International Inc.

Business Summary November 30, 2009

CORPORATE OVERVIEW. ENSCO International is an international offshore oil and gas contract drilling company. As of February 2009, ESV's offshore drilling fleet was comprised of 43 jackup rigs; two active semisubmersible rigs (and six more under construction); and one barge rig. ESV lost one of its former jackup rigs, the Ensco 74, during Hurricane Ike in September 2008, and the rig is presumed sunk. The company is one of the leading international providers of offshore contract drilling services, operating in North and South America, Europe/Africa, and the Asia/Pacific Rim region. As of February 2009, the total backlog of contract drilling work was approximately $4.0 billion, of which approximately 47% was from semisubmersibles, with the remaining 53% from jackups. Business operations are conducted through four segments: Deepwater (which includes only the two current active semis); Asia Pacific (19 jackups as of February 2009); North & South America (14 jackups); and Europe/Africa (10 jackups). Of the six ultra-deepwater semisubmersibles then under construction, the next (the Ensco 8501) is slated for delivery in the second quarter of 2009; the Ensco 8502, announced in September at a projected capital cost of $385 million, is due in the first quarter of 2010; and the Ensco 8503 is

due in the fourth quarter of 2010. During 2008, ESV entered into agreements to build three additional 8500-class floaters (the Ensco 8504, Ensco 8505 and Ensco 8506) which will be due between the second half of 2011 and the second half of 2012.

In Asia Pacific (43% of 2008 contract drilling revenues, and 44% of 2008 operating income), ESV experienced utilization of 95%, down from 99% in 2007. Average dayrates, however, rose to $152,981 from $131,384. In North & South America (21%, 18%), rig utilization was up markedly in 2008, to 97% from 79%, while average dayrates fell slightly to $101,534 from $104,318. In Europe/Africa (33%, 35%), rig utilization advanced to 96% from 93%, and average dayrates rose to $221,164 from $198,551.

Company Financials Fiscal Year Ended Dec. 31

Per Share Data ($)	2008	2007	2006	2005	2004	2003	2002	2001	2000	1999
Tangible Book Value	30.61	23.74	18.97	14.32	12.14	11.55	10.85	10.70	9.59	9.05
Cash Flow	9.51	7.99	6.11	2.92	1.69	1.61	1.29	2.41	1.32	0.76
Earnings	8.17	6.74	4.96	1.86	0.69	0.71	0.42	1.50	0.61	-0.05
S&P Core Earnings	8.17	6.72	4.96	1.79	0.64	0.64	0.30	1.34	NA	NA
Dividends	0.10	0.10	0.10	0.10	0.10	0.10	0.10	0.10	0.10	0.10
Payout Ratio	1%	1%	2%	5%	14%	14%	24%	7%	16%	NM
Prices:High	83.24	67.61	58.75	50.34	34.15	31.10	35.50	44.49	43.13	25.00
Prices:Low	22.38	45.00	37.36	29.25	24.95	23.58	20.87	12.81	20.25	8.75
P/E Ratio:High	10	10	12	27	49	44	85	30	71	NM
P/E Ratio:Low	3	7	8	16	36	33	50	9	33	NM

Income Statement Analysis (Million $)	2008	2007	2006	2005	2004	2003	2002	2001	2000	1999
Revenue	2,450	2,144	1,814	1,047	768	791	698	817	534	364
Operating Income	1,596	1,400	1,192	573	323	316	290	442	230	102
Depreciation, Depletion and Amortization	190	184	175	161	150	135	124	124	98.7	98.2
Interest Expense	21.6	32.3	16.5	28.8	36.6	36.7	31.1	32.8	13.4	19.3
Pretax Income	1,402	1,254	1,011	391	140	149	87.1	292	125	5.20
Effective Tax Rate	17.3%	20.9%	25.0%	27.4%	25.8%	28.2%	31.9%	29.0%	31.8%	NM
Net Income	1,160	992	759	284	104	107	59.3	207	85.4	6.70
S&P Core Earnings	1,160	990	759	273	94.8	96.1	42.5	182	NA	NA

Balance Sheet & Other Financial Data (Million $)	2008	2007	2006	2005	2004	2003	2002	2001	2000	1999
Cash	790	630	566	269	267	354	147	279	107	165
Current Assets	1,401	1,129	987	578	494	543	388	461	289	273
Total Assets	5,830	4,969	4,334	3,618	3,322	3,183	3,062	2,324	2,108	1,978
Current Liabilities	428	504	385	231	216	187	198	149	117	135
Long Term Debt	274	291	309	475	527	550	548	462	422	371
Common Equity	4,677	3,752	3,216	2,533	2,182	2,081	1,967	1,440	1,329	1,241
Total Capital	5,292	4,395	3,881	3,354	3,084	2,977	2,847	2,162	1,981	1,829
Capital Expenditures	772	520	529	478	305	187	227	145	256	248
Cash Flow	1,350	1,176	934	445	254	242	183	332	184	105
Current Ratio	3.3	2.2	2.6	2.5	2.3	2.9	2.0	3.1	2.5	2.0
% Long Term Debt of Capitalization	5.2	6.6	7.9	14.2	17.1	18.5	19.2	21.4	21.3	20.3
% Return on Assets	21.5	21.3	19.1	8.2	3.2	3.4	2.2	9.4	4.2	0.3
% Return on Equity	27.5	28.5	26.4	12.0	4.9	5.3	3.5	15.0	6.7	0.5

Data as orig reptd.; bef. results of disc opers/spec. items. Per share data adj. for stk. divs.; EPS diluted. E-Estimated. NA-Not Available. NM-Not Meaningful. NR-Not Ranked. UR-Under Review.

Office: 500 North Akard Street, Dallas, TX, USA 75201-3331.
Telephone: 214-397-3000.
Email: hrstaff@enscous.com
Website: http://www.enscous.com

Chrmn, Pres & CEO: D.W. Rabun
COO & EVP: W.S. Chadwick, Jr.
SVP & CFO: J.W. Swent, III
Treas: R. Yi

Treas: M.B. Howe
Investor Contact: R.A. LeBlanc (214-397-3011)
Board Members: D. M. Carmichael, J. R. Clark, C. C. Gaut, G. W. Haddock, T. L. Kelly, II, D. W. Rabun, K. O. Rattie, R. M. Rodriguez, P. E. Rowsey, III

Founded: 1978
Domicile: Delaware
Employees: 3,947

STANDARD &POOR'S

Entergy Corp.

S&P Recommendation **BUY** ★★★★☆	Price $78.50 (as of Nov 27, 2009)	12-Mo. Target Price $88.00	Investment Style Large-Cap Blend

GICS Sector Utilities
Sub-Industry Electric Utilities

Summary This electric utility holding company serves 2.6 million customers in Arkansas, Louisiana, Mississippi, and Texas.

Key Stock Statistics (Source S&P, Vickers, company reports)

52-Wk Range	$86.61– 59.87	S&P Oper. EPS 2009**E**	6.32	Market Capitalization(B)	$14.831	Beta	0.64
Trailing 12-Month EPS	$5.54	S&P Oper. EPS 2010**E**	6.86	Yield (%)	3.82	S&P 3-Yr. Proj. EPS CAGR(%)	5
Trailing 12-Month P/E	14.2	P/E on S&P Oper. EPS 2009**E**	12.4	Dividend Rate/Share	$3.00	S&P Credit Rating	BBB
$10K Invested 5 Yrs Ago	$13,660	Common Shares Outstg. (M)	188.9	Institutional Ownership (%)	79		

Price Performance

30-Week Mov. Avg. · · · 10-Week Mov. Avg. – – **GAAP Earnings vs. Previous Year** Volume Above Avg. STARS
12-Mo. Target Price — Relative Strength — ▲ Up ▼ Down ► No Change Below Avg. ★

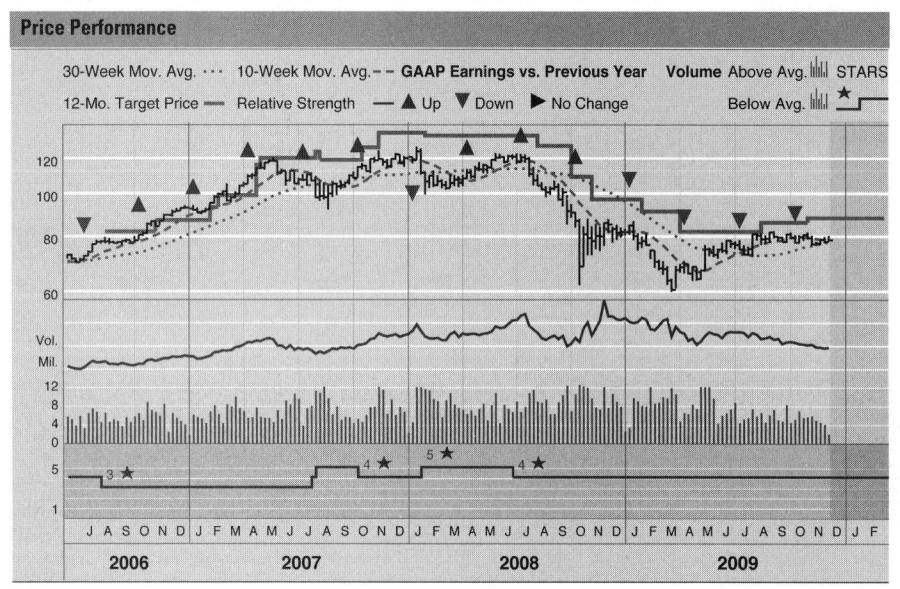

Options: ASE, CBOE, P, Ph

Analysis prepared by **Justin McCann** on October 23, 2009, when the stock traded at **$ 80.89**.

Highlights

▶ Due to pending state regulatory decisions and financing concerns, it is uncertain as to when ETR's planned tax-free spinoff of its non-utility nuclear assets (to a company named Enexus Energy), and the equally owned joint venture (EquaGen) to be formed with Enexus, can be implemented. ETR hopes regulatory approvals will be received by the end of 2009, and says it is ready to launch the spinoff once the regulatory and financial issues have been resolved.

▶ Excluding $0.26 of net one-time charges, we expect operating EPS in 2009 to decline nearly 3% from 2008's $6.51. This would reflect the impact of lower spot market power prices and additional refueling and unplanned plant outages at the nuclear business, as well as a significant impairment of decommissioning trust investments. We also see customer demand at the utility operations being affected by the weak economy, particularly in the industrial segment.

▶ Assuming a still combined entity, we project operating EPS in 2010 to increase more than 8% from anticipated results in 2009. The increase would be driven by a gradual recovery in the economy and power markets, fewer plant outages, and fewer average shares outstanding.

Investment Rationale/Risk

▶ We expect the stock to continue to recover from its multi-year low reached in March. We think the sharp drop reflected the weakening economy, a decline in power prices, and the crisis in the credit markets. ETR's plan to spin off its non-utility nuclear operations should enable the new company (Enexus) to realize higher growth and P/E multiples than ETR would as a single, combined entity. We also expect the retained regulated utilities to achieve shareholder value with a targeted 70% to 75% dividend payout, annual EPS growth of 6% to 8%, and fewer shares through a new share buyback program combined with a post-spinoff exchange of Enexus shares for Entergy shares.

▶ Risks to our recommendation and target price include a sharp drop in the margins of ETR's non-regulated operations, unanticipated problems with its nuclear facilities, and a decline in the average P/E of the group as a whole.

▶ Should it occur, we believe ETR's spinoff of its non-utility nuclear assets would benefit the stock. With the stock down around 2% year-to-date, the recent dividend yield was about 3.7%. Our 12-month target price is $88, a premium-to-peers P/E of 12.8X our 2010 EPS estimate.

Qualitative Risk Assessment

LOW	MEDIUM	HIGH

Our risk assessment reflects the steady cash flow we expect from most of the regulated utilities and the nuclear operations, offset by uncertainties related to the recovery of the economy and the wholesale power markets.

Quantitative Evaluations

S&P Quality Ranking   A

D	C	B-	B	B+	A-	A	A+

Relative Strength Rank   MODERATE

50

LOWEST = 1   HIGHEST = 99

Revenue/Earnings Data

Revenue (Million $)

	1Q	2Q	3Q	4Q	Year
2009	2,789	2,521	2,937	--	--
2008	2,865	3,264	3,964	3,001	13,094
2007	2,600	2,769	3,289	2,825	11,484
2006	2,568	2,629	3,255	2,481	10,932
2005	2,323	2,710	3,130	2,652	10,106
2004	2,252	2,485	2,964	2,424	10,124

Earnings Per Share ($)

	1Q	2Q	3Q	4Q	Year
2009	1.19	1.14	2.32	E1.41	E6.32
2008	1.56	1.37	2.41	0.89	6.23
2007	1.03	1.32	2.30	0.96	5.60
2006	0.93	1.27	1.83	1.32	5.36
2005	0.79	1.33	1.65	0.59	4.40
2004	0.88	1.14	1.22	0.68	3.93

Fiscal year ended Dec. 31. Next earnings report expected: Early February. EPS Estimates based on S&P Operating Earnings; historical GAAP earnings are as reported.

Dividend Data (Dates: mm/dd Payment Date: mm/dd/yy)

Amount ($)	Date Decl.	Ex-Div. Date	Stk. of Record	Payment Date
0.750	01/30	02/09	02/11	03/02/09
0.750	04/07	05/11	05/13	06/01/09
0.750	07/31	08/10	08/12	09/01/09
0.750	10/30	11/09	11/12	12/01/09

Dividends have been paid since 1988. Source: Company reports.

Please read the Required Disclosures and Analyst Certification on the last page of this report.

The **McGraw-Hill** Companies

Stock Report | November 28, 2009 | NYS Symbol: **ETR**

Entergy Corp.

STANDARD &POOR'S

Business Summary October 23, 2009

CORPORATE OVERVIEW. Entergy is an integrated energy company primarily engaged in electric power production and retail electric distribution operations. It owns and operates power plants with about 30,000 megawatts (MW) of electric generating capacity, and is the second largest nuclear power generator in the U.S. As the holding company for Entergy Arkansas, Entergy Gulf States Louisiana, Entergy Louisiana, Entergy Mississippi, Entergy New Orleans, and Entergy Texas. Entergy Corp. provides electricity to 2.7 million U.S. retail customers. ETR also owns System Energy Resources, which has a 90% interest in the Grand Gulf 1 nuclear plant. The non-utility nuclear business owns and operates five nuclear plants in the northeastern U.S., selling mainly to wholesale customers.

IMPACT OF MAJOR DEVELOPMENTS. On November 5, 2007, Entergy announced that it planned to spin off to shareholders the company's non-utility nuclear business. On April 25, 2008, ETR announced that the name of the spun-off company would be Enexus Energy Corp. Entergy also announced that it and Enexus intend to form an equally owned joint venture, to be named EquaGen L.L.C., that will be involved in the operation of the new company's nuclear assets and which will offer ancillary nuclear services to third parties. The company has deferred the spinoff and joint venture transactions until capital market conditions improve. The spinoff transaction is expected to be tax-free for both the company and the shareholders.

Hurricanes Katrina and Rita in 2005 caused catastrophic damage to large portions of ETR's service territories in Louisiana, Mississippi and Texas, including the effect of extensive flooding in and around greater New Orleans. As of December 31, 2008, Entergy had received $277 million on its Katrina and Rita insurance claims. The company expects to receive any remaining insurance recovery related to Hurricanes Katrina and Rita in 2009.

On December 31, 2007, Entergy's Gulf States utility completed a jurisdictional separation into two vertically integrated utilities, Entergy Gulf States Louisiana and Entergy Texas. Entergy Gulf States Louisiana was allocated 58.1% of the former entity's assets, and Energy Texas, 41.9%.

On May 8, 2007, Entergy New Orleans emerged from Chapter 11 bankruptcy. This followed the approval of the company's plan of reorganization by the U.S. Bankruptcy Court for the Eastern District of Louisiana. The utility had filed for Chapter 11 reorganization in September 2005, soon after the devastation caused by Hurricane Katrina. Under the reorganization plan, all creditors would be fully compensated.

Company Financials Fiscal Year Ended Dec. 31

Per Share Data ($)	2008	2007	2006	2005	2004	2003	2002	2001	2000	1999
Tangible Book Value	40.08	38.76	38.59	35.49	36.43	36.38	33.61	33.74	31.83	29.71
Earnings	6.23	5.60	5.36	4.40	3.93	3.42	2.64	3.13	2.97	2.25
S&P Core Earnings	5.64	5.74	5.54	4.49	3.99	3.70	2.14	2.21	NA	NA
Dividends	3.00	2.58	2.16	2.16	1.89	1.60	1.34	1.28	1.22	1.20
Payout Ratio	48%	46%	40%	49%	48%	47%	51%	41%	41%	53%
Prices:High	127.48	125.00	94.03	79.22	68.67	57.24	46.85	44.67	43.88	33.50
Prices:Low	61.93	89.60	66.78	64.48	50.64	42.26	32.12	32.56	15.94	23.69
P/E Ratio:High	20	22	18	18	17	17	18	14	15	15
P/E Ratio:Low	10	16	12	15	13	12	12	10	5	11

Income Statement Analysis (Million $)										
Revenue	13,094	11,484	10,932	10,106	10,124	9,195	8,305	9,621	10,016	8,773
Depreciation	1,031	1,132	888	856	896	851	839	721	785	745
Maintenance	NA	NA	NA	NA	NA	NA	NA	NA	NA	NA
Fixed Charges Coverage	3.92	3.49	3.36	3.69	3.54	2.66	2.23	2.25	2.83	2.34
Construction Credits	69.8	67.8	63.8	75.1	65.3	75.9	57.0	48.0	56.0	52.0
Effective Tax Rate	33.1%	30.7%	28.1%	36.6%	28.2%	37.6%	32.1%	38.5%	40.3%	37.5%
Net Income	1,221	1,135	1,133	969	933	813	623	727	711	595
S&P Core Earnings	1,108	1,162	1,171	961	922	856	487	495	NA	NA

Balance Sheet & Other Financial Data (Million $)										
Gross Property	38,591	36,302	33,366	32,437	32,055	31,181	32,964	32,403	29,865	28,178
Capital Expenditures	2,435	1,578	1,586	1,458	1,411	1,569	1,580	1,380	1,494	1,196
Net Property	22,660	21,194	19,651	19,426	18,915	18,561	20,657	20,597	18,501	17,279
Capitalization:Long Term Debt	11,174	9,728	8,809	8,838	7,034	7,498	7,458	7,536	8,014	7,253
Capitalization:% Long Term Debt	57.4	54.3	50.8	53.2	44.5	45.2	47.6	49.1	52.2	49.3
Capitalization:Preferred	311	311	345	Nil	365	334	359	361	335	338
Capitalization:% Preferred	1.60	1.70	1.99	Nil	2.31	2.01	2.29	2.35	2.18	2.30
Capitalization:Common	7,967	7,863	8,198	7,761	8,400	8,773	7,839	7,456	7,003	7,118
Capitalization:% Common	NA	44.0	47.2	46.8	53.2	52.8	50.1	48.6	45.6	48.4
Total Capital	26,343	24,625	23,531	22,399	21,266	21,805	20,355	19,399	19,095	18,539
% Operating Ratio	87.6	87.1	88.7	63.3	87.6	89.4	85.8	88.6	89.0	88.3
% Earned on Net Property	10.7	10.3	9.2	9.3	8.8	8.1	5.8	8.1	8.6	7.3
% Return on Revenue	9.3	9.9	10.4	9.6	9.2	8.8	7.5	7.6	7.1	6.8
% Return on Invested Capital	7.3	7.7	7.0	6.6	6.5	2.4	7.7	7.6	7.1	7.0
% Return on Common Equity	15.4	14.1	14.2	11.7	10.6	9.5	7.8	9.7	9.6	7.8

Data as orig reptd.; bef. results of disc opers/spec. items. Per share data adj. for stk. divs.; EPS diluted. E-Estimated. NA-Not Available. NM-Not Meaningful. NR-Not Ranked. UR-Under Review.

Office: 639 Loyola Ave, New Orleans, LA 70113-3125.
Telephone: 504-576-4000.
Website: http://www.entergy.com
Chrmn & CEO: J.W. Leonard

Pres & COO: R.J. Smith
EVP & CFO: L.P. Denault
EVP & General Counsel: R.D. Sloan
SVP & Chief Acctg Officer: T. Bunting, Jr.

Investor Contact: N. Morovich (504-576-5506)
Board Members: M. S. Bateman, W. Blount, G. W. Edwards, A. Herman, D. C. Hintz, J. W. Leonard, S. L. Levenick, S. C. Myers, J. R. Nichols, W. A. Percy, II, W. J. Tauzin, S. V. Wilkinson

Founded: 1989
Domicile: Delaware
Employees: 14,669

EOG Resources Inc.

STANDARD &POOR'S

S&P Recommendation BUY ★★★★☆	Price $87.23 (as of Nov 27, 2009)	12-Mo. Target Price $108.00	Investment Style Large-Cap Growth

GICS Sector Energy
Sub-Industry Oil & Gas Exploration & Production

Summary One of the largest independent exploration and production companies in the world, this U.S. company is focused on onshore natural gas production in North America.

Key Stock Statistics (Source S&P, Vickers, company reports)

52-Wk Range	$95.86– 45.03	S&P Oper. EPS 2009**E**	1.46	Market Capitalization(B)	$22.013	Beta	0.96
Trailing 12-Month EPS	$2.42	S&P Oper. EPS 2010**E**	3.61	Yield (%)	0.66	S&P 3-Yr. Proj. EPS CAGR(%)	-6
Trailing 12-Month P/E	36.1	P/E on S&P Oper. EPS 2009**E**	59.7	Dividend Rate/Share	$0.58	S&P Credit Rating	A-
$10K Invested 5 Yrs Ago	$23,567	Common Shares Outstg. (M)	252.4	Institutional Ownership (%)	92		

Price Performance

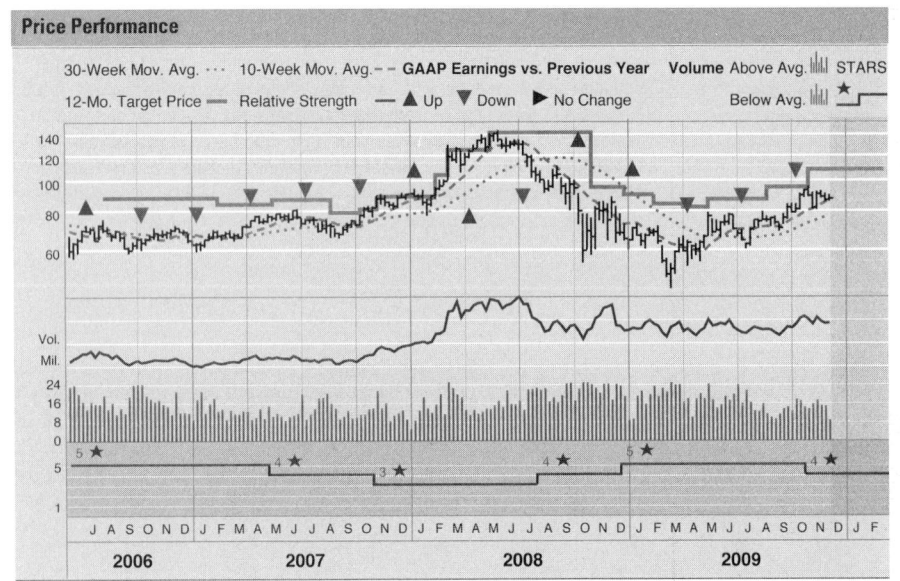

30-Week Mov. Avg. ··· 10-Week Mov. Avg. − − GAAP Earnings vs. Previous Year   Volume Above Avg. ▨▨ STARS
12-Mo. Target Price ▬ Relative Strength   ▲ Up ▼ Down ► No Change   Below Avg. ▨▨

Options: ASE, CBOE, P, Ph

Analysis prepared by **Michael Kay** on October 28, 2009, when the stock traded at **$ 86.77**.

Highlights

▶ Production rose 16% in 2008, driven by natural gas increases in the Barnett Shale, the Gulf Coast, the North Dakota Bakken and Mid-Continent. In the Bakken, EOG sees strong oil reserves from its large position in the Parshall field, which has driven oil production up over 60%. EOG recently began producing from three wells in the Horn River Shale Basin of British Columbia. We see production growth of 5% in 2009, on a 20% boost to oil volume, before resuming double-digit growth in 2010. EOG has increased oil activity due to weak gas markets.

▶ While industry costs have been rising, EOG has kept increases low versus peers through relatively efficient operations in North America natural gas basins. As a result, EOG estimates its North Dakota Bakken, Barnett Shale and Uinta Basin plays offer stronger returns relative to other North American developments.

▶ After 2008 EPS of $9.71 (with a non-cash derivative gain of $1.88 and a $0.34 asset sale gain), we see 2009 EPS of $1.98 ($0.91 derivative loss in first six months) on lower oil and gas price forecasts and $3.46 in 2010 on production and price gains. EOG spent $4.9 billion on drilling in 2008 and has set a 2009 budget of $3.1 billion.

Investment Rationale/Risk

▶ EOG raised spending to organically lift production growth, focused on plays such as the Barnett Shale and the Bakken Oil Shale. We think expertise in horizontal drilling and technology will aid onshore production growth. In 2008, EOG announced several new onshore plays in the U.S. and expanded the Barnett Shale into a promising new oil play. In May 2008, EOG identified a natural gas play in the Mid-Continent region. EOG also scaled back operations in Trinidad. With drilling capex cutbacks expected for 2009, we believe an attractive cost and debt structure, coupled with a low-risk production profile, makes EOG shares attractive.

▶ Risks to our recommendation and target price include changes in economic conditions, lower oil and gas prices, increased costs, and difficulty replacing reserves.

▶ We value EOG on proven reserve NAV estimates and do not factor in EOG's significant resource play potential. We blend our NAV estimate of $112 with DCF ($103; WACC, 10%; terminal growth 3%) and relative metrics to arrive at our 12-month target price of $108. We remain positive on EOG's earnings and production potential as well as its financial flexibility.

Qualitative Risk Assessment

LOW	MEDIUM	HIGH

Our risk assessment of EOG is based on its participation in a very competitive, capital-intensive and cyclical industry, partly offset by our view of its significant net acreage position, active drilling program and history of relatively low operating costs.

Quantitative Evaluations

S&P Quality Ranking A-

D	C	B-	B	B+	A-	A	A+

Relative Strength Rank MODERATE

68

LOWEST = 1   HIGHEST = 99

Revenue/Earnings Data

Revenue (Million $)

	1Q	2Q	3Q	4Q	Year
2009	1,158	827.5	1,007	--	--
2008	1,101	1,875	3,220	1,105	6,529
2007	875.2	1,055	990.5	1,251	4,191
2006	1,085	919.1	968.3	932.5	3,904
2005	688.2	783.9	934.5	1,214	3,620
2004	464.3	519.0	594.2	693.7	2,271

Earnings Per Share ($)

2009	0.63	-0.07	0.02	E0.88	E1.46
2008	0.96	0.71	6.20	1.85	9.72
2007	0.88	1.24	0.82	1.44	4.37
2006	1.73	1.34	1.21	0.96	5.24
2005	0.83	1.02	1.40	1.88	5.13
2004	0.42	0.60	0.71	0.85	2.58

Fiscal year ended Dec. 31. Next earnings report expected: Early February. EPS Estimates based on S&P Operating Earnings; historical GAAP earnings are as reported.

Dividend Data (Dates: mm/dd Payment Date: mm/dd/yy)

Amount ($)	Date Decl.	Ex-Div. Date	Stk. of Record	Payment Date
0.135	12/16	01/14	01/16	01/30/09
0.145	02/04	04/14	04/16	04/30/09
0.145	04/30	07/15	07/17	07/31/09
0.145	09/03	10/14	10/16	10/30/09

Dividends have been paid since 1990. Source: Company reports.

Please read the Required Disclosures and Analyst Certification on the last page of this report.

EOG Resources Inc.

STANDARD &POOR'S

Business Summary October 28, 2009

CORPORATE OVERVIEW. EOG Resources, Inc. (EOG), a Delaware corporation organized in 1985, together with its subsidiaries, explores for, develops, produces and markets natural gas and crude oil primarily in major producing basins in the U.S., Canada, offshore Trinidad, the U.K. North Sea, and other select regions.

As EOG begins to operate in regions with limited infrastructure, the company is placing more emphasis on gathering and processing operations to support its production activities. This has resulted in the subsidiary formation of Pecan Pipeline Co. and Pecan Pipeline (North Dakota), Inc.

Proved oil and gas reserves rose 12%, to 8.689 trillion cubic feet equivalent (Tcfe; 84% natural gas, 76% developed), in 2008. Also, we estimate EOG has exhibited a three-year reserve CAGR of 12%. About 71% of EOG's 2008 proved reserves were in the U.S., 15% in Canada, 14% in Trinidad, and less than 1% in other international. We estimate EOG's 2008 organic reserve replacement at 252% and reserve replacement cost at $2.70 per Mcf. This compares to a three-year reserve replacement of 233% and three-year reserve replacement cost of $2.49 per Mcf. Oil and gas production rose 16%, to 1.988 billion cubic feet equivalent (Bcfe) per day (82% natural gas), in 2008. Production growth came from a 60% boost in oil volumes due to the development of EOG's Bakken properties and a 20% rise in domestic natural gas production.

MARKET PROFILE. One of the largest independent exploration and production companies in the world, EOG has focused on onshore natural gas operations, primarily in the U.S. and Canada. Substantial portions of its reserves are in long-lived fields with well-established production characteristics.

In the U.S., EOG has interests in the Barnett Shale play of the Fort Worth Basin, including Johnson, Montague, Clay and Archer Counties; the Upper Gulf Coast area covering East Texas, Louisiana and Mississippi; Permian Basin, Rocky Mountain area, including the Uinta Basin, Williston Basin and Bakken play in North Dakota; the Mid-Continent area including the Hugoton-Deep play in the Southwest Kansas/Oklahoma Panhandle and the Cleveland Horizontal play in the Texas Panhandle; South Texas and the Gulf of Mexico; and the Marcellus Shale in Pennsylvania.

In Canada, EOG operates through its subsidiary, EOG Resources Canada, Inc. (EOGRC), with operations focused in the Southeast Alberta/Southwest Saskatchewan shallow natural gas trends; the Pembina/Highvale area of Central Alberta; the Grand Prairie/Wapiti area of Northwest Alberta; the Waskada area in Southwest Manitoba; and the Horn River Basin in northeastern British Columbia.

Company Financials Fiscal Year Ended Dec. 31

Per Share Data ($)	2008	2007	2006	2005	2004	2003	2002	2001	2000	1999
Tangible Book Value	36.11	28.68	22.76	17.21	11.97	8.95	6.64	6.47	5.27	4.11
Cash Flow	15.79	9.27	8.56	7.81	4.69	3.73	2.02	3.32	3.17	3.61
Earnings	9.72	4.37	5.24	5.13	2.58	1.83	0.33	1.65	1.12	2.00
S&P Core Earnings	9.39	4.37	5.21	5.08	2.54	1.77	0.26	1.60	NA	NA
Dividends	0.47	0.33	0.22	0.15	0.12	0.09	0.08	0.08	0.07	0.06
Payout Ratio	5%	8%	4%	3%	5%	5%	25%	5%	6%	3%
Prices:High	144.99	91.63	86.91	82.00	38.25	23.76	22.08	27.75	28.34	12.69
Prices:Low	54.42	59.21	56.31	32.05	21.23	17.85	15.01	12.90	6.84	7.19
P/E Ratio:High	15	21	17	16	15	13	68	17	25	6
P/E Ratio:Low	6	14	11	6	8	10	46	8	6	4

Income Statement Analysis (Million $)										
Revenue	6,529	4,191	3,904	3,620	2,271	1,745	1,095	1,655	1,490	801
Operating Income	5,144	2,802	1,895	1,992	979	697	648	1,181	697	18.2
Depreciation, Depletion and Amortization	1,520	1,213	817	654	504	442	398	392	370	460
Interest Expense	51.7	76.1	43.2	62.5	63.1	58.7	59.7	45.1	61.0	61.8
Pretax Income	3,747	1,631	1,913	1,965	926	654	120	631	634	568
Effective Tax Rate	35.0%	33.2%	32.0%	35.9%	32.5%	33.1%	27.2%	36.9%	37.3%	NM
Net Income	2,437	1,090	1,300	1,260	625	437	87.2	399	397	569
S&P Core Earnings	2,353	1,083	1,281	1,238	605	412	62.4	376	NA	NA

Balance Sheet & Other Financial Data (Million $)										
Cash	331	54.2	218	644	21.0	4.44	9.85	2.51	20.2	24.8
Current Assets	2,108	1,292	1,350	1,563	587	396	395	272	394	201
Total Assets	15,951	12,089	9,402	7,753	5,799	4,749	3,814	3,414	3,001	2,611
Current Liabilities	1,765	1,474	1,255	1,172	632	477	276	311	370	219
Long Term Debt	1,860	1,185	733	859	1,078	1,109	1,145	856	859	990
Common Equity	9,015	6,985	5,547	4,217	2,847	2,098	1,524	1,495	1,234	982
Total Capital	13,688	10,246	7,846	6,298	4,925	4,125	3,478	3,050	2,580	2,346
Capital Expenditures	5,195	3,679	2,819	1,725	1,417	1,204	714	974	603	403
Cash Flow	3,956	2,296	2,106	1,906	1,118	868	474	780	756	1,028
Current Ratio	1.2	0.9	1.1	1.3	0.9	0.8	1.4	0.9	1.1	0.9
% Long Term Debt of Capitalization	13.6	14.5	9.3	13.6	21.9	26.9	32.9	28.1	33.3	42.2
% Return on Assets	17.4	10.1	15.2	18.6	11.8	10.2	2.4	12.4	14.1	20.2
% Return on Equity	30.5	17.3	26.4	35.5	24.9	23.4	5.0	28.4	34.8	50.3

Data as orig reptd.; bef. results of disc opers/spec. items. Per share data adj. for stk. divs.; EPS diluted. E-Estimated. NA-Not Available. NM-Not Meaningful. NR-Not Ranked. UR-Under Review.

Office: 1111 Bagby St Lbby 2, Houston, TX 77002-2551.
Telephone: 877-363-3647.
Email: ir@eogresources.com
Website: http://www.eogresources.com

Chrmn & CEO: M.G. Papa
COO: G.L. Thomas
SVP & General Counsel: F.J. Plaeger, II
CFO & Chief Acctg Officer: T.K. Driggers

Chief Admin Officer: P.L. Edwards
Investor Contact: M.A. Baldwin (713-651-6364)
Board Members: G. A. Alcorn, C. R. Crisp, J. C. Day, M. G. Papa, H. L. Steward, D. F. Textor, F. G. Wisner

Founded: 1985
Domicile: Delaware
Employees: 2,100

The McGraw·Hill Companies

STANDARD &POOR'S

E TRADE Financial Corporation

S&P Recommendation **HOLD** ★★★★★	Price $1.59 (as of Nov 27, 2009)	12-Mo. Target Price $2.00	Investment Style Large-Cap Growth

GICS Sector Financials
Sub-Industry Investment Banking & Brokerage

Summary This company provides online discount brokerage, mortgage and banking services, primarily to retail customers.

Key Stock Statistics (Source S&P, Vickers, company reports)

52-Wk Range	$2.90– 0.59	S&P Oper. EPS 2009**E**	-1.28	Market Capitalization(B)	$2.966	Beta	2.08
Trailing 12-Month EPS	$-1.94	S&P Oper. EPS 2010**E**	0.01	Yield (%)	Nil	S&P 3-Yr. Proj. EPS CAGR(%)	NM
Trailing 12-Month P/E	NM	P/E on S&P Oper. EPS 2009**E**	NM	Dividend Rate/Share	Nil	S&P Credit Rating	CCC
$10K Invested 5 Yrs Ago	$1,097	Common Shares Outstg. (M)	1,865.5	Institutional Ownership (%)	44		

Price Performance

30-Week Mov. Avg. · · ·   10-Week Mov. Avg. - -   **GAAP Earnings vs. Previous Year**   Volume Above Avg. ▯▮▯ STARS
12-Mo. Target Price —   Relative Strength   ▲ Up ▼ Down ▶ No Change   Below Avg. ▯▯▯

Options: ASE, CBOE, P, Ph

Analysis prepared by **Matthew Albrecht** on November 02, 2009, when the stock traded at **$ 1.46**.

Highlights

▶ We view ETFC's decision to refocus on its core retail segment competencies as prudent, although we believe significant damage to its balance sheet and future earnings power has already taken place, which puts it in a weaker position relative to peers. Nevertheless, problems at ETFC's bank have not driven away brokerage clients, in our view, as total accounts at the end of September were up 8% over the prior year and up modestly over the prior month. Furthermore, daily average revenue trades were up 7% year over year, though they fell sequentially.

▶ In the third quarter, ETFC recorded loan loss provisions of $347 million, the fourth straight quarterly decline after peaking in the 2008 third quarter. We expect loss provisions to decline slightly going forward as the economy gains steam and loan modifications take effect. ETFC currently maintains a 6.72% Tier-1 ratio, near its stated goal of 6%. We view ETFC's $550 million secondary offering and convertible bond debt exchange as very dilutive, but necessary to bolster capital ratios.

▶ We project a per-share loss of $1.28 in 2009 and EPS of $0.01 in 2010.

Investment Rationale/Risk

▶ We see the overhang from ETFC's remaining mortgage assets offsetting relative strength elsewhere. While we believe new account growth has lagged that of its online brokerage competitors, we think its recent balance sheet restructuring will raise confidence. We are encouraged that the change in the number of home equity loans in the special mention category has turned negative. It appears to us that ETFC home equity loan deterioration has reached a plateau. Yet, ETFC's one-to-four family mortgage book remains weak, in our view, as there was another strong inflow into the special mention category in the second quarter. While concerning, we think it is not as damaging as the home equity portfolio delinquencies, because losses are offset by the collateral value of the home.

▶ Risks to our opinion and target price include greater-than-expected declines in retail trading volume and client assets, and larger writedowns in the remaining mortgage portfolio.

▶ Our 12-month target price of $2.00 is a slight discount to our projection for ETFC's book value, and the stock trades at a discount to peer multiples.

Qualitative Risk Assessment

LOW	MEDIUM	**HIGH**

Our risk assessment reflects our concerns about significant industry volatility and ETFC's exposure to residential mortgage and home equity loans, partially offset by our view of its strong client relationships.

Quantitative Evaluations

S&P Quality Ranking   **C**

D	**C**	B-	B	B+	A-	A	A+

Relative Strength Rank   **MODERATE**

49

LOWEST = 1   HIGHEST = 99

Revenue/Earnings Data

Revenue (Million $)

	1Q	2Q	3Q	4Q	Year
2009	295.3	232.4	575.3	--	--
2008	529.1	532.3	377.7	486.4	1,926
2007	645.0	663.5	321.2	-2,008	-378.0
2006	598.4	611.4	581.8	628.9	2,420
2005	417.4	387.7	419.8	478.9	1,704
2004	400.5	380.9	337.1	409.5	1,947

Earnings Per Share ($)

	1Q	2Q	3Q	4Q	Year
2009	-0.41	-0.22	-0.66	E-0.04	E-1.28
2008	-0.20	-0.24	-0.60	-0.50	-1.59
2007	0.39	0.37	-0.14	-3.98	-3.40
2006	0.33	0.36	0.34	0.40	1.44
2005	0.27	0.29	0.29	0.31	1.16
2004	0.23	0.24	0.21	0.24	0.92

Fiscal year ended Dec. 31. Next earnings report expected: Late January. EPS Estimates based on S&P Operating Earnings; historical GAAP earnings are as reported.

Dividend Data

No cash dividends have been paid.

Please read the Required Disclosures and Analyst Certification on the last page of this report.

The McGraw-Hill Companies

E TRADE Financial Corporation

STANDARD &POOR'S

Business Summary November 02, 2009

CORPORATE OVERVIEW. E Trade Financial Corporation is one of the industry's leading online financial services concerns. The company provides online discount brokerage and banking services, primarily to retail customers. Although most of the company's business is done over the Internet, ETFC also serves customers through branches, automated and live telephone service, and Internet-enabled wireless devices. Retail customers can move money electronically between brokerage, banking and lending accounts. As of December 31, 2008, ETFC had about 4.4 million total retail accounts.

Brokerage customers can buy and sell stocks, bonds, options, futures, and over 7,000 non-proprietary mutual funds. Customers can also obtain streaming quotes and charts, access real-time market commentary and research reports, and perform personalized portfolio tracking. Brokerage customers can obtain margin loans collateralized by their securities. The company uses sophisticated proprietary transaction-enabling technology to automate traditionally labor-intensive transactions. The brokerage business continues to be the primary point of introduction for the majority of ETFC's customers, which are typically self-directed investors.

Through its Banking segment, the company has historically offered residential mortgage products, home equity loans and home equity lines of credit (HELOCs). However, in view of the housing-led recession, ETFC made the decision to exit all loan origination channels in 2008.

In late 2003, the Banking segment began sweeping Brokerage customer money market balances into an FDIC-insured Sweep Deposit Account (SDA) product, which lowered its cost of funds. At the end of 2008, ETFC had $9.6 billion in the SDA product, up from $4.3 billion at the end of 2003. ETFC's loan portfolio consists of first mortgages, the majority of which are adjustable-rate, home equity lines of credit, second mortgage loan products, and consumer loans for RVs, marine, automobile, and credit card loans. Going forward, we expect the asset composition of this segment to change significantly as ETFC completes its restructuring plan announced in September 2007 and realigns its focus on its core retail business.

Company Financials Fiscal Year Ended Dec. 31

Per Share Data ($)	2008	2007	2006	2005	2004	2003	2002	2001	2000	1999
Tangible Book Value	0.47	1.01	3.87	2.07	4.58	3.73	2.68	2.54	4.43	3.81
Cash Flow	-1.43	-3.10	1.61	1.36	1.07	0.55	1.20	-0.28	0.37	-0.09
Earnings	-1.59	-3.40	1.44	1.16	0.92	0.55	0.30	-0.81	-0.06	-0.23
S&P Core Earnings	-1.45	-3.26	1.33	0.88	0.66	0.27	0.27	-0.86	NA	NA
Dividends	Nil	Nil	Nil	Nil	Nil	Nil	Nil	Nil	Nil	Nil
Payout Ratio	Nil	Nil	Nil	Nil	Nil	Nil	Nil	Nil	Nil	Nil
Prices:High	5.48	26.08	27.76	21.71	15.40	12.91	12.64	15.38	34.25	72.25
Prices:Low	0.79	3.15	18.81	10.53	9.51	3.65	2.81	4.07	6.66	12.74
P/E Ratio:High	NM	NM	19	19	17	23	42	NM	NM	NM
P/E Ratio:Low	NM	NM	13	9	10	7	9	NM	NM	NM

Income Statement Analysis (Million $)	2008	2007	2006	2005	2004	2003	2002	2001	2000	1999
Commissions	516	694	625	459	350	337	302	407	739	356
Interest Income	2,470	3,570	2,775	1,650	1,146	893	946	1,160	960	196
Total Revenue	3,128	2,978	3,840	2,537	2,077	2,009	1,903	2,062	1,973	695
Interest Expense	1,202	2,133	1,527	853	558	532	609	832	630	73.4
Pretax Income	-1,279	-2,178	929	676	514	310	194	-310	104	-91.5
Effective Tax Rate	36.7%	33.8%	32.5%	34.0%	31.6%	36.2%	43.9%	NM	81.8%	NM
Net Income	-809	-1,442	627	446	351	203	107	-271	19.2	-54.4
S&P Core Earnings	-742	-1,378	580	339	247	101	96.1	-291	NA	NA

Balance Sheet & Other Financial Data (Million $)	2008	2007	2006	2005	2004	2003	2002	2001	2000	1999
Total Assets	48,538	56,846	53,739	44,568	31,033	26,049	21,534	18,172	17,317	3,927
Cash Items	5,051	1,778	1,212	844	940	921	2,223	1,601	301	189
Receivables	2,791	7,179	7,636	7,174	3,035	2,298	1,500	2,139	6,543	2,913
Securities Owned	10,862	11,385	13,922	12,565	12,589	9,876	8,702	4,726	985	189
Securities Borrowed	Nil	Nil	Nil	Nil	Nil	Nil	Nil	Nil	NA	NA
Due Brokers & Customers	3,753	5,515	7,825	7,316	3,619	3,696	2,792	2,700	6,056	2,824
Other Liabilities	35,090	38,033	NA	NA	NA	NA	NA	NA	NA	NA
Capitalization:Debt	7,104	10,469	7,166	6,189	586	695	907	605	3,336	Nil
Capitalization:Equity	2,592	2,829	4,196	3,400	2,228	1,918	1,506	1,571	1,857	914
Capitalization:Total	9,696	13,298	11,363	9,589	2,814	2,614	2,412	2,175	5,192	914
% Return on Revenue	NM	NM	20.7	68.4	18.0	11.8	5.4	NM	1.6	NM
% Return on Assets	NM	NM	1.3	1.2	1.2	0.9	0.5	NM	0.2	NM
% Return on Equity	NM	NM	16.5	15.9	16.9	11.9	7.0	NM	1.2	NM

Data as orig reptd.; bef. results of disc opers/spec. items. Per share data adj. for stk. divs.; EPS diluted. Total net revenues reported in quarterly table. E-Estimated. NA-Not Available. NM-Not Meaningful. NR-Not Ranked. UR-Under Review.

Office: 135 E 57th St, New York, NY 10022-2050.
Telephone: 646-521-4300.
Email: ir@etrade.com
Website: http://www.etrade.com

Chrmn & CEO: D.H. Layton
Vice Chrmn: S.H. Willard
COO, EVP & CIO: G. Framke
EVP, CFO & Chief Acctg Officer: B.P. Nolop

EVP, Secy & General Counsel: K.A. Roessner
Board Members: R. Druskin, R. D. Fisher, K. C. Griffin, G. A. Hayter, F. W. Kanner, D. H. Layton, M. K. Parks, C. C. Raffaeli, L. E. Randall, J. L. Sclafani, D. L. Weaver, S. H. Willard
Founded: 1982
Domicile: Delaware
Employees: 3,249

The McGraw-Hill Companies

EQT Corp

STANDARD &POOR'S

S&P Recommendation	HOLD ★★★☆☆	Price $40.70 (as of Nov 27, 2009)	12-Mo. Target Price $44.00	Investment Style Large-Cap Growth

GICS Sector Utilities
Sub-Industry Gas Utilities

Summary This energy company focuses on natural gas production, transmission and distribution, and energy management services.

Key Stock Statistics (Source S&P, Vickers, company reports)

52-Wk Range	$46.80– 26.09	S&P Oper. EPS 2009**E**	1.49	Market Capitalization(B)	$5.328	Beta	0.84
Trailing 12-Month EPS	$1.03	S&P Oper. EPS 2010**E**	1.83	Yield (%)	2.16	S&P 3-Yr. Proj. EPS CAGR(%)	3
Trailing 12-Month P/E	39.5	P/E on S&P Oper. EPS 2009**E**	27.3	Dividend Rate/Share	$0.88	S&P Credit Rating	BBB
$10K Invested 5 Yrs Ago	$15,303	Common Shares Outstg. (M)	130.9	Institutional Ownership (%)	83		

Price Performance

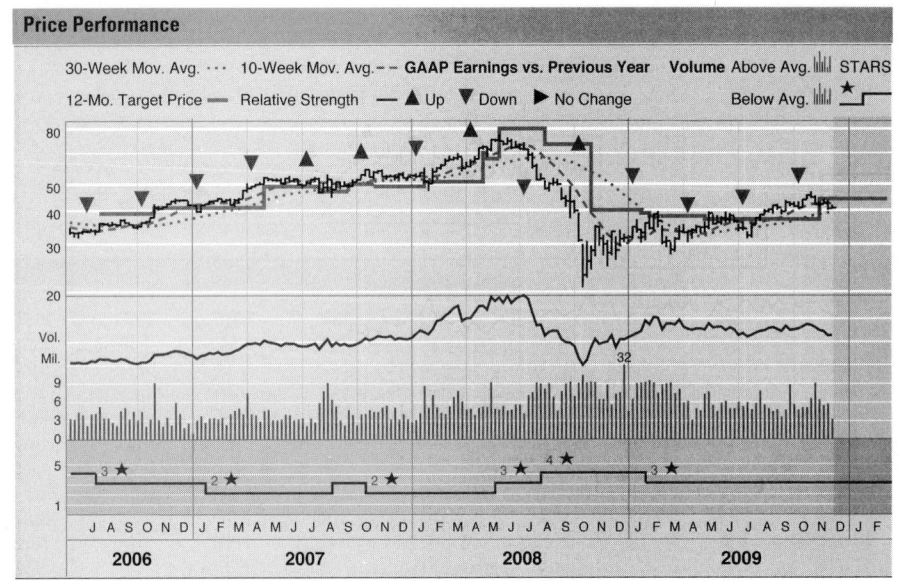

30-Week Mov. Avg. · · · 10-Week Mov. Avg. – – GAAP Earnings vs. Previous Year Volume Above Avg. STARS
12-Mo. Target Price — Relative Strength ▲ Up ▼ Down ► No Change Below Avg.

Options: ASE, CBOE, P, Ph

Analysis prepared by **Christopher B. Muir** on November 10, 2009, when the stock traded at **$ 43.32**.

Highlights

► We expect 2009 revenues to fall 17%, driven by lower average realized commodity prices during the year at its exploration and production business. We see 2009 revenues from these unregulated businesses falling 26%. However, we forecast revenues will rise 6.3% in 2010 as we anticipate stabilizing commodity prices and increasing volumes. We see unregulated revenues rising 6.9% in 2010.

► We anticipate that 2009 operating margins will rise to 31.3% from 26.2%, on wider gross margins from lower production costs and prices of gas and lower per-revenue non-fuel operating expenses, partly offset by rising per-revenue depreciation and depletion expense. We see pretax margins rising slightly to 23.6% from 23.2%, less than operating margins, as we expect interest expense to rise, partly offset by higher non-operating income. We see operating and pretax margins in 2010 of 34.0% and 26.8%, respectively.

► We project 2009 operating EPS, excluding $0.21 in net nonrecurring losses, of $1.49, down 17% from $1.79, excluding $0.20 in net nonrecurring gains, in 2008. Our 2010 EPS estimate is $1.83, up 23%.

Investment Rationale/Risk

► We like EQT's horizontal drilling program, which includes re-entry wells into existing fields. We believe results have been positive in the program so far. We expect EQT to use cash generated by recent non-core asset sales for additional investment in E&P operations. Much of the company's expansion has been in the Huron shale, but we think it also has opportunities and has shown good early results in the Berea Sandstone wells, in the Devonian shale re-entry wells, and in the Marcellus shale. However, we note that exploration and drilling expenses have been rising.

► Risks to our opinion and target price include lower-than-expected E&P production growth, energy prices and utility income, as well as higher-than-expected interest rates.

► EQT's shares recently traded at 23.7X our 2010 EPS estimate, a 66% premium to gas distribution peers. Our 12-month target price of $44 is 24.0X our 2010 EPS estimate, a 95% premium to our peer target. We believe the premium is warranted by our expectation for strong EPS growth driven by its unregulated businesses, partly offset by the riskier nature of the company's unregulated businesses.

Qualitative Risk Assessment

LOW	MEDIUM	HIGH

Our risk assessment is based on our view that the company's riskier exploration and production and energy marketing operations are balanced by its regulated gas businesses.

Quantitative Evaluations

S&P Quality Ranking B+

D	C	B-	B	B+	A-	A	A+

Relative Strength Rank MODERATE

36

LOWEST = 1 HIGHEST = 99

Revenue/Earnings Data

Revenue (Million $)

	1Q	2Q	3Q	4Q	Year
2009	469.4	238.0	218.4	--	--
2008	535.8	334.0	297.8	408.9	1,576
2007	456.6	293.2	226.8	384.8	1,361
2006	430.1	251.2	232.8	353.8	1,268
2005	401.3	230.2	229.4	392.9	1,254
2004	400.4	240.6	205.9	344.7	1,192

Earnings Per Share ($)

2009	0.55	0.20	0.02	E0.50	E1.49
2008	0.57	0.42	0.73	0.26	2.00
2007	0.46	0.87	0.27	0.49	2.10
2006	0.59	0.36	0.26	0.56	1.77
2005	0.60	0.47	0.37	0.65	2.09
2004	0.55	1.03	0.29	0.35	2.22

Fiscal year ended Dec. 31. Next earnings report expected: Late January. EPS Estimates based on S&P Operating Earnings; historical GAAP earnings are as reported.

Dividend Data (Dates: mm/dd Payment Date: mm/dd/yy)

Amount ($)	Date Decl.	Ex-Div. Date	Stk. of Record	Payment Date
0.220	01/21	02/12	02/17	03/01/09
0.220	04/23	05/06	05/08	06/01/09
0.220	07/08	08/05	08/07	09/01/09
0.220	10/21	11/04	11/06	12/01/09

Dividends have been paid since 1950. Source: Company reports.

Please read the Required Disclosures and Analyst Certification on the last page of this report.

The McGraw·Hill Companies

EQT Corp

STANDARD &POOR'S

Business Summary November 10, 2009

CORPORATE OVERVIEW. Equitable Resources Inc. (EQT) is a vertically integrated energy company operating through three business segments: Equitable Production (EP), Equitable Midstream (EM) and Equitable Distribution (ED). The EP unit (54% of 2008 operating income) is engaged in exploration and production of natural gas and oil, chiefly in the Appalachian Basin. The EM unit (29%) provides gathering, processing, transmission and storage services to EP and independent third parties. Its transmission system is located throughout north central West Virginia and southwestern Pennsylvania, and its gas gathering assets are located in Kentucky, West Virginia, Virginia and Pennsylvania. The ED unit (13%) operates a regulated natural gas utility in southwestern Pennsylvania and a small gathering system in Pennsylvania, and provides off-system sales activities.

CORPORATE STRATEGY. The ED unit is focused on earning a competitive return on its asset base through regulatory mechanisms and operational efficiency. ED believes it can achieve earnings growth by establishing a reputation for excellent customer service, effectively managing its capital spending, improving the efficiency of its work force through superior work management, and continuing to leverage technology throughout its operations. In 2008, ED

filed a base rate case and agreed to a settlement of the rate case that requested a $38 million increase in revenues. In January 2009, the settlement was approved by an administrative law judge.

The EP unit's business strategy is to focus on increased drilling and development in the Appalachian basin. ES also plans to create additional reserve potential through emerging development investments. To achieve maximum value from its existing assets, EP drills multilateral and stacked multilateral horizontal wells, refracs existing wells and drills re-entry wells where low pressured vertical shale wells were previously drilled.

The EM unit's strategy focuses on building a long-term growth platform to facilitate the development of EP's growing reserve base in the Huron play, and provides opportunities to sell capacity to third parties by connecting wells to existing midstream infrastructure in an effort to fill existing capacity.

Company Financials Fiscal Year Ended Dec. 31

Per Share Data ($)	2008	2007	2006	2005	2004	2003	2002	2001	2000	1999
Tangible Book Value	15.67	11.52	7.78	2.96	6.75	7.33	5.83	6.18	4.86	4.42
Cash Flow	3.06	2.99	2.59	2.94	2.88	3.40	1.72	1.70	1.54	1.24
Earnings	2.00	2.10	1.77	2.09	2.22	1.37	1.18	1.15	0.80	0.50
S&P Core Earnings	2.08	1.45	1.79	1.59	1.33	1.35	1.11	1.09	NA	NA
Dividends	0.88	0.88	0.87	0.82	0.72	0.49	0.34	0.31	0.29	0.29
Payout Ratio	44%	42%	49%	39%	32%	35%	28%	27%	37%	59%
Prices:High	76.14	56.75	44.48	41.18	30.59	21.71	18.78	20.25	16.69	9.75
Prices:Low	20.71	39.26	31.59	27.89	21.05	17.22	14.34	13.00	8.06	5.81
P/E Ratio:High	38	27	25	20	14	16	16	18	21	19
P/E Ratio:Low	10	19	18	13	9	13	12	11	10	12

Income Statement Analysis (Million $)	2008	2007	2006	2005	2004	2003	2002	2001	2000	1999
Revenue	1,576	1,361	1,268	1,254	1,192	1,047	1,069	1,764	1,652	1,063
Operating Income	602	432	470	445	388	380	352	328	312	243
Depreciation	137	110	100	93.5	83.1	78.1	69.4	73.2	97.8	101
Interest Expense	58.4	54.4	47.1	44.4	49.2	45.8	38.8	41.1	75.7	37.1
Pretax Income	411	402	326	412	424	257	235	240	163	108
Effective Tax Rate	37.7%	35.9%	33.7%	37.2%	33.7%	31.9%	33.0%	36.6%	35.0%	36.3%
Net Income	256	257	216	259	280	174	151	152	106	69.1
S&P Core Earnings	266	177	219	197	168	170	141	143	NA	NA

Balance Sheet & Other Financial Data (Million $)	2008	2007	2006	2005	2004	2003	2002	2001	2000	1999
Cash	Nil	81.7	Nil	75.0	Nil	37.3	17.7	92.6	52.0	18.0
Current Assets	927	742	701	1,097	653	550	430	613	615	327
Total Assets	5,330	3,937	3,257	3,342	3,197	2,940	2,437	2,519	2,456	1,790
Current Liabilities	1,043	1,519	1,080	2,092	1,015	703	552	612	877	430
Long Term Debt	1,249	754	754	763	618	681	586	396	413	423
Common Equity	2,050	1,097	946	354	875	965	779	846	694	643
Total Capital	3,304	2,252	2,038	1,142	1,990	2,118	1,728	1,621	1,370	1,267
Capital Expenditures	1,344	777	405	276	202	222	218	133	124	102
Cash Flow	392	367	316	352	363	430	220	225	204	170
Current Ratio	0.9	0.5	0.6	0.5	0.6	0.8	0.8	1.0	0.7	0.8
% Long Term Debt of Capitalization	37.8	33.5	37.0	66.9	31.0	32.2	33.9	24.4	30.1	33.4
% Net Income of Revenue	16.2	18.9	17.0	20.6	23.5	16.6	14.1	8.6	6.4	6.5
% Return on Assets	5.5	7.2	6.5	7.9	9.1	6.5	6.1	6.1	5.0	3.8
% Return on Equity	16.2	25.2	33.2	42.1	30.4	19.9	18.5	19.7	15.9	10.2

Data as orig reptd.; bef. results of disc opers/spec. items. Per share data adj. for stk. divs.; EPS diluted. E-Estimated. NA-Not Available. NM-Not Meaningful. NR-Not Ranked. UR-Under Review.

Office: 225 N Shore Dr, Pittsburgh, PA 15212-5860.
Telephone: 412-553-5700.
Website: http://www.eqt.com
Chrmn & CEO: M.S. Gerber

Pres & COO: D.L. Porges
SVP & CFO: P.P. Conti
Chief Acctg Officer & Cntlr: T.Z. Bone
Secy: K.L. Sachse

Investor Contact: P.J. Kane (412-553-7833)
Board Members: V. A. Bailey, P. G. Behrman, A. B. Cary, Jr., M. S. Gerber, B. S. Jeremiah, G. L. Miles, Jr., D. L. Porges, J. E. Rohr, D. S. Shapira, L. T. Todd, Jr., J. W. Whalen

Founded: 1926
Domicile: Pennsylvania
Employees: 1,680

The McGraw-Hill Companies

Equifax Inc.

STANDARD
&POOR'S

S&P Recommendation HOLD ★★★☆☆	Price $28.82 (as of Nov 27, 2009)	12-Mo. Target Price $29.00	Investment Style Large-Cap Growth

GICS Sector Industrials
Sub-Industry Research & Consulting Services

Summary This company is a leading worldwide source of consumer and commercial credit information.

Key Stock Statistics (Source S&P, Vickers, company reports)

52-Wk Range	$29.62– 19.63	S&P Oper. EPS 2009**E**	2.26	Market Capitalization(B)	$3.645	Beta	1.12
Trailing 12-Month EPS	$1.86	S&P Oper. EPS 2010**E**	2.33	Yield (%)	0.56	S&P 3-Yr. Proj. EPS CAGR(%)	10
Trailing 12-Month P/E	15.5	P/E on S&P Oper. EPS 2009**E**	12.8	Dividend Rate/Share	$0.16	S&P Credit Rating	BBB+
$10K Invested 5 Yrs Ago	$10,457	Common Shares Outstg. (M)	126.5	Institutional Ownership (%)	78		

Price Performance

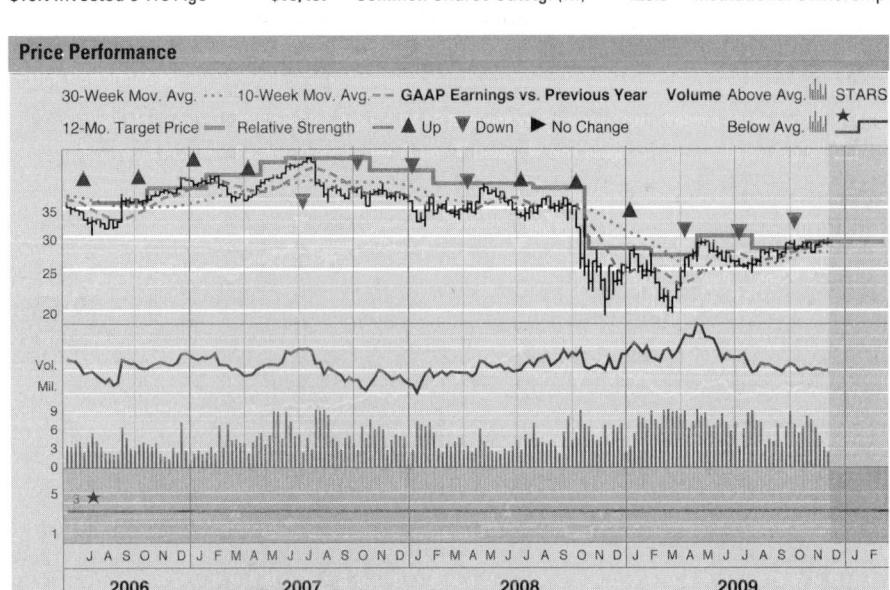

30-Week Mov. Avg. · · · 10-Week Mov. Avg. · - **GAAP Earnings vs. Previous Year** Volume Above Avg. STARS
12-Mo. Target Price — Relative Strength ▲ Up ▼ Down ► No Change Below Avg.

Options: ASE, P, Ph

Analysis prepared by **Zaineb Bokhari** on October 27, 2009, when the stock traded at **$ 28.38**.

Highlights

▶ We see a sales recovery for many of EFX's core products strongly tied to a recovery in the global economy. As a result, we think sales will decline by about 7% in 2009 to $1.8 billion. We think year-to-year comparisons should ease, however, late in the year. We expect limited acquisition activity as EFX focuses more on fine-tuning existing operations, cutting costs and repaying outstanding debt. We project sales growth of approximately 3% in 2010.

▶ EFX has flattened and realigned its organizational structure, yielding cost savings. However, we expect declining sales to offset these benefits. Expense reduction measures should continue throughout 2009 as EFX seeks to preserve operating margins in the face of declining sales. Thus, we look for narrower operating margins in 2009. We see modestly wider operating margins in 2010 as sales growth likely resumes.

▶ We expect interest expense to remain high following issuance/assumption of debt from the company's acquisition of TALX, but see some decline as EFX pays down debt. We estimate operating EPS of $2.26 in 2009 (before acquisition-related intangibles), rising to $2.33 in 2010.

Investment Rationale/Risk

▶ International markets have offered attractive avenues for growth, in our view, particularly in Latin America. We see this being negatively impacted, however, by unfavorable currency fluctuations and by the weakness in the global economy, especially in Europe. EFX's largest and most profitable segment, U.S. Consumer Information Solutions, has been in a decline since late 2007 and we expect this to continue throughout 2009. We look for a rising contribution from TALX, but expect this to limit near-term operating margin expansion from expense reductions. We are optimistic about settlement and analytical tools and services, which we consider to be counter-cyclical.

▶ Risks to our recommendation and target price include increasing competition from the other major credit bureaus and data providers. In view of the economic backdrop, we are also concerned about a further slowdown in EFX's North American Direct and Credit Marketing segments and well as in international markets.

▶ Our 12-month target price of $29 is derived by applying a 12.5X P/E multiple, within the three-year average range for EFX shares of 11.0X-16.7X, to our 2010 EPS estimate.

Qualitative Risk Assessment

LOW	MEDIUM	HIGH

Our risk assessment reflects our view that a majority of the company's domestic operations are relatively mature, and have exposure to the financial services sector. We are also concerned about the weak global economy, particularly in Europe, offset by our positive outlook for the company's Latin American operations, which we see expanding faster than its domestic operations.

Quantitative Evaluations

S&P Quality Ranking B+

D	C	B-	B	B+	A-	A	A+

Relative Strength Rank MODERATE

61

LOWEST = 1 HIGHEST = 99

Revenue/Earnings Data

Revenue (Million $)

	1Q	2Q	3Q	4Q	Year
2009	452.9	455.4	451.9	--	--
2008	503.1	501.9	484.1	446.6	1,936
2007	405.1	454.5	492.5	490.9	1,843
2006	374.0	387.7	394.6	390.0	1,546
2005	343.4	363.4	375.3	361.3	1,443
2004	309.9	315.4	319.9	327.6	1,273

Earnings Per Share ($)

2009	0.43	0.47	0.47	E0.54	E2.26
2008	0.50	0.54	0.56	0.50	2.09
2007	0.54	0.51	0.48	0.49	2.02
2006	0.48	0.53	0.61	0.50	2.12
2005	0.44	0.47	0.47	0.48	1.86
2004	0.38	0.58	0.40	0.42	1.78

Fiscal year ended Dec. 31. Next earnings report expected: Early February. EPS Estimates based on S&P Operating Earnings; historical GAAP earnings are as reported.

Dividend Data (Dates: mm/dd Payment Date: mm/dd/yy)

Amount ($)	Date Decl.	Ex-Div. Date	Stk. of Record	Payment Date
0.040	02/06	02/18	02/20	03/13/09
0.040	05/08	05/21	05/26	06/15/09
0.040	08/14	08/21	08/25	09/15/09
0.040	11/06	11/20	11/24	12/15/09

Dividends have been paid since 1914. Source: Company reports.

Please read the Required Disclosures and Analyst Certification on the last page of this report.

The McGraw-Hill Companies

Equifax Inc.

STANDARD
&POOR'S

Business Summary October 27, 2009

CORPORATE OVERVIEW. Equifax is one of three global providers of consumer and commercial credit information. Equifax collects, organizes and manages credit, financial, demographic and marketing information regarding individuals and businesses, which the company collects from various sources. These sources include financial or credit granting institutions (which provide accounts receivable information), government organizations and consumers. The company maintains information in proprietary databases regarding consumers and businesses worldwide. EFX amasses and processes this data using proprietary systems, and makes the data available to customers in various formats.

Products and services include consumer credit information, information database management, marketing information, business credit information, decisioning and analytical tools, and identity verification services that enable businesses to make informed decisions about extending credit or providing services, managing portfolio risk, and developing marketing strategies. According to the company, EFX allows consumers to manage and protect their financial affairs through products that the company sells directly to individuals using the Internet.

Equifax derived 80% of operating revenue from North America in 2008, unchanged from 2007. The U.S. accounted for 74% of operating revenues in 2008, unchanged from 2007, while EFX's Canadian Consumer business accounted for 6% of total revenues in 2008 (also unchanged from 2007). The company's largest segment, U.S. Consumer Information Solutions (46% of revenues in 2008, down from 53% in 2007), includes Consumer Information Solutions (credit information regarding individuals; 31% of 2008 revenues, down from 35% in 2007), Mortgage Reporting Solutions (credit loan origination information; 4%, 4%), Credit Marketing Services (7%, 8%) and Direct Marketing Services (5%, 6%). Other North American operating segments include Personal Solutions (credit information sales to consumers; 8%, 8%) and Commercial Solutions (credit information concerning businesses; 4%, 4%). TALX, acquired in May 2007 (employment, income verification and human resources outsourcing services) accounted for just under 16% of revenues in 2008 (10%).

Company Financials Fiscal Year Ended Dec. 31

Per Share Data ($)	2008	2007	2006	2005	2004	2003	2002	2001	2000	1999
Tangible Book Value	NM	NM	NM	NM	NM	NM	NM	NM	NM	NM
Cash Flow	2.60	2.48	2.76	2.49	2.39	2.00	1.96	1.61	2.77	2.44
Earnings	2.09	2.02	2.12	1.86	1.78	1.31	1.39	0.84	1.68	1.55
S&P Core Earnings	1.90	2.02	2.07	1.88	1.59	1.18	1.04	0.52	NA	NA
Dividends	0.16	0.16	0.16	0.15	0.11	0.08	0.08	0.25	0.37	0.36
Payout Ratio	8%	8%	8%	8%	6%	6%	6%	29%	22%	23%
Prices:High	39.95	46.30	41.64	39.00	28.46	27.59	31.30	38.76	36.50	39.88
Prices:Low	19.38	35.22	30.15	26.97	22.60	17.84	18.95	18.60	19.88	20.13
P/E Ratio:High	19	23	20	21	16	21	23	46	22	26
P/E Ratio:Low	9	17	14	14	13	14	14	22	12	13

Income Statement Analysis (Million $)										
Revenue	1,936	1,843	1,546	1,443	1,273	1,225	1,109	1,139	1,966	1,773
Operating Income	560	548	519	504	459	438	432	420	604	540
Depreciation	66.3	62.0	82.8	82.2	81.1	95.3	80.5	106	149	125
Interest Expense	71.3	58.5	31.9	35.6	34.9	39.6	41.2	47.8	76.0	61.0
Pretax Income	412	431	420	396	388	286	317	205	385	366
Effective Tax Rate	32.3%	35.3%	33.6%	36.5%	38.1%	36.5%	39.0%	41.7%	40.8%	41.0%
Net Income	273	273	275	247	237	179	191	117	228	216
S&P Core Earnings	247	273	268	248	211	162	146	73.6	NA	NA

Balance Sheet & Other Financial Data (Million $)										
Cash	58.2	81.6	67.8	37.5	52.1	39.3	30.5	33.2	89.4	137
Current Assets	354	425	345	280	300	286	286	358	605	609
Total Assets	3,260	3,524	1,791	1,832	1,557	1,553	1,507	1,423	2,070	1,840
Current Liabilities	318	547	582	295	457	355	428	276	426	505
Long Term Debt	1,187	1,165	174	464	399	663	691	694	994	934
Common Equity	1,312	1,399	838	820	524	372	221	244	384	393
Total Capital	2,715	2,842	1,083	1,410	961	1,079	938	1,026	1,467	1,400
Capital Expenditures	111	119	52.0	17.2	16.5	14.6	12.8	13.0	37.1	39.0
Cash Flow	339	335	357	329	318	274	272	224	377	341
Current Ratio	1.1	0.8	0.6	1.0	0.7	0.8	0.7	1.3	1.4	1.2
% Long Term Debt of Capitalization	43.7	41.0	16.1	32.9	41.5	61.5	73.7	67.6	67.7	66.7
% Net Income of Revenue	14.1	14.8	17.8	17.1	18.6	14.6	17.2	10.3	11.6	12.2
% Return on Assets	8.0	10.3	15.2	14.5	15.3	11.7	13.1	7.1	11.7	11.8
% Return on Equity	20.1	24.4	33.1	36.7	53.0	60.3	82.4	37.4	76.1	49.7

Data as orig reptd.; bef. results of disc opers/spec. items. Per share data adj. for stk. divs.; EPS diluted. E-Estimated. NA-Not Available. NM-Not Meaningful. NR-Not Ranked. UR-Under Review.

Office: 1550 Peachtree St NW, Atlanta, GA 30309.
Telephone: 404-885-8000.
Email: investor@equifax.com
Website: http://www.equifax.com

Chrmn & CEO: R.F. Smith
COO: A.S. Bodea
SVP, Chief Acctg Officer & Cntlr: N.M. King
CFO: L. Adrean

Secy: D.C. Arvidson
Board Members: W. W. Canfield, J. Copeland, Jr., R. D. Daleo, W. W. Driver, Jr., M. L. Feidler, L. P. Humann, S. S. Marshall, J. A. McKinley, Jr., R. F. Smith, M. B. Templeton

Founded: 1913
Domicile: Georgia
Employees: 6,500

The McGraw-Hill Companies

Equity Residential

STANDARD
&POOR'S

S&P Recommendation SELL ★ ★ ☆ ☆ ☆

Price	12-Mo. Target Price	Investment Style
$30.91 (as of Nov 27, 2009)	$24.00	Large-Cap Value

GICS Sector Financials
Sub-Industry Residential REITS

Summary This equity real estate investment trust owns and operates a nationally diversified portfolio of apartment properties.

Key Stock Statistics (Source S&P, Vickers, company reports)

52-Wk Range	$34.91–15.68	S&P FFO/Sh. 2009E	2.18	Market Capitalization(B)	$8.536	Beta	1.38
Trailing 12-Month FFO/Share	NA	S&P FFO/Sh. 2010E	1.95	Yield (%)	4.37	S&P 3-Yr. FFO/Sh. Proj. CAGR(%)	-5
Trailing 12-Month P/FFO	NA	P/FFO on S&P FFO/Sh. 2009E	14.2	Dividend Rate/Share	$1.35	S&P Credit Rating	BBB+
$10K Invested 5 Yrs Ago	$11,669	Common Shares Outstg. (M)	276.1	Institutional Ownership (%)	93		

Price Performance

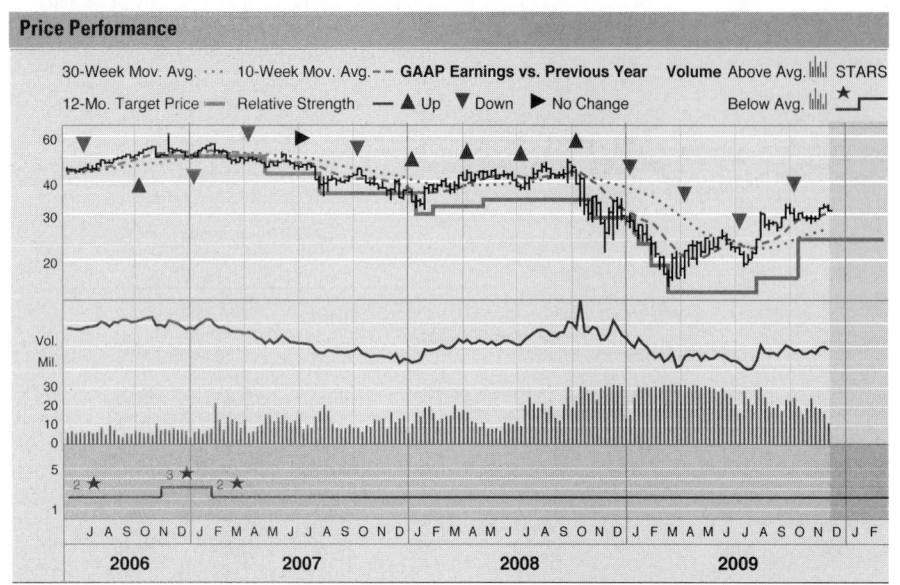

30-Week Mov. Avg. ··· 10-Week Mov. Avg. - - **GAAP Earnings vs. Previous Year** Volume Above Avg. STARS
12-Mo. Target Price — Relative Strength — ▲ Up ▼ Down ► No Change   Below Avg. ★

Options: ASE, CBOE, Ph

Analysis prepared by **Royal F. Shepard, CFA** on November 02, 2009, when the stock traded at **$ 28.31**.

Highlights

► We think EQR's tenants are pushing back on rental rate increases due to concerns about the U.S. job market and economy. We estimate average rental rates will decline 2%-3% in 2009, driven by declines of close to 10% on new leases. For 2010, we anticipate further revenue pressure during the first half as lower rents roll through EQR's portfolio. However, an improved job picture and a limited amount of new competitive supply may set the stage for a modest recovery in the second half of 2010, in our view.

► We expect EQR to dispose of about $900 million in assets in 2009, resulting in dilution to reported earnings on a per-share basis. For 2010, we think EQR could become a net buyer of assets as economic conditions improve and depending on available acquisition opportunities.

► We project 2009 FFO per share of $2.18, falling to $1.95 in 2010. Our outlook reflects rental rate contraction as leases roll over, dilution from dispositions, and additional shares outstanding. We see 2009 property level expenses remaining essentially flat, benefiting from a recent decline in utility bills. EQR cut its third-quarter cash dividend by 30%, to $1.35 annually, to better match expected taxable income.

Investment Rationale/Risk

► We like EQR's long-term focus on coastal markets, which have favorable demographic trends. However, we think job losses in its core New York City, Los Angeles, and South Florida markets will be a drag on near-term operating results. We expect lower effective rents to roll through the portfolio until mid-2010. Also, we do not expect an active development pipeline to contribute positively until late 2010 or 2011. Recently at about 14.7X our 2010 FFO per share outlook, EQR is trading at a premium to peers, which we view as unwarranted.

► Risks to our recommendation and target price include faster-than-anticipated job growth, an improved housing market resulting in less rental competition from single-family homes, and an increase in property values due to investor demand.

► Our 12-month target price of $24 is based on a multiple of 12.3X our 2010 FFO per share estimate of $1.95, a modest discount to peers. We arrive at intrinsic value of $24 using a discount rate of 10.6% and a terminal growth rate of 3%.

Qualitative Risk Assessment

LOW	MEDIUM	HIGH

Our risk assessment reflects our view that EQR is one of the largest, most diversified residential REITs and has below-average financial leverage and strong coverage of fixed charges.

Quantitative Evaluations

S&P Quality Ranking B+

D	C	B-	B	B+	A-	A	A+

Relative Strength Rank STRONG

76

LOWEST = 1   HIGHEST = 99

Revenue/FFO Data

Revenue (Million $)

	1Q	2Q	3Q	4Q	Year
2009	515.1	505.2	492.8	--	--
2008	507.4	525.6	536.9	533.3	2,103
2007	483.2	507.2	522.6	528.1	2,038
2006	470.5	490.6	511.5	517.9	1,990
2005	461.6	478.9	495.5	518.9	1,955
2004	443.9	474.7	483.5	487.4	1,890

FFO Per Share ($)

2009	0.57	E0.58	E0.53	E0.50	E2.18
2008	0.59	0.64	0.65	0.29	2.18
2007	0.55	0.60	0.58	0.67	2.39
2006	0.56	0.61	0.62	0.49	2.27
2005	0.74	0.56	0.56	0.66	2.52
2004	0.52	0.56	0.50	0.56	2.14

Fiscal year ended Dec. 31. Next earnings report expected: Early February. FFO Estimates based on S&P Funds From Operations Est..

Dividend Data (Dates: mm/dd Payment Date: mm/dd/yy)

Amount ($)	Date Decl.	Ex-Div. Date	Stk. of Record	Payment Date
0.483	12/10	12/18	12/22	01/09/09
0.483	02/16	03/12	03/16	04/09/09
0.483	05/28	06/11	06/15	07/10/09
0.338	09/08	09/17	09/21	10/09/09

Dividends have been paid since 1993. Source: Company reports.

Please read the Required Disclosures and Analyst Certification on the last page of this report.

The McGraw-Hill Companies

Equity Residential

STANDARD &POOR'S

Business Summary November 02, 2009

CORPORATE OVERVIEW. Equity Residential is one of the largest publicly held owners of multi-family properties. Structured as a real estate investment trust (REIT), it owns, manages and operates properties through its 93.4% interest in its operating limited partnership. At December 31, 2008, EQR owned or had interests in 548 multi-family properties with 147,244 units in 23 states. The trust adopted its current name in May 2002.

During 2006, EQR sold a majority of its ranch style properties, leaving a focus on garden and mid-rise/high-rise assets. Garden-style properties have two or three floors, while mid-rise/high-rise properties have more than three floors. At the end of December 2008, the trust's largest geographic markets as measured by net operating income were the New York Metro Area (10.0%), Washington DC/N. Virginia (8.8%), South Florida (8.4%), Los Angeles (7.8%), and Seattle/Tacoma (7.5%). Average occupancy during the fourth quarter of 2008 was 94.3%, just behind 94.4% for the same period in 2007.

MARKET PROFILE. The U.S. housing market is highly fragmented and is broadly characterized by two types of housing units, multifamily and single-family. At the end of 2008, the U.S. Census Bureau estimated that there were 130.84 million housing units in the country, an increase of 1.7% from 2007. Partially due to the high fragmentation, and the fact that residents have the option of

either being owners or tenants (renters), the housing market can be highly competitive. Main demand drivers for apartments are household formation and employment growth. We estimate 0.7 million new households were formed in 2008. Supply is created by new housing unit construction, which could consist of single-family homes, or multifamily apartment buildings or condominiums. We estimate that 0.90 million housing units were started in 2008, down about 26% from 2007. Multifamily housing starts, for structures with more than 5 units, dropped significantly less, declining about 4.5%.

With apartment tenants on relatively short leases compared to those of commercial and industrial properties, we believe apartment REITs are generally more sensitive to changes in market conditions than REITs in other property categories. Results could be hurt by new construction that adds new space in excess of actual demand. Trends in home price affordability also affect both rent levels and the level of new construction, since the relative price attractiveness of owning versus renting is an important factor in consumer decision making.

Company Financials Fiscal Year Ended Dec. 31

Per Share Data ($)	2008	2007	2006	2005	2004	2003	2002	2001	2000	1999
Tangible Book Value	17.55	17.79	18.58	16.65	15.28	15.43	15.57	16.20	20.82	16.33
Earnings	0.09	0.23	0.20	0.51	0.37	0.43	0.78	1.36	1.67	1.15
S&P Core Earnings	0.10	0.21	0.20	0.51	0.34	0.41	0.72	1.38	NA	NA
Dividends	1.93	1.87	1.79	1.74	1.73	1.73	1.73	1.68	1.58	1.47
Payout Ratio	NM	NM	NM	NM	NM	NM	222%	124%	94%	128%
Prices:High	49.00	56.46	61.50	42.17	36.75	30.30	30.96	30.45	28.63	24.19
Prices:Low	21.27	33.79	38.84	30.70	26.65	23.12	21.55	24.80	19.34	19.06
P/E Ratio:High	NM	NM	NM	83	99	70	40	22	17	21
P/E Ratio:Low	NM	NM	NM	60	72	54	28	18	12	17

Income Statement Analysis (Million $)										
Rental Income	2,092	2,029	1,981	1,944	1,878	1,809	1,970	2,075	1,960	1,712
Mortgage Income	Nil	Nil	Nil	Nil	Nil	Nil	Nil	8.79	11.2	12.6
Total Income	2,103	2,038	1,990	1,955	1,890	1,823	1,994	2,171	2,030	1,753
General Expenses	890	883	881	925	870	802	841	924	812	673
Interest Expense	489	495	436	391	349	333	343	361	388	341
Provision for Losses	Nil	Nil	Nil	Nil	Nil	Nil	Nil	Nil	Nil	Nil
Depreciation	591	588	563	508	484	444	462	457	450	409
Net Income	40.9	93.0	101	152	135	212	302	474	555	394
S&P Core Earnings	26.4	58.3	59.5	98.5	74.5	86.4	194	374	NA	NA

Balance Sheet & Other Financial Data (Million $)										
Cash	891	71.0	260	88.8	83.5	49.6	540	449	417	114
Total Assets	16,535	15,690	15,062	14,099	12,645	11,467	11,811	12,236	12,264	11,716
Real Estate Investment	18,690	18,333	17,235	16,597	14,864	12,874	13,046	13,016	12,591	12,239
Loss Reserve	Nil	Nil	Nil	Nil	Nil	Nil	Nil	Nil	Nil	Nil
Net Investment	15,129	15,163	14,217	13,709	12,264	10,578	10,934	11,297	11,239	11,168
Short Term Debt	863	680	921	NA	NA	NA	334	699	Nil	250
Capitalization:Debt	9,638	8,829	7,136	7,032	5,642	4,836	5,050	5,044	5,706	5,224
Capitalization:Equity	4,789	4,853	5,498	4,891	4,436	4,345	4,251	4,447	4,436	4,195
Capitalization:Total	14,954	14,929	13,432	12,850	10,714	10,452	10,858	11,094	11,938	11,186
% Earnings & Depreciation/Assets	3.9	4.4	4.5	4.9	5.1	5.6	6.4	7.6	8.3	7.2
Price Times Book Value:High	2.8	3.2	3.3	2.5	2.4	2.0	2.0	1.9	1.4	1.5
Price Times Book Value:Low	1.2	1.9	2.1	1.8	1.7	1.5	1.4	1.5	0.9	1.2

Data as orig reptd.; bef. results of disc opers/spec. items. Per share data adj. for stk. divs.; EPS diluted. E-Estimated. NA-Not Available. NM-Not Meaningful. NR-Not Ranked. UR-Under Review.

Office: Two North Riverside Plaza, Chicago, IL 60606.
Telephone: 312-474-1300.
Email: investorrelations@eqrworld.com
Website: http://www.equityresidential.com

Chrmn: S. Zell
Pres & CEO: D.J. Neithercut
Vice Chrmn: G.A. Spector
COO: D.S. Santee

EVP & CFO: M.J. Parrell
Investor Contact: M. McKenna
Trustees: J. W. Alexander, C. L. Atwood, B. A. Knox, J. H. Lynford, J. E. Neal, D. J. Neithercut, S. Z. Rosenberg, G. A. Spector, B. J. White, S. Zell

Founded: 1993
Domicile: Maryland
Employees: 4,700

Exelon Corp

STANDARD &POOR'S

S&P Recommendation	BUY ★★★★☆	Price $47.66 (as of Nov 27, 2009)	12-Mo. Target Price $60.00	Investment Style Large-Cap Blend

GICS Sector Utilities
Sub-Industry Electric Utilities

Summary Exelon, the holding company for Philadelphia-based PECO Energy and Chicago-based ComEd, is the largest nuclear operator in the U.S.

Key Stock Statistics (Source S&P, Vickers, company reports)

52-Wk Range	$58.98– 38.41	S&P Oper. EPS 2009E	4.09	Market Capitalization(B)	$31.426	Beta	0.58
Trailing 12-Month EPS	$4.29	S&P Oper. EPS 2010E	4.04	Yield (%)	4.41	S&P 3-Yr. Proj. EPS CAGR(%)	1
Trailing 12-Month P/E	11.1	P/E on S&P Oper. EPS 2009E	11.7	Dividend Rate/Share	$2.10	S&P Credit Rating	BBB
$10K Invested 5 Yrs Ago	$13,141	Common Shares Outstg. (M)	659.4	Institutional Ownership (%)	66		

Price Performance

30-Week Mov. Avg. ···   10-Week Mov. Avg. - -   **GAAP Earnings vs. Previous Year**   Volume Above Avg. STARS
12-Mo. Target Price —   Relative Strength —   ▲ Up   ▼ Down   ▶ No Change   Below Avg.

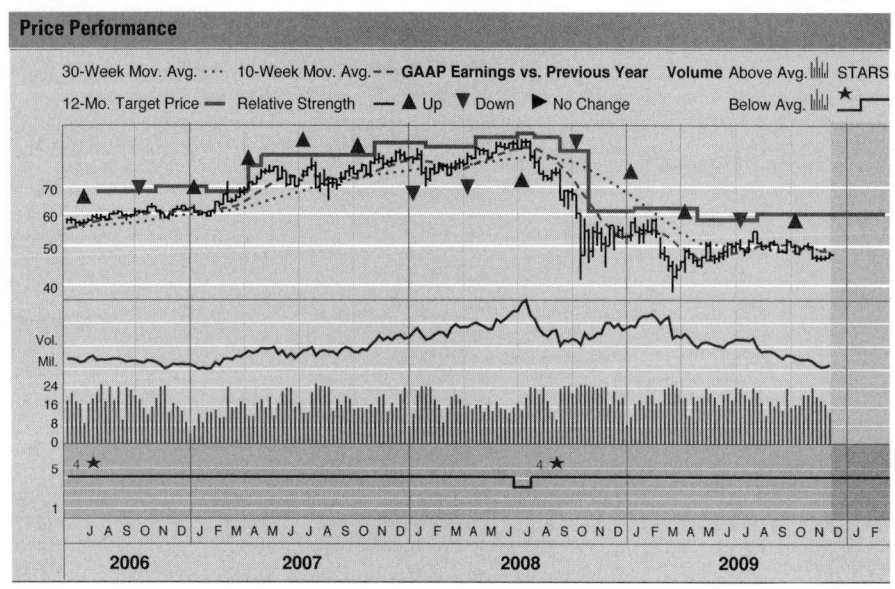

Options: ASE, CBOE, P, Ph

Analysis prepared by **Justin McCann** on September 29, 2009, when the stock traded at **$ 50.00.**

Highlights

► We expect operating EPS in 2009 (excluding $0.17 of net one-time charges) to decline more than 1% from 2008 operating EPS of $4.20 (which excluded $0.10 of net one-time charges), reflecting the weak economy and power market, with lower commodity prices and higher nuclear fuel costs resulting in lower margins at the power generating segment. We expect the rate increases at ComEd and PECO to be largely offset by a decline in demand.

► We expect operating EPS in 2010 to decline about 2% from anticipated results in 2009, despite a projected $350 million decline in O&M expenses. However, we project solid growth for 2011, due to the planned shift to market-based power contracts with PECO Energy.

► Following the termination of its fixed exchange ratio acquisition offer to the shareholders of NRG Energy (NRG 27, Buy), we do not expect EXC to initiate another merger attempt in the current market environment. It intends to seek internally generated growth and is working to develop a plan for an independent transmission company and is also planning to add 1,300 to 1,500 megawatts of new nuclear capacity through uprates at its existing plants.

Investment Rationale/Risk

► Following a sharp plunge in early 2009, the stock has rebounded more than 30% from its multi-year low reached in March. We think the shares had been hurt by weakness in the economy and power markets, the crisis in the credit markets, and the extreme downturn and volatility in the stock market. We believe the strong recovery has reflected both the recovery of the broader market, as well as the termination of the attempted acquisition of NRG Energy, which would have included the uncertainties related to the consolidation of the company and the assumption of more than $8 billion of NRG debt.

► Risks to our recommendation and target price include an extended economic recession, sharply reduced wholesale power margins, and a drop in the average peer P/E of the sector.

► With the rebound in the shares, the recent dividend yield was about 4.2%, roughly in line with that of other utility holding companies that we think have potential for long-term, above-peers earnings growth. Our 12-month target price is $60, a premium-to-peers P/E of 14.8X our EPS estimate for 2010. We believe the premium is warranted by Exelon's leading position in the nuclear power industry.

Qualitative Risk Assessment

LOW	MEDIUM	HIGH

Our risk assessment reflects our view of Exelon's strong and steady cash flow from the regulated PECO Energy and ComEd utilities, as well as the healthy earnings and cash flow from very profitable but higher-risk power generating and energy marketing operations.

Quantitative Evaluations

S&P Quality Ranking B+

D	C	B-	B	B+	A-	A	A+

Relative Strength Rank MODERATE

41

LOWEST = 1   HIGHEST = 99

Revenue/Earnings Data

Revenue (Million $)

	1Q	2Q	3Q	4Q	Year
2009	4,722	4,141	4,339	--	--
2008	4,517	4,622	5,228	4,493	18,859
2007	4,829	4,501	5,032	4,554	18,916
2006	3,861	3,697	4,401	3,696	15,655
2005	3,561	3,484	4,473	3,838	15,357
2004	3,722	3,550	3,865	3,378	14,515

Earnings Per Share ($)

2009	1.08	0.99	1.14	E0.90	E4.09
2008	0.88	1.13	1.06	1.04	4.10
2007	1.01	1.03	1.15	0.84	4.03
2006	0.59	0.95	-0.07	0.87	2.35
2005	0.77	0.76	1.07	-1.19	1.40
2004	0.57	0.76	0.86	0.54	2.75

Fiscal year ended Dec. 31. Next earnings report expected: Late January. EPS Estimates based on S&P Operating Earnings; historical GAAP earnings are as reported.

Dividend Data (Dates: mm/dd Payment Date: mm/dd/yy)

Amount ($)	Date Decl.	Ex-Div. Date	Stk. of Record	Payment Date
0.525	01/27	02/11	02/13	03/10/09
0.525	04/29	05/13	05/15	06/10/09
0.525	07/28	08/12	08/14	09/10/09
0.525	10/28	11/10	11/13	12/10/09

Dividends have been paid since 1902. Source: Company reports.

Please read the Required Disclosures and Analyst Certification on the last page of this report.

The McGraw·Hill Companies

Exelon Corp

STANDARD
&POOR'S

Business Summary September 29, 2009

CORPORATE OVERVIEW. Exelon Corp. was formed in October 2000 through the acquisition by Philadelphia-based PECO Energy of Chicago-based Unicom Corp. The company, along with its subsidiaries, is engaged in the energy delivery, generation and other businesses. Exelon operates in three business segments: Generation, PECO, and ComEd (Commonwealth Edison). Segment contributions to consolidated net income from ongoing operations in 2008 were: Generation, $2,258 million ($2,025 million in 2007); PECO, $325 million ($507 million); ComEd, $165 million ($165 million), and other, a loss of $67 million (earnings of $29 million).

IMPACT OF MAJOR DEVELOPMENTS. On July 21, 2009, Exelon terminated its unsolicited offer to acquire all of the outstanding common shares of NRG Energy (NRG $27, Buy), one of the leading competitive wholesale power generators in the United States, with net generating capacity of 24,315 megawatts as

of December 31, 2008. The termination immediately followed NRG shareholder rejection of directors proposed by Exelon to the NRG board, as well as the expansion of that board. The original proposal, made on October 19, 2008, had offered a fixed exchange ratio of 0.485 of an EXC share for each NRG share. However, on July 2, 2009, Exelon increased its offer by 12.4% to a fixed exchange ratio of 0.545 of an EXC share for each NRG share. If the attempted merger had been completed, the combined company would have been the largest power company in the U.S. in terms of assets, market capitalization, enterprise value and generating capacity.

Company Financials Fiscal Year Ended Dec. 31

Per Share Data ($)	2008	2007	2006	2005	2004	2003	2002	2001	2000	1999
Tangible Book Value	12.58	11.86	11.08	8.48	7.10	5.77	4.26	4.51	3.18	4.57
Earnings	4.10	4.03	2.35	1.40	2.75	1.20	2.58	2.20	1.44	1.58
S&P Core Earnings	3.32	3.92	3.49	3.01	2.79	1.74	1.64	1.49	NA	NA
Dividends	2.02	1.76	2.00	1.60	1.53	0.96	0.88	0.91	0.46	0.50
Payout Ratio	49%	44%	85%	114%	56%	80%	34%	41%	32%	32%
Prices:High	92.13	86.83	63.62	57.46	44.90	33.31	28.50	35.13	35.50	25.25
Prices:Low	41.23	58.74	51.13	41.77	30.92	23.04	18.92	19.38	16.50	15.38
P/E Ratio:High	22	22	27	41	16	28	11	16	25	16
P/E Ratio:Low	10	15	22	30	11	19	7	9	11	10
Income Statement Analysis (Million $)										
Revenue	18,859	18,916	15,655	15,357	14,515	15,812	14,955	15,140	7,499	5,437
Depreciation	2,308	1,520	1,487	1,334	1,305	1,126	1,340	1,449	458	237
Maintenance	NA	NA	NA	NA	NA	NA	NA	NA	NA	NA
Fixed Charges Coverage	5.88	6.03	5.19	4.88	3.94	2.19	3.56	2.98	2.94	3.24
Construction Credits	NA	NA	NA	NA	NA	NA	NA	NA	Nil	4.00
Effective Tax Rate	32.7%	34.7%	43.1%	49.8%	27.5%	29.4%	37.4%	39.7%	27.3%	36.6%
Net Income	2,717	2,726	1,590	951	1,841	793	1,670	1,416	907	619
S&P Core Earnings	2,197	2,656	2,358	2,035	1,865	1,142	1,062	962	NA	NA
Balance Sheet & Other Financial Data (Million $)										
Gross Property	34,055	31,964	30,025	29,853	28,711	27,578	25,904	21,526	19,886	9,412
Capital Expenditures	3,117	2,674	2,418	2,165	1,921	1,954	2,150	2,041	752	491
Net Property	25,813	24,153	22,775	21,981	21,482	20,630	17,134	13,742	12,936	5,045
Capitalization:Long Term Debt	12,592	12,052	11,998	11,760	12,235	13,576	14,580	13,492	14,398	6,098
Capitalization:% Long Term Debt	53.3	54.3	54.6	56.3	56.5	61.5	65.3	62.1	66.6	75.6
Capitalization:Preferred	Nil	Nil	Nil	Nil	Nil	Nil	Nil	Nil	Nil	193
Capitalization:% Preferred	Nil	Nil	Nil	Nil	Nil	Nil	Nil	Nil	Nil	2.39
Capitalization:Common	11,047	10,137	9,973	9,125	9,423	8,503	7,742	8,230	7,215	1,773
Capitalization:% Common	46.7	45.7	45.4	43.7	43.5	38.5	34.7	37.9	33.4	22.0
Total Capital	28,578	27,270	27,395	25,964	26,463	26,724	26,325	26,341	26,352	10,760
% Operating Ratio	78.9	83.0	80.3	80.5	81.1	82.2	73.1	83.9	80.5	80.7
% Earned on Net Property	21.2	19.9	15.7	12.5	16.3	11.4	21.3	25.2	17.0	28.6
% Return on Revenue	14.4	14.4	10.2	6.2	12.7	5.0	11.2	9.4	12.1	11.4
% Return on Invested Capital	17.5	13.5	12.1	11.4	10.3	10.2	10.2	9.8	9.8	10.3
% Return on Common Equity	25.7	27.1	16.7	10.2	20.5	9.8	21.1	18.3	20.2	25.1

Data as orig reptd.; bef. results of disc opers/spec. items. Per share data adj. for stk. divs.; EPS diluted. E-Estimated. NA-Not Available. NM-Not Meaningful. NR-Not Ranked. UR-Under Review.

Office: 10 S Dearborn St, Chicago, IL 60603-2300.
Telephone: 312-394-7398.
Website: http://www.exeloncorp.com
Chrmn & CEO: J.W. Rowe

Pres: C.M. Crane
EVP & General Counsel: A.L. Zopp
SVP & CFO: M.F. Hilzinger
SVP & Secy: K.K. Combs

Investor Contact: C. Patterson (312-394-7234)
Board Members: J. A. Canning, Jr., M. W. D'Alessio, N. DeBenedictis, B. DeMars, N. A. Diaz, S. L. Gin, R. B. Greco, P. L. Joskow, R. W. Mies, J. M. Palms, W. C. Richardson, T. J. Ridge, J. W. Rogers, Jr., J. W. Rowe, S. D. Steinour, D. Thompson

Founded: 1887
Domicile: Pennsylvania
Employees: 19,610

The McGraw-Hill Companies

Expedia Inc

STANDARD &POOR'S

S&P Recommendation HOLD ★★★☆☆	Price $25.21 (as of Nov 27, 2009)	12-Mo. Target Price $26.00	Investment Style Large-Cap Blend

GICS Sector Consumer Discretionary
Sub-Industry Internet Retail

Summary Expedia is one of the world's largest online travel-services companies. Businesses include Expedia, Hotels.com, Hotwire and TripAdvisor.

Key Stock Statistics (Source S&P, Vickers, company reports)

52-Wk Range	$27.37– 6.31	S&P Oper. EPS 2009**E**	0.98	Market Capitalization(B)	$6.634	Beta	2.32
Trailing 12-Month EPS	$-8.91	S&P Oper. EPS 2010**E**	1.45	Yield (%)	Nil	S&P 3-Yr. Proj. EPS CAGR(%)	12
Trailing 12-Month P/E	NM	P/E on S&P Oper. EPS 2009**E**	25.7	Dividend Rate/Share	Nil	S&P Credit Rating	BBB-
$10K Invested 5 Yrs Ago	NA	Common Shares Outstg. (M)	288.8	Institutional Ownership (%)	81		

Price Performance

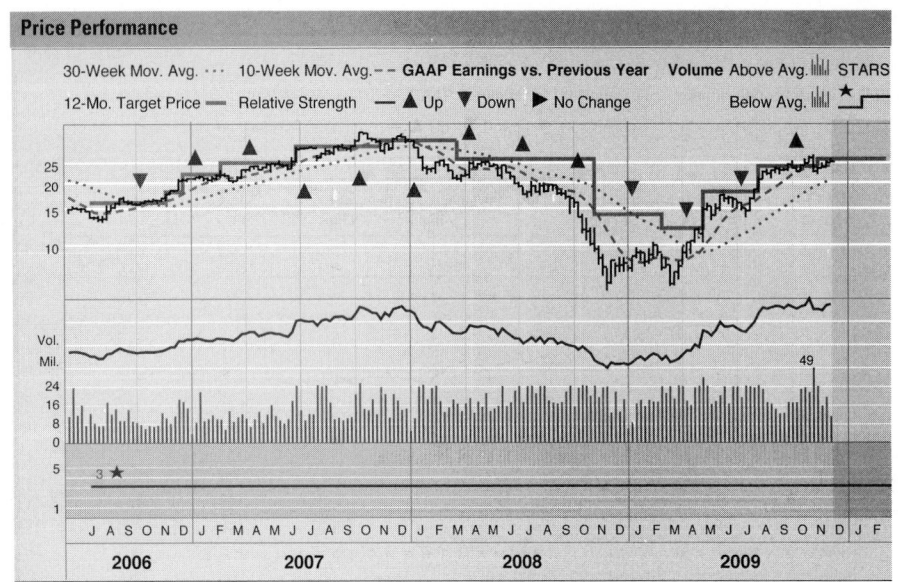

30-Week Mov. Avg. ···· 10-Week Mov. Avg. – – **GAAP Earnings vs. Previous Year** Volume Above Avg. STARS
12-Mo. Target Price — Relative Strength — ▲ Up ▼ Down ▶ No Change Below Avg.

Options: ASE, CBOE, P, Ph

Analysis prepared by **Scott H. Kessler** on November 02, 2009, when the stock traded at **$ 22.67**.

Highlights

▶ We believe EXPE is among the worldwide leaders in the Internet travel segment and will benefit from the continuing migration of associated purchases online. However, we think global economic uncertainty and substantial exposure to Europe, where currency uncertainties are notable, are worrisome. We project that revenues will decline 1% in 2009, notwithstanding secular growth trends and projected market share gains, and increase 6% in 2010.

▶ We estimate that annual operating income before amortization (OIBA) and net margins bottomed in 2006, partly due to considerable sales and marketing expenses and technology investments, which yielded benefits into 2008. We expect cost-cutting and expense-containment efforts to aid 2009 and 2010 margins.

▶ In mid-2007, EXPE repurchased 25 million shares (8% of those outstanding as of June 2007) at $29 apiece, after a larger buyback was scaled back due to issues in the credit market. EXPE had $959 million in cash and investments as of September 2009, and $895 million of long-term debt. In the second quarter of 2009, EXPE repaid a tapped $650 million credit facility.

Investment Rationale/Risk

▶ We believe EXPE has some of the Internet's best-known travel franchises (including Expedia, Hotels.com and TripAdvisor), some well-positioned and strong international operations, and a healthy domestic business. We also think it has done a good job over the past few quarters of seizing upon opportunities and executing relatively well. However, we believe the company faces many challenges, including significant economic uncertainty and related weakened consumer sentiment, a maturing online travel market in the U.S., and significant competition worldwide.

▶ Risks to our recommendation and target price include a notable further weakening of global or domestic consumer sentiment or spending, and increasing competitive and/or pricing pressures.

▶ Our discounted cash flow model has assumptions including a weighted average cost of capital of 10.6%, annual free cash flow growth averaging 12% over the next five years, and a perpetuity growth rate of 3%. These inputs yield an intrinsic value of around $26, which is our 12-month target price.

Qualitative Risk Assessment

LOW	MEDIUM	HIGH

Our risk assessment reflects what we believe is a maturing online travel market in the U.S., an intensely competitive landscape, and relatively low barriers to entry.

Quantitative Evaluations

S&P Quality Ranking NR

D	C	B-	B	B+	A-	A	A+

Relative Strength Rank STRONG

81

LOWEST = 1   HIGHEST = 99

Revenue/Earnings Data

Revenue (Million $)

	1Q	2Q	3Q	4Q	Year
2009	635.7	769.8	852.4	--	--
2008	687.8	795.1	833.3	620.8	2,937
2007	550.5	689.9	759.6	665.3	2,665
2006	493.9	598.5	613.9	531.3	2,238
2005	485.1	555.0	584.1	494.8	2,119
2004	413.3	487.0	503.8	439.0	1,843

Earnings Per Share ($)

2009	0.14	0.14	0.40	E0.30	E0.98
2008	0.17	0.33	0.33	-9.60	-8.63
2007	0.11	0.30	0.32	0.22	0.94
2006	0.06	0.27	0.17	0.20	0.70
2005	0.12	--	0.23	0.07	0.65
2004	--	--	0.17	0.13	0.37

Fiscal year ended Dec. 31. Next earnings report expected: Mid February. EPS Estimates based on S&P Operating Earnings; historical GAAP earnings are as reported.

Dividend Data

No cash dividends have been paid.

Expedia Inc

STANDARD &POOR'S

Business Summary November 02, 2009

CORPORATE OVERVIEW. Expedia, Inc. leverages its portfolio of brands to target a broad range of travelers interested in different travel options. EXPE provides a wide selection of travel products and services, from simple discounted travel to more complex luxury trips. The company's offerings primarily include airline tickets, hotel reservations, car rentals, cruise arrangements, and destination services.

The company's localized Expedia-branded websites (focused on the U.S., as well as Australia, Austria, Canada, Denmark, France, Germany, Ireland, Italy, Japan, the Netherlands, New Zealand, Norway, Spain, Sweden, and the U.K.) offer a large variety of travel products and services. Expedia websites also serve as the travel channel on MSN.com. Expedia Corporate Travel is a full-service travel management firm available to corporate travelers in the U.S., Canada, China, and Europe. Hotels.com provides a multitude of lodging options to travelers, from traditional hotels, to vacation rentals. Part of Hotels.com's strategy is to position itself as a hotel expert offering premium content about lodging properties. These businesses are planning to provide other travel products and services. Hotwire.com is a discount travel website that offers deals to travelers willing to make purchases without knowing certain itinerary details such as brand, time of departure, and hotel address. eLong (LONG 12, NR) is a majority-owned online travel services company based in

and focused on China (see below for more details).

TripAdvisor is an online travel content destination, with search and directory features, guidebook reviews, and user opinions. We believe TripAdvisor is an extremely valuable asset, not only because we believe it constitutes the Internet's largest and most active travel-related social networking property, but also because it diversifies EXPE operations away from transactions and into media and advertising. Expansion in China has been a major focus of TripAdvisor, with entry into the market in April 2009 with the launch of DaoDao.com (a localized reviews and community website for Chinese travelers), and the proposed acquisition of Kuxun.cn (the second-largest online travel-related website in China) in October 2009.

In December 2004, IAC/InterActiveCorp (IACI 19, Hold) announced a plan to spin off what became EXPE. In August 2005, EXPE was spun off as a separate publicly traded company.

Company Financials Fiscal Year Ended Dec. 31

Per Share Data ($)	2008	2007	2006	2005	2004	2003	2002	2001	2000	1999
Tangible Book Value	NM	NM	NM	NM	NA	NA	NA	NA	NA	NA
Cash Flow	-8.13	1.38	1.40	1.82	NA	NA	NA	NA	NA	NA
Earnings	-8.63	0.94	0.70	0.65	0.37	NA	NA	NA	NA	NA
S&P Core Earnings	-2.48	0.94	0.79	0.69	0.48	0.27	0.26	-1.04	NA	NA
Dividends	Nil	Nil	Nil	Nil	NA	NA	NA	NA	NA	NA
Payout Ratio	Nil	Nil	Nil	Nil	NA	NA	NA	NA	NA	NA
Prices:High	31.88	35.28	27.55	27.50	NA	NA	NA	NA	NA	NA
Prices:Low	6.00	19.97	12.87	18.49	NA	NA	NA	NA	NA	NA
P/E Ratio:High	NM	38	39	42	NA	NA	NA	NA	NA	NA
P/E Ratio:Low	NM	21	18	28	NA	NA	NA	NA	NA	NA

Income Statement Analysis (Million $)										
Revenue	2,937	2,665	2,238	2,119	1,843	2,340	1,499	NA	NA	NA
Operating Income	713	666	648	678	NA	NA	NA	NA	NA	NA
Depreciation	146	137	249	407	157	104	61.4	NA	NA	NA
Interest Expense	72.0	52.9	17.3	Nil	7.45	NA	NA	NA	NA	NA
Pretax Income	-2,515	497	385	414	219	256	209	NA	NA	NA
Effective Tax Rate	NM	40.9%	36.2%	44.9%	40.0%	38.0%	39.4%	NA	NA	NA
Net Income	-2,518	296	245	229	131	111	76.7	NA	NA	NA
S&P Core Earnings	-722	296	275	244	163	92.3	34.2	-98.1	NA	NA

Balance Sheet & Other Financial Data (Million $)										
Cash	758	634	853	297	232	882	NA	NA	NA	NA
Current Assets	1,199	1,046	1,183	590	569	NA	NA	NA	NA	NA
Total Assets	5,894	8,295	8,269	7,757	7,803	8,755	NA	NA	NA	NA
Current Liabilities	1,566	1,774	1,400	1,438	1,515	NA	NA	NA	NA	NA
Long Term Debt	1,545	1,085	500	Nil	NA	NA	NA	NA	NA	NA
Common Equity	2,328	4,818	5,904	5,734	5,820	7,554	NA	NA	NA	NA
Total Capital	4,115	6,316	6,835	6,174	8,171	7,554	NA	NA	NA	NA
Capital Expenditures	160	86.7	92.6	52.3	53.4	46.2	46.5	NA	NA	NA
Cash Flow	-2,372	433	494	636	NA	NA	NA	NA	NA	NA
Current Ratio	0.8	0.6	0.8	0.4	0.4	2.0	NA	NA	NA	NA
% Long Term Debt of Capitalization	37.5	17.2	7.3	Nil	Nil	Nil	Nil	NA	NA	NA
% Net Income of Revenue	NM	11.1	10.9	10.8	7.1	4.8	5.1	NA	NA	NA
% Return on Assets	NM	3.6	3.1	2.6	1.8	NA	NA	NA	NA	NA
% Return on Equity	NM	5.5	4.2	3.3	2.1	NA	NA	NA	NA	NA

Data as orig reptd.; bef. results of disc opers/spec. items. Per share data adj. for stk. divs.; EPS diluted. E-Estimated. NA-Not Available. NM-Not Meaningful. NR-Not Ranked. UR-Under Review.

Office: 333 108th Ave NE, Bellevue, WA 98004-5703.
Telephone: 425-679-7200.
Website: http://www.expedia.com
Chrmn: B. Diller

Pres & CEO: D. Khosrowshahi
Vice Chrmn: V.A. Kaufman
CEO: E. Blachford
EVP & CFO: M.B. Adler

Investor Contact: S. Haas (425-679-7852)
Board Members: A. G. Battle, B. Diller, J. L. Dolgen, W. R. Fitzgerald, C. A. Jacobson, V. A. Kaufman, P. Kern, D. Khosrowshahi, J. C. Malone, J. A. Tazon

Founded: 1996
Domicile: Delaware
Employees: 8,050

Expeditors International of Washington Inc

STANDARD &POOR'S

S&P Recommendation	**BUY** ★★★★☆	Price $32.10 (as of Nov 27, 2009)	12-Mo. Target Price $43.00	Investment Style Large-Cap Growth

GICS Sector Industrials
Sub-Industry Air Freight & Logistics

Summary This company is a global air and ocean freight forwarder and customs broker.

Key Stock Statistics (Source S&P, Vickers, company reports)

52-Wk Range	$38.10– 23.86	S&P Oper. EPS 2009**E**	1.10	Market Capitalization(B)	$6.807	Beta	0.63
Trailing 12-Month EPS	$1.15	S&P Oper. EPS 2010**E**	1.25	Yield (%)	1.18	S&P 3-Yr. Proj. EPS CAGR(%)	15
Trailing 12-Month P/E	27.9	P/E on S&P Oper. EPS 2009**E**	29.2	Dividend Rate/Share	$0.38	S&P Credit Rating	NA
$10K Invested 5 Yrs Ago	$12,464	Common Shares Outstg. (M)	212.1	Institutional Ownership (%)	95		

Price Performance

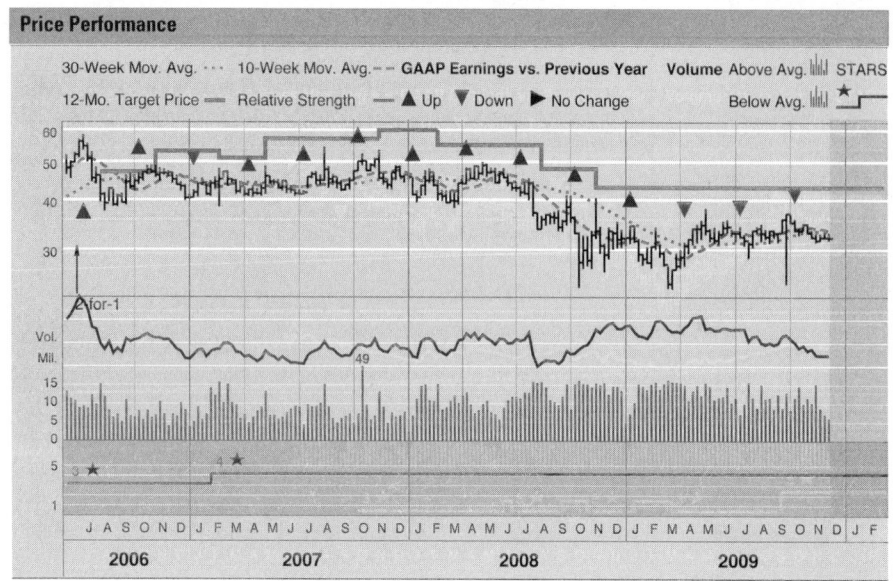

30-Week Mov. Avg. ···· 10-Week Mov. Avg. --- **GAAP Earnings vs. Previous Year** Volume Above Avg. STARS
12-Mo. Target Price — Relative Strength ▲ Up ▼ Down ► No Change Below Avg. ★

2006 | 2007 | 2008 | 2009

Options: ASE, CBOE, P, Ph

Analysis prepared by **Jim Corridore** on November 11, 2009, when the stock traded at **$ 32.81.**

Qualitative Risk Assessment

LOW	MEDIUM	HIGH

Our risk assessment reflects that EXPD operates in a highly cyclical industry and is exposed to currency and global economic risk. We see its communication style as an additional risk. However, we think EXPD has a diversified stream of air, ocean and customs businesses, and we also believe the balance sheet is strong, with no debt and a relatively large amount of cash.

Quantitative Evaluations

S&P Quality Ranking   **A+**

D	C	B-	B	B+	A-	A	A+

Relative Strength Rank   **MODERATE**

35

LOWEST = 1   HIGHEST = 99

Highlights

► We expect 2010 net revenues to rise about 10%, versus our estimate of an approximate 15% decline in 2009. Net revenue growth in 2010 should benefit from overall improving volumes in the early stages of a global economic recovery. In addition, EXPD should see better pricing in air and ocean freight. We look for Europe and Asia to lag the recovery in the U.S. by about six months. Volumes and pricing in the U.S. should start to show modest improvement in the first half and strengthen significantly in the second half of 2010.

► We project margins in 2010 benefiting from improving volumes and continued reductions in ocean and air transportation rates, reflecting new ocean freight capacity that has recently come on line, as well as excess ocean and air shipping capacity. Partly offsetting this are likely to be continued legal costs related to a Department of Justice Investigation related to potential anti-competitive practices, as well as some pressure on SG&A expenses.

► We forecast 2010 EPS of $1.25, which would represent 14% growth over our 2009 EPS estimate of $1.10. Our EPS estimate for 2009 represents a 20% decline from 2008's EPS of $1.37.

Investment Rationale/Risk

► With EXPD trading below our 12-month target price, our recommendation is buy. While the logistics sector is likely to suffer from the continuing weak U.S. and global economies, we believe EXPD's diversified revenue base, geographical reach and shipping mode will allow it to outperform peers. A debt-free balance sheet and our view of strong long-term earnings and cash flow growth potential are additional positives. We also expect improved investor sentiment for EXPD and other logistics stocks on signs of an improving U.S. economy.

► Risks to our recommendation and target price include any worsening of the global economy. We also see management's communication style, in which it mainly answers questions through 8-K filings, as a risk, in that it may not allow investors to react quickly enough to potentially important news. The company could be hit with a large judgment related to the current Department of Justice investigation into anti-competitive practices.

► Our 12-month target price of $43 values the stock at about 34X our 2010 EPS estimate of $1.25, compared to a five-year historical P/E range of 24.1X-55.0X EPS.

Revenue/Earnings Data

Revenue (Million $)

	1Q	2Q	3Q	4Q	Year
2009	912.7	895.4	1,037	--	--
2008	1,307	1,454	1,565	1,307	5,634
2007	1,119	1,259	1,411	1,447	5,235
2006	1,025	1,129	1,230	1,242	4,626
2005	825.2	928.0	1,046	1,102	3,902
2004	686.9	798.7	897.2	934.8	3,318

Earnings Per Share ($)

2009	0.27	0.25	0.27	E0.31	E1.10
2008	0.30	0.32	0.39	0.36	1.37
2007	0.27	0.30	0.34	0.32	1.21
2006	0.24	0.25	0.29	0.28	1.06
2005	0.17	0.20	0.25	0.36	0.98
2004	0.15	0.17	0.20	0.20	0.71

Fiscal year ended Dec. 31. Next earnings report expected: Mid February. EPS Estimates based on S&P Operating Earnings; historical GAAP earnings are as reported.

Dividend Data (Dates: mm/dd Payment Date: mm/dd/yy)

Amount ($)	Date Decl.	Ex-Div. Date	Stk. of Record	Payment Date
0.160	11/05	11/26	12/01	12/15/08
0.190	05/07	05/28	06/01	06/15/09
0.190	11/03	11/27	12/01	12/15/09

Dividends have been paid since 1993. Source: Company reports.

Please read the Required Disclosures and Analyst Certification on the last page of this report.

The McGraw-Hill Companies

Expeditors International of Washington Inc

STANDARD
&POOR'S

Business Summary November 11, 2009

CORPORATE OVERVIEW. With an international network supporting the movement and strategic positioning of goods, Expeditors International of Washington is engaged in the business of providing global logistics services to customers diversified in terms of industry specialization and geographic location. In each of its U.S. offices, and in many international offices, the company acts as a customs broker, and also provides additional services, including distribution management, vendor consolidation, cargo insurance, purchase order management, and customized logistics information. EXPD does not compete for domestic freight, overnight courier, or small parcel business, and does not own aircraft or steamships. The company has historically pursued a strategy emphasizing organic growth supplemented by strategic acquisitions. As of February 2009, EXPD had a network of 180 full-service offices, 69 satellite locations and four international service centers located on six continents.

Shipments of computer components, other electronic equipment, housewares, sporting goods, machine parts and toys comprise a significant percentage of the company's business. Import customers include computer retailers and distributors of consumer electronics, department store chains, clothing and shoe wholesalers. Historically, no single customer has accounted for over 5% of revenues.

Air freight services accounted for 36% of net revenues in 2008. EXPD typically acts either as a freight consolidator (purchasing cargo space on airlines and reselling it to customers at lower rates than the airline would charge customers directly), or as an agent for the airlines (receiving shipments from suppliers, and consolidating and forwarding them to the airlines). Shipments are usually characterized by a high value-to-weight ratio, a need for rapid delivery, or both. The company estimates that its average air freight consolidation weighs 3,500 lbs. to 4,500 lbs. Because shipping by air is relatively expensive compared with ocean transportation, air shipments are generally categorized by a high value-to-weight ratio, the need for rapid delivery, or both.

The company's strategy to not own aircraft is based on its view that the ownership of aircraft would subject EXPD to undue business risks, including large capital outlays, increased fixed operating costs, problems of fully utilizing aircraft and competition with airlines. EXPD relies on commercial aircraft to transport its shipments.

Company Financials Fiscal Year Ended Dec. 31

Per Share Data ($)	2008	2007	2006	2005	2004	2003	2002	2001	2000	1999
Tangible Book Value	6.38	5.69	4.95	4.21	3.70	2.98	2.49	2.01	1.76	1.40
Cash Flow	1.56	1.39	1.27	1.12	0.82	0.67	0.62	0.55	0.48	0.37
Earnings	1.37	1.21	1.06	0.98	0.71	0.56	0.52	0.45	0.38	0.28
S&P Core Earnings	1.37	1.21	1.06	0.85	0.59	0.46	0.44	0.39	NA	NA
Dividends	0.32	0.28	0.22	0.15	0.11	0.08	0.06	0.04	0.04	0.03
Payout Ratio	23%	23%	21%	15%	16%	14%	12%	10%	9%	9%
Prices:High	49.92	54.46	58.32	36.37	29.20	20.42	17.22	16.48	15.03	11.59
Prices:Low	24.05	38.31	32.83	23.59	17.85	14.81	12.47	10.49	8.16	5.08
P/E Ratio:High	36	45	55	37	41	36	33	37	40	42
P/E Ratio:Low	18	32	31	24	25	26	24	24	21	18

Income Statement Analysis (Million $)										
Revenue	5,634	5,235	4,626	3,902	3,318	2,625	2,297	1,653	1,695	1,445
Operating Income	515	463	411	337	268	211	194	170	150	114
Depreciation	41.6	40.0	35.4	32.3	26.7	24.4	22.7	23.5	22.5	20.8
Interest Expense	0.18	Nil	0.20	0.31	0.04	0.19	0.18	0.52	0.43	1.07
Pretax Income	500	450	396	320	250	196	178	154	133	94.6
Effective Tax Rate	39.4%	40.0%	40.6%	29.6%	35.4%	36.4%	36.8%	37.0%	37.7%	37.5%
Net Income	301	269	235	219	156	122	113	97.2	83.0	59.2
S&P Core Earnings	301	269	235	187	130	98.4	92.7	83.8	NA	NA

Balance Sheet & Other Financial Data (Million $)										
Cash	742	575	511	464	409	296	212	219	169	71.2
Current Assets	1,573	1,535	1,342	1,202	1,046	762	605	511	523	382
Total Assets	2,101	2,069	1,822	1,566	1,364	1,041	880	688	662	512
Current Liabilities	670	770	709	613	524	392	356	274	230	229
Long Term Debt	Nil	Nil	Nil	Nil	Nil	Nil	Nil	Nil	Nil	Nil
Common Equity	1,366	1,227	1,070	914	807	646	524	415	362	282
Total Capital	1,430	1,299	1,113	954	840	649	524	415	362	282
Capital Expenditures	59.7	82.8	141	90.8	66.2	20.7	81.4	37.4	25.6	26.6
Cash Flow	343	309	271	251	183	146	135	121	106	80.0
Current Ratio	2.4	2.0	1.9	2.0	2.0	1.9	1.7	1.9	2.3	1.7
% Long Term Debt of Capitalization	Nil	Nil	Nil	Nil	Nil	Nil	Nil	Nil	Nil	Nil
% Net Income of Revenue	5.3	5.1	5.1	5.6	4.7	4.6	4.9	5.9	4.9	4.1
% Return on Assets	14.4	13.8	13.9	14.9	13.0	12.7	14.3	14.4	13.9	12.9
% Return on Equity	23.2	23.4	23.6	25.4	21.5	20.9	24.0	25.0	25.8	23.7

Data as orig reptd.; bef. results of disc opers/spec. items. Per share data adj. for stk. divs.; EPS diluted. E-Estimated. NA-Not Available. NM-Not Meaningful. NR-Not Ranked. UR-Under Review.

Office: 1015 Third Avenue, Seattle, WA 98104-1190.
Telephone: 206-674-3400.
Website: http://www.expeditors.com
Chrmn & CEO: P.J. Rose

Pres & COO: R. Gates
SVP & Cntlr: C.J. Lynch
SVP & CIO: J.S. Musser
CFO & Chief Acctg Officer: B.S. Powell

Investor Contact: R.J. Gates (206-674-3400)
Board Members: M. A. Emmert, R. Gates, D. P. Kourkoumelis, M. J. Malone, J. W. Meisenbach, P. J. Rose, L. Wang, R. R. Wright

Founded: 1979
Domicile: Washington
Employees: 12,580

The McGraw-Hill Companies

Express Scripts Inc

S&P Recommendation	**STRONG BUY** ★★★★★	Price $85.74 (as of Nov 27, 2009)	12-Mo. Target Price $97.00	Investment Style Large-Cap Growth

GICS Sector Health Care
Sub-Industry Health Care Services

Summary This company offers prescription benefits and disease state management services.

Key Stock Statistics (Source S&P, Vickers, company reports)

52-Wk Range	$88.58– 42.75	S&P Oper. EPS 2009**E**	3.41	Market Capitalization(B)	$23.554	Beta	0.91
Trailing 12-Month EPS	$3.13	S&P Oper. EPS 2010**E**	4.03	Yield (%)	Nil	S&P 3-Yr. Proj. EPS CAGR(%)	15
Trailing 12-Month P/E	27.4	P/E on S&P Oper. EPS 2009**E**	25.1	Dividend Rate/Share	Nil	S&P Credit Rating	BBB
$10K Invested 5 Yrs Ago	$49,340	Common Shares Outstg. (M)	274.7	Institutional Ownership (%)	87		

Price Performance

30-Week Mov. Avg. · · · 10-Week Mov. Avg. - - **GAAP Earnings vs. Previous Year** Volume Above Avg. STARS
12-Mo. Target Price — Relative Strength — ▲ Up ▼ Down ► No Change Below Avg. ★

2-for-1

Vol.
Mil.

J A S O N D J F M A M J J A S O N D J F M A M J J A S O N D J F M A M J J A S O N D J F
2006   2007   2008   2009

Options: ASE, CBOE, P

Analysis prepared by **Phillip M. Seligman** on November 09, 2009, when the stock traded at **$ 85.91**.

Highlights

▶ ESRX has agreed to acquire WellPoint's (WLP 52, Buy) in-house PBM unit, subject to closing conditions. Until the transaction closes, we continue to follow ESRX in its current form. On that basis, we expect 2009 revenues to grow by 1.1%, to about $22.2 billion, as gains from new accounts and higher prices outweigh the increasing penetration of low-priced generic drugs, 0.5% fewer prescriptions due to tough economic conditions, and client losses. Looking ahead, we forecast revenues to rise by 2.3% in 2010, on 3.0% more prescriptions, with revenue growth tempered by generic drug penetration.

▶ Our model reflects the financing transactions for the pending acquisition since they have occurred. We include 25.45 million additional shares, interest income from their sale at $61 a share, and interest costs from $2.5 billion of senior notes. We assume they will be redeemed and that share buybacks will occur in 2010 if the acquisition does not close. Meanwhile, we see EBITDA margins continuing to expand.

▶ Our 2009 non-GAAP EPS estimate is $3.41, before $0.37 of one-time costs, versus 2008's $3.13, before $0.03 of one-time costs. We look for EPS of $4.03 in 2010.

Investment Rationale/Risk

▶ Despite the dilutive impact of financing transactions and not accounting for any acquisitions, our recommendation is strong buy. We think a strong generic drug launch cycle we see through 2015 and opportunities presented by health care reform, should it occur, provide healthy long-term earnings growth for PBMs including ESRX. We particularly like ESRX's agreement to acquire WLP's PBM unit, which should boost its claims volumes by 50% and, we believe, improve its competitive position. Before transaction costs and intangibles amortization, ESRX sees the deal as accretive from the start, and upon 12-18 months integration, adding over $1 billion in EBITDA. We are also encouraged that it has been experiencing a strong selling season, winning 238 accounts so far for 2010, including eight major ones.

▶ Risks to our recommendation and target price include increased government oversight, loss of key clients, and failure of the proposed WLP PBM acquisition.

▶ We derive our 12-month target price of $97 by applying an above-peer P/E-to-growth ratio of 1.6X, assuming three-year EPS growth of 15% and our 2010 EPS estimate.

Qualitative Risk Assessment

LOW	**MEDIUM**	HIGH

Our risk assessment reflects our view of rising drug demand, and the company's improving financial performance and healthy operating cash flow. However, we believe intense competition and increased government regulation of pharmacy benefits managers (PBMs), which we view as likely, could result in changes in industry conditions.

Quantitative Evaluations

S&P Quality Ranking   B+

D	C	B-	B	**B+**	A-	A	A+

Relative Strength Rank   STRONG

82

LOWEST = 1   HIGHEST = 99

Revenue/Earnings Data

Revenue (Million $)

	1Q	2Q	3Q	4Q	Year
2009	5,423	5,503	5,619	--	--
2008	5,491	5,530	5,451	5,506	21,978
2007	4,540	4,600	4,519	4,694	18,274
2006	4,380	4,421	4,330	4,529	17,660
2005	3,839	3,944	3,848	4,635	16,266
2004	3,628	3,780	3,768	3,940	15,115

Earnings Per Share ($)

2009	0.86	0.74	0.71	E0.86	E3.41
2008	0.70	0.76	0.81	0.83	3.10
2007	0.49	0.57	0.56	0.65	2.28
2006	0.35	0.38	0.42	0.54	1.67
2005	0.29	0.34	0.34	0.38	1.34
2004	0.22	0.21	0.20	0.27	0.90

Fiscal year ended Dec. 31. Next earnings report expected: Late February. EPS Estimates based on S&P Operating Earnings; historical GAAP earnings are as reported.

Dividend Data

No cash dividends have been paid.

Please read the Required Disclosures and Analyst Certification on the last page of this report.

Express Scripts Inc

STANDARD
&POOR'S

Business Summary November 09, 2009

CORPORATE OVERVIEW. Express Scripts is one of the largest U.S. pharmacy benefits managers (PBMs). Its PBM services (82.9% of 2008 revenue, versus 83.4% in 2007) include retail network pharmacy management, mail pharmacy services, benefit design consultation, drug utilization review, formulary management, disease management, and compliance and therapy management for thousands of client groups that include health insurers, third-party administrators, employers, union-sponsored benefit plans and government health programs.

The SAAS segment (17.1%, versus 16.6%) comprises specialty operations of CuraScript, and its SDS and PMG service lines. The segment's services include delivery of injectable drugs to patient homes, physician offices, and clinics, third-party logistics services, and bio-pharma services including reimbursement and customized logistics solutions. The segment also includes distribution of specialty pharmaceuticals requiring special handling or packaging; distribution of pharmaceuticals to low-income patients through manufacturer-sponsored branded and company-sponsored generic patient assistance programs; and distribution of sample units to physicians and verification of practitioner licensure. The infusion business was reclassified as discontinued

operations in 2007's fourth quarter.

Revenues are generated primarily from the delivery of prescription drugs through 60,000 contracted retail pharmacies, three home delivery fulfillment pharmacies, and eight specialty drug pharmacies, as of December 31, 2008. Revenues from the delivery of prescription drugs to members represented 98.7% of revenues in 2008, versus 98.6% in 2007. Revenues from services, such as the administration of some clients' retail pharmacy networks, and certain services provided by SAAS comprised the remainder.

The five largest clients accounted for 18.2% of revenues in 2008, compared to 18.1% in 2007. In 2008, ESRX processed 379.6 million network pharmacy claims, 40.8 million home delivery pharmacy claims and 4.3 million SAAS claims, versus 379.9 million, 40.8 million and 4.7 million, respectively, in 2007.

Company Financials Fiscal Year Ended Dec. 31

Per Share Data ($)	2008	2007	2006	2005	2004	2003	2002	2001	2000	1999
Tangible Book Value	NM	NM	NM	NM	NM	NM	NM	NM	NM	NM
Cash Flow	3.48	2.64	2.03	1.62	1.12	0.97	0.90	0.64	0.23	0.78
Earnings	3.10	2.28	1.67	1.34	0.90	0.79	0.64	0.39	-0.03	0.53
S&P Core Earnings	3.12	2.24	1.67	1.30	0.87	0.75	0.60	0.36	NA	NA
Dividends	Nil	Nil	Nil	Nil	Nil	Nil	Nil	Nil	Nil	Nil
Payout Ratio	Nil	Nil	Nil	Nil	Nil	Nil	Nil	Nil	Nil	Nil
Prices:High	79.10	74.40	47.50	45.40	20.30	18.86	16.48	15.36	13.38	13.19
Prices:Low	48.37	32.32	29.40	18.27	14.58	11.58	9.66	8.71	3.56	5.55
P/E Ratio:High	26	33	28	34	23	24	26	39	NM	25
P/E Ratio:Low	16	14	18	14	16	15	15	22	NM	10

Income Statement Analysis (Million $)

	2008	2007	2006	2005	2004	2003	2002	2001	2000	1999
Revenue	21,978	18,274	17,660	16,266	15,115	13,295	12,261	9,329	6,787	4,288
Operating Income	1,390	1,177	925	727	563	503	454	317	279	241
Depreciation	97.7	97.5	101	84.0	70.0	54.0	82.0	80.1	78.6	74.0
Interest Expense	77.6	108	95.7	37.0	41.7	41.4	42.2	34.2	47.9	60.0
Pretax Income	1,214	945	740	615	451	405	330	208	-4.47	265
Effective Tax Rate	35.8%	36.5%	35.9%	35.0%	38.3%	38.2%	38.2%	39.9%	NM	40.7%
Net Income	780	600	474	400	278	251	204	125	-8.02	157
S&P Core Earnings	784	592	474	389	270	239	192	115	NA	NA

Balance Sheet & Other Financial Data (Million $)

	2008	2007	2006	2005	2004	2003	2002	2001	2000	1999
Cash	539	437	131	478	166	396	191	178	53.2	283
Current Assets	2,044	1,968	1,772	2,257	1,443	1,560	1,394	1,213	998	1,066
Total Assets	5,509	5,256	5,108	5,493	3,600	3,409	3,207	2,500	2,277	2,487
Current Liabilities	2,722	2,475	2,429	2,394	1,813	1,626	1,544	1,246	1,116	1,100
Long Term Debt	1,340	1,760	1,270	1,401	412	455	563	346	396	636
Common Equity	1,078	696	1,125	1,465	1,196	1,194	1,003	832	705	699
Total Capital	2,732	2,735	2,395	2,866	1,608	1,649	1,565	1,178	1,102	1,335
Capital Expenditures	85.8	75.0	66.8	60.0	51.5	53.1	61.3	57.3	80.2	37.0
Cash Flow	877	698	575	484	348	305	286	205	70.6	231
Current Ratio	0.8	0.8	0.7	0.9	0.8	1.0	0.9	1.0	0.9	1.0
% Long Term Debt of Capitalization	49.1	64.4	53.0	48.9	25.6	27.6	35.9	29.4	36.0	47.6
% Net Income of Revenue	3.6	3.3	2.7	2.5	1.8	1.9	1.7	1.3	NM	3.7
% Return on Assets	14.5	11.6	8.9	8.8	7.9	7.6	7.1	5.2	NM	8.8
% Return on Equity	87.9	65.9	36.6	30.1	23.3	22.8	22.2	16.3	NM	33.2

Data as orig reptd.; bef. results of disc opers/spec. items. Per share data adj. for stk. divs.; EPS diluted. E-Estimated. NA-Not Available. NM-Not Meaningful. NR-Not Ranked. UR-Under Review.

Office: 1 Express Way, Saint Louis, MO 63121-1824.
Telephone: 314-996-0900.
Email: investor.relations@express-scripts.com
Website: http://www.express-scripts.com

Chrmn, Pres & CEO: G. Paz
EVP & CFO: J.L. Hall
EVP, Secy & General Counsel: K.J. Ebling
Investor Contact: D. Myers (314-810-3115)

Chief Acctg Officer & Cntlr: K. Elliott
Board Members: G. G. Benanav, F. J. Borelli, M. Breen, N. J. LaHowchic, T. P. MacMahon, F. Mergenthaler, W. Myers, Jr., J. O. Parker, Jr., G. Paz, S. K. Skinner, S. Sternberg, B. Toan

Founded: 1986
Domicile: Delaware
Employees: 10,820

STANDARD &POOR'S

Exxon Mobil Corp

S&P Recommendation	**STRONG BUY** ★ ★ ★ ★ ★	Price $74.87 (as of Nov 27, 2009)	12-Mo. Target Price $88.00	Investment Style Large-Cap Blend

GICS Sector Energy
Sub-Industry Integrated Oil & Gas

Summary XOM, formed through the merger of Exxon and Mobil in late 1999, is the world's largest publicly owned integrated oil company.

Key Stock Statistics (Source S&P, Vickers, company reports)

52-Wk Range	$83.64–61.86	S&P Oper. EPS 2009E	3.88	Market Capitalization(B)	$355.429	Beta	0.46
Trailing 12-Month EPS	$4.29	S&P Oper. EPS 2010E	5.96	Yield (%)	2.24	S&P 3-Yr. Proj. EPS CAGR(%)	-4
Trailing 12-Month P/E	17.5	P/E on S&P Oper. EPS 2009E	19.3	Dividend Rate/Share	$1.68	S&P Credit Rating	AAA
$10K Invested 5 Yrs Ago	$15,987	Common Shares Outstg. (M)	4,747.3	Institutional Ownership (%)	47		

Price Performance

30-Week Mov. Avg. ···· 10-Week Mov. Avg. - - GAAP Earnings vs. Previous Year Volume Above Avg. STARS
12-Mo. Target Price — Relative Strength ▲ Up ▼ Down ► No Change Below Avg.

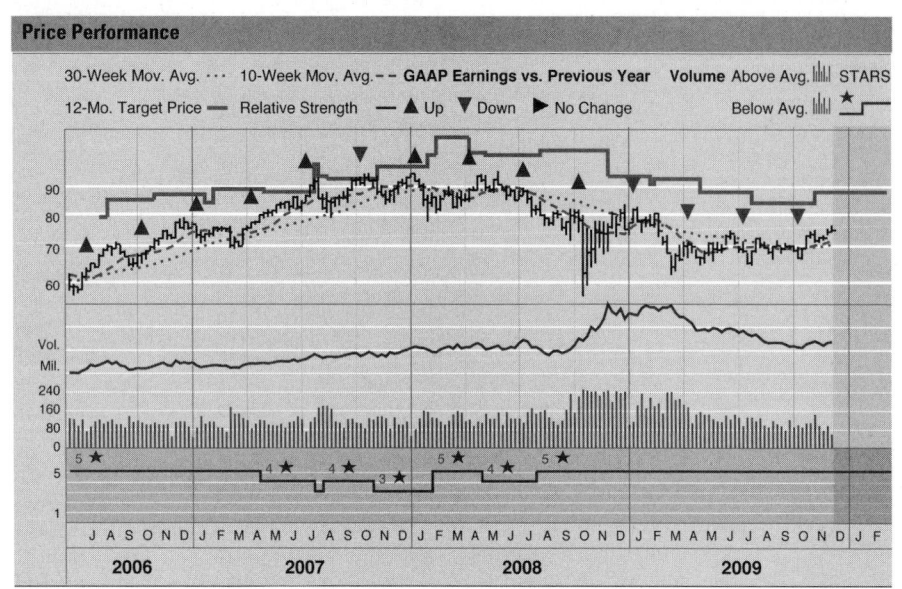

Options: ASE, CBOE, P, Ph

Analysis prepared by **Tina J. Vital** on October 29, 2009, when the stock traded at **$73.52.**

Qualitative Risk Assessment

LOW	MEDIUM	HIGH

Our risk assessment reflects our view of the company's diversified and strong business profile in volatile, cyclical and capital-intensive segments of the energy industry. We view ExxonMobil's earnings stability and corporate governance practices as above average.

Quantitative Evaluations

S&P Quality Ranking A+

D	C	B-	B	B+	A-	A	A+

Relative Strength Rank STRONG

72

LOWEST = 1   HIGHEST = 99

Revenue/Earnings Data

Revenue (Million $)

	1Q	2Q	3Q	4Q	Year
2009	64,028	74,457	82,260	--	--
2008	116,854	138,072	137,737	84,696	477,359
2007	87,223	98,350	102,337	116,642	404,552
2006	86,317	96,024	96,268	86,858	377,635
2005	82,051	88,568	100,717	99,662	370,680
2004	67,602	70,693	76,375	83,357	298,035

Earnings Per Share ($)

2009	0.92	0.81	0.98	E1.14	E3.88
2008	2.03	2.22	2.86	1.55	8.69
2007	1.62	1.83	1.70	2.14	7.28
2006	1.37	1.72	1.77	1.76	6.62
2005	1.22	1.20	1.58	1.71	5.71
2004	0.83	0.88	0.88	1.30	3.89

Fiscal year ended Dec. 31. Next earnings report expected: Early February. EPS Estimates based on S&P Operating Earnings; historical GAAP earnings are as reported.

Highlights

► XOM has nine major project start-ups slated for 2009 (Qatar's Qatargas II Train 4 and 5, Qatar's RasGas Train 6 and 7, Qatar's Al Khaleej Gas Phase 2, the U.S. Piceance Phase 1, Norway Tyrihans, plus LNG terminals in Italy and the U.K.), nine in 2010-11, and 35 thereafter. We forecast over 3% per annum oil & gas production growth in 2008-13. However, we expect flat growth in 2009 on reduced demand, to about 3.95 million boe per day, with a ramp-up of about 2% in 2010.

► On the downstream, reduced product demand has resulted in narrowed refining margins. While we consider XOM to be a highly efficient and complex refiner, once market conditions improve, we look for XOM to rationalize its relatively less efficient units. We expect U.S. Gulf Coast 3-2-1 crack spreads to narrow about 16% in 2009, but widen about 7% in 2010.

► Operating EPS excluded $0.03 of net special gains in the 2009 first nine months. We expect after-tax operating earnings to drop 57% in 2009 on reduced demand and lower oil & gas prices, before rebounding 52% in 2010 on an improved economic outlook.

Investment Rationale/Risk

► XOM has enjoyed a superior degree of earnings and dividend growth and stability (as evidenced by its S&P Quality Ranking of A+). We believe the company will benefit from "big-pocket" upstream growth opportunities in deepwater, liquefied natural gas (LNG), and ventures with state-owned oil companies. We think XOM's advanced technology permits project development in a timely and cost efficient manner. In addition, we see its upstream E&P benefiting from a strong pipeline of long-lived resources, and its downstream unit benefiting over the long term from its complex refineries, which offer feedstock flexibility and the processing of lower-cost feedstocks.

► Risks to our recommendation and target price include deterioration in economic, industry and operating conditions, such as difficulty replacing reserves and increased production costs.

► Blending our discounted cash flow ($93 per share; assuming a WACC of 6.9% and terminal growth of 3%) and relative market valuations, our 12-month target price is $88 per share, representing an expected enterprise value of 7.2X our 2010 EBITDA estimate, a premium to U.S. supermajor oil peers.

Dividend Data (Dates: mm/dd Payment Date: mm/dd/yy)

Amount ($)	Date Decl.	Ex-Div. Date	Stk. of Record	Payment Date
0.400	01/28	02/06	02/10	03/10/09
0.420	04/29	05/11	05/13	06/10/09
0.420	07/29	08/11	08/13	09/10/09
0.420	10/28	11/09	11/12	12/10/09

Dividends have been paid since 1882. Source: Company reports.

Please read the Required Disclosures and Analyst Certification on the last page of this report.

The McGraw·Hill Companies

Exxon Mobil Corp

Business Summary October 29, 2009

CORPORATE OVERVIEW. In late 1999, the FTC allowed Exxon and Mobil to re-unite, creating Exxon Mobil Corp. (XOM). ExxonMobil's businesses include oil and natural gas exploration and production (9% of 2008 sales; 76% of 2008 segment earnings); refining and marketing (83%; 18%); chemicals (8%; 6%); and other operations, such as electric power generation, coal and minerals.

Including non-consolidated equity interest, proved oil and gas reserves declined about 3.0% to 21.11 billion barrel oil equivalent (boe; 48% liquids), as of year-end 2008. In addition, proved Canadian oil sands reserves rose 170% to 1.871 billion barrels (84% attributable to Imperial Oil Ltd.) as of year-end 2008. Including oil sands and non-consolidated interests, liquids production declined 8.8%, to 2.405 million b/d in 2008, and natural gas production available for sale declined 3.1%, to 9.095 billion cubic feet per day (Bcf/d) in 2008. Using data from John S. Herold, we estimate XOM's three-year (2005-2007) reserve replacement at 134%, above the peer average; its three-year finding and development cost at $7.34 per boe, below the peer average; its proved ac-

quisition costs at $0.51 per boe, below the peer average; and its reserve replacement costs at $6.39 per boe, below the peer average.

As of year-end 2008, the company had an ownership interest in 37 refineries with 6.21 million b/d of atmospheric distillation capacity (U.S. 32%, Europe 28%, Asia Pacific 27%, Canada 8%, and Latin America/other 5%).

MANAGEMENT. We believe XOM is one of the best managed companies in the energy sector. In January 2006, Lee R. Raymond retired and Rex W. Tillerson became chairman and CEO. We expect Mr. Tillerson to benefit from plans made by Mr. Raymond over the past 12 years, and we see Mr. Tillerson's diplomatic skills as playing an important role in enhancing those plans.

Company Financials Fiscal Year Ended Dec. 31

Per Share Data ($)	2008	2007	2006	2005	2004	2003	2002	2001	2000	1999
Tangible Book Value	22.70	22.62	19.87	18.13	15.90	13.69	11.13	10.74	10.21	9.13
Cash Flow	11.08	9.48	8.89	7.34	5.38	4.50	2.84	3.32	3.43	2.30
Earnings	8.69	7.28	6.62	5.71	3.89	3.15	1.61	2.18	2.27	1.13
S&P Core Earnings	8.64	7.40	6.75	5.72	4.01	3.03	1.52	2.03	NA	NA
Dividends	1.55	1.37	1.28	1.14	1.06	0.98	0.92	0.91	0.88	0.84
Payout Ratio	18%	19%	19%	20%	27%	31%	57%	42%	39%	74%
Prices:High	96.12	95.27	79.00	65.96	52.05	41.13	44.58	45.84	47.72	43.63
Prices:Low	56.51	69.02	56.42	49.25	39.91	31.58	29.75	35.01	34.94	32.16
P/E Ratio:High	11	13	12	12	13	13	28	21	21	39
P/E Ratio:Low	7	9	9	9	10	10	18	16	15	29

Income Statement Analysis (Million $)										
Revenue	477,359	404,552	377,635	370,680	298,035	246,738	204,506	213,488	232,748	185,527
Operating Income	78,669	156,810	150,107	59,255	45,639	32,230	23,280	29,602	33,309	17,921
Depreciation, Depletion and Amortization	12,379	12,250	11,416	10,253	9,767	9,047	8,310	7,944	8,130	8,304
Interest Expense	673	957	654	496	638	207	398	293	589	695
Pretax Income	81,750	71,479	68,453	60,231	42,017	32,660	17,719	24,688	27,493	11,295
Effective Tax Rate	44.7%	41.8%	40.8%	38.7%	37.9%	33.7%	36.7%	36.5%	40.3%	28.7%
Net Income	45,220	40,610	39,500	36,130	25,330	20,960	11,011	15,105	15,990	7,910
S&P Core Earnings	44,959	41,250	40,263	36,164	26,089	20,214	10,418	14,042	NA	NA

Balance Sheet & Other Financial Data (Million $)										
Cash	32,007	34,500	32,848	28,671	18,531	10,626	7,229	6,547	7,081	1,761
Current Assets	72,266	85,963	75,777	73,342	60,377	45,960	38,291	35,681	40,399	31,141
Total Assets	228,052	242,082	219,015	208,335	195,256	174,278	152,644	143,174	149,000	144,521
Current Liabilities	49,100	58,312	48,817	46,307	42,981	38,386	33,175	30,114	38,191	38,733
Long Term Debt	7,025	7,183	6,645	6,220	5,013	4,756	6,655	7,099	7,280	8,402
Common Equity	112,965	121,762	113,844	111,186	101,756	89,915	74,597	73,161	70,757	63,466
Total Capital	144,274	156,126	141,340	138,284	131,813	118,171	100,504	99,444	97,709	91,807
Capital Expenditures	19,318	15,387	15,462	13,839	11,986	12,859	11,437	9,989	8,446	10,849
Cash Flow	57,599	52,860	50,916	46,383	35,097	30,007	19,321	23,049	24,120	16,178
Current Ratio	1.5	1.5	1.6	1.6	1.4	1.2	1.2	1.2	1.1	0.8
% Long Term Debt of Capitalization	4.9	4.6	4.7	4.4	3.8	4.0	6.6	7.1	7.5	9.2
% Return on Assets	19.2	17.6	18.5	17.9	13.7	12.8	7.4	10.3	10.9	5.6
% Return on Equity	38.5	34.5	35.1	33.9	26.4	25.5	14.9	21.0	23.8	12.6

Data as orig reptd.; bef. results of disc opers/spec. items. Per share data adj. for stk. divs.; EPS diluted. E-Estimated. NA-Not Available. NM-Not Meaningful. NR-Not Ranked. UR-Under Review.

Office: 5959 Las Colinas Blvd, Irving, TX 75039-2298.
Telephone: 972-444-1000.
Website: http://www.exxonmobil.com
Chrmn, Pres & CEO: R.W. Tillerson

SVP, CFO & Treas: D.D. Humphreys
Chief Acctg Officer & Cntlr: P.T. Mulva
Secy: D.S. Rosenthal
General Counsel: C.W. Matthews

Board Members: M. J. Boskin, L. R. Faulkner, K. C. Frazier, W. W. George, R. C. King, M. C. Nelson, S. J. Palmisano, S. S. Reinemund, R. W. Tillerson, E. E. Whitacre, Jr.

Founded: 1870
Domicile: New Jersey
Employees: 79,900

Family Dollar Stores Inc.

| S&P Recommendation **STRONG BUY** ★★★★★ | Price $31.02 (as of Nov 27, 2009) | 12-Mo. Target Price $40.00 | Investment Style Large-Cap Blend |

GICS Sector Consumer Discretionary
Sub-Industry General Merchandise Stores

Summary This company operates a chain of more than 6,650 retail discount stores in 44 states across the U.S.

Key Stock Statistics (Source S&P, Vickers, company reports)

52-Wk Range	$35.00– 21.79	S&P Oper. EPS 2010**E**	2.30	Market Capitalization(B)	$4.306	Beta	0.15
Trailing 12-Month EPS	$2.07	S&P Oper. EPS 2011**E**	2.58	Yield (%)	1.74	S&P 3-Yr. Proj. EPS CAGR(%)	12
Trailing 12-Month P/E	15.0	P/E on S&P Oper. EPS 2010**E**	13.5	Dividend Rate/Share	$0.54	S&P Credit Rating	NA
$10K Invested 5 Yrs Ago	$10,758	Common Shares Outstg. (M)	138.8	Institutional Ownership (%)	95		

Price Performance

30-Week Mov. Avg. · · · ·   10-Week Mov. Avg. – – –   **GAAP Earnings vs. Previous Year**   Volume Above Avg. ▮▮▮ STARS
12-Mo. Target Price —   Relative Strength —   ▲ Up   ▼ Down   ► No Change   Below Avg. ▮▮▮ ★

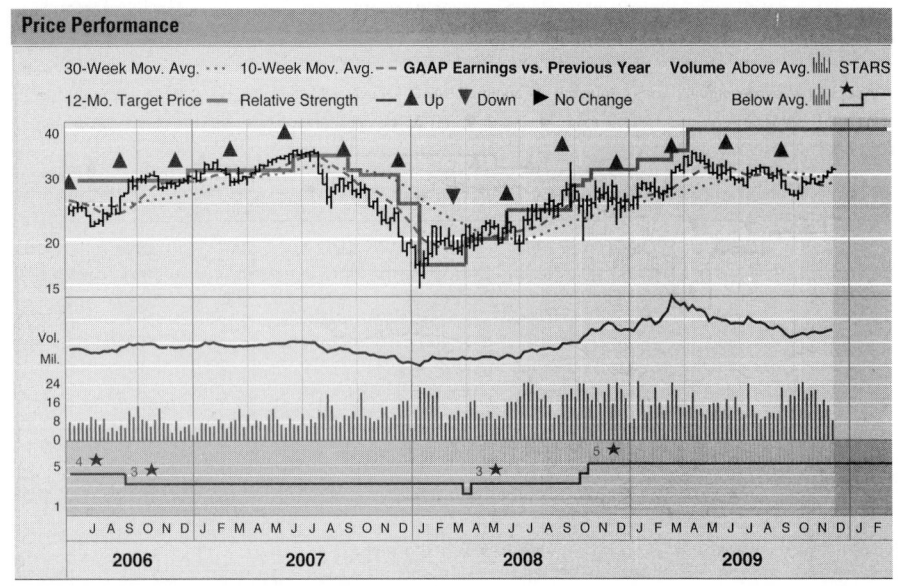

Options: ASE, CBOE, P, Ph

Analysis prepared by **Jason N. Asaeda** on October 08, 2009, when the stock traded at **$ 28.21**.

Highlights

► We expect net sales to increase 5% in FY 10 (Aug.), to $7.79 billion, supported by a projected 4% same-store sales gain and FDO's plan to open about 200 new stores. We expect the company to attract cost-conscious consumers with its value-priced assortment of everyday necessities, including food, personal care products, and household cleaners. We also think "surprise finds" in fashion and seasonal merchandise will draw "treasure" hunters.

► While we anticipate increased sales penetration of lower-margin consumables, we see gross margins widening on lower inventory shrinkage and higher initial mark-ups, reflecting global sourcing efforts and sharper pricing. We also look for FDO to tightly control inventories of more discretionary categories to limit its markdown exposure.

► We foresee higher insurance expense and incentive compensation costs, as well as investments by the company to upgrade store technology and to improve the in-store shopping experience. However, we expect FDO to leverage most other SG&A expenses off of same-store sales gains. Assuming limited share buybacks, we see EPS of $2.30 in FY 10.

Investment Rationale/Risk

► In the FY 09 fourth quarter, same-store sales rose 1%. While missing our 3% growth projection, we note that FDO anniversaried a tough year-ago 5.6% gain that was supported by fiscal stimulus checks. Sales were also hurt this summer by the company's decision to aggressively reformat about half of its stores. We expect the resulting expanded selection of consumables and improved shopping convenience of these stores to yield higher sales productivity and earnings in FY 10. We also view FDO's finances and balance sheet as healthy, and expect the company to generate free cash that it can use, in part, for new store openings and investments in what we view to be promising long-term growth initiatives.

► Risks to our recommendation and target price include sales shortfalls due to changes in consumer confidence, spending habits, and buying preferences; merchandise availability; and increased promotional activity by competitors.

► We derive our 12-month target price of $40 by applying a forward P/E multiple of 17.2X, a 10% discount to FDO's 10-year historical average of 19.1X, to our calendar 2010 EPS estimate of $2.35.

Qualitative Risk Assessment

| LOW | MEDIUM | HIGH |

Our risk assessment reflects our view of FDO's high-quality earnings, as reflected in its S&P Quality Ranking of A+, healthy balance sheet, and strong cash flow generation. We also believe demand for the company's merchandise is generally stable and not affected by changes in the economy, except for more discretionary categories.

Quantitative Evaluations

S&P Quality Ranking A+

| D | C | B- | B | B+ | A- | A | **A+** |

Relative Strength Rank STRONG

80

LOWEST = 1   HIGHEST = 99

Revenue/Earnings Data

Revenue (Million $)

	1Q	2Q	3Q	4Q	Year
2009	1,754	1,992	1,843	1,811	7,401
2008	1,683	1,833	1,702	1,766	6,984
2007	1,600	1,947	1,655	1,632	6,834
2006	1,511	1,736	1,570	1,578	6,395
2005	1,380	1,587	1,428	1,430	5,825
2004	1,245	1,403	1,310	1,324	5,282

Earnings Per Share ($)

2009	0.42	0.60	0.62	0.43	2.07
2008	0.37	0.45	0.46	0.38	1.66
2007	0.36	0.60	0.40	0.26	1.62
2006	0.32	0.35	0.37	0.21	1.26
2005	0.32	0.48	0.32	0.18	1.30
2004	0.37	0.47	0.43	0.26	1.53

Fiscal year ended Aug. 31. Next earnings report expected: Early January. EPS Estimates based on S&P Operating Earnings; historical GAAP earnings are as reported.

Dividend Data (Dates: mm/dd Payment Date: mm/dd/yy)

Amount ($)	Date Decl.	Ex-Div. Date	Stk. of Record	Payment Date
0.135	01/15	03/11	03/13	04/15/09
0.135	04/09	06/11	06/15	07/15/09
0.135	08/27	09/11	09/15	10/15/09
0.135	11/18	12/11	12/15	01/15/10

Dividends have been paid since 1976. Source: Company reports.

Please read the Required Disclosures and Analyst Certification on the last page of this report.

The McGraw-Hill Companies

Family Dollar Stores Inc.

STANDARD &POOR'S

Business Summary October 08, 2009

CORPORATE OVERVIEW. Family Dollar Stores Inc. (FDO) operates a chain of over 6,650 retail discount stores in 44 states. The company describes its typical customer as a woman in her mid-40s who is the head of her household and has an annual income of under $30,000. Family Dollar stores carry an assortment of hardlines and softlines priced from under $1 to $10 and are operated on a self-service basis, with limited advertising support and promotional activity. The once cash-only stores now accept PIN-based debit card payments in most locations. Food stamp and credit card acceptance is also being rolled out. In our view, broader tender options offer the company an opportunity to improve its share of customer wallet as shopping is more convenient and available cash does not limit basket size.

Store inventory is comprised of both regularly available merchandise, which provides consistency in product offerings, and a frequently changing selection of brands and products that FDO acquires through closeouts and manufacturer overruns at discounted wholesale prices. Low product costs and store overhead enable the company to sell its value-priced merchandise profitably.

PRIMARY BUSINESS DYNAMICS. FDO's primary growth drivers are same-store sales and chain expansion. In FY 09 (Aug.), same-store sales rose 4.0%, reflecting an increase in average customer transaction value and higher customer traffic, as measured by the company in number of register transactions. In our opinion, customers are spending more due to an expanded assortment of consumables and "treasure hunt" items that add an element of excitement and interest to the shopping experience. FDO has also increased its marketing efforts to emphasize the value and shopping convenience it offers.

While core customers are spending more per store visit, they are also shopping less often due to macroeconomic concerns. However, we think the company is gaining incremental business from middle-income customers trading down from higher-priced retailers for everyday basics. In the company's view, the economic downturn hurt low income consumers first and the hardest, and is now impacting higher-income consumers.

Company Financials Fiscal Year Ended Aug. 31

Per Share Data ($)	2009	2008	2007	2006	2005	2004	2003	2002	2001	2000
Tangible Book Value	10.38	8.98	8.19	8.04	8.64	8.13	7.61	6.66	5.57	4.66
Cash Flow	NA	2.72	2.59	2.13	1.99	2.10	1.94	1.69	1.49	1.31
Earnings	2.07	1.66	1.62	1.26	1.30	1.53	1.43	1.25	1.10	1.00
S&P Core Earnings	2.07	1.66	1.71	1.44	1.21	1.45	1.39	1.22	1.08	NA
Dividends	0.52	0.48	0.44	0.40	0.36	0.32	0.28	0.25	0.23	0.22
Payout Ratio	25%	29%	27%	31%	28%	21%	20%	20%	21%	21%
Prices:High	35.00	32.50	35.42	30.91	35.25	39.66	44.13	37.25	31.35	24.50
Prices:Low	24.02	14.62	17.95	21.57	19.40	25.09	25.46	23.75	18.38	14.25
P/E Ratio:High	17	20	22	24	27	26	31	30	29	25
P/E Ratio:Low	12	9	11	17	15	16	18	19	17	14

Income Statement Analysis (Million $)	2009	2008	2007	2006	2005	2004	2003	2002	2001	2000
Revenue	7,401	6,984	6,834	6,395	5,825	5,282	4,750	4,163	3,665	3,133
Operating Income	NA	515	532	452	458	512	478	419	366	325
Depreciation	160	150	144	135	115	97.9	88.3	77.0	67.7	54.5
Interest Expense	NA	15.4	17.0	13.1	Nil	Nil	Nil	Nil	Nil	Nil
Pretax Income	451	362	382	311	343	414	390	342	298	271
Effective Tax Rate	35.4%	35.6%	36.4%	37.3%	36.5%	36.6%	36.5%	36.5%	36.5%	36.5%
Net Income	291	233	243	195	218	263	247	217	190	172
S&P Core Earnings	291	233	257	223	202	250	241	213	186	NA

Balance Sheet & Other Financial Data (Million $)	2009	2008	2007	2006	2005	2004	2003	2002	2001	2000
Cash	445	159	87.0	79.7	105	150	207	220	21.8	43.6
Current Assets	NA	1,344	1,537	1,419	1,355	1,225	1,156	1,056	807	751
Total Assets	2,843	2,662	2,624	2,523	2,410	2,167	1,986	1,755	1,400	1,244
Current Liabilities	NA	1,069	1,130	986	895	714	595	531	390	412
Long Term Debt	250	250	250	250	Nil	Nil	Nil	Nil	Nil	Nil
Common Equity	1,440	1,254	1,175	1,208	2,187	1,360	1,533	1,245	959	798
Total Capital	1,690	1,555	1,494	1,537	2,274	1,454	1,612	1,314	1,009	832
Capital Expenditures	155	168	132	192	229	218	220	187	163	172
Cash Flow	NA	383	387	330	332	361	336	294	257	227
Current Ratio	1.5	1.3	1.4	1.4	1.5	1.7	1.9	2.0	2.1	1.8
% Long Term Debt of Capitalization	14.8	16.1	16.7	16.2	Nil	Nil	Nil	Nil	Nil	Nil
% Net Income of Revenue	3.9	3.3	3.5	3.1	3.7	5.0	5.2	5.2	5.2	5.5
% Return on Assets	10.6	8.8	9.4	7.9	9.4	12.7	13.2	13.8	14.3	14.7
% Return on Equity	21.6	19.2	20.3	8.9	10.6	19.7	17.8	18.9	21.6	23.1

Data as orig reptd.; bef. results of disc opers/spec. items. Per share data adj. for stk. divs.; EPS diluted. E-Estimated. NA-Not Available. NM-Not Meaningful. NR-Not Ranked. UR-Under Review.

Office: 10401 Monroe Rd, Matthews, NC 28105.
Telephone: 704-847-6961.
Website: http://www.familydollar.com
Chrmn & CEO: H.R. Levine

Pres & COO: R.J. Kelly
SVP & CFO: K.T. Smith
SVP & Chief Acctg Officer: C.M. Sowers
SVP, Secy & General Counsel: J.C. Snyder, Jr.

Investor Contact: K.F. Rawlins (704-849-7496)
Board Members: M. R. Bernstein, P. L. Davies, S. A. Decker, E. C. Dolby, G. A. Eisenberg, H. R. Levine, G. R. Mahoney, Jr., J. G. Martin, H. Morgan, D. Pond

Founded: 1959
Domicile: Delaware
Employees: 47,000

The McGraw·Hill Companies

Fastenal Company

STANDARD &POOR'S

S&P Recommendation	STRONG BUY ★★★★★	Price $37.02 (as of Nov 27, 2009)	12-Mo. Target Price $51.00	Investment Style Large-Cap Growth

GICS Sector Industrials
Sub-Industry Trading Companies & Distributors

Summary This company distributes fasteners and other industrial and construction supplies through over 2,300 stores throughout the U.S. and in a few foreign countries.

Key Stock Statistics (Source S&P, Vickers, company reports)

52-Wk Range	$41.67–25.87	S&P Oper. EPS 2009**E**	1.25	Market Capitalization(B)	$5.491	Beta	0.97
Trailing 12-Month EPS	$1.36	S&P Oper. EPS 2010**E**	1.45	Yield (%)	1.94	S&P 3-Yr. Proj. EPS CAGR(%)	-3
Trailing 12-Month P/E	27.2	P/E on S&P Oper. EPS 2009**E**	29.6	Dividend Rate/Share	$0.72	S&P Credit Rating	NA
$10K Invested 5 Yrs Ago	$12,748	Common Shares Outstg. (M)	148.3	Institutional Ownership (%)	86		

Price Performance

30-Week Mov. Avg. · · · · 10-Week Mov. Avg. - - - **GAAP Earnings vs. Previous Year** Volume Above Avg. ▐▌▌ STARS
12-Mo. Target Price — Relative Strength — ▲ Up ▼ Down ► No Change Below Avg. ▐▌▌ ★

Options: ASE, CBOE, P

Analysis prepared by **Michael W. Jaffe** on October 12, 2009, when the stock traded at **$ 38.83**.

Highlights

► We forecast sales to increase 4% in 2010. Sales have been very soft to date in 2009, limited by the very weak U.S. economy. We see these trends continuing for a while longer, but believe that early signs of economic stabilization will lead to a bottoming of FAST's business in late 2009 or early 2010. We anticipate that situation bringing a modest sales recovery in 2010. We also look for market share gains, expanded product offerings, and the conversion of sites to a more customer-friendly format to assist FAST's top line.

► We expect FAST's sales details to shift in coming periods, under its current strategy (announced in July 2007) of slowing its rate of store growth while increasing the size of the sales staff at its stores.

► We look for wider net margins in 2010, on the modest improvement that we expect in sales trends. We also see margins benefiting from what we believe will be an ongoing aggressive effort by FAST to keep staff expenses in check and to negotiate more favorable store leases upon their renewal. Our 2009 and 2010 forecasts compare with operating income of $1.91 a share in 2008.

Investment Rationale/Risk

► We see soft conditions in the U.S. economy and markets served by the company causing operating challenges for FAST for a while longer. However, we expect its business to bottom in coming months (average sales to manufacturing customers rose sequentially in each month but one from May through September, but sales for non-residential construction continued to weaken). We are also very positive about FAST's longer-term outlook under its new business strategy of larger sales staffs and fewer store openings. Combined with valuation considerations, we view FAST as undervalued.

► Risks to our recommendation and target price include an even longer downturn in the U.S. economy than we expect, and an unsuccessful change in the company's business model.

► The shares recently traded about 27X our 2010 EPS estimate, a large premium to the S&P 500, but in the lower half of FAST's range for the past decade. Given Fastenal's typically strong profit growth, and our very positive views of its recent strategy change and its management effort, we think a higher P/E multiple is merited. Our 12-month target price is $51, or 35X our 2010 EPS forecast.

Qualitative Risk Assessment

LOW	MEDIUM	HIGH

Our risk assessment for FAST reflects our view of its consistent generation of solid levels of free cash flow, a healthy balance sheet with no long-term debt, and a very well run business model, with a strong focus on growth and cost controls. This is offset by the cyclical nature of FAST's business and uncertainties in its recently announced change in business model, to one with less store unit growth and larger sales staffs.

Quantitative Evaluations

S&P Quality Ranking A

D	C	B-	B	B+	A-	A	A+

Relative Strength Rank MODERATE

48

LOWEST = 1   HIGHEST = 99

Revenue/Earnings Data

Revenue (Million $)

	1Q	2Q	3Q	4Q	Year
2009	489.3	474.9	489.3	--	--
2008	566.2	604.2	625.0	545.0	2,340
2007	489.2	519.7	533.8	519.2	2,062
2006	431.7	458.8	470.1	448.7	1,809
2005	353.8	383.3	402.2	384.0	1,523
2004	284.2	310.1	325.7	318.5	1,238

Earnings Per Share ($)

2009	0.33	0.29	0.32	E0.31	E1.25
2008	0.46	0.51	0.49	0.42	1.88
2007	0.36	0.40	0.41	0.38	1.55
2006	0.32	0.34	0.36	0.30	1.32
2005	0.25	0.29	0.31	0.26	1.10
2004	0.19	0.23	0.23	0.22	0.86

Fiscal year ended Dec. 31. Next earnings report expected: Late January. EPS Estimates based on S&P Operating Earnings; historical GAAP earnings are as reported.

Dividend Data (Dates: mm/dd Payment Date: mm/dd/yy)

Amount ($)	Date Decl.	Ex-Div. Date	Stk. of Record	Payment Date
.27 Spl.	11/18	12/03	12/05	12/15/08
0.350	01/19	02/11	02/16	02/27/09
0.370	07/10	08/13	08/17	08/28/09

Dividends have been paid since 1991. Source: Company reports.

Please read the Required Disclosures and Analyst Certification on the last page of this report.

The McGraw-Hill Companies

Stock Report | November 28, 2009 | NNM Symbol: **FAST**

Fastenal Company

**STANDARD
&POOR'S**

Business Summary October 12, 2009

CORPORATE OVERVIEW. Fastenal, which sells industrial and construction supplies, began operations in 1967, with a plan to supply threaded fasteners in small- to medium-size cities. It later changed its business plan to include some sites in large cities. At the end of 2008, FAST had 2,311 stores in all 50 states, Puerto Rico, Canada, Mexico, Singapore, China and the Netherlands (2,097 in the U.S.), up 7.0% from 2,160 sites a year earlier. The company's store count had grown to 2,352 at September 30, 2009. About two-thirds of the company's stores were opened in the past decade, and FAST has closed only 19 stores in its history (with three later reopened). FAST distributes products to its store sites from 14 distribution centers, with 11 located throughout the U.S., two in Canada and one in Mexico. Threaded fasteners accounted for 46% of 2008 sales (46% in 2007).

The company offered 10 product lines at the end of 2008, and planned to add more lines in the future. Its original product line now consists of about 382,000 different types of threaded fasteners and supplies. Other product lines offered include 128,000 different types of tools and equipment; 226,000 different cutting tool blades and abrasives; 58,000 types of fluid transfer components and accessories for hydraulic and pneumatic power, plumbing, and heating, ventilating and air-conditioning; 15,000 types of material handling, storage and packaging products; 14,000 kinds of janitorial supplies, chemicals and paint;

23,000 types of electrical supplies; 30,000 welding supply items; 25,000 different safety supplies; and 9,000 types of metals, alloys and materials. FAST sells mostly to customers in the construction industry, and in the manufacturing market for both OEMs and maintenance and repair operations. Its construction customers serve general construction, electrical, plumbing, sheet metal, and road contractor markets.

Most products sold are made by other companies. No supplier accounted for over 5% of FAST's 2008 purchases. No customer accounts for a significant portion of total sales.

COMPETITIVE LANDSCAPE. Fastenal's business is highly competitive. Competition includes both large distributors located primarily in large cities and smaller distributors located in many of the cities in which the company has stores. FAST believes that the principal competitive factors affecting the markets for its products are customer service and convenience.

Company Financials Fiscal Year Ended Dec. 31

Per Share Data ($)	2008	2007	2006	2005	2004	2003	2002	2001	2000	1999
Tangible Book Value	7.68	6.76	6.10	5.19	4.51	3.80	3.30	2.80	2.37	1.86
Cash Flow	2.14	1.79	1.54	1.29	1.02	0.69	0.60	0.56	0.61	0.51
Earnings	1.88	1.55	1.32	1.10	0.86	0.56	0.50	0.46	0.53	0.43
S&P Core Earnings	1.91	1.55	1.32	1.10	0.86	0.55	0.45	0.47	NA	NA
Dividends	0.79	0.44	0.40	0.31	0.20	0.11	0.03	0.02	0.02	0.01
Payout Ratio	42%	28%	30%	28%	23%	19%	5%	5%	4%	2%
Prices:High	56.48	52.94	49.32	41.96	32.25	25.50	21.68	18.25	18.33	15.14
Prices:Low	30.08	33.05	33.18	25.54	21.94	13.76	13.31	11.73	8.92	8.41
P/E Ratio:High	30	30	37	38	37	46	44	40	34	35
P/E Ratio:Low	16	21	25	23	26	25	27	26	17	19

Income Statement Analysis (Million $)	2008	2007	2006	2005	2004	2003	2002	2001	2000	1999
Revenue	2,340	2,062	1,809	1,523	1,238	995	905	818	746	609
Operating income	498	414	354	297	231	156	131	127	141	117
Depreciation	39.3	37.4	33.5	29.0	23.6	20.4	16.9	15.0	11.8	11.8
Interest Expense	Nil	Nil	Nil	Nil	Nil	Nil	Nil	Nil	Nil	0.06
Pretax Income	451	378	321	269	208	136	121	114	131	106
Effective Tax Rate	38.0%	38.4%	38.0%	38.0%	37.1%	38.3%	38.3%	38.3%	38.6%	38.5%
Net Income	280	233	199	167	131	84.1	74.8	70.7	80.7	65.5
S&P Core Earnings	284	233	199	167	131	82.6	68.5	70.3	NA	NA

Balance Sheet & Other Financial Data (Million $)	2008	2007	2006	2005	2004	2003	2002	2001	2000	1999
Cash	86.7	57.4	33.9	70.1	74.5	95.6	51.4	68.5	32.7	28.1
Current Assets	975	881	768	649	538	454	396	341	293	227
Total Assets	1,304	1,163	1,039	890	1,308	652	559	475	402	319
Current Liabilities	148	138	104	91.5	71.2	60.9	47.1	40.6	36.6	33.7
Long Term Debt	Nil	Nil	Nil	Nil	Nil	Nil	Nil	Nil	Nil	Nil
Common Equity	1,142	1,010	922	784	684	577	504	425	359	282
Total Capital	1,156	1,025	935	798	699	591	516	435	366	285
Capital Expenditures	95.3	55.8	77.6	65.9	52.7	50.2	42.7	45.3	36.7	39.2
Cash Flow	319	270	233	196	155	105	91.8	85.1	92.5	77.2
Current Ratio	6.6	6.4	7.4	7.1	7.6	7.5	8.4	8.4	8.0	6.8
% Long Term Debt of Capitalization	Nil	Nil	Nil	Nil	Nil	Nil	Nil	Nil	Nil	Nil
% Net Income of Revenue	12.0	11.3	11.0	11.0	10.6	8.5	8.3	8.6	10.8	10.7
% Return on Assets	22.7	21.1	20.6	20.0	10.9	13.9	14.5	16.0	22.4	23.0
% Return on Equity	26.0	24.1	23.3	22.7	20.8	15.6	16.1	17.9	25.2	26.2

Data as orig reptd.; bef. results of disc opers/spec. items. Per share data adj. for stk. divs.; EPS diluted. E-Estimated. NA-Not Available. NM-Not Meaningful. NR-Not Ranked. UR-Under Review.

Office: 2001 Theurer Boulevard, Winona, MN 55987-0978.
Telephone: 507-454-5374.
Email: info@fastenal.com
Website: http://www.fastenal.com

Chrmn: R.A. Kierlin
Pres & CEO: W.D. Oberton
EVP, CFO, Chief Acctg Officer & Treas: D.L. Florness

Board Members: M. J. Ancius, M. J. Dolan, M. M. Gostomski, R. A. Kierlin, H. L. Miller, W. D. Oberton, S. A. Satterlee, S. M. Slaggie, R. K. Wisecup

Founded: 1968
Domicile: Minnesota
Employees: 13,634

The McGraw-Hill Companies

Federated Investors Inc.

STANDARD &POOR'S

S&P Recommendation HOLD ★★★☆☆	Price $25.60 (as of Nov 27, 2009)	12-Mo. Target Price $29.00	Investment Style Large-Cap Growth

GICS Sector Financials
Sub-Industry Asset Management & Custody Banks

Summary This leading U.S. investment management company has a strong market share in money market products.

Key Stock Statistics (Source S&P, Vickers, company reports)

52-Wk Range	$28.10–15.80	S&P Oper. EPS 2009**E**	1.95	Market Capitalization(B)	$2.622	Beta	0.78
Trailing 12-Month EPS	$2.00	S&P Oper. EPS 2010**E**	2.19	Yield (%)	3.75	S&P 3-Yr. Proj. EPS CAGR(%)	2
Trailing 12-Month P/E	12.8	P/E on S&P Oper. EPS 2009**E**	13.1	Dividend Rate/Share	$0.96	S&P Credit Rating	NA
$10K Invested 5 Yrs Ago	$10,742	Common Shares Outstg. (M)	102.4	Institutional Ownership (%)	78		

Price Performance

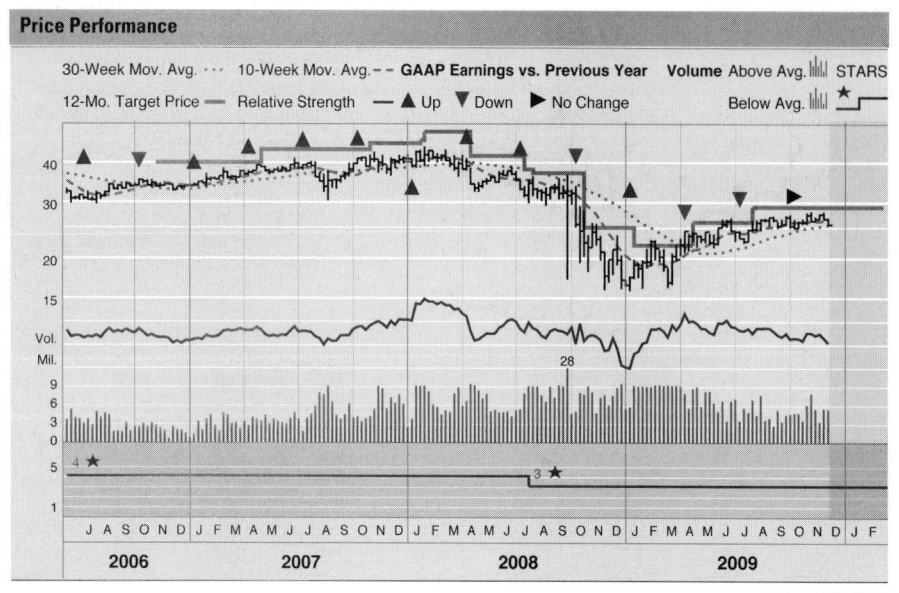

30-Week Mov. Avg. · · · · 10-Week Mov. Avg. - - **GAAP Earnings vs. Previous Year** Volume Above Avg. STARS
12-Mo. Target Price — Relative Strength — ▲ Up ▼ Down ▶ No Change Below Avg.

Options: ASE, CBOE

Analysis prepared by **Matthew Albrecht** on October 29, 2009, when the stock traded at **$ 27.17**.

Highlights

► We believe government guarantees and new regulations under discussion should improve confidence in the money market industry. Increased barriers to entry into the money market industry may also improve the company's footing. Federated benefited from volatility in the markets earlier this year, as money market and ultra-short-term bond products saw strong flows from investors, but we think investors have a renewed appetite for risk, and we expect outflows from money market mutual funds. Its challenge will be to retain client assets in its equity and bond products, and it has pursued small acquisitions to broaden its lineup. We expect continued pressure on management fee rates due to an unfavorable asset mix and fee waivers.

► We expect the marketing and distribution costs associated with growth in the managed asset base to pressure the pretax margin this year, particularly early in the year. We also look for compensation to rise on a relative basis, putting further pressure on margins.

► We forecast EPS of $1.95 in 2009 and $2.19 in 2010, aided by modest share repurchases.

Investment Rationale/Risk

► We view a discounted valuation on the shares relative to peers as appropriate, given the firm's focus on lower-margined money market funds. We view favorably the company's direct sales force and strong relationships with wholesalers and intermediaries in our valuation. We also like moves to increase FII's exposure to equities, which should help margins. We have a positive view of the company's common share repurchase program, which should help results.

► Risks to our recommendation and target price include increased competition, lower short-term interest rates, and weaker equity fund performance. From a corporate governance perspective, we would like to see a greater percentage of independent directors on the board.

► The shares benefited from market volatility, which had investors seeking safe havens for their cash, and outperformed their peer group over the past year. The stock recently traded at about 13.9X our 2009 EPS estimate. Our 12-month target price of $29 is equal to 13.4X our forward 12-month earnings estimate of $2.16, a discount to peers.

Qualitative Risk Assessment

LOW	MEDIUM	HIGH

Our risk assessment reflects the company's relatively narrow product offering and significant competition from larger, more diversified fund management companies.

Quantitative Evaluations

S&P Quality Ranking A

D	C	B-	B	B+	A-	A	A+

Relative Strength Rank MODERATE

35

LOWEST = 1   HIGHEST = 99

Revenue/Earnings Data

Revenue (Million $)

	1Q	2Q	3Q	4Q	Year
2009	310.6	306.9	293.6	--	--
2008	305.7	310.3	305.9	301.8	1,224
2007	264.4	276.5	286.0	300.3	1,128
2006	238.8	236.4	243.9	259.7	978.9
2005	205.4	220.7	241.4	241.8	909.2
2004	220.7	213.1	205.2	208.1	847.0

Earnings Per Share ($)

2009	0.34	0.52	0.56	E0.53	E1.95
2008	0.55	0.55	0.56	0.54	2.20
2007	0.50	0.54	0.57	0.52	2.12
2006	0.43	0.44	0.43	0.51	1.80
2005	0.07	0.35	0.61	0.48	1.51
2004	0.46	0.44	0.43	0.29	1.62

Fiscal year ended Dec. 31. Next earnings report expected: Late January. EPS Estimates based on S&P Operating Earnings; historical GAAP earnings are as reported.

Dividend Data (Dates: mm/dd Payment Date: mm/dd/yy)

Amount ($)	Date Decl.	Ex-Div. Date	Stk. of Record	Payment Date
0.240	01/22	02/04	02/06	02/13/09
0.240	04/23	05/06	05/08	05/15/09
0.240	07/23	08/06	08/10	08/14/09
0.240	10/22	11/05	11/09	11/13/09

Dividends have been paid since 1998. Source: Company reports.

Please read the Required Disclosures and Analyst Certification on the last page of this report.

The **McGraw·Hill** Companies

Federated Investors Inc.

STANDARD
&POOR'S

Business Summary October 29, 2009

CORPORATE OVERVIEW. A leading provider of investment management products and related financial services, Federated Investors (FII) has been in the mutual fund business for more than 40 years. The company is one of the largest mutual fund managers in the United States, based on assets under management. Assets under management at the end of 2008 totaled $407 billion, up from $302 billion at the end of 2007.

Federated manages assets across a wide range of asset categories, including increasing participation in fast-growing areas such as equity and international investments. It is among the industry leaders in money market funds, based on assets under management, and offers one of the industry's most comprehensive product lines. Assets under management by class at the end of 2008 included money market (87% of total), equity (7%), and fixed income (6%). By product type, mutual funds represented about 89% of total assets under management, with the balance held in separately managed accounts.

CORPORATE STRATEGY. Over the past several years, Federated has added

several investment professionals and strengthened its equity and fixed-income product portfolio, in our opinion. The company has more than 170 investment professionals, which includes portfolio managers, analysts and traders. The company ended 2007 with 148 mutual funds and various separately managed accounts. FII has managed institutional separate accounts since 1973, and is focused on growing its managed account business for high-net-worth individuals with investable equity assets of $100,000 or more.

Federated believes that it benefits from a developing industry trend toward intermediary-assisted sales (sales of mutual fund products through a financial intermediary), driven by the wide array of options now available to investors, and by a need for financial planning advice that has resulted from a recent increase in the average household's financial assets.

Company Financials Fiscal Year Ended Dec. 31

Per Share Data ($)	2008	2007	2006	2005	2004	2003	2002	2001	2000	1999
Tangible Book Value	NM	0.53	0.39	1.59	1.36	2.05	1.46	0.79	0.86	0.62
Cash Flow	2.44	2.37	2.07	1.75	1.79	1.95	1.90	1.65	1.40	1.10
Earnings	2.20	2.12	1.80	1.51	1.62	1.71	1.74	1.44	1.27	0.96
S&P Core Earnings	2.23	2.16	1.80	1.67	1.70	1.67	1.69	1.46	NA	NA
Dividends	0.93	0.81	0.69	0.58	0.41	0.30	0.22	0.22	0.14	0.11
Payout Ratio	42%	38%	38%	38%	26%	17%	12%	15%	11%	11%
Prices:High	45.01	43.35	40.17	38.11	33.79	31.90	36.18	32.80	31.69	14.12
Prices:Low	15.80	30.31	29.56	26.99	26.72	23.85	23.43	23.31	12.46	10.04
P/E Ratio:High	20	20	22	25	21	19	21	23	25	15
P/E Ratio:Low	7	14	16	18	16	14	13	16	10	10

Income Statement Analysis (Million $)	2008	2007	2006	2005	2004	2003	2002	2001	2000	1999
Income Interest	0.38	5.60	2.51	8.73	3.39	2.15	2.40	9.74	19.0	13.9
Income Other	4.10	1.20	7.02	0.05	-0.11	0.00	2.27	706	662	587
Total Income	1,224	1,128	979	909	847	823	711	716	681	601
General Expenses	863	770	694	634	530	531	399	388	394	364
Interest Expense	5.20	5.40	8.19	17.9	21.0	4.71	4.79	29.7	34.2	31.8
Depreciation	24.5	25.6	24.1	24.0	19.0	20.6	19.2	26.0	15.8	18.1
Net Income	222	217	191	163	179	191	204	173	155	124
S&P Core Earnings	225	222	191	181	188	187	199	175	NA	NA

Balance Sheet & Other Financial Data (Million $)	2008	2007	2006	2005	2004	2003	2002	2001	2000	1999
Cash	45.4	146	119	246	258	234	151	73.5	150	171
Receivables	24.0	37.3	23.3	45.8	33.8	38.3	31.2	32.6	36.9	35.2
Cost of Investments	13.2	25.9	16.2	38.4	2.10	1.53	1.00	4.60	85.3	66.4
Total Assets	847	841	810	897	955	879	530	432	705	673
Loss Reserve	Nil	Nil	Nil	Nil	Nil	Nil	Nil	0.32	0.09	0.18
Short Term Debt	0.05	Nil	Nil	Nil	Nil	Nil	Nil	Nil	14.3	14.3
Capitalization:Debt	157	63.0	113	160	285	328	59.2	55.0	394	394
Capitalization:Equity	423	574	529	540	458	396	341	237	148	119
Capitalization:Total	613	667	671	723	767	744	416	299	583	551
Price Times Book Value:High	NM	81.8	103	24.0	24.8	15.6	24.8	41.5	36.7	22.0
Price Times Book Value:Low	NM	57.2	76.0	17.0	19.6	11.6	16.0	29.5	14.5	16.0
Cash Flow	246	243	215	187	198	212	223	199	171	142
% Expense/Operating Revenue	70.5	68.3	71.7	71.7	65.1	65.1	56.7	58.4	62.9	65.9
% Earnings & Depreciation/Assets	29.1	29.4	25.2	20.2	19.5	25.3	46.4	35.0	24.8	22.7

Data as orig reptd.; bef. results of disc opers/spec. items. Per share data adj. for stk. divs.; EPS diluted. E-Estimated. NA-Not Available. NM-Not Meaningful. NR-Not Ranked. UR-Under Review.

Office: Federated Investors Tower, Pittsburgh, PA 15222-3779.
Telephone: 412-288-1900.
Email: investors@federatedinv.com
Website: http://www.FederatedInvestors.com

Chrmn: J.F. Donahue
Pres & CEO: J.C. Donahue
Vice Chrmn: G.J. Ceresino
Vice Chrmn, EVP, Secy & General Counsel: J.W. McGonigle

CFO & Treas: T.R. Donahue
Investor Contact: R. Hanley (412-288-1920)
Board Members: L. E. Auriana, G. J. Ceresino, J. F. Donahue, J. C. Donahue, M. J. Farrell, D. M. Kelly, J. W. McGonigle, J. L. Murdy, E. G. O'Connor

Founded: 1955
Domicile: Pennsylvania
Employees: 1,381

The McGraw-Hill Companies

FedEx Corp.

STANDARD &POOR'S

S&P Recommendation **BUY** ★★★★☆	Price	12-Mo. Target Price	Investment Style
	$82.65 (as of Nov 27, 2009)	$90.00	Large-Cap Growth

GICS Sector Industrials
Sub-Industry Air Freight & Logistics

Summary This company provides guaranteed domestic and international air express, residential and business ground package delivery, heavy freight and logistics services.

Key Stock Statistics (Source S&P, Vickers, company reports)

52-Wk Range	$85.43– 34.02	S&P Oper. EPS 2010**E**	3.26	Market Capitalization(B)	$25.830	Beta	1.09
Trailing 12-Month EPS	$-0.34	S&P Oper. EPS 2011**E**	4.21	Yield (%)	0.53	S&P 3-Yr. Proj. EPS CAGR(%)	8
Trailing 12-Month P/E	NM	P/E on S&P Oper. EPS 2010**E**	25.4	Dividend Rate/Share	$0.44	S&P Credit Rating	BBB
$10K Invested 5 Yrs Ago	$8,840	Common Shares Outstg. (M)	312.5	Institutional Ownership (%)	80		

Price Performance

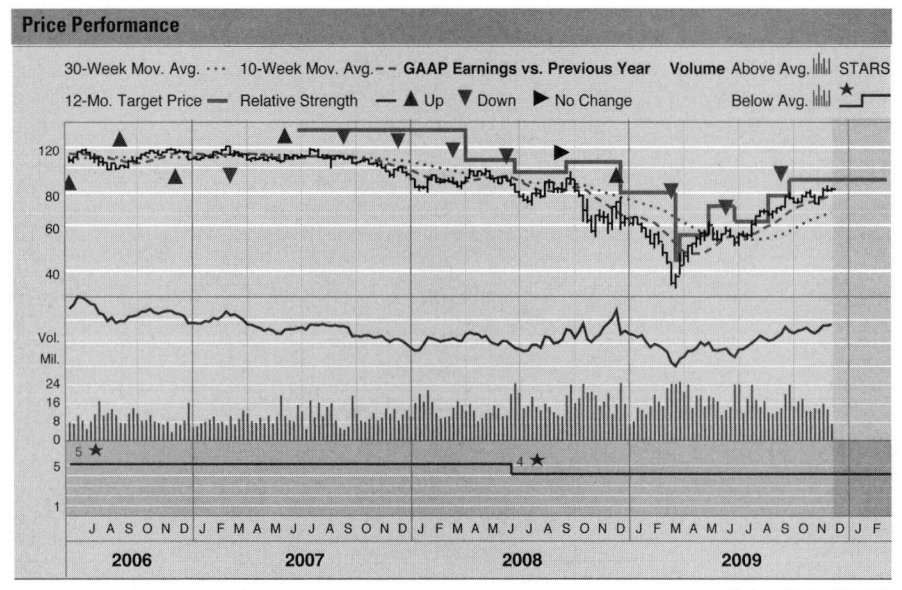

30-Week Mov. Avg. ···· 10-Week Mov. Avg. – – GAAP Earnings vs. Previous Year   Volume Above Avg. STARS
12-Mo. Target Price — Relative Strength — ▲ Up ▼ Down ▶ No Change   Below Avg.

Options: ASE, CBOE, P, PH

Analysis prepared by **Jim Corridore** on September 18, 2009, when the stock traded at **$ 76.46**.

Highlights

► We expect FY 10 (May) revenues to decline 8%. We expect to see strengthening in the second half of the fiscal year on easier comparisons along with our view that global GDP will likely to start to improve by that time. We think FedEx Ground is likely to benefit from the exit of DHL from the U.S. business and expansion of home delivery. We see Express revenues down 10%, Ground flat, and Freight down 11%. FDX recently announced a 5.9% general rate increase for calendar 2010, but we think it will have trouble fully passing this through to customers.

► We think operating margins will be hurt by a mix shift toward more deferred products and rising personnel costs at Ground due to changes related to disputes over the independent contractor model. We also expect a margin impact from a leveraging a lower revenue base over FDX's fixed cost infrastructure. The company is attempting to push lower-margin shipments into ground and freight channels, which could aid margins over the long term.

► We forecast FY 10 operating EPS of $3.26, a 13% decline from FY 09's $3.76 (excluding $3.45 a share of one-time charges).

Investment Rationale/Risk

► While we think FDX's results are likely to be hurt by the weak U.S. economy, we believe the shares will benefit from increased interest in logistics stocks on signs of economic improvement. We are encouraged by signs of volume improvement which we think could signal that the economic recovery is starting to gain traction. As we expect that over the next three to five years EPS to increase faster than the overall market, we think the shares deserve to trade at a premium valuation to the S&P 500.

► Risks to our recommendation and target price include a possible price war on excess industry capacity. If recent challenges to the company's independent contractor are successful, or attempts to overturn the U.S. Railway Labor Act come to fruition, the company would likely incur higher labor costs.

► Our 12-month target price of $90 values the shares at 27.6X our FY 10 EPS estimate of $3.26, the high end of the company's five-year historical P/E range of 13.7X-27.6X, to reflect our view that earnings are near trough levels.

Qualitative Risk Assessment

LOW	MEDIUM	HIGH

Our risk assessment reflects our view of the company's strong and stable balance sheet, healthy cash flow generation, and strong earnings growth potential amid the inherent cyclicality of its business.

Quantitative Evaluations

S&P Quality Ranking B+

D	C	B-	B	B+	A-	A	A+

Relative Strength Rank STRONG
85
LOWEST = 1   HIGHEST = 99

Revenue/Earnings Data

Revenue (Million $)

	1Q	2Q	3Q	4Q	Year
2010	8,009	--	--	--	--
2009	9,970	9,538	8,137	7,852	35,497
2008	9,199	9,451	9,437	9,866	37,953
2007	8,545	8,926	8,592	9,151	35,214
2006	7,707	8,090	8,003	8,494	32,294
2005	6,975	7,334	7,339	7,715	29,363

Earnings Per Share ($)

	1Q	2Q	3Q	4Q	Year
2010	0.58	E0.85	E0.90	E0.93	E3.26
2009	1.23	1.58	0.31	-2.82	0.31
2008	1.23	1.54	1.26	-0.78	3.60
2007	1.53	1.64	1.35	1.96	6.48
2006	1.10	1.53	1.38	1.82	5.83
2005	1.08	1.15	1.03	1.46	4.72

Fiscal year ended May 31. Next earnings report expected: Mid December. EPS Estimates based on S&P Operating Earnings; historical GAAP earnings are as reported.

Dividend Data (Dates: mm/dd Payment Date: mm/dd/yy)

Amount ($)	Date Decl.	Ex-Div. Date	Stk. of Record	Payment Date
0.110	02/13	03/09	03/11	04/01/09
0.110	06/08	06/16	06/18	07/01/09
0.110	08/14	09/08	09/10	10/01/09
0.110	11/20	12/10	12/14	01/04/10

Dividends have been paid since 2002. Source: Company reports.

FedEx Corp.

Business Summary September 18, 2009

CORPORATE OVERVIEW. FedEx Corp. provides global time-definite air express services for packages, documents and freight in more than 220 countries, and ground-based delivery of small packages in North America. In addition, the company offers expedited critical shipment delivery, customs brokerage solutions, less-than-truckload (LTL) freight transportation, and customized logistics. In February 2004, FDX paid $2.4 billion in cash for Kinko's, which operates about 1,200 copy centers that also provide business services. Kinko's has annual revenues of about $2 billion. Kinko's joined three other FedEx companies: Express, Ground, and Freight.

CORPORATE STRATEGY. The company intends to leverage and extend the FedEx brand and to provide customers with seamless access to its entire

portfolio of integrated transportation services. Sales and marketing activities are coordinated among operating companies. Advanced information technology makes it convenient for customers to use the full range of FedEx services and provides a single point of contact for customers to access shipment tracking, customer service and invoicing information. The company intends to continue to operate independent express, ground and freight networks, but has increased its emphasis on having the individual business units work together to compete more effectively.

Company Financials Fiscal Year Ended May 31

Per Share Data ($)	2009	2008	2007	2006	2005	2004	2003	2002	2001	2000
Tangible Book Value	36.15	35.92	29.73	28.39	22.36	17.45	21.03	18.38	16.20	14.33
Cash Flow	6.64	9.84	12.20	10.83	9.48	7.28	7.20	6.89	6.35	6.23
Earnings	0.31	3.60	6.48	5.83	4.72	2.76	2.74	2.39	1.99	2.32
S&P Core Earnings	-0.16	2.77	6.32	5.60	4.48	2.61	1.38	0.95	0.44	NA
Dividends	0.40	0.36	0.36	0.32	0.28	0.22	0.20	Nil	Nil	Nil
Payout Ratio	129%	10%	6%	5%	6%	8%	7%	Nil	Nil	Nil
Calendar Year	2008	2007	2006	2005	2004	2003	2002	2001	2000	1999
Prices:High	99.46	121.42	120.01	105.82	100.92	78.05	61.35	53.48	49.85	61.88
Prices:Low	53.90	89.01	96.50	76.81	64.84	47.70	42.75	33.15	30.56	34.88
P/E Ratio:High	NM	34	19	18	21	28	22	22	25	27
P/E Ratio:Low	NM	25	15	13	14	17	16	14	15	15

Income Statement Analysis (Million $)	2009	2008	2007	2006	2005	2004	2003	2002	2001	2000
Revenue	35,497	37,953	35,214	32,294	29,363	24,710	22,487	20,607	19,629	18,257
Operating Income	3,926	4,903	5,018	4,564	3,933	3,250	2,822	2,804	2,347	2,376
Depreciation	1,975	1,946	1,742	1,550	1,462	1,375	1,351	1,364	1,276	1,155
Interest Expense	156	182	136	142	160	136	118	139	144	106
Pretax Income	677	2,016	3,215	2,899	2,313	1,319	1,338	1,160	928	1,138
Effective Tax Rate	85.5%	44.2%	37.3%	37.7%	37.4%	36.5%	38.0%	37.5%	37.0%	39.5%
Net Income	98.0	1,125	2,016	1,806	1,449	838	830	725	584	688
S&P Core Earnings	-49.6	868	1,966	1,733	1,376	790	415	286	130	NA

Balance Sheet & Other Financial Data (Million $)	2009	2008	2007	2006	2005	2004	2003	2002	2001	2000
Cash	2,292	1,539	1,569	1,937	1,039	1,046	538	331	121	68.0
Current Assets	7,116	7,244	6,629	6,464	5,269	4,970	3,941	3,665	3,449	3,285
Total Assets	24,244	25,633	24,000	22,690	20,404	19,134	15,385	13,812	13,340	11,527
Current Liabilities	4,524	5,368	5,428	5,473	4,734	4,732	3,335	2,942	3,250	2,891
Long Term Debt	1,930	1,506	2,662	1,592	2,427	2,837	1,709	1,800	1,900	1,776
Common Equity	13,626	14,526	12,656	11,511	9,588	8,036	7,288	6,545	5,900	4,785
Total Capital	16,209	16,534	16,215	14,470	13,221	12,054	9,879	8,944	8,256	6,906
Capital Expenditures	2,459	2,947	2,882	2,518	2,236	1,271	1,511	1,615	1,893	1,627
Cash Flow	2,073	3,071	3,758	3,356	2,911	2,213	2,181	2,089	1,860	1,843
Current Ratio	1.6	1.4	1.2	1.2	1.1	1.1	1.2	1.2	1.1	1.1
% Long Term Debt of Capitalization	11.9	8.7	16.4	11.0	18.3	23.5	17.2	20.1	23.0	25.7
% Net Income of Revenue	0.3	3.0	5.7	5.6	4.9	3.4	3.7	3.5	3.0	3.8
% Return on Assets	0.4	4.5	8.6	8.4	7.3	4.9	5.7	5.3	4.7	6.2
% Return on Equity	0.7	8.3	16.7	17.1	16.4	10.9	11.8	11.7	10.9	14.6

Data as orig reptd.; bef. results of disc opers/spec. items. Per share data adj. for stk. divs.; EPS diluted. E-Estimated. NA-Not Available. NM-Not Meaningful. NR-Not Ranked. UR-Under Review.

Office: 942 South Shady Grove Road, Memphis, TN 38120-4117.
Telephone: 901-818-7500.
Website: http://www.fedex.com
Chrmn, Pres & CEO: F.W. Smith

Investor Contact: A.B. Graf, Jr. (901-818-7388)
EVP & CFO: A.B. Graf, Jr.
EVP, Secy & General Counsel: C.P. Richards
EVP & CIO: R.B. Carter

Board Members: J. L. Barksdale, J. A. Edwardson, J. L. Estrin, J. R. Hyde, III, S. A. Jackson, S. R. Loranger, G. W. Loveman, S. C. Schwab, F. W. Smith, J. I. Smith, D. P. Steiner, P. S. Walsh
Founded: 1971
Domicile: Delaware
Employees: 140,000

Fidelity National Information Services Inc

STANDARD &POOR'S

S&P Recommendation	HOLD ★★★☆☆	Price $22.53 (as of Nov 27, 2009)	12-Mo. Target Price $27.00	Investment Style Large-Cap Growth

GICS Sector Information Technology
Sub-Industry Data Processing & Outsourced Services

Summary This company is a leading provider of core processing services and products to financial institutions.

Key Stock Statistics (Source S&P, Vickers, company reports)

52-Wk Range	$26.00– 15.20	S&P Oper. EPS 2009**E**	1.73	Market Capitalization(B)	$8.392	Beta	0.63
Trailing 12-Month EPS	$0.98	S&P Oper. EPS 2010**E**	1.92	Yield (%)	0.89	S&P 3-Yr. Proj. EPS CAGR(%)	12
Trailing 12-Month P/E	23.0	P/E on S&P Oper. EPS 2009**E**	13.0	Dividend Rate/Share	$0.20	S&P Credit Rating	NA
$10K Invested 5 Yrs Ago	NA	Common Shares Outstg. (M)	372.5	Institutional Ownership (%)	49		

Price Performance

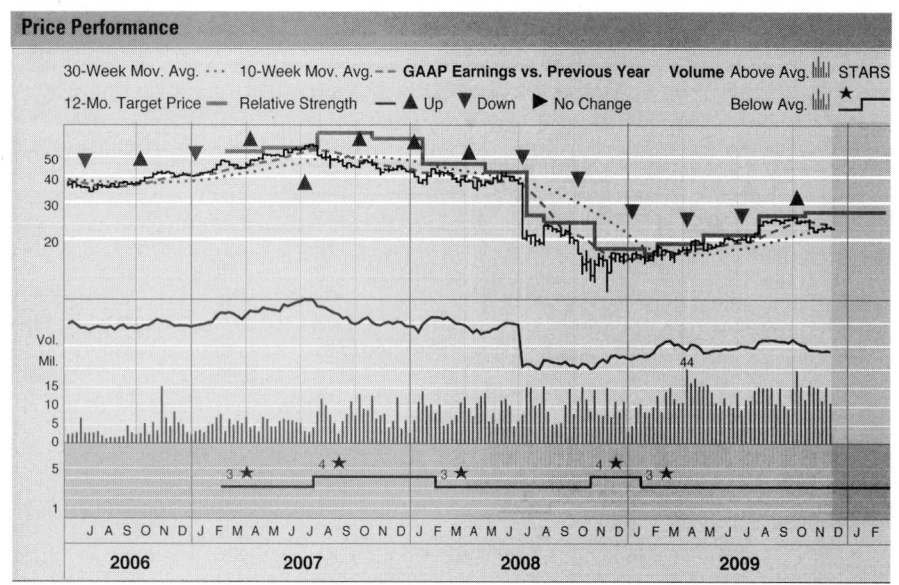

30-Week Mov. Avg. ··· 10-Week Mov. Avg. -- **GAAP Earnings vs. Previous Year** Volume Above Avg. STARS
12-Mo. Target Price — Relative Strength — ▲ Up ▼ Down ► No Change Below Avg.

Options: ASE, CBOE, P, Ph

Analysis prepared by **Zaineb Bokhari** on November 18, 2009, when the stock traded at **$ 23.49**.

Highlights

► We expect revenues to rise 10% in 2009, to $3.8 billion, aided by the October 2009 acquisition of Metavante. We are optimistic about the scale and heft the acquisition added to the company, and we expect ample opportunity to cross-sell add-on service to the large combined base of core processing customers. We currently project a 45% rise in 2010 revenues, reflecting contributions from Metavante.

► We look for notably wider operating margins in 2009 and 2010, reflecting internal cost containment, scale benefits from the acquisition of Metavante and the anticipated achievement of targeted annual cost synergies, the majority of which are expected to be realized in 2010. We also expect improved margins in the company's international operations.

► Our 2009 adjusted EPS estimate is $1.73, up from an adjusted $1.49 in 2008. Our estimate excludes projected M&A and restructuring charges and purchase price amortization. We project EPS of $1.92 for 2010.

Investment Rationale/Risk

► We expect FIS, a large and focused provider of core transaction processing, credit and debit card processing, e-banking, electronic bill payment and item processing, to continue its cost-cutting efforts as it targets efficiencies in existing and acquired operations amid a weak economic environment. The recent purchase of Metavante will boost year-to-year revenue growth comparisons, and existing contracts should allow the combined entity to generate recurring revenues. We think the company is well managed, and we believe the recent acquisition, while not without risk, will support rising long-term profitability and organic growth.

► Risks to our recommendation and target price include ongoing consolidation among financial services clients, which could lead to business loss or disruption. We are also concerned about FIS's exposure to community banks, which could be more vulnerable to the depressed U.S. economy.

► We apply a 14X multiple to our 2010 EPS estimate to derive our $27 target price, below the recent 16X mean for data processing and outsourced services peers, reflecting integration risks.

Qualitative Risk Assessment

LOW	MEDIUM	HIGH

Our risk assessment reflects uncertainty regarding the company's exposure to the financial services industry and ongoing acquisition integration risks. While the company's transaction processing business offers a considerable base of recurring revenues, recent M&A and spin-off transactions have made an objective analysis of long-term historical financials somewhat challenging.

Quantitative Evaluations

S&P Quality Ranking NR

D	C	B-	B	B+	A-	A	A+

Relative Strength Rank MODERATE

36

LOWEST = 1   HIGHEST = 99

Revenue/Earnings Data

Revenue (Million $)

	1Q	2Q	3Q	4Q	Year
2009	797.8	834.8	850.7	--	--
2008	1,291	1,339	893.8	862.0	3,446
2007	1,124	1,176	1,168	1,330	4,758
2006	900.9	1,022	1,081	1,129	4,133
2005	262.5	276.0	282.8	295.9	1,117
2004	538.6	603.4	514.5	675.0	1,040

Earnings Per Share ($)

2009	0.18	0.31	0.35	E0.49	E1.73
2008	0.35	0.38	0.24	0.26	0.61
2007	0.30	0.75	1.02	0.55	2.60
2006	0.23	0.34	0.41	0.39	1.37
2005	0.34	0.40	0.36	0.57	1.66
2004	--	--	0.37	0.27	0.92

Fiscal year ended Dec. 31. Next earnings report expected: Mid February. EPS Estimates based on S&P Operating Earnings; historical GAAP earnings are as reported.

Dividend Data (Dates: mm/dd Payment Date: mm/dd/yy)

Amount ($)	Date Decl.	Ex-Div. Date	Stk. of Record	Payment Date
0.050	02/10	03/12	03/16	03/30/09
0.050	04/28	06/12	06/16	06/30/09
0.050	07/21	09/14	09/16	09/30/09
0.050	10/20	12/14	12/16	12/30/09

Dividends have been paid since 2006. Source: Company reports.

Please read the Required Disclosures and Analyst Certification on the last page of this report.

The McGraw-Hill Companies

Fidelity National Information Services Inc

Business Summary November 18, 2009

CORPORATE OVERVIEW. Fidelity National Information Services, Inc. (FIS) was formed via the combination, on February 1, 2006, of the information processing subsidiary of Fidelity National Financial (FNF), a leading provider of title and specialty insurance, and Certegy, a provider of card and check processing services. As a result of the combination, the company is a leading provider of technology solutions, processing services, and information-based services to the financial industry. Until recently, FIS operated in two main business segments: Transaction Processing Services (TPS) and Lender Processing Services (LPS). On July 2, 2008, FIS completed the spin-off of Lender Processing Services to shareholders. After this spin-off, FIS served 14,000 financial institution customers in more than 90 countries. In 2008, the company derived 22% of revenues from international customers.

The company's segments were recast in late 2008 as: Financial Solutions, Payment Solutions and International. Financial Solutions segment includes products and services that address the core processing needs of clients such as banks, credit unions, commercial and automotive lenders, and independent community banks. Core processing solutions include applications used to process deposits, loans, and other central services provided to customers of a financial institution. Channel solutions, which include applications that improve customer interaction are also included in this segment. These include

customer-facing channels through which customers access an institution's products and services, such as ATMs, and the Internet, as well as call centers. Other solutions offered include decision management solutions, which aid in the management of accounts throughout their lifecycle, applications that support wholesale and commercial banking, and assist in the evaluation and management of auto loans. Other solutions offered through this segment support risk management and fraud detection, branch automation and compliance. In 2008, the Financial Solutions segment accounted for almost 34% of total revenues.

Through its Payment Solutions segment, FIS offers payment and electronic funds services to banks, credit unions and other financial institutions. Segment offerings include: debit and electronic funds transfer processing, Internet banking and bill payment, merchant processing, item processing, credit card production and activation, fraud management, check authorization and pre-paid card management and administration services. Revenues from this segment comprised 44% of 2008 revenues.

Company Financials Fiscal Year Ended Dec. 31

Per Share Data ($)	2008	2007	2006	2005	2004	2003	2002	2001	2000	1999
Tangible Book Value	NM	NM	NM	3.53	0.55	NA	NA	NA	NA	NA
Cash Flow	2.03	4.04	3.66	2.48	2.40	NA	NA	NA	NA	NA
Earnings	0.61	2.60	1.37	1.66	0.92	NA	NA	NA	NA	NA
S&P Core Earnings	0.70	1.72	1.37	0.98	0.94	1.00	NA	NA	NA	NA
Dividends	0.20	0.20	0.20	Nil	Nil	NA	NA	NA	NA	NA
Payout Ratio	33%	8%	15%	Nil	Nil	NA	NA	NA	NA	NA
Prices:High	43.83	57.80	42.62	NA	NA	NA	NA	NA	NA	NA
Prices:Low	11.15	39.99	33.50	NA	NA	NA	NA	NA	NA	NA
P/E Ratio:High	72	22	31	NA	NA	NA	NA	NA	NA	NA
P/E Ratio:Low	18	15	24	NA	NA	NA	NA	NA	NA	NA

Income Statement Analysis (Million $)										
Revenue	3,446	4,758	4,133	1,117	1,040	1,945	654	418	NA	NA
Operating Income	710	1,030	1,025	248	227	NA	NA	NA	NA	NA
Depreciation	276	284	434	51.9	47.4	144	18.6	9.45	NA	NA
Interest Expense	148	201	193	12.8	12.9	NA	NA	NA	NA	NA
Pretax Income	179	813	409	174	168	362	106	53.8	NA	NA
Effective Tax Rate	32.2%	37.0%	36.7%	39.5%	37.0%	38.8%	37.3%	40.9%	NA	NA
Net Income	117	510	259	106	106	207	58.2	31.0	NA	NA
S&P Core Earnings	135	338	259	196	189	200	NA	NA	NA	NA

Balance Sheet & Other Financial Data (Million $)										
Cash	221	355	212	138	86.7	100	56.5	NA	NA	NA
Current Assets	1,180	1,830	1,301	445	409	NA	NA	NA	NA	NA
Total Assets	7,490	9,795	7,631	972	922	2,371	556	NA	NA	NA
Current Liabilities	852	1,254	881	234	290	NA	NA	NA	NA	NA
Long Term Debt	2,409	4,275	2,948	228	274	10.5	18.9	NA	NA	NA
Common Equity	3,538	3,781	3,548	459	300	1,904	295	NA	NA	NA
Total Capital	6,212	8,194	6,892	716	614	1,958	392	NA	NA	NA
Capital Expenditures	76.7	114	122	63.6	40.9	57.3	3.35	0.50	NA	NA
Cash Flow	393	795	693	157	153	NA	NA	NA	NA	NA
Current Ratio	1.4	1.5	1.5	1.9	1.4	1.4	1.6	NA	NA	NA
% Long Term Debt of Capitalization	37.3	51.3	42.8	31.8	44.6	0.5	4.8	Nil	NA	NA
% Net Income of Revenue	3.4	10.7	6.3	9.4	10.2	10.6	8.9	7.4	NA	NA
% Return on Assets	1.4	5.9	4.4	11.1	12.4	14.1	NA	NA	NA	NA
% Return on Equity	3.2	14.8	12.2	27.5	37.7	18.8	NA	NA	NA	NA

Data as orig reptd.; bef. results of disc opers/spec. items. Per share data adj. for stk. divs.; EPS diluted. E-Estimated. NA-Not Available. NM-Not Meaningful. NR-Not Ranked. UR-Under Review.

Office: 601 Riverside Ave, Jacksonville, FL 32204-2901.
Telephone: 904-854-8100.
Website: http://www.fidelityinfoservices.com
Pres & CEO: F.R. Martire

COO & EVP: G. Norcross
EVP & CFO: M. Hayford
EVP, Secy & General Counsel: R.G. Cook
CTO: B. Hurdis

Board Members: W. P. Foley, II, T. M. Hagerty, K. W. Hughes, D. K. Hunt, S. A. James, L. A. Kennedy, F. R. Martire, R. N. Massey, J. Neary

Founded: 2001
Domicile: Georgia
Employees: 26,000

Fifth Third Bancorp

STANDARD &POOR'S

S&P Recommendation	HOLD ★★★☆☆	Price $9.57 (as of Nov 27, 2009)	12-Mo. Target Price $11.00	Investment Style Large-Cap Blend

GICS Sector Financials
Sub-Industry Regional Banks

Summary A diversified financial services company, with $116 billion in assets, FITB operates 1,306 branches in Ohio, Kentucky, Indiana, Michigan, Illinois, Florida, Tennessee, West Virginia, Pennsylvania, Missouri, Georgia and North Carolina.

Key Stock Statistics (Source S&P, Vickers, company reports)

52-Wk Range	$11.20–1.01	S&P Oper. EPS 2009E	0.78	Market Capitalization(B)	$7.611	Beta	2.39
Trailing 12-Month EPS	$-2.35	S&P Oper. EPS 2010E	0.08	Yield (%)	0.42	S&P 3-Yr. Proj. EPS CAGR(%)	NM
Trailing 12-Month P/E	NM	P/E on S&P Oper. EPS 2009E	12.3	Dividend Rate/Share	$0.04	S&P Credit Rating	BBB
$10K Invested 5 Yrs Ago	$2,258	Common Shares Outstg. (M)	795.3	Institutional Ownership (%)	73		

Price Performance

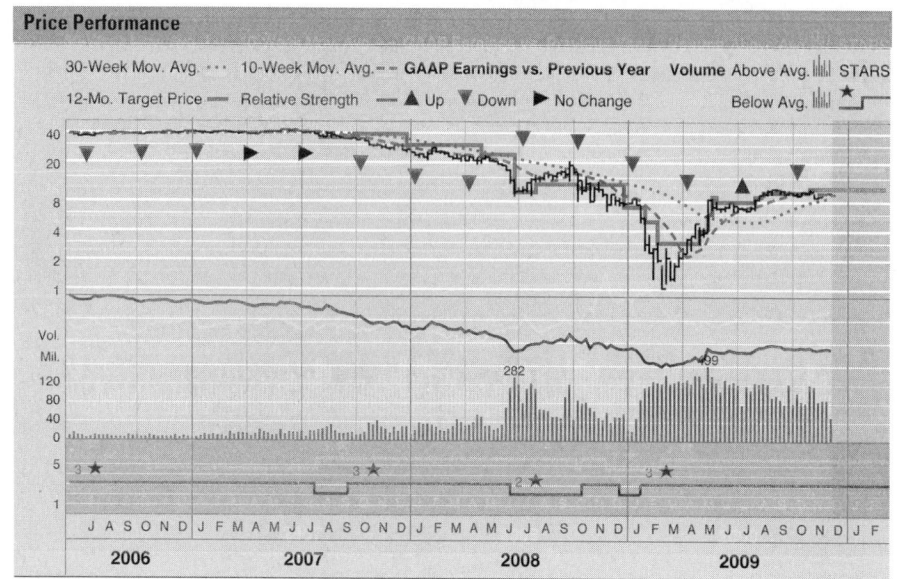

30-Week Mov. Avg. · · · 10-Week Mov. Avg. – – GAAP Earnings vs. Previous Year Volume Above Avg. ılıll STARS
12-Mo. Target Price — Relative Strength ▲ Up ▼ Down ► No Change Below Avg. ılıll ★

Options: ASE, CBOE, P, Ph

Analysis prepared by **Erik Oja** on October 27, 2009, when the stock traded at **$ 9.52**.

Highlights

▶ For 2009, we expect mortgage banking fees of $521 million, up from $199 million in 2008. However, much of the transaction processing business, which had revenues of $913 million in 2008, has been transferred to a joint venture. Excluding the revenues which were transferred, and gains, we expect core noninterest income to grow 12% in 2009, driven by mortgage banking revenues. However, due to the economic slowdown, we forecast a 6.5% decline in net interest income, to $3.3 billion.

▶ Nonperforming loans at the end of the third quarter of $2.95 billion comprised 3.75% of total loans, up 14% from the end of the second quarter, a growth rate in-line with industry peers. FITB is addressing its credit quality issues with mortgage modifications, and the sale of certain problem credits, but we think this will take several more quarters. We expect loan loss provisions of $3.35 billion in 2009, based on our expectations for net chargeoffs of $2.40 billion, plus $950 million of reserve building. For 2010, we expect $1.5 billion in provisions.

▶ For 2009, 2010 and 2011, we expect EPS of $0.75, $0.07 and $0.84, respectively.

Investment Rationale/Risk

▶ During the third quarter, FITB reported net interest income of $874 million and fairly good core fee income of $538 million, as well as above-peers capital ratios and reserves to nonperforming loans ratios. Tangible common equity is now at 6.98% of tangible assets, up from 6.67% at June 30, both above peers. However, since FITB has nearly 55% of its loan portfolio in commercial lending, including residential construction, we think commercial lending credit deterioration will continue into mid-2010, likely depressing earnings until 2011 at the earliest, by our calculations. Therefore, we value the shares on a price-to-tangible book value basis, relative to banking peers and relative to credit quality. On this basis, we think FITB should trade slightly above 1.0X tangible book value.

▶ Risks to our recommendation and target price include a faster than expected decline in economic conditions in the Midwest, and higher than forecast deposit costs.

▶ Our 12-month target price of $11 is equal to 1.15X tangible book value, slightly below peers, and 13.1X our 2011 EPS estimate, above peers.

Qualitative Risk Assessment

LOW	MEDIUM	HIGH

Our risk assessment for FITB reflects numerous credit challenges in the company's Florida and Michigan loan portfolios, partly offset by our view of its solid fee income businesses and strong customer base.

Quantitative Evaluations

S&P Quality Ranking B+

D	C	B-	B	B+	A-	A	A+

Relative Strength Rank MODERATE

45

LOWEST = 1　　　　HIGHEST = 99

Revenue/Earnings Data

Revenue (Million $)

	1Q	2Q	3Q	4Q	Year
2009	1,875	3,762	2,020	--	--
2008	2,311	1,929	2,265	2,048	8,554
2007	2,108	2,202	2,251	2,126	8,479
2006	2,015	2,132	2,196	1,765	8,108
2005	1,752	1,850	1,905	1,988	7,495
2004	1,617	1,749	1,654	1,560	6,579

Earnings Per Share ($)

2009	-0.04	1.15	-0.20	E-0.16	E0.78
2008	0.54	-0.37	-0.14	-3.82	-3.94
2007	0.65	0.69	0.61	0.07	1.99
2006	0.65	0.69	0.68	0.12	2.12
2005	0.72	0.75	0.71	0.60	2.77
2004	0.75	0.79	0.83	0.31	2.68

Fiscal year ended Dec. 31. Next earnings report expected: Late January. EPS Estimates based on S&P Operating Earnings; historical GAAP earnings are as reported.

Dividend Data (Dates: mm/dd Payment Date: mm/dd/yy)

Amount ($)	Date Decl.	Ex-Div. Date	Stk. of Record	Payment Date
0.010	12/16	12/29	12/31	01/22/09
0.010	03/17	03/27	03/31	04/23/09
0.010	06/17	06/26	06/30	07/23/09
0.010	09/15	09/28	09/30	10/22/09

Dividends have been paid since 1952. Source: Company reports.

The McGraw-Hill Companies

Fifth Third Bancorp

STANDARD &POOR'S

Business Summary October 27, 2009

CORPORATE OVERVIEW. FITB is divided into five segments: commercial banking, branch banking, consumer lending, investment advisors, and processing solutions. Commercial banking provides a comprehensive range of financial services and products to large and middle-market businesses, governments and professional customers. In addition to traditional lending and depository offerings, commercial banking products and services include cash management, foreign exchange and international trade finance, derivatives and capital markets services, asset-based lending, real estate finance, public finance, commercial leasing, and syndicated finance.

Branch banking offers depository and loan products, such as checking and savings accounts, home equity lines of credit, credit cards, and loans for automobiles and other personal financing needs, plus products designed to meet the specific needs of small businesses, including cash management services.

Consumer lending includes mortgage and home equity lending activities and other indirect lending activities. Mortgage and home equity lending activities include the origination, retention and servicing of mortgage and home equity loans or lines of credit, sales and securitizations of those loans or pools of

loans or lines of credit and all associated hedging activities. Other indirect lending activities include loans to consumers through dealers and federal and private student education loans.

Investment advisors provides a full range of investment alternatives for individuals, companies and not-for-profit organizations. Primary services include trust, asset management, retirement plans and custody. Fifth Third Securities, Inc., an indirect wholly owned subsidiary, offers full-service retail brokerage services to individual clients and broker dealer services to the institutional marketplace. Fifth Third Asset Management, Inc., an indirect wholly owned subsidiary, provides asset management services and also advises a proprietary family of mutual funds, Fifth Third Funds. Fifth Third Processing Solutions provides electronic funds transfer, debit, credit and merchant transaction processing, operates the Jeanie ATM network, and provides other data processing services to affiliated and unaffiliated customers.

Company Financials Fiscal Year Ended Dec. 31

Per Share Data ($)	2008	2007	2006	2005	2004	2003	2002	2001	2000	1999
Tangible Book Value	7.87	11.11	13.78	12.72	13.33	13.46	13.12	13.09	10.50	8.79
Earnings	-3.94	1.99	2.12	2.77	2.68	2.97	2.76	1.86	1.83	1.43
S&P Core Earnings	-2.36	2.19	2.14	2.78	2.69	2.84	2.56	1.63	NA	NA
Dividends	0.04	1.70	1.58	1.46	1.31	1.13	0.98	0.83	0.70	0.56
Payout Ratio	NM	85%	75%	53%	49%	38%	36%	45%	38%	39%
Prices:High	28.58	43.32	41.57	48.12	60.00	62.15	69.70	64.77	60.88	50.29
Prices:Low	6.32	24.82	35.86	35.04	45.32	47.05	55.26	45.69	29.33	38.58
P/E Ratio:High	NM	22	20	17	22	21	25	35	33	35
P/E Ratio:Low	NM	12	17	13	17	16	20	25	16	27

Income Statement Analysis (Million $)										
Net Interest Income	3,514	3,009	2,873	2,965	3,012	2,905	2,700	2,433	1,470	1,405
Tax Equivalent Adjustment	22.0	24.0	26.0	31.0	36.0	39.0	39.5	45.5	93.0	73.0
Non Interest Income	2,870	2,494	1,657	2,461	2,502	2,399	2,047	1,626	1,013	876
Loan Loss Provision	4,560	628	343	330	268	399	247	236	89.0	134
% Expense/Operating Revenue	55.5%	55.3%	67.1%	53.6%	53.5%	46.0%	51.9%	57.7%	45.1%	47.7%
Pretax Income	-2,664	1,537	1,627	2,208	2,237	2,547	2,432	1,653	1,275	1,026
Effective Tax Rate	NM	30.0%	27.2%	29.8%	31.8%	31.6%	31.2%	33.3%	32.3%	34.9%
Net Income	-2,113	1,076	1,184	1,549	1,525	1,722	1,635	1,101	863	668
% Net Interest Margin	3.54	3.36	3.06	3.23	3.48	3.62	3.96	3.82	3.77	3.99
S&P Core Earnings	-1,301	1,183	1,191	1,555	1,529	1,650	1,513	965	NA	NA

Balance Sheet & Other Financial Data (Million $)										
Money Market Assets	1,191	171	187	117	77.0	55.0	312	225	198	355
Investment Securities	13,088	11,032	12,218	22,471	25,474	29,402	25,828	20,748	15,827	12,817
Commercial Loans	50,479	40,412	36,114	33,214	30,601	28,242	22,614	10,839	12,382	11,141
Other Loans	30,877	39,841	39,485	38,024	29,207	25,493	23,314	30,709	13,570	14,746
Total Assets	119,764	110,962	100,669	105,225	94,456	91,143	80,894	71,026	45,857	41,589
Demand Deposits	29,113	36,179	36,908	39,020	37,288	31,899	11,139	10,595	5,604	8,011
Time Deposits	49,500	39,266	32,472	13,656	20,938	25,196	41,069	35,259	25,344	18,072
Long Term Debt	13,585	12,857	12,558	15,227	13,983	9,063	8,179	7,030	4,034	1,977
Common Equity	7,836	9,152	10,013	9,437	8,915	8,516	8,466	7,630	4,891	4,306
% Return on Assets	NM	1.0	1.2	1.6	1.6	2.0	2.2	1.6	2.0	1.7
% Return on Equity	NM	11.2	12.2	16.9	17.3	20.3	20.3	15.4	19.2	16.6
% Loan Loss Reserve	3.3	1.1	1.0	1.0	1.2	1.4	1.4	1.4	1.4	4.9
% Loans/Deposits	107.0	106.8	108.8	105.6	103.7	94.9	94.4	95.4	85.6	100.4
% Equity to Assets	7.4	9.1	9.4	9.2	9.5	9.9	10.6	10.2	10.3	10.3

Data as orig reptd.; bef. results of disc opers/spec. items. Per share data adj. for stk. divs.; EPS diluted. E-Estimated. NA-Not Available. NM-Not Meaningful. NR-Not Ranked. UR-Under Review.

Office: 38 Fountain Square Plaza, Cincinnati, OH 45263.
Telephone: 513-534-5300.
Website: http://www.53.com
Chrmn, Pres & CEO: K.T. Kabat

COO & EVP: G.D. Carmichael
EVP & CFO: D.T. Poston
EVP, Secy & General Counsel: P.L. Reynolds
SVP & Treas: M. Sankaran

Investor Contact: C.G. Marshall (800-972-3030)
Board Members: D. F. Allen, U. L. Bridgeman, Jr., E. Brumback, M. Crawford, J. P. Hackett, G. R. Heminger, A. M. Hill, J. Hoover, K. T. Kabat, R. L. Koch, II, M. D. Livingston, H. G. Meijer, J. E. Rogers, J. J. Schiff, Jr., D. S. Taft, T. W. Traylor, M. C. Williams

Founded: 1862
Domicile: Ohio
Employees: 21,476

The **McGraw-Hill** Companies

FirstEnergy Corp.

STANDARD &POOR'S

S&P Recommendation	HOLD ★★★☆☆	Price $42.61 (as of Nov 27, 2009)	12-Mo. Target Price $44.00	Investment Style Large-Cap Blend

GICS Sector Utilities
Sub-Industry Electric Utilities

Summary This electric utility holding company serves about 4.5 million customers in portions of Ohio, Pennsylvania and New Jersey.

Key Stock Statistics (Source S&P, Vickers, company reports)

52-Wk Range	$58.31– 35.26	S&P Oper. EPS 2009**E**	3.75	Market Capitalization(B)	$12.989	Beta	0.52
Trailing 12-Month EPS	$3.59	S&P Oper. EPS 2010**E**	3.60	Yield (%)	5.16	S&P 3-Yr. Proj. EPS CAGR(%)	-4
Trailing 12-Month P/E	11.9	P/E on S&P Oper. EPS 2009**E**	11.4	Dividend Rate/Share	$2.20	S&P Credit Rating	BBB
$10K Invested 5 Yrs Ago	$11,930	Common Shares Outstg. (M)	304.8	Institutional Ownership (%)	70		

Price Performance

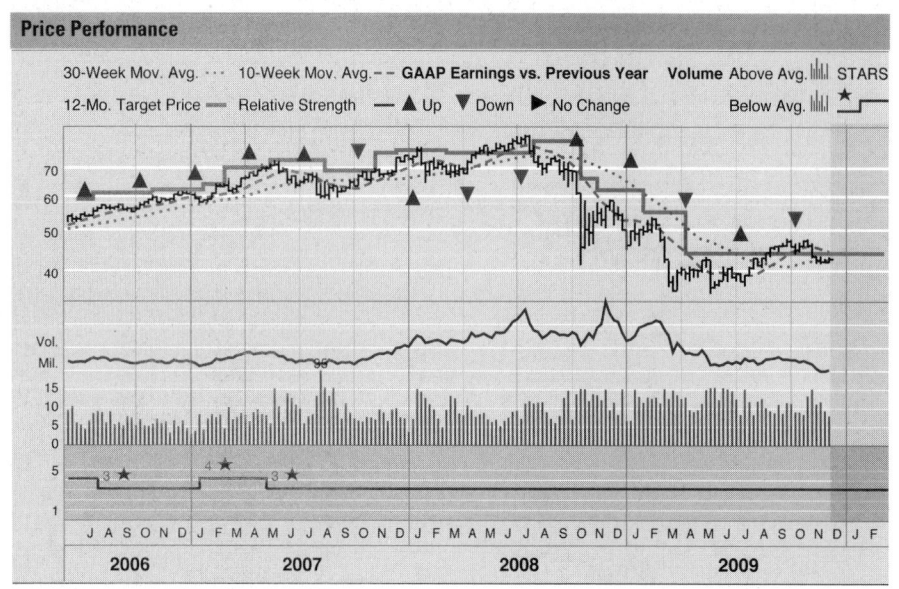

30-Week Mov. Avg. · · · 10-Week Mov. Avg. - - - **GAAP Earnings vs. Previous Year** Volume Above Avg. STARS
12-Mo. Target Price — Relative Strength — ▲ Up ▼ Down ► No Change Below Avg.

Options: ASE, CBOE, P, Ph

Analysis prepared by **Justin McCann** on September 09, 2009, when the stock traded at **$ 46.33**.

Qualitative Risk Assessment

LOW	MEDIUM	HIGH

Our risk assessment reflects the strong and steady cash flow we expect from the company's regulated electric utility subsidiaries; its low-cost baseload power generation in Ohio and Pennsylvania; its low-risk transmission distribution operations in New Jersey and Pennsylvania; and its rate certainty in Ohio. This is partially offset by the company's below-average production performance from nuclear operations and our view of its high level of debt and environmental spending.

Quantitative Evaluations

S&P Quality Ranking A-

D	C	B-	B	B+	A-	A	A+

Relative Strength Rank MODERATE

37

LOWEST = 1   HIGHEST = 99

Highlights

▶ Excluding net one-time charges of $0.13, we expect 2009 operating EPS to decline about 17% from 2008's $4.57, which excluded $0.20 of net one-time charges. We believe the decline will reflect the weakness in the economy and the power markets, where power prices and margins are down due to excess generating capacity and reduced demand. We also look for earnings to be hurt by increased pension costs, and the expiration of a favorable third-party power supply contract. This should be partially offset by the benefit of rate increases in Ohio.

▶ For 2010, we expect operating EPS to decline nearly 5% from anticipated results in 2009, as projected higher generation margins and distribution sales, lower operation and maintenance expenses, and a full year of the Ohio rate increases are more than offset by a rise in fuel and purchased power costs, taxes and depreciation expense, and higher financing costs.

▶ FE took a regulatory asset impairment charge of about $139 million ($0.46 a share) in the first quarter of 2009. This reflected an agreement by FE's CEI utility to negate the $216 million balance of the Regulatory Transition Charge it had been scheduled to recover through 2010.

Investment Rationale/Risk

▶ After rebounding about 30% from its multi-year low reached in March, the stock was recently down around 4% year to date. The shares were hurt, in our view, by sharply lower EPS expectations due to the weak economy and wholesale power markets, as well as the crisis in the credit markets and its potential impact on FE's cost of capital. We believe the rebound has reflected the recovery in the broader market. While the stock could remain volatile, we believe it is fairly valued at recent levels.

▶ Risks to our recommendation and target price include the possibility of higher-than-anticipated or inadequately hedged replacement power costs, as well as a reduction in the average P/E of FE's electric utility peers.

▶ While we do not expect dividend increases during the current economic slowdown, we believe the company will still target future annual increases of 4% to 5% and a dividend payout ratio of 50% to 60%. The targeted growth rate is above both the industry's expected dividend growth rate and FE's own expected long-term EPS growth rate of 3% to 4%. Our 12-month target price of $44 reflects a modest premium-to-peers P/E of 12.2X our EPS estimate for 2010.

Revenue/Earnings Data

Revenue (Million $)

	1Q	2Q	3Q	4Q	Year
2009	3,334	3,271	3,408	--	--
2008	3,277	3,245	3,904	3,201	13,195
2007	2,973	3,109	3,641	3,079	12,802
2006	2,705	2,751	3,365	2,680	11,501
2005	2,813	2,900	3,588	2,892	11,989
2004	3,183	3,150	3,536	2,950	12,453

Earnings Per Share ($)

2009	0.39	1.36	0.77	E0.76	E3.75
2008	0.90	0.85	1.54	1.09	4.37
2007	0.92	1.10	1.34	0.87	4.22
2006	0.67	0.93	1.40	0.84	3.82
2005	0.42	0.54	1.01	0.67	2.65
2004	0.53	0.62	0.91	0.61	2.66

Fiscal year ended Dec. 31. Next earnings report expected: Late February. EPS Estimates based on S&P Operating Earnings; historical GAAP earnings are as reported.

Dividend Data (Dates: mm/dd Payment Date: mm/dd/yy)

Amount ($)	Date Decl.	Ex-Div. Date	Stk. of Record	Payment Date
0.550	12/16	02/04	02/06	03/01/09
0.550	03/17	05/05	05/07	06/01/09
0.550	07/21	08/05	08/07	09/01/09
0.550	09/15	11/04	11/06	12/01/09

Dividends have been paid since 1930. Source: Company reports.

Please read the Required Disclosures and Analyst Certification on the last page of this report.

The McGraw-Hill Companies

FirstEnergy Corp.

STANDARD &POOR'S

Business Summary September 09, 2009

CORPORATE OVERVIEW. FirstEnergy (FE) is a diversified energy company involved in the generation, transmission and distribution of electricity as well as energy management and related services. The company operates primarily through two core business segments: Regulated Services, which is comprised of seven electric utility operating companies and provides transmission and distribution services, and Power Supply Management Services, which owns and operates the generation assets and wholesale purchase of electricity, energy management and other energy-related services. The electric utilities accounted for 88.5% of revenues in 2008, with the remaining 11.5% contributed by the unregulated businesses.

MARKET PROFILE. FirstEnergy's utility subsidiaries serve approximately 4.5 million customers within an area of 36,100 square miles in Ohio, Pennsylvania and New Jersey. As of December 31, 2008, the company's power generating facilities had demonstrated net capacity of 14,173 megawatts (MW) of electricity, with coal plants accounting for approximately 56% of the total; nuclear 28%; oil and natural gas peaking units 14%; and other 2%.

In October 2005, four of FE's utility subsidiaries completed an intra-system transfer of 8,132 megawatts of fossil and hydroelectric generation assets to FirstEnergy Generation Corp. for $1.6 billion. The transfer was part of the transitional plans approved by both the Ohio and Pennsylvania public utility commissions requiring the separation of the generation assets from the distribution businesses. Under a June 2006 coal supply agreement between FE's generation subsidiary and CONSOL Energy (CNX), CNX would supply a total of more than 128 million tons of high-BTU coal for the 20-year period 2009 through 2028. The agreement replaced an earlier agreement that ran through 2020, and should result in the shipment of an additional two million tons per year. While we expect FE to benefit from its low-cost fuel sources, with industrial customers accounting for a significant portion of its customer base, we believe it has a greater-than-peers vulnerability to a significant downturn in the regional economy.

Company Financials Fiscal Year Ended Dec. 31

Per Share Data ($)	2008	2007	2006	2005	2004	2003	2002	2001	2000	1999
Tangible Book Value	8.88	11.06	9.83	9.63	7.70	6.55	4.11	6.04	11.42	10.47
Earnings	4.37	4.22	3.82	2.65	2.66	1.39	2.33	2.84	2.69	2.50
S&P Core Earnings	3.28	3.80	3.71	2.56	2.77	1.61	1.69	2.36	NA	NA
Dividends	2.20	2.00	1.80	1.67	1.50	1.50	1.50	1.13	1.50	1.50
Payout Ratio	50%	47%	47%	63%	56%	108%	64%	40%	56%	60%
Prices:High	84.00	74.98	61.70	53.36	43.41	38.90	39.12	36.98	32.13	33.19
Prices:Low	41.20	57.77	47.75	37.70	35.24	25.82	24.85	25.10	18.00	22.13
P/E Ratio:High	19	18	16	20	16	28	17	13	12	13
P/E Ratio:Low	9	14	13	14	13	19	11	9	7	9

Income Statement Analysis (Million $)	2008	2007	2006	2005	2004	2003	2002	2001	2000	1999
Revenue	13,195	12,802	11,501	11,989	12,453	12,307	12,152	7,999	7,029	6,320
Depreciation	789	1,657	1,457	1,870	1,756	1,282	1,106	890	934	938
Maintenance	NA	NA	NA	NA	NA	NA	NA	NA	NA	NA
Fixed Charges Coverage	4.02	3.95	3.78	3.39	3.25	1.88	2.25	2.85	2.71	2.62
Construction Credits	NA	NA	NA	NA	NA	NA	24.5	35.5	27.1	13.4
Effective Tax Rate	36.7%	40.3%	38.7%	46.3%	43.4%	49.0%	44.5%	42.0%	38.6%	41.0%
Net Income	1,342	1,309	1,258	873	874	422	686	655	599	568
S&P Core Earnings	1,005	1,177	1,211	841	911	492	496	546	NA	NA

Balance Sheet & Other Financial Data (Million $)	2008	2007	2006	2005	2004	2003	2002	2001	2000	1999
Gross Property	28,544	25,731	24,722	23,790	22,892	22,374	21,231	20,589	12,839	15,013
Capital Expenditures	2,888	1,633	1,315	1,208	846	856	998	852	588	625
Net Property	17,723	15,383	14,667	13,998	13,478	13,269	12,680	12,428	7,575	9,093
Capitalization:Long Term Debt	9,100	8,869	8,535	8,339	10,348	9,789	11,636	12,508	6,552	6,906
Capitalization:% Long Term Debt	52.3	49.7	48.6	47.1	53.7	53.1	62.0	62.8	58.5	60.2
Capitalization:Preferred	Nil	Nil	Nil	184	335	352	Nil	Nil	Nil	Nil
Capitalization:% Preferred	Nil	Nil	Nil	1.04	1.74	1.91	Nil	Nil	Nil	Nil
Capitalization:Common	8,283	8,977	9,035	9,188	8,589	8,289	7,120	7,399	4,653	4,564
Capitalization:% Common	47.7	50.3	51.4	51.9	44.6	45.0	38.0	37.2	41.5	39.8
Total Capital	19,546	20,517	20,310	20,437	21,597	20,608	21,360	22,852	13,540	13,970
% Operating Ratio	85.4	84.9	84.3	89.0	87.3	90.4	86.6	50.8	37.8	82.0
% Earned on Net Property	16.7	18.7	18.2	15.0	16.5	11.2	17.4	16.8	18.1	16.7
% Return on Revenue	10.2	10.2	10.9	7.3	7.0	3.4	5.6	8.2	8.5	9.0
% Return on Invested Capital	10.2	10.1	9.6	7.3	7.4	6.5	7.4	21.8	32.0	7.8
% Return on Common Equity	15.6	14.5	13.8	9.8	10.4	5.5	9.5	10.9	13.0	12.6

Data as orig reptd.; bef. results of disc opers/spec. items. Per share data adj. for stk. divs.; EPS diluted. E-Estimated. NA-Not Available. NM-Not Meaningful. NR-Not Ranked. UR-Under Review.

Office: 76 South Main Street, Akron, OH 44308-1890.
Telephone: 800-736-3402.
Website: http://www.firstenergycorp.com
Chrmn: G.M. Smart

Pres & CEO: A.J. Alexander
EVP & CFO: M.T. Clark
EVP & General Counsel: L.L. Vespoli
Chief Acctg Officer & Cntlr: H.L. Wagner

Investor Contact: R.E. Seeholzer (800-736-3402)
Board Members: P. T. Addison, A. J. Alexander, M. Anderson, C. Cartwright, W. T. Cottle, R. B. Heisler, Jr., E. J. Novak, Jr., C. A. Rein, G. M. Smart, W. M. Taylor, J. T. Williams

Founded: 1996
Domicile: Ohio
Employees: 14,698

First Horizon National Corp

STANDARD &POOR'S

S&P Recommendation	HOLD ★★★☆☆	Price $13.22 (as of Nov 27, 2009)	12-Mo. Target Price $13.00	Investment Style Large-Cap Blend

GICS Sector Financials
Sub-Industry Regional Banks

Summary FHN (formerly First Tennessee National) owns First Tennessee Bank and First Horizon Home Loan Corporation.

Key Stock Statistics (Source S&P, Vickers, company reports)

52-Wk Range	$14.82– 6.56	S&P Oper. EPS 2009E	-1.56	Market Capitalization(B)	$2.891	Beta	0.28
Trailing 12-Month EPS	$-1.48	S&P Oper. EPS 2010E	-0.89	Yield (%)	Nil	S&P 3-Yr. Proj. EPS CAGR(%)	NM
Trailing 12-Month P/E	NM	P/E on S&P Oper. EPS 2009E	NM	Dividend Rate/Share	Nil	S&P Credit Rating	BBB-
$10K Invested 5 Yrs Ago	$4,043	Common Shares Outstg. (M)	218.7	Institutional Ownership (%)	71		

Price Performance

30-Week Mov. Avg. — 10-Week Mov. Avg. - - GAAP Earnings vs. Previous Year Volume Above Avg. STARS
12-Mo. Target Price — Relative Strength ▲ Up ▼ Down ► No Change Below Avg. ★

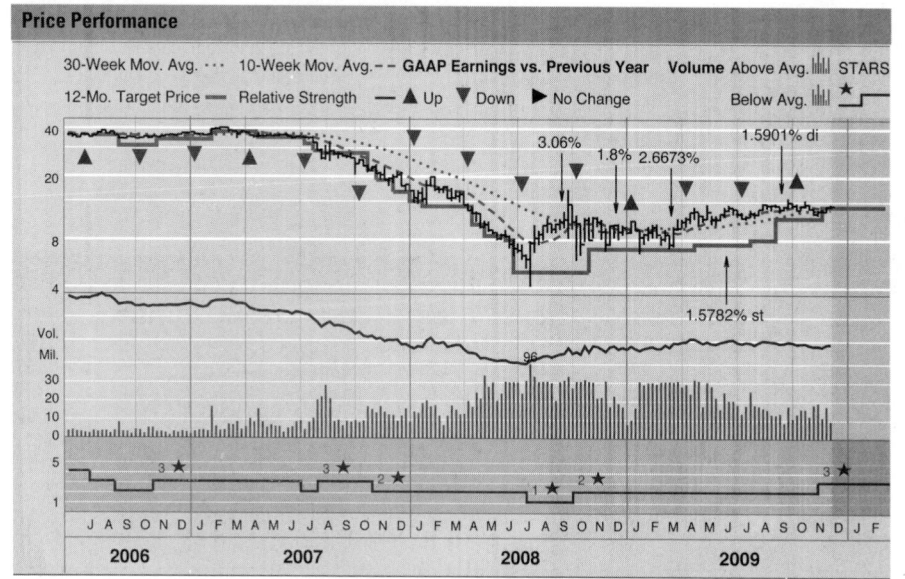

Options: P, Ph

Qualitative Risk Assessment

LOW	MEDIUM	HIGH

Our risk assessment reflects FHN's exposure to a weak residential real estate market, with significant holdings of riskier construction and home equity loans, which we believe are especially vulnerable to rising unemployment.

Quantitative Evaluations

S&P Quality Ranking **A-**

D	C	B-	B	B+	A-	A	A+

Relative Strength Rank **STRONG**

71

LOWEST = 1   HIGHEST = 99

Revenue/Earnings Data

Revenue (Million $)

	1Q	2Q	3Q	4Q	Year
2009	2,015	547.8	540.2	--	--
2008	925.5	814.5	688.4	669.6	3,098
2007	866.4	875.2	786.1	638.5	3,166
2006	731.0	913.6	930.4	921.0	3,496
2005	728.3	781.8	867.0	862.9	3,240
2004	624.1	630.1	627.8	647.9	2,530

Earnings Per Share ($)

	1Q	2Q	3Q	4Q	Year
2009	-0.38	-0.57	-0.20	E-0.43	E-1.56
2008	-0.05	-0.10	-0.58	-0.29	-1.05
2007	0.49	0.15	-0.10	-1.80	-1.26
2006	0.03	0.74	0.48	0.54	3.25
2005	0.76	0.72	0.81	0.78	3.08
2004	0.83	0.83	0.80	0.73	3.18

Fiscal year ended Dec. 31. Next earnings report expected: Mid January. EPS Estimates based on S&P Operating Earnings; historical GAAP earnings are as reported.

Highlights

► The STARS recommendation for FHN has recently been changed to 3 (hold) from 2 (sell) and the 12-month target price has recently been changed to $13.00 from $11.00. The Highlights section of this Stock Report will be updated accordingly.

Investment Rationale/Risk

► The Investment Rationale/Risk section of this Stock Report will be updated shortly. For the latest News story on FHN from MarketScope, see below.

► 11/11/09 02:02 pm ET ... S&P RAISES RECOMMENDATION ON FIRST HORIZON NATIONAL TO HOLD FROM SELL (FHN 12.38***): The FHN shares have fallen about 8% since reaching a relative high in mid-October, vs. a 0.45% decline for the S&P 500 over the same time period. On a recent increase in banking valuation multiples, we are raising our target price to $13, up $2, and we are basing it on a 1.35X multiple on our 12/31 tangible book value per share estimate of $9.59, in-line with regional banking peers, and warranted, we think, by what we see as FHN's relatively strong capital position, partly offset by its exposure to riskier home equity loans. / E.Oja

Dividend Data (Dates: mm/dd Payment Date: mm/dd/yy)

Amount ($)	Date Decl.	Ex-Div. Date	Stk. of Record	Payment Date
1.837 Stk.	10/22	12/10	12/12	01/01/09
2.6673%	01/26	03/11	03/13	04/01/09
1.497%	10/20	12/09	12/11	01/01/10

Dividends have been paid since 1895. Source: Company reports.

First Horizon National Corp

Business Summary October 28, 2009

CORPORATE OVERVIEW. First Horizon National (formerly First Tennessee National) is a Memphis, TN-based regional bank. FHN is one of the 40 largest bank holding companies in the U.S. in terms of asset size, with $31.0 billion in assets at December 31, 2008. FHN provides diversified financial services through five business segments. Three of the segments reflect the common activities and operations of aggregated business segments across the various delivery channels: regional banking, capital markets, and mortgage banking. National specialty lending consists of traditional consumer and construction lending activities in national markets outside of FHN's Tennessee-based market footprint, and those operations largely were discontinued in 2008. In addition, the corporate segment provides essential support within the corporation. During 2008, 62% of revenues came from fee income, versus 52% in 2007.

Regional banking contributed 35% of revenues in 2008 (versus 51% in 2007), capital markets 26% (23%), national specialty lending 7% (15%), mortgage banking 27% (10%), and corporate 5% (1%).

As of December 2008, FHN's subsidiaries had over 200 business locations in 15 U.S. states, Hong Kong, and Tokyo. FHN had 202 financial center bank branch locations in three states: 191 branches in 17 Tennessee counties, including all of the major metropolitan areas of the state; 2 branches in Georgia; and 9 branches in Mississippi. FHN was in the top 20 nationally in mortgage loan originations and the top 15 in mortgage loan servicing, at December 31, 2007 (latest available data), as reported by Inside Mortgage Finance.

CORPORATE STRATEGY. Beginning in 2007, and continuing throughout 2008, FHN conducted a review of business practices with the goal of improving overall profitability and productivity. In order to redeploy capital to higher-return businesses, origination through national construction lending operations was discontinued. FHN sold the national mortgage origination and servicing platforms, including servicing on $19.1 billion of unpaid principal balance; and the sale of most of the First Horizon Bank branches outside of the bank's Tennessee-based market footprint was completed.

Company Financials Fiscal Year Ended Dec. 31

Per Share Data ($)	2008	2007	2006	2005	2004	2003	2002	2001	2000	1999
Tangible Book Value	8.72	13.43	15.29	13.67	13.25	12.08	10.72	9.24	8.83	7.67
Earnings	-1.05	-1.25	3.25	3.08	3.18	3.26	2.60	2.26	1.59	1.72
S&P Core Earnings	-1.22	-0.88	1.76	2.82	2.94	2.87	2.24	1.62	NA	NA
Dividends	0.36	1.62	1.62	1.57	1.47	1.17	0.94	0.82	0.79	0.68
Payout Ratio	NM	NM	50%	51%	46%	36%	36%	36%	50%	40%
Prices:High	20.19	40.88	38.75	40.30	43.77	43.63	36.89	33.73	26.37	40.82
Prices:Low	4.07	15.88	33.38	31.29	36.70	32.01	26.77	24.40	14.34	24.63
P/E Ratio:High	NM	NM	12	13	14	13	14	15	17	24
P/E Ratio:Low	NM	NM	10	10	12	10	10	11	9	14

Income Statement Analysis (Million $)

	2008	2007	2006	2005	2004	2003	2002	2001	2000	1999
Net Interest Income	895	941	997	984	856	806	753	686	598	590
Tax Equivalent Adjustment	1.35	0.69	NA	1.17	1.10	1.26	1.50	2.10	2.60	3.00
Non Interest Income	1,491	861	1,233	1,400	1,342	1,638	1,550	1,321	1,068	1,121
Loan Loss Provision	1,080	273	83.1	67.7	48.3	86.7	92.2	93.5	67.4	57.9
% Expense/Operating Revenue	93.3%	102.3%	78.2%	70.1%	68.4%	67.1%	71.3%	67.7%	75.5%	74.4%
Pretax Income	-350	-316	338	645	667	719	558	494	337	379
Effective Tax Rate	NM	NM	25.8%	31.6%	31.9%	34.2%	32.5%	33.2%	31.0%	34.8%
Net Income	-193	-175	251	441	454	473	376	330	233	248
% Net Interest Margin	2.95	2.82	2.93	3.08	3.62	3.78	4.33	4.27	3.73	3.80
S&P Core Earnings	-244	-128	261	423	438	434	337	248	NA	NA

Balance Sheet & Other Financial Data (Million $)

	2008	2007	2006	2005	2004	2003	2002	2001	2000	1999
Money Market Assets	980,149	1,129	1,221	3,629	1,676	1,182	1,157	877	380	430
Investment Securities	3,125	3,033	3,890	2,912	2,681	2,470	2,700	2,526	2,839	3,101
Commercial Loans	7,864	8,435	8,338	9,899	7,730	6,904	5,723	5,598	5,327	4,431
Other Loans	13,414	13,669	13,767	10,702	8,698	7,087	5,622	4,685	4,912	4,933
Total Assets	31,022	37,015	37,918	36,579	29,772	24,507	23,823	20,617	18,555	18,373
Demand Deposits	3,957	5,055	5,448	10,027	4,995	4,540	5,149	4,010	2,847	2,798
Time Deposits	10,285	11,977	14,766	13,411	14,788	11,140	10,564	9,596	9,342	8,560
Long Term Debt	4,768	6,825	6,132	3,733	2,617	1,117	1,074	3,066	3,119	459
Common Equity	2,497	2,136	2,462	2,312	2,041	1,850	1,691	1,478	1,384	1,241
% Return on Assets	NM	NM	0.7	1.3	1.7	2.0	1.7	1.7	1.3	1.3
% Return on Equity	NM	NM	10.4	20.3	23.1	26.7	23.8	23.0	17.7	21.1
% Loan Loss Reserve	4.0	1.5	0.9	0.8	0.7	0.9	0.9	1.1	1.2	1.2
% Loans/Deposits	149.4	118.7	123.6	106.8	109.2	108.2	102.7	100.6	98.2	100.5
% Equity to Assets	6.8	6.1	6.5	6.6	7.2	7.3	7.1	7.3	7.1	6.3

Data as orig reptd.; bef. results of disc opers/spec. items. Per share data adj. for stk. divs.; EPS diluted. E-Estimated. NA-Not Available. NM-Not Meaningful. NR-Not Ranked. UR-Under Review.

Office: 165 Madison Avenue, Memphis, TN 38103. **Telephone:** 901-523-4444. **Website:** http://www.fhnc.com **Chrmn:** M.D. Rose

Pres & CEO: D.B. Jordan **EVP & CFO:** W.C. Losch, III **EVP & CTO:** M. McDougall **EVP & Chief Acctg Officer:** J.F. Keen

Investor Contact: D. Miller (901-523-4162) **Board Members:** R. B. Carter, S. F. Cooper, M. A. Emkes, J. A. Haslam, III, D. B. Jordan, R. B. Martin, V. R. Palmer, C. V. Reed, M. D. Rose, W. B. Sansom, L. Yancy, III

Founded: 1968 **Domicile:** Tennessee **Employees:** 6,095

First Solar Inc

STANDARD &POOR'S

S&P Recommendation	HOLD ★★★☆☆	Price	12-Mo. Target Price	Investment Style
		$120.30 (as of Nov 27, 2009)	$135.00	Large-Cap Blend

GICS Sector Industrials
Sub-Industry Electrical Components & Equipment

Summary This company produces solar modules using a proprietary thin film semiconductor technology.

Key Stock Statistics (Source S&P, Vickers, company reports)

52-Wk Range	$207.51– 100.90	S&P Oper. EPS 2009E	7.36	Market Capitalization(B)	$10.238	Beta	1.62
Trailing 12-Month EPS	$7.50	S&P Oper. EPS 2010E	6.30	Yield (%)	Nil	S&P 3-Yr. Proj. EPS CAGR(%)	25
Trailing 12-Month P/E	16.0	P/E on S&P Oper. EPS 2009E	16.3	Dividend Rate/Share	Nil	S&P Credit Rating	NA
$10K Invested 5 Yrs Ago	NA	Common Shares Outstg. (M)	85.1	Institutional Ownership (%)	57		

Price Performance

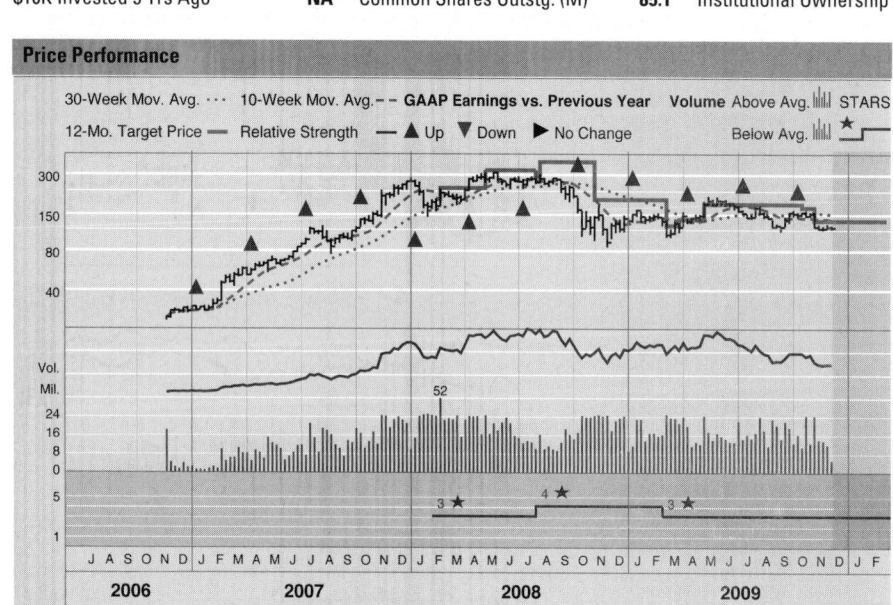

30-Week Mov. Avg. · · · 10-Week Mov. Avg. – – GAAP Earnings vs. Previous Year   Volume Above Avg. STARS
12-Mo. Target Price — Relative Strength — ▲ Up ▼ Down ▶ No Change   Below Avg. ★

Options: ASE, CBOE

Analysis prepared by **Angelo Zino** on October 30, 2009, when the stock traded at **$ 122.80**.

Highlights

▸ We expect sales to rise 61% in 2009 and 27% in 2010, on higher solar module sales, as FSLR continues to expand its capacity. We see higher volume from capacity expansion offset somewhat by lower prices, partly due to solar module oversupply and aggressive competition from China-based silicon module manufacturers. We think FSLR continues to generate new orders and believe utility pipelines will develop into substantial volume by late 2010.

▸ We forecast annual gross margins of 51% in 2009 and 40% in 2010, as lower selling prices are partly offset by higher volume and reduced manufacturing costs. We forecast pricing declines of 24% in 2009 and 21% in 2010. We think FSLR can lower its cost per watt, from $0.87 currently to $0.65 by 2012, through greater scale and manufacturing efficiencies. FSLR's modules had a conversion efficiency ratio of 11.0% at the end of September 2009.

▸ FSLR is offering rebates in Germany so that it can sustain its market share, as silicon module makers are rapidly reducing prices. However, we expect margins to suffer through discounted prices and think FSLR will likely have less control of its panel prices going forward.

Investment Rationale/Risk

▸ Although a difficult financial environment and rising supply pose uncertainties in solar markets, we think First Solar is well positioned to prosper long term. We view its April 2009 purchase of OptiSolar's solar project pipeline as an important step in developing a major footprint in projects with utilities. However, we see risk to FSLR's high gross margins should peers drive module prices to cash cost levels, forcing FSLR to lower prices at a steeper pace. In our view, however, default risk and project financing remain risks to sales. We also note uncertainty regarding German feed-in-tariffs.

▸ Risks to our recommendation and target price include potential inefficient execution of FSLR's aggressive capacity expansion plan, and falling prices.

▸ Our 12-month target price of $135 is based on a price-to-earnings multiple of 21.4X our 2010 EPS projection, above peers. We believe FSLR merits a premium valuation, based on our view of the company as a leader in bringing out a solar energy product with low production costs. Also, we view FSLR's balance sheet and margins as considerably stronger than peers.

Qualitative Risk Assessment

LOW	MEDIUM	**HIGH**

Our risk assessment reflects our view of the highly competitive nature of First Solar's business, the relatively early stages of the business cycle for alternative energy sources, and a high degree of execution risk in the company's aggressive capacity expansion plans. We also have concerns that over 40% of the company's common stock is held by the estate of John T. Walton and affiliates, which have considerable control over operation of the company's business.

Quantitative Evaluations

S&P Quality Ranking   NR

D	C	B-	B	B+	A-	A	A+

Relative Strength Rank   WEAK

16

LOWEST = 1   HIGHEST = 99

Revenue/Earnings Data

Revenue (Million $)

	1Q	2Q	3Q	4Q	Year
2009	418.2	525.9	480.9	--	--
2008	196.9	267.0	348.7	433.7	1,246
2007	66.95	77.22	159.0	200.8	504.0
2006	13.62	27.86	40.79	52.70	135.0
2005	8.53	9.37	16.59	13.58	48.06
2004	--	--	--	--	13.52

Earnings Per Share ($)

2009	1.99	2.11	1.79	E1.48	E7.36
2008	0.57	0.85	1.20	1.61	4.24
2007	0.07	0.58	0.58	0.77	2.03
2006	-0.12	-0.05	0.07	0.12	0.07
2005	-0.02	-0.01	0.03	-0.14	-0.13
2004	--	--	--	--	-0.39

Fiscal year ended Dec. 31. Next earnings report expected: Late February. EPS Estimates based on S&P Operating Earnings; historical GAAP earnings are as reported.

Dividend Data

No cash dividends have been paid.

Stock Report | November 28, 2009 | NNM Symbol: **FSLR**

First Solar Inc

**STANDARD
&POOR'S**

Business Summary October 30, 2009

CORPORATE OVERVIEW. First Solar designs and manufactures solar modules using a proprietary thin film semiconductor technology. The company's solar modules employ a thin layer of cadmium telluride semiconductor material to convert sunlight into electricity. In less than three hours, FSLR is able to transform a two foot by four foot sheet of glass into a complete solar module, using about 1% of the semiconductor material needed to produce crystalline silicon solar modules. Its production process eliminates the multiple supply chain operators, and expensive and time-consuming batch processing steps that are used to make a crystalline silicon solar module. During 2008, the company derived 94% of its revenues from customers headquartered in the European Union (primarily Germany, which accounted for 74% of FSLR's revenues).

CORPORATE STRATEGY. As of year-end 2008, FSLR manufactured its solar modules and conducted its research and development activities at a total of 19 production lines at plants in Perrysburg, OH , Frankfurt/Oder, Germany, and Kulim, Malaysia. During 2008, FSLR produced 504 MW of solar modules, including 173.6 MW in the fourth quarter. Upon the completion of its fourth plant in Malaysia, and the expansion of its Perrysburg, OH, plant (both expected in 2009), First Solar will have annual manufacturing capacity of about 1.15 GW.

First Solar's manufacturing costs totaled $0.98 per watt in 2008's fourth quarter, down 12% from the year-earlier level. The company's average manufac-

turing cost for the full year was $1.08 per watt, versus $1.23 in 2007, also a 12% reduction. The company has noted that its objective is to become, by 2010, the first solar-module manufacturer to offer a product that competes on a non-subsidized basis with the price of retail electricity in key markets in North America, Europe and Asia.

In April 2009, First Solar closed on a deal to buy the solar project pipeline of privately held OptiSolar, for about $400 million in stock. The transaction, which greatly expanded FSLR's penetration of the U.S. utility solar power market, consisted of a 550 MW solar development project under a power purchase agreement with PG&E Corp., a project pipeline of 1.3 GW of utility contracts under negotiation, and land rights on 136,000 acres.

LEGAL/REGULATORY ISSUES. The United States, Canada and countries in Europe and Asia have adopted a variety of government subsidies to allow renewable sources of electricity to compete with conventional sources of electricity, such as fossil fuels.

Company Financials Fiscal Year Ended Dec. 31

Per Share Data ($)	2008	2007	2006	2005	2004	2003	2002	2001	2000	1999
Tangible Book Value	18.12	13.54	5.69	NM	NA	NA	NA	NA	NA	NA
Cash Flow	4.99	2.35	0.21	-0.07	NA	NA	NA	NA	NA	NA
Earnings	4.24	2.03	0.07	-0.13	-0.39	-0.78	NA	NA	NA	NA
S&P Core Earnings	4.24	2.03	0.06	-0.09	NA	NA	NA	NA	NA	NA
Dividends	Nil	Nil	Nil	Nil	NA	NA	NA	NA	NA	NA
Payout Ratio	Nil	Nil	Nil	Nil	NA	NA	NA	NA	NA	NA
Prices:High	317.00	283.00	30.00	NA	NA	NA	NA	NA	NA	NA
Prices:Low	85.28	27.54	20.00	NA	NA	NA	NA	NA	NA	NA
P/E Ratio:High	75	NM	NM	NA	NA	NA	NA	NA	NA	NA
P/E Ratio:Low	20	NM	NM	NA	NA	NA	NA	NA	NA	NA

Income Statement Analysis (Million $)	2008	2007	2006	2005	2004	2003	2002	2001	2000	1999
Revenue	1,246	504	135	48.1	13.5	3.21	NA	NA	NA	NA
Operating Income	501	162	13.0	-1.41	NA	NA	NA	NA	NA	NA
Depreciation	61.5	24.8	10.2	3.38	1.94	1.50	NA	NA	NA	NA
Interest Expense	7.39	6.07	4.36	0.42	NA	NA	NA	NA	NA	NA
Pretax Income	464	156	9.18	-6.55	-16.8	-28.0	NA	NA	NA	NA
Effective Tax Rate	24.9%	NM	56.7%	NM	NA	NA	NA	NA	NA	NA
Net Income	348	158	3.97	-6.55	-16.8	-28.0	NA	NA	NA	NA
S&P Core Earnings	348	158	3.97	-6.55	NA	NA	NA	NA	NA	NA

Balance Sheet & Other Financial Data (Million $)	2008	2007	2006	2005	2004	2003	2002	2001	2000	1999
Cash	792	637	308	17.0	3.77	NA	NA	NA	NA	NA
Current Assets	1,077	803	389	26.6	NA	NA	NA	NA	NA	NA
Total Assets	2,115	1,371	579	102	41.8	NA	NA	NA	NA	NA
Current Liabilities	382	186	52.1	33.9	NA	NA	NA	NA	NA	NA
Long Term Debt	164	68.9	61.1	28.6	13.7	NA	NA	NA	NA	NA
Common Equity	1,513	1,097	411	13.1	22.6	NA	NA	NA	NA	NA
Total Capital	1,712	1,166	523	41.7	36.3	NA	NA	NA	NA	NA
Capital Expenditures	459	242	153	42.5	7.73	14.9	NA	NA	NA	NA
Cash Flow	410	183	14.2	-3.18	NA	NA	NA	NA	NA	NA
Current Ratio	2.8	4.3	7.5	0.8	2.3	NA	NA	NA	NA	NA
% Long Term Debt of Capitalization	9.6	5.9	11.7	68.5	37.7	NA	NA	NA	NA	NA
% Net Income of Revenue	28.0	31.4	2.9	NM	NM	NM	NA	NA	NA	NA
% Return on Assets	20.0	16.2	1.2	NM	NM	NA	NA	NA	NA	NA
% Return on Equity	26.7	21.0	1.9	NM	NA	NA	NA	NA	NA	NA

Data as orig reptd.; bef. results of disc opers/spec. items. Per share data adj. for stk. divs.; EPS diluted. E-Estimated. NA-Not Available. NM-Not Meaningful. NR-Not Ranked. UR-Under Review.

Office: 350 W Washington St Ste 600, Tempe, AZ 85281-1496.
Telephone: 602-414-9300.
Email: info@firstsolar.com
Website: http://www.firstsolar.com

Chrmn: M.J. Ahearn
Pres: B. Sohn
CEO: R.J. Gillette
EVP & Secy: J.T. Gaffney

CFO: J. Meyerhoff
Investor Contact: L. Polizzotto (602-414-9315)
Board Members: M. J. Ahearn, R. J. Gillette, C. Kennedy, J. F. Nolan, J. T. Presby, P. H. Stebbins, M. T. Sweeney, J. H. Villarreal

Founded: 1999
Domicile: Delaware
Employees: 3,524

Fiserv Inc

S&P Recommendation BUY ★★★★☆	**Price** $46.29 (as of Nov 27, 2009)	**12-Mo. Target Price** $57.00	**Investment Style** Large-Cap Growth

GICS Sector Information Technology
Sub-Industry Data Processing & Outsourced Services

Summary This company provides account processing and integrated information management systems for financial institutions. In December 2007, it acquired CheckFree Corp. for $4.4 billion.

Key Stock Statistics (Source S&P, Vickers, company reports)

52-Wk Range	$50.91– 29.46	S&P Oper. EPS 2009**E**	3.65	Market Capitalization(B)	$7.124	Beta	1.08
Trailing 12-Month EPS	$2.69	S&P Oper. EPS 2010**E**	4.05	Yield (%)	Nil	S&P 3-Yr. Proj. EPS CAGR(%)	11
Trailing 12-Month P/E	17.2	P/E on S&P Oper. EPS 2009**E**	12.7	Dividend Rate/Share	Nil	S&P Credit Rating	BBB
$10K Invested 5 Yrs Ago	$11,936	Common Shares Outstg. (M)	153.9	Institutional Ownership (%)	81		

Price Performance

30-Week Mov. Avg. · · · 10-Week Mov. Avg. - - GAAP Earnings vs. Previous Year Volume Above Avg. STARS
12-Mo. Target Price — Relative Strength — ▲ Up ▼ Down ► No Change Below Avg.

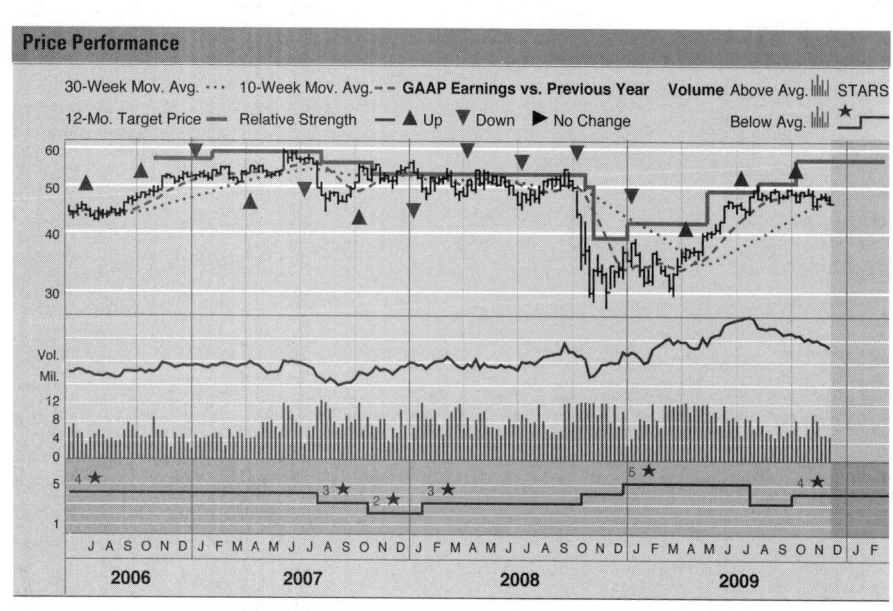

Options: ASE, CBOE, Ph

Analysis prepared by **Scott H. Kessler** on October 29, 2009, when the stock traded at **$ 46.67.**

Highlights

► We project a decline of 13% in 2009 adjusted net revenues, reflecting an unfavorable spending backdrop, offset somewhat by market share gains and cross-selling efforts. We see uncertainties related to continuing challenges and consolidation in the financial services segment, but are encouraged by notable recurring revenues. We see a 3% gain in 2010 adjusted net revenues.

► Historically, FISV has used free cash flow to make acquisitions intended to broaden its offerings and customer base. Acquisitions once accounted for about 50% of FISV's revenue growth. However, in recent years FISV has de-emphasized acquisitions and focused cross-selling and margin-improvement efforts.

► In December 2007, FISV acquired CheckFree Corp. for $4.4 billion. We believe CheckFree notably expanded FISV's offerings, technology, and customer base, and will contribute to material market share gains. In January 2008, FISV sold Fiserv Health for $721 million. In July 2008, FISV sold 51% of its insurance unit for $510 million in after-tax proceeds.

Investment Rationale/Risk

► Notwithstanding FISV's substantial exposure to financial services, which has increased on a percentage basis in recent years, we believe its size and footprint, diversified customer base, and considerable recurring revenues are appealing. We also think the recent financial crisis could prove beneficial for new opportunities, especially as FISV pursues international business.

► Risks to our recommendation and target price include weaker demand than we expect for financial services technology offerings, segment consolidation negatively affecting existing contracts or new business prospects, and sustained weakness in internal growth rates.

► Comparisons to the P/E and P/E-to-growth rate multiples of data processing companies in the S&P 1500 yield a price of $52. Our DCF model (including assumptions of a discount rate of 9.3%, average growth of 10% over the next five years, and a terminal growth rate of 3%) leads to an intrinsic value calculation of $69. Weighting these considerations results in our 12-month target price of $57.

Qualitative Risk Assessment

LOW	MEDIUM	HIGH

Our risk assessment reflects our view of FISV's notable size, market position and flexible balance sheet, offset by what we consider its relatively modest internal growth rate and active acquisition strategy.

Quantitative Evaluations

S&P Quality Ranking B+

D	C	B-	B	B+	A-	A	A+

Relative Strength Rank MODERATE

35

LOWEST = 1 HIGHEST = 99

Revenue/Earnings Data

Revenue (Million $)

	1Q	2Q	3Q	4Q	Year
2009	1,044	1,032	992.0	--	--
2008	1,310	1,295	1,080	1,061	4,739
2007	1,219	1,180	1,174	1,110	3,922
2006	1,097	1,093	1,157	1,198	4,544
2005	973.1	996.4	1,012	1,078	4,059
2004	937.5	946.0	958.1	966.4	3,730

Earnings Per Share ($)

2009	0.65	0.73	0.80	E0.96	E3.65
2008	0.59	0.60	0.45	0.45	2.12
2007	0.66	0.62	0.72	0.54	2.42
2006	0.64	0.63	0.63	0.61	2.49
2005	0.71	0.59	0.58	0.80	2.68
2004	0.49	0.49	0.53	0.49	2.00

Fiscal year ended Dec. 31. Next earnings report expected: Early February. EPS Estimates based on S&P Operating Earnings; historical GAAP earnings are as reported.

Dividend Data

No cash dividends have been paid.

Fiserv Inc

Business Summary October 29, 2009

CORPORATE OVERVIEW. At the end of 2006, Fiserv made some adjustments to its operating segments. Most notably, it created a new insurance services unit, which included the old health plan management services segment, and insurance operations that were previously classified in the financial institutions segment.

In December 2007, the company bought CheckFree Corp., entering the electronic payments area. In January 2008, FISV sold Fiserv Health, and most of its health-related businesses. In July 2008, FISV sold a majority stake of its insurance segment.

The financial segment (accounting for 45% of revenues in 2008, and 53% of revenues in 2007) provides solutions to thousands of financial institutions, including banks, credit unions, leasing and finance companies, and savings institutions. Many offerings are sold as an integrated suite to clients, and could include core processing (allowing for account servicing and management information functionality for banks, thrifts and credit unions), lending and item

processing (providing for the clearing of paper and imaged checks), payments processing (enabling FISV clients to provide their customers with services such as home-banking and bill payment offerings), and a variety of industry-specific products and services.

In December 2007, FISV acquired CheckFree for $4.4 billion, and thus created the Payments unit (45%, 27%). The segment's financial e-commerce products enable consumers to review bank accounts and receive and pay bills electronically. In 2008, the business processed 1.3 billion transactions and delivered 300 million electronic bills. We believe the CheckFree acquisition has bolstered FISV's base of offerings, technology and customers, and see notable cross-selling potential.

Company Financials Fiscal Year Ended Dec. 31

Per Share Data ($)	2008	2007	2006	2005	2004	2003	2002	2001	2000	1999
Tangible Book Value	NM	NM	NM	NM	0.96	NM	2.60	2.60	2.18	1.57
Cash Flow	2.85	2.88	3.62	3.62	2.94	2.48	2.09	1.86	1.33	1.18
Earnings	2.12	2.42	2.49	2.68	2.00	1.61	1.37	1.09	0.93	0.73
S&P Core Earnings	2.47	2.42	2.50	2.28	1.91	1.47	1.26	1.00	NA	NA
Dividends	Nil	Nil	Nil	Nil	Nil	Nil	Nil	Nil	Nil	Nil
Payout Ratio	Nil	Nil	Nil	Nil	Nil	Nil	Nil	Nil	Nil	Nil
Prices:High	56.80	59.85	53.60	46.89	41.01	40.77	47.24	44.61	42.75	27.17
Prices:Low	27.75	44.16	40.29	36.33	32.20	27.23	22.50	29.08	16.21	16.08
P/E Ratio:High	27	25	21	17	21	25	34	41	46	37
P/E Ratio:Low	13	18	16	14	16	17	16	27	17	22

Income Statement Analysis (Million $)

	2008	2007	2006	2005	2004	2003	2002	2001	2000	1999
Revenue	4,739	3,922	4,544	4,059	3,730	3,034	2,569	1,890	1,654	1,408
Operating Income	1,046	836	943	925	845	704	734	501	429	347
Depreciation	119	78.0	199	179	185	172	141	148	70.1	86.3
Interest Expense	260	76.0	41.0	27.8	24.9	22.9	17.8	12.1	22.1	19.4
Pretax Income	625	661	710	818	641	516	436	347	300	234
Effective Tax Rate	44.6%	38.3%	37.6%	37.5%	38.4%	39.0%	39.0%	40.0%	41.0%	41.0%
Net Income	346	408	443	511	395	315	266	208	177	138
S&P Core Earnings	403	408	443	435	377	288	246	191	NA	NA

Balance Sheet & Other Financial Data (Million $)

	2008	2007	2006	2005	2004	2003	2002	2001	2000	1999
Cash	232	309	185	184	516	203	227	136	98.9	80.6
Current Assets	2,145	4,204	NA	NA	NA	NA	NA	NA	NA	NA
Total Assets	9,331	11,846	6,208	6,040	8,383	7,214	6,439	5,322	5,586	5,308
Current Liabilities	2,047	3,754	NA	NA	NA	NA	NA	NA	NA	NA
Long Term Debt	3,850	5,405	747	595	505	699	483	343	335	326
Common Equity	2,594	2,467	2,426	2,466	2,564	2,200	1,828	1,605	1,252	1,091
Total Capital	6,974	7,933	3,173	3,227	3,204	2,990	2,357	1,948	1,622	1,477
Capital Expenditures	199	160	187	165	161	143	142	68.0	73.0	69.7
Cash Flow	465	486	642	691	580	487	407	356	247	224
Current Ratio	1.1	1.1	1.6	1.4	5.0	0.9	1.0	1.1	1.1	1.1
% Long Term Debt of Capitalization	55.2	66.5	23.6	18.4	15.8	23.4	20.5	17.6	20.7	22.1
% Net Income of Revenue	7.3	10.4	9.8	12.6	10.6	10.4	10.4	11.0	10.7	9.8
% Return on Assets	3.3	4.5	7.2	7.1	5.1	4.6	4.5	3.8	3.2	3.0
% Return on Equity	13.7	16.7	18.1	20.3	16.6	15.6	15.5	14.6	15.1	13.9

Data as orig reptd.; bef. results of disc opers/spec. items. Per share data adj. for stk. divs.; EPS diluted. E-Estimated. NA-Not Available. NM-Not Meaningful. NR-Not Ranked. UR-Under Review.

Office: 255 Fiserv Drive, Brookfield, WI 53045.
Telephone: 262-879-5000.
Email: general_info@fiserv.com
Website: http://www.fiserv.com

Chrmn: D.F. Dillon
Pres & CEO: J. Yabuki
Vice Chrmn: P.J. Kight
EVP, CFO, Chief Acctg Officer & Treas: T.J. Hirsch

EVP, Chief Admin Officer, Secy & General Counsel: C.W. Sprague
Investor Contact: D. Banks (262-879-5055)
Board Members: D. F. Dillon, D. P. Kearney, P. J. Kight, G. J. Levy, D. J. O'Leary, G. M. Renwick, K. M. Robak, D. R. Simons, T. Wertheimer, J. Yabuki

Founded: 1984
Domicile: Wisconsin
Employees: 20,000

FLIR Systems Inc

STANDARD &POOR'S

S&P Recommendation HOLD ★★★☆☆

Price	12-Mo. Target Price	Investment Style
$28.79 (as of Nov 27, 2009)	$32.00	Large-Cap Growth

GICS Sector Information Technology
Sub-Industry Electronic Equipment Manufacturers

Summary This company designs, manufactures, and markets thermal imaging and broadcast camera systems for use in commercial and government markets.

Key Stock Statistics (Source S&P, Vickers, company reports)

52-Wk Range	$32.31– 18.81	S&P Oper. EPS 2009E	1.46	Market Capitalization(B)	$4.370	Beta	1.04
Trailing 12-Month EPS	$1.48	S&P Oper. EPS 2010E	1.60	Yield (%)	Nil	S&P 3-Yr. Proj. EPS CAGR(%)	14
Trailing 12-Month P/E	19.5	P/E on S&P Oper. EPS 2009E	19.7	Dividend Rate/Share	Nil	S&P Credit Rating	NR
$10K Invested 5 Yrs Ago	$19,828	Common Shares Outstg. (M)	151.8	Institutional Ownership (%)	98		

Price Performance

30-Week Mov. Avg. · · · · 10-Week Mov. Avg. – – **GAAP Earnings vs. Previous Year** Volume Above Avg. STARS
12-Mo. Target Price — Relative Strength — ▲ Up ▼ Down ► No Change Below Avg.

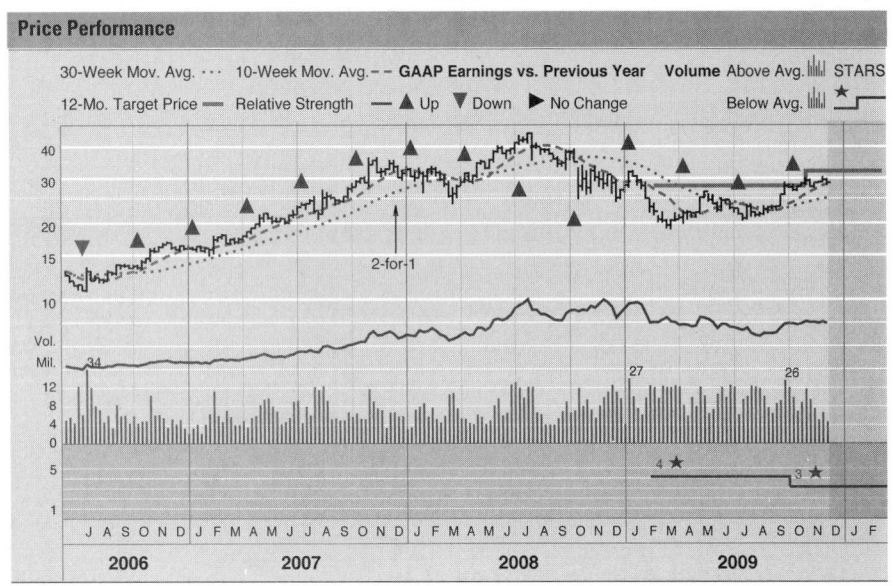

Options: ASE, CBOE, P, Ph

Analysis prepared by **Dylan Cathers** on October 22, 2009, when the stock traded at **$ 28.48**.

Highlights

► We see revenues rising 7.5% in 2009, and increasing 9% in 2010. We believe that there are notable sales opportunities with the U.S. military and other government agencies as the military increases its technological capabilities. Further, we think growth for more commercial products will accelerate as product prices decrease and the economy improves. Still, we believe near-term orders may be volatile as the Iraq war will likely wind down and ongoing macroeconomic headwinds may cause private customers to delay new purchases.

► We project that gross margins will remain in the mid-to-high 50% range over the foreseeable future, reflecting our expectation that pricing for FLIR's government applications will remain relatively stable and that FLIR will reduce and manage costs effectively. As sales advance, we think operating leverage will contribute to a wider operating margin in 2009 versus last year.

► We look for EPS of $1.46 in 2009, increasing to $1.60 in 2010. Our projections assume 32% and 33% effective tax rates, respectively, and a modest decline in the diluted share count.

Investment Rationale/Risk

► We believe FLIR has a profitable business model and notable growth opportunities, and we think that sales will not only hold up during the economic downturn, but will accelerate at a brisk pace during the upturn. We anticipate healthy sales growth, margins, and free cash flows contributing to attractive returns. Our forecasts reflect notable risks we see related to government spending, contract wins, and the traction of growth for commercial applications.

► Risks to our recommendation and target price include a sharper-than-anticipated decrease in military spending on infrared related technology, formidable competition, economic headwinds, and financial risks.

► Our 12-month target price of $32 is based on our relative valuation analysis. We arrive at our target price using a roughly peer-average P/E ratio of 20X our 2010 EPS estimate, which is towards the low end of FLIR's range of 14X-44X over the past four years.

Qualitative Risk Assessment

LOW	MEDIUM	HIGH

Our risk assessment reflects the uncertainty of government spending on infrared-related technologies balanced by the long nature of government contracts, helping to reduce business risk. The company carries long-term debt, but has also exhibited healthy profitability and cash flows, in our view, balancing the financial risk.

Quantitative Evaluations

S&P Quality Ranking B

D	C	B-	B	B+	A-	A	A+

Relative Strength Rank STRONG

73

LOWEST = 1   HIGHEST = 99

Revenue/Earnings Data

Revenue (Million $)

	1Q	2Q	3Q	4Q	Year
2009	272.0	278.0	285.6	--	--
2008	236.9	261.0	276.7	302.4	1,077
2007	161.4	184.3	191.1	242.6	779.4
2006	117.3	138.6	133.2	185.9	575.0
2005	108.3	131.0	113.0	156.3	508.6
2004	108.9	119.3	110.8	143.7	482.7

Earnings Per Share ($)

2009	0.33	0.35	0.38	E0.40	E1.46
2008	0.24	0.29	0.35	0.41	1.28
2007	0.18	0.19	0.23	0.30	0.89
2006	0.09	0.14	0.18	0.26	0.66
2005	0.10	0.16	0.11	0.22	0.58
2004	0.09	0.12	0.11	0.16	0.47

Fiscal year ended Dec. 31. Next earnings report expected: Early February. EPS Estimates based on S&P Operating Earnings; historical GAAP earnings are as reported.

Dividend Data

No cash dividends have been paid.

Please read the Required Disclosures and Analyst Certification on the last page of this report.

The McGraw-Hill Companies

FLIR Systems Inc

Business Summary October 22, 2009

CORPORATE OVERVIEW. A leading infrared technology company, FLIR Systems, Inc. (FLIR) uses its expertise in product design, infrared imagers, optics, lasers, image processing, systems integration and other technologies, to develop and produce sophisticated thermal and multi-sensor imaging systems used in various applications in commercial, industrial, and government markets. In addition to offering a variety of systems configurations to suit customer's requirements, the company also sells more general, commercial applications.

FLIR's business is organized by three divisions (from largest to smallest based on percentage of 2008 sales): Government Systems (53%), Thermography (30%), Commercial Vision Systems (17%).

The Government Systems division is focused on government contracts and markets where high performance is required. Products are often customized for specific applications, and frequently incorporate additional sensors, including visible light cameras, low light cameras, laser rangefinders, laser illuminators and laser designators. These products are used in applications such as surveillance, force protection, drug interdiction, search and rescue, special operations and target designation. Prices range from $30,000 for hand-

held and fixed security systems to over $1 million for advanced stabilized laser designation systems.

The Thermography division sells products for commercial and industrial applications where imaging and temperature together are required, and include specialized cameras with analytical and image processing capabilities to less expensive cameras for less demanding applications. Prices for these cameras range from $3,000 to $150,000.

The Commercial Vision Systems division is focused on emerging commercial markets for infrared imaging technology where the primary need is to see at night or in adverse conditions. The company notes that demand from markets, such as commercial security and automotive, has grown rapidly as the cost of infrared technology has declined. CVS products range in price from under $2,000 for an OEM imaging core to more than $450,000 for a high definition airborne electronic news gathering broadcast system.

Company Financials Fiscal Year Ended Dec. 31

Per Share Data ($)	2008	2007	2006	2005	2004	2003	2002	2001	2000	1999
Tangible Book Value	3.95	2.88	1.51	1.18	0.85	1.13	1.13	0.67	0.11	0.33
Cash Flow	1.50	1.02	0.92	0.77	0.53	0.39	0.33	0.26	-0.14	-0.39
Earnings	1.28	0.89	0.66	0.58	0.47	0.32	0.29	0.20	-0.23	-0.48
S&P Core Earnings	1.28	0.89	0.66	0.51	0.38	0.27	0.19	0.16	NA	NA
Dividends	Nil	Nil	Nil	Nil	Nil	Nil	Nil	Nil	Nil	Nil
Payout Ratio	Nil	Nil	Nil	Nil	Nil	Nil	Nil	Nil	Nil	Nil
Prices:High	45.49	36.43	17.02	18.18	16.67	9.25	7.44	6.19	2.41	2.97
Prices:Low	23.68	14.81	10.73	10.23	8.74	5.13	3.42	0.52	0.38	1.38
P/E Ratio:High	36	41	26	31	35	29	26	31	NM	NM
P/E Ratio:Low	19	17	16	18	19	16	12	3	NM	NM

Income Statement Analysis (Million $)										
Revenue	1,077	779	575	509	483	312	261	214	186	179
Operating Income	324	218	158	142	124	69.8	56.4	44.8	-1.11	-27.1
Depreciation	40.0	25.9	20.6	15.6	14.8	6.26	6.20	7.50	9.72	9.90
Interest Expense	8.99	10.2	8.96	7.92	8.09	4.86	1.68	9.42	12.0	7.84
Pretax Income	295	191	133	122	99.9	63.8	48.9	28.7	-22.3	-52.1
Effective Tax Rate	30.9%	28.5%	23.9%	25.7%	28.4%	30.0%	15.0%	9.77%	NM	NM
Net Income	204	137	101	90.8	71.5	44.7	41.6	25.9	-26.1	-54.4
S&P Core Earnings	204	137	101	78.4	57.6	38.4	27.6	20.5	NA	NA

Balance Sheet & Other Financial Data (Million $)										
Cash	289	204	139	107	121	198	46.6	15.5	11.9	4.26
Current Assets	812	656	486	406	367	382	174	140	122	139
Total Assets	1,244	1,024	798	694	619	450	234	185	167	196
Current Liabilities	172	166	170	90.1	88.7	70.3	52.6	71.0	56.5	135
Long Term Debt	190	227	207	206	205	204	Nil	Nil	75.5	1.50
Common Equity	840	623	399	369	313	165	172	105	29.0	56.2
Total Capital	1,036	833	608	586	519	369	172	105	105	57.2
Capital Expenditures	27.6	44.1	43.0	34.0	13.9	14.6	6.60	4.24	7.28	7.47
Cash Flow	244	163	121	106	86.3	51.0	47.8	33.4	-16.3	-44.5
Current Ratio	4.7	4.0	2.9	4.5	4.1	5.4	3.3	2.0	2.2	1.0
% Long Term Debt of Capitalization	18.4	25.0	34.0	35.2	39.6	55.4	Nil	Nil	72.2	2.6
% Net Income of Revenue	18.9	17.5	17.5	17.8	14.8	14.3	15.9	12.1	NM	NM
% Return on Assets	18.0	15.0	13.6	13.7	13.4	13.1	19.8	14.7	NM	NM
% Return on Equity	27.8	26.8	26.7	26.6	29.9	26.5	30.0	38.7	NM	NM

Data as orig reptd.; bef. results of disc opers/spec. items. Per share data adj. for stk. divs.; EPS diluted. E-Estimated. NA-Not Available. NM-Not Meaningful. NR-Not Ranked. UR-Under Review.

Office: 27700 SW Parkway Ave Ste A, Wilsonville, OR 97070-8238.
Telephone: 503-498-3547.
Email: investor@flir.com
Website: http://www.flir.com

Chrmn, Pres & CEO: E. Lewis
SVP, CFO & Chief Acctg Officer: S.M. Bailey
SVP, Secy & General Counsel: W.W. Davis
Investor Contact: A.L. Trunzo (503-498-3547)

Board Members: J. D. Carter, W. W. Crouch, J. C. Hart, E. Lewis, A. L. MacDonald, M. T. Smith, J. W. Wood, Jr., S. Wynne

Founded: 1978
Domicile: Oregon
Employees: 1,943

Flowserve Corp.

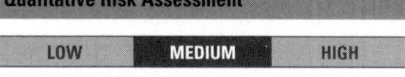

STANDARD &POOR'S

S&P Recommendation	STRONG BUY ★★★★★	Price $100.20 (as of Nov 27, 2009)	12-Mo. Target Price $115.00	Investment Style Large-Cap Growth

GICS Sector Industrials
Sub-Industry Industrial Machinery

Summary This company is a global manufacturer of industrial pumps and related equipment for the chemical, oil & gas and power industries.

Key Stock Statistics (Source S&P, Vickers, company reports)

52-Wk Range	$108.85– 37.86	S&P Oper. EPS 2009**E**	8.50	Market Capitalization(B)	$5.596	Beta	1.52
Trailing 12-Month EPS	$7.69	S&P Oper. EPS 2010**E**	9.25	Yield (%)	1.08	S&P 3-Yr. Proj. EPS CAGR(%)	28
Trailing 12-Month P/E	13.0	P/E on S&P Oper. EPS 2009**E**	11.8	Dividend Rate/Share	$1.08	S&P Credit Rating	BB+
$10K Invested 5 Yrs Ago	$40,538	Common Shares Outstg. (M)	55.8	Institutional Ownership (%)	93		

Price Performance

30-Week Mov. Avg. ··· 10-Week Mov. Avg. – – GAAP Earnings vs. Previous Year Volume Above Avg. ▮▮▮ STARS
12-Mo. Target Price — Relative Strength — ▲ Up ▼ Down ► No Change Below Avg. ▮▮▮ ★

Options: ASE, CBOE, Ph

Analysis prepared by **Stewart Scharf** on November 02, 2009, when the stock traded at **$ 97.98**.

Highlights

► Following a low single digit decline we see in organic sales in 2009 (before about 4% negative foreign currency effect), we expect demand to improve sequentially during 2010, as global market conditions begin to recover. We see near-term softness in the flow control and flow solutions segments in the chemical, oil & gas and general industries markets, while further growth is likely in the pump division, especially for aftermarket products. We also see growth in renewable energy.

► In our view, gross margins will expand to near 36% in 2009, from 35.3% in 2008, with further expansion seen in 2010, based on pricing and operational initiatives, improved fixed cost absorption, and a greater mix of higher-end products. We see adjusted EBITDA margins widening from our near 18% projection for 2009 (15% in 2008), as FLS focuses on cost-cutting initiatives and plant realignments, including head count reduction and optimizing certain non-strategic facilities.

► We estimate a higher effective tax rate of 27% for 2009, and operating EPS of $8.50 (before $0.90 realignment charge), rising 8.8% to $9.25 in 2010.

Investment Rationale/Risk

► Our strong buy recommendation is based on our valuation metrics, as well as our favorable perception of FLS's strong balance sheet and diversified business model, and signs of increased bidding activity for large projects.

► Risks to our recommendation and target price include significant delays and/or project cancellations due to customer spending cutbacks, especially in the oil & gas and power sectors; a shortage of skilled labor; geopolitical issues in developing regions; a weak euro; and problems with internal controls over financial reporting.

► The shares trade at 10.5X our 2010 EPS estimate, a steep discount to our projected P/E for S&P's Industrial Machinery group, which we attribute to FLS's cyclical project business and exposure to the volatile oil & gas and power markets. Our DCF model, which assumes a terminal growth rate of 4.0% and a weighted average cost of capital of 12.5%, indicates intrinsic value of about $110. Our relative metrics, including enterprise value to EBITDA and P/E-to-EPS growth, suggest a value of $120. Blending these metrics, we arrive at our 12-month target price of $115.

Qualitative Risk Assessment

LOW	MEDIUM	HIGH

Our risk assessment reflects the company's exposure to cyclical end markets, foreign exchange swings based on its significant proportion of foreign sales, and past problems filing financial statements in a timely manner. We think these factors are offset by its leading position in many markets, strong cash flows, favorable leverage ratio, and limited interest rate risk due to hedges.

Quantitative Evaluations

S&P Quality Ranking B

D	C	B-	B	B+	A-	A	A+

Relative Strength Rank MODERATE

62

LOWEST = 1   HIGHEST = 99

Revenue/Earnings Data

Revenue (Million $)

	1Q	2Q	3Q	4Q	Year
2009	1,025	1,090	1,051	--	--
2008	993.3	1,158	1,154	1,169	4,473
2007	803.4	930.7	919.2	1,109	3,763
2006	653.9	752.9	770.8	883.5	3,061
2005	616.1	691.2	649.5	738.5	2,695
2004	605.1	648.5	652.1	732.5	2,638

Earnings Per Share ($)

	1Q	2Q	3Q	4Q	Year
2009	1.64	1.92	2.07	E2.44	E8.50
2008	1.53	2.13	2.04	2.03	7.74
2007	0.59	1.11	1.10	1.67	4.47
2006	0.32	0.58	0.49	0.58	2.00
2005	0.05	0.33	0.08	0.36	0.82
2004	0.13	0.10	0.11	0.02	0.36

Fiscal year ended Dec. 31. Next earnings report expected: Late February. EPS Estimates based on S&P Operating Earnings; historical GAAP earnings are as reported.

Dividend Data (Dates: mm/dd Payment Date: mm/dd/yy)

Amount ($)	Date Decl.	Ex-Div. Date	Stk. of Record	Payment Date
0.270	02/25	03/23	03/25	04/08/09
0.270	05/15	06/22	06/24	07/08/09
0.270	08/25	09/21	09/23	10/07/09
0.270	11/23	12/21	12/23	01/06/10

Dividends have been paid since 2007. Source: Company reports.

Please read the Required Disclosures and Analyst Certification on the last page of this report.

The McGraw-Hill Companies

Flowserve Corp.

Business Summary November 02, 2009

CORPORATE OVERVIEW. Flowserve Corp., which was formed through the 1997 merger of Durco International Inc. and BW/IP, Inc., is one of the world's leading providers of fluid motion and control products and services. The company manufactures engineered and industrial pumps, seals and valves, and also provides related flow management services. Customers use fluid motion and control products to regulate the movement of liquids or gases through processing systems in their facilities. Industries served include oil and gas, chemical, power generation, water treatment and general industrial.

Principal markets for the company's products are oil and gas (39% of bookings in 2008), general industrial (23%), chemical (17%), power generation (15%) and water treatment (6%). On a geographic basis, 2008 revenue broke down as follows: North America 35%; Europe 28%, Middle East and Africa 11%; Asia Pacific 18%; and Latin America 8%. The company does not use forward currency contracts to hedge future cash flows.

The company's Pump division (55% of 2008 sales) manufactures engineered and industrial pumps and pump systems, replacement parts and related equipment. The segment's products are primarily used by companies in the oil & gas, chemical processing, power generation, water treatment and general

industrial markets. Pump systems and components are produced at 26 plants worldwide. FLS manufactures over 150 different pump models, ranging from simple fractional horsepower industrial pumps to high horsepower engineered pumps (over 30,000 horsepower). Aftermarket services through the company's global network are provided in 79 service centers in 28 countries. The company's Flow Control division (31%) designs manual valves, control valves, nuclear valves, actuators and other equipment that provide flow control-related services. These products are typically utilized within a flow control system to control the flow of liquids or gases. FLS's Flow Solutions division (15%) manufactures mechanical seals, sealing systems and parts. Seals are used on a variety of rotating equipment, including pumps, mixers, compressors, steam turbines and other specialty equipment. The division's products are used primarily by companies in the oil & gas, chemical processing, mineral and ore processing, and general industrial end markets.

Company Financials Fiscal Year Ended Dec. 31

Per Share Data ($)	2008	2007	2006	2005	2004	2003	2002	2001	2000	1999
Tangible Book Value	7.56	5.42	0.47	NM	NM	NM	NM	NM	NM	5.66
Cash Flow	9.12	5.82	3.30	2.07	1.68	2.36	2.29	2.29	1.91	1.37
Earnings	7.74	4.47	2.00	0.82	0.36	0.96	1.16	0.42	0.40	0.32
S&P Core Earnings	7.47	4.39	2.14	0.87	0.41	0.95	0.82	-0.08	NA	NA
Dividends	1.00	0.60	Nil	Nil	Nil	Nil	Nil	Nil	Nil	0.56
Payout Ratio	13%	13%	Nil	Nil	Nil	Nil	Nil	Nil	Nil	175%
Prices:High	145.45	102.74	61.06	39.75	28.18	22.93	35.09	33.30	23.50	21.56
Prices:Low	37.18	48.73	39.63	23.69	18.64	10.40	7.58	18.70	10.56	15.00
P/E Ratio:High	19	23	31	48	78	24	30	79	59	67
P/E Ratio:Low	5	11	20	29	52	11	7	45	26	47

Income Statement Analysis (Million $)										
Revenue	4,473	3,763	3,061	2,695	2,638	2,404	2,251	1,918	1,538	1,061
Operating Income	675	488	296	260	229	260	274	204	204	101
Depreciation	79.1	77.7	71.0	69.9	73.2	77.6	65.3	73.9	57.0	39.6
Interest Expense	51.3	60.1	65.7	74.1	81.0	84.2	92.9	118	70.3	15.5
Pretax Income	590	360	187	83.3	59.6	73.8	92.1	25.6	23.2	18.2
Effective Tax Rate	25.0%	29.0%	39.1%	44.5%	66.2%	28.4%	34.4%	36.2%	34.0%	33.3%
Net Income	442	256	114	46.2	20.2	52.9	60.4	16.4	15.3	12.2
S&P Core Earnings	427	252	122	48.9	22.5	52.4	42.7	-3.30	NA	NA

Balance Sheet & Other Financial Data (Million $)										
Cash	472	371	67.0	92.9	63.8	53.5	49.3	21.5	42.3	30.5
Current Assets	2,332	1,897	1,303	1,071	1,050	1,091	1,031	898	898	454
Total Assets	4,024	3,520	2,869	2,576	2,634	2,801	2,608	2,052	2,110	838
Current Liabilities	1,608	1,250	884	695	708	633	492	417	434	196
Long Term Debt	546	550	557	653	658	880	1,056	996	1,111	198
Common Equity	1,368	1,293	1,021	832	870	821	756	411	305	308
Total Capital	1,924	1,856	1,577	1,485	1,528	1,701	1,811	1,407	1,416	506
Capital Expenditures	127	89.0	73.5	49.3	45.2	28.8	30.9	35.2	27.7	40.5
Cash Flow	522	333	185	116	93.3	130	126	90.2	72.3	51.8
Current Ratio	1.5	1.5	1.5	1.5	1.5	1.7	2.1	2.2	2.1	2.3
% Long Term Debt of Capitalization	28.3	29.6	35.3	44.0	43.0	51.7	58.3	70.8	78.5	39.1
% Net Income of Revenue	9.9	6.8	3.7	1.7	0.8	2.2	2.7	0.9	1.0	1.1
% Return on Assets	11.7	8.0	4.2	1.8	0.8	2.0	2.6	0.8	1.0	1.4
% Return on Equity	33.3	22.1	12.2	5.4	2.4	6.9	10.4	4.6	5.0	3.7

Data as orig reptd.; bef. results of disc opers/spec. items. Per share data adj. for stk. divs.; EPS diluted. E-Estimated. NA-Not Available. NM-Not Meaningful. NR-Not Ranked. UR-Under Review.

Office: 5215 N O Connor Blvd Ste 2300, Irving, TX, USA 75039-3726.
Telephone: 972-443-6500.
Website: http://www.flowserve.com
Chrmn: J.O. Rollans

Pres & CEO: M.A. Blinn
Vice Chrmn: L.M. Kling
SVP, Secy & General Counsel: R.F. Shuff
SVP & CIO: A.J. Beall

Investor Contact: P. Fehlman (972-443-6517)
Board Members: M. A. Blinn, G. J. Delly, R. L. Fix, J. R. Friedery, J. E. Harlan, M. F. Johnston, L. M. Kling, R. J. Mills, C. M. Rampacek, J. O. Rollans, W. C. Rusnack, K. E. Sheehan

Founded: 1912
Domicile: New York
Employees: 15,000

Fluor Corp.

STANDARD &POOR'S

S&P Recommendation	BUY ★★★★☆	Price $43.07 (as of Nov 27, 2009)	12-Mo. Target Price $55.00	Investment Style Large-Cap Blend

GICS Sector Industrials
Sub-Industry Construction & Engineering

Summary Fluor is one of the world's largest engineering, procurement, and construction companies.

Key Stock Statistics (Source S&P, Vickers, company reports)

52-Wk Range	$58.62– 30.21	S&P Oper. EPS 2009**E**	3.90	Market Capitalization(B)	$7.709	Beta	1.42
Trailing 12-Month EPS	$4.01	S&P Oper. EPS 2010**E**	3.50	Yield (%)	1.16	S&P 3-Yr. Proj. EPS CAGR(%)	16
Trailing 12-Month P/E	10.7	P/E on S&P Oper. EPS 2009**E**	11.0	Dividend Rate/Share	$0.50	S&P Credit Rating	A-
$10K Invested 5 Yrs Ago	$17,169	Common Shares Outstg. (M)	179.0	Institutional Ownership (%)	86		

Price Performance

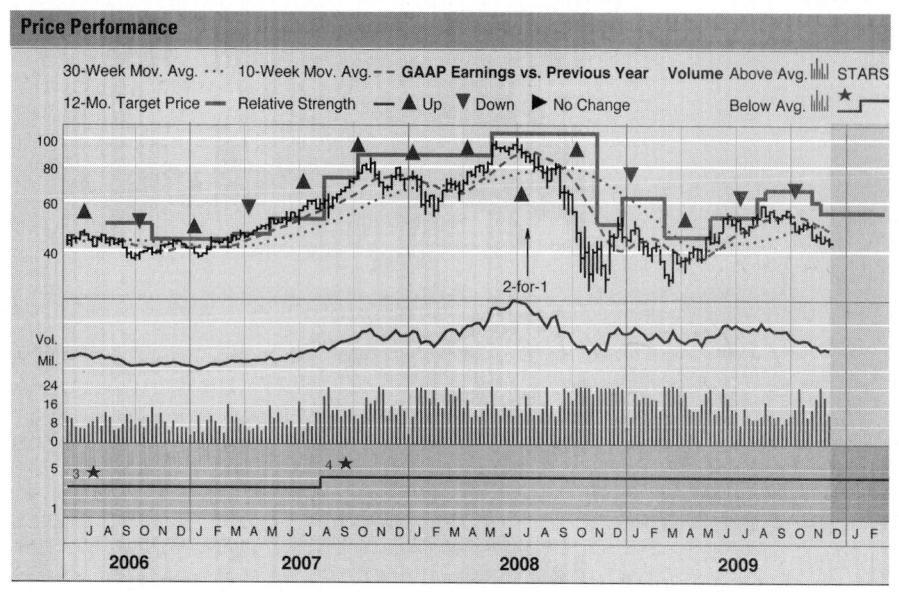

30-Week Mov. Avg. · · · 10-Week Mov. Avg. - - GAAP Earnings vs. Previous Year Volume Above Avg. STARS
12-Mo. Target Price — Relative Strength — ▲ Up ▼ Down ► No Change Below Avg.

2-for-1

Options: ASE, CBOE, P, Ph

Analysis prepared by **Stewart Scharf** on November 12, 2009, when the stock traded at **$ 44.11**.

Highlights

▶ We project a modest decline in revenues for 2009, with new orders picking up sequentially during 2010 as global markets gradually recover. We still see delays and cancellations, and timing issues affecting quarterly results. However, long-term prospects are favorable, in our view, for upstream oil & gas projects abroad, and government and mining projects. We expect power awards to remain weak due to an uncertain U.S. energy policy, while global services spending remains challenging near term.

▶ We see larger, higher-margin new awards during 2010, especially in the upstream and petrochemicals oil & gas markets, and mining sector. We expect operating margins to expand somewhat, from our 5.5% projection for 2009, based a better mix, and lower overhead and compensation expenses, despite some oil & gas projects transitioning to the lower-margin construction phase. We believe the company will still prioritize profit growth and return on assets (ROA) ahead of expected margin improvement.

▶ We forecast an effective tax rate of near 37% through 2010, and EPS of $3.90, falling to $3.50 in 2010.

Investment Rationale/Risk

▶ Our buy recommendation is based on our valuation models, along with our view of FLR's favorable long-term prospects, especially overseas, and strong balance sheet. Despite customer cautiousness, we see stronger bookings in 2010 as customers are likely to resume their long-term capital investing plans.

▶ Risks to our recommendation and target price include project delays and cancellations based on challenging market conditions, labor shortages, negative foreign currency effect, credit market issues, sharply lower oil prices, and timing issues for new awards.

▶ Our 12-month target price of $55 is derived from a blend of our relative and discounted cash flow (DCF) metrics. Based on various relative metrics, we use a modest premium-to-peers P/E of 14.3X our 2010 EPS estimate, reflecting FLR's strong global prospect list and diversified business model, resulting in a value of $50. Our DCF model, which assumes a 3.5% terminal growth rate and an 8.3% weighted average cost of capital, suggests the stock's intrinsic value is $60.

Qualitative Risk Assessment

LOW	MEDIUM	HIGH

Our risk assessment reflects tight credit markets, and project delays and cancellations, along with geopolitical issues as more projects are in unstable regions of the world. This is offset by our view of FLR's strong balance sheet, modest debt levels, and diverse project mix and customer base.

Quantitative Evaluations

S&P Quality Ranking   B+

D	C	B-	B	B+	A-	A	A+

Relative Strength Rank   WEAK

18

LOWEST = 1   HIGHEST = 99

Revenue/Earnings Data

Revenue (Million $)

	1Q	2Q	3Q	4Q	Year
2009	5,798	4,293	5,420	--	--
2008	4,807	5,574	5,674	6,072	22,326
2007	3,642	4,222	4,155	4,712	16,691
2006	3,625	3,456	3,364	3,633	14,079
2005	2,860	2,920	3,419	3,963	13,161
2004	2,063	2,214	2,363	2,740	9,380

Earnings Per Share ($)

	1Q	2Q	3Q	4Q	Year
2009	1.13	0.93	0.89	E0.96	E3.90
2008	0.75	1.13	1.01	1.04	3.93
2007	0.47	0.52	0.51	1.42	2.93
2006	0.50	0.37	0.16	0.45	1.48
2005	0.28	-0.10	0.76	0.37	1.31
2004	0.29	0.27	0.29	0.29	1.13

Fiscal year ended Dec. 31. Next earnings report expected: Late February. EPS Estimates based on S&P Operating Earnings; historical GAAP earnings are as reported.

Dividend Data (Dates: mm/dd Payment Date: mm/dd/yy)

Amount ($)	Date Decl.	Ex-Div. Date	Stk. of Record	Payment Date
0.125	02/05	03/04	03/06	04/02/09
0.125	05/06	06/03	06/05	07/02/09
0.125	07/31	09/02	09/04	10/02/09
0.125	10/30	12/02	12/04	01/05/10

Dividends have been paid since 1974. Source: Company reports.

Please read the Required Disclosures and Analyst Certification on the last page of this report.

The **McGraw·Hill** Companies

Fluor Corp.

Business Summary November 12, 2009

CORPORATE OVERVIEW. Fluor Corp. is one of the world's largest engineering, procurement, construction and maintenance companies. It has five principal operating segments. The Oil and Gas segment provides services to oil, gas, refining, chemical, polymer and petrochemical customers. Industrial and Infrastructure provides EPC services to businesses, including industrial, commercial, telecommunications, mining and technology. Global Services provides operations and maintenance support, and equipment and outsourcing, through TRS Staffing Solutions. Government Services provides support services to the federal government and other government parties.

Contributions to revenues and operating profits in 2008 were as follows: Oil and Gas, 58% of revenues and operating profits of $724 million; Industrial and Infrastructure, 15% and $208 million; Power, 9% and $75 million; Global Services, 12% and $229 million; and Government, 6% and $52 million.

Total backlog of $28 billion at September 30, 2009, fell 23% from a year earlier, but rose 12% sequentially. During the first nine months of 2009, FLR removed $5.3 billion from its backlog, including $2.1 billion in the first quarter from a canceled Kuwait refinery project. The backlog at the end of the 2009 third quarter was divided by segment as follows: Oil and Gas $13.1 billion, down 43% from a year ago; Industrial and Infrastructure $9.7 billion, up 14%; Power $1.5 billion, down 6%; Global Services $2.4 billion, down 11%; and Government

Services $1.3 billion, up 44%. Backlog by geographic region was: U.S. 39%; the Americas 23%; Europe, Africa and the Middle East 26%; and Asia-Pacific (including Australia) 12%. Backlog includes a long cycle of larger projects that tend to take three to five years to complete, versus earlier smaller projects which had an 18-to-36 month cycle. As of September 30, 2009, FLR's percentage of fixed price work in its backlog had decreased to about 21% (near 30% a year ago), with most in infrastructure and power, while oil & gas is primarily cost reimbursable. The company expects an increase in fixed-price projects, although with mainly front-end work and negotiated lump sum contracts, the added risk should be minimal.

FLR received new awards of $15 billion in the first nine months of 2009, down 28% from a year. New awards by segment were: Oil and Gas, $6.1 billion, down 51% from a year ago (accounting for 40% of total awards); Industrial and Infrastructure, $5.3 billion, up 6% (35%); Government, $2 billion, up 79% (13%); Global Services, $992 million, down 42% (7%); and Power, $767 million, up 6% (5%).

Company Financials Fiscal Year Ended Dec. 31

Per Share Data ($)	2008	2007	2006	2005	2004	2003	2002	2001	2000	1999
Tangible Book Value	14.23	12.39	9.39	8.92	7.45	6.26	5.38	4.79	9.98	9.64
Cash Flow	4.82	3.74	2.18	1.91	1.68	1.61	1.55	1.26	2.69	2.78
Earnings	3.93	2.93	1.48	1.31	1.13	1.12	1.07	0.81	0.66	0.69
S&P Core Earnings	3.49	2.93	1.50	1.31	1.04	1.17	0.90	0.57	NA	NA
Dividends	0.50	0.20	0.10	0.32	0.32	0.32	0.32	0.32	0.50	0.40
Payout Ratio	13%	7%	7%	24%	28%	29%	30%	40%	76%	58%
Prices:High	101.37	86.08	51.93	39.55	27.60	20.41	22.48	31.60	24.25	23.25
Prices:Low	28.60	37.61	36.76	25.06	18.05	13.33	10.03	15.60	11.97	13.09
P/E Ratio:High	26	29	35	30	25	18	21	39	37	34
P/E Ratio:Low	7	13	25	19	16	12	9	19	18	19
Income Statement Analysis (Million $)										
Revenue	22,326	16,691	14,079	13,161	9,380	8,806	9,959	8,972	9,970	12,417
Operating Income	1,160	755	504	396	370	344	332	258	451	654
Depreciation	163	147	126	104	91.9	79.7	78.0	71.9	312	318
Interest Expense	11.9	24.0	23.0	16.3	15.4	10.1	8.93	25.0	26.3	50.9
Pretax Income	1,114	649	382	300	281	268	261	185	142	186
Effective Tax Rate	35.4%	17.8%	31.0%	24.1%	33.6%	33.0%	34.8%	31.1%	29.8%	44.0%
Net Income	720	533	263	227	187	180	170	128	99.8	104
S&P Core Earnings	639	533	267	226	171	188	143	90.2	NA	NA
Balance Sheet & Other Financial Data (Million $)										
Cash	2,108	1,714	976	789	605	497	753	573	69.4	210
Current Assets	4,669	4,060	3,324	3,108	2,723	2,214	1,941	1,851	1,448	1,910
Total Assets	6,424	5,796	4,875	4,574	3,970	3,449	3,142	3,091	3,653	4,886
Current Liabilities	3,163	2,860	2,406	2,339	1,764	1,829	1,756	1,811	1,620	2,204
Long Term Debt	17.7	325	187	92.0	348	44.7	17.6	17.6	17.6	318
Common Equity	2,671	2,274	1,730	1,631	1,336	1,082	884	789	1,609	1,581
Total Capital	2,689	2,292	1,918	1,723	1,683	1,126	901	807	1,627	2,061
Capital Expenditures	300	284	274	213	104	79.2	63.0	148	284	504
Cash Flow	884	680	390	331	279	259	248	200	412	422
Current Ratio	1.5	1.4	1.4	1.3	1.5	1.2	1.1	1.0	0.9	0.9
% Long Term Debt of Capitalization	0.7	0.8	9.8	5.3	20.7	4.0	2.0	2.2	1.1	15.4
% Net Income of Revenue	3.2	3.2	1.9	1.7	2.0	2.0	1.7	1.4	1.0	0.8
% Return on Assets	11.8	10.0	5.6	5.3	5.0	5.4	5.4	4.4	2.3	2.1
% Return on Equity	29.1	26.6	15.7	15.3	15.4	18.3	20.3	18.0	6.3	6.7

Data as orig reptd.; bef. results of disc opers/spec. items. Per share data adj. for stk. divs.; EPS diluted. E-Estimated. NA-Not Available. NM-Not Meaningful. NR-Not Ranked. UR-Under Review.

Office: 6700 Las Colinas Blvd, Irving, TX 75039-2902.
Telephone: 469-398-7000.
Email: investor@fluor.com
Website: http://www.fluor.com

Chrmn & CEO: A.L. Boeckmann
COO: D.T. Seaton
EVP & CIO: R.F. Barnard
SVP, CFO & Chief Acctg Officer: D.M. Steuert

Chief Admin Officer: G.C. Gilkey
Investor Contact: K. Lockwood (469-398-7220)
Board Members: I. Adesida, P. K. Barker, A. L. Boeckmann, P. J. Fluor, J. T. Hackett, K. Kresa, D. R. O'Hare, J. W. Prueher, N. H. Sultan, P. S. Watson, S. H. Woolsey

Founded: 1924
Domicile: Delaware
Employees: 42,119

STANDARD &POOR'S

FMC Corp.

S&P Recommendation	HOLD ★★★★★	Price	12-Mo. Target Price	Investment Style
		$55.32 (as of Nov 27, 2009)	$55.00	Large-Cap Value

GICS Sector Materials
Sub-Industry Diversified Chemicals

Summary This company is a diversified producer of industrial, specialty and agricultural chemicals.

Key Stock Statistics (Source S&P, Vickers, company reports)

52-Wk Range	$58.13–34.00	S&P Oper. EPS 2009**E**	4.10	Market Capitalization(B)	$4.000	Beta	1.04
Trailing 12-Month EPS	$2.90	S&P Oper. EPS 2010**E**	4.55	Yield (%)	0.90	S&P 3-Yr. Proj. EPS CAGR(%)	10
Trailing 12-Month P/E	19.1	P/E on S&P Oper. EPS 2009**E**	13.5	Dividend Rate/Share	$0.50	S&P Credit Rating	BBB+
$10K Invested 5 Yrs Ago	$23,351	Common Shares Outstg. (M)	72.3	Institutional Ownership (%)	89		

Price Performance

30-Week Mov. Avg. ···· 10-Week Mov. Avg. – – GAAP Earnings vs. Previous Year   Volume Above Avg. STARS
12-Mo. Target Price — Relative Strength — ▲ Up ▼ Down ► No Change   Below Avg.

Options: ASE, CBOE, P, Ph

Analysis prepared by **Richard O'Reilly, CFA** on November 02, 2009, when the stock traded at **$ 50.42**.

Highlights

► We expect operating EPS of $4.55 in 2010, versus a projected $4.10 for 2009. We believe industrial chemicals profits in 2009 will decline about 55%, including a large drop in the first half, as reduced demand in glass, paper and pulp and detergent markets and higher raw material costs outweigh higher prices for soda ash and peroxygens. We see some recovery in industrial chemicals profits in 2010 assuming price gains in soda ash and the European phosphate business.

► Specialty chemicals sales and profits should again increase modestly in 2010, on expected sales growth in biopolymers and recovery in lithium volumes. We look for continued sales and profit growth in the pesticide unit following projected gains in 2009, reflecting increases in most regions on new product introductions and productivity improvement.

► We see interest expense in 2010 increasing from $26 million seen for 2009. Pension expense should also be greater, but we expect the effective tax rate to be similar to the 32% forecast for 2009. The repurchase of stock in 2009 should have a favorable EPS impact.

Investment Rationale/Risk

► Our Hold opinion is based on valuation. We project a rebound in EPS in 2010 on further profit gains in pesticides and specialty chemicals. Industrial chemicals should show improved profitability, assuming better demand and higher soda ash and phosphate prices. We believe FMC's balance sheet will allow it to make bolt-on acquisitions in the specialty businesses while continuing stock buybacks.

► Risks to our recommendation and target price include higher-than-expected raw material and energy costs, unplanned production outages and interruptions, adverse weather conditions, adverse economic conditions in Brazil (15% of annual sales), and the company's inability to maintain or increase industrial chemicals selling prices and receive approvals for new specialty chemical and pesticide products.

► Based on our 2010 estimates, the stock trades at P/E and cash flow multiples similar to those of comparable-sized chemical companies. Our 12-month target price of $55 is based on a P/E multiple of 12X our 2010 EPS estimate, a typical historical discount to the company's peer group.

Qualitative Risk Assessment

LOW	MEDIUM	HIGH

Our risk assessment reflects the company's diversified product mix and leading domestic market positions in many product lines, offset by the cyclical nature of the industrial chemicals business and geographic exposure to the Brazilian farm economy.

Quantitative Evaluations

S&P Quality Ranking B-

D	C	B-	B	B+	A-	A	A+

Relative Strength Rank MODERATE

67

LOWEST = 1   HIGHEST = 99

Revenue/Earnings Data

Revenue (Million $)

	1Q	2Q	3Q	4Q	Year
2009	690.5	700.3	713.3	--	--
2008	750.2	806.6	820.8	737.7	3,115
2007	674.1	657.9	626.6	674.3	2,633
2006	594.1	592.3	572.2	588.4	2,347
2005	552.4	565.5	510.0	522.2	2,150
2004	505.7	534.3	497.5	513.7	2,051

Earnings Per Share ($)

2009	1.00	1.01	0.47	E0.88	E4.10
2008	1.31	1.20	1.13	0.69	4.35
2007	0.71	0.19	0.54	0.60	2.02
2006	0.48	0.44	0.49	0.43	1.84
2005	0.46	0.43	-0.04	0.57	1.42
2004	0.10	0.55	0.40	1.27	2.35

Fiscal year ended Dec. 31. Next earnings report expected: Early February. EPS Estimates based on S&P Operating Earnings; historical GAAP earnings are as reported.

Dividend Data (Dates: mm/dd Payment Date: mm/dd/yy)

Amount ($)	Date Decl.	Ex-Div. Date	Stk. of Record	Payment Date
0.125	12/05	12/29	12/31	01/15/09
0.125	02/20	03/27	03/31	04/16/09
0.125	04/28	06/26	06/30	07/16/09
0.125	07/24	09/28	09/30	10/15/09

Dividends have been paid since 2006. Source: Company reports.

Please read the Required Disclosures and Analyst Certification on the last page of this report.

The McGraw-Hill Companies

FMC Corp.

STANDARD
&POOR'S

Business Summary November 02, 2009

CORPORATE OVERVIEW. FMC Corp. concentrates solely on its chemicals businesses, consisting of pesticides, and industrial and specialty chemicals. International operations provided 68% of 2008 sales; Brazil alone accounted for 15% of sales.

Industrial chemicals accounted for 42% of sales and 34% of profits in 2008. FMC is North America's largest producer of natural soda ash (about 50% of annual sales) and hydrogen peroxide (15%), and is a major European producer of phosphates, peroxygens, zeolites, silicates, and sulfur derivatives through Foret, S.A. (35%). The segment had posted three years of substantial earnings growth after its cyclical low in 2003, reflecting significantly higher selling prices and increased earnings at the former Astaris joint venture, before easing in 2007 as higher raw material costs more than offset increased sales. Profits more than doubled in 2008 on higher selling prices and improved power markets in Europe.

In November 2005, FMC and its partner sold their equally owned Astaris phosphorus chemicals joint venture for $225 million. In 2004, Astaris completed a restructuring program, including the closure of four facilities, achieving annual cost savings of $40 million.

Agricultural products (34%, 41%) consist of insecticides, herbicides, and fungicides for crop protection and pest control. The segment in 2008 achieved its sixth consecutive year of record sales and profits. Insecticides (including Founce, Furadan and Capture) account for about 64% of sales; almost 80% of segment sales are derived outside the U.S. Herbicide sales (42%) have grown significantly over the past several years. FMC's herbicides primarily target niche uses and include two product lines (sulfentrazone and carfentrazone) introduced in the late 1990s.

In the specialty chemicals segment (24%, 25%), FMC BioPolymer (about 70% of segment sales) is the world's leading producer of carrageenan, alginate, and microcrystalline cellulose (over 50% share), used for pharmaceutical ingredients, food stabilizers and thickeners, and personal care and household products. FMC believes that carrageenan and microcrystalline cellulose are growing faster than the overall food ingredients market. The company is also the leading maker of lithium compounds (30% of segment sales), with only two other global integrated lithium producers. We expect high single digit percentage growth for lithium use in pharmaceuticals, and low double digit growth in energy storage.

Company Financials Fiscal Year Ended Dec. 31

Per Share Data ($)	2008	2007	2006	2005	2004	2003	2002	2001	2000	1999
Tangible Book Value	9.19	15.24	11.17	10.53	9.55	6.12	3.94	1.64	4.99	3.97
Cash Flow	5.75	3.49	3.50	3.21	4.19	2.33	2.68	-2.79	5.79	6.20
Earnings	4.35	2.02	1.84	1.42	2.35	0.56	1.01	-4.93	2.81	3.29
S&P Core Earnings	3.42	1.79	1.99	0.97	2.22	0.30	0.40	-4.94	NA	NA
Dividends	0.48	0.41	0.36	Nil	Nil	Nil	Nil	Nil	Nil	Nil
Payout Ratio	11%	20%	20%	Nil	Nil	Nil	Nil	Nil	Nil	Nil
Prices:High	80.23	59.00	38.99	31.94	25.25	17.43	21.15	42.00	38.59	37.63
Prices:Low	28.53	35.63	25.87	21.63	16.48	7.11	11.45	22.83	23.03	19.63
P/E Ratio:High	18	29	21	23	11	31	21	NM	14	11
P/E Ratio:Low	7	18	14	15	7	13	11	NM	8	6

Income Statement Analysis (Million $)										
Revenue	3,115	2,633	2,347	2,150	2,051	1,921	1,853	1,943	3,926	4,111
Operating Income	656	507	461	416	363	321	306	323	565	557
Depreciation	106	114	132	136	134	125	119	132	189	181
Interest Expense	38.6	41.4	42.0	62.3	80.9	96.1	73.0	63.0	99.7	117
Pretax Income	472	195	153	201	135	40.9	89.9	-471	227	281
Effective Tax Rate	26.6%	14.9%	NM	41.0%	NM	NM	19.4%	NM	19.9%	21.0%
Net Income	330	157	145	111	176	39.8	69.1	-306	177	216
S&P Core Earnings	259	139	157	75.9	166	21.4	27.4	-307	NA	NA

Balance Sheet & Other Financial Data (Million $)										
Cash	52.4	75.5	166	206	212	57.0	364	23.4	25.1	64.0
Current Assets	1,433	1,194	1,068	1,067	1,073	1,010	1,176	820	1,330	1,417
Total Assets	2,976	2,733	2,735	2,740	2,978	2,829	2,872	2,477	3,746	3,996
Current Liabilities	759	751	702	659	820	728	875	1,079	1,400	1,576
Long Term Debt	593	420	524	640	822	1,033	1,036	652	872	945
Common Equity	903	1,064	1,056	1,026	942	654	406	219	800	744
Total Capital	1,561	1,542	1,638	1,717	1,816	1,736	1,487	915	1,720	1,735
Capital Expenditures	175	115	116	93.5	85.4	87.0	83.9	146	240	236
Cash Flow	436	271	277	247	310	164	188	-175	366	397
Current Ratio	1.9	1.6	1.5	1.6	1.3	1.4	1.3	0.8	0.9	0.9
% Long Term Debt of Capitalization	38.0	27.2	32.0	37.3	45.3	59.5	69.7	71.2	50.7	54.5
% Net Income of Revenue	10.6	6.0	6.2	5.2	8.6	2.1	3.7	NM	4.5	5.3
% Return on Assets	11.5	5.7	5.3	3.9	6.0	1.4	2.6	NM	4.6	5.3
% Return on Equity	33.5	15.0	13.9	11.3	22.0	7.0	22.1	NM	23.0	29.3

Data as orig reptd.; bef. results of disc opers/spec. items. Per share data adj. for stk. divs.; EPS diluted. E-Estimated. NA-Not Available. NM-Not Meaningful. NR-Not Ranked. UR-Under Review.

Office: 1735 Market St, Philadelphia, PA 19103-7597.
Telephone: 215-299-6000.
Email: investor-info@fmc.com
Website: http://www.fmc.com

Chrmn, Pres & CEO: W.G. Walter
SVP & CFO: W.K. Foster
Chief Acctg Officer & Cntlr: G.R. Wood
Treas: T.C. Deas, Jr.

Secy & General Counsel: A.E. Utecht
Investor Contact: B. Arndt (215-299-6266)
Board Members: P. A. Buffler, G. P. D'Aloia, C. S. Greer, D. Kempthorne, E. J. Mooney, P. J. Norris, R. C. Pallash, E. J. Sosa, V. R. Volpe, Jr., W. G. Walter

Founded: 1884
Domicile: Delaware
Employees: 5,000

The McGraw-Hill Companies

FMC Technologies Inc

STANDARD &POOR'S

S&P Recommendation	HOLD ★★★☆☆	Price	12-Mo. Target Price	Investment Style
		$53.83 (as of Nov 27, 2009)	$60.00	Large-Cap Growth

GICS Sector Energy
Sub-Industry Oil & Gas Equipment & Services

Summary This company is a leading provider of oilfield services capital equipment, particularly for subsea equipment used in deepwater energy exploration and development.

Key Stock Statistics (Source S&P, Vickers, company reports)

52-Wk Range	$59.48– 20.88	S&P Oper. EPS 2009E	2.86	Market Capitalization(B)	$6.577	Beta	1.19
Trailing 12-Month EPS	$2.85	S&P Oper. EPS 2010E	2.64	Yield (%)	Nil	S&P 3-Yr. Proj. EPS CAGR(%)	11
Trailing 12-Month P/E	18.9	P/E on S&P Oper. EPS 2009E	18.8	Dividend Rate/Share	Nil	S&P Credit Rating	NA
$10K Invested 5 Yrs Ago	NA	Common Shares Outstg. (M)	122.2	Institutional Ownership (%)	98		

Price Performance

30-Week Mov. Avg. · · · 10-Week Mov. Avg. - - **GAAP Earnings vs. Previous Year** Volume Above Avg. ▮▮▮ STARS
12-Mo. Target Price — Relative Strength — ▲ Up ▼ Down ► No Change   Below Avg. ▮▮▮ ★

Options: ASE, P, Ph

Analysis prepared by **Stewart Glickman, CFA** on November 20, 2009, when the stock traded at **$ 55.59**.

Highlights

► Energy Production Systems backlog at September 2009 was $3.0 billion, up from $2.8 billion at the end of June, with subsea backlog comprising the vast majority ($2.4 billion). While new order flow into backlog may be choppy in 2009, we think the recent recovery in crude oil prices to above $70 per barrel raises the likelihood of improved order flow in 2010. While the book-to-bill ratio at Energy Production Systems fell to 0.41 in the fourth quarter, it had improved to the 0.78 range in the first nine months of 2009, and we expect further gains through 2010. Continued thawing in credit markets should also help improve order flows.

► FTI booked 17 subsea trees in the third quarter, a solid uptick over the seven trees booked in the June quarter. We remain of the opinion that major projects, such as in Brazil, will ultimately be funded, and we view FTI as among the best positioned in the industry to capitalize on these opportunities.

► Excluding discontinued operations, we see a revenue decline of 3.0% in 2009, followed by a 2.3% recovery in 2010. We see EPS of $2.86 in 2009 and $2.64 in 2010.

Investment Rationale/Risk

► FTI has had two straight quarters of solid execution, which it attributes in part to leveraging opportunities in the supply chain. With the supply chain likely to tighten in the near-term, we do not expect the recent strength in margins to continue, but to narrow modestly in 2010. Near-term, we see some downside risk to its North American surface control business, given chronically weak natural gas prices, but this area accounts for only a small portion of the revenue base. In FTI's more significant subsea space, we note that the company has a strong installed base, and we see it as well positioned to benefit from a secular trend toward deepwater development.

► Risks to our recommendation and target price include reduced subsea activity, lower energy prices, unexpected contract cancellations, and appreciation of the U.S. dollar.

► Our DCF model, assuming free cash flow growth of 16%, terminal growth of 3%, and a WACC of 11%, shows intrinsic value of $65. Applying a premium multiples of 13X to estimated 2010 EBITDA and 15X projected 2010 cash flow, and blending with our DCF model, our 12-month target price is $60.

Qualitative Risk Assessment

LOW	MEDIUM	HIGH

Our risk assessment reflects the company's exposure to crude oil and natural gas prices and capital spending decisions by oil and gas producers, and its commitment to technological innovation in oilfield services. This is offset by improving visibility in the subsea systems business, given FTI's multi-year order backlog.

Quantitative Evaluations

S&P Quality Ranking   NR

D	C	B-	B	B+	A-	A	A+

Relative Strength Rank   MODERATE

54

LOWEST = 1   HIGHEST = 99

Revenue/Earnings Data

Revenue (Million $)

	1Q	2Q	3Q	4Q	Year
2009	1,053	1,104	1,088	--	--
2008	1,294	1,454	1,128	1,205	4,551
2007	979.9	1,153	1,136	1,364	4,615
2006	826.6	949.2	938.3	1,077	3,791
2005	681.6	812.5	776.1	956.5	3,227
2004	562.7	671.5	700.0	833.5	2,768

Earnings Per Share ($)

2009	0.56	0.84	0.73	E0.73	E2.86
2008	0.62	0.81	0.72	0.74	2.72
2007	0.45	0.55	0.60	0.70	2.30
2006	0.34	0.45	0.44	0.47	1.51
2005	Nil	0.21	0.33	0.22	0.75
2004	0.10	0.18	0.16	0.41	0.84

Fiscal year ended Dec. 31. Next earnings report expected: Mid February. EPS Estimates based on S&P Operating Earnings; historical GAAP earnings are as reported.

Dividend Data

No cash dividends have been paid.

Please read the Required Disclosures and Analyst Certification on the last page of this report.

The McGraw-Hill Companies

FMC Technologies Inc

STANDARD
&POOR'S

Business Summary November 20, 2009

CORPORATE OVERVIEW. FMC Technologies is a global provider of high technology solutions for the energy industry. The company designs, manufactures and services advanced systems and products such as subsea production and processing systems, surface wellhead production systems, high pressure fluid control equipment, measurement solutions, and marine loading systems for the oil & gas industry. Operations are separated into two reportable segments: Energy Production Systems, and Energy Processing Systems. Together, these two segments comprise Energy Systems. Approximately 24% of total 2008 revenues were derived in the United States, followed by Norway, with 23%. In July 2008, the company spun off its former FoodTech and Airport Systems segments to John Bean Technologies (JBT $11, Not Rated), rendering the remainder of FTI as a pure-play energy services company that specializes in capital equipment. These former segments are now classified under discontinued operations.

The Energy Production Systems segment (81% of 2008 revenues, and 72% of 2008 segment operating profits) is a global leader in production systems that control the flow of oil and gas from producing wells. Approximately 80% of this segment's revenue base is derived from sales of subsea systems. Subsea systems are placed on the seafloor, and are used to control the flow of oil or gas from the reservoir to a host facility (such as floating production facility, a fixed platform, or an onshore facility). Many systems that the company provides are used in exploration, development and production of crude oil and

natural gas reserves located in deepwater environments, with water depths greater than 1,000 ft. The remaining 20% of this segment's revenue base is derived from surface production systems (or trees). The company is also involved in subsea separation systems, which helps to separate the flow of oil, gas and water more efficiently. Lastly, FTI is advancing the development of subsea processing, an emerging technology in the industry, which would enable separation at the seabed and thus be more cost-efficient for customers. This technology was introduced commercially in the North Sea in 2007.

The Energy Processing Systems segment (19%, 28%) designs, manufactures and supplies technologically advanced high pressure valves and fittings for oilfield services customers. FTI also builds and supplies liquid and gas measurement and transportation equipment and systems to customers involved in upstream, midstream and downstream operations. Products include the WECO/Chiksan line of flowline products, which pump fracturing fluids into a well during the well servicing process, or that pump cement during the completion of new wells. Other product lines include flow meters, fluid loading and transfer systems, material handling systems, and blending and transfer systems.

Company Financials Fiscal Year Ended Dec. 31

Per Share Data ($)	2008	2007	2006	2005	2004	2003	2002	2001	2000	1999
Tangible Book Value	3.78	5.79	5.18	3.82	3.45	1.81	1.40	0.55	0.14	NA
Cash Flow	3.22	2.85	2.01	1.21	1.30	1.01	0.85	0.75	0.91	NA
Earnings	2.72	2.30	1.51	0.75	0.84	0.57	0.48	0.30	0.46	NA
S&P Core Earnings	2.52	2.20	1.49	0.56	0.58	0.51	0.27	0.17	NA	NA
Dividends	Nil	Nil	Nil	Nil	Nil	Nil	Nil	Nil	NA	NA
Payout Ratio	Nil	Nil	Nil	Nil	Nil	Nil	Nil	Nil	NA	NA
Prices:High	83.18	67.78	35.95	22.11	17.25	12.30	11.92	11.24	NA	NA
Prices:Low	20.27	27.57	21.69	14.31	10.99	8.97	7.15	5.50	NA	NA
P/E Ratio:High	31	29	24	29	21	22	25	37	NA	NA
P/E Ratio:Low	7	12	14	19	13	16	15	18	NA	NA

Income Statement Analysis (Million $)	2008	2007	2006	2005	2004	2003	2002	2001	2000	1999
Revenue	4,551	4,615	3,791	3,227	2,768	2,307	2,072	1,928	1,875	1,953
Operating Income	596	524	375	198	174	174	154	149	165	NA
Depreciation	64.9	73.4	70.8	65.9	63.5	57.7	48.6	57.8	59.1	62.3
Interest Expense	1.50	21.5	11.8	9.00	Nil	10.1	14.1	14.1	18.8	3.50
Pretax Income	506	465	299	165	160	108	92.5	63.5	78.4	110
Effective Tax Rate	30.0%	33.7%	28.3%	34.1%	26.4%	28.8%	28.3%	38.0%	22.8%	30.5%
Net Income	353	308	212	106	117	75.6	64.1	39.4	60.5	76.5
S&P Core Earnings	327	294	208	78.3	81.3	68.3	36.1	21.6	NA	NA

Balance Sheet & Other Financial Data (Million $)	2008	2007	2006	2005	2004	2003	2002	2001	2000	1999
Cash	340	130	79.5	153	124	29.0	32.4	28.0	12.0	40.1
Current Assets	2,444	2,104	1,690	1,428	1,217	949	813	755	740	NA
Total Assets	3,586	3,211	2,488	2,096	1,894	1,591	1,363	1,438	1,408	1,473
Current Liabilities	1,963	1,785	1,208	1,058	995	845	728	681	613	NA
Long Term Debt	472	122	213	253	160	201	175	194	250	NA
Common Equity	696	1,022	886	706	669	442	322	418	379	722
Total Capital	1,181	1,151	1,107	965	835	650	502	616	629	722
Capital Expenditures	165	203	139	91.8	50.2	65.2	68.1	67.6	NA	40.9
Cash Flow	418	381	282	172	180	133	113	97.2	120	NA
Current Ratio	1.3	1.2	1.4	1.3	1.2	1.1	1.1	1.1	1.2	1.1
% Long Term Debt of Capitalization	40.0	10.6	19.2	26.2	19.2	30.9	34.9	31.5	39.7	Nil
% Net Income of Revenue	7.8	6.7	5.6	3.3	4.2	3.3	3.1	2.0	3.2	3.9
% Return on Assets	10.4	10.8	9.2	5.3	6.7	5.1	4.6	2.8	NA	NA
% Return on Equity	41.1	32.2	26.7	15.4	20.7	19.8	16.8	7.5	NA	NA

Data as orig reptd.; bef. results of disc opers/spec. items. Per share data adj. for stk. divs.; EPS diluted. E-Estimated. NA-Not Available. NM-Not Meaningful. NR-Not Ranked. UR-Under Review.

Office: 1803 Gears Rd, Houston, TX 77067-4003.
Telephone: 281-591-4000.
Website: http://www.fmctechnologies.com
Chrmn, Pres & CEO: P.D. Kinnear

EVP & CFO: W.H. Schumann, III
Chief Admin Officer: M.T. Seaman
Chief Acctg Officer & Cntlr: J.A. Nutt
Treas: A.T. Melin

Investor Contact: R. Cherry (281-591-4560)
Board Members: M. Bowlin, P. J. Burguieres, C. M.
Devine, T. Enger, C. S. Farley, T. M. Hamilton, P. D.
Kinnear, E. J. Mooney, J. H. Netherland, Jr., R. A.
Pattarozzi, J. M. Ringler

Founded: 2000
Domicile: Delaware
Employees: 9,800

The McGraw·Hill Companies

Ford Motor Co

STANDARD &POOR'S

S&P Recommendation HOLD ★★★☆☆	Price	12-Mo. Target Price	Investment Style
	$8.73 (as of Nov 27, 2009)	$9.00	Large-Cap Value

GICS Sector Consumer Discretionary
Sub-Industry Automobile Manufacturers

Summary The world's third largest producer of cars and trucks, Ford also has automotive financing and insurance operations.

Key Stock Statistics (Source S&P, Vickers, company reports)

52-Wk Range	$9.14–1.50	S&P Oper. EPS 2009E	-0.10	Market Capitalization(B)	$28.252	Beta		2.56
Trailing 12-Month EPS	$-1.43	S&P Oper. EPS 2010E	0.30	Yield (%)	Nil	S&P 3-Yr. Proj. EPS CAGR(%)		NM
Trailing 12-Month P/E	NM	P/E on S&P Oper. EPS 2009E	NM	Dividend Rate/Share	Nil	S&P Credit Rating		B-
$10K Invested 5 Yrs Ago	$6,592	Common Shares Outstg. (M)	3,307.1	Institutional Ownership (%)	47			

Price Performance

30-Week Mov. Avg. ··· 10-Week Mov. Avg. — GAAP Earnings vs. Previous Year   Volume Above Avg. STARS
12-Mo. Target Price — Relative Strength — ▲ Up ▼ Down ▶ No Change   Below Avg. ★

Options: ASE, CBOE, P, Ph

Analysis prepared by **Efraim Levy, CFA** on November 16, 2009, when the stock traded at **$ 8.65**.

Highlights

► We see Ford's total revenues falling 21% in 2009, due to lower demand in the U.S., Europe and elsewhere, excess capacity, and lower pickup truck demand. The financial services segment has historically been an important contributor to sales and earnings, but we think it will be less profitable in 2010. We expect revenues to rise about 6% in 2010, as industry volume recovers, offset by lower financial services revenues.

► In 2010, we see margins benefiting from improved volume, more efficient use of production capacity and past cost-cutting efforts, partly offset by higher raw material costs. In our view, Ford's brand has benefited because it did not tap government financial aid and because of some new products.

► In 2009, we expect losses and sizable cash outlays as Ford restructures amid declining North American and global sales. Despite the recent rejection of further union concessions, we see F's contracts with the UAW enhancing profitability by about $2.5 billion a year starting in 2010. The agreements include unprecedented union givebacks in terms of benefits and work rules, customized to F's needs.

Investment Rationale/Risk

► We think Ford's president and CEO has made a noticeable positive difference in Ford's improvement efforts. However, while we are less confident in his or Ford's ability to consistently bring to market successful vehicles -- one of the company's most important challenges, in our view, we do see progress in bolstering the company's image.

► Risks to our opinion and target price include increased competitive challenges, a greater than expected decline in demand and production, weaker than projected financial services income, a greater drop in cash balances than we expect, and failure of one or more key suppliers. We are also concerned about Ford's corporate governance, with Ford family members having greater voting rights than other shareholders.

► As of September 30, 2009, total stockholders' equity was negative. The stock recently traded at a price-to-sales (P/S) multiple below that of F's largest Japanese peers. In light of our view that the worst may be behind Ford and based on historical and peer comparative P/E multiples, our 12-month target price is $9.00, equal to about 30X projected 2010 EPS.

Qualitative Risk Assessment

LOW	MEDIUM	HIGH

Our risk assessment reflects the highly cyclical nature of Ford's markets as well as our view of the current and long-term challenges it faces, including weak industry demand, intensifying competition, high fixed and legacy costs, and a weak balance sheet.

Quantitative Evaluations

S&P Quality Ranking C

D	C	B-	B	B+	A-	A	A+

Relative Strength Rank STRONG

92

LOWEST = 1   HIGHEST = 99

Revenue/Earnings Data

Revenue (Million $)

	1Q	2Q	3Q	4Q	Year
2009	24,778	27,189	30,892	--	--
2008	43,513	38,600	32,100	29,200	139,300
2007	43,019	44,200	41,100	44,100	172,455
2006	41,055	41,965	37,110	40,318	160,123
2005	45,136	44,548	40,856	46,549	177,089
2004	44,691	42,802	38,996	44,930	171,652

Earnings Per Share ($)

2009	-0.60	0.69	0.29	E0.21	E-0.10
2008	0.05	-3.88	-0.06	-2.46	-6.41
2007	-0.15	0.30	-0.19	-1.33	-1.40
2006	-0.64	-0.14	-2.79	-2.98	-6.72
2005	0.58	0.47	-0.16	0.21	1.14
2004	0.95	0.57	0.25	0.03	1.80

Fiscal year ended Dec. 31. Next earnings report expected: Mid January. EPS Estimates based on S&P Operating Earnings; historical GAAP earnings are as reported.

Dividend Data

No cash dividends have been paid since 2006.

Please read the Required Disclosures and Analyst Certification on the last page of this report.

The McGraw-Hill Companies

Ford Motor Co

Business Summary November 16, 2009

CORPORATE OVERVIEW. Ford is the world's third largest motor vehicle manufacturer. It produces cars and trucks, and many of the vehicles' plastic, glass and electronic components, and replacement parts. It also owns a 14% stake in Mazda Motor Corp. Financial services include Ford Motor Credit (automotive financing and insurance) and American Road Insurance Co.

In recent years, Ford's margins have been pressured by an increase in competition -- primarily from Asian companies -- and a shift away from the more profitable large pickup truck and SUV segments to smaller, less profitable crossover utility vehicles (CUVs). We think this is likely to continue to hurt Ford's market share, at least until the company can introduce more of its own CUVs.

The company's business and product portfolio has changed several times in recent years as Ford sought to optimize its financial health and performance. In December 2005, Ford sold its Hertz Corp. unit for about $15 billion, including around $5.6 billion in cash proceeds. We believe the sale diluted EPS in 2006, as Hertz had contributed $0.16 per share to EPS in 2004 and $0.19 in the first nine months of 2005, according to company estimates. In 1999, the company acquired the car operations of AB Volvo for $6.45 billion. In 2000, Ford ac-

quired Land Rover from BMW Group for $1.9 billion. In June 2008, the company sold Jaguar and Land Rover to Tata Motors for $2.3 billion, but used about $600 million of the proceeds to fund the Jaguar and Land Rover pension plans. In late 2008, the company reduced its stake in Mazda from 33% to 13.8%.

CORPORATE STRATEGY. Challenged by a shrinking U.S. market share and more recently by lower industry volume, the company has announced restructuring plans in recent years in an attempt to lower its costs. However, even as Ford works to reduce its costs, the company now faces expenses stemming from assistance F is giving its former in-house parts manufacturing unit, Visteon Corp. In October 2005, Ford acquired 23 money-losing plants and facilities from Visteon. Ford is working to sell or close most of these facilities. It also provided financial assistance to Visteon. In exchange, it received warrants to purchase Visteon common shares.

Company Financials Fiscal Year Ended Dec. 31

Per Share Data ($)	2008	2007	2006	2005	2004	2003	2002	2001	2000	1999
Tangible Book Value	NM	0.70	NM	3.68	4.60	2.30	NM	NM	6.10	16.60
Cash Flow	2.49	5.26	-6.71	7.62	9.12	8.31	8.45	5.78	13.46	13.36
Earnings	-6.41	-1.40	-6.72	1.14	1.80	0.50	0.15	-3.02	3.59	5.86
S&P Core Earnings	-7.69	-0.94	-5.58	0.64	1.80	1.03	-1.16	-4.56	NA	NA
Dividends	Nil	Nil	0.35	0.40	0.40	0.40	0.40	1.05	2.30	1.88
Payout Ratio	Nil	Nil	NM	35%	22%	80%	NM	NM	64%	32%
Prices:High	8.79	9.70	9.48	14.75	17.34	17.33	18.23	31.42	57.25	67.88
Prices:Low	1.01	6.65	1.06	7.57	12.61	6.58	6.90	14.70	21.69	46.25
P/E Ratio:High	NM	NM	NM	13	10	35	NM	NM	16	12
P/E Ratio:Low	NM	NM	NM	7	7	13	NM	NM	6	8

Income Statement Analysis (Million $)										
Revenue	139,300	172,455	160,123	177,089	171,652	164,196	163,420	162,412	170,064	162,558
Operating Income	16,199	21,189	8,286	21,052	24,945	24,770	25,034	22,941	34,530	29,311
Depreciation	20,329	13,158	16,453	14,042	13,052	14,297	15,177	15,922	14,849	9,254
Interest Expense	9,682	10,927	8,783	7,643	7,071	7,690	8,824	10,848	10,902	9,076
Pretax Income	-14,303	-3,746	-15,051	1,996	4,853	1,370	953	-7,584	8,234	11,026
Effective Tax Rate	NM	NM	NM	NM	19.3%	9.85%	31.7%	NM	32.9%	33.3%
Net Income	-14,580	-2,764	-12,615	2,228	3,634	921	284	-5,453	5,410	7,237
S&P Core Earnings	-17,458	-1,866	-10,472	1,146	3,637	1,905	-2,202	-8,266	NA	NA

Balance Sheet & Other Financial Data (Million $)										
Cash	15,181	50,031	50,366	39,082	33,018	33,642	30,521	15,028	16,490	23,585
Total Assets	218,328	279,264	278,554	269,476	292,654	304,594	289,357	276,543	284,421	276,229
Long Term Debt	153,497	107,478	144,373	94,428	106,540	119,751	125,806	121,430	99,560	78,734
Total Debt	154,688	168,530	172,049	154,332	172,973	179,804	167,892	168,009	166,229	152,738
Common Equity	-17,311	5,628	-3,465	12,957	16,045	11,651	5,590	7,786	18,610	27,537
Capital Expenditures	6,696	6,022	6,848	7,517	6,745	7,749	7,278	7,008	8,348	8,535
Cash Flow	5,648	10,394	-12,615	16,270	16,686	15,218	15,446	10,454	20,244	16,476
% Return on Assets	NM	NM	NM	0.8	1.2	0.3	0.1	NM	2.0	2.8
% Return on Equity	NM	NM	NM	15.4	26.2	10.7	4.0	NM	23.3	28.4
% Long Term Debt of Capitalization	111.7	93.9	83.7	82.9	82.2	87.5	87.8	87.2	78.3	68.6

Data as orig reptd.; bef. results of disc opers/spec. items. Per share data adj. for stk. divs.; EPS diluted. E-Estimated. NA-Not Available. NM-Not Meaningful. NR-Not Ranked. UR-Under Review.

Office: 1 American Rd, Dearborn, MI 48126-2798.
Telephone: 313-322-3000.
Website: http://www.ford.com
Chrmn & COO: W.C. Ford, Jr.

Pres & CEO: A.R. Mulally
EVP & CFO: L.W. Booth
CTO: G. Schmidt
Treas: N.M. Schloss

Investor Contact: L. Heck (313-594-0613)
Board Members: S. G. Butler, K. A. Casiano, A. F. Earley, Jr., E. B. Ford, II, W. C. Ford, Jr., R. A. Gephardt, I. O. Hockaday, Jr., R. A. Manoogian, E. R. Marram, A. R. Mulally, H. A. Neal, G. L. Shaheen, J. L. Thornton

Founded: 1903
Domicile: Delaware
Employees: 213,000

Forest Laboratories Inc.

STANDARD &POOR'S

S&P Recommendation **HOLD** ★★★☆☆	Price $30.56 (as of Nov 27, 2009)	12-Mo. Target Price $31.00	Investment Style Large-Cap Growth

GICS Sector Health Care
Sub-Industry Pharmaceuticals

Summary This company develops and makes branded and generic ethical drug products, sold primarily in the U.S., Puerto Rico, and Western and Eastern Europe.

Key Stock Statistics (Source S&P, Vickers, company reports)

52-Wk Range	$31.14–18.37	S&P Oper. EPS 2010**E**	3.47	Market Capitalization(B)	$9.222	Beta	0.73
Trailing 12-Month EPS	$2.41	S&P Oper. EPS 2011**E**	3.77	Yield (%)	Nil	S&P 3-Yr. Proj. EPS CAGR(%)	7
Trailing 12-Month P/E	12.7	P/E on S&P Oper. EPS 2010**E**	8.8	Dividend Rate/Share	Nil	S&P Credit Rating	NA
$10K Invested 5 Yrs Ago	$7,895	Common Shares Outstg. (M)	301.8	Institutional Ownership (%)	93		

Price Performance

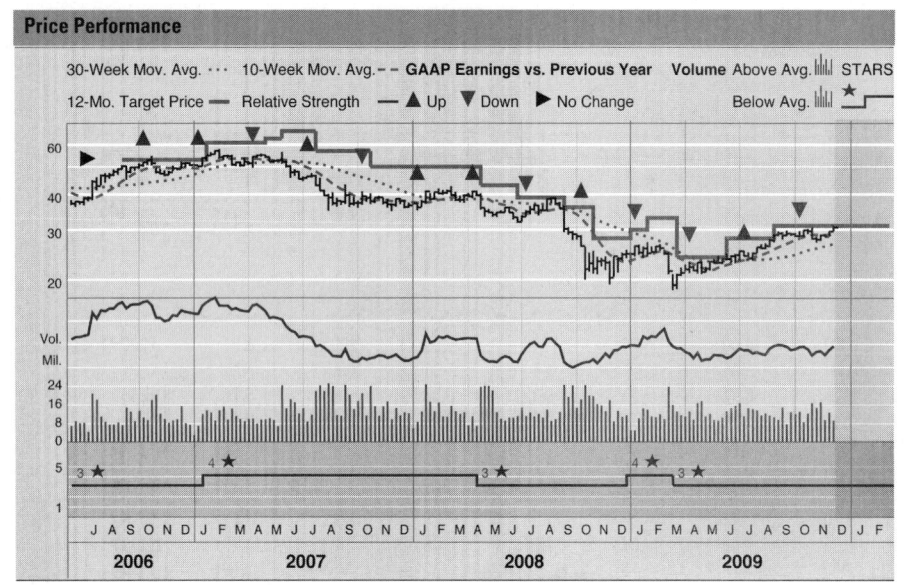

Options: ASE, CBOE, P, Ph

Analysis prepared by **Herman B. Saftlas** on November 23, 2009, when the stock traded at **$ 29.88**.

Highlights

► We expect revenues to rise about 7% in FY 10 (Mar.). Key sales drivers should be Namenda Alzheimer's treatment, helped by greater market penetration and price increases, and Bystolic, a new enhanced beta blocker for heart disease. We see Bystolic sales expanding 2.6X, to $180 million, reflecting greater market penetration and an anticipated new congestive heart failure indication. Recently launched Savella, a new drug for fibromyalgia, should contribute some $45 million to sales. However, we look for lower sales of Lexapro in a highly generics-dominated antidepressant market.

► We forecast that FY 10 gross margins will hold relatively steady with FY 09's 77.5%. We expect SG&A expenses as a percentage of revenues to be modestly below the FY 09 level, but R&D expenditures will likely increase about 15%. We forecast modestly lower income from Benicar, a heart drug that FRX co-markets with Sankyo.

► After a projected effective tax rate of about 21.5%, versus an adjusted 21.1%, we estimate non-GAAP EPS of $3.47 for FY 10, versus $3.46 in FY 09. We forecast EPS of $3.77 for FY 11.

Investment Rationale/Risk

► Forest recently in-licensed U.S. marketing rights from Swiss drugmaker Nycomed for Daxas, a novel treatment for chronic obstructive pulmonary disorder. FRX also formed a partnership with AstraZeneca (AZN 45, Hold) to co-develop and market FRX's new cephalosporin antibiotic outside of the U.S., Canada and Japan. We see potentially significant future revenues from these products, as well as from other pipeline compounds such as linaclotide for irritable bowel syndrome and cariprazine for schizophrenia. We believe these and other new drugs should largely offset anticipated patent expirations on Lexapro in 2012 and Namenda in 2015.

► Risks to our recommendation and target price include greater-than-expected competition in principal markets, as well as possible setbacks in the R&D pipeline.

► Our 12-month target price of $31 applies a discount-to-peers P/E multiple of 8.9X to our FY 10 estimate. This valuation is also supported by our DCF model, which assumes decelerating cash flow growth over the next 10 years, a WACC of 8%, and terminal growth of 1%, and leads to an intrinsic value of $31.

Qualitative Risk Assessment

LOW	MEDIUM	HIGH

Our risk assessment reflects our view of the company's recent legal victory against generic challengers to its important Lexapro patent. We also think its R&D pipeline shows much promise. However, Forest's relatively small size among big pharma competitors and our view of its somewhat limited product line represent negative risk factors.

Quantitative Evaluations

S&P Quality Ranking B+

D	C	B-	B	B+	A-	A	A+

Relative Strength Rank STRONG

82

LOWEST = 1   HIGHEST = 99

Revenue/Earnings Data

Revenue (Million $)

	1Q	2Q	3Q	4Q	Year
2010	1,008	1,013	--	--	--
2009	947.9	972.8	972.4	951.9	3,845
2008	928.3	919.0	998.2	990.9	3,718
2007	816.3	847.0	893.0	885.4	3,442
2006	711.8	736.5	757.8	756.3	2,962
2005	782.4	869.7	818.9	640.6	3,114

Earnings Per Share ($)

2010	0.87	0.62	E0.87	E0.88	E3.47
2009	0.79	0.80	0.62	0.31	2.52
2008	0.83	0.71	0.96	0.55	3.06
2007	0.62	0.75	0.78	-0.75	1.41
2006	0.62	0.59	0.57	0.28	2.08
2005	0.60	0.79	0.70	0.15	2.25

Fiscal year ended Mar. 31. Next earnings report expected: Late January. EPS Estimates based on S&P Operating Earnings; historical GAAP earnings are as reported.

Dividend Data

No cash dividends have been paid.

Forest Laboratories Inc.

STANDARD &POOR'S

Business Summary November 23, 2009

CORPORATE OVERVIEW. Forest Laboratories is a leading producer of niche-oriented branded and generic prescription pharmaceuticals. Most of Forest's products were developed in collaboration with licensing partners. Product sales accounted for 93% of total revenues in FY 09 (Mar.), contract revenues for 5%, and other income for 2%.

Lexapro antidepressant is the FRX's single most important product. A single enanitomer version of Celexa (an older, off-patent FRX antidepressant), Lexapro is an advanced selective serotonin reuptake inhibitor (SSRI) indicated for both depression and generalized anxiety disorder. Lexapro had sales of $2.3 billion in FY 09, unchanged from FY 08. As of April 30, 2009, Lexapro accounted for 16% of the SSRI/SNRI antidepressant market. FRX in-licensed Lexapro from H. Lundbeck A/S, a Danish drug firm. FRX's Lexapro's patent expires in March 2012.

FRX's second most important product is Namenda (licensed from Merz Pharmaceuticals of Germany), a treatment for moderate to severe Alzheimer's disease. Sales of Namenda were $949 million in FY 09, up from $830 million in FY 08. As of the end of April 2009, Namenda accounted for about 34% of the Alzheimer's prescription drug market.

The company's third largest drug is Benicar, an antihypertensive co-promoted with Sankyo. FRX booked income of about $196 million from Benicar in FY 09, down from $212 million in FY 08. In January 2008, FRX launched Bystolic, a novel beta blocker antihypertensive that was in-licensed from Mylan Laboratories. Bystolic had sales of $69 million in FY 09. Other products include Tiazac antihypertensive, Aerobid asthma drug, Campral for alcohol addiction, Combunox for severe pain and other drugs.

COMPETITIVE LANDSCAPE. The U.S. antidepressant drug market totaled about $11 billion in 2008, based on estimates by Standard & Poor's. We expect this market to shrink in terms of dollar sales over the coming years, reflecting the impact of inexpensive generic versions of many patent-expired branded antidepressants. Pfizer's Zoloft antidepressant lost patent protection in 2006, and Wyeth's patent on Effexor antidepressant expired in 2008. Generics now largely comprise previously branded Prozac and Paxil antidepressant markets.

Company Financials Fiscal Year Ended Mar. 31

Per Share Data ($)	2009	2008	2007	2006	2005	2004	2003	2002	2001	2000
Tangible Book Value	11.94	10.19	8.93	7.69	8.21	8.03	5.66	3.75	2.60	1.79
Cash Flow	2.84	3.34	1.55	2.20	2.32	2.01	1.80	1.06	0.71	0.44
Earnings	2.52	3.06	1.41	2.08	2.25	1.95	1.66	0.91	0.59	0.32
S&P Core Earnings	2.53	3.01	1.41	1.97	2.15	1.85	1.58	0.74	0.47	NA
Dividends	Nil	Nil	Nil	Nil	Nil	Nil	Nil	Nil	Nil	Nil
Payout Ratio	Nil	Nil	Nil	Nil	Nil	Nil	Nil	Nil	Nil	Nil
Calendar Year	2008	2007	2006	2005	2004	2003	2002	2001	2000	1999
Prices:High	42.76	57.97	54.70	45.21	78.81	63.23	54.99	41.60	35.33	15.44
Prices:Low	19.23	34.89	36.18	32.46	36.10	41.85	32.12	23.25	14.34	10.31
P/E Ratio:High	17	19	39	22	35	32	33	46	60	48
P/E Ratio:Low	8	11	26	16	16	21	19	26	24	32

Income Statement Analysis (Million $)										
Revenue	3,845	3,718	3,442	2,962	3,114	2,650	2,207	1,567	1,181	882
Operating Income	989	1,179	754	701	1,164	929	833	490	318	181
Depreciation	96.5	86.7	45.4	40.7	25.4	22.2	51.6	54.6	43.3	40.6
Interest Expense	Nil	Nil	Nil	Nil	Nil	Nil	Nil	Nil	Nil	Nil
Pretax Income	971	1,210	709	870	1,185	937	821	470	299	157
Effective Tax Rate	20.9%	20.0%	35.9%	18.5%	29.2%	21.5%	24.2%	28.1%	28.0%	28.4%
Net Income	768	968	454	709	839	736	622	338	215	113
S&P Core Earnings	771	953	454	673	800	697	589	272	170	NA

Balance Sheet & Other Financial Data (Million $)										
Cash	2,581	1,777	1,353	1,323	1,619	2,131	1,556	893	506	355
Current Assets	3,786	2,908	2,423	2,207	2,708	2,916	2,255	1,195	884	645
Total Assets	5,197	4,525	3,653	3,120	3,705	3,863	2,918	1,952	1,447	1,098
Current Liabilities	818	611	628	421	564	564	605	325	224	211
Long Term Debt	Nil	Nil	Nil	Nil	Nil	Nil	Nil	Nil	Nil	Nil
Common Equity	4,115	3,715	3,025	2,698	3,132	3,256	2,352	1,625	1,222	885
Total Capital	4,115	3,716	3,026	2,699	3,141	3,258	2,354	1,627	1,223	887
Capital Expenditures	40.6	34.9	30.0	55.0	89.0	102	79.6	36.4	30.9	35.3
Cash Flow	864	1,055	500	749	864	758	674	393	258	153
Current Ratio	4.6	4.8	3.9	5.2	4.8	4.8	4.0	3.7	4.0	3.1
% Long Term Debt of Capitalization	Nil	Nil	Nil	Nil	Nil	Nil	Nil	Nil	Nil	Nil
% Net Income of Revenue	20.0	26.0	13.5	24.3	26.9	27.8	28.2	21.6	18.2	12.8
% Return on Assets	15.8	23.7	13.4	20.8	22.2	21.7	25.5	19.9	16.7	11.4
% Return on Equity	19.6	28.7	15.9	24.3	26.3	26.2	31.3	23.7	20.4	13.8

Data as orig reptd.; bef. results of disc opers/spec. items. Per share data adj. for stk. divs.; EPS diluted. E-Estimated. NA-Not Available. NM-Not Meaningful. NR-Not Ranked. UR-Under Review.

Office: 909 3rd Ave, New York, NY 10022-4748.
Telephone: 212-421-7850.
Email: investor.relations@frx.com
Website: http://www.frx.com

Chrmn & CEO: H. Solomon
Pres & COO: L.S. Olanoff
SVP & CFO: F.I. Perier, Jr.
Secy: W.J. Candee, III

Investor Contact: F.J. Murdolo (212-224-6714)
Board Members: N. Basgoz, W. J. Candee, III, G. S. Cohan, D. L. Goldwasser, K. E. Goodman, L. S. Olanoff, L. Salans, H. Solomon

Founded: 1956
Domicile: Delaware
Employees: 5,225

The McGraw·Hill Companies

Fortune Brands Inc.

STANDARD &POOR'S

S&P Recommendation **HOLD** ★★★☆☆	Price $38.42 (as of Nov 27, 2009)	12-Mo. Target Price $46.00	Investment Style Large-Cap Blend

GICS Sector Consumer Discretionary
Sub-Industry Housewares & Specialties

Summary This diversified holding company has interests in consumer businesses that include home improvement, spirits, and golf-related products.

Key Stock Statistics (Source S&P, Vickers, company reports)

52-Wk Range	$46.77– 17.67	S&P Oper. EPS 2009**E**	2.35	Market Capitalization(B)	$5.776	Beta	1.63
Trailing 12-Month EPS	$-0.33	S&P Oper. EPS 2010**E**	2.80	Yield (%)	1.98	S&P 3-Yr. Proj. EPS CAGR(%)	5
Trailing 12-Month P/E	NM	P/E on S&P Oper. EPS 2009**E**	16.3	Dividend Rate/Share	$0.76	S&P Credit Rating	BBB-
$10K Invested 5 Yrs Ago	NA	Common Shares Outstg. (M)	150.3	Institutional Ownership (%)	72		

Price Performance

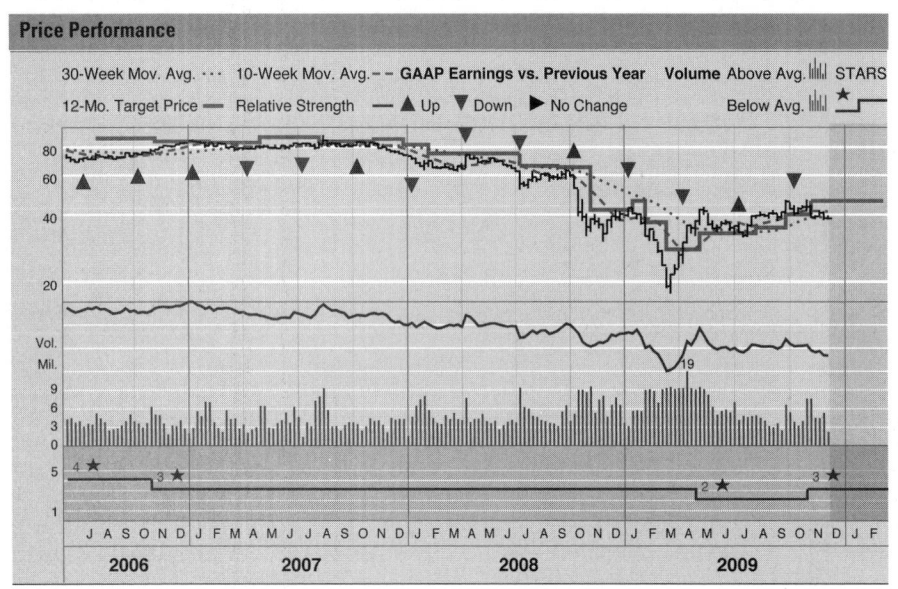

- 30-Week Mov. Avg. · · ·   10-Week Mov. Avg. – –   GAAP Earnings vs. Previous Year   Volume Above Avg. ▮▮▮ STARS
- 12-Mo. Target Price —   Relative Strength —   ▲ Up   ▼ Down   ▶ No Change   Below Avg. ▮▮▮ ★

Options: ASE, CBOE, P, Ph

Analysis prepared by **Loran Braverman, CFA** on October 23, 2009, when the stock traded at **$ 43.83**.

Highlights

► For 2009, we project a total company sales decline of 13%, including a negative foreign currency impact, with all segments down: Spirits -1%; Home & Hardware -21%; and Golf -12%. Weakness in U.S. and international discretionary spending has hurt even the Spirits segment, which we think of as "recession-resistant," not "recession-proof," compared to the other more cyclical segments. We think that, for the most part, FO appears to be holding its market shares overall. For 2010, our sales growth forecast is 3%.

► For 2009, we look for the operating margin, before restructuring charges, to narrow at least 270 basis points (which follows upon 2008's almost 300 bp decline), as worsening operating leverage offsets benefits from restructuring programs and moderating commodity costs. We look for a partial recovery in the operating margin in 2010.

► We expect operating EPS of $2.35 in 2009, down from operating EPS of $3.79 in 2008. Both EPS figures exclude restructuring and one-term charges, and 2008 also excludes asset impairment charges. Our 2010 EPS estimate is $2.80.

Investment Rationale/Risk

► Our hold opinion reflects our view that the stock price accurately reflects FO's near-term outlook. We remain concerned about consumer spending in many international markets and continuing weakness in the home repair and re-modeling business in the U.S. Due to the early termination in August 2008 of FO's Absolut Vodka distribution agreement, FO no longer reports noncash recognition of about $27 million in annual deferred gains. In April 2009, FO announced a reduction in its quarterly dividend to $0.19, from $0.44.

► Risks to our recommendation and target price include a delayed recovery in the economy, higher interest rates, and weak consumer acceptance of new products.

► Our 12-month target price of $46 is based on a blend of our historical and peer analyses. Our historical analysis applies a P/E in line with the 10-year historical average to our 2010 EPS estimate, implying a value of $45. Our sum-of-the-parts peer analysis, weighted by our relative segmental 2010 projected operating income percentages, applies a P/E of 16.8X, implying a value of $47.

Qualitative Risk Assessment

LOW	**MEDIUM**	HIGH

FO's businesses -- spirits, golf and home & hardware (primarily for the remodeling market) -- are usually less cyclical than many other consumer-related businesses. However, the depth of the economic downturn here and in many major international markets has significantly affected FO's results.

Quantitative Evaluations

S&P Quality Ranking   B

D	C	B-	**B**	B+	A-	A	A+

Relative Strength Rank   WEAK

29

LOWEST = 1   HIGHEST = 99

Revenue/Earnings Data

Revenue (Million $)

	1Q	2Q	3Q	4Q	Year
2009	1,338	1,617	1,593	--	--
2008	1,711	1,967	1,922	1,628	7,105
2007	1,909	2,293	2,145	2,215	8,563
2006	2,017	2,257	2,219	2,277	8,769
2005	1,518	1,783	1,802	1,959	7,061
2004	1,708	1,890	1,812	1,912	7,321

Earnings Per Share ($)

2009	0.05	0.66	0.82	E0.58	E2.35
2008	0.69	0.17	2.01	-1.83	1.07
2007	0.78	1.47	1.33	1.22	4.79
2006	1.15	1.63	0.98	1.65	5.42
2005	0.95	1.22	0.52	1.17	3.87
2004	0.92	1.11	1.52	1.68	5.23

Fiscal year ended Dec. 31. Next earnings report expected: Late January. EPS Estimates based on S&P Operating Earnings; historical GAAP earnings are as reported.

Dividend Data (Dates: mm/dd Payment Date: mm/dd/yy)

Amount ($)	Date Decl.	Ex-Div. Date	Stk. of Record	Payment Date
0.440	01/28	02/09	02/11	03/02/09
0.190	04/28	05/11	05/13	06/01/09
0.190	07/28	08/10	08/12	09/01/09
0.190	10/01	11/02	11/04	12/01/09

Dividends have been paid since 1905. Source: Company reports.

Fortune Brands Inc.

STANDARD
&POOR'S

Business Summary October 23, 2009

CORPORATE OVERVIEW. Fortune Brands is a holding company with subsidiaries that produce spirits, home and hardware products, and golf products.

Spirits (formerly Spirits & Wine) (33% of total sales and 57% of operating company contributions before corporate expenses and asset impairment and restructuring charges) are sold through the Beam Global Spirits & Wine subsidiary. Leading brands include Jim Beam bourbon whiskey, DeKuyper cordials, Gilbey's gin, Kamchatka vodka, and Maker's Mark bourbon. Principal markets are the U.S., the U.K., and Australia, with markets outside the U.S. accounting ror about 48% of the segment's sales.

In July 2005, the company acquired various spirits and wine brands from Pernod Ricard, which in turn were acquired by Pernod from Allied Domecq PLC. This transaction more than doubled the sales of FO's Spirits & Wine segment. In 2007, the U.S. wine businesses were sold; we believe they had annualized sales of about $225 million. In August 2008, Pernod Ricard, which purchased the Absolut Vodka brand earlier in 2008, agreed to pay FO $230 million for an early termination of FO's distribution agreement for Absolut and other brands. Also, Pernod Ricard agreed to sell the Cruzan Rum brand, already distributed by FO, to FO for $103 million.

Major units of FO's Home & Hardware products segment (49%, 32%) include MasterBrand Cabinets, Moen, Master Lock, Waterloo and Therma-Tru. While we believe that more of the segment's sales go into the remodeling market than the new housing market, the segment has been affected by the current, deeply depressed housing market.

Golf products (18%, 11%) operations are conducted through Acushnet, a leading producer of golf balls (Titleist, Pinnacle), golf shoes (FootJoy), golf clubs (Cobra, Titleist), and golf gloves. Other products include bags, carts, dress and athletic shoes, socks and accessories.

In 2008, net sales by geographic region for FO, based on country of destination, were the United States, with 70% of net sales, Canada 7%, the United Kingdom 6%, Australia 3%, Spain 2% and all other 12%.

Company Financials Fiscal Year Ended Dec. 31

Per Share Data ($)	2008	2007	2006	2005	2004	2003	2002	2001	2000	1999
Tangible Book Value	NM	NM	NM	NM	NM	NM	NM	2.06	0.89	0.83
Cash Flow	2.74	6.58	7.37	5.35	6.70	5.14	4.57	3.89	0.63	-3.96
Earnings	1.07	4.79	5.42	3.87	5.23	3.86	3.41	2.49	-0.88	-5.35
S&P Core Earnings	1.66	4.62	5.47	3.73	4.58	3.79	3.14	2.38	NA	NA
Dividends	1.72	1.62	1.50	1.38	1.26	1.14	1.02	0.97	0.93	0.89
Payout Ratio	161%	34%	28%	36%	24%	30%	30%	39%	NM	NM
Prices:High	74.44	90.80	85.96	96.18	80.50	71.80	57.86	40.54	33.25	45.88
Prices:Low	30.24	72.13	68.45	73.50	66.10	40.60	36.85	28.38	19.19	29.38
P/E Ratio:High	70	19	16	25	15	19	17	16	NM	NM
P/E Ratio:Low	28	15	13	19	13	11	11	11	NM	NM

Income Statement Analysis (Million $)	2008	2007	2006	2005	2004	2003	2002	2001	2000	1999
Revenue	7,105	8,563	8,769	7,061	7,321	6,215	5,678	5,679	5,845	5,525
Operating Income	1,313	1,712	1,777	1,715	1,374	1,142	1,011	870	938	853
Depreciation	263	280	298	224	221	193	179	219	237	231
Interest Expense	237	294	332	159	87.9	73.8	74.1	96.8	134	107
Pretax Income	188	1,120	1,209	926	1,086	884	756	492	38.9	-721
Effective Tax Rate	47.6%	30.9%	25.7%	35.0%	26.1%	32.7%	28.3%	19.2%	NM	NM
Net Income	165	750	830	582	784	579	526	386	-138	-891
S&P Core Earnings	255	722	837	559	684	567	484	367	NA	NA

Balance Sheet & Other Financial Data (Million $)	2008	2007	2006	2005	2004	2003	2002	2001	2000	1999
Cash	163	204	183	93.6	165	105	15.4	48.7	20.9	72.0
Current Assets	3,468	3,781	3,930	3,193	2,642	2,282	1,903	1,970	2,265	2,313
Total Assets	12,092	13,957	14,668	13,202	7,884	7,445	5,822	5,301	5,764	6,417
Current Liabilities	1,190	2,094	2,515	2,818	2,036	2,134	1,515	1,258	2,040	2,003
Long Term Debt	4,689	4,374	5,035	4,890	1,240	1,243	200	950	1,152	1,205
Common Equity	4,692	5,680	4,722	3,639	3,203	2,712	2,305	2,094	2,127	2,728
Total Capital	9,393	11,138	11,458	9,788	5,207	4,664	2,983	3,444	3,343	3,991
Capital Expenditures	176	267	266	222	242	194	194	207	227	241
Cash Flow	421	1,029	1,128	805	1,005	772	704	605	99.0	-661
Current Ratio	2.9	1.8	1.6	1.1	1.3	1.1	1.3	1.6	1.1	1.2
% Long Term Debt of Capitalization	49.9	38.7	43.9	50.0	23.8	26.6	6.7	27.6	34.5	30.2
% Net Income of Revenue	2.3	8.7	9.5	8.2	10.7	9.3	9.3	6.8	NM	NM
% Return on Assets	1.3	5.2	6.0	5.5	10.2	8.7	9.5	7.0	NM	NM
% Return on Equity	3.2	14.4	19.9	17.2	26.5	23.1	23.9	18.3	NM	NM

Data as orig reptd.; bef. results of disc opers/spec. items. Per share data adj. for stk. divs.; EPS diluted. E-Estimated. NA-Not Available. NM-Not Meaningful. NR-Not Ranked. UR-Under Review.

Office: 520 Lake Cook Rd, Deerfield, IL 60015-5611.
Telephone: 847-484-4400.
Email: investorrelations@fortunebrands.com
Website: http://www.fortunebrands.com

Chrmn, Pres & CEO: B.A. Carbonari
SVP & CFO: C.P. Omtvedt
SVP & Treas: M. Hausberg
SVP, Secy & General Counsel: M.A. Roche

Cntlr: E.A. Wiertel
Board Members: B. A. Carbonari, R. A. Goldstein, A. F. Hackett, P. Leroy, A. D. MacKay, A. M. Tatlock, D. M. Thomas, R. V. Waters, III, N. H. Wesley, P. M. Wilson

Founded: 1904
Domicile: Delaware
Employees: 27,100

The McGraw·Hill Companies

FPL Group Inc.

STANDARD
&POOR'S

S&P Recommendation	STRONG BUY ★★★★★	Price	12-Mo. Target Price	Investment Style
		$51.58 (as of Nov 27, 2009)	$64.00	Large-Cap Blend

GICS Sector Utilities
Sub-Industry Electric Utilities

Summary FPL Group is the holding company for Florida Power & Light and NextEra Energy Resources (formerly FPL Energy).

Key Stock Statistics (Source S&P, Vickers, company reports)

52-Wk Range	$60.61– 41.48	S&P Oper. EPS 2009E	4.15	Market Capitalization(B)	$21.320	Beta	0.64
Trailing 12-Month EPS	$4.13	S&P Oper. EPS 2010E	4.62	Yield (%)	3.66	S&P 3-Yr. Proj. EPS CAGR(%)	10
Trailing 12-Month P/E	12.5	P/E on S&P Oper. EPS 2009E	12.4	Dividend Rate/Share	$1.89	S&P Credit Rating	A
$10K Invested 5 Yrs Ago	$16,662	Common Shares Outstg. (M)	413.3	Institutional Ownership (%)	66		

Price Performance

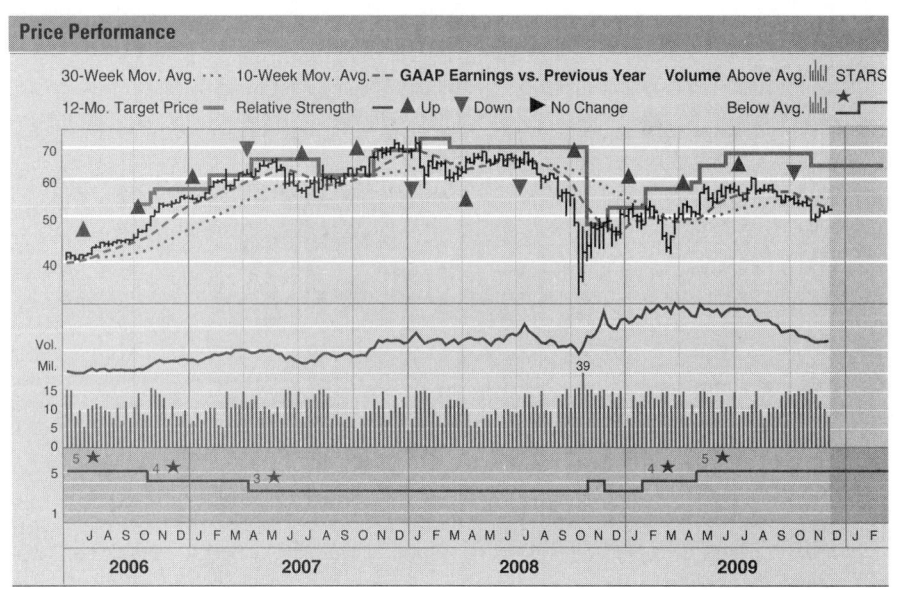

30-Week Mov. Avg. ···· 10-Week Mov. Avg. – – – GAAP Earnings vs. Previous Year   Volume Above Avg. STARS
12-Mo. Target Price — Relative Strength — ▲ Up ▼ Down ▶ No Change   Below Avg.

Options: ASE, CBOE, P, Ph

Analysis prepared by **Justin McCann** on October 28, 2009, when the stock traded at **$ 50.81**.

Highlights

► Excluding one-time charges of $0.14, we expect 2009 operating EPS to grow 8% from 2008's $3.84. This should reflect new wind power investments and related tax credits, and renewed higher-margin power contracts at NextEra Energy Resources, partially offset by flat customer accounts at the FP&L utility and a weak market for the gas generation assets in Texas.

► We believe EPS growth in 2010 will again be driven by new wind power investments and tax credits at NextEra Energy Resources, partially restricted by the weak gas merchant market in Texas. The outlook for FP&L, however, will be dependent upon a regulatory ruling on its nearly $1.3 billion rate increase request, as well as the timing and extent of a recovery in Florida's economy and housing market.

► On October 27, 2009, FPL placed into service the 25 megawatt Desoto Solar Energy Center, the largest solar photovoltaic power plant in the U.S. It will produce enough electricity to serve approximately 3,000 homes. With two additional solar projects scheduled to be placed into operation toward the end of next year, FPL expects to have 110 megawatts of installed solar capacity by the end of 2010.

Investment Rationale/Risk

► We believe the shares will benefit from the expansion of FPL's wind and solar power projects and from the tax credits provided by the passage of the federal stimulus package, which could add $0.10 to $0.15 to annual EPS over the next several years. While the stock has been restricted by the uncertainty related to FP&L's rate increase request, as well as the continuing weakness in the Florida economy and housing market, we believe the shares will benefit from the growth prospects we still see for NextEra Energy Resources, with above-average total return over the next 12 months.

► Risks to our recommendation and target price include an unfavorable regulatory ruling on FP&L's rate case, lower-than-expected results from the unregulated NextEra Energy Resources business, and a reduction in the average P/E for the electric utility sector as a whole.

► We expect the company to sustain average annual dividend growth of about 8% over the next few years. Our 12-month target price is $64, a premium-to-peers P/E of 13.9X our 2010 EPS estimate, with the premium warranted, in our view, by the company being the national leader in the development of wind and solar power.

Qualitative Risk Assessment

LOW	MEDIUM	HIGH

Our risk assessment reflects our view of FPL's strong and steady cash flows from its Florida Power & Light utility, which enjoys well above average customer growth, and a generally supportive regulatory environment. We believe this largely offsets the fast-growing but higher-risk cash flows from its independent power subsidiary.

Quantitative Evaluations

S&P Quality Ranking   A

D	C	B-	B	B+	A-	A	A+

Relative Strength Rank   MODERATE

38

LOWEST = 1   HIGHEST = 99

Revenue/Earnings Data

Revenue (Million $)

	1Q	2Q	3Q	4Q	Year
2009	3,705	3,811	4,473	--	--
2008	3,434	3,585	5,387	4,003	16,410
2007	3,075	3,929	4,575	3,683	15,263
2006	3,584	3,809	4,694	3,623	15,710
2005	2,437	2,741	3,504	3,164	11,846
2004	2,331	2,619	2,983	2,589	10,522

Earnings Per Share ($)

2009	0.90	0.91	1.31	E0.89	E4.15
2008	0.62	0.52	1.92	1.01	4.07
2007	0.38	1.01	1.33	0.56	3.27
2006	0.64	0.60	1.32	0.67	3.23
2005	0.36	0.52	0.87	0.53	2.29
2004	0.39	0.72	0.88	0.47	2.46

Fiscal year ended Dec. 31. Next earnings report expected: Late January. EPS Estimates based on S&P Operating Earnings; historical GAAP earnings are as reported.

Dividend Data (Dates: mm/dd Payment Date: mm/dd/yy)

Amount ($)	Date Decl.	Ex-Div. Date	Stk. of Record	Payment Date
0.473	02/13	02/25	02/27	03/16/09
0.473	05/22	06/03	06/05	06/15/09
0.473	07/24	08/26	08/28	09/15/09
0.473	10/16	11/24	11/27	12/15/09

Dividends have been paid since 1944. Source: Company reports.

Please read the Required Disclosures and Analyst Certification on the last page of this report.

FPL Group Inc.

STANDARD &POOR'S

Business Summary October 28, 2009

CORPORATE OVERVIEW. FPL Group, one of the largest providers of electricity-related services in the U.S., is the holding company for Florida Power & Light Co. (FP&L), a regulated and vertically integrated utility, and NextEra Energy Resources (formerly FPL Energy), a wholesale generator of electricity with operations in 25 states.

MARKET PROFILE. Florida Power & Light provides electricity to about 4.5 million customers in an area covering nearly all of Florida's eastern seaboard, as well as the southern part of the state. As is true of most states in the Southeast, Florida has shown little interest in restructuring its electric utility industry. Although there have been efforts to introduce a competitive wholesale generation market within the state, there has not been any legislation that would allow it to take place, and we do not expect to see any within the next several years.

Electric revenues by customer class in 2008 were: residential 53%; commercial 40%; industrial 3%; and other 4%. Given its unusually low level of exposure to industrial customers, we consider the company to normally be much less vulnerable to economic downturns. However, after experiencing average annual customer growth over the previous 10 years, FP&L started to experience a slowdown in retail customer growth in 2007, as well as a decline in non-weather-related usage, and in 2008, retail customer growth had declined to 0.2%. We do not expect to see a recovery in this growth until there is a broader recovery in the state's economy.

Company Financials Fiscal Year Ended Dec. 31

Per Share Data ($)	2008	2007	2006	2005	2004	2003	2002	2001	2000	1999
Tangible Book Value	28.57	26.35	24.52	21.52	20.24	18.93	17.46	17.09	15.89	15.00
Earnings	4.07	3.27	3.23	2.29	2.46	2.51	2.01	2.31	2.07	2.04
S&P Core Earnings	3.84	3.04	3.00	2.06	2.17	2.21	1.52	1.83	NA	NA
Dividends	1.78	1.64	1.50	1.42	1.30	1.20	1.16	1.12	1.08	1.04
Payout Ratio	44%	50%	46%	62%	53%	48%	58%	48%	52%	51%
Prices:High	73.75	72.77	55.57	48.11	38.05	34.04	32.66	35.81	36.50	30.97
Prices:Low	33.81	53.72	37.81	35.90	30.10	26.78	22.50	25.61	18.19	20.56
P/E Ratio:High	18	22	17	21	15	14	16	16	18	15
P/E Ratio:Low	8	16	12	16	12	11	11	11	9	10
Income Statement Analysis (Million $)										
Revenue	16,410	15,263	15,710	11,846	10,522	9,630	8,311	8,475	7,082	6,438
Depreciation	1,579	1,261	1,185	1,285	1,198	1,105	952	983	1,032	1,040
Maintenance	NA	NA	NA	NA	NA	NA	NA	NA	NA	NA
Fixed Charges Coverage	3.43	3.18	3.30	2.87	3.26	3.95	4.52	4.51	4.55	4.96
Construction Credits	35.0	23.0	21.0	28.0	37.0	NA	NA	NA	Nil	Nil
Effective Tax Rate	21.5%	21.9%	23.7%	23.5%	23.1%	29.2%	26.0%	32.7%	32.3%	31.7%
Net Income	1,639	1,312	1,281	885	887	893	695	781	704	697
S&P Core Earnings	1,547	1,218	1,187	797	782	786	527	616	NA	NA
Balance Sheet & Other Financial Data (Million $)										
Gross Property	45,528	41,040	36,152	33,351	31,720	30,272	26,505	23,388	21,022	19,554
Capital Expenditures	4,989	1,826	1,763	1,616	1,394	1,383	1,277	1,544	1,299	861
Net Property	32,411	28,652	24,499	22,463	21,226	20,297	14,304	11,662	9,934	9,264
Capitalization:Long Term Debt	13,833	11,280	9,591	8,039	8,027	8,728	6,016	5,084	4,202	3,704
Capitalization:% Long Term Debt	54.2	51.2	49.1	48.6	51.6	55.6	47.4	45.8	42.9	40.8
Capitalization:Preferred	Nil	Nil	Nil	Nil	Nil	Nil	Nil	Nil	Nil	Nil
Capitalization:% Preferred	Nil	Nil	Nil	Nil	Nil	Nil	Nil	Nil	Nil	Nil
Capitalization:Common	11,681	10,735	9,930	8,499	7,537	6,967	6,688	6,015	5,593	5,370
Capitalization:% Common	45.8	48.8	50.9	51.4	48.4	44.4	52.6	54.2	57.1	59.2
Total Capital	29,745	25,836	22,953	19,615	15,645	17,850	14,444	12,629	11,442	10,337
% Operating Ratio	85.5	87.5	87.1	88.6	87.8	87.9	85.7	87.6	86.3	88.0
% Earned on Net Property	9.3	8.6	8.9	6.7	7.1	8.1	9.5	10.3	12.9	18.2
% Return on Revenue	10.0	8.6	8.2	7.5	8.4	9.3	8.4	9.2	9.9	10.8
% Return on Invested Capital	8.4	8.2	10.9	8.6	9.2	8.1	9.0	9.6	9.7	11.4
% Return on Common Equity	14.6	12.7	13.9	11.0	12.0	13.4	10.7	13.5	12.8	13.3

Data as orig reptd.; bef. results of disc opers/spec. items. Per share data adj. for stk. divs.; EPS diluted. E-Estimated. NA-Not Available. NM-Not Meaningful. NR-Not Ranked. UR-Under Review.

Office: 700 Universe Boulevard, Juno Beach, FL 33408-0420.
Telephone: 561-694-4000.
Website: http://www.fplgroup.com
Chrmn & CEO: L. Hay, III

Pres & COO: J.L. Robo
EVP & CFO: A. Pimentel, Jr.
EVP & General Counsel: C.E. Sieving
Chief Acctg Officer & Cntlr: K.M. Davis

Investor Contact: P. Cutler (800-222-4511)
Board Members: S. S. Barrat, R. Beall, II, J. H. Brown, J. L. Camaren, J. B. Ferguson, L. Hay, III, T. Jennings, O. D. Kingsley, Jr., R. E. Schupp, W. H. Swanson, M. H. Thaman, H. E. Tookes, II, P. R. Tregurtha

Founded: 1984
Domicile: Florida
Employees: 15,300

The McGraw-Hill Companies

Franklin Resources Inc.

STANDARD &POOR'S

S&P Recommendation BUY ★★★★☆	Price $108.97 (as of Nov 27, 2009)	12-Mo. Target Price $134.00	Investment Style Large-Cap Growth

GICS Sector Financials
Sub-Industry Asset Management & Custody Banks

Summary This company is one of the world's largest asset managers, serving retail, institutional, and high-net-worth clients.

Key Stock Statistics (Source S&P, Vickers, company reports)

52-Wk Range	$116.39– 37.11	S&P Oper. EPS 2010E	6.37	Market Capitalization(B)	$24.981	Beta		1.50
Trailing 12-Month EPS	$3.87	S&P Oper. EPS 2011E	NA	Yield (%)	0.77	S&P 3-Yr. Proj. EPS CAGR(%)		4
Trailing 12-Month P/E	28.2	P/E on S&P Oper. EPS 2010E	17.1	Dividend Rate/Share	$0.84	S&P Credit Rating		AA-
$10K Invested 5 Yrs Ago	$18,248	Common Shares Outstg. (M)	229.3	Institutional Ownership (%)	50			

Price Performance

30-Week Mov. Avg. · · · 10-Week Mov. Avg. – – GAAP Earnings vs. Previous Year Volume Above Avg. STARS
12-Mo. Target Price — Relative Strength — ▲ Up ▼ Down ► No Change Below Avg.

Options: ASE, CBOE, P, Ph

Analysis prepared by **Matthew Albrecht** on November 02, 2009, when the stock traded at **$ 104.63**.

Highlights

► Assets under management have rebounded sharply since March lows, boosted by net asset inflows and equity market gains. Plus, with equity gains outpacing fixed income returns, the improved mix of assets should result in a higher management fee rate. Net flows remain strongest into fixed income funds, though equity trends continue to improve and outflows from money market funds may continue as investors renew their appetite for risk. We also note that fund performance has improved across asset classes, which should help sales. A return to investment gains, compared to losses in the past few quarters, has helped results although performance fee income will likely remain weak. Now facing easier comparisons, we think higher average asset balances will help revenues advance about 30% in FY 10 (Sep.).

► Top line growth should allow for much improved margins in FY 10. Lower headcount versus year ago levels should help lower compensation accruals, but improving asset flows will limit the expansion of the underwriting and distribution margin.

► We see EPS of $6.37 in FY 10.

Investment Rationale/Risk

► We think the shares have traded at a discount to peers due to the relative underperformance of BEN's funds over the past few years, offsetting what we view as its relatively strong balance sheet. We have a favorable view of BEN's strong operating free cash flow and diversification. We think the earnings power of the firm has returned, taking into account improved relative performance, a return to positive net flows from clients, and severe cost cutting.

► Risks to our recommendation and target price include potential depreciation in global equity, bond and currency markets that would materially hinder growth in assets under management and inflows.

► The shares recently traded at 16.5X our FY 10 EPS estimate, a discount to the rising multiples of comparable peers and in line with BEN's historical multiple. Our 12-month target price of $134 is equal to about 21X our FY 10 earnings estimate, a premium to the historical multiple, but in line with peers.

Qualitative Risk Assessment

LOW	MEDIUM	HIGH

Our risk assessment reflects our view of the company's strong operating margins, well capitalized balance sheet, and international exposure, offset by concerns about uneven client flow trends and recent declines in relative investment performance.

Quantitative Evaluations

S&P Quality Ranking B+

D	C	B-	B	B+	A-	A	A+

Relative Strength Rank STRONG

72

LOWEST = 1   HIGHEST = 99

Revenue/Earnings Data

Revenue (Million $)

	1Q	2Q	3Q	4Q	Year
2009	969.3	912.3	1,074	1,239	4,194
2008	1,686	1,504	1,522	1,321	6,032
2007	1,428	1,509	1,640	1,629	6,206
2006	1,181	1,255	1,317	1,297	5,051
2005	986.0	1,051	1,110	1,163	4,310
2004	809.7	879.0	867.8	881.7	3,438

Earnings Per Share ($)

2009	0.52	0.48	1.29	1.60	3.87
2008	2.12	1.54	1.71	1.28	6.67
2007	1.67	1.73	1.86	1.76	7.03
2006	1.21	0.74	1.41	1.49	4.86
2005	0.92	0.85	1.00	1.28	4.06
2004	0.67	0.68	0.69	0.74	2.78

Fiscal year ended Sep. 30. Next earnings report expected: Late January. EPS Estimates based on S&P Operating Earnings; historical GAAP earnings are as reported.

Dividend Data (Dates: mm/dd Payment Date: mm/dd/yy)

Amount ($)	Date Decl.	Ex-Div. Date	Stk. of Record	Payment Date
0.210	12/12	12/29	12/31	01/09/09
0.210	03/11	03/27	03/31	04/14/09
0.210	06/16	06/26	06/30	07/10/09
0.210	09/17	10/01	10/05	10/15/09

Dividends have been paid since 1981. Source: Company reports.

Please read the Required Disclosures and Analyst Certification on the last page of this report.

The McGraw-Hill Companies

Franklin Resources Inc.

STANDARD
&POOR'S

Business Summary November 02, 2009

CORPORATE OVERVIEW. Franklin Resources is one of the largest U.S. money managers, with $507.3 billion in assets under management at the end of FY 08 (Sep.), down from $645.9 billion at the end of FY 07. At the end of FY 08, equity-based investments accounted for 52% of assets under management, fixed income investments 28%, hybrid funds 19%, and money funds 1%. We think that a potential decline in the dollar relative to other major currencies would aid BEN, due to the high percentage of assets invested globally. Conversely, the company's results may be challenged by a declining U.S. dollar relative to major currencies. At the end of FY 08, about 28% of assets under management were held by investors domiciled outside the U.S.

The company's sponsored investment products are distributed under five distinct names: Franklin, Templeton, Mutual Series, Bissett and Fiduciary. The Franklin family of funds is best known for its bond funds, although it includes a range of equity and balanced products. The Templeton family of funds is known for its global investment strategies and value style. Mutual Series funds are primarily known for their value-oriented equity focus. The Bissett family of mutual funds operates in Canada, and serves a broad range of clients, primarily institutions. We are impressed with BEN's broad range of investment products, but we think the company lacks a compelling roster of growth equity products. BEN has targeted key market segments, including re-

tail (58% of assets at the end of FY 08) and institutional and international (42%).

The company generates the majority of its revenue from investment management and related services provided to its retail and institutional mutual funds, and to its institutional, high net-worth and separately managed accounts. Investment management and related services include fund administration, shareholder services, transfer agency, underwriting, distribution, custodial, trustee, and other fiduciary services. Investment management fees depend on the level of client assets under management, and it earns higher revenues and income from equity assets, generally, and a shift in assets from equity to fixed income or balanced funds reduces revenue. Underwriting and distribution fees consist of sales charges and commissions derived from sales of sponsored investment products and distribution fees. It also generates fees from investment management services for high net worth individuals and families through Fiduciary Trust.

Company Financials Fiscal Year Ended Sep. 30

Per Share Data ($)	2009	2008	2007	2006	2005	2004	2003	2002	2001	2000
Tangible Book Value	NA	21.72	21.49	18.57	14.39	12.23	9.31	8.69	7.23	7.37
Cash Flow	NA	7.57	7.82	5.86	5.02	3.51	2.67	2.35	2.79	3.13
Earnings	3.87	6.67	7.03	4.86	4.06	2.78	1.97	1.65	1.91	2.28
S&P Core Earnings	NA	6.77	6.64	4.72	3.97	2.47	1.70	1.56	1.61	NA
Dividends	0.83	0.75	0.57	0.36	0.40	0.33	0.29	0.28	0.26	0.24
Payout Ratio	21%	11%	8%	7%	10%	12%	15%	17%	14%	11%
Prices:High	116.39	129.08	145.59	114.98	98.86	71.45	52.25	44.48	48.30	45.63
Prices:Low	37.11	45.52	108.46	80.16	63.56	46.85	29.99	27.90	30.85	24.63
P/E Ratio:High	30	19	21	24	24	26	27	27	25	20
P/E Ratio:Low	10	7	15	16	16	17	15	17	16	11
Income Statement Analysis (Million $)										
Income Interest	NA	Nil	Nil	NA	NA	NA	NA	NA	NA	NA
Income Other	NA	Nil	Nil	NA	NA	NA	NA	NA	NA	NA
Total Income	4,194	6,032	6,206	5,051	4,310	3,438	2,624	2,519	2,355	2,340
General Expenses	NA	3,933	4,138	3,417	3,004	NA	NA	NA	NA	NA
Interest Expense	NA	15.8	23.2	29.2	34.0	30.7	19.9	12.3	10.6	14.0
Depreciation	NA	215	199	215	17.5	NA	NA	NA	NA	200
Net Income	897	1,588	1,773	1,268	1,058	702	503	433	485	562
S&P Core Earnings	NA	1,612	1,674	1,229	1,033	622	432	410	407	NA
Balance Sheet & Other Financial Data (Million $)										
Cash	NA	2,528	3,584	3,613	3,152	2,917	1,054	981	569	746
Receivables	NA	1,062	1,106	711	549	444	441	393	603	693
Cost of Investments	NA	916	1,065	NA	1,566	NA	NA	NA	NA	NA
Total Assets	NA	9,177	9,943	9,500	8,894	8,228	6,971	6,423	6,266	4,042
Loss Reserve	NA	Nil	Nil	NA	Nil	NA	NA	NA	NA	NA
Short Term Debt	NA	13.3	420	168	169	NA	0.29	7.80	NA	NA
Capitalization:Debt	NA	118	162	628	1,208	1,196	1,109	595	566	294
Capitalization:Equity	NA	7,074	7,332	6,685	5,684	5,107	4,310	4,267	3,978	2,965
Capitalization:Total	NA	7,416	7,750	7,620	7,204	6,615	5,622	5,037	4,544	3,260
Price Times Book Value:High	NA	5.9	6.8	6.2	6.9	NA	5.5	5.1	NA	NA
Price Times Book Value:Low	NA	2.1	5.2	4.3	4.4	NA	3.2	3.2	NA	NA
Cash Flow	NA	1,803	1,972	1,483	1,075	NA	NA	NA	NA	762
% Expense/Operating Revenue	NA	65.2	66.7	67.7	70.1	NA	NA	NA	NA	NA
% Earnings & Depreciation/Assets	NA	18.9	20.3	16.1	12.6	NA	NA	NA	NA	NA

Data as orig reptd.; bef. results of disc opers/spec. items. Per share data adj. for stk. divs.; EPS diluted. E-Estimated. NA-Not Available. NM-Not Meaningful. NR-Not Ranked. UR-Under Review.

Office: One Franklin Parkway, San Mateo, CA 94403.
Telephone: 650-312-2000.
Website: http://www.franklintempleton.com
Chrmn: C.B. Johnson

Pres & CEO: G.E. Johnson
Vice Chrmn: R.H. Johnson, Jr.
COO & CTO: J.J. Bolt
EVP, CFO, Chief Acctg Officer & Treas: K.A. Lewis

Board Members: S. H. Armacost, C. Crocker, J. R. Hardiman, F. W. Hellman, R. D. Joffe, C. B. Johnson, G. E. Johnson, R. H. Johnson, Jr., T. H. Kean, S. C. Ratnathicam, P. M. Sacerdote, L. Stein, A. M. Tatlock

Founded: 1947
Domicile: Delaware
Employees: 8,809

Freeport-McMoran Copper & Gold Inc.

STANDARD &POOR'S

S&P Recommendation BUY ★★★★☆	**Price** $84.14 (as of Nov 27, 2009)	**12-Mo. Target Price** $107.00

GICS Sector Materials
Sub-Industry Diversified Metals & Mining

Summary FCX is the world's second largest copper producer.

Key Stock Statistics (Source S&P, Vickers, company reports)

52-Wk Range	$87.35– 15.70	S&P Oper. EPS 2009**E**	5.25	Market Capitalization(B)	$36.170	Beta	1.82
Trailing 12-Month EPS	$-31.23	S&P Oper. EPS 2010**E**	6.72	Yield (%)	0.71	S&P 3-Yr. Proj. EPS CAGR(%)	7
Trailing 12-Month P/E	NM	P/E on S&P Oper. EPS 2009**E**	16.0	Dividend Rate/Share	$0.60	S&P Credit Rating	BBB-
$10K Invested 5 Yrs Ago	$25,220	Common Shares Outstg. (M)	429.9	Institutional Ownership (%)	82		

Price Performance

- 30-Week Mov. Avg. · · · 10-Week Mov. Avg. - - GAAP Earnings vs. Previous Year Volume Above Avg. STARS
- 12-Mo. Target Price — Relative Strength — ▲ Up ▼ Down ► No Change Below Avg.

Options: ASE, CBOE, P, Ph

Analysis prepared by **Leo J. Larkin** on October 22, 2009, when the stock traded at **$ 80.35**.

Qualitative Risk Assessment

LOW	**MEDIUM**	HIGH

Our risk assessment reflects the company's exposure to cyclical demand for copper and gold, along with sizable debt incurred in the merger with Phelps Dodge. Offsetting this is FCX's large share of the global copper market.

Quantitative Evaluations

S&P Quality Ranking B-

D	C	**B-**	B	B+	A-	A	A+

Relative Strength Rank STRONG

90

LOWEST = 1   HIGHEST = 99

Revenue/Earnings Data

Revenue (Million $)

	1Q	2Q	3Q	4Q	Year
2009	2,602	3,684	4,144	--	--
2008	5,672	5,441	4,616	2,067	17,796
2007	2,303	5,807	5,066	4,184	16,939
2006	1,086	1,426	1,636	1,642	5,791
2005	803.1	902.9	983.3	1,490	4,179
2004	360.2	486.3	600.6	924.8	2,372

Earnings Per Share ($)

2009	0.11	1.38	2.07	E1.69	E5.25
2008	2.64	2.24	1.31	-36.76	-29.72
2007	2.02	2.62	1.85	1.07	7.41
2006	1.23	1.74	1.67	1.99	6.63
2005	0.70	0.91	0.86	2.19	4.67
2004	-0.10	-0.30	0.10	1.08	0.85

Fiscal year ended Dec. 31. Next earnings report expected: Late January. EPS Estimates based on S&P Operating Earnings; historical GAAP earnings are as reported.

Highlights

► We think that higher copper and gold prices will offset reduced output of both metals and permit a 16% sales gain in 2010, versus a projected drop of 20% in 2009. The estimated gain will also reflect a rise in the price and production of molybdenum. Our copper price outlook is based on our forecast for a rebound in global copper demand from 2009's depressed levels and a gradual decline in metal exchange inventories. Our estimate for higher copper demand is based on the IHS Global Insight forecast for world economic growth of 1.8% in 2010, versus an estimated decrease of 2.2% in 2009. Our expectation for a higher gold price in 2010 assumes continued low short-term interest rates worldwide and currency volatility.

► Benefiting mostly from higher prices, we look for an increase in operating profit in 2010. After interest expense, taxes and more shares outstanding, we project EPS of $6.72 in 2010, versus EPS of $5.25 estimated for 2009.

► Longer term, we expect earnings and reserves to increase on a secular rise in copper demand and expansions at existing mines.

Investment Rationale/Risk

► For the long term, we think rising secular demand for durable goods in China and India, along with less rapid increases in the supply of copper, will support generally higher prices, sales, earnings and reserves. We believe that the depletion of existing mines will offset production from new mines and keep copper supply tight over the course of the business cycle. We think FCX, as the world's second largest copper producer, is well positioned to capitalize on rising demand and prices for copper with expansion projects in Africa and further development of existing mines. Also, we see earnings being aided on a projected rise in the price of gold and a rebound in the price of molybdenum. We think FCX is attractively valued, recently trading at about 11.8X our 2010 EPS estimate.

► Risks to our opinion and target price include a decline in the price of copper in 2010 instead of the increase we project.

► Our 12-month target price of $107 assumes that FCX will trade at 15.9X our 2010 EPS estimate, which is toward the low end of the stock's historical range of the past 10 years, and about in line with the P/E we apply to peers.

Dividend Data (Dates: mm/dd Payment Date: mm/dd/yy)

Amount ($)	Date Decl.	Ex-Div. Date	Stk. of Record	Payment Date
Div Susp	12/03	--	--	12/03/08

Dividends have been paid since 2003. Source: Company reports.

Please read the Required Disclosures and Analyst Certification on the last page of this report.

The McGraw·Hill Companies

Freeport-McMoran Copper & Gold Inc.

Business Summary October 22, 2009

CORPORATE OVERVIEW. Freeport-McMoRan Copper & Gold is the world's second largest copper producer and is a major producer of gold and molybdenum. FCX has 12 producing mines located in Indonesia, North America, and South America along with exploration projects in Africa.

Copper production totaled 4.0 billion pounds in 2008, versus 3.9 billion pounds in 2007; and gold production totaled 1.3 million oz., versus 2.3 million oz. in 2007. Molybdenum production was 73 million pounds in 2008, versus 70 million pounds in 2007. In 2008, North America accounted for 36% of copper production, South America 37%, and Indonesia 27%.

At year-end 2008, consolidated proven and probable reserves totaled 102.0 billion pounds of copper, 40.0 million ounces of gold, and 2.48 billion pounds of

molybdenum. Some 35% of FCX's copper reserves were in Indonesia, about 32% were in South America, 28% were in North America and some 5% were in Africa. About 96% of FCX's gold reserves were in Indonesia, with the balance located in South America. Some 84% of molybdenum reserves are primarily in North America, with the remaining in South America. At the end of 2007, FCX's consolidated proven and probable reserves totaled 93.2 billion pounds of copper, 41.0 million ounces of gold and 2.0 billion pounds of molybdenum.

Company Financials Fiscal Year Ended Dec. 31

Per Share Data ($)	2008	2007	2006	2005	2004	2003	2002	2001	2000	1999
Tangible Book Value	4.43	28.56	6.83	3.98	0.36	4.23	NM	NM	NM	NM
Cash Flow	-25.02	10.03	7.33	5.38	1.96	2.52	2.67	2.49	2.09	2.39
Earnings	-29.72	7.41	6.63	4.67	0.85	1.07	0.89	0.53	0.26	0.61
S&P Core Earnings	-14.14	7.26	6.56	4.63	0.48	1.03	0.84	0.49	NA	NA
Dividends	1.81	1.25	1.25	1.25	0.85	0.27	Nil	Nil	Nil	Nil
Payout Ratio	NM	17%	19%	27%	100%	25%	Nil	Nil	Nil	Nil
Prices:High	127.24	120.20	72.20	56.35	44.90	46.74	20.83	17.15	21.44	21.38
Prices:Low	15.70	48.85	43.10	31.52	27.76	16.01	9.95	8.31	6.75	9.13
P/E Ratio:High	NM	16	11	12	53	44	23	32	82	35
P/E Ratio:Low	NM	7	7	7	33	15	11	16	26	15

Income Statement Analysis (Million $)	2008	2007	2006	2005	2004	2003	2002	2001	2000	1999
Revenue	17,796	16,939	5,791	4,179	2,372	2,212	1,910	1,839	1,869	1,887
Operating Income	-4,711	7,801	3,096	2,429	823	1,054	901	827	778	876
Depreciation	1,782	1,246	228	252	206	231	260	284	284	293
Interest Expense	706	660	75.6	132	148	197	171	174	205	194
Pretax Income	-13,294	6,133	2,826	2,037	574	584	450	359	273	381
Effective Tax Rate	NM	39.1%	42.5%	44.9%	57.6%	57.9%	54.6%	56.6%	58.4%	51.4%
Net Income	-11,067	2,942	1,457	995	202	197	168	113	77.0	136
S&P Core Earnings	-5,396	2,672	1,381	919	77.7	167	123	70.8	NA	NA

Balance Sheet & Other Financial Data (Million $)	2008	2007	2006	2005	2004	2003	2002	2001	2000	1999
Cash	872	1,626	907	764	551	464	7.84	7.59	7.97	6.70
Current Assets	5,233	5,903	2,151	2,022	1,460	1,100	638	548	569	564
Total Assets	23,271	40,661	5,390	5,550	5,087	4,718	4,192	4,212	3,951	4,083
Current Liabilities	3,158	3,869	972	1,369	698	632	538	628	634	515
Long Term Debt	7,284	7,180	661	1,003	1,874	2,076	1,961	2,133	1,988	2,033
Common Equity	2,083	14,259	1,345	743	63.6	776	-83.2	-246	-312	-153
Total Capital	16,643	33,953	4,119	3,971	4,189	3,925	3,514	3,464	3,204	3,453
Capital Expenditures	2,708	1,755	251	143	141	139	188	167	292	161
Cash Flow	-9,559	3,980	1,624	1,186	363	401	391	360	323	394
Current Ratio	1.7	1.5	2.2	1.5	2.1	1.7	1.2	0.9	0.9	1.1
% Long Term Debt of Capitalization	43.8	26.9	16.0	25.2	44.7	52.9	55.8	61.6	62.0	58.9
% Net Income of Revenue	NM	17.4	25.2	23.8	8.5	8.9	8.8	6.1	4.1	7.2
% Return on Assets	NM	11.9	26.6	18.7	4.1	4.4	4.0	2.8	1.9	3.3
% Return on Equity	NM	35.0	133.7	231.7	37.3	49.0	NM	NM	NM	NM

Data as orig reptd.; bef. results of disc opers/spec. items. Per share data adj. for stk. divs.; EPS diluted. E-Estimated. NA-Not Available. NM-Not Meaningful. NR-Not Ranked. UR-Under Review.

Office: 1 N Central Ave, Phoenix, AZ 85004-4414.
Telephone: 602-366-8100.
Email: ir@fmi.com
Website: http://www.fcx.com

Chrmn: J.R. Moffett
Pres & CEO: R.C. Adkerson
Vice Chrmn: B.M. Rankin, Jr.
Investor Contact: K.L. Quirk

EVP, CFO & Treas: K.L. Quirk
Board Members: R. C. Adkerson, R. J. Allison, Jr., R. A. Day, G. J. Ford, H. D. Graham, Jr., J. B. Johnston, C. C. Krulak, B. L. Lackey, J. C. Madonna, D. E. McCoy, G. K. McDonald, J. R. Moffett, B. M. Rankin, Jr., J. S. Roy, S. H. Siegele, J. T. Wharton

Founded: 1987
Domicile: Delaware
Employees: 29,484

Frontier Communications Corp

STANDARD &POOR'S

S&P Recommendation BUY ★★★★☆	Price $7.91 (as of Nov 27, 2009)	12-Mo. Target Price $9.00	Investment Style Large-Cap Value

GICS Sector Telecommunication Services
Sub-Industry Integrated Telecommunication Services

Summary Frontier provides wireline communications services including voice services to 2.2 million customers in rural areas and small and medium-sized cities in the U.S. In May 2009, the company announced plans to combine with assets from Verizon Communications.

Key Stock Statistics (Source S&P, Vickers, company reports)

52-Wk Range	$9.00– 5.32	S&P Oper. EPS 2009E	0.58	Market Capitalization(B)	$2.471	Beta	0.82
Trailing 12-Month EPS	$0.48	S&P Oper. EPS 2010E	0.64	Yield (%)	12.64	S&P 3-Yr. Proj. EPS CAGR(%)	3
Trailing 12-Month P/E	16.5	P/E on S&P Oper. EPS 2009E	13.6	Dividend Rate/Share	$1.00	S&P Credit Rating	BB
$10K Invested 5 Yrs Ago	$6,475	Common Shares Outstg. (M)	312.3	Institutional Ownership (%)	51		

Price Performance

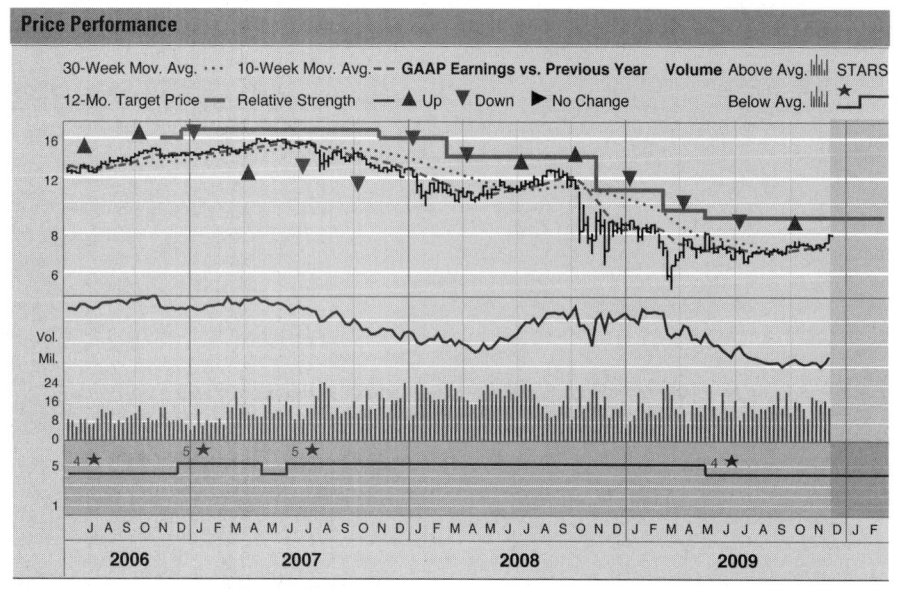

- 30-Week Mov. Avg. ··· 10-Week Mov. Avg. - - **GAAP Earnings vs. Previous Year** Volume Above Avg. STARS
- 12-Mo. Target Price — Relative Strength — ▲ Up ▼ Down ► No Change Below Avg.

Options: CBOE, P, Ph

Analysis prepared by **Todd Rosenbluth** on November 09, 2009, when the stock traded at **$ 7.44**.

Qualitative Risk Assessment

LOW	MEDIUM	HIGH

Our risk assessment for Frontier Communications reflects the rural, less competitive nature of its operations and what we see as the strong and stable cash flow that supports its dividend policy, offset by sensitivity to the U.S. economy and the company's acquisition strategy.

Quantitative Evaluations

S&P Quality Ranking B-

D	C	B-	B	B+	A-	A	A+

Relative Strength Rank STRONG

85

LOWEST = 1   HIGHEST = 99

Highlights

▶ We expect revenues of $2.13 billion in 2009 and $2.07 billion in 2010, as additional DSL and video penetration is offset by lower access and network charges due to a decline in universal service support and access line weakness. We believe line losses will continue due to macroeconomic pressure as unemployment levels rise in core markets, although we losses have slowed since mid-2009.

▶ We think EBITDA margins will narrow slightly to 53% in 2009 and hold steady in 2010, remaining among the industry's best. We expect benefits from work force cuts and automation of services, but we see this being outweighed by increased promotional activities for introductory service bundles and weakness in higher-margin voice services.

▶ Even with a decrease in depreciation charges, we see EPS being held back with the absence of share repurchase activity relative to prior years. We forecast EPS of $0.58 in 2009 and $0.64 in 2010. Our estimates exclude any costs or revenues from the pending Verizon transaction.

Investment Rationale/Risk

▶ We believe FTR generates strong cash flow to support its dividend and view the terms of the pending combination with rural wireline operations from Verizon favorably. We think FTR will have opportunities for cost savings, broadband growth, and debt and dividend payout develeraging assuming a smooth closing in mid-2010. However, we see risks for FTR both as a standalone company, and upon deal closing, with potential pressure on margins as costs and management attention are needed to complete the deal, which will triple its size. We believe FTR has a strong track record in small deal integration and in generating high revenues per household.

▶ Risks to our recommendation and target price include failure to complete the pending Verizon deal; not retaining customers in existing and acquired markets; and greater costs to complete the transaction.

▶ Our 12-month target price of $9 is based on an EV/EBITDA multiple of 6.6X, in line with rural telecom peers and down slightly from historical levels to reflect risks. At our target price, FTR's dividend yield would be above average.

Revenue/Earnings Data

Revenue (Million $)

	1Q	2Q	3Q	4Q	Year
2009	538.0	532.1	526.8	--	--
2008	569.2	562.6	557.9	547.4	2,237
2007	556.2	578.8	575.8	577.2	2,288
2006	506.9	506.9	507.2	504.4	2,025
2005	537.2	531.8	537.4	556.1	2,162
2004	558.5	544.1	545.4	545.0	2,193

Earnings Per Share ($)

2009	0.12	0.09	0.17	E0.17	E0.58
2008	0.14	0.15	0.15	0.11	0.57
2007	0.21	0.12	0.14	0.18	0.65
2006	0.13	0.29	0.16	0.20	0.78
2005	0.11	0.13	0.11	0.23	0.59
2004	0.15	0.08	-0.04	0.05	0.23

Fiscal year ended Dec. 31. Next earnings report expected: Late February. EPS Estimates based on S&P Operating Earnings; historical GAAP earnings are as reported.

Dividend Data (Dates: mm/dd Payment Date: mm/dd/yy)

Amount ($)	Date Decl.	Ex-Div. Date	Stk. of Record	Payment Date
0.250	02/06	03/05	03/09	03/31/09
0.250	05/13	06/05	06/09	06/30/09
0.250	07/30	09/04	09/09	09/30/09
0.250	10/28	12/07	12/09	12/31/09

Dividends have been paid since 2004. Source: Company reports.

Frontier Communications Corp

Business Summary November 09, 2009

CORPORATE OVERVIEW. Frontier Communications (formerly Citizens Communications) provides wireline services to rural areas and small and medium-sized towns and cities in 24 states, including Arizona, California, New York and Pennsylvania. FTR is an incumbent local exchange carrier (ILEC) for 2.15 million access lines as of September 2009 (with 64% used by residential customers), including lines acquired in two deals in 2007. The company also had 621,000 DSL subscribers, up 9% from a year earlier.

In May 2009, FTR announced plans to combine with wireline assets that are to be spun out by Verizon Communications, subject to necessary approvals, in a stock and debt assumption deal valued originally at $8.6 billion; we believe the agreed price is equal to a fair 4.5X trailing EBITDA multiple. The Verizon properties, in 14 states, include 4.3 million access lines, and 1.1 million DSL and FiOS customers as of September 2009, which helped generate revenues of $4.3 billion and EBITDA of $1.9 billion (44% margin) in 2008. FTR, which expects $500 million in expense savings largely in the second year following closing, plans to issue new stock and assume $3.3 billion of debt to complete the deal around mid-2010.

CORPORATE STRATEGY. In 2009, FTR has focused on expanding by providing rural local residential phone customers with enhanced services as well as long-distance (64% of total lines at end of 2008), DSL and satellite video. At the end of September 2009, FTR had DSL penetration of 45% of its residential access lines (29% of total lines) and wholesale satellite video penetration of 12%. The company reduced operating expenses through the consolidation of call centers, enabling some employees to work from home, and billing consolidation, helping to keep its EBITDA margin wider than rural peers that also receive regulatory support.

COMPETITIVE LANDSCAPE. We believe FTR faces challenges from cable telephony and wireless that led to its 6.3% access line erosion in the 12 months ended September 2009 (an improvement from the 7.1% as of March 2009). In the 12 months ended September 2009, the soon-to-be-combined Verizon assets lost 11.5% of their access lines. FTR competes with cable providers such as Time Warner in its most competitive Rochester, NY, market, and Comcast in California, which began to offer telephony services in 2006, along with other cable providers in its smallest markets. As of late 2008, approximately 65% of FTR's operating territory faced cable telephony competition, and we think this rate will increase to 70% in 2009.

Company Financials Fiscal Year Ended Dec. 31

Per Share Data ($)	2008	2007	2006	2005	2004	2003	2002	2001	2000	1999
Tangible Book Value	NM	NM	NM	NM	NM	NM	NM	NM	4.09	7.36
Cash Flow	2.34	2.30	2.25	2.26	2.09	2.37	-0.24	2.08	1.30	1.45
Earnings	0.57	0.65	0.78	0.59	0.23	0.42	-2.93	-0.28	-0.15	0.45
S&P Core Earnings	0.45	0.52	0.64	0.59	0.19	0.68	-2.89	-0.58	NA	NA
Dividends	1.00	1.00	1.00	1.00	0.50	Nil	Nil	Nil	Nil	Nil
Payout Ratio	175%	154%	128%	169%	NM	Nil	Nil	Nil	Nil	Nil
Prices:High	12.94	16.05	14.95	14.05	14.80	13.40	11.52	15.88	19.00	14.31
Prices:Low	6.35	12.03	11.97	12.08	11.37	8.81	2.51	8.20	12.50	7.25
P/E Ratio:High	23	25	19	24	62	32	NM	NM	NM	32
P/E Ratio:Low	11	19	15	20	47	21	NM	NM	NM	16

Income Statement Analysis (Million $)

	2008	2007	2006	2005	2004	2003	2002	2001	2000	1999
Revenue	2,237	2,288	2,025	2,162	2,193	2,445	2,669	2,457	1,802	1,087
Operating Income	1,214	1,251	1,121	1,149	1,148	1,173	1,179	927	549	8.07
Depreciation	562	546	476	542	573	595	756	632	388	262
Interest Expense	363	384	336	339	379	423	478	386	194	93.2
Pretax Income	289	343	390	285	85.5	189	-1,238	-78.7	-44.0	158
Effective Tax Rate	36.8%	37.4%	35.0%	29.6%	15.6%	35.5%	NM	NM	NM	40.8%
Net Income	183	215	254	200	72.2	122	-823	-63.9	-40.1	117
S&P Core Earnings	146	171	206	201	57.7	198	-811	-164	NA	NA

Balance Sheet & Other Financial Data (Million $)

	2008	2007	2006	2005	2004	2003	2002	2001	2000	1999
Cash	164	226	1,041	266	167	584	393	57.7	31.2	37.1
Current Assets	468	524	1,273	542	450	896	1,201	2,533	2,263	309
Total Assets	6,889	7,256	6,791	6,412	6,668	7,689	8,147	10,554	6,955	5,772
Current Liabilities	383	446	426	617	418	536	771	1,567	992	467
Long Term Debt	4,722	4,739	4,461	3,999	4,267	4,397	5,159	5,736	3,264	2,309
Common Equity	519	998	1,058	1,042	1,362	1,415	1,172	1,946	1,720	1,920
Total Capital	5,245	6,446	6,033	5,366	5,629	6,259	6,468	8,112	5,474	4,700
Capital Expenditures	288	316	269	268	276	278	469	531	537	485
Cash Flow	744	761	730	742	645	717	-67.5	568	348	380
Current Ratio	1.2	1.2	3.0	0.9	1.1	1.7	1.6	1.6	2.3	0.7
% Long Term Debt of Capitalization	90.0	82.6	73.9	74.5	75.8	70.2	79.8	70.7	59.6	49.1
% Net Income of Revenue	8.2	9.4	12.5	9.3	3.3	5.0	NM	NM	NM	10.8
% Return on Assets	2.6	3.1	3.8	3.1	1.0	1.5	NM	NM	NM	2.1
% Return on Equity	24.1	20.9	24.2	16.7	5.2	9.4	NM	NM	NM	6.5

Data as orig reptd.; bef. results of disc opers/spec. items. Per share data adj. for stk. divs.; EPS diluted. E-Estimated. NA-Not Available. NM-Not Meaningful. NR-Not Ranked. UR-Under Review.

Office: 3 High Ridge Park, Stamford, CT 06905-1337.
Telephone: 203-614-5600.
Email: citizens@cnz.com
Website: http://www.czn.net

Chrmn, Pres & CEO: M. Wilderotter
COO & EVP: D.J. McCarthy
EVP & CFO: D.R. Shassian
SVP & Chief Acctg Officer: R.J. Larson

SVP, Secy & General Counsel: H.E. Glassman
Board Members: K. Q. Abernathy, L. T. Barnes, Jr., P. C. Bynoe, J. Finard, L. W. Fitt, W. M. Kraus, H. L. Schrott, L. D. Segil, D. H. Ward, M. Wick, III, M. Wilderotter

Founded: 1927
Domicile: Delaware
Employees: 5,671

The McGraw-Hill Companies

GameStop Corp.

STANDARD &POOR'S

S&P Recommendation	**STRONG BUY** ★ ★ ★ ★ ★	Price $25.32 (as of Nov 27, 2009)	12-Mo. Target Price $32.00	Investment Style Large-Cap Growth

GICS Sector Consumer Discretionary
Sub-Industry Computer & Electronics Retail

Summary This company is the largest U.S. video game and PC entertainment software specialty retailer, and operates over 6,000 stores worldwide.

Key Stock Statistics (Source S&P, Vickers, company reports)

52-Wk Range	$32.82–18.01	S&P Oper. EPS 2010**E**	2.57	Market Capitalization(B)	$4.170	Beta	1.03
Trailing 12-Month EPS	$2.35	S&P Oper. EPS 2011**E**	2.82	Yield (%)	Nil	S&P 3-Yr. Proj. EPS CAGR(%)	10
Trailing 12-Month P/E	10.8	P/E on S&P Oper. EPS 2010**E**	9.9	Dividend Rate/Share	Nil	S&P Credit Rating	NA
$10K Invested 5 Yrs Ago	$23,336	Common Shares Outstg. (M)	164.7	Institutional Ownership (%)	97		

Price Performance

Options: ASE, CBOE, Ph

Analysis prepared by **Michael Souers** on November 23, 2009, when the stock traded at **$ 25.49**.

Highlights

► We see FY 11 (Jan.) revenues rising 5.5%, following our projection of a 5.1% advance in FY 10. We expect this growth to be driven by the opening of about 400 new stores worldwide and flat comp-store sales. We continue to project that GME's used game business will thrive in the current challenging economic environment, and also expect a strong lineup of new software in calendar 2010. We look for price cuts on next-generation consoles to stem recent declines of hardware sales, although we do expect a sales decline for this category.

► We forecast gross margins will widen modestly in FY 11 due to an expected shift in product mix to new and used software from hardware following a significant ramp-up in the installed base. We see operating margins widening approximately 30 basis points, driven by gross margin improvement, partially offset by the deleveraging of SG&A expenses due to flat projected comp-store sales results.

► After a slight decline in interest expense, we project FY 11 EPS of $2.82, a 9.7% increase from the $2.57 we project the company to earn in FY 10, excluding debt extinguishment expense.

Investment Rationale/Risk

► We think the video game industry continues to benefit from a growth cycle unprecedented in strength, and we expect near-term earnings growth from GME despite the slowdown in consumer spending. Long term, we believe the electronic game industry will benefit from hardware platform technology evolution, a growing used video game market, and broadening demographic appeal, but we have concerns that online gaming may take some share from the retail market. Nonetheless, we consider the shares' valuation to be compelling, with GME trading at about 9X our FY 11 EPS estimate, a significant discount to the S&P 500.

► Risks to our opinion and target price include a slowdown in consumer spending, inventory shortages, an inability to successfully manage new store openings or merger integration, the threat of online gaming emerging as a viable alternative for gamers, and corporate governance issues including the existence of a non-shareholder-approved "poison pill."

► Our 12-month target price of $32, about 11X our FY 11 EPS estimate, is based on our DCF analysis, which assumes a weighted average cost of capital of 10.8% and terminal growth of 3.0%.

Qualitative Risk Assessment

LOW	MEDIUM	HIGH

Our risk assessment reflects the company's leading market share position, offset by industry cyclicality, as growth is partly dependent on the timing of new hardware and software releases.

Quantitative Evaluations

S&P Quality Ranking   NR

D	C	B-	B	B+	A-	A	A+

Relative Strength Rank   MODERATE

57

LOWEST = 1   HIGHEST = 99

Revenue/Earnings Data

Revenue (Million $)

	1Q	2Q	3Q	4Q	Year
2010	1,981	1,739	1,835	--	--
2009	1,814	1,804	1,696	3,492	8,806
2008	1,279	1,338	1,611	2,866	7,094
2007	1,040	963.4	1,012	2,304	5,319
2006	474.7	415.9	534.2	1,667	3,092
2005	371.7	345.6	416.7	708.7	1,843

Earnings Per Share ($)

2010	0.42	0.23	0.31	E1.59	E2.57
2009	0.37	0.34	0.28	1.39	2.38
2008	0.15	0.34	0.31	1.14	1.75
2007	0.08	0.02	0.09	0.81	1.00
2006	0.10	0.07	-0.02	0.55	0.81
2005	0.06	0.07	0.11	0.32	0.53

Fiscal year ended Jan. 31. Next earnings report expected: Late March. EPS Estimates based on S&P Operating Earnings; historical GAAP earnings are as reported.

Dividend Data

No cash dividends have been paid.

GameStop Corp.

STANDARD &POOR'S

Business Summary November 23, 2009

CORPORATE OVERVIEW. GameStop is the world's largest retailer of video game products and PC entertainment software. The company sells new and used video game hardware, video game software and accessories, as well as PC entertainment software, related accessories and other merchandise. As of January 31, 2009, GameStop operated 6,207 stores in the U.S., Australia, Canada and Europe, primarily under the names GameStop and EB Games. Of the total store count, 4,331 stores are located in the U.S., with the remaining 1,876 located internationally.

In October 2005, GameStop acquired close peer Electronics Boutique Holding Corp., which essentially doubled the company's market share in video game retailing. In November 2008, GME purchased Micromania, the leading retailer of video and computer games in France, with 332 locations.

MARKET PROFILE. According to NPD Group, Inc., a market research firm, the U.S. electronic games industry generated approximately $22 billion in 2008, and, according to the International Development Group, retail sales of video game hardware and software and PC entertainment software totaled $19.8 billion in Europe. The Entertainment Software Association (ESA) estimates that 65% of all American head of households play video or computer games, and

that the average game player is 35 years old. We believe that trends such as hardware platform technology evolution and a broadening demographic appeal will continue to propel growth in this industry.

In addition, as the installed base of video game hardware platforms has increased, and new hardware platforms are introduced, a rising used video game market has evolved in the U.S. We believe that GameStop is the leading retailer of used video games in the world, with the broadest selection of used video game products for both current and previous generation platforms. We think that the company's focus on the used game market enables GameStop to differentiate itself from mass merchants, toy stores and consumer electronics retailers that sell video game products. We note that the used game business, which represented 23% of FY 09 (Jan.) sales, generates significantly higher gross margins than the company average. For example, used game products generated a gross margin of approximately 48% in FY 09, compared to 6% for hardware and 26% for the total company.

Company Financials Fiscal Year Ended Jan. 31

Per Share Data ($)	2009	2008	2007	2006	2005	2004	2003	2002	2001	2000
Tangible Book Value	1.17	2.80	NM	NM	2.19	2.41	2.02	NM	NM	NA
Cash Flow	3.24	2.54	1.69	1.34	0.85	0.77	0.62	0.47	0.14	NA
Earnings	2.38	1.75	1.00	0.81	0.53	0.53	0.44	0.09	-0.17	-0.43
S&P Core Earnings	2.33	1.75	1.00	0.76	0.92	0.47	0.37	0.09	NA	NA
Dividends	Nil	Nil	Nil	Nil	Nil	Nil	Nil	Nil	Nil	NA
Payout Ratio	Nil	Nil	Nil	Nil	Nil	Nil	Nil	Nil	Nil	NA
Calendar Year	2008	2007	2006	2005	2004	2003	2002	2001	2000	1999
Prices:High	62.29	63.77	29.21	19.21	11.76	9.52	12.15	NA	NA	NA
Prices:Low	16.91	24.95	15.57	9.27	7.19	3.75	4.46	NA	NA	NA
P/E Ratio:High	26	36	29	24	22	18	28	NA	NA	NA
P/E Ratio:Low	7	14	16	12	14	7	10	NA	NA	NA

Income Statement Analysis (Million $)	2009	2008	2007	2006	2005	2004	2003	2002	2001	2000
Revenue	8,806	7,094	5,319	3,092	1,843	1,579	1,353	1,121	757	553
Operating Income	825	632	450	273	163	133	110	64.4	27.8	NA
Depreciation	145	130	110	66.7	37.0	28.9	22.6	30.3	22.0	8.09
Interest Expense	50.5	61.6	84.7	37.9	2.16	0.66	1.37	19.6	23.0	NA
Pretax Income	634	441	254	160	98.9	105	87.7	14.6	-17.8	-5.51
Effective Tax Rate	37.2%	34.6%	37.8%	37.0%	38.4%	39.7%	40.2%	52.4%	NM	38.0%
Net Income	398	288	158	101	60.9	63.5	52.4	6.96	-12.0	-3.42
S&P Core Earnings	390	288	158	94.1	53.2	55.6	44.1	6.76	NA	NA

Balance Sheet & Other Financial Data (Million $)	2009	2008	2007	2006	2005	2004	2003	2002	2001	2000
Cash	578	857	652	402	171	205	232	80.8	8.70	6.61
Current Assets	1,818	1,795	1,440	1,121	424	473	416	237	138	NA
Total Assets	4,513	3,776	3,350	3,015	915	899	804	607	510	308
Current Liabilities	1,563	1,261	1,087	888	314	284	247	206	140	NA
Long Term Debt	546	574	844	963	24.3	Nil	Nil	400	385	204
Common Equity	2,300	1,862	1,376	1,115	543	594	549	-3.99	-20.6	-8.57
Total Capital	2,845	2,437	2,220	2,091	588	612	554	399	367	195
Capital Expenditures	183	176	134	111	98.3	63.0	39.5	20.5	25.1	16.4
Cash Flow	543	419	268	167	97.9	92.4	75.0	37.3	10.0	NA
Current Ratio	1.2	1.4	1.3	1.3	1.4	1.7	1.7	1.2	1.0	0.7
% Long Term Debt of Capitalization	19.2	23.6	38.0	46.1	4.1	Nil	Nil	100.2	105.0	104.4
% Net Income of Revenue	4.5	4.1	3.0	3.3	3.3	4.0	3.9	0.6	NM	NM
% Return on Assets	9.6	8.1	5.0	5.1	6.7	7.5	7.4	1.2	NM	NA
% Return on Equity	19.1	17.8	12.7	12.2	10.7	11.1	19.2	NM	NM	NA

Data as orig reptd.; bef. results of disc opers/spec. items. Per share data adj. for stk. divs.; EPS diluted. E-Estimated. NA-Not Available. NM-Not Meaningful. NR-Not Ranked. UR-Under Review.

Office: 625 Westport Pkwy, Grapevine, TX 76051-6740.
Telephone: 817-424-2000.
Email: investorrelations@gamestop.com
Website: http://www.gamestop.com

Chrmn: R.R. Fontaine
Vice Chrmn & CEO: D.A. Dematteo
COO: J.P. Raines
EVP & CFO: D.W. Carlson

SVP & Chief Acctg Officer: R.A. Lloyd
Investor Contact: M. Hodges (817-424-2000)
Board Members: J. L. Davis, D. A. Dematteo, R. R. Fontaine, S. Koonin, L. Riggio, M. N. Rosen, S. M. Shern, S. Steinberg, G. R. Szczepanski, E. A. Volkwein, L. S. Zilavy

Founded: 1994
Domicile: Delaware
Employees: 56,000

The McGraw·Hill Companies

Gannett Co Inc.

STANDARD &POOR'S

S&P Recommendation **HOLD** ★★★★★	Price $10.32 (as of Nov 27, 2009)	12-Mo. Target Price $15.00	Investment Style Large-Cap Blend

GICS Sector Consumer Discretionary
Sub-Industry Publishing

Summary Gannett publishes 85 daily U.S. newspapers, about 850 non-daily publications in the U.S., and more than 200 U.K. titles, and operates 23 TV stations in the U.S.

Key Stock Statistics (Source S&P, Vickers, company reports)

52-Wk Range	$14.18–1.85	S&P Oper. EPS 2009E	1.78	Market Capitalization(B)	$2.438	Beta	2.74
Trailing 12-Month EPS	$-19.37	S&P Oper. EPS 2010E	1.85	Yield (%)	1.55	S&P 3-Yr. Proj. EPS CAGR(%)	6
Trailing 12-Month P/E	NM	P/E on S&P Oper. EPS 2009E	5.8	Dividend Rate/Share	$0.16	S&P Credit Rating	BB
$10K Invested 5 Yrs Ago	$1,521	Common Shares Outstg. (M)	236.2	Institutional Ownership (%)	99		

Price Performance

30-Week Mov. Avg. · · · 10-Week Mov. Avg. - - GAAP Earnings vs. Previous Year   Volume Above Avg. ▥▥ STARS
12-Mo. Target Price — Relative Strength — ▲ Up ▼ Down ► No Change   Below Avg. ▥▥ ★

Options: ASE, CBOE, P, Ph

Analysis prepared by **Joseph Agnese** on October 26, 2009, when the stock traded at **$12.35**.

Highlights

► We see print publishing revenues remaining soft in 2009 and 2010 given weak economic environments in the U.S. and the U.K., and we expect classified advertising to continue to migrate online. We expect broadcast revenue to rise in the low single digits in 2010, following our estimate of an 18% drop in 2009 in the absence of the Olympics and the election year advertising of 2008. Overall, we expect a revenue drop of about 18% this year, moderating to a 5% decline in 2010. GCI has taken preemptive action to deal with weakening demand, including unpaid furloughs, and reducing hard copy circulation for some subscribers, but is expanding 24/7 digital channels.

► We forecast an EBIT margin of 13.9% in 2009, down from 19.4% in 2008, but rising to 15.0% in 2010. We see the benefits of staff reduction initiatives and significantly lower print costs being more than offset by negative operating leverage from lower revenues.

► We forecast 2010 EPS of $1.85, up from our estimate of operating EPS of $1.78 in 2009, which excludes severance, facility closures, asset impairments and writedowns, legal settlements and other one-time items.

Investment Rationale/Risk

► We remain concerned by what we see as a secular decline in newspaper advertising, especially as the company garners only about 6% of its revenues from online operations. We are also concerned by negative trends in the U.S. and U.K. economies that should continue to hurt classified advertising. On a positive note, with strong operating cash flow and a high free cash flow/equity yield, we think there is long-term value in what we see as GCI's strong free cash flow generating capabilities.

► Risks to our recommendation and target price include a worse than expected decline in U.S. GDP, lower audience ratings at network-affiliated TV stations, and a weakening of the British pound versus the U.S. dollar.

► Our 12-month target price of $15 is derived by applying a peer median enterprise value-to-EBITDA ratio of 6.5X to our 2010 EBITDA estimate of $1.0 billion. This multiple is at the low end of the company's historical range, which we think is appropriate given significant cyclical, secular and operating challenges we believe the company is facing.

Qualitative Risk Assessment

LOW	MEDIUM	**HIGH**

Our risk assessment reflects a highly competitive and weak advertising environment along with significant industry upheaval as consumers increasingly opt to get their news online and for free. This is only partly offset, in our vies, by GCI's strong free cash flow and profitability as well as its relatively low cost of capital.

Quantitative Evaluations

S&P Quality Ranking B+

D	C	B-	B	**B+**	A-	A	A+

Relative Strength Rank MODERATE

41

LOWEST = 1   HIGHEST = 99

Revenue/Earnings Data

Revenue (Million $)

	1Q	2Q	3Q	4Q	Year
2009	1,378	1,413	1,337	--	--
2008	1,677	1,718	1,637	1,735	6,768
2007	1,871	1,928	1,756	1,897	7,439
2006	1,883	2,028	1,915	2,208	8,033
2005	1,768	1,911	1,865	2,055	7,599
2004	1,730	1,873	1,816	1,962	7,381

Earnings Per Share ($)

2009	0.34	0.30	0.31	E0.62	E1.78
2008	0.84	-10.03	0.69	0.69	-29.11
2007	0.90	1.24	1.01	1.06	4.17
2006	0.99	1.31	1.11	1.51	4.90
2005	1.03	1.34	1.13	1.44	4.92
2004	1.00	1.30	1.18	1.47	4.92

Fiscal year ended Dec. 31. Next earnings report expected: Early February. EPS Estimates based on S&P Operating Earnings; historical GAAP earnings are as reported.

Dividend Data (Dates: mm/dd Payment Date: mm/dd/yy)

Amount ($)	Date Decl.	Ex-Div. Date	Stk. of Record	Payment Date
0.040	02/25	03/04	03/06	04/01/09
0.040	04/28	06/03	06/05	07/01/09
0.040	07/28	09/09	09/11	10/01/09
0.040	10/28	12/09	12/11	01/04/10

Dividends have been paid since 1929. Source: Company reports.

Gannett Co Inc.

STANDARD &POOR'S

Business Summary October 26, 2009

CORPORATE OVERVIEW. Gannett is the largest newspaper publisher in the U.S. The company publishes newspapers, operates broadcasting stations, runs Web sites in connection with its newspaper and broadcast operations, and is engaged in marketing, commercial printing, a newswire service, data services, and news programming.

The newspaper publishing segment (84% of 2008 revenues) consists of the operations of 85 daily newspapers and about 850 non-daily publications. The segment includes the publication of USA TODAY, the nation's largest selling daily newspaper. The company's strategy for non-daily publications is to target these products at communities of interest, defined by geography, demographics or lifestyle. In the U.K., the company is the second largest regional publisher via its wholly owned subsidiary, Newsquest plc, generating $988 million in 2008 revenues. Newspaper publishing revenues are derived principally from the sale of advertising (74% of 2008 revenues), circulation revenues (21%) and commercial printing (5%). Within the advertising category, revenues were derived from retail (47%), national (16%) and classified (37%) advertising.

In 2008, with the purchase of a controlling interest in Careerbuilder, GCI began reporting a separate digital segment (4% of 2008 revenues). The segment also

includes PointRoll, an Internet ad services business, Planet Discover, a provider of local, integrated online search and advertising technology, commercial printing, newswire, marketing and data services operations. GCI's Online Internet Audience in January 2009 was 27 million unique visitors, about 16% of the Internet audience as measured by Nielsen//NetRatings.

The broadcast segment (12% of 2008 revenues) consists of 23 network-affiliated TV stations, including 12 NBC, six CBS, three ABC affiliates and two MyNetworkTV affiliates, and Captivate Network, a national news and entertainment network that delivers programming and full-motion video advertising through video screens located in office tower elevators across North America. The principal sources of GCI's television revenues are: local advertising focusing on the immediate geographic area of the stations; national advertising, compensation paid by the networks for carrying commercial network programs; advertising on the stations' Web sites; and payments by advertisers to television stations for other services, such as the production of advertising material. Captivate derives its revenue principally from national advertising.

Company Financials Fiscal Year Ended Dec. 31

Per Share Data ($)	2008	2007	2006	2005	2004	2003	2002	2001	2000	1999
Tangible Book Value	NM	NM	NM	NM	NM	NM	NM	NM	NM	NM
Cash Flow	-27.96	5.38	6.07	6.24	6.14	5.30	5.13	4.78	4.99	3.87
Earnings	-29.11	4.17	4.90	4.92	4.92	4.46	4.31	3.12	3.63	3.26
S&P Core Earnings	-0.17	4.01	4.86	4.43	4.45	4.23	3.70	2.39	NA	NA
Dividends	1.60	1.42	1.20	1.12	1.04	0.98	0.94	0.90	0.86	0.81
Payout Ratio	NM	34%	24%	23%	21%	22%	22%	29%	24%	25%
Prices:High	39.00	63.50	64.97	82.41	91.38	89.63	79.90	71.14	81.56	83.63
Prices:Low	5.00	34.34	51.65	58.37	78.84	66.70	62.76	53.00	48.38	60.63
P/E Ratio:High	NM	15	13	17	19	20	19	23	22	26
P/E Ratio:Low	NM	8	11	12	16	15	15	17	13	19

Income Statement Analysis (Million $)										
Revenue	6,768	7,439	8,033	7,599	7,381	6,711	6,422	6,344	6,222	5,260
Operating Income	1,477	2,005	2,275	2,322	2,392	2,213	2,149	2,034	2,190	1,843
Depreciation	262	282	277	274	244	232	215	444	376	169
Interest Expense	191	260	288	211	141	139	146	222	219	94.6
Pretax Income	-1,715	1,449	1,719	1,818	1,995	1,840	1,765	1,371	1,609	1,527
Effective Tax Rate	NM	32.7%	32.5%	33.4%	34.0%	34.2%	34.3%	39.4%	39.6%	39.8%
Net Income	-1,783	976	1,161	1,211	1,317	1,211	1,160	831	972	919
S&P Core Earnings	-40.6	939	1,151	1,092	1,191	1,150	998	638	NA	NA

Balance Sheet & Other Financial Data (Million $)										
Cash	99.0	77.3	94.3	163	136	67.2	90.4	141	193	46.2
Current Assets	1,246	1,343	1,532	1,462	1,371	1,223	1,133	1,178	1,302	1,075
Total Assets	7,797	15,888	16,224	15,743	15,399	14,706	13,733	13,096	12,980	9,006
Current Liabilities	1,153	962	1,117	1,096	1,005	962	959	1,128	1,174	884
Long Term Debt	3,817	4,098	5,210	5,438	4,608	3,835	4,547	5,080	5,748	2,463
Common Equity	1,056	9,017	8,382	7,571	8,164	8,423	6,912	5,736	5,103	4,630
Total Capital	5,083	13,832	14,319	13,897	13,685	13,094	12,138	11,319	11,126	7,572
Capital Expenditures	165	171	201	263	280	281	275	325	351	258
Cash Flow	-6,385	1,258	1,438	1,486	1,561	1,443	1,375	1,275	1,348	1,089
Current Ratio	1.1	1.4	1.4	1.3	1.4	1.3	1.2	1.0	1.1	1.2
% Long Term Debt of Capitalization	75.1	29.6	36.4	39.1	33.7	29.3	37.5	44.9	51.7	32.5
% Net Income of Revenue	NM	13.1	14.4	15.9	17.8	18.0	18.1	13.1	15.6	17.5
% Return on Assets	NM	6.1	7.3	7.8	8.8	8.5	8.6	6.4	8.8	11.5
% Return on Equity	NM	11.2	14.6	15.4	15.9	15.8	18.3	15.3	20.0	21.4

Data as orig reptd.; bef. results of disc opers/spec. items. Per share data adj. for stk. divs.; EPS diluted. E-Estimated. NA-Not Available. NM-Not Meaningful. NR-Not Ranked. UR-Under Review.

Office: 7950 Jones Branch Dr, McLean, VA 22107-0910.
Telephone: 703-854-6000.
Email: gcishare@gannett.com
Website: http://www.gannett.com

Chrmn, Pres & CEO: C. Dubow
EVP & CFO: G.C. Martore
SVP, Secy & General Counsel: T.A. Mayman
Treas: M.A. Hart

Investor Contact: J. Heinz (703-854-6917)
Board Members: C. Dubow, H. D. Elias, A. H. Harper, J. Louis, M. Magner, S. K. McCune, D. M. McFarland, D. E. Shalala, N. Shapiro, K. H. Williams
Founded: 1906
Domicile: Delaware
Employees: 41,500

The **McGraw·Hill** Companies

Gap Inc. (The)

STANDARD &POOR'S

S&P Recommendation **HOLD** ★★★☆☆	Price $22.03 (as of Nov 27, 2009)	12-Mo. Target Price $25.00	Investment Style Large-Cap Blend

GICS Sector Consumer Discretionary
Sub-Industry Apparel Retail

Summary This specialty apparel retailer operates Gap, Banana Republic and Old Navy stores, offering casual clothing to moderate, upscale and value-oriented market segments.

Key Stock Statistics (Source S&P, Vickers, company reports)

52-Wk Range	$23.36– 9.56	S&P Oper. EPS 2010**E**	1.48	Market Capitalization(B)	$15.373	Beta	1.18
Trailing 12-Month EPS	$1.41	S&P Oper. EPS 2011**E**	1.60	Yield (%)	1.54	S&P 3-Yr. Proj. EPS CAGR(%)	8
Trailing 12-Month P/E	15.6	P/E on S&P Oper. EPS 2010**E**	14.9	Dividend Rate/Share	$0.34	S&P Credit Rating	BB+
$10K Invested 5 Yrs Ago	$10,375	Common Shares Outstg. (M)	697.8	Institutional Ownership (%)	64		

Price Performance

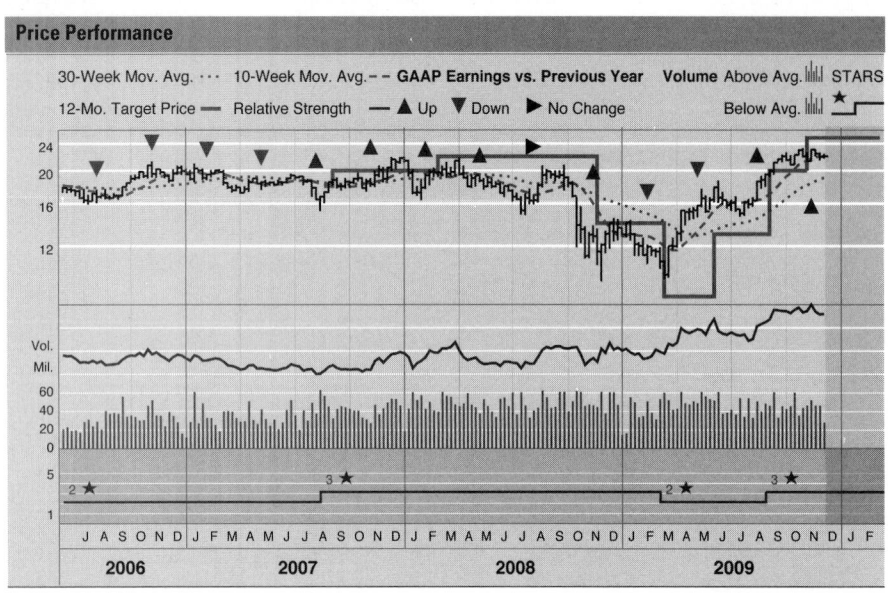

30-Week Mov. Avg. ··· 10-Week Mov. Avg. -- **GAAP Earnings vs. Previous Year** Volume Above Avg. STARS
12-Mo. Target Price — Relative Strength — ▲ Up ▼ Down ▶ No Change Below Avg. ★

Options: ASE, CBOE, P, Ph

Analysis prepared by **Marie Driscoll, CFA** on November 02, 2009, when the stock traded at **$ 21.34**.

Highlights

► We believe GPS's brands are mature and overdistributed, resulting in weak sales trends since FY 05 (Jan.). FY 09 sales declined 8%, to $14.5 billion (down 12% on a comp-store basis after a 4% comp decline in FY 08).

► We look for FY 10 sales to drop 5%; comps for the April and July quarters declined 8%. We expect modest sales improvement in the FY 10 second half, and see flat sales in FY 11. We believe Old Navy is in the nascent stage of a turn-around, but expect increased competition for Banana Republic and continued lackluster top-line results at Gap NA and Gap International to mitigate consolidated gains. We see FY 10 on-line (e-commerce) sales up 10%, benefiting from new brands Athleta and Piperlime.

► We expect gross margin improvement of 110 basis points (bps) in FY 10 to 38.6%, as improved merchandise margins outweigh deleveraging of occupancy costs. We see a 10 bps increase in the SG&A expense ratio with the deleveraging of fixed and home office expenses, resulting in a projected 11.6% EBIT margin. In FY 11, we look for about 90 bps of EBIT margin expansion, reflecting sourcing benefits to merchandise margins.

Investment Rationale/Risk

► Quarterly same-store sales comparisons have been negative for the past 20 quarters. We see traction at Old Navy with a 4% July-quarter comp decline versus a 16% drop in the prior-year quarter and note that September traffic rose 5% at Old Navy. With continued marketing support, we think Old Navy is well positioned to capture share this holiday season. We expect negative sales comparisons at Gap and Banana to restrict stock performance in FY 10.

► Risks to our recommendation and target price include significantly worse-than-expected same-store sales trends and a substantially slower-than-expected global economic recovery and a resulting further slowdown in consumer spending on discretionary purchases.

► Our 12-month target price of $25 assumes that GPS will trade at about 16X our FY 11 EPS estimate, about a 5% discount to the forward multiple for GPS's specialty apparel peers, based on our expectation that GPS will continue to disappoint investors with its monthly sales reports over the next 12 months.

Qualitative Risk Assessment

LOW	**MEDIUM**	HIGH

Our risk assessment reflects our view of GPS's strong cash flow and balance sheet, offset by weakness in its two largest brands and increased competition.

Quantitative Evaluations

S&P Quality Ranking   A-

D	C	B-	B	B+	**A-**	A	A+

Relative Strength Rank   MODERATE

66

LOWEST = 1   HIGHEST = 99

Revenue/Earnings Data

Revenue (Million $)

	1Q	2Q	3Q	4Q	Year
2010	3,127	3,245	3,589	--	--
2009	3,384	3,499	3,561	4,082	14,526
2008	3,549	3,685	3,854	4,675	15,763
2007	3,441	3,716	3,856	4,930	15,943
2006	3,626	3,716	3,860	4,821	16,023
2005	3,668	3,721	3,980	4,898	16,267

Earnings Per Share ($)

2010	0.31	0.33	0.44	E0.41	E1.48
2009	0.34	0.32	0.35	0.34	1.34
2008	0.25	0.32	0.30	0.35	1.09
2007	0.28	0.15	0.23	0.27	0.93
2006	0.31	0.30	0.24	0.39	1.24
2005	0.33	0.21	0.28	0.40	1.21

Fiscal year ended Jan. 31. Next earnings report expected: Early March. EPS Estimates based on S&P Operating Earnings; historical GAAP earnings are as reported.

Dividend Data (Dates: mm/dd Payment Date: mm/dd/yy)

Amount ($)	Date Decl.	Ex-Div. Date	Stk. of Record	Payment Date
0.085	02/25	04/06	04/08	04/29/09
0.085	05/20	07/06	07/08	07/29/09
0.085	10/02	10/09	10/14	10/28/09
0.085	11/18	01/04	01/06	01/27/10

Dividends have been paid since 1976. Source: Company reports.

Please read the Required Disclosures and Analyst Certification on the last page of this report.

The McGraw-Hill Companies

Gap Inc. (The)

Business Summary November 02, 2009

CORPORATE OVERVIEW. Gap, Inc. is a specialty retailer that operates stores selling casual apparel, accessories, and personal care products for men, women and children. As of January 31, 2009, it operated 3,190 stores: 1,227 Gap North America; 573 Banana Republic North America; 1,076 Old Navy North America; and 314 international locations, with 39.5 million sq. ft. of total retail space. In FY 09 (Jan.), international retail locations accounted for an estimated 10% of sales.

MARKET PROFILE. GPS participates in the men's, women's and children's apparel market, which generated approximately $200 billion at U.S. retail in 2008 (a 3.8% decline from 2007), according to ND Fashion world consumer estimated data. The apparel market is fragmented, with national brands marketed by 20 companies accounting for about 30% of total apparel sales, and the remaining 70% comprised of smaller and/or private label "store" brands. The market is mature, in our view, with demand largely mirroring population growth, and fashion trends accounting for a modicum of incremental volume. Deflationary pricing pressure is a function of channel competition and pro-

duction steadily moving offshore to low-cost producers in India, Asia and China, in our view. S&P forecasts an 5% to 8% drop in 2009 apparel sales.

COMPETITIVE LANDSCAPE. By channel, specialty stores account for the largest share of apparel sales, at 31% in 2008, according to NPD. Mass merchants (e.g., Walmart and Target) came in second, at 21%, and department stores came in third, at 15%, down from 19% in 2003. National chains (e.g., Sears and JC Penney) captured 14% of 2008 apparel sales, and off-price retailers (e.g., TJX and Ross Stores) were at 9% and the only retail channel to grow in 2008, + 5.2%. The remaining 11% was divided among factory outlets and direct and e-mail pure plays. GPS is the largest U.S. specialty retailer, with an estimated 20% of the channel's volume.

Company Financials Fiscal Year Ended Jan. 31

Per Share Data ($)	2009	2008	2007	2006	2005	2004	2003	2002	2001	2000
Tangible Book Value	6.04	11.50	9.58	6.33	5.73	5.33	4.12	3.48	3.43	2.63
Cash Flow	2.25	1.89	1.57	1.93	1.79	1.71	1.43	0.93	1.67	1.75
Earnings	1.34	1.09	0.93	1.24	1.21	1.09	0.54	-0.01	1.00	1.26
S&P Core Earnings	1.34	1.09	0.93	1.15	1.13	1.03	0.50	-0.10	0.86	NA
Dividends	0.32	0.32	0.20	0.09	0.09	0.09	0.09	0.09	0.09	0.09
Payout Ratio	24%	29%	22%	7%	7%	8%	17%	NM	9%	7%
Calendar Year	2008	2007	2006	2005	2004	2003	2002	2001	2000	1999
Prices:High	21.89	22.02	21.39	22.70	25.72	23.47	17.14	34.98	53.75	52.69
Prices:Low	9.41	15.20	15.91	15.90	18.12	12.01	8.35	11.12	18.50	30.81
P/E Ratio:High	16	20	23	18	21	22	32	NM	54	42
P/E Ratio:Low	7	14	17	13	15	11	15	NM	18	24

Income Statement Analysis (Million $)	2009	2008	2007	2006	2005	2004	2003	2002	2001	2000
Revenue	14,526	15,763	15,943	16,023	16,267	15,854	14,455	13,848	13,674	11,635
Operating Income	2,199	1,984	1,701	2,370	2,705	2,543	1,794	1,148	2,035	2,253
Depreciation	651	635	530	625	620	664	781	810	590	436
Interest Expense	9.00	36.0	49.0	45.0	167	234	249	109	74.9	31.8
Pretax Income	1,584	1,406	1,264	1,793	1,872	1,683	801	242	1,382	1,785
Effective Tax Rate	39.0%	38.3%	38.5%	37.9%	38.6%	38.8%	40.4%	NM	36.5%	36.9%
Net Income	967	867	778	1,113	1,150	1,030	477	-7.76	877	1,127
S&P Core Earnings	967	867	776	1,033	1,073	978	439	-89.1	760	NA

Balance Sheet & Other Financial Data (Million $)	2009	2008	2007	2006	2005	2004	2003	2002	2001	2000
Cash	1,715	1,939	2,644	2,987	7,139	2,261	3,389	1,036	409	450
Current Assets	4,005	4,086	5,029	5,239	6,304	6,689	5,740	3,045	2,648	2,198
Total Assets	7,564	7,838	8,544	8,821	10,048	10,343	9,902	7,591	7,013	5,189
Current Liabilities	2,158	2,433	2,272	1,942	2,242	2,492	2,727	2,056	2,799	1,753
Long Term Debt	Nil	50.0	188	513	1,886	2,487	2,896	1,961	780	785
Common Equity	4,387	4,274	5,174	5,425	4,936	4,783	3,658	3,010	2,928	2,233
Total Capital	4,437	4,324	5,362	5,938	6,822	7,270	6,554	4,971	3,708	3,018
Capital Expenditures	431	682	572	600	442	272	303	940	1,859	1,239
Cash Flow	1,618	1,502	1,308	1,738	1,770	1,694	1,258	803	1,468	1,563
Current Ratio	1.9	1.7	2.2	2.7	2.8	2.7	2.1	1.5	0.9	1.3
% Long Term Debt of Capitalization	Nil	1.2	3.5	8.6	27.6	34.2	44.2	39.5	21.0	26.0
% Net Income of Revenue	6.7	5.5	4.9	6.9	7.1	6.5	3.3	NM	6.4	9.7
% Return on Assets	12.6	10.6	9.0	11.8	11.1	10.2	5.4	NM	14.4	24.6
% Return on Equity	22.3	18.4	14.7	21.5	24.0	24.4	14.3	NM	34.0	59.2

Data as orig reptd.; bef. results of disc opers/spec. items. Per share data adj. for stk. divs.; EPS diluted. E-Estimated. NA-Not Available. NM-Not Meaningful. NR-Not Ranked. UR-Under Review.

Office: 2 Folsom St, San Francisco, CA 94105-1205.
Telephone: 650-952-4400 .
Email: investor_relations@gap.com
Website: http://www.gapinc.com

Chrmn & CEO: G.K. Murphy
COO: A. Peck
EVP, CFO & Chief Acctg Officer: S.L. Simmons
SVP & Secy: M. Banks

Investor Contact: E. Price (415-427-2360)
Board Members: A. D. Bellamy, D. De Sole, R. J. Fisher, W. S. Fisher, B. L. Martin, J. P. Montoya, G. K. Murphy, J. Schneider, M. A. Shattuck, III, K. C. Youngblood

Founded: 1969
Domicile: Delaware
Employees: 134,000

General Dynamics Corp

STANDARD &POOR'S

S&P Recommendation	HOLD ★★★☆☆	Price $67.08 (as of Nov 27, 2009)	12-Mo. Target Price $70.00	Investment Style Large-Cap Growth

GICS Sector Industrials
Sub-Industry Aerospace & Defense

Summary General Dynamics is the world's sixth largest military contractor and also one of the world's biggest makers of corporate jets.

Key Stock Statistics (Source S&P, Vickers, company reports)

52-Wk Range	$68.84– 35.28	S&P Oper. EPS 2009**E**	6.20	Market Capitalization(B)	$25.880	Beta		1.20
Trailing 12-Month EPS	$6.17	S&P Oper. EPS 2010**E**	6.45	Yield (%)	2.27	S&P 3-Yr. Proj. EPS CAGR(%)		4
Trailing 12-Month P/E	10.9	P/E on S&P Oper. EPS 2009**E**	10.8	Dividend Rate/Share	$1.52	S&P Credit Rating		A
$10K Invested 5 Yrs Ago	$13,515	Common Shares Outstg. (M)	385.8	Institutional Ownership (%)	77			

Price Performance

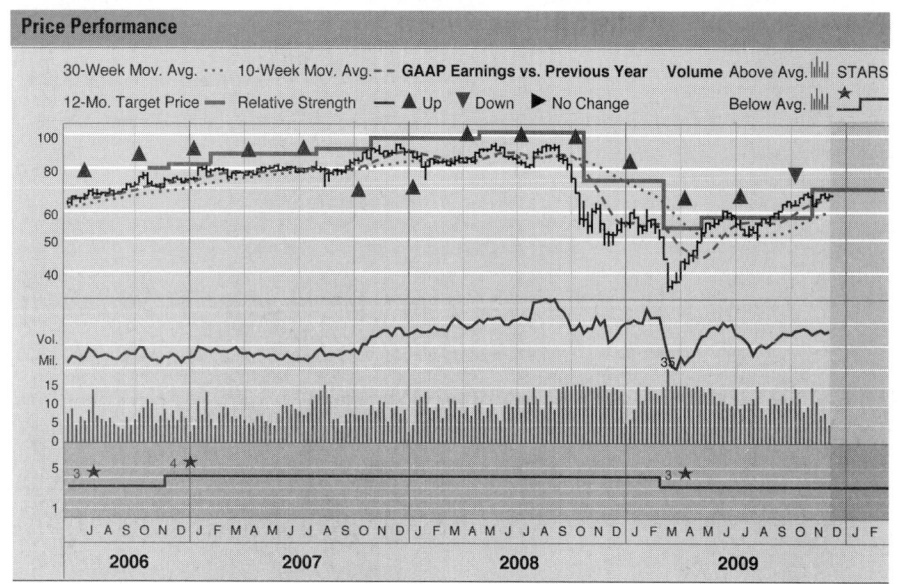

30-Week Mov. Avg. · · · 10-Week Mov. Avg. – – GAAP Earnings vs. Previous Year Volume Above Avg. STARS
12-Mo. Target Price — Relative Strength — ▲ Up ▼ Down ► No Change Below Avg. ★

Options: ASE, CBOE, Ph

Analysis prepared by **Richard Tortoriello** on November 03, 2009, when the stock traded at **$ 62.31**.

Highlights

► We estimate that sales will increase about 9% in 2009, driven by strong growth in Combat Systems and Marine Systems. For 2010, we project a 6% rise, with more even growth across Combat Systems, Marine, and Information Systems & Technology. We see Combat Systems growth driven by demand for ground vehicles and upgrades (Stryker, Abrams) and weapons systems and ammunition. We expect Marine growth to be fueled by a government-planned production increase from one to two nuclear submarines per year in 2011, and demand for DDG-1000 and Littoral combat ships and T-AKE combat-logistics ships.

► We project a 2009 operating margin of about 11.4%, versus 12.5% recorded in 2008, primarily reflecting anticipated lower margins in Aerospace, as well as lower Combat Systems margins, due to a change in product mix (the absence of significant MRAP vehicle production in 2009). We expect operating margins in 2010 to be flat with 2009 levels.

► We project EPS of $6.20 in 2009 and $6.45 in 2010. GD generated $6.61 in free cash flow per share in 2008, and we look for free cash flow above net income in 2009.

Investment Rationale/Risk

► Although growth at GD over the past few years has been fueled to a significant extent by Aerospace, we expect growth going forward to be driven increasingly by its defense segments, due to sharply declining demand for business jets. We see GD benefiting from growth in Marine, due to funding for new Virginia Class submarines, and moderate long-term growth in Combat Systems and IS&T, but we see the longer-term outlook for U.S. defense budget growth as weak, on a ballooning overall budget deficit and shifting military priorities.

► Risks to our recommendation and target price include the potential for cuts in military budgets and failure of GD to perform well on existing contracts or to win new contracts, as well as a greater-than-expected deterioration in GD's business jet backlog.

► Our 12-month target price of $70 is based on an enterprise value to estimated 2010 EBITDA multiple of 9.5X, below GD's 10-year average of 11X, but above GD's 20-year average of 8X. Given our view of GD's strong business execution and long-term business-jet prospects, we believe a near-average multiple is warranted for the shares.

Qualitative Risk Assessment

LOW	MEDIUM	HIGH

Our risk assessment for GD is based on the company's long-term record of consistent earnings and dividend growth, as reflected in its S&P Quality Ranking of A+. In addition, we note the company's conservative capitalization, with a debt-to-total capital ratio of 21% as of September 2009.

Quantitative Evaluations

S&P Quality Ranking   A+

D	C	B-	B	B+	A-	A	A+

Relative Strength Rank   STRONG

74

LOWEST = 1   HIGHEST = 99

Revenue/Earnings Data

Revenue (Million $)

	1Q	2Q	3Q	4Q	Year
2009	8,264	8,100	7,719	--	--
2008	7,005	7,303	7,140	7,852	29,300
2007	6,300	6,591	6,834	7,515	27,240
2006	5,546	5,934	6,069	6,514	24,063
2005	4,819	5,214	5,380	5,831	21,244
2004	4,661	4,666	4,661	5,190	19,178

Earnings Per Share ($)

2009	1.53	1.61	1.48	E1.57	E6.20
2008	1.42	1.60	1.59	1.62	6.22
2007	1.07	1.27	1.34	1.42	5.10
2006	0.95	1.03	1.08	1.13	4.20
2005	0.85	0.85	0.92	1.00	3.63
2004	0.66	0.73	0.79	0.82	2.99

Fiscal year ended Dec. 31. Next earnings report expected: Late January. EPS Estimates based on S&P Operating Earnings; historical GAAP earnings are as reported.

Dividend Data (Dates: mm/dd Payment Date: mm/dd/yy)

Amount ($)	Date Decl.	Ex-Div. Date	Stk. of Record	Payment Date
0.350	12/03	01/14	01/16	02/06/09
0.380	03/04	04/07	04/10	05/08/09
0.380	06/03	06/30	07/02	08/07/09
0.380	08/05	10/07	10/09	11/13/09

Dividends have been paid since 1979. Source: Company reports.

Please read the Required Disclosures and Analyst Certification on the last page of this report.

The McGraw-Hill Companies

General Dynamics Corp

STANDARD &POOR'S

Business Summary November 03, 2009

CORPORATE OVERVIEW. General Dynamics is the world's sixth largest defense contractor and the second largest maker of corporate jets by revenues. The company conducts business through four segments.

Information Systems & Technology (IS&T; 34% of sales and 29% of operating profits in 2008) primarily makes sophisticated electronics for land-, sea- and air-based weapons systems. Customers also include federal civilian agencies and commercial customers. The segment was created in 1998, and has grown through 27 acquisitions and internal development. The group's three principal markets are tactical and strategic mission systems (primarily secure communications systems), information technology and mission services, and intelligence mission systems, which provides specialized intelligence, surveillance, and reconnaissance equipment and services. Primary competitors are the IT divisions of Northrop Grumman, Lockheed Martin and Boeing.

Combat Systems (28% of sales and 30% of operating profit) makes, repairs and supports wheeled and tracked armored vehicles and munitions. Product lines include wheeled armored combat and tactical vehicles; tracked main battle tanks and infantry fighting vehicles; guns and ammunition-handling systems; ammunition and ordnance; mobile bridge systems; armor; chemical, bio-

logical, and explosion detection systems; spare parts; etc. Reflecting the U.S. Army's desire to transform itself into a highly agile fighting force, demand is expected to slow for tanks, but to accelerate for its various wheeled combat vehicles. Major current programs include the M1 Abrams tank (upgrade programs), the Stryker wheeled combat vehicle, and the Expeditionary Fighting Vehicle. CS's main competitor is BAE Systems' Land & Armaments division.

Aerospace (19% and 27%) makes the well-known Gulfstream business jet. Based on revenues, Gulfstream is the world's second-largest corporate jet maker, slightly behind Canada-based Bombardier. Textron's Cessna division, France's Dassault Aviation, and Hawker Beechcraft Corp. are also significant competitors. Gulfstream sells business jets primarily to the high end of the market. In 2008, Gulfstream introduced the ultra-large, ultra-long range G650 and the super-mid-size G250, which GD says offers the largest cabin, longest range, and fastest speed in its class. The G250 is scheduled for service entry in 2011 and the G650 in 2012.

Company Financials Fiscal Year Ended Dec. 31

Per Share Data ($)	2008	2007	2006	2005	2004	2003	2002	2001	2000	1999
Tangible Book Value	NM	0.46	0.25	1.40	NM	NM	2.81	1.92	3.22	1.64
Cash Flow	6.97	5.78	5.16	4.48	3.57	3.20	3.14	2.99	2.80	2.66
Earnings	6.22	5.10	4.20	3.63	2.99	2.50	2.59	2.33	2.24	2.18
S&P Core Earnings	5.16	4.90	4.08	3.34	2.81	2.34	1.62	1.57	NA	NA
Dividends	1.34	1.10	0.66	0.78	0.70	0.63	0.59	0.55	0.51	0.47
Payout Ratio	22%	22%	16%	22%	23%	25%	23%	24%	23%	22%
Prices:High	95.13	94.55	77.98	61.14	54.99	45.40	55.59	48.00	39.50	37.72
Prices:Low	47.81	70.61	56.68	48.80	42.48	25.00	36.63	30.25	18.13	23.09
P/E Ratio:High	15	19	19	17	18	18	21	21	18	17
P/E Ratio:Low	8	14	13	13	14	10	14	13	8	11
Income Statement Analysis (Million $)										
Revenue	29,300	27,240	24,063	21,244	19,178	16,617	13,829	12,163	10,356	8,959
Operating Income	3,954	3,391	3,009	2,539	2,173	1,744	1,795	1,756	1,555	1,396
Depreciation	301	278	384	342	232	277	213	271	226	193
Interest Expense	133	131	101	154	157	98.0	45.0	56.0	60.0	34.0
Pretax Income	3,604	3,047	2,527	2,100	1,785	1,372	1,584	1,424	1,262	1,126
Effective Tax Rate	31.2%	31.7%	32.3%	30.1%	32.6%	27.3%	33.6%	33.8%	28.6%	21.8%
Net Income	2,478	2,080	1,710	1,468	1,203	997	1,051	943	901	880
S&P Core Earnings	2,054	1,999	1,663	1,354	1,130	931	658	636	NA	NA
Balance Sheet & Other Financial Data (Million $)										
Cash	1,621	3,155	1,604	2,331	976	860	328	442	177	270
Current Assets	11,950	12,298	9,880	9,173	7,287	6,394	5,098	4,893	3,551	3,491
Total Assets	28,373	25,733	22,376	19,591	17,544	16,183	11,731	11,069	7,987	7,774
Current Liabilities	10,360	9,164	7,824	6,907	5,374	5,616	4,582	4,579	2,901	3,453
Long Term Debt	3,113	2,118	2,774	2,781	3,291	3,296	718	724	162	169
Common Equity	10,053	11,768	9,827	8,145	7,189	5,921	5,199	4,528	3,820	3,171
Total Capital	13,265	13,886	12,601	10,926	10,480	9,217	5,917	5,252	3,982	3,340
Capital Expenditures	490	474	334	279	266	224	264	356	288	197
Cash Flow	2,779	2,358	2,094	1,810	1,435	1,274	1,264	1,214	1,127	1,073
Current Ratio	1.2	1.3	1.3	1.3	1.4	1.1	1.1	1.1	1.2	1.0
% Long Term Debt of Capitalization	23.5	15.3	22.0	25.5	31.4	35.8	12.1	13.8	4.1	5.1
% Net Income of Revenue	8.5	7.6	7.1	6.9	6.3	6.0	7.6	7.8	8.7	9.8
% Return on Assets	9.2	8.6	8.1	7.9	7.1	7.1	9.2	9.9	11.4	12.6
% Return on Equity	22.7	19.3	19.0	19.1	18.4	17.9	21.6	22.6	25.8	31.5

Data as orig reptd.; bef. results of disc opers/spec. items. Per share data adj. for stk. divs.; EPS diluted. E-Estimated. NA-Not Available. NM-Not Meaningful. NR-Not Ranked. UR-Under Review.

Office: 2941 Fairview Park Dr Ste 100, Falls Church, VA 22042-4513.
Telephone: 703-876-3000.
Website: http://www.generaldynamics.com
Chrmn: N.D. Chabraja

Pres & CEO: J.L. Johnson
SVP & CFO: L.H. Redd
SVP, Secy & General Counsel: D.A. Savner
Chief Admin Officer: W. Oliver

Investor Contact: A. Gilliland (703-876-3748)
Board Members: N. D. Chabraja, J. S. Crown, W. P. Fricks, G. A. Joulwan, P. G. Kaminski, J. M. Keane, L. L. Lyles, J. C. Reyes, R. Walmsley

Founded: 1899
Domicile: Delaware
Employees: 92,300

General Electric Co

STANDARD &POOR'S

| S&P Recommendation | **BUY** ★★★★☆ | Price $15.94 (as of Nov 27, 2009) | 12-Mo. Target Price $19.00 | Investment Style Large-Cap Blend |

GICS Sector Industrials
Sub-Industry Industrial Conglomerates

Summary This conglomerate sells products ranging from jet engines and gas turbines to consumer appliances, railroad locomotives and medical equipment. It also owns NBC Universal, and is one of the world's largest providers of consumer and commercial financing.

Key Stock Statistics (Source S&P, Vickers, company reports)

52-Wk Range	$19.30–5.73	S&P Oper. EPS 2009**E**	0.96	Market Capitalization(B)	$169.721	Beta		1.55
Trailing 12-Month EPS	$1.08	S&P Oper. EPS 2010**E**	0.90	Yield (%)	2.51	S&P 3-Yr. Proj. EPS CAGR(%)		NM
Trailing 12-Month P/E	14.8	P/E on S&P Oper. EPS 2009**E**	16.6	Dividend Rate/Share	$0.40	S&P Credit Rating		AA+
$10K Invested 5 Yrs Ago	$5,430	Common Shares Outstg. (M)	10,647.5	Institutional Ownership (%)	50			

Price Performance

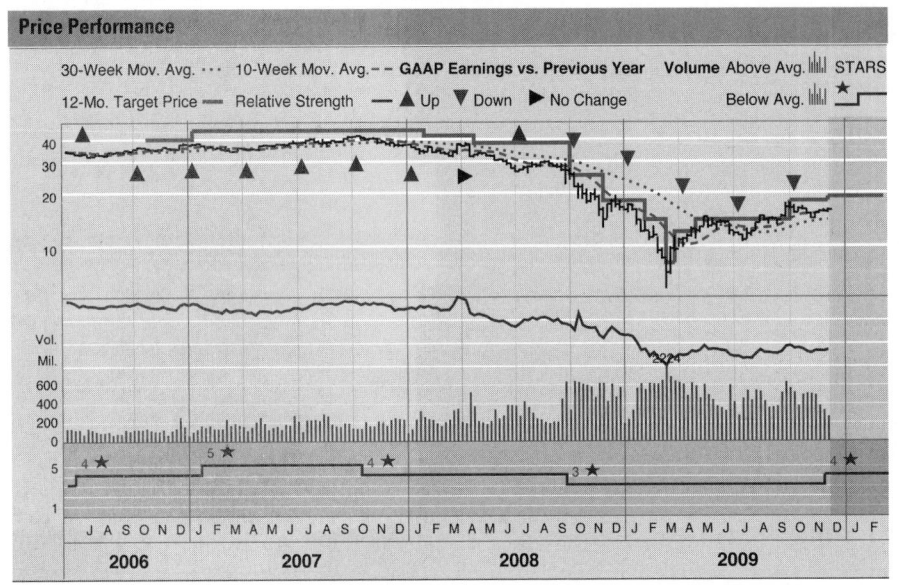

30-Week Mov. Avg. · · · 10-Week Mov. Avg. – – **GAAP Earnings vs. Previous Year** Volume Above Avg. STARS
12-Mo. Target Price — Relative Strength — ▲ Up ▼ Down ▶ No Change Below Avg.

Options: ASE, CBOE, P, Ph

Analysis prepared by **Richard Tortoriello** on November 23, 2009, when the stock traded at **$15.59**.

Highlights

► We project a 16% revenue decline in 2009, driven by double-digit declines in Capital Finance, as GE shrinks its finance portfolio, and in Consumer & Industrial. For 2010, we forecast a 7% decrease, reflecting an additional double-digit decline in Capital Finance, as well as much smaller declines in GE's industrial businesses driven by anticipated low order rates in late 2009 and early 2010. We see order rates across GE's businesses recovering in 2010, as we expect significant improvement in the global economy.

► We see operating margins narrowing to 9.5% in 2009, from 13.0% in 2008, primarily due to a significant profit decline in Capital Finance, where we expect sharply increased provisions for loan losses to drive operating margins down to near 0% in the fourth quarter of the year. For 2010, we project a slight increase in operating margin, to 9.7%, as we expect continued loan loss provisioning to be offset by efficiency improvements in GE's industrial businesses.

► We estimate EPS of $0.96 in 2009, declining to $0.90 in 2010.

Investment Rationale/Risk

► We see the following trends supporting our view of stock price appreciation over the next 12 months: continued good growth in emerging economies including China, Brazil, and Middle Eastern countries; our belief that GE will see significant effects from U.S. stimulus spending in 2010; stabilization in commercial air traffic, which we see as leading to growth in aerospace aftermarket demand; rising oil prices spurring demand in GE's oil & gas businesses; and continued signs of improvement in global economies and financial markets. Given this backdrop, we view current below-historical-average valuations for GE as attractive.

► Risks to our recommendation and target price include the possibility of a shallower economic upturn than we anticipate, as well as greater-than-expected credit losses at Capital Finance.

► Our 12-month target price of $19 reflects an enterprise value to estimated 2010 EBITDA multiple of 8.5X. This level is modestly above a 23-year low multiple (i.e., as far back as our data goes) of 7.5X, and well below a historical average of 16.5X.

Qualitative Risk Assessment

| LOW | **MEDIUM** | HIGH |

Our risk assessment reflects our view of GE's long-term record of steady growth in earnings, cash flow and dividends, which we attribute to good management of a diversified portfolio of growing and profitable businesses, offset by recent financial market turmoil, which has caused GE to access the capital markets.

Quantitative Evaluations

S&P Quality Ranking   A

| D | C | B- | B | B+ | A- | **A** | A+ |

Relative Strength Rank   STRONG

75

LOWEST = 1   HIGHEST = 99

Revenue/Earnings Data

Revenue (Million $)

	1Q	2Q	3Q	4Q	Year
2009	38,411	39,082	37,799	--	--
2008	42,243	46,891	47,234	46,213	182,515
2007	39,200	42,384	42,534	48,588	172,738
2006	37,370	39,243	40,286	44,621	163,391
2005	39,409	40,960	41,580	40,705	149,702
2004	33,350	37,035	38,272	43,706	152,363

Earnings Per Share ($)

2009	0.26	0.26	0.22	E0.22	E0.96
2008	0.44	0.54	0.45	0.36	1.78
2007	0.44	0.52	0.50	0.68	2.20
2006	0.40	0.48	0.48	0.64	1.99
2005	0.33	0.41	0.43	0.55	1.72
2004	0.32	0.38	0.38	0.51	1.59

Fiscal year ended Dec. 31. Next earnings report expected: Late January. EPS Estimates based on S&P Operating Earnings; historical GAAP earnings are as reported.

Dividend Data (Dates: mm/dd Payment Date: mm/dd/yy)

Amount ($)	Date Decl.	Ex-Div. Date	Stk. of Record	Payment Date
0.310	12/16	12/24	12/29	01/26/09
0.310	02/06	02/19	02/23	04/27/09
0.100	06/12	06/18	06/22	07/27/09
0.100	09/04	09/17	09/21	10/26/09

Dividends have been paid since 1899. Source: Company reports.

Please read the Required Disclosures and Analyst Certification on the last page of this report.

The McGraw·Hill Companies

General Electric Co

**STANDARD
&POOR'S**

Business Summary November 23, 2009

CORPORATE OVERVIEW. This multi-industry, heavy-equipment, media and financing giant does business through five segments: Energy Infrastructure, Technology Infrastructure, NBC Universal, Capital Finance, and Consumer & Industrial. Revenue by geographic region in 2008: U.S. 47%, Europe 24%, Pacific Basin 13%, Americas 8%, Middle East and Africa 5%, and Other 3%.

The Energy Infrastructure segment (21% of segment sales and 23% of segment operating profits in 2008) consists of GE's Energy, Oil & Gas and Water & Process Technologies businesses. Major products include gas turbines, wind turbines, solar technology, integrated coal gasification systems, and nuclear power plants, through joint ventures with Hitachi and Toshiba (the Energy business line); surface and subsea drilling and production systems, equipment for floating production platforms, compressors, turbines, and pressure control equipment (Oil & Gas); and water treatment solutions for industrial and municipal water systems (Water & Process Technologies). GE provides extensive aftermarket services for its equipment.

Technology Infrastructure (26% of sales and 31% of operating profits) includes the Healthcare, Aviation, Enterprise Solutions and Transportation business lines. Healthcare makes and services a wide variety of medical imaging

products, including X-ray, digital mammography, computed tomography, magnetic resonance and molecular imaging technologies. Aviation primarily makes and services jet engines for commercial and military aircraft. Enterprise Solutions offers products that improve customers' profitability and productivity, including sensor systems, security and life-cycle technologies, power system protection and control, plant automation, and embedded computer systems. Transportation makes and services locomotives, motors and electrical drive systems for a variety of industries, and gearing technology for applications such as wind turbines.

NBC Universal (9%, 12%) principally provides broadcast network television services to affiliated television stations within the U.S.; the production of live and recorded TV programs; the production and distribution of motion pictures; the operation of TV broadcasting stations; the ownership of several cable/satellite networks around the world; the operation of theme parks; and investment and programming activities in multimedia and the Internet.

Company Financials Fiscal Year Ended Dec. 31

Per Share Data ($)	2008	2007	2006	2005	2004	2003	2002	2001	2000	1999
Tangible Book Value	0.75	2.38	2.52	2.64	2.55	2.40	1.76	2.34	2.32	1.68
Cash Flow	2.92	3.21	2.90	2.53	2.39	2.24	2.11	2.11	2.04	1.74
Earnings	1.78	2.20	1.99	1.72	1.59	1.55	1.51	1.41	1.27	1.07
S&P Core Earnings	1.57	2.07	1.90	1.66	1.54	1.41	1.10	0.98	NA	NA
Dividends	0.93	1.15	1.03	0.91	0.82	0.77	0.73	0.66	0.57	0.49
Payout Ratio	52%	52%	52%	53%	52%	50%	48%	47%	45%	46%
Prices:High	38.52	42.15	38.49	37.34	37.75	32.42	41.84	53.55	60.50	53.17
Prices:Low	12.58	33.90	32.06	32.67	28.88	21.30	21.40	28.50	41.65	31.35
P/E Ratio:High	22	19	19	22	24	21	28	38	48	50
P/E Ratio:Low	7	15	16	19	18	14	14	20	33	29

Income Statement Analysis (Million $)										
Revenue	182,515	172,738	163,391	149,702	152,363	134,187	131,698	125,913	129,853	111,630
Operating Income	57,897	69,594	53,972	46,840	40,262	36,792	35,431	38,200	38,329	32,646
Depreciation	11,492	10,278	9,158	8,538	8,385	6,956	5,998	7,089	7,736	6,691
Interest Expense	26,209	23,787	19,286	15,187	11,907	10,432	10,216	11,062	11,720	10,013
Pretax Income	19,782	27,514	25,528	23,115	21,034	20,194	19,217	20,049	18,873	15,577
Effective Tax Rate	5.32%	15.0%	15.5%	16.7%	16.7%	21.4%	19.6%	27.8%	30.3%	31.1%
Net Income	18,089	22,468	20,666	18,275	16,593	15,589	15,133	14,128	12,735	10,717
S&P Core Earnings	15,939	21,155	19,701	17,548	16,138	14,195	11,038	9,889	NA	NA

Balance Sheet & Other Financial Data (Million $)										
Cash	12,300	17,578	14,275	9,011	150,864	133,388	125,772	110,099	99,534	90,312
Current Assets	NA	NA	NA	NA	NA	NA	NA	NA	NA	NA
Total Assets	797,800	795,337	697,239	673,342	750,330	647,483	575,244	495,023	437,006	405,200
Current Liabilities	NA	NA	NA	NA	NA	NA	NA	NA	NA	NA
Long Term Debt	330,067	319,015	260,804	212,281	213,161	170,004	140,632	79,806	82,132	71,427
Common Equity	104,700	115,559	112,314	109,354	110,284	79,180	63,706	54,824	50,492	42,557
Total Capital	448,263	454,722	394,867	346,019	354,242	267,611	222,328	148,975	146,250	128,436
Capital Expenditures	16,010	17,870	16,650	14,441	13,118	9,767	13,351	15,520	13,967	15,502
Cash Flow	29,506	32,746	29,824	26,813	24,978	22,545	21,131	21,217	20,471	17,408
Current Ratio	2.0	1.9	1.8	1.9	1.7	1.7	1.5	1.2	1.3	1.2
% Long Term Debt of Capitalization	73.6	70.2	66.0	61.3	60.2	63.5	63.3	53.6	56.2	55.6
% Net Income of Revenue	9.9	13.2	12.8	12.2	10.8	11.6	11.5	11.2	9.8	9.6
% Return on Assets	2.3	3.0	3.0	2.6	2.4	2.5	2.8	3.0	3.0	2.8
% Return on Equity	16.4	19.7	18.6	16.6	17.5	21.8	25.5	26.8	27.4	26.3

Data as orig reptd.; bef. results of disc opers/spec. items. Per share data adj. for stk. divs.; EPS diluted. E-Estimated. NA-Not Available. NM-Not Meaningful. NR-Not Ranked. UR-Under Review.

Office: 3135 Easton Tpke, Fairfield, CT 06828-0001.
Telephone: 203-373-2211.
Website: http://www.ge.com
Chrmn & CEO: J. Immelt

Pres: P. Ehrenheim
Vice Chrmn: J. Krenicki, Jr.
Vice Chrmn: M. Neal
Vice Chrmn: J.G. Rice

Investor Contact: D. Janki
Board Members: W. G. Beattie, J. I. Cash, Jr., W. Castell, A. M. Fudge, S. Hockfield, J. Immelt, A. Jung, J. Krenicki, Jr., A. Lafley, R. W. Lane, R. S. Larsen, R. B. Lazarus, J. J. Mulva, M. Neal, S. A. Nunn, R. S. Penske, J. G. Rice, K. S. Sherin, R. J. Swieringa, D. A. Warner, III

Founded: 1892
Domicile: New York
Employees: 323,000

The McGraw-Hill Companies

General Mills Inc.

STANDARD &POOR'S

| S&P Recommendation **STRONG BUY** ★★★★★ | Price $68.10 (as of Nov 27, 2009) | 12-Mo. Target Price $72.00 | Investment Style Large-Cap Blend |

GICS Sector Consumer Staples
Sub-Industry Packaged Foods & Meats

Summary This company is a major producer of packaged consumer food products, including Big G cereals and Betty Crocker desserts/baking mixes.

Key Stock Statistics (Source S&P, Vickers, company reports)

52-Wk Range	$69.10– 46.37	S&P Oper. EPS 2010**E**	4.45	Market Capitalization(B)	$22.240	Beta	0.30
Trailing 12-Month EPS	$4.26	S&P Oper. EPS 2011**E**	4.80	Yield (%)	2.76	S&P 3-Yr. Proj. EPS CAGR(%)	9
Trailing 12-Month P/E	16.0	P/E on S&P Oper. EPS 2010**E**	15.3	Dividend Rate/Share	$1.88	S&P Credit Rating	BBB+
$10K Invested 5 Yrs Ago	$17,378	Common Shares Outstg. (M)	326.6	Institutional Ownership (%)	73		

Price Performance

30-Week Mov. Avg. ··· 10-Week Mov. Avg. - - **GAAP Earnings vs. Previous Year** Volume Above Avg. ▊▊▊ STARS
12-Mo. Target Price ▬ Relative Strength ▬ ▲ Up ▼ Down ▶ No Change Below Avg. ▊▊▊ ★

Options: ASE, CBOE, P, Ph

Analysis prepared by **Tom Graves, CFA** on September 24, 2009, when the stock traded at **$ 63.89**.

Highlights

▶ In FY 10 (May), we look for net sales to advance no more than modestly from the $14.7 billion reported for FY 09, which included a 53rd week. We anticipate that FY 10 will be bolstered by investments in consumer marketing. Also, currency fluctuation translation could affect reported sales; in FY 10's first quarter, we saw a negative impact.

▶ We expect margin pressure from ingredient costs to ease in FY 10, and operating margins to receive support from productivity gains. Excluding some special items, we look for FY 10 EPS of $4.45, up from operating EPS of $3.98 in FY 09. Our FY 10 estimate includes $0.06 of costs related to restructuring, impairment and other exit costs, following an estimated $0.08 of such costs in FY 09. For FY 11, we see EPS of $4.80.

▶ Special items in FY 09 reported results included a negative impact of $0.22 a share from mark-to-market valuation of certain commodity positions, which we generally view as recognition of future commodity-related operating costs. GIS also had an $0.11 net gain related to divestitures, an $0.08 gain from an insurance settlement, and a $0.15 expense related to a tax item.

Investment Rationale/Risk

▶ We expect GIS's important U.S. Retail segment to benefit from consumers eating more at home. Also, we generally like the company's brand strength, which we think will provide some protection from competitive pressure presented by less expensive private label products. We believe that GIS has opportunities to bolster longer-term profit margins through a focus on such areas as manufacturing and spending efficiency, global sourcing and sales mix. We look for GIS to continue generating free cash flow, with a portion being used for dividends and stock repurchases.

▶ Risks to our recommendation and target price include competitive pressures, disappointing consumer acceptance of new products, higher-than-expected commodity cost inflation, and an inability to achieve sales and earnings growth forecasts.

▶ Our 12-month target price of $72 reflects a modest P/E premium, based on our calendar 2009 EPS estimates, to what we project, on average, for a group of other packaged food stocks. GIS shares recently had an indicated dividend yield of 2.9%.

Qualitative Risk Assessment

| LOW | MEDIUM | HIGH |

Our risk assessment reflects the relatively stable nature of the company's end markets, strong cash flows, and an S&P Quality Ranking of A- that reflects GIS's historical earnings and dividend growth.

Quantitative Evaluations

S&P Quality Ranking A-

| D | C | B- | B | B+ | A- | A | A+ |

Relative Strength Rank STRONG

78

LOWEST = 1   HIGHEST = 99

Revenue/Earnings Data

Revenue (Million $)

	1Q	2Q	3Q	4Q	Year
2010	3,519	--	--	--	--
2009	3,497	4,011	3,537	3,646	14,691
2008	3,072	3,703	3,406	3,471	13,652
2007	2,860	3,467	3,054	3,061	12,442
2006	2,662	3,273	2,860	2,845	11,640
2005	2,585	3,168	2,772	2,719	11,244

Earnings Per Share ($)

2010	1.25	E1.35	E0.97	E0.85	E4.45
2009	0.79	1.09	0.85	1.07	3.80
2008	0.80	1.14	1.23	0.53	3.71
2007	0.74	1.08	0.74	0.62	3.18
2006	0.64	0.97	0.68	0.61	2.90
2005	0.45	0.92	0.58	1.14	3.08

Fiscal year ended May 31. Next earnings report expected: Mid December. EPS Estimates based on S&P Operating Earnings; historical GAAP earnings are as reported.

Dividend Data (Dates: mm/dd Payment Date: mm/dd/yy)

Amount ($)	Date Decl.	Ex-Div. Date	Stk. of Record	Payment Date
0.430	12/08	01/08	01/12	02/02/09
0.430	03/09	04/07	04/09	05/01/09
0.470	06/29	07/08	07/10	08/03/09
0.470	09/21	10/07	10/12	11/02/09

Dividends have been paid since 1898. Source: Company reports.

Please read the Required Disclosures and Analyst Certification on the last page of this report.

The McGraw-Hill Companies

General Mills Inc.

STANDARD
&POOR'S

Business Summary September 24, 2009

CORPORATE OVERVIEW. General Mills (GIS) is the second largest U.S. producer of ready-to-eat breakfast cereals, and a leading producer of other well-known packaged consumer foods. The U.S. Retail segment, which accounted for 68% of net sales in FY 09 (May), includes cereals, refrigerated yogurt, soup, dinners, vegetables, dough products, baking products, snacks, and organic products. The Bakeries and Foodservice segment (14%) includes products sold to distributors, convenience stores, restaurant operators, and cafeterias. The International segment (18%) includes products manufactured in the U.S. for export, mainly to Caribbean and Latin American markets, as well as products manufactured for sale to GIS international joint ventures.

Major cereal brands include Cheerios, Wheaties, Lucky Charms, Total and Chex. Other consumer packaged food products include baking mixes (e.g., Betty Crocker, Bisquick); dry dinners; Progresso soups, Green Giant canned and frozen vegetables; snacks; Pillsbury refrigerated and frozen dough products, frozen pizza; Yoplait and Colombo yogurt; Haagen-Dazs ice cream; and Cascadian Farm and Muir Glen organic products. Some products may be mar-

keted under licensing arrangements with other parties. GIS also has a grain merchandising operation that holds inventories carried at fair market value, and uses derivatives to hedge its net inventory position and minimize its market exposures.

During FY 09, Wal-Mart Stores, Inc., and affiliates accounted for 21% of GIS's consolidated net sales.

GIS joint ventures include a 50% equity interest in Cereal Partners Worldwide (CPW), a joint venture with Nestle S.A. that manufactures and markets cereal products outside the U.S. and Canada; and a 50% equity interest in Haagen-Dazs Japan, Inc., which manufactures, distributes and markets Haagen-Dazs ice cream products and frozen novelties.

Company Financials Fiscal Year Ended May 31

Per Share Data ($)	2009	2008	2007	2006	2005	2004	2003	2002	2001	2000
Tangible Book Value	NM	NM	NM	NM	NM	NM	NM	NM	NM	NM
Cash Flow	5.12	5.06	4.59	3.99	4.11	3.79	3.39	2.21	3.04	2.68
Earnings	3.80	3.71	3.18	2.90	3.08	2.75	2.43	1.35	2.28	2.00
S&P Core Earnings	2.88	3.29	3.03	2.72	2.17	2.43	1.74	0.55	1.79	NA
Dividends	1.57	1.44	1.44	1.34	1.24	1.10	1.10	1.10	1.10	1.10
Payout Ratio	41%	39%	42%	46%	40%	40%	45%	81%	48%	55%
Calendar Year	2008	2007	2006	2005	2004	2003	2002	2001	2000	1999
Prices:High	72.01	61.52	59.23	53.89	49.96	49.66	51.73	52.86	45.31	43.94
Prices:Low	51.00	54.17	47.05	44.67	43.01	41.43	37.38	37.26	29.38	32.50
P/E Ratio:High	19	17	19	19	16	18	21	39	20	22
P/E Ratio:Low	13	15	15	15	14	15	15	28	13	16

Income Statement Analysis (Million $)	2009	2008	2007	2006	2005	2004	2003	2002	2001	2000
Revenue	14,691	13,652	12,442	11,640	11,244	11,070	10,506	7,949	7,078	6,700
Operating Income	2,727	2,687	2,515	2,420	2,435	2,442	2,290	1,569	1,392	1,308
Depreciation	454	459	418	424	443	399	365	296	223	209
Interest Expense	417	422	427	427	488	537	589	445	223	168
Pretax Income	2,025	1,917	1,704	1,631	1,904	1,583	1,377	700	1,015	950
Effective Tax Rate	35.6%	32.5%	32.9%	33.2%	34.9%	33.4%	33.4%	34.1%	34.5%	35.3%
Net Income	1,304	1,295	1,144	1,090	1,240	1,055	917	461	665	614
S&P Core Earnings	988	1,142	1,089	1,024	863	931	652	189	512	NA

Balance Sheet & Other Financial Data (Million $)	2009	2008	2007	2006	2005	2004	2003	2002	2001	2000
Cash	750	674	417	647	573	751	703	975	64.1	25.6
Current Assets	3,535	3,620	3,054	3,176	3,055	3,215	3,179	3,437	1,408	1,190
Total Assets	17,875	19,042	18,184	18,207	18,066	18,448	18,227	16,540	5,091	4,574
Current Liabilities	3,606	4,856	5,845	6,138	4,184	2,757	3,444	5,747	2,209	2,529
Long Term Debt	5,755	4,349	3,218	2,415	4,255	7,410	7,516	5,591	2,221	1,760
Common Equity	5,175	6,216	5,319	5,772	5,676	5,248	4,175	3,576	52.2	-289
Total Capital	11,680	12,261	11,109	11,145	12,915	14,730	13,652	9,727	2,696	1,859
Capital Expenditures	563	522	460	360	414	628	711	506	308	268
Cash Flow	1,758	1,754	1,562	1,514	1,683	1,454	1,282	757	888	823
Current Ratio	1.0	0.8	0.5	0.5	0.7	1.2	0.9	0.6	0.6	0.5
% Long Term Debt of Capitalization	49.3	35.4	28.9	21.7	32.9	50.3	55.1	57.5	82.4	94.7
% Net Income of Revenue	8.9	9.5	9.2	9.4	11.0	9.5	8.7	5.8	9.4	9.2
% Return on Assets	7.1	7.0	6.3	6.0	6.8	5.8	5.3	4.3	13.8	14.1
% Return on Equity	22.9	22.5	20.6	18.7	22.7	22.4	23.7	25.4	NM	NM

Data as orig reptd.; bef. results of disc opers/spec. items. Per share data adj. for stk. divs.; EPS diluted. E-Estimated. NA-Not Available. NM-Not Meaningful. NR-Not Ranked. UR-Under Review.

Office: 1 General Mills Blvd, Minneapolis, MN 55426-1348.
Telephone: 763-764-7600.
Website: http://www.generalmills.com
Chrmn, Pres & CEO: K.J. Powell

EVP & CFO: D.L. Mulligan
EVP, Secy & General Counsel: R.A. Palmore
CTO: P.C. Erickson
Chief Acctg Officer & Cntlr: R.O. Lund

Investor Contact: K. Wenker (800-245-5703)
Board Members: B. H. Anderson, R. K. Clark, P. Danos, W. T. Esrey, R. V. Gilmartin, J. R. Hope, H. G. Miller, H. O. Ochoa-Brillembourg, S. Odland, K. J. Powell, L. E. Quam, M. D. Rose, R. L. Ryan, D. A. Terrell

Founded: 1928
Domicile: Delaware
Employees: 30,000

Genuine Parts Co

STANDARD &POOR'S

S&P Recommendation **STRONG BUY** ★★★★★	Price $36.13 (as of Nov 27, 2009)	12-Mo. Target Price $47.00	Investment Style Large-Cap Blend

GICS Sector Consumer Discretionary
Sub-Industry Distributors

Summary This company is a leading wholesale distributor of automotive replacement parts, industrial parts and supplies, and office products.

Key Stock Statistics (Source S&P, Vickers, company reports)

52-Wk Range	$40.50– 24.93	S&P Oper. EPS 2009**E**	2.38	Market Capitalization(B)	$5.765	Beta	0.74
Trailing 12-Month EPS	$2.43	S&P Oper. EPS 2010**E**	2.59	Yield (%)	4.43	S&P 3-Yr. Proj. EPS CAGR(%)	2
Trailing 12-Month P/E	14.9	P/E on S&P Oper. EPS 2009**E**	15.2	Dividend Rate/Share	$1.60	S&P Credit Rating	NA
$10K Invested 5 Yrs Ago	$9,931	Common Shares Outstg. (M)	159.6	Institutional Ownership (%)	73		

Price Performance

30-Week Mov. Avg. · · · 10-Week Mov. Avg. - - GAAP Earnings vs. Previous Year Volume Above Avg. ▓ STARS
12-Mo. Target Price — Relative Strength ▲ Up ▼ Down ▶ No Change Below Avg. ▓ ★

Options: ASE, P, Ph

Analysis prepared by **Efraim Levy, CFA** on October 21, 2009, when the stock traded at **$ 37.85**.

Highlights

▶ We expect revenues to drop 9.5% in 2009. We think pricing will remain competitive, and we foresee operating margins narrowing in 2009 as lower revenues should squeeze profits despite cost-cutting initiatives. We forecast a sales increase of 1.7% in 2010, as we think most segments will have sales growth.

▶ We expect longer-term prospects for GPC's auto parts segment to be enhanced by the rising number and increasing complexity of vehicles. The median vehicle age in the U.S. is currently more than nine years. We believe GPC will benefit from an expanding market share, as long-term industry consolidation continues to drive out smaller participants. We also think GPC will use its distribution strength to leverage sales of acquired parts companies.

▶ EPS of $2.92 in 2008 includes a charge of about $0.07 for pension plan losses. We think the company's solid balance sheet, low debt, and strong cash flow provide the ability and resources to help accelerate earnings growth over the longer term. We see GPC using cash flow to repurchase shares, invest in the business, make modest-sized acquisitions, and increase the dividend.

Investment Rationale/Risk

▶ Based on our 2010 EPS estimate, the stock's recent P/E of about 14.5X is below the average for peers, as depressed earnings for peers has increased the group average P/E. In normal economic conditions we think a premium for GPC is warranted by the company's greater earnings stability. We view GPC as financially strong. Earnings quality appears high to us, and an above-average dividend yield adds to GPC's total return potential.

▶ Risks to our recommendation and target price include weaker-than-expected demand for the company's products and a slower-than-anticipated improvement in operating margins.

▶ Our 12-month target price of $47 is based on a weighted blend of our relative and discounted cash flow (DCF) metrics. On a relative basis, we assume a P/E of about 18X applied to our 2010 EPS estimate of $2.59, reflecting historical and peer P/E comparisons, leading to a value of nearly $47. Our DCF model, which assumes a weighted average cost of capital of 9.0%, a compound annual growth rate of 4.5% over the next 15 years, and a terminal growth rate of 3%, calculates an intrinsic value of $47.

Qualitative Risk Assessment

LOW	MEDIUM	HIGH

Our risk assessment reflects GPC's long-term record of rising sales and earnings and what we view as strong corporate leadership and a healthy balance sheet.

Quantitative Evaluations

S&P Quality Ranking A

D	C	B-	B	B+	A-	A	A+

Relative Strength Rank MODERATE

42

LOWEST = 1   HIGHEST = 99

Revenue/Earnings Data

Revenue (Million $)

	1Q	2Q	3Q	4Q	Year
2009	2,445	2,535	2,607	--	--
2008	2,739	2,873	2,882	2,520	11,015
2007	2,649	2,770	2,798	2,627	10,843
2006	2,554	2,662	2,700	2,543	10,458
2005	2,342	2,476	2,556	2,410	9,783
2004	2,197	2,298	2,349	2,253	9,097

Earnings Per Share ($)

2009	0.56	0.65	0.67	E0.50	E2.38
2008	0.75	0.81	0.81	0.55	2.92
2007	0.71	0.76	0.76	0.75	2.98
2006	0.66	0.70	0.71	0.70	2.76
2005	0.61	0.63	0.63	0.63	2.50
2004	0.57	0.58	0.56	0.55	2.25

Fiscal year ended Dec. 31. Next earnings report expected: Mid February. EPS Estimates based on S&P Operating Earnings; historical GAAP earnings as reported.

Dividend Data (Dates: mm/dd Payment Date: mm/dd/yy)

Amount ($)	Date Decl.	Ex-Div. Date	Stk. of Record	Payment Date
0.400	01/23	03/04	03/06	04/01/09
0.400	04/20	06/03	06/05	07/01/09
0.400	08/17	09/02	09/04	10/01/09
0.400	11/16	12/02	12/04	01/04/10

Dividends have been paid since 1948. Source: Company reports.

Genuine Parts Co

**STANDARD
&POOR'S**

Business Summary October 21, 2009

CORPORATE OVERVIEW. Genuine Parts is the leading independent U.S. distributor of automotive replacement parts. It operates 58 NAPA warehouse distribution centers in the U.S., about 1,100 company-owned jobbing stores, three Rayloc auto parts rebuilding plants, four Balkamp distribution centers, two Altrom import parts distribution centers, 13 heavy vehicle parts distribution centers and facilities and one JI Chicago distribution center. It also has operations in Canada and Mexico. The company has been expanding via a combination of internal growth and acquisitions.

The automotive parts segment (48% of 2008 revenues, 45% of profits) serves about 5,800 NAPA Auto Parts stores, including about 1,100 company-owned stores, selling to garages, service stations, car and truck dealers, fleet operators, leasing companies, bus and truck lines, etc.

The industrial parts segment (32%, 34%) distributes around three million industrial replacement parts and related supply items, including bearings, power transmission equipment replacement parts, including hydraulic and pneumatic products, material handling components, agricultural and irrigation

equipment, and related items from locations in the U.S. and Canada.

Through S. P. Richards Co., the office products group (16%, 17%) distributes more than 40,000 office product items, including information processing supplies and office furniture, machines and supplies to office suppliers, from facilities in the U.S. and Canada.

The EIS electrical/electronics materials group (4%, 4%) was formed via the 1998 acquisition of EIS, Inc., for $200 million. EIS is a wholesale distributor of material and supplies to the electrical and electronic industries.

The U.S. accounted for almost 88% of sales in 2008. Canada contributed 11%, and Mexico represented 1%.

Company Financials Fiscal Year Ended Dec. 31

Per Share Data ($)	2008	2007	2006	2005	2004	2003	2002	2001	2000	1999
Tangible Book Value	13.58	15.86	4.82	15.21	14.21	12.95	11.88	10.97	10.50	9.80
Cash Flow	3.46	3.49	3.18	2.87	2.61	2.42	2.50	2.21	2.72	2.61
Earnings	2.92	2.98	2.76	2.50	2.25	2.03	2.10	1.71	2.20	2.11
S&P Core Earnings	2.54	2.98	2.76	2.40	2.22	1.95	1.80	1.53	NA	NA
Dividends	1.56	1.46	1.35	1.25	1.20	1.18	1.16	1.14	1.10	1.03
Payout Ratio	53%	49%	49%	50%	53%	58%	55%	67%	50%	49%
Prices:High	46.28	51.68	48.34	46.64	44.32	33.75	38.80	37.94	26.69	35.75
Prices:Low	29.92	46.00	40.00	40.75	32.03	27.20	27.10	23.91	18.25	22.25
P/E Ratio:High	16	17	18	19	20	17	18	22	12	17
P/E Ratio:Low	10	15	14	16	14	13	13	14	8	11

Income Statement Analysis (Million $)	2008	2007	2006	2005	2004	2003	2002	2001	2000	1999
Revenue	11,015	10,843	10,458	9,783	9,097	8,449	8,259	8,221	8,370	7,982
Operating Income	889	926	870	804	698	641	676	656	739	718
Depreciation	88.7	87.7	73.4	65.5	62.2	69.0	70.2	85.8	92.3	90.0
Interest Expense	31.7	31.3	31.6	29.6	Nil	Nil	Nil	Nil	Nil	Nil
Pretax Income	768	822	771	709	636	572	606	496	647	628
Effective Tax Rate	38.1%	37.8%	38.3%	38.3%	37.8%	38.1%	39.3%	40.1%	40.4%	39.9%
Net Income	475	506	475	437	396	354	368	297	385	378
S&P Core Earnings	414	506	475	420	388	339	316	265	NA	NA

Balance Sheet & Other Financial Data (Million $)	2008	2007	2006	2005	2004	2003	2002	2001	2000	1999
Cash	67.8	232	136	189	135	15.4	20.0	85.8	27.7	45.7
Current Assets	3,871	4,053	3,835	3,807	3,633	3,418	3,336	3,146	3,019	2,895
Total Assets	4,786	4,774	4,497	4,772	4,455	4,116	4,020	4,207	4,142	3,930
Current Liabilities	1,287	1,548	1,199	1,249	1,133	1,017	1,070	919	988	916
Long Term Debt	500	250	500	500	500	625	675	836	771	702
Common Equity	2,324	2,717	2,550	2,694	2,544	2,312	2,130	2,345	2,261	2,178
Total Capital	2,893	3,033	3,111	3,408	3,212	3,100	2,950	3,287	3,154	3,014
Capital Expenditures	105	116	126	85.7	72.1	73.9	64.8	41.9	71.1	88.3
Cash Flow	564	594	549	503	458	423	438	383	478	468
Current Ratio	3.0	2.6	3.2	3.0	3.2	3.4	3.1	3.4	3.1	3.2
% Long Term Debt of Capitalization	17.3	8.2	16.1	14.7	15.6	20.2	22.9	25.4	24.4	23.3
% Net Income of Revenue	4.3	4.7	4.5	4.5	4.3	4.2	4.4	3.6	4.6	4.7
% Return on Assets	10.0	10.9	10.3	9.5	9.2	8.6	8.9	7.1	9.5	10.0
% Return on Equity	18.9	19.2	18.1	16.7	16.3	15.9	16.4	12.9	17.4	17.9

Data as orig reptd.; bef. results of disc opers/spec. items. Per share data adj. for stk. divs.; EPS diluted. E-Estimated. NA-Not Available. NM-Not Meaningful. NR-Not Ranked. UR-Under Review.

Office: 2999 Cir 75 Pkwy, Atlanta, GA 30339.
Telephone: 770-953-1700.
Website: http://www.genpt.com
Chrmn, Pres & CEO: T. Gallagher

Vice Chrmn, EVP, CFO & Chief Acctg Officer: J.W. Nix
COO: M.D. Orr
SVP & Treas: F.M. Howard
SVP & Secy: C.B. Yancey

Board Members: M. B. Bullock, J. E. Douville, T. Gallagher, G. C. Guynn, J. D. Johns, M. M. Johns, J. H. Lanier, W. B. Needham, J. W. Nix, L. L. Prince, G. W. Rollins

Founded: 1928
Domicile: Georgia
Employees: 30,300

Genworth Financial Inc

STANDARD &POOR'S

S&P Recommendation	HOLD ★★★★★	Price $10.68 (as of Nov 27, 2009)	12-Mo. Target Price $12.00	Investment Style Large-Cap Blend

GICS Sector Financials
Sub-Industry Multi-line Insurance

Summary This insurance holding company serves lifestyle protection, retirement income, investment and mortgage insurance needs around the world.

Key Stock Statistics (Source S&P, Vickers, company reports)

52-Wk Range	$13.68–0.78	S&P Oper. EPS 2009**E**	0.43	Market Capitalization(B)	$5.218	Beta		3.65
Trailing 12-Month EPS	$-1.88	S&P Oper. EPS 2010**E**	1.22	Yield (%)	Nil	S&P 3-Yr. Proj. EPS CAGR(%)		-26
Trailing 12-Month P/E	NM	P/E on S&P Oper. EPS 2009**E**	24.8	Dividend Rate/Share	Nil	S&P Credit Rating		BBB
$10K Invested 5 Yrs Ago	$4,348	Common Shares Outstg. (M)	488.6	Institutional Ownership (%)	74			

Price Performance

30-Week Mov. Avg. ··· 10-Week Mov. Avg. – – GAAP Earnings vs. Previous Year Volume Above Avg. |||| STARS
12-Mo. Target Price — Relative Strength ▲ Up ▼ Down ► No Change Below Avg. |||| ★

Options: ASE, CBOE, P, Ph

Analysis prepared by **Bret Howlett** on November 11, 2009, when the stock traded at **$ 11.56**.

Highlights

► We expect strong earnings growth in 2010 as GNW benefits from lower losses at U.S. mortgage Insurance (MI), and cost-cutting initiatives. We expect the fundamentals in Retirement & Protection will be weak, characterized by lower sales and product outflows, narrower margins, partially offset by higher investment income. GNW has scaled back production in fixed annuities and guaranteed investment contracts to preserve capital, and has shifted focus in distributing its annuities and traditional life products, which we think will hurt margins. We believe life insurance earnings will be down on higher funding costs, lower long term care sales and an elevated benefit ratio, partially offset by rate increases on the in-force block.

► We forecast losses in U.S. MI as mortgage delinquencies rise, although loss mitigation efforts should lead to betters earnings results. We expect international earnings to increase 12% on the improving housing markets of Canada and Australia, and rate increases for Lifestyle products.

► We forecast operating EPS of $0.43 in 2009 and $1.22 in 2010, excluding realized investment gains or losses.

Investment Rationale/Risk

► Although GNW currently trades at a steep discount to the life insurance group, our hold opinion reflects our view that the company's limited financial flexibility, continued losses in the U.S. mortgage insurance business, and elevated impairments in its investment portfolio will continue to weigh on the shares. While we believe GNW's capital and liquidity positions are weak relative to peers, its financial position has recently improved amid better credit markets and the IPO of 43% of its Canadian MI business. Since GNW still has sizable exposure to RMBS and CMBS, we expect market concerns regarding the credit environment to result in share price volatility. However, we think capital, housing, and credit market problems are largely reflected in the valuation.

► Risks to our recommendation and target price include a continued low interest rate environment; increased investment portfolio risks; high concentrations of product line sales associated with certain third parties; and a prolonged slowdown in the housing market.

► Our 12-month target price of $12, about 0.5X our 2010 book value per share estimate, is below the company's historical average multiple.

Qualitative Risk Assessment

LOW	MEDIUM	HIGH

Our risk assessment reflects significant exposure of the mortgage insurance business to the U.S. housing market, which may result in volatility. In addition, GNW is vulnerable to investment losses and has a weaker capital position than peers, in our view. Our assessment also reflects the unfavorable operating environment for GNW's life insurance subsidiaries.

Quantitative Evaluations

S&P Quality Ranking NR

D	C	B-	B	B+	A-	A	A+

Relative Strength Rank MODERATE

58

LOWEST = 1   HIGHEST = 99

Revenue/Earnings Data

Revenue (Million $)

	1Q	2Q	3Q	4Q	Year
2009	1,734	2,483	2,391	--	--
2008	2,753	2,398	2,168	2,629	9,948
2007	2,710	2,765	2,875	2,775	11,125
2006	2,625	2,754	2,804	2,846	11,029
2005	2,611	2,610	2,628	2,655	10,504
2004	3,024	2,921	2,470	2,642	11,057

Earnings Per Share ($)

2009	-1.08	-0.11	0.04	E0.16	E0.43
2008	0.27	-0.25	-0.60	-0.74	-1.32
2007	0.69	0.70	0.76	0.41	2.58
2006	0.69	0.68	0.65	0.81	2.83
2005	0.65	0.60	0.64	0.64	2.52
2004	0.53	0.55	0.55	0.70	2.34

Fiscal year ended Dec. 31. Next earnings report expected: Early February. EPS Estimates based on S&P Operating Earnings; historical GAAP earnings are as reported.

Dividend Data

The most recent payment was $0.10 a share in October 2008.

The McGraw·Hill Companies

Genworth Financial Inc

STANDARD &POOR'S

Business Summary November 11, 2009

CORPORATE OVERVIEW. Genworth Financial, Inc., carved out from General Electric (GE) in May 2004, is a U.S. insurance company with an expanding international presence. As of February 2009, GNW had operations in 25 countries and offered products and services to over 15 million consumers. The company believed it was one of the largest providers of private mortgage insurance outside the U.S. based on new insurance written. In addition, GNW believed that in the U.S. it was the largest individual provider of long-term care insurance, the second largest provider of fixed immediate annuities, based on total premiums and deposits, and the fifth largest provider of mortgage insurance, based on new insurance written.

The company conducts its business through three major segments. The first segment is retirement and protection (63% of 2008 total revenues excluding institutional, 68% of 2007 total revenues). This segment is comprised of wealth management (3.0%, 3.0%); retirement income (11%, 17%); spread-based institutional (reported a $333 million loss, 4.6%); life insurance (14%, 18%); and long-term care (35%, 26%). The second segment is international (28%, 24%).

This segment consists of the company's mortgage insurance business in Canada, Australia and Europe, in addition to proposals for other target countries for mortgage insurance. The segment also includes payment protection insurance, which helps consumers meet their payment obligations in the event of illness, involuntary unemployment, disability or death. The third segment is U.S. mortgage insurance (8.0%, 7.2%). The mortgage insurance business facilitates home ownership by enabling borrowers to buy homes with low down payment mortgages. These products also help financial institutions manage their capital efficiently by reducing the capital required for low down payment mortgages. The company also has a corporate and other segment (0.2%, 0.6%), which includes unallocated corporate income and expenses, results of a small, non-core business, and most interest and other financing expenses.

Company Financials Fiscal Year Ended Dec. 31

Per Share Data ($)	2008	2007	2006	2005	2004	2003	2002	2001	2000	1999
Tangible Book Value	15.71	31.64	24.20	24.51	21.69	20.18	NA	NA	NA	NA
Operating Earnings	NA	NA	NA	NA	NA	NA	NA	NA	NA	NA
Earnings	-1.32	2.58	2.83	2.52	2.34	1.82	NA	NA	NA	NA
S&P Core Earnings	1.45	3.04	2.92	2.52	2.29	1.96	NA	NA	NA	NA
Dividends	0.40	0.37	0.32	0.27	0.07	NA	NA	NA	NA	NA
Relative Payout	NM	14%	11%	11%	3%	NA	NA	NA	NA	NA
Prices:High	25.57	37.16	36.47	35.25	27.84	NA	NA	NA	NA	NA
Prices:Low	0.70	23.26	31.00	25.72	18.75	NA	NA	NA	NA	NA
P/E Ratio:High	NM	14	13	14	12	NA	NA	NA	NA	NA
P/E Ratio:Low	NM	9	11	10	8	NA	NA	NA	NA	NA

Income Statement Analysis (Million $)	2008	2007	2006	2005	2004	2003	2002	2001	2000	1999
Life Insurance in Force	677	670	NA	NA	NA	NA	NA	NA	NA	NA
Premium Income:Life A & H	NA	NA	NA	NA	NA	6,252	NA	NA	NA	NA
Premium Income:Casualty/Property.	NA	NA	NA	NA	NA	Nil	NA	NA	NA	NA
Net Investment Income	3,730	4,135	3,837	3,536	3,648	2,928	NA	NA	NA	NA
Total Revenue	9,948	11,125	11,029	10,504	11,057	9,775	11,229	11,101	10,226	NA
Pretax Income	-942	1,606	1,918	1,798	1,638	1,263	1,791	1,821	1,851	NA
Net Operating Income	NA	NA	NA	NA	NA	NA	NA	NA	NA	NA
Net Income	-572	1,154	1,324	1,221	1,145	892	1,380	1,231	1,275	NA
S&P Core Earnings	624	1,359	1,369	1,221	1,126	956	NA	NA	NA	NA

Balance Sheet & Other Financial Data (Million $)	2008	2007	2006	2005	2004	2003	2002	2001	2000	1999
Cash & Equivalent	7,497	5,369	3,222	2,608	2,125	1,630	1,569	881	NA	NA
Premiums Due	NA	16,483	NA	NA	NA	NA	NA	NA	NA	NA
Investment Assets:Bonds	42,871	55,154	55,448	53,791	52,424	50,081	NA	NA	NA	NA
Investment Assets:Stocks	234	366	NA	367	374	387	NA	NA	NA	NA
Investment Assets:Loans	10,096	10,604	9,985	8,908	7,275	6,794	NA	NA	NA	NA
Investment Assets:Total	55,322	67,131	73,519	66,573	65,747	61,749	72,080	62,977	NA	NA
Deferred Policy Costs	7,786	7,034	NA	5,586	5,020	4,421	NA	NA	NA	NA
Total Assets	107,201	114,315	110,871	105,292	103,878	100,216	117,357	103,998	NA	NA
Debt	8,849	7,558	3,921	3,336	3,042	3,016	NA	NA	NA	NA
Common Equity	8,926	13,478	13,330	13,310	12,866	12,258	16,752	14,165	NA	NA
Combined Loss-Expense Ratio	198.0	93.0	49.0	48.0	50.0	51.0	39.0	50.0	42.0	NA
% Return on Revenue	NM	10.4	12.0	11.6	10.4	9.1	12.3	11.1	12.5	NA
% Return on Equity	NM	8.6	2.2	9.3	8.0	6.0	8.9	NA	NA	NA
% Investment Yield	6.1	6.1	5.8	5.7	5.2	5.4	5.9	12.4	NA	NA

Data as orig reptd.; bef. results of disc opers/spec. items. Per share data adj. for stk. divs.; EPS diluted. E-Estimated. NA-Not Available. NM-Not Meaningful. NR-Not Ranked. UR-Under Review.

Office: 6620 West Broad Street, Richmond, VA 23230.
Telephone: 804-281-6000.
Email: investorinfo@genworth.com
Website: http://www.genworth.com

Chrmn, Pres & CEO: M.D. Fraizer
SVP & CFO: P.B. Kelleher
SVP, Secy & General Counsel: L.E. Roday
SVP & CIO: S.J. McKay

Chief Acctg Officer & Cntlr: A.R. Corbin
Investor Contact: C. English (804-662-2614)
Board Members: F. J. Borelli, M. D. Fraizer, N. J. Karch, J. R. Kerrey, R. J. Lavizzo-Mourey, C. B. Mead, T. E. Moloney, J. A. Parke, J. S. Riepe, B. Toan, T. B. Wheeler

Founded: 2003
Domicile: Delaware
Employees: 6,000

Genzyme Corp

STANDARD &POOR'S

S&P Recommendation HOLD ★★★☆☆	Price $51.07 (as of Nov 27, 2009)	12-Mo. Target Price $53.00	Investment Style Large-Cap Growth

GICS Sector Health Care
Sub-Industry Biotechnology

Summary This biopharmaceutical concern makes human therapeutic and diagnostic products. Its leading product is Cerezyme, a drug to treat rare disorder Gaucher disease.

Key Stock Statistics (Source S&P, Vickers, company reports)

52-Wk Range	$73.75– 47.09	S&P Oper. EPS 2009**E**	1.73	Market Capitalization(B)	$13.553	Beta	0.31
Trailing 12-Month EPS	$1.75	S&P Oper. EPS 2010**E**	3.13	Yield (%)	Nil	S&P 3-Yr. Proj. EPS CAGR(%)	19
Trailing 12-Month P/E	29.2	P/E on S&P Oper. EPS 2009**E**	29.5	Dividend Rate/Share	Nil	S&P Credit Rating	A-
$10K Invested 5 Yrs Ago	$9,116	Common Shares Outstg. (M)	265.4	Institutional Ownership (%)	94		

Price Performance

30-Week Mov. Avg. · · · 10-Week Mov. Avg. - - GAAP Earnings vs. Previous Year Volume Above Avg. STARS
12-Mo. Target Price — Relative Strength ▲ Up ▼ Down ▶ No Change Below Avg.

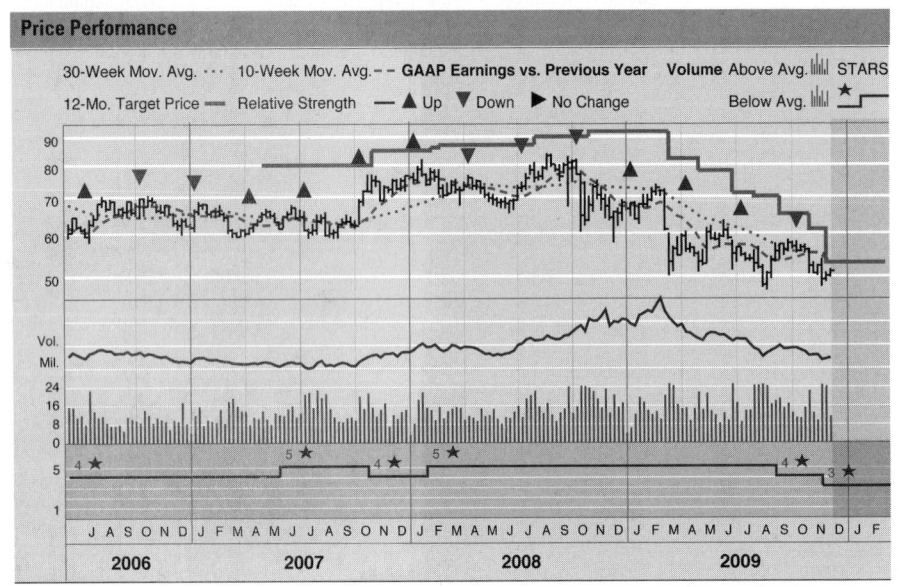

Options: ASE, CBOE, P, Ph

Analysis prepared by **Steven Silver** on November 19, 2009, when the stock traded at **$ 49.64**.

Qualitative Risk Assessment

LOW	MEDIUM	HIGH

Our risk assessment reflects our view that Genzyme's manufacturing facility challenges in 2009 underscore the complexity that is inherent for companies producing biologic drugs. Though we view GENZ's portfolio of therapeutic products and diagnostic businesses as diverse, the shortage of main revenue generator Cerezyme is likely to result in new entrants to the Gaucher disease treatment market. We believe such competition could mitigate the benefits of product diversity.

Quantitative Evaluations

S&P Quality Ranking B-

D	C	B-	B	B+	A-	A	A+

Relative Strength Rank MODERATE

33

LOWEST = 1 HIGHEST = 99

Highlights

► We expect 2009 revenues to decline 2% to $4.5 billion, impacted by lost sales of Cerezyme and Fabrazyme due to the mid-2009 Allston plant closure. We look for revenue growth of 21% in 2010, to $5.45 billion. We see ongoing regulatory scrutiny over its facilities delaying approval of larger scale Myozyme production, which we view as key to diversifying revenues, amid looming competition to sales leader Cerezyme. We are encouraged, however, by the recent advancement of next-generation Gaucher disease drug GENZ-112638 to Phase III study.

► We expect 2009 and 2010 operating margins of 13% and 25%, respectively, down from 2008's 29% due to the Allston plant closure, but we look for margins to recover as plant production and drug availability return to historical levels. We see strong operational cash flows funding share repurchase programs, new drug licensing/acquisition deals, and capital investments.

► Our 2009 and 2010 EPS estimates of $1.73 and $3.13, respectively, include previously withheld amortization of intangible assets and other one-time items, upon the company's revision of its adjusted EPS figures.

Investment Rationale/Risk

► We recently downgraded our recommendation on the shares to Hold, from Buy, reflecting concern over lingering manufacturing issues related to GENZ's Allston Landing plant, which has disrupted key drug production and supplies and, we believe, hastened new competition to Cerezyme. We see GENZ investing heavily in its facilities, but we expect share volatility until clarity emerges. In our view, GENZ has a diverse product roster and has aggressively supported its long-term pipeline by licensing novel clinical assets. We view key growth catalysts as Campath, in Phase III study for multiple sclerosis, in-licensed Phase III cholesterol-lowering drug mipomersen, and securing U.S. approval of large-scale Myozyme production.

► Risks to our recommendation and target price include continued manufacturing issues limiting product supply or prompting drug recalls over safety, clinical or regulatory setbacks to the new product pipeline and any slowdown in sales growth for key marketed products.

► Our 12-month target price of $53 is 17X our 2010 EPS estimate of $3.13, about 0.9X our three-year projected growth rate, a discount to profitable sector peers given manufacturing challenges.

Revenue/Earnings Data

Revenue (Million $)

	1Q	2Q	3Q	4Q	Year
2009	1,149	1,229	1,058	--	--
2008	1,100	1,171	1,160	1,174	4,605
2007	883.2	933.4	960.2	1,037	3,814
2006	730.8	793.4	808.6	854.2	3,187
2005	630.0	668.1	708.1	728.7	2,735
2004	491.3	549.6	569.2	591.1	2,201

Earnings Per Share ($)

2009	0.70	0.68	0.06	E0.16	E1.73
2008	0.52	0.25	0.42	0.31	1.50
2007	0.57	0.51	0.58	0.29	1.74
2006	0.37	0.49	0.06	-1.02	-0.06
2005	0.36	0.46	0.43	0.39	1.65
2004	0.29	0.33	0.41	-0.68	0.37

Fiscal year ended Dec. 31. Next earnings report expected: Mid February. EPS Estimates based on S&P Operating Earnings; historical GAAP earnings are as reported.

Dividend Data

No cash dividends have been paid.

Genzyme Corp

STANDARD
&POOR'S

Business Summary November 19, 2009

CORPORATE OVERVIEW. Genzyme develops, manufactures and markets therapeutic and diagnostic products. Its leading product is Cerezyme, an enzyme replacement therapy (ERT) for Gaucher disease, a debilitating genetic disorder that causes fatigue, anemia and bone erosion. In 2008, Cerezyme sales totaled $1.24 billion, 9% higher than 2007, accounting for 26% of sales, down from 30% in 2007. Cerezyme's patents expire in 2013. Phase III studies of potential successor, orally administered GENZ-112638, started in late 2009.

Renagel, which reduces elevated serum phosphorus levels in kidney dialysis patients, and Renvela, its buffered form which was launched in early 2008, generated $678 million in 2008 sales (up 13% over 2007). In November 2009, GENZ discontinued study on an advanced phosphate binder intended as a successor to Renvela when it failed to outperform Renvela. Key Renagel/Renvela patents expire around 2014.

Fabrazyme is approved for treating Fabry disease, a rare genetic disorder. Fabrazyme sales were $494 million in 2008, up 17% over 2007's $424 million;

Myozyme is approved for treating Pompe disease, a rare and often fatal disorder that afflicts an estimated 10,000 patients worldwide and generated 2008 sales of $296 million, up from $201 million, despite production constraints. The drug was approved at 4000 liter scale in Europe in February 2009, but has seen delays in FDA approval at 2000 liter scale (to be called Lumizyme) as FDA has scrutinized GENZ's risk mitigation plans and plant conditions. Biosurgery unit sales are led by Synvisc, an injectable biomaterial to treat knee osteoarthritis by improving joint lubrication. Synvisc sales were $263 million in 2008, 9% higher than in 2007. A single-injection version, Synvisc-One, was approved in Europe in late 2007 and in the U.S. in early 2009.

Genzyme's genetics and diagnostics division generated 2008 sales of $360 million, 25% higher than 2007's $287 million.

Company Financials Fiscal Year Ended Dec. 31

Per Share Data ($)	2008	2007	2006	2005	2004	2003	2002	2001	2000	1999
Tangible Book Value	15.70	13.73	10.91	7.99	8.11	6.31	NM	6.10	4.05	5.54
Cash Flow	2.79	2.92	2.00	2.67	1.24	0.41	1.16	0.75	0.91	1.27
Earnings	1.50	1.74	-0.06	1.65	0.37	0.42	0.81	0.19	0.68	1.00
S&P Core Earnings	1.50	1.94	0.32	1.23	-0.03	-0.26	0.59	0.02	NA	NA
Dividends	Nil	Nil	Nil	Nil	Nil	Nil	Nil	Nil	Nil	Nil
Payout Ratio	Nil	Nil	Nil	Nil	Nil	Nil	Nil	Nil	Nil	Nil
Prices:High	83.97	76.90	75.34	77.82	59.14	52.45	58.55	64.00	51.88	31.56
Prices:Low	57.61	58.71	54.64	55.15	40.67	28.45	15.64	34.34	19.84	15.38
P/E Ratio:High	56	44	NM	47	NM	NM	72	NM	77	32
P/E Ratio:Low	38	34	NM	33	NM	NM	19	NM	29	15

Income Statement Analysis (Million $)										
Revenue	4,605	3,814	3,187	2,735	2,201	1,714	1,080	982	752	635
Operating Income	1,303	1,183	913	915	717	463	318	380	-185	280
Depreciation	375	338	541	285	205	160	96.0	118	41.2	50.2
Interest Expense	23.4	26.7	15.5	19.6	38.2	26.6	17.8	23.2	14.2	19.9
Pretax Income	623	732	-63.1	641	222	2.82	207	56.5	-179	226
Effective Tax Rate	32.8%	34.9%	NM	29.2%	63.7%	NM	27.3%	93.1%	51.9%	37.3%
Net Income	421	480	-16.8	441	86.5	-67.6	151	3.88	85.9	142
S&P Core Earnings	420	535	90.4	326	-6.61	-61.0	125	5.25	NA	NA

Balance Sheet & Other Financial Data (Million $)										
Cash	974	947	492	292	481	293	373	167	136	94.5
Current Assets	2,516	2,609	1,990	1,665	1,634	1,323	1,100	721	605	605
Total Assets	8,937	8,302	7,191	6,879	6,069	5,005	3,556	3,225	2,499	1,400
Current Liabilities	914	1,502	651	550	624	392	275	243	167	117
Long Term Debt	23.2	717	810	816	811	1,415	600	600	454	273
Common Equity	7,335	6,613	5,661	5,150	4,380	2,936	2,586	2,280	1,750	1,008
Total Capital	7,331	6,727	6,481	6,301	5,417	4,558	3,268	2,961	2,329	1,280
Capital Expenditures	598	413	334	19.2	187	260	220	171	72.6	52.9
Cash Flow	796	818	524	726	292	92.9	247	122	127	192
Current Ratio	2.8	1.7	3.1	3.0	2.6	3.4	4.0	3.0	3.6	5.2
% Long Term Debt of Capitalization	1.7	1.7	12.5	12.9	15.0	30.1	18.4	20.3	31.1	21.3
% Net Income of Revenue	9.1	12.6	NM	16.1	3.9	NM	14.0	0.4	11.4	22.4
% Return on Assets	4.9	6.2	NM	6.8	1.6	NM	4.4	0.2	4.0	10.1
% Return on Equity	6.0	7.8	NM	9.3	2.4	NM	6.2	0.1	5.5	14.6

Data as orig reptd.; bef. results of disc opers/spec. items. Per share data adj. for stk. divs.; EPS diluted. E-Estimated. NA-Not Available. NM-Not Meaningful. NR-Not Ranked. UR-Under Review.

Office: 500 Kendall St, Cambridge, MA 02142-1108.
Telephone: 617-252-7570.
Email: information@genzyme.com
Website: http://www.genzyme.com

Chrmn, Pres & CEO: H.A. Termeer
COO: M.R. Bamforth
EVP & CFO: M.S. Wyzga
EVP & Secy: P. Wirth

SVP & CSO: A.E. Smith
Investor Contact: P. Flanigan (617-768-6563)
Board Members: D. A. Berthiaume, G. K. Boudreaux, R. J. Carpenter, C. L. Cooney, V. J. Dzau, C. Mack, III, C. Mcgillicudy, III, R. F. Syron, H. A. Termeer

Founded: 1991
Domicile: Massachusetts
Employees: 11,000

Gilead Sciences Inc

**STANDARD
&POOR'S**

S&P Recommendation	**STRONG BUY** ★★★★★	Price	12-Mo. Target Price	Investment Style
		$46.56 (as of Nov 27, 2009)	$59.00	Large-Cap Growth

GICS Sector Health Care
Sub-Industry Biotechnology

Summary This biopharmaceutical company is engaged in the discovery, development and commercialization of treatments to fight viral, bacterial and fungal infections.

Key Stock Statistics (Source S&P, Vickers, company reports)

52-Wk Range	$53.28– 40.62	S&P Oper. EPS 2009**E**	2.82	Market Capitalization(B)	$41.901	Beta	0.43
Trailing 12-Month EPS	$2.59	S&P Oper. EPS 2010**E**	3.10	Yield (%)	Nil	S&P 3-Yr. Proj. EPS CAGR(%)	17
Trailing 12-Month P/E	18.0	P/E on S&P Oper. EPS 2009**E**	16.5	Dividend Rate/Share	Nil	S&P Credit Rating	NA
$10K Invested 5 Yrs Ago	$26,983	Common Shares Outstg. (M)	899.9	Institutional Ownership (%)	91		

Price Performance

30-Week Mov. Avg. · · · 10-Week Mov. Avg. - - GAAP Earnings vs. Previous Year   Volume Above Avg. |||| STARS

12-Mo. Target Price — Relative Strength — ▲ Up ▼ Down ▶ No Change   Below Avg. |||| ★

Options: ASE, CBOE, P, Ph

Analysis prepared by **Steven Silver** on October 26, 2009, when the stock traded at **$ 43.16**.

Highlights

▶ We see 2009 revenues of $6.9 billion, which would represent a 29% increase over 2008, and forecast 12% growth in 2010 to about $7.7 billion. We view favorably GILD's expanding U.S. HIV drug market share, with 70% of HIV patients and 80% of all treatment-naive HIV patients on a tenofovir (Viread)-based treatment. We think further share expansion is likely, given recent safety concerns with rival GlaxoSmithKline's abacavir. We are encouraged by Atripla's European rollout, now available in its five largest markets, after launching in France in mid-2009.

▶ We forecast operating margins of around 50% in 2009 and 2010. We have a favorable view of GILD's robust pipeline, despite maintaining lower investment in R&D as a percentage of sales to its sector peers. We believe GILD is disciplined in managing expenses, as it has supported the launch of new products such as Letairis, which requires a comprehensive risk management program.

▶ Our 2009 EPS estimate is $2.82, and 2010's is $3.10. We see GILD as well positioned to support EPS growth through share repurchases and effective cost management.

Investment Rationale/Risk

▶ We view GILD as a core biotech holding with strong fundamentals, as it has generated $2.1 billion in cash flows through the third quarter of 2009, amid challenging global economic conditions. We expect near-term results to be boosted by increased Tamiflu royalties, as the drug is used to combat the global swine flu outbreak. We believe GILD is well positioned to acquire growth assets, as evidenced by the early 2009 $1.4 billion purchase of CV Therapeutics for its cardiovascular products and infrastructure, which we expect to aid in diversifying GILD's product sales beyond its HIV franchise in the coming years. We also note recent pipeline advancement, with next-generation anti-viral therapies nearing late-stage study.

▶ Risks to our recommendation and target price include any slowdown in GILD's HIV product sales from competition or patent challenges, and failure to secure FDA approval of its pipeline candidates.

▶ Our 12-month target price of $59 is 19X our 2010 EPS estimate, a premium-to-peers PEG multiple of about 1.1X on our long-term growth rate of 17% to reflect GILD's dominant HIV market position and strong cash flows.

Qualitative Risk Assessment

LOW	MEDIUM	**HIGH**

Our risk assessment reflects Gilead's dependence on the growth of its anti-HIV drug portfolio. Also, the company operates in a highly competitive market, and failure to successfully commercialize its pipeline candidates could diminish growth expectations in the future.

Quantitative Evaluations

S&P Quality Ranking B-

D	C	**B-**	B	B+	A-	A	A+

Relative Strength Rank MODERATE

60

LOWEST = 1   HIGHEST = 99

Revenue/Earnings Data

Revenue (Million $)

	1Q	2Q	3Q	4Q	Year
2009	1,530	1,647	1,801	--	--
2008	1,258	1,278	1,371	1,428	5,336
2007	1,028	1,048	1,059	1,095	4,230
2006	692.9	685.3	748.7	899.2	3,026
2005	430.4	495.3	493.5	609.3	2,028
2004	309.1	319.7	326.2	369.6	1,325

Earnings Per Share ($)

2009	0.63	0.61	0.72	E0.80	E2.82
2008	0.51	0.46	0.53	0.60	2.10
2007	0.43	0.42	0.42	0.41	1.68
2006	0.28	0.28	-0.06	-1.81	-1.30
2005	0.17	0.21	0.19	0.29	0.86
2004	0.13	0.12	0.13	0.12	0.50

Fiscal year ended Dec. 31. Next earnings report expected: Late January. EPS Estimates based on S&P Operating Earnings; historical GAAP earnings are as reported.

Dividend Data

No cash dividends have been paid.

Please read the Required Disclosures and Analyst Certification on the last page of this report.

The McGraw·Hill Companies

Gilead Sciences Inc

Business Summary October 26, 2009

CORPORATE OVERVIEW. Gilead Sciences (GILD) focuses on the research, development and marketing of anti-infective medications, with a primary focus on treatments for HIV.

Truvada continues to be GILD's sales leader, with sales of $2.11 billion in 2008, 33% above 2007's $1.59 billion. Truvada, approved in 2004, is a once-daily combination tablet formulated with previous-generation drugs Viread and Emtriva. Emtriva was the lead product of Triangle Pharmaceuticals, acquired in 2003. Viread was approved in 2001 to treat HIV patients who had become resistant to other reverse transcriptase inhibitors, as well as naive patients in front-line treatment settings. Viread sales were $621 million in 2008, up from $613 million in 2007.

In late 2004, GILD and Bristol-Myers Squibb (BMY) formed a joint venture for a combination tablet with Truvada and BMY's Sustiva. The formulation, marketed as Atripla, was approved and launched in July 2006. GILD books Atripla sales and then pays BMY its 37% share for the Sustiva portion of the drug, which GILD counts as cost of goods on its financial statements. Atripla generated 2008 sales of $1.57 billion, up 74% from $903 million in 2007. Atripla re-

ceived EU approval in December 2007 and began to be launched in 2008. As of June 2009, Atripla was available in all five of the largest European markets, after a recent launch in France.

Hepsera was approved for treatment of hepatitis B in the U.S. and EU in September 2002 and March 2003, respectively. GILD recorded $341 million of Hepsera sales in 2008, up 13% from $303 million in 2007. However, we expect sales declines for Hepsera, following the August 2008 FDA approval of GILD's Viread in treating chronic hepatitis B.

AmBisome is a liposomal formulation of amphotericin B, an antifungal agent that attacks a broad variety of life-threatening fungal infections. AmBisome is also approved by the FDA to treat cryptococcal meningitis in AIDS patients. Sales were $290 million in 2008, up 10% from $263 million in 2007.

Company Financials Fiscal Year Ended Dec. 31

Per Share Data ($)	2008	2007	2006	2005	2004	2003	2002	2001	2000	1999
Tangible Book Value	4.56	3.71	1.97	3.30	2.09	1.17	0.72	0.58	0.47	0.42
Cash Flow	2.15	1.71	-1.24	0.90	0.51	-0.06	0.10	0.08	-0.04	-0.08
Earnings	2.10	1.68	-1.30	0.86	0.50	-0.09	0.09	0.06	-0.06	-0.10
S&P Core Earnings	2.10	1.67	-1.29	0.78	0.39	-0.17	0.01	-0.14	NA	NA
Dividends	Nil	Nil	Nil	Nil	Nil	Nil	Nil	Nil	Nil	Nil
Payout Ratio	Nil	Nil	Nil	Nil	Nil	Nil	Nil	Nil	Nil	Nil
Prices:High	57.63	47.90	35.00	28.26	19.55	17.65	10.00	9.21	7.38	5.97
Prices:Low	35.60	30.96	26.24	15.20	12.88	7.81	6.52	3.11	2.70	2.20
P/E Ratio:High	27	29	NM	33	39	NM	NM	NM	NM	NM
P/E Ratio:Low	17	18	NM	18	26	NM	NM	NM	NM	NM

Income Statement Analysis (Million $)

	2008	2007	2006	2005	2004	2003	2002	2001	2000	1999
Revenue	5,336	4,230	3,026	2,028	1,325	868	467	234	196	169
Operating Income	2,741	2,201	1,683	1,148	656	361	95.4	-106	-40.3	-39.2
Depreciation	51.7	36.9	47.3	36.8	24.4	20.9	14.4	14.7	12.0	12.6
Interest Expense	12.1	13.5	20.4	0.44	7.35	21.9	13.9	14.0	Nil	6.52
Pretax Income	2,726	2,261	-644	1,158	656	-168	73.4	55.3	-41.9	-65.6
Effective Tax Rate	26.5%	29.0%	NM	30.0%	31.5%	NM	1.77%	7.48%	NM	NM
Net Income	2,011	1,615	-1,190	814	449	-72.0	72.1	51.2	-43.1	-66.5
S&P Core Earnings	2,008	1,610	-1,188	737	354	-133	8.55	-108	NA	NA

Balance Sheet & Other Financial Data (Million $)

	2008	2007	2006	2005	2004	2003	2002	2001	2000	1999
Cash	3,240	1,172	937	2,324	1,254	707	942	583	513	294
Current Assets	4,300	3,028	2,429	3,092	1,850	1,266	1,184	708	594	372
Total Assets	7,019	5,835	4,086	3,765	2,156	1,555	1,288	795	678	437
Current Liabilities	1,221	736	764	455	253	186	105	80.1	58.2	47.9
Long Term Debt	1,300	1,301	1,300	241	0.23	345	595	250	252	84.8
Common Equity	4,152	3,460	1,816	3,028	1,871	1,003	571	452	351	297
Total Capital	5,672	4,772	3,169	3,277	1,871	1,348	1,166	703	603	382
Capital Expenditures	115	78.7	105	2,226	51.4	38.6	17.6	26.3	15.6	12.5
Cash Flow	2,063	1,652	-1,143	851	474	-51.1	86.5	65.9	-31.1	-53.9
Current Ratio	3.5	4.1	3.2	6.8	7.3	6.8	11.3	8.8	10.2	7.8
% Long Term Debt of Capitalization	22.9	27.2	41.0	7.3	NM	25.6	51.0	35.6	41.8	22.2
% Net Income of Revenue	37.7	38.2	NM	40.1	33.9	NM	15.4	21.9	NM	NM
% Return on Assets	31.3	32.6	NM	27.5	24.2	NM	6.9	6.9	NM	NM
% Return on Equity	52.8	61.2	NM	33.2	31.3	NM	14.1	12.7	NM	NM

Data as orig reptd.; bef. results of disc opers/spec. items. Per share data adj. for stk. divs.; EPS diluted. E-Estimated. NA-Not Available. NM-Not Meaningful. NR-Not Ranked. UR-Under Review.

Office: 333 Lakeside Drive, Foster City, CA 94404.
Telephone: 650-574-3000.
Email: investor_relations@gilead.com
Website: http://www.gilead.com

Chrmn & CEO: J.C. Martin
Pres & COO: J.F. Milligan
EVP & CSO: N.W. Bischofberger
SVP, CFO & Chief Acctg Officer: R.L. Washington

Investor Contact: S. Hubbard (650 522-5715)
Board Members: P. Berg, J. F. Cogan, E. Davignon, J. M. Denny, C. A. Hills, K. Loften, K. E. Lofton, J. W. Madigan, J. C. Martin, G. E. Moore, N. G. Moore, R. J. Whitley, G. E. Wilson

Founded: 1987
Domicile: Delaware
Employees: 3,441

Goldman Sachs Group Inc. (The)

STANDARD &POOR'S

S&P Recommendation BUY ★★★★☆

Price	$164.16 (as of Nov 27, 2009)
12-Mo. Target Price	$216.00
Investment Style	Large-Cap Growth

GICS Sector Financials
Sub-Industry Investment Banking & Brokerage

Summary Goldman Sachs is one of the world's leading investment banking and securities companies.

Key Stock Statistics (Source S&P, Vickers, company reports)

52-Wk Range	$193.60– 59.13	S&P Oper. EPS 2009**E**	18.95	Market Capitalization(B)	$84.392	Beta	1.42
Trailing 12-Month EPS	$4.47	S&P Oper. EPS 2010**E**	21.37	Yield (%)	0.85	S&P 3-Yr. Proj. EPS CAGR(%)	75
Trailing 12-Month P/E	36.7	P/E on S&P Oper. EPS 2009**E**	8.7	Dividend Rate/Share	$1.40	S&P Credit Rating	A
$10K Invested 5 Yrs Ago	$16,350	Common Shares Outstg. (M)	514.1	Institutional Ownership (%)	77		

Price Performance

30-Week Mov. Avg. · · · 10-Week Mov. Avg. - - **GAAP Earnings vs. Previous Year** Volume Above Avg. STARS
12-Mo. Target Price — Relative Strength — ▲ Up ▼ Down ► No Change Below Avg. ★

Options: ASE, CBOE, P, Ph

Analysis prepared by **Matthew Albrecht** on October 20, 2009, when the stock traded at **$185.50**.

Highlights

► An equity market rebound off of market lows and the reopening of fixed income markets signals an improved operating environment, in our view. We think M&A backlogs have improved, demand for restructuring advice remains strong, and the IPO market has started to show signs of life. Still, lower asset balances and reduced volume should continue to pressure results in asset management and prime brokerage operations. We think trading results thus far reflect the company's ability and willingness to take on risk when some competitors may be pulling back, but profitability could decline if trades get more crowded. We expect writedowns from legacy commercial and residential mortgage securities exposure to decrease, but principal investments may see further declines. We look for top- and bottom-line rebounds in 2009, absent significant writedowns.

► We look for compensation to approximate 48% of net revenues. We expect non-compensation costs to decline after cost-cutting measures, and the pretax margin should expand in 2009.

► We estimate EPS of $18.95 in 2009 and $21.37 in 2010, including the dilution from 2009 share sales.

Investment Rationale/Risk

► The shares have traditionally traded at a premium to peers, which we believe reflects the company's global reach, significant operating leverage, client relationships, peer-best return on equity and what we see as a solid balance sheet. We think its balance sheet strength compared to peers gives it a head start on gaining market share in a recovery, and we view the shares as attractive.

► Risks to our recommendation and target price include stock and bond market depreciation, sharply higher interest rates, widening credit spreads, and greater regulatory scrutiny. We think GS's global business model also adds risk due to its exposure to geopolitical issues.

► The shares recently traded at about 9.8X our 2009 EPS estimate and approximately 1.7X current book value per share, discounts to historical multiples and the S&P 500. Our 12-month target price of $216 is based on a price-to-book value multiple of about 1.8X applied to our 12-month forward book value projection of $120, a premium to peers but a discount to its historical multiple.

Qualitative Risk Assessment

LOW	**MEDIUM**	HIGH

Our risk assessment reflects our view of the company's global footprint and strong client relationships, offset by industry cyclicality and its high leverage ratio.

Quantitative Evaluations

S&P Quality Ranking B+

D	C	B-	B	**B+**	A-	A	A+

Relative Strength Rank WEAK

27

LOWEST = 1 HIGHEST = 99

Revenue/Earnings Data

Revenue (Million $)

	1Q	2Q	3Q	4Q	Year
2009	11,880	1,428	1,310	--	--
2008	18,629	17,643	13,625	3,682	53,579
2007	22,280	20,351	23,803	21,534	87,968
2006	17,246	18,002	15,979	18,126	69,353
2005	9,964	8,949	12,333	12,145	43,391
2004	7,905	7,676	6,803	7,455	29,839

Earnings Per Share ($)

	1Q	2Q	3Q	4Q	Year
2009	3.39	4.93	5.25	E5.38	E18.95
2008	3.23	4.58	1.81	-4.97	4.47
2007	6.67	4.93	1.81	7.01	24.73
2006	5.08	4.78	3.26	6.59	19.69
2005	2.94	1.71	3.25	3.35	11.21
2004	2.50	2.31	1.74	2.36	8.92

Fiscal year ended Dec. 31. Next earnings report expected: Late December. EPS Estimates based on S&P Operating Earnings; historical GAAP earnings are as reported.

Dividend Data (Dates: mm/dd Payment Date: mm/dd/yy)

Amount ($)	Date Decl.	Ex-Div. Date	Stk. of Record	Payment Date
0.467	12/16	02/20	02/24	03/26/09
q	04/13	05/21	05/26	06/25/09
0.350	07/14	08/21	08/25	09/24/09
0.350	10/15	11/30	12/02	12/30/09

Dividends have been paid since 1999. Source: Company reports.

The McGraw-Hill Companies

Goldman Sachs Group Inc. (The)

STANDARD &POOR'S

Business Summary October 20, 2009

CORPORATE OVERVIEW. Goldman Sachs (GS) is a global investment banking, securities and investment management firm that provides a wide range of services to corporations, financial institutions, governments and high-net-worth individuals. GS operates through three core businesses: Trading and Principal Investments, Investment Banking, and Asset Management and Securities Services.

The Trading and Principal Investments business (41% of FY 08-Nov. net revenues) facilitates customer transactions with a diverse group of corporations, financial institutions, governments and individuals, and takes proprietary positions through market making in, and trading of, fixed income and equity products, currencies, commodities and derivatives. The activities of the Trading and Principal Investments business can be grouped under three segments: Fixed Income, Currency and Commodities (FICC); Equities; and Principal Investments. The FICC business makes markets in and trades interest rate and credit products, mortgage-backed securities, loans and other asset-backed securities, currencies and commodities. The Equities business makes markets in, trades, and acts as a specialist for equities and equity-related products. It

generates commissions from executing and clearing client transactions on major stock, options, and futures exchanges worldwide through its Equities customer franchise and clearing activities.

The Principal Investments business primarily represents net revenues from corporate and real estate merchant banking investments. These net revenues are from four primary sources -- returns on corporate and real estate investments, its investment in the convertible preferred stock of Sumitomo Mitsui Financial Group, Inc. (SMFG), its investment in the ordinary shares of Industrial and Commercial Bank of China Limited (ICBC), and overrides. Overrides represent net revenues from the increased share of the income and gains derived from GS's merchant banking funds when the return on a fund's investments exceeds certain threshold returns.

Company Financials Fiscal Year Ended Dec. 31

Per Share Data ($)	2008	2007	2006	2005	2004	2003	2002	2001	2000	1999
Tangible Book Value	104.56	101.62	119.66	52.15	52.14	45.73	40.18	38.30	34.15	22.65
Cash Flow	7.24	27.68	20.78	12.22	9.90	6.97	5.20	5.39	6.94	6.27
Earnings	4.47	24.73	19.69	11.21	8.92	5.87	4.03	4.26	6.00	5.27
S&P Core Earnings	4.40	24.76	19.72	11.12	8.63	5.26	3.30	3.60	NA	NA
Dividends	1.40	1.40	1.30	1.00	1.00	0.74	0.48	0.48	0.48	0.24
Payout Ratio	31%	6%	7%	9%	11%	13%	12%	11%	8%	4%
Prices:High	215.05	250.70	206.70	134.99	110.88	100.78	97.25	120.00	133.63	94.81
Prices:Low	47.41	157.38	124.23	94.75	83.29	61.02	58.57	63.27	65.50	53.00
P/E Ratio:High	27	10	10	12	12	17	24	28	22	17
P/E Ratio:Low	6	6	6	8	9	10	15	15	11	10

Income Statement Analysis (Million $)										
Commissions	5,179	12,286	10,140	6,689	5,941	4,317	3,273	3,020	2,307	Nil
Interest Income	35,633	45,968	35,186	21,250	11,914	10,751	11,269	16,620	17,396	12,722
Total Revenue	53,579	87,968	69,353	43,391	29,839	23,623	22,854	31,138	33,000	25,363
Interest Expense	31,357	41,981	31,688	18,153	8,888	7,600	8,868	15,327	16,410	12,018
Pretax Income	2,336	17,604	14,560	8,273	6,676	4,445	3,253	3,696	5,020	1,992
Effective Tax Rate	0.60%	34.1%	34.5%	32.0%	31.8%	32.4%	35.0%	37.5%	38.9%	NM
Net Income	2,322	11,599	9,537	5,626	4,553	3,005	2,114	2,310	3,067	2,708
S&P Core Earnings	2,009	11,419	9,416	5,560	4,406	2,693	1,737	1,949	NA	NA

Balance Sheet & Other Financial Data (Million $)										
Total Assets	884,547	1,119,796	838,201	706,804	531,379	403,799	355,574	312,218	289,760	250,491
Cash Items	122,404	131,821	87,283	61,666	52,544	36,802	25,211	29,043	21,002	12,190
Receivables	428,889	425,596	312,355	75,381	52,545	36,377	28,938	33,463	159,019	150,154
Securities Owned	33,325	452,595	416,687	238,043	183,880	160,719	129,775	108,885	95,260	81,809
Securities Borrowed	17,060	28,624	22,208	23,331	19,394	17,528	12,238	81,579	40,211	49,352
Due Brokers & Customers	254,043	318,453	223,874	188,318	161,221	109,028	95,590	97,297	82,148	59,534
Other Liabilities	23,216	38,907	31,866	13,830	10,360	8,144	6,002	7,129	11,116	110,508
Capitalization:Debt	168,220	164,174	122,842	100,007	80,696	57,482	38,711	31,016	31,395	20,952
Capitalization:Equity	47,898	39,700	32,686	26,252	25,079	21,632	19,003	18,231	16,530	10,145
Capitalization:Total	232,589	206,974	189,521	128,009	105,775	79,114	57,714	49,247	47,925	31,097
% Return on Revenue	4.3	13.1	13.8	13.0	15.3	12.7	9.3	7.4	9.3	10.7
% Return on Assets	0.2	1.1	1.2	0.9	1.0	0.8	0.6	0.8	1.1	1.2
% Return on Equity	4.7	32.0	31.9	21.9	19.5	14.8	11.4	13.3	23.0	30.4

Data as orig reptd.; bef. results of disc opers/spec. items. Per share data adj. for stk. divs.; EPS diluted. Prior to 2009, fiscal year ended November 30. E-Estimated. NA-Not Available. NM-Not Meaningful. NR-Not Ranked. UR-Under Review.

Office: 85 Broad Street, New York, NY 10004.
Telephone: 212-902-1000.
Email: gs-investor-relations@gs.com
Website: http://www.gs.com

Chrmn & CEO: L.C. Blankfein
Pres & COO: G.D. Cohn
Vice Chrmn: J.M. Evans
EVP, CFO & CTO: D.A. Viniar

EVP & Secy: E.E. Stecher
Investor Contact: J. Andrews (212-357-2674)
Auditor: PricewaterhouseCoopers
Board Members: L. C. Blankfein, J. H. Bryan, Jr., G. D. Cohn, C. Dahlback, J. M. Evans, S. Friedman, W. W. George, R. K. Gupta, J. A. Johnson, L. D. Juliber, L. N. Mittal, J. J. Schiro, R. J. Simmons, S. Wang

Founded: 1869
Domicile: Delaware
Employees: 30,067

The McGraw-Hill Companies

Goodrich Corp

STANDARD &POOR'S

S&P Recommendation	BUY ★★★★☆	Price $60.07 (as of Nov 27, 2009)	12-Mo. Target Price $64.00	Investment Style Large-Cap Value

GICS Sector Industrials
Sub-Industry Aerospace & Defense

Summary This company is one of the world's largest providers of equipment, parts, and services to the large commercial, regional, business, and military jet markets.

Key Stock Statistics (Source S&P, Vickers, company reports)

52-Wk Range	$62.17– 29.95	S&P Oper. EPS 2009E	4.45	Market Capitalization(B)	$7.470	Beta	1.24
Trailing 12-Month EPS	$5.27	S&P Oper. EPS 2010E	4.60	Yield (%)	1.80	S&P 3-Yr. Proj. EPS CAGR(%)	0
Trailing 12-Month P/E	11.4	P/E on S&P Oper. EPS 2009E	13.5	Dividend Rate/Share	$1.08	S&P Credit Rating	BBB+
$10K Invested 5 Yrs Ago	$21,291	Common Shares Outstg. (M)	124.4	Institutional Ownership (%)	84		

Price Performance

- 30-Week Mov. Avg. · · ·   10-Week Mov. Avg.   — GAAP Earnings vs. Previous Year   Volume Above Avg. STARS
- 12-Mo. Target Price —   Relative Strength —   ▲ Up   ▼ Down   ► No Change   Below Avg. ★

Options: ASE, CBOE, P, Ph

Analysis prepared by **Richard Tortoriello** on October 27, 2009, when the stock traded at **$ 56.42**.

Highlights

► We project a revenue decline of 4.5% in 2009, but growth of 3% in 2010, the latter reflecting our forecast for improvement in the global economy. For 2010, we expect the following trends: a moderate increase in large commercial OEM sales, primarily due to initial production on the 787; further moderate sales declines in business and regional jet sales; increased military and space sales; and, a significant increase in large commercial aftermarket sales. We expect global air traffic to begin to increase in 2010 and note our view that GR is well-positioned on newer aircraft, which should be the first to be put back into service.

► We expect operating margins to decline to 15.7% in 2009, from 17.2% in 2008, primarily due to inefficiencies from lower volume. For 2010, we project a slight improvement to 15.8%.

► We estimate 2009 EPS of $4.45, down from EPS of $5.33 in 2008, but we see growth to $4.60 in 2010. We expect free cash flow (cash generated from operations less capital expenditures) of well over $3.00 per share in 2009.

Investment Rationale/Risk

► Although we expect results to be constrained by slow aftermarket demand, we see signs of improvement in international air and freight traffic, which we believe bodes well for future business at GR. Total aftermarket sales rose 16% in 2007, but slowed to 9% in 2008, and we look for a double-digit decline in aftermarket revenues in 2009, but expect growth of about 6% in 2010. Although we expect significant order cancellations and deferrals at both Boeing and Airbus, we believe very large order backlogs, as well as the first delivery of the Boeing 787, which we believe will occur by late-2010, will mean production cuts will be modest.

► Risks to our recommendation and target price include the potential for a prolonged global economic decline, the possibility of slowing defense industry orders, and operational and other missteps at GR.

► Our 12-month target price of $64 is based on an enterprise value to estimated 2010 EBITDA multiple of about 8.0X. Over the past 10 years, GR's average EV-to-EBITDA multiple has been 7.8X. With strong signs of economic improvement, we believe an average multiple is appropriate for the shares.

Qualitative Risk Assessment

LOW	MEDIUM	HIGH

Our risk assessment reflects GR's history of cyclical earnings growth and its long record of dividend payments, offset by a lack of growth in dividends, as reflected by an S&P Quality Ranking of B+ (average). We also take into account GR's long-term debt to capital ratio of 37%, as of September 2009, which is slightly above average for peers in the aerospace & defense sub-industry.

Quantitative Evaluations

S&P Quality Ranking B+

D	C	B-	B	B+	A-	A	A+

Relative Strength Rank STRONG

80

LOWEST = 1   HIGHEST = 99

Revenue/Earnings Data

Revenue (Million $)

	1Q	2Q	3Q	4Q	Year
2009	1,696	1,700	1,647	--	--
2008	1,745	1,849	1,772	1,695	7,062
2007	1,589	1,622	1,602	1,668	6,392
2006	1,424	1,483	1,436	1,535	5,878
2005	1,276	1,353	1,371	1,398	5,397
2004	1,162	1,134	1,167	1,262	4,725

Earnings Per Share ($)

	1Q	2Q	3Q	4Q	Year
2009	1.35	1.15	1.12	E0.82	E4.45
2008	1.21	1.44	1.33	1.35	5.33
2007	0.78	0.98	1.10	1.05	3.89
2006	1.59	0.64	0.80	0.78	3.80
2005	0.46	0.51	0.49	0.51	1.97
2004	0.26	0.32	0.41	0.30	1.30

Fiscal year ended Dec. 31. Next earnings report expected: Early February. EPS Estimates based on S&P Operating Earnings; historical GAAP earnings are as reported.

Dividend Data (Dates: mm/dd Payment Date: mm/dd/yy)

Amount ($)	Date Decl.	Ex-Div. Date	Stk. of Record	Payment Date
0.250	02/17	02/26	03/02	04/01/09
0.250	04/21	05/28	06/01	07/01/09
0.250	07/21	08/28	09/01	10/01/09
0.270	10/13	11/27	12/01	01/04/10

Dividends have been paid since 1939. Source: Company reports.

Please read the Required Disclosures and Analyst Certification on the last page of this report.

The McGraw-Hill Companies

Goodrich Corp

Business Summary October 27, 2009

CORPORATE OVERVIEW. Goodrich Corp., a global aircraft components maker and services provider, is also a leading supplier of systems and products to the global defense and aerospace markets. Operations are divided into three segments.

Nacelles and Interior Systems (35% of revenues and 53% of operating profits in 2008) manufactures products and provides maintenance, repair and overhaul associated with aircraft engines, including thrust reversers, cowlings, nozzles and their components (a nacelle is the structure that surrounds an aircraft engine and includes all of the foregoing items), and aircraft interior products, including slides, seats, and cargo and lighting systems. N&IS's largest customers include Airbus, Boeing, Rolls-Royce and global airlines. Primary competitors in this market include Aircelle (a subsidiary of SAFRAN), GE, and Spirit Aerosystems.

Actuation and Landing Systems (37% and 25%) provides systems, components and related services pertaining to aircraft taxi, takeoff, flight control, landing and stopping, as well as engine components, including fuel delivery systems and rotating assemblies. Key products include actuation systems, which use linear, rotary or fly-by-wire actuation to control movement; landing gear; aircraft wheels and brakes. A&LS and Messier-Dowty (a division of France-based SNECMA) each control about 50% of the global landing gear market.

Competitors in other markets include Honeywell (wheels and brakes), Parker Hannifin (actuation), and United Technologies (actuation).

The unit is also a major global provider of aircraft maintenance, repair and overhaul (MRO) services. A&LS's MRO customers mostly comprise the world's major airlines and aircraft leasing companies. Primary aircraft maintenance competitors include TIMCO Aviation Services, SIA Engineering Co., Singapore Technologies and Lufthansa Technik.

Electronic Systems (28% and 22%) produces a wide array of systems and components that provide flight performance measurements, flight management information, engine controls, fuel controls, electrical power systems, and safety data, as well as reconnaissance and surveillance systems. Key products include sensor systems: aircraft and engine sensors that provide critical measurements for flight control, cockpit information, and engine control systems; and power systems: aircraft electrical power for large commercial airplanes, business jets, and helicopters. Competitors include Honeywell, Thales, United Technologies, and BAE Systems.

Company Financials Fiscal Year Ended Dec. 31

Per Share Data ($)	2008	2007	2006	2005	2004	2003	2002	2001	2000	1999
Tangible Book Value	2.42	7.15	1.31	NM	NM	NM	NM	4.66	3.48	1.41
Cash Flow	7.00	5.48	5.78	3.79	3.18	2.18	3.31	3.28	4.39	3.62
Earnings	5.33	3.89	3.80	1.97	1.30	0.33	1.57	1.65	2.68	1.53
S&P Core Earnings	4.23	3.77	3.94	2.10	1.57	0.42	0.42	0.41	NA	NA
Dividends	0.93	0.83	1.00	0.80	0.80	0.80	0.88	1.10	1.10	1.10
Payout Ratio	17%	21%	26%	41%	62%	242%	56%	67%	41%	72%
Prices:High	71.14	75.74	47.45	45.82	33.90	30.30	34.45	44.50	43.13	45.69
Prices:Low	25.11	44.97	37.15	30.11	26.60	12.20	14.17	15.91	21.56	21.00
P/E Ratio:High	13	19	12	23	26	92	22	27	16	30
P/E Ratio:Low	5	12	10	15	20	37	9	10	8	14
Income Statement Analysis (Million $)										
Revenue	7,062	6,392	5,878	5,397	4,725	4,383	3,910	4,185	4,364	5,538
Operating Income	1,313	1,086	886	759	636	515	586	666	830	973
Depreciation	212	205	240	226	223	219	184	174	193	231
Interest Expense	117	130	126	131	143	163	117	118	129	138
Pretax Income	967	717	462	375	199	61.3	259	271	443	316
Effective Tax Rate	30.3%	30.8%	NM	31.8%	21.7%	37.2%	36.0%	34.8%	35.4%	46.3%
Net Income	674	496	481	244	156	38.5	166	177	286	170
S&P Core Earnings	535	482	499	260	189	48.6	44.9	44.7	NA	NA
Balance Sheet & Other Financial Data (Million $)										
Cash	370	406	201	251	298	378	150	85.8	77.5	66.4
Current Assets	3,668	3,549	3,008	2,425	2,357	2,087	2,008	1,921	3,080	2,101
Total Assets	7,483	7,534	6,901	6,454	6,218	5,890	5,990	4,638	5,718	5,456
Current Liabilities	1,841	1,743	1,633	1,615	1,565	1,401	1,554	1,159	2,147	1,511
Long Term Debt	1,410	1,563	1,722	1,742	1,899	2,137	2,254	1,432	1,590	1,788
Common Equity	2,091	2,579	1,977	1,473	1,343	1,194	933	1,361	1,227	1,293
Total Capital	3,564	4,313	3,756	3,215	3,276	3,330	3,187	2,808	2,819	3,208
Capital Expenditures	285	283	257	216	152	125	107	191	148	246
Cash Flow	885	701	721	470	379	258	349	351	479	400
Current Ratio	2.0	2.0	1.8	1.5	1.5	1.5	1.3	1.7	1.4	1.4
% Long Term Debt of Capitalization	39.6	36.2	45.8	54.2	58.0	64.2	70.7	51.0	56.4	55.7
% Net Income of Revenue	9.5	7.8	8.2	4.5	3.3	0.9	4.2	4.2	6.6	3.1
% Return on Assets	9.0	6.9	7.2	3.8	2.6	0.6	3.0	3.6	5.3	3.2
% Return on Equity	28.8	21.8	27.9	17.3	12.3	3.6	14.5	13.7	22.7	13.4

Data as orig reptd.; bef. results of disc opers/spec. items. Per share data adj. for stk. divs.; EPS diluted. E-Estimated. NA-Not Available. NM-Not Meaningful. NR-Not Ranked. UR-Under Review.

Office: Four Coliseum Centre, Charlotte, NC 28217-4578.
Telephone: 704-423-7000.
Website: http://www.goodrich.com
Chrmn, Pres & CEO: M.O. Larsen

EVP & CFO: S.E. Kuechle
Chief Admin Officer & General Counsel: T.G. Linnert
CTO: J. Witowski
Chief Acctg Officer & Cntlr: S. Cottrill

Investor Contact: P. Gifford (704-423-5517)
Board Members: C. Corvi, D. C. Creel, G. A. Davidson, Jr., H. E. DeLoach, Jr., J. W. Griffith, W. R. Holland, J. P. Jumper, M. O. Larsen, L. W. Newton, D. E. Olesen, A. M. Rankin, Jr., A. T. Young

Founded: 1912
Domicile: New York
Employees: 25,000

Goodyear Tire & Rubber Co

STANDARD &POOR'S

S&P Recommendation BUY ★★★★☆	**Price** $13.69 (as of Nov 27, 2009)	**12-Mo. Target Price** $19.00	**Investment Style** Large-Cap Blend

GICS Sector Consumer Discretionary
Sub-Industry Tires & Rubber

Summary GT is the largest U.S. manufacturer of tires, and one of the biggest worldwide. Operations also include rubber and plastic products and chemicals.

Key Stock Statistics (Source S&P, Vickers, company reports)

52-Wk Range	$18.84– 3.17	S&P Oper. EPS 2009**E**	-1.24	Market Capitalization(B)	$3.315	Beta		3.03
Trailing 12-Month EPS	$-3.37	S&P Oper. EPS 2010**E**	1.22	Yield (%)	Nil	S&P 3-Yr. Proj. EPS CAGR(%)		-21
Trailing 12-Month P/E	NM	P/E on S&P Oper. EPS 2009**E**	NM	Dividend Rate/Share	Nil	S&P Credit Rating		BB-
$10K Invested 5 Yrs Ago	$10,952	Common Shares Outstg. (M)	242.2	Institutional Ownership (%)	77			

Price Performance

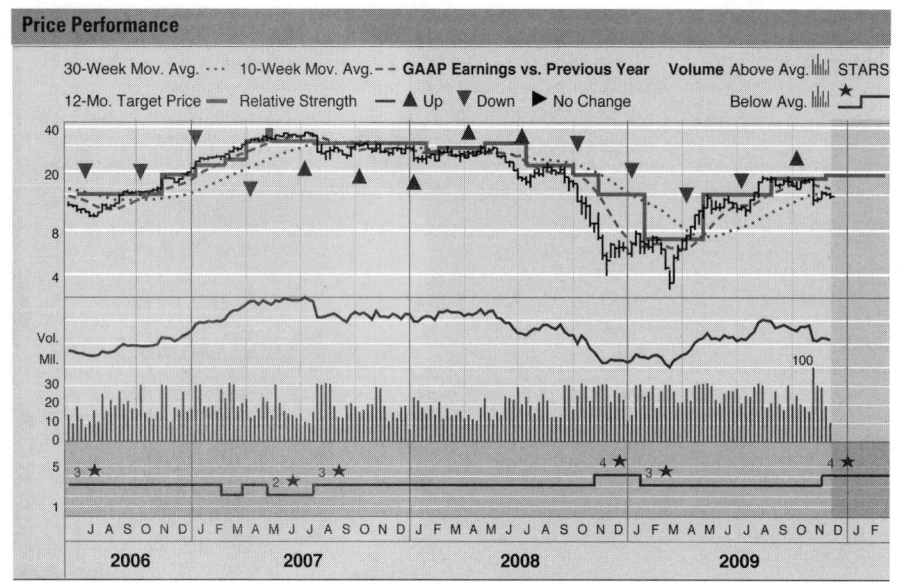

30-Week Mov. Avg. · · · 10-Week Mov. Avg. – – GAAP Earnings vs. Previous Year Volume Above Avg. STARS
12-Mo. Target Price — Relative Strength — ▲ Up ▼ Down ► No Change Below Avg. ★

Options: ASE, CBOE, P, Ph

Analysis prepared by **Efraim Levy, CFA** on November 19, 2009, when the stock traded at **$14.33**.

Highlights

▶ With a weak global economy, sharp vehicle production cuts, and reduced miles driven in key markets, we expect GT's sales to fall nearly 19% in 2009. The sales decline should be limited by the introduction of about 50 new tire products during the year. Although margins should be aided by higher selling prices and expense reductions from restructuring activities, we think weaker production will more than offset these factors. We expect global vehicle production to rise in 2010 and spur a return to profitability for Goodyear. We expect higher volume and increased prices to drive sales 13% higher in 2010.

▶ Along with higher volume, we expect higher prices in 2010 and past and current cost-cutting actions to offset an expected increase in raw material costs, including oil. We see reductions in higher-cost plant capacity and a shift to Asia-based production leading to savings.

▶ We expect GT to save $100 million on an annualized basis now that the courts have approved the transfer of union health care benefits to union responsibility. We expect additional savings from restructuring actions.

Investment Rationale/Risk

▶ GT has been extending its debt maturities, and we see a $350 million convertible debt offering helping liquidity, as should $833 million of net proceeds from the May 2007 equity issuance. While we have increased confidence in GT's near-term liquidity, including paying off its 2009 debt maturities, we regard liquidity challenges from debt and employee retirement obligations as matters of concern for the long term. There is no long-term debt due in 2010.

▶ Risks to our recommendation and target price include an increase in GT's need for cash, weaker-than-anticipated demand for tires, lower-than-expected cost savings, an inability to get expected price increases and higher-than-projected raw material costs. We also see risk of production disruption in the event of a failure of key industry participants.

▶ We expect losses and negative cash flow in 2009, even before cash contributions to fund GT's pension plan. However, we expect a rebound to profitability in 2010. Applying a P/E multiple of about 15.5X, based on historical levels and rising peer multiples, to our 2010 estimate of $1.22, we derive our 12-month target price of $19.

Qualitative Risk Assessment

LOW	MEDIUM	HIGH

Our risk assessment reflects the highly cyclical nature of the company's markets as well as the current and long-term challenges that we believe GT faces due to its highly leveraged balance sheet, intensifying competition, high fixed costs, and legacy costs.

Quantitative Evaluations

S&P Quality Ranking B-

D	C	B-	B	B+	A-	A	A+

Relative Strength Rank WEAK

20

LOWEST = 1 HIGHEST = 99

Revenue/Earnings Data

Revenue (Million $)

	1Q	2Q	3Q	4Q	Year
2009	3,536	3,943	4,385	--	--
2008	4,942	5,239	5,172	4,135	19,488
2007	4,499	4,921	5,064	5,160	19,644
2006	4,856	5,142	5,284	4,976	20,258
2005	4,767	4,992	5,030	4,934	19,723
2004	4,302	4,519	4,714	4,835	18,370

Earnings Per Share ($)

2009	-1.38	-0.92	0.30	E0.13	E-1.24
2008	0.60	0.31	0.13	-1.37	-0.32
2007	-0.61	0.14	0.67	0.26	0.66
2006	0.37	0.01	-0.27	-2.02	-1.86
2005	0.35	0.34	0.70	-0.23	1.21
2004	-0.44	0.17	0.20	0.62	0.63

Fiscal year ended Dec. 31. Next earnings report expected: Mid February. EPS Estimates based on S&P Operating Earnings; historical GAAP earnings are as reported.

Dividend Data

Dividends were last paid in 2002.

The **McGraw·Hill** Companies

Goodyear Tire & Rubber Co

STANDARD
&POOR'S

Business Summary November 19, 2009

CORPORATE OVERVIEW. Goodyear Tire & Rubber is the largest U.S. manufacturer of tires, and one of the largest worldwide. Operations also include rubber and plastic products and chemicals. GT holds the leading market share in North America, Latin America, China and India.

With the sale of substantially all of its engineered products business in July 2007, the results of that segment have been classified as discontinued operations.

In February 2008, Goodyear formed a new strategic business unit, Europe, Middle East and Africa (EMEA). These regions collectively had about $7.2 billion in revenues in 2007, making the unit the second largest, after North America, in terms of sales. The company began reporting the new segment results in the 2008 first quarter.

CORPORATE STRATEGY. The company plans to achieve more than $2.0 billion in aggregate cost savings from 2006 through 2009 through a four-point plan. Sources of savings are expected to include continuous improvement in

processes, increased low-cost country sourcing, high-cost capacity reductions and reduced SG&A expenses, including ongoing savings from the master labor agreement with the United Steel Workers.

The company sometimes uses joint ventures to facilitate the growth of its business. In 1999, GT and Sumitomo Rubber Industries (SRI) completed a global alliance that again made GT the world's leading tire manufacturer. GT created a European joint venture with SRI. GT and SRI owned 75% and 25%, respectively, of both the North American and European joint ventures. In Japan, the ownership ratio is reversed.

GT and Pacific Dunlop Ltd. participate in equally owned joint ventures in South Pacific Tyres, an Australian partnership, and South Pacific Tyres N.Z. Ltd., a New Zealand company.

Company Financials Fiscal Year Ended Dec. 31

Per Share Data ($)	2008	2007	2006	2005	2004	2003	2002	2001	2000	1999
Tangible Book Value	0.74	8.58	NM	NM	NM	NM	NM	14.06	18.49	19.87
Cash Flow	2.42	3.25	1.95	4.16	3.87	-0.62	-3.01	2.71	4.22	5.18
Earnings	-0.32	0.66	-1.86	1.21	0.63	-4.58	-6.62	-1.27	0.26	1.52
S&P Core Earnings	-1.48	1.15	-0.88	2.61	0.84	-3.32	-8.16	-3.09	NA	NA
Dividends	Nil	Nil	Nil	Nil	Nil	Nil	0.48	1.02	1.20	1.20
Payout Ratio	Nil	Nil	Nil	Nil	Nil	Nil	NM	NM	NM	79%
Prices:High	30.10	36.90	21.35	18.59	15.01	8.19	28.85	32.10	31.63	66.75
Prices:Low	3.93	21.40	9.75	11.24	7.06	3.35	6.50	17.37	15.60	25.50
P/E Ratio:High	NM	56	NM	15	24	NM	NM	NM	NM	44
P/E Ratio:Low	NM	32	NM	9	11	NM	NM	NM	NM	17

Income Statement Analysis (Million $)

	2008	2007	2006	2005	2004	2003	2002	2001	2000	1999
Revenue	19,488	19,644	20,258	19,723	18,370	15,119	13,850	14,147	14,417	12,881
Operating Income	1,434	1,677	1,256	1,706	1,457	-549	915	916	1,173	1,094
Depreciation	660	614	675	630	629	693	603	637	630	582
Interest Expense	397	566	451	411	369	296	241	292	283	179
Pretax Income	186	464	-113	584	381	-655	37.9	-273	92.3	337
Effective Tax Rate	112.4%	55.0%	NM	42.8%	54.6%	NM	NM	NM	20.0%	16.5%
Net Income	-77.0	139	-330	239	115	-802	-1,106	-204	40.3	241
S&P Core Earnings	-355	253	-157	522	142	-584	-1,362	-495	NA	NA

Balance Sheet & Other Financial Data (Million $)

	2008	2007	2006	2005	2004	2003	2002	2001	2000	1999
Cash	1,894	3,654	3,899	2,178	1,968	1,565	947	959	253	241
Current Assets	8,340	10,172	10,179	8,680	8,632	6,988	5,227	5,255	5,467	5,261
Total Assets	15,226	17,191	17,029	15,627	16,533	15,006	13,147	13,513	13,568	13,103
Current Liabilities	4,779	4,664	4,666	4,811	5,113	3,686	4,071	3,327	4,226	3,960
Long Term Debt	4,132	4,329	6,563	4,742	449	4,826	2,989	3,204	2,350	2,348
Common Equity	1,022	2,850	-758	73.0	72.8	-13.1	651	2,864	3,503	3,617
Total Capital	6,550	8,456	7,015	5,910	1,774	5,639	4,380	6,855	6,698	6,856
Capital Expenditures	1,049	739	671	634	519	375	458	435	614	805
Cash Flow	583	753	345	869	744	-109	-503	433	671	823
Current Ratio	1.8	2.2	2.2	1.8	1.7	1.9	1.3	1.6	1.3	1.3
% Long Term Debt of Capitalization	62.6	51.2	93.6	80.2	25.3	85.6	68.2	46.7	35.1	34.2
% Net Income of Revenue	NM	0.7	NM	1.2	0.6	NM	NM	NM	0.3	1.9
% Return on Assets	NM	0.8	NM	1.5	0.7	NM	NM	NM	0.3	2.0
% Return on Equity	NM	13.3	NM	325.2	565.5	NM	NM	NM	1.1	6.5

Data as orig reptd.; bef. results of disc opers/spec. items. Per share data adj. for stk. divs.; EPS diluted. E-Estimated. NA-Not Available. NM-Not Meaningful. NR-Not Ranked. UR-Under Review.

Office: 1144 East Market Street, Akron, OH, USA 44316-0001.
Telephone: 330-796-2121.
Email: goodyear.investor.relations@goodyear.com
Website: http://www.goodyear.com

Chrmn, Pres & CEO: R.J. Keegan
COO: R.J. Kramer
EVP & CFO: D.R. Wells
SVP & CTO: J. Kihn

SVP & Treas: D.J. Audia
Investor Contact: G. Dooley (330-796-6704)
Board Members: J. C. Boland, J. A. Firestone, R. J. Keegan, W. A. McCollough, D. Morrison, R. O'Neal, S. D. Peterson, S. A. Streeter, G. C. Sullivan, T. H. Weidemeyer, M. R. Wessel

Founded: 1898
Domicile: Ohio
Employees: 74,700

Google Inc

STANDARD &POOR'S

S&P Recommendation	HOLD ★ ★ ★ ☆ ☆	Price $579.76 (as of Nov 27, 2009)	12-Mo. Target Price $600.00	Investment Style Large-Cap Growth

GICS Sector Information Technology
Sub-Industry Internet Software & Services

Summary GOOG, which completed its initial public offering in August 2004, is the world's largest Internet company. It specializes in online search and advertising.

Key Stock Statistics (Source S&P, Vickers, company reports)

52-Wk Range	**$587.06– 262.58**	S&P Oper. EPS 2009**E**	**19.56**	Market Capitalization(B)	**$140.286**	Beta	**1.12**
Trailing 12-Month EPS	**$15.50**	S&P Oper. EPS 2010**E**	**22.11**	Yield (%)	**Nil**	S&P 3-Yr. Proj. EPS CAGR(%)	**14**
Trailing 12-Month P/E	**37.4**	P/E on S&P Oper. EPS 2009**E**	**29.6**	Dividend Rate/Share	**Nil**	S&P Credit Rating	**NA**
$10K Invested 5 Yrs Ago	**$32,318**	Common Shares Outstg. (M)	**317.3**	Institutional Ownership (%)	**81**		

Price Performance

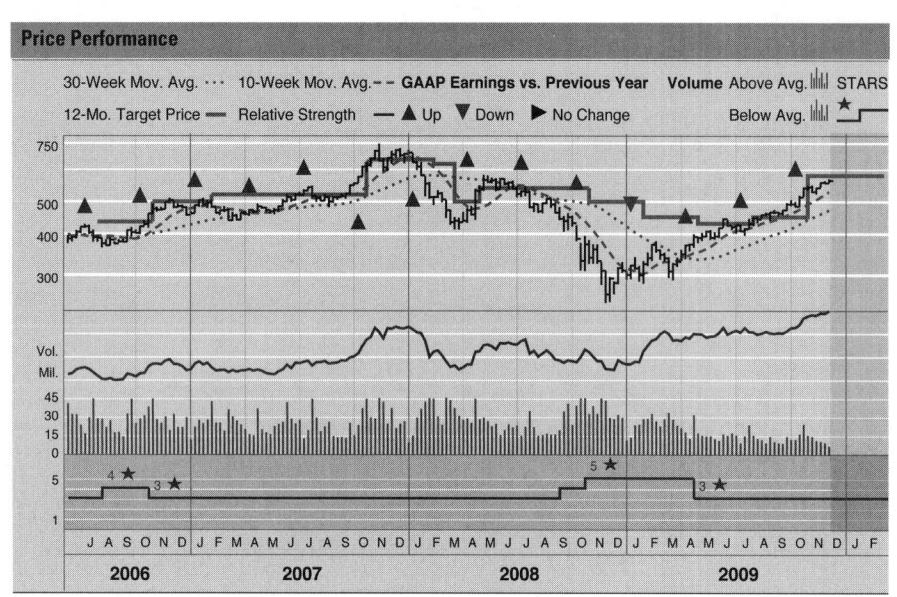

30-Week Mov. Avg. · · · 10-Week Mov. Avg. - - **GAAP Earnings vs. Previous Year** Volume Above Avg. STARS
12-Mo. Target Price — Relative Strength — ▲ Up ▼ Down ▶ No Change Below Avg.

Options: ASE, CBOE, P, Ph

Analysis prepared by **Scott H. Kessler** on October 20, 2009, when the stock traded at **$ 548.85**.

Highlights

► We believe that gross revenues will rise 7% in 2009 and 14% in 2010, benefiting from greater spending on Internet advertising, the appeal of search advertising, some market share gains, and international expansion. We think GOOG continues to face challenges in many of its businesses not centered on its more traditional Internet search offerings. We believe the tough economic climate poses difficulties, but that GOOG is relatively well positioned.

► We think the annual operating margin will improve in 2009, reflecting less reliance on large content partners and a relatively new and aggressive focus on cost containment and cutting. However, we see the margin as flat in 2010, owing in part to continuing investments in expansion and R&D. Although revenues had been adversely affected by currency fluctuations, we believe a relatively new hedging program has largely aided profits, and a recently weaker dollar could contribute as well.

► Our EPS estimates include notable expenses related to stock-based compensation. We foresee only moderate growth in diluted outstanding shares through 2010.

Investment Rationale/Risk

► We believe competitive pressures and concerns about GOOG's size/power could detract from revenue growth. Nonetheless, its business model has been resilient, in our view. We are constructive on efforts to broaden its offerings, especially with Web applications (Apps) and mobile services, but believe in some cases it has paid excessive prices to do so. In November 2006, GOOG acquired YouTube for $1.8 billion in stock, and in March 2008 it purchased DoubleClick for $3.2 billion.

► Risks to our opinion and target price include possible market share losses, possible industry consolidation intended to better compete with GOOG, new offerings or partnerships that do not succeed as some expect, and challenges related to legal/regulatory issues.

► Our DCF model includes assumptions of a weighted average cost of capital of 9.5%, five-year average annual growth of 14%, and a perpetuity growth rate of 3%, and yields an intrinsic value of roughly $600, which is our 12-month target price. GOOG generates billions of dollars in annual free cash flow and recently had about $22 billion in cash and marketable securities and no debt.

Qualitative Risk Assessment

LOW	MEDIUM	HIGH

Our risk assessment reflects what we see as the Internet segment's emerging nature and relatively low barriers to entry, significant and mounting competition, substantial and increasing investment and related new offerings, our view of somewhat lacking corporate governance practices, and notable share-price volatility.

Quantitative Evaluations

S&P Quality Ranking NR

D	C	B-	B	B+	A-	A	A+

Relative Strength Rank STRONG

88

LOWEST = 1 HIGHEST = 99

Revenue/Earnings Data

Revenue (Million $)

	1Q	2Q	3Q	4Q	Year
2009	5,509	5,523	5,945	--	--
2008	5,186	5,367	5,541	5,701	21,796
2007	3,664	3,872	4,231	4,827	16,594
2006	2,254	2,456	2,690	3,206	10,605
2005	1,257	1,385	1,578	1,919	6,139
2004	651.6	700.2	805.9	1,032	3,189

Earnings Per Share ($)

	1Q	2Q	3Q	4Q	Year
2009	4.49	4.66	5.13	E5.28	E19.56
2008	4.12	3.92	4.06	1.21	13.31
2007	3.18	2.93	3.38	3.79	13.29
2006	1.95	2.33	2.36	3.29	9.94
2005	1.29	1.19	1.32	1.22	5.02
2004	0.24	0.30	0.19	0.71	1.46

Fiscal year ended Dec. 31. Next earnings report expected: Late January. EPS Estimates based on S&P Operating Earnings; historical GAAP earnings are as reported.

Dividend Data

No cash dividends have been paid.

Please read the Required Disclosures and Analyst Certification on the last page of this report.

The McGraw-Hill Companies

Google Inc

Business Summary October 20, 2009

CORPORATE OVERVIEW. Google is a global technology company whose stated mission is to organize the world's information and make it universally accessible and useful. GOOG has amassed and maintains what we believe is the Internet's largest index of information (consisting of billions of items, including Web pages, images and videos), and makes most of it freely accessible and usable to anyone with online access. GOOG's websites are a leading Internet destination, and its brand is one of the most recognized in the world. International sources contributed 53% of revenues in the 2009 third quarter, versus 51% in the prior-year period.

GOOG's advertising program, called AdWords, enables advertisers to present online ads when users are searching for related information. Advertisers employ GOOG's tools to create text-based ads, bid on keywords that trigger dis-

play of their ads, and set daily spending budgets. Ads are ranked for presentation based on the maximum cost per click set by the advertiser, click-through rates, and other factors used to determine ad relevance. This process is designed to favor the most relevant ads. GOOG's AdSense technology enables Google Network websites to provide targeted ads from AdWords advertisers.

Advertising accounted for 97% of revenues in the third quarters of both 2009 and 2008. Google websites accounted for 67% of third-quarter revenues in 2009 and 2008. Google Network websites contributed 30% during both periods.

Company Financials Fiscal Year Ended Dec. 31

Per Share Data ($)	2008	2007	2006	2005	2004	2003	2002	2001	2000	1999
Tangible Book Value	71.09	63.67	49.02	31.20	10.25	7.66	NA	NA	NA	NA
Cash Flow	18.01	16.36	11.79	5.90	1.93	0.75	NA	NA	NA	NA
Earnings	13.31	13.29	9.94	5.02	1.46	0.51	0.45	0.04	-0.22	-0.14
S&P Core Earnings	15.54	13.18	9.92	4.68	1.85	0.40	0.44	NA	NA	NA
Dividends	Nil	Nil	Nil	Nil	Nil	NA	NA	NA	NA	NA
Payout Ratio	Nil	Nil	Nil	Nil	Nil	NA	NA	NA	NA	NA
Prices:High	697.37	747.24	513.00	446.21	201.60	NA	NA	NA	NA	NA
Prices:Low	247.30	437.00	331.55	172.57	85.00	NA	NA	NA	NA	NA
P/E Ratio:High	52	56	52	89	NM	NA	NA	NA	NA	NA
P/E Ratio:Low	19	33	33	34	NM	NA	NA	NA	NA	NA

Income Statement Analysis (Million $)	2008	2007	2006	2005	2004	2003	2002	2001	2000	1999
Revenue	21,796	16,594	10,605	6,139	3,189	1,466	440	86.4	19.1	0.22
Operating Income	8,219	6,052	3,550	2,274	970	393	204	21.0	NA	NA
Depreciation	1,492	968	572	257	129	50.2	18.0	10.0	NA	NA
Interest Expense	Nil	1.30	0.26	0.78	0.86	1.93	2.57	1.76	NA	NA
Pretax Income	5,854	5,674	4,011	2,142	650	347	185	10.1	-14.7	-6.08
Effective Tax Rate	27.8%	26.0%	23.3%	31.6%	38.6%	69.5%	46.1%	30.6%	Nil	Nil
Net Income	4,227	4,204	3,077	1,465	399	106	99.7	6.99	-14.7	-6.08
S&P Core Earnings	4,933	4,170	3,071	1,366	503	103	97.4	NA	NA	NA

Balance Sheet & Other Financial Data (Million $)	2008	2007	2006	2005	2004	2003	2002	2001	2000	1999
Cash	15,846	14,219	11,244	8,034	2,132	1,712	146	33.6	19.1	20.0
Current Assets	20,178	17,289	13,040	9,001	2,693	NA	232	NA	NA	NA
Total Assets	31,768	25,336	18,473	10,272	3,313	2,492	286	84.5	46.9	25.8
Current Liabilities	2,302	2,036	1,305	745	340	NA	89.5	NA	NA	NA
Long Term Debt	Nil	Nil	Nil	Nil	Nil	NA	6.50	NA	NA	NA
Common Equity	28,239	22,690	17,040	9,419	2,929	2,181	130	NA	NA	NA
Total Capital	28,251	22,690	17,080	9,454	2,929	603	178	50.2	27.2	20.0
Capital Expenditures	2,358	2,403	1,903	838	319	177	37.2	13.1	NA	NA
Cash Flow	5,719	5,172	3,649	1,722	528	156	118	17.0	NA	NA
Current Ratio	8.8	8.5	10.0	12.1	7.9	2.4	2.6	NA	NA	NA
% Long Term Debt of Capitalization	Nil	Nil	Nil	Nil	Nil	Nil	3.7	Nil	NA	NA
% Net Income of Revenue	19.4	25.3	29.0	23.9	12.5	7.2	22.7	8.1	NM	NM
% Return on Assets	14.8	19.1	21.4	21.6	19.1	18.2	NA	NA	NA	NA
% Return on Equity	16.6	21.1	23.3	23.7	23.0	31.4	NA	NA	NA	NA

Data as orig reptd.; bef. results of disc opers/spec. items. Per share data adj. for stk. divs.; EPS diluted. E-Estimated. NA-Not Available. NM-Not Meaningful. NR-Not Ranked. UR-Under Review.

Office: 1600 Amphitheatre Parkway, Mountain View, CA 94043.
Telephone: 650-253-0000.
Email: info@google.com
Website: http://www.google.com

Chrmn & CEO: E.E. Schmidt
COO: U. Holzle
SVP & CFO: P. Pichette
SVP, Secy & General Counsel: D. Drummond

CTO: S. Brin
Investor Contact: M. Shim (650-253-7663)
Board Members: S. Brin, L. Doerr, III, J. L. Hennessy, A. Mather, P. S. Otellini, L. Page, E. E. Schmidt, K. Shriram, S. M. Tilghman

Employees: 20,222

Grainger (W W) Inc.

S&P Recommendation HOLD ★ ★ ★ ★ ★

Price	12-Mo. Target Price	Investment Style
$97.46 (as of Nov 27, 2009)	$105.00	Large-Cap Blend

GICS Sector Industrials
Sub-Industry Trading Companies & Distributors

Summary Grainger is the largest global distributor of industrial and commercial supplies such as hand tools, electric motors, light bulbs and janitorial items.

Key Stock Statistics (Source S&P, Vickers, company reports)

52-Wk Range	$102.54–59.95	S&P Oper. EPS 2009E	5.10	Market Capitalization(B)	$7.243	Beta	0.98
Trailing 12-Month EPS	$5.79	S&P Oper. EPS 2010E	5.60	Yield (%)	1.89	S&P 3-Yr. Proj. EPS CAGR(%)	5
Trailing 12-Month P/E	16.8	P/E on S&P Oper. EPS 2009E	19.1	Dividend Rate/Share	$1.84	S&P Credit Rating	AA+
$10K Invested 5 Yrs Ago	$17,183	Common Shares Outstg. (M)	74.3	Institutional Ownership (%)	75		

Price Performance

30-Week Mov. Avg. ··· 10-Week Mov. Avg. – – GAAP Earnings vs. Previous Year Volume Above Avg. STARS
12-Mo. Target Price — Relative Strength — ▲ Up ▼ Down ► No Change Below Avg. ★

Options: ASE, CBOE, P, Ph

Analysis prepared by **Stewart Scharf** on November 20, 2009, when the stock traded at **$ 96.87**.

Highlights

► We project a near 10% sales decline in 2009, with low single digit organic growth likely in 2010, as demand in the U.S. heavy manufacturing, contractor, reseller and retail markets gradually begins to recover. In Canada, gas, forestry and manufacturing sales should also pick up, while strength continues in Mexico and other foreign regions. Recent consolidations in Japan and India, and an acquisition, should add 3% to total sales growth in 2010.

► We believe gross margins will expand by about 50 basis points in 2009, to 41.5%, as price hikes and supply chain cost savings outweigh lower volume rebates and a less favorable product mix. We see EBITDA margins narrowing to 12.4%, from 13% in 2008, as costs for customer incentive programs and sales force expansion offset work force reductions. However, operating margins should expand by about 50 basis points in 2010, based on cost controls and synergies from acquisitions.

► For 2009, we see a slightly higher effective tax rate near 39%, and operating EPS of $5.10 (before a $0.05 restructuring charge and a $0.37 gain), advancing 10% in 2010, to $5.60.

Investment Rationale/Risk

► Our hold opinion is based on valuation, as well as our view of still soft, albeit improving, market trends, with better sales comparisons starting in late 2009. In our view, GWW will continue to increase market share via acquisitions and product-line expansion, targeting more small to mid-size customers and overseas ventures.

► Risks to our recommendation and target price include a further significant downturn in industrial production and economic conditions; a negative impact from entering new markets; the need to maintain a large customer base; and a stronger U.S. dollar mainly versus the peso and Canadian dollar.

► Our 12-month target price of $105 is based on a blend of our relative and DCF analyses. Based on price-to-EBITDA and P/E-to-EPS growth ratios, we believe GWW deserves a below-peer but above historical P/E multiple near 18X our 2010 EPS estimate, which leads to a value of $100. Our DCF-based model, assuming a 3.5% terminal growth rate and an 8.3% weighted average cost of capital, indicates intrinsic value of $110.

Qualitative Risk Assessment

LOW	MEDIUM	HIGH

Our risk assessment reflects uncertain economic conditions, pricing pressures, and possible facilities disruptions or shutdowns. This is offset by GWW's S&P Quality Ranking of A+, which indicates the highest level of sustained dividend and earnings growth.

Quantitative Evaluations

S&P Quality Ranking A+

D	C	B-	B	B+	A-	A	A+

Relative Strength Rank STRONG

73

LOWEST = 1   HIGHEST = 99

Revenue/Earnings Data

Revenue (Million $)

	1Q	2Q	3Q	4Q	Year
2009	1,465	1,533	1,590	--	--
2008	1,661	1,757	1,839	1,593	6,850
2007	1,547	1,601	1,659	1,612	6,418
2006	1,419	1,483	1,520	1,462	5,884
2005	1,335	1,373	1,428	1,391	5,527
2004	1,228	1,256	1,301	1,265	5,050

Earnings Per Share ($)

2009	1.25	1.21	1.88	E1.18	E5.10
2008	1.43	1.43	1.79	1.39	6.04
2007	1.17	1.21	1.29	1.28	4.94
2006	0.93	1.02	1.16	1.13	4.24
2005	0.79	0.89	0.97	1.13	3.78
2004	0.69	0.72	0.74	0.98	3.13

Fiscal year ended Dec. 31. Next earnings report expected: Late January. EPS Estimates based on S&P Operating Earnings; historical GAAP earnings are as reported.

Dividend Data (Dates: mm/dd Payment Date: mm/dd/yy)

Amount ($)	Date Decl.	Ex-Div. Date	Stk. of Record	Payment Date
0.400	01/28	02/05	02/09	03/01/09
0.460	04/29	05/07	05/11	06/01/09
0.460	07/29	08/06	08/10	09/01/09
0.460	10/28	11/05	11/09	12/01/09

Dividends have been paid since 1965. Source: Company reports.

Grainger (W W) Inc.

STANDARD &POOR'S

Business Summary November 20, 2009

CORPORATE OVERVIEW. W.W. Grainger distributes facilities maintenance and other industrial and commercial supplies, including pumps, tools, motors, and electrical and safety products. The company holds a 4% share of the estimated $140 billion North American facilities maintenance market. It has more than 600 branches, 18 distribution centers, and multiple websites. Starting in 2006, the company began reporting its Canadian branch-based business as a separate segment: Acklands-Grainger. The branch-based business segment mainly consists of 416 U.S. brick and mortar branch stores, 158 Canadian branches, and 17 Will Call Express branches, as well as 23 stores in Mexico, two stores in Puerto Rico, and one branch each in China and Panama. Six Will Call Express locations in China were closed in the third quarter of 2008. These branches sell company-made -- as well as third-party -- industrial supplies, via in-store catalogs and Internet services. GWW estimates China's market for facilities maintenance supplies at $38 billion, and projects that it will exceed $70 billion by 2014.

In 2008, the branch-based unit accounted for 83% of sales and had a pretax return on invested capital (ROIC) of 38.7%. The Acklands unit (157 branches as of mid-2009) accounted for 11% of sales, with ROIC of 12.9%. Lab Safety, a direct marketer of safety and other industrial products, was responsible for 6.6% of sales, with ROIC of 29.5%. In the first quarter of 2009, the Lab Safety

business was integrated into the U.S. branch-based unit.

Approximately 24% of GWW's sales in 2008 consisted of private label items. Approximately 18% of sales were derived from heavy manufacturing, 19% commercial, 17% government, 13% contractor, 9% light manufacturing, 7% retail, 5% reseller, 4% agriculture and mining, and 8% other.

The company's 2009 catalog features nearly 233,000 products, a 27% increase from 183,000 products in 2008, and triple the amount of four years ago. It projects nearly 300,000 products in the 2010 catalog.

No shares were repurchased in the second or third quarters of 2009, following the buyback of 1.9 million shares for $128 million in the first quarter. In 2008, the company bought back 5.7 million shares for $394 million. Approximately 5.5 million shares remain under GWW's repurchase authorization. In the first quarter of 2009, the company incurred a $0.03 a share charge for severance costs related to staff reductions. It also recorded a $0.01 charge due to an accounting change.

Company Financials Fiscal Year Ended Dec. 31

Per Share Data ($)	2008	2007	2006	2005	2004	2003	2002	2001	2000	1999
Tangible Book Value	24.35	23.47	23.40	23.47	20.89	18.43	16.92	15.51	14.67	14.00
Cash Flow	7.52	6.25	5.35	4.85	4.06	3.28	3.30	2.73	3.01	2.85
Earnings	6.04	4.94	4.24	3.78	3.13	2.46	2.50	1.84	2.05	1.92
S&P Core Earnings	6.13	4.94	4.26	3.65	2.96	2.36	2.29	1.87	NA	NA
Dividends	1.55	1.34	1.11	0.92	0.79	0.74	0.72	0.70	0.67	0.63
Payout Ratio	26%	27%	26%	24%	25%	30%	29%	38%	33%	33%
Prices:High	93.99	98.60	79.95	72.45	66.99	53.30	59.40	48.99	56.88	58.13
Prices:Low	58.86	68.77	60.60	51.65	45.00	41.40	39.20	29.51	24.31	36.88
P/E Ratio:High	16	20	19	19	21	22	24	27	28	30
P/E Ratio:Low	10	14	14	14	14	17	16	16	12	19

Income Statement Analysis (Million $)										
Revenue	6,850	6,418	5,884	5,527	5,050	4,667	4,644	4,754	4,977	4,534
Operating Income	906	782	679	617	525	463	467	461	426	406
Depreciation	117	111	101	98.1	85.6	76.1	75.9	83.7	90.6	88.4
Interest Expense	15.8	4.37	1.93	1.86	4.39	6.02	6.16	10.7	24.4	15.6
Pretax Income	773	682	603	533	445	381	398	297	332	304
Effective Tax Rate	38.5%	38.4%	36.4%	35.0%	35.5%	40.4%	40.8%	41.3%	41.8%	40.5%
Net Income	475	420	383	346	287	227	235	175	193	181
S&P Core Earnings	482	420	385	336	272	217	213	177	NA	NA

Balance Sheet & Other Financial Data (Million $)										
Cash	396	134	361	545	429	403	209	169	63.4	62.7
Current Assets	2,144	1,801	1,862	1,998	1,755	1,633	1,485	1,393	1,483	1,471
Total Assets	3,513	3,094	3,046	3,108	2,810	2,625	2,437	2,331	2,460	2,565
Current Liabilities	762	826	706	727	662	707	586	554	747	871
Long Term Debt	488	4.90	4.90	4.90	Nil	4.90	120	118	125	125
Common Equity	2,034	2,098	2,178	2,289	2,068	1,845	1,668	1,603	1,537	1,481
Total Capital	2,543	27,720	2,189	2,301	2,072	1,850	1,787	1,723	1,663	1,654
Capital Expenditures	169	189	128	112	128	74.1	134	100	65.5	114
Cash Flow	592	531	484	444	372	303	311	258	284	269
Current Ratio	2.8	2.2	2.6	2.7	2.6	2.3	2.5	2.5	2.0	1.7
% Long Term Debt of Capitalization	19.2	NM	0.2	0.2	Nil	0.3	6.7	6.9	7.5	7.6
% Net Income of Revenue	6.9	6.6	6.5	6.3	5.7	4.9	5.1	3.7	3.9	4.0
% Return on Assets	14.4	13.7	12.5	11.7	10.6	9.0	9.9	7.3	7.7	7.7
% Return on Equity	23.0	19.7	17.2	15.9	14.7	12.9	14.4	11.1	12.8	13.1

Data as orig reptd.; bef. results of disc opers/spec. items. Per share data adj. for stk. divs.; EPS diluted. E-Estimated. NA-Not Available. NM-Not Meaningful. NR-Not Ranked. UR-Under Review.

Office: 100 Grainger Pkwy, Lake Forest, IL 60045.
Telephone: 847-535-1000.
Website: http://www.grainger.com
Chrmn, Pres & CEO: J.T. Ryan

Vice Chrmn: P.O. Loux
SVP & CFO: R.L. Jadin
SVP & General Counsel: J.L. Howard
Chief Acctg Officer & Cntlr: G.S. Irving

Investor Contact: W.D. Chapman (847-535-0881)
Board Members: B. P. Anderson, W. H. Gantz, V. A. Hailey, W. Hall, R. L. Keyser, S. L. Levenick, P. O. Loux, J. W. McCarter, Jr., N. Novich, M. J. Roberts, G. L. Rogers, J. T. Ryan, J. D. Slavik, H. B. Smith

Founded: 1927
Domicile: Illinois
Employees: 18,334

Halliburton Co

STANDARD &POOR'S

S&P Recommendation HOLD ★★★☆☆	Price $29.09 (as of Nov 27, 2009)	12-Mo. Target Price $30.00	Investment Style Large-Cap Growth

GICS Sector Energy
Sub-Industry Oil & Gas Equipment & Services

Summary This leading oilfield services company provides products and services to the global energy industry.

Key Stock Statistics (Source S&P, Vickers, company reports)

52-Wk Range	$32.00– 12.80	S&P Oper. EPS 2009E	1.30	Market Capitalization(B)	$26.237	Beta	1.54
Trailing 12-Month EPS	$0.76	S&P Oper. EPS 2010E	1.24	Yield (%)	1.24	S&P 3-Yr. Proj. EPS CAGR(%)	-23
Trailing 12-Month P/E	38.3	P/E on S&P Oper. EPS 2009E	22.4	Dividend Rate/Share	$0.36	S&P Credit Rating	A
$10K Invested 5 Yrs Ago	$15,083	Common Shares Outstg. (M)	901.9	Institutional Ownership (%)	81		

Price Performance

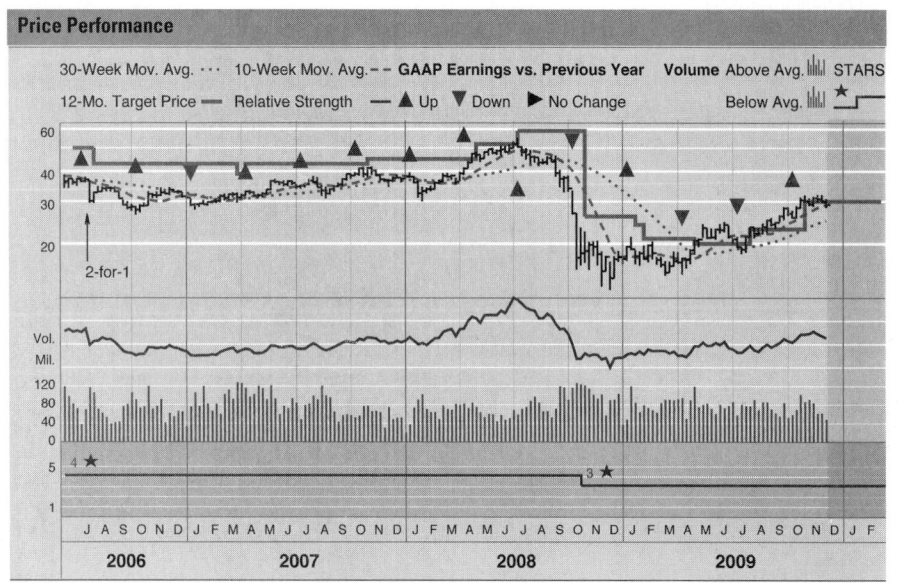

30-Week Mov. Avg. ···   10-Week Mov. Avg. - -   **GAAP Earnings vs. Previous Year**   Volume Above Avg. STARS
12-Mo. Target Price —   Relative Strength —   ▲ Up   ▼ Down   ► No Change   Below Avg.

Options: ASE, CBOE, P, Ph

Analysis prepared by **Stewart Glickman, CFA** on November 02, 2009, when the stock traded at **$ 29.10**.

Highlights

▶ We think HAL's North American operating margins bottomed in the third quarter, but expect this segment's margins to remain relatively weak (compared to 2008 levels) in the high single digit range through 2010. We remain concerned about natural gas prices remaining low, as well as excess supply of pressure pumping capacity in North America, a key franchise for HAL. However, we believe that upstream customers' cautious approach to capital spending will loosen, particularly outside North America, and so we see the beginnings of a recovery during 2010. We see about a 32% fall in HAL's 2009 North American revenues, and a 9% drop outside North America, with Latin America to yield the smallest decline.

▶ HAL should see continued benefits in 2010 from the ongoing shift in resources to overseas markets, although we see international margins coming under modest pricing pressure as customers continue to vie for cost reductions from their suppliers.

▶ For 2009, we see a revenue decline of 19%, with a 1% recovery in 2010. We expect EPS of $1.32 in 2009 (down 39% versus 2008), followed by $1.24 in 2010.

Investment Rationale/Risk

▶ We remain unenthusiastic on prospects for fourth quarter 2009 upstream capital spending, although we do see a recovery in 2010. In the near term, we think that HAL (and its major competitors) will see deceleration in demand growth for oilfield services in North America, which is likely to weigh on both revenues and margins. Long term, we think HAL is well positioned to benefit from a trend toward services with higher technology content, as well as interest in North American unconventional resource plays, which typically yield higher service intensity.

▶ Risks to our recommendation and target price include reduced oil and gas drilling activity; lower-than-expected oil and natural gas prices; and political risk, especially in regard to hydraulic fracturing in the U.S.

▶ Our DCF model, assuming free cash flow growth of about 18% per year for 10 years, a WACC of 11.3% and terminal growth of 3%, shows intrinsic value of $30. Using peer-average multiples of 11X estimated 2010 EBITDA and 13X projected 2010 cash flow, and blending these results with our DCF model, our 12-month target price is $30.

Qualitative Risk Assessment

LOW	MEDIUM	HIGH

Our risk assessment reflects HAL's exposure to volatile crude oil and natural gas prices, leverage to the North American oilfield services market, and political risk associated with operating in frontier regions such as West Africa and the Middle East. A partial offset is HAL's strong number two position in oilfield services.

Quantitative Evaluations

S&P Quality Ranking B

D	C	B-	B	B+	A-	A	A+

Relative Strength Rank MODERATE

61

LOWEST = 1   HIGHEST = 99

Revenue/Earnings Data

Revenue (Million $)

	1Q	2Q	3Q	4Q	Year
2009	3,907	3,494	3,588	--	--
2008	4,029	4,487	4,853	4,910	18,279
2007	3,422	3,735	3,928	4,179	15,264
2006	5,184	5,545	5,831	6,016	22,576
2005	4,938	5,163	5,095	5,798	20,994
2004	5,519	4,956	4,790	5,201	20,466

Earnings Per Share ($)

2009	0.42	0.29	0.29	E0.29	E1.30
2008	0.64	0.68	-0.02	0.87	2.17
2007	0.52	0.63	0.79	0.74	2.66
2006	0.45	0.48	0.58	0.65	2.16
2005	0.36	0.38	0.48	1.04	2.27
2004	0.09	-0.07	0.21	0.20	0.44

Fiscal year ended Dec. 31. Next earnings report expected: Late January. EPS Estimates based on S&P Operating Earnings; historical GAAP earnings are as reported.

Dividend Data (Dates: mm/dd Payment Date: mm/dd/yy)

Amount ($)	Date Decl.	Ex-Div. Date	Stk. of Record	Payment Date
0.090	02/11	02/27	03/03	03/20/09
0.090	05/20	05/28	06/01	06/19/09
0.090	07/16	08/31	09/02	09/22/09
0.090	11/09	12/01	12/03	12/23/09

Dividends have been paid since 1947. Source: Company reports.

Halliburton Co

**STANDARD
&POOR'S**

Business Summary November 02, 2009

CORPORATE OVERVIEW. Halliburton is a leading global provider of oilfield services to the energy industry, and until April 2007, provided engineering and construction expertise to energy, industrial and governmental customers. In 2006, HAL was comprised of two main business units: the Energy Services Group (ESG), and the KBR unit. In April 2007, HAL effected the complete separation of KBR via a split-off of its 135.6 million share stake in KBR in exchange for HAL shares. Under the transaction, HAL exchanged its stake in KBR for about 85.3 million shares of HAL which were retired as treasury stock in early April. Following the separation, HAL was transformed into a pure-play oilfield services company. In the second half of 2007, the company reorganized its four ESG operating segments into two new segments: Completion & Production (54% of 2008 revenues excluding KBR, and 56% of 2008 operating income excluding KBR), and Drilling & Evaluation (46%, 44%). Results from the former KBR segment have been reclassified under discontinued operations. Geographically, HAL generated 46% of its total 2008 revenues from North America, followed by Europe/CIS/West Africa (24%), Middle East/Asia (17%) and Latin America (13%). Approximately 64% of HAL's North American revenues in 2008 were derived from C&P activity.

CORPORATE STRATEGY. Subsequent to the split-off, with HAL's financial

obligations to KBR for the Barracuda-Caratinga project and the Foreign Corrupt Practices Act (FCPA) investigations limited by terms of the Master Separation Agreement with KBR, we view HAL's exposure to such issues as reduced. While we expect HAL to defend its strong market position in North America, we believe that future capital expenditures will increasingly flow to the Eastern Hemisphere, which we see as growing faster in the long term. In 2007, HAL moved its corporate headquarters to Dubai, from Houston, which we view as symbolic of the growing importance of the Eastern Hemisphere to company operations.

UPCOMING CATALYSTS. Geographically, North America remains the dominant source of revenue for HAL, and is the primary driver for the Completion & Production segment. However, results in the Drilling & Evaluation segment are likely to be increasingly drawn from overseas, in our view, given expectations that offshore rig demand will show the strongest growth outside of North America.

Company Financials Fiscal Year Ended Dec. 31

Per Share Data ($)	2008	2007	2006	2005	2004	2003	2002	2001	2000	1999
Tangible Book Value	NA	8.72	6.61	5.46	3.55	2.14	3.25	4.65	3.90	3.98
Cash Flow	2.99	3.27	2.66	2.76	1.01	0.98	0.18	1.26	0.77	1.53
Earnings	2.17	2.66	2.16	2.27	0.44	0.39	-0.40	0.64	0.21	0.34
S&P Core Earnings	2.10	2.64	2.12	2.11	0.37	0.34	-0.52	0.33	NA	NA
Dividends	0.36	0.35	0.30	0.25	0.25	0.25	0.25	0.25	0.25	0.25
Payout Ratio	17%	13%	14%	11%	57%	64%	NM	39%	119%	75%
Prices:High	55.38	41.95	41.99	34.89	20.85	13.60	10.83	24.63	27.59	25.88
Prices:Low	12.80	27.65	26.33	18.59	12.90	8.60	4.30	5.47	16.13	14.06
P/E Ratio:High	26	16	19	15	48	35	NM	38	NM	77
P/E Ratio:Low	6	10	12	8	30	22	NM	9	NM	42

Income Statement Analysis (Million $)										
Revenue	18,279	15,264	22,576	20,994	20,466	16,271	12,572	13,046	11,856	14,765
Operating Income	4,703	4,029	3,875	2,972	1,291	1,191	363	1,615	789	1,069
Depreciation, Depletion and Amortization	738	583	527	504	509	518	505	531	503	599
Interest Expense	160	154	175	207	229	139	113	147	146	144
Pretax Income	3,163	3,460	3,449	2,492	651	612	-228	954	335	1,012
Effective Tax Rate	38.3%	26.2%	33.2%	3.17%	37.0%	38.2%	NM	40.3%	38.5%	21.1%
Net Income	1,961	2,524	2,272	2,357	385	339	-346	551	188	755
S&P Core Earnings	1,893	2,505	2,220	2,181	320	299	-445	287	NA	NA

Balance Sheet & Other Financial Data (Million $)										
Cash	1,124	2,235	4,379	2,391	2,808	1,815	1,107	290	231	466
Current Assets	7,411	7,573	11,183	9,327	9,962	7,919	5,560	5,573	5,568	6,022
Total Assets	14,385	13,135	16,820	15,010	15,796	15,463	12,844	10,966	10,103	10,728
Current Liabilities	2,781	2,411	4,727	4,437	7,064	6,542	3,272	2,908	3,826	3,693
Long Term Debt	2,586	2,627	2,786	2,813	3,593	3,415	1,181	1,403	1,049	1,056
Common Equity	7,725	6,866	7,376	6,372	3,932	2,547	3,558	4,752	5,618	4,287
Total Capital	10,330	9,587	10,609	9,330	7,633	6,062	4,810	6,196	6,705	5,496
Capital Expenditures	1,824	1,583	891	651	575	515	764	797	578	593
Cash Flow	2,699	3,107	2,799	2,861	894	857	159	1,082	691	1,354
Current Ratio	2.7	3.1	2.4	2.1	1.4	1.2	1.7	1.9	1.5	1.6
% Long Term Debt of Capitalization	26.9	27.4	26.3	30.2	47.1	56.3	24.6	22.6	15.6	19.2
% Return on Assets	14.3	16.9	14.3	15.3	2.5	2.4	NM	5.2	1.9	6.9
% Return on Equity	26.9	35.4	33.1	45.7	14.4	11.1	NM	12.7	3.7	18.1

Data as orig reptd.; bef. results of disc opers/spec. items. Per share data adj. for stk. divs.; EPS diluted. E-Estimated. NA-Not Available. NM-Not Meaningful. NR-Not Ranked. UR-Under Review.

Office: 1401 McKinney St Ste 2400, Houston, TX 77010-4040.
Telephone: 713-759-2600.
Email: investors@halliburton.com
Website: http://www.halliburton.com

Chrmn, Pres & CEO: D.J. Lesar
EVP & CFO: M.A. McCollum
EVP & General Counsel: A.O. Cornelison, Jr.
SVP & Treas: C.W. Nunez

Chief Admin Officer: L. Pope
Investor Contact: C. Garcia (713-759-2688)
Board Members: A. Bennett, J. R. Boyd, M. Carroll, N. K. Dicciani, S. M. Gillis, J. T. Hackett, D. J. Lesar, R. A. Malone, J. Martin, J. A. Precourt, D. L. Reed

Founded: 1919
Domicile: Delaware
Employees: 57,000

The McGraw-Hill Companies

Harley-Davidson Inc.

STANDARD &POOR'S

S&P Recommendation	SELL ★★★★★	Price	12-Mo. Target Price	Investment Style
		$28.69 (as of Nov 27, 2009)	$20.00	Large-Cap Growth

GICS Sector Consumer Discretionary
Sub-Industry Motorcycle Manufacturers

Summary This leading maker of heavyweight motorcycles also produces a line of motorcycle parts and accessories.

Key Stock Statistics (Source S&P, Vickers, company reports)

52-Wk Range	$29.25– 7.99	S&P Oper. EPS 2009**E**	0.58	Market Capitalization(B)	$6.726	Beta	2.27
Trailing 12-Month EPS	$1.04	S&P Oper. EPS 2010**E**	1.24	Yield (%)	1.39	S&P 3-Yr. Proj. EPS CAGR(%)	-19
Trailing 12-Month P/E	27.6	P/E on S&P Oper. EPS 2009**E**	49.5	Dividend Rate/Share	$0.40	S&P Credit Rating	BBB
$10K Invested 5 Yrs Ago	$5,567	Common Shares Outstg. (M)	234.4	Institutional Ownership (%)	86		

Price Performance

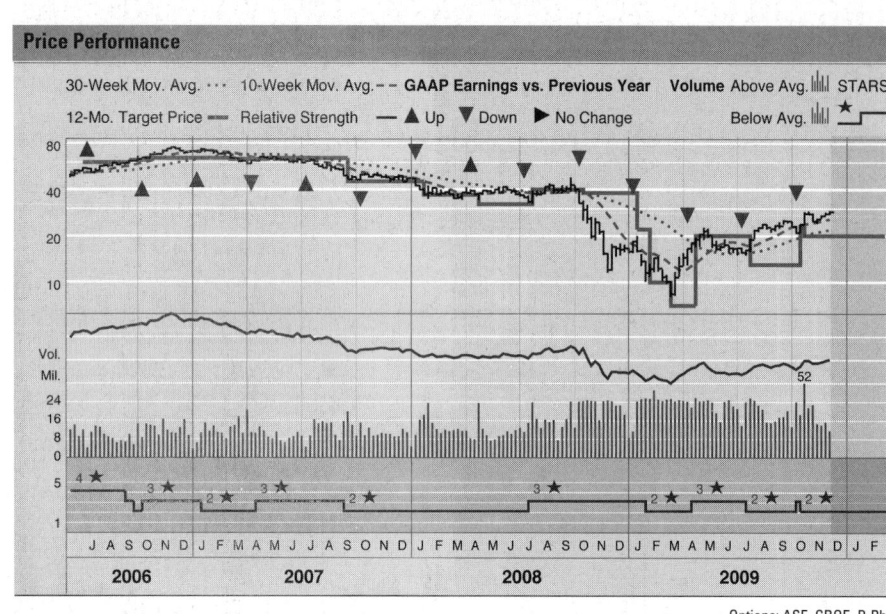

30-Week Mov. Avg. ··· 10-Week Mov. Avg. - - **GAAP Earnings vs. Previous Year** Volume Above Avg. STARS
12-Mo. Target Price — Relative Strength — ▲ Up ▼ Down ▶ No Change Below Avg.

Options: ASE, CBOE, P, Ph

Analysis prepared by **Erik Kolb** on October 20, 2009, when the stock traded at **$ 28.43**.

Highlights

▶ In October 2009, HOG reported plans to ship 35,000 to 40,000 new Harley-Davidson motorcycles in the fourth quarter, a 48%-54% decrease from a year earlier, and 222,000 to 227,000 for the full year, a 25%-27% reduction from 2008. Given current demand, we question whether these projections are still too high.

▶ We look for revenues to fall 23% in 2009, as HOG attempts to reduce currently bloated inventory levels. We see the company reducing shipments through temporary plant shutdowns and adjustments to production rates. We estimate EPS of $0.58 in 2009. In 2010, we expect a 4.4% revenue decline, and coupled with further cost cuts, our EPS estimate is $1.24.

▶ Cash and equivalents have been steadily increasing since December 31, 2005, when levels stood at $141 million. HOG had cash equivalents totaling about $1.524 billion as of September 27, 2009. In 2008, the company repurchased 6.4 million shares of its common stock at a cost of $250.4 million, implying an average price of $39.13, well above the current price.

Investment Rationale/Risk

▶ Although we continue to view positively HOG's strong brand, we expect worldwide motorcycle sales to be weak in the near term as the economic slowdown will likely continue to pressure domestic sales. We think recent cost-cutting efforts are notable, but we believe further improvements at the York, PA manufacturing facility are needed for the company to remain competitive, or HOG says the entire facility could be moved. Our liquidity concerns have largely abated, but we will keep a close watch on HOG's financial service arm, Harley-Davidson Financial Services (HDFS). HOG cut its dividend 70% in the first quarter of 2009 to conserve cash.

▶ Risks to our recommendation and target price include the possibility that consumers will increase their discretionary spending more than we expect and that demand for HOG bikes will be substantially higher than we anticipate.

▶ Our 12-month target price of $20 is based on relative valuation, in which we apply a P/E multiple of 16.0X to our 2010 EPS projection of $1.24. This multiple is roughly in line with peers.

Qualitative Risk Assessment

LOW	MEDIUM	HIGH

Our risk assessment reflects our view that this company's market leadership position and strong brand will help offset the prospect that an aging U.S. population will limit future domestic demand for motorcycles.

Quantitative Evaluations

S&P Quality Ranking A

D	C	B-	B	B+	A-	A	A+

Relative Strength Rank STRONG

91

LOWEST = 1   HIGHEST = 99

Revenue/Earnings Data

Revenue (Million $)

	1Q	2Q	3Q	4Q	Year
2009	1,291	1,154	1,121	--	--
2008	1,306	1,573	1,423	1,293	5,594
2007	1,179	1,620	1,541	1,386	5,727
2006	1,285	1,377	1,636	1,503	5,801
2005	1,235	1,333	1,431	1,342	5,342
2004	1,166	1,328	1,301	1,221	5,015

Earnings Per Share ($)

2009	0.50	0.08	0.11	E-0.12	E0.58
2008	0.79	0.95	0.71	0.34	2.79
2007	0.74	1.14	1.07	0.78	3.74
2006	0.86	0.91	1.20	0.97	3.93
2005	0.77	0.84	0.96	0.84	3.41
2004	0.68	0.83	0.77	0.71	3.00

Fiscal year ended Dec. 31. Next earnings report expected: Late January. EPS Estimates based on S&P Operating Earnings; historical GAAP earnings are as reported.

Dividend Data (Dates: mm/dd Payment Date: mm/dd/yy)

Amount ($)	Date Decl.	Ex-Div. Date	Stk. of Record	Payment Date
0.330	12/09	12/17	12/19	12/30/08
0.100	02/12	03/03	03/05	03/19/09
0.100	04/25	06/02	06/04	06/19/09
0.100	09/10	09/24	09/28	10/08/09

Dividends have been paid since 1993. Source: Company reports.

Harley-Davidson Inc.

STANDARD &POOR'S

Business Summary October 20, 2009

CORPORATE OVERVIEW. Harley-Davidson is a leading supplier of heavy-weight motorcycles (engine displacement exceeding about 651 cubic centimeters). The company also sells motorcycle parts, accessories, clothing and collectibles, and has a sizable financial services business.

HOG manufactures five families of Harley-Davidson brand motorcycles: Sportster, Dyna, Softail, Touring and VRSC. As of early 2009, the engines in these product lines ranged in size from 883 cc to 1800 cc. The company's 2009 model year line-up includes 31 models of Harley-Davidson heavyweight motorcycles, with domestic manufacturer's suggested retail prices ranging from $6,595 to $20,195. Also, as of early 2009, HOG was offering some limited-edition custom motorcycles having suggested retail prices ranging from $24,995 to $33,495. In 2008, HOG shipped 303,479 Harley-Davidson brand motorcycles, down from 330,619 in 2007. HOG shipped 13,119 Buell motorcycles in 2008, up from 11,513 in 2007.

CORPORATE STRATEGY. We expect the company to focus on both current owners of HOG motorcycles and on potential new customers. We believe that many purchasers of a new Harley-Davidson motorcycle previously owned a

HOG bike. We expect HOG's marketing focus to include international markets, where we project that HOG's opportunities for growth are stronger than they are in the U.S. In 2008, HOG's international sales totaled about $1.75 billion (31% of total sales), up from $1.52 billion (27%) in 2008.

HOG has in the past earned sizable profits from financial services it provides to independent dealers and to retail customers of those dealers. During 2008, Harley-Davidson Financial Services financed 53.5% of the new Harley-Davidson motorcycles retailed by independent dealers in the United States, as compared to 55% in 2007.

In August 2008, HOG completed its acquisition of 100% of MV Agusta Group, an Italian motorcycle manufacturer, for total consideration of $109 million. In 2007, MVAG shipped 5,819 motorcycles. HOG did not disclose how many units MVAG shipped in 2008.

Company Financials Fiscal Year Ended Dec. 31

Per Share Data ($)	2008	2007	2006	2005	2004	2003	2002	2001	2000	1999
Tangible Book Value	8.49	16.32	10.46	11.05	10.73	9.63	7.21	5.64	4.47	3.65
Cash Flow	3.83	4.55	4.87	4.25	3.72	3.18	2.48	1.93	1.56	1.23
Earnings	2.79	3.74	3.93	3.41	3.00	2.50	1.90	1.43	1.13	0.87
S&P Core Earnings	2.57	3.76	3.95	3.44	2.98	2.51	1.85	1.34	NA	NA
Dividends	1.29	1.06	0.81	0.63	0.41	0.20	0.14	0.12	0.10	0.09
Payout Ratio	46%	28%	21%	18%	13%	8%	7%	8%	9%	10%
Prices:High	48.05	74.03	75.87	62.49	63.75	52.51	57.25	55.99	50.63	32.03
Prices:Low	11.54	44.37	47.86	44.40	45.20	35.01	42.60	32.00	29.53	21.38
P/E Ratio:High	NA	17	19	18	21	21	30	39	45	37
P/E Ratio:Low	4	12	12	13	15	14	22	22	26	25

Income Statement Analysis (Million $)										
Revenue	5,594	5,727	5,801	5,342	5,015	4,624	4,091	3,363	2,906	2,453
Operating Income	1,441	1,721	1,431	1,676	1,576	1,346	1,059	816	648	530
Depreciation	242	204	214	206	214	197	176	153	133	114
Interest Expense	141	81.5	Nil	Nil	Nil	Nil	Nil	Nil	Nil	Nil
Pretax Income	1,034	1,448	1,624	1,488	1,379	1,166	886	673	549	421
Effective Tax Rate	36.7%	35.5%	35.8%	35.5%	35.5%	34.7%	34.5%	35.0%	36.6%	36.5%
Net Income	655	934	1,043	960	890	761	580	438	348	267
S&P Core Earnings	604	940	1,048	969	881	763	564	411	NA	NA

Balance Sheet & Other Financial Data (Million $)										
Cash	594	405	897	1,046	1,612	1,323	796	635	420	183
Total Assets	7,829	5,657	5,532	5,255	5,483	4,923	3,861	3,118	2,436	2,112
Long Term Debt	2,176	980	87.0	1,000	800	670	380	380	355	280
Total Debt	3,915	2,100	87.0	1,205	1,295	794	763	597	445	461
Common Equity	2,116	2,375	2,757	3,084	3,218	2,958	2,233	1,756	1,406	1,161
Capital Expenditures	232	242	220	198	214	227	324	204	204	166
Cash Flow	897	1,138	1,257	1,165	1,104	958	756	591	481	381
% Return on Assets	9.7	16.7	19.3	17.9	17.1	17.3	16.6	15.8	15.3	13.3
% Return on Equity	29.2	36.4	35.7	30.5	28.8	29.3	29.1	27.7	27.1	24.4
% Long Term Debt of Capitalization	50.7	29.2	3.1	23.6	19.7	17.8	14.4	17.6	20.2	19.4

Data as orig reptd.; bef. results of disc opers/spec. items. Per share data adj. for stk. divs.; EPS diluted. E-Estimated. NA-Not Available. NM-Not Meaningful. NR-Not Ranked. UR-Under Review.

Office: 3700 W Juneau Ave, Milwaukee, WI 53208.
Telephone: 414-342-4680.
Email: investor_relations@harley-davidson.com
Website: http://www.harley-davidson.com

Chrmn: B.K. Allen
Pres & CEO: K.E. Wandell
EVP, Secy & General Counsel: G.A. Lione
CFO: J. Olin

Chief Acctg Officer: M. Kornetzke
Investor Contact: T.E. Bergmann (414-342-4680)
Board Members: B. K. Allen, R. I. Beattie, M. F. Brooks, G. H. Conrades, J. C. Green, D. A. James, S. Levinson, N. T. Linebarger, G. L. Miles, Jr., J. A. Norling, K. E. Wandell, J. Zeitz

Founded: 1903
Domicile: Wisconsin
Employees: 10,100

Harman International Industries Inc.

STANDARD &POOR'S

S&P Recommendation **STRONG SELL** ★☆☆☆☆	Price $36.21 (as of Nov 27, 2009)	12-Mo. Target Price $27.00	Investment Style Large-Cap Growth

GICS Sector Consumer Discretionary
Sub-Industry Consumer Electronics

Summary This company manufactures and markets high-fidelity audio products and electronic systems targeted at OEM, consumer, and professional markets.

Key Stock Statistics (Source S&P, Vickers, company reports)

52-Wk Range	$40.33–9.17	S&P Oper. EPS 2010**E**	-0.16	Market Capitalization(B)	$2.512	Beta		2.23
Trailing 12-Month EPS	$-7.38	S&P Oper. EPS 2011**E**	0.71	Yield (%)	Nil	S&P 3-Yr. Proj. EPS CAGR(%)		NM
Trailing 12-Month P/E	NM	P/E on S&P Oper. EPS 2010**E**	NM	Dividend Rate/Share	Nil	S&P Credit Rating		B+
$10K Invested 5 Yrs Ago	$2,895	Common Shares Outstg. (M)	69.4	Institutional Ownership (%)	NM			

Price Performance

30-Week Mov. Avg. ··· 10-Week Mov. Avg. - - **GAAP Earnings vs. Previous Year** Volume Above Avg. STARS
12-Mo. Target Price — Relative Strength — ▲ Up ▼ Down ► No Change Below Avg.

2006   2007   2008   2009

Options: ASE, CBOE, P, Ph

Analysis prepared by **Michael Souers** on November 09, 2009, when the stock traded at **$ 38.69**.

Highlights

► We see FY 10 (Jun.) revenues rising 4.4%, following a 30% decline in FY 09. We see this increase being driven by a slight uptick in automotive sales, including the positive benefit of the 'cash for clunkers' program, as well as by favorable foreign currency translation. In addition, HAR has captured several audio and infotainment awards, which should lead to sales growth over the next couple of years. Offsetting these positive drivers is a weak global economy, which we expect to pressure consumer spending over the near term.

► HAR has identified $400 million in cost savings across engineering, sourcing, and manufacturing, and we expect these efforts to be ongoing. In FY 10, given our outlook of a moderating decline in revenues, we see the substantial cost-cutting leading to a modest widening of operating margins.

► Excluding $0.09 in goodwill impairment and restructuring charges, we project a net operating loss of $0.16 per share in FY 10, an improvement from the $1.01 net loss incurred in FY 09, excluding $6.18 in goodwill impairment and restructuring charges. We project EPS of $0.71 in FY 11.

Investment Rationale/Risk

► We think HAR's plans to sharply reduce costs have paid off, and we expect much-improved operating margins as a result. In addition, we think HAR's selection by Toyota to provide infotainment systems for its vehicles sold in Europe is a major boon for future sales. Nevertheless, we continue to project a weak global economic recovery, with only a modest improvement in automotive sales over the next couple of years. We think earnings visibility remains low, and think the shares are significantly overvalued, trading at over 50X our FY 11 EPS estimate. Following a rapid recent increase in the share price that we think largely ignores inherent risks, our recommendation is strong sell.

► Risks to our recommendation and target price include lower-than-anticipated research and development costs, an improvement in automotive sales, an increase in overall consumer discretionary spending, and unfavorable foreign currency translation.

► We derive our 12-month target price of $27 from our discounted cash flow analysis. Our model assumes a weighted average cost of capital of 10.1% and a terminal growth rate of 3.0%.

Qualitative Risk Assessment

LOW	MEDIUM	**HIGH**

Our risk assessment reflects our view of HAR's strong balance sheet, offset by its large customer concentration in the automotive segment and sensitivity to the cyclical automobile industry.

Quantitative Evaluations

S&P Quality Ranking   B

D	C	B-	**B**	B+	A-	A	A+

Relative Strength Rank   **STRONG**

82

LOWEST = 1   HIGHEST = 99

Revenue/Earnings Data

Revenue (Million $)

	1Q	2Q	3Q	4Q	Year
2010	757.4	--	--	--	--
2009	869.2	755.9	598.3	667.7	2,891
2008	947.0	1,066	1,033	1,067	4,113
2007	825.5	931.7	882.8	911.1	3,551
2006	754.7	832.7	801.5	859.1	3,248
2005	691.7	788.6	742.6	808.0	3,031

Earnings Per Share ($)

2010	-0.14	E0.05	E-0.13	E-0.03	E-0.16
2009	0.40	-5.41	-1.14	-1.05	-7.19
2008	0.55	0.68	-0.06	0.54	1.73
2007	0.85	1.22	1.07	1.58	4.72
2006	0.79	1.07	0.94	0.95	3.75
2005	0.48	0.92	0.90	1.01	3.31

Fiscal year ended Jun. 30. Next earnings report expected: Early February. EPS Estimates based on S&P Operating Earnings; historical GAAP earnings are as reported.

Dividend Data (Dates: mm/dd Payment Date: mm/dd/yy)

Amount ($)	Date Decl.	Ex-Div. Date	Stk. of Record	Payment Date
0.013	02/04	02/11	02/15	03/02/09
Div	04/29	04/29	--	04/29/09
Suspended				

Source: Company reports.

Please read the Required Disclosures and Analyst Certification on the last page of this report.

The **McGraw·Hill** Companies

Harman International Industries Inc.

STANDARD &POOR'S

Business Summary November 09, 2009

CORPORATE OVERVIEW. HAR has four operating segments: Automotive (70% of FY 09 (Jun.) sales), Professional (17%), Consumer (12%) and Other (1%). Within Automotive, HAR designs, manufactures and markets audio, electronic and infotainment systems to be installed as original equipment by automotive manufacturers. Infotainment systems are a combination of information and entertainment components that may include or control GPS navigation, traffic information, voice-activated telephone and climate control, rear seat entertainment, wireless Internet access, hard disk recording, MP3 playback, and high-end branded audio systems. Brand names include JBL, Infinity, Mark Levinson, Harmon/Kardon, Logic 7, Lexicon and Becker. Customers include Daimler, Chrysler, BMW, Toyota/Lexus, Audi/VW, Porsche, Land Rover, Hyundai, PSA Peugeot Citroen and Jaguar. HAR also produces an infotainment system for Harley-Davidson motorcycles, and produces personal navigation devices that are primarily sold in Europe. HAR believes its competitive position is enhanced by the company's technical expertise in designing and integrating acoustics, navigation, speech recognition and human-machine interfaces into complete infotainment systems uniquely adapted to the specific requirements of each automotive model.

In the Consumer segment, HAR makes audio, video and electronic systems for home, mobile and multimedia applications. Mobile products include an array of aftermarket systems to deliver audio entertainment and navigation in vehicles. Products for multimedia applications are primarily focused on enhancing sound for Apple's iPods and iPhones, computers, headphones and MP3 players. Brands include AKG, JBL, Infinity, Harman/Kardon and Mark Levinson. The Professional segment produces loudspeakers and electronics used by audio professionals in concert halls, stadiums, and other buildings for recording, broadcast, cinema and music reproduction applications. In August 2008, the company installed sound systems at venues in China for the Olympics. Brands include JBL Professional, Soundcraft, AKG, Crown, Lexicon, DigiTech, dbx, BSS and Studer.

Company Financials Fiscal Year Ended Jun. 30

Per Share Data ($)	2009	2008	2007	2006	2005	2004	2003	2002	2001	2000
Tangible Book Value	12.87	15.44	16.71	12.82	10.74	9.43	6.66	5.04	4.33	4.69
Cash Flow	-4.68	4.18	6.64	5.66	4.99	3.80	2.85	2.00	1.48	1.95
Earnings	-7.19	1.73	4.72	3.75	3.31	2.27	1.55	0.85	0.48	1.03
S&P Core Earnings	-3.50	1.79	4.75	3.75	3.28	2.27	1.51	0.76	0.41	NA
Dividends	0.04	0.05	0.05	0.05	0.05	0.05	0.05	0.05	0.05	0.04
Payout Ratio	NM	3%	1%	1%	2%	2%	3%	6%	10%	4%
Prices:High	40.33	73.75	125.13	115.85	130.45	131.74	75.35	32.65	23.31	25.18
Prices:Low	9.17	9.87	69.48	74.65	68.54	66.12	26.15	19.09	11.64	13.75
P/E Ratio:High	NM	43	27	31	39	58	49	38	49	24
P/E Ratio:Low	NM	6	15	20	21	29	17	22	24	13

Income Statement Analysis (Million $)										
Revenue	2,891	4,113	3,551	3,248	3,031	2,711	2,229	1,826	1,717	1,678
Operating Income	-31.2	351	514	527	470	360	255	181	138	186
Depreciation	147	152	127	130	119	106	88.5	78.1	67.2	64.6
Interest Expense	15.3	21.2	1.50	13.0	10.5	17.2	22.6	22.4	25.0	18.5
Pretax Income	-520	124	382	376	335	228	142	80.2	45.1	103
Effective Tax Rate	NM	13.8%	18.4%	32.4%	30.6%	30.6%	26.0%	28.2%	28.2%	29.1%
Net Income	-423	108	314	255	233	158	105	57.5	32.4	72.8
S&P Core Earnings	-206	111	316	256	231	158	102	51.5	27.3	NA

Balance Sheet & Other Financial Data (Million $)										
Cash	591	223	106	292	291	378	148	116	2.75	4.36
Current Assets	1,511	1,439	1,233	1,249	1,183	1,204	968	877	709	671
Total Assets	2,492	2,827	2,509	2,355	2,187	1,989	1,704	1,480	1,162	1,138
Current Liabilities	744	907	816	869	729	662	487	433	350	361
Long Term Debt	629	427	57.7	179	331	388	498	470	Nil	255
Common Equity	974	1,340	1,510	1,228	1,061	875	656	527	423	486
Total Capital	1,603	1,767	1,568	1,410	1,392	1,263	1,154	999	424	742
Capital Expenditures	79.9	139	175	131	176	135	116	114	88.1	80.4
Cash Flow	-275	260	441	385	352	264	194	136	99.6	137
Current Ratio	2.0	1.6	1.5	1.4	1.6	1.8	2.0	2.0	2.0	1.9
% Long Term Debt of Capitalization	39.2	24.2	3.7	12.7	23.8	30.7	43.2	47.1	Nil	34.3
% Net Income of Revenue	NM	2.6	8.8	7.9	7.7	5.8	4.7	3.1	1.9	4.3
% Return on Assets	NM	4.0	12.9	11.2	11.2	8.6	6.6	4.4	2.8	6.6
% Return on Equity	NM	7.6	22.8	22.3	24.1	20.6	17.8	12.1	7.1	15.3

Data as orig reptd.; bef. results of disc opers/spec. items. Per share data adj. for stk. divs.; EPS diluted. E-Estimated. NA-Not Available. NM-Not Meaningful. NR-Not Ranked. UR-Under Review.

Office: 400 Atlantic Street, Stamford, CT 06901.
Telephone: 203-328-3500.
Website: http://www.harman.com
Chrmn & CEO: D.C. Paliwal

EVP & CFO: H.K. Parker
CTO: S. Lawande
Chief Acctg Officer: J. Peter
Treas: R.C. Ryan

Investor Contact: S.B. Robinson (202-393-1101)
Board Members: B. F. Carroll, H. Einsmann, R. K. Gupta, A. M. Korologos, E. H. Meyer, D. C. Paliwal, K. Reiss, H. S. Runtagh, G. G. Steel

Founded: 1980
Domicile: Delaware
Employees: 9,482

Harris Corp

STANDARD &POOR'S

S&P Recommendation **HOLD** ★★★☆☆	Price $43.84 (as of Nov 27, 2009)	12-Mo. Target Price $42.00	Investment Style Large-Cap Growth

GICS Sector Information Technology
Sub-Industry Communications Equipment

Summary This company focuses on communications equipment for voice, data, and video applications for commercial and governmental customers.

Key Stock Statistics (Source S&P, Vickers, company reports)

52-Wk Range	$45.41–26.11	S&P Oper. EPS 2010E	3.86	Market Capitalization(B)	$5.774	Beta	0.90
Trailing 12-Month EPS	$0.18	S&P Oper. EPS 2011E	4.10	Yield (%)	2.01	S&P 3-Yr. Proj. EPS CAGR(%)	8
Trailing 12-Month P/E	NM	P/E on S&P Oper. EPS 2010E	11.4	Dividend Rate/Share	$0.88	S&P Credit Rating	BBB+
$10K Invested 5 Yrs Ago	NA	Common Shares Outstg. (M)	131.7	Institutional Ownership (%)	86		

Price Performance

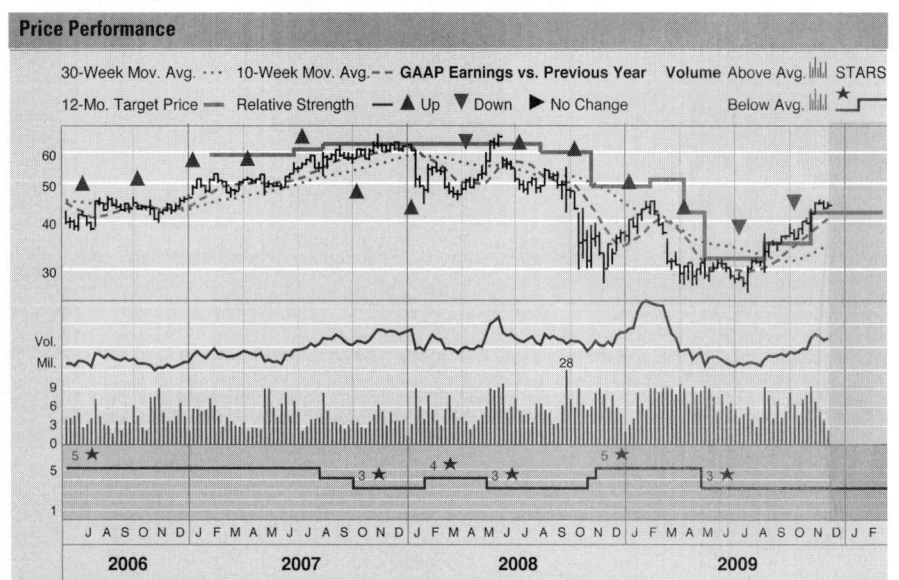

30-Week Mov. Avg. · · · 10-Week Mov. Avg. - - GAAP Earnings vs. Previous Year   Volume Above Avg. STARS
12-Mo. Target Price — Relative Strength   ▲ Up ▼ Down ► No Change   Below Avg. ★

Options: ASE, CBOE, P, Ph

Analysis prepared by **Todd Rosenbluth** on November 02, 2009, when the stock traded at **$ 41.72**.

Highlights

► With Harris Stratex spun off in May 2009, and factoring in the acquired assets from Tyco Electronics, we forecast revenues of $5.2 billion in FY 10 and $5.5 billion in FY 11. We expect prior pressure on the RF Communications segment to wane beginning in the FY 10 second quarter, as orders for tactical radios to U.S. military agencies has picked up. Meanwhile, we see flat FY 10 revenues for the government communications segment as key projects are completed and newer ones are first worked on.

► Gross margins held steady in FY 09 at 31%, but we expect improvement to 33% in FY 10 as higher volumes in RF Communications and cost reductions in other segments provide a boost. We expect HRS to keep its SG&A costs well contained, which should help the operating margin to expand to 16% in FY 10.

► We estimate operating EPS of $3.86 in FY 10 down slightly from $3.89 achieved in FY 09. Second-quarter FY 09 results included a $1.37 asset impairment charge for Stratex that has since been spun off. We see EPS of $4.10 in FY 11.

Investment Rationale/Risk

► Visibility into the company's order demand for its radios has improved following FY 09 weakness, and we believe the company's revenue and earnings will normalize in FY 10. However, growth prospects this fiscal year for the government communications segment remain limited, in our view. We believe long-term trends favor growth in HRS's core segments, as local and federal government agencies focus on improving the technological capabilities of their communications systems, and we see the recent segment acquisition from Tyco as a positive; we think HRS's balance sheet allows it the flexibility to expand via acquisitions.

► Risks to our recommendation and target price include reduced funding for U.S. government contracts, lower capital spending by service operators, and delays or missed contract orders.

► Based on projected 8% EPS growth over the next three years and a discount-to-peers P/E of about 11X our FY 10 EPS estimate, we arrive at our 12-month target price of $42. We believe HRS's dividend yield lends support to the shares.

Qualitative Risk Assessment

LOW	MEDIUM	HIGH

With most of sales coming from federal governments and government agencies, we believe HRS is exposed to uneven sales patterns and fixed-price contract risks, which may affect profitability. However, we think HRS's balance sheet and competitive position is strong.

Quantitative Evaluations

S&P Quality Ranking   B+

D	C	B-	B	B+	A-	A	A+

Relative Strength Rank   STRONG

88

LOWEST = 1   HIGHEST = 99

Revenue/Earnings Data

Revenue (Million $)

	1Q	2Q	3Q	4Q	Year
2010	1,203	--	--	--	--
2009	1,173	1,333	1,205	1,294	5,005
2008	1,231	1,318	1,330	1,433	5,311
2007	946.8	1,016	1,072	1,208	4,243
2006	759.7	841.6	881.1	992.4	3,475
2005	669.4	737.2	772.1	821.9	3,001

Earnings Per Share ($)

2010	0.79	E0.99	E1.00	E1.08	E3.86
2009	0.89	1.06	1.02	-0.64	2.35
2008	0.73	0.83	0.78	0.91	3.26
2007	0.60	0.67	1.52	0.63	3.43
2006	0.36	0.22	0.52	0.61	1.71
2005	0.29	0.33	0.40	0.44	1.46

Fiscal year ended Jun. 30. Next earnings report expected: Early February. EPS Estimates based on S&P Operating Earnings; historical GAAP earnings are as reported.

Dividend Data (Dates: mm/dd Payment Date: mm/dd/yy)

Amount ($)	Date Decl.	Ex-Div. Date	Stk. of Record	Payment Date
Stk.	04/01	05/11	05/13	05/27/09
0.200	04/24	05/28	06/01	06/15/09
0.220	08/28	09/04	09/09	09/18/09
0.220	10/23	11/18	11/20	12/04/09

Dividends have been paid since 1941. Source: Company reports.

Please read the Required Disclosures and Analyst Certification on the last page of this report.

The **McGraw-Hill** Companies

Harris Corp

Business Summary November 02, 2009

CORPORATE OVERVIEW. Harris Corp. is an international communications equipment company that focuses on providing product, system and service solutions for commercial and governmental customers including communications networks, antennas, aviation electronics, and handheld radios. The company operates under three main business segments: government communications systems, RF communications (which includes the tactical hardheld radios and now includes the recently acquired wireless systems business from Tyco Electronics) and broadcast communications. In FY 09 (Jun.), 40% of revenues from tactical radios were from non-U.S. markets, up from 27% a year earlier.

PRIMARY BUSINESS DYNAMICS. The government communications systems (GCS) segment, which contributed 54% of revenues in FY 09, develops prototypes and designs, and develops and produces state-of-the-art airborne, space-borne and terrestrial communications, information processing systems for the Federal Aviation Administration, the U.S. Census Bureau, the Department of Defense (DoD) and other governmental agencies. The government segment has a diverse portfolio of more than 300 programs. In January 2008, Harris won business with the U.S. Air Force in a six-year contract that could be worth more than $400 million. In the fourth quarter of FY 09, HRS was awarded a ten-year contract Geostationary Operatonal Environmental Satellite Series and a separate 10-year contract military communications contract

with the US Army. During the first quarter of FY 10, orders were consistent with revenues, but were up from a year earlier. The Multimax business, acquired in 2007, is part of this segment.

The RF Communications segment (35% of revenues) supplies secure wireless voice and data communications products, systems and networks to the U.S. DoD and other federal and state agencies, and foreign government defense agencies. The segment offers a line of secure tactical radio products and systems for person-transportable, mobile, strategic fixed-site and shipboard applications used by military personnel. As of March 2009, orders on a fiscal year to date basis were down 37% from a year earlier, hurt by what HRS said is a delay in two major orders; one order is with the U.S. Army and the other from the Iraq Ministry of Defense. In addition, HRS indicated in May 2009 that pressure on DoD budgets is slowing procurements for defense products and systems such as its radios. But June quarter orders improved, with particular gains outside of the U.S, and they rose further in the September quarter, signaling to HRS that the delays were in the past.

Company Financials Fiscal Year Ended Jun. 30

Per Share Data ($)	2009	2008	2007	2006	2005	2004	2003	2002	2001	2000
Tangible Book Value	0.20	2.69	NM	3.90	5.79	7.96	7.21	7.05	6.82	8.75
Cash Flow	3.68	4.46	4.75	2.53	1.94	1.36	0.87	1.04	0.75	0.68
Earnings	2.35	3.26	3.43	1.71	1.46	0.94	0.45	0.63	0.16	0.17
S&P Core Earnings	3.14	3.19	2.74	1.74	1.43	0.90	0.31	0.28	-0.45	NA
Dividends	0.80	0.60	0.44	0.32	0.24	0.20	0.16	0.10	0.10	0.05
Payout Ratio	34%	18%	13%	19%	16%	21%	36%	16%	63%	29%
Prices:High	45.41	66.71	66.94	49.78	45.78	34.58	19.74	19.35	18.50	19.69
Prices:Low	26.11	27.56	45.85	37.69	26.94	18.92	12.68	12.05	10.40	10.38
P/E Ratio:High	19	20	20	29	31	37	44	31	NM	NM
P/E Ratio:Low	11	8	13	22	18	20	28	19	65	61

Income Statement Analysis (Million $)										
Revenue	5,005	5,311	4,243	3,475	3,001	2,519	2,093	1,876	1,955	1,807
Operating Income	972	958	676	505	393	264	142	153	167	108
Depreciation	178	164	135	98.4	71.4	55.1	56.4	55.1	79.7	68.6
Interest Expense	52.8	55.8	41.1	36.5	24.0	24.5	24.9	26.7	34.8	25.2
Pretax Income	485	638	661	381	298	180	90.1	125	72.4	38.5
Effective Tax Rate	35.6%	31.6%	28.9%	37.5%	32.2%	30.2%	34.0%	34.0%	70.4%	35.1%
Net Income	312	444	480	238	202	126	59.5	82.6	21.4	25.0
S&P Core Earnings	417	435	382	243	199	120	40.8	36.5	-60.5	NA

Balance Sheet & Other Financial Data (Million $)										
Cash	285	392	409	181	378	644	466	278	250	811
Current Assets	1,859	2,047	1,829	1,428	1,318	1,554	1,358	1,154	1,222	1,629
Total Assets	4,465	4,559	4,406	3,142	2,457	2,226	2,080	1,859	1,960	2,327
Current Liabilities	1,110	995	1,638	752	590	543	496	426	460	556
Long Term Debt	1,177	832	409	700	401	401	402	283	384	383
Common Equity	1,869	2,274	1,904	1,662	1,439	1,279	1,188	1,150	1,115	1,374
Total Capital	3,046	3,466	2,701	2,390	1,867	1,683	1,590	1,433	1,500	1,757
Capital Expenditures	98.7	113	88.8	102	75.0	66.4	73.0	45.9	55.2	81.3
Cash Flow	490	609	616	336	274	181	116	138	101	93.6
Current Ratio	1.7	2.1	1.1	1.9	2.2	2.9	2.7	2.7	2.7	2.9
% Long Term Debt of Capitalization	38.6	24.0	15.1	29.3	21.5	23.9	25.3	19.8	25.6	21.8
% Net Income of Revenue	6.2	8.4	11.3	6.8	6.7	5.0	2.8	4.4	1.1	1.4
% Return on Assets	6.9	9.9	12.7	8.5	8.6	5.8	3.0	4.3	1.0	0.9
% Return on Equity	15.1	21.3	26.9	15.3	14.9	10.2	5.1	7.3	1.7	1.7

Data as orig reptd.; bef. results of disc opers/spec. items. Per share data adj. for stk. divs.; EPS diluted. E-Estimated. NA-Not Available. NM-Not Meaningful. NR-Not Ranked. UR-Under Review.

Office: 1025 W. NASA Boulevard, Melbourne, FL 32919.
Telephone: 321-727-9100.
Website: http://www.harris.com
Chrmn, Pres & CEO: H.L. Lance

COO & EVP: R.K. Henry
SVP & CFO: G.L. McArthur
CTO: R.K. Buchanan
Chief Acctg Officer: L.A. Schwartz

Investor Contact: P. Padgett (321-727-9383)
Board Members: T. A. Dattilo, T. D. Growcock, L. Hay, III, K. L. Katen, S. Kaufman, L. F. Kenne, H. L. Lance, D. B. Rickard, J. C. Stoffel, G. T. Swienton, H. E. Tookes, II

Founded: 1916
Domicile: Delaware
Employees: 15,400

Hartford Financial Services Group Inc. (The)

STANDARD &POOR'S

S&P Recommendation	HOLD ★★★☆☆	Price	12-Mo. Target Price	Investment Style
		$23.72 (as of Nov 27, 2009)	$28.00	Large-Cap Blend

GICS Sector Financials
Sub-Industry Multi-line Insurance

Summary One of the largest U.S. multi-line insurance holding companies, HIG is a leading writer of individual variable annuities in the U.S.

Key Stock Statistics (Source S&P, Vickers, company reports)

52-Wk Range	$29.59–3.33	S&P Oper. EPS 2009E	0.70	Market Capitalization(B)	$9.085	Beta	3.40
Trailing 12-Month EPS	$-7.13	S&P Oper. EPS 2010E	3.60	Yield (%)	0.84	S&P 3-Yr. Proj. EPS CAGR(%)	-31
Trailing 12-Month P/E	NM	P/E on S&P Oper. EPS 2009E	33.9	Dividend Rate/Share	$0.20	S&P Credit Rating	BBB
$10K Invested 5 Yrs Ago	$4,216	Common Shares Outstg. (M)	383.0	Institutional Ownership (%)	63		

Price Performance

30-Week Mov. Avg. ··· 10-Week Mov. Avg. -- GAAP Earnings vs. Previous Year Volume Above Avg. STARS
12-Mo. Target Price — Relative Strength — ▲ Up ▼ Down ► No Change Below Avg. ★

Options: ASE, CBOE, P, Ph

Analysis prepared by **Bret Howlett** on November 13, 2009, when the stock traded at **$ 24.81**.

Qualitative Risk Assessment

LOW	MEDIUM	HIGH

Our risk assessment reflects our view of HIG's vulnerability to further credit writedowns, DAC charge-offs, and potential dilution of shares stemming from the capital infusion from Allianz, and the company's decision to accept TARP funds from the government. Also, we think HIG could face the need for additional capital if the economy or stock market were to decline substantially.

Quantitative Evaluations

S&P Quality Ranking B

D	C	B-	B	B+	A-	A	A+

Relative Strength Rank MODERATE

37

LOWEST = 1   HIGHEST = 99

Highlights

► We expect the fundamentals in HIG's life operations to remain weak in 2010, although we believe market share losses in some businesses will stabilize. We forecast double-digit earnings growth in Individual Markets, as HIG shifts its focus to traditional life products. We forecast variable annuities sales and flows to remain well below historical levels due to product changes, although we expect better earnings grow on higher fee income and reserve releases. We forecast International earnings to decline as HIG has stopped marketing variable annuities in Japan. We view favorably the fundamentals in Retirement, and forecast higher 401k, employee benefits, and mutual fund sales.

► We believe HIG's P&C unit is well positioned and will provide stability to earnings. We expect written premiums to decline slightly and the combined ratio to be around 93%. Our forecast assumes personal lines earned premiums rising 4%, small commercial lines premiums falling 3%, and middle-market commercial lines premiums declining 3%.

► We estimate operating EPS of $0.70 in 2009 and $3.60 in 2010, excluding realized investment gains or losses.

Investment Rationale/Risk

► We believe that what we see as HIG's reduced financial strength will hurt it competitively, however we think the challenges facing the company are reflected in its stock price. HIG trades at a substantial discount to its peers. We believe HIG's balance sheet is more exposed to investment losses than the life group as a whole, but we view positively the improvement in HIG's life subsidiary risk-based capital ratio, access to $3.4 billion in TARP funds, and $900 million raised through a common equity offering. However, we think a meaningful decline in the equity markets could result in further deferred acquisition cost charges and reserve increases related to variable annuities. Going forward, we think the fundamentals in HIG's P&C unit are strong, and we expect improvements in many of its life businesses in 2010.

► Risks to our recommendation and target price include deteriorating claim trends, increased premium price competition, and a significant worsening in the credit quality of HIG's investment portfolio.

► Our 12-month target price of $28 assumes the shares will trade at about 0.7X our 2010 book value, below the peer average.

Revenue/Earnings Data

Revenue (Million $)

	1Q	2Q	3Q	4Q	Year
2009	5,394	7,637	5,230	--	--
2008	1,544	7,503	-393.0	565.0	9,219
2007	6,759	7,660	5,823	5,674	25,916
2006	6,543	4,971	7,407	7,579	26,500
2005	6,002	6,064	7,307	7,710	27,083
2004	5,732	5,444	5,416	6,101	22,693

Earnings Per Share ($)

2009	-3.77	-0.06	-0.79	E0.90	E0.70
2008	0.46	1.73	-8.74	-2.71	-8.99
2007	2.71	1.96	2.68	1.88	9.24
2006	2.34	1.52	2.39	2.42	8.69
2005	2.21	1.98	1.76	1.51	7.44
2004	2.01	1.46	1.66	2.08	7.20

Fiscal year ended Dec. 31. Next earnings report expected: Early February. EPS Estimates based on S&P Operating Earnings; historical GAAP earnings are as reported.

Dividend Data (Dates: mm/dd Payment Date: mm/dd/yy)

Amount ($)	Date Decl.	Ex-Div. Date	Stk. of Record	Payment Date
0.050	02/10	02/26	03/02	04/01/09
0.050	05/15	05/28	06/01	07/01/09
0.050	07/16	08/31	09/02	10/01/09
0.050	10/21	11/27	12/01	01/04/10

Dividends have been paid since 1996. Source: Company reports.

Please read the Required Disclosures and Analyst Certification on the last page of this report.

The McGraw-Hill Companies

Hartford Financial Services Group Inc. (The)

STANDARD &POOR'S

Business Summary November 13, 2009

CORPORATE OVERVIEW. Hartford Financial Services Group (HIG) is a multi-line insurer and one of the largest providers of investment, life insurance, and property and casualty insurance products in the U.S. Revenues totaled $9.2 billion in 2008 (down from $25.7 billion in 2007). HIG's P&C operations reported revenues of $10.2 billion and the life insurance unit reported a loss of $1.2 billion.

HIG's property-casualty operation provides a wide range of commercial, personal, specialty and reinsurance coverages. It constitutes one of the largest U.S. property-casualty insurance organizations, and is the endorsed provider of automobile and homeowners coverages to members of AARP. Earned premiums of $10.3 billion in 2008 were derived from personal lines (38%), small commercial lines (26%), middle-market commercial lines (22%) and specialty commercial (14%).

HIG's life insurance operations are conducted by Hartford Life. Total assets under management declined to $298 billion in 2008 from $372 billion in 2007. The Retail Investment Products Group generated revenues of $3.5 billion (25% of total life revenues in 2008 excluding investment income) and provides an

array of investment and savings products to individual investors, including annuities, mutual funds, 401(k) plans and 529 college savings plans. Group Benefits generated $5.5 billion of revenues (40%) and offers short- and long-term disability insurance, group life and accident insurance, and other specialty products to employers. The Individual Life segment generated revenues of $1.2 billion (8%) and offers an array of life insurance, including variable universal life, universal life, whole life and term life insurance. The Institutional Solutions Group generated revenues of $2.0 billion (14%) and provides customized wealth creation and financial protection solutions for institutions, corporations and high-net-worth individuals. The Retirement Plans Group generated revenues of $676 million (5%) and provides retirement plans for corporate clients and non-profit organizations. The International unit generated $1.0 billion of revenues (7%) and offers fixed and variable annuities in Japan, Brazil and the U.K.

Company Financials Fiscal Year Ended Dec. 31

Per Share Data ($)	2008	2007	2006	2005	2004	2003	2002	2001	2000	1999
Tangible Book Value	26.18	55.69	53.12	45.05	42.58	34.80	35.31	29.87	32.88	25.07
Operating Earnings	NA	NA	NA	NA	NA	-0.93	4.96	3.00	4.29	3.68
Earnings	-8.99	9.24	8.69	7.44	7.20	-0.33	3.97	2.27	4.36	3.79
S&P Core Earnings	4.11	11.27	8.98	7.62	6.52	-1.15	4.27	2.22	NA	NA
Dividends	1.91	2.03	1.70	1.17	1.13	1.09	1.05	1.01	0.97	0.90
Relative Payout	NM	22%	20%	16%	16%	NM	26%	44%	22%	24%
Prices:High	87.88	106.23	94.03	89.49	69.57	59.27	70.24	71.15	80.00	66.44
Prices:Low	4.16	83.00	79.24	65.35	52.73	31.64	37.25	45.50	29.38	36.50
P/E Ratio:High	NM	11	11	12	10	NM	18	31	18	18
P/E Ratio:Low	NM	9	9	9	7	NM	9	20	7	10

Income Statement Analysis (Million $)										
Life Insurance in Force	195,464	179,483	164,227	764,293	139,889	704,369	629,028	534,489	585,582	527,285
Premium Income:Life A & H	15,503	15,619	15,023	14,359	13,566	11,891	4,884	4,903	4,565	4,069
Premium Income:Casualty/Property.	NA	NA	NA	NA	NA	8,805	8,114	7,266	6,975	6,488
Net Investment Income	-6,005	5,359	6,515	8,231	5,162	3,233	2,953	2,850	2,674	2,627
Total Revenue	9,219	25,916	26,500	27,083	22,693	18,733	15,907	15,147	14,703	13,528
Pretax Income	-4,591	4,005	3,602	2,985	2,523	-550	1,068	354	1,418	1,235
Net Operating Income	NA	NA	NA	NA	NA	-253	1,250	724	962	837
Net Income	-2,749	2,949	2,745	2,274	2,138	-91.0	1,000	549	974	862
S&P Core Earnings	1,290	3,598	2,839	2,335	1,936	-315	1,078	538	NA	NA

Balance Sheet & Other Financial Data (Million $)										
Cash & Equivalent	1,811	2,011	1,424	1,273	1,148	462	377	353	227	182
Premiums Due	3,604	3,681	3,675	6,360	6,178	9,043	7,706	2,432	6,874	2,071
Investment Assets:Bonds	65,112	81,657	80,755	76,440	75,100	61,263	48,889	40,046	34,492	32,875
Investment Assets:Stocks	32,278	38,777	31,132	25,495	14,466	565	917	1,349	1,056	1,286
Investment Assets:Loans	8,677	7,471	5,369	3,747	2,662	2,512	2,934	3,317	3,610	4,222
Investment Assets:Total	118,531	131,086	119,173	106,935	94,408	65,847	54,530	46,689	40,669	39,141
Deferred Policy Costs	13,248	11,742	10,268	9,702	8,509	7,599	6,689	6,420	5,305	5,038
Total Assets	287,583	360,361	326,710	285,557	259,735	225,853	182,043	181,238	171,532	167,051
Debt	7,033	3,951	3,762	4,048	4,308	4,613	4,064	3,377	3,105	2,798
Common Equity	9,268	19,204	18,876	15,325	14,238	11,639	10,734	9,013	7,464	5,466
Combined Loss-Expense Ratio	90.7	90.8	89.3	93.2	95.3	98.0	99.2	112.4	102.4	103.3
% Return on Revenue	NM	11.4	10.4	8.4	9.4	NM	6.3	3.6	6.6	6.4
% Return on Equity	NM	15.5	16.1	15.4	16.5	NM	10.1	6.7	15.1	14.5
% Investment Yield	4.8	4.3	5.8	8.2	6.4	5.4	5.8	6.5	6.7	6.3

Data as orig reptd.; bef. results of disc opers/spec. items. Per share data adj. for stk. divs.; EPS diluted. E-Estimated. NA-Not Available. NM-Not Meaningful. NR-Not Ranked. UR-Under Review.

Office: 1 Hartford Plz, Hartford, CT 06155-0001.
Telephone: 860-547-5000.
Website: http://www.thehartford.com
Chrmn & CEO: L.E. McGee

Pres: J.C. Andrade
EVP & CFO: L.H. Zlatkus
EVP & General Counsel: A.J. Kreczko
SVP, Chief Acctg Officer & Cntlr: B.A. Bombara

Investor Contact: R. Costello (860-547-8480)
Board Members: R. B. Allardice, III, T. Fetter, E. J. Kelly, III, L. E. McGee, G. J. McGovern, M. G. Morris, C. B. Strauss, H. P. Swygert

Founded: 1810
Domicile: Delaware
Employees: 31,000

Hasbro Inc.

STANDARD &POOR'S

S&P Recommendation	BUY ★★★★☆	Price	12-Mo. Target Price
		$29.34 (as of Nov 27, 2009)	$34.00

GICS Sector Consumer Discretionary
Sub-Industry Leisure Products

Summary This large toy company has brands that include Monopoly, Playskool and Tonka, as well as various items related to categories such as Star Wars and Pokemon.

Key Stock Statistics (Source S&P, Vickers, company reports)

52-Wk Range	$30.32– 21.14	S&P Oper. EPS 2009E	2.22	Market Capitalization(B)	$4.061	Beta	1.08
Trailing 12-Month EPS	$2.01	S&P Oper. EPS 2010E	2.23	Yield (%)	2.73	S&P 3-Yr. Proj. EPS CAGR(%)	5
Trailing 12-Month P/E	14.6	P/E on S&P Oper. EPS 2009E	13.2	Dividend Rate/Share	$0.80	S&P Credit Rating	BBB
$10K Invested 5 Yrs Ago	$17,301	Common Shares Outstg. (M)	138.4	Institutional Ownership (%)	86		

Price Performance

Legend: 30-Week Mov. Avg. · · · 10-Week Mov. Avg. - - GAAP Earnings vs. Previous Year · Volume Above Avg. STARS · 12-Mo. Target Price — Relative Strength — ▲ Up ▼ Down ► No Change · Below Avg.

Options: ASE, CBOE, P, Ph

Analysis prepared by **Erik Kolb** on October 22, 2009, when the stock traded at **$ 27.96**.

Highlights

► We see net revenues decreasing 1.4% in 2009, to $3.91 billion, and we forecast a 1.5% increase in 2010, to $3.96 billion. Although we think HAS will face a difficult selling environment this year as consumers reduce discretionary spending, we believe toy sales will hold up better than other areas. New product introductions, especially in the boys category, as well as continued Nerf strength, bode well, in our view. HAS should benefit from summer movie releases GI Joe and Transformers 2, but we think related toy sales will be modest compared to recent blockbusters. Elsewhere, we see royalties generated from the Electronic Arts agreement ramping up modestly in 2009 and beyond.

► We expect operating margins to rise about 180 basis points in 2009, to 14.1%, and we see an increase of 110 basis points in 2010, to 15.2%, as an improved product mix, modest pricing increases, and the initial EA licensing contribution outweigh rising production costs at Chinese facilities and higher advertising expenses.

► We estimate operating EPS of $2.22 and $2.23 in 2009 and 2010, respectively.

Investment Rationale/Risk

► We think HAS is well positioned to increase its market share in the toy category, particularly as the company increases the use of technology in its offerings and makes toys more interactive, but given the weakened economy, we think near-term consumer spending habits are less certain. We believe HAS has strong cash flow and an improved balance sheet, which should enable the company to continue its ongoing share repurchase program. Although we view positively the recent Discovery Communications joint venture, it will likely be $0.25 to $0.30 dilutive to EPS in 2010.

► Risks to our recommendation and target price include more store closings and tight inventory management at toy retailers, weaker than expected consumer spending, poorly received new toy introductions, and increased competition in the consumer electronic toy category from larger consumer electronics manufacturers.

► Our 12-month target price of $34 applies a multiple of about 15.5X to a blend of our 2009 and 2010 EPS estimates, below HAS's historical average, but roughly in line with toy industry peer averages.

Qualitative Risk Assessment

LOW	MEDIUM	HIGH

Our risk assessment takes into account our view of HAS's strong market share position and healthy balance sheet, offset by intense industry rivalry and the concentrated buying power of U.S. toy retailers.

Quantitative Evaluations

S&P Quality Ranking A-

D	C	B-	B	B+	A-	A	A+

Relative Strength Rank STRONG

74

LOWEST = 1 HIGHEST = 99

Revenue/Earnings Data

Revenue (Million $)

	1Q	2Q	3Q	4Q	Year
2009	621.3	792.2	1,279	--	--
2008	704.2	784.3	1,302	1,231	4,022
2007	625.3	691.4	1,223	1,298	3,838
2006	468.2	527.8	1,039	1,116	3,151
2005	454.9	572.4	988.1	1,072	3,088
2004	474.3	516.4	947.3	1,060	2,998

Earnings Per Share ($)

	1Q	2Q	3Q	4Q	Year
2009	0.14	0.26	0.99	E0.84	E2.22
2008	0.25	0.25	0.89	0.62	2.00
2007	0.19	0.03	0.95	0.84	1.97
2006	-0.03	0.07	0.58	0.62	1.29
2005	-0.02	0.13	0.47	0.48	1.09
2004	0.03	0.06	0.43	0.44	0.96

Fiscal year ended Dec. 31. Next earnings report expected: Early February. EPS Estimates based on S&P Operating Earnings; historical GAAP earnings are as reported.

Dividend Data (Dates: mm/dd Payment Date: mm/dd/yy)

Amount ($)	Date Decl.	Ex-Div. Date	Stk. of Record	Payment Date
0.200	12/04	01/30	02/03	02/17/09
0.200	02/05	04/29	05/01	05/15/09
0.200	05/21	07/30	08/03	08/17/09
0.200	10/01	10/29	11/02	11/16/09

Dividends have been paid since 1981. Source: Company reports.

Please read the Required Disclosures and Analyst Certification on the last page of this report.

The McGraw-Hill Companies

Hasbro Inc.

STANDARD & POOR'S

Business Summary October 22, 2009

CORPORATE OVERVIEW. Hasbro is a worldwide leader in children's and family leisure time and entertainment products and services, including the design, manufacture and marketing of games and toys ranging from traditional to high-tech. Some of the company's widely recognized core brands, both internationally and in the U.S., are Playskool, Tonka, Super Soaker, Milton Bradley, Parker Brothers, Tiger And Wizards of the Coast. Offerings in the games segment include traditional board games, hand-held electronic, trading card, plug and play and DVD games, as well as electronic learning aids and puzzles. Toy offerings include boys' action figures, vehicles and playsets, girls' toys, electronic toys, plush products, preschool toys and infant products, children's consumer electronics, electronic interactive products and toy related specialty products.

Part of HAS's growth strategy includes licensing, which has been successful in the past for HAS. In 2008, revenues generated from the sale of Star Wars products produced under its license with Lucas Licensing and Lucasfilm represented approximately 7.8% of total company revenues. In January 2006, HAS completed a licensing agreement with Marvel Entertainment, Inc. to produce action figures and other toys and games based on their library of intel-

lectual property, including Spiderman and the Fantastic 4. Products related to this license began shipping late in 2006, with full ramp-up realized in 2007. In 2008, Marvel accounted for 5.7% of revenues and Transformers for 9.5%.

MARKET PROFILE. According to the NPD Group, a leading consumer and retail information provider, retail sales in the U.S. toy industry decreased approximately 3.1% to $21.64 billion in 2008, versus $22.32 billion generated in 2007. This compares to a 5.8% rise in U.S. HAS sales for 2008. Although total industry sales declined, certain subcategories that HAS participates in performed well, contributing to the company's market share gains. In particular, Boys' toys rose approximately 5.8% to $1.1 billion, and Girls' toys increased 14% to $790 million. Excluding HAS's international sales, we estimate that the company had approximately an 11% market share in the U.S. toy industry in 2008.

Company Financials Fiscal Year Ended Dec. 31

Per Share Data ($)	2008	2007	2006	2005	2004	2003	2002	2001	2000	1999
Tangible Book Value	2.50	2.95	3.34	3.61	3.01	1.32	0.08	NM	NM	0.64
Cash Flow	3.05	2.86	2.35	2.20	1.75	2.37	0.95	1.66	0.69	2.31
Earnings	2.00	1.97	1.29	1.09	0.96	0.98	0.43	0.35	-0.82	0.93
S&P Core Earnings	1.91	1.96	1.29	1.02	0.90	0.93	0.44	0.19	NA	NA
Dividends	0.76	0.60	0.45	0.33	0.21	0.12	0.12	0.12	0.24	0.23
Payout Ratio	39%	30%	35%	30%	22%	12%	28%	34%	NM	25%
Prices:High	41.68	33.49	27.69	22.35	23.33	22.63	17.30	18.44	18.94	37.00
Prices:Low	21.57	25.25	17.00	17.75	16.90	11.23	9.87	10.31	8.38	16.88
P/E Ratio:High	21	17	21	21	24	23	40	53	NM	40
P/E Ratio:Low	11	13	13	16	18	11	23	29	NM	18

Income Statement Analysis (Million $)	2008	2007	2006	2005	2004	2003	2002	2001	2000	1999
Revenue	4,022	3,838	3,151	3,088	2,998	3,139	2,816	2,856	3,787	4,232
Operating Income	660	686	523	491	439	509	309	435	268	669
Depreciation	166	157	147	180	146	240	89.3	226	264	277
Interest Expense	47.1	34.6	27.5	30.5	31.7	52.5	77.5	104	114	69.3
Pretax Income	441	462	341	311	260	244	104	96.2	-226	274
Effective Tax Rate	30.5%	28.0%	32.6%	31.8%	24.6%	28.3%	27.9%	36.8%	NM	31.0%
Net Income	307	333	230	212	196	175	75.1	60.8	-145	189
S&P Core Earnings	293	332	230	199	184	166	79.1	33.8	NA	NA

Balance Sheet & Other Financial Data (Million $)	2008	2007	2006	2005	2004	2003	2002	2001	2000	1999
Cash	630	774	715	942	725	521	495	233	127	280
Current Assets	1,714	1,888	1,718	1,830	1,718	1,509	1,432	1,369	1,580	2,132
Total Assets	3,169	3,237	3,097	3,301	3,241	3,163	3,143	3,369	3,828	4,463
Current Liabilities	800	888	906	911	1,149	930	967	759	1,240	2,071
Long Term Debt	710	710	495	496	303	687	857	1,166	1,168	421
Common Equity	1,391	1,385	1,538	1,723	1,640	1,405	1,191	1,353	1,327	1,879
Total Capital	2,107	2,095	2,033	2,219	1,942	2,092	2,049	2,519	2,495	2,300
Capital Expenditures	117	91.5	82.1	70.6	79.2	63.1	58.7	50.0	125	107
Cash Flow	473	490	377	392	342	415	164	287	120	466
Current Ratio	2.1	2.1	1.9	2.0	1.5	1.6	1.5	1.8	1.3	1.0
% Long Term Debt of Capitalization	33.7	33.8	24.3	22.3	15.6	32.8	41.8	46.3	46.8	18.3
% Net Income of Revenue	7.6	8.7	7.3	6.9	6.5	5.6	2.7	2.1	NM	4.5
% Return on Assets	9.6	10.5	7.2	6.5	6.1	5.6	2.3	1.7	NM	4.6
% Return on Equity	22.1	22.8	14.1	12.6	12.9	13.5	5.9	4.5	NM	9.9

Data as orig reptd.; bef. results of disc opers/spec. items. Per share data adj. for stk. divs.; EPS diluted. E-Estimated. NA-Not Available. NM-Not Meaningful. NR-Not Ranked. UR-Under Review.

Office: 1027 Newport Ave, Pawtucket, RI, USA 02861-2500.
Telephone: 401-431-8697.
Website: http://www.hasbro.com
Chrmn: A.J. Verrecchia

Pres & CEO: B. Goldner
Vice Chrmn: A.R. Batkin
COO & EVP: D.D. Hargreaves
SVP & Treas: M.R. Trueb

Investor Contact: K.A. Warren (401-727-5401)
Board Members: B. L. Anderson, A. R. Batkin, F. J. Biondi, Jr., K. A. Bronfin, J. M. Connors, Jr., M. W. Garrett, E. G. Gee, B. Goldner, J. M. Greenberg, A. G. Hassenfeld, T. A. Leinbach, E. M. Philip, P. Stern, A. J. Verrecchia

Founded: 1926
Domicile: Rhode Island
Employees: 5,900

HCP Inc

STANDARD &POOR'S

S&P Recommendation HOLD ★★★☆☆	**Price** $29.73 (as of Nov 27, 2009)	**12-Mo. Target Price** $31.00	**Investment Style** Large-Cap Value

GICS Sector Financials
Sub-Industry Specialized REITS

Summary This equity-oriented real estate investment trust, based in California, has direct or joint venture investments in health care-related facilities across the U.S.

Key Stock Statistics (Source S&P, Vickers, company reports)

52-Wk Range	$31.09– 14.93	S&P FFO/Sh. 2009**E**	2.14	Market Capitalization(B)	$8.715	Beta	1.43
Trailing 12-Month FFO/Share	**NA**	S&P FFO/Sh. 2010**E**	2.20	Yield (%)	6.19	S&P 3-Yr. FFO/Sh. Proj. CAGR(%)	-2
Trailing 12-Month P/FFO	**NA**	P/FFO on S&P FFO/Sh. 2009**E**	13.9	Dividend Rate/Share	$1.84	S&P Credit Rating	BBB
$10K Invested 5 Yrs Ago	**$12,820**	Common Shares Outstg. (M)	293.1	Institutional Ownership (%)	83		

Price Performance

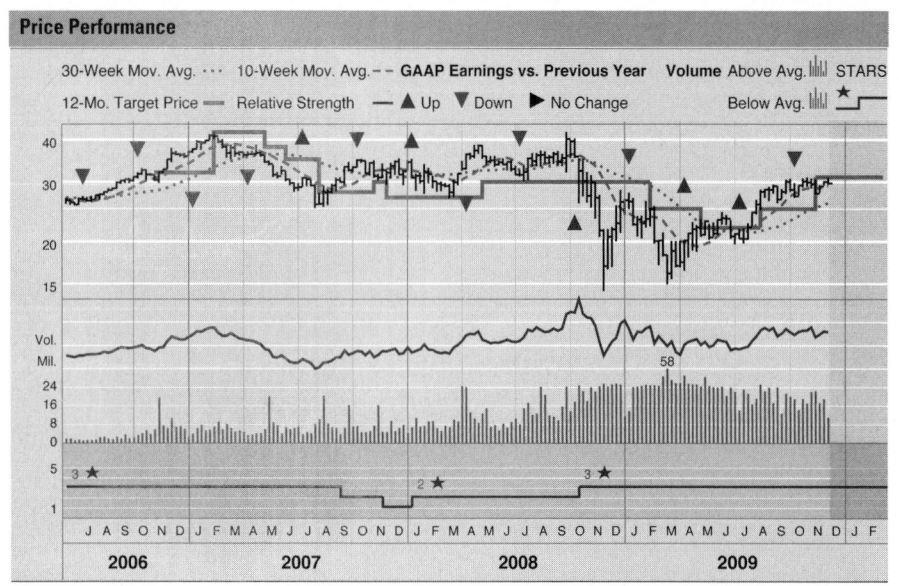

- 30-Week Mov. Avg. ···
- 10-Week Mov. Avg. - -
- **GAAP Earnings vs. Previous Year**
- Volume Above Avg. ⏐⏐⏐⏐ STARS
- 12-Mo. Target Price —
- Relative Strength —
- ▲ Up ▼ Down ▶ No Change
- Below Avg. ⏐⏐⏐⏐

Options: CBOE

Analysis prepared by **Robert McMillan** on November 04, 2009, when the stock traded at **$ 29.16**.

Highlights

▶ We believe HCP has assembled a portfolio of health care properties that is well diversified in terms of asset type, geography, and tenant base. With its core focus on senior housing, we think HCP will benefit from increased demand driven by the aging baby boomer population.

▶ Following a 23% rise in 2008 on acquisitions, we see revenue growth in HCP's need-based businesses advancing fractionally in 2009 and 2.3% in 2010. During the third quarter of 2009, growth in net operating income in the life sciences (+18.3%), medical office building (+8.4%) and skilled nursing (+3.7%) portfolios offset declines in senior housing (-4.2%) and hospital (-11.6%), leading to 3.3% overall growth in net operating income. We see management limiting HCP's exposure to the hospital sector, which faces ongoing and sustained operating pressures; we think it will focus on acquisitions in the life sciences and medical office building sectors.

▶ We forecast per-share funds from operations (FFO) of $2.14 (or $1.71 including non-recurring items) in 2009 and $2.20 in 2010.

Investment Rationale/Risk

▶ We like the predictable nature of HCP's long-term oriented, needs-oriented businesses, and believe the stock correlates less with macroeconomic trends than most other REITs. Amid economic uncertainty, we favor what we see as HCP's stable revenue stream with minimal short-term lease expirations and an improving balance sheet. Although the portfolio has been resilient during the recession, we do not see rapid growth once the economy rebounds, unless management significantly accelerates its acquisition activities.

▶ Risks to our recommendation and target price include a faster-than-expected decline in senior housing occupancy, and an decrease in government reimbursement rates.

▶ The stock recently traded at 13.7X trailing 12-month FFO per share. Our 12-month target price of $31 is 14.0X our forward four-quarter FFO per share estimate of $2.18, a modest multiple by historical standards, but reasonable, we believe, given HCP's portfolio and operating performance. We expect a widening of the valuation multiple to be driven by continued improvement in operating results.

Qualitative Risk Assessment

LOW	**MEDIUM**	HIGH

Our risk assessment reflects HCP's position as a major and diversified owner of health care-related properties, offset by our view of its leveraged financial position.

Quantitative Evaluations

S&P Quality Ranking   B+

D	C	B-	B	**B+**	A-	A	A+

Relative Strength Rank   MODERATE

70

LOWEST = 1   HIGHEST = 99

Revenue/FFO Data

Revenue (Million $)

	1Q	2Q	3Q	4Q	Year
2009	251.6	267.3	255.3	--	--
2008	252.2	251.4	269.9	263.3	1,026
2007	223.8	223.2	262.5	273.1	1,001
2006	126.5	127.5	130.2	234.9	619.1
2005	108.4	118.5	124.4	127.7	477.3
2004	96.56	106.1	110.7	115.5	428.7

FFO Per Share ($)

	1Q	2Q	3Q	4Q	Year
2009	0.56	0.55	0.52	E0.54	E2.14
2008	0.55	0.51	0.71	0.48	2.25
2007	0.50	0.58	0.52	0.54	2.14
2006	0.53	0.47	0.50	0.35	1.82
2005	0.44	0.47	0.50	0.48	1.89
2004	0.41	0.44	0.37	0.45	1.66

Fiscal year ended Dec. 31. Next earnings report expected: Mid February. FFO Estimates based on S&P Funds From Operations Est..

Dividend Data (Dates: mm/dd Payment Date: mm/dd/yy)

Amount ($)	Date Decl.	Ex-Div. Date	Stk. of Record	Payment Date
0.460	02/02	02/05	02/09	02/23/09
0.460	04/23	05/01	05/05	05/21/09
0.460	07/29	08/04	08/06	08/19/09
0.460	10/29	11/05	11/09	11/24/09

Dividends have been paid since 1985. Source: Company reports.

Please read the Required Disclosures and Analyst Certification on the last page of this report.

The McGraw·Hill Companies

HCP Inc

STANDARD &POOR'S

Business Summary November 04, 2009

CORPORATE OVERVIEW. Organized in 1985 to qualify as a real estate invest-ment trust (REIT), HCP Inc is a self-administered REIT that invests exclusively in health care real estate throughout the U.S. It leases its single-tenant build-ings to health care operators on a long-term basis, and its multi-tenant build-ings to health care providers under various market terms. HCP invests in prop-erties directly, through joint ventures, and provides secured financing to facil-ity operators, depending on the dynamics of the investment opportunity.

At December 31, 2008, HCP's real estate investments consisted of 594 facili-ties, including 20 hospitals, 51 skilled nursing facilities, 239 senior housing fa-cilities, 188 medical office buildings, and 96 life science facilities. HCP saw this portfolio shrink in 2008 as it significantly reduced its exposure in the hos-pital segment with $438 million of dispositions. All told, dispositions totaled $656 million in 2008. At year end, mezzanine loans and other debt investments aggregated $1.2 billion.

CORPORATE STRATEGY. HCP's investment strategy is based on three princi-ples: opportunistic investing, portfolio diversification, and a balance sheet that we view as conservative. The company completes real estate transactions when they are expected to drive profitable growth and create long-term stockholder value.

A key to HCP's strategy is maintaining a diversified portfolio of health care-

related real estate. The trust believes that diversification within the health care industry reduces the likelihood that a single event will materially harm its business. This allows HCP to take advantage of opportunities in different mar-kets, based on individual market dynamics. We view HCP as one of the most diversified health care REITs in terms of geography, property type and tenant base. The company's largest tenants are Brookdale Senior Living, Sunrise Se-nior Living, Tenet Healthcare, HCA, Inc., and HCR ManorCare. During 2008, HCP had one tenant accounting for more than 10% of revenues -- Sunrise Se-nior Living.

HCP routinely acquires and disposes of properties in order to enhance the overall value of its portfolio. However, in the midst of the economic downturn in 2008, HCP became more conservative, with only $228 million in investments. The bulk of these investments (69%) were in the life sciences segment for construction and other capital expenditures. We expect HCP to continue to be very selective with regard to investment spending across the various areas of its portfolio in 2009.

Company Financials Fiscal Year Ended Dec. 31

Per Share Data ($)	2008	2007	2006	2005	2004	2003	2002	2001	2000	1999
Tangible Book Value	17.35	14.45	12.47	7.82	8.41	8.82	8.46	8.62	8.55	9.00
Earnings	0.77	0.67	0.57	1.02	1.03	0.94	0.97	0.89	1.07	1.13
S&P Core Earnings	0.65	0.67	0.57	1.02	1.02	0.94	0.96	0.88	NA	NA
Dividends	1.82	1.78	1.70	1.68	1.67	1.66	1.63	1.55	1.10	1.39
Payout Ratio	NM	NM	NM	165%	162%	177%	169%	174%	103%	124%
Prices:High	42.16	42.11	37.84	28.92	29.67	25.85	22.54	19.52	15.22	16.56
Prices:Low	14.26	25.11	25.12	23.13	20.00	16.53	17.90	14.63	11.53	10.84
P/E Ratio:High	55	63	66	28	29	27	23	22	14	15
P/E Ratio:Low	19	37	44	23	19	18	19	16	11	10

Income Statement Analysis (Million $)										
Rental Income	962	836	557	452	389	349	332	311	307	190
Mortgage Income	Nil	Nil	Nil	Nil	Nil	Nil	Nil	Nil	23.0	25.2
Total Income	1,026	983	619	477	429	400	360	332	330	225
General Expenses	268	257	137	91.1	79.3	63.4	51.1	43.3	41.0	27.8
Interest Expense	348	357	213	107	89.1	90.7	78.0	78.5	86.7	57.7
Provision for Losses	Nil	Nil	Nil	Nil	Nil	Nil	Nil	Nil	Nil	Nil
Depreciation	315	274	144	107	87.0	79.1	75.7	84.1	72.6	47.9
Net Income	204	161	107	159	158	155	137	121	113	96.2
S&P Core Earnings	155	140	85.5	138	136	118	112	94.5	NA	NA

Balance Sheet & Other Financial Data (Million $)										
Cash	57.6	133	764	69.9	81.1	228	41.2	30.2	81.2	55.3
Total Assets	11,850	12,522	10,013	3,597	3,103	3,036	2,748	2,431	2,399	2,469
Real Estate Investment	10,186	9,979	7,463	3,856	3,351	2,992	2,796	2,535	2,389	2,423
Loss Reserve	Nil	Nil	Nil	Nil	Nil	Nil	Nil	Nil	Nil	Nil
Net Investment	9,358	9,250	6,867	3,242	2,816	2,506	2,371	2,195	2,101	2,193
Short Term Debt	150	500	NA	NA	NA	NA	NA	NA	4.30	3.79
Capitalization:Debt	5,685	7,027	4,318	1,837	1,242	1,407	1,334	358	1,155	960
Capitalization:Equity	4,916	3,819	3,009	1,115	1,134	1,155	1,006	972	870	925
Capitalization:Total	10,601	11,454	7,774	3,386	2,783	2,965	2,686	1,674	2,339	2,201
% Earnings & Depreciation/Assets	9.4	3.9	3.6	7.9	8.0	8.1	8.2	8.5	7.6	7.5
Price Times Book Value:High	2.4	2.9	3.0	3.7	3.5	2.9	2.7	2.3	1.8	1.8
Price Times Book Value:Low	0.8	1.7	2.0	3.0	2.4	1.9	2.1	1.7	1.3	1.2

Data as orig reptd.; bef. results of disc opers/spec. items. Per share data adj. for stk. divs.; EPS diluted. E-Estimated. NA-Not Available. NM-Not Meaningful. NR-Not Ranked. UR-Under Review.

Office: 3760 Kilroy Airport Way Ste 300, Long Beach, CA 90806-6862.
Telephone: 562-733-5100.
Email: investorrelations@hcpi.com
Website: http://www.hcpi.com

Chrmn, Pres, CEO & COO: J.F. Flaherty, III
EVP, CFO & Treas: T.M. Herzog
EVP, Chief Admin Officer, Secy & General Counsel: E.J.Garvey, D. B. Henry, L. E. Martin, M. D. McKee, H. M. Henning
SVP & Chief Acctg Officer: S.A. Anderson

Investor Contact: M.A. Wallace
Board Members: R. Fanning, Jr., J. F. Flaherty, III, C. N. Messmer, Jr., P. L. Rhein, K. B. Roath, R. M. Rosenberg, J. P. Sullivan

Founded: 1985
Domicile: Maryland
Employees: 144

The **McGraw-Hill** Companies

Health Care REIT Inc.

STANDARD &POOR'S

S&P Recommendation **HOLD** ★★★☆☆	Price $42.80 (as of Nov 27, 2009)	12-Mo. Target Price $45.00	Investment Style Large-Cap Value

GICS Sector Financials
Sub-Industry Specialized REITS

Summary This REIT invests in health care facilities, including senior housing, specialty care, and medical office buildings.

Key Stock Statistics (Source S&P, Vickers, company reports)

52-Wk Range	$45.74–25.86	S&P FFO/Sh. 2009E	3.12	Market Capitalization(B)	$5.265	Beta	1.04
Trailing 12-Month FFO/Share	NA	S&P FFO/Sh. 2010E	3.19	Yield (%)	6.36	S&P 3-Yr. FFO/Sh. Proj. CAGR(%)	6
Trailing 12-Month P/FFO	NA	P/FFO on S&P FFO/Sh. 2009E	13.7	Dividend Rate/Share	$2.72	S&P Credit Rating	BBB-
$10K Invested 5 Yrs Ago	$16,840	Common Shares Outstg. (M)	123.0	Institutional Ownership (%)	78		

Price Performance

30-Week Mov. Avg. ···· 10-Week Mov. Avg. - - **GAAP Earnings vs. Previous Year** Volume Above Avg. STARS
12-Mo. Target Price — Relative Strength — ▲ Up ▼ Down ▶ No Change Below Avg.

Options: CBOE, Ph

Analysis prepared by **Robert McMillan** on November 09, 2009, when the stock traded at **$ 42.14**.

Highlights

▶ We believe HCN has assembled a portfolio of health care properties that is well diversified in terms of asset type, geography, and tenant base. With its core focus on senior housing, we think HCN will benefit from increased demand driven by the aging baby boomer population. However, we have some near-term concerns about weak fundamentals in this sector, as we see the challenging economy and weak residential real estate market straining those consumers looking to transition into senior housing.

▶ Amid a soft economy, HCN's diverse portfolio, which is dominated by needs-based facilities, has remained resilient. We see revenues growing 5% in 2009 and in 2010, driven by stabilizing trends among the facilities operators at HCN's properties. During the third quarter, revenues per unit rose in its assisted living, independent living and skilled nursing facilities, while occupancy levels in the medical office building portfolio declined to 90.0% at the end of the third quarter from 91.5% and its net operating income rose 1.1%.

▶ We forecast per-share funds from operations (FFO) of $2.86 (or $3.12 excluding non-recurring items)in 2009, and $3.19 in 2010.

Investment Rationale/Risk

▶ We like the predictable nature of HCN's long-term triple net lease revenue stream, and believe the stock correlates less with macroeconomic trends than most other REITs. Amid economic uncertainty, we favor what we see as HCN's stable revenue stream with minimal short-term lease expirations, a solid balance sheet, and relatively a secure dividend payout. We view the shares as fairly valued.

▶ Risks to our opinion and target price include a slower-than-expected economic recovery, and decreased government reimbursement rates.

▶ The stock recently traded at about 13.0X trailing 12-month FFO per share. The shares and the valuation multiple have been volatile recently on concerns, in our view, about the state of the economy. Our 12-month target price of $43 is about 14.3X our forward four-quarter FFO estimate of $3.01, a modest multiple by historical standards, but reasonable, we believe, given HCN's portfolio and operating performance. We expect a widening of the valuation multiple to be driven by continued improvement in operating results. HCN's recent decision to commence a tender offer for some of its outstanding debt should further help reduce leverage.

Qualitative Risk Assessment

LOW	MEDIUM	HIGH

Our risk assessment reflects HCN's position as an owner of a large and diversified portfolio of health care-related properties that are leased under long-term contracts and provide what we see as a steady and predictable stream of income, offset by relatively low rent coverage ratios in certain segments.

Quantitative Evaluations

S&P Quality Ranking A-

D	C	B-	B	B+	A-	A	A+

Relative Strength Rank MODERATE

49

LOWEST = 1   HIGHEST = 99

Revenue/FFO Data

Revenue (Million $)

	1Q	2Q	3Q	4Q	Year
2009	144.3	141.7	145.1	--	--
2008	127.8	133.1	143.2	147.1	551.0
2007	110.4	117.7	124.4	133.5	486.0
2006	76.01	78.64	80.39	87.79	322.8
2005	65.84	66.05	71.99	77.97	281.9
2004	60.96	59.33	63.63	68.79	251.4

FFO Per Share ($)

	1Q	2Q	3Q	4Q	Year
2009	0.81	0.80	0.77	E0.74	E3.12
2008	0.81	0.87	0.86	0.83	3.38
2007	0.76	0.78	0.79	0.80	3.16
2006	0.71	0.74	0.73	0.77	2.86
2005	0.72	0.36	0.77	0.76	2.65
2004	0.70	0.69	0.73	0.71	2.82

Fiscal year ended Dec. 31. Next earnings report expected: Late February. FFO Estimates based on S&P Funds From Operations Est..

Dividend Data (Dates: mm/dd Payment Date: mm/dd/yy)

Amount ($)	Date Decl.	Ex-Div. Date	Stk. of Record	Payment Date
0.680	01/29	02/05	02/09	02/20/09
0.680	04/30	05/07	05/11	05/20/09
0.680	07/30	08/06	08/10	08/20/09
0.680	10/29	11/05	11/09	11/20/09

Dividends have been paid since 1971. Source: Company reports.

Health Care REIT Inc.

STANDARD &POOR'S

Business Summary November 09, 2009

CORPORATE OVERVIEW. Health Care REIT is a self-administered equity REIT that invests in health care facilities offering skilled nursing, assisted living, medical office buildings, independent living, and specialty care services. HCN's investments are primarily real estate property leased to operators under long-term operating leases or financed with operators under long-term mortgages.

As of December 31, 2008, HCN had nearly $6.5 billion of gross real estate investments comprising 600 facilities and loan receivables of $483 million on an additional 33 properties. As of December 31, 2008, HCN's portfolio included 186 assisted living facilities, 225 skilled nursing facilities, 63 independent living/continuing care retirement communities, 128 medical office buildings, and 31 specialty care facilities.

An assisted living facility is a combination of housing, personalized supportive services, and health care designed to meet the needs of those who require help with the activities of daily living. Skilled nursing facilities provide inpatient skilled nursing and personal care services as well as rehabilitative, restorative and transitional medical services. Specialty care facilities include acute care hospitals, long-term acute care hospitals, and other specialty care

hospitals. Medical office buildings are office and clinical facilities designed for the use of physicians and other health care professionals.

CORPORATE STRATEGY. HCN invests mainly in long-term care facilities managed by experienced operators, and diversifies its investment portfolio by operator and by geographic location. Each facility, which includes the land, building, improvements and related rights owned by HCN is leased to an operator pursuant to a long-term operating lease. In order to better diversify the risk of any one facility, a large percentage of HCN's leased properties is subject to master leases. The leases generally cover multiple facilities under one lease and have a fixed term of 12 to 15 years and contain one or more five to 15-year renewal options. The tenants are required to repair, rebuild and maintain the leased properties. With its Windrose Medical acquisition in late 2006, HCN expanded its portfolio to include medical office buildings, which are generally structured as long-term gross leases, where HCN is responsible for all or a portion of the property operating expenses.

Company Financials Fiscal Year Ended Dec. 31

Per Share Data ($)	2008	2007	2006	2005	2004	2003	2002	2001	2000	1999
Tangible Book Value	27.90	24.26	27.04	19.85	24.23	20.43	19.20	18.57	19.04	19.52
Earnings	1.35	1.26	1.32	1.06	1.38	1.44	1.47	1.52	1.91	2.21
S&P Core Earnings	1.35	1.26	1.32	1.06	1.38	1.41	1.46	1.51	NA	NA
Dividends	2.70	2.28	2.88	2.46	2.39	2.34	2.34	2.34	2.34	2.27
Payout Ratio	NM	182%	NM	NM	173%	163%	159%	154%	122%	103%
Prices:High	53.98	48.55	43.02	39.20	40.88	36.10	31.82	26.40	19.25	26.63
Prices:Low	30.14	35.08	32.80	31.15	27.70	24.84	24.02	16.06	13.81	14.69
P/E Ratio:High	40	39	33	37	30	25	22	17	10	12
P/E Ratio:Low	22	28	25	29	20	17	16	11	7	7

Income Statement Analysis (Million $)										
Rental Income	501	450	300	253	226	177	134	99.0	88.3	72.7
Mortgage Income	40.1	25.8	18.8	24.0	22.8	20.8	26.5	31.3	41.1	48.1
Total Income	551	486	323	282	251	201	163	135	135	129
General Expenses	91.2	75.1	27.1	17.2	16.6	11.5	9.67	8.08	7.41	7.36
Interest Expense	131	135	94.8	80.1	72.0	54.1	41.1	32.0	34.6	26.9
Provision for Losses	0.01	Nil	1.00	1.20	1.20	2.87	1.00	1.00	1.00	0.60
Depreciation	156	146	93.1	80.0	73.0	51.1	39.3	30.2	22.7	17.9
Net Income	150	125	104	79.2	84.9	75.7	67.4	60.8	68.1	75.6
S&P Core Earnings	127	100	82.0	57.4	71.9	62.4	54.4	46.8	NA	NA

Balance Sheet & Other Financial Data (Million $)										
Cash	23.4	30.3	36.2	36.2	19.8	125	9.55	9.83	2.84	2.13
Total Assets	6,193	5,214	4,281	2,972	2,550	2,183	1,594	1,270	1,157	1,271
Real Estate Investment	6,463	5,498	4,477	3,131	2,667	2,153	1,643	1,301	1,180	1,264
Loss Reserve	7.50	7.41	7.41	6.46	5.26	7.83	4.96	6.86	5.86	5.60
Net Investment	5,854	5,013	4,123	2,850	2,442	1,992	1,524	1,214	1,121	1,222
Short Term Debt	39.7	70.3	71.7	2.60	6.28	45.8	0.40	12.6	10.0	35.0
Capitalization:Debt	2,824	2,634	2,126	1,498	1,180	967	676	479	420	504
Capitalization:Equity	2,922	2,074	1,640	1,154	1,052	1,029	770	608	549	557
Capitalization:Total	6,046	5,048	4,107	2,929	2,515	2,117	1,574	1,236	1,128	1,211
% Earnings & Depreciation/Assets	5.4	6.1	5.4	5.7	6.6	6.7	7.5	7.5	7.5	8.0
Price Times Book Value:High	1.9	2.0	1.6	2.0	1.7	1.7	1.7	1.4	1.0	0.8
Price Times Book Value:Low	1.1	1.4	1.2	1.6	1.1	1.2	1.3	0.9	0.7	0.6

Data as orig reptd.; bef. results of disc opers/spec. items. Per share data adj. for stk. divs.; EPS diluted. E-Estimated. NA-Not Available. NM-Not Meaningful. NR-Not Ranked. UR-Under Review.

Office: One Seagate Ste 1500, Toledo, OH 43604-1541.
Telephone: 419-247-2800.
Website: http://www.hcreit.com
Chrmn, Pres & CEO: G.L. Chapman

Vice Chrmn: F.S. Klipsch
EVP & CFO: S.A. Estes
EVP & General Counsel: J.H. Miller
SVP & Treas: M.A. Crabtree

Investor Contact: S.A. Estes (419-247-2800)
Board Members: W. C. Ballard, Jr., P. C. Borra, G. L. Chapman, T. J. Derosa, J. H. Donahue, P. J. Grua, F. S. Klipsch, S. M. Oster, J. R. Otten, R. S. Trumbull

Founded: 1970
Domicile: Delaware
Employees: 208

The McGraw-Hill Companies

Heinz (H J) Co

STANDARD & POOR'S

S&P Recommendation BUY ★★★★☆

Price	12-Mo. Target Price	Investment Style
$42.42 (as of Nov 27, 2009)	$43.00	Large-Cap Blend

GICS Sector Consumer Staples
Sub-Industry Packaged Foods & Meats

Summary This company produces a wide variety of food products worldwide, with a major presence in the U.S. in condiments, frozen potatoes, and convenience meals.

Key Stock Statistics (Source S&P, Vickers, company reports)

52-Wk Range	$43.70–30.51	S&P Oper. EPS 2010**E**	2.85	Market Capitalization(B)	$13.370	Beta	0.63
Trailing 12-Month EPS	$2.85	S&P Oper. EPS 2011**E**	3.02	Yield (%)	3.96	S&P 3-Yr. Proj. EPS CAGR(%)	4
Trailing 12-Month P/E	14.9	P/E on S&P Oper. EPS 2010**E**	14.9	Dividend Rate/Share	$1.68	S&P Credit Rating	BBB
$10K Invested 5 Yrs Ago	$13,447	Common Shares Outstg. (M)	315.2	Institutional Ownership (%)	67		

Price Performance

30-Week Mov. Avg. · · · 10-Week Mov. Avg. – – **GAAP Earnings vs. Previous Year** Volume Above Avg. STARS
12-Mo. Target Price — Relative Strength — ▲ Up ▼ Down ▶ No Change Below Avg.

Options: ASE, CBOE, P

Analysis prepared by **Tom Graves, CFA** on September 23, 2009, when the stock traded at **$ 40.42.**

Highlights

► We look for FY 10 (Apr.) net sales to rise modestly from the $10.1 billion reported for FY 09, reflecting a prospective negative impact from the value of the U.S. dollar relative to foreign currencies, especially the British pound and the euro. In FY 09, 60% of HNZ's net external sales came from outside the U.S., including 16% from the United Kingdom. In FY 10, we expect HNZ's overall pricing to be up, but much less than the 7.0% increase on FY 09.

► In FY 10, we forecast that profit margins will be bolstered by productivity gains. However, we see some risk of Heinz-branded products losing market share, with price-sensitive consumers shifting to less expensive private label products. Including an expected negative impact from currency fluctuation, we estimate FY 10 EPS of $2.78, down from the $2.90 reported for FY 09. For FY 11, we look for EPS of $3.00.

► We expect HNZ's strategy to include a focus on innovation investment in its core brands, growth in emerging markets, reducing or controlling costs, and leveraging the company's global scale.

Investment Rationale/Risk

► Our buy recommendation on the shares reflects our view that the stock will receive support from HNZ's above-average dividend yield, and what we see as some underlying strength in HNZ's business. However, in the year ahead, we anticipate that currency fluctuation will be more of a drag on profits than it has been in the recent past. In FY 09, with currency hedging contracts, we believe HNZ limited the extent to which currency fluctuation (i.e., a stronger U.S. dollar) could adversely affect reported profits. In FY 09, currency movements had a negative 6.6% impact on HNZ's reported sales.

► Risks to our recommendation and target price include competitive product and pricing pressures, adverse currency fluctuation, raw material cost inflation, and unfavorable consumer acceptance of new product introductions.

► Our 12-month target price of $43 reflects our view that the shares should trade at about 16.2X our estimated calendar 2009 EPS of $2.65, or a modest premium to the target P/E that we expect, on average, for a group of other food stocks. HNZ shares recently had an indicated dividend yield of about 4.2%.

Qualitative Risk Assessment

LOW	MEDIUM	HIGH

Our risk assessment for H. J. Heinz reflects the relatively stable nature of the company's end markets, our view of its strong cash flow, and corporate governance practices that we believe are favorable relative to peers.

Quantitative Evaluations

S&P Quality Ranking B+

D	C	B-	B	B+	A-	A	A+

Relative Strength Rank STRONG

76

LOWEST = 1   HIGHEST = 99

Revenue/Earnings Data

Revenue (Million $)

	1Q	2Q	3Q	4Q	Year
2010	2,468	--	--	--	--
2009	2,583	2,613	2,415	2,538	10,148
2008	2,248	2,523	2,611	2,688	10,071
2007	2,060	2,232	2,295	2,414	9,002
2006	2,110	2,339	2,187	2,400	8,643
2005	2,003	2,200	2,261	2,448	8,912

Earnings Per Share ($)

	1Q	2Q	3Q	4Q	Year
2010	0.67	E0.73	E0.77	E0.65	E2.85
2009	0.72	0.87	0.76	0.76	2.90
2008	0.72	0.71	0.68	0.61	2.63
2007	0.58	0.59	0.66	0.55	2.38
2006	0.45	0.50	0.40	Nil	1.29
2005	0.55	0.56	0.50	0.58	2.08

Fiscal year ended Apr. 30. Next earnings report expected: NA. EPS Estimates based on S&P Operating Earnings; historical GAAP earnings are as reported.

Dividend Data (Dates: mm/dd Payment Date: mm/dd/yy)

Amount ($)	Date Decl.	Ex-Div. Date	Stk. of Record	Payment Date
0.415	03/11	03/20	03/24	04/10/09
0.420	05/28	06/22	06/24	07/10/09
0.420	08/12	09/18	09/22	10/10/09
0.420	11/11	12/18	12/22	01/10/10

Dividends have been paid since 1911. Source: Company reports.

Heinz (H J) Co

STANDARD
&POOR'S

Business Summary September 23, 2009

CORPORATE OVERVIEW. Although largely known for its familiar ketchup, H.J. Heinz boasts many other branded food products, ranging from Ore-Ida frozen potatoes to Weight Watchers frozen dinners. In FY 09 (Apr.), the North American Consumer Products segment represented 31% of sales, while Europe accounted for 33%, Asia/Pacific for 16%, U.S. Foodservice for 15%, and Rest of World for 5%. Also, in FY 09, one customer, Wal-Mart Stores Inc., accounted for 11% of HNZ's sales.

The company's revenues are generated via the manufacture and sale of products in the following categories: ketchup and sauces (42% of FY 09 sales); meals and snacks (43%); infant/nutrition (11%); and other products (4%). Brands or trademarks utilized by HNZ include Heinz, Classico, Weight Watchers (licensed), Smart Ones, Boston Market (licensed), and Ore-Ida.

CORPORATE STRATEGY. In August 2009, HNZ reiterated guidance for FY 10, which excluded a prospective impact from currency fluctuation. On this basis, HNZ said that the company was projecting sales growth of 4% to 6%, and EPS

growth of 5% to 8%. However, a strong U.S. dollar relative to such currencies as the euro and the U.K. pound could adversely affect FY 10 financial results. Also, HNZ stated that it expected operating free cash flow in FY 10 of $850 million to $900 million.

HNZ said that emerging markets could generate as much as 20% of its total sales by FY 13, compared with 14% in FY 09.

Heinz has focused on exiting non-strategic business operations. In the fourth quarter of FY 06, the company completed the sale of its European seafood business and its Tegel poultry business in New Zealand. HNZ's portfolio realignment has resulted in the divesture of about 20 non-core product lines and businesses and has generated proceeds of about $1 billion.

Company Financials Fiscal Year Ended Apr. 30

Per Share Data ($)	2009	2008	2007	2006	2005	2004	2003	2002	2001	2000
Tangible Book Value	NM	NM	NM	NM	NM	NM	NM	NM	NM	NM
Cash Flow	3.76	3.49	3.88	2.07	2.82	2.86	2.17	3.22	2.26	3.32
Earnings	2.90	2.63	2.38	1.29	2.08	2.20	1.57	2.36	1.41	2.47
S&P Core Earnings	2.55	2.26	2.36	1.72	2.29	2.11	1.43	1.99	1.31	NA
Dividends	1.52	1.52	1.20	1.14	1.10	1.08	1.61	1.55	1.45	1.40
Payout Ratio	52%	58%	50%	88%	53%	49%	88%	65%	102%	56%
Calendar Year	2008	2007	2006	2005	2004	2003	2002	2001	2000	1999
Prices:High	53.00	53.00	46.75	39.13	40.61	36.82	43.48	47.94	48.00	58.81
Prices:Low	35.26	35.26	33.42	33.64	34.53	28.90	29.60	36.90	30.81	39.50
P/E Ratio:High	18	20	20	30	20	17	24	20	34	24
P/E Ratio:Low	12	13	14	26	17	13	16	16	22	16
Income Statement Analysis (Million $)										
Revenue	10,148	10,071	9,002	8,643	8,912	8,415	8,237	9,431	9,430	9,408
Operating Income	1,765	1,847	1,946	1,377	1,607	1,613	1,389	1,892	1,282	1,575
Depreciation	272	279	500	264	252	234	215	302	299	306
Interest Expense	340	333	333	316	232	212	224	294	333	270
Pretax Income	1,296	1,218	1,124	693	1,059	1,169	869	1,279	673	1,464
Effective Tax Rate	28.8%	30.6%	29.6%	36.2%	30.5%	33.3%	36.1%	34.8%	26.5%	39.2%
Net Income	923	845	792	443	736	779	555	834	495	891
S&P Core Earnings	812	725	784	587	809	747	500	702	458	NA
Balance Sheet & Other Financial Data (Million $)										
Cash	373	618	653	445	1,084	1,180	802	207	139	138
Current Assets	2,945	3,326	3,019	2,704	3,646	3,611	3,284	3,374	3,117	3,170
Total Assets	9,664	10,565	10,033	9,738	10,578	9,877	9,225	10,278	9,035	8,851
Current Liabilities	2,063	2,670	2,505	2,018	2,587	2,469	1,926	2,509	3,655	2,126
Long Term Debt	5,076	4,406	4,414	4,357	4,122	4,538	4,776	4,643	3,015	3,936
Common Equity	1,220	1,888	2,280	2,049	2,614	8,841	2,876	1,719	1,374	1,596
Total Capital	6,701	7,013	7,256	7,045	7,359	13,797	8,252	7,197	4,642	5,804
Capital Expenditures	292	302	245	231	241	232	154	213	411	452
Cash Flow	1,195	1,123	1,291	707	988	1,013	770	1,136	794	1,197
Current Ratio	1.4	1.3	1.2	1.3	1.4	1.5	1.7	1.3	0.9	1.5
% Long Term Debt of Capitalization	75.8	62.8	60.8	61.8	56.0	32.9	57.9	64.5	64.9	67.8
% Net Income of Revenue	9.1	8.4	8.8	5.1	8.3	9.3	6.7	8.8	5.2	9.5
% Return on Assets	9.1	8.2	8.0	4.4	7.2	8.2	5.7	8.6	5.5	10.5
% Return on Equity	59.4	45.3	34.0	19.0	26.3	8.9	17.9	53.9	33.3	52.4

Data as orig reptd.; bef. results of disc opers/spec. items. Per share data adj. for stk. divs.; EPS diluted. E-Estimated. NA-Not Available. NM-Not Meaningful. NR-Not Ranked. UR-Under Review.

Office: 1 Ppg Pl, Pittsburgh, PA 15222-5415.
Telephone: 412-456-5700.
Website: http://www.heinz.com
Chrmn: S. Clark

Pres & CEO: W.R. Johnson
EVP & CFO: A.B. Winkleblack
EVP & General Counsel: T.N. Bobby
SVP, Chief Acctg Officer & Cntlr: E.J. McMenamin

Investor Contact: M.R. Nollen
Board Members: C. E. Bunch, S. Clark, L. S. Coleman, Jr., J. G. Drosdick, E. E. Holiday, W. R. Johnson, C. Kendle, D. R. O'Hare, N. Peltz, D. H. Reilley, L. Swann, T. J. Usher, M. F. Weinstein

Founded: 1869
Domicile: Pennsylvania
Employees: 32,400

Hershey Co (The)

STANDARD &POOR'S

S&P Recommendation HOLD ★★★☆☆

Price $35.60 (as of Nov 27, 2009)	**12-Mo. Target Price** $40.00	**Investment Style** Large-Cap Growth

GICS Sector Consumer Staples
Sub-Industry Packaged Foods & Meats

Summary Hershey is a major producer of chocolate and confectionery products.

Key Stock Statistics (Source S&P, Vickers, company reports)

52-Wk Range	$42.25– 30.27	S&P Oper. EPS 2009E	2.14	Market Capitalization(B)	$5.946	Beta		0.32
Trailing 12-Month EPS	$1.71	S&P Oper. EPS 2010E	2.27	Yield (%)	3.34	S&P 3-Yr. Proj. EPS CAGR(%)		7
Trailing 12-Month P/E	20.8	P/E on S&P Oper. EPS 2009E	16.6	Dividend Rate/Share	$1.19	S&P Credit Rating		A
$10K Invested 5 Yrs Ago	$7,762	Common Shares Outstg. (M)	227.7	Institutional Ownership (%)	71			

Price Performance

30-Week Mov. Avg. ···· 10-Week Mov. Avg. – – GAAP Earnings vs. Previous Year Volume Above Avg. STARS
12-Mo. Target Price — Relative Strength — ▲ Up ▼ Down ► No Change Below Avg.

Options: ASE, CBOE, P, Ph

Analysis prepared by **Tom Graves, CFA** on October 26, 2009, when the stock traded at **$ 38.01**.

Highlights

► We look for HSY's sales to increase moderately in 2010 from the $5.3 billion estimated for 2009, including a favorable impact from increased advertising expenditures in 2009. Near term, we expect year-to-year U.S. sales comparisons to continue to reflect higher product prices, which are likely to limit volumes.

► With recent increases in cocoa prices, we see the prospect of some commodity cost pressure in 2010. However, we have been impressed by recent profit margin improvement at HSY, and we expect that 2010 will benefit from supply chain efficiencies and productivity gains. However, on a year-to-year basis, we do not anticipate that HSY will have as much incremental savings from a supply chain transformation program in 2010 as we expect there will be 2009.

► We estimate that EPS, before special items, will total $2.27 in 2010, up from the $2.14 that we anticipate for 2009. This excludes business re-alignment and impairment charges, which we expect will total $0.26 to $0.32 a share, compared to $0.52 of such charges in 2008.

Investment Rationale/Risk

► We see HSY's plan for an improved supply chain bolstering longer-term profit growth prospects. We expect a portion of anticipated manufacturing savings to be spent on areas such as brand support, new products, and overseas expansion. In terms of corporate governance, we are concerned about the company's dual class capital structure with unequal voting rights.

► Risks to our recommendation and target price include the possibility that sales will be weaker than we anticipate; that profit margins will be less favorable; and that new products or cost-saving efforts execute worse than expected.

► Our 12-month target price of $40 is based on a P/E of about 18.7X our 2009 EPS estimate of $2.14. With what we view as signs of the company making progress, we believe the shares merit about a 20% P/E premium to what we expect, on average, from a group of other packaged food stocks. Also, HSY shares recently had an indicated dividend yield of about 3.1%.

Qualitative Risk Assessment

LOW	MEDIUM	HIGH

Our risk assessment reflects what we see as the relative stability of Hershey's primary end markets, the strength of its U.S. business, and the strength of its balance sheet and cash flow.

Quantitative Evaluations

S&P Quality Ranking B+

D	C	B-	B	B+	A-	A	A+

Relative Strength Rank WEAK

24

LOWEST = 1 HIGHEST = 99

Revenue/Earnings Data

Revenue (Million $)

	1Q	2Q	3Q	4Q	Year
2009	1,236	1,171	1,484	--	--
2008	1,160	1,105	1,490	1,377	5,133
2007	1,153	1,052	1,399	1,342	4,947
2006	1,140	1,052	1,416	1,337	4,944
2005	1,126	988.5	1,368	1,353	4,836
2004	1,013	893.7	1,255	1,268	4,429

Earnings Per Share ($)

2009	0.33	0.31	0.71	E0.60	E2.14
2008	0.28	0.18	0.54	0.36	1.36
2007	0.40	0.01	0.27	0.24	0.93
2006	0.50	0.41	0.78	0.65	2.34
2005	0.47	0.39	0.48	0.70	1.99
2004	0.41	0.56	0.66	0.68	2.30

Fiscal year ended Dec. 31. Next earnings report expected: Late January. EPS Estimates based on S&P Operating Earnings; historical GAAP earnings are as reported.

Dividend Data (Dates: mm/dd Payment Date: mm/dd/yy)

Amount ($)	Date Decl.	Ex-Div. Date	Stk. of Record	Payment Date
0.298	02/17	02/23	02/25	03/13/09
0.298	04/29	05/20	05/25	06/15/09
0.298	08/04	08/21	08/25	09/15/09
0.298	10/09	11/23	11/25	12/15/09

Dividends have been paid since 1930. Source: Company reports.

Please read the Required Disclosures and Analyst Certification on the last page of this report.

The McGraw-Hill Companies

Hershey Co (The)

STANDARD &POOR'S

Business Summary October 26, 2009

CORPORATE OVERVIEW. The Hershey Co. produces and distributes a variety of chocolate, confectionery and grocery products. The company's brands include Hershey's Kisses and Reese's.

CORPORATE STRATEGY. In February 2007, HSY announced a supply chain transformation program that is expected to be at least largely completed by December 2009. In 2009's first nine months, HSY had $0.19 a share of charges related to the supply chain transformation program. Also, in October 2009, HSY estimated that this program will incur pretax charges and non-recurring project implementation costs (likely including asset write-offs) of $640 million to $665 million, which includes $55 million to $65 million of non-cash pension settlement charges. Under the program, HSY is expected to significantly increase manufacturing capacity utilization by reducing the number of its production lines; outsource the production of low value-added items; and construct a production facility in Mexico. As a result of the transformation program, we expect HSY to be targeting ongoing annual savings of $170 million to $190 million, at least the bulk of which we look to be generated by 2010. HSY planned to invest a portion of these savings in strategic growth initiatives.

We expect that HSY's strategy will include focus on, and advertising support for, core brands that have provided about 60% of U.S. sales.

In 2008, if special items are excluded, HSY had EPS of $1.88, compared with $2.08 in 2007, and $2.37 in 2006. In July 2009, HSY said that it expected 2009 charges of $0.24 to $0.33 a share, including possible non-cash pension settlement charges.

In 2008, there were special charges of $0.38 related to the supply chain transformation program, $0.13 related to intangible trademark values (primarily Mauna Loa), and $0.01 related to a business realignment in Brazil. In 2007, there were special charges of $1.10 a share related to the supply chain program, and $0.05 a share of business realignment and impairment charges related to HSY's business in Brazil.

In 2008, 14.4% of HSY's net sales were from businesses outside the U.S., up from 13.8% in 2007. Longer term, we expect international expansion to include a focus on emerging markets in Asia, particularly India and China, Mexico, and selected markets in South America.

Company Financials Fiscal Year Ended Dec. 31

Per Share Data ($)	2008	2007	2006	2005	2004	2003	2002	2001	2000	1999
Tangible Book Value	NM	NM	0.18	1.63	2.03	3.29	3.55	2.65	2.57	2.34
Cash Flow	2.11	2.27	3.17	2.96	3.17	2.44	2.17	1.44	1.84	2.21
Earnings	1.36	0.93	2.34	1.99	2.30	1.76	1.46	0.75	1.21	1.63
S&P Core Earnings	1.22	1.14	2.26	1.94	2.23	1.73	1.37	0.94	NA	NA
Dividends	1.19	1.14	1.03	0.93	0.84	0.72	0.63	0.58	0.54	0.50
Payout Ratio	87%	122%	44%	47%	36%	41%	43%	78%	45%	31%
Prices:High	44.32	56.75	57.65	67.37	56.75	39.33	39.75	35.08	33.22	32.44
Prices:Low	32.10	38.21	48.20	52.49	37.28	30.35	28.23	27.56	18.88	22.88
P/E Ratio:High	33	61	25	34	25	22	27	47	27	20
P/E Ratio:Low	24	41	21	26	16	17	19	37	16	14

Income Statement Analysis (Million $)	2008	2007	2006	2005	2004	2003	2002	2001	2000	1999
Revenue	5,133	4,947	4,944	4,836	4,429	4,173	4,120	4,557	4,221	3,971
Operating Income	941	1,047	1,207	1,175	1,092	992	904	812	799	722
Depreciation	171	311	200	218	190	181	178	190	176	163
Interest Expense	105	119	116	89.5	66.5	63.5	60.7	71.5	81.0	77.3
Pretax Income	492	340	877	773	836	733	638	344	547	728
Effective Tax Rate	36.7%	37.1%	36.2%	36.2%	29.3%	36.6%	36.7%	39.7%	38.8%	36.8%
Net Income	311	214	559	493	591	465	404	207	335	460
S&P Core Earnings	279	264	540	482	573	455	377	258	NA	NA

Balance Sheet & Other Financial Data (Million $)	2008	2007	2006	2005	2004	2003	2002	2001	2000	1999
Cash	37.1	129	97.1	67.2	54.8	115	298	134	32.0	118
Current Assets	1,345	1,427	1,418	1,409	1,182	1,132	1,264	1,168	1,295	1,280
Total Assets	3,635	4,247	4,158	4,295	3,798	3,583	3,481	3,247	3,448	3,347
Current Liabilities	1,270	1,619	1,454	1,518	1,285	586	547	606	767	713
Long Term Debt	1,506	1,280	1,248	943	691	968	852	877	878	878
Common Equity	318	593	683	1,021	1,089	1,280	1,372	1,147	1,175	1,099
Total Capital	1,860	2,084	2,218	2,364	2,109	2,626	2,572	2,280	2,353	2,303
Capital Expenditures	263	190	183	181	182	219	133	160	138	115
Cash Flow	482	525	759	711	781	646	581	398	511	624
Current Ratio	1.1	0.9	1.0	0.9	0.9	1.9	2.3	1.9	1.7	1.8
% Long Term Debt of Capitalization	81.0	61.4	56.3	39.9	32.7	36.9	33.1	38.5	37.3	38.1
% Net Income of Revenue	6.1	4.3	11.3	10.2	13.3	11.1	9.8	4.5	7.9	11.6
% Return on Assets	7.9	5.1	13.3	12.2	16.0	13.2	12.0	6.2	9.8	13.6
% Return on Equity	68.4	33.6	65.8	45.7	46.4	35.1	32.0	17.8	29.4	43.0

Data as orig reptd.; bef. results of disc opers/spec. items. Per share data adj. for stk. divs.; EPS diluted. E-Estimated. NA-Not Available. NM-Not Meaningful. NR-Not Ranked. UR-Under Review.

Office: 100 Crystal A Dr, Hershey, PA 17033-9790.
Telephone: 717-534-4200.
Website: http://www.hersheys.com
Chrmn: J.E. Nevels

Pres & CEO: D.J. West
SVP & CFO: H. Alfonso
SVP, Secy & General Counsel: B.H. Snyder
SVP & CIO: G.F. Davis

Investor Contact: M.K. Pogharian (717-534-7556)
Board Members: R. F. Cavanaugh, C. A. Davis, J. E. Nevels, T. J. Ridge, D. L. Shedlarz, D. J. West, L. S. Zimmerman

Founded: 1894
Domicile: Delaware
Employees: 14,400

The McGraw-Hill Companies

Hess Corp

STANDARD &POOR'S

S&P Recommendation **BUY** ★★★★☆	Price $57.80 (as of Nov 27, 2009)	12-Mo. Target Price $67.00	Investment Style Large-Cap Blend

GICS Sector Energy
Sub-Industry Integrated Oil & Gas

Summary This integrated oil and natural gas company has exploration and production activities worldwide, and markets refined petroleum products on the U.S. East Coast.

Key Stock Statistics (Source S&P, Vickers, company reports)

52-Wk Range	$69.74– 35.50	S&P Oper. EPS 2009**E**	1.85	Market Capitalization(B)	$18.905	Beta	0.92
Trailing 12-Month EPS	$0.95	S&P Oper. EPS 2010**E**	3.98	Yield (%)	0.69	S&P 3-Yr. Proj. EPS CAGR(%)	-12
Trailing 12-Month P/E	60.8	P/E on S&P Oper. EPS 2009**E**	31.2	Dividend Rate/Share	$0.40	S&P Credit Rating	BBB-
$10K Invested 5 Yrs Ago	$20,163	Common Shares Outstg. (M)	327.1	Institutional Ownership (%)	80		

Price Performance

- 30-Week Mov. Avg. ···· 10-Week Mov. Avg. -- **GAAP Earnings vs. Previous Year** Volume Above Avg. ▮▮▮ STARS
- 12-Mo. Target Price — Relative Strength — ▲ Up ▼ Down ▶ No Change Below Avg. ▮▮▮ ★

Options: ASE, CBOE, Ph

Analysis prepared by **Tina J. Vital** on October 30, 2009, when the stock traded at **$ 54.74**.

Highlights

► While we expect the refining market will continue to struggle over the next 12-months, we see HES's earnings being driven by its upstream exploration & production business, which is oil-focused and should benefit from our expectations for higher oil prices. We project HES's oil & gas production will increase over 7% to near 409,000 boe per day in 2009, and over 5% in 2010. The JDA Phase 2 natural gas project in the Gulf of Thailand started up in November, and the Shenzi development in the deepwater Gulf of Mexico is ramping up, and the Pangkah Oil & LPG project in Indonesia is slated to start up late in 2009.

► On the downstream, refining margins and light-heavy crude differentials have narrowed on a global economic slowdown. Using data from the IHS Global Insight, we expect U.S. industry-wide refining margins to narrow about 16% in 2009 before widening about 7% in 2010.

► After-tax operating earnings excluded $0.13 of net special gains in the 2009 first nine months, and we look for these earnings to drop about 76% in 2009 on projected lower prices, before rebounding about 115% in 2010 on an improved economic outlook and cost initiatives.

Investment Rationale/Risk

► We believe that HES's upstream cost position has improved, with its three-year (2005-07) average costs below the peer average. Further, we think increased spending has improved HES's exploration success. Successful wells were drilled by HES in Australia, Libya, and Egypt during 2008, and HES continued appraisals of the Pony and Tubular Bells discoveries in the deepwater Gulf of Mexico and added to its acreage in the U.S. Gulf of Mexico and Indonesia. Exploratory wells continued to be drilled offshore Brazil and Australia. In July 2009, HES wrote-off costs associated with a well offshore Brazil and two wells in the Gulf of Mexico.

► Risks to our recommendation and target price include deterioration in economic and industrial conditions, and the company's potential inability to replace oil and gas reserves.

► A blend of our discounted cash flow ($71 per share value assuming a WACC of 9.0% and terminal growth of 3%) and relative market valuations leads to our 12-month target price of $67, representing an expected enterprise value multiple of 5.1X our 2010 EBITDA estimate, in line with peers.

Qualitative Risk Assessment

LOW	MEDIUM	HIGH

Our risk assessment reflects HES's diversified business profile in volatile, cyclical, and capital-intensive segments of the energy industry. While we see risk from its investments in politically troubled locales, offsets include its improved, relatively low cost structure in exploration and production.

Quantitative Evaluations

S&P Quality Ranking B+

D	C	B-	B	B+	A-	A	A+

Relative Strength Rank MODERATE

64

LOWEST = 1 HIGHEST = 99

Revenue/Earnings Data

Revenue (Million $)

	1Q	2Q	3Q	4Q	Year
2009	6,915	6,751	7,270	--	--
2008	10,667	11,717	11,398	7,383	41,165
2007	7,319	7,421	7,451	9,456	31,647
2006	7,159	6,718	7,035	7,155	28,067
2005	4,956	4,963	5,769	7,059	22,747
2004	4,488	3,803	3,830	4,612	16,733

Earnings Per Share ($)

	1Q	2Q	3Q	4Q	Year
2009	-0.18	0.31	1.05	E0.81	E1.85
2008	2.34	2.76	2.37	-0.23	7.24
2007	1.17	1.75	1.23	1.59	5.74
2006	2.21	1.79	0.94	1.13	6.07
2005	0.71	0.92	0.87	1.44	3.98
2004	0.92	0.92	0.58	0.74	3.17

Fiscal year ended Dec. 31. Next earnings report expected: Late January. EPS Estimates based on S&P Operating Earnings; historical GAAP earnings as reported.

Dividend Data (Dates: mm/dd Payment Date: mm/dd/yy)

Amount ($)	Date Decl.	Ex-Div. Date	Stk. of Record	Payment Date
0.100	12/03	12/17	12/19	01/02/09
0.100	03/04	03/12	03/16	03/31/09
0.100	06/05	06/12	06/16	06/30/09
0.100	09/09	09/16	09/18	09/30/09

Dividends have been paid since 1922. Source: Company reports.

Please read the Required Disclosures and Analyst Certification on the last page of this report.

The McGraw·Hill Companies

Hess Corp

Business Summary October 30, 2009

CORPORATE OVERVIEW. Hess Corp. (HES; formerly Amerada Hess Corp.) has two operating segments: Exploration and Production (24% of 2008 revenues; 90% of 2008 net income), and Marketing and Refining (76%; 10%). Business is conducted in the U.S., Europe, Africa, Asia and elsewhere. As of May 2009, the Hess family owned about 11% of the common shares.

Oil and gas production rose 1% in 2008, to 381,000 barrels of oil equivalent (boe) per day (70% liquids). Net proved oil and gas reserves rose 7.7%, to 1.43 billion boe (57% developed, 68% liquids). Using data from John S. Herold, an oil industry consultant, we estimate HES's three-year (2005-07) average proved acquisition costs at $3.01 per boe, below the peer average; its three-year finding and development costs at $19.86 per boe, below the peer average; its three-year reserve replacement costs at $14.68 per boe, below the peer average; and its three-year reserve replacement at 181%, below the peer average. We estimate HES's 2008 reserve replacement rate at 172%, and its organic replacement rate at 62%.

HES's refining earnings are mainly derived from its 50% ownership in the refining joint venture HOVENSA, formed in October 1998 with a subsidiary of

Petroleos de Venezuela S.A. (PdVSA) in the U.S. Virgin Islands. Refining operations at HOVENSA consist of crude units (500,000 b/d), a fluid catalytic cracker (150,000 b/d), and a delayed coker (58,000 b/d). In addition, HES owns and operates a 65,000 b/d fluid catalytic cracking facility in Port Reading, NJ, to produce gasoline and heating oil.

As of year-end 2008, HOVENSA had a long-term supply contract with PdVSA to purchase 115,000 b/d of Venezuelan Merey heavy crude oil. PdVSA also supplies 155,000 b/d of Venezuelan Mesa medium gravity crude oil to HOVENSA under a long-term supply contract. The remaining crude oil requirements are purchased mainly under contracts of one year or less from third parties, and through spot purchases on the open market. After sales of refined products by HOVENSA to third parties, the company purchases 50% of HOVENSA's remaining production at market prices.

Company Financials Fiscal Year Ended Dec. 31

Per Share Data ($)	2008	2007	2006	2005	2004	2003	2002	2001	2000	1999
Tangible Book Value	34.31	26.67	21.77	16.61	14.34	13.62	12.17	14.70	14.59	11.17
Cash Flow	13.86	10.99	9.80	7.11	6.18	5.61	4.17	7.04	6.43	4.02
Earnings	9.93	5.74	6.07	3.98	3.17	1.72	-0.83	3.42	3.79	1.62
S&P Core Earnings	7.12	5.83	5.38	3.78	3.06	1.75	-1.28	3.25	NA	NA
Dividends	0.30	0.40	0.40	0.40	0.40	0.40	0.40	0.40	0.20	0.20
Payout Ratio	3%	7%	7%	10%	13%	23%	NM	12%	5%	12%
Prices:High	137.00	105.85	56.45	47.50	31.30	19.07	28.23	30.13	25.42	22.10
Prices:Low	35.50	45.96	37.62	25.94	17.75	13.71	16.47	17.92	15.94	14.58
P/E Ratio:High	14	18	9	12	10	11	NM	9	7	14
P/E Ratio:Low	4	8	6	7	6	8	NM	5	4	9

Income Statement Analysis (Million $)										
Revenue	41,165	31,647	28,067	22,747	16,733	14,480	12,093	13,413	11,993	7,039
Operating Income	7,207	5,259	4,812	2,967	2,769	2,127	2,382	2,399	2,264	1,214
Depreciation, Depletion and Amortization	2,154	1,678	1,224	1,025	970	1,053	1,320	967	714	648
Interest Expense	267	306	201	224	241	293	269	194	162	158
Pretax Income	4,700	3,704	4,040	2,226	1,558	781	-51.0	1,438	1,672	702
Effective Tax Rate	49.8%	50.5%	52.6%	44.2%	37.7%	40.2%	NM	36.4%	38.8%	37.6%
Net Income	2,360	1,832	1,916	1,242	970	467	-218	914	1,023	438
S&P Core Earnings	2,320	1,865	1,657	1,131	888	468	-339	870	NA	NA

Balance Sheet & Other Financial Data (Million $)										
Cash	908	607	383	315	877	518	197	37.0	312	41.0
Current Assets	7,332	6,926	5,848	5,290	4,335	3,186	2,756	3,946	4,115	1,828
Total Assets	28,908	26,131	22,404	19,115	16,312	13,983	13,262	15,369	10,274	7,728
Current Liabilities	7,730	8,024	6,739	6,447	4,697	2,669	2,553	3,718	3,538	1,579
Long Term Debt	3,812	3,918	3,745	3,759	3,785	3,868	4,976	5,283	1,985	2,287
Common Equity	12,307	9,774	8,111	6,272	5,583	5,326	8,498	4,907	3,883	3,038
Total Capital	18,360	16,054	13,955	11,446	10,566	10,352	14,518	11,301	6,378	5,767
Capital Expenditures	4,438	3,578	3,844	2,341	1,521	1,358	1,404	2,501	938	797
Cash Flow	4,514	3,510	3,096	2,219	1,892	1,515	1,102	1,881	1,737	1,086
Current Ratio	1.0	0.9	0.9	0.8	0.9	1.2	1.1	1.1	1.2	1.2
% Long Term Debt of Capitalization	20.8	24.4	26.8	32.8	35.8	37.4	34.3	46.7	31.1	39.7
% Return on Assets	8.6	7.5	9.2	7.0	6.4	3.4	NM	7.1	11.4	5.6
% Return on Equity	21.4	20.5	26.0	20.1	16.9	9.7	NM	20.8	29.6	15.4

Data as orig reptd.; bef. results of disc opers/spec. items. Per share data adj. for stk. divs.; EPS diluted. E-Estimated. NA-Not Available. NM-Not Meaningful. NR-Not Ranked. UR-Under Review.

Office: 1185 Avenue Of The Americas, New York, NY 10036.
Telephone: 212-997-8500.
Email: investorrelations@hess.com
Website: http://www.hess.com

Chrmn & CEO: J.B. Hess
SVP, CFO & Chief Acctg Officer: J.P. Rielly
SVP & General Counsel: T.B. Goodell
CTO: S. Heck

Treas: S. Mehra
Investor Contact: J.R. Wilson (212-536-8940)
Board Members: S. W. Bodman, III, N. F. Brady, J. B. Collins, II, J. B. Hess, G. P. Hill, E. E. Holiday, T. H. Kean, R. J. Lavizzo-Mourey, C. G. Matthews, J. H. Mullin, III, F. A. Olson, F. B. Walker, R. N. Wilson, E. H. von Metzsch

Founded: 1920
Domicile: Delaware
Employees: 13,500

Hewlett-Packard Co

STANDARD &POOR'S

S&P Recommendation **STRONG BUY** ★★★★★	Price $49.07 (as of Nov 27, 2009)	12-Mo. Target Price $62.00	Investment Style Large-Cap Blend

GICS Sector Information Technology
Sub-Industry Computer Hardware

Summary This leading maker of computer products, including printers, servers and PCs, has a large service and support network.

Key Stock Statistics (Source S&P, Vickers, company reports)

52-Wk Range	$51.43– 25.39	S&P Oper. EPS 2010**E**	4.45	Market Capitalization(B)	$116.348	Beta		1.05
Trailing 12-Month EPS	$3.14	S&P Oper. EPS 2011**E**	4.90	Yield (%)	0.65	S&P 3-Yr. Proj. EPS CAGR(%)		13
Trailing 12-Month P/E	15.6	P/E on S&P Oper. EPS 2010**E**	11.0	Dividend Rate/Share	$0.32	S&P Credit Rating		A
$10K Invested 5 Yrs Ago	$25,507	Common Shares Outstg. (M)	2,371.1	Institutional Ownership (%)	75			

Price Performance

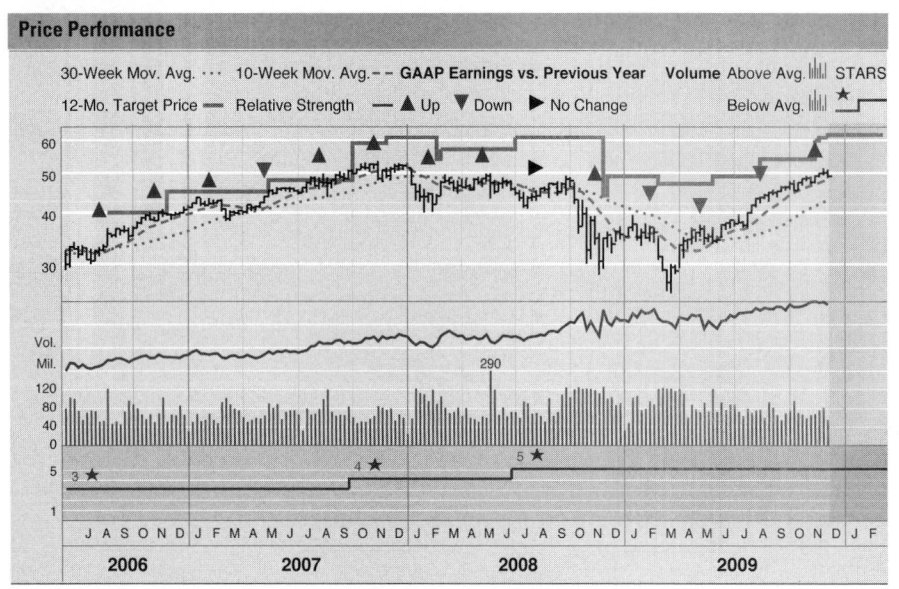

30-Week Mov. Avg. ···· 10-Week Mov. Avg. - - **GAAP Earnings vs. Previous Year** Volume Above Avg. STARS
12-Mo. Target Price — Relative Strength ▲ Up ▼ Down ▶ No Change Below Avg.

Options: ASE, CBOE, P, Ph

Analysis prepared by **Thomas W. Smith, CFA** on November 25, 2009, when the stock traded at **$ 50.15**.

Highlights

▶ We estimate revenue will grow 5% in FY 10 (Oct.) and 5% in FY 11. We project economic headwinds seen in FY 09 will fade in FY 10, spurring spending on information technology goods and services. The company has recently been gaining market share in PCs, and we think this pattern will continue over the next 12 months.

▶ On November 11, the company agreed to acquire 3Com Corp. (COMS 7.40, Hold) for approximately $2.7 billion in cash. Directors of both companies have approved the deal, which is expected to close in the first half of calendar 2010, subject to approvals from regulators and customary closing conditions. We expect operating margins, excluding acquisition-related charges, to widen in FY 10, based on higher volumes and cost savings from the integration of EDS operations acquired in late FY 08.

▶ We estimate operating EPS, excluding restructuring charges and pending acquisitions, of $4.45 for FY 10 (Oct.) and $4.90 for FY 11. We expect a strategy favoring share buybacks to continue, lending some support to per share results.

Investment Rationale/Risk

▶ We believe that HPQ has the potential to gain market share in PCs, servers, printers, and IT services. The company has made substantial progress in cost reduction, by our analysis. We think the acquisition of EDS dramatically broadened the services segment and thus enabled HPQ to offer better one-stop shopping for global enterprises' information technology needs. We believe the pending acquisition of 3Com, if completed as planned, will further enhance the one-stop shopping appeal of HPQ.

▶ Risks to our recommendation and target price include HPQ's ability to effectively close and integrate acquisitions. A trend we foresee for a rebound in U.S. economic growth and spending on technology equipment could prove weaker than we have forecast.

▶ We apply a target multiple near 14X, toward the low end of the four-year historical range for HPQ and at a discount to the recent average of about 17X for Information Technology Sector companies in the S&P 500, to our FY 10 operating EPS estimate of $4.45 to arrive at our 12-month target price of $62.

Qualitative Risk Assessment

LOW	**MEDIUM**	HIGH

Our risk assessment reflects the intensely price competitive environment in the computer hardware industry and potential integration risk from planned and completed acquisitions, balanced by our view of the company's broad worldwide customer base and its successful efforts in reducing its cost structure.

Quantitative Evaluations

S&P Quality Ranking   B+

D	C	B-	B	**B+**	A-	A	A+

Relative Strength Rank   MODERATE

70

LOWEST = 1   HIGHEST = 99

Revenue/Earnings Data

Revenue (Million $)

	1Q	2Q	3Q	4Q	Year
2009	28,800	27,351	27,451	30,777	114,552
2008	28,467	28,262	28,032	33,603	118,364
2007	25,082	25,534	25,377	28,293	104,286
2006	22,659	22,554	21,890	24,555	91,658
2005	21,454	21,570	20,759	22,913	86,696
2004	19,514	20,113	18,889	21,389	79,905

Earnings Per Share ($)

2009	0.75	0.70	0.67	0.99	3.14
2008	0.80	0.81	0.80	0.84	3.25
2007	0.55	0.65	0.80	0.81	2.68
2006	0.42	0.66	0.48	0.60	2.18
2005	0.32	0.33	0.03	0.14	0.82
2004	0.30	0.29	0.19	0.37	1.15

Fiscal year ended Oct. 31. Next earnings report expected: Mid February. EPS Estimates based on S&P Operating Earnings; historical GAAP earnings are as reported.

Dividend Data (Dates: mm/dd Payment Date: mm/dd/yy)

Amount ($)	Date Decl.	Ex-Div. Date	Stk. of Record	Payment Date
0.080	02/06	03/09	03/11	04/01/09
0.080	06/01	06/08	06/10	07/01/09
0.080	07/23	09/14	09/16	10/07/09
0.080	11/19	12/14	12/16	01/06/10

Dividends have been paid since 1965. Source: Company reports.

Please read the Required Disclosures and Analyst Certification on the last page of this report.

The McGraw·Hill Companies

Hewlett-Packard Co

**STANDARD
&POOR'S**

Business Summary November 25, 2009

CORPORATE OVERVIEW. Hewlett-Packard provides personal computers, printers, enterprise server and storage technology, and a wide range of related products and services to individual and enterprise customers worldwide. Revenues in FY 08 (Oct.) came almost 78% from products and 22% from services. In the first quarter of FY 09, about 30% of revenues came from the Services segment, reflecting the first full quarter with acquired Electronic Data Systems (EDS) operations.

Ongoing work force restructurings have enabled HPQ to develop a global delivery structure that has improved margins by taking advantage of low-cost technical expertise. The cost and efficiency campaign has been led by former NCR Corp. CEO Mark Hurd, who was named CEO and president of HPQ effective April 1, 2005. In addition, Mr. Hurd took over the chairman's role in late September 2006.

The breadth of the company's customer base is illustrated by the almost 69% of FY 08 revenues that came from outside the U.S. Further, no single customer accounted for more than 10% of sales in FY 08.

The company reports in seven segments. Three segments accounting for over one-third of sales are often grouped together as the Technology Solutions Group. These include Enterprise Storage and Servers, representing approximately 16% of FY 08 sales, HP Services 19%, and HP software 2%. Other segments include the Personal Systems Group, representing about 35% of FY 08 sales, the Imaging and Printing Group 25%, HP Financial Services 2%, and Corporate investments 1%.

PRIMARY BUSINESS DYNAMICS. Large corporations and small offices/home offices are the primary drivers of spending on information technology products and services. Industrywide trends, exchange rates and distribution channels influence HPQ's financial performance. Most players sell broad product lines and have a global sourcing and distribution system.

Company Financials Fiscal Year Ended Oct. 31

Per Share Data ($)	2009	2008	2007	2006	2005	2004	2003	2002	2001	2000
Tangible Book Value	NA	NM	4.91	6.57	6.04	6.06	6.08	5.35	7.20	7.30
Cash Flow	NA	4.56	3.67	3.00	1.63	1.93	1.65	0.48	1.01	2.37
Earnings	3.14	3.25	2.68	2.18	0.82	1.15	0.83	-0.37	0.32	1.73
S&P Core Earnings	NA	2.97	2.56	2.10	0.74	0.94	0.65	-0.65	0.16	NA
Dividends	0.32	0.32	0.32	0.32	0.32	0.32	0.32	0.32	0.32	0.32
Payout Ratio	10%	10%	12%	15%	39%	28%	39%	NM	100%	18%
Prices:High	51.43	50.98	53.48	41.70	30.25	26.28	23.90	24.12	37.95	77.75
Prices:Low	25.39	28.23	38.15	28.37	18.89	16.08	14.18	10.75	12.50	29.13
P/E Ratio:High	16	16	20	19	37	23	29	NM	NM	45
P/E Ratio:Low	8	9	14	13	23	14	17	NM	NM	17

Income Statement Analysis (Million $)	2009	2008	2007	2006	2005	2004	2003	2002	2001	2000
Revenue	114,552	118,364	104,286	91,658	86,696	79,905	73,061	56,588	45,226	48,782
Operating Income	NA	14,196	11,773	9,372	7,520	7,017	6,713	4,570	3,192	5,257
Depreciation	4,773	3,367	2,705	2,353	2,344	2,395	2,527	2,119	1,369	1,368
Interest Expense	NA	467	289	249	334	247	277	212	234	233
Pretax Income	9,415	10,473	9,177	7,191	3,543	4,196	2,888	-1,052	702	4,625
Effective Tax Rate	18.6%	20.5%	20.9%	13.8%	32.3%	16.7%	12.1%	NM	11.1%	23.0%
Net Income	7,660	8,329	7,264	6,198	2,398	3,497	2,539	-923	624	3,561
S&P Core Earnings	NA	7,598	6,913	5,992	2,150	2,886	1,983	-1,635	285	NA

Balance Sheet & Other Financial Data (Million $)	2009	2008	2007	2006	2005	2004	2003	2002	2001	2000
Cash	13,334	10,246	11,293	16,400	13,911	12,663	14,188	11,192	4,197	3,415
Current Assets	NA	51,728	47,402	48,264	43,334	42,901	40,996	36,075	21,305	23,244
Total Assets	114,799	113,331	88,699	81,981	77,317	76,138	74,708	70,710	32,584	34,009
Current Liabilities	NA	52,939	39,260	2,490	31,460	28,588	26,630	24,310	13,964	15,197
Long Term Debt	13,980	7,676	4,997	2,490	3,392	4,623	6,494	6,035	3,729	3,402
Common Equity	40,517	38,942	38,526	38,144	37,176	37,564	37,746	36,262	13,953	14,209
Total Capital	54,497	49,292	43,523	40,634	40,568	42,187	44,240	42,297	17,682	17,611
Capital Expenditures	3,695	2,990	3,040	2,536	1,995	2,126	1,995	1,710	1,527	1,737
Cash Flow	NA	11,696	9,969	8,551	4,742	5,892	5,066	1,196	1,993	4,929
Current Ratio	1.2	1.0	1.2	1.3	1.4	1.5	1.5	1.5	1.5	1.5
% Long Term Debt of Capitalization	25.7	15.4	11.5	6.1	8.4	11.0	14.7	14.3	21.1	19.3
% Net Income of Revenue	6.7	7.0	7.0	6.8	2.8	4.4	3.5	NM	1.4	7.3
% Return on Assets	6.7	8.3	8.5	7.8	3.1	4.6	3.5	NM	1.9	10.3
% Return on Equity	19.3	21.5	19.0	16.5	6.4	9.3	6.9	NM	4.4	21.9

Data as orig reptd.; bef. results of disc opers/spec. items. Per share data adj. for stk. divs.; EPS diluted. E-Estimated. NA-Not Available. NM-Not Meaningful. NR-Not Ranked. UR-Under Review.

Office: 3000 Hanover Street, Palo Alto, CA 94304-1112.
Telephone: 650-857-1501.
Website: http://www.hp.com
Chrmn, Pres & CEO: M. Hurd

EVP & CFO: C.A. Lesjak
EVP & Chief Admin Officer: P.J. Bocian
EVP & CTO: S.V. Robison
EVP & General Counsel: M.J. Holston

Investor Contact: B. Humphries (650-857-3342)
Board Members: M. L. Andreessen, L. T. Babbio, Jr., S. Baldauf, R. L. Gupta, J. Hammergren, M. Hurd, J. Hyatt, J. R. Joyce, R. L. Ryan, L. S. Salhany, G. Thompson

Founded: 1939
Domicile: Delaware
Employees: 321,000

The **McGraw-Hill** Companies

Home Depot Inc. (The)

STANDARD &POOR'S

S&P Recommendation HOLD ★★★☆☆

Price	12-Mo. Target Price	Investment Style
$27.61 (as of Nov 27, 2009)	$27.00	Large-Cap Blend

GICS Sector Consumer Discretionary
Sub-Industry Home Improvement Retail

Summary HD operates a chain of over 2,200 retail warehouse-type stores, selling a wide variety of home improvement products for the do-it-yourself and home remodeling markets.

Key Stock Statistics (Source S&P, Vickers, company reports)

52-Wk Range	$28.44– 17.49	S&P Oper. EPS 2010**E**	1.55	Market Capitalization(B)	$47.063	Beta	0.66
Trailing 12-Month EPS	$1.34	S&P Oper. EPS 2011**E**	1.62	Yield (%)	3.26	S&P 3-Yr. Proj. EPS CAGR(%)	7
Trailing 12-Month P/E	20.6	P/E on S&P Oper. EPS 2010**E**	17.8	Dividend Rate/Share	$0.90	S&P Credit Rating	BBB+
$10K Invested 5 Yrs Ago	$7,180	Common Shares Outstg. (M)	1,704.6	Institutional Ownership (%)	69		

Price Performance

30-Week Mov. Avg. · · · 10-Week Mov. Avg. - - **GAAP Earnings vs. Previous Year** Volume Above Avg. STARS
12-Mo. Target Price — Relative Strength — ▲ Up ▼ Down ► No Change Below Avg. ★

Options: ASE, CBOE, P, Ph

Analysis prepared by **Michael Souers** on November 19, 2009, when the stock traded at **$ 27.07**.

Highlights

► We expect retail sales to increase 1.0% in FY 11 (Jan.), following our projection of an 8.3% decline in FY 10. We see this rise reflecting 5-10 net new retail store additions, including international store openings, and a possible slight increase in same-store sales. We project a slow recovery in the housing market in calendar 2010, and we expect the tightening of consumer credit to also adversely affect near-term sales for home improvement retailers, particularly on big-ticket remodeling projects.

► We see FY 11 operating margins widening 40 basis points, driven by a rational pricing environment, continued tight expense control, supply chain benefits from the recent investment in rapid deployment centers, and an improving mix. We expect these factors to be partially offset by the deleveraging of fixed expenses due to our projection of flattish same-store sales.

► We expect slightly lower interest expense and taxes at an effective rate of 35.5%. We project FY 11 EPS of $1.62, a 4.5% increase from the $1.55 we project for FY 10, excluding store rationalization charges.

Investment Rationale/Risk

► At about 17X our FY 11 EPS estimate, HD recently traded in line with key peer Lowe's (LOW 21, Hold). We expect the housing market to recover gradually over the coming year, and we believe HD will reap the rewards from an accelerated focus on customer service. Favorable demographic trends such as the aging of houses and low interest rates should help support home remodeling efforts over the longer term. Although we are concerned that the bleak housing market and the outlook for consumer spending will limit share price upside over the near term, we favor what we see as HD's strong balance sheet, financial flexibility, and abundant free cash flow generation.

► Risks to our recommendation and target price include a sharp or protracted slowdown in the U.S. economy; a large hike in interest rates; and unfavorable currency movements.

► Our 12-month target price of $27, which is equal to about 17X our FY 11 EPS estimate, is derived from our DCF model, which assumes a weighted average cost of capital of 9.5% and a terminal growth rate of 3.0%.

Qualitative Risk Assessment

LOW	MEDIUM	HIGH

Our risk assessment for Home Depot reflects our view of ample opportunities for growth in the professional market domestically and the retail business overseas, and an S&P Quality Ranking of A. This is partially offset by the cyclical nature of the home improvement retail industry, which is reliant on economic growth.

Quantitative Evaluations

S&P Quality Ranking   A

D	C	B-	B	B+	A-	A	A+

Relative Strength Rank   STRONG

71

LOWEST = 1   HIGHEST = 99

Revenue/Earnings Data

Revenue (Million $)

	1Q	2Q	3Q	4Q	Year
2010	16,175	19,071	16,361	--	--
2009	17,907	20,990	17,784	14,607	71,288
2008	21,585	22,184	18,961	17,659	77,349
2007	21,461	26,026	23,085	20,265	90,837
2006	18,973	22,305	20,744	19,489	81,511
2005	17,550	19,960	18,772	16,812	73,094

Earnings Per Share ($)

2010	0.30	0.66	0.41	E0.12	E1.55
2009	0.21	0.71	0.45	-0.03	1.37
2008	0.53	0.71	0.59	0.40	2.27
2007	0.70	0.90	0.73	0.46	2.79
2006	0.57	0.82	0.72	0.60	2.72
2005	0.49	0.70	0.60	0.47	2.26

Fiscal year ended Jan. 31. Next earnings report expected: Late February. EPS Estimates based on S&P Operating Earnings; historical GAAP earnings are as reported.

Dividend Data (Dates: mm/dd Payment Date: mm/dd/yy)

Amount ($)	Date Decl.	Ex-Div. Date	Stk. of Record	Payment Date
0.225	02/26	03/10	03/12	03/26/09
0.225	05/28	06/09	06/11	06/25/09
0.225	08/20	09/01	09/03	09/17/09
0.225	11/19	12/01	12/03	12/17/09

Dividends have been paid since 1987. Source: Company reports.

Please read the Required Disclosures and Analyst Certification on the last page of this report.

The McGraw-Hill Companies

Home Depot Inc. (The)

STANDARD &POOR'S

Business Summary November 19, 2009

CORPORATE OVERVIEW. Home Depot is the world's largest home improvement retailer, with revenues in excess of $70 billion. At February 1, 2009, HD operated 2,233 Home Depot stores (176 in Canada, 74 in Mexico and 12 in China). On January 26, 2009, the company announced the planned closing of 34 EXPO Design Centers, five Yardbirds stores in California, and two THD Design Centers as part of HD's continued focus on its core business.

Home Depot stores average approximately 105,000 sq. ft., plus 23,000 sq. ft. of garden center and storage space. They stock 30,000 to 40,000 items, including brand name and proprietary items. Home Depot stores serve three primary customer groups: Do-It-Yourself (DIY) customers, typically homeowners who complete their own projects and installations; Do-It-For-Me (DIFM) customers, usually homeowners who purchase materials and hire third parties to complete the project and/or installation; and Professional customers, consisting of professional remodelers, general contractors, repairpeople and tradespeople. By product group, plumbing, electrical and kitchen (31% of FY 09 (Jan.) revenues) represented HD's largest source of revenue, followed by hardware and seasonal (29%), building materials, lumber and millwork (22%) and paint, flooring and wall covering (18%).

CORPORATE STRATEGY. We believe HD is in a period of transition after years of expanding rapidly as a big-box retailer. We expect Home Depot to confront a rapidly saturating domestic market by accelerating its expansion efforts abroad. Domestically, HD is increasing its focus on service and customer retention as a means to gain market share.

At the end of 2006, Home Depot acquired The Home Way, a Chinese home improvement retailer, including 12 stores in six cities. We expect HD to either exit the Chinese market in FY 10 or to embark on an aggressive expansion of stores over the next several years.

In August 2007, Home Depot closed the sale of HD Supply for $8.3 billion, recognizing a $4 million loss, net of tax. In connection with the sale, it purchased a 12.5% equity interest in the newly formed HD Supply for $325 million, and guaranteed a $1.0 billion senior secured loan of HD Supply.

Company Financials Fiscal Year Ended Jan. 31

Per Share Data ($)	2009	2008	2007	2006	2005	2004	2003	2002	2001	2000
Tangible Book Value	9.81	9.75	11.81	11.12	9.54	9.56	8.39	7.53	6.32	5.22
Cash Flow	2.43	3.19	3.65	3.45	2.85	2.35	1.95	1.62	1.35	1.19
Earnings	1.37	2.27	2.79	2.72	2.26	1.88	1.56	1.29	1.10	1.00
S&P Core Earnings	1.43	2.27	2.79	2.68	2.19	1.78	1.46	1.18	1.01	NA
Dividends	0.90	0.68	0.68	0.40	0.33	0.26	0.21	0.17	0.16	0.11
Payout Ratio	66%	30%	24%	15%	15%	14%	13%	13%	15%	11%
Calendar Year	2008	2007	2006	2005	2004	2003	2002	2001	2000	1999
Prices:High	31.08	42.01	43.95	43.98	44.30	37.89	52.60	53.73	70.00	69.75
Prices:Low	17.05	25.57	32.85	34.56	32.34	20.10	23.01	30.30	34.69	34.58
P/E Ratio:High	23	19	16	16	20	20	41	43	64	70
P/E Ratio:Low	12	11	12	13	14	11	18	24	32	35

Income Statement Analysis (Million $)										
Revenue	71,288	77,349	90,837	81,511	73,094	64,816	58,247	53,553	45,738	38,434
Operating Income	7,093	9,032	11,435	10,942	9,245	7,922	6,733	5,696	4,792	4,258
Depreciation	1,783	1,702	1,762	1,579	1,319	1,076	903	764	601	463
Interest Expense	644	742	427	143	70.0	62.0	37.0	28.0	21.0	28.0
Pretax Income	3,590	6,620	9,308	9,282	7,912	6,843	5,872	4,957	4,217	3,804
Effective Tax Rate	35.6%	36.4%	38.1%	37.1%	36.8%	37.1%	37.6%	38.6%	38.8%	39.0%
Net Income	2,312	4,210	5,761	5,838	5,001	4,304	3,664	3,044	2,581	2,320
S&P Core Earnings	2,418	4,210	5,761	5,751	4,843	4,067	3,414	2,780	2,364	NA

Balance Sheet & Other Financial Data (Million $)										
Cash	525	457	614	793	506	2,826	2,188	2,477	167	168
Current Assets	13,362	14,674	18,000	15,346	14,190	13,328	11,917	10,361	7,777	6,390
Total Assets	41,164	44,324	52,263	44,482	38,907	34,437	30,011	26,394	21,385	17,081
Current Liabilities	11,153	12,706	12,931	12,901	10,529	9,554	8,035	6,501	4,385	3,656
Long Term Debt	9,667	10,983	11,237	2,302	1,807	545	1,049	1,022	1,318	537
Common Equity	17,777	17,714	25,030	26,909	24,158	22,407	19,802	18,082	15,004	12,341
Total Capital	28,794	28,982	36,272	29,713	25,976	23,461	20,853	19,105	16,334	12,914
Capital Expenditures	1,847	3,558	3,542	3,881	3,948	3,508	2,749	3,393	3,558	2,581
Cash Flow	4,095	5,912	7,523	7,417	6,320	5,380	4,567	3,808	3,182	2,783
Current Ratio	1.2	1.2	1.4	1.2	1.3	1.4	1.5	1.6	1.8	1.7
% Long Term Debt of Capitalization	33.1	38.2	31.8	8.7	7.8	3.5	6.1	6.4	9.2	5.7
% Net Income of Revenue	3.2	5.4	6.3	7.2	6.8	6.6	6.3	5.7	5.6	6.0
% Return on Assets	5.4	8.7	11.9	14.0	13.6	13.4	13.0	12.7	13.4	15.2
% Return on Equity	13.0	19.7	22.2	22.9	21.5	20.4	19.3	18.4	18.9	22.0

Data as orig reptd.; bef. results of disc opers/spec. items. Per share data adj. for stk. divs.; EPS diluted. E-Estimated. NA-Not Available. NM-Not Meaningful. NR-Not Ranked. UR-Under Review.

Office: 2455 Paces Ferry Rd, N.W., Atlanta, GA 30339-1834.
Telephone: 770-433-8211.
Website: http://www.homedepot.com
Chrmn & CEO: F.S. Blake

Pres: A.M. Campbell
COO: M.D. Powers
EVP, CFO & Chief Acctg Officer: C.B. Tome
EVP, Secy & General Counsel: J.A. VanWoerkom

Investor Contact: D. Dayhoff (770-384-2666)
Board Members: F. D. Ackerman, D. H. Batchelder, F. S. Blake, A. Bousbib, G. D. Brenneman, A. P. Carey, J. L. Clendenin, A. M. Codina, M. A. Hart, III, B. Hill, L. P. Jackson, Jr., K. L. Katen, C. X. Laporte

Founded: 1978
Domicile: Delaware
Employees: 322,000

The **McGraw-Hill** Companies

Honeywell International Inc.

STANDARD &POOR'S

S&P Recommendation	STRONG BUY ★★★★★	Price $38.48 (as of Nov 27, 2009)	12-Mo. Target Price $45.00	Investment Style Large-Cap Value

GICS Sector Industrials
Sub-Industry Aerospace & Defense

Summary The world's largest maker of cockpit controls, small jet engines and climate control equipment, HON also makes industrial materials and automotive products.

Key Stock Statistics (Source S&P, Vickers, company reports)

52-Wk Range	$40.55–23.06	S&P Oper. EPS 2009E	2.83	Market Capitalization(B)	$29.362	Beta	1.33
Trailing 12-Month EPS	$2.90	S&P Oper. EPS 2010E	2.75	Yield (%)	3.14	S&P 3-Yr. Proj. EPS CAGR(%)	3
Trailing 12-Month P/E	13.3	P/E on S&P Oper. EPS 2009E	13.6	Dividend Rate/Share	$1.21	S&P Credit Rating	A
$10K Invested 5 Yrs Ago	$12,179	Common Shares Outstg. (M)	763.0	Institutional Ownership (%)	74		

Price Performance

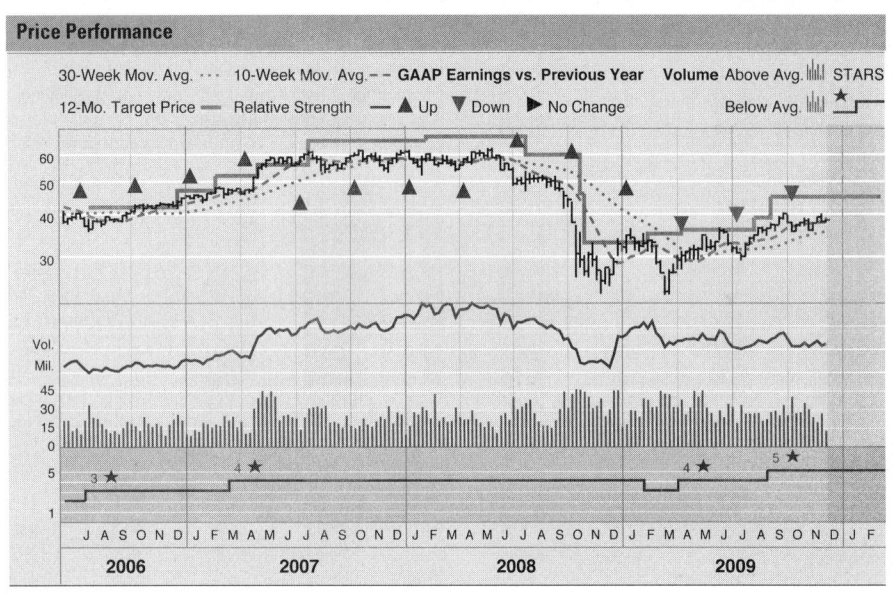

30-Week Mov. Avg. ···· 10-Week Mov. Avg. – – GAAP Earnings vs. Previous Year   Volume Above Avg. STARS
12-Mo. Target Price — Relative Strength — ▲ Up ▼ Down ▶ No Change   Below Avg.

Options: ASE, CBOE, P, Ph

Analysis prepared by **Richard Tortoriello** on October 29, 2009, when the stock traded at **$ 37.12**.

Highlights

► We project a 15% sales decline in 2009, as we see a prolonged global economic downturn affecting all of HON's businesses. For 2010, we project a 2% sales increase. Specifically, we expect 8% growth in Transportation, off depressed revenue levels, as we see sales improving, aided by platform wins in Turbo. We also expect 3% to 4% bounce backs in Automation & Control Systems and in Specialty Materials. We project a 3% decline in Aerospace, as we see the business jet market as slow to recover.

► We project a 30 basis point drop in operating margins in 2009, to 13.0%, as productivity improvements and restructuring (primarily employee reductions) are offset by volume declines. We are modeling a margin decline to 12.6% in 2010, on increased pension expense.

► We project EPS of $2.83 in 2009, with a modest decline to $2.75 in 2010. We expect HON to generate what we view as strong free cash flow of $3.1 billion (over $4.00 per share) in 2009, versus $3.2 billion ($4.30 per share) in 2008.

Investment Rationale/Risk

► We see HON's emphasis on building environmental and lighting controls and its turbocharger products as benefiting from what we view as a strong global trend toward energy efficiency. In aerospace, we continue to expect global fleet sizes to rise, over the long term, as air travel increases in developing economies. At the same time, we view HON's valuations as below historical averages on a variety of measures. We believe that current valuations offer investors the ability to own a world-class global industrial company at a compelling price.

► Risks to our recommendation and target price include a stronger or longer-than-expected downturn in the global economy, higher-than-projected pension liabilities, and less-than-anticipated restructuring benefits.

► Our 12-month target price of $45 is based on an enterprise value to EBITDA multiple of 8.5X, using our 2010 EBITDA estimate of $4.5 billion. This multiple is below the 20-year average EV-to-EBITDA multiple for HON of 9.1X, on our view that we are still early in an economic recovery and substantial risks remain.

Qualitative Risk Assessment

LOW	MEDIUM	HIGH

Our risk assessment reflects what we believe is above-average exposure to market movements, economic cycles, currency fluctuations and raw material costs. This is offset by what we view as HON's strong balance sheet and its ability to generate significant amounts of cash.

Quantitative Evaluations

S&P Quality Ranking B+

D	C	B-	B	B+	A-	A	A+

Relative Strength Rank MODERATE

66

LOWEST = 1   HIGHEST = 99

Revenue/Earnings Data

Revenue (Million $)

	1Q	2Q	3Q	4Q	Year
2009	7,570	7,566	7,700	--	--
2008	8,895	9,674	9,275	8,712	36,556
2007	8,041	8,538	8,735	9,275	34,589
2006	7,241	7,898	7,952	8,276	31,367
2005	6,453	7,026	6,899	7,275	27,653
2004	6,178	6,388	6,395	6,640	25,601

Earnings Per Share ($)

2009	0.54	0.60	0.80	E0.89	E2.83
2008	0.85	0.96	0.97	0.97	3.76
2007	0.66	0.78	0.81	0.91	3.16
2006	0.51	0.63	0.66	0.72	2.51
2005	0.42	0.33	0.51	0.61	1.86
2004	0.34	0.42	0.43	0.30	1.49

Fiscal year ended Dec. 31. Next earnings report expected: Early February. EPS Estimates based on S&P Operating Earnings; historical GAAP earnings are as reported.

Dividend Data (Dates: mm/dd Payment Date: mm/dd/yy)

Amount ($)	Date Decl.	Ex-Div. Date	Stk. of Record	Payment Date
0.303	02/12	02/18	02/20	03/10/09
0.303	04/27	05/18	05/20	06/10/09
0.303	07/31	08/18	08/20	09/10/09
0.303	10/30	11/18	11/20	12/10/09

Dividends have been paid since 1887. Source: Company reports.

Please read the Required Disclosures and Analyst Certification on the last page of this report.

The McGraw-Hill Companies

Honeywell International Inc.

STANDARD &POOR'S

Business Summary October 29, 2009

CORPORATE OVERVIEW. Honeywell International Inc., an aerospace and industrial conglomerate with $33 billion in estimated 2009 revenues, conducts business through four operating segments. HON generated about 49% of sales from products sold outside of the U.S. in 2008, primarily in Europe (29%), Canada, Asia (10%), and Latin America. Sales to the U.S. government accounted for 12% of total sales in 2008.

The Aerospace segment (35% of 2008 revenues and 46% of operating profits) makes a variety of products for commercial and military aircraft, including cockpit controls and other avionics, flight safety systems, auxiliary power units, environmental controls, electric power systems, lighting, and wheels and brakes. It is also a leading maker of jet engines for regional and business jet manufacturers, and makes space and military products and subsystems. The Aerospace segment is also a major player in the estimated $57 billion global aircraft maintenance, repair and overhaul (MRO) industry, and distributes aircraft hardware.

HON's Automation and Control Solutions segment (38% of revenues and 32% of operating profits) is a leading global producer of environmental and combustion controls, sensing controls, security and life safety products and services, and process automation and building solutions and services for homes, buildings, and industrial facilities. Building solutions and services include energy management, security and asset management, building information services, and HVAC and building control.

The Specialty Materials segment (14% and 14%) makes specialty chemicals and fibers. Products include fluorine products, specialty films and additives, advanced fibers and composites, intermediates, specialty chemicals, electronic materials and chemicals, and catalysts, absorbents, and equipment and technologies for the petrochemical and refining industries. HON sells its industrial materials primarily to the petrochemical, food, pharmaceutical, and electronic packaging industries.

The Transportation Systems segment (13% and 8%) consists of a portfolio of brand name car care products, such as FRAM filters, Prestone antifreeze, Autolite spark plugs, and Simoniz car waxes. The unit is also a leading manufacturer of turbochargers for passenger cars and commercial vehicles and braking products.

Company Financials Fiscal Year Ended Dec. 31

Per Share Data ($)	2008	2007	2006	2005	2004	2003	2002	2001	2000	1999
Tangible Book Value	NM	NM	0.09	1.95	4.70	4.46	2.52	3.45	4.71	4.95
Cash Flow	4.97	4.24	3.59	2.74	2.24	2.25	0.53	1.02	3.28	2.99
Earnings	3.76	3.16	2.51	1.86	1.49	1.56	-0.27	-0.12	2.05	1.90
S&P Core Earnings	2.14	3.15	2.62	1.83	1.42	1.57	0.15	-0.26	NA	NA
Dividends	1.10	1.00	0.91	1.03	0.75	0.75	0.75	0.75	0.75	0.68
Payout Ratio	29%	32%	36%	55%	50%	48%	NM	NM	37%	36%
Prices:High	62.99	62.29	45.77	39.50	38.46	33.50	40.95	53.90	60.50	68.63
Prices:Low	23.24	43.14	35.24	32.68	31.23	20.20	18.77	22.15	32.13	37.81
P/E Ratio:High	17	20	18	21	26	21	NM	NM	30	36
P/E Ratio:Low	6	14	14	18	21	13	NM	NM	16	20

Income Statement Analysis (Million $)										
Revenue	36,556	34,589	31,367	27,653	25,601	23,103	22,274	23,652	25,023	23,735
Operating Income	5,444	4,561	3,855	3,178	2,350	2,513	2,573	1,085	3,794	2,905
Depreciation	903	837	794	697	650	595	671	926	995	881
Interest Expense	482	456	374	356	331	335	344	405	481	265
Pretax Income	3,801	3,321	2,798	2,323	1,680	1,647	-945	-422	2,398	2,248
Effective Tax Rate	26.6%	26.4%	25.7%	31.9%	23.8%	18.0%	NM	NM	30.8%	31.5%
Net Income	2,792	2,444	2,078	1,581	1,281	1,344	-220	NA	1,659	1,541
S&P Core Earnings	1,590	2,445	2,168	1,554	1,225	1,363	119	-207	NA	NA

Balance Sheet & Other Financial Data (Million $)										
Cash	2,065	1,829	1,224	1,234	3,586	2,950	2,021	1,393	1,196	1,991
Current Assets	13,263	13,685	12,304	11,962	12,820	11,523	10,195	9,894	10,661	10,422
Total Assets	35,490	33,805	30,941	32,294	31,062	29,344	27,559	24,226	25,175	23,527
Current Liabilities	12,289	11,941	10,135	10,430	8,739	6,783	6,574	6,220	7,214	8,272
Long Term Debt	5,865	5,419	3,909	3,082	4,069	4,961	4,719	4,731	3,941	2,457
Common Equity	7,187	9,222	9,720	11,254	11,252	7,243	8,925	9,170	9,707	8,599
Total Capital	13,750	15,375	13,981	14,839	15,718	12,520	14,063	14,776	14,821	11,920
Capital Expenditures	884	767	733	684	629	655	671	876	853	986
Cash Flow	3,695	3,281	2,872	2,278	1,931	1,939	451	827	2,654	2,422
Current Ratio	1.1	1.2	1.2	1.1	1.5	1.7	1.6	1.6	1.5	1.3
% Long Term Debt of Capitalization	42.7	35.2	28.0	20.8	25.9	39.6	33.6	32.0	26.6	20.6
% Net Income of Revenue	7.6	7.0	6.6	5.7	5.0	5.8	NM	NM	6.6	6.5
% Return on Assets	8.1	7.5	6.5	5.0	4.2	4.7	NM	NM	6.8	6.7
% Return on Equity	34.0	25.8	20.3	14.0	11.7	21.1	NM	NM	18.1	18.5

Data as orig reptd.; bef. results of disc opers/spec. items. Per share data adj. for stk. divs.; EPS diluted. E-Estimated. NA-Not Available. NM-Not Meaningful. NR-Not Ranked. UR-Under Review.

Office: 101 Columbia Rd, Morristown, NJ 07960-4640.
Telephone: 973-455-2000.
Website: http://www.honeywell.com
Chrmn & CEO: D.M. Cote

COO & CTO: L.E. Kittelberger
SVP & CFO: D.J. Anderson
SVP & General Counsel: K.L. Adams
Chief Acctg Officer & Cntlr: K.A. Winters

Investor Contact: M. Grainger (973-455-2222)
Board Members: G. Bethune, D. M. Cote, D. S. Davis, L. F. Deily, C. R. Hollick, J. C. Pardo, G. Paz, B. T. Sheares, J. R. Stafford, T. P. Stafford, M. W. Wright

Founded: 1920
Domicile: Delaware
Employees: 128,000

Hormel Foods Corp

STANDARD &POOR'S

S&P Recommendation	HOLD ★★★☆☆	Price $37.56 (as of Nov 27, 2009)	12-Mo. Target Price $40.00	Investment Style Large-Cap Blend

GICS Sector Consumer Staples
Sub-Industry Packaged Foods & Meats

Summary This company is a leading processor of branded, convenience meat products (primarily pork) for the consumer market.

Key Stock Statistics (Source S&P, Vickers, company reports)

52-Wk Range	$40.46– 24.81	S&P Oper. EPS 2010**E**	2.68	Market Capitalization(B)	$5.041	Beta	0.41
Trailing 12-Month EPS	$2.53	S&P Oper. EPS 2011**E**	NA	Yield (%)	2.24	S&P 3-Yr. Proj. EPS CAGR(%)	8
Trailing 12-Month P/E	14.9	P/E on S&P Oper. EPS 2010**E**	14.0	Dividend Rate/Share	$0.84	S&P Credit Rating	A
$10K Invested 5 Yrs Ago	$13,402	Common Shares Outstg. (M)	134.2	Institutional Ownership (%)	28		

Price Performance

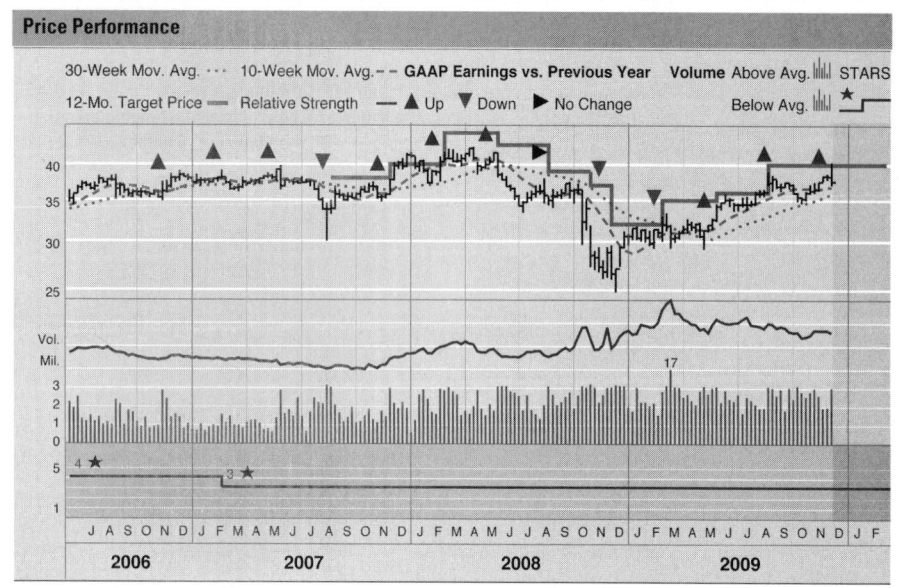

30-Week Mov. Avg. ··· 10-Week Mov. Avg. – – GAAP Earnings vs. Previous Year Volume Above Avg. STARS
12-Mo. Target Price — Relative Strength ▲ Up ▼ Down ► No Change Below Avg. ★

Options: Ph

Analysis prepared by **Tom Graves, CFA** on September 28, 2009, when the stock traded at **$ 36.05**.

Highlights

▶ In FY 10 (Oct.), we look for revenues to increase moderately from the $6.6 billion that we project for FY 09. We expect refrigerated food sales to be bolstered by increased demand for value-added products. We think the strength of HRL's brands should help to protect them from market share loss to less expensive private label products provided by others. Also, we look for HRL to benefit from less commodity cost pressure.

▶ Near-term, we see a prospect of continued weakness in foodservice demand, and a potential impact on pork sales from fears of H1N1 virus. However, we were impressed by the extent to which HRL recently expanded year-to-year profit margins in most of its business segments during a period in which sales declined.

▶ We look for FY 10 EPS to increase about 8%, to $2.65 a share, up from the $2.45 that we estimate for FY 09. Also, in the first nine months of FY 09, HRL spent $13.9 million on stock repurchase, compared with $56.5 million in the year-ago period. At the end of the quarter, authorization remained to buy back 1.8 million shares.

Investment Rationale/Risk

▶ At July 26, 2009, HRL had cash and equivalents totaling $295.1 million. We expect that HRL to be looking for opportunities to make strategic acquisitions. Also, over time, we expect HRL to be able to increase the importance of non-U.S. sales, including a larger presence in some Asian markets. As a producer of protein products, including the Spam brand, we think that HRL should have opportunities to benefit from rising incomes and changing lifestyles in some developing markets. Overall, non-U.S. sales accounted for only 5% HRL's total in FY 08.

▶ Risks to our recommendation and target price include weaker-than-expected demand, market share losses to private label competition, and higher-than-expected turkey feed costs.

▶ We think the company is well positioned for long-term growth, with profitability expected to benefit as higher-margin, value-added products become a larger part of its business. Our 12-month target price of $40 is based on a P/E that is moderately below a five-year average for the stock. The shares have an indicated dividend yield of 2.1%.

Qualitative Risk Assessment

LOW	MEDIUM	**HIGH**

Our risk assessment reflects the company's cyclical operations, which are significantly affected by exposure to commodity crop and meat markets.

Quantitative Evaluations

S&P Quality Ranking A+

D	C	B-	B	B+	A-	A	**A+**

Relative Strength Rank MODERATE

60

LOWEST = 1   HIGHEST = 99

Revenue/Earnings Data

Revenue (Million $)

	1Q	2Q	3Q	4Q	Year
2009	1,689	1,595	1,574	1,675	6,534
2008	1,621	1,594	1,678	1,862	6,755
2007	1,504	1,505	1,520	1,664	6,193
2006	1,416	1,365	1,407	1,557	5,745
2005	1,271	1,310	1,355	1,478	5,414
2004	1,136	1,143	1,156	1,345	4,780

Earnings Per Share ($)

2009	0.60	0.59	0.57	0.77	2.53
2008	0.64	0.56	0.38	0.50	2.08
2007	0.54	0.49	0.38	0.73	2.17
2006	0.50	0.48	--	0.64	2.05
2005	0.46	0.40	0.37	0.59	1.82
2004	0.37	0.38	0.40	0.50	1.65

Fiscal year ended Oct. 31. Next earnings report expected: Mid February. EPS Estimates based on S&P Operating Earnings; historical GAAP earnings are as reported.

Dividend Data (Dates: mm/dd Payment Date: mm/dd/yy)

Amount ($)	Date Decl.	Ex-Div. Date	Stk. of Record	Payment Date
0.190	03/24	04/15	04/18	05/15/09
0.190	05/19	07/15	07/18	08/15/09
0.190	10/05	10/21	10/24	11/15/09
0.210	11/24	01/20	01/23	02/15/10

Dividends have been paid since 1928. Source: Company reports.

Please read the Required Disclosures and Analyst Certification on the last page of this report.

The McGraw-Hill Companies

Hormel Foods Corp

Business Summary September 28, 2009

CORPORATE OVERVIEW. Probably best known for its ubiquitous Spam, Hormel Foods is a diversified producer of consumer foods. Founded in 1891 as George A. Hormel & Company, the company got its start as a processor of meat products, principally pork. Over the years, it has expanded its business both internally and through acquisitions. In our view, although pork and turkey remain the major raw material for Hormel products, the company has emphasized for several years the manufacture and distribution of branded, consumer packaged items over the commodity fresh meat business closely associated with its business of the past.

The company operates under the grocery products, refrigerated foods, Jennie-O Turkey Store, specialty foods, and other business segments. The grocery product segment (14% of FY 08 (Oct.) revenues and 28% of operating income) processes, markets and sells shelf-stable food products predominately in the retail market. The refrigerated foods segment (52%; 39%), including meat products and food service business units, processes, markets and sells branded and unbranded pork products for the retail, food service, and fresh customer markets. Jennie-O Turkey Store (19%; 15%) processes, markets and sells branded and unbranded turkey products to the retail, food service and fresh customer markets. The specialty foods segment (11%; 13%) packages and sells various sugar and sugar substitute products, salt and pepper prod-

ucts. The "other" segment (4%; 5%) produces, markets and sells company products internationally through Dan's Prize Inc. and Hormel Foods International operating segments.

CORPORATE STRATEGY. We expect the company to be viewing strategic acquisitions as a prospective use of cash. In June 2008, the company acquired Boca Grande Foods, Inc., a manufacturer and distributor of liquid portion products in Georgia. In March 2006, HRL acquired Valley Fresh, a manufacturer of canned ready-to-eat chicken products and a distributor of pre-cooked chicken products. In November 2006, the company acquired Sag's Products, a processor and marketer of branded, premium gourmet sausages and specialty cooked meats. In December 2006, HRL acquired Pro vena Foods, a provider of pepperoni and pasta to pizza makers and packaged food manufacturers. In April 2005, HRL acquired Lloyd's Barbecue Company, a manufacturer of barbecue products. In March 2005, the company purchased Mark-Lynn Foods Inc., a manufacturer and distributor of a variety of food products.

Company Financials Fiscal Year Ended Oct. 31

Per Share Data ($)	2009	2008	2007	2006	2005	2004	2003	2002	2001	2000
Tangible Book Value	NA	9.20	8.31	8.04	6.77	6.43	5.36	5.41	4.45	5.64
Cash Flow	NA	2.92	3.08	2.92	2.64	2.33	1.96	1.94	1.95	1.67
Earnings	2.53	2.08	2.17	2.05	1.82	1.65	1.33	1.35	1.30	1.20
S&P Core Earnings	NA	1.88	2.15	NA	1.88	1.61	1.22	1.10	1.23	NA
Dividends	0.76	0.74	0.60	0.56	0.52	0.45	0.42	0.39	0.37	0.35
Payout Ratio	30%	36%	28%	27%	29%	27%	32%	29%	28%	29%
Prices:High	40.46	42.77	41.82	39.09	35.44	32.11	27.49	28.20	27.35	20.97
Prices:Low	29.16	24.81	30.04	31.88	29.16	24.90	19.93	20.02	17.00	13.63
P/E Ratio:High	16	21	19	19	19	19	21	21	21	17
P/E Ratio:Low	12	12	14	16	16	15	15	15	13	11
Income Statement Analysis (Million $)										
Revenue	6,534	6,755	6,193	5,745	5,414	4,780	4,200	3,910	4,124	3,675
Operating Income	NA	624	611	567	534	448	393	394	390	328
Depreciation	127	115	127	121	115	94.8	88.0	83.2	90.2	65.9
Interest Expense	NA	28.0	27.7	25.6	27.7	27.1	31.9	31.4	28.0	14.9
Pretax Income	525	458	470	431	405	365	289	294	285	264
Effective Tax Rate	34.7%	37.6%	35.7%	33.5%	37.4%	36.5%	35.8%	35.6%	36.0%	35.6%
Net Income	343	286	302	286	253	232	186	189	182	170
S&P Core Earnings	NA	258	300	NA	263	225	171	155	173	NA
Balance Sheet & Other Financial Data (Million $)										
Cash	385	155	150	172	170	289	98.0	310	186	107
Current Assets	NA	1,438	1,232	1,142	1,041	1,029	824	962	883	711
Total Assets	3,692	3,616	3,394	3,060	2,822	2,534	2,393	2,220	2,163	1,642
Current Liabilities	NA	781	665	585	583	464	442	410	420	343
Long Term Debt	350	350	350	350	350	362	395	410	462	146
Common Equity	2,123	2,008	1,885	1,803	1,575	1,399	1,253	1,115	993	874
Total Capital	2,473	2,358	2,235	2,153	1,925	1,765	1,659	1,525	1,455	1,020
Capital Expenditures	92.0	126	126	142	107	80.4	67.1	64.5	77.1	100
Cash Flow	NA	400	429	407	369	326	274	273	273	236
Current Ratio	2.3	1.8	1.9	2.0	1.8	2.2	1.9	2.3	2.1	2.1
% Long Term Debt of Capitalization	14.2	14.9	15.6	16.3	18.2	20.5	23.8	26.9	31.8	14.3
% Net Income of Revenue	5.3	4.2	4.8	5.0	4.7	4.8	4.4	4.8	4.4	4.6
% Return on Assets	9.4	8.2	9.3	9.7	9.5	9.4	8.1	8.6	9.6	10.2
% Return on Equity	16.6	14.7	16.3	16.8	17.0	17.5	15.7	18.0	19.5	19.9

Data as orig reptd.; bef. results of disc opers/spec. items. Per share data adj. for stk. divs.; EPS diluted. E-Estimated. NA-Not Available. NM-Not Meaningful. NR-Not Ranked. UR-Under Review.

Office: 1 Hormel Place, Austin, MN 55912-3680.
Telephone: 507-437-5611.
Website: http://www.hormel.com
Chrmn, Pres & CEO: J.M. Ettinger

SVP & CFO: J.H. Feragen
SVP & General Counsel: J.W. Cavanaugh
Chief Acctg Officer & Cntlr: J.N. Sheehan
Treas: R.G. Gentzler

Investor Contact: K.C. Jones (507-437-5248)
Board Members: T. K. Crews, J. M. Ettinger, J. H. Feragen, S. Marvin, J. L. Morrison, E. A. Murano, R. C. Nakasone, S. K. Nestegard, R. D. Pearson, D. A. Pippins, H. C. Smith, J. G. Turner

Founded: 1891
Domicile: Delaware
Employees: 19,100

Hospira Inc

STANDARD &POOR'S

| S&P Recommendation | HOLD ★★★☆☆ | Price $47.05 (as of Nov 27, 2009) | 12-Mo. Target Price $48.00 | Investment Style Large-Cap Growth |

GICS Sector Health Care
Sub-Industry Health Care Equipment

Summary Spun off from Abbott Laboratories in May 2004, this company provides a variety of hospital products, including injectable generic drugs, pumps, and syringes.

Key Stock Statistics (Source S&P, Vickers, company reports)

52-Wk Range	$48.25– 21.21	S&P Oper. EPS 2009E	2.87	Market Capitalization(B)	$7.630	Beta	0.86
Trailing 12-Month EPS	$2.54	S&P Oper. EPS 2010E	3.20	Yield (%)	Nil	S&P 3-Yr. Proj. EPS CAGR(%)	13
Trailing 12-Month P/E	18.5	P/E on S&P Oper. EPS 2009E	16.4	Dividend Rate/Share	Nil	S&P Credit Rating	BBB+
$10K Invested 5 Yrs Ago	$14,589	Common Shares Outstg. (M)	162.2	Institutional Ownership (%)	82		

Price Performance

30-Week Mov. Avg. · · · 10-Week Mov. Avg. - - - GAAP Earnings vs. Previous Year   Volume Above Avg. ▌▐▐ STARS
12-Mo. Target Price ▬ Relative Strength ▬ ▲ Up ▼ Down ► No Change   Below Avg. ▐▐▌ ★

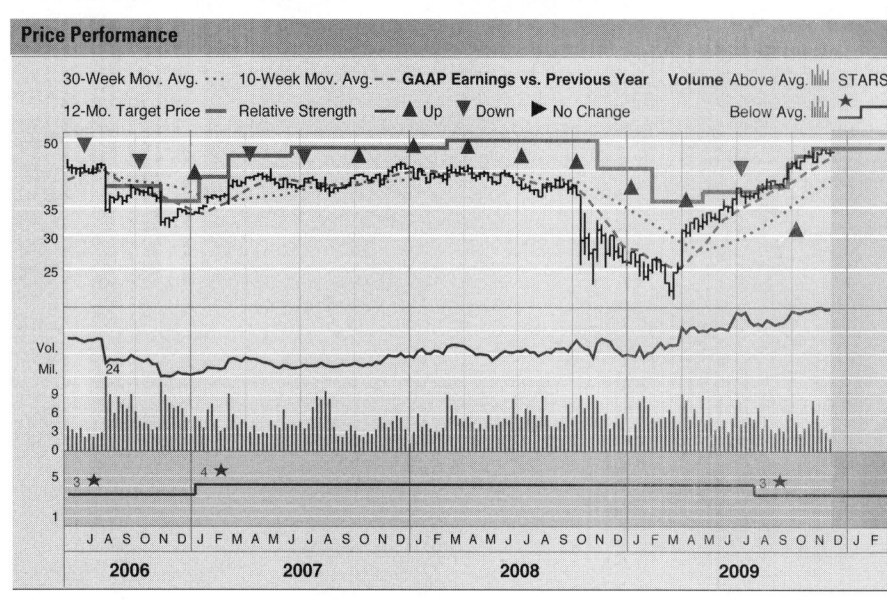

Options: ASE, CBOE, P, Ph

Analysis prepared by **Jeffrey Englander, CFA** on November 11, 2009, when the stock traded at **$ 47.94**.

Highlights

► We expect revenues to increase about 3% in 2009, reflecting the rationalization of underperforming operations and rollout of Oxaliplatin. We look for sales to increase about 4% in 2010 as Oxaliplatin sales pulled into 2009 impact 2010, but other new product growth accelerates. We see sales being driven by HSP's renewed focus on its core specialty injectables, the introduction of Oxaliplatin and high-dose Heparin, and progress in the medication management business. We also expect rising international penetration from the 2007 Mayne Pharma acquisition, and incremental new sales in the contract manufacturing business.

► We project operating expenses to decline as a percentage of sales in both 2009 and 2010, as HSP continues to focus on cost controls and realizes the benefits of Project Fuel (HSP's new cost optimization program). We look for HSP to gradually transition to higher-margin products, particularly in its medication management systems business. We expect HSP's EBITDA margins to increase to near 40% in both 2009 and 2010 reflecting the impact of Project Fuel.

► We see operating EPS of $2.87 in 2009 and $3.20 in 2010, excluding restructuring charges.

Investment Rationale/Risk

► We look for HSP to benefit from its increased emphasis on strategic assets and operational efficiency under Project Fuel. In addition, we expect ongoing, albeit gradually slower, growth in the medication management systems business, a strong pipeline of new products and anticipated launches in 2009, as well as increased international sales. We see unappreciated potential in its biogeneric portfolio, where HSP, with its partner Stada, launched its first biogeneric (a generic EPO with trade name Retacrit) in Europe in the first quarter of 2008, and expects to launch a second biogeneric by 2010.

► Risks to our recommendation and target price include the failure to gain approval or slower-than-anticipated approval for injectable drugs and biogenerics, lower-than-anticipated drug pricing, and a decrease in demand for medication delivery products.

► Our 12-month target price of $48 assumes that HSP will trade at approximately 15X our 2010 EPS estimate of $3.20, a narrower discount to the historical P/E ratio afforded peers, given HSP's improving operating performance and margins.

Qualitative Risk Assessment

| LOW | MEDIUM | HIGH |

Our risk assessment reflects HSP's broad product portfolio, which reduces dependence on any one product category. We see stable demand for hospital products, given our belief that demand for hospital services will remain strong. However, we see minimal growth overall for this industry.

Quantitative Evaluations

S&P Quality Ranking   NR

| D | C | B- | B | B+ | A- | A | A+ |

Relative Strength Rank   STRONG

78

LOWEST = 1   HIGHEST = 99

Revenue/Earnings Data

Revenue (Million $)

	1Q	2Q	3Q	4Q	Year
2009	859.7	956.9	1,008	--	--
2008	888.7	901.6	925.5	913.7	3,630
2007	782.8	869.4	838.0	946.1	3,436
2006	664.3	629.9	646.6	706.5	2,689
2005	662.1	618.5	656.6	646.2	2,627
2004	609.0	667.4	656.1	700.3	2,645

Earnings Per Share ($)

	1Q	2Q	3Q	4Q	Year
2009	1.03	0.16	0.71	E0.64	E2.87
2008	0.41	0.43	0.51	0.65	1.99
2007	-0.19	0.20	0.37	0.47	0.85
2006	0.49	0.34	0.35	0.30	1.48
2005	0.49	0.44	0.37	0.16	1.46
2004	0.43	0.80	0.39	0.31	1.92

Fiscal year ended Dec. 31. Next earnings report expected: Mid February. EPS Estimates based on S&P Operating Earnings; historical GAAP earnings are as reported.

Dividend Data

No cash dividends have been paid.

Please read the Required Disclosures and Analyst Certification on the last page of this report.

The McGraw-Hill Companies

Hospira Inc

STANDARD & POOR'S

Business Summary November 11, 2009

CORPORATE OVERVIEW. Hospira (HSP) was created on May 3, 2004, as a spinoff from Abbott Laboratories. Abbott shareholders received one share of Hospira for every 10 shares of Abbott. HSP provides medication delivery systems and specialty pharmaceuticals to hospitals, clinics and physicians. The legal separation to become a standalone company was completed in the second quarter of 2006.

Hospira has operations in the Americas (77% of 2008 revenues); Europe, the Middle East and Africa (16%); and Asia-Pacific (7.0%). The company operates 16 manufacturing facilities domestically and internationally.

Operating segments include specialty injectable pharmaceuticals -- including specialty injectables and biogenerics (2008 sales of $1,821.7 million, 50% of sales); medication management systems -- principally infusion pumps as well as related software and services ($1,118.50 million, 31%); and other pharma-

ceuticals -- encompassing large volume I.V. solutions, nutritionals and contract manufacturing services ($689.3 million, 19%), with the balance of sales from other devices. Major competitors include APP Pharmaceuticals, Baxter International, Becton, Dickinson, Edwards Lifesciences, Fresenius AG and Patheon.

The specialty injectable pharmaceuticals division provides over 200 generic injectable drugs available in a wide array of dosages and formulations. Therapeutic areas of focus include cardiovascular, anesthesia, anti-infectives, analgesics, and other.

Company Financials Fiscal Year Ended Dec. 31

Per Share Data ($)	2008	2007	2006	2005	2004	2003	2002	2001	2000	1999
Tangible Book Value	1.28	NM	8.03	7.57	5.74	NM	NA	NA	NA	NA
Cash Flow	3.55	2.32	2.45	2.42	2.84	NA	NA	NA	NA	NA
Earnings	1.99	0.85	1.48	1.46	1.92	1.65	NA	NA	NA	NA
S&P Core Earnings	1.89	0.79	1.45	1.35	1.31	1.46	NA	NA	NA	NA
Dividends	Nil	Nil	Nil	Nil	Nil	NA	NA	NA	NA	NA
Payout Ratio	Nil	Nil	Nil	Nil	Nil	NA	NA	NA	NA	NA
Prices:High	44.00	44.64	47.99	45.10	34.86	NA	NA	NA	NA	NA
Prices:Low	23.00	33.60	31.15	28.35	24.02	NA	NA	NA	NA	NA
P/E Ratio:High	22	53	32	31	18	NA	NA	NA	NA	NA
P/E Ratio:Low	12	40	21	19	13	NA	NA	NA	NA	NA

Income Statement Analysis (Million $)	2008	2007	2006	2005	2004	2003	2002	2001	2000	1999
Revenue	3,630	3,436	2,689	2,627	2,645	2,624	2,603	2,514	2,348	NA
Operating Income	836	763	506	493	509	506	NA	NA	NA	NA
Depreciation	252	235	157	156	146	146	134	123	133	NA
Interest Expense	124	145	31.0	28.3	18.8	Nil	NA	NA	NA	NA
Pretax Income	408	188	324	322	412	359	352	390	421	NA
Effective Tax Rate	21.3%	27.2%	26.9%	26.8%	26.7%	27.5%	30.0%	30.0%	29.5%	NA
Net Income	321	137	237	236	302	260	247	273	297	NA
S&P Core Earnings	304	128	233	217	206	231	187	NA	NA	NA

Balance Sheet & Other Financial Data (Million $)	2008	2007	2006	2005	2004	2003	2002	2001	2000	1999
Cash	484	241	322	521	200	Nil	NA	NA	NA	NA
Current Assets	2,149	1,841	1,523	1,561	1,198	1,075	NA	NA	NA	NA
Total Assets	5,074	5,085	2,848	2,789	2,343	2,250	2,154	2,133	NA	NA
Current Liabilities	1,048	794	606	596	536	360	NA	NA	NA	NA
Long Term Debt	1,834	2,243	702	695	699	Nil	NA	NA	NA	NA
Common Equity	1,776	1,745	1,361	1,328	984	1,453	1,334	1,461	NA	NA
Total Capital	3,636	3,980	2,066	2,027	1,687	1,453	1,334	1,461	NA	NA
Capital Expenditures	164	211	235	256	229	197	191	200	199	NA
Cash Flow	573	372	393	392	447	406	NA	NA	NA	NA
Current Ratio	2.1	2.3	2.5	2.6	2.2	3.0	2.4	2.8	NA	NA
% Long Term Debt of Capitalization	50.5	55.6	34.0	34.3	41.4	Nil	Nil	Nil	Nil	NA
% Net Income of Revenue	8.8	4.0	8.8	9.0	11.4	9.9	9.5	10.9	12.7	NA
% Return on Assets	6.3	3.5	8.4	9.2	13.1	11.8	11.5	NA	NA	NA
% Return on Equity	18.2	8.8	17.6	20.4	24.7	18.7	17.7	NA	NA	NA

Data as orig reptd.; bef. results of disc opers/spec. items. Per share data adj. for stk. divs.; EPS diluted. E-Estimated. NA-Not Available. NM-Not Meaningful. NR-Not Ranked. UR-Under Review.

Office: 275 North Field Drive, Lake Forest, IL 60045.
Telephone: 847-937-6100.
Chrmn & CEO: C.B. Begley
COO: T.C. Kearney

SVP & CFO: T.E. Werner
SVP & CSO: S. Ramachandra
SVP, Secy & General Counsel: B.J. Smith
Investor Contact: L. McHugh (224-212-2363)

Board Members: I. W. Bailey, II, C. B. Begley, B. L. Bowles, C. Curran, R. W. Hale, R. A. Matricaria, J. J. Sokolov, J. C. Staley, H. Von Prondzynski, M. F. Wheeler

Founded: 2003
Domicile: Delaware
Employees: 14,500

Host Hotels & Resorts Inc

STANDARD &POOR'S

S&P Recommendation **SELL** ★★☆☆☆	Price $10.06 (as of Nov 27, 2009)	12-Mo. Target Price $9.00	Investment Style Large-Cap Value

GICS Sector Financials
Sub-Industry Specialized REITS

Summary This real estate investment trust owns a portfolio of luxury and upper-upscale full-service hotels.

Key Stock Statistics (Source S&P, Vickers, company reports)

52-Wk Range	$12.20– 3.08	S&P FFO/Sh. 2009E	0.75	Market Capitalization(B)	$6.214	Beta	2.43
Trailing 12-Month FFO/Share	NA	S&P FFO/Sh. 2010E	0.95	Yield (%)	NA	S&P 3-Yr. FFO/Sh. Proj. CAGR(%)	-2
Trailing 12-Month P/FFO	NA	P/FFO on S&P FFO/Sh. 2009E	13.4	Dividend Rate/Share	NA	S&P Credit Rating	BB-
$10K Invested 5 Yrs Ago	$7,772	Common Shares Outstg. (M)	617.7	Institutional Ownership (%)	89		

Price Performance

30-Week Mov. Avg. · · · 10-Week Mov. Avg. - - ► Volume Above Avg. STARS
12-Mo. Target Price — Relative Strength — ▲ Up ▼ Down ► No Change Below Avg.

Options: ASE, CBOE, P, Ph

Analysis prepared by **Royal F. Shepard, CFA** on October 15, 2009, when the stock traded at **$11.76**.

Highlights

► We think harsh economic conditions will continue to present challenges for hotel owners into early 2010. Industry statistics, in addition to HST's results thus far in 2009, indicate that operating metrics continue to deteriorate. We believe both leisure and business travelers are reducing the number and length of hotel stays, and thereby putting significant pressure on average room rates.

► In the third quarter, HST's comparable revenue per available room (RevPAR) fell nearly 21.3%, reflecting a 460 basis point (bps) decrease in occupancy rates, and a significant drop in demand for resort properties. Reflecting slack demand, average daily room rates fell 14.8%. We expect somewhat smaller declines through the first the first half of 2010, before a recovery in the second half as economic trends improve. For the full year, we think RevPAR will increase modestly. Operating margins should also benefit from lower utility costs in late 2009 and in 2010, partially offset by increasing personnel and insurance costs.

► Our 2009 FFO estimate of $0.75 a share excludes non-cash impairment and interest charges, including $0.25 in the first nine months.

Investment Rationale/Risk

► We expect overall industry growth rates to remain negative through the first half of 2010, and we believe HST will see negative growth for several of its key fundamentals. Despite current market turmoil, we believe HST will be well positioned to eventually increase profits given its high quality portfolio and strong capital raising efforts, including $130 million in new equity raised during the third quarter. We believe HST has the liquidity to meet its $480 million of debt obligations coming due through the end of 2010. Nevertheless, we believe HST's performance will be hindered by a highly uncertain economic climate. HST has declared a fourth quarter dividend of $0.25 a share, with only $0.03 in cash.

► Risks to our recommendation and target price include a faster than expected recovery in demand for business and leisure travel in conjunction with an overall economic turnaround.

► Our 12-month target price of $9.00 is based on a multiple of 9.5X our 2010 FFO estimate of $0.95 a share, close to the average of the hotel REIT sector.

Qualitative Risk Assessment

LOW	MEDIUM	HIGH

Our risk assessment reflects the highly cyclical nature of the lodging industry and the volatility that this may create in earnings and dividends. We think HST's large and well diversified portfolio provides a partial offset.

Quantitative Evaluations

S&P Quality Ranking B-

D	C	B-	B	B+	A-	A	A+

Relative Strength Rank MODERATE

34

LOWEST = 1   HIGHEST = 99

Revenue/FFO Data

Revenue (Million $)

	1Q	2Q	3Q	4Q	Year
2009	882.0	1,064	912.0	--	--
2008	1,058	1,417	1,168	1,634	5,278
2007	1,031	1,385	1,201	1,809	5,437
2006	840.0	1,195	1,119	1,734	4,888
2005	802.0	976.0	831.0	1,272	3,881
2004	777.0	898.0	784.0	1,181	3,640

FFO Per Share ($)

2009	0.10	0.12	E0.11	E0.27	E0.75
2008	0.33	0.56	0.31	0.53	1.74
2007	0.30	0.48	0.38	0.75	1.91
2006	0.27	0.39	0.28	0.44	1.53
2005	0.19	0.22	0.19	0.35	1.15
2004	0.13	0.02	0.06	0.35	0.77

Fiscal year ended Dec. 31. Next earnings report expected: Mid February. FFO Estimates based on S&P Funds From Operations Est..

Dividend Data (Dates: mm/dd Payment Date: mm/dd/yy)

Amount ($)	Date Decl.	Ex-Div. Date	Stk. of Record	Payment Date
0.050	12/16	12/29	12/31	01/15/09
0.250	09/14	11/04	11/06	12/18/09
Omitted	02/18	--	--	02/18/09

Dividends have been paid since 2005. Source: Company reports.

Please read the Required Disclosures and Analyst Certification on the last page of this report.

The McGraw-Hill Companies

Host Hotels & Resorts Inc

**STANDARD
&POOR'S**

Business Summary October 15, 2009

CORPORATE OVERVIEW. Host Hotels & Resorts operates as a self-managed and self-administered real estate investment trust (REIT). At December 31, 2008, HST owned a portfolio consisting of 116 luxury and upper-upscale hotels containing approximately 63,000 rooms. HST's hotels operate under a number of well known brands, including Marriott, Ritz-Carlton, Hyatt, Sheraton, Swissotel, Four Seasons, Hilton, Fairmont and Westin. Seventy-five of the company's properties were operated under the Marriott brand name. HST also holds a minority interest in a joint venture that owns 11 hotels in Europe with approximately 3,500 rooms. HST is geographically diversified, with hotels in most of the major metropolitan areas. The company's locations primarily include central business districts of major cities, airport areas, and resort/conference destinations.

HST's hotel revenue has traditionally experienced moderate seasonality, with a greater percentage of revenue falling in the second and fourth quarters. In addition, the fourth quarter reflects 16 or 17 weeks of results, versus 12 weeks in each of the first three fiscal quarters.

MARKET PROFILE. We believe the lodging industry's strong recovery following the post-September 11, 2001, downturn is clearly over. In the early part of 2004, the industry began to see positive trends in the three key metrics for lodging companies: occupancy, average daily rate (ADR), and revenue per available room (RevPAR). Along with strong demand for both business and leisure travel, lodging companies benefited from a limited new supply of rooms. A number of factors kept the supply pipeline slow, including, in our view, the depressed demand environment in 2002 and 2003, increasing construction costs, difficulty obtaining construction financing, and the demand for alternative real estate such as condo conversions.

According to industry data provider Smith Travel Research, the U.S. lodging industry experienced a 1.9% RevPAR decline in 2008, compared to growth of 5.7% in 2007, 7.5% in 2006, 8.4% in 2005, and 7.8% in 2004. The ADR grew 2.4% in 2008, versus 6.2% growth in 2007, while occupancy declined to 60.4% in 2008, from 63.1% in 2007. In 2008, we believe overall room supply increased 3%-3.5% based on a room count of 4.7 million. In 2009, Smith Travel projects a 3.9% decrease in occupancy, a 2% decline in ADR, and a 5.9% reduction in RevPAR.

Company Financials Fiscal Year Ended Dec. 31

Per Share Data ($)	2008	2007	2006	2005	2004	2003	2002	2001	2000	1999
Tangible Book Value	10.32	10.22	9.83	NM	5.64	5.57	4.87	4.77	5.50	5.82
Earnings	0.71	1.01	0.60	0.30	-0.31	-0.92	-0.24	0.09	0.64	0.87
S&P Core Earnings	0.70	0.92	0.57	0.27	-0.31	-0.95	-0.25	0.09	NA	NA
Dividends	0.65	0.80	0.71	0.41	0.10	Nil	Nil	0.78	0.86	0.63
Payout Ratio	92%	79%	118%	137%	NM	Nil	Nil	NM	106%	72%
Prices:High	18.81	28.98	25.79	19.24	17.40	12.33	12.25	13.95	12.93	14.81
Prices:Low	4.77	16.55	18.77	15.46	11.16	6.07	7.50	6.22	8.00	7.38
P/E Ratio:High	26	29	43	64	NM	NM	NM	NM	20	17
P/E Ratio:Low	7	16	31	52	NM	NM	NM	NM	13	8

Income Statement Analysis (Million $)										
Rental Income	NA	120	119	111	106	100	101	126	1,390	1,295
Mortgage Income	Nil	Nil	Nil	Nil	Nil	Nil	Nil	Nil	Nil	Nil
Total Income	5,278	5,426	4,888	3,881	3,640	3,448	3,680	3,754	1,473	1,295
General Expenses	3,955	4,007	3,665	2,936	2,812	2,765	2,823	2,821	337	318
Interest Expense	341	422	450	443	483	523	498	492	465	467
Provision for Losses	Nil	Nil	Nil	Nil	Nil	Nil	Nil	Nil	Nil	Nil
Depreciation	582	517	459	368	354	367	372	378	331	289
Net Income	402	550	309	138	-64.0	-225	-29.0	53.0	159	196
S&P Core Earnings	386	490	276	98.0	-106	-267	-65.0	20.0	NA	NA

Balance Sheet & Other Financial Data (Million $)										
Cash	508	553	524	225	416	838	627	608	566	326
Total Assets	11,951	11,812	11,808	8,245	8,421	8,592	8,316	8,338	8,396	8,202
Real Estate Investment	15,038	14,288	13,897	10,382	9,924	9,511	9,193	8,828	8,599	8,329
Loss Reserve	Nil	Nil	Nil	Nil	Nil	Nil	Nil	Nil	Nil	Nil
Net Investment	10,739	10,588	10,584	7,434	7,274	7,085	7,031	6,999	7,110	49.0
Short Term Debt	410	261	268	NA	NA	NA	NA	148	54.0	180
Capitalization:Debt	5,542	5,364	5,610	5,370	5,523	3,976	5,638	5,929	5,743	5,386
Capitalization:Equity	5,420	5,344	5,125	2,176	2,058	1,797	1,271	1,270	1,225	1,309
Capitalization:Total	11,239	11,021	11,045	7,932	8,126	6,112	7,471	7,748	7,649	7,448
% Earnings & Depreciation/Assets	8.3	9.0	7.6	6.0	3.4	1.7	4.1	5.2	5.9	5.9
Price Times Book Value:High	1.8	2.8	2.6	NM	3.1	2.2	2.5	2.9	2.4	2.5
Price Times Book Value:Low	0.5	1.6	1.9	NM	2.0	1.1	1.5	1.3	1.5	1.3

Data as orig reptd.; bef. results of disc opers/spec. items. Per share data adj. for stk. divs.; EPS diluted. E-Estimated. NA-Not Available. NM-Not Meaningful. NR-Not Ranked. UR-Under Review.

Office: 6903 Rockledge Drive, Bethesda, MD 20817.
Telephone: 240-744-5121.
Website: http://www.hosthotels.com
Chrmn: R.E. Marriott

Pres & CEO: W.E. Walter
EVP, CFO & Treas: L.K. Harvey
EVP, Secy & General Counsel: E.A. Abdoo
Investor Contact: G.J. Larson (240-744-5120)

Board Members: R. M. Baylis, W. W. Brittain, Jr., T. C. Golden, A. M. Korologos, R. E. Marriott, J. B. Morse, Jr., G. H. Smith, W. E. Walter

Founded: 1927
Domicile: Maryland
Employees: 215

Block (H&R) Inc.

STANDARD &POOR'S

S&P Recommendation HOLD ★ ★ ★ ☆ ☆	Price $20.39 (as of Nov 27, 2009)	12-Mo. Target Price $22.00	Investment Style Large-Cap Blend

GICS Sector Consumer Discretionary
Sub-Industry Specialized Consumer Services

Summary This diversified company provides a wide range of financial products and services, including income tax preparation, business, consulting, and retail banking services.

Key Stock Statistics (Source S&P, Vickers, company reports)

52-Wk Range	$23.27– 13.73	S&P Oper. EPS 2010**E**	1.59	Market Capitalization(B)	$6.837	Beta		0.50
Trailing 12-Month EPS	$1.44	S&P Oper. EPS 2011**E**	1.70	Yield (%)	2.94	S&P 3-Yr. Proj. EPS CAGR(%)		6
Trailing 12-Month P/E	14.2	P/E on S&P Oper. EPS 2010**E**	12.8	Dividend Rate/Share	$0.60	S&P Credit Rating		BBB
$10K Invested 5 Yrs Ago	$9,893	Common Shares Outstg. (M)	335.3	Institutional Ownership (%)	89			

Price Performance

30-Week Mov. Avg. · · · · 10-Week Mov. Avg. - - **GAAP Earnings vs. Previous Year** Volume Above Avg. STARS
12-Mo. Target Price — Relative Strength — ▲ Up ▼ Down ▶ No Change Below Avg. ★

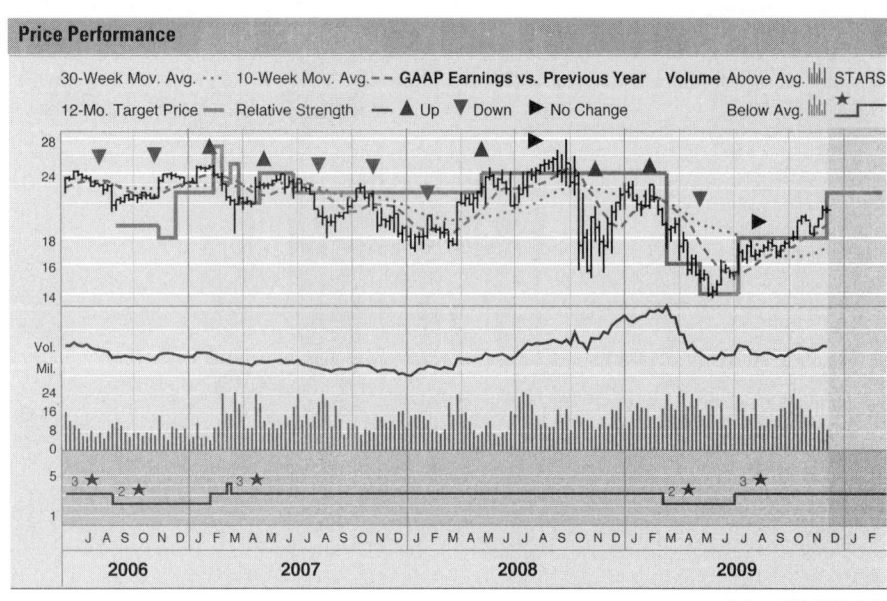

Options: ASE, CBOE, P, Ph

Qualitative Risk Assessment

LOW	MEDIUM	HIGH

Despite HRB's leading tax preparer position in its market, our risk assessment reflects uncertainty surrounding a pending IRS ruling regarding a case on refund anticipation loan products. We are also concerned about internal accounting control issues, which in 2006 caused HRB to restate almost three years of results.

Quantitative Evaluations

S&P Quality Ranking B+

D	C	B-	B	B+	A-	A	A+

Relative Strength Rank STRONG

84

LOWEST = 1   HIGHEST = 99

Revenue/Earnings Data

Revenue (Million $)

	1Q	2Q	3Q	4Q	Year
2010	275.5	--	--	--	--
2009	271.9	351.5	993.5	2,467	4,084
2008	381.2	434.8	972.6	2,615	4,404
2007	342.8	396.1	931.2	2,351	4,021
2006	615.0	605.0	1,157	2,496	4,873
2005	482.7	539.3	1,032	2,357	4,420

Earnings Per Share ($)

2010	-0.39	E-0.41	E0.11	E2.28	E1.59
2009	-0.39	-0.40	0.20	2.09	1.53
2008	-0.39	-0.42	0.03	2.11	1.39
2007	-0.36	-0.38	0.07	1.81	1.15
2006	-0.08	-0.25	0.04	1.77	1.47
2005	-0.13	-0.16	0.28	1.83	1.88

Fiscal year ended Apr. 30. Next earnings report expected: Early December. EPS Estimates based on S&P Operating Earnings; historical GAAP earnings are as reported.

Highlights

► The 12-month target price for HRB has recently been changed to $22.00 from $18.00. The Highlights section of this Stock Report will be updated accordingly.

Investment Rationale/Risk

► The Investment Rationale/Risk section of this Stock Report will be updated shortly. For the latest News story on HRB from MarketScope, see below.

► 11/25/09 12:25 pm ET ... S&P MAINTAINS HOLD OPINION ON SHARES OF H&R BLOCK (HRB 20.59***): Ahead of HRB's Oct-Q earnings report on 12/8, we expect HRB to have focused on its core tax-preparation business. But given still relatively weak consumer spending patterns, we see risks from e-filings and competition from independent firms. For FY 10 (Apr), we now see a 2.2% total revenue decline, versus our previous 3% growth forecast. We widen our Oct-Q loss estimate a penny to $0.41. On adjustments, we also reduce our FY 10 EPS to $1.59 from $1.65. Separately, we are raising our 12-month target price to $22 from $18 on updated peer EBITDA comparisons. /E.Kolb

Dividend Data (Dates: mm/dd Payment Date: mm/dd/yy)

Amount ($)	Date Decl.	Ex-Div. Date	Stk. of Record	Payment Date
0.150	11/25	12/10	12/12	01/02/09
0.150	02/23	03/09	03/11	04/01/09
0.150	05/07	06/08	06/10	07/01/09
0.150	07/28	09/08	09/10	10/01/09

Dividends have been paid since 1962. Source: Company reports.

Block (H&R) Inc.

STANDARD
&POOR'S

Business Summary September 15, 2009

CORPORATE OVERVIEW. HRB provides various financial products and services, which the company believes are complementary. In FY 09 (Apr.), Tax Services accounted for 74.3% of revenues and 106.5% of profits, Business Services 21.9% and 11.4%, and Consumer Financial Services 3.5% and -1.7%; the corporate division accounted for 0.3% and -16.2%.

The Tax Services division served about 24 million clients in FY 09 vs. 24.6 million clients in FY 08 and 24 million in FY 07. HRB's revenues related directly to the RAL program totaled $141 million in FY 09 or 3.5% of consolidated revenues. There were 12,923 company-owned and franchised U.S. H&R Block offices at April 30, 2009. In addition, HRB offers tax preparation services at hundreds of H&R Block Premium offices for more complex returns. International operations are located primarily in Australia, and Canada, with combined company owned and franchise offices numbering 1,571 at April 30, 2009. Tax Services also offers online tax preparation, tax preparation software, and guarantee programs.

HRB also provides wealth management, accounting, tax and consulting services, and tax, and capital market services.

MARKET PROFILE. HRB's largest segment, Tax Services, competes with other tax service chains, professional CPA/accounting firms, "mom and pop" local tax service providers and do-it-yourselfers DIYers). In addition, HRB and some other online tax service product providers participate in the Free Filing Alliance, which offers free online federal return preparation with no income limitations. We believe HRB competes successfully by offering many services at what customers believe is an acceptable price-to-value relationship. These services include: the convenience of the largest retail tax office network in the U.S.; a "Peace of Mind" Guarantee" (POM) whereby HRB commits to representing its clients if they are audited by the IRS, and assuming the cost of additional taxes resulting from errors attributable to an HRB tax professional; "Refund Anticipation Loans" and "Refund Anticipation Checks" and a service whereby DIYers using HRB's online service can have an HRB tax professional check their returns and receive the POM guarantee. By offering increased value, HRB has been able to raise its rates 5%-7% annually since 2002.

Company Financials Fiscal Year Ended Apr. 30

Per Share Data ($)	2009	2008	2007	2006	2005	2004	2003	2002	2001	2000
Tangible Book Value	0.51	NM	0.74	1.90	1.64	1.41	1.69	0.73	0.67	0.32
Cash Flow	1.90	1.83	1.62	2.05	2.43	2.42	2.02	1.57	2.61	1.01
Earnings	1.53	1.39	1.15	1.47	1.88	1.95	1.58	1.16	0.76	0.64
S&P Core Earnings	1.53	1.40	1.15	1.53	1.76	1.85	1.44	1.07	0.73	NA
Dividends	0.56	0.53	0.49	0.54	0.39	0.39	0.35	0.29	0.27	0.26
Payout Ratio	37%	38%	42%	37%	21%	20%	22%	25%	35%	40%
Calendar Year	2008	2007	2006	2005	2004	2003	2002	2001	2000	1999
Prices:High	27.97	24.95	25.75	30.00	30.50	27.89	26.75	23.19	12.38	14.88
Prices:Low	15.00	17.57	19.80	22.99	22.08	17.64	14.50	9.16	6.73	9.50
P/E Ratio:High	18	18	22	20	16	14	17	20	16	23
P/E Ratio:Low	10	13	17	16	12	9	9	8	9	15

Income Statement Analysis (Million $)										
Revenue	4,084	4,404	4,021	4,873	4,420	4,206	3,780	3,318	3,002	2,452
Operating Income	963	871	810	128	215	1,411	240	987	913	704
Depreciation	122	146	150	192	184	172	162	155	206	147
Interest Expense	1.65	243	46.9	49.1	62.4	84.6	92.6	116	243	154
Pretax Income	839	745	636	827	1,018	1,164	987	717	473	412
Effective Tax Rate	38.9%	39.0%	41.1%	40.7%	37.5%	39.5%	41.2%	39.4%	41.5%	38.9%
Net Income	513	454	374	490	636	704	580	434	277	252
S&P Core Earnings	514	458	374	509	593	665	527	400	268	NA

Balance Sheet & Other Financial Data (Million $)										
Cash	1,655	729	1,254	1,088	1,617	1,617	1,337	617	326	442
Current Assets	2,571	2,382	3,454	2,824	3,071	2,961	2,747	2,245	2,271	3,864
Total Assets	5,360	5,623	7,499	5,989	5,539	5,380	4,604	4,231	4,122	5,699
Current Liabilities	2,398	3,096	5,176	2,893	2,209	2,472	1,897	1,880	1,988	3,520
Long Term Debt	1,107	1,032	520	418	923	546	822	868	871	872
Common Equity	1,406	988	1,414	2,148	1,976	1,897	1,664	1,369	1,174	1,219
Total Capital	2,546	2,131	1,934	2,565	2,899	2,443	2,486	2,238	2,045	2,091
Capital Expenditures	97.9	106	161	251	209	128	151	112	90.0	113
Cash Flow	635	600	525	682	820	876	742	590	482	399
Current Ratio	1.1	0.8	0.7	1.0	1.4	1.2	1.4	1.2	1.1	1.1
% Long Term Debt of Capitalization	43.5	48.4	26.9	16.3	31.8	22.3	33.1	38.8	42.6	41.7
% Net Income of Revenue	12.6	10.3	9.3	12.4	14.3	16.7	21.4	13.1	9.2	10.3
% Return on Assets	9.3	6.9	5.6	8.5	11.8	13.9	13.1	10.4	5.6	6.6
% Return on Equity	42.9	37.8	21.0	23.9	33.5	39.6	38.2	34.2	23.1	22.1

Data as orig reptd.; bef. results of disc opers/spec. items. Per share data adj. for stk. divs.; EPS diluted. E-Estimated. NA-Not Available. NM-Not Meaningful. NR-Not Ranked. UR-Under Review.

Office: 1 H&R Block Way, Kansas City, MO 64105.
Telephone: 816-854-3000.
Email: investorrelations@hrblock.com
Website: http://www.hrblock.com

Chrmn: R.C. Breeden
Pres: D. Nelson
Pres & CEO: R.P. Smyth
SVP, CFO & Treas: B.S. Shulman

SVP, Secy & General Counsel: B.J. Woram
Investor Contact: S. Dudley (816-854-4505)
Board Members: A. Bennett, T. M. Bloch, R. C. Breeden, R. A. Gerard, L. J. Lauer, D. B. Lewis, T. D. Seip, L. E. Shaw, Jr., R. P. Smyth, C. Wood

Founded: 1946
Domicile: Missouri
Employees: 133,700

Hudson City Bancorp Inc

STANDARD &POOR'S

S&P Recommendation	BUY ★★★★☆	Price $12.95 (as of Nov 27, 2009)	12-Mo. Target Price $16.00	Investment Style Large-Cap Blend

GICS Sector Financials
Sub-Industry Thrifts & Mortgage Finance

Summary Hudson City Bancorp, through Hudson City Savings Bank, operates over 100 branches in the New York metropolitan area. It caters to high median household income counties and focuses on jumbo mortgage loan funding, largely through time deposits.

Key Stock Statistics (Source S&P, Vickers, company reports)

52-Wk Range	$16.50–7.46	S&P Oper. EPS 2009E	1.07	Market Capitalization(B)	$6.348	Beta	0.64
Trailing 12-Month EPS	$1.05	S&P Oper. EPS 2010E	1.17	Yield (%)	4.63	S&P 3-Yr. Proj. EPS CAGR(%)	14
Trailing 12-Month P/E	12.3	P/E on S&P Oper. EPS 2009E	12.1	Dividend Rate/Share	$0.60	S&P Credit Rating	NA
$10K Invested 5 Yrs Ago	$12,106	Common Shares Outstg. (M)	490.2	Institutional Ownership (%)	73		

Price Performance

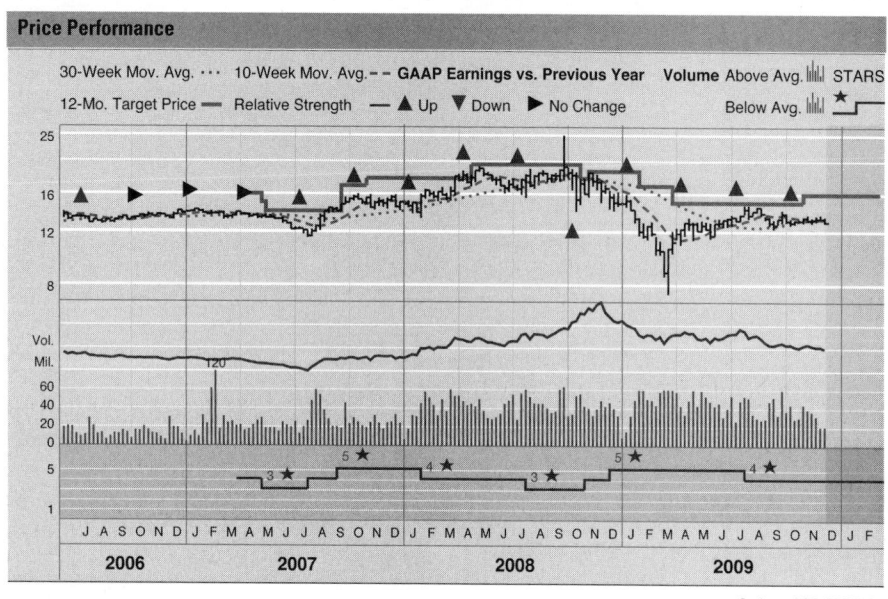

30-Week Mov. Avg. · · · 10-Week Mov. Avg. – – GAAP Earnings vs. Previous Year   Volume Above Avg. STARS
12-Mo. Target Price — Relative Strength   ▲ Up ▼ Down ► No Change   Below Avg. ★

Options: ASE, CBOE, Ph

Analysis prepared by **Kevin Cole, CFA** on October 22, 2009, when the stock traded at **$ 13.11**.

Highlights

► We anticipate that continued loan growth will result in revenues increasing 35% in 2009 and 6.8% in 2010, versus 45% in 2008. We see loan growth moderating in 2010 due to a lack of qualified borrowers and increasing competition in the jumbo loan market. We expect net interest margin to expand to 2.25% and 2.31% in 2009 and 2010, respectively, from 1.94% in 2008. Our forecasts assume that HCBK will continue to lower its reliance on higher cost borrowing and garner deposits at attractive yields.

► We look for HCBK's efficiency ratio to remain among the best in the industry, averaging a little more than 20%. However, we look for provisions to increase sharply in 2009, before leveling in 2010, as HCBK builds its reserve, which grew to 37% of nonperformers at September 30, 2009, from only 29% at June 30, 2009. We see chargeoffs rising through 2010, largely due to the more lengthy default and foreclosure process associated with lower loan-to-value mortgages.

► Assuming an effective tax rate of 39.5%, we see EPS of $1.07 in 2009 and $1.17 in 2010, up from 2008's $0.90.

Investment Rationale/Risk

► We believe that HCBK will benefit from relatively high jumbo mortgage spreads, as the effects of actions by the Federal Reserve to buy large quantities of mortgage-backed securities remain largely confined to the conforming market. However, we believe that HCBK is currently under-reserved, and will need to increase provisions through the first quarter of 2010. With a tangible equity to tangible assets ratio of 8.70% as of September 30, 2009, we believe HCBK has adequate capital to continue pursuing its risk-averse growth strategy. We think HCBK's avoidance of subprime, option-ARM and high-LTV loans will enable it to weather the current housing price decline better than most.

► Risks to our opinion and target price include greater-than-expected job losses in the New York City metropolitan area, competition significantly increasing in the jumbo loan market, and a severe deterioration in prime loans.

► Our 12-month target price of $16 equates to roughly 1.5X HCBK's tangible book value of $10.43 a share. This multiple is above peers, but warranted, we believe, by what we see as HCBK's strong credit quality.

Qualitative Risk Assessment

LOW	MEDIUM	HIGH

Our risk assessment reflects our view of the solid credit quality of HCBK's loan portfolio and its history of profitability. While the company operates in a highly competitive and fragmented industry, companies in the industry tend to produce relatively stable financial results.

Quantitative Evaluations

S&P Quality Ranking   A

D	C	B-	B	B+	A-	A	A+

Relative Strength Rank   MODERATE

38

LOWEST = 1   HIGHEST = 99

Revenue/Earnings Data

Revenue (Million $)

	1Q	2Q	3Q	4Q	Year
2009	725.6	754.4	746.7	--	--
2008	615.5	648.8	683.5	714.0	2,662
2007	481.2	513.3	550.3	590.0	2,135
2006	361.0	385.6	423.7	449.0	1,621
2005	257.5	280.5	315.2	333.8	1,187
2004	216.7	224.7	239.2	251.1	931.6

Earnings Per Share ($)

2009	0.26	0.26	0.28	E0.28	E1.07
2008	0.18	0.22	0.25	0.25	0.90
2007	0.13	0.14	0.15	0.16	0.58
2006	0.13	0.13	0.13	0.13	0.53
2005	0.11	0.11	0.13	0.13	0.48
2004	0.09	0.10	0.11	0.11	0.40

Fiscal year ended Dec. 31. Next earnings report expected: Late January. EPS Estimates based on S&P Operating Earnings; historical GAAP earnings are as reported.

Dividend Data (Dates: mm/dd Payment Date: mm/dd/yy)

Amount ($)	Date Decl.	Ex-Div. Date	Stk. of Record	Payment Date
0.140	01/21	02/05	02/09	02/28/09
0.150	04/21	05/06	05/08	05/30/09
0.150	07/21	08/05	08/07	08/29/09
0.150	10/21	11/04	11/06	11/27/09

Dividends have been paid since 1999. Source: Company reports.

Please read the Required Disclosures and Analyst Certification on the last page of this report.

The McGraw-Hill Companies

Hudson City Bancorp Inc

STANDARD &POOR'S

Business Summary October 22, 2009

CORPORATE OVERVIEW. New Jersey-based Hudson City Bancorp, Inc. (HCBK), a community- and consumer-oriented retail savings bank holding company, offers traditional deposit products, residential real estate mortgage loans and consumer loans. In addition, HCBK purchases mortgages, mortgage-backed securities, securities issued by the U.S. government and government-sponsored agencies and other investments permitted by applicable laws and regulations. HCBK is the holding company of its only subsidiary, Hudson City Savings Bank. The company's revenues are derived principally from interest on mortgage loans & mortgage-backed securities and interest & dividends on investment securities. The bank's primary sources of funds are customer deposits, borrowings, scheduled amortization and prepayments of mortgage loans and mortgage-backed securities, maturities and calls of investment securities and funds provided by operations.

PRIMARY BUSINESS DYNAMICS. As of December 31, 2008, HCBK had total loans of $29.42 billion. Hudson's loan portfolio primarily consists of one-to-four family residential first mortgage loans. HCBK's first mortgage loans totaled $29.03 billion as of December 31, 2008, representing 98.7% of the total loan portfolio. Of the first mortgage loans outstanding at that date, fixed-rate mort-

gage loans represented 75.7%, while adjustable-rate mortgage loans accounted for the remaining 24.3%. HCBK's loan portfolio also includes multi-family and commercial mortgage loans, construction loans and consumer and other loans, which primarily consist of fixed-rate second mortgage loans and home equity credit lines. The company does not originate or purchase sub-prime loans, negative amortization loans or option ARM loans.

CORPORATE STRATEGY. HCBK seeks to continue its growth by focusing on the origination and purchase of mortgage loans, while purchasing mortgage-backed securities and investment securities as a supplement. It intends to fund its growth with customer deposits and borrowed funds. The company aims to increase customer deposits by continuing to offer desirable products at competitive rates and by opening new branch offices. HCBK continues to focus on high median household income counties, in line with its jumbo mortgage loan and consumer deposit business model.

Company Financials Fiscal Year Ended Dec. 31

Per Share Data ($)	2008	2007	2006	2005	2004	2003	2002	2001	2000	1999
Tangible Book Value	9.77	9.22	8.54	8.83	2.35	2.18	2.14	2.03	2.04	NA
Earnings	0.90	0.58	0.53	0.48	0.40	0.35	0.32	0.21	0.16	NA
S&P Core Earnings	0.89	0.58	0.53	0.47	0.39	0.34	0.31	0.20	NA	NA
Dividends	0.60	0.33	0.30	0.27	0.22	0.16	0.11	0.07	0.03	NA
Payout Ratio	67%	57%	57%	56%	54%	47%	34%	35%	21%	NA
Prices:High	25.05	16.08	14.09	12.61	12.79	12.00	6.71	4.14	3.16	NA
Prices:Low	13.28	11.45	11.90	10.09	9.79	5.79	4.04	2.72	1.97	NA
P/E Ratio:High	28	28	27	26	32	35	21	20	19	NA
P/E Ratio:Low	15	20	22	21	24	17	13	13	12	NA
Income Statement Analysis (Million $)										
Net Interest Income	942	647	613	562	485	401	388	287	254	NA
Loan Loss Provision	19.5	4.80	Nil	0.07	0.79	0.90	1.50	1.88	2.13	NA
Non Interest Income	8.50	7.27	6.29	5.27	16.6	5.34	5.95	4.69	4.54	NA
Non Interest Expenses	198	168	159	128	118	103	93.5	81.8	79.0	NA
Pretax Income	733	482	461	442	382	327	301	208	177	NA
Effective Tax Rate	39.2%	38.6%	37.3%	37.6%	37.4%	36.6%	36.3%	35.3%	35.3%	NA
Net Income	446	296	289	276	239	207	192	135	115	NA
% Net Interest Margin	1.96	1.64	1.96	2.35	3.66	2.65	3.10	2.87	2.90	2.98
S&P Core Earnings	440	294	287	272	235	204	186	128	NA	NA
Balance Sheet & Other Financial Data (Million $)										
Total Assets	54,163	44,424	35,507	28,075	20,146	17,033	14,145	11,427	9,380	NA
Loans	29,441	24,198	19,069	15,037	11,328	8,766	6,932	5,932	4,841	NA
Deposits	18,464	15,153	13,416	11,383	11,477	10,454	9,139	7,913	6,604	NA
Capitalization:Debt	30,225	24,141	16,966	11,350	7,150	5,150	3,600	2,150	650	NA
Capitalization:Equity	4,949	4,611	4,930	5,201	1,403	1,329	1,316	1,289	1,465	NA
Capitalization:Total	35,174	28,752	21,896	16,551	8,553	6,479	4,916	3,439	2,115	NA
% Return on Assets	0.9	0.7	0.9	1.1	1.3	1.3	1.5	1.3	1.3	NA
% Return on Equity	9.3	6.2	5.7	8.4	17.5	15.7	14.7	9.8	7.8	NA
% Loan Loss Reserve	0.2	0.1	0.2	0.2	0.2	0.2	0.4	0.4	0.5	NA
% Risk Based Capital	21520.0	24.8	31.0	41.3	17.5	7.5	26.8	32.0	43.0	NA
Price Times Book Value:High	NA	1.1	1.6	1.4	5.4	5.5	3.1	2.0	1.5	NA
Price Times Book Value:Low	NA	0.8	1.4	1.1	4.2	2.7	1.9	1.3	0.9	NA

Data as orig reptd.; bef. results of disc opers/spec. items. Per share data adj. for stk. divs.; EPS diluted. E-Estimated. NA-Not Available. NM-Not Meaningful. NR-Not Ranked. UR-Under Review.

Office: 80 W Century Rd, Paramus, NJ, USA 07652-1405.
Telephone: 201-967-1900.
Website: http://www.hcbk.com
Chrmn, Pres & CEO: R.E. Hermance, Jr.

COO & EVP: D.J. Salamone
EVP & CFO: J.C. Kranz
Investor Contact: S. Munhall (201-967-8290)

Board Members: M. W. Azzara, W. G. Bardel, S. A. Belair, V. H. Bruni, W. J. Cosgrove, R. E. Hermance, Jr., D. O. Quest, D. J. Salamone, J. G. Sponholz

Founded: 1868
Domicile: Delaware
Employees: 1,496

Humana Inc.

STANDARD &POOR'S

S&P Recommendation BUY ★★★★☆	Price $41.73 (as of Nov 27, 2009)	12-Mo. Target Price $45.00	Investment Style Large-Cap Growth

GICS Sector Health Care
Sub-Industry Managed Health Care

Summary This company provides a broad range of managed health care services to more than 10.3 million individuals.

Key Stock Statistics (Source S&P, Vickers, company reports)

52-Wk Range	$46.01– 18.57	S&P Oper. EPS 2009**E**	6.15	Market Capitalization(B)	$7.087	Beta	1.31
Trailing 12-Month EPS	$5.71	S&P Oper. EPS 2010**E**	5.35	Yield (%)	Nil	S&P 3-Yr. Proj. EPS CAGR(%)	9
Trailing 12-Month P/E	7.3	P/E on S&P Oper. EPS 2009**E**	6.8	Dividend Rate/Share	Nil	S&P Credit Rating	BBB-
$10K Invested 5 Yrs Ago	$17,251	Common Shares Outstg. (M)	169.8	Institutional Ownership (%)	89		

Price Performance

30-Week Mov. Avg. ··· 10-Week Mov. Avg. — **GAAP Earnings vs. Previous Year** Volume Above Avg. STARS
12-Mo. Target Price — Relative Strength — ▲ Up ▼ Down ▶ No Change Below Avg. ★

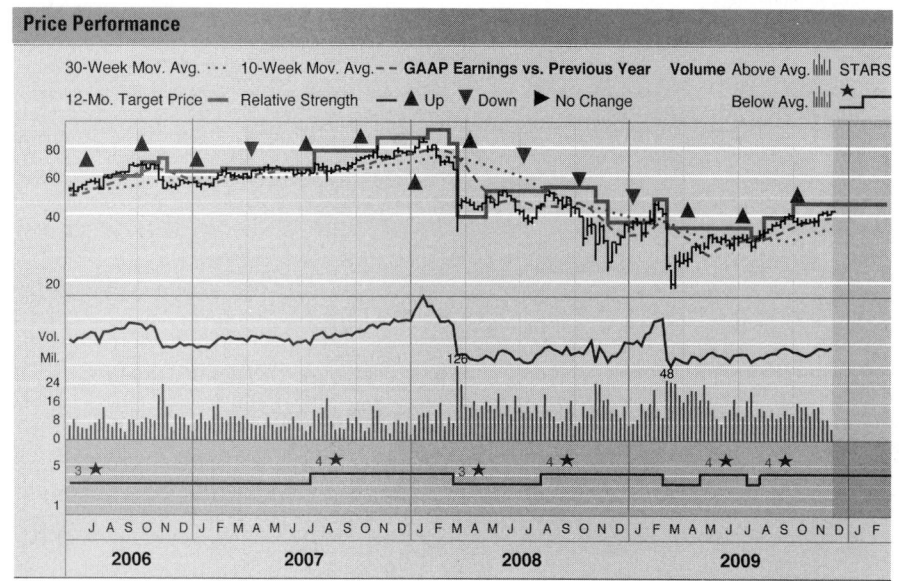

Options: ASE, CBOE, Ph

Analysis prepared by **Phillip M. Seligman** on November 12, 2009, when the stock traded at **$ 41.71**.

Qualitative Risk Assessment

LOW	MEDIUM	HIGH

Our risk assessment reflects HUM's heavy reliance on Medicare Advantage (MA) for growth. We also believe that intense competition will continue to limit commercial enrollment growth.

Quantitative Evaluations

S&P Quality Ranking B+

D	C	B-	B	B+	A-	A	A+

Relative Strength Rank STRONG

86

LOWEST = 1   HIGHEST = 99

Revenue/Earnings Data

Revenue (Million $)

	1Q	2Q	3Q	4Q	Year
2009	7,712	7,899	7,717	--	--
2008	6,960	7,351	7,148	7,488	28,946
2007	6,205	6,427	6,320	6,339	25,290
2006	4,704	5,407	5,650	5,655	21,417
2005	3,887	3,546	3,821	3,663	14,418
2004	3,287	3,431	3,176	3,210	13,104

Earnings Per Share ($)

2009	1.22	1.67	1.78	E1.48	E6.15
2008	0.47	1.24	1.09	1.03	3.83
2007	0.42	1.28	1.78	1.43	4.91
2006	0.50	0.53	0.95	0.92	2.90
2005	0.54	0.51	0.30	0.39	1.87
2004	0.41	0.50	0.52	0.29	1.72

Fiscal year ended Dec. 31. Next earnings report expected: Early February. EPS Estimates based on S&P Operating Earnings; historical GAAP earnings are as reported.

Dividend Data

No cash dividends have been paid since 1993.

Highlights

► We think operating revenues will rise 7.8% in 2009 to over $30.7 billion, from 2008's $28.5 billion. Drivers for 2009 include 65,000 additional Medicare Advantage (MA) members, but 1.15 million fewer members in the Medicare standalone PDP program, 72,000 fewer Medicaid members, 200,000 fewer commercial members, and no change in TRICARE enrollment. For 2010, we look for operating revenues to grow by 5% to over $32.3 billion, with higher premium rates and 210,000 more MA members by year end, offset by 175,000 fewer PDP members, 145,000 fewer commercial members, no change in Medicaid enrollment and the loss of the TRICARE account in the fourth quarter.

► We expect the consolidated medical cost ratio (MCR) will decline by 150 basis points (bps) in 2009, as PDP repricing and benefit changes and the institution of premiums in MA private fee-for-service (PFFS) plans outweigh the impact from increased utilization of provider services. But we expect it to rise by 130 bps in 2010 mainly on the pending MA premium rate cut.

► We estimate operating EPS of $6.15 in 2009, and $5.35 in 2010 before a $0.20-$0.30 charge related to the exit from the TRICARE contract.

Investment Rationale/Risk

► We expect HUM to manage through the pending 2010 MA rate reduction and see it benefiting from certain rivals' planned MA market exits. Moreover, as long as current and prospective members view HUM's MA plans as more attractive to seniors in price and/or service than other rivals' plans or traditional Medicare, we think it will continue to add members. Meanwhile, we are encouraged that HUM has been attracting new members and transitioning its PFFS members to its PPOs and HMOs prior to the end of PFFS in 2011. On the downside, HUM is poised to lose its TRICARE contract as of October 2010, which we believe reduces future cash flow, but not enough to significantly crimp its financial flexibility. HUM filed a formal protest, but we think it will seek ways to compensate for the pending loss of the multi-billion-dollar contract, and that it has the financial wherewithal to do so.

► Risks to our recommendation and target price include intensified competition, a medical cost spike, and MA rate cuts.

► Our 12-month target price of $45 assumes a below-peer forward multiple of 8.5X applied to our 2010 EPS estimate.

Please read the Required Disclosures and Analyst Certification on the last page of this report.

The McGraw-Hill Companies

Humana Inc.

STANDARD
&POOR'S

Business Summary November 12, 2009

CORPORATE OVERVIEW. Humana is one of the largest managed care organizations, with medical membership of 10,317,000 (8,356,600 excluding Medicare Prescription Drug Program (PDP) enrollment) as of September 30, 2009, versus 11,559,100 (8,492,500) at December 31, 2008.

The Commercial segment consists of members enrolled in products marketed to employer groups and individuals, including fully insured medical (1,860,700 versus 1,978,600), administrative services only (ASO; 1,566,200 versus 1,642,000), and specialty (7,262,900 versus 6,817,800). Health maintenance organizations (HMOs; 9.1% of total premium and fee revenues in 2008) require members to use only doctors in their networks and generally reimburse providers on a capitated basis. Preferred provider organizations (PPOs; 12.6%) allow members the option to go to doctors outside of the network, with the members paying a portion of the provider's fees. ASO products (1.2%), which include HMOs, PPOs and consumer-directed health plans, are offered to employers that self-insure their employee health plans. Specialty products (3.3%) include dental, group and individual life, and short-term disability.

The Government segment consists of Medicare Advantage (MA; HMO: 591,000 versus 557,300; PPO: 348,000 versus 181,100; private fee-for-service, or

PFFS: 575,800 versus 697,500); Medicare PDP (Standard: 751,800 versus 1,471,800, Enhanced: 1,087,300 versus 1,439,800, Complete: 121,300 versus 155,000); Medicaid (insured: 399,800 versus 385,400; ASO: 0 versus 85,700), and the Dept. of Defense health program, TRICARE (fully insured: 1,754,300 versus 1,736,400; ASO: 1,260,800 versus 1,228,300).

In 2008, MA revenues were $13.8 billion (48.3% of premium and fee revenues) and Medicare PDP revenues were $3.4 billion (11.9%). As of April 2008 (latest available), MA plans included 14 local HMOs, 41 local PPOs, a regional PPO in 25 states, and private fee-for-service (PFFS) programs in 50 states. HUM also offered the Medicare Prescription Drug Program in 50 states.

The Medicaid unit (2.1%) has contracts in Puerto Rico and Florida.

HUM's current TRICARE South Region contract (fully insured: 11.3%; administrative services fees: 0.3%) covers beneficiaries in 10 states.

Company Financials Fiscal Year Ended Dec. 31

Per Share Data ($)	2008	2007	2006	2005	2004	2003	2002	2001	2000	1999
Tangible Book Value	12.99	13.91	10.46	7.41	7.52	6.54	5.09	4.33	3.43	2.75
Cash Flow	5.13	6.00	3.79	2.68	2.45	2.20	1.57	1.67	1.42	-1.53
Earnings	3.83	4.91	2.90	1.87	1.72	1.41	0.85	0.70	0.54	-2.28
S&P Core Earnings	4.14	4.87	2.64	1.99	1.55	1.23	0.87	0.63	NA	NA
Dividends	Nil	Nil	Nil	Nil	Nil	Nil	Nil	Nil	Nil	Nil
Payout Ratio	Nil	Nil	Nil	Nil	Nil	Nil	Nil	Nil	Nil	Nil
Prices:High	88.10	81.50	68.24	55.70	31.02	23.39	17.45	15.63	15.81	20.75
Prices:Low	22.33	51.00	41.08	28.92	15.20	8.68	9.78	8.38	4.75	5.88
P/E Ratio:High	23	17	24	30	18	17	21	22	29	NM
P/E Ratio:Low	6	10	14	15	9	6	12	12	9	NM

Income Statement Analysis (Million $)	2008	2007	2006	2005	2004	2003	2002	2001	2000	1999
Revenue	28,946	25,290	21,417	14,418	13,104	12,226	11,261	10,195	10,395	9,959
Operating Income	1,293	1,543	974	590	415	489	384	114	171	59.0
Depreciation	220	185	149	129	118	127	121	162	147	124
Interest Expense	80.3	68.9	63.1	39.3	23.2	17.4	17.0	25.0	29.0	33.0
Pretax Income	993	1,289	762	422	416	345	210	183	114	-404
Effective Tax Rate	34.8%	35.3%	36.0%	26.9%	32.7%	33.6%	32.0%	36.1%	21.1%	NM
Net Income	647	834	487	308	280	229	143	117	90.0	-382
S&P Core Earnings	699	826	443	330	252	200	145	104	NA	NA

Balance Sheet & Other Financial Data (Million $)	2008	2007	2006	2005	2004	2003	2002	2001	2000	1999
Cash	1,970	5,676	1,740	732	580	931	721	651	2,067	2,485
Current Assets	8,396	8,733	7,333	4,206	3,596	3,321	2,795	2,623	2,499	3,064
Total Assets	13,042	12,879	10,127	6,870	5,658	5,293	4,600	4,404	4,167	4,900
Current Liabilities	5,184	5,792	5,192	3,220	2,327	2,265	2,390	2,307	2,665	3,164
Long Term Debt	1,937	1,688	1,269	514	637	643	340	315	Nil	324
Common Equity	4,457	4,029	3,054	2,474	2,090	1,836	1,606	1,508	1,374	1,268
Total Capital	6,394	5,717	4,323	2,988	2,727	2,479	1,946	1,823	1,374	1,592
Capital Expenditures	262	239	193	166	114	101	112	115	135	89.0
Cash Flow	868	1,018	636	437	398	356	264	279	237	-258
Current Ratio	1.6	1.5	1.4	1.3	1.5	1.5	1.2	1.1	0.9	1.0
% Long Term Debt of Capitalization	30.3	29.5	29.4	17.2	23.3	25.9	17.5	17.3	Nil	20.4
% Net Income of Revenue	2.2	3.3	2.3	2.1	102.6	1.9	1.3	1.2	0.9	NM
% Return on Assets	5.0	7.3	5.7	4.9	5.1	4.5	3.2	2.7	2.0	NM
% Return on Equity	15.3	23.5	17.5	13.5	14.3	13.3	9.2	8.2	6.8	NM

Data as orig reptd.; bef. results of disc opers/spec. items. Per share data adj. for stk. divs.; EPS diluted. E-Estimated. NA-Not Available. NM-Not Meaningful. NR-Not Ranked. UR-Under Review.

Office: 500 W Main St, Louisville, KY 40202-4268.
Telephone: 502-580-1000.
Website: http://www.humana.com
Chrmn: D.A. Jones, Jr.

Pres & CEO: M.B. McCallister
COO & SVP: J.E. Murray
SVP, CFO & Treas: J.H. Bloem
SVP & General Counsel: C.M. Todoroff

Investor Contact: R.C. Nethery (502-580-3644)
Board Members: F. A. D'Amelio, W. R. Dunbar, K. J. Hilzinger, D. A. Jones, Jr., M. B. McCallister, W. J. McDonald, W. E. Mitchell, J. J. O'Brien, M. T. Peterson, W. A. Reynolds

Founded: 1964
Domicile: Delaware
Employees: 28,900

The McGraw-Hill Companies

Huntington Bancshares Inc

STANDARD
&POOR'S

S&P Recommendation	HOLD ★ ★ ★ ☆ ☆	Price $3.59 (as of Nov 27, 2009)	12-Mo. Target Price $4.00	Investment Style Large-Cap Blend

GICS Sector Financials
Sub-Industry Regional Banks

Summary This regional bank holding company has a network of branches throughout the Midwest.

Key Stock Statistics (Source S&P, Vickers, company reports)

52-Wk Range	$8.26– 1.00	S&P Oper. EPS 2009**E**	-6.12	Market Capitalization(B)	$2.567	Beta	1.79
Trailing 12-Month EPS	$-7.43	S&P Oper. EPS 2010**E**	-0.26	Yield (%)	1.11	S&P 3-Yr. Proj. EPS CAGR(%)	NM
Trailing 12-Month P/E	NM	P/E on S&P Oper. EPS 2009**E**	NM	Dividend Rate/Share	$0.04	S&P Credit Rating	BB+
$10K Invested 5 Yrs Ago	$1,871	Common Shares Outstg. (M)	715.1	Institutional Ownership (%)	63		

Price Performance

30-Week Mov. Avg. · · · · 10-Week Mov. Avg. – – **GAAP Earnings vs. Previous Year** Volume Above Avg. ▌▍▌ STARS
12-Mo. Target Price —— Relative Strength —— ▲ Up ▼ Down ► No Change Below Avg. ▍▍ ★

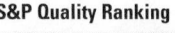

Options: CBOE, Ph

Analysis prepared by **Erik Oja** on October 29, 2009, when the stock traded at **$ 4.01.**

Highlights

► We expect HBAN to earn $1.41 billion of net interest income in 2009, down 8.1%. We see a good net interest spread environment, currently offsetting the negative impacts of nonperforming loans and weak loan growth. We expect these effects to reverse at different times in 2010, beginning with the relatively wide spread, followed by improvements in loan growth and credit quality, and we are forecasting net interest income of $1.37 billion in 2010, down 2.8%. We forecast 2009 fee income, before securities gains and losses, to be $832 million, a 12.6% increase from $739 million in 2008, driven by strong results in mortgage banking.

► Non-accrual loans at the end of the third quarter rose nearly 20.0% to $2.18 billion, or 5.59% of total loans and leases, from $1.82 billion, or 4.66% of total loans at the end of the second quarter. We estimate HBAN will take $1.55 billion of loan loss provisions in 2009, based on our expectations for net chargeoffs of $1.357 billion, plus $193 million of reserve building. For 2010, we expect provisions of $957 million.

► For 2009 and 2010, we expect losses per share of $6.12 and $0.26. We expect earnings to finally turn positive in 2011, and forecast $0.40 per share.

Investment Rationale/Risk

► We see the next four quarters as a race between capital deterioration caused by credit losses, versus earnings from banking and fee income, with the outcome dependent on whether or not the economy of HBAN's midwestern lending territory further deteriorates. In 2009, HBAN has raised $1.603 billion of additional capital, mostly from the sale of common shares, thus raising its tangible common equity ratio to an above-peers 6.46% at September 30. We see capital levels as sufficient for the foreseeable future, though we expect credit losses to bring down capital levels in each of the next four quarters, and we project a tangible common equity ratio of 5.80% in the third quarter of 2010, and rising thereafter.

► Risks to our recommendation and target price include higher-than-expected loan losses, and additional common stock offerings.

► Our 12-month target price of $4 is 0.70X tangible book value per share of $5.75, about 50% below regional banking peers, but we see this valuation multiple as in line with banks that are similarly struggling with credit quality. Our target price of $4 equates to 10.0X our 2011 EPS estimate of $0.40, slightly below peers.

Qualitative Risk Assessment

LOW	MEDIUM	**HIGH**

Our risk assessment reflects HBAN's Midwestern lending exposure and possible needs for additional regulatory capital.

Quantitative Evaluations

S&P Quality Ranking **B**

D	C	B-	**B**	B+	A-	A	A+

Relative Strength Rank **WEAK**

16

LOWEST = 1   HIGHEST = 99

Revenue/Earnings Data

Revenue (Million $)

	1Q	2Q	3Q	4Q	Year
2009	809.1	829.0	809.9	--	--
2008	971.2	933.1	853.6	729.6	3,505
2007	689.1	698.7	1,056	985.0	3,420
2006	624.3	684.9	636.9	685.5	2,632
2005	544.2	558.5	581.6	589.8	2,274
2004	553.6	542.3	527.9	542.2	2,166

Earnings Per Share ($)

2009	-6.79	-0.40	-0.33	E-0.24	E-6.12
2008	0.35	0.25	0.17	-1.20	-0.44
2007	0.40	0.34	0.38	-0.65	0.25
2006	0.45	0.46	0.65	0.37	1.92
2005	0.41	0.45	0.47	0.44	1.77
2004	0.45	0.47	0.40	0.39	1.71

Fiscal year ended Dec. 31. Next earnings report expected: Late January. EPS Estimates based on S&P Operating Earnings; historical GAAP earnings are as reported.

Dividend Data (Dates: mm/dd Payment Date: mm/dd/yy)

Amount ($)	Date Decl.	Ex-Div. Date	Stk. of Record	Payment Date
0.010	01/22	03/11	03/13	04/01/09
0.010	04/21	06/10	06/12	07/01/09
0.010	07/22	09/09	09/11	10/01/09
0.010	10/21	12/16	12/18	01/04/10

Dividends have been paid since 1912. Source: Company reports.

Please read the Required Disclosures and Analyst Certification on the last page of this report.

Huntington Bancshares Inc

STANDARD &POOR'S

Business Summary October 29, 2009

CORPORATE OVERVIEW. Huntington Bancshares Inc. (HBAN) is a multi-state diversified financial holding company focused on the Midwest region of the United States. It provides full-service commercial and consumer banking services, mortgage banking services, automobile financing, equipment leasing, investment management, trust services, and brokerage services. The company also offers insurance services.

The regional banking line of business provides traditional banking products and services to consumer, small business and commercial customers located in its eight operating regions within the six states of Ohio, Pennsylvania, Michigan, West Virginia, Indiana and Kentucky. It provides these services through a banking network of 600 branches, over 1,400 ATMs, along with Internet and telephone banking channels. It also provides certain services outside of these five states, including mortgage banking and equipment leasing. Each region is further divided into retail and commercial banking units.

On July 2, 2007, HBAN completed the acquisition of Sky Financial Group for $3.052 billion, in a 90% stock, 10% cash deal, on friendly terms. Under the terms of the deal, HBAN paid 1.098 shares of HBAN for each share of Sky Financial, and issued approximately 131.3 million shares of its own stock to acquire Sky Financial's 119.6 million outstanding shares. These 131.3 million new shares represented a 55% increase in HBAN's share count at the time. The merger added nearly $13 billion in loans to HBAN's June 30, 2007, level of $26.8 billion, and added $13.1 billion in total deposits to HBAN's June 30, 2007, level of $24.6 billion.

Company Financials Fiscal Year Ended Dec. 31

Per Share Data ($)	2008	2007	2006	2005	2004	2003	2002	2001	2000	1999
Tangible Book Value	6.27	7.14	10.12	11.41	10.02	8.99	8.95	6.77	9.43	8.66
Earnings	-0.44	0.25	1.92	1.77	1.71	1.67	1.49	0.71	1.32	1.65
S&P Core Earnings	-0.52	0.32	1.95	1.73	1.66	1.56	0.67	0.60	NA	NA
Dividends	0.04	1.06	1.00	0.85	0.75	0.67	0.64	0.72	0.74	0.68
Payout Ratio	NM	NM	52%	48%	44%	40%	43%	101%	56%	41%
Prices:High	14.87	24.14	24.97	25.41	25.38	22.55	21.77	19.28	21.82	30.89
Prices:Low	4.37	13.50	22.56	20.97	20.89	17.78	16.00	12.63	12.52	19.49
P/E Ratio:High	NM	97	13	14	15	14	15	27	17	19
P/E Ratio:Low	NM	54	12	12	12	11	11	18	9	12

Income Statement Analysis (Million $)	2008	2007	2006	2005	2004	2003	2002	2001	2000	1999
Net Interest Income	1,532	1,302	1,019	962	911	849	984	996	942	1,042
Tax Equivalent Adjustment	20.2	19.3	16.0	13.4	NA	9.68	5.21	6.35	8.31	9.42
Non Interest Income	707	706	634	640	803	1,064	680	509	494	561
Loan Loss Provision	1,057	644	65.2	81.3	55.1	164	227	309	90.5	88.4
% Expense/Operating Revenue	57.0%	62.5%	60.0%	60.5%	65.5%	64.3%	50.6%	67.4%	61.7%	56.6%
Pretax Income	-296	22.6	514	544	553	524	589	173	460	615
Effective Tax Rate	NM	NM	10.3%	24.2%	27.8%	26.4%	38.4%	NM	28.6%	31.3%
Net Income	-114	75.2	461	412	399	386	363	179	328	422
% Net Interest Margin	3.25	3.36	3.29	3.33	3.33	3.49	4.19	4.02	3.73	4.11
S&P Core Earnings	-190	96.8	467	405	388	360	165	152	NA	NA

Balance Sheet & Other Financial Data (Million $)	2008	2007	2006	2005	2004	2003	2002	2001	2000	1999
Money Market Assets	419	1,965	551	105	960	138	86.6	118	143	28.9
Investment Securities	4,384	4,500	4,363	4,527	4,239	4,929	3,411	2,862	4,107	4,889
Commercial Loans	23,639	22,308	12,354	10,845	10,303	9,486	9,336	10,415	8,887	8,452
Other Loans	16,553	17,746	13,799	13,627	13,257	11,590	11,619	11,187	11,723	12,216
Total Assets	54,312	54,697	35,329	32,765	32,565	30,484	27,579	28,500	28,599	29,037
Demand Deposits	9,560	5,372	3,616	3,390	3,392	2,987	3,074	3,741	3,505	7,594
Time Deposits	32,466	32,371	21,432	19,020	17,376	15,500	14,425	16,446	16,272	11,613
Long Term Debt	6,871	6,955	4,513	4,597	6,227	6,808	3,304	3,039	3,338	4,269
Common Equity	5,349	5,949	3,014	2,594	2,538	2,275	2,304	2,416	2,366	2,182
% Return on Assets	NM	0.2	1.4	1.3	1.3	1.3	1.3	0.6	1.1	1.5
% Return on Equity	NM	1.7	16.6	16.0	16.6	17.3	15.4	7.5	14.4	19.5
% Loan Loss Reserve	2.2	1.4	1.0	-0.7	1.1	1.6	1.7	1.8	1.4	-1.4
% Loans/Deposits	108.3	105.4	105.5	171.3	114.5	115.2	122.8	110.1	105.0	106.5
% Equity to Assets	10.4	10.0	8.2	7.8	7.6	7.7	8.4	8.4	7.9	7.6

Data as orig reptd.; bef. results of disc opers/spec. items. Per share data adj. for stk. divs.; EPS diluted. E-Estimated. NA-Not Available. NM-Not Meaningful. NR-Not Ranked. UR-Under Review.

Office: 41 S High St, Columbus, OH 43287.
Telephone: 614-480-8300.
Website: http://www.huntington.com
Chrmn, Pres & CEO: S.D. Steinour

EVP, CFO & Treas: D.R. Kimble
EVP, Secy & General Counsel: R.A. Cheap
Investor Contact: D.R. Kimble (614-480-5676)

Board Members: D. M. Casto, III, M. J. Endres, M. Fennell, J. B. Gerlach, Jr., D. J. Hilliker, D. P. Lauer, J. A. Levy, W. J. Lhota, G. E. Little, G. P. Mastroianni, D. L. Porteous, K. H. Ransier, W. R. Robertson, S. D. Steinour

Founded: 1966
Domicile: Maryland
Employees: 10,951

Illinois Tool Works Inc.

STANDARD &POOR'S

| S&P Recommendation **HOLD** ★★★☆☆ | Price $48.66 (as of Nov 27, 2009) | 12-Mo. Target Price $53.00 | Investment Style Large-Cap Growth |

GICS Sector Industrials
Sub-Industry Industrial Machinery

Summary This diversified manufacturer operates a portfolio of about 750 industrial and consumer businesses throughout the world.

Key Stock Statistics (Source S&P, Vickers, company reports)

52-Wk Range	$51.16–25.60	S&P Oper. EPS 2009**E**	1.82	Market Capitalization(B)	$24.374	Beta	1.03
Trailing 12-Month EPS	$1.34	S&P Oper. EPS 2010**E**	2.68	Yield (%)	2.55	S&P 3-Yr. Proj. EPS CAGR(%)	10
Trailing 12-Month P/E	36.3	P/E on S&P Oper. EPS 2009**E**	26.7	Dividend Rate/Share	$1.24	S&P Credit Rating	A+
$10K Invested 5 Yrs Ago	$11,284	Common Shares Outstg. (M)	500.9	Institutional Ownership (%)	85		

Price Performance

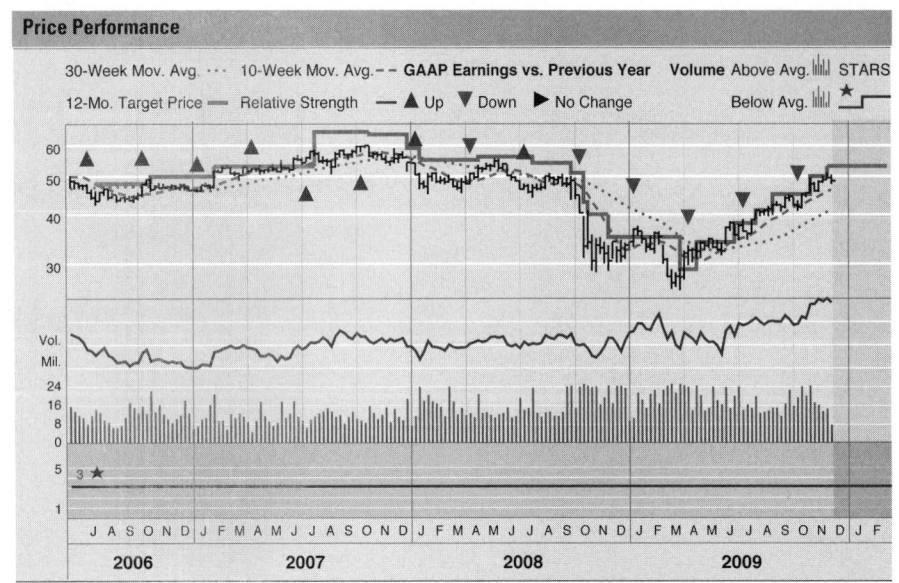

30-Week Mov. Avg. ··· 10-Week Mov. Avg. -- **GAAP Earnings vs. Previous Year** Volume Above Avg. STARS
12-Mo. Target Price — Relative Strength — ▲ Up ▼ Down ▶ No Change Below Avg.

Options: ASE, CBOE, Ph

Analysis prepared by **Mathew Christy, CFA** on November 18, 2009, when the stock traded at **$ 50.28**.

Highlights

► Excluding discontinued operations, we see revenues falling nearly 20% in 2009, given declining organic growth in ITW's end markets and the negative impact of currency translation. We see weak end-market conditions due to reductions in North American auto production, construction activity and industrial activity, along with slowing international economic growth. For 2010, however, we forecast revenue growth of nearly 6%, based on our forecast for better economic conditions and acquisitions, and we expect improved industrial activity and auto production to lead to better revenue results.

► We expect the operating margin in 2009 to contract due to acquisition and restructuring costs, increased input costs, lower pricing, and lower operating leverage. In 2010, we forecast an improvement in the operating margin due mainly to better operating leverage, production rates, and benefits associated with cost-cutting initiatives.

► With steady interest expense and a stable tax rate, we forecast EPS of $1.82 and $2.68 in 2009 and 2010, respectively.

Investment Rationale/Risk

► We expect lower results in 2009 due to the weak global economy and reduced end-market activity in the automotive and construction industries, along with generally lower industrial activity. However, results have begun to improve sequentially, and S&P forecasts a resumption of economic growth in 2010. We expect ITW to benefit from the end of inventory destocking, acquisitions, and marginal benefits from infrastructure stimulus spending programs. We believe the shares are appropriately valued at recent levels.

► Risks to our recommendation and target price include lower than expected industrial activity and/or capital spending; acquisition execution risk; and further slowing of construction activity and/or automotive markets.

► Our 12-month target price of $53 represents a blend of two valuation metrics. Our discounted cash flow model, which assumes 3% growth in perpetuity and a 9.6% weighted average cost of capital, indicates intrinsic value of about $50. In terms of relative valuation, we apply a target multiple of about 20X, ahead of peers, to our 2010 EPS estimate, suggesting a value of $55.

Qualitative Risk Assessment

| LOW | MEDIUM | HIGH |

Our risk assessment reflects an S&P Quality Ranking of A, a balance sheet that we see as strong with a relatively low level of debt, and free cash flow that has averaged about 97% of net income over the past 10 years.

Quantitative Evaluations

S&P Quality Ranking A

| D | C | B- | B | B+ | A- | **A** | A+ |

Relative Strength Rank STRONG

79

LOWEST = 1   HIGHEST = 99

Revenue/Earnings Data

Revenue (Million $)

	1Q	2Q	3Q	4Q	Year
2009	2,914	3,393	3,580	--	--
2008	4,139	4,570	4,148	3,678	15,869
2007	3,759	4,160	4,094	4,244	16,171
2006	3,297	3,579	3,538	3,641	14,055
2005	3,074	3,296	3,258	3,294	12,922
2004	2,710	3,002	2,967	3,052	11,731

Earnings Per Share ($)

2009	-0.06	0.36	0.60	E0.62	E1.82
2008	0.57	1.01	0.85	0.54	3.04
2007	0.71	0.90	0.89	0.87	3.28
2006	0.65	0.81	0.78	0.77	3.01
2005	0.53	0.65	0.72	0.71	2.60
2004	0.47	0.58	0.55	0.61	2.20

Fiscal year ended Dec. 31. Next earnings report expected: Late January. EPS Estimates based on S&P Operating Earnings; historical GAAP earnings are as reported.

Dividend Data (Dates: mm/dd Payment Date: mm/dd/yy)

Amount ($)	Date Decl.	Ex-Div. Date	Stk. of Record	Payment Date
0.310	02/13	03/27	03/31	04/14/09
0.310	05/08	06/26	06/30	07/14/09
0.310	08/07	09/28	09/30	10/14/09
0.310	10/30	12/29	12/31	01/12/10

Dividends have been paid since 1933. Source: Company reports.

Illinois Tool Works Inc.

STANDARD &POOR'S

Business Summary November 18, 2009

CORPORATE OVERVIEW. Illinois Tool Works (ITW) operates about 750 small industrial businesses in a highly decentralized structure that places responsibility on managers at the lowest level possible, in an attempt to focus each business unit on the needs of particular customers. Each business unit manager is held strictly accountable for the results of his or her individual business.

ITW is diversified not only by customer and industry, but also by geographic region, with about 41% of revenues derived from overseas. At the end of 2008, ITW diversified its business segmentation beyond its former four reporting segments and now reports on the basis of eight reportable segments, including Industrial Packaging, Power Systems and Electronics, Transportation, Construction Products, Food Equipment, Decorative Surfaces, Polymers & Fluids and All Other.

The Industrial Packaging segment (16% of revenues and 12% of operating income in 2008; 10.6% operating profit margin) produces steel, plastic and paper products used for bundling, shipping and protecting transported goods. In 2008, major segments served were the primary metals (28%), general industrial (22%), construction (12%) and food and beverage (12%) markets.

The Power Systems & Electronics segment (15% and 20%; 20%) produces equipment and consumables associated with specialty power conversion, metallurgy and electronics. In 2008, this segment primarily served the general industrial (43%), electronics (19%) and construction (9%) markets.

The Transportation segment (15% and 12%; 11.8%) produces components, fasteners, fluids and polymers for transportation-related applications. In 2008, this segment primarily served the automotive original equipment manufacturers (65%) and auto aftermarket (23%).

The Construction segment (13% and 10%; 12%) produces fasteners and related fastening tools for wood applications; anchors, fasteners and related tools for concrete and wood applications; metal plate truss components and related equipment and software; and packaged hardware fasteners, anchors and other products for retail.

Company Financials Fiscal Year Ended Dec. 31

Per Share Data ($)	2008	2007	2006	2005	2004	2003	2002	2001	2000	1999
Tangible Book Value	2.78	7.37	6.94	6.89	7.59	8.22	6.90	5.42	4.82	4.64
Cash Flow	3.71	4.22	3.79	3.26	2.78	2.18	2.01	1.94	2.25	1.94
Earnings	3.04	3.28	3.01	2.60	2.20	1.69	1.51	1.31	1.58	1.38
S&P Core Earnings	2.84	3.27	3.03	2.60	2.13	1.63	1.38	1.13	NA	NA
Dividends	1.18	0.98	0.92	0.61	0.52	0.47	0.45	0.42	0.38	0.34
Payout Ratio	39%	30%	30%	23%	24%	28%	30%	32%	24%	25%
Prices:High	55.59	60.00	53.54	47.32	48.35	42.35	38.90	36.00	34.50	41.00
Prices:Low	28.50	45.60	41.54	39.25	36.46	27.28	27.52	24.58	24.75	29.06
P/E Ratio:High	18	18	18	18	22	25	26	27	22	30
P/E Ratio:Low	9	14	14	15	17	16	18	19	16	21

Income Statement Analysis (Million $)										
Revenue	15,869	16,171	14,055	12,922	11,731	10,036	9,468	9,293	9,984	9,333
Operating Income	2,690	3,147	2,865	2,558	2,410	1,940	1,812	1,692	1,977	1,830
Depreciation	351	523	444	383	353	307	306	386	413	343
Interest Expense	152	102	85.6	87.0	69.2	70.7	68.5	68.1	72.4	67.5
Pretax Income	2,191	2,581	2,445	2,182	1,999	1,576	1,434	1,231	1,478	1,353
Effective Tax Rate	27.8%	29.3%	29.8%	31.5%	33.0%	34.0%	35.0%	34.8%	35.2%	37.8%
Net Income	1,583	1,826	1,718	1,495	1,340	1,040	932	802	958	841
S&P Core Earnings	1,476	1,818	1,729	1,493	1,299	1,009	851	691	NA	NA

Balance Sheet & Other Financial Data (Million $)										
Cash	743	828	590	370	667	1,684	1,058	282	151	233
Current Assets	5,924	6,166	5,206	4,112	4,322	4,783	3,879	3,163	3,329	3,273
Total Assets	15,213	15,526	13,880	11,446	11,352	11,193	10,623	9,822	9,603	9,060
Current Liabilities	4,876	2,960	2,637	2,001	1,851	1,489	1,567	1,518	1,818	2,045
Long Term Debt	1,244	2,299	956	958	921	920	1,460	1,267	1,549	1,361
Common Equity	7,663	9,351	9,018	7,547	7,628	7,874	6,649	6,041	5,401	4,815
Total Capital	9,022	11,501	9,973	8,505	8,549	8,795	8,109	7,308	6,950	6,176
Capital Expenditures	355	353	301	293	283	258	271	257	314	336
Cash Flow	1,935	2,349	2,162	1,878	1,693	1,347	1,238	1,189	1,371	1,184
Current Ratio	1.2	2.1	2.0	2.1	2.3	3.2	2.5	2.1	1.8	1.6
% Long Term Debt of Capitalization	13.8	16.8	9.6	11.3	10.8	10.5	18.0	17.3	22.3	22.0
% Net Income of Revenue	10.0	11.3	12.2	11.6	11.4	10.4	9.8	8.6	9.6	9.0
% Return on Assets	10.3	12.4	13.6	13.1	11.9	9.5	9.1	8.3	10.3	9.7
% Return on Equity	18.6	19.9	20.7	19.7	17.3	14.3	14.7	14.0	18.8	18.6

Data as orig reptd.; bef. results of disc opers/spec. items. Per share data adj. for stk. divs.; EPS diluted. E-Estimated. NA-Not Available. NM-Not Meaningful. NR-Not Ranked. UR-Under Review.

Office: 3600 W. Lake Avenue, Glenview, IL 60026-5811.
Telephone: 847-724-7500.
Website: http://www.itw.com
Chrmn & CEO: D.B. Speer

SVP, CFO & Cntlr: R.D. Kropp
SVP, Secy & General Counsel: J.H. Wooten, Jr.
CTO: M.W. Croll
Chief Acctg Officer: R. Scheuneman

Investor Contact: J. Brooklier (847-657-4104)
Board Members: W. F. Aldinger, III, M. D. Brailsford, S. M. Crown, D. H. Davis, Jr., R. C. McCormack, R. S. Morrison, J. A. Skinner, H. B. Smith, D. B. Speer, P. B. Strobel

Founded: 1912
Domicile: Delaware
Employees: 65,000

The McGraw-Hill Companies

IMS Health Inc

STANDARD &POOR'S

S&P Recommendation **HOLD** ★★★☆☆	Price $21.38 (as of Nov 27, 2009)	12-Mo. Target Price $22.00	Investment Style Large-Cap Growth

GICS Sector Health Care
Sub-Industry Health Care Technology

Summary This provider of information solutions to the health care sector agreed in November 2009, to be acquired for $22 a share in cash.

Key Stock Statistics (Source S&P, Vickers, company reports)

52-Wk Range	$21.68– 11.12	S&P Oper. EPS 2009**E**	1.55	Market Capitalization(B)	$3.901	Beta	0.96
Trailing 12-Month EPS	$1.57	S&P Oper. EPS 2010**E**	1.70	Yield (%)	0.56	S&P 3-Yr. Proj. EPS CAGR(%)	6
Trailing 12-Month P/E	13.6	P/E on S&P Oper. EPS 2009**E**	13.8	Dividend Rate/Share	$0.12	S&P Credit Rating	NA
$10K Invested 5 Yrs Ago	$9,817	Common Shares Outstg. (M)	182.4	Institutional Ownership (%)	87		

Price Performance

30-Week Mov. Avg. ··· 10-Week Mov. Avg. – – **GAAP Earnings vs. Previous Year** Volume Above Avg. STARS
12-Mo. Target Price — Relative Strength — ▲ Up ▼ Down ▶ No Change Below Avg. ★

Options: CBOE, P, Ph

Analysis prepared by **Michael W. Jaffe** on November 11, 2009, when the stock traded at **$ 21.09**.

Highlights

► IMS Health agreed in November 2009, to be acquired for $22 a share in cash, subject to necessary approvals, by investment funds managed by TPG Capital and the CPP Investment Board. In its current state, we see RX's revenues increasing 4% in 2010. We expect demand for RX's services to remain limited in 2010 by the likelihood of ongoing below historical growth in the global pharmaceutical market and a high level of patent expirations. However, in light of recent signs of some recovery in RX's primary pharmaceutical client base, we expect a modest increase in sales in 2010. We believe these seemingly better market conditions are related to what we think are the early stages of a global economic recovery.

► We expect slightly wider margins in 2010, as we see early benefits of recently announced restructuring initiatives outweighing the impact of our outlook for still below historical client trends.

► Our 2009 operating EPS forecast excludes $0.06 a share of net charges in the first three quarters, with charges from a new restructuring plan largely offset by credits from tax and foreign exchange hedge items.

Investment Rationale/Risk

► We believe the $22 a share takeover bid that RX accepted in November 2009, is an appropriate valuation. Since we think the company shopped itself around before agreeing to the bid, we do not expect competing offers. IMS Health has been facing challenging business trends in its client base, as sales growth has slowed at many pharmaceutical companies in recent years. However, we have a favorable view of RX's efforts to boost operating efficiencies and cut costs through ongoing restructuring actions, and business recently seemed to be getting a little more favorable at its client base.

► Risks to our recommendation and target price include the withdrawal of the buyout pact, and weaker-than-anticipated conditions in RX's client markets.

► The $22 a share takeover proposal accepted by RX values the company at about 13X our 2010 EPS estimate, or slightly above the bottom part of its historical range. We believe this is a fair valuation, on our view that RX's business has experienced a worsening of secular trends, but is still a solid cash generator whose client base seems poised for a modest business recovery. Our 12-month target price is $22.

Qualitative Risk Assessment

LOW	MEDIUM	HIGH

Our risk assessment reflects our view of RX's usually solid levels of free cash flow, offset by the company's relatively high level of debt leverage. Also, income statements typically have numerous one-time items, which we view as raising questions about the quality of earnings.

Quantitative Evaluations

S&P Quality Ranking B+

D	C	B-	B	**B+**	A-	A	A+

Relative Strength Rank STRONG

96

LOWEST = 1 HIGHEST = 99

Revenue/Earnings Data

Revenue (Million $)

	1Q	2Q	3Q	4Q	Year
2009	526.9	522.8	540.8	--	--
2008	574.2	600.7	573.7	580.9	2,330
2007	510.4	537.5	538.8	605.9	2,193
2006	446.2	486.2	482.7	543.5	1,959
2005	411.0	433.3	432.8	477.7	1,755
2004	361.6	379.6	384.2	443.7	1,569

Earnings Per Share ($)

2009	0.73	0.34	-0.05	E0.46	E1.55
2008	0.32	0.42	0.41	0.54	1.70
2007	0.43	0.36	0.29	0.09	1.18
2006	0.56	0.30	0.34	0.32	1.53
2005	0.13	0.41	0.30	0.38	1.22
2004	0.34	0.27	0.28	0.32	1.20

Fiscal year ended Dec. 31. Next earnings report expected: Early February. EPS Estimates based on S&P Operating Earnings; historical GAAP earnings are as reported.

Dividend Data (Dates: mm/dd Payment Date: mm/dd/yy)

Amount ($)	Date Decl.	Ex-Div. Date	Stk. of Record	Payment Date
0.030	02/10	02/26	03/02	03/27/09
0.030	04/21	04/29	05/01	06/05/09
0.030	07/20	08/05	08/07	09/04/09
0.030	10/20	11/04	11/06	12/04/09

Dividends have been paid since 1997. Source: Company reports.

Stock Report | November 28, 2009 | NYS Symbol: RX

IMS Health Inc

STANDARD
&POOR'S

Business Summary November 11, 2009

CORPORATE OVERVIEW. In November 2009, IMS Health agreed to be acquired by investment funds managed by TPG Capital (a private equity firm) and the CPP Investment Board (the Canada Pension Plan), under which the funds would pay $22 a share in cash for each IMS share, and would also assume the company's debt. The planned transaction had fully committed financing, and was expected to close in 2010's first quarter, subject to approval by IMS shareholders and regulators, and other customary closing conditions. IMS Health is a global provider of market intelligence to the pharmaceutical and health care industries, with operations covering more than 100 countries (64% of revenues from foreign operations in 2008). IMS provides critical business intelligence, including information, analytics and consulting services. This includes offerings in the areas of sales force effectiveness (45% of revenues in 2008), portfolio optimization (28%), and launch, brand management and other (27%).

The company's sales force effectiveness services are used principally by pharmaceutical manufacturers to measure, forecast and optimize the effectiveness and efficiency of sales representatives, and to focus on sales and marketing efforts. They include sales territory and prescription tracking reports.

RX's portfolio optimization services provide customers with the intelligence and tools to identify and optimize pharmaceutical product portfolios, including currently marketed products and the new product pipeline. Integrating prescriptions, sales, disease/treatment and industry intelligence, RX's portfolio optimization services provide a comprehensive picture of the worldwide market. The company's offerings include pharmaceutical, medical, hospital and prescription audits.

In the area of launch, brand management and other services, RX's offerings combine information and analytical tools to address client needs relevant to each stage in the life of a pharmaceutical product. The areas covered include brand planning, pricing and market access, promotion management, and performance management.

Company Financials Fiscal Year Ended Dec. 31

Per Share Data ($)	2008	2007	2006	2005	2004	2003	2002	2001	2000	1999
Tangible Book Value	NM	NM	NM	NM	NM	NM	0.13	0.24	NM	0.51
Cash Flow	2.18	1.57	1.88	1.67	1.65	0.87	1.14	0.69	0.69	1.10
Earnings	1.70	1.18	1.53	1.22	1.20	0.56	0.93	0.46	0.39	0.78
S&P Core Earnings	1.58	1.14	1.36	1.09	0.95	0.47	0.82	0.52	NA	NA
Dividends	0.12	0.12	0.12	0.08	0.08	0.08	0.08	0.08	0.08	0.08
Payout Ratio	7%	10%	8%	7%	7%	14%	9%	17%	21%	10%
Prices:High	25.50	33.12	30.13	28.60	26.80	25.07	22.59	30.50	28.69	39.19
Prices:Low	9.63	21.20	23.94	22.01	20.16	13.68	12.90	17.30	14.25	21.50
P/E Ratio:High	15	28	20	23	22	45	24	66	74	50
P/E Ratio:Low	6	18	16	18	17	24	14	38	37	28

Income Statement Analysis (Million $)										
Revenue	2,330	2,193	1,959	1,755	1,569	1,382	1,428	1,333	1,424	1,398
Operating Income	601	557	524	543	517	437	510	494	459	439
Depreciation	89.6	77.7	73.8	105	93.5	75.1	61.8	69.2	92.0	100
Interest Expense	47.2	37.9	40.4	22.7	19.5	15.4	14.4	18.1	17.6	7.59
Pretax Income	415	357	449	454	415	305	397	177	257	152
Effective Tax Rate	25.0%	32.3%	29.7%	37.5%	31.2%	54.4%	32.9%	21.7%	54.7%	NM
Net Income	311	234	316	284	285	139	266	138	116	250
S&P Core Earnings	290	226	282	252	226	116	236	155	NA	NA

Balance Sheet & Other Financial Data (Million $)										
Cash	216	218	157	363	460	385	415	268	119	116
Current Assets	773	840	693	821	937	779	827	657	569	607
Total Assets	2,087	2,244	1,907	1,973	1,891	1,644	1,619	1,368	1,243	1,451
Current Liabilities	541	635	543	549	554	837	679	635	827	723
Long Term Debt	1,404	1,203	975	611	627	152	325	150	Nil	Nil
Common Equity	-256	-40.3	33.9	415	256	190	222	218	147	494
Total Capital	1,251	1,264	1,110	1,126	984	443	727	513	282	619
Capital Expenditures	36.4	61.2	27.5	52.0	22.5	23.7	44.4	34.3	33.4	33.0
Cash Flow	401	312	389	389	379	214	328	208	208	351
Current Ratio	1.4	1.3	1.3	1.5	1.7	0.9	1.2	1.0	0.7	0.8
% Long Term Debt of Capitalization	112.2	95.2	87.9	54.3	63.7	34.3	44.7	29.2	Nil	Nil
% Net Income of Revenue	13.4	10.7	16.1	16.2	18.2	10.1	18.6	10.4	8.2	17.9
% Return on Assets	NA	11.3	16.3	14.7	16.1	8.5	17.8	10.3	8.7	15.8
% Return on Equity	NA	NM	140.6	84.7	128.2	67.6	120.8	86.0	34.7	38.0

Data as orig reptd.; bef. results of disc opers/spec. items. Per share data adj. for stk. divs.; EPS diluted. E-Estimated. NA-Not Available. NM-Not Meaningful. NR-Not Ranked. UR-Under Review.

Office: 901 Main Ave, Norwalk, CT 06851-1170.
Telephone: 203-845-5200.
Website: http://www.imshealth.com
Chrmn, Pres & CEO: D.R. Carlucci

Vice Chrmn: G.V. Pajot
SVP & CFO: L.G. Katz
SVP & General Counsel: H.A. Ashman
Chief Acctg Officer & Cntlr: H. Bhangdia

Investor Contact: D. Peck (203-845-5237)
Board Members: D. R. Carlucci, C. L. Clemente, J. D. Edwards, K. E. Giusti, H. Lockhart, G. V. Pajot, M. B. Puckett, B. T. Sheares, W. C. Vanfaasen, B. W. Wise

Founded: 1998
Domicile: Delaware
Employees: 7,500

Redistribution or reproduction is prohibited without written permission. Copyright ©2009 The McGraw-Hill Companies, Inc.

The McGraw-Hill Companies

Integrys Energy Group Inc

STANDARD &POOR'S

S&P Recommendation	SELL ★★☆☆☆	Price	12-Mo. Target Price	Investment Style
		$38.15 (as of Nov 27, 2009)	$30.00	Large-Cap Blend

GICS Sector Utilities
Sub-Industry Multi-Utilities

Summary This utility holding company serves about 485,000 regulated electric and 1,674,000 regulated gas customers. The company also operates an unregulated energy supply and services business.

Key Stock Statistics (Source S&P, Vickers, company reports)

52-Wk Range	$45.10– 19.44	S&P Oper. EPS 2009**E**	2.38	Market Capitalization(B)	$2.915	Beta	0.86
Trailing 12-Month EPS	$-0.89	S&P Oper. EPS 2010**E**	2.60	Yield (%)	7.13	S&P 3-Yr. Proj. EPS CAGR(%)	-4
Trailing 12-Month P/E	NM	P/E on S&P Oper. EPS 2009**E**	16.0	Dividend Rate/Share	$2.72	S&P Credit Rating	A-
$10K Invested 5 Yrs Ago	$10,048	Common Shares Outstg. (M)	76.4	Institutional Ownership (%)	49		

Price Performance

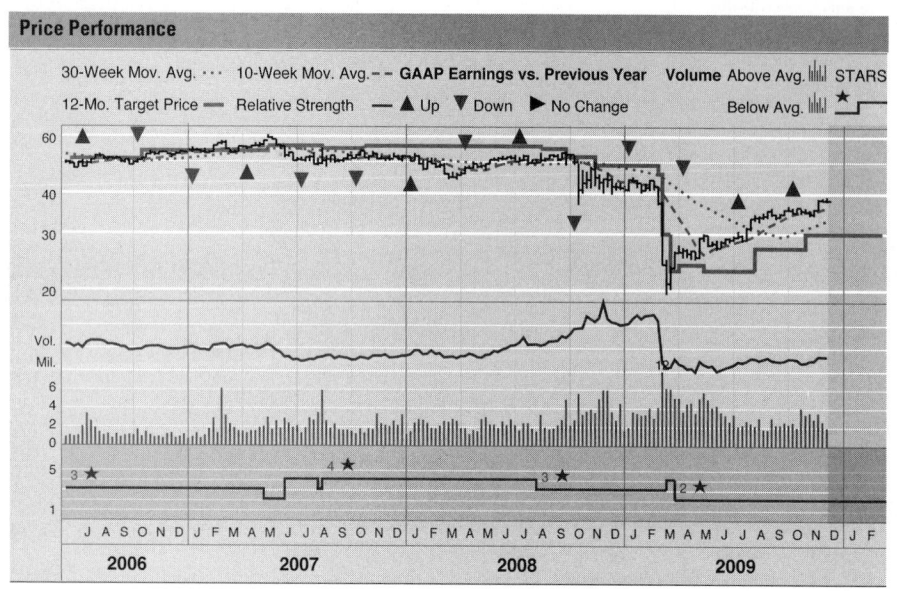

- 30-Week Mov. Avg. · · · 10-Week Mov. Avg. - - GAAP Earnings vs. Previous Year Volume Above Avg. ⅡⅢ STARS
- 12-Mo. Target Price — Relative Strength — ▲ Up ▼ Down ▶ No Change Below Avg. ⅠⅢ ★

2006 2007 2008 2009

Options: P, Ph

Analysis prepared by **Christopher B. Muir** on October 22, 2009, when the stock traded at **$ 35.39**.

Highlights

▶ We expect 2009 revenues to drop 36%. We see utility revenues falling 15%, reflecting lower commodity prices and a weaker economy. We project a 46% decline in unregulated revenues, reflecting the scaling back of the company's unregulated operations. In 2010, we see revenues falling 25% due to continued reductions in the unregulated businesses.

▶ Our operating profit margin forecasts are 4.4% for 2009 and 5.8% for 2010, versus 2008's 3.0%, as we expect lower per-revenue fuel costs to be partly offset by higher per-revenue non-fuel operating expenses. Our pretax profit margin estimates (3.4% for 2009 and 4.9% for 2010, versus 2008's 2.4%) indicate less improvement, as we see interest expense falling at a slower rate than revenues and lower non-operating income.

▶ Our 2009 EPS estimate is $2.38 (excluding net charges of $3.39), down 22% from 2008's $3.04 (which excludes net charges of $1.44), due to the scaling back of unregulated businesses. We see EPS of $2.60 in 2010, up 9.2%, helped by lower interest costs.

Investment Rationale/Risk

▶ We think TEG has made some good acquisitions recently, but it has announced it would scale back and/or sell its unregulated businesses. As a result, TEG expects to have a substantial increase in cash balances due to the return of capital, which we think will be used to maintain its dividend as well as to lower debt. TEG also said it would consider stock repurchases with any excess cash.

▶ Risks to our recommendation and target price include higher-than-expected economic activity, merger savings and share repurchases, and lower-than-expected interest rates.

▶ TEG recently traded at 13.8X our 2010 EPS estimate, a 15% premium to its multi-utility peers. Our 12-month target price of $30 is 11.5X our 2010 estimate, a small discount to our average peer forecast. We think it will take TEG until 2019 to lower its 100%-plus payout ratio to about 60%, a level that is closer to the multi-utility peer average, assuming 5% EPS growth from a 2010 base and no dividend growth. We see rate increases and interest cost reductions being the only near-term EPS growth source for TEG.

Qualitative Risk Assessment

LOW	MEDIUM	HIGH

Our risk assessment reflects what we see as a balanced portfolio of operations, which includes lower risk gas and electric utility businesses as well as higher risk unregulated wholesale and retail energy marketing services.

Quantitative Evaluations

S&P Quality Ranking B+

D	C	B-	B	B+	A-	A	A+

Relative Strength Rank STRONG

81

LOWEST = 1 HIGHEST = 99

Revenue/Earnings Data

Revenue (Million $)

	1Q	2Q	3Q	4Q	Year
2009	3,201	1,428	1,298	--	--
2008	3,989	3,417	3,223	3,418	14,048
2007	2,747	2,362	2,123	3,062	10,292
2006	1,996	1,475	1,555	1,865	6,891
2005	1,462	1,328	1,757	2,391	6,826
2004	1,373	1,046	1,073	1,399	4,891

Earnings Per Share ($)

	1Q	2Q	3Q	4Q	Year
2009	-2.35	0.45	0.63	E0.63	E2.38
2008	1.77	-0.31	-0.77	0.27	1.58
2007	2.01	-0.53	0.14	1.19	2.48
2006	1.44	0.97	0.63	0.50	3.50
2005	1.62	0.62	1.25	0.53	4.11
2004	1.22	0.26	0.99	1.60	4.07

Fiscal year ended Dec. 31. Next earnings report expected: Late February. EPS Estimates based on S&P Operating Earnings; historical GAAP earnings are as reported.

Dividend Data (Dates: mm/dd Payment Date: mm/dd/yy)

Amount ($)	Date Decl.	Ex-Div. Date	Stk. of Record	Payment Date
0.680	02/17	02/25	02/27	03/20/09
0.680	05/13	05/27	05/29	06/20/09
0.680	07/09	08/27	08/31	09/19/09
0.680	10/13	11/25	11/30	12/19/09

Dividends have been paid since 1940. Source: Company reports.

Please read the Required Disclosures and Analyst Certification on the last page of this report.

The McGraw-Hill Companies

Integrys Energy Group Inc

STANDARD &POOR'S

Business Summary October 22, 2009

CORPORATE OVERVIEW. Integrys Energy Group (TEG) is a holding company with regulated and unregulated business units. As of December 31, 2008, the company's subsidiaries were organized in three operating segments: electric utility, gas utility, and Integrys Energy Services, Inc. (ESI). A holding company and other segment includes operations that do not fit into the other segments, including nonutility operations of the regulated utilities. In 2008, ESI was the largest contributor to TEG's revenues, at 69%. The electric utility segment contributed 9%, while the gas utility segment contributed 22%.

The electric utility segment includes the electric operations of Wisconsin Public Service Corporation (WPSC) and Upper Peninsula Power Company (UPPCO). The gas utility segment includes the gas operations of WPSC, Michigan Gas Utilities Corporation (MGUC), Minnesota Energy Resources Corporation (MERC), The Peoples Gas Light and Coke Company (PGL); and North Shore Gas Company (NSG). Integrys Energy Services is an unregulated subsidiary that operates electric generation facilities and energy marketing operations and provides energy generation and management services.

IMPACT OF MAJOR DEVELOPMENTS. On February 25, TEG announced that it intends to either fully or partially divest of its ESI segment, or reduce its size,

risk, and financial requirements in response to increased collateral requirements. Its short-term strategy will be to reduce and refocus its financial, credit, and risk capital on those aspects of ESI's business that yield the highest return, with consideration given toward lower risk. Longer term, assuming ESI is not sold, it will be a smaller segment that requires significantly less capital, parental guarantees, and overall financial liquidity. TEG intends to reduce the invested capital at ESI in 2009 from $1 billion to $600 million by December 31, 2009, and the invested capital for the segment's nonregulated energy marketing business segment is expected to be insignificant by December 31, 2010. TEG says that it could use cash returned to it to reduce debt, repurchase shares, or both. In any event, we think TEG will keep enough cash to maintain the dividend. On September 21, 2009, TEG sold its Canadian marketing business for an undisclosed sum and said that it would be able to reduce collateral postings by $300 million as a result of the transaction.

Company Financials Fiscal Year Ended Dec. 31

Per Share Data ($)	2008	2007	2006	2005	2004	2003	2002	2001	2000	1999
Tangible Book Value	28.22	29.97	28.36	31.69	29.12	27.25	24.48	22.91	20.42	19.97
Earnings	1.58	2.48	3.50	4.11	4.07	3.24	3.42	2.74	2.53	2.24
S&P Core Earnings	0.73	2.49	3.58	2.86	3.82	3.12	1.48	0.99	NA	NA
Dividends	2.68	2.50	2.28	2.24	2.20	2.16	2.12	2.08	2.04	2.00
Payout Ratio	170%	101%	62%	55%	54%	67%	62%	76%	81%	89%
Prices:High	53.92	60.63	57.75	60.00	50.53	46.80	42.68	36.80	39.00	35.75
Prices:Low	36.91	48.10	47.39	47.67	43.50	36.80	30.47	31.00	22.63	24.44
P/E Ratio:High	34	24	16	15	12	14	12	13	15	16
P/E Ratio:Low	23	19	13	12	11	11	9	11	9	11

Income Statement Analysis (Million $)										
Revenue	14,048	10,292	6,891	6,826	4,891	4,321	2,675	2,676	1,952	516
Depreciation	235	195	106	142	107	138	98.0	86.6	99.8	83.7
Maintenance	NA	NA	NA	NA	NA	NA	NA	NA	73.0	60.6
Fixed Charges Coverage	2.07	2.57	2.85	3.80	4.31	3.55	3.97	2.32	2.14	3.03
Construction Credits	NA	NA	NA	NA	NA	NA	NA	NA	4.46	3.62
Effective Tax Rate	29.6%	32.2%	23.3%	20.7%	16.1%	22.0%	18.5%	5.83%	8.23%	33.3%
Net Income	122	181	152	148	153	114	109	77.6	67.0	59.6
S&P Core Earnings	56.4	179	152	111	144	103	47.1	28.2	NA	NA

Balance Sheet & Other Financial Data (Million $)										
Gross Property	7,483	7,066	3,961	3,099	3,308	3,065	3,186	2,979	2,716	2,444
Capital Expenditures	533	393	342	414	290	176	229	249	191	273
Net Property	4,773	4,464	2,535	2,044	2,003	1,829	1,610	1,464	1,351	1,319
Capitalization:Long Term Debt	2,339	2,316	1,338	918	866	923	926	829	761	686
Capitalization:% Long Term Debt	43.0	41.7	46.6	41.3	42.0	47.9	53.7	53.7	58.4	56.1
Capitalization:Preferred	Nil	Nil	Nil	Nil	Nil	Nil	Nil	Nil	Nil	Nil
Capitalization:% Preferred	Nil	Nil	Nil	Nil	Nil	Nil	Nil	Nil	Nil	Nil
Capitalization:Common	3,100	3,236	1,534	1,304	1,114	1,003	798	716	543	536
Capitalization:% Common	57.0	58.3	53.4	58.7	58.0	52.1	46.3	46.3	41.6	43.9
Total Capital	5,911	6,085	2,970	2,317	2,062	2,024	1,816	1,635	1,428	1,359
% Operating Ratio	98.6	97.3	97.0	98.2	96.7	97.8	95.3	96.2	94.5	195.4
% Earned on Net Property	5.5	10.5	10.9	9.2	9.9	7.4	9.8	7.6	8.6	59.2
% Return on Revenue	0.9	1.8	2.2	2.2	3.1	2.6	4.1	2.9	3.4	11.5
% Return on Invested Capital	4.7	7.7	9.4	25.0	18.6	9.3	10.1	9.1	9.1	8.2
% Return on Common Equity	3.8	7.5	10.5	13.3	14.5	12.8	14.5	12.3	12.4	11.3

Data as orig reptd.; bef. results of disc opers/spec. items. Per share data adj. for stk. divs.; EPS diluted. E-Estimated. NA-Not Available. NM-Not Meaningful. NR-Not Ranked. UR-Under Review.

Office: 130 E Randolph St, Chicago, IL 60601-6207.
Telephone: 800-699-1269.
Email: investor@integrysgroup.com
Website: http://www.integrysgroup.com

Exec Chrmn: L.L. Weyers
Pres & CEO: C.A. Schrock
SVP & CFO: J.P. O'Leary
VP & Treas: B.A. Johnson

VP & Cntlr: D.L. Ford
Investor Contact: S.P. Eschbach (312-228-5408)
Board Members: K. E. Bailey, R. A. Bemis, W. J. Brodsky, A. J. Budney, Jr., P. S. Cafferty, E. Carnahan, R. C. Gallagher, K. M. Hasselblad-Pascale, J. W. Higgins, J. L. Kemerling, M. E. Lavin, W. F. Protz, Jr., C. A. Schrock, L. L. Weyers

Founded: 1883
Domicile: Wisconsin
Employees: 5,191

The **McGraw·Hill** Companies

Intel Corp

STANDARD &POOR'S

S&P Recommendation	BUY ★★★★☆	Price $19.11 (as of Nov 27, 2009)	12-Mo. Target Price $24.00	Investment Style Large-Cap Growth

GICS Sector Information Technology
Sub-Industry Semiconductors

Summary This company is the world's largest manufacturer of microprocessors, the central processing units of PCs, and also produces other semiconductor products.

Key Stock Statistics (Source S&P, Vickers, company reports)

52-Wk Range	$21.27–12.05	S&P Oper. EPS 2009E	0.68	Market Capitalization(B)	$105.525	Beta	1.18
Trailing 12-Month EPS	$0.41	S&P Oper. EPS 2010E	1.40	Yield (%)	3.30	S&P 3-Yr. Proj. EPS CAGR(%)	5
Trailing 12-Month P/E	46.6	P/E on S&P Oper. EPS 2009E	28.1	Dividend Rate/Share	$0.63	S&P Credit Rating	A+
$10K Invested 5 Yrs Ago	$9,230	Common Shares Outstg. (M)	5,522.0	Institutional Ownership (%)	65		

Price Performance

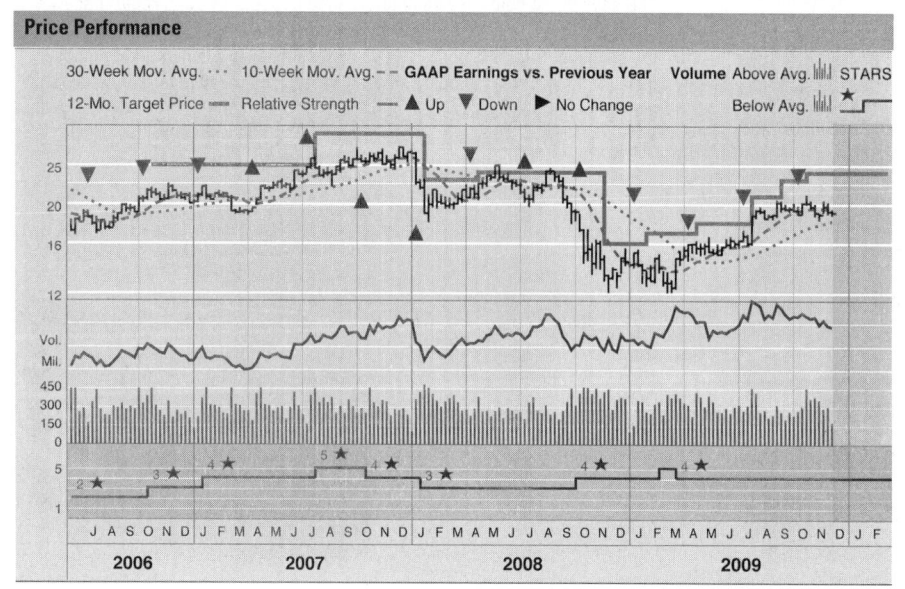

Options: ASE, CBOE, P, Ph

Analysis prepared by **Clyde Montevirgen** on November 13, 2009, when the stock traded at **$ 19.72**.

Highlights

▶ We think sales will rise 12% in 2010, after a projected 7% decline in 2009. We believe INTC's customers have begun replenishing inventories and accelerating their build plans in anticipation of stronger demand, which should provide a boost for chip orders. We expect Intel's latest and soon-to-be-released chips to outperform competitors' offerings, which should lead to market share gains in higher-end segments, helping preserve average selling prices. Furthermore, we see INTC's Atom processor and upcoming graphics releases providing additional growth opportunities.

▶ We forecast gross margins widening to 57% in 2010, from an estimated 55% in 2009. We see higher volume and plant utilization, as well as lower startup costs and one-time charges, offsetting the impact of falling selling prices. Similarly, we think operating margins will expand to about 27% in 2010, from an anticipated 15% in 2009 (which includes a $1.45 billion fine imposed by the European Commission and a $1.25 billion payment to AMD), as sales grow faster than expenses.

▶ Our EPS projections include company-guided gains/losses and modest share count declines.

Investment Rationale/Risk

▶ We expect declining earnings this year, as Intel and the semiconductor industry face strong macroeconomic headwinds and soft computer demand, especially from enterprises. However, we still think Intel has the best competitive position in our semiconductor coverage universe, a strong balance sheet, and healthy free cash flows, and carries lower business and financial risks than most other chipmakers. As demand recovers and after Intel ramps up new production lines, which should yield leading-technology chips and cost benefits, we see the company in an even better competitive position, with a larger market share in higher-end segments, new market opportunities with Atom and embedded chips, and better profitability.

▶ Risks to our recommendation and target price include lower-than-expected demand for PCs, accelerated ASP erosion, and less-than-anticipated traction for the company's latest chips.

▶ Our 12-month target price of $24 reflects our discounted cash flow analysis, which assumes a WACC of about 11% and a terminal growth rate of 4%.

Qualitative Risk Assessment

LOW	MEDIUM	HIGH

Our risk assessment reflects Intel's exposure to the sales cycles of the semiconductor industry and demand trends for personal computers, offset by its large size, long corporate history, and its low debt levels compared to peers.

Quantitative Evaluations

S&P Quality Ranking B+

D	C	B-	B	B+	A-	A	A+

Relative Strength Rank MODERATE

42

LOWEST = 1   HIGHEST = 99

Revenue/Earnings Data

Revenue (Million $)

	1Q	2Q	3Q	4Q	Year
2009	7,145	8,024	9,389	--	--
2008	9,673	9,470	10,217	8,226	37,586
2007	8,852	8,680	10,090	10,712	38,334
2006	8,940	8,009	8,739	9,694	35,382
2005	9,434	9,231	9,960	10,201	38,826
2004	8,091	8,049	8,471	9,598	34,209

Earnings Per Share ($)

	1Q	2Q	3Q	4Q	Year
2009	0.12	-0.07	0.33	E0.31	E0.68
2008	0.25	0.28	0.35	0.04	0.92
2007	0.28	0.22	0.30	0.38	1.18
2006	0.23	0.15	0.22	0.26	0.86
2005	0.35	0.33	0.32	0.40	1.40
2004	0.26	0.27	0.30	0.33	1.16

Fiscal year ended Dec. 31. Next earnings report expected: Mid January. EPS Estimates based on S&P Operating Earnings; historical GAAP earnings are as reported.

Dividend Data (Dates: mm/dd Payment Date: mm/dd/yy)

Amount ($)	Date Decl.	Ex-Div. Date	Stk. of Record	Payment Date
0.140	01/23	02/04	02/07	03/01/09
0.140	03/19	05/05	05/07	06/01/09
0.140	07/16	08/05	08/07	09/01/09
0.140	09/10	11/04	11/07	12/01/09

Dividends have been paid since 1992. Source: Company reports.

The McGraw-Hill Companies

Intel Corp

Business Summary November 13, 2009

CORPORATE OVERVIEW. Intel is the world's largest semiconductor chipmaker based on revenue and unit shipments, and is well known for its dominant market share in microprocessors for personal computers (PCs). The company has three main operating segments: Digital Enterprise Group, Mobility Group, and Other Products.

The Digital Enterprise Group (55% of 2008 total sales) makes products that are incorporated into desktop and nettop computers, enterprise computing servers and workstations, a broad range of embedded applications, and other products that help make up the infrastructure of the Internet. DEG serves the broad desktop computing market, including consumer and enterprise desktops, as well as the enterprise, and embedded and communications market segments. Revenues from microprocessors within DEG represented 43% of total sales in 2008.

The Mobility Group (42%) makes microprocessors and related chipsets designed for the notebook and netbook market segments, wireless connectivity products, and energy-efficient products designed for the MID and ultra-mobile PC market segments. Intel's Centrino and Centrino 2 mobile platform, consisting of a processor, chipset, and wireless network connection, represented most of the revenue for the Mobility Group. Revenues from microprocessors

within MG represented 42% of total sales in 2008.

The Other Products segment (3%) includes the NAND Solution Group, which offers NAND flash memory primarily used in memory cards and system-level applications, the Digital Home Group, and Digital Health Group.

CORPORATE STRATEGY. Intel's stated mission is to be the pre-eminent supplier of silicon chips and platform solutions to the worldwide digital economy. Owning over 80% of total microprocessors shipped in late 2008, the company is a clear share leader in the worldwide microprocessor market. Although INTC has a sizable lead over competitors, runner-up Advanced Micro Devices (AMD), with about a 20% market share, has effectively increased its presence over the past couple of years. In 2005, when Intel was focusing on creating faster microprocessors, AMD went in a different direction and focused on creating chips that were not only fast but also power efficient, a quality that became increasingly attractive to enterprises with large energy bills and to laptop customers facing short battery lives, among others.

Company Financials Fiscal Year Ended Dec. 31

Per Share Data ($)	2008	2007	2006	2005	2004	2003	2002	2001	2000	1999
Tangible Book Value	6.18	6.51	5.70	5.46	5.57	5.26	4.74	4.59	4.67	4.14
Cash Flow	1.72	1.98	1.65	2.15	1.91	1.62	1.25	1.13	2.20	1.57
Earnings	0.92	1.18	0.86	1.40	1.16	0.85	0.46	0.19	1.51	1.05
S&P Core Earnings	0.96	1.18	0.77	1.22	0.99	0.83	0.35	0.11	NA	NA
Dividends	0.55	0.45	0.40	0.32	0.16	0.08	0.08	0.08	0.07	0.07
Payout Ratio	60%	38%	47%	23%	14%	9%	17%	42%	4%	7%
Prices:High	26.34	27.99	26.63	28.84	34.60	34.51	36.78	38.59	75.81	44.75
Prices:Low	12.06	18.75	16.75	21.94	19.64	14.88	12.95	18.96	29.81	25.06
P/E Ratio:High	29	24	31	21	30	41	80	NM	50	42
P/E Ratio:Low	13	16	19	16	17	18	28	NM	20	24

Income Statement Analysis (Million $)										
Revenue	37,586	38,334	35,382	38,826	34,209	30,141	26,764	26,539	33,726	29,389
Operating Income	14,283	13,643	10,861	16,685	15,019	13,225	9,746	8,923	15,339	13,756
Depreciation	4,619	4,798	4,654	4,595	4,889	5,070	5,344	6,469	4,835	3,597
Interest Expense	8.00	15.0	1,202	19.0	50.0	62.0	84.0	56.0	35.0	36.0
Pretax Income	7,686	9,166	7,068	12,610	10,417	7,442	4,204	2,183	15,141	11,228
Effective Tax Rate	31.2%	23.9%	28.6%	31.3%	27.8%	24.2%	25.9%	40.9%	30.4%	34.9%
Net Income	5,292	6,976	5,044	8,664	7,516	5,641	3,117	1,291	10,535	7,314
S&P Core Earnings	5,521	6,978	4,518	7,555	6,374	5,467	2,332	740	NA	NA

Balance Sheet & Other Financial Data (Million $)										
Cash	11,843	15,363	6,598	7,324	8,407	7,971	7,404	7,970	2,976	3,695
Current Assets	19,871	23,885	18,280	21,194	24,058	22,882	18,925	17,633	21,150	17,819
Total Assets	50,715	55,651	48,368	48,314	48,143	47,143	44,224	44,395	47,945	43,849
Current Liabilities	7,818	8,571	8,514	9,234	8,006	6,879	6,595	6,570	8,650	7,099
Long Term Debt	1,886	1,980	1,848	2,106	703	936	929	1,050	707	955
Common Equity	39,088	42,762	36,752	36,182	38,579	37,846	35,468	35,830	37,322	32,535
Total Capital	41,020	45,153	38,865	38,991	40,137	40,264	37,629	37,825	39,295	36,750
Capital Expenditures	5,197	5,000	5,779	5,818	3,843	3,656	4,703	7,309	6,674	3,403
Cash Flow	9,911	11,774	9,698	13,259	12,405	10,711	8,461	7,760	15,370	10,911
Current Ratio	2.5	2.8	2.1	2.3	3.0	3.3	2.9	2.7	2.4	2.5
% Long Term Debt of Capitalization	4.6	4.4	4.8	5.4	1.8	2.3	2.5	2.8	1.8	2.6
% Net Income of Revenue	14.1	18.2	14.3	22.3	22.0	18.7	11.6	4.9	31.2	24.9
% Return on Assets	10.0	13.4	10.4	18.0	15.8	12.3	7.0	2.8	23.0	19.4
% Return on Equity	12.9	17.6	13.8	23.2	19.7	15.4	8.7	3.5	30.1	26.0

Data as orig reptd.; bef. results of disc opers/spec. items. Per share data adj. for stk. divs.; EPS diluted. E-Estimated. NA-Not Available. NM-Not Meaningful. NR-Not Ranked. UR-Under Review.

Office: 2200 Mission College Boulevard, Santa Clara, CA 95054-1549.
Telephone: 408-765-8080.
Website: http://www.intc.com
Chrmn: J.E. Shaw

Pres & CEO: P.S. Otellini
EVP & Chief Admin Officer: A. Bryant
SVP & General Counsel: D. Melamed
CFO & Chief Acctg Officer: S.J. Smith

Investor Contact: R. Gallegos (408-765-5374)
Board Members: C. Barshefsky, S. Decker, J. J. Donahoe, R. E. Hundt, P. S. Otellini, J. Plummer, D. S. Pottruck, J. E. Shaw, J. L. Thornton, F. D. Yeary, D. B. Yoffie

Founded: 1968
Domicile: Delaware
Employees: 83,900

IntercontinentalExchange Inc

STANDARD &POOR'S

S&P Recommendation	HOLD ★★★☆☆	Price	12-Mo. Target Price	Investment Style
		$104.82 (as of Nov 27, 2009)	$108.00	Large-Cap Growth

GICS Sector Financials
Sub-Industry Specialized Finance

Summary ICE is a fully electronic marketplace that offers exchange-based and over-the-counter trading of a variety of energy and soft commodity products.

Key Stock Statistics (Source S&P, Vickers, company reports)

52-Wk Range	$121.93–50.10	S&P Oper. EPS 2009**E**	4.49	Market Capitalization(B)	$7.679	Beta	1.43
Trailing 12-Month EPS	$3.80	S&P Oper. EPS 2010**E**	5.35	Yield (%)	Nil	S&P 3-Yr. Proj. EPS CAGR(%)	14
Trailing 12-Month P/E	27.6	P/E on S&P Oper. EPS 2009**E**	23.3	Dividend Rate/Share	Nil	S&P Credit Rating	NA
$10K Invested 5 Yrs Ago	NA	Common Shares Outstg. (M)	73.3	Institutional Ownership (%)	87		

Price Performance

30-Week Mov. Avg. ··· 10-Week Mov. Avg. - - **GAAP Earnings vs. Previous Year** Volume Above Avg. STARS
12-Mo. Target Price — Relative Strength ▲ Up ▼ Down ► No Change Below Avg. ★

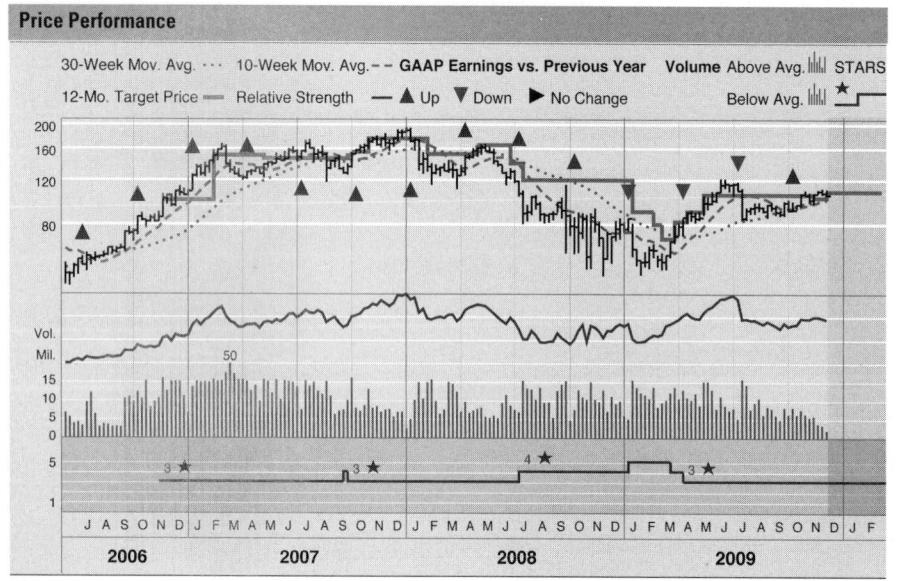

Options: ASE, CBOE, P, Ph

Analysis prepared by **Rafay Khalid, CFA** on November 23, 2009, when the stock traded at **$ 106.77**.

Highlights

► By embracing electronic trading and being an innovator with its centrally cleared over-the-counter (OTC) offerings, ICE has established itself as a leading marketplace for trading energy products. Nevertheless, de-leveraging by hedge funds and banks and the possibility that increased regulation in the form of position limits and more scarce hedge exemptions increases the risk of volumes receding. However, results thus far in 2009 seem to indicate that energy market trading volumes have resilience despite the headwinds.

► In 2009, we forecast the popular U.K.-based oil futures contracts will generate positive volume growth and what we view as strong growth in U.S. derivatives. But we expect OTC energy derivatives contracts will be weak in 2009. In addition, we project higher expenses, primarily related to recent acquisitions and new initiatives. As a result, we forecast operating margins will decline to 53.2% from 60.7% in 2008, but then partially rebound to 56.1% in 2010.

► We estimate operating EPS of $4.49 in 2009 and $5.35 in 2010.

Investment Rationale/Risk

► While near-term earnings visibility is somewhat cloudy stemming from uncertainty about trading volumes and potential regulatory changes, we are positive about ICE's long-term prospects. Momentum from ICE's agreement with nine major banks regarding their support of a central credit-default swap (CDS) clearinghouse has ramped up since ICE began clearing operations on March 9. We expect CDS clearing to be slightly accretive in 2009, and expect greater growth in 2010. In the long term, we believe centralized clearing and exchange-based trading of most derivatives will be commonplace and will allow ICE to leverage its low fixed-cost structure. In addition, we are encouraged by the launch of CDS clearing in Europe, and in the U.S. we see improvements in agriculture volumes giving rise to increasing revenues due to their high rates per contract relative to other products.

► Risks to our recommendation and target price include slower trading volumes, enhanced regulatory scrutiny, and increasing competition.

► Our 12-month target price of $108 is based on a historical average P/E of 20.2X our 2010 EPS projection.

Qualitative Risk Assessment

LOW	MEDIUM	HIGH

Our risk assessment reflects the potential volatility in results due to changes in energy product trading volumes, recent acquisition activity in the sector, and a changing regulatory environment.

Quantitative Evaluations

S&P Quality Ranking NR

D	C	B-	B	B+	A-	A	A+

Relative Strength Rank MODERATE

69

LOWEST = 1   HIGHEST = 99

Revenue/Earnings Data

Revenue (Million $)

	1Q	2Q	3Q	4Q	Year
2009	231.6	250.4	256.3	--	--
2008	207.2	197.2	201.4	207.3	813.1
2007	126.6	136.7	151.7	159.3	574.3
2006	73.59	73.59	94.66	95.26	313.8
2005	31.83	37.53	45.24	41.26	155.9
2004	24.21	26.26	29.45	28.50	108.4

Earnings Per Share ($)

2009	0.98	0.97	1.18	E1.21	E4.49
2008	1.29	1.19	1.04	0.67	4.17
2007	0.80	0.75	0.93	0.90	3.39
2006	0.33	0.52	0.73	0.81	2.40
2005	0.17	-0.13	0.05	-0.48	0.39
2004	0.09	0.10	0.13	0.09	0.41

Fiscal year ended Dec. 31. Next earnings report expected: Mid February. EPS Estimates based on S&P Operating Earnings; historical GAAP earnings are as reported.

Dividend Data

No cash dividends have been paid.

Please read the Required Disclosures and Analyst Certification on the last page of this report.

The McGraw-Hill Companies

IntercontinentalExchange Inc

STANDARD &POOR'S

Business Summary November 23, 2009

CORPORATE OVERVIEW. IntercontinentalExchange, Inc. operates a fully electronic marketplace offering exchange-based and over-the-counter (OTC) trading of a variety of energy products, and is the leading global exchange for soft commodities. The company's primary products include futures contracts for Brent crude oil and West Texas Intermediate crude oil, OTC trading of Henry Hub natural gas contracts, and various soft commodity futures. ICE provides trading for financial settlement and contracts for physical delivery of the underlying commodity.

ICE was formed in May 2000 to provide a platform for OTC energy trading. In June 2001, the company acquired the International Petroleum Exchange (IPE), which was mainly a floor-based futures exchange. In early 2002, the company introduced the industry's first cleared OTC contract through its partnership with LCH.Clearnet. In April 2005, ICE closed the IPE trading floor and moved to an entirely electronic marketplace. In January 2007, ICE acquired the New York Board of Trade (NYBOT) for approximately $1.1 billion. NYBOT, which has been renamed ICE Futures U.S., is a leading soft commodity exchange for products such as sugar, coffee, cocoa, orange juice, pulp and cotton, as well as several financial products. In 2008, ICE derived approximately 85% of its revenue from commission fees associated with trading its products on its exchange and OTC platforms. ICE generates a majority of its trading commissions from a relatively small amount of crude, gas oil, and North American power futures and OTC contracts.

We view ICE's move to offer cleared OTC contracts as one of the key growth drivers for the OTC business. Transaction fees for cleared OTC contracts grew from $6.0 million in 2003 to over $274 million in 2008, and now represent about 62% of OTC revenue, up from 14% in 2003. By offering cleared contracts for the traditionally bilaterally settled OTC market, we believe ICE has helped to simplify and reduce the credit risk for OTC transactions, facilitating greater trading activity.

COMPETITIVE LANDSCAPE. ICE's principal competitor in the energy market is the New York Mercantile Exchange (NYMEX). In August 2008, NYMEX merged with the Chicago Mercantile Exchange. ICE also faces global competition from a number of natural gas and power exchanges and OTC brokers. We believe competition is based on a number of factors, including the depth and liquidity of markets, transaction costs, reliability, and clearing and settlement support.

Company Financials Fiscal Year Ended Dec. 31

Per Share Data ($)	2008	2007	2006	2005	2004	2003	2002	2001	2000	1999
Tangible Book Value	NM	NM	6.42	2.82	2.56	NA	NA	NA	NA	NA
Cash Flow	5.03	3.85	2.63	1.04	0.73	0.72	0.89	NA	NA	NA
Earnings	4.17	3.39	2.40	0.39	0.41	0.37	0.37	NA	NA	NA
S&P Core Earnings	4.31	3.30	2.39	0.82	0.32	0.18	NA	NA	NA	NA
Dividends	Nil	Nil	Nil	Nil	NA	NA	NA	NA	NA	NA
Payout Ratio	Nil	Nil	Nil	Nil	NA	NA	NA	NA	NA	NA
Prices:High	193.87	194.92	113.85	44.21	NA	NA	NA	NA	NA	NA
Prices:Low	49.69	108.15	36.00	26.00	NA	NA	NA	NA	NA	NA
P/E Ratio:High	46	57	47	NM	NA	NA	NA	NA	NA	NA
P/E Ratio:Low	12	32	15	NM	NA	NA	NA	NA	NA	NA

Income Statement Analysis (Million $)										
Revenue	813	574	314	156	108	93.7	125	NA	NA	NA
Operating Income	556	397	218	91.1	49.4	38.3	65.3	NA	NA	NA
Depreciation	62.3	32.7	13.7	15.1	17.0	19.3	14.4	NA	NA	NA
Interest Expense	19.6	18.6	0.23	0.61	0.14	0.08	0.40	NA	NA	NA
Pretax Income	474	358	213	60.0	33.7	19.9	25.4	NA	NA	NA
Effective Tax Rate	36.4%	32.9%	32.6%	32.6%	34.7%	32.7%	33.8%	NA	NA	NA
Net Income	301	241	143	40.4	21.9	13.4	34.7	NA	NA	NA
S&P Core Earnings	311	234	143	43.8	17.0	9.81	NA	NA	NA	NA

Balance Sheet & Other Financial Data (Million $)										
Cash	287	280	204	32.6	89.2	56.9	NA	NA	NA	NA
Current Assets	12,553	1,142	341	164	NA	NA	NA	NA	NA	NA
Total Assets	14,960	2,796	493	266	208	215	NA	NA	NA	NA
Current Liabilities	12,312	911	37.9	26.4	NA	NA	NA	NA	NA	NA
Long Term Debt	336	184	Nil	Nil	Nil	NA	NA	NA	NA	NA
Common Equity	2,006	1,477	454	233	221	186	NA	NA	NA	NA
Total Capital	2,544	1,770	454	238	221	186	NA	NA	NA	NA
Capital Expenditures	30.5	43.3	12.4	8.61	1.70	1.61	14.8	NA	NA	NA
Cash Flow	363	273	157	55.5	38.9	39.3	49.1	NA	NA	NA
Current Ratio	1.0	1.3	9.0	6.2	2.9	5.9	NA	NA	NA	NA
% Long Term Debt of Capitalization	13.2	10.4	Nil	Nil	Nil	Nil	Nil	NA	NA	NA
% Net Income of Revenue	37.0	41.9	45.5	25.9	20.3	14.3	27.8	NA	NA	NA
% Return on Assets	3.4	14.6	37.7	NM	10.4	NA	NA	NA	NA	NA
% Return on Equity	17.3	24.9	41.6	NM	13.1	NA	NA	NA	NA	NA

Data as orig reptd.; bef. results of disc opers/spec. items. Per share data adj. for stk. divs.; EPS diluted. E-Estimated. NA-Not Available. NM-Not Meaningful. NR-Not Ranked. UR-Under Review.

Office: 2100 RiverEdge Parkway, Atlanta, GA 30328.
Telephone: 770-857-4700.
Email: ir@theice.com
Website: http://www.theice.com

Chrmn & CEO: J.C. Sprecher
Pres & COO: C.A. Vice
SVP, CFO & Chief Acctg Officer: S.A. Hill
SVP & CTO: E.D. Marcial

SVP, Secy & General Counsel: J.H. Short
Investor Contact: K. Loeffler (770-857-4726)
Board Members: C. R. Crisp, J. Forneri, F. W. Hatfield, T. F. Martell, M. C. McCarthy, R. Reid, F. V. Salerno, F. W. Schneider, F. W. Schoenhut, J. C. Sprecher, J. A. Sprieser, V. Tese

Founded: 2000
Domicile: Delaware
Employees: 795

The McGraw-Hill Companies

International Business Machines Corp

STANDARD &POOR'S

S&P Recommendation **STRONG BUY** ★★★★★	Price $125.70 (as of Nov 27, 2009)	12-Mo. Target Price $163.00	Investment Style Large-Cap Growth

GICS Sector Information Technology
Sub-Industry Computer Hardware

Summary IBM's global capabilities include information technology services, software, computer hardware equipment, fundamental research, and related financing.

Key Stock Statistics (Source S&P, Vickers, company reports)

52-Wk Range	$128.94– 75.31	S&P Oper. EPS 2009**E**	9.97	Market Capitalization(B)	$165.120	Beta	0.81
Trailing 12-Month EPS	$9.74	S&P Oper. EPS 2010**E**	11.25	Yield (%)	1.75	S&P 3-Yr. Proj. EPS CAGR(%)	12
Trailing 12-Month P/E	12.9	P/E on S&P Oper. EPS 2009**E**	12.6	Dividend Rate/Share	$2.20	S&P Credit Rating	A+
$10K Invested 5 Yrs Ago	$14,287	Common Shares Outstg. (M)	1,313.6	Institutional Ownership (%)	59		

Price Performance

30-Week Mov. Avg. · · · 10-Week Mov. Avg. - - **GAAP Earnings vs. Previous Year**   Volume Above Avg. ▥▥ STARS
12-Mo. Target Price — Relative Strength — ▲ Up ▼ Down ▶ No Change   Below Avg. ▥▥ ★

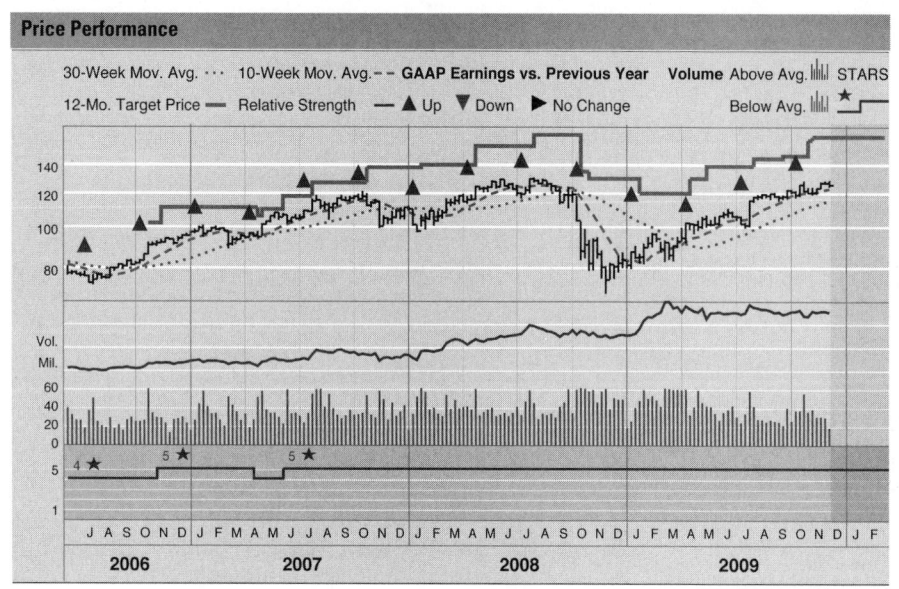

Options: ASE, CBOE, P, Ph

Analysis prepared by **Thomas W. Smith, CFA** on October 29, 2009, when the stock traded at **$ 121.50**.

Highlights

▶ We expect revenues to decrease about 8% in 2009, reflecting a slower growing global economy and negative currency effects. We then project a 4% revenue increase for 2010 as we see economic conditions gradually improving. We believe the Services segments will continue to gain traction, given a $134 billion services order backlog at the end of September 2009. We project growth in IBM's Software segment, reflecting recent acquisitions, including Cognos, Platform Solutions, ILOG, and Exeros. We look for softness in Systems and Technology segment sales, as hardware is being hit especially hard in an IT industry downturn.

▶ We look for gross margins to widen to 45.8% in 2009 and 46.6% in 2010, from 44.1% in 2008, on ongoing cost reduction efforts and an improved sales mix. We think pretax margins will expand as well. Effective tax rates should benefit from more international business.

▶ We estimate EPS of $9.97 for 2009 and $11.25 for 2010. About $9.2 billion of board authorizations for buybacks was in place as of October 27, 2009, and we expect share buybacks to bolster EPS.

Investment Rationale/Risk

▶ IBM's results should benefit from relatively strong revenue growth in emerging markets and a widening of margins reflecting cost cutting and improved profitability in more mature markets. We expect per-share results to benefit from lower interest expenses as debt is reduced, lower effective tax rates as business shifts overseas, and from share buybacks.

▶ Risks to our recommendation and target price include a preliminary investigation of the mainframe computer market by the Department of Justice begun in early October 2009. Pricing pressure and product transitions also pose risks.

▶ Our 12-month target price of $163 reflects a target P/E near 15X, which is toward the middle of the recent five-year historical range for IBM, applied to our 12-month forward EPS estimate of $10.84. Our target P/E is also at a discount to the 16.6X P/E of Information Technology Sector companies in the S&P 500 Index based on 2010 earnings estimates. We view the stock's valuation as compelling given IBM's economies of scale and relatively steady earnings performance.

Qualitative Risk Assessment

LOW	MEDIUM	HIGH

Our risk assessment reflects what we view as IBM's competitively positioned solutions offerings, global market presence, and significant economies of scale, offset by what we see as an intensely competitive pricing environment.

Quantitative Evaluations

S&P Quality Ranking A

D	C	B-	B	B+	A-	A	A+

Relative Strength Rank MODERATE

66

LOWEST = 1   HIGHEST = 99

Revenue/Earnings Data

Revenue (Million $)

	1Q	2Q	3Q	4Q	Year
2009	21,711	23,250	23,566	--	--
2008	24,502	26,820	25,302	27,006	103,630
2007	22,029	23,772	24,119	28,866	98,786
2006	20,659	21,890	22,617	26,257	91,424
2005	22,908	22,270	21,529	24,427	91,134
2004	22,175	23,098	23,349	27,671	96,293

Earnings Per Share ($)

	1Q	2Q	3Q	4Q	Year
2009	1.70	2.32	2.40	E3.55	E9.97
2008	1.65	1.98	2.05	3.28	8.93
2007	1.21	1.55	1.68	2.80	7.18
2006	1.08	1.30	1.45	2.30	6.06
2005	0.85	1.14	0.94	2.01	4.91
2004	0.93	1.16	1.06	1.81	4.94

Fiscal year ended Dec. 31. Next earnings report expected: Late January. EPS Estimates based on S&P Operating Earnings; historical GAAP earnings are as reported.

Dividend Data (Dates: mm/dd Payment Date: mm/dd/yy)

Amount ($)	Date Decl.	Ex-Div. Date	Stk. of Record	Payment Date
0.500	01/27	02/06	02/10	03/10/09
0.550	04/28	05/06	05/08	06/10/09
0.550	07/28	08/06	08/10	09/10/09
0.550	10/27	11/06	11/10	12/10/09

Dividends have been paid since 1916. Source: Company reports.

Please read the Required Disclosures and Analyst Certification on the last page of this report.

The McGraw-Hill Companies

International Business Machines Corp

STANDARD &POOR'S

Business Summary October 29, 2009

CORPORATE OVERVIEW. With a corporate history dating back to 1911, International Business Machines has grown to be a major contributor to each major category that comprises the total information technology market: hardware, software, and services. The company is a leading server vendor, among the largest software vendors (behind Microsoft Corp.), and has the largest global services organization.

The company strives for innovation as a means of product differentiation, and had a research and development budget of $6.3 billion in 2008, up from $6.2 billion in 2007. IBM reports being awarded over 4,000 patents in 2008, more than any other company.

The global scope of operations is reflected in the mix of revenue sources in 2008, with the Americas representing about 41%, EMEA 36%, Asia Pacific 20%, and an OEM category 3%. Regional growth was stronger outside the Americas in 2008 on a dollar reporting basis, but was stronger in the Americas on a constant currency basis. Revenue from the Americas grew at a 4% (4% in constant currency) pace in 2008, while revenue from EMEA grew 7% (3%), and revenue from Asia Pacific grew 8% (2%), compared to a 5% (2%) rate for

all IBM. The company's revenue from the so-called BRIC countries (Brazil, Russia, India and China) grew 18% (15%) in 2008.

CORPORATE STRATEGY. IBM has evolved from being a computer hardware vendor to a systems, services and software company. While computer hardware (included in the Systems and Technology segment) accounted for about 19% of sales in 2008 (22% of sales in 2007), IBM has emphasized -- through acquisitions and investments -- services and software. These areas serving adjacent markets to hardware have gained momentum as IBM leverages its ability to offer total solutions to customers. IBM's focus on higher value added segments such as services, at 57% of 2008 sales (55% of 2007 sales), and software 21% (20%) resulted in these areas together representing almost 78% of revenue in 2008. Global financing represented approximately 3% (3%) of 2008 revenues, and is primarily used to leverage IBM's financial structuring and portfolio management, and to expand the customer base.

Company Financials Fiscal Year Ended Dec. 31

Per Share Data ($)	2008	2007	2006	2005	2004	2003	2002	2001	2000	1999
Tangible Book Value	NM	8.72	8.93	13.97	11.86	12.36	10.84	12.96	11.08	10.65
Cash Flow	12.49	10.22	9.39	8.10	7.82	7.01	5.61	7.08	6.95	7.40
Earnings	8.93	7.18	6.06	4.91	4.94	4.34	3.07	4.35	4.44	4.12
S&P Core Earnings	6.04	6.94	5.88	3.93	4.06	3.00	0.08	1.33	NA	NA
Dividends	1.90	1.50	1.10	0.78	0.70	0.63	0.59	0.55	0.51	0.47
Payout Ratio	21%	21%	18%	16%	14%	15%	19%	13%	11%	11%
Prices:High	130.93	121.46	97.88	99.10	100.43	94.54	126.39	124.70	134.94	139.19
Prices:Low	69.50	88.77	72.73	71.85	90.82	73.17	54.01	83.75	80.06	80.88
P/E Ratio:High	15	17	16	20	20	22	41	29	30	34
P/E Ratio:Low	8	12	12	15	18	17	18	19	18	20

Income Statement Analysis (Million $)	2008	2007	2006	2005	2004	2003	2002	2001	2000	1999
Revenue	103,630	98,786	91,424	91,134	96,293	89,131	81,186	85,866	88,396	87,548
Operating Income	21,680	18,765	16,912	14,564	15,890	14,790	11,175	14,115	16,147	18,086
Depreciation	4,930	4,405	4,983	5,188	4,915	4,701	4,379	4,820	4,513	6,159
Interest Expense	1,477	1,431	278	220	139	145	145	238	717	727
Pretax Income	16,715	14,489	13,317	12,226	12,028	10,874	7,524	10,953	11,534	11,757
Effective Tax Rate	26.2%	28.1%	29.3%	34.6%	29.8%	30.0%	29.1%	29.5%	29.8%	34.4%
Net Income	12,334	10,418	9,416	7,994	8,448	7,613	5,334	7,723	8,093	7,712
S&P Core Earnings	8,340	10,072	9,116	6,395	6,923	5,270	111	2,302	NA	NA

Balance Sheet & Other Financial Data (Million $)	2008	2007	2006	2005	2004	2003	2002	2001	2000	1999
Cash	12,907	16,146	10,656	13,686	10,570	7,647	5,975	6,393	3,722	5,831
Current Assets	49,004	53,177	44,660	45,661	46,970	44,998	41,652	42,461	43,880	43,155
Total Assets	109,524	120,431	103,234	105,748	109,183	104,457	96,484	88,313	88,349	87,495
Current Liabilities	42,435	44,310	40,091	35,152	39,798	37,900	34,550	35,119	36,406	39,578
Long Term Debt	22,689	23,039	13,780	15,425	14,828	16,986	19,986	15,963	18,371	14,124
Common Equity	13,465	28,470	28,506	33,098	29,747	27,864	22,782	23,614	20,624	20,264
Total Capital	45,096	51,509	42,286	48,523	44,575	44,850	42,768	39,577	38,995	36,236
Capital Expenditures	4,171	4,630	4,362	3,842	4,368	4,393	4,753	5,660	5,616	5,959
Cash Flow	17,264	14,823	14,399	13,182	13,363	12,314	9,713	12,533	12,586	13,851
Current Ratio	1.2	1.2	1.1	1.3	1.2	1.2	1.2	1.2	1.2	1.1
% Long Term Debt of Capitalization	71.6	44.7	32.6	31.7	33.3	37.9	46.7	40.3	47.1	39.2
% Net Income of Revenue	11.9	10.6	10.3	8.8	8.8	8.5	6.6	9.0	9.2	8.8
% Return on Assets	10.7	9.3	9.0	7.4	7.9	7.6	5.7	8.7	9.2	8.9
% Return on Equity	58.8	36.6	30.6	24.7	29.3	30.1	23.1	35.1	39.7	39.0

Data as orig reptd.; bef. results of disc opers/spec. items. Per share data adj. for stk. divs.; EPS diluted. E-Estimated. NA-Not Available. NM-Not Meaningful. NR-Not Ranked. UR-Under Review.

Office: New Orchard Road, Armonk, NY 10504.
Telephone: 914-499-1900.
Website: http://www.ibm.com
Chrmn, Pres & CEO: S.J. Palmisano

SVP & CFO: M. Loughridge
SVP & General Counsel: R.C. Weber
Treas: M.J. Schroeter
Secy: A. Bonzani

Investor Contact: T.S. Shaughnessy (914-499-1900)   **Founded:** 1910
Board Members: A. J. Belda, C. P. Black, W. Brody, K. I.   **Domicile:** New York
Chenault, M. L. Eskew, S. A. Jackson, W. J. McNerney,   **Employees:** 398,455
Jr., T. Nishimuro, J. W. Owens, S. J. Palmisano, J. E.
Spero, S. Taurel, L. Zambrano

International Flavors & Fragrances Inc.

STANDARD
&POOR'S

S&P Recommendation HOLD ★★★☆☆	Price $40.32 (as of Nov 27, 2009)	12-Mo. Target Price $42.00	Investment Style Large-Cap Growth

GICS Sector Materials
Sub-Industry Specialty Chemicals

Summary This leading producer of flavors and fragrances used in a wide variety of consumer goods derives over two-thirds of sales and earnings from operations outside the U.S.

Key Stock Statistics (Source S&P, Vickers, company reports)

52-Wk Range	$41.70–24.96	S&P Oper. EPS 2009**E**	2.64	Market Capitalization(B)	$3.187	Beta	0.87
Trailing 12-Month EPS	$2.50	S&P Oper. EPS 2010**E**	2.90	Yield (%)	2.48	S&P 3-Yr. Proj. EPS CAGR(%)	8
Trailing 12-Month P/E	16.1	P/E on S&P Oper. EPS 2009**E**	15.3	Dividend Rate/Share	$1.00	S&P Credit Rating	BBB
$10K Invested 5 Yrs Ago	$11,150	Common Shares Outstg. (M)	79.0	Institutional Ownership (%)	80		

Price Performance

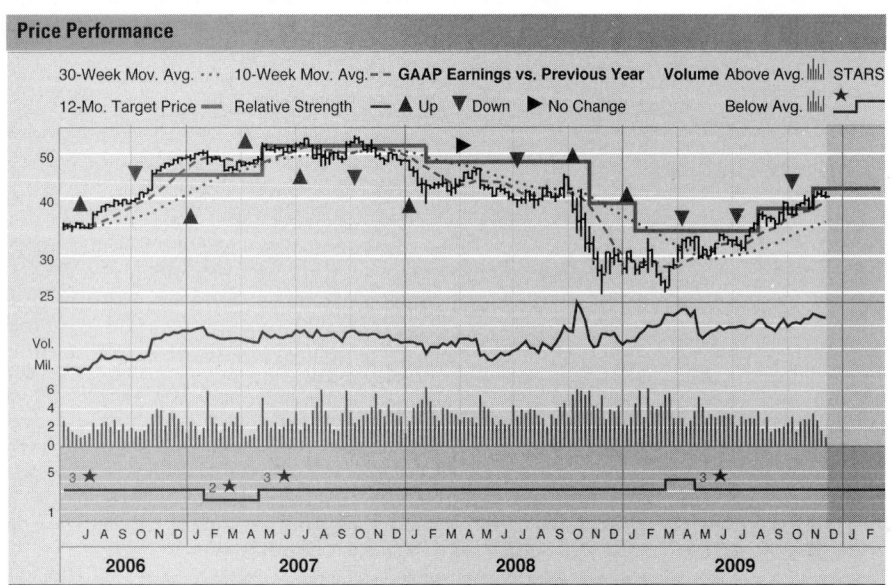

- 30-Week Mov. Avg. · · · 10-Week Mov. Avg. – – GAAP Earnings vs. Previous Year   Volume Above Avg. STARS
- 12-Mo. Target Price — Relative Strength — ▲ Up ▼ Down ▶ No Change   Below Avg. ★

Options: CBOE

Analysis prepared by **Richard O'Reilly, CFA** on November 06, 2009, when the stock traded at **$ 40.25**.

Highlights

- ► We expect sales in 2010 to increase by about 5%, aided by favorable currency exchange rates, following a modest decline expected for 2009, which includes unfavorable exchange rates and slowdowns in domestic and European consumer markets earlier in the year. We believe that IFF in 2009 continued to gain share with major customers based on a high win rate of new business, but we expect the retail environment for fine fragrances to remain challenging in late 2009.

- ► We forecast a gross margin of about 40.5% in 2010, assuming a decline in raw material and freight costs beginning in late 2009, up from 40.0% seen for 2009, which reflects sales softness for high margin fine fragrances.

- ► We expect a decline in interest expense in 2009, excluding a $4 million charge in the first quarter for the settlement of an interest rate swap. We project that the effective tax rate for 2010 will be about 27%, up from 2009. Our EPS estimate for 2009 excludes $0.20 of special and restructuring charges

Investment Rationale/Risk

- ► We expect the company to be helped in 2010 by a high win rate of new business, especially in flavors, while currency exchange rates should turn into a favorable tailwind on EPS. We believe IFF has strong cash flows and ample liquidity, including revolving credit facilities.

- ► Risks to our recommendation and target price include increased economic and political uncertainties in global markets, greater currency fluctuations, an inability to maintain close relationships with customers, lack of customers' success in new product launches, and unexpected increases in raw material costs.

- ► The shares, with a dividend yield of about 2.5%, recently traded at a P/E of about 14X our 2010 EPS estimate. We think the stock will perform in line with the S&P 500 over the next 12 months, reflecting what we see as a favorable EPS outlook for 2010. Assuming a P/E multiple closer to peers, our 12-month target price is $42.

Qualitative Risk Assessment

LOW	MEDIUM	HIGH

Our risk assessment reflects our view of the stable nature of the company's businesses and end markets, and its leadership product positions, offset by a somewhat concentrated customer base.

Quantitative Evaluations

S&P Quality Ranking   A-

D	C	B-	B	B+	A-	A	A+

Relative Strength Rank   STRONG

73

LOWEST = 1   HIGHEST = 99

Revenue/Earnings Data

Revenue (Million $)

	1Q	2Q	3Q	4Q	Year
2009	599.6	568.3	612.6	--	--
2008	596.6	636.1	617.5	539.1	2,389
2007	566.1	573.7	583.3	553.5	2,277
2006	511.4	530.5	539.1	514.3	2,095
2005	523.1	515.6	493.1	461.7	1,993
2004	535.0	524.2	506.2	468.2	2,034

Earnings Per Share ($)

2009	0.60	0.61	0.66	E0.57	E2.64
2008	0.69	0.83	0.73	0.62	2.87
2007	0.69	0.87	0.67	0.58	2.82
2006	0.58	0.67	0.70	0.53	2.48
2005	0.55	0.60	0.72	0.16	2.04
2004	0.59	0.59	0.44	0.43	2.05

Fiscal year ended Dec. 31. Next earnings report expected: Early February. EPS Estimates based on S&P Operating Earnings; historical GAAP earnings are as reported.

Dividend Data (Dates: mm/dd Payment Date: mm/dd/yy)

Amount ($)	Date Decl.	Ex-Div. Date	Stk. of Record	Payment Date
0.250	12/09	12/17	12/19	01/06/09
0.250	03/10	03/18	03/20	04/03/09
0.250	04/28	06/18	06/22	07/07/09
0.250	07/28	09/17	09/21	10/05/09

Dividends have been paid since 1956. Source: Company reports.

Please read the Required Disclosures and Analyst Certification on the last page of this report.

International Flavors & Fragrances Inc.

STANDARD &POOR'S

Business Summary November 06, 2009

CORPORATE OVERVIEW. International Flavors & Fragrances, founded in 1909, is a leading global maker of products used by other manufacturers to enhance the aromas and tastes of consumer products. The November 2000 purchase of Bush Boake Allen Inc. (BOA) for $970 million boosted annual sales to nearly $2 billion.

IFF receives more than 70% of its sales outside the U.S. In 2008, North America contributed 25% of sales; Europe 38%; Latin America 14%; and Asia-Pacific 23%.

Fragrance products accounted for 54% of sales and 50% of operating profits in 2008. Fragrances are used in the manufacture of soaps, detergents, cosmetic creams, lotions and powders, lipsticks, after shave lotions, deodorants, hair preparations, air fresheners, perfumes and colognes and other consumer products. Most major U.S. companies in these industries are IFF customers. Cosmetics (including perfumes and toiletries) and household products (soaps and detergents) are the two largest customer groups.

Flavor products account for IFF's remaining sales and profits. Flavors are sold principally to the food, beverage and other industries for use in consumer products such as soft drinks, candies, cake mixes, desserts, prepared foods, dietary foods, dairy products, drink powders, pharmaceuticals, oral care products, alcoholic beverages and tobacco. Two of the largest customers for flavor products are major U.S. producers of prepared foods and beverages.

By category, 46% of sales in 2008 were from flavor compounds, 23% functional fragrances (for personal care and household products), 19% fine fragrances and beauty care (perfumes, colognes and toiletries), and 12% ingredients.

The company uses both synthetic and natural ingredients in its compounds. IFF manufactures most of the synthetic ingredients, of which a substantial portion (45% in 2008) is sold to others. It has had a consistent commitment to R&D spending, and anticipates that R&D expense will approximate 9% of annual sales over the next several years. R&D is conducted in 32 laboratories in 24 countries.

Company Financials Fiscal Year Ended Dec. 31

Per Share Data ($)	2008	2007	2006	2005	2004	2003	2002	2001	2000	1999
Tangible Book Value	NM	NM	1.78	1.54	1.28	NM	NM	NM	NM	8.19
Cash Flow	3.82	3.77	3.46	3.07	3.01	2.77	2.72	2.47	1.90	2.06
Earnings	2.87	2.82	2.48	2.04	2.05	1.83	1.84	1.20	1.22	1.53
S&P Core Earnings	2.29	2.75	2.35	2.04	1.82	1.70	1.37	0.70	NA	NA
Dividends	0.96	0.88	0.77	0.73	0.69	0.63	0.60	0.60	1.52	1.52
Payout Ratio	33%	31%	31%	36%	33%	34%	33%	50%	125%	99%
Prices:High	48.01	54.75	49.88	42.90	43.20	36.61	37.45	31.69	37.94	48.50
Prices:Low	24.72	45.71	32.53	31.19	32.77	29.18	26.05	19.75	14.69	33.63
P/E Ratio:High	17	19	20	21	21	20	20	26	31	32
P/E Ratio:Low	9	16	13	15	16	16	14	16	12	22

Income Statement Analysis (Million $)										
Revenue	2,389	2,277	2,095	1,993	2,034	1,902	1,809	1,844	1,463	1,439
Operating Income	452	452	421	382	433	415	396	409	322	338
Depreciation	76.0	82.8	89.7	91.9	91.0	86.7	84.5	123	69.3	56.4
Interest Expense	74.0	41.5	25.5	24.0	24.0	28.5	37.0	70.4	25.1	5.15
Pretax Income	281	329	313	246	281	252	266	188	184	243
Effective Tax Rate	18.1%	24.8%	27.7%	21.6%	30.2%	31.5%	34.0%	38.2%	33.2%	33.5%
Net Income	230	247	227	193	196	173	176	116	123	162
S&P Core Earnings	183	241	214	193	174	161	131	68.5	NA	NA

Balance Sheet & Other Financial Data (Million $)										
Cash	179	152	115	273	32.6	12.1	14.9	48.5	129	62.1
Current Assets	1,161	1,190	1,080	1,191	961	903	867	896	1,019	835
Total Assets	2,762	2,727	2,479	2,638	2,363	2,307	2,233	2,268	2,489	1,401
Current Liabilities	451	539	447	1,203	400	526	359	560	1,179	370
Long Term Debt	1,154	1,060	791	131	669	690	1,007	939	417	3.83
Common Equity	573	617	873	915	910	743	575	524	631	858
Total Capital	1,727	1,677	1,665	1,047	1,579	1,433	1,582	1,508	1,152	895
Capital Expenditures	85.4	65.6	58.3	93.4	70.6	6.40	81.8	52.0	60.7	102
Cash Flow	306	330	316	285	287	259	260	239	192	218
Current Ratio	2.6	2.2	2.4	1.0	2.4	1.7	2.4	1.6	0.9	2.3
% Long Term Debt of Capitalization	66.8	63.2	47.5	12.5	42.4	48.2	63.7	62.3	36.2	0.4
% Net Income of Revenue	9.6	10.9	10.8	9.7	9.6	9.1	9.7	6.3	8.4	11.3
% Return on Assets	8.4	9.1	8.9	7.7	8.4	7.6	7.8	4.9	6.3	11.6
% Return on Equity	38.6	33.2	26.0	21.1	23.7	26.2	32.0	20.1	16.5	18.0

Data as orig reptd.; bef. results of disc opers/spec. items. Per share data adj. for stk. divs.; EPS diluted. E-Estimated. NA-Not Available. NM-Not Meaningful. NR-Not Ranked. UR-Under Review.

Office: 521 W 57th St, New York, NY 10019-2960.
Telephone: 212-765-5500.
Email: investor.relations@iff.com
Website: http://www.iff.com

Chrmn & CEO: D.D. Tough
Pres: B.M. Tansky
EVP & CFO: K. Berryman
SVP, Secy & General Counsel: D.M. Meany

Treas: C.D. Weller
Investor Contact: Y. Rudich (212-708-7164)
Board Members: M. H. Adame, M. Bottoli, L. B. Buck, J. M. Cook, P. A. Georgescu, A. A. Herzan, H. W. Howell, Jr., K. M. Hudson, A. C. Martinez, B. M. Tansky, D. D. Tough

Founded: 1909
Domicile: New York
Employees: 5,300

The McGraw-Hill Companies

International Game Technology

STANDARD &POOR'S

S&P Recommendation	HOLD ★★★☆☆	Price $19.41 (as of Nov 27, 2009)	12-Mo. Target Price $21.00	Investment Style Large-Cap Growth

GICS Sector Consumer Discretionary
Sub-Industry Casinos & Gaming

Summary This company is a leading maker of gaming machines and proprietary software systems for gaming machine networks.

Key Stock Statistics (Source S&P, Vickers, company reports)

52-Wk Range	$23.30– 6.81	S&P Oper. EPS 2010E	0.90	Market Capitalization(B)	$5.751	Beta	1.77
Trailing 12-Month EPS	$0.51	S&P Oper. EPS 2011E	NA	Yield (%)	1.24	S&P 3-Yr. Proj. EPS CAGR(%)	7
Trailing 12-Month P/E	38.1	P/E on S&P Oper. EPS 2010E	21.6	Dividend Rate/Share	$0.24	S&P Credit Rating	BBB
$10K Invested 5 Yrs Ago	$5,960	Common Shares Outstg. (M)	296.3	Institutional Ownership (%)	88		

Price Performance

30-Week Mov. Avg. · · · · 10-Week Mov. Avg. ~ — **GAAP Earnings vs. Previous Year** Volume Above Avg. ▨▨▨ STARS
12-Mo. Target Price — Relative Strength — ▲ Up ▼ Down ► No Change Below Avg. ▨▨▨ ★

Options: ASE, CBOE

Analysis prepared by **Esther Y. Kwon, CFA** on November 09, 2009, when the stock traded at **$ 20.51**.

Highlights

► In FY 10 (Sep.), we see revenues rising at a low single digit rate after about a 16% drop in FY 09 on a slight pickup in spending by operators to refresh stale floors and potential expansion of gaming in cash-strapped states looking for additional sources of revenue. We expect gaming operations growth to lag product sales growth as IGT loses share to its competitors in this arena.

► As unit growth resumes, we see product gross margins expanding to over 50% and gaming gross margins exceeding 61%. On restructuring benefits, we forecast SG&A and R&D expenses remaining about flat with FY 09 levels. Overall, we project operating margin expansion of about 300 basis points and EPS of $0.90 in FY 10, versus operating EPS of $0.87 in FY 09.

► In May 2009, IGT issued $850 million in convertible notes due May 2014 and entered into hedging transactions on its common stock and separate warrant transactions with hedge counterparties. These actions may affect share count depending on the stock price.

Investment Rationale/Risk

► In the near term, we are concerned about market share losses and revenue declines in gross gaming revenues at casino operator customers, which we think may result in purchasing delays or price competition among equipment manufacturers. There has also been excessive management turnover recently at IGT, which we think will make a turnaround more difficult. Effective April 1, 2009, former director Patti Hart, who has held several high level positions at technology companies, was named president and CEO, replacing T.J. Matthews, who remains chairman.

► Risks to our recommendation and target price include prospects for growth from new or expanded gaming markets becoming less favorable than we anticipate.

► Our 12-month target price of $21 reflects a P/E about in line with IGT's recent historical average of 25X, but a premium to the S&P 500. We see limited near-term catalysts for the shares, given market share losses, new management and questions about the speed and scope of developing demand for new gaming machines and systems.

Qualitative Risk Assessment

LOW	MEDIUM	HIGH

Our risk assessment reflects the company's industry-leading position as a supplier of gaming machines. We expect the company to generate free cash flow, with at least some of it used for stock repurchases. This is offset by our projection that IGT will continue to spend heavily on research and development and our view that growth prospects depend on regulatory factors and technology changes, including the legalization of gaming markets.

Quantitative Evaluations

S&P Quality Ranking B+

D	C	B-	B	B+	A-	A	A+

Relative Strength Rank MODERATE

36

LOWEST = 1   HIGHEST = 99

Revenue/Earnings Data

Revenue (Million $)

	1Q	2Q	3Q	4Q	Year
2009	601.6	475.7	522.1	514.6	2,114
2008	645.8	573.2	677.4	632.2	2,529
2007	642.3	609.7	706.5	662.9	2,621
2006	616.2	644.4	612.4	638.7	2,512
2005	641.2	551.0	579.6	607.6	2,379
2004	608.1	636.1	618.9	621.7	2,485

Earnings Per Share ($)

2009	0.22	0.13	0.22	-0.07	0.51
2008	0.36	0.22	0.35	0.18	1.10
2007	0.35	0.38	0.41	0.38	1.51
2006	0.34	0.35	0.33	0.33	1.34
2005	0.33	0.26	0.32	0.30	1.20
2004	0.33	0.32	0.38	0.15	1.18

Fiscal year ended Sep. 30. Next earnings report expected: Late January. EPS Estimates based on S&P Operating Earnings; historical GAAP earnings are as reported.

Dividend Data (Dates: mm/dd Payment Date: mm/dd/yy)

Amount ($)	Date Decl.	Ex-Div. Date	Stk. of Record	Payment Date
0.145	12/23	12/31	01/05	01/19/09
0.060	03/03	03/20	03/24	04/07/09
0.060	05/19	06/12	06/16	07/10/09
0.060	08/04	09/03	09/08	10/09/09

Dividends have been paid since 2003. Source: Company reports.

Please read the Required Disclosures and Analyst Certification on the last page of this report.

The McGraw-Hill Companies

International Game Technology

Business Summary November 09, 2009

CORPORATE OVERVIEW. International Game Technology (IGT) is a leading maker of gaming machines. In addition to selling machines, IGT's business includes the placement of machines from which it receives recurring revenues.

In FY 08 (Sep.), 47% of IGT revenues came from product sales, compared to 48% in FY 07, with the remainder from gaming operations, including progressive systems.

Product sales in FY 08 included the sale of 72,700 machines, down from 105,900 machines in FY 07, and down from 112,000 in FY 06. FY 08 sales included 35,000 for North America versus 43,000 and 51,100 in FY 07 and FY 06, respectively. Shipments to international markets totaled 37,700, down from 62,900 machines in FY 07 and 61,900 in FY 06. International sales may include some lower-priced machines with relatively low-value prizes. In addition to machines for casinos, IGT has made video gaming terminals (VGTs) for government-sponsored programs, including lotteries.

IGT's gaming operations segment includes the placement of games in both casinos and government-sponsored gaming markets, under a variety of recurring revenue pricing arrangements, including wide-area progressive systems, standalone participation and flat fee, equipment leasing and rental, as well as hybrid pricing or premium products that include a product sale and a recurring fee.

CORPORATE STRATEGY. In FY 08, IGT's research and development spending totaled $223.1 million (about 8.8% of revenues), up from $202.2 million (7.7%) in FY 07, and up from $188.6 million (7.5%) in FY 06. We expect that the company's ability to develop successful machines and games, with features that appeal to gamblers and casinos, will be a significant factor in the amount of product sales it has.

PRIMARY BUSINESS DYNAMICS. We see opportunities for IGT gaming machines including: racetracks in Indiana; a new opening in the Las Vegas locals market, East Side Cannery; the expansion of Native American casinos in California, Connecticut and Oklahoma; and, the continued build out in Pennsylvania. Longer term, resort openings in Las Vegas and Atlantic City, as well as Singapore, should also drive demand for slots.

Overall, during the next few years, we expect a shift toward sales or licensing of server-based games to become more evident, creating opportunities for increased IGT revenues from sales or licensing of replacement machines or games for use in such locations as U.S. casinos.

Company Financials Fiscal Year Ended Sep. 30

Per Share Data ($)	2009	2008	2007	2006	2005	2004	2003	2002	2001	2000
Tangible Book Value	NA	NM	0.29	2.06	1.56	1.98	1.42	0.55	0.40	NM
Cash Flow	NA	2.03	2.30	1.99	1.78	1.56	1.45	1.23	0.91	0.67
Earnings	0.51	1.10	1.51	1.34	1.20	1.18	1.07	0.80	0.70	0.50
S&P Core Earnings	NA	1.20	1.47	1.33	1.15	1.11	1.02	0.79	0.67	NA
Dividends	0.33	0.57	0.52	0.50	0.48	0.30	0.18	Nil	Nil	Nil
Payout Ratio	64%	51%	34%	37%	40%	25%	16%	Nil	Nil	Nil
Prices:High	23.30	49.41	48.79	46.76	34.63	47.12	37.00	20.03	17.99	12.34
Prices:Low	6.81	7.03	33.57	30.12	24.20	28.22	18.05	11.94	8.93	4.36
P/E Ratio:High	46	45	32	35	29	40	35	25	26	25
P/E Ratio:Low	13	6	22	22	20	24	17	15	13	9

Income Statement Analysis (Million $)										
Revenue	2,114	2,529	2,621	2,512	2,379	2,485	2,128	1,848	1,199	1,004
Operating Income	NA	947	1,066	960	886	964	800	646	315	343
Depreciation	277	286	266	235	222	150	134	146	63.3	54.4
Interest Expense	NA	102	77.6	50.8	58.1	90.5	117	117	102	102
Pretax Income	238	591	805	747	681	653	599	110	339	245
Effective Tax Rate	37.4%	42.0%	36.9%	36.6%	35.9%	34.2%	37.3%	NM	37.0%	36.0%
Net Income	149	343	508	474	437	430	375	277	214	157
S&P Core Earnings	NA	371	493	470	415	405	357	273	204	NA

Balance Sheet & Other Financial Data (Million $)										
Cash	168	266	261	295	289	765	1,316	424	364	245
Current Assets	NA	1,470	1,287	1,376	1,437	1,510	2,078	1,195	968	814
Total Assets	4,388	4,557	4,168	3,903	3,864	3,873	4,185	3,316	1,923	1,624
Current Liabilities	NA	737	692	1,247	1,218	560	945	511	371	259
Long Term Debt	2,170	2,247	1,503	200	200	792	1,146	971	985	992
Common Equity	967	909	1,453	2,042	1,906	1,977	1,687	1,433	296	96.6
Total Capital	3,142	3,156	2,956	2,242	2,106	2,768	2,833	2,413	1,281	1,088
Capital Expenditures	257	298	344	311	239	211	30.8	33.8	34.7	18.5
Cash Flow	NA	628	774	709	659	580	509	423	277	211
Current Ratio	2.0	2.0	1.9	1.1	1.2	2.7	2.2	2.3	2.6	3.1
% Long Term Debt of Capitalization	69.1	71.2	50.9	8.9	9.5	28.6	40.4	40.3	76.9	91.1
% Net Income of Revenue	7.1	13.6	19.4	18.9	18.3	17.3	17.6	15.0	17.8	15.6
% Return on Assets	3.3	7.9	12.6	12.2	11.3	10.7	10.0	10.6	12.1	9.3
% Return on Equity	15.9	29.0	29.1	24.0	22.5	23.5	24.1	32.0	109.0	92.6

Data as orig reptd.; bef. results of disc opers/spec. items. Per share data adj. for stk. divs.; EPS diluted. E-Estimated. NA-Not Available. NM-Not Meaningful. NR-Not Ranked. UR-Under Review.

Office: 9295 Prototype Drive, Reno, NV 89521.
Telephone: 775-448-7777.
Website: http://www.igt.com
Chrmn: T.J. Matthews

Pres & CEO: P.S. Hart
COO: A. Ciorciari
Investor Contact: P.W. Cavanaugh (866-296-4232)
EVP, CFO & Treas: P.W. Cavanaugh

Board Members: R. A. Bittman, R. R. Burt, P. S. Hart, R. A. Mathewson, T. J. Matthews, R. J. Miller, F. B. Rentschler, D. E. Roberson, P. G. Satre
Founded: 1980
Domicile: Nevada
Employees: 5,800

International Paper Co

STANDARD &POOR'S

S&P Recommendation	BUY ★★★★☆	Price $24.85 (as of Nov 27, 2009)	12-Mo. Target Price $29.00	Investment Style Large-Cap Value

GICS Sector Materials
Sub-Industry Paper Products

Summary This company is a leading worldwide producer and distributor of printing papers and packaging products.

Key Stock Statistics (Source S&P, Vickers, company reports)

52-Wk Range	$25.92– 3.93	S&P Oper. EPS 2009**E**	0.80	Market Capitalization(B)	$10.762	Beta	2.37
Trailing 12-Month EPS	$-2.42	S&P Oper. EPS 2010**E**	1.10	Yield (%)	0.40	S&P 3-Yr. Proj. EPS CAGR(%)	-9
Trailing 12-Month P/E	NM	P/E on S&P Oper. EPS 2009**E**	31.1	Dividend Rate/Share	$0.10	S&P Credit Rating	BBB
$10K Invested 5 Yrs Ago	$7,042	Common Shares Outstg. (M)	433.1	Institutional Ownership (%)	81		

Price Performance

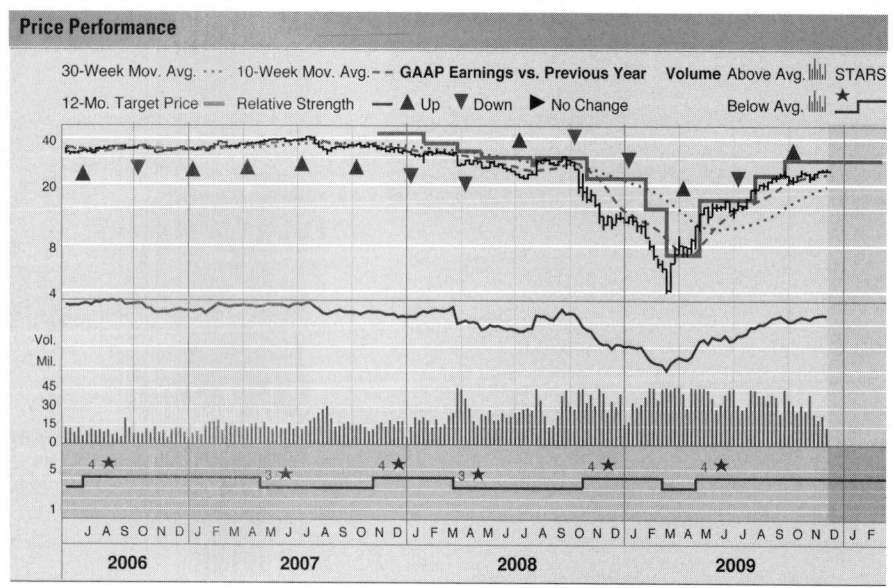

30-Week Mov. Avg. · · · 10-Week Mov. Avg. — GAAP Earnings vs. Previous Year Volume Above Avg. STARS
12-Mo. Target Price — Relative Strength ▲ Up ▼ Down ▶ No Change Below Avg. ★

Options: ASE, CBOE, P, Ph

Analysis prepared by **Stuart J. Benway, CFA** on November 03, 2009, when the stock traded at **$ 22.91**.

Highlights

▶ We forecast sales in 2009 to decline 5%-7% as demand for printing papers and linerboard is likely to be lower due to expected economic weakness and reduced employment. In 2010, we look for a sales rebound of 3%-5% as volume should improve along with renewed growth in the economy. We also expect prices to rise modestly after falling for much of 2009.

▶ We project operating margins from continuing operations to narrow modestly in 2009, resulting from underutilized capacity, as well as from lower prices for most products. Significantly higher pension expense is also likely to put pressure on margins. Partially offsetting this, in our view, will be lower prices for energy. Net margins are likely to be helped by significant gains from alternative fuel credits. We expect margins to improve in 2010 on permanent cost reductions.

▶ We see operating EPS of $0.80 for 2009 excluding unusual items, a significant decline from the $2.02 earned in 2008, but a better result than we expect for many of its competitors. We project an improvement to $1.10 in 2010.

Investment Rationale/Risk

▶ IP has made many moves in recent years aimed at focusing on faster-growing regions and higher return businesses, but the weak economy is hurting its ability to fully capitalize on these moves. The company has investments and joint ventures in Brazil, China, and Russia that we believe will contribute meaningfully to earnings when the economy recovers. Cost synergies from the major linerboard acquisition are also being realized sooner than originally expected, and debt levels are being reduced quickly.

▶ Risks to our recommendation and target price include a lack of economic recovery, worse-than-projected demand and pricing trends for uncoated paper and packaging, further declines in the value of its pension assets, and the failure of new ventures to achieve targeted returns.

▶ Our discounted cash flow model, which assumes an 8.4% weighted average cost of capital, reduced capital expenditures and solid free cash flow generation over the next several years, and a 2.5% terminal growth rate, calculates intrinsic value of $29, which is our 12-month target price.

Qualitative Risk Assessment

LOW	MEDIUM	HIGH

IP operates in a cyclical and capital-intensive industry and is affected by changes in industrial production, interest rates, and economic growth. However, this is offset as it is one of the largest companies in the sector, and has greater economies of scale than many of its competitors.

Quantitative Evaluations

S&P Quality Ranking B

D	C	B-	B	B+	A-	A	A+

Relative Strength Rank STRONG

84

LOWEST = 1   HIGHEST = 99

Revenue/Earnings Data

Revenue (Million $)

	1Q	2Q	3Q	4Q	Year
2009	5,668	5,802	5,919	--	--
2008	5,668	5,807	6,808	6,546	24,829
2007	5,217	5,291	5,541	5,841	21,890
2006	5,668	6,270	5,867	5,324	21,995
2005	6,011	5,916	6,036	6,134	24,097
2004	6,138	6,229	6,578	6,603	25,548

Earnings Per Share ($)

2009	0.61	0.32	0.87	E0.15	E0.80
2008	0.35	0.54	0.35	-1.08	0.17
2007	1.02	0.46	0.52	0.80	2.81
2006	0.14	0.24	0.23	4.53	2.65
2005	0.22	0.19	1.48	-0.17	1.74
2004	0.10	0.13	0.42	0.32	0.98

Fiscal year ended Dec. 31. Next earnings report expected: Late January. EPS Estimates based on S&P Operating Earnings; historical GAAP earnings are as reported.

Dividend Data (Dates: mm/dd Payment Date: mm/dd/yy)

Amount ($)	Date Decl.	Ex-Div. Date	Stk. of Record	Payment Date
0.250	01/13	02/11	02/16	03/16/09
0.025	03/02	05/14	05/18	06/15/09
0.025	07/14	08/13	08/17	09/15/09
0.025	10/13	11/12	11/16	12/15/09

Dividends have been paid since 1946. Source: Company reports.

International Paper Co

Business Summary November 03, 2009

CORPORATE OVERVIEW. International Paper is the world's largest paper and forest products company. According to Pulp & Paper magazine, its market share is about 25% in uncoated free sheet (UFS), used in copiers and for envelopes and forms, giving it the number-two position in that major category. It is the largest linerboard producer, used to make corrugated boxes, with nearly 30% of the market. It also manufactures bleached paperboard used to package cosmetics, food, beverages, and pharmaceuticals, and is the second-largest boxboard producer in the U.S., with a share of 11%.

IMPACT OF MAJOR DEVELOPMENTS. On March 17, 2008, International Paper agreed to acquire the corrugated packaging business of Weyerhaeuser for $6 billion in cash and closed the deal on August 4, 2008. Because the transaction is a purchase of assets rather than stock, IP said that it would realize a tax benefit with a net present value of approximately $1.4 billion. This business had sales in 2007 of $5.2 billion and EBITDA of $670 million. IP originally expected to generate $400 million of synergies on an annual basis after three years but reached that target in the first 12 months. These savings have come from reduced overhead, improved logistics, greater efficiency, and better customer mix. The deal gives IP just under a 30% share of the North American corrugated packaging market. We think the move is a good strategic fit for IP,

and it is reducing debt from the acquisition faster than initially expected.

MARKET PROFILE. IP operates in a highly cyclical and capital-intensive industry. Demand for the company's products is dependent on a number of factors, including industrial non-durable goods production, consumer spending, commercial printing and advertising activity, white collar employment levels, and movements in currency exchange rates. Historical prices for paper and wood products have been volatile, and, despite its size, IP has had only a limited direct influence over the timing and extent of price changes for its products. Pricing is significantly affected by the relationship between supply and demand, and supply is mainly influenced by fluctuations in available manufacturing capacity. Technology seems to be having an impact on paper demand, especially in uncoated free sheet, where demand has grown more slowly than the economy in recent years. We doubt the trend is likely to improve in the near term considering the weakness in the worldwide economy.

Company Financials Fiscal Year Ended Dec. 31

Per Share Data ($)	2008	2007	2006	2005	2004	2003	2002	2001	2000	1999
Tangible Book Value	5.01	14.08	11.10	6.75	6.69	6.01	4.31	7.78	11.89	18.65
Cash Flow	0.19	5.31	4.99	4.38	4.19	4.07	3.90	1.51	4.28	4.16
Earnings	0.17	2.81	2.65	1.74	0.98	0.66	0.61	-2.37	0.82	0.48
S&P Core Earnings	0.12	2.45	1.13	1.67	0.84	0.51	0.92	-2.25	NA	NA
Dividends	1.00	1.00	1.00	1.00	1.00	1.00	1.00	1.00	1.00	1.00
Payout Ratio	588%	36%	38%	57%	102%	152%	164%	NM	122%	NM
Prices:High	33.77	41.57	37.98	42.59	45.01	43.32	46.20	43.31	60.00	59.50
Prices:Low	10.20	31.05	30.69	26.97	37.12	33.09	31.35	30.70	26.31	39.50
P/E Ratio:High	NM	15	14	24	46	66	76	NM	73	NM
P/E Ratio:Low	NM	11	12	15	38	50	51	NM	32	NM

Income Statement Analysis (Million $)										
Revenue	24,829	21,890	21,995	24,097	25,548	25,179	24,976	26,363	28,180	24,573
Operating Income	2,717	2,796	2,609	3,228	3,251	3,293	3,576	3,305	5,432	3,061
Depreciation	1,347	1,086	1,158	1,376	1,565	1,644	1,587	1,870	1,916	1,520
Interest Expense	572	483	651	593	743	766	783	929	791	541
Pretax Income	235	1,654	3,188	586	746	346	371	-1,265	497	448
Effective Tax Rate	68.9%	25.1%	59.3%	NM	27.6%	NM	NM	NM	23.5%	19.2%
Net Income	70.0	1,215	1,282	859	478	315	295	-1,142	142	199
S&P Core Earnings	55.0	1,058	539	819	402	242	444	-1,091	NA	NA

Balance Sheet & Other Financial Data (Million $)										
Cash	1,144	905	1,624	1,641	2,596	2,363	1,074	1,224	1,198	453
Current Assets	7,360	6,735	8,637	7,409	9,319	9,337	7,738	8,312	10,455	7,241
Total Assets	28,252	24,159	24,034	28,771	34,217	35,525	33,792	37,158	42,109	30,268
Current Liabilities	4,755	3,842	4,641	4,844	4,872	6,803	4,579	5,374	7,413	4,382
Long Term Debt	11,246	6,620	6,531	11,023	14,132	13,450	13,042	14,262	14,453	9,325
Common Equity	5,508	8,672	10,839	8,351	8,254	8,237	7,374	10,291	12,034	10,304
Total Capital	16,215	18,172	19,816	20,311	25,631	25,085	25,435	29,804	32,541	24,554
Capital Expenditures	1,002	1,288	1,009	1,155	1,262	1,166	1,009	1,049	1,352	1,139
Cash Flow	78.0	2,301	2,440	2,235	2,043	1,959	1,882	728	2,058	1,719
Current Ratio	1.6	1.8	1.9	1.5	1.9	1.4	1.7	1.5	1.4	1.7
% Long Term Debt of Capitalization	69.3	41.7	33.0	54.3	55.1	53.6	51.3	47.9	44.4	38.0
% Net Income of Revenue	0.3	5.6	5.8	3.6	1.9	1.3	1.2	NM	0.5	0.8
% Return on Assets	0.3	5.0	4.9	2.7	1.4	0.9	0.8	NM	0.4	0.6
% Return on Equity	1.0	14.6	13.4	10.3	5.8	4.0	3.3	NM	1.3	1.9

Data as orig reptd.; bef. results of disc opers/spec. items. Per share data adj. for stk. divs.; EPS diluted. E-Estimated. NA-Not Available. NM-Not Meaningful. NR-Not Ranked. UR-Under Review.

Office: 6400 Poplar Ave, Memphis, TN 38197-0198.
Telephone: 901-419-7000.
Email: comm@ipaper.com
Website: http://www.internationalpaper.com

Chrmn & CEO: J.V. Faraci
SVP & CFO: T.S. Nicholls
SVP, Secy & General Counsel: M.A. Smith
SVP & CIO: J.N. Balboni

CTO: T.S. Joseph
Investor Contact: T.A. Cleves (901-419-7566)
Board Members: D. J. Bronczek, L. L. Elsenhans, J. V. Faraci, S. G. Gibara, S. J. Mobley, J. L. Townsend, III, J. F. Turner, W. G. Walter, A. Weisser, J. S. Whisler

Founded: 1898
Domicile: New York
Employees: 61,700

Interpublic Group of Companies Inc. (The)

STANDARD
&POOR'S

S&P Recommendation SELL ★★☆☆☆	Price $6.46 (as of Nov 27, 2009)	12-Mo. Target Price $5.50	Investment Style Large-Cap Blend

GICS Sector Consumer Discretionary
Sub-Industry Advertising

Summary Interpublic is one of the world's largest organizations of advertising agencies and marketing communications companies.

Key Stock Statistics (Source S&P, Vickers, company reports)

52-Wk Range	$7.77– 3.08	S&P Oper. EPS 2009**E**	0.27	Market Capitalization(B)	$3.140	Beta	1.46
Trailing 12-Month EPS	$0.36	S&P Oper. EPS 2010**E**	0.32	Yield (%)	Nil	S&P 3-Yr. Proj. EPS CAGR(%)	9
Trailing 12-Month P/E	17.9	P/E on S&P Oper. EPS 2009**E**	23.9	Dividend Rate/Share	Nil	S&P Credit Rating	B+
$10K Invested 5 Yrs Ago	$5,197	Common Shares Outstg. (M)	486.1	Institutional Ownership (%)	100		

Price Performance

30-Week Mov. Avg. · · · 10-Week Mov. Avg. - - **GAAP Earnings vs. Previous Year** Volume Above Avg. STARS
12-Mo. Target Price — Relative Strength — ▲ Up ▼ Down ► No Change Below Avg. ★

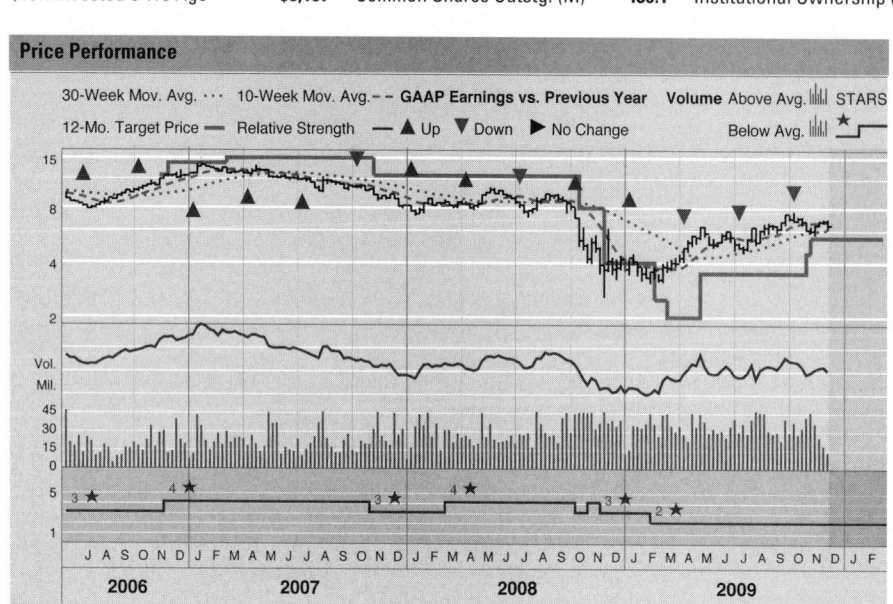

Options: ASE, CBOE, Ph

Analysis prepared by **Joseph Agnese** on November 04, 2009, when the stock traded at **$ 6.29.**

Highlights

► The ongoing contraction in global advertising continued into the third quarter of 2009, leading to a 16.5% decline in revenues. Excluding acquisitions and foreign currency translation effects, organic revenues fell 11.8%. We forecast a 14% decrease in 2009 revenues, reflecting an expected 10% fall in organic revenue and a 5% negative forex effect. In 2010, we see revenues rising 2.0% as the global economy stabilizes and as forex comparisons ease in the fourth quarter.

► Despite having reduced headcount by 5,100 employees, or about 11% of IPG's workforce, since September 2008, the ratio of staff costs as a percentage of revenue was 68.8% through the third quarter, versus 64.4% in the year-earlier period. Office and general expense through the first three quarters fell 13.4% organically. For 2009, we expect the staff cost ratio to rise to 66.3% of revenues from 62.4%, and office and general expense to decrease to 28.1% of revenues from 29.0%. We see the office and general expense trend continuing in 2010 as staff costs stabilize.

► We expect EPS of $0.27 in 2009, rising to $0.32 in 2010.

Investment Rationale/Risk

► Our sell opinion reflects our view that advertising fundamentals will remain weak into at least 2010 on declining or sluggish economic conditions in most regions of the world. We believe our view is supported by IPG's commentary that the global economic and financial situation was weighing negatively on marketers' spending plans. In international markets, we expect weaker revenue in 2009 despite share gains in certain markets.

► Risks to our recommendation and target price include unexpected new business wins, positive accounting-related developments, a faster-than-expected U.S. economic recovery, and lower-than-expected severance expenses or professional fees.

► Our 12-month target price of $5.50 is derived by applying an enterprise value/EBITDA multiple of 6.0X to our 2010 EBITDA estimate of approximately $637 million. This reflects a modest discount to peers due to differences in the mix of revenue sources, as well as our view that much of IPG's return to profitability in recent years had been driven by acquisitions and the weak dollar.

Qualitative Risk Assessment

LOW	MEDIUM	HIGH

Our risk assessment reflects our view of a highly competitive advertising industry, and economic cyclicality associated with advertising spending, partly offset by what we see as a moderately conservative balance sheet structure and structural improvements in profitability for IPG.

Quantitative Evaluations

S&P Quality Ranking B-

D	C	B-	B	B+	A-	A	A+

Relative Strength Rank MODERATE

43

LOWEST = 1   HIGHEST = 99

Revenue/Earnings Data

Revenue (Million $)

	1Q	2Q	3Q	4Q	Year
2009	1,325	1,474	1,427	--	--
2008	1,485	1,836	1,740	1,902	6,963
2007	1,359	1,653	1,560	1,983	6,554
2006	1,327	1,533	1,454	1,877	6,191
2005	1,328	1,611	1,440	1,896	6,274
2004	1,389	1,513	1,519	1,966	6,387

Earnings Per Share ($)

2009	-0.16	0.04	0.03	E0.31	E0.27
2008	-0.15	0.17	0.08	0.39	0.52
2007	-0.29	0.24	-0.06	0.31	0.26
2006	-0.43	0.09	-0.03	0.11	-0.20
2005	-0.36	0.01	-0.25	-0.10	-0.70
2004	-0.21	-0.23	-1.22	0.22	-1.36

Fiscal year ended Dec. 31. Next earnings report expected: Early March. EPS Estimates based on S&P Operating Earnings; historical GAAP earnings are as reported.

Dividend Data

No cash dividends have been paid since 2002.

Please read the Required Disclosures and Analyst Certification on the last page of this report.

Interpublic Group of Companies Inc. (The)

STANDARD &POOR'S

Business Summary November 04, 2009

CORPORATE OVERVIEW. The Interpublic Group of Companies, along with its subsidiaries, is one of the world's largest advertising and marketing services companies, made up of communication agencies around the world that deliver custom marketing solutions to clients. These agencies cover the spectrum of marketing disciplines and specialties, from traditional services such as consumer advertising and direct marketing, to emerging services such as mobile and search engine marketing.

The company generates revenue from planning, creating and placing advertising in various media and from planning and executing other communications or marketing programs. IPG also receives commissions from clients for planning and supervising work done by outside contractors in the physical preparation of finished print advertisements and the production of TV and radio commercials and other forms of advertising. In addition, IPG derives revenue in a number of other ways, including the planning and placement in media of advertising produced by unrelated advertising agencies, the creation and publication of brochures, billboards, point of sale materials and direct marketing pieces for clients, the planning and carrying out of specialized marketing research, public relations campaigns, and creating and managing special events at which client products are featured.

IPG has two reportable segments: the McCann Worldgroup unit, comprised of

Draftfcb, Lowe, Momentum, McCann Healthcare, media agencies and other standalone agencies, and the Constituent Management Group (CMG), which is made up of the bulk of IPG's specialist marketing service offerings. Draftfcb was formed from the merger of two IPG companies in 2006, and is focused on consumer advertising and behavioral, data-driven direct marketing. Lowe is a creative advertising agency operating in the world's largest advertising markets. McCann Worldgroup is a marketing communications company that consists of McCann Erickson Advertising, MRM Worldwide for relationship marketing and digital expertise, Momentum for experiential marketing, and McCann Healthcare for health care communications, as well as various other brands.

Mediabrands was installed in recent years to oversee all media operations in order to align the company's media networks with its global brand agencies. Also, in recent years the company has focused on making strategic investments, including a number of acquisitions in Brazil, India, Russia, and China, or "BRIC" countries.

Company Financials Fiscal Year Ended Dec. 31

Per Share Data ($)	2008	2007	2006	2005	2004	2003	2002	2001	2000	1999
Tangible Book Value	NM	NM	NM	NM	NM	NM	NM	NM	NM	NM
Cash Flow	0.85	0.63	0.21	-0.30	-0.91	-0.90	0.83	-0.36	1.99	1.77
Earnings	0.52	0.26	-0.20	-0.70	-1.36	-1.43	0.26	-1.37	1.15	1.11
S&P Core Earnings	0.51	0.29	-0.18	-0.62	-0.82	-0.84	0.36	-0.60	NA	NA
Dividends	Nil	Nil	Nil	Nil	Nil	Nil	0.38	0.38	0.37	0.33
Payout Ratio	Nil	Nil	Nil	Nil	Nil	Nil	146%	NM	32%	30%
Prices:High	10.47	13.94	12.83	13.80	17.31	16.50	34.98	47.44	57.69	58.38
Prices:Low	2.57	7.91	7.79	9.08	10.47	7.20	9.85	18.25	32.69	34.41
P/E Ratio:High	20	54	NM	NM	NM	NM	NM	NM	50	53
P/E Ratio:Low	5	30	NM	NM	NM	NM	NM	NM	28	31

Income Statement Analysis (Million $)	2008	2007	2006	2005	2004	2003	2002	2001	2000	1999
Revenue	6,963	6,554	6,191	6,274	6,387	5,863	6,204	6,727	5,626	4,427
Operating Income	780	547	341	156	589	719	762	1,113	1,096	791
Depreciation	173	177	174	169	185	204	218	372	263	190
Interest Expense	212	237	219	182	172	173	146	165	109	66.4
Pretax Income	475	243	2.00	-173	-261	-330	271	-519	672	592
Effective Tax Rate	33.0%	24.2%	NM	NM	NM	NM	51.8%	NM	40.7%	39.9%
Net Income	295	168	-36.7	-272	-545	-553	99.5	-505	359	322
S&P Core Earnings	265	150	-75.8	-265	-363	-325	136	-217	NA	NA

Balance Sheet & Other Financial Data (Million $)	2008	2007	2006	2005	2004	2003	2002	2001	2000	1999
Cash	2,275	2,083	1,957	2,192	1,970	2,006	933	935	748	1,018
Current Assets	7,488	7,686	7,209	7,497	7,637	7,350	6,322	6,467	6,026	5,768
Total Assets	12,125	12,458	11,864	11,945	12,272	12,235	11,794	11,515	10,238	8,727
Current Liabilities	6,877	7,121	6,663	6,857	7,563	6,625	7,090	6,434	6,106	5,637
Long Term Debt	1,787	2,044	2,249	2,183	Nil	2,192	1,818	2,481	1,505	867
Common Equity	1,951	1,807	1,416	1,047	1,345	2,721	2,100	2,384	2,046	2,407
Total Capital	4,517	4,376	4,236	4,178	1,773	5,356	3,988	4,953	3,637	3,394
Capital Expenditures	138	148	128	141	194	160	183	268	202	150
Cash Flow	441	317	89.3	-129	-380	-349	317	-133	622	512
Current Ratio	1.1	1.1	1.1	1.1	1.0	1.1	0.9	1.0	1.0	1.0
% Long Term Debt of Capitalization	39.5	46.7	53.1	52.3	Nil	40.9	45.6	50.1	41.4	25.5
% Net Income of Revenue	4.2	2.6	NM	NM	NM	NM	1.6	NM	6.4	7.3
% Return on Assets	2.4	1.4	NM	NM	NM	NM	0.9	NM	3.7	4.1
% Return on Equity	14.2	10.4	NM	NM	NM	NM	5.1	NM	18.8	14.7

Data as orig reptd.; bef. results of disc opers/spec. items. Per share data adj. for stk. divs.; EPS diluted. E-Estimated. NA-Not Available. NM-Not Meaningful. NR-Not Ranked. UR-Under Review.

Office: 1114 Avenue Of The Americas, New York, NY 10036.
Telephone: 212-704-1200.
Website: http://www.interpublic.com
Chrmn & CEO: M.I. Roth

EVP & CFO: F. Mergenthaler
SVP, Chief Acctg Officer & Cntlr: C.F. Carroll
SVP & Treas: E.T. Johnson
SVP, Secy & General Counsel: N.J. Camera

Investor Contact: J. Leshne (212-704-1439)
Board Members: F. J. Borelli, R. K. Brack, Jr., J. E. Carter-Miller, J. M. Considine, R. A. Goldstein, H. J. Greeniaus, M. J. Guilfoile, W. T. Kerr, M. I. Roth, D. M. Thomas

Founded: 1902
Domicile: Delaware
Employees: 45,000

The McGraw-Hill Companies

Intuitive Surgical Inc

&POOR'S

S&P Recommendation **HOLD** ★★★☆☆	Price $280.11 (as of Nov 27, 2009)	12-Mo. Target Price $275.00	Investment Style Large-Cap Blend

GICS Sector Health Care
Sub-Industry Health Care Equipment

Summary This company has developed the da Vinci Surgical System, which uses advanced robotics and computerized visualization technology for minimally invasive surgeries.

Key Stock Statistics (Source S&P, Vickers, company reports)

52-Wk Range	$283.09– 84.86	S&P Oper. EPS 2009**E**	5.63	Market Capitalization(B)	$10.698	Beta	2.08
Trailing 12-Month EPS	$5.24	S&P Oper. EPS 2010**E**	6.98	Yield (%)	Nil	S&P 3-Yr. Proj. EPS CAGR(%)	20
Trailing 12-Month P/E	53.5	P/E on S&P Oper. EPS 2009**E**	49.8	Dividend Rate/Share	Nil	S&P Credit Rating	NA
$10K Invested 5 Yrs Ago	$78,971	Common Shares Outstg. (M)	38.2	Institutional Ownership (%)	93		

Price Performance

30-Week Mov. Avg. ···· 10-Week Mov. Avg. - - **GAAP Earnings vs. Previous Year** Volume Above Avg. STARS
12-Mo. Target Price — Relative Strength — ▲ Up ▼ Down ▶ No Change Below Avg.

Options: ASE, CBOE, Ph

Analysis prepared by **Jeffrey Englander, CFA** on November 04, 2009, when the stock traded at **$250.54**.

Highlights

► We see sales increasing about 16% in 2009 and 18% in 2010, based on increasing sales of the new da Vinci Si system, higher procedure volumes, and greater instrument sales outside the U.S. While the company's sales growth has slowed from that of recent years, reflecting increased pressure on hospital capital expenditure budgets, we believe the degree of deceleration in cutbacks in hospital budgets may be gradually slowing.

► We look for gross margins of just over 71% in 2009, aided by higher service margins and reduced instrument costs, which we see being offset by lower system selling prices and the cost of expanding manufacturing. We anticipate that the company will incur higher SG&A costs and modestly higher R&D expenditures as a percentage of sales amid slowing revenue growth. For 2010, we look for gross margins to expand modestly, reflecting the higher margins of the Da Vinci Si system. We look for an effective tax rate of 41% in 2009 and 38% in 2010.

► With demand appearing to stabilize, we forecast adjusted EPS of $5.63 in 2009 and $6.98 in 2010, excluding the impact of deferred revenue from upgrades to the da Vinci Si system.

Investment Rationale/Risk

► We think ISRG's technology represents the leading edge in minimally invasive surgery and will continue to gain validity through use in a growing number of surgical procedures. However, we see results in 2009 being challenged by constrained hospital spending and the da Vinci systems' high sales price. On the positive side, we see signs that some facilities are using the da Vinci technology to differentiate themselves and drive volumes amid challenging market conditions. At recent levels, we see the shares' valuation reflecting the company's growth prospects.

► Risks to our recommendation and target price include increased equipment pricing pressures, lower sales of da Vinci systems than we project, and more restrictive credit conditions, which could hinder customers' ability to expand their capital expenditure budgets.

► As we believe the rate of decline in hospital capex has slowed, we think ISRG can return to growth rates at the upper end of its peer group. Our target price of $275 assumes a PEG ratio of about 2.0X based on our 2010 EPS estimate, a premium to peers reflecting ISRG's relative growth rate and differentiated product.

Qualitative Risk Assessment

LOW	MEDIUM	HIGH

Our risk assessment reflects risks that we see as specific to a maker of medical devices such as ISRG, including those associated with protecting its intellectual property rights, compliance with regulations of U.S. and foreign health agencies, and legal liability for injury that may result from use of the company's products, such as inappropriate or "off-label" use.

Quantitative Evaluations

S&P Quality Ranking   B-

D	C	B-	B	B+	A-	A	A+

Relative Strength Rank   STRONG

89

LOWEST = 1   HIGHEST = 99

Revenue/Earnings Data

Revenue (Million $)

	1Q	2Q	3Q	4Q	Year
2009	188.4	260.6	280.1	--	--
2008	118.2	219.2	236.0	231.6	874.9
2007	114.2	140.3	156.9	189.5	600.8
2006	77.26	87.03	95.83	112.6	372.7
2005	41.61	52.76	60.87	72.10	227.3
2004	27.06	31.06	35.49	45.19	138.8

Earnings Per Share ($)

2009	0.72	1.62	1.64	E1.74	E5.63
2008	1.12	1.28	1.44	1.27	5.12
2007	0.62	0.79	1.04	1.24	3.70
2006	0.38	0.44	0.45	0.62	1.89
2005	0.25	0.40	0.55	1.31	2.51
2004	0.02	0.14	0.17	0.32	0.67

Fiscal year ended Dec. 31. Next earnings report expected: Late January. EPS Estimates based on S&P Operating Earnings; historical GAAP earnings are as reported.

Dividend Data

No cash dividends have been paid.

Intuitive Surgical Inc

STANDARD
&POOR'S

Business Summary November 04, 2009

Intuitive Surgical (ISRG) has designed the da Vinci Surgical System, a product that incorporates advanced robotics and computerized visualization technologies to improve the ability of surgeons to perform complex, minimally invasive procedures. As of 2008 year end, the company had an installed base of 1,111 da Vinci Surgical Systems, and surgeons using the company's technology had successfully completed about 136,000 surgical procedures of various types, including urologic, gynecologic, cardiothoracic and general surgery.

The da Vinci Surgical System consists of a surgeon's console, a patient-side cart, a high performance vision system, and proprietary wristed instruments. By placing computer-enhanced technology between the surgeon and patient, ISRG believes da Vinci lets surgeons perform better surgery in a manner never before experienced. The system translates a surgeon's natural hand movements on instrument controls on a console into corresponding micro-movements of instruments positioned inside the patient through small puncture incisions (ports). It gives a surgeon the intuitive control, range of motion, fine tissue manipulation capability, and 3-D visualization characteristics of open surgery, while simultaneously allowing use of the small ports of minimally invasive surgery. During 2008, surgeons using ISRG products performed

about 73,000 prostatectomy procedures and 34,000 hysterectomy procedures worldwide.

Intuitive's strategy is targeted at establishing Intuitive surgery as the standard for complex surgical procedures and many other procedures. Over time, the company hopes to broaden the number of procedures performed using the da Vinci Surgical System and to educate surgeons and hospitals about the benefits of Intuitive surgery.

The da Vinci System is covered by over 255 U.S. patents and 46 foreign patents that are licensed or owned by the company. The manufacture, marketing, and use of Class II medical devices such as the da Vinci System is governed by extensive regulations administered by the FDA, which we think act as significant barriers to entry by competitors.

Company Financials Fiscal Year Ended Dec. 31

Per Share Data ($)	2008	2007	2006	2005	2004	2003	2002	2001	2000	1999
Tangible Book Value	28.07	19.61	12.55	8.64	4.83	3.87	3.46	4.14	4.86	5.42
Cash Flow	5.74	4.04	2.15	2.64	0.82	-0.23	-0.80	-0.76	-1.42	-1.46
Earnings	5.12	3.70	1.89	2.51	0.67	-0.41	-1.02	-0.94	-1.56	-1.58
S&P Core Earnings	5.31	3.70	1.89	2.14	0.39	-0.57	-1.10	-1.14	NA	NA
Dividends	Nil	Nil	Nil	Nil	Nil	Nil	Nil	Nil	Nil	NA
Payout Ratio	Nil	Nil	Nil	Nil	Nil	Nil	Nil	Nil	Nil	NA
Prices:High	357.98	359.59	139.50	124.79	40.60	18.61	22.50	29.56	38.13	NA
Prices:Low	110.35	86.20	85.63	35.69	15.08	7.34	11.20	6.00	10.75	NA
P/E Ratio:High	70	97	74	50	61	NM	NM	NM	NM	NA
P/E Ratio:Low	22	23	45	14	23	NM	NM	NM	NM	NA

Income Statement Analysis (Million $)	2008	2007	2006	2005	2004	2003	2002	2001	2000	1999
Revenue	875	601	373	227	139	91.7	72.0	51.7	26.6	10.2
Operating Income	336	220	117	73.6	26.3	-7.73	-16.3	-17.3	-20.7	-18.1
Depreciation	25.1	13.0	10.0	4.86	5.10	4.15	3.89	3.12	1.60	1.44
Interest Expense	Nil	Nil	Nil	0.02	0.09	0.20	0.20	0.27	0.40	0.41
Pretax Income	335	237	120	73.8	24.2	-9.62	-18.4	-16.7	-18.5	-18.4
Effective Tax Rate	39.1%	39.1%	40.0%	NM	3.00%	NM	NM	NM	NM	NM
Net Income	204	145	72.0	94.1	23.5	-9.62	-18.4	-16.7	-18.5	-18.4
S&P Core Earnings	212	145	72.0	80.1	13.6	-13.6	-20.0	-20.3	NA	NA

Balance Sheet & Other Financial Data (Million $)	2008	2007	2006	2005	2004	2003	2002	2001	2000	1999
Cash	902	427	34.4	5.51	5.77	11.3	17.6	10.5	22.7	95.5
Current Assets	704	610	374	209	177	152	78.6	89.2	104	NA
Total Assets	1,475	1,040	672	502	354	315	91.6	100	112	106
Current Liabilities	165	132	80.7	58.0	38.4	34.2	26.1	21.3	19.8	NA
Long Term Debt	Nil	Nil	Nil	Nil	Nil	0.70	1.84	0.77	1.86	2.47
Common Equity	1,267	889	590	443	315	279	63.7	78.3	90.7	93.2
Total Capital	1,267	889	590	443	315	280	65.5	79.1	92.6	95.6
Capital Expenditures	62.5	20.3	15.9	30.1	22.4	2.53	5.79	5.53	3.56	0.93
Cash Flow	229	158	82.1	99.0	28.6	-5.47	-14.5	-13.6	-16.9	-17.0
Current Ratio	4.3	4.6	4.6	3.6	4.6	4.4	3.0	4.2	5.2	3.3
% Long Term Debt of Capitalization	Nil	Nil	Nil	Nil	Nil	0.2	2.8	1.0	2.0	2.6
% Net Income of Revenue	23.4	24.1	19.3	41.4	16.9	NM	NM	NM	NM	NM
% Return on Assets	16.3	16.9	12.3	22.0	7.0	NM	NM	NM	NM	NM
% Return on Equity	19.0	19.6	14.0	24.9	7.9	NM	NM	NM	NM	NM

Data as orig reptd.; bef. results of disc opers/spec. items. Per share data adj. for stk. divs.; EPS diluted. E-Estimated. NA-Not Available. NM-Not Meaningful. NR-Not Ranked. UR-Under Review.

Office: 1266 Kifer Rd, Sunnyvale, CA, USA 94086-5304.
Telephone: 408-523-2100 .
Email: ir@intusurg.com
Website: http://www.intuitivesurgical.com

Chrmn & CEO: L.M. Smith
Pres & COO: G.S. Guthart
SVP, CFO & Chief Acctg Officer: M.L. Mohr
SVP & General Counsel: M.J. Meltzer

Cntlr: J.J. Skoglund
Board Members: R. W. Duggan, D. K. Grossman, G. S. Guthart, E. H. Halvorson, A. J. Levy, F. D. Loop, H. E. Rubash, L. M. Smith, G. J. Stalk, Jr.

Founded: 1995
Domicile: Delaware
Employees: 1,049

The McGraw-Hill Companies

Intuit Inc

STANDARD &POOR'S

S&P Recommendation HOLD ★★★★★		**Price** $29.27 (as of Nov 27, 2009)	**12-Mo. Target Price** $31.00	**Investment Style** Large-Cap Growth

GICS Sector Information Technology
Sub-Industry Application Software

Summary This company develops and markets small business accounting and management, tax preparation, and personal finance software.

Key Stock Statistics (Source S&P, Vickers, company reports)

52-Wk Range	$31.29– 20.18	S&P Oper. EPS 2010E	1.66	Market Capitalization(B)	$9.423	Beta	0.81
Trailing 12-Month EPS	$1.31	S&P Oper. EPS 2011E	1.89	Yield (%)	Nil	S&P 3-Yr. Proj. EPS CAGR(%)	13
Trailing 12-Month P/E	22.3	P/E on S&P Oper. EPS 2010E	17.6	Dividend Rate/Share	Nil	S&P Credit Rating	BBB
$10K Invested 5 Yrs Ago	$13,611	Common Shares Outstg. (M)	321.9	Institutional Ownership (%)	86		

Price Performance

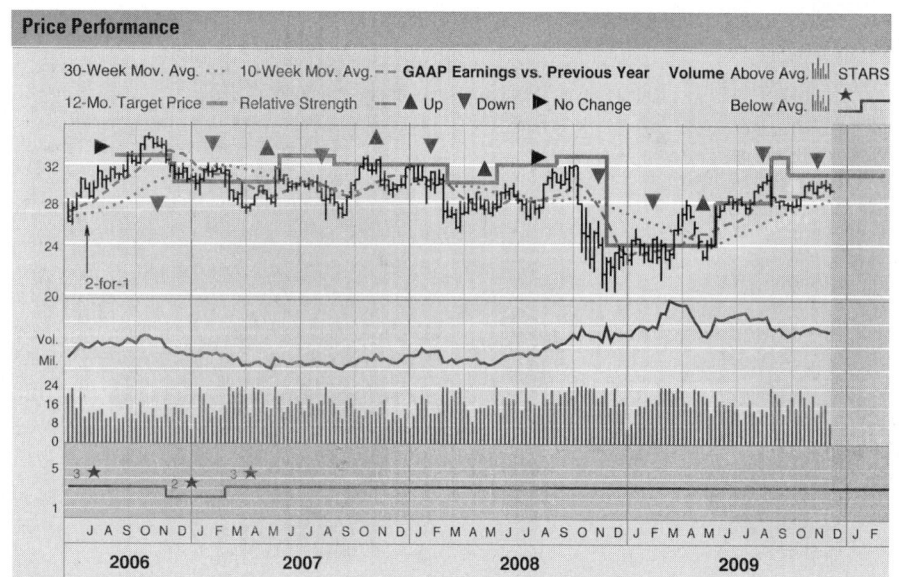

30-Week Mov. Avg. · · · 10-Week Mov. Avg. — - **GAAP Earnings vs. Previous Year** Volume Above Avg. STARS
12-Mo. Target Price — Relative Strength — ▲ Up ▼ Down ► No Change Below Avg. ★

Options: ASE, CBOE, P, Ph

Analysis prepared by **Zaineb Bokhari** on November 25, 2009, when the stock traded at **$ 29.46**.

Highlights

► We estimate that sales will rise 7% in FY 10 (July) to $3.4 billion, and be aided by acquisition of PayCycle in July 2009. We forecast 7% sales growth for INTU's tax business, supported by rising usage of online consumer tax preparation offerings. We expect small business segment sales to rise 6%, aided by recent acquisitions. We expect QuickBooks sales to remain flat as a weak economic environment restricts new business formation. We expect sales overall to rise 8% in FY 11.

► We expect INTU to continue to exercise cost discipline but see FY 10 non-GAAP operating margins remaining essentially flat as INTU absorbs the recent acquisition of Mint.com. Organically, we expect the company to benefit from selective hiring and a recent work force reduction. It is also actively evaluating sales and marketing expenditures relative to their benefits. We look for a further modest widening in FY 11.

► We estimate operating EPS of $1.66 for FY 10, excluding $0.14 of amortization and acquisition-related expense but including projected stock-based compensation expense. Our FY 11 estimate is $1.89.

Investment Rationale/Risk

► Our hold recommendation reflects our view that INTU's small business segment is vulnerable in a weak economic environment. While its tax franchise is less vulnerable, we expect rising competition for that business. We are encouraged by market share gains in the online consumer tax and small business segments. We expect recent acquisitions and new products and services to help drive sales growth. The recent sale of non-core businesses will partly offset this growth but allow for better focus of corporate resources, in our view. All told, we believe the stock is fairly valued at recent levels.

► Risks to our recommendation and target price include increased competition in the consumer tax market and a material worsening of the economic environment leading to elevated losses in INTU's small business segment. We are also concerned about potential acquisition integration issues.

► Our 12-month target price of $31 is 18.5X our FY 10 operating EPS estimate, modestly below the 19.2X average three-year P/E multiple that we calculate for the shares, reflecting our view of weak organic growth for the small business franchise and competitive pressures.

Qualitative Risk Assessment

LOW	MEDIUM	HIGH

Our risk assessment reflects our view of the company's strong market position within the consumer and professional tax segments and its solid balance sheet. However, this is tempered by our concern about the potential for further slowing in the company's small business segment as the economy remains weak.

Quantitative Evaluations

S&P Quality Ranking   B+

D	C	B-	B	B+	A-	A	A+

Relative Strength Rank   MODERATE

50
LOWEST = 1   HIGHEST = 99

Revenue/Earnings Data

Revenue (Million $)

	1Q	2Q	3Q	4Q	Year
2010	493.0	--	--	--	--
2009	481.4	791.0	1,434	475.8	3,183
2008	444.9	834.9	1,313	478.2	3,071
2007	350.5	750.6	1,139	432.7	2,673
2006	304.1	742.7	952.6	342.9	2,342
2005	266.0	662.6	849.5	301.8	2,038

Earnings Per Share ($)

	1Q	2Q	3Q	4Q	Year
2010	-0.21	E0.24	E1.70	E-0.16	E1.66
2009	-0.16	0.26	1.47	-0.22	1.35
2008	-0.14	0.34	1.33	-0.19	1.33
2007	-0.17	0.40	1.04	-0.19	1.25
2006	-0.17	0.43	0.84	-0.06	1.05
2005	-0.11	0.39	0.81	-0.06	1.00

Fiscal year ended Jul. 31. Next earnings report expected: Mid February. EPS Estimates based on S&P Operating Earnings; historical GAAP earnings are as reported.

Dividend Data

No cash dividends have been paid.

The McGraw-Hill Companies

Intuit Inc

Business Summary November 25, 2009

CORPORATE OVERVIEW. Intuit is a leading provider of accounting, financial management, personal finance and tax software for consumers and small businesses. The company's flagship products include QuickBooks, TurboTax, Lacerte, and Quicken, among others. In FY 09 (Jul.), the company had four main product categories, which contained seven segments. The company's Small Business Group includes Financial Management Solutions (formerly Quickbooks), Employee Management Solutions (formerly Payroll), and Payment Solutions (formerly Payments) segment. Its Tax product group includes Consumer Tax and Accounting Professional segments; other segments include: Financial Institutions, and Other Businesses.

Financial Management Solutions (which accounted for 18% of total net revenues in FY 09) includes products and services that provide bookkeeping capabilities and business management tools. INTU offers QuickBooks Simple Start for very small, less complex businesses; QuickBooks Pro, for slightly larger businesses and QuickBooks Pro for Mac; QuickBooks Premier, to support businesses that need advanced accounting capabilities and business planning tools; and QuickBooks Enterprise Solutions, designed for mid-sized companies. INTU also offers an online version of QuickBooks and Premier and Enterprise versions that cater to specific industries, including Manufacturing, Wholesale, Retail, Non-Profit, Contractor, and Professional Services.

Employee Management Solutions (11%) consists of solutions including outsourced payroll services QuickBooks Payroll in different varieties and QuickBooks Online Payroll, for use with QuickBooks Online Edition. Direct deposit and electronic tax payment and filing services are available with some of these offerings for additional fees. Payment Solutions (9%) segment includes credit card, debit card, electronic benefits, check guarantee and gift card processing, Web-based transaction processing services for online merchants as well as customer service, charge-back retrieval and support, and fraud and loss prevention screening.

Consumer Tax (31%) segment is centered on TurboTax. TurboTax software enables individuals and small businesses to prepare and file income tax returns using computers. TurboTax for the Web allows individuals to prepare tax returns online. Versions of TurboTax Premier software are designed to address the special income tax needs of different types of users, including investors, those planning for retirement, and rental property owners. Electronic tax filing services are also provided.

Company Financials Fiscal Year Ended Jul. 31

Per Share Data ($)	2009	2008	2007	2006	2005	2004	2003	2002	2001	2000
Tangible Book Value	1.35	0.32	0.66	3.41	3.61	2.75	3.44	4.02	4.15	4.00
Cash Flow	NA	1.97	1.51	1.34	1.31	1.03	0.81	0.30	-0.09	1.23
Earnings	1.35	1.33	1.25	1.05	1.00	0.79	0.82	0.16	-0.24	0.73
S&P Core Earnings	1.35	1.22	1.19	1.04	0.86	0.61	0.41	NA	-0.32	NA
Dividends	Nil	Nil	Nil	Nil	Nil	Nil	Nil	Nil	Nil	Nil
Payout Ratio	Nil	Nil	Nil	Nil	Nil	Nil	Nil	Nil	Nil	Nil
Prices:High	31.29	32.00	33.10	35.98	27.97	26.63	26.95	27.52	23.69	45.00
Prices:Low	21.07	20.18	26.14	23.99	18.62	17.92	16.65	17.26	11.31	12.88
P/E Ratio:High	23	24	26	34	28	34	33	NM	NM	62
P/E Ratio:Low	16	15	21	23	19	23	20	NM	NM	18

Income Statement Analysis (Million $)	2009	2008	2007	2006	2005	2004	2003	2002	2001	2000
Revenue	3,183	3,071	2,673	2,342	2,038	1,868	1,651	1,358	1,261	1,094
Operating Income	NA	891	773	677	659	561	461	343	265	200
Depreciation	275	216	135	104	118	97.0	76.5	59.9	59.9	213
Interest Expense	NA	52.3	27.1	Nil	Nil	Nil	Nil	Nil	Nil	Nil
Pretax Income	653	698	696	610	556	453	393	84.9	-96.5	513
Effective Tax Rate	31.4%	35.2%	36.1%	38.0%	32.6%	30.0%	33.0%	17.9%	NM	40.4%
Net Income	447	451	443	377	375	317	263	69.8	-97.1	306
S&P Core Earnings	446	414	422	372	323	245	172	-0.77	-129	NA

Balance Sheet & Other Financial Data (Million $)	2009	2008	2007	2006	2005	2004	2003	2002	2001	2000
Cash	1,347	828	255	180	83.8	27.2	1,207	452	535	643
Current Assets	NA	1,774	1,952	1,817	1,614	1,517	1,669	1,995	2,148	2,129
Total Assets	4,826	4,667	4,252	2,770	2,716	2,696	2,790	2,963	2,962	2,879
Current Liabilities	NA	1,467	1,160	1,016	1,003	857	796	733	788	807
Long Term Debt	998	1,000	998	15.4	17.5	5.77	29.3	14.6	12.4	0.54
Common Equity	2,556	2,073	2,035	1,738	1,695	1,822	1,965	2,216	2,170	4,143
Total Capital	3,556	3,079	3,034	1,754	1,713	1,828	1,994	2,230	2,182	4,143
Capital Expenditures	182	306	105	44.6	38.2	52.3	50.4	42.6	77.1	94.9
Cash Flow	NA	667	538	482	493	414	340	130	-37.2	519
Current Ratio	1.8	1.2	1.7	1.8	1.6	1.8	2.1	2.7	2.7	2.6
% Long Term Debt of Capitalization	28.1	32.5	32.9	0.9	1.0	0.3	1.5	0.7	0.6	0.0
% Net Income of Revenue	14.1	14.7	16.6	16.1	18.4	17.0	15.9	5.1	NM	27.9
% Return on Assets	9.4	10.1	24.1	13.8	13.8	11.6	9.2	2.4	NM	11.4
% Return on Equity	19.3	22.0	23.5	22.0	21.3	16.7	12.6	3.2	NM	8.4

Data as orig reptd.; bef. results of disc opers/spec. items. Per share data adj. for stk. divs.; EPS diluted. E-Estimated. NA-Not Available. NM-Not Meaningful. NR-Not Ranked. UR-Under Review.

Office: 2700 Coast Ave, Mountain View, CA 94043-1140.
Telephone: 650-944-6000.
Email: investor_relations@intuit.com
Website: http://www.intuit.com

Chrmn: W.V. Campbell
Pres & CEO: B.D. Smith
SVP & CFO: R.N. Williams
SVP & CTO: P. Halvorsen

SVP, Secy & General Counsel: L.A. Fennell
Investor Contact: K. Patel (650-944-3560)
Board Members: S. M. Bennett, C. W. Brody, W. V. Campbell, S. D. Cook, D. B. Greene, M. R. Hallman, W. H. Harris, Jr., S. N. Johnson, E. A. Kangas, D. D. Powell, S. Sclavos, B. D. Smith

Founded: 1984
Domicile: Delaware
Employees: 7,800

Invesco Ltd

S&P Recommendation BUY ★★★★☆

Price	12-Mo. Target Price	Investment Style
$21.68 (as of Nov 27, 2009)	$28.00	Large-Cap Blend

GICS Sector Financials
Sub-Industry Asset Management & Custody Banks

Summary This diversified investment manager offers an array of investment options to individuals and institutions through offices around the world.

Key Stock Statistics (Source S&P, Vickers, company reports)

52-Wk Range	$24.07–9.33	S&P Oper. EPS 2009E	0.78	Market Capitalization(B)	$9.296	Beta	1.70
Trailing 12-Month EPS	$0.59	S&P Oper. EPS 2010E	1.32	Yield (%)	1.89	S&P 3-Yr. Proj. EPS CAGR(%)	8
Trailing 12-Month P/E	36.8	P/E on S&P Oper. EPS 2009E	27.8	Dividend Rate/Share	$0.41	S&P Credit Rating	BBB+
$10K Invested 5 Yrs Ago	$18,411	Common Shares Outstg. (M)	428.8	Institutional Ownership (%)	82		

Price Performance

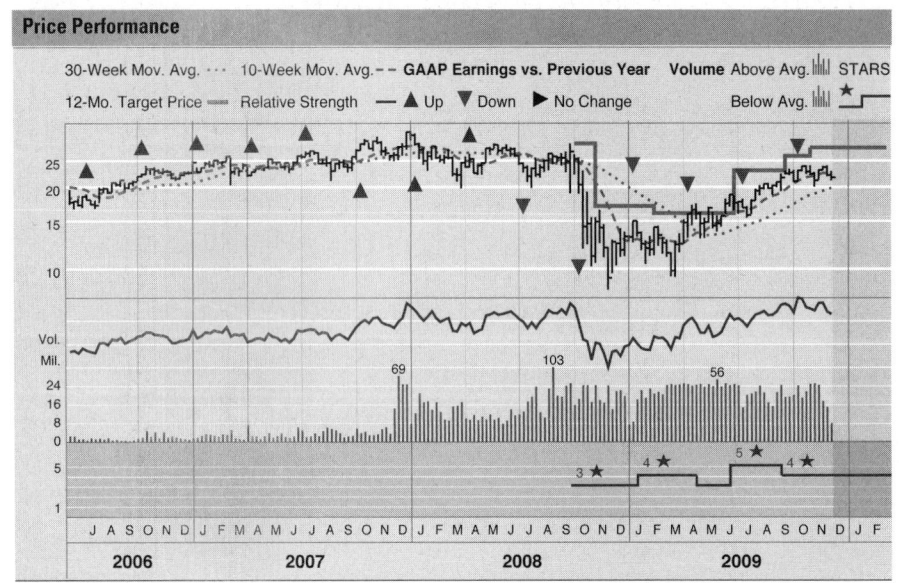

Analysis prepared by **Matthew Albrecht** on October 22, 2009, when the stock traded at **$ 22.96**.

Highlights

► Invesco will acquire the retail asset management business from Morgan Stanley (MS 34, Hold) for about $1.5 billion in cash and stock. The deal brings IVZ $119 billion in client assets across product classes, and more importantly, should give the firm an improved distribution platform with access to Morgan Stanley Smith Barney brokers. Still, lower average asset balances and an unfavorable asset mix will likely keep pressure on revenues throughout 2009, though we expect assets under management to recover and end up 20% versus 2008. Client flows have resumed, and we expect continued positive flows into 2010. Revenues are likely to decline over 20% in 2009 before a double digit improvement in 2010.

► We think IVZ's variable cost structure, combined with cost-cutting measures and headcount reductions, will help mitigate the impact of sharply lower revenues on margins in the current year, with a marked improvement likely in 2010. We see distribution costs coming down on a percentage basis, but those costs could rebound on a recovery in fund flows.

► We see EPS of $0.78 in 2009 and $1.32 in 2010.

Investment Rationale/Risk

► We think that Invesco, with its broad product offerings and global reach, is in position to attract and retain client assets. While the firm's asset base is weighted toward equities, it also has achieved international diversification, and its customer base is composed of both retail and institutional clients. We have a positive view of Invesco's corporate governance policies, including the independence of the majority of directors and separation of the chairman and chief executive roles. As we think the current valuation understates the firm's future earnings power, our recommendation is buy.

► Risks to our recommendation and target price include equity and bond market depreciation, poor relative investment performance, and increased government regulation within the industry.

► IVZ recently traded at about 17.2X our 2010 earnings estimate, a discount to its peer group average multiple. Our 12-month target price of $28 assumes a 22.6X multiple applied to our forward 12-month earnings estimate of $1.24, in line with the forward multiples of peers and IVZ's historical multiple.

Qualitative Risk Assessment

LOW	MEDIUM	HIGH

Our risk assessment reflects our view of the company's strong market share, broad product base and improving investment performance, offset by economic and industry cyclicality, the firm's bias toward equity products, and recent relative fund underperformance.

Quantitative Evaluations

S&P Quality Ranking NR

D	C	B-	B	B+	A-	A	A+

Relative Strength Rank MODERATE

40

LOWEST = 1   HIGHEST = 99

Revenue/Earnings Data

Revenue (Million $)

	1Q	2Q	3Q	4Q	Year
2009	548.6	625.1	705.8	--	--
2008	910.4	935.6	827.2	634.4	3,308
2007	900.2	979.0	976.6	1,023	3,879
2006	584.1	588.1	587.1	655.3	2,415
2005	537.8	547.8	536.2	551.4	2,173
2004	530.4	525.7	508.2	576.9	2,224

Earnings Per Share ($)

2009	0.08	0.18	0.24	E0.28	E0.78
2008	0.39	0.41	0.33	0.08	1.21
2007	0.38	0.43	0.41	0.43	1.64
2006	0.26	0.30	0.26	0.40	1.20
2005	0.18	0.18	0.18	-0.02	0.52
2004	0.04	0.03	-0.84	Nil	-0.84

Fiscal year ended Dec. 31. Next earnings report expected: Early February. EPS Estimates based on S&P Operating Earnings; historical GAAP earnings are as reported.

Dividend Data (Dates: mm/dd Payment Date: mm/dd/yy)

Amount ($)	Date Decl.	Ex-Div. Date	Stk. of Record	Payment Date
0.100	10/27	11/24	11/26	12/17/08
0.103	01/30	05/18	05/20	06/03/09
0.103	07/24	08/17	08/19	09/02/09
0.103	10/16	11/16	11/18	12/02/09

Dividends have been paid since 1995. Source: Company reports.

Please read the Required Disclosures and Analyst Certification on the last page of this report.

Invesco Ltd

STANDARD
&POOR'S

Business Summary October 22, 2009

CORPORATE OVERVIEW. Invesco is an independent global investment management company that provides an array of investment choices for retail, institutional and high-net-worth clients around the globe. It is incorporated under the laws of Bermuda, and it is headquartered in Atlanta, Georgia. Prior to May 2007, the company was called AMVESCAP PLC, formed through the 1997 merger of Invesco and AIM. Through its subsidiaries, it offers equity, fixed income, and alternative strategies to investors domiciled throughout the world. Assets under management (AUM) totaled $357 billion at December 31, 2008. Retail assets accounted for 42% of AUM, institutional assets were 54% of the total, and assets in the private wealth management unit accounted for the remaining 4%. Clients domiciled in the U.S. accounted for 65% of AUM at the end of 2008, U.K. clients owned 16%, and clients in Canada, Europe, and Asia each represented less than 10% of assets.

The company distributes its products utilizing a number of brands through various distribution channels. Its retail products are distributed through Invesco AIM in the U.S., Invesco Trimark in Canada, Invesco Perpetual in the U.K., Invesco in Europe and Asia, and PowerShares for exchange traded funds (ETFs). Retail products are primarily distributed through third parties, including broker-dealers, retirement platforms, financial advisors and insurance companies. Its assets in China are managed through its joint-venture called In-

vesco Great Wall. It offers a full array of investment options, including money market, fixed income, balanced, equity and alternative fund choices.

Its institutional clients are served throughout the world through Invesco and Invesco AIM. It offers a range of products, including equities, fixed income, real estate, financial structures and absolute return strategies. Private equity options are offered through W.L. Ross & Co. A global salesforce distributes products and provides service to clients around the world. Clients include public entities, corporate, union, non-profit, endowments, foundations, and financial institutions.

Invesco's private wealth management services are offered through Atlantic Trust. It provides high-net-worth individuals with personalized service, including financial counseling, estate planning, asset allocation, investment management, private equity, trust, custody and other services. It had offices in 11 cities at December 31, 2008.

Company Financials Fiscal Year Ended Dec. 31

Per Share Data ($)	2008	2007	2006	2005	2004	2003	2002	2001	2000	1999
Tangible Book Value	NM	NM	NM	NM	NM	NM	NM	NM	NM	NM
Cash Flow	1.33	1.85	1.37	0.76	-0.60	0.80	0.89	1.27	1.65	1.26
Earnings	1.21	1.64	1.20	0.52	-0.84	-0.08	0.06	0.54	1.22	0.88
Dividends	0.52	0.37	0.36	0.33	0.32	0.37	0.36	0.30	0.46	0.27
Payout Ratio	43%	23%	30%	63%	NM	NM	NM	56%	38%	31%
Prices:High	31.40	32.25	25.04	15.92	17.33	18.16	31.80	48.00	61.19	23.40
Prices:Low	8.35	26.10	15.46	11.15	9.62	7.65	7.62	16.20	20.60	14.40
P/E Ratio:High	3	20	21	31	NM	NM	NM	89	51	27
P/E Ratio:Low	1	16	13	21	NM	NM	NM	30	17	16
Income Statement Analysis (Million $)										
Revenue	3,308	3,879	2,415	2,173	1,158	1,158	1,345	1,620	1,629	1,072
Operating Income	795	1,058	853	595	-63.3	362	427	591	591	393
Depreciation	47.6	64.1	67.6	94.5	45.6	200	210	206	110	77.4
Interest Expense	76.9	71.3	81.3	85.1	44.1	48.3	52.6	55.9	51.6	44.7
Pretax Income	657	1,244	755	360	-138	36.4	102	280	446	283
Effective Tax Rate	35.9%	28.7%	35.0%	40.7%	NM	NM	83.5%	44.8%	35.3%	36.0%
Net Income	482	674	490	212	-173	-17.3	16.9	155	289	181
Balance Sheet & Other Financial Data (Million $)										
Cash	658	1,130	924	1,957	369	393	424	209	466	250
Current Assets	2,379	4,194	3,497	2,706	1,385	1,297	1,150	785	1,152	926
Total Assets	9,757	12,925	9,292	7,578	3,907	4,110	4,138	4,432	4,296	1,827
Current Liabilities	2,103	3,641	3,582	2,523	1,253	1,070	1,139	641	764	706
Long Term Debt	862	1,276	973	1,212	683	730	596	844	960	659
Common Equity	5,690	6,591	4,270	3,613	1,863	2,232	2,283	2,282	2,103	437
Total Capital	7,458	8,988	5,248	4,872	2,590	2,993	2,918	3,126	3,063	1,096
Capital Expenditures	84.1	36.7	37.7	38.2	27.6	36.6	54.6	68.0	62.0	56.7
Cash Flow	529	738	558	307	-128	183	227	361	399	258
Current Ratio	1.1	1.2	1.0	1.1	1.1	1.2	1.0	1.2	1.5	1.3
% Long Term Debt of Capitalization	11.6	14.2	18.5	24.9	26.4	24.4	20.4	27.0	31.3	60.2
% Net Income of Revenue	14.6	17.4	20.3	9.8	NM	NM	1.3	9.6	17.7	16.9
% Return on Assets	5.9	5.3	5.8	2.8	NM	NM	0.4	3.6	9.4	10.5
% Return on Equity	7.8	10.6	12.4	5.9	NM	NM	0.7	7.1	22.7	47.2

Data as orig reptd.; bef. results of disc opers/spec. items. Per share data adj. for stk. divs.; EPS diluted. Prior to 2005 balance sheet and income statement in pounds. E-Estimated. NA-Not Available. NM-Not Meaningful. NR-Not Ranked. UR-Under Review.

Office: 1360 Peachtree St NE, Atlanta, GA 30309-3233.
Telephone: 404-892-0896.
Email: AMVESCAPContactUs@amvescap.com
Website: http://www.invesco.com

Chrmn: R.D. Adams
Pres & CEO: M.L. Flanagan
CFO: L.M. Starr
Chief Admin Officer: C.D. Meadows

Chief Acctg Officer: D.A. Hartley
Investor Contact: M.S. Perman (44-0-20-7065-3942)
Board Members: R. D. Adams, J. Banham, J. R. Canion, M. L. Flanagan, B. F. Johnson, III, D. Kessler, E. P. Lawrence, J. T. Presby, J. I. Robertson

Founded: 1935
Domicile: Bermuda
Employees: 5,325

Iron Mountain Inc

STANDARD &POOR'S

S&P Recommendation	HOLD ★★★☆☆	Price $24.52 (as of Nov 27, 2009)	12-Mo. Target Price $28.00	Investment Style Large-Cap Growth

GICS Sector Industrials
Sub-Industry Diversified Support Services

Summary This company provides information protection and storage services.

Key Stock Statistics (Source S&P, Vickers, company reports)

52-Wk Range	$32.04– 16.91	S&P Oper. EPS 2009**E**	0.90	Market Capitalization(B)	$4.986	Beta	0.93
Trailing 12-Month EPS	$0.79	S&P Oper. EPS 2010**E**	1.06	Yield (%)	Nil	S&P 3-Yr. Proj. EPS CAGR(%)	11
Trailing 12-Month P/E	31.0	P/E on S&P Oper. EPS 2009**E**	27.2	Dividend Rate/Share	Nil	S&P Credit Rating	BB-
$10K Invested 5 Yrs Ago	$12,260	Common Shares Outstg. (M)	203.4	Institutional Ownership (%)	94		

Price Performance

30-Week Mov. Avg. · · · · 10-Week Mov. Avg. – – **GAAP Earnings vs. Previous Year** Volume Above Avg. STARS
12-Mo. Target Price — Relative Strength — ▲ Up ▼ Down ► No Change Below Avg.

3-for-2

Options: CBOE, P, Ph

Analysis prepared by **Dylan Cathers** on November 04, 2009, when the stock traded at **$ 24.87**.

Highlights

► We believe that revenues will decline 1.5% in 2009, primarily reflecting soft demand for the company's services offerings during the first three quarters of the year. We think the weakening of the U.S. dollar during the past few months should aid results going forward. We continue to foresee weakness in international markets, partially offset by modest growth in the North American market in 2009. In 2010, we look for growth of 5%, on gains in the North American physical and worldwide digital segments. Over the long term, we think revenue growth will be spurred by a rigorous regulatory environment (which requires documents to be stored and accessible for what we consider relatively long periods of time), as well as by selective acquisitions.

► We see operating margins widening in 2009, with further modest gains likely in 2010, based on increased operational efficiencies and lower costs, partially offset by weak sales of higher-margin services.

► Our operating EPS estimates are $0.90 for 2009, excluding one-time items, and $1.06 for 2010. This compares to $0.78 in 2008, excluding $0.38 of one-time items.

Investment Rationale/Risk

► Our hold opinion is based on valuation. We believe IRM's brand, customer base and business model are competitive advantages over the long term. Nonetheless, we think weaker recycled paper prices and higher levels of destructions (which adversely affects growth in storage) will continue to limit sales and earnings growth in the near term. In addition, we continue to have concerns about a longer sales cycle, weak demand, and pricing pressure as we believe customers will reduce costs amid the still difficult economic environment.

► Risks to our recommendation and target price include slower growth in corporate storage spending than we project, lower-than-expected recycled paper prices, further deterioration in overseas markets, and less favorable foreign currency rates.

► Our 12-month target price of $28 is based on our P/E analysis. We use a peer-premium multiple of 26.4X our 2010 EPS estimate. While we believe the stability of IRM's business merits a peer-premium valuation, our P/E ratio is near a four-year historical low for the company.

Qualitative Risk Assessment

LOW	MEDIUM	HIGH

Our risk assessment reflects our view of IRM's diversified and significant recurring revenue base, offset by notable and growing competition and a substantial amount of debt on its balance sheet.

Quantitative Evaluations

S&P Quality Ranking   **B**

D	C	B-	B	B+	A-	A	A+

Relative Strength Rank   **WEAK**

25

LOWEST = 1   HIGHEST = 99

Revenue/Earnings Data

Revenue (Million $)

	1Q	2Q	3Q	4Q	Year
2009	723.4	746.0	764.9	--	--
2008	749.4	768.9	784.3	752.6	3,055
2007	632.5	668.7	701.8	727.0	2,730
2006	563.7	581.6	595.6	609.5	2,350
2005	501.4	511.9	526.5	538.4	2,078
2004	433.9	445.4	459.3	478.9	1,818

Earnings Per Share ($)

2009	0.14	0.43	0.21	E0.22	E0.90
2008	0.17	0.18	0.06	0.01	0.40
2007	0.17	0.19	0.25	0.14	0.76
2006	0.13	0.19	0.13	0.18	0.64
2005	0.11	0.13	0.18	0.15	0.57
2004	0.12	0.11	0.09	0.15	0.48

Fiscal year ended Dec. 31. Next earnings report expected: Late February. EPS Estimates based on S&P Operating Earnings; historical GAAP earnings are as reported.

Dividend Data

No cash dividends have been paid.

Please read the Required Disclosures and Analyst Certification on the last page of this report.

The McGraw-Hill Companies

Iron Mountain Inc

STANDARD
&POOR'S

Business Summary November 04, 2009

CORPORATE OVERVIEW. We view Iron Mountain as the global leader in information protection and storage services. IRM helps organizations reduce related costs and risks. Specifically, the company offers records-management and data protection solutions, and helps address information challenges including rising storage costs, litigation, regulatory compliance, and disaster recovery.

Revenues are generated by providing storage for a variety of information media formats, core records management services, data and recovery offerings, information destruction services, and an expanding menu of complementary products and services to a diverse customer base. Core services, which are highly recurring in nature, primarily consist of the collection, handling, and transportation of stored records and information. In 2008, IRM's storage and core service revenues represented about 86% of total revenues.

As of year-end 2008, IRM had more than 120,000 corporate clients around the world, including more than 90% of the Fortune 1000 and over 90% of the FTSE 1000. The company provides services in 37 countries and operates over 1,000

records management facilities. The share of international contributions to IRM's revenue has crept up to 32% for 2008, from 31% in 2007, 30% for 2006 and 28% for 2005.

The customer base is diversified by industry, with commercial, legal, banking, healthcare, accounting, financial, entertainment, and government organizations all represented. Further, no single customer represented more than 2% of revenue for 2008 or either of the two prior years.

CORPORATE STRATEGY. Primary growth drivers include increasing revenues from existing customers, adding new clients, introducing new products and services (such as secure shredding, electronic vaulting and digital archiving), and acquisitions.

Company Financials Fiscal Year Ended Dec. 31

Per Share Data ($)	2008	2007	2006	2005	2004	2003	2002	2001	2000	1999
Tangible Book Value	NM	NM	NM	NM	NM	NM	NM	NM	NM	NM
Cash Flow	1.83	1.99	1.71	1.54	1.31	1.12	0.91	0.64	0.57	0.57
Earnings	0.40	0.76	0.64	0.57	0.48	0.43	0.35	-0.17	-0.14	-0.01
S&P Core Earnings	0.40	0.69	0.61	0.55	0.46	0.43	0.33	-0.17	NA	NA
Dividends	Nil	Nil	Nil	Nil	Nil	Nil	Nil	Nil	Nil	Nil
Payout Ratio	Nil	Nil	Nil	Nil	Nil	Nil	Nil	Nil	Nil	Nil
Prices:High	37.13	38.85	29.91	30.06	23.39	18.06	15.20	13.54	11.65	11.70
Prices:Low	16.71	25.05	22.64	17.77	17.22	13.44	8.95	9.37	8.22	7.44
P/E Ratio:High	93	51	47	52	49	41	44	NM	NM	NM
P/E Ratio:Low	42	33	35	31	36	31	26	NM	NM	NM

Income Statement Analysis (Million $)	2008	2007	2006	2005	2004	2003	2002	2001	2000	1999
Revenue	3,055	2,730	2,350	2,078	1,818	1,501	1,319	1,171	986	520
Operating Income	791	699	611	575	507	441	364	302	257	130
Depreciation	291	249	214	192	164	135	110	154	127	65.4
Interest Expense	237	229	195	184	186	150	137	135	118	54.4
Pretax Income	225	223	224	197	167	157	120	-8.13	-18.0	9.84
Effective Tax Rate	63.6%	30.9%	41.8%	41.4%	41.7%	42.5%	41.1%	NM	NM	NM
Net Income	82.0	153	129	114	94.2	84.6	67.0	-32.2	-24.9	-1.06
S&P Core Earnings	82.4	139	122	110	91.9	83.4	63.5	-31.7	NA	NA

Balance Sheet & Other Financial Data (Million $)	2008	2007	2006	2005	2004	2003	2002	2001	2000	1999
Cash	278	133	45.4	53.4	31.9	74.7	56.3	21.4	6.20	3.83
Current Assets	976	822	680	554	501	472	367	309	237	144
Total Assets	6,357	6,308	5,210	4,766	4,442	3,892	3,231	2,860	2,659	1,317
Current Liabilities	730	766	639	592	515	585	428	359	314	150
Long Term Debt	3,207	3,213	2,606	2,504	2,439	1,974	1,662	1,461	1,314	603
Common Equity	1,803	1,795	1,553	1,370	1,219	1,066	945	886	924	489
Total Capital	5,050	5,389	4,444	4,105	3,877	3,262	2,748	2,459	2,320	1,150
Capital Expenditures	387	386	382	272	232	204	197	197	169	98.7
Cash Flow	373	402	343	306	258	219	177	121	102	64.4
Current Ratio	1.3	1.1	1.1	0.9	1.0	0.8	0.9	0.9	0.8	1.0
% Long Term Debt of Capitalization	63.5	64.2	58.6	61.0	62.9	60.5	60.5	59.4	56.6	52.4
% Net Income of Revenue	2.7	5.6	5.5	5.5	5.2	5.6	5.1	NM	NM	NM
% Return on Assets	1.3	2.7	2.6	2.5	2.3	2.4	2.2	NM	NM	NM
% Return on Equity	4.6	9.1	8.8	8.8	8.2	8.4	7.3	NM	NM	NM

Data as orig reptd.; bef. results of disc opers/spec. items. Per share data adj. for stk. divs.; EPS diluted. E-Estimated. NA-Not Available. NM-Not Meaningful. NR-Not Ranked. UR-Under Review.

Office: 745 Atlantic Ave, Boston, MA 02111-2717.
Telephone: 617-535-4766.
Website: http://www.ironmountain.com
Chrmn: C.R. Reese

Pres: R. Venkata
Pres & CEO: R.T. Brennan
EVP, CFO & Chief Acctg Officer: B.P. McKeon
SVP, Secy & General Counsel: E.W. Cloutier

Investor Contact: S.P. Golden (617-535-4766)
Board Members: C. H. Bailey, C. R. Boden, R. T. Brennan, K. P. Dauten, P. Halvorsen, M. W. Lamach, A. D. Little, C. R. Reese, V. J. Ryan, L. A. Tucker

Founded: 1951
Domicile: Delaware
Employees: 21,000

ITT Corp

STANDARD &POOR'S

S&P Recommendation	STRONG BUY ★★★★★	Price $51.85 (as of Nov 27, 2009)	12-Mo. Target Price $61.00	Investment Style Large-Cap Growth

GICS Sector Industrials
Sub-Industry Aerospace & Defense

Summary This company is a diversified industrial manufacturer of advanced technology products.

Key Stock Statistics (Source S&P, Vickers, company reports)

52-Wk Range	$56.95–31.94	S&P Oper. EPS 2009**E**	3.75	Market Capitalization(B)	$9.473	Beta		1.11
Trailing 12-Month EPS	$3.45	S&P Oper. EPS 2010**E**	4.20	Yield (%)	1.64	S&P 3-Yr. Proj. EPS CAGR(%)		14
Trailing 12-Month P/E	15.0	P/E on S&P Oper. EPS 2009**E**	13.8	Dividend Rate/Share	$0.85	S&P Credit Rating		BBB+
$10K Invested 5 Yrs Ago	$12,797	Common Shares Outstg. (M)	182.7	Institutional Ownership (%)	81			

Price Performance

- 30-Week Mov. Avg. ···· 10-Week Mov. Avg. - - GAAP Earnings vs. Previous Year Volume Above Avg. STARS
- 12-Mo. Target Price — Relative Strength — ▲ Up ▼ Down ▶ No Change Below Avg.

Options: ASE, CBOE, Ph

Highlights

- ► The 12-month target price for ITT has recently been changed to $61.00 from $64.00. The Highlights section of this Stock Report will be updated accordingly.

Investment Rationale/Risk

- ► The Investment Rationale/Risk section of this Stock Report will be updated shortly. For the latest News story on ITT from MarketScope, see below.

- ► 10/30/09 12:09 pm ET ... S&P REITERATES STRONG BUY OPINION ON SHARES OF ITT (ITT 50.81*****): ITT posts adjusted Q3 EPS from continuing operations of $1.03 vs. $1.11, and above our $0.96 estimate. Results exclude a $0.71 per share charge for estimated future asbestos payments, much higher than previously indicated. We believe this is the primary drag on the shares today. However, we do not expect its impact to be material to ITT. Rather, we view ITT's balance sheet and cash flows as able to support acquisitions, share buybacks, dividend increases, and asbestos claims. Separately, we cut our target price by $3 to $61 on a revised blend of P/E and DCF analysis. / E.Levy-CFA

Qualitative Risk Assessment

LOW	MEDIUM	HIGH

Our risk assessment reflects our view of ITT's favorable growth prospects in most of the markets it serves and our view of its strong management team and solid balance sheet. This is offset by our outlook for U.S. defense spending growth, which we think may slow in coming years.

Quantitative Evaluations

S&P Quality Ranking A-

D	C	B-	B	B+	A-	A	A+

Relative Strength Rank MODERATE

53

LOWEST = 1 HIGHEST = 99

Revenue/Earnings Data

Revenue (Million $)

	1Q	2Q	3Q	4Q	Year
2009	2,557	2,780	2,698	--	--
2008	2,806	3,064	2,879	2,945	11,695
2007	2,070	2,223	2,181	2,529	9,003
2006	1,792	1,964	2,001	2,051	7,808
2005	1,776	1,874	1,828	1,950	7,427
2004	1,511	1,647	1,663	1,943	6,764

Earnings Per Share ($)

	1Q	2Q	3Q	4Q	Year
2009	1.01	1.10	0.36	E1.01	E3.75
2008	0.93	1.22	1.20	0.96	4.23
2007	0.74	1.08	0.92	0.70	3.44
2006	0.55	0.72	0.75	0.65	2.67
2005	0.65	0.70	0.79	-0.48	1.67
2004	0.47	0.60	0.58	0.66	2.32

Fiscal year ended Dec. 31. Next earnings report expected: Early February. EPS Estimates based on S&P Operating Earnings; historical GAAP earnings are as reported.

Dividend Data (Dates: mm/dd Payment Date: mm/dd/yy)

Amount ($)	Date Decl.	Ex-Div. Date	Stk. of Record	Payment Date
0.213	02/20	03/02	03/04	04/01/09
0.213	05/12	05/20	05/22	07/01/09
0.213	08/06	08/19	08/21	10/01/09
0.213	10/06	11/10	11/13	01/01/10

Dividends have been paid since 1996. Source: Company reports.

Please read the Required Disclosures and Analyst Certification on the last page of this report.

The McGraw-Hill Companies

ITT Corp

STANDARD
&POOR'S

Business Summary September 09, 2009

CORPORATE OVERVIEW. ITT Corp. (name changed from ITT Industries in July 2006) is primarily a producer of defense electronics and fluid technology products.

Fluid technology products (nearly 33% of 2008 sales) include pumps, valves, heat exchangers, mixers and fluid measuring instruments and controls for residential, agricultural, commercial, municipal and industrial applications. The fluid technology segment became the world's largest pump manufacturer (formerly third largest) following its 1997 acquisition of Goulds Pumps, Inc.

Defense electronics and services (nearly 54%) are sold to the military and to government agencies. Products include traffic control systems, jamming devices that guard military planes against radar guided missiles, digital combat radios, night vision devices, radar, satellite instruments and other.

Motion & flow control products (nearly 14%) include switches and valves for industrial and aerospace applications, products for the marine and leisure markets, and fluid handling materials such as tubing systems and connectors

for various automotive and industrial markets for the transportation industry.

CORPORATE STRATEGY. The company seeks to expand revenues through a combination of internal growth and acquisitions. We expect the company to continue its tradition of successful acquisition integrations.

At the same time, ITT plans to divest operations that do not fit its strategic goals or provide adequate returns. A recent example is the 2007 divestiture of the switch components operations, which accounted for about half of the electronics segment's 2006 revenues.

We expect the company to increase revenues via new products, expanded markets and acquisitions.

Company Financials Fiscal Year Ended Dec. 31

Per Share Data ($)	2008	2007	2006	2005	2004	2003	2002	2001	2000	1999
Tangible Book Value	NM	NM	1.72	1.38	NM	0.78	NM	NM	NM	NM
Cash Flow	5.74	4.45	3.58	2.71	3.37	3.08	2.94	2.37	2.59	2.25
Earnings	4.23	3.44	2.67	1.67	2.32	2.08	2.03	1.20	1.47	1.27
S&P Core Earnings	2.65	3.35	2.74	2.28	2.13	1.94	0.69	-0.18	NA	NA
Dividends	0.70	0.56	0.55	0.36	0.34	0.32	0.30	0.30	0.30	0.30
Payout Ratio	17%	16%	21%	22%	15%	15%	15%	25%	20%	24%
Prices:High	69.73	73.44	58.73	58.05	43.36	37.70	35.43	26.00	19.81	20.75
Prices:Low	34.75	56.30	45.34	40.24	35.52	25.06	22.90	17.78	11.19	15.25
P/E Ratio:High	16	21	22	35	19	18	17	22	13	16
P/E Ratio:Low	8	16	17	24	15	12	11	15	8	12

Income Statement Analysis (Million $)	2008	2007	2006	2005	2004	2003	2002	2001	2000	1999
Revenue	11,695	9,003	7,808	7,427	6,764	5,627	4,985	4,676	4,829	4,632
Operating Income	1,566	1,229	1,024	985	871	559	706	707	695	592
Depreciation	278	185	172	197	199	188	171	213	202	181
Interest Expense	141	115	86.2	75.0	50.4	Nil	68.8	85.5	93.1	84.8
Pretax Income	1,088	898	727	448	610	531	509	333	420	370
Effective Tax Rate	28.7%	29.6%	31.3%	29.8%	28.3%	26.3%	25.3%	35.0%	37.0%	37.0%
Net Income	775	633	500	314	438	391	380	217	265	233
S&P Core Earnings	485	616	512	429	400	364	129	-31.7	NA	NA

Balance Sheet & Other Financial Data (Million $)	2008	2007	2006	2005	2004	2003	2002	2001	2000	1999
Cash	965	1,840	937	451	263	414	202	121	88.7	182
Current Assets	4,064	4,930	3,348	2,772	2,329	2,106	1,701	1,459	1,506	1,628
Total Assets	10,480	11,553	7,430	7,063	7,277	5,938	5,390	4,508	4,611	4,530
Current Liabilities	4,031	5,456	2,759	2,560	2,446	1,687	1,730	1,897	2,233	2,110
Long Term Debt	468	3,566	500	516	543	461	492	456	408	479
Common Equity	3,060	3,945	3,362	2,723	2,343	1,848	1,137	1,376	1,211	1,099
Total Capital	3,541	4,637	3,863	3,240	2,886	2,309	1,630	1,832	1,620	1,578
Capital Expenditures	249	239	177	179	165	154	153	174	181	228
Cash Flow	1,054	818	671	511	636	579	551	430	466	414
Current Ratio	1.0	0.9	1.2	1.1	1.0	1.2	1.0	0.8	0.7	0.8
% Long Term Debt of Capitalization	13.3	10.9	13.0	15.9	18.8	20.0	30.2	24.9	25.2	30.3
% Net Income of Revenue	6.6	7.0	6.4	4.2	6.5	6.9	7.6	4.6	5.5	5.0
% Return on Assets	7.0	6.7	6.9	4.4	6.6	6.9	7.7	4.8	5.8	4.9
% Return on Equity	22.1	18.6	16.1	12.4	20.9	26.2	30.2	16.8	22.9	19.4

Data as orig reptd.; bef. results of disc opers/spec. items. Per share data adj. for stk. divs.; EPS diluted. E-Estimated. NA-Not Available. NM-Not Meaningful. NR-Not Ranked. UR-Under Review.

Office: 1133 Westchester Ave, White Plains, NY 10604-3516.
Telephone: 914-641-2000.
Website: http://www.itt.com
Chrmn, Pres & CEO: S.R. Loranger

SVP & CFO: D.L. Ramos
SVP & CTO: B.L. Reichelderfer
SVP & Treas: D.E. Foley
Chief Acctg Officer: J.M. Klettner

Investor Contact: P.J. Milligan
Board Members: C. J. Crawford, C. A. Gold, R. F. Hake, J. J. Hamre, P. J. Kern, S. R. Loranger, F. T. MacInnis, S. N. Mohapatra, L. S. Sanford, M. I. Tambakeras

Founded: 1920
Domicile: Indiana
Employees: 40,800

The McGraw·Hill Companies

Jabil Circuit Inc

STANDARD &POOR'S

S&P Recommendation BUY ★★★★☆

Price	12-Mo. Target Price	Investment Style
$13.34 (as of Nov 27, 2009)	$16.00	Large-Cap Growth

GICS Sector Information Technology
Sub-Industry Electronic Manufacturing Services

Summary This company manufactures circuit board assemblies for international OEMs in the computing, peripheral, storage, communications, networking, and industrial markets.

Key Stock Statistics (Source S&P, Vickers, company reports)

52-Wk Range	$15.45– 3.10	S&P Oper. EPS 2010**E**	0.70	Market Capitalization(B)	$2.857	Beta	1.97
Trailing 12-Month EPS	$-5.63	S&P Oper. EPS 2011**E**	0.95	Yield (%)	2.10	S&P 3-Yr. Proj. EPS CAGR(%)	NM
Trailing 12-Month P/E	NM	P/E on S&P Oper. EPS 2010**E**	19.1	Dividend Rate/Share	$0.28	S&P Credit Rating	BB+
$10K Invested 5 Yrs Ago	$5,767	Common Shares Outstg. (M)	214.2	Institutional Ownership (%)	88		

Price Performance

30-Week Mov. Avg. ···   10-Week Mov. Avg. --   **GAAP Earnings vs. Previous Year**   Volume Above Avg.▏▍▏ STARS
12-Mo. Target Price —   Relative Strength   ▲ Up ▼ Down ► No Change   Below Avg.▏▍▏ ★

J A S O N D J F M A M J J A S O N D J F M A M J J A S O N D J F M A M J J A S O N D J F

2006   2007   2008   2009

Options: ASE, CBOE, P, Ph

Analysis prepared by **Thomas W. Smith, CFA** on September 30, 2009, when the stock traded at **$ 13.24**.

Highlights

► We forecast revenue to increase 4% for FY 10 (Aug.), and 6% in FY 11, reflecting our projection of a recovery for the EMS industry from a deep downturn. We see the potential for new business wins and a continued push into low-cost geographies providing some offset to a sluggish global economy. While JBL benefits from providing end-to-end solutions to a well-diversified customer base, we believe some rivals have even greater scale efficiencies.

► We expect gross margins to widen to 7.0% in FY 10, and 7.1% in FY 11, aided by rising volumes and an improved cost structure resulting from restructuring activities. The company announced September 28, 2009, that its ongoing workforce reduction plan would reduce staff by 4,500, higher than the 3,000 previously planned.

► We see JBL benefiting from favorable tax jurisdictions in offshore locations. On an operating basis excluding restructuring-related charges, but including stock options expense that we estimate near $0.22 a year, we project EPS of $0.70 for FY 10, and $0.95 for FY 11.

Investment Rationale/Risk

► We think that an economic downturn that subdued sales for JBL in FY 09 will abate in FY 10, permitting better results for the company. We believe a push by the company to diversify its business mix away from lower-margin consumer business should aid margins ahead. Cost savings from restructurings should also help, in our opinion. We view these volatile shares as attractively valued in the context of an industry upturn that we project.

► Risks to our recommendation and target price include fewer market share gains than we project, slower implementation of new contracts and facilities than we expect, and less smooth acquisition restructuring than we foresee.

► We apply our target price-to-book ratio of 2.8X, which is in the lower half of a five-year historical range for JBL, to our estimate of tangible book value per share of $6.12 to derive a valuation of about $17. Our P/E analysis yields a lower valuation, and we blend the measures to arrive at our 12-month target price of $16.

Qualitative Risk Assessment

LOW	MEDIUM	**HIGH**

Our risk assessment reflects our view of the historically volatile nature of the electronic manufacturing services industry as well as what we see as the company's relatively high exposure to fluctuations in commodity prices.

Quantitative Evaluations

S&P Quality Ranking   B-

D	C	**B-**	B	B+	A-	A	A+

Relative Strength Rank   MODERATE

58

LOWEST = 1   HIGHEST = 99

Revenue/Earnings Data

Revenue (Million $)

	1Q	2Q	3Q	4Q	Year
2009	3,383	2,887	2,615	2,800	11,685
2008	3,368	3,059	3,088	3,265	12,780
2007	3,224	2,935	3,002	3,130	12,291
2006	2,404	2,315	2,592	2,954	10,265
2005	1,833	1,716	1,938	2,037	7,524
2004	1,509	1,492	1,626	1,626	6,253

Earnings Per Share ($)

	1Q	2Q	3Q	4Q	Year
2009	-1.34	-4.19	-0.14	0.03	-5.63
2008	0.30	-0.12	0.19	0.28	0.65
2007	0.20	0.07	0.03	0.06	0.35
2006	0.37	0.32	0.30	-0.22	0.77
2005	0.27	0.22	0.29	0.34	1.12
2004	0.20	0.19	0.19	0.22	0.81

Fiscal year ended Aug. 31. Next earnings report expected: Late December. EPS Estimates based on S&P Operating Earnings; historical GAAP earnings are as reported.

Dividend Data (Dates: mm/dd Payment Date: mm/dd/yy)

Amount ($)	Date Decl.	Ex-Div. Date	Stk. of Record	Payment Date
0.070	01/23	02/12	02/17	03/02/09
0.070	04/23	05/13	05/15	06/01/09
0.070	07/16	08/13	08/17	09/01/09
0.070	10/23	11/12	11/16	12/01/09

Dividends have been paid since 2006. Source: Company reports.

Please read the Required Disclosures and Analyst Certification on the last page of this report.

The McGraw-Hill Companies

Jabil Circuit Inc

STANDARD
&POOR'S

Business Summary September 30, 2009

CORPORATE OVERVIEW. This provider of electronic manufacturing services (EMS) works with customers in a variety of industries at facilities around the world. Among the many services Jabil Circuit offers are design and engineering, component selection and procurement, automated assembly, product testing, parallel global production, enclosure services, systems assembly, direct-order fulfillment, and aftermarket services.

Since September 1, 2007, the company reports in three operating segments: Electronic Manufacturing Services (EMS) represented 64% of sales in FY 08 (Aug.), Consumer represented 31%, and Aftermarket Services (AMS) represented 5%. Within the EMS segment, industry sectors served include Automotive, at 4% of FY 08 total sales, Computing and Storage 13%, Instrumentation and Medical 18%, Networking 21%, Telecommunications 6%, and Other 2%. Within the Consumer segment, Display represented 7% of FY 08 total sales, Mobility 12%, and Peripherals 12%. Notably among trends within the company's focus, revenue from the Mobility operations has been decreasing over

the past two years, to 12% in FY 08, from 21% of total sales in FY 06.

In FY 08, Cisco Systems and Hewlett-Packard were the only customers accounting for more than 10% of sales, with Cisco at 16% (15% of FY 07 sales) and Hewlett at 11% (under 10% of FY 07 sales). Among other large customers are Nokia Corp., which accounted for 13% of FY 07 sales, IBM, Motorola, Network Appliance, NEC, Royal Philips Electronics, and Tellabs. In FY 08, the five largest customers represented 47% of sales, and 44 customers accounted for 90% of JBL's revenues. Overall, we believe the company faces some risk from reliance on large customer accounts. However, this is typical within the EMS industry and we think the company has made some progress in broadening its customer base over the past three years.

Company Financials Fiscal Year Ended Aug. 31

Per Share Data ($)	2009	2008	2007	2006	2005	2004	2003	2002	2001	2000
Tangible Book Value	6.15	6.90	5.97	8.26	8.22	7.29	6.06	6.63	6.43	6.68
Cash Flow	NA	1.99	1.51	1.71	2.18	1.89	1.32	1.11	1.35	1.31
Earnings	-5.63	0.65	0.35	0.77	1.12	0.81	0.21	0.17	0.59	0.78
S&P Core Earnings	-0.73	0.64	0.35	0.77	0.64	0.59	0.04	NA	0.46	NA
Dividends	0.28	0.28	0.28	0.14	Nil	Nil	Nil	Nil	Nil	Nil
Payout Ratio	NM	43%	80%	18%	Nil	Nil	Nil	Nil	Nil	Nil
Prices:High	15.45	18.78	27.86	43.70	39.00	32.40	31.66	26.79	40.99	68.00
Prices:Low	3.10	4.77	14.27	22.01	21.80	19.18	21.20	11.13	14.00	18.63
P/E Ratio:High	NM	29	80	57	35	40	NM	NM	69	87
P/E Ratio:Low	NM	7	41	29	19	24	NM	65	24	24

Income Statement Analysis (Million $)										
Revenue	11,685	12,780	12,291	10,265	7,524	6,253	4,729	3,545	4,331	3,558
Operating Income	NA	582	494	522	507	439	369	296	353	317
Depreciation	292	276	240	199	220	222	224	188	155	99.3
Interest Expense	NA	94.3	86.1	23.5	24.8	19.4	17.0	13.1	5.86	7.61
Pretax Income	-1,005	157	94.5	225	276	198	37.0	44.8	166	213
Effective Tax Rate	NM	16.0%	22.6%	26.9%	16.1%	15.5%	NM	22.4%	28.7%	31.5%
Net Income	-1,165	134	73.2	165	232	167	43.0	34.7	119	146
S&P Core Earnings	-152	131	73.9	165	134	122	8.12	-0.11	93.4	NA

Balance Sheet & Other Financial Data (Million $)										
Cash	876	773	664	774	796	621	700	641	431	338
Current Assets	NA	4,139	3,666	3,679	2,686	2,183	2,094	1,588	1,447	1,387
Total Assets	5,318	7,032	6,295	5,412	4,077	3,329	3,245	2,548	2,358	2,018
Current Liabilities	NA	3,048	2,991	2,701	1,568	1,159	1,263	593	505	692
Long Term Debt	1,037	1,100	760	330	327	305	297	355	362	25.0
Common Equity	1,435	2,716	2,443	2,294	2,135	1,819	1,588	1,507	1,414	1,270
Total Capital	2,677	3,832	3,226	2,632	2,462	2,125	1,905	1,903	1,813	1,323
Capital Expenditures	292	338	302	280	257	218	117	85.5	309	333
Cash Flow	NA	410	313	363	452	389	267	223	274	245
Current Ratio	1.4	1.4	1.2	1.4	1.7	1.9	1.7	2.7	2.9	2.0
% Long Term Debt of Capitalization	38.7	28.7	23.6	12.5	13.3	14.4	15.6	18.6	20.0	1.9
% Net Income of Revenue	NM	1.1	0.6	1.6	3.1	2.7	0.9	1.0	2.7	4.1
% Return on Assets	NM	2.0	1.3	3.5	6.3	5.1	1.5	1.4	5.4	9.5
% Return on Equity	NM	5.2	3.1	7.4	11.7	9.8	2.8	2.4	8.8	15.8

Data as orig reptd.; bef. results of disc opers/spec. items. Per share data adj. for stk. divs.; EPS diluted. E-Estimated. NA-Not Available. NM-Not Meaningful. NR-Not Ranked. UR-Under Review.

Office: 10560 Dr. Martin Luther King Jr. Street North, St. Petersburg, FL 33716.
Telephone: 727-577-9749.
Email: investor_relations@jabil.com
Website: http://www.jabil.com

Chrmn: W.D. Morean
Pres & CEO: T.L. Main
Vice Chrmn: T.A. Sansone
COO: M.T. Mondello

CFO & Chief Acctg Officer: F.I. Alexander
Investor Contact: B. Walters (727-803-3349)
Board Members: M. S. Lavitt, T. L. Main, W. D. Morean, L. J. Murphy, F. A. Newman, S. A. Raymund, T. A. Sansone, D. Stout, K. A. Walters

Founded: 1969
Domicile: Delaware
Employees: 61,000

STANDARD &POOR'S

Jacobs Engineering Group Inc.

S&P Recommendation	STRONG BUY ★★★★★	Price	12-Mo. Target Price	Investment Style
		$35.58 (as of Nov 27, 2009)	$52.00	Large-Cap Growth

GICS Sector Industrials
Sub-Industry Construction & Engineering

Summary This company provides engineering, construction and maintenance services to private industry and federal government agencies on a worldwide basis.

Key Stock Statistics (Source S&P, Vickers, company reports)

52-Wk Range	$54.71–30.16	S&P Oper. EPS 2010E	2.50	Market Capitalization(B)	$4.424	Beta	1.48
Trailing 12-Month EPS	$3.21	S&P Oper. EPS 2011E	3.15	Yield (%)	Nil	S&P 3-Yr. Proj. EPS CAGR(%)	-2
Trailing 12-Month P/E	11.1	P/E on S&P Oper. EPS 2010E	14.2	Dividend Rate/Share	Nil	S&P Credit Rating	NA
$10K Invested 5 Yrs Ago	$15,736	Common Shares Outstg. (M)	124.3	Institutional Ownership (%)	79		

Price Performance

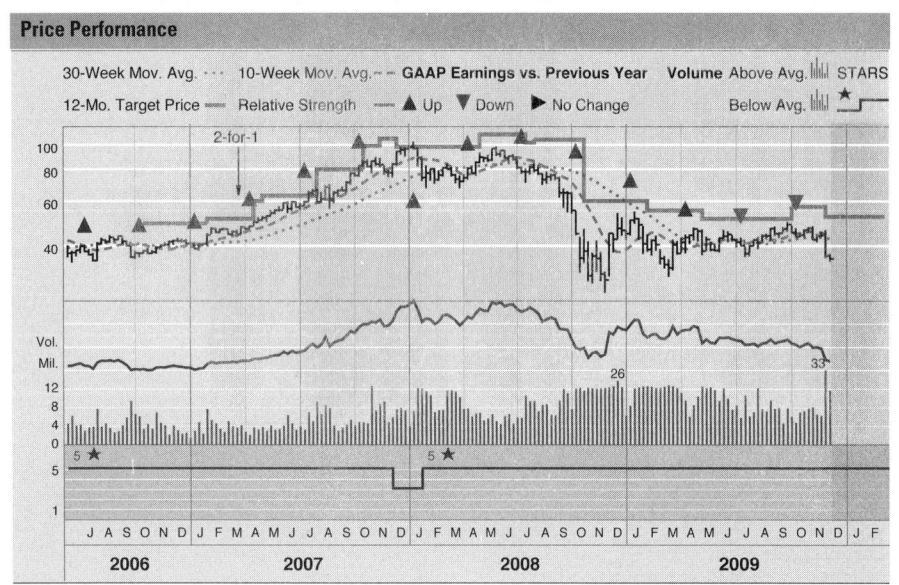

30-Week Mov. Avg. · · · · 10-Week Mov. Avg. - - - **GAAP Earnings vs. Previous Year** Volume Above Avg. STARS
12-Mo. Target Price — Relative Strength — ▲ Up ▼ Down ▶ No Change Below Avg.

Options: ASE, CBOE, Ph

Analysis prepared by **Stewart Scharf** on November 19, 2009, when the stock traded at **$36.58**.

Highlights

► We expect revenue to decline in the high-single digits in FY 10 (Sep.), driven by fewer bookings for refining, oil & gas and other private sector projects, as well project cancellations. However, we believe higher oil prices and improving global economic trends will lead to a resurgence in orders, while government and U.S. stimulus spending contribute to public infrastructure growth. We also see further expansion and strength in the Middle East and India, while JEC continues to focus on attractively-priced accretive acquisitions.

► In our view, gross margins will narrow in FY 10, from 13.7% in FY 09, driven by competitive pricing pressures in the private sector. Margins should begin to improve sequentially later in the fiscal year due in part to a better mix, while we believe operating margins will expand on increased global engineering work at low-cost centers (mainly in India), synergies and other cost control efforts, as JEC focuses on driving down SG&A expense.

► We expect the effective tax rate to remain near 36% in FY 10, with operating EPS of $2.50, climbing to $3.15 in FY 11.

Investment Rationale/Risk

► We base our Strong Buy opinion on our valuation metrics, along with the company's diversified customer and geographic base, and preferred relationship business model which focuses on relatively small, lower-risk projects rather than the competitively bid large lump-sum projects that are basically the industry standard.

► Risks to our recommendation and target price include a prolonged global economic downturn; project delays or cancellations based on customer liquidity issues or sharply lower oil prices; an inability to outsource skilled labor overseas; and a lack of acquisition opportunities.

► Our discounted cash flow (DCF) model suggests an intrinsic value of $59, assuming a perpetuity growth rate of 4% and a weighted average cost of capital (WACC) of about 8%. Based on relative metrics, our view of more favorable prospects later in FY 10, and JEC's relatively low-risk business model, we apply an above-peer and market P/E of 18X our FY 10 EPS estimate, resulting in a value of $45. Blending these metrics, we arrive at our 12-month target price of $52.

Qualitative Risk Assessment

LOW	MEDIUM	HIGH

Our risk assessment reflects the cyclical nature of the company's various markets, its growth-by-acquisition strategy, changes in global political conditions, timing issues related to new awards, and fluctuations in interest rates and foreign currencies. These factors are offset by what we see as JEC's strong cash position and virtually no debt.

Quantitative Evaluations

S&P Quality Ranking B+

D	C	B-	B	B+	A-	A	A+

Relative Strength Rank WEAK

10

LOWEST = 1   HIGHEST = 99

Revenue/Earnings Data

Revenue (Million $)

	1Q	2Q	3Q	4Q	Year
2009	3,233	2,975	2,707	2,553	11,467
2008	2,472	2,665	2,919	3,197	11,252
2007	2,019	2,092	2,084	2,280	8,474
2006	1,683	1,832	1,926	1,979	7,421
2005	1,283	1,383	1,449	1,519	5,635
2004	1,135	1,124	1,120	1,216	4,594

Earnings Per Share ($)

2009	0.94	0.88	0.76	0.63	3.21
2008	0.79	0.80	0.87	0.92	3.38
2007	0.51	0.55	0.61	0.68	2.35
2006	0.36	0.37	0.42	0.49	1.64
2005	0.28	0.31	0.34	0.36	1.29
2004	0.29	0.31	0.26	0.26	1.13

Fiscal year ended Sep. 30. Next earnings report expected: Late January. EPS Estimates based on S&P Operating Earnings; historical GAAP earnings are as reported.

Dividend Data

No cash dividends have been paid since 1984.

Please read the Required Disclosures and Analyst Certification on the last page of this report.

The McGraw-Hill Companies

Jacobs Engineering Group Inc.

STANDARD
&POOR'S

Business Summary November 19, 2009

CORPORATE OVERVIEW. Jacobs Engineering focuses on providing a broad range of technical, professional and construction services to a large number of industrial, commercial and governmental clients worldwide. The company offers project services; consulting services; operations and maintenance services; and construction services via offices primarily in North America, Europe, Asia and Australia. In November 2007, the company was moved into the S&P 500 Index from S&P's MidCap 400 Index.

In FY 09 (Sep.), revenues by sector were: refining (downstream), 35%; national government (environmental, defense and NASA), 21%; chemicals, 11%; pharmaBio (pharmaceutical and biotech), 8%; oil and gas (upstream), 8%; infrastructure, 8%; buildings, 5%; and pulp and paper, high tech, food and consumer products, 4%. The higher-margin technical professional services component accounted for 48% of revenues and 54% of backlog in FY 09, with the balance derived from field services (construction). At October 2, 2009, backlog was $15.2 billion, down 9% from a year earlier. The company generally realizes about 60% to 65% of its backlog as revenues during any 12-month period. About 40% of revenues is generated from operations outside of the U.S. However, JEC is targeting a near 50/50 split of foreign versus domestic revenues within a few years.

Project services include the engineering and design of process plants and high-technology facilities. Construction services offers traditional field services to private and public sector clients. Process, scientific and systems consulting includes market analyses to determine the feasibility of a project. Operations and maintenance services include all tasks required to keep a process plant in day-to-day operation.

In FY 08 (latest available), revenues derived from agencies of the U.S. government accounted for 16.8% of the total, up from 16.6% in FY 07. JEC sees total federal contracts (about 40%) gradually rising to 50% of its business. Cost-reimbursable projects accounted for 86% of the FY 08 total, down from 88% in FY 07.

At the end of FY 08, the company's pension plans were underfunded by $234 million, up from $110 million a year earlier.

Company Financials Fiscal Year Ended Sep. 30

Per Share Data ($)	2009	2008	2007	2006	2005	2004	2003	2002	2001	2000
Tangible Book Value	13.19	10.28	8.42	7.36	5.10	4.04	4.00	2.73	2.55	2.15
Cash Flow	NA	3.97	2.85	2.04	1.70	1.44	1.45	1.31	1.16	0.86
Earnings	3.21	3.38	2.35	1.64	1.29	1.13	1.14	0.99	0.81	0.48
S&P Core Earnings	3.01	3.08	2.38	1.68	1.16	1.02	0.91	0.75	0.53	NA
Dividends	Nil	Nil	Nil	Nil	Nil	Nil	Nil	Nil	Nil	Nil
Payout Ratio	Nil	Nil	Nil	Nil	Nil	Nil	Nil	Nil	Nil	Nil
Prices:High	54.71	103.29	99.62	46.64	34.71	24.11	24.97	21.45	18.92	12.30
Prices:Low	30.16	26.00	38.25	33.90	22.33	18.43	17.48	13.05	10.56	6.55
P/E Ratio:High	17	31	42	29	27	21	22	22	24	25
P/E Ratio:Low	9	8	16	21	17	16	15	13	13	14

Income Statement Analysis (Million $)	2009	2008	2007	2006	2005	2004	2003	2002	2001	2000
Revenue	11,467	11,252	8,474	7,421	5,635	4,594	4,616	4,556	3,957	3,419
Operating Income	NA	716	498	350	288	232	232	207	183	165
Depreciation	86.3	73.1	55.7	48.3	46.4	34.2	35.4	35.1	38.9	40.1
Interest Expense	NA	4.41	8.00	7.50	6.47	3.57	3.25	7.50	11.7	11.4
Pretax Income	625	657	449	305	236	198	197	169	138	81.3
Effective Tax Rate	36.0%	36.0%	36.0%	35.5%	36.0%	35.0%	35.0%	35.0%	36.5%	37.3%
Net Income	400	421	287	197	151	129	128	110	87.8	51.0
S&P Core Earnings	374	383	290	202	136	118	102	82.3	57.5	NA

Balance Sheet & Other Financial Data (Million $)	2009	2008	2007	2006	2005	2004	2003	2002	2001	2000
Cash	1,034	604	613	434	240	100	126	48.5	49.3	65.8
Current Assets	NA	2,750	2,278	1,818	1,337	1,084	970	975	946	851
Total Assets	4,429	4,278	3,389	2,854	2,354	2,071	1,671	1,674	1,557	1,384
Current Liabilities	NA	1,577	1,276	1,041	785	686	611	740	701	684
Long Term Debt	0.74	55.7	40.0	77.7	89.6	78.8	17.8	85.7	164	147
Common Equity	2,626	2,245	1,844	1,423	1,141	1,005	842	690	592	496
Total Capital	2,650	2,386	1,884	1,508	1,237	1,089	865	781	761	648
Capital Expenditures	55.5	115	64.6	54.0	43.9	37.1	25.8	37.2	28.8	44.4
Cash Flow	NA	494	343	245	197	163	163	145	127	91.1
Current Ratio	2.2	1.7	1.8	1.7	1.7	1.6	1.6	1.3	1.4	1.2
% Long Term Debt of Capitalization	Nil	2.3	2.1	5.2	7.2	7.2	2.1	11.0	21.6	22.7
% Net Income of Revenue	3.5	3.7	3.3	2.7	2.7	2.8	2.8	2.4	2.2	1.5
% Return on Assets	NA	11.0	9.1	7.5	6.8	6.9	7.7	6.8	6.0	3.9
% Return on Equity	NA	20.6	17.5	15.2	14.1	14.0	16.7	17.1	16.1	10.8

Data as orig reptd.; bef. results of disc opers/spec. items. Per share data adj. for stk. divs.; EPS diluted. E-Estimated. NA-Not Available. NM-Not Meaningful. NR-Not Ranked. UR-Under Review.

Office: 1111 South Arroyo Parkway, Pasadena, CA, USA 91105.
Telephone: 626-578-3500.
Website: http://www.jacobs.com
Chrmn: N. Watson

Pres & CEO: C.L. Martin
COO: T.R. Hammond
EVP, CFO, Chief Admin Officer & Treas: J. Prosser, Jr.
SVP, Chief Acctg Officer & Cntlr: N.G. Thawerbhoy

Investor Contact: J.W. Prosser, Jr. (626-578-6803)
Board Members: J. R. Bronson, J. F. Coyne, R. C. Davidson, Jr., E. V. Fritzky, R. B. Gwyn, J. P. Jumper, C. L. Martin, B. Montoya, T. M. Niles, P. J. Robertson, N. Watson, L. F. levinson

Founded: 1957
Domicile: Delaware
Employees: 53,200

Janus Capital Group Inc

**STANDARD
&POOR'S**

S&P Recommendation **BUY** ★★★★☆	Price $12.70 (as of Nov 27, 2009)	12-Mo. Target Price $18.00	Investment Style Large-Cap Blend

GICS Sector Financials
Sub-Industry Asset Management & Custody Banks

Summary Janus is an investment management company focused on equity growth and quantitative strategies.

Key Stock Statistics (Source S&P, Vickers, company reports)

52-Wk Range	$16.06– 3.73	S&P Oper. EPS 2009**E**	0.35	Market Capitalization(B)	$2.312	Beta	2.73
Trailing 12-Month EPS	$-4.88	S&P Oper. EPS 2010**E**	0.82	Yield (%)	0.31	S&P 3-Yr. Proj. EPS CAGR(%)	5
Trailing 12-Month P/E	NM	P/E on S&P Oper. EPS 2009**E**	36.3	Dividend Rate/Share	$0.04	S&P Credit Rating	BB+
$10K Invested 5 Yrs Ago	$7,804	Common Shares Outstg. (M)	182.0	Institutional Ownership (%)	82		

Price Performance

30-Week Mov. Avg. · · · 10-Week Mov. Avg. - - **GAAP Earnings vs. Previous Year**   Volume Above Avg. ▌▌▌ STARS
12-Mo. Target Price — Relative Strength — ▲ Up ▼ Down ► No Change   Below Avg. ▌▌▌ ★

Options: CBOE, P, Ph

Analysis prepared by **Matthew Albrecht** on October 27, 2009, when the stock traded at **$ 14.30**.

Highlights

► Asset totals now reflect recent equity market strength and improved investor sentiment. Janus and Perkins long-term funds have seen flow trends improve, while poor relative performance has caused investors to withdrawal funds from its quant-based INTECH funds. We believe its traditional funds have seen performance improve, and that the company will now benefit from improved distribution channels and increased penetration into the institutional market. We expect depressed average asset balances to continue to pressure management fee income and revenues throughout 2009, but market gains should boost results in 2010.

► We look for compensation to be at least 40% of net revenues this year, which is above historical norms. We forecast this percentage to decline somewhat in 2010. Cost-cutting measures have already helped reduce non-compensation expenses, but rising compensation costs will likely reduce margins for the year. We expect interest costs to continue to weigh on results, but seed investment losses have declined.

► We see EPS of $0.35 in 2009 and $0.82 in 2010.

Investment Rationale/Risk

► As of September 30, 2009, 79%, 88% and 86% of firm-wide mutual funds were in the top half of their categories on a one-, three- and five-year performance basis, respectively, and we think an improvement in fund performance has attracted client assets. Investor preference for growth products and JNS's strong fund performance warrant a premium multiple in an improving investment environment, in our opinion. While we think caution is warranted as the company is less diversified than many peers, an improved economic outlook and recent strength in equity markets brightens our view, and our recommendation is buy.

► Risks to our recommendation and target price include potential equity and bond market depreciation, and increased competition. We are concerned about Janus' corporate governance practices and would like to see a higher proportion of independent directors.

► The shares recently traded at about 41.6X our 2009 EPS estimate, a steep premium to the peer group average. Our 12-month target price of $18 is equal to 23.1X our forward 12-month earnings forecast of $0.78, a slight premium to peer multiples.

Qualitative Risk Assessment

LOW	MEDIUM	HIGH

Our risk assessment reflects the company's lack of product diversification, previous regulatory issues, and turnover of investment personnel.

Quantitative Evaluations

S&P Quality Ranking   B-

D	C	B-	B	B+	A-	A	A+

Relative Strength Rank   WEAK

24

LOWEST = 1   HIGHEST = 99

Revenue/Earnings Data

Revenue (Million $)

	1Q	2Q	3Q	4Q	Year
2009	170.3	200.2	227.6	--	--
2008	281.2	304.2	275.4	177.1	1,038
2007	247.9	273.0	284.6	311.5	1,117
2006	256.1	254.6	250.1	265.9	1,027
2005	239.0	229.3	237.5	247.3	953.1
2004	274.4	258.8	237.8	239.8	1,011

Earnings Per Share ($)

2009	0.02	0.10	0.05	E0.18	E0.35
2008	0.24	0.40	0.16	0.05	0.86
2007	0.20	0.28	0.29	0.30	1.07
2006	0.17	0.15	0.15	0.19	0.66
2005	0.09	0.12	0.15	0.05	0.40
2004	-0.10	0.54	0.20	0.08	0.73

Fiscal year ended Dec. 31. Next earnings report expected: Late January. EPS Estimates based on S&P Operating Earnings; historical GAAP earnings are as reported.

Dividend Data (Dates: mm/dd Payment Date: mm/dd/yy)

Amount ($)	Date Decl.	Ex-Div. Date	Stk. of Record	Payment Date
0.040	05/01	05/13	05/15	05/29/09

Dividends have been paid since 2000. Source: Company reports.

Please read the Required Disclosures and Analyst Certification on the last page of this report.

The **McGraw·Hill** Companies

Janus Capital Group Inc

Business Summary October 27, 2009

CORPORATE OVERVIEW. Janus Capital Group, a single-branded global asset management company, was created through the January 1, 2003 merger of Janus Capital Corp. into its parent company, Stilwell Financial Inc., which had been spun off from Kansas City Southern Industries in July 2000 via a stock offering. The company had total assets under management of $123.5 billion at the end of 2008, down sharply from $206.7 billion at the end of 2007. The company distributes its products through one global distribution network directly to investors, and through advisers and financial intermediaries.

Wholly owned Janus Capital Management focuses on growth equities, and uses both fundamental and quantitative investment research. It also offers core, international, specialty fixed-income, and money market products. Its largest funds include Janus Fund (JANSX), Janus Worldwide (JAWWX) and Janus Twenty (JAVLX).

The company owns 89.5% (and is in the process of upping its stake to 92%,

per contractual obligations with the founders) of Enhanced Investment Technologies, LLC (INTECH), which focuses on mathematically driven equity investing strategies. INTECH's assets under management totaled $42.4 billion at the end of 2008, up from $7.3 billion at the end of 2002. INTECH, which manages assets for large institutions and endowments, seeks to achieve long-term returns that outperform a passive index, while controlling risks and trading costs.

JNS owns about 80% of Perkins Investment Management LLC (formerly Perkins, Wolf, McDonnell and Co.), which focuses on value investing and sub-advises a number of Janus's small- and mid-cap value products. Perkins had $9.1 billion in client assets at the end of 2008.

Company Financials Fiscal Year Ended Dec. 31

Per Share Data ($)	2008	2007	2006	2005	2004	2003	2002	2001	2000	1999
Tangible Book Value	NM	NM	NM	0.88	1.43	1.00	NM	NM	3.50	NA
Cash Flow	1.04	1.21	0.93	0.64	0.99	4.46	0.70	1.93	3.30	1.51
Earnings	0.86	1.07	0.66	0.40	0.73	4.17	0.38	1.31	2.90	1.31
S&P Core Earnings	1.10	1.05	0.61	0.42	0.32	1.60	0.42	1.18	NA	NA
Dividends	0.04	0.04	0.04	0.04	0.04	0.04	0.05	0.04	0.01	NA
Payout Ratio	5%	4%	6%	10%	5%	1%	13%	3%	NM	NA
Prices:High	36.88	37.08	24.20	20.59	17.90	19.00	29.24	46.63	54.50	NA
Prices:Low	5.18	19.35	15.50	12.75	12.60	9.46	8.97	18.20	30.75	NA
P/E Ratio:High	43	35	37	51	25	5	77	36	19	NA
P/E Ratio:Low	6	18	23	32	17	2	24	14	11	NA

Income Statement Analysis (Million $)	2008	2007	2006	2005	2004	2003	2002	2001	2000	1999
Revenue	1,038	1,117	1,027	953	1,011	995	1,145	1,556	2,248	1,212
Operating Income	362	375	267	224	264	396	441	872	1,118	554
Depreciation	28.8	24.9	47.1	50.1	60.4	67.6	72.3	131	81.2	35.4
Interest Expense	75.5	58.8	32.3	28.6	38.4	60.5	57.8	34.8	7.70	5.90
Pretax Income	216	330	237	176	272	895	320	620	1,202	587
Effective Tax Rate	31.9%	35.3%	34.5%	38.6%	33.9%	NM	72.6%	35.1%	35.5%	36.8%
Net Income	138	192	134	87.8	170	956	84.7	302	664	313
S&P Core Earnings	178	189	124	92.5	74.1	367	92.4	276	NA	NA

Balance Sheet & Other Financial Data (Million $)	2008	2007	2006	2005	2004	2003	2002	2001	2000	1999
Cash	408	691	560	553	527	1,223	161	237	364	324
Current Assets	584	954	925	1,004	1,065	1,466	346	478	641	525
Total Assets	3,337	3,564	3,538	3,629	3,768	4,332	3,322	3,392	1,581	1,232
Current Liabilities	157	227	186	268	155	301	185	881	196	163
Long Term Debt	1,106	1,128	537	262	378	769	856	400	Nil	Nil
Common Equity	1,608	1,724	2,306	2,581	2,735	2,661	1,508	1,363	1,058	815
Total Capital	2,752	3,272	3,261	3,283	3,553	3,997	3,097	2,466	1,342	1,024
Capital Expenditures	20.1	16.7	17.0	23.6	26.5	23.9	16.3	34.3	107	50.5
Cash Flow	167	217	181	138	230	1,023	157	433	745	348
Current Ratio	3.7	4.2	5.0	3.7	6.9	4.9	1.9	0.5	3.3	3.2
% Long Term Debt of Capitalization	41.2	39.3	16.5	8.0	10.6	19.2	27.6	16.2	Nil	Nil
% Net Income of Revenue	13.3	17.2	13.0	9.2	16.8	96.1	7.4	19.4	29.5	25.8
% Return on Assets	4.0	5.4	3.7	2.4	4.2	25.0	2.5	12.2	47.2	30.5
% Return on Equity	8.3	9.5	5.5	3.3	6.3	45.9	5.9	25.0	70.9	46.2

Data as orig reptd.; bef. results of disc opers/spec. items. Per share data adj. for stk. divs.; EPS diluted. E-Estimated. NA-Not Available. NM-Not Meaningful. NR-Not Ranked. UR-Under Review.

Office: 151 Detroit St, Denver, CO 80206-4928.
Telephone: 303-333-3863.
Website: http://www.janus.com
Chrmn: S.L. Scheid

CEO: T.K. Armour
EVP & CFO: G.A. Frost
EVP, Chief Admin Officer, Secy & General Counsel: K.D. Howes
SVP & Treas: S.S. Grace

Board Members: T. K. Armour, P. F. Balser, G. A. Cox, J. Diermeier, J. Fredericks, D. R. Gatzek, L. E. Kochard, R. T. Parry, J. Patton, L. H. Rowland, G. S. Schafer, S. L. Scheid, R. J. Skidelskiy

Founded: 1998
Domicile: Delaware
Employees: 1,164

STANDARD &POOR'S

JDS Uniphase Corp

S&P Recommendation	HOLD ★★★☆☆	Price	12-Mo. Target Price	Investment Style
		$7.43 (as of Nov 27, 2009)	$8.00	Large-Cap Blend

GICS Sector Information Technology
Sub-Industry Communications Equipment

Summary This company manufactures fiber optic products and communications test and measurement solutions.

Key Stock Statistics (Source S&P, Vickers, company reports)

52-Wk Range	$8.38–2.21	S&P Oper. EPS 2010**E**	0.05	Market Capitalization(B)	$1.621	Beta	2.11
Trailing 12-Month EPS	$-4.06	S&P Oper. EPS 2011**E**	0.20	Yield (%)	Nil	S&P 3-Yr. Proj. EPS CAGR(%)	12
Trailing 12-Month P/E	NM	P/E on S&P Oper. EPS 2010**E**	NM	Dividend Rate/Share	Nil	S&P Credit Rating	NA
$10K Invested 5 Yrs Ago	$2,939	Common Shares Outstg. (M)	218.1	Institutional Ownership (%)	68		

Price Performance

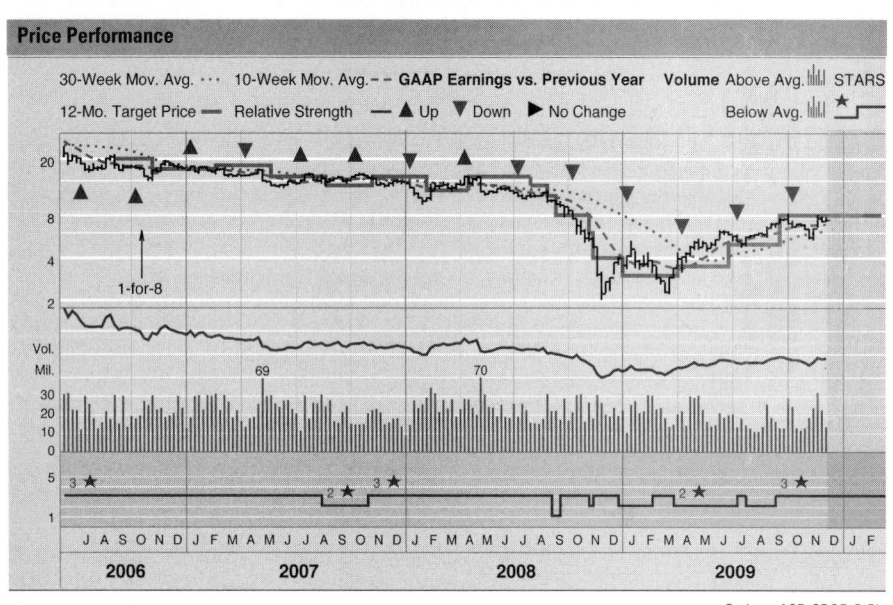

30-Week Mov. Avg. ··· 10-Week Mov. Avg. -- **GAAP Earnings vs. Previous Year** Volume Above Avg. |||| STARS
12-Mo. Target Price — Relative Strength — ▲ Up ▼ Down ► No Change Below Avg. |||| ★

1-for-8

Options: ASE, CBOE, P, Ph

Analysis prepared by **Ari Bensinger** on November 25, 2009, when the stock traded at **$ 7.81**.

Highlights

► Following a 15% decline in FY 09 (Jun.), we see sales decreasing 2% in FY 10, owing to continued weak demand for optical components as customers work through excess inventory. We see a modest sales recovery, however, in the test measurement and advanced optical segments as the macroeconomic environment begins to improve. We remain optimistic about the growth prospects related to tunable lasers and ROADMs.

► The company is in the midst of a major restructuring program. As a result of a favorable product mix and the implementation of lean manufacturing initiatives, we believe FY 10 gross margins will widen roughly 100 basis points, to 44%. We see FY 10 operating expenses declining markedly from FY 09 on continued cost cutting.

► After minimal taxes due to loss carryovers and a sharp decline in interest income on lower interest rates, we project FY 10 operating EPS of $0.05, including $0.20 of projected stock option expense, versus the $0.05 loss per share posted in FY 09, which excludes $3.97 of non-recurring items, the majority related to a goodwill impairment charge.

Investment Rationale/Risk

► We view the shares as fairly valued. Although near-term visibility remains limited, improved booking and order activity give us increased confidence that industry demand is recovering. We are encouraged with JDSU's cost management progress, and believe FY 11 operating margins will nearly double, year over year, to 5%. We see a continued rapid rise in network bandwidth demand acting as a solid underlying growth driver for JDSU over the long term.

► Risks to our recommendation and target price include a prolonged downturn in telecom capital spending, market share losses, and slower-than-expected margin improvement.

► Our 12-month target price of $8 is based largely on 1.5X our FY 10 sales per share estimate and 2X the company's book value, multiples that are in line with the peer mean. We see material operating leverage in the business model, but believe the shares, recently trading at 25X our FY 11 EPS estimate of $0.18, after adding $3 cash per share and excluding associated interest income of $0.02, already reflect a successful operational turnaround.

Qualitative Risk Assessment

LOW	MEDIUM	HIGH

Our risk assessment reflects the highly competitive nature of the communications equipment industry, and the company's dependence on telecom carrier spending, which tends to be uneven due to the uncertain timing of network projects and upgrades.

Quantitative Evaluations

S&P Quality Ranking C

D	C	B-	B	B+	A-	A	A+

Relative Strength Rank STRONG
87
LOWEST = 1 HIGHEST = 99

Revenue/Earnings Data

Revenue (Million $)

	1Q	2Q	3Q	4Q	Year
2010	297.8	--	--	--	--
2009	380.7	357.0	280.6	276.1	1,294
2008	356.7	399.2	383.9	390.3	1,530
2007	318.1	366.3	361.7	350.7	1,397
2006	258.3	312.9	314.9	318.2	1,204
2005	194.5	180.5	166.3	170.9	712.2

Earnings Per Share ($)

	1Q	2Q	3Q	4Q	Year
2010	-0.14	E0.02	ENil	E0.04	E0.05
2009	-0.08	-3.28	-0.39	-0.27	-4.02
2008	-0.03	0.09	-0.03	-0.13	-0.10
2007	-0.08	0.10	-0.07	-0.08	-0.12
2006	-0.32	-0.24	0.02	-0.24	-0.72
2005	-0.16	-0.24	-0.24	-0.80	-1.44

Fiscal year ended Jun. 30. Next earnings report expected: Early February. EPS Estimates based on S&P Operating Earnings; historical GAAP earnings are as reported.

Dividend Data

No cash dividends have been paid.

Please read the Required Disclosures and Analyst Certification on the last page of this report.

The **McGraw-Hill** Companies

JDS Uniphase Corp

STANDARD &POOR'S

Business Summary November 25, 2009

CORPORATE OVERVIEW. JDS Uniphase supplies optical components, as well as communications test and measurement solutions for the communications market. The company also leverages its optical science capabilities on non-communications applications, offering products for display, security, medical environmental instrumentation, decorative, aerospace and defense applications.

The company operates in three principal segments: communications test and measurement (47% of FY 09 (Jun.) revenue); communications and commercial optical products (37%); and advanced optical technologies (16%).

PRIMARY BUSINESS DYNAMICS. The communications test and measurement segment provides instruments, software, systems and services that help communications equipment manufacturers and service providers accelerate the deployment of broadband networks and services from the core of the network to the home, including deployment over fiber to the curb, node or premise and digital networks. Solutions focus primarily on lab and production test platforms, field test instrumentation and software, and network and service as-

surance systems.

The communications and commercial optical product group supplies the basic building blocks for fiber optic networks, which enable the rapid transmission of large amounts of data over long distances via light waves through fiber optic components, modules and subsystems. Transmission products include optical transceivers, optical transponders, and their supporting components such as modulators and source lasers. Transport products primarily consist of amplifiers and reconfigurable optical add/drop multiplexers (ROADMs) and their supporting components such as pump lasers, passive devices, and array waveguides. The segment also offers a broad portfolio of lasers used by customers in markets and applications such as biotechnology and graphics imaging, remote sensing, and materials processing and precision machining.

Company Financials Fiscal Year Ended Jun. 30

Per Share Data ($)	2009	2008	2007	2006	2005	2004	2003	2002	2001	2000
Tangible Book Value	2.44	2.73	2.80	2.72	5.76	7.12	7.92	11.44	22.24	20.88
Cash Flow	-3.35	0.55	0.48	-0.46	-1.11	-0.32	-4.82	-42.21	-370.58	0.52
Earnings	-4.02	-0.10	-0.12	-0.72	-1.44	-0.64	-5.28	-52.00	-411.20	-10.08
S&P Core Earnings	-0.52	-0.12	-0.21	-0.88	-2.24	-2.56	-7.84	-32.88	-175.60	NA
Dividends	Nil	Nil	Nil	Nil	Nil	Nil	Nil	Nil	Nil	Nil
Payout Ratio	Nil	Nil	Nil	Nil	Nil	Nil	Nil	Nil	Nil	Nil
Prices:High	8.38	15.33	17.99	34.40	26.08	47.08	37.68	82.72	519.50	1227
Prices:Low	2.21	2.01	12.41	13.93	10.56	22.72	19.84	12.64	40.96	296.00
P/E Ratio:High	NM	NM	NM	NM	NM	NM	NM	NM	NM	NM
P/E Ratio:Low	NM	NM	NM	NM	NM	NM	NM	NM	NM	NM

Income Statement Analysis (Million $)	2009	2008	2007	2006	2005	2004	2003	2002	2001	2000
Revenue	1,294	1,530	1,397	1,204	712	636	676	1,098	3,233	1,430
Operating Income	39.8	87.6	36.8	-107	-83.9	-58.5	-306	-374	-62.5	446
Depreciation	145	145	128	57.4	61.3	55.9	79.2	1,645	5,542	951
Interest Expense	7.70	8.80	7.10	27.7	Nil	Nil	Nil	Nil	Nil	0.50
Pretax Income	-869	-19.3	-24.3	-152	-255	-128	-920	-8,501	-56,494	-830
Effective Tax Rate	NM	NM	NM	NM	NM	NM	NM	NM	NM	NM
Net Income	-866	-21.7	-26.3	-151	-261	-113	-934	-8,738	-56,122	-905
S&P Core Earnings	-111	-27.5	-45.7	-181	-394	-446	-1,399	-5,534	-23,966	NA

Balance Sheet & Other Financial Data (Million $)	2009	2008	2007	2006	2005	2004	2003	2002	2001	2000
Cash	685	874	363	365	511	328	242	412	763	319
Current Assets	1,108	1,429	1,661	1,805	1,588	1,866	1,515	1,857	3,036	1,973
Total Assets	1,670	2,906	3,025	3,065	2,080	2,422	2,138	3,005	12,245	26,389
Current Liabilities	310	445	348	422	240	350	423	483	848	647
Long Term Debt	325	427	808	900	467	465	Nil	5.50	12.8	41.0
Common Equity	861	1,817	1,736	1,584	1,335	1,571	1,671	2,471	10,706	24,779
Total Capital	1,186	2,267	2,544	2,484	1,802	2,063	1,699	2,519	11,392	25,722
Capital Expenditures	54.7	51.7	75.7	67.2	35.8	66.4	47.2	133	732	280
Cash Flow	-722	123	102	-93.8	-200	-56.7	-855	-7,093	-50,580	46.0
Current Ratio	3.6	3.2	4.8	4.3	6.6	5.3	3.6	3.8	3.6	3.0
% Long Term Debt of Capitalization	27.4	18.8	31.8	36.2	25.9	22.5	Nil	0.2	0.1	0.2
% Net Income of Revenue	NM	NM	NM	NM	NM	NM	NM	NM	NM	NM
% Return on Assets	NM	NM	NM	NM	NM	NM	NM	NM	NM	NM
% Return on Equity	NM	NM	NM	NM	NM	NM	NM	NM	NM	NM

Data as orig reptd.; bef. results of disc opers/spec. items. Per share data adj. for stk. divs.; EPS diluted. E-Estimated. NA-Not Available. NM-Not Meaningful. NR-Not Ranked. UR-Under Review.

Office: 430 N McCarthy Blvd, Milpitas, CA 95035-5116.
Telephone: 408-546-5000.
Email: investor.relations@jdsu.com
Website: http://www.jdsu.com

Chrmn: M.A. Kaplan
Pres & CEO: T.H. Waechter
Vice Chrmn: K.J. Kennedy
Investor Contact: D. Vellequette (408-546-4445)

EVP & CFO: D. Vellequette
Board Members: R. E. Belluzzo, H. L. Covert, Jr., B. D. Day, P. A. Herscher, M. A. Jabbar, M. A. Kaplan, K. J. Kennedy, R. T. Liebhaber, C. S. Skrzypczak, T. H. Waechter

Founded: 1979
Domicile: Delaware
Employees: 4,000

Johnson Controls Inc.

STANDARD
&POOR'S

S&P Recommendation BUY ★★★★☆

Price $26.93 (as of Nov 27, 2009)	**12-Mo. Target Price** $30.00	**Investment Style** Large-Cap Blend

GICS Sector Consumer Discretionary
Sub-Industry Auto Parts & Equipment

Summary This company supplies building controls and energy management systems, automotive seating, and batteries.

Key Stock Statistics (Source S&P, Vickers, company reports)

52-Wk Range	$28.34–8.35	S&P Oper. EPS 2010**E**	1.45	Market Capitalization(B)	$16.036	Beta		1.82
Trailing 12-Month EPS	$-0.57	S&P Oper. EPS 2011**E**	NA	Yield (%)	1.93	S&P 3-Yr. Proj. EPS CAGR(%)		10
Trailing 12-Month P/E	NM	P/E on S&P Oper. EPS 2010**E**	18.6	Dividend Rate/Share	$0.52	S&P Credit Rating		BBB
$10K Invested 5 Yrs Ago	$14,058	Common Shares Outstg. (M)	595.5	Institutional Ownership (%)	90			

Price Performance

30-Week Mov. Avg. · · · 10-Week Mov. Avg. – – GAAP Earnings vs. Previous Year Volume Above Avg. ||||| STARS
12-Mo. Target Price — Relative Strength ▲ Up ▼ Down ► No Change Below Avg. ||||| ★

Options: ASE, CBOE, Ph

Highlights

► The STARS recommendation for JCI has recently been changed to 4 (buy) from 2 (sell) and the 12-month target price has recently been changed to $30.00 from $23.00. The Highlights section of this Stock Report will be updated accordingly.

Investment Rationale/Risk

► The Investment Rationale/Risk section of this Stock Report will be updated shortly. For the latest News story on JCI from MarketScope, see below.

► 10/27/09 10:21 am ET … S&P REITERATES BUY OPINION ON SHARES OF JOHNSON CONTROLS (JCI 25.08****): JCI posts adjusted Sep-Q EPS of $0.52, in line with 10/13 guidance. JCI maintained its FY 10 (Sep.) EPS outlook of $1.35-$1.45. We see $1.45. In FY 10, we expect all segments to see improved demand. Automotive sales should benefit from rising industry volume and a post-"clunkers" replenishment of vehicle inventories. The controls business should benefit from improving economies as well as stimulus program projects starting in the second half of FY 10. Margins should benefit from cost cutting. With a target price of $30, we would purchase for total return potential. / ELevy-CFA

Qualitative Risk Assessment

LOW	MEDIUM	HIGH

Our risk assessment reflects our view of favorable growth prospects in the building controls markets that JCI serves and what we see as a strong management team and a healthy balance sheet, offset by the challenges faced by the automotive operations.

Quantitative Evaluations

S&P Quality Ranking A

D	C	B-	B	B+	A-	A	A+

Relative Strength Rank STRONG

72

LOWEST = 1   HIGHEST = 99

Revenue/Earnings Data

Revenue (Million $)

	1Q	2Q	3Q	4Q	Year
2009	7,336	6,315	6,979	7,867	28,497
2008	9,484	9,406	9,865	9,307	38,062
2007	8,210	8,492	8,911	9,011	34,624
2006	7,528	8,167	8,390	8,150	32,235
2005	6,618	6,899	7,062	6,900	27,479
2004	6,384	6,620	6,792	6,757	26,553

Earnings Per Share ($)

2009	-1.02	-0.32	0.26	0.47	-0.57
2008	0.39	0.48	0.73	0.03	1.63
2007	0.28	0.44	0.66	0.77	2.16
2006	0.29	0.28	0.57	0.62	1.75
2005	0.28	0.09	0.44	0.50	1.30
2004	0.29	0.27	0.38	0.47	1.41

Fiscal year ended Sep. 30. Next earnings report expected: Mid January. EPS Estimates based on S&P Operating Earnings; historical GAAP earnings are as reported.

Dividend Data (Dates: mm/dd Payment Date: mm/dd/yy)

Amount ($)	Date Decl.	Ex-Div. Date	Stk. of Record	Payment Date
0.130	01/21	03/11	03/13	04/02/09
0.130	05/20	06/10	06/12	07/02/09
0.130	07/22	09/09	09/11	10/02/09
0.130	11/18	12/09	12/11	01/04/10

Dividends have been paid since 1887. Source: Company reports.

Johnson Controls Inc.

STANDARD &POOR'S

Business Summary October 02, 2009

CORPORATE OVERVIEW. Johnson Controls, founded in 1885, is a leading manufacturer of automotive interior systems, automotive batteries and automated building control systems. It also provides facility management services for commercial buildings. In FY 08 (Sep.), the automotive segment accounted for 63% of sales and 54% of income, with the balance coming from controls and facility management.

The automotive interior segment manufactures interior products and systems, including complete seats and seating components for North American and European car and light-truck manufacturers. The segment has grown rapidly in recent years, gaining contracts to produce seats formerly manufactured in-house by automakers, and expanding in Europe. Seating accounted for 48% of sales in FY 08.

The power solutions unit, the largest automotive battery operation in North America, makes lead-acid batteries primarily for the automotive replacement market and for OEMs. Batteries accounted for about 15% of FY 08 sales and the unit is expanding operations in Europe.

The building efficiency (formerly called controls) segment manufactures, in-

stalls and services controls and control systems, principally for nonresidential buildings, which are used for temperature and energy management, and fire safety and security maintenance. The segment also includes custom engineering, installation and servicing of process control systems and a growing facilities management business. Building efficiency sales accounted for 37% of FY 08 revenues. As of September 2008, JCI had an unearned backlog of building systems and services contracts totaling $4.7 billion.

Government building trends promoting facility management outsourcing and energy efficiency programs are creating additional opportunities, in our view.

Ford, GM, Chrysler LLC and Toyota accounted for an aggregate of 28% of FY 08 U.S sales, although none of the companies individually accounted for more than 10% of sales overall. We expect the share of revenues from the three U.S.-based customers to shrink as the company expands its sales outside the U.S. and with non-domestic customers expanding in the U.S.

Company Financials Fiscal Year Ended Sep. 30

Per Share Data ($)	2009	2008	2007	2006	2005	2004	2003	2002	2001	2000
Tangible Book Value	NA	3.63	3.38	1.10	3.52	1.93	1.27	0.74	1.17	0.61
Cash Flow	NA	2.93	3.38	2.95	2.41	2.48	2.17	1.97	1.77	1.79
Earnings	-0.57	1.63	2.16	1.75	1.30	1.41	1.20	1.06	0.85	0.85
S&P Core Earnings	NA	1.39	2.16	1.74	1.31	1.42	1.16	0.89	0.70	NA
Dividends	0.52	0.63	0.33	0.37	0.33	0.30	0.24	0.22	0.21	0.19
Payout Ratio	NM	39%	15%	21%	26%	21%	20%	21%	24%	22%
Prices:High	28.34	36.52	44.46	30.00	25.07	21.33	19.37	15.53	13.78	10.85
Prices:Low	8.35	13.65	28.09	22.12	17.52	16.52	11.96	11.52	8.66	7.64
P/E Ratio:High	NM	22	21	17	19	15	16	15	16	13
P/E Ratio:Low	NM	8	13	13	13	12	10	11	10	9
Income Statement Analysis (Million $)										
Revenue	28,497	38,062	34,624	32,235	27,479	26,553	22,646	20,103	18,427	17,155
Operating Income	NA	2,744	2,527	2,184	1,913	1,918	1,720	1,639	1,477	1,427
Depreciation	745	783	732	705	636	617	558	517	516	462
Interest Expense	NA	270	277	248	121	111	114	122	129	128
Pretax Income	-318	1,324	1,607	1,138	1,003	1,212	1,058	1,006	867	856
Effective Tax Rate	NM	24.2%	18.7%	5.54%	20.4%	26.0%	31.0%	34.6%	38.7%	39.6%
Net Income	-338	979	1,295	1,033	757	818	683	600	478	472
S&P Core Earnings	NA	833	1,292	1,025	764	818	650	497	385	NA
Balance Sheet & Other Financial Data (Million $)										
Cash	761	384	674	293	171	170	136	262	375	276
Current Assets	NA	10,676	10,872	9,264	7,139	6,377	5,620	4,946	4,544	4,277
Total Assets	23,983	25,318	24,105	21,921	16,144	15,091	13,127	11,165	9,912	9,428
Current Liabilities	NA	9,810	9,920	8,146	6,841	6,602	5,584	4,806	4,580	4,510
Long Term Debt	3,168	3,201	3,255	4,166	1,578	1,631	1,777	1,827	1,395	1,315
Common Equity	9,121	9,411	8,907	7,355	6,058	5,206	4,164	3,396	2,862	2,447
Total Capital	12,490	12,890	11,290	11,650	7,831	7,106	6,260	5,515	4,588	3,891
Capital Expenditures	647	807	828	711	664	862	664	496	622	547
Cash Flow	NA	1,762	2,027	1,738	1,394	1,434	1,234	1,110	985	924
Current Ratio	1.1	1.1	1.1	1.1	1.0	1.0	1.0	1.0	1.0	0.9
% Long Term Debt of Capitalization	25.4	24.8	28.8	35.8	20.1	22.9	28.4	33.1	30.4	33.8
% Net Income of Revenue	NM	2.6	3.7	3.2	2.8	3.1	3.0	3.0	2.6	2.8
% Return on Assets	NM	4.0	5.6	5.4	4.9	5.8	5.6	5.7	4.9	5.2
% Return on Equity	NM	10.7	15.9	15.4	13.4	17.4	17.9	18.9	17.7	20.2

Data as orig reptd.; bef. results of disc opers/spec. items. Per share data adj. for stk. divs.; EPS diluted. E-Estimated. NA-Not Available. NM-Not Meaningful. NR-Not Ranked. UR-Under Review.

Office: 5757 N. Green Bay Avenue, Milwaukee, WI 53209-4408.
Telephone: 414-524-1200.
Website: http://www.johnsoncontrols.com
Chrmn, Pres & CEO: S.A. Roell

EVP & CFO: R.B. McDonald
Chief Acctg Officer & Cntlr: S.M. Kreh
Treas: F.A. Voltolina
Secy & General Counsel: J.D. Okarma

Investor Contact: G.Z. Ponczak (414-524-1200)
Board Members: D. Abney, D. W. Archer, R. L. Barnett, N. A. Black, R. A. Cornog, R. Goodman, J. A. Joerres, W. H. Lacy, S. J. Morcott, E. C. Reyes-Retana, S. A. Roell

Founded: 1900
Domicile: Wisconsin
Employees: 140,000

Johnson & Johnson

STANDARD &POOR'S

S&P Recommendation **BUY** ★★★★☆	Price $62.89 (as of Nov 27, 2009)	12-Mo. Target Price $70.00	Investment Style Large-Cap Growth

GICS Sector Health Care
Sub-Industry Pharmaceuticals

Summary This company is a leader in the pharmaceutical, medical device and consumer products industries.

Key Stock Statistics (Source S&P, Vickers, company reports)

52-Wk Range	$63.44– 46.25	S&P Oper. EPS 2009E	4.56	Market Capitalization(B)	$173.520	Beta	0.55
Trailing 12-Month EPS	$4.58	S&P Oper. EPS 2010E	4.90	Yield (%)	3.12	S&P 3-Yr. Proj. EPS CAGR(%)	6
Trailing 12-Month P/E	13.7	P/E on S&P Oper. EPS 2009E	13.8	Dividend Rate/Share	$1.96	S&P Credit Rating	AAA
$10K Invested 5 Yrs Ago	$11,837	Common Shares Outstg. (M)	2,759.1	Institutional Ownership (%)	63		

Price Performance

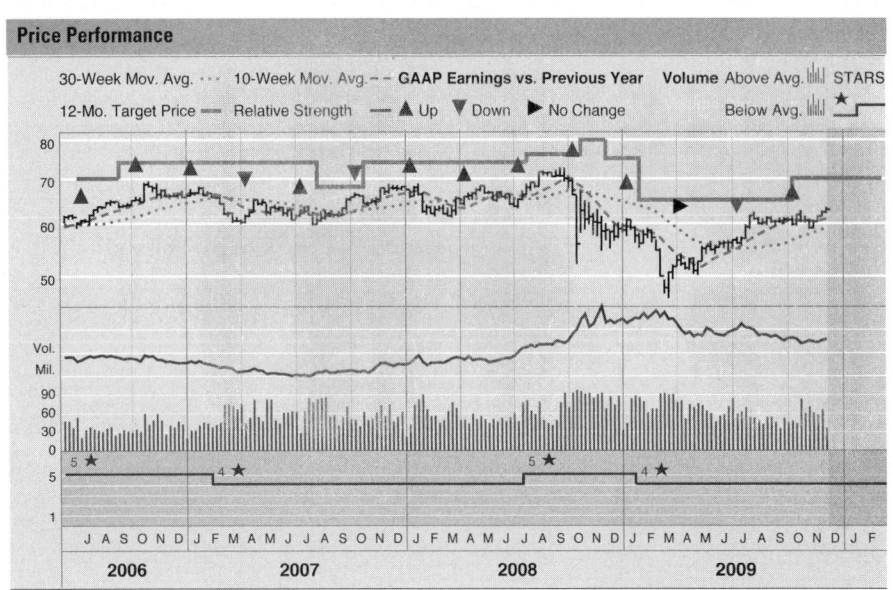

30-Week Mov. Avg. ··· 10-Week Mov. Avg. – – GAAP Earnings vs. Previous Year Volume Above Avg. STARS
12-Mo. Target Price — Relative Strength — ▲ Up ▼ Down ► No Change Below Avg.

Options: ASE, CBOE, P, Ph

Analysis prepared by **Herman B. Saftlas** on October 16, 2009, when the stock traded at **$ 60.94**.

Highlights

► After a 4% decline seen for 2009, we expect revenues to rise about 6% in 2010, helped by projected gains in key business segments, and likely improved currency exchange. Despite expected ongoing generic erosion in Risperdal and Topamax, we see growth in pharmaceutical sales in 2010, supported by gains in Remicade and Levaquin, and contributions from new drugs such as Simponi for severe arthritis and Xarelto anti-clotting agent. New cardiovascular and orthopedic products are expected to bolster device sales, while consumer sales should benefit from firming in the general economy.

► We look for 2010 gross margins to show modest expansion over 2009's projected 70.9%, reflecting better volume and manufacturing efficiencies. Profitability should also benefit from reduced staffing levels and other operating economies. We expect anticipated dilution from recent acquisitions to be offset by cost reduction measures.

► After a projected tax rate of about 23.5% (similar to our estimate for 2009), we expect operating EPS of $4.90 for 2010, up from the $4.56 that we estimate for 2009. We see EPS reaching $5.40 in 2011.

Investment Rationale/Risk

► We believe JNJ's diversified sales base across drugs, medical devices and consumer products, along with its decentralized business model, has served it well in the past, and should continue to do so in the years ahead. In our view, JNJ's recent vaccine, aesthetics and bio-surgical products acquisitions are part of a strategy to diversify into new long-term opportunities in the face of challenging prospects in drugs. Ongoing cost restructurings augur well for the future, in our opinion. We also see promise in the R&D pipeline, especially for Xarelto, Simponi, and new influenza vaccines.

► Risks to our recommendation and target price include faster-than-expected generic erosion in several drug lines, an inability to sustain growth in the device area, possible pipeline disappointments, and adverse foreign exchange.

► Our 12-month target price of $70 applies a P/E of 14.3X to our 2010 EPS estimate, a valuation that is roughly in line with peer large capitalization, diversified health care stocks. Our DCF analysis also shows intrinsic value of $70, assuming a 7.7% WACC and 2% terminal growth.

Qualitative Risk Assessment

LOW	MEDIUM	HIGH

Our risk assessment reflects our belief that JNJ has products that are largely immune from economic cycles, has modest reliance on any single product category or customer for sustained growth, and enjoys competitive advantages owing to its large financial resources, business scale and global sales capabilities.

Quantitative Evaluations

S&P Quality Ranking   A+

D	C	B-	B	B+	A-	A	A+

Relative Strength Rank   STRONG

71

LOWEST = 1   HIGHEST = 99

Revenue/Earnings Data

Revenue (Million $)

	1Q	2Q	3Q	4Q	Year
2009	15,026	15,239	15,081	--	--
2008	16,194	16,450	15,921	15,182	63,747
2007	15,037	15,131	14,970	15,957	61,095
2006	12,992	13,363	13,287	13,682	53,324
2005	12,832	12,762	12,310	12,610	50,514
2004	11,559	11,484	11,553	12,752	47,348

Earnings Per Share ($)

2009	1.26	1.15	1.20	E0.95	E4.56
2008	1.26	1.17	1.17	0.97	4.57
2007	0.88	1.05	0.88	0.82	3.63
2006	1.10	0.95	0.94	0.74	3.73
2005	0.97	0.89	0.87	0.73	3.46
2004	0.83	0.82	0.78	0.41	2.84

Fiscal year ended Dec. 31. Next earnings report expected: Late January. EPS Estimates based on S&P Operating Earnings; historical GAAP earnings are as reported.

Dividend Data (Dates: mm/dd Payment Date: mm/dd/yy)

Amount ($)	Date Decl.	Ex-Div. Date	Stk. of Record	Payment Date
0.460	01/05	02/20	02/24	03/10/09
0.490	04/23	05/21	05/26	06/09/09
0.490	07/20	08/21	08/25	09/08/09
0.490	10/22	11/20	11/24	12/08/09

Dividends have been paid since 1944. Source: Company reports.

Johnson & Johnson

STANDARD
&POOR'S

Business Summary October 16, 2009

CORPORATE OVERVIEW. Johnson & Johnson ranks as one of the largest and most diversified health care firms, with products spanning across the pharmaceutical and medical device industries. The company is also a major participant in the global consumer products business, and, in December 2006, purchased the consumer products unit of Pfizer for $16.6 billion.

The pharmaceutical segment (39% of 2008 sales) includes products in therapeutic areas including anti-infective, anti-psychotic, cardiovascular, contraceptive, dermatology, gastrointestinal, hematology, immunology, neurology, oncology, pain management, urology and virology. In 2008, eight products each generated at least $1 billion of sales: Risperdal/Risperdal Consta ($3.4 billion, down 24% from 2007), Procrit/Eprex ($2.5 billion, down 15%), Remicade ($3.7 billion, up 13%), Topamax ($2.7 billion, up 11%), Floxin/Levaquin ($1.6 billion, up down 3%), Duragesic ($1.0 billion, down 11%), Aciphex/Pariet ($1.2 billion, down 15%), and Concerta ($1.2 billion, up 21%). U.S. patent protection on Risperdal expired in June 2008, and the patent on Topamax expires in March 2009.

The medical devices and diagnostics segment (36%) sells a wide range of products, including Ethicon's wound care, surgical sports medicine and women's health care products; Cordis's circulatory disease management products; Lifescan's blood glucose monitoring products; Ortho-Clinical Diagnostic's professional diagnostic products; Depuy's orthopaedic joint reconstruction and spinal products; and Vistakon's disposable contact lenses.

The consumer segment (25%) primarily sells personal care products, including nonprescription drugs, adult skin and hair care products, baby care products, oral care products, first aid products, women's health products, and nutritional products. Major brands include Band-Aid Brand Adhesive Bandages, Imodium A-D antidiarrheal, Johnson's Baby line of products, Neutrogena skin and hair care products, and Tylenol pain reliever.

Company Financials Fiscal Year Ended Dec. 31

Per Share Data ($)	2008	2007	2006	2005	2004	2003	2002	2001	2000	1999
Tangible Book Value	5.35	5.13	3.67	8.64	6.72	5.17	4.53	4.97	4.15	3.11
Cash Flow	5.57	4.59	4.57	4.20	3.58	3.01	2.67	2.35	2.23	1.98
Earnings	4.57	3.63	3.73	3.46	2.84	2.40	2.16	1.84	1.70	1.47
S&P Core Earnings	4.17	3.61	3.65	3.38	2.77	2.26	1.99	1.66	NA	NA
Dividends	1.80	1.62	1.46	1.28	1.10	0.93	0.80	0.70	0.62	0.55
Payout Ratio	39%	45%	39%	37%	39%	39%	37%	38%	36%	37%
Prices:High	72.76	68.75	69.41	69.99	64.25	59.08	65.89	60.97	52.97	53.44
Prices:Low	52.06	59.72	56.65	59.76	49.25	48.05	41.40	40.25	33.06	38.50
P/E Ratio:High	16	19	19	20	23	25	31	33	31	36
P/E Ratio:Low	11	16	15	17	17	20	19	22	19	26

Income Statement Analysis (Million $)										
Revenue	63,747	61,095	53,324	50,514	47,348	41,862	36,298	33,004	29,139	27,471
Operating Income	19,001	17,990	15,886	15,464	14,987	12,740	11,340	9,490	7,992	7,370
Depreciation	2,832	2,777	2,177	2,093	2,124	1,869	1,662	1,605	1,515	1,444
Interest Expense	582	426	63.0	54.0	187	207	160	153	146	197
Pretax Income	16,929	13,283	14,587	13,656	12,838	10,308	9,291	7,898	6,622	5,753
Effective Tax Rate	23.5%	20.4%	24.2%	23.8%	33.7%	30.2%	29.0%	28.2%	27.5%	27.6%
Net Income	12,949	10,576	11,053	10,411	8,509	7,197	6,597	5,668	4,800	4,167
S&P Core Earnings	11,832	10,534	10,814	10,161	8,263	6,785	6,052	5,090	NA	NA

Balance Sheet & Other Financial Data (Million $)										
Cash	12,809	9,315	4,084	16,138	12,884	9,523	7,596	8,941	6,013	4,320
Current Assets	34,377	29,945	22,975	31,394	27,320	22,995	19,266	18,473	15,450	13,200
Total Assets	84,912	80,954	70,556	58,025	53,317	48,263	40,556	38,488	31,321	29,163
Current Liabilities	20,852	19,837	19,161	12,635	13,927	13,448	11,449	8,044	7,140	7,454
Long Term Debt	8,120	7,074	2,014	2,017	2,565	2,955	2,022	2,217	2,037	2,450
Common Equity	42,511	43,319	61,266	37,871	31,813	26,869	22,697	24,233	18,808	16,213
Total Capital	52,063	51,886	64,599	40,099	34,781	30,604	25,362	26,943	21,100	18,950
Capital Expenditures	3,066	2,942	2,666	2,632	2,175	2,262	2,099	1,731	1,646	1,728
Cash Flow	15,781	13,353	13,230	12,504	10,633	9,066	8,259	7,273	6,315	5,611
Current Ratio	1.7	1.5	1.2	2.5	2.0	1.7	1.7	2.3	2.2	1.8
% Long Term Debt of Capitalization	15.6	13.6	3.1	5.0	7.4	9.7	8.0	8.2	9.7	12.9
% Net Income of Revenue	20.3	17.3	20.7	20.6	18.0	17.2	18.2	17.2	16.5	15.2
% Return on Assets	15.6	14.9	17.1	18.7	16.8	16.2	16.7	15.6	15.9	14.8
% Return on Equity	30.2	20.2	19.8	29.9	29.0	29.0	28.1	25.4	27.4	27.5

Data as orig reptd.; bef. results of disc opers/spec. items. Per share data adj. for stk. divs.; EPS diluted. E-Estimated. NA-Not Available. NM-Not Meaningful. NR-Not Ranked. UR-Under Review.

Office: One Johnson & Johnson Plaza, New Brunswick, NJ 08933.
Telephone: 732-524-0400.
Website: http://www.jnj.com
Chrmn & CEO: W.C. Weldon

CFO: D.J. Caruso
CSO: T.J. Torphy
Chief Acctg Officer & Cntlr: S.J. Cosgrove
Treas: J.A. Papa

Investor Contact: L. Mehrotra (732-524-6491)
Board Members: M. S. Coleman, J. G. Cullen, M. M. Johns, A. G. Langbo, S. L. Lindquist, A. M. Mulcahy, L. F. Mullin, W. D. Perez, C. Prince, III, D. Satcher, W. C. Weldon

Founded: 1887
Domicile: New Jersey
Employees: 118,700

JPMorgan Chase & Co.

STANDARD &POOR'S

S&P Recommendation **STRONG BUY** ★★★★★	Price $42.49 (as of Nov 30, 2009)	12-Mo. Target Price $57.00	Investment Style Large-Cap Value

GICS Sector Financials
Sub-Industry Other Diversified Financial Services

Summary This leading global financial services company has assets of $2.3 trillion and operations in more than 50 countries.

Key Stock Statistics (Source S&P, Vickers, company reports)

52-Wk Range	$47.47– 14.96	S&P Oper. EPS 2009**E**	2.30	Market Capitalization(B)	$167.438	Beta	1.11
Trailing 12-Month EPS	$1.60	S&P Oper. EPS 2010**E**	3.38	Yield (%)	0.47	S&P 3-Yr. Proj. EPS CAGR(%)	20
Trailing 12-Month P/E	26.6	P/E on S&P Oper. EPS 2009**E**	18.5	Dividend Rate/Share	$0.20	S&P Credit Rating	A+
$10K Invested 5 Yrs Ago	$12,769	Common Shares Outstg. (M)	3,940.7	Institutional Ownership (%)	73		

Price Performance

30-Week Mov. Avg. ··· 10-Week Mov. Avg. – – **GAAP Earnings vs. Previous Year** Volume Above Avg.▐▌▌ STARS
12-Mo. Target Price — Relative Strength ▲ Up ▼ Down ► No Change Below Avg.▐▌▌ ★

Options: ASE, CBOE, P, Ph

Analysis prepared by **Stuart Plesser** on November 03, 2009, when the stock traded at **$ 42.24**.

Highlights

► We look for revenue to rise over 50% in 2009 (due largely to the acquisition of Washington Mutual), but increase only 2.8% in 2010, as net interest margins should narrow. We see low single digit average earning asset growth, as loans will likely decline due to a dearth of qualified borrowers. JPM should continue to gain market share in investment banking due to the exit of weaker players. Net interest income will likely be flat in 2010 due to a contraction in the net interest margin, assuming the Fed raises rates in 2010.

► We look for provisions to decline about 12.5% in 2010 from a projected 69% increase in 2009, assuming JPM adds to reserves commensurate with net chargeoffs (we are not assuming a reserve release in 2010). We think JPM's reserve ratios are strong, and at 4.69% of loans, are near the top of the peer range. JPM's exposure to leveraged loans and Alt-A securities has been reduced in recent quarters, and we do not see significant writedowns in coming periods. We expect expenses to amount to roughly 53.5% of revenues in 2009 and 2010.

► Assuming no share buybacks, we estimate EPS of $2.30 in 2009 and $3.38 in 2010.

Investment Rationale/Risk

► Although we think JPM is well reserved for tough credit conditions, rising chargeoffs will likely continue at least through the fourth quarter of 2009. At that point, we expect provision building to ease, which should translate into higher EPS. JPM has already paid back government TARP capital of $25 billion, which should give it an advantage over competition due to lower restrictions regarding compensation and the ability to take higher risk. We think JPM's exposure to additional securities writedowns is limited. We see a decline in provisions in relation to chargeoffs as the next potential catalyst for the shares. Notably, sequential chargeoffs rose at a slower rate in third quarter, signaling, in our view, a possible end to further deterioration in JPM's loan portfolio.

► Risks to our recommendation and target price include legal and regulatory risk; integration risk; unexpected further turmoil in the credit markets; a sharper-than-expected economic downturn; and a flattening of the yield curve.

► Our 12-month target price of $57 is equal to 2.22X JPM's current tangible book value, in line with historical levels, as we think credit risk has been mitigated.

Qualitative Risk Assessment

LOW	MEDIUM	HIGH

Our risk assessment reflects our view of the company's well-reserved balance sheet, diversified lines of business and strong capital ratios. We believe JPM's diversity in its geographic presence and product offerings provides significant protection from a local or regional downturn.

Quantitative Evaluations

S&P Quality Ranking   B

D	C	B-	**B**	B+	A-	A	A+

Relative Strength Rank   MODERATE
      45
LOWEST = 1   HIGHEST = 99

Revenue/Earnings Data

Revenue (Million $)

	1Q	2Q	3Q	4Q	Year
2009	29,584	29,502	30,145	--	--
2008	26,763	26,634	23,069	25,025	101,491
2007	29,486	30,082	16,112	28,104	116,353
2006	23,477	24,175	24,957	26,693	99,302
2005	19,054	18,691	21,048	21,109	79,902
2004	11,625	11,227	16,546	17,483	56,931

Earnings Per Share ($)

	1Q	2Q	3Q	4Q	Year
2009	0.40	0.28	0.80	E0.77	E2.30
2008	0.68	0.54	-0.06	-0.28	0.84
2007	1.34	1.20	0.97	0.86	4.38
2006	0.86	0.98	0.90	1.26	3.82
2005	0.63	0.28	0.71	0.76	2.38
2004	0.92	-0.27	0.39	0.46	1.55

Fiscal year ended Dec. 31. Next earnings report expected: Mid January. EPS Estimates based on S&P Operating Earnings; historical GAAP earnings are as reported.

Dividend Data (Dates: mm/dd Payment Date: mm/dd/yy)

Amount ($)	Date Decl.	Ex-Div. Date	Stk. of Record	Payment Date
0.380	12/09	01/02	01/06	01/31/09
0.050	02/23	04/02	04/06	04/30/09
0.050	05/19	07/01	07/06	07/31/09
0.050	09/15	10/02	10/06	10/31/09

Dividends have been paid since 1827. Source: Company reports.

JPMorgan Chase & Co.

STANDARD &POOR'S

Business Summary November 03, 2009

CORPORATE OVERVIEW. JPMorgan Chase's operations are divided into six major business lines: Investment Banking, Retail Financial Services (RFS), Card Services (CS), Commercial Banking (CB), Treasury & Securities Services (TSS), and Asset Management (AM), as well as a Corporate/Private Equity segment.

JPM is one of the world's leading investment banks, with clients consisting of corporations, financial institutions, governments, and institutional investors worldwide. Its products and services include advising on corporate strategy and structure, equity and debt capital raising, sophisticated risk management, research, market making in cash securities and derivative instruments and prime brokerage and research.

RFS includes Home Finance, Consumer & Small Business Banking, Auto & Education Finance and Insurance. At year-end 2008, RFS had over 5,400 bank branches, and 4,500 ATMs. In 2008, JPM added 2,322 branches on a net basis, versus 73 in 2007, primarily due to the acquisition of Washington Mutual.

CS had over 168 million cards in circulation and $190 billion in managed loans as of December 31, 2008. Card Services offers a wide variety of products to

satisfy the needs of its card members, including cards issued on behalf of many well-known partners, such as major airlines, hotels, universities, retailers, and other financial institutions.

CB provides lending, treasury services, investment banking and investment management services to corporations, municipalities, financial institutions and not-for-profit entities.

TSS offers transaction, investment and information services to support the needs of corporations, issuers and institutional investors worldwide. TSS reported assets under custody of $13.2 trillion in 2008, up 17% from 2007.

AM provides investment management to retail and institutional investors, financial intermediaries and high-net-worth families and individuals globally. Assets under management reached $1.1 trillion in AM in 2008.

Company Financials Fiscal Year Ended Dec. 31

Per Share Data ($)	2008	2007	2006	2005	2004	2003	2002	2001	2000	1999
Tangible Book Value	19.27	18.77	16.11	15.88	14.77	14.77	15.82	12.54	12.95	18.59
Earnings	0.84	4.38	3.82	2.38	1.55	3.24	0.80	0.81	2.86	4.18
S&P Core Earnings	0.67	4.44	3.88	2.76	2.25	3.12	0.65	0.34	NA	NA
Dividends	1.52	1.44	1.36	1.36	1.36	1.36	1.36	1.34	1.23	1.06
Payout Ratio	NM	33%	34%	57%	88%	42%	170%	165%	43%	25%
Prices:High	50.63	53.25	49.00	40.56	43.84	38.26	39.68	57.33	67.17	60.75
Prices:Low	19.69	40.15	37.88	32.92	34.62	20.13	15.26	29.04	32.38	43.87
P/E Ratio:High	60	12	12	17	28	12	50	71	23	15
P/E Ratio:Low	23	9	9	14	22	6	19	36	11	10

Income Statement Analysis (Million $)										
Net Interest Income	38,779	26,406	21,242	19,831	16,761	12,337	11,526	10,802	9,512	8,744
Tax Equivalent Adjustment	579	377	NA	269	NA	NA	NA	NA	NA	NA
Non Interest Income	28,937	44,802	17,959	34,702	26,336	19,473	16,525	17,382	23,193	13,372
Loan Loss Provision	20,979	6,864	3,270	3,483	NA	NA	4,331	3,185	1,377	1,621
% Expense/Operating Revenue	60.0%	58.6%	97.7%	66.5%	85.6%	73.0%	81.2%	82.7%	69.8%	55.3%
Pretax Income	2,773	22,805	19,886	12,215	6,194	10,028	2,519	2,566	8,733	8,375
Effective Tax Rate	NM	32.6%	31.4%	30.6%	27.9%	33.0%	34.0%	33.0%	34.4%	35.0%
Net Income	3,699	15,365	13,649	8,483	4,466	6,719	1,663	1,719	5,727	5,446
% Net Interest Margin	2.87	2.39	2.16	2.19	2.27	2.10	2.09	1.99	1.87	2.98
S&P Core Earnings	2,409	15,563	13,852	9,802	6,456	6,439	1,290	698	NA	NA

Balance Sheet & Other Financial Data (Million $)										
Money Market Assets	713,098	662,306	506,262	432,358	390,168	329,739	314,110	265,875	293,429	115,168
Investment Securities	329,943	169,634	172,022	128,578	149,675	109,328	126,834	105,537	117,494	61,513
Commercial Loans	111,654	238,210	188,372	150,111	135,067	83,097	91,548	104,864	119,460	88,120
Other Loans	610,080	281,164	294,755	269,037	267,047	136,421	124,816	112,580	96,590	88,039
Total Assets	2,175,052	1,562,147	1,351,520	1,198,942	1,157,248	770,912	758,800	693,575	715,348	406,105
Demand Deposits	210,899	135,748	140,443	143,075	136,188	79,465	82,029	76,974	62,713	55,529
Time Deposits	790,681	604,980	498,345	411,916	385,268	247,027	222,724	216,676	216,652	186,216
Long Term Debt	270,683	197,878	117,358	119,886	105,718	54,782	45,190	44,172	47,788	20,690
Common Equity	134,945	123,221	115,790	107,072	105,314	45,145	41,297	40,090	40,818	22,689
% Return on Assets	0.2	1.1	1.1	0.7	0.5	0.9	0.2	0.2	0.8	1.4
% Return on Equity	2.9	12.9	12.2	8.0	5.9	15.4	4.0	4.1	15.2	23.6
% Loan Loss Reserve	3.1	1.8	1.5	1.7	1.8	2.1	2.5	2.1	1.7	2.0
% Loans/Deposits	73.8	72.6	75.6	75.5	77.1	67.2	71.0	74.0	77.3	72.9
% Equity to Assets	6.9	8.2	8.7	9.0	7.8	5.7	5.6	5.7	5.4	5.9

Data as orig reptd.; bef. results of disc opers/spec. items. Per share data adj. for stk. divs.; EPS diluted. E-Estimated. NA-Not Available. NM-Not Meaningful. NR-Not Ranked. UR-Under Review.

Office: 270 Park Ave, New York, NY 10017-2070.
Telephone: 212-270-6000.
Website: http://www.jpmorganchase.com
Chrmn, Pres & CEO: J. Dimon

Vice Chrmn: B.J. Taylor
Vice Chrmn: M. Breuer
EVP & CFO: M.J. Cavanagh
EVP & General Counsel: S.M. Cutler

Investor Contact: J. Bates (212-270-7318)
Board Members: C. C. Bowles, M. Breuer, S. B. Burke, D. M. Cote, J. S. Crown, J. Dimon, E. Futter, W. H. Gray, III, L. P. Jackson, Jr., D. C. Novak, L. R. Raymond, W. C. Weldon

Founded: 1823
Domicile: Delaware
Employees: 224,961

Juniper Networks Inc

STANDARD &POOR'S

S&P Recommendation HOLD ★★★☆☆	Price $25.67 (as of Nov 27, 2009)	12-Mo. Target Price $29.00	Investment Style Large-Cap Blend

GICS Sector Information Technology
Sub-Industry Communications Equipment

Summary This company provides Internet Protocol networking products and services, with a specific emphasis on telecom routing solutions.

Key Stock Statistics (Source S&P, Vickers, company reports)

52-Wk Range	$28.74– 12.43	S&P Oper. EPS 2009E	0.70	Market Capitalization(B)	$13.488	Beta		1.40
Trailing 12-Month EPS	$0.43	S&P Oper. EPS 2010E	0.90	Yield (%)	Nil	S&P 3-Yr. Proj. EPS CAGR(%)		15
Trailing 12-Month P/E	59.7	P/E on S&P Oper. EPS 2009E	36.7	Dividend Rate/Share	Nil	S&P Credit Rating		NR
$10K Invested 5 Yrs Ago	$9,058	Common Shares Outstg. (M)	525.4	Institutional Ownership (%)	98			

Price Performance

30-Week Mov. Avg. · · · 10-Week Mov. Avg. - - **GAAP Earnings vs. Previous Year** Volume Above Avg. STARS
12-Mo. Target Price — Relative Strength — ▲ Up ▼ Down ► No Change Below Avg.

Options: ASE, CBOE, P, Ph

Analysis prepared by **Ari Bensinger** on October 26, 2009, when the stock traded at **$ 27.44**.

Highlights

► Following a projected 8% decline in 2009, we see sales advancing 10% during 2010, on higher demand for carrier network infrastructure products, as well as increased market penetration in the enterprise sector. We are optimistic about recent portfolio enhancements and new product introductions, specifically the launch of a new ethernet switch and core router.

► We foresee 2010 gross margins widening roughly 150 basis points from the prior year, to 67%, largely reflecting lower manufacturing costs and a favorable product mix shift, partly offset by industry pricing pressure. Despite aggressive R&D investment, we believe JNPR will manage 2010 costs prudently, and expect operating expenses to grow at a slower rate than sales.

► We believe 2010 operating margins will be near 23%. After flat interest income and a stable tax rate of 28%, we look for 2010 operating EPS of $0.90, up from the $0.70 that we forecast for 2009. Our 2009 and 2010 estimates include projected stock option expense of $0.16 and $0.20, respectively.

Investment Rationale/Risk

► We are encouraged by the company's increased customer traction in the newly entered enterprise market, and believe new product upgrades will help boost carrier sales. We see the continued rapid increase in IP traffic acting as a strong underlying growth driver for the networking industry. Even so, we think the shares, recently trading above peers on a P/E and price-to-sales basis, adequately reflect the large market opportunity that we see available for JNPR.

► Risks to our recommendation and target price include a prolonged decline in carrier spending, routing market share losses, and slower-than-expected sales traction in the enterprise sector.

► Our 12-month target price of $29 translates to a P/E of 32X our 2010 EPS estimate and 4.3X our 2010 sales forecast, valuation metrics that are above the peer mean, warranted, we believe, by JNPR's strong position in the fast-growing IP networking sector. Using our three-year earnings growth estimate of 15%, our target price represents a forward P/E-to-growth (PEG) ratio of 2.1X, in line with the industry average.

Qualitative Risk Assessment

LOW	MEDIUM	HIGH

Our risk assessment reflects the highly competitive nature of the industry and execution risks related to the company's planned expansion into the enterprise market.

Quantitative Evaluations

S&P Quality Ranking **B**

D	C	B-	B	B+	A-	A	A+

Relative Strength Rank **MODERATE**

47

LOWEST = 1   HIGHEST = 99

Revenue/Earnings Data

Revenue (Million $)

	1Q	2Q	3Q	4Q	Year
2009	764.2	786.4	823.9	--	--
2008	822.9	879.0	947.0	923.5	3,572
2007	626.9	664.9	735.1	809.2	2,836
2006	566.7	567.5	573.6	595.8	2,304
2005	449.1	493.0	546.4	575.5	2,064
2004	224.1	306.9	375.0	430.1	1,336

Earnings Per Share ($)

2009	-0.01	0.03	0.16	E0.23	E0.70
2008	0.20	0.22	0.27	0.25	0.93
2007	0.11	0.15	0.15	0.22	0.62
2006	0.13	-2.13	0.10	0.12	-1.76
2005	0.13	0.15	0.14	0.17	0.59
2004	0.08	-0.02	0.08	0.11	0.25

Fiscal year ended Dec. 31. Next earnings report expected: Late January. EPS Estimates based on S&P Operating Earnings; historical GAAP earnings are as reported.

Dividend Data

No cash dividends have been paid.

Juniper Networks Inc

Business Summary October 26, 2009

CORPORATE OVERVIEW. Juniper Networks, founded in 1996, makes secure Internet Protocol (IP) networking solutions that are designed to address the needs at the core and at the edge of the network, and for wireless access. The company's core product is IP backbone routers for service providers. The acquisition of NetScreen in 2004 added a broad family of network security solutions aimed at enterprises, service providers, and government entities.

The service provider market accounted for 72% of total revenue in 2008, with the remainder of sales derived from the enterprise market. JNPR enjoys good customer diversification, having sold its products to all of the 100 largest service providers in the world, with no single customer accounting for more than 10% of total sales in 2008. Nokia Siemens Networks accounted for more than 10% of total sales during 2006 and 2007.

During 2008, international revenue represented 51% of total sales, down from 53% in 2007. Operations are organized into three operating segments: infrastructure, service layer technologies (SLT), and service.

PRIMARY BUSINESS DYNAMICS. The infrastructure segment (76% of total sales in 2008) primarily offers scalable router products that are used to control and direct network traffic from the core, through the edge, aggregation and the customer premise equipment level. The company has experienced an in-

creased demand for infrastructure products due to the adoption and expansion of IP networks as a result of peer-to-peer interaction, increased broadband usage, video, and IP television.

Infrastructure products include the M-series and T-series routers, geared to service providers, offering carrier class reliability and scalability. The M-series, which can be deployed at the edge of operator networks, in small and medium core networks, includes the M320, M160, M40e, M20, M10i and M7i platforms. The MX-Series addresses the Carrier Ethernet market. The T-series, T1600, T640 and T320, and TX Matrix are primarily designed for core IP infrastructures. Other product platforms include E-series and J-series (wireless routers, developed through JNPR's joint venture with Ericsson). In January 2008, the company introduced the EX-series family of Ethernet switches. Products run on JNPR's JUNOS Internet software, and are differentiated from their competition in that they also feature the company's high-performance, ASIC-based packet forwarding technology.

Company Financials Fiscal Year Ended Dec. 31

Per Share Data ($)	2008	2007	2006	2005	2004	2003	2002	2001	2000	1999
Tangible Book Value	4.26	3.09	4.08	3.04	2.89	1.48	1.18	2.36	1.87	1.47
Cash Flow	1.23	0.96	-1.46	0.82	0.52	0.27	-0.16	0.42	0.53	-0.01
Earnings	0.93	0.62	-1.76	0.59	0.25	0.10	-0.34	-0.04	0.43	-0.05
S&P Core Earnings	0.96	0.60	-0.27	0.26	0.12	-0.06	-0.51	-0.38	NA	NA
Dividends	Nil	Nil	Nil	Nil	Nil	Nil	Nil	Nil	Nil	Nil
Payout Ratio	Nil	Nil	Nil	Nil	Nil	Nil	Nil	Nil	Nil	Nil
Prices:High	33.30	37.95	22.63	27.65	31.25	19.38	23.01	145.00	244.50	64.06
Prices:Low	3.29	17.21	12.09	19.65	18.75	6.88	4.15	8.90	48.83	5.67
P/E Ratio:High	36	61	NM	47	NM	NM	NM	NM	NM	NM
P/E Ratio:Low	14	28	NM	33	NM	NM	NM	NM	NM	NM

Income Statement Analysis (Million $)	2008	2007	2006	2005	2004	2003	2002	2001	2000	1999
Revenue	3,572	2,836	2,304	2,064	1,336	701	547	887	674	103
Operating Income	876	610	496	595	376	141	42.2	205	249	-9.31
Depreciation	167	193	173	139	145	70.0	63.0	148	34.8	5.31
Interest Expense	2.90	1.70	3.59	3.93	5.38	39.1	55.6	61.4	52.7	Nil
Pretax Income	729	511	-897	502	219	59.0	-115	16.5	230	-6.61
Effective Tax Rate	29.8%	29.3%	NM	29.5%	38.0%	33.6%	NM	NM	35.8%	NM
Net Income	512	361	-1,001	354	136	39.2	-120	-13.4	148	-9.03
S&P Core Earnings	527	353	-156	156	65.9	-25.6	-180	-122	NA	NA

Balance Sheet & Other Financial Data (Million $)	2008	2007	2006	2005	2004	2003	2002	2001	2000	1999
Cash	2,192	1,956	1,596	918	713	396	194	607	563	158
Current Assets	2,816	2,555	2,522	1,818	1,414	691	681	1,126	1,349	378
Total Assets	7,187	6,885	7,368	8,027	7,000	2,411	2,615	2,390	2,103	513
Current Liabilities	1,057	1,380	763	627	503	291	242	242	216	55.7
Long Term Debt	Nil	Nil	400	400	Nil	558	942	1,150	1,120	Nil
Common Equity	5,901	5,354	6,115	6,900	5,993	1,562	1,431	997	730	458
Total Capital	5,901	5,354	6,515	7,300	5,993	2,120	2,373	2,147	1,850	458
Capital Expenditures	165	147	102	98.2	63.2	19.4	36.1	241	35.0	10.0
Cash Flow	679	554	-828	493	281	109	-56.6	134	183	-3.73
Current Ratio	2.7	1.9	3.3	2.9	2.8	2.4	2.8	4.6	6.2	6.8
% Long Term Debt of Capitalization	Nil	Nil	6.1	5.5	Nil	26.3	39.7	53.6	60.5	Nil
% Net Income of Revenue	14.3	12.7	NM	17.2	10.2	5.6	NM	NM	22.0	NM
% Return on Assets	7.3	5.1	NM	4.7	2.9	1.6	NM	NM	11.3	NM
% Return on Equity	9.1	6.3	NM	5.5	3.6	2.6	NM	NM	24.9	NM

Data as orig reptd.; bef. results of disc opers/spec. items. Per share data adj. for stk. divs.; EPS diluted. E-Estimated. NA-Not Available. NM-Not Meaningful. NR-Not Ranked. UR-Under Review.

Office: 1194 North Mathilda Avenue, Sunnyvale, CA 94089.
Telephone: 408-745-2000.
Email: investor-relations@juniper.net
Website: http://www.juniper.net

Chrmn & Pres: S.G. Kriens
Vice Chrmn & CTO: P. Sindhu
CEO: K.R. Johnson
COO: M.J. Rose

EVP & CFO: R.M. Denholm
Board Members: B. Calderoni, M. B. Cranston, K. R. Johnson, S. G. Kriens, J. M. Lawrie, W. F. Meehan, III, S. Sclavos, P. Sindhu, W. R. Stensrud

Founded: 1996
Domicile: Delaware
Employees: 7,014

KB Home

STANDARD &POOR'S

S&P Recommendation **HOLD** ★★★☆☆	Price $13.62 (as of Nov 27, 2009)	12-Mo. Target Price $15.00	Investment Style Large-Cap Blend

GICS Sector Consumer Discretionary
Sub-Industry Homebuilding

Summary This large, diversified homebuilder has operations in most of the largest markets in the U.S.

Key Stock Statistics (Source S&P, Vickers, company reports)

52-Wk Range	$20.70– 7.85	S&P Oper. EPS 2009**E**	-3.30	Market Capitalization(B)	$1.040	Beta	1.82
Trailing 12-Month EPS	$-6.63	S&P Oper. EPS 2010**E**	-1.50	Yield (%)	1.84	S&P 3-Yr. Proj. EPS CAGR(%)	NM
Trailing 12-Month P/E	NM	P/E on S&P Oper. EPS 2009**E**	NM	Dividend Rate/Share	$0.25	S&P Credit Rating	BB-
$10K Invested 5 Yrs Ago	$3,339	Common Shares Outstg. (M)	76.3	Institutional Ownership (%)	NM		

Price Performance

30-Week Mov. Avg. · · · 10-Week Mov. Avg. – – GAAP Earnings vs. Previous Year Volume Above Avg. STARS
12-Mo. Target Price — Relative Strength — ▲ Up ▼ Down ► No Change Below Avg. ★

Options: ASE, CBOE, P, Ph

Analysis prepared by **Kenneth M. Leon, CPA** on October 07, 2009, when the stock traded at **$ 15.00**.

Highlights

► Following an estimated revenue decline of 42% in FY 09 (Nov.), we forecast that KB Home revenues will rebound 19% in FY 10 with the introduction of new smaller homes. We believe KBH, like many homebuilders, is beginning to show positive sequential growth in orders and sales, but at a pace that will not lead to profitability, in our opinion, for the next 12 months.

► The company responded to the depressed new housing market by booking $2.7 billion of asset writedowns in FY 07 for home inventory, acquisitions, and investments in joint ventures. KBH booked $221 million of asset writeoffs in the fourth quarter and a total of $816 million in FY 08. In the first nine months of FY 09, KBH booked only $130 million of asset impairments.

► With $1.2 billion in cash at August 31, 2009, we believe KBH can survive what we view as its concentrated position in the weaker West and Southeast regions. KBH may begin to acquire, in our opinion, low priced land to expand new communities in FY 10. Including asset writedowns, we estimate losses per share of $3.30 for FY 09 and $1.50 for FY 10.

Investment Rationale/Risk

► With a sales backlog value that declined from $6 billion in early FY 06 to $734 million at August 31, 2009, but up from $521 million at the end of FY 08, we believe KBH's sales comparisons will begin to improve with higher net new orders, although we think price pressure in its markets will delay profitability. However, we think KBH, with $1.2 billion in cash, can meet its debt obligations.

► Risks to our recommendation and target price include key factors that would reduce buyers' confidence levels, such as less affordable mortgage rates, delays in employment gains, and less favorable home affordability than we project. With KBH focused on entry-level and move-up products, we think the expiration of the federal tax credit and credit availability overall are risks.

► With the shares falling 27% from mid-September 2009 highs, we increased our opinion to hold from sell in early October. Our 12-month target price of $15 is based on a target price-to-book value multiple just under 1.9X -- near the mid-point of the historical range for KBH reflecting a wider risk premium, and near other large builders -- applied to our 12-month forward book value estimate near $8.00.

Qualitative Risk Assessment

LOW	MEDIUM	HIGH

Our risk assessment reflects our opinion that market conditions remain challenging, although are improving from the past 12 months, and that a housing turnaround leading to positive growth is not likely until 2010. KBH has taken large writeoffs to adjust inventory, land, and goodwill to its view of market value. Partly offsetting these risks is KBH's cash and borrowing capacity.

Quantitative Evaluations

S&P Quality Ranking B+

D	C	B-	B	B+	A-	A	A+

Relative Strength Rank WEAK

15

LOWEST = 1 HIGHEST = 99

Revenue/Earnings Data

Revenue (Million $)

	1Q	2Q	3Q	4Q	Year
2009	307.4	384.5	458.5	--	--
2008	794.2	639.1	681.6	919.0	3,034
2007	1,389	1,413	1,544	2,071	6,417
2006	2,192	2,592	2,674	3,546	11,004
2005	1,636	2,130	2,525	3,150	9,442
2004	1,353	1,570	1,748	2,381	7,053

Earnings Per Share ($)

	1Q	2Q	3Q	4Q	Year
2009	-0.75	-1.03	-0.87	E-0.65	E-3.30
2008	-3.47	-3.30	-1.87	-3.96	-12.59
2007	0.14	-2.26	-6.19	-9.99	-18.33
2006	2.01	2.45	1.90	-0.64	5.82
2005	1.41	2.06	2.55	3.51	9.53
2004	0.88	1.20	1.42	2.21	5.70

Fiscal year ended Nov. 30. Next earnings report expected: Mid January. EPS Estimates based on S&P Operating Earnings; historical GAAP earnings are as reported.

Dividend Data (Dates: mm/dd Payment Date: mm/dd/yy)

Amount ($)	Date Decl.	Ex-Div. Date	Stk. of Record	Payment Date
0.063	01/22	02/03	02/05	02/19/09
0.063	04/02	05/05	05/07	05/21/09
0.063	07/09	08/04	08/06	08/20/09
0.063	10/01	11/03	11/05	11/19/09

Dividends have been paid since 1986. Source: Company reports.

Please read the Required Disclosures and Analyst Certification on the last page of this report.

The McGraw·Hill Companies

KB Home

Business Summary October 07, 2009

CORPORATE OVERVIEW. From its base in California, KB Home has become one of the five largest single-family homebuilders in the country. In doing so, it has helped establish what has become the industry model for rapid growth: using the acquisition of smaller builders as platforms for growth into new markets. Since 1993, KBH has expanded into Nevada, Arizona, Colorado, New Mexico, Texas, Florida, Georgia, North Carolina, South Carolina, Illinois and Indiana.

KBH entered Georgia and North Carolina in March 2003, through the acquisition of Colony Homes; re-entered Illinois through the September 2003 takeover of Zale Homes in Chicago; South Carolina through the January 2004 purchase of Palmetto Traditional Homes; and Indiana through the June 2004 purchase of Dura Builders.

In FY 08 (Nov.), the company delivered a total of 12,438 homes, down from 32,124 in FY 06 and 23,743 in FY 07. KBH's FY 09 first quarter net unit deliveries were only 1,445 homes. The company reports in four geographic segments. In FY 08, the West Coast accounted for 24% of unit deliveries (21% in FY 07), the Southwest 19% (20%), Central 27% (27%), and the Southeast 30% (32%).

Reflecting housing market conditions that show significant slowing, the number of lots under option was reduced to 11,511 at year-end FY 08, from 20,643 a year before. Similarly bracing for a slower market ahead, the company reduced its total lots owned or under option to 47,023 as of year-end FY 08, from 65,708 at year-end FY 07 and 130,548 at year-end FY 06.

At the end of FY 08, KBH's backlog totaled 2,269 units, representing $521 million. These levels were down 64% and 65%, respectively, from a year earlier. Backlog increased in FY 09's second quarter to 3,804 units, or $796 million, from $559 million at the end of the first quarter. In our opinion, a 9.7% decline in average selling prices (ASP) in FY 08 reflected a credit crunch that negatively affected mortgage availability and homebuyer demand. ASP improved to $239,700 in FY 09's third quarter, from $210,700 in the first quarter.

Company Financials Fiscal Year Ended Nov. 30

Per Share Data ($)	2008	2007	2006	2005	2004	2003	2002	2001	2000	1999
Tangible Book Value	10.69	23.06	30.09	27.50	19.34	14.63	11.25	8.95	6.63	5.35
Cash Flow	-12.47	-18.10	6.11	9.76	5.96	4.65	3.77	3.32	3.14	1.95
Earnings	-12.59	-18.33	5.82	9.53	5.70	4.40	3.58	2.75	2.62	1.54
S&P Core Earnings	-12.00	-17.41	5.61	9.28	11.32	8.69	7.00	5.32	NA	NA
Dividends	0.81	1.00	1.00	0.56	0.15	0.15	0.15	0.15	0.15	0.15
Payout Ratio	NM	NM	17%	6%	3%	3%	4%	5%	6%	10%
Prices:High	28.99	56.08	81.99	85.45	53.76	37.48	27.20	20.72	19.16	15.13
Prices:Low	6.90	18.44	37.89	49.25	30.14	21.28	18.57	12.34	8.41	8.38
P/E Ratio:High	NM	NM	14	9	9	9	8	8	7	10
P/E Ratio:Low	NM	NM	7	5	5	5	5	4	3	5

Income Statement Analysis (Million $)										
Revenue	3,034	6,417	11,004	9,442	7,053	5,851	5,031	4,574	3,931	3,836
Operating Income	-777	1,329	790	1,387	796	584	539	448	373	333
Depreciation	9.32	19.8	24.2	20.5	21.8	21.5	17.2	43.9	41.3	40.0
Interest Expense	146	Nil	18.8	24.0	22.7	30.2	44.2	59.5	50.9	45.0
Pretax Income	-968	-1,461	766	1,374	787	580	486	352	329	257
Effective Tax Rate	NM	NM	28.1%	33.0%	30.1%	31.5%	31.9%	31.3%	26.6%	30.7%
Net Income	-976	-1,415	482	842	481	371	314	214	210	147
S&P Core Earnings	-930	-1,344	465	808	467	357	302	207	NA	NA

Balance Sheet & Other Financial Data (Million $)										
Cash	1,251	1,325	655	145	234	138	330	281	33.1	28.0
Current Assets	NA	NA	NA	NA	NA	NA	NA	NA	NA	NA
Total Assets	4,044	5,706	9,014	7,747	5,836	4,236	4,026	3,693	2,829	2,664
Current Liabilities	NA	NA	NA	NA	NA	NA	NA	NA	NA	NA
Long Term Debt	1,662	2,162	3,027	2,433	2,048	1,393	1,181	1,111	1,208	1,308
Common Equity	831	1,851	2,923	2,852	2,056	1,593	1,274	1,092	655	676
Total Capital	2,493	4,013	6,139	5,429	4,231	3,075	2,530	2,267	1,919	1,994
Capital Expenditures	NA	0.69	22.1	24.0	23.2	13.1	31.1	12.2	18.5	19.0
Cash Flow	-967	-1,397	503	863	503	392	332	258	251	187
Current Ratio	2.9	2.9	2.7	3.0	3.1	2.7	3.5	3.7	4.1	3.4
% Long Term Debt of Capitalization	66.7	53.8	49.3	44.8	48.4	45.3	46.7	49.0	62.9	65.6
% Net Income of Revenue	NM	NM	4.4	8.9	6.8	6.3	6.2	4.7	5.3	3.8
% Return on Assets	NM	NM	5.8	12.4	9.5	9.0	8.1	6.6	7.6	6.5
% Return on Equity	NM	NM	16.9	34.3	26.4	25.9	26.6	24.5	31.6	25.6

Data as orig reptd.; bef. results of disc opers/spec. items. Per share data adj. for stk. divs.; EPS diluted. E-Estimated. NA-Not Available. NM-Not Meaningful. NR-Not Ranked. UR-Under Review.

Office: 10990 Wilshire Blvd, Los Angeles, CA 90024-3913.
Telephone: 310-231-4000.
Website: http://www.kbhome.com
Chrmn: S.F. Bollenbach

Pres & CEO: J. Mezger
EVP & CFO: R.P. Silcock
EVP, Secy & General Counsel: W.C. Shiba
SVP, Chief Acctg Officer & Cntlr: W.R. Hollinger

Investor Contact: K. Masuda (310-893-7434)
Board Members: S. F. Bollenbach, R. W. Burkle, T. W. Finchem, K. M. Jastrow, II, R. L. Johnson, M. Lora, M. G. McCaffery, J. Mezger, L. Moonves, L. G. Nogales

Founded: 1957
Domicile: Delaware
Employees: 1,600

Kellogg Co

S&P Recommendation BUY ★★★★☆	Price $52.97 (as of Nov 27, 2009)	12-Mo. Target Price $55.00	Investment Style Large-Cap Growth

GICS Sector Consumer Staples
Sub-Industry Packaged Foods & Meats

Summary Kellogg is a leading producer of ready-to-eat cereal, and also sells convenience foods such as cookies, crackers, cereal bars, fruit snacks, and frozen waffles.

Key Stock Statistics (Source S&P, Vickers, company reports)

52-Wk Range	$54.05–35.64	S&P Oper. EPS 2009**E**	3.18	Market Capitalization(B)	$20.098	Beta	0.51
Trailing 12-Month EPS	$3.17	S&P Oper. EPS 2010**E**	3.60	Yield (%)	2.83	S&P 3-Yr. Proj. EPS CAGR(%)	9
Trailing 12-Month P/E	16.7	P/E on S&P Oper. EPS 2009**E**	16.7	Dividend Rate/Share	$1.50	S&P Credit Rating	BBB+
$10K Invested 5 Yrs Ago	$13,282	Common Shares Outstg. (M)	379.4	Institutional Ownership (%)	88		

Price Performance

Options: CBOE, Ph

Analysis prepared by **Tom Graves, CFA** on October 30, 2009, when the stock traded at **$ 51.38**.

Highlights

► In 2010, we look for sales to increase moderately from the $12.6 billion estimated for 2009, including a contribution from both pricing and volume. In 2009, we see Kellogg's sales comparison negatively affected by a currency translation impact on international sales from a stronger U.S. dollar, and the absence of a 53rd week. Also, in both 2010 and 2009, we look for much less margin pressure from commodity cost increases than we think there was in 2008.

► We think that Kellogg will receive benefits from cost-reduction projects in 2010, but that it will also incur expenses related to such initiatives. We anticipate that these costs will total about $0.15 a share in 2009, down from an estimated $0.26 in 2009. In addition, we expect 2009 to include about a $0.05 a share negative impact connected to a peanut-related product recall, similar to such an impact in 2008's fourth quarter. Overall, we look for Kellogg's pretax operating margin to widen in both 2010 and 2009.

► We estimate net income in 2010 of $1.35 billion ($3.60 a share, on fewer shares), up from the $1.22 billion ($3.18) projected for 2009.

Investment Rationale/Risk

► We recently upgraded our recommendation on the shares to Buy, from Hold. Looking ahead, we expect sales of Kellogg products to benefit from marketing support and product innovation. We think that this activity will lessen the risk of consumers trading down to less expensive private label products.

► Risks to our recommendation and target price include competitive pressures in Kellogg's businesses, consumer acceptance of new product introductions, commodity cost inflation, and the company's inability to achieve sales and earnings growth forecasts.

► In our view, the prospect of strong company cash flow (after capital expenditures) should help give the stock some appeal. In 2009, we expect cash flow to total about $1.2 billion. Our 12-month target price of $55 reflects our view that the stock should receive a P/E valuation (approximately 15.3X estimated 2010 EPS) that is a moderate premium to the average P/E that we expect from a group of other packaged foods stocks. Also, with its September 2009 payment, Kellogg increased its quarterly dividend about 10%. The stock recently had an indicated dividend yield of about 2.9%.

Qualitative Risk Assessment

LOW	MEDIUM	HIGH

Our risk assessment for Kellogg Company reflects the relatively stable nature of the company's end markets, what we consider its strong balance sheet and cash flow, and corporate governance practices that we think are favorable versus peers.

Quantitative Evaluations

S&P Quality Ranking A

D	C	B-	B	B+	A-	A	A+

Relative Strength Rank STRONG

76

LOWEST = 1   HIGHEST = 99

Revenue/Earnings Data

Revenue (Million $)

	1Q	2Q	3Q	4Q	Year
2009	3,169	3,229	3,277	--	--
2008	3,258	3,343	3,288	2,933	12,822
2007	2,963	3,015	3,004	2,794	11,776
2006	2,727	2,774	2,822	2,584	10,907
2005	2,572	2,587	2,623	2,394	10,177
2004	2,391	2,387	2,445	2,391	9,614

Earnings Per Share ($)

2009	0.84	0.92	0.94	E0.51	E3.18
2008	0.81	0.82	0.89	0.47	2.98
2007	0.80	0.75	0.76	0.44	2.76
2006	0.68	0.67	0.70	0.45	2.51
2005	0.61	0.62	0.66	0.47	2.36
2004	0.53	0.57	0.59	0.45	2.14

Fiscal year ended Dec. 31. Next earnings report expected: Early February. EPS Estimates based on S&P Operating Earnings; historical GAAP earnings are as reported.

Dividend Data (Dates: mm/dd Payment Date: mm/dd/yy)

Amount ($)	Date Decl.	Ex-Div. Date	Stk. of Record	Payment Date
0.340	02/20	02/27	03/03	03/17/09
0.340	04/23	05/28	06/01	06/16/09
0.375	07/24	08/28	09/01	09/15/09
0.375	10/23	11/30	12/02	12/15/09

Dividends have been paid since 1923. Source: Company reports.

Please read the Required Disclosures and Analyst Certification on the last page of this report.

The McGraw-Hill Companies

Kellogg Co

STANDARD
&POOR'S

Business Summary October 30, 2009

CORPORATE OVERVIEW. Kellogg Co., incorporated in 1922, is a leading producer of ready-to-eat cereal. The company has expanded its operations to include convenience food products such as Pop-Tarts toaster pastries, Eggo frozen waffles, Nutri-Grain cereal bars, and Rice Krispies Treats squares.

With the 2001 acquisition of the Keebler Foods Co., the company also markets cookies, crackers and other convenience food products under brand names such as Keebler, Cheez-It, Murray and Famous Amos, and manufactures private label cookies, crackers and other products.

Sales contributions by geographic region in 2008 were: North America 66%, Europe 20%, Latin America 8%, and Asia Pacific 6%. In 2008, cereal sold through North American retail channels represented 24% of total net sales, while international cereal sales represented 28%. Other sales categories included North American retail snacks (31%), North American frozen and specialty channels (11%), and international convenience foods (6%).

In 2008, Kellogg's top five customers accounted for about 33% of net sales collectively, and about 42% of U.S. net sales. Kellogg's largest customer, Wal-Mart Stores, Inc., and its affiliates, accounted for about 20% of net sales during 2008.

Kellogg's expenditures for research and development were about $181 million in 2008, and $179 million in 2007.

Company Financials Fiscal Year Ended Dec. 31

Per Share Data ($)	2008	2007	2006	2005	2004	2003	2002	2001	2000	1999
Tangible Book Value	NM	NM	NM	NM	NM	NM	NM	NM	1.21	1.28
Cash Flow	3.96	3.69	3.39	3.30	3.15	2.83	2.60	2.26	2.16	1.54
Earnings	2.98	2.76	2.51	2.36	2.14	1.92	1.75	1.18	1.45	0.83
S&P Core Earnings	2.48	2.74	2.62	2.29	2.10	1.86	1.24	0.77	NA	NA
Dividends	1.30	1.49	1.14	1.06	1.01	1.01	1.01	1.01	1.00	0.96
Payout Ratio	44%	54%	45%	45%	47%	53%	58%	86%	69%	116%
Prices:High	58.51	56.89	50.95	46.99	45.32	38.57	37.00	34.00	32.00	42.25
Prices:Low	40.32	48.68	42.41	42.35	37.00	27.85	29.02	24.25	20.75	30.00
P/E Ratio:High	20	21	20	20	21	20	21	29	22	51
P/E Ratio:Low	14	18	17	18	17	15	17	21	14	36
Income Statement Analysis (Million $)										
Revenue	12,822	11,776	10,907	10,177	9,614	8,812	8,304	8,853	6,955	6,984
Operating Income	2,431	2,347	2,119	2,142	2,091	1,917	1,857	1,640	1,367	1,361
Depreciation	375	372	353	392	410	373	348	439	291	288
Interest Expense	314	324	307	300	309	371	391	352	138	119
Pretax Income	1,633	1,547	1,471	1,425	1,366	1,170	1,144	804	868	537
Effective Tax Rate	29.7%	28.7%	31.7%	31.2%	34.8%	32.7%	37.0%	40.1%	32.3%	37.0%
Net Income	1,148	1,103	1,004	980	891	787	721	482	588	338
S&P Core Earnings	955	1,093	1,047	953	875	763	510	312	NA	NA
Balance Sheet & Other Financial Data (Million $)										
Cash	255	524	411	219	417	141	101	2,318	204	151
Current Assets	2,521	2,717	2,427	2,197	2,122	1,797	1,763	1,902	1,607	1,569
Total Assets	10,946	11,397	10,714	10,575	10,790	10,231	10,219	10,369	4,896	4,809
Current Liabilities	3,552	4,044	4,020	3,163	2,846	2,766	3,015	2,208	2,493	1,588
Long Term Debt	4,068	3,276	3,053	3,703	3,893	4,265	4,519	5,619	709	1,613
Common Equity	1,448	2,526	2,069	2,284	2,257	1,443	895	871	898	813
Total Capital	5,816	6,443	5,122	5,986	6,150	5,709	5,415	6,491	1,607	2,426
Capital Expenditures	461	472	453	374	279	247	254	277	231	266
Cash Flow	1,523	1,475	1,357	1,372	1,301	1,160	1,069	921	878	626
Current Ratio	0.7	0.7	0.6	0.7	0.7	0.6	0.6	0.9	0.6	1.0
% Long Term Debt of Capitalization	69.9	50.9	59.6	61.9	63.3	74.7	83.5	86.6	44.1	66.5
% Net Income of Revenue	9.0	9.4	9.2	9.6	9.3	8.9	8.7	5.4	8.5	4.8
% Return on Assets	10.3	10.0	9.4	9.3	8.5	7.7	7.0	6.3	12.1	6.9
% Return on Equity	57.8	48.0	46.1	43.2	48.1	67.3	81.6	54.5	68.7	39.7

Data as orig reptd.; bef. results of disc opers/spec. items. Per share data adj. for stk. divs.; EPS diluted. E-Estimated. NA-Not Available. NM-Not Meaningful. NR-Not Ranked. UR-Under Review.

Office: One Kellogg Sq, Battle Creek, MI, USA 49016-3599.
Telephone: 269-961-2000.
Website: http://www.kelloggcompany.com
Chrmn: J.M. Jenness

Pres & CEO: A.D. MacKay
COO, EVP & CFO: J.A. Bryant
SVP & CIO: R.E. Bruch
CTO: M. Bath

Investor Contact: J. Wittenberg (269-961-9089)
Board Members: B. S. Carson, J. T. Dillon, G. Gund, J. M. Jenness, D. A. Johnson, D. R. Knauss, A. M. Korologos, A. D. MacKay, R. M. Rebolledo, S. K. Speirn, R. A. Steele, J. L. Zabriskie

Founded: 1906
Domicile: Delaware
Employees: 32,394

KeyCorp

STANDARD &POOR'S

S&P Recommendation	HOLD ★★★☆☆	Price	12-Mo. Target Price	Investment Style
		$5.57 (as of Nov 27, 2009)	$7.50	Large-Cap Value

GICS Sector Financials
Sub-Industry Regional Banks

Summary This multi-regional bank holding company operates about 985 branch offices in Ohio, New York, Washington State, Oregon, Maine, Indiana, and eight other states.

Key Stock Statistics (Source S&P, Vickers, company reports)

52-Wk Range	$9.82– 4.40	S&P Oper. EPS 2009**E**	-2.74	Market Capitalization(B)	$4.894	Beta	0.54
Trailing 12-Month EPS	$-3.19	S&P Oper. EPS 2010**E**	-1.70	Yield (%)	0.72	S&P 3-Yr. Proj. EPS CAGR(%)	NM
Trailing 12-Month P/E	NM	P/E on S&P Oper. EPS 2009**E**	NM	Dividend Rate/Share	$0.04	S&P Credit Rating	BBB+
$10K Invested 5 Yrs Ago	$2,031	Common Shares Outstg. (M)	878.6	Institutional Ownership (%)	70		

Price Performance

30-Week Mov. Avg. · · · 10-Week Mov. Avg. - - **GAAP Earnings vs. Previous Year** Volume Above Avg. STARS
12-Mo. Target Price — Relative Strength ▲ Up ▼ Down ► No Change Below Avg.

Options: ASE, CBOE, P, Ph

Analysis prepared by **Stuart Plesser** on October 29, 2009, when the stock traded at **$ 5.88.**

Highlights

► We forecast that KEY's loan portfolio will contract modestly in 2010, following a projected 18.5% decrease in 2009, reflecting softness in the U.S. economy and KEY exiting specified loan portfolios. We think KEY's net interest margin will improve in coming quarters, as we think interest rates have bottomed and higher yielding deposits will come due. We look for a net interest margin of 2.78% in 2010, versus projected 2.71% in 2009. Our estimate is for a modest increase in fee income in 2010, reflecting a pickup in fee-driven businesses.

► Non-performing loans totaled 3.68% of total loans at the end of the third quarter, up from 3.09% at the end of the second quarter. Annualized chargeoffs rose to 3.59% of loans from 2.93% in the previous quarter, reflecting deterioration of KEY's commercial loan portfolio. We estimate an annualized chargeoff rate of 4.50% in 2010, due to a further deterioration of its commercial portfolio. We see loan loss provisions of $2.8 billion in 2010, versus $3.2 billion projected for 2009.

► Assuming share dilution of roughly 55%, we project per share losses of $2.74 in 2009 and $1.70 in 2010.

Investment Rationale/Risk

► KEY recently raised $1.7 billion of common equity, and we now believe the company has sufficient capital. KEY's tangible book value per share (TBV) currently totals $8.29 after the capital raise. Based on our loss estimates, we look for KEY's TBV to decline another $2.14 per share to $6.15. At current levels, we think the risk/reward metrics for the stock are appropriate. Although we look for KEY's commercial loan portfolio to deteriorate in the quarters ahead and will contribute to losses, we expect KEY's net interest margin to increase in coming quarters, reflecting historically low interest rates.

► Risks to our recommendation and target price include a slower-than-expected economic recovery and higher-than-expected commercial writedowns, causing elevated provisions.

► Our 12-month target price of $7.50 is derived by applying a below-historical 1.20X multiple to our projected tangible book value estimate of $6.15. We think this multiple is warranted given the weak credit quality of KEY's loan book.

Qualitative Risk Assessment

LOW	MEDIUM	HIGH

Our risk assessment reflects our view of ongoing losses, a likely further decline in its lending credit quality, and the possibility that credit deterioration may result in the need to raise additional capital.

Quantitative Evaluations

S&P Quality Ranking   B-

D	C	B-	B	B+	A-	A	A+

Relative Strength Rank   WEAK

24

LOWEST = 1   HIGHEST = 99

Revenue/Earnings Data

Revenue (Million $)

	1Q	2Q	3Q	4Q	Year
2009	1,524	1,709	1,322	--	--
2008	1,882	1,435	1,620	1,562	6,434
2007	2,022	2,044	1,872	1,935	7,621
2006	1,732	1,872	1,932	1,971	7,507
2005	1,565	1,602	1,705	1,823	6,695
2004	1,370	1,358	1,388	1,448	5,564

Earnings Per Share ($)

2009	-1.09	-0.69	-0.50	E-0.46	E-2.74
2008	0.55	-2.70	-0.07	-1.12	-3.35
2007	0.89	0.85	0.57	0.06	2.38
2006	0.66	0.75	0.74	0.76	2.91
2005	0.64	0.70	0.67	0.72	2.73
2004	0.59	0.58	0.61	0.51	2.30

Fiscal year ended Dec. 31. Next earnings report expected: Late January. EPS Estimates based on S&P Operating Earnings; historical GAAP earnings are as reported.

Dividend Data (Dates: mm/dd Payment Date: mm/dd/yy)

Amount ($)	Date Decl.	Ex-Div. Date	Stk. of Record	Payment Date
0.063	01/15	02/27	03/03	03/13/09
0.010	05/22	05/29	06/02	06/15/09
0.010	07/20	08/28	09/01	09/15/09
0.010	11/19	11/27	12/01	12/15/09

Dividends have been paid since 1963. Source: Company reports.

KeyCorp

STANDARD &POOR'S

Business Summary October 29, 2009

CORPORATE OVERVIEW. KEY owns KeyBank, located in Ohio, New York, Washington, Oregon, Maine, Colorado, Indiana, Utah, Idaho, Vermont, Alaska, Michigan, Florida and Kentucky. The company has two business groups: Community Banking and National Banking.

The Community Banking segment generates about 65% of total revenues, and houses Regional Banking and Commercial Banking.

National Banking generates about 35% of total revenues, and houses Real Estate Capital and Corporate Banking Services, Equipment Finance, Institutional and Capital Markets, and Consumer Finance.

MARKET PROFILE. As of June 30, 2008 (latest available FDIC data), KEY had 997 branches and $61.0 billion in deposits, with about 56% of its deposits and 46% of its branches concentrated in Ohio and New York, according to our calculation. In Ohio, KEY had 231 branches, $19.3 billion in deposits, and a deposit market share of about 8.5%, which ranks fifth. In New York, KEY had 228

branches, $15.1 billion in deposits, and a deposit market share of about 2.0%, which ranks tenth. In Washington State, KEY had 153 branches, $7.9 billion in deposits, and a deposit market share of about 7.0%, which ranks fifth. In Oregon, KEY had 64 branches, $3.4 billion in deposits, and a deposit market share of about 6.9%, which ranks sixth. In Maine, KEY had 63 branches, $2.6 billion in deposits, and a deposit market share of about 13.2%, which ranks second. In Indiana, KEY had 64 branches, $2.7 billion in deposits, and a deposit market share of about 3.0%, which ranks sixth. In Colorado, KEY had 50 branches, $2.9 billion in deposits, and a deposit market share of about 3.5%, which ranks seventh. In addition, KEY had a number three ranking in Idaho, and a number five market ranking in Vermont and a number four ranking in Alaska. Finally, KEY had offices in Utah, Michigan and Florida, with a small presence in Kentucky.

Company Financials Fiscal Year Ended Dec. 31

Per Share Data ($)	2008	2007	2006	2005	2004	2003	2002	2001	2000	1999
Tangible Book Value	11.87	16.39	15.99	15.05	13.91	13.87	13.34	11.85	12.39	11.13
Earnings	-3.35	2.38	2.91	2.73	2.30	2.12	2.27	0.37	2.30	2.45
S&P Core Earnings	-2.54	2.12	2.93	2.72	2.41	2.12	2.10	0.43	NA	NA
Dividends	1.00	1.46	1.38	1.30	1.24	1.22	1.20	1.18	1.12	1.04
Payout Ratio	NM	61%	47%	48%	54%	58%	53%	NM	49%	42%
Prices:High	27.23	39.90	38.63	35.00	34.50	29.41	29.40	29.25	28.50	38.13
Prices:Low	4.99	21.04	32.90	30.10	28.23	22.31	20.98	20.49	15.56	21.00
P/E Ratio:High	NM	17	13	13	15	14	13	79	12	16
P/E Ratio:Low	NM	9	11	11	12	11	9	55	7	9

Income Statement Analysis (Million $)										
Net Interest Income	2,409	2,769	2,815	2,790	2,637	2,725	2,749	2,825	2,730	2,787
Tax Equivalent Adjustment	-454	99.0	103	121	94.0	71.0	120	45.0	28.0	32.0
Non Interest Income	1,805	2,264	2,126	2,077	1,742	1,749	1,763	1,690	2,222	2,265
Loan Loss Provision	1,835	529	150	143	185	501	553	1,350	490	348
% Expense/Operating Revenue	68.2%	64.5%	62.4%	64.5%	62.8%	60.3%	57.3%	64.5%	58.6%	60.0%
Pretax Income	-1,134	1,221	1,643	1,588	1,388	1,242	1,312	259	1,517	1,684
Effective Tax Rate	NM	22.9%	27.4%	28.9%	31.3%	27.3%	25.6%	39.4%	33.9%	34.3%
Net Income	-1,468	941	1,193	1,129	954	903	976	157	1,002	1,107
% Net Interest Margin	2.16	3.46	3.67	3.69	3.64	3.80	3.97	3.81	3.69	3.93
S&P Core Earnings	-1,143	840	1,198	1,125	1,006	898	896	179	NA	NA

Balance Sheet & Other Financial Data (Million $)										
Money Market Assets	1,289	1,056	Nil	Nil	NA	NA	NA	NA	NA	NA
Investment Securities	9,988	7,860	NA	NA	NA	NA	NA	NA	NA	NA
Commercial Loans	36,299	52,705	48,306	39,291	43,276	36,189	36,612	38,063	39,610	36,672
Other Loans	38,402	18,748	17,520	20,078	25,188	26,522	25,845	25,246	27,295	27,550
Total Assets	104,531	99,983	92,337	93,126	90,739	84,487	85,202	80,938	87,270	83,395
Demand Deposits	29,584	38,663	13,553	13,335	11,581	11,175	10,630	23,128	9,076	8,607
Time Deposits	35,676	24,436	45,563	45,430	39,683	39,683	38,716	21,667	39,573	34,626
Long Term Debt	14,995	11,957	14,533	13,939	14,846	15,294	16,865	15,842	15,404	17,124
Common Equity	7,408	7,746	7,703	7,598	7,117	6,969	6,835	6,155	6,623	6,389
% Return on Assets	NM	1.0	1.3	1.2	1.1	1.1	1.2	0.2	1.2	1.4
% Return on Equity	NM	12.2	15.6	15.3	13.5	13.1	15.0	2.5	15.4	17.6
% Loan Loss Reserve	2.5	1.7	1.4	1.4	1.7	2.2	2.3	2.7	1.5	1.4
% Loans/Deposits	112.2	111.8	117.5	118.9	118.4	123.3	126.6	138.0	137.5	148.5
% Equity to Assets	7.4	8.0	8.3	8.0	8.0	8.1	7.8	7.6	7.6	7.7

Data as orig reptd.; bef. results of disc opers/spec. items. Per share data adj. for stk. divs.; EPS diluted. E-Estimated. NA-Not Available. NM-Not Meaningful. NR-Not Ranked. UR-Under Review.

Office: 127 Public Square, Cleveland, OH 44114-1306.
Telephone: 216-689-6300.
Website: http://www.key.com
Chrmn & CEO: H.L. Meyer, III

Vice Chrmn & Chief Admin Officer: T.C. Stevens
EVP & CFO: J.B. Weeden
EVP & Chief Acctg Officer: R.L. Morris
EVP & Treas: J.M. Vayda

Board Members: W. G. Bares, E. P. Campbell, J. A. Carrabba, C. Cartwright, A. M. Cutler, H. J. Dallas, R. A. Gillis, K. Manos, L. E. Martin, E. R. Menasce, H. L. Meyer, III, B. R. Sanford, T. C. Stevens, P. G. Ten Eyck, II

Founded: 1849
Domicile: Ohio
Employees: 18,095

Kimberly-Clark Corp

STANDARD &POOR'S

S&P Recommendation HOLD ★★★☆☆

Price	**12-Mo. Target Price**	**Investment Style**	
$65.56 (as of Nov 27, 2009)	$69.00	Large-Cap Blend	

GICS Sector Consumer Staples
Sub-Industry Household Products

Summary This leading consumer products company's global tissue, personal care and health care brands include Huggies, Pull-Ups, Kotex, Depend, Kleenex, Scott and Kimberly-Clark.

Key Stock Statistics (Source S&P, Vickers, company reports)

52-Wk Range	$66.20– 43.05	S&P Oper. EPS 2009**E**	4.72	Market Capitalization(B)	$27.232	Beta		0.46
Trailing 12-Month EPS	$4.36	S&P Oper. EPS 2010**E**	5.21	Yield (%)	3.66	S&P 3-Yr. Proj. EPS CAGR(%)		8
Trailing 12-Month P/E	15.0	P/E on S&P Oper. EPS 2009**E**	13.9	Dividend Rate/Share	$2.40	S&P Credit Rating		A
$10K Invested 5 Yrs Ago	$12,390	Common Shares Outstg. (M)	415.4	Institutional Ownership (%)	74			

Price Performance

- 30-Week Mov. Avg. ···
- 10-Week Mov. Avg. - -
- **GAAP Earnings vs. Previous Year**
- Volume Above Avg. ▮▮▮ STARS
- 12-Mo. Target Price —
- Relative Strength —
- ▲ Up ▼ Down ► No Change
- Below Avg. ▮▮▮ ★

Options: ASE, CBOE, P

Analysis prepared by **Loran Braverman, CFA** on October 22, 2009, when the stock traded at **$ 63.10**.

Highlights

► We forecast 2009 sales to decline 2% (including a -5% impact from foreign currency), with all segments except health care seen having flat or lower sales on a reported basis. We look for higher growth from developing and emerging markets than developed markets. For 2010, our sales growth projection is 6%, including a small positive foreign currency impact.

► Excluding restructuring costs, the operating margin declined 160 basis points (bps) in 2008 despite cost reduction programs and higher prices. KMB had substantial commodity cost pressures, as well as planned strategic investments in advertising and promotions and higher pension expense. We see the operating margin wider by 180 bps in 2009, with moderation of commodity cost pressures and cost cutting offsetting higher pension expense and foreign currency translation charges. We expect further margin improvement in 2010.

► We project EPS in 2009 of $4.72, excluding costs associated with the June 2009 plan to streamline the organization. KMB had operating EPS of $4.14 in 2008 (excluding restructuring charges). Our 2010 estimate is $5.21.

Investment Rationale/Risk

► We think continuing intense competition in developed countries and in consumer tissue and personal care categories will somewhat offset KMB's efforts to support sales growth by expanding in non-traditional (for KMB) categories and focusing on certain developing markets. Also, while we have seen substantial moderation of commodity cost pressures in mid-2009, some costs have begun to rise again. However, we have started to see more benefits from the strategic cost reduction program begun in late 2005 and other cost containment programs.

► Risks to our recommendation and target price include increased promotional activity in the consumer paper category, higher commodity costs, a lack of product innovation, unfavorable foreign currency shifts, and decreased consumer acceptance of KMB's products.

► Our 12-month target price of $69 is based on a blend of our historical and relative analyses. Our historical analysis suggests a value of $73, using a P/E towards the low end of the 10-year range applied to our 2009 EPS forecast of $4.72. Our peer analysis applies a discount to the group average, implying a value of $66.

Qualitative Risk Assessment

LOW	MEDIUM	HIGH

Our risk assessment reflects the generally static demand for household and personal care products, which is usually not affected by changes in the economy or geopolitical factors.

Quantitative Evaluations

S&P Quality Ranking   A

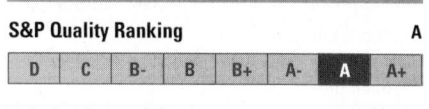

D	C	B-	B	B+	A-	A	A+

Relative Strength Rank   **STRONG**

83

LOWEST = 1   HIGHEST = 99

Revenue/Earnings Data

Revenue (Million $)

	1Q	2Q	3Q	4Q	Year
2009	4,493	4,727	4,913	--	--
2008	4,813	5,006	4,998	4,598	19,415
2007	4,385	4,502	4,621	4,758	18,266
2006	4,068	4,161	4,210	4,307	16,747
2005	3,906	3,987	4,001	4,009	15,903
2004	3,712	3,687	3,783	3,901	15,083

Earnings Per Share ($)

2009	0.98	0.97	1.40	E1.17	E4.72
2008	1.04	1.01	0.99	1.01	4.06
2007	0.98	1.00	1.04	1.07	4.09
2006	0.60	0.82	0.79	1.05	3.25
2005	0.93	0.88	0.68	0.82	3.31
2004	0.88	0.88	0.87	0.92	3.55

Fiscal year ended Dec. 31. Next earnings report expected: Late January. EPS Estimates based on S&P Operating Earnings; historical GAAP earnings are as reported.

Dividend Data (Dates: mm/dd Payment Date: mm/dd/yy)

Amount ($)	Date Decl.	Ex-Div. Date	Stk. of Record	Payment Date
0.600	02/27	03/04	03/06	04/02/09
0.600	04/30	06/03	06/05	07/02/09
0.600	08/03	09/02	09/04	10/02/09
0.600	11/18	12/02	12/04	01/05/10

Dividends have been paid since 1935. Source: Company reports.

Please read the Required Disclosures and Analyst Certification on the last page of this report.

The **McGraw-Hill** Companies

Kimberly-Clark Corp

STANDARD
&POOR'S

Business Summary October 22, 2009

CORPORATE OVERVIEW. Kimberly-Clark, best known for brands such as Kleenex, Scott, Huggies and Kotex, sells consumer and other products in more than 150 countries. After operating as a broadly diversified enterprise, KMB made a major transition since the early 1990s, transforming itself into a global consumer products company. The company further developed its health care business through the acquisitions of Technol Medical Products, Ballard Medical Products, and Safeskin Corp. Reflecting more than 30 strategic acquisitions and 20 strategic divestitures since 1992, KMB has become a leading global manufacturer of tissue, personal care and health care products, manufactured in 39 countries. In 2004, KMB distributed to its shareholders all of the outstanding shares of Neenah Paper, Inc., which was formed in 2004 to facilitate the spin-off of KMB's U.S. fine paper and technical paper businesses and its Canadian pulp mills.

KMB classifies its business into four reportable global segments: Personal Care; Consumer Tissue; K-C Professional & Other; and Health Care. In 2008, Personal Care contributed 43% of sales and 59% of segment operating profits; Consumer Tissue 35% and 21%; K-C Professional & Other 16% and 15%; and Health Care 6% and 5%.

In 2008, sales by geographic region were: U.S. 50%; Canada 3%; Europe 18%;

and Asia, Latin America and other 29%. Wal-Mart Stores, Inc. is KMB's single largest customer, accounting for about 14% of net sales in 2008 and in 2007 and about 13% in 2006.

CORPORATE STRATEGY. In mid-2003, KMB introduced a new strategic plan called the Global Business Plan (GBP), which involves prioritizing growth opportunities and applying greater financial discipline to KMB's global operations. The annual goals established by the GBP are: top-line growth of 3%-5%; EPS growth in the mid- to high-single digits; an operating margin improvement of 40 to 50 basis points; capital spending of 5%-6% of net sales; an ROIC improvement of 40 to 50 basis points; and dividend increases in the high single digits to the low double digits. On average, in the 2004 through 2007 period, we believe KMB met or exceeded all these goals but an operating margin improvement, which was adversely affected by unusually high inflationary cost pressures. Also, under the GBP, capital allocation focused on more targeted expansion activity and an increased emphasis on innovation and cost reduction.

Company Financials Fiscal Year Ended Dec. 31

Per Share Data ($)	2008	2007	2006	2005	2004	2003	2002	2001	2000	1999
Tangible Book Value	2.45	5.92	7.10	6.22	8.13	8.21	6.65	7.10	7.04	7.12
Cash Flow	5.91	5.90	5.34	5.08	5.32	4.80	4.60	1.39	4.55	4.17
Earnings	4.06	4.09	3.25	3.31	3.55	3.33	3.24	3.02	3.34	3.09
S&P Core Earnings	3.57	4.09	3.32	3.32	3.56	3.35	2.74	2.49	NA	NA
Dividends	2.32	2.12	1.96	1.80	1.60	1.36	1.20	1.12	1.08	1.03
Payout Ratio	57%	52%	60%	54%	45%	41%	37%	37%	32%	33%
Prices:High	69.69	72.79	68.58	68.29	69.00	59.30	66.79	72.19	73.25	69.56
Prices:Low	50.27	63.79	56.59	55.60	56.19	42.92	45.30	52.06	42.00	44.81
P/E Ratio:High	17	18	21	21	19	18	21	24	22	23
P/E Ratio:Low	12	16	17	17	16	13	14	17	13	15

Income Statement Analysis (Million $)										
Revenue	19,415	18,266	16,747	15,903	15,083	14,348	13,566	14,524	13,982	13,007
Operating Income	3,414	3,553	3,034	3,155	3,358	3,158	3,170	3,162	3,203	2,815
Depreciation	775	806	933	844	800	746	707	740	673	586
Interest Expense	318	283	220	190	163	168	182	192	222	213
Pretax Income	2,455	2,488	2,064	2,106	2,328	2,153	2,411	2,319	2,622	2,441
Effective Tax Rate	25.2%	21.6%	22.7%	20.8%	20.8%	23.9%	27.7%	27.8%	28.9%	29.9%
Net Income	1,698	1,823	1,500	1,581	1,770	1,694	1,686	1,610	1,801	1,668
S&P Core Earnings	1,495	1,820	1,533	1,581	1,777	1,708	1,424	1,329	NA	NA

Balance Sheet & Other Financial Data (Million $)										
Cash	364	762	361	364	594	291	495	405	207	323
Current Assets	5,813	6,097	5,270	4,783	4,962	4,438	4,274	3,922	3,790	3,562
Total Assets	18,074	18,440	17,067	16,303	17,018	16,780	15,586	15,008	14,480	12,816
Current Liabilities	4,752	4,929	5,016	4,643	4,537	3,919	4,038	4,168	4,574	3,846
Long Term Debt	4,882	4,394	3,069	3,352	3,021	3,301	3,398	2,962	Nil	1,927
Common Equity	3,878	5,224	6,097	5,558	6,630	6,766	5,650	5,647	5,767	5,093
Total Capital	10,852	11,476	9,981	9,878	10,859	10,366	10,158	9,923	7,036	8,101
Capital Expenditures	906	989	972	710	535	878	871	1,100	1,170	786
Cash Flow	2,473	2,629	2,432	2,425	2,571	2,440	2,393	740	2,474	2,254
Current Ratio	1.2	1.2	1.1	1.0	1.1	1.1	1.1	0.9	0.8	0.9
% Long Term Debt of Capitalization	44.9	38.3	30.8	33.9	27.8	31.8	33.4	29.9	Nil	23.8
% Net Income of Revenue	8.8	10.0	9.0	9.9	11.7	11.8	12.4	11.1	12.9	12.8
% Return on Assets	9.3	10.3	9.0	9.5	10.5	10.5	11.0	10.9	13.2	13.6
% Return on Equity	37.3	32.2	25.7	25.9	26.4	27.3	29.8	28.2	33.2	37.1

Data as orig reptd.; bef. results of disc opers/spec. items. Per share data adj. for stk. divs.; EPS diluted. E-Estimated. NA-Not Available. NM-Not Meaningful. NR-Not Ranked. UR-Under Review.

Office: P.O. Box 619100, Dallas, TX 75261-9100.
Telephone: 972-281-1200.
Website: http://www.kimberly-clark.com
Chrmn, Pres & CEO: T.J. Falk

SVP & CFO: M.A. Buthman
Chief Acctg Officer: R.J. Vest
Secy: T.C. Everett
Investor Contact: M.D. Masseth (972-281-1478)

Board Members: J. R. Alm, D. Beresford, J. F. Bergstrom, A. E. Bru, R. W. Decherd, T. J. Falk, M. C. Jemison, J. M. Jenness, I. C. Read, L. J. Rice, M. J. Shapiro, G. C. Sullivan

Founded: 1872
Domicile: Delaware
Employees: 53,000

The McGraw-Hill Companies

Kimco Realty Corp

STANDARD &POOR'S

S&P Recommendation	HOLD ★★★☆☆	Price	12-Mo. Target Price	Investment Style
		$11.85 (as of Nov 27, 2009)	$14.00	Large-Cap Blend

GICS Sector Financials
Sub-Industry Retail REITS

Summary This real estate investment trust is one of the largest U.S. owners and operators of neighborhood and community shopping centers.

Key Stock Statistics (Source S&P, Vickers, company reports)

52-Wk Range	$20.90– 6.33	S&P FFO/Sh. 2009E	1.32	Market Capitalization(B)	$4.464	Beta	2.00
Trailing 12-Month FFO/Share	NA	S&P FFO/Sh. 2010E	1.12	Yield (%)	5.40	S&P 3-Yr. FFO/Sh. Proj. CAGR(%)	-19
Trailing 12-Month P/FFO	NA	P/FFO on S&P FFO/Sh. 2009E	9.0	Dividend Rate/Share	$0.64	S&P Credit Rating	BBB+
$10K Invested 5 Yrs Ago	$5,404	Common Shares Outstg. (M)	376.7	Institutional Ownership (%)	90		

Price Performance

30-Week Mov. Avg. ···· 10-Week Mov. Avg. – – GAAP Earnings vs. Previous Year   Volume Above Avg. STARS
12-Mo. Target Price — Relative Strength — ▲ Up ▼ Down ► No Change   Below Avg.

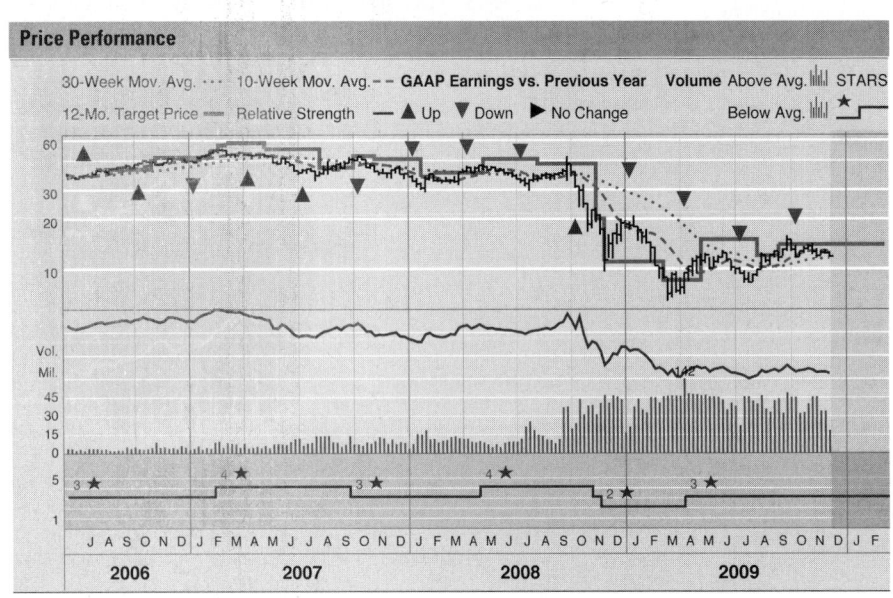

Options: ASE, CBOE, P, Ph

Analysis prepared by **Robert McMillan** on November 05, 2009, when the stock traded at **$ 11.83**.

Highlights

► We expect the trust to continue to benefit from what we view as a successful strategy of operating neighborhood and community shopping centers in North America and expanding into high-growth international markets via joint ventures.

► We look for total revenues, after rising 12% in 2008, to advance 1.3% in 2009 and 5.9% in 2010 on higher rents at established properties. Operating trends appear to be stabilizing. Occupancy of KIM's total portfolio dropped to about 92.3% at the end of the third quarter, from about 95.3% a year earlier; it was above the prior quarter's 92.2%. We believe that a rebound in retailer demand for new as well as existing space, on top of limited new construction, will help results in 2010. Rents on new and renewal leases in the U.S. rose 1.3% during the third quarter. We also see continued growth in Canada and Latin America (driven in part by Wal-Mart's continued expansion) as well as acquisitions helping KIM's long term growth.

► We project FFO per share of $0.85 (or $1.32 excluding impairments) for 2009 and $1.12 for 2010.

Investment Rationale/Risk

► We believe that KIM, one of the largest owners and operators of neighborhood and community shopping centers in the U.S. with a broad array of established relationships, will generate above-average rent growth in the long term. Near term, though, we think an expected drop in development stemming from the weak economy and credit crunch will restrict the shares.

► Risks to our recommendation and target price include slower-than-expected growth in retailer expansion and rental rates, higher-than-expected retailer bankruptcies, and a sharp drop in development activities.

► The shares recently traded at about 7.9X trailing 12-month FFO per share. Our 12-month target price of $14 is equal to about 13.0X our forward 12-month FFO estimate of $1.12. We believe the stock has been volatile over the past year in part due to concerns about the soft economy, a rise in store closures, and declines in transaction volumes. We think the valuation multiple will expand over time as KIM shows that its core portfolio, anchored by long-term leases, continues to grow. Further, KIM's recent equity offering, although dilutive, eases our concerns about the company's liquidity.

Qualitative Risk Assessment

LOW	MEDIUM	HIGH

Our risk assessment reflects our view of KIM's strong fundamentals, healthy credit quality, and diversified customer base. We also believe KIM's diversity in its geographic presence helps provide significant protection from a local or regional downturn.

Quantitative Evaluations

S&P Quality Ranking   A

D	C	B-	B	B+	A-	A	A+

Relative Strength Rank   WEAK

29

LOWEST = 1   HIGHEST = 99

Revenue/FFO Data

Revenue (Million $)

	1Q	2Q	3Q	4Q	Year
2009	208.0	203.3	205.5	--	--
2008	190.5	199.9	208.6	213.6	824.7
2007	158.3	170.8	210.3	179.7	750.6
2006	138.1	147.9	150.7	157.3	653.0
2005	129.3	126.7	129.6	137.0	580.6
2004	139.9	129.7	122.7	124.7	517.0

FFO Per Share ($)

2009	0.43	0.31	0.30	E0.28	E1.32
2008	0.64	0.66	0.37	0.04	2.02
2007	0.78	0.71	0.57	0.53	2.59
2006	0.53	0.54	0.56	0.58	2.21
2005	0.53	0.54	0.56	0.55	2.00
2004	0.47	0.48	0.50	0.45	1.78

Fiscal year ended Dec. 31. Next earnings report expected: Early February. FFO Estimates based on S&P Funds From Operations Est..

Dividend Data (Dates: mm/dd Payment Date: mm/dd/yy)

Amount ($)	Date Decl.	Ex-Div. Date	Stk. of Record	Payment Date
0.440	02/05	04/02	04/06	04/15/09
0.060	07/06	07/01	07/06	07/15/09
0.060	07/30	10/01	10/05	10/15/09
0.160	11/04	12/30	01/04	01/15/10

Dividends have been paid since 1992. Source: Company reports.

Kimco Realty Corp

STANDARD &POOR'S

Business Summary November 05, 2009

Kimco Realty specializes in the acquisition, development and management of shopping centers that it believes are well located and have strong growth potential. At the end of 2008, KIM had interests in 1,950 properties, totaling approximately 182.2 million square feet of gross leasable area (GLA) located in 45 states, Canada, Mexico, Puerto Rico, Brazil, Chile and Peru. The trust's ownership interests in real estate consist of its consolidated portfolio and portfolios where it owns an economic interest, such as properties in its investment management programs, where it partners with institutional investors and also retains management.

The trust's investment objective has been to increase cash flow, current income, and, consequently, the value of its existing portfolio of properties, and to seek continued growth through the strategic re-tenanting, renovation and expansion of its existing centers, and through the selective acquisition of established income-producing real estate properties and properties requiring significant re-tenanting and redevelopment. These properties are mainly located in neighborhood and community shopping centers in geographic regions in which KIM currently operates.

For KIM as well as other retail-oriented REITs, we believe that location and the financial health and growth of its retail tenants are among the most important factors affecting the success of its portfolio. KIM's neighborhood and community shopping center properties are designed to attract local area customers and typically are anchored by a discount department store, a supermarket or a drugstore tenant offering day-to-day necessities rather than high-priced luxury items. The trust seeks to reduce operating and leasing risks through diversification achieved by the geographic distribution of its properties and a large tenant base. At December 31, 2008, the single largest neighborhood and community shopping center accounted for 1.0% of annualized base rental revenues and 0.9% of total shopping center GLA. At December 31, 2008, the five largest tenants were The Home Depot, TJX Companies, Sears Holdings, Kohl's and Wal-Mart.

Company Financials Fiscal Year Ended Dec. 31

Per Share Data ($)	2008	2007	2006	2005	2004	2003	2002	2001	2000	1999
Tangible Book Value	14.66	15.40	13.24	9.70	9.17	8.87	8.04	7.95	7.26	6.98
Earnings	0.69	1.33	1.36	1.40	1.19	1.04	1.10	1.08	0.96	0.82
S&P Core Earnings	0.69	1.33	1.36	1.40	1.18	1.03	1.08	1.07	NA	NA
Dividends	0.24	1.52	1.38	1.27	1.16	1.10	1.05	0.98	0.91	0.79
Payout Ratio	35%	114%	101%	91%	97%	105%	96%	91%	95%	96%
Prices:High	47.80	53.60	47.13	33.35	29.64	22.93	16.94	17.03	14.92	13.58
Prices:Low	9.56	33.74	32.02	25.90	19.77	15.13	12.98	13.58	10.92	10.29
P/E Ratio:High	69	40	35	24	25	22	15	16	16	17
P/E Ratio:Low	14	25	24	18	17	14	12	13	11	13

Income Statement Analysis (Million $)	2008	2007	2006	2005	2004	2003	2002	2001	2000	1999
Rental Income	759	682	594	523	517	480	451	469	459	434
Mortgage Income	Nil	14.2	18.8	NA	NA	NA	NA	NA	NA	NA
Total Income	825	751	653	581	517	480	451	469	466	434
General Expenses	118	104	164	128	111	104	9.15	89.7	138	136
Interest Expense	213	214	173	128	108	103	86.9	89.4	92.1	83.6
Provision for Losses	Nil	Nil	Nil	Nil	Nil	Nil	Nil	Nil	Nil	Nil
Depreciation	204	190	141	106	102	86.2	76.7	74.2	71.1	67.4
Net Income	225	362	343	334	282	247	249	237	205	177
S&P Core Earnings	178	342	333	322	268	222	227	209	NA	NA

Balance Sheet & Other Financial Data (Million $)	2008	2007	2006	2005	2004	2003	2002	2001	2000	1999
Cash	136	87.5	1,616	1,018	757	581	36.0	93.8	19.1	28.1
Total Assets	9,397	9,098	7,869	5,535	4,747	4,604	3,757	3,385	3,171	3,007
Real Estate Investment	7,819	7,325	6,002	4,560	4,877	4,137	3,399	3,201	3,112	2,951
Loss Reserve	Nil	Nil	Nil	Nil	Nil	Nil	Nil	Nil	Nil	Nil
Net Investment	6,659	6,348	5,195	3,820	4,242	3,569	2,882	2,748	2,720	2,627
Short Term Debt	186	281	209	NA	NA	570	147	123	4.60	229
Capitalization:Debt	4,371	3,936	3,378	2,397	1,860	1,585	1,430	1,205	1,321	1,021
Capitalization:Equity	3,974	3,894	3,366	2,387	2,236	2,135	1,906	1,889	1,703	1,604
Capitalization:Total	8,691	8,279	7,170	4,907	4,203	3,820	3,431	3,103	3,039	2,640
% Earnings & Depreciation/Assets	4.6	6.5	7.2	8.5	8.2	8.0	9.1	9.5	8.9	8.1
Price Times Book Value:High	3.3	3.5	3.6	3.4	3.2	2.6	2.1	2.1	2.1	2.0
Price Times Book Value:Low	0.7	2.2	2.4	2.7	2.2	1.7	1.6	1.7	1.5	1.5

Data as orig reptd.; bef. results of disc opers/spec. items. Per share data adj. for stk. divs.; EPS diluted. E-Estimated. NA-Not Available. NM-Not Meaningful. NR-Not Ranked. UR-Under Review.

Office: 3333 New Hyde Park Road, New Hyde Park, NY 11042-0020.
Telephone: 800-285-4626.
Email: ir@kimcorealty.com
Website: http://www.kimcorealty.com

Chrmn & CEO: M. Cooper
Pres & Vice Chrmn: D.B. Henry
COO & EVP: D.R. Lukes
EVP, CFO & Chief Admin Officer: M.V. Pappagallo

SVP, Chief Acctg Officer & Treas: G.G. Cohen
Investor Contact: B. Pooley (866-831-4297)
Board Members: M. Cooper, P. E. Coviello, R. G. Dooley, J. Grills, D. B. Henry, F. P. Hughes, F. Lourenso, R. B. Saltzman

Founded: 1966
Domicile: Maryland
Employees: 734

King Pharmaceuticals Inc.

STANDARD
&POOR'S

S&P Recommendation HOLD ★★★☆☆	Price $11.95 (as of Nov 27, 2009)	12-Mo. Target Price $13.00	Investment Style Large-Cap Blend

GICS Sector Health Care
Sub-Industry Pharmaceuticals

Summary This company makes and markets a line of prescription pharmaceuticals. In December 2008, King acquired Alpharma, another specialty drugmaker, for $1.6 billion in cash.

Key Stock Statistics (Source S&P, Vickers, company reports)

52-Wk Range	$12.19– 5.86	S&P Oper. EPS 2009E	1.10	Market Capitalization(B)	$2.966	Beta	0.74
Trailing 12-Month EPS	$-1.93	S&P Oper. EPS 2010E	1.15	Yield (%)	Nil	S&P 3-Yr. Proj. EPS CAGR(%)	5
Trailing 12-Month P/E	NM	P/E on S&P Oper. EPS 2009E	10.9	Dividend Rate/Share	Nil	S&P Credit Rating	BB
$10K Invested 5 Yrs Ago	$10,093	Common Shares Outstg. (M)	248.2	Institutional Ownership (%)	96		

Price Performance

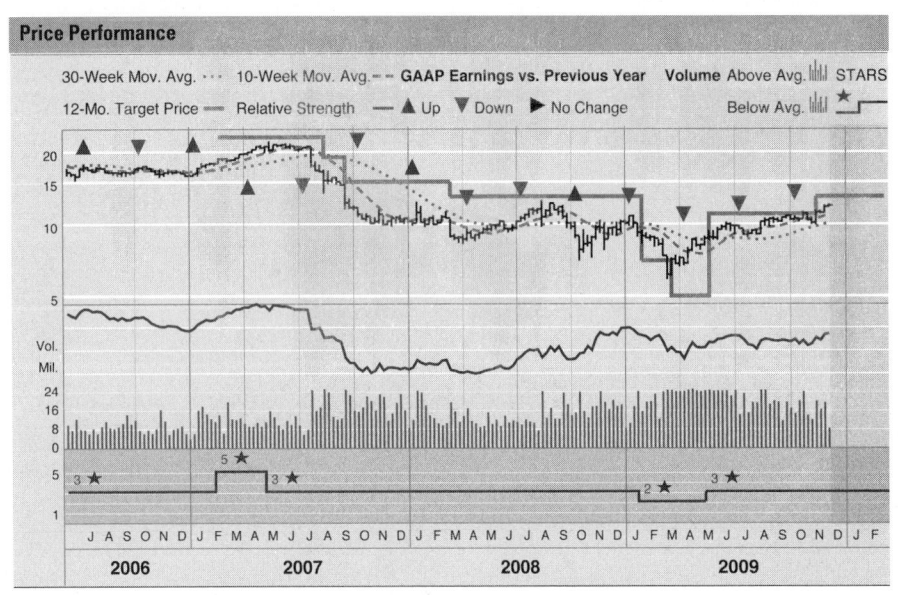

30-Week Mov. Avg. · · · 10-Week Mov. Avg. - - GAAP Earnings vs. Previous Year Volume Above Avg. STARS
12-Mo. Target Price — Relative Strength — ▲ Up ▼ Down ► No Change Below Avg.

Options: ASE, CBOE, P, Ph

Analysis prepared by **Herman B. Saftlas** on November 19, 2009, when the stock traded at **$ 11.81**.

Highlights

▶ We expect 2010 revenues to increase modestly from the $1.8 billion forecasted for 2009. Key positive sales drivers should be recently launched Embeda abuse-deterrent morphine pain drug, and growth of the Flector pain patch. Sales at Meridian Medical should be helped by new products. However, we see lower sales for older drugs such as Skelaxin and Thrombin JMI, which are expected to be impacted by increased competitive pressures. Sales of animal health products are likely to be little changed from the $355 million we forecast for 2009.

▶ We project gross margins to contract slightly from the 68% that we estimate for 2009, impacted by a less favorable sales mix. But we are assuming the SG&A and R&D cost ratios will remain steady. Depreciation is expected to rise, but interest costs will probably decline, by our analysis.

▶ After a projected effective tax rate similar to the 37% we see for 2009, we forecast cash EPS of $1.15 for 2010, up from the $1.10 that we forecast for 2009. Results exclude goodwill amortization associated with the Alpharma acquisition.

Investment Rationale/Risk

▶ We believe that King has made major investments in new treatments for pain, which we think will drive growth in the years ahead and help to offset anticipated generic erosion in older products. In line with this strategy, KG acquired Alpharma in late 2008, which brought it the Flector pain patch, and recently launched Embeda abuse deterrent morphine-based pain drug. Alpharma should also provide annual synergies estimated at about $80 billion. However, our enthusiasm for the stock is tempered by anticipated near term generic erosion in the key Skelaxin line. We also note recent regulatory delays with KG's other abuse-resistant drug Remoxy.

▶ Risks to our recommendation and target price include possible difficulties in integrating and achieving EPS accretion from Alpharma, sooner than expected generic erosion in Skelaxin, and pipeline disappointments.

▶ Our target price of $13 applies a peer P/E of 11.3X to our 2010 EPS estimate. Our DCF model, which assumes slowing cash flow growth, a WACC of 8.5%, and terminal growth of 1%, also indicates intrinsic value of about $13.

Qualitative Risk Assessment

LOW	MEDIUM	HIGH

Our risk assessment reflects King Pharmaceuticals' reliance on in-licensing drugs from other companies and on aggressive marketing for its sales growth. KG recently lost patent protection on its Altace heart drug, and faces increased competitive pressures in other lines. We think the recent purchase of Alpharma makes strategic sense, but we see KG facing further execution risk in integrating the acquisition.

Quantitative Evaluations

S&P Quality Ranking   B-

D	C	B-	B	B+	A-	A	A+

Relative Strength Rank   STRONG

89

LOWEST = 1   HIGHEST = 99

Revenue/Earnings Data

Revenue (Million $)

	1Q	2Q	3Q	4Q	Year
2009	429.1	445.0	463.4	--	--
2008	432.0	396.9	388.5	347.7	1,565
2007	516.0	542.7	544.9	533.3	2,137
2006	484.2	499.7	491.7	512.9	1,989
2005	368.6	462.9	518.0	423.3	1,773
2004	291.5	275.1	394.7	342.6	1,304

Earnings Per Share ($)

2009	-0.04	0.15	0.17	E0.25	E1.10
2008	0.36	0.18	0.35	-2.25	-1.37
2007	0.48	0.26	-0.17	0.18	0.75
2006	0.21	0.46	0.37	0.15	1.19
2005	0.28	0.08	0.50	-0.39	0.48
2004	-0.01	-0.27	-0.01	0.06	-0.21

Fiscal year ended Dec. 31. Next earnings report expected: Late February. EPS Estimates based on S&P Operating Earnings; historical GAAP earnings are as reported.

Dividend Data

No cash dividends have been paid.

King Pharmaceuticals Inc.

STANDARD &POOR'S

Business Summary November 19, 2009

CORPORATE OVERVIEW. King Pharmaceuticals is a vertically integrated branded drug company. A key part of its business strategy consists of the acquisition of drugs being divested by large global pharmaceutical companies. To date, King has successfully acquired and commercialized more than 35 branded products, and has introduced several product line extensions. In late December 2008, KG completed the acquisition of Alpharma Inc. for $1.6 billion in cash.

Revenues from King's legacy businesses (excluding Alpharma) were derived as follows in 2008: branded pharmaceuticals 81%; Meridian Medical Technologies (a maker of auto-injectors) 13%; and royalties from licensed drugs, contract manufacturing and other 6%.

King's largest selling drug is Skelaxin (sales of $446 million in 2008), a muscle relaxant indicated for the relief of discomforts associated with acute, painful musculoskeletal conditions. Other key neuroscience products include Avinza ($135 million), a once-daily, extended-release formulation of morphine sulfate for severe pain; and Flector Patch ($129 million), a topical non-steroidal, anti-inflammatory patch for the treatment of acute pain due to minor strains, sprains and contusions.

Other important pharmaceutical products consist of Thrombin-JMI ($255 mil-

lion), a drug used to control minor bleeding during surgery; Altace ($166 million), an off-patent heart drug used to treat hypertension and congestive heart failure; and Levoxyl ($73 million), a treatment for thyroid disorders. Other drugs include Sonata anti-insomnia agent, Bicillin anti-infective, Synercid injectable antibiotic; and Intall multi-dose inhaler asthma treatment. Impacted by generic erosion, sales of Altace fell 74% in 2008. Sales of Levoxyl declined 27%.

The Meridian Medical Technologies division markets auto-injectors, which are pre-filled, pen-like devices that allow patients or caregivers to automatically inject precise drug dosages.

KG markets its branded drugs to general/family practitioners, internal medicine physicians, cardiologists, and hospitals across the U.S. Pursuant to a major cost restructuring put in place in 2007, the company terminated about 20% of its total work force, primarily through a reduction in sales personnel. About 72% of sales in 2008 were derived from three key drug wholesalers: McKesson Corp. (30%), Cardinal/Bindley (28%), and AmerisourceBergen Corp. (14%).

Company Financials Fiscal Year Ended Dec. 31

Per Share Data ($)	2008	2007	2006	2005	2004	2003	2002	2001	2000	1999
Tangible Book Value	3.22	6.51	5.41	3.66	7.67	0.68	2.90	3.47	0.85	NM
Cash Flow	-0.76	1.43	1.79	1.09	0.46	0.95	0.98	1.20	0.66	1.12
Earnings	-1.37	0.75	1.19	0.48	-0.21	0.44	0.74	0.99	0.47	0.47
S&P Core Earnings	-1.35	0.78	1.31	0.47	-0.06	0.41	0.71	0.94	NA	NA
Dividends	Nil	Nil	Nil	Nil	Nil	Nil	Nil	Nil	Nil	Nil
Payout Ratio	Nil	Nil	Nil	Nil	Nil	Nil	Nil	Nil	Nil	Nil
Prices:High	12.60	22.25	20.00	17.99	20.62	18.13	42.13	46.05	41.63	34.00
Prices:Low	6.98	9.75	15.15	7.50	10.01	9.46	15.00	24.79	14.81	6.46
P/E Ratio:High	NM	30	17	37	NM	41	57	47	88	72
P/E Ratio:Low	NM	13	13	16	NM	22	20	25	31	14

Income Statement Analysis (Million $)	2008	2007	2006	2005	2004	2003	2002	2001	2000	1999
Revenue	1,565	2,137	1,989	1,773	1,304	1,521	1,128	872	620	348
Operating Income	584	834	700	551	272	403	426	429	326	155
Depreciation	148	167	148	147	162	125	59.3	48.0	41.9	26.9
Interest Expense	8.51	8.10	9.86	11.9	12.6	13.4	12.4	12.7	37.0	55.4
Pretax Income	-202	251	424	178	-58.0	177	268	371	192	73.0
Effective Tax Rate	NM	27.0%	32.0%	34.5%	NM	40.2%	31.8%	37.2%	45.4%	37.5%
Net Income	-333	183	289	117	-50.6	106	183	233	105	45.7
S&P Core Earnings	-328	191	318	115	-13.1	98.4	175	222	NA	NA

Balance Sheet & Other Financial Data (Million $)	2008	2007	2006	2005	2004	2003	2002	2001	2000	1999
Cash	947	1,366	114	48.5	359	146	815	924	76.4	8.50
Current Assets	1,669	1,820	1,673	1,248	1,127	946	1,262	1,238	317	131
Total Assets	4,258	3,427	3,330	2,965	2,924	3,178	2,751	2,507	1,282	806
Current Liabilities	1,007	453	618	971	689	669	370	151	105	89.8
Long Term Debt	963	400	400	Nil	345	345	345	346	99.0	553
Common Equity	2,177	2,511	2,289	1,973	1,849	2,042	1,931	1,908	988	148
Total Capital	3,580	2,911	2,689	1,973	2,194	2,387	2,310	2,292	1,104	716
Capital Expenditures	57.5	49.6	45.8	53.3	55.1	51.2	73.6	40.2	25.1	8.80
Cash Flow	-185	350	436	264	111	230	242	281	147	22.6
Current Ratio	1.7	4.0	2.7	1.3	1.6	1.4	3.4	8.2	3.0	1.5
% Long Term Debt of Capitalization	26.9	13.7	14.9	Nil	15.7	14.5	14.9	15.1	9.0	77.2
% Net Income of Revenue	NM	8.6	14.5	6.6	NM	7.0	16.2	26.7	16.9	13.1
% Return on Assets	NM	5.4	9.2	4.0	NM	3.6	6.9	12.3	8.5	6.2
% Return on Equity	NM	7.6	13.5	6.1	NM	5.3	9.5	16.1	14.1	36.7

Data as orig reptd.; bef. results of disc opers/spec. items. Per share data adj. for stk. divs.; EPS diluted. E-Estimated. NA-Not Available. NM-Not Meaningful. NR-Not Ranked. UR-Under Review.

Office: 501 Fifth Street, Bristol, TN 37620-2304.
Telephone: 423-989-8000.
Email: investorrelations@kingpharm.com
Website: http://www.kingpharm.com

Chrmn, Pres & CEO: B.A. Markison
CFO & Chief Acctg Officer: J. Squicciarino
CSO: E.G. Carter
Secy & General Counsel: J.W. Elrod

Investor Contact: J.J. Howarth
Board Members: E. W. Deavenport, Jr., E. M. Greetham, P. A. Incarnati, G. D. Jordan, B. A. Markison, R. Moyer, D. G. Rooker, T. G. Wood

Founded: 1993
Domicile: Tennessee
Employees: 3,392

The McGraw-Hill Companies

KLA Tencor Corp

S&P Recommendation BUY ★★★★☆	**Price** $31.92 (as of Nov 27, 2009)	**12-Mo. Target Price** $40.00	**Investment Style** Large-Cap Growth

GICS Sector Information Technology
Sub-Industry Semiconductor Equipment

Summary This company is the world's leading manufacturer of yield monitoring and process control systems for the semiconductor industry.

Key Stock Statistics (Source S&P, Vickers, company reports)

52-Wk Range	$37.71– 15.28	S&P Oper. EPS 2010**E**	1.09	Market Capitalization(B)	$5.455	Beta	1.86
Trailing 12-Month EPS	$-3.07	S&P Oper. EPS 2011**E**	2.01	Yield (%)	1.88	S&P 3-Yr. Proj. EPS CAGR(%)	NM
Trailing 12-Month P/E	NM	P/E on S&P Oper. EPS 2010**E**	29.3	Dividend Rate/Share	$0.60	S&P Credit Rating	BBB
$10K Invested 5 Yrs Ago	$7,525	Common Shares Outstg. (M)	170.9	Institutional Ownership (%)	95		

Price Performance

30-Week Mov. Avg. ···	10-Week Mov. Avg. - - **GAAP Earnings vs. Previous Year**	Volume Above Avg. ▪▪▪ STARS
12-Mo. Target Price —	Relative Strength — ▲ Up ▼ Down ▶ No Change	Below Avg. ▪▪▪ ★

Options: ASE, CBOE, P, Ph

Analysis prepared by **Angelo Zino** on November 03, 2009, when the stock traded at **$ 31.56**.

Highlights

▶ After a 40% revenue drop in FY 09 (Jun.), we see sales rising 11% in FY 10 and 24% in FY 11. We are encouraged by improving profitability from chipmakers and rebounding memory prices. We think some leading-edge customers are moving ahead with capital investment plans and see new product releases in areas like reticle inspection aiding sales. Going forward, we see greater memory spending and capacity expansion. Foundry customers accounted for 76% of orders in the September quarter.

▶ We forecast an annual gross margin of 53% in FY 10 compared to 56% in FY 09. We view KLAC's yield management and process control systems as only moderately susceptible to pricing pressure due to the critical value they add to semiconductor customers. We think KLAC's quarterly breakeven revenue level is around $325 million. We project gross and operating margins to eventually surpass previous peak levels.

▶ We project operating EPS of $1.09 in FY 10, which excludes $0.04 in non-recurring charges, and EPS of $2.01 in FY 11. We think KLAC could begin repurchasing shares should industry conditions remain sustainable.

Investment Rationale/Risk

▶ We view KLAC's competitive position in both inspection and metrology as strong, and we see long-term growth in yield management and process control. We view positively its leading market share position in its respective markets and solid business model. In our opinion, the company is well positioned to manage current industry conditions and benefit from the next cyclical upturn. We expect the yield monitoring and process control systems products to fare better than other types of front-end semiconductor equipment. We think the transition to lower nanometer nodes will cause yield and defectivity challenges, which we believe will stimulate customers to increase spending.

▶ Risks to our recommendation and target price include an industry downturn, competition pressuring KLAC's market share position, and a weakening of the global economy.

▶ Our 12-month target price of $40 is based on a price-to-sales (P/S) multiple of 3.6X our calendar year 2010 sales per share estimate of $11.18. This is a premium to larger front-end semiconductor equipment peers warranted, we think, by KLAC's higher margin potential and lower sales volatility.

Qualitative Risk Assessment

LOW	MEDIUM	HIGH

Our risk assessment reflects the company's exposure to the cyclicality of the semiconductor equipment industry and changes in relevant technologies, only partially offset by limited pricing pressure and our view of KLAC's strong market position, size, and financial condition.

Quantitative Evaluations

S&P Quality Ranking   B-

D	C	B-	B	B+	A-	A	A+

Relative Strength Rank   MODERATE

33

LOWEST = 1   HIGHEST = 99

Revenue/Earnings Data

Revenue (Million $)

	1Q	2Q	3Q	4Q	Year
2010	342.7	--	--	--	--
2009	532.5	396.6	309.6	281.5	1,520
2008	693.0	635.8	602.2	590.7	2,522
2007	629.4	649.3	716.2	736.4	2,731
2006	484.3	487.7	519.7	579.0	2,071
2005	518.8	532.9	541.6	491.9	2,085

Earnings Per Share ($)

2010	0.12	E0.26	E0.30	E0.37	E1.09
2009	0.11	-2.57	-0.49	-0.15	-3.07
2008	0.46	0.45	0.61	0.43	1.95
2007	0.67	0.44	0.76	0.75	2.61
2006	0.37	0.38	0.47	0.65	1.86
2005	0.58	0.61	0.61	0.52	2.32

Fiscal year ended Jun. 30. Next earnings report expected: Late January. EPS Estimates based on S&P Operating Earnings; historical GAAP earnings are as reported.

Dividend Data (Dates: mm/dd Payment Date: mm/dd/yy)

Amount ($)	Date Decl.	Ex-Div. Date	Stk. of Record	Payment Date
0.150	02/19	02/26	03/02	03/09/09
0.150	05/05	05/13	05/15	06/01/09
0.150	08/06	08/13	08/17	09/01/09
0.150	11/04	11/12	11/16	12/01/09

Dividends have been paid since 2005. Source: Company reports.

KLA Tencor Corp

STANDARD
&POOR'S

Business Summary November 03, 2009

CORPORATE OVERVIEW. KLA-Tencor (KLAC) is the world's leading manufacturer of yield management and process monitoring systems for the semiconductor industry.

Maximizing yields, or the number of good die (chips) per wafer, is a key goal in manufacturing integrated circuits (ICs). Higher yields increase revenues obtained for each semiconductor wafer processed. As IC line widths decrease, yields become more sensitive to microscopic-sized defects. KLAC's systems are used to improve yields by identifying defects, analyzing them to determine process problems and patterns, and facilitate corrective actions. These systems monitor subsequent results to ensure that problems have been contained. With in-line systems, corrections can be made while the wafer is still in the production line, rather than waiting for end-of-process testing and feedback.

KLAC offers a broad range of inspection and yield management. The company's wafer inspection systems include unpatterned and patterned wafer inspection tools used to find, count and characterize particles and pattern defects on wafers both in engineering applications and in-line at various stages during the semiconductor manufacturing process. KLAC's brightfield inspection systems are extremely sensitive to small defects and capture a large range of defect types, which is critical as customers move to 45nm and smaller production.

Reticle inspection systems look for defects on the quartz plates used in copying circuit designs onto an IC during the photolithography process. Film measurement products measure a variety of optical and electrical properties of thin films. Scanning electron beam microscopes (SEMs) can measure the critical dimensions (CDs) of tiny semiconductor features. For chip manufacturing below 90nm, e-beam inspection is becoming increasingly important, not only during the research and development phase, where the highest levels of sensitivity are needed to highlight and eradicate potential design problems, but also in production, where dedicated high-speed e-beam inspection systems.

At the end of FY 08 (Jun.), KLAC's revenues by geographic region were divided as follows: United States 21% (24% in FY 07), Europe & Israel 12% (10%), Japan 24% (22%), Taiwan 23% (20%), Korea 9% (11%), and Asia Pacific 11% (13%). No customer accounted for greater than 10% of revenues during FY 08 or FY 07.

Company Financials Fiscal Year Ended Jun. 30

Per Share Data ($)	2009	2008	2007	2006	2005	2004	2003	2002	2001	2000
Tangible Book Value	10.00	11.96	16.00	17.56	15.49	13.34	11.56	10.70	9.38	9.11
Cash Flow	2.34	2.58	3.15	2.20	2.67	1.62	1.07	1.45	2.22	1.65
Earnings	-3.07	1.95	2.61	1.86	2.32	1.21	0.70	1.10	1.93	1.32
S&P Core Earnings	-1.48	2.05	2.64	1.89	1.88	0.77	0.12	0.49	1.45	NA
Dividends	0.60	0.60	0.48	0.48	0.12	Nil	Nil	Nil	Nil	Nil
Payout Ratio	NM	31%	18%	26%	5%	Nil	Nil	Nil	Nil	Nil
Prices:High	37.71	48.35	62.67	55.03	55.00	62.82	61.25	70.58	61.00	97.75
Prices:Low	15.28	14.81	46.59	38.38	37.39	35.02	31.20	25.16	28.61	25.50
P/E Ratio:High	NM	25	24	30	24	52	88	64	32	74
P/E Ratio:Low	NM	8	18	21	16	29	45	23	15	19
Income Statement Analysis (Million $)										
Revenue	1,520	2,522	2,731	2,071	2,085	1,497	1,323	1,637	2,104	1,499
Operating Income	-7.00	708	699	379	653	380	201	314	512	370
Depreciation	124	116	109	69.4	70.9	82.9	71.4	69.6	55.6	63.3
Interest Expense	55.3	10.8	Nil	Nil	Nil	Nil	0.39	Nil	Nil	Nil
Pretax Income	-603	560	680	378	627	325	181	287	513	353
Effective Tax Rate	NM	35.9%	22.1%	NM	25.0%	24.9%	24.0%	24.8%	27.2%	28.1%
Net Income	-523	359	528	380	467	244	137	216	373	254
S&P Core Earnings	-251	379	535	386	377	156	22.4	96.5	281	NA
Balance Sheet & Other Financial Data (Million $)										
Cash	1,330	1,579	1,711	2,326	2,195	1,876	1,488	1,334	697	844
Current Assets	2,399	3,036	3,253	3,543	3,203	2,192	1,806	1,619	1,897	1,552
Total Assets	3,610	4,848	4,623	4,576	3,986	3,539	2,867	2,718	2,745	2,204
Current Liabilities	564	950	1,073	1,002	932	912	651	687	984	495
Long Term Debt	745	745	Nil	Nil	Nil	Nil	Nil	Nil	Nil	Nil
Common Equity	2,184	2,982	3,550	3,568	3,045	2,628	2,216	2,030	1,760	1,709
Total Capital	2,930	3,726	3,550	3,573	3,055	2,628	2,216	2,030	1,760	1,709
Capital Expenditures	22.2	57.3	83.8	73.8	59.7	55.5	134	68.7	162	78.7
Cash Flow	-399	475	637	450	538	327	209	286	429	317
Current Ratio	4.3	3.2	3.0	3.5	3.4	2.4	2.8	2.4	1.9	3.1
% Long Term Debt of Capitalization	25.4	20.0	Nil	Nil	Nil	Nil	Nil	Nil	Nil	Nil
% Net Income of Revenue	NM	14.2	19.3	18.4	22.4	16.3	10.4	13.2	17.7	16.9
% Return on Assets	NM	7.6	11.5	8.8	12.4	7.6	4.9	7.9	15.1	13.4
% Return on Equity	NM	11.0	14.8	11.4	16.5	10.1	6.5	11.4	21.5	17.3

Data as orig reptd.; bef. results of disc opers/spec. items. Per share data adj. for stk. divs.; EPS diluted. E-Estimated. NA-Not Available. NM-Not Meaningful. NR-Not Ranked. UR-Under Review.

Office: 1 Technology Dr, Milpitas, CA 95035-7916.
Telephone: 408-875-3000.
Website: http://www.tencor.com
Chrmn: E.W. Barnholt

Pres & CEO: R.P. Wallace
EVP & CFO: M.P. Dentinger
EVP & CTO: B. Tsai
SVP & Chief Acctg Officer: V.A. Kirloskar

Investor Contact: W. Lin (408-875-3000)
Board Members: R. P. Akins, E. W. Barnholt, R. T. Bond, B. Calderoni, J. T. Dickson, S. Kaufman, K. J. Kennedy, K. M. Patel, R. P. Wallace, D. C. Wang

Founded: 1975
Domicile: Delaware
Employees: 4,900

The McGraw-Hill Companies

Kohl's Corp

STANDARD &POOR'S

S&P Recommendation **BUY** ★★★★☆	Price $54.45 (as of Nov 27, 2009)	12-Mo. Target Price $66.00	Investment Style Large-Cap Growth

GICS Sector Consumer Discretionary
Sub-Industry Department Stores

Summary This company operates about 1,059 specialty department stores in 49 states, featuring moderately priced apparel, shoes, accessories, and products for the home.

Key Stock Statistics (Source S&P, Vickers, company reports)

52-Wk Range	$60.89–28.35	S&P Oper. EPS 2010**E**	3.05	Market Capitalization(B)	$16.639	Beta	1.02
Trailing 12-Month EPS	$2.93	S&P Oper. EPS 2011**E**	3.35	Yield (%)	Nil	S&P 3-Yr. Proj. EPS CAGR(%)	9
Trailing 12-Month P/E	18.6	P/E on S&P Oper. EPS 2010**E**	17.9	Dividend Rate/Share	Nil	S&P Credit Rating	BBB+
$10K Invested 5 Yrs Ago	$11,124	Common Shares Outstg. (M)	305.6	Institutional Ownership (%)	92		

Price Performance

30-Week Mov. Avg. · · ·   10-Week Mov. Avg. – – –   **GAAP Earnings vs. Previous Year**   Volume Above Avg. ▮▮▮ STARS
12-Mo. Target Price —   Relative Strength —   ▲ Up   ▼ Down   ▶ No Change   Below Avg. ▮▮▮ ★

Options: ASE, CBOE, P, Ph

Analysis prepared by **Jason N. Asaeda** on November 12, 2009, when the stock traded at **$ 54.71**.

Highlights

► We project net sales will reach $16.98 billion in FY 10 (Jan.) and $17.82 billion in FY 11, supported by expansion. KSS recently completed opening 56 stores in FY 10, including 31 locations in California, and we expect at least 30 new stores in FY 11. We see the company continuing its efforts to inject newness into its assortments, including new brands such as Dana Buchman and LC Lauren Conran that were launched this year, to flow receipts more frequently in season, and to allocate apparel inventory according to size profiles for individual stores. Weighing these positive factors against our view of weak consumer spending, we see same-store sales down 1% in FY 10 and flat in FY 11.

► While we look for KSS to maintain a highly promotional calendar, we expect annual gross margin improvement on increased penetration of higher-margin private and exclusive brands, and lower clearance levels as a result of tight inventory controls. We also look for the company to aggressively manage its cost structure. However, we anticipate limited expense leverage on projected same-store sales.

► Assuming no share buyback activity, we see EPS of $3.05 in FY 10 and $3.35 in FY 11.

Investment Rationale/Risk

► Our buy recommendation on the shares is based on valuation. KSS remains one of the fastest-growing department store chains, with the highest operating margin within its peer group. Over the past three years, the company's focus on more exclusive, higher-quality brands and products, lifestyle merchandising, and efforts to better tailor assortments to reflect regional market preferences have supported improving sales and margins. While FY 10 should be a challenging year for KSS, we look for the company to gain market share on the strength of its value pricing strategy, ongoing efforts to inject newness into its assortments, and expansion.

► Risks to our recommendation and target price include sales shortfalls due to unforeseen shifts in fashion trends and further weakening of consumer spending levels. We also see risk of increasingly cost-conscious consumers trading down to discounters such as Wal-Mart Stores (WMT 53, strong buy).

► Our 12-month target price of $66 is based on an EV/EBITDA multiple of 8.6X, KSS's 10-year historical average, applied to our FY 11 EBITDA estimate of $2.42 billion.

Qualitative Risk Assessment

LOW	MEDIUM	HIGH

Our risk assessment reflects our view of KSS's improving sales, increasing market share in the moderate department store sector, and healthy balance sheet and cash flow, offset by uncertainty over consumer discretionary spending in light of economic conditions and debt levels.

Quantitative Evaluations

S&P Quality Ranking B+

D	C	B-	B	B+	A-	A	A+

Relative Strength Rank MODERATE

42

LOWEST = 1   HIGHEST = 99

Revenue/Earnings Data

Revenue (Million $)

	1Q	2Q	3Q	4Q	Year
2010	3,638	3,806	4,051	--	--
2009	3,624	3,725	3,804	5,235	16,389
2008	3,572	3,589	3,825	5,487	16,474
2007	3,185	3,291	3,637	5,431	15,544
2006	2,743	2,888	3,119	4,652	13,402
2005	2,380	2,498	2,744	4,079	11,701

Earnings Per Share ($)

2010	0.45	0.75	0.63	E1.22	E3.05
2009	0.49	0.77	0.52	1.10	2.88
2008	0.64	0.77	0.61	1.31	3.39
2007	0.48	0.69	0.68	1.48	3.31
2006	0.36	0.54	0.45	1.08	2.43
2005	0.32	0.45	0.41	0.94	2.12

Fiscal year ended Jan. 31. Next earnings report expected: Early February. EPS Estimates based on S&P Operating Earnings; historical GAAP earnings are as reported.

Dividend Data

No cash dividends have been paid.

Kohl's Corp

STANDARD &POOR'S

Business Summary November 12, 2009

CORPORATE OVERVIEW. Kohl's (KSS), with its "Expect Great Things" line, has positioned itself as a preferred shopping destination for busy women. Its traditional customers are married women aged 25 to 54. The company's stores feature easy-to-shop layouts and emphasize moderately priced exclusive and national brand family apparel and shoes, accessories, cosmetics, home furnishings, and housewares. KSS uses a "nine-box grid" merchandising strategy. Product assortments fall into three categories, "good," "better," and "best," differentiated by price and quality, and also reflect three distinct customer styles: the "classic" customer who wants a coordinated look without bending the rules; the "updated" customer who likes classic styles with a twist; and the more fashion-forward "contemporary" customer.

PRIMARY BUSINESS DYNAMICS. KSS is one of the fastest-growing retail chains in the U.S. From FY 04 through FY 09, the company increased its selling square footage at a compound annual growth rate (CAGR) of 13% as it expanded its store count from 542 to 1,004. KSS opened 19 stores this spring and 37 stores this fall, for a total of 56 new stores in FY 10. As we see this level of expansion unlikely to be matched by other department stores, we think the company is in a position to potentially capture market share, particularly in California. KSS also completed 51 store remodels during FY 10, compared to

36 stores in FY 09, and is targeting at least 65 store remodels in FY 11.

From a merchandising standpoint, we believe KSS fell behind competitors such as J.C. Penney and Macy's in delivering newness and better quality merchandise sought by its customers in FY 04. Since then, however, we have seen the company prove itself capable of creating a more compelling sales mix by investing in new contemporary brands such as Candie's in juniors and young girls, and by entering the beauty business. KSS also responded successfully, in our view, to dress clothing trends in FY 06 with the launch of Chaps (by Ralph Lauren) in men's career casual sportswear.

In FY 07, the company filled out its contemporary apparel offerings, and expanded its most popular brands into additional product categories (e.g., Chaps into women's and boys), creating true lifestyle brands. We think these rollouts complemented KSS's ongoing efforts to capture more share of wallet among empty nesters aged 45 to 54 and single women aged 25 to 34.

Company Financials Fiscal Year Ended Jan. 31

Per Share Data ($)	2009	2008	2007	2006	2005	2004	2003	2002	2001	2000
Tangible Book Value	21.41	21.77	18.32	16.62	13.78	11.60	9.85	7.78	6.21	4.70
Cash Flow	4.65	4.80	4.47	3.42	2.95	2.43	2.41	1.93	1.48	1.05
Earnings	2.88	3.39	3.31	2.43	2.12	1.72	1.87	1.35	1.10	0.78
S&P Core Earnings	2.89	3.39	3.31	2.43	2.04	1.62	1.78	1.38	1.04	NA
Dividends	Nil	Nil	Nil	Nil	Nil	Nil	Nil	Nil	Nil	Nil
Payout Ratio	Nil	Nil	Nil	Nil	Nil	Nil	Nil	Nil	Nil	Nil
Calendar Year	2008	2007	2006	2005	2004	2003	2002	2001	2000	1999
Prices:High	56.00	79.55	75.54	58.90	54.10	65.44	78.83	72.24	66.50	40.63
Prices:Low	24.28	44.16	42.78	43.63	39.59	42.40	44.00	41.95	33.50	28.63
P/E Ratio:High	19	23	23	24	26	38	42	54	60	52
P/E Ratio:Low	8	13	13	18	19	25	24	31	30	37

Income Statement Analysis (Million $)										
Revenue	16,389	16,474	15,544	13,402	11,701	10,282	9,120	7,489	6,152	4,557
Operating Income	2,077	2,257	2,202	1,755	1,525	1,260	1,282	1,002	779	537
Depreciation	541	452	388	339	288	237	191	152	128	83.3
Interest Expense	140	98.7	74.4	72.1	64.1	75.2	59.4	57.4	Nil	29.5
Pretax Income	1,425	1,742	1,774	1,346	1,174	950	1,034	800	605	421
Effective Tax Rate	37.9%	37.8%	37.5%	37.4%	37.8%	37.8%	37.8%	38.0%	38.5%	38.7%
Net Income	885	1,084	1,109	842	730	591	643	496	372	258
S&P Core Earnings	885	1,084	1,109	842	703	557	608	471	349	NA

Balance Sheet & Other Financial Data (Million $)										
Cash	676	664	620	127	117	113	90.1	107	124	12.6
Current Assets	3,700	3,724	3,401	4,266	3,643	3,025	3,284	2,464	1,922	1,367
Total Assets	11,334	10,560	9,041	9,153	7,979	6,698	6,316	4,930	3,855	2,915
Current Liabilities	1,815	1,771	1,919	1,746	1,456	1,122	1,508	880	723	634
Long Term Debt	2,053	2,052	1,040	1,046	1,103	1,076	1,059	1,095	803	495
Common Equity	6,739	6,102	5,603	5,957	4,967	4,191	3,512	2,791	2,203	1,686
Total Capital	9,112	8,416	6,887	7,221	6,367	5,504	4,743	4,001	3,090	2,247
Capital Expenditures	1,014	1,542	1,142	799	890	832	716	662	481	625
Cash Flow	1,426	1,536	1,496	1,181	1,019	828	835	648	500	341
Current Ratio	2.0	2.1	1.8	2.4	2.5	2.7	2.2	2.8	2.7	2.2
% Long Term Debt of Capitalization	22.5	24.4	15.7	14.5	17.3	19.5	22.3	27.4	26.0	22.0
% Net Income of Revenue	5.4	6.6	7.1	6.3	6.2	5.7	7.1	6.6	6.0	5.7
% Return on Assets	8.1	11.1	12.2	9.8	10.0	9.1	11.4	11.3	10.9	10.6
% Return on Equity	13.8	18.5	19.2	15.3	16.0	15.3	20.4	19.9	19.1	18.1

Data as orig reptd.; bef. results of disc opers/spec. items. Per share data adj. for stk. divs.; EPS diluted. E-Estimated. NA-Not Available. NM-Not Meaningful. NR-Not Ranked. UR-Under Review.

Office: N56W17000 Ridgewood Dr, Menomonee Falls, WI 53051-5660.
Telephone: 262-703-7000.
Website: http://www.kohls.com
Chrmn, Pres & CEO: K. Mansell

Investor Contact: W.S. McDonald (262-703-1893)
EVP, CFO & Chief Acctg Officer: W.S. McDonald
EVP, Secy & General Counsel: R.D. Schepp

Board Members: P. Boneparth, S. Burd, J. F. Herma, D. E. Jones, W. S. Kellogg, K. Mansell, L. Montgomery, F. V. Sica, P. M. Sommerhauser, S. A. Streeter, S. E. Watson

Founded: 1986
Domicile: Wisconsin
Employees: 126,000

The McGraw-Hill Companies

Kraft Foods Inc.

S&P Recommendation **SELL** ★★★★★	Price $26.64 (as of Nov 27, 2009)	12-Mo. Target Price $25.00	Investment Style Large-Cap Blend

GICS Sector Consumer Staples
Sub-Industry Packaged Foods & Meats

Summary Kraft Foods is one of the world's largest branded food and beverage companies.

Key Stock Statistics (Source S&P, Vickers, company reports)

52-Wk Range	**$29.84– 20.81**	S&P Oper. EPS 2009**E**	**2.00**	Market Capitalization(B)	**$39.316**	Beta	**0.64**
Trailing 12-Month EPS	**$1.70**	S&P Oper. EPS 2010**E**	**2.18**	Yield (%)	**4.35**	S&P 3-Yr. Proj. EPS CAGR(%)	**8**
Trailing 12-Month P/E	**15.7**	P/E on S&P Oper. EPS 2009**E**	**13.3**	Dividend Rate/Share	**$1.16**	S&P Credit Rating	**A-**
$10K Invested 5 Yrs Ago	**$9,044**	Common Shares Outstg. (M)	**1,475.8**	Institutional Ownership (%)	**72**		

Price Performance

30-Week Mov. Avg. ···· 10-Week Mov. Avg. – – GAAP Earnings vs. Previous Year   Volume Above Avg. STARS
12-Mo. Target Price — Relative Strength — ▲ Up ▼ Down ► No Change   Below Avg.

Options: ASE, CBOE, P, Ph

Analysis prepared by **Tom Graves, CFA** on November 09, 2009, when the stock traded at **$ 26.58**.

Highlights

▶ In November 2009, KFT said that it would offer to acquire confectionery company Cadbury plc in a stock-and-cash transaction that we value at about $17 billion. Based on a recent KFT share price, about 58% of the transaction's value would be in KFT stock, and the remainder would be in cash. Cadbury said that its board recommends shareholders reject the offer, and added that it would be communicating to provide more detail why it believes the offer falls well short of reflecting Cadbury's value.

▶ Earlier, KFT outlined some potential cost synergies related to a possible acquisition of Cadbury, and indicated that a combination of the two companies could lead to some upwardly revised long-term growth targets for KFT.

▶ In 2010, for KFT as currently constituted, we look for at least modest revenue growth, including less of a negative impact from currency exchange rate fluctuation. For the company as currently constituted, we estimate 2010 EPS at $2.18, up from the $2.00 we estimate for 2009. This is up from $1.81 from continuing operations in 2008, which excluded some special items.

Investment Rationale/Risk

▶ We believe that a multi-year KFT restructuring program, expected to produce annual savings of $1.4 billion, has positioned the company better for growth.

▶ Risks to our recommendation and target price include a better than anticipated outcome to KFT's interest in acquiring Cadbury, more favorable than expected commodity costs and currency exchange rates, and market share gains.

▶ We are wary about the price that KFT might be willing to pay to acquire Cadbury. As announced on November 9, KFT's offer would be for a price comprised of about 58% stock and 42% cash. We are concerned that KFT may increase the offer price in an effort to gain approval from Cadbury shareholders. We see Cadbury offering strategic value for KFT (e.g., geographic diversity). However, in our view, this is more than offset by acquisition price risk. Our 12-month target price of $25 for KFT is a discount P/E (excluding Cadbury) to what we expect from a group of packaged food stocks. KFT shares recently had an indicated dividend yield of about 4.3%.

Qualitative Risk Assessment

LOW	**MEDIUM**	HIGH

Our risk assessment reflects the risks that we see KFT facing from competitive conditions, and other factors such as commodity costs and currency exchange rates. This is offset by the relatively stable nature of the company's end markets, by our expectation of relatively good company cash flow, and by KFT's leading market share positions.

Quantitative Evaluations

S&P Quality Ranking   **NR**

D	C	B-	B	B+	A-	A	A+

Relative Strength Rank   **MODERATE**

43

LOWEST = 1   HIGHEST = 99

Revenue/Earnings Data

Revenue (Million $)

	1Q	2Q	3Q	4Q	Year
2009	9,396	10,162	9,803	--	--
2008	10,372	11,176	10,462	10,767	42,201
2007	8,586	9,205	9,054	10,396	37,241
2006	8,123	8,619	8,243	9,371	34,356
2005	8,059	8,334	8,057	9,663	34,113
2004	7,575	8,091	7,718	8,784	32,168

Earnings Per Share ($)

2009	0.45	0.56	0.55	E0.44	E2.00
2008	0.42	0.48	0.36	0.06	1.23
2007	0.43	0.44	0.38	0.38	1.63
2006	0.61	0.41	0.45	0.38	1.85
2005	0.41	0.45	0.40	0.46	1.72
2004	0.32	0.40	0.45	0.40	1.55

Fiscal year ended Dec. 31. Next earnings report expected: Early February. EPS Estimates based on S&P Operating Earnings; historical GAAP earnings are as reported.

Dividend Data (Dates: mm/dd Payment Date: mm/dd/yy)

Amount ($)	Date Decl.	Ex-Div. Date	Stk. of Record	Payment Date
0.290	12/11	12/23	12/26	01/13/09
0.290	03/12	03/23	03/25	04/08/09
0.290	05/20	06/26	06/30	07/14/09
0.290	09/10	09/28	09/30	10/14/09

Dividends have been paid since 2001. Source: Company reports.

Please read the Required Disclosures and Analyst Certification on the last page of this report.

Kraft Foods Inc.

STANDARD
&POOR'S

Business Summary November 09, 2009

CORPORATE OVERVIEW. Kraft Foods is one of the world's largest branded food and beverage companies. In 2008, North American business segments accounted for $24.0 billion, or approximately 57%, of total company net revenues. Kraft International had net revenues of $18.2 billion (43%).

Business segments include U.S. Beverages (7.1% of 2008 net revenues), U.S. Cheese (9.5%), U.S. Convenient Meals (10%), U.S. Grocery (8.0%), U.S. Snacks (12%), Canada and North America Foodservice (10%), European Union (27%), and Developing Markets (17%). Also, Wal-Mart Stores, Inc., and affiliates accounted for about 16% of KFT's net revenues in 2008.

We believe that Kraft has at least eight or nine brands with annual revenue of at least about $1 billion each. These include Kraft cheeses, dinners and dressings; Oscar Mayer meats; Philadelphia cream cheese; Maxwell House coffee; Nabisco cookies and crackers and its Oreo brand; Jacobs coffees; Milka chocolates; and LU biscuits.

Divestitures by KFT have included its Post cereal business in 2008; hot cereal assets and trademarks, which were sold in the first quarter of 2007; and its pet snacks brand and assets, which were sold in the third quarter of 2006.

CORPORATE STRATEGY. In November 2009, KFT said that it would offer to acquire confectionery company Cadbury plc with a stock-and-cash transaction that we value at about $17 billion. Based on a recent KFT share price, about

58% of the transaction's value would be in KFT stock, and the remainder would be in cash. Cadbury said that its board recommends shareholders reject the offer, and added that it would be communicating to provide more detail why it believes the offer falls well short of reflecting Cadbury's value.

In 2008, KFT completed a five-year restructuring program whose objectives were to leverage global scale, realign and lower cost structure, and optimize capacity. In August 2009, KFT said that as part of the program, it incurred $3.0 billion of pretax charges, reflecting asset disposals, and severance and implementation costs. KFT said it would use cash to pay for $2.0 billion of the $3.0 billion in charges. Earlier, KFT said it anticipated reaching cumulative annualized savings of $1.4 billion for the total program.

In 2009's second quarter, KFT reversed $35 million of restructuring program charges, and recorded a $17 million loss on the divestiture of a plant. In August 2009, KFT said that since the inception of the restructuring program, it had paid cash for $1.6 billion of the $3.0 billion in charges, including $80 million in the first half of 2009. At June 30, 2009, KFT had an accrual of $399 million, and had eliminated about 16,000 positions.

Company Financials Fiscal Year Ended Dec. 31

Per Share Data ($)	2008	2007	2006	2005	2004	2003	2002	2001	2000	1999
Tangible Book Value	NM	NM	NM	NM	NM	NM	NM	NM	NM	NA
Cash Flow	1.88	2.18	2.39	2.27	2.07	2.48	2.37	2.19	2.02	NA
Earnings	1.23	1.63	1.85	1.72	1.55	2.01	1.96	1.17	1.03	1.21
S&P Core Earnings	1.01	1.65	1.80	1.74	1.53	1.93	1.65	0.81	NA	NA
Dividends	1.12	1.04	0.96	0.87	0.77	0.66	0.56	0.26	NA	NA
Payout Ratio	91%	64%	52%	51%	50%	33%	29%	22%	NA	NA
Prices:High	34.97	37.20	36.67	35.65	36.06	39.40	43.95	35.57	NA	NA
Prices:Low	24.75	29.95	27.44	27.88	29.45	26.35	32.50	29.50	NA	NA
P/E Ratio:High	28	23	20	21	23	20	22	30	NA	NA
P/E Ratio:Low	20	18	15	16	19	13	17	25	NA	NA

Income Statement Analysis (Million $)

	2008	2007	2006	2005	2004	2003	2002	2001	2000	1999
Revenue	42,201	37,241	34,356	34,113	32,168	31,010	29,723	33,875	34,679	26,797
Operating Income	6,116	5,794	6,065	6,002	6,108	6,786	6,892	6,526	6,284	NA
Depreciation	986	886	898	879	879	813	716	1,642	1,722	1,030
Interest Expense	1,272	701	510	636	666	678	854	1,437	NA	NA
Pretax Income	2,577	3,730	4,016	4,116	3,946	5,346	5,267	3,447	3,214	3,040
Effective Tax Rate	28.3%	30.5%	23.7%	29.4%	32.3%	34.9%	35.5%	45.4%	44.4%	42.3%
Net Income	1,849	2,590	3,060	2,904	2,669	3,476	3,394	1,882	1,787	1,753
S&P Core Earnings	1,529	2,640	2,963	2,930	2,632	3,337	2,861	1,308	NA	NA

Balance Sheet & Other Financial Data (Million $)

	2008	2007	2006	2005	2004	2003	2002	2001	2000	1999
Cash	1,244	567	239	316	282	514	215	162	191	95.0
Current Assets	11,366	10,737	8,254	8,153	9,722	8,124	7,456	7,006	NA	NA
Total Assets	63,078	67,993	55,574	57,628	59,928	59,285	57,100	55,798	52,071	30,336
Current Liabilities	11,044	17,086	10,473	8,724	9,078	7,861	7,169	8,875	NA	NA
Long Term Debt	18,589	12,902	7,081	8,475	9,723	11,591	10,416	13,134	15,677	7,035
Common Equity	22,200	27,295	28,555	29,593	29,911	28,530	25,832	23,478	22,755	13,461
Total Capital	41,554	45,073	39,566	44,135	45,484	45,977	41,676	41,643	38,432	20,559
Capital Expenditures	1,367	1,241	1,169	1,171	1,006	1,085	1,184	1,101	1,151	860
Cash Flow	2,835	3,476	3,958	3,783	3,548	4,289	4,110	3,524	3,509	NA
Current Ratio	1.0	0.6	0.8	0.9	1.1	1.0	1.0	0.8	0.9	1.1
% Long Term Debt of Capitalization	44.7	28.6	17.9	19.2	21.4	25.2	25.0	31.5	40.8	34.2
% Net Income of Revenue	4.4	7.0	8.9	8.5	8.3	11.2	11.4	5.6	5.2	6.5
% Return on Assets	2.8	4.2	5.4	4.9	4.5	6.0	6.0	3.5	4.9	NA
% Return on Equity	7.5	9.3	10.5	9.8	9.1	12.8	13.8	10.0	14.6	NA

Data as orig reptd.; bef. results of disc opers/spec. items. Per share data adj. for stk. divs.; EPS diluted. E-Estimated. NA-Not Available. NM-Not Meaningful. NR-Not Ranked. UR-Under Review.

Office: Three Lakes Drive, Northfield, IL 60093.
Telephone: 847-646-2000.
Website: http://www.kraft.com
Chrmn & CEO: I. Rosenfeld

COO: D.A. Brearton
EVP & CFO: T.R. McLevish
SVP & Cntlr: K.H. Jones
SVP & Cntlr: J.K. Harris

Board Members: A. Banga, M. M. Hart, L. D. Juliber, M. Ketchum, R. A. Lerner, J. C. Pope, F. G. Reynolds, I. Rosenfeld, D. C. Wright, F. G. Zarb

Founded: 2000
Domicile: Virginia
Employees: 98,000

The McGraw-Hill Companies

Kroger Co. (The)

STANDARD &POOR'S

S&P Recommendation	HOLD ★★★☆☆	Price $22.87 (as of Nov 27, 2009)	12-Mo. Target Price $21.00	Investment Style Large-Cap Blend

GICS Sector Consumer Staples
Sub-Industry Food Retail

Summary This supermarket operator, with about 2,500 stores in 31 states, also operates convenience stores, jewelry stores, supermarket fuel centers, and food processing plants.

Key Stock Statistics (Source S&P, Vickers, company reports)

52-Wk Range	$27.79– 19.39	S&P Oper. EPS 2010E	1.95	Market Capitalization(B)	$14.884	Beta	0.42
Trailing 12-Month EPS	$1.95	S&P Oper. EPS 2011E	2.10	Yield (%)	1.66	S&P 3-Yr. Proj. EPS CAGR(%)	8
Trailing 12-Month P/E	11.7	P/E on S&P Oper. EPS 2010E	11.7	Dividend Rate/Share	$0.38	S&P Credit Rating	BBB
$10K Invested 5 Yrs Ago	$14,773	Common Shares Outstg. (M)	650.8	Institutional Ownership (%)	78		

Price Performance

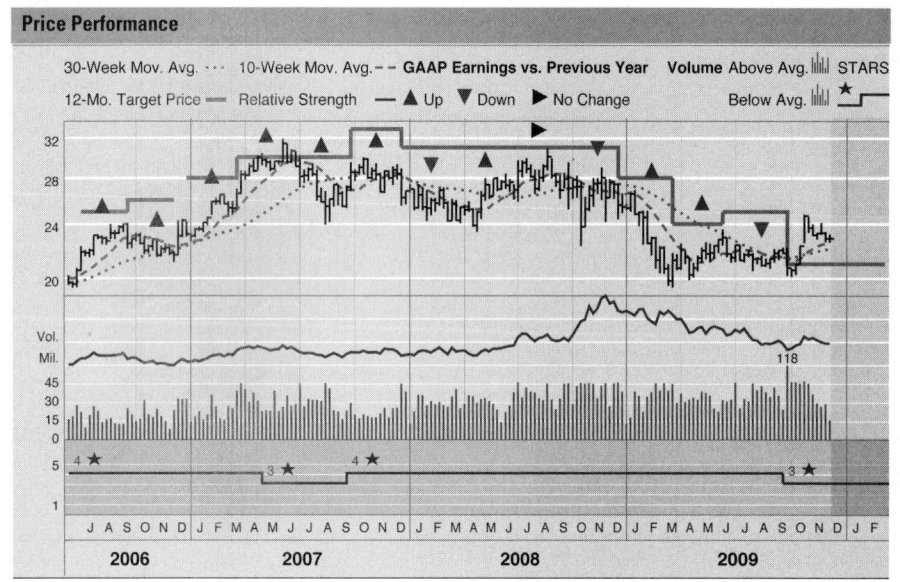

30-Week Mov. Avg. · · · 10-Week Mov. Avg. – – **GAAP Earnings vs. Previous Year** Volume Above Avg. STARS
12-Mo. Target Price — Relative Strength ▲ Up ▼ Down ▶ No Change Below Avg. ★

Options: ASE, CBOE, P

Analysis prepared by **Joseph Agnese** on September 15, 2009, when the stock traded at **$ 20.34**.

Highlights

▶ We expect sales to decrease slightly to approximately $75.9 billion in FY 10 (Jan.), from $76.0 billion in FY 09, reflecting lower retail fuel prices and about 2.0% square footage growth and 2.5% identical-store sales gains (excluding fuel). We expect sales to reflect food cost inflation of 1.0% to 2.0% and market share gains, offset by significantly lower retail gasoline prices.

▶ We believe EBIT margins will widen slightly as increased sales leverage (excluding fuel), a more stable promotional spending budget, and cost-saving opportunities that we forecast in areas such as administration, labor, shrinkage, warehousing and transportation are partially offset by the company's pursuit of a price reduction strategy and product cost inflation in the low single digits. In addition, we believe merchandising and service improvements will help the company compete against lower-priced mass merchants.

▶ After benefits from fewer shares outstanding due to an active repurchase program, we expect FY 10 EPS to increase 2.6%, to $1.95, from $1.90 in FY 09.

Investment Rationale/Risk

▶ We recently downgraded our recommendation on the shares to hold, from buy, as we believe increased industry pricing pressures and commodity price deflation will pressure margins over the next 12 months. However, we think the company will continue to gain market share due to its position as a low-priced food retailer and its strategy of boosting sales through targeted marketing, price reductions, and improved service levels.

▶ Risks to our recommendation and target price include potential weakness in the economy that would cause consumers to become more price conscious, increased price competition, and losses of market share to new competitors.

▶ Our 12-month target price of $21 is based on our P/E analysis and supported by our EV/EBITDA valuation. Reflecting our view of KR's stable earnings growth and defensive positioning in a weak economic environment, we think the shares should trade at about 9.9X our FY 11 EPS estimate of $2.10, in line with its three year historical median, leading to a projected value of $21. Our target price is supported by applying a 4.7X multiple, in line with its closest peers, to our FY 11 EBITDA estimate of $4.2 billion.

Qualitative Risk Assessment

LOW	MEDIUM	HIGH

Our risk assessment reflects our view of the company's diversification through multiple format offerings, strong market share positions, and potential opportunities from industry consolidation.

Quantitative Evaluations

S&P Quality Ranking B

D	C	B-	B	B+	A-	A	A+

Relative Strength Rank MODERATE

57

LOWEST = 1 HIGHEST = 99

Revenue/Earnings Data

Revenue (Million $)

	1Q	2Q	3Q	4Q	Year
2010	22,799	17,735	--	--	--
2009	23,107	18,053	17,580	17,260	76,000
2008	20,726	16,139	16,135	17,235	70,235
2007	19,415	15,138	14,999	16,859	66,111
2006	17,948	13,865	14,021	14,720	60,553
2005	16,905	12,980	12,854	13,695	56,434

Earnings Per Share ($)

2010	0.66	0.39	E0.35	E0.56	E1.95
2009	0.58	0.42	0.36	0.53	1.90
2008	0.47	0.42	0.37	0.48	1.69
2007	0.42	0.29	0.30	0.54	1.54
2006	0.40	0.27	0.25	0.39	1.31
2005	0.35	0.19	0.19	-0.89	-0.14

Fiscal year ended Jan. 31. Next earnings report expected: Early December. EPS Estimates based on S&P Operating Earnings; historical GAAP earnings are as reported.

Dividend Data (Dates: mm/dd Payment Date: mm/dd/yy)

Amount ($)	Date Decl.	Ex-Div. Date	Stk. of Record	Payment Date
0.090	01/23	02/11	02/13	03/01/09
0.090	03/12	05/13	05/15	06/01/09
0.090	06/25	08/12	08/14	09/01/09
0.095	09/17	11/12	11/16	12/01/09

Dividends have been paid since 2006. Source: Company reports.

Kroger Co. (The)

STANDARD
&POOR'S

Business Summary September 15, 2009

CORPORATE OVERVIEW. Kroger is one of the largest U.S. supermarket chains, with 2,481 supermarkets as of February 2009. The company's principal operating format is combination food and drug stores (combo stores). In addition to combo stores, KR also operates multi-department stores, marketplace stores, price-impact warehouses, convenience stores, fuel centers, jewelry stores, and food processing plants. Total food store square footage was approximately 147 million as of January 31, 2009.

Retail food stores are operated under three formats: combo stores, multi-department stores, and price-impact warehouse stores. Combo stores are considered neighborhood stores, and include many specialty departments, such as whole health sections, pharmacies, general merchandise, pet centers, and perishables, such as fresh seafood and organic produce. Combo banners include Kroger, Ralphs, King Soopers, City Market, Dillons, Smith's, Fry's, QFC, Hilander, Owen's, Jay C, Baker's, Pay Less and Gerbes.

Multi-department stores offer one-stop shopping, are significantly larger in size than combo stores, and sell a wider selection of general merchandise items, including apparel, home fashion and furnishings, electronics, automotive, toys, and fine jewelry. Multi-department formats include Fred Meyer, Fry's Marketplace, Smith's Marketplace and Kroger Marketplace. Many combination and multi-department stores include a fuel center.

Price-impact warehouse stores offer everyday low prices, plus promotions for a wide selection of grocery and health and beauty care items. Price-impact warehouse stores include Food 4 Less and Foods Co.

Company Financials Fiscal Year Ended Jan. 31

Per Share Data ($)	2009	2008	2007	2006	2005	2004	2003	2002	2001	2000
Tangible Book Value	4.48	7.07	5.61	3.04	1.85	1.18	0.36	NM	NM	NM
Cash Flow	4.08	3.64	3.30	3.04	1.57	2.02	2.93	2.44	2.11	1.86
Earnings	1.90	1.69	1.54	1.31	-0.14	0.42	1.56	1.26	1.04	0.74
S&P Core Earnings	1.74	1.70	1.59	1.27	0.99	0.98	1.40	1.12	0.96	NA
Dividends	0.29	0.20	Nil	Nil	Nil	Nil	Nil	Nil	Nil	Nil
Payout Ratio	15%	12%	Nil	Nil	Nil	Nil	Nil	Nil	Nil	Nil
Calendar Year	2008	2007	2006	2005	2004	2003	2002	2001	2000	1999
Prices:High	30.99	31.94	24.48	20.88	19.67	19.70	23.81	27.66	27.94	34.91
Prices:Low	22.30	22.94	18.05	15.15	14.65	12.05	11.00	19.60	14.06	14.88
P/E Ratio:High	16	19	16	16	NM	47	15	22	27	47
P/E Ratio:Low	12	14	12	12	NM	29	7	16	14	20

Income Statement Analysis (Million $)

	2009	2008	2007	2006	2005	2004	2003	2002	2001	2000
Revenue	76,000	70,235	66,111	60,553	56,434	53,791	51,760	50,098	49,000	45,352
Operating Income	3,918	3,657	3,508	3,300	3,003	3,147	3,676	3,567	3,397	3,125
Depreciation	1,442	1,356	1,272	1,265	1,256	1,209	1,087	973	907	961
Interest Expense	485	474	488	510	557	604	600	648	675	652
Pretax Income	1,966	1,827	1,748	1,525	290	770	1,973	1,711	1,508	1,129
Effective Tax Rate	36.5%	35.4%	36.2%	37.2%	NM	59.1%	37.5%	39.0%	41.6%	43.5%
Net Income	1,249	1,181	1,115	958	-100	315	1,233	1,043	880	638
S&P Core Earnings	1,140	1,193	1,155	928	720	745	1,105	914	816	NA

Balance Sheet & Other Financial Data (Million $)

	2009	2008	2007	2006	2005	2004	2003	2002	2001	2000
Cash	263	918	803	210	144	159	171	161	161	281
Current Assets	7,206	7,114	6,755	6,466	6,406	5,619	5,566	5,512	5,416	5,531
Total Assets	23,211	22,299	21,215	20,482	20,491	20,184	20,102	19,087	18,190	17,966
Current Liabilities	7,629	8,689	7,581	6,715	6,316	5,586	5,608	5,485	5,591	5,728
Long Term Debt	7,505	6,529	6,154	6,678	7,900	8,116	8,222	8,412	8,210	8,045
Common Equity	5,176	4,914	4,923	4,390	3,540	4,011	3,850	3,502	3,089	2,683
Total Capital	12,913	11,810	11,799	11,911	12,379	13,117	12,072	11,914	11,299	10,728
Capital Expenditures	2,149	2,126	1,683	1,306	1,634	2,000	1,891	2,139	1,623	1,701
Cash Flow	2,691	2,537	2,387	2,223	1,156	1,524	2,320	2,016	1,787	1,599
Current Ratio	1.0	0.8	0.9	1.0	1.0	1.0	1.0	1.0	1.0	1.0
% Long Term Debt of Capitalization	56.3	55.3	55.6	56.1	63.8	61.9	68.1	70.6	72.7	75.0
% Net Income of Revenue	1.6	1.7	1.7	1.6	NM	0.6	2.4	2.1	1.8	1.4
% Return on Assets	5.5	5.4	5.4	4.7	NM	1.6	6.3	5.6	4.9	3.7
% Return on Equity	24.8	24.0	24.0	23.9	NM	8.0	33.5	31.6	30.5	27.7

Data as orig reptd.; bef. results of disc opers/spec. items. Per share data adj. for stk. divs.; EPS diluted. E-Estimated. NA-Not Available. NM-Not Meaningful. NR-Not Ranked. UR-Under Review.

Office: 1014 Vine St, Cincinnati, OH 45202.
Telephone: 513-762-4000.
Email: investors@kroger.com
Website: http://www.kroger.com

Chrmn & CEO: D.B. Dillon
Pres, Vice Chrmn & COO: W.R. McMullen
EVP, Secy & General Counsel: P.W. Heldman
SVP & CFO: J.M. Schlotman

SVP & CIO: C.T. Hjelm
Investor Contact: C. Fike (513-762-4969)
Board Members: R. V. Anderson, R. D. Beyer, D. B. Dillon, S. J. Kropf, J. T. Lamacchia, D. B. Lewis, D. W. McGeorge, W. R. McMullen, J. P. Montoya, C. R. Moore, S. M. Phillips, S. R. Rogel, J. A. Runde, R. L. Sargent, B. Shackouls

Founded: 1883
Domicile: Ohio
Employees: 326,000

Laboratory Corporation of America Holdings

STANDARD &POOR'S

S&P Recommendation BUY ★★★★☆	Price $73.29 (as of Nov 27, 2009)	12-Mo. Target Price $84.00	Investment Style Large-Cap Growth

GICS Sector Health Care
Sub-Industry Health Care Services

Summary This clinical laboratory organization offers a broad range of clinical tests through a national network of laboratories.

Key Stock Statistics (Source S&P, Vickers, company reports)

52-Wk Range	$74.80–53.25	S&P Oper. EPS 2009E	4.89	Market Capitalization(B)	$7.783	Beta	0.51
Trailing 12-Month EPS	$4.77	S&P Oper. EPS 2010E	5.40	Yield (%)	Nil	S&P 3-Yr. Proj. EPS CAGR(%)	12
Trailing 12-Month P/E	15.4	P/E on S&P Oper. EPS 2009E	15.0	Dividend Rate/Share	Nil	S&P Credit Rating	BBB+
$10K Invested 5 Yrs Ago	$15,304	Common Shares Outstg. (M)	106.2	Institutional Ownership (%)	94		

Price Performance

30-Week Mov. Avg. · · · 10-Week Mov. Avg. – – GAAP Earnings vs. Previous Year Volume Above Avg. STARS
12-Mo. Target Price — Relative Strength ▲ Up ▼ Down ► No Change Below Avg. ★

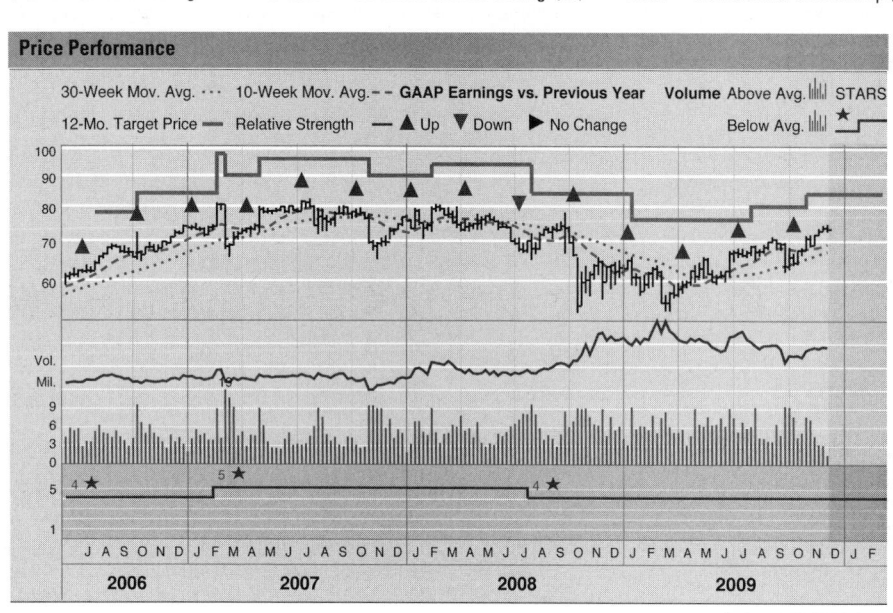

Options: ASE, CBOE, P, Ph

Analysis prepared by **Jeffrey Loo, CFA** on October 27, 2009, when the stock traded at **$ 70.60**.

Highlights

► We expect 2009 and 2010 sales to rise 4% and 5%, respectively, to $4.68 billion and $4.92 billion, on solid growth in esoteric testing, partially offset by a significant decline in drug of abuse testing due to higher unemployment amid the challenging economic environment. We think lower drug testing will adversely affect testing volume by 1% in 2009, but believe the rate of decline is moderating; we also note that it is a low-margin business. We expect 2009 gross margins to improve 60 basis points (bps) and operating margins to rebound 100 bps following last year's 230 bps decline due to consolidation of its lower-margin Canadian joint venture and efforts to control costs. However, we expect bad debt will remain at around 5.3%.

► In the first three quarters 2009, LH made $16.4 million in transition payments to UnitedHealthcare. We expect transition payments to stop by the end of 2009.

► LH continues to buy back shares, with about 8.4 million repurchased since 2008. As of September 2009 LH had about $180.2 million remaining in its repurchase program. We forecast EPS of $4.89 for 2009 and $5.40 for 2010.

Investment Rationale/Risk

► Amid a challenging economic environment, higher unemployment levels and slower volume growth, we believe LH's core lab testing business is fundamentally sound. Although we see continued lower employee-related drug testing adversely affecting sales, we believe the level of decline is moderating. The shares were recently trading at 13.1X our 2010 EPS forecast, well below historical levels, and are undervalued, in our view. Given the current environment, we believe LH is well positioned to acquire smaller labs at reasonable values to supplement organic growth. We also think LH will be able to maintain industry-leading margins by cutting costs and through leverage.

► Risks to our recommendation and target price include greater-than-expected pricing pressure and a significant slowdown in doctor visits, leading to lower test volume.

► Our 12-month target price of $84 is based on our DCF analysis (assuming a weighted average cost of capital of 9.1% and a terminal growth rate of 3%) and a P/E-to-growth (PEG) ratio of 1.3X applied to our 2010 EPS estimate, in line with peers.

Qualitative Risk Assessment

LOW	MEDIUM	HIGH

Our risk assessment reflects LH's leadership position in a large, mature industry, its broad geographic service area with clients in all 50 states, and our view of its diverse and balanced payer mix.

Quantitative Evaluations

S&P Quality Ranking   B+

D	C	B-	B	B+	A-	A	A+

Relative Strength Rank   STRONG

75

LOWEST = 1   HIGHEST = 99

Revenue/Earnings Data

Revenue (Million $)

	1Q	2Q	3Q	4Q	Year
2009	1,156	1,189	1,185	--	--
2008	1,103	1,148	1,135	1,119	4,505
2007	998.7	1,043	1,021	1,006	4,068
2006	878.6	903.7	909.9	898.6	3,591
2005	799.1	853.3	852.9	822.3	3,328
2004	752.5	784.3	781.5	766.5	3,085

Earnings Per Share ($)

2009	1.22	1.24	1.21	E1.15	E4.89
2008	1.14	0.92	1.00	1.08	4.16
2007	0.98	1.05	0.92	0.98	3.93
2006	0.76	0.87	0.81	0.81	3.24
2005	0.67	0.74	0.66	0.64	2.71
2004	0.58	0.66	0.66	0.58	2.45

Fiscal year ended Dec. 31. Next earnings report expected: Mid February. EPS Estimates based on S&P Operating Earnings; historical GAAP earnings are as reported.

Dividend Data

No cash dividends have been paid.

The McGraw·Hill Companies

Laboratory Corporation of America Holdings

STANDARD &POOR'S

Business Summary October 27, 2009

CORPORATE OVERVIEW. Laboratory Corporation of America Holdings is the second largest independent U.S. clinical laboratory. Clinical laboratory tests are used by medical professionals in routine testing, patient diagnosis, and in the monitoring and treatment of disease. As of December 2007, LH had 37 primary testing facilities and more than 1,600 service sites consisting of branches, patient service centers, and STAT laboratories that have the ability to perform certain routine tests quickly and report results to the physician immediately. The company's laboratory services involve the testing of both bodily fluids and human tissues. LH offers more than 4,400 different tests, consisting of routine tests and specialty and niche testing (esoteric). The most frequently administered routine tests include blood chemistry analyses, urinalysis, blood cell counts, pap tests, HIV tests, microbiology cultures and procedures, and alcohol and other substance abuse tests. The company's esoteric tests include testing for infectious diseases, allergies, diagnostic genetics, identity, and oncology. An average of 440,000 specimens were being processed daily as of December 2008, with routine testing results generally available within 24 hours.

The company provides testing services to a broad range of health care providers, including independent physicians, hospitals, HMOs and other managed care groups, and governmental and other institutions. During 2008, no client accounted for over 4% of net sales. Most testing services are billed to a party other than the physician or other authorized person who ordered the test. Payers other than the direct patient include insurance companies, managed care organizations, Medicare and Medicaid. Client-billed accounted for 28% of revenue in 2008 (27% in 2007), and generated an average of $33.65 ($31.60 in 2007) in revenue per requisition; patients-billed 9% (9% in 2007) and $165.00 ($158.84 in 2007); managed care clients 44% (46% in 2007) and $35.80 ($35.74 in 2007); and Medicare, Medicaid and Insurance 19% (18% in 2007) and $42.40 ($40.66 in 2007). In May 2005, the company acquired Esoterix, Inc., a provider of specialty reference testing. In February 2005, LH bought US Labs, located in Irvine, CA. In March 2004, LH purchased laboratory operations in Poughkeepsie, NY, and Atlanta, GA, from MDS Diagnostic Services. In July 2007, LH acquired DSI Labs, expanding its operations in southwest Florida.

Company Financials Fiscal Year Ended Dec. 31

Per Share Data ($)	2008	2007	2006	2005	2004	2003	2002	2001	2000	1999
Tangible Book Value	NM	NM	NM	NM	1.04	0.27	2.67	0.83	0.09	NM
Cash Flow	5.75	5.26	4.80	4.24	3.33	3.18	2.47	2.03	1.74	0.19
Earnings	4.16	3.93	3.24	2.71	2.45	2.22	1.77	1.29	0.81	0.29
S&P Core Earnings	4.04	3.89	3.21	2.53	2.25	2.04	1.56	1.15	NA	NA
Dividends	Nil	Nil	Nil	Nil	Nil	Nil	Nil	Nil	Nil	Nil
Payout Ratio	Nil	Nil	Nil	Nil	Nil	Nil	Nil	Nil	Nil	Nil
Prices:High	80.77	82.32	74.30	55.00	50.03	37.72	52.38	45.68	45.75	9.69
Prices:Low	52.93	65.13	52.58	44.63	36.70	22.21	18.51	24.88	7.81	3.13
P/E Ratio:High	19	21	23	20	20	17	30	35	57	33
P/E Ratio:Low	13	17	16	16	15	10	10	19	10	11
Income Statement Analysis (Million $)										
Revenue	4,505	4,068	3,591	3,328	3,085	2,939	2,508	2,200	1,919	1,699
Operating Income	1,070	989	853	785	736	671	554	472	340	234
Depreciation	178	161	155	150	139	136	102	104	89.6	84.5
Interest Expense	72.0	56.6	47.8	34.4	36.1	40.9	19.2	27.0	38.5	41.6
Pretax Income	786	802	721	641	615	540	432	332	208	106
Effective Tax Rate	39.2%	40.6%	40.1%	39.7%	41.0%	40.6%	41.1%	45.0%	46.0%	38.0%
Net Income	465	477	432	386	363	321	255	183	112	65.4
S&P Core Earnings	451	472	428	368	339	295	226	162	NA	NA
Balance Sheet & Other Financial Data (Million $)										
Cash	220	166	51.5	45.4	187	123	56.4	149	48.8	40.3
Current Assets	1,033	938	887	702	740	658	597	624	512	500
Total Assets	4,670	4,368	4,001	3,876	3,601	3,415	2,612	1,930	1,667	1,590
Current Liabilities	547	968	931	888	301	758	229	201	312	246
Long Term Debt	1,601	1,078	603	604	892	361	522	509	354	483
Common Equity	1,688	1,725	1,977	1,886	1,999	1,896	1,612	1,085	877	176
Total Capital	3,460	3,310	2,989	2,899	3,213	2,530	2,133	1,594	1,231	1,217
Capital Expenditures	157	143	116	93.6	95.0	83.6	74.3	88.1	55.5	69.4
Cash Flow	642	638	587	536	502	457	356	287	167	99.5
Current Ratio	1.9	1.0	1.0	0.8	2.5	0.9	2.6	3.1	1.6	2.0
% Long Term Debt of Capitalization	46.2	32.6	20.2	20.9	27.8	14.3	24.4	31.9	28.7	39.7
% Net Income of Revenue	10.3	11.7	12.0	11.6	11.8	10.9	10.2	8.3	5.8	3.9
% Return on Assets	10.3	11.4	11.0	10.3	10.3	10.7	11.2	10.2	6.9	4.0
% Return on Equity	27.2	25.8	22.3	19.9	18.6	18.3	18.9	18.6	14.8	9.1

Data as orig reptd.; bef. results of disc opers/spec. items. Per share data adj. for stk. divs.; EPS diluted. E-Estimated. NA-Not Available. NM-Not Meaningful. NR-Not Ranked. UR-Under Review.

Office: 358 South Main Street, Burlington, NC 27215.
Telephone: 336-229-1127.
Website: http://www.labcorp.com
Chrmn, Pres & CEO: D.P. King

COO & EVP: J.T. Boyle, Jr.
EVP, CFO, Chief Acctg Officer & Treas: W.B. Hayes
SVP, Secy & General Counsel: F.S. Eberts, III
SVP & CIO: L.L. Fonseca

Investor Contact: S. Fleming (336-436-4879)
Board Members: K. B. Anderson, J. Belingard, D. P. King, W. E. Lane, T. P. MacMahon, R. E. Mittelstaedt, Jr., A. H. Rubenstein, M. K. Weikel, R. S. Williams

Founded: 1971
Domicile: Delaware
Employees: 28,000

STANDARD &POOR'S

Estee Lauder Companies Inc. (The)

S&P Recommendation	HOLD ★★★☆☆	Price $46.99 (as of Nov 27, 2009)	12-Mo. Target Price $48.00	Investment Style Large-Cap Growth

GICS Sector Consumer Staples
Sub-Industry Personal Products

Summary This company is one of the world's leading manufacturers and marketers of skin care, makeup and fragrance products.

Key Stock Statistics (Source S&P, Vickers, company reports)

52-Wk Range	$49.23– 19.81	S&P Oper. EPS 2010E	2.14	Market Capitalization(B)	$5.576	Beta	1.16
Trailing 12-Month EPS	$1.56	S&P Oper. EPS 2011E	2.46	Yield (%)	1.17	S&P 3-Yr. Proj. EPS CAGR(%)	10
Trailing 12-Month P/E	30.1	P/E on S&P Oper. EPS 2010E	22.0	Dividend Rate/Share	$0.55	S&P Credit Rating	A
$10K Invested 5 Yrs Ago	$11,424	Common Shares Outstg. (M)	196.7	Institutional Ownership (%)	94		

Price Performance

30-Week Mov. Avg. ···· 10-Week Mov. Avg. ‒ ‒ **GAAP Earnings vs. Previous Year** Volume Above Avg. STARS
12-Mo. Target Price — Relative Strength ▲ Up ▼ Down ► No Change Below Avg.

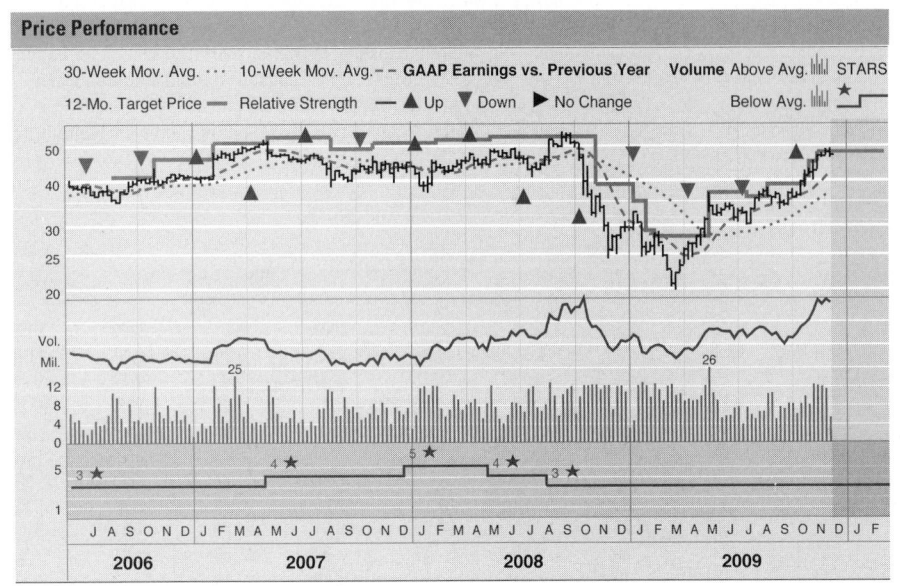

Options: ASE, CBOE, Ph

Analysis prepared by **Loran Braverman, CFA** on November 02, 2009, when the stock traded at **$ 42.50**.

Highlights

► In February 2009, EL outlined a four-year strategy that builds on its strengths as a brand builder and innovator and more sharply focuses on its execution capabilities and lowering its cost bases. Elements of the plan include expanding market share; increasing non-U.S. sales; improving operating margins; cutting costs; and writing off restructuring and other one-time costs. In September 2009, EL announced the closing of global wholesale distribution of its Prescriptives Brand by January 31, 2010.

► In FY 09 (Jun.), sales fell 7%, including a -5% impact from foreign currency. We forecast a positive trend in year-to-year quarterly sales comparisons in FY 10, with improvement in both underlying sales and foreign exchange impact, for an overall gain of 3.5%. For FY 10, we think the benefits from the restructuring and right-sizing efforts will allow for substantial recovery from FY 09's 330 basis point decline in the segmental operating margin, despite our modest sales growth forecast.

► Our FY 10 operating EPS estimate is $2.14, versus FY 09's $1.42, excluding restructuring charges. Our FY 11 estimate is $2.46.

Investment Rationale/Risk

► Our hold recommendation reflects our view that EL's long-term growth prospects are adequately reflected in the stock price. We are concerned about a prolonged consumer spending slowdown in some major Western Europe markets, Japan and the U.S. Also, EL has historically had much more quarterly earnings volatility than many of the companies in our universe.

► Risks to our recommendation and target price include a prolonged decline in the economies in EL's major country markets, slow consumer acceptance of new products, and unfavorable foreign exchange translation. We are concerned about EL's corporate governance practices given the majority voting power of insiders.

► Our 12-month target price of $48 is based on our DCF model and our historical and peer analyses. Our DCF model assumes a 9.3% weighted average cost of capital and a 3% terminal growth rate, implying a value of $53. Our historical analysis suggests a value of $52 based on a multiple in line with the 10-year average, applied to our calendar 2010 EPS estimate of $2.07. Our peer analysis uses a P/E of 19.4X, a premium to the peer average, and values the stock at $40.

Qualitative Risk Assessment

LOW	MEDIUM	HIGH

Our risk assessment reflects our view of EL's market share advantage, leading brands, scale leverage, and strong balance sheet. This is partly offset by its exposure to short-term factors such as changes in the retail industry, geopolitical events, and consumer spending.

Quantitative Evaluations

S&P Quality Ranking B+

D	C	B-	B	B+	A-	A	A+

Relative Strength Rank STRONG

91

LOWEST = 1   HIGHEST = 99

Revenue/Earnings Data

Revenue (Million $)

	1Q	2Q	3Q	4Q	Year
2010	1,833	--	--	--	--
2009	1,904	2,041	1,697	1,683	7,324
2008	1,710	2,309	1,880	2,012	7,911
2007	1,594	1,991	1,691	1,762	7,038
2006	1,497	1,784	1,578	1,605	6,464
2005	1,504	1,750	1,538	1,544	6,336

Earnings Per Share ($)

	1Q	2Q	3Q	4Q	Year
2010	0.71	E0.84	E0.23	E0.22	E2.14
2009	0.26	0.80	0.14	-0.09	1.10
2008	0.20	1.14	0.46	0.61	2.40
2007	0.27	0.99	0.45	0.45	2.16
2006	0.28	0.70	0.28	0.23	1.49
2005	0.41	0.60	0.46	0.30	1.78

Fiscal year ended Jun. 30. Next earnings report expected: Early February. EPS Estimates based on S&P Operating Earnings; historical GAAP earnings are as reported.

Dividend Data (Dates: mm/dd Payment Date: mm/dd/yy)

Amount ($)	Date Decl.	Ex-Div. Date	Stk. of Record	Payment Date
0.550	11/06	11/26	12/01	12/17/08
0.550	11/13	11/25	11/30	12/16/09

Dividends have been paid since 1996. Source: Company reports.

Please read the Required Disclosures and Analyst Certification on the last page of this report.

The McGraw-Hill Companies

Estee Lauder Companies Inc. (The)

STANDARD
&POOR'S

Business Summary November 02, 2009

CORPORATE OVERVIEW. The Estee Lauder Companies was founded in 1946 by Estee and Joseph Lauder. EL has grown into one of the world's largest manufacturers and marketers of skin care, makeup and fragrance products, sold in more than 140 countries and territories worldwide. EL has historically been a dominant player in the high-end fragrance and cosmetic categories, with brand names such as Estee Lauder, Clinique, Aramis, Prescriptives, Origins, M.A.C, Bobbi Brown, La Mer, Aveda, Stila, Jo Malone, and Bumble and Bumble. EL is also the global licensee for fragrances and cosmetics sold under the Tommy Hilfiger, Donna Karan, Michael Kors and Sean Jean brands. Each brand is distinctly positioned within the cosmetics market, according to the company.

EL reports sales and operating income by three regions. The Americas accounted for 47% of sales and 23% of profits in FY 09 (Jun.), Europe, the Middle East and Africa 35% of sales and 45% of profits, and Asia/Pacific 18% and 32%, respectively.

The skin care division (39% of FY 09 net sales) addresses various skin care needs of women and men. Products include moisturizers, creams, lotions, cleansers, sun screens and self-tanning products. The makeup division (39%) manufactures, markets and sells a full array of makeup products, including lipsticks, mascaras, foundations, eye shadows, nail polishes and powders.

The fragrance division (16%) offers a variety of fragrance products, including eau de parfum sprays and colognes, as well as lotions, powders, creams and soaps that are based on a particular fragrance. The products of the hair care division (5%) are offered mainly in salons and in freestanding retail stores and include styling products, shampoos, conditioners and finishing sprays. Other is less than 1%.

As is customary in the cosmetics industry, EL accepts returns of its products from retailers under certain conditions. In recognition of this practice and in according with generally accepted accounting principals, EL reports sales on a net basis, which is computed by deducting the amount of actual returns received and an amount established for anticipated returns from gross sales. As a percentage of gross sales, returns were 4.4% in FY 09 and in FY 08, 4.2% in FY 07 and 5.0% in FY 06.

In FY 09, Macy's, Inc. accounted for 11% of EL's accounts receivable and 12% of consolidated net sales.

Company Financials Fiscal Year Ended Jun. 30

Per Share Data ($)	2009	2008	2007	2006	2005	2004	2003	2002	2001	2000
Tangible Book Value	3.71	3.86	2.23	4.29	6.79	4.35	2.92	3.20	2.64	1.77
Cash Flow	2.39	3.66	3.16	2.41	2.64	2.45	2.01	1.46	1.82	1.73
Earnings	1.10	2.40	2.16	1.49	1.78	1.62	1.26	0.78	1.17	1.20
S&P Core Earnings	1.01	2.28	2.18	1.52	1.69	1.51	1.17	0.70	1.01	NA
Dividends	0.55	0.55	0.50	0.40	0.40	0.30	0.20	0.20	0.20	0.15
Payout Ratio	50%	23%	23%	27%	22%	19%	16%	26%	17%	12%
Prices:High	49.23	54.75	52.31	43.60	47.50	49.34	40.20	38.80	44.35	55.88
Prices:Low	19.81	24.24	38.41	32.79	29.98	37.55	25.73	25.20	29.25	33.75
P/E Ratio:High	45	23	24	29	27	30	32	50	38	47
P/E Ratio:Low	18	10	18	22	17	23	20	32	25	28

Income Statement Analysis (Million $)	2009	2008	2007	2006	2005	2004	2003	2002	2001	2000
Revenue	7,324	7,911	7,038	6,464	6,336	5,790	5,118	4,744	4,608	4,367
Operating Income	812	1,059	958	910	917	836	712	614	706	645
Depreciation	254	248	207	198	197	192	175	162	156	129
Interest Expense	75.7	66.8	38.9	23.8	13.9	27.1	8.10	9.80	12.3	17.1
Pretax Income	343	744	711	596	707	617	474	332	483	499
Effective Tax Rate	33.8%	34.9%	35.9%	43.6%	41.2%	37.7%	33.9%	34.5%	36.0%	37.0%
Net Income	218	474	449	325	406	375	320	213	307	314
S&P Core Earnings	200	450	453	332	390	351	274	171	245	NA

Balance Sheet & Other Financial Data (Million $)	2009	2008	2007	2006	2005	2004	2003	2002	2001	2000
Cash	864	402	254	369	553	612	364	547	347	320
Current Assets	2,913	2,787	2,239	2,177	2,303	2,199	1,845	1,928	1,739	1,619
Total Assets	5,177	5,011	4,126	3,784	3,886	3,708	3,350	3,417	3,219	3,043
Current Liabilities	1,459	1,699	1,501	1,438	1,498	1,322	1,054	960	857	902
Long Term Debt	1,388	1,078	1,028	432	451	462	284	404	411	418
Common Equity	1,640	1,653	1,199	1,622	1,693	1,733	1,424	1,462	1,352	1,160
Total Capital	3,052	2,758	2,248	2,079	2,160	2,211	2,080	2,226	2,123	1,939
Capital Expenditures	280	358	312	261	230	207	163	203	192	181
Cash Flow	472	722	656	523	603	567	471	351	440	420
Current Ratio	2.0	1.6	1.5	1.5	1.5	1.7	1.8	2.0	2.0	1.8
% Long Term Debt of Capitalization	45.5	39.1	45.7	20.8	20.9	20.9	13.6	18.1	19.4	21.6
% Net Income of Revenue	3.0	6.0	6.4	5.0	6.4	6.5	6.2	4.5	6.7	7.2
% Return on Assets	4.3	10.4	11.3	8.5	10.7	10.6	9.5	6.4	9.8	10.8
% Return on Equity	13.3	33.2	31.8	19.6	23.7	23.8	20.5	13.4	22.6	27.9

Data as orig reptd.; bef. results of disc opers/spec. items. Per share data adj. for stk. divs.; EPS diluted. E-Estimated. NA-Not Available. NM-Not Meaningful. NR-Not Ranked. UR-Under Review.

Office: 767 5th Avenue, New York, NY 10153-0023.
Telephone: 212-572-4200.
Email: irdept@estee.com
Website: http://www.elcompanies.com

Chrmn: W.P. Lauder
Pres & CEO: F. Freda
EVP, CFO & Chief Acctg Officer: R.W. Kunes
EVP & General Counsel: S.E. Moss

SVP & Secy: S.G. Smul
Investor Contact: D. D'Andrea (212-572-4384)
Board Members: C. Barshefsky, R. M. Bravo, F. Freda, P. J. Fribourg, M. L. Hobson, I. O. Hockaday, Jr., A. Lauder, J. Lauder, L. A. Lauder, W. P. Lauder, R. D. Parsons, B. S. Sternlicht, L. F. de Rothschild

Founded: 1946
Domicile: Delaware
Employees: 31,300

Leggett & Platt Inc

STANDARD &POOR'S

S&P Recommendation	HOLD ★★★☆☆	Price $19.57 (as of Nov 27, 2009)	12-Mo. Target Price $22.00	Investment Style Large-Cap Blend

GICS Sector Consumer Discretionary
Sub-Industry Home Furnishings

Summary This company makes a broad line of bedding and furniture components and other home, office and commercial furnishings, as well as diversified products for non-furnishings markets.

Key Stock Statistics (Source S&P, Vickers, company reports)

52-Wk Range	$21.44– 10.03	S&P Oper. EPS 2009E	0.80	Market Capitalization(B)	$2.977	Beta	1.10
Trailing 12-Month EPS	$0.36	S&P Oper. EPS 2010E	1.20	Yield (%)	5.31	S&P 3-Yr. Proj. EPS CAGR(%)	12
Trailing 12-Month P/E	54.4	P/E on S&P Oper. EPS 2009E	24.5	Dividend Rate/Share	$1.04	S&P Credit Rating	A-
$10K Invested 5 Yrs Ago	$8,140	Common Shares Outstg. (M)	152.1	Institutional Ownership (%)	77		

Price Performance

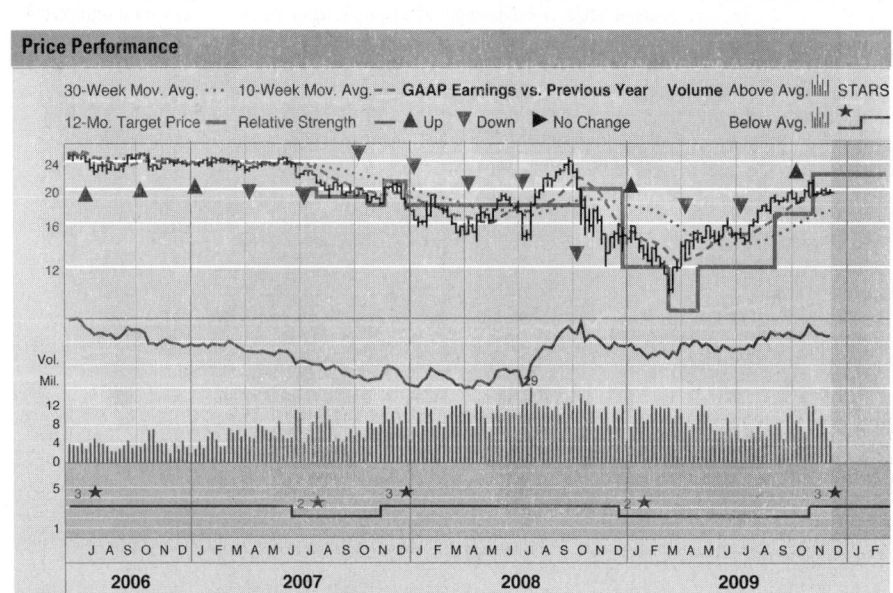

- 30-Week Mov. Avg. · · · 10-Week Mov. Avg. - - GAAP Earnings vs. Previous Year   Volume Above Avg. STARS
- 12-Mo. Target Price — Relative Strength ▲ Up ▼ Down ► No Change   Below Avg.

Options: ASE, Ph

Analysis prepared by **Kenneth M. Leon, CPA** on October 23, 2009, when the stock traded at **$ 19.41**.

Highlights

► With a slower recovery expected in some of LEG's addressable markets and following an estimated revenue decline of 26% in 2009, we forecast that revenues will rebound 8.3% in 2010 and 10% in 2011. All of LEG's markets remained weak during the third quarter, particularly the office furniture and residential furnishings markets, but we anticipate a recovery in the year ahead.

► Despite lower shipment volumes, LEG has been able to reduce total costs to realize wider margins. With stable or lower raw material costs (such as steel), we project gross margins of 22% to 23% in both 2010 and 2011, compared to an estimated 20.8% in 2009, and 17% in 2008. As a percentage of total sales, we model SG&A expenses at 11% for 2009 and the next two years, as the company tries to stimulate new sales, compared to 10.4% in 2008.

► With LEG eliminating underperforming operations, we estimate operating margins will widen to 9.2% in 2009 and 11% in 2010, from 6.6% in 2008. Assuming one to two million shares of net repurchases, our EPS estimates are $0.80 for 2009, $1.20 for 2010 and $1.40 for 2011.

Investment Rationale/Risk

► We believe LEG's customer markets will stabilize and recover in 2010, even though the general economy may recover faster. We see some of LEG's business segments beginning to move to double-digit sales growth by late 2010 or 2011. Despite near-term headwinds, the company expects to generate more than $500 million of operating cash in 2009.

► Risks to our recommendation and target price include a prolonged recession and weak market conditions leading to further sales declines in home furnishings and commercial fixtures, unexpected increases in raw material costs, fuel and energy, and less focus on cost controls that lead to narrower margins than we forecast.

► Applying a forward P/E multiple of 18.3X to our 2010 EPS estimate of $1.20, slightly above peers to reflect the company's leading market share position, we arrive at our 12-month target price of $22. Our target multiple is at the upper end of LEG's five-year historical range, reflecting the company's high cyclical profile.

Qualitative Risk Assessment

LOW	MEDIUM	HIGH

Our risk assessment takes into account our view of LEG's long history of profitability and strong free cash flow, offset by the cyclicality of the industry. We believe the company markets its products to some lagging industries relative to the general economy, which may lead to a slower sales recovery.

Quantitative Evaluations

S&P Quality Ranking B

D	C	B-	B	B+	A-	A	A+

Relative Strength Rank MODERATE

64

LOWEST = 1   HIGHEST = 99

Revenue/Earnings Data

Revenue (Million $)

	1Q	2Q	3Q	4Q	Year
2009	718.1	757.4	809.9	--	--
2008	998.3	1,063	1,132	882.5	4,076
2007	1,064	1,316	1,325	1,054	4,306
2006	1,378	1,403	1,415	1,311	5,505
2005	1,301	1,310	1,349	1,340	5,299
2004	1,187	1,278	1,338	1,282	5,086

Earnings Per Share ($)

	1Q	2Q	3Q	4Q	Year
2009	0.06	0.12	0.34	E0.28	E0.80
2008	0.23	0.25	0.29	-0.05	0.73
2007	0.31	0.30	0.36	-0.71	0.28
2006	0.33	0.45	0.45	0.38	1.61
2005	0.37	0.41	0.28	0.24	1.30
2004	0.32	0.39	0.41	0.33	1.45

Fiscal year ended Dec. 31. Next earnings report expected: Early February. EPS Estimates based on S&P Operating Earnings; historical GAAP earnings are as reported.

Dividend Data (Dates: mm/dd Payment Date: mm/dd/yy)

Amount ($)	Date Decl.	Ex-Div. Date	Stk. of Record	Payment Date
0.250	02/19	03/11	03/13	04/15/09
0.250	05/07	06/11	06/15	07/15/09
0.260	08/06	09/11	09/15	10/15/09
0.260	11/05	12/11	12/15	01/15/10

Dividends have been paid since 1939. Source: Company reports.

Please read the Required Disclosures and Analyst Certification on the last page of this report.

The McGraw-Hill Companies

Leggett & Platt Inc

Business Summary October 23, 2009

CORPORATE OVERVIEW. Leggett & Platt, founded in 1883, is a diversified manufacturer that conceives, designs and produces a wide range of engineered components and products that can be found in most homes, offices, retail stores and automobiles.

LEG's business is organized into five business segments. Residential Furnishings, which accounted for 52% of 2008 sales (53% in 2007) consists of Bedding, Home Furniture & Consumer Products, and Fabric and Carpet Underlay. The Commercial Fixturing & Components segment (17%; 19%) consists of Fixture & Display and Office Furniture Components. Industrial Materials (16%; 12%) consists of Wire and Tubing, while Specialized Products (15%; 16%) consists of Automotive, Machinery and Commercial Vehicles.

Although no customer accounted for more than 5% of total company revenues in 2008 and 2007, one customer provided 13% and 12% of Specialized Products sales in 2008 and 2007, respectively.

PRIMARY BUSINESS DYNAMICS. In the past 20 years, about two-thirds of LEG's sales growth has come from acquisitions. Over the past 10 years, the average acquisition target had revenues of $15 million to $20 million, which the company believes serves to minimize the risk of any single acquisition. In 2008, LEG generated $436 million in cash from operations, down from 2007's

$614 million; the company expects it will need about $300 million annually to fund capital expenditures and dividends. LEG expects to use much of the excess cash to repurchase shares.

In 2007, LEG acquired three businesses in the Commercial Fixturing & Components ($20 million annual sales), Industrial Materials ($50 million) and Specialized Products ($30 million) segments. In Industrial Materials, LEG bought a maker of coated wire products, including racks for dishwashers. In Specialized Products, LEG bought a company that designs and assembles docking stations that secure computer and other electronic equipment in vehicles. In Commercial Fixturing & Components, LEG bought a company located in China that makes office furniture components.

In 2006, LEG acquired five businesses representing $75 million in annualized sales, all within the Residential Furnishings segment. The largest acquisition was a maker of rubber carpet underlay, a product type that accounts for 6% of LEG's overall revenue. In addition, the company divested five businesses in 2006 with annualized sales of about $45 million.

Company Financials Fiscal Year Ended Dec. 31

Per Share Data ($)	2008	2007	2006	2005	2004	2003	2002	2001	2000	1999
Tangible Book Value	3.72	5.73	5.72	5.55	6.38	5.62	5.36	4.81	4.61	4.50
Cash Flow	1.42	1.16	2.67	2.18	2.35	1.89	1.99	1.92	2.18	2.19
Earnings	0.73	0.28	1.61	1.30	1.45	1.05	1.17	0.94	1.32	1.45
S&P Core Earnings	0.60	0.90	1.57	1.27	1.38	1.02	1.11	0.85	NA	NA
Dividends	1.00	0.78	0.84	0.63	0.58	0.54	0.50	0.48	0.42	0.35
Payout Ratio	137%	NM	52%	48%	40%	51%	43%	51%	32%	24%
Prices:High	24.60	24.73	27.04	29.61	30.68	23.69	27.40	24.45	22.56	28.31
Prices:Low	12.03	17.14	21.93	18.19	21.19	17.16	18.60	16.85	14.19	18.63
P/E Ratio:High	34	88	17	23	21	23	23	26	17	20
P/E Ratio:Low	16	61	14	14	15	16	16	18	11	13

Income Statement Analysis (Million $)										
Revenue	4,076	4,306	5,505	5,299	5,086	4,388	4,272	4,114	4,276	3,779
Operating Income	371	492	666	605	622	520	582	558	660	650
Depreciation	116	157	175	171	177	167	165	197	173	149
Interest Expense	48.4	58.6	56.2	46.7	45.9	46.9	42.1	58.8	66.3	43.0
Pretax Income	188	128	435	356	423	315	364	297	419	463
Effective Tax Rate	34.6%	60.3%	30.9%	29.4%	32.5%	34.7%	35.9%	36.9%	36.9%	37.2%
Net Income	123	51.0	300	251	285	206	233	188	264	291
S&P Core Earnings	102	161	291	245	272	202	221	169	NA	NA

Balance Sheet & Other Financial Data (Million $)										
Cash	165	205	132	64.9	491	444	225	187	37.3	20.6
Current Assets	1,307	1,834	1,894	1,763	2,065	1,819	1,488	1,422	1,405	1,256
Total Assets	3,162	4,073	4,265	4,053	4,197	3,890	3,501	3,413	3,373	2,978
Current Liabilities	524	800	691	738	960	626	598	457	477	432
Long Term Debt	851	1,001	1,060	922	779	1,012	809	978	988	787
Common Equity	1,653	2,133	2,351	2,249	2,313	2,114	1,977	1,867	1,794	1,646
Total Capital	2,539	3,176	3,478	3,230	3,178	3,221	2,865	2,909	2,854	2,502
Capital Expenditures	118	149	166	164	157	137	124	128	170	159
Cash Flow	239	208	476	422	463	373	398	384	437	440
Current Ratio	2.5	2.3	2.7	2.4	2.2	2.9	2.5	3.1	2.9	2.9
% Long Term Debt of Capitalization	33.5	31.5	30.5	28.5	24.5	31.4	28.2	33.6	34.6	31.5
% Net Income of Revenue	3.0	1.2	5.5	4.7	5.6	4.7	5.5	4.6	6.2	7.7
% Return on Assets	3.4	1.2	7.2	6.1	7.1	5.6	6.7	5.5	8.3	10.5
% Return on Equity	6.5	2.3	13.1	11.0	12.9	10.1	12.1	10.3	15.4	18.8

Data as orig reptd.; bef. results of disc opers/spec. items. Per share data adj. for stk. divs.; EPS diluted. E-Estimated. NA-Not Available. NM-Not Meaningful. NR-Not Ranked. UR-Under Review.

Office: No. 1 Leggett Road, Carthage, MO 64836-9649.
Telephone: 417-358-8131.
Email: invest@leggett.com
Website: http://www.leggett.com

Chrmn: R.T. Fisher
Pres & CEO: D.S. Haffner
COO & EVP: K.G. Glassman
SVP & CFO: M.C. Flanigan

SVP, Secy & General Counsel: E.C. Jett
Investor Contact: D.M. DeSonier (417-358-8131)
Board Members: R. E. Brunner, R. Clark, R. T. Enloe, III, R. T. Fisher, K. G. Glassman, D. S. Haffner, J. W. McClanathan, J. C. Odom, M. E. Purnell, Jr., P. A. Wood

Founded: 1883
Domicile: Missouri
Employees: 20,600

Legg Mason Inc

STANDARD &POOR'S

S&P Recommendation SELL ★★☆☆☆	Price $28.10 (as of Nov 27, 2009)	12-Mo. Target Price $28.00	Investment Style Large-Cap Growth

GICS Sector Financials
Sub-Industry Asset Management & Custody Banks

Summary This diversified investment manager serves individual and institutional investors through offices around the United States.

Key Stock Statistics (Source S&P, Vickers, company reports)

52-Wk Range	$33.70– 10.35	S&P Oper. EPS 2010**E**	1.33	Market Capitalization(B)	$4.565	Beta	2.11
Trailing 12-Month EPS	$-11.88	S&P Oper. EPS 2011**E**	1.90	Yield (%)	0.43	S&P 3-Yr. Proj. EPS CAGR(%)	NM
Trailing 12-Month P/E	NM	P/E on S&P Oper. EPS 2010**E**	21.1	Dividend Rate/Share	$0.12	S&P Credit Rating	BBB+
$10K Invested 5 Yrs Ago	$4,492	Common Shares Outstg. (M)	162.4	Institutional Ownership (%)	92		

Price Performance

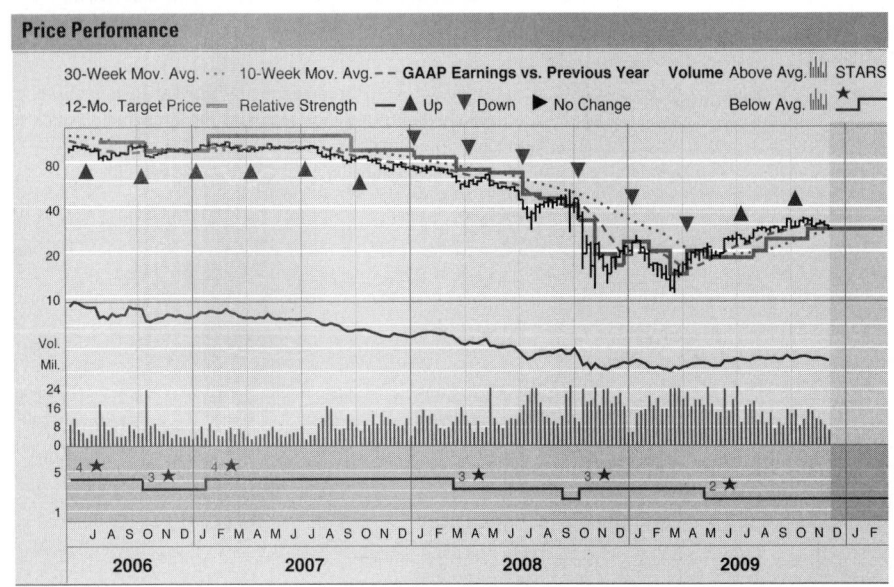

30-Week Mov. Avg. · · · 10-Week Mov. Avg. - - **GAAP Earnings vs. Previous Year** Volume Above Avg. STARS
12-Mo. Target Price — Relative Strength — ▲ Up ▼ Down ► No Change Below Avg.

Options: ASE, CBOE, P, Ph

Analysis prepared by **Matthew Albrecht** on October 27, 2009, when the stock traded at **$ 30.64**.

Highlights

► We project assets under management will grow 16% in FY 10 (Mar.) after a drop of more than 30% in FY 09. We believe LM's funds continue to underperform versus peers, and investor redemptions continue to outpace new sales. Equity markets remain below peak levels, resulting in an unfavorable asset mix favoring fixed income and money market products, reducing the average management fee rate. LM is expanding its distribution network around the globe and extending its reach with wirehouses, but we do not anticipate a return to positive flows until fund performance improves. We expect a decline in operating revenues for FY 10, based on lower average asset balances.

► The distribution expense ratio remains slightly below historical levels because of reduced fund sales, and will likely approximate 41% in FY 10. The elimination of structured investment vehicle (SIV) investments has helped eliminate costs related to their support, and headcount reductions and other cost controls will help the pretax margin expand, in our view.

► We forecast EPS of $1.33 in FY 10 and $1.90 in FY 11.

Investment Rationale/Risk

► We think some of Legg Mason's flagship funds, hurt by a number of high profile investments gone sour, have seen improved relative performance since equity markets bottomed in March 2009. Still, longer term track records compare unfavorably to peers and benchmarks, and outflows from products continue. We believe, however, that the sale of SIV exposures has improved the outlook for LM's balance sheet and eliminated a significant overhang weighing on the stock. Nevertheless, we think that the shares deserve a discounted valuation relative to peers due to consistent net outflows and poor relative performance, and our recommendation is sell.

► Risks to our recommendation and target price include stock market appreciation, improved relative investment performance, and a return to net inflows.

► The shares recently traded at 23.2X our FY 10 EPS estimate, a premium to their historical multiples. Our 12-month target price of $28 is derived by applying a P/E multiple of 18.1X to our forward 12-month earnings estimate of $1.55, a discount to forward peer multiples, but in line with LM's historical multiple.

Qualitative Risk Assessment

LOW	MEDIUM	**HIGH**

Our risk assessment reflects our view of the company's strong market share, offset by its poor recent relative investment performance, weakening balance sheet, and industry cyclicality.

Quantitative Evaluations

S&P Quality Ranking   B+

D	C	B-	B	**B+**	A-	A	A+

Relative Strength Rank   WEAK

27

LOWEST = 1   HIGHEST = 99

Revenue/Earnings Data

Revenue (Million $)

	1Q	2Q	3Q	4Q	Year
2010	613.1	659.9	--	--	--
2009	1,054	966.1	720.0	617.2	3,357
2008	1,206	1,172	1,187	1,069	4,634
2007	1,038	1,031	1,133	1,142	4,344
2006	437.7	466.4	689.0	1,052	2,645
2005	554.9	585.5	658.3	690.8	2,490

Earnings Per Share ($)

2010	0.35	0.30	E0.31	E0.37	E1.33
2009	-0.22	-0.74	-10.55	-2.29	-13.85
2008	1.32	1.23	1.07	-1.81	1.86
2007	1.08	1.00	1.21	1.19	4.48
2006	0.93	0.75	0.77	1.04	3.30
2005	0.76	0.81	0.98	0.98	3.53

Fiscal year ended Mar. 31. Next earnings report expected: Late January. EPS Estimates based on S&P Operating Earnings; historical GAAP earnings are as reported.

Dividend Data (Dates: mm/dd Payment Date: mm/dd/yy)

Amount ($)	Date Decl.	Ex-Div. Date	Stk. of Record	Payment Date
0.240	01/27	03/10	03/12	04/13/09
0.030	05/05	06/12	06/16	07/13/09
0.030	07/28	10/06	10/08	10/26/09
0.030	10/27	12/14	12/16	01/11/10

Dividends have been paid since 1983. Source: Company reports.

Please read the Required Disclosures and Analyst Certification on the last page of this report.

Legg Mason Inc

STANDARD
&POOR'S

Business Summary October 27, 2009

CORPORATE OVERVIEW. Legg Mason is a holding company which, through subsidiaries, is principally engaged in providing asset management and other related financial services to individuals, institutions, corporations, governments, and government agencies. We are pleased with the company's recent efforts to focus on its asset management business, which we think makes LM a much larger, broader, and more focused asset management company. At the end of FY 08 (Mar.), total assets under management were about $950 billion, down from about $969 billion a year earlier. Headquartered in Baltimore, MD, LM's offices are mainly in the U.S., as well as in the U.K., Canada and Singapore. At the end of March 2008, fixed income assets represented 53% of total assets under management, equity assets 29%, and liquidity assets 18%. We are pleased with the company's success in diversifying its product offerings, but would like to see more sector and industry-specific mutual funds.

We think LM has a diverse collection of asset management subsidiaries, which include Western Asset, Legg Mason Capital Management, Brandywine,

and Permal. LM's Asset Management business provides asset management services to institutional and individual clients and investment advisory services to company-sponsored investment funds. Investment products include proprietary mutual funds ranging from money market and fixed income funds to equity funds managed in a wide variety of investing styles, non-U.S. funds, and a number of unregistered, alternative investment products. LM's mutual funds group sponsors domestic and international equity, fixed income and money market mutual funds, closed-end funds, and other proprietary funds. Legg Mason Value Trust (LMVTX), managed by Bill Miller, had been the only equity mutual fund to have surpassed the S&P 500 Index for 15 straight years, with the streak ending in 2006. We do not doubt his investment strategy, however, and we still believe the fund will outperform the market frequently.

Company Financials Fiscal Year Ended Mar. 31

Per Share Data ($)	2009	2008	2007	2006	2005	2004	2003	2002	2001	2000
Tangible Book Value	NM	NM	NM	NM	11.66	6.50	3.32	1.52	8.25	7.07
Cash Flow	-12.86	2.84	5.95	3.90	3.83	2.62	1.85	1.49	1.53	1.56
Earnings	-13.85	1.86	4.48	3.30	3.53	2.64	1.85	1.49	1.53	1.55
S&P Core Earnings	-8.12	1.86	4.48	3.25	3.41	2.57	1.63	1.35	1.44	NA
Dividends	0.96	0.81	0.69	0.40	0.37	0.29	0.29	0.23	0.20	0.18
Payout Ratio	NM	44%	15%	12%	11%	11%	15%	16%	13%	12%
Calendar Year	2008	2007	2006	2005	2004	2003	2002	2001	2000	1999
Prices:High	75.33	110.17	140.00	129.00	73.70	56.77	38.10	37.99	40.17	28.58
Prices:Low	11.09	68.35	81.01	68.10	48.95	29.47	24.74	22.83	20.46	17.62
P/E Ratio:High	NM	59	31	39	21	22	21	25	26	18
P/E Ratio:Low	NM	37	18	21	14	11	13	15	13	11

Income Statement Analysis (Million $)										
Commissions	Nil	Nil	Nil	Nil	358	344	317	331	359	363
Interest Income	56.3	77.0	58.9	48.0	119	84.3	109	168	282	223
Total Revenue	3,357	4,634	4,344	2,645	2,490	2,004	1,615	1,579	1,536	1,371
Interest Expense	150	83.0	71.5	52.6	80.8	63.2	87.1	127	175	134
Pretax Income	-3,156	444	1,044	703	659	472	308	253	266	239
Effective Tax Rate	NM	39.7%	38.1%	39.2%	38.0%	38.5%	38.1%	39.6%	41.2%	40.4%
Net Income	-1,948	268	646	434	408	291	191	153	156	143
S&P Core Earnings	-1,142	268	646	421	394	283	168	138	146	NA

Balance Sheet & Other Financial Data (Million $)										
Total Assets	9,321	11,830	9,604	9,302	8,219	7,263	6,067	5,940	4,688	4,785
Cash Items	1,421	2,557	1,184	1,023	3,554	3,744	3,274	2,970	2,498	1,628
Receivables	1,204	764	852	850	1,564	1,458	1,155	1,230	1,333	1,652
Securities Owned	336	489	273	142	1,298	870	419	458	374	774
Securities Borrowed	Nil	Nil	Nil	Nil	588	488	220	280	253	688
Due Brokers & Customers	Nil	Nil	Nil	Nil	3,419	3,657	75.0	35.0	2,955	15.2
Other Liabilities	NA	1,216	1,079	1,633	1,108	764	462	410	328	334
Capitalization:Debt	2,965	1,826	1,108	1,166	811	794	787	877	219	339
Capitalization:Equity	4,454	6,621	6,678	5,850	2,293	1,560	1,248	1,075	917	752
Capitalization:Total	7,679	8,802	8,229	7,016	3,104	2,354	2,035	1,952	1,136	1,091
% Return on Revenue	NM	5.8	14.9	16.4	19.2	17.5	14.7	12.3	13.3	14.1
% Return on Assets	NM	2.5	6.8	5.0	5.3	4.4	3.2	2.9	3.3	3.5
% Return on Equity	NM	4.1	10.2	10.7	21.2	20.7	16.4	15.4	18.7	21.8

Data as orig reptd.; bef. results of disc opers/spec. items. Per share data adj. for stk. divs.; EPS diluted. E-Estimated. NA-Not Available. NM-Not Meaningful. NR-Not Ranked. UR-Under Review.

Office: 100 Light Street, Baltimore, MD 21202-1099.
Telephone: 410-539-0000.
Website: http://www.leggmason.com
Chrmn, Pres & CEO: M.R. Fetting

EVP & Chief Admin Officer: J.A. Sullivan
SVP, CFO & Treas: C.J. Daley, Jr.
Investor Contact: A. Magleby (410-454-5246)

Board Members: H. L. Adams, R. E. Angelica, D. Beresford, M. R. Fetting, R. P. Hearn, B. W. Huff, J. E. Koerner, III, C. G. Krongard, E. Lee, S. C. Nuttall, N. Peltz, W. A. Reed, M. M. Richardson, R. W. Schipke, K. L. Schmoke, N. J. St. George, R. M. Tarola

Founded: 1899
Domicile: Maryland
Employees: 3,890

Lennar Corp

STANDARD &POOR'S

S&P Recommendation	STRONG BUY ★★★★★	Price	12-Mo. Target Price	Investment Style
		$12.86 (as of Nov 27, 2009)	$19.00	Large-Cap Blend

GICS Sector Consumer Discretionary
Sub-Industry Homebuilding

Summary LEN, one of the largest, most geographically diversified U.S. home builders, concentrates on moderately priced homes.

Key Stock Statistics (Source S&P, Vickers, company reports)

52-Wk Range	$17.66–5.54	S&P Oper. EPS 2009**E**	-3.07	Market Capitalization(B)	$1.955	Beta	1.81
Trailing 12-Month EPS	$-7.68	S&P Oper. EPS 2010**E**	Nil	Yield (%)	1.24	S&P 3-Yr. Proj. EPS CAGR(%)	NM
Trailing 12-Month P/E	NM	P/E on S&P Oper. EPS 2009**E**	NM	Dividend Rate/Share	$0.16	S&P Credit Rating	BB-
$10K Invested 5 Yrs Ago	$3,017	Common Shares Outstg. (M)	183.3	Institutional Ownership (%)	89		

Price Performance

30-Week Mov. Avg. ··· 10-Week Mov. Avg. - - **GAAP Earnings vs. Previous Year**   Volume Above Avg. STARS
12-Mo. Target Price — Relative Strength — ▲ Up ▼ Down ▶ No Change   Below Avg. ★

Options: ASE, CBOE, P, Ph

Analysis prepared by **Kenneth M. Leon, CPA** on October 05, 2009, when the stock traded at **$ 13.22**.

Highlights

► Following an estimated revenue decline of 37% in FY 09 (Nov.), we project that revenues will rebound 7% in FY 10, reflecting a slow but steady U.S. housing recovery. Home deliveries and average selling prices are beginning to ease from sharp declines in early 2009. With improved demand in the third quarter of FY 09, we believe a higher backlog of contracts should lead to expanded home deliveries in FY 10.

► We believe LEN currently faces uncertain housing demand, but there are signs of improvement with increased traffic to its communities and first-time buyers taking advantage of affordable pricing combined with federal tax credit incentives. We see LEN beginning to acquire land at low prices for new communities.

► We also see the size of LEN's asset writeoffs declining or leveling off, with $296 million taken in the first nine months of FY 09, compared to $559 million in all of FY 08. We estimate a loss per share of $3.07 in FY 09, excluding any potential inventory writedowns, and breakeven in FY 10.

Investment Rationale/Risk

► After $4.4 billion of asset impairments since the beginning of 2006, we believe writeoffs will continue, albeit at a lower level, in FY 09. We think LEN's joint venture with Morgan Stanley (formed in December 2007), whereby that firm paid $525 million to LEN for an 80% equity stake in acquired land, was beneficial to the company. As of August 31, 2009, LEN had $1.34 billion in cash to support its working capital and debt obligations.

► Risks to our recommendation and target price include a prolonged housing recession further impairing new home purchases, higher mortgage rates, and weak demand without the $8,000 federal tax credit for first time homebuyers that expires November 30, 2009.

► Following $3.9 billion of asset impairments in FY 07 and $559 million in FY 08, we believe the company's net tangible book value of $13.60 may still decline in FY 09 on further asset impairments. Applying a price-to-book value multiple of slightly below 1.4X, using a wider risk premium that is near that of large homebuilders, our 12-month target price is $19.

Qualitative Risk Assessment

LOW	MEDIUM	HIGH

Our risk assessment reflects that despite LEN being among the least leveraged homebuilders in our coverage universe, the company's off balance sheet operations, including a 50%-owned development joint venture and a relatively high level of land controlled through option contracts, suggest to us that more effort is required to reduce its risk exposure in these areas.

Quantitative Evaluations

S&P Quality Ranking   B

D	C	B-	**B**	B+	A-	A	A+

Relative Strength Rank   WEAK

24

LOWEST = 1   HIGHEST = 99

Revenue/Earnings Data

Revenue (Million $)

	1Q	2Q	3Q	4Q	Year
2009	593.1	891.9	720.7	--	--
2008	1,063	1,128	1,107	1,278	4,575
2007	2,792	2,876	2,342	2,177	10,187
2006	3,241	4,578	4,182	4,266	16,267
2005	2,406	2,933	3,498	5,030	13,867
2004	1,863	2,343	2,748	3,551	10,505

Earnings Per Share ($)

2009	-0.98	-0.76	-0.97	E-0.38	E-3.07
2008	-0.56	-0.76	-0.56	-5.12	-7.00
2007	0.43	-1.55	-3.25	-7.92	-12.31
2006	1.58	2.00	1.30	-1.24	3.69
2005	1.17	1.55	2.06	3.54	8.17
2004	0.84	1.22	1.36	2.29	5.70

Fiscal year ended Nov. 30. Next earnings report expected: Mid December. EPS Estimates based on S&P Operating Earnings; historical GAAP earnings are as reported.

Dividend Data (Dates: mm/dd Payment Date: mm/dd/yy)

Amount ($)	Date Decl.	Ex-Div. Date	Stk. of Record	Payment Date
0.040	01/13	01/30	02/03	02/13/09
0.040	04/15	05/01	05/05	05/20/09
0.040	06/30	07/20	07/22	08/05/09
0.040	10/06	10/21	10/23	11/13/09

Dividends have been paid since 1978. Source: Company reports.

Lennar Corp

STANDARD
&POOR'S

Business Summary October 05, 2009

CORPORATE OVERVIEW. Lennar Corp., one of the largest homebuilders in the U.S. (based on FY 08 (Nov.) U.S. home closings), constructs homes for first-time, move-up and active adult buyers, and also provides various financial services. It takes part in all phases of planning and building, and subcontracts nearly all development and construction work. LEN sells homes primarily from models it has designed and constructed. During FY 08, these homes had an average sales price of $270,000. As of August 31, 2009, the average sales price of new orders was approximately $239,000.

The financial services division provides mortgage financing, title insurance, closing services and insurance agency services for LEN homebuyers and others, and sells the loans it originates in the secondary mortgage market.

CORPORATE STRATEGY. Lennar greatly expanded its operations through the May 2000 purchase of U.S. Home Corp. (UH), and maintained an active acquisition program for several years. The company entered the North Carolina and South Carolina markets, and extended its positions in Colorado and Arizona, through the acquisition of various operations of Fortress Group in two separate transactions in late 2001 and mid-2002. It expanded its California business by acquiring Pacific Century Homes and Cambridge Homes (combined annual

deliveries of about 2,000 homes) in 2002.

In 2005, the company entered the metropolitan New York City and Boston markets by acquiring rights to develop a portfolio of properties in New Jersey facing mid-town Manhattan and waterfront properties near Boston. It also entered the Reno, NV, market through the acquisition of Barker Coleman. In addition, LEN expanded its presence in Jacksonville through the acquisition of Admiral Homes that same year.

IMPACT OF MAJOR DEVELOPMENTS. To improve its liquidity and financial condition during FY 09, the company was involved in both a debt repurchase and a new debt issuance. LEN retired $281 million of 7 5/8% senior notes due March 2009 and issued $400 million of 12.25% senior notes due 2017 in April 2009. In May 2009, LEN issued 12.8 million common shares for gross proceeds of $126.3 million, to be used for general corporate purposes.

Company Financials Fiscal Year Ended Nov. 30

Per Share Data ($)	2008	2007	2006	2005	2004	2003	2002	2001	2000	1999
Tangible Book Value	16.12	25.67	34.42	32.09	24.05	20.68	15.71	12.14	8.92	7.08
Cash Flow	-6.69	-11.95	4.03	8.60	5.98	5.11	4.32	3.45	2.23	1.69
Earnings	-7.00	-12.31	3.69	8.17	5.70	4.65	3.86	3.01	1.82	1.37
S&P Core Earnings	-7.44	-12.36	3.62	8.10	5.63	4.61	3.83	2.90	NA	NA
Dividends	0.52	0.64	0.64	0.57	0.39	0.14	0.03	0.03	0.03	0.03
Payout Ratio	NM	NM	17%	7%	7%	3%	1%	1%	1%	2%
Prices:High	22.73	56.54	66.44	68.86	57.20	50.90	31.99	24.94	19.69	13.94
Prices:Low	3.42	14.00	38.66	50.30	40.30	24.10	21.60	15.52	7.63	6.53
P/E Ratio:High	NM	NM	18	8	10	11	8	8	11	10
P/E Ratio:Low	NM	NM	10	6	7	5	6	5	4	5

Income Statement Analysis (Million $)										
Revenue	4,575	10,187	16,267	13,867	10,505	8,908	7,320	6,029	4,707	3,119
Operating Income	-353	-2,626	941	2,124	1,426	1,158	1,094	868	533	382
Depreciation	49.8	57.0	56.5	79.6	55.6	54.5	72.4	68.7	58.5	47.7
Interest Expense	148	Nil	Nil	Nil	Nil	141	146	120	98.6	48.9
Pretax Income	-566	-3,081	956	2,205	1,519	1,207	876	679	376	285
Effective Tax Rate	NM	NM	36.5%	37.0%	37.8%	37.8%	37.8%	38.5%	39.0%	39.5%
Net Income	-1,109	-1,942	594	1,344	946	751	545	418	229	173
S&P Core Earnings	-1,178	-1,948	582	1,331	934	744	541	404	NA	NA

Balance Sheet & Other Financial Data (Million $)										
Cash	1,091	642	778	910	1,322	1,201	731	824	288	83.3
Current Assets	NA	NA	NA	NA	NA	NA	NA	NA	NA	NA
Total Assets	7,425	9,103	12,408	12,541	9,165	6,775	5,756	4,714	3,778	2,058
Current Liabilities	NA	NA	NA	NA	NA	NA	NA	NA	NA	NA
Long Term Debt	2,117	2,295	2,614	2,565	2,918	1,552	1,521	1,488	1,240	524
Common Equity	2,623	3,822	5,702	5,251	4,053	3,264	2,229	1,659	1,229	881
Total Capital	4,906	6,146	8,283	7,895	6,971	4,816	3,751	3,147	2,468	1,405
Capital Expenditures	1.40	Nil	26.8	21.7	27.4	29.6	4.09	13.1	16.0	15.3
Cash Flow	-1,059	-1,885	650	1,424	1,001	806	618	487	288	220
Current Ratio	7.2	5.5	4.3	5.9	3.0	3.3	2.9	3.6	2.5	2.8
% Long Term Debt of Capitalization	43.2	37.3	31.2	32.5	41.9	32.2	40.6	47.3	50.2	37.3
% Net Income of Revenue	NM	NM	3.7	9.7	9.0	8.4	7.4	6.9	4.9	5.5
% Return on Assets	NM	NM	4.8	12.4	11.9	12.0	10.4	9.8	7.9	8.7
% Return on Equity	NM	NM	10.8	28.9	25.8	27.4	28.0	28.9	21.7	21.6

Data as orig reptd.; bef. results of disc opers/spec. items. Per share data adj. for stk. divs.; EPS diluted. E-Estimated. NA-Not Available. NM-Not Meaningful. NR-Not Ranked. UR-Under Review.

Office: 700 NW 107th Ave, Miami, FL 33172.
Telephone: 305-559-4000.
Website: http://www.lennar.com
Pres & CEO: S. Miller

COO: J.M. Jaffe
CFO: B.E. Gross
Chief Acctg Officer & Cntlr: D.M. Collins
Treas: D.J. Bessette

Investor Contact: M.H. Ames (800-741-4663)
Board Members: I. Bolotin, S. L. Gerard, S. W. Hudson, D. J. Kaiserman, R. K. Landon, S. Lapidus, S. Miller, D. E. Shalala, J. Sonnenfeld

Founded: 1954
Domicile: Delaware
Employees: 4,704

Leucadia National Corp

STANDARD &POOR'S

S&P Recommendation **HOLD** ★★★☆☆	Price $21.36 (as of Nov 27, 2009)	12-Mo. Target Price $26.00	Investment Style Large-Cap Growth

GICS Sector Financials
Sub-Industry Multi-Sector Holdings

Summary This diversified holding company has subsidiaries engaged in manufacturing, real estate, medical product development, gaming entertainment, mining, and energy.

Key Stock Statistics (Source S&P, Vickers, company reports)

52-Wk Range	$26.47– 10.26	S&P Oper. EPS 2009**E**	2.75	Market Capitalization(B)	$5.193	Beta		1.81
Trailing 12-Month EPS	$-9.15	S&P Oper. EPS 2010**E**	1.00	Yield (%)	Nil	S&P 3-Yr. Proj. EPS CAGR(%)		NM
Trailing 12-Month P/E	NM	P/E on S&P Oper. EPS 2009**E**	7.8	Dividend Rate/Share	Nil	S&P Credit Rating		BB+
$10K Invested 5 Yrs Ago	$10,539	Common Shares Outstg. (M)	243.1	Institutional Ownership (%)	63			

Price Performance

30-Week Mov. Avg. · · · 10-Week Mov. Avg. – – **GAAP Earnings vs. Previous Year** Volume Above Avg. STARS
12-Mo. Target Price — Relative Strength — ▲ Up ▼ Down ► No Change Below Avg.

Options: ASE, CBOE, Ph

Analysis prepared by **Stuart J. Benway, CFA** on November 10, 2009, when the stock traded at **$ 23.17**.

Highlights

► We see revenues falling 5% to 10% in 2009. Sales should benefit from an acquisition in the telecom segment. However, these gains will likely be offset by sharply lower sales in timber remanufacturing, plastics, and property management services, which are being hurt by economic weakness in the United States. An expected stronger real estate market should lead to sales recovery of 10% to 15% in 2010.

► Leucadia has scaled back its investments in financial entities and is working to conserve cash during this weak environment. We believe investments it has in mining, auto finance, and investment banking will recover moderately in 2009. In 2010, spending could increase on medical product and energy project development.

► Our forecast is for earnings of $2.75 a share in 2009, following an operating loss of $3.55 per share in 2008 (excluding charges). We see EPS of $1.00 in 2010. We expect LUK to have a very uneven earnings pattern due to frequent changes in the number and types of businesses it operates, as well as changes in the value of its investments.

Investment Rationale/Risk

► Leucadia has a strong long-term record of increasing its book value, we think given its strategy and success of finding assets that are out of favor or are troubled, and therefore selling at a discount to their inherent value. However, this trend has been disrupted in recent years due to the broad-based decline in equity markets. We expect gradual additional recovery in the companies investments in coming quarters.

► Risks to our recommendation and target price include reliance on the two top executives for most of the company's investment decisions, and the potential for further declines in the value of the company's holdings due to the impact of tight credit markets and overall economic weakness.

► Book value per share at Leucadia rose at a compound annual growth rate of nearly 26% from 2003 through 2007. However, stated book value dropped sharply in 2008 to $11.22 per share due to the decline in the stock market. Our 12-month target price of $28 is calculated by applying a 1.6X multiple, in line with historical levels, to our 2010 book value per share estimate of $17.50.

Qualitative Risk Assessment

LOW	**MEDIUM**	HIGH

Our risk assessment reflects the broad diversity of the company's investments and what we view as a strong management team, offset by exposure to certain development stage businesses.

Quantitative Evaluations

S&P Quality Ranking C

D	**C**	B-	B	B+	A-	A	A+

Relative Strength Rank WEAK

21

LOWEST = 1   HIGHEST = 99

Revenue/Earnings Data

Revenue (Million $)

	1Q	2Q	3Q	4Q	Year
2009	245.0	273.1	280.8	--	--
2008	324.9	337.6	251.6	166.6	1,081
2007	197.2	344.0	331.2	282.6	1,155
2006	291.6	224.4	170.2	176.4	862.7
2005	121.3	258.7	343.3	317.9	1,041
2004	509.7	569.6	633.6	549.2	2,262

Earnings Per Share ($)

2009	-0.59	1.67	1.40	E0.27	E2.75
2008	-0.43	-0.76	0.37	-11.72	-11.19
2007	0.04	0.12	0.01	1.87	2.09
2006	0.37	0.17	0.02	0.03	0.60
2005	-0.03	5.23	0.22	-0.10	5.36
2004	-0.06	0.17	0.34	0.24	0.70

Fiscal year ended Dec. 31. Next earnings report expected: Early March. EPS Estimates based on S&P Operating Earnings; historical GAAP earnings are as reported.

Dividend Data

No cash dividends have been paid since 2007.

Leucadia National Corp

**STANDARD
&POOR'S**

Business Summary November 10, 2009

CORPORATE OVERVIEW. Leucadia National is a diversified holding company that is involved in a wide variety of businesses, including timber and plastics manufacturing, telecommunications, real estate activities, medical product development, and winery operations. The company also owns equity interests in operating businesses and investment partnerships including gaming entertainment, land-based contract oil and gas drilling, real estate activities, and development of a copper mine in Spain and a major iron ore project in Australia. In addition, Leucadia has significant investments in several partnerships that invest in domestic and international debt and equity securities. Revenues by major business segment in 2008 were as follows: Telecommunications 42%; Idaho Timber 22%; Conwed Plastics 10%; property management and services 13%; and gaming 11%.

CORPORATE STRATEGY. Leucadia's approach to its investments is to focus on return on investment and cash flow to build long-term shareholder value. Management continuously evaluates the retention and disposition of its existing operations, and investigates possible acquisition targets. In selecting potential acquisitions, LUK seeks assets and companies that are troubled or out of favor, and that are selling below apparent value as a result. We expect the

composition of Leucadia's assets to change continuously as certain businesses are divested and others are acquired.

PRIMARY BUSINESS DYNAMICS. Leucadia's telecommunications business is conducted through STi Prepaid and consists primarily of prepaid international long distance calling cards. Consumers located in the U.S. who make international calls often use calling cards because they provide lower rates than those offered by traditional long distance providers. STi Prepaid's cards are primarily marketed to ethnic communities in urban areas. Through its Idaho Timber business, the company remanufactures dimension lumber that is used in general construction and home improvement. Idaho Timber purchases low quality lumber and upgrades it into higher grade products through cutting, trimming and planing. This unit also makes boards for home centers and decking products. Demand in this business is closely tied to the level of housing starts and home size.

Company Financials Fiscal Year Ended Dec. 31

Per Share Data ($)	2008	2007	2006	2005	2004	2003	2002	2001	2000	1999
Tangible Book Value	10.87	24.66	17.72	16.87	17.32	10.04	8.78	7.05	7.26	6.58
Cash Flow	-10.91	2.26	0.75	NA	NA	NA	NA	NA	NA	NA
Earnings	-11.19	2.09	0.60	5.36	0.70	0.46	0.91	0.39	0.69	1.09
S&P Core Earnings	-11.27	2.06	NA	4.69	0.05	0.42	1.05	0.27	NA	NA
Dividends	Nil	0.25	0.25	0.13	0.13	0.08	0.08	0.08	0.08	4.53
Payout Ratio	Nil	12%	42%	2%	18%	18%	9%	21%	12%	NM
Prices:High	56.90	52.67	32.62	24.64	23.50	15.40	13.42	11.90	12.50	11.13
Prices:Low	12.19	26.52	23.26	16.20	15.02	10.86	9.21	8.77	6.88	6.71
P/E Ratio:High	NM	25	54	5	34	34	15	31	18	10
P/E Ratio:Low	NM	13	39	3	21	24	10	22	10	6
Income Statement Analysis (Million $)										
Revenue	936	1,155	863	1,041	2,262	556	242	375	715	710
Operating Income	-147	58.1	222	NA	NA	NA	NA	NA	NA	NA
Depreciation	65.4	49.8	43.6	190	233	65.7	18.7	17.5	21.4	15.4
Interest Expense	145	112	79.4	68.4	96.8	43.6	33.5	55.2	57.7	50.7
Pretax Income	-906	-79.0	172	93.0	132	42.9	13.2	53.7	193	243
Effective Tax Rate	NM	708.9%	24.4%	NM	NM	NM	NM	NM	37.6%	18.3%
Net Income	-2,579	481	130	1,224	152	84.4	153	64.8	115	193
S&P Core Earnings	-2,598	473	-9.43	1,071	5.47	77.7	177	45.7	NA	NA
Balance Sheet & Other Financial Data (Million $)										
Cash	604	1,440	3,430	3,063	2,781	2,033	1,044	1,183	1,613	1,467
Current Assets	867	1,720	1,366	NA	NA	NA	NA	NA	NA	NA
Total Assets	5,198	8,127	5,304	5,261	4,800	4,397	2,542	2,577	3,144	3,070
Current Liabilities	563	460	327	NA	NA	NA	NA	NA	NA	NA
Long Term Debt	1,833	2,004	975	987	1,484	1,155	328	424	412	491
Common Equity	2,677	5,570	3,893	3,662	2,259	2,134	1,487	1,195	1,204	1,122
Total Capital	4,777	7,596	4,887	4,665	3,760	3,307	1,893	1,666	1,631	1,720
Capital Expenditures	76.1	135	111	136	97.4	84.7	NA	NA	NA	NA
Cash Flow	-2,514	531	173	NA	NA	NA	NA	NA	NA	NA
Current Ratio	1.5	3.7	4.2	4.7	3.1	2.1	8.4	5.6	4.5	3.5
% Long Term Debt of Capitalization	38.4	26.4	19.9	20.8	38.8	34.7	17.5	25.7	24.4	28.6
% Net Income of Revenue	NM	41.6	15.7	117.6	6.8	15.2	63.1	16.2	16.8	27.3
% Return on Assets	NM	77.2	2.5	24.3	3.3	2.4	6.0	2.3	3.7	5.5
% Return on Equity	NM	10.2	3.4	41.4	6.9	4.7	11.4	5.4	9.9	13.0

Data as orig reptd.; bef. results of disc opers/spec. items. Per share data adj. for stk. divs.; EPS diluted. E-Estimated. NA-Not Available. NM-Not Meaningful. NR-Not Ranked. UR-Under Review.

Office: 315 Park Ave S, New York, NY 10010.
Telephone: 212-460-1900.
Chrmn & CEO: I.M. Cumming
Pres & COO: J.S. Steinberg

CFO: J.A. Orlando
Chief Acctg Officer & Cntlr: B.L. Lowenthal
Treas: R.J. Nittoli
Investor Contact: L.E. Ulbrandt (212-460-1900)

Board Members: I. M. Cumming, P. M. Dougan, A. J. Hirschfield, J. E. Jordan, J. C. Keil, J. C. Nichols, III, J. S. Steinberg

Founded: 1854
Domicile: New York
Employees: 3,584

Lexmark International Inc.

STANDARD &POOR'S

S&P Recommendation BUY ★★★★☆	Price $25.19 (as of Nov 27, 2009)	12-Mo. Target Price $30.00	Investment Style Large-Cap Growth

GICS Sector Information Technology
Sub-Industry Computer Storage & Peripherals

Summary Lexmark develops, manufactures and supplies laser and inkjet printers and associated consumable supplies for the office and home markets.

Key Stock Statistics (Source S&P, Vickers, company reports)

52-Wk Range	$29.16– 14.23	S&P Oper. EPS 2009E	2.66	Market Capitalization(B)	$1.967	Beta	1.10
Trailing 12-Month EPS	$1.32	S&P Oper. EPS 2010E	2.30	Yield (%)	Nil	S&P 3-Yr. Proj. EPS CAGR(%)	NA
Trailing 12-Month P/E	19.1	P/E on S&P Oper. EPS 2009E	9.5	Dividend Rate/Share	Nil	S&P Credit Rating	NA
$10K Invested 5 Yrs Ago	$2,947	Common Shares Outstg. (M)	78.1	Institutional Ownership (%)	NM		

Price Performance

30-Week Mov. Avg. · · · · 10-Week Mov. Avg. – – GAAP Earnings vs. Previous Year   Volume Above Avg. ▮▮▮ STARS
12-Mo. Target Price — Relative Strength — ▲ Up ▼ Down ▶ No Change   Below Avg. ▮▮▮ ★

Options: ASE, CBOE, P, Ph

Analysis prepared by **Thomas W. Smith, CFA** on October 20, 2009, when the stock traded at **$ 26.30**.

Highlights

▶ We project revenues will decline 17% in 2009, continuing a multi-year trend of weakening top-line performance. We then forecast revenues to increase 3% in 2010, reflecting our projection for improvement in presently sluggish global economic conditions. We see new products aiding sales in the context of very competitive printer markets.

▶ We look for operating margins to narrow in 2009, as the company follows through on several restructuring efforts, before widening in 2010. In January 2009, LXK announced a restructuring plan affecting 375 staff positions, and in April the company announced a plant closing in Mexico and other actions affecting 360 positions. In October 2009, LXK announced further restructuring affecting 825 jobs.

▶ We expect modest effective tax rates, reflecting shifts in the siting of operations, to aid results. We estimate operating EPS, excluding restructuring charges, of $2.66 for 2009 and $2.35 for 2010. We foresee few share buybacks until printer industry demand picks up.

Investment Rationale/Risk

▶ We recently upgraded our recommendation on the shares to buy, from hold. We view LXK as attractively valued in light of new product introductions and potential cost reductions that could help earnings despite a period of weak printer industry demand that we foresee lasting through 2009 but improving in 2010. We think that LXK owns some important intellectual property, and should be able to expand its branded products and laser printer businesses when the economy picks up.

▶ Risks to our recommendation and target price include the possibility that competition from Hewlett-Packard (HPQ 49, Strong Buy) will be more than we anticipate, that savings from restructuring will come in below our estimates, and that penetration of high-growth segments will be slower than we project.

▶ Our 12-month target price of $30 is based on our P/E analysis. We apply a target P/E of 13.5X, which is toward the low end of an historical range for LXK to reflect a slow revenue environment that we foresee, to our 12-month forward operating EPS estimate of $2.21.

Qualitative Risk Assessment

LOW	MEDIUM	HIGH

Our risk assessment reflects what we see as a difficult competitive pricing environment in the printer market, offset by our view of LXK's strides in improving its product portfolio and cost position.

Quantitative Evaluations

S&P Quality Ranking   B

D	C	B-	B	B+	A-	A	A+

Relative Strength Rank   STRONG

82

LOWEST = 1   HIGHEST = 99

Revenue/Earnings Data

Revenue (Million $)

	1Q	2Q	3Q	4Q	Year
2009	944.1	904.6	958.0	--	--
2008	1,175	1,139	1,131	1,084	4,528
2007	1,261	1,208	1,195	1,310	4,974
2006	1,275	1,229	1,235	1,369	5,108
2005	1,358	1,283	1,216	1,365	5,222
2004	1,256	1,248	1,266	1,544	5,314

Earnings Per Share ($)

2009	0.76	0.22	0.13	E0.58	E2.66
2008	1.07	0.89	0.42	0.23	2.69
2007	0.95	0.67	0.48	1.04	3.14
2006	0.78	0.74	0.85	0.91	3.27
2005	0.96	0.64	0.59	0.71	2.91
2004	0.91	1.02	1.17	1.18	4.28

Fiscal year ended Dec. 31. Next earnings report expected: Late January. EPS Estimates based on S&P Operating Earnings; historical GAAP earnings are as reported.

Dividend Data

No cash dividends have been paid.

Please read the Required Disclosures and Analyst Certification on the last page of this report.

The McGraw·Hill Companies

Lexmark International Inc.

STANDARD &POOR'S

Business Summary October 20, 2009

CORPORATE OVERVIEW. Lexmark shook up the printer industry with the introduction of the first desktop color printer priced under $100 with its November 1997 launch of the $99 color inkjet printer, aimed at building brand awareness and an installed base. We think LXK's competitive advantage in the past was its low cost structure and its ability to price aggressively. However, in recent years, it has been on the defensive, in our view, as peers have undercut its prices and LXK's product mix was not focused on some of the more compelling printer areas. Going forward, LXK management believes that its commitment to R&D should bear fruit and help revive unit growth and subsequently high-margin supplies sales, but we view this as a multi-year process. New products in 2008 included over 40 new laser product models and 15 new inkjet products.

The company operates mainly in two segments -- Printing Solutions and Services (formerly the Business market) and Imaging Solutions (formerly the Consumer market). Printing Solutions and Services offers mainly laser products and represented 69% of sales in 2008 (65% of 2007 sales) and saw a revenue

decline of 1%. Laser printer hardware unit shipments decreased 7% in 2008, despite growth in laser multi-function printers. Imaging Solutions represented 26% of 2008 sales (30% of 2007 sales), and suffered a 22% revenue decline. Inkjet hardware unit shipments fell 45% in 2008, partly because of a planned transition to a more favorable printer product mix that could potentially boost usage of associated consumable products.

Lexmark distributes to business customers via many channels, including the company's network of authorized distributors. The company distributes to consumers through retail outlets worldwide. The company also sells through alliances and OEM arrangements. One customer, Dell, accounted for 13% of revenues in 2008, down from 14% in 2007 and 15% in 2006.

Company Financials Fiscal Year Ended Dec. 31

Per Share Data ($)	2008	2007	2006	2005	2004	2003	2002	2001	2000	1999
Tangible Book Value	10.45	15.76	10.67	12.77	NM	17.46	NM	8.25	6.11	6.24
Cash Flow	4.97	5.13	5.21	4.21	5.29	4.48	3.84	2.98	2.80	2.89
Earnings	2.69	3.14	3.27	2.91	4.28	3.34	2.79	2.05	2.13	2.32
S&P Core Earnings	2.36	3.10	3.28	2.52	3.94	3.04	2.27	1.57	NA	NA
Dividends	Nil	Nil	Nil	Nil	Nil	Nil	Nil	Nil	Nil	Nil
Payout Ratio	Nil	Nil	Nil	Nil	Nil	Nil	Nil	Nil	Nil	Nil
Prices:High	37.88	73.20	74.68	86.62	97.50	79.65	69.50	70.75	135.88	104.00
Prices:Low	22.13	32.35	44.09	39.33	76.00	56.57	41.94	40.81	28.75	42.09
P/E Ratio:High	14	23	23	30	23	24	25	35	64	45
P/E Ratio:Low	8	10	13	14	18	17	15	20	13	18

Income Statement Analysis (Million $)	2008	2007	2006	2005	2004	2003	2002	2001	2000	1999
Revenue	4,528	4,974	5,108	5,222	5,314	4,755	4,356	4,143	3,807	3,452
Operating Income	573	564	715	692	867	743	643	525	548	557
Depreciation	203	191	201	159	135	149	138	126	91.2	80.1
Interest Expense	28.9	13.0	12.1	11.2	12.3	12.5	9.00	14.8	12.8	10.7
Pretax Income	276	350	459	554	746	594	496	318	396	459
Effective Tax Rate	12.9%	13.9%	26.3%	35.7%	23.8%	26.0%	26.0%	13.9%	28.0%	30.6%
Net Income	240	301	338	356	569	439	367	274	285	319
S&P Core Earnings	211	297	340	308	524	399	298	210	NA	NA

Balance Sheet & Other Financial Data (Million $)	2008	2007	2006	2005	2004	2003	2002	2001	2000	1999
Cash	973	796	551	889	1,567	1,196	498	90.7	68.5	93.9
Current Assets	2,063	2,067	1,830	2,170	3,001	2,444	1,799	1,493	1,244	1,089
Total Assets	3,265	3,121	2,849	3,330	4,124	3,450	2,808	2,450	2,073	1,703
Current Liabilities	1,258	1,497	1,324	1,234	1,468	1,183	1,099	931	979	736
Long Term Debt	649	Nil	150	150	150	149	149	149	149	149
Common Equity	812	1,278	1,035	1,429	2,083	1,643	1,082	1,076	777	659
Total Capital	1,461	1,278	1,185	1,578	2,232	1,792	1,231	1,225	926	808
Capital Expenditures	218	183	200	201	198	93.8	112	214	297	220
Cash Flow	443	492	539	515	704	588	505	399	377	399
Current Ratio	1.6	1.4	1.4	1.8	2.0	2.1	1.6	1.6	1.3	1.5
% Long Term Debt of Capitalization	44.4	Nil	12.6	9.5	6.7	8.3	12.1	12.2	16.1	18.4
% Net Income of Revenue	5.3	6.1	6.6	6.8	10.7	9.2	8.4	6.6	7.5	9.2
% Return on Assets	7.5	10.1	11.0	9.6	15.0	14.0	13.9	12.1	15.1	20.0
% Return on Equity	23.0	26.0	27.5	20.3	30.5	32.2	34.0	29.5	39.7	51.5

Data as orig reptd.; bef. results of disc opers/spec. items. Per share data adj. for stk. divs.; EPS diluted. E-Estimated. NA-Not Available. NM-Not Meaningful. NR-Not Ranked. UR-Under Review.

Office: 740 West New Circle Rd, Lexington, KY 40550.
Telephone: 859-232-2000.
Website: http://www.lexmark.com
Chrmn & CEO: P.J. Curlander

EVP, CFO & Chief Acctg Officer: J.W. Gamble, Jr.
Treas: B. Frost
Secy & General Counsel: R.J. Patton
Investor Contact: J. Morgan (859-232-5568)

Board Members: T. Beck, P. J. Curlander, W. R. Fields, R. E. Gomory, S. R. Hardis, J. F. Hardymon, R. Holland, Jr., M. L. Mann, M. J. Maples, J. L. Montupet, K. P. Seifert

Founded: 1990
Domicile: Delaware
Employees: 14,000

The McGraw-Hill Companies

Life Technologies Corp

STANDARD &POOR'S

S&P Recommendation	STRONG BUY ★★★★★	Price $49.95 (as of Nov 27, 2009)	12-Mo. Target Price $65.00	Investment Style Large-Cap Growth

GICS Sector Health Care
Sub-Industry Life Sciences Tools & Services

Summary This company develops and manufactures research products and instruments for biotechnology and biopharmaceutical researchers.

Key Stock Statistics (Source S&P, Vickers, company reports)

52-Wk Range	$51.33– 20.00	S&P Oper. EPS 2009**E**	2.94	Market Capitalization(B)	$8.908	Beta	0.83
Trailing 12-Month EPS	$-0.39	S&P Oper. EPS 2010**E**	3.25	Yield (%)	Nil	S&P 3-Yr. Proj. EPS CAGR(%)	14
Trailing 12-Month P/E	NM	P/E on S&P Oper. EPS 2009**E**	17.0	Dividend Rate/Share	Nil	S&P Credit Rating	NA
$10K Invested 5 Yrs Ago	$16,388	Common Shares Outstg. (M)	178.3	Institutional Ownership (%)	93		

Price Performance

30-Week Mov. Avg. · · · 10-Week Mov. Avg. - - **GAAP Earnings vs. Previous Year**   Volume Above Avg. STARS
12-Mo. Target Price — Relative Strength ▲ Up ▼ Down ► No Change   Below Avg. ★

2-for-1

Options: ASE, CBOE, P, Ph

Analysis prepared by **Jeffrey Loo, CFA** on October 30, 2009, when the stock traded at **$ 48.68**.

Highlights

► In 2009, we expect pro forma sales, inclusive of a 2% adverse foreign exchange impact, to rise 4% to $3.26 billion. We expect organic sales in molecular diagnostics to rise 5%, genetic systems to advance 6% with a decline in capillary electrophoresis systems and robust double-digit gains in the SOLiD system, and Cell System sales to decline 1%. We see a 30 basis point (bps) rise in gross margins as better pricing is partially offset by lower royalties. We see operating margins improving 280 bps, aided by cost saving synergies. In 2010 we expect sales to rise 6% to $3.45 billion.

► In September, LIFE agreed to sell its ownership stake in its mass spectrometry unit, which accounted for $525 million in 2008 sales, to Danaher Corporation (DHR 81, buy), for $450 million, subject to approvals. The deal is expected to close in the fourth quarter. This unit is a joint venture with MDS Inc., with sales and income accounted for under the equity method. We estimate the joint venture accounts for about $30 million in annual income. We expect LIFE to use the sales proceeds to pay down debt.

► We estimate EPS of $2.94 in 2009 and $3.25 in 2010.

Investment Rationale/Risk

► We think the shares, recently trading at 14.8X our 2010 EPS forecast and at a 1.0 P/E-to-growth ratio, well below historical levels, are undervalued. We believe LIFE is well positioned within its end-markets, and think it has a solid platform for expansion in high-growth markets within genomics, proteomics, and cell biology. We see continued robust growth for its genomic analyzer, the SOLiD system and expect improvement in consumable sales in 2010 as we believe the impact from global economic challenges will not significantly affect these sales. We think LIFE will benefit significantly from the $10 billion increase in the NIH budget included in the economic stimulus package with the initial benefits starting in the fourth quarter of 2009 and accelerating in 2010.

► Risks to our recommendation and target price include a slowdown in pharmaceutical and biotech R&D spending.

► Our 12-month target price of $65 is based on a 1.4X P/E-to-growth ratio, slightly ahead of peers, based on our 2010 EPS estimate and a projected growth rate of 14%. We believe a premium is warranted given our view that LIFE has an above average industry growth profile.

Qualitative Risk Assessment

LOW	MEDIUM	HIGH

Our risk assessment reflects LIFE's diverse product portfolio and broad geographic client base. The life sciences industry is highly competitive, and companies need to develop new innovative products to remain viable, as technology is rapidly changing. Although life sciences is LIFE's main market, the company also sells products to the environmental, food safety, and industrial markets.

Quantitative Evaluations

S&P Quality Ranking B-

D	C	B-	B	B+	A-	A	A+

Relative Strength Rank STRONG

75

LOWEST = 1   HIGHEST = 99

Revenue/Earnings Data

Revenue (Million $)

	1Q	2Q	3Q	4Q	Year
2009	775.7	832.8	800.7	--	--
2008	350.2	367.8	361.4	540.6	1,620
2007	308.7	321.7	315.0	336.5	1,282
2006	309.0	313.6	311.0	329.8	1,263
2005	277.1	306.5	289.6	325.3	1,198
2004	251.3	254.0	256.3	262.2	1,024

Earnings Per Share ($)

2009	0.09	0.22	0.22	E0.69	E2.94
2008	0.60	0.55	0.26	-0.89	0.29
2007	0.31	0.31	0.32	0.41	1.35
2006	0.18	0.18	-1.27	-1.04	-1.86
2005	0.41	0.11	0.21	0.44	1.17
2004	0.10	0.18	0.26	0.28	0.82

Fiscal year ended Dec. 31. Next earnings report expected: Mid February. EPS Estimates based on S&P Operating Earnings; historical GAAP earnings are as reported.

Dividend Data

No cash dividends have been paid.

Please read the Required Disclosures and Analyst Certification on the last page of this report.

The McGraw-Hill Companies

Life Technologies Corp

STANDARD & POOR'S

Business Summary October 30, 2009

CORPORATE OVERVIEW. Life Technologies Inc. was formed through Invitrogen Corporation's (IVGN) $5.1 billion acquisition of Applied Biosystems Inc. (ABI) in November 2008. Prior to the transaction, Invitrogen had annual sales of about $1.3 billion and Applied Biosystems had annual sales of about $2.2 billion. Invitrogen develops, manufactures and markets a broad line of tool kits and reagents, and provides other products and services, including informatics software and contract research services, used in life sciences research and the commercial manufacture of biopharmaceutical products. IVGN's revenue consisted of about 99% consumables and services and 1% instrument reagent systems. Applied Biosystems develops and manufactures instrument-based systems, consumables and reagents, and software and related services for the life sciences industry, as well as for the food safety, environmental and other industrial end-markets. ABI's revenue consisted of 19% Mass Spectrometry instrument sales, 21% Instrument Reagent Systems, and 60% Consumable and Services. Life Technologies is now one of the largest companies within the life sciences industry based on annual revenue. LIFE's expected revenue breakdown is 12% Mass Spectrometry instrument sales, 14% Instrument Reagent Systems, and 74% Consumables and Services.

LIFE has an extensive product portfolio offering end-to-end workflow solutions. Products primarily from IVGN's portfolio are used for sample prepara-

tion and sample processing, while ABI's instrumentation is used for detection and analysis and data interpretation. IVGN has two main units -- BioDiscovery and Cell Culture Systems. The BioDiscovery segment serves governmental and academic laboratories as well as biotechnology and pharmaceutical firms engaged in research of biological and genetic substances. The Cell Culture Systems segment primarily serves companies that are engaged in the commercialization of such substances; these concerns typically require large amounts of biologic or genetic materials or the growth media used in their manufacture. The company produces cell culture products under the GIBCO brand. These products include a variety of sera, culture media and reagents. Some of these substances are used in the manufacture of genetically engineered products, and are produced in large-scale commercial production facilities. The BioDiscovery segment provides products and services used for initial gene cloning and manipulation of DNA, examining RNA levels and regulating gene expression in cells, and capturing, separating and analyzing proteins. These products include reagents and tool kits to simplify and improve gene acquisition, cloning, expression and analysis.

Company Financials Fiscal Year Ended Dec. 31

Per Share Data ($)	2008	2007	2006	2005	2004	2003	2002	2001	2000	1999
Tangible Book Value	NM	NM	NM	NM	0.47	3.49	5.31	4.62	2.94	3.23
Cash Flow	1.57	2.74	-0.28	2.44	1.95	1.66	1.28	1.33	0.62	0.25
Earnings	0.29	1.35	-1.86	1.17	0.82	0.58	0.45	-1.41	-0.90	0.20
S&P Core Earnings	0.26	1.35	0.70	0.86	0.49	0.27	0.15	-1.75	NA	NA
Dividends	Nil	Nil	Nil	Nil	Nil	Nil	Nil	Nil	Nil	Nil
Payout Ratio	Nil	Nil	Nil	Nil	Nil	Nil	Nil	Nil	Nil	Nil
Prices:High	49.00	49.58	38.33	44.25	41.00	35.47	31.35	42.97	49.75	33.69
Prices:Low	19.56	27.96	27.35	30.07	23.10	14.02	12.62	19.25	18.00	6.00
P/E Ratio:High	NM	37	NM	38	50	61	70	NM	NM	NM
P/E Ratio:Low	NM	21	NM	26	28	24	28	NM	NM	NM

Income Statement Analysis (Million $)										
Revenue	1,620	1,282	1,263	1,198	1,024	778	649	629	246	68.3
Operating Income	431	320	286	305	284	203	172	148	35.0	15.6
Depreciation	133	136	162	160	147	111	87.7	287	91.8	2.72
Interest Expense	43.0	28.0	32.4	34.2	32.2	28.6	24.1	11.3	8.94	0.24
Pretax Income	154	179	-163	174	121	85.1	71.2	-137	-54.5	10.2
Effective Tax Rate	80.6%	27.1%	NM	24.0%	26.8%	28.6%	31.2%	NM	NM	34.7%
Net Income	30.0	130	-191	132	88.8	60.1	47.7	-148	-54.3	6.67
S&P Core Earnings	27.0	131	71.4	94.7	52.8	28.1	15.4	-183	NA	NA

Balance Sheet & Other Financial Data (Million $)										
Cash	336	671	367	435	198	589	547	995	431	102
Current Assets	1,612	1,090	798	1,151	1,332	1,287	968	1,204	672	123
Total Assets	8,914	3,330	3,183	3,877	3,614	3,166	2,615	2,667	2,369	136
Current Liabilities	1,007	234	248	512	196	126	141	127	153	9.20
Long Term Debt	3,504	1,151	1,152	1,152	1,300	1,055	672	676	179	0.72
Common Equity	3,400	1,765	1,630	2,042	1,913	1,807	1,643	1,683	1,778	126
Total Capital	7,542	3,019	2,883	3,335	3,367	3,023	2,427	2,525	2,194	126
Capital Expenditures	81.9	78.3	61.1	71.8	39.1	32.2	51.5	44.2	22.7	2.75
Cash Flow	163	266	-29.3	292	236	171	135	139	37.5	9.38
Current Ratio	1.6	4.7	3.2	2.3	6.8	10.2	6.9	9.5	4.4	13.4
% Long Term Debt of Capitalization	46.5	38.1	40.0	34.5	38.6	34.9	27.7	26.8	8.2	0.6
% Net Income of Revenue	1.9	10.2	NM	11.0	8.7	7.7	7.3	NM	NM	9.8
% Return on Assets	0.5	4.0	NM	3.5	2.6	2.1	1.8	NM	NM	8.0
% Return on Equity	1.2	7.7	NM	6.7	4.8	3.5	2.9	NM	NM	10.2

Data as orig reptd.; bef. results of disc opers/spec. items. Per share data adj. for stk. divs.; EPS diluted. E-Estimated. NA-Not Available. NM-Not Meaningful. NR-Not Ranked. UR-Under Review.

Office: 5791 Van Allen Way, Carlsbad, CA 92008-7321.
Telephone: 760-603-7200.
Website: http://www.lifetechnologies.com
Chrmn & CEO: G.T. Lucier

COO & Co-Pres: M.P. Stevenson
SVP & CFO: D.F. Hoffmeister
CSO: J.A. Finlay
Chief Acctg Officer: K.R. Richard

Investor Contact: A. Clardy (760-603-7200)
Board Members: G. F. Adam, Jr., R. V. Dittamore, D. W. Grimm, B. S. Iyer, A. J. Levine, W. H. Longfield, B. G. Lorimier, G. T. Lucier, R. A. Matricaria, P. A. Peterson, W. A. Reynolds, W. S. Shanahan, D. C. U'Prichard

Founded: 1987
Domicile: Delaware
Employees: 9,700

Eli Lilly and Co

STANDARD &POOR'S

S&P Recommendation **HOLD** ★★★☆☆	Price $36.90 (as of Nov 27, 2009)	12-Mo. Target Price $37.00	Investment Style Large-Cap Blend

GICS Sector Health Care
Sub-Industry Pharmaceuticals

Summary This leading producer of prescription drugs offers a wide range of treatments for neurological disorders, diabetes, cancer, and other conditions. The company also sells animal health products.

Key Stock Statistics (Source S&P, Vickers, company reports)

52-Wk Range	$40.78–27.21	S&P Oper. EPS 2009**E**	4.40	Market Capitalization(B)	$42.399	Beta	0.79
Trailing 12-Month EPS	$-0.20	S&P Oper. EPS 2010**E**	4.75	Yield (%)	5.31	S&P 3-Yr. Proj. EPS CAGR(%)	7
Trailing 12-Month P/E	NM	P/E on S&P Oper. EPS 2009**E**	8.4	Dividend Rate/Share	$1.96	S&P Credit Rating	AA
$10K Invested 5 Yrs Ago	$8,125	Common Shares Outstg. (M)	1,149.0	Institutional Ownership (%)	76		

Price Performance

30-Week Mov. Avg. ··· 10-Week Mov. Avg. – – GAAP Earnings vs. Previous Year Volume Above Avg. STARS
12-Mo. Target Price — Relative Strength ▲ Up ▼ Down ▶ No Change   Below Avg.

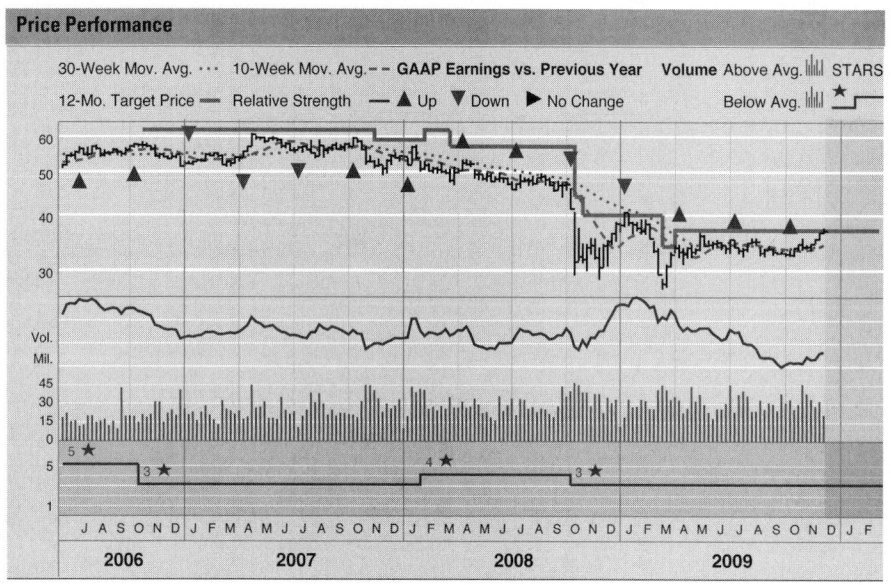

Options: ASE, CBOE, P, Ph

Analysis prepared by **Herman B. Saftlas** on November 04, 2009, when the stock traded at **$33.71**.

Highlights

▶ We forecast a revenue increase of about 6% in 2010, from the $21.5 billion that we forecast for 2009, lifted by growth in several lines and more favorable foreign exchange. Sales of Cymbalta should show continued growth, boosted by expanded direct-to-consumer advertising, new indications, and expansion in foreign markets. We also see gains in other drugs such as Humalog, Cialis and Alimta. Sales of Zyprexa will probably be modestly lower, while sales of Gemzar are expected to come under generic competition. Animal health sales should be modestly higher.

▶ We look for 2010 gross margins to show modest attrition from an indicated 81% in 2009, adversely affected by a less favorable product mix. R&D costs are also expected to rise sharply on stepped up spending on new drugs. However, we expect lower SG&A spending, benefiting from ongoing cost reduction.

▶ After a projected rise in the tax rate to 22%, from an indicated 21% in 2009, we project operating EPS of $4.55 for 2010, up from an indicated $4.40 in 2009, excluding acquisition-related charges and other nonrecurring items.

Investment Rationale/Risk

▶ Lilly faces a major patent cliff starting with the loss of U.S. patent protection on Zyprexa in 2011. We believe LLY is addressing this issue through stepped up new drug development activities and acquisitions. In 2008, Lilly acquired ImClone Systems, which gave it access to Erbitux, an anticancer drug that we expect to grow in the years ahead. Although expected to be dilutive in 2011, Imclone expanded LLY's biologics base and has provided cost synergies. However, we see somewhat limited prospects for LLY's new Effient anti-clotting agent, which has been linked with bleeding risks.

▶ Risks to our recommendation and target price include greater-than-expected competitive pressures, as well as failure to develop and commercialize new drugs.

▶ Our 12-month target price of $37 applies a below-peers multiple of 8.4X to our 2009 EPS estimate, which we believe is reasonable given the impending patent cliff. Our DCF model, which assumes decelerating cash flow growth over the next 10 years, a WACC of 7.0%, and perpetuity growth of 1%, also indicates intrinsic value of $37. The dividend recently yielded 5.8%.

Qualitative Risk Assessment

LOW	**MEDIUM**	HIGH

Our risk assessment reflects generic challenges to the company's branded patents, and drug development and regulatory risks. This is offset by our view of LLY's diverse drug portfolio, limited patent expiration exposure, and robust pipeline.

Quantitative Evaluations

S&P Quality Ranking   **B**

D	C	B-	**B**	B+	A-	A	A+

Relative Strength Rank   **STRONG**

82

LOWEST = 1   HIGHEST = 99

Revenue/Earnings Data

Revenue (Million $)

	1Q	2Q	3Q	4Q	Year
2009	5,047	5,293	5,562	--	--
2008	4,808	5,150	5,210	5,211	20,378
2007	4,226	4,631	4,587	5,190	18,634
2006	3,715	3,867	3,864	4,245	15,691
2005	3,497	3,668	3,601	3,879	14,645
2004	3,377	3,556	3,280	3,644	13,858

Earnings Per Share ($)

2009	1.20	1.06	0.86	E0.89	E4.40
2008	0.97	0.88	-0.43	-3.31	-1.89
2007	0.47	0.61	0.85	0.78	2.71
2006	0.77	0.76	0.80	0.12	2.45
2005	0.68	-0.23	0.73	0.66	1.83
2004	0.37	0.60	0.69	Nil	1.66

Fiscal year ended Dec. 31. Next earnings report expected: Late January. EPS Estimates based on S&P Operating Earnings; historical GAAP earnings are as reported.

Dividend Data (Dates: mm/dd Payment Date: mm/dd/yy)

Amount ($)	Date Decl.	Ex-Div. Date	Stk. of Record	Payment Date
0.490	12/15	02/11	02/13	03/10/09
0.490	04/20	05/13	05/15	06/10/09
0.490	06/22	08/12	08/15	09/10/09
0.490	10/19	11/10	11/13	12/10/09

Dividends have been paid since 1885. Source: Company reports.

Eli Lilly and Co

Business Summary November 04, 2009

CORPORATE OVERVIEW. Eli Lilly and Co. is a leading maker of prescription drugs, offering a wide range of treatments for neurological disorders, diabetes, cancer, and other conditions. Animal health products are also sold. Foreign sales accounted for about 46% of total revenues in 2008.

LLY's largest selling drug is Zyprexa, a treatment for schizophrenia and bipolar disorder that offers clinical advantages over older antipsychotic drugs. Sales of Zyprexa totaled $4.7 billion in 2008, down from $4.8 billion in 2007. LLY also offers Symbyax, a combination of Zyprexa and Prozac, to treat bipolar depression.

In August 2004, the company launched Cymbalta, a potent antidepressant. Cymbalta works on two body chemicals involved in depression -- serotonin and norepinephrine -- while most conventional antidepressants affect only serotonin. Sales of Cymbalta climbed to $2.7 billion in 2008, from $2.2 billion in 2007, reflecting greater market penetration and expanded indications.

Diabetes care products (sales of $4.6 billion in 2008) include Humulin, a human insulin produced through recombinant DNA technology; Humalog, a rapid-

acting injectable human insulin analog; Iletin, an animal-source insulin; and Actos, an oral agent for Type 2 diabetes that is manufactured by Takeda Chemical Industries of Japan and co-marketed by Lilly and Takeda. In May 2005, the FDA approved Byetta (generically known as exenatide) for Type 2 diabetes. Lilly shares in the profits from Byetta with Amylin Pharmaceuticals, co-developer of the drug.

Other important drugs are Gemzar, a treatment for lung cancer and pancreatic cancer (sales of $1.7 billion); Cialis, a treatment for erectile dysfunction ($1.4 billion); Evista, a drug used to prevent and treat osteoporosis in postmenopausal women ($1.1 billion); Alimta, a treatment for lung cancer ($1.2 billion); Forteo for severe osteoporosis ($779 million); and Humatrope, a recombinant human growth hormone ($468 million). Animal health products ($1.1 billion) include cattle feed additives, antibiotics and related items.

Company Financials Fiscal Year Ended Dec. 31

Per Share Data ($)	2008	2007	2006	2005	2004	2003	2002	2001	2000	1999
Tangible Book Value	2.45	10.64	9.70	9.55	9.51	8.69	7.37	6.32	5.37	4.49
Cash Flow	-1.05	3.49	3.06	2.41	2.21	2.87	2.85	2.91	3.18	2.70
Earnings	-1.89	2.71	2.45	1.83	1.66	2.37	2.50	2.58	2.79	2.30
S&P Core Earnings	-1.38	2.78	2.90	1.85	1.42	2.09	1.96	2.17	NA	NA
Dividends	1.88	1.70	1.60	1.52	1.42	1.34	1.24	1.12	1.04	0.92
Payout Ratio	NM	63%	65%	83%	86%	57%	50%	43%	37%	40%
Prices:High	57.52	61.00	59.24	60.98	76.95	73.89	81.09	95.00	109.00	97.75
Prices:Low	28.62	49.09	50.19	49.47	50.34	52.77	43.75	70.01	54.00	60.56
P/E Ratio:High	NM	23	24	33	46	31	32	37	39	42
P/E Ratio:Low	NM	18	20	27	30	22	17	27	19	26

Income Statement Analysis (Million $)										
Revenue	20,378	18,634	15,691	14,645	13,858	12,583	11,078	11,543	10,862	10,003
Operating Income	6,525	5,658	4,927	4,375	4,256	4,050	3,821	4,185	3,996	3,803
Depreciation	925	855	802	726	598	548	493	455	436	440
Interest Expense	277	324	Nil	105	274	61.0	79.7	147	182	242
Pretax Income	-1,308	3,877	3,418	2,718	2,942	3,262	3,458	3,552	3,859	3,245
Effective Tax Rate	NM	23.8%	22.1%	26.3%	38.5%	21.5%	21.7%	20.9%	20.8%	21.5%
Net Income	-2,072	2,953	2,663	2,002	1,810	2,561	2,708	2,809	3,058	2,547
S&P Core Earnings	-1,523	3,028	3,153	2,016	1,558	2,261	2,128	2,359	NA	NA

Balance Sheet & Other Financial Data (Million $)										
Cash	5,926	4,831	3,109	3,007	5,365	2,756	1,946	2,702	4,115	3,700
Current Assets	12,453	12,257	9,694	10,796	12,836	8,759	7,804	6,939	7,943	7,056
Total Assets	29,213	26,788	21,955	24,581	24,867	21,678	19,042	16,434	14,691	12,825
Current Liabilities	13,110	5,268	5,086	5,716	7,594	5,551	5,064	5,203	4,961	3,935
Long Term Debt	4,616	4,594	3,494	5,764	4,492	4,688	4,358	3,132	2,634	2,812
Common Equity	6,735	13,664	11,081	11,000	10,920	9,765	8,274	7,104	8,682	5,013
Total Capital	11,771	18,545	14,638	17,459	16,032	14,453	12,632	10,236	11,407	7,962
Capital Expenditures	947	1,082	1,078	1,298	1,898	1,707	1,131	884	678	528
Cash Flow	-1,147	3,808	3,465	2,728	2,408	3,109	3,201	3,264	3,494	2,986
Current Ratio	1.0	2.3	1.9	1.9	1.7	1.6	1.5	1.3	1.6	1.8
% Long Term Debt of Capitalization	39.2	24.8	23.9	33.0	28.0	32.4	34.5	30.6	23.1	35.3
% Net Income of Revenue	NM	15.9	17.0	13.7	13.1	20.4	24.4	24.3	28.2	25.5
% Return on Assets	NM	12.1	11.4	8.1	7.8	12.6	15.3	18.1	22.2	20.0
% Return on Equity	NM	24.0	24.2	18.1	17.5	28.4	35.2	42.7	44.7	53.9

Data as orig reptd.; bef. results of disc opers/spec. items. Per share data adj. for stk. divs.; EPS diluted. E-Estimated. NA-Not Available. NM-Not Meaningful. NR-Not Ranked. UR-Under Review.

Office: Lilly Corporate Center, Indianapolis, IN 46285.
Telephone: 317-276-2000.
Website: http://www.lilly.com
Chrmn, Pres & CEO: J.C. Lechleiter

CEO: J. Millon
SVP & CFO: D.W. Rice
SVP & General Counsel: R.A. Armitage
CSO & CTO: S.M. Paul

Investor Contact: P. Johnson (317-277-0001)
Board Members: R. Alvarez, W. Bischoff, D. M. Edgar, M. L. Eskew, M. Feldstein, J. E. Fyrwald, A. G. Gilman, R. D. Hoover, K. N. Horn, J. C. Lechleiter, E. R. Marram, D. R. Oberhelman, F. G. Prendergast, K. P. Seifert

Founded: 1876
Domicile: Indiana
Employees: 40,450

Limited Brands Inc.

STANDARD &POOR'S

S&P Recommendation HOLD ★★★☆☆	Price	12-Mo. Target Price	Investment Style
	$16.92 (as of Nov 27, 2009)	$19.00	Large-Cap Blend

GICS Sector Consumer Discretionary
Sub-Industry Apparel Retail

Summary This specialty retailer of women's apparel, lingerie, and personal care and beauty products operates about 3,000 specialty stores.

Key Stock Statistics (Source S&P, Vickers, company reports)

52-Wk Range	$19.99–5.98	S&P Oper. EPS 2010**E**	1.01	Market Capitalization(B)	$5.443	Beta	1.67
Trailing 12-Month EPS	$0.33	S&P Oper. EPS 2011**E**	1.13	Yield (%)	3.55	S&P 3-Yr. Proj. EPS CAGR(%)	8
Trailing 12-Month P/E	51.3	P/E on S&P Oper. EPS 2010**E**	16.8	Dividend Rate/Share	$0.60	S&P Credit Rating	BB
$10K Invested 5 Yrs Ago	$8,204	Common Shares Outstg. (M)	321.7	Institutional Ownership (%)	75		

Price Performance

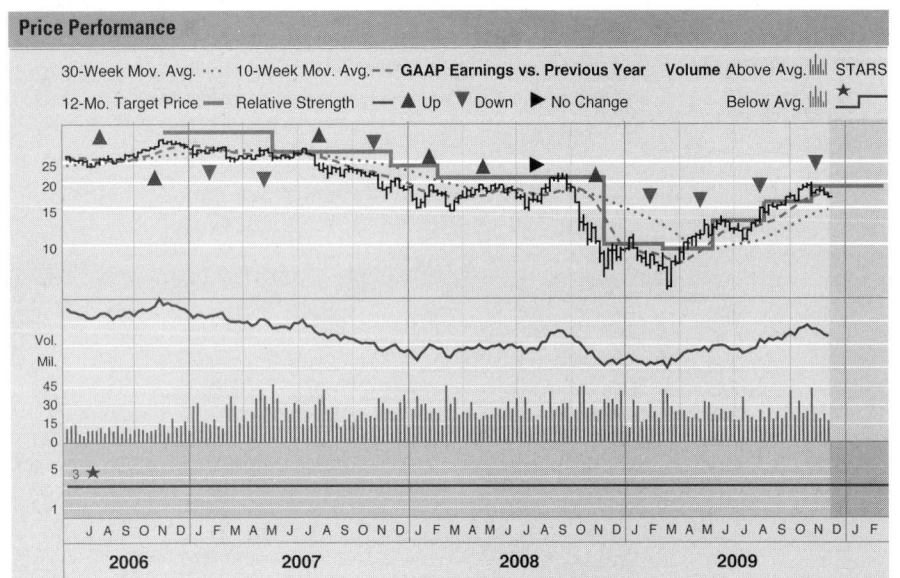

30-Week Mov. Avg. ···· 10-Week Mov. Avg. – – GAAP Earnings vs. Previous Year Volume Above Avg. STARS
12-Mo. Target Price — Relative Strength — ▲ Up ▼ Down ▶ No Change Below Avg.

Options: ASE, CBOE, P, Ph

Analysis prepared by **Marie Driscoll, CFA** on November 03, 2009, when the stock traded at **$ 17.78**.

Highlights

► LTD entered FY 10 (Jan.) with tightly managed inventories (down 34% per square foot in the past two years), a $150 million reduction in the expense base, and an approximate 58% cut to capital expenditures as it manages through the current consumer slowdown, which S&P forecasts will extend into 2010. Long-term growth opportunities include potential line extensions, sub-brands, and global expansion for Victoria's Secret and Bath & Body Works, the company's intimates and personal care retail brands. However, we see heightened category competition weakening near-term results.

► We project FY 10 (Jan.) sales of $8.43 billion, down 6%, reflecting a 5% same-store sales drop, flat direct sales, and a modest store opening schedule. LTD reported a 7% same-store sales decline for the first 35 weeks of FY 10, versus a 7% decline in the same period a year ago. We see a 2% sales drop in FY 11.

► We see 20 basis points of operating margin expansion in FY 10, to 8.1%, on reduced inventory investment and improved merchandise margins, modestly offset by deleveraging of fixed costs on reduced sales productivity. We see 80 basis points of margin expansion in FY 11.

Investment Rationale/Risk

► We see no near-term catalyst for share outperformance, with the shares recently trading at about 17.6X our FY 11 EPS estimate. We expect LTD to focus on controlling costs and improving the merchandise margin in FY 10, with a growth strategy of developing new concepts. La Senza (acquired in FY 08) launched LTD into the international intimate apparel market and should provide a platform for further global expansion, which we believe will be important given the relative maturity of LTD's many domestic retail concepts. The dividend recently provided a yield of about 3.4%.

► Risks to our recommendation and target price include fashion and inventory risk, weakening trends in consumer spending, integration risk with La Senza, and weak same-store sales trends. With an estimated 65%+ of LTD's profits earned in the fiscal fourth quarter, we think earnings risk is heightened.

► We employ DCF methodology to derive our 12-month target price of $19, incorporating a 10% WACC and 3% terminal growth rate. On a P/E basis, this represents 19X our FY 11 EPS estimate, in line with peers.

Qualitative Risk Assessment

LOW	MEDIUM	HIGH

Our risk assessment reflects LTD's strong cash flow, offset by execution risk in the company's attempt to re-position its Victoria's Secret brand in an increasingly competitive marketplace.

Quantitative Evaluations

S&P Quality Ranking B+

D	C	B-	B	B+	A-	A	A+

Relative Strength Rank MODERATE

42

LOWEST = 1   HIGHEST = 99

Revenue/Earnings Data

Revenue (Million $)

	1Q	2Q	3Q	4Q	Year
2010	1,725	2,067	1,777	--	--
2009	1,925	2,284	1,843	2,991	9,043
2008	2,311	2,624	1,923	3,276	10,134
2007	2,077	2,454	2,115	4,025	10,671
2006	1,975	2,291	1,892	3,542	9,699
2005	1,975	2,211	1,891	3,328	9,408

Earnings Per Share ($)

	1Q	2Q	3Q	4Q	Year
2010	-0.01	0.23	-0.05	E0.75	E1.01
2009	0.28	0.30	0.01	0.05	0.65
2008	0.13	0.30	-0.03	1.10	1.89
2007	0.25	0.28	0.06	1.08	1.68
2006	0.16	0.20	Nil	1.28	1.62
2005	0.06	0.31	0.16	0.87	1.47

Fiscal year ended Jan. 31. Next earnings report expected: Late February. EPS Estimates based on S&P Operating Earnings; historical GAAP earnings are as reported.

Dividend Data (Dates: mm/dd Payment Date: mm/dd/yy)

Amount ($)	Date Decl.	Ex-Div. Date	Stk. of Record	Payment Date
0.150	02/02	02/25	02/27	03/13/09
0.150	05/28	06/04	06/08	06/16/09
0.150	08/07	08/26	08/28	09/11/09
0.150	11/05	11/24	11/27	12/11/09

Dividends have been paid since 1970. Source: Company reports.

Please read the Required Disclosures and Analyst Certification on the last page of this report.

The McGraw-Hill Companies

Limited Brands Inc.

STANDARD &POOR'S

Business Summary November 03, 2009

CORPORATE OVERVIEW. Limited Brands (formerly The Limited) is a specialty retailer that conducts its business in two primary segments: Victoria's Secret, a women's intimate apparel, personal care products and accessories retail brand; and Bath & Body Works, a personal care and home fragrance products retail brand. At January 31, 2009, the store base consisted of 1,043 Victoria's Secret, 322 La Senza and 1,638 Bath & Body Works locations. LTD also operates five Henri Bendel stores and six BBW Canada stores. The company adopted its current name in May 2002.

In FY 08 (Jan.), LTD attempted to divest its apparel businesses and sold a 67% interest in Express and a 75% interest in The Limited for a net gain of $250 million. The divested apparel businesses generated $870 million of revenues in the FY 08 first half, accounting for 9% of FY 08 consolidated sales. Victoria's Secret accounted for 55%, and Bath & Body Works for 25%. The remaining 11% was Mast Industries external sales to third parties, including second-half sales to the divested apparel businesses.

Victoria's Secret (VS) is the leading specialty retailer of women's intimate apparel and beauty products, with FY 09 sales of $5.6 billion, which includes $1.5

billion at Victoria's Secret Direct, a catalog and e-commerce retailer of women's intimate and other apparel and beauty products and $490 million at La Senza. Bath & Body Works (BBW) is a specialty retailer of personal care and home fragrance products. FY 09 sales were $2.4 billion, including White Barn Candle Company.

MARKET PROFILE. The mature and fragmented U.S. women's apparel market generated about $109 billion at retail in 2008, according to NPD Fashionworld consumer estimated data. S&P forecasts that apparel sales will decline about 8% in 2009, following a 4% drop in 2008 and 4% gains in 2006 and 2007, based on NPD data. For 2009, we see reduced demand reflecting a weak economy with increased unemployment and deflationary pricing driving reduced apparel spending. The domestic personal care market is mature as well, with the demand function reflecting population trends in addition to the development of new categories.

Company Financials Fiscal Year Ended Jan. 31

Per Share Data ($)	2009	2008	2007	2006	2005	2004	2003	2002	2001	2000
Tangible Book Value	NM	NM	2.34	1.69	1.31	6.78	5.93	6.40	5.43	5.00
Cash Flow	1.77	2.82	2.46	2.45	2.17	1.90	1.48	1.83	1.58	1.61
Earnings	0.65	1.89	1.68	1.62	1.47	1.36	0.95	0.94	0.96	1.00
S&P Core Earnings	0.86	1.47	1.68	1.57	1.27	1.03	0.94	0.80	0.91	NA
Dividends	0.60	0.79	0.60	0.48	0.40	0.40	0.30	0.30	0.30	0.30
Payout Ratio	92%	42%	36%	30%	27%	29%	32%	32%	31%	30%
Calendar Year	2008	2007	2006	2005	2004	2003	2002	2001	2000	1999
Prices:High	22.16	30.03	32.60	25.50	27.89	18.46	22.34	21.29	27.88	25.31
Prices:Low	6.90	16.50	21.62	18.81	17.35	10.88	12.53	9.00	14.44	13.75
P/E Ratio:High	34	16	19	16	19	14	24	23	29	25
P/E Ratio:Low	11	9	13	12	12	8	13	10	15	14

Income Statement Analysis (Million $)

	2009	2008	2007	2006	2005	2004	2003	2002	2001	2000
Revenue	9,043	10,134	10,671	9,699	9,408	8,934	8,445	9,363	10,105	9,766
Operating Income	1,095	1,232	1,492	1,285	1,360	1,246	1,148	1,025	1,148	1,169
Depreciation	377	352	316	299	333	28.3	276	277	272	272
Interest Expense	181	149	102	94.0	58.0	62.0	30.0	34.0	58.0	78.0
Pretax Income	450	1,107	1,097	960	1,116	1,166	843	968	828	905
Effective Tax Rate	51.9%	37.1%	38.5%	30.3%	36.8%	38.5%	40.5%	39.8%	40.0%	41.0%
Net Income	220	718	675	669	705	717	496	519	428	461
S&P Core Earnings	291	561	675	638	609	540	492	352	406	NA

Balance Sheet & Other Financial Data (Million $)

	2009	2008	2007	2006	2005	2004	2003	2002	2001	2000
Cash	1,173	1,018	500	1,208	1,161	3,129	2,262	1,375	563	817
Current Assets	2,867	2,919	2,771	2,784	2,684	4,433	3,606	2,682	2,068	2,285
Total Assets	6,972	7,437	7,093	6,346	6,089	7,873	7,246	4,719	4,088	4,126
Current Liabilities	1,255	1,374	1,709	1,575	1,451	1,392	1,259	1,319	1,000	1,236
Long Term Debt	2,897	2,905	1,665	1,669	1,646	648	547	250	400	400
Common Equity	1,874	2,219	2,955	2,471	2,335	5,266	4,860	2,744	2,317	2,147
Total Capital	4,985	5,354	4,864	4,319	4,191	6,048	5,532	3,171	2,860	2,666
Capital Expenditures	479	749	548	480	431	293	306	337	446	375
Cash Flow	597	1,070	991	968	1,038	1,000	772	796	700	733
Current Ratio	2.3	2.1	1.6	1.8	1.8	3.2	2.9	2.0	2.1	1.8
% Long Term Debt of Capitalization	58.1	54.3	35.5	38.6	39.3	10.7	9.9	7.9	14.0	15.0
% Net Income of Revenue	2.4	7.1	6.3	6.9	7.5	8.0	5.9	5.5	4.2	4.7
% Return on Assets	3.1	9.9	10.1	10.8	10.1	9.5	8.0	11.8	10.4	10.7
% Return on Equity	10.8	27.8	24.9	27.9	18.6	14.2	13.0	20.5	19.2	21.4

Data as orig reptd.; bef. results of disc opers/spec. items. Per share data adj. for stk. divs.; EPS diluted. E-Estimated. NA-Not Available. NM-Not Meaningful. NR-Not Ranked. UR-Under Review.

Office: Three Limited Parkway, Columbus, OH 43216.
Telephone: 614-415-7000.
Website: http://www.limitedbrands.com
Chrmn & CEO: L.H. Wexner

EVP & CFO: S.B. Burgdoerfer
EVP & Chief Admin Officer: M.R. Redgrave
SVP, Secy & General Counsel: S.P. Fried
CTO: J.J. Ricker

Investor Contact: T.J. Faber ()
Board Members: D. S. Hersch, J. L. Heskett, D. A. James, D. T. Kollat, W. R. Loomis, Jr., J. H. Miro, J. Swartz, A. R. Tessler, A. S. Wexner, L. H. Wexner, R. Zimmerman

Founded: 1967
Domicile: Delaware
Employees: 90,900

Lincoln National Corp

STANDARD &POOR'S

S&P Recommendation **BUY** ★ ★ ★ ★ ★	Price	12-Mo. Target Price	Investment Style
	$22.81 (as of Nov 27, 2009)	$30.00	Large-Cap Value

GICS Sector Financials
Sub-Industry Life & Health Insurance

Summary This company offers annuities, life insurance, mutual funds, asset management, and related advisory services to affluent individuals.

Key Stock Statistics (Source S&P, Vickers, company reports)

52-Wk Range	$28.10– 4.90	S&P Oper. EPS 2009**E**	3.13	Market Capitalization(B)	$6.890	Beta	2.81
Trailing 12-Month EPS	$-4.13	S&P Oper. EPS 2010**E**	3.50	Yield (%)	0.18	S&P 3-Yr. Proj. EPS CAGR(%)	-13
Trailing 12-Month P/E	NM	P/E on S&P Oper. EPS 2009**E**	7.3	Dividend Rate/Share	$0.04	S&P Credit Rating	A-
$10K Invested 5 Yrs Ago	$5,636	Common Shares Outstg. (M)	302.1	Institutional Ownership (%)	77		

Price Performance

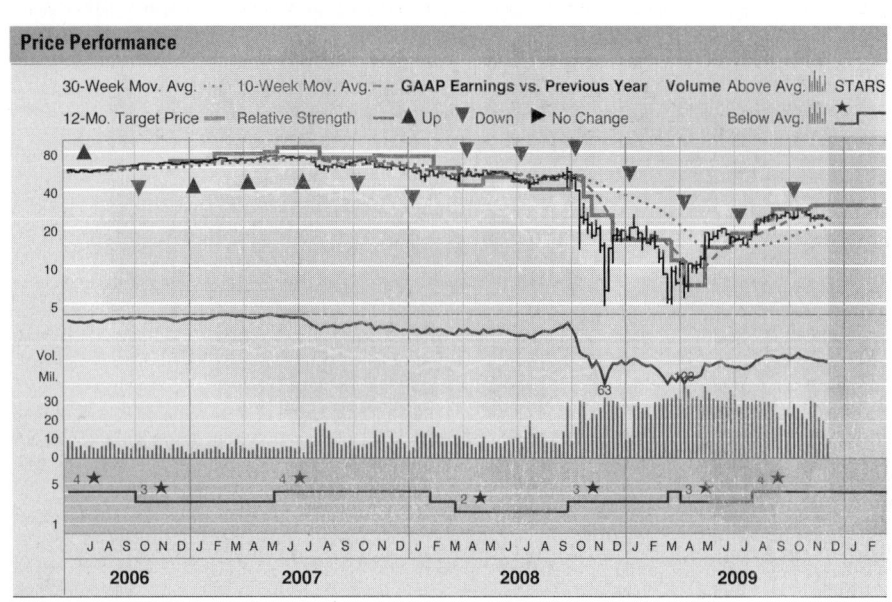

30-Week Mov. Avg. · · · 10-Week Mov. Avg. ─ **GAAP Earnings vs. Previous Year** Volume Above Avg. ▪▪▫ STARS
12-Mo. Target Price ─ Relative Strength ─ ▲ Up ▼ Down ▶ No Change Below Avg. ▪▫▫ ★

Options: ASE, CBOE, P, Ph

Analysis prepared by **Bret Howlett** on November 09, 2009, when the stock traded at **$ 24.81**.

Highlights

▶ We see operating earnings increasing in the high single-digits in Life Insurance in 2010, led by strong sales of term life and universal life products, and a pick-up in alternative investment income. We expect earnings in Annuities to benefit from solid sales of variable annuities (VA), and better investment spreads in the fixed and index annuity businesses, but we believe sales growth will moderate for fixed products. If the equity markets continue to appreciate going forward, we believe earnings will be boosted by a favorable deferred acquisition cost (DAC) unlocking and reserve releases related to LNC's VA guarantees.

▶ We remain cautious in our earnings outlook in the Group Protection segment since higher unemployment and a weak macro environment in 2010 could pressure sales and increase the loss ratio. We forecast earnings to rise in the high single-digits in the Defined Contribution unit due to better net flows, improved investment spreads and higher investment income.

▶ We forecast operating EPS of $3.13 in 2009 and $3.50 in 2010. Our estimates exclude realized investment gains or losses.

Investment Rationale/Risk

▶ Our Buy recommendation is based on our belief that LNC's valuation is attractive, with the stock recently trading at a sizable discount to the group. In addition, we believe the recent rebound in credit and equity markets, $2.1 billion raised through common stock and debt offerings, and participation in TARP have considerably strengthened the company's capital position. With nearly 40% of LNC's earnings derived from the equity markets, we believe the recent appreciation in the stock market has restored the core earnings power of the franchise. We expect LNC's business fundamentals to improve in 2010 driven by the strength of its internal sales force, a strong brand name, and partnerships with third-party distribution channels.

▶ Risks to our opinion and target price include a significant decline in equity markets, narrower-than-expected product spreads, deterioration in life insurance and annuity sales, instability in the credit markets, investment impairments, and the potential for a dilutive equity raise to repay TARP funds.

▶ Our 12-month target price of $30 is 0.8X LNC's 2009 book value, below the historical multiple.

Qualitative Risk Assessment

LOW	MEDIUM	**HIGH**

Our risk assessment reflects LNC's significant exposure to the equity markets and potential for further investment losses. We also believe weak credit and equity markets have limited the company's financial flexibility. As a partial offset, we think the company's capital position has benefited from its decision to accept TARP funds, and recent successful equity and debt issuances.

Quantitative Evaluations

S&P Quality Ranking B+

D	C	B-	B	**B+**	A-	A	A+

Relative Strength Rank WEAK

29

LOWEST = 1 HIGHEST = 99

Revenue/Earnings Data

Revenue (Million $)

	1Q	2Q	3Q	4Q	Year
2009	2,245	1,952	2,081	--	--
2008	2,592	2,582	2,436	2,273	9,883
2007	2,670	2,740	2,681	2,606	10,594
2006	1,417	2,496	2,487	2,658	9,063
2005	1,313	1,373	1,413	1,388	5,488
2004	1,259	1,359	1,406	1,347	5,371

Earnings Per Share ($)

2009	-2.27	Nil	0.21	E0.85	E3.13
2008	1.12	0.48	0.58	-1.98	0.24
2007	1.42	1.37	1.21	0.89	4.82
2006	1.24	1.23	1.29	1.36	5.13
2005	1.01	1.13	1.30	1.28	4.72
2004	0.86	1.04	1.12	1.07	4.09

Fiscal year ended Dec. 31. Next earnings report expected: Early February. EPS Estimates based on S&P Operating Earnings; historical GAAP earnings are as reported.

Dividend Data (Dates: mm/dd Payment Date: mm/dd/yy)

Amount ($)	Date Decl.	Ex-Div. Date	Stk. of Record	Payment Date
0.010	02/24	04/07	04/09	05/01/09
0.010	05/14	07/08	07/10	08/01/09
0.010	08/06	10/07	10/09	11/01/09
0.010	11/05	01/07	01/11	02/01/10

Dividends have been paid since 1920. Source: Company reports.

Lincoln National Corp

STANDARD &POOR'S

Business Summary November 09, 2009

CORPORATE OVERVIEW. Lincoln National is a holding company with subsidiaries that operate multiple insurance and investment management businesses. Primary operating subsidiaries include The Lincoln National Life Insurance Company, First Penn-Pacific Life Insurance Company, Lincoln Life & Annuity Company of New York, Delaware Management Holdings, Inc., Lincoln National (UK) plc, Lincoln Financial Advisors (LFA), a retail distribution unit, and Lincoln Financial Distributors (LFD), a wholesale distribution unit.

Following the acquisition of Jefferson-Pilot in April 2006, LNC's segments were restructured. In 2008, LNC's businesses were realigned again and operations are now divided into five business segments: Retirement Solutions (33% of 2008 operating revenue), Insurance Solutions (55%), Investment Management (4.1%), Lincoln U.K. (3.1%), and Other Operations (4.1%).

The Retirement Solutions segment offers products through two segments: Annuities and Defined Contribution. LNC offers guaranteed benefit riders on some of its variable annuity products including the guaranteed death benefit (GDB), a guaranteed withdrawal benefit (GWB), and a guaranteed income benefit (GIB). The Defined Contribution segment provides employers tax-deferred retirement savings plans for their employees mainly through 403 (b) and 401 (k) plans. LNC offers a number of savings products including individu-

al and group variable annuities, group fixed annuities and mutual funds. In addition, the company provides a variety of plan services including record keeping, compliance testing and participant education.

The Insurance Solutions segment provides products through its Life Insurance and Group Protection businesses. The life insurance business targets the affluent market, and underwrites and sells universal life, variable universal life, interest-sensitive whole life, corporate-owned life insurance (COLI), term-life insurance, and linked products such as universal life linked with long-term care benefits. The Group Protection business offers group non-medical insurance products to the employer marketplace.

The Investment Management segment offers retail and institutional mutual funds, separate and managed accounts, 529 college savings plans, and retirement plans and services, including 401(k) plans and administration services through Delaware Investments.

Company Financials Fiscal Year Ended Dec. 31

Per Share Data ($)	2008	2007	2006	2005	2004	2003	2002	2001	2000	1999
Tangible Book Value	15.13	15.20	27.92	22.47	22.25	18.74	15.62	14.10	11.06	5.59
Operating Earnings	NA	NA	NA	NA	NA	NA	2.56	3.56	3.27	2.32
Earnings	0.24	4.82	5.13	4.72	4.09	2.85	0.49	3.13	3.19	2.30
S&P Core Earnings	1.83	4.78	5.05	4.71	3.78	4.36	1.16	3.10	NA	NA
Dividends	1.66	1.58	1.52	1.46	1.40	1.34	1.28	1.22	1.16	1.10
Payout Ratio	NM	31%	30%	31%	34%	47%	NM	39%	36%	48%
Prices:High	59.99	74.72	66.72	54.41	50.38	41.32	53.65	52.75	56.38	57.50
Prices:Low	4.76	54.40	52.00	41.59	39.98	24.73	25.11	38.00	22.63	36.00
P/E Ratio:High	NM	15	13	12	12	14	NM	17	18	25
P/E Ratio:Low	NM	11	10	9	10	9	NM	12	7	16

Income Statement Analysis (Million $)										
Life Insurance in Force	781,400	748,200	702,600	339,100	325,700	307,800	873,595	651,900	637,100	516,600
Premium Income:Life	4,271	4,258	3,354	2,069	1,882	1,694	1,730	2,907	3,064	2,721
Premium Income:A & H	1,054	941	656	1.30	3.52	3.98	20.3	341	410	698
Net Investment Income	4,208	4,384	3,981	2,702	2,704	2,639	2,608	2,680	2,747	2,808
Total Revenue	9,883	10,594	9,063	5,488	5,371	5,284	4,635	6,381	6,852	6,798
Pretax Income	-25.6	1,874	1,811	1,075	1,036	1,048	1.62	764	836	570
Net Operating Income	NA	NA	NA	NA	NA	NA	474	689	639	457
Net Income	61.8	1,321	1,316	831	732	767	91.6	606	621	460
S&P Core Earnings	475	1,311	1,298	831	675	782	215	600	NA	NA

Balance Sheet & Other Financial Data (Million $)										
Cash & Equivalent	5,546	2,508	2,487	2,838	2,187	2,234	2,227	3,659	2,474	2,429
Premiums Due	481	401	356	343	233	352	213	400	297	260
Investment Assets:Bonds	48,935	56,276	55,853	33,443	34,701	32,769	32,767	28,346	27,450	27,689
Investment Assets:Stocks	288	518	701	3,391	3,399	3,319	337	471	550	604
Investment Assets:Loans	10,639	10,258	10,144	5,525	5,728	6,119	6,151	6,475	6,624	6,628
Investment Assets:Total	67,341	71,922	71,488	43,168	44,507	42,778	40,000	36,113	35,369	35,578
Deferred Policy Costs	11,936	9,580	8,420	4,092	3,445	3,192	2,971	2,885	3,071	2,800
Total Assets	163,136	191,435	178,494	124,788	116,219	106,745	93,133	98,001	99,844	103,096
Debt	6,758	5,168	4,116	1,333	1,083	1,459	1,512	1,336	1,457	1,457
Common Equity	7,976	11,718	71,017	6,384	6,175	5,811	5,296	5,263	4,953	4,264
% Return on Revenue	0.6	12.5	14.5	15.1	13.6	14.5	2.0	9.5	9.1	6.8
% Return on Assets	0.0	0.7	0.1	0.1	0.1	0.1	0.1	0.6	0.6	0.5
% Return on Equity	0.6	11.1	2.3	13.2	12.2	13.8	1.7	11.9	13.5	0.4
% Investment Yield	6.2	6.1	6.8	6.1	6.8	7.1	6.9	7.5	7.7	7.6

Data as orig reptd.; bef. results of disc opers/spec. items. Per share data adj. for stk. divs.; EPS diluted. E-Estimated. NA-Not Available. NM-Not Meaningful. NR-Not Ranked. UR-Under Review.

Office: 150 N Radnor Chester Rd Ste A305, Radnor, PA 19087-5238.
Telephone: 484-583-1400.
Email: investorrelations@lnc.com
Website: http://www.lfg.com

Chrmn: J.P. Barrett
Pres & CEO: D.R. Glass
EVP & CFO: F.J. Crawford
EVP & Chief Admin Officer: C.C. Cornelio

SVP & General Counsel: D.L. Schoff
Board Members: W. J. Avery, J. P. Barrett, W. H. Cunningham, D. R. Glass, G. W. Henderson, III, E. G. Johnson, M. L. Lachman, M. F. Mee, W. P. Payne, P. S. Pittard, D. A. Stonecipher, I. Tidwell

Founded: 1905
Domicile: Indiana
Employees: 9,696

The McGraw-Hill Companies

Linear Technology Corp

STANDARD &POOR'S

S&P Recommendation	STRONG BUY ★★★★★	Price $26.91 (as of Nov 27, 2009)	12-Mo. Target Price $32.00	Investment Style Large-Cap Growth

GICS Sector Information Technology
Sub-Industry Semiconductors

Summary This company manufactures high-performance linear integrated circuits.

Key Stock Statistics (Source S&P, Vickers, company reports)

52-Wk Range	$28.99– 18.19	S&P Oper. EPS 2010E	1.24	Market Capitalization(B)	$6.004	Beta	1.01
Trailing 12-Month EPS	$1.23	S&P Oper. EPS 2011E	1.32	Yield (%)	3.27	S&P 3-Yr. Proj. EPS CAGR(%)	-2
Trailing 12-Month P/E	21.9	P/E on S&P Oper. EPS 2010E	21.7	Dividend Rate/Share	$0.88	S&P Credit Rating	NA
$10K Invested 5 Yrs Ago	$7,901	Common Shares Outstg. (M)	223.1	Institutional Ownership (%)	99		

Price Performance

30-Week Mov. Avg. · · · 10-Week Mov. Avg. - - GAAP Earnings vs. Previous Year   Volume Above Avg. STARS
12-Mo. Target Price — Relative Strength — ▲ Up ▼ Down ► No Change   Below Avg.

Analysis prepared by **Clyde Montevirgen** on October 15, 2009, when the stock traded at **$ 27.40**.

Options: ASE, CBOE, P, Ph

Highlights

▶ We think revenues will rise 5% in FY 10 (Jun.), versus an 18% drop in FY 09. Although the weak global economy has hurt demand, we believe sales have troughed and are starting to recover. Near-term results should be supported by healthy computer and communications orders, in our view. As government stimulus spending flows out, we see industrial orders providing a lift to sales because of LLTC's large exposure to this end-market. Over the longer term, we believe that the proliferation of portable electronic devices and market share gains will aid revenue advances.

▶ We look for gross margins to widen to 76% in FY 10, from 75% in FY 09, due largely to higher plant utilization as demand recovers, and a more favorable sales mix. As we think operating leverage will improve with increasing sales, we expect operating margins to expand from the high 30% level at the end of FY 09 to around 43% by the end of FY 10.

▶ Our EPS projections assume an effective tax rate of around 30%, and include over $0.20 of stock-based compensation.

Investment Rationale/Risk

▶ Our strong buy opinion reflects our view of the company's solid and profitable business model, and anticipated catalysts related to recovering demand in currently weak markets, such as industrials. One of the better-run semiconductor companies, in our view, with relatively high margins, LLTC has been able to effectively manage through the downturn and maintain above-peer profitability. We believe LLTC offers generally less business risk than peers, and has more than enough cash and healthy free cash flows to reduce financial risks related to its leverage. Furthermore, it recently had a dividend yield of about 3.1%. Although the stock trades at a premium to peers, we believe that LLTC's longer-term growth is not yet fully discounted.

▶ Risks to our recommendation and target price include increasing competition, higher-than-anticipated operating expenses, and a longer-than-expected economic downturn.

▶ Our 12-month target price of $32 is based on our discounted cash flow analysis, which assumes a weighted average cost of capital of 9% and a terminal growth rate of 4%.

Qualitative Risk Assessment

LOW	MEDIUM	HIGH

Our risk assessment reflects the company's exposure to the sales cycles of the semiconductor industry. This is offset by stabilizing factors such as a high level of proprietary circuit design content, a varied customer base, diverse end markets, and wider margins than most competitors.

Quantitative Evaluations

S&P Quality Ranking   A-

D	C	B-	B	B+	A-	A	A+

Relative Strength Rank   MODERATE

52

LOWEST = 1   HIGHEST = 99

Revenue/Earnings Data

Revenue (Million $)

	1Q	2Q	3Q	4Q	Year
2010	236.1	--	--	--	--
2009	310.4	249.2	200.9	208.0	968.5
2008	281.5	288.7	297.9	307.1	1,175
2007	292.1	267.9	255.0	268.1	1,083
2006	256.0	265.2	278.9	292.9	1,093
2005	253.0	250.1	290.7	255.8	1,050

Earnings Per Share ($)

2010	0.27	E0.30	E0.32	E0.33	E1.24
2009	0.48	0.43	0.25	0.25	1.41
2008	0.40	0.41	0.44	0.46	1.71
2007	0.37	0.34	0.32	0.36	1.39
2006	0.31	0.33	0.35	0.37	1.37
2005	0.33	0.33	0.39	0.34	1.38

Fiscal year ended Jun. 30. Next earnings report expected: Mid January. EPS Estimates based on S&P Operating Earnings; historical GAAP earnings are as reported.

Dividend Data (Dates: mm/dd Payment Date: mm/dd/yy)

Amount ($)	Date Decl.	Ex-Div. Date	Stk. of Record	Payment Date
0.220	01/13	02/11	02/13	02/25/09
0.220	04/14	05/13	05/15	05/27/09
0.220	07/21	08/12	08/14	08/26/09
0.220	10/13	11/10	11/13	11/25/09

Dividends have been paid since 1992. Source: Company reports.

Linear Technology Corp

STANDARD
&POOR'S

Business Summary October 15, 2009

CORPORATE OVERVIEW. Linear Technology Corp. (LLTC) designs, makes and markets a broad line of high-performance standard linear integrated circuits (ICs) that address a wide range of real-world signal processing applications. Its principal product lines include operational and high-speed amplifiers, voltage regulators, voltage references, data converters, interface circuits, and other linear circuits, including buffers, battery monitors, comparators, drivers and filters.

LLTC's products are used in a wide variety of applications, including wireless and wireline telecommunications, networking, satellite systems, notebook and desk-top PCs, computer peripherals, video/multimedia, industrial instrumentation, medical devices, and high-end consumer products such as digital cameras and MP3 players.

The company has consistently expanded its customer base throughout its history. LLTC initially served primarily an industrial customer base, with a high percentage of revenues from the military market. Since the late 1980s, new products led to growth in the PC and hand-held device markets, and commu-

nication and networking markets contributed to growth significantly in recent years. The company now sells its products to more than 15,000 original equipment manufacturers directly or through a sales distributor channel. Its largest customer in FY 08 (Jun.) was the distributor Arrow Electronics, which accounted for 12% of total revenue. No other single company comprised over 10% of sales.

Linear has fabrication plants in Camas, WA, and Milpitas, CA. The company currently produces semiconductors on six-inch diameter (150 millimeter) wafers. Processed wafers are then shipped to its assembly plant in Penang, Malaysia, or other independent assembly contractors for "back-end" functions such as separating and packaging. The chips are then sent to its Singapore facility for final testing and inspection. The process from manufacturing to final testing can take up to 16 weeks.

Company Financials Fiscal Year Ended Jun. 30

Per Share Data ($)	2009	2008	2007	2006	2005	2004	2003	2002	2001	2000
Tangible Book Value	NM	NM	NM	6.94	6.55	5.87	5.80	5.63	5.59	4.20
Cash Flow	1.63	1.93	1.56	1.53	1.53	1.17	0.88	0.74	1.39	0.95
Earnings	1.41	1.71	1.39	1.37	1.38	1.02	0.74	0.60	1.29	0.88
S&P Core Earnings	1.41	1.71	1.39	1.37	0.99	0.79	0.50	0.40	1.10	NA
Dividends	0.86	0.78	0.66	0.50	0.36	0.28	0.21	0.17	0.13	0.08
Payout Ratio	61%	46%	47%	36%	26%	27%	28%	28%	10%	9%
Prices:High	28.99	37.77	38.84	39.35	41.67	45.09	44.80	47.50	65.13	74.75
Prices:Low	20.26	17.69	29.62	27.80	32.83	34.01	24.76	18.92	29.45	35.06
P/E Ratio:High	21	22	28	29	30	44	61	79	50	85
P/E Ratio:Low	14	10	21	20	24	33	33	32	23	40

Income Statement Analysis (Million $)										
Revenue	968	1,175	1,083	1,093	1,050	807	607	512	973	706
Operating Income	464	617	575	613	638	485	340	271	582	399
Depreciation	48.0	48.1	50.7	49.3	48.8	48.7	45.9	46.3	35.8	25.0
Interest Expense	52.3	57.8	12.1	Nil	Nil	Nil	Nil	Nil	Nil	Nil
Pretax Income	407	541	570	617	620	462	333	278	611	417
Effective Tax Rate	23.0%	28.4%	27.8%	30.5%	30.0%	29.0%	29.0%	29.0%	30.0%	31.0%
Net Income	314	388	412	429	434	328	237	198	427	288
S&P Core Earnings	314	388	412	429	311	253	161	132	366	NA

Balance Sheet & Other Financial Data (Million $)										
Cash	869	967	156	541	323	204	136	212	321	230
Current Assets	1,089	1,246	861	2,077	2,007	1,832	1,776	1,728	1,728	1,310
Total Assets	1,422	1,584	1,219	2,391	2,286	2,088	2,057	1,988	2,017	1,507
Current Liabilities	125	175	180	237	208	203	162	169	202	169
Long Term Debt	1,406	1,700	1,700	Nil	Nil	Nil	Nil	Nil	Nil	Nil
Common Equity	-267	-434	-708	2,104	2,007	1,811	1,815	1,781	1,782	1,322
Total Capital	1,202	1,308	1,005	2,104	2,007	1,811	1,815	1,819	1,815	1,339
Capital Expenditures	39.1	35.3	62.0	69.4	62.1	20.7	6.61	17.9	128	80.3
Cash Flow	362	436	462	478	483	377	282	244	463	313
Current Ratio	8.7	7.1	4.8	8.8	9.7	9.0	11.0	10.2	8.5	7.8
% Long Term Debt of Capitalization	116.9	130.0	169.2	Nil	Nil	Nil	Nil	Nil	Nil	Nil
% Net Income of Revenue	32.4	33.0	38.0	39.2	41.3	40.7	39.0	38.6	43.9	40.8
% Return on Assets	20.9	27.7	22.8	18.3	19.8	15.8	11.7	9.9	24.3	22.5
% Return on Equity	NM	NM	59.0	20.9	22.7	18.1	13.2	11.1	27.5	25.8

Data as orig reptd.; bef. results of disc opers/spec. items. Per share data adj. for stk. divs.; EPS diluted. E-Estimated. NA-Not Available. NM-Not Meaningful. NR-Not Ranked. UR-Under Review.

Office: 1630 McCarthy Boulevard, Milpitas, CA 95035-7487.
Telephone: 408-432-1900.
Website: http://www.linear.com
Chrmn: R.H. Swanson, Jr.

CEO: L. Maier
COO: A.R. McCann
Investor Contact: P. Coghlan (408-432-1900)
CFO, Chief Acctg Officer & Secy: P. Coghlan

Board Members: D. S. Lee, L. Maier, R. M. Moley, R. H. Swanson, Jr., T. S. Volpe

Founded: 1981
Domicile: Delaware
Employees: 3,821

Lockheed Martin Corp

STANDARD &POOR'S

S&P Recommendation	SELL ★★☆☆☆	Price $77.10 (as of Nov 27, 2009)	12-Mo. Target Price $65.00	Investment Style Large-Cap Growth

GICS Sector Industrials
Sub-Industry Aerospace & Defense

Summary This company is the world's largest military weapons manufacturer and is also a significant supplier to NASA and other government agencies.

Key Stock Statistics (Source S&P, Vickers, company reports)

52-Wk Range	$87.06– 57.41	S&P Oper. EPS 2009**E**	7.58	Market Capitalization(B)	$29.358	Beta	0.99
Trailing 12-Month EPS	$7.65	S&P Oper. EPS 2010**E**	7.50	Yield (%)	3.27	S&P 3-Yr. Proj. EPS CAGR(%)	-3
Trailing 12-Month P/E	10.1	P/E on S&P Oper. EPS 2009**E**	10.2	Dividend Rate/Share	$2.52	S&P Credit Rating	A-
$10K Invested 5 Yrs Ago	$14,326	Common Shares Outstg. (M)	380.8	Institutional Ownership (%)	89		

Price Performance

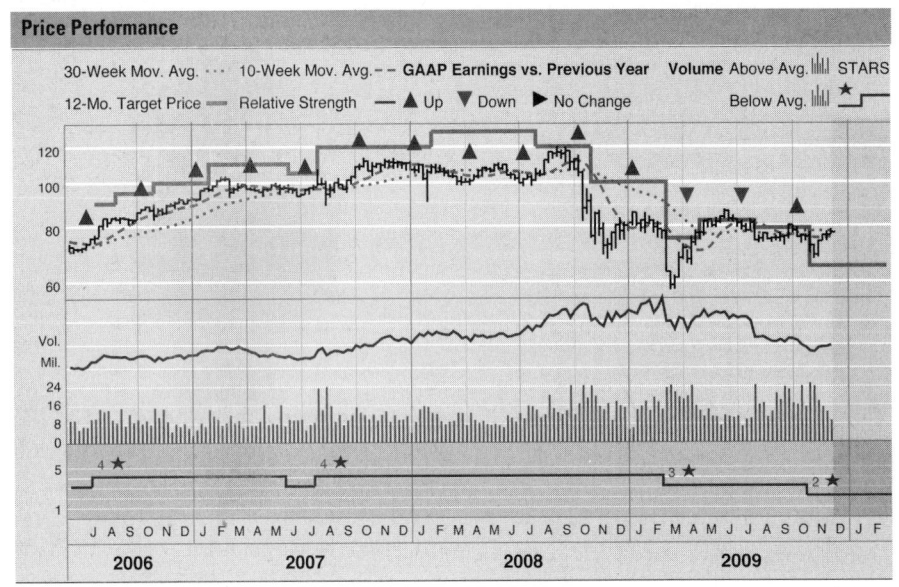

30-Week Mov. Avg. · · · 10-Week Mov. Avg. - - **GAAP Earnings vs. Previous Year** Volume Above Avg. STARS
12-Mo. Target Price — Relative Strength — ▲ Up ▼ Down ▶ No Change Below Avg.

Options: ASE, CBOE, P, Ph

Analysis prepared by **Richard Tortoriello** on October 23, 2009, when the stock traded at **$ 72.25**.

Highlights

▶ We project a 5% revenue increase in 2009, and a 3% increase in 2010. We see 2010 sales up in all four segments, with the highest growth in Aeronautics (3%), and lower growth in Information Systems & Global Services, Electronic Systems, and Space Systems. We expect F-35 revenue to increase in 2011 and beyond as the program transitions from low-rate initial production to full production, but expect margins on the F-35 program to remain low until production processes have matured.

▶ We expect operating margins to narrow to 9.8% in 2009, from 12% in 2008, and to narrow further to 9.4% in 2010. One primary drag we see on operating margins is increased pension expense. However, we note that our estimate suggests margins at IS&GS will narrow to 8.4% in 2009, from 9.3% in 2008 and 2007. We believe these margins declines are partly due to price pressure on new contracts.

▶ We estimate that EPS will decline to $7.58 in 2009, and to $7.50 in 2010. We expect free cash flow per share to be significantly above earnings per share in 2009.

Investment Rationale/Risk

▶ Although we see significant long-term opportunities for Lockheed in Aeronautics (LMT expects nearly $20 billion in annual revenue from the F-35 by 2015) and in international military sales, we view the outlook for U.S. defense budget growth, the largest driver of LMT's earnings, as weak. Specifically, we see a ballooning U.S. budget deficit and changing military priorities as likely to shift funding away from large military programs. We also see the government putting increasing emphasis on low price for new contracts. As a result, despite our view of valuations that are low historically, we would sell the shares.

▶ Risks to our recommendation and target price include the potential for unexpected increases in defense spending and the possibility that the government's defense budgets could favor LMT.

▶ Our 12-month target price of $65 is based on an enterprise value multiple of 5X our 2010 EBITDA estimate. This multiple is below a 20-year average EV-to-EBITDA multiple for LMT of 8X, but above an historical low of 4X, due to our view of a likely decline in U.S. defense spending.

Qualitative Risk Assessment

LOW	**MEDIUM**	HIGH

Our risk assessment reflects the company's leading position in military markets and our view of a healthy balance sheet, with long-term debt representing about 27% of LMT's total capitalization as of September 2009. However, our risk evaluation also factors the dependence of Lockheed's business on government funding, which can change with political and economic priorities.

Quantitative Evaluations

S&P Quality Ranking   B+

D	C	B-	B	**B+**	A-	A	A+

Relative Strength Rank   MODERATE

68

LOWEST = 1   HIGHEST = 99

Revenue/Earnings Data

Revenue (Million $)

	1Q	2Q	3Q	4Q	Year
2009	10,373	11,236	11,056	--	--
2008	9,983	11,039	10,577	11,132	42,731
2007	9,275	10,651	11,095	10,841	41,862
2006	9,214	9,961	9,605	10,840	39,620
2005	8,488	9,295	9,201	10,229	37,213
2004	8,347	8,776	8,438	9,965	35,526

Earnings Per Share ($)

2009	1.68	1.88	2.07	E1.97	E7.58
2008	1.75	2.15	1.92	2.05	7.86
2007	1.60	1.82	1.80	1.89	7.10
2006	1.34	1.34	1.46	1.68	5.80
2005	0.83	1.02	0.96	1.29	4.10
2004	0.65	0.66	0.69	0.83	2.83

Fiscal year ended Dec. 31. Next earnings report expected: Late January. EPS Estimates based on S&P Operating Earnings; historical GAAP earnings are as reported.

Dividend Data (Dates: mm/dd Payment Date: mm/dd/yy)

Amount ($)	Date Decl.	Ex-Div. Date	Stk. of Record	Payment Date
0.570	01/22	02/26	03/02	03/27/09
0.570	04/23	05/28	06/01	06/26/09
0.570	06/25	08/28	09/01	09/25/09
0.630	09/24	11/27	12/01	12/31/09

Dividends have been paid since 1995. Source: Company reports.

Please read the Required Disclosures and Analyst Certification on the last page of this report.

The McGraw-Hill Companies

Lockheed Martin Corp

STANDARD
&POOR'S

Business Summary October 23, 2009

CORPORATE OVERVIEW. Lockheed Martin is the world's largest military weapons maker. During 2008, the company derived 84% of its net sales from the U.S. government, including both Department of Defense (DoD) and non-DoD agencies. Sales to foreign governments were 13% of net sales, with 3% of net sales to commercial and other customers. Lockheed Martin conducts business through four operating segments:

The Aeronautics segment (27% of revenues and 29% of operating profits in 2008) primarily makes fighter jets and military transport planes. Major development and production programs include the F-35 Lightning II, the F-22 Raptor, the F-16 Fighting Falcon, and the C-130J Super Hercules transport. In addition, LMT's "Skunk Works" research & development laboratory is well known for its advanced R&D efforts. It is currently focused on unmanned military aircraft, among other initiatives.

Electronic Systems (27% and 30%) primarily makes land-, sea- and air-based missiles and missile defense systems. Other offerings include various electronic surveillance and reconnaissance systems. About 41% of the segment's 2007 sales came from maritime systems & sensors, with another 38% coming from missiles & fire control products. Major current programs include the Terminal High-Altitude Area Defense System (THAAD), the Patriot Advanced Capability (PAC-3) missile, the AEGIS Ballistic Missile Defense system, and the Arrowhead fire control system for the Apache helicopter.

Space Systems (19% and 19%) mostly makes satellites, strategic and defensive missile systems and space transportation systems. Satellites include both government and commercial products. Space transportation systems include NASA's next-generation space flight systems, including the Orion crew exploration vehicle. Satellites accounted for 63% of segment sales in 2008. LMT is the prime contractor for the Space-Based Infrared System (SBIRS) missile detection program and the Advanced Extremely High Frequency (AEHF) communications system. LMT's 50/50 joint venture with Boeing, the United Launch Alliance, provides satellite launch services to the U.S. government.

Information Systems & Global Services (27% and 22%) is engaged in a wide variety of information technology, IT services, and other technology services to federal agencies and other customers. Major product lines/programs include: transformational communication systems; mission & combat support solutions; civil agency programs (including the U.S. Census); the FAA Automated Flight Service Station; the FBI's Sentinel IT program; mission planning and launch services for NASA's Orion project; other NASA programs; and military and space efforts.

Company Financials Fiscal Year Ended Dec. 31

Per Share Data ($)	2008	2007	2006	2005	2004	2003	2002	2001	2000	1999
Tangible Book Value	NM	NM	NM	NM	NM	NM	NM	NM	NM	NM
Cash Flow	9.92	9.02	7.55	5.68	4.39	3.69	2.40	2.08	1.36	3.30
Earnings	7.86	7.10	5.80	4.10	2.83	2.34	1.18	0.18	-1.05	1.92
S&P Core Earnings	4.07	6.65	5.70	4.11	3.23	2.20	-0.78	-2.29	NA	NA
Dividends	1.83	1.47	1.25	1.05	0.91	0.58	0.44	0.44	0.44	0.88
Payout Ratio	23%	21%	22%	26%	32%	25%	37%	NM	NM	46%
Prices:High	120.30	113.74	93.24	65.46	61.77	58.95	71.52	52.98	37.58	46.00
Prices:Low	67.38	88.86	62.52	52.54	43.10	40.64	45.85	31.00	16.50	16.38
P/E Ratio:High	15	16	16	16	22	25	61	NM	NM	24
P/E Ratio:Low	9	13	11	13	15	17	39	NM	NM	9

Income Statement Analysis (Million $)										
Revenue	42,731	41,862	39,620	37,213	35,526	31,824	26,578	23,990	25,329	25,530
Operating Income	5,494	5,032	4,198	3,242	2,624	2,585	2,507	2,366	2,582	2,634
Depreciation	845	819	764	705	656	609	558	823	968	969
Interest Expense	341	352	361	370	425	487	581	700	919	809
Pretax Income	4,702	4,368	3,592	2,616	1,664	1,532	577	188	286	1,200
Effective Tax Rate	31.6%	30.6%	29.6%	30.2%	23.9%	31.3%	7.63%	58.0%	NM	38.6%
Net Income	3,217	3,033	2,529	1,825	1,266	1,053	533	79.0	-424	737
S&P Core Earnings	1,666	2,844	2,486	1,830	1,448	994	-353	-989	NA	NA

Balance Sheet & Other Financial Data (Million $)										
Cash	2,229	2,981	1,912	2,244	1,060	1,010	2,738	912	1,505	455
Current Assets	10,683	10,940	10,164	10,529	8,953	9,401	10,626	10,778	11,259	10,696
Total Assets	33,434	28,926	28,231	27,744	25,554	26,175	25,758	27,654	30,349	30,012
Current Liabilities	10,542	9,871	9,553	9,428	8,566	8,893	9,821	9,689	10,175	8,812
Long Term Debt	3,563	4,303	4,405	4,784	5,104	6,072	6,217	7,422	9,065	11,427
Common Equity	2,865	9,805	6,884	7,867	7,021	6,756	5,865	6,443	7,160	6,361
Total Capital	6,428	14,108	11,289	12,651	12,125	12,828	12,082	14,857	16,961	17,788
Capital Expenditures	926	940	893	865	769	687	662	619	500	669
Cash Flow	4,062	3,852	3,293	2,530	1,922	1,662	1,091	902	544	1,266
Current Ratio	1.0	1.1	1.1	1.1	1.0	1.1	1.1	1.1	1.1	1.2
% Long Term Debt of Capitalization	55.4	30.5	39.0	37.8	42.1	47.3	51.5	50.0	53.4	64.2
% Net Income of Revenue	7.5	7.3	6.4	4.9	3.6	3.3	2.0	0.3	NM	2.9
% Return on Assets	10.3	10.6	9.0	6.8	4.9	4.0	2.0	0.3	NM	2.5
% Return on Equity	50.8	36.4	34.3	24.5	18.4	16.7	8.7	1.2	NM	11.8

Data as orig reptd.; bef. results of disc opers/spec. items. Per share data adj. for stk. divs.; EPS diluted. E-Estimated. NA-Not Available. NM-Not Meaningful. NR-Not Ranked. UR-Under Review.

Office: 6801 Rockledge Drive, Bethesda, MD 20817.
Telephone: 301-897-6000.
Website: http://www.lockheedmartin.com
Chrmn, Pres & CEO: R.J. Stevens

Pres: M.S. Williams
COO: R. Nakamoto
EVP & CFO: B.L. Tanner
SVP & CTO: R. Johnson

Board Members: E. Aldridge, Jr., N. D. Archibald, D. Burritt, J. O. Ellis, Jr., G. S. King, J. M. Loy, D. H. McCorkindale, J. W. Ralston, F. Savage, J. Schneider, A. Stevens, R. J. Stevens, J. R. Ukropina

Founded: 1909
Domicile: Maryland
Employees: 146,000

Loews Corp

STANDARD &POOR'S

| S&P Recommendation **BUY** ★★★★☆ | Price $35.00 (as of Nov 27, 2009) | 12-Mo. Target Price $39.00 | Investment Style Large-Cap Value |

GICS Sector Financials
Sub-Industry Multi-line Insurance

Summary This conglomerate includes holdings in property/casualty insurance, offshore drilling, hotels, and natural gas pipelines.

Key Stock Statistics (Source S&P, Vickers, company reports)

52-Wk Range	$36.66– 17.40	S&P Oper. EPS 2009**E**	1.35	Market Capitalization(B)	$15.037	Beta	1.33
Trailing 12-Month EPS	$-1.83	S&P Oper. EPS 2010**E**	3.89	Yield (%)	0.71	S&P 3-Yr. Proj. EPS CAGR(%)	2
Trailing 12-Month P/E	NM	P/E on S&P Oper. EPS 2009**E**	25.9	Dividend Rate/Share	$0.25	S&P Credit Rating	A
$10K Invested 5 Yrs Ago	$15,895	Common Shares Outstg. (M)	429.6	Institutional Ownership (%)	53		

Price Performance

30-Week Mov. Avg. ···· 10-Week Mov. Avg. – – **GAAP Earnings vs. Previous Year** Volume Above Avg. STARS
12-Mo. Target Price — Relative Strength — ▲ Up ▼ Down ► No Change Below Avg.

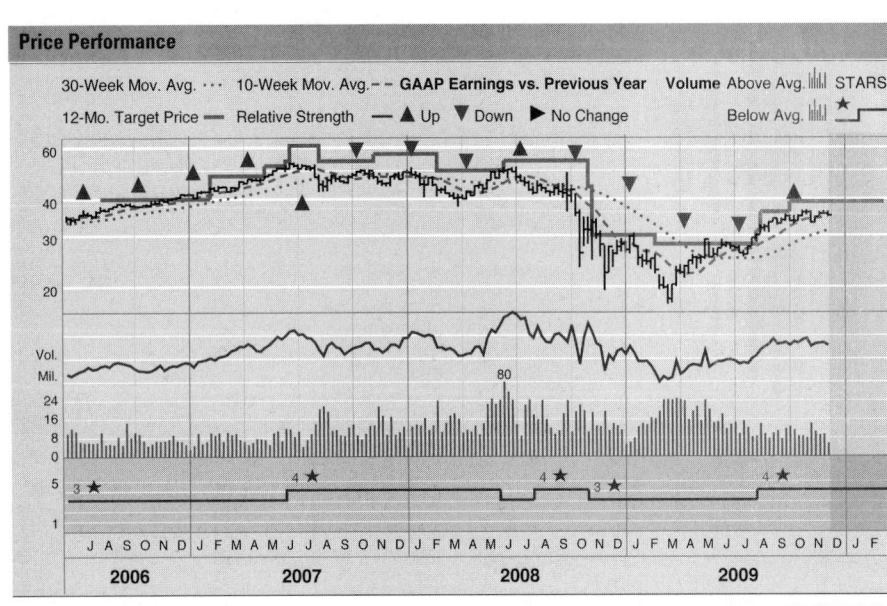

Options: ASE, CBOE, P, Ph

Analysis prepared by **Bret Howlett** on November 12, 2009, when the stock traded at **$ 35.58**.

Highlights

► We see revenues increasing around 8% in 2010 at L's principal subsidiary, 90%-owned CNA Financial (CNA 22, Hold), as we expect it to benefit from an improving P&C rate environment and higher investment income. We view positively CNA's solid track record of favorable reserve releases, which we believe reflects its strong underwriting. We expect utilization rates to stabilize at 50%-owned Diamond Offshore (DO 102, Buy), and its robust backlog and low capital spending needs should provide solid earnings visibility. We forecast considerably higher operating earnings for 74%-owned Boardwalk Pipeline Partners (BWP), as pipeline maintenance issues are resolved and natural gas storage capacity expands.

► We expect operating earnings to decline roughly 10% at CNA on lower new business production due to the tough pricing environment and a normalization of catastrophe losses. We believe the recovery in the credit markets could allow CNA to pay back L's preferred stock investment in 2010. We forecast double digit earnings growth for L's hotel business.

► Our forecast of EPS from continuing operations is $1.35 for 2009 and $3.89 for 2010.

Investment Rationale/Risk

► Our buy recommendation is based on our forecast for improved fundamentals in L's subsidiaries. At current levels, we view L's valuation as attractive. We believe the strength in the financial markets has reduced the risks related to L's investment portfolio and CNA's capital position, and we expect the company to deploy excess cash by repurchasing its shares, undertaking new business ventures, and investing in the debt markets. We see the operating environment improving for CNA, and we believe the down-phase in the commercial underwriting pricing cycle will stabilize or reverse. We think a rebound in oil prices will boost income at L's energy subsidiaries and that HighMount will benefit from a rebound in production.

► Risks to our recommendation and target price include a decline in the level of oil and gas production at Diamond Offshore; higher-than-projected catastrophe losses; greater-than-expected losses in the investment portfolio; asbestos and environmental losses at CNA; and a slowdown in consumer spending affecting Loews Hotels.

► Our 12-month target price of $39 is 10X our 2010 EPS estimate, below historical multiples.

Qualitative Risk Assessment

| LOW | MEDIUM | HIGH |

Our risk assessment for Loews reflects exposure to investment losses from its CNA Financial subsidiary, regulatory risks, litigation risk, and catastrophe losses. This is offset by its diversified group of holdings and substantial free cash flow.

Quantitative Evaluations

S&P Quality Ranking   B

| D | C | B- | B | B+ | A- | A | A+ |

Relative Strength Rank   MODERATE

62

LOWEST = 1   HIGHEST = 99

Revenue/Earnings Data

Revenue (Million $)

	1Q	2Q	3Q	4Q	Year
2009	3,023	3,534	3,738	--	--
2008	3,612	3,922	2,970	2,743	13,247
2007	4,660	4,637	4,653	4,567	18,380
2006	4,245	4,277	4,507	4,882	17,911
2005	3,741	4,031	4,138	4,108	16,018
2004	3,491	3,915	3,785	4,051	15,242

Earnings Per Share ($)

	1Q	2Q	3Q	4Q	Year
2009	-1.49	0.78	1.08	E0.98	E1.35
2008	0.77	1.00	-0.33	-2.20	-0.82
2007	1.19	0.96	0.76	0.71	3.64
2006	0.86	0.85	0.93	1.15	3.80
2005	0.53	0.68	0.42	0.07	1.69
2004	0.02	0.66	0.40	0.80	1.88

Fiscal year ended Dec. 31. Next earnings report expected: Early February. EPS Estimates based on S&P Operating Earnings; historical GAAP earnings are as reported.

Dividend Data (Dates: mm/dd Payment Date: mm/dd/yy)

Amount ($)	Date Decl.	Ex-Div. Date	Stk. of Record	Payment Date
0.063	02/10	02/26	03/02	03/13/09
0.063	05/12	05/28	06/01	06/12/09
0.063	08/11	08/28	09/01	09/14/09
0.063	11/10	11/25	11/30	12/11/09

Dividends have been paid since 1967. Source: Company reports.

Loews Corp

STANDARD
&POOR'S

Business Summary November 12, 2009

CORPORATE OVERVIEW. Loews Corp. is a holding company with interests in property/casualty insurance (CNA Financial Corp., 90% stake), hotels (Loews Hotels Holding Corp.), offshore oil and gas drilling (Diamond Offshore Drilling, Inc., 50%), exploration, production and marketing of natural gas and natural gas liquids (HighMount Exploration & Production LLC), and interstate natural gas pipelines (Boardwalk Pipeline Partners, LP, 74%).

CNA Financial Corp. (NYSE: CNA; 59% of consolidated total revenues in 2008) is an insurance holding company with subsidiaries that primarily consist of property and casualty insurance companies. The company serves small, medium and large businesses as well as associations, professionals and groups. CNA's The Loews Hotels division (2.9%) owns and/or operates 18 hotels in the U.S. and Canada. Diamond Offshore (NYSE: DO; 26%) operates 45

offshore drilling rigs that are chartered on a contract basis for fixed terms by energy exploration companies. Boardwalk Pipeline Partners (NYSE: BWP; 6.4%) owns and operates three interstate natural gas pipeline systems, Gulf Crossing Pipeline Company, Gulf South Pipeline and Texas Gas Transmission. HighMount Exploration & Production LLC (5.8%) is involved in the exploration, production and marketing of natural gas, NGLs (predominantly ethane and propane) and oil. Other activities reported a consolidated revenue loss of $36 million in 2008.

Company Financials Fiscal Year Ended Dec. 31

Per Share Data ($)	2008	2007	2006	2005	2004	2003	2002	2001	2000	1999
Tangible Book Value	27.93	25.44	NM	NM	21.35	NM	19.88	16.23	18.28	15.24
Operating Earnings	NA	NA	NA	NA	NA	NA	1.71	-2.27	1.90	1.01
Earnings	-0.82	3.64	3.80	1.69	1.88	-1.30	1.50	-0.92	3.15	0.80
S&P Core Earnings	1.57	3.76	3.65	1.49	2.17	-2.00	2.63	-2.47	NA	NA
Dividends	0.25	0.25	0.18	0.20	0.20	0.20	0.20	0.19	0.17	0.17
Relative Payout	NM	7%	5%	12%	11%	NM	13%	NM	5%	21%
Prices:High	51.51	53.46	42.18	32.90	23.67	16.49	20.77	24.17	34.98	17.42
Prices:Low	19.39	40.21	30.42	22.35	16.36	12.75	12.50	13.68	12.75	9.75
P/E Ratio:High	NM	15	11	19	13	NM	14	NM	11	22
P/E Ratio:Low	NM	11	8	13	9	NM	8	NM	4	12

Income Statement Analysis (Million $)										
Life Insurance in Force	NA	14,090	15,652	20,548	56,645	388,968	437,751	497,732	534,781	469,990
Premium Income:Life A & H	611	618	641	704	901	2,275	3,382	4,351	4,549	4,502
Premium Income:Casualty/Property.	6,539	6,866	6,962	6,865	7,304	6,935	6,828	5,010	6,923	8,775
Net Investment Income	1,581	2,891	2,915	2,099	1,869	1,732	1,867	2,145	2,388	2,175
Total Revenue	13,247	18,380	17,911	16,018	15,242	16,461	17,495	19,417	21,338	21,465
Pretax Income	587	4,575	1,237	1,016	1,822	-751	1,647	-813	3,206	945
Net Operating Income	NA	NA	NA	NA	NA	NA	1,099	-1,328	1,134	658
Net Income	-182	2,481	760	623	1,231	-468	983	-536	1,877	521
S&P Core Earnings	749	2,014	2,024	831	1,205	-1,112	1,594	-1,447	NA	NA

Balance Sheet & Other Financial Data (Million $)										
Cash & Equivalent	2,030	141	132	151	220	181	185	181	195	184
Premiums Due	11,672	11,677	12,423	15,314	18,807	20,468	16,601	19,453	15,302	13,529
Investment Assets:Bonds	29,451	34,663	37,570	33,381	33,502	28,781	27,434	31,191	27,244	27,924
Investment Assets:Stocks	1,185	1,347	1,309	1,107	664	888	1,121	1,646	2,683	4,024
Investment Assets:Loans	Nil	Nil	Nil	Nil	Nil	Nil	NA	NA	NA	NA
Investment Assets:Total	38,450	47,923	52,020	43,547	44,299	42,515	40,137	41,159	40,396	40,633
Deferred Policy Costs	1,125	1,161	1,190	1,197	1,268	2,533	2,551	2,424	2,418	2,436
Total Assets	69,857	76,079	75,325	69,548	73,750	77,881	70,520	75,251	70,877	69,464
Debt	8,187	6,900	1,230	1,627	5,980	2,032	5,652	5,920	6,040	5,706
Common Equity	13,126	17,591	15,580	-201	45,428	-729	11,235	9,649	11,191	9,978
Combined Loss-Expense Ratio	109.0	110.1	109.1	120.3	105.9	146.6	110.3	158.6	113.6	120.9
% Return on Revenue	NM	13.5	4.2	3.9	8.1	14.2	5.6	NM	8.8	2.4
% Return on Equity	NM	15.0	14.2	2.6	2.8	NM	8.1	NM	4.9	5.2
% Investment Yield	3.7	5.8	6.1	2.6	4.3	4.2	4.6	5.2	5.9	5.2

Data as orig reptd.; bef. results of disc opers/spec. items. Per share data adj. for stk. divs.; EPS diluted. E-Estimated. NA-Not Available. NM-Not Meaningful. NR-Not Ranked. UR-Under Review.

Office: 667 Madison Ave, New York, NY 10065-8087.
Telephone: 212-521-2000.
Website: http://www.loews.com
Co-Chrmn: J.M. Tisch

Co-Chrmn: A. Tisch
Pres & CEO: J.S. Tisch
SVP & CFO: P.W. Keegan
SVP, Secy & General Counsel: G.W. Garson

Investor Contact: D. Daugherty (212-521-2788)
Board Members: A. E. Berman, J. L. Bower, C. M. Diker, P. J. Fribourg, W. L. Harris, P. A. Laskawy, K. Miller, G. R. Scott, A. Tisch, J. S. Tisch, J. M. Tisch

Founded: 1954
Domicile: Delaware
Employees: 19,100

Lorillard Inc

STANDARD &POOR'S

S&P Recommendation **BUY** ★★★★☆	Price $78.91 (as of Nov 27, 2009)	12-Mo. Target Price $81.00	Investment Style Large-Cap Blend

GICS Sector Consumer Staples
Sub-Industry Tobacco

Summary Lorillard is the third largest U.S. tobacco company and the leading manufacturer and marketer of menthol cigarettes.

Key Stock Statistics (Source S&P, Vickers, company reports)

52-Wk Range	$81.76– 52.50	S&P Oper. EPS 2009**E**	5.76	Market Capitalization(B)	$12.676	Beta	0.49
Trailing 12-Month EPS	$5.77	S&P Oper. EPS 2010**E**	6.22	Yield (%)	5.07	S&P 3-Yr. Proj. EPS CAGR(%)	7
Trailing 12-Month P/E	13.7	P/E on S&P Oper. EPS 2009**E**	13.7	Dividend Rate/Share	$4.00	S&P Credit Rating	BBB-
$10K Invested 5 Yrs Ago	$28,867	Common Shares Outstg. (M)	160.6	Institutional Ownership (%)	100		

Price Performance

30-Week Mov. Avg. · · · 10-Week Mov. Avg. - - **GAAP Earnings vs. Previous Year** Volume Above Avg. STARS
12-Mo. Target Price — Relative Strength — ▲ Up ▼ Down ▶ No Change Below Avg. ★

Analysis prepared by **Esther Y. Kwon, CFA** on October 27, 2009, when the stock traded at **$ 76.48**.

Highlights

► Lorillard, formerly a division of Loews Corp., was spun off in June 2008. Its operating performance had previously been followed as a tracking stock (Loews Corp. - Carolina Group; CG).

► We see discount brand volumes, which rose 39% in 2008, posting strong growth through 2009, resulting in deterioration in gross margins, but this should be more than offset by a recent price increase across the company's brands. Although we believe marketing costs and pension expense will rise, we see only a modest increase in selling, general and administrative expenses. We expect operating margins to remain flat. In 2010, we project continued robust growth in discount brands and forecast lower gross margins as discount brands become a higher proportion of total sales. We see operating margins narrowing slightly in 2010.

► On significantly reduced investment income, we estimate 2009 EPS of $5.76, up from 2008 EPS of $5.27. In 2010, we forecast EPS of $6.22. On July 27, the board of directors approved an additional $750 million share repurchase program after the $250 million approved in May.

Investment Rationale/Risk

► We view positively LO's continued market share gains for its leading brand, Newport, in both the menthol and premium categories. We believe efforts to increase its investment in this brand will result in long-term volume growth ahead of peers, less promotional activity, and higher average prices, and we have become less concerned about the impact of last year's New York state cigarette excise tax hike on volumes.

► Risks to our recommendation and target price include increasing menthol competition in the premium and deep discount segments, a slowdown in industry volume trends, and a worsening of the litigation environment.

► Applying a below recent average P/E multiple of 13X to our 2010 estimate, we arrive at our 12-month target price of $81. Our target P/E multiple is a premium to those of Altria (MO 18, Strong Buy) and Reynolds American (RAI 48, Buy). While we are concerned about relatively high geographic concentration and see more limited margin expansion potential, we think LO is attractive given its separation from Loews, which should be supportive to the shares, as well as its total return potential.

Qualitative Risk Assessment

LOW	MEDIUM	HIGH

Our risk assessment reflects the relatively stable revenue and income streams enjoyed by the tobacco industry, offset by significant ongoing litigation.

Quantitative Evaluations

S&P Quality Ranking NR

D	C	B-	B	B+	A-	A	A+

Relative Strength Rank MODERATE

65

LOWEST = 1 HIGHEST = 99

Revenue/Earnings Data

Revenue (Million $)

	1Q	2Q	3Q	4Q	Year
2009	767.0	1,033	953.0	--	--
2008	932.0	886.0	936.0	912.0	3,492
2007	947.3	1,055	1,044	957.0	3,281
2006	880.8	998.6	1,016	936.7	3,866
2005	--	--	--	916.0	3,640
2004	776.1	868.0	887.4	832.5	3,388

Earnings Per Share ($)

2009	1.09	1.71	1.44	E1.51	E5.76
2008	1.00	1.25	1.38	1.53	5.15
2007	1.08	1.30	1.34	1.18	5.16
2006	0.86	1.09	1.17	1.26	4.46
2005	0.68	0.82	0.99	1.11	3.62
2004	0.59	0.70	0.92	0.93	3.15

Fiscal year ended Dec. 31. Next earnings report expected: Early February. EPS Estimates based on S&P Operating Earnings; historical GAAP earnings are as reported.

Dividend Data (Dates: mm/dd Payment Date: mm/dd/yy)

Amount ($)	Date Decl.	Ex-Div. Date	Stk. of Record	Payment Date
0.920	02/18	02/26	03/02	03/12/09
0.920	05/21	05/28	06/01	06/12/09
1.000	08/14	08/28	09/01	09/11/09
1.000	11/12	11/27	12/01	12/11/09

Dividends have been paid since 2002. Source: Company reports.

Please read the Required Disclosures and Analyst Certification on the last page of this report.

The **McGraw-Hill** Companies

Lorillard Inc

**STANDARD
&POOR'S**

Business Summary October 27, 2009

CORPORATE OVERVIEW. The company produces and markets cigarettes primarily in the U.S. The tobacco used in Lorillard cigarettes includes burley leaf, flue-cured tobacco grown in the U.S. and abroad, and aromatic tobacco grown primarily in Turkey and other Near Eastern countries. Through Alliance One International, Inc., Lorillard directs the purchase of more than 80% of its U.S. leaf tobacco needs. The company stores the various types and grades of its tobacco in 29 warehouses at its Danville, VA, facility. Its sole manufacturing plant, located in Greensboro, NC, has an annual production capacity of about 43 billion cigarettes. Lorillard, formerly a division of Loews Corp., was spun off in June 2008.

The company primarily sells its cigarettes to distributors that resell them to chain store organizations and government agencies. As of December 31, 2008, Lorillard had approximately 600 direct buying customers servicing more than 400,000 retail accounts. Lorillard does not sell cigarettes directly to consumers. During 2008, 2007, 2006 and 2005, sales made by Lorillard to McLane

Company, Inc. comprised 26%, 24%, 23% and 21%, respectively, of Lorillard's revenues. No other customer accounted for more than 10% of sales.

REGULATORY ENVIRONMENT. Lorillard's business operations are subject to a variety of federal, state and local laws and regulations governing, among other things, the publication of health warnings on cigarette packaging, advertising and sales of tobacco products, restrictions on smoking in public places, and fire safety standards. The U.S. cigarette industry faces a number of issues that have affected and may continue to affect its operations, including substantial litigation that seeks billions of dollars of damages. As of February 20, 2009, Lorillard was a defendant in about 5,825 cases facing the industry.

Company Financials Fiscal Year Ended Dec. 31

Per Share Data ($)	2008	2007	2006	2005	2004	2003	2002	2001	2000	1999
Tangible Book Value	3.76	6.34	NM	NM	NM	NM	NM	NA	NA	NA
Cash Flow	5.34	NA	NA	NA	NA	8.08	NA	NA	NA	NA
Earnings	5.15	5.16	4.46	3.62	3.15	2.76	3.50	NA	NA	NA
S&P Core Earnings	4.91	5.31	4.46	3.63	3.13	3.31	2.92	NA	NA	NA
Dividends	2.75	1.82	1.82	1.82	1.82	1.81	1.34	NA	NA	NA
Payout Ratio	53%	35%	41%	50%	58%	66%	38%	NA	NA	NA
Prices:High	89.21	92.79	64.83	46.06	30.00	28.10	34.05	NA	NA	NA
Prices:Low	53.30	64.00	43.83	28.47	22.49	17.18	16.80	NA	NA	NA
P/E Ratio:High	17	18	15	13	10	10	10	NA	NA	NA
P/E Ratio:Low	10	12	10	8	7	6	5	NA	NA	NA

Income Statement Analysis (Million $)	2008	2007	2006	2005	2004	2003	2002	2001	2000	1999
Revenue	3,492	3,281	3,866	3,640	3,388	3,288	3,798	3,868	NA	NA
Operating Income	1,465	1,392	1,352	1,156	1,041	934	NA	NA	NA	NA
Depreciation	32.0	40.0	47.0	48.0	40.0	NA	NA	NA	NA	NA
Interest Expense	NA	74.0	116	141	158	183	178	0.70	NA	NA
Pretax Income	1,434	1,318	1,237	1,016	884	751	1,121	1,105	NA	NA
Effective Tax Rate	38.2%	35.1%	38.5%	38.6%	38.2%	37.7%	39.2%	39.0%	NA	NA
Net Income	887	855	760	623	546	468	682	673	NA	NA
S&P Core Earnings	845	577	417	252	184	138	117	672	NA	NA

Balance Sheet & Other Financial Data (Million $)	2008	2007	2006	2005	2004	2003	2002	2001	2000	1999
Cash	1,191	2.00	1.50	2.50	36.0	1.90	2.20	1.70	NA	NA
Current Assets	1,962	NA	NA	NA	NA	NA	NA	NA	NA	NA
Total Assets	2,322	2,702	2,861	2,897	2,278	2,725	2,927	2,769	NA	NA
Current Liabilities	1,273	NA	NA	NA	NA	NA	NA	NA	NA	NA
Long Term Debt	Nil	424	1,230	1,627	1,871	2,032	2,438	Nil	NA	NA
Common Equity	635	685	0.16	-201	-502	-729	-884	1,275	NA	NA
Total Capital	631	1,109	1,230	1,426	1,369	1,303	1,555	1,275	NA	NA
Capital Expenditures	44.0	51.0	29.7	31.2	50.8	56.4	51.7	41.2	NA	NA
Cash Flow	919	NA	NA	NA	NA	NA	NA	NA	NA	NA
Current Ratio	1.5	1.8	1.8	1.7	NA	NA	NA	NA	NA	NA
% Long Term Debt of Capitalization	Nil	38.2	100.0	114.1	136.7	156.0	156.8	Nil	NA	NA
% Net Income of Revenue	25.4	26.1	19.7	17.1	16.1	14.2	17.9	17.4	NA	NA
% Return on Assets	36.0	30.7	26.4	22.0	19.8	16.6	23.9	NA	NA	NA
% Return on Equity	107.7	203.4	5.4	NM	NM	NM	348.6	NA	NA	NA

Data as orig reptd.; bef. results of disc opers/spec. items. Per share data adj. for stk. divs.; EPS diluted. Prior to June 11, 2008, data and historical prices reflect the former Loews Corp-Carolina Group. E-Estimated. NA-Not Available. NM-Not Meaningful. NR-Not Ranked. UR-Under Review.

Office: 714 Green Valley Rd, Greensboro, NC 27408-7018.
Telephone: 339-335-7000.
Email: ir@loews.com
Website: http://www.loews.com

Chrmn, Pres & CEO: M.L. Orlowsky
EVP & CFO: D.H. Taylor
SVP, Chief Acctg Officer & Treas: T.R. Staab
SVP, Secy & General Counsel: R.S. Milstein

Treas: H. Lewis
Investor Contact: P.W. Keegan (212-521-2000)
Board Members: R. C. Almon, V. W. Colbert, D. E. Dangoor, K. D. Dietz, M. L. Orlowsky, R. W. Roedel, D. H. Taylor, N. Travis

Founded: 1969
Domicile: Delaware
Employees: 2,800

The McGraw-Hill Companies

Lowe's Companies Inc.

STANDARD
&POOR'S

S&P Recommendation HOLD ★★★☆☆	Price $21.96 (as of Nov 27, 2009)	12-Mo. Target Price $22.00	Investment Style Large-Cap Growth

GICS Sector Consumer Discretionary
Sub-Industry Home Improvement Retail

Summary This company retails building materials and supplies, lumber, hardware, and appliances through about 1,600 stores in 49 states and Canada.

Key Stock Statistics (Source S&P, Vickers, company reports)

52-Wk Range	$24.09– 13.00	S&P Oper. EPS 2010**E**	1.21	Market Capitalization(B)	$32.447	Beta	0.96
Trailing 12-Month EPS	$1.19	S&P Oper. EPS 2011**E**	1.25	Yield (%)	1.64	S&P 3-Yr. Proj. EPS CAGR(%)	7
Trailing 12-Month P/E	18.5	P/E on S&P Oper. EPS 2010**E**	18.1	Dividend Rate/Share	$0.36	S&P Credit Rating	A+
$10K Invested 5 Yrs Ago	$8,074	Common Shares Outstg. (M)	1,477.6	Institutional Ownership (%)	82		

Price Performance

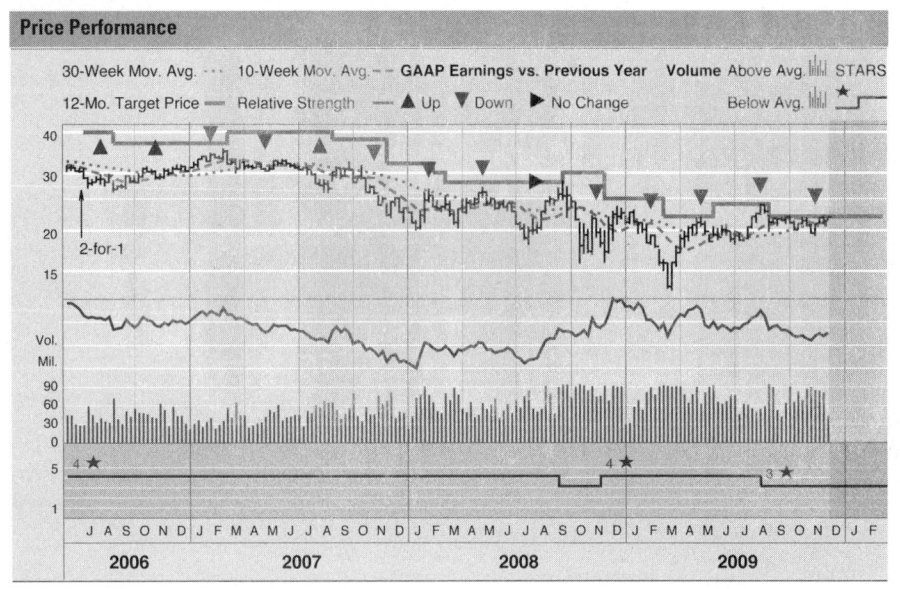

30-Week Mov. Avg. · · · 10-Week Mov. Avg. – – **GAAP Earnings vs. Previous Year** Volume Above Avg. STARS
12-Mo. Target Price — Relative Strength — ▲ Up ▼ Down ► No Change Below Avg. ★

Options: ASE, CBOE, P, Ph

Analysis prepared by **Michael Souers** on November 19, 2009, when the stock traded at **$ 21.31**.

Highlights

► We forecast a sales increase of 3.4% in FY 11 (Jan.), following our projection of a 2.5% decline in FY 10. We expect this rise to be driven by an estimated 50-60 net new store openings, representing a 3%-4% increase in total square footage, along with flat same-store-sales results. We expect the housing market to remain under pressure throughout much of 2010, and continue to project weak consumer spending, particularly on big-ticket home remodeling projects.

► We project FY 11 operating margins will increase slightly, as lower sourcing costs, a rational pricing environment and improving product mix shift are only partially offset by increasing payroll expenses and a deleveraging of expenses due to flat same-store sales results.

► We project a slight increase in interest expense, a tax rate of 37.5% and a slight rise in the diluted share count. We forecast FY 11 EPS of $1.25, a 3.3% increase from the $1.21 we project the company to earn in FY 10, excluding $0.03 of charges related to the canceling of certain future store openings and an unrelated tax benefit.

Investment Rationale/Risk

► We think the aging of homes and relatively high home ownership rates are powerful long-term demographic drivers that will help mitigate the continued weakness in housing turnover we see for 2010. However, with home refinancings and home equity loans likely to be somewhat sparse in the near to medium term, we expect home remodeling activity, particularly on big projects, to remain weak. While housing turnover appears to be nearing a bottom, we do not expect a significant recovery in 2010. We think the shares are fairly valued, trading at about 17X our FY 11 EPS estimate, in what we expect to be the cyclical earnings trough.

► Risks to our recommendation and target price include a sharp slowdown in the economy, a large rise in long term interest rates, and failure by LOW to execute its metro market expansion strategy.

► At about 17X our FY 11 EPS estimate, LOW shares recently traded in line with key peer Home Depot (HD 27, Hold). Our 12-month target price of $22 is derived from our discounted cash flow analysis, which assumes a weighted average cost of capital of 9.5% and a terminal growth rate of 3.0%.

Qualitative Risk Assessment

LOW	MEDIUM	HIGH

Our risk assessment reflects the cyclical nature of the home improvement retail industry, which is reliant on economic growth, offset by our view of ample opportunities for retail growth both domestically and abroad, and an S&P Quality Ranking of A, reflecting LOW's consistent historical earnings and dividend growth.

Quantitative Evaluations

S&P Quality Ranking   A

D	C	B-	B	B+	A-	A	A+

Relative Strength Rank   STRONG

75

LOWEST = 1   HIGHEST = 99

Revenue/Earnings Data

Revenue (Million $)

	1Q	2Q	3Q	4Q	Year
2010	11,832	13,844	11,375	--	--
2009	12,009	14,509	11,728	9,984	48,230
2008	12,172	14,167	11,565	10,379	48,283
2007	11,921	13,389	11,211	10,406	46,927
2006	9,913	11,929	10,592	10,808	43,243
2005	8,681	10,169	9,064	8,550	36,464

Earnings Per Share ($)

2010	0.32	0.51	0.23	E0.11	E1.21
2009	0.41	0.64	0.33	0.11	1.49
2008	0.48	0.64	0.43	0.28	1.86
2007	0.53	0.60	0.46	0.40	1.99
2006	0.37	0.52	0.41	0.44	1.73
2005	0.28	0.44	0.32	0.32	1.36

Fiscal year ended Jan. 31. Next earnings report expected: Late February. EPS Estimates based on S&P Operating Earnings; historical GAAP earnings are as reported.

Dividend Data (Dates: mm/dd Payment Date: mm/dd/yy)

Amount ($)	Date Decl.	Ex-Div. Date	Stk. of Record	Payment Date
0.085	03/23	04/15	04/17	05/01/09
0.090	05/29	07/15	07/17	07/31/09
0.090	08/24	10/14	10/16	10/30/09
0.090	11/16	01/15	01/20	02/03/10

Dividends have been paid since 1961. Source: Company reports.

Please read the Required Disclosures and Analyst Certification on the last page of this report.

Lowe's Companies Inc.

STANDARD
&POOR'S

Business Summary November 19, 2009

CORPORATE OVERVIEW. Lowe's Companies is the world's second largest home improvement retailer, with nearly $50 billion in revenues generated in FY 09 (Jan.). It focuses on retail do-it-yourself (DIY) customers, do-it-for-me (DIFM) customers who utilize LOW's installation services, and commercial business customers. Lowe's offers a complete line of products and services for home decorating, maintenance, repair, remodeling, and the maintenance of commercial buildings.

As of January 30, 2009, LOW operated 1,649 stores in 50 states and Canada, representing approximately 187 million sq. ft. of selling space. The company has three primary prototype stores--117,000-square-foot and 103,000-square-foot stores for larger markets and a 94,000-square-foot store used primarily to serve smaller markets. Both prototypes include a lawn and garden center, averaging an additional 31,000 square feet for larger stores and 26,000 square feet for smaller stores. Of the total stores operating at January 30, 2009, approximately 88% were owned, including stores on leased land, while the remaining 12% were leased from unaffiliated third parties. Typical LOW stores stock more than 40,000 items, with hundreds of thousands of

items available through the company's special order system.

CORPORATE STRATEGY. LOW is focusing much of its future expansion on metropolitan markets with populations of 500,000 or more. The company expects that the majority of its FY 10 expansion plans will be comprised of the 103,000 square-foot stores in larger markets (in place of 117,000 square-foot formats in an effort to be more cost-efficient), but it also plans to open 94,000 square-foot stores in smaller to mid-sized markets.

Lowe's opened five new stores in Canada in 2008, bringing its Canadian store count to 11, and will continue its expansion in FY 10. Additionally, LOW plans on expanding into Mexico, with two stores expected to open in Monterrey in 2009.

Company Financials Fiscal Year Ended Jan. 31

Per Share Data ($)	2009	2008	2007	2006	2005	2004	2003	2002	2001	2000
Tangible Book Value	12.28	11.04	10.31	9.15	7.45	6.55	5.31	4.30	3.59	3.07
Cash Flow	2.54	2.77	2.73	2.44	1.92	1.68	1.32	0.98	0.79	0.66
Earnings	1.49	1.86	1.99	1.73	1.36	1.16	0.93	0.65	0.52	0.44
S&P Core Earnings	1.50	1.86	1.99	1.73	1.33	1.13	0.87	0.61	0.50	NA
Dividends	0.29	0.18	0.11	0.08	0.06	0.06	0.04	0.04	0.04	0.03
Payout Ratio	19%	10%	6%	4%	4%	5%	5%	0%	7%	7%
Calendar Year	2008	2007	2006	2005	2004	2003	2002	2001	2000	1999
Prices:High	28.49	35.74	34.83	34.85	30.27	30.21	25.00	24.44	16.81	16.61
Prices:Low	15.76	21.01	26.15	25.36	22.95	16.69	16.25	10.94	8.56	10.75
P/E Ratio:High	19	19	17	20	22	26	27	38	32	38
P/E Ratio:Low	11	11	13	15	17	14	18	17	16	25

Income Statement Analysis (Million $)										
Revenue	48,230	48,283	46,927	43,243	36,464	30,838	26,491	22,111	18,779	15,906
Operating Income	5,333	6,071	6,314	5,715	4,878	3,959	3,186	2,332	1,811	1,511
Depreciation	1,539	1,366	1,162	1,051	920	781	645	534	409	337
Interest Expense	356	304	238	158	176	180	203	199	146	123
Pretax Income	3,506	4,511	4,998	4,506	3,536	2,998	2,359	1,624	1,283	1,065
Effective Tax Rate	37.4%	37.7%	37.9%	38.5%	38.5%	37.9%	37.6%	37.0%	36.9%	36.8%
Net Income	2,195	2,809	3,105	2,771	2,176	1,862	1,471	1,023	810	673
S&P Core Earnings	2,204	2,809	3,105	2,763	2,134	1,801	1,386	968	773	NA

Balance Sheet & Other Financial Data (Million $)										
Cash	661	530	796	423	813	1,624	1,126	799	456	491
Current Assets	9,251	8,686	8,314	7,831	6,974	6,687	5,568	4,920	4,175	3,710
Total Assets	32,686	30,869	27,767	24,682	21,209	19,042	16,109	13,736	11,376	9,012
Current Liabilities	8,022	7,751	6,539	5,832	5,719	4,368	3,578	3,017	2,929	2,386
Long Term Debt	5,039	5,576	4,325	3,499	3,060	3,678	3,736	3,734	2,698	1,727
Common Equity	18,055	16,098	15,725	14,339	11,535	10,309	8,302	6,675	5,494	4,695
Total Capital	23,754	22,344	20,785	18,573	15,331	14,644	12,516	10,713	8,443	6,622
Capital Expenditures	3,322	4,010	3,916	3,379	2,927	2,444	2,362	2,199	2,332	1,472
Cash Flow	3,734	4,175	4,267	3,822	3,096	2,643	2,116	1,557	1,219	1,010
Current Ratio	1.2	1.1	1.3	1.3	1.2	1.5	1.6	1.6	1.4	1.6
% Long Term Debt of Capitalization	21.2	25.0	21.6	18.8	20.0	25.1	29.8	34.9	32.0	26.1
% Net Income of Revenue	4.6	5.8	6.6	6.4	6.0	6.0	5.6	4.6	4.3	4.2
% Return on Assets	6.9	9.6	11.9	12.1	10.9	10.6	9.9	8.2	7.9	8.4
% Return on Equity	12.9	17.7	20.7	21.4	20.0	20.0	19.6	16.8	15.9	16.2

Data as orig reptd.; bef. results of disc opers/spec. items. Per share data adj. for stk. divs.; EPS diluted. E-Estimated. NA-Not Available. NM-Not Meaningful. NR-Not Ranked. UR-Under Review.

Office: 1000 Lowes Blvd, Mooresville, NC 28117-8520.
Telephone: 704-758-1000.
Website: http://www.lowes.com
Chrmn & CEO: R.A. Niblock

Pres & COO: L.D. Stone
EVP & CFO: R.F. Hull, Jr.
SVP & Chief Acctg Officer: M.V. Hollifield
SVP, Secy, General Counsel & CCO: G.M. Keener, Jr.

Investor Contact: P. Taaffe (704-758-2033)
Board Members: D. W. Bernauer, L. L. Berry, P. C. Browning, D. Hudson, R. A. Ingram, R. L. Johnson, M. O. Larsen, R. K. Lochridge, R. A. Niblock, S. F. Page, O. T. Sloan, Jr.

Founded: 1952
Domicile: North Carolina
Employees: 229,000

The **McGraw·Hill** Companies

L-3 Communications Holdings Inc

STANDARD &POOR'S

S&P Recommendation	**HOLD** ★★★☆☆	Price $78.45 (as of Nov 27, 2009)	12-Mo. Target Price $80.00	Investment Style Large-Cap Blend

GICS Sector Industrials
Sub-Industry Aerospace & Defense

Summary This company is a provider of intelligence, surveillance, and reconnaissance systems; secure communications systems; aircraft modernization, training and government services; and, other defense, intelligence, and security products.

Key Stock Statistics (Source S&P, Vickers, company reports)

52-Wk Range	$82.65–57.12	S&P Oper. EPS 2009E	7.52	Market Capitalization(B)	$9.118	Beta	0.85
Trailing 12-Month EPS	$8.00	S&P Oper. EPS 2010E	8.00	Yield (%)	1.78	S&P 3-Yr. Proj. EPS CAGR(%)	4
Trailing 12-Month P/E	9.8	P/E on S&P Oper. EPS 2009E	10.4	Dividend Rate/Share	$1.40	S&P Credit Rating	BBB-
$10K Invested 5 Yrs Ago	$11,558	Common Shares Outstg. (M)	116.2	Institutional Ownership (%)	82		

Price Performance

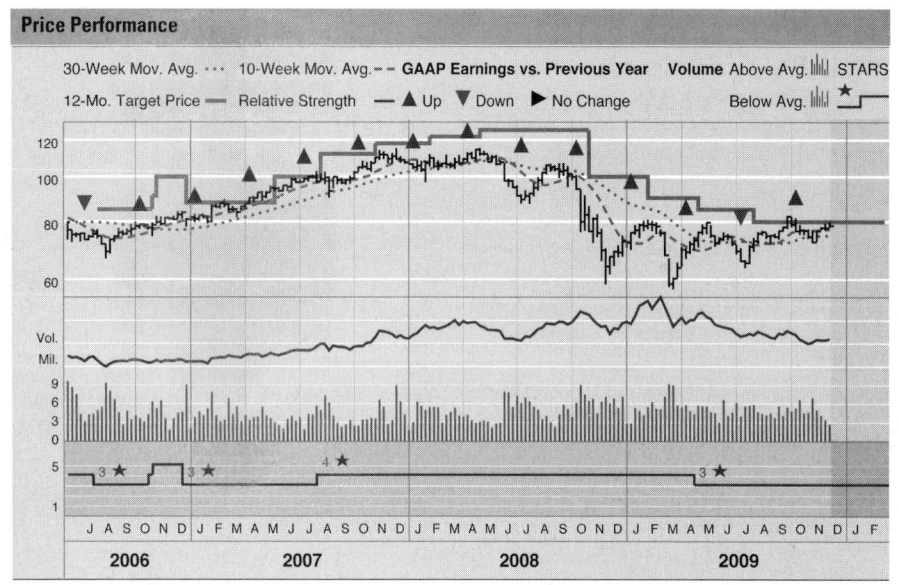

Legend:
30-Week Mov. Avg. · · · 10-Week Mov. Avg. - - GAAP Earnings vs. Previous Year   Volume Above Avg. STARS
12-Mo. Target Price — Relative Strength — ▲ Up ▼ Down ► No Change   Below Avg. ★

Options: ASE, CBOE, P

Analysis prepared by **Richard Tortoriello** on November 02, 2009, when the stock traded at **$ 73.21**.

Highlights

► We anticipate revenue gain of 3.2% in 2009, and project further growth of about 3% in 2010. We see 2010 growth driven primarily by C3ISR, where we are modeling a 12% increase, due to our view of high government demand for intelligence, surveillance, and reconnaissance products. We also project 5% growth in Specialized Products, on a variety of military products and systems. We expect modest declines (about 3%) in Government Services and Aircraft Modernization & Maintenance.

► We project operating margins of 10.5% in 2009, flat with 2008 margins, as LLL absorbs increased pension expense, due primarily to the recent stock market decline. For 2010, we anticipate a moderate increase in operating margins to 10.7%.

► We project EPS of $7.52 in 2009, down about 3% from 2008's level, due to the absence of a $0.57 net special gain recorded in the second quarter of 2008. For 2010, we project 6% growth to $8.00. We project free cash flow per share of near $10.00 in 2009.

Investment Rationale/Risk

► Following the June 2006 death of L-3's founder, we see L-3 as much more conservatively run, in terms of acquisitions activity. Consequently, we see sales and profit growth slowing significantly from previous high levels. Although we think L-3's mix of defense electronics and specialized military products and government services are well matched with current military priorities, we see a pull-out of U.S. troops from Iraq and our overall expectation of no real growth in the U.S. defense budget going forward as preventing the shares from outperforming.

► Risks to our recommendation and target price include the potential for delays and/or cuts in military budgets and failure to perform well on existing contracts or to win new contracts.

► Our 12-month target price of $80 is based on an enterprise value to estimated 2010 EBITDA multiple of about 6.5X, below an average historical multiple of 12X, but in line with multiples we are using to value other defense contractors. We believe the likelihood of a troop drawdown from Iraq and slower-than-historical growth at LLL warrant this multiple.

Qualitative Risk Assessment

LOW	**MEDIUM**	HIGH

Our risk assessment reflects our view of LLL's strong historical record of earnings growth, offset by the company's moderately high financial leverage, and risks inherent in its dependence on government spending.

Quantitative Evaluations

S&P Quality Ranking   A-

D	C	B-	B	B+	**A-**	A	A+

Relative Strength Rank   MODERATE

66

LOWEST = 1   HIGHEST = 99

Revenue/Earnings Data

Revenue (Million $)

	1Q	2Q	3Q	4Q	Year
2009	3,636	3,929	3,842	--	--
2008	3,506	3,722	3,662	4,011	14,901
2007	3,300	3,408	3,448	3,806	13,961
2006	2,904	3,083	3,105	3,385	12,477
2005	1,963	2,076	2,506	2,900	9,445
2004	1,522	1,680	1,784	1,911	6,897

Earnings Per Share ($)

2009	1.66	1.90	2.12	E1.84	E7.52
2008	1.54	2.24	1.73	2.21	7.72
2007	1.29	1.49	1.56	1.63	5.98
2006	1.13	0.40	1.31	1.37	4.22
2005	0.86	0.99	1.11	1.24	4.20
2004	0.67	0.81	0.93	1.01	3.33

Fiscal year ended Dec. 31. Next earnings report expected: Late January. EPS Estimates based on S&P Operating Earnings; historical GAAP earnings are as reported.

Dividend Data (Dates: mm/dd Payment Date: mm/dd/yy)

Amount ($)	Date Decl.	Ex-Div. Date	Stk. of Record	Payment Date
0.350	02/05	02/17	02/19	03/16/09
0.350	04/28	05/14	05/18	06/15/09
0.350	07/14	08/13	08/17	09/15/09
0.350	10/06	11/13	11/17	12/15/09

Dividends have been paid since 2004. Source: Company reports.

Please read the Required Disclosures and Analyst Certification on the last page of this report.

The McGraw-Hill Companies

L-3 Communications Holdings Inc

STANDARD &POOR'S

Business Summary November 02, 2009

CORPORATE OVERVIEW. L-3 Communications (LLL), an acquisitive $16 billion in estimated 2009 revenues maker of military and homeland security electronics, conducts business through four operating segments.

The Command, Control, Communications, Intelligence, Surveillance, and Reconnaissance (C3ISR) business segment (17% of sales and 16% of operating income in 2008), specializes in signals intelligence (SIGINT) and communications intelligence (COMINT) products. These products provide troops the ability to collect and analyze unknown electronic signals from command centers, communications nodes and air defense systems for real-time situation awareness and response. C3ISR also provides C3 systems, networked communications systems, and secure communications products for military and other U.S. government agencies and foreign governments.

The Government Services segment (29% of sales and 27% of operating profits) provides a wide range of engineering, technical, information technology, advisory, training, and support services to the Department of Defense (DoD), Dept. of State, Dept. of Justice, U.S. Government intelligence agencies, and allied foreign governments. Major services include communication software support; high-end engineering and information systems support for command, control, communications and ISR architectures; developing and managing

programs in the U.S. and internationally that focus on teaching, training and education, logistics, strategic planning, leadership development, etc.; human intelligence support; command and control systems for maritime and expeditionary warfare; intelligence solutions support to the DoD and U.S. government intelligence agencies; and conventional high-end enterprise IT support, systems, and services to the DoD and U.S. federal agencies.

The Aircraft Modernization & Maintenance segment (18% of sales and 16% of operating profits) provides modernization, upgrades and sustainment, maintenance and logistics support services for military and various government aircraft and other platforms. Services are sold primarily to the U.S. DoD, the Canadian Department of National Defense, and other allied foreign governments. Major products and services include aircraft and vehicle modernization, including engineering, modification, maintenance, logistics, and upgrades; aviation life-cycle management services for various military fixed and rotary wing aircraft; and aerospace and other technical services related to large fleet support.

Company Financials Fiscal Year Ended Dec. 31

Per Share Data ($)	2008	2007	2006	2005	2004	2003	2002	2001	2000	1999
Tangible Book Value	NM	NM	NM	NM	NM	NM	NM	NM	NM	NM
Cash Flow	9.16	7.53	5.30	5.46	4.27	3.52	2.96	2.37	2.25	16.75
Earnings	7.72	5.98	4.22	4.20	3.33	2.71	2.29	1.48	1.18	0.88
S&P Core Earnings	6.24	5.68	4.93	4.07	3.22	2.66	1.87	1.08	NA	NA
Dividends	1.20	1.00	0.75	0.50	0.40	Nil	Nil	Nil	Nil	Nil
Payout Ratio	16%	17%	18%	12%	12%	Nil	Nil	Nil	Nil	Nil
Prices:High	115.33	115.29	88.50	84.84	77.26	51.83	66.78	49.04	39.66	27.13
Prices:Low	58.49	79.26	66.50	64.66	49.31	34.22	40.60	30.35	17.84	17.13
P/E Ratio:High	15	19	21	20	23	19	29	33	33	31
P/E Ratio:Low	8	13	16	15	15	13	18	21	15	20

Income Statement Analysis (Million $)										
Revenue	14,901	13,961	12,477	9,445	6,897	5,062	4,011	2,347	1,910	1,405
Operating Income	1,771	1,645	1,376	1,150	868	676	530	362	297	204
Depreciation	197	196	136	153	119	95.4	75.9	87.0	74.3	53.7
Interest Expense	271	296	296	204	145	133	122	86.4	93.0	60.6
Pretax Income	1,462	1,183	835	798	606	437	336	191	134	95.4
Effective Tax Rate	34.3%	35.3%	35.7%	35.1%	35.5%	35.7%	35.0%	37.1%	38.3%	38.5%
Net Income	949	756	526	509	382	278	212	115	82.7	58.7
S&P Core Earnings	768	719	615	493	370	274	171	82.0	NA	NA

Balance Sheet & Other Financial Data (Million $)										
Cash	867	780	348	394	653	135	135	361	32.7	42.8
Current Assets	4,961	4,763	3,930	3,644	2,808	1,938	1,639	1,239	830	568
Total Assets	14,630	14,391	13,287	11,909	7,781	6,493	5,242	3,335	2,464	1,634
Current Liabilities	2,707	2,582	2,376	1,854	1,176	924	697	524	469	318
Long Term Debt	4,548	4,547	4,535	4,634	2,190	2,457	1,848	1,315	1,095	605
Common Equity	5,836	5,989	5,306	4,491	3,800	2,574	2,202	1,214	693	583
Total Capital	10,462	10,857	10,069	9,325	6,067	5,108	4,123	2,599	1,788	1,188
Capital Expenditures	218	157	156	120	80.5	82.9	62.1	48.1	33.6	23.5
Cash Flow	1,126	952	662	661	501	373	288	202	157	112
Current Ratio	1.8	1.9	1.7	2.0	2.4	2.1	2.4	2.4	1.8	1.8
% Long Term Debt of Capitalization	43.4	41.8	45.0	49.7	36.1	48.1	44.8	50.6	61.3	50.9
% Net Income of Revenue	6.4	5.4	4.2	5.4	5.5	5.5	5.3	4.9	4.3	4.2
% Return on Assets	6.5	5.5	4.2	5.2	5.3	4.7	5.0	4.0	4.0	4.0
% Return on Equity	16.1	13.4	10.7	12.3	12.0	11.6	12.4	12.1	13.0	13.3

Data as orig reptd.; bef. results of disc opers/spec. items. Per share data adj. for stk. divs.; EPS diluted. E-Estimated. NA-Not Available. NM-Not Meaningful. NR-Not Ranked. UR-Under Review.

Office: 600 3rd Ave, New York, NY 10016.
Telephone: 212-697-1111.
Website: http://www.L3com.com
Chrmn, Pres & CEO: M.T. Strianese

COO: D.T. Butler, III
SVP, Secy & General Counsel: S. Post
CFO: R.G. D'Ambrosio
Chief Admin Officer: S.M. Sheridan

Investor Contact: E. Boyriven (212-850-5600)
Board Members: C. R. Canizares, T. A. Corcoran, L. Kramer, R. B. Millard, J. M. Shalikashvili, A. L. Simon, M. T. Strianese, A. H. Washkowitz, J. P. White

Founded: 1997
Domicile: Delaware
Employees: 65,000

LSI Corp

STANDARD &POOR'S

| S&P Recommendation | **BUY** ★★★★☆ | Price $5.42 (as of Nov 27, 2009) | 12-Mo. Target Price $6.50 | Investment Style Large-Cap Blend |

GICS Sector Information Technology
Sub-Industry Semiconductors

Summary This leading supplier of complex, high-performance semiconductors and storage systems acquired Agere Systems in April 2007.

Key Stock Statistics (Source S&P, Vickers, company reports)

52-Wk Range	$6.06– 2.39	S&P Oper. EPS 2009**E**	0.10	Market Capitalization(B)	$3.540	Beta	1.80
Trailing 12-Month EPS	$-1.11	S&P Oper. EPS 2010**E**	0.40	Yield (%)	Nil	S&P 3-Yr. Proj. EPS CAGR(%)	12
Trailing 12-Month P/E	NM	P/E on S&P Oper. EPS 2009**E**	54.2	Dividend Rate/Share	Nil	S&P Credit Rating	NR
$10K Invested 5 Yrs Ago	$9,982	Common Shares Outstg. (M)	653.2	Institutional Ownership (%)	81		

Price Performance

30-Week Mov. Avg. ··· 10-Week Mov. Avg. – – GAAP Earnings vs. Previous Year Volume Above Avg. ▎▍▎ STARS
12-Mo. Target Price — Relative Strength — ▲ Up ▼ Down ► No Change Below Avg. ▎▍▎ ★

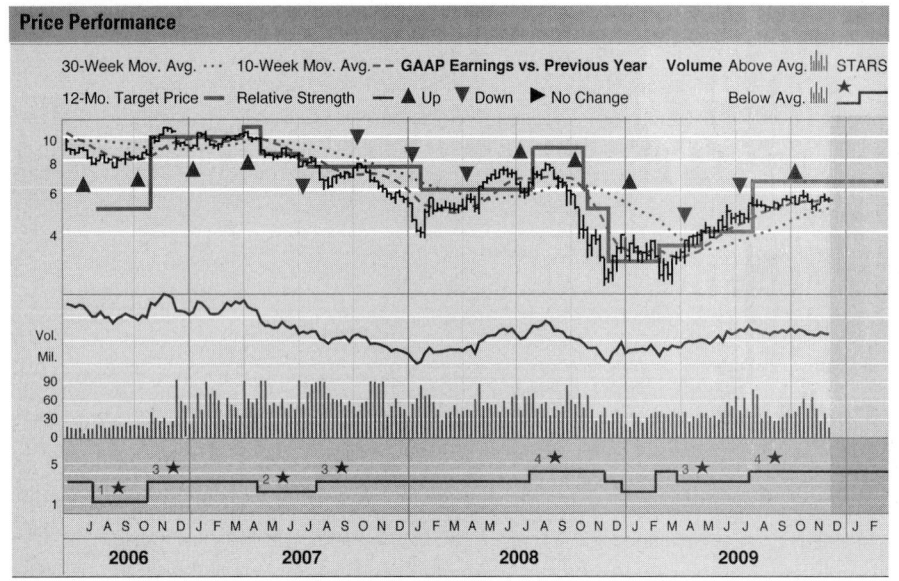

Options: ASE, CBOE, P, Ph

Analysis prepared by **Clyde Montevirgen** on October 30, 2009, when the stock traded at **$ 5.30**.

Highlights

► We project that revenues will decline about 17% in 2009, reflecting weak IT spending environment amid the difficult economy. While we believe the company will achieve new design wins in storage semiconductors and systems product categories during 2009, we think revenues from these new designs will start to ramp up next year when we see businesses increasing spending. We are also assuming healthy PC growth, supporting the company's hard disk drive and related businesses. As a result, we forecast revenue growth of 13% in 2010.

► We see non-GAAP gross margins widening to 44% in 2010 from a projected 43% in 2009, reflecting our expectation of a more favorable product mix and better product margins in its businesses. We believe LSI will look to grow expenses at a slower pace than sales, and anticipate the adjusted operating margin expanding to 10% in 2010 from an estimated 2% in 2009, on operating leverage.

► Our per-share operating estimates include a notable tax benefit in 2009 and essentially no taxes in 2010.

Investment Rationale/Risk

► Our buy recommendation reflects our view of improving fundamentals and attractive valuations. We believe that the company will benefit from an anticipated improvement in IT spending in coming years as companies look to refresh their server and storage capacities and as they upgrade to hardware with the latest microprocessors and operating systems. Although we see increasing expenses for compensation as business conditions improve, we think the company will keep a tight control over expenses, especially employee headcount, and believe that operating leverage will contribute to earnings power.

► Risks to our recommendation and target price include a slower ramp up of new product sales, disruptions in the supply chain, and higher-than-expected operating expenses.

► Our 12-month target price of $6.50 reflects a price-to-earnings multiple of 16X, which is around the industry average and justified by our view of earnings growth, applied to our 2010 EPS estimate.

Qualitative Risk Assessment

| LOW | MEDIUM | **HIGH** |

LSI is subject to the sales cycles of the semiconductor industry and consumer electronics and data storage end markets. The company faces competition from makers of programmable logic devices as well as from many custom logic chip makers.

Quantitative Evaluations

S&P Quality Ranking   C

| D | **C** | B- | B | B+ | A- | A | A+ |

Relative Strength Rank   MODERATE

55

LOWEST = 1   HIGHEST = 99

Revenue/Earnings Data

Revenue (Million $)

	1Q	2Q	3Q	4Q	Year
2009	482.3	520.7	578.4	--	--
2008	660.8	692.1	714.3	610.0	2,677
2007	465.4	669.9	727.4	740.9	2,604
2006	475.9	489.6	493.0	523.7	1,982
2005	450.0	481.3	481.7	506.2	1,919
2004	452.4	447.9	380.2	419.7	1,700

Earnings Per Share ($)

	1Q	2Q	3Q	4Q	Year
2009	-0.16	-0.09	0.08	E0.06	E0.10
2008	-0.02	-0.02	0.02	-0.94	-0.96
2007	0.07	-0.50	-0.20	-2.88	-3.87
2006	0.03	0.13	0.11	0.14	0.42
2005	0.01	0.06	-0.19	0.09	-0.01
2004	0.02	0.02	-0.73	-0.51	-1.21

Fiscal year ended Dec. 31. Next earnings report expected: Late January. EPS Estimates based on S&P Operating Earnings; historical GAAP earnings are as reported.

Dividend Data

No cash dividends have been paid.

LSI Corp

Business Summary October 30, 2009

CORPORATE OVERVIEW. LSI Corp. (formerly LSI Logic) is best known as a leading supplier of application-specific and standard integrated circuits, and since 1998 has diversified into storage components. In March 2006, the company announced plans to focus on growth opportunities in storage and consumer markets. Following its 2007 merger with Agere Systems, and divestiture of its consumer and mobility business segments, LSI focuses on two main segments: semiconductors and storage systems.

In 2008, the semiconductor segment accounted for 67% of revenues, compared to 68% in 2007; and storage systems represented 33% (32%). Revenues for the semiconductor group were up 0.9% in 2008, while storage systems revenues increased 6.9%.

MARKET PROFILE. Customers are generally electronic original equipment manufacturers (OEMs). LSI focuses on larger companies that make products in high volume.

The company emphasizes complex system-on-a-chip products that employ its CoreWare design methodology. Using sophisticated electronic design automation tools, customers add product features to pre-wired cores of industry-standard architecture protocols and algorithms that are electronically stitched together on a single chip. CoreWare methodology is based on application-specific integrated circuit (ASIC) technology: these semiconductors are designed to satisfy particular customer requirements. LSI is a large player in the global ASIC market, competing with companies such as IBM, Philips Electronics, Texas Instruments and Broadcom.

Company Financials Fiscal Year Ended Dec. 31

Per Share Data ($)	2008	2007	2006	2005	2004	2003	2002	2001	2000	1999
Tangible Book Value	0.44	1.12	2.24	1.66	1.38	2.39	2.80	3.15	5.96	5.21
Cash Flow	-0.50	-3.48	0.62	0.36	-0.75	-0.12	0.15	-1.32	1.81	1.62
Earnings	-0.96	-3.87	0.42	-0.01	-1.21	-0.82	-0.79	-2.84	0.70	0.52
S&P Core Earnings	-0.68	-1.80	0.35	-0.20	-1.51	-1.33	-1.36	-3.47	NA	NA
Dividends	Nil	Nil	Nil	Nil	Nil	Nil	Nil	Nil	Nil	Nil
Payout Ratio	Nil	Nil	Nil	Nil	Nil	Nil	Nil	Nil	Nil	Nil
Prices:High	7.97	10.68	11.81	10.75	11.50	12.90	18.60	26.10	90.38	35.69
Prices:Low	2.36	5.06	7.41	4.92	4.01	3.78	3.97	9.70	16.30	8.06
P/E Ratio:High	NM	NM	28	NM	NM	NM	NM	NM	NM	69
P/E Ratio:Low	NM	NM	18	NM	NM	NM	NM	NM	NM	16

Income Statement Analysis (Million $)										
Revenue	2,677	2,604	1,982	1,919	1,700	1,693	1,817	1,785	2,738	2,089
Operating Income	287	168	236	283	172	171	155	-157	815	568
Depreciation	298	253	82.3	146	177	263	349	533	404	367
Interest Expense	34.9	31.0	24.3	25.3	25.3	30.7	52.0	44.6	41.6	40.0
Pretax Income	-595	-2,475	185	20.9	-439	-284	-291	-1,030	380	224
Effective Tax Rate	NM	NM	8.46%	NM	NM	NM	NM	NM	37.6%	29.0%
Net Income	-622	-2,487	170	-5.62	-464	-309	-292	-992	237	159
S&P Core Earnings	-449	-1,157	140	-80.0	-582	-505	-507	-1,214	NA	NA

Balance Sheet & Other Financial Data (Million $)										
Cash	1,119	1,398	328	265	219	270	449	757	236	251
Current Assets	1,799	2,193	1,636	1,620	1,365	1,390	1,626	1,769	2,072	1,288
Total Assets	3,344	4,396	2,852	2,796	2,874	3,448	4,143	4,626	4,197	3,207
Current Liabilities	798	762	527	743	396	391	398	510	627	475
Long Term Debt	350	718	350	350	782	866	1,241	1,336	846	672
Common Equity	1,441	2,485	1,896	1,628	1,618	2,042	2,300	2,480	2,498	1,856
Total Capital	2,036	3,388	2,246	1,978	2,400	2,916	3,665	3,995	3,481	2,610
Capital Expenditures	135	103	58.7	48.1	52.8	78.2	39.0	224	277	205
Cash Flow	-324	-2,234	252	141	-287	-45.8	57.0	-459	641	526
Current Ratio	2.3	2.9	3.1	2.2	3.4	3.6	4.1	3.5	3.3	2.7
% Long Term Debt of Capitalization	17.2	21.2	15.6	17.7	32.6	29.7	33.8	33.4	24.3	25.7
% Net Income of Revenue	NM	NM	8.6	NM	NM	NM	NM	NM	8.6	7.6
% Return on Assets	NM	NM	6.0	NM	NM	NM	NM	NM	6.4	5.3
% Return on Equity	NM	NM	9.6	NM	NM	NM	NM	NM	10.9	9.4

Data as orig reptd.; bef. results of disc opers/spec. items. Per share data adj. for stk. divs.; EPS diluted. E-Estimated. NA-Not Available. NM-Not Meaningful. NR-Not Ranked. UR-Under Review.

Office: 1621 Barber Lane, Milpitas, CA 95035.
Telephone: 408-433-8000.
Email: investorrelations@lsil.com
Website: http://www.lsi.com

Chrmn: G. Reyes
Pres & CEO: A.Y. Talwalkar
EVP, CFO, Chief Admin Officer & Chief Acctg Officer: B. Look
EVP, Secy & General Counsel: J.F. Rankin

Investor Contact: S. Shah (610-712-5471)
Board Members: C. A. Haggerty, R. Hill, J. H. Miner, A. Netravali, M. J. O'Rourke, G. Reyes, M. G. Strachan, A. Y. Talwalkar, S. M. Whitney

Founded: 1980
Domicile: Delaware
Employees: 5,488

Macy's Inc

STANDARD
&POOR'S

S&P Recommendation	HOLD ★★★☆☆	Price $16.97 (as of Nov 27, 2009)	12-Mo. Target Price $19.00	Investment Style Large-Cap Blend

GICS Sector Consumer Discretionary
Sub-Industry Department Stores

Summary This company operates more than 850 department stores under the Macy's and Bloomingdale's names.

Key Stock Statistics (Source S&P, Vickers, company reports)

52-Wk Range	$20.84– 6.27	S&P Oper. EPS 2010**E**	1.10	Market Capitalization(B)	$7.136	Beta	1.98
Trailing 12-Month EPS	$-11.60	S&P Oper. EPS 2011**E**	1.35	Yield (%)	1.18	S&P 3-Yr. Proj. EPS CAGR(%)	7
Trailing 12-Month P/E	NM	P/E on S&P Oper. EPS 2010**E**	15.4	Dividend Rate/Share	$0.20	S&P Credit Rating	BB
$10K Invested 5 Yrs Ago	$6,286	Common Shares Outstg. (M)	420.5	Institutional Ownership (%)	90		

Price Performance

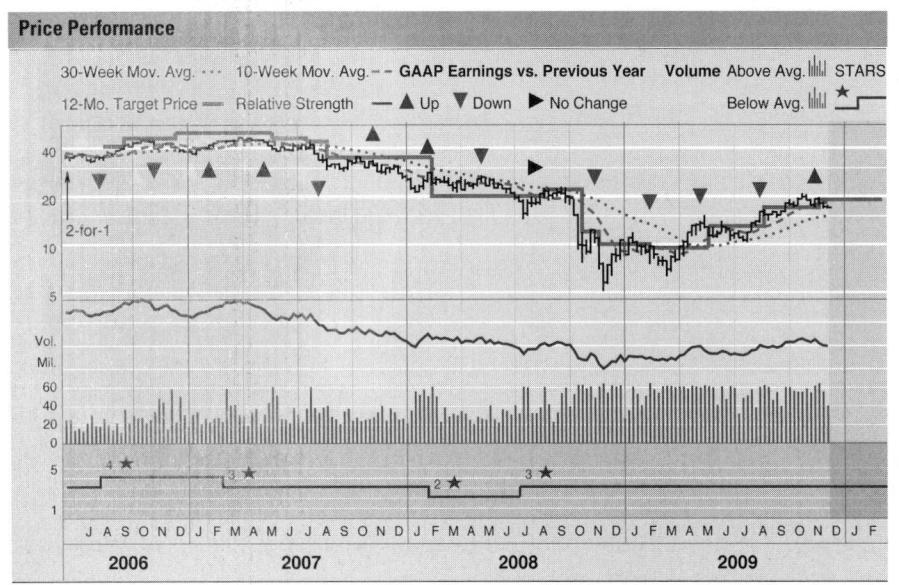

30-Week Mov. Avg. ···· · 10-Week Mov. Avg. – – GAAP Earnings vs. Previous Year Volume Above Avg. STARS
12-Mo. Target Price — Relative Strength — ▲ Up ▼ Down ► No Change Below Avg.

Options: ASE, CBOE, P, Ph

Analysis prepared by **Jason N. Asaeda** on November 12, 2009, when the stock traded at **$ 17.89**.

Highlights

► We project net sales of $23.5 billion in both FY 10 (Jan.) and FY 11. In February 2009, M announced plans to expand nationwide "My Macy's," an initiative aimed at accelerating same-store sales growth through custom-tailoring of merchandise assortments, size ranges, marketing programs and shopping experiences to the needs of core customers surrounding each Macy's store. While we see promise in My Macy's, given perceived execution challenges and our view of difficult retail conditions, we project same-store sales to decline about 6% in FY 10 and to be approximately flat in FY 11. We anticipate modest square footage growth annually.

► We expect sales growth in private label merchandise to partially offset gross margin pressure from planned promotional activity. The company also projects cost savings of approximately $250 million in FY 10 and about $400 million annually beginning in FY 11 from recently announced restructuring activities.

► Assuming no share buybacks, we see EPS of $1.10 in FY 10, which excludes estimated restructuring-related costs of $400 million, and $1.35 in FY 11.

Investment Rationale/Risk

► Our hold recommendation is based on valuation. In the FY 10 third quarter, same-store sales declined 3.6%, representing a significant improvement over the first half of the year. We believe M's sales recovery is being supported by favorable customer response to new private/exclusive label offerings, a stronger value message in marketing, and growth in the macys.com and bloomingdales.com online businesses. We expect M to benefit from easier same-store sales comparisons through the first half of FY 11 and see initial payoff of the company's localization initiatives at Macy's starting in the spring.

► Risks to our recommendation and target price include a loss of business due to lackluster merchandising or uncompetitive pricing. Our corporate governance concerns include the non-disclosure of specific hurdle rates for performance-based equity awards and of stock ownership by executives.

► Our 12-month target price of $19 is based on an EV/EBITDA multiple of 6.2X, M's 10-year historical average, applied to our FY 11 EBITDA estimate of $2.6 billion.

Qualitative Risk Assessment

LOW	MEDIUM	HIGH

Our risk assessment reflects merchandise localization challenges and an uncertain outlook for consumer discretionary spending, partly offset by our view of M's strong brand and geographical presence in a consolidating industry.

Quantitative Evaluations

S&P Quality Ranking   B-

D	C	B-	B	B+	A-	A	A+

Relative Strength Rank   MODERATE

36

LOWEST = 1   HIGHEST = 99

Revenue/Earnings Data

Revenue (Million $)

	1Q	2Q	3Q	4Q	Year
2010	5,199	5,164	5,277	--	--
2009	5,747	5,718	5,493	7,934	24,892
2008	5,921	5,892	5,906	8,594	26,313
2007	5,930	5,995	5,886	9,159	26,970
2006	3,641	3,623	5,785	9,571	22,390
2005	3,517	3,548	3,491	5,074	15,630

Earnings Per Share ($)

2010	-0.21	0.02	-0.08	E1.09	E1.10
2009	-0.14	0.17	-0.10	-11.33	-11.40
2008	0.11	0.17	0.08	1.73	2.01
2007	-0.13	0.51	0.03	1.45	1.80
2006	0.36	0.84	0.89	1.23	3.16
2005	0.26	0.22	0.21	1.28	1.93

Fiscal year ended Jan. 31. Next earnings report expected: Late February. EPS Estimates based on S&P Operating Earnings; historical GAAP earnings are as reported.

Dividend Data (Dates: mm/dd Payment Date: mm/dd/yy)

Amount ($)	Date Decl.	Ex-Div. Date	Stk. of Record	Payment Date
0.050	02/02	03/11	03/13	04/01/09
0.050	05/15	06/11	06/15	07/01/09
0.050	08/21	09/11	09/15	10/01/09
0.050	10/23	12/11	12/15	01/04/10

Dividends have been paid since 2003. Source: Company reports.

Please read the Required Disclosures and Analyst Certification on the last page of this report.

The McGraw-Hill Companies

Macy's Inc

STANDARD
&POOR'S

Business Summary November 12, 2009

CORPORATE OVERVIEW. In February 2005, Macy's Inc. (formerly Federated Department Stores, Inc.) and The May Department Stores Co. announced merger plans. At that time, May was in need of new leadership to revive its business, and M was in the midst of a successful turnaround and on the lookout for acquisitions that would expand its presence in underserved markets. Both companies viewed the merger as a win-win proposition, as M would roll out its profit-driving merchandising, pricing, and service initiatives to May's stores, and May would extend M's presence into 15 new states.

As a result of the $17 billion May merger, which closed in August 2005, M is now the fourth largest U.S. mass merchandiser in annual revenues, with over 840 department stores in 45 states under the Macy's and Bloomingdale's names.

CORPORATE STRATEGY. Since 2005, M has focused on three key priorities to better position its business for long-term growth: growing "better" and "afford-

able luxury" assortments, with an emphasis on private label merchandise; improving customer perceptions of fair value in less discounted prices; and enriching the overall shopping experience. With its merger with May, the company also expanded its core Macy's brand nationwide.

Going forward, M sees an opportunity to accelerate the sales performance in about 400 former May locations that were rebranded Macy's on September 9, 2006. As part of its efforts to increase public awareness of Macy's, which contributes about 90% of the company's revenues, M changed its corporate name to Macy's, Inc. from Federated Department Stores, Inc. on June 1, 2007. On that date, the company's shares also began trading under the ticker symbol "M" (replacing "FD") on the New York Stock Exchange.

Company Financials Fiscal Year Ended Jan. 31

Per Share Data ($)	2009	2008	2007	2006	2005	2004	2003	2002	2001	2000
Tangible Book Value	0.44	NM	5.56	5.34	16.55	NM	13.47	12.16	12.47	11.26
Cash Flow	-8.37	4.90	4.11	4.29	4.09	3.92	3.31	2.94	1.32	3.49
Earnings	-11.40	2.01	1.80	3.16	1.93	1.86	1.61	1.30	-0.45	1.81
S&P Core Earnings	-3.23	1.90	1.62	2.21	1.83	1.69	1.24	0.91	0.25	NA
Dividends	0.39	0.51	0.45	0.26	0.19	Nil	Nil	Nil	Nil	Nil
Payout Ratio	NM	25%	25%	8%	10%	Nil	Nil	Nil	Nil	Nil
Calendar Year	2008	2007	2006	2005	2004	2003	2002	2001	2000	1999
Prices:High	28.47	46.70	45.01	39.03	29.08	25.30	22.13	24.95	26.94	28.53
Prices:Low	5.07	24.70	32.38	27.10	21.40	11.76	11.80	13.03	10.50	18.22
P/E Ratio:High	NM	23	25	12	15	14	14	19	NM	16
P/E Ratio:Low	NM	12	18	9	11	6	7	10	NM	10

Income Statement Analysis (Million $)										
Revenue	24,892	26,313	26,970	22,390	15,630	15,264	15,435	15,651	18,407	17,716
Operating Income	2,680	3,167	2,910	3,087	2,143	2,047	2,019	1,923	2,239	2,443
Depreciation	1,278	1,304	1,265	974	743	706	676	657	727	742
Interest Expense	599	588	520	422	299	266	311	331	444	368
Pretax Income	-4,938	1,320	1,446	2,044	1,116	1,084	1,048	780	113	1,346
Effective Tax Rate	NM	31.1%	31.7%	32.8%	38.3%	36.1%	39.1%	33.6%	NM	40.9%
Net Income	-48,003	909	988	1,373	689	693	638	518	-184	795
S&P Core Earnings	-1,366	860	888	967	655	628	490	364	102	NA

Balance Sheet & Other Financial Data (Million $)										
Cash	1,306	583	1,211	248	868	925	716	636	322	218
Current Assets	6,740	6,324	7,422	10,145	7,510	7,452	7,154	7,280	8,700	8,522
Total Assets	22,145	27,789	29,550	33,168	14,885	14,550	14,441	15,044	17,012	17,692
Current Liabilities	5,126	5,360	6,359	7,590	4,301	3,883	3,601	3,714	4,869	4,552
Long Term Debt	8,733	9,087	7,847	8,860	2,637	3,151	3,408	3,859	4,374	4,589
Common Equity	4,646	9,907	12,254	13,519	6,167	5,940	5,762	5,564	5,822	6,552
Total Capital	14,498	20,440	21,829	24,083	10,003	10,089	10,168	10,768	11,589	12,585
Capital Expenditures	761	994	1,317	568	467	508	568	615	742	770
Cash Flow	-3,525	2,213	2,253	2,347	1,432	1,399	1,314	1,175	543	1,537
Current Ratio	1.3	1.2	1.2	1.3	1.7	1.9	2.0	2.0	1.8	1.9
% Long Term Debt of Capitalization	60.2	44.5	39.0	36.8	26.4	31.2	33.5	35.8	37.7	36.5
% Net Income of Revenue	NM	3.5	3.7	6.1	4.4	4.5	4.1	3.3	NM	4.5
% Return on Assets	NM	3.2	3.2	5.7	4.7	4.8	4.2	3.4	NM	5.1
% Return on Equity	NM	8.2	7.7	13.9	11.4	11.8	11.3	9.1	NM	13.0

Data as orig reptd.; bef. results of disc opers/spec. items. Per share data adj. for stk. divs.; EPS diluted. E-Estimated. NA-Not Available. NM-Not Meaningful. NR-Not Ranked. UR-Under Review.

Office: 7 W Seventh St, Cincinnati, OH 45202.
Telephone: 513-579-7000.
Website: http://www.fds.com
Chrmn, Pres & CEO: T.J. Lundgren

Vice Chrmn: R.J. Borneo
Investor Contact: K.M. Hoguet (212-494-1602)
EVP & CFO: K.M. Hoguet
SVP & Secy: D.J. Broderick

Board Members: S. F. Bollenbach, D. Connelly, M. Feldberg, S. Levinson, T. J. Lundgren, J. Neubauer, J. A. Pichler, J. M. Roche, M. S. Traub, C. Weatherup, M. C. Whittington, K. M. von der Heyden

Founded: 1858
Domicile: Delaware
Employees: 188,000

Marathon Oil Corp

STANDARD &POOR'S

| S&P Recommendation | BUY ★★★★☆ | Price $32.63 (as of Nov 27, 2009) | 12-Mo. Target Price $38.00 | Investment Style Large-Cap Blend |

GICS Sector Energy
Sub-Industry Integrated Oil & Gas

Summary One of the largest integrated oil companies in the U.S., Marathon also has international oil and gas exploration and production operations, and domestic refining, marketing and transportation operations.

Key Stock Statistics (Source S&P, Vickers, company reports)

52-Wk Range	$35.71– 20.05	S&P Oper. EPS 2009**E**	2.34	Market Capitalization(B)	$23.135	Beta	1.27
Trailing 12-Month EPS	$1.50	S&P Oper. EPS 2010**E**	3.52	Yield (%)	2.94	S&P 3-Yr. Proj. EPS CAGR(%)	-15
Trailing 12-Month P/E	21.8	P/E on S&P Oper. EPS 2009**E**	13.9	Dividend Rate/Share	$0.96	S&P Credit Rating	BBB+
$10K Invested 5 Yrs Ago	$18,403	Common Shares Outstg. (M)	709.0	Institutional Ownership (%)	80		

Price Performance

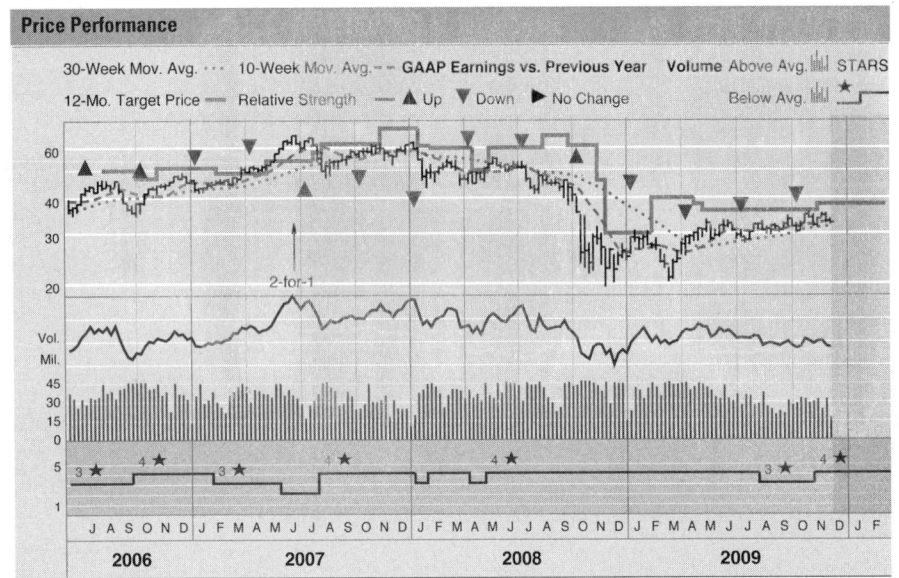

30-Week Mov. Avg. · · · · 10-Week Mov. Avg. – – 12-Mo. Target Price — Relative Strength — GAAP Earnings vs. Previous Year ▲ Up ▼ Down ▶ No Change Volume Above Avg. STARS Below Avg. ★

2006 2007 2008 2009

Options: ASE, CBOE, P, Ph

Analysis prepared by **Tina J. Vital** on November 04, 2009, when the stock traded at **$ 33.01**.

Highlights

▶ With resumed production from Gulf of Mexico shut-ins and contributions from start-ups in the Gulf of Mexico and Norway, we expect oil and gas production available for sale to increase more than 5% in 2009. Combined with new international developments and emerging U.S. onshore shale plays, we expect over 6% per annum oil and gas production available for sale growth between 2008 and 2013.

▶ On the downstream, the global economic slowdown has sharply reduced the demand for refined petroleum fuels. As a result, crude oil and product prices have dropped, and refining margins and light-heavy crude differentials have narrowed; we expect this trend to continue into the fourth quarter. Overall, we look for U.S. industrywide refining margins to narrow about 16% in 2009 before widening about 7% in 2010.

▶ First nine months operating EPS included $0.20 of net gains related to sale of assets and derivatives. We expect after-tax operating earnings to fall about 68% in 2009 on lower projected prices, before rebounding about 59% in 2010 on an improved economic outlook.

Investment Rationale/Risk

▶ MRO has increased its exposure to higher-growth but politically challenging regions such as Africa, and has focused on larger exploration and production projects in the deepwater Gulf of Mexico and in western Canada). In July 2008, MRO evaluated the potential separation of its exploration and production and refining and marketing units into two independent, publicly traded companies, but in February 2009, it concluded that it was in the best interests of its shareholders to remain a fully integrated energy company. While we see increased earnings stability as an integrated business, we look for reduced upstream investment going forward.

▶ Risks to our recommendation and target price include adverse economic, industry and operating conditions, rising industry costs, and difficulty replacing reserves.

▶ Blending our discounted cash flow ($37 per share, assuming a WACC of 10.2% and terminal growth of 3%) and relative market valuations, our 12-month target price is $38, representing an expected enterprise value of 4.1X our 2010 EBITDA estimate, a discount to peers.

Qualitative Risk Assessment

| LOW | MEDIUM | HIGH |

Our risk assessment reflects our view of the company's diversified and solid business profile in volatile and cyclical segments of the energy industry. We consider MRO's earnings stability to be good, and its corporate governance practices sound.

Quantitative Evaluations

S&P Quality Ranking B+

| D | C | B- | B | B+ | A- | A | A+ |

Relative Strength Rank MODERATE

43

LOWEST = 1   HIGHEST = 99

Revenue/Earnings Data

Revenue (Million $)

	1Q	2Q	3Q	4Q	Year
2009	9,080	13,358	13,104	--	--
2008	18,100	20,617	21,841	13,064	72,128
2007	12,869	16,736	16,762	18,185	64,552
2006	16,418	18,179	16,492	13,807	64,896
2005	12,932	16,019	17,248	17,314	63,673
2004	10,652	12,514	12,249	14,183	49,598

Earnings Per Share ($)

2009	0.40	0.48	0.55	E0.78	E2.34
2008	1.02	1.08	2.90	-0.06	4.95
2007	1.04	2.24	1.49	0.94	5.68
2006	1.07	2.04	2.26	1.53	6.87
2005	0.47	0.96	1.04	1.74	4.25
2004	0.42	0.51	0.32	0.62	1.86

Fiscal year ended Dec. 31. Next earnings report expected: Mid January. EPS Estimates based on S&P Operating Earnings; historical GAAP earnings are as reported.

Dividend Data (Dates: mm/dd Payment Date: mm/dd/yy)

Amount ($)	Date Decl.	Ex-Div. Date	Stk. of Record	Payment Date
0.240	02/02	02/13	02/18	03/10/09
0.240	04/29	05/18	05/20	06/10/09
0.240	07/29	08/17	08/19	09/10/09
0.240	10/28	11/16	11/18	12/10/09

Dividends have been paid since 1991. Source: Company reports.

Please read the Required Disclosures and Analyst Certification on the last page of this report.

The McGraw-Hill Companies

Marathon Oil Corp

STANDARD &POOR'S

Business Summary November 04, 2009

CORPORATE OVERVIEW. As one of the largest integrated oil companies in the U.S., Marathon Oil (MRO; formerly USX-Marathon Group, a part of USX Corp.) is engaged in four operating segments: Exploration and Production (E&P; 16% of 2008 revenues; 61% of 2008 segment income); Oil Sands Mining (OSM; 1%; 6%), Refining, Marketing and Transportation (RM&T; 83%; 26%); and Integrated Gas (IG; less than 1%; 7%).

The E&P segment conducts exploration in the U.S., Angola, Norway and Indonesia, and production activities in the U.S., the U.K., Norway, Ireland, Equatorial Guinea and Libya. Excluding oil sands, proved oil and gas reserves declined 2.4% to 1.195 billion barrel oil equivalent (boe; 76% developed, 53% liquids) in 2008. Proved bitumen reserves from the oil sands segment declined 7.8% to 388 million barrels in 2008. Oil and gas volume sales rose 8.5% to 381,000 boe per day (boe/d; 55% liquids) in 2008. Using data from John S. Herold, we estimate MRO's three-year (2005-07) finding and development costs at $25.89 per boe, above the peer average; its three-year proved acqui-

sition costs at $10.42 per boe, above the peer average; its three-year reserve replacement costs at $16.04 per boe, below the peer average; and its three-year reserve replacement rate at 244%, above the peer average. Excluding oil sands, we estimate MRO's 2008 organic reserve replacement at 80% of production.

Through MRO's 2007 acquisition of Western Oil Sands Inc. (WTO) for about US$6.9 billion, MRO gained a 20% interest in the Athabasca Oil Sands Project (AOSP) in Alberta, Canada. The venture produces bitumen from oil sands deposits and upgrades the bitumen to synthetic crude oil. As a result, MRO's directors approved a $1.9 billion Heavy Oil Upgrading Project at its Detroit refinery.

Company Financials Fiscal Year Ended Dec. 31

Per Share Data ($)	2008	2007	2006	2005	2004	2003	2002	2001	2000	1999
Tangible Book Value	28.16	22.59	18.72	13.90	11.17	9.20	7.57	7.99	7.77	7.70
Cash Flow	8.00	7.91	9.30	6.14	3.57	3.53	2.80	4.12	2.69	2.59
Earnings	4.95	5.68	6.87	4.25	1.86	1.63	0.86	2.13	0.70	1.05
S&P Core Earnings	5.77	5.69	6.85	4.20	1.91	1.63	0.69	2.21	NA	NA
Dividends	0.96	0.92	0.77	0.61	0.52	0.48	0.46	0.46	0.44	0.42
Payout Ratio	19%	16%	11%	14%	28%	29%	53%	75%	63%	40%
Prices:High	63.22	67.04	49.37	36.34	21.30	16.81	15.15	16.87	15.19	16.94
Prices:Low	19.34	41.50	31.01	17.76	15.15	9.93	9.41	12.48	10.34	9.81
P/E Ratio:High	13	12	7	9	11	10	18	28	22	16
P/E Ratio:Low	4	7	5	4	8	6	11	20	15	9
Income Statement Analysis (Million $)										
Revenue	72,128	64,552	64,896	63,673	49,598	40,963	31,464	33,019	34,487	24,212
Operating Income	9,237	7,598	9,932	6,660	8,379	2,988	2,253	4,215	3,521	1,997
Depreciation, Depletion and Amortization	2,178	1,613	1,518	1,358	1,217	1,175	1,201	1,236	1,245	950
Interest Expense	50.0	290	108	145	161	238	288	196	260	290
Pretax Income	6,973	6,846	8,969	5,157	2,509	1,898	1,098	2,781	1,412	1,425
Effective Tax Rate	49.4%	42.4%	44.8%	33.5%	29.0%	30.8%	35.4%	27.3%	34.1%	22.7%
Net Income	3,528	3,948	4,957	3,051	1,257	1,012	536	1,318	432	654
S&P Core Earnings	4,112	3,953	4,949	3,013	1,290	1,014	428	1,367	NA	NA
Balance Sheet & Other Financial Data (Million $)										
Cash	1,285	1,199	2,585	2,617	3,369	1,396	488	657	340	111
Current Assets	8,403	10,587	10,096	9,383	8,867	6,040	4,479	4,411	4,985	4,102
Total Assets	42,686	42,746	30,831	28,498	23,423	19,482	17,812	16,129	15,232	15,705
Current Liabilities	7,753	11,260	8,061	8,154	5,253	4,207	3,659	3,468	4,012	3,149
Long Term Debt	7,087	6,084	6,084	3,061	4,057	4,085	4,410	3,432	4,196	3,504
Common Equity	21,409	19,223	14,607	11,705	8,111	6,075	5,082	4,940	4,845	4,800
Total Capital	31,826	28,696	20,083	17,868	16,411	12,171	12,908	11,632	12,235	11,552
Capital Expenditures	7,146	4,466	3,433	2,890	2,237	1,892	1,574	1,639	1,669	1,378
Cash Flow	5,706	5,500	6,475	4,409	2,474	2,187	1,737	2,546	1,677	1,604
Current Ratio	1.1	0.9	1.3	1.2	1.7	1.4	1.2	1.3	1.2	1.3
% Long Term Debt of Capitalization	22.3	21.2	15.2	20.7	24.7	33.6	34.2	29.5	34.3	30.3
% Return on Assets	8.3	10.7	16.7	11.8	5.9	5.4	3.2	7.9	2.8	4.3
% Return on Equity	17.4	23.3	37.7	30.8	17.7	18.1	10.7	22.4	9.0	14.4

Data as orig reptd.; bef. results of disc opers/spec. items. Per share data adj. for stk. divs.; EPS diluted. E-Estimated. NA-Not Available. NM-Not Meaningful. NR-Not Ranked. UR-Under Review.

Office: 5555 San Felipe St Bsmt, Houston, TX 77056-2701.
Telephone: 713-629-6600.
Website: http://www.marathon.com
Chrmn: T.J. Usher

Pres & CEO: C.P. Cazalot, Jr.
EVP & CFO: J.F. Clark
Chief Acctg Officer & Cntlr: M.K. Stewart
Treas: P.C. Reinbolt

Investor Contact: H. Thill (713-296-4140)
Board Members: G. H. Boyce, C. P. Cazalot, Jr., D. A. Daberko, W. L. Davis, S. A. Jackson, P. Lader, C. R. Lee, M. E. Phelps, D. H. Reilley, S. E. Schofield, J. W. Snow, T. J. Usher

Founded: 1901
Domicile: Delaware
Employees: 30,360

Marriott International Inc.

STANDARD &POOR'S

| S&P Recommendation | **STRONG SELL** ★ ☆ ☆ ☆ ☆ | Price $25.26 (as of Nov 27, 2009) | 12-Mo. Target Price $13.00 | Investment Style Large-Cap Growth |

GICS Sector Consumer Discretionary
Sub-Industry Hotels, Resorts & Cruise Lines

Summary MAR's lodging brands include over 3,350 properties, most of which are managed by the company or are operated by others through franchise relationships.

Key Stock Statistics (Source S&P, Vickers, company reports)

52-Wk Range	$28.40– 12.09	S&P Oper. EPS 2009**E**	0.60	Market Capitalization(B)	$9.024	Beta	1.51
Trailing 12-Month EPS	$-1.30	S&P Oper. EPS 2010**E**	0.65	Yield (%)	Nil	S&P 3-Yr. Proj. EPS CAGR(%)	-10
Trailing 12-Month P/E	NM	P/E on S&P Oper. EPS 2009**E**	42.2	Dividend Rate/Share	Nil	S&P Credit Rating	BBB-
$10K Invested 5 Yrs Ago	$9,319	Common Shares Outstg. (M)	357.2	Institutional Ownership (%)	68		

Price Performance

30-Week Mov. Avg. ··· 10-Week Mov. Avg. – – **GAAP Earnings vs. Previous Year** Volume Above Avg. ▮▮▮ STARS
12-Mo. Target Price — Relative Strength — ▲ Up ▼ Down ▶ No Change Below Avg. ▮▮▮ ★

Options: ASE, CBOE, P, Ph

Analysis prepared by **Mark S. Basham** on November 04, 2009, when the stock traded at **$ 25.34**.

Highlights

► We see global systemwide RevPAR (revenue per available room) declining 18% to 20% in 2009. Our outlook for North America is for percentage declines at the low end of this range, while outside North America we expect a drop of slightly more than 20%. Results also reflect the addition of about 30,000 rooms to the portfolio, a 5.4% increase.

► We project that franchise fees, management fees, and revenues from owned hotels combined will decline 22% in 2009. We estimate timeshare results, net of expenses and loan loss provisions, will show a $30 million loss, excluding impairment charges of $752 million. We expect EBITDA from ongoing operations to decrease 44% in 2009, to $630 million, from $1.12 billion in 2008. Excluding non-recurring items, we estimate operating EPS will fall 60%, to $0.60, from $1.51 in 2008.

► We expect base management fees will rise 5% to 6% in 2010, on a 4% increase in room demand and additions to the hotel portfolio. Incentive fees are likely to remain under pressure, while we see a return to profitability in the timeshare segment. We estimate EBITDA of $635 million and forecast a rise in EPS to $0.65.

Investment Rationale/Risk

► Our Strong Sell opinion reflects our view that global hotel industry fundamentals are likely to remain weaker far longer than we had earlier expected, with a full recovery unlikely until at least 2012. We believe MAR's growth strategy could increase financing risks and stress its capital structure. We also think the financial health of MAR's hotel owner and franchise partners pose potential risks.

► Risks to our recommendation and target price include the prospects for a shorter and milder global economic downturn than we currently expect, raising the possibility of an earlier industry rebound. Property development could slow dramatically during this period of global financial distress, which would generally be a long-term positive.

► Our 12-month target price of $13 is based on an enterprise value of about 12X estimated 2010 EBITDA of $635 million, and assumes debt reduction of approximately $625 million during 2009. MAR has substituted a stock dividend in recent periods for its cash dividend in order to preserve cash.

Qualitative Risk Assessment

| LOW | MEDIUM | **HIGH** |

Our risk assessment reflects our view that MAR is subject to not only improving cyclical economic factors, but also ongoing weakness in industry fundamentals, with the latter outweighing the former, so that a material increase in earnings may be difficult for some time. While we expect internal cash flow to be sufficient to finance future minimum capital needs, outside capital, particularly to finance timeshare receivables, is likely to be more costly, if available at all.

Quantitative Evaluations

S&P Quality Ranking A

| D | C | B- | B | B+ | A- | **A** | A+ |

Relative Strength Rank MODERATE

39

LOWEST = 1 HIGHEST = 99

Revenue/Earnings Data

Revenue (Million $)

	1Q	2Q	3Q	4Q	Year
2009	2,495	2,562	2,471	--	--
2008	2,947	3,185	2,963	3,784	12,879
2007	2,836	3,122	2,943	4,089	12,990
2006	2,705	2,891	2,703	3,861	12,160
2005	2,534	2,661	2,714	3,641	11,550
2004	2,252	2,402	2,304	3,141	10,099

Earnings Per Share ($)

2009	-0.06	0.10	-1.31	E0.23	E0.60
2008	0.33	0.41	0.26	-0.03	0.98
2007	0.40	0.43	0.31	0.61	1.74
2006	0.38	0.43	0.33	0.51	1.65
2005	0.30	0.29	0.32	0.53	1.43
2004	0.23	0.33	0.27	0.39	1.22

Fiscal year ended Dec. 31. Next earnings report expected: Mid February. EPS Estimates based on S&P Operating Earnings; historical GAAP earnings are as reported.

Dividend Data (Dates: mm/dd Payment Date: mm/dd/yy)

Amount ($)	Date Decl.	Ex-Div. Date	Stk. of Record	Payment Date
0.088	02/05	03/30	04/01	04/29/09
Stk.	05/01	06/23	06/25	07/30/09
Stk.	08/06	08/18	08/20	09/03/09
Stk.	11/05	11/17	11/19	12/03/09

Dividends have been paid since 1998. Source: Company reports.

Marriott International Inc.

STANDARD
&POOR'S

Business Summary November 04, 2009

CORPORATE OVERVIEW. Marriott International's lodging and timeshare businesses included 3,362 properties with 586,515 rooms or suites as of September 11, 2009. This compared with 3,178 properties with 560,681 rooms or suites as of January 2, 2009. Of the 3,362 properties, approximately 2,850 were located in the U.S.

At year-end 2008, MAR had 1,093 properties (280,100 rooms or suites) that MAR operated under long-term management or lease agreements, and had six owned properties (1,448). With its management agreements, the company typically earns a base fee, and may receive an incentive management fee that is based on hotel profits. MAR also had 2,079 franchised properties, with 279,133 rooms, that were operated by other parties.

By brand (including franchises), as of year-end 2008, MAR's business included 531 Marriott Hotels & Resorts, Marriott Conference Centers or JW Marriott Hotels & Resorts properties; 70 Ritz-Carlton hotels; 141 Renaissance hotels; 808 Courtyard hotels; 569 Fairfield Inn properties; 208 SpringHill Suites properties, 573 Residence Inn hotels; 163 TownPlace Suites properties; two Bulgari Hotel & Resorts properties, 67 timeshare properties; and 46 residential units. Two brands for which the first properties are in planning or development are Nickelodeon Resorts by Marriott, and Edition, a global boutique hotel brand for which the company has partnered with hotelier Ian Schrager.

In 2008, MAR's North American full-service lodging segment, which included Marriott full-service and Renaissance businesses, accounted for 44% of total revenues, while North American limited service accounted for 17%. In addition, international accounted for 12%, luxury 13%, and timeshare and other 14%.

The company's international presence as of year-end 2008 included: 106 properties (25,475 rooms or suites) in Europe, 61 in the British Isles (11,783) 99 properties (34,339) in Asia, 34 (10,080) in the Middle East or Africa, 122 (27,694) in the Americas ex-U.S., and eight (2,353) in Australia.

CORPORATE STRATEGY. In the third quarter of 2009, MAR determined that in response to difficult business conditions and a lack of consumer confidence, it would alter it timeshare strategy to stimulate sales, accelerate cash flow, and minimize future investment spending. These changes included price reductions and a cessation of most future development, and resulted in pretax charges of $752 million during the quarter.

Company Financials Fiscal Year Ended Dec. 31

Per Share Data ($)	2008	2007	2006	2005	2004	2003	2002	2001	2000	1999
Tangible Book Value	NM	1.40	2.85	4.47	5.79	5.11	4.52	3.52	2.77	2.11
Cash Flow	1.48	2.23	2.30	1.82	1.66	1.28	1.21	0.88	1.31	1.03
Earnings	0.98	1.74	1.65	1.43	1.22	0.96	0.86	0.46	0.93	0.75
S&P Core Earnings	0.98	1.76	1.55	1.24	0.99	0.67	0.76	0.35	NA	NA
Dividends	0.33	0.28	0.24	0.20	0.16	0.15	0.14	0.13	0.12	0.10
Payout Ratio	34%	16%	14%	14%	13%	15%	16%	28%	12%	13%
Prices:High	37.48	51.44	47.79	35.01	31.65	23.34	22.97	24.98	21.51	22.01
Prices:Low	11.75	31.00	31.97	28.69	20.10	14.12	12.98	13.50	12.92	14.34
P/E Ratio:High	38	29	29	24	26	24	27	55	23	28
P/E Ratio:Low	12	18	19	20	16	15	15	30	14	18

Income Statement Analysis (Million $)	2008	2007	2006	2005	2004	2003	2002	2001	2000	1999
Revenue	12,879	12,990	12,160	11,550	10,099	9,014	8,441	10,152	10,017	8,739
Operating Income	1,120	1,385	1,199	739	643	537	634	779	997	828
Depreciation	190	197	188	184	166	160	187	222	195	162
Interest Expense	218	184	124	106	99.0	110	86.0	109	100	61.0
Pretax Income	694	1,137	997	717	654	488	471	370	757	637
Effective Tax Rate	50.4%	39.0%	28.7%	13.1%	15.3%	NM	6.79%	36.2%	36.7%	37.2%
Net Income	359	697	717	668	594	476	439	236	479	400
S&P Core Earnings	364	711	680	579	484	330	381	180	NA	NA

Balance Sheet & Other Financial Data (Million $)	2008	2007	2006	2005	2004	2003	2002	2001	2000	1999
Cash	134	332	193	203	770	229	198	817	334	489
Current Assets	3,368	3,572	3,314	2,010	1,946	1,235	1,744	2,130	1,415	1,600
Total Assets	8,903	8,942	8,588	8,530	8,668	8,177	8,296	9,107	8,237	7,324
Current Liabilities	2,533	2,876	2,522	1,992	2,356	1,770	2,207	1,802	1,917	1,743
Long Term Debt	2,975	2,790	1,818	1,681	836	1,391	1,553	2,815	2,016	1,676
Common Equity	1,380	1,429	2,618	3,252	4,081	3,838	3,573	3,478	3,267	2,908
Total Capital	4,366	4,219	4,436	4,944	4,929	5,398	5,232	6,293	5,283	4,584
Capital Expenditures	357	671	529	780	181	210	292	560	1,095	929
Cash Flow	549	894	905	852	760	636	626	458	674	562
Current Ratio	1.3	1.2	1.3	1.0	0.8	0.7	0.8	1.2	0.7	0.9
% Long Term Debt of Capitalization	68.1	66.1	41.0	34.0	16.9	25.7	29.7	44.7	38.2	36.6
% Net Income of Revenue	2.8	5.3	5.9	5.8	5.9	5.3	5.2	2.3	4.8	4.6
% Return on Assets	4.0	7.9	8.4	7.8	7.1	5.8	5.0	2.7	6.2	5.9
% Return on Equity	25.6	34.4	24.4	18.2	15.0	12.8	12.5	7.0	15.5	14.6

Data as orig reptd.; bef. results of disc opers/spec. items. Per share data adj. for stk. divs.; EPS diluted. E-Estimated. NA-Not Available. NM-Not Meaningful. NR-Not Ranked. UR-Under Review.

Office: 10400 Fernwood Road, Bethesda, MD 20817-1102.
Telephone: 301-380-3000.
Website: http://www.marriott.com
Chrmn & CEO: J.W. Marriott, Jr.

Pres & COO: A.M. Sorenson
Vice Chrmn: J.W. Marriott, III
Vice Chrmn: W.J. Shaw
EVP, CFO & Chief Acctg Officer: C. Berquist

Investor Contact: T. Marder (301-380-2553)
Board Members: M. K. Bush, L. Kellner, D. L. Lee, J. W. Marriott, III, J. W. Marriott, Jr., G. Munoz, H. J. Pearce, S. S. Reinemund, W. M. Romney, W. M. Romney, W. J. Shaw, L. M. Small

Founded: 1971
Domicile: Delaware
Employees: 146,000

The McGraw-Hill Companies

Marshall & Ilsley Corp

STANDARD &POOR'S

S&P Recommendation **BUY** ★★★★☆	Price $5.43 (as of Nov 27, 2009)	12-Mo. Target Price $6.00	Investment Style Large-Cap Blend

GICS Sector Financials
Sub-Industry Regional Banks

Summary This bank holding company operates in Wisconsin, Missouri, Arizona, Minnesota, Indiana, Florida, and three other states.

Key Stock Statistics (Source S&P, Vickers, company reports)

52-Wk Range	$14.85–2.98	S&P Oper. EPS 2009**E**	-2.11	Market Capitalization(B)	$2.849	Beta	1.54
Trailing 12-Month EPS	$-8.48	S&P Oper. EPS 2010**E**	-0.66	Yield (%)	0.74	S&P 3-Yr. Proj. EPS CAGR(%)	NM
Trailing 12-Month P/E	NM	P/E on S&P Oper. EPS 2009**E**	NM	Dividend Rate/Share	$0.04	S&P Credit Rating	A
$10K Invested 5 Yrs Ago	$1,880	Common Shares Outstg. (M)	524.7	Institutional Ownership (%)	67		

Price Performance

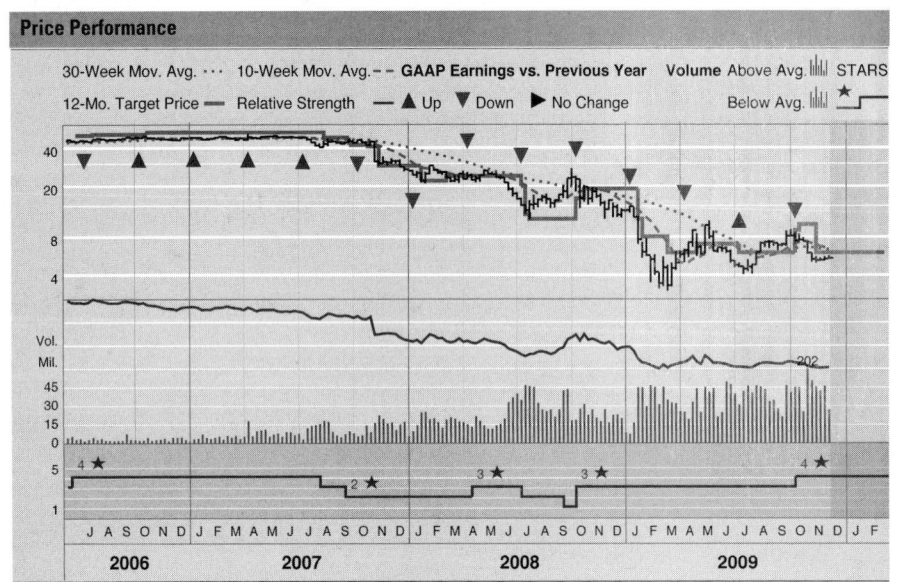

30-Week Mov. Avg. · · · 10-Week Mov. Avg. — GAAP Earnings vs. Previous Year Volume Above Avg. STARS
12-Mo. Target Price — Relative Strength — ▲ Up ▼ Down ▶ No Change Below Avg.

Options: ASE, CBOE, P, Ph

Analysis prepared by **Erik Oja** on November 04, 2009, when the stock traded at **$ 5.20**.

Qualitative Risk Assessment

LOW	**MEDIUM**	HIGH

Our risk assessment reflects our view of the company's large-cap valuation, and its history of profitability, offset by the risk that credit quality may suffer from continuing downtrends in the Sunbelt and Midwest.

Quantitative Evaluations

S&P Quality Ranking A-

D	C	B-	B	B+	**A-**	A	A+

Relative Strength Rank WEAK

15

LOWEST = 1 HIGHEST = 99

Revenue/Earnings Data

Revenue (Million $)

	1Q	2Q	3Q	4Q	Year
2009	820.5	895.7	171.8	--	--
2008	1,090	1,002	982.5	951.5	4,169
2007	1,386	1,438	1,474	3,873	4,398
2006	1,139	1,290	1,381	1,317	5,128
2005	895.1	975.8	1,014	1,076	3,963
2004	702.5	728.0	792.2	882.5	3,112

Earnings Per Share ($)

2009	-0.44	-0.83	-0.68	E-0.42	E-2.11
2008	0.56	-1.52	0.32	-7.25	-7.92
2007	0.83	0.83	0.85	-0.09	1.87
2006	0.72	0.74	0.92	0.79	3.17
2005	0.73	0.81	0.78	0.78	3.10
2004	0.65	0.67	0.69	0.76	2.77

Fiscal year ended Dec. 31. Next earnings report expected: Mid January. EPS Estimates based on S&P Operating Earnings; historical GAAP earnings are as reported.

Highlights

► We expect MI to earn $1.51 billion of net interest income in 2009, down 15%. We see a good net interest spread environment, currently offsetting the negative impacts of nonperforming loans and weak loan growth. We expect each of these effects to reverse at different times in 2010, beginning with the relatively wide spread, followed by improvements in loan growth and credit quality, and we are forecasting net interest income of $1.44 billion in 2010, down 4.6%. We forecast 2009 fee income, before securities gains and losses, to be $763 million, a 4.4% increase from $731 million in 2008, driven by gains on sales of mortgage loans.

► We see loan loss provisions in 2009 totaling about $1.99 billion, based on our expectation of net chargeoffs of 3.50% of loans, plus reserve building of $250 million. For 2010, we expect loan loss provisions of $1.12 billion, based on net chargeoffs of 2.25% of loans, with no reserve building. In 2011, we expect loan loss provisions to moderate to $115 million per quarter, a level we see as low enough to generate positive earnings per share in each quarter.

► We look for losses per share of $2.11 in 2009 and $0.66 in 2010, and EPS of $0.27 in 2011.

Investment Rationale/Risk

► MI recently raised another $863 million in equity capital, for a total of $1.415 billion raised in 2009, thus raising its tangible common equity ratio to an above-peers 8.04% at September 30, by our calculations. We see capital levels as sufficient for the foreseeable future, though we expect credit losses to bring down capital levels in each of the next five quarters, and we project an above-peers tangible common equity ratio of 7.45% in the fourth quarter of 2010, but rising thereafter. While MI appears expensive on a price to earnings valuation at 19.5X our 2011 EPS estimate of $0.27, we see MI as inexpensive on price to book, at only 0.65X our December 31, 2010 tangible book value per share estimate of $8.16, in our view, overly below peers with similar credit quality levels.

► Risks to our recommendation and target price include higher-than-expected net chargeoffs and loan loss provisions.

► Our 12-month target price of $6 is based on a below-peers 0.74X our December 30, 2010 tangible book value per share estimate of $8.16, reflecting MI's credit challenges, offset by our expectations for credit quality improvements in 2010.

Dividend Data (Dates: mm/dd Payment Date: mm/dd/yy)

Amount ($)	Date Decl.	Ex-Div. Date	Stk. of Record	Payment Date
0.010	02/19	02/26	03/02	03/13/09
0.010	04/28	05/27	05/29	06/12/09
0.010	08/20	08/28	09/01	09/11/09
0.010	10/15	11/25	11/30	12/11/09

Dividends have been paid since 1938. Source: Company reports.

Please read the Required Disclosures and Analyst Certification on the last page of this report.

The **McGraw-Hill** Companies

Marshall & Ilsley Corp

STANDARD &POOR'S

Business Summary November 04, 2009

CORPORATE OVERVIEW. Marshall & Ilsley Corp. owns banking subsidiaries with operations in Wisconsin and the metropolitan areas of Phoenix and Tucson, AZ, Minneapolis/St. Paul, MN, St. Louis, MO, Las Vegas, NV, and Naples and Bonita Springs, FL. MI also owns nonbanking subsidiaries that are related or incidental to banking. The company also has other business operations that include trust services, residential mortgage banking, capital markets, brokerage and insurance, commercial leasing, commercial mortgage banking and community development investments.

PRIMARY BUSINESS DYNAMICS. In early 2007, MI announced that it would separate MI and Metavante Corporation into two separate publicly held companies by the end of 2007. Warburg Pincus, a global private equity investor, invested $625 million to acquire an equity stake of 25% in Metavante Corp. MI shareholders own the remaining 75% of Metavante. By the terms of the deal, each share of the "old" MI was entitled to receive one share of "new" Marshall & Ilsley Corp., plus one-third of a share of Metavante Corp. MI received a cash infusion of about $1.665 billion, which may be invested, used to improve MI's capital ratios, buy back shares or increase the dividend. This deal closed on November 1, 2007.

Starting in the 1990s, the company made several sizable bank acquisitions, mostly in Wisconsin. Beginning in 2000, it shifted its bank acquisition focus outside Wisconsin. Between 1994 and 1998, the company acquired six Wisconsin banks, with assets totaling $9.3 billion, for $2.0 billion. In 2001 and 2002, MI acquired three banks in Minnesota and one bank in Missouri, with combined assets of $4.3 billion, for a total of $994 million. On April 3, 2006, MI closed its acquisition of Gold Banc Corp. in Kansas, with assets of $4.1 billion, for $715 million. On March 1, 2006, the company completed its acquisition of Trustcorp Financial in Missouri, with assets of $705 million, for $181 million. On December 4, 2006, MI announced the pending acquisition of United Heritage Bank of Orlando, for $217 million; this deal closed on April 2, 2007. On February 12, 2007, MI announced the acquisition of Excel Bank Corp. for $101 million, and this transaction closed July 2, 2007. MI's most recent acquisition was First Indiana Corp., for $538 million cash, on January 3, 2008.

Company Financials Fiscal Year Ended Dec. 31

Per Share Data ($)	2008	2007	2006	2005	2004	2003	2002	2001	2000	1999
Tangible Book Value	20.71	19.82	11.51	9.02	7.76	9.96	8.61	9.00	9.06	8.12
Earnings	-7.92	1.87	3.17	3.10	2.77	2.38	2.16	1.54	1.45	1.57
S&P Core Earnings	-2.06	1.87	3.17	2.99	2.66	2.28	2.07	1.49	NA	NA
Dividends	1.27	1.20	1.05	0.93	0.81	0.70	0.55	0.57	0.52	0.47
Payout Ratio	NM	64%	33%	30%	29%	29%	25%	37%	36%	30%
Prices:High	29.07	51.48	49.10	47.40	44.70	38.46	32.12	32.12	31.13	36.38
Prices:Low	10.90	26.04	40.83	40.05	35.67	24.60	23.11	23.54	19.13	27.19
P/E Ratio:High	NM	28	15	15	16	16	15	21	22	23
P/E Ratio:Low	NM	14	13	13	13	10	11	15	13	17

Income Statement Analysis (Million $)										
Net Interest Income	1,781	1,616	1,490	1,233	1,132	1,057	1,006	843	673	705
Tax Equivalent Adjustment	27.8	28.2	NA	33.3	NA	NA	32.2	31.2	31.0	28.7
Non Interest Income	733	729	1,906	1,704	1,411	1,194	1,089	1,020	978	850
Loan Loss Provision	2,038	320	50.6	44.8	38.0	63.0	74.4	54.1	30.4	25.4
% Expense/Operating Revenue	117.8%	56.1%	63.6%	62.2%	62.7%	64.5%	61.9%	68.1%	65.4%	64.2%
Pretax Income	-2,503	711	1,196	1,090	945	758	719	501	470	528
Effective Tax Rate	NM	30.1%	32.4%	33.3%	33.6%	28.3%	33.2%	32.6%	32.5%	32.9%
Net Income	-2,043	497	808	727	627	544	480	338	317	355
% Net Interest Margin	3.12	3.14	3.27	3.31	3.52	3.65	3.96	3.67	2.81	3.58
S&P Core Earnings	-533	496	808	705	605	519	453	319	NA	NA

Balance Sheet & Other Financial Data (Million $)										
Money Market Assets	749	587	293	330	191	163	250	947	163	175
Investment Securities	7,669	7,818	7,473	6,320	6,085	5,607	5,209	4,464	5,848	5,575
Commercial Loans	14,880	26,526	23,717	19,023	16,646	14,254	6,586	10,815	9,649	4,754
Other Loans	35,105	19,770	17,917	14,866	12,810	10,896	17,011	8,480	7,938	11,580
Total Assets	63,824	59,849	56,230	46,213	40,437	34,373	32,875	27,254	26,078	24,370
Demand Deposits	6,880	6,174	6,112	5,525	15,005	4,715	4,462	3,559	3,130	2,831
Time Deposits	34,143	29,017	27,972	22,149	11,450	17,555	15,932	12,934	16,119	13,604
Long Term Debt	9,614	9,873	8,026	6,669	5,027	2,735	2,284	1,560	921	665
Common Equity	7,748	7,033	6,151	4,769	3,970	3,329	3,037	2,536	3,200	2,117
% Return on Assets	NM	0.9	1.6	1.7	1.7	1.6	1.6	1.3	1.3	1.5
% Return on Equity	NM	7.5	14.7	16.6	17.1	17.1	17.4	13.8	10.6	13.8
% Loan Loss Reserve	2.4	1.1	1.0	1.1	1.2	1.4	1.4	1.4	1.3	1.4
% Loans/Deposits	121.9	125.8	123.0	123.5	111.6	113.1	117.2	117.0	91.4	99.4
% Equity to Assets	10.9	11.4	10.7	9.9	9.8	9.5	9.2	9.0	11.9	11.0

Data as orig reptd.; bef. results of disc opers/spec. items. Per share data adj. for stk. divs.; EPS diluted. E-Estimated. NA-Not Available. NM-Not Meaningful. NR-Not Ranked. UR-Under Review.

Office: 770 N Water St, Milwaukee, WI 53202.
Telephone: 414-765-7801.
Website: http://www.micorp.com
Chrmn: D.J. Kuester

Pres & CEO: M.F. Furlong
SVP & CFO: G.A. Smith
SVP, Chief Admin Officer & General Counsel: R.J. Erickson
SVP, Chief Acctg Officer & Cntlr: P.R. Justiliano

Investor Contact: D.L. Urban (414-765-7853)
Board Members: A. N. Baur, J. F. Chait, J. Daniels, Jr., M. F. Furlong, T. D. Kellner, D. J. Kuester, D. J. Lubar, K. C. Lyall, J. A. Mellowes, R. J. O'Toole, S. W. Orr, Jr., P. M. Platten, III, J. S. Shiely, G. E. Wardeberg, J. B. Wigdale.

Founded: 1959
Domicile: Wisconsin
Employees: 10,191

The **McGraw-Hill** Companies

Marsh & McLennan Companies Inc.

STANDARD &POOR'S

S&P Recommendation HOLD ★★★☆☆	Price $22.26 (as of Nov 27, 2009)	12-Mo. Target Price $23.00	Investment Style Large-Cap Blend

GICS Sector Financials
Sub-Industry Insurance Brokers

Summary This global professional services concern provides risk and insurance services, investment management, and consulting services through its operating companies.

Key Stock Statistics (Source S&P, Vickers, company reports)

52-Wk Range	$25.58–17.18	S&P Oper. EPS 2009**E**	1.41	Market Capitalization(B)	$1.173	Beta	0.84
Trailing 12-Month EPS	$0.53	S&P Oper. EPS 2010**E**	1.78	Yield (%)	3.59	S&P 3-Yr. Proj. EPS CAGR(%)	22
Trailing 12-Month P/E	42.0	P/E on S&P Oper. EPS 2009**E**	15.8	Dividend Rate/Share	$0.80	S&P Credit Rating	BBB-
$10K Invested 5 Yrs Ago	$8,965	Common Shares Outstg. (M)	52.7	Institutional Ownership (%)	77		

Price Performance

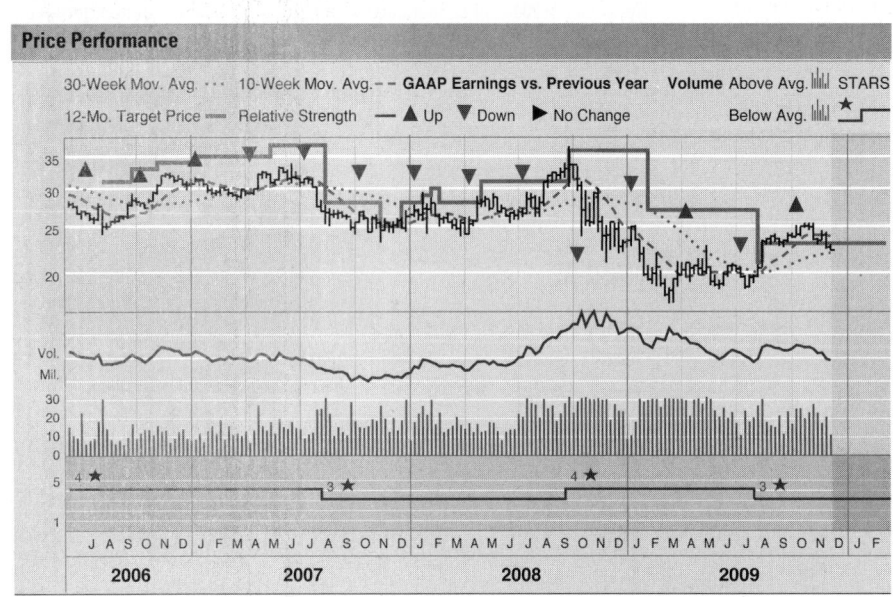

30-Week Mov. Avg. ···· 10-Week Mov. Avg. ─ ─ **GAAP Earnings vs. Previous Year** Volume Above Avg. STARS
12-Mo. Target Price ── Relative Strength ── ▲ Up ▼ Down ▶ No Change Below Avg. ★

Options: ASE, CBOE, P, Ph

Analysis prepared by **Bret Howlett** on November 09, 2009, when the stock traded at **$ 23.37**.

Highlights

► We anticipate organic revenue growth of 3% at risk & insurance in 2010, driven by our expectation of an improvement in commercial P&C pricing. We also see profits at risk & insurance benefiting from double digit revenue growth at Guy Carpenter, partially offset by weakness in European business. We estimate that consulting revenues will decline by 5% due to MMC's exposure to economically sensitive industries. We believe profitability will improve in the risk technology segment due to restructuring initiatives at Kroll, and expect overall revenues to increase in the second half. We are encouraged by MMC's client retention rates and new business production.

► MMC's cost reduction initiatives have exceeded our estimate so far in 2009 and we think the adjusted operating margin for risk & insurance will improve to 22% in 2010. We expect MMC to continue its aggressive expense mangement, and forecast at least $100 million of cost savings in 2010. We believe MMC's financial position is strong and that it is well positioned to capitalize on M&A opportunities.

► We forecast EPS from continuing operations of $1.41 in 2009 and $1.78 in 2010.

Investment Rationale/Risk

► While we believe MMC is making progress with its restructuring initiatives, and think it will benefit from an improved insurance pricing environment , we expect its economically sensitive consulting business to be a drag on earnings growth. MMC has been aggressively cutting costs at Mercer, Oliver Wyman and Kroll, but its consulting businesses contribute nearly half of the company's revenues, and could present earnings challenges, in our view. Still, we view favorably MMC's organic growth outlook, new business production and improving customer retention rates despite a weak environment. We see considerable room for margin expansion given cost-cutting efforts, restructured operations, and top-line growth.

► Risks to our recommendation and target price include lower-than-expected revenue on rate increases; deteriorating client retention; lower-than-projected cost savings from restructurings and layoffs; lower-than-anticipated cost savings and growth at Kroll; and unfavorable legal and regulatory developments.

► Our 12-month target price is $23, about 12.9X our estimate of 2010 EPS, below MMC's historical multiples.

Qualitative Risk Assessment

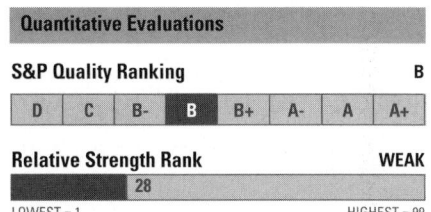

LOW	MEDIUM	HIGH

Our risk assessment reflects the company's leading market share position, diversified businesses and global scale, offset by regulatory scrutiny and business model changes as a result of contingent commissions, and potential impairment charges related to goodwill. We believe MMC is more exposed to the weak economy than peers due to its sizable consulting businesses.

Quantitative Evaluations

S&P Quality Ranking   **B**

D	C	B-	B	B+	A-	A	A+

Relative Strength Rank   **WEAK**

28

LOWEST = 1   HIGHEST = 99

Revenue/Earnings Data

Revenue (Million $)

	1Q	2Q	3Q	4Q	Year
2009	2,629	2,629	2,523	--	--
2008	3,047	3,048	2,838	2,662	11,587
2007	2,812	2,819	2,794	2,925	11,350
2006	3,016	2,970	2,872	3,063	11,921
2005	3,070	2,977	2,779	2,826	11,652
2004	3,196	3,028	2,950	2,985	12,159

Earnings Per Share ($)

	1Q	2Q	3Q	4Q	Year
2009	0.35	-0.32	0.40	E0.40	E1.41
2008	-0.41	0.11	0.03	0.14	-0.13
2007	0.41	0.25	0.15	0.17	0.98
2006	0.43	0.31	0.32	0.39	1.45
2005	0.24	0.30	0.11	0.03	0.67
2004	0.83	0.73	0.04	-1.29	0.33

Fiscal year ended Dec. 31. Next earnings report expected: Mid February. EPS Estimates based on S&P Operating Earnings; historical GAAP earnings are as reported.

Dividend Data (Dates: mm/dd Payment Date: mm/dd/yy)

Amount ($)	Date Decl.	Ex-Div. Date	Stk. of Record	Payment Date
0.200	01/21	01/28	01/30	02/17/09
0.200	03/18	04/07	04/09	05/15/09
0.200	05/21	07/08	07/10	08/17/09
0.200	09/17	10/07	10/09	11/16/09

Dividends have been paid since 1923. Source: Company reports.

Please read the Required Disclosures and Analyst Certification on the last page of this report.

The **McGraw·Hill** Companies

Marsh & McLennan Companies Inc.

STANDARD
&POOR'S

Business Summary November 09, 2009

CORPORATE OVERVIEW. Marsh & McLennan is one of the world's largest insurance brokers and provides advice and solutions in areas of risk, strategy and human capital. In 2008, total revenues exceeded $11.5 billion, with MMC providing its services in more than 100 countries.

The insurance brokerage industry has suffered in recent years from probes into bid rigging and contingent commissions. We believe recent settlements and corporate restructurings have improved the outlook at MMC, but ongoing legal and regulatory proceedings and uncertainty regarding implementing a new business model remains a risk.

MMC operates in three main segments: risk and insurance services, risk consulting and technology, and consulting. Risk and insurance services (47% of operating segment revenues in 2008; 49% in 2007) includes insurance services, reinsurance services and risk capital holdings, risk management and consulting, insurance broking, and insurance program management. Reinsurance broking and catastrophe and financial modeling services are provided under the Guy Carpenter name. Risk consulting and technology (9.0% in 2008;

8.7% in 2007) is conducted under the Kroll name. Consulting and human resource outsourcing (45% in 2008; 43% in 2007) is offered under the Mercer and Oliver Wyman Group names.

LEGAL/REGULATORY ISSUES. In April 2004, Putnam entered into the final settlements of charges by the SEC and the Massachusetts Secretary of the Commonwealth related to alleged short-term trading of Putnam mutual funds by employees in their personal accounts. Under the settlements, Putnam agreed, without admitting or denying the charges, to pay $110 million in penalties and restitution, and to implement a number of remedial actions. In March 2005, an independent consultant concluded that Putnam should pay fund shareholders $108.5 million, of which $83.5 million was in addition to previous settlement amounts.

Company Financials Fiscal Year Ended Dec. 31

Per Share Data ($)	2008	2007	2006	2005	2004	2003	2002	2001	2000	1999
Tangible Book Value	NM	0.13	NM	NM	NM	NM	NM	NM	9.47	NM
Cash Flow	0.61	1.80	2.34	1.58	1.18	3.52	3.10	2.61	2.94	2.07
Earnings	-0.13	0.98	1.45	0.67	0.33	2.81	2.45	1.70	2.05	1.31
S&P Core Earnings	-0.12	0.86	1.30	0.38	1.11	2.29	1.60	0.91	NA	NA
Dividends	0.80	0.76	0.68	0.68	0.99	1.18	1.09	1.03	0.95	0.85
Payout Ratio	NM	71%	47%	101%	NM	42%	44%	61%	46%	65%
Prices:High	36.82	33.90	32.73	34.25	49.69	54.97	57.30	59.03	67.84	48.38
Prices:Low	20.96	23.12	24.00	26.67	22.75	38.27	34.61	39.50	35.25	28.56
P/E Ratio:High	NM	35	23	51	NM	19	23	35	33	37
P/E Ratio:Low	NM	24	17	40	NM	14	14	23	17	22

Income Statement Analysis (Million $)										
Revenue	11,587	11,350	11,921	11,652	12,159	11,588	10,440	9,943	10,157	9,157
Operating Income	1,561	1,586	1,946	1,386	2,073	2,887	2,633	2,283	2,179	1,859
Depreciation	382	442	488	490	456	391	359	520	488	400
Interest Expense	220	267	303	332	219	185	160	196	247	233
Pretax Income	79.0	847	1,219	571	450	2,335	2,133	1,590	1,955	1,247
Effective Tax Rate	173.4%	34.8%	31.8%	33.6%	57.6%	33.0%	35.0%	37.7%	38.5%	41.8%
Net Income	-69.0	538	818	369	176	1,540	1,365	974	1,181	726
S&P Core Earnings	-57.9	462	732	211	590	1,254	890	525	NA	NA

Balance Sheet & Other Financial Data (Million $)										
Cash	1,685	2,133	2,089	2,020	1,396	665	546	537	240	428
Current Assets	4,784	5,454	5,834	5,262	4,887	3,901	3,664	3,792	3,639	3,283
Total Assets	15,221	17,359	18,137	17,892	18,337	15,053	13,855	13,293	13,769	13,021
Current Liabilities	3,386	3,493	5,549	4,351	4,735	4,089	3,863	3,938	4,119	4,318
Long Term Debt	3,194	3,604	3,860	5,044	4,691	2,910	2,891	2,334	2,347	2,357
Common Equity	5,722	7,822	5,819	5,360	5,056	5,451	5,018	5,173	5,228	4,170
Total Capital	8,916	11,426	9,679	10,404	9,747	8,361	7,909	7,507	7,575	6,527
Capital Expenditures	386	378	307	345	376	436	423	433	472	358
Cash Flow	313	980	1,306	859	632	1,931	1,724	1,494	1,669	1,126
Current Ratio	1.4	1.6	1.1	1.2	1.0	1.0	0.9	1.0	0.9	0.8
% Long Term Debt of Capitalization	35.8	31.5	39.9	48.5	48.1	34.8	36.6	31.1	31.0	36.1
% Net Income of Revenue	NM	4.7	6.9	3.2	1.4	13.3	13.1	9.8	11.6	7.9
% Return on Assets	NM	3.0	4.5	2.0	1.1	10.7	10.1	7.2	8.8	5.8
% Return on Equity	NM	7.9	14.6	7.1	3.4	29.4	26.8	18.7	25.1	18.5

Data as orig reptd.; bef. results of disc opers/spec. items. Per share data adj. for stk. divs.; EPS diluted. E-Estimated. NA-Not Available. NM-Not Meaningful. NR-Not Ranked. UR-Under Review.

Office: 1166 Avenue Of The Americas, New York, NY 10036-2708.
Telephone: 212-345-5000.
Email: shareowner-svcs@email.bankofny.com
Website: http://www.mmc.com

Chrmn: S.R. Hardis
Pres & CEO: B. Duperreault
Vice Chrmn: M. Neely
EVP & CFO: V.A. Wittman

EVP & General Counsel: P.J. Beshar
Investor Contact: M.B. Bartley (212-345-5000)
Board Members: L. M. Baker, Jr., Z. W. Carter, B. Duperreault, O. Fanjul Martin, S. R. Hardis, G. S. King, I. B. Lang, B. P. Nolop, M. D. Oken, D. A. Olsen, M. Schapiro, A. Simmons

Founded: 1923
Domicile: Delaware
Employees: 54,400

The McGraw-Hill Companies

Masco Corp

STANDARD &POOR'S

| S&P Recommendation **BUY** ★★★★☆ | Price $13.53 (as of Nov 27, 2009) | 12-Mo. Target Price $17.00 | Investment Style Large-Cap Blend |

GICS Sector Industrials
Sub-Industry Building Products

Summary This company is one of the world's leading makers of faucets, cabinets, coatings, and other consumer brand-name home improvement and building products.

Key Stock Statistics (Source S&P, Vickers, company reports)

52-Wk Range	$15.50– 3.64	S&P Oper. EPS 2009**E**	0.25	Market Capitalization(B)	$4.859	Beta	2.19
Trailing 12-Month EPS	$-1.43	S&P Oper. EPS 2010**E**	0.50	Yield (%)	2.22	S&P 3-Yr. Proj. EPS CAGR(%)	33
Trailing 12-Month P/E	NM	P/E on S&P Oper. EPS 2009**E**	54.1	Dividend Rate/Share	$0.30	S&P Credit Rating	BBB
$10K Invested 5 Yrs Ago	$4,522	Common Shares Outstg. (M)	359.1	Institutional Ownership (%)	87		

Price Performance

30-Week Mov. Avg. · · · 10-Week Mov. Avg. – – GAAP Earnings vs. Previous Year   Volume   Above Avg. STARS
12-Mo. Target Price — Relative Strength — ▲ Up ▼ Down ► No Change   Below Avg.   ★

Options: ASE, CBOE, P, Ph

Analysis prepared by **Michael W. Jaffe** on November 09, 2009, when the stock traded at **$ 13.25**.

Highlights

► We expect sales to increase by 4% in 2010. Results have weakened sharply over the past three years, hurt mostly by a very soft U.S. housing market, and much slower big-ticket consumer spending. Moreover, sales have turned much lower in Europe, on economic woes. We see these factors crimping sales for somewhat longer, but based on our belief that government stimulus is finally starting to stabilize housing markets, we expect a modest sales upturn in 2010. We think the strongest sales performance in 2010 is likely to come in the decorative architectural products segment, as we see do-it-yourself home improvement being one of the first places for spending to pick up.

► We see margins improving in 2010, on our outlook for the start of a housing market recovery, and a likely positive impact from foreign currency, as the U.S. dollar has greatly weakened over the past year. We see incremental benefits from the company's cost cutting efforts, particularly major headcount reductions.

► Our 2009 EPS estimate excludes $0.13 of charges recorded in the first nine months of the year.

Investment Rationale/Risk

► MAS has been hurt for a prolonged period by very soft U.S. housing and home improvement markets, and Europe's major economic downturn. Yet, we see MAS's business starting to recover over the next year, on aggressive stimulus actions put in place by the government over the past year. We also think MAS was wise to sharply cut its dividend in early 2009, and its recent amendment of debt covenants puts MAS in better financial order, in our view. Our valuation model finds MAS shares undervalued.

► Risks to our recommendation and target price include a longer than expected U.S. housing downturn, and weaker than expected performance in foreign markets served by MAS.

► With MAS in what we view as the final stages of a severe business downturn, we think price-to-sales analysis is the best method of valuing its shares. The shares recently traded at a little under 0.6X projected sales per share, based on our $8.1 billion sales forecast for 2010. We think that valuation, which falls below MAS's traditional trough valuation, is too low, based on our view that its business is in the process of stabilizing. Our 12-month target price is $17, or 0.75X projected sales per share.

Qualitative Risk Assessment

| LOW | MEDIUM | HIGH |

Our risk assessment for Masco reflects its generation of strong levels of free cash flow during most business cycles, and what we view as a good business model. However, it also operates in a very cyclical area, as evidenced by the recent major downturn in its operating performance.

Quantitative Evaluations

S&P Quality Ranking   B

| D | C | B- | B | B+ | A- | A | A+ |

Relative Strength Rank   MODERATE

64

LOWEST = 1   HIGHEST = 99

Revenue/Earnings Data

Revenue (Million $)

	1Q	2Q	3Q	4Q	Year
2009	1,819	2,036	2,094	--	--
2008	2,446	2,640	2,528	1,979	9,600
2007	2,865	3,148	3,059	2,698	11,770
2006	3,167	3,370	3,295	2,946	12,778
2005	2,914	3,286	3,296	3,146	12,642
2004	2,806	3,061	3,173	3,034	12,074

Earnings Per Share ($)

2009	-0.23	0.15	0.14	E0.06	E0.25
2008	0.07	0.20	0.10	-1.45	-1.08
2007	0.37	0.50	0.57	-0.39	1.06
2006	0.50	0.53	0.57	-0.48	1.15
2005	0.47	0.62	0.60	0.34	2.03
2004	0.52	0.65	0.64	0.23	2.04

Fiscal year ended Dec. 31. Next earnings report expected: Mid February. EPS Estimates based on S&P Operating Earnings; historical GAAP earnings are as reported.

Dividend Data (Dates: mm/dd Payment Date: mm/dd/yy)

Amount ($)	Date Decl.	Ex-Div. Date	Stk. of Record	Payment Date
0.235	12/10	01/07	01/09	02/09/09
0.075	03/27	04/07	04/09	05/11/09
0.075	06/26	07/07	07/10	08/10/09
0.075	09/11	10/07	10/09	11/09/09

Dividends have been paid since 1944. Source: Company reports.

The McGraw·Hill Companies

Masco Corp

STANDARD &POOR'S

Business Summary November 09, 2009

CORPORATE OVERVIEW. Masco is one of the largest U.S. makers of brand name consumer products for home improvement and new construction markets; it derives most of its revenues from the sale of faucets, kitchen and bath cabinets, plumbing supplies and architectural coatings. Operations are focused on North America (78% of 2008 sales) and Europe (most of the rest). Home Depot contributed 21% of 2008 sales (20% in 2007).

The plumbing products division (32% of 2008 sales) is a major global faucet maker. Masco revolutionized faucets in 1954 with the Delta line, and also offers the Peerless, Brizo and Newport Brass brands, among others. In addition, the division offers other bath products, including plumbing fittings and valves, bathtubs and shower enclosures, and spa items; brand names include Aqua Glass and HotSpring. The cabinets and related products division (24%) makes cabinetry for kitchen, bath, storage, home office and home entertainment applications, featuring the Kraftmaid, Tvilum-Scanbirk and Merillat brands. According to the company, it is the largest U.S. maker of kitchen and bath cabinetry.

Masco sells decorative architectural items (17%), including paints and stains, and decorative bath and shower accessories. Trade names include Behr in paints and stains and Franklin Brass in bath and shower. It also supplies and installs insulation products and other building products (19%) such as gutters, fireplaces, garage doors and framing components, and sells other specialty products (7%), such as windows, patio doors and electric staple guns.

MANAGEMENT. In July 2007, Richard Manoogian, Masco's chairman and CEO, gave up his CEO duties and moved into a new post as executive chairman. Based on Mr. Manoogian's recommendation, Timothy Wadhams, Masco's senior vice president and CFO since 2001, was appointed to the CEO role. In addition, Alan Barry, Masco's president, stepped down from his post at the end of 2007, when he reached normal retirement age, with Mr. Wadhams also assuming that title.

Company Financials Fiscal Year Ended Dec. 31

Per Share Data ($)	2008	2007	2006	2005	2004	2003	2002	2001	2000	1999
Tangible Book Value	NM	NM	0.54	0.88	1.54	1.36	1.31	1.30	2.78	3.14
Cash Flow	-0.41	1.71	1.76	2.66	2.56	2.00	1.85	1.02	1.84	1.68
Earnings	-1.08	1.06	1.15	2.03	2.04	1.51	1.33	0.42	1.31	1.28
S&P Core Earnings	0.23	1.56	2.17	2.17	2.25	1.67	1.52	1.12	NA	NA
Dividends	0.93	0.91	0.86	0.78	0.66	0.58	0.55	0.52	0.49	0.45
Payout Ratio	NM	86%	75%	38%	32%	38%	41%	125%	37%	35%
Prices:High	23.50	34.72	33.70	38.43	37.02	28.44	29.43	26.94	27.00	33.69
Prices:Low	6.82	20.89	25.85	27.15	25.88	16.59	17.25	17.76	14.50	22.50
P/E Ratio:High	NM	33	29	19	18	19	22	64	21	26
P/E Ratio:Low	NM	20	22	13	13	11	13	42	11	18

Income Statement Analysis (Million $)										
Revenue	9,600	11,770	12,778	12,642	12,074	10,936	9,419	8,358	7,243	6,307
Operating Income	780	1,419	1,700	1,881	1,944	1,738	1,683	1,309	1,295	1,093
Depreciation	236	241	244	241	237	244	220	269	238	182
Interest Expense	228	258	240	247	217	262	237	239	191	120
Pretax Income	-211	770	900	1,412	1,518	1,216	1,031	301	893	904
Effective Tax Rate	NM	43.6%	45.8%	36.7%	37.5%	38.1%	33.8%	34.0%	33.8%	37.0%
Net Income	-382	397	461	872	930	740	682	199	592	570
S&P Core Earnings	80.1	582	866	936	1,027	816	779	528	NA	NA

Balance Sheet & Other Financial Data (Million $)										
Cash	1,028	922	1,958	1,964	1,256	795	1,067	312	169	231
Current Assets	3,300	3,808	5,115	5,123	4,402	3,804	3,950	2,627	2,308	2,110
Total Assets	9,483	10,907	12,325	12,559	12,541	12,149	12,050	9,183	7,744	6,635
Current Liabilities	1,547	1,908	3,389	2,894	2,147	2,099	1,932	1,237	1,078	846
Long Term Debt	3,915	3,966	3,533	3,915	4,187	3,848	4,316	3,628	3,018	2,431
Common Equity	2,846	4,025	4,471	4,848	5,596	5,456	5,294	4,120	3,426	3,137
Total Capital	7,323	7,991	8,004	9,665	9,783	9,304	9,610	7,747	6,444	5,788
Capital Expenditures	200	248	388	282	310	271	285	274	388	351
Cash Flow	-146	638	705	1,113	1,167	984	902	468	830	751
Current Ratio	2.1	2.0	1.5	1.8	2.1	1.8	2.0	2.1	2.1	2.5
% Long Term Debt of Capitalization	53.5	49.6	44.1	40.5	42.8	41.4	44.9	46.8	46.8	42.0
% Net Income of Revenue	NM	3.4	3.6	6.9	7.7	6.8	7.2	2.4	8.2	9.0
% Return on Assets	NM	3.4	3.7	6.9	7.5	6.1	6.5	2.3	8.2	9.3
% Return on Equity	NM	9.4	9.9	17.0	16.6	13.8	14.7	5.3	18.0	19.3

Data as orig reptd.; bef. results of disc opers/spec. items. Per share data adj. for stk. divs.; EPS diluted. E-Estimated. NA-Not Available. NM-Not Meaningful. NR-Not Ranked. UR-Under Review.

Office: 21001 Van Born Road, Taylor, MI 48180.
Telephone: 313-274-7400.
Website: http://www.masco.com
Chrmn: R.A. Manoogian

Pres & CEO: T. Wadhams
COO & EVP: D.J. Demarie, Jr.
CFO & Treas: J.G. Sznewajs
Chief Acctg Officer & Cntlr: W.T. Anderson

Investor Contact: M.C. Duey (313-274-7400)
Board Members: D. W. Archer, T. G. Denomme, A. F. Earley, Jr., V. G. Istock, D. L. Johnston, J. M. Losh, R. A. Manoogian, L. A. Payne, M. A. Van Lokeren, T. Wadhams

Founded: 1929
Domicile: Delaware
Employees: 39,000

Massey Energy Co

STANDARD &POOR'S

S&P Recommendation SELL ★★☆☆☆	Price $37.59 (as of Nov 27, 2009)	12-Mo. Target Price $32.00

GICS Sector Energy
Sub-Industry Coal & Consumable Fuels

Summary Massey Energy is the fourth largest U.S. coal producer with about 20% of production sold into the metallurgical coal markets.

Key Stock Statistics (Source S&P, Vickers, company reports)

52-Wk Range	$41.14–9.62	S&P Oper. EPS 2009E	1.21	Market Capitalization(B)	$3.216	Beta		2.12
Trailing 12-Month EPS	$1.58	S&P Oper. EPS 2010E	1.76	Yield (%)	0.64	S&P 3-Yr. Proj. EPS CAGR(%)		20
Trailing 12-Month P/E	23.8	P/E on S&P Oper. EPS 2009E	31.1	Dividend Rate/Share	$0.24	S&P Credit Rating		NA
$10K Invested 5 Yrs Ago	$10,763	Common Shares Outstg. (M)	85.5	Institutional Ownership (%)	88			

Price Performance

30-Week Mov. Avg. · · · 10-Week Mov. Avg. — GAAP Earnings vs. Previous Year Volume Above Avg. STARS
12-Mo. Target Price — Relative Strength — ▲ Up ▼ Down ▶ No Change Below Avg. ★

Options: ASE, CBOE, P, Ph

Analysis prepared by **Mathew Christy, CFA** on November 19, 2009, when the stock traded at **$ 37.59**.

Highlights

- Following a 24% revenue increase in 2008, we expect a 6% decline in 2009, based on a projected 6% drop in coal volumes and about a 1% increase in average realized coal prices. Our forecast is based on significant declines in both metallurgical and industrial coal volume, partly offset by gains in thermal coal volumes from higher production rates and market share gains. In addition, we expect greater volume due to MEE's renegotiation of contracts struck in 2008 at prices much higher than current spot market rates. In 2010, we forecast about a 7% increase in revenues as we look for somewhat higher pricing and volumes in the year.

- We think operating margins will narrow in 2009 due to lower productivity on decreased coal volume production and nearly flat pricing, and as we see production costs rising about 8%. In 2010, we project operating margins will increase somewhat over 2009 levels due to better production rates and higher operating leverage.

- On steady tax rates projected for both 2009 and 2010, we estimate operating EPS of $1.21 in 2009 and $1.76 in 2010.

Investment Rationale/Risk

- Our recent downgrade is based on valuation and is despite our expectation for a gradual recovery in the coal markets. Despite this view, we believe that a recovery will be uneven, noting that thermal coal inventories at 70 days of supply, high Chinese inventories/possible overcapacity in steel production, and lower commercial construction activity may limit coal demand. In addition, we believe the shares are overvalued at 7X our 2010 EV/EBITDA estimate, equal to the peer average but relative to a historic discount.

- Risks to our recommendation and target price include higher-than-expected coal prices, production volumes and productivity; more robust demand growth for metallurgical coal; and, positive outcomes as it relates to EPA rulings and other legislation.

- Our 12-month target price of $32 is based on a relative peer valuation analysis. We apply an EV/EBITDA multiple of 6X, below the peer average, to our 2010 EBITDA estimate, suggesting a $32 value. We believe that a below-peers average multiple is appropriate due to MEE's historical discount to the overall group.

Qualitative Risk Assessment

LOW	MEDIUM	HIGH

Our risk assessment reflects the cyclicality of the coal market, MEE's and the industry's high fixed-cost structure, the concentration of company reserves in the central Appalachian region, the heavy regulation of the industry and its utilities end market, and recent lawsuits pending against the company.

Quantitative Evaluations

S&P Quality Ranking B-

D	C	B-	B	B+	A-	A	A+

Relative Strength Rank STRONG
94
LOWEST = 1   HIGHEST = 99

Revenue/Earnings Data

Revenue (Million $)

	1Q	2Q	3Q	4Q	Year
2009	768.1	697.6	641.6	--	--
2008	644.6	826.8	763.3	755.0	2,990
2007	607.3	617.8	603.4	585.0	2,414
2006	559.5	556.1	555.9	548.4	2,220
2005	570.0	582.5	533.7	518.0	2,204
2004	410.9	466.7	436.7	452.4	1,767

Earnings Per Share ($)

2009	0.51	0.24	0.19	E0.27	E1.21
2008	0.52	-1.16	0.64	0.63	0.68
2007	0.40	0.43	0.27	0.06	1.17
2006	0.08	0.04	0.30	0.10	0.51
2005	0.59	0.44	0.28	-2.37	-1.33
2004	-0.03	0.16	0.03	0.02	0.18

Fiscal year ended Dec. 31. Next earnings report expected: Early February. EPS Estimates based on S&P Operating Earnings; historical GAAP earnings are as reported.

Dividend Data (Dates: mm/dd Payment Date: mm/dd/yy)

Amount ($)	Date Decl.	Ex-Div. Date	Stk. of Record	Payment Date
0.060	02/18	03/13	03/17	03/31/09
0.060	05/19	06/12	06/16	06/30/09
0.060	08/18	09/14	09/16	09/30/09
0.060	11/09	12/15	12/17	12/31/09

Dividends have been paid since 2001. Source: Company reports.

Please read the Required Disclosures and Analyst Certification on the last page of this report.

The McGraw-Hill Companies

Massey Energy Co

STANDARD &POOR'S

Business Summary November 19, 2009

CORPORATE OVERVIEW. Massey Energy (formerly Fluor Corp.) produces low-sulfur coal for electric generation, steel-making, and various industrial applications. In November 2000, the company spun off Fluor Corp., which assumed all of its non-coal businesses. The spinoff was accomplished through the distribution to MEE common stockholders of all Fluor common stock. The company declared a special dividend of one Fluor common share for every MEE share held of record on November 30, 2000. MEE is the fourth largest U.S. coal company, by our calculation, and the largest in the central Appalachian region. It produces, processes and sells bituminous, low-sulfur coal of steam and metallurgical grades from 46 underground mines and 20 surface mines in West Virginia, Kentucky and Virginia. Its steam coal is primarily purchased by utilities and industrial clients as fuel for power plants. Its metallurgical coal is used primarily to make coke for use in the manufacture of steel. Coal sold rose to 40.9 million tons in 2008, from 39.8 million tons in 2007. Revenue per ton increased to $61.78, from $50.13. Average cash cost per ton was $48.57, up from $43.10. In 2008, approximately 97% of coal sales volumes was sold under long-term contracts.

The breakdown of tonnage sold by end market in 2008 was as follows: electric utilities, 66%; metallurgical (steel industry sector), 24%; and general industrial, 10%. In 2008, Constellation Energy Commodities Group, Inc. accounted for 11% of total produced coal revenue. The company produces coal using four distinct mining methods: underground room and pillar, underground longwall, surface, and highwall. Use of continuous miner machines in the room and pillar method of underground mining accounted for 43% of production in 2008, underground longwall mining operations provided 3% of production, surface mining accounted for 47%, and highwall 7%. MEE estimated that it had total recoverable reserves of about 2.3 billion tons as of December 31, 2008. The company projected that 62% of its reserves were comprised of coal containing less than 1% sulfur. Low-sulfur coal is vital to utility customers seeking to reduce emissions and reduce costs of compliance with the Clean Air Act.

Company Financials Fiscal Year Ended Dec. 31

Per Share Data ($)	2008	2007	2006	2005	2004	2003	2002	2001	2000	1999
Tangible Book Value	12.13	10.17	8.60	10.26	10.16	10.05	10.73	11.55	NM	NM
Cash Flow	3.93	4.22	3.34	1.74	3.12	2.20	2.35	2.38	3.39	3.28
Earnings	0.68	1.17	0.51	-1.33	0.18	-0.43	-0.44	-0.07	1.07	1.01
S&P Core Earnings	2.55	1.09	0.27	-1.83	0.14	-0.60	-0.33	-0.30	NA	NA
Dividends	0.21	0.17	0.16	0.16	0.16	0.16	0.16	0.12	Nil	NA
Payout Ratio	31%	15%	31%	NM	89%	NM	NM	NM	Nil	NA
Prices:High	95.70	37.99	44.34	57.00	36.96	21.60	22.41	28.95	13.19	NA
Prices:Low	10.05	16.01	18.77	31.80	17.99	7.30	4.55	11.25	9.94	NA
P/E Ratio:High	NM	32	87	NM	NM	NM	NM	NM	12	NA
P/E Ratio:Low	NM	14	37	NM	NM	NM	NM	NM	9	NA

Income Statement Analysis (Million $)										
Revenue	2,990	2,414	2,220	2,204	1,767	1,553	1,630	1,432	1,141	1,114
Operating Income	647	433	348	426	280	179	181	191	268	307
Depreciation	269	246	231	235	225	196	208	181	171	168
Interest Expense	89.9	85.8	86.1	67.1	60.7	48.3	35.3	34.2	0.35	0.80
Pretax Income	60.3	130	45.0	-75.4	-5.64	-60.7	-57.5	-15.9	122	153
Effective Tax Rate	6.80%	27.3%	7.57%	NM	NM	NM	NM	NM	35.5%	32.4%
Net Income	56.2	94.1	41.6	-102	13.9	-32.3	-32.6	-5.42	78.8	103
S&P Core Earnings	211	87.6	22.8	-140	10.6	-44.8	-24.0	-22.1	NA	NA

Balance Sheet & Other Financial Data (Million $)										
Cash	646	365	239	319	123	88.8	2.73	5.66	6.93	8.05
Current Assets	1,236	887	800	1,044	791	703	510	458	384	287
Total Assets	3,676	2,861	2,741	2,986	2,651	2,377	2,241	2,271	2,161	1,980
Current Liabilities	504	368	355	374	332	259	573	542	275	243
Long Term Debt	1,464	1,103	1,102	1,103	900	784	286	300	Nil	Nil
Common Equity	1,037	784	697	841	777	759	808	861	1,375	1,277
Total Capital	2,618	2,041	1,916	2,177	1,894	1,770	1,339	1,411	1,629	1,503
Capital Expenditures	737	270	298	347	347	164	135	248	205	230
Cash Flow	325	340	272	133	238	164	175	176	250	271
Current Ratio	2.5	2.4	2.3	2.8	2.4	2.7	0.9	0.8	1.4	1.2
% Long Term Debt of Capitalization	55.9	54.0	57.5	50.6	47.5	44.3	21.4	21.3	Nil	Nil
% Net Income of Revenue	1.9	3.9	1.9	NM	NM	NM	NM	NM	6.9	9.3
% Return on Assets	1.7	3.4	1.5	NM	NM	NM	NM	NM	3.8	5.4
% Return on Equity	6.2	12.7	5.4	NM	NM	NM	NM	NM	5.9	8.4

Data as orig reptd.; bef. results of disc opers/spec. items. Per share data adj. for stk. divs.; EPS diluted. E-Estimated. NA-Not Available. NM-Not Meaningful. NR-Not Ranked. UR-Under Review.

Office: 4 North 4th Street, Richmond, VA 23219.
Telephone: 804-788-1800.
Website: http://www.masseyenergyco.com
Chrmn & CEO: D.L. Blankenship

Pres: B.F. Phillips, Jr.
COO & SVP: J.C. Adkins
CFO: E.B. Tolbert
Chief Admin Officer: J.M. Poma

Board Members: D. L. Blankenship, J. B. Crawford, R. H. Foglesong, R. M. Gabrys, B. R. Inman, B. T. Judge, D. R. Moore, B. F. Phillips, Jr., S. C. Suboleski
Founded: 1912
Domicile: Delaware
Employees: 6,743

MasterCard Inc

STANDARD &POOR'S

| S&P Recommendation **BUY** ★★★★☆ | Price $235.59 (as of Nov 27, 2009) | 12-Mo. Target Price $280.00 | Investment Style Large-Cap Growth |

GICS Sector Information Technology
Sub-Industry Data Processing & Outsourced Services

Summary MasterCard is a global leader in transaction processing and brand licensing providing services in over 210 countries and territories. The company has more than 25 million acceptance locations.

Key Stock Statistics (Source S&P, Vickers, company reports)

52-Wk Range	$242.93– 117.06	S&P Oper. EPS 2009**E**	11.22	Market Capitalization(B)	$25.862	Beta	1.18
Trailing 12-Month EPS	$10.75	S&P Oper. EPS 2010**E**	12.95	Yield (%)	0.25	S&P 3-Yr. Proj. EPS CAGR(%)	19
Trailing 12-Month P/E	21.9	P/E on S&P Oper. EPS 2009**E**	21.0	Dividend Rate/Share	$0.60	S&P Credit Rating	NA
$10K Invested 5 Yrs Ago	NA	Common Shares Outstg. (M)	129.8	Institutional Ownership (%)	96		

Price Performance

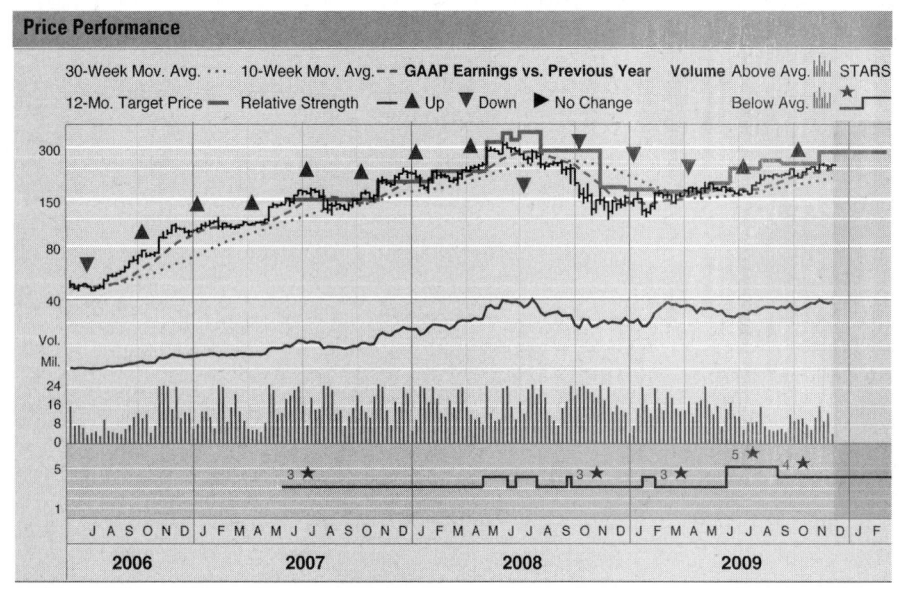

30-Week Mov. Avg. · · ·   10-Week Mov. Avg. – –   **GAAP Earnings vs. Previous Year**   Volume Above Avg. STARS
12-Mo. Target Price —   Relative Strength —   ▲ Up ▼ Down ▶ No Change   Below Avg. ★

Options: ASE, CBOE, P, Ph

Analysis prepared by **Stuart Plesser** on November 03, 2009, when the stock traded at **$ 217.60**.

Highlights

▶ We project revenue to advance 2% in 2009, followed by a 9% increase in 2010, mainly reflecting our expectations for a pickup in growth of both gross dollar volume (GDV) and processed transactions. We forecast more emphasis on international growth, as U.S. GDV will likely grow at a slower rate. While we anticipate that spending growth will be tempered due to high unemployment rates, especially in the U.S., we look favorably upon continued growth of transactions, which we think points to a secular trend in credit card usage.

▶ We anticipate that expenses in 2010 will be up from projected 2009 levels, as MA's cost-cutting initiatives will likely be more than offset by a higher marketing budget. Even so, we forecast that operating margins will improve in 2010 on lower expenses as a percentage of revenue. Indeed, we are particularly encouraged by the strong operating leverage of the company's business model. Longer term, we see expansion of revenue growth emanating from a bigger push for MA's debit and prepaid cards.

▶ Our EPS estimated for 2009 is $11.22, with an increase to $12.95 in 2010.

Investment Rationale/Risk

▶ We believe there are plenty of opportunities for MA to generate strong growth in the longer term, including international expansion, debit card growth, and prepaid cards. We expect transaction volumes to remain solid despite a general slowdown in consumer spending, as consumers shift to greater credit usage. Cross border fees will likely rise at a more robust rate in 2010 as international travel picks up. We think MA is a good inflation hedge as a large portion of its revenue is based on the dollar amount of customer transactions.

▶ Risks to our recommendation and target price include a further deterioration in domestic consumer spending, a significant rise in unemployment that would pressure spending, negative outcomes concerning possible regulatory issues, and further consolidation of MA's customer base.

▶ Our 12-month target price of $280 is about 21.6X our 2010 EPS estimate of $12.95, a discount to its historical average and Visa (V 77, Hold), which we think is justified by MA's lower exposure to debit cards and fewer cards outstanding.

Qualitative Risk Assessment

| LOW | MEDIUM | HIGH |

Our risk assessment reflects what we view as an oligopolistic market environment, tempered somewhat by pending litigation risks and an evolving competitive environment.

Quantitative Evaluations

S&P Quality Ranking NR

| D | C | B- | B | B+ | A- | A | A+ |

Relative Strength Rank STRONG
83
LOWEST = 1   HIGHEST = 99

Revenue/Earnings Data

Revenue (Million $)

	1Q	2Q	3Q	4Q	Year
2009	1,156	1,280	1,364	--	--
2008	1,182	1,247	1,338	1,225	4,992
2007	915.1	997.0	1,083	1,073	4,068
2006	738.5	846.5	902.0	839.2	3,326
2005	658.2	771.9	791.6	715.9	2,938
2004	594.3	647.3	667.8	683.9	2,593

Earnings Per Share ($)

	1Q	2Q	3Q	4Q	Year
2009	2.80	2.67	3.45	E2.27	E11.22
2008	3.38	-5.74	-1.49	1.84	-1.95
2007	1.57	1.85	2.31	2.26	8.00
2006	0.94	-2.30	1.42	0.30	0.37
2005	0.93	1.20	1.06	-0.53	2.67
2004	0.74	0.66	0.98	0.01	2.38

Fiscal year ended Dec. 31. Next earnings report expected: Early February. EPS Estimates based on S&P Operating Earnings; historical GAAP earnings are as reported.

Dividend Data (Dates: mm/dd Payment Date: mm/dd/yy)

Amount ($)	Date Decl.	Ex-Div. Date	Stk. of Record	Payment Date
0.150	12/02	01/07	01/09	02/10/09
0.150	02/03	04/08	04/13	05/08/09
0.150	06/09	07/08	07/10	08/10/09
0.150	09/21	10/07	10/09	11/10/09

Dividends have been paid since 2006. Source: Company reports.

Please read the Required Disclosures and Analyst Certification on the last page of this report.

The McGraw-Hill Companies

MasterCard Inc

STANDARD &POOR'S

Business Summary November 03, 2009

CORPORATE OVERVIEW. MasterCard Incorporated (MA), a leading global payment solutions company, provides a variety of services in support of the credit, debit and related payment programs of about 25,000 financial institutions. MA follows a three-tiered business model as a franchisor, processor and advisor. The company, through its businesses, develops and markets payment solutions, processes payment transactions, and provides consulting services to its customers and merchants. MA manages a family of payment card brands, including MasterCard, MasterCard Electronic, Maestro, and Cirrus, which it licenses to its customers.

MasterCard generates revenues from two sources: operations fees and assessments. The company follows a "four-party" payment system, which typically involves four parties in addition to the company: the cardholder, the merchant, the issuer (the cardholder's bank) and the acquirer (the merchant's bank). Issuers typically pay operations fees and assessments, while acquirers principally pay assessments on gross dollar volume (GDV) or cards and, to a lesser extent, certain operations fees.

MA charges operations fees to its customers for providing transaction processing and other payment-related services. Operations fees include core authorization, clearing and settlement fees, cross-border and currency con-

version fees, switch fees, connectivity fees and other operations fees, such as acceptance development fees, warning bulletins, holograms, fees for compliance programs, and user-pay fees for a variety of transaction enhancement services. The company charges assessments based on customers' GDV of activity on the cards that carry its brands, and rates vary by region. GDV includes the aggregated dollar amount of usage (purchases, cash disbursements, balance transfers and convenience checks) on MasterCard-branded cards.

On an aggregate basis, MA received approximately 75% of its revenues in connection with operations fees and approximately 25% in connection with assessments in 2008. The company processed 21.0 billion transactions (including PIN-based online transactions) during 2008, an 11.8% increase over the number of transactions processed in 2007. GDV on cards carrying the MasterCard brand, as reported by MA's customers, increased 11.5% year over year to approximately $2.5 trillion in 2008.

Company Financials Fiscal Year Ended Dec. 31

Per Share Data ($)	2008	2007	2006	2005	2004	2003	2002	2001	2000	1999
Tangible Book Value	9.56	18.79	13.90	6.99	NA	NA	NA	NA	NA	NA
Cash Flow	-1.50	8.37	NA	NA	NA	NA	NA	NA	NA	NA
Earnings	-1.95	8.00	0.37	2.67	2.38	-3.91	1.35	1.98	1.65	NA
S&P Core Earnings	9.37	5.77	0.53	2.97	2.56	1.06	NA	NA	NA	NA
Dividends	0.60	0.54	0.09	Nil	NA	NA	NA	NA	NA	NA
Payout Ratio	NM	7%	24%	Nil	NA	NA	NA	NA	NA	NA
Prices:High	320.30	227.18	108.60	NA	NA	NA	NA	NA	NA	NA
Prices:Low	113.05	95.30	39.00	NA	NA	NA	NA	NA	NA	NA
P/E Ratio:High	NM	28	NM	NA	NA	NA	NA	NA	NA	NA
P/E Ratio:Low	NM	12	NM	NA	NA	NA	NA	NA	NA	NA

Income Statement Analysis (Million $)

	2008	2007	2006	2005	2004	2003	2002	2001	2000	1999
Revenue	4,992	4,068	3,326	2,938	2,593	2,231	1,892	1,611	1,445	NA
Operating Income	2,007	1,161	713	NA	NA	NA	NA	NA	NA	NA
Depreciation	59.1	49.3	43.5	110	123	120	90.5	70.0	59.4	NA
Interest Expense	104	57.3	61.2	NA	NA	NA	NA	NA	NA	NA
Pretax Income	-383	1,671	294	407	324	-612	158	229	193	NA
Effective Tax Rate	NM	35.0%	82.9%	34.5%	26.5%	36.1%	26.5%	39.7%	42.5%	NA
Net Income	-254	1,086	50.2	267	238	-391	116	142	118	NA
S&P Core Earnings	1,230	782	72.8	297	257	107	NA	NA	NA	NA

Balance Sheet & Other Financial Data (Million $)

	2008	2007	2006	2005	2004	2003	2002	2001	2000	1999
Cash	2,247	2,970	2,484	1,282	1,138	911	872	670	NA	NA
Current Assets	4,312	4,592	3,577	NA	NA	NA	NA	NA	NA	NA
Total Assets	6,476	6,260	5,082	3,701	3,265	2,901	2,261	1,486	NA	NA
Current Liabilities	2,990	2,363	1,812	NA	NA	NA	NA	NA	NA	NA
Long Term Debt	19.4	150	230	229	230	230	80.1	80.1	NA	NA
Common Equity	1,927	3,027	2,364	1,169	975	699	1,023	607	NA	NA
Total Capital	2,026	3,253	2,665	1,403	1,209	933	1,104	687	NA	NA
Capital Expenditures	75.6	81.6	61.2	43.9	30.5	76.3	54.2	57.9	113	NA
Cash Flow	-195	1,135	NA	NA	NA	NA	NA	NA	NA	NA
Current Ratio	1.4	1.9	2.0	1.4	1.5	1.4	1.6	1.7	NA	NA
% Long Term Debt of Capitalization	1.0	4.6	8.8	16.4	19.0	24.6	7.3	11.7	Nil	NA
% Net Income of Revenue	NM	26.7	1.5	9.1	9.2	NM	6.2	8.8	8.2	NA
% Return on Assets	NM	19.2	1.1	7.7	7.7	NM	6.2	NA	NA	NA
% Return on Equity	NM	40.3	2.8	24.9	28.5	NM	14.3	NA	NA	NA

Data as orig reptd.; bef. results of disc opers/spec. items. Per share data adj. for stk. divs.; EPS diluted. E-Estimated. NA-Not Available. NM-Not Meaningful. NR-Not Ranked. UR-Under Review.

Office: 2000 Purchase Street, Purchase, NY 10577.
Telephone: 914-249-2000.
Website: http://www.mastercard.com
Chrmn: R.N. Haythornthwaite

Pres & COO: A. Banga
CEO: R.W. Selander
CFO: M. Hund-Mejean
CTO: M. Manchisi

Investor Contact: B. Gasper (914-249-4565)
Board Members: S. Barzi, D. R. Carlucci, S. J. Freiberg, B. S. Fung, R. N. Haythornthwaite, N. J. Karch, J. O. Lagunes, M. R. Olivie, M. Schwartz, R. W. Selander, E. T. Suning, J. P. Tai

Founded: 1966
Domicile: Delaware
Employees: 5,500

Mattel Inc.

STANDARD &POOR'S

S&P Recommendation BUY ★★★★☆

Price	12-Mo. Target Price	Investment Style
$19.57 (as of Nov 27, 2009)	$22.00	Large-Cap Blend

GICS Sector Consumer Discretionary
Sub-Industry Leisure Products

Summary This large toy company's brands and products include Barbie dolls, Fisher-Price toys, American Girl dolls and books, and Hot Wheels.

Key Stock Statistics (Source S&P, Vickers, company reports)

52-Wk Range	$21.05– 10.36	S&P Oper. EPS 2009E	1.21	Market Capitalization(B)	$7.074	Beta	1.14
Trailing 12-Month EPS	$1.04	S&P Oper. EPS 2010E	1.69	Yield (%)	3.83	S&P 3-Yr. Proj. EPS CAGR(%)	19
Trailing 12-Month P/E	18.8	P/E on S&P Oper. EPS 2009E	16.2	Dividend Rate/Share	$0.75	S&P Credit Rating	BBB-
$10K Invested 5 Yrs Ago	$12,816	Common Shares Outstg. (M)	361.5	Institutional Ownership (%)	94		

Price Performance

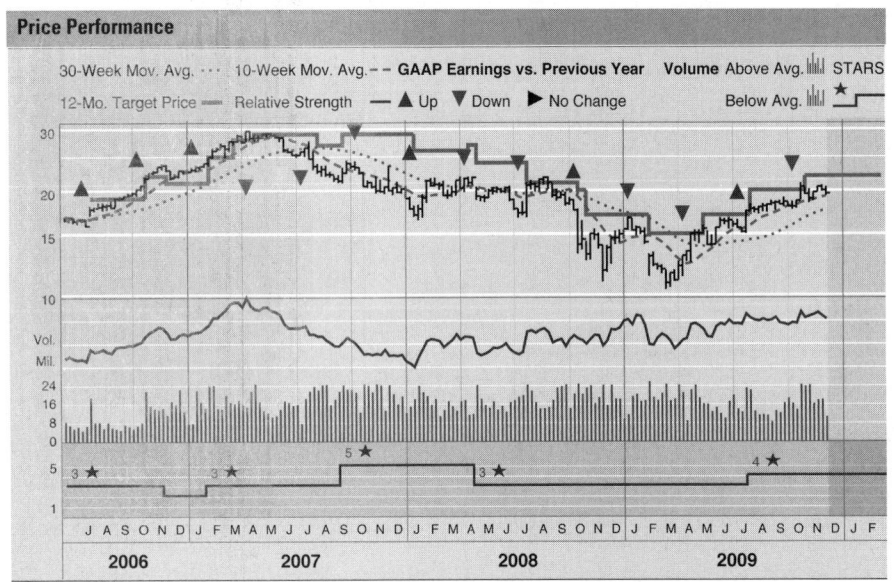

30-Week Mov. Avg. · · · 10-Week Mov. Avg. – – GAAP Earnings vs. Previous Year   Volume Above Avg. STARS
12-Mo. Target Price — Relative Strength — ▲ Up ▼ Down ► No Change   Below Avg.

Options: CBOE, P, Ph

Analysis prepared by **Erik Kolb** on October 21, 2009, when the stock traded at **$ 19.90**.

Highlights

► Against the backdrop of a weak economic outlook and reduced consumer spending on toys, we see revenues decreasing 6.4% in 2009, compared to a 2008 drop of 8.7%. We expect a 9.4% decline at Mattel Boys & Girls and a 5.0% drop at Fisher Price segments as sales are negatively impacted by lower consumer demand, especially internationally. Currency translations will also likely hurt. We expect Barbie to remain a key product but for the overall fashion doll category to remain weak globally. Thus, while domestic Barbie sales will likely benefit from recent advertising efforts, we see increased competition from other product lines such as Hannah Montana. We look for total revenue growth of 0.3% in 2010.

► We see gross profit margins of 49.2% in 2009, up from 45.4% in 2008, as productivity initiatives related to reducing headcount and administrative expenses are partially offset by continued external cost pressures, such as higher raw material and transportation costs, and foreign exchange. Price increases should help modestly. We expect margins of 48.0% in 2010.

► We project 2009 EPS of $1.21, versus $1.05 in 2008, and our 2010 estimate is $1.69.

Investment Rationale/Risk

► We have confidence in MAT's portfolio of leading consumer brands and its strong cash flow, and think that the company is effectively handling a difficult environment that will likely remain depressed into 2010. Indeed, cost-cutting efforts appear to be notably benefiting the bottom line. Also, efforts to market to lower price points seem well placed. But we think some products, particularly in the Fisher-Price segment, are seeing some near-term weakness. In 2007, MAT recalled a substantial number of toys, some of which contained lead paint and were produced in China by third-party manufacturers, but we believe the company will be able to restore consumer confidence in the safety of its products.

► Risks to our recommendation and target price include an uncertain toy retailing environment and the possibility of continued toy store closings, an inability to reinvigorate the top line, continued cost pressures, and a material impact from the 2007 toy recalls.

► Our 12-month target price of $22 is based on a P/E multiple of 15.0X, roughly in line with peers and slightly below historical averages, applied to a blend of our 2009 and 2010 EPS estimates.

Qualitative Risk Assessment

LOW	MEDIUM	HIGH

Our risk assessment reflects our favorable view of MAT's leading market share position and strong balance sheet, offset by our negative view of the intense industry rivalry and concentrated buying power of U.S. toy retailers.

Quantitative Evaluations

S&P Quality Ranking   B

D	C	B-	B	B+	A-	A	A+

Relative Strength Rank   MODERATE

64

LOWEST = 1   HIGHEST = 99

Revenue/Earnings Data

Revenue (Million $)

	1Q	2Q	3Q	4Q	Year
2009	785.7	898.2	1,792	--	--
2008	919.3	1,112	1,946	1,940	5,918
2007	940.3	1,003	1,839	2,189	5,970
2006	793.3	957.7	1,790	2,109	5,650
2005	783.1	886.8	1,666	1,843	5,179
2004	780.9	804.0	1,667	1,850	5,103

Earnings Per Share ($)

	1Q	2Q	3Q	4Q	Year
2009	-0.14	0.06	0.63	E0.66	E1.21
2008	-0.13	0.03	0.66	0.49	1.05
2007	0.03	0.06	0.61	0.89	1.54
2006	0.08	0.10	0.62	0.75	1.53
2005	0.02	-0.23	0.55	0.69	1.01
2004	0.02	0.06	0.61	0.68	1.35

Fiscal year ended Dec. 31. Next earnings report expected: Early February. EPS Estimates based on S&P Operating Earnings; historical GAAP earnings are as reported.

Dividend Data (Dates: mm/dd Payment Date: mm/dd/yy)

Amount ($)	Date Decl.	Ex-Div. Date	Stk. of Record	Payment Date
0.750	11/21	12/03	12/05	12/18/08
0.750	11/12	11/25	11/30	12/17/09

Dividends have been paid since 1990. Source: Company reports.

Please read the Required Disclosures and Analyst Certification on the last page of this report.

The McGraw-Hill Companies

Mattel Inc.

Business Summary October 21, 2009

CORPORATE OVERVIEW. Mattel markets a wide variety of toy products on a worldwide basis. Brands are grouped in the following categories: Mattel Girls & Boys Brands, Fisher-Price Brands and American Girl Brands. Mattel brands include Barbie, Polly Pocket, Disney Classics, Hot Wheels, Matchbox and Tyco R/C vehicles and playsets, Nickelodeon, Harry Potter, Yu-Gi-Oh!, Batman, Justice League, and Megaman, among others. Fisher-Price brands include Fisher-Price, Power Wheels, Sesame Street, Little People, Winnie the Pooh, Rescue Heroes, Barney, See 'N Say, Dora the Explorer, BabyGear, and View-Master. American Girl brand products are sold directly to consumers, and its children's publications are sold to certain retailers. Brand names include American Girl Today, the American Girls Collection, Just Like You and Bitty Baby.

MAT operates in the U.S. and internationally. Revenues from the international segment provided 49% of consolidated gross sales in 2008. In the international segment, the geographic breakdown was as follows: Europe, 53% of 2008 sales; Latin America, 31%; Asia Pacific, 9%; and Other, 7%.

CORPORATE STRATEGY. We believe that two key elements of MAT's growth strategy are to build its brands and cut costs. With declining sales in its core Barbie brand, MAT has been focused on reinvigorating this product line, while driving growth in other key brands. To further leverage its brands, MAT also

pursues licensing arrangements and strategic partnerships, which we think helps to extend its portfolio of brands into areas outside of traditional toys.

In early August 2007, MAT reported a recall of 967,000 plastic preschool toys made by a Chinese vendor because of an excessive amount of lead paint and announced that it would cut its already announced second-quarter operating income by $30 million. Two weeks afterward, MAT announced an additional recall involving die-cast cars and other toys involving magnets. Then, in early September, MAT announced a third recall of toys that contain an excessive amount of lead, including Barbie Doll accessories. MAT's 2007 third-quarter results included $40 million in charges related to the product recalls. This included a $13.3 million increase in reserves due primarily to higher product return rates, $9.1 million in reserves for subsequent product recalls and $17 million in incremental legal, advertising and administrative costs. We remain concerned, but we believe the impact on worldwide sales will be minimal and that MAT will be able to restore consumer confidence in the safety of its products. In December 2008, MAT settled litigation with 39 U.S. states, agreeing to pay $12 million related to the recalls, to be divided among the states.

Company Financials Fiscal Year Ended Dec. 31

Per Share Data ($)	2008	2007	2006	2005	2004	2003	2002	2001	2000	1999
Tangible Book Value	2.97	4.04	4.13	3.51	3.97	3.49	2.92	1.46	0.59	1.36
Cash Flow	1.51	1.97	1.98	1.44	1.79	1.63	1.47	1.31	1.00	0.73
Earnings	1.05	1.54	1.53	1.01	1.35	1.22	1.03	0.71	0.40	-0.21
S&P Core Earnings	1.06	1.54	1.55	0.88	1.25	1.14	1.00	0.66	NA	NA
Dividends	0.75	0.75	0.65	0.50	0.45	0.40	0.05	0.05	0.27	0.34
Payout Ratio	71%	49%	42%	50%	33%	33%	5%	7%	67%	NM
Prices:High	21.99	29.71	23.98	21.64	19.79	23.20	22.36	19.92	15.13	30.31
Prices:Low	10.89	18.83	14.75	14.52	15.94	18.57	15.05	13.52	8.94	11.69
P/E Ratio:High	21	19	16	21	15	19	22	28	38	NM
P/E Ratio:Low	10	12	10	14	12	15	15	19	22	NM

Income Statement Analysis (Million $)										
Revenue	5,918	5,970	5,650	5,179	5,103	4,960	4,885	4,804	4,670	5,515
Operating Income	761	1,011	901	840	913	974	934	881	652	671
Depreciation	170	170	172	175	182	184	192	263	256	390
Interest Expense	81.9	71.0	79.9	76.5	77.8	80.6	114	155	153	152
Pretax Income	488	703	684	652	696	741	621	430	225	-111
Effective Tax Rate	22.2%	14.7%	13.3%	36.0%	17.7%	27.4%	26.8%	27.7%	24.5%	NM
Net Income	380	600	593	417	573	538	455	311	170	-82.4
S&P Core Earnings	380	601	600	359	531	502	439	288	NA	NA

Balance Sheet & Other Financial Data (Million $)										
Cash	618	901	1,206	998	1,157	1,153	1,267	617	232	275
Current Assets	2,387	2,593	2,850	2,413	2,637	2,395	2,389	2,093	1,751	2,420
Total Assets	4,675	4,805	4,956	4,372	4,756	4,511	4,460	4,541	4,313	5,127
Current Liabilities	1,260	1,570	1,583	1,463	1,727	1,468	1,649	1,597	1,502	1,818
Long Term Debt	750	550	636	525	400	589	640	1,021	1,242	1,184
Common Equity	2,117	2,307	2,433	2,102	2,386	2,216	1,979	1,738	1,403	1,963
Total Capital	2,915	2,857	3,069	2,627	2,786	2,805	2,619	2,759	2,645	3,147
Capital Expenditures	199	147	64.1	137	144	101	167	101	162	212
Cash Flow	550	770	765	592	755	721	647	573	427	304
Current Ratio	1.9	1.7	1.8	1.6	1.5	1.6	1.4	1.3	1.2	1.3
% Long Term Debt of Capitalization	25.7	19.3	20.7	20.0	14.4	21.0	24.4	37.0	47.0	37.6
% Net Income of Revenue	6.4	10.0	10.5	8.1	11.2	10.8	9.3	6.5	3.6	NM
% Return on Assets	8.0	12.3	12.7	9.1	12.4	12.0	10.1	7.0	3.8	NM
% Return on Equity	17.2	25.3	26.2	18.6	24.9	25.6	24.5	19.8	10.1	NM

Data as orig reptd.; bef. results of disc opers/spec. items. Per share data adj. for stk. divs.; EPS diluted. E-Estimated. NA-Not Available. NM-Not Meaningful. NR-Not Ranked. UR-Under Review.

Office: 333 Continental Boulevard, El Segundo, CA 90245-5012.
Telephone: 310-252-2000.
Website: http://www.mattel.com
Chrmn & CEO: R.A. Eckert

COO: T.A. Debrowski
SVP, Chief Acctg Officer & Cntlr: H.S. Topham
SVP, Secy & General Counsel: R. Normile
CFO: K.M. Farr

Board Members: M. J. Dolan, R. A. Eckert, F. D. Fergusson, T. M. Friedman, R. Gelbart, D. Ng, V. M. Prabhu, A. L. Rich, R. L. Sargent, D. A. Scarborough, C. Sinclair, G. C. Sullivan, K. B. White

Founded: 1945
Domicile: Delaware
Employees: 29,000

MBIA Inc.

S&P Recommendation HOLD ★★★☆☆

Price $3.40 (as of Nov 27, 2009)	**12-Mo. Target Price** $5.00	**Investment Style** Large-Cap Blend

GICS Sector Financials
Sub-Industry Property & Casualty Insurance

Summary This company provides financial guarantee insurance and related services to public finance clients and financial institutions around the world.

Key Stock Statistics (Source S&P, Vickers, company reports)

52-Wk Range	$72.80–2.17	S&P Oper. EPS 2009**E**	-4.98	Market Capitalization(B)	$0.707	Beta	2.47
Trailing 12-Month EPS	$-1.42	S&P Oper. EPS 2010**E**	0.22	Yield (%)	Nil	S&P 3-Yr. Proj. EPS CAGR(%)	NM
Trailing 12-Month P/E	NM	P/E on S&P Oper. EPS 2009**E**	NM	Dividend Rate/Share	Nil	S&P Credit Rating	BB-
$10K Invested 5 Yrs Ago	$606	Common Shares Outstg. (M)	208.0	Institutional Ownership (%)	74		

Price Performance

30-Week Mov. Avg. · · · · 10-Week Mov. Avg. – – – **GAAP Earnings vs. Previous Year** Volume Above Avg. STARS

12-Mo. Target Price — Relative Strength — ▲ Up ▼ Down ► No Change   Below Avg.

Options: ASE, CBOE, P, Ph

Analysis prepared by **Cathy A. Seifert** on November 23, 2009, when the stock traded at **$ 3.56**.

Highlights

► We expect earned premiums to decline in 2009 amid an expected drop in the level of refunded premiums. Premiums could rise modestly in 2010 if the underlying book of business remains intact. Earned premiums declined 5.7%, year to year, in the first nine months of 2009, as a 13% rise in scheduled earned premiums was offset by a 50% decline in refunded premiums. Total operating revenues (which exclude investment gains/losses) should remain under pressure in coming periods amid an expected drop in fee and investment income.

► Operating margins are expected to remain under pressure in 2009 and 2010, largely due to an expected ongoing elevated level of loss costs amid significantly increased claims related to mortgage-backed securities that MBIA insured. Loss and loss adjustment expenses equaled 34.6% of earned premiums in the first nine months of 2009, versus 207% in the 2008 period.

► We forecast an operating loss per share of $4.98 in 2009 and operating EPS of $0.22 in 2010. These estimates exclude the impact of mark-to-market adjustments on credit derivative portfolios. MBIA reported net losses of $12.29 a share for 2008 and $15.17 a share for 2007.

Investment Rationale/Risk

► At recent levels, the shares were trading at a discount to the company's September 30, 2009, tangible book value (excluding goodwill and deferred acquisition costs), which we've calculated to be $9.76 a share (on a fully diluted basis). We view positively MBIA's planned restructuring, including the formation of a separate municipal bond insurance unit. However, our outlook is tempered by our concerns that continued deterioration in underwriting results and claim trends could further pressure results, and that MBIA may have to raise additional (and likely dilutive) capital we believe will be needed to adequately restore its financial strength.

► Risks to our opinion and target price include a greater-than-expected impact from MBIA's exposure to the mortgage-related structured finance market, and a heightening of concerns over its capital adequacy and its future business prospects.

► Our 12-month target price of $5 assumes that the shares will trade at a discount to estimated 2009 year end tangible book value. We caution that book values may vary greatly due to mark-to-market accounting mandates.

Qualitative Risk Assessment

LOW	MEDIUM	**HIGH**

Our risk assessment reflects our view that the company faces a number of challenges as it seeks to maintain and rebuild its business. In addition to risks associated with interest rate fluctuations and macro credit trends, we believe MBIA faces a high degree of "reputation risk," driven primarily by concerns the company may face additional challenges after losing its top-tier financial strength rating.

Quantitative Evaluations

S&P Quality Ranking   B

D	C	B-	**B**	B+	A-	A	A+

Relative Strength Rank   WEAK

5

LOWEST = 1   HIGHEST = 99

Revenue/Earnings Data

Revenue (Million $)

	1Q	2Q	3Q	4Q	Year
2009	1,929	992.1	-620.2	--	--
2008	-2,943	3,355	319.8	-1,589	-856.6
2007	369.6	779.1	428.3	-2,220	-384.7
2006	351.8	689.2	707.4	693.3	2,712
2005	326.0	339.3	605.2	600.0	2,301
2004	327.5	340.4	476.0	345.5	2,001

Earnings Per Share ($)

	1Q	2Q	3Q	4Q	Year
2009	3.36	4.30	-3.49	E-1.48	E-4.98
2008	-13.03	7.14	-3.48	-5.30	-12.29
2007	1.46	1.61	-0.29	-18.55	-15.17
2006	1.45	1.61	1.58	1.30	5.95
2005	1.52	1.37	1.05	1.34	5.19
2004	1.42	1.47	1.29	1.36	5.61

Fiscal year ended Dec. 31. Next earnings report expected: Early March. EPS Estimates based on S&P Operating Earnings; historical GAAP earnings are as reported.

Dividend Data

No cash dividends have been paid since 2007.

Please read the Required Disclosures and Analyst Certification on the last page of this report.

The McGraw-Hill Companies

MBIA Inc.

STANDARD &POOR'S

Business Summary November 23, 2009

CORPORATE OVERVIEW. MBIA Inc. (MBI), provides financial guarantee insurance and related advisory and portfolio services for the public and structured finance markets.

MBI offers insurance for new issues of municipal bonds, and for bonds traded in the secondary market, including bonds held in unit investment trusts and mutual funds. The economic value of municipal bond insurance to the governmental unit or agency offering bonds is a saving in interest costs reflecting the difference in yield on an insured bond from that on the same bond if uninsured.

At December 31, 2008, the net par value of the company's insured debt obligations was $786.5 billion, of which general obligation municipal bonds accounted for 32%, utility bonds 12%, tax-backed bonds 9%, transportation bonds 7%, health care bonds 3%, other U.S. municipal bonds 7%, non-U.S. municipal obligations 4%, U.S. structured finance obligations (asset/mortgage backed) 18%, and international structured finance 8%. Of the $786.5 billion of net outstanding insured debt obligations at December 31, 2008, 18% had been issued

by nationally diversified entities, 12% had been issued outside the U.S., 12% had been issued by California, 7% by New York, 5% by Florida, 4% each by Texas and Illinois, and 3% by New Jersey.

MBI in recent years has expanded its presence in the structured finance (or asset-backed) markets, although activity in many areas of this unit slowed considerably in 2008. At December 31, 2008, the net par value of the company's structured finance portfolio equaled $203.6 billion (and is included in the aggregate portfolio of $786.5 billion). Collateralized debt obligations (CDOs) accounted for 61% of the structured finance portfolio, while residential mortgage-backed obligations equaled 16%, commercial mortgage-backed obligations 3%, consumer asset-backed (including auto loans, student loans and manufactured housing loans) 5%, and corporate asset-backed obligations accounted for the remaining 15%.

Company Financials Fiscal Year Ended Dec. 31

Per Share Data ($)	2008	2007	2006	2005	2004	2003	2002	2001	2000	1999
Tangible Book Value	4.32	24.76	53.15	48.36	46.63	42.87	37.32	31.56	27.86	23.01
Operating Earnings	NA	NA	NA	NA	5.25	4.80	4.27	3.88	3.41	3.15
Earnings	-12.29	-15.17	5.95	5.19	5.61	5.61	3.98	3.91	3.55	2.13
S&P Core Earnings	-7.05	-15.48	5.88	5.75	5.33	5.25	3.91	3.81	NA	NA
Dividends	Nil	1.36	1.24	1.12	0.96	0.80	0.68	0.60	0.55	0.53
Payout Ratio	Nil	NM	21%	22%	17%	14%	17%	15%	15%	25%
Prices:High	19.75	76.02	73.49	64.00	67.34	60.72	60.11	57.49	50.79	47.92
Prices:Low	3.50	17.79	56.00	49.07	52.55	34.14	34.93	36.00	24.21	30.08
P/E Ratio:High	NM	NM	12	12	12	11	15	15	14	23
P/E Ratio:Low	NM	NM	9	9	9	6	9	9	7	14

Income Statement Analysis (Million $)										
Premium Income	850	824	836	843	822	733	589	524	446	443
Net Investment Income	1,551	2,184	1,863	492	474	447	442	413	394	359
Other Revenue	-1,544	-3,290	13.5	1,458	704	590	120	197	217	605
Total Revenue	-857	-283	2,712	2,301	2,001	1,770	1,151	1,134	1,057	964
Pretax Income	-3,727	-3,066	1,133	1,016	1,130	1,149	793	791	715	388
Net Operating Income	NA	NA	NA	NA	NA	NA	NA	NA	NA	NA
Net Income	-2,673	-1,922	813	712	813	814	587	583	529	321
S&P Core Earnings	-1,534	-1,961	804	789	773	761	577	568	NA	NA

Balance Sheet & Other Financial Data (Million $)										
Cash & Equivalent	2,280	854	796	629	678	452	298	297	246	229
Premiums Due	217	326	363	408	505	536	522	507	NA	NA
Investment Assets:Bonds	11,224	29,589	27,756	23,747	19,680	17,391	16,195	14,087	11,737	10,274
Investment Assets:Stocks	Nil	Nil	Nil	Nil	Nil	Nil	Nil	Nil	Nil	Nil
Investment Assets:Loans	Nil	Nil	Nil	Nil	Nil	Nil	Nil	Nil	Nil	Nil
Investment Assets:Total	20,639	42,066	46,399	40,562	41,556	27,707	17,095	14,516	12,233	10,694
Deferred Policy Costs	561	473	450	427	360	320	302	278	274	252
Total Assets	29,657	47,415	39,763	34,561	33,027	30,268	18,852	16,200	13,894	12,264
Debt	10,527	15,412	13,619	10,033	8,877	8,870	1,033	805	795	689
Common Equity	994	3,656	7,204	6,592	6,579	6,259	5,493	4,783	4,223	3,513
Property & Casualty:Loss Ratio	NA	105.2	9.7	10.0	10.0	9.2	9.4	9.3	6.2	12.3
Property & Casualty:Expense Ratio	27.8	23.6	26.6	24.9	22.0	12.8	16.8	13.4	22.1	23.6
Property & Casualty Combined Ratio	157.5	128.6	36.3	34.9	32.0	22.0	26.2	22.7	28.3	35.9
% Return on Revenue	NM	NM	30.0	31.0	40.6	46.0	51.0	51.4	50.0	33.2
% Return on Equity	NM	NM	11.8	10.8	12.7	13.8	11.4	13.0	13.7	8.8

Data as orig reptd.; bef. results of disc opers/spec. items. Per share data adj. for stk. divs.; EPS diluted. E-Estimated. NA-Not Available. NM-Not Meaningful. NR-Not Ranked. UR-Under Review.

Office: 113 King Street, Armonk, NY 10504-1610.
Telephone: 914-273-4545.
Website: http://www.mbia.com
Chrmn: D.P. Kearney

CEO: J.W. Brown, Jr.
COO & Co-Pres: W.C. Fallon
EVP, Secy & General Counsel: R.D. Wertheim
CFO, Chief Admin Officer & Co-Pres: C. Chaplin

Investor Contact: G. Diamond (914-765-3190)
Board Members: J. W. Brown, Jr., D. A. Coulter, C. L. Gaudiani, D. P. Kearney, K. Lee, L. H. Meyer, C. R. Rinehart, T. Shasta, R. C. Vaughan

Founded: 1973
Domicile: Connecticut
Employees: 420

McAfee Inc

STANDARD &POOR'S

S&P Recommendation BUY ★★★★☆

Price	12-Mo. Target Price	Investment Style
$39.92 (as of Nov 27, 2009)	$50.00	Large-Cap Growth

GICS Sector Information Technology
Sub-Industry Systems Software

Summary This company develops network security and management software products.

Key Stock Statistics (Source S&P, Vickers, company reports)

52-Wk Range	$45.68– 26.15	S&P Oper. EPS 2009**E**	1.14	Market Capitalization(B)	$6.297	Beta	1.18
Trailing 12-Month EPS	$1.04	S&P Oper. EPS 2010**E**	1.56	Yield (%)	Nil	S&P 3-Yr. Proj. EPS CAGR(%)	16
Trailing 12-Month P/E	38.4	P/E on S&P Oper. EPS 2009**E**	35.0	Dividend Rate/Share	Nil	S&P Credit Rating	NA
$10K Invested 5 Yrs Ago	$14,490	Common Shares Outstg. (M)	157.7	Institutional Ownership (%)	93		

Price Performance

30-Week Mov. Avg. ··· 10-Week Mov. Avg. -- **GAAP Earnings vs. Previous Year** Volume Above Avg. STARS
12-Mo. Target Price — Relative Strength — ▲ Up ▼ Down ▶ No Change Below Avg. ★

Options: ASE, CBOE, P, Ph

Analysis prepared by **Jim Yin** on November 11, 2009, when the stock traded at **$ 43.19**.

Highlights

▶ We project that revenues will increase 20% and 12% in 2009 and 2010, respectively, compared to 22% growth in 2008. Our projection of slower revenue growth reflects our view of a slow recovery in IT spending. We estimate overall IT spending will rise 4% in 2010, following a 6% decline seen for 2009. However, we believe the security software segment will be less affected than other IT sectors as security software is viewed as mission critical. We expect MFE to gain market share in the corporate business segment through a broader product portfolio.

▶ We expect gross margins of 75% in 2009 and 2010, down from 76% in 2008. We project operating expenses to decline to 63% and 60% of revenues in 2009 and 2010, respectively, down from 64% in 2008, due to cost synergies achieved from recent acquisitions and better economies of scale. We see the operating margin widening to 12.0% and 14.8% in 2009 and 2010, respectively, from 11.8% in 2008, on higher revenues and cost savings.

▶ Our EPS estimates for 2009 and 2010 are $1.14 and $1.56, respectively, compared to $1.08 in 2008. The expected increases reflect our forecast of higher revenues and operating margins.

Investment Rationale/Risk

▶ We recently downgraded our recommendation to buy, from strong buy, on valuation. We think overall IT spending will remain weak in the first half of 2010 given the uncertainty of the economic recovery. However, we think security software will be less affected than other IT sectors given its mission-critical nature. We expect MFE to gain market share because of its financial flexibility to make acquisitions that will strengthen its product offerings. Also, the company has been improving its operating margins as a result of cost savings from recent acquisitions.

▶ Risks to our opinion and target price include a weaker than expected economic recovery and intense competition in the Internet security software sector as competitors broaden product offerings.

▶ Our 12-month target price of $50 is based on a blend of our discounted cash flow (DCF) and P/E analyses. Our DCF model assumes a 12% WACC and 3% terminal growth, yielding an intrinsic value of $55. From our P/E analysis, we derive a value of $45 based on an industry P/E-to-growth ratio of 1.8X, or 29X our 2010 EPS estimate of $1.56.

Qualitative Risk Assessment

LOW	MEDIUM	HIGH

Our risk assessment reflects our view of the highly competitive security software market, rapid technological obsolescence, and a slow recovery in IT spending.

Quantitative Evaluations

S&P Quality Ranking B-

D	C	B-	B	B+	A-	A	A+

Relative Strength Rank WEAK

27

LOWEST = 1   HIGHEST = 99

Revenue/Earnings Data

Revenue (Million $)

	1Q	2Q	3Q	4Q	Year
2009	447.7	468.7	485.3	--	--
2008	369.6	396.8	409.7	424.0	1,600
2007	314.9	314.8	322.0	356.5	1,308
2006	275.2	277.6	287.1	305.2	1,145
2005	235.7	245.4	252.9	253.3	987.3
2004	219.1	225.7	221.6	244.2	910.5

Earnings Per Share ($)

2009	0.34	0.18	0.23	E0.39	E1.14
2008	0.18	0.30	0.32	0.29	1.08
2007	0.28	0.30	0.39	0.07	1.02
2006	0.25	0.19	0.19	0.21	0.84
2005	0.21	0.25	0.13	0.23	0.82
2004	0.33	0.06	0.70	0.23	1.31

Fiscal year ended Dec. 31. Next earnings report expected: Mid February. EPS Estimates based on S&P Operating Earnings; historical GAAP earnings are as reported.

Dividend Data

No cash dividends have been paid.

Please read the Required Disclosures and Analyst Certification on the last page of this report.

The **McGraw·Hill** Companies

McAfee Inc

STANDARD
&POOR'S

Business Summary November 11, 2009

CORPORATE OVERVIEW. MFE is a leading supplier of computer security software that helps home users, businesses, government agencies and service providers protect their systems and networks from potential threats around the world. The company was incorporated in 1992 as an application service provider (ASP) targeted at consumers and small to medium-sized businesses. It merged with Network General Corporation in December 1997 to become Network Associates, Inc. The company adopted its current name in June 2004, and began trading on the New York Stock Exchange under the symbol MFE.

MFE provides integrated solutions that help its customers solve problems, enhance security and reduce costs. The company's major product lines are system security, network security and vulnerability and risk management. Its system security products protect both consumer and corporate computer systems including laptops and other mobile devices from malicious attacks such as viruses and spyware. The products also safeguard sensitive data stored in mobile devices from leaking to the public that occurs through theft. MFE's mobile security offerings also limit the spread of mobile malware, inappropriate content, and unsolicited messaging.

MFE's network security products provide the same type of protection as its

system security products, but are focused on the enterprise IT infrastructure. Network protection encompasses firewall, intrusion prevention, and email and data loss protection security appliances. It also includes McAfee SiteAdvisor, which warns Internet users of potential harmful websites.

MFE's vulnerability and risk management offerings help companies meet regulatory statues, resolve policy issues, conduct audits and identify risks such as non-compliant personal computers connecting to the internal network.

MFE markets its products to commercial and government customers through resellers and distributors. The top 10 distributors typically account for 35%-55% of total revenue. The two largest distributors, Ingram Micro and Tech Data Corp., together accounted for approximately 27% of total revenue in 2008. For the consumer market, MFE sells its products through original equipment manufacturers, retail stores and online. The company generated approximately 47%, 48% and 45% of its revenue outside of North America in 2008, 2007 and 2006, respectively.

Company Financials Fiscal Year Ended Dec. 31

Per Share Data ($)	2008	2007	2006	2005	2004	2003	2002	2001	2000	1999
Tangible Book Value	1.74	6.32	4.90	5.58	4.04	2.09	2.55	1.85	2.16	2.82
Cash Flow	1.86	1.53	1.27	1.20	1.65	0.75	1.03	0.04	-0.09	-0.57
Earnings	1.08	1.02	0.84	0.82	1.31	0.36	0.80	-0.74	-0.74	-1.15
S&P Core Earnings	1.14	1.02	0.83	0.81	0.28	0.05	0.62	-1.58	NA	NA
Dividends	Nil	Nil	Nil	Nil	Nil	Nil	Nil	Nil	Nil	Nil
Payout Ratio	Nil	Nil	Nil	Nil	Nil	Nil	Nil	Nil	Nil	Nil
Prices:High	40.97	41.66	277.60	33.24	33.55	20.70	30.50	27.84	37.19	67.50
Prices:Low	24.72	27.74	287.10	20.35	14.90	10.42	8.14	3.56	3.25	10.06
P/E Ratio:High	38	41	1145	41	26	58	38	NM	NM	NM
P/E Ratio:Low	23	27	23	25	11	29	10	NM	NM	NM

Income Statement Analysis (Million $)										
Revenue	1,600	1,308	1,145	987	911	936	1,043	834	746	684
Operating Income	348	286	210	280	146	157	257	29.9	-61.9	-75.4
Depreciation	124	84.4	70.0	64.9	66.7	62.8	53.7	108	90.1	81.5
Interest Expense	Nil	Nil	Nil	Nil	5.32	7.54	25.1	24.7	18.2	17.3
Pretax Income	222	229	184	182	316	73.1	130	-91.4	-97.8	-131
Effective Tax Rate	22.5%	27.2%	25.1%	23.5%	28.9%	18.1%	NM	NM	NM	NM
Net Income	172	167	137	139	225	59.9	128	-102	-103	-160
S&P Core Earnings	181	166	136	139	37.3	9.42	102	-217	NA	NA

Balance Sheet & Other Financial Data (Million $)										
Cash	594	733	606	1,045	524	508	674	749	361	389
Current Assets	1,405	1,408	1,177	1,568	966	961	1,194	1,083	621	676
Total Assets	3,453	3,414	2,800	2,643	2,238	2,120	2,045	1,627	1,385	1,479
Current Liabilities	1,329	1,178	1,030	869	706	545	882	541	424	390
Long Term Debt	Nil	Nil	Nil	Nil	Nil	347	356	579	396	379
Common Equity	1,752	1,905	1,427	1,455	1,201	888	770	445	519	660
Total Capital	1,752	1,905	1,427	1,455	1,201	1,236	1,126	1,061	934	1,059
Capital Expenditures	48.8	33.6	44.0	28.9	25.4	60.0	59.4	31.5	54.0	20.5
Cash Flow	296	251	207	204	292	123	182	5.67	-12.6	-78.4
Current Ratio	1.1	1.2	1.1	1.8	1.4	1.8	1.4	2.0	1.5	1.7
% Long Term Debt of Capitalization	Nil	Nil	Nil	Nil	Nil	28.1	31.6	54.5	42.4	35.8
% Net Income of Revenue	10.8	12.8	11.9	14.1	24.7	7.2	12.3	NM	NM	NM
% Return on Assets	5.0	5.4	5.0	5.7	10.3	2.9	7.0	NM	NM	NM
% Return on Equity	9.4	10.0	9.5	10.5	21.5	7.2	23.1	NM	NM	NM

Data as orig reptd.; bef. results of disc opers/spec. items. Per share data adj. for stk. divs.; EPS diluted. E-Estimated. NA-Not Available. NM-Not Meaningful. NR-Not Ranked. UR-Under Review.

Office: 3965 Freedom Circle, Santa Clara, CA 95054.
Telephone: 408-988-3832.
Email: ir@nai.com
Website: http://www.mcafee.com

Chrmn: C. Robel
Pres & CEO: D.G. DeWalt
COO & CFO: A.A. Pimentel
EVP & CTO: G. Kurtz

EVP, Secy & General Counsel: M.D. Cochran
Investor Contact: K. Doherty (917-842-0334)
Board Members: C. Bass, T. E. Darcy, D. G. DeWalt, L. G. Denend, J. A. Miller, D. J. O'Leary, R. W. Pangia, C. Robel, A. Zingale

Founded: 1989
Domicile: Delaware
Employees: 5,600

McCormick & Company Inc

STANDARD &POOR'S

S&P Recommendation HOLD ★★★☆☆	Price $35.78 (as of Nov 27, 2009)	12-Mo. Target Price $36.00	Investment Style Large-Cap Growth

GICS Sector Consumer Staples
Sub-Industry Packaged Foods & Meats

Summary This company primarily produces spices, seasonings and flavorings for the retail food, food service and industrial markets. Trademarks include McCormick and Schilling.

Key Stock Statistics (Source S&P, Vickers, company reports)

52-Wk Range	$36.61– 28.08	S&P Oper. EPS 2009E	2.33	Market Capitalization(B)	$4.240	Beta	0.45
Trailing 12-Month EPS	$2.01	S&P Oper. EPS 2010E	2.47	Yield (%)	2.91	S&P 3-Yr. Proj. EPS CAGR(%)	8
Trailing 12-Month P/E	17.8	P/E on S&P Oper. EPS 2009E	15.4	Dividend Rate/Share	$1.04	S&P Credit Rating	A-
$10K Invested 5 Yrs Ago	$10,767	Common Shares Outstg. (M)	130.9	Institutional Ownership (%)	78		

Price Performance

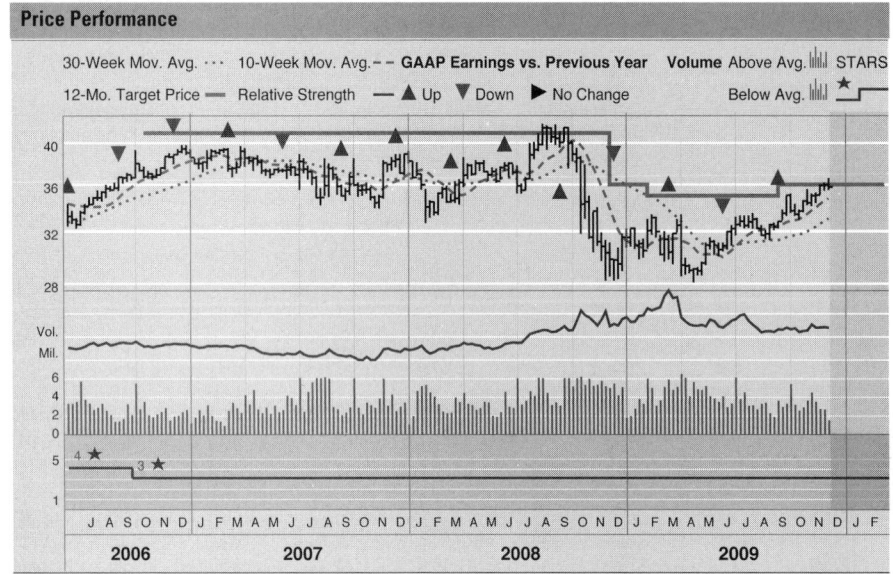

30-Week Mov. Avg. · · · 10-Week Mov. Avg. – – GAAP Earnings vs. Previous Year Volume Above Avg. STARS
12-Mo. Target Price — Relative Strength ▲ Up ▼ Down ► No Change Below Avg.

Options: Ph

Analysis prepared by **Loran Braverman, CFA** on September 29, 2009, when the stock traded at **$ 34.10**.

Highlights

▶ In FY 09 (Nov.), with the full-year inclusion of the Lawry's business (acquired in July 2008), we look for net sales to increase modestly from the $3.18 billion reported for FY 08, with the comparison limited by an adverse impact from currency exchange rate fluctuation. We expect a portion of MKC's business to benefit from U.S. consumers increasingly eating at home, but product demand from restaurants may weaken. Our sales growth forecast for FY 10 is 6%.

▶ We expect profit margins (before restructuring charges) to be bolstered by easing input costs, plus productivity and restructuring benefits. Excluding special items, we project FY 09 EPS of $2.33, up from $2.14 in FY 08. In FY 09, we look for MKC to have restructuring charges totaling about $0.05 a share, compared to special items that had a net negative impact of about $0.20 a share in FY 08. For FY 10, we estimate EPS of $2.47.

▶ As of May 31, 2009, MKC had $39 million remaining of a $400 million share repurchase authorization. However, for the near term, in view of the Lawry's acquisition, we expect MKC to emphasize debt repayment as a use of cash.

Investment Rationale/Risk

▶ We believe the recent Lawry's acquisition represented a logical expansion for MKC into a related business. Excluding any special items, we expect the acquisition to be accretive to EPS in FY 09. For the company as a whole, we think longer-term prospects to generate free cash flow are favorable. With respect to its restructuring program, MKC had about $11 million of incremental cost savings in FY 08, following $35 million in FY 07 and $10 million in FY 06.

▶ Risks to our recommendation and target price include competitive pressures in MKC's businesses, consumer acceptance of new product introductions, and commodity cost inflation. In terms of corporate governance, the company has a dual class capital structure with unequal voting rights, which we view unfavorably.

▶ Our 12-month target price of $36 is based on a blend of our historical and relative analyses. Our historical analysis suggests a P/E of 16.7X our FY 09 operating EPS estimate of $2.33, for a $39 value. Our peer analysis applies a P/E of 14.6X, close to the peer average, for a $34 value. We use for peers a mixture of small and mid-capitalization stocks in the food industry or the flavoring and/or coloring business.

Qualitative Risk Assessment

LOW	MEDIUM	HIGH

Our risk assessment reflects the relatively stable nature of the company's end markets, our view of its strong balance sheet and cash flow, and an S&P Quality Ranking of A+, which reflects historical stability of earnings and dividends.

Quantitative Evaluations

S&P Quality Ranking   A+

D	C	B-	B	B+	A-	A	A+

Relative Strength Rank   STRONG

71

LOWEST = 1   HIGHEST = 99

Revenue/Earnings Data

Revenue (Million $)

	1Q	2Q	3Q	4Q	Year
2009	718.5	757.3	791.7	--	--
2008	724.0	764.1	781.6	906.9	3,177
2007	652.6	687.2	716.2	860.1	2,916
2006	609.7	639.9	663.1	803.7	2,716
2005	603.6	628.6	622.7	737.1	2,592
2004	572.4	596.2	613.5	744.1	2,526

Earnings Per Share ($)

2009	0.44	0.38	0.57	E0.90	E2.33
2008	0.39	0.41	0.52	0.62	1.94
2007	0.33	0.31	0.43	0.67	1.73
2006	0.11	0.46	0.32	0.62	1.50
2005	0.26	0.31	0.35	0.65	1.56
2004	0.27	0.30	0.33	0.62	1.52

Fiscal year ended Nov. 30. Next earnings report expected: Late January. EPS Estimates based on S&P Operating Earnings; historical GAAP earnings are as reported.

Dividend Data (Dates: mm/dd Payment Date: mm/dd/yy)

Amount ($)	Date Decl.	Ex-Div. Date	Stk. of Record	Payment Date
0.240	03/25	04/02	04/06	04/20/09
0.240	06/23	07/01	07/06	07/20/09
0.240	09/22	09/30	10/02	10/16/09
0.260	11/24	12/29	12/31	01/15/10

Dividends have been paid since 1925. Source: Company reports.

Please read the Required Disclosures and Analyst Certification on the last page of this report.

The McGraw-Hill Companies

McCormick & Company Inc

Business Summary September 29, 2009

CORPORATE OVERVIEW. Founded by Willoughby M. McCormick in 1889, McCormick & Co. is the world's largest spice company, with operations in the manufacture, marketing and distribution of spices, seasonings, flavorings and other specialty food products. The company markets its products to retail food, foodservice and industrial markets under the McCormick and Schilling names.

McCormick's consumer segment, which accounted for 58% of sales and 81% of operating profits (before restructuring and impairment charges) in FY 08 (Nov.), sells spices, herbs, extracts, seasoning blends, sauces, marinades and specialty foods to the consumer food market. The industrial segment (42%, 19%) sells seasoning blends, natural spices and herbs, wet flavors, coating systems and compound flavors to food manufacturers and the food service industry, both directly and through distributors. Many spices and herbs purchased by the company are imported into the U.S., although significant quantities of some materials, such as paprika, dehydrated vegetables, onion and garlic, and food ingredients other than spices and herbs, originate in the U.S.

MKC says that many of its products are prepared from confidential formulas developed by its research laboratories and product development teams. Ex-

penditures for research and development were $51.0 million in FY 08, compared to $49.3 million in FY 07.

CORPORATE STRATEGY. We see MKC aiming to improve profitability with cost reduction efforts and a focus on higher-margin, higher-value-added products.

A restructuring program was announced in 2005, and the company says that in its third year (FY 08), annual savings reached $56 million, including an incremental $11 million in FY 08. We expect the restructuring plan to be completed in FY 09. Also, we expect the restructuring plan to include the consolidation of global manufacturing, the rationalization of distribution facilities, efforts to improve its go-to-market strategy, the elimination of administrative redundancies, and the rationalization of joint venture partnerships. We believe a portion of the savings may be invested in potential growth drivers such as brand advertising.

Company Financials Fiscal Year Ended Nov. 30

Per Share Data ($)	2008	2007	2006	2005	2004	2003	2002	2001	2000	1999
Tangible Book Value	NM	NM	NM	NM	0.45	0.28	0.62	NM	NM	1.70
Cash Flow	2.50	2.36	2.14	2.10	2.11	1.85	1.73	1.57	1.43	1.12
Earnings	1.94	1.73	1.50	1.56	1.52	1.40	1.26	1.05	0.99	0.72
S&P Core Earnings	1.70	1.81	1.40	1.51	1.43	1.28	1.12	0.90	NA	NA
Dividends	0.88	0.80	0.72	0.64	0.56	0.46	0.37	0.40	0.38	0.34
Payout Ratio	45%	46%	48%	41%	37%	33%	29%	38%	38%	48%
Prices:High	42.06	39.73	39.82	39.14	38.94	30.21	27.25	23.27	18.88	17.31
Prices:Low	28.21	33.89	30.09	28.95	28.60	21.71	20.70	17.00	11.88	13.31
P/E Ratio:High	22	23	27	25	26	22	22	22	19	24
P/E Ratio:Low	15	20	20	19	19	16	16	16	12	19

Income Statement Analysis (Million $)	2008	2007	2006	2005	2004	2003	2002	2001	2000	1999
Revenue	3,177	2,916	2,716	2,592	2,526	2,270	2,320	2,372	2,124	2,007
Operating Income	496	468	429	429	402	366	353	324	287	252
Depreciation	73.5	83.0	86.8	74.6	72.0	65.3	66.8	73.0	61.3	57.4
Interest Expense	57.6	61.0	53.7	48.2	41.0	38.6	43.6	52.9	39.7	32.4
Pretax Income	356	302	270	316	308	286	257	212	204	163
Effective Tax Rate	28.2%	30.4%	24.0%	30.6%	28.9%	29.1%	28.9%	29.7%	32.6%	36.8%
Net Income	256	230	202	215	215	199	180	147	138	103
S&P Core Earnings	224	240	189	208	202	182	158	126	NA	NA

Balance Sheet & Other Financial Data (Million $)	2008	2007	2006	2005	2004	2003	2002	2001	2000	1999
Cash	38.9	46.0	49.0	30.3	70.3	25.1	47.3	31.3	23.9	12.0
Current Assets	968	983	899	800	864	762	725	636	620	491
Total Assets	3,220	2,788	2,568	2,273	2,370	2,148	1,931	1,772	1,660	1,189
Current Liabilities	1,034	861	780	699	773	713	673	714	1,027	471
Long Term Debt	885	574	570	464	465	449	454	454	160	241
Common Equity	1,055	1,085	933	800	890	755	592	463	359	382
Total Capital	1,988	1,669	1,575	1,293	1,386	1,226	1,046	943	523	628
Capital Expenditures	85.8	79.0	84.8	73.8	69.8	91.6	111	112	53.6	49.3
Cash Flow	329	313	289	290	287	265	247	220	199	161
Current Ratio	0.9	1.1	1.2	1.1	1.1	1.1	1.1	0.9	0.6	1.0
% Long Term Debt of Capitalization	44.5	34.3	37.8	35.9	33.6	36.6	43.4	48.2	30.6	38.5
% Net Income of Revenue	8.1	7.8	7.4	8.3	8.5	8.8	7.8	6.2	6.5	5.1
% Return on Assets	8.5	8.5	8.4	9.3	9.5	9.8	9.7	8.5	9.7	8.4
% Return on Equity	23.9	22.7	23.3	25.4	26.1	29.6	34.1	35.7	37.1	26.8

Data as orig reptd.; bef. results of disc opers/spec. items. Per share data adj. for stk. divs.; EPS diluted. E-Estimated. NA-Not Available. NM-Not Meaningful. NR-Not Ranked. UR-Under Review.

Office: 18 Loveton Circle, Sparks, MD 21152-6000.
Telephone: 410-771-7301.
Website: http://www.mccormick.com
Chrmn, Pres & CEO: A.D. Wilson

EVP & CFO: G.M. Stetz, Jr.
SVP, Chief Acctg Officer & Cntlr: K.A. Kelly, Jr.
SVP & Treas: P.C. Beard
SVP, Secy & General Counsel: W.G. Carpenter

Investor Contact: J. Brooks (410-771-7244)
Board Members: J. P. Bilbrey, J. T. Brady, J. M. Fitzpatrick, F. A. Hrabowski, III, M. D. Mangan, J. W. McGrath, M. M. Preston, G. A. Roche, W. E. Stevens, A. D. Wilson

Founded: 1889
Domicile: Maryland
Employees: 7,500

McDonald's Corp

STANDARD &POOR'S

S&P Recommendation **BUY** ★★★★☆	Price $63.60 (as of Nov 27, 2009)	12-Mo. Target Price $70.00	Investment Style Large-Cap Growth

GICS Sector Consumer Discretionary
Sub-Industry Restaurants

Summary MCD is the largest fast-food restaurant company in the world, with over 32,000 restaurants in 118 countries.

Key Stock Statistics (Source S&P, Vickers, company reports)

52-Wk Range	$64.75–50.44	S&P Oper. EPS 2009E	4.05	Market Capitalization(B)	$68.636	Beta	0.65
Trailing 12-Month EPS	$3.87	S&P Oper. EPS 2010E	4.20	Yield (%)	3.46	S&P 3-Yr. Proj. EPS CAGR(%)	7
Trailing 12-Month P/E	16.4	P/E on S&P Oper. EPS 2009E	15.7	Dividend Rate/Share	$2.20	S&P Credit Rating	A
$10K Invested 5 Yrs Ago	$23,760	Common Shares Outstg. (M)	1,079.2	Institutional Ownership (%)	70		

Price Performance

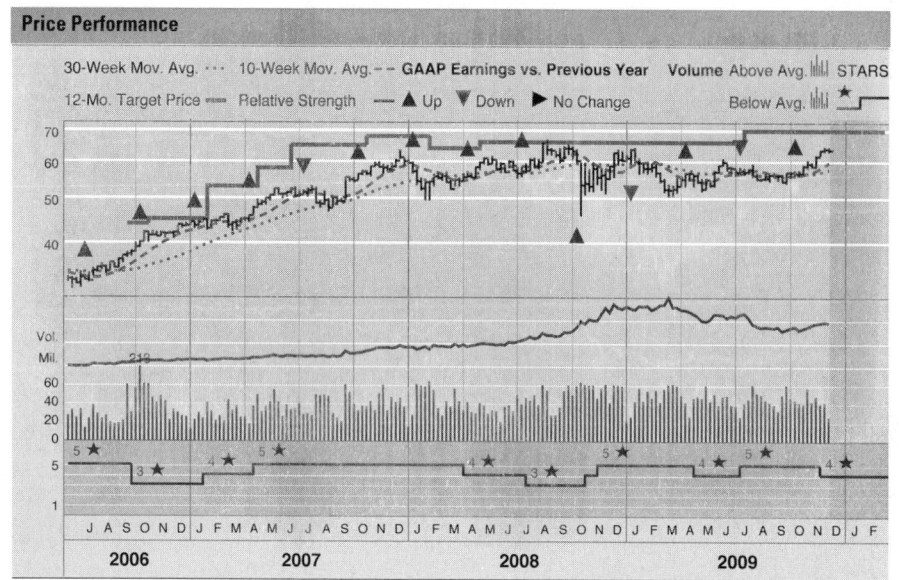

30-Week Mov. Avg. · · · 10-Week Mov. Avg. – – GAAP Earnings vs. Previous Year   Volume Above Avg. STARS
12-Mo. Target Price — Relative Strength ▲ Up ▼ Down ► No Change   Below Avg.

Options: ASE, CBOE, P, Ph

Analysis prepared by **Mark S. Basham** on November 16, 2009, when the stock traded at **$63.58**.

Highlights

► We project that revenues in 2009 will increase about 2%, exclusive of negative forex effects equal to about 7%. Systemwide sales in the U.S. are expected to be up 4.5%, while they are likely to climb 8% and 7% in local currencies in Europe and Asia Pacific/Middle East/Africa, respectively. We expect the net number of systemwide restaurants to increase about 2% in 2009.

► We estimate 2009 operating EPS, aided by stock repurchases, will increase 9.8%, to $4.05 from $3.67 in 2008, which excluded a $0.09 gain on the sale of the company's minority stake in the Pret a Manger chain. We expect negative currency effects in 2009 of about $0.16 a share, including a positive effect of $0.06 a share in the fourth quarter.

► For 2010, we expect revenues to rise 3% to 4%, while systemwide sales rise 4% to 5%, exclusive of forex effects. MCD expects about 1,000 (gross) new restaurants will open systemwide in 2010. We estimate that EPS will increase 3.7%, to $4.20. Assumptions include that margins will be stable, as will commodity food costs, and that MCD will continue buying back its shares.

Investment Rationale/Risk

► Our buy recommendation reflects our view that the shares are likely to be seen as somewhat of a defensive play against further risks to a global economic rebound, although after recent gains in the share price, we think that somewhat more modest upside remains. We also believe the $2.20 per share annual cash dividend is an additional attraction to owning the shares.

► Risks to our recommendation and target price include higher-than-expected food costs, poor customer acceptance of MCD's new menu offerings, and exchange rate risk in light of MCD's substantial international business.

► Our 12-month target price of $70 is based on a forward P/E of approximately 17X applied to our 2010 EPS estimate of $4.20, a slight premium to the peer group average. Our target price is supported by our discounted cash flow model, which assumes free cash flow growth of 5% over the 2009-2012 period that then gradually declines to a perpetuity growth rate of 2.0%, and a weighted average cost of equity of 9.8%. The 2009 fourth quarter increase in the annual dividend rate to $2.20 results in a 3.5% dividend yield at recent stock prices.

Qualitative Risk Assessment

LOW	**MEDIUM**	HIGH

McDonald's competes in the global fast food industry, where it has a very strong brand name presence. However, results can vary widely due to fluctuations in food costs, competitive discounting, and exchange rate volatility. We recently lowered our risk assessment to medium, as it appears global economic weakness may have started to subside.

Quantitative Evaluations

S&P Quality Ranking A-

D	C	B-	B	B+	**A-**	A	A+

Relative Strength Rank **STRONG**

81

LOWEST = 1   HIGHEST = 99

Revenue/Earnings Data

Revenue (Million $)

	1Q	2Q	3Q	4Q	Year
2009	5,077	5,647	6,047	--	--
2008	5,615	6,075	6,267	5,565	23,522
2007	5,293	5,839	5,901	5,754	22,787
2006	4,914	5,367	5,671	5,634	21,586
2005	4,803	5,096	5,327	5,235	20,460
2004	4,400	4,729	4,926	5,010	19,065

Earnings Per Share ($)

2009	0.87	0.98	1.15	E1.05	E4.05
2008	0.81	1.04	1.05	0.87	3.76
2007	0.63	-0.59	0.83	1.06	1.93
2006	0.46	0.56	0.67	0.61	2.30
2005	0.56	0.42	0.58	0.48	2.04
2004	0.40	0.47	0.61	0.31	1.79

Fiscal year ended Dec. 31. Next earnings report expected: Late January. EPS Estimates based on S&P Operating Earnings; historical GAAP earnings are as reported.

Dividend Data (Dates: mm/dd Payment Date: mm/dd/yy)

Amount ($)	Date Decl.	Ex-Div. Date	Stk. of Record	Payment Date
0.500	01/22	02/26	03/02	03/16/09
0.500	05/27	06/04	06/08	06/22/09
0.500	07/23	08/28	09/01	09/15/09
0.550	09/24	11/27	12/01	12/15/09

Dividends have been paid since 1976. Source: Company reports.

Please read the Required Disclosures and Analyst Certification on the last page of this report.

The McGraw·Hill Companies

McDonald's Corp

**STANDARD
&POOR'S**

Business Summary November 16, 2009

CORPORATE OVERVIEW. With one of the world's most widely known brand names, McDonald's operates and franchises of more than 32,000 restaurants in 118 countries. Systemwide sales totaled $70.7 billion in 2008, up from $64.1 billion in 2007.

In the U.S., the McDonald's chain leads the $157 billion quick-service restaurant industry. With U.S. systemwide sales of $30 billion, its domestic business is several times larger than its closest competitors, Burger King and Wendy's Old Fashioned Hamburgers. MCD's international segment has supplied much of its earnings growth over the past two decades, and, in 2008, contributed 53% of operating income (before corporate expenses and one-time charges). All restaurants are operated by MCD, franchisees, or affiliates under joint venture agreements.

In August 2007, the company completed the sale of its existing businesses in Brazil, Argentina, Mexico, Puerto Rico, Venezuela and 13 other countries in Latin America and the Caribbean to a developmental licensee (the Latam transaction). The company recorded impairment charges totaling approximately $1.7 billion, substantially all of which was non-cash. The charges included approximately $892 million for the difference between the net book value of the Latam business and the approximately $680 million in cash proceeds, and $773 million in foreign currency translation losses previously included in

comprehensive income.

CORPORATE STRATEGY. In 2009, the company will continue its "Plan to Win" corporate strategy that it commenced in 2003. This strategy focuses on product development and investment in existing properties, rather than on expansion and price discounting. MCD's stated operating priorities include fixing operating inadequacies in existing restaurants; taking a more integrated and focused approach to growth, with an emphasis on increasing sales, margins and returns in existing restaurants; and ensuring the correct operating structure and resources, aligned behind focusing priorities that create benefits for its customers and restaurants.

A significant part of the new corporate strategy was to de-emphasize Partner Brands concepts in order to focus on the McDonald's brand. In 2006 and 2007, MCD disposed of interests in the Chipotle Mexican Grill restaurant concept as well as the Boston Market chain, and it sold its minority interest in Pret a Manger in 2008.

Company Financials Fiscal Year Ended Dec. 31

Per Share Data ($)	2008	2007	2006	2005	2004	2003	2002	2001	2000	1999
Tangible Book Value	10.00	11.14	11.01	10.45	9.74	8.18	6.88	6.30	5.86	6.20
Cash Flow	4.78	2.87	3.29	3.05	2.73	2.08	1.59	2.08	2.20	2.07
Earnings	3.76	1.93	2.30	2.04	1.79	1.18	0.77	1.25	1.46	1.39
S&P Core Earnings	3.60	1.88	2.28	2.00	1.66	0.96	0.51	1.01	NA	NA
Dividends	1.63	1.50	1.00	0.67	0.55	0.40	0.24	0.23	0.22	0.20
Payout Ratio	43%	78%	43%	33%	31%	34%	31%	18%	15%	14%
Prices:High	67.00	63.69	44.68	35.69	32.96	27.01	30.72	35.06	43.63	49.56
Prices:Low	45.79	42.31	31.73	27.36	24.54	12.12	15.17	24.75	26.38	35.94
P/E Ratio:High	18	33	19	17	18	23	40	28	30	36
P/E Ratio:Low	12	22	14	13	14	10	20	20	18	26

Income Statement Analysis (Million $)										
Revenue	23,522	22,787	21,586	20,460	19,065	17,141	15,406	14,870	14,243	13,259
Operating Income	7,445	6,683	5,829	5,243	4,742	3,980	3,164	3,983	4,144	4,171
Depreciation	1,162	1,145	1,250	1,250	1,201	1,148	1,051	1,086	1,011	956
Interest Expense	535	417	402	356	358	388	360	452	430	396
Pretax Income	6,158	3,572	4,166	3,702	3,202	2,346	1,662	2,330	2,882	2,884
Effective Tax Rate	30.0%	34.6%	31.0%	29.7%	28.9%	35.7%	40.3%	29.8%	31.4%	32.5%
Net Income	4,313	2,335	2,873	2,602	2,279	1,508	992	1,637	1,977	1,948
S&P Core Earnings	4,127	2,277	2,848	2,540	2,100	1,226	667	1,328	NA	NA

Balance Sheet & Other Financial Data (Million $)										
Cash	2,063	1,981	2,136	4,260	1,380	493	330	418	422	420
Current Assets	3,518	3,582	3,625	5,850	2,858	1,885	1,715	1,819	1,662	1,572
Total Assets	28,462	29,392	29,024	29,989	27,838	25,525	23,971	22,535	21,683	20,983
Current Liabilities	2,538	4,499	3,008	4,036	3,521	2,486	2,422	2,248	2,361	3,274
Long Term Debt	10,186	7,310	8,417	8,937	8,357	9,343	9,704	8,556	7,844	5,632
Common Equity	13,383	15,280	15,458	15,146	14,202	11,982	10,281	9,488	9,204	9,639
Total Capital	24,514	23,551	24,941	25,060	23,340	22,340	20,988	19,156	18,133	16,445
Capital Expenditures	2,136	1,947	1,742	1,607	1,419	1,307	2,004	1,906	1,945	1,868
Cash Flow	5,475	3,480	4,123	3,852	3,480	2,656	2,043	2,723	2,988	2,904
Current Ratio	1.4	0.8	1.2	1.4	0.8	0.8	0.7	0.8	0.7	0.5
% Long Term Debt of Capitalization	41.6	31.0	33.7	35.7	35.8	41.8	46.2	44.7	43.3	34.2
% Net Income of Revenue	18.3	10.3	13.3	12.7	12.0	8.8	6.4	11.0	13.9	14.7
% Return on Assets	NA	8.9	9.7	9.0	8.5	6.1	4.3	7.4	9.3	9.6
% Return on Equity	NA	15.2	18.8	17.7	17.4	13.5	10.0	17.5	21.0	20.4

Data as orig reptd.; bef. results of disc opers/spec. items. Per share data adj. for stk. divs.; EPS diluted. E-Estimated. NA-Not Available. NM-Not Meaningful. NR-Not Ranked. UR-Under Review.

Office: McDonald's Plaza, Oak Brook, IL 60523.
Telephone: 630-623-3000.
Website: http://www.mcdonalds.com
Chrmn: A.J. McKenna

Pres & COO: R. Alvarez
Vice Chrmn & CEO: J.A. Skinner
EVP & CFO: P.J. Bensen
EVP, Secy & General Counsel: G. Santona

Investor Contact: M.K. Shaw (630-623-7559)
Board Members: R. Alvarez, S. E. Arnold, R. A. Eckert, E. Hernandez, Jr., J. P. Jackson, R. H. Lenny, W. E. Massey, A. J. McKenna, C. D. McMillan, S. A. Penrose, J. W. Rogers, Jr., J. A. Skinner, R. W. Stone, M. D. White

Founded: 1948
Domicile: Delaware
Employees: 400,000

McGraw-Hill Companies Inc. (The)

STANDARD
&POOR'S

S&P Recommendation	**NOT RANKED**	Price	Investment Style
		$30.45 (as of Nov 27, 2009)	Large-Cap Growth

GICS Sector Consumer Discretionary
Sub-Industry Publishing

Summary This leading information services organization serves worldwide markets in education, business, industry, other professions and government.

Key Stock Statistics (Source S&P, Vickers, company reports)

52-Wk Range	$34.10– 17.22	S&P Oper. EPS 2009**E**	**NA**	Market Capitalization(B)	$9.589	Beta	1.13
Trailing 12-Month EPS	$2.17	S&P Oper. EPS 2010**E**	**NA**	Yield (%)	2.96	S&P 3-Yr. Proj. EPS CAGR(%)	
Trailing 12-Month P/E	14.0	P/E on S&P Oper. EPS 2009**E**	**NA**	Dividend Rate/Share	$0.90	S&P Credit Rating	**NR**
$10K Invested 5 Yrs Ago	$7,608	Common Shares Outstg. (M)	314.9	Institutional Ownership (%)	75		

Price Performance

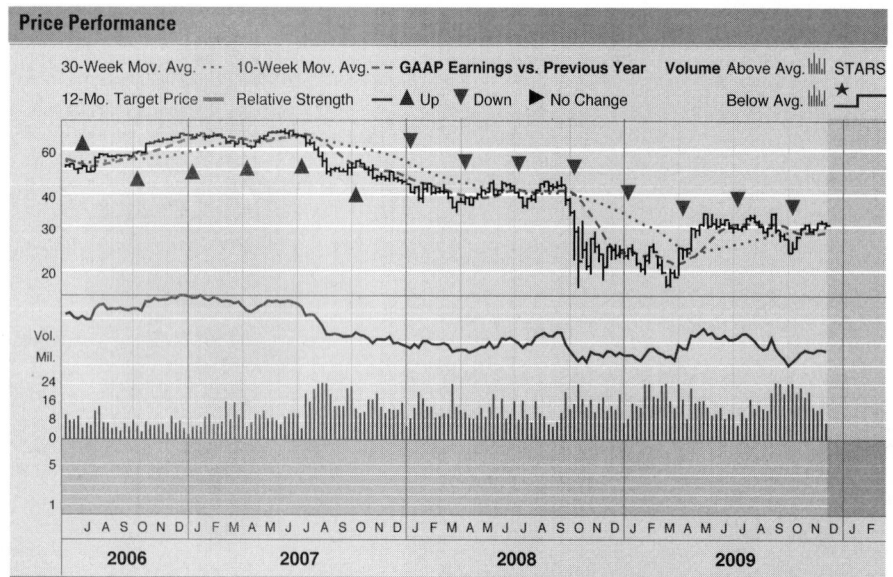

30-Week Mov. Avg. · · · · 10-Week Mov. Avg. - - **GAAP Earnings vs. Previous Year** Volume Above Avg. STARS
12-Mo. Target Price — Relative Strength — ▲ Up ▼ Down ▶ No Change Below Avg.

Options: ASE, CBOE, P, Ph

Analysis prepared by **Tom Graves, CFA** on October 29, 2009, when the stock traded at **$ 29.90**.

Highlights

► In October 2009, MHP said it had agreed to sell BusinessWeek to Bloomberg L.P., with the transaction expected to close in the fourth quarter. In July 2009, MHP reported a second quarter charge of $0.03 a share, including employee severance costs related to a work force reduction of about 550 positions, and a reversal of some severance estimates related to prior restructuring initiatives. The second quarter also included a $0.03 a share loss on the divestiture of MHP's Vista Research business.

► In late October 2009, excluding the second quarter restructuring charge, the loss related to the sale of its Vista business, and a projected $0.02 gain on the sale of BusinessWeek, MHP said it expects 2009 EPS at the top end of a $2.20 to $2.25 guidance range. Excluding restructuring charges and the loss on Vista, MHP expects profit margin declines in all three of its operating segments in 2009.

► At September 30, 2009, MHP had gross debt of $1.2 billion, and $957 million of cash and equivalents.

Investment Rationale/Risk

► In late October 2009, MHP said it expects 2009 free cash flow (after investments, dividends, and a recent pension contribution) to exceed $500 million, compared to $455.2 million in 2008. Also, MHP said that pre-publication investments are expected to be about $200 million in 2009, down from $254 million in 2008. MHP anticipated 2009 expenditures for property and equipment of $75 million to $80 million, down from $106 million in 2008; and depreciation and amortization charges of $445 million to $450 million, compared to $449 million in 2008.

► MHP noted in its 2008 10-K report filed with the SEC in February 2009 that possible risk factors for the company include a reduction in the volume of debt securities issued in capital markets, changes in educational funding, and possible loss of market share or revenue due to competition or regulation.

► Standard & Poor's is a division of MHP, and provides no EPS estimates, target price or recommendation for the company.

Qualitative Risk Assessment

A Qualitative Risk Assessment is not available for this company.

Quantitative Evaluations

S&P Quality Ranking NR

D	C	B-	B	B+	A-	A	A+

Relative Strength Rank MODERATE

69

LOWEST = 1   HIGHEST = 99

Revenue/Earnings Data

Revenue (Million $)

	1Q	2Q	3Q	4Q	Year
2009	1,148	1,465	1,876	--	--
2008	1,218	1,673	2,049	1,415	6,355
2007	1,296	1,718	2,188	1,570	6,772
2006	1,141	1,528	1,993	1,594	6,255
2005	1,029	1,456	1,977	1,541	6,004
2004	919.9	1,246	1,723	1,362	5,251

Earnings Per Share ($)

2009	0.20	0.52	1.07	--	--
2008	0.25	0.66	1.23	0.37	2.51
2007	0.40	0.79	1.34	0.43	2.94
2006	0.20	0.60	1.06	0.56	2.40
2005	0.21	0.51	1.00	0.50	2.21
2004	0.20	0.43	0.85	0.49	1.96

Fiscal year ended Dec. 31. Next earnings report expected: Late January. EPS Estimates based on S&P Operating Earnings; historical GAAP earnings are as reported.

Dividend Data (Dates: mm/dd Payment Date: mm/dd/yy)

Amount ($)	Date Decl.	Ex-Div. Date	Stk. of Record	Payment Date
0.225	01/28	02/23	02/25	03/11/09
0.225	04/29	05/22	05/27	06/10/09
0.225	07/29	08/24	08/26	09/10/09
0.225	10/28	11/23	11/25	12/10/09

Dividends have been paid since 1937. Source: Company reports.

McGraw-Hill Companies Inc. (The)

STANDARD
&POOR'S

Business Summary October 29, 2009

CORPORATE OVERVIEW. The McGraw-Hill Companies, Inc. is a leading provider of information products and services to business, professional and education markets worldwide. The company believes that through acquisitions, new product and service development, and a strong commitment to customer service, many of its business units have grown to be leaders in their respective fields. Well known brands include Standard & Poor's, Platts, F.W. Dodge and Sweet's.

The Financial Services segment (42% of revenues and 72% of segment operating profit in 2008) operates under the Standard & Poor's brand and provides credit ratings, evaluation services, and analyses globally on corporations, financial institutions, securitized and project financings, and local, state and sovereign governments. The company believes it is the world's leading provider of credit analysis and information, incorporating the largest global network of credit ratings professionals. In 2005, MHP acquired majority ownership of Crisil Limited, a leading provider of credit ratings, financial news and risk and policy advisory services in India. In 2004, MHP acquired privately owned Capital IQ, a provider of information solutions to the global investment and financial services communities. In May 2009, MHP announced the sale of its Vista Research business to Guidepoint Global, LLC. MHP had acquired Vista, a leading provider of primary research, in 2005. In February 2007, MHP

announced the sale of its mutual fund data business to Morningstar, Inc.

McGraw-Hill Education (42%, 22%) is comprised of two operating groups -- the School Education Group (SEG) and the Higher Education, Professional and International Group (HPI). SEG provides educational and professional materials in the U.S. to the pre-K to 12th grade market, and is a leading provider of assessment and reporting services. In July 2004, MHP acquired The Grow Network, a privately held company now part of SEG that provides assessment reporting and customized content for states and large school districts across the U.S.

HPI serves a global market offering e-books, on-line tutoring, customized course websites and subscription services, as well as traditional materials for college, university and post-graduate courses. Professional operations focus on professional, reference and trade publishing for medical, business, engineering and other professions. International operations cover markets worldwide with locally developed and English-language materials.

Company Financials Fiscal Year Ended Dec. 31

Per Share Data ($)	2008	2007	2006	2005	2004	2003	2002	2001	2000	1999
Tangible Book Value	NM	NM	1.00	2.04	2.72	2.24	0.94	0.09	0.17	1.12
Cash Flow	3.07	3.41	2.85	3.21	2.98	2.84	1.71	2.04	2.13	1.85
Earnings	2.51	2.94	2.40	2.21	1.96	1.79	1.48	0.96	1.21	1.07
S&P Core Earnings	2.29	2.89	2.38	2.05	1.80	1.44	1.15	0.60	NA	NA
Dividends	0.88	0.82	0.73	0.66	0.60	0.54	0.51	0.49	0.47	0.43
Payout Ratio	35%	28%	30%	30%	31%	30%	34%	51%	39%	40%
Prices:High	47.13	72.50	69.25	53.97	46.06	35.00	34.85	35.44	33.84	31.56
Prices:Low	17.15	43.46	46.37	40.51	34.55	25.87	25.36	24.35	20.94	23.56
P/E Ratio:High	19	25	29	24	23	20	24	37	28	29
P/E Ratio:Low	7	15	19	18	18	14	17	25	17	22

Income Statement Analysis (Million $)										
Revenue	6,355	6,772	6,255	6,004	5,251	4,828	4,788	4,646	4,281	3,992
Operating Income	1,607	1,846	1,580	1,749	1,467	1,369	1,037	1,044	1,128	984
Depreciation	178	161	162	385	393	403	89.6	421	362	308
Interest Expense	75.6	40.6	13.6	5.20	5.79	7.10	22.5	55.1	52.8	42.0
Pretax Income	1,279	1,623	1,405	1,360	1,169	1,130	905	615	767	698
Effective Tax Rate	37.5%	37.5%	37.2%	37.9%	35.3%	39.1%	36.3%	38.7%	38.5%	39.0%
Net Income	799	1,014	882	844	756	688	577	377	472	426
S&P Core Earnings	729	995	874	786	694	552	446	233	NA	NA

Balance Sheet & Other Financial Data (Million $)										
Cash	472	396	353	749	681	696	58.2	53.5	3.17	6.49
Current Assets	2,303	2,333	2,258	2,591	2,448	2,256	1,674	1,813	1,802	1,554
Total Assets	6,080	6,357	6,043	6,396	5,863	5,394	5,032	5,161	4,931	4,089
Current Liabilities	2,531	2,657	2,468	2,225	1,969	1,994	1,775	1,876	1,781	1,525
Long Term Debt	1,198	1,197	0.31	0.34	0.51	0.39	459	834	818	355
Common Equity	1,282	1,607	7,785	3,113	4,952	2,557	2,202	1,884	1,761	1,691
Total Capital	2,480	2,943	7,936	3,432	5,185	2,758	2,861	2,908	2,742	2,182
Capital Expenditures	106	230	127	120	139	115	70.0	117	97.7	154
Cash Flow	978	1,175	1,044	1,230	1,149	1,091	666	798	834	734
Current Ratio	0.9	0.9	0.9	1.2	1.2	1.1	0.9	1.0	1.0	1.0
% Long Term Debt of Capitalization	48.2	40.7	NM	0.0	0.0	0.0	16.0	28.7	29.8	16.3
% Net Income of Revenue	12.6	15.0	14.1	14.1	14.4	14.2	12.0	8.1	11.0	10.7
% Return on Assets	12.8	16.3	14.2	13.8	13.5	13.2	11.3	7.5	10.4	10.8
% Return on Equity	55.3	47.3	12.8	27.7	16.5	29.1	28.2	20.5	27.7	26.3

Data as orig reptd.; bef. results of disc opers/spec. items. Per share data adj. for stk. divs.; EPS diluted. E-Estimated. NA-Not Available. NM-Not Meaningful. NR-Not Ranked. UR-Under Review.

Office: 1221 Avenue Of The Americas, New York, NY 10020-1095.
Telephone: 212-512-2000.
Email: investor_relations@mcgraw-hill.com
Website: http://www.mcgraw-hill.com

Chrmn, Pres & CEO: H. McGraw, III
EVP & CFO: R.J. Bahash
EVP & General Counsel: K.M. Vittor
EVP & CIO: B.D. Marcus

SVP, Chief Acctg Officer & Cntlr: E. Korakis
Investor Contact: D.S. Rubin (212-512-4321)
Board Members: P. A. Armella, W. Bischoff, D. N. Daft, L. K. Lorimer, R. P. McGraw, H. McGraw, III, H. O. Ochoa-Brillembourg, M. Rake, E. B. Rust, Jr., K. L. Schmoke, S. Taurel

Founded: 1899
Domicile: New York
Employees: 21,649

McKesson Corp

STANDARD
&POOR'S

S&P Recommendation	STRONG BUY ★★★★★	Price	12-Mo. Target Price	Investment Style
		$62.75 (as of Nov 27, 2009)	$73.00	Large-Cap Blend

GICS Sector Health Care
Sub-Industry Health Care Distributors

Summary This company (formerly McKesson HBOC) provides pharmaceutical supply management and information technologies to a broad range of health care customers.

Key Stock Statistics (Source S&P, Vickers, company reports)

52-Wk Range	$64.98–31.34	S&P Oper. EPS 2010**E**	4.55	Market Capitalization(B)	$16.816	Beta	0.85
Trailing 12-Month EPS	$3.10	S&P Oper. EPS 2011**E**	4.85	Yield (%)	0.76	S&P 3-Yr. Proj. EPS CAGR(%)	8
Trailing 12-Month P/E	20.2	P/E on S&P Oper. EPS 2010**E**	13.8	Dividend Rate/Share	$0.48	S&P Credit Rating	BBB+
$10K Invested 5 Yrs Ago	$22,274	Common Shares Outstg. (M)	268.0	Institutional Ownership (%)	87		

Price Performance

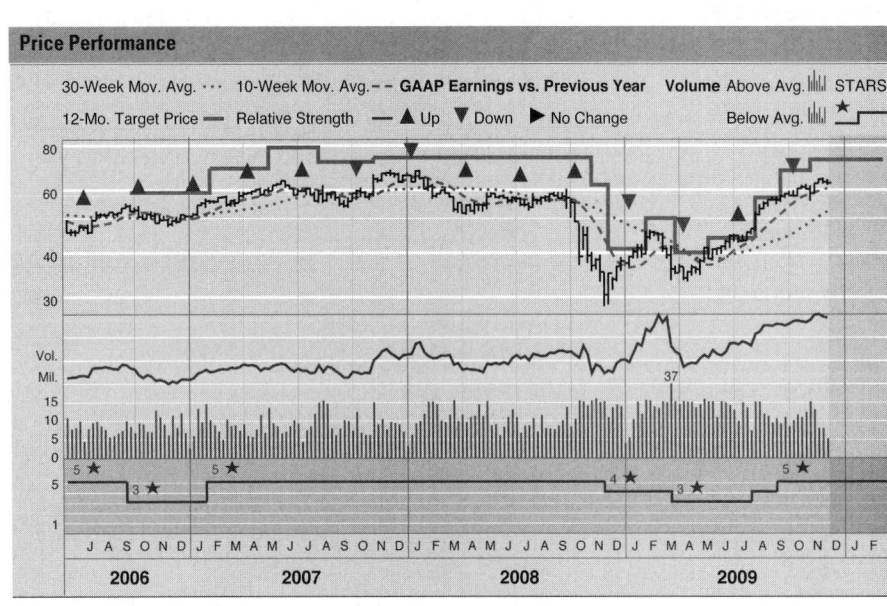

30-Week Mov. Avg. ··· 10-Week Mov. Avg. - - GAAP Earnings vs. Previous Year Volume Above Avg. STARS
12-Mo. Target Price — Relative Strength — ▲ Up ▼ Down ► No Change Below Avg.

Options: ASE, CBOE, P, Ph

Analysis prepared by **Phillip M. Seligman** on November 04, 2009, when the stock traded at **$ 60.74**.

Highlights

► For FY 10 (Mar.), we forecast companywide revenues to rise 1.6%, following FY 09's 4.8% increase. Drivers we see include 1.5% higher drug distribution (part of McKesson Distribution Solutions, MDS) revenues, down from FY 09's 4.9% advance, as gains from existing accounts and a May 2008 acquisition are offset by the loss of two buying group customers that accounted for $3 billion in volume, and generic drugs' low prices. We see 6.7% higher medical-surgical (also part of MDS) sales, above that unit's 5.9% growth in FY 09, partly related to the H1N1 flu outbreak, and 2.2% McKesson Technology Solutions (MTS) revenue growth, following a 2.7% rise in FY 09, on hospitals' capital spending cutbacks.

► We expect firmwide operating margins to widen slightly in FY 10, as the margin benefits from generic drug penetration, cost controls and flu-related sales outweigh the impact of slower IT sales and sell-margin pressure.

► We project FY 10 operating EPS of $4.55, versus FY 09's $3.88 before $0.89 in net one-time costs. We look for EPS of $4.85 in FY 11.

Investment Rationale/Risk

► We remain encouraged by what we view as MCK's bright prospects. We believe the U.S. Centers for Disease Control's choice of MCK as the exclusive distributor of the H1N1 flu vaccine gives the company some prestige in the competitive drug distribution space. We also view the high-margin MTS segment as poised to benefit greatly from stimulus-related spending, and assume bookings from hospitals will start in late FY 10/early FY 11. Moreover, assuming health care reform eventually occurs, we see more people able to afford pharmaceuticals. Meanwhile, excluding the customer losses, MCK has been matching the market in pharmaceutical distribution revenue growth, while earnings benefit from an improved product mix and cost control initiatives. Elsewhere, we are encouraged by what we see as MCK's healthy cash flow, which should provide financial flexibility.

► Risks to our recommendation and target price include the loss of major accounts and unfavorable regulatory changes.

► Our 12-month target price of $73 is derived by applying an above-peers P/E of 15.3X to our calendar 2010 EPS estimate of $4.78.

Qualitative Risk Assessment

LOW	MEDIUM	HIGH

Our risk assessment reflects our view of MCK's improving profitability and the growing demand for its highly profitable IT products and services, offset by our belief that the company is more price competitive than peers and that future drugmaker-distributor contract negotiations might be less favorable for distributors.

Quantitative Evaluations

S&P Quality Ranking B+

D	C	B-	B	B+	A-	A	A+

Relative Strength Rank STRONG

78

LOWEST = 1   HIGHEST = 99

Revenue/Earnings Data

Revenue (Million $)

	1Q	2Q	3Q	4Q	Year
2010	26,657	27,130	--	--	--
2009	26,704	26,574	27,130	26,224	106,632
2008	24,528	24,450	26,494	26,231	101,703
2007	23,315	22,386	23,111	24,165	92,977
2006	20,968	21,515	22,510	23,057	88,050
2005	19,187	19,934	20,782	20,612	80,515

Earnings Per Share ($)

2010	1.06	1.11	E1.19	E1.23	E4.55
2009	0.83	1.17	-0.07	1.01	2.99
2008	0.77	0.83	0.68	1.05	3.32
2007	0.60	0.94	0.79	0.85	3.17
2006	0.55	0.49	0.61	0.70	2.34
2005	0.55	0.29	-2.26	0.85	-0.53

Fiscal year ended Mar. 31. Next earnings report expected: Late January. EPS Estimates based on S&P Operating Earnings; historical GAAP earnings are as reported.

Dividend Data (Dates: mm/dd Payment Date: mm/dd/yy)

Amount ($)	Date Decl.	Ex-Div. Date	Stk. of Record	Payment Date
0.120	01/21	02/26	03/02	04/01/09
0.120	05/27	06/08	06/10	07/01/09
0.120	07/22	08/28	09/01	10/01/09
0.120	10/30	11/27	12/01	01/04/10

Dividends have been paid since 1995. Source: Company reports.

Please read the Required Disclosures and Analyst Certification on the last page of this report.

The McGraw·Hill Companies

McKesson Corp

STANDARD
&POOR'S

Business Summary November 04, 2009

CORPORATE OVERVIEW. McKesson Corp. is a leading distributor of medical products and supplies and health care information technology products and services. Beginning in FY 08 (Mar.), MCK started reporting its results in two segments:

McKesson Distribution Solutions (MDS; 97.1% of FY 09 revenue on a pro forma basis) includes what was previously reported as Pharmaceutical Solutions and Medical-Surgical Solutions, with the exception of its Payor business. The pharmaceutical distribution unit primarily distributes ethical and proprietary drugs and health and beauty care, and focuses on three customer segments: retail independent pharmacies, retail chains, and institutions, in all 50 states and Canada. The medical-surgical distribution unit provides medical-surgical supplies, equipment, logistics and related services to alternate-site health care providers, including physicians' offices, long-term care and home care. Through its investment in Parata Systems, MDS also markets automated pharmacy systems to hospitals and retail pharmacies.

McKesson Technology Solutions (MTS; 2.9%) consists primarily of the former

Provider Technologies segment and the aforementioned Payor business. MTS delivers enterprise-wide patient care, clinical, financial, supply chain, and strategic management software solutions, pharmacy automation for hospitals, as well as connectivity, outsourcing and other services, to health care organizations throughout North America, the United Kingdom and other European countries. Its customers include hospitals, physicians, home care providers, retail pharmacies and payors.

CORPORATE STRATEGY. Distribution agreements between distributors and most drugmakers have transitioned toward a more fee-based approach, with the distributors appropriately and predictably compensated for distribution and related logistic and administrative services and data, in our opinion. MCK and its peers see over 80% of their drugmaker compensation as fixed and not dependent upon drug price inflation.

Company Financials Fiscal Year Ended Mar. 31

Per Share Data ($)	2009	2008	2007	2006	2005	2004	2003	2002	2001	2000
Tangible Book Value	4.83	10.42	9.10	13.36	12.47	12.66	10.57	9.81	8.55	8.40
Cash Flow	3.89	4.09	4.14	3.28	0.32	2.94	2.65	2.20	0.72	1.37
Earnings	2.99	3.32	3.17	2.34	-0.53	2.19	1.90	1.43	-0.15	0.66
S&P Core Earnings	4.16	3.33	3.16	2.07	1.93	1.29	1.24	0.87	-0.39	NA
Dividends	0.24	0.24	0.24	0.24	0.24	0.24	0.24	0.24	0.24	0.31
Payout Ratio	8%	7%	8%	10%	NM	11%	13%	17%	NM	46%
Calendar Year	2008	2007	2006	2005	2004	2003	2002	2001	2000	1999
Prices:High	68.40	68.43	55.10	52.89	35.90	37.14	42.09	41.50	37.00	89.75
Prices:Low	28.27	50.80	44.60	30.13	22.61	22.61	24.99	23.40	16.00	18.56
P/E Ratio:High	23	21	17	23	NM	17	22	29	NM	NM
P/E Ratio:Low	9	15	14	13	NM	10	13	16	NM	NM

Income Statement Analysis (Million $)										
Revenue	106,632	101,703	92,977	88,050	80,515	69,506	57,121	50,006	42,010	36,734
Operating Income	1,951	1,736	1,553	1,425	1,260	1,216	1,134	923	454	359
Depreciation	261	231	295	266	251	232	204	208	246	201
Interest Expense	144	142	99.0	94.0	118	120	121	119	118	120
Pretax Income	1,064	1,457	1,297	1,158	-240	911	855	601	9.60	307
Effective Tax Rate	22.7%	32.1%	25.4%	36.4%	NM	29.1%	34.3%	30.4%	NM	39.7%
Net Income	823	989	968	737	-157	646	562	419	-42.7	185
S&P Core Earnings	1,159	991	964	650	565	380	364	255	-113	NA

Balance Sheet & Other Financial Data (Million $)										
Cash	2,109	1,362	1,954	2,142	1,809	718	534	563	446	606
Current Assets	18,671	17,786	17,856	16,919	15,332	13,004	11,254	10,699	9,164	7,966
Total Assets	25,267	24,603	23,943	20,975	18,775	16,240	14,353	13,324	11,530	10,373
Current Liabilities	15,606	15,348	15,126	13,515	11,793	9,456	7,974	7,588	6,550	5,122
Long Term Debt	2,290	1,795	1,803	965	1,202	1,210	1,487	1,485	1,232	1,440
Common Equity	6,193	6,121	6,273	5,907	5,275	5,165	4,529	3,940	3,493	4,213
Total Capital	8,483	7,916	8,076	6,872	6,477	6,375	6,016	5,425	4,724	5,653
Capital Expenditures	195	195	126	167	140	115	116	132	159	145
Cash Flow	1,084	1,220	1,263	1,003	94.2	879	766	626	203	386
Current Ratio	1.2	1.2	1.2	1.3	1.3	1.4	1.4	1.4	1.4	1.6
% Long Term Debt of Capitalization	27.0	22.7	22.3	14.0	18.6	19.0	24.7	27.4	26.1	25.5
% Net Income of Revenue	0.8	1.0	1.0	0.8	NM	0.9	1.0	0.8	NM	0.5
% Return on Assets	3.3	4.1	4.3	3.7	NM	4.2	4.1	3.4	NM	1.9
% Return on Equity	13.4	16.0	15.9	13.2	NM	13.3	13.3	11.3	NM	4.8

Data as orig reptd.; bef. results of disc opers/spec. items. Per share data adj. for stk. divs.; EPS diluted. E-Estimated. NA-Not Available. NM-Not Meaningful. NR-Not Ranked. UR-Under Review.

Office: One Post St McKesson Plaza, San Francisco, CA 94104-5296.
Telephone: 415-983-8300.
Email: investors@mckesson.com
Website: http://www.mckesson.com

Chrmn, Pres & CEO: J. Hammergren
EVP & CFO: J. Campbell
EVP, CTO & CIO: R. Spratt
EVP, Secy & General Counsel: L.E. Seeger

Chief Acctg Officer & Cntlr: N.A. Rees
Investor Contact: J.C. Campbell (800-826-9360)
Board Members: A. Bryant, W. A. Budd, J. Hammergren, A. F. Irby, III, M. C. Jacobs, M. L. Knowles, D. M. Lawrence, E. A. Mueller, J. E. Shaw

Founded: 1994
Domicile: Delaware
Employees: 32,500

MeadWestvaco Corp

STANDARD &POOR'S

S&P Recommendation **BUY** ★★★★☆	Price $26.46 (as of Nov 27, 2009)	12-Mo. Target Price $26.00	Investment Style Large-Cap Value

GICS Sector Materials
Sub-Industry Paper Products

Summary This company is primarily a major producer of paperboard packaging used in a variety of consumer markets.

Key Stock Statistics (Source S&P, Vickers, company reports)

52-Wk Range	$27.43– 7.53	S&P Oper. EPS 2009**E**	0.65	Market Capitalization(B)	$4.528	Beta	1.73
Trailing 12-Month EPS	$0.92	S&P Oper. EPS 2010**E**	0.90	Yield (%)	3.48	S&P 3-Yr. Proj. EPS CAGR(%)	20
Trailing 12-Month P/E	28.8	P/E on S&P Oper. EPS 2009**E**	40.7	Dividend Rate/Share	$0.92	S&P Credit Rating	BBB
$10K Invested 5 Yrs Ago	$9,424	Common Shares Outstg. (M)	171.1	Institutional Ownership (%)	85		

Price Performance

30-Week Mov. Avg. ···· 10-Week Mov. Avg. -- **GAAP Earnings vs. Previous Year** Volume Above Avg. ▮▮▮ STARS
12-Mo. Target Price — Relative Strength — ▲ Up ▼ Down ▶ No Change   Below Avg. ▮▮▮ ★

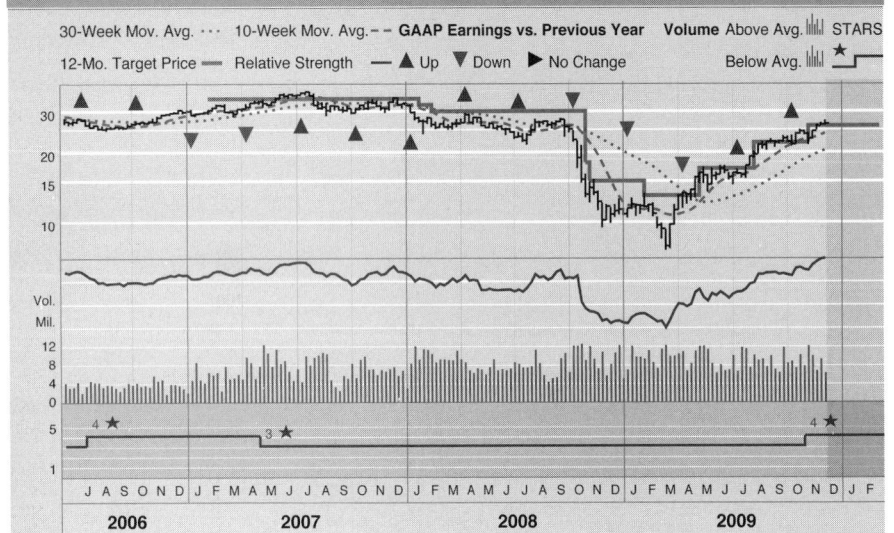

Options: ASE, CBOE, P

Analysis prepared by **Stuart J. Benway, CFA** on October 30, 2009, when the stock traded at **$ 23.35**.

Highlights

► We expect sales to rebound by about 5% in 2010 after an expected 10% decline in 2009. Demand for media and office products is likely to be weak due to secular declines in usage for CDs, DVDs and time management products. MWV has also shut several facilities and eliminated certain product lines. However, we expect economic activity to improve moderately in 2010, which should boost demand for beverage packaging and home and garden supplies.

► We anticipate continuing margin improvement in 2010. Weak demand in 2009 prompted management to reduce its product line and close several manufacturing facilities. We expect the lower costs from reduced overhead and improved manufacturing efficiencies to bolster margins in 2010. Our forecast is for operating margins to widen to 6.5% in 2010 from an estimated 5.5% in 2009 and 2.2% in 2008.

► Our operating EPS forecast for 2009 is $0.65 (excluding charges), and for 2010 we forecast $0.90, including modest land sales gains, which could be significant in certain quarters.

Investment Rationale/Risk

► We believe that volume trends in the packaging sector will remain subdued in the near term due to reduced compact disc sales, an increased emphasis on packaging reduction, and weak economic output. However, we think that MWV has valuable land that it will sell gradually over the long term, and is well positioned in certain higher-growth packaging markets. MWV's strong position in emerging markets and its moves to eliminate low-margin product lines should also aid long-term growth.

► Risks to our recommendation and target price include a weaker-than-expected global economy, softer-than-projected demand and pricing trends for the company's packaging grades, and a renewed rise in energy and raw material costs.

► Our discounted cash flow model, which assumes a weighted average cost of capital of 9.2%, large non-cash depreciation charges, solid cash flow generation in 2010, and growth in perpetuity of 3%, values the shares at $26, which is our 12-month target price.

Qualitative Risk Assessment

LOW	MEDIUM	HIGH

MWV operates in a moderately cyclical and seasonal sector and is subject to swings in certain commodity prices. However, it has some pricing power due to its high market share, and its debt levels are low relative to many of its peers.

Quantitative Evaluations

S&P Quality Ranking B-

D	C	B-	B	B+	A-	A	A+

Relative Strength Rank STRONG

90

LOWEST = 1   HIGHEST = 99

Revenue/Earnings Data

Revenue (Million $)

	1Q	2Q	3Q	4Q	Year
2009	1,354	1,432	1,627	--	--
2008	1,518	1,709	1,811	1,599	6,637
2007	1,552	1,706	1,796	1,852	6,906
2006	1,434	1,570	1,751	1,775	6,530
2005	1,373	1,587	1,583	1,627	6,170
2004	1,833	2,095	2,148	2,151	8,227

Earnings Per Share ($)

2009	-0.46	0.72	0.74	E0.17	E0.65
2008	-0.05	0.33	0.26	-0.09	0.46
2007	-0.09	0.17	0.66	0.82	1.55
2006	0.02	-0.04	0.31	0.23	0.52
2005	0.08	-0.06	0.30	0.33	0.62
2004	-0.01	0.24	0.52	-2.45	-1.73

Fiscal year ended Dec. 31. Next earnings report expected: Late January. EPS Estimates based on S&P Operating Earnings; historical GAAP earnings are as reported.

Dividend Data (Dates: mm/dd Payment Date: mm/dd/yy)

Amount ($)	Date Decl.	Ex-Div. Date	Stk. of Record	Payment Date
0.230	01/26	02/03	02/05	03/02/09
0.230	04/27	05/05	05/07	06/01/09
0.230	06/23	07/30	08/03	09/01/09
0.230	11/17	11/24	11/27	12/01/09

Dividends have been paid since 1892. Source: Company reports.

Please read the Required Disclosures and Analyst Certification on the last page of this report.

The McGraw-Hill Companies

MeadWestvaco Corp

STANDARD &POOR'S

Business Summary October 30, 2009

CORPORATE OVERVIEW. Through a series of mergers and divestitures, Mead-Westvaco has molded itself into one of the largest producers of packaging products in the world, and it is also a major supplier of consumer and office products and specialty chemicals. The Packaging Resources segment (38% of 2008 revenues) produces bleached paperboard, coated paperboard, kraft paperboard, linerboard and saturating kraft, and packaging for consumer products including beverage and dairy, cosmetics, tobacco, pharmaceuticals, and health care products. Some of the company's major customers include Altria, Anheuser-Busch, Coca-Cola and Procter & Gamble. The Consumer Solutions segment (36%) sells a full range of consumer packaging products, including printed plastic packaging and injection-molded products used for packaging DVDs, CDs, cosmetics, and pharmaceuticals, and plastic dispensing and spraying systems for worldwide personal care, health care, fragrance, and lawn and garden markets. The Consumer and Office Products segment (15%) makes, markets and distributes school and office products, time management products, and envelopes. The Specialty Chemicals segment (8%) produces, markets and distributes specialty chemicals derived from sawdust and other by-products of the pulp and papermaking process. These chemicals include activated carbon, printing ink resins, emulsifiers used in asphalt paving, and

dyestuffs. Real estate and corporate and other accounted for 3% of sales in 2008. The company also owns about 800,000 acres of forest lands in the U.S.

MARKET PROFILE. MeadWestvaco is the largest producer of paperboard, also known as folding boxboard or cartonboard, in North America, with a share of about 16%, according to Pulp & Paper magazine. The market is somewhat fragmented, with more than 15 companies accounting for at least a 1% share, although the top three producers control 36% of the industry. Unlike containerboard, paperboard has a bendable quality for creasing, scoring and shaping, and usually packages single items meant for consumer purchase. It is used in a variety of consumer applications where print quality, strength and customer appeal are important. Folding carton demand is primarily driven by consumer spending and industrial production. We believe the company's market position, technical expertise and product line diversity give it a moderate level of control over pricing.

Company Financials Fiscal Year Ended Dec. 31

Per Share Data ($)	2008	2007	2006	2005	2004	2003	2002	2001	2000	1999
Tangible Book Value	9.37	13.52	14.74	14.58	18.44	19.89	20.44	17.34	23.17	21.65
Cash Flow	2.91	4.13	3.37	3.17	1.87	3.60	3.49	4.29	5.63	3.90
Earnings	0.46	1.56	0.52	0.62	-1.73	-0.01	-0.01	0.87	2.53	1.11
S&P Core Earnings	-0.68	0.21	-0.11	0.27	-2.67	-0.81	-1.37	-1.04	NA	NA
Dividends	0.92	0.92	0.92	0.92	0.92	0.92	0.92	0.88	0.88	0.88
Payout Ratio	NM	599%	177%	148%	NM	NM	NM	101%	35%	79%
Prices:High	31.44	36.50	30.85	34.33	34.34	29.83	36.50	32.10	34.75	33.50
Prices:Low	9.44	28.39	24.76	25.06	25.16	21.37	15.57	22.68	24.06	20.81
P/E Ratio:High	68	23	59	55	NM	NM	NM	37	14	30
P/E Ratio:Low	21	18	48	40	NM	NM	NM	26	10	19
Income Statement Analysis (Million $)										
Revenue	6,637	6,906	6,530	6,170	8,227	7,553	7,242	3,935	3,663	2,802
Operating Income	734	893	743	818	1,042	855	859	677	869	601
Depreciation	423	473	517	491	726	724	674	347	314	280
Interest Expense	210	219	211	208	278	291	309	208	192	124
Pretax Income	79.0	400	98.0	135	-454	-29.0	-15.0	119	404	148
Effective Tax Rate	NM	28.8%	5.10%	11.9%	NM	NM	NM	25.6%	36.9%	24.9%
Net Income	80.0	285	93.0	119	-349	-2.00	-3.00	88.2	255	111
S&P Core Earnings	-118	36.7	-22.1	50.6	-539	-164	-264	-104	NA	NA
Balance Sheet & Other Financial Data (Million $)										
Cash	549	245	156	297	270	225	372	81.2	255	109
Current Assets	2,161	2,167	2,015	2,030	2,562	2,426	2,431	1,016	1,064	738
Total Assets	8,455	9,837	9,285	8,908	11,681	12,487	12,921	6,787	6,570	4,897
Current Liabilities	1,274	1,455	1,465	1,042	1,751	1,501	1,620	701	567	425
Long Term Debt	2,309	2,375	2,372	2,417	3,427	3,969	4,233	2,660	2,687	1,502
Common Equity	2,967	3,708	3,533	3,483	4,317	4,768	4,831	2,341	2,333	2,171
Total Capital	6,195	7,311	7,082	7,052	9,249	10,415	10,821	6,009	5,927	4,472
Capital Expenditures	288	347	302	305	407	393	377	290	214	229
Cash Flow	503	758	610	610	377	722	671	436	569	392
Current Ratio	1.7	1.5	1.4	1.9	1.5	1.6	1.5	1.4	1.9	1.7
% Long Term Debt of Capitalization	37.3	32.5	33.5	34.3	37.1	38.1	39.1	44.3	45.3	33.6
% Net Income of Revenue	1.2	4.1	1.4	1.9	NM	NM	NM	2.2	7.0	4.0
% Return on Assets	0.9	3.0	1.0	1.2	NM	NM	NM	1.3	4.4	2.2
% Return on Equity	2.4	7.9	2.7	3.1	NM	NM	NM	3.8	11.3	5.0

Data as orig reptd.; bef. results of disc opers/spec. items. Per share data adj. for stk. divs.; EPS diluted. E-Estimated. NA-Not Available. NM-Not Meaningful. NR-Not Ranked. UR-Under Review.

Office: 11013 West Broad St, Glen Allen, VA 23060-5937.
Telephone: 804-327-5200.
Website: http://www.meadwestvaco.com
Chrmn & CEO: J.A. Luke, Jr.

Pres: J.A. Buzzard
SVP & CFO: E.M. Rajkowski
SVP, Secy & General Counsel: W.L. Willkie, II
CTO: M.T. Watkins

Investor Contact: E.M. Rajkowski (804-327-5200)
Board Members: M. E. Campbell, T. W. Cole, Jr., J. G. Kaiser, R. B. Kelson, J. M. Kilts, S. J. Kropf, D. S. Luke, J. A. Luke, Jr., R. C. McCormack, T. H. Powers, E. M. Straw, L. J. Styslinger, Jr., J. L. Warner

Founded: 1846
Domicile: Delaware
Employees: 22,000

The McGraw-Hill Companies

Medco Health Solutions Inc.

STANDARD &POOR'S

S&P Recommendation	STRONG BUY ★★★★★	Price $62.49 (as of Nov 27, 2009)	12-Mo. Target Price $72.00	Investment Style Large-Cap Blend

GICS Sector Health Care
Sub-Industry Health Care Services

Summary Medco, spun off from Merck & Co. in August 2003, is the largest U.S. pharmacy benefit manager (PBM) in terms of revenues and script count.

Key Stock Statistics (Source S&P, Vickers, company reports)

52-Wk Range	$63.32– 36.46	S&P Oper. EPS 2009**E**	2.82	Market Capitalization(B)	$29.793	Beta	0.47
Trailing 12-Month EPS	$2.45	S&P Oper. EPS 2010**E**	3.38	Yield (%)	Nil	S&P 3-Yr. Proj. EPS CAGR(%)	19
Trailing 12-Month P/E	25.5	P/E on S&P Oper. EPS 2009**E**	22.2	Dividend Rate/Share	Nil	S&P Credit Rating	BBB
$10K Invested 5 Yrs Ago	$33,417	Common Shares Outstg. (M)	476.8	Institutional Ownership (%)	77		

Price Performance

30-Week Mov. Avg. · · · 10-Week Mov. Avg. — **GAAP Earnings vs. Previous Year** Volume Above Avg. STARS
12-Mo. Target Price ▬ Relative Strength — ▲ Up ▼ Down ► No Change Below Avg. ★

Options: ASE, CBOE, P, Ph

Analysis prepared by **Phillip M. Seligman** on November 12, 2009, when the stock traded at **$ 61.79**.

Highlights

► We expect revenues to rise by more than 16% in 2009, to $59.6 billion, and another 7.6% in 2010, to slightly under $64.1 billion. Drivers we see include a 99% retention rate of existing business, net new business of more than $8.0 billion for 2009 and over $4.0 billion garnered for 2010 as of November 3, 2009, and brand-name drug price inflation. But we also see growth tempered by the weak economy and the penetration of generic drugs, which carry lower prices but wider margins than branded drugs.

► We believe EBITDA per adjusted prescription, a measure of PBM profitability, will be down modestly, following 2008's 16% growth, since 2009 account wins have lower mail penetration rates and MHS lost accounts with higher mail order volumes. Assuming an improved mail and generic drug penetration and well-controlled SG&A costs, we think EBITDA per adjusted prescription can rise by 10% to 11% in 2010.

► We look for operating EPS before amortization charges of $2.82 in 2009, versus 2008's $2.34, and we see $3.38 in 2010. MHS expects $0.13 from generic drug launches in 2009 and $0.25 in 2010.

Investment Rationale/Risk

► We view the fundamentals of the PBM space as bright, as health plans, governments and employers seek to control drug costs. We believe the weak economy will continue to pressure drug utilization but spur increasing generic drug and mail utilization, which saves consumers money while benefiting PBM margins. Looking ahead, we believe MHS has significant opportunities to expand generic drug mail penetration of its new 2009 accounts, and we expect the company and peers to benefit from pending patent losses of additional brand name drugs. We also view certain health care reform proposals, including an approval pathway for biogenerics, as providing opportunities for PBMs. Elsewhere, we view MHS's cash flow as healthy, providing financial flexibility.

► Risks to our recommendation and target price include intensifying competition and more regulatory oversight.

► Our 12-month target price of $72 is derived by applying a P/E-to-growth ratio of 1.13X, assuming three-year EPS growth of 19%, to our 2010 operating EPS estimate. The PEG ratio reflects MHS's historical discount to peers.

Qualitative Risk Assessment

LOW	MEDIUM	HIGH

Our risk assessment reflects rising drug demand and our view of MHS's improving financial performance and declining debt leverage. However, we believe that intense competition and increased government regulation of pharmacy benefit managers, which we view as likely, could slow long-term progress in profits.

Quantitative Evaluations

S&P Quality Ranking NR

D	C	B-	B	B+	A-	A	A+

Relative Strength Rank STRONG

86

LOWEST = 1 HIGHEST = 99

Revenue/Earnings Data

Revenue (Million $)

	1Q	2Q	3Q	4Q	Year
2009	14,834	14,930	14,795	--	--
2008	12,963	12,775	12,559	12,961	51,258
2007	11,160	11,050	10,919	11,379	44,506
2006	10,564	10,589	10,461	10,930	42,544
2005	8,743	8,999	9,325	10,803	37,871
2004	8,906	8,836	8,697	8,913	35,352

Earnings Per Share ($)

	1Q	2Q	3Q	4Q	Year
2009	0.58	0.64	0.69	E0.75	E2.82
2008	0.50	0.51	0.58	0.54	2.13
2007	0.47	0.38	0.39	0.38	1.63
2006	0.08	0.28	0.31	0.39	1.05
2005	0.24	0.24	0.26	0.29	1.03
2004	0.19	0.23	0.22	0.24	0.88

Fiscal year ended Dec. 31. Next earnings report expected: Late February. EPS Estimates based on S&P Operating Earnings; historical GAAP earnings are as reported.

Dividend Data

No cash dividends have been paid.

Medco Health Solutions Inc.

STANDARD & POOR'S

Business Summary November 12, 2009

CORPORATE OVERVIEW. Medco Health Solutions was spun off to Merck & Co. (MRK) shareholders in a tax-free transaction on August 19, 2003. The company is one of the largest U.S. pharmacy benefit managers (PBMs). It provides programs and services to clients and members of PBMs, and to physicians and pharmacies that they use.

In 2008, MHS processed about 796 million adjusted prescriptions (with one mail-order prescription is the equivalent of three retail prescriptions), compared to 748 million in 2007. Revenues and net income are derived from: rebates and discounts on prescription drugs from pharmaceutical manufacturers; competitive discounts from retail pharmacies; the negotiation of favorable client pricing, including rebate sharing terms; the shift in dispensing volumes from retail to home delivery; and the provision of services in a cost-efficient manner.

Rebates from brand-name pharmaceutical manufacturers, which are reflect-

ed as a reduction in cost of product net revenues, totaled $4,447 million in 2008, $3,561 million in 2007 and $3,417 million in 2006, with formulary rebates representing 54.7%, 50.1% and 51.9% of total rebates, respectively, and market share rebates reflecting the remainder. The increases in rebates reflect improved formulary management and patient compliance, as well as favorable pharmaceutical manufacturer rebate contract revisions, and volume from new 2008 clients, partially offset by lower rebates as a result of brand-name drug volumes that have converted to generic drugs. MHS retained about $806 million, or 18.1%, of total rebates in 2008, $547 million, or 15.4%, in 2007, and $670 million, or 19.6%, in 2006.

Company Financials Fiscal Year Ended Dec. 31

Per Share Data ($)	2008	2007	2006	2005	2004	2003	2002	2001	2000	1999
Tangible Book Value	NM	NM	NM	NM	0.49	NM	NM	0.85	0.66	NA
Cash Flow	2.98	2.33	1.69	1.63	1.56	1.31	1.07	1.08	0.94	NA
Earnings	2.13	1.63	1.05	1.03	0.88	0.79	0.59	0.48	0.40	NA
S&P Core Earnings	2.11	1.62	1.21	0.93	0.74	0.52	0.54	0.36	NA	NA
Dividends	Nil	Nil	Nil	Nil	Nil	Nil	NA	NA	NA	NA
Payout Ratio	Nil	Nil	Nil	Nil	Nil	Nil	NA	NA	NA	NA
Prices:High	54.63	51.67	32.06	28.98	20.95	19.00	NA	NA	NA	NA
Prices:Low	29.80	26.26	23.54	20.28	14.70	10.10	NA	NA	NA	NA
P/E Ratio:High	26	32	31	28	24	24	NA	NA	NA	NA
P/E Ratio:Low	14	16	22	20	17	13	NA	NA	NA	NA

Income Statement Analysis (Million $)	2008	2007	2006	2005	2004	2003	2002	2001	2000	1999
Revenue	51,258	44,506	42,544	37,871	35,352	34,265	32,959	29,071	22,266	NA
Operating Income	2,461	2,000	1,470	1,350	1,244	1,025	886	837	731	NA
Depreciation	443	397	392	358	378	283	257	323	289	NA
Interest Expense	234	134	65.9	73.9	Nil	Nil	73.5	Nil	Nil	NA
Pretax Income	1,791	1,503	1,012	953	806	729	547	518	448	NA
Effective Tax Rate	38.4%	39.3%	37.7%	36.8%	40.3%	41.6%	41.7%	50.5%	51.6%	NA
Net Income	1,103	912	630	602	482	426	319	257	217	NA
S&P Core Earnings	1,092	908	726	544	404	279	287	188	NA	NA

Balance Sheet & Other Financial Data (Million $)	2008	2007	2006	2005	2004	2003	2002	2001	2000	1999
Cash	1,002	844	818	888	1,146	638	203	16.3	NA	NA
Current Assets	7,098	6,303	5,855	5,061	4,320	3,760	3,044	2,534	NA	NA
Total Assets	17,011	16,218	14,388	13,703	10,542	10,263	9,714	9,252	8,915	NA
Current Liabilities	5,798	5,129	4,827	3,761	2,645	2,605	2,370	1,809	NA	NA
Long Term Debt	4,003	2,894	866	944	1,093	1,346	1,385	Nil	Nil	NA
Common Equity	5,958	6,875	7,504	7,724	5,719	5,080	4,738	6,268	6,358	NA
Total Capital	11,026	10,937	9,531	9,882	6,812	7,604	7,305	7,423	7,502	NA
Capital Expenditures	287	178	151	132	98.1	125	235	322	251	NA
Cash Flow	1,546	1,309	1,022	960	859	709	576	580	506	NA
Current Ratio	1.2	1.2	1.2	1.3	1.6	1.4	1.3	1.4	NA	NA
% Long Term Debt of Capitalization	36.3	26.5	9.1	9.6	16.0	17.7	19.0	Nil	Nil	NA
% Net Income of Revenue	2.2	2.1	1.5	1.6	1.4	1.2	1.0	0.9	1.0	NA
% Return on Assets	6.6	6.0	4.4	5.0	4.6	4.2	NA	2.8	NA	NA
% Return on Equity	17.2	12.7	8.3	9.0	8.9	7.3	NA	4.1	NA	NA

Data as orig reptd.; bef. results of disc opers/spec. items. Per share data adj. for stk. divs.; EPS diluted. E-Estimated. NA-Not Available. NM-Not Meaningful. NR-Not Ranked. UR-Under Review.

Office: 100 Parsons Pond Drive, Franklin Lakes, NJ 07417-2603.
Telephone: 201-269-3400.
Website: http://www.medco.com
Chrmn & CEO: D.B. Snow, Jr.

Pres & COO: K.O. Klepper
SVP & CFO: R.J. Rubino
SVP, Chief Acctg Officer & Cntlr: G.R. Cappucci
SVP, Secy & General Counsel: T.M. Moriarty

Board Members: H. W. Barker, Jr., J. L. Cassis, M. Goldstein, C. M. Lillis, M. S. Potter, W. Roper, D. B. Snow, Jr., D. D. Stevens, B. J. Wilson

Founded: 1983
Domicile: Delaware
Employees: 21,800

The McGraw-Hill Companies

Medtronic Inc.

S&P Recommendation	BUY ★★★★☆	Price $42.44 (as of Nov 30, 2009)	12-Mo. Target Price $47.00	Investment Style Large-Cap Growth

GICS Sector Health Care
Sub-Industry Health Care Equipment

Summary This global medical device manufacturer has leadership positions in the pacemaker, defibrillator, orthopedic, diabetes management and other medical markets.

Key Stock Statistics (Source S&P, Vickers, company reports)

52-Wk Range	$43.65– 24.06	S&P Oper. EPS 2010E	3.22	Market Capitalization(B)	$46.973	Beta	0.65
Trailing 12-Month EPS	$1.99	S&P Oper. EPS 2011E	3.41	Yield (%)	1.93	S&P 3-Yr. Proj. EPS CAGR(%)	12
Trailing 12-Month P/E	21.3	P/E on S&P Oper. EPS 2010E	13.2	Dividend Rate/Share	$0.82	S&P Credit Rating	AA-
$10K Invested 5 Yrs Ago	$9,447	Common Shares Outstg. (M)	1,106.8	Institutional Ownership (%)	76		

Price Performance

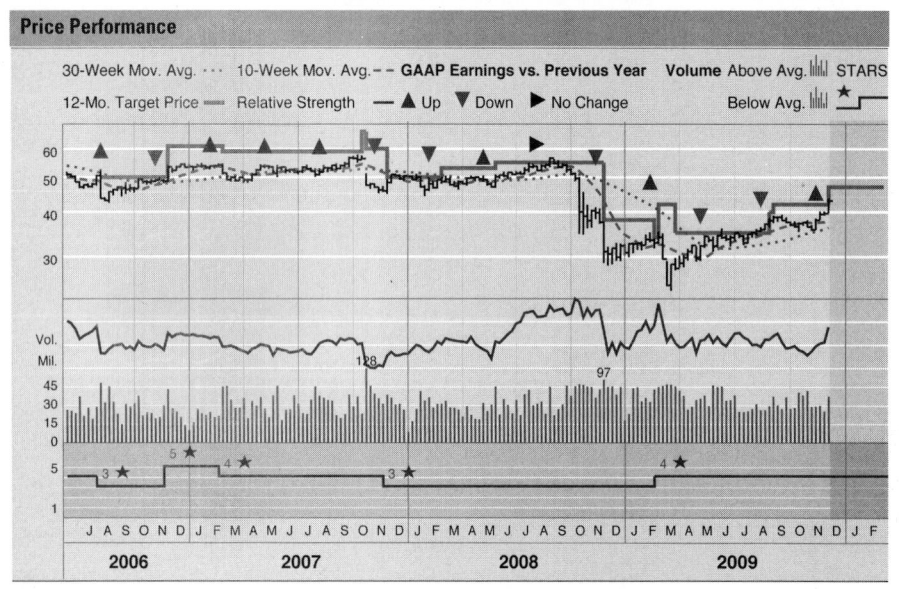

30-Week Mov. Avg. ··· 10-Week Mov. Avg. ‒ ‒ GAAP Earnings vs. Previous Year   Volume Above Avg. STARS
12-Mo. Target Price — Relative Strength — ▲ Up ▼ Down ▶ No Change   Below Avg. ★

Options: ASE, CBOE, P, Ph

Analysis prepared by **Jeffrey Englander, CFA** on November 30, 2009, when the stock traded at **$ 42.36**.

Highlights

► We expect FY 10 (Apr.) sales growth of approximately 9%, including low to mid single digit increases in the cardiac rhythm management and spine divisions, with high single digits to low double digits in cardiovascular, neuromodulation and diabetes divisions. We look for MDT to be able to achieve constant currency growth of 5%-8%, and expect a positive low single digit impact from currency. For FY 11, we look for total revenues to grow approximately 6%, including currency impact.

► In FY 10, we look for gross margins to expand to the upper end of MDT's goal of 75.5%-76.0%, driven by ongoing cost optimization efforts. We look for R&D to increase modestly from FY 09 levels relative to sales, driven by additions to R&D head count. We expect SG&A costs to decline from FY 09 levels as a percentage of sales, reflecting optimization of IT initiatives and outsourcing of certain functions.

► We see FY 10 operating EPS of $3.22, up from $2.92 in FY 09, and forecast $3.41 in FY 11, excluding approximately $0.06-$0.07 of acquisition-related dilution. We assume approximately 1,100 shares outstanding for both years.

Investment Rationale/Risk

► We believe the global ICD market will expand about 4% in 2009 and 7% in 2010 aided by the resolution of product safety issues and steady sales growth overseas. In our view, MDT has significant growth opportunities in the cardiac stent markets, driven by rising demand for its Endeavor drug-coated product in Europe and the U.S. We also look for contributions from the launch of new heart valve products, and we think the diabetes franchise will continue to grow at an annual rate in excess of 20%.

► Risks to our opinion and target price include a loss of share in key markets, unfavorable patent litigation, adverse reimbursement rate changes, and further weakness in the U.S. ICD market.

► Although we anticipate competitive pressures in the ICD and cardiac stent categories, we think investors will gravitate toward the stock amid global economic weakness, attracted by MDT's product line diversity and ability to generate high levels of free cash flow. Our 12-month target price of $47 is about 15X our FY 10 EPS estimate, a very modest discount to peers given our view of MDT's more consistent and improving growth prospects and relative stability of its core ICD and CRM markets.

Qualitative Risk Assessment

LOW	MEDIUM	HIGH

Our risk assessment reflects MDT's exposure to intensely competitive areas of the medical equipment markets, which are typically characterized by relatively short product life cycles, pricing pressures, and the threat of new market entrants. However, we believe this is offset by MDT's many competitive advantages due to the scale of its operations and sales force, product breadth, and what we see as its financial strength.

Quantitative Evaluations

S&P Quality Ranking A-

D	C	B-	B	B+	A-	A	A+

Relative Strength Rank STRONG

90

LOWEST = 1   HIGHEST = 99

Revenue/Earnings Data

Revenue (Million $)

	1Q	2Q	3Q	4Q	Year
2010	3,933	3,838	--	--	--
2009	3,706	3,570	3,494	3,829	14,599
2008	3,127	3,124	3,405	3,860	13,515
2007	2,897	3,075	3,048	3,280	12,299
2006	2,690	2,765	2,770	3,077	11,292
2005	2,346	2,400	2,531	2,778	10,055

Earnings Per Share ($)

2010	0.40	0.78	E0.76	E0.89	E3.22
2009	0.66	0.51	0.65	0.11	1.93
2008	0.66	0.58	0.07	0.72	1.95
2007	0.51	0.59	0.61	0.70	2.41
2006	0.26	0.67	0.55	0.62	2.09
2005	0.43	0.44	0.45	0.16	1.48

Fiscal year ended Apr. 30. Next earnings report expected: Mid February. EPS Estimates based on S&P Operating Earnings; historical GAAP earnings are as reported.

Dividend Data (Dates: mm/dd Payment Date: mm/dd/yy)

Amount ($)	Date Decl.	Ex-Div. Date	Stk. of Record	Payment Date
0.188	10/16	12/30	01/02	01/23/09
0.188	02/19	04/01	04/03	04/24/09
0.205	06/18	07/08	07/10	07/31/09
0.205	08/27	10/07	10/09	10/30/09

Dividends have been paid since 1977. Source: Company reports.

Medtronic Inc.

STANDARD
&POOR'S

Business Summary November 30, 2009

CORPORATE OVERVIEW. Medtronic has leading positions in medical device categories, including cardiac rhythm management, spinal, vascular, neurology and cardiac surgery.

Cardiac rhythm management products (34% of FY 09 (Apr.) revenues) include implantable pacemakers to treat slow or irregular heartbeats. Bradycardia systems include pacemakers, leads and accessories. Some models are non-invasively programmed by a physician to adjust sensing, electrical pulse intensity, duration, rate and other factors, as well as pacers that can sense in both upper and lower heart chambers and produce appropriate impulses. In May 2005, FDA approval was received for EnRhythm, the company's newest dual-chamber pacemaker, and the first to offer an exclusive pacing mode, called Managed Ventricular Pacing, which enables the device to be programmed to minimize pacing pulses to the right ventricle.

Implantable cardioverter defibrillators (ICDs) treat abnormally fast heart beats by monitoring the heart; when a rapid rhythm is detected, electrical impulses or shocks are delivered. Cardiac resynchronization therapy (CRT) devices synchronize contractions of multiple heart chambers. The company's InSynch ICD offers CRT for heart failure, as well as advanced defibrillation capabilities for patients also at risk for potentially lethal tachyarrhythmias that may lead to cardiac arrest. The Insynch Marquis system combines the cardiac resynchronization of InSynch devices with defibrillation therapies of the Marquis ICD platform.

Company Financials Fiscal Year Ended Apr. 30

Per Share Data ($)	2009	2008	2007	2006	2005	2004	2003	2002	2001	2000
Tangible Book Value	1.95	1.62	4.56	2.98	4.26	3.18	2.21	1.10	3.53	2.61
Cash Flow	2.55	2.51	2.91	2.54	1.86	1.96	1.64	1.07	1.10	1.10
Earnings	1.93	1.95	2.41	2.09	1.48	1.60	1.30	0.80	0.85	0.90
S&P Core Earnings	2.12	2.12	2.44	2.00	1.65	1.46	1.10	0.76	0.91	NA
Dividends	0.50	0.44	0.39	0.34	0.29	0.25	0.25	0.20	0.12	0.15
Payout Ratio	26%	23%	16%	16%	20%	16%	19%	25%	14%	16%
Calendar Year	2008	2007	2006	2005	2004	2003	2002	2001	2000	1999
Prices:High	56.97	57.99	59.87	58.91	53.70	52.92	50.69	60.81	62.00	44.63
Prices:Low	28.33	44.87	42.37	48.70	43.99	42.90	32.50	36.64	32.75	29.94
P/E Ratio:High	30	30	25	28	36	33	39	72	61	50
P/E Ratio:Low	15	23	18	23	30	27	25	43	32	33

Income Statement Analysis (Million $)

	2009	2008	2007	2006	2005	2004	2003	2002	2001	2000
Revenue	14,599	13,515	12,299	11,292	10,055	9,087	7,665	6,411	5,552	5,015
Operating Income	5,276	4,728	4,322	4,248	3,907	3,583	3,062	2,479	2,176	1,871
Depreciation	699	637	583	544	463	443	408	330	297	243
Interest Expense	217	NA	228	Nil	55.1	56.5	7.20	Nil	74.0	13.0
Pretax Income	2,772	2,885	3,515	3,161	2,544	2,797	2,341	1,524	1,549	1,630
Effective Tax Rate	17.4%	22.7%	20.3%	19.4%	29.1%	29.9%	31.7%	35.4%	32.5%	32.6%
Net Income	2,291	2,231	2,802	2,547	1,804	1,959	1,600	984	1,046	1,099
S&P Core Earnings	2,392	2,423	2,841	2,450	2,006	1,790	1,347	936	1,121	NA

Balance Sheet & Other Financial Data (Million $)

	2009	2008	2007	2006	2005	2004	2003	2002	2001	2000
Cash	1,676	1,613	1,256	2,994	2,232	1,594	1,470	411	1,030	448
Current Assets	7,460	7,322	7,918	10,377	7,422	5,313	4,606	3,488	3,757	3,013
Total Assets	23,605	22,198	19,512	19,665	16,617	14,111	12,321	10,905	7,039	5,669
Current Liabilities	3,147	3,535	2,563	4,406	3,380	4,241	1,813	3,985	1,359	992
Long Term Debt	6,772	5,700	5,578	5,486	1,973	1.10	1,980	9.50	13.0	14.0
Common Equity	12,973	11,536	10,977	9,383	10,450	9,077	7,906	6,431	5,510	4,491
Total Capital	19,570	17,330	16,555	14,891	12,901	9,486	10,191	6,674	5,523	4,520
Capital Expenditures	498	513	573	407	452	425	380	386	440	342
Cash Flow	2,868	2,868	3,385	3,090	2,267	2,402	2,008	1,314	1,343	1,342
Current Ratio	2.4	2.1	3.1	2.4	2.2	1.3	2.5	0.9	2.8	3.0
% Long Term Debt of Capitalization	34.3	33.3	33.7	36.8	15.3	0.0	19.4	0.1	0.2	0.3
% Net Income of Revenue	15.7	16.5	22.8	22.6	17.9	21.6	20.9	15.3	18.8	21.9
% Return on Assets	10.0	10.7	14.3	14.0	11.7	14.8	13.8	11.0	16.5	20.6
% Return on Equity	18.7	19.8	27.5	25.7	18.5	23.1	22.3	16.5	20.9	26.6

Data as orig reptd.; bef. results of disc opers/spec. items. Per share data adj. for stk. divs.; EPS diluted. E-Estimated. NA-Not Available. NM-Not Meaningful. NR-Not Ranked. UR-Under Review.

Office: 710 Medtronic Parkway, Minneapolis, MN 55432-5604.
Telephone: 763-514-4000.
Website: http://www.medtronic.com
Chrmn & CEO: W.A. Hawkins, III

Pres: P.A. Moothathamby
COO: H.J. Dallas
SVP, CFO & Chief Acctg Officer: G.L. Ellis
SVP & CSO: R. Kuntz

Investor Contact: J. Warren (763-505-2696)
Board Members: R. H. Anderson, D. L. Calhoun, V. J. Dzau, W. A. Hawkins, III, S. A. Jackson, J. T. Lenehan, D. M. O'Leary, K. J. Powell, R. C. Pozen, J. Rosso, J. Schuler

Founded: 1957
Domicile: Minnesota
Employees: 41,000

MEMC Electronic Materials Inc.

S&P Recommendation **STRONG BUY** ★★★★★	Price $12.06 (as of Nov 27, 2009)	12-Mo. Target Price $17.00	Investment Style Large-Cap Growth

GICS Sector Information Technology
Sub-Industry Semiconductor Equipment

Summary This company is a worldwide producer of silicon wafers used in semiconductors for microelectronic applications. It also provides silicon materials to the solar industry.

Key Stock Statistics (Source S&P, Vickers, company reports)

52-Wk Range	$21.36–11.32	S&P Oper. EPS 2009**E**	-0.06	Market Capitalization(B)	$2.696	Beta	1.60
Trailing 12-Month EPS	$0.06	S&P Oper. EPS 2010**E**	0.31	Yield (%)	Nil	S&P 3-Yr. Proj. EPS CAGR(%)	-10
Trailing 12-Month P/E	NM	P/E on S&P Oper. EPS 2009**E**	NM	Dividend Rate/Share	Nil	S&P Credit Rating	NA
$10K Invested 5 Yrs Ago	$11,125	Common Shares Outstg. (M)	223.6	Institutional Ownership (%)	88		

Price Performance

30-Week Mov. Avg. · · · 10-Week Mov. Avg. – – **GAAP Earnings vs. Previous Year** Volume Above Avg. STARS
12-Mo. Target Price — Relative Strength — ▲ Up ▼ Down ▶ No Change Below Avg. ★

Options: ASE, CBOE, P, Ph

Analysis prepared by **Angelo Zino** on November 16, 2009, when the stock traded at **$ 13.07**.

Highlights

► We see sales declining 44% in 2009, reflecting a sharp decrease in wafer sales to both the semiconductor and solar industries, before rebounding 23% in 2010. While we see the potential of WFR raising prices for its semiconductor wafers in 2010, we expect solar wafer pricing to continue to be hindered by excess supply. We look for polysilicon prices to drop to about $50/kg by the middle of 2010 before stabilizing. Going forward, we see the rate of decline slowing considerably for solar wafers.

► We project annual gross margins of 10% in 2009 and 17% in 2010. We expect margins to be pressured by solar customers renegotiating long-term contracts at lower prices and an ongoing decline in polysilicon spot prices. We believe WFR's plan to close two facilities by early 2011 in an effort to drive down costs will result in annual savings of $55 million. Cash costs related to the moves are anticipated to be $73 million to $78 million. We expect operating expenses, excluding restructuring costs, to comprise about 16% of sales in 2009 and 12% in 2010.

► We view positively WFR's intent to purchase SunEdison, as it provides exposure to the solar end-market and more attractive margins.

Investment Rationale/Risk

► We expect sales and margins will benefit from rising semiconductor capacity utilization levels and wafer starts in 2010. We expect semiconductor wafer pricing to stabilize and possibly rise, which should aid margins, but we continue to see pricing pressure related to the solar industry, as excess supply persists. WFR has signed long-term solar agreements with Suntech, Gintech, Conergy and Tainergy. WFR had $1.24 billion, or $5.53 per share, of cash, and minimal debt at September 30, 2009.

► Risks to our recommendation and target price include faster expansion of industry capacity than we expect, changes in governmental policy related to alternative energy technology, a further slowdown in the global economy, and slower-than-expected growth.

► Our 12-month target price of $17 is based on a price/sales multiple of 2.7X our 2010 sales per share forecast of $6.18, which is a premium to both semiconductor and solar peers, warranted, in our view, by WFR's superior financial position. This multiple is modestly below WFR's three- and five-year moving averages.

Qualitative Risk Assessment

LOW	MEDIUM	HIGH

Our risk assessment reflects WFR's exposure to the historical cyclicality of the semiconductor equipment industry and intense competition, partly offset by what we view as WFR's strong market position and size.

Quantitative Evaluations

S&P Quality Ranking B-

D	C	B-	B	B+	A-	A	A+

Relative Strength Rank WEAK

10

LOWEST = 1 HIGHEST = 99

Revenue/Earnings Data

Revenue (Million $)

	1Q	2Q	3Q	4Q	Year
2009	214.0	282.9	310.0	--	--
2008	501.4	531.4	546.0	425.7	2,005
2007	440.4	472.7	472.8	535.9	1,922
2006	341.6	370.5	408.0	420.6	1,541
2005	250.9	272.3	280.7	303.4	1,107
2004	228.8	255.5	275.3	268.4	1,028

Earnings Per Share ($)

	1Q	2Q	3Q	4Q	Year
2009	0.01	0.01	-0.29	E Nil	E-0.06
2008	-0.18	0.76	0.80	0.33	1.71
2007	0.58	0.70	0.65	1.62	3.56
2006	0.29	0.36	0.40	0.56	1.61
2005	0.25	0.18	0.45	0.22	1.10
2004	0.16	0.27	0.27	0.31	1.02

Fiscal year ended Dec. 31. Next earnings report expected: Late January. EPS Estimates based on S&P Operating Earnings; historical GAAP earnings are as reported.

Dividend Data

No cash dividends have been paid.

MEMC Electronic Materials Inc.

STANDARD &POOR'S

Business Summary November 16, 2009

CORPORATE OVERVIEW. MEMC Electronic Materials, Inc. (WFR) is a global leader in the manufacture of silicon wafers. The company designs, manufactures and provides wafers and intermediate products for use in the semiconductor, solar and related industries. WFR operates manufacturing facilities in every major semiconductor manufacturing region, including Europe, Japan, Malaysia, South Korea, Taiwan, and the U.S. Its customers include virtually all of the world's major semiconductor device manufacturers, such as the major memory, microprocessor, and applications specific integrated circuit (ASIC) manufacturers, as well as the world's largest foundries.

WFR's products include prime polish wafers, epitaxial wafers and test and monitor wafers. In 2009, it intends to begin shipping commercial quantities of silicon-on-insulator (SOI) wafers. WFR's prime wafer is a polished, highly refined, pure wafer with an ultraflat and ultraclean surface. The majority of these wafers are manufactured with a sophisticated chemical-mechanical polishing process that removes defects and leaves an extremely smooth surface. WFR's epitaxial, or epi, wafers consist of a thin silicon layer grown on the polished surface of the wafer. The epitaxial layer usually has different electrical properties from the underlying wafer, which provides customers with better isolation between circuit elements than a polished wafer, and the ability to tailor the wafer to the specific demands of the device.

WFR supplies test/monitor wafers to customers for their use in testing semiconductor manufacturing lines and processes. Although test/monitor wafers are essentially the same as prime wafers with respect to cleanliness, it has some less rigorous requirements, allowing WFR to produce some of the test/monitor wafers from the portion of the silicon ingot that does not meet customer specifications. A SOI wafer is a new type of starting material for the chip making process. SOI wafers have three layers: a thin surface layer of silicon where the transistors are formed, an underlying layer of insulating material, and a support bulk silicon wafer. Transistors built within the top silicon layer typically switch signals faster, run at lower voltages, and are much less vulnerable to signal noise from background cosmic ray particles.

The company markets its products primarily through a global direct sales force, with about 65% of 2008 sales in the Asia-Pacific region, 24% in the U.S., and 11% in Europe. WFR has a network of customer service and support centers globally. In 2008, Suntech Power Holding, Samsung Electronics and Gintech Energy each accounted for greater than 10% of total revenues.

Company Financials Fiscal Year Ended Dec. 31

Per Share Data ($)	2008	2007	2006	2005	2004	2003	2002	2001	2000	1999
Tangible Book Value	9.27	8.98	5.23	3.21	2.13	0.94	NM	NM	4.61	5.55
Cash Flow	2.15	3.90	1.91	1.35	1.22	0.68	0.09	-4.65	1.86	0.12
Earnings	1.71	3.56	1.61	1.10	1.02	0.53	-0.17	-7.51	-0.62	-2.43
S&P Core Earnings	1.68	3.57	1.62	1.06	0.96	0.49	-0.33	-7.60	NA	NA
Dividends	Nil	Nil	Nil	Nil	Nil	Nil	Nil	Nil	Nil	Nil
Payout Ratio	Nil	Nil	Nil	Nil	Nil	Nil	Nil	Nil	Nil	Nil
Prices:High	91.45	96.08	48.90	24.68	13.28	14.51	11.50	11.90	24.25	21.62
Prices:Low	10.00	39.51	22.60	10.70	7.33	7.00	2.25	1.05	6.25	5.37
P/E Ratio:High	53	27	30	17	13	27	NM	NM	NM	NM
P/E Ratio:Low	6	11	14	7	7	13	NM	NM	NM	NM

Income Statement Analysis (Million $)										
Revenue	2,005	1,922	1,541	1,107	1,028	781	687	618	872	694
Operating Income	969	929	629	314	304	174	114	-9.69	161	0.11
Depreciation	103	79.3	70.3	57.2	44.1	31.0	34.2	169	173	159
Interest Expense	2.60	2.40	2.43	7.26	13.5	12.9	73.4	78.4	78.8	66.1
Pretax Income	590	1,112	590	252	175	162	20.8	-259	-65.6	-222
Effective Tax Rate	33.4%	25.4%	36.4%	NM	NM	22.7%	NM	NM	NM	NM
Net Income	390	826	369	249	226	117	-5.07	-489	-43.4	-151
S&P Core Earnings	385	827	370	240	212	108	-41.9	-529	NA	NA

Balance Sheet & Other Financial Data (Million $)										
Cash	1,137	1,316	528	126	92.3	96.9	166	107	94.8	28.6
Current Assets	1,454	1,590	900	436	390	365	364	264	410	276
Total Assets	2,940	2,887	1,766	1,148	1,010	727	632	549	1,891	1,725
Current Liabilities	473	444	258	225	216	244	286	222	324	190
Long Term Debt	26.1	25.6	29.4	34.8	116	59.3	161	145	943	870
Common Equity	2,085	2,035	1,167	711	443	194	-24.7	-9.74	366	433
Total Capital	2,146	2,096	1,235	791	605	317	194	186	1,384	1,346
Capital Expenditures	303	276	148	163	150	85.2	22.0	7.00	57.8	49.3
Cash Flow	490	906	440	307	270	148	12.1	-324	130	7.60
Current Ratio	3.1	3.6	3.5	1.9	1.8	1.5	1.3	1.2	1.3	1.5
% Long Term Debt of Capitalization	1.2	1.2	2.4	4.4	19.2	18.7	82.9	77.8	68.1	64.6
% Net Income of Revenue	19.5	43.0	24.0	22.5	22.0	14.9	NM	NM	NM	NM
% Return on Assets	13.4	35.5	25.3	22.9	26.0	17.2	NM	NM	NM	NM
% Return on Equity	19.0	51.6	39.3	43.2	71.1	138.1	NM	NM	NM	NM

Data as orig reptd.; bef. results of disc opers/spec. items. Per share data adj. for stk. divs.; EPS diluted. E-Estimated. NA-Not Available. NM-Not Meaningful. NR-Not Ranked. UR-Under Review.

Office: 501 Pearl Drive, St. Peters, MO 63376.
Telephone: 636-474-5000.
Email: invest@memc.com
Website: http://www.memc.com

Chrmn: J.W. Marren
Pres & CEO: A.R. Chatila
SVP & CFO: T. Oliver
Secy & General Counsel: B.D. Kohn

Investor Contact: B. Michalek (636-474-5443)
Board Members: P. Blackmore, R. J. Boehlke, A. R. Chatila, E. T. Hernandez, J. W. Marren, C. D. Marsh, M. McNamara, W. E. Stevens, M. Turner, Jr., J. B. Williams

Founded: 1984
Domicile: Delaware
Employees: 4,900

The McGraw-Hill Companies

Merck & Co Inc.

STANDARD &POOR'S

S&P Recommendation	BUY ★★★★☆	Price $36.29 (as of Nov 27, 2009)	12-Mo. Target Price $38.00	Investment Style Large-Cap Blend

GICS Sector Health Care
Sub-Industry Pharmaceuticals

Summary One of the world's largest drugmakers, MRK acquired Schering-Plough in November 2009 for about $41 billion in cash and stock.

Key Stock Statistics (Source S&P, Vickers, company reports)

52-Wk Range	$36.96– 20.05	S&P Oper. EPS 2009**E**	3.15	Market Capitalization(B)	$76.542	Beta	0.84
Trailing 12-Month EPS	$3.82	S&P Oper. EPS 2010**E**	3.40	Yield (%)	4.19	S&P 3-Yr. Proj. EPS CAGR(%)	2
Trailing 12-Month P/E	9.5	P/E on S&P Oper. EPS 2009**E**	11.5	Dividend Rate/Share	$1.52	S&P Credit Rating	AA-
$10K Invested 5 Yrs Ago	$16,328	Common Shares Outstg. (M)	2,109.2	Institutional Ownership (%)	79		

Price Performance

30-Week Mov. Avg. ··· 10-Week Mov. Avg. - - **GAAP Earnings vs. Previous Year** Volume Above Avg.|||| STARS
12-Mo. Target Price — Relative Strength — ▲ Up ▼ Down ▶ No Change   Below Avg.|||| ★

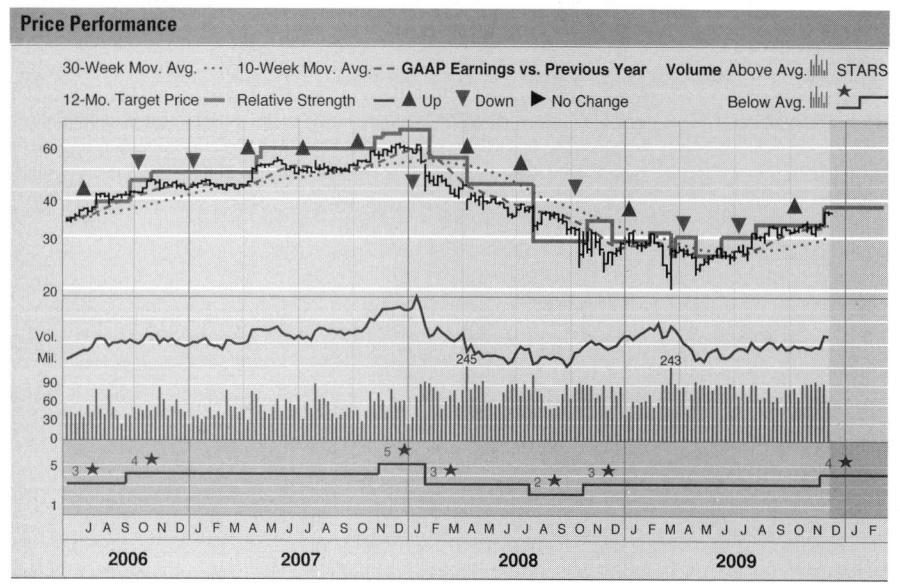

Options: ASE, CBOE, P, Ph

Analysis prepared by **Herman B. Saftlas** on November 16, 2009, when the stock traded at **$ 33.81**.

Qualitative Risk Assessment

LOW	**MEDIUM**	HIGH

Our risk assessment reflects challenges to branded patents, new drug development, and regulatory risks. In addition, MRK's Vytorin/Zetia franchise has been affected by disappointing clinical trial results. However, we see significant synergies accruing from the recent acquisition of Schering-Plough. We also think MRK has one of the stronger R&D pipelines in the sector.

Quantitative Evaluations

S&P Quality Ranking   B+

D	C	B-	B	**B+**	A-	A	A+

Relative Strength Rank   STRONG
89
LOWEST = 1   HIGHEST = 99

Revenue/Earnings Data

Revenue (Million $)

	1Q	2Q	3Q	4Q	Year
2009	5,385	5,900	6,050	--	--
2008	5,822	6,052	5,944	6,032	23,850
2007	5,769	6,111	6,074	6,243	24,198
2006	5,410	5,772	5,410	6,044	22,636
2005	5,362	5,468	5,416	5,766	22,012
2004	5,631	6,022	5,538	5,748	22,939

Earnings Per Share ($)

	1Q	2Q	3Q	4Q	Year
2009	0.67	0.74	1.61	E0.68	E3.15
2008	1.52	0.82	0.51	0.78	3.64
2007	0.78	0.77	0.70	-0.74	1.49
2006	0.69	0.69	0.43	0.22	2.03
2005	0.62	0.33	0.65	0.51	2.10
2004	1.06	1.26	1.28	0.50	2.61

Fiscal year ended Dec. 31. Next earnings report expected: Early February. EPS Estimates based on S&P Operating Earnings; historical GAAP earnings are as reported.

Highlights

▶ With MRK's recent acquisition of Schering-Plough, we project total 2010 revenues of $45 billion, up from $23.5 billion indicated for 2009. In our opinion, key established Merck drivers should be Singulair, Januvia/Janumet and viral vaccines. Among Schering's products, we see gains in Nasonex and Remicade. We project relatively flat sales of Vytorin and Zetia cholesterol drugs, reflecting lingering effects of past disappointing clinical data. Sales of Cozaar/Hyzaar are expected to decline sharply due to patent expirations.

▶ By our analysis, gross margins will likely narrow in 2010, partly reflecting the inclusion of Schering's relatively low margin animal health and consumer products lines. The SG&A and R&D cost ratios will probably decline, helped by merger synergies and other cost streamlining measures, but interest expense is expected to rise sharply.

▶ After a projected effective tax rate similar to the 22% that we estimate for 2009, we project 2010 non-GAAP EPS of about $3.40, up from $3.26 estimated for 2009.

Investment Rationale/Risk

▶ We view the early November 2009 acquisition of rival drugmaker Schering-Plough for $41 billion in cash and stock as a major transforming event for Merck. In our opinion, this merger should expand and diversify Merck's revenue base ahead of impending patent expirations on Cozaar/Hyzaar and Singulair, and provide annual cost synergies of close to $3.5 billion by 2011. Schering-Plough has also beefed up Merck's R&D pipeline, which now consists of 15 projects in late-stage Phase III clinical trials. We expect the merger to be modestly accretive in 2010.

▶ Risks to our opinion and target price include failure to successfully integrate Schering-Plough, uncertainties with respect to Remicade/Simponi litigation with Johnson & Johnson, and possible pipeline setbacks.

▶ Our 12-month target price of $38 applies a peer parity level P/E of 11.2X to our $3.40 operating EPS estimate for 2010. The dividend, which we expect to be maintained, recently yielded a generous 4.6%.

Dividend Data (Dates: mm/dd Payment Date: mm/dd/yy)

Amount ($)	Date Decl.	Ex-Div. Date	Stk. of Record	Payment Date
0.380	02/24	03/04	03/06	04/01/09
0.380	05/27	06/04	06/08	07/01/09
0.380	07/28	09/02	09/04	10/01/09
0.380	11/24	12/11	12/15	01/08/10

Dividends have been paid since 1935. Source: Company reports.

Please read the Required Disclosures and Analyst Certification on the last page of this report.

The McGraw·Hill Companies

Merck & Co Inc.

STANDARD &POOR'S

Business Summary November 16, 2009

CORPORATE OVERVIEW. Merck & Co. is a leading global drugmaker, producing a wide range of prescription drugs in many therapeutic classes in the U.S. and abroad. Foreign operations accounted for 44% of total pharmaceutical and vaccine sales in 2008. In early November 2009, MRK acquired rival drugmaker Schering-Plough for about $41 billion in cash and stock. Schering earned $2.5 billion from operations on sales of $13.5 billion in the first three quarters of 2009.

MRK's largest-selling products include Singulair (sales of $4.3 billion in 2008), a treatment for asthma and seasonal allergic rhinitis; Cozaar/Hyzaar ($3.6 billion), treatments for high blood pressure and congestive heart failure; Fosamax ($1.6 billion), a drug for osteoporosis (a bone-thinning disease that affects postmenopausal women); and Januvia/Janumet ($1.7 billion), treatments for type 2 diabetes.

Merck is also a leading maker of vaccines, which accounted for 17% of sales in 2008. Key vaccines include Gardasil ($1.4 billion) for human papillomavirus, the main cause of cervical cancer; RotaTeq pediatric vaccine, and Zostavax for shingles.

With the recent purchase of Schering-Plough, Merck gained total rights to Ze-

tia -- a cholesterol therapy that works by blocking cholesterol absorption in the intestines -- as well as Vytorin, a combination pill containing both Zocor and Zetia. In 2008, Vytorin had sales of $2.4 billion ($2.8 billion in 2007), and Zetia had sales of $2.3 billion ($2.4 billion in 2007). OTC medications such as Pepcid AC are offered through a venture with Johnson & Johnson. Through a venture with AstraZeneca, Merck books sales of Nexium and other drugs.

MARKET PROFILE. The dollar value of the global pharmaceutical market is projected to grow 4%-6% in 2010, from an estimated $775 billion to $785 billion in 2009, according to IMS Health. Worldwide industry revenue growth has slowed in recent years, reflecting the effects of tighter reimbursements from key managed care markets, the loss of patent protection on blockbuster drugs, weakened global economies, and relatively sluggish new product flow. Much of the projected growth in 2010 should come from emerging markets. Sales in North America are expected to grow 3%-5%, but sales in Europe are projected to grow about 1%-3%, according to IMS.

Company Financials Fiscal Year Ended Dec. 31

Per Share Data ($)	2008	2007	2006	2005	2004	2003	2002	2001	2000	1999
Tangible Book Value	7.97	11.76	7.00	7.48	7.03	6.13	4.88	3.77	3.23	2.43
Cash Flow	4.30	2.19	3.06	2.88	3.29	3.51	3.79	3.77	3.44	3.02
Earnings	3.64	1.49	2.03	2.10	2.61	2.92	3.14	3.14	2.90	2.45
S&P Core Earnings	2.78	2.85	2.28	2.09	2.56	2.71	2.81	2.87	NA	NA
Dividends	1.52	1.52	1.52	1.52	1.49	1.45	1.41	1.37	1.26	1.10
Payout Ratio	42%	102%	75%	72%	57%	50%	45%	44%	43%	45%
Prices:High	61.18	61.62	46.37	35.36	49.33	63.50	64.50	95.25	96.69	87.38
Prices:Low	22.82	42.35	31.81	25.50	25.60	40.57	38.50	56.80	52.00	60.94
P/E Ratio:High	17	41	23	17	19	22	21	30	33	36
P/E Ratio:Low	6	28	16	12	10	14	12	18	18	25

Income Statement Analysis (Million $)

	2008	2007	2006	2005	2004	2003	2002	2001	2000	1999
Revenue	23,850	24,198	22,636	22,012	22,939	22,486	51,790	47,716	40,363	32,714
Operating Income	7,854	7,779	5,955	7,567	8,074	9,912	11,361	11,192	10,686	9,056
Depreciation	1,415	1,528	2,268	1,708	1,451	1,314	1,488	1,464	1,277	1,145
Interest Expense	251	384	375	386	294	351	391	465	484	317
Pretax Income	9,808	3,492	6,342	7,486	8,129	9,220	10,428	10,693	10,133	8,842
Effective Tax Rate	20.4%	2.73%	28.2%	36.5%	26.6%	26.7%	29.3%	29.2%	29.6%	30.9%
Net Income	7,808	3,275	4,434	4,631	5,813	6,590	7,150	7,282	6,822	5,891
S&P Core Earnings	5,958	6,255	4,973	4,582	5,699	6,089	6,395	6,649	NA	NA

Balance Sheet & Other Financial Data (Million $)

	2008	2007	2006	2005	2004	2003	2002	2001	2000	1999
Cash	5,486	8,231	5,915	9,585	2,879	1,201	2,243	2,144	2,537	2,022
Current Assets	19,305	15,045	15,230	21,049	13,475	11,527	14,834	12,962	13,353	11,259
Total Assets	47,196	48,351	44,570	44,846	42,573	40,588	47,561	44,007	39,910	35,635
Current Liabilities	14,319	12,258	12,723	13,304	11,744	9,570	12,375	11,544	9,710	8,759
Long Term Debt	3,943	3,916	5,551	5,126	4,692	5,096	4,879	4,799	3,601	3,144
Common Equity	18,758	18,185	17,560	17,917	17,288	15,576	18,200	16,050	14,832	13,242
Total Capital	25,118	24,903	25,517	25,449	24,387	24,588	28,008	25,686	23,454	19,847
Capital Expenditures	1,298	1,011	980	1,403	1,726	1,916	2,370	2,725	2,728	2,561
Cash Flow	9,223	4,803	6,702	6,339	7,264	7,904	8,638	8,746	8,099	7,035
Current Ratio	1.4	1.2	1.2	1.6	1.1	1.2	1.2	1.1	1.4	1.3
% Long Term Debt of Capitalization	15.5	15.7	21.8	20.1	19.2	20.7	17.4	18.7	15.4	15.8
% Net Income of Revenue	32.7	13.5	19.6	21.0	25.3	29.3	13.8	15.3	16.9	18.0
% Return on Assets	16.3	7.1	9.9	10.6	14.0	15.0	15.6	17.3	18.1	17.4
% Return on Equity	42.3	18.3	25.0	26.3	35.4	39.0	41.7	47.2	48.6	20.1

Data as orig reptd.; bef. results of disc opers/spec. items. Per share data adj. for stk. divs.; EPS diluted. E-Estimated. NA-Not Available. NM-Not Meaningful. NR-Not Ranked. UR-Under Review.

Office: 2000 Galloping Hill Road, Kenilworth, NJ 07033.
Telephone: 908-298-4000.
Website: http://www.merck.com
Chrmn, Pres & CEO: R.T. Clark

Pres: R.S. Bowles, III
EVP & CFO: P.N. Kellogg
EVP & General Counsel: B.N. Kuhlik
EVP & CIO: J.C. Scalet

Investor Contact: G. Bell (908-423-5185)
Board Members: L. A. Brun, T. R. Cech, R. T. Clark, T. H. Glocer, S. F. Goldstone, W. B. Harrison, Jr., H. R. Jacobson, W. N. Kelley, R. B. Lazarus, C. E. Represas, T. E. Shenk, A. M. Tatlock, S. O. Thier, W. P. Weeks, P. C. Wendell

Founded: 1891
Domicile: New Jersey
Employees: 51,000

The McGraw-Hill Companies

Meredith Corp

STANDARD &POOR'S

S&P Recommendation HOLD ★★★☆☆	Price $27.27 (as of Nov 27, 2009)	12-Mo. Target Price $32.00	Investment Style Large-Cap Growth

GICS Sector Consumer Discretionary
Sub-Industry Publishing

Summary This company derives the bulk of its earnings from publishing magazines (primarily Better Homes and Gardens and Ladies' Home Journal) and the ownership of 12 TV stations.

Key Stock Statistics (Source S&P, Vickers, company reports)

52-Wk Range	$33.17– 10.60	S&P Oper. EPS 2010E	1.80	Market Capitalization(B)	$0.986	Beta	1.78
Trailing 12-Month EPS	$-2.38	S&P Oper. EPS 2011E	2.26	Yield (%)	3.30	S&P 3-Yr. Proj. EPS CAGR(%)	20
Trailing 12-Month P/E	NM	P/E on S&P Oper. EPS 2010E	15.2	Dividend Rate/Share	$0.90	S&P Credit Rating	NA
$10K Invested 5 Yrs Ago	$5,740	Common Shares Outstg. (M)	45.3	Institutional Ownership (%)	NM		

Price Performance

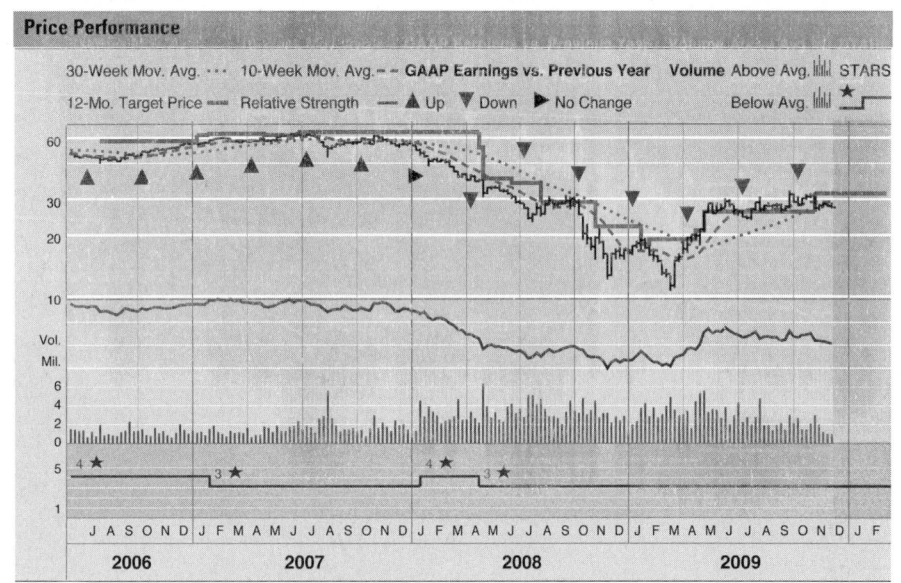

30-Week Mov. Avg. ···· 10-Week Mov. Avg. — GAAP Earnings vs. Previous Year   Volume Above Avg. STARS
12-Mo. Target Price — Relative Strength — ▲ Up ▼ Down ► No Change   Below Avg. ★

Options: ASE

Analysis prepared by **Joseph Agnese** on October 30, 2009, when the stock traded at **$ 27.10**.

Highlights

► We forecast overall advertising revenues will decline sharply in the first half of FY 10 (Jun.) due to a weak macroeconomic environment. In view of a soft retail sales environment, and the closing of Country Home magazine, effective with the March 2009 issue, we also project a significant reduction in circulation revenues. Still, we see annual growth in retransmission fees and in revenues from MDP's highly profitable brand licensing, video production and integrated marketing businesses. All told, we project total revenues of $1.34 billion in FY 10, down 5.9% from FY 09.

► Given expected negative operating leverage from lower revenues and company expectations for $10 million in pension expense, we forecast operating margin contraction in FY 10. However, margin expansion should be supported in the second half of FY 10 as we expect stabilization in publishing and broadcasting advertising and continued expense reductions.

► We see operating EPS falling to $1.80 in FY 10 (excluding $0.06 in one-time tax benefits) from operating EPS of $2.00 in FY 09, excluding restructuring charges of $0.21.

Investment Rationale/Risk

► We expect MDP to continue to supplement organic growth with selective acquisitions. We also believe recent licensing deals demonstrate the company's ability to leverage its strong brands into incremental and profitable revenue streams. In addition, we see incremental revenue growth opportunities for MDP in its non-core advertising categories. However, our optimism is tempered by a difficult economic environment that we see hurting the company's core advertising revenues and reducing earnings in the near term.

► Risks to our opinion and target price include a longer-than-expected advertising downturn. We also are concerned about MDP's corporate governance, as we do not believe policies such as a dual class voting structure are in the best interests of common shareholders.

► We believe MDP, with a more conservative debt/EBITDA ratio than peers in an adverse economic environment, should trade at a 15% premium to peers average enterprise value (EV)/ EBITDA of 8.0X. Applying a ratio of 9.2X to our 2010 EBITDA estimate of $194 million yields our 12-month target price of $32.

Qualitative Risk Assessment

LOW	MEDIUM	HIGH

Our risk assessment reflects a highly competitive environment for advertising among publishers and other media, offset by our view of the company's consistent record of earnings growth and incremental growth opportunities we see in brand licensing and integrated marketing.

Quantitative Evaluations

S&P Quality Ranking B+

D	C	B-	B	B+	A-	A	A+

Relative Strength Rank WEAK

29

LOWEST = 1   HIGHEST = 99

Revenue/Earnings Data

Revenue (Million $)

	1Q	2Q	3Q	4Q	Year
2010	332.4	--	--	--	--
2009	370.1	361.3	337.6	345.9	1,409
2008	404.1	396.3	401.0	385.2	1,587
2007	386.4	399.4	337.6	428.5	1,616
2006	390.3	386.0	394.9	426.4	1,598
2005	288.9	294.6	305.5	332.4	1,221

Earnings Per Share ($)

2010	0.40	E0.36	E0.52	E0.58	E1.80
2009	0.42	0.39	0.55	-3.64	-2.28
2008	0.68	0.73	0.98	0.41	2.82
2007	0.62	0.73	1.08	1.01	3.44
2006	0.52	0.58	0.97	0.97	2.86
2005	0.46	0.52	0.69	0.83	2.50

Fiscal year ended Jun. 30. Next earnings report expected: Late January. EPS Estimates based on S&P Operating Earnings; historical GAAP earnings are as reported.

Dividend Data (Dates: mm/dd Payment Date: mm/dd/yy)

Amount ($)	Date Decl.	Ex-Div. Date	Stk. of Record	Payment Date
0.225	02/02	02/25	02/27	03/13/09
0.225	05/14	05/27	05/29	06/15/09
0.225	08/12	08/27	08/31	09/15/09
0.225	11/05	11/25	11/30	12/15/09

Dividends have been paid since 1930. Source: Company reports.

Meredith Corp

STANDARD
&POOR'S

Business Summary October 30, 2009

CORPORATE OVERVIEW. Meredith Corp. is a diversified media and marketing company with operations in publishing (80% of FY 08 (Jun.) revenues) and broadcasting (20%). Advertising accounted for about 60% of total revenues, followed by magazine circulation (20%) and other (20%).

The publishing segment focuses on the home and family market. Meredith has more than 25 subscription-based magazines, including Better Homes and Gardens, Family Circle, Ladies' Home Journal and approximately 150 special interest publications. The segment also includes book publishing, integrated marketing, a large consumer database, 26 websites, brand licensing and other related activities. Books are published under the Better Homes and Gardens trademark and under licensed trademarks such as The Home Depot books. Meredith Integrated Marketing offers integrated promotional, database management, relationship and direct marketing capabilities for corporate customers. In April 2006, Meredith acquired O'Grady Meyers (OGM), an interactive marketing services agency that specializes in online customer relationship marketing. Overall FY 08 publishing segment revenues were derived from

advertising (50%), circulation (25%) and other (25%).

The broadcasting segment consists of 12 network-affiliated TV stations, one AM radio station, related interactive media operations, and video related operations. Broadcasting affiliations consist of CBS (six stations), FOX (three), MyNetwork TV (two), and NBC (one). The segment also includes 26 websites and video related operations. Local and national advertising contributed approximately 97% of segment revenues in FY 08, and the company states that 30% to 40% of a market's television ad revenues are generated by local news on major network-affiliated stations. The other 3% of revenues comes primarily from broadcast retransmission fees. Given current industry trends, we expect the company to negotiate substantially higher retransmission fees when most of its retransmission agreements expire in FY 09.

Company Financials Fiscal Year Ended Jun. 30

Per Share Data ($)	2009	2008	2007	2006	2005	2004	2003	2002	2001	2000
Tangible Book Value	NM	NM	NM	NM	NM	NM	NM	NM	NM	NM
Cash Flow	-1.33	3.85	4.94	3.76	3.19	2.82	2.40	3.64	2.39	3.01
Earnings	-2.28	2.82	3.44	2.86	2.50	2.14	1.78	1.79	1.39	1.35
S&P Core Earnings	1.85	2.69	3.48	2.84	2.49	2.01	1.64	0.92	0.92	NA
Dividends	0.88	0.80	0.69	0.60	0.52	0.43	0.37	0.35	0.33	0.16
Payout Ratio	NM	28%	20%	20%	21%	20%	22%	20%	24%	12%
Prices:High	33.17	55.08	63.41	57.29	54.33	55.94	50.32	47.75	38.97	41.06
Prices:Low	10.60	12.06	48.15	45.04	44.51	48.24	47.09	33.42	26.50	22.38
P/E Ratio:High	NM	20	18	20	22	26	28	27	28	30
P/E Ratio:Low	NM	4	14	16	18	23	26	19	19	17

Income Statement Analysis (Million $)										
Revenue	1,409	1,587	1,616	1,598	1,221	1,162	1,080	988	1,053	1,097
Operating Income	202	317	365	312	263	238	209	212	204	249
Depreciation	42.6	49.2	73.8	45.7	35.3	35.2	31.4	93.8	51.6	87.6
Interest Expense	20.8	22.4	27.2	30.2	Nil	22.7	27.8	33.2	32.9	34.9
Pretax Income	-155	220	263	237	209	181	149	149	116	128
Effective Tax Rate	NM	39.1%	35.7%	39.0%	38.7%	38.7%	38.7%	38.7%	38.7%	44.3%
Net Income	-103	134	169	145	128	111	91.1	91.4	71.3	71.0
S&P Core Earnings	83.4	128	171	144	127	104	83.5	46.8	47.6	NA

Balance Sheet & Other Financial Data (Million $)										
Cash	27.9	37.6	39.2	30.7	29.8	58.7	22.3	28.2	36.3	22.9
Current Assets	340	403	453	432	304	314	268	272	291	289
Total Assets	1,669	2,060	2,090	2,041	1,491	1,466	1,437	1,460	1,438	1,440
Current Liabilities	349	443	487	464	439	371	297	307	371	359
Long Term Debt	380	410	375	515	125	225	375	385	400	455
Common Equity	609	788	833	698	652	589	501	508	448	423
Total Capital	1,053	1,337	1,375	1,338	871	912	948	985	907	926
Capital Expenditures	23.5	29.6	42.6	29.2	23.8	24.5	26.6	23.4	56.0	39.4
Cash Flow	-59.9	183	243	190	163	146	123	185	123	159
Current Ratio	1.0	0.9	0.9	0.9	0.7	0.8	0.9	0.9	0.8	0.8
% Long Term Debt of Capitalization	36.1	30.7	27.3	38.5	14.4	24.7	39.6	39.1	44.1	49.1
% Net Income of Revenue	NM	8.5	10.4	9.1	10.5	9.5	8.4	9.3	6.8	6.5
% Return on Assets	NM	6.5	8.2	8.2	8.7	7.6	6.3	6.3	5.0	5.0
% Return on Equity	NM	16.6	22.1	21.5	20.3	20.4	18.1	19.1	16.4	17.0

Data as orig reptd.; bef. results of disc opers/spec. items. Per share data adj. for stk. divs.; EPS diluted. E-Estimated. NA-Not Available. NM-Not Meaningful. NR-Not Ranked. UR-Under Review.

Office: 1716 Locust Street, Des Moines, IA 50309-3023.
Telephone: 515-284-3000.
Website: http://www.meredith.com
Chrmn: W.T. Kerr

Pres & CEO: S.M. Lacy
CFO & Chief Acctg Officer: J.H. Ceryanec
Secy & General Counsel: J.S. Zieser
Investor Contact: S.V. Radia (515-284-3357)

Board Members: H. M. Bount, M. S. Coleman, J. R. Craigie, A. H. Drewes, D. M. Frazier, F. B. Henry, J. W. Johnson, W. T. Kerr, S. M. Lacy, P. A. Marineau, E. E. Tallett

Founded: 1902
Domicile: Iowa
Employees: 3,280

Metlife Inc.

STANDARD &POOR'S

S&P Recommendation BUY ★★★★☆	Price $33.28 (as of Nov 27, 2009)	12-Mo. Target Price $43.00	Investment Style Large-Cap Blend

GICS Sector Financials
Sub-Industry Life & Health Insurance

Summary This company is a leading publicly traded diversified U.S. life insurance and financial services concern.

Key Stock Statistics (Source S&P, Vickers, company reports)

52-Wk Range	$41.45–11.37	S&P Oper. EPS 2009E	2.90	Market Capitalization(B)	$27.249	Beta	1.95
Trailing 12-Month EPS	$-2.10	S&P Oper. EPS 2010E	4.10	Yield (%)	2.22	S&P 3-Yr. Proj. EPS CAGR(%)	-13
Trailing 12-Month P/E	NM	P/E on S&P Oper. EPS 2009E	11.5	Dividend Rate/Share	$0.74	S&P Credit Rating	A-
$10K Invested 5 Yrs Ago	$9,123	Common Shares Outstg. (M)	818.8	Institutional Ownership (%)	61		

Price Performance

30-Week Mov. Avg. · · · 10-Week Mov. Avg. - - **GAAP Earnings vs. Previous Year** Volume Above Avg. STARS
12-Mo. Target Price — Relative Strength — ▲ Up ▼ Down ► No Change Below Avg.

Options: ASE, CBOE, P

Analysis prepared by **Bret Howlett** on November 05, 2009, when the stock traded at **$ 33.81**.

Highlights

► We forecast premiums in Individual to rise roughly 9% in 2010 due to strong variable annuity and traditional life sales. We expect production to drop in the Universal and Variable Life businesses. We project premiums in Institutional to grow in the mid single-digits as the weakened macro environment should temper growth in sales and flows in Retirement and Savings and Group life. We believe variable income should boost revenue growth substantially in the second half of 2010 as income from hedge funds and real estate JVs picks up.

► We believe the international segment will continue to be the biggest growth driver for MET and expect premiums to increase in the double-digits (excluding the impact of foreign currency). We look for Korea, Mexico, and Japan to contribute to operating profits, as MET focuses on increasing sales, expanding marketing efforts, making strategic acquisitions, and developing new partnerships. We expect investment spreads to improve as more cash is shifted to higher yielding securities.

► We estimate operating EPS of $2.90 in 2009, and operating EPS of $4.10 in 2010. Our estimates exclude realized investment gains or losses.

Investment Rationale/Risk

► We believe MET is well positioned to capture market share in the current environment given its strong capital position, scale, diverse businesses, distribution capabilities, and global reach. While we expect elevated credit impairments to suppress net income over the near-term, we think MET's investment portfolio is less vulnerable to the weak economy versus peers, and that it holds enough excess capital to absorb investment losses. We believe MET is poised to generated a double-digit ROE in 2010 due to a rebound in variable income, and as it reduces its defensive liquidity position and puts cash to work in higher yielding investments. We expect earnings growth to be boosted by expense reduction initiatives, strong net flows in many businesses, and better investment spreads.

► Risks to our recommendation and target price include credit and interest rate risk; a decline in the equity markets; the potential need for additional capital; and, exposure to asbestos-related liability claims.

► Our 12-month target price of $43 is about 1.1X our estimated 2010 book value per share projection, below MET's historical multiples.

Qualitative Risk Assessment

LOW	MEDIUM	HIGH

Our risk assessment reflects our view of the company's consistent earnings growth, strong brand identity, diversified product offerings, and geographic footprint, offset by the potential for further losses in its investment portfolio and vulnerability to a declines in the equity markets.

Quantitative Evaluations

S&P Quality Ranking B+

D	C	B-	B	B+	A-	A	A+

Relative Strength Rank WEAK

26

LOWEST = 1   HIGHEST = 99

Revenue/Earnings Data

Revenue (Million $)

	1Q	2Q	3Q	4Q	Year
2009	10,216	8,266	10,238	--	--
2008	13,027	13,715	13,378	13,962	50,989
2007	12,908	13,216	13,053	13,830	53,007
2006	11,565	11,387	12,551	12,893	48,396
2005	10,257	10,961	12,012	11,546	44,776
2004	9,426	9,479	10,047	10,062	39,014

Earnings Per Share ($)

	1Q	2Q	3Q	4Q	Year
2009	-0.75	-1.74	-0.79	E0.95	E2.90
2008	0.84	1.26	1.42	1.15	4.55
2007	1.29	1.47	1.25	1.44	5.44
2006	0.92	0.74	1.19	1.00	3.85
2005	1.08	1.36	0.96	0.77	4.16
2004	0.86	1.11	0.93	0.68	3.59

Fiscal year ended Dec. 31. Next earnings report expected: Early February. EPS Estimates based on S&P Operating Earnings; historical GAAP earnings are as reported.

Dividend Data (Dates: mm/dd Payment Date: mm/dd/yy)

Amount ($)	Date Decl.	Ex-Div. Date	Stk. of Record	Payment Date
0.740	10/29	11/06	11/10	12/15/08
0.740	10/29	11/05	11/09	12/14/09

Dividends have been paid since 2000. Source: Company reports.

Please read the Required Disclosures and Analyst Certification on the last page of this report.

The McGraw·Hill Companies

Metlife Inc.

STANDARD
&POOR'S

Business Summary November 05, 2009

CORPORATE OVERVIEW. MetLife (MET) is one of the largest insurance and financial services companies in the U.S. The company benefits from a strong brand, a solid financial position, and a large distribution network, in our view. According to the American Council of Life Insurers, MetLife was the largest life insurer in 2007, based on total assets. As of February 2006, MetLife had access to 71% of the world's life insurance markets, up from 36% in 2004. Formerly a mutual insurance company, MetLife demutualized and issued publicly traded stock in April 2000.

MET is organized into five business segments: institutional, individual, auto and home, international, and reinsurance. The institutional segment accounted for 49% of consolidated revenues in 2008 (41% in 2007), the individual segment 30% (29%), the auto and home segment 6.5% (5.9%), the international segment 13% (9.9%). Corporate and other activities, including MetLife Bank operations, accounted for 2.1% (2.9%) of consolidated revenues in 2008.

CORPORATE STRATEGY. In June 2008, MET said it planned to exit the reinsur-

ance business and announced that it intended to spin off most of its 52% stake in Reinsurance Group of America (RGA) in a tax-free exchange offer. Under the terms of the transaction, MET accepted 23,093,689 shares of its common stock in exchange for 29,243,539 shares of RGA Class B stock. In September 2008, MET completed the transaction.

On July 1, 2005, MET acquired Travelers Life & Annuity from Citigroup, Inc. and substantially all of Citigroup's international insurance businesses for $11.8 billion, including approximately $1 billion in MET shares and $10.8 billion in cash. The Travelers acquisition greatly enhanced MET's size and scope in its core businesses and led to strong top-line growth in its international operations, in our view.

Company Financials Fiscal Year Ended Dec. 31

Per Share Data ($)	2008	2007	2006	2005	2004	2003	2002	2001	2000	1999
Tangible Book Value	19.54	34.79	35.64	32.06	31.16	27.94	24.83	22.43	21.53	NA
Operating Earnings	NA	NA	NA	NA	NA	NA	NA	NA	NA	NA
Earnings	4.55	5.44	3.85	4.16	3.59	2.57	1.58	0.62	1.49	1.21
S&P Core Earnings	2.42	5.91	5.01	4.12	3.41	2.87	2.06	0.91	NA	NA
Dividends	0.74	0.74	0.59	0.52	0.46	0.23	0.21	0.20	0.20	NA
Payout Ratio	16%	14%	15%	13%	13%	9%	13%	32%	13%	NA
Prices:High	65.50	71.23	60.00	52.57	41.27	34.14	34.85	36.63	36.50	NA
Prices:Low	15.72	58.48	48.00	37.29	32.30	23.51	20.60	24.70	14.25	NA
P/E Ratio:High	14	13	16	13	11	13	22	59	24	NA
P/E Ratio:Low	3	11	12	9	9	9	13	40	10	NA

Income Statement Analysis (Million $)										
Life Insurance in Force	NA	6,135,797	5,707,215	5,125,427	4,346,898	3,875,110	2,679,870	2,419,341	2,572,261	NA
Premium Income:Life	NA	19,254	18,368	17,399	15,341	14,065	13,070	11,611	11,224	NA
Premium Income:A & H	NA	5,666	4,991	4,489	4,016	3,537	3,052	2,744	2,377	NA
Net Investment Income	NA	19,006	17,192	14,910	12,418	11,636	11,329	11,923	11,768	7,639
Total Revenue	50,989	53,007	49,746	44,869	39,014	36,147	33,147	31,928	31,947	19,244
Pretax Income	5,090	6,279	4,221	4,399	3,779	2,630	1,671	739	1,416	1,357
Net Operating Income	NA	NA	NA	NA	NA	NA	NA	NA	NA	NA
Net Income	3,510	4,280	3,105	3,139	2,708	1,943	1,155	473	953	918
S&P Core Earnings	1,811	4,495	3,867	3,123	2,574	2,144	1,512	697	NA	NA

Balance Sheet & Other Financial Data (Million $)										
Cash & Equivalent	25,153	13,998	10,454	7,054	6,389	5,919	4,411	9,535	5,484	4,097
Premiums Due	NA	14,607	14,490	12,186	6,696	7,047	7,669	6,437	8,343	6,552
Investment Assets:Bonds	NA	242,242	243,428	230,050	176,763	167,752	140,553	115,398	112,979	75,252
Investment Assets:Stocks	NA	6,829	5,890	4,163	2,188	1,598	1,348	3,063	2,193	2,006
Investment Assets:Loans	NA	57,449	52,467	47,170	41,305	34,998	33,666	31,893	30,109	16,805
Investment Assets:Total	297,158	334,734	324,689	301,709	234,985	218,099	188,335	162,222	156,527	105,187
Deferred Policy Costs	NA	21,521	20,851	19,641	14,336	12,943	11,727	11,167	10,618	4,416
Total Assets	501,678	558,562	527,715	481,645	356,808	326,841	277,385	256,898	255,018	226,791
Debt	NA	19,535	13,759	12,022	5,944	5,703	5,690	4,884	3,516	3,350
Common Equity	23,733	35,178	33,797	29,100	22,824	21,149	17,385	16,062	16,389	13,873
% Return on Revenue	6.9	8.1	6.2	7.0	6.9	5.4	3.5	1.5	3.0	4.8
% Return on Assets	0.7	0.8	0.6	0.7	0.8	0.6	0.4	0.2	0.4	0.4
% Return on Equity	11.9	12.0	9.4	11.8	12.3	10.1	6.9	2.9	6.3	5.9
% Investment Yield	5.3	5.8	5.5	5.6	6.8	5.7	6.5	7.5	8.0	7.2

Data as orig reptd.; bef. results of disc opers/spec. items. Per share data adj. for stk. divs.; EPS diluted. E-Estimated. NA-Not Available. NM-Not Meaningful. NR-Not Ranked. UR-Under Review.

Office: 200 Park Ave, New York, NY 10166-0188.
Telephone: 212-578-2211.
Website: http://www.metlife.com
Chrmn, Pres & CEO: C.R. Henrikson

Pres: R.A. Liddy
COO & CTO: M.R. Morris
EVP & CFO: W.J. Wheeler
EVP & Chief Admin Officer: R.A. Fattori

Board Members: S. M. Burwell, E. Castro-Wright, B. A. Dole, Jr., C. W. Grise, M. Haydel, C. R. Henrikson, R. G. Hubbard, J. M. Keane, A. F. Kelly, Jr., J. M. Kilts, C. R. Kinneyxxx, H. B. Price, D. Satcher, K. J. Sicchitano, W. C. Steere, Jr., L. C. Wang
Founded: 1999
Domicile: Delaware
Employees: 57,000

The McGraw-Hill Companies

MetroPCS Communications Inc

STANDARD
&POOR'S

S&P Recommendation BUY ★★★★☆	Price $6.32 (as of Nov 27, 2009)	12-Mo. Target Price $12.00	Investment Style Large-Cap Blend

GICS Sector Telecommunication Services
Sub-Industry Wireless Telecommunication Services

Summary This company provides wireless services primarily to the youth and minority markets under the brand name MetroPCS.

Key Stock Statistics (Source S&P, Vickers, company reports)

52-Wk Range	$18.98– 5.65	S&P Oper. EPS 2009**E**	0.54	Market Capitalization(B)	$2.227	Beta	0.47
Trailing 12-Month EPS	$0.45	S&P Oper. EPS 2010**E**	0.82	Yield (%)	Nil	S&P 3-Yr. Proj. EPS CAGR(%)	15
Trailing 12-Month P/E	14.0	P/E on S&P Oper. EPS 2009**E**	11.7	Dividend Rate/Share	Nil	S&P Credit Rating	NA
$10K Invested 5 Yrs Ago	NA	Common Shares Outstg. (M)	352.4	Institutional Ownership (%)	60		

Price Performance

30-Week Mov. Avg. ··· 10-Week Mov. Avg. – – GAAP Earnings vs. Previous Year Volume Above Avg. STARS
12-Mo. Target Price — Relative Strength — ▲ Up ▼ Down ▶ No Change Below Avg.

Analysis prepared by **James Moorman, CFA** on November 10, 2009, when the stock traded at **$ 5.88**.

Highlights

► We believe subscriber revenues will increase 28% in 2009 and 9% in 2010, following a 27% advance in 2008, with growth driven by new market launches, such as Las Vegas (late March 2008), Philadelphia (July 1, 2008), Boston (February 4, 2009), and New York (February 4, 2009). We expect the majority of new subscribers to come from expansion markets, but look for a resurgence in the core markets. However, we are concerned that adverse economic conditions could pressure net additions and average revenue per user (ARPU) in the latter part of this year.

► We expect EBITDA margins on service revenue to contract to 31.0% in 2009, from 32.1% in 2008, before expanding to 34.2% in 2010. We believe the market launches will entail higher selling and marketing costs, and we expect equipment costs to rise as higher handset subsidies are used to lure new subscribers.

► We look for higher depreciation charges in 2009 stemming from PCS's market launches. We estimate EPS of $0.54 in 2009 and $0.82 in 2010, following operating EPS of $0.52 in 2008.

Investment Rationale/Risk

► Our buy opinion reflects our outlook for 20% EBITDA growth in 2010, despite a competitive wireless industry. Further, we believe the proposed acquisition of Virgin Mobile (VM 4, Hold) by Sprint Nextel (S 3, Buy) could help reduce some of the competitive pressures in the competitive prepaid segment. We believe that the recent national roaming agreement and license exchange with wireless peer Leap Wireless (LEAP 13, Buy) means that a merger between the two is likely off the table for the near term. For now, we think PCS will trade on fundamentals, and we believe the shares are attractive at current levels.

► Risks to our recommendation and target price include weaker-than-expected net customer growth, higher-than-expected churn, pressure on EBITDA margins, and debt issuance.

► Our 12-month target price of $12 is derived from an enterprise value-to-EBITDA multiple of 6.0X 2010 projected results, in line with the peer average. We expect the shares to be volatile.

Qualitative Risk Assessment

LOW	MEDIUM	HIGH

Our risk assessment reflects the competitive nature of the wireless market and the company's focus on the prepaid market, partly offset by our view of its relatively strong balance sheet.

Quantitative Evaluations

S&P Quality Ranking NR

D	C	B-	B	B+	A-	A	A+

Relative Strength Rank WEAK

10

LOWEST = 1   HIGHEST = 99

Revenue/Earnings Data

Revenue (Million $)

	1Q	2Q	3Q	4Q	Year
2009	795.3	859.6	895.6	--	--
2008	662.4	678.8	686.7	723.6	2,752
2007	536.7	551.2	556.7	591.1	2,236
2006	329.5	368.2	396.1	453.1	1,547
2005	236.0	250.7	263.6	288.2	1,038
2004	173.0	--	--	--	748.3

Earnings Per Share ($)

2009	0.12	0.07	0.21	E0.16	E0.54
2008	0.11	0.14	0.13	0.04	0.42
2007	0.11	0.17	0.15	-0.10	0.28
2006	0.04	0.06	0.08	-0.08	0.18
2005	0.26	0.47	0.03	0.05	0.62
2004	0.02	--	--	--	0.33

Fiscal year ended Dec. 31. Next earnings report expected: Late February. EPS Estimates based on S&P Operating Earnings; historical GAAP earnings are as reported.

Dividend Data

No cash dividends have been paid.

MetroPCS Communications Inc

**STANDARD
&POOR'S**

Business Summary November 10, 2009

CORPORATE OVERVIEW. Metro PCS offers digital wireless services in the U.S. under the MetroPCS brand. The company's services are based on the Code Division Multiple Access (CDMA 1xRTT) technology. PCS offers unlimited service for a flat rate to customer segments that we believe are underserved by traditional wireless carriers. The company sells handsets that are equipped with color screens, camera phones and other features to facilitate digital data transmission. In the third quarter of 2009, equipment sales accounted for 9% of total revenues, while service revenues contributed 91%. PCS provided services to roughly 6.3 million subscribers at the end of September 2009, up from 4.8 million a year earlier.

In the second half of 2006, the company won eight licenses costing a total of $1.4 billion in Auction 66, the Advanced Wireless Services auction, covering roughly 126 million potential customers, including areas where PCS already provides service. The company recently expanded its coverage with launches in New York, Philadelphia, Boston and Las Vegas and plans to buildout these markets to cover 40 million POPs in 2009 and 2010. In March 2008, PCS participated in the 700 MHz spectrum auction and won a license covering the Boston market for roughly $360 million.

In September 2007, PCS announced a stock-based offer to merge with Leap Wireless (LEAP 13, Buy), a regional prepaid wireless carrier. The terms of the

deal, equal to 2.75 shares of PCS for every LEAP share, originally valued LEAP at $5.5 billion, or $75 a share. In November 2007, PCS withdrew its offer. In September 2008, PCS and LEAP announced a national roaming agreement and spectrum swap. As part of the agreement, both companies also settled all outstanding litigation. Hence, we do not expect a merger in the near term as PCS is in the middle of its market launches and may gain a stronger bargaining position once the launches begin to reap results.

PRIMARY BUSINESS DYNAMICS. In the third quarter of 2009, PCS added 66,157 net subscribers, and had a monthly churn rate of 5.8% and average revenue per user (ARPU) of $41.08, up 0.9% from a year earlier. In the second and third quarters of any given year, PCS's churn rate tends to increase and customer growth slows, but this is likely to be more pronounced in 2009 due to economic issues, including less disposable income. The company's customer profile is skewed toward first-time users, with roughly 55% of its customers fitting into that category. About 90% of its subscribers use their wireless phone as their primary phone service.

Company Financials Fiscal Year Ended Dec. 31

Per Share Data ($)	2008	2007	2006	2005	2004	2003	2002	2001	2000	1999
Tangible Book Value	NM	NM	NM	NA	NA	NA	NA	NA	NA	NA
Cash Flow	1.14	0.91	0.54	NA	NA	NA	NA	NA	NA	NA
Earnings	0.42	0.28	0.18	0.62	0.33	0.01	0.57	-0.48	NA	NA
S&P Core Earnings	0.51	0.47	0.18	0.17	NA	NA	NA	NA	NA	NA
Dividends	Nil	Nil	NA	NA	NA	NA	NA	NA	NA	NA
Payout Ratio	Nil	Nil	NA	NA	NA	NA	NA	NA	NA	NA
Prices:High	21.86	40.87	NA	NA	NA	NA	NA	NA	NA	NA
Prices:Low	10.23	13.77	NA	NA	NA	NA	NA	NA	NA	NA
P/E Ratio:High	52	NM	NA	NA	NA	NA	NA	NA	NA	NA
P/E Ratio:Low	24	NM	NA	NA	NA	NA	NA	NA	NA	NA

Income Statement Analysis (Million $)										
Revenue	2,752	2,236	1,547	1,038	748	451	129	NA	NA	NA
Operating Income	742	639	381	292	193	84.0	-95.9	NA	NA	NA
Depreciation	255	178	135	87.9	62.2	42.4	21.5	0.21	NA	NA
Interest Expense	179	202	116	58.0	19.0	11.1	6.72	10.5	16.1	NA
Pretax Income	279	224	90.5	326	112	31.7	156	-45.2	-20.6	NA
Effective Tax Rate	46.5%	55.1%	40.6%	39.1%	42.0%	51.1%	16.4%	NA	NA	NA
Net Income	149	100	53.8	199	64.9	15.5	130	-45.2	-20.6	NA
S&P Core Earnings	182	164	59.5	55.2	NA	NA	NA	NA	NA	NA

Balance Sheet & Other Financial Data (Million $)										
Cash	698	1,470	1,375	503	59.4	236	61.7	42.7	NA	NA
Current Assets	1,044	1,733	NA	NA	NA	NA	NA	NA	NA	NA
Total Assets	6,422	5,806	NA	2,159	965	902	563	324	NA	NA
Current Liabilities	742	580	NA	NA	NA	NA	NA	NA	NA	NA
Long Term Debt	3,058	2,986	2,596	903	171	182	41.4	48.6	NA	NA
Common Equity	2,034	1,849	1,730	368	125	84.9	76.1	-52.9	NA	NA
Total Capital	5,116	5,130	4,326	1,744	712	660	422	119	NA	NA
Capital Expenditures	955	768	551	278	251	117	212	134	0.09	NA
Cash Flow	405	271	164	NA	NA	NA	NA	NA	NA	NA
Current Ratio	1.4	3.0	NA	2.6	1.0	1.5	0.9	0.3	NA	NA
% Long Term Debt of Capitalization	59.8	58.2	NA	51.8	24.0	27.6	9.8	40.8	NA	NA
% Net Income of Revenue	5.4	4.5	NA	19.1	8.7	4.5	110.7	NA	NA	NA
% Return on Assets	2.4	2.0	NA	12.7	7.0	2.8	31.4	NA	NA	NA
% Return on Equity	7.7	8.2	NA	80.5	61.7	25.6	NA	NA	NA	NA

Data as orig reptd.; bef. results of disc opers/spec. items. Per share data adj. for stk. divs.; EPS diluted. E-Estimated. NA-Not Available. NM-Not Meaningful. NR-Not Ranked. UR-Under Review.

Office: 2250 Lakeside Blvd, Richardson, TX 75082-4304.
Telephone: 214-570-5800.
Website: http://www.metropcs.com
Chrmn, Pres & CEO: R.D. Linquist

COO: T.C. Keys
EVP & CFO: J.B. Carter, II
EVP, Secy & General Counsel: M.A. Stachiw
SVP, Chief Acctg Officer & Cntlr: C.B. Kornegay

Investor Contact: J. Mathias (214-570-4641)
Board Members: R. A. Anderson, W. M. Barnes, J. F. Callahan, Jr., M. P. Cole, C. C. Landry, R. D. Linquist, A. C. Patterson, J. N. Perry, Jr.

Founded: 2004
Domicile: Delaware
Employees: 3,200

The McGraw-Hill Companies

Microchip Technology Inc

STANDARD
&POOR'S

S&P Recommendation	STRONG BUY ★★★★★	Price $26.05 (as of Nov 27, 2009)	12-Mo. Target Price $33.00	Investment Style Large-Cap Growth

GICS Sector Information Technology
Sub-Industry Semiconductors

Summary This company supplies microcontrollers and analog and other semiconductor products for a wide variety of high-volume embedded control applications.

Key Stock Statistics (Source S&P, Vickers, company reports)

52-Wk Range	$28.11– 16.23	S&P Oper. EPS 2010E	0.97	Market Capitalization(B)	$4.783	Beta	1.04
Trailing 12-Month EPS	$0.92	S&P Oper. EPS 2011E	1.39	Yield (%)	5.22	S&P 3-Yr. Proj. EPS CAGR(%)	5
Trailing 12-Month P/E	28.3	P/E on S&P Oper. EPS 2010E	26.9	Dividend Rate/Share	$1.36	S&P Credit Rating	NA
$10K Invested 5 Yrs Ago	$10,991	Common Shares Outstg. (M)	183.6	Institutional Ownership (%)	NM		

Price Performance

30-Week Mov. Avg. ··· 10-Week Mov. Avg. - - — **GAAP Earnings vs. Previous Year** Volume Above Avg. ▂▃▅ STARS
12-Mo. Target Price — Relative Strength — ▲ Up ▼ Down ▶ No Change Below Avg. ▁▂▃ ★

Options: ASE, CBOE, Ph

Analysis prepared by **Clyde Montevirgen** on November 11, 2009, when the stock traded at **$ 26.66.**

Highlights

▶ We expect sales to rebound 2% in FY 10 (Mar.) after a 13% decrease in FY 09. Although the macroeconomic slowdown has hurt orders, we believe sales growth will be supported by the business and product cycles. We see more share gains in the 8-bit and 16-bit microcontroller (MCU) markets putting the company in a good position to outperform competitors as demand conditions improve, and we expect MCHP's analog business to grow faster than peers as well. For FY 11, we project a 21% advance in sales.

▶ We expect non-GAAP gross margins to narrow to 54% in FY 10, from 57% in FY 09, reflecting generally lower plant utilization than experienced last year, when the peak of the cycle occurred. Similarly, we look for non-GAAP operating margins to narrow to about 23% in FY 10, from 27% in FY 09, as we see expenses rising faster than revenues. However, we think that profitability will improve each quarter and estimate a 29% operating margin for FY 11.

▶ Our EPS estimates assume a 14% effective tax rate, exclude a few cents in non-recurring expenses, and include over $0.15 in stock-based compensation.

Investment Rationale/Risk

▶ We view MCHP as having a profitable business model featuring unusually diverse end-markets and a low cost structure. MCHP is a share leader in the 8-bit MCU business, and we believe it will continue to take share in that market as well as further penetrate the 16-bit MCU and analog markets. We think MCHP faces less risk than peers due to its ability to reduce volatility in earnings through effectively managing sales and expenses. In addition to our expectation for share price appreciation, we see the recent dividend yield of around 5% providing compelling total return potential.

▶ Risks to our recommendation and target price include industry cyclicality, global operations, numerous competitors, and the challenges of entering new markets for 16-bit MCUs.

▶ Our 12-month target price of $33 is based on a weighted blend of valuation metrics. We apply a price-to-sales multiple of 5.8X, near the historical average, to our forward 12-month sales per share forecast, implying a value of $32. We also utilize a discounted cash flow model, which assumes a 10% weighted average cost of capital and a terminal growth rate of 4%, resulting in an intrinsic value of $35.

Qualitative Risk Assessment

LOW	MEDIUM	HIGH

Our risk assessment reflects the cyclicality of the semiconductor industry, offset by the company's very broad customer base and end-markets and its low cost structure.

Quantitative Evaluations

S&P Quality Ranking B+

D	C	B-	B	B+	A-	A	A+

Relative Strength Rank MODERATE

55

LOWEST = 1 HIGHEST = 99

Revenue/Earnings Data

Revenue (Million $)

	1Q	2Q	3Q	4Q	Year
2010	193.0	226.7	--	--	--
2009	268.2	269.7	192.2	173.3	903.3
2008	264.1	258.7	252.6	260.4	1,036
2007	262.6	267.9	251.0	258.2	1,040
2006	218.5	227.3	234.9	247.2	927.9
2005	212.8	220.7	205.4	208.1	846.9

Earnings Per Share ($)

	1Q	2Q	3Q	4Q	Year
2010	0.15	0.24	E0.29	E0.29	E0.97
2009	0.40	0.41	0.40	0.12	1.33
2008	0.36	0.27	0.38	0.40	1.40
2007	0.35	0.36	0.33	0.57	1.62
2006	0.29	0.31	0.19	0.35	1.13
2005	0.21	0.29	0.25	0.27	1.01

Fiscal year ended Mar. 31. Next earnings report expected: Late January. EPS Estimates based on S&P Operating Earnings; historical GAAP earnings are as reported.

Dividend Data (Dates: mm/dd Payment Date: mm/dd/yy)

Amount ($)	Date Decl.	Ex-Div. Date	Stk. of Record	Payment Date
0.339	01/29	02/11	02/13	02/27/09
0.339	05/07	05/19	05/21	06/04/09
0.339	08/06	08/18	08/20	09/03/09
0.340	11/04	11/16	11/18	12/02/09

Dividends have been paid since 2002. Source: Company reports.

Please read the Required Disclosures and Analyst Certification on the last page of this report.

The McGraw-Hill Companies

Microchip Technology Inc

STANDARD &POOR'S

Business Summary November 11, 2009

CORPORATE OVERVIEW. Microchip Technology Inc. (MCHP) develops and manufactures specialized chips used in a wide variety of embedded control applications. MCHP is a leading microcontroller company, having shipped over 7 billion PIC microcontrollers since 1990. MCHP also offers a broad range of high-performance linear, mixed-signal, power management, thermal management, battery management, and interface devices, and serial EEPROMs.

Microcontrollers are low-cost components that form the brains of the vast majority of electronic devices, except for PCs. MCHP's signature products include a broad family of proprietary 8- and 16-bit field programmable microcontrollers under the PIC name, designed for applications requiring high performance, fast time-to-market, and user programmability. The company offers a comprehensive set of low-cost and easy-to-learn application development tools that let system designers program a PIC microcontroller for specific applications.

By main product lines, microcontrollers provided 81.0% of sales in FY 09 (Mar.) (80.4% in FY 08), memory products 9.9% (11.6%), and analog and interface products 9.1% (8.0%). Average selling prices are relatively stable for the microcontrollers and for analog products with significant proprietary content, which is about half the analog segment. Pricing for some of its commodity-type products, such as EEPROMs, tend to fluctuate.

Foreign sales accounted for 75% of FY 09 net sales, similar to FY 08 results. By major region, FY 09 sales came from Asia (46.2%), Europe (28.5%), and the Americas (25.3%). Approximately 23% of FY 09 sales were sourced from China, including Hong Kong, and Taiwan accounted for about 10% of sales. About 64% of net sales in FY 09 were made through distributors.

Company Financials Fiscal Year Ended Mar. 31

Per Share Data ($)	2009	2008	2007	2006	2005	2004	2003	2002	2001	2000
Tangible Book Value	5.18	5.39	9.03	7.89	6.95	6.19	5.58	5.36	4.80	3.52
Cash Flow	1.85	1.87	2.14	1.64	1.58	1.32	1.00	0.98	1.20	0.93
Earnings	1.33	1.40	1.62	1.13	1.01	0.65	0.47	0.45	0.69	0.56
S&P Core Earnings	1.35	1.48	1.62	1.05	0.89	0.47	0.30	0.28	0.57	NA
Dividends	1.21	0.97	0.57	0.21	0.11	0.04	0.04	Nil	Nil	Nil
Payout Ratio	91%	69%	35%	18%	11%	6%	9%	Nil	Nil	Nil
Calendar Year	2008	2007	2006	2005	2004	2003	2002	2001	2000	1999
Prices:High	38.37	42.46	38.56	34.98	34.88	36.50	33.99	28.29	34.39	22.81
Prices:Low	16.28	27.50	30.63	24.06	25.12	17.85	15.02	14.00	12.92	7.54
P/E Ratio:High	29	30	24	31	35	56	72	62	50	41
P/E Ratio:Low	12	20	19	21	25	27	32	31	19	14

Income Statement Analysis (Million $)										
Revenue	903	1,036	1,040	928	847	699	651	571	716	496
Operating Income	336	427	464	567	400	314	286	232	304	204
Depreciation	96.1	98.2	116	111	120	142	111	109	104	68.5
Interest Expense	24.3	0.75	0.75	5.42	1.97	0.94	0.25	0.49	0.57	0.75	1.05
Pretax Income	237	351	401	359	277	178	128	127	196	140
Effective Tax Rate	NM	15.2%	11.0%	32.5%	22.9%	22.8%	22.3%	25.5%	27.2%	27.0%
Net Income	249	298	357	242	214	137	99.7	94.8	143	102
S&P Core Earnings	253	314	357	226	190	100	63.5	58.2	117	NA

Balance Sheet & Other Financial Data (Million $)										
Cash	1,390	1,325	167	565	68.7	105	53.9	281	130	188
Current Assets	1,743	1,718	1,085	1,119	1,075	884	609	549	372	365
Total Assets	2,421	2,512	2,270	2,351	1,818	1,622	1,428	1,276	1,161	812
Current Liabilities	156	191	256	609	307	270	215	168	195	169
Long Term Debt	1,149	1,150	Nil	Nil	Nil	Nil	Nil	Nil	Nil	Nil
Common Equity	991	1,036	2,004	1,726	1,486	1,321	1,179	1,076	943	624
Total Capital	2,192	2,208	2,013	1,741	1,510	1,351	1,212	1,107	966	643
Capital Expenditures	102	69.8	60.0	76.3	63.2	63.5	80.4	44.7	441	212
Cash Flow	345	396	473	353	334	279	211	204	247	171
Current Ratio	11.2	9.0	4.2	1.8	3.5	3.3	2.8	3.3	1.9	2.2
% Long Term Debt of Capitalization	52.4	52.1	Nil	Nil	Nil	Nil	Nil	Nil	Nil	Nil
% Net Income of Revenue	27.6	28.8	34.3	26.1	25.2	19.6	15.3	16.6	20.0	20.6
% Return on Assets	10.1	12.5	15.5	11.6	12.4	9.0	7.4	7.8	14.1	15.5
% Return on Equity	24.6	19.6	19.1	15.1	15.2	11.0	8.8	9.4	17.8	20.8

Data as orig reptd.; bef. results of disc opers/spec. items. Per share data adj. for stk. divs.; EPS diluted. E-Estimated. NA-Not Available. NM-Not Meaningful. NR-Not Ranked. UR-Under Review.

Office: 2355 West Chandler Boulevard, Chandler, AZ 85224-6199.
Telephone: 480-792-7200.
Email: ir@mail.microchip.com
Website: http://www.microchip.com

Chrmn, Pres & CEO: S. Sanghi
COO & EVP: G. Moorthy
CFO & Chief Acctg Officer: J.E. Bjornholt
Secy & General Counsel: K. Van Herk

Investor Contact: G. Parnell (480-792-7374)
Board Members: M. W. Chapman, L. Day, IV, A. Hugo-Martinez, W. Meyercord, S. Sanghi

Founded: 1989
Domicile: Delaware
Employees: 4,895

Micron Technology Inc.

STANDARD &POOR'S

S&P Recommendation BUY ★★★★☆	**Price** $7.30 (as of Nov 27, 2009)	**12-Mo. Target Price** $10.00	**Investment Style** Large-Cap Value

GICS Sector Information Technology
Sub-Industry Semiconductors

Summary This company is a manufacturer of semiconductor memory products, including DRAM and NAND flash memory, as well as image sensors.

Key Stock Statistics (Source S&P, Vickers, company reports)

52-Wk Range	$9.13– 1.75	S&P Oper. EPS 2010E	-0.10	Market Capitalization(B)	$6.204	Beta	1.06
Trailing 12-Month EPS	$-2.29	S&P Oper. EPS 2011E	NA	Yield (%)	Nil	S&P 3-Yr. Proj. EPS CAGR(%)	NM
Trailing 12-Month P/E	NM	P/E on S&P Oper. EPS 2010E	NM	Dividend Rate/Share	Nil	S&P Credit Rating	B
$10K Invested 5 Yrs Ago	$6,404	Common Shares Outstg. (M)	849.8	Institutional Ownership (%)	94		

Price Performance

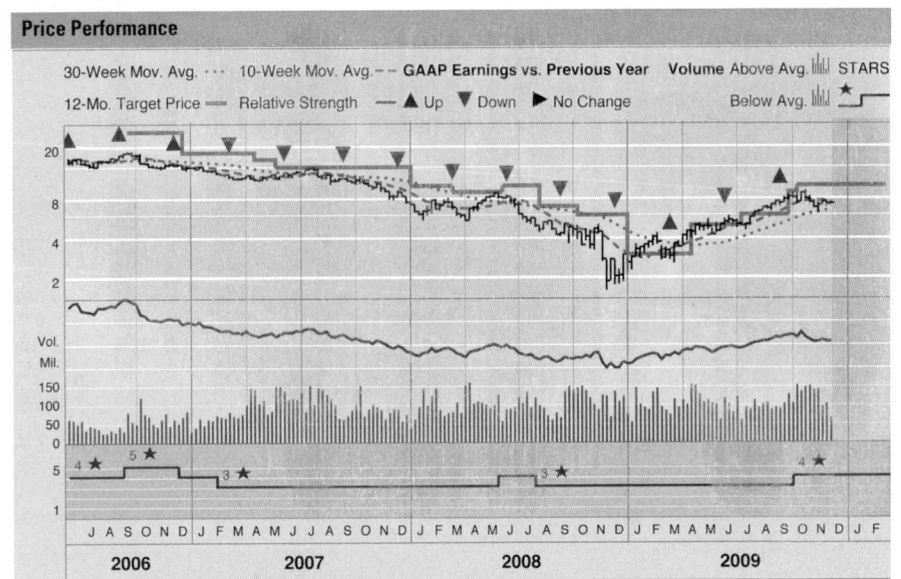

30-Week Mov. Avg. · · · 10-Week Mov. Avg. ‑ ‑ **GAAP Earnings vs. Previous Year** Volume Above Avg. STARS
12-Mo. Target Price — Relative Strength — ▲ Up ▼ Down ► No Change Below Avg.

Options: ASE, CBOE, P, Ph

Analysis prepared by **Clyde Montevirgen** on October 02, 2009, when the stock traded at **$ 7.44**.

Highlights

► We think revenues will grow 35% in FY 10 (Aug.), after an 18% decrease in FY 09. We expect average selling prices for DRAM and NAND chips to improve from recent levels due to improving industry dynamics, including consolidation and joint ventures, bankruptcy of weaker memory chipmakers, reduced production, and more prudent capital expenditures. We anticipate healthy demand and bit-growth supported by computers, mobile phones and flash-based portable media players.

► We expect gross margins of 15% in FY 10, versus the -9% seen in FY 09, largely based on our view of improving ASPs and healthy bit growth. We also believe that gross margins will benefit from improving capacity utilization, assuming that demand will pick up in FY 10. We see operating margins of 2% in FY 10, an improvement from the -35% in FY 09, which includes notable impairment, restructuring and other operating expenses.

► Our estimates assume low effective tax rates and include stock-based compensation.

Investment Rationale/Risk

► We believe Micron is in a better financial position than some competitors, and we think it will be among the survivors after a projected industry shakeout. The company has invested in new manufacturing technology that could reduce per-unit costs when demand recovers, which we see aiding long-term margins. With a more favorable pricing environment, we think Micron will turn profitable in coming quarters, and believe that relative multiples will rise as a result.

► Risks to our opinion and target price include notable financial risks, worse-than-expected sales of computers and consumer electronic products, excessive inventory, and lower-than-anticipated unit cost reductions.

► Our 12-month target price of $10 is based on a price-to-sales multiple of about 1.3X applied to our forward 12-month sales per share estimate. We believe that a below-historical average multiple is warranted by our view of weaker growth compared to sales performance in previous upcycles, and the high risk of further ASP deterioration.

Qualitative Risk Assessment

LOW	MEDIUM	HIGH

Micron is subject to semiconductor industry cyclicality and to sudden changes in pricing for commodity memory products. It is a relatively large semiconductor company and is the lone American survivor in the global DRAM industry, which has been consolidating in recent years.

Quantitative Evaluations

S&P Quality Ranking C

D	C	B-	B	B+	A-	A	A+

Relative Strength Rank MODERATE

42

LOWEST = 1   HIGHEST = 99

Revenue/Earnings Data

Revenue (Million $)

	1Q	2Q	3Q	4Q	Year
2009	1,402	993.0	1,106	1,302	4,803
2008	1,535	1,359	1,498	1,449	5,841
2007	1,530	1,427	1,294	1,437	5,688
2006	1,362	1,225	1,312	1,373	5,272
2005	1,260	1,308	1,054	1,258	4,880
2004	1,107	991.0	1,117	1,189	4,404

Earnings Per Share ($)

2009	-0.91	-0.97	-0.36	-0.10	-2.29
2008	-0.34	-1.01	-0.30	-0.45	-2.10
2007	0.15	-0.07	-0.29	-0.21	-0.42
2006	0.09	0.27	0.12	0.08	0.57
2005	0.23	0.17	-0.20	0.07	0.29
2004	Nil	-0.04	0.13	0.14	0.24

Fiscal year ended Aug. 31. Next earnings report expected: Late December. EPS Estimates based on S&P Operating Earnings; historical GAAP earnings are as reported.

Dividend Data

No cash dividends have been paid since 1996.

Micron Technology Inc.

Business Summary October 02, 2009

CORPORATE OVERVIEW. Micron Technology is a global manufacturer and marketer of dynamic random access memory (DRAM), NAND flash memory, and complementary metal-oxide semiconductor (CMOS) image sensors. The company's products are used in an increasingly broad range of electronic devices, including personal computers, workstations, network servers, mobile phones, digital still cameras, MP3 players and other consumer electronics products. About 50% of FY 08 (Aug.) total sales were to the computing market. Intel accounted for 19% of the company's FY 08 sales.

The company has been in the DRAM business since 1980, and is currently one of the world's largest DRAM suppliers. DRAM products are high-density, low-cost per bit, random access memory devices that provide high-speed data storage and retrieval. Micron offers DRAM products with a variety of performance, pricing, and other characteristics. The company's DRAM products may be classified as core DRAM or specialty memory.

Micron has two segments -- memory, which includes both DRAM and NAND

flash memory, and imaging. The memory segment comprised 89% of total revenues in FY 08. By memory type, DRAM sales accounted for 54% of the total in FY 08, down from 65% in the previous fiscal year, reflecting an expansion into flash memory and CMOS image sensors over the last couple of years. NAND flash memory sales comprised 35% of sales in FY 08, reflecting growing market demand for memory devices that can retain memory when the power is turned off, for use in handheld electronic devices such as digital still cameras.

The imaging segment made up 11% of total revenues in FY 08. This segment's main product is the CMOS image sensor. Micron offers a broad range of image sensors, including lower-end pixel resolutions from its VGA (video graphics array) products to its higher resolution 9-megapixel products. The company's main image sensor customers are camera module integrators.

Company Financials Fiscal Year Ended Aug. 31

Per Share Data ($)	2009	2008	2007	2006	2005	2004	2003	2002	2001	2000
Tangible Book Value	5.08	7.56	9.00	9.64	9.07	8.73	7.68	9.93	11.59	11.34
Cash Flow	NA	0.57	1.81	2.33	2.07	2.13	-0.10	0.45	1.00	4.13
Earnings	-2.29	-2.10	-0.42	0.57	0.29	0.24	-2.11	-1.51	-0.88	2.56
S&P Core Earnings	-2.27	-1.54	-0.38	0.40	-0.12	-0.09	-2.60	-2.14	-1.06	NA
Dividends	Nil	Nil	Nil	Nil	Nil	Nil	Nil	Nil	Nil	Nil
Payout Ratio	Nil	Nil	Nil	Nil	Nil	Nil	Nil	Nil	Nil	Nil
Prices:High	9.13	8.97	14.31	18.65	14.82	18.25	15.66	39.50	49.61	97.50
Prices:Low	2.55	1.59	7.11	13.12	9.32	10.89	6.60	9.50	16.39	28.00
P/E Ratio:High	NM	NM	NM	33	51	76	NM	NM	NM	38
P/E Ratio:Low	NM	NM	NM	23	32	45	NM	NM	NM	11

Income Statement Analysis (Million $)	2009	2008	2007	2006	2005	2004	2003	2002	2001	2000
Revenue	4,803	5,841	5,688	5,272	4,880	4,404	3,091	2,589	3,936	7,336
Operating Income	NA	887	1,381	1,631	1,458	1,445	133	152	138	3,288
Depreciation	2,139	2,056	1,718	1,281	1,265	1,218	1,210	1,177	1,114	994
Interest Expense	NA	95.0	40.0	25.0	46.9	36.0	36.5	17.1	16.7	104
Pretax Income	-1,944	-1,611	-168	433	199	232	-1,200	-998	-960	2,317
Effective Tax Rate	NM	NM	NM	4.16%	5.34%	32.2%	NM	NM	NM	34.4%
Net Income	-1,835	-1,619	-320	408	188	157	-1,273	-907	-521	1,504
S&P Core Earnings	-1,819	-1,190	-290	288	-75.8	-62.2	-1,578	-1,288	-626	NA

Balance Sheet & Other Financial Data (Million $)	2009	2008	2007	2006	2005	2004	2003	2002	2001	2000
Cash	1,485	1,362	2,192	1,431	525	486	570	398	469	702
Current Assets	NA	3,779	5,234	5,101	2,926	2,639	2,037	2,119	3,138	4,904
Total Assets	11,455	13,430	14,818	12,221	8,006	7,760	7,158	7,555	8,363	9,632
Current Liabilities	NA	1,598	2,026	1,661	979	972	993	753	687	1,648
Long Term Debt	2,674	2,451	1,987	405	1,020	1,028	997	361	445	934
Common Equity	4,654	6,178	7,752	8,114	5,847	5,615	5,038	6,367	7,135	6,432
Total Capital	9,738	11,503	12,371	10,115	6,902	6,685	6,035	6,727	7,599	7,899
Capital Expenditures	488	2,529	3,603	1,365	1,065	1,081	822	760	1,489	1,188
Cash Flow	NA	437	1,398	1,689	1,453	1,375	-63.3	270	593	2,499
Current Ratio	1.8	2.4	2.6	3.1	3.0	2.7	2.1	2.8	4.6	3.0
% Long Term Debt of Capitalization	27.5	21.3	16.1	4.0	14.8	15.4	16.5	5.4	5.9	11.8
% Net Income of Revenue	NM	NM	NM	7.7	3.9	3.6	NM	NM	NM	20.5
% Return on Assets	NM	NM	NM	4.0	2.4	2.1	NM	NM	NM	18.1
% Return on Equity	NM	NM	NM	5.8	3.3	3.0	NM	NM	NM	28.9

Data as orig reptd.; bef. results of disc opers/spec. items. Per share data adj. for stk. divs.; EPS diluted. E-Estimated. NA-Not Available. NM-Not Meaningful. NR-Not Ranked. UR-Under Review.

Office: 8000 South Federal Way, Boise, ID 83716-9632.
Telephone: 208-368-4000.
Email: invrel@micron.com
Website: http://www.micron.com

Chrmn & CEO: S.R. Appleton
Pres & COO: D.M. Durcan
CFO & Chief Acctg Officer: R.C. Foster
Treas: P. Morali

Secy & General Counsel: R.W. Lewis
Investor Contact: K.A. Bedard (208-368-4400)
Board Members: T. Aoki, S. R. Appleton, J. W. Bageley, R. L. Bailey, M. Johnson, L. Mondry, R. E. Switz

Founded: 1978
Domicile: Delaware
Employees: 18,200

Microsoft Corp

STANDARD
&POOR'S

S&P Recommendation	HOLD ★★★☆☆	Price $29.22 (as of Nov 27, 2009)	12-Mo. Target Price $30.00	Investment Style Large-Cap Growth

GICS Sector Information Technology
Sub-Industry Systems Software

Summary Microsoft, the world's largest software company, develops PC software, including the Windows operating system, and the Office application suite.

Key Stock Statistics (Source S&P, Vickers, company reports)

52-Wk Range	$30.14–14.87	S&P Oper. EPS 2010**E**	1.67	Market Capitalization(B)	$259.448	Beta	0.92
Trailing 12-Month EPS	$1.54	S&P Oper. EPS 2011**E**	1.77	Yield (%)	1.78	S&P 3-Yr. Proj. EPS CAGR(%)	9
Trailing 12-Month P/E	19.0	P/E on S&P Oper. EPS 2010**E**	17.5	Dividend Rate/Share	$0.52	S&P Credit Rating	AAA
$10K Invested 5 Yrs Ago	$11,915	Common Shares Outstg. (M)	8,879.1	Institutional Ownership (%)	61		

Price Performance

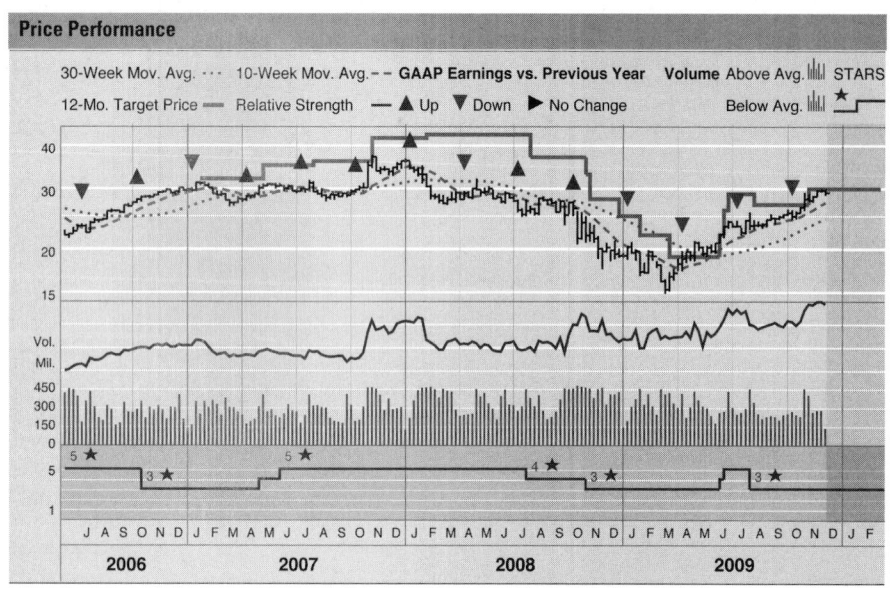

30-Week Mov. Avg. · · · 10-Week Mov. Avg. - - **GAAP Earnings vs. Previous Year**   Volume Above Avg. STARS
12-Mo. Target Price — Relative Strength   ▲ Up ▼ Down ► No Change   Below Avg.

Options: ASE, CBOE, P, Ph

Analysis prepared by **Jim Yin** on November 03, 2009, when the stock traded at **$ 27.56**.

Highlights

► We expect revenues to decrease 0.8% in FY 10 (Jun.), compared to a 3.3% decline in FY 09, reflecting our view of weak corporate and consumer spending even as the global economy recovers. We see client revenue rising 3.1% in FY 10, based on a high single-digit growth in PC sales in 2010 offset by lower selling prices in emerging and laptop markets. We project that server and tools revenue will rise 2.4%, and 1.8% for the Microsoft Business in FY 10 reflecting a sluggish recovery in corporate IT spending. We estimate Entertainment and Devices division (EDD) revenue will fall 8.5% in FY 10, on lower royalties from games developed for Xbox.

► We look for gross margins to narrow to 78% in FY 10 from 79% in FY 09, reflecting modest pricing pressure on its operating systems and increased spending in the online services group. We see operating margins rising slightly to 33.2% in FY 10, from 32.9% in FY 09, as a result of further cost reductions.

► We estimate EPS of $1.67 in FY 10, up from $1.62 in FY 09, reflecting our forecast for slightly higher operating margins and fewer shares outstanding.

Investment Rationale/Risk

► Our hold recommendation reflects our view of an economic upturn and new product announcements, offset by our concern about a slow recovery in corporate IT spending. Although we see a stronger global economy in 2010, we think companies will remain cautious. We project a mere 4% increase in IT spending in 2010. MSFT has been slowing the rate of loss of market share for the desktop operating system, but we think further loss will be abated with the release of Windows 7. We also think Bing, the company's new web search engine, will gain traction.

► Risks to our recommendation and target price include lower-than-projected PC sales, further weakness in the global economy, and failure to achieve cost synergies from acquisitions.

► Our 12-month target price of $30 is based on a weighted blend of our discounted cash flow (DCF) and P/E analyses. Our DCF model assumes an 11.1% weighted average cost of capital and 3% terminal growth rate, yielding an intrinsic value of $33. Our P/E analysis derives a value of $27, based on an industry P/E-to-growth ratio of 1.8X, or 16X our FY 10 EPS estimate of $1.67.

Qualitative Risk Assessment

LOW	MEDIUM	HIGH

Our risk assessment reflects our concern about a sluggish economic recovery, market share losses in Internet search engine, and potential difficulties releasing new products in a timely manner, mitigated by the company's current leading market positions and financial strength.

Quantitative Evaluations

S&P Quality Ranking   B+

D	C	B-	B	B+	A-	A	A+

Relative Strength Rank   STRONG

84

LOWEST = 1   HIGHEST = 99

Revenue/Earnings Data

Revenue (Million $)

	1Q	2Q	3Q	4Q	Year
2010	12,920	--	--	--	--
2009	15,061	16,629	13,648	13,099	58,437
2008	13,762	16,367	14,454	15,837	60,420
2007	10,811	12,542	14,398	13,371	51,122
2006	9,741	11,837	10,900	11,804	44,282
2005	9,189	10,818	9,620	10,161	39,788

Earnings Per Share ($)

2010	0.40	E0.48	E0.38	E0.41	E1.67
2009	0.48	0.47	0.33	0.34	1.62
2008	0.45	0.50	0.47	0.46	1.87
2007	0.35	0.26	0.50	0.31	1.42
2006	0.29	0.34	0.29	0.28	1.20
2005	0.23	0.32	0.23	0.34	1.12

Fiscal year ended Jun. 30. Next earnings report expected: Late January. EPS Estimates based on S&P Operating Earnings; historical GAAP earnings are as reported.

Dividend Data (Dates: mm/dd Payment Date: mm/dd/yy)

Amount ($)	Date Decl.	Ex-Div. Date	Stk. of Record	Payment Date
0.130	12/10	02/17	02/19	03/12/09
0.130	03/09	05/19	05/21	06/18/09
0.130	06/10	08/18	08/20	09/10/09
0.130	09/18	11/17	11/19	12/10/09

Dividends have been paid since 2003. Source: Company reports.

Please read the Required Disclosures and Analyst Certification on the last page of this report.

The McGraw-Hill Companies

Microsoft Corp

Business Summary November 03, 2009

CORPORATE OVERVIEW. Microsoft is the world's largest software maker, primarily as a result of its dominant position in operating systems, which run 90% of all PCs currently in use, and business productivity applications, where its Office productivity suite has over 400 million users. The combination of these two strongholds provides MSFT with a strong barrier to entry for competitors, in our opinion. With MSFT generating over $1 billion every month in free cash flow, it had $31.4 billion in cash and investments as of June 2009, despite having paid out more than $130 billion for dividends and share buybacks from FY 04 to FY 09 (Jun.).

MARKET PROFILE. According to IDC, global spending on packaged software totaled $211.3 billion in 2005, with MSFT's share totaling $35.0 billion or 17% of the total market. IDC expects the system infrastructure market, which comprises roughly half of MSFT's software revenues, to expand at a compound annual growth rate (CAGR) of 9.1% from 2005 through 2010. The applications market, which constitutes more than a third of revenues, is expected to increase 7.0%, and the application development and deployment market, more than 10% of revenues, is forecast to rise 7.1%. We look for MSFT to expand at slightly faster rates for the most part, as the Windows platform continues to gain market share.

CORPORATE STRATEGY. The company has been slowly shifting its business strategy from a PC-centric computing environment to a computing platform in which diverse devices will access information on the Internet. MSFT has termed it as "cloud computing." In the coming years, MSFT will focus on creating seamless user experiences across multiple devices, from PCs to cell phones to PDAs to home entertainment consoles and devices, for all the various tasks users engage in, from communications to productivity to e-commerce to entertainment. It also envisions delivering multiple levels of different services, some of which may be free or advertising-supported, some of which will have low prices, and some at higher pricing points, depending on the needs of the user. MSFT believes software must be sold both as an application, which resides on a user's system or network, and as a service, with the application and data residing on its servers with users gaining access via the Internet.

Company Financials Fiscal Year Ended Jun. 30

Per Share Data ($)	2009	2008	2007	2006	2005	2004	2003	2002	2001	2000
Tangible Book Value	2.84	2.43	2.71	3.55	4.14	6.55	5.34	2.05	4.39	3.92
Cash Flow	1.90	2.07	1.57	1.28	1.20	0.86	1.05	0.80	0.83	0.92
Earnings	1.62	1.87	1.42	1.20	1.12	0.75	0.92	0.71	0.66	0.85
S&P Core Earnings	1.63	1.99	1.38	1.27	1.20	0.83	0.75	0.65	0.58	NA
Dividends	0.50	0.43	0.39	0.34	3.32	0.16	0.08	Nil	Nil	Nil
Payout Ratio	31%	23%	27%	28%	NM	21%	9%	Nil	Nil	Nil
Prices:High	30.14	35.96	37.50	30.26	28.25	30.20	30.00	35.31	38.08	59.31
Prices:Low	14.87	17.50	26.60	21.46	23.82	24.86	22.55	20.71	21.44	20.13
P/E Ratio:High	19	19	26	25	25	40	33	50	58	70
P/E Ratio:Low	9	9	19	18	21	33	25	29	32	24

Income Statement Analysis (Million $)										
Revenue	58,437	60,420	51,122	44,282	39,788	36,835	32,187	28,365	25,296	22,956
Operating Income	23,255	25,877	19,964	17,375	15,416	10,220	14,656	12,994	13,256	11,685
Depreciation	2,562	1,872	1,440	903	855	1,186	1,439	1,084	1,536	748
Interest Expense	NA	NA	Nil	Nil	Nil	Nil	Nil	Nil	Nil	Nil
Pretax Income	19,821	23,814	20,101	18,262	16,628	12,196	14,726	11,513	11,525	14,275
Effective Tax Rate	26.5%	25.8%	30.0%	31.0%	26.3%	33.0%	32.1%	32.0%	33.0%	34.0%
Net Income	14,569	17,681	14,065	12,599	12,254	8,168	9,993	7,829	7,721	9,421
S&P Core Earnings	14,650	18,873	13,643	13,329	13,107	9,042	8,155	7,051	6,518	NA

Balance Sheet & Other Financial Data (Million $)										
Cash	29,907	21,171	6,111	6,714	4,851	15,982	6,438	3,016	3,922	4,846
Current Assets	49,280	43,242	40,168	49,010	48,737	70,566	58,973	48,576	39,637	30,308
Total Assets	77,888	72,793	63,171	69,597	70,815	92,389	79,571	67,646	59,257	52,150
Current Liabilities	27,034	29,886	23,754	22,442	16,877	14,969	13,974	12,744	11,132	9,755
Long Term Debt	3,746	1.00	Nil	Nil	Nil	Nil	Nil	Nil	Nil	Nil
Common Equity	39,558	36,286	31,097	40,104	48,115	74,825	61,020	52,180	47,289	41,368
Total Capital	43,304	36,287	31,097	40,104	48,115	74,825	62,751	52,578	48,125	42,753
Capital Expenditures	3,119	3,182	2,264	1,578	812	1,109	891	770	1,103	879
Cash Flow	17,131	19,553	15,505	13,502	13,109	9,354	11,432	8,913	9,257	10,156
Current Ratio	1.8	1.5	1.7	2.2	2.9	4.7	4.2	3.8	3.6	3.1
% Long Term Debt of Capitalization	8.7	NM	Nil	Nil	Nil	Nil	Nil	Nil	Nil	Nil
% Net Income of Revenue	24.9	29.3	27.5	28.5	30.8	22.2	31.0	27.6	30.5	41.0
% Return on Assets	19.3	26.0	21.2	17.9	14.8	9.4	13.6	12.4	13.9	20.8
% Return on Equity	38.4	52.5	39.5	28.6	19.9	11.7	17.7	15.7	17.4	27.3

Data as orig reptd.; bef. results of disc opers/spec. items. Per share data adj. for stk. divs.; EPS diluted. E-Estimated. NA-Not Available. NM-Not Meaningful. NR-Not Ranked. UR-Under Review.

Office: 1 Microsoft Way, Redmond, WA 98052-8300.
Telephone: 425-882-8080.
Email: msft@microsoft.com
Website: http://www.microsoft.com

Chrmn: W.H. Gates, III
CEO: S.A. Ballmer
COO: B.K. Turner
SVP & CFO: C.P. Liddell

SVP, Secy & General Counsel: B.L. Smith
Investor Contact: F. Brod (800-285-7772)
Board Members: S. A. Ballmer, D. Dublon, W. H. Gates, III, R. V. Gilmartin, R. Hastings, M. M. Klawe, D. F. Marquardt, C. H. Noski, H. Panke

Founded: 1975
Domicile: Washington
Employees: 93,000

Millipore Corp

STANDARD &POOR'S

| S&P Recommendation | BUY ★★★★☆ | Price $67.85 (as of Nov 27, 2009) | 12-Mo. Target Price $82.00 | Investment Style Large-Cap Growth |

GICS Sector Health Care
Sub-Industry Life Sciences Tools & Services

Summary This company provides technologies, tools and services for the discovery, development and production of new therapeutic drugs.

Key Stock Statistics (Source S&P, Vickers, company reports)

52-Wk Range	$72.99–43.42	S&P Oper. EPS 2009**E**	3.95	Market Capitalization(B)	$3.773	Beta	0.66
Trailing 12-Month EPS	$3.08	S&P Oper. EPS 2010**E**	4.38	Yield (%)	Nil	S&P 3-Yr. Proj. EPS CAGR(%)	13
Trailing 12-Month P/E	22.0	P/E on S&P Oper. EPS 2009**E**	17.2	Dividend Rate/Share	Nil	S&P Credit Rating	BB+
$10K Invested 5 Yrs Ago	$13,972	Common Shares Outstg. (M)	55.6	Institutional Ownership (%)	99		

Price Performance

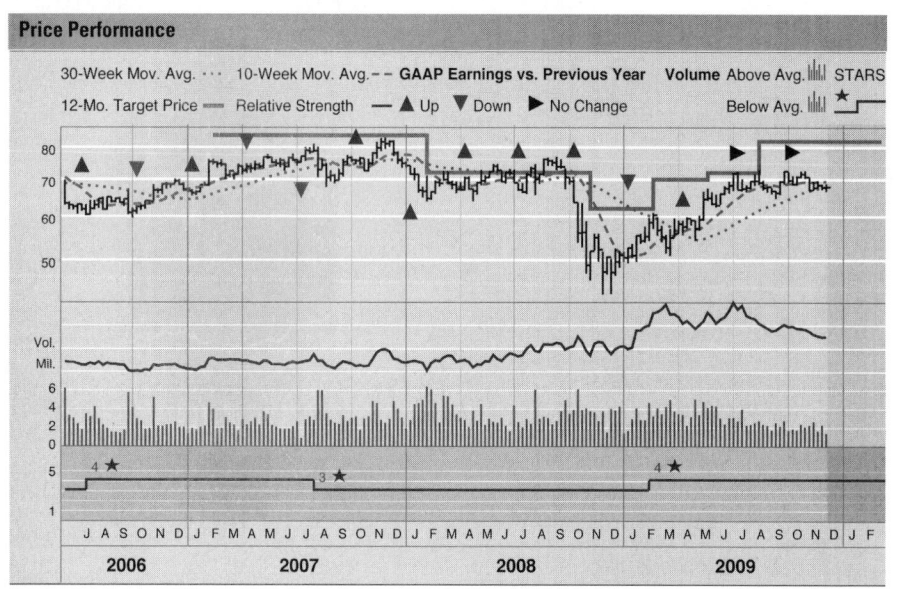

30-Week Mov. Avg. ··· 10-Week Mov. Avg. -- **GAAP Earnings vs. Previous Year** Volume Above Avg. ▮▮▮ STARS
12-Mo. Target Price — Relative Strength — ▲ Up ▼ Down ► No Change Below Avg. ▮▮▮ ★

Options: ASE, CBOE, P, Ph

Analysis prepared by **Jeffrey Loo, CFA** on November 10, 2009, when the stock traded at **$ 68.85.**

Highlights

► We see 2009 organic sales rising 6%, but we believe foreign exchange will adversely affect sales by 2%. With a 1% contribution from the 2009 Guava Technologies acquisition, we see overall sales growth of 3%, to $1.65 billion. The Bioprocess unit has returned to growth in 2009 after a challenging 2008, as large biotech clients adjusted inventory, resulting in soft demand. We think this inventory adjustment, which began in mid-2007, is complete, and we now see normal ordering patterns. We also see the bioprocess unit benefiting from strong demand for products used to manufacture H1N1 flu vaccine. Within Bioscience, we see solid demand for drug discovery and life sciences, particularly from academic facilities. In 2010, we see sales growing 6% to $1.75 billion.

► We expect gross margins to improve 150 basis points (bps) in 2009, aided by new and higher-margin products, and but see operating margins rising 120 bps on higher R&D costs. While we think MIL's net debt ($775 million at September 30, 2009) continues to hurt net margins, we see good progress paying down the debt.

► Our 2009 and 2010 operating EPS estimates are $3.95 and $4.38, respectively.

Investment Rationale/Risk

► We think companies such as MIL, which primarily supply consumables and do not rely on instrument sales, are better positioned to withstand the challenging economic environment. Approximately 90% of MIL's sales are derived from consumables and services. Although we see cost cutting within R&D departments, we think consumable sales will be only moderately affected, and we believe MIL, through its internal and external product expansion and diversification, is well positioned to gain market share. We also see several growth catalysts, including the expected significant increase in biologic license application filings in 2009, which should aid MIL's Bioprocess unit this year and beyond, and the $10 billion NIH funding from the economic stimulus package should benefit the academic and government end-markets.

► Risks to our recommendation and target price include greater-than-expected deterioration in the pharmaceutical and biotech R&D spending environment.

► Our 12-month target price of $82 is based on a peer P/E-to-growth (PEG) ratio of about 1.4X, with a three-year EPS growth rate of 13%, applied to our 2010 EPS estimate.

Qualitative Risk Assessment

| LOW | MEDIUM | HIGH |

Our risk assessment reflects MIL's broad product line and geographic reach, offset by a highly competitive marketplace and the company's proactive acquisition strategy, which we believe increases its risk profile.

Quantitative Evaluations

S&P Quality Ranking　　　　　　　B

| D | C | B- | B | B+ | A- | A | A+ |

Relative Strength Rank　　　　MODERATE

41

LOWEST = 1　　　　　　　　　HIGHEST = 99

Revenue/Earnings Data

Revenue (Million $)

	1Q	2Q	3Q	4Q	Year
2009	407.9	408.6	411.9	--	--
2008	396.2	414.2	395.0	396.8	1,602
2007	372.0	383.2	371.2	405.2	1,532
2006	268.4	273.8	330.1	383.1	1,255
2005	250.2	245.0	293.6	256.3	991.0
2004	222.5	224.7	210.7	225.4	883.3

Earnings Per Share ($)

2009	0.95	0.72	0.71	E0.93	E3.95
2008	0.59	0.72	0.71	0.60	2.62
2007	0.49	0.52	0.66	0.82	2.48
2006	0.64	0.54	0.27	0.34	1.79
2005	0.64	0.47	0.44	0.02	1.55
2004	0.55	0.57	0.50	0.49	2.10

Fiscal year ended Dec. 31. Next earnings report expected: Early February. EPS Estimates based on S&P Operating Earnings; historical GAAP earnings are as reported.

Dividend Data

No cash dividends have been paid since January 2002.

Please read the Required Disclosures and Analyst Certification on the last page of this report.

The **McGraw·Hill** Companies

Millipore Corp

STANDARD
&POOR'S

Business Summary November 10, 2009

COMPANY OVERVIEW. Millipore provides tools and services for the development and production of therapeutic drugs. MIL focuses on solutions for drug manufacturing and other production processes, and on research and development tools for the life science industry. MIL's offerings include consumable products, capital equipment, and services sold mainly to pharmaceutical, biotechnology and life science research companies. In 2008, consumables and services accounted for about 90% of sales, with the remaining 10% from hardware. The company sells more than 5,000 products, including process filtration and chromatography products, hardware components and systems used to manufacture and process biopharmaceuticals, process monitoring tools to test for contamination, laboratory sample preparation products, and laboratory water products used to create ultra pure water for laboratory analysis and clinical testing.

The company concentrates its in-house R&D on the development of new products and has augmented its product offerings and research capabilities through acquisitions and alliances, including the $1.5 billion acquisition of Serologicals in July 2006. MIL has said that its operations could be affected by an increasing number of biologic therapeutics being developed and approved over time, since its products are used in research laboratories, drug development programs, and drug manufacturing. According to the company, the drug industry is developing about 2,200 biologic compounds, including about 565 antibodies.

MIL sells its products through a global sales network. In the U.S., it mainly uses a direct sales force and Web site sales. Outside the U.S., MIL has subsidiaries and branches in more than 30 countries, and also employs independent distributors. Revenues by geographic region were as follows: the Americas 39% in 2008 (42% in 2007), Europe 43% (41%), and Asia-Pacific (the majority derived from Japan) 19% (17%). Competitors include Amersham Biosciences, Apogent Technologies (now part of Thermo Fisher Scientific), Pall Corp., Qiagen, and United States Filter Corp.

Company Financials Fiscal Year Ended Dec. 31

Per Share Data ($)	2008	2007	2006	2005	2004	2003	2002	2001	2000	1999
Tangible Book Value	NM	NM	NM	12.74	12.24	8.72	5.16	7.60	5.25	2.36
Cash Flow	4.99	4.73	3.16	2.53	2.99	2.88	2.39	1.96	3.51	2.40
Earnings	2.62	2.48	1.79	1.55	2.10	2.06	1.67	1.32	2.53	1.42
S&P Core Earnings	2.53	2.48	1.81	1.43	1.27	1.67	1.41	1.08	NA	NA
Dividends	Nil	Nil	Nil	Nil	Nil	Nil	Nil	0.44	0.44	0.44
Payout Ratio	Nil	Nil	Nil	Nil	Nil	Nil	Nil	33%	17%	31%
Prices:High	76.92	83.20	76.95	67.95	57.20	49.37	60.95	66.85	77.38	42.13
Prices:Low	43.36	65.29	59.58	42.01	42.13	29.90	27.25	42.65	36.25	23.44
P/E Ratio:High	29	34	43	44	27	24	36	51	31	30
P/E Ratio:Low	17	26	33	27	20	15	16	32	14	17

Income Statement Analysis (Million $)	2008	2007	2006	2005	2004	2003	2002	2001	2000	1999
Revenue	1,602	1,532	1,255	991	883	800	704	657	954	771
Operating Income	386	376	219	195	182	166	160	150	216	149
Depreciation	132	124	74.4	50.7	44.5	40.5	35.0	30.7	46.1	44.3
Interest Expense	60.8	69.0	45.3	6.71	9.45	16.5	19.0	25.3	26.9	30.2
Pretax Income	178	152	120	138	130	112	104	78.4	154	82.4
Effective Tax Rate	16.1%	8.15%	17.8%	41.7%	19.1%	10.1%	22.0%	19.0%	22.4%	21.9%
Net Income	146	136	97.0	80.2	106	101	80.8	63.5	119	64.3
S&P Core Earnings	141	136	97.9	74.6	64.0	82.0	68.5	51.8	NA	NA

Balance Sheet & Other Financial Data (Million $)	2008	2007	2006	2005	2004	2003	2002	2001	2000	1999
Cash	115	36.2	77.5	651	152	147	101	62.5	58.4	51.1
Current Assets	752	690	709	1,067	541	516	390	312	465	359
Total Assets	2,752	2,777	2,771	1,647	1,014	951	786	916	875	793
Current Liabilities	247	282	402	243	163	222	134	134	235	270
Long Term Debt	1,129	1,260	1,316	552	147	216	334	320	300	313
Common Equity	1,278	1,137	948	792	639	461	288	394	305	177
Total Capital	2,413	2,412	2,286	1,350	793	677	622	759	605	490
Capital Expenditures	76.5	102	110	86.4	63.7	71.9	79.3	72.3	52.2	31.3
Cash Flow	278	260	171	131	150	141	116	94.2	165	109
Current Ratio	3.0	2.5	1.8	4.4	3.3	2.3	2.9	2.3	2.0	1.3
% Long Term Debt of Capitalization	46.7	52.2	57.6	40.9	18.5	31.9	53.7	42.1	49.6	63.9
% Net Income of Revenue	9.1	8.9	7.7	8.1	12.0	12.6	11.5	9.7	12.5	8.3
% Return on Assets	5.3	4.9	4.4	6.0	10.7	11.5	9.3	7.3	14.3	8.3
% Return on Equity	12.1	13.1	11.1	11.2	19.1	26.9	23.7	18.2	49.4	41.4

Data as orig reptd.; bef. results of disc opers/spec. items. Per share data adj. for stk. divs.; EPS diluted. E-Estimated. NA-Not Available. NM-Not Meaningful. NR-Not Ranked. UR-Under Review.

Office: 290 Concord Road, Billerica, MA 01821.
Telephone: 978-715-4321 .
Website: http://www.millipore.com
Chrmn, Pres & CEO: M.D. Madaus

COO: P.C. Kershaw
CFO: C.F. Wagner, Jr.
CSO: D.W. Harris
Chief Acctg Officer & Cntlr: A.L. Mattacchione

Investor Contact: J. Young (978-715-1527)
Board Members: D. Bellus, R. C. Bishop, M. D. Booth, R. Classon, M. A. Hendricks, M. H. Hoffman, M. D. Madaus, J. F. Reno, E. M. Scolnick, K. E. Welke

Founded: 1954
Domicile: Massachusetts
Employees: 5,900

Molex Inc

STANDARD & POOR'S

S&P Recommendation **BUY** ★★★★☆	Price $18.88 (as of Nov 27, 2009)	12-Mo. Target Price $24.00	Investment Style Large-Cap Growth

GICS Sector Information Technology
Sub-Industry Electronic Manufacturing Services

Summary This company makes electrical and electronic devices primarily for OEMs in the computer, telecommunications, home appliance, and home entertainment industries.

Key Stock Statistics (Source S&P, Vickers, company reports)

52-Wk Range	$22.41– 9.68	S&P Oper. EPS 2010**E**	0.85	Market Capitalization(B)	$1.804	Beta	1.55
Trailing 12-Month EPS	$-2.17	S&P Oper. EPS 2011**E**	1.20	Yield (%)	3.23	S&P 3-Yr. Proj. EPS CAGR(%)	-6
Trailing 12-Month P/E	NM	P/E on S&P Oper. EPS 2010**E**	22.2	Dividend Rate/Share	$0.61	S&P Credit Rating	NA
$10K Invested 5 Yrs Ago	$7,206	Common Shares Outstg. (M)	173.7	Institutional Ownership (%)	64		

Price Performance

30-Week Mov. Avg. ··· 10-Week Mov. Avg. --- GAAP Earnings vs. Previous Year   Volume Above Avg. STARS
12-Mo. Target Price — Relative Strength — ▲ Up ▼ Down ► No Change   Below Avg. ★

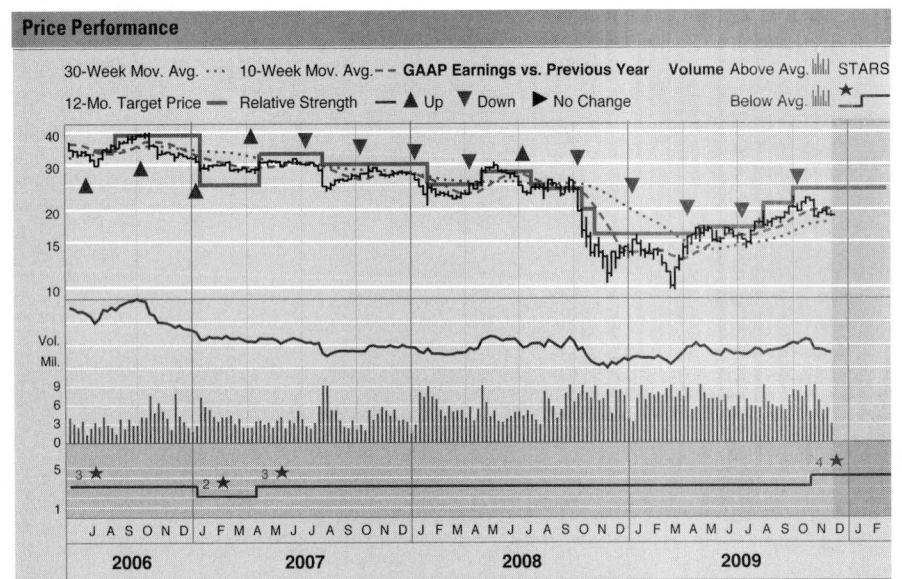

Options: CBOE, P, Ph

Analysis prepared by **Stewart Scharf** on October 29, 2009, when the stock traded at **$ 19.31**.

Highlights

► We expect revenues to continue to improve sequentially, and advance in the mid-to-high single digits in FY 10 (Jun.), driven by a return to favorable demand trends for consumer electronics, telecom and data products, especially in Asia, and a weaker U.S. dollar. We still expect global markets to remain challenging, but also see a recovery in the automotive and industrial sectors.

► We look for gross margins to expand during FY 10, from 25.4% in FY 09, based on a better mix from new products and absorption of overhead as production levels pick up. A softer U.S. dollar will likely have a negative impact on margins, while a hedging program should partially mitigate higher gold and copper prices. In our view, adjusted EBITDA margins should also improve during FY 10, from 12.4% in FY 09, reflecting cost-cutting initiatives and additional savings from a restructuring program that MOLX expects to complete in late FY 10.

► We project a lower effective tax rate of 31% in FY 10, and operating EPS of $0.85 (before about $0.32 of restructuring charges), advancing in FY 11 to $1.20.

Investment Rationale/Risk

► We recently upgraded our recommendation on the shares to Buy, from Hold, based on our valuation metrics and signs of a sequential rebound in order rates. We project potential cost benefits from a restructuring plan and other cost reductions.

► Risks to our recommendation and target price include a significant rise in copper, gold, and plastics prices; adverse foreign exchange rates; and a prolonged global economic downturn. Corporate governance practices are also a concern to us as MOLX has two classes of stock, and the board of directors consists mostly of insiders.

► Based on a blend of our relative and DCF valuation metrics, our 12-month target price is $24. Our relative metrics, including historical average price-to-sales and three-year PEG ratios, lead us to a P/E multiple of 25X our FY 10 EPS estimate, a premium to peers but on par with MOLX's five-year average historical forward P/E, valuing the shares at $21. Our DCF analysis, which assumes a 10.3% cost of capital (WACC) and a 3% terminal growth rate, suggests an intrinsic value of $27.

Qualitative Risk Assessment

LOW	MEDIUM	HIGH

Our risk assessment reflects the cyclicality in MOLX's global markets, price and product competition, volatile raw material costs, and fluctuating foreign currency exchange rates. However, we view the company's balance sheet as strong.

Quantitative Evaluations

S&P Quality Ranking   B

D	C	B-	B	B+	A-	A	A+

Relative Strength Rank   MODERATE

34

LOWEST = 1   HIGHEST = 99

Revenue/Earnings Data

Revenue (Million $)

	1Q	2Q	3Q	4Q	Year
2010	674.0	--	--	--	--
2009	839.0	666.7	505.5	570.6	2,582
2008	792.6	841.6	822.3	871.9	3,328
2007	829.6	837.5	807.0	791.9	3,266
2006	659.8	697.4	720.3	783.8	2,861
2005	640.2	651.8	612.8	643.8	2,549

Earnings Per Share ($)

2010	-0.07	E0.20	E0.22	E0.25	E0.85
2009	0.25	-0.50	-0.34	-1.27	-1.84
2008	0.29	0.33	0.28	0.29	1.19
2007	0.41	0.36	0.35	0.18	1.30
2006	0.25	0.31	0.33	0.38	1.26
2005	0.29	0.27	0.24	0.03	0.81

Fiscal year ended Jun. 30. Next earnings report expected: Late January. EPS Estimates based on S&P Operating Earnings; historical GAAP earnings are as reported.

Dividend Data (Dates: mm/dd Payment Date: mm/dd/yy)

Amount ($)	Date Decl.	Ex-Div. Date	Stk. of Record	Payment Date
0.153	08/01	12/29	12/31	01/26/09
0.153	08/01	03/27	03/31	04/27/09
0.153	08/01	06/26	06/30	07/27/09
0.153	08/01	09/28	09/30	10/26/09

Dividends have been paid since 1976. Source: Company reports.

Molex Inc

STANDARD
&POOR'S

Business Summary October 29, 2009

CORPORATE OVERVIEW. Molex is the world's second largest connector maker, operating 43 plants in 18 countries, and offering more than 100,000 products.

MOLX's products include electrical and electronic devices such as terminals, cable assemblies, interconnection systems, fiber-optic interconnection systems, and mechanical and electronic switches. In FY 09 (Jun.), these products were sold to the following industries: data products (21%), telecommunications (26%), consumer products (21%), automotive (14%), industrial (15%), and other (3%). Revenues by segment were: Connector, 69%; Custom & Electrical, 31%; and Corporate and other, less than 1%.

MOLX sells primarily to original equipment manufacturers (OEMs), subcontractors and suppliers. Customers include Arrow, Cisco, Dell, Ford, General Motors, Hewlett-Packard, IBM, Matsushita, Motorola and Nokia. The highly fragmented $36 billion global connector industry has grown at a compound annual rate (CAGR) of 6% over the past 25 years, although sales were projected to decline 25% in calendar 2009.

Net revenues outside the U.S. accounted for 73% of the FY 09 total. About 54% of net revenues were generated in Asia/Pacific (including 24% in China and 17% in Japan), 19% in Europe and 27% in the Americas. About 52% of manufacturing capacity is in lower-cost regions such as Eastern Europe, Mexico and China.

At September 30, 2009, order backlog was $304 million, up 20% on a sequential basis. New orders in the first quarter of FY 10 were $724 million, down 9% from a year earlier but up 26% sequentially, driven by orders in the Asia/Pacific. The 1.07 book-to-bill ratio remained positive, and was up from 1.01 in the prior period. in FY 09, the company generated 22% of sales from new products (introduced within the past 36 months), launching 194 new products. MOLX's annual target range is 20% to 30%.

In the first half of FY 09, the company bought back 1,607,000 of its Class A common shares and 2.9 million common shares for $77 million. Subsequently, MOLX suspended the buyback plan based on adverse economic conditions. About $123 million remains under the authorization.

In FY 09, MOLX incurred a pretax restructuring charge of $131 million ($0.57 per share, after taxes), a pretax charge of $20 million for impairments ($0.07), and after-tax goodwill impairment charges of $264 million ($1.51).

Company Financials Fiscal Year Ended Jun. 30

Per Share Data ($)	2009	2008	2007	2006	2005	2004	2003	2002	2001	2000
Tangible Book Value	10.89	12.66	10.64	11.60	10.78	10.05	9.10	8.64	8.25	7.83
Cash Flow	-0.40	2.58	2.58	2.41	2.02	2.10	1.62	1.53	2.13	2.11
Earnings	-1.84	1.19	1.30	1.26	0.81	0.92	0.44	0.39	1.03	1.12
S&P Core Earnings	-0.36	1.13	1.30	1.27	0.76	0.85	0.39	0.39	1.01	NA
Dividends	0.61	0.45	0.30	0.23	0.15	0.10	0.10	0.10	0.10	0.07
Payout Ratio	NM	38%	23%	18%	19%	11%	23%	26%	10%	6%
Prices:High	22.41	30.61	32.34	40.10	30.00	36.10	35.12	39.61	48.00	63.75
Prices:Low	9.68	10.29	23.50	25.63	23.75	27.07	19.98	19.43	25.76	34.19
P/E Ratio:High	NM	26	25	32	37	39	80	NM	47	57
P/E Ratio:Low	NM	22	18	20	29	29	45	50	25	31

Income Statement Analysis (Million $)										
Revenue	2,582	3,328	3,266	2,861	2,549	2,247	1,843	1,712	2,366	2,217
Operating Income	321	599	596	552	481	450	-120	324	498	512
Depreciation	252	252	238	215	231	228	229	224	218	196
Interest Expense	Nil	Nil	Nil	Nil	Nil	Nil	Nil	Nil	Nil	Nil
Pretax Income	-319	339	338	329	217	240	110	93.2	291	324
Effective Tax Rate	NM	36.4%	28.8%	28.0%	28.8%	26.5%	22.5%	17.9%	30.0%	31.1%
Net Income	-321	215	241	237	154	176	84.9	76.5	204	222
S&P Core Earnings	-62.1	205	241	238	143	164	76.1	76.7	200	NA

Balance Sheet & Other Financial Data (Million $)										
Cash	468	510	461	486	498	339	350	313	208	241
Current Assets	1,448	1,783	1,591	1,548	1,374	1,169	962	915	892	1,023
Total Assets	2,942	3,600	3,316	2,973	2,728	2,572	2,335	2,254	2,214	2,247
Current Liabilities	714	649	531	595	470	428	356	360	374	475
Long Term Debt	30.3	146	128	8.81	9.98	14.0	16.9	17.8	25.5	21.6
Common Equity	2,063	2,677	2,523	2,281	2,168	2,066	1,897	1,828	1,766	1,706
Total Capital	2,093	2,823	2,651	2,290	2,180	2,081	1,914	1,846	1,793	1,734
Capital Expenditures	178	235	297	277	231	190	171	172	376	337
Cash Flow	-69.4	468	479	452	385	404	314	300	422	419
Current Ratio	2.0	2.8	3.0	2.6	2.9	2.7	2.7	2.5	2.4	2.2
% Long Term Debt of Capitalization	1.5	5.2	4.8	0.4	0.5	0.7	0.9	1.0	1.4	1.2
% Net Income of Revenue	NM	6.5	7.4	8.3	6.1	7.8	4.6	4.5	8.6	10.0
% Return on Assets	NM	6.2	7.7	8.3	5.8	7.2	3.7	3.4	9.1	10.7
% Return on Equity	NM	8.3	10.0	10.7	7.3	8.9	4.6	4.3	11.7	13.9

Data as orig reptd.; bef. results of disc opers/spec. items. Per share data adj. for stk. divs.; EPS diluted. E-Estimated. NA-Not Available. NM-Not Meaningful. NR-Not Ranked. UR-Under Review.

Office: 2222 Wellington Court, Lisle, IL 60532.
Telephone: 630-969-4550.
Website: http://www.molex.com
Co-Chrmn: J.H. Krehbie, Jr.

Co-Chrmn: F.A. Krehbiel
Pres & COO: L. McCarthy
Vice Chrmn & CEO: M.P. Slark
Investor Contact: D.D. Johnson (630-969-4550)

Board Members: M. J. Birck, M. L. Collins, A. Dhebar, E.
D. Jannotta, J. H. Krehbie, Jr., F. L. Krehbiel, F. A.
Krehbiel, D. L. Landsittel, J. W. Laymon, D. G. Lubin, J.
S. Metcalf, R. J. Potter, M. P. Slark

Founded: 1938
Domicile: Delaware
Employees: 25,240

Molson Coors Brewing Co

STANDARD &POOR'S

S&P Recommendation **BUY** ★★★★☆	Price $45.01 (as of Nov 27, 2009)	12-Mo. Target Price $52.00	Investment Style Large-Cap Blend

GICS Sector Consumer Staples
Sub-Industry Brewers

Summary TAP, the fifth largest brewer in the world, was formed in early 2005 via the combination of Adolph Coors Co. and Molson, Inc.

Key Stock Statistics (Source S&P, Vickers, company reports)

52-Wk Range	$51.33– 30.76	S&P Oper. EPS 2009**E**	3.86	Market Capitalization(B)	$7.155	Beta	0.85
Trailing 12-Month EPS	$3.24	S&P Oper. EPS 2010**E**	3.57	Yield (%)	2.13	S&P 3-Yr. Proj. EPS CAGR(%)	8
Trailing 12-Month P/E	13.9	P/E on S&P Oper. EPS 2009**E**	11.7	Dividend Rate/Share	$0.96	S&P Credit Rating	BBB-
$10K Invested 5 Yrs Ago	$13,666	Common Shares Outstg. (M)	185.0	Institutional Ownership (%)	85		

Price Performance

30-Week Mov. Avg. · · · · 10-Week Mov. Avg. – – – **GAAP Earnings vs. Previous Year** Volume Above Avg. STARS
12-Mo. Target Price — Relative Strength — ▲ Up ▼ Down ► No Change Below Avg.

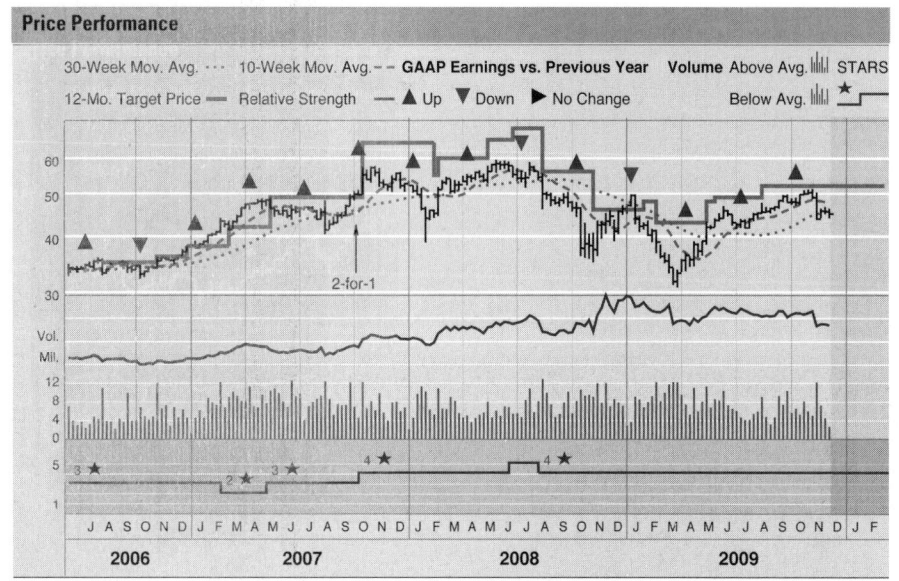

2-for-1

Options: CBOE, P, Ph

Analysis prepared by **Esther Y. Kwon, CFA** on November 10, 2009, when the stock traded at **$ 44.75**.

Highlights

► In June 2008, TAP combined its U.S. operations in a joint venture with SABMiller, with accounting on an equity interest basis. By pooling breweries, distribution resources and brand marketing, the companies believe they can achieve $500 million of cost synergies annually in three years.

► As a result of the joint venture, we see 2009 sales falling about 40%. We expect continued growth for Coors Light, Blue Moon and Keystone Light in the U.S., partially offsetting volume drops for Miller brands. We look for continued pressures in the U.K. market to hurt overall sales growth, but expect improvement as the Scottish and Newcastle brewing agreement ramps up volume. Due to the JV, we see increased profits on a full year of MillerCoors equity operations and accelerated cost reductions of about $240 million in 2009. In 2010, we see profits from the MillerCoors equity operations rising at just under a double-digit rate.

► On an effective tax rate of about 3% compared to slightly over 20% in 2008, we estimate 2009 operating EPS of $3.86, before special items, versus 2008's adjusted $2.77. In 2010, we forecast EPS of $3.57 on a 23% tax rate.

Investment Rationale/Risk

► We had been concerned about raw materials inflation, particularly in Canada and the U.K., where TAP has limited ability to hedge adverse impact, but recent declines in key commodities have made us more positive on TAP's outlook. We project improving results based on new business and easing comparisons in the U.K. in 2009 and from continuing strength in core brands Coors Light, Keystone Light and Blue Moon in the U.S. However, we are somewhat concerned with weak volumes in Canada in light of increased price competition. Still, we view the shares as undervalued at recent levels.

► Risks to our opinion and target price include a weakening of Coors Light volumes in the U.S. and Canada, an inability to successfully raise prices, and heightened competitive pressures, particularly in Canada. Commodity cost increases could pose additional risks. We see significant execution risk in the joint venture.

► Our 12-month target price of $52 is based on our P/E analysis. Applying a forward P/E multiple of 14.5X, below TAP's recent average, to our 2010 EPS estimate, we derive a value of $52.

Qualitative Risk Assessment

LOW	MEDIUM	HIGH

Our risk assessment reflects the stable revenue streams of the brewing industry, in which TAP is a major player, offset by our corporate governance concerns with respect to TAP's multi-class stock structure and its more than 50% controlling family interest.

Quantitative Evaluations

S&P Quality Ranking   A-

D	C	B-	B	B+	A-	A	A+

Relative Strength Rank   MODERATE

31

LOWEST = 1   HIGHEST = 99

Revenue/Earnings Data

Revenue (Million $)

	1Q	2Q	3Q	4Q	Year
2009	559.0	798.9	853.7	--	--
2008	1,357	1,757	921.1	739.2	4,774
2007	1,229	1,676	1,685	1,600	6,191
2006	1,154	1,583	1,577	1,531	5,845
2005	1,048	1,547	1,527	1,385	5,507
2004	923.5	1,151	1,104	1,127	4,306

Earnings Per Share ($)

2009	0.43	1.01	1.31	E1.07	E3.86
2008	0.25	0.50	0.92	0.49	2.16
2007	0.11	1.02	0.74	0.96	2.84
2006	-0.11	0.91	0.71	0.65	2.16
2005	-0.24	0.56	0.76	0.20	1.44
2004	0.07	0.95	0.84	0.73	2.60

Fiscal year ended Dec. 31. Next earnings report expected: Mid February. EPS Estimates based on S&P Operating Earnings; historical GAAP earnings are as reported.

Dividend Data (Dates: mm/dd Payment Date: mm/dd/yy)

Amount ($)	Date Decl.	Ex-Div. Date	Stk. of Record	Payment Date
0.200	02/20	02/25	02/27	03/16/09
0.240	05/15	05/27	05/29	06/15/09
0.240	08/05	08/27	08/31	09/15/09
0.240	11/12	11/25	11/30	12/15/09

Dividends have been paid since 1970. Source: Company reports.

Please read the Required Disclosures and Analyst Certification on the last page of this report.

The **McGraw·Hill** Companies

Molson Coors Brewing Co

Business Summary November 10, 2009

CORPORATE OVERVIEW. Molson Coors Brewing Company was formed in February 2005 by the combination of Adolph Coors Co. and Canadian brewer Molson, Inc. The transaction resulted in each Molson Class B voting share being converted to shares with 0.126 voting rights and 0.234 non-voting rights of Molson Coors stock, and each Molson Class A converted to shares with a 0.360 non-voting share of Molson Coors. In June 2008, Molson Coors and SABMiller formed a joint venture of each company's United States and Puerto Rican operations. The deal gave TAP a 50% voting and 42% economic interest.

Molson Inc. was the world's 14th largest brewer in 2004, pre-merger, with operations in Canada, Brazil and the United States. A global brewer with C$3.5 billion in gross annual sales, Molson traces its roots back to 1786, making it North America's oldest beer brand. Adolph Coors Co. was the third largest U.S. brewer, with a 10.3% share of the U.S. beer market in 2004, selling 32.7 million barrels of beer and other malt beverage products, up 3% from the level of 2003. The company was founded in 1873.

TAP's stable of well known U.S. brands includes Coors Light, Original Coors, and Coors Non-Alcoholic premium beers; above-premium brews such as

George Killian's Irish Red and Blue Moon Belgian White Ale, and Aspen Edge; and lower-priced beers, including Extra Gold, Keystone Premium, Keystone Light, and Keystone Ice. Coors produces Zima and Zima Citrus malt-based beverages. Brands sold primarily in Canada include Molson Canadian, Molson Dry, Molson Export, Creemore Springs, Rickard's Red Ale, Carling and Pilsner. Brands sold primarily in the U.K. include Carling, Coors Fine Light Beer, Worthington's Caffrey's, Reef, Screamers, and Stones. Approximately 74% of TAP's 2008 volume was sold in the United States segment, 12% in the Canada segment, and 14% in the Europe segment.

CORPORATE STRATEGY. We look favorably on TAP's strategy to gain market share in each area by cross marketing its products. We are particularly pleased with the gains we see for Coors Light brand in Canada, where it now has a 13% market share, making it the largest selling light beer and second largest selling beer brand in Canada.

Company Financials Fiscal Year Ended Dec. 31

Per Share Data ($)	2008	2007	2006	2005	2004	2003	2002	2001	2000	1999
Tangible Book Value	4.13	NM	NM	NM	1.72	NM	NM	12.03	12.16	11.03
Cash Flow	3.63	4.74	4.68	3.89	6.13	5.71	5.36	3.28	3.19	2.88
Earnings	2.16	2.84	2.16	1.44	2.60	2.39	2.21	1.66	1.47	1.23
S&P Core Earnings	1.03	2.53	1.87	1.07	2.13	2.10	0.77	0.68	NA	NA
Dividends	0.76	0.64	0.64	0.64	0.41	0.41	0.41	0.40	0.36	0.32
Payout Ratio	35%	23%	31%	44%	16%	17%	19%	24%	25%	26%
Prices:High	59.51	57.70	38.50	40.00	40.06	32.41	35.08	40.59	41.16	32.91
Prices:Low	35.00	37.56	30.38	28.69	26.87	22.93	25.25	21.33	18.69	22.63
P/E Ratio:High	28	20	18	28	15	14	16	25	28	27
P/E Ratio:Low	16	13	15	20	10	10	11	13	13	18
Income Statement Analysis (Million $)										
Revenue	4,774	6,191	5,845	5,507	4,306	4,000	3,776	2,429	2,414	2,057
Operating Income	874	1,099	1,097	960	609	551	535	296	295	271
Depreciation	273	346	438	393	268	244	230	121	129	124
Interest Expense	104	136	143	131	72.4	81.2	70.9	2.01	6.41	4.36
Pretax Income	515	534	472	295	308	254	257	198	170	151
Effective Tax Rate	20.0%	0.78%	17.5%	17.0%	30.9%	31.2%	37.0%	37.9%	35.3%	38.7%
Net Income	400	515	374	230	197	175	162	123	110	92.3
S&P Core Earnings	190	459	324	172	161	154	56.1	50.7	NA	NA
Balance Sheet & Other Financial Data (Million $)										
Cash	216	377	182	39.4	123	19.4	59.2	310	120	164
Current Assets	1,107	1,777	1,458	1,468	1,268	1,079	1,054	607	498	613
Total Assets	10,417	13,452	11,603	11,799	4,658	4,486	4,297	1,740	1,629	1,546
Current Liabilities	986	1,736	1,800	2,237	1,177	1,134	1,148	518	379	393
Long Term Debt	1,832	2,261	2,130	2,137	894	1,160	1,383	20.0	105	105
Common Equity	5,980	7,149	5,817	5,325	1,601	1,267	982	951	932	842
Total Capital	7,822	10,059	8,601	8,151	2,682	2,623	2,522	1,033	1,127	1,025
Capital Expenditures	231	428	446	406	212	240	240	245	154	134
Cash Flow	674	861	812	623	465	418	392	244	239	216
Current Ratio	1.1	1.0	0.8	0.7	1.1	1.0	0.9	1.2	1.3	1.6
% Long Term Debt of Capitalization	23.4	22.5	24.8	26.2	33.3	44.2	54.9	1.9	9.3	10.2
% Net Income of Revenue	8.4	8.3	6.4	4.2	4.6	4.4	4.3	5.1	4.5	4.5
% Return on Assets	3.4	4.1	3.2	2.8	4.3	4.0	5.4	7.3	6.9	6.1
% Return on Equity	6.1	7.9	6.7	6.7	13.7	15.5	16.7	13.1	12.4	11.4

Data as orig reptd.; bef. results of disc opers/spec. items. Per share data adj. for stk. divs.; EPS diluted. E-Estimated. NA-Not Available. NM-Not Meaningful. NR-Not Ranked. UR-Under Review.

Office: 1225 17th St, Denver, CO 80202-5534.
Telephone: 303-279-6565.
Website: http://www.molsoncoors.com
Chrmn: P.H. Coors

Pres & CEO: P.S. Swinburn
Vice Chrmn: A. Molson
SVP, Secy & General Counsel: S.D. Walker
CFO: S. Glendinning

Investor Contact: D. Dunnewald (303-279-6565)
Board Members: F. Bellini, R. G. Brewer, J. E. Cleghorn, P. H. Coors, C. M. Herington, F. W. Hobbs, A. Molson, G. E. Molson, I. Napier, D. P. Obrien, M. E. Osborn, P. H. Patsley, H. Riley, P. S. Swinburn

Founded: 1873
Domicile: Delaware
Employees: 14,000

Monsanto Co

STANDARD &POOR'S

S&P Recommendation HOLD ★★★☆☆

Price	12-Mo. Target Price	Investment Style
$79.50 (as of Nov 27, 2009)	$84.00	Large-Cap Blend

GICS Sector Materials
Sub-Industry Fertilizers & Agricultural Chemicals

Summary This company is a global provider of agricultural products and integrated solutions for farmers.

Key Stock Statistics (Source S&P, Vickers, company reports)

52-Wk Range	$93.35– 65.60	S&P Oper. EPS 2010**E**	3.20	Market Capitalization(B)	$43.332	Beta	0.71
Trailing 12-Month EPS	$3.80	S&P Oper. EPS 2011**E**	4.12	Yield (%)	1.33	S&P 3-Yr. Proj. EPS CAGR(%)	16
Trailing 12-Month P/E	20.9	P/E on S&P Oper. EPS 2010**E**	24.8	Dividend Rate/Share	$1.06	S&P Credit Rating	A+
$10K Invested 5 Yrs Ago	$36,659	Common Shares Outstg. (M)	545.1	Institutional Ownership (%)	79		

Price Performance

30-Week Mov. Avg. · · · 10-Week Mov. Avg. – – **GAAP Earnings vs. Previous Year** Volume Above Avg. STARS
12-Mo. Target Price — Relative Strength ▲ Up ▼ Down ▶ No Change Below Avg.

Options: ASE, CBOE, P

Analysis prepared by **Kevin Kirkeby** on November 12, 2009, when the stock traded at **$ 74.35.**

Qualitative Risk Assessment

LOW	MEDIUM	HIGH

Our risk assessment reflects MON's exposure to global agricultural markets and currencies, adverse weather, unfavorable legal and regulatory developments, and risks relating to the enforcement of intellectual property rights. This is offset by relatively low exposure to economic cycles and our view of consistent cash flow generation.

Quantitative Evaluations

S&P Quality Ranking B+

D	C	B-	B	B+	A-	A	A+

Relative Strength Rank STRONG

73

LOWEST = 1   HIGHEST = 99

Revenue/Earnings Data

Revenue (Million $)

	1Q	2Q	3Q	4Q	Year
2009	2,649	4,035	3,161	1,879	11,724
2008	2,049	3,727	3,538	2,051	11,365
2007	1,539	2,609	2,842	1,573	8,563
2006	1,405	2,200	2,348	1,391	7,344
2005	1,072	1,908	2,040	1,274	6,294
2004	1,028	1,492	1,679	1,258	5,457

Earnings Per Share ($)

2009	0.98	1.97	1.25	-0.43	3.78
2008	0.45	2.00	1.46	-0.32	3.59
2007	0.17	0.99	1.02	-0.52	1.66
2006	0.11	0.80	0.61	-0.25	1.27
2005	-0.24	0.68	0.08	-0.24	0.29
2004	-0.15	0.29	0.43	-0.07	0.51

Fiscal year ended Aug. 31. Next earnings report expected: Early January. EPS Estimates based on S&P Operating Earnings; historical GAAP earnings are as reported.

Highlights

► We forecast revenues will decline 2% in FY 10 (Aug.), based on farmers maintaining relatively stable corn and soybean acreage domestically, but a sharp decline in global glyphosate prices. In the face of rising supplies and aggressive pricing tactics by competitors, we believe MON shifted away from its premium pricing strategy for Roundup herbicides. Still, we anticipate that it continues to achieve market share gains and higher average prices through the rollout of next generation seeds.

► While we still expect MON to aggressively manage production costs in its Roundup unit, the magnitude of price cuts, in our view, will lead to a narrowing in overall margins during FY 10. Further, we expect little change in actual amounts spent on research and development, as well as in the selling, general and administrative line item. Still, we see margins in the seeds and traits segment widening as double and triple stacked varieties become a larger portion of the sales mix.

► Our EPS estimate for FY 10 of $3.20 excludes the $0.15 to $0.18 in restructuring charges the company expects to take in the coming year.

Investment Rationale/Risk

► MON shares trade at a valuation premium to the S&P 500, reflecting what we see as above-average earnings growth prospects over the coming decade. We expect the primary contributors to be the introduction of next-generation seeds, and development of its smaller product segments. Also, we anticipate that recent trait approvals will boost crop penetration outside the United States. However, given uncertainty regarding both glyphosate profitability and the yield benefit of its new corn seeds, we believe the stock is fairly valued.

► Risks to our recommendation and target price include unfavorable weather affecting planting and crop mix, further declines in grain or fertilizer prices, and greater U.S. regulatory scrutiny.

► Our DCF model, which assumes a 10.4% cost of equity and annual free cash flow growth averaging 16% for five years, slowing to 4% terminal growth thereafter, calculates intrinsic value approaching $83. Our relative valuation model targets a four-quarter forward P/E multiple of 26.0X, which is above the 5-year historical average, and produces a value near $86. Blending these two metrics results in our 12-month target price of $84.

Dividend Data (Dates: mm/dd Payment Date: mm/dd/yy)

Amount ($)	Date Decl.	Ex-Div. Date	Stk. of Record	Payment Date
0.240	12/08	01/07	01/09	01/30/09
0.265	01/14	04/01	04/03	04/24/09
0.265	06/09	06/30	07/02	07/24/09
0.265	08/05	10/07	10/09	10/30/09

Dividends have been paid since 2001. Source: Company reports.

Please read the Required Disclosures and Analyst Certification on the last page of this report.

The McGraw-Hill Companies

Monsanto Co

STANDARD & POOR'S

Business Summary November 12, 2009

CORPORATE OVERVIEW. Monsanto (MON) produces leading seed brands and develops biotechnology traits that assist farmers in controlling insects and weeds, and provides other seed companies with genetic material and biotech traits. MON's Roundup herbicides are used for agricultural, industrial and residential weed control, and are sold in more than 80 countries.

MARKET PROFILE. The company operates in two segments: agricultural productivity, and seeds and genomics. Agricultural productivity (38% of sales and 33% of gross profits in FY 09 (Aug.)) consists of MON's crop protection products (Roundup herbicide and other glyphosate products), its animal agriculture, and the Roundup lawn and garden products. In FY 09, Roundup and other glyphosate-based herbicides accounted for 30% of total sales. Patent protection for the active ingredient in Roundup herbicides expired in the U.S. in 2000. Since then, MON has repositioned itself as one of the lowest cost producers in an effort to mitigate declining herbicide pricing and margins.

Seeds and genomics (62% of sales and 67% of gross profits) consists of the

global seeds and related traits businesses, and technology platforms based on plant genomics, which increases the speed and power of genetic research. MON's seeds and genomics segment focuses on corn, soybeans and other oilseeds, cotton and wheat. Given the loss of patent protection for Roundup, we believe MON has focused on capturing value and profitability in its patent-protected seeds and traits business, and expanded its product line through its acquisition of Seminis in 2005 and De Ruiter in 2008, among other smaller purchases. De Ruiter is a leader in the protected-culture segment of the vegetable seeds market, where MON had little presence. Given this trend, we think that the growth and margin outlook for MON's seeds and genomics segment is superior to that of its agricultural productivity segment.

Company Financials Fiscal Year Ended Aug. 31

Per Share Data ($)	2009	2008	2007	2006	2005	2004	2003	2002	2001	2000
Tangible Book Value	10.02	8.59	6.35	6.95	5.99	7.71	7.26	7.24	7.84	7.24
Cash Flow	NA	4.61	2.61	2.25	1.21	1.37	0.56	1.12	1.61	1.40
Earnings	3.78	3.59	1.66	1.27	0.29	0.51	-0.02	0.25	0.57	0.34
S&P Core Earnings	3.60	3.27	1.72	1.36	0.67	0.68	0.61	0.01	0.52	NA
Dividends	1.01	0.77	0.48	0.39	0.33	0.27	0.25	0.24	0.23	Nil
Payout Ratio	27%	21%	29%	30%	113%	53%	NM	98%	40%	Nil
Prices:High	93.35	145.80	116.25	53.49	39.93	28.22	14.45	17.00	19.40	13.69
Prices:Low	66.57	63.47	49.10	37.91	25.00	14.04	6.78	6.60	13.44	9.88
P/E Ratio:High	25	41	70	42	NM	55	NM	69	34	40
P/E Ratio:Low	18	18	30	30	86	28	NM	27	24	29

Income Statement Analysis (Million $)	2009	2008	2007	2006	2005	2004	2003	2002	2001	2000
Revenue	11,724	11,365	8,563	7,344	6,294	5,457	3,373	4,673	5,462	5,493
Operating Income	NA	3,458	2,138	1,694	1,503	1,254	768	882	1,335	1,216
Depreciation	548	573	527	519	488	452	302	460	554	546
Interest Expense	NA	132	139	134	115	91.0	57.0	59.0	99.0	214
Pretax Income	2,967	2,926	1,336	1,055	261	402	-38.0	202	463	334
Effective Tax Rate	28.5%	30.7%	30.1%	32.2%	39.8%	32.6%	NM	36.1%	35.9%	47.6%
Net Income	2,098	2,007	922	698	157	271	-11.0	129	297	175
S&P Core Earnings	1,997	1,830	951	745	363	362	317	5.45	277	NA

Balance Sheet & Other Financial Data (Million $)	2009	2008	2007	2006	2005	2004	2003	2002	2001	2000
Cash	1,956	1,613	866	1,460	525	1,037	511	428	307	131
Current Assets	NA	7,609	5,084	5,461	4,644	4,931	4,962	4,424	4,797	4,973
Total Assets	17,874	17,993	12,983	11,728	10,579	9,164	9,461	8,890	11,429	11,726
Current Liabilities	NA	4,439	3,075	2,279	2,159	1,894	1,944	1,810	2,377	2,757
Long Term Debt	1,724	1,792	1,150	1,639	1,458	1,075	1,258	851	893	962
Common Equity	10,056	9,374	7,503	6,680	5,613	5,258	5,156	5,180	7,483	7,341
Total Capital	11,780	11,370	8,653	8,319	7,071	6,333	6,414	6,031	8,376	8,303
Capital Expenditures	916	918	509	370	281	210	114	224	382	582
Cash Flow	NA	2,580	1,449	1,217	645	723	291	589	851	721
Current Ratio	2.1	1.7	1.7	2.4	2.2	2.6	2.6	2.4	2.0	1.8
% Long Term Debt of Capitalization	14.6	15.8	13.3	19.7	20.6	17.0	19.6	14.1	10.7	11.6
% Net Income of Revenue	17.9	17.7	10.8	9.5	2.5	5.0	NM	2.8	5.4	3.2
% Return on Assets	11.7	13.0	7.5	6.3	1.6	2.9	NM	1.3	2.6	1.5
% Return on Equity	21.6	23.8	13.0	11.2	2.9	5.2	NM	2.0	4.0	2.9

Data as orig reptd.; bef. results of disc opers/spec. items. Per share data adj. for stk. divs.; EPS diluted. E-Estimated. NA-Not Available. NM-Not Meaningful. NR-Not Ranked. UR-Under Review.

Office: 800 North Lindbergh Boulevard, St. Louis, MO 63167-0001.
Telephone: 314-694-1000.
Email: info@monsanto.com
Website: http://www.monsanto.com

Chrmn, Pres & CEO: H. Grant
EVP & CFO: C.M. Casale
EVP & CTO: R.T. Fraley
SVP, Secy & General Counsel: D.F. Snively

Chief Acctg Officer & Cntlr: R.B. Clark
Investor Contact: S.L. Foster (314-694-8148)
Board Members: F. V. AtLee, III, J. W. Bachmann, D. L. Chicoine, J. Fields, H. Grant, A. H. Harper, G. S. King, C. S. McMillan, W. U. Parfet, G. H. Poste, R. J. Stevens

Founded: 2000
Domicile: Delaware
Employees: 27,000

Monster Worldwide Inc

STANDARD &POOR'S

S&P Recommendation BUY ★★★★☆

Price	12-Mo. Target Price	Investment Style
$14.92 (as of Nov 27, 2009)	$20.00	Large-Cap Blend

GICS Sector Industrials
Sub-Industry Human Resource & Employment Services

Summary Monster Worldwide operates a multinational online career network. It also provides offerings to help consumers develop and direct their careers.

Key Stock Statistics (Source S&P, Vickers, company reports)

52-Wk Range	$19.28– 5.95	S&P Oper. EPS 2009**E**	0.05	Market Capitalization(B)	$1.875	Beta	2.13
Trailing 12-Month EPS	$0.41	S&P Oper. EPS 2010**E**	0.30	Yield (%)	Nil	S&P 3-Yr. Proj. EPS CAGR(%)	-21
Trailing 12-Month P/E	36.4	P/E on S&P Oper. EPS 2009**E**	NM	Dividend Rate/Share	Nil	S&P Credit Rating	NA
$10K Invested 5 Yrs Ago	$5,435	Common Shares Outstg. (M)	125.7	Institutional Ownership (%)	NM		

Price Performance

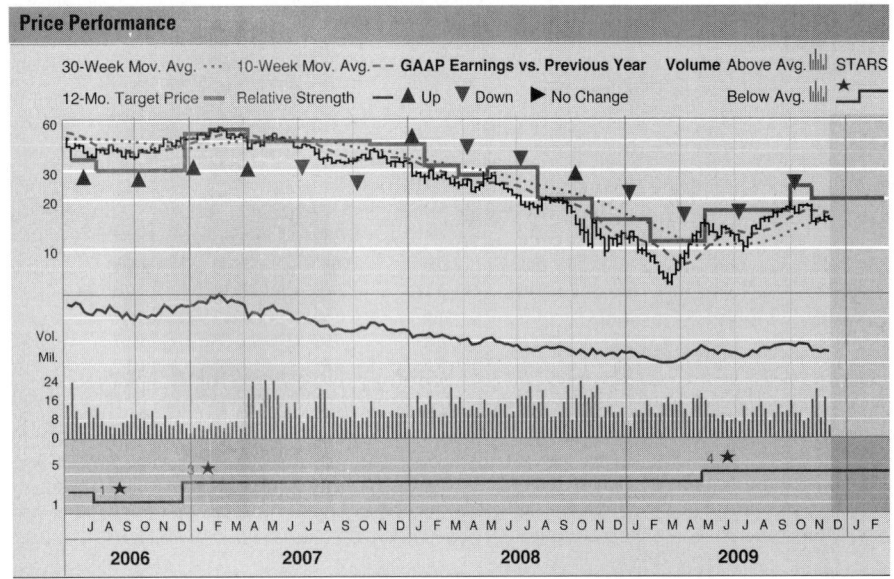

30-Week Mov. Avg. · · · · 10-Week Mov. Avg. – – **GAAP Earnings vs. Previous Year** Volume Above Avg. ▮▮▮ STARS
12-Mo. Target Price — Relative Strength — ▲ Up ▼ Down ▶ No Change Below Avg. ▮▮▮ ★

Options: ASE, CBOE, P

Qualitative Risk Assessment

LOW	MEDIUM	HIGH

Our risk assessment reflects the cyclicality of the help wanted industry, as it strongly correlates with the economy. In addition, foreign operations carry operating and exchange rate risks.

Quantitative Evaluations

S&P Quality Ranking B-

D	C	B-	B	B+	A-	A	A+

Relative Strength Rank WEAK

27

LOWEST = 1 HIGHEST = 99

Revenue/Earnings Data

Revenue (Million $)

	1Q	2Q	3Q	4Q	Year
2009	254.4	223.1	214.5	--	--
2008	366.5	354.3	332.2	290.7	1,344
2007	329.0	331.2	337.1	354.0	1,351
2006	257.0	275.2	285.9	298.6	1,117
2005	232.1	239.0	249.3	266.6	986.9
2004	182.4	202.1	224.2	236.8	845.5

Earnings Per Share ($)

	1Q	2Q	3Q	4Q	Year
2009	-0.09	-0.01	0.27	E0.01	E0.05
2008	0.19	0.15	0.36	0.24	0.94
2007	0.30	0.21	0.25	0.36	1.13
2006	0.26	0.29	0.31	0.31	1.17
2005	0.19	0.21	0.25	0.28	0.92
2004	0.11	0.14	0.18	0.20	0.62

Fiscal year ended Dec. 31. Next earnings report expected: Late January. EPS Estimates based on S&P Operating Earnings; historical GAAP earnings are as reported.

Highlights

➤ The 12-month target price for MWW has recently been changed to $20.00 from $24.00. The Highlights section of this Stock Report will be updated accordingly.

Investment Rationale/Risk

➤ The Investment Rationale/Risk section of this Stock Report will be updated shortly. For the latest News story on MWW from MarketScope, see below.

➤ 10/29/09 12:23 pm ET ... S&P MAINTAINS BUY OPINION ON SHARES OF MONSTER WORLD-WIDE (MWW 15.64****): Q3 adjusted EPS of $0.01 vs. $0.40 is $0.02 below our forecast, as revenues fell 35% on soft global recruitment demand. But we think MWW is doing a good job reducing costs and updating its services, and will likely post solid EPS gains when labor markets recover. We cut our '09 EPS estimate by $0.05 to $0.05, and '10's by $0.20 to $0.30. Despite our estimate cuts, we think government stimulus is bringing labor markets to a trough. We cut our target price by $4 to $20, 2.7X our reduced '10 revenue forecast of $940 million, and similar to prior business rebounds. /M.Jaffe

Dividend Data

No cash dividends have been paid.

Monster Worldwide Inc

STANDARD
&POOR'S

Business Summary September 24, 2009

CORPORATE OVERVIEW. Monster Worldwide is a leading online recruitment and career management services provider through its Monster.com Web site. MWW's clients range from Fortune 100 companies, to small and medium-sized enterprises and government agencies. During 2008, the company derived 47% of its revenues from its Monster Careers North America division, 43% from Monster Careers International, and 10% from its Advertising & Fees division. No client accounts for more than 5% of MWW's revenues.

Among the most visited brands on the Internet, the Monster network is designed to connect companies with qualified job seekers, offering innovative technology and services that provide greater control over the recruiting process. As of late 2008, the Monster.com network was available in about 40 countries.

Monster's job search, resume posting services and basic networking are free to the job seeker. It also offers premium career services to job seekers at a

fee, including resume writing, resume priority listing, and premium networking. MWW charges a fee to employers and human resources professionals who want to post jobs, search its resume database, and use its career site hosting and other ancillary services.

The company's Internet Advertising & Fees division provides consumers with content, services and offers, to help them manage the development and direction of their current and future careers. The majority of its services are free to users and are primarily available in North America at present, although MWW plans to expand its offerings across its global network. Revenues for the division are derived mostly from lead generation, display advertising, and products sold to consumers for a fee.

Company Financials Fiscal Year Ended Dec. 31

Per Share Data ($)	2008	2007	2006	2005	2004	2003	2002	2001	2000	1999
Tangible Book Value	0.85	3.97	3.65	1.47	0.27	0.18	2.02	2.61	5.16	0.18
Cash Flow	1.42	1.49	1.47	1.22	0.92	0.31	-0.46	1.28	1.11	0.35
Earnings	0.94	1.13	1.17	0.92	0.62	0.06	-0.96	0.61	0.53	-0.09
S&P Core Earnings	1.16	1.13	1.17	0.47	0.37	-0.08	-1.48	0.10	NA	NA
Dividends	Nil	Nil	Nil	Nil	Nil	Nil	Nil	Nil	Nil	Nil
Payout Ratio	Nil	Nil	Nil	Nil	Nil	Nil	Nil	Nil	Nil	Nil
Prices:High	32.66	54.79	59.99	42.03	34.25	29.65	48.13	68.73	94.69	80.50
Prices:Low	8.91	31.07	34.75	22.44	17.60	7.63	7.94	25.21	45.00	18.50
P/E Ratio:High	35	48	51	46	55	NM	NM	NM	NM	NM
P/E Ratio:Low	9	27	30	24	28	NM	NM	NM	NM	NM

Income Statement Analysis (Million $)	2008	2007	2006	2005	2004	2003	2002	2001	2000	1999
Revenue	1,344	1,351	1,117	987	846	680	1,115	1,448	1,292	766
Operating Income	284	303	270	214	152	101	112	262	222	109
Depreciation	58.0	47.0	39.8	38.0	37.6	28.0	55.5	76.0	62.6	35.0
Interest Expense	NA	Nil	Nil	Nil	Nil	Nil	4.90	10.6	9.49	17.0
Pretax Income	179	232	241	179	112	23.6	-130	125	114	-1.50
Effective Tax Rate	36.2%	36.5%	36.3%	35.8%	34.6%	69.0%	NM	46.1%	50.5%	NM
Net Income	114	147	154	115	73.1	7.32	-107	69.0	56.9	-7.40
S&P Core Earnings	141	147	154	59.2	44.0	-8.08	-165	11.4	NA	NA

Balance Sheet & Other Financial Data (Million $)	2008	2007	2006	2005	2004	2003	2002	2001	2000	1999
Cash	224	578	58.7	320	198	142	192	341	572	57.0
Current Assets	683	1,185	1,124	773	704	567	809	1,006	1,248	557
Total Assets	1,917	2,078	1,970	1,679	1,544	1,122	1,631	2,206	1,992	945
Current Liabilities	724	829	826	697	731	640	799	930	853	565
Long Term Debt	0.01	0.23	0.42	15.7	34.0	2.09	3.93	9.13	28.0	71.0
Common Equity	1,047	1,117	1,110	920	756	468	813	1,229	1,058	281
Total Capital	1,072	1,136	1,143	981	789	470	817	1,238	1,086	352
Capital Expenditures	93.6	64.1	55.6	39.8	24.3	21.6	46.7	73.6	78.9	40.4
Cash Flow	173	194	193	153	111	35.4	-51.0	145	119	27.6
Current Ratio	0.9	1.4	1.4	1.1	1.0	0.9	1.0	1.1	1.5	1.0
% Long Term Debt of Capitalization	Nil	0.0	0.0	1.6	4.3	0.4	0.5	0.7	2.6	19.6
% Net Income of Revenue	8.5	10.9	13.8	11.7	8.6	1.1	NM	4.8	4.4	NM
% Return on Assets	5.7	7.3	8.4	7.1	5.5	0.5	NM	3.2	3.7	NM
% Return on Equity	10.6	13.2	15.0	13.7	11.9	1.1	NM	6.0	8.2	NM

Data as orig reptd.; bef. results of disc opers/spec. items. Per share data adj. for stk. divs.; EPS diluted. E-Estimated. NA-Not Available. NM-Not Meaningful. NR-Not Ranked. UR-Under Review.

Office: 622 Third Ave, New York, NY 10017-6707.
Telephone: 212-351-7000.
Email:
corporate.communications@monsterworldwide.com
Website: http://www.monsterworldwide.com

Chrmn, Pres & CEO: S. Iannuzzi
EVP & CFO: T.T. Yates
EVP & Chief Admin Officer: L. Poulos
EVP & CIO: D. Dejanovic

SVP & Chief Acctg Officer: J.M. Langrock
Investor Contact: T.T. Yates
Board Members: R. J. Chrenc, J. R. Gaulding, E. Giambastiani, Jr., S. Iannuzzi, R. J. Kramer, R. Tunioli, T. T. Yates

Founded: 1967
Domicile: Delaware
Employees: 6,950

Moody's Corp.

STANDARD &POOR'S

S&P Recommendation	**HOLD** ★★★☆☆	Price $22.94 (as of Nov 27, 2009)	12-Mo. Target Price $27.00	Investment Style Large-Cap Growth

GICS Sector Financials
Sub-Industry Specialized Finance

Summary Moody's is a leading global credit rating, research and risk analysis concern.

Key Stock Statistics (Source S&P, Vickers, company reports)

52-Wk Range	$31.79– 15.57	S&P Oper. EPS 2009**E**	1.65	Market Capitalization(B)	$5.425	Beta	1.30
Trailing 12-Month EPS	$1.64	S&P Oper. EPS 2010**E**	1.80	Yield (%)	1.74	S&P 3-Yr. Proj. EPS CAGR(%)	-2
Trailing 12-Month P/E	14.0	P/E on S&P Oper. EPS 2009**E**	13.9	Dividend Rate/Share	$0.40	S&P Credit Rating	NA
$10K Invested 5 Yrs Ago	$5,891	Common Shares Outstg. (M)	236.5	Institutional Ownership (%)	84		

Price Performance

30-Week Mov. Avg. · · · 10-Week Mov. Avg. - - **GAAP Earnings vs. Previous Year** Volume Above Avg. STARS
12-Mo. Target Price — Relative Strength — ▲ Up ▼ Down ▶ No Change Below Avg. ★

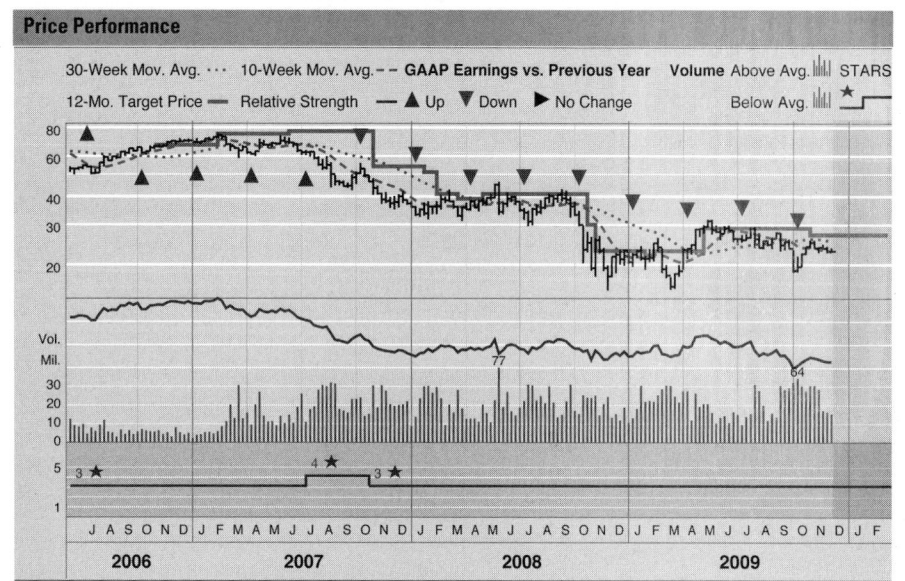

Options: ASE, CBOE, P, Ph

Analysis prepared by **Royal F. Shepard, CFA** on November 04, 2009, when the stock traded at **$ 23.59.**

Highlights

► We think revenue trends have begun to stabilize, following a 22% decline in 2008. Demand for structured finance products is likely to remain tepid until the housing recovery gains additional traction, in our view. On the back of a resurgence in corporate debt issuance, however, we estimate a 2% decline in overall 2009 revenues followed by a 4% increase in 2010. We also expect modest growth for analytical services, including software.

► We forecast a widening in operating margins to 41.3% in 2010, from 39.8% seen in 2009, due to a higher revenue basis. In our view, tight control of discretionary operating expenses will largely offset outlays for heightened regulatory compliance. The bottom line, in our estimation, may also benefit moderately from a lower effective tax rate as an increased percentage of earnings comes from non-U.S. tax jurisdictions.

► Our 2010 EPS estimate of $1.80, down from $1.65 seen in 2009, assumes MCO does not reactivate its $1.4 billion authorization for share repurchases. We exclude non-recurring restructuring costs, including $0.04 a share through the first nine months of 2009.

Investment Rationale/Risk

► We believe MCO's credit ratings business has significant barriers to entry, which should help maintain steady cash flow despite increased spending for regulatory compliance. We also expect growth to come from capital markets development overseas, acquisitions, and analytical services. We think the economic environment in the U.S. and Europe is beginning to improve, particularly for the corporate finance sector. Increased regulatory scrutiny and potential investor litigation could detract from efforts to expand advisory services.

► Risks to our opinion and target price include a greater-than-anticipated decline in the volume of debt issued in domestic and global capital markets, regulatory changes that increase competition, and persistently high long-term interest rates.

► Our 12-month target price of $27 is based primarily on applying a 9.5X EV/EBITDA multiple to our 2010 EBITDA estimate of $790 million. This multiple is at the low end of MCO's historical average, which we think is appropriate given an uncertain regulatory outlook. Our DCF model yields an intrinsic value of $28, assuming a 10.2% WACC and 3.0% terminal growth.

Qualitative Risk Assessment

LOW	**MEDIUM**	HIGH

Our risk assessment reflects Moody's significant market share in the high barrier to entry ratings industry, and what we consider the company's net positive balance sheet cash position, offset by ratings business sensitivity to higher interest rates, and the possibility of regulatory reform designed to increase competition.

Quantitative Evaluations

S&P Quality Ranking B+

D	C	B-	B	**B+**	A-	A	A+

Relative Strength Rank MODERATE

33

LOWEST = 1 HIGHEST = 99

Revenue/Earnings Data

Revenue (Million $)

	1Q	2Q	3Q	4Q	Year
2009	408.9	450.7	451.8	--	--
2008	430.7	487.6	433.4	403.7	1,755
2007	583.0	646.1	525.0	504.9	2,259
2006	440.2	511.4	495.5	590.0	2,037
2005	390.5	446.8	421.1	473.2	1,732
2004	331.2	357.6	357.9	391.6	1,438

Earnings Per Share ($)

2009	0.38	0.46	0.42	E0.33	E1.65
2008	0.48	0.55	0.46	0.37	1.87
2007	0.62	0.95	0.51	0.49	2.58
2006	0.49	0.59	0.55	0.97	2.58
2005	0.39	0.47	0.48	0.50	1.84
2004	0.34	0.34	0.32	0.40	1.40

Fiscal year ended Dec. 31. Next earnings report expected: Early February. EPS Estimates based on S&P Operating Earnings; historical GAAP earnings are as reported.

Dividend Data (Dates: mm/dd Payment Date: mm/dd/yy)

Amount ($)	Date Decl.	Ex-Div. Date	Stk. of Record	Payment Date
0.100	12/17	02/18	02/20	03/10/09
0.100	04/29	05/18	05/20	06/10/09
0.100	07/29	08/18	08/20	09/10/09
0.100	10/29	11/18	11/20	12/10/09

Dividends have been paid since 1934. Source: Company reports.

Please read the Required Disclosures and Analyst Certification on the last page of this report.

The McGraw-Hill Companies

Moody's Corp.

STANDARD
&POOR'S

Business Summary November 04, 2009

CORPORATE PROFILE. Moody's Investors Service and the Dun & Bradstreet (D&B) operating company were separated into stand-alone entities on September 30, 2000. Old D&B changed its name to Moody's Corp. (MCO), and new D&B assumed the name Dun & Bradstreet Corp. (DNB).

Moody's is a provider of credit ratings, research and analysis covering debt instruments and securities in the global capital markets, and a provider of quantitative credit assessment services, credit training services and credit process software to banks and other financial institutions. Moody's credit ratings and research help investors analyze the credit risks associated with fixed-income securities. Beyond credit rating services for issuers, Moody's provides research services, data, and analytic tools that are utilized by institutional investors and other credit and capital markets professionals.

Moody's provides ratings and credit research on governmental and commercial entities in more than 110 countries, and its customers include a wide range of corporate and governmental issuers of securities as well as institutional investors, depositors, creditors, investment banks, commercial banks, and other financial intermediaries. In 2008, 48.1% of total revenues were derived from non-U.S. markets.

Moody's operates in two reportable segments: Moody's Investors Service (MIS), and Moody's Analytics. Moody's Investors Service consists of core credit ratings services, including four ratings groups: structured finance (53% of 2008 segment revenues), corporate finance (20%), financial institutions and sovereign risk (14%), and public finance (12%). MIS revenues are derived from the originators and issuers of such transaction, typically known as a Issuer-Fee Model. The ratings groups generate revenue mainly from the assignment of credit ratings on fixed-income instruments in the debt markets.

Moody's Analytics (MA), formerly Moody's KMV, provides a variety of credit risk processing and credit risk management products for banks and investors in credit-sensitive assets in about 120 countries. In addition, MA distributes investor-oriented research and data developed by MIS as part of its credit rating business. MA estimates that more than 30,000 clients access its data and research, primarily through the Moody's research web site.

Company Financials Fiscal Year Ended Dec. 31

Per Share Data ($)	2008	2007	2006	2005	2004	2003	2002	2001	2000	1999
Tangible Book Value	NM	NM	NM	0.30	0.39	NM	NM	NM	NM	NM
Cash Flow	2.06	2.73	2.72	1.95	1.51	1.30	1.00	0.72	0.54	1.21
Earnings	1.94	2.58	2.58	1.84	1.40	1.20	0.92	0.66	0.49	0.78
S&P Core Earnings	1.85	2.61	2.26	1.83	1.35	1.12	0.85	0.64	NA	NA
Dividends	0.38	0.32	0.28	0.20	0.15	0.09	0.07	0.11	0.28	0.37
Payout Ratio	20%	12%	11%	11%	11%	8%	7%	17%	57%	47%
Prices:High	46.36	76.09	73.29	62.50	43.86	30.43	26.20	20.55	18.09	20.00
Prices:Low	15.41	35.05	49.76	39.55	29.85	19.75	17.90	12.78	11.31	11.69
P/E Ratio:High	24	29	28	34	31	25	29	31	37	26
P/E Ratio:Low	8	14	19	21	21	17	20	19	23	15
Income Statement Analysis (Million $)										
Revenue	1,755	2,259	2,037	1,732	1,438	1,247	1,023	797	602	1,972
Operating Income	818	1,222	1,138	975	820	696	563	416	305	621
Depreciation	46.7	41.2	39.5	35.2	34.1	32.6	25.0	17.0	16.6	141
Interest Expense	73.7	62.2	15.2	21.0	16.2	21.8	21.0	16.5	3.60	5.00
Pretax Income	726	1,117	1,261	935	771	656	517	382	284	457
Effective Tax Rate	37.0%	37.2%	40.2%	40.0%	44.9%	44.6%	44.1%	44.4%	44.2%	39.1%
Net Income	458	702	754	561	425	364	289	212	159	256
S&P Core Earnings	452	710	662	558	413	340	269	203	NA	NA
Balance Sheet & Other Financial Data (Million $)										
Cash	253	441	408	486	606	269	40.0	163	119	113
Current Assets	809	989	1,002	1,052	1,023	569	272	371	278	785
Total Assets	1,772	1,715	1,498	1,457	1,376	941	631	505	398	1,786
Current Liabilities	1,393	1,349	700	579	837	432	462	359	253	1,415
Long Term Debt	750	600	300	300	Nil	300	300	300	300	Nil
Common Equity	-996	-784	167	309	318	-32.1	-327	-304	-283	-417
Total Capital	-244	-184	467	609	318	268	-27.0	-4.10	17.5	-115
Capital Expenditures	84.4	182	31.1	31.3	21.3	17.9	18.0	14.8	12.3	44.1
Cash Flow	504	743	793	596	459	397	314	229	175	397
Current Ratio	0.6	0.7	1.4	1.8	1.2	1.3	0.6	1.0	1.1	0.6
% Long Term Debt of Capitalization	NM	-326.8	64.2	49.2	Nil	112.0	NM	NM	NM	Nil
% Net Income of Revenue	26.1	31.1	37.0	32.4	29.6	29.2	28.2	26.6	26.3	13.0
% Return on Assets	26.3	43.7	51.0	39.4	36.5	46.3	50.9	47.0	47.1	14.3
% Return on Equity	NM	NM	316.2	178.9	297.9	NM	NM	NM	NM	NM

Data as orig reptd.; bef. results of disc opers/spec. items. Per share data adj. for stk. divs.; EPS diluted. E-Estimated. NA-Not Available. NM-Not Meaningful. NR-Not Ranked. UR-Under Review.

Office: 250 Greenwich St, New York, NY 10007-2140.
Telephone: 212-553-0300.
Website: http://www.moodys.com
Chrmn & CEO: R.W. McDaniel, Jr.

EVP & CFO: L.S. Huber
SVP, Chief Acctg Officer & Cntlr: J. McCabe
SVP & General Counsel: J.J. Goggins
SVP & CIO: P.F. Rotella

Investor Contact: L. Westlake (212-553-7179)
Board Members: B. L. Anderson, J. D. Duffie, R. R. Glauber, E. Kist, C. Mack, III, R. W. McDaniel, Jr., H. A. McKinnell, Jr., C. Mcgillicudy, III, N. S. Newcomb, J. K. Wulff

Founded: 1998
Domicile: Delaware
Employees: 3,900

Morgan Stanley

S&P Recommendation HOLD ★★★☆☆	Price $30.51 (as of Nov 27, 2009)	12-Mo. Target Price $36.00	Investment Style Large-Cap Blend

GICS Sector Financials
Sub-Industry Investment Banking & Brokerage

Summary Morgan Stanley is among the largest financial services firms in the U.S., with operations in investment banking, securities, and investment and wealth management.

Key Stock Statistics (Source S&P, Vickers, company reports)

52-Wk Range	$35.78–10.85	S&P Oper. EPS 2009E	-0.93	Market Capitalization(B)	$41.476	Beta	1.39
Trailing 12-Month EPS	$1.45	S&P Oper. EPS 2010E	3.48	Yield (%)	0.66	S&P 3-Yr. Proj. EPS CAGR(%)	37
Trailing 12-Month P/E	21.0	P/E on S&P Oper. EPS 2009E	NM	Dividend Rate/Share	$0.20	S&P Credit Rating	A
$10K Invested 5 Yrs Ago	NA	Common Shares Outstg. (M)	1,359.4	Institutional Ownership (%)	74		

Price Performance

30-Week Mov. Avg. · · · 10-Week Mov. Avg. – – **GAAP Earnings vs. Previous Year** Volume Above Avg. STARS
12-Mo. Target Price — Relative Strength — ▲ Up ▼ Down ► No Change Below Avg. ★

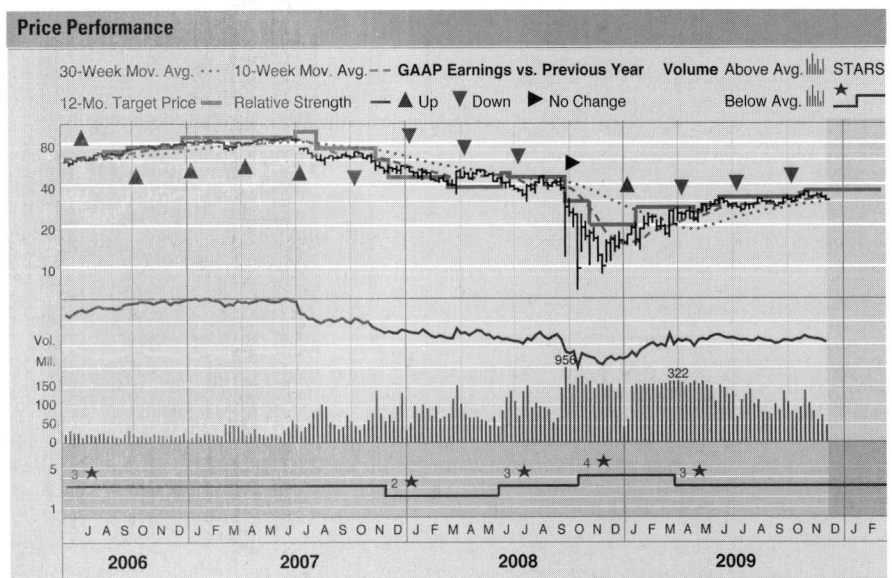

Options: ASE, CBOE, P, Ph

Analysis prepared by **Matthew Albrecht** on October 23, 2009, when the stock traded at **$ 35.00**.

Highlights

► Trading results have picked up, suggesting the firm is again willing to take on balance sheet risk, in our view. Despite narrowing spreads, with interest rates still low, margins in the business can still be attractive. The outlook for investment banking has brightened, by our analysis, and advisory revenues should increase throughout 2010, augmenting improved underwriting income. We expect better asset management results, with the firm focusing on institutional clients. Plus, wealth management results should see continued improvement as the Morgan Stanley Smith Barney joint venture gains steam. We think MS is on solid financial footing now, with sufficient excess capital and credit spreads on its own debt that have narrowed to near pre-crisis levels.

► Debt valuation adjustments will likely continue to weigh on results in the near term. Compensation costs will remain elevated on a relative basis in 2009, before returning to near 50% of net revenues in 2010, in our view. Cost cuts elsewhere should help to mitigate the margin compression.

► We expect a per-share loss of $0.93 in 2009 and EPS of $3.48 in 2010.

Investment Rationale/Risk

► We think the creation of the joint venture with Smith Barney and the sizeable resulting brokerage force will provide some long-term revenue stability. We believe trends in the Institutional Securities segment have improved, with a pickup in investment banking activity and a better trading environment, and we think a global footprint will continue to provide business opportunities. We are also encouraged because MS was able to raise capital relatively easily to repay TARP funds and pass the U.S. government "stress test." But we think the company still lags peers at this point in the recovery, and view the shares as appropriately valued.

► Risks to our recommendation and target price include stock and bond market depreciation and widening credit spreads, as well as additional industry regulation.

► MS recently traded at a discount to the overall market and its historical average multiples. Our 12-month target price of $36 is about 1.3X our 12-month forward book value per share projection, a discount to comparable peer multiples.

Qualitative Risk Assessment

LOW	MEDIUM	HIGH

Our risk assessment reflects our favorable view of the company's diversification by product and by region, offset by our concerns about corporate governance and our view that certain segments lack competitive advantages.

Quantitative Evaluations

S&P Quality Ranking B

D	C	B-	B	B+	A-	A	A+

Relative Strength Rank MODERATE

32

LOWEST = 1 HIGHEST = 99

Revenue/Earnings Data

Revenue (Million $)

	1Q	2Q	3Q	4Q	Year
2009	5,417	1,881	1,408	--	--
2008	21,184	16,523	16,699	1,829	62,264
2007	23,192	26,195	21,230	14,711	85,328
2006	18,119	19,062	20,055	19,473	76,551
2005	11,641	11,845	13,157	15,525	52,081
2004	9,992	9,802	9,854	10,420	39,549

Earnings Per Share ($)

2009	-0.57	-1.37	0.38	E0.63	E-0.93
2008	1.45	0.95	1.32	-2.24	1.54
2007	2.17	2.24	1.32	-3.61	2.37
2006	1.50	1.85	1.75	2.08	7.09
2005	1.23	0.86	1.09	1.69	4.81
2004	1.11	1.10	0.78	1.09	4.08

Fiscal year ended Dec. 31. Next earnings report expected: Mid December. EPS Estimates based on S&P Operating Earnings; historical GAAP earnings are as reported.

Dividend Data (Dates: mm/dd Payment Date: mm/dd/yy)

Amount ($)	Date Decl.	Ex-Div. Date	Stk. of Record	Payment Date
0.017	--	04/22	04/28	04/30/09
0.017	04/22	04/28	04/30	05/15/09
0.050	07/22	07/29	07/31	08/14/09
0.050	10/21	10/28	10/30	11/13/09

Dividends have been paid since 1993. Source: Company reports.

Please read the Required Disclosures and Analyst Certification on the last page of this report.

The McGraw-Hill Companies

Morgan Stanley

STANDARD &POOR'S

Business Summary October 23, 2009

CORPORATE OVERVIEW. Morgan Stanley is a global financial services firm that provides a comprehensive suite of products to a diverse group of clients and customers, including corporations, governments, financial institutions and individuals. MS currently has three operating segments: Institutional Securities, Global Wealth Management Group and Asset Management.

The Institutional Securities segment includes capital raising; financial advisory services; corporate lending; sales, trading, financing and market-making activities for equity and fixed-income securities and related products such as foreign exchange and commodities; benchmark indices and risk management analytics; research; and investment activities. The investment banking business is included in this segment, and includes capital raising activities, financial advisory services and corporate lending. This business is one of the largest in the world, ranking second globally during its fiscal year in announced mergers and acquisitions, third in initial public offerings, and tenth in global debt issuance. This segment accounted for approximately 67% of net revenues FY 08 (Nov.).

The Global Wealth Management Group provides brokerage and investment advisory services; financial and wealth planning services; annuity and insurance products; credit and other lending products; banking and cash management services; retirement services; and trust and fiduciary services. It provides these services to clients through a network of more than 8,000 global representatives, overseeing $546 billion in client assets at the end of FY 08. The segment accounted for about 28% of net revenues in FY 08. This unit was recently spun off to create a market-leading retail brokerage force with Citigroup's (C: 5, Buy) Smith Barney unit, in which Morgan Stanley holds a 51% controlling stake, with the option to increase its ownership following the third anniversary of the transaction.

Company Financials Fiscal Year Ended Dec. 31

Per Share Data ($)	2008	2007	2006	2005	2004	2003	2002	2001	2000	1999
Tangible Book Value	27.24	25.75	34.89	25.23	23.93	21.52	19.43	17.36	16.91	14.79
Earnings	1.54	2.37	7.09	4.81	4.08	3.45	2.69	3.19	4.73	4.10
S&P Core Earnings	1.07	2.17	7.12	5.00	4.18	3.48	2.38	2.84	NA	NA
Dividends	1.08	1.08	1.08	1.08	1.00	0.92	0.92	0.92	0.80	0.48
Payout Ratio	70%	46%	15%	22%	25%	27%	34%	29%	17%	12%
Prices:High	53.40	90.95	83.40	60.51	62.83	58.78	60.02	90.49	110.00	71.44
Prices:Low	6.71	47.25	54.52	47.66	46.54	32.46	28.80	35.75	58.63	35.41
P/E Ratio:High	8	38	12	13	15	17	22	28	23	17
P/E Ratio:Low	1	20	8	10	11	9	11	11	12	9

Income Statement Analysis (Million $)										
Net Interest Income	3,202	2,781	3,279	3,750	3,731	2,935	3,896	3,348	3,058	2,365
Non Interest Income	21,537	25,245	45,558	23,906	20,959	19,189	16,549	19,600	24,179	20,110
Loan Loss Provision	Nil	831	756	878	925	1,267	1,336	1,052	810	529
Non Interest Expenses	22,452	24,858	23,614	20,857	18,333	16,636	15,725	17,264	18,746	14,281
% Expense/Operating Revenue	49.9%	96.0%	84.6%	84.2%	80.8%	79.9%	81.3%	84.6%	79.5%	75.7%
Pretax Income	2,287	3,394	10,772	7,050	6,312	5,334	4,633	5,684	8,526	7,728
Effective Tax Rate	21.0%	24.5%	30.4%	26.4%	28.6%	29.0%	35.5%	36.5%	36.0%	38.0%
Net Income	1,807	2,563	7,497	5,192	4,509	3,787	2,988	3,610	5,456	4,791
% Net Interest Margin	NA	NA	NA	NA	NA	5.40	5.50	5.57	6.08	8.47
S&P Core Earnings	1,163	2,284	7,511	5,401	4,624	3,830	2,658	3,203	NA	NA

Balance Sheet & Other Financial Data (Million $)										
Money Market Assets	72,777	126,887	174,866	174,330	123,041	78,205	76,910	54,618	50,992	70,366
Investment Securities	233,542	457,192	680,484	304,172	260,640	228,904	185,588	164,011	130,818	112,042
Earning Assets:Total Loans	6,528	11,629	24,173	23,754	21,169	20,384	24,322	20,955	21,870	20,229
Total Assets	658,812	1,045,409	1,120,645	898,523	775,410	602,843	529,499	482,628	426,794	366,967
Demand Deposits	36,673	27,186	14,872	2,629	1,117	1,264	1,441	1,741	1,589	1,458
Time Deposits	6,082	3,993	13,471	16,034	12,660	11,575	12,316	10,535	10,341	8,939
Long Term Debt	141,466	190,624	144,978	110,465	95,286	68,410	43,985	40,851	36,830	28,604
Common Equity	31,676	30,169	34,264	29,248	28,272	24,933	21,951	20,437	18,796	16,344
% Return on Assets	0.2	0.2	0.7	0.6	0.7	0.7	0.6	0.8	1.4	1.4
% Return on Equity	5.8	7.7	23.5	18.9	16.9	16.2	14.1	18.2	30.3	30.3
% Loan Loss Reserve	Nil	Nil	3.3	3.5	4.5	4.9	3.8	4.0	3.6	3.7
% Loans/Deposits	24.5	78.0	85.2	127.3	153.7	158.8	176.8	170.7	183.3	229.2
% Loans/Assets	1.1	2.1	2.3	2.7	3.0	3.9	4.5	4.7	5.4	6.2
% Equity to Assets	3.6	3.0	3.1	3.3	3.9	4.1	4.2	4.3	4.5	4.4

Data as orig reptd.; bef. results of disc opers/spec. items. Per share data adj. for stk. divs.; EPS diluted. Prior to 2009, fiscal year ended November 30. E-Estimated. NA-Not Available. NM-Not Meaningful. NR-Not Ranked. UR-Under Review.

Office: 1585 Broadway, New York, NY 10036.
Telephone: 212-761-4000.
Website: http://www.morganstanley.com
Chrmn & CEO: J. Mack

EVP & CFO: T.C. Kelleher
EVP, Chief Admin Officer & Secy: T.R. Nides
EVP & General Counsel: G.G. Lynch
CTO: P. Heller

Investor Contact: W. Pike (212-761-0008)
Board Members: R. J. Bostock, E. B. Bowles, H. Davies, J. H. Hance, Jr., N. Hirano, C. R. Kidder, J. Mack, F. P. McClean, D. T. Nicolaisen, C. H. Noski, H. Olayan, C. E. Phillips, Jr., O. G. Sexton, L. D. Tyson, F. B. Whittemore

Auditor: Deloitte & Touche
Founded: 1981
Domicile: Delaware
Employees: 46,964

The **McGraw·Hill** Companies

Motorola Inc.

STANDARD &POOR'S

S&P Recommendation BUY ★★★★☆

Price $8.20 (as of Nov 27, 2009)	**12-Mo. Target Price** $12.00

Investment Style Large-Cap Blend

GICS Sector Information Technology
Sub-Industry Communications Equipment

Summary Motorola provides wireless and networking equipment for cable, fixed-line, and wireless service providers. In early 2008, MOT announced plans to spin off its handset unit as a separate company but has since delayed the possible action beyond 2009.

Key Stock Statistics (Source S&P, Vickers, company reports)

52-Wk Range	$9.45–2.98	S&P Oper. EPS 2009E	0.01	Market Capitalization(B)	$18.950	Beta	1.88
Trailing 12-Month EPS	$-1.69	S&P Oper. EPS 2010E	0.28	Yield (%)	Nil	S&P 3-Yr. Proj. EPS CAGR(%)	10
Trailing 12-Month P/E	NM	P/E on S&P Oper. EPS 2009E	NM	Dividend Rate/Share	Nil	S&P Credit Rating	BB+
$10K Invested 5 Yrs Ago	$5,112	Common Shares Outstg. (M)	2,310.9	Institutional Ownership (%)	80		

Price Performance

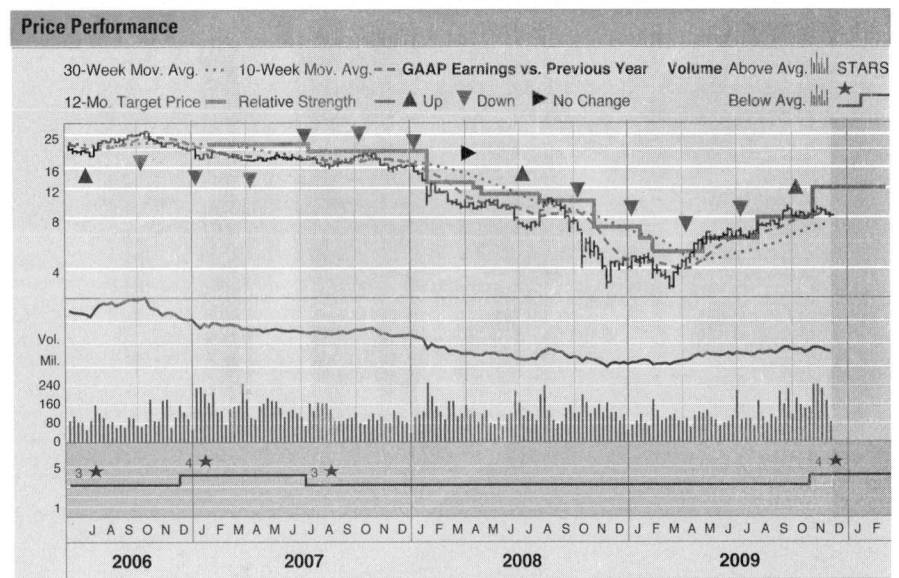

30-Week Mov. Avg. · · · 10-Week Mov. Avg. - - GAAP Earnings vs. Previous Year Volume Above Avg. STARS
12-Mo. Target Price — Relative Strength — ▲ Up ▼ Down ▶ No Change Below Avg.

Options: ASE, CBOE, P, Ph

Analysis prepared by **James Moorman, CFA** on October 30, 2009, when the stock traded at **$ 8.83**.

Highlights

► Following a sales decline of 18% in 2008, we expect a further 25% decrease in 2009 before a 14% recovery in 2010, resulting from weakness in MOT's still large Mobile Devices unit. We see almost a 50% decrease in volumes being partially offset by an 11% increase in average selling prices. We expect the Home and Networks Mobility unit (21% annual revenue decline seen for 2009) to see some pressure in the fourth quarter, and Enterprise Mobility (-13%) to also improve through the remainder of 2009 and into 2010.

► Despite pressure on sales, we expect gross margins to improve to 31.9% in 2009 and 34.0% in 2010, from 28% in 2008, as MOT improves its handset manufacturing process and focuses on higher margin smartphones. We believe that Home and Networks Mobility profitability will improve as 2009 progresses as it becomes a bigger piece of the pie.

► After an operating loss per share of $0.21 in 2008, we expect EPS of $0.01 in 2009 and $0.28 in 2010, including projected stock option expense.

Investment Rationale/Risk

► We are encouraged by MOT's efforts to lower costs and consolidate its mobile device operations as it seeks to return the business to profitability. We believe MOT will focus more on the high-end smartphone market, which could mean lower volumes but higher selling prices and margins. However, we believe execution will not only take time, but will be difficult in light of stiff competition. We anticipate operating strength in non-handset operations persisting despite some pressure on customer spending. We believe that management is still considering a potential spinoff of the Mobile Devices segment.

► Risks to our recommendation and target price include execution risks involving the handset unit, failure to successfully introduce and ship new handset products, increasing competition in the handset and smartphone market and a slowdown in telecom equipment capital spending.

► Based on a below-peers enterprise value-to-sales multiple of 1.05X our 2010 estimate, our 12-month target price is $12. We believe the shares are attractive at current levels.

Qualitative Risk Assessment

LOW | **MEDIUM** | HIGH

Our risk assessment reflects the company's exposure to the economic health of the telecom and broadband industries and risks related to high-volume manufacturing and distribution to service providers. This is offset by our view of MOT's strong cash balance.

Quantitative Evaluations

S&P Quality Ranking C

D | **C** | B- | B | B+ | A- | A | A+

Relative Strength Rank MODERATE
46
LOWEST = 1 HIGHEST = 99

Revenue/Earnings Data

Revenue (Million $)

	1Q	2Q	3Q	4Q	Year
2009	5,371	5,497	5,453	--	--
2008	7,448	8,082	7,480	7,136	30,146
2007	9,433	8,732	8,811	9,646	36,622
2006	9,608	10,876	10,603	11,792	42,879
2005	8,161	8,825	9,424	10,433	36,843
2004	7,441	7,541	7,499	8,842	31,323

Earnings Per Share ($)

2009	-0.13	-0.01	0.01	E0.08	E0.01
2008	-0.09	Nil	-0.18	-1.61	-1.87
2007	-0.09	-0.02	0.02	0.05	-0.05
2006	0.26	0.54	0.29	0.21	1.30
2005	0.28	0.38	0.69	0.47	1.82
2004	0.19	0.25	0.18	0.28	0.90

Fiscal year ended Dec. 31. Next earnings report expected: Early February. EPS Estimates based on S&P Operating Earnings; historical GAAP earnings are as reported.

Dividend Data (Dates: mm/dd Payment Date: mm/dd/yy)

Amount ($)	Date Decl.	Ex-Div. Date	Stk. of Record	Payment Date
0.050	11/12	12/11	12/15	01/15/09

Dividends have been paid since 1942. Source: Company reports.

Motorola Inc.

STANDARD
&POOR'S

Business Summary October 30, 2009

CORPORATE OVERVIEW. Motorola provides wireless and networking equipment for cable and telecom service providers. We believe all these markets are exposed to increased buyer's power due to the industry consolidation of service providers. The Mobile Devices segment (31% of sales in the third quarter of 2009, down from 41% a year earlier) manufactures wireless handsets for GSM and CDMA standards. With the sale of 160 million handsets in 2007, 100 million in 2008 and 43.1 million in the first nine months of 2009, we estimate that MOT's global handset market share declined to 13%, 6.5% and 5.5%, respectively, from 22% in 2006. The Mobile Devices segment had an operating loss in 2008, even as MOT reduced inventory.

In October 2008, MOT announced efforts to revamp its handset software platforms to reduce its cost structure and better align its offerings with customer demand for both smartphones and low-end handsets; we believe this will result in a number of product cancellations. We also think this will result in further pressure on handset volumes in the fourth quarter of 2009. In early 2009, MOT announced an additional work force reduction. We also expect the company to move away from the low-end handset business and focus more on the high-end smartphone market.

The remainder of MOT's revenues come from the Home and Networks Mobility (37%) and Enterprise Mobility (32%) segments. Within Home and Networks, during the third quarter of 2009, MOT shipped 3.3 million digital entertainment devices used primarily by U.S. telecom and cable companies. In addition, MOT provided infrastructure for CDMA, GSM and iDEN wireless networks. Within Enterprise Mobility, sales to the government and public safety segments remain a large percentage of the total.

COMPETITIVE LANDSCAPE. Within the handset market, we see ongoing pressure from diversified manufacturers such as Nokia and Samsung and smartphone specialists such as Apple and Research in Motion that have been gaining market share as consumers look to use their phones for data services.

Company Financials Fiscal Year Ended Dec. 31

Per Share Data ($)	2008	2007	2006	2005	2004	2003	2002	2001	2000	1999
Tangible Book Value	2.42	4.28	7.15	6.67	5.45	5.43	4.85	6.07	8.50	8.89
Cash Flow	-1.51	0.35	1.53	2.06	1.15	1.09	-0.17	-0.63	1.70	1.60
Earnings	-1.87	-0.05	1.30	1.82	0.90	0.38	-1.09	-1.78	0.58	0.44
S&P Core Earnings	-1.16	0.07	1.24	1.18	0.78	0.08	-0.93	-2.23	NA	NA
Dividends	0.20	0.20	0.19	0.16	0.16	0.16	0.16	0.16	0.16	0.16
Payout Ratio	NM	NM	15%	9%	18%	42%	NM	NM	28%	37%
Prices:High	16.20	20.91	26.30	24.99	20.89	14.40	17.12	25.13	61.54	49.83
Prices:Low	3.00	14.87	18.66	14.48	13.83	7.59	7.30	10.50	15.81	20.85
P/E Ratio:High	NM	NM	20	14	23	38	NM	NM	NM	NM
P/E Ratio:Low	NM	NM	14	8	15	20	NM	NM	NM	NM

Income Statement Analysis (Million $)										
Revenue	30,146	36,622	42,879	36,843	31,323	27,058	26,679	30,004	37,580	30,931
Operating Income	703	1,349	4,675	4,851	3,887	2,694	2,059	-2,595	4,544	3,279
Depreciation	829	906	558	613	659	1,667	2,108	2,552	2,522	2,182
Interest Expense	313	365	335	325	199	295	668	645	494	305
Pretax Income	-2,536	-390	4,610	6,520	3,252	1,293	-3,446	-5,511	2,231	1,168
Effective Tax Rate	NM	73.1%	29.3%	29.5%	32.6%	30.9%	NM	NM	40.9%	30.1%
Net Income	-4,163	-105	3,261	4,599	2,191	893	-2,485	-3,937	1,318	817
S&P Core Earnings	-2,641	186	3,132	2,964	1,899	164	-2,084	-4,893	NA	NA

Balance Sheet & Other Financial Data (Million $)										
Cash	6,979	8,606	15,416	14,641	10,556	7,877	6,507	6,082	3,301	3,345
Current Assets	17,363	22,222	30,975	27,869	21,082	17,907	17,134	17,149	19,885	16,503
Total Assets	27,887	34,812	38,593	35,649	30,889	32,098	31,152	33,398	42,343	37,327
Current Liabilities	10,620	12,500	15,425	12,488	10,573	9,433	9,810	9,698	16,257	12,416
Long Term Debt	4,092	3,991	2,704	3,806	4,578	7,161	7,674	8,857	4,778	3,573
Common Equity	9,525	15,447	17,142	16,673	13,331	12,689	11,239	13,691	18,612	16,344
Total Capital	13,602	20,371	19,846	20,479	17,909	19,850	18,913	22,548	24,894	23,398
Capital Expenditures	504	527	649	583	494	655	607	1,321	4,131	2,684
Cash Flow	-3,415	801	3,819	5,212	2,850	2,560	-377	-1,385	3,840	2,999
Current Ratio	1.6	1.8	2.0	2.2	2.0	1.9	1.7	1.8	1.2	1.3
% Long Term Debt of Capitalization	30.1	19.6	13.6	18.6	25.6	36.1	40.6	39.3	19.2	15.3
% Net Income of Revenue	NM	NM	7.6	12.5	7.0	3.3	NM	NM	3.5	2.6
% Return on Assets	NM	NM	8.8	13.8	7.0	2.8	NM	NM	3.2	2.5
% Return on Equity	NM	NM	19.3	30.7	16.8	7.5	NM	NM	7.1	5.7

Data as orig reptd.; bef. results of disc opers/spec. items. Per share data adj. for stk. divs.; EPS diluted. E-Estimated. NA-Not Available. NM-Not Meaningful. NR-Not Ranked. UR-Under Review.

Office: 1303 East Algonquin Road, Schaumburg, IL 60196.
Telephone: 800-262-8509.
Email: investors@motorola.com
Website: http://www.motorola.com

Chrmn: D.W. Dorman
Pres & Co-CEO: G.Q. Brown
Co-CEO: S.K. Jha
EVP, Secy & General Counsel: A.P. Lawson

SVP, CFO, Chief Acctg Officer & Cntlr: E.J. Fitzpatrick
Investor Contact: D. Lindroth (847-576-6899)
Board Members: G. Q. Brown, D. W. Dorman, W. R. Hambrecht, S. K. Jha, J. C. Lewent, K. A. Meister, T. J. Meredith, S. C. Scott, III, J. Stengel, T. Vinciquerra, D. A. Warner, III, J. A. White, III, A. Wilton

Founded: 1928
Domicile: Delaware
Employees: 64,000

The *McGraw·Hill* Companies

M&T Bank Corp

STANDARD &POOR'S

S&P Recommendation	HOLD ★★★★★	Price $63.85 (as of Nov 27, 2009)	12-Mo. Target Price $70.00	Investment Style Large-Cap Blend

GICS Sector Financials
Sub-Industry Regional Banks

Summary This bank holding company for M&T Bank has offices in New York, Pennsylvania, Maryland, Virginia, West Virginia, New Jersey, Delaware, and Washington, DC.

Key Stock Statistics (Source S&P, Vickers, company reports)

52-Wk Range	$70.96–29.11	S&P Oper. EPS 2009**E**	2.66	Market Capitalization(B)	$7.540	Beta	0.91
Trailing 12-Month EPS	$2.75	S&P Oper. EPS 2010**E**	3.97	Yield (%)	4.39	S&P 3-Yr. Proj. EPS CAGR(%)	6
Trailing 12-Month P/E	23.2	P/E on S&P Oper. EPS 2009**E**	24.0	Dividend Rate/Share	$2.80	S&P Credit Rating	A-
$10K Invested 5 Yrs Ago	$7,035	Common Shares Outstg. (M)	118.1	Institutional Ownership (%)	80		

Price Performance

30-Week Mov. Avg. · · · 10-Week Mov. Avg. - - **GAAP Earnings vs. Previous Year** Volume Above Avg. ▐▌▌ STARS
12-Mo. Target Price — Relative Strength — ▲ Up ▼ Down ▶ No Change Below Avg. ▐▌▌ ★

Options: ASE, CBOE, P, Ph

Analysis prepared by **Stuart Plesser** on October 22, 2009, when the stock traded at **$ 67.17**.

Highlights

▶ We expect loan growth to remain sluggish in 2010, reflecting business conditions in the Northeast, as well as MTB's cautionary stance on credit quality. The net interest margin should stabilize at 3.60% but may head lower if the Fed increases short-term interest rates during 2010. We expect non-interest income to be up 15% in 2010, reflecting MTB's recent acquisition of Provident Bankshares and better results at Bayview, offset by likely lower mortgage banking revenue.

▶ We expect MTB's non-interest expense to total revenue to remain low relative to other regional banks of similar size. Our 2010 estimate is 61.0%, versus 64.7% projected for 2009, a figure that is distorted somewhat by the writedown of securities and high FDIC costs. We expect loan loss provisions to decline 6% in 2010 from the $620 million we project for 2009, assuming chargeoffs peak around the middle of 2010. Although commercial chargeoffs are of concern, we think MTB's higher underwriting standards separate it from peers.

▶ We expect minimal share repurchases in 2010. We project EPS of $2.66 in 2009 versus $5.01 in 2008, and see $3.97 in 2010.

Investment Rationale/Risk

▶ We believe MTB will continue to benefit from a flight to quality and increase its deposit base. MTB has weathered the credit storm well versus peers, as reflected in the third quarter chargeoff rate of only 1.07% of loans. We think net chargeoffs will peak in mid-2010 at about 1.20% of average loans. As a result, we think provisions will decline in 2010 versus 2009 but still remain elevated. Although its Bayview commercial lending operations continue to lose money, we don't expect an impairment charge on the acquisition. We think MTB will gradually build capital levels through 2010 to be in line with peers. We view MTB as a well run bank, and view the shares as fairly valued at 17X our 2010 EPS estimate, in line with historical levels.

▶ Risks to our opinion and target price include a narrower-than-expected net interest margin increase and worse-than-expected credit quality.

▶ Our 12-month target price of $70 is about 17.6X our 2010 EPS estimate, above historical levels, which we think is warranted as 2010 earnings will likely lag normalized earnings potential due to elevated provisions.

Qualitative Risk Assessment

LOW	MEDIUM	HIGH

Our risk assessment reflects the company's large-cap valuation, its history of profitability, its low chargeoff levels relative to peers, and its ability to build capital through income generation.

Quantitative Evaluations

S&P Quality Ranking A-

D	C	B-	B	B+	A-	A	A+

Relative Strength Rank MODERATE

57

LOWEST = 1 HIGHEST = 99

Revenue/Earnings Data

Revenue (Million $)

	1Q	2Q	3Q	4Q	Year
2009	886.9	949.1	978.8	--	--
2008	1,197	1,089	915.1	1,016	4,217
2007	1,098	1,161	1,146	1,073	4,478
2006	1,030	1,076	1,127	1,127	4,360
2005	872.6	921.9	942.3	1,002	3,738
2004	774.3	792.9	828.0	846.5	3,242

Earnings Per Share ($)

	1Q	2Q	3Q	4Q	Year
2009	0.49	0.36	0.97	E0.85	E2.66
2008	1.82	1.44	0.82	0.92	5.01
2007	1.57	1.95	1.83	0.60	5.95
2006	1.77	1.87	1.85	1.88	7.37
2005	1.62	1.69	1.64	1.78	6.73
2004	1.30	1.53	1.56	1.62	6.00

Fiscal year ended Dec. 31. Next earnings report expected: Late January. EPS Estimates based on S&P Operating Earnings; historical GAAP earnings are as reported.

Dividend Data (Dates: mm/dd Payment Date: mm/dd/yy)

Amount ($)	Date Decl.	Ex-Div. Date	Stk. of Record	Payment Date
0.700	02/18	02/25	02/27	03/31/09
0.700	05/20	05/28	06/01	06/30/09
0.700	08/18	08/28	09/01	09/30/09
0.700	11/17	11/27	12/01	12/31/09

Dividends have been paid since 1979. Source: Company reports.

Please read the Required Disclosures and Analyst Certification on the last page of this report.

The **McGraw·Hill** Companies

M&T Bank Corp

STANDARD
&POOR'S

Business Summary October 22, 2009

CORPORATE OVERVIEW. M&T Bank Corporation is a New York-based bank holding company with $65.8 billion in assets as of December 31, 2008. Its principal subsidiary is M&T Bank, a New York State chartered bank that focuses its lending on consumers and small- and medium-sized businesses in the Mid-Atlantic region. It also owns M&T Bank, National Association (N.A.), a national banking association that offers selected deposit and loan products on a nationwide basis through direct mail and telephone marketing, and operates other subsidiaries that provide insurance, securities, investments, leasing, mortgage, mortgage reinsurance, real estate and other financial products and services.

Following MTB's acquisition of Allfirst Financial Inc., a bank holding company in Baltimore, MD, from Allied Irish Banks, p.l.c. (AIB) on April 1, 2003, AIB gained a 22.5% stake in MTB. As of December 31, 2008, the foreign bank owned 24.2% of MTB's common stock. As long as AIB maintains a significant ownership in MTB, each bank will have representation on the other's board.

MARKET PROFILE. As of June 30, 2008, MTB had 691 branches and $36.5 billion in deposits, with about 58% of its deposits and 42% of its branches concentrated in New York, according to the Federal Deposit Insurance Corporation. In addition, 97.7% of MTB's deposits and 95.9% of branches were concentrated in the three adjoining states of New York, Pennsylvania, and Maryland. In New York, MTB had 291 branches, $21.0 billion in deposits, and a deposit market share of about 2.75%, ranking eighth. In Pennsylvania, MTB had 220 branches, $7.2 billion in deposits, and a deposit market share of about 2.7%, ranking tenth. In Maryland, MTB has 152 branches, $7.4 billion in deposits, and a deposit market share of about 7.7%, ranking fifth. Finally, MTB has a small presence in the District of Columbia, Virginia, West Virginia and Delaware.

Company Financials Fiscal Year Ended Dec. 31

Per Share Data ($)	2008	2007	2006	2005	2004	2003	2002	2001	2000	1999
Tangible Book Value	24.21	30.62	30.05	25.56	24.52	21.43	20.23	17.84	16.10	14.88
Earnings	5.01	5.95	7.37	6.73	6.00	4.95	5.07	3.82	3.44	3.28
S&P Core Earnings	4.63	5.87	7.36	6.64	5.97	4.95	4.60	3.40	NA	NA
Dividends	2.80	2.60	2.25	1.75	1.60	1.20	1.05	1.00	0.62	0.45
Payout Ratio	56%	44%	31%	26%	27%	24%	21%	26%	18%	14%
Prices:High	108.53	125.13	124.98	112.50	108.75	98.98	90.05	82.11	68.42	58.25
Prices:Low	52.20	77.39	105.72	96.71	82.90	74.71	67.70	59.80	35.70	40.60
P/E Ratio:High	22	21	17	17	18	20	18	21	20	18
P/E Ratio:Low	10	13	14	14	14	15	13	16	10	12

Income Statement Analysis (Million $)										
Net Interest Income	1,940	1,850	1,818	1,794	1,735	1,599	1,248	1,158	854	759
Tax Equivalent Adjustment	21.9	20.8	NA	17.3	NA	16.3	14.0	17.5	10.5	7.71
Non Interest Income	939	1,059	1,043	978	940	831	513	476	325	282
Loan Loss Provision	412	192	80.0	88.0	95.0	131	122	104	NA	44.5
% Expense/Operating Revenue	54.4%	55.9%	54.2%	53.2%	56.7%	59.6%	51.9%	57.4%	61.6%	59.4%
Pretax Income	740	964	1,232	1,171	1,067	851	716	584	446	418
Effective Tax Rate	24.9%	32.1%	31.9%	33.2%	32.3%	32.5%	32.3%	35.2%	35.9%	36.5%
Net Income	556	654	839	782	723	574	485	378	286	266
% Net Interest Margin	3.38	3.60	3.70	3.77	3.88	4.09	4.36	4.23	4.02	4.02
S&P Core Earnings	514	646	838	772	718	574	440	336	NA	NA

Balance Sheet & Other Financial Data (Million $)										
Money Market Assets	649	348	143	211	199	250	380	84.4	57.8	1,286
Investment Securities	7,919	8,962	7,371	8,400	8,475	7,259	3,955	3,024	3,310	1,901
Commercial Loans	27,397	25,715	23,165	23,940	22,886	20,869	14,522	14,071	13,399	6,141
Other Loans	21,963	22,637	20,042	16,614	15,758	15,169	11,415	11,117	9,571	11,431
Total Assets	65,816	64,876	57,065	55,146	52,939	49,826	33,175	31,450	28,949	22,409
Demand Deposits	8,856	9,322	8,820	9,044	9,246	10,150	5,101	4,634	4,218	2,844
Time Deposits	32,584	31,944	25,660	28,056	26,183	20,756	16,564	16,946	16,014	12,530
Long Term Debt	12,075	10,318	6,891	5,586	6,349	5,535	4,497	3,462	3,415	1,744
Common Equity	6,217	6,485	6,281	5,876	5,730	5,717	3,182	2,939	38.0	44.5
% Return on Assets	0.9	1.1	1.5	1.4	1.4	1.4	1.5	1.3	1.1	1.2
% Return on Equity	8.4	10.3	13.8	13.5	12.6	12.9	15.8	13.4	12.7	15.6
% Loan Loss Reserve	1.6	1.6	1.5	1.6	1.6	1.7	1.7	1.7	1.6	-2.0
% Loans/Deposits	115.1	112.1	107.6	108.7	108.4	108.0	119.7	116.7	112.4	115.4
% Equity to Assets	9.7	10.5	10.8	10.7	11.1	10.8	9.5	9.3	8.8	7.9

Data as orig reptd.; bef. results of disc opers/spec. items. Per share data adj. for stk. divs.; EPS diluted. E-Estimated. NA-Not Available. NM-Not Meaningful. NR-Not Ranked. UR-Under Review.

Office: 1 M And T Plz, Buffalo, NY 14203-2399.
Telephone: 716-842-5445.
Email: ir@mandtbank.com
Website: http://www.mandtbank.com

Chrmn & CEO: R.G. Wilmers
Pres: M.J. Czarnecki
Vice Chrmn: J.G. Pereira
Vice Chrmn: R.E. Sadler, Jr.

Vice Chrmn: M. Pinto
Investor Contact: D.J. MacLeod (716-842-5138)
Board Members: B. D. Baird, R. J. Bennett, C. A. Bontempo, R. T. Brady, M. D. Buckley, T. J. Cunningham, III, M. J. Czarnecki, C. E. Doherty, G. N. Geisel, P. W. Hodgson, R. G. King, R. B. Newman, II, J. G. Pereira, M. Pinto, R. E. Sadler, Jr., E. Sheehy, S. G. Sheetz, H. L. Washington, R. G. Wilmers

Founded: 1969
Domicile: New York
Employees: 13,620

The **McGraw·Hill** Companies

Murphy Oil Corp

STANDARD &POOR'S

S&P Recommendation	BUY ★★★★☆	Price $56.70 (as of Nov 27, 2009)	12-Mo. Target Price $71.00	Investment Style Large-Cap Blend

GICS Sector Energy
Sub-Industry Integrated Oil & Gas

Summary This international integrated oil company has exploration and production interests worldwide, and refining and marketing operations in the U.S.

Key Stock Statistics (Source S&P, Vickers, company reports)

52-Wk Range	$65.12–35.55	S&P Oper. EPS 2009E	2.90	Market Capitalization(B)	$10.826	Beta	0.94
Trailing 12-Month EPS	$3.36	S&P Oper. EPS 2010E	5.44	Yield (%)	1.76	S&P 3-Yr. Proj. EPS CAGR(%)	-10
Trailing 12-Month P/E	16.9	P/E on S&P Oper. EPS 2009E	19.6	Dividend Rate/Share	$1.00	S&P Credit Rating	BBB
$10K Invested 5 Yrs Ago	$14,126	Common Shares Outstg. (M)	190.9	Institutional Ownership (%)	80		

Price Performance

30-Week Mov. Avg. ··· 10-Week Mov. Avg. – – GAAP Earnings vs. Previous Year Volume Above Avg. STARS
12-Mo. Target Price — Relative Strength — ▲ Up ▼ Down ▶ No Change Below Avg.

Options: ASE, CBOE, P, Ph

Analysis prepared by **Tina J. Vital** on November 12, 2009, when the stock traded at **$ 60.34**.

Qualitative Risk Assessment

LOW	MEDIUM	HIGH

Our risk assessment reflects our view of MUR's moderate financial policies and integrated operations in a volatile, cyclical and capital-intensive segment of the energy industry. We believe its low reserve-to-production ratio limits its operating flexibility, increasing dependence on long-term projects.

Quantitative Evaluations

S&P Quality Ranking   A-

D	C	B-	B	B+	A-	A	A+

Relative Strength Rank   WEAK

28

LOWEST = 1   HIGHEST = 99

Revenue/Earnings Data

Revenue (Million $)

	1Q	2Q	3Q	4Q	Year
2009	3,446	4,556	5,184	--	--
2008	6,533	8,363	8,186	4,431	27,513
2007	3,435	4,614	4,781	5,610	18,424
2006	2,991	3,799	4,153	3,364	14,307
2005	2,415	2,950	3,317	3,195	11,877
2004	1,628	2,096	2,291	2,301	8,360

Earnings Per Share ($)

2009	0.37	0.84	0.98	E0.82	E2.90
2008	2.14	3.22	3.04	0.83	9.22
2007	0.58	1.32	1.04	1.07	4.01
2006	0.60	1.13	1.18	0.46	3.37
2005	0.60	1.85	1.18	0.82	4.46
2004	0.43	0.90	0.62	0.71	2.66

Fiscal year ended Dec. 31. Next earnings report expected: Late January. EPS Estimates based on S&P Operating Earnings; historical GAAP earnings are as reported.

Highlights

▶ MUR's third quarter oil and gas production climbed 28%, to 162,004 barrels of oil equivalent per day (boe/d), on ramp-ups and the absence of last year's hurricane shut-ins, but missed our estimate on maintenance issues. With three projects starting up in the 2009 second half -- Thunder Hawk in the Gulf of Mexico (commenced July 2009), Azurite offshore the Republic of Congo (August 2009), and Sarawak offshore Malaysia (September 2009) -- we look for oil and gas production to increase about 28%, to 163,000 boe/d, in 2009, and about 18% in 2010.

▶ First nine months operating expenses dropped 42% on contract renegotiations and cost initiatives; we look for operating expenses to drop about 28% in 2009. On the downstream, we expect U.S. Gulf Coast 3-2-1 crack spreads to narrow about 16% in 2009 before widening about 7% in 2010.

▶ First nine months EPS excluded $0.10 in special gains and $0.51 from discontinued operations. We expect after-tax operating earnings to drop about 68% in 2009 on lower projected prices, before rebounding about 87% in 2010 on an improved economic outlook.

Investment Rationale/Risk

▶ With an oil focus and three major oil and gas projects started in the 2009 second half, we look for MUR to benefit from our expectations for higher oil prices. While MUR's primary focus is in the U.S. in the deepwater Gulf of Mexico, its international stakes have added growth opportunities. MUR's Kikeh project offshore Malaysia has improved its upstream prospects, and so far in 2009, the company has announced discoveries offshore Congo, Malaysia and the Gulf of Mexico. We estimate MUR's 2008 organic reserve replacement at a solid 105%, albeit below the peer average.

▶ Risks to our recommendation and target price include unfavorable changes to economic, industry and operating conditions, such as difficulty in replacing oil and gas reserves.

▶ Blending our discounted cash flow ($71 per share, assuming a WACC of 10.7% and terminal growth of 3%) and relative market valuations, leads to our 12-month target price of $71. This represents an expected enterprise value of about 5.1X our 2010 EBITDA estimate, in line with the peer average.

Dividend Data (Dates: mm/dd Payment Date: mm/dd/yy)

Amount ($)	Date Decl.	Ex-Div. Date	Stk. of Record	Payment Date
0.250	02/04	02/12	02/17	03/02/09
0.250	04/01	05/13	05/15	06/01/09
0.250	08/05	08/13	08/17	09/01/09
0.250	10/07	11/10	11/13	12/01/09

Dividends have been paid since 1961. Source: Company reports.

Murphy Oil Corp

STANDARD &POOR'S

Business Summary November 12, 2009

CORPORATE OVERVIEW. Originally incorporated in Louisiana in 1950 as Murphy Corp., the company was reincorporated in Delaware in 1964 under the name Murphy Oil Corp. (MUR). As an international integrated oil and gas company, MUR explores for oil and gas worldwide, and has refining and marketing interests in the U.S. The company operates in two business segments: Exploration and Production (15% of 2008 revenues; 84% of 2008 segment income), and Refining and Marketing (85%; 16%).

The Exploration and Production segment produces oil and gas in the U.S., Canada, the U.K. North Sea, Malaysia and Ecuador, and explores worldwide. In the U.S., the company has interests in eight oil and gas fields (six in the deepwater Gulf of Mexico, two onshore Louisiana), four operated by MUR and four by others. MUR's primary focus in the U.S. is in the deepwater Gulf of Mexico, where its primary asset is the Medusa field (60% stake; 36% of 2008 oil and gas production) in the Mississippi Canyon Block 538/582.

In Canada, MUR owns an interest in three nonoperated long-lived assets, the Hibernia (6.5%) and Terra Nova (12%) fields offshore Newfoundland and Syncrude Canada Ltd. (5%) in northern Alberta. In addition, the company owns interests in two heavy oil areas and one natural gas area in the Western Canadian Sedimentary Basin (WCSB). Through 2008, the company had acquired approximately 84,000 acres of mineral rights in northeastern British Columbia in an area named Tupper. First production of natural gas a Tupper was in December 2008, and volumes are expected to ramp up in 2009.

In Malaysia, the company has majority interests in seven separate production-sharing contracts (PSCs) and serves as operator. In 2002, MUR made an important discovery at the Kikeh field (80%) in deepwater Block K, offshore Sabah, and added another important discovery at Kakap in 2004. The company also has interests in the U.K. sector of the North Sea, offshore Ecuador and offshore the Republic of Congo.

Proved oil and gas reserves declined 2.0%, to 271.2 million barrels of oil equivalent (boe; 64% liquids, 45% developed), in 2008. Synthetic oil reserves rose 2.5%, to 131.6 million barrels. Oil and gas production climbed 25%, to 127,507 boe per day (93% liquids), reflecting the ramp-up at the Kikeh field in Malaysia. Using data from John S. Herold, we estimate MUR's three-year (2005-07) proved acquisition costs at $0.32 per boe, below the peer average; its three-year finding and development costs at $28.61 per boe, above peers; its three-year reserve replacement costs at $28.49 per boe, above peers; and its three-year reserve replacement at 123%, solid but below the peer average. We estimate MUR's 2008 organic reserve replacement at 105%.

Company Financials Fiscal Year Ended Dec. 31

Per Share Data ($)	2008	2007	2006	2005	2004	2003	2002	2001	2000	1999
Tangible Book Value	32.73	25.99	21.37	18.38	14.16	10.27	8.41	7.99	6.72	5.87
Cash Flow	13.48	6.75	5.40	6.57	4.38	3.39	2.16	3.07	2.87	1.80
Earnings	9.22	4.01	3.37	4.46	2.66	1.63	0.53	1.82	1.69	0.67
S&P Core Earnings	8.55	4.03	3.32	3.85	2.40	1.40	0.39	1.30	NA	NA
Dividends	0.88	0.68	0.52	0.45	0.43	0.40	0.39	0.38	0.36	0.35
Payout Ratio	9%	17%	16%	10%	16%	25%	73%	21%	21%	53%
Prices:High	101.47	85.94	60.18	57.07	43.69	34.35	24.86	21.96	17.27	15.41
Prices:Low	35.55	45.45	44.72	37.80	28.45	19.27	15.95	13.81	12.05	8.22
P/E Ratio:High	11	21	18	13	16	21	47	12	10	23
P/E Ratio:Low	4	11	13	8	11	12	30	8	7	12

Income Statement Analysis (Million $)	2008	2007	2006	2005	2004	2003	2002	2001	2000	1999
Revenue	27,513	18,439	14,307	11,877	8,360	5,345	3,967	4,479	4,639	2,037
Operating Income	3,640	1,845	1,514	1,854	1,110	781	492	768	723	400
Depreciation, Depletion and Amortization	850	523	384	397	321	328	300	229	213	204
Interest Expense	43.7	75.5	9.48	8.77	34.1	20.5	27.0	19.0	16.3	20.3
Pretax Income	2,850	1,237	1,028	1,372	805	419	152	506	465	179
Effective Tax Rate	37.9%	38.1%	37.9%	38.9%	38.3%	28.1%	35.7%	34.6%	34.3%	32.9%
Net Income	1,771	767	638	838	496	301	97.5	331	306	120
S&P Core Earnings	1,643	772	630	725	448	259	71.4	236	NA	NA

Balance Sheet & Other Financial Data (Million $)	2008	2007	2006	2005	2004	2003	2002	2001	2000	1999
Cash	666	674	543	585	536	252	165	82.7	133	34.1
Current Assets	2,846	2,887	2,107	1,839	1,629	1,039	854	599	817	593
Total Assets	12,205	10,536	7,446	6,369	5,458	4,713	3,886	3,259	3,134	2,446
Current Liabilities	1,888	2,109	1,311	1,287	1,205	810	718	560	745	488
Long Term Debt	1,026	1,516	840	610	613	1,090	863	521	525	393
Common Equity	6,314	5,066	4,053	3,461	2,649	1,951	1,594	1,498	1,260	1,057
Total Capital	8,183	7,526	5,498	4,685	3,263	3,463	2,784	2,322	2,014	1,604
Capital Expenditures	2,186	1,949	1,192	1,246	938	938	834	814	512	387
Cash Flow	2,590	1,290	1,022	1,235	818	630	398	560	519	324
Current Ratio	1.5	1.4	1.6	1.4	1.4	1.3	1.2	1.1	1.1	1.2
% Long Term Debt of Capitalization	12.5	20.2	15.3	13.0	18.8	31.5	31.0	22.4	26.1	24.5
% Return on Assets	15.6	8.5	9.2	14.2	9.8	7.0	2.7	10.4	11.0	5.2
% Return on Equity	31.1	16.8	17.0	27.4	21.6	17.0	6.3	24.0	26.4	11.8

Data as orig reptd.; bef. results of disc opers/spec. items. Per share data adj. for stk. divs.; EPS diluted. E-Estimated. NA-Not Available. NM-Not Meaningful. NR-Not Ranked. UR-Under Review.

Office: 200 Peach Street, El Dorado, AR 71730-7000.
Telephone: 870-862-6411.
Email: murphyoil@murphyoilcorp.com
Website: http://www.murphyoilcorp.com

Chrmn: W.C. Nolan, Jr.
Pres & CEO: D.M. Wood
EVP & General Counsel: S.A. Cosse
SVP & CFO: K.G. Fitzgerald

Chief Acctg Officer & Cntlr: J.W. Eckart
Investor Contact: M. West (870-864-6315)
Board Members: F. W. Blue, C. P. Deming, R. A. Hermes, J. V. Kelley, R. M. Murphy, W. C. Nolan, Jr., I. B. Ramberg, N. E. Schmale, D. J. Smith, C. G. Theus, D. M. Wood

Founded: 1950
Domicile: Delaware
Employees: 8,277

The *McGraw-Hill* Companies

Stock Report | November 30, 2009 | NNM Symbol: **MYL** | **MYL** is in the S&P 500

Mylan Inc

**STANDARD
&POOR'S**

| **S&P Recommendation** STRONG BUY ★★★★★ | **Price** $17.87 (as of Nov 30, 2009) | **12-Mo. Target Price** $22.00 | **Investment Style** Large-Cap Growth |

GICS Sector Health Care
Sub-Industry Pharmaceuticals

Summary This leading manufacturer of generic pharmaceuticals produces a broad range of generic drugs in varying strengths. In October 2007, Mylan acquired the generic drug division of German drugmaker Merck KGaA for some $7.0 billion in cash.

Key Stock Statistics (Source S&P, Vickers, company reports)

52-Wk Range	$18.45– 8.69	S&P Oper. EPS 2009**E**	1.26	Market Capitalization(B)	$5.461	Beta	0.52
Trailing 12-Month EPS	$0.16	S&P Oper. EPS 2010**E**	1.55	Yield (%)	Nil	S&P 3-Yr. Proj. EPS CAGR(%)	30
Trailing 12-Month P/E	NM	P/E on S&P Oper. EPS 2009**E**	14.2	Dividend Rate/Share	Nil	S&P Credit Rating	BB
$10K Invested 5 Yrs Ago	$9,979	Common Shares Outstg. (M)	305.6	Institutional Ownership (%)	98		

Price Performance

30-Week Mov. Avg. ··· 10-Week Mov. Avg. - - GAAP Earnings vs. Previous Year Volume Above Avg. STARS
12-Mo. Target Price — Relative Strength — ▲ Up ▼ Down ▶ No Change Below Avg. ★

Options: ASE, CBOE, P, Ph

Analysis prepared by **Herman B. Saftlas** on November 30, 2009, when the stock traded at **$ 17.89.**

Highlights

► We forecast 2010 revenues of $5.4 billion, up from $5.0 billion that we expect in 2009. We see sales growth in 2010 driven by gains in existing lines, as well as by new products such as recently launched generic versions of Prevacid heartburn treatment. In total, MYL has some 125 ANDAs pending FDA review, of which 36 represent potential first-to-file opportunities with six months of marketing exclusivity. In Mylan's branded segment, we see robust growth for EpiPen, an auto-injector treatment for potential life-threatening allergic reactions.

► We look for gross margins in 2010 to show modest expansion on the projected better volume and productivity enhancements. We also see tight control of SG&A costs and R&D spending, helped by ongoing merger synergies (over $300 million expected to be realized in 2010). However, the effective tax rate is expected to rise to about 32%, from 30% indicated for 2009.

► After projected lower preferred dividend payments, we see 2010 cash EPS of $1.55, up from $1.26 in 2009, before acquisition-related charges and other items.

Investment Rationale/Risk

► We believe MYL's efforts to expand its base through the acquisitions of Merck KGaA's generic business and Matrix Laboratories hold much long-term promise. Besides broadening MYL's geographic reach, these deals also provided access to in-house sourcing of active pharmaceutical ingredients and generic biologics. MYL also recently formed a venture with India's Biocon to develop biogenerics. We expect accrued merger synergies to exceed $300 million by the end of 2010. We also think MYL is well positioned to benefit from the robust growth that we project for the generics market.

► Risks to our recommendation and target price include possible problems integrating the Merck KGaA business, as well as cash flow risks that could threaten MYL's ability to manage its high debt load.

► MYL shares are valued in line with peers on an EV/EBITDA basis. Our 12-month target price of $22 applies a modest premium to peers multiple of 14.2X to our 2010 EPS estimate. This is supported by our DCF model, which assumes a WACC of 8% and perpetuity growth of 1%, and also shows intrinsic value in the $22 area.

Qualitative Risk Assessment

| LOW | **MEDIUM** | HIGH |

Our risk assessment reflects risks inherent in the generic pharmaceutical business, which include the ability to successfully develop generic products, obtain regulatory approvals and legally challenge branded patents. However, we believe these risks are offset at Mylan, given its wide and diverse generic portfolio and promising branded drugs business. We also think the acquisition of Merck KGaA's generic business holds long-term promise.

Quantitative Evaluations

S&P Quality Ranking A-

| D | C | B- | B | B+ | **A-** | A | A+ |

Relative Strength Rank STRONG
87
LOWEST = 1 HIGHEST = 99

Revenue/Earnings Data

Revenue (Million $)

	1Q	2Q	3Q	4Q	Year
2009	1,181	1,267	1,264	--	--
2008	1,074	1,203	1,657	1,203	5,138
2007	356.1	366.7	401.8	487.3	1,612
2006	323.4	298.0	311.3	324.6	1,257
2005	339.0	307.0	291.0	316.4	1,253
2004	331.4	360.1	349.8	333.4	1,375

Earnings Per Share ($)

2009	0.23	0.19	-0.13	E0.29	E1.26
2008	-1.46	-0.03	0.45	-0.13	-1.05
2007	0.35	0.36	0.63	-0.31	0.99
2006	0.16	0.16	0.22	0.27	0.79
2005	0.30	0.18	0.13	0.14	0.74
2004	0.31	0.33	0.31	0.27	1.21

Fiscal year ended Dec. 31. Next earnings report expected: Mid February. EPS Estimates based on S&P Operating Earnings; historical GAAP earnings are as reported.

Dividend Data

Dividends were suspended in 2008.

Please read the Required Disclosures and Analyst Certification on the last page of this report.

The McGraw-Hill Companies

Redistribution or reproduction is prohibited without written permission. Copyright ©2009 The McGraw-Hill Companies, Inc.

Mylan Inc

STANDARD
&POOR'S

Business Summary November 30, 2009

CORPORATE PROFILE. Mylan Laboratories is a leading manufacturer of generic pharmaceutical products in finished tablet, capsule and powder dosage forms. Generic drugs are the chemical equivalents of branded drugs, and are marketed after patents on the primary products expire. Generics are typically sold at prices significantly below those of comparable branded products.

Generics accounted for some 82% of operating revenues in 2008, specialty products for 9%, and Matrix Laboratories for 9%. MYL markets more than 570 products throughout the world. The U.S. generic division markets about 204 generic products, primarily solid oral dose drugs encompassing a wide variety of therapeutic categories. Some 22 generics are extended-release drugs. UDL Laboratories is the largest U.S. repackager of pharmaceuticals in unit dose formats, which are used primarily in hospitals, nursing homes and similar settings. Mylan Technologies develops and markets products using transdermal drug delivery systems.

IMPACT OF MAJOR DEVELOPMENTS. In October 2007, Mylan acquired a generic drug business from German drugmaker Merck KGaA (referred to as Merck Generics) that markets several hundred products. The operation has a strong presence in key foreign generic markets, including France, the U.K.,

Japan, Canada and Australia. Under terms of the acquisition agreement, MYL has rights to purchase Merck KGaA's generic businesses in 17 additional countries in Latin America, Europe and Asia until October 2009.

As part of the Merck Generics acquisition, MYL also acquired Dey, a producer of branded specialty respiratory and allergy drugs. Key Dey products are EpiPen, an auto-injector treatment for allergic reactions; and DuoNeb, a nebulized treatment for COPD.

In January 2007, MYL acquired about 72% of the voting shares of Indian drugmaker Matrix Laboratories for about $776 million in cash. Matrix is the second largest maker of active pharmaceutical ingredients (APIs) in the world. Matrix produces high-quality APIs for Mylan's own generics, as well as for third parties. In March 2009, MYL said it planned to buy the remaining interest in Matrix.

Company Financials Fiscal Year Ended Dec. 31

Per Share Data ($)	2008	2007	2006	2005	2004	2003	2002	2001	2000	1999
Tangible Book Value	NM	2.75	2.76	6.03	5.30	4.39	3.97	2.97	3.00	2.49
Cash Flow	0.33	1.27	0.99	0.91	1.37	1.11	1.07	0.28	0.65	0.50
Earnings	-1.05	0.99	0.79	0.74	1.21	0.97	0.91	0.13	0.52	0.43
S&P Core Earnings	0.25	-4.50	0.78	0.64	1.05	0.89	0.84	0.40	NA	NA
Dividends	Nil	0.24	0.12	0.10	0.08	0.08	0.07	0.07	0.07	0.07
Payout Ratio	Nil	24%	15%	14%	7%	18%	8%	55%	14%	17%
Prices:High	15.49	22.90	25.00	21.69	26.35	28.75	16.56	16.94	14.33	14.22
Prices:Low	5.75	12.93	18.65	15.21	14.24	15.56	11.15	8.96	7.11	7.58
P/E Ratio:High	NM	23	25	27	36	24	17	19	NM	27
P/E Ratio:Low	NM	13	19	19	19	13	12	12	NM	14

Income Statement Analysis (Million $)										
Revenue	5,138	1,612	1,257	1,253	1,375	1,269	1,104	847	790	721
Operating Income	1,359	586	347	321	504	452	441	209	259	224
Depreciation	422	61.5	46.8	45.1	44.3	40.6	46.1	42.4	35.7	26.9
Interest Expense	357	52.3	31.3	Nil	Nil	Nil	Nil	Nil	Nil	Nil
Pretax Income	-47.8	426	275	312	513	427	408	58.0	243	192
Effective Tax Rate	NM	48.9%	32.8%	34.8%	34.7%	36.1%	36.3%	36.0%	36.5%	40.0%
Net Income	-181	217	185	204	335	272	260	37.1	154	115
S&P Core Earnings	75.6	-1,156	184	175	286	247	241	113	NA	NA

Balance Sheet & Other Financial Data (Million $)										
Cash	599	1,427	518	808	687	687	617	285	303	260
Current Assets	3,175	2,412	1,192	1,528	1,318	1,228	1,062	879	687	583
Total Assets	10,410	4,254	1,871	2,136	1,875	1,745	1,617	1,466	1,341	1,207
Current Liabilities	1,545	701	265	246	174	266	175	291	87.8	96.4
Long Term Debt	5,165	1,655	685	19.3	19.1	19.9	21.9	23.3	30.6	26.8
Common Equity	2,704	1,649	4,242	2,786	2,600	1,446	1,607	1,133	1,204	1,060
Total Capital	8,443	3,390	4,948	2,830	2,642	1,479	1,646	1,175	1,253	1,110
Capital Expenditures	165	162	104	90.7	118	32.6	20.6	24.7	28.8	16.7
Cash Flow	101	279	231	249	379	313	306	79.5	190	142
Current Ratio	2.1	3.4	4.5	6.2	7.6	4.6	6.1	3.0	7.8	6.0
% Long Term Debt of Capitalization	61.2	48.8	13.8	0.7	0.7	1.3	1.3	2.0	2.4	2.4
% Net Income of Revenue	NM	13.5	14.7	16.2	24.3	21.5	23.6	4.4	19.5	16.0
% Return on Assets	NM	7.1	9.2	10.1	18.5	16.2	16.9	2.6	12.1	11.2
% Return on Equity	NM	17.8	5.3	7.6	14.1	19.1	17.7	3.2	13.6	12.8

Data as orig reptd.; bef. results of disc opers/spec. items. Per share data adj. for stk. divs.; EPS diluted. E-Estimated. NA-Not Available. NM-Not Meaningful. NR-Not Ranked. UR-Under Review.

Office: 1500 Corporate Dr, Canonsburg, PA 15317-8580.
Telephone: 724-514-1800.
Email: investor_relations@mylan.com
Website: http://www.mylan.com

Chrmn & CEO: R.J. Coury
Pres: H. Bresch
Vice Chrmn: R. Piatt
COO & EVP: R. Malik

EVP & CFO: J.L. Varney
Investor Contact: K. King (724-514-1800)
Board Members: W. Cameron, R. J. Coury, N. Dimick, D. J. Leech, J. Maroon, M. W. Parrish, R. Piatt, N. Prasad, C. B. Todd, R. L. Vanderveen

Founded: 1970
Domicile: Pennsylvania
Employees: 15,000

Nabors Industries Ltd

STANDARD &POOR'S

| **S&P Recommendation** HOLD ★★★☆☆ | **Price** $20.57 (as of Nov 27, 2009) | **12-Mo. Target Price** $26.00 | **Investment Style** Large-Cap Growth |

GICS Sector Energy
Sub-Industry Oil & Gas Drilling

Summary This Bermuda company, based in Barbados, is the world's largest oil and gas land drilling contractor.

Key Stock Statistics (Source S&P, Vickers, company reports)

52-Wk Range	$24.07– 8.25	S&P Oper. EPS 2009**E**	1.30	Market Capitalization(B)	$5.827	Beta	1.66
Trailing 12-Month EPS	$-0.25	S&P Oper. EPS 2010**E**	0.86	Yield (%)	Nil	S&P 3-Yr. Proj. EPS CAGR(%)	-35
Trailing 12-Month P/E	NM	P/E on S&P Oper. EPS 2009**E**	15.8	Dividend Rate/Share	Nil	S&P Credit Rating	A-
$10K Invested 5 Yrs Ago	$7,799	Common Shares Outstg. (M)	283.3	Institutional Ownership (%)	87		

Price Performance

30-Week Mov. Avg. · · · 10-Week Mov. Avg. – – **GAAP Earnings vs. Previous Year** Volume Above Avg. STARS
12-Mo. Target Price — Relative Strength — ▲ Up ▼ Down ► No Change Below Avg.

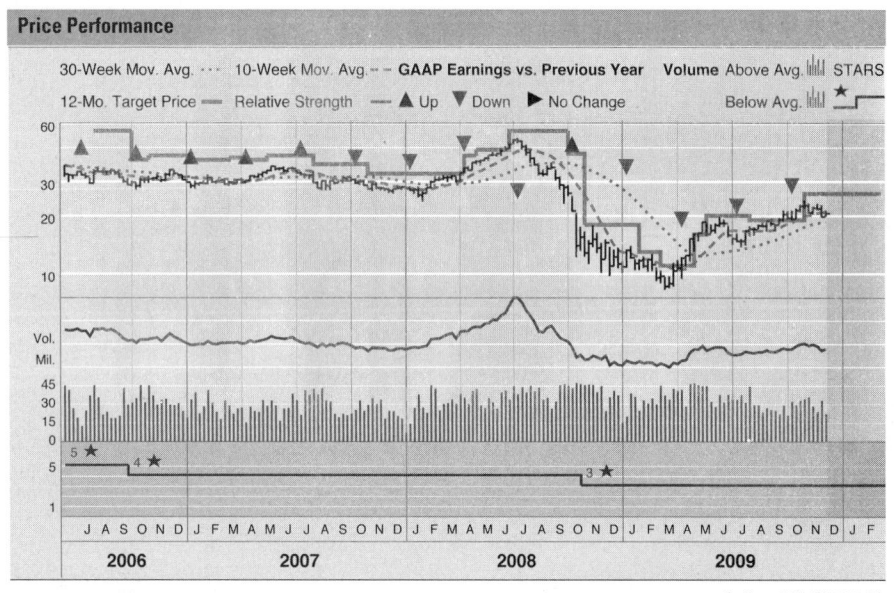

Options: ASE, CBOE, P, Ph

Analysis prepared by **Michael Kay** on October 29, 2009, when the stock traded at **$ 22.23**.

Highlights

► Third-quarter cash margins fell $577 per day, to $9,673, on lower revenue and higher costs. NBR had an average of 137 working rigs, and 22 idle rigs under contract, versus about 260 rigs last year. NBR believes the rig count bottomed out in the third quarter. The company is seeing better demand for its newbuilds, which are more efficient and produce better margins per rig. With a dominant position in U.S. shale, NBR stands to further improve market share when natural gas markets strengthen, in our view.

► Disappointing international performance has driven our expectations lower. However, NBR sees 14 new international rigs in 2009 and expects that business to bottom out in another quarter or two. We also see opportunities in Canadian natural gas shale drilling.

► We see 2009 and 2010 EPS of $1.30 and $0.86, respectively, versus 2008 operating EPS of $3.04 (excluding $1.43 in mainly impairments, and a $0.32 tax benefit), on lower utilization and declines in U.S. land drilling margins. We expect NBR to cut capex to $1 billion in 2009 and to $600 million in 2010. We believe the company, with $1.2 billion in cash, can fund $250 million in debt due in 2009.

Investment Rationale/Risk

► North American onshore drilling faces challenges due to capacity additions, spending cutbacks and an overall decline in drilling activity. While we view NBR as somewhat protected through long-term contracts, its emphasis on larger operators, and segment diversification, we expect volatility in the sector amid continued market turmoil. In our view, NBR has strong drilling prospects related to unconventional natural gas plays, given technology advantages and its newbuild program. NBR expects the international segment to benefit from the start-up of some offshore jackup rigs.

► Risks to our recommendation and target price include reduced oil and natural gas prices; lower land drilling dayrates; slower-than-expected deliveries of new rigs; and rising cost inflation.

► Shares of land drillers have recovered in 2009, but a weaker outlook for dayrates and utilization, uncertain economic conditions, the ongoing credit crisis and weak natural gas fundamentals have us cautious on the sector. Blending valuations of 8X our 2010 EBITDA estimate, 6X our 2010 cash flow projection, and 25X our 2010 EPS estimate, we arrive at our 12-month target price of $26.

Qualitative Risk Assessment

LOW	MEDIUM	HIGH

Our risk assessment reflects NBR's sensitivity to volatile crude oil and natural gas prices (especially the latter), capital spending decisions made by oil and gas producing customers, and the rising number of newbuild land rigs on order. Partly offsetting these risks is NBR's diversified fleet, including overseas operations, and its leadership position in the industry.

Quantitative Evaluations

S&P Quality Ranking NR

D	C	B-	B	B+	A-	A	A+

Relative Strength Rank MODERATE

44

LOWEST = 1 HIGHEST = 99

Revenue/Earnings Data

Revenue (Million $)

	1Q	2Q	3Q	4Q	Year
2009	1,143	867.9	791.9	--	--
2008	1,322	1,282	1,455	1,475	5,512
2007	1,277	1,128	1,226	1,309	4,941
2006	1,164	1,144	1,244	1,329	4,943
2005	783.7	786.1	893.3	1,016	3,551
2004	607.7	546.7	585.7	701.0	2,394

Earnings Per Share ($)

	1Q	2Q	3Q	4Q	Year
2009	0.44	-0.68	0.10	E0.18	E1.30
2008	0.81	0.67	0.73	-0.30	1.93
2007	0.92	0.79	0.68	0.78	3.13
2006	0.79	0.77	1.02	0.97	3.40
2005	0.40	0.41	0.56	0.65	2.00
2004	0.23	0.15	0.24	0.34	0.96

Fiscal year ended Dec. 31. Next earnings report expected: Late February. EPS Estimates based on S&P Operating Earnings; historical GAAP earnings are as reported.

Dividend Data

No cash dividends have been paid.

The *McGraw-Hill* Companies

Nabors Industries Ltd

STANDARD &POOR'S

Business Summary October 29, 2009

CORPORATE OVERVIEW. The world's largest land drilling contractor, Nabors Industries Ltd. owns a fleet of about 528 land drilling rigs. Formed as a Bermuda-exempt company in December 2001, but operating continuously in the drilling sector since the early 1900s, Nabors conducts oil, gas and geothermal land drilling operations in the lower 48 U.S. states, Alaska and Canada, and internationally, mainly in South and Central America, the Middle East and Africa. NBR actively markets approximately 592 land workover and well servicing rigs in the U.S. Southwest and West, and approximately 171 well servicing and workover rigs in Canada. In addition, it markets 37 platform, 13 jackup and three barge rigs in the Gulf of Mexico and international markets; these rigs provide well servicing, workover and drilling services. NBR also has a 51% ownership interest in a joint venture in Saudi Arabia, which actively markets 9 rigs.

The contract drilling segment (94% of 2008 revenues) provides drilling, workover, well servicing and related services in the U.S. (including the lower 48, Alaska and offshore), Canada, and internationally. During 2008, 38% of

contract drilling revenues served customers in the Lower 48, either for land drilling or land well-servicing. Well servicing and workover services are provided for existing wells where some form of artificial lift is required to bring oil to the surface. To supplement its primary business, NBR offers ancillary well-site services, such as oilfield management, engineering, transportation, construction, maintenance, and well logging. As of December 2008, NBR had a fleet of 29 marine transportation and support vessels, primarily in the Gulf of Mexico, Trinidad, and the Middle East, providing marine transportation of drilling materials, supplies and crews for offshore rig operations and support for other offshore facilities. The supply vessels are used as freight-carrying vessels for bringing drill pipe, tubing, casing, drilling mud, and other equipment to drilling rigs and production platforms.

Company Financials Fiscal Year Ended Dec. 31

Per Share Data ($)	2008	2007	2006	2005	2004	2003	2002	2001	2000	1999
Tangible Book Value	15.96	14.84	11.46	10.83	8.68	7.35	6.39	5.89	5.51	4.76
Cash Flow	4.24	5.01	4.77	3.04	1.84	1.36	1.06	1.59	0.94	0.53
Earnings	1.93	3.13	3.40	2.00	0.96	0.63	0.41	1.09	0.45	0.12
Dividends	Nil	Nil	Nil	Nil	Nil	Nil	Nil	Nil	Nil	Nil
Payout Ratio	Nil	Nil	Nil	Nil	Nil	Nil	Nil	Nil	Nil	Nil
Prices:High	50.58	36.42	41.35	39.94	27.13	22.93	24.99	31.56	30.24	15.63
Prices:Low	9.72	26.00	27.26	23.10	20.01	16.10	13.07	9.00	14.06	5.38
P/E Ratio:High	26	12	12	20	28	37	62	29	68	NM
P/E Ratio:Low	5	8	8	12	21	26	32	8	32	NM

Income Statement Analysis (Million $)										
Revenue	5,512	4,941	4,943	3,551	2,394	1,880	1,466	2,121	1,327	639
Operating Income	1,264	1,750	1,952	1,304	626	438	351	0.69	377	155
Depreciation, Depletion and Amortization	658	540	409	339	300	235	195	190	152	99.9
Interest Expense	91.6	63.6	46.6	44.8	48.5	70.7	67.1	60.7	35.4	30.4
Pretax Income	802	1,135	1,471	874	336	175	141	542	227	45.6
Effective Tax Rate	31.2%	21.1%	30.6%	25.8%	9.94%	NM	13.7%	35.9%	40.2%	39.3%
Net Income	551	896	1,021	649	302	192	121	348	135	27.7

Balance Sheet & Other Financial Data (Million $)										
Cash	584	767	701	565	1,253	1,532	1,331	919	551	112
Current Assets	2,167	2,205	2,505	2,617	1,581	1,516	1,370	1,031	1,018	461
Total Assets	10,468	10,103	9,142	7,230	5,863	5,603	5,064	4,152	3,137	2,398
Current Liabilities	1,129	1,494	854	1,352	1,199	598	751	330	279	265
Long Term Debt	3,888	3,306	4,004	1,252	1,202	1,986	1,615	1,568	855	483
Common Equity	4,692	4,514	3,537	3,758	2,929	2,490	2,158	1,858	1,806	1,470
Total Capital	9,339	8,363	8,125	5,727	4,517	4,849	4,175	3,711	2,759	2,046
Capital Expenditures	1,490	2,014	1,927	907	544	353	317	701	301	82.1
Cash Flow	1,209	1,436	1,430	987	603	427	317	538	288	128
Current Ratio	1.9	1.5	2.9	1.9	1.3	2.5	1.8	3.1	3.6	1.7
% Long Term Debt of Capitalization	41.6	39.5	49.3	21.9	26.6	41.0	38.7	42.2	31.0	23.6
% Return on Assets	5.4	9.3	12.5	9.9	5.3	3.6	2.6	9.5	4.9	1.4
% Return on Equity	12.0	22.3	28.0	19.4	11.2	8.3	6.0	19.0	8.3	2.4

Data as orig reptd.; bef. results of disc opers/spec. items. Per share data adj. for stk. divs.; EPS diluted. E-Estimated. NA-Not Available. NM-Not Meaningful. NR-Not Ranked. UR-Under Review.

Office: 8 Par-La-Ville Road, Hamilton, Bermuda HM08.
Telephone: 441-292-1510.
Website: http://www.nabors.com
Chrmn & CEO: E.M. Isenberg

Pres, Vice Chrmn & COO: A.G. Petrello
CFO, Chief Acctg Officer & Cntlr: R.C. Wood
Secy: M.D. Andrews
Investor Contact: D.A. Smith (281-775-8038)

Board Members: W. T. Comfort, III, E. M. Isenberg, J. V. Lombardi, J. L. Payne, A. G. Petrello, M. M. Sheinfeld, M. J. Whitman
Founded: 1968
Domicile: Bermuda
Employees: 22,992

The McGraw-Hill Companies

Nasdaq OMX Group Inc (The)

STANDARD &POOR'S

S&P Recommendation **BUY** ★★★★☆	Price $18.78 (as of Nov 27, 2009)	12-Mo. Target Price $25.00	Investment Style Large-Cap Blend

GICS Sector Financials
Sub-Industry Specialized Finance

Summary This leading global exchange group delivers trading, exchange technology, securities listing, and public company services across six continents.

Key Stock Statistics (Source S&P, Vickers, company reports)

52-Wk Range	$27.66–17.51	S&P Oper. EPS 2009**E**	1.82	Market Capitalization(B)	$3.964	Beta	1.05
Trailing 12-Month EPS	$1.24	S&P Oper. EPS 2010**E**	2.03	Yield (%)	Nil	S&P 3-Yr. Proj. EPS CAGR(%)	13
Trailing 12-Month P/E	15.2	P/E on S&P Oper. EPS 2009**E**	10.3	Dividend Rate/Share	Nil	S&P Credit Rating	BBB-
$10K Invested 5 Yrs Ago	NA	Common Shares Outstg. (M)	211.1	Institutional Ownership (%)	62		

Price Performance

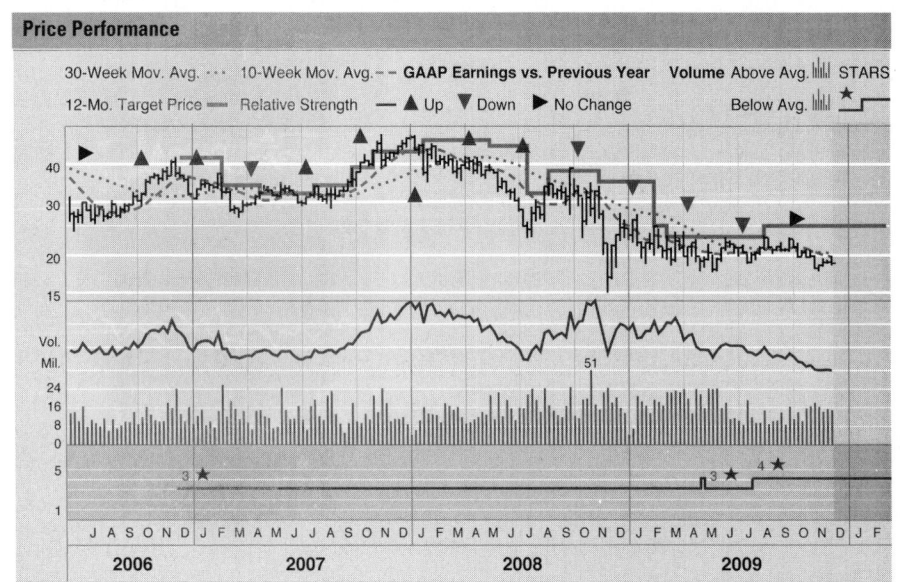

30-Week Mov. Avg. ···· 10-Week Mov. Avg. ─ **GAAP Earnings vs. Previous Year**   Volume Above Avg. ▥ STARS
12-Mo. Target Price ─ Relative Strength — ▲ Up ▼ Down ▶ No Change   Below Avg. ▥ ★

Options: ASE, CBOE, P, Ph

Analysis prepared by **Rafay Khalid, CFA** on November 18, 2009, when the stock traded at **$ 18.88**.

Highlights

▶ We project that revenues will decline 5.3% in 2009. Our outlook reflects our expectation for stabilization in NDAQ's U.S. cash equities market share during 2009. While we believe the company's new pricing scheme will help gain market share, we believe it will slightly lower revenues in 2009. We forecast the company's market technology business segment will experience solid growth, on our view of increasing customer orders. We forecast revenue growth of about 3% in 2010.

▶ From a margin perspective, we are encouraged that NDAQ is working to establish multiple clearing facilities in the U.S. and Europe to take advantage of their fixed-cost structure, and enabling diminishing marginal costs. Based on merger synergies and other cost-cutting, we see operating margins, excluding merger expenses, improving to 18.3% in 2009 and 20.9% in 2010, from 18.0% in 2008.

▶ Our operating EPS estimates are $1.82 for 2009 and $2.03 in 2010, both exclude one-time items. This compares to operating EPS of $1.95 in 2008, excluding one-time items.

Investment Rationale/Risk

▶ Our buy opinion is primarily based on valuation. We believe NDAQ has made solid progress in integrating its recent acquisitions and establishing new opportunities such as interest rate swap clearing through its subsidiary, IDCG, which has garnered significant participant interest. We expect the company to financially benefit from its initiative to introduce central clearing to all Nordic cash equity markets and diversify its revenue stream away from just cash equities. NDAQ claims that its ban on flash trading beginning in September is immaterial to its results, which we view positively.

▶ Risks to our recommendation and target price include a decrease in trading volumes, lower-than-expected revenue ramp up from new initiatives, changes in the regulatory environment driving increased competition, and integration risk related to acquisitions.

▶ We keep our 12-month target price of $25, using a historical average P/E ratio of 12.5X our 2010 EPS forecast. We note that NDAQ's P/E ratio is at a slight discount to its most comparable peer, NYSE Euronext (NYX 26, Hold).

Qualitative Risk Assessment

LOW	MEDIUM	**HIGH**

Our risk assessment reflects the potential volatility in results due to changes in equity trading volumes, the potential impact of future regulatory changes, and the uncertainty surrounding NDAQ's international strategy.

Quantitative Evaluations

S&P Quality Ranking   NR

D	C	B-	B	B+	A-	A	A+

Relative Strength Rank   WEAK

29

LOWEST = 1   HIGHEST = 99

Revenue/Earnings Data

Revenue (Million $)

	1Q	2Q	3Q	4Q	Year
2009	895.0	889.0	810.0	--	--
2008	813.8	821.5	990.3	1,024	3,649
2007	562.0	558.2	652.0	664.5	2,437
2006	396.2	411.0	402.9	447.2	1,658
2005	180.2	219.7	220.5	259.6	879.9
2004	128.4	120.0	124.0	168.1	540.4

Earnings Per Share ($)

2009	0.44	0.33	0.28	E0.45	E1.82
2008	0.69	0.48	0.28	0.17	1.56
2007	0.14	0.39	2.41	0.57	3.46
2006	0.16	0.13	0.22	0.43	0.95
2005	0.13	0.13	0.16	0.15	0.57
2004	0.02	0.02	-0.08	-0.10	-0.14

Fiscal year ended Dec. 31. Next earnings report expected: Late February. EPS Estimates based on S&P Operating Earnings; historical GAAP earnings are as reported.

Dividend Data

No cash dividends have been paid.

Nasdaq OMX Group Inc (The)

STANDARD &POOR'S

Business Summary November 18, 2009

CORPORATE OVERVIEW. Nasdaq OMX Group is a leading global exchange group that delivers trading, exchange technology, securities listing and public company services across six continents. In the U.S., it operates The Nasdaq Stock Market, the largest electronic equity securities market in the country, with 3,800 listed companies as of December 31, 2008. NDAQ's matched volume in all U.S. securities was 666 billion in 2008, up from 442 billion in 2007. The company earns revenue from a number of products and services including trade execution, reselling market data, listing fees, intellectual property licensing, and corporate client services.

NDAQ's business is divided into three segments - Market Services, Issuer Services, and Market Technology. In 2008, Market Services accounted for approximately 88% of the company's revenue. This segment consists of NDAQ's U.S. and European transaction-based business, market data, and broker services. The largest portion of Market Services segment is transaction fees NDAQ receives for executing trades on its electronic platform. A smaller revenue source is the fees the company earns from aggregating and reselling trade and quote information from its systems.

Issuer Services, which accounts for about 9% of revenues, includes fees from its securities listings business and other financial products. Revenues in this segment are primarily derived from annual fees from companies whose

shares are listed on the Nasdaq Stock Market, fees for listing additional shares, and fees for new listings (initial public offerings). Issuer services also generates revenue from developing and licensing the NDAQ brand. Market technology made up 3% of the NDAQ's revenues in 2008. This segment offers systems solutions, which support trading, clearing and settlement, and information dissemination for a variety of instruments including equities and derivatives.

COMPETITIVE LANDSCAPE. We see NDAQ competing with other domestic exchanges, primarily the NYSE Euronext (NYX), for company listings, and competing with these exchanges, regional exchanges and electronic communication networks (ECNs) for trade execution volume. While consolidation, particularly among ECNs, has decreased the number of domestic competitors, we believe technology advancements and regulatory changes have kept the U.S. equity exchange business highly competitive. We think NDAQ competes on the basis of liquidity, speed and price in its core trade execution services. NDAQ plans to be the low price provider in the market for trade execution, and we expect it to continue offering lower listing fees than the NYSE.

Company Financials Fiscal Year Ended Dec. 31

Per Share Data ($)	2008	2007	2006	2005	2004	2003	2002	2001	2000	1999
Tangible Book Value	NM	7.54	2.44	NM	NM	2.04	NA	NA	NA	NA
Cash Flow	2.02	3.65	1.20	1.08	0.99	0.57	NA	NA	NA	NA
Earnings	1.56	3.46	0.95	0.57	-0.14	-0.68	0.40	0.35	1.34	0.86
S&P Core Earnings	1.75	1.62	0.96	0.53	-0.19	-0.69	0.31	NA	NA	NA
Dividends	Nil	Nil	Nil	Nil	Nil	Nil	NA	NA	NA	NA
Payout Ratio	Nil	Nil	Nil	Nil	Nil	Nil	NA	NA	NA	NA
Prices:High	49.90	50.47	46.75	45.23	NA	NA	NA	NA	NA	NA
Prices:Low	14.96	26.57	23.91	8.15	NA	NA	NA	NA	NA	NA
P/E Ratio:High	32	15	49	79	NM	NA	NA	NA	NA	NA
P/E Ratio:Low	10	8	25	14	NM	NA	NA	NA	NA	NA

Income Statement Analysis (Million $)	2008	2007	2006	2005	2004	2003	2002	2001	2000	1999
Revenue	3,649	2,437	1,658	880	540	590	799	857	868	634
Operating Income	758	440	288	181	85.0	126	NA	NA	NA	NA
Depreciation	92.6	38.9	45.1	67.0	76.0	90.0	97.9	93.4	65.6	43.7
Interest Expense	86.6	72.9	91.1	20.0	11.0	19.0	NA	NA	NA	NA
Pretax Income	524	794	212	106	2.60	-66.0	71.7	73.1	254	145
Effective Tax Rate	38.6%	34.7%	40.2%	41.8%	29.3%	NM	57.3%	52.4%	41.3%	40.4%
Net Income	320	518	128	62.0	1.80	-45.0	43.1	40.5	150	86.2
S&P Core Earnings	355	238	129	50.5	-15.2	-54.1	26.4	NA	NA	NA

Balance Sheet & Other Financial Data (Million $)	2008	2007	2006	2005	2004	2003	2002	2001	2000	1999
Cash	793	1,325	1,950	165	58.0	149	445	522	516	175
Current Assets	5,435	1,682	2,313	597	406	530	NA	NA	NA	NA
Total Assets	12,695	2,979	3,716	2,047	815	851	1,176	1,326	1,075	578
Current Liabilities	5,061	411	461	325	208	238	NA	NA	NA	NA
Long Term Debt	2,294	118	1,493	1,185	265	265	430	289	25.0	25.0
Common Equity	4,242	2,208	1,457	253	157	27.0	137	518	765	352
Total Capital	7,224	2,419	3,066	1,533	452	467	705	812	805	377
Capital Expenditures	54.7	18.5	21.0	25.0	26.0	32.0	85.4	123	187	106
Cash Flow	412	557	172	129	77.8	45.0	NA	NA	NA	NA
Current Ratio	1.1	4.1	5.0	1.8	2.0	2.2	2.4	2.8	3.2	2.1
% Long Term Debt of Capitalization	31.8	4.9	50.6	77.2	58.6	56.7	60.9	35.5	3.1	6.6
% Net Income of Revenue	8.8	21.3	7.7	7.0	0.0	NM	5.4	4.7	17.3	13.6
% Return on Assets	4.1	15.5	4.4	4.3	0.0	NM	3.5	3.4	18.2	NA
% Return on Equity	9.9	28.3	15.8	30.2	6.7	NM	13.2	6.3	26.9	NA

Data as orig reptd.; bef. results of disc opers/spec. items. Per share data adj. for stk. divs.; EPS diluted. E-Estimated. NA-Not Available. NM-Not Meaningful. NR-Not Ranked. UR-Under Review.

Office: 1 Liberty Plz, New York, NY 10006.
Telephone: 212-401-8700.
Website: http://www.nasdaq.com
Chrmn: H.F. Baldwin

Vice Chrmn: U. Backstrom
CEO: R. Greifeld
EVP & CFO: A. Friedman
EVP & General Counsel: E.S. Knight

Investor Contact: V. Palmiere (212-401-8742)
Board Members: U. Backstrom, H. F. Baldwin, M. L. Baum, M. Casey, L. Gorman, R. Greifeld, G. H. Hutchins, B. Kantola, E. Kazim, J. D. Markese, H. M. Nielsen, T. F. O'Neill, J. S. Riepe, M. R. Splinter, L. Wedenborn, D. L. Wince-Smith

Founded: 1979
Domicile: Delaware
Employees: 2,507

National Oilwell Varco Inc

S&P Recommendation **BUY** ★★★★☆	Price $43.30 (as of Nov 27, 2009)	12-Mo. Target Price $57.00	Investment Style Large-Cap Growth

GICS Sector Energy
Sub-Industry Oil & Gas Equipment & Services

Summary This company designs and manufactures drill rig equipment, provides downhole tools and services, and also provides supply chain integration services to the upstream oil and gas industry.

Key Stock Statistics (Source S&P, Vickers, company reports)

52-Wk Range	$50.17– 18.80	S&P Oper. EPS 2009**E**	3.29	Market Capitalization(B)	$18.114	Beta	1.39
Trailing 12-Month EPS	$3.98	S&P Oper. EPS 2010**E**	3.43	Yield (%)	0.92	S&P 3-Yr. Proj. EPS CAGR(%)	-3
Trailing 12-Month P/E	10.9	P/E on S&P Oper. EPS 2009**E**	13.2	Dividend Rate/Share	$0.40	S&P Credit Rating	A-
$10K Invested 5 Yrs Ago	$23,412	Common Shares Outstg. (M)	418.3	Institutional Ownership (%)	83		

Price Performance

30-Week Mov. Avg. · · · 10-Week Mov. Avg. — **GAAP Earnings vs. Previous Year** Volume Above Avg. STARS
12-Mo. Target Price — Relative Strength — ▲ Up ▼ Down ► No Change Below Avg.

2-for-1

Options: ASE, CBOE, P

Analysis prepared by **Stewart Glickman, CFA** on November 20, 2009, when the stock traded at **$ 43.07**.

Highlights

► At the end of September, total backlog stood at $7.3 billion, down $1.4 billion sequentially, as third quarter new orders (net of cancellations) of $261 million were about 16% of the revenues out of backlog. We note, however, that additions to backlog are inherently lumpy; given the amount of work slated to be done in key markets such as Brazil, and NOV's key role in the oilfield capital equipment market, we think order and thus backlog recovery is mainly a question of timing. We expect NOV to exit 2009 with a backlog of roughly $6.5 billion, and note that management anticipates some of the Brazil work likely to be awarded in mid-2010.

► We see significantly lower 2009 revenues in the Petroleum Services & Supplies segment, but a recovery in 2010. We estimate that perhaps one-third of this segment is exposed to customers choosing to cannibalize inventories on idled projects (e.g., drill pipe), and projects with lower margins given high exposure to North America.

► We see revenues falling 8.1% in 2009, and down 2.1% in 2010. We see EPS of $3.29 in 2009, but on higher margins, see EPS of $3.43 in 2010.

Investment Rationale/Risk

► We view NOV as an attractive play on the growing need for new rig equipment, particularly for deepwater and unconventional natural gas developments. While the current book of 145 rigs either on order or under construction (68 jackups, 40 semisubmersibles, and 37 drillships) implies about a 23% addition to the existing marketed fleet, we think that currently unsatisfied demand (especially for deepwater-capable equipment) will absorb most new additions.

► Risks to our opinion and target price include lower-than-expected prices for crude oil and natural gas; a slowdown in drilling activity; delays in meeting capital equipment orders; and unexpected contract cancellations.

► Our discounted cash flow (DCF) model, assuming free cash flow growth of 14%, terminal growth of 3% and a WACC of 12.8%, yields an intrinsic value of $56. We see ROIC of about 10% in 2010, below NOV's capital equipment peers, so we think a modest discount is merited. Based on an assumed 10.0X multiple of enterprise value to projected 2010 EBITDA, 11.5X estimated 2010 cash flow (below peers), and our DCF model, our 12-month target price is $57.

Qualitative Risk Assessment

LOW	MEDIUM	HIGH

Our risk assessment reflects NOV's exposure to volatile crude oil and natural gas prices, and capital spending decisions made by its contract driller and exploration and production customers. Offsetting these risks is what we view as NOV's leading industry position as a manufacturer of rig capital equipment.

Quantitative Evaluations

S&P Quality Ranking   B+

D	C	B-	B	B+	A-	A	A+

Relative Strength Rank   MODERATE

56

LOWEST = 1   HIGHEST = 99

Revenue/Earnings Data

Revenue (Million $)

	1Q	2Q	3Q	4Q	Year
2009	3,481	3,010	3,087	--	--
2008	2,685	3,324	3,612	3,810	13,431
2007	2,166	2,385	2,580	2,659	9,789
2006	1,512	1,657	1,778	2,079	7,026
2005	814.9	1,216	1,237	1,377	4,645
2004	496.2	533.5	618.9	669.5	2,318

Earnings Per Share ($)

	1Q	2Q	3Q	4Q	Year
2009	1.13	0.53	0.92	E0.72	E3.29
2008	1.11	1.04	1.31	1.40	4.90
2007	0.78	0.90	1.02	1.05	3.76
2006	0.34	0.42	0.50	0.68	1.94
2005	0.17	0.18	0.25	0.29	0.91
2004	0.07	0.13	0.16	0.29	0.64

Fiscal year ended Dec. 31. Next earnings report expected: Early February. EPS Estimates based on S&P Operating Earnings; historical GAAP earnings are as reported.

Dividend Data (Dates: mm/dd Payment Date: mm/dd/yy)

Amount ($)	Date Decl.	Ex-Div. Date	Stk. of Record	Payment Date
1.0 Spl.	11/17	11/30	12/02	12/16/09
0.100	11/17	11/30	12/02	12/16/09

Dividends have been paid since 2009. Source: Company reports.

Please read the Required Disclosures and Analyst Certification on the last page of this report.

The McGraw·Hill Companies

National Oilwell Varco Inc

STANDARD &POOR'S

Business Summary November 20, 2009

CORPORATE OVERVIEW. Formerly known as National-Oilwell, this company changed its name to National Oilwell Varco (NOV) on March 14, 2005, following the completion of the merger with Varco International. NOV, a worldwide designer, manufacturer and marketer of comprehensive systems and components used in oil and gas drilling and production, as well as a provider of downhole tools and services, also provides supply chain integration services to the upstream oil and gas industry. The company estimates that more than 90% of the mobile offshore rig fleet and the majority of the world's larger land rigs (2,000 horsepower and greater) manufactured in the past 20 years use drawworks, mud pumps and other drilling components manufactured by NOV.

The combined company generated 2008 revenues of about $13.4 billion, and operating income of $2.9 billion, for an operating margin of approximately 21.6%. The company's Rig Technology segment ($7.5 billion of revenue in 2008, and $2.0 billion of 2008 segment operating income) designs, manufactures and sells drilling systems and components for both land and offshore drilling rigs, as well as complete land drilling and well servicing rigs. The major mechanical components include drawworks, mud pumps, power swivels, SCR houses,

solids control equipment, traveling equipment and rotary tables. Many of these components are designed specifically for applications in offshore, extended reach and deep land drilling. This equipment is installed on new rigs and is often replaced during the upgrade and refurbishment of existing rigs. As of December 31, 2008, total backlog in this segment was about $11.1 billion, up about 23% from one year earlier.

The company's Petroleum Services & Supplies segment ($4.6 billion, $1.2 billion) provides a variety of consumable goods and services used in the drilling, completion, workover and remediation of oil and gas wells, service pipelines, flowlines, and other oilfield tubular goods. Products include transfer pumps, solids control systems, drilling motors and other downhole tools, rig instrumentation systems, and mud pump consumables. Following the April 2008 acquisition of Grant Prideco, this segment now offers drill pipe and drill bits.

Company Financials Fiscal Year Ended Dec. 31

Per Share Data ($)	2008	2007	2006	2005	2004	2003	2002	2001	2000	1999
Tangible Book Value	NA	9.65	5.91	4.20	3.33	2.49	2.17	3.19	2.72	1.90
Cash Flow	5.90	4.19	2.39	1.27	0.89	0.68	0.60	0.87	0.30	0.21
Earnings	4.90	3.76	1.94	0.91	0.64	0.45	0.45	0.64	0.08	0.02
S&P Core Earnings	4.89	3.76	1.94	0.90	0.58	0.41	0.38	0.57	NA	NA
Dividends	NA	Nil	Nil	Nil	Nil	Nil	Nil	Nil	Nil	Nil
Payout Ratio	NA	Nil	Nil	Nil	Nil	Nil	Nil	Nil	Nil	Nil
Prices:High	NA	82.00	38.80	34.17	18.69	12.43	14.41	20.62	19.84	9.25
Prices:Low	NA	26.88	25.81	16.54	10.83	8.75	7.60	6.20	7.00	4.25
P/E Ratio:High	NA	22	20	38	29	28	32	32	NM	NM
P/E Ratio:Low	NA	7	13	18	17	19	17	10	NM	NM

Income Statement Analysis (Million $)										
Revenue	13,431	9,789	7,026	4,645	2,318	2,005	1,522	1,747	1,150	745
Operating Income	3,419	2,198	1,280	623	213	198	159	228	97.6	45.1
Depreciation, Depletion and Amortization	401	153	161	115	44.0	39.2	25.0	38.9	35.0	23.2
Interest Expense	67.3	50.3	48.7	52.9	38.4	38.9	27.3	24.9	Nil	Nil
Pretax Income	2,961	2,029	1,049	430	132	117	112	168	27.0	4.52
Effective Tax Rate	33.5%	33.3%	33.9%	32.3%	14.6%	28.9%	35.0%	38.1%	51.4%	66.4%
Net Income	1,952	1,337	684	287	110	76.8	73.1	104	13.1	1.52
S&P Core Earnings	1,947	1,338	685	283	99.2	69.3	61.6	93.6	NA	NA

Balance Sheet & Other Financial Data (Million $)										
Cash	1,543	1,842	957	209	143	74.2	118	43.2	42.5	12.4
Current Assets	9,657	7,594	4,966	2,998	1,537	1,246	1,115	909	743	478
Total Assets	21,399	12,115	9,019	6,679	2,599	2,243	1,969	1,472	1,279	782
Current Liabilities	5,624	4,027	2,665	1,187	800	452	346	277	263	176
Long Term Debt	870	738	835	836	350	594	595	300	222	196
Common Equity	12,637	6,661	5,024	4,194	1,296	1,090	933	868	767	395
Total Capital	15,728	8,026	6,283	5,428	1,767	1,753	1,592	1,188	1,006	597
Capital Expenditures	379	252	200	105	39.0	32.4	24.8	27.4	24.6	15.4
Cash Flow	2,353	1,490	845	402	154	116	98.1	143	48.2	24.8
Current Ratio	1.7	1.9	1.9	2.5	1.9	2.8	3.2	3.3	2.8	2.7
% Long Term Debt of Capitalization	5.5	9.2	13.3	15.4	19.8	33.9	37.3	25.3	22.1	32.8
% Return on Assets	NA	12.7	8.7	6.2	4.6	3.6	4.2	7.6	1.2	0.2
% Return on Equity	20.2	22.9	14.8	10.5	9.2	7.6	8.1	12.7	1.9	0.4

Data as orig reptd.; bef. results of disc opers/spec. items. Per share data adj. for stk. divs.; EPS diluted. E-Estimated. NA-Not Available. NM-Not Meaningful. NR-Not Ranked. UR-Under Review.

Office: 7909 Parkwood Circle Dr, Houston, TX 77036-6565.
Telephone: 713-346-7500.
Email: investor.relations@natoil.com
Website: http://www.natoil.com

Chrmn, Pres & CEO: M.A. Miller, Jr.
EVP & CFO: C.C. Williams
SVP, Secy & General Counsel: D.W. Rettig
CTO: H. Kverneland

Chief Acctg Officer & Cntlr: R.W. Blanchard
Board Members: G. L. Armstrong, R. E. Beauchamp, B. A. Guill, D. Harrison, R. L. Jarvis, E. Mattson, M. A. Miller, Jr., J. A. Smisek

Founded: 1987
Domicile: Delaware
Employees: 40,205

National Semiconductor Corp

STANDARD &POOR'S

S&P Recommendation	BUY ★★★★☆	Price $14.47 (as of Nov 27, 2009)	12-Mo. Target Price $19.00	Investment Style Large-Cap Growth

GICS Sector Information Technology
Sub-Industry Semiconductors

Summary This company is a leading manufacturer of a broad line of semiconductors, including analog, digital and mixed-signal integrated circuits.

Key Stock Statistics (Source S&P, Vickers, company reports)

52-Wk Range	$16.20–9.06	S&P Oper. EPS 2010E	0.60	Market Capitalization(B)	$3.424	Beta	1.24
Trailing 12-Month EPS	$0.10	S&P Oper. EPS 2011E	0.80	Yield (%)	2.21	S&P 3-Yr. Proj. EPS CAGR(%)	-9
Trailing 12-Month P/E	NM	P/E on S&P Oper. EPS 2010E	24.1	Dividend Rate/Share	$0.32	S&P Credit Rating	BB+
$10K Invested 5 Yrs Ago	$9,337	Common Shares Outstg. (M)	236.6	Institutional Ownership (%)	89		

Price Performance

30-Week Mov. Avg. ···· 10-Week Mov. Avg. - - GAAP Earnings vs. Previous Year   Volume Above Avg. STARS
12-Mo. Target Price — Relative Strength — ▲ Up ▼ Down ► No Change   Below Avg.

Options: ASE, CBOE, P, Ph

Analysis prepared by **Clyde Montevirgen** on September 14, 2009, when the stock traded at **$14.92**.

Qualitative Risk Assessment

LOW	MEDIUM	**HIGH**

NSM operates in the semiconductor industry, which tends to be cyclical. Sudden slowdowns can result from downturns in demand for electronics or from chip inventory buildup and industry overcapacity.

Quantitative Evaluations

S&P Quality Ranking B-

D	C	**B-**	B	B+	A-	A	A+

Relative Strength Rank MODERATE

69

LOWEST = 1   HIGHEST = 99

Revenue/Earnings Data

Revenue (Million $)

	1Q	2Q	3Q	4Q	Year
2010	314.4	--	--	--	--
2009	465.6	421.6	292.4	280.8	1,460
2008	471.5	499.0	453.4	462.0	1,886
2007	541.4	501.6	431.0	455.9	1,930
2006	493.8	544.0	547.7	572.6	2,158
2005	548.0	448.9	449.2	467.0	1,913

Earnings Per Share ($)

	1Q	2Q	3Q	4Q	Year
2010	0.13	E0.12	E0.15	E0.21	E0.60
2009	0.33	0.16	0.09	-0.28	0.31
2008	0.33	0.33	0.29	0.34	1.26
2007	0.35	0.27	0.22	0.28	1.12
2006	0.24	0.32	0.37	0.34	1.26
2005	0.31	0.24	0.21	0.36	1.11

Fiscal year ended May 31. Next earnings report expected: Early December. EPS Estimates based on S&P Operating Earnings; historical GAAP earnings are as reported.

Highlights

► We expect sales to fall 7% in FY 10 (May), after a decline of 23% in FY 09. We believe there are near-term headwinds due to NSM's exposure to industrial markets and general macroeconomic weakness. However, the company has cut lower-margin product lines and transformed its product portfolio, now consisting of higher-margin chips for faster-growing markets. We see power management products, new solar and light-emitting diode (LED) products and better penetration in end markets, where it currently has limited exposure, supporting healthy long-term revenue advances.

► We forecast gross margins to narrow to 61% in FY 10, about two percentage points below FY 09 results. Although we think NSM has done a good job improving its product portfolio and manufacturing efficiency, we see slower orders leading to lower plant utilization as NSM adjusts production to meet lower demand and target inventory levels. We expect operating margins to rise to 19% in FY 10, from 12% in FY 09, reflecting fewer one-time expenses.

► Our projections assume an effective tax rate of around 30% and include stock-based compensation.

Investment Rationale/Risk

► Our buy opinion reflects our view of anticipated margin expansion and growth. There are near-term headwinds related to weak macroeconomic conditions, which we think will limit sales growth. However, we believe NSM is taking appropriate actions to reduce its cost structure in light of lower sales levels, and will begin to show quarterly improvements in profitability. As sales rise, operating leverage should provide more earnings power, in our view. NSM also has growth opportunities with new solar and LED products that we believe could add notable incremental sales opportunities.

► Risks to our recommendation and target price include a longer-than-expected recession, a worse-than-expected impact from product mix, and ineffective restructuring execution.

► Our 12-month target price of $19 is based on price/sales (P/S) and discounted cash flow metrics. We apply a P/S multiple of around 3X, near the historical average to reflect our view of rebounding sales, to our forward 12-month sales per share estimate to derive a value of $19. Our DCF model, which assumes a WACC of 9% and 4% terminal growth, suggests an intrinsic value of $20.

Dividend Data (Dates: mm/dd Payment Date: mm/dd/yy)

Amount ($)	Date Decl.	Ex-Div. Date	Stk. of Record	Payment Date
0.080	09/25	12/11	12/15	01/05/09
0.080	03/11	03/19	03/23	04/14/09
0.080	06/11	06/18	06/22	07/13/09
0.080	09/10	09/17	09/21	10/12/09

Dividends have been paid since 2005. Source: Company reports.

Please read the Required Disclosures and Analyst Certification on the last page of this report.

National Semiconductor Corp

STANDARD &POOR'S

Business Summary September 14, 2009

CORPORATE OVERVIEW. National Semiconductor designs, develops, makes and markets a wide range of semiconductor products. Leading-edge products include power management circuits, display drivers, audio and operational amplifiers, communication interface products and data conversion solutions.

The company targets a broad range of markets and applications such as wireless handsets, medical applications, displays, automotive applications, networks, test and measurement applications, industrial markets, and a broad range of portable applications. Most of its products are analog and mixed-signal integrated circuits, comprising about 98% of FY 08 (May) total revenue.

NSM classifies its product lines in two groups, Power Management and Analog Signal Path. The Power Management group makes products that convert and manage power consumption in electronic systems. The Analog Signal Path group makes analog technology that is used during the path that information or data enters the electronic products, is conditioned, converted and processed to the point it is sent out. This technology is used to connect and convert analog signals to digital information.

The company markets its products globally to original equipment manufacturers (OEMs) and original design manufacturers through a direct sales force. In FY 08, 58% of sales were to its top 10 customers. NSM listed three large customers, including distributors Avnet (which accounted for 15% of NSM's FY 08 sales) and Arrow (12%), and handset OEM Nokia (11%). Some 54% of FY 08 revenues came from distributors.

CORPORATE STRATEGY. National Semiconductor's CEO, Brian Halla, who joined the company in 1996, has led an effort to form a "new" NSM. The company's expertise has been primarily in analog intensive, digital and mixed-signal complex integrated circuits. In 1996, NSM spun off its logic, memory and discrete products (considered commodity-type components) as a separate company, Fairchild Semiconductor. The company now focuses on high-end analog chips.

Wafer fabrication is concentrated in two facilities in the U.S. and one in Scotland. Nearly all product assembly and final test operations are performed in several facilities in Asia. The Singapore assembly and test facility is scheduled for closure in 2007; most operations were transferred to the Malaysia and China plants during FY 06.

Company Financials Fiscal Year Ended May 31

Per Share Data ($)	2009	2008	2007	2006	2005	2004	2003	2002	2001	2000
Tangible Book Value	0.50	0.59	5.43	5.57	5.65	4.21	4.18	4.46	4.70	4.63
Cash Flow	0.82	NA	1.56	1.72	1.63	1.27	0.54	0.31	1.30	2.33
Earnings	0.31	1.26	1.12	1.26	1.11	0.74	-0.09	-0.34	0.65	1.64
S&P Core Earnings	0.28	1.24	1.11	1.21	1.15	0.26	-0.59	-0.84	0.29	NA
Dividends	0.20	0.14	0.10	0.04	Nil	Nil	Nil	Nil	Nil	Nil
Payout Ratio	65%	11%	9%	3%	Nil	Nil	Nil	Nil	Nil	Nil
Calendar Year	2008	2007	2006	2005	2004	2003	2002	2001	2000	1999
Prices:High	24.75	29.69	30.93	28.75	24.35	22.63	18.65	17.55	42.97	25.94
Prices:Low	9.02	21.54	20.56	18.36	11.85	6.27	4.98	9.85	8.56	4.44
P/E Ratio:High	80	24	28	23	22	31	NM	NM	66	16
P/E Ratio:Low	29	17	18	15	11	8	NM	NM	13	3

Income Statement Analysis (Million $)

	2009	2008	2007	2006	2005	2004	2003	2002	2001	2000
Revenue	1,460	1,886	1,930	2,158	1,913	1,983	1,673	1,495	2,113	2,140
Operating Income	447	404	642	844	626	582	248	81.9	517	550
Depreciation	120	133	145	166	194	210	229	230	243	264
Interest Expense	72.7	85.5	Nil	Nil	Nil	Nil	Nil	3.90	5.00	17.9
Pretax Income	114	451	531	695	410	334	-23.3	-123	307	642
Effective Tax Rate	35.5%	26.4%	29.3%	35.4%	NM	14.7%	NM	NM	19.4%	2.32%
Net Income	73.3	332	375	449	415	285	-33.3	-122	246	628
S&P Core Earnings	66.9	326	372	433	430	102	-215	-298	108	NA

Balance Sheet & Other Financial Data (Million $)

	2009	2008	2007	2006	2005	2004	2003	2002	2001	2000
Cash	700	737	829	932	867	643	802	681	818	850
Current Assets	1,087	1,172	1,291	1,541	1,514	1,246	1,281	1,073	1,275	1,468
Total Assets	1,963	2,149	2,202	2,511	2,504	2,280	2,245	2,289	2,362	2,382
Current Liabilities	276	309	300	398	285	461	367	404	472	628
Long Term Debt	1,227	1,415	20.6	21.1	23.0	Nil	19.9	20.4	26.0	48.6
Common Equity	177	197	1,749	1,926	2,062	1,681	1,706	1,781	1,768	1,643
Total Capital	1,467	1,674	1,769	1,947	2,085	1,681	1,726	1,802	1,794	1,692
Capital Expenditures	83.7	111	107	163	96.6	215	171	138	228	170
Cash Flow	193	465	520	616	610	495	195	109	489	891
Current Ratio	4.0	3.8	4.3	3.9	5.3	2.7	3.5	2.7	2.7	2.3
% Long Term Debt of Capitalization	83.7	84.5	1.2	1.1	1.1	Nil	1.2	1.1	1.4	2.9
% Net Income of Revenue	5.0	17.6	19.4	20.8	21.7	14.4	NM	NM	11.6	29.3
% Return on Assets	3.6	15.3	15.9	17.9	17.4	12.6	NM	NM	10.3	28.4
% Return on Equity	39.2	34.2	20.4	22.6	22.1	16.8	NM	NM	14.4	49.3

Data as orig reptd.; bef. results of disc opers/spec. items. Per share data adj. for stk. divs.; EPS diluted. E-Estimated. NA-Not Available. NM-Not Meaningful. NR-Not Ranked. UR-Under Review.

Office: 2900 Semiconductor Dr, Santa Clara, CA 95052-8090.
Telephone: 408-721-5000.
Email: invest.group@nsc.com
Website: http://www.national.com

Chrmn & CEO: B.L. Halla
Pres & COO: D. Macleod
SVP & CFO: L. Chew
SVP, Secy & General Counsel: T.M. DuChene

CTO: M. Yegnashankaran
Investor Contact: R.E. Debarr ()
Board Members: S. R. Appleton, G. P. Arnold, R. J. Danzig, J. T. Dickson, R. J. Frankenberg, B. L. Halla, M. A. Maidique, E. McCracken, R. C. McGeary

Founded: 1959
Domicile: Delaware
Employees: 5,800

The McGraw-Hill Companies

NetApp Inc

STANDARD & POOR'S

| S&P Recommendation | HOLD ★★★☆☆ | Price $30.83 (as of Nov 27, 2009) | 12-Mo. Target Price $35.00 | Investment Style Large-Cap Growth |

GICS Sector Information Technology
Sub-Industry Computer Storage & Peripherals

Summary This company provides storage hardware, software and services to a variety of enterprise customers.

Key Stock Statistics (Source S&P, Vickers, company reports)

52-Wk Range	$31.50–11.66	S&P Oper. EPS 2010**E**	1.05	Market Capitalization(B)	$10.370	Beta	1.50
Trailing 12-Month EPS	$0.46	S&P Oper. EPS 2011**E**	1.47	Yield (%)	Nil	S&P 3-Yr. Proj. EPS CAGR(%)	15
Trailing 12-Month P/E	67.0	P/E on S&P Oper. EPS 2010**E**	29.4	Dividend Rate/Share	Nil	S&P Credit Rating	NA
$10K Invested 5 Yrs Ago	$10,158	Common Shares Outstg. (M)	336.4	Institutional Ownership (%)	99		

Price Performance

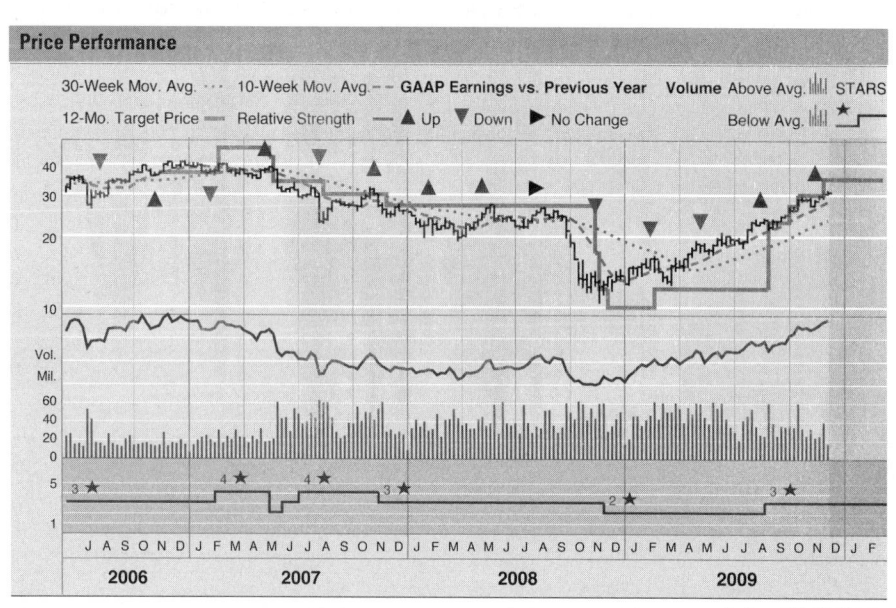

30-Week Mov. Avg. · · · 10-Week Mov. Avg. - - - **GAAP Earnings vs. Previous Year** Volume Above Avg. STARS
12-Mo. Target Price — Relative Strength — ▲ Up ▼ Down ▶ No Change Below Avg.

Options: ASE, CBOE, P, Ph

Analysis prepared by **Jim Yin** on November 20, 2009, when the stock traded at **$ 30.17**.

Highlights

► We expect revenues to increase 7.7% and 9.5% in FY 10 (Apr.) and FY 11, respectively. Although we forecast a sluggish recovery for IT spending in 2010, we expect the data storage market segment to rebound more quickly than other IT sectors given the severity of the cutback during the downturn. We also believe NTAP will gain market share due to new product introductions and a stronger distribution partnership with IBM.

► We project gross margins of 66% in both FY 10 and FY 11, versus 58.4% in FY 09, based on our outlook for a favorable product mix and lower component costs. We believe NTAP will keep a tight control over employee head count. As a result, we see operating margins widening to 12% in FY 10 and 15% in FY 11, from 1.4% in FY 09.

► We estimate EPS of $1.05 in FY 10 and $1.47 in FY 11, compared to $0.26 in FY 09. Our estimates include $0.35 of amortization of intangibles and stock-based compensation expense in both FY 10 and FY 11. In addition to stronger demand, we think earnings will be helped by better cost containment and lower restructuring charges.

Investment Rationale/Risk

► Our hold recommendation is based on valuation, following significant price appreciation. We believe the rise is warranted given our view of an improving economy. We expect overall IT spending to rise 4% in 2010. We believe the data storage market segment will grow faster than the overall IT industry and that NTAP will gain market share with new products. Also, we think NTAP has a strong balance sheet, with net cash of $2.0 billion as of October 2009, providing the company financial flexibility to make strategic acquisitions.

► Risks to our recommendation and target price include a weaker-than-expected economic recovery, lower IT spending, and significant loss of market share.

► Our 12-month target price of $35 is based on a blend of our discounted cash flow (DCF) and enterprise value (EV)-to-sales analyses. Our DCF model assumes a weighted average cost of capital of 13% and 3% terminal growth, and yields an intrinsic value of $34. We apply an EV-to-sales multiple of 2.6X, near the company's historical average, to our FY 11 sales estimate of $4.0 billion to derive a $36 valuation.

Qualitative Risk Assessment

| LOW | MEDIUM | HIGH |

Our risk assessment takes into account our view of a sluggish IT spending environment, the historical volatility of the data storage industry, and the rapid pace of technological change that typifies the industry.

Quantitative Evaluations

S&P Quality Ranking B

| D | C | B- | **B** | B+ | A- | A | A+ |

Relative Strength Rank STRONG
91
LOWEST = 1   HIGHEST = 99

Revenue/Earnings Data

Revenue (Million $)

	1Q	2Q	3Q	4Q	Year
2010	838.0	910.0	--	--	--
2009	868.8	911.6	746.3	879.6	3,406
2008	689.2	792.2	884.0	937.7	3,303
2007	621.3	652.5	729.3	801.2	2,804
2006	448.4	483.1	537.0	598.0	2,066
2005	358.4	375.2	412.7	451.8	1,598

Earnings Per Share ($)

2010	0.15	0.27	E0.30	E0.32	E1.05
2009	0.11	0.15	-0.23	0.23	0.26
2008	0.11	0.23	0.29	0.26	0.86
2007	0.14	0.22	0.17	0.23	0.77
2006	0.16	0.18	0.20	0.15	0.69
2005	0.13	0.15	0.16	0.16	0.59

Fiscal year ended Apr. 30. Next earnings report expected: Mid February. EPS Estimates based on S&P Operating Earnings; historical GAAP earnings are as reported.

Dividend Data

No cash dividends have been paid.

NetApp Inc

STANDARD &POOR'S

Business Summary November 20, 2009

CORPORATE OVERVIEW. NetApp Inc. (formerly known as Network Appliance) is a provider of enterprise-level storage hardware and data-management software products and services. NTAP's solutions help global enterprises meet major information technology challenges such as managing the continuing growth in the volume of data, scaling existing infrastructure, complying with regulatory regimes, and security corporate networks and information.

The NTAP family of modular and scalable networked systems provides seamless access to a full range of enterprise data for users working with a variety of platforms, including Fibre Channel (FC), network-attached storage (NAS), storage area network (SAN), and iSCSI environments, as well as online data residing in central locations. NTAP refers to this as fabric-attached storage (FAS). Products include the 200, 900, 3000 and 6000 series.

NTAP's V-Series is a network-based solution that consolidates storage arrays from different suppliers, enabling unified SAN and file access to data stored in heterogeneous FC SAN storage arrays. The V-Series family supports products from Hewlett-Packard, Hitachi and IBM.

CORPORATE STRATEGY. NearStore products focus on optimizing data protection and retention applications. This system offers an alternative to customers by providing faster data access than off-line storage at a significantly lower cost than primary storage. Offerings in this category include the Virtual Tape Library (VTL), a disk-to-disk backup appliance that appears as a tape library to a back-up software application.

The NetCache suite of solutions is designed to manage, control and improve access to Web-based information. Working with a range of software partners, NetCache provides large enterprises with the ability to manage Internet access and security. It essentially enables IT managers to control user access to information, based on profiles, actions, timing, etc.

Company Financials Fiscal Year Ended Apr. 30

Per Share Data ($)	2009	2008	2007	2006	2005	2004	2003	2002	2001	2000
Tangible Book Value	2.82	2.72	3.56	3.62	3.67	2.91	2.75	2.39	2.21	1.54
Cash Flow	0.77	1.26	1.05	0.90	0.77	0.58	0.38	0.14	0.33	0.26
Earnings	0.26	0.86	0.77	0.69	0.59	0.42	0.22	0.01	0.21	0.21
S&P Core Earnings	0.71	0.84	0.73	0.45	0.39	0.16	-0.28	-0.77	-0.52	NA
Dividends	Nil	Nil	Nil	Nil	Nil	Nil	Nil	Nil	Nil	Nil
Payout Ratio	Nil	Nil	Nil	Nil	Nil	Nil	Nil	Nil	Nil	Nil
Calendar Year	2008	2007	2006	2005	2004	2003	2002	2001	2000	1999
Prices:High	27.49	40.89	41.56	34.98	34.99	26.69	27.95	74.98	152.75	45.94
Prices:Low	10.39	22.51	25.85	22.50	15.92	9.26	5.18	6.00	33.88	9.53
P/E Ratio:High	NM	48	54	51	59	64	NM	NM	NM	NM
P/E Ratio:Low	NM	26	34	33	27	22	NM	NM	NM	NM

Income Statement Analysis (Million $)										
Revenue	3,406	3,303	2,804	2,066	1,598	1,170	892	798	1,006	579
Operating Income	410	464	387	395	319	228	146	76.5	179	121
Depreciation	171	144	111	81.8	65.6	59.5	57.4	65.3	42.3	15.7
Interest Expense	26.9	Nil	11.6	1.28	Nil	Nil	Nil	Nil	Nil	Nil
Pretax Income	44.8	383	360	350	276	170	97.8	2.53	133	114
Effective Tax Rate	NM	19.1%	17.2%	23.9%	18.3%	10.8%	21.8%	NM	43.7%	35.5%
Net Income	86.5	310	298	266	226	152	76.5	3.03	74.9	73.8
S&P Core Earnings	235	303	282	175	148	59.5	-98.0	-256	-167	NA

Balance Sheet & Other Financial Data (Million $)										
Cash	2,604	1,164	489	461	194	241	284	211	272	279
Current Assets	3,439	2,067	2,241	2,033	1,576	1,089	853	679	636	533
Total Assets	5,453	4,071	3,658	3,261	2,373	1,877	1,319	1,109	1,036	592
Current Liabilities	1,679	1,414	1,188	917	520	344	265	216	219	113
Long Term Debt	1,430	173	Nil	138	4.47	4.86	3.10	3.73	0.15	0.05
Common Equity	1,662	1,700	1,989	1,923	1,661	1,416	987	858	804	479
Total Capital	3,092	1,873	1,989	2,061	1,665	1,421	990	862	805	479
Capital Expenditures	290	188	166	133	93.6	48.6	61.3	284	83.7	40.8
Cash Flow	257	454	409	348	291	212	134	47.4	117	89.5
Current Ratio	2.1	1.5	1.9	2.2	3.0	3.2	3.2	3.2	2.9	4.7
% Long Term Debt of Capitalization	46.2	9.2	Nil	6.7	0.3	0.3	0.3	0.4	0.0	0.0
% Net Income of Revenue	2.5	9.4	10.6	12.9	14.1	13.0	8.6	0.4	7.4	12.7
% Return on Assets	1.8	8.0	8.6	9.5	10.6	9.5	6.3	0.3	9.2	15.7
% Return on Equity	5.2	16.8	15.2	14.9	14.7	12.7	8.3	0.4	11.7	19.1

Data as orig reptd.; bef. results of disc opers/spec. items. Per share data adj. for stk. divs.; EPS diluted. E-Estimated. NA-Not Available. NM-Not Meaningful. NR-Not Ranked. UR-Under Review.

Office: 495 East Java Drive, Sunnyvale, CA 94089.
Telephone: 408-822-6000.
Email: investor_relations@netapp.com
Website: http://www.netapp.com

Chrmn: D. Warmenhoven
Pres & CEO: T. Georgens
Investor Contact: S. Gomo ()
EVP, CFO & Chief Acctg Officer: S. Gomo

SVP & CSO: S. Kleiman
Board Members: J. R. Allen, A. L. Earhart, T. Georgens, E. R. Kozel, M. Leslie, N. G. Moore, G. T. Shaheen, D. T. Valentine, R. T. Wall, D. Warmenhoven

Founded: 1992
Domicile: Delaware
Employees: 7,976

Newell Rubbermaid Inc.

STANDARD &POOR'S

S&P Recommendation	HOLD ★★★☆☆	Price	12-Mo. Target Price	Investment Style
		$14.65 (as of Nov 27, 2009)	$17.00	Large-Cap Value

GICS Sector Consumer Discretionary
Sub-Industry Housewares & Specialties

Summary This high volume, brand name consumer products concern has grown through acquisitions. Major product lines include housewares, home furnishings, office products and hardware.

Key Stock Statistics (Source S&P, Vickers, company reports)

52-Wk Range	$16.10– 4.51	S&P Oper. EPS 2009**E**	1.31	Market Capitalization(B)	$4.068	Beta	1.87
Trailing 12-Month EPS	$-0.11	S&P Oper. EPS 2010**E**	1.40	Yield (%)	1.37	S&P 3-Yr. Proj. EPS CAGR(%)	5
Trailing 12-Month P/E	NM	P/E on S&P Oper. EPS 2009**E**	11.2	Dividend Rate/Share	$0.20	S&P Credit Rating	BBB-
$10K Invested 5 Yrs Ago	$7,443	Common Shares Outstg. (M)	277.7	Institutional Ownership (%)	90		

Price Performance

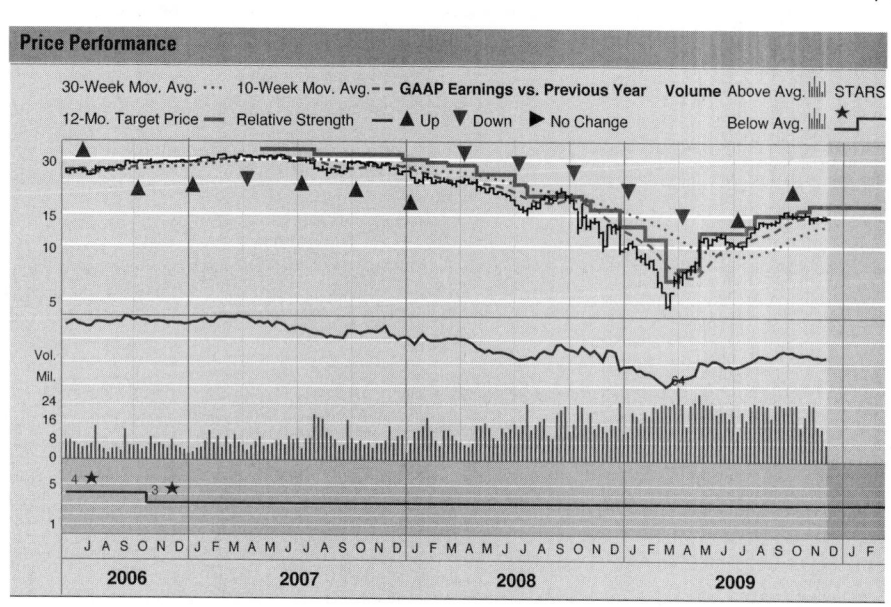

30-Week Mov. Avg. ··· 10-Week Mov. Avg. - - **GAAP Earnings vs. Previous Year** Volume Above Avg. ||||| STARS
12-Mo. Target Price — Relative Strength — ▲ Up ▼ Down ▶ No Change   Below Avg. |||||

Options: ASE, CBOE, P

Analysis prepared by **Loran Braverman, CFA** on October 28, 2009, when the stock traded at **$ 13.80**.

Highlights

► For 2009, we see overall sales down 14%, with negative foreign currency translation of 2% and planned product line exits of 6%. Using the revised 2009 segmentation, we project Office Products sales down 16%, Tools, Hardware & Commercial Products down 17%, and Home & Family down 11% (helped by an acquisition made in 2008). Our 2010 sales projection is 2%.

► In 2008, commodity cost pressures and weak sales contributed to a 330 basis point narrowing in the pre-corporate overhead operating margin. For 2009, we think moderation in commodity cost pressures and gross margin benefits from product line exits will more than offset negative sales leverage, allowing the operating margin to rise by 270 bps. We also assume lower interest & other expense and a 33% tax rate. For 2010, we see further operating margin improvement.

► We estimate that operating EPS will be $1.31 in 2009, about flat with 2008's $1.22. In May 2009, NWL cut its quarterly dividend to $0.05, from $0.105, which itself had been slashed from $0.21 earlier in the year. Our 2010 EPS estimate is $1.40.

Investment Rationale/Risk

► We think the stock price adequately reflects NWL's improved longer-term growth prospects but a current difficult environment. We believe the company, under new leadership, is poised for better innovation and efficiency. NWL has been exiting lower-margin, often resin-intensive product lines and investing in what we think are more profitable categories. In our view, NWL should be able to gain market share through better consumer research and greater product innovation.

► Risks to our recommendation and target price include poor consumer acceptance of new products, a prolonged weak consumer spending environment, a low level of cost savings from the company's reorganization program, negative currency translation and a material increase in prices of key raw materials.

► Our 12-month target price of $17 is a blend of our historical and relative analyses. Our historical model uses a P/E of 13.3X our 2010 EPS estimate, a discount to the 10-year median, to arrive at a $19 value. Our relative analysis uses a peer-average multiple for a $16 value.

Qualitative Risk Assessment

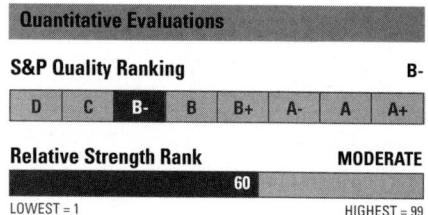

LOW	MEDIUM	HIGH

Our risk assessment reflects that housewares companies' products are generally affordable, low-priced goods that are usually modestly affected by swings in the economy. However, there is a greater level of import competition for commodity-type goods.

Quantitative Evaluations

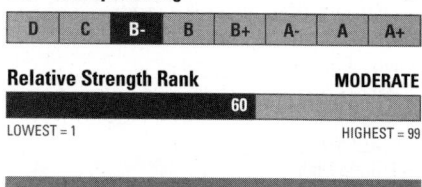

S&P Quality Ranking   B-

D	C	B-	B	B+	A-	A	A+

Relative Strength Rank   MODERATE

LOWEST = 1   60   HIGHEST = 99

Revenue/Earnings Data

Revenue (Million $)

	1Q	2Q	3Q	4Q	Year
2009	1,204	1,504	1,449	--	--
2008	1,434	1,825	1,760	1,452	6,471
2007	1,384	1,693	1,687	1,643	6,407
2006	1,343	1,634	1,586	1,638	6,201
2005	1,363	1,646	1,585	1,749	6,343
2004	1,541	1,736	1,672	1,809	6,748

Earnings Per Share ($)

2009	0.12	0.37	0.28	E0.26	E1.31
2008	0.21	0.33	0.20	-0.93	-0.19
2007	0.23	0.51	0.61	0.36	1.72
2006	0.47	0.49	0.41	0.33	1.71
2005	0.33	0.30	0.37	0.31	1.29
2004	0.12	0.21	-0.86	0.45	-0.07

Fiscal year ended Dec. 31. Next earnings report expected: Late January. EPS Estimates based on S&P Operating Earnings; historical GAAP earnings are as reported.

Dividend Data (Dates: mm/dd Payment Date: mm/dd/yy)

Amount ($)	Date Decl.	Ex-Div. Date	Stk. of Record	Payment Date
0.105	02/12	02/25	02/27	03/13/09
0.050	05/07	05/27	05/29	06/15/09
0.050	08/06	08/27	08/31	09/15/09
0.050	11/12	11/25	11/30	12/15/09

Dividends have been paid since 1946. Source: Company reports.

Please read the Required Disclosures and Analyst Certification on the last page of this report.

Newell Rubbermaid Inc.

Business Summary October 28, 2009

CORPORATE OVERVIEW. Newell Rubbermaid is a global manufacturer and marketer of name brand consumer products and their commercial extensions, serving a wide array of retail channels including department stores, warehouse clubs, home centers, hardware stores, commercial distributors, office superstores, contract stationers, automotive stores and small superstores. As of April 2009, NWL recategorized its four business segments into three: Office Products (31% of 2008 sales, 30% of segment operating profits), Tools, Hardware & Commercial Products (28%, 39%), and Home & Family (41%, 31%). About 31% of 2008 sales were made outside the U.S. Sales to Wal-Mart Stores, Inc. and its subsidiaries amounted to about 13% of sales in 2008.

The global business units (GBUs) that formerly comprised the Cleaning, Organization & Decor segment, that is Home Products, Foodservice Products, Commercial Products and Decor, have been intergated into two of the three remaining segments. Brands include Rubbermaid, Brute, Roughneck, TakeAlongs, Levolor and Kirsch. The Rubbermaid Food & Home Products and Decor GBUs are now included in Home & Family segment. Also, the Amerock brand, which was previously part of the Tools & Hardware segment, has been integrated into the Decor GBU.

The office products segment is comprised of the following GBUs: Markers, Highlighters & Art Products, Everyday Writing & Coloring, Technology, Fine Writing & Luxury Accessories and Office Organization. Brands include Sharpie, Paper-Mate, Waterman, Parker, and DYMO.

The tools & hardware business is composed of the following GBUs: Industrial Products & Services, Construction Accessories, Construction Tools and Cabinet, Window & Door. It sells hand tools, power tool accessories, propane torches, manual paint applicator products, cabinet hardware, and window hardware under brand names such as Irwin, Lenox, and BernzOmatic.

The home & family segment also includes the following GBUs: Culinary Lifestyle, Baby & Parenting Essentials and Beauty & Style. Brand names include Calphalon, Katana and Goody.

Company Financials Fiscal Year Ended Dec. 31

Per Share Data ($)	2008	2007	2006	2005	2004	2003	2002	2001	2000	1999
Tangible Book Value	NM	NM	NM	NM	NM	NM	NM	0.44	0.97	2.38
Cash Flow	0.29	2.18	2.41	2.07	0.84	0.84	2.21	2.22	2.57	1.30
Earnings	-0.19	1.72	1.71	1.29	-0.07	-0.17	1.16	0.99	1.57	0.34
S&P Core Earnings	0.71	1.73	1.73	1.22	0.56	0.39	0.86	0.71	NA	NA
Dividends	0.84	0.84	0.84	0.84	0.84	0.84	0.84	0.84	0.84	0.80
Payout Ratio	NM	49%	49%	65%	NM	NM	72%	85%	54%	235%
Prices:High	25.94	32.19	29.98	25.69	26.41	32.00	36.70	29.50	31.88	52.00
Prices:Low	9.13	24.22	23.25	20.50	19.05	20.27	26.11	20.50	18.25	25.25
P/E Ratio:High	NM	19	18	20	NM	NM	32	30	20	NM
P/E Ratio:Low	NM	14	14	16	NM	NM	23	21	12	NM

Income Statement Analysis (Million $)										
Revenue	6,471	6,407	6,201	6,343	6,748	7,750	7,454	6,909	6,935	6,413
Operating Income	752	970	916	843	870	992	1,033	966	1,173	862
Depreciation	131	143	193	214	249	278	281	329	293	272
Interest Expense	147	132	155	142	130	140	111	137	130	100
Pretax Income	1.80	632	515	418	86.3	20.1	495	443	685	231
Effective Tax Rate	NM	23.7%	8.58%	14.8%	NM	NM	31.7%	34.2%	38.5%	58.7%
Net Income	-51.8	479	471	356	-19.1	-46.6	312	265	422	95.4
S&P Core Earnings	196	481	476	333	153	108	232	190	NA	NA

Balance Sheet & Other Financial Data (Million $)										
Cash	275	329	201	116	506	144	55.1	6.80	31.7	102
Current Assets	2,394	2,652	2,477	2,473	3,012	3,000	3,080	2,851	2,897	2,739
Total Assets	6,793	6,683	6,311	6,446	6,666	7,481	7,389	7,266	7,262	6,724
Current Liabilities	2,206	2,564	1,897	1,798	1,871	2,022	2,614	2,534	1,551	1,630
Long Term Debt	2,118	1,197	1,972	2,430	2,424	2,869	2,357	1,865	2,815	1,956
Common Equity	1,614	2,247	1,890	1,643	1,764	2,016	2,064	2,433	2,449	2,697
Total Capital	4,485	3,445	3,863	4,073	4,189	4,887	4,426	4,373	5,358	4,738
Capital Expenditures	158	157	138	92.2	122	300	252	250	317	200
Cash Flow	79.3	622	664	570	230	232	592	593	714	367
Current Ratio	1.1	1.0	1.3	1.4	1.6	1.5	1.2	1.1	1.9	1.7
% Long Term Debt of Capitalization	47.2	34.8	51.1	59.7	57.9	58.7	53.2	42.7	52.5	41.3
% Net Income of Revenue	NM	7.5	7.6	5.6	NM	NM	4.2	3.8	6.1	1.5
% Return on Assets	NM	7.4	7.4	5.4	NM	NM	4.3	3.6	6.0	1.5
% Return on Equity	NM	23.2	26.6	20.9	NM	NM	13.9	10.8	16.4	3.4

Data as orig reptd.; bef. results of disc opers/spec. items. Per share data adj. for stk. divs.; EPS diluted. E-Estimated. NA-Not Available. NM-Not Meaningful. NR-Not Ranked. UR-Under Review.

Office: 10B Glenlake Pkwy NE Ste 300, Atlanta, GA 30328-7266.
Telephone: 770-418-7000.
Email: investor.relations@newellco.com
Website: http://www.newellrubbermaid.com

Chrmn: W. Marohn
Pres & CEO: M. Ketchum
EVP & CFO: J.P. Robinson
SVP, Secy & General Counsel: D.L. Matschullat

SVP & CIO: G.C. Steele
Investor Contact: N. O'Donnell (770-418-7723)
Board Members: T. E. Clarke, S. S. Cowen, M. T. Cowhig, E. Cuthbert-Millett, D. De Sole, M. Ketchum, W. Marohn, C. A. Montgomery, M. B. Polk, S. J. Strobel, M. A. Todman, R. Viault

Founded: 1903
Domicile: Delaware
Employees: 20,400

Newmont Mining Corp

STANDARD &POOR'S

S&P Recommendation HOLD ★★★☆☆

Price	$53.35 (as of Nov 27, 2009)
12-Mo. Target Price	$56.00
Investment Style	Large-Cap Growth

GICS Sector Materials
Sub-Industry Gold

Summary Newmont is one of the world's largest gold producers, and is also engaged in the production of copper.

Key Stock Statistics (Source S&P, Vickers, company reports)

52-Wk Range	$54.94–26.80	S&P Oper. EPS 2009E	2.54	Market Capitalization(B)	$25.630	Beta	0.48
Trailing 12-Month EPS	$1.60	S&P Oper. EPS 2010E	3.11	Yield (%)	0.75	S&P 3-Yr. Proj. EPS CAGR(%)	27
Trailing 12-Month P/E	33.3	P/E on S&P Oper. EPS 2009E	21.0	Dividend Rate/Share	$0.40	S&P Credit Rating	BBB+
$10K Invested 5 Yrs Ago	$11,396	Common Shares Outstg. (M)	480.4	Institutional Ownership (%)	84		

Price Performance

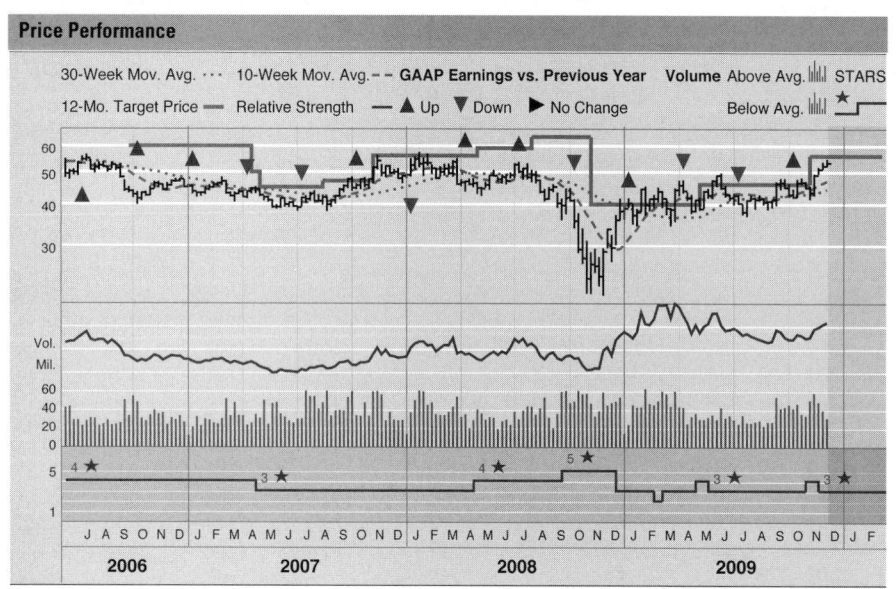

Options: ASE, CBOE, P, Ph

Analysis prepared by **Leo J. Larkin** on November 17, 2009, when the stock traded at **$52.57**.

Highlights

▶ Following a projected gain of 18% in 2009, we look for an 11% sales rise in 2010. In 2010, we expect a higher average price for both gold and copper compared with 2009, and look for higher gold production as increases from the Boddington and Batu Hijau mines more than offset declines in Nevada and Peru. We think that copper production will approximate 2009's projected level of 481 million pounds. We expect that continued low short-term interest rates worldwide and volatility in the world's major currencies will support another rise in the gold price in 2010. We believe that a gradual decline in metal exchange inventories and a rebound in global demand will boost the copper price.

▶ Reflecting expected higher gold output and increased prices for both metals, we look for higher operating profit. After interest expense, taxes and more shares outstanding, we estimate EPS of $3.11 in 2010, versus operating EPS of $2.54 projected for 2009, which excludes unusual items totaling $0.12.

▶ Longer term, we see EPS and reserves being aided by a projected rise in the price of gold, further consolidation of the industry, acquisitions, and expansion projects.

Investment Rationale/Risk

▶ With the acquisitions of Boddington and Miramar Mining, we see NEM's growth prospects as more secure. Also, with its output exposed to the spot gold price, NEM is well positioned for a continued bull market in gold, in our view. We believe that gold will remain in a bull market for several reasons: we expect the gap between consumption and production to persist as production worldwide stagnates; we think gold and gold shares will be viewed as attractive alternative investments, given our view that financial asset returns will continue to trail the high levels seen in the late 1990s; and we believe that currency instability will increase gold's role as a monetary reserve asset. But with NEM recently trading with only modest upside to our target price, we would hold, but not add to, positions.

▶ Risks to our recommendation and target price include a drop in the price of gold and copper in 2010 instead of the increase we currently project.

▶ Applying a P/E multiple of 18X to our 2010 EPS estimate, at the low end of its historical range and at a discount to its major peer, we arrive at our 12-month target price of $56.

Qualitative Risk Assessment

LOW	MEDIUM	HIGH

Our risk assessment reflects Newmont's exposure to the cyclical markets for copper and gold. This is offset by our view of its moderate balance sheet leverage and our expectation that the company should begin to generate positive free cash flow in 2009.

Quantitative Evaluations

S&P Quality Ranking C

D	C	B-	B	B+	A-	A	A+

Relative Strength Rank STRONG
92
LOWEST = 1   HIGHEST = 99

Revenue/Earnings Data

Revenue (Million $)

	1Q	2Q	3Q	4Q	Year
2009	1,552	1,602	2,049	--	--
2008	1,943	1,522	1,392	1,342	6,199
2007	1,256	1,302	1,646	1,410	5,526
2006	1,132	1,293	1,102	1,460	4,987
2005	945.0	998.0	1,158	1,305	4,406
2004	1,122	1,009	1,163	1,230	4,524

Earnings Per Share ($)

2009	0.40	0.35	0.79	E0.88	E2.54
2008	0.80	0.61	0.39	0.02	1.82
2007	0.15	-0.90	0.72	-2.03	-2.13
2006	0.46	0.34	0.59	0.47	1.86
2005	0.19	0.19	0.29	0.16	0.83
2004	0.30	0.08	0.29	0.43	1.10

Fiscal year ended Dec. 31. Next earnings report expected: Mid February. EPS Estimates based on S&P Operating Earnings; historical GAAP earnings are as reported.

Dividend Data (Dates: mm/dd Payment Date: mm/dd/yy)

Amount ($)	Date Decl.	Ex-Div. Date	Stk. of Record	Payment Date
0.100	02/18	03/04	03/06	03/27/09
0.100	04/29	06/03	06/05	06/26/09
0.100	07/22	09/03	09/08	09/28/09
0.100	10/28	12/04	12/08	12/29/09

Dividends have been paid since 1934. Source: Company reports.

Newmont Mining Corp

STANDARD
&POOR'S

Business Summary November 17, 2009

CORPORATE OVERVIEW. Newmont Mining Corp. is one of the world's largest gold producers. It has significant assets and operations in the United States, Australia, Peru, Indonesia, Ghana, Canada, Bolivia, New Zealand and Mexico. The company has two large development projects in Ghana, West Africa. Newmont is also engaged in the production of copper, principally through its Batu Hijau operation in Indonesia.

Proven and probable gold reserves totaled 85 million oz. at the end of 2008 using a gold price of $725 an oz., versus 86.5 million oz. at the end of 2007, using a gold price assumption of $575 an oz.

At year-end 2008, 28.1 million oz. of NEM's gold reserves were located in Nevada, 12.8 million oz. in Peru, 17.0 million oz. in Ghana, 20.9 million oz. in Australia/New Zealand, 4.1 million oz. in Indonesia, and 2.1 million oz. in other operations located in Mexico and Bolivia.

Copper reserves totaled 7.8 billion lbs. at the end of 2008, using a copper price assumption of $2.00 per lb., versus 7.6 billion lbs. at the end of 2007, using a copper price assumption of $1.75 per lb. Equity copper sales totaled 130 million lbs. in 2008, versus 204 million lbs. in 2007.

In 2008, 35% of Newmont's equity gold sales came from the United States, 30% from Peru, 19% from Australia/New Zealand, 5% from Indonesia and 8% from Ghana. Equity gold sales totaled 5.2 million oz. in 2008, versus 5.3 million oz. in 2007.

As of December 31, 2008, 26% of the company's total long-lived assets were located in the U.S., 14% in Canada, 13% in Peru, 20% in Australia/New Zealand, 17% in Indonesia, 9% in Ghana and 1% other.

CORPORATE STRATEGY. NEM's main strategy is to increase its portfolio of low-cost, long-life mines. In 2007's second quarter, NEM incurred a charge to eliminate its remaining gold hedges, as it anticipates higher gold prices over the longer term, and seeks to provide shareholders with maximum leverage to the price of gold.

Company Financials Fiscal Year Ended Dec. 31

Per Share Data ($)	2008	2007	2006	2005	2004	2003	2002	2001	2000	1999
Tangible Book Value	15.20	16.27	14.98	12.27	11.02	8.39	2.77	7.49	8.58	8.66
Cash Flow	3.56	-0.59	3.27	2.27	2.66	2.60	1.75	1.38	1.61	1.58
Earnings	1.82	-2.13	1.86	0.83	1.10	1.23	0.39	-0.16	-0.06	0.15
S&P Core Earnings	1.86	0.42	1.45	0.79	1.22	1.05	0.25	-0.26	NA	NA
Dividends	0.40	0.40	0.40	0.40	0.30	0.17	0.12	0.12	0.12	0.12
Payout Ratio	22%	NM	22%	48%	28%	14%	31%	NM	NM	80%
Prices:High	57.55	56.35	62.72	53.93	50.20	50.28	32.75	25.23	28.38	30.06
Prices:Low	21.17	38.01	39.84	34.90	34.70	24.08	18.52	14.00	12.75	16.38
P/E Ratio:High	32	NM	34	65	46	41	84	NM	NM	NM
P/E Ratio:Low	12	NM	21	42	32	20	47	NM	NM	NM
Income Statement Analysis (Million $)										
Revenue	6,199	5,526	4,987	4,406	4,524	3,214	2,658	1,656	1,555	1,399
Operating Income	2,057	2,041	2,059	1,621	1,878	1,219	852	435	502	493
Depreciation	789	695	636	644	697	564	506	300	293	240
Interest Expense	149	155	97.0	98.0	97.6	88.6	130	86.4	79.6	62.6
Pretax Income	1,271	-353	1,627	1,068	1,102	890	268	-10.2	94.2	112
Effective Tax Rate	8.89%	NM	26.1%	29.4%	25.0%	23.2%	7.43%	NM	12.1%	12.9%
Net Income	829	-963	840	374	490	510	150	-23.3	-10.5	24.8
S&P Core Earnings	847	192	657	356	540	435	96.7	-52.8	NA	NA
Balance Sheet & Other Financial Data (Million $)										
Cash	447	1,292	1,275	1,899	1,726	1,459	402	149	60.3	55.3
Current Assets	2,361	2,672	2,642	3,036	2,721	2,360	1,113	709	512	534
Total Assets	15,839	15,598	15,601	13,992	12,771	11,050	10,155	4,062	3,510	3,383
Current Liabilities	1,596	1,500	1,739	1,350	1,101	834	693	486	291	274
Long Term Debt	3,373	2,683	Nil	1,733	1,311	887	1,701	1,090	976	1,014
Common Equity	7,102	7,548	9,865	8,376	7,938	7,385	5,419	1,469	1,466	1,452
Total Capital	12,896	12,705	10,963	11,489	10,500	9,251	8,132	2,955	2,695	2,627
Capital Expenditures	1,881	1,670	1,551	1,226	718	501	300	402	378	221
Cash Flow	1,618	-268	1,476	1,018	1,187	1,075	652	269	283	264
Current Ratio	1.5	1.8	1.5	2.2	2.5	2.8	1.6	1.5	1.8	2.0
% Long Term Debt of Capitalization	26.2	21.1	Nil	15.1	12.5	9.6	20.9	40.3	36.2	38.6
% Net Income of Revenue	13.4	NM	16.8	8.5	10.8	15.9	5.7	NM	NM	1.8
% Return on Assets	5.3	NM	5.7	2.8	4.2	4.8	2.1	NM	NM	0.7
% Return on Equity	11.3	NM	9.0	4.5	6.4	8.0	4.4	NM	NM	1.7

Data as orig reptd.; bef. results of disc opers/spec. items. Per share data adj. for stk. divs.; EPS diluted. E-Estimated. NA-Not Available. NM-Not Meaningful. NR-Not Ranked. UR-Under Review.

Office: 6363 S Fiddlers Green Cir, Greenwood Village, CO 80111-4917.
Telephone: 303-863-7414.
Website: http://www.newmont.com
Chrmn: V.A. Calarco

Pres & CEO: R.T. O'Brien
COO: B.A. Hill
EVP & CFO: R.D. Ball
CFO: D.B. Russell

Investor Contact: J. Seaberg (303-837-5743)
Board Members: G. A. Barton, V. A. Calarco, J. A. Carrabba, N. Doyle, V. M. Hagen, M. S. Hamson, R. J. Miller, R. T. O'Brien, J. B. Prescott, D. C. Roth, J. V. Taranik, S. R. Thompson

Founded: 1916
Domicile: Delaware
Employees: 15,450

The McGraw-Hill Companies

New York Times Co (The)

STANDARD &POOR'S

S&P Recommendation **SELL** ★★☆☆☆	Price	12-Mo. Target Price	Investment Style
	$8.76 (as of Nov 27, 2009)	$9.00	Large-Cap Blend

GICS Sector Consumer Discretionary
Sub-Industry Publishing

Summary This diversified communications company publishes newspapers, operates radio and television stations, and has equity holdings in newsprint and paper mills.

Key Stock Statistics (Source S&P, Vickers, company reports)

52-Wk Range	$11.05– 3.44	S&P Oper. EPS 2009**E**	0.13	Market Capitalization(B)	$1.259	Beta	1.59
Trailing 12-Month EPS	$-0.30	S&P Oper. EPS 2010**E**	0.28	Yield (%)	Nil	S&P 3-Yr. Proj. EPS CAGR(%)	50
Trailing 12-Month P/E	NM	P/E on S&P Oper. EPS 2009**E**	67.4	Dividend Rate/Share	Nil	S&P Credit Rating	B
$10K Invested 5 Yrs Ago	$2,465	Common Shares Outstg. (M)	144.5	Institutional Ownership (%)	72		

Price Performance

30-Week Mov. Avg. · · · 10-Week Mov. Avg. - - **GAAP Earnings vs. Previous Year** Volume Above Avg. STARS
12-Mo. Target Price — Relative Strength — ▲ Up ▼ Down ▶ No Change Below Avg.

Options: ASE, CBOE, P, Ph

Analysis prepared by **Joseph Agnese** on November 16, 2009, when the stock traded at **$ 9.56**.

Highlights

▶ We believe NYT's revenues will fare better than those of other pure-play peers exposed to cyclical and secular challenges in the print publishing industry, but its Internet revenues, previously fast-growing, were down 9.2% through the first nine months in 2009. For full-year 2010, we expect advertising revenues to decline 11%, circulation revenues to be up 1.0% (reflecting higher prices and lower volumes), and total revenues to drop 6.1%.

▶ We expect the operating margin to widen slightly in 2010, reflecting significantly lower newsprint costs and continued reductions in labor costs, partially offset by sales deleveraging. We look for notably higher interest expense as debt maturing in 2009 had to be refinanced at much higher rates.

▶ We see EPS of $0.28 in 2010, up significantly from our estimate of $0.13 in 2009. Our EPS numbers include severance costs, which we view as operational due to ongoing restructuring activity at NYT, but exclude a $0.07 loss on leases in 2009.

Investment Rationale/Risk

▶ In recent months, NYT reduced its capital expenditures budget, cut costs, suspended its dividend (February 2009), entered into two private loan agreements totaling $250 million (January 2009), did a sale-leaseback on part of its headquarters space (March 2009) and announced interest in selling other assets. While near-term pressures from refinancing issues may be lessened, we still see no near-term catalyst for the stock given the difficult print ad revenue environment that we expect to persist for the foreseeable future.

▶ Risks to our recommendation and target price include significant improvement in the health of the New York City and Boston economies, where NYT derives most of its newspaper advertising revenues.

▶ Our 12-month target price of $9 is derived from a blend of our historical and relative enterprise value/EBITDA models. Our historical model applies a multiple of 6.8X to our 2010 EBITDA estimate of $299 million to value the stock at $8.00. Our relative analysis uses a multiple of 9.2X, a premium to peers, to reach a $10.50 valuation.

Qualitative Risk Assessment

LOW	MEDIUM	HIGH

Our risk assessment reflects our view of a highly competitive advertising environment for publishers and other media.

Quantitative Evaluations

S&P Quality Ranking B-

D	C	B-	B	B+	A-	A	A+

Relative Strength Rank STRONG
74
LOWEST = 1   HIGHEST = 99

Revenue/Earnings Data

Revenue (Million $)

	1Q	2Q	3Q	4Q	Year
2009	609.0	584.5	570.6	--	--
2008	747.9	741.9	687.0	772.1	2,949
2007	786.0	788.9	754.4	865.8	3,195
2006	799.2	819.6	739.6	931.5	3,290
2005	805.6	845.1	791.1	931.0	3,373
2004	801.9	823.9	773.8	903.9	3,304

Earnings Per Share ($)

2009	-0.52	-0.27	-0.25	E0.37	E0.13
2008	Nil	0.15	-0.01	0.19	-0.46
2007	0.14	0.15	0.10	0.37	0.76
2006	0.21	0.37	0.06	-4.59	-3.93
2005	0.76	0.42	0.16	0.49	1.82
2004	0.38	0.50	0.33	0.75	1.96

Fiscal year ended Dec. 31. Next earnings report expected: Late January. EPS Estimates based on S&P Operating Earnings; historical GAAP earnings are as reported.

Dividend Data (Dates: mm/dd Payment Date: mm/dd/yy)

Amount ($)	Date Decl.	Ex-Div. Date	Stk. of Record	Payment Date
0.060	11/20	11/26	12/01	12/15/08

Source: Company reports.

The McGraw-Hill Companies

New York Times Co (The)

STANDARD &POOR'S

Business Summary November 16, 2009

CORPORATE OVERVIEW. The New York Times Company is a media company that includes newspapers, Internet businesses, a radio station, investments in paper mills and other investments. In 2008, NYT classified its businesses into two segments, the News Media Group (about 96% of revenues) and About.com (4%).

The News Media Group primarily consists of The New York Times, the International Herald Tribune, The Boston Globe, the Worcester Telegram & Gazette, 15 daily newspapers in Alabama, California, Florida, Louisiana, North Carolina and South Carolina, and related print and digital businesses, such as NYT.com. The majority of the News Media Group's revenue comes from advertising sold in its newspapers and other publications and on its Web sites. In 2008, revenues were derived from national advertising (51%), classified (21%), retail and pre-print (24%), and other (4%). We note that as one of only three national newspapers (along with USA Today and The Wall Street Journal), the New York Times garners a disproportionate amount of its advertising from national advertisers relative to most other newspapers. According to TNS Media Intelligence, the New York Times had a 50% market share of national advertising revenue among national newspapers in 2008.

The About group consists of the websites About.com, ConsumerSearch.com, UCompareHealthCare.com and Caloriecount.about.com. About.com provides users with information and advice on thousands of topics, and the site was one of the top 20 most visited Web sites in 2008. About.com generates revenues through display advertising relevant to adjacent content, cost-per-click advertising, and e-commerce. ConsumerSearch.com is a leading online aggregator and publisher of reviews of consumer products. UCompareHealthCare.com provides Web-based interactive tools to enable users to measure the quality of certain healthcare services. Caloriecount.about.com offers weight loss tools and nutritional information.

NYT also owns equity interests in a Canadian newsprint company and a supercalendered paper manufacturing partnership in Maine; 17.5% of New England Sports Ventures, LLC (NESV), which owns the Boston Red Sox, Fenway Park and adjacent real estate, approximately 80% of the New England Sports Network (the regional cable sports network that televises the Red Sox games) and 50% of Roush Fenway Racing, a NASCAR team; and an equity interest in Metro Boston LLC (Metro Boston), which publishes a free daily newspaper catering to young professionals and students in the Boston metropolitan area.

Company Financials Fiscal Year Ended Dec. 31

Per Share Data ($)	2008	2007	2006	2005	2004	2003	2002	2001	2000	1999
Tangible Book Value	NM	1.16	0.25	NM	NM	NM	NM	NM	NM	0.83
Cash Flow	0.51	1.82	-2.76	2.81	2.94	2.95	2.93	2.48	3.65	2.83
Earnings	-0.46	0.76	-3.93	1.82	1.96	1.98	1.94	1.26	2.32	1.73
S&P Core Earnings	-1.04	0.91	1.13	1.41	1.62	1.77	1.35	0.72	NA	NA
Dividends	0.75	0.87	0.69	0.65	0.61	0.57	0.53	0.49	0.45	0.41
Payout Ratio	NM	114%	NM	36%	31%	29%	27%	39%	19%	24%
Prices:High	21.14	26.90	28.98	40.90	49.23	49.06	53.00	47.98	49.88	49.94
Prices:Low	4.95	16.02	21.54	26.09	38.47	43.29	38.60	35.48	32.63	26.50
P/E Ratio:High	NM	35	NM	22	25	25	27	38	21	29
P/E Ratio:Low	NM	21	NM	14	20	22	20	28	14	15

Income Statement Analysis (Million $)										
Revenue	2,949	3,195	3,290	3,373	3,304	3,227	3,079	3,016	3,489	3,131
Operating Income	302	492	464	502	657	687	698	568	864	769
Depreciation	139	153	170	144	147	148	153	194	228	197
Interest Expense	50.8	59.1	50.7	49.2	44.2	44.8	48.7	51.4	64.1	52.5
Pretax Income	-71.4	185	-552	446	477	500	491	340	673	538
Effective Tax Rate	NM	41.2%	NM	40.4%	38.5%	39.6%	39.0%	40.5%	40.9%	42.4%
Net Income	-66.1	109	-568	266	293	303	300	202	398	310
S&P Core Earnings	-149	129	164	205	242	268	208	116	NA	NA

Balance Sheet & Other Financial Data (Million $)										
Cash	56.8	51.5	72.4	44.9	42.4	39.4	37.0	52.0	69.0	63.9
Current Assets	624	664	1,185	658	614	603	563	560	611	615
Total Assets	3,402	3,473	3,856	4,533	3,950	3,805	3,634	3,439	3,607	3,496
Current Liabilities	1,033	976	1,298	1,067	1,120	760	736	861	877	674
Long Term Debt	580	679	795	898	471	726	729	599	637	598
Common Equity	504	978	820	1,516	1,401	1,392	1,362	1,150	1,281	1,449
Total Capital	1,180	1,663	1,621	2,683	2,139	2,350	2,164	1,813	2,024	2,188
Capital Expenditures	167	380	332	221	154	121	161	90.4	85.3	73.4
Cash Flow	73.3	262	-398	409	439	450	453	396	626	508
Current Ratio	0.6	0.7	0.9	0.6	0.5	0.8	0.8	0.7	0.7	0.9
% Long Term Debt of Capitalization	49.1	40.8	49.1	33.5	22.0	30.9	33.7	33.0	31.5	27.3
% Net Income of Revenue	NM	3.4	NM	7.9	8.9	9.4	9.7	6.7	11.4	9.9
% Return on Assets	NM	3.0	NM	6.3	7.5	8.1	8.5	5.7	11.2	8.9
% Return on Equity	NM	12.1	NM	18.2	21.0	22.7	23.9	16.6	29.1	20.8

Data as orig reptd.; bef. results of disc opers/spec. items. Per share data adj. for stk. divs.; EPS diluted. E-Estimated. NA-Not Available. NM-Not Meaningful. NR-Not Ranked. UR-Under Review.

Office: 620 8th Ave, New York, NY 10018-1618.
Telephone: 212-556-1234.
Website: http://www.nytco.com
Chrmn: A.O. Sulzberger, Jr.

Pres & CEO: J.L. Robinson
Vice Chrmn: M. Golden
SVP & CFO: R. Caputo
SVP, Chief Acctg Officer & Cntlr: R.A. Benten

Investor Contact: C.J. Mathis (212-556-1981)
Board Members: R. E. Cesan, D. H. Cohen, R. E. Denham, L. Dolnick, S. W. Dryfoos, S. Galloway, M. Golden, J. A. Kohlberg, D. G. Lepore, D. E. Liddle, E. R. Marram, T. Middelhoff, J. L. Robinson, A. O. Sulzberger, Jr., D. A. Toben

Founded: 1896
Domicile: New York
Employees: 9,346

The McGraw-Hill Companies

News Corp

STANDARD &POOR'S

S&P Recommendation	HOLD ★★★☆☆	Price $11.54 (as of Nov 27, 2009)	12-Mo. Target Price $14.00	Investment Style Large-Cap Blend

GICS Sector Consumer Discretionary
Sub-Industry Movies & Entertainment

Summary This leading media conglomerate, with controlling interests in leading content and distribution assets across the globe, including Fox Entertainment, SKY Italia, BSkyB and STAR Asia, acquired Dow Jones in late 2007.

Key Stock Statistics (Source S&P, Vickers, company reports)

52-Wk Range	$13.09– 4.95	S&P Oper. EPS 2010**E**	0.76	Market Capitalization(B)	$21.020	Beta		1.56
Trailing 12-Month EPS	$-1.27	S&P Oper. EPS 2011**E**	0.90	Yield (%)	1.04	S&P 3-Yr. Proj. EPS CAGR(%)		8
Trailing 12-Month P/E	NM	P/E on S&P Oper. EPS 2010**E**	15.2	Dividend Rate/Share	$0.12	S&P Credit Rating		BBB+
$10K Invested 5 Yrs Ago	$6,828	Common Shares Outstg. (M)	2,620.0	Institutional Ownership (%)	87			

Price Performance

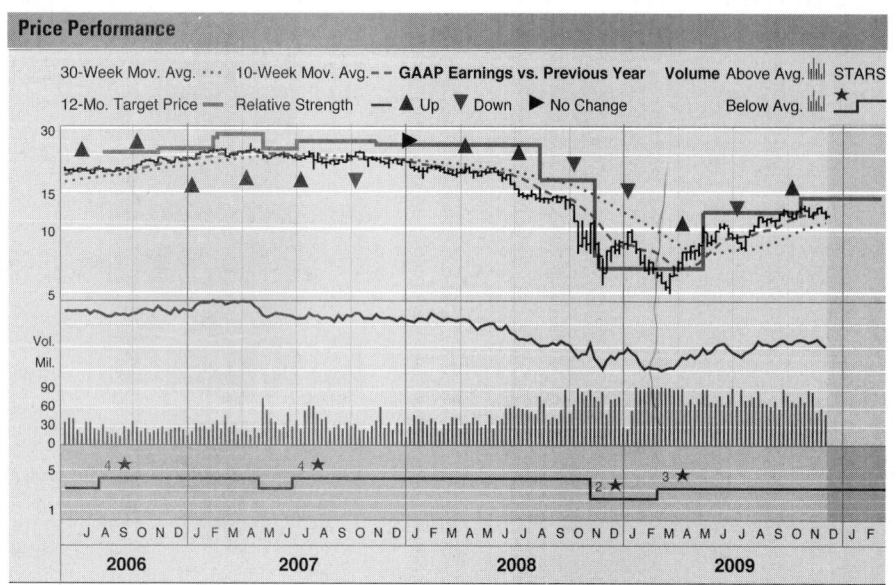

30-Week Mov. Avg. · · · 10-Week Mov. Avg. – – **GAAP Earnings vs. Previous Year** Volume Above Avg. ▮▮▮ STARS
12-Mo. Target Price — Relative Strength — ▲ Up ▼ Down ► No Change Below Avg. ▮▮▮ ★

Analysis prepared by **Tuna N. Amobi, CFA, CPA** on November 20, 2009, when the stock traded at **$ 12.08.**

Options: ASE, CBOE, P, Ph

Highlights

▶ We estimate total revenues will advance about 3% in FY 10 (Jun.) to $31.3 billion -- mainly on continued strong growth in cable networks' affiliate fees (Fox News, Fox International, FX, Big 10, RSNs) and solid home video sales from a number of key franchises (Ice Age, X-Men). With further continued improvement in TV ads for both the cable and broadcast networks, we expect 5% growth in FY 11, to nearly $32.6 billion, also reflecting moderating growth for the Sky Italia satellite TV unit, and relatively stagnant growth for the print divisions (magazines, inserts, book publishing, newspapers).

▶ With the benefit of increased operating leverage on recent restructuring initiatives, we view management's FY 10 guidance for high single digit to low double digit EBIT growth as readily achievable. Improved results at the MySpace unit and other digital media businesses could also factor into further FY 11 margin expansion.

▶ We forecast about 13% and 17% total adjusted EBIT growth in FY 10 and FY 11, respectively, to $3.9 billion and $4.6 billion. After interest expense and a 35% effective tax rate, we see operating EPS of $0.76 and $0.90.

Investment Rationale/Risk

▶ After a very challenging FY 09 on a sharp consumer spending slowdown, we think NWSA's stronger-than-expected FY 10 first quarter results (on standout film and cable networks units) showed improvements in the underlying advertising, content and subscriptions businesses. Following a sizable FY 09 writedown of the Dow Jones acquisition, the company's plans to convert its online news sites to a paying model (recently suggested by CEO Rupert Murdoch) could portend a near-term strategic shift for its core newspapers businesses. We see a strong financial profile with ample liquidity -- recently $7.8 billion+ of cash.

▶ Risks to our recommendation and target price include a slower-than-expected economic recovery; secular hurdles for the print brands; continued challenges for MySpace; a sharp decline for Fox ratings; potential succession and governance issues with the Murdoch family; dilutive acquisitions; and currency exposure.

▶ Our PEG-based 12-month target price is $14, blending EV/EBITDA and sum-of-the-parts analyses (including equity affiliates). Cash and equivalents recently approximated $3 a share.

Qualitative Risk Assessment

LOW	**MEDIUM**	HIGH

Our risk assessment reflects the company's portfolio of leading properties with balanced business and geographic diversification, and our view of its strong balance sheet, offset by a high cyclical ad exposure, film volatility, currency risk, and some corporate governance issues.

Quantitative Evaluations

S&P Quality Ranking   A-

D	C	B-	B	B+	**A-**	A	A+

Relative Strength Rank   MODERATE

38

LOWEST = 1   HIGHEST = 99

Revenue/Earnings Data

Revenue (Million $)

	1Q	2Q	3Q	4Q	Year
2010	7,199	--	--	--	--
2009	7,509	7,871	7,373	7,670	30,423
2008	7,067	8,590	8,750	8,589	32,996
2007	5,914	7,844	7,530	7,367	28,655
2006	5,682	6,665	6,198	6,782	25,327
2005	5,191	6,562	6,043	6,108	23,859

Earnings Per Share ($)

2010	0.22	E0.17	E0.17	E0.20	E0.76
2009	0.20	-2.45	1.04	-0.08	-1.29
2008	0.23	0.27	0.91	0.43	1.81
2007	0.28	0.27	0.29	0.30	1.14
2006	0.19	0.22	0.27	0.24	0.92
2005	0.22	0.14	0.14	0.23	0.73

Fiscal year ended Jun. 30. Next earnings report expected: Early February. EPS Estimates based on S&P Operating Earnings; historical GAAP earnings are as reported.

Dividend Data (Dates: mm/dd Payment Date: mm/dd/yy)

Amount ($)	Date Decl.	Ex-Div. Date	Stk. of Record	Payment Date
0.060	02/05	03/09	03/11	04/15/09
0.060	08/05	09/04	09/09	10/14/09

Dividends have been paid since 1995. Source: Company reports.

News Corp

Business Summary November 20, 2009

CORPORATE OVERVIEW. News Corp., once a small publisher of Australian newspapers, has grown into one of the world's premier media conglomerates. In December 2004, the company moved its domicile to the U.S., followed in March 2005 by a tender offer for the public's 18% minority stake in its Fox Entertainment Group, which we believe helped to simplify its corporate structure. Dow Jones was acquired in December 2007.

Key U.S. assets include Fox film studio and 20th Century Fox TV; Fox broadcast network and TV stations; Fox News, FX and regional sports networks (including FSN Ohio, FSN Florida and 40% of FSN Bay Area); HarperCollins (book publishers); the New York Post newspaper; and an inserts business. International assets include several newspaper businesses in the U.K. and Australia (including The Times, The Sun, News of the World and The Australian); the wholly owned DBS provider SKY Italia; a 39% controlling stake in U.K. DBS provider BSkyB; a 40% stake in Sky Deutschland; and other associated entities in Asia, Australia and Latin America. About 55% of FY 09 (Jun.) revenues were derived from the U.S. and Canada, 31% from Europe, and 14% from Australasia/other.

CORPORATE STRATEGY. Over the past few years, NWS has completed a number of strategic acquisitions and divestitures. In December 2007, the company acquired Dow Jones in a $5.7 billion transaction. In February 2009, NWS divested its 38.4% stake in DirecTV, plus three regional sports networks and $550 million of cash, in exchange for Liberty Media's 16.3% voting stake.

In 2005, the company acquired MySpace.com, a leading social networking site, for about $650 million (now the core of its Fox Interactive Media unit, which also includes IGN Entertainment and Scout Media). Revenues at the Fox Interactive Media's MySpace have reflected a multi-year search deal with Google through 2010, providing for a minimum revenue guarantee of $900 million over its term. NWS's TV shows are also available from Apple's iTunes and mobile content destination Mobizzo.

Company Financials Fiscal Year Ended Jun. 30

Per Share Data ($)	2009	2008	2007	2006	2005	2004	2003	2002	2001	2000
Tangible Book Value	NM	NM	2.37	1.86	1.81	1.85	NM	0.68	3.34	0.76
Cash Flow	-0.86	2.22	1.38	1.62	1.40	0.79	0.65	-2.39	-0.01	0.48
Earnings	-1.29	1.81	1.14	0.92	0.73	0.58	0.46	-2.75	0.32	0.39
S&P Core Earnings	0.53	1.39	1.00	0.83	0.66	0.52	0.51	-1.10	NA	NA
Dividends	0.12	0.12	0.12	0.13	0.11	0.10	0.08	0.07	0.07	0.07
Payout Ratio	NM	7%	11%	14%	14%	17%	17%	NM	22%	18%
Prices:High	13.09	20.55	25.40	21.94	18.88	18.77	15.54	13.60	18.70	28.59
Prices:Low	4.95	5.43	19.00	15.17	13.94	14.57	9.33	7.54	9.80	13.44
P/E Ratio:High	NM	11	22	24	26	32	34	NM	58	73
P/E Ratio:Low	NM	3	17	16	19	25	20	NM	31	34

Income Statement Analysis (Million $)	2009	2008	2007	2006	2005	2004	2003	2002	2001	2000
Revenue	30,423	32,996	28,655	25,327	23,859	29,428	29,913	29,014	25,578	22,443
Operating Income	4,696	6,482	5,331	4,643	4,329	5,146	4,372	4,291	3,799	2,913
Depreciation	1,138	1,207	879	775	765	844	776	749	706	562
Interest Expense	927	970	843	791	736	958	1,094	1,384	1,358	1,248
Pretax Income	-5,539	7,321	5,306	4,405	3,561	3,855	3,000	-10,959	-562	1,587
Effective Tax Rate	NM	24.6%	34.2%	34.6%	34.3%	32.3%	25.8%	NM	NM	20.7%
Net Income	-3,378	5,387	3,426	2,812	2,128	2,312	1,808	-11,962	-746	1,259
S&P Core Earnings	1,379	4,142	3,171	2,663	2,017	1,563	1,303	-2,718	NA	NA

Balance Sheet & Other Financial Data (Million $)	2009	2008	2007	2006	2005	2004	2003	2002	2001	2000
Cash	6,540	4,662	7,654	5,783	6,470	6,217	6,746	6,337	5,615	4,638
Current Assets	15,836	14,362	15,906	13,123	12,779	15,012	14,861	14,647	16,173	13,127
Total Assets	53,121	62,308	62,343	56,649	54,692	73,738	67,747	71,441	84,961	65,585
Current Liabilities	10,639	9,182	7,494	6,373	6,649	10,437	9,303	11,005	9,776	9,008
Long Term Debt	12,204	13,230	12,147	11,385	10,087	12,972	14,480	15,275	23,345	18,396
Common Equity	23,224	28,623	32,922	29,874	29,377	39,387	31,834	34,101	42,050	29,389
Total Capital	39,455	48,303	51,530	46,740	44,500	59,473	53,867	54,743	70,940	51,056
Capital Expenditures	1,101	1,443	1,308	976	901	517	551	505	1,113	671
Cash Flow	-2,240	6,594	4,305	3,587	2,883	3,156	2,584	-11,213	-40.0	1,598
Current Ratio	1.5	1.6	2.1	2.1	1.9	1.4	1.6	1.3	1.7	1.5
% Long Term Debt of Capitalization	31.9	27.4	23.6	24.4	22.7	21.8	26.9	27.9	32.9	36.0
% Net Income of Revenue	NM	16.3	12.0	11.1	8.9	7.9	6.0	NM	NM	5.6
% Return on Assets	NM	8.6	5.8	5.1	4.1	3.3	2.6	NM	NM	2.1
% Return on Equity	NM	17.5	10.9	9.5	8.4	6.5	5.5	NM	NM	4.0

Data as orig reptd.; bef. results of disc opers/spec. items. Per share data adj. for stk. divs.; EPS diluted. Income and balance sheet data in Australian $ prior to 2005. E-Estimated. NA-Not Available. NM-Not Meaningful. NR-Not Ranked. UR-Under Review.

Office: 1211 Avenue Of The Americas, New York, NY 10036-8701.
Telephone: 212-852-7000.
Website: http://www.newscorp.com
Chrmn & CEO: K.R. Murdoch

Pres, Vice Chrmn & COO: C. Carey
EVP, CFO & Chief Acctg Officer: D.F. DeVoe
EVP & General Counsel: L.A. Jacobs
SVP & Cntlr: R. Gannon

Investor Contact: R. Nolte (212-852-7017)
Board Members: J. M. Aznar, N. Bancroft, P. L. Barnes, C. Carey, K. E. Cowley, D. F. DeVoe, V. D. Dinh, R. Eddington, M. Hurd, A. S. Knight, J. Murdoch, K. R. Murdoch, L. K. Murdoch, T. J. Perkins, A. M. Siskind, J. L. Thornton

Founded: 1922
Domicile: Delaware
Employees: 55,000

Nicor Inc.

STANDARD &POOR'S

S&P Recommendation	**BUY** ★★★★☆	Price $39.11 (as of Nov 27, 2009)	12-Mo. Target Price $41.00	Investment Style Large-Cap Blend

GICS Sector Utilities
Sub-Industry Gas Utilities

Summary This holding company's Nicor Gas subsidiary is one of the largest U.S. distributors of natural gas.

Key Stock Statistics (Source S&P, Vickers, company reports)

52-Wk Range	$40.21–27.50	S&P Oper. EPS 2009**E**	2.80	Market Capitalization(B)	$1.769	Beta	0.33
Trailing 12-Month EPS	$2.82	S&P Oper. EPS 2010**E**	3.10	Yield (%)	4.76	S&P 3-Yr. Proj. EPS CAGR(%)	7
Trailing 12-Month P/E	13.9	P/E on S&P Oper. EPS 2009**E**	14.0	Dividend Rate/Share	$1.86	S&P Credit Rating	AA
$10K Invested 5 Yrs Ago	$13,143	Common Shares Outstg. (M)	45.2	Institutional Ownership (%)	56		

Price Performance

30-Week Mov. Avg. · · ·   10-Week Mov. Avg. - -   **GAAP Earnings vs. Previous Year**   Volume Above Avg.⽶ STARS
12-Mo. Target Price —   Relative Strength — ▲ Up ▼ Down ▶ No Change   Below Avg.⽶ ★

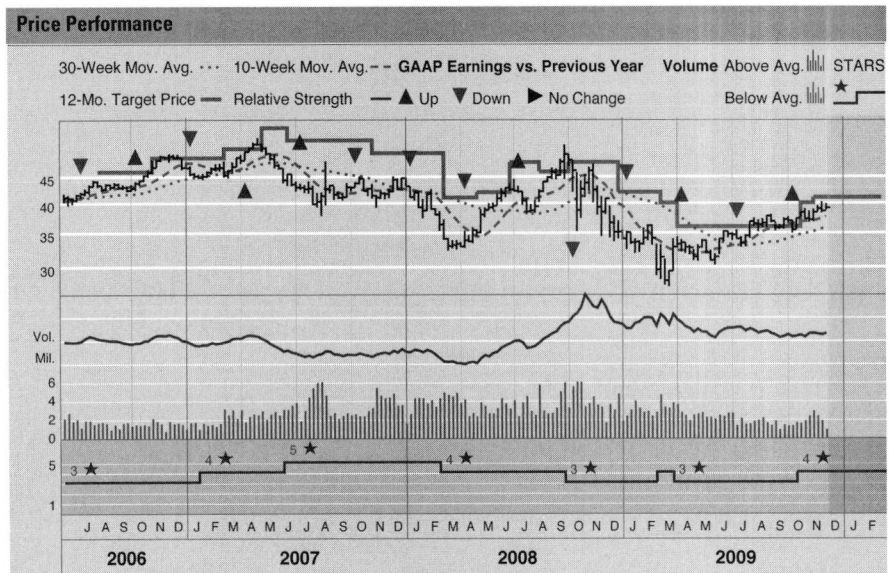

Options: P

Analysis prepared by **Christopher B. Muir** on November 11, 2009, when the stock traded at **$ 38.92.**

Highlights

▶ We see revenues falling 23% in 2009. We expect utility revenues to decline as a result of lower gas prices and customer usage, partly offset by customer growth and a large rate hike. We project a 16% drop in revenues at the Tropical Shipping unit due to the economic slowdown. Revenues at the Other Energy Ventures segment should grow slowly, in our view. In 2010, we see the full-year effects of rate increases helping revenues rise by 3.8%.

▶ We project operating margins of 7.2% in 2009 and 7.7% in 2010, up from 4.9% in 2008, reflecting lower per-revenue cost of gas, partly offset by higher per-revenue non-utility operating costs. We expect other expense categories to grow about as fast as revenues. We forecast pretax margins of 6.2% in 2009 and 6.8% in 2010, up from 4.3% in 2008, a slower increase in 2009 than observed with operating margins as we see higher interest expense.

▶ We estimate EPS of $2.80 in 2009, excluding a net one-time gain of $0.09, up 6.1% from 2008's $2.64. Our 2010 EPS projection is $3.10, a rise of 11%.

Investment Rationale/Risk

▶ Our 2009 projected payout ratio of 67% is higher than the peer average of around 54%. However, we think the dividend is safe, and the shares recently yielded about 4.8%. GAS was granted rate increases of $69 million effective April 2009 and $11 million effective October 2009, which we expect to result in a payout ratio of about 60% in 2010 based on our EPS estimate. Should economic growth in the U.S. recover, we see strong earnings growth returning to GAS's unregulated businesses.

▶ Risks to our recommendation and target price include a weak economy in GAS's service territory, higher-than-expected interest rates, and slower-than-projected growth in unregulated operations.

▶ The stock recently traded at about 12.5X our 2010 EPS estimate, a 12% discount to its natural gas utility peers. Our 12-month target price of $41 equates to a multiple of 13.2X our 2010 EPS estimate, about a 1% premium to our peer forecast. We think this valuation is warranted by our view of no dividend increases through the end of 2010 and relatively moderate EPS and dividend growth after 2010, offset by what we see as an extremely strong balance sheet.

Qualitative Risk Assessment

LOW	MEDIUM	HIGH

Our risk assessment reflects the low-risk nature of the company's main subsidiary, a regulated natural gas distribution company, slightly offset by the higher-risk nature of its much smaller competitive operations. The company benefits from being the lone delivery agent of natural gas to customers within its service territory.

Quantitative Evaluations

S&P Quality Ranking   **B**

D	C	B-	**B**	B+	A-	A	A+

Relative Strength Rank   **STRONG**

72

LOWEST = 1   HIGHEST = 99

Revenue/Earnings Data

Revenue (Million $)

	1Q	2Q	3Q	4Q	Year
2009	1,111	447.6	325.6	--	--
2008	1,596	699.8	440.3	1,041	3,777
2007	1,335	556.9	365.2	919.5	3,176
2006	1,319	451.3	351.1	838.2	2,960
2005	1,180	484.4	336.0	1,358	3,358
2004	1,116	429.5	299.9	894.6	2,740

Earnings Per Share ($)

2009	0.96	0.50	0.30	E1.12	E2.80
2008	0.91	0.64	0.03	1.05	2.63
2007	1.04	0.40	0.32	1.23	2.99
2006	0.99	0.19	0.39	1.29	2.87
2005	0.99	0.75	-0.06	1.40	3.07
2004	0.44	0.36	-0.26	1.08	1.70

Fiscal year ended Dec. 31. Next earnings report expected: Late February. EPS Estimates based on S&P Operating Earnings; historical GAAP earnings are as reported.

Dividend Data (Dates: mm/dd Payment Date: mm/dd/yy)

Amount ($)	Date Decl.	Ex-Div. Date	Stk. of Record	Payment Date
0.465	02/19	03/27	03/31	05/01/09
0.465	04/23	06/26	06/30	08/01/09
0.465	07/23	09/28	09/30	11/01/09
0.465	11/20	12/29	12/31	02/01/10

Dividends have been paid since 1954. Source: Company reports.

Please read the Required Disclosures and Analyst Certification on the last page of this report.

The McGraw-Hill Companies

Nicor Inc.

STANDARD &POOR'S

Business Summary November 11, 2009

CORPORATE OVERVIEW. Nicor Inc. is a holding company, whose principal subsidiaries are Northern Illinois Gas Company (doing business as Nicor Gas Company), one of the nation's largest distributors of natural gas, and Tropical Shipping, a transporter of containerized freight in the Bahamas and the Caribbean region. Nicor also owns several energy-related ventures, including Nicor Services and Nicor Solutions, which provide energy-related products and services to retail markets, and Nicor Enerchange, a wholesale natural gas marketing company.

PRIMARY BUSINESS DYNAMICS. Nicor seeks earnings growth through investment in unregulated operations, including its Tropical Shipping and Other Energy Ventures divisions. However, the company's main operating segment remains its regulated gas utility operations.

As of the end of 2008, Nicor Gas (67% of 2008 segment operating profits) served 2.2 million customers in a service area that covers most of northern Illinois, excluding Chicago. In 2008, gas deliveries climbed to 498.1 billion cubic feet (Bcf), from 468.3 Bcf in 2007. The company has an extensive storage and transmission system that is directly connected to eight interstate pipelines, and includes eight owned underground gas storage facilities, with

about 150 Bcf of annual storage capacity. In addition, Nicor Gas has about 40 Bcf of purchased storage from an affiliated party under contracts that expire between 2012 and 2013.

Nicor Gas also operates the Chicago Hub, which provides natural gas storage and transmission-related services to marketers and other gas distribution companies, but revenues are passed on directly to Nicor Gas's customers.

GAS's Tropical Shipping unit (21%) is one of the largest containerized cargo carriers in the Caribbean, with a fleet of 11 owned and six chartered vessels, with total container capacity of about 5,600 20-foot equivalent units (TEU), serving 25 ports. Total volumes shipped in 2008 were 197,100 TEU, down from 206,600 TEU in 2007 and 203,100 TEU in 2006. However, revenues per TEU remained relatively high at $2,158 in 2008 versus $1,955 in 2007 and $1,961 in 2006.

Company Financials Fiscal Year Ended Dec. 31

Per Share Data ($)	2008	2007	2006	2005	2004	2003	2002	2001	2000	1999
Tangible Book Value	21.02	20.51	19.43	18.36	16.99	17.15	16.55	16.39	15.56	16.76
Cash Flow	6.40	6.64	6.44	6.55	5.05	5.73	6.00	6.46	4.12	5.58
Earnings	2.63	2.99	2.87	3.07	1.70	2.48	2.88	3.17	1.00	2.62
S&P Core Earnings	2.11	2.74	2.83	2.47	1.97	2.45	2.30	1.99	NA	NA
Dividends	1.86	1.86	1.86	1.86	1.86	1.86	1.84	1.76	1.66	1.54
Payout Ratio	71%	62%	65%	61%	109%	75%	64%	56%	166%	59%
Prices:High	51.99	53.66	49.92	42.97	39.65	39.30	49.00	42.38	43.88	42.94
Prices:Low	32.35	37.80	38.72	35.50	32.04	23.70	18.09	34.00	29.38	31.19
P/E Ratio:High	20	18	17	14	23	16	17	13	44	16
P/E Ratio:Low	12	13	13	12	19	10	6	11	29	12
Income Statement Analysis (Million $)										
Revenue	3,777	3,176	2,960	3,358	2,740	2,663	1,897	2,544	2,298	1,615
Operating Income	356	372	366	202	138	189	227	244	507	352
Depreciation	171	166	160	155	149	144	138	149	144	140
Interest Expense	40.1	38.2	49.8	48.0	41.6	37.3	38.5	44.9	48.6	45.1
Pretax Income	164	184	174	171	105	169	186	217	61.1	190
Effective Tax Rate	27.1%	26.6%	26.3%	20.3%	28.7%	35.2%	31.0%	33.8%	23.6%	34.6%
Net Income	120	135	128	136	75.1	110	128	144	46.7	124
S&P Core Earnings	96.2	124	127	110	87.7	108	102	90.4	NA	NA
Balance Sheet & Other Financial Data (Million $)										
Cash	95.5	91.9	41.1	119	12.9	50.3	75.2	10.7	55.8	42.5
Current Assets	1,339	1,024	911	1,346	1,021	916	708	518	915	508
Total Assets	4,784	4,252	4,090	4,391	3,975	3,797	2,899	2,575	2,885	2,452
Current Liabilities	1,668	1,276	1,142	1,623	1,174	1,069	1,099	826	1,312	746
Long Term Debt	449	423	498	486	495	497	396	446	347	436
Common Equity	973	945	873	811	749	755	728	728	708	788
Total Capital	1,822	1,769	1,787	1,751	1,873	1,813	1,514	1,548	1,173	1,539
Capital Expenditures	250	173	592	202	190	181	193	186	158	154
Cash Flow	290	301	288	291	224	253	266	292	191	264
Current Ratio	0.8	0.8	0.8	0.8	0.9	0.9	0.6	0.6	0.7	0.7
% Long Term Debt of Capitalization	24.6	23.9	27.9	27.7	26.4	27.4	26.1	28.8	29.6	28.3
% Net Income of Revenue	3.2	4.3	4.3	4.5	2.7	4.1	6.7	5.6	2.0	7.7
% Return on Assets	2.1	3.2	3.0	11.4	7.8	3.3	4.7	5.3	1.8	5.1
% Return on Equity	12.5	14.9	15.2	17.4	9.9	14.8	12.3	20.0	6.2	16.0

Data as orig reptd.; bef. results of disc opers/spec. items. Per share data adj. for stk. divs.; EPS diluted. E-Estimated. NA-Not Available. NM-Not Meaningful. NR-Not Ranked. UR-Under Review.

Office: 1844 Ferry Road, Naperville, IL 60563-9600.
Telephone: 630-305-9500.
Website: http://www.nicorinc.com
Chrmn, Pres & CEO: R.M. Strobel

EVP & CFO: R.L. Hawley
SVP, Secy & General Counsel: P.C. Gracey, Jr.
Chief Acctg Officer & Cntlr: K.K. Pepping
Treas: D.M. Ruschau

Investor Contact: K.D. Brunner (630-388-2529)
Board Members: R. M. Beavers, Jr., B. P. Bickner, J. H. Birdsall, III, N. R. Bobins, B. J. Gaines, R. A. Jean, D. J. Keller, R. E. Martin, G. R. Nelson, A. J. Olivera, J. E. Rau, J. C. Staley, R. M. Strobel

Founded: 1953
Domicile: Illinois
Employees: 3,900

The McGraw-Hill Companies

NIKE Inc.

STANDARD &POOR'S

S&P Recommendation **BUY** ★★★★★	Price $65.05 (as of Nov 27, 2009)	12-Mo. Target Price $70.00	Investment Style Large-Cap Growth

GICS Sector Consumer Discretionary
Sub-Industry Footwear

Summary NIKE is the world's leading designer and marketer of high-quality athletic footwear, athletic apparel, and accessories.

Key Stock Statistics (Source S&P, Vickers, company reports)

52-Wk Range	$66.35–38.24	S&P Oper. EPS 2010E	3.95	Market Capitalization(B)	$25.481	Beta	0.87
Trailing 12-Month EPS	$3.04	S&P Oper. EPS 2011E	4.20	Yield (%)	1.66	S&P 3-Yr. Proj. EPS CAGR(%)	6
Trailing 12-Month P/E	21.4	P/E on S&P Oper. EPS 2010E	16.5	Dividend Rate/Share	$1.08	S&P Credit Rating	A+
$10K Invested 5 Yrs Ago	$16,485	Common Shares Outstg. (M)	487.0	Institutional Ownership (%)	91		

Price Performance

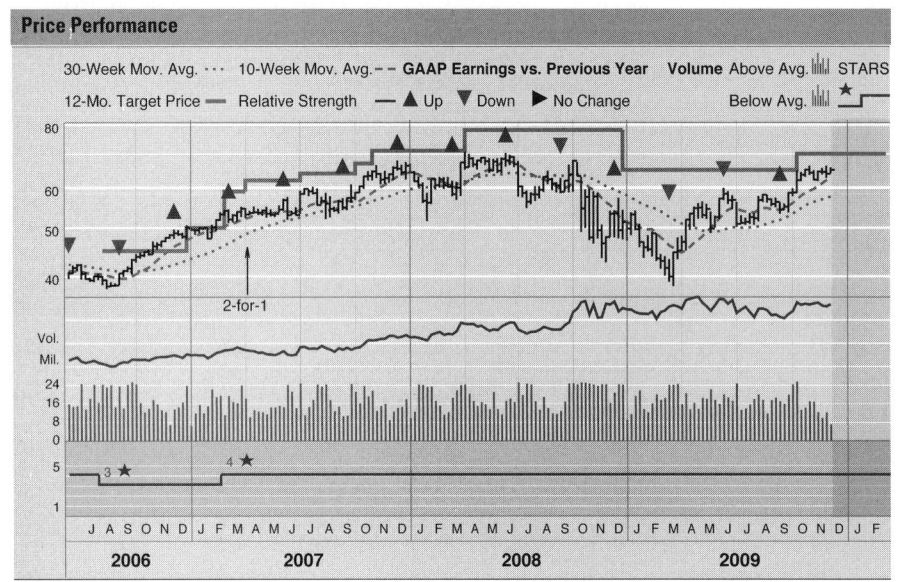

30-Week Mov. Avg. · · · 10-Week Mov. Avg. – – GAAP Earnings vs. Previous Year Volume Above Avg. STARS
12-Mo. Target Price — Relative Strength — ▲ Up ▼ Down ► No Change Below Avg.

Options: ASE, CBOE, P, Ph

Analysis prepared by **Marie Driscoll, CFA** on October 02, 2009, when the stock traded at **$ 62.08.**

Highlights

► We see FY 10 (May) sales down 1%, reflecting a weak global consumer and currency, but we think NKE's broad geographic exposure, with nearly 60% of sales outside the U.S., positions it well for growth, while mitigating its overall risk. China is NKE's second largest market, with $1.7 billion in sales in FY 09. Despite the consumer pullback in the U.S., NKE entered FY 10 with U.S. future orders off just 4%.

► NKE's FY 09 companywide restructuring resulted in a 5% work force reduction, at a cost of $195 million, which we believe should benefit FY 10 profitability by a similar amount. We see about 100 bps of operating margin expansion in FY 10, to 13.8%. We expect cost containment efforts via attempts to hold SG&A spending flat, as NKE reduces management layers and leverages support services globally.

► NKE had $3.6 billion in cash and short-term investments at the end of August 2009 ($6/share net of debt), and generates strong free cash flow. We expect NKE to maintain its dividend while suspending its share buyback program as part of a cash conservation policy.

Investment Rationale/Risk

► Over the past three years, NKE has more than doubled its quarterly dividend and repurchased nearly $3.3 billion of its shares. We see strong fundamentals and a dominant global brand with exceptional international growth opportunities supporting the share price. Moreover, NKE has launched key marketing and sales strategies that are designed to more closely align the company and sales with key markets. NKE entered FY 10 with future orders down 12% for the Nike brand (-5% excluding currency impact); this metric improved sequentially in the first quarter, to -4% ex-currency. We expect NKE to pick up market share in most product categories as consumers tend to opt for established brands in uncertain environments.

► Risks to our recommendation and target price include a severe economic slowdown domestically and a greater-than-expected moderation in consumer spending. International risks include economic weakness, supply disruptions, and unfavorable currency fluctuations.

► Our 12-month target price of $70 is equal to about 18X our FY 10 EPS estimate of $3.95, at the low end of the 14X to 26X range in which the stock has traded over the past five years.

Qualitative Risk Assessment

LOW	MEDIUM	HIGH

Our risk assessment reflects what we see as NKE's strong financial and operating metrics, offset by an increasingly competitive global marketplace and prospects for slowing consumer spending in the U.S.

Quantitative Evaluations

S&P Quality Ranking A+

D	C	B-	B	B+	A-	A	A+

Relative Strength Rank STRONG

77

LOWEST = 1   HIGHEST = 99

Revenue/Earnings Data

Revenue (Million $)

	1Q	2Q	3Q	4Q	Year
2010	4,799	--	--	--	--
2009	5,432	4,590	4,441	4,713	19,176
2008	4,655	4,340	4,544	5,088	18,627
2007	4,194	3,822	3,927	4,383	16,326
2006	3,862	3,475	3,613	4,005	14,955
2005	3,562	3,148	3,308	3,721	13,740

Earnings Per Share ($)

	1Q	2Q	3Q	4Q	Year
2010	1.04	E0.82	E1.00	E1.10	E3.95
2009	1.03	0.80	0.50	0.70	3.03
2008	1.12	0.71	0.92	0.98	3.74
2007	0.74	0.64	0.68	0.86	2.93
2006	0.81	0.57	0.62	0.64	2.64
2005	0.61	0.49	0.51	0.65	2.24

Fiscal year ended May 31. Next earnings report expected: Mid December. EPS Estimates based on S&P Operating Earnings; historical GAAP earnings are as reported.

Dividend Data (Dates: mm/dd Payment Date: mm/dd/yy)

Amount ($)	Date Decl.	Ex-Div. Date	Stk. of Record	Payment Date
0.250	02/12	03/05	03/09	04/01/09
0.250	05/12	06/04	06/08	07/01/09
0.250	08/10	09/03	09/08	10/01/09
0.270	11/19	12/03	12/07	01/04/10

Dividends have been paid since 1984. Source: Company reports.

NIKE Inc.

STANDARD &POOR'S

Business Summary October 02, 2009

CORPORATE OVERVIEW. Nike Inc. is the world's largest supplier of athletic footwear, with an estimated 50% of this $20 billion market (at wholesale). Sports apparel and equipment are also sold under the Nike banner, and the company's Other segment (13% of sales) houses its affiliated brands including Cole Haan, Converse, Hurley Nike Golf and Umbro.

MARKET PROFILE. Innovation, marketing and the sports cycle drive the global footwear and athletic apparel markets, in our view. Technologically superior performance products, we think, convey the idea of extraordinary ability to the wearer and are the root of the marketing campaigns aimed at lifestyle consumers (individuals attracted to a brand's attributes of an active lifestyle regardless of sports participation). The global market for athletic apparel is several times as large as the footwear market, and totals over $100 billion, according to industry sources. An estimated 30% of this market consists of active sports apparel (purchased with the intent to be used in an active sport), and the remainder is lifestyle or casual wear. We see apparel representing a significant opportunity for NKE via its brand extensions and market penetra-

tion. According to NPD Fashionworld consumer estimated data, U.S. athletic footwear sales dropped about 3.8% in 2008, to $18.6 billion, following several years of low single digit gains. We estimate frequent technological innovation enables manufacturers to hold and increase prices while building brand equity. S&P projects a low single digit annual decline for these markets in 2009. In the first three months of 2009 sales were off 2% at $4.2 billion.

COMPETITIVE LANDSCAPE. Both the athletic footwear and apparel markets are fragmented, providing opportunities for growing market share, in our view. Significant domestic footwear retail channels in 2008 include athletic footwear specialty shops (8% market share), sporting goods stores (6%), and discounters or mass merchants (14%).

Company Financials Fiscal Year Ended May 31

Per Share Data ($)	2009	2008	2007	2006	2005	2004	2003	2002	2001	2000
Tangible Book Value	16.54	13.51	12.93	11.23	9.77	8.14	7.22	6.39	5.77	5.05
Cash Flow	3.74	4.36	3.51	3.17	2.72	2.22	1.83	3.51	1.44	1.37
Earnings	3.03	3.74	2.93	2.64	2.24	1.76	1.39	1.23	1.08	1.04
S&P Core Earnings	3.56	3.67	2.89	2.56	2.14	1.68	1.31	1.16	1.03	NA
Dividends	0.83	0.68	0.56	0.45	0.45	0.34	0.26	0.24	0.24	0.24
Payout Ratio	27%	18%	19%	17%	20%	19%	19%	20%	22%	23%
Calendar Year	2008	2007	2006	2005	2004	2003	2002	2001	2000	1999
Prices:High	70.60	67.93	50.60	45.77	46.22	34.27	32.14	30.03	28.50	33.47
Prices:Low	42.68	47.46	37.76	37.55	32.91	21.19	19.27	17.75	12.91	19.38
P/E Ratio:High	23	18	17	17	21	20	26	24	26	32
P/E Ratio:Low	14	13	13	14	15	12	16	14	12	19

Income Statement Analysis (Million $)										
Revenue	19,176	18,627	16,326	14,955	13,740	12,253	10,697	9,893	9,489	8,995
Operating Income	2,802	2,747	2,402	23,912	2,151	1,802	1,485	1,291	1,212	1,150
Depreciation	347	313	270	282	257	252	239	224	197	188
Interest Expense	40.2	67.1	Nil	Nil	39.7	40.3	42.9	47.6	58.7	45.0
Pretax Income	1,957	2,503	2,200	2,142	1,860	1,450	1,123	2,035	921	919
Effective Tax Rate	24.0%	24.8%	32.2%	35.0%	34.9%	34.8%	34.1%	17.2%	36.0%	37.0%
Net Income	1,487	1,883	1,492	1,392	1,212	946	740	1,686	590	579
S&P Core Earnings	1,748	1,848	1,472	1,346	1,148	897	698	632	559	NA

Balance Sheet & Other Financial Data (Million $)										
Cash	3,455	2,776	1,857	954	1,388	828	634	576	304	254
Current Assets	9,734	8,839	8,077	7,359	6,351	5,512	4,680	4,158	3,625	3,596
Total Assets	13,250	12,443	10,688	9,870	8,794	7,892	6,714	6,443	5,820	5,857
Current Liabilities	3,277	3,322	2,584	2,623	1,999	2,009	2,015	1,836	1,787	2,140
Long Term Debt	437	441	Nil	Nil	687	682	552	626	436	470
Common Equity	8,693	7,825	7,025	6,285	5,644	4,782	3,991	3,839	3,495	3,136
Total Capital	9,130	8,267	7,026	6,286	6,332	5,464	4,543	4,465	3,931	3,607
Capital Expenditures	456	449	314	334	257	214	186	283	318	420
Cash Flow	1,834	2,196	1,761	1,674	1,469	1,198	979	1,909	787	767
Current Ratio	3.0	2.7	3.1	2.8	3.2	2.7	2.3	2.3	2.0	1.7
% Long Term Debt of Capitalization	4.8	5.3	Nil	Nil	10.9	12.5	12.1	14.0	11.1	13.0
% Net Income of Revenue	7.8	10.1	9.1	9.3	8.8	7.7	6.9	17.0	6.2	6.4
% Return on Assets	11.6	16.3	14.5	14.9	14.5	12.9	11.3	27.5	10.1	10.4
% Return on Equity	18.0	25.4	22.4	23.3	23.2	21.6	18.9	46.0	17.8	17.9

Data as orig reptd.; bef. results of disc opers/spec. items. Per share data adj. for stk. divs.; EPS diluted. E-Estimated. NA-Not Available. NM-Not Meaningful. NR-Not Ranked. UR-Under Review.

Office: 1 Bowerman Dr, Beaverton, OR 97005-0979.
Telephone: 503-641-6453.
Website: http://www.nikebiz.com
Chrmn: P. Knight

Pres & CEO: M.G. Parker
COO: G.M. DeStefano
CFO: D.W. Blair
Chief Acctg Officer & Cntlr: B.F. Pliska

Investor Contact: P.M. Catlett (800-640-8007)
Board Members: J. G. Connors, J. K. Conway, T. D. Cook, R. D. DeNunzio, A. B. Graf, Jr., D. G. Houser, P. Knight, J. C. Lechleiter, M. G. Parker, J. A. Rodgers, O. Smith, J. R. Thompson, Jr., P. M. Wise

Founded: 1964
Domicile: Oregon
Employees: 34,300

The McGraw-Hill Companies

NiSource Inc.

**STANDARD
&POOR'S**

S&P Recommendation **SELL** ★★☆☆☆	Price $14.21 (as of Nov 27, 2009)	12-Mo. Target Price $12.00	Investment Style Large-Cap Value

GICS Sector Utilities
Sub-Industry Multi-Utilities

Summary NI, the third largest U.S. gas distribution utility and the fourth largest gas pipeline company, also provides electric utility services.

Key Stock Statistics (Source S&P, Vickers, company reports)

52-Wk Range	$14.58–7.79	S&P Oper. EPS 2009**E**	1.04	Market Capitalization(B)	$3.918	Beta	0.80
Trailing 12-Month EPS	$1.05	S&P Oper. EPS 2010**E**	1.15	Yield (%)	6.47	S&P 3-Yr. Proj. EPS CAGR(%)	-6
Trailing 12-Month P/E	13.5	P/E on S&P Oper. EPS 2009**E**	13.7	Dividend Rate/Share	$0.92	S&P Credit Rating	BBB-
$10K Invested 5 Yrs Ago	$8,441	Common Shares Outstg. (M)	275.8	Institutional Ownership (%)	83		

Price Performance

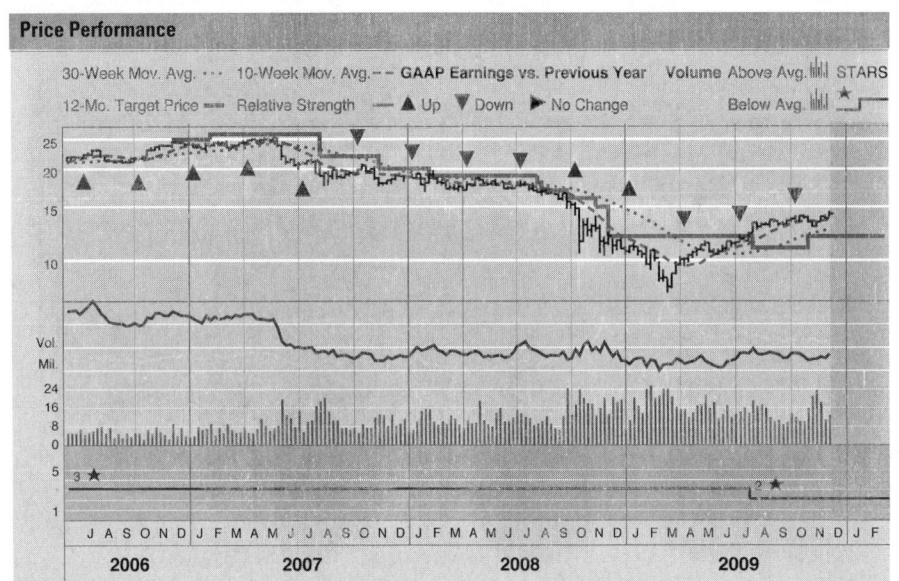

Options: ASE, CBOE, Ph

Analysis prepared by **Christopher B. Muir** on October 21, 2009, when the stock traded at **$ 13.77**.

Highlights

► We see total revenues falling 22% in 2009 and rising 1.2% in 2010. For the regulated utilities, we expect 2009 to be affected by lower gas prices and declining customer usage due to conservation, partly offset by multiple rate increases and customer growth. Gas transmission and storage revenues should benefit from slightly higher short-term transportation and storage volumes, as well as a new pipeline. We see non-regulated revenues contracting due to lower commodity prices, partly offset by higher marketing volumes.

► We expect operating margins of 12.8% in 2009 and 13.2% in 2010, versus 2008's 10.1%. We anticipate lower per-revenue fuel and purchased power costs, partly offset by higher per-revenue non-fuel costs in 2009. We see pretax margins of 7.0% in 2009 and 7.4% in 2010, versus 6.0% in 2008. In 2009, we project higher interest expense as well as lower non-operating income.

► Our 2009 operating EPS estimate, excluding $0.05 of nonrecurring charges, is $1.04, down 16% from 2008's $1.23, which excludes $0.11 of nonrecurring gains. Our 2010 forecast is $1.15, up 11%.

Investment Rationale/Risk

► We view NI's utility service territory as having relatively slow, but stable, customer growth, and we see no near-term impetus for base revenue growth outside of rate increases. NI has several rate cases filed, and the potential exists for at least one rate hike in 2009, in our view. Depreciation charges are rising as a result of capital spending programs now in place, and operations and maintenance costs have increased as a result of electric plant maintenance activities. We do not expect any meaningful EPS growth from a 2008 base year until after 2010, at which point we believe a growth rate of 5% is achievable.

► Risks to our recommendation and target price include wider power margins, unusually cold winter weather, lower natural gas prices, and lower interest rates.

► The stock recently traded at 12X our 2010 EPS estimate, a 3% premium to multi-utility peers. Our 12-month target price of $12 is 10.5X our 2010 EPS estimate -- a 9% discount to our peer target. We believe this is warranted by what we view as an absence of near-term EPS and dividend growth prospects and relatively slow longer-term EPS growth.

Qualitative Risk Assessment

LOW	MEDIUM	HIGH

Our risk assessment reflects the company's reliance on fairly stable regulated sources of earnings including gas distribution, gas transmission, and electric utility services.

Quantitative Evaluations

S&P Quality Ranking   **B**

D	C	B-	B	B+	A-	A	A+

Relative Strength Rank   **STRONG**

78

LOWEST = 1   HIGHEST = 99

Revenue/Earnings Data

Revenue (Million $)

	1Q	2Q	3Q	4Q	Year
2009	2,720	1,009	884.8	--	--
2008	3,290	1,792	1,409	2,386	8,874
2007	2,894	1,577	1,241	2,245	7,940
2006	2,972	1,312	1,156	2,050	7,490
2005	2,683	1,356	1,165	2,695	7,899
2004	2,473	1,245	979.8	1,968	6,666

Earnings Per Share ($)

2009	0.58	-0.03	-0.03	E0.37	E1.04
2008	0.69	0.08	0.12	0.46	1.34
2007	0.76	0.11	0.03	0.24	1.14
2006	0.63	0.08	0.10	0.33	1.14
2005	0.77	0.03	-0.02	0.27	1.04
2004	0.82	0.13	0.08	0.58	1.62

Fiscal year ended Dec. 31. Next earnings report expected: Early February. EPS Estimates based on S&P Operating Earnings; historical GAAP earnings are as reported.

Dividend Data (Dates: mm/dd Payment Date: mm/dd/yy)

Amount ($)	Date Decl.	Ex-Div. Date	Stk. of Record	Payment Date
0.230	01/09	01/28	01/30	02/20/09
0.230	03/24	04/28	04/30	05/20/09
0.230	05/12	07/29	07/31	08/20/09
0.230	08/26	10/28	10/30	11/20/09

Dividends have been paid since 1987. Source: Company reports.

Please read the Required Disclosures and Analyst Certification on the last page of this report.

The McGraw-Hill Companies

Business Summary October 21, 2009

CORPORATE OVERVIEW. NiSource is the third largest U.S. natural gas distributor (measured by customers served), the fourth largest owner of U.S. natural gas interstate pipelines (by route miles), and one of the largest owners of underground natural gas storage. It also provides electric utility services in northern Indiana. The company's operating divisions include Gas Distribution (36% of year end-2008 segment operating income), Gas Transmission and Storage (40%), Electric Operations (24%), and Other Operations (less than 0%).

Gas Distribution operations provide gas utility service to 3.3 million customers in seven states. The division owns and operates 57,466 miles of pipeline, 28,479 acres of underground storage, 90 underground storage wells and 75.9 million gallons of liquefied natural gas storage facilities. In 2008, total sales and transportation volumes were 923 MM Dth, up from 907 MM Dth in 2007. Deliveries were 30% to residential customers, 19% to commercial customers, 40% to industrial customers and 11% to off-system sales and other customers.

Gas Transmission and Storage operates 15,658 miles of interstate natural gas pipelines and 826,000 acres of underground storage systems with a capacity of about 629 billion cubic feet (Bcf). In 2008, total throughput was 1,522 MM Dth, up 9.4% from 2007 due to increased transportation deliveries on Columbia Transmission related to Hardy Storage field operations being in service for a

full year, as well as incremental throughput from new interconnects along the Columbia Gulf and Columbia Transmission pipeline systems. The division has recently completed Millennium Pipeline and Hardy Storage projects and is engaged in other projects. The Millennium project is a 182-mile, 0.53 MM Dth/day pipeline across southern New York State. The 12 Bcf Hardy storage project in West Virginia is expected to be fully operational in 2009. NI said it is in the process of a potential separation of Columbia Gas into a master limited partnership structure, but we do not expect any action until the economy and financial markets improve.

NI's Northern Indiana subsidiary, NIPSCO, generates and distributes electricity for 457,325 electric utility customers. The utility operates three coal-fired plants (2,574 MW), six gas-fired plants (738 MW), and two hydroelectric plants (10 MW). In 2008, the utility generated 81.6% of its electric requirements, and purchased 18.4%. NI has said it was considering a possible sale of this business.

Company Financials Fiscal Year Ended Dec. 31

Per Share Data ($)	2008	2007	2006	2005	2004	2003	2002	2001	2000	1999
Tangible Book Value	2.63	3.58	3.29	2.79	2.14	0.70	NM	NM	NM	9.88
Cash Flow	3.40	3.17	3.16	3.04	3.54	3.53	4.70	4.07	3.84	NA
Earnings	1.34	1.14	1.14	1.04	1.62	1.63	2.00	1.01	1.08	1.27
S&P Core Earnings	0.83	1.09	1.13	1.20	1.62	1.67	1.43	0.32	NA	NA
Dividends	0.92	0.92	0.92	0.92	0.92	1.10	1.16	1.16	1.08	1.02
Payout Ratio	69%	78%	81%	88%	57%	67%	58%	115%	100%	80%
Prices:High	19.82	25.43	24.80	25.50	22.82	21.97	24.99	32.55	31.50	30.94
Prices:Low	10.35	17.49	19.51	20.44	19.65	16.39	14.51	18.25	12.75	16.38
P/E Ratio:High	15	22	22	25	14	13	12	32	29	24
P/E Ratio:Low	8	15	17	20	12	10	7	18	12	13

Income Statement Analysis (Million $)										
Revenue	8,874	7,940	7,490	7,899	6,666	6,247	6,492	9,459	6,031	3,145
Operating Income	1,468	1,493	880	1,520	1,072	1,116	1,203	1,009	568	773
Depreciation	567	559	549	545	510	497	574	642	374	311
Interest Expense	380	418	7,304	425	408	469	533	605	325	184
Pretax Income	555	484	484	433	671	662	680	416	298	269
Effective Tax Rate	33.4%	35.6%	35.3%	34.5%	35.9%	35.4%	34.4%	44.1%	43.7%	33.5%
Net Income	370	312	314	284	430	426	426	212	147	160
S&P Core Earnings	229	298	310	324	429	437	305	67.9	NA	NA

Balance Sheet & Other Financial Data (Million $)										
Cash	20.6	95.4	33.1	69.4	30.1	27.3	56.2	128	193	43.5
Current Assets	3,411	2,455	2,783	3,061	2,286	2,063	1,869	2,567	4,918	NA
Total Assets	20,032	18,005	18,157	17,959	16,988	16,624	16,897	17,374	19,697	6,835
Current Liabilities	4,583	3,393	3,821	3,843	3,602	2,609	4,177	4,729	6,893	NA
Long Term Debt	5,944	5,594	5,146	5,271	4,917	6,075	5,448	6,214	6,148	2,320
Common Equity	4,729	5,077	5,014	4,933	4,787	4,416	4,175	3,469	3,415	1,354
Total Capital	12,223	12,234	11,775	11,866	11,448	10,490	11,581	11,515	11,483	4,903
Capital Expenditures	970	788	637	590	517	575	622	668	366	341
Cash Flow	937	871	863	829	940	923	1,000	854	521	NA
Current Ratio	0.7	0.7	0.7	0.8	0.6	0.8	0.4	0.5	0.7	0.5
% Long Term Debt of Capitalization	48.6	45.7	43.7	44.4	42.9	57.9	47.0	54.0	53.5	60.3
% Net Income of Revenue	4.2	3.9	4.2	3.6	6.5	6.8	6.6	2.2	2.4	5.1
% Return on Assets	1.9	1.7	1.7	1.6	2.6	2.5	2.5	1.1	1.1	2.7
% Return on Equity	7.5	6.2	6.3	5.8	9.3	9.9	11.1	6.2	6.2	12.8

Data as orig reptd.; bef. results of disc opers/spec. items. Per share data adj. for stk. divs.; EPS diluted. E-Estimated. NA-Not Available. NM-Not Meaningful. NR-Not Ranked. UR-Under Review.

Office: 801 East 86th Avenue, Merrillville, IN, USA 46410-6272.
Telephone: 877-647-5990.
Email: questions@nisource.com
Website: http://www.nisource.com

Chrmn: I.M. Rolland
Pres & CEO: R.C. Skaggs, Jr.
EVP & CFO: S.P. Smith
EVP & General Counsel: C.J. Hightman

Chief Admin Officer: V.G. Sistovaris
Investor Contact: D.J. Vajda (877-647-5990)
Board Members: R. A. Abdoo, S. C. Beering, D. E. Foster, M. E. Jesanis, M. R. Kittrell, W. L. Nutter, D. S. Parker, I. M. Rolland, R. C. Skaggs, Jr., R. L. Thompson, C. Y. Woo

Founded: 1912
Domicile: Delaware
Employees: 7,981

Noble Energy Inc

STANDARD &POOR'S

| S&P Recommendation | BUY ★★★★☆ | Price $64.92 (as of Nov 27, 2009) | 12-Mo. Target Price $83.00 | Investment Style Large-Cap Growth |

GICS Sector Energy
Sub-Industry Oil & Gas Exploration & Production

Summary This independent exploration and production company (formerly Noble Affiliates) is engaged in the exploration, production and marketing of oil and natural gas worldwide.

Key Stock Statistics (Source S&P, Vickers, company reports)

52-Wk Range	$74.02–37.15	S&P Oper. EPS 2009E	1.52	Market Capitalization(B)	$11.262	Beta	0.91
Trailing 12-Month EPS	$0.93	S&P Oper. EPS 2010E	3.85	Yield (%)	1.11	S&P 3-Yr. Proj. EPS CAGR(%)	-11
Trailing 12-Month P/E	69.8	P/E on S&P Oper. EPS 2009E	42.7	Dividend Rate/Share	$0.72	S&P Credit Rating	BBB
$10K Invested 5 Yrs Ago	$21,103	Common Shares Outstg. (M)	173.5	Institutional Ownership (%)	94		

Price Performance

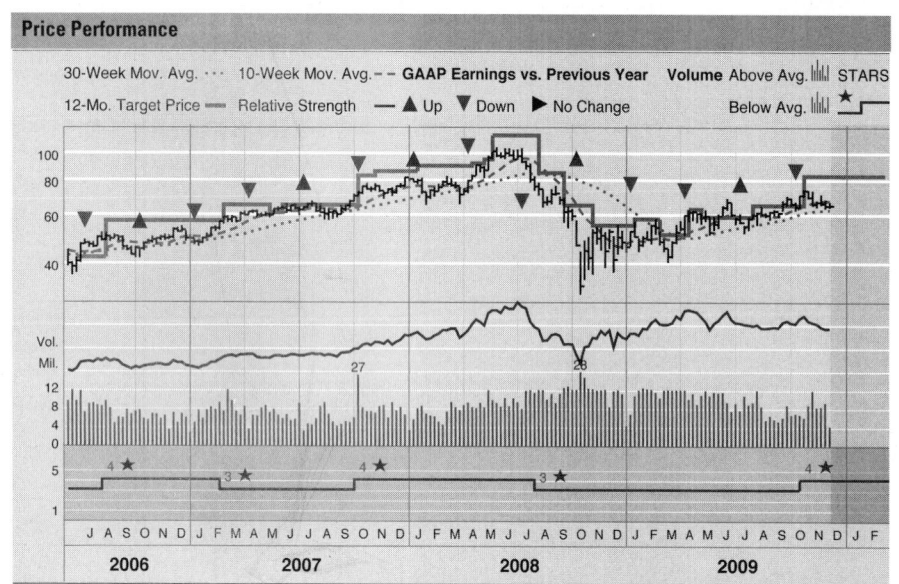

Options: ASE, CBOE, P, Ph

Analysis prepared by **Michael Kay** on October 20, 2009, when the stock traded at **$73.21**.

Qualitative Risk Assessment

LOW | MEDIUM | **HIGH**

Our risk assessment reflects our view of NBL's aggressive financial profile, and a satisfactory business profile limited by participation in the cyclical, competitive and capital-intensive exploration and production sector, and by U.S. and international oil and gas operations that carry heightened political and operational risk.

Quantitative Evaluations

S&P Quality Ranking B+

D | C | B- | B | **B+** | A- | A | A+

Relative Strength Rank MODERATE
38
LOWEST = 1   HIGHEST = 99

Revenue/Earnings Data

Revenue (Million $)

	1Q	2Q	3Q	4Q	Year
2009	441.0	491.0	596.0	--	--
2008	1,025	1,205	1,098	573.0	3,901
2007	742.6	794.2	813.8	921.5	3,272
2006	712.0	772.6	741.3	714.2	2,940
2005	368.2	485.4	632.1	701.0	2,187
2004	317.6	335.2	320.2	378.2	1,351

Earnings Per Share ($)

2009	-1.09	-0.33	0.61	E0.90	E1.52
2008	1.20	-0.84	5.37	1.72	7.58
2007	1.22	1.21	1.28	1.73	5.45
2006	1.26	-0.17	1.75	0.94	3.79
2005	0.92	0.91	0.99	1.18	4.12
2004	0.65	0.60	0.68	0.73	2.70

Fiscal year ended Dec. 31. Next earnings report expected: Mid February. EPS Estimates based on S&P Operating Earnings; historical GAAP earnings are as reported.

Highlights

► On the development of Rocky Mountain assets, the start-up of Gulf of Mexico (GOM) projects and Phase II at Dumbarton in the North Sea, and increased sales in Israel, 2008 production rose 9%. In 2009, we expect the completion of an LNG plant and higher West Africa volumes to help offset production declines from the disposal of GOM assets. NBL has reduced drilling activity in the Piceance, but continues to drill the Wattenberg field in Colorado. In 2009, development spending will focus on international and deepwater GOM and high return domestic onshore projects, while exploration spending is to focus on projects in West Africa, Israel, and the deepwater GOM.

► Despite our outlook for a severe drop in industry service costs for 2009 on increased capacity brought about by lower industry capex, we see NBL's lease operating expense increasing slightly due to projects in West Africa.

► NBL's 2009 capital budget is $1.6 billion, down from $2.3 billion in 2008. We see 2009 EPS of $1.40 (with $1.10 unrealized derivative charge), versus EPS of $8.66 (with $1.69 unrealized derivative gain) in 2008, on lower oil and gas prices, and $3.35 in 2010, on improved prices.

Investment Rationale/Risk

► In our view, acquisitions have extended NBL's reserve life and made reserve replacement efforts less dependent on non-operated projects. We view NBL as a low-cost and geographically balanced producer with financial flexibility. In 2009, we see U.S. gas drilling projects, mainly in the Rockies, shelved in favor of high impact international targets, where spending is expected to total 30% of 2009's budget. We expect NBL share performance to reflect oil and gas prices, which remain highly volatile, but we see potential catalysts in exploration. In 2008, NBL made large discoveries at Gunflint in GOM, Tamar in Israel, and Carmen in Equatorial Guinea.

► Risks to our recommendation and target price include declines in oil and gas prices and production, and an inability to replace reserves.

► We discount unproven resource potential and value NBL on proven reserve NAV estimates. Our 12-month target price of $83 blends our proved NAV estimate of $82 with our DCF model ($84, assuming a WACC of 10.8% and terminal growth of 3%) and above peer-average relative valuations, given our view of a strong balance sheet and reserve growth potential.

Dividend Data (Dates: mm/dd Payment Date: mm/dd/yy)

Amount ($)	Date Decl.	Ex-Div. Date	Stk. of Record	Payment Date
0.180	01/27	02/05	02/09	02/23/09
0.180	04/27	05/07	05/11	05/26/09
0.180	07/28	08/06	08/10	08/24/09
0.180	10/27	11/05	11/09	11/23/09

Dividends have been paid since 1975. Source: Company reports.

Noble Energy Inc

STANDARD
&POOR'S

Business Summary October 20, 2009

CORPORATE OVERVIEW. Noble Energy is a large international independent exploration and production concern, engaged in exploration, production and marketing of oil and natural gas. The company has operations in the U.S. (offshore the Gulf of Mexico and California, the Gulf Coast region, the Mid-Continent region, and the Rocky Mountain region) and internationally (in Argentina, China, Ecuador, Equatorial Guinea, the Mediterranean Sea, and the North Sea).

As of December 31, 2008, NBL had estimated proved reserves of 5.18 Bcfe, of which 64% was natural gas and 69% was proved developed. This compares with estimated proved reserves of 5.28 Bcfe, 63% natural gas and 74% proved developed, at the end of 2007, a 2% decline. Reserves declined due to negative price revisions resulting from lower commodity prices at the end of 2008 versus 2007. We forecast NBL's reserve life to be 11 years, compared to 12.1 years at the end of 2006.

In February 2009, NBL estimated its 2008 reserve replacement, excluding negative price revisions, at 147%. Including revisions, we estimate NBL organically replaced 67% of its production and 87% including acquisitions. Companywide at year-end 2008, reserves were 864 million BOE, and reserve additions from all sources were 115 million BOE, at a finding and development cost of $20.38 per BOE. NBL's production grew 9% in 2008. NBL has been reducing its investment in the Gulf of Mexico's conventional shallow shelf and shifting its

domestic offshore exploration focus to deepwater Gulf of Mexico areas. NBL is now a larger, more-diversified company with greater opportunities for both domestic and international growth, in our view, through high-impact exploration drilling as well as lower-risk exploitation projects.

IMPACT OF MAJOR DEVELOPMENTS. On July 14, 2006, NBL closed on a $625 million sale of its Gulf of Mexico shelf assets to Coldren Resources LP. After-tax cash proceeds from the sale totaled $504 million, including proceeds received from parties that exercised preferential rights to purchase certain minor properties.

On May 16, 2005, NBL acquired Patina Oil and Gas Corp. As a result of the transaction, NBL incurred about $1.7 billion of debt in the deal. We estimate that the Patina merger extended NBL's reserve life and made its reserve replacement less dependent on international and Gulf of Mexico projects operated by other companies. The Patina acquisition remains a major transaction in NBL's history, exposing NBL to more unconventional gas and Western U.S. gas markets.

Company Financials Fiscal Year Ended Dec. 31

Per Share Data ($)	2008	2007	2006	2005	2004	2003	2002	2001	2000	1999
Tangible Book Value	31.95	23.51	19.35	12.68	12.37	9.38	8.80	8.86	7.58	5.99
Cash Flow	12.17	9.65	7.27	6.61	5.26	3.47	2.62	3.64	3.72	2.65
Earnings	7.58	5.45	3.79	4.12	2.70	0.78	0.16	1.17	1.69	0.43
S&P Core Earnings	7.52	5.42	3.05	4.08	2.58	0.70	0.08	1.08	NA	NA
Dividends	0.66	0.44	0.28	0.15	0.10	0.09	0.08	0.08	0.08	0.08
Payout Ratio	9%	8%	7%	4%	4%	11%	52%	7%	5%	19%
Prices:High	105.11	81.71	54.64	48.75	32.30	23.00	20.38	25.55	24.19	17.50
Prices:Low	30.89	46.04	36.14	27.78	21.33	16.19	13.33	13.75	9.59	9.56
P/E Ratio:High	14	15	14	12	12	29	NM	22	14	41
P/E Ratio:Low	4	8	9	7	8	21	NM	12	6	22

Income Statement Analysis (Million $)										
Revenue	3,901	3,272	2,940	2,187	1,351	1,011	1,444	1,572	1,381	887
Operating Income	2,295	2,029	2,019	1,423	884	539	376	535	550	352
Depreciation, Depletion and Amortization	791	728	623	391	309	309	285	284	231	255
Interest Expense	69.0	130	117	87.5	48.2	47.0	47.7	26.0	31.6	43.0
Pretax Income	2,061	1,368	1,096	969	516	142	42.6	225	299	77.6
Effective Tax Rate	34.5%	31.0%	38.1%	33.3%	39.2%	36.5%	58.6%	40.5%	36.0%	36.3%
Net Income	1,350	944	678	646	314	89.9	17.7	134	192	49.5
S&P Core Earnings	1,340	938	548	640	305	81.0	8.88	123	NA	NA

Balance Sheet & Other Financial Data (Million $)										
Cash	1,140	660	153	110	180	62.4	15.4	73.2	23.2	2.93
Current Assets	2,158	1,569	1,069	1,176	734	478	310	352	271	148
Total Assets	12,384	10,831	9,589	8,878	3,443	2,843	2,730	2,480	1,879	1,450
Current Liabilities	1,174	1,636	1,184	1,240	665	655	472	381	325	184
Long Term Debt	2,241	1,851	1,801	2,031	880	776	977	837	525	445
Common Equity	6,309	4,809	4,114	3,231	1,460	1,074	1,009	1,010	850	2,134
Total Capital	10,724	8,644	7,673	5,262	2,524	2,013	2,188	2,024	1,492	2,662
Capital Expenditures	1,971	1,415	1,357	786	661	527	596	739	537	123
Cash Flow	2,141	1,672	1,301	1,036	623	399	303	418	422	304
Current Ratio	1.8	1.0	0.9	0.9	1.1	0.7	0.7	0.9	0.8	0.8
% Long Term Debt of Capitalization	20.9	21.4	23.5	38.6	34.9	38.6	44.6	41.4	35.2	16.7
% Return on Assets	11.6	9.2	7.3	10.5	10.0	3.2	0.7	6.1	11.6	3.2
% Return on Equity	24.3	51.7	18.8	27.5	24.8	8.6	1.7	14.4	25.0	2.2

Data as orig reptd.; bef. results of disc opers/spec. items. Per share data adj. for stk. divs.; EPS diluted. E-Estimated. NA-Not Available. NM-Not Meaningful. NR-Not Ranked. UR-Under Review.

Office: 100 Glenborough Drive, Houston, TX 77067.
Telephone: 281-872-3100.
Email: info@nobleenergyinc.com
Website: http://www.nobleenergyinc.com

Chrmn & CEO: C.D. Davidson
Pres & COO: D.L. Stover
SVP & CFO: K.M. Fisher
SVP, Secy & General Counsel: A.J. Johnson

Chief Acctg Officer: F. Bruning
Investor Contact: D. Larson (281-872-3100)
Board Members: J. L. Berenson, M. A. Cawley, E. F. Cox, C. D. Davidson, T. J. Edelman, E. P. Grubman, K. L. Hedrick, S. D. Urban, W. T. Van Kleef

Auditor: KPMG
Founded: 1969
Domicile: Delaware

The McGraw-Hill Companies

Nordstrom Inc.

STANDARD &POOR'S

S&P Recommendation HOLD ★★★☆☆

Price	12-Mo. Target Price	Investment Style
$34.02 (as of Nov 27, 2009)	$35.00	Large-Cap Growth

GICS Sector Consumer Discretionary
Sub-Industry Department Stores

Summary This specialty retailer of apparel and accessories, widely known for its emphasis on service, operates about 183 stores in 28 states.

Key Stock Statistics (Source S&P, Vickers, company reports)

52-Wk Range	$36.52– 10.11	S&P Oper. EPS 2010E	1.85	Market Capitalization(B)	$7.374	Beta	1.81
Trailing 12-Month EPS	$1.54	S&P Oper. EPS 2011E	2.35	Yield (%)	1.88	S&P 3-Yr. Proj. EPS CAGR(%)	13
Trailing 12-Month P/E	22.1	P/E on S&P Oper. EPS 2010E	18.4	Dividend Rate/Share	$0.64	S&P Credit Rating	BBB+
$10K Invested 5 Yrs Ago	$16,538	Common Shares Outstg. (M)	216.8	Institutional Ownership (%)	76		

Price Performance

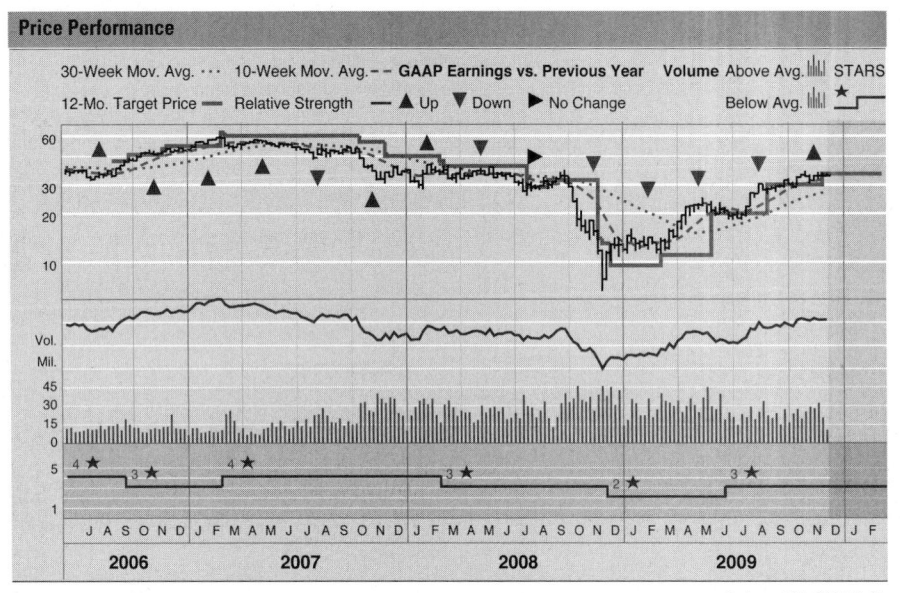

Options: ASE, CBOE, P, Ph

Analysis prepared by **Jason N. Asaeda** on November 16, 2009, when the stock traded at **$ 33.99**.

Highlights

► Following a projected 6% decline in FY 10 (Jan.), we look for flat same-store sales in FY 11. We see JWN weathering the economic downturn by focusing on its most productive brands and improving the value proposition through reported 10% lower average prices (excluding cosmetics) at its full-line stores. We also think the company is meeting the needs of increasingly cost-conscious shoppers through expansion of its off-price Nordstrom Rack business. JWN plans to open three full-line and 16 Rack stores in FY 10 and an additional three full-line and 15 Rack units in FY 11. All told, we project net sales of $8.09 billion in FY 10 and $8.47 billion in FY 11, versus FY 09's $8.27 billion.

► We look for the company to drive annual gross margin expansion by keeping inventory aligned with sales trends. However, while we expect JWN to remain focused on cost savings initiatives, we anticipate limited expense leverage in FY 10 given our projection of a decline for same-store sales. We also anticipate higher bad debt expense in FY 10 on a forecasted increase in credit card account delinquencies.

► Assuming no share repurchase activity, we see EPS of $1.85 in FY 10 and $2.35 in FY 11.

Investment Rationale/Risk

► Our hold recommendation is based on valuation. While JWN's outlook for consumer spending remains guarded, we think the company can sustain the recent improvement in its sales trend this holiday season and into FY 11 on favorable customer response to its sharper pricing and in-flow of newness and fashion. Also, with same-store inventory down 12% at the end of the third quarter, versus a same-store sales decline of 1.2%, we think the company is effectively managing its inventory and expect JWN to continue to report lower markdown and clearance levels. In addition, we see a consistent customer-focused shopping experience across the company's full-line store base, expansion of Nordstrom Rack, suspended share repurchases, and a disciplined approach to capital spending as underlying positives to JWN's business.

► Risks to our recommendation and target price include a loss of business due to lackluster merchandising and uncompetitive pricing.

► We arrive at our 12-month target price of $35 by applying JWN's 10-year historical median forward P/E multiple of 14.9X to our FY 11 EPS estimate.

Qualitative Risk Assessment

LOW	MEDIUM	HIGH

Our risk assessment reflects our view of JWN's improving sales and profit margins, increasing market share in the better department store sector, and healthy balance sheet and cash flow. This is offset by uncertainty over consumer discretionary spending in light of higher interest rates and debt levels.

Quantitative Evaluations

S&P Quality Ranking A-

D	C	B-	B	B+	A-	A	A+

Relative Strength Rank STRONG

80

LOWEST = 1   HIGHEST = 99

Revenue/Earnings Data

Revenue (Million $)

	1Q	2Q	3Q	4Q	Year
2010	1,792	2,232	1,963	--	--
2009	1,949	2,359	1,879	2,386	8,573
2008	1,954	2,390	1,970	2,514	8,828
2007	1,787	2,270	1,872	2,631	8,561
2006	1,654	2,106	1,666	2,296	7,723
2005	1,535	1,953	1,542	2,100	7,131

Earnings Per Share ($)

2010	0.37	0.48	0.38	E0.62	E1.85
2009	0.54	0.65	0.33	0.31	1.83
2008	0.60	0.65	0.68	0.92	2.88
2007	0.48	0.67	0.52	0.89	2.55
2006	0.38	0.53	0.39	0.69	1.98
2005	0.24	0.38	0.27	0.50	1.39

Fiscal year ended Jan. 31. Next earnings report expected: Late February. EPS Estimates based on S&P Operating Earnings; historical GAAP earnings are as reported.

Dividend Data (Dates: mm/dd Payment Date: mm/dd/yy)

Amount ($)	Date Decl.	Ex-Div. Date	Stk. of Record	Payment Date
0.160	02/17	02/25	02/27	03/16/09
0.160	05/19	05/27	05/29	06/15/09
0.160	08/18	08/27	08/31	09/15/09
0.160	11/18	11/25	11/30	12/15/09

Dividends have been paid since 1971. Source: Company reports.

Please read the Required Disclosures and Analyst Certification on the last page of this report.

The McGraw-Hill Companies

Nordstrom Inc.

STANDARD &POOR'S

Business Summary November 16, 2009

CORPORATE OVERVIEW. In our view, Nordstrom (JWN) is the clear leader in the U.S. better department store sector, reflecting its focus on high-quality, differentiated merchandise; personalized customer service; and a consistent upscale shopping experience across its entire Nordstrom store base. The company derives its revenues from retail, credit and direct sales channels. JWN formerly owned Faconnable, a wholly owned wholesaler and retailer of high-quality men's, women's and boy's apparel and accessories. In FY 09 (Jan.), merchandise category sales were: women's apparel 34%; shoes 21%; men's apparel 16%; women's accessories 12%; cosmetics 11%; children's apparel 3%; and other 3%.

IMPACT OF MAJOR DEVELOPMENTS. JWN spends about $150 million annually on information technology (IT). In FY 03, the company invested in a perpetual inventory system that has enabled its merchant teams to more accurately forecast sales trends and to better track and plan store-level inventory and expenses, resulting in improved sales performance and profitability, in our

opinion. In FY 05, JWN put into place a new point of sales system that includes Personal Book, a tool that allows salespeople to tailor service to the needs of each customer by organizing and tracking customer preferences, purchases, and contact information. The company has noted that Personal Book has driven incremental sales volume.

In July 2007, JWN agreed to sell Faconnable to M1 Group, a Lebanon-based, family-owned diversified business, for $210 million. As part of the agreement, JWN will continue to buy Faconnable merchandise at historical levels for at least the next three years and will continue to offer Faconnable in Nordstrom stores. The company realized a gain of $33.9 million on the sale ($0.09 per share, after-tax), which closed in the third quarter of FY 08.

Company Financials Fiscal Year Ended Jan. 31

Per Share Data ($)	2009	2008	2007	2006	2005	2004	2003	2002	2001	2000
Tangible Book Value	5.37	4.81	7.90	7.26	6.10	5.40	4.55	4.38	4.06	4.49
Cash Flow	3.21	3.95	3.62	2.98	2.31	1.78	1.24	1.27	1.16	1.44
Earnings	1.83	2.88	2.55	1.98	1.39	0.88	0.38	0.46	0.39	0.73
S&P Core Earnings	1.84	2.80	2.55	1.93	2.62	1.67	0.62	0.80	0.83	NA
Dividends	0.54	0.42	0.32	0.24	0.21	0.21	0.19	0.18	0.16	0.18
Payout Ratio	30%	15%	13%	12%	15%	23%	50%	38%	41%	24%
Calendar Year	2008	2007	2006	2005	2004	2003	2002	2001	2000	1999
Prices:High	40.59	59.70	51.40	39.00	23.68	17.75	13.44	11.49	17.25	22.41
Prices:Low	6.61	30.46	31.77	22.71	16.55	7.50	7.80	6.90	7.06	10.84
P/E Ratio:High	22	21	20	20	17	20	35	25	44	31
P/E Ratio:Low	4	11	12	11	12	9	20	15	18	15

Income Statement Analysis (Million $)										
Revenue	8,272	8,828	8,561	7,723	7,131	6,492	5,975	5,634	5,529	5,124
Operating Income	1,072	1,503	1,195	1,010	817	585	424	363	335	467
Depreciation	302	269	285	276	265	251	234	218	203	194
Interest Expense	145	71.7	62.4	45.3	85.4	91.0	86.2	73.5	63.0	54.0
Pretax Income	648	1,173	1,106	885	647	398	196	204	167	332
Effective Tax Rate	38.1%	39.1%	38.7%	37.7%	39.2%	39.0%	47.1%	39.0%	38.9%	38.9%
Net Income	401	715	678	551	393	243	104	125	102	203
S&P Core Earnings	403	697	677	536	373	229	83.9	107	109	NA

Balance Sheet & Other Financial Data (Million $)										
Cash	72.0	358	403	463	361	476	208	331	25.0	27.0
Current Assets	3,217	3,361	2,742	2,874	2,572	2,455	2,073	2,055	1,813	1,565
Total Assets	5,661	5,600	4,822	4,921	4,605	4,466	4,096	4,049	3,608	3,062
Current Liabilities	1,601	1,635	1,433	1,623	1,341	1,050	870	948	951	867
Long Term Debt	2,214	2,236	624	628	929	1,605	1,342	1,351	1,100	747
Common Equity	1,210	1,115	2,169	2,093	1,789	1,634	1,372	1,314	1,229	1,185
Total Capital	3,435	3,612	2,792	2,720	2,718	3,239	2,714	2,666	2,329	1,932
Capital Expenditures	563	501	264	272	247	258	328	390	321	305
Cash Flow	703	984	963	828	658	494	338	342	305	397
Current Ratio	2.0	2.1	1.9	1.8	1.9	2.3	2.4	2.2	1.9	1.8
% Long Term Debt of Capitalization	64.2	61.9	22.3	23.1	34.2	49.5	49.4	50.7	47.2	38.7
% Net Income of Revenue	4.9	8.1	7.9	7.1	5.5	3.7	1.7	2.2	1.8	4.0
% Return on Assets	7.1	13.7	13.9	11.6	8.6	5.7	2.5	3.3	3.1	6.6
% Return on Equity	34.5	43.6	31.8	28.4	23.0	16.2	7.7	9.8	8.5	16.3

Data as orig reptd.; bef. results of disc opers/spec. items. Per share data adj. for stk. divs.; EPS diluted. E-Estimated. NA-Not Available. NM-Not Meaningful. NR-Not Ranked. UR-Under Review.

Office: 1617 6th Ave, Seattle, WA 98101-1707.
Telephone: 206-628-2111.
Email: invrelations@nordstrom.com
Website: http://www.nordstrom.com

Chrmn: E. Hernandez, Jr.
Pres: B.W. Nordstrom
EVP & CFO: M. Koppel
EVP & Chief Admin Officer: D.F. Little

EVP, Secy & General Counsel: R.B. Sari
Investor Contact: C. Holloway (206-303-3200)
Board Members: P. J. Campbell, E. Hernandez, Jr., R. G. Miller, B. W. Nordstrom, E. B. Nordstrom, P. E. Nordstrom, P. G. Satre, R. D. Walter, A. A. Winter

Founded: 1901
Domicile: Washington
Employees: 51,000

The McGraw-Hill Companies

Norfolk Southern Corp

STANDARD
&POOR'S

S&P Recommendation	BUY ★★★★☆	Price $51.19 (as of Nov 27, 2009)	12-Mo. Target Price $55.00	Investment Style Large-Cap Blend

GICS Sector Industrials
Sub-Industry Railroads

Summary This railroad operates 21,200 route miles serving 22 eastern states, the District of Columbia, and Ontario, Canada.

Key Stock Statistics (Source S&P, Vickers, company reports)

52-Wk Range	$52.84– 26.69	S&P Oper. EPS 2009E	2.79	Market Capitalization(B)	$18.832	Beta	1.10
Trailing 12-Month EPS	$3.16	S&P Oper. EPS 2010E	3.90	Yield (%)	2.66	S&P 3-Yr. Proj. EPS CAGR(%)	10
Trailing 12-Month P/E	16.2	P/E on S&P Oper. EPS 2009E	18.3	Dividend Rate/Share	$1.36	S&P Credit Rating	BBB+
$10K Invested 5 Yrs Ago	$16,446	Common Shares Outstg. (M)	367.9	Institutional Ownership (%)	68		

Price Performance

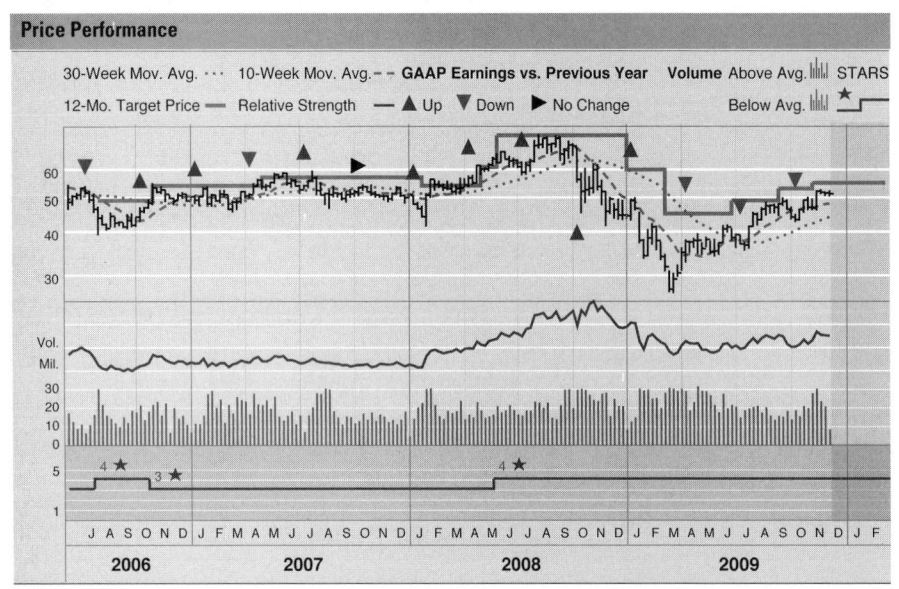

30-Week Mov. Avg. · · ·   10-Week Mov. Avg. - - - **GAAP Earnings vs. Previous Year**   Volume Above Avg. STARS
12-Mo. Target Price —   Relative Strength —   ▲ Up   ▼ Down   ▶ No Change   Below Avg.

Options: ASE, CBOE, P, Ph

Analysis prepared by **Kevin Kirkeby** on October 29, 2009, when the stock traded at **$ 47.13**.

Highlights

► We expect revenues to decline 25% in 2009, with volumes down 19% and yield, including fuel pass-throughs, accounting for the difference. However, with auto and steel production starting to come back on line, we think volumes of metallurgical coal bottomed in early 2009 and will improve into 2010. Our forecast for 2010 of 10% revenue growth is based on a 4% rise in yield and a 5% increase in carloadings, aided by a general improvement in the economy. We expect fuel surcharges to add 1% to revenues in 2010, after representing an expected 12% headwind in 2009.

► We see the operating margin widening in 2010, on improved fixed cost coverage as volumes are forecast to rise, and expense controls. While we see higher depreciation charges and a contractual wage hike, we think this will be offset by cost savings from the deployment of new locomotives and higher capacity railcars. Also, we expect railcar lease expenses to decline as contracts are allowed to expire, given the large number of cars in inventory.

► Our EPS estimate for 2009 of $2.74 excludes $0.06 in one-time tax benefits. We forecast EPS of $3.90 in 2010.

Investment Rationale/Risk

► Medium-term trends in NSC's primary markets remain favorable and support rising traffic, in our opinion. We see investments in its network improving capacity on heavily trafficked lanes like the Heartland and Crescent corridors, and leading to greater conversion of truck traffic over to rail. Weighing the ongoing economic uncertainty against the sequential improvement in volumes achieved by NSC since the start of July, we believe a valuation in line with peers, and above the historical average, is warranted.

► Risks to our recommendation and target price include a renewed worsening in manufacturing and the economy, unfavorable changes in regulatory framework, rising competition in its shorter routes where trucks are able to compete effectively, and a prolonged period of low natural gas prices that encourages utilities to use less coal in their overall fuel mix.

► Blending a P/E of 15.0X our 2010 EPS estimate, above the five-year average, with our DCF model, which assumes an 11.2% cost of equity, 11% average net income growth over the next five years, and a 3.5% terminal growth rate (yielding an intrinsic value of $51), we arrive at our 12-month target price of $55.

Qualitative Risk Assessment

LOW	MEDIUM	HIGH

Our risk assessment reflects what we see as NSC's exposure to economic cycles, regulations, labor and fuel costs, significant capital expenditure requirements, and challenges in maintaining system fluidity, offset by our view of a diverse customer base, historically positive free cash flow, and moderate financial leverage.

Quantitative Evaluations

S&P Quality Ranking A-

D	C	B-	B	B+	A-	A	A+

Relative Strength Rank STRONG

81

LOWEST = 1   HIGHEST = 99

Revenue/Earnings Data

Revenue (Million $)

	1Q	2Q	3Q	4Q	Year
2009	1,943	1,857	2,063	--	--
2008	2,500	2,765	2,894	2,502	10,661
2007	2,247	2,378	2,353	2,454	9,432
2006	2,303	2,392	2,393	2,319	9,407
2005	1,961	2,154	2,155	2,257	8,527
2004	1,693	1,813	1,857	1,949	7,312

Earnings Per Share ($)

2009	0.47	0.66	0.81	E0.85	E2.79
2008	0.76	1.18	1.37	1.21	4.52
2007	0.71	0.98	1.02	1.02	3.68
2006	0.72	0.89	1.02	0.95	3.57
2005	0.47	1.04	0.73	0.87	3.11
2004	0.40	0.54	0.72	0.65	2.31

Fiscal year ended Dec. 31. Next earnings report expected: Late January. EPS Estimates based on S&P Operating Earnings; historical GAAP earnings are as reported.

Dividend Data (Dates: mm/dd Payment Date: mm/dd/yy)

Amount ($)	Date Decl.	Ex-Div. Date	Stk. of Record	Payment Date
0.340	01/27	02/04	02/06	03/10/09
0.340	04/21	04/29	05/01	06/10/09
0.340	07/28	08/05	08/07	09/10/09
0.340	10/27	11/04	11/06	12/10/09

Dividends have been paid since 1901. Source: Company reports.

Please read the Required Disclosures and Analyst Certification on the last page of this report.

The McGraw-Hill Companies

Norfolk Southern Corp

STANDARD
&POOR'S

Business Summary October 29, 2009

CORPORATE OVERVIEW. Norfolk Southern provides rail transportation service in the eastern U.S., operating over 21,000 miles of road, with an extensive intermodal and coal service network and a significant general freight business, including an automotive business that is the largest in North America. NSC owns 58% of Conrail's shares, with CSX holding the remainder, and holds 50% voting rights. NSC and CSX operate separate portions of Conrail's rail routes and assets. NSC's non-rail activities include real estate and natural resources.

NSC's intermodal business represented 19% of 2008 freight revenues. Although it was the second largest contributor to revenues, intermodal was the largest category by volume at 41% of total carloads. This was the third highest percentage among the Class I rails in 2008. Coal, which we believe is NSC's most profitable segment, accounted for 29% of 2008 freight revenues, and 23% of carloads. Most of this traffic, which is delivered primarily to power utilities, originates from the Appalachian coal fields. However, the company has been increasing the number of carloads it carries that originated in the Illinois Basin and the Powder River Basin. General merchandise, sensitive to U.S. GDP trends, provided 52% of freight revenues in 2008. Within this category are chemicals and automotive shipments, representing 12% and 8% of 2008

freight revenues, respectively. We consider NSC to have considerable exposure to the auto market since it serves 24 assembly plants, fourteen of which belong to the domestic manufacturers Ford, Chrysler and General Motors.

COMPETITIVE LANDSCAPE. The U.S. rail industry has an oligopoly-like structure, with over 80% of revenues generated by the four largest railroads: NSC and CSX Corp. operating on the East Coast, and Union Pacific Corp. and Burlington Northern Santa Fe Corp. operating on the West Coast. Railroads simultaneously compete for customers while cooperating by sharing assets, interfacing systems, and completing customer movements. NSC, for example, is a net payer of equipment rents as it takes on more freight originated by other carriers than it hands off to them at its major gateways. Likewise, NSC has formed separate joint ventures with Kansas City Southern and Pan Am Railways that enhance its access along certain corridors in exchange for much needed capital investments.

Company Financials Fiscal Year Ended Dec. 31

Per Share Data ($)	2008	2007	2006	2005	2004	2003	2002	2001	2000	1999
Tangible Book Value	26.23	27.12	24.19	22.66	19.98	17.83	16.71	15.78	15.17	15.53
Cash Flow	6.63	5.63	5.50	5.02	3.83	2.40	2.50	2.27	1.80	1.91
Earnings	4.52	3.68	3.57	3.11	2.31	1.05	1.18	0.94	0.45	0.63
S&P Core Earnings	4.21	3.48	3.43	2.97	2.13	0.95	0.70	0.41	NA	NA
Dividends	1.22	0.96	0.68	0.48	0.46	0.30	0.26	0.24	0.80	0.80
Payout Ratio	27%	26%	19%	15%	20%	29%	22%	26%	178%	127%
Prices:High	75.53	59.77	57.71	45.81	36.69	24.62	26.98	24.11	22.75	36.44
Prices:Low	41.36	45.38	39.10	29.60	20.38	17.35	17.20	13.41	11.94	19.63
P/E Ratio:High	17	16	16	15	16	23	23	26	51	58
P/E Ratio:Low	9	12	11	10	9	17	15	14	27	31

Income Statement Analysis (Million $)										
Revenue	10,661	9,406	9,407	8,527	7,312	6,468	6,270	6,170	6,159	5,195
Operating Income	3,901	3,334	3,307	2,904	2,311	1,592	1,158	1,521	1,150	1,207
Depreciation	804	775	750	787	609	528	515	514	517	489
Interest Expense	457	482	493	500	506	497	518	553	551	561
Pretax Income	2,750	2,237	2,230	1,697	1,302	586	706	553	250	351
Effective Tax Rate	37.6%	34.6%	33.6%	24.5%	29.1%	29.9%	34.8%	34.5%	31.2%	31.9%
Net Income	1,716	1,464	1,481	1,281	923	411	460	362	172	239
S&P Core Earnings	1,595	1,377	1,417	1,224	849	365	270	155	NA	NA

Balance Sheet & Other Financial Data (Million $)										
Cash	618	206	527	289	579	284	184	204	Nil	37.0
Current Assets	1,999	1,675	2,400	2,650	1,967	1,425	1,299	1,047	849	1,371
Total Assets	26,297	26,144	26,028	25,861	24,750	20,596	19,956	19,418	18,976	19,250
Current Liabilities	2,105	1,948	2,093	1,921	2,201	1,801	1,853	2,386	1,887	1,924
Long Term Debt	6,316	6,132	6,109	6,616	6,863	6,800	7,006	7,027	7,339	7,556
Common Equity	9,597	9,727	9,615	9,289	7,990	6,976	6,500	6,090	5,824	5,932
Total Capital	22,295	22,290	22,168	22,525	21,403	17,008	16,561	15,943	15,958	16,225
Capital Expenditures	1,558	1,341	1,178	1,025	1,041	720	689	746	731	912
Cash Flow	2,520	2,239	2,231	2,068	1,532	939	975	876	689	728
Current Ratio	1.0	0.9	1.1	1.4	0.9	0.8	0.7	0.4	0.4	0.7
% Long Term Debt of Capitalization	28.3	27.5	27.6	29.4	32.1	40.0	42.3	44.1	46.0	46.6
% Net Income of Revenue	16.1	15.6	15.7	15.0	12.6	6.4	7.3	5.9	2.8	4.6
% Return on Assets	6.5	5.6	5.7	5.1	4.1	2.0	2.3	1.9	0.9	1.3
% Return on Equity	17.8	15.1	15.7	14.8	12.3	6.1	7.3	6.1	2.9	4.0

Data as orig reptd.; bef. results of disc opers/spec. items. Per share data adj. for stk. divs.; EPS diluted. E-Estimated. NA-Not Available. NM-Not Meaningful. NR-Not Ranked. UR-Under Review.

Office: 3 Commercial Pl, Norfolk, VA 23510-2191.
Telephone: 757-629-2680.
Website: http://www.nscorp.com
Chrmn, Pres & CEO: C.W. Moorman, IV

COO & EVP: M.D. Manion
EVP & CFO: J.A. Squires
EVP & CIO: D.H. Butler
Chief Admin Officer: J.P. Rathbone

Investor Contact: M. Parkerson (757-533-4939)
Board Members: G. L. Baliles, D. A. Carp, G. R. Carter, A. D. Correll, L. Hilliard, K. N. Horn, B. M. Joyce, S. F. Leer, M. D. Lockhart, C. W. Moorman, IV, J. P. Reason

Founded: 1980
Domicile: Virginia
Employees: 30,709

Northeast Utilities

STANDARD &POOR'S

S&P Recommendation	BUY ★★★★☆	Price $24.00 (as of Nov 27, 2009)	12-Mo. Target Price $26.00	Investment Style Large-Cap Blend

GICS Sector Utilities
Sub-Industry Electric Utilities

Summary This utility holding company serves Connecticut, western Massachusetts, and New Hampshire.

Key Stock Statistics (Source S&P, Vickers, company reports)

52-Wk Range	$25.31– 19.01	S&P Oper. EPS 2009**E**	1.85	Market Capitalization(B)	$4.211	Beta	0.49
Trailing 12-Month EPS	$1.89	S&P Oper. EPS 2010**E**	1.90	Yield (%)	3.96	S&P 3-Yr. Proj. EPS CAGR(%)	3
Trailing 12-Month P/E	12.7	P/E on S&P Oper. EPS 2009**E**	13.0	Dividend Rate/Share	$0.95	S&P Credit Rating	BBB
$10K Invested 5 Yrs Ago	$15,519	Common Shares Outstg. (M)	175.5	Institutional Ownership (%)	77		

Price Performance

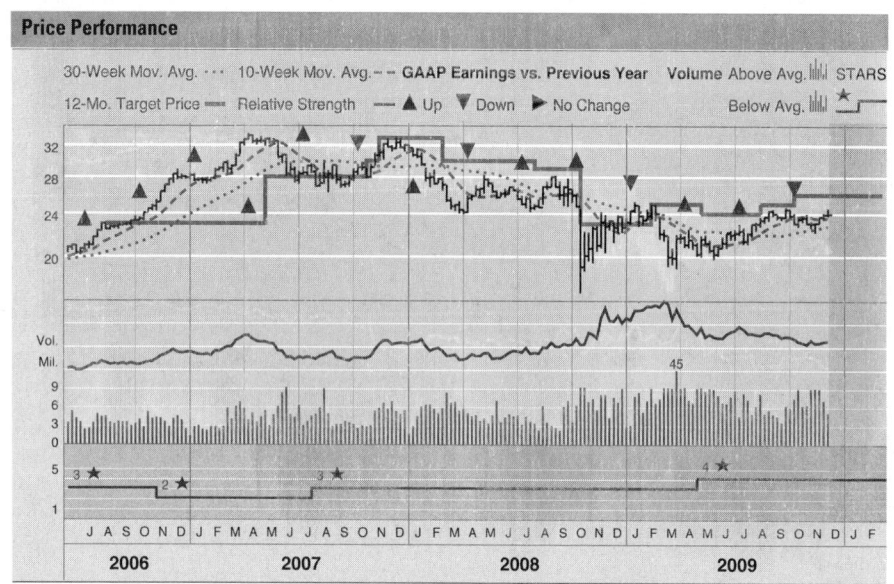

30-Week Mov. Avg. · · · 10-Week Mov. Avg. — — GAAP Earnings vs. Previous Year Volume Above Avg. STARS
12-Mo. Target Price — Relative Strength — ▲ Up ▼ Down ▶ No Change   Below Avg.

Options: Ph

Analysis prepared by **Justin McCann** on September 28, 2009, when the stock traded at **$ 24.02**.

Highlights

▶ We expect 2009 operating EPS to increase only slightly from 2008's $1.86. We believe EPS growth in 2009 will be restricted by more shares outstanding, higher operating expenses, milder weather, and a weak economy, which is expected to result in lower demand and an increase in uncollectible accounts. We believe the regulated distribution and generating companies will earn about $0.97 a share in 2009, the transmission business about $0.91, and the competitive businesses about $0.05, with the parent company recording a loss of about $0.05.

▶ For 2010, we project operating EPS to increase about 5% from anticipated results in 2009. While we expect only a gradual recovery in the regional economy, we believe earnings will benefit from growth in the transmission operations as well as return to more normal weather.

▶ On June 30, 2009, PSNH filed with the New Hampshire Public Utility Commission (PUC) for a $51 million increase in its distribution rates effective August 1, 2009. On July 6, PSNH entered into a settlement agreement with the PUC staff for a temporary $25.6 million increase effective as of August 1, but which will be subject to reconciliation with the PUC's final ruling.

Investment Rationale/Risk

▶ With the shares having recovered more than 20% from their 2009 low, the stock is down less than 1% year to date. The shares had been hurt, we believe, by the crisis in the financial markets and the downturn in the economy, as well as by the company's reduced EPS outlook for 2009. Following the recent rebound, the stock could be restricted over the short term, but we believe it will benefit over the next 12 months, as investors focus on NU's investments in its transmission system. We think the company is attractive for above-average total return.

▶ Risks to our investment recommendation and target price include worse-than-expected earnings from the company's transmission operations, and/or a sharp decrease in the average peer group P/E multiple.

▶ Following the recent rebound in the shares, as well as the 12% payment increase in early 2009, the dividend was recently yielding around 4.0%, which, while well below the recent peer average yield of approximately 4.9%, has become more competitive. Our 12-month target price is $26, a premium-to-peers P/E of about 13.1X our EPS estimate for 2010.

Qualitative Risk Assessment

LOW	MEDIUM	HIGH

Our risk assessment reflects the steady cash flow we expect from regulated electric and gas utility operations, a generally healthy economy in most of NU's service territories, and a relatively supportive regulatory environment. It also reflects the company's exit from its nonregulated and high-risk wholesale energy marketing and energy services businesses.

Quantitative Evaluations

S&P Quality Ranking — B

D	C	B-	B	B+	A-	A	A+

Relative Strength Rank — MODERATE

64

LOWEST = 1   HIGHEST = 99

Revenue/Earnings Data

Revenue (Million $)

	1Q	2Q	3Q	4Q	Year
2009	1,593	1,224	1,306	--	--
2008	1,520	1,325	1,507	1,448	5,800
2007	1,704	1,392	1,451	1,276	5,822
2006	2,147	1,671	1,594	1,483	6,884
2005	2,265	1,551	1,755	1,878	7,397
2004	1,838	1,525	1,668	1,656	6,687

Earnings Per Share ($)

2009	0.60	0.47	0.37	E0.42	E1.85
2008	0.38	0.37	0.47	0.46	1.67
2007	0.50	0.30	0.32	0.47	1.58
2006	-0.13	0.09	0.67	0.19	0.82
2005	-0.91	-0.21	-0.71	-0.08	-1.74
2004	0.53	0.18	0.30	-0.26	0.91

Fiscal year ended Dec. 31. Next earnings report expected: Mid February. EPS Estimates based on S&P Operating Earnings; historical GAAP earnings are as reported.

Dividend Data (Dates: mm/dd Payment Date: mm/dd/yy)

Amount ($)	Date Decl.	Ex-Div. Date	Stk. of Record	Payment Date
0.238	02/10	02/25	03/01	03/31/09
0.238	04/14	05/28	06/01	06/30/09
0.238	07/14	08/28	09/01	09/30/09
0.238	10/13	11/27	12/01	12/31/09

Dividends have been paid since 1999. Source: Company reports.

Please read the Required Disclosures and Analyst Certification on the last page of this report.

The McGraw·Hill Companies

Northeast Utilities

STANDARD
&POOR'S

Business Summary September 28, 2009

CORPORATE OVERVIEW. Northeast Utilities (NU) is a holding company that provides electricity and gas services through its utility subsidiaries. The company's electric subsidiaries include The Connecticut Light & Power Company, Public Service Company of New Hampshire, and Western Massachusetts Electric Company. NU distributes natural gas through its Yankee Gas Services Company subsidiary. Yankee Gas operates the largest natural gas distribution system in Connecticut. NU Enterprises Inc., the nonregulated subsidiary of NU, owns a number of competitive energy and related businesses. In 2008, the electric distribution segment accounted for 81.3% of consolidated revenues (84.6% in 2007); the gas distribution segment, 10.0% (8.8%); the transmission segment, 6.8% (4.9%); and the competitive businesses, 1.9% (1.7%).

CORPORATE STRATEGY. NU implemented a key strategic shift in the exiting of almost all of its competitive businesses, which has enabled it to place sub-

stantially more focus on its regulated companies. Management's long-term strategic goal is to meet the reliability needs of customers and to deliver value to shareholders. We see the continuing expansion of the electricity transmission business as being the key factor in the company's overall growth. NU's transmission rate base at the end of 2008 was approximately $2.4 billion, up from around $1.5 billion at the end of 2006. The company expects its transmission rate base to grow to about $2.463 billion at the end of 2009, $2.576 billion at the end of 2010, $3.378 billion at the end of 2011, $4.251 billion at the end of 2012, and $5.044 billion at the end of 2013.

Company Financials Fiscal Year Ended Dec. 31

Per Share Data ($)	2008	2007	2006	2005	2004	2003	2002	2001	2000	1999
Tangible Book Value	17.54	16.81	16.28	13.98	14.87	14.68	14.20	13.79	12.73	15.50
Earnings	1.67	1.58	0.82	-1.74	0.91	0.95	1.18	1.96	1.55	0.26
S&P Core Earnings	1.11	1.55	0.93	-1.59	0.96	1.13	-0.77	-3.68	NA	NA
Dividends	0.83	0.78	0.72	0.68	0.63	0.58	0.52	0.45	0.40	0.10
Payout Ratio	49%	49%	88%	NM	69%	61%	44%	23%	26%	38%
Prices:High	31.62	33.62	28.90	21.95	20.27	20.32	20.70	24.35	24.56	22.00
Prices:Low	17.16	26.21	19.07	17.30	17.17	13.13	12.66	16.59	18.00	13.56
P/E Ratio:High	19	21	35	NM	22	21	18	12	16	85
P/E Ratio:Low	10	17	23	NM	19	14	11	8	12	52
Income Statement Analysis (Million $)										
Revenue	5,800	5,822	6,884	7,397	6,687	6,069	5,216	6,874	5,877	4,471
Depreciation	279	265	445	614	528	540	667	983	515	899
Maintenance	254	212	194	200	188	232	263	259	256	340
Fixed Charges Coverage	2.33	2.25	1.23	-0.26	1.63	1.72	1.10	-0.24	2.00	0.63
Construction Credits	NA	NA	NA	NA	NA	NA	NA	Nil	Nil	8.40
Effective Tax Rate	28.8%	30.3%	NM	NM	30.7%	33.1%	35.1%	39.5%	43.0%	69.4%
Net Income	261	251	126	-229	117	121	152	266	205	34.2
S&P Core Earnings	173	240	144	-209	122	143	-99.7	-500	NA	NA
Balance Sheet & Other Financial Data (Million $)										
Gross Property	10,978	9,892	8,857	8,969	8,247	7,674	7,213	7,241	10,588	10,036
Capital Expenditures	1,255	1,115	872	752	644	532	492	443	414	330
Net Property	8,208	7,230	6,242	6,417	5,864	5,430	4,728	3,822	3,547	3,947
Capitalization:Long Term Debt	4,219	3,600	4,254	4,494	4,453	4,387	4,186	4,311	2,228	2,693
Capitalization:% Long Term Debt	58.3	55.3	60.3	64.9	66.0	66.0	64.3	65.9	50.1	56.4
Capitalization:Preferred	Nil	Nil	Nil	Nil	Nil	Nil	Nil	116	Nil	Nil
Capitalization:% Preferred	Nil	Nil	Nil	Nil	Nil	Nil	Nil	1.78	Nil	Nil
Capitalization:Common	3,020	2,914	2,798	2,429	2,297	2,264	2,211	2,118	2,219	2,083
Capitalization:% Common	41.7	44.7	39.7	35.1	34.0	34.0	33.9	32.4	49.9	43.6
Total Capital	9,175	8,527	8,184	8,325	8,283	8,042	8,056	8,156	6,285	6,704
% Operating Ratio	91.6	92.6	95.4	99.3	96.1	93.8	96.2	104.0	90.9	97.4
% Earned on Net Property	7.7	8.0	3.5	NM	7.3	8.3	6.1	NM	12.4	6.8
% Return on Revenue	4.5	4.3	1.8	NM	1.7	2.0	2.9	3.9	3.5	0.8
% Return on Invested Capital	6.1	8.6	4.6	1.1	4.8	4.7	5.5	8.2	8.4	4.4
% Return on Common Equity	8.8	8.6	4.8	NM	5.1	5.4	7.0	11.9	8.9	1.7

Data as orig reptd.; bef. results of disc opers/spec. items. Per share data adj. for stk. divs.; EPS diluted. E-Estimated. NA-Not Available. NM-Not Meaningful. NR-Not Ranked. UR-Under Review.

Northern Trust Corp

S&P Recommendation HOLD ★★★☆☆	Price $47.69 (as of Nov 27, 2009)	12-Mo. Target Price $61.00	Investment Style Large-Cap Growth

GICS Sector Financials
Sub-Industry Asset Management & Custody Banks

Summary Northern Trust is a leading provider of fiduciary, asset management, and private banking services.

Key Stock Statistics (Source S&P, Vickers, company reports)

52-Wk Range	$66.08–39.09	S&P Oper. EPS 2009**E**	3.07	Market Capitalization(B)	$11.517	Beta	0.83
Trailing 12-Month EPS	$3.79	S&P Oper. EPS 2010**E**	3.61	Yield (%)	2.35	S&P 3-Yr. Proj. EPS CAGR(%)	18
Trailing 12-Month P/E	12.6	P/E on S&P Oper. EPS 2009**E**	15.5	Dividend Rate/Share	$1.12	S&P Credit Rating	AA-
$10K Invested 5 Yrs Ago	$11,072	Common Shares Outstg. (M)	241.5	Institutional Ownership (%)	78		

Price Performance

30-Week Mov. Avg. · · · · 10-Week Mov. Avg. - - - **GAAP Earnings vs. Previous Year** Volume Above Avg. ▙▟▌ STARS
12-Mo. Target Price — Relative Strength — ▲ Up ▼ Down ► No Change Below Avg. ▙▟▌ ★▁

Options: ASE, CBOE, P, Ph

Analysis prepared by **Stuart Plesser** on October 26, 2009, when the stock traded at **$ 51.94**.

Highlights

► In 2010, we look for double-digit average earning asset growth amid new business wins. We look for net interest income to improve assuming the Fed will increase rates sometime in 2010, as NTRS' spreads should benefit from a rate increase. All told, we look for revenue to increase 3.6% in 2010, versus a projected 8.4% decline in 2009. We expect new business wins to increase in light of disruptions at competitors. We forecast an 8% increase in non-interest expense in 2010, as incentive compensation will likely rise in line with higher revenue.

► Asset quality deteriorated in 2009, with nonperforming assets as a percentage of total loans and other real estate owned at 1.07% at the end of the third quarter, which will likely result in continued elevated provisions. However, new international business growth should help offset rising chargeoffs. We expect Northern Trust's private client business to make up an increasing portion of its business. We anticipate a slightly lower effective tax rate due to NTRS's increasing international exposure.

► Assuming a roughly 5% increase in shares in 2009, we estimate EPS of $3.07 in 2009. For 2010, we look for EPS of $3.61.

Investment Rationale/Risk

► We have a positive view of NTRS's product and geographic diversity. We believe the company's leading position in the affluent market should result in above peer-average revenue. We are also encouraged by the defensive positioning of its securities portfolio. Recent market advances should result in higher funds under management. We also look for the net interest margin to widen as NTRS invests funds a bit more aggressively. NTRS's investment portfolio is highly conservative and should result in limited write-downs, by our analysis. However, we think NTRS's current valuation takes into account most of the positives that we foresee.

► Risks to our recommendation and target price include failure to generate new business from existing and new clients, a significant decline in economic activity, and legal and regulatory risks.

► Over the past five years, on average, the shares have traded at 21X NTRS's trailing 12-month EPS. Our 12-month target price of $61 is equal to approximately 16.8X our 2010 EPS estimate of $3.61, a discount to the historical average, warranted, we think, by slower growth prospects.

Qualitative Risk Assessment

LOW	MEDIUM	HIGH

Our risk assessment reflects what we see as solid business fundamentals and a strong customer base. We view NTRS as well-diversified geographically and able to withstand the economic downturn.

Quantitative Evaluations

S&P Quality Ranking A-

D	C	B-	B	B+	A-	A	A+

Relative Strength Rank WEAK

17

LOWEST = 1   HIGHEST = 99

Revenue/Earnings Data

Revenue (Million $)

	1Q	2Q	3Q	4Q	Year
2009	1,010	1,140	--	--	--
2008	1,204	1,434	1,314	1,373	5,678
2007	1,250	1,338	1,385	1,699	5,395
2006	1,030	1,134	1,117	1,192	4,473
2005	792.9	902.4	912.0	947.1	3,554
2004	680.9	695.9	686.7	765.6	2,829

Earnings Per Share ($)

2009	0.61	0.95	0.77	E0.74	E3.07
2008	1.71	0.96	-0.67	1.47	3.47
2007	0.84	0.92	0.93	0.55	3.24
2006	0.74	0.76	0.74	0.77	3.00
2005	0.63	0.68	0.67	0.67	2.64
2004	0.57	0.59	0.52	0.59	2.26

Fiscal year ended Dec. 31. Next earnings report expected: Late January. EPS Estimates based on S&P Operating Earnings; historical GAAP earnings are as reported.

Dividend Data (Dates: mm/dd Payment Date: mm/dd/yy)

Amount ($)	Date Decl.	Ex-Div. Date	Stk. of Record	Payment Date
0.280	02/17	03/06	03/10	04/01/09
0.280	04/21	06/08	06/10	07/01/09
0.280	07/21	09/08	09/10	10/01/09
0.280	10/20	12/08	12/10	01/04/10

Dividends have been paid since 1896. Source: Company reports.

Please read the Required Disclosures and Analyst Certification on the last page of this report.

Northern Trust Corp

STANDARD
&POOR'S

Business Summary October 26, 2009

CORPORATE OVERVIEW. Northern Trust Corp. (NTRS) organizes its services globally around its two principal business units: Corporate and Institutional Services (C&IS) and Personal Financial Services (PFS). C&IS is a leading worldwide provider of asset servicing, asset management and related services to corporate and public entity retirement funds, foundation and endowment clients, fund managers, insurance companies and government funds. C&IS also offers a full range of commercial banking services through the bank, placing special emphasis on developing and supporting institutional relationships in two target markets: large and mid-sized corporations and financial institutions (both U.S. and non-U.S.). Asset servicing, asset management and related services encompass a full range of capabilities including: global master trust and custody, trade, settlement, and reporting; fund administration; cash management; and investment risk and performance analytical services.

In 2005, NTRS completed its acquisition of the Financial Services Group Limited (FSG) from Baring Asset Management Holdings Limited. The purchase of

FSG brought to C&IS expanded capabilities in institutional fund administration, custody, trust and related services as well as new capabilities in hedge fund and private equity administration, in our view.

PFS provides personal trust, investment management, custody and philanthropic services; financial consulting; guardianship and estate administration; qualified retirement plans; brokerage services; and private and business banking. PFS focuses on high net worth individuals and families, business owners, executives, professionals, retirees and established privately held businesses in its target markets. PFS also includes the Wealth Management Group, which provides customized products and services to meet the complex financial needs of families and individuals in the U.S. and throughout the world, with assets typically exceeding $200 million.

Company Financials Fiscal Year Ended Dec. 31

Per Share Data ($)	2008	2007	2006	2005	2004	2003	2002	2001	2000	1999
Tangible Book Value	NA	18.50	15.53	14.72	14.14	13.88	13.04	11.97	10.54	9.25
Earnings	3.47	3.24	3.00	2.64	2.26	1.89	1.97	2.11	2.08	1.74
S&P Core Earnings	3.31	3.69	3.04	2.51	2.19	1.63	1.64	1.82	NA	NA
Dividends	1.12	1.03	0.94	0.86	0.78	0.70	0.68	0.64	0.56	0.48
Payout Ratio	32%	32%	31%	33%	35%	37%	35%	30%	27%	28%
Prices:High	88.92	83.17	61.40	55.00	51.35	48.75	62.67	82.25	92.13	54.63
Prices:Low	33.88	56.52	49.12	41.60	38.40	27.64	30.41	41.40	46.75	40.16
P/E Ratio:High	26	26	20	21	23	26	32	39	44	31
P/E Ratio:Low	10	17	16	16	17	15	15	20	22	23

Income Statement Analysis (Million $)										
Net Interest Income	4,164	832	730	661	561	548	602	595	569	519
Tax Equivalent Adjustment	49.8	62.5	64.8	60.9	54.4	52.4	48.7	52.6	53.3	38.6
Non Interest Income	3,032	2,326	2,018	1,783	1,711	1,542	1,537	1,580	1,537	1,235
Loan Loss Provision	115	18.0	15.0	2.50	-15.0	2.50	37.5	66.5	24.0	12.5
% Expense/Operating Revenue	32.6%	77.0%	69.6%	69.2%	65.9%	68.1%	67.2%	61.8%	62.6%	62.8%
Pretax Income	1,276	1,061	1,024	888	754	631	669	732	730	616
Effective Tax Rate	37.7%	31.5%	35.0%	34.2%	33.1%	32.9%	33.2%	33.4%	33.6%	34.3%
Net Income	795	727	665	584	505	423	447	488	485	405
% Net Interest Margin	1.76	1.67	1.73	1.79	1.66	1.73	1.93	2.02	2.02	2.05
S&P Core Earnings	747	828	674	561	491	365	369	418	NA	NA

Balance Sheet & Other Financial Data (Million $)										
Money Market Assets	NA	25,051	16,790	16,036	13,168	9,565	9,332	10,546	5,865	3,439
Investment Securities	NA	8,888	12,365	11,109	9,042	9,471	6,594	6,331	7,270	6,244
Commercial Loans	8,254	7,907	6,515	5,064	4,498	4,702	5,137	5,767	5,708	5,485
Other Loans	NA	17,433	16,094	14,905	13,445	13,111	12,927	12,213	12,437	9,890
Total Assets	82,054	67,611	60,712	53,414	45,277	41,450	39,478	39,665	36,022	28,708
Demand Deposits	11,824	10,118	9,315	7,427	6,377	5,767	6,602	7,110	5,375	4,945
Time Deposits	NA	41,095	34,505	31,093	24,681	20,503	19,460	17,909	17,453	16,426
Long Term Debt	5,359	5,721	2,421	2,791	1,340	1,341	1,284	1,485	1,356	1,427
Common Equity	6,389	4,509	3,944	3,601	3,296	3,055	2,880	2,653	2,342	2,055
% Return on Assets	1.1	1.1	1.2	3.0	1.2	1.0	1.1	1.3	1.5	1.4
% Return on Equity	14.6	17.2	17.6	42.7	15.9	14.2	16.1	19.4	21.8	20.7
% Loan Loss Reserve	0.7	0.6	0.6	0.6	0.7	0.8	0.9	0.9	0.9	1.0
% Loans/Deposits	50.9	50.5	51.6	51.8	57.8	67.8	69.3	71.9	79.5	71.9
% Equity to Assets	6.3	6.6	6.6	7.0	7.3	7.3	7.0	6.6	6.8	6.8

Data as orig reptd.; bef. results of disc opers/spec. items. Per share data adj. for stk. divs.; EPS diluted. E-Estimated. NA-Not Available. NM-Not Meaningful. NR-Not Ranked. UR-Under Review.

Office: 50 S La Salle St, Chicago, IL 60603-1003.
Telephone: 312-630-6000.
Website: http://www.northerntrust.com
Chrmn, Pres & CEO: F.H. Waddell

EVP & Chief Admin Officer: T.P. Moen
EVP & CTO: N. Krishnamurthy
EVP, Chief Acctg Officer & Cntlr: A.B. Blake
EVP & Treas: W.R. Dodds, Jr.

Investor Contact: S.L. Fradkin
Board Members: L. W. Bynoe, N. D. Chabraja, S. M. Crown, D. Jain, A. L. Kelly, R. W. Lane, R. C. McCormack, E. J. Mooney, J. W. Rowe, H. B. Smith, W. D. Smithburg, E. J. Sosa, C. A. Tribbett, III, F. H. Waddell

Founded: 1889
Domicile: Delaware
Employees: 12,200

Northrop Grumman Corp

STANDARD &POOR'S

S&P Recommendation	HOLD ★★★☆☆	Price	12-Mo. Target Price	Investment Style
		$55.00 (as of Nov 27, 2009)	$53.00	Large-Cap Blend

GICS Sector Industrials
Sub-Industry Aerospace & Defense

Summary This company is the world's third largest producer of military arms and equipment, and also has a large government IT services business.

Key Stock Statistics (Source S&P, Vickers, company reports)

52-Wk Range	$56.46– 33.81	S&P Oper. EPS 2009**E**	5.14	Market Capitalization(B)	$17.256	Beta	1.01
Trailing 12-Month EPS	$-3.90	S&P Oper. EPS 2010**E**	5.45	Yield (%)	3.13	S&P 3-Yr. Proj. EPS CAGR(%)	0
Trailing 12-Month P/E	NM	P/E on S&P Oper. EPS 2009**E**	10.7	Dividend Rate/Share	$1.72	S&P Credit Rating	BBB+
$10K Invested 5 Yrs Ago	$10,982	Common Shares Outstg. (M)	313.8	Institutional Ownership (%)	90		

Price Performance

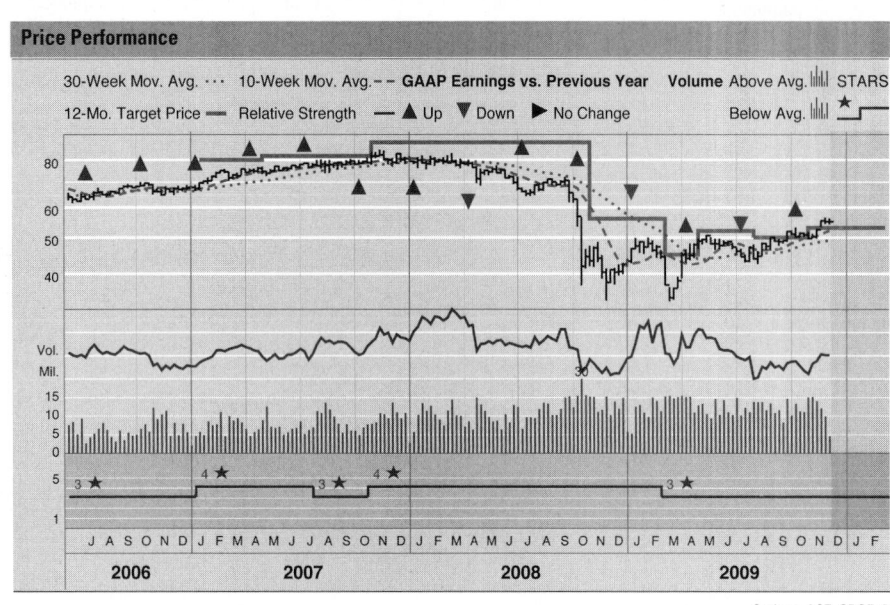

Options: ASE, CBOE, P

Analysis prepared by **Richard Tortoriello** on October 29, 2009, when the stock traded at **$ 50.58**.

Highlights

► We estimate revenue growth of about 3% in 2009, following a 7% increase in 2008. We expect growth across NOC's business segments in 2009, with the exception of Shipbuilding. We see particular growth in Technical Services and Electronic Systems. For 2010, we also project 3% growth, and expect improvement in Shipbuilding.

► We expect operating margins to deteriorate significantly in 2009 (excluding a goodwill impairment and another special write-down taken in 2008), due primarily to a large projected increase in pension expense. We estimate 2009 operating margins of 9.0%, versus 9.7% in 2008. However, we see the pension headwind abating somewhat in 2010, and project margins will rise to 9.4%.

► We project EPS of $5.14 in 2009, down from operating EPS of $5.84 in 2008, which excludes two large special charges, but we expect a rebound to $5.45 in 2010.

Investment Rationale/Risk

► NOC's funded backlog rose substantially in 2008, and remains elevated in 2009, in our view. We continue to expect long-term growth in Shipbuilding and Aerospace, led by the Virginia Class Submarine and various manned and unmanned aircraft programs. However, we expect a ballooning U.S. budget deficit, as well as shifting military priorities, will lead to cuts in large military programs over the long term. Along these lines, the fiscal 2010 defense budget proposes a slowing in production of several ship-building programs, including the Navy Aircraft Carrier program, for which NOC is the prime contractor.

► Risks to our recommendation and target price include the potential for large cuts in military budgets, and failure to perform well on existing contracts or to win new contracts.

► Our 12-month target price of $53 is based on an enterprise value to estimated 2009 EBITDA multiple of about 5X. This multiple is above a 10-year low of 4X, but below a 10-year average of 8X and a 20-year average near 9X. We believe the below average valuation is appropriate due to our view of flat to declining U.S. defense budgets going forward.

Qualitative Risk Assessment

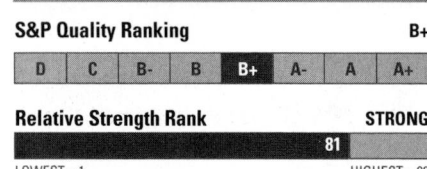

LOW	MEDIUM	HIGH

Our risk assessment reflects our view of NOC's typically strong levels of cash flow and a solid balance sheet with a relatively low level of debt. This is offset by the cyclical nature of the company's business, particularly its dependence on government defense programs.

Quantitative Evaluations

S&P Quality Ranking   B+

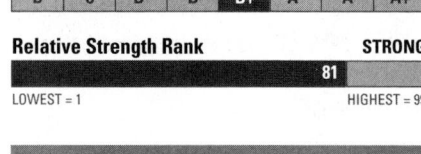

D	C	B-	B	B+	A-	A	A+

Relative Strength Rank   STRONG

81

LOWEST = 1   HIGHEST = 99

Revenue/Earnings Data

Revenue (Million $)

	1Q	2Q	3Q	4Q	Year
2009	8,320	8,957	8,726	--	--
2008	7,724	8,628	8,381	9,154	33,887
2007	7,340	7,926	7,928	8,824	32,018
2006	7,093	7,601	7,433	8,021	30,148
2005	7,453	7,962	7,446	7,860	30,721
2004	7,105	7,374	7,408	7,846	29,853

Earnings Per Share ($)

	1Q	2Q	3Q	4Q	Year
2009	1.17	1.21	1.52	E1.27	E5.14
2008	0.76	1.40	1.50	-7.76	-3.83
2007	1.11	1.33	1.41	1.32	5.16
2006	1.03	1.26	0.87	1.29	4.44
2005	1.08	1.00	0.80	0.92	3.81
2004	0.63	0.79	0.80	0.81	2.99

Fiscal year ended Dec. 31. Next earnings report expected: Early February. EPS Estimates based on S&P Operating Earnings; historical GAAP earnings are as reported.

Dividend Data (Dates: mm/dd Payment Date: mm/dd/yy)

Amount ($)	Date Decl.	Ex-Div. Date	Stk. of Record	Payment Date
0.400	02/18	02/26	03/02	03/14/09
0.430	05/20	05/28	06/01	06/13/09
0.430	07/16	08/27	08/31	09/12/09
0.430	10/19	11/25	11/30	12/12/09

Dividends have been paid since 1951. Source: Company reports.

Northrop Grumman Corp

STANDARD &POOR'S

Business Summary October 29, 2009

CORPORATE OVERVIEW. This $35 billion in estimated 2009 revenues defense electronics, aerospace, and warship-making giant, which operated through five reportable segments in 2008, conducts most of its business with the U.S. government, principally the Department of Defense. NOC also transacts with foreign governments and makes commercial sales both domestically and overseas. In January 2009, the company reorganized its reported business segments into five from a previous seven. The new segment structure is reported below.

The Information & Services (28% of 2008 revenue) provides products and services in the areas of command, control, communications, computers, and intelligence (C4I); missile and air defense; airborne reconnaissance; intelligence management and processing; decision support systems; information technology (IT) systems engineering; and systems integration. It consists of six areas of business: Command, Control and Communications (C3); Intelligence, Surveillance, and Reconnaissance (ISR); Intelligence; Civilian Agencies; Commercial, State & Local (CS&L); and Defense.

The Technical Services segment (7% of revenue) is a leading provider of logistics, infrastructure, and sustainment support, while also providing a wide array of technical services including training and simulation. It consists of three business areas: Systems Support (SSG); Training & Simulation (TSG); and Life Cycle Optimization & Engineering (LCOE).

The Aerospace Systems segment (28% of revenue) is a developer, integrator, producer, and supporter of manned and unmanned aircraft, spacecraft, high-energy laser systems, microelectronics and other systems and subsystems critical to maintaining the nation's security and leadership in science and technology. It consists of four business areas: Strike & Surveillance Systems (S&SS); Space Systems (SS); Battle Management & Engagement Systems (BM&ES); and Advanced Programs & Technology (AP&T).

Company Financials Fiscal Year Ended Dec. 31

Per Share Data ($)	2008	2007	2006	2005	2004	2003	2002	2001	2000	1999
Tangible Book Value	NM	NM	NM	NM	NM	NM	NM	NM	NM	NM
Cash Flow	-1.71	7.09	6.34	5.94	5.01	4.05	5.29	6.31	7.08	6.23
Earnings	-3.83	5.16	4.44	3.81	2.99	2.16	2.86	2.40	4.41	3.47
S&P Core Earnings	1.44	4.09	3.67	2.84	2.63	2.42	-0.95	-2.85	NA	NA
Dividends	1.57	1.48	1.16	1.01	0.89	0.80	0.80	0.80	0.80	0.80
Payout Ratio	NM	29%	26%	27%	30%	37%	28%	33%	18%	23%
Prices:High	83.40	85.21	71.37	60.26	58.15	50.55	67.50	55.28	46.94	37.97
Prices:Low	33.96	66.23	59.10	51.10	46.91	41.50	43.60	38.20	21.31	23.50
P/E Ratio:High	NM	17	16	16	19	23	24	23	11	11
P/E Ratio:Low	NM	13	13	13	16	19	15	16	5	7

Income Statement Analysis (Million $)										
Revenue	33,887	32,018	30,148	30,721	29,853	26,206	17,206	13,558	7,618	8,995
Operating Income	3,920	3,716	3,159	2,951	2,740	1,538	1,391	1,649	1,479	1,358
Depreciation	708	710	705	773	734	682	525	645	381	389
Interest Expense	295	336	347	388	431	497	422	373	175	224
Pretax Income	-368	2,686	2,276	2,044	1,615	1,131	1,009	699	975	762
Effective Tax Rate	NM	32.9%	31.2%	32.3%	32.3%	28.6%	30.9%	38.9%	35.9%	36.6%
Net Income	-1,281	1,803	1,567	1,383	1,093	808	697	427	625	483
S&P Core Earnings	481	1,426	1,288	1,026	961	892	-223	-487	NA	NA

Balance Sheet & Other Financial Data (Million $)										
Cash	1,504	963	1,015	1,605	1,230	342	1,412	464	319	142
Current Assets	7,189	6,772	6,719	7,549	6,907	5,745	15,835	4,589	2,526	2,793
Total Assets	30,197	33,373	32,009	34,214	33,361	33,009	42,266	20,886	9,622	9,285
Current Liabilities	7,424	6,432	6,753	7,974	6,223	6,361	11,373	5,132	2,688	2,464
Long Term Debt	3,443	4,268	3,992	3,881	5,116	5,410	9,398	5,033	1,605	2,000
Common Equity	11,920	17,687	16,615	16,825	16,970	15,785	14,322	7,391	3,919	3,257
Total Capital	15,363	22,285	20,957	21,651	22,942	22,067	24,209	13,443	5,800	5,321
Capital Expenditures	681	685	737	824	672	635	538	393	274	201
Cash Flow	-573	2,513	2,272	2,156	1,827	1,490	1,222	1,072	1,006	872
Current Ratio	1.0	1.1	1.0	0.9	1.1	0.9	1.4	0.9	0.9	1.1
% Long Term Debt of Capitalization	22.4	19.2	19.0	17.9	22.3	24.5	38.8	37.4	27.7	37.6
% Net Income of Revenue	NM	5.6	5.2	4.5	3.7	3.1	4.1	3.1	8.2	5.4
% Return on Assets	NM	5.5	4.7	4.1	3.3	2.1	2.2	2.8	6.6	5.1
% Return on Equity	NM	10.5	9.4	8.2	6.6	5.4	6.4	7.6	17.4	15.8

Data as orig reptd.; bef. results of disc opers/spec. items. Per share data adj. for stk. divs.; EPS diluted. E-Estimated. NA-Not Available. NM-Not Meaningful. NR-Not Ranked. UR-Under Review.

Office: 1840 Century Park E, Los Angeles, CA 90067-2199.
Telephone: 310-553-6262.
Email: investor_relations@mail.northgrum.com
Website: http://www.northropgrumman.com

Chrmn & CEO: R.D. Sugar
Pres & COO: W.G. Bush
CFO: J.F. Palmer
Chief Admin Officer: I.V. Ziskin

CTO: A.C. Livanos
Investor Contact: P. Gregory (310-201-1634)
Board Members: W. G. Bush, L. W. Coleman, T. B. Fargo, V. Fazio, D. E. Felsinger, S. E. Frank, B. S. Gordon, M. Kleiner, K. J. Krapek, R. B. Myers, A. L. Peters, K. W. Sharer, R. D. Sugar

Founded: 1939
Domicile: Delaware
Employees: 123,600

The McGraw-Hill Companies

Novell Inc

STANDARD &POOR'S

S&P Recommendation **HOLD** ★★★★★	Price $3.90 (as of Nov 27, 2009)	12-Mo. Target Price $5.00	Investment Style Large-Cap Blend

GICS Sector Information Technology
Sub-Industry Systems Software

Summary This company is a leading vendor of directory-enabled networking software, with its NetWare product line and Linux-based offerings.

Key Stock Statistics (Source S&P, Vickers, company reports)

52-Wk Range	$4.98– 2.97	S&P Oper. EPS 2009**E**	0.18	Market Capitalization(B)	$1.353	Beta	0.92
Trailing 12-Month EPS	$0.08	S&P Oper. EPS 2010**E**	0.21	Yield (%)	Nil	S&P 3-Yr. Proj. EPS CAGR(%)	5
Trailing 12-Month P/E	48.8	P/E on S&P Oper. EPS 2009**E**	21.7	Dividend Rate/Share	Nil	S&P Credit Rating	NA
$10K Invested 5 Yrs Ago	$6,446	Common Shares Outstg. (M)	346.8	Institutional Ownership (%)	69		

Price Performance

30-Week Mov. Avg. · · · · 10-Week Mov. Avg. - - - **GAAP Earnings vs. Previous Year** Volume Above Avg. STARS
12-Mo. Target Price — Relative Strength — ▲ Up ▼ Down ► No Change Below Avg. ★

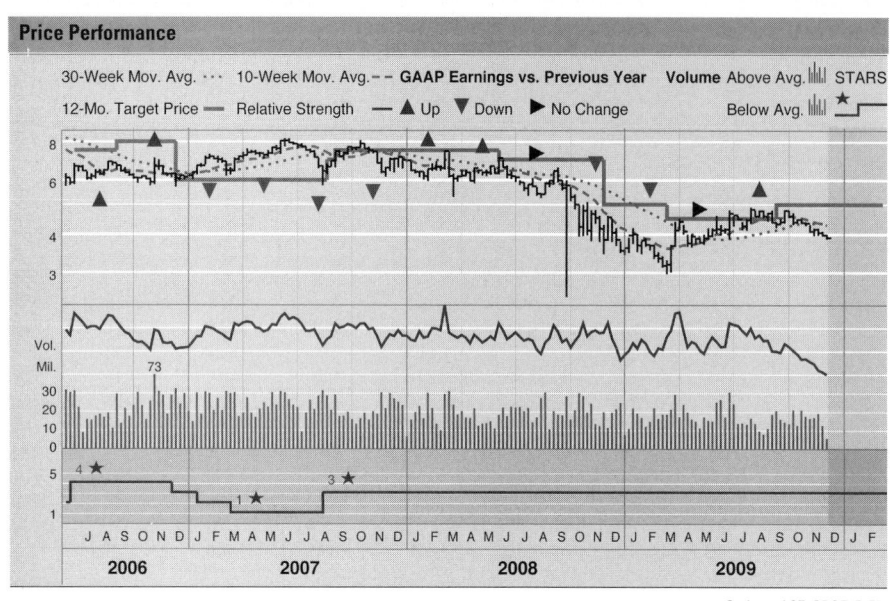

Options: ASE, CBOE, P, Ph

Analysis prepared by **Jim Yin** on September 01, 2009, when the stock traded at **$ 4.35**.

Highlights

► We estimate that total revenues will increase 0.7% in FY 10 (Oct.), following a 9.6% decline seen for FY 09. The expected increase in FY 10 reflects our view of an economic recovery in 2010, partially offset by continued weakness in NOVL's legacy products. We see a 20% rise in FY 10 open platform solutions revenue, as the company expands its presence in the Linux and open source software markets. NOVL should benefit from its partnership with Microsoft (MSFT 25, Hold), as many customers signed up for multi-year service agreements following the two companies' announced alliance.

► We expect gross margins in FY 10 to stay at 79%, the same percentage projected for FY 09. Total operating expenses should decrease as a result of further head count reductions and lower research and development expenses, partially offset by increased stock-based compensation. We see FY 10 operating margins widening to 13%, from 9.1% expected in FY 09.

► We estimate EPS of $0.21 in FY 10, compared to $0.18 seen in FY 09. The expected improvement reflects our view of better operating margins and a lower effective tax rate.

Investment Rationale/Risk

► Our hold recommendation reflects our concern about NOVL's ability to transform itself into a solutions provider in a mixed operating system environment through its NetWare business, which has been declining. We believe the company needs to continue developing solutions in areas such as system integration to counter increased competition from Red Hat (RHT 23, Sell) and Oracle (ORCL 22, Hold). However, the company has stabilized its NetWare product revenue and improved operating margins in recent quarters. We also believe NOVL's net cash and investments of $893 million, or about $2.58 per share, as of April 30, 2009, will lend some support to the share price.

► Risks to our opinion and target price include slower-than-expected growth in Linux products, lower-than-expected cost savings from cost-cutting initiatives, and a slowdown in the global economy.

► Our 12-month target price of $5 is based on an enterprise value/sales ratio of 1.0X, which is below the industry average of 2.1X. We believe this discount is appropriate in view of our projections for revenue and lower profitability than peers.

Qualitative Risk Assessment

LOW	MEDIUM	**HIGH**

Our risk assessment reflects the volatile market conditions in the Linux and open source software markets, the continuing decline in sales of NOVL's NetWare products, and our belief that NOVL is having difficulty gaining sufficient traction in Linux to offset the decrease in NetWare revenues.

Quantitative Evaluations

S&P Quality Ranking   C

D	**C**	B-	B	B+	A-	A	A+

Relative Strength Rank   **WEAK**

21

LOWEST = 1   HIGHEST = 99

Revenue/Earnings Data

Revenue (Million $)

	1Q	2Q	3Q	4Q	Year
2009	214.9	215.6	216.1	--	--
2008	230.9	235.7	245.2	244.7	956.5
2007	218.4	232.4	236.8	244.9	932.5
2006	274.4	278.3	241.4	244.9	967.3
2005	290.1	297.1	290.2	320.3	1,198
2004	267.1	293.6	304.6	300.7	1,166

Earnings Per Share ($)

	1Q	2Q	3Q	4Q	Year
2009	0.03	0.04	0.05	E0.05	E0.18
2008	0.04	0.04	-0.04	-0.05	-0.04
2007	-0.04	Nil	-0.04	-0.03	-0.08
2006	Nil	0.01	0.03	0.06	0.02
2005	0.90	-0.04	Nil	-0.01	0.86
2004	0.03	-0.04	0.06	0.03	0.08

Fiscal year ended Oct. 31. Next earnings report expected: Early December. EPS Estimates based on S&P Operating Earnings; historical GAAP earnings are as reported.

Dividend Data

No cash dividends have been paid.

Please read the Required Disclosures and Analyst Certification on the last page of this report.

Novell Inc

Business Summary September 01, 2009

CORPORATE OVERVIEW. Novell Inc. (NOVL) is a provider of software and services that help customers manage their information technology infrastructure. The company's legacy products are based on its proprietary network operating system, NetWare. Sales of NetWare have been declining, and IDC, an independent market research firm, expects NetWare revenue to decrease at a 32% CAGR (compound annual growth rate) from 2006 through 2011.

In the past few years, NOVL has embraced and promoted Linux and open source computing. The company is the second largest provider of Linux operating systems and subsystems, capturing 29% of the market by revenue in 2007 according to IDC, up from 21% in 2004. As a result of increased use of open source software in enterprise applications, NOVL has repositioned the company as a solution provider in a mixed operating system environment that includes open source and proprietary technologies, thus reducing reliance on its legacy products, such as NetWare.

NOVL reorganized into four product-related business units and a consulting unit. The four business unit segments are open platform solutions, which encompasses SUSE Linux operating system; identity and security management,

which helps to provide secured logon and protect information assets; systems and resource management, which includes software to manage multiple infrastructure resources in a virtual environment; and workgroup, which helps customers to collaborate across the enterprise.

CORPORATE STRATEGY. NOVL relies on a series of alliances and partnerships to drive sales growth; its partners include IBM, HP, Dell, Intel, Oracle, SAP, AMD, CA, EMC and Adobe. NOVL believes it has created an ecosystem around it to combine its strengths with those of its partners; however, these partners are also counted among the strategic partners of many other software firms, and we doubt the partnerships provide a significant competitive advantage. In addition, NOVL's go-to market strategy embraces both a direct and indirect sales channel, with the indirect channel including independent distributors, value-added resellers, systems integrators and hardware OEMs.

Company Financials Fiscal Year Ended Oct. 31

Per Share Data ($)	2008	2007	2006	2005	2004	2003	2002	2001	2000	1999
Tangible Book Value	1.32	2.05	1.86	2.42	1.39	1.89	2.31	2.98	3.80	4.57
Cash Flow	0.08	0.04	0.15	0.98	0.22	-0.27	-0.09	-0.53	0.39	0.75
Earnings	-0.04	-0.08	0.02	0.86	0.08	-0.44	-0.28	-0.79	0.15	0.55
S&P Core Earnings	0.01	-0.09	-0.02	-0.11	-0.07	-0.45	-0.47	-1.27	NA	NA
Dividends	Nil	Nil	Nil	Nil	Nil	Nil	Nil	Nil	Nil	Nil
Payout Ratio	Nil	Nil	Nil	Nil	Nil	Nil	Nil	Nil	Nil	Nil
Prices:High	7.59	8.26	9.83	9.27	14.24	10.77	5.64	9.13	44.56	41.19
Prices:Low	2.49	5.76	5.70	4.94	5.62	2.14	1.57	2.96	4.88	16.06
P/E Ratio:High	NM	NM	NM	11	NM	NM	NM	NM	NM	75
P/E Ratio:Low	NM	NM	NM	6	NM	NM	NM	NM	33	29

Income Statement Analysis (Million $)										
Revenue	957	933	967	1,198	1,166	1,105	1,134	1,040	1,162	1,273
Operating Income	90.7	30.4	27.8	99.3	140	52.3	103	46.1	98.2	293
Depreciation	40.4	40.4	47.0	56.3	53.5	61.1	68.8	86.7	81.9	70.2
Interest Expense	23.4	25.9	8.02	9.63	Nil	Nil	Nil	Nil	Nil	Nil
Pretax Income	22.9	8.40	30.9	466	75.0	-55.0	-92.2	-277	70.7	244
Effective Tax Rate	153.9%	NM	75.3%	19.2%	23.7%	NM	NM	NM	30.0%	21.8%
Net Income	-12.3	-26.3	7.63	377	57.2	-162	-103	-262	49.5	191
S&P Core Earnings	3.64	-29.5	-8.34	-52.6	-30.8	-167	-172	-384	NA	NA

Balance Sheet & Other Financial Data (Million $)										
Cash	1,068	1,080	676	811	434	752	636	705	698	895
Current Assets	1,386	2,154	1,761	2,009	1,535	1,031	920	1,027	1,007	1,336
Total Assets	2,269	2,854	2,450	2,762	2,292	1,568	1,665	1,904	1,712	1,942
Current Liabilities	900	822	686	753	693	626	592	611	455	440
Long Term Debt	4.00	600	600	600	600	Nil	Nil	Nil	Nil	Nil
Common Equity	1,088	1,158	1,105	1,386	963	934	1,066	1,271	1,245	1,492
Total Capital	1,218	1,758	1,718	2,004	1,599	941	1,074	1,293	1,257	1,503
Capital Expenditures	37.7	25.2	26.7	30.8	27.0	39.5	27.6	33.3	57.8	69.2
Cash Flow	28.1	14.1	54.6	433	84.6	-101	-34.3	-175	131	261
Current Ratio	1.5	2.6	2.6	2.7	2.2	1.6	1.6	1.7	2.2	3.0
% Long Term Debt of Capitalization	0.4	34.1	34.9	29.9	37.5	Nil	Nil	Nil	Nil	Nil
% Net Income of Revenue	NM	NM	0.8	31.5	4.9	NM	NM	NM	4.3	15.0
% Return on Assets	NM	NM	0.3	14.9	3.0	NM	NM	NM	2.7	9.9
% Return on Equity	NM	NM	0.6	32.1	3.3	NM	NM	NM	3.6	12.8

Data as orig reptd.; bef. results of disc opers/spec. items. Per share data adj. for stk. divs.; EPS diluted. E-Estimated. NA-Not Available. NM-Not Meaningful. NR-Not Ranked. UR-Under Review.

Office: 404 Wyman St Ste 500, Waltham, MA 02451-1212.
Telephone: 781-464-8000.
Website: http://www.novell.com
Chrmn: R.L. Crandall

Pres & CEO: R.W. Hovsepian
EVP & CTO: J. Jaffe
SVP, CFO, Chief Acctg Officer & Cntlr: D.C. Russell
SVP, Secy & General Counsel: S.N. Semel

Investor Contact: E.M. Hennessy (781-464-8553)
Board Members: A. Aiello, Jr., F. Corrado, R. L. Crandall, G. G. Greenfield, J. H. Hamilton, R. W. Hovsepian, P. Jones, C. B. Malone, R. L. Nolan, T. G. Plaskett, J. W. Poduska, K. B. White

Founded: 1983
Domicile: Delaware
Employees: 4,000

Novellus Systems Inc

STANDARD
&POOR'S

S&P Recommendation **BUY** ★★★★☆	Price $20.72 (as of Nov 27, 2009)	12-Mo. Target Price $26.00	Investment Style Large-Cap Growth

GICS Sector Information Technology
Sub-Industry Semiconductor Equipment

Summary This company manufactures, markets, and services automated wafer fabrication systems for the deposition of thin films.

Key Stock Statistics (Source S&P, Vickers, company reports)

52-Wk Range	$23.17–11.20	S&P Oper. EPS 2009**E**	-0.57	Market Capitalization(B)	$2.010	Beta	1.39
Trailing 12-Month EPS	$-2.60	S&P Oper. EPS 2010**E**	1.25	Yield (%)	Nil	S&P 3-Yr. Proj. EPS CAGR(%)	NM
Trailing 12-Month P/E	NM	P/E on S&P Oper. EPS 2009**E**	NM	Dividend Rate/Share	Nil	S&P Credit Rating	NA
$10K Invested 5 Yrs Ago	$7,397	Common Shares Outstg. (M)	97.0	Institutional Ownership (%)	86		

Price Performance

30-Week Mov. Avg. · · · 10-Week Mov. Avg. — — **GAAP Earnings vs. Previous Year** Volume Above Avg. STARS
12-Mo. Target Price — Relative Strength — ▲ Up ▼ Down ► No Change Below Avg.

Options: ASE, CBOE, P, Ph

Analysis prepared by **Angelo Zino** on November 20, 2009, when the stock traded at **$ 20.89**.

Highlights

► We anticipate sales rebounding 62% in 2010 following our projection for a 38% decline in 2009, as we see industry conditions improving. We believe that memory supply and demand balance has improved, and think rising memory prices and stabilizing customer sales may result in an increase in advanced technology spending by some customers. We believe NVLS's recent surge in bookings is primarily due to rising foundry orders and transition to DDR3 technology and currently foresee a boost in NAND flash memory spending by late 2010.

► We look for annual gross margins of 38% in 2009 and 47% in 2010. Going forward, we expect the gross margin to expand, driven by higher system sales from low levels and benefits from cost-cutting efforts. We expect NVLS to keep quarterly operating expenses below $80 million at a revenue level below $250 million; at levels above that we expect operating expenses to run at about 28% to 33% of sales.

► We see an operating loss per share of $0.57 in 2009, excluding $0.34 from non-recurring charges, and EPS of $1.25 in 2010. NVLS believes it can achieve $1.2 billion in sales and $2.00 in EPS in 2011.

Investment Rationale/Risk

► Our buy recommendation reflects valuation and expectations for industry conditions to continue to recover, as we see foundries and memory customers now looking to spend on advanced technology purchases. We positively view steep cost cutting efforts and NVLS's plan to close its Oregon facility. As business conditions and customer utilization rates improve, we expect some customers to start investing in capacity expansion. We think production cuts by memory makers have helped reduce excess capacity and have led to a more favorable pricing environment. We see rational investing from memory customers but expect sales within its industrial segment to remain sluggish.

► Risks to our recommendation and target price include a longer-than-expected semiconductor equipment downturn, weaker-than-projected global economic growth, and higher-than-expected R&D expense growth.

► We apply a price-to-sales multiple of 2.5X, below peers, to our 2010 sales per share estimate of $10.50 to arrive at our 12-month target price of $26. We calculate that large front-end semiconductor equipment manufacturers recently traded at a 2010 P/S ratio of 2.6X.

Qualitative Risk Assessment

LOW	MEDIUM	**HIGH**

Our risk assessment reflects the historical cyclicality of the semiconductor equipment industry, the lack of visibility in the medium term, the dynamic nature of semiconductor technology, and intense competition. We believe these risks are partially offset by our view of the company's strong market position, size, and financial condition.

Quantitative Evaluations

S&P Quality Ranking B-

D	C	**B-**	B	B+	A-	A	A+

Relative Strength Rank MODERATE

52

LOWEST = 1   HIGHEST = 99

Revenue/Earnings Data

Revenue (Million $)

	1Q	2Q	3Q	4Q	Year
2009	98.91	119.2	176.9	--	--
2008	314.7	257.7	250.1	188.5	1,011
2007	397.0	416.3	393.3	363.5	1,570
2006	365.9	410.1	444.0	438.5	1,659
2005	339.7	329.6	338.9	332.3	1,340
2004	262.9	338.2	415.9	340.3	1,357

Earnings Per Share ($)

2009	-0.69	-0.52	-0.04	E0.34	E-0.57
2008	0.15	-0.02	0.01	-1.36	-1.18
2007	0.42	0.45	0.41	0.47	1.75
2006	0.18	0.42	0.57	0.34	1.49
2005	0.22	0.24	0.17	0.17	0.80
2004	0.11	0.25	0.45	0.27	1.06

Fiscal year ended Dec. 31. Next earnings report expected: Early February. EPS Estimates based on S&P Operating Earnings; historical GAAP earnings are as reported.

Dividend Data

No cash dividends have been paid.

Novellus Systems Inc

STANDARD &POOR'S

Business Summary November 20, 2009

CORPORATE OVERVIEW. Novellus is the second largest maker of deposition equipment used to deposit conductive and insulating layers on semiconductor wafers to form integrated circuits (ICs). The company entered the market for wafer surface preparation equipment in 2001. NVLS also entered the chemical mechanical planarization (CMP) equipment market in 2002. These two types of equipment are complementary to deposition equipment.

NVLS's product line of deposition equipment includes chemical vapor deposition (CVD), physical vapor deposition (PVD) and electrochemical deposition (ECD), all of which are used to form the layers of wiring and insulation, known as the interconnect, of ICs. High-density plasma CVD (HDP) and plasma-enhanced CVD (PECVD) systems employ chemical plasma to deposit all of the insulating layers and some of the conductive layers on the surface of a wafer. PVD systems deposit conductive layers through a process known as sputtering, where ions of an inert gas such as argon are electrically accelerated in a high vacuum toward a target of pure metal, such as tantalum or copper. ECD systems are used to build the copper conductive layers on wafers.

Although NVLS's original tool sets established it as a leader in CVD, the company has centered its product strategy on the emergence of the copper inter-connect market. Copper has lower resistance and capacitance values than aluminum, the conductive metal generally used in ICs, offering increased speed and decreased chip size. The company's SABRE tool offers a complete solution for the deposition of copper interconnects and holds the leading market share in copper.

Surface preparation products, including photoresist strip and clean, are becoming more important with the industry's migration to copper interconnects. Surface preparation systems remove photoresist and other potential contaminants from a wafer before proceeding with the next deposition step. CMP systems polish the surface of a wafer after a deposition step to create a flat topography before moving on to subsequent manufacturing steps. Since copper is more difficult to polish and smooth than previous generation aluminum interconnects, and low-k dielectrics are much more porous than predecessors, NVLS's products in this category have become very important, in our view.

Company Financials Fiscal Year Ended Dec. 31

Per Share Data ($)	2008	2007	2006	2005	2004	2003	2002	2001	2000	1999
Tangible Book Value	11.73	11.98	12.54	11.29	11.06	12.42	12.69	13.04	11.49	6.47
Cash Flow	-0.53	2.30	2.05	1.39	1.66	0.43	0.45	1.32	2.04	0.89
Earnings	-1.18	1.75	1.49	0.80	1.06	-0.03	0.15	0.97	1.75	0.64
S&P Core Earnings	-0.11	1.71	1.47	0.43	0.74	-0.42	-0.33	0.52	NA	NA
Dividends	Nil	Nil	Nil	Nil	Nil	Nil	Nil	Nil	Nil	Nil
Payout Ratio	Nil	Nil	Nil	Nil	Nil	Nil	Nil	Nil	Nil	Nil
Prices:High	27.66	34.97	35.00	30.77	44.52	45.50	54.48	58.70	70.25	42.79
Prices:Low	10.26	25.40	22.28	20.83	22.89	24.93	19.40	25.37	24.94	14.96
P/E Ratio:High	NM	20	23	38	42	NM	NM	61	40	67
P/E Ratio:Low	NM	15	15	26	22	NM	NM	26	14	23

Income Statement Analysis (Million $)										
Revenue	1,011	1,570	1,659	1,340	1,357	925	840	1,339	1,174	593
Operating Income	81.1	329	388	228	308	56.5	46.3	273	328	130
Depreciation	63.3	66.9	69.7	82.8	89.3	69.6	44.3	51.9	40.1	29.8
Interest Expense	7.02	6.38	4.29	3.51	2.13	0.91	1.02	1.15	2.34	1.70
Pretax Income	-107	315	339	159	223	-15.3	22.9	209	342	114
Effective Tax Rate	NM	32.1%	44.2%	30.6%	29.8%	NM	NM	31.0%	31.0%	33.0%
Net Income	-116	214	189	110	157	-5.03	22.9	144	236	76.6
S&P Core Earnings	-10.0	209	186	59.8	108	-67.2	-50.7	81.6	NA	NA

Balance Sheet & Other Financial Data (Million $)										
Cash	471	593	58.5	649	106	497	616	551	571	182
Current Assets	1,043	1,224	1,505	1,364	1,369	1,572	1,634	2,517	1,827	733
Total Assets	1,638	2,077	2,362	2,290	2,402	2,339	2,494	3,010	2,015	910
Current Liabilities	305	329	361	344	324	221	382	1,138	505	140
Long Term Debt	Nil	143	128	125	161	Nil	Nil	Nil	Nil	Nil
Common Equity	1,247	1,529	1,835	1,779	1,862	2,072	2,056	1,872	1,511	770
Total Capital	1,248	1,700	1,963	1,904	2,023	2,072	2,075	1,872	1,511	770
Capital Expenditures	17.9	33.2	39.4	44.7	31.7	31.1	26.8	80.0	68.5	28.8
Cash Flow	-52.4	281	259	193	246	64.5	67.2	196	276	106
Current Ratio	3.4	3.7	4.2	4.0	4.2	7.1	4.3	2.2	3.6	5.2
% Long Term Debt of Capitalization	Nil	8.4	6.5	6.6	8.0	Nil	Nil	Nil	Nil	Nil
% Net Income of Revenue	NM	13.6	11.4	8.2	11.5	NM	2.7	10.8	20.1	12.9
% Return on Assets	NM	9.6	8.1	4.7	6.6	NM	0.8	5.5	16.1	10.5
% Return on Equity	NM	12.7	10.5	6.0	8.0	NM	1.2	8.2	20.7	13.4

Data as orig reptd.; bef. results of disc opers/spec. items. Per share data adj. for stk. divs.; EPS diluted. E-Estimated. NA-Not Available. NM-Not Meaningful. NR-Not Ranked. UR-Under Review.

Office: 4000 North First Street, San Jose, CA 95134-1568.
Telephone: 408-943-9700.
Email: info@novellus.com
Website: http://www.novellus.com

Chrmn & CEO: R. Hill
COO: G. Addiego
EVP, CFO & Chief Admin Officer: J.C. Benzing
EVP & CTO: F.E. Chen

SVP, Secy & General Counsel: M.J. Collins
Investor Contact: R. Yim (408-943-9700)
Board Members: N. R. Bonke, Y. A. El-Mansy, R. Hill, J. D. Litster, Y. Nishi, G. G. Possley, A. D. Rhoads, W. R. Spivey, J. D. Ulster, D. A. Whitaker

Founded: 1984
Domicile: California
Employees: 3,048

The McGraw-Hill Companies

Nucor Corp

STANDARD &POOR'S

S&P Recommendation HOLD ★★★☆☆	Price $41.81 (as of Nov 27, 2009)	12-Mo. Target Price $49.00	Investment Style Large-Cap Blend

GICS Sector Materials
Sub-Industry Steel

Summary As the largest minimill steelmaker in the U.S., Nucor has one of the most diverse product lines of any steelmaker in the Americas.

Key Stock Statistics (Source S&P, Vickers, company reports)

52-Wk Range	$51.08– 29.84	S&P Oper. EPS 2009E	-1.13	Market Capitalization(B)	$13.162	Beta		1.20
Trailing 12-Month EPS	$-0.77	S&P Oper. EPS 2010E	3.39	Yield (%)	3.35	S&P 3-Yr. Proj. EPS CAGR(%)		-3
Trailing 12-Month P/E	NM	P/E on S&P Oper. EPS 2009E	NM	Dividend Rate/Share	$1.40	S&P Credit Rating		A
$10K Invested 5 Yrs Ago	$18,387	Common Shares Outstg. (M)	314.8	Institutional Ownership (%)	79			

Price Performance

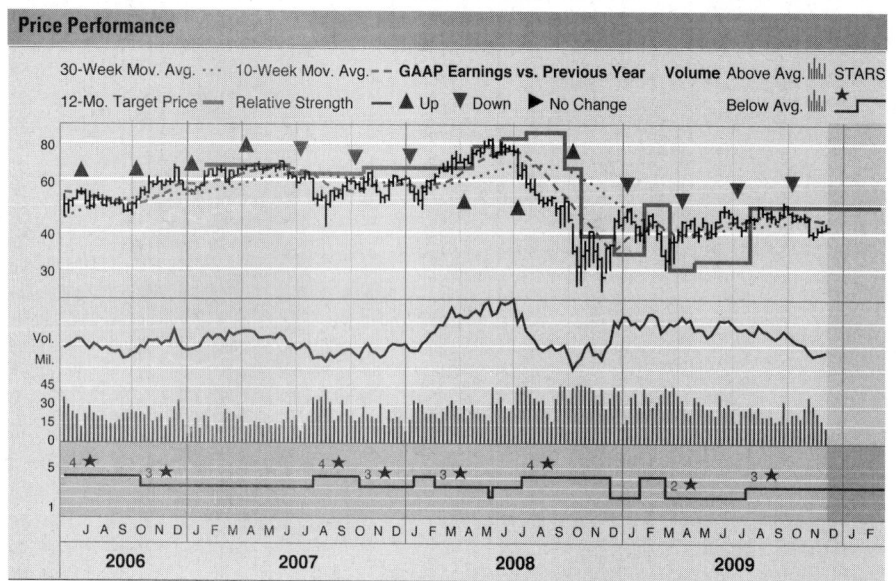

30-Week Mov. Avg. · · · 10-Week Mov. Avg. – – **GAAP Earnings vs. Previous Year** Volume Above Avg. STARS
12-Mo. Target Price — Relative Strength — ▲ Up ▼ Down ► No Change Below Avg. ★

Options: ASE, CBOE, P, Ph

Analysis prepared by **Leo J. Larkin** on October 23, 2009, when the stock traded at **$ 44.30.**

Highlights

► Following a projected decline of 53% in 2009, we look for a 29% sales rise in 2010 on a rebound in shipment volume and prices. Our projections rest on several assumptions. First, S&P forecasts 1.8% GDP growth in 2010, versus a 2.7% decline in GDP estimated for 2009. Second, S&P expects an 17.8% decline in non-residential construction spending, versus projected drop of 19.5% forecasted for 2009. We see this easing downward pressure on sales of structural steel products for construction markets as well as sales of fabricated building products. Third, after destocking for most of 2009, we believe that distributors will rebuild inventories in 2010, leading to better demand for most steel products. Lastly, a projected upturn in domestic steel production will lift sales of scrap products.

► We expect margin recovery on higher volume, increased prices, and moderation of input costs. After interest expense and taxes, we project EPS of $3.39 in 2010, versus a per share loss of $1.13 estimated for 2009.

► Longer term, we see EPS rising on industry consolidation, acquisitions, and better control of raw material costs.

Investment Rationale/Risk

► We see Nucor's long-term EPS rising on the consolidation of the global steel industry. With the industry becoming more consolidated, a greater concentration of production among fewer companies should result in greater pricing power and more production discipline. In turn, this should result in generally less volatile sales and EPS over the business cycle. Also, we see EPS rising on better raw material cost control and a gradually improving mix. Higher EPS should enable NUE to generate enough free cash flow to buy back shares, increase the dividend, and make acquisitions. Thanks to disciplined working capital management, Nucor was free cash flow positive in 2009's first nine months despite posting a net loss.

► Risks to our opinion and target price include the possibility that steel and scrap prices will decline in 2010 instead of rise as we project.

► Our 12-month target price of $49 is based on our view that the shares will trade at a P/E of 14.5X our 2010 EPS estimate. On this projected multiple, NUE would trade at a small premium to the P/E we apply to peers. We believe NUE warrants a premium given what we view as its stronger balance sheet vis-a-vis rivals.

Qualitative Risk Assessment

LOW	MEDIUM	HIGH

Our risk assessment reflects that despite Nucor's exposure to cyclical markets such as non-residential construction, the company has a solid share of the markets in which it competes, a very low ratio of total debt to assets, and a very diverse product mix.

Quantitative Evaluations

S&P Quality Ranking B

D	C	B-	B	B+	A-	A	A+

Relative Strength Rank MODERATE

34

LOWEST = 1   HIGHEST = 99

Revenue/Earnings Data

Revenue (Million $)

	1Q	2Q	3Q	4Q	Year
2009	2,654	2,478	3,120	--	--
2008	4,974	7,091	7,448	4,151	23,663
2007	3,769	4,168	4,259	4,397	16,593
2006	3,545	3,806	3,931	3,469	14,751
2005	3,323	3,145	3,026	3,207	12,701
2004	2,286	2,762	3,240	3,089	11,376

Earnings Per Share ($)

2009	-0.60	-0.42	-0.10	E-0.01	E-1.13
2008	1.41	1.94	2.31	0.34	5.98
2007	1.26	1.14	1.29	1.26	4.94
2006	1.21	1.45	1.68	1.35	5.68
2005	1.10	1.02	0.93	1.09	4.13
2004	0.36	0.79	1.30	1.06	3.51

Fiscal year ended Dec. 31. Next earnings report expected: Early December. EPS Estimates based on S&P Operating Earnings; historical GAAP earnings are as reported.

Dividend Data (Dates: mm/dd Payment Date: mm/dd/yy)

Amount ($)	Date Decl.	Ex-Div. Date	Stk. of Record	Payment Date
0.350	12/09	12/29	12/31	02/11/09
0.350	02/18	03/27	03/31	05/12/09
0.350	06/02	06/26	06/30	08/11/09
0.350	09/03	09/28	09/30	11/11/09

Dividends have been paid since 1973. Source: Company reports.

Please read the Required Disclosures and Analyst Certification on the last page of this report.

The McGraw·Hill Companies

Nucor Corp

Business Summary October 23, 2009

CORPORATE OVERVIEW. Nucor is the largest U.S. minimill steelmaker. In 2008, production was 20.4 million tons, and outside shipments were 18.2 million tons.

CORPORATE STRATEGY. Nucor's growth strategy involves four initiatives. The first is to optimize existing operations. The second is to make strategic acquisitions. The third involves construction of new plants and development of new technologies for markets where the company believes it has a major cost advantage. The fourth initiative is to expand globally through joint ventures that leverage new technologies.

MARKET PROFILE. The primary factors affecting demand for steel products are economic growth in general and growth in demand for durable goods in particular. The two largest end markets for steel products in the U.S. are autos and construction. In 2008, these two markets accounted for 35% of shipments in the U.S. market. Other end markets include appliances, containers, machinery, and oil and gas. Distributors, also known as service centers, ac-

counted for 25% of industry shipments in the U.S. market in 2008. Distributors are the largest single market for the steel industry in the U.S. Because distributors sell to a wide variety of OEMs, it is impossible to trace the final destination of much of the industry's shipments. Consequently, demand for steel from the auto, construction and other industries may be higher than the shipment data would suggest. Construction accounts for some 60% of the demand for Nucor's products, oil and gas 15%, autos and appliances 15%, and other markets 10%. In terms of production, the size of the U.S. market was 100.7 million tons in 2008, and Nucor's market share was 20.4%. In the U.S. market, consumption decreased at a compound annual growth rate (CAGR) of 1.8% from 1999 through 2008. Global steel production was 1.33 billion metric tons in 2008. Consumption grew at a CAGR of 6.4% from 1998 through 2007.

Company Financials Fiscal Year Ended Dec. 31

Per Share Data ($)	2008	2007	2006	2005	2004	2003	2002	2001	2000	1999
Tangible Book Value	16.72	13.18	15.56	13.80	10.84	7.45	7.43	7.07	6.87	6.49
Cash Flow	7.78	6.38	7.05	5.43	4.72	1.36	1.50	1.29	1.74	1.44
Earnings	5.98	4.94	5.68	4.13	3.51	0.20	0.52	0.36	0.95	0.70
S&P Core Earnings	6.19	4.94	5.68	4.09	3.49	0.15	0.46	0.33	NA	NA
Dividends	NA	0.63	0.40	0.30	0.24	0.20	0.19	0.17	0.15	0.13
Payout Ratio	9%	13%	7%	7%	7%	100%	37%	47%	16%	18%
Prices:High	83.56	69.93	67.55	35.11	27.74	14.70	17.54	14.13	14.11	15.45
Prices:Low	25.25	41.62	33.63	22.78	13.04	8.76	9.00	8.36	7.38	10.41
P/E Ratio:High	14	14	12	9	8	73	34	39	15	22
P/E Ratio:Low	4	8	6	6	4	44	17	23	8	15

Income Statement Analysis (Million $)	2008	2007	2006	2005	2004	2003	2002	2001	2000	1999
Revenue	23,663	16,593	14,751	12,701	11,377	6,266	4,802	4,139	4,586	4,009
Operating Income	3,849	2,980	3,240	2,497	2,216	468	601	469	737	631
Depreciation	549	428	364	375	383	364	307	289	259	257
Interest Expense	135	51.1	Nil	4.20	22.4	24.6	22.9	22.0	24.1	20.5
Pretax Income	3,104	2,547	2,913	2,127	1,812	90.8	310	174	478	379
Effective Tax Rate	30.9%	30.7%	32.1%	33.2%	33.6%	4.51%	22.0%	35.0%	35.0%	35.5%
Net Income	1,831	1,472	1,758	1,310	1,121	62.8	162	113	311	245
S&P Core Earnings	1,895	1,472	1,758	1,296	1,114	47.9	143	101	NA	NA

Balance Sheet & Other Financial Data (Million $)	2008	2007	2006	2005	2004	2003	2002	2001	2000	1999
Cash	2,355	1,576	786	1,838	779	350	219	462	491	572
Current Assets	6,397	5,073	4,675	4,072	3,175	1,621	1,424	1,374	1,381	1,539
Total Assets	13,874	9,826	7,885	7,139	6,133	4,492	4,381	3,759	3,722	3,730
Current Liabilities	1,854	1,582	1,450	1,256	1,066	630	592	484	558	531
Long Term Debt	3,086	2,250	922	922	924	904	879	460	460	390
Common Equity	7,929	5,113	4,826	4,280	3,456	2,342	2,323	2,201	2,131	2,262
Total Capital	11,523	7,651	5,987	5,396	4,553	3,423	3,419	2,946	2,904	2,934
Capital Expenditures	1,019	520	338	331	286	215	244	261	415	375
Cash Flow	2,380	1,900	2,122	1,685	1,505	427	469	402	570	501
Current Ratio	3.5	3.2	3.2	3.2	3.0	2.6	2.4	2.8	2.5	2.9
% Long Term Debt of Capitalization	26.8	29.4	15.4	17.1	20.3	26.4	25.7	15.6	15.9	13.3
% Net Income of Revenue	7.7	8.9	11.9	10.3	9.9	1.0	3.4	2.7	6.8	6.1
% Return on Assets	15.5	16.6	23.4	19.7	21.1	1.4	4.0	3.0	8.3	7.0
% Return on Equity	28.1	29.6	38.6	33.9	38.7	2.7	5.1	5.2	14.2	11.3

Data as orig reptd.; bef. results of disc opers/spec. items. Per share data adj. for stk. divs.; EPS diluted. E-Estimated. NA-Not Available. NM-Not Meaningful. NR-Not Ranked. UR-Under Review.

Office: 1915 Rexford Rd, Charlotte, NC 28211-3441.
Telephone: 704-366-7000.
Email: info@nucor.com
Website: http://www.nucor.com

Chrmn, Pres & CEO: D.R. DiMicco
COO: J.J. Ferriola
EVP, CFO & Treas: T.S. Lisenby
Secy: A.R. Eagle

Cntlr: J.D. Frias
Board Members: P. C. Browning, C. C. Daley, Jr., D. R. DiMicco, H. B. Gantt, V. F. Haynes, J. D. Hlavacek, B. L. Kasriel, C. J. Kearney, J. H. Walker

Founded: 1940
Domicile: Delaware
Employees: 21,700

NVIDIA Corp

STANDARD &POOR'S

S&P Recommendation HOLD ★★★☆☆

Price	12-Mo. Target Price	Investment Style
$12.79 (as of Nov 27, 2009)	$16.00	Large-Cap Growth

GICS Sector Information Technology
Sub-Industry Semiconductors

Summary This company develops and markets 3D graphics processors for personal computers, workstations and digital entertainment platforms.

Key Stock Statistics (Source S&P, Vickers, company reports)

52-Wk Range	$16.58–6.74	S&P Oper. EPS 2010**E**	-0.23	Market Capitalization(B)	$7.097	Beta	1.77
Trailing 12-Month EPS	$-0.64	S&P Oper. EPS 2011**E**	0.57	Yield (%)	Nil	S&P 3-Yr. Proj. EPS CAGR(%)	NM
Trailing 12-Month P/E	NM	P/E on S&P Oper. EPS 2010**E**	NM	Dividend Rate/Share	Nil	S&P Credit Rating	NR
$10K Invested 5 Yrs Ago	$19,320	Common Shares Outstg. (M)	554.9	Institutional Ownership (%)	84		

Price Performance

30-Week Mov. Avg. · · ·   10-Week Mov. Avg. – – **GAAP Earnings vs. Previous Year**   Volume Above Avg. STARS
12-Mo. Target Price —   Relative Strength —   ▲ Up ▼ Down ▶ No Change   Below Avg. ★

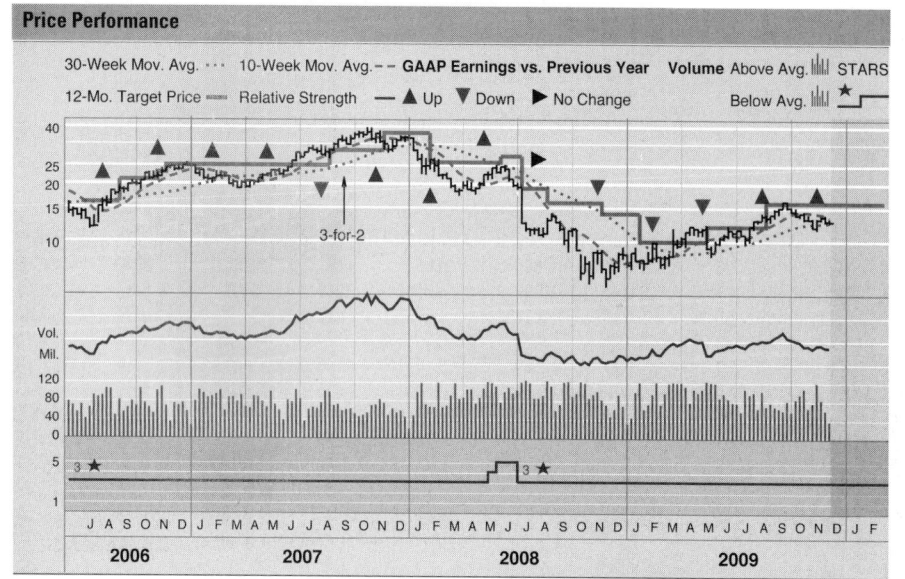

Options: ASE, CBOE, P, Ph

Analysis prepared by **Clyde Montevirgen** on November 10, 2009, when the stock traded at **$ 13.03.**

Highlights

▶ We see FY 10 (Jan.) sales down 5%, after a 16% drop in FY 09. Although we think long-term drivers, such as the growth of graphics-intensive applications, remain intact, we see near-term results limited by slow computer growth. We are also concerned about slowing sales of desktop computers as laptops gain popularity. But with our view of NVDA's strong brand recognition and technologically leading higher-end products, we think it will gain market share in various graphics related markets.

▶ We believe gross margins will widen to the 40% range over the next few quarters, as older inventory sells off and as workstation product orders recover. Various impairments and charges contributed to weak operating margins early in the fiscal year, but we expect them to expand as sales increase and gross margins improve. All told, we see an FY 10 operating margin of around -5%, versus -2% for FY 09.

▶ We see a per share loss of $0.23 (operating EPS of $0.15, excluding non-recurring charges related to the tender offer to buy out stock options) for FY 10, compared to a $0.05 loss for FY 09.

Investment Rationale/Risk

▶ Our hold recommendation reflects our view of weak profitability balanced by fair valuations, and a strong balance sheet. NVIDIA has become a market share leader due to its favorable brand awareness among gamers, strong computer growth, and increasing graphics intensity in applications. We think NVDA's quality products will help it take share in high-end markets that use graphics-intensive applications. However, we see margins remaining at low levels over the next couple of quarters because of a less favorable sales mix, slowing demand for desktop computers, and upcoming releases of innovative graphics products from formidable competitors.

▶ Risks to our opinion and target price include worse than anticipated desktop sales, slower than expected inventory digestion, and market-share loss.

▶ Our 12-month target price of $16 is based on our price-to-sales analysis. We apply a price-to-sales multiple of about 2.4X, below the mid-point of NVDA's historical average to account for our view of uninspiring sales results, to our forward 12-month sales per share estimate.

Qualitative Risk Assessment

LOW	MEDIUM	HIGH

Our risk assessment reflects the cyclicality of the semiconductor industry and of demand trends for electronics goods that benefit from advanced visual displays, and revenue volatility resulting from wins and losses of deals with big accounts.

Quantitative Evaluations

S&P Quality Ranking B

D	C	B-	B	B+	A-	A	A+

Relative Strength Rank MODERATE

32

LOWEST = 1   HIGHEST = 99

Revenue/Earnings Data

Revenue (Million $)

	1Q	2Q	3Q	4Q	Year
2010	664.2	776.5	903.2	--	--
2009	1,153	892.7	897.7	481.1	3,425
2008	844.3	935.3	1,116	1,203	4,098
2007	681.8	687.5	820.6	878.9	3,069
2006	583.9	574.8	583.4	633.6	2,376
2005	471.9	456.1	515.6	566.5	2,010

Earnings Per Share ($)

2010	-0.37	-0.19	0.19	E0.12	E-0.23
2009	0.30	-0.22	0.11	-0.27	-0.05
2008	0.22	-0.22	0.38	0.42	1.32
2007	0.15	0.15	0.18	0.27	0.77
2006	0.12	0.14	0.12	0.18	0.55
2005	0.04	0.01	0.05	0.09	0.19

Fiscal year ended Jan. 31. Next earnings report expected: Mid February. EPS Estimates based on S&P Operating Earnings; historical GAAP earnings are as reported.

Dividend Data

No cash dividends have been paid.

The McGraw·Hill Companies

Stock Report | November 28, 2009 | NNM Symbol: **NVDA**

NVIDIA Corp

Business Summary November 10, 2009

CORPORATE OVERVIEW. NVIDIA Corp. designs, develops and markets high-performance graphics processing units (GPUs), media and communications processors (MCPs), handheld GPUs, and related software for PCs and digital entertainment platforms, ranging from professional workstations to video game consoles to handheld electronic devices. The company's products are designed to generate realistic, interactive graphics on consumer and professional computing devices. It aims to be the leading supplier of performance GPUs, MCPs and handheld GPUs.

NVDA has four major product line operating segments: the graphics processing units business, the professional solutions business (PSB), the media and communications processor (MCP) business, and the consumer product business (CPB).

Interactive 3D graphics displays are an integral part of many computing applications for workstations, consumer and commercial desktop and laptop PCs, personal digital assistants, cellular phones, and gaming consoles. NVDA's products are designed into products offered by nearly all leading PC OEMs.

The company supplied graphics chips for Microsoft's Xbox video game console, but lost to rival AMD/ATI Technologies for the GPU for the next-generation Xbox. However, the company presently supplies GPU products for Sony's PlayStation 3 video game console.

CORPORATE STRATEGY. NVDA's goal is to become the leading supplier of performance GPUs, MCPs, and handheld GPUs and application processors. The elements behind the strategy include: building award-winning and architecturally compatible graphics and media products for various platforms; targeting leading OEMs, ODMs, and system builders; sustaining technology and product leadership in graphics and media products; increasing market share; creating synergy by combining expertise in graphics and media; and using its intellectual property and resources to enter into license and development contracts.

Company Financials Fiscal Year Ended Jan. 31

Per Share Data ($)	2009	2008	2007	2006	2005	2004	2003	2002	2001	2000
Tangible Book Value	3.49	4.35	3.32	2.52	2.08	1.83	1.81	1.52	0.93	0.34
Cash Flow	0.28	1.54	0.95	0.73	0.38	0.30	0.29	0.43	0.24	0.14
Earnings	-0.05	1.32	0.77	0.55	0.19	0.14	0.18	0.34	0.21	0.09
S&P Core Earnings	-0.05	1.31	0.79	0.42	0.03	-0.00	-0.22	0.10	0.12	NA
Dividends	Nil	Nil	Nil	Nil	Nil	Nil	Nil	Nil	Nil	Nil
Payout Ratio	Nil	Nil	Nil	Nil	Nil	Nil	Nil	Nil	Nil	Nil
Calendar Year	2008	2007	2006	2005	2004	2003	2002	2001	2000	1999
Prices:High	34.25	39.67	25.97	12.83	9.12	9.25	24.22	23.42	14.67	3.96
Prices:Low	5.75	18.69	11.45	6.82	3.10	3.11	2.40	4.71	2.92	1.00
P/E Ratio:High	NM	30	34	23	48	65	NM	68	71	42
P/E Ratio:Low	NM	14	15	12	16	22	NM	14	14	11

Income Statement Analysis (Million $)	2009	2008	2007	2006	2005	2004	2003	2002	2001	2000
Revenue	3,425	4,098	3,069	2,376	2,010	1,823	1,909	1,369	735	375
Operating Income	334	976	593	452	216	172	202	299	146	63.4
Depreciation	185	136	108	98.0	103	82.0	58.2	43.5	15.7	9.00
Interest Expense	0.41	0.05	0.02	0.07	0.16	12.0	Nil	16.2	4.85	Nil
Pretax Income	-43.0	901	494	360	125	86.7	151	253	147	56.2
Effective Tax Rate	NM	11.5%	9.37%	16.0%	20.0%	14.1%	39.7%	30.0%	31.9%	32.1%
Net Income	-30.0	798	448	303	100	74.4	90.8	177	100	38.1
S&P Core Earnings	-30.4	798	460	230	14.6	-1.44	-104	49.4	54.7	NA

Balance Sheet & Other Financial Data (Million $)	2009	2008	2007	2006	2005	2004	2003	2002	2001	2000
Cash	1,255	1,809	1,118	950	670	604	1,028	791	674	61.6
Current Assets	2,168	2,889	2,032	1,549	1,305	1,053	1,352	1,234	930	173
Total Assets	3,351	3,748	2,675	1,915	1,629	1,399	1,617	1,503	1,017	203
Current Liabilities	779	967	639	439	421	334	379	433	110	76.2
Long Term Debt	25.6	Nil	Nil	Nil	Nil	0.86	305	306	300	1.46
Common Equity	2,395	2,618	2,007	1,458	1,178	1,051	933	764	406	125
Total Capital	2,420	2,705	2,007	1,466	1,199	1,061	1,238	1,070	706	126
Capital Expenditures	408	188	145	79.6	67.3	128	63.1	97.0	36.3	11.6
Cash Flow	155	933	556	401	203	156	149	220	114	50.0
Current Ratio	2.8	3.0	3.2	3.5	3.1	3.2	3.6	2.8	8.4	2.3
% Long Term Debt of Capitalization	1.1	Nil	Nil	Nil	Nil	0.1	24.6	28.6	42.4	1.2
% Net Income of Revenue	NM	19.5	14.6	12.7	5.0	4.1	4.8	12.9	13.4	10.9
% Return on Assets	NM	24.8	19.4	17.1	6.6	4.9	5.8	14.0	16.1	25.9
% Return on Equity	NM	34.5	25.6	23.0	9.0	7.5	10.7	30.2	36.9	42.9

Data as orig reptd.; bef. results of disc opers/spec. items. Per share data adj. for stk. divs.; EPS diluted. E-Estimated. NA-Not Available. NM-Not Meaningful. NR-Not Ranked. UR-Under Review.

Office: 2701 San Tomas Expressway, Santa Clara, CA 95050.
Telephone: 408-486-2000.
Email: ir@nvidia.com
Website: http://www.nvidia.com

Pres & CEO: J. Huang
COO: D. Shoquist
EVP, CFO & Chief Acctg Officer: D.L. White
EVP, Secy & General Counsel: D.M. Shannon

CSO: B. Dally
Investor Contact: M. Hara (408-486-2511)
Board Members: T. Coxe, J. C. Gaither, J. Huang, H. C. Jones, Jr., W. J. Miller, M. L. Perry, B. B. Seawell, M. A. Stevens

Founded: 1993
Domicile: Delaware
Employees: 5,420

Redistribution or reproduction is prohibited without written permission. Copyright ©2009 The McGraw-Hill Companies, Inc.

The McGraw-Hill Companies

NYSE Euronext

STANDARD &POOR'S

S&P Recommendation	HOLD ★★★☆☆	Price $25.24 (as of Nov 27, 2009)	12-Mo. Target Price $30.00	Investment Style Large-Cap Growth

GICS Sector Financials
Sub-Industry Specialized Finance

Summary This holding company operates six cash equities exchanges and six derivatives exchanges in six countries.

Key Stock Statistics (Source S&P, Vickers, company reports)

52-Wk Range	$31.93– 14.52	S&P Oper. EPS 2009E	2.01	Market Capitalization(B)	$6.562	Beta	1.74
Trailing 12-Month EPS	$-4.96	S&P Oper. EPS 2010E	2.30	Yield (%)	4.75	S&P 3-Yr. Proj. EPS CAGR(%)	-6
Trailing 12-Month P/E	NM	P/E on S&P Oper. EPS 2009E	12.6	Dividend Rate/Share	$1.20	S&P Credit Rating	AA
$10K Invested 5 Yrs Ago	NA	Common Shares Outstg. (M)	260.0	Institutional Ownership (%)	57		

Price Performance

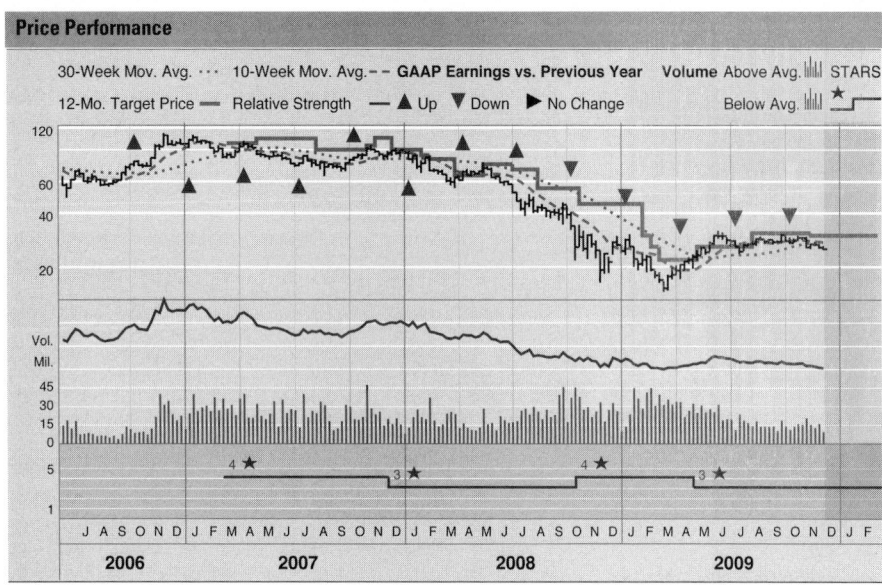

Analysis prepared by **Rafay Khalid, CFA** on November 02, 2009, when the stock traded at **$ 25.90**.

Highlights

► We project that revenues will decline 6.6% in 2009. Our outlook reflects our expectation for continued market share losses in the cash equities segment, which generated 49% of 2008 revenues. However, we believe NYX's market share will stabilize in 2010, as the company is making significant progress reducing order execution times. In addition, we believe NYX's new initiatives will continue to generate revenue growth in 2010. As a result, we forecast revenue growth of 3.7% in 2010.

► In 2009, we foresee the company's cost-cutting program helping to reduce fixed expenses, which exclude one-time items, liquidity payments, and routing fees. However, we forecast an increase in expenses related to new initiatives and liquidity payments during 2009. We expect the company to keep a tight control over expenses in 2010. As a result, we see adjusted operating margins declining to 21.1% in 2009, from 29.4% in 2008, but then partially rebounding to 23.1% in 2010.

► Our operating EPS estimates are $2.01 for 2009 and $2.30 for 2010, excluding one-time items. This compares to operating EPS of $3.04 in 2008.

Investment Rationale/Risk

► We believe NYX is taking the right steps to position itself for what we view as a globally competitive exchange environment including initiatives such as its move to UTP-Direct, a universal trading platform; block trading in the U.S. and Europe; and the shift to the designated market maker model from the specialist model on the NYSE trading floor. We believe incentives to attract liquidity to NYX's exchanges may benefit NYX in the long term, once it has increased market share. Yet, in the interim, we forecast margin compression and lower earnings in 2009. We see NYX using its derivatives clearinghouse, Liffe, to aggressively attract market players to build market share in OTC derivative products in both Europe and the U.S. Nevertheless, we caution that about 75% of NYX's transaction volume still comes from lower-margin cash trading, indicating that NYX is still in a transition phase.

► Risks to our recommendation and target price include execution risk related to growth initiatives, and lower than expected trading volumes.

► Our 12-month target price of $30 is based on a two-year historical average P/E ratio of 13.1X our 2010 EPS forecast.

Qualitative Risk Assessment

LOW	MEDIUM	HIGH

Our risk assessment reflects the potential volatility in results due to changes in equity and equity options trading volumes, the impact of current and future regulatory changes, and the integration of a number of recent acquisitions.

Quantitative Evaluations

S&P Quality Ranking NR

D	C	B-	B	B+	A-	A	A+

Relative Strength Rank WEAK
23
LOWEST = 1   HIGHEST = 99

Revenue/Earnings Data

Revenue (Million $)

	1Q	2Q	3Q	4Q	Year
2009	1,112	1,125	1,048	--	--
2008	1,191	1,112	1,159	1,177	4,474
2007	702.0	1,078	1,198	1,180	3,602
2006	478.9	659.5	602.9	658.5	2,376
2005	282.8	262.5	301.9	301.9	1,667
2004	263.4	259.2	283.4	283.4	1,044

Earnings Per Share ($)

2009	0.40	-0.70	0.48	E0.50	E2.01
2008	0.87	0.73	0.64	-5.08	-2.81
2007	0.43	0.62	0.97	0.59	2.70
2006	0.24	0.39	0.43	0.29	1.36
2005	--	--	0.01	-0.17	0.58
2004	--	--	--	--	--

Fiscal year ended Dec. 31. Next earnings report expected: Early February. EPS Estimates based on S&P Operating Earnings; historical GAAP earnings are as reported.

Dividend Data (Dates: mm/dd Payment Date: mm/dd/yy)

Amount ($)	Date Decl.	Ex-Div. Date	Stk. of Record	Payment Date
0.300	06/19	03/11	03/13	03/31/09
0.300	05/01	06/11	06/15	06/30/09
0.300	05/01	09/11	09/15	09/30/09
0.300	05/01	12/11	12/15	12/31/09

Dividends have been paid since 2007. Source: Company reports.

Please read the Required Disclosures and Analyst Certification on the last page of this report.

The McGraw-Hill Companies

NYSE Euronext

STANDARD &POOR'S

Business Summary November 02, 2009

CORPORATE OVERVIEW. NYSE Euronext (NYX) is a holding company created by the combination of NYSE Group and Euronext on April 4, 2007. NYX operates the world's largest and most liquid exchange group and offers a diverse array of financial products and services. The company, which brings together six cash equities exchanges in five countries and six derivatives exchanges in six countries, offers listings, trading in cash equities, equity and interest rate derivatives, bonds and the distribution of market data. As of December 31, 2008, NYX combined listed companies represented over $16.7 trillion in total market capitalization. In addition, there were 1,201 new listings in 2008, and IPOs raised $27.1 billion on NYX's markets.

NYX generates revenue primarily from transactions, company listing fees, market data, regulatory fees, and exchange licenses. The company also records activity assessment revenue, which is a pass through netted against section 31 fee expense. We have excluded this revenue line item when examining NYX's revenue from operations. Following the combination of the NYSE with Archipelago (now NYSE Arca), transaction fees have become the largest revenue driver for NYX (68% of total revenue in 2008). Transaction revenue is generated from fees paid for trading on NYX's exchanges, and benefits from

higher trading volumes. Market data is NYX's second largest revenue contributor (8.8%) and includes real time information related to price, transaction or order data of all instruments traded on the cash and derivatives markets on NYX's exchanges. Listing fees (8.1%) include initial fees charged for companies listing on one of NYX's exchanges and an ongoing annual listing fee. We view transactional revenue as the key growth driver for NYX moving forward.

CORPORATE STRATEGY. We believe NYX is in the middle of a transformational phase as it fully integrates the NYSE Arca assets with the NYSE, transitions the NYSE from a floor-based trading system to a hybrid floor/electronic model, completes its merger with Euronext, and readies for significant regulatory and structural changes in U.S. and European equity and equity options trading. We expect the number and scope of ongoing projects and regulatory changes to likely make for uneven financial performance and difficult historical and peer comparisons over the coming quarters.

Company Financials Fiscal Year Ended Dec. 31

Per Share Data ($)	2008	2007	2006	2005	2004	2003	2002	2001	2000	1999
Tangible Book Value	NM	NM	3.51	NA	NA	NA	NA	NA	NA	NA
Cash Flow	-1.86	3.76	2.27	1.50	NA	NA	NA	NA	NA	NA
Earnings	-2.81	2.70	1.36	0.58	NA	NA	NA	NA	NA	NA
S&P Core Earnings	0.92	2.55	1.28	0.35	0.31	NA	NA	NA	NA	NA
Dividends	1.15	0.75	Nil	NA	NA	NA	NA	NA	NA	NA
Payout Ratio	NM	28%	Nil	NA	NA	NA	NA	NA	NA	NA
Prices:High	87.70	109.50	112.00	NA	NA	NA	NA	NA	NA	NA
Prices:Low	16.33	64.26	48.62	NA	NA	NA	NA	NA	NA	NA
P/E Ratio:High	NM	41	82	NA	NA	NA	NA	NA	NA	NA
P/E Ratio:Low	NM	24	36	NA	NA	NA	NA	NA	NA	NA

Income Statement Analysis (Million $)										
Revenue	4,474	4,158	2,376	1,667	1,044	1,034	1,018	1,035	NA	NA
Operating Income	1,403	1,228	424	3.18	NA	NA	NA	NA	NA	NA
Depreciation	253	252	136	143	95.7	67.6	61.9	60.6	NA	NA
Interest Expense	150	129	Nil	Nil	NA	NA	NA	NA	NA	NA
Pretax Income	-645	921	328	176	NA	87.3	42.1	52.8	NA	NA
Effective Tax Rate	NM	27.5%	36.7%	47.6%	NA	41.7%	27.8%	33.6%	NA	NA
Net Income	-745	643	205	90.0	NA	49.6	28.1	31.8	NA	NA
S&P Core Earnings	244	609	193	54.1	42.3	NA	NA	NA	NA	NA

Balance Sheet & Other Financial Data (Million $)										
Cash	1,013	973	298	328	930	880	963	963	NA	NA
Current Assets	2,026	2,278	1,443	1,204	NA	NA	NA	NA	NA	NA
Total Assets	13,948	16,618	3,466	3,154	NA	1,777	1,757	1,730	NA	NA
Current Liabilities	2,582	3,462	832	823	NA	NA	NA	NA	NA	NA
Long Term Debt	1,787	522	Nil	Nil	NA	NA	NA	NA	NA	NA
Common Equity	6,556	9,384	1,669	1,366	NA	952	896	882	NA	NA
Total Capital	8,770	12,469	1,934	1,646	801	983	921	910	NA	NA
Capital Expenditures	376	182	97.8	NA	84.6	68.5	113	89.0	NA	NA
Cash Flow	-492	895	341	233	NA	NA	NA	NA	NA	NA
Current Ratio	0.8	0.7	1.7	1.5	2.6	2.9	3.4	3.0	NA	NA
% Long Term Debt of Capitalization	21.4	4.2	Nil	Nil	Nil	Nil	Nil	Nil	NA	NA
% Net Income of Revenue	NM	15.5	8.6	5.4	2.9	4.8	2.8	3.1	NA	NA
% Return on Assets	NM	6.4	7.2	NA	1.6	2.8	1.6	NA	NA	NA
% Return on Equity	NM	11.6	16.6	NA	3.5	5.4	3.2	NA	NA	NA

Data as orig reptd.; bef. results of disc opers/spec. items. Per share data adj. for stk. divs.; EPS diluted. E-Estimated. NA-Not Available. NM-Not Meaningful. NR-Not Ranked. UR-Under Review.

Office: 11 Wall Street, New York, NY 10005.
Telephone: 212-656-3000.
Website: http://www.nyse.com
Chrmn: J. Hessels

Vice Chrmn: M.N. Carter
CEO: D.L. Niederauer
EVP & CFO: M.S. Geltzeiler
EVP & Chief Admin Officer: A.T. Brandman

Investor Contact: S.C. Davidson (212-656-2183)
Board Members: E. L. Brown, M. N. Carter, P. M. Cloherty, G. Cox, S. M. Hefes, J. Hessels, D. Hoenn, S. A. Jackson, D. M. McFarland, J. J. McNulty, D. L. Niederauer, B. J. Peterbroeck, A. M. Rivlin, R. S. Salgado, J. Theodore, R. W. Van Tets, B. Williamson

Founded: 2006
Domicile: Delaware
Employees: 3,757

Occidental Petroleum Corp

STANDARD & POOR'S

S&P Recommendation	**BUY** ★★★★☆	Price $81.20 (as of Nov 27, 2009)	12-Mo. Target Price $90.00	Investment Style Large-Cap Blend

GICS Sector Energy
Sub-Industry Integrated Oil & Gas

Summary As one of the largest oil and gas companies in the U.S., OXY has global operations in exploration and production. Its subsidiary OxyChem is the largest U.S. merchant marketer of chlorine and caustic soda.

Key Stock Statistics (Source S&P, Vickers, company reports)

52-Wk Range	$85.20–41.27	S&P Oper. EPS 2009**E**	3.39	Market Capitalization(B)	$65.907	Beta	1.03
Trailing 12-Month EPS	$2.99	S&P Oper. EPS 2010**E**	6.06	Yield (%)	1.63	S&P 3-Yr. Proj. EPS CAGR(%)	-4
Trailing 12-Month P/E	27.2	P/E on S&P Oper. EPS 2009**E**	24.0	Dividend Rate/Share	$1.32	S&P Credit Rating	A
$10K Invested 5 Yrs Ago	$29,386	Common Shares Outstg. (M)	811.7	Institutional Ownership (%)	79		

Price Performance

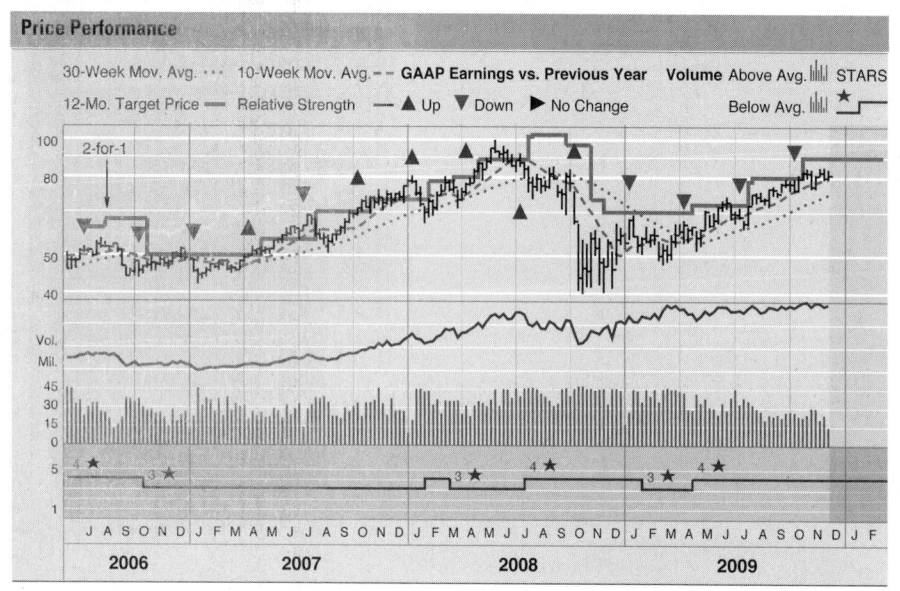

- 30-Week Mov. Avg. · · · 10-Week Mov. Avg. - - GAAP Earnings vs. Previous Year Volume Above Avg. STARS
- 12-Mo. Target Price — Relative Strength ▲ Up ▼ Down ► No Change Below Avg. ★

Options: ASE, CBOE, P, Ph

Analysis prepared by **Tina J. Vital** on October 27, 2009, when the stock traded at **$81.19**.

Highlights

▶ We expect oil and gas sales volumes to increase about 7% to average near 643,000 boe per day in 2009 and over 2% in 2010, driven by domestic operations in Kern County, CA and the Permian Basin, and internationally in Oman and the Dolphin project. In October, OXY said it was part of an Eni-led consortium awarded a license to develop the giant Zubair oil field in Iraq (current oil production at 195,000 boe per day, with plateau production of 1.125 million boe per day within seven years).

▶ We estimate that OXY's finding & development costs are above the peer average. Oil and gas cash production costs (excluding taxes) averaged $10.15 per boe in the third quarter, versus $10.17 in the second quarter. We expect that these cash production costs will decline over 25% in 2009 on reduced demand, contract renegotiations, and internal efforts.

▶ First nine months 2009 operating EPS excluded net special charges of $0.05. We expect after-tax operating earnings to drop about 62% in 2009, on reduced demand, before rebounding about 79% in 2010 on an improved economic outlook.

Investment Rationale/Risk

▶ With an oil focus and no refining business, and a strong pipeline of development projects, we expect OXY to benefit from expectations for higher oil prices. OXY's oil and gas operations are focused on long-lived reserves (California and Permian Basin), but we expect future growth to be driven by international projects, such as in the Middle East, Latin America, and North Africa. We estimate OXY replaced about 152% of its overall production in 2008, but its organic replacement was only 57%, reflecting additions in the U.S. and Oman.

▶ Risks to our recommendation and target price include a worsening of economic, industrial, and operating conditions, including increased geopolitical risk and difficulty replacing reserves.

▶ Blending our discounted cash flow ($93 per share; assuming a WACC of 10.5% and terminal growth of 3%) and relative market valuations, our 12-month target price is $90 per share, representing an expected enterprise value of about 6.7X our 2010 EBITDA estimate, a premium to peers.

Qualitative Risk Assessment

LOW	MEDIUM	HIGH

Our risk assessment reflects our view of OXY's strong business profile and modest financial risk profile. The company has a large, geographically diverse reserve base, predictable production, and substantial liquidity. However, we believe its strengths are limited by participation in volatile, competitive and capital-intensive businesses, and a penchant for debt-financed acquisitions.

Quantitative Evaluations

S&P Quality Ranking A-

D	C	B-	B	B+	A-	A	A+

Relative Strength Rank MODERATE

68

LOWEST = 1   HIGHEST = 99

Revenue/Earnings Data

Revenue (Million $)

	1Q	2Q	3Q	4Q	Year
2009	3,103	3,687	4,104	--	--
2008	6,020	7,116	7,060	4,021	24,217
2007	4,015	4,411	4,841	5,517	18,784
2006	4,396	4,599	4,522	4,144	17,661
2005	3,303	3,518	4,057	4,330	15,208
2004	2,557	2,724	3,005	3,082	11,368

Earnings Per Share ($)

	1Q	2Q	3Q	4Q	Year
2009	0.45	0.84	1.14	E0.90	E3.39
2008	2.20	2.79	2.78	0.55	8.33
2007	1.38	1.36	1.57	1.74	6.05
2006	1.34	1.39	1.35	1.08	5.15
2005	1.04	1.89	2.12	1.40	6.45
2004	0.62	0.73	0.94	0.96	3.25

Fiscal year ended Dec. 31. Next earnings report expected: Late January. EPS Estimates based on S&P Operating Earnings; historical GAAP earnings are as reported.

Dividend Data (Dates: mm/dd Payment Date: mm/dd/yy)

Amount ($)	Date Decl.	Ex-Div. Date	Stk. of Record	Payment Date
0.320	02/05	03/06	03/10	04/15/09
0.330	04/30	06/08	06/10	07/15/09
0.330	07/16	09/08	09/10	10/15/09
0.330	10/08	12/08	12/10	01/15/10

Dividends have been paid since 1975. Source: Company reports.

Please read the Required Disclosures and Analyst Certification on the last page of this report.

Occidental Petroleum Corp

Business Summary October 27, 2009

CORPORATE OVERVIEW. One of the largest oil and gas companies in the U.S., Occidental Petroleum Corp. (OXY) engages in oil and gas exploration and production in three main regions: the U.S. (63% of 2008 sales), the Middle East/North Africa (26%), Latin America (9%), and other regions (2%). OxyChem, a wholly owned subsidiary, manufactures and markets chlor-alkali products and vinyls, and is the largest merchant marketer of chlorine and caustic soda in the U.S.

OXY's businesses operate in three segments: Oil and Gas (75% of 2008 net sales; 90% of 2008 earnings), Chemicals (21%; 6%), and Midstream, Marketing and Other (1%; 4%). In early 2008, OXY reclassified its midstream assets (marketing, gas processing, pipelines, power generation, and CO2 source fields and facilities) out of its Oil and Gas segment into a new segment called Midstream, Marketing and Other.

The Oil and Gas segment explores for, develops, produces and markets crude oil and natural gas. Oil and gas sales volumes rose 5.4%, to 601,000 boe per day (77% liquids), in 2008. Proved oil and gas reserves (including other interests) rose 3.9%, to 2.98 billion barrels of oil equivalent (boe; 74% developed, 74% liquids) at year-end 2008. Using data from John S. Herold, an industry research firm, we estimate OXY's three-year (2005-07) proved acquisition costs at $12.09 per boe, below the peer average; three-year finding and develop-

ment costs at $16.19 per boe, above peers; three-year reserve replacement costs at $14.31, above peers; and three-year reserve replacement at 180%, below the peer average. We estimate OXY's 2008 overall replacement rate at 152%, and its organic replacement rate at 57%.

OxyChem manufactures and markets basic chemicals, vinyls, and performance chemicals, focused on the chlorovinyls chain beginning with chlorine. As of year-end 2008, the company owned and operated chemical plants at 21 domestic sites in the U.S., and at three international sites in Brazil, Canada and Chile.

MARKET PROFILE. OXY's oil and gas operations are focused on large, long-lived "legacy" oil and gas assets, such as those in California (such as the Elk Hills oil and gas field) and the Permian Basin (OXY was the largest producer in the Permian Basin as of year-end 2007), which tend to have moderate decline rates, enhanced secondary and tertiary recovery opportunities and economies of scale that lead to cost-effective production.

Company Financials Fiscal Year Ended Dec. 31

Per Share Data ($)	2008	2007	2006	2005	2004	2003	2002	2001	2000	1999
Tangible Book Value	33.69	27.63	22.84	18.69	13.30	10.25	8.35	7.53	6.45	4.79
Cash Flow	12.31	8.86	7.71	8.26	4.93	3.56	2.87	2.88	3.35	1.92
Earnings	8.33	6.05	5.15	6.45	3.25	2.06	1.54	1.59	2.13	0.79
S&P Core Earnings	8.28	5.19	4.97	5.78	3.26	2.03	1.28	1.70	NA	NA
Dividends	1.21	0.94	NA	0.65	0.41	0.52	0.50	0.50	0.50	0.50
Payout Ratio	15%	16%	NA	10%	13%	25%	33%	32%	23%	63%
Prices:High	100.04	79.25	NA	44.90	30.38	21.49	15.38	15.55	12.78	12.28
Prices:Low	39.93	42.06	NA	27.09	20.98	13.59	11.49	10.94	7.88	7.31
P/E Ratio:High	12	13	NA	7	9	10	10	10	6	16
P/E Ratio:Low	5	7	NA	4	6	7	7	7	4	9

Income Statement Analysis (Million $)										
Revenue	24,217	18,784	17,661	15,208	11,368	9,326	7,338	13,985	13,574	7,610
Operating Income	14,652	10,044	9,664	7,860	5,573	4,281	3,119	3,638	3,826	1,831
Depreciation, Depletion and Amortization	3,267	2,356	2,042	1,485	1,303	1,177	1,012	971	901	805
Interest Expense	26.0	396	291	293	260	332	295	392	518	498
Pretax Income	11,468	8,660	8,012	7,365	4,389	2,884	1,662	1,892	3,196	1,257
Effective Tax Rate	40.4%	40.5%	43.3%	27.4%	38.9%	42.5%	25.4%	29.8%	45.1%	50.2%
Net Income	6,839	5,078	4,435	5,272	2,606	1,595	1,163	1,186	1,569	568
S&P Core Earnings	6,803	4,360	4,280	4,729	2,607	1,568	963	1,273	NA	NA

Balance Sheet & Other Financial Data (Million $)										
Cash	1,777	1,964	1,339	2,189	1,449	683	146	199	97.0	214
Current Assets	7,172	8,595	6,006	6,574	4,431	2,474	1,873	1,483	2,067	1,688
Total Assets	41,537	36,519	32,355	26,108	21,391	18,168	16,548	17,850	19,414	14,125
Current Liabilities	6,134	6,266	4,724	4,280	3,423	2,526	2,235	1,890	2,740	1,967
Long Term Debt	2,073	1,742	2,619	2,873	3,345	3,993	4,452	4,528	5,658	4,854
Common Equity	27,300	22,823	19,184	15,032	10,550	7,929	6,318	5,634	4,774	3,523
Total Capital	32,058	26,923	24,470	19,207	15,470	13,235	12,085	13,489	13,977	9,372
Capital Expenditures	9,365	3,497	3,005	2,423	1,843	1,601	1,236	1,401	952	601
Cash Flow	10,106	7,434	6,477	6,757	3,909	2,772	2,175	2,157	2,470	1,366
Current Ratio	1.2	1.4	1.3	1.5	1.3	1.0	0.8	0.8	0.8	0.9
% Long Term Debt of Capitalization	6.5	6.5	10.7	15.0	21.6	30.2	36.8	33.6	40.5	51.8
% Return on Assets	17.5	14.7	15.2	22.2	13.2	9.2	6.8	6.4	9.4	3.9
% Return on Equity	27.3	24.2	25.9	41.2	28.2	22.4	19.5	22.8	37.8	16.9

Data as orig reptd.; bef. results of disc opers/spec. items. Per share data adj. for stk. divs.; EPS diluted. E-Estimated. NA-Not Available. NM-Not Meaningful. NR-Not Ranked. UR-Under Review.

Office: 10889 Wilshire Boulevard, Los Angeles, CA 90024-4201.
Telephone: 310-208-8800.
Email: investorrelations_newyork@oxy.com
Website: http://www.oxy.com

Chrmn & CEO: R.R. Irani
Pres & CFO: S.I. Chazen
EVP, Secy & General Counsel: D.P. de Brier
Chief Acctg Officer & Cntlr: R. Pineci

Treas: J.R. Havert
Investor Contact: C.G. Stavros (212-603-8184)
Board Members: S. Abraham, R. W. Burkle, J. S. Chalsty, E. P. Djerejian, J. E. Feick, C. M. Gutierrez, R. R. Irani, I. W. Maloney, A. B. Poladian, R. Segovia, A. R. Syriani, R. Tomich, W. L. Weisman

Founded: 1920
Domicile: Delaware
Employees: 10,400

Office Depot Inc

STANDARD &POOR'S

S&P Recommendation **SELL** ★★☆☆☆	Price $6.28 (as of Nov 27, 2009)	12-Mo. Target Price $4.00	Investment Style Large-Cap Growth

GICS Sector Consumer Discretionary
Sub-Industry Specialty Stores

Summary Office Depot is a leading operator of office products superstores and mail order catalogs.

Key Stock Statistics (Source S&P, Vickers, company reports)

52-Wk Range	$7.84– 0.59	S&P Oper. EPS 2009**E**	-0.48	Market Capitalization(B)	$1.725	Beta	3.41
Trailing 12-Month EPS	$-7.66	S&P Oper. EPS 2010**E**	-0.53	Yield (%)	Nil	S&P 3-Yr. Proj. EPS CAGR(%)	NM
Trailing 12-Month P/E	NM	P/E on S&P Oper. EPS 2009**E**	NM	Dividend Rate/Share	Nil	S&P Credit Rating	B
$10K Invested 5 Yrs Ago	$3,738	Common Shares Outstg. (M)	274.7	Institutional Ownership (%)	69		

Price Performance

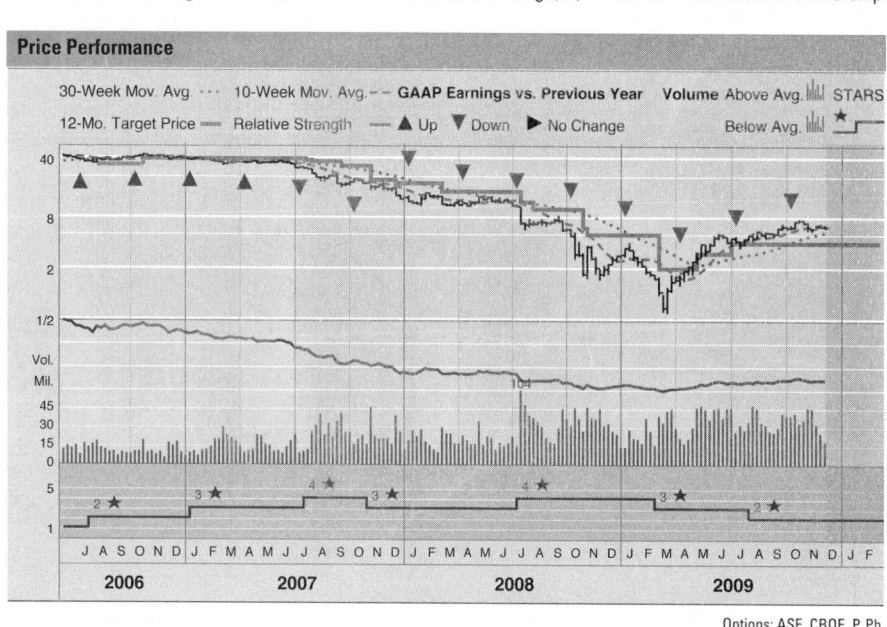

30-Week Mov. Avg. ··· 10-Week Mov. Avg. - - **GAAP Earnings vs. Previous Year** Volume Above Avg. ⊪⊪ STARS
12-Mo. Target Price — Relative Strength — ▲ Up ▼ Down ► No Change Below Avg. ⊪⊪ ★

Options: ASE, CBOE, P, Ph

Analysis prepared by **Michael Souers** on November 03, 2009, when the stock traded at **$ 5.75**.

Highlights

► We expect sales to fall 1.1% in 2010, following our projection of a 17% decrease in 2009. We forecast a slight decline in same-store-sales, following a projected 14% decrease in 2009. We also look for a slight drop in sales in the U.S. contract business, as we expect business conditions to remain challenging, particularly for small to medium-sized companies.

► We project a slight widening of gross margins in 2010, reflecting inventory optimization, a reduction in promotional activity and a continued push toward selling higher-margin private label brands. However, we continue to expect a product mix shift to lower-margin goods, which should partially offset this improvement. We expect ODP's operating margins to narrow slightly on expense de-leverage from declining same-store-sales.

► We estimate a net loss of $0.53 per share in 2010, a slight deterioration from our 2009 operating net loss estimate of $0.48 per share, which excludes charges for deferred tax asset valuation and write-downs related to store closures and other restructuring charges.

Investment Rationale/Risk

► We think poor execution, liquidity concerns, and macro-related challenges have created an overhang of uncertainty on the shares, leading to a significant drop in the share price from about $13 over the past year. While we think the company has sufficient liquidity to weather a multi-year economic downturn given current credit availability and the recent cash infusion by private equity firm BC Partners (for $350 million in convertible preferred stock), we do not foresee any positive catalyst for the shares. We are also concerned that the retail market for office supply stores has reached saturation levels, providing little opportunity for future growth.

► Risks to our recommendation and target price include a greater-than-expected increase in capital spending by businesses, solid same-store sales gains in ODP's North American Retail division, and favorable currency fluctuations.

► Our 12-month target price of $4 is based on our DCF analysis, which assumes a weighted average cost of capital of 9.6% and a terminal growth rate of 3.0%.

Qualitative Risk Assessment

LOW	MEDIUM	HIGH

Our risk assessment reflects the cyclical nature of the office supply retailing industry, which is highly dependent on consumer and business spending, and the company's fairly large exposure to international markets.

Quantitative Evaluations

S&P Quality Ranking B-

D	C	B-	B	B+	A-	A	A+

Relative Strength Rank MODERATE

55

LOWEST = 1   HIGHEST = 99

Revenue/Earnings Data

Revenue (Million $)

	1Q	2Q	3Q	4Q	Year
2009	3,225	2,824	3,029	--	--
2008	3,962	3,605	3,658	3,271	14,496
2007	4,094	3,632	3,935	3,867	15,528
2006	3,816	3,495	3,857	3,843	15,011
2005	3,703	3,364	3,493	3,719	14,279
2004	3,605	3,162	3,328	3,469	13,565

Earnings Per Share ($)

2009	-0.20	-0.31	-1.51	E-0.28	E-0.48
2008	0.25	-0.01	-0.02	-5.64	-5.42
2007	0.55	0.38	0.43	0.07	1.43
2006	0.43	0.41	0.47	0.48	1.79
2005	0.37	0.31	-0.15	0.34	0.87
2004	0.37	0.25	0.28	0.17	1.06

Fiscal year ended Dec. 31. Next earnings report expected: Late February. EPS Estimates based on S&P Operating Earnings; historical GAAP earnings are as reported.

Dividend Data

No cash dividends have been paid.

Office Depot Inc

STANDARD &POOR'S

Business Summary November 03, 2009

CORPORATE OVERVIEW. Office Depot is a global supplier of office products and services. It generated net sales of $14.5 billion in 2008 to customers and businesses of all sizes through three business segments: the North American Retail division (42% of revenues), the North American Business Solutions division (29%), and the International division (29%). Sales by product group were as follows: supplies 61%; technology 25%; and furniture and other 14%.

At January 24, 2009, ODP's North American Retail division operated 1,267 office supply stores in 49 states, the District of Columbia, Puerto Rico, and Canada. North American Retail sells a broad assortment of merchandise, including brand name and private brand office supplies, business machines and computers, computer software, office furniture, and other business-related products through its chain of office supply stores. Most stores also contain a copy and print center that offers printing, reproduction mailing, shipping, and other services. Also, during 2008, ODP announced the national availability of a PC support and network installation service that provides customers with in-home, in-office and in-store support for their technology needs.

ODP's North American Business Solutions division provides office supply products and services directly to businesses, selling branded and private label products by means of a dedicated sales force, through catalogs and electronically through its Internet sites. Its direct business is tailored to serve small- to medium-sized customers, while its contract business serves the office supply needs of predominantly medium-sized to Fortune 100 customers.

ODP's International division served customers in 48 countries outside the U.S. and Canada through 162 company-owned stores and 186 additional stores operating under licensing and joint venture agreements as of December 31, 2008. It also participates in 98 franchised stores in South Korea and Thailand.

Company Financials Fiscal Year Ended Dec. 31

Per Share Data ($)	2008	2007	2006	2005	2004	2003	2002	2001	2000	1999
Tangible Book Value	4.78	6.20	5.11	6.26	6.96	5.77	6.61	5.28	4.66	5.06
Cash Flow	-4.49	2.46	2.76	1.72	1.92	1.75	1.59	1.27	0.86	1.08
Earnings	-5.42	1.43	1.79	0.87	1.06	0.96	0.98	0.66	0.16	0.69
S&P Core Earnings	-0.95	1.42	1.74	0.86	1.03	0.91	0.92	0.58	NA	NA
Dividends	Nil	Nil	Nil	Nil	Nil	Nil	Nil	Nil	Nil	Nil
Payout Ratio	Nil	Nil	Nil	Nil	Nil	Nil	Nil	Nil	Nil	Nil
Prices:High	15.54	39.66	46.52	31.76	19.50	18.50	21.96	18.70	14.88	26.00
Prices:Low	1.45	13.08	30.64	16.50	13.87	10.28	10.60	7.13	5.88	9.00
P/E Ratio:High	NM	28	26	37	18	19	22	28	93	38
P/E Ratio:Low	NM	9	17	19	13	11	11	11	37	13

Income Statement Analysis (Million $)										
Revenue	14,496	15,528	15,011	14,279	13,565	12,359	11,357	11,154	11,570	10,263
Operating Income	266	797	998	750	799	719	707	562	433	615
Depreciation	254	282	279	268	269	248	201	199	206	169
Interest Expense	68.3	63.1	40.8	32.4	61.1	54.8	46.2	44.3	33.9	26.1
Pretax Income	-1,578	459	727	362	461	445	479	314	92.5	414
Effective Tax Rate	NM	13.7%	29.0%	24.3%	27.3%	32.1%	35.0%	36.0%	46.6%	37.8%
Net Income	-1,479	396	516	274	336	302	311	201	49.3	258
S&P Core Earnings	-260	392	500	270	327	286	292	178	NA	NA

Balance Sheet & Other Financial Data (Million $)										
Cash	156	223	174	703	794	791	877	563	151	219
Current Assets	3,122	3,716	3,455	3,530	3,916	3,577	3,210	2,806	2,699	2,631
Total Assets	5,268	7,257	6,570	6,099	6,767	6,145	4,766	4,332	4,196	4,276
Current Liabilities	2,626	2,973	2,970	2,469	2,618	2,277	1,992	2,102	1,908	1,944
Long Term Debt	689	607	571	569	584	829	412	318	598	321
Common Equity	1,363	3,084	2,610	2,739	3,223	2,794	2,297	1,848	1,601	1,908
Total Capital	1,770	3,707	3,197	3,308	3,957	3,868	2,774	2,230	2,200	2,229
Capital Expenditures	369	461	343	261	391	212	202	207	268	396
Cash Flow	-1,225	678	795	542	605	550	512	400	255	426
Current Ratio	1.2	1.3	1.2	1.4	1.5	1.6	1.6	1.3	1.4	1.4
% Long Term Debt of Capitalization	38.9	16.4	17.9	17.2	14.8	21.4	14.9	14.2	27.2	14.4
% Net Income of Revenue	NM	2.6	3.4	1.9	2.5	2.4	2.7	1.8	0.4	2.5
% Return on Assets	NM	5.7	8.1	4.2	5.2	5.5	6.8	4.7	1.2	6.2
% Return on Equity	NM	13.9	19.3	9.2	11.2	11.9	15.0	11.7	2.8	13.1

Data as orig reptd.; bef. results of disc opers/spec. items. Per share data adj. for stk. divs.; EPS diluted. E-Estimated. NA-Not Available. NM-Not Meaningful. NR-Not Ranked. UR-Under Review.

Office: 6600 N Military Trl, Boca Raton, FL 33496-2434.
Telephone: 561-438-4800.
Email: investor.relations@officedepot.com
Website: http://www.officedepot.com
Chrmn & CEO: S. Odland
EVP & CFO: M.D. Newman
EVP, Secy & General Counsel: E.D. Garcia
SVP, Chief Acctg Officer & Cntlr: M.E. Hutchens
SVP & CIO: T. Toews
Investor Contact: B. Turcotte (561-438-3657)
Board Members: L. A. Ault, III, N. R. Austrian, J. Bateman, D. W. Bernauer, M. J. Evans, D. I. Fuente, B. J. Gaines, M. M. Hart, W. Hedrick, K. Mason, S. Odland, J. S. Rubin, R. Svider
Founded: 1986
Domicile: Delaware
Employees: 43,000

Omnicom Group Inc.

STANDARD &POOR'S

S&P Recommendation	SELL ★★★★★	Price $36.41 (as of Nov 27, 2009)	12-Mo. Target Price $34.00	Investment Style Large-Cap Growth

GICS Sector Consumer Discretionary
Sub-Industry Advertising

Summary This company owns the DDB Worldwide, BBDO Worldwide and TBWA Worldwide advertising agency networks; and more than 100 marketing and specialty services firms.

Key Stock Statistics (Source S&P, Vickers, company reports)

52-Wk Range	$39.11– 20.09	S&P Oper. EPS 2009E	2.56	Market Capitalization(B)	$11.332	Beta		1.04
Trailing 12-Month EPS	$2.70	S&P Oper. EPS 2010E	2.52	Yield (%)	1.65	S&P 3-Yr. Proj. EPS CAGR(%)		-2
Trailing 12-Month P/E	13.5	P/E on S&P Oper. EPS 2009E	14.2	Dividend Rate/Share	$0.60	S&P Credit Rating		A-
$10K Invested 5 Yrs Ago	$9,450	Common Shares Outstg. (M)	311.2	Institutional Ownership (%)	87			

Price Performance

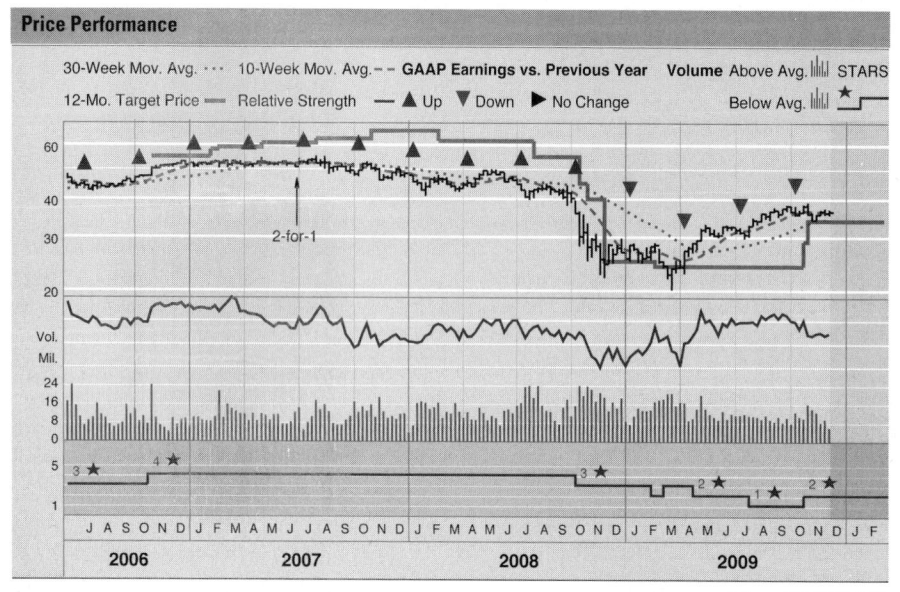

30-Week Mov. Avg. · · · 10-Week Mov. Avg. - - GAAP Earnings vs. Previous Year   Volume Above Avg. | STARS
12-Mo. Target Price — Relative Strength   ▲ Up ▼ Down ► No Change   Below Avg. |

Options: ASE, CBOE, P, Ph

Analysis prepared by **Joseph Agnese** on November 19, 2009, when the stock traded at **$ 36.18**.

Highlights

► Organic revenues declined 9.4% through the first nine months of 2009, in line with our expectations. In the U.S., organic revenues fell 11.4%. A 15% negative forex effect was evident in the 19% decline seen in the Eurozone and the 27% drop in the U.K. In other markets, revenues decreased 16%. Acquisitions contributed 0.3% to revenues.

► Business was weak in the first nine months of 2009 across numerous sectors, most notably automotive. For the remainder of 2009, comparisons go up against 2008 levels that were boosted by the Olympics and the U.S. elections. We forecast a 2009 revenue decrease of 12%, including negative forex effects of about 5%.

► Our outlook for 2010-2012 is for limited growth, if any, as clients go through bankruptcy, commission rates come under pressure, and the traditional ad agency business model is challenged by new ways of measuring ad effectiveness. For 2010, we see revenues declining 0.3%, with EPS declining 1.6% to $2.52 from our estimate of $2.56 in 2009.

Investment Rationale/Risk

► Reflecting our belief that the company is poorly positioned in adverse secular and cyclical environment, we believe the shares remain overvalued. Our valuation incorporates our view that the global economy will remain weak well into 2010, with only sluggish growth into 2011. Despite OMC's efforts to maintain margins by cutting costs, we expect margins to remain flat as we think these efforts will not be sufficient to widen margins. Further cost cuts will likely have a negative effect on winning new and retaining existing business.

► Risks to our recommendation and target price include stronger-than-expected global GDP, acquisitions that may boost results, and a return to healthy credit markets.

► We derive our 12-month target price of $34 by applying an EV/EBITDA multiple of 7.5X to our 2010 EBITDA estimate of $1.63 billion. This multiple is close to the low end of OMC's historical range, which we believe is appropriate given the still-elevated level of risk we see in the economy.

Qualitative Risk Assessment

LOW	MEDIUM	HIGH

Our risk assessment primarily reflects a highly competitive advertising industry, partly offset by OMC's diversified geographic and product revenue sources coupled with its position as the world's largest advertising agency by revenue, and our view of its strong track record of EPS and free cash flow growth.

Quantitative Evaluations

S&P Quality Ranking   A+

D	C	B-	B	B+	A-	A	A+

Relative Strength Rank   MODERATE

56

LOWEST = 1   HIGHEST = 99

Revenue/Earnings Data

Revenue (Million $)

	1Q	2Q	3Q	4Q	Year
2009	2,747	2,871	2,838	--	--
2008	3,195	3,477	3,316	3,371	13,360
2007	2,841	3,126	3,101	3,626	12,694
2006	2,563	2,823	2,774	3,216	11,377
2005	2,403	2,616	2,523	2,939	10,481
2004	2,231	2,408	2,319	2,789	9,747

Earnings Per Share ($)

2009	0.53	0.75	0.53	E0.76	E2.56
2008	0.65	0.96	0.69	0.88	3.17
2007	0.55	0.84	0.62	0.96	2.95
2006	0.47	0.71	0.52	0.81	2.50
2005	0.41	0.62	0.45	0.71	2.18
2004	0.36	0.55	0.40	0.64	1.94

Fiscal year ended Dec. 31. Next earnings report expected: Mid February. EPS Estimates based on S&P Operating Earnings; historical GAAP earnings are as reported.

Dividend Data (Dates: mm/dd Payment Date: mm/dd/yy)

Amount ($)	Date Decl.	Ex-Div. Date	Stk. of Record	Payment Date
0.150	12/05	12/15	12/17	01/05/09
0.150	02/13	03/04	03/06	04/03/09
0.150	05/19	06/05	06/09	07/06/09
0.150	07/16	09/16	09/18	10/02/09

Dividends have been paid since 1986. Source: Company reports.

Please read the Required Disclosures and Analyst Certification on the last page of this report.

Omnicom Group Inc.

STANDARD &POOR'S

Business Summary November 19, 2009

CORPORATE OVERVIEW. Omnicom Group, a global advertising and marketing services company, is one of the world's largest corporate communications companies. OMC is comprised of more than 1,500 subsidiary agencies, operating in over 100 countries. It operates as three independent global agency networks: the BBDO Worldwide Network, the DDB Worldwide Network, and the TBWA Worldwide Network. Each agency network has its own clients, and the networks compete with each other in the same markets.

OMC's companies provide an extensive range of services, which it groups into four disciplines: traditional media advertising (43% of 2008 revenues), customer relationship management (38%), public relations (9.5%), and specialty communications (9.5%). In 2007 (latest available), the company's 10 and 100 largest clients accounted for approximately 16.7% and 46.2% of consolidated revenue, respectively. The largest client accounted for about 2.8% of 2007 revenues; no other single client accounted for more than 2.4% of revenues. Operations cover the major regions of North America, the U.K., Europe, the Middle East, Africa, Latin America, the Far East and Australia. In 2008, 52% of revenues were derived from the U.S., 22% from euro-denominated markets, 10% from the U.K., and 16% from other international markets.

The services in these categories include but are not limited to: advertising, brand consultancy, crisis communications, database management, digital and interactive marketing, direct marketing, directory advertising, experiential marketing, field marketing, health care communications, in-store design, investor relations, marketing research, media planning and buying, organizational communications, product placement, promotional marketing, public relations, recruitment communications, reputation consulting, retail marketing, and sports and event marketing.

In our opinion, the breadth, depth and diversity of OMC's business reduces exposure to any single industry, and to an economic reversal in any world region. It also provides the company with significant opportunities to benefit from growth in non-advertising services, such as public relations and event marketing, expenditures for which are growing faster than those for traditional advertising.

Company Financials Fiscal Year Ended Dec. 31

Per Share Data ($)	2008	2007	2006	2005	2004	2003	2002	2001	2000	1999
Tangible Book Value	NM	NM	NM	NM	NM	NM	NM	NM	NM	NM
Cash Flow	3.75	3.45	3.13	2.71	2.40	2.10	2.03	1.88	1.81	1.30
Earnings	3.17	2.95	2.50	2.18	1.94	1.80	1.72	1.35	1.37	1.01
S&P Core Earnings	3.17	2.95	2.50	2.18	1.92	1.69	1.56	1.24	NA	NA
Dividends	0.60	0.50	0.50	0.46	0.45	0.40	0.40	0.39	0.35	0.30
Payout Ratio	19%	17%	20%	21%	23%	22%	23%	29%	26%	30%
Prices:High	50.16	55.45	53.03	45.74	44.41	43.80	48.68	49.10	50.47	53.75
Prices:Low	22.02	45.82	39.38	37.88	33.22	23.25	18.25	29.55	34.06	27.97
P/E Ratio:High	16	19	21	21	23	24	28	36	37	53
P/E Ratio:Low	7	16	16	17	17	13	11	22	25	28

Income Statement Analysis (Million $)										
Revenue	13,360	12,694	11,377	10,481	9,747	8,621	7,536	6,889	6,154	5,131
Operating Income	1,872	1,823	1,674	1,515	1,388	1,289	1,224	1,179	1,065	821
Depreciation	183	164	190	175	172	124	120	211	187	97.1
Interest Expense	125	107	125	78.0	51.1	57.9	45.5	72.8	76.5	84.9
Pretax Income	1,657	1,624	1,422	1,308	1,196	1,137	1,087	908	923	689
Effective Tax Rate	32.8%	33.1%	32.8%	33.3%	33.1%	33.5%	34.5%	38.8%	40.0%	39.7%
Net Income	1,000	976	864	791	724	676	643	503	499	363
S&P Core Earnings	1,000	976	866	790	715	631	584	456	NA	NA

Balance Sheet & Other Financial Data (Million $)										
Cash	1,112	1,841	1,740	836	1,166	1,529	667	472	517	576
Current Assets	8,565	10,504	9,647	7,967	8,095	7,286	5,637	5,234	5,367	4,712
Total Assets	17,318	19,272	18,164	15,920	16,002	14,499	11,820	10,617	9,891	9,018
Current Liabilities	9,754	11,227	10,296	8,700	8,744	7,762	6,840	6,644	6,625	6,009
Long Term Debt	3,054	3,055	3,055	2,357	2,358	2,537	1,945	1,340	1,245	712
Common Equity	3,523	4,092	3,871	3,948	4,079	3,466	2,569	2,178	1,548	1,553
Total Capital	6,810	7,563	7,562	6,921	6,949	6,394	4,687	3,677	2,970	2,708
Capital Expenditures	212	223	178	163	160	141	117	149	150	130
Cash Flow	1,183	1,140	1,054	966	896	800	763	714	685	460
Current Ratio	0.9	0.9	0.9	0.9	0.9	0.9	0.8	0.8	0.8	0.8
% Long Term Debt of Capitalization	42.9	40.4	40.4	34.1	33.9	39.7	41.5	36.4	41.9	26.3
% Net Income of Revenue	7.5	7.7	7.6	7.5	7.4	7.8	8.5	7.3	8.1	7.1
% Return on Assets	5.5	5.2	5.1	5.0	4.7	5.1	5.7	4.9	5.3	4.5
% Return on Equity	26.3	24.5	22.1	19.7	18.8	22.4	27.1	27.0	32.2	27.9

Data as orig reptd.; bef. results of disc opers/spec. items. Per share data adj. for stk. divs.; EPS diluted. E-Estimated. NA-Not Available. NM-Not Meaningful. NR-Not Ranked. UR-Under Review.

Office: 437 Madison Ave Bsmt, New York, NY 10022-7000.
Telephone: 212-415-3600.
Email: IR@OmnicomGroup.com
Website: http://www.omnicomgroup.com

Chrmn: B.A. Crawford
Pres & CEO: J. Wren
Vice Chrmn: T. Love
Investor Contact: R.J. Weisenburger

EVP & CFO: R.J. Weisenburger
Board Members: A. R. Batkin, R. C. Clark, L. S. Coleman, Jr., E. M. Cook, B. A. Crawford, S. Denison, M. A. Henning, T. Love, J. R. Murphy, J. R. Purcell, L. J. Rice, G. L. Roubos, J. Wren

Founded: 1944
Domicile: New York
Employees: 68,000

The McGraw-Hill Companies

Oracle Corp

**STANDARD
&POOR'S**

S&P Recommendation HOLD ★★★☆☆	**Price** $22.09 (as of Nov 27, 2009)	**12-Mo. Target Price** $24.00	**Investment Style** Large-Cap Growth

GICS Sector Information Technology
Sub-Industry Systems Software

Summary This company is a leading supplier of enterprise database management systems and business applications.

Key Stock Statistics (Source S&P, Vickers, company reports)

52-Wk Range	$22.95–13.80	S&P Oper. EPS 2010**E**	1.46	Market Capitalization(B)	$110.741	Beta	0.91
Trailing 12-Month EPS	$1.11	S&P Oper. EPS 2011**E**	1.61	Yield (%)	0.91	S&P 3-Yr. Proj. EPS CAGR(%)	13
Trailing 12-Month P/E	19.9	P/E on S&P Oper. EPS 2010**E**	15.1	Dividend Rate/Share	$0.20	S&P Credit Rating	A
$10K Invested 5 Yrs Ago	$17,579	Common Shares Outstg. (M)	5,013.2	Institutional Ownership (%)	59		

Price Performance

30-Week Mov. Avg. · · · 10-Week Mov. Avg. - - **GAAP Earnings vs. Previous Year** Volume Above Avg. ▮▮▮ STARS
12-Mo. Target Price — Relative Strength — ▲ Up ▼ Down ▶ No Change Below Avg. ▮▮▮ ★

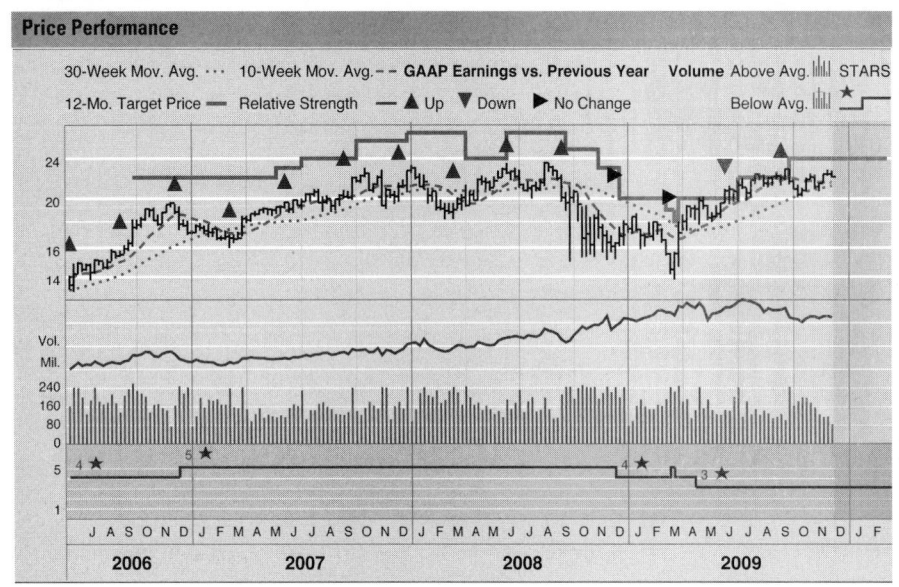

Options: ASE, CBOE, P, Ph

Analysis prepared by **Zaineb Bokhari** on September 18, 2009, when the stock traded at **$ 21.64**.

Highlights

► We expect revenues to stay essentially flat at $23.5 billion in FY 10 (May). We think the weak global economy has dampened spending by enterprises on new licenses. As a result, we project FY 10 license revenues will decline 6%, to $6.7 billion, following FY 09's 5% decline. We forecast growth for software license updates and support, which we think customers are less likely to curtail than licenses. Our outlook also reflects some currency headwinds. In April, ORCL agreed to acquire Sun Microsystems (JAVA 9, Hold) for $9.50 per share, subject to approvals. Our current estimates do not include the impact of this proposed transaction.

► In view of ORCL's success in expanding operating margins while integrating past acquisitions, we expect targeted cost synergies and scale benefits to be achieved, and we look for non-GAAP operating margins to widen to 48% in FY 10, from about 46% in FY 09. We expect margins to flatten in FY 11.

► We estimate non-GAAP EPS of $1.46 in FY 10 and $1.61 in FY 11. We exclude $0.24 of amortization and other items from our estimates.

Investment Rationale/Risk

► We think ORCL enjoys a strong market position and generates considerable free cash flow. We expect ORCL's broad product portfolio, geographic diversity, and sizable maintenance revenue streams to enable it to weather the current downturn, although we expect growth to slow considerably. We expect cost discipline, targeted acquisition-related synergies, and lower variable sales compensation to help increase operating margins. We think the company's planned acquisition of Sun Microsystems takes ORCL far afield from its core software business and is fraught with risk. We see it significantly changing ORCL's margin profile.

► Risks to our recommendation and target price include notable acquisition integration risk, intense competition, and pricing pressure.

► Our 12-month target price of $24 is based on a blend of our relative and intrinsic valuation measures. In our discounted cash flow analysis, we assume a 9.2% weighted average cost of capital and 3% terminal growth rate, which yields an intrinsic value of approximately $26. For our P/E analysis, we apply a 15X multiple to our forward 12-month EPS estimate of $1.48, resulting in a price of $22.

Qualitative Risk Assessment

LOW	MEDIUM	HIGH

Our risk assessment reflects potential acquisition integration risks following a series of large purchases over the past several years. This is offset by our favorable view of ORCL's balance sheet, free cash flow, and deep management bench.

Quantitative Evaluations

S&P Quality Ranking B+

D	C	B-	B	B+	A-	A	A+

Relative Strength Rank MODERATE

61

LOWEST = 1   HIGHEST = 99

Revenue/Earnings Data

Revenue (Million $)

	1Q	2Q	3Q	4Q	Year
2010	5,054	--	--	--	--
2009	5,331	5,607	5,453	6,861	23,252
2008	4,529	5,313	5,349	7,239	22,430
2007	3,591	4,163	4,414	5,828	17,996
2006	2,768	3,292	3,470	4,851	14,380
2005	2,215	2,756	2,950	3,878	11,799

Earnings Per Share ($)

2010	0.22	E0.34	E0.35	E0.48	E1.46
2009	0.21	0.25	0.26	0.38	1.09
2008	0.16	0.25	0.26	0.39	1.06
2007	0.13	0.18	0.20	0.31	0.81
2006	0.10	0.15	0.14	0.24	0.64
2005	0.10	0.16	0.10	0.20	0.55

Fiscal year ended May 31. Next earnings report expected: Mid December. EPS Estimates based on S&P Operating Earnings; historical GAAP earnings are as reported.

Dividend Data (Dates: mm/dd Payment Date: mm/dd/yy)

Amount ($)	Date Decl.	Ex-Div. Date	Stk. of Record	Payment Date
0.050	03/18	04/06	04/08	05/08/09
0.050	06/22	07/13	07/15	08/13/09
0.050	09/16	10/09	10/14	11/04/09

Dividends have been paid since 2009. Source: Company reports.

The McGraw·Hill Companies

Oracle Corp

Business Summary September 18, 2009

CORPORATE OVERVIEW. Oracle Corp., a leading provider of enterprise software, is organized into two businesses: software and services. The software business is further divided into: new software licenses (30% of revenues in FY 09 and 34% of revenues in FY 08) and software license updates, and product support (51% and 46% of revenue in FY 09 and FY 08, respectively). The services business is divided into consulting (14%, 15%), On Demand (3%, 3%), and education (1%, 2%). Oracle's software products fall into two broad categories: database and middleware, and application software. Database and middleware products accounted for 68% of total software revenues in FY 09 (65% in FY 08).

MARKET PROFILE. We expect enterprises to scale back spending on information technology in 2009, as the global economy slows. Until recently, regions outside the U.S. offset slower domestic growth, but we think these economies have since weakened. We think companies will also be impacted by the recent volatility in foreign exchange rates. We expect corporate spending on software to rise slightly, likely in the low single-digits for 2009, mainly due to maintenance contracts. Large enterprise software deals are sporadic and

tend to be susceptible to delays and disruptions due to long sales cycles and the increasing number of approvals needed to close such deals. This should be more pronounced in the current weak economic environment. As a result, we think visibility will be limited and that quarters will be back-end loaded. We think software vendors face intense competition and pricing pressure as they close deals.

With some exceptions, we favor large software providers with significant installed bases and diversified technology assets over smaller best-of-breed vendors. We see installed bases as key, because we think deeper penetration into existing customers is a less expensive way to grow. We think corporate buyers are evaluating not just the initial cost of the software, but also the long-term cost of support and viability of the vendor. We believe this favors diversified software vendors.

Company Financials Fiscal Year Ended May 31

Per Share Data ($)	2009	2008	2007	2006	2005	2004	2003	2002	2001	2000
Tangible Book Value	NM	NM	NM	0.13	0.09	1.55	1.21	1.13	1.12	1.15
Cash Flow	1.48	1.34	1.03	0.79	0.63	0.55	0.49	0.45	0.50	1.10
Earnings	1.09	1.06	0.81	0.64	0.55	0.50	0.43	0.39	0.44	1.05
S&P Core Earnings	1.09	1.05	0.80	0.62	0.52	0.46	0.37	0.34	0.36	NA
Dividends	Nil	Nil	Nil	Nil	Nil	Nil	Nil	Nil	Nil	Nil
Payout Ratio	Nil	Nil	Nil	Nil	Nil	Nil	Nil	Nil	Nil	Nil
Calendar Year	2008	2007	2006	2005	2004	2003	2002	2001	2000	1999
Prices:High	23.62	23.31	19.75	14.51	15.51	14.03	17.50	35.00	46.47	28.34
Prices:Low	15.00	15.97	12.06	11.25	9.78	10.64	7.25	10.16	21.50	5.25
P/E Ratio:High	22	22	24	23	28	28	41	90	NM	27
P/E Ratio:Low	14	15	15	18	18	21	17	26	NM	5

Income Statement Analysis (Million $)										
Revenue	23,252	22,430	17,996	14,380	11,799	10,156	9,475	9,673	10,860	10,130
Operating Income	10,531	9,489	726	5,764	4,802	4,098	3,767	3,934	4,124	3,472
Depreciation	1,976	1,480	1,127	806	425	234	327	363	347	391
Interest Expense	630	24.0	343	169	135	21.0	16.0	20.0	24.0	18.9
Pretax Income	7,834	7,834	5,986	4,810	4,051	3,945	3,425	3,408	3,971	10,123
Effective Tax Rate	28.6%	29.5%	28.6%	29.7%	28.8%	32.0%	32.6%	34.7%	35.5%	37.8%
Net Income	5,593	5,521	4,274	3,381	2,886	2,681	2,307	2,224	2,561	6,297
S&P Core Earnings	5,593	5,481	4,224	3,237	2,750	2,459	2,049	1,923	2,119	NA

Balance Sheet & Other Financial Data (Million $)										
Cash	12,624	11,043	7,020	7,605	4,802	4,138	4,737	3,095	4,449	7,429
Current Assets	18,581	18,103	12,883	11,974	8,479	11,336	9,227	8,728	8,963	10,883
Total Assets	47,416	47,268	34,572	29,029	20,687	12,763	11,064	10,800	11,030	13,077
Current Liabilities	9,149	10,029	9,387	6,930	8,063	4,272	4,158	3,960	3,917	5,862
Long Term Debt	9,237	10,234	6,235	5,735	159	163	175	298	301	301
Common Equity	25,090	23,025	16,919	15,012	10,837	7,995	6,320	6,117	6,278	6,461
Total Capital	35,682	34,628	24,275	21,311	12,006	8,217	6,681	6,619	6,906	7,028
Capital Expenditures	529	243	319	236	188	189	291	278	313	263
Cash Flow	7,569	7,001	5,401	4,187	3,311	2,915	2,634	2,587	2,908	6,611
Current Ratio	2.0	1.8	1.4	1.7	1.1	2.7	2.2	2.2	2.3	1.9
% Long Term Debt of Capitalization	26.2	29.7	25.7	26.9	1.3	2.0	2.6	4.5	4.4	4.3
% Net Income of Revenue	24.1	24.6	22.7	23.5	24.4	26.4	24.3	23.0	23.6	62.2
% Return on Assets	11.8	13.5	13.4	13.6	17.3	22.6	21.1	20.4	21.2	61.9
% Return on Equity	23.3	27.6	26.8	26.2	30.7	37.5	37.1	35.9	40.2	124.0

Data as orig reptd.; bef. results of disc opers/spec. items. Per share data adj. for stk. divs.; EPS diluted. E-Estimated. NA-Not Available. NM-Not Meaningful. NR-Not Ranked. UR-Under Review.

Office: 500 Oracle Parkway, Redwood Shores, CA 94065-1675.
Telephone: 650-506-7000.
Email: investor_us@oracle.com
Website: http://www.oracle.com

Chrmn: J.O. Henley
Pres: S.A. Catz
Pres: C.E. Phillips, Jr.
CEO: L.J. Ellison

EVP & CFO: J. Epstein
Investor Contact: K. Bond (650-607-0349)
Board Members: J. S. Berg, H. R. Bingham, M. J. Boskin, S. A. Catz, B. R. Chizen, G. H. Conrades, L. J. Ellison, H. Garcia-Molina, J. O. Henley, J. F. Kemp, D. L. Lucas, C. E. Phillips, Jr., N. Seligman

Founded: 1977
Domicile: Delaware
Employees: 86,000

O'Reilly Automotive Inc

STANDARD &POOR'S

S&P Recommendation	BUY ★★★★☆	Price $38.99 (as of Nov 27, 2009)	12-Mo. Target Price $44.00	Investment Style Large-Cap Growth

GICS Sector Consumer Discretionary
Sub-Industry Automotive Retail

Summary This company is one of the largest U.S. retailers of car parts and accessories.

Key Stock Statistics (Source S&P, Vickers, company reports)

52-Wk Range	$42.93– 23.68	S&P Oper. EPS 2009**E**	2.23	Market Capitalization(B)	$5.349	Beta	0.47
Trailing 12-Month EPS	$2.03	S&P Oper. EPS 2010**E**	2.54	Yield (%)	Nil	S&P 3-Yr. Proj. EPS CAGR(%)	15
Trailing 12-Month P/E	19.2	P/E on S&P Oper. EPS 2009**E**	17.5	Dividend Rate/Share	Nil	S&P Credit Rating	NA
$10K Invested 5 Yrs Ago	$17,695	Common Shares Outstg. (M)	137.2	Institutional Ownership (%)	96		

Price Performance

30-Week Mov. Avg. · · · · 10-Week Mov. Avg. – – **GAAP Earnings vs. Previous Year** Volume Above Avg. STARS
12-Mo. Target Price — Relative Strength — ▲ Up ▼ Down ▶ No Change Below Avg. ★

Options: ASE, CBOE, Ph

Analysis prepared by **Michael Souers** on November 06, 2009, when the stock traded at **$ 37.78**.

Highlights

► We look for sales to increase 8% in 2010, following our projections of a 37% advance in 2009, which includes growth from the July 2008 acquisition of CSK Auto. We expect this growth to be driven by the opening of about 175 net new stores and by a same-store sales increase of approximately 3%. We believe challenging macro conditions will lead consumers to defer vehicle maintenance when possible, but that industry tailwinds such as the increasing age of vehicles and a recent uptick in miles driven should support continued growth.

► We think operating margins will widen modestly in 2010, as the conversion of CSK Auto stores should drive increased cost synergies. Also, we see continued efficiency improvements from current distribution centers and increased buying power with vendors. We expect modest comp-store growth to leverage SG&A expenses in 2010.

► Assuming a 38.3% effective tax rate and a slightly higher diluted share count, we forecast 2010 EPS of $2.54, a 14% increase from our operating EPS projection of $2.23 in 2009, which excludes $0.02 of acquisition-related charges.

Investment Rationale/Risk

► We expect ORLY to outpace the industry in terms of square footage, sales and EPS growth over the next few years, and we like its dual sales strategy focused on commercial as well as retail customers. In addition, we think ORLY's strong recent execution bodes well for continued market share gains in a fragmented industry. We also favor the acquisition of CSK Auto, and expect significant revenue and cost benefits to result over the longer term. We view the shares, trading at about 15X our 2010 EPS estimate, a slight discount to the S&P MidCap 400, as attractive.

► Risks to our recommendation and target price include an increase in new car sales and declines in miles driven. Our concerns with regard to corporate governance include ORLY's board of directors being controlled by a large percentage of insiders as well as a non-shareholder approved "poison pill" anti-takeover plan.

► Our 12-month target price of $44 is based on our DCF model, which assumes a weighted average cost of capital of 9.9% and a terminal growth rate of 3.5%.

Qualitative Risk Assessment

LOW	**MEDIUM**	HIGH

Our risk assessment reflects the cyclical nature of the auto parts retailing industry. However, what we see as the company's stronger-than-average balance sheet and its large opportunity for continued domestic expansion offset the industry risk, in our opinion.

Quantitative Evaluations

S&P Quality Ranking   B+

D	C	B-	B	**B+**	A-	A	A+

Relative Strength Rank   MODERATE

70

LOWEST = 1   HIGHEST = 99

Revenue/Earnings Data

Revenue (Million $)

	1Q	2Q	3Q	4Q	Year
2009	1,164	1,251	1,258	--	--
2008	646.2	704.4	1,111	1,115	3,577
2007	613.2	643.1	661.8	604.3	2,522
2006	536.6	591.2	597.1	558.3	2,283
2005	466.2	521.2	542.9	515.0	2,045
2004	403.3	435.2	455.2	427.6	1,721

Earnings Per Share ($)

	1Q	2Q	3Q	4Q	Year
2009	0.46	0.62	0.63	E0.50	E2.23
2008	0.40	0.48	0.31	0.32	1.49
2007	0.42	0.45	0.46	0.35	1.67
2006	0.35	0.43	0.42	0.35	1.55
2005	0.30	0.38	0.42	0.35	1.45
2004	0.25	0.31	0.30	0.20	1.06

Fiscal year ended Dec. 31. Next earnings report expected: Mid February. EPS Estimates based on S&P Operating Earnings; historical GAAP earnings are as reported.

Dividend Data

No cash dividends have been paid.

O'Reilly Automotive Inc

STANDARD &POOR'S

Business Summary November 06, 2009

CORPORATE OVERVIEW. O'Reilly Automotive is the third-largest specialty retailer of automotive aftermarket parts, tools, supplies, equipment and accessories in the United States, with 3,285 stores in 38 states, as of December 31, 2008. This includes the July 2008 acquisition of CSK Auto, one of the largest specialty retailers of auto parts in the Western U.S., with 1,342 stores operating under four brand names: Checker Auto Parts, Schuck's Auto Supply, Kragen Auto Parts, and Murray's Discount Auto Parts. ORLY's stores carry, on average, about 19,100 SKUs, and average approximately 6,900 total square feet in size.

The company's stores carry an extensive product line of new and remanufactured automotive hard parts (alternators, starters, fuel pumps, water pumps, brake shoes and pads), maintenance items (oil, antifreeze, fluids, filters, lighting, engine additives, appearance products), accessories (floor mats, seat covers), and a complete line of autobody paint, automotive tools, and professional service equipment. Merchandise consists of nationally recognized brands and a wide variety of private label products. ORLY offers engine machining services through its stores, but does not sell tires nor does it perform automotive repairs or installations.

ORLY currently operates 18 distribution centers, in Georgia, Michigan, Montana, Texas, Iowa, California, Indiana, Missouri, Oklahoma, Arkansas, Alabama, Tennessee, Minnesota and Washington. Inventory management and distribution systems electronically link each of ORLY's stores to a distribution center, providing for efficient inventory control and management. The distribution system provides each of the stores with same day or overnight access to over 116,000 SKUs, many of which are hard-to-find items.

CORPORATE STRATEGY. The company has a dual market strategy, targeting do-it-yourself (DIY) customers as well as professional installers. ORLY believes this gives it a competitive advantage, allowing the company to target a larger base of consumers of automotive aftermarket parts; capitalize on existing retail and distribution infrastructure; operate profitably not only in large metropolitan markets but also in less densely populated areas, which typically attract fewer competitors; and enhance service levels to the DIY market by offering a broad selection of products and extensive product knowledge required by professional installers. In 2008, 52% of sales were to the DIY market, and 48% to professional installers. O'Reilly seeks to aggressively add new stores to achieve greater penetration in existing markets and to expand into new, contiguous ones.

Company Financials Fiscal Year Ended Dec. 31

Per Share Data ($)	2008	2007	2006	2005	2004	2003	2002	2001	2000	1999
Tangible Book Value	11.16	13.38	11.97	10.19	8.56	7.18	6.10	5.27	4.50	3.97
Cash Flow	2.41	2.35	2.11	1.95	1.54	1.31	1.11	0.92	0.74	0.64
Earnings	1.49	1.67	1.55	1.45	1.05	0.92	0.77	0.63	0.50	0.46
S&P Core Earnings	1.48	1.67	1.55	1.27	1.97	1.67	1.39	1.15	NA	NA
Dividends	Nil	Nil	Nil	Nil	Nil	Nil	Nil	Nil	Nil	Nil
Payout Ratio	Nil	Nil	Nil	Nil	Nil	Nil	Nil	Nil	Nil	Nil
Prices:High	32.68	38.84	38.30	32.53	23.54	22.45	18.63	19.22	13.63	13.66
Prices:Low	20.00	30.43	27.49	21.98	18.03	11.46	12.05	7.75	4.13	8.94
P/E Ratio:High	22	23	25	22	22	24	24	31	27	30
P/E Ratio:Low	13	18	18	15	17	12	16	12	8	19

Income Statement Analysis (Million $)	2008	2007	2006	2005	2004	2003	2002	2001	2000	1999
Revenue	3,577	2,522	2,283	2,045	1,721	1,512	1,312	1,092	890	754
Operating Income	462	384	347	310	245	208	175	144	65.2	94.8
Depreciation	117	78.9	64.9	57.2	54.3	42.4	36.9	30.5	24.8	17.9
Interest Expense	28.5	6.28	4.32	5.06	4.70	6.86	9.25	9.09	8.36	5.34
Pretax Income	303	307	282	251	188	160	131	107	83.2	73.0
Effective Tax Rate	38.4%	36.9%	36.9%	34.6%	37.3%	37.5%	37.4%	37.8%	37.8%	37.5%
Net Income	186	194	178	164	118	100	82.0	66.4	51.7	45.6
S&P Core Earnings	186	194	178	143	110	90.9	74.8	60.9	NA	NA

Balance Sheet & Other Financial Data (Million $)	2008	2007	2006	2005	2004	2003	2002	2001	2000	1999
Cash	31.3	58.4	29.9	31.4	69.0	21.1	29.3	15.0	9.20	9.79
Current Assets	1,875	1,102	1,001	911	813	687	631	551	449	364
Total Assets	4,193	2,280	1,977	1,714	1,432	1,188	1,009	857	716	610
Current Liabilities	1,054	529	434	486	334	246	147	121	153	115
Long Term Debt	718	75.2	110	25.5	100	121	190	166	90.5	90.7
Common Equity	2,282	1,592	1,364	1,181	973	784	651	556	464	403
Total Capital	3,000	1,695	1,512	1,249	1,112	935	857	731	558	495
Capital Expenditures	342	283	229	205	173	136	102	68.5	82.0	86.0
Cash Flow	303	273	243	221	172	142	119	96.9	76.5	63.5
Current Ratio	1.8	2.1	2.3	1.9	2.4	2.8	4.3	4.5	2.9	3.2
% Long Term Debt of Capitalization	24.1	4.4	7.3	2.0	9.0	12.9	22.2	22.7	16.2	18.3
% Net Income of Revenue	5.2	7.7	7.8	8.0	6.8	6.6	6.2	6.1	5.8	6.1
% Return on Assets	5.8	9.1	9.6	10.4	9.1	9.1	8.8	8.4	7.8	8.3
% Return on Equity	9.6	13.1	14.2	15.3	13.3	14.0	13.6	13.0	11.9	14.7

Data as orig reptd.; bef. results of disc opers/spec. items. Per share data adj. for stk. divs.; EPS diluted. E-Estimated. NA-Not Available. NM-Not Meaningful. NR-Not Ranked. UR-Under Review.

Office: 233 S Patterson Ave, Springfield, MO 65802.
Telephone: 417-862-6708.
Website: http://www.oreillyauto.com
Chrmn: D. O'Reilly

Vice Chrmn: C.H. O'Reilly, Jr.
Vice Chrmn: L.P. O'Reilly
CEO & Co-Pres: G.L. Henslee
COO & Co-Pres: T.F. Wise

Investor Contact: T.G. McFall
Board Members: J. D. Burchfield, P. R. Lederer, J. R. Murphy, D. O'Reilly, L. P. O'Reilly, C. H. O'Reilly, Jr., R. O'Reilly-Wooten, R. Rashkow

Founded: 1957
Domicile: Missouri
Employees: 40,735

The McGraw-Hill Companies

Owens-Illinois Inc.

STANDARD &POOR'S

S&P Recommendation **BUY** ★★★★☆	Price $31.87 (as of Nov 27, 2009)	12-Mo. Target Price $44.00	Investment Style Large-Cap Blend

GICS Sector Materials
Sub-Industry Metal & Glass Containers

Summary This company is a large global maker of glass bottles and containers.

Key Stock Statistics (Source S&P, Vickers, company reports)

52-Wk Range	$39.56–9.53	S&P Oper. EPS 2009**E**	3.00	Market Capitalization(B)	$5.370	Beta	2.14
Trailing 12-Month EPS	$0.53	S&P Oper. EPS 2010**E**	3.65	Yield (%)	Nil	S&P 3-Yr. Proj. EPS CAGR(%)	7
Trailing 12-Month P/E	60.1	P/E on S&P Oper. EPS 2009**E**	10.6	Dividend Rate/Share	Nil	S&P Credit Rating	BB
$10K Invested 5 Yrs Ago	$16,023	Common Shares Outstg. (M)	168.5	Institutional Ownership (%)	93		

Price Performance

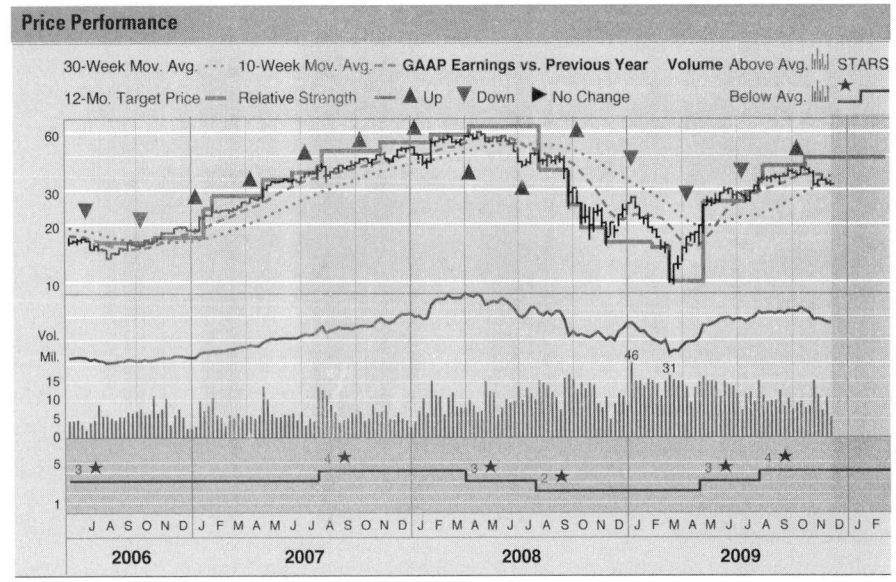

30-Week Mov. Avg. · · · 10-Week Mov. Avg. – – GAAP Earnings vs. Previous Year Volume Above Avg. STARS
12-Mo. Target Price — Relative Strength — ▲ Up ▼ Down ► No Change Below Avg.

Options: ASE, CBOE, P, Ph

Analysis prepared by **Stewart Scharf** on November 10, 2009, when the stock traded at **$ 34.72**.

Qualitative Risk Assessment

LOW	**MEDIUM**	HIGH

Our risk assessment reflects ongoing asbestos claims and volatile commodity costs, offset by our view of sound corporate governance practices and an improving balance sheet.

Quantitative Evaluations

S&P Quality Ranking   B-

D	C	**B-**	B	B+	A-	A	A+

Relative Strength Rank   WEAK

24

LOWEST = 1   HIGHEST = 99

Revenue/Earnings Data

Revenue (Million $)

	1Q	2Q	3Q	4Q	Year
2009	1,519	1,807	1,875	--	--
2008	1,961	2,211	2,009	1,705	7,885
2007	1,684	1,997	1,928	1,957	7,567
2006	1,688	1,946	1,912	1,877	7,422
2005	1,663	1,853	1,808	1,756	7,090
2004	1,268	1,417	1,718	1,726	6,128

Earnings Per Share ($)

2009	0.27	0.88	0.74	E0.56	E3.00
2008	1.02	1.33	0.46	-1.38	1.48
2007	0.31	0.92	0.45	0.06	1.78
2006	0.12	0.24	0.02	-0.71	-0.32
2005	0.73	0.53	0.34	-5.86	-4.26
2004	0.29	0.52	0.40	-0.25	1.00

Fiscal year ended Dec. 31. Next earnings report expected: Late January. EPS Estimates based on S&P Operating Earnings; historical GAAP earnings are as reported.

Dividend Data

No cash dividends have been paid.

Highlights

► We expect net sales to decline at least 12% in 2009, with weak glass container shipments in North America, Europe and, especially, South America and a negative foreign currency effect outweighing higher prices. We see a sequential rebound during 2010 leading to a return to growth for the full year as global markets begin to recover.

► In our view, gross margins should expand in 2010, from our 22.5% projection for 2009 (21.3% in 2008), based on contractual price hikes and a better mix, less volatile energy and other inflationary costs, and a weaker U.S. dollar. We see production being more in line with demand, following temporary and permanent plant shutdowns, and we project wider operating (EBITDA) margins, based on strategic footprint alignment initiatives.

► We forecast lower interest expense and a higher effective tax rate of about 26.5% for 2009. We estimate operating EPS of $3.00 (before at least $0.55 of restructuring and other charges), advancing to $3.65 in 2010.

Investment Rationale/Risk

► Our buy recommendation is based on our view that global market conditions will gradually rebound during 2010, combined with our valuation metrics. We still see challenging markets near term, but we expect OI to benefit over the longer term from growth in emerging markets and new strategic initiatives aimed at improving its footprint in the glass business.

► Risks to our recommendation and target price include a prolonged global market downturn, a stronger U.S. dollar versus the euro and the Australian dollar, another sharp rise in commodity prices, more inventory de-stocking, and fewer long-term contract extensions.

► Our relative valuations use a multiple of 11.5X our 2010 EPS estimate -- close to other companies in S&P's Metal & Glass group but at a discount to our projected P/E for the S&P 500 -- which values the shares at $42. Our DCF model, assuming an 8.5% weighted average cost of capital and 3% terminal growth, derives intrinsic value of $46. Using a blend of these metrics, we arrive at our 12-month target price of $44.

Owens-Illinois Inc.

STANDARD &POOR'S

Business Summary November 10, 2009

CORPORATE OVERVIEW. In 2005, Owens-Illinois began operating under the name O-I as part of a transformation strategy begun in 2004 to leverage its global capabilities, broaden its market base, and focus on its core glass container business. OI believes it is the world's largest manufacturer of glass packaging products. It has 79 glass manufacturing plants in 21 countries, and has acquired 17 glass container businesses since 1990, in regions that include Europe, South America and Asia/Pacific. In 2008, geographic sales were: North America 28%; Europe 45%; Asia/Pacific 12%; and South America 15%. The company accounts for about 50% of the glass containers produced worldwide.

OI plans to further reduce inventory levels to bring supply more in line with demand. We expect the company to focus on improving its operational and capital performance, while integrating operations in Europe and cutting production capacity there by 5%. OI maintains a hedging program, with about 50% of natural gas hedged in North America. In Europe, the company enters into fixed-price contracts for 50% of its energy spend. As of October 2009, OI was entering the final stages of contract negotiations with several large North American customers, which is expected to include provisions for more rapid pass-throughs of volatile commodity costs such as energy. As of late 2009, 25% of North American volume was sold under customer contracts that in-clude clauses for OI to quickly pass through costs. In 2008, currency translation added $276 million to sales growth and $0.25 to EPS, based on a weaker U.S. dollar mainly against the euro and Australian dollar. However, a headwind in the 2008 fourth quarter resulted in a negative $195 million effect on sales and $0.13 on EPS. In the first nine months of 2009, the stronger U.S. dollar had a $526 million negative effect on sales and $0.27 on operating EPS, although the trend has been reversing as the dollar weakens.

In the first nine months of 2009, OI incurred pretax restructuring charges of $113 million ($0.52 a share, after tax), plus other charges of $5.2 million ($0.03). In 2008, OI incurred pretax restructuring and asset impairment charges of $133 million ($0.65 per share, after tax) and asbestos-related charges of $250 million ($1.47). In 2007, non-GAAP EPS of $2.94 excluded net charges of $1.16, comprised of $0.68 of asbestos-related charges, a $0.51 loss from natural gas hedge contracts, and a $0.05 charge related to deferred finance fees, net of an $0.08 gain from foreign tax credits. In 2006, non-GAAP EPS of $0.83 excluded total charges of $1.15.

Company Financials Fiscal Year Ended Dec. 31

Per Share Data ($)	2008	2007	2006	2005	2004	2003	2002	2001	2000	1999
Tangible Book Value	NM	NM	NM	NM	NM	NM	NM	NM	NM	NM
Cash Flow	3.99	4.18	2.53	-0.99	3.91	-3.67	2.84	5.08	0.83	4.39
Earnings	1.48	1.78	-0.32	-4.26	1.00	-6.89	-0.08	2.33	-2.00	1.79
S&P Core Earnings	0.39	1.47	0.36	-0.89	1.22	0.04	-1.45	-0.92	NA	NA
Dividends	Nil	Nil	Nil	Nil	Nil	Nil	Nil	Nil	Nil	Nil
Payout Ratio	Nil	Nil	Nil	Nil	Nil	Nil	Nil	Nil	Nil	Nil
Prices:High	60.60	50.97	22.60	27.50	23.89	15.50	19.19	10.08	24.88	33.44
Prices:Low	15.20	18.48	13.10	17.50	10.80	7.51	9.55	3.62	2.50	19.31
P/E Ratio:High	8	29	NM	NM	24	NM	NM	4	NM	19
P/E Ratio:Low	2	10	NM	NM	11	NM	NM	2	NM	11

Income Statement Analysis (Million $)	2008	2007	2006	2005	2004	2003	2002	2001	2000	1999
Revenue	7,885	7,567	7,422	7,090	6,128	6,059	5,640	5,403	5,552	5,523
Operating Income	1,529	1,432	-1,100	1,297	1,185	1,175	1,281	1,173	245	1,064
Depreciation	431	423	469	480	436	473	428	403	413	404
Interest Expense	253	339	488	467	475	491	422	434	487	426
Pretax Income	558	507	143	-219	210	-1,091	16.6	667	-392	498
Effective Tax Rate	42.4%	29.2%	NM	NM	2.81%	NM	NM	42.9%	NM	37.3%
Net Income	252	299	-27.5	-622	172	-991	9.40	361	-270	299
S&P Core Earnings	60.3	226	55.4	-134	185	5.85	-213	-135	NA	NA

Balance Sheet & Other Financial Data (Million $)	2008	2007	2006	2005	2004	2003	2002	2001	2000	1999
Cash	405	448	223	247	278	163	126	156	230	257
Current Assets	2,445	2,695	2,433	2,282	2,401	2,122	1,887	1,987	2,082	2,110
Total Assets	7,977	9,325	9,321	9,522	10,737	9,531	9,869	10,107	10,343	10,756
Current Liabilities	2,003	2,530	2,366	1,822	1,907	1,363	1,297	1,232	1,318	1,273
Long Term Debt	2,940	3,014	4,719	5,019	5,168	5,333	5,268	5,330	5,730	5,733
Common Equity	1,041	1,735	-83.9	271	1,092	551	1,218	1,699	1,428	1,893
Total Capital	4,311	5,562	5,407	6,110	7,065	6,617	7,359	8,106	8,005	8,685
Capital Expenditures	362	293	320	404	437	432	496	365	481	650
Cash Flow	677	701	420	-163	586	-539	416	742	121	681
Current Ratio	1.2	1.1	1.0	1.3	1.3	1.6	1.5	1.6	1.6	1.7
% Long Term Debt of Capitalization	68.2	54.2	87.3	82.1	73.1	80.6	71.6	65.8	71.6	66.0
% Net Income of Revenue	3.2	4.0	NM	NM	2.8	NM	0.2	6.7	NM	5.4
% Return on Assets	2.9	3.0	NM	NM	1.7	NM	0.1	3.5	NM	2.7
% Return on Equity	18.1	33.9	NM	NM	18.3	NM	0.6	21.7	NM	14.2

Data as orig reptd.; bef. results of disc opers/spec. items. Per share data adj. for stk. divs.; EPS diluted. E-Estimated. NA-Not Available. NM-Not Meaningful. NR-Not Ranked. UR-Under Review.

Office: 1 Michael Owens Way, Perrysburg, OH 43551-2999.
Telephone: 567-336-5000.
Website: http://www.o-i.com
Chrmn, Pres & CEO: A.P. Stroucken

COO & CTO: R.E. Lachmiller
SVP & CFO: E.C. White
SVP, Secy & General Counsel: J.W. Baehren
Treas: M.J. Gannon

Investor Contact: S. Sekpeh (567-336-2355)
Board Members: G. F. Colter, J. L. Geldmacher, P. S. Hellman, D. H. Ho, A. D. Kelly, H. R. Kravis, J. J. McMackin, Jr., C. A. McNeill, Jr., H. H. Roberts, A. P. Stroucken, H. H. Wehmeier, D. K. Williams, T. L. Young

Founded: 1903
Domicile: Delaware
Employees: 23,000

The McGraw·Hill Companies

PACCAR Inc

STANDARD &POOR'S

S&P Recommendation **HOLD** ★★★☆☆	Price $37.21 (as of Nov 27, 2009)	12-Mo. Target Price $39.00	Investment Style Large-Cap Blend

GICS Sector Industrials
Sub-Industry Construction & Farm Machinery & Heavy Trucks

Summary This heavy-duty truck manufacturer produces the well known Peterbilt and Kenworth brand heavy-duty highway trucks.

Key Stock Statistics (Source S&P, Vickers, company reports)

52-Wk Range	$40.26– 20.38	S&P Oper. EPS 2009**E**	0.22	Market Capitalization(B)	$13.526	Beta	1.34
Trailing 12-Month EPS	$0.49	S&P Oper. EPS 2010**E**	0.95	Yield (%)	0.97	S&P 3-Yr. Proj. EPS CAGR(%)	1
Trailing 12-Month P/E	75.9	P/E on S&P Oper. EPS 2009**E**	NM	Dividend Rate/Share	$0.36	S&P Credit Rating	AA-
$10K Invested 5 Yrs Ago	$12,616	Common Shares Outstg. (M)	363.5	Institutional Ownership (%)	59		

Price Performance

Options: ASE, CBOE, P, Ph

Analysis prepared by **Jim Corridore** on October 30, 2009, when the stock traded at **$ 37.65.**

Highlights

► We expect the overall operating environment to start to show some improvement in early 2010. We project revenues will decline 40% in 2009, and grow about 10% in 2010 off a depressed revenue base. We expect the North American market for heavy trucks to start improving in early 2010, driven by fleet owners replacing older vehicles and positioning their fleets ahead of a more stringent set of emission standards scheduled to take effect in 2010. We expect a recovery in Europe in mid-2010, lagging the North American economy by about six months.

► We expect margins to narrow sharply in 2009, as PCAR is forced to leverage fixed costs over a smaller revenue base, and due to pricing pressure. This should be partly offset by lower raw material costs, restructuring actions and cost controls. We expect margins to benefit in 2010 from improving volumes and ongoing benefit from recent cost cutting actions to cut costs. Within the financial services segment, we expect results in both years to be pressured by rising provisions for credit losses and reduced finance margins.

► We estimate EPS of $0.22 for 2009 and $0.95 for 2010.

Investment Rationale/Risk

► While we see weak demand in both the North American and international truck markets, reflecting the weak global economy, we think demand is likely near a trough. We believe the shares have already largely discounted the current weak environment, and we think the stock could see increased investor interest if signs of a strengthening U.S. economy start to emerge. However, the shares are already trading at the high end of their historical P/E range based on our 2010 EPS estimate, which we think will limit upside potential.

► Risks to our recommendation and target price include a longer duration to the current sharp downturn than we are currently forecasting, potential supply disruptions; foreign exchange volatility; and potential increases in raw material costs.

► Our 12-month target price of $39 values the shares at 41X our 2010 EPS estimate of $95, above the high end of PCAR's historical P/E range, reflecting our view that earnings are likely near a trough in 2009 and should start to improve in 2010.

Qualitative Risk Assessment

LOW	MEDIUM	HIGH

Our risk assessment for Paccar reflects the highly cyclical nature of the heavy-duty (Class 8) truck market, offset by our view of a strong balance sheet with a relatively low amount of manufacturing debt and a geographical sales mix that is increasingly diversified.

Quantitative Evaluations

S&P Quality Ranking B+

D	C	B-	B	B+	A-	A	A+

Relative Strength Rank MODERATE

43

LOWEST = 1 HIGHEST = 99

Revenue/Earnings Data

Revenue (Million $)

	1Q	2Q	3Q	4Q	Year
2009	1,985	1,846	2,000	--	--
2008	3,938	4,113	4,005	2,917	14,973
2007	3,985	3,716	3,762	3,759	15,222
2006	3,852	3,937	3,959	3,968	16,454
2005	3,422	3,555	3,541	3,426	14,057
2004	2,501	2,787	2,775	3,190	11,396

Earnings Per Share ($)

2009	0.07	0.07	0.04	E0.07	E0.22
2008	0.79	0.86	0.82	0.31	2.78
2007	0.97	0.79	0.81	0.71	3.29
2006	0.90	0.98	1.07	1.01	3.97
2005	0.69	0.62	0.79	0.81	2.92
2004	0.46	0.60	0.63	0.61	2.29

Fiscal year ended Dec. 31. Next earnings report expected: Early February. EPS Estimates based on S&P Operating Earnings; historical GAAP earnings are as reported.

Dividend Data (Dates: mm/dd Payment Date: mm/dd/yy)

Amount ($)	Date Decl.	Ex-Div. Date	Stk. of Record	Payment Date
0.180	12/09	02/17	02/19	03/03/09
0.180	04/28	05/15	05/19	06/05/09
0.090	07/07	08/14	08/18	09/08/09
0.090	09/15	11/17	11/19	12/07/09

Dividends have been paid since 1943. Source: Company reports.

Please read the Required Disclosures and Analyst Certification on the last page of this report.

The McGraw-Hill Companies

PACCAR Inc

**STANDARD
&POOR'S**

Business Summary October 30, 2009

CORPORATE OVERVIEW. Originally incorporated in 1924 as the Pacific Car and Foundry Company, and tracing its roots back to the Seattle Car Manufacturing Company, PACCAR has grown into a multinational company with principal businesses that include the design, manufacture and distribution of high-quality light, medium and heavy-duty commercial trucks and related aftermarket parts. The company's heavy-duty (Class 8) diesel trucks are marketed under the Peterbilt, Kenworth, DAF and Foden names. In addition, through its Peterbilt and Kenworth divisions, PCAR competes in the North American medium-duty (Class 6/7) markets and the European light/medium (6 to 15 metric ton) commercial vehicle market with DAF cab-over-engine trucks.

In 2008, the company's truck production and related aftermarket parts distribution businesses accounted for 90% of revenues and 84% of operating income. Segment profit margins in 2008, 2007, 2006 and 2005 were 8.5%, 9.7%, 1.9%, and 11.5%, respectively; in the previous cycle, during the boom years of

2000, 1999 and 1998, segment profit margins were 6.9%, 9.0% and 7.4%, respectively.

Like other big truck makers, the company aims to capitalize on a growing trend toward truck leasing and financing. The Finance Services segment accounted for 10% of 2008 revenues, but generated 16% of operating income; it posted 17%, 24%, 26%, and 26%, operating margins in 2008, 2007, 2006, and 2005, respectively. In 2008, 2007, 2006 and 2005, provisions for loan losses were $103 million, $41 million, $34 million, $40 million, and $18 million, respectively.

Company Financials Fiscal Year Ended Dec. 31

Per Share Data ($)	2008	2007	2006	2005	2004	2003	2002	2001	2000	1999
Tangible Book Value	13.36	13.66	11.98	10.27	9.61	7.36	6.08	5.64	5.64	5.13
Cash Flow	4.56	4.70	5.12	3.87	3.09	2.00	1.50	0.91	1.54	1.85
Earnings	2.78	3.29	3.97	2.92	2.29	1.33	0.95	0.45	1.13	1.46
S&P Core Earnings	2.63	3.24	3.97	2.92	2.25	1.32	0.89	0.37	NA	NA
Dividends	0.82	0.83	0.64	0.39	0.33	0.46	0.29	0.24	0.24	0.47
Payout Ratio	29%	25%	16%	13%	15%	35%	30%	53%	21%	32%
Prices:High	55.54	65.75	46.17	36.17	36.19	25.95	15.70	13.68	10.72	12.44
Prices:Low	21.96	42.15	30.12	28.13	22.05	12.37	9.09	8.44	7.16	7.80
P/E Ratio:High	20	20	12	12	16	20	17	31	9	9
P/E Ratio:Low	8	13	8	10	10	9	10	19	6	5

Income Statement Analysis (Million $)	2008	2007	2006	2005	2004	2003	2002	2001	2000	1999
Revenue	14,973	15,222	16,454	14,057	11,396	8,195	7,219	6,089	7,437	9,021
Operating Income	2,859	2,932	3,136	2,572	1,972	1,313	1,012	672	1,122	1,243
Depreciation	649	526	435	370	315	268	218	180	156	147
Interest Expense	NA	737	573	445	331	3.50	249	275	294	223
Pretax Income	1,464	1,764	2,175	1,774	1,368	806	574	255	665	923
Effective Tax Rate	30.5%	30.4%	31.2%	36.1%	33.7%	34.6%	35.2%	32.0%	33.6%	36.8%
Net Income	1,018	1,227	1,496	1,133	907	527	372	174	442	584
S&P Core Earnings	962	1,208	1,496	1,134	889	523	349	145	NA	NA

Balance Sheet & Other Financial Data (Million $)	2008	2007	2006	2005	2004	2003	2002	2001	2000	1999
Cash	2,075	1,948	2,628	2,290	2,220	1,724	1,308	1,062	910	1,059
Current Assets	3,643	3,919	4,200	3,508	3,332	2,599	2,102	1,834	1,861	2,119
Total Assets	16,250	17,228	16,107	13,715	12,228	9,940	8,703	7,914	8,271	7,933
Current Liabilities	1,829	2,503	2,738	2,182	2,151	1,482	1,258	1,134	1,268	1,534
Long Term Debt	19.3	3,039	498	936	2,314	1,557	1,552	1,547	1,655	1,475
Common Equity	4,847	5,013	4,456	3,901	3,762	3,246	2,601	2,253	2,249	2,111
Total Capital	4,866	8,052	4,954	4,837	6,077	4,803	4,152	3,800	3,904	3,585
Capital Expenditures	1,550	1,267	312	300	232	111	78.8	83.9	143	256
Cash Flow	1,667	1,754	1,931	1,503	1,222	794	590	354	598	730
Current Ratio	2.0	1.6	1.5	1.6	1.5	1.8	1.7	1.6	1.5	1.4
% Long Term Debt of Capitalization	0.3	37.7	10.1	19.3	38.1	32.4	37.4	40.7	42.4	41.1
% Net Income of Revenue	6.8	8.1	9.1	8.1	8.0	6.4	5.2	2.9	5.9	6.5
% Return on Assets	6.1	7.4	10.0	8.7	8.2	5.6	4.5	2.1	5.5	7.9
% Return on Equity	20.7	25.9	35.8	29.6	25.9	18.0	15.3	7.7	20.3	30.1

Data as orig reptd.; bef. results of disc opers/spec. items. Per share data adj. for stk. divs.; EPS diluted. E-Estimated. NA-Not Available. NM-Not Meaningful. NR-Not Ranked. UR-Under Review.

Office: 777 106th Avenue NE, Bellevue, WA 98004-5027.
Telephone: 425-468-7400.
Website: http://www.paccar.com
Chrmn & CEO: M.C. Pigott

Pres: J. Cardillo
Vice Chrmn & CFO: T.E. Plimpton
Chief Acctg Officer & Cntlr: M.T. Barkley
Secy: J.M. D'Amato

Investor Contact: R. Easton
Board Members: A. J. Carnwath, J. Fluke, Jr., K. S. Hachigian, S. F. Page, R. T. Parry, J. M. Pigott, M. C. Pigott, T. E. Plimpton, W. G. Reed, Jr., G. M. Spierkel, W. R. Staley, C. R. Williamson

Founded: 1905
Domicile: Delaware
Employees: 18,700

The McGraw-Hill Companies

Pactiv Corp

STANDARD &POOR'S

S&P Recommendation BUY ★★★★☆	**Price** $24.10 (as of Nov 27, 2009)	**12-Mo. Target Price** $31.00	**Investment Style** Large-Cap Growth

GICS Sector Materials
Sub-Industry Metal & Glass Containers

Summary Spun off by Tenneco in 1999, this company is a leading provider of specialty packaging and consumer products.

Key Stock Statistics (Source S&P, Vickers, company reports)

52-Wk Range	$27.71– 10.62	S&P Oper. EPS 2009**E**	2.45	Market Capitalization(B)	$3.189	Beta	1.06
Trailing 12-Month EPS	$2.58	S&P Oper. EPS 2010**E**	2.50	Yield (%)	Nil	S&P 3-Yr. Proj. EPS CAGR(%)	15
Trailing 12-Month P/E	9.3	P/E on S&P Oper. EPS 2009**E**	9.8	Dividend Rate/Share	Nil	S&P Credit Rating	BBB
$10K Invested 5 Yrs Ago	$9,745	Common Shares Outstg. (M)	132.3	Institutional Ownership (%)	85		

Price Performance

30-Week Mov. Avg. · · · 10-Week Mov. Avg. - - **GAAP Earnings vs. Previous Year** Volume Above Avg. STARS
12-Mo. Target Price — Relative Strength — ▲ Up ▼ Down ► No Change Below Avg.

Options: ASE, CBOE, Ph

Analysis prepared by **Stewart Scharf** on October 23, 2009, when the stock traded at **$ 24.70**.

Highlights

► We expect sales to decline close to 7% in 2009, primarily reflecting unfavorable pricing resulting from price adjustments to match lower raw material costs, and lower volume of Hefty waste bags. We expect pricing initiatives and contractual pass throughs to offset rising resin costs into 2010, and see further growth in 2010 in the foodservice segment, especially for cups and cutlery, while consumer tableware sales remain strong.

► We project that gross margins (before D&A) in 2009 will approach 34%, versus 26% in 2008, reflecting a favorable spread between selling prices and raw material costs, and lower operating costs. We see operating margins (EBITDA) expanding further in 2010, from our 24% projection for 2009 (near 18% for 2008), mainly due to price hikes and prior cost-cutting initiatives, which should outweigh higher advertising expense and incentive compensation accruals

► We project a higher effective tax rate of 37% for 2009, and operating EPS of $2.45 (including an estimated $0.17 of pension income), and we forecast an advance to $2.50 for 2010.

Investment Rationale/Risk

► Our buy recommendation is based on our valuation models, as well as our expectations for a sequential rebound in unit volume as economic conditions recover, and better pricing. We project strong cash flow and improved working capital.

► Risks to our recommendation and target price include volatile resin prices, and market share loss as customers continue to purchase lower-priced packaging products. Regarding corporate governance, we are somewhat concerned that the positions of chairman and CEO are held by the same person.

► Our DCF model, which assumes a 3% terminal growth rate and a 7.5% weighted average cost of capital (WACC), produces an intrinsic value of $33. Based on relative metrics, we apply a P/E of 11.5X to our 2010 EPS estimate, a modest discount to peers, to arrive at a value of $29. We think this P/E, which is below PTV's five-year historical average, is warranted, based on a consumer shift to more private label waste bags and other products. We blend our DCF valuation with relative metrics to arrive at our 12-month target price of $31.

Qualitative Risk Assessment

LOW	MEDIUM	HIGH

Our risk assessment reflects a customer shift to private-label products due to the soft economy, supplier and customer consolidation, pension plan costs, and volatile raw material costs. However, we believe the balance sheet is strong as the company generates cash to pay down debt and pursue acquisitions.

Quantitative Evaluations

S&P Quality Ranking B-

D	C	B-	B	B+	A-	A	A+

Relative Strength Rank MODERATE

41

LOWEST = 1 HIGHEST = 99

Revenue/Earnings Data

Revenue (Million $)

	1Q	2Q	3Q	4Q	Year
2009	766.0	901.0	839.0	--	--
2008	808.0	951.0	925.0	883.0	3,567
2007	677.0	828.0	872.0	876.0	3,253
2006	680.0	750.0	749.0	738.0	2,917
2005	613.0	707.0	695.0	741.0	2,756
2004	775.0	858.0	865.0	884.0	3,382

Earnings Per Share ($)

2009	0.69	0.73	0.54	E0.49	E2.45
2008	0.27	0.49	0.40	0.52	1.67
2007	0.43	0.52	0.45	0.45	1.84
2006	0.35	0.49	0.75	0.39	1.98
2005	0.14	0.24	0.28	0.30	0.96
2004	Nil	0.33	0.37	0.31	1.01

Fiscal year ended Dec. 31. Next earnings report expected: Late January. EPS Estimates based on S&P Operating Earnings; historical GAAP earnings are as reported.

Dividend Data

No cash dividends have been paid.

The McGraw·Hill Companies

Pactiv Corp

STANDARD
&POOR'S

Business Summary October 23, 2009

CORPORATE OVERVIEW. Pactiv Corp., a global supplier of specialty packaging and consumer products, derives more than 80% of its sales from markets in which it holds the No. 1 or No. 2 market share position. It operates 43 manufacturing plants in North America and one in Germany. It also has a 62.5%-owned joint venture corrugated-converting facility and a 51%-owned folding carton operation in China. In 2008, 96% of sales were generated in North America (91% in the U.S.). Wal-Mart accounted for 21% of total sales.

After discontinuing the protective and flexible packaging division during 2005, PTV operated two units: consumer products (Hefty) and foodservice/food packaging. Consumer products sales accounted for 38% of total sales in 2008 ($212 million of operating income, before restructuring charges of $5 million), and foodservice/food packaging 62% ($246 million, before $10 million of restructuring charges). In June 2007, PTV acquired Prairie Packaging Inc., a manufacturer of disposable tableware products with sales of over $500 million, broadening its cups and cutlery business.

The company manufactures consumer products such as plastic storage bags and waste bags; foam and molded fiber disposable tableware; and disposable aluminum cookware. It sells many products under recognized brand names such as Hefty, Baggies and Kordite. Hefty products include, One-Zip, Zoo Pals,

The Gripper, Cinch Sak, Ultra Flex, Kitchen Fresh, Hearty Meals, E-Z Foil and Easy Grip. In early 2007, PTV rolled out Hefty One Zip travel bags for liquid carry-on items at airports and OneZip big bags for storing or transporting large items. The company expects new product innovations to generate $100 million in annual retail sales over the next few years.

PTV makes food packaging products for the food processing industry, including molded fiber egg cartons, foam meat trays, aluminum containers, and modified atmosphere packaging. The company also offers tableware products such as plates, bowls, cups, and takeout-service containers made from microwaveable plastic, foam, molded fiber, paperboard and aluminum.

The company estimates that a 1% change in resin costs equates to a $0.03 effect on EPS on an annualized basis, assuming no pricing actions.

PTV incurred pretax restructuring charges of $16 million ($0.08 a share, after taxes) in 2008.

Company Financials Fiscal Year Ended Dec. 31

Per Share Data ($)	2008	2007	2006	2005	2004	2003	2002	2001	2000	1999
Tangible Book Value	NM	NM	0.68	0.23	0.98	0.77	1.79	4.91	3.79	2.19
Cash Flow	3.04	3.08	3.02	1.94	2.10	2.24	2.35	2.14	1.84	0.43
Earnings	1.67	1.84	1.98	0.96	1.01	1.21	1.37	1.03	0.70	-0.67
S&P Core Earnings	0.14	1.51	1.71	0.56	0.64	1.00	-0.23	-0.57	NA	NA
Dividends	Nil	Nil	Nil	Nil	Nil	Nil	Nil	Nil	Nil	Nil
Payout Ratio	Nil	Nil	Nil	Nil	Nil	Nil	Nil	Nil	Nil	Nil
Prices:High	29.52	36.91	36.53	25.58	25.73	24.03	24.47	18.10	13.31	14.50
Prices:Low	18.97	22.79	21.50	16.50	19.80	17.55	15.35	11.26	7.50	9.31
P/E Ratio:High	18	20	18	27	25	20	18	18	19	NM
P/E Ratio:Low	11	12	11	17	20	15	11	11	11	NM

Income Statement Analysis (Million $)										
Revenue	3,567	3,253	2,917	2,756	3,382	3,138	2,880	2,812	3,134	2,921
Operating Income	649	644	568	452	954	630	617	574	570	498
Depreciation	181	165	145	146	169	163	158	177	185	184
Interest Expense	108	98.0	73.0	82.0	101	96.0	96.0	107	134	146
Pretax Income	342	381	391	224	244	314	367	284	207	-159
Effective Tax Rate	35.1%	35.4%	29.2%	36.2%	36.9%	37.6%	39.8%	41.5%	44.0%	NM
Net Income	221	244	277	143	155	195	220	165	113	-112
S&P Core Earnings	18.5	200	239	82.3	96.9	160	-36.1	-91.1	NA	NA

Balance Sheet & Other Financial Data (Million $)										
Cash	80.0	95.0	181	172	222	140	127	41.0	26.0	12.0
Current Assets	785	797	838	820	1,079	982	904	740	900	866
Total Assets	3,692	3,765	2,758	2,820	3,741	3,706	3,412	4,060	4,341	4,588
Current Liabilities	333	460	549	456	984	474	501	459	512	920
Long Term Debt	1,345	1,574	771	869	869	1,336	1,224	1,211	1,560	1,741
Common Equity	640	1,226	853	820	1,083	1,061	897	1,689	1,539	1,350
Total Capital	2,000	3,032	1,753	1,802	2,209	2,617	2,282	3,502	3,595	3,432
Capital Expenditures	136	151	78.0	121	100	112	126	145	135	1,129
Cash Flow	402	409	422	289	324	358	378	342	298	72.0
Current Ratio	2.4	1.7	1.5	1.8	1.1	2.1	1.8	1.6	1.8	0.9
% Long Term Debt of Capitalization	67.3	51.9	44.0	48.2	39.3	51.1	53.6	34.6	43.4	50.7
% Net Income of Revenue	6.2	7.5	9.5	5.2	4.6	6.2	7.6	5.9	3.6	NM
% Return on Assets	5.9	7.5	9.9	4.4	4.2	5.5	5.9	4.0	2.5	NM
% Return on Equity	23.7	23.5	33.1	15.0	14.5	19.9	17.0	10.2	7.8	NM

Data as orig reptd.; bef. results of disc opers/spec. items. Per share data adj. for stk. divs.; EPS diluted. E-Estimated. NA-Not Available. NM-Not Meaningful. NR-Not Ranked. UR-Under Review.

Office: 1900 West Field Court, Lake Forest, IL 60045-4828.
Telephone: 847-482-2000.
Email: investorrelations@pactiv.com
Website: http://www.pactiv.com

Chrmn, Pres & CEO: R.L. Wambold
SVP & CFO: E.T. Walters
Chief Acctg Officer & Cntlr: D.E. King
Secy & General Counsel: J.E. Doyle

Investor Contact: C. Hanneman (847-482-2429)
Board Members: L. D. Brady, II, K. D. Brookser, R. J. Darnall, M. R. Henderson, N. T. Linebarger, R. B. Porter, R. L. Wambold, N. H. Wesley

Founded: 1965
Domicile: Delaware
Employees: 12,000

Pall Corp

STANDARD &POOR'S

S&P Recommendation HOLD ★★★☆☆		**Price** $32.13 (as of Nov 27, 2009)	**12-Mo. Target Price** $35.00

GICS Sector Industrials
Sub-Industry Industrial Machinery

Summary This company is a leading producer of filters for the health care, aerospace, microelectronics, and other industries.

Key Stock Statistics (Source S&P, Vickers, company reports)

52-Wk Range	$35.23– 18.20	S&P Oper. EPS 2010**E**	1.95	Market Capitalization(B)	$3.756	Beta		1.08
Trailing 12-Month EPS	$1.64	S&P Oper. EPS 2011**E**	2.20	Yield (%)	1.81	S&P 3-Yr. Proj. EPS CAGR(%)		4
Trailing 12-Month P/E	19.6	P/E on S&P Oper. EPS 2010**E**	16.5	Dividend Rate/Share	$0.58	S&P Credit Rating		BBB
$10K Invested 5 Yrs Ago	$12,520	Common Shares Outstg. (M)	116.9	Institutional Ownership (%)	88			

Price Performance

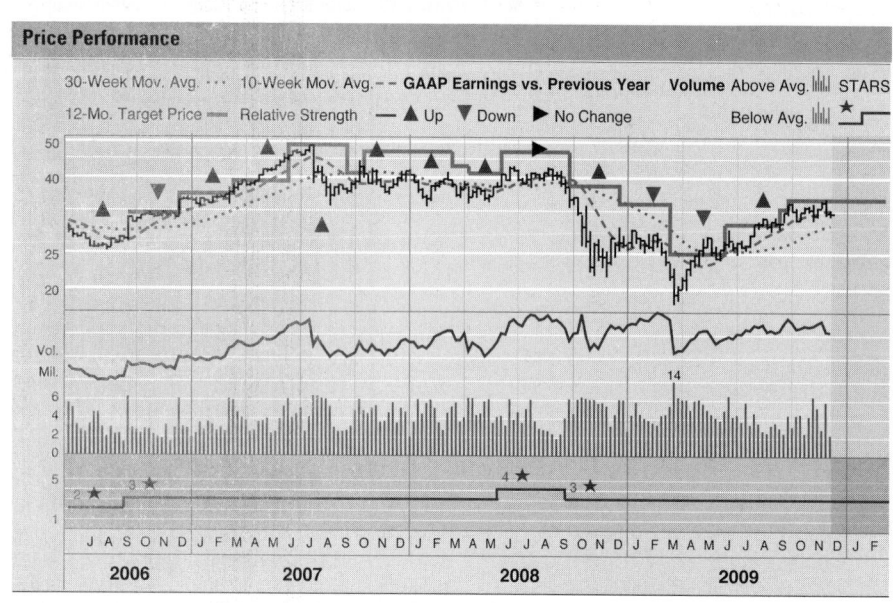

30-Week Mov. Avg. · · · · 10-Week Mov. Avg. - - - **GAAP Earnings vs. Previous Year** Volume Above Avg. ▥ STARS

12-Mo. Target Price — Relative Strength — ▲ Up ▼ Down ▶ No Change Below Avg. ▥ ★

Options: CBOE, Ph

Analysis prepared by **Stewart Scharf** on September 16, 2009, when the stock traded at **$33.17**.

Highlights

▶ Although we believe global markets will remain soft in the near term, we expect further sequential growth in microelectronics, as well as in other industrial sectors, especially in the second half of FY 10 (Jul.), as global economic conditions recover. In our view, demand for semiconductors and consumer electronics products will pick up, while we look for further growth in the blood filtration market and biopharmaceuticals, which should benefit from increased demand for consumables. Additionally, we see more demand in the municipal water market.

▶ We project gross margins to improve in FY 10, from 47.3% in FY 09, based on pricing initiatives, cost savings from workforce reductions, product line rationalizations and a better mix due to fewer sales of the lower-margin systems. We expect operating margins (EBITDA) to expand from 16.7% FY 09, on improved productivity and additional cost-cutting initiatives.

▶ We forecast a lower effective tax rate of about 30% for FY 10, and see operating EPS of $1.95, advancing by 13% to $2.20 in FY 11.

Investment Rationale/Risk

▶ Our hold opinion on the shares is based on our view of still challenging, albeit recovering, global markets, offset somewhat by PLL's diverse geographic and market base. We see favorable trends in some core businesses, and expect PLL to continue to focus on rationalizations.

▶ Risks to our recommendation and target price include an extended cyclical downturn in semiconductors, negative foreign currency translations, and a significant rise in raw material costs. We have some corporate governance concerns based on financial reporting errors that led to seven years of restated earnings, although internal controls now appear to be sound.

▶ Our relative valuation results in a value of $33 using a P/E of 17X our FY 10 EPS estimate, a steep discount to PLL's five-year historical forward average but on par with that of S&P's Industrial Machinery sub-industry group. Our intrinsic value estimate of $37 is based on our DCF model, which assumes a terminal growth rate of 3.5% and a weighted average cost of capital of 8.5%. Blending these metrics, our 12-month target price is $35.

Qualitative Risk Assessment

LOW	MEDIUM	HIGH

Our risk assessment reflects the historically cyclical semiconductor sector, PLL's exposure to foreign markets, and a pending settlement with the IRS and other civil lawsuits related to understating tax payments, even though the SEC inquiry and restatements have been completed. Also, an IRS audit and U.S. Attorney inquiry are still pending. This is offset by our view of PLL's reduced debt levels and positive cash generation.

Quantitative Evaluations

S&P Quality Ranking   B+

D	C	B-	B	B+	A-	A	A+

Relative Strength Rank   MODERATE

47

LOWEST = 1   HIGHEST = 99

Revenue/Earnings Data

Revenue (Million $)

	1Q	2Q	3Q	4Q	Year
2009	578.0	543.3	555.9	652.0	2,329
2008	561.0	625.8	661.7	723.2	2,572
2007	499.3	544.9	559.4	646.3	2,250
2006	431.2	478.4	510.0	597.3	2,017
2005	414.7	469.5	493.5	524.5	1,902
2004	374.3	428.1	463.9	504.5	1,771

Earnings Per Share ($)

2009	0.36	0.33	0.37	0.58	1.64
2008	0.29	0.39	0.51	0.57	1.76
2007	0.13	0.36	0.40	0.57	1.03
2006	0.20	0.26	0.20	0.50	1.16
2005	0.17	0.26	0.35	0.34	1.12
2004	0.19	0.20	0.37	0.44	1.20

Fiscal year ended Jul. 31. Next earnings report expected: Early December. EPS Estimates based on S&P Operating Earnings; historical GAAP earnings are as reported.

Dividend Data (Dates: mm/dd Payment Date: mm/dd/yy)

Amount ($)	Date Decl.	Ex-Div. Date	Stk. of Record	Payment Date
0.145	01/22	01/29	02/02	02/16/09
0.145	04/01	04/22	04/24	05/08/09
0.145	07/16	08/04	08/06	08/20/09
0.145	09/21	10/07	10/09	10/29/09

Dividends have been paid since 1974. Source: Company reports.

Please read the Required Disclosures and Analyst Certification on the last page of this report.

The **McGraw·Hill** Companies

Pall Corp

STANDARD &POOR'S

Business Summary September 16, 2009

CORPORATE OVERVIEW. Pall Corp. is a global producer of filters for health care, aerospace and industrial markets. Pall divides these markets into the following subsegments: Medical and BioPharmaceuticals (the Life Sciences segment), Energy, Water & Process Technologies, Aerospace & Transportation, and Microelectronics (the Industrial segment). The company's Industrial group includes machinery and equipment, food and beverage, fuels and chemicals, power generation, and municipal water. System sales account for about 13% of revenues.

The Industrial segment (60% of revenues in FY 09; $186 million of profits) makes filters and separation products for three markets. Aerospace & Transportation (21% of the segment's sales) includes both commercial and military markets. Energy, Water & Process Technologies (64%) produces filters for the aluminum, paper, automobile, oil, gas, chemical, petrochemical and power industries. Microelectronics (15%) makes products for the semiconductor, data storage and photographic film industries. Consumer electronics accounted for about 40% of division sales in FY 09, up from 25% in 2000. Main competitors in the Energy, Water & Process Technologies group include 3M's CUNO, General Electric's GE Infrastructure unit, Siemens's U.S. Filter, Rohm & Haas (acquired by Dow Chemical in 2009), and Parker-Hannifin. More than 90% of systems sales are in this segment.

The Life Sciences segment contributed 40% of total revenues ($200 million in operating profits) in FY 09. The BioPharmaceuticals division makes filter products used in the development of drugs, and food and beverage filters that help produce yeast- and bacteria-free water. The rapidly expanding blood division offers hospitals and blood centers blood filters that reduce leukocyte (white cells) and other bloodborne viral contaminants, such as bacteria. Biopharmaceutical sales accounted for nearly 59% of the segment's total sales in FY 09, while medical products (blood and cardiovascular filtration) accounted for the balance. PLL estimates the market potential for medical filters at $4.3 billion.

In FY 09, the Western Hemisphere accounted for 33% of sales, Europe for 41%, and Asia for 26%. In FY 09, pro forma EPS was $1.77, excluding $0.19 of severance and other rationalizations costs, and a $0.06 tax benefit. Negative foreign currency impacted EPS by $0.17. In FY 08, pro forma EPS was $1.97, before restructuring charges of $0.21.

Company Financials Fiscal Year Ended Jul. 31

Per Share Data ($)	2009	2008	2007	2006	2005	2004	2003	2002	2001	2000
Tangible Book Value	6.57	6.94	6.14	7.21	6.73	6.21	5.16	NM	6.29	5.41
Cash Flow	NA	2.51	1.78	1.92	1.85	1.90	1.51	1.19	1.53	1.68
Earnings	1.64	1.76	1.03	1.16	1.12	1.20	0.83	0.59	0.95	1.18
S&P Core Earnings	1.55	1.67	1.05	1.22	1.13	1.16	0.70	0.42	0.83	NA
Dividends	0.42	0.50	0.35	0.53	0.38	0.27	0.36	0.52	0.68	0.50
Payout Ratio	26%	28%	34%	46%	34%	23%	43%	88%	71%	42%
Prices:High	35.23	43.19	49.00	35.57	31.52	29.80	27.00	24.48	26.25	25.00
Prices:Low	18.20	21.61	33.23	25.26	25.21	22.00	15.01	14.68	17.50	17.13
P/E Ratio:High	21	25	48	31	28	25	33	41	28	21
P/E Ratio:Low	11	12	32	22	23	18	18	25	18	15

Income Statement Analysis (Million $)										
Revenue	2,329	2,572	2,250	2,017	1,902	1,771	1,614	1,291	1,235	1,224
Operating Income	NA	483	NA	341	337	320	299	215	256	274
Depreciation	89.4	93.2	94.0	95.7	90.9	88.9	83.9	74.0	71.5	63.4
Interest Expense	NA	50.9	NA	23.0	26.0	20.5	24.4	14.3	16.6	14.1
Pretax Income	271	326	261	210	181	198	143	100.0	150	188
Effective Tax Rate	27.8%	33.3%	51.1%	30.8%	22.2%	23.4%	27.9%	26.7%	21.5%	22.2%
Net Income	196	217	128	145	141	152	103	73.2	118	147
S&P Core Earnings	185	205	131	153	142	148	87.4	52.1	102	NA

Balance Sheet & Other Financial Data (Million $)										
Cash	414	454	443	318	165	199	127	105	54.9	81.0
Current Assets	NA	1,660	NA	1,377	1,160	1,070	938	916	779	753
Total Assets	2,841	2,957	2,709	2,553	2,265	2,140	2,017	2,027	1,549	1,507
Current Liabilities	NA	574	NA	531	457	419	421	438	314	438
Long Term Debt	578	747	592	640	510	489	490	620	359	224
Common Equity	1,115	1,139	1,061	1,179	1,140	1,054	935	820	770	761
Total Capital	1,692	1,890	1,654	1,826	1,660	1,559	1,439	1,478	1,149	1,006
Capital Expenditures	133	124	97.8	96.0	86.2	61.3	62.2	69.9	77.8	66.5
Cash Flow	NA	310	NA	241	232	241	187	147	190	210
Current Ratio	2.2	2.9	1.9	2.6	2.5	2.6	2.2	2.1	2.5	1.7
% Long Term Debt of Capitalization	34.1	39.4	35.8	35.0	30.7	31.3	34.0	41.9	31.2	22.3
% Net Income of Revenue	8.4	8.5	5.7	7.2	7.4	8.6	6.4	5.7	9.6	12.0
% Return on Assets	6.8	7.7	4.9	6.0	6.3	7.3	5.1	4.1	7.7	9.8
% Return on Equity	17.4	19.8	11.4	12.5	12.8	15.2	11.8	9.2	15.4	19.7

Data as orig reptd.; bef. results of disc opers/spec. items. Per share data adj. for stk. divs.; EPS diluted. E-Estimated. NA-Not Available. NM-Not Meaningful. NR-Not Ranked. UR-Under Review.

Office: 25 Harbor Park Drive, Port Washington, NY 11050.
Telephone: 516-484-5400.
Email: invrel@pall.com
Website: http://www.pall.com

Chrmn & CEO: E. Krasnoff
Pres & COO: D.B. Stevens, Jr.
SVP, Secy & General Counsel: S. Marino
CFO & Treas: L. McDermott

Chief Acctg Officer & Cntlr: F. Moschella
Investor Contact: P. Iannucci (516-801-9848)
Board Members: D. J. Carroll, Jr., R. B. Coutts, C. W. Grise, U. S. Haynes, Jr., R. L. Hoffman, E. Krasnoff, D. N. Longstreet, E. W. Martin, Jr., K. L. Plourde, E. L. Snyder, E. Travaglianti

Founded: 1946
Domicile: New York
Employees: 10,200

Parker-Hannifin Corp

STANDARD &POOR'S

S&P Recommendation **STRONG BUY** ★★★★★	Price $53.57 (as of Nov 27, 2009)	12-Mo. Target Price $68.00	Investment Style Large-Cap Blend

GICS Sector Industrials
Sub-Industry Industrial Machinery

Summary This company is a global maker of industrial pumps, valves, and hydraulics. Its products are used in everything from jet engines to trucks and autos and utility turbines.

Key Stock Statistics (Source S&P, Vickers, company reports)

52-Wk Range	$59.36–27.69	S&P Oper. EPS 2010**E**	1.76	Market Capitalization(B)	$8.608	Beta	1.45
Trailing 12-Month EPS	$2.06	S&P Oper. EPS 2011**E**	2.60	Yield (%)	1.87	S&P 3-Yr. Proj. EPS CAGR(%)	NM
Trailing 12-Month P/E	26.0	P/E on S&P Oper. EPS 2010**E**	30.4	Dividend Rate/Share	$1.00	S&P Credit Rating	A
$10K Invested 5 Yrs Ago	$11,440	Common Shares Outstg. (M)	160.7	Institutional Ownership (%)	80		

Price Performance

30-Week Mov. Avg. · · · 10-Week Mov. Avg. – – – GAAP Earnings vs. Previous Year ▬ Volume Above Avg. STARS
12-Mo. Target Price ▬ Relative Strength ▬ ▲ Up ▼ Down ► No Change Below Avg.

Options: ASE, CBOE, Ph

Analysis prepared by **Richard Tortoriello** on October 23, 2009, when the stock traded at **$57.11**.

Highlights

► We estimate an 11% drop in FY 10 (Jun.) revenue, after a 15% decline in FY 09, on the effects of a sustained global recession. PH's order rates dropped 20% in the December 2008 quarter, 34% in the March 2009 quarter and 38% in the June quarter, as the global recession steepened. However, order declines moderated somewhat to 25% in the September quarter, and with signs of economic improvement in the U.S. and globally, we believe the worst of the order downturn is over. We expect revenue to rise 7% in FY 11.

► We see segment operating margins narrowing to 8.3% in FY 10, from 9.7% in FY 09 and 14.1% in FY 08, due to declining volume and resulting manufacturing inefficiencies. PH continues to take restructuring and cost cuts to preserve cash flow, and we believe these actions will lead to increased operating leverage at PH when the global economy recovers. We are modeling operating margins of 9.7% in FY 11.

► We project EPS of $1.76 in FY 10 and $2.60 in FY 11. PH generated $5.27 per share of free cash flow in FY 09, well above EPS of $3.13, and we expect the company to continue to seek to maximize cash generation.

Investment Rationale/Risk

► Although orders from PH's diversified industrial base have declined sharply, we believe the worst of the order declines is over, and we see order rates stabilizing in late 2009 and increasing in 2010. At the same time, we note that the shares remain 30% below their 2008 highs and are well under 20-year historical average valuations on price to free cash flow and enterprise value to EBITDA. Given that we think PH's operating leverage will enable it to achieve substantial earnings growth in an economic recovery, and given our strong positive view of management, we see the shares as compelling.

► Risks to our recommendation and target price include the potential for worsening in the global economy, an extended downturn in the aerospace market, and operational or other missteps at PH.

► Our 12-month target price of $68 is based on an enterprise value to EBITDA multiple of 12X our FY 11 EBITDA estimate. Although well above PH's historical average EV to EBITDA ratio of 8.1X, we believe it is appropriate as our FY 11 estimate represents less than half of peak earnings, and we expect earnings to continue to expand as an economic recovery unfolds.

Qualitative Risk Assessment

LOW	MEDIUM	HIGH

Our risk assessment reflects the highly cyclical nature of the company's industrial and aviation markets, volatile energy costs, and a competitive environment. This is offset by our view of PH's favorable earnings and dividend track record.

Quantitative Evaluations

S&P Quality Ranking A-

D	C	B-	B	B+	A-	A	A+

Relative Strength Rank MODERATE

55

LOWEST = 1 HIGHEST = 99

Revenue/Earnings Data

Revenue (Million $)

	1Q	2Q	3Q	4Q	Year
2010	2,237	--	--	--	--
2009	3,065	2,689	2,345	2,211	10,309
2008	2,787	2,829	3,183	3,347	12,146
2007	2,552	2,511	2,781	2,874	10,718
2006	2,114	2,158	2,498	2,617	9,386
2005	1,947	1,943	2,142	2,211	8,215

Earnings Per Share ($)

	1Q	2Q	3Q	4Q	Year
2010	0.45	E0.32	E0.50	E0.49	E1.76
2009	1.50	0.96	0.33	0.31	3.13
2008	1.33	1.23	1.49	1.47	5.53
2007	1.17	1.09	1.19	1.23	4.67
2006	0.79	0.71	0.97	1.03	3.52
2005	0.74	0.63	0.79	0.89	3.03

Fiscal year ended Jun. 30. Next earnings report expected: Late January. EPS Estimates based on S&P Operating Earnings; historical GAAP earnings are as reported.

Dividend Data (Dates: mm/dd Payment Date: mm/dd/yy)

Amount ($)	Date Decl.	Ex-Div. Date	Stk. of Record	Payment Date
0.250	01/29	02/17	02/19	03/06/09
0.250	04/23	05/19	05/21	06/05/09
0.250	08/13	08/20	08/24	09/04/09
0.250	10/28	11/17	11/19	12/04/09

Dividends have been paid since 1949. Source: Company reports.

The McGraw-Hill Companies

Parker-Hannifin Corp

STANDARD &POOR'S

Business Summary October 23, 2009

CORPORATE OVERVIEW. Parker-Hannifin is one of the world's largest makers of components that control the flow of industrial fluids. It is also a major global maker of components that move and/or control the operation of a variety of machinery and equipment. In addition to motion control products, PH also produces fluid purification, fluid and fuel control, process instrumentation, air conditioning, refrigeration, electromagnetic shielding, and thermal management products and systems. PH's offerings include a wide range of valves, pumps, hydraulics, filters and related products. The company's components are used in everything from jet engines to medical devices, farm tractors and utility turbines.

Although U.S. markets still account for most of the company's revenues, PH has been expanding its overseas presence in recent years. International sales accounted for 41% of total revenue in FY 09 (Jun.), and 45% in FY 08.

PH's Industrial business (74% of FY 09 sales and 74% of segment operating earnings) makes valves, pumps, filters, seals and hydraulic components for a broad range of industries, as well as pneumatic and electromechanical components and systems. The company's industrial components are sold to manufacturers (as part of original equipment) and to end users (as replacement

parts). Replacement part sales are generally more profitable than original equipment sales. PH's industrial components are designed for both standard and custom specifications. Custom-made components are typically more profitable than standard components. The industrial business is reported as two segments: Industrial North America (36% of sales and 39% of operating profits) and Industrial International (38% and 35%). Sales through distributors account for about half of PH's total industrial business.

Aerospace (18% of sales and 26% of segment operating profits) primarily makes hydraulic, pneumatic and fuel equipment used in civilian and military airframes and jet engines. It also makes aircraft wheels and brakes for small planes and military aircraft. PH sells aircraft components to aircraft manufacturers as new equipment, and to end-users (such as airlines) as replacement parts. As with industrial components, aircraft-related replacement parts sales are generally more profitable than are original equipment sales.

Company Financials Fiscal Year Ended Jun. 30

Per Share Data ($)	2009	2008	2007	2006	2005	2004	2003	2002	2001	2000
Tangible Book Value	0.07	8.59	10.69	9.75	9.23	9.39	7.63	8.18	8.95	9.96
Cash Flow	5.32	7.43	6.45	5.07	4.50	3.34	2.57	2.37	3.53	3.44
Earnings	3.13	5.53	4.67	3.52	3.03	1.94	1.12	0.75	1.99	2.21
S&P Core Earnings	2.71	5.10	4.77	3.83	3.08	2.00	0.61	0.37	1.19	NA
Dividends	1.00	0.84	0.69	0.61	0.52	0.51	0.49	0.48	0.47	0.34
Payout Ratio	32%	15%	15%	17%	17%	26%	44%	64%	23%	15%
Prices:High	59.36	86.91	86.56	58.67	50.82	52.28	39.87	36.59	33.40	36.00
Prices:Low	27.69	31.29	50.41	43.44	37.87	34.49	23.88	23.01	20.27	20.67
P/E Ratio:High	19	16	19	17	17	27	36	49	17	16
P/E Ratio:Low	9	6	11	12	12	18	21	31	10	9

Income Statement Analysis (Million $)	2009	2008	2007	2006	2005	2004	2003	2002	2001	2000
Revenue	10,309	12,146	10,718	9,386	8,215	7,107	6,411	6,149	5,980	5,355
Operating Income	1,196	1,773	1,513	1,263	1,100	817	639	628	836	829
Depreciation	358	325	295	281	265	253	259	282	265	206
Interest Expense	112	99.0	83.4	75.8	67.0	73.4	81.6	82.0	90.4	59.2
Pretax Income	681	1,327	1,159	900	756	494	297	218	534	562
Effective Tax Rate	25.4%	28.4%	28.4%	NM	27.6%	30.0%	34.0%	40.3%	35.5%	34.5%
Net Income	509	949	830	638	548	346	196	130	344	368
S&P Core Earnings	441	876	846	694	557	357	107	65.0	204	NA

Balance Sheet & Other Financial Data (Million $)	2009	2008	2007	2006	2005	2004	2003	2002	2001	2000
Cash	188	326	173	172	336	184	246	46.0	23.7	68.5
Current Assets	3,124	4,096	3,386	3,139	2,786	2,537	2,397	2,236	2,196	2,153
Total Assets	9,856	10,387	8,441	8,173	6,899	6,257	5,986	5,733	5,338	4,646
Current Liabilities	2,006	2,183	1,925	1,681	1,336	1,260	1,424	1,360	1,413	1,186
Long Term Debt	1,840	1,952	1,087	1,059	938	954	966	1,089	857	702
Common Equity	4,280	5,259	4,712	4,241	3,340	2,982	2,521	2,584	2,529	2,309
Total Capital	6,393	7,374	5,913	5,419	4,314	4,015	3,508	3,750	3,518	3,089
Capital Expenditures	271	280	238	198	157	142	158	207	345	230
Cash Flow	866	1,274	1,125	919	813	599	455	412	609	575
Current Ratio	1.6	1.9	1.8	1.9	2.1	2.0	1.7	1.6	1.6	1.8
% Long Term Debt of Capitalization	28.8	26.5	18.4	19.6	21.8	23.8	27.5	29.0	24.4	22.7
% Net Income of Revenue	4.9	7.8	7.7	6.8	6.7	4.9	3.1	2.1	5.8	6.9
% Return on Assets	5.0	10.1	10.0	8.5	8.3	5.6	3.3	2.3	6.9	8.8
% Return on Equity	10.7	19.1	18.5	16.8	17.3	12.6	7.7	5.1	14.2	17.7

Data as orig reptd.; bef. results of disc opers/spec. items. Per share data adj. for stk. divs.; EPS diluted. E-Estimated. NA-Not Available. NM-Not Meaningful. NR-Not Ranked. UR-Under Review.

Office: 6035 Parkland Boulevard, Cleveland, OH 44124-4141.
Telephone: 216-896-3000.
Website: http://www.parker.com
Chrmn, Pres & CEO: D.E. Washkewicz

CFO & Chief Admin Officer: T.K. Pistell
CTO: M.C. Maxwell
Chief Acctg Officer & Cntlr: J.P. Marten
Investor Contact: P.J. Huggins (216-896-2240)

Board Members: L. Harty, W. E. Kassling, R. J. Kohlhepp, G. Mazzalupi, K. Muller, C. M. Obourn, J. M. Scaminace, W. R. Schmitt, M. I. Tambakeras, J. L. Wainscott, D. E. Washkewicz

Founded: 1924
Domicile: Ohio
Employees: 51,639

The McGraw-Hill Companies

Patterson Companies Inc

STANDARD
&POOR'S

S&P Recommendation BUY ★★★★☆	Price $25.86 (as of Nov 27, 2009)	12-Mo. Target Price $32.00	Investment Style Large-Cap Growth

GICS Sector Health Care
Sub-Industry Health Care Distributors

Summary This company is one of the largest distributors of dental supplies in North America and also sells veterinary supplies and rehabilitative equipment.

Key Stock Statistics (Source S&P, Vickers, company reports)

52-Wk Range	$28.34– 16.08	S&P Oper. EPS 2010E	1.75	Market Capitalization(B)	$3.163	Beta	0.84
Trailing 12-Month EPS	$1.70	S&P Oper. EPS 2011E	1.95	Yield (%)	Nil	S&P 3-Yr. Proj. EPS CAGR(%)	8
Trailing 12-Month P/E	15.2	P/E on S&P Oper. EPS 2010E	14.8	Dividend Rate/Share	Nil	S&P Credit Rating	NA
$10K Invested 5 Yrs Ago	$6,390	Common Shares Outstg. (M)	122.3	Institutional Ownership (%)	69		

Price Performance

30-Week Mov. Avg. · · · 10-Week Mov. Avg. – – **GAAP Earnings vs. Previous Year** Volume Above Avg. STARS
12-Mo. Target Price — Relative Strength — ▲ Up ▼ Down ► No Change Below Avg.

Options: CBOE, Ph

Analysis prepared by **Phillip M. Seligman** on November 19, 2009, when the stock traded at **$ 26.15**.

Highlights

► We project that PDCO's sales will rise 5.6% in FY 10 (Apr.) to $3.27 billion, mainly on the October 2008 acquisition of the regional companion-pet supply distributor and the April 2009 acquisition of a U.K. rehab products distributor. We forecast slightly lower dental consumable sales, as the market appears to have stabilized somewhat amid a still-weak U.S. economy. We also expect basic dental equipment sales to remain depressed, but high-tech equipment sales to show relative strength, aided by promotion activity, including financing. Elsewhere, we expect rehab supply sales to benefit from the U.K. acquisition.

► We expect gross margins to decline slightly in FY 10, as the pressure from higher veterinary supplies volumes as a percentage of sales outweighs margin gains in the dental and rehab businesses. But we expect the SG&A cost ratio to narrow modestly, as several cost-reduction initiatives, including a wage freeze, outweigh the costs of acquisition-integration efforts.

► We look for EPS of $1.75 in FY 10, versus FY 09's $1.72, and $1.95 in FY 11.

Investment Rationale/Risk

► PDCO appears to us to be gaining market share in high-tech dental equipment sales, likely because dentists view its products as offering rapid rates of return on investment. But we continue to expect weakness in basic dental equipment persisting over the next few quarters amid the soft economy. Meanwhile, its veterinary consumables business continues to realize better organic growth than we expected. Elsewhere, we see the rehab supply segment benefiting from an aging baby-boomer population and more active lifestyles, and are encouraged by PDCO's view that the rehab market has recently started firming and the company is garnering market share. We also view PDCO's cash flow as healthy, providing financial flexibility, and believe its moves to expand its salesforces, product offerings, and value-added platforms strengthen it competitively.

► Risks to our recommendation and target price include worse than expected performance in PDCO's operating segments.

► Our 12-month target price of $32 is based on a peer-level P/E of 17X our calendar 2010 EPS estimate of $1.89. The P/E is below PDCO's historical levels.

Qualitative Risk Assessment

LOW	MEDIUM	HIGH

Our risk assessment is based on our view of PDCO's strong long-term record of earnings growth, offset by the impact that the economy and consumer confidence (both currently weak) can have on consumer demand for the services of the company's dental, medical, and veterinary clients.

Quantitative Evaluations

S&P Quality Ranking   B+

D	C	B-	B	B+	A-	A	A+

Relative Strength Rank   MODERATE

44

LOWEST = 1   HIGHEST = 99

Revenue/Earnings Data

Revenue (Million $)

	1Q	2Q	3Q	4Q	Year
2010	789.6	815.0	--	--	--
2009	743.9	759.5	811.0	779.9	3,094
2008	701.4	742.0	777.0	778.4	2,999
2007	655.5	694.3	709.5	739.1	2,798
2006	595.9	641.7	682.4	695.2	2,615
2005	577.9	578.2	638.0	627.3	2,421

Earnings Per Share ($)

2010	0.38	0.41	E0.47	E0.49	E1.75
2009	0.39	0.40	0.45	0.46	1.69
2008	0.39	0.39	0.45	0.51	1.69
2007	0.30	0.35	0.43	0.44	1.51
2006	0.31	0.32	0.39	0.41	1.43
2005	0.29	0.31	0.36	0.36	1.32

Fiscal year ended Apr. 30. Next earnings report expected: Mid February. EPS Estimates based on S&P Operating Earnings; historical GAAP earnings are as reported.

Dividend Data

No cash dividends have been paid.

Patterson Companies Inc

STANDARD &POOR'S

Business Summary November 19, 2009

CORPORATE OVERVIEW. Patterson Companies (formerly Patterson Dental), one of two large distributors of dental products in North America, is a full-service supplier to dentists, dental laboratories, institutions, physicians, and other health care professionals. Through the July 2001 acquisition of J.A. Webster, PDCO became the second largest U.S. distributor of companion-pet veterinary supplies. Also, through the August 2003 acquisition of AbilityOne Products Corp. (now Patterson Medical), PDCO became the largest distributor of non-wheelchair assistive products for patient rehabilitation in the U.S. and the U.K.

PDCO's Patterson Dental subsidiary, 70.3% of FY 09 (Apr.) sales, versus 72.7% in FY 08, provides a broad range of consumables (X-ray film, restorative materials, and sterilization products), advanced technology dental equipment, practice management software, and office forms and stationery. It has a 35% share of a $6 billion market.

Consumables and printed products accounted for 56.0% of dental supply sales in FY 09, slightly below FY 08's 55.8%. The company offers its own private label line of anesthetics, instruments, preventative and restorative products, as well as brand name supplies, including X-ray film, protective clothing, toothbrushes, and other dental accessories. Printed products include insurance and billing forms, stationery, appointment books, and other stock office supply products.

PDCO offers a wide range of dental equipment, which accounted for 33.6% of dental supply sales in FY 09, down from 34.1% in FY 08. The product line includes X-ray machines, sterilizers, dental chairs, dental lights and diagnostic equipment. Two of PDCO's fastest growing product lines are the CEREC chair-side ceramic dental-restorative system and digital radiography (X-ray) systems. CEREC sales slowed in FY 07 and FY 08's first half, but picked up afterward. Not only do we think that dentists were awaiting the launch of a rival's system, but, in addition, the manufacturer of CEREC had production glitches. However, sales of digital radiography systems slowed sharply in FY 08's final quarter.

Other products, which accounted for 10.4% of dental supply sales in FY 09 and 10.1% in FY 08, include software services, equipment installation and repair, dental office design, and equipment financing.

Company Financials Fiscal Year Ended Apr. 30

Per Share Data ($)	2009	2008	2007	2006	2005	2004	2003	2002	2001	2000
Tangible Book Value	1.79	1.01	3.70	2.73	1.95	0.76	3.66	2.85	2.64	2.08
Cash Flow	1.88	1.84	1.70	1.60	1.52	1.27	0.94	0.80	0.65	0.55
Earnings	1.69	1.69	1.51	1.43	1.32	1.09	0.85	0.70	0.57	0.48
S&P Core Earnings	1.69	1.69	1.51	1.39	1.30	1.08	0.84	0.70	0.57	NA
Dividends	Nil	Nil	Nil	Nil	Nil	Nil	Nil	Nil	Nil	Nil
Payout Ratio	Nil	Nil	Nil	Nil	Nil	Nil	Nil	Nil	Nil	Nil
Calendar Year	2008	2007	2006	2005	2004	2003	2002	2001	2000	1999
Prices:High	37.78	40.08	38.28	53.85	44.20	35.75	27.56	21.03	17.25	12.53
Prices:Low	15.75	28.32	29.61	33.21	29.70	17.71	19.00	13.75	8.13	8.28
P/E Ratio:High	22	24	25	38	33	33	32	30	31	26
P/E Ratio:Low	9	17	20	23	22	16	22	20	14	17

Income Statement Analysis (Million $)

	2009	2008	2007	2006	2005	2004	2003	2002	2001	2000
Revenue	3,094	2,999	2,798	2,615	2,421	1,969	1,657	1,416	1,156	1,040
Operating Income	369	379	361	347	329	262	192	161	391	205
Depreciation	22.9	19.5	25.5	23.7	26.9	19.4	12.8	14.3	11.1	10.2
Interest Expense	30.2	0.12	14.2	13.4	15.1	9.60	0.07	0.11	0.12	0.13
Pretax Income	320	357	330	317	293	240	186	152	122	103
Effective Tax Rate	37.6%	37.1%	36.8%	37.4%	37.4%	37.6%	37.6%	37.4%	37.4%	37.4%
Net Income	200	225	208	198	184	150	116	95.3	76.5	64.5
S&P Core Earnings	200	225	208	194	180	147	115	95.3	76.5	NA

Balance Sheet & Other Financial Data (Million $)

	2009	2008	2007	2006	2005	2004	2003	2002	2001	2000
Cash	158	308	242	224	233	287	195	126	160	113
Current Assets	938	985	886	847	800	778	606	529	443	351
Total Assets	2,129	2,076	1,940	1,912	1,685	1,589	824	718	549	452
Current Liabilities	334	466	377	410	322	264	184	198	133	113
Long Term Debt	525	525	130	210	302	480	0.13	Nil	Nil	Nil
Common Equity	1,186	1,005	1,379	1,243	1,015	802	634	514	409	330
Total Capital	1,250	1,660	1,563	1,502	1,363	1,325	634	514	409	330
Capital Expenditures	32.3	36.0	19.5	49.2	31.5	19.6	11.4	11.1	10.0	15.4
Cash Flow	223	244	234	222	211	169	129	110	87.6	74.7
Current Ratio	2.8	2.1	2.3	2.1	2.5	2.9	3.3	2.7	3.3	3.1
% Long Term Debt of Capitalization	42.0	33.1	8.3	14.0	22.1	36.2	Nil	Nil	Nil	Nil
% Net Income of Revenue	6.5	7.5	7.4	7.6	7.6	7.6	7.0	6.7	6.6	6.2
% Return on Assets	9.5	11.2	10.8	11.0	11.2	12.4	15.1	15.0	15.3	15.6
% Return on Equity	18.2	18.9	15.9	17.6	20.2	20.8	20.3	20.7	20.7	21.6

Data as orig reptd.; bef. results of disc opers/spec. items. Per share data adj. for stk. divs.; EPS diluted. E-Estimated. NA-Not Available. NM-Not Meaningful. NR-Not Ranked. UR-Under Review.

Office: 1031 Mendota Heights Road, St. Paul, MN 55120-1419.
Telephone: 612-686-1600.
Email: investors@pattersondental.com
Website: http://www.pattersondental.com
Chrmn: P.L. Frechette
Pres & CEO: J.W. Wiltz
COO: D.H. Peckskamp
EVP, CFO, Chief Acctg Officer & Treas: R.S. Armstrong
Secy & General Counsel: M.L. Levitt
Board Members: J. D. Buck, R. E. Ezerski, P. L. Frechette, A. B. Lacy, C. Reich, E. A. Rudnick, H. C. Slavkin, L. C. Vinney, J. W. Wiltz
Founded: 1877
Domicile: Minnesota
Employees: 7,010

The McGraw-Hill Companies

Paychex Inc

STANDARD &POOR'S

S&P Recommendation	SELL ★ ★ ☆ ☆ ☆	Price $31.33 (as of Nov 27, 2009)	12-Mo. Target Price $26.00	Investment Style Large-Cap Growth

GICS Sector Information Technology
Sub-Industry Data Processing & Outsourced Services

Summary Paychex provides payroll accounting services to small- and medium-sized concerns throughout the U.S.

Key Stock Statistics (Source S&P, Vickers, company reports)

52-Wk Range	$31.85–20.31	S&P Oper. EPS 2010E	1.37	Market Capitalization(B)	$11.322	Beta	0.83
Trailing 12-Month EPS	$1.41	S&P Oper. EPS 2011E	1.47	Yield (%)	3.96	S&P 3-Yr. Proj. EPS CAGR(%)	4
Trailing 12-Month P/E	22.2	P/E on S&P Oper. EPS 2010E	22.9	Dividend Rate/Share	$1.24	S&P Credit Rating	NA
$10K Invested 5 Yrs Ago	$10,815	Common Shares Outstg. (M)	361.4	Institutional Ownership (%)	72		

Price Performance

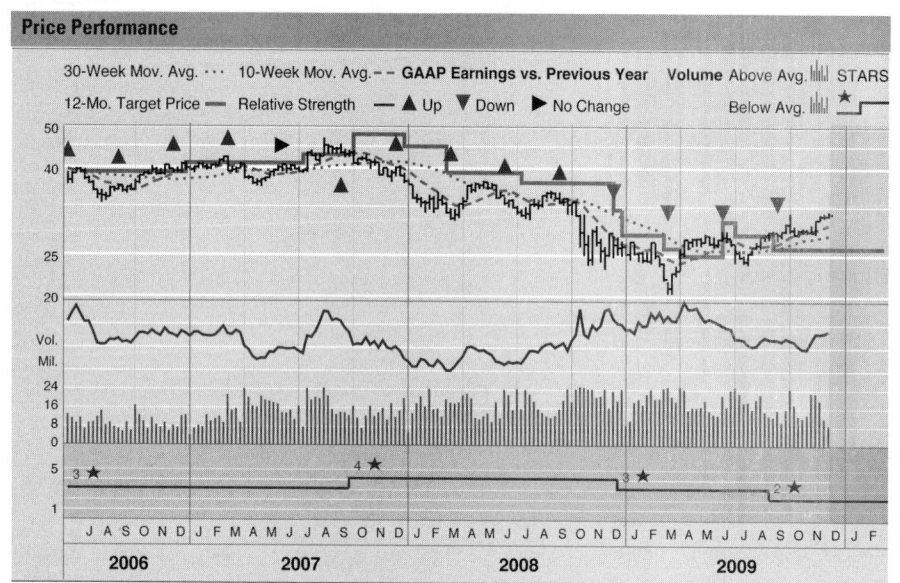

- 30-Week Mov. Avg. · · · 10-Week Mov. Avg. - - **GAAP Earnings vs. Previous Year** Volume Above Avg. | STARS
- 12-Mo. Target Price — Relative Strength — ▲ Up ▼ Down ▶ No Change Below Avg. | ★

Options: ASE, CBOE, Ph

Analysis prepared by **Dylan Cathers** on September 28, 2009, when the stock traded at **$ 28.78**.

Highlights

► After revenue growth of 0.8% in FY 09 (May), we think revenues will decline by 4% in FY 10. We believe PAYX will experience a full-year decline in its core payroll services business, as it is affected by problems among its clients, including an increased number of bankruptcies, fewer hires, and more clients moving to non-processing status. Also, HR services growth is slowing. Interest on funds held for clients should be down sharply again this fiscal year, due to lower short-term interest rates, although PAYX may shift its investment strategy slightly to try to capture more yield. We look for revenue growth of 3.5% in FY 11.

► We think operating margins will be down slightly in FY 10. We believe expenses from rising personnel levels, fewer checks per client, and increased sales efforts will be partially offset by solid cost controls, reduced attrition levels, and high customer retention rates.

► In December 2007, PAYX completed a $1 billion share repurchase plan. This, along with an increased dividend, is still adversely affecting corporate investment income. We estimate EPS of $1.37 in FY 10 and $1.47 in FY 11.

Investment Rationale/Risk

► Our sell recommendation is based on valuation, as the shares recently traded at a notable premium to peers. We believe that near-term results will be adversely affected by the difficult economic and employment environment in the U.S. Further, we think that elevated unemployment rates will linger into 2011. Longer term, we see PAYX's earnings benefiting from solid execution, increased sales of higher-value services, and strong profitability.

► Risks to our recommendation and target price include a faster pickup in the economy, leading to increased hiring by small and mid-sized businesses; greater-than-expected margin improvements from cost-containment initiatives; a faster push into wider-margin HR outsourcing; and slower penetration of Automatic Data Processing (ADP 38, Hold) into the small office market.

► To arrive at our 12-month target price of $26, we apply a peer-premium P/E of 18.6X to our calendar 2010 EPS estimate of $1.40. We believe a premium is warranted, given the company's strong balance sheet, with no debt and over $1.30 per share in cash, and cash flows.

Qualitative Risk Assessment

LOW	MEDIUM	HIGH

Our risk assessment reflects what we see as the company's strong balance sheet and regular cash inflows, offset by the highly competitive nature of the outsourcing industry as well as the threat of new entrants into the human resources segment.

Quantitative Evaluations

S&P Quality Ranking   A+

D	C	B-	B	B+	A-	A	A+

Relative Strength Rank   STRONG

81

LOWEST = 1   HIGHEST = 99

Revenue/Earnings Data

Revenue (Million $)

	1Q	2Q	3Q	4Q	Year
2010	500.2	--	--	--	--
2009	534.1	524.2	528.6	495.9	2,083
2008	507.1	307.8	532.2	519.2	2,066
2007	459.4	455.0	485.3	487.4	1,887
2006	403.7	399.8	430.6	440.5	1,675
2005	345.0	347.3	373.9	379.0	1,445

Earnings Per Share ($)

	1Q	2Q	3Q	4Q	Year
2010	0.34	E0.34	E0.34	E0.35	E1.37
2009	0.41	0.39	0.36	0.32	1.48
2008	0.40	0.40	0.39	0.38	1.56
2007	0.35	0.35	0.33	0.32	1.39
2006	0.30	0.30	0.30	0.32	1.22
2005	0.23	0.23	0.24	0.27	0.97

Fiscal year ended May 31. Next earnings report expected: Mid December. EPS Estimates based on S&P Operating Earnings; historical GAAP earnings are as reported.

Dividend Data (Dates: mm/dd Payment Date: mm/dd/yy)

Amount ($)	Date Decl.	Ex-Div. Date	Stk. of Record	Payment Date
0.310	01/09	01/28	02/01	02/16/09
0.310	04/09	04/29	05/01	05/15/09
0.310	07/08	07/30	08/03	08/17/09
0.310	10/13	10/29	11/02	11/16/09

Dividends have been paid since 1988. Source: Company reports.

Please read the Required Disclosures and Analyst Certification on the last page of this report.

The McGraw·Hill Companies

Paychex Inc

Business Summary September 28, 2009

CORPORATE OVERVIEW. Paychex is a leading provider of payroll processing, human resources and benefits services. The company was founded in 1971, and began by serving the payroll accounting services of businesses with fewer than 200 employees. It currently has more than 100 locations and serves over 572,000 clients throughout the U.S.

The company's payroll segment prepares payroll checks, earnings statements, internal accounting records, all federal, state and local payroll tax returns, and provides collection and remittance of payroll obligations. PAYX's tax filing and payment services provide automatic tax filing and payment, preparation and submission of tax returns, plus deposit of funds with tax authorities. Employee Payment Services provides a variety of ways for businesses to pay employees.

In our opinion, PAYX has shown an ability to expand its client base and increase the use of ancillary services, which we believe will lead to consistent growth for its mainstay payroll segment.

The Human Resources/Professional Employer Organization (HRS/PEO) segment provides employee benefits, management and human resources ser-

vices. The Paychex Administrative Services (PAS) product offers businesses a bundled package that includes payroll, employer compliance, and human resource and employee benefit administration. PAYX also offers 401(k) plan services.

MARKET PROFILE. The worldwide market for HR services totaled $104.6 billion in calendar 2008, according to market researcher IDC. Between 2008 and 2013, IDC expects this area to post a compound annual growth rate (CAGR) of 5.6%, with the market in the U.S. increasing at a CAGR of 5.7% from $50.4 billion in 2008. For the more narrow U.S. payroll services market, where we believe Automatic Data Processing is the market leader, IDC sees a CAGR of 4.8% between 2008 and 2013. In contrast, in the U.S. market for business process outsourcing (BPO) services, IDC expects a CAGR of 6.8% over the same time frame.

Company Financials Fiscal Year Ended May 31

Per Share Data ($)	2009	2008	2007	2006	2005	2004	2003	2002	2001	2000
Tangible Book Value	2.30	1.91	3.87	3.12	2.40	1.88	1.55	2.43	2.00	1.50
Cash Flow	1.72	1.78	1.54	1.39	1.13	1.02	0.89	0.80	0.75	0.57
Earnings	1.48	1.56	1.39	1.22	0.97	0.80	0.78	0.73	0.68	0.51
S&P Core Earnings	1.48	1.55	1.41	1.17	0.93	0.80	0.72	0.66	0.65	NA
Dividends	1.20	0.79	0.61	0.51	0.47	0.44	0.33	0.33	0.22	0.18
Payout Ratio	81%	51%	44%	42%	48%	55%	56%	45%	32%	35%
Calendar Year	2008	2007	2006	2005	2004	2003	2002	2001	2000	1999
Prices:High	37.47	47.14	42.37	43.37	39.12	40.54	42.15	51.00	61.25	29.92
Prices:Low	23.22	35.96	32.98	28.60	28.83	23.76	20.39	28.27	24.17	15.71
P/E Ratio:High	25	30	30	36	40	51	54	70	90	59
P/E Ratio:Low	16	23	24	23	30	30	26	39	36	31

Income Statement Analysis (Million $)										
Revenue	2,083	2,066	1,887	1,675	1,445	1,294	1,099	955	870	728
Operating Income	891	909	775	716	596	516	444	393	700	283
Depreciation	85.8	80.6	73.4	66.5	62.0	82.8	43.4	29.5	26.4	23.9
Interest Expense	Nil	Nil	Nil	Nil	Nil	Nil	Nil	Nil	Nil	Nil
Pretax Income	812	855	743	675	546	450	432	395	364	275
Effective Tax Rate	34.3%	32.6%	30.7%	31.1%	32.5%	32.6%	32.0%	30.5%	30.0%	31.0%
Net Income	534	576	515	465	369	303	293	275	255	190
S&P Core Earnings	533	572	537	445	353	304	272	252	243	NA

Balance Sheet & Other Financial Data (Million $)										
Cash	492	393	79.4	137	281	219	79.9	61.9	45.8	47.1
Current Assets	4,240	4,466	4,861	4,444	3,689	3,280	3,033	2,815	2,791	2,363
Total Assets	5,127	5,310	6,247	5,549	4,379	3,950	3,691	2,953	2,907	2,456
Current Liabilities	3,702	4,037	4,237	3,838	2,942	2,722	2,588	2,023	2,144	1,887
Long Term Debt	Nil	Nil	Nil	Nil	Nil	Nil	Nil	Nil	Nil	Nil
Common Equity	1,341	1,197	1,985	1,670	1,411	1,235	1,077	924	745	563
Total Capital	1,341	1,197	1,994	1,686	1,429	1,249	1,084	924	745	563
Capital Expenditures	64.7	82.3	79.0	81.1	70.7	50.6	60.2	54.4	45.3	32.9
Cash Flow	619	657	589	531	431	386	337	304	281	214
Current Ratio	1.2	1.1	1.1	1.2	1.3	1.2	1.2	1.4	1.3	1.3
% Long Term Debt of Capitalization	Nil	Nil	Nil	Nil	Nil	Nil	Nil	Nil	Nil	Nil
% Net Income of Revenue	25.6	27.9	27.3	27.8	25.5	23.4	26.7	28.7	29.3	26.1
% Return on Assets	10.2	10.0	8.7	9.1	8.9	7.9	8.8	9.4	9.5	8.8
% Return on Equity	42.0	36.6	28.2	30.2	27.9	26.2	29.3	32.6	38.7	38.0

Data as orig reptd.; bef. results of disc opers/spec. items. Per share data adj. for stk. divs.; EPS diluted. E-Estimated. NA-Not Available. NM-Not Meaningful. NR-Not Ranked. UR-Under Review.

Office: 911 Panorama Trail South, Rochester, NY 14625-2396.
Telephone: 585-385-6666.
Website: http://www.paychex.com
Chrmn: T. Golisano

Pres & CEO: J. Judge
COO: M. Mucci
SVP, CFO, Chief Acctg Officer & Secy: J.M. Morphy
General Counsel: S.L. Schaeffer

Investor Contact: T.J. Allen (585-383-3406)
Board Members: D. J. Flaschen, T. Golisano, G. M. Inman, P. A. Joseph, J. Judge, J. M. Tucci, J. M. Velli

Founded: 1979
Domicile: Delaware
Employees: 12,500

Peabody Energy Corp

STANDARD &POOR'S

S&P Recommendation `HOLD` ★★★☆☆	Price $44.56 (as of Nov 27, 2009)	12-Mo. Target Price $47.00	Investment Style Large-Cap Blend

GICS Sector Energy
Sub-Industry Coal & Consumable Fuels

Summary BTU is the world's largest public coal company, with 10.2 billion tons of coal reserves. Its coal fuels about 10% of the electricity generated in the U.S. and 2% worldwide.

Key Stock Statistics (Source S&P, Vickers, company reports)

52-Wk Range	$47.64– 16.65	S&P Oper. EPS 2009E	1.58	Market Capitalization(B)	$11.935	Beta	1.48
Trailing 12-Month EPS	$2.43	S&P Oper. EPS 2010E	2.76	Yield (%)	0.63	S&P 3-Yr. Proj. EPS CAGR(%)	8
Trailing 12-Month P/E	18.3	P/E on S&P Oper. EPS 2009E	28.2	Dividend Rate/Share	$0.28	S&P Credit Rating	BB+
$10K Invested 5 Yrs Ago	NA	Common Shares Outstg. (M)	267.8	Institutional Ownership (%)	76		

Price Performance

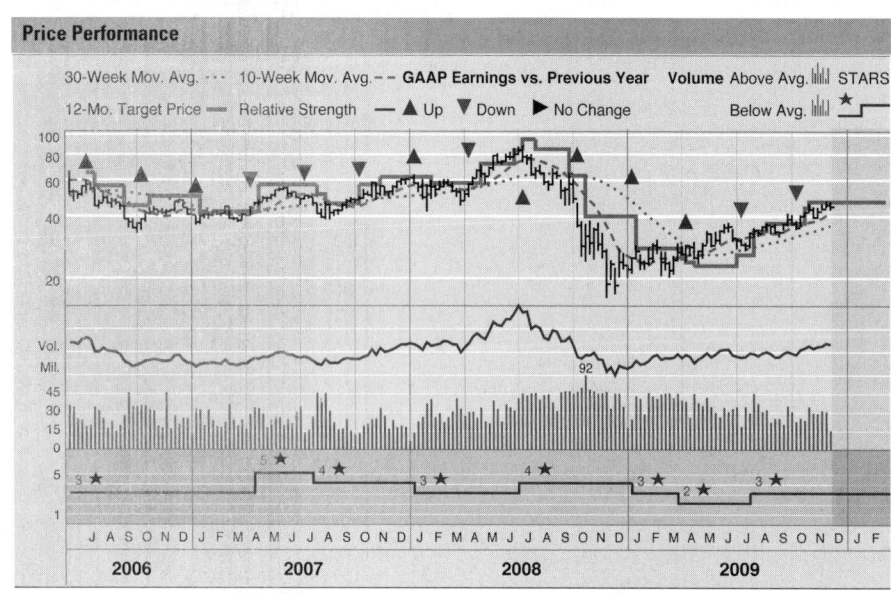

30-Week Mov. Avg. · · · · 10-Week Mov. Avg. - - **GAAP Earnings vs. Previous Year** Volume Above Avg. STARS
12-Mo. Target Price — Relative Strength — ▲ Up ▼ Down ► No Change Below Avg. ★

Options: ASE, CBOE, P, Ph

Analysis prepared by **Mathew Christy, CFA** on October 27, 2009, when the stock traded at **$ 42.31**.

Highlights

► We expect revenues to fall about 7.5% in 2009 and see per-ton prices decreasing about 3%, as higher-priced legacy contracts are offset by re-openers and reduced prices on customer rene-gotiations. In addition, we look for total coal volumes to decline somewhat more than 4% and anticipate lower production across BTU's regions, as high coal inventories, low natural gas prices and slowing electricity production reduce demand. In 2010, we see volumes falling 2% and pricing gains of about 11%, leading to overall revenue growth of 9%.

► We look for the 2009 EBITDA margin to contract to somewhat more than 21%, mainly due to lower volumes, continued increases in total production costs per ton, and lower overall realized coal pricing, partly offset by a reduction in higher-cost coal production. In 2010, we forecast an increase in the EBITDA margin mainly due to better operating leverage off of higher prices and moderate production cost growth.

► On higher projected taxes, we estimate EPS of $1.58 in 2009 and $2.76 in 2010.

Investment Rationale/Risk

► Despite our view that BTU will experience lower coal pricing and production in 2009, we believe the coal markets are in the process of bottoming and note that utility coal inventories have recently declined somewhat while steel producers look to be increasing production, which is likely to help drive demand for metallurgical coal. In addition, we believe BTU's focus on Western and international assets will help solidify its profile in growing and profitable markets. We view BTU's shares as appropriately valued, recently trading at about 8.4X our 2010 EBITDA estimate, somewhat above the five-year historical average.

► Risks to our recommendation and target price include further declines in coal and natural gas prices, lower productivity and production, higher production costs, and higher coal market inventories.

► Our 12-month target price of $47 is based on our relative peer valuation analysis. We apply an EV/EBITDA multiple of 8.7X to our 2010 EBITDA per share estimate, ahead of BTU's industry peer multiples due to the company's size, diversity, historical valuation premium and international growth strategy.

Qualitative Risk Assessment

LOW	**MEDIUM**	HIGH

Our risk assessment reflects the industry's high cyclicality and extensive regulation, the potential for geological difficulties with mines, transportation problems, volatility in the prices of competing fuels, and a narrow customer focus. This is offset by the company's leading market position and geographically well diversified coal holdings.

Quantitative Evaluations

S&P Quality Ranking NR

D	C	B-	B	B+	A-	A	A+

Relative Strength Rank STRONG

86

LOWEST = 1   HIGHEST = 99

Revenue/Earnings Data

Revenue (Million $)

	1Q	2Q	3Q	4Q	Year
2009	1,460	1,341	1,667	--	--
2008	1,276	1,531	1,906	1,881	6,593
2007	1,365	1,322	1,494	1,212	4,575
2006	1,312	1,316	1,265	1,363	5,256
2005	1,077	1,109	1,224	1,235	4,644
2004	788.6	920.1	923.1	1,024	3,632

Earnings Per Share ($)

2009	0.51	0.32	0.41	E0.35	E1.58
2008	0.26	0.89	1.38	1.11	3.63
2007	0.33	0.40	0.12	0.71	1.56
2006	0.48	0.57	0.53	0.65	2.23
2005	0.20	0.36	0.42	0.61	1.58
2004	0.10	0.16	0.17	0.27	0.70

Fiscal year ended Dec. 31. Next earnings report expected: Late January. EPS Estimates based on S&P Operating Earnings; historical GAAP earnings are as reported.

Dividend Data (Dates: mm/dd Payment Date: mm/dd/yy)

Amount ($)	Date Decl.	Ex-Div. Date	Stk. of Record	Payment Date
0.060	01/28	02/09	02/11	03/04/09
0.060	04/16	04/28	04/30	05/21/09
0.060	07/24	08/05	08/07	08/28/09
0.070	10/22	11/03	11/05	11/27/09

Dividends have been paid since 2001. Source: Company reports.

Please read the Required Disclosures and Analyst Certification on the last page of this report.

The McGraw-Hill Companies

Peabody Energy Corp

STANDARD
&POOR'S

Business Summary October 27, 2009

CORPORATE OVERVIEW. Peabody Energy Corp. (BTU) was founded in 1883 as Peabody, Daniels and Co., a retail coal supplier. BTU is currently the world's largest private sector coal company. In 2008, it produced over 225 million tons of coal, with U.S. operations producing more than 201 million tons, or about a 17% share of U.S. production, by our calculation, and 23.9 million tons produced in Australia. BTU sold 256 million tons of coal to 329 electricity generating and industrial plants in 21 countries, and fueled the generation of nearly 10% of all electricity in the U.S., and 2% of all electricity in the world. At December 31, 2008, BTU had 9.2 billion tons of proven and probable coal reserves. BTU owns majority interests in 30 coal operations located in the Western and Midwestern U.S. coal producing regions and in Australia. It also owns a minority interest in one Venezuelan mine through a joint venture agreement. In 2008, 84% of the U.S. mining operation's coal sales were shipped from the U.S. West, and the remaining 16% from the Midwest. Most production in the West is low sulfur coal from the Powder River Basin, which has seen the fastest growth of all U.S. coal regions, according to the Energy Information Administration (EIA). In the West, the company owns and operates mines in Arizona, Colorado, New Mexico and Wyoming. In the Midwest, BTU owns and

operates mines in Illinois and Indiana.

In 2008, 82% of sales were to U.S. electricity generators, 2% to the U.S. industrial sector, and 16% to foreign customers. About 90% of 2008 coal sales were under long-term contracts with an average volume-weighted term of approximately five years, with terms ranging from one to 17 years. As of January 31, 2009, the company had 9 million to 11 million and 62 million to 74 million tons of total unpriced planned production for 2009 and 2010, respectively. In addition to its mining operations, BTU markets and trades coal and emission allowances. Total tons traded amounted to 31.2 million in 2008 (24.1 million tons in 2007). Other energy-related businesses include coalbed methane production, transportation services, and the development of coal-fueled generation plants.

Company Financials Fiscal Year Ended Dec. 31

Per Share Data ($)	2008	2007	2006	2005	2004	2003	2002	2001	2000	1999
Tangible Book Value	10.96	9.33	7.95	8.27	3.33	5.18	5.16	4.98	5.72	NA
Cash Flow	5.31	2.91	3.63	2.76	0.88	1.26	1.57	0.96	3.12	NA
Earnings	3.63	1.56	2.23	1.58	0.70	0.19	0.49	0.10	0.74	0.10
S&P Core Earnings	3.36	1.42	2.00	1.43	0.63	0.11	0.27	-0.03	NA	NA
Dividends	0.24	0.24	0.24	0.17	0.13	0.11	0.10	0.05	0.05	NA
Payout Ratio	7%	15%	11%	11%	19%	59%	20%	53%	7%	NA
Prices:High	88.69	62.55	76.29	43.48	21.70	10.75	7.69	9.51	NA	NA
Prices:Low	16.00	36.20	32.94	18.37	9.10	6.13	4.38	5.55	NA	NA
P/E Ratio:High	24	40	34	28	31	57	16	NM	NA	NA
P/E Ratio:Low	4	23	15	12	13	32	9	NM	NA	NA

Income Statement Analysis (Million $)										
Revenue	6,593	4,575	5,256	4,644	3,632	2,829	2,717	2,027	2,670	2,387
Operating Income	1,774	827	884	703	519	385	390	276	405	NA
Depreciation	454	362	377	316	270	234	232	175	241	210
Interest Expense	226	237	143	103	96.8	98.5	102	89.0	198	180
Pretax Income	1,177	341	531	426	153	-3.18	78.8	29.0	153	26.0
Effective Tax Rate	15.8%	NM	NM	0.23%	NM	NM	NM	12.9%	27.9%	51.6%
Net Income	985	421	601	423	178	41.5	106	19.0	103	10.7
S&P Core Earnings	910	383	541	382	160	23.9	58.5	-5.74	NA	NA

Balance Sheet & Other Financial Data (Million $)										
Cash	450	45.3	327	503	390	118	71.2	39.0	67.7	194
Current Assets	1,971	1,927	1,274	1,325	1,055	683	550	527	630	NA
Total Assets	9,822	9,668	9,514	6,852	6,179	5,280	5,140	5,151	5,209	7,024
Current Liabilities	1,856	2,187	1,368	1,023	774	632	632	684	777	NA
Long Term Debt	3,139	3,139	3,168	1,383	1,406	1,173	982	985	1,369	2,470
Common Equity	2,904	2,520	2,339	2,178	1,725	1,132	1,081	1,040	631	495
Total Capital	6,061	5,975	5,735	3,902	3,526	2,742	2,599	2,590	2,613	3,052
Capital Expenditures	486	649	478	384	267	156	209	194	151	196
Cash Flow	1,439	783	978	739	448	276	338	194	344	NA
Current Ratio	1.1	0.9	0.9	1.3	1.4	1.1	0.9	0.8	0.8	1.4
% Long Term Debt of Capitalization	51.9	52.5	55.2	35.4	39.9	42.8	37.8	38.0	52.4	81.6
% Net Income of Revenue	14.9	9.2	11.4	9.1	4.9	NM	3.9	0.1	3.8	0.5
% Return on Assets	10.1	4.4	7.3	6.5	3.1	NM	2.1	0.3	1.9	0.2
% Return on Equity	36.3	17.3	26.6	21.7	12.5	NM	10.0	2.3	18.0	1.0

Data as orig reptd.; bef. results of disc opers/spec. items. Per share data adj. for stk. divs.; EPS diluted. E-Estimated. NA-Not Available. NM-Not Meaningful. NR-Not Ranked. UR-Under Review.

Office: 701 Market St, St. Louis, MO 63101-1826.
Telephone: 314-342-3400.
Email: publicrelations@peabodyenergy.com
Website: http://www.peabodyenergy.com

Chrmn & CEO: G.H. Boyce
Pres: R.A. Navarre
COO & EVP: E. Ford
EVP, CFO & Chief Acctg Officer: M.C. Crews

EVP & Chief Admin Officer: S.D. Fiehler
Investor Contact: C. Morrow (314-342-7900)
Board Members: G. H. Boyce, W. A. Coley, W. E. James, R. B. Karn, III, M. F. Keeth, H. E. Lentz, Jr., R. A. Malone, W. C. Rusnack, J. F. Turner, S. A. Van Trease, A. H. Washkowitz

Founded: 1883
Domicile: Delaware
Employees: 7,200

The **McGraw-Hill** Companies

J. C. Penney Company Inc.

STANDARD &POOR'S

S&P Recommendation BUY ★★★★☆	Price $29.57 (as of Nov 27, 2009)	12-Mo. Target Price $38.00	Investment Style Large-Cap Blend

GICS Sector Consumer Discretionary
Sub-Industry Department Stores

Summary This company is the leading mall-based family department store operator in the U.S., with over 1,100 retail locations and catalog/Internet operations.

Key Stock Statistics (Source S&P, Vickers, company reports)

52-Wk Range	$37.21– 13.71	S&P Oper. EPS 2010**E**	1.11	Market Capitalization(B)	$6.975	Beta		1.75
Trailing 12-Month EPS	$1.14	S&P Oper. EPS 2011**E**	1.50	Yield (%)	2.71	S&P 3-Yr. Proj. EPS CAGR(%)		-8
Trailing 12-Month P/E	25.9	P/E on S&P Oper. EPS 2010**E**	26.6	Dividend Rate/Share	$0.80	S&P Credit Rating		BB
$10K Invested 5 Yrs Ago	$7,948	Common Shares Outstg. (M)	235.9	Institutional Ownership (%)	92			

Price Performance

30-Week Mov. Avg. ···· 10-Week Mov. Avg. — — **GAAP Earnings vs. Previous Year** Volume Above Avg. STARS
12-Mo. Target Price — Relative Strength — ▲ Up ▼ Down ▶ No Change Below Avg.

Options: ASE, CBOE, P

Analysis prepared by **Jason N. Asaeda** on November 16, 2009, when the stock traded at **$ 31.00**.

Highlights

▶ In our view, middle-income consumers, JCP's target demographic, are increasingly making mostly need-based purchases in response to macroeconomic concerns. As such, we see net sales declining to $17.6 billion in FY 10 (Jan.) and $17.3 billion in FY 11. However, we look for the company to continue to invest prudently in new brands and products in support of growth. We also expect JCP to maintain healthy cash flow in a soft sales environment by reducing capital spending on expansion. The company opened 17 new stores in FY 10 and plans to open five new stores in FY 11.

▶ As we expect JCP to keep inventory aligned with sales trends, we look for increased selling at regular promotional prices and lower clearance levels to drive annual gross margin gains. We also expect the company to remain focused on cost savings initiatives. But we think it will be difficult to leverage expenses off our projection of same-store sales declines of 6.5% in FY 10 and 3% in FY 11.

▶ Also factoring in projected non-cash pension expense of approximately $300 million in FY 10 and $250 million in FY 11, we see EPS of $1.11 and $1.50 in the respective years.

Investment Rationale/Risk

▶ Our buy recommendation is based on valuation. We see JCP aggressively managing inventories, expenses and cash flow while continuing to invest prudently in new brands, the "Sephora inside JCPenney" concept (155 locations as of October 31, 2009), and off-mall expansion in support of growth. We are encouraged by the company's report of positive customer response to new women's contemporary fashion apparel brands such as she said and I "Heart" Ronson and the new Cindy Crawford Style home furnishings brand, which has eased our concerns over merchandising risk, as well as improved sales trends in California, where we think JCP is gaining former Mervyn's customers.

▶ Risk to our recommendation and target price include sales shortfalls due to unforeseen shifts in fashion trends and cost-conscious consumers trading down to discounters such as Wal-Mart Stores (WMT 53, Strong Buy) for basic apparel and home merchandise.

▶ Our 12-month target price of $38 is based on an EV/EBITDA multiple of 8.3X, JCP's 10-year historical average, applied to our FY 11 EBITDA estimate of $1.3 billion.

Qualitative Risk Assessment

LOW	MEDIUM	HIGH

Our risk assessment reflects our view of JCP's strong brand and increasing market share in the moderate department store sector, offset by a challenging macroeconomic environment that has led to weakening sales and profit trends in recent quarters.

Quantitative Evaluations

S&P Quality Ranking — B

D	C	B-	**B**	B+	A-	A	A+

Relative Strength Rank — WEAK
24
LOWEST = 1 — HIGHEST = 99

Revenue/Earnings Data

Revenue (Million $)

	1Q	2Q	3Q	4Q	Year
2010	3,884	3,943	4,179	--	--
2009	4,127	4,282	4,318	5,759	18,486
2008	4,350	4,391	4,729	6,390	19,860
2007	4,220	4,238	4,781	6,664	19,903
2006	4,192	3,981	4,479	6,203	18,781
2005	4,033	3,857	4,461	6,073	18,424

Earnings Per Share ($)

2010	-0.11	Nil	0.11	E0.86	E1.11
2009	0.54	0.52	0.55	0.93	2.54
2008	1.04	0.52	1.17	1.93	4.91
2007	0.90	0.75	1.26	2.00	4.88
2006	0.63	0.46	0.94	1.92	3.83
2005	0.38	0.23	0.53	1.16	2.23

Fiscal year ended Jan. 31. Next earnings report expected: Late February. EPS Estimates based on S&P Operating Earnings; historical GAAP earnings are as reported.

Dividend Data (Dates: mm/dd Payment Date: mm/dd/yy)

Amount ($)	Date Decl.	Ex-Div. Date	Stk. of Record	Payment Date
0.200	12/10	01/07	01/09	02/02/09
0.200	03/26	04/07	04/09	05/01/09
0.200	05/15	07/08	07/10	08/03/09
0.200	09/18	10/07	10/09	11/02/09

Dividends have been paid since 1922. Source: Company reports.

Please read the Required Disclosures and Analyst Certification on the last page of this report.

The McGraw·Hill Companies

J. C. Penney Company Inc.

STANDARD
&POOR'S

Business Summary November 16, 2009

CORPORATE OVERVIEW. In our view, JCP is the leading mall-based family department store operator, with 1,109 JCPenney stores in 49 states and Puerto Rico, as of October 8, 2009. We think the company is also adeptly addressing the needs of time-strapped shoppers with the shopping convenience afforded by its direct business, comprised of JCPenney catalogs and the jcpenney.com web site, as well as its growing off-mall retail presence.

CORPORATE STRATEGY. From FY 01 (Jan.) to FY 06, JCP executed a turnaround plan to improve the profitability of its JCPenney stores. The company focused on delivering competitive, fashionable merchandise assortments; developing a compelling and appealing marketing program; improving store environments; reducing its expense structure; and attracting and retaining an experienced and professional work force. In support of these objectives, JCP moved from decentralized to centralized merchandising, marketing and operating functions, and invested in a new store distribution network and in new merchandise planning, allocation and replenishment systems.

With what we view as the success of its turnaround, JCP has mapped out a new long-range plan for making JCPenney the preferred shopping choice for "Middle America," which it defines as customers aged 35 to 54 with annual household incomes of $35,000 to $85,000. Key strategies include offering styles that make an emotional connection with the customer; making it easier for the customer to shop seamlessly across store/catalog/Internet channels; creating and sustaining a customer-focused culture; and using the off-mall store format to expand the company's presence in high-potential markets. JCP sees the potential for up to 400 new stores, relocations or expansions on a long-term basis.

Company Financials Fiscal Year Ended Jan. 31

Per Share Data ($)	2009	2008	2007	2006	2005	2004	2003	2002	2001	2000
Tangible Book Value	18.09	23.93	18.97	17.20	17.92	18.54	12.04	11.46	NM	14.28
Cash Flow	4.65	6.80	6.57	5.79	3.33	2.68	3.45	3.00	0.36	3.87
Earnings	2.54	4.91	4.88	3.83	2.23	1.21	1.25	0.32	-2.29	1.16
S&P Core Earnings	1.15	4.37	4.66	3.77	2.26	1.24	0.66	0.15	-2.47	NA
Dividends	0.80	0.72	0.50	0.50	0.50	0.50	0.50	0.50	0.50	2.19
Payout Ratio	31%	15%	10%	13%	22%	41%	40%	156%	NM	188%
Calendar Year	2008	2007	2006	2005	2004	2003	2002	2001	2000	1999
Prices:High	51.42	87.18	82.49	57.99	41.82	26.42	27.75	29.50	22.50	54.44
Prices:Low	13.95	39.98	54.18	40.26	25.29	15.57	14.07	10.50	8.63	17.69
P/E Ratio:High	20	18	17	15	19	22	22	92	NM	47
P/E Ratio:Low	5	8	11	11	11	13	11	33	NM	15

Income Statement Analysis (Million $)										
Revenue	18,486	19,860	19,903	18,781	18,424	17,786	32,347	32,004	31,846	32,510
Operating Income	1,579	2,268	2,277	1,949	1,680	1,184	1,681	1,473	873	1,681
Depreciation	469	426	389	372	368	394	667	717	695	710
Interest Expense	268	278	270	169	233	261	388	386	427	673
Pretax Income	910	1,723	1,792	1,444	1,020	546	584	203	-886	531
Effective Tax Rate	37.7%	35.9%	36.7%	32.3%	34.6%	33.3%	36.5%	43.8%	NM	36.7%
Net Income	567	1,105	1,134	977	667	345	371	114	-568	336
S&P Core Earnings	258	986	1,081	960	662	345	171	41.0	-650	NA

Balance Sheet & Other Financial Data (Million $)										
Cash	2,352	2,471	2,747	3,016	4,687	2,994	2,474	2,840	944	1,233
Current Assets	6,220	6,751	6,648	6,702	8,427	6,515	8,353	8,677	7,257	8,472
Total Assets	12,011	14,309	12,673	12,461	14,127	18,300	17,867	18,048	19,742	20,888
Current Liabilities	2,794	3,338	3,492	2,762	3,447	3,754	4,159	4,499	4,235	4,465
Long Term Debt	3,505	3,505	3,010	3,444	3,464	5,114	4,940	5,179	5,448	5,844
Common Equity	4,155	5,312	4,288	4,007	4,856	5,121	6,037	5,766	5,860	6,782
Total Capital	7,659	10,280	8,504	8,738	9,638	11,756	12,701	12,539	12,843	14,087
Capital Expenditures	969	1,243	772	535	412	373	658	631	648	631
Cash Flow	1,036	1,531	1,523	1,349	1,023	733	1,011	802	94.0	1,010
Current Ratio	2.2	2.0	1.9	2.4	2.4	1.7	2.0	1.9	1.7	1.9
% Long Term Debt of Capitalization	45.8	34.1	41.2	39.4	35.9	43.5	38.9	41.3	42.4	41.5
% Net Income of Revenue	3.1	5.6	5.7	5.2	3.6	2.0	1.1	0.4	NM	1.0
% Return on Assets	4.3	8.2	9.0	7.3	4.1	2.0	2.1	0.1	NM	1.5
% Return on Equity	12.0	23.0	27.3	22.0	13.1	6.1	5.8	1.9	NM	4.5

Data as orig reptd.; bef. results of disc opers/spec. items. Per share data adj. for stk. divs.; EPS diluted. E-Estimated. NA-Not Available. NM-Not Meaningful. NR-Not Ranked. UR-Under Review.

Office: 6501 Legacy Drive, Plano, TX 75024-3698.
Telephone: 972-431-1000.
Website: http://www.jcpenney.net
Chrmn & CEO: M.E. Ullman, III

EVP & CFO: R.B. Cavanaugh
EVP & Chief Admin Officer: M.T. Theilmann
EVP, Secy & General Counsel: J.L. Dhillon
EVP & CIO: T.M. Nealon

Investor Contact: P. Sanchez (972-431-5575)
Board Members: C. C. Barrett, M. A. Burns, M. K. Clark, T. J. Engibous, K. B. Foster, B. Osborne, J. A. Rein, L. H. Roberts, J. G. Teruel, R. G. Turner, M. E. Ullman, III, M. B. West

Founded: 1902
Domicile: Delaware
Employees: 147,000

People's United Financial Inc

STANDARD &POOR'S

S&P Recommendation	BUY ★★★★☆	Price	12-Mo. Target Price	Investment Style
		$16.37 (as of Nov 27, 2009)	$20.00	Large-Cap Blend

GICS Sector Financials
Sub-Industry Thrifts & Mortgage Finance

Summary This company provides banking and financial services in four states, with most of its business concentrated in Connecticut.

Key Stock Statistics (Source S&P, Vickers, company reports)

52-Wk Range	$18.73– 14.72	S&P Oper. EPS 2009**E**	0.32	Market Capitalization(B)	$5.701	Beta	0.12
Trailing 12-Month EPS	$0.34	S&P Oper. EPS 2010**E**	0.38	Yield (%)	3.73	S&P 3-Yr. Proj. EPS CAGR(%)	4
Trailing 12-Month P/E	48.2	P/E on S&P Oper. EPS 2009**E**	51.2	Dividend Rate/Share	$0.61	S&P Credit Rating	A-
$10K Invested 5 Yrs Ago	$15,223	Common Shares Outstg. (M)	348.3	Institutional Ownership (%)	77		

Price Performance

30-Week Mov. Avg. · · · 10-Week Mov. Avg. ‑ ‑ **GAAP Earnings vs. Previous Year** Volume Above Avg. STARS
12-Mo. Target Price — Relative Strength — ▲ Up ▼ Down ► No Change Below Avg.

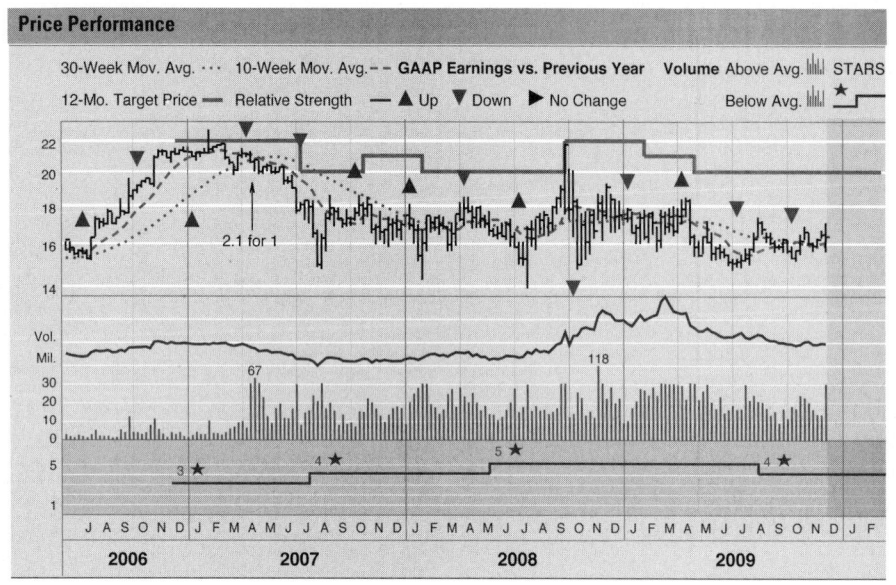

Options: ASE, CBOE, Ph

Analysis prepared by **Stuart Plesser** on November 23, 2009, when the stock traded at **$ 16.47**.

Qualitative Risk Assessment

LOW	MEDIUM	HIGH

Our risk assessment reflects our view of the good credit quality of PBCT's loan portfolio and its history of profitability, offset by execution risk, mostly stemming from the investment of the proceeds from the company's second-step conversion.

Quantitative Evaluations

S&P Quality Ranking B

D	C	B-	B	B+	A-	A	A+

Relative Strength Rank MODERATE

60

LOWEST = 1 HIGHEST = 99

Revenue/Earnings Data

Revenue (Million $)

	1Q	2Q	3Q	4Q	Year
2009	267.4	277.2	272.1	--	--
2008	337.2	300.9	296.6	286.1	1,221
2007	193.0	233.0	239.6	226.8	892.4
2006	179.5	183.5	161.4	195.9	729.5
2005	157.2	164.3	172.7	185.5	679.7
2004	141.7	143.7	149.6	152.9	587.9

Earnings Per Share ($)

2009	0.08	0.08	0.08	E0.08	E0.32
2008	0.05	0.13	0.14	0.11	0.42
2007	0.11	0.05	0.20	0.16	0.51
2006	0.11	0.11	0.05	0.13	0.40
2005	0.10	0.10	0.11	0.11	0.42
2004	-0.26	0.08	0.08	0.09	-0.02

Fiscal year ended Dec. 31. Next earnings report expected: Late January. EPS Estimates based on S&P Operating Earnings; historical GAAP earnings are as reported.

Highlights

► We believe a modest increase in average earning assets, combined with a slight widening of the net interest margin assuming interest rates rise in 2010, will result in a 1.0% increase in revenue in 2010. Our 2010 estimates include a net interest margin of 3.25%, up five basis points from the projected 2009 level, assuming rate increases.

► We see expenses declining modestly in 2010, assuming continued cost-cutting efforts from the Chittenden acquisition and no further special FDIC assessment. All told, we look for expenses to increase to 75.0% of revenue in 2010, down from a projected 76% in 2009. Asset quality deteriorated in the third quarter due to a deepening downturn in the credit cycle. We expect 2009 provisions of roughly $57 million, but a decline to only $34 million in 2010, assuming the credit downturn eases by the end of 2009 or the beginning of 2010. We see reserve building ending in early 2010.

► Assuming an effective tax rate of 31.0% and a slight increase in shares outstanding, we estimate 2009 EPS of $0.32. Based on a widening net interest margin, we look for EPS of $0.38 in 2010.

Investment Rationale/Risk

► People's United Financial completed its second-step conversion in April 2007, raising $3.4 billion. It then purchased Chittenden (CHZ) for $1.9 billion in a cash/stock deal that closed in early January 2008. PBCT's liquidity has hurt its net interest margin, but it is beginning to put its excess funds to work. It recently announced the planned acquisition of Financial Federal Corporation (FIF 27, NR) for $738 million, which would give PBCT additional exposure to high-yielding equipment leasing. The deal, expected to close in the first quarter of 2010 pending necessary approvals, should be accretive to earnings with an internal rate of return above 20%. We expect further deals to follow, as PBCT will likely continue to put its excess liquidity to work.

► Risks to our recommendation and target price include possible integration problems related to the Chittenden acquisition, and pursuing a poorly priced acquisition.

► Our 12-month target price of $20 is based on a roughly 1.87X multiple of current tangible book value of $10.77 per share, a premium to regional bank peers, warranted, in our view, by PBCT's strong balance sheet.

Dividend Data (Dates: mm/dd Payment Date: mm/dd/yy)

Amount ($)	Date Decl.	Ex-Div. Date	Stk. of Record	Payment Date
0.150	01/22	01/28	02/01	02/15/09
0.153	04/16	04/29	05/01	05/15/09
0.153	07/16	07/29	08/01	08/15/09
0.153	10/15	10/28	11/01	11/15/09

Dividends have been paid since 1993. Source: Company reports.

Please read the Required Disclosures and Analyst Certification on the last page of this report.

The McGraw-Hill Companies

People's United Financial Inc

STANDARD
&POOR'S

Business Summary November 23, 2009

CORPORATE OVERVIEW. People's United Financial (formerly People's Bank of Connecticut), formed in 1842, is a state-chartered stock savings bank headquartered in Bridgeport, CT. As of December 31, 2008, assets totaled roughly $20.2 billion. The company offers a full range of financial services to individual, corporate and municipal customers. In addition to traditional banking activities, People's provides specialized services tailored to specific markets, including personal, institutional and employee benefits; cash management; and municipal banking and finance. PBCT offers brokerage, financial advisory services and life insurance through its People's Securities subsidiary and Chittenden Securities; equipment financing through People's Capital and Leasing (PCLC); and other insurance services through R.C. Knox and Company, Inc. and Chittenden Insurance Group, LLC Services are delivered through a network of over 300 branches in Connecticut, Massachusetts, New Hampshire, Vermont, Maine and New York, including 79 full-service supermarket branches, 43 investment and brokerage offices, nine PCLC offices, 16 commercial banking offices, and over 400 ATMs.

PBCT has increased its residential mortgage and home equity lending activities in the contiguous markets of New York and Massachusetts. In addition, PBCT maintains a loan production office in Massachusetts, and PCLC maintains a sales presence in six states to support its equipment financing operations outside of New England. Within the Commercial Banking division, PBCT maintains a national credits group, which has participated in commercial loans and real estate loans to borrowers in various industries on a national scale.

PRIMARY BUSINESS DYNAMICS. As of December 31, 2008, total loans of $14.6 billion were 22% residential real estate loans (versus 36% in 2007); 29% commercial loans (29%); 34% commercial real estate (21%); and 15% consumer loans (14%).

As of December 31, 2008, deposits comprised 97.5% of funding costs versus 99.3% at December 31, 2007. At year-end 2008, deposits consisted of non-interest 22% (versus 24% in 2007); low interest 44% (34%); and time deposits 34% (42%).

Company Financials Fiscal Year Ended Dec. 31

Per Share Data ($)	2008	2007	2006	2005	2004	2003	2002	2001	2000	1999
Tangible Book Value	10.87	15.06	8.68	3.98	5.53	4.55	2.83	2.82	2.61	2.25
Earnings	0.42	0.51	0.40	0.42	-0.02	0.22	0.19	0.30	0.37	0.38
S&P Core Earnings	0.37	0.51	0.41	0.41	-0.01	0.22	0.16	0.09	NA	NA
Dividends	0.58	0.52	0.46	0.41	0.45	0.32	0.30	0.28	0.25	0.22
Payout Ratio	138%	102%	115%	96%	NM	148%	158%	96%	68%	57%
Prices:High	21.76	22.81	21.62	16.07	14.12	7.20	5.94	6.01	5.71	6.83
Prices:Low	13.92	14.78	14.29	11.43	6.88	5.13	4.37	4.37	3.47	4.07
P/E Ratio:High	52	45	54	38	NM	33	31	20	15	18
P/E Ratio:Low	33	29	36	27	NM	23	23	15	9	11

Income Statement Analysis (Million $)										
Net Interest Income	636	487	382	370	327	320	351	354	385	338
Loan Loss Provision	26.2	8.00	3.40	8.60	13.3	48.6	77.7	101	59.9	54.5
Non Interest Income	303	180	175	172	155	252	251	339	290	282
Non Interest Expenses	654	439	347	343	479	436	441	441	453	414
Pretax Income	208	225	180	190	-14.2	86.9	80.4	133	166	170
Effective Tax Rate	32.8%	33.6%	32.2%	33.7%	NM	26.6%	31.1%	34.8%	34.5%	34.3%
Net Income	140	149	122	126	-5.60	63.8	55.4	86.7	108	112
% Net Interest Margin	3.62	4.12	3.87	3.68	3.33	2.95	3.40	4.33	4.47	4.26
S&P Core Earnings	124	147	124	124	-4.16	63.9	46.6	27.2	NA	NA

Balance Sheet & Other Financial Data (Million $)										
Total Assets	20,168	13,555	10,687	10,933	10,718	11,672	12,261	11,891	11,571	10,738
Loans	14,566	8,877	9,298	8,498	7,861	8,122	7,336	6,931	7,345	6,970
Deposits	14,269	8,881	9,083	9,083	8,862	8,714	8,426	7,983	7,761	7,191
Capitalization:Debt	368	65.4	65.3	109	122	1,162	1,165	1,478	1,824	1,046
Capitalization:Equity	5,176	4,445	1,340	1,289	1,200	1,002	940	935	882	782
Capitalization:Total	5,544	4,511	1,405	1,398	1,322	2,164	2,104	2,413	2,706	1,828
% Return on Assets	0.8	1.2	1.1	1.2	NM	0.5	0.5	0.7	1.0	1.1
% Return on Equity	2.9	5.2	9.3	10.1	NM	6.6	5.9	9.5	13.0	13.7
% Loan Loss Reserve	1.1	0.8	0.8	0.9	0.9	1.4	1.5	1.6	1.4	1.5
% Risk Based Capital	13400.0	33.4	16.1	16.4	16.7	13.1	12.5	12.3	11.6	10.9
Price Times Book Value:High	2.0	1.5	2.5	4.0	2.6	1.6	2.1	2.1	2.2	3.0
Price Times Book Value:Low	1.3	1.0	1.6	2.9	1.2	1.1	1.5	1.6	1.3	1.8

Data as orig reptd.; bef. results of disc opers/spec. items. Per share data adj. for stk. divs.; EPS diluted. E-Estimated. NA-Not Available. NM-Not Meaningful. NR-Not Ranked. UR-Under Review.

Office: 850 Main St, Bridgeport, CT 06604-4904.
Telephone: 203-338-7171.
Website: http://www.peoples.com
Chrmn: G. Carter

Pres & CEO: P.R. Sherringham
COO: M.K. Vitelli
EVP & CFO: P.D. Burner
EVP & Chief Admin Officer: J.P. Barnes

Investor Contact: J. Shaw
Board Members: C. P. Baron, G. Carter, J. K. Dwight, J. Franklin, E. S. Groark, J. M. Hansen, R. M. Hoyt, J. J. Lowney, Jr., M. W. Richards, P. R. Sherringham, J. A. Thomas

Founded: 1842
Domicile: Connecticut
Employees: 4,754

Pepco Holdings Inc.

STANDARD &POOR'S

S&P Recommendation	HOLD ★★★☆☆	Price $16.02 (as of Nov 27, 2009)	12-Mo. Target Price $15.00	Investment Style Large-Cap Blend

GICS Sector Utilities
Sub-Industry Electric Utilities

Summary This electric utility holding company was formed through the 2002 merger of Potomac Electric Power Co. (Pepco) and Conectiv.

Key Stock Statistics (Source S&P, Vickers, company reports)

52-Wk Range	$18.71– 10.07	S&P Oper. EPS 2009E	0.98	Market Capitalization(B)	$3.550	Beta	0.56
Trailing 12-Month EPS	$1.20	S&P Oper. EPS 2010E	1.36	Yield (%)	6.74	S&P 3-Yr. Proj. EPS CAGR(%)	-5
Trailing 12-Month P/E	13.4	P/E on S&P Oper. EPS 2009E	16.3	Dividend Rate/Share	$1.08	S&P Credit Rating	BBB
$10K Invested 5 Yrs Ago	$9,567	Common Shares Outstg. (M)	221.6	Institutional Ownership (%)	52		

Price Performance

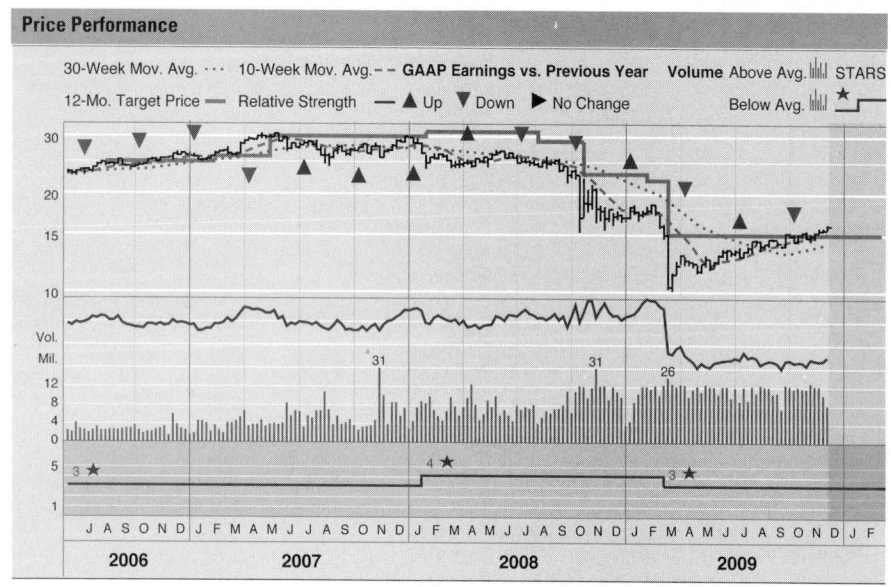

30-Week Mov. Avg. · · · 10-Week Mov. Avg. - - GAAP Earnings vs. Previous Year Volume Above Avg. STARS
12-Mo. Target Price — Relative Strength — ▲ Up ▼ Down ▶ No Change Below Avg.

Options: Ph

Analysis prepared by **Justin McCann** on November 06, 2009, when the stock traded at **$ 15.42.**

Qualitative Risk Assessment

LOW	MEDIUM	HIGH

Our risk assessment reflects our view of the steady cash flows expected from the regulated electric transmission and distribution businesses, which account for approximately 70% of consolidated cash flows and reflect a healthy economy in the company's service territories. We believe this should largely offset the less predictable earnings and cash flow from the company's unregulated wholesale and retail power marketing businesses.

Quantitative Evaluations

S&P Quality Ranking B

D	C	B-	B	B+	A-	A	A+

Relative Strength Rank STRONG

82

LOWEST = 1   HIGHEST = 99

Revenue/Earnings Data

Revenue (Million $)

	1Q	2Q	3Q	4Q	Year
2009	2,520	2,065	2,539	--	--
2008	2,641	2,518	3,060	2,481	10,700
2007	2,179	2,084	2,770	2,333	9,366
2006	1,952	1,917	2,590	1,905	8,363
2005	1,805	1,712	2,489	2,063	8,066
2004	1,764	1,692	2,047	1,720	7,222

Earnings Per Share ($)

2009	0.21	0.11	0.56	E0.26	E0.98
2008	0.49	0.07	0.59	0.32	1.47
2007	0.27	0.30	0.87	0.29	1.72
2006	0.29	0.27	0.54	0.19	1.30
2005	0.24	0.34	0.90	0.43	1.91
2004	0.30	0.53	0.64	0.03	1.47

Fiscal year ended Dec. 31. Next earnings report expected: Early March. EPS Estimates based on S&P Operating Earnings; historical GAAP earnings are as reported.

Dividend Data (Dates: mm/dd Payment Date: mm/dd/yy)

Amount ($)	Date Decl.	Ex-Div. Date	Stk. of Record	Payment Date
0.270	05/26	12/08	12/10	12/31/08
0.270	01/22	09/08	09/10	09/30/09
0.270	10/22	12/08	12/10	12/31/09

Dividends have been paid since 1904. Source: Company reports.

Highlights

► Excluding net one-time gains of $0.16, we expect operating EPS in 2009 to decline about 49% from 2008's $1.93. In addition to more shares outstanding, EPS in 2009 is being hurt by higher operating, pension and interest expenses at the utilities, as well as the much milder than normal weather. We see margins being severely pressured at Conectiv due to substantially reduced demand amid the weak economy, and the decline and reduced level of volatility in power prices. However. we expect earnings at Pepco Energy Services to be relatively flat, as higher interest expense related to its credit and collateral facilities should be largely offset by lower electric and gas supply costs.

► For 2010, we expect operating EPS to rebound more than 35% from the sharp decline projected for 2009. We believe this will reflect a return to more normal weather, and a gradual recovery in the economy and the power markets.

► In September 2009, the Public Service Commission for the District of Columbia approved Pepco's proposed revenue decoupling rate structure effective as of November 1, 2009. In connection with the approval, it reduced Pepco's authorized return on equity from 10.0% to 9.5%.

Investment Rationale/Risk

► The stock is down nearly 14% year to date, but has rebounded over 50% from its 2009 low. The shares fell sharply after POM said that its Pepco Energy Services (PES) unit was losing customers to competitors, and that it was reviewing all of its options for this business. We believe the stock was also hurt by the crisis in the credit markets, and the impact of the economic downturn and weak power market. We believe the strong rebound has reflected the improved outlook for PES and the recovery in the broader market, but expect the stock to consolidate its recent level over the next 12 months.

► Risks to our recommendation and target price include the potential inability to fund a significant rise in collateral requirements; much weaker than expected earnings from the unregulated Conectiv Energy and Pepco Energy Services; and the potential for a significant shift in the average P/E of the group as a whole.

► Despite the strong rebound in the company's shares, the recent yield from the dividend (around 7.0%) was still well above the recent average peer yield of about 5.0%. Our 12-month target price is $15, reflecting a discount-to-peers P/E of 11X our EPS estimate for 2010.

Pepco Holdings Inc.

STANDARD
&POOR'S

Business Summary November 06, 2009

CORPORATE OVERVIEW. Pepco Holdings (POM) is an energy holding company involved in two principal business operations: power delivery and competitive energy. POM's power delivery business, which provides transmission and distribution of electricity and distribution of natural gas, contributed 49.3% of the company's consolidated operating revenues in 2008. Its operations are conducted through three regulated utility subsidiaries: Potomac Electric Power Company (Pepco), Delmarva Power & Light Company (DPL), and Atlantic City Electric Company (ACE). POM's competitive energy business provides non-regulated generation, marketing and supply of electricity and natural gas, and related energy management services through the Conectiv Energy and Pepco Energy Services (PES) subsidiaries. In 2008, the competitive energy business contributed 50.7% of consolidated operating revenues.

CORPORATE STRATEGY. The company's business strategy is to stay focused

on the low-risk, stable, power delivery business. It intends to achieve earnings growth in this business by investing more than $5 billion in its transmission and distribution infrastructure over the next five years. POM also seeks to supplement these utility earnings through its competitive energy businesses, which are serving the wholesale and retail markets primarily within the PJM Regional Transmission Organization. However, POM has been reviewing its strategic options regarding PES's retail energy supply business, which has been experiencing reduced levels of both new and retained retail customers, as the cost of capital related to PES's rising collateral requirements has made its retail pricing less competitive than competitors.

Company Financials Fiscal Year Ended Dec. 31

Per Share Data ($)	2008	2007	2006	2005	2004	2003	2002	2001	2000	1999
Tangible Book Value	12.69	13.01	11.48	11.34	10.28	9.12	9.20	17.01	16.77	16.05
Earnings	1.47	1.72	1.30	1.91	1.47	0.63	1.61	1.50	2.96	1.98
S&P Core Earnings	1.08	1.60	1.28	1.37	1.38	0.87	1.31	1.20	NA	NA
Dividends	0.54	1.04	1.04	1.00	1.00	1.00	0.92	1.17	1.66	1.66
Payout Ratio	37%	60%	80%	52%	68%	159%	57%	78%	56%	84%
Prices:High	29.64	30.71	26.99	24.46	21.71	20.56	23.83	24.90	27.88	31.75
Prices:Low	15.27	24.20	21.79	20.26	16.94	16.10	15.37	20.08	19.06	21.25
P/E Ratio:High	20	18	21	13	15	33	15	17	9	16
P/E Ratio:Low	10	14	17	11	12	26	10	13	6	11

Income Statement Analysis (Million $)										
Revenue	10,700	9,366	8,363	8,066	7,222	7,271	4,325	2,503	2,624	2,476
Depreciation	377	366	413	423	441	422	240	171	248	273
Maintenance	NA	NA	NA	NA	NA	NA	NA	NA	NA	NA
Fixed Charges Coverage	2.42	2.41	2.25	2.37	2.06	1.43	2.47	3.06	4.32	2.71
Construction Credits	NA	NA	NA	NA	NA	NA	NA	NA	NA	NA
Effective Tax Rate	35.9%	36.0%	39.4%	41.3%	40.1%	38.0%	37.1%	33.1%	49.2%	31.7%
Net Income	300	334	248	362	259	108	211	168	352	247
S&P Core Earnings	219	311	246	259	241	147	171	130	NA	NA

Balance Sheet & Other Financial Data (Million $)										
Gross Property	12,926	12,307	11,820	11,384	11,045	10,747	10,625	4,367	4,339	6,862
Capital Expenditures	781	623	475	467	517	564	504	245	226	200
Net Property	8,314	7,877	7,577	7,312	7,088	6,965	6,798	2,758	2,776	4,602
Capitalization:Long Term Debt	5,378	4,735	4,367	4,885	5,128	5,373	5,122	1,722	1,985	2,992
Capitalization:% Long Term Debt	56.2	54.1	54.7	57.7	60.4	63.7	62.2	45.9	50.4	59.8
Capitalization:Preferred	Nil	Nil	Nil	Nil	Nil	63.2	111	210	90.3	100
Capitalization:% Preferred	Nil	Nil	Nil	Nil	Nil	0.75	1.35	5.59	2.29	2.00
Capitalization:Common	4,190	4,018	3,612	3,584	3,366	3,003	2,996	1,823	1,863	1,910
Capitalization:% Common	43.8	45.9	45.3	42.3	39.6	35.6	36.4	48.5	47.3	38.2
Total Capital	11,883	10,903	10,134	10,455	10,532	8,439	9,833	4,282	4,384	6,105
% Operating Ratio	94.4	93.7	93.2	92.4	91.6	92.6	90.3	87.1	91.9	81.4
% Earned on Net Property	9.5	10.0	9.3	12.6	11.0	18.6	16.4	27.5	16.0	10.0
% Return on Revenue	2.8	3.6	3.0	4.5	3.6	1.5	4.9	6.7	13.4	10.0
% Return on Invested Capital	5.5	6.0	6.2	8.0	6.7	8.3	6.4	9.6	11.8	7.6
% Return on Common Equity	7.3	8.8	6.9	10.5	8.1	3.4	8.7	8.9	18.4	12.6

Data as orig reptd.; bef. results of disc opers/spec. items. Per share data adj. for stk. divs.; EPS diluted. E-Estimated. NA-Not Available. NM-Not Meaningful. NR-Not Ranked. UR-Under Review.

Office: 701 Ninth Street N.W., Washington, DC 20068.
Telephone: 202-872-2000.
Email: shareholder@pepco.com
Website: http://www.pepcoholdings.com

Chrmn, Pres & CEO: J.M. Rigby
SVP & CFO: P.H. Barry
Chief Acctg Officer & Cntlr: R.K. Clark
Treas: K.M. McGowan

Secy: E.S. Rogers
Investor Contact: E.J. Bourscheid (202-872-2797)
Board Members: J. B. Dunn, IV, T. C. Golden, P. T. Harker, F. O. Heintz, B. J. Krumsiek, G. F. MacCormack, L. C. Nussdorf, J. M. Rigby, F. K. Ross, P. A. Schneider, L. Silverman

Founded: 1896
Domicile: Delaware
Employees: 5,474

PepsiCo Inc

STANDARD &POOR'S

S&P Recommendation HOLD ★★★☆☆

Price $62.30 (as of Nov 27, 2009)	**12-Mo. Target Price** $62.00	**Investment Style** Large-Cap Growth

GICS Sector Consumer Staples
Sub-Industry Soft Drinks

Summary This company is a major international producer of branded beverage and snack food products.

Key Stock Statistics (Source S&P, Vickers, company reports)

52-Wk Range	$63.27– 43.78	S&P Oper. EPS 2009E	3.73	Market Capitalization(B)	$97.216	Beta	0.51
Trailing 12-Month EPS	$3.33	S&P Oper. EPS 2010E	4.11	Yield (%)	2.89	S&P 3-Yr. Proj. EPS CAGR(%)	8
Trailing 12-Month P/E	18.7	P/E on S&P Oper. EPS 2009E	16.7	Dividend Rate/Share	$1.80	S&P Credit Rating	A+
$10K Invested 5 Yrs Ago	$13,600	Common Shares Outstg. (M)	1,560.4	Institutional Ownership (%)	66		

Price Performance

30-Week Mov. Avg. · · · 10-Week Mov. Avg. - - GAAP Earnings vs. Previous Year Volume Above Avg. STARS
12-Mo. Target Price — Relative Strength ▲ Up ▼ Down ► No Change Below Avg. ★

Options: ASE, CBOE, P, Ph

Analysis prepared by **Esther Y. Kwon, CFA** on October 09, 2009, when the stock traded at **$ 60.39**.

Qualitative Risk Assessment

LOW	MEDIUM	HIGH

Our risk assessment reflects the relatively stable nature of the company's end markets, strong cash flow, leading global market positions, corporate governance practices that we view as favorable versus peers, and an S&P Quality Ranking of A+, reflecting superior long-term earnings and dividend growth.

Quantitative Evaluations

S&P Quality Ranking A+

D	C	B-	B	B+	A-	A	A+

Relative Strength Rank MODERATE
69
LOWEST = 1   HIGHEST = 99

Revenue/Earnings Data

Revenue (Million $)

	1Q	2Q	3Q	4Q	Year
2009	8,263	10,592	11,080	--	--
2008	8,333	10,945	11,244	12,729	43,251
2007	7,350	9,607	10,171	12,346	39,474
2006	7,205	8,599	8,950	10,383	35,137
2005	6,585	7,697	8,184	10,096	32,562
2004	6,131	7,070	7,257	8,803	29,261

Earnings Per Share ($)

	1Q	2Q	3Q	4Q	Year
2009	0.72	1.06	1.09	E0.89	E3.73
2008	0.70	1.05	0.99	0.46	3.21
2007	0.65	0.94	1.06	0.77	3.41
2006	0.60	0.80	0.88	1.06	3.34
2005	0.53	0.70	0.51	0.65	2.39
2004	0.46	0.61	0.79	0.55	2.41

Fiscal year ended Dec. 31. Next earnings report expected: Mid February. EPS Estimates based on S&P Operating Earnings; historical GAAP earnings are as reported.

Highlights

► In 2009, we see net sales falling 1.4%, as volume growth in beverages and snacks, led by international, is more than offset by adverse foreign exchange and somewhat sluggish North America trends. This is a considerable slowdown from 10% growth in 2008 when sales were boosted by positive currency tailwinds. At Frito-Lay North America where volumes were hurt by substantial price hikes, we project a pickup in volumes in the second half of the year as PEP begins adding 20% more product in its packages while holding prices steady.

► We expect operating margins to improve as 2009 progresses. PEP recently implemented its Productivity for Growth restructuring aimed at saving more than $1.2 billion over the next three years with $350 to $400 million of savings to be realized in 2009. We also see moderating commodity inflation lifting margins later in the year.

► We estimate 2009 operating EPS of $3.73, up from 2008's $3.66. We assume that foreign exchange will have about a mid-single digit percentage negative impact on growth and that PEP will not repurchase any shares in anticipation of closing its bottler acquisitions. For 2010, we project EPS of $4.11.

Investment Rationale/Risk

► Although we view favorably PEP's international growth opportunities and healthy cash flow growth, we remain cautious about sluggish Americas beverage trends and potential integration risk stemming from its proposed acquisition of two of its bottlers, which it expects to complete in late 2009 or early 2010. Long term, we like PEP's prospects. In addition to the company's leading market positions, we view PEP's product innovation strategy as trend-setting for the industry. Its focus on health and wellness should continue to drive the top line.

► Risks to our recommendation and target price include unfavorable weather conditions in the company's markets and increased competitive activity. As PEP boosts its exposure to foreign markets, political and currency risks also increase.

► Our relative valuation model, derived from an analysis of peer P/Es and historical P/E multiples, indicates a valuation of $62, which is our 12-month target price. This reflects a P/E multiple on projected 2010 EPS below the low end of the recent historical range of 19X to 27X.

Dividend Data (Dates: mm/dd Payment Date: mm/dd/yy)

Amount ($)	Date Decl.	Ex-Div. Date	Stk. of Record	Payment Date
0.425	02/06	03/04	03/06	03/31/09
0.450	05/05	06/03	06/05	06/30/09
0.450	07/17	09/02	09/04	09/30/09
0.450	11/13	12/02	12/04	01/04/10

Dividends have been paid since 1952. Source: Company reports.

Please read the Required Disclosures and Analyst Certification on the last page of this report.

The McGraw-Hill Companies

PepsiCo Inc

STANDARD & POOR'S

Business Summary October 09, 2009

CORPORATE OVERVIEW. Originally incorporated in 1919, PepsiCo is a leader in the global snack and beverage industry. The company manufactures, markets and sells a variety of salty, convenient, sweet and grain-based snacks, carbonated and non-carbonated beverages, and foods. PepsiCo is organized into six business segments: Frito-Lay North America (FLNA), Quaker Foods North America (QFNA), Latin America Foods (LAF), PepsiCo Beverages America (PAB), United Kingdom & Europe (UKEU) and Middle East, Africa and Asia (MEAA). The company's North American divisions operate in the U.S. and Canada. PepsiCo operates in over 200 countries, and international revenues (including Latin America) accounted for over 40% of its net revenue and over 34% of its operating profits.

FLNA (29% of 2008 net revenue, 37% of operating profits before corporate overhead) produces the best-selling line of snack foods in the U.S., including Fritos brand corn chips, Lay's and Ruffles potato chips, Doritos and Tostitos tortilla chips, Cheetos cheese-flavored snacks, Rold Gold pretzels, SunChips multigrain snacks, Grandma's cookies, Quaker Fruit and Oatmeal bars, Quaker Chewy granola bars, Lay's Stax potato crisps, Cracker Jack candy-coated popcorn and Quaker Quakes corn and rice snacks. FLNA branded products are sold to independent distributors and retailers. Products are transported from Frito-Lay's manufacturing plants to major distribution centers, principally by company-owned trucks.

PAB (25%, 26%) manufactures or uses contract manufacturers, markets and sells beverage concentrates, fountain syrups and finished goods, under the brands Pepsi, Mountain Dew, Gatorade, Tropicana Pure Premium, Sierra Mist, SoBe Life Water, Tropicana juice drinks, Propel, Naked juice drinks and Izze. PBNA also manufactures, markets and sells ready-to-drink tea and coffee products through joint ventures with Lipton and Starbucks. In addition, it markets the Aquafina water brand and licenses it to its bottlers.

UKEU (15%,10%) manufactures, markets and sells salty and sweet snack brands including Lay's, Walkers, Doritos, Cheetos and Ruffles as well as beverage concentrates, fountain syrups and finished goods under brands including Pepsi, 7Up and Tropicana. In Russia, through its purchase of Lebedyansky it manufactures and sells the leading juice brand. The division also manufactures, on its own or through contract manufacturers, markets and sells many Quaker brand products.

Company Financials Fiscal Year Ended Dec. 31

Per Share Data ($)	2008	2007	2006	2005	2004	2003	2002	2001	2000	1999
Tangible Book Value	3.36	6.80	1.93	2.17	1.96	3.82	2.37	1.90	1.91	1.48
Cash Flow	4.14	4.27	4.30	3.25	2.45	2.75	2.47	2.07	2.13	2.06
Earnings	3.21	3.41	3.34	2.39	2.41	2.05	1.85	1.47	1.48	1.37
S&P Core Earnings	2.99	3.38	3.30	2.37	2.44	2.03	1.54	1.20	NA	NA
Dividends	1.65	1.43	1.16	1.01	0.85	0.63	0.60	0.58	0.56	0.53
Payout Ratio	51%	42%	35%	42%	35%	31%	32%	39%	38%	39%
Prices:High	79.79	79.00	65.99	60.34	55.71	48.88	53.50	50.46	49.94	42.56
Prices:Low	49.74	61.89	56.00	51.34	45.30	36.24	34.00	40.25	29.69	30.13
P/E Ratio:High	25	23	20	25	23	24	29	34	34	31
P/E Ratio:Low	15	18	17	21	19	18	18	27	20	22

Income Statement Analysis (Million $)	2008	2007	2006	2005	2004	2003	2002	2001	2000	1999
Revenue	43,251	39,474	35,137	32,562	29,261	26,971	25,112	26,935	20,438	20,367
Operating Income	8,964	8,596	7,845	7,230	6,673	6,208	6,066	5,490	4,185	3,915
Depreciation	1,486	1,426	1,406	1,308	1,264	1,221	1,112	1,082	960	1,032
Interest Expense	329	224	239	256	167	163	178	219	221	363
Pretax Income	7,021	7,631	6,989	6,382	5,546	4,992	4,868	4,029	3,210	3,656
Effective Tax Rate	26.8%	25.8%	19.3%	36.1%	24.7%	28.5%	31.9%	33.9%	32.0%	43.9%
Net Income	5,142	5,658	5,642	4,078	4,174	3,568	3,313	2,662	2,183	2,050
S&P Core Earnings	4,781	5,602	5,565	4,028	4,191	3,543	2,749	2,164	NA	NA

Balance Sheet & Other Financial Data (Million $)	2008	2007	2006	2005	2004	2003	2002	2001	2000	1999
Cash	2,277	910	1,651	1,716	1,280	820	1,638	683	864	964
Current Assets	10,806	10,151	9,130	10,454	8,639	6,930	6,413	5,853	4,604	4,173
Total Assets	35,994	34,628	29,930	31,727	27,987	25,327	23,474	21,695	18,339	17,551
Current Liabilities	8,787	7,753	6,860	9,406	6,752	6,415	6,052	4,998	3,935	3,788
Long Term Debt	7,858	4,203	2,550	2,313	2,397	1,702	2,187	2,651	2,346	2,812
Common Equity	12,203	17,325	15,327	14,210	13,572	11,896	9,250	8,648	7,249	6,881
Total Capital	20,190	22,174	18,446	17,998	17,226	14,837	13,196	12,821	10,956	10,902
Capital Expenditures	2,446	2,430	2,068	1,736	1,387	1,345	1,437	1,324	1,067	1,118
Cash Flow	6,626	7,084	7,047	5,384	4,109	4,786	4,421	3,744	3,143	3,082
Current Ratio	1.2	1.3	1.3	1.1	1.3	1.1	1.1	1.2	1.2	1.1
% Long Term Debt of Capitalization	38.9	18.9	13.8	12.9	13.9	11.5	16.6	20.7	21.4	25.8
% Net Income of Revenue	11.9	14.3	16.1	12.5	14.3	13.2	13.2	9.9	10.7	10.1
% Return on Assets	14.6	17.5	18.3	13.7	15.7	14.6	14.7	12.5	12.2	10.2
% Return on Equity	34.8	34.6	38.2	29.4	22.3	33.3	37.0	32.8	30.9	30.9

Data as orig reptd.; bef. results of disc opers/spec. items. Per share data adj. for stk. divs.; EPS diluted. E-Estimated. NA-Not Available. NM-Not Meaningful. NR-Not Ranked. UR-Under Review.

Office: 700 Anderson Hill Road, Purchase, NY 10577.
Telephone: 914-253-2000.
Website: http://www.pepsico.com
Chrmn, Pres & CEO: I. Nooyi

SVP, Chief Acctg Officer & Cntlr: P. Bridgman
SVP & Treas: T. Hilado
SVP, Secy & General Counsel: L.D. Thompson
CFO: R. Goodman

Board Members: S. L. Brown, I. M. Cook, D. Dublon, V. J. Dzau, R. L. Hunt, A. Ibarguen, A. C. Martinez, I. Nooyi, S. P. Rockefeller, J. J. Schiro, L. G. Trotter, D. L. Vasella, M. D. White
Founded: 1916
Domicile: North Carolina
Employees: 198,000

The McGraw-Hill Companies

Pepsi Bottling Group Inc.

STANDARD &POOR'S

S&P Recommendation	HOLD ★★★☆☆	Price $37.93 (as of Nov 27, 2009)	12-Mo. Target Price $38.00	Investment Style Large-Cap Blend

GICS Sector Consumer Staples
Sub-Industry Soft Drinks

Summary This company is the world's largest manufacturer, seller, and distributor of carbonated and non-carbonated Pepsi-Cola beverages.

Key Stock Statistics (Source S&P, Vickers, company reports)

52-Wk Range	$38.24– 16.36	S&P Oper. EPS 2009**E**	2.46	Market Capitalization(B)	$8.266	Beta		1.30
Trailing 12-Month EPS	$1.16	S&P Oper. EPS 2010**E**	2.64	Yield (%)	1.90	S&P 3-Yr. Proj. EPS CAGR(%)		8
Trailing 12-Month P/E	32.7	P/E on S&P Oper. EPS 2009**E**	15.4	Dividend Rate/Share	$0.72	S&P Credit Rating		A
$10K Invested 5 Yrs Ago	$14,928	Common Shares Outstg. (M)	218.0	Institutional Ownership (%)	55			

Price Performance

30-Week Mov. Avg. · · · 10-Week Mov. Avg. – – **GAAP Earnings vs. Previous Year** **Volume** Above Avg. ▌▊▎ STARS
12-Mo. Target Price — Relative Strength — ▲ Up ▼ Down ▶ No Change Below Avg. ▌▊▎ ★

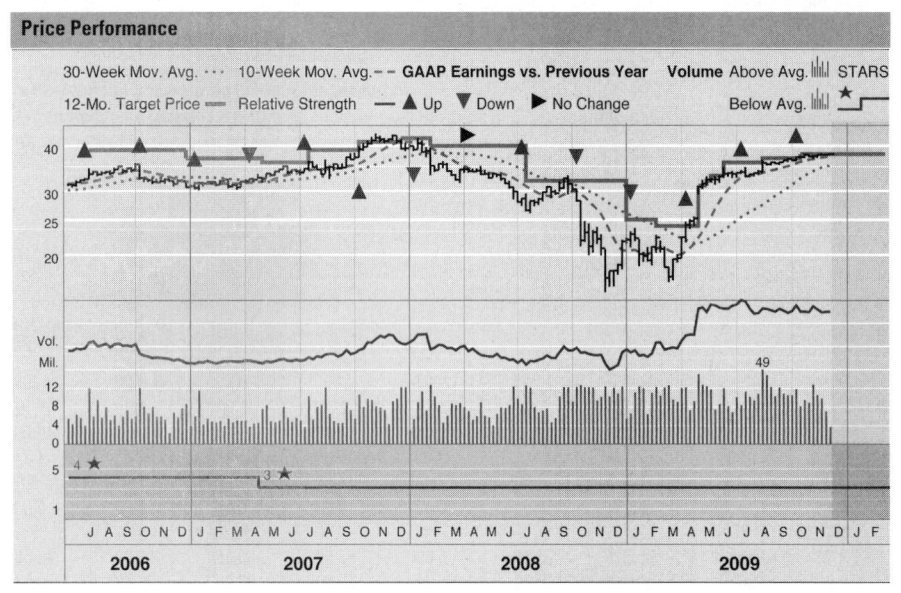

Analysis prepared by **Esther Y. Kwon, CFA** on October 06, 2009, when the stock traded at **$ 37.34**.

Options: ASE, CBOE, P, Ph

Highlights

► In 2009, we expect net revenues to slip about 5%, primarily on a negative foreign currency impact and flat to lower comparable worldwide volume comparisons, partially offset by a 4% to 5% rise in net revenue per case in the U.S. We expect overall category growth to be negative on sluggish carbonated soft drink (CSD) trends, weak non-CSD trends, and accelerated declines in unflavored water for PBG as it focuses on profitability rather than volume. By geographic segment, we see lower volume in the U.S. and a low single-digit rise in Europe.

► We look for margins to be aided by cost-saving and efficiency initiatives. However, we think higher raw material and packaging costs will lead to higher cost of goods sold per case in the first half of 2009, although we expect costs to be more favorable in the second half. We project operating margin expansion based on improving gross margins on moderating commodity costs and $265 million of cost savings, partially offset by higher pension expenses.

► On a lower effective tax rate of approximately 28% compared to over 33% in 2008, we forecast EPS of $2.46 this year. In 2010, we estimate EPS of $2.64.

Investment Rationale/Risk

► On August 4, PBG entered into a merger agreement to be acquired by PepsiCo (PEP 56, Buy) for a revised offer of $36.50 cash or 0.6432 shares of PEP stock, subject to proration such that the aggregate consideration should be 50% cash and 50% common stock, as well as necessary approvals. Previously, on April 20, PEP offered to buy the remaining shares of PBG it did not already own for $14.75 in cash plus 0.283 of a share of PEP. On May 4, PBG rejected that offer as grossly inadequate.

► Risks to our recommendation and target price include failure to consummate its acquisition, rising competitive pressures in Mexico, increasing commodity cost pressures, inability to meet volume and revenue growth targets, and unfavorable weather conditions. In terms of corporate governance, PBG has a dual class capital structure with unequal voting rights, which we view unfavorably.

► Our 12-month target price of $38 is based on the value of PepsiCo's 0.6432 shares of PEP stock. This is supported by the all cash offer of $36.50 per share.

Qualitative Risk Assessment

LOW	MEDIUM	HIGH

Our risk assessment reflects the relatively stable nature of the company's end markets, strong cash flow and market share positions, and its relationship with corporate partner PepsiCo.

Quantitative Evaluations

S&P Quality Ranking A

D	C	B-	B	B+	A-	A	A+

Relative Strength Rank MODERATE

66

LOWEST = 1 HIGHEST = 99

Revenue/Earnings Data

Revenue (Million $)

	1Q	2Q	3Q	4Q	Year
2009	2,507	3,274	3,633	--	--
2008	2,651	3,522	3,814	3,809	13,796
2007	2,466	3,360	3,729	4,036	13,591
2006	2,367	3,138	3,460	3,765	12,730
2005	2,147	2,862	3,214	3,662	11,885
2004	2,067	2,675	2,934	3,230	10,906

Earnings Per Share ($)

2009	0.27	0.96	1.14	E0.55	E2.46
2008	0.12	0.78	1.06	-1.28	0.74
2007	0.12	0.70	1.12	0.35	2.29
2006	0.14	0.61	0.86	0.55	2.16
2005	0.15	0.59	0.82	0.30	1.86
2004	0.19	0.53	0.73	0.29	1.73

Fiscal year ended Dec. 31. Next earnings report expected: Mid February. EPS Estimates based on S&P Operating Earnings; historical GAAP earnings are as reported.

Dividend Data (Dates: mm/dd Payment Date: mm/dd/yy)

Amount ($)	Date Decl.	Ex-Div. Date	Stk. of Record	Payment Date
0.170	02/09	03/04	03/06	03/31/09
0.180	03/26	06/03	06/06	06/30/09
0.180	07/22	09/02	09/04	09/30/09
0.180	10/08	12/02	12/04	01/04/10

Dividends have been paid since 1999. Source: Company reports.

Please read the Required Disclosures and Analyst Certification on the last page of this report.

The McGraw·Hill Companies

Pepsi Bottling Group Inc.

STANDARD & POOR'S

Business Summary October 06, 2009

CORPORATE OVERVIEW. The Pepsi Bottling Group is the world's largest manufacturer, seller and distributor of carbonated and non-carbonated Pepsi-Cola beverages. The company was separated from PepsiCo (PEP: buy, $50) via a March 1999 IPO. As of January 23, 2009, PepsiCo's ownership represented 40.2% of the voting power of all classes of PBG's voting stock. In addition, PEP owned a 6.6% interest in Bottling Group, LLC, PBG's main operating subsidiary.

The company has exclusive rights to manufacture, sell and distribute Pepsi-Cola beverages in all or a portion of 42 states, the District of Columbia, nine Canadian provinces, Spain, Greece, Turkey, Mexico and Russia. In 2008, approximately 75% of PBG's net revenues were generated in the U.S. and Canada, 15% were derived from Europe, and the remaining 10% came from Mexico.

The company's brands include some of the world's best recognized trademarks, and include Pepsi, Diet Pepsi, Diet Pepsi Max, Mountain Dew, Lipton, Sierra Mist, Tropicana juice drinks, Mug Root Beer, SoBe, Dole, Aquafina, Starbucks Frappuccino and Mirinda, which are bottled under licenses from PepsiCo or PepsiCo joint ventures. In some markets, PBG also has the rights to bottle and sell non-PEP beverages such as Dr Pepper and Squirt.

In 2008, about 74% of sales volume in the U.S. and Canada was from carbonated beverages while 69% and 52% of sales in Europe and Mexico, respectively, were from carbonated products.

The company has established an extensive production and distribution system to deliver products directly to stores without using wholesalers or middlemen. In Europe, PBG uses a combination of direct store distribution and distribution through wholesalers, depending on local market conditions. At December 31, 2008, it operated 96 soft production facilities worldwide, as well as 485 distribution facilities. PBG also owns or leases and operates approximately 38,500 vehicles, and owns more than 2 million coolers and soft drink dispensing and vending machines.

Company Financials Fiscal Year Ended Dec. 31

Per Share Data ($)	2008	2007	2006	2005	2004	2003	2002	2001	2000	1999
Tangible Book Value	NM	NM	NM	NM	NM	NM	NM	NM	NM	NM
Cash Flow	3.80	5.16	4.84	4.38	3.99	3.57	3.00	2.77	2.23	2.43
Earnings	0.74	2.29	2.16	1.86	1.73	1.52	1.46	1.03	0.77	0.46
S&P Core Earnings	1.81	2.40	2.27	1.71	1.64	1.42	1.18	0.78	NA	NA
Dividends	0.65	0.53	0.52	0.29	0.16	0.04	0.04	0.04	0.04	0.02
Payout Ratio	88%	23%	24%	16%	9%	3%	3%	4%	5%	4%
Prices:High	42.02	43.38	35.83	30.35	31.40	27.62	34.80	25.00	21.25	12.63
Prices:Low	15.78	30.13	27.99	26.00	24.00	17.00	21.65	15.81	8.13	7.75
P/E Ratio:High	57	19	17	16	18	18	24	24	28	27
P/E Ratio:Low	21	13	13	14	14	11	15	15	11	17

Income Statement Analysis (Million $)										
Revenue	13,796	13,591	12,730	11,885	10,906	10,265	9,216	8,443	7,982	7,505
Operating Income	1,822	1,793	1,666	1,653	1,568	1,524	1,349	1,190	1,025	901
Depreciation	673	669	649	630	593	568	451	514	435	505
Interest Expense	316	305	266	250	230	239	191	194	192	202
Pretax Income	334	803	740	772	745	710	700	482	397	209
Effective Tax Rate	33.5%	22.0%	21.5%	32.0%	31.1%	33.5%	31.6%	28.2%	34.0%	33.5%
Net Income	162	532	522	466	457	422	428	305	229	118
S&P Core Earnings	398	559	549	431	435	394	347	229	NA	NA

Balance Sheet & Other Financial Data (Million $)										
Cash	966	647	629	502	305	1,235	222	277	318	190
Current Assets	3,141	3,086	2,749	2,412	2,039	3,039	1,737	1,548	1,584	1,493
Total Assets	12,982	13,115	11,927	11,524	10,793	11,544	10,027	7,857	7,736	7,619
Current Liabilities	3,083	2,215	2,051	2,598	1,581	2,478	1,248	1,081	967	947
Long Term Debt	4,784	4,770	4,754	3,939	4,489	4,493	4,523	3,285	3,271	3,268
Common Equity	1,343	2,615	2,084	2,043	1,949	1,881	1,824	1,601	1,646	1,563
Total Capital	8,241	9,714	8,671	7,899	8,298	8,191	7,960	6,226	6,295	6,287
Capital Expenditures	760	854	725	715	717	644	623	593	515	560
Cash Flow	835	1,201	1,171	1,096	1,050	990	879	819	664	623
Current Ratio	1.0	1.4	1.3	0.9	1.3	1.2	1.4	1.4	1.6	1.6
% Long Term Debt of Capitalization	58.1	49.1	54.8	49.9	54.1	54.9	56.8	52.8	52.0	51.9
% Net Income of Revenue	1.2	3.9	4.1	3.9	4.2	4.1	4.6	3.6	2.9	1.6
% Return on Assets	1.2	4.3	4.5	4.1	4.1	3.9	4.8	3.9	3.0	1.6
% Return on Equity	8.2	22.6	25.3	23.3	23.9	22.8	25.0	18.8	14.3	17.8

Data as orig reptd.; bef. results of disc opers/spec. items. Per share data adj. for stk. divs.; EPS diluted. E-Estimated. NA-Not Available. NM-Not Meaningful. NR-Not Ranked. UR-Under Review.

Office: 1 Pepsi Way, Somers, NY 10589-2212.
Telephone: 914-767-6000.
Email: shareholder.relations@pepsi.com
Website: http://www.pbg.com

Chrmn & CEO: E. Foss
Pres: R. Shabel
COO: V.L. Crawford
SVP & CFO: A.H. Drewes

SVP, Secy & General Counsel: S.M. Rapp
Investor Contact: M. Settino (914-767-7216)
Board Members: L. G. Alvarado, B. H. Beracha, J. C. Compton, E. Foss, I. D. Hall, S. D. Kronick, B. J. McGarvie, J. A. Quelch, J. G. Teruel, C. M. Trudell

Founded: 1999
Domicile: Delaware
Employees: 66,800

The McGraw-Hill Companies

PerkinElmer Inc.

STANDARD &POOR'S

S&P Recommendation HOLD ★ ★ ★ ☆ ☆

Price	12-Mo. Target Price	Investment Style
$18.99 (as of Nov 27, 2009)	$20.00	Large-Cap Value

GICS Sector Health Care
Sub-Industry Life Sciences Tools & Services

Summary This diversified technology company provides advanced scientific and technical products and services worldwide to pharmaceutical and industrial markets.

Key Stock Statistics (Source S&P, Vickers, company reports)

52-Wk Range	$21.09– 10.88	S&P Oper. EPS 2009E	1.24	Market Capitalization(B)	$2.217	Beta	0.90
Trailing 12-Month EPS	$0.65	S&P Oper. EPS 2010E	1.34	Yield (%)	1.47	S&P 3-Yr. Proj. EPS CAGR(%)	12
Trailing 12-Month P/E	29.2	P/E on S&P Oper. EPS 2009E	15.3	Dividend Rate/Share	$0.28	S&P Credit Rating	BBB
$10K Invested 5 Yrs Ago	$9,750	Common Shares Outstg. (M)	116.8	Institutional Ownership (%)	92		

Price Performance

30-Week Mov. Avg. ··· 10-Week Mov. Avg. - - **GAAP Earnings vs. Previous Year** Volume Above Avg. ▮▮▮ STARS
12-Mo. Target Price — Relative Strength — ▲ Up ▼ Down ▶ No Change Below Avg. ▮▮▮ ★

Options: ASE, CBOE, Ph

Analysis prepared by **Jeffrey Loo, CFA** on November 05, 2009, when the stock traded at **$ 18.89**.

Highlights

▶ We see 2009 sales declining 8% to $1.79 billion, amid challenging economic conditions adversely affecting several of PKI's end-markets. We expect slow instrument sales within its healthcare and industrial end-markets throughout 2009 and into early 2010. Also, due to funding constraints, several states have not expanded the number of neonatal tests, thereby limiting potential growth, though we see modest growth. We expect research-related consumables to increase in the low single-digits and food safety-related sales to benefit from new regulations. We expect 2009 gross margins to improve 60 basis points (bps) on a higher-margin product mix and lower instrument sales. Still, we project operating margins will decline 70 bps on lower sales, despite cost controls. We see improvement in 2010 and forecast a sales rise of 3%.

▶ In September PKI acquired SYM-BIO Lifescience, a China-based diagnostics company, and Surendra Genetic Labs, an India-based company focused on neonatal and maternal health. We expect these deals to increase PKI's access in these growing markets.

▶ Excluding intangible amortization, we estimate 2009 and 2010 operating EPS of $1.24 and $1.34.

Investment Rationale/Risk

▶ We believe the challenging economic environment will materially affect sales, but we expect PKI's end-markets to stabilize in early 2010. On a longer-term basis, we see significant benefits from PKI's R&D investments, recent acquisitions, and portfolio restructuring. We think PKI will continue to make strategic deals to increase the product offering and expand geographic access. Acquisitions, product development efforts, and recent divestitures will allow PKI to focus on the faster-growing, higher-margin end-markets, in our view. We believe the shares, recently trading at about 14.2X our 2010 EPS forecast and at a 1.2X P/E-to-growth ratio, both in line with peers, are fairly valued.

▶ Risks to our recommendation and target price include a greater-than-anticipated decline in instrument sales, and for PKI's industrial end-markets.

▶ Our 12-month target price of $20 is based on a blend of our discounted cash flow analysis, assuming a weighted average cost of capital of 10.8% and a terminal growth rate of 3%, and our relative valuation analysis, using a P/E-to-growth ratio of 1.25X and our 2010 EPS estimate, in line with peers.

Qualitative Risk Assessment

LOW	MEDIUM	HIGH

Our risk assessment reflects PKI's broad product mix and diverse global client base. However, the company has been actively restructuring its business units and product portfolio, which we believe could increase operating risks.

Quantitative Evaluations

S&P Quality Ranking **B**

D	C	B-	B	B+	A-	A	A+

Relative Strength Rank **MODERATE**

47

LOWEST = 1   HIGHEST = 99

Revenue/Earnings Data

Revenue (Million $)

	1Q	2Q	3Q	4Q	Year
2009	431.6	434.6	437.1	--	--
2008	482.3	528.6	505.1	495.0	1,937
2007	402.9	437.3	435.7	511.5	1,787
2006	355.5	377.0	386.9	427.0	1,546
2005	358.2	368.0	360.0	387.7	1,474
2004	392.6	412.6	403.4	478.6	1,687

Earnings Per Share ($)

	1Q	2Q	3Q	4Q	Year
2009	0.13	0.20	0.14	E0.40	E1.24
2008	0.20	0.27	0.37	0.29	1.06
2007	0.12	0.28	0.26	0.46	1.11
2006	0.17	0.21	0.23	0.33	0.94
2005	0.12	0.23	0.20	-0.05	0.51
2004	0.11	0.17	0.19	0.29	0.75

Fiscal year ended Dec. 31. Next earnings report expected: Late January. EPS Estimates based on S&P Operating Earnings; historical GAAP earnings are as reported.

Dividend Data (Dates: mm/dd Payment Date: mm/dd/yy)

Amount ($)	Date Decl.	Ex-Div. Date	Stk. of Record	Payment Date
0.070	01/28	04/15	04/17	05/08/09
0.070	06/12	07/15	07/17	08/07/09
0.070	07/21	10/21	10/23	11/13/09
0.070	10/21	01/20	01/22	02/12/10

Dividends have been paid since 1965. Source: Company reports.

Please read the Required Disclosures and Analyst Certification on the last page of this report.

The McGraw-Hill Companies

PerkinElmer Inc.

STANDARD
&POOR'S

Business Summary November 05, 2009

CORPORATE OVERVIEW. PerkinElmer is a global technology company with operations in more than 125 countries. It develops, manufactures and provides scientific instruments, consumables and services to the pharmaceutical, biomedical, environmental testing, food and consumer safety testing, and general industrial markets. Collectively, these markets are commonly referred to as the health sciences and industrial sciences markets. In 2005, PKI operated three business segments within its end markets: Life and Analytical Sciences, Optoelectronics, and Fluid Sciences. However, in 2005 and 2006, PKI divested its Fluid Sciences unit in an effort to focus on the health sciences market, which PKI believes has greater growth and profitability potential. The health sciences market includes all of the businesses in the Life and Analytical Sciences unit and the medical imaging, medical sensors and lighting business in the Optoelectronics unit. The industrial sciences market includes the remaining businesses in Optoelectronics. In 2009, PKI again realigned its business units to Human Health and Environmental Health and plans to divest its specialty lighting business, which includes xenon flashtubes, ceramic xenon light sources, and laser pump sources.

Human Health provides drug discovery, genetic screening, reagents, consum-

ables and services. Its instruments are used for scientific research and clinical applications. For drug discovery, PKI offers a wide range of instrumentation, software and consumables, including reagents, based on its core expertise in fluorescent, chemiluminescent and radioactive labeling, and the detection of nucleic acids and proteins. For genetic screening laboratories, it provides software, reagents and analysis tools to test for various inherited disorders. For chemical analysis, the company offers analytical tools employing technologies such as molecular and atomic spectroscopy, high-pressure liquid chromatography, gas chromatography and thermal analysis.

Environmental Health unit makes products for environmental safety and security and includes digital imaging, sensor and specialty lighting components to customers in biomedical, consumer products and other specialty end-markets. PKI supplies amorphous silicon digital X-ray detectors, a technology for medical imaging and radiation therapy.

Company Financials Fiscal Year Ended Dec. 31

Per Share Data ($)	2008	2007	2006	2005	2004	2003	2002	2001	2000	1999
Tangible Book Value	NM	NM	0.45	1.91	NM	NM	NM	NM	NM	NM
Cash Flow	1.81	1.76	1.52	1.03	1.35	1.07	0.58	0.77	1.62	1.01
Earnings	1.06	1.11	0.94	0.51	0.75	0.43	-0.03	-0.01	1.32	0.31
S&P Core Earnings	0.91	1.03	0.91	0.40	0.63	0.25	-0.34	-0.68	NA	NA
Dividends	0.28	0.28	0.28	0.28	0.28	0.28	0.28	0.28	0.28	0.28
Payout Ratio	26%	25%	30%	55%	37%	65%	NM	NM	21%	92%
Prices:High	29.95	30.00	24.17	24.02	23.28	18.71	36.30	52.31	60.50	22.50
Prices:Low	12.70	21.28	16.31	17.92	15.05	7.22	4.28	21.28	19.00	12.75
P/E Ratio:High	28	27	26	47	31	44	NM	NM	46	74
P/E Ratio:Low	12	19	17	35	20	17	NM	NM	14	42

Income Statement Analysis (Million $)	2008	2007	2006	2005	2004	2003	2002	2001	2000	1999
Revenue	1,937	1,787	1,546	1,474	1,687	1,535	1,505	1,330	1,695	1,363
Operating Income	287	249	221	229	253	211	131	196	263	177
Depreciation	88.3	78.0	69.2	67.0	76.2	80.2	76.6	80.5	79.1	66.1
Interest Expense	25.2	15.3	9.16	74.3	38.0	Nil	Nil	Nil	Nil	28.3
Pretax Income	147	151	151	66.7	137	80.9	-8.55	34.2	144	44.9
Effective Tax Rate	14.4%	11.5%	21.5%	0.19%	28.2%	32.0%	NM	NM	40.4%	36.8%
Net Income	126	134	118	66.5	98.3	55.0	-4.14	-0.62	86.1	28.4
S&P Core Earnings	109	124	114	53.8	81.3	31.2	-43.1	-71.3	NA	NA

Balance Sheet & Other Financial Data (Million $)	2008	2007	2006	2005	2004	2003	2002	2001	2000	1999
Cash	179	203	199	502	208	202	317	138	126	127
Current Assets	831	843	745	999	748	766	991	997	893	815
Total Assets	2,935	2,949	2,510	2,693	2,576	2,608	2,836	2,919	2,260	1,715
Current Liabilities	516	548	477	495	446	452	698	708	718	852
Long Term Debt	509	516	152	243	365	544	614	598	583	115
Common Equity	1,568	1,575	1,578	1,651	1,460	1,349	1,252	1,364	728	551
Total Capital	2,077	2,159	1,730	1,894	1,825	1,893	1,866	1,962	1,312	666
Capital Expenditures	43.3	47.0	44.5	25.1	19.0	16.6	37.8	88.7	70.6	41.1
Cash Flow	214	212	188	134	174	135	72.4	79.9	165	94.5
Current Ratio	1.6	1.5	1.6	2.0	1.7	1.7	1.4	1.4	1.2	1.0
% Long Term Debt of Capitalization	24.5	23.9	8.8	12.8	20.0	28.7	32.9	30.5	44.5	17.3
% Net Income of Revenue	6.5	7.5	7.7	4.5	5.8	3.6	NM	NM	5.1	2.1
% Return on Assets	4.3	4.9	4.5	2.5	3.8	2.0	NM	NM	4.3	2.0
% Return on Equity	8.0	8.5	7.3	4.3	7.0	4.2	NM	NM	13.5	6.0

Data as orig reptd.; bef. results of disc opers/spec. items. Per share data adj. for stk. divs.; EPS diluted. E-Estimated. NA-Not Available. NM-Not Meaningful. NR-Not Ranked. UR-Under Review.

Office: 940 Winter St, Waltham, MA 02451-1457.
Telephone: 781-663-6900.
Website: http://www.perkinelmer.com
Chrmn, Pres & CEO: R. Friel

SVP, CFO & Chief Acctg Officer: F.A. Wilson
SVP & Chief Admin Officer: R.F. Walsh
SVP & CSO: D.R. Marshak
SVP, Secy & General Counsel: J.S. Goldberg

Board Members: R. Friel, N. A. Lopardo, A. P. Michas, J. C. Mullen, V. L. Sato, G. Schmergel, K. J. Sicchitano, P. J. Sullivan, G. R. Tod

Founded: 1947
Domicile: Massachusetts
Employees: 7,900

The McGraw-Hill Companies

Pfizer Inc.

STANDARD &POOR'S

S&P Recommendation **BUY** ★★★★☆	Price $18.17 (as of Nov 30, 2009)	12-Mo. Target Price $21.00	Investment Style Large-Cap Blend

GICS Sector Health Care
Sub-Industry Pharmaceuticals

Summary The world's largest pharmaceutical company, Pfizer produces a wide range of drugs across a broad therapeutic spectrum. In mid-October 2009, PFE acquired rival drugmaker Wyeth for some $68 billion in cash and stock.

Key Stock Statistics (Source S&P, Vickers, company reports)

52-Wk Range	$18.90–11.62	S&P Oper. EPS 2009**E**	2.03	Market Capitalization(B)	$146.623	Beta		0.73
Trailing 12-Month EPS	$1.20	S&P Oper. EPS 2010**E**	2.20	Yield (%)	3.52	S&P 3-Yr. Proj. EPS CAGR(%)		1
Trailing 12-Month P/E	15.1	P/E on S&P Oper. EPS 2009**E**	9.0	Dividend Rate/Share	$0.64	S&P Credit Rating		AA
$10K Invested 5 Yrs Ago	$8,458	Common Shares Outstg. (M)	8,069.5	Institutional Ownership (%)	60			

Price Performance

30-Week Mov. Avg. ··· 10-Week Mov. Avg. - - **GAAP Earnings vs. Previous Year**   Volume Above Avg. STARS
12-Mo. Target Price — Relative Strength —   ▲ Up ▼ Down ▶ No Change   Below Avg. ★

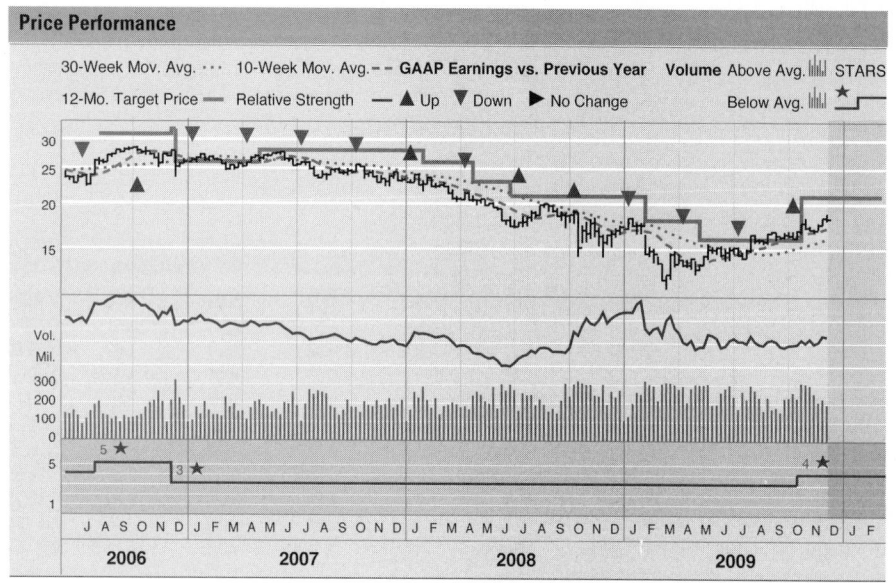

Options: ASE, CBOE, P, Ph

Analysis prepared by **Herman B. Saftlas** on November 30, 2009, when the stock traded at **$ 18.28.**

Highlights

▶ Bolstered by the full year inclusion of Wyeth (acquired in mid-October 2009), we project revenues to climb to $67 billion in 2010, from the $49.5 billion that we forecast for 2009. With respect to key products, we see growth in newer lines such as Lyrica neuropathic pain drug. We also expect volume gains in Zyvox, Sutent, Viagra and Geodon. Principal Wyeth growth drivers, in our opinion, should be Prevnar vaccines and Enbrel TNF inhibitor, boosted by new indications and greater market penetration. We also see modest growth in continuing animal health and consumer product lines.

▶ We think gross margins to narrow somewhat in 2010, reflecting a less favorable sales mix and merger costs. However, we see SG&A and R&D cost ratios improving, driven by aggressive cost streamlinng measures. However, merger-related interest expense is expected to be sharply higher.

▶ After a projected tax rate in 2010 similar to the 30% indicated for 2009, we see adjusted operating EPS in 2010 increasing to $2.20, from an estimated $2.03 in 2009, despite a projected 15% increase in shares outstanding.

Investment Rationale/Risk

▶ We view the $68 billion acquisition of Wyeth in October 2009 a transformational event for Pfizer. Wyeth brings to PFE a broad and diverse drug portfolio, with particular emphasis in biologics, immunology and vaccines, areas where PFE has been seeking to expand. In our opinion, existing Wyeth products, along new pipeline opportunities should largely offset impending generic erosion in Lipitor in 2011. Despite expected initial dilution, we see the combination revitalizing PFE's top line, as well as providing an estimated $4 billion in cost synergies, on top of the $2 billion in savings that Pfizer expects from streamlining legacy operations.

▶ Risks to our recommendation and target price include an inability to achieve planned synergies from Wyeth, and possible pipeline setbacks.

▶ Our 12-month target price of $21 applies a below peers P/E of 9.5X to our 2010 EPS estimate. Our target price is also close to our calculation of intrinsic value, derived from our DCF model, which assumes slowing cash flow growth over the next few years, a WACC of 7.2%, and a terminal growth rate of 1%.

Qualitative Risk Assessment

LOW	MEDIUM	HIGH

Our risk assessment reflects PFE's leading position in the global pharmaceutical market, which we believe affords important competitive operating and financial advantages. While we believe PFE's recent acquisition of Wyeth will bolster sales and margins ahead of major patent expirations in 2011, we remain uncertain if PFE will able to realize all of its key strategic objectives from the deal.

Quantitative Evaluations

S&P Quality Ranking B+

D	C	B-	B	B+	A-	A	A+

Relative Strength Rank STRONG

81

LOWEST = 1   HIGHEST = 99

Revenue/Earnings Data

Revenue (Million $)

	1Q	2Q	3Q	4Q	Year
2009	10,867	10,984	11,621	--	--
2008	11,848	12,129	11,973	12,346	48,296
2007	12,474	11,084	11,990	12,870	48,418
2006	11,747	11,741	12,280	12,603	48,371
2005	13,091	12,425	12,189	13,592	51,298
2004	12,487	12,274	12,831	14,924	52,516

Earnings Per Share ($)

2009	0.40	0.33	0.43	E0.50	E2.03
2008	0.41	0.41	0.33	0.03	1.19
2007	0.48	0.19	0.12	0.40	1.18
2006	0.55	0.31	0.44	0.21	1.52
2005	0.04	0.47	0.22	0.37	1.09
2004	0.30	0.38	0.43	0.39	1.49

Fiscal year ended Dec. 31. Next earnings report expected: Late January. EPS Estimates based on S&P Operating Earnings; historical GAAP earnings are as reported.

Dividend Data (Dates: mm/dd Payment Date: mm/dd/yy)

Amount ($)	Date Decl.	Ex-Div. Date	Stk. of Record	Payment Date
0.320	12/15	02/04	02/06	03/03/09
0.160	04/23	05/06	05/08	06/02/09
0.160	06/25	08/05	08/07	09/02/09
0.160	10/22	11/04	11/06	12/01/09

Dividends have been paid since 1901. Source: Company reports.

The **McGraw·Hill** Companies

Stock Report | November 30, 2009 | NYS Symbol: **PFE**

Pfizer Inc.

STANDARD
&POOR'S

Business Summary November 30, 2009

CORPORATE OVERVIEW. Pfizer stands out above its peers in the $780 billion global pharmaceutical sector, in our opinion. Growth over the past 10 years was largely augmented by two major acquisitions -- Warner-Lambert Co. in 2000 and Pharmacia Corp. in 2003 -- as well as by in-licensed products. The business was significantly expanded with the acquisition of Wyeth in October 2009.

Pfizer's drug portfolio is unmatched in terms of breadth and depth in the global drug market, by our analysis. Principal cardiovasculars include Lipitor, the world's largest-selling cholesterol-lowering agent as well as the biggest drug in any therapeutic category in 2008 (sales of $12.4 billion in 2008), and antihypertensives such as off-patent Norvasc ($2.2 billion), and Caduet ($589 million), a combination of Lipitor and Norvasc. Key central nervous system medicines include Lyrica, a treatment for nerve pain and epileptic seizures ($2.6 billion); and Geodon, an antipsychotic ($1.0 billion). Infectious disease drugs consist of Zyvox ($1.1 billion), a treatment for severe bacterial infections, and Vfend ($743 million), an antifungal. Foreign sales accounted for 57% of total revenues in 2008.

Other drugs sold include Celebrex COX-2 inhibitor for arthritis and pain (sales of $2.5 billion); Viagra for male erectile dysfunction ($1.9 billion); Xalatan/Xal-

com, for glaucoma ($1.7 billion); Detrol and LA/Detrol, treatments for incontinence ($1.2 billion); Chantix ($846 million) for smoking cessation, and anti-cancer agents ($2.6 billion). The animal health division ($2.8 billion in sales) offers one of the largest-selling and broadest product lines in its field. Principal products include feed additives, vaccines, antibiotics, antihelmintics, and other veterinary products.

MARKET PROFILE. The dollar value of the drug market is projected to grow about 4%-6% in 2010, from an estimated $775 billion to $785 in 2009, according to IMS Health. Worldwide pharmaceutical industry revenue growth has slowed in recent years, reflecting the effects of tighter reimbursements from key managed care markets, the loss of patent protection on blockbuster drugs, weakened global economies and relatively sluggish new product flow. Much of the projected growth in 2010 should come from emerging markets. Sales in North America are expected to grow 3%-5%, but sales in Europe are projected to grow about 1%-3%, according to IMS.

Company Financials Fiscal Year Ended Dec. 31

Per Share Data ($)	2008	2007	2006	2005	2004	2003	2002	2001	2000	1999
Tangible Book Value	2.71	4.93	3.65	1.91	1.48	0.85	3.04	2.64	2.26	2.11
Cash Flow	1.94	1.93	2.24	1.84	2.16	0.78	1.64	1.39	0.74	0.96
Earnings	1.19	1.18	1.52	1.09	1.49	0.22	1.47	1.22	0.59	0.82
S&P Core Earnings	1.42	1.14	1.53	1.02	1.45	0.29	1.35	1.09	NA	NA
Dividends	1.28	1.16	0.96	0.76	0.68	0.60	0.52	0.44	0.36	0.31
Payout Ratio	108%	98%	63%	70%	46%	273%	35%	36%	61%	37%
Prices:High	24.24	27.73	28.60	29.21	38.89	36.92	42.46	46.75	49.25	50.04
Prices:Low	14.26	22.24	22.16	20.27	21.99	27.90	25.13	34.00	30.00	31.54
P/E Ratio:High	20	23	19	27	26	NM	29	38	83	61
P/E Ratio:Low	12	19	15	19	15	NM	17	28	51	38

Income Statement Analysis (Million $)										
Revenue	48,296	48,418	48,371	51,298	52,516	45,188	32,373	32,259	29,574	16,204
Operating Income	21,925	19,983	19,575	20,501	22,117	17,061	13,436	12,147	9,758	5,091
Depreciation	5,090	5,200	5,293	5,576	5,093	4,078	1,036	1,068	968	542
Interest Expense	562	440	488	488	359	290	279	432	401	236
Pretax Income	9,694	9,278	13,028	11,534	14,007	3,263	11,796	10,329	5,781	4,448
Effective Tax Rate	17.0%	11.0%	15.3%	29.7%	19.0%	49.7%	22.1%	24.8%	35.4%	28.0%
Net Income	8,026	8,213	11,024	8,094	11,332	1,639	9,181	7,752	3,718	3,199
S&P Core Earnings	9,538	7,963	11,048	7,588	11,030	2,147	8,441	6,862	NA	NA

Balance Sheet & Other Financial Data (Million $)										
Cash	23,731	25,475	1,827	2,247	1,808	1,520	1,878	1,036	1,099	739
Current Assets	43,076	46,849	46,949	41,896	39,694	29,741	24,781	18,450	17,187	11,191
Total Assets	111,148	115,268	114,837	117,565	123,684	116,775	46,356	39,153	33,510	20,574
Current Liabilities	27,009	21,835	21,389	28,448	26,458	23,657	18,555	13,640	11,981	9,185
Long Term Debt	7,963	7,314	5,546	6,347	7,279	5,755	3,140	2,609	1,123	525
Common Equity	57,483	64,917	71,217	65,458	68,085	65,158	19,950	18,293	16,076	8,887
Total Capital	66,640	80,134	84,919	82,214	88,189	84,370	23,454	21,354	17,579	9,713
Capital Expenditures	1,701	1,880	2,050	2,106	2,601	2,641	1,758	2,203	2,191	1,561
Cash Flow	13,113	13,409	16,317	13,661	16,417	5,710	10,217	8,820	4,686	3,741
Current Ratio	1.6	2.2	2.2	1.5	1.5	1.3	1.3	1.4	1.4	1.2
% Long Term Debt of Capitalization	11.6	9.1	6.5	7.7	8.3	6.8	13.4	12.2	6.4	5.4
% Net Income of Revenue	16.6	17.0	22.8	15.8	21.6	3.6	28.4	24.0	12.6	19.7
% Return on Assets	7.1	7.1	9.5	6.7	9.4	2.0	21.5	21.3	11.5	16.5
% Return on Equity	13.1	12.1	16.1	12.1	17.0	3.8	48.0	45.1	24.8	36.2

Data as orig reptd.; bef. results of disc opers/spec. items. Per share data adj. for stk. divs.; EPS diluted. E-Estimated. NA-Not Available. NM-Not Meaningful. NR-Not Ranked. UR-Under Review.

Office: 235 East 42nd Street, New York, NY 10017-5703.
Telephone: 212-573-2323.
Website: http://www.pfizer.com
Chrmn & CEO: J.B. Kindler

COO & CFO: F.A. D'Amelio
SVP, Chief Acctg Officer & Cntlr: L.V. Cangialosi
SVP & General Counsel: A.W. Schulman
Investor Contact: J. Davis (212-733-0717)

Board Members: D. A. Ausiello, M. S. Brown, M. A. Burns, R. N. Burt, W. D. Cornwell, W. H. Gray, III, C. J. Horner, S. N. Johnson, J. M. Kilts, J. B. Kindler, G. A. Lorch, D. G. Mead, S. W. Sanger, W. C. Steere, Jr.

Founded: 1849
Domicile: Delaware
Employees: 81,800

The McGraw·Hill Companies

PG&E Corp

STANDARD &POOR'S

S&P Recommendation	HOLD ★★★☆☆	Price	12-Mo. Target Price	Investment Style
		$42.14 (as of Nov 27, 2009)	$42.00	Large-Cap Blend

GICS Sector Utilities
Sub-Industry Multi-Utilities

Summary This energy holding company is the parent of Pacific Gas & Electric Co., which emerged from a bankruptcy reorganization in April 2004.

Key Stock Statistics (Source S&P, Vickers, company reports)

52-Wk Range	$43.21–33.61	S&P Oper. EPS 2009**E**	3.19	Market Capitalization(B)	$15.632	Beta	0.33
Trailing 12-Month EPS	$3.84	S&P Oper. EPS 2010**E**	3.36	Yield (%)	3.99	S&P 3-Yr. Proj. EPS CAGR(%)	7
Trailing 12-Month P/E	11.0	P/E on S&P Oper. EPS 2009**E**	13.2	Dividend Rate/Share	$1.68	S&P Credit Rating	BBB+
$10K Invested 5 Yrs Ago	$14,667	Common Shares Outstg. (M)	371.0	Institutional Ownership (%)	69		

Price Performance

30-Week Mov. Avg. ···   10-Week Mov. Avg. – –   **GAAP Earnings vs. Previous Year**   Volume Above Avg. STARS
12-Mo. Target Price —   Relative Strength —   ▲ Up   ▼ Down   ► No Change   Below Avg.

Options: ASE, CBOE, P

Analysis prepared by **Justin McCann** on November 09, 2009, when the stock traded at **$ 41.69**.

Highlights

► Excluding net one-time gains of $0.08, we expect operating EPS in 2009 to increase about 8% from 2008's $2.95, which excluded a $0.68 benefit from a multi-year tax settlement. We believe the increase in 2009 operating earnings will be driven by higher electric revenues resulting from Pacific Gas & Electric's pre-approved rate base transmission and generation investments, as well as through the realization of energy efficiency incentive revenues.

► For 2010, we expect operating EPS to increase more than 5% from anticipated results in 2009. PG&E is in the third year of its four-year General Rate Case, in which the CPUC had authorized a net 4.5% increase in its electric and gas rates that remain in effect through the end of 2010. Hearings for the 2011 General Rate Case are expected to begin in the summer of 2010.

► On May 13, 2009, Pacific Gas & Electric announced that it had entered into a series of contracts to purchase 1,300 megawatts of solar thermal power from an independent power producer. The first of these plants is expected to begin operation in 2012. California law requires its electric utilities to purchase 30% of their power from renewable resources by 2017.

Investment Rationale/Risk

► The stock is up around 8% year to date. Although the shares have underperformed PCG's gas utility peers, they have outperformed its electric utility peers. With the authorized decoupling of revenues from electric demand (so as to promote energy efficiencies), earnings are not impacted by the decline in demand. The stock recently traded at a premium to the company's peers (based on our 2010 EPS estimates), but we expect it to trade at a slightly smaller premium over the next 12 months.

► Risks to our recommendation and target price include a much worse than expected earnings performance, and/or a major decline in the average P/E multiple of the peer group.

► Reflecting the weakness of the utility sector, the company's P/E multiple has fallen from about 15.6X our EPS estimate for 2008 in early December 2007, to approximately 12.2X 2020's forecast. With the April increase in the dividend payment, the recent yield was around 4.1%. However, this still is a discount to the peer yield (recently about 5.0%). We keep our 12-month target price of $42, reflecting a modest premium-to-peers P/E of 12.5X our EPS estimate for 2010.

Qualitative Risk Assessment

LOW	MEDIUM	HIGH

Our risk assessment reflects our view of the company's strong and steady cash flow from the regulated Pacific Gas & Electric subsidiary, its much improved balance sheet and credit profile, a healthy economy in its service territory, and a greatly improved regulatory environment.

Quantitative Evaluations

S&P Quality Ranking   B

D	C	B-	**B**	B+	A-	A	A+

Relative Strength Rank   MODERATE

63

LOWEST = 1   HIGHEST = 99

Revenue/Earnings Data

Revenue (Million $)

	1Q	2Q	3Q	4Q	Year
2009	3,431	3,194	3,235	--	--
2008	3,733	3,578	3,674	3,643	14,628
2007	3,356	3,187	3,279	3,415	13,237
2006	3,148	3,017	3,168	3,206	12,539
2005	2,669	2,498	2,804	3,732	11,703
2004	2,722	2,749	2,623	2,986	11,080

Earnings Per Share ($)

	1Q	2Q	3Q	4Q	Year
2009	0.67	1.02	0.82	E0.76	E3.19
2008	0.62	0.80	0.83	0.97	3.22
2007	0.71	0.74	0.77	0.56	2.78
2006	0.60	0.65	1.09	0.43	2.76
2005	0.54	0.70	0.62	0.49	2.34
2004	7.15	0.88	0.53	0.44	8.97

Fiscal year ended Dec. 31. Next earnings report expected: Late February. EPS Estimates based on S&P Operating Earnings; historical GAAP earnings are as reported.

Dividend Data (Dates: mm/dd Payment Date: mm/dd/yy)

Amount ($)	Date Decl.	Ex-Div. Date	Stk. of Record	Payment Date
0.390	12/17	12/29	12/31	01/15/09
0.420	02/24	03/27	03/31	04/15/09
0.420	06/17	06/26	06/30	07/15/09
0.420	09/17	09/28	09/30	10/15/09

Dividends have been paid since 2005. Source: Company reports.

Please read the Required Disclosures and Analyst Certification on the last page of this report.

The **McGraw·Hill** Companies

PG&E Corp

**STANDARD
&POOR'S**

Business Summary November 09, 2009

CORPORATE OVERVIEW. PG&E Corporation (PCG) is an energy-based holding company that conducts its business through Pacific Gas and Electric Company, a public utility operating in northern and central California. The utility's business consists of four main operational units: electricity and natural gas distribution, electricity generation, gas transmission, and electricity transmission. The utility is primarily regulated by the California Public Utilities Commission (CPUC) and the Federal Energy Regulatory Commission (FERC).

CORPORATE STRATEGY. To support anticipated customer growth and the improvement of its existing services, Pacific Gas & Electric plans to make major capital additions to its infrastructure. The utility is also devoting substantial resources to the building and expansion of its transmission lines, which has become the fastest growing part of its business. It has proposed constructing additional gas and electric transmission arteries so as to create access to new supplies of renewable energy and new sources of natural gas. In addition to maintaining its ongoing investment in its existing hydroelectric and nuclear facilities, the company is planning to build three new state-of-the-art

power plants that are scheduled to come on line in 2009 and 2010, and to generate enough power for around 950,000 homes.

MARKET PROFILE. PG&E's electricity and gas distribution network covers 70,000 square miles and 47 of the 58 counties in California. The utility served approximately 5.1 million electricity distribution customers and about 4.3 million natural gas distribution customers as of December 31, 2008. In 2008, commercial customers accounted for about 39% of electricity deliveries, residential 36%, industrial 18%, and agricultural and other 7%. Transport-only customers accounted for about 63% of natural gas deliveries in 2008, residential 26%, and commercial 11%. As of December 31, 2008, the company had $40.5 billion of total assets.

Company Financials Fiscal Year Ended Dec. 31

Per Share Data ($)	2008	2007	2006	2005	2004	2003	2002	2001	2000	1999
Tangible Book Value	25.97	25.80	20.89	19.67	20.60	10.11	8.92	11.87	8.74	19.13
Earnings	3.22	2.78	2.76	2.34	8.97	1.96	-0.15	2.99	-9.18	0.04
S&P Core Earnings	1.91	2.53	2.64	2.45	9.00	2.05	-1.08	1.59	NA	NA
Dividends	1.56	1.44	1.32	1.23	Nil	Nil	Nil	Nil	1.20	1.20
Payout Ratio	48%	52%	48%	53%	Nil	Nil	Nil	Nil	NM	NM
Prices:High	45.68	52.17	48.17	40.10	34.46	27.98	23.75	20.94	31.81	34.00
Prices:Low	26.67	42.58	36.25	31.83	25.90	11.69	8.00	6.50	17.00	20.25
P/E Ratio:High	14	19	17	17	4	14	NM	7	NM	NM
P/E Ratio:Low	8	15	13	14	3	6	NM	2	NM	NM
Income Statement Analysis (Million $)										
Revenue	14,628	13,237	12,539	11,703	11,080	10,435	12,495	22,959	26,232	20,820
Depreciation	1,863	1,770	1,709	1,735	1,497	1,222	1,309	1,068	3,659	1,780
Maintenance	NA	NA	NA	NA	NA	NA	NA	NA	NA	NA
Fixed Charges Coverage	3.21	3.03	3.09	3.48	2.75	2.23	2.94	2.48	3.01	2.99
Construction Credits	NA	NA	NA	NA	NA	NA	NA	NA	NA	Nil
Effective Tax Rate	26.4%	34.9%	35.9%	37.6%	39.2%	36.7%	NM	35.8%	NM	95.0%
Net Income	1,184	1,006	991	904	3,820	791	-57.0	1,090	-3,324	13.0
S&P Core Earnings	720	940	972	974	3,828	830	-404	580	NA	NA
Balance Sheet & Other Financial Data (Million $)										
Gross Property	39,833	36,584	34,214	32,030	30,509	29,222	31,179	33,012	28,469	28,067
Capital Expenditures	3,628	2,769	2,402	1,804	1,559	1,698	3,032	2,665	1,758	1,584
Net Property	26,261	23,656	21,785	19,955	18,989	18,107	16,928	19,167	16,591	16,776
Capitalization:Long Term Debt	10,786	10,005	8,885	9,794	8,311	9,924	11,590	9,527	5,516	9,484
Capitalization:% Long Term Debt	53.5	53.9	53.2	57.5	49.0	70.2	76.2	68.8	63.5	57.9
Capitalization:Preferred	Nil	Nil	Nil	Nil	Nil	Nil	Nil	Nil	Nil	Nil
Capitalization:% Preferred	Nil	Nil	Nil	Nil	Nil	Nil	Nil	Nil	Nil	Nil
Capitalization:Common	9,377	8,553	7,811	7,240	8,633	4,215	3,613	4,322	3,172	6,886
Capitalization:% Common	46.5	46.1	46.8	42.5	51.0	29.8	23.8	31.2	36.5	42.1
Total Capital	23,654	21,710	19,642	20,238	20,596	15,122	16,786	15,668	10,536	19,748
% Operating Ratio	87.4	88.1	87.6	87.8	102.2	80.4	67.2	90.3	84.1	90.9
% Earned on Net Property	9.1	9.3	10.1	10.1	38.4	14.6	31.2	15.0	34.7	5.1
% Return on Revenue	8.1	7.6	7.9	7.7	34.5	7.6	NM	4.7	NM	0.1
% Return on Invested Capital	8.4	8.6	8.7	7.3	15.6	13.9	22.8	16.7	29.1	9.7
% Return on Common Equity	13.2	12.3	13.2	11.4	59.5	20.2	NM	29.1	NM	0.2

Data as orig reptd.; bef. results of disc opers/spec. items. Per share data adj. for stk. divs.; EPS diluted. E-Estimated. NA-Not Available. NM-Not Meaningful. NR-Not Ranked. UR-Under Review.

Office: 1 Mkt Spear Tower St Ste 2400, San Francisco, CA 94105-1415.
Telephone: 415-267-7000.
Email: invrel@pg-corp.com
Website: http://www.pgecorp.com

Chrmn, Pres & CEO: P.A. Darbee
SVP & CFO: K.M. Harvey
SVP & General Counsel: H. Park
Treas: N. Bijur

Secy: L.Y. Cheng
Investor Contact: L.Y. Cheng (415-267-7070)
Board Members: D. R. Andrews, L. Chew, C. L. Cox, P. A. Darbee, M. C. Herringer, R. H. Kimmel, R. Meserve, F. E. Miller, R. G. Parra, B. L. Rambo, B. L. Williams

Founded: 1995
Domicile: California
Employees: 21,667

The McGraw-Hill Companies

Philip Morris International Inc

STANDARD &POOR'S

S&P Recommendation **BUY** ★★★★☆	Price $49.99 (as of Nov 27, 2009)	12-Mo. Target Price $56.00	Investment Style Large-Cap Blend

GICS Sector Consumer Staples
Sub-Industry Tobacco

Summary This company, comprising the international operations spun off by Altria in early 2008, is the largest publicly traded manufacturer and marketer of tobacco products.

Key Stock Statistics (Source S&P, Vickers, company reports)

52-Wk Range	$52.35–32.04	S&P Oper. EPS 2009**E**	3.27	Market Capitalization(B)	$95.215	Beta		NA
Trailing 12-Month EPS	$3.16	S&P Oper. EPS 2010**E**	3.75	Yield (%)	4.64	S&P 3-Yr. Proj. EPS CAGR(%)		10
Trailing 12-Month P/E	15.8	P/E on S&P Oper. EPS 2009**E**	15.3	Dividend Rate/Share	$2.32	S&P Credit Rating		A
$10K Invested 5 Yrs Ago	NA	Common Shares Outstg. (M)	1,904.7	Institutional Ownership (%)	71			

Price Performance

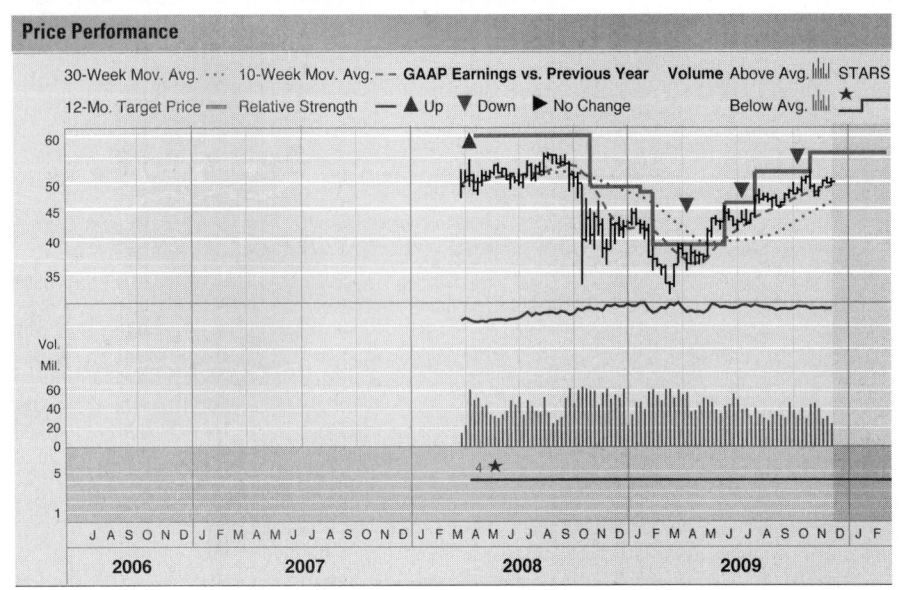

30-Week Mov. Avg. · · · 10-Week Mov. Avg. – – **GAAP Earnings vs. Previous Year** Volume Above Avg. STARS
12-Mo. Target Price — Relative Strength — ▲ Up ▼ Down ▶ No Change Below Avg. ★

Options: ASE, CBOE, Ph

Analysis prepared by **Esther Y. Kwon, CFA** on October 19, 2009, when the stock traded at **$ 51.73**.

Highlights

▶ We estimate a net revenue decline of approximately 5% in 2009, as positive pricing is more than offset by lower volumes and negative foreign currency. With growing health concerns, smoking bans and higher taxes, we look for a mid single-digit percentage decline in consumption in Western Europe, offset by mid-single digit growth in emerging markets. In 2010, we look for revenues to rise about 12%.

▶ With its spin-off, PM embarked on an extensive three-year cost reduction program, which we calculate will widen operating margins on net savings of about $1 billion. Operations planning, procurement and supply chain initiatives, along with productivity savings through elimination of less profitable SKUs and streamlining of product specifications, should account for the majority of the savings, with the consolidation of common functions and back office operations accounting for the remainder.

▶ On an effective tax rate of 29%, we estimate 2009 operating EPS of $3.22, down about 3% from 2008's $3.32. In 2010, we project a return to growth with EPS of $3.75. Over the two years, we look for share repurchases of at least $13 billion.

Investment Rationale/Risk

▶ Separated from operations in the U.S. and the regulatory and litigation risk of that market, PM will, in our view, be better positioned to innovate, tailor offerings to higher-growth emerging markets, achieve cost savings, and incentivize managers. We think PM's low penetration of markets with potentially high cigarette consumption, such as China, India and Vietnam, also provides attractive opportunities. In addition, the spin-off provided PM with currency for acquisitions. We believe its high cash flow generation is supportive of regular stock repurchases and its indicated dividend yield of over 4%.

▶ Risks to our recommendation and target price include execution risk, higher-than-expected excise taxes or regulatory constraints, greater-than-expected price competition, and commodity cost inflation.

▶ Our 12-month target price of $56 is based on a blend of comparative and historical forward P/E and EV/EBITDA multiples. Considering PM's scale, growth prospects and brand equity, we believe a premium to its international tobacco peers, but a discount to global consumer products companies, is appropriate. We assign a 15X P/E to our 2010 EPS estimate of $3.75.

Qualitative Risk Assessment

LOW	MEDIUM	HIGH

Our risk assessment reflects the geographic diversity of the company's operations and end-markets and its participation in a generally stable industry, producing ample free cash flow. Health concerns, excise tax increases, extensive regulation and, to some extent, litigation have limited the growth prospects for the industry, but have also kept barriers to entry high.

Quantitative Evaluations

S&P Quality Ranking NR

D	C	B-	B	B+	A-	A	A+

Relative Strength Rank MODERATE

66

LOWEST = 1   HIGHEST = 99

Revenue/Earnings Data

Revenue (Million $)

	1Q	2Q	3Q	4Q	Year
2009	5,597	6,134	6,587	--	--
2008	6,330	6,709	6,953	6,122	25,705
2007	5,549	5,835	5,916	5,498	55,096
2006	5,228	5,346	5,412	4,926	20,794
2005	--	--	--	--	20,013
2004	--	--	--	--	17,583

Earnings Per Share ($)

2009	0.74	0.79	0.93	E0.77	E3.27
2008	0.89	0.80	1.01	0.71	3.32
2007	0.69	--	--	--	2.75
2006	--	--	--	--	--
2005	--	--	--	--	--
2004	--	--	--	--	--

Fiscal year ended Dec. 31. Next earnings report expected: Early February. EPS Estimates based on S&P Operating Earnings; historical GAAP earnings are as reported.

Dividend Data (Dates: mm/dd Payment Date: mm/dd/yy)

Amount ($)	Date Decl.	Ex-Div. Date	Stk. of Record	Payment Date
0.540	12/16	12/23	12/26	01/09/09
0.540	03/12	03/23	03/25	04/09/09
0.540	06/10	06/22	06/24	07/10/09
0.580	09/15	09/24	09/28	10/09/09

Dividends have been paid since 2008. Source: Company reports.

Please read the Required Disclosures and Analyst Certification on the last page of this report.

The McGraw·Hill Companies

Philip Morris International Inc

**STANDARD
&POOR'S**

Business Summary October 19, 2009

CORPORATE OVERVIEW. Philip Morris International is the world's largest publicly traded manufacturer and marketer of tobacco products, with a 15.6% share of 2008 international market volumes, unchanged from 2007, according to Philip Morris estimates. Excluding China, PM's estimated market share was 25.8% and 25.2% in 2008 and 2007, respectively. PM sold 869.8 billion cigarettes in 2008, with the Marlboro brand contributing about 36% of total PM volume, up from 848.6 billion in 2007. Other brands include L&M, Parliament, Virginia Slims, Muratti and Chesterfield; low price brands such as Bond Street, Red & White and Next; and local brands such as Diana, Petra, f6, Assos and Delicados.

The geographic breakdown of 2008 revenue was as follows: European Union 47.6%; Eastern Europe, Middle East & Africa 23.3%; Asia 19.2%; and Latin America 10%. Adjusted operating income (on revenues minus excise taxes) from the European Union was 45.4% of the company total, followed by Eastern Europe, Middle East & Africa (29.9%), Asia (19.7%), and Latin America (5.0%)

CORPORATE STRATEGY. Philip Morris International's strategy for growth includes both organic growth and acquisition. Using its existing brands, PM plans to introduce new packaging, new blends and other line extensions across its portfolio and in existing and new markets. It sees four major markets -- China, India, Bangladesh and Vietnam -- where it has little or no presence and which account for approximately 40% of total international cigarette consumption as opportunities. We estimate China alone accounts for about one-third of the total market. In addition, PM plans on spending about half of its R&D budget to develop next-generation products that meet consumer preferences and that could cause less harm than traditional tobacco products.

PM also plans to evaluate potential acquisitions and other business development opportunities. In September 2008, it acquired Rothmans Inc., Canada's second largest tobacco company, for C$2.0 billion.

Acquisitions in 2007 included the purchase of an additional stake in a Pakistan cigarette manufacturer, Lakson Tobacco Company, and an additional stake in its Mexican tobacco business from Group Carso. In addition, PM reached an agreement with China National Tobacco Corporation in 2005 for the licensed production of Marlboro in China and the establishment of an international joint venture to support the distribution of a portfolio of Chinese brands in international markets and explore other business development opportunities.

Company Financials Fiscal Year Ended Dec. 31

Per Share Data ($)	2008	2007	2006	2005	2004	2003	2002	2001	2000	1999
Tangible Book Value	NM	2.31	NA	NA	NA	NA	NA	NA	NA	NA
Cash Flow	3.72	3.10	NA	NA	NA	NA	NA	NA	NA	NA
Earnings	3.32	2.75	NA	NA	NA	NA	NA	NA	NA	NA
S&P Core Earnings	3.30	2.91	2.81	NA	NA	NA	NA	NA	NA	NA
Dividends	1.54	Nil	NA	NA	NA	NA	NA	NA	NA	NA
Payout Ratio	46%	Nil	NA	NA	NA	NA	NA	NA	NA	NA
Prices:High	56.26	NA	NA	NA	NA	NA	NA	NA	NA	NA
Prices:Low	33.30	NA	NA	NA	NA	NA	NA	NA	NA	NA
P/E Ratio:High	17	NA	NA	NA	NA	NA	NA	NA	NA	NA
P/E Ratio:Low	10	NA	NA	NA	NA	NA	NA	NA	NA	NA

Income Statement Analysis (Million $)	2008	2007	2006	2005	2004	2003	2002	2001	2000	1999
Revenue	25,705	55,096	20,794	20,013	17,583	NA	NA	NA	NA	NA
Operating Income	11,174	9,685	NA	NA	NA	NA	NA	NA	NA	NA
Depreciation	842	748	658	527	459	NA	NA	NA	NA	NA
Interest Expense	528	209	NA	NA	NA	NA	NA	NA	NA	NA
Pretax Income	9,937	8,572	8,226	7,641	6,478	NA	NA	NA	NA	NA
Effective Tax Rate	28.1%	28.9%	22.2%	24.0%	27.2%	NA	NA	NA	NA	NA
Net Income	6,890	5,821	6,146	5,620	4,570	NA	NA	NA	NA	NA
S&P Core Earnings	6,852	6,153	5,904	NA	NA	NA	NA	NA	NA	NA

Balance Sheet & Other Financial Data (Million $)	2008	2007	2006	2005	2004	2003	2002	2001	2000	1999
Cash	1,531	1,284	1,676	1,209	NA	NA	NA	NA	NA	NA
Current Assets	14,939	14,423	NA	NA	NA	NA	NA	NA	NA	NA
Total Assets	32,972	31,414	26,120	23,135	NA	NA	NA	NA	NA	NA
Current Liabilities	10,144	8,465	NA	NA	NA	NA	NA	NA	NA	NA
Long Term Debt	11,377	5,578	2,222	4,141	NA	NA	NA	NA	NA	NA
Common Equity	7,500	14,700	14,267	10,307	NA	NA	NA	NA	NA	NA
Total Capital	19,086	21,481	16,634	14,593	NA	NA	NA	NA	NA	NA
Capital Expenditures	1,099	1,072	886	736	711	NA	NA	NA	NA	NA
Cash Flow	7,732	6,569	NA	NA	NA	NA	NA	NA	NA	NA
Current Ratio	1.5	1.7	1.7	1.6	NA	NA	NA	NA	NA	NA
% Long Term Debt of Capitalization	59.6	26.0	13.4	28.4	Nil	NA	NA	NA	NA	NA
% Net Income of Revenue	26.8	10.6	29.6	28.1	26.0	NA	NA	NA	NA	NA
% Return on Assets	21.2	NA	25.0	NA	NA	NA	NA	NA	NA	NA
% Return on Equity	60.2	NA	50.0	NA	NA	NA	NA	NA	NA	NA

Data as orig reptd.; bef. results of disc opers/spec. items. Per share data adj. for stk. divs.; EPS diluted. Data for 2007 are pro forma. E-Estimated. NA-Not Available. NM-Not Meaningful. NR-Not Ranked. UR-Under Review.

Office: 120 Park Ave, New York, NY 10017.
Telephone: 917-663-2000.
Website: http://www.pmintl.com
Chrmn & CEO: L.C. Camilleri

Vice Chrmn: M. Cabiallavetta
Vice Chrmn & General Counsel: C.R. Wall
COO: A. Calantzopoulos
EVP & CFO: H.G. Waldemer

Board Members: H. Brown, M. Cabiallavetta, L. C. Camilleri, J. D. Fishburn, G. MacKay, S. Marchionne, L. A. Noto, C. Slim Helu, C. R. Wall, S. Wolf

Founded: 1987
Domicile: Virginia
Employees: 75,600

Pinnacle West Capital Corp

STANDARD &POOR'S

S&P Recommendation HOLD ★★★☆☆

Price	12-Mo. Target Price	Investment Style
$34.90 (as of Nov 27, 2009)	$34.00	Large-Cap Value

GICS Sector Utilities
Sub-Industry Electric Utilities

Summary This utility holding company is the parent of Arizona Public Service (APS), Arizona's largest electric utility.

Key Stock Statistics (Source S&P, Vickers, company reports)

52-Wk Range	$35.48– 22.32	S&P Oper. EPS 2009E	2.31	Market Capitalization(B)	$3.535	Beta	0.61
Trailing 12-Month EPS	$0.59	S&P Oper. EPS 2010E	2.92	Yield (%)	6.02	S&P 3-Yr. Proj. EPS CAGR(%)	-2
Trailing 12-Month P/E	59.2	P/E on S&P Oper. EPS 2009E	15.1	Dividend Rate/Share	$2.10	S&P Credit Rating	BBB-
$10K Invested 5 Yrs Ago	$10,045	Common Shares Outstg. (M)	101.3	Institutional Ownership (%)	78		

Price Performance

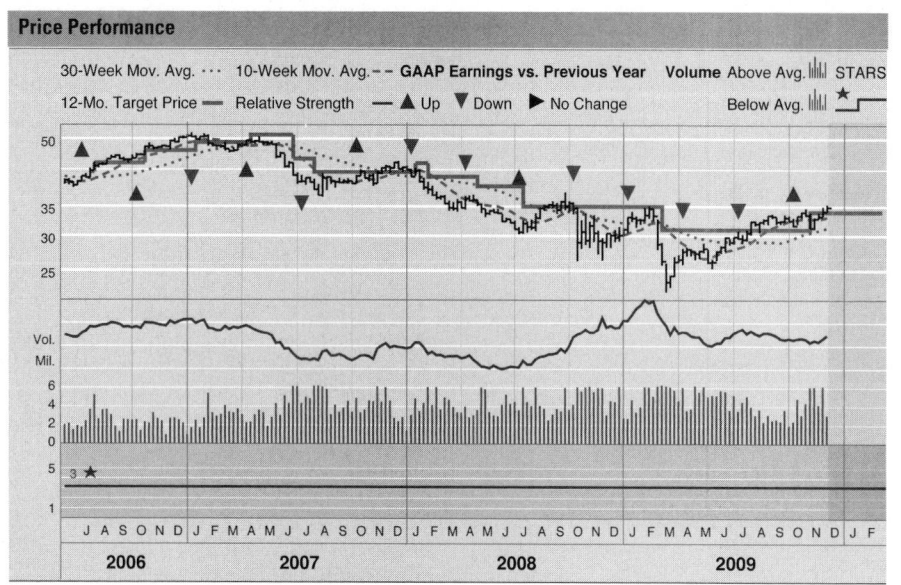

- 30-Week Mov. Avg.   ⋯ 10-Week Mov. Avg. – – **GAAP Earnings vs. Previous Year**   **Volume** Above Avg. STARS
- 12-Mo. Target Price — Relative Strength   — ▲ Up ▼ Down ► No Change   Below Avg.

Options: P

Analysis prepared by **Justin McCann** on November 04, 2009, when the stock traded at **$ 32.16**.

Highlights

▶ Excluding $0.99 of one-time charges, we expect EPS in 2009 to decline nearly 5% from 2008 on-going EPS of $2.42. With the abnormally mild first quarter being partially offset by a hotter than normal third quarter, our 2009 estimate projects higher operating, interest and depreciation charges related to the infrastructure development program at Arizona Public Service, partially offset by an interim rate increase.

▶ For 2010, we expect EPS from continuing operations to increase more than 25% from anticipated results for 2009. In addition to an assumed return to normal weather, the projected 2010 increase reflects a full year of the interim rate increase implemented in 2009, as well as expected benefits to be realized from the company's cost reduction program.

▶ PNW recorded after-tax impairment charges of about $123 million ($1.26 a share) in the first quarter of 2009. The charges primarily reflected the company's decision to dispose of a significant portion of its real estate assets in 2009 due to the distressed conditions in the local real estate and credit markets. Beginning in the second quarter of 2009, the affected properties were reclassified as discontinued operations.

Investment Rationale/Risk

▶ The stock has rebounded sharply from its year-to-date low and we expect it to stabilize at around its recent level. In addition to the weakness in the electric utility sector, the stock had been hurt, in our view, by the weak local economy and real estate market, and the uncertainty as to whether regulators will authorize a rate increase that would enable APS to recover the costs of its infrastructure expansion. We believe the strong rebound in the shares has reflected both the recovery in the broader market as well as the well-above-peers yield (which had risen to above 9%) from the dividend, to which PNW has confirmed its commitment.

▶ Risks to our recommendation and target price include a negative ruling on PNW's rate case and a sharp decline in the average P/E multiple of the group as a whole.

▶ The company discontinued its long-standing policy of raising the annual dividend $0.10 a year with the December 2007 payment. Despite the strong rebound in the shares, the yield from the dividend (recently at 6.7%) was still well-above peers (5.2%). Our 12-month target price of $34 reflects a modest discount-to-peers P/E of about 11.7X our EPS estimate for 2010.

Qualitative Risk Assessment

LOW	MEDIUM	HIGH

Our risk assessment reflects the steady cash flow that we project from the electric utility operations of Arizona Public Service, which has one of the fastest-growing service territories in the U.S. While the regulatory environment has often been difficult, we do not expect to see the general strength of the utility significantly impeded by regulatory rulings. This should help offset the less-predictable earnings stream from the real estate business and the power marketing and trading operations.

Quantitative Evaluations

S&P Quality Ranking B

D	C	B-	B	B+	A-	A	A+

Relative Strength Rank STRONG

79

LOWEST = 1   HIGHEST = 99

Revenue/Earnings Data

Revenue (Million $)

	1Q	2Q	3Q	4Q	Year
2009	629.4	840.1	1,143	--	--
2008	736.7	926.2	1,080	624.2	3,367
2007	695.1	863.4	1,206	759.1	3,524
2006	670.2	925.0	1,076	730.1	3,402
2005	585.4	755.3	955.6	691.7	2,988
2004	574.4	722.7	886.8	734.7	2,900

Earnings Per Share ($)

2009	-1.52	0.70	1.85	E0.09	E2.31
2008	-0.05	1.13	1.49	-0.46	2.12
2007	0.16	0.78	1.99	-0.03	2.96
2006	0.12	1.11	1.84	0.10	3.17
2005	0.32	0.88	0.86	0.24	2.31
2004	0.33	0.78	1.14	0.32	2.57

Fiscal year ended Dec. 31. Next earnings report expected: Late February. EPS Estimates based on S&P Operating Earnings; historical GAAP earnings are as reported.

Dividend Data (Dates: mm/dd Payment Date: mm/dd/yy)

Amount ($)	Date Decl.	Ex-Div. Date	Stk. of Record	Payment Date
0.525	01/21	01/29	02/02	03/02/09
0.525	04/22	04/29	05/01	06/01/09
0.525	07/22	07/30	08/03	09/01/09
0.525	10/21	10/29	11/02	12/01/09

Dividends have been paid since 1993. Source: Company reports.

Please read the Required Disclosures and Analyst Certification on the last page of this report.

Pinnacle West Capital Corp

STANDARD &POOR'S

Business Summary November 04, 2009

CORPORATE OVERVIEW. Pinnacle West Capital, formed in 1985, is the holding company for Arizona Public Service (APS), which, with about 1.1 million customers, is Arizona's largest electric utility. PNW's other major subsidiaries are APS Energy Services, which provides competitive energy services, including wholesale marketing and trading, and SunCor, which is engaged in real estate development and investment activities. In 2008, the regulated electricity segment accounted for 92.9% of PNW's consolidated revenues (compared to 82.8% in 2007); the marketing and trading segment 2.0% (9.7%); the real estate segment 3.9% (6.1%); and other 1.2% (1.4%).

MARKET PROFILE. APS provides vertically integrated retail and wholesale service to the entire state of Arizona, with the exception of Tucson and about 50% of the Phoenix area. In 2008, residential customers accounted for 46.4% of the utility's total electric revenues (48.3% in 2007); commercial customers 39.4% (39.5%); industrial customers 6.0% (6.0%); off-system sales 2.8% (1.7%); and other wholesale and other 5.4% (4.5%). APS has a 29.1% owned or leased interest in the Palo Verde Nuclear Generating Station's Units 1, 2 and 3. It has a 100% interest in Units 1, 2 and 3 and a 15% interest in Units 4 and 5 of the coal-fueled Four Corners Steam Generating Station; and a 14.0% interest in Units 1, 2 and 3 of the coal-fueled Navajo Steam Generating Station (NGS). Consolidated fuel sources for APS in 2008 were: coal, 37.4% (36.8% in 2007); nuclear, 24.2% (21.5%); purchased power, 20.3% (23.3%); nuclear, 24.2%

(21.5%); and gas, 18.1% (18.4%). With APS dependent on purchased power for so much of its fuel sources, we believe that its earnings can be significantly affected by the price of natural gas and by the time lags involved in being authorized to recover the difference between its actual fuel costs and the rates the company is allowed to charge its customers.

SunCor develops residential, commercial and industrial real estate projects in Arizona, Idaho, New Mexico and Utah. The company, which had total assets of $547 million at the end of 2008, has been hurt by the impact of the housing crisis in Arizona. In 2008, SunCor's operating revenues declined to $131 million, from $213 million in 2007 and $400 million in 2006, and after net income of $24 million in 2007 and $61 million in 2006, it reported a net loss of $26 million in 2008. To reduce around $175 million of its outstanding debt, SunCor's directors authorized, on March 27, 2009, a series of strategic transactions to dispose of the company's homebuilding operations, master-planned communities and golf courses in 2009. The company expects to reclassify most of the affected properties as discontinued operations beginning in the second quarter of 2009.

Company Financials Fiscal Year Ended Dec. 31

Per Share Data ($)	2008	2007	2006	2005	2004	2003	2002	2001	2000	1999
Tangible Book Value	32.85	34.11	34.48	34.58	30.99	29.81	28.23	29.46	28.09	26.00
Earnings	2.12	2.96	3.17	2.31	2.57	2.52	2.53	3.85	3.56	1.97
S&P Core Earnings	1.76	2.71	3.00	2.00	2.15	2.43	1.65	3.00	NA	NA
Dividends	2.10	2.10	2.03	1.93	1.83	1.73	1.63	1.53	1.43	1.33
Payout Ratio	99%	71%	64%	83%	71%	68%	64%	40%	40%	67%
Prices:High	42.92	51.67	51.00	46.68	45.84	40.48	46.68	50.70	52.69	43.38
Prices:Low	26.27	36.79	38.31	39.81	36.30	28.34	21.70	37.65	25.69	30.19
P/E Ratio:High	20	17	16	20	18	16	18	13	15	22
P/E Ratio:Low	12	12	12	17	14	11	9	10	7	15

Income Statement Analysis (Million $)										
Revenue	3,367	3,524	3,402	2,988	2,900	2,818	2,637	4,551	3,690	2,423
Depreciation	424	373	359	348	401	438	425	428	394	386
Maintenance	NA	NA	NA	NA	NA	NA	NA	NA	NA	NA
Fixed Charges Coverage	2.41	3.37	3.23	2.77	2.75	2.43	2.64	3.80	3.95	3.61
Construction Credits	18.6	21.2	14.3	11.2	4.89	14.2	NA	NA	NA	11.7
Effective Tax Rate	23.5%	33.6%	33.0%	36.2%	35.4%	31.4%	39.1%	39.5%	42.5%	38.4%
Net Income	214	299	317	223	235	231	215	327	302	270
S&P Core Earnings	178	273	300	193	197	223	140	255	NA	NA

Balance Sheet & Other Financial Data (Million $)										
Gross Property	13,396	12,762	11,679	11,200	18,280	10,470	16,316	9,285	8,383	7,805
Capital Expenditures	954	919	738	634	538	693	896	1,041	659	343
Net Property	8,917	8,437	7,882	7,577	14,914	7,310	12,842	5,907	5,133	4,779
Capitalization:Long Term Debt	3,032	3,127	3,233	2,608	2,585	2,898	2,882	2,673	1,955	2,206
Capitalization:% Long Term Debt	46.8	47.0	48.4	43.2	46.7	50.6	51.8	51.7	45.1	50.0
Capitalization:Preferred	Nil	Nil	Nil	Nil	Nil	Nil	Nil	Nil	Nil	Nil
Capitalization:% Preferred	Nil	Nil	Nil	Nil	Nil	Nil	Nil	Nil	Nil	Nil
Capitalization:Common	3,446	3,532	3,446	3,425	2,950	2,830	2,686	2,499	2,383	2,206
Capitalization:% Common	53.2	53.0	51.6	56.8	53.3	49.4	48.2	48.3	54.9	50.0
Total Capital	7,881	7,902	7,905	7,259	6,763	7,057	6,777	6,237	5,481	5,599
% Operating Ratio	86.2	86.7	85.6	82.4	85.8	86.6	81.7	89.9	87.7	83.1
% Earned on Net Property	6.1	7.6	8.0	6.8	3.4	6.8	4.2	24.6	13.6	12.2
% Return on Revenue	6.3	8.5	9.3	7.5	8.1	8.2	8.2	7.2	8.2	11.1
% Return on Invested Capital	5.2	6.2	7.2	8.0	6.9	6.2	7.7	7.9	8.2	7.5
% Return on Common Equity	6.1	8.6	9.2	7.0	8.1	8.4	8.3	13.4	13.2	12.3

Data as orig reptd.; bef. results of disc opers/spec. items. Per share data adj. for stk. divs.; EPS diluted. E-Estimated. NA-Not Available. NM-Not Meaningful. NR-Not Ranked. UR-Under Review.

Office: 400 N 5th St Frnt, Phoenix, AZ 85004-3903.
Telephone: 602-250-1000.
Website: http://www.pinnaclewest.com
Chrmn, Pres, CEO & COO: D.E. Brandt

EVP, Secy & General Counsel: D.P. Falck
SVP & CFO: J.R. Hatfield
Chief Acctg Officer & Cntlr: B.M. Gomez
Treas: C.N. Froggatt

Investor Contact: R. Hickman (602-250-5668)
Board Members: E. N. Basha, Jr., D. E. Brandt, S. Clark-Johnson, M. L. Gallagher, P. Grant, R. A. Herberger, Jr., W. S. Jamieson, Jr., H. S. Lopez, K. L. Munro, B. J. Nordstrom, W. D. Parker, W. J. Post, W. L. Stewart

Founded: 1920
Domicile: Arizona
Employees: 7,500

Pioneer Natural Resources Co

STANDARD &POOR'S

S&P Recommendation HOLD ★★★☆☆	Price $41.25 (as of Nov 27, 2009)	12-Mo. Target Price $44.00	Investment Style Large-Cap Blend

GICS Sector Energy
Sub-Industry Oil & Gas Exploration & Production

Summary This company explores for and produces oil and natural gas in the U.S., Canada and Africa.

Key Stock Statistics (Source S&P, Vickers, company reports)

52-Wk Range	$46.39– 11.88	S&P Oper. EPS 2009**E**	-0.78	Market Capitalization(B)	$4.757	Beta	1.93
Trailing 12-Month EPS	$-1.44	S&P Oper. EPS 2010**E**	1.62	Yield (%)	0.19	S&P 3-Yr. Proj. EPS CAGR(%)	-9
Trailing 12-Month P/E	NM	P/E on S&P Oper. EPS 2009**E**	NM	Dividend Rate/Share	$0.08	S&P Credit Rating	BB+
$10K Invested 5 Yrs Ago	$11,800	Common Shares Outstg. (M)	115.3	Institutional Ownership (%)	89		

Price Performance

30-Week Mov. Avg. · · · 10-Week Mov. Avg. - - GAAP Earnings vs. Previous Year   Volume Above Avg. STARS
12-Mo. Target Price — Relative Strength   ▲ Up ▼ Down ► No Change   Below Avg. ★

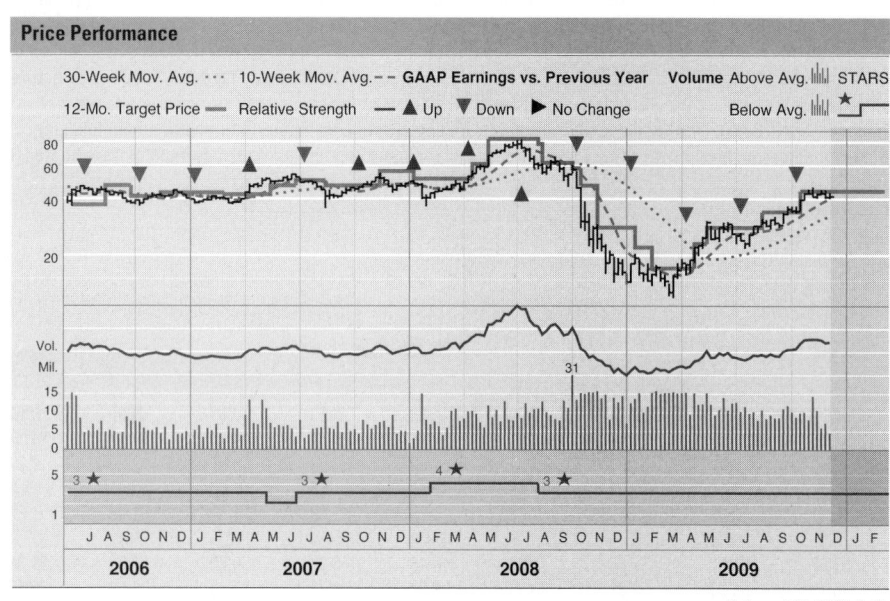

Options: ASE, CBOE, P, Ph

Analysis prepared by **Michael Kay** on October 13, 2009, when the stock traded at **$ 40.79**.

Highlights

► Oil and gas production rose 11% in 2008, driven by the Spraberry field, the Raton Basin, and the Edwards Trend. Our outlook has been tempered by lower oil and gas prices and drilling activity levels, shut-ins from hurricanes and PXD's lower capital budget for 2009. In October, PXD initiated production from its most prolific well at the South Coast Gas Project in Africa and drilled its first two wells in the Pierre Shale. In 2008, PXD commenced production at Oooguruk in Alaska's North Slope, where drilling results have been better than expected. We see production growth of 1% in 2009 and a 4% decline in 2010 on lower drilling activity spurred by recent weakness in natural gas prices.

► PXD's 2009 drilling budget stands at $300 million, down from 2008's $1.3 billion, as lower oil and gas prices have caused a reduction in drilling. It has halted drilling in Tunisia.

► After 2008 operating EPS of $3.09 (excluding $1.23 in one-time charges), up 42% on production and price gains, we see lower prices and a $0.55 non-cash derivative loss in the first half generating a 2009 loss per share of $0.63. We see EPS of $1.62 in 2010, on improved fundamentals.

Investment Rationale/Risk

► We view PXD, after a lengthy restructuring, as an onshore producer with strong production growth prospects and impending project start-ups. In 2008, PXD saw a combined 20% boost in production from its new core regions at the Spraberry, Raton and Edwards fields. PXD reported limited hurricane damage to its own facilities, but has seen minor shut-ins from a third-party facility that was damaged. We expect near-term asset sales at mature properties to reduce debt. PXD saw a slight drop in year-end reserves due to price revisions.

► Risks to our recommendation and target price include negative changes to economic, industrial and operating conditions, such as rising costs or increased geopolitical risk.

► Shares of PXD are up well over 100% in 2009 as higher oil prices and improved cost structure have led to the outperformance versus peers, in our view. We blend our proven reserve NAV estimate of $48 with relative metrics to arrive at our 12-month target price of $44. We expect PXD to trade in line with peers, and our hold opinion reflects the unusually high risk we see in the E&P sector, high relative debt levels and finding and development costs.

Qualitative Risk Assessment

LOW	MEDIUM	HIGH

Our risk assessment reflects what we see as PXD's aggressive financial risk profile in a volatile and capital-intensive segment of the energy industry. While its reserves are characterized by long production life, its lifting costs have been rising with the elimination of lower-cost Gulf of Mexico production.

Quantitative Evaluations

S&P Quality Ranking   B

D	C	B-	B	B+	A-	A	A+

Relative Strength Rank   STRONG

79

LOWEST = 1   HIGHEST = 99

Revenue/Earnings Data

Revenue (Million $)

	1Q	2Q	3Q	4Q	Year
2009	373.8	370.7	410.0	--	--
2008	584.2	653.3	612.2	453.4	2,277
2007	367.3	444.7	490.4	530.9	1,833
2006	396.5	413.9	432.6	389.8	1,633
2005	550.9	592.6	568.2	622.2	2,216
2004	435.5	435.9	441.7	519.5	1,833

Earnings Per Share ($)

2009	-0.13	-0.82	-0.17	E0.08	E-0.78
2008	1.07	1.32	-0.02	-0.54	1.86
2007	0.25	0.29	0.77	0.71	1.99
2006	-0.01	0.52	0.64	0.22	1.36
2005	0.58	0.72	0.74	1.07	3.02
2004	0.50	0.58	0.67	0.69	2.46

Fiscal year ended Dec. 31. Next earnings report expected: Late January. EPS Estimates based on S&P Operating Earnings; historical GAAP earnings are as reported.

Dividend Data (Dates: mm/dd Payment Date: mm/dd/yy)

Amount ($)	Date Decl.	Ex-Div. Date	Stk. of Record	Payment Date
0.040	03/05	03/27	03/31	04/14/09
0.040	08/27	09/28	09/30	10/09/09

Dividends have been paid since 2004. Source: Company reports.

Pioneer Natural Resources Co

STANDARD
&POOR'S

Business Summary October 13, 2009

CORPORATE OVERVIEW. This independent oil and gas exploration and pro-duction company has an asset base anchored by the Spraberry oil field in West Texas, the Hugoton gas field in Kansas, the West Panhandle gas field in the Texas Panhandle, and the Raton gas field in southern Colorado. Comple-menting these areas, Pioneer Natural Resources has oil and gas exploration, development and production activities in the onshore Gulf Coast area, Alaska, South Africa and Tunisia. Given increasing capital costs and diminishing drilling success, PXD recently sold its deepwater Gulf of Mexico, Argentina and Canadian assets.

As of December 31, 2008, PXD had estimated proved reserves of 959.6 MM-BOE, of which 52% consisted of natural gas, and 48% crude oil and natural gas liquids. This compares to estimated proved reserves of 963.8 MMBOE, of which 52% was comprised of natural gas, 48% crude oil and natural gas liq-uids at year-end 2007. We estimate PXD's 2008 reserve life to be 21.5 years, compared to 23.3 years at the end of 2007. The expected decline in year-end 2008 reserves versus 2007 is a result of negative price revisions due to the se-vere decline in crude oil and natural gas prices.

MARKET PROFILE. PXD's addressable markets include onshore North Ameri-

can operations (97% of 2008 reserves), with some emerging fields in Africa. These assets are characterized by long reserve lives (generally reserve-to-production ratios in excess of 10 years), with most production in the form of natural gas. Given these characteristics, PXD competes in a fragmented on-shore natural gas market that has continued along a rationalization path over the past eight years, in our view. PXD competes with much larger onshore players. These producers increasingly employ unconventional drilling and production techniques to successfully boost production, in our opinion. Such unconventional resource plays include basin-centered tight gas formations, and fractured shale formations, which are characterized by a low proportion of exploration capital expenditures, resulting in relatively low risk resource acquisition capability. In our view, the main driver of value in these resource plays is the development of drilling techniques in a basin that are repeatable, increasing productivity organically and moving reserves characterized as probable and possible to the proven category.

Company Financials Fiscal Year Ended Dec. 31

Per Share Data ($)	2008	2007	2006	2005	2004	2003	2002	2001	2000	1999
Tangible Book Value	28.56	24.38	22.01	14.82	19.55	14.75	11.73	12.37	9.19	7.72
Cash Flow	6.66	5.40	4.17	7.01	6.96	6.63	2.32	3.27	3.82	2.13
Earnings	1.86	1.99	1.36	3.02	2.46	3.33	0.43	1.04	1.65	-0.22
S&P Core Earnings	1.82	1.57	1.34	2.00	2.41	3.26	0.32	0.93	NA	NA
Dividends	0.30	0.27	0.25	0.22	0.20	Nil	Nil	Nil	Nil	Nil
Payout Ratio	16%	14%	18%	7%	8%	Nil	Nil	Nil	Nil	Nil
Prices:High	82.21	54.87	54.46	56.35	37.50	32.90	27.50	23.05	20.63	13.19
Prices:Low	14.03	35.51	36.43	32.91	29.27	22.76	16.10	12.62	6.75	5.00
P/E Ratio:High	44	28	40	19	15	10	64	22	12	NM
P/E Ratio:Low	8	18	27	11	12	7	37	12	4	NM

Income Statement Analysis (Million $)										
Revenue	2,277	1,833	1,633	2,216	1,833	1,299	702	847	853	645
Operating Income	1,256	1,019	757	1,262	1,191	804	351	433	475	344
Depreciation, Depletion and Amortization	569	415	360	568	575	391	216	223	215	236
Interest Expense	154	168	107	128	103	91.4	95.8	132	162	170
Pretax Income	448	355	309	715	479	331	54.1	108	158	-21.9
Effective Tax Rate	45.9%	31.7%	44.2%	40.8%	34.7%	NM	9.35%	3.73%	NM	NM
Net Income	221	242	172	424	313	395	49.1	104	164	-22.5
S&P Core Earnings	217	192	170	280	307	386	36.4	92.2	NA	NA

Balance Sheet & Other Financial Data (Million $)										
Cash	48.3	12.2	7.03	18.8	7.26	19.3	8.49	14.3	26.2	34.8
Current Assets	487	765	537	624	312	205	147	256	191	183
Total Assets	9,163	8,617	7,355	7,329	6,647	3,952	3,455	3,271	2,954	2,929
Current Liabilities	695	994	887	1,033	544	430	275	228	217	197
Long Term Debt	2,964	2,755	1,497	2,058	2,569	1,604	1,669	1,577	1,579	1,745
Common Equity	3,582	3,043	2,985	2,217	2,832	1,760	1,375	1,285	905	775
Total Capital	8,083	7,028	5,654	4,276	5,927	3,376	3,052	2,876	2,512	2,563
Capital Expenditures	1,403	2,204	1,499	1,123	616	688	615	530	300	11.9
Cash Flow	790	657	532	992	888	786	265	326	379	214
Current Ratio	0.7	0.8	0.6	0.6	0.6	0.5	0.5	1.1	0.9	0.9
% Long Term Debt of Capitalization	36.7	39.2	26.5	48.1	43.3	47.5	54.7	54.8	62.8	68.1
% Return on Assets	2.5	3.0	2.3	6.0	5.9	10.7	1.5	3.3	5.6	NM
% Return on Equity	6.7	8.0	6.6	16.8	13.6	25.2	3.7	9.5	19.6	NM

Data as orig reptd.; bef. results of disc opers/spec. items. Per share data adj. for stk. divs.; EPS diluted. E-Estimated. NA-Not Available. NM-Not Meaningful. NR-Not Ranked. UR-Under Review.

Office: 5205 N O' Connor Blvd Ste 200, Irving, TX 75039.
Telephone: 972-444-9001.
Email: ir@pxd.com
Website: http://www.pxd.com

Chrmn & CEO: S.D. Sheffield
Pres & COO: T.L. Dove
EVP & CFO: R.P. Dealy
EVP & General Counsel: M.S. Berg

Chief Admin Officer: L.N. Paulsen
Investor Contact: F.E. Hopkins (972-969-4065)
Board Members: T. D. Arthur, E. Buchanan, A. F. Cates, R. H. Gardner, A. Lundquist, C. E. Ramsey, Jr., S. J. Reiman, F. A. Risch, S. D. Sheffield, J. A. Watson

Founded: 1997
Domicile: Delaware
Employees: 1,824

Pitney Bowes Inc.

STANDARD &POOR'S

S&P Recommendation	BUY ★★★★☆	Price	12-Mo. Target Price	Investment Style
		$23.27 (as of Nov 27, 2009)	$31.00	Large-Cap Growth

GICS Sector Industrials
Sub-Industry Office Services & Supplies

Summary PBI, the world's largest maker of mailing systems, also provides production and document management equipment and facilities management services.

Key Stock Statistics (Source S&P, Vickers, company reports)

52-Wk Range	$27.46– 17.62	S&P Oper. EPS 2009**E**	2.27	Market Capitalization(B)	$4.820	Beta	0.93
Trailing 12-Month EPS	$1.93	S&P Oper. EPS 2010**E**	2.60	Yield (%)	6.19	S&P 3-Yr. Proj. EPS CAGR(%)	10
Trailing 12-Month P/E	12.1	P/E on S&P Oper. EPS 2009**E**	10.3	Dividend Rate/Share	$1.44	S&P Credit Rating	A
$10K Invested 5 Yrs Ago	$6,457	Common Shares Outstg. (M)	207.1	Institutional Ownership (%)	84		

Price Performance

30-Week Mov. Avg. · · · 10-Week Mov. Avg. - - GAAP Earnings vs. Previous Year Volume Above Avg. STARS
12-Mo. Target Price — Relative Strength ▲ Up ▼ Down ► No Change Below Avg.

Options: CBOE, P, Ph

Analysis prepared by **Thomas W. Smith, CFA** on November 04, 2009, when the stock traded at **$ 24.83**.

Highlights

► We look for revenues to decrease 10% in 2009 and then rise 4% in 2010, based largely on our outlook for moderating global economic growth in 2009 to turn higher in 2010. We believe several product partnerships are helping the company expand sales opportunities and extend its marketing reach into Asia. We expect the Mailstream Services segment to outperform the Mailstream Solutions segment.

► We see gross margins dipping toward 51.1% in 2009, from about 52.4% in 2008, as a less-favorable business mix combines with little change in volume. We expect operating margins to narrow in 2009, but eventually widen in 2010 as cost savings from restructurings are more fully realized. The company has been paying down debt in recent quarters. Results have recently been aided by share buybacks, but we project that the company will repurchase few shares until economic conditions improve

► We estimate 2009 operating EPS of $2.27, excluding restructuring charges. We expect EPS to improve to $2.60 in 2010.

Investment Rationale/Risk

► PBI has a large recurring revenue stream and a leadership position within its market, in our view. Despite our projection for weak demand for office equipment to limit near-term sales potential, we expect synergies from acquisitions, and from new product introductions focusing on digital technology, to aid future growth. Restructurings should aid margins. Share price declines since September 2008 have helped lift the dividend yield to over 5%, which is about twice the yield for Industrial Sector peers.

► Risks to our recommendation and target price include increased competition in the document management outsourcing market. Postal regulatory changes in key countries are also a risk factor. Currency fluctuations may affect earnings reported in dollars.

► Our 12-month target price of $31 is based mainly on our P/E analysis. We apply a target P/E of 12.5, a discount to Industrials Sector peers in the S&P 500 Index and toward the low end of a historical range for PBI to reflect near-term revenue weakness we foresee, to our 12-month forward EPS estimate of $2.52.

Qualitative Risk Assessment

LOW	MEDIUM	HIGH

Our risk assessment reflects our view of PBI's steady cash flow, recurring revenue streams, consistent dividend increases and share buybacks. However, we think these factors are offset by a lackluster rate of revenue growth and integration risk associated with recent acquisitions.

Quantitative Evaluations

S&P Quality Ranking   B+

D	C	B-	B	B+	A-	A	A+

Relative Strength Rank   MODERATE

32

LOWEST = 1   HIGHEST = 99

Revenue/Earnings Data

Revenue (Million $)

	1Q	2Q	3Q	4Q	Year
2009	1,380	1,378	1,357	--	--
2008	1,574	1,588	1,548	1,553	6,262
2007	1,414	1,543	1,508	1,664	6,130
2006	1,362	1,389	1,433	1,546	5,730
2005	1,318	1,360	1,356	1,458	5,492
2004	1,172	1,206	1,218	1,362	4,957

Earnings Per Share ($)

2009	0.49	0.54	0.51	E0.66	E2.27
2008	0.58	0.63	0.48	0.45	2.13
2007	0.66	0.69	0.59	-0.32	1.63
2006	0.60	0.54	0.64	0.73	2.51
2005	0.64	0.60	0.62	0.41	2.27
2004	0.54	0.58	0.58	0.35	2.05

Fiscal year ended Dec. 31. Next earnings report expected: Early February. EPS Estimates based on S&P Operating Earnings; historical GAAP earnings are as reported.

Dividend Data (Dates: mm/dd Payment Date: mm/dd/yy)

Amount ($)	Date Decl.	Ex-Div. Date	Stk. of Record	Payment Date
0.360	02/05	02/18	02/20	03/12/09
0.360	04/13	05/13	05/15	06/12/09
0.360	07/13	08/12	08/14	09/12/09
0.360	11/06	11/18	11/20	12/12/09

Dividends have been paid since 1934. Source: Company reports.

Please read the Required Disclosures and Analyst Certification on the last page of this report.

Pitney Bowes Inc.

STANDARD &POOR'S

Business Summary November 04, 2009

CORPORATE OVERVIEW. In business since 1920, Pitney Bowes is a major global provider of mail processing equipment and integrated mail solutions. The company's postage meters and other offerings help business customers optimize the flow of physical and electronic mail, documents and packages. The company operates seven business units within two business groups known as Mailstream Solutions and Mailstream Services.

The Mailstream Solutions segment, which accounted for 70% of 2008 revenue (72% in 2007), is comprised of four units. The first, U.S. Mailing, includes U.S. revenue and related expenses from the sale, rental and financing of mail finishing, mail creation, shipping equipment and software, services, and payment solutions. The second, International Mailing, includes non-U.S. revenue and related expenses from activities similar to those of the first unit. The third unit, Production Mail, includes the worldwide sales, service and financing of high-speed production mail systems and sorting equipment. The fourth unit, Software, includes the worldwide sales and support services of non-equipment-based mailing and customer communication and location intelligence software.

The Mailstream Services segment (30%, 28%) is made up of three units. The first, Management Services, includes worldwide facilities management services, secure mail services, reprographic, document management, litigation support, eDiscovery and other services. The second, Mail Services, offers presort mail services and cross-border mail services. The third, Marketing Services, focuses on direct marketing campaign services, web-tools for customization of promotional mail, and other marketing consulting services.

Reviewing revenue sources by product category, Business Services is the largest area, representing 31% of 2008 revenues, following by Equipment Sales 20%, Financing 12%, Support Services 12%, Rentals 12%, Software 6%, and Supplies 6%.

Company Financials Fiscal Year Ended Dec. 31

Per Share Data ($)	2008	2007	2006	2005	2004	2003	2002	2001	2000	1999
Tangible Book Value	NM	NM	NM	NM	NM	NM	0.10	1.05	4.34	5.28
Cash Flow	3.60	3.37	4.21	3.70	3.36	3.32	2.98	3.44	3.55	4.05
Earnings	2.13	1.63	2.51	2.27	2.05	2.10	1.81	2.08	2.18	2.42
S&P Core Earnings	1.67	1.61	2.50	2.09	1.94	1.87	1.34	0.81	NA	NA
Dividends	1.40	1.32	1.28	1.24	1.22	1.20	1.18	1.16	1.14	1.02
Payout Ratio	66%	81%	51%	55%	60%	57%	65%	56%	52%	42%
Prices:High	39.98	49.70	47.97	47.50	46.97	42.75	44.41	44.70	54.13	73.31
Prices:Low	20.83	36.40	40.18	40.34	38.88	29.45	28.55	32.00	24.00	40.88
P/E Ratio:High	19	30	19	21	23	20	25	21	25	30
P/E Ratio:Low	10	22	16	18	19	14	16	15	11	17

Income Statement Analysis (Million $)	2008	2007	2006	2005	2004	2003	2002	2001	2000	1999
Revenue	6,262	6,130	5,730	5,492	4,957	4,577	4,410	4,122	3,881	4,433
Operating Income	1,437	1,549	1,487	1,435	1,352	1,291	1,276	1,046	1,316	1,526
Depreciation	307	383	363	332	307	289	264	317	321	412
Interest Expense	229	251	228	214	172	168	185	193	201	184
Pretax Income	713	661	914	867	699	721	619	766	803	985
Effective Tax Rate	34.3%	42.4%	36.6%	39.3%	31.3%	31.4%	29.3%	32.9%	29.9%	33.1%
Net Income	447	361	566	527	481	495	438	514	563	659
S&P Core Earnings	352	357	564	485	456	440	324	199	NA	NA

Balance Sheet & Other Financial Data (Million $)	2008	2007	2006	2005	2004	2003	2002	2001	2000	1999
Cash	398	440	239	244	316	294	315	232	198	254
Current Assets	3,033	3,320	2,919	2,742	2,693	2,513	2,553	2,557	2,627	3,343
Total Assets	8,827	9,550	8,480	10,621	9,821	8,891	8,732	8,318	7,901	8,223
Current Liabilities	3,243	3,556	2,747	2,911	3,294	2,647	3,350	3,083	2,882	2,873
Long Term Debt	3,935	3,802	4,232	3,850	3,109	3,151	2,317	2,419	2,192	2,308
Common Equity	-189	642	698	1,301	1,289	1,086	852	890	1,283	1,624
Total Capital	4,405	5,302	5,287	7,074	4,399	5,898	4,706	4,584	4,704	5,015
Capital Expenditures	237	265	328	292	317	286	225	256	269	305
Cash Flow	754	744	929	858	787	784	702	832	884	1,071
Current Ratio	0.9	0.9	1.1	0.9	0.8	0.9	0.8	0.8	0.9	1.2
% Long Term Debt of Capitalization	89.3	71.7	80.0	54.4	70.7	53.4	49.2	52.8	46.6	46.0
% Net Income of Revenue	7.2	5.9	9.9	11.2	9.7	10.8	9.9	12.5	14.5	14.9
% Return on Assets	4.9	4.0	5.9	5.1	5.1	5.6	5.1	6.3	7.0	8.3
% Return on Equity	NM	53.9	54.9	40.7	40.5	51.1	50.3	47.3	38.7	40.3

Data as orig reptd.; bef. results of disc opers/spec. items. Per share data adj. for stk. divs.; EPS diluted. E-Estimated. NA-Not Available. NM-Not Meaningful. NR-Not Ranked. UR-Under Review.

Office: 1 Elmcroft Rd, Stamford, CT 06926-0700.
Telephone: 203-351-6858.
Email: investorrelations@pb.com
Website: http://www.pb.com

Chrmn, Pres & CEO: M. Martin
EVP & CFO: M. Monahan
EVP & General Counsel: V.A. O'Meara
SVP & CTO: J.E. Wall

SVP & CIO: G.E. Buoncontri
Investor Contact: C.F. McBride (203-351-6349)
Board Members: R. C. Adkins, L. G. Alvarado, A. M. Busquet, A. S. Fuchs, E. Green, J. H. Keyes, M. Martin, J. S. McFarlane, E. R. Menasce, M. I. Roth, D. L. Shedlarz, D. B. Snow, Jr., R. E. Weissman

Founded: 1920
Domicile: Delaware
Employees: 35,140

Plum Creek Timber Co Inc.

STANDARD &POOR'S

S&P Recommendation	HOLD ★ ★ ★ ☆ ☆	Price	12-Mo. Target Price	Investment Style
		$33.51 (as of Nov 27, 2009)	$34.00	Large-Cap Blend

GICS Sector Financials
Sub-Industry Specialized REITS

Summary Plum Creek Timber Co., a real estate investment trust (REIT), is the largest private timberland owner in the United States, with more than 7 million acres of timberlands in 19 states.

Key Stock Statistics (Source S&P, Vickers, company reports)

52-Wk Range	$37.89– 22.88	S&P Oper. EPS 2009**E**	1.40	Market Capitalization(B)	$5.456	Beta	1.07
Trailing 12-Month EPS	$1.84	S&P Oper. EPS 2010**E**	1.10	Yield (%)	5.01	S&P 3-Yr. Proj. EPS CAGR(%)	-2
Trailing 12-Month P/E	18.2	P/E on S&P Oper. EPS 2009**E**	23.9	Dividend Rate/Share	$1.68	S&P Credit Rating	BBB-
$10K Invested 5 Yrs Ago	$11,001	Common Shares Outstg. (M)	162.8	Institutional Ownership (%)	73		

Price Performance

30-Week Mov. Avg. · · · 10-Week Mov. Avg. - - **GAAP Earnings vs. Previous Year** Volume Above Avg. ▍▎▍ STARS
12-Mo. Target Price — Relative Strength — ▲ Up ▼ Down ▶ No Change   Below Avg. ▍▎▍ ★

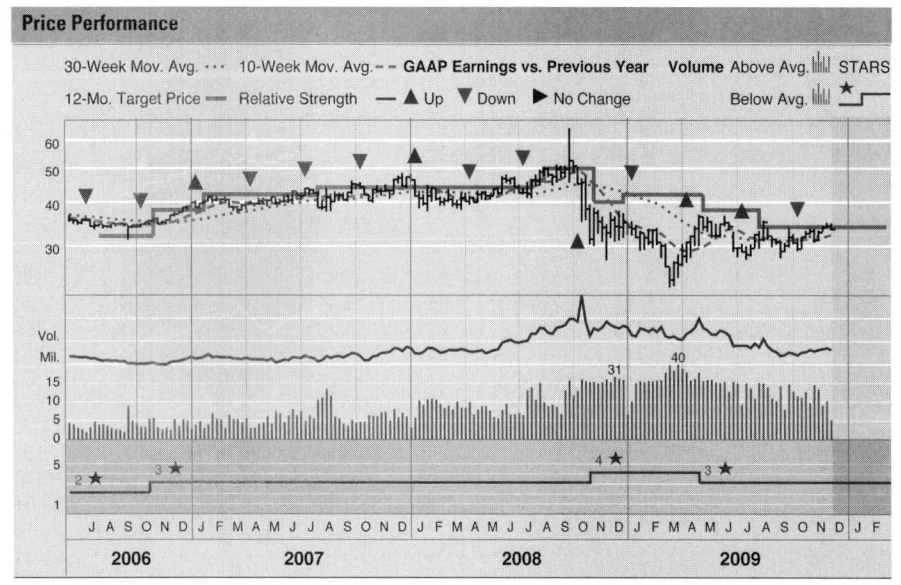

Options: CBOE, P, Ph

Analysis prepared by **Stuart J. Benway, CFA** on October 28, 2009, when the stock traded at **$ 32.11**.

Highlights

▶ S&P projects that housing starts will decline 36% in 2009. We expect this to prevent any sustained rise in sawlog prices, although pulpwood demand is expected to remain fairly stable. In 2010, we expect housing to rebound, which should lead to modestly improved demand and prices for timber. However, rural land sales are expected to decline due to lower sales of large tracts in Montana. Overall, we expect revenues to fall about 20% this year and to decline about 5% in 2010.

▶ We think that average wood product prices in 2009 will be below those of 2008 before improving modestly in 2010, as demand from the housing market continues to be weak. Margins are expected to decrease in the timberland operations in 2009, and we look for a larger loss in wood products. We see PCL capturing improved prices for its higher and better use land sales over the long term.

▶ Our 2009 operating EPS estimate is $1.40, and for 2010 we forecast $1.10, with the decline due to reduced gains on expected land sales. We note that the timing of real estate transactions will likely create quarterly volatility.

Investment Rationale/Risk

▶ We believe PCL has significant value in its land holdings, and we expect real estate to become a rising source of earnings in coming years. It plans to develop 210,000 acres of land over the next 15 years, and we estimate that these properties can be sold at high margin levels. Over the next two years, PCL plans to sell 180,000 acres in Montana. However, demand and prices for timber are likely to remain well below historical averages due to expected sustained weakness in the housing market.

▶ Risks to our recommendation and target price include renewed declines in log demand and prices due to weakness in the U.S. housing market, and lower-than-projected profits on sales of higher and better use land.

▶ Using a sum-of-the-parts analysis, which recognizes the different values of PCL's land holdings, we value the shares at $38. Our dividend discount model, which assumes a $1.68 payout in 2010, a required rate of return of 10.0%, and constant dividend growth of 4%, indicates that the stock has an intrinsic value of $28. Our 12-month target price of $34 is a blend of these measures.

Qualitative Risk Assessment

LOW	MEDIUM	HIGH

Our risk assessment reflects that Plum Creek operates in a cyclical industry, with demand for its products tied to residential construction and paper manufacturing. It is subject to movements in interest rates, economic conditions and currency, and prices for its products have historically been volatile. However, it is a major landowner, and its debt levels are relatively low.

Quantitative Evaluations

S&P Quality Ranking   B

D	C	B-	B	B+	A-	A	A+

Relative Strength Rank   MODERATE

68

LOWEST = 1   HIGHEST = 99

Revenue/Earnings Data

Revenue (Million $)

	1Q	2Q	3Q	4Q	Year
2009	470.0	272.0	294.0	--	--
2008	363.0	376.0	414.0	461.0	1,614
2007	369.0	395.0	407.0	504.0	1,675
2006	414.0	380.0	454.0	379.0	1,627
2005	400.0	358.0	427.0	391.0	1,576
2004	497.0	341.0	363.0	327.0	1,528

Earnings Per Share ($)

2009	0.95	0.19	0.12	E0.12	E1.40
2008	0.22	0.18	0.40	0.57	1.37
2007	0.25	0.33	0.34	0.68	1.60
2006	0.50	0.34	0.51	0.39	1.74
2005	0.56	0.37	0.52	0.34	1.79
2004	0.84	0.31	0.42	0.28	1.84

Fiscal year ended Dec. 31. Next earnings report expected: Early February. EPS Estimates based on S&P Operating Earnings; historical GAAP earnings are as reported.

Dividend Data (Dates: mm/dd Payment Date: mm/dd/yy)

Amount ($)	Date Decl.	Ex-Div. Date	Stk. of Record	Payment Date
0.420	02/10	02/18	02/20	03/06/09
0.420	05/05	05/13	05/15	05/29/09
0.420	08/04	08/12	08/14	08/31/09
0.420	11/03	11/12	11/16	11/30/09

Dividends have been paid since 1989. Source: Company reports.

Please read the Required Disclosures and Analyst Certification on the last page of this report.

The McGraw·Hill Companies

Plum Creek Timber Co Inc.

STANDARD &POOR'S

Business Summary October 28, 2009

CORPORATE OVERVIEW. Plum Creek Timber Co., a real estate investment trust (REIT), is the largest private timberland owner in the United States, with more than 7 million acres of timberlands in 19 states. In addition, the trust operates several wood products manufacturing facilities and is actively involved in land purchases and sales. The company conducts operations through four business segments: the timber operation accounted for 47% of 2008 revenues, manufacturing (25%), real estate (27%), and other (1%). The Northern Resources portion of the timber segment encompasses 3.7 million acres of timberlands, in Maine, Michigan, Montana, New Hampshire, Oregon, Vermont, Washington, West Virginia, and Wisconsin. The Southern Resources portion of the timber segment consists of 3.7 million acres of timberlands in Alabama, Arkansas, Florida, Georgia, Louisiana, Mississippi, North Carolina, Oklahoma, South Carolina, and Texas.

MARKET PROFILE. The timber industry provides raw materials and manages resources for the paper and forest products industry. Harvested logs are sold to third-party mills that produce lumber, plywood, oriented strand board, and pulp and paper products. There are six primary end markets for most of the timber harvested in the United States: new housing construction, home repair

and remodeling, products for industrial uses, raw material for the manufacture of pulp and paper, wood fiber for energy production, and logs for export.

The demand for timber is directly related to the underlying demand for pulp and paper products, lumber, panels, and other wood products. The demand for pulp and paper is largely driven by population growth, per-capita income levels, and industry capacity. The demand for lumber and manufactured wood products is primarily affected by the level of new residential construction activity and repair and remodeling activity, which, in turn, is affected by changes in general economic and demographic factors, including population growth and interest rates for home mortgages and construction loans. The market for wood fiber used in paper production and wood products manufacturing is very diverse, with many manufacturers of various sizes. We therefore believe that Plum Creek has only limited control over the prices that it can charge for timber and wood products.

Company Financials Fiscal Year Ended Dec. 31

Per Share Data ($)	2008	2007	2006	2005	2004	2003	2002	2001	2000	1999
Tangible Book Value	9.47	12.06	11.80	12.62	12.19	11.57	12.04	12.21	7.46	7.70
Cash Flow	2.10	2.37	2.45	1.92	2.46	1.63	1.82	3.00	2.47	3.10
Earnings	1.37	1.60	1.74	1.79	1.84	1.04	1.26	2.58	1.91	1.72
S&P Core Earnings	1.35	1.61	1.67	1.78	1.82	1.04	1.24	2.57	NA	NA
Dividends	1.26	1.68	1.60	1.52	1.42	1.40	1.49	2.85	2.28	2.28
Payout Ratio	2%	105%	92%	85%	77%	135%	118%	110%	119%	133%
Prices:High	65.00	48.45	40.00	39.63	39.45	30.75	31.98	30.00	29.81	32.13
Prices:Low	27.33	37.13	31.21	33.40	27.30	20.88	18.92	23.30	21.50	23.13
P/E Ratio:High	47	30	23	22	21	30	25	12	16	19
P/E Ratio:Low	20	23	18	19	15	20	15	9	11	13

Income Statement Analysis (Million $)	2008	2007	2006	2005	2004	2003	2002	2001	2000	1999
Revenue	1,614	1,675	1,627	1,576	1,528	1,196	1,137	598	209	461
Operating Income	453	558	571	561	586	410	443	305	166	206
Depreciation	125	134	128	113	114	107	105	55.0	38.9	59.7
Interest Expense	148	147	133	109	111	117	103	54.0	46.8	63.5
Pretax Income	206	277	328	339	366	186	235	196	132	100
Effective Tax Rate	NM	NM	3.90%	2.30%	7.40%	NM	0.85%	NM	NM	NM
Net Income	233	280	315	331	339	192	233	338	132	113
S&P Core Earnings	229	281	301	329	336	193	229	336	NA	NA

Balance Sheet & Other Financial Data (Million $)	2008	2007	2006	2005	2004	2003	2002	2001	2000	1999
Cash	369	240	301	395	376	260	246	193	181	115
Current Assets	699	456	513	574	499	405	378	306	195	133
Total Assets	4,780	4,664	4,661	4,812	4,378	4,387	4,289	4,122	1,250	1,251
Current Liabilities	307	303	281	375	184	168	155	149	180	74.2
Long Term Debt	2,807	2,376	1,617	1,524	1,853	2,031	1,839	1,667	560	643
Common Equity	1,572	1,901	2,089	2,325	2,240	2,119	2,222	2,247	507	533
Total Capital	4,383	4,297	3,731	3,888	4,138	4,187	4,105	3,952	1,066	1,176
Capital Expenditures	189	Nil	86.0	89.0	70.0	246	231	59.0	21.7	25.6
Cash Flow	358	414	443	444	453	299	338	393	171	173
Current Ratio	2.3	1.5	1.8	1.5	2.7	2.4	2.4	2.1	1.1	1.8
% Long Term Debt of Capitalization	64.0	55.3	43.3	39.1	44.8	48.5	44.8	42.2	52.5	54.7
% Net Income of Revenue	14.4	16.7	19.3	21.0	22.2	16.1	20.5	56.5	63.1	24.6
% Return on Assets	4.9	6.0	6.6	7.2	7.7	4.4	5.5	11.8	10.5	8.4
% Return on Equity	13.4	14.0	14.2	14.5	15.6	8.8	10.4	28.3	25.4	24.2

Data as orig reptd.; bef. results of disc opers/spec. items. Per share data adj. for stk. divs.; EPS diluted. E-Estimated. NA-Not Available. NM-Not Meaningful. NR-Not Ranked. UR-Under Review.

Office: 999 3rd Ave Ste 4300, Seattle, WA 98104-4096.
Telephone: 206-467-3600.
Email: info@plumcreek.com
Website: http://www.plumcreek.com

Chrmn: J.F. Morgan
Pres & CEO: R.R. Holley
COO & EVP: T.M. Lindquist
SVP & CFO: D.W. Lambert

SVP, Secy & General Counsel: J.A. Kraft
Investor Contact: J. Hobbs (800-858-5347)
Board Members: R. R. Holley, R. Josephs, J. G. McDonald, R. B. McLeod, J. F. Morgan, J. H. Scully, S. C. Tobias, M. A. White

Founded: 1989
Domicile: Delaware
Employees: 1,740

PNC Financial Services Group Inc.

STANDARD &POOR'S

S&P Recommendation HOLD ★★★☆☆	Price $55.38 (as of Nov 27, 2009)	12-Mo. Target Price $60.00	Investment Style Large-Cap Value

GICS Sector Financials
Sub-Industry Regional Banks

Summary This bank holding company conducts regional banking, wholesale banking and asset management in 13 eastern states, with concentration in Pennsylvania, Ohio, Indiana, Maryland and Kentucky.

Key Stock Statistics (Source S&P, Vickers, company reports)

52-Wk Range	$57.86– 16.20	S&P Oper. EPS 2009E	2.93	Market Capitalization(B)	$25.386	Beta	1.23
Trailing 12-Month EPS	$1.69	S&P Oper. EPS 2010E	3.53	Yield (%)	0.72	S&P 3-Yr. Proj. EPS CAGR(%)	27
Trailing 12-Month P/E	32.8	P/E on S&P Oper. EPS 2009E	18.9	Dividend Rate/Share	$0.40	S&P Credit Rating	A
$10K Invested 5 Yrs Ago	$12,033	Common Shares Outstg. (M)	458.4	Institutional Ownership (%)	73		

Price Performance

30-Week Mov. Avg. · · · 10-Week Mov. Avg. - - GAAP Earnings vs. Previous Year Volume Above Avg. STARS
12-Mo. Target Price — Relative Strength — ▲ Up ▼ Down ► No Change Below Avg.

Options: ASE, CBOE, Ph

Analysis prepared by **Erik Oja** on November 23, 2009, when the stock traded at **$ 56.20.**

Highlights

► We expect PNC to generate net interest income of about $8.89 billion in 2009 and $8.64 billion in 2010, and fee income, ex-gains and losses, of $6.69 billion in 2009 and $5.98 billion in 2010.

► Merger savings from the National City acquisition totaled $460 million in the first three quarters of 2009. PNC expects $1.2 billion or more of total savings from the NCC merger, and we estimate that the $740 million remaining savings will be spread over the next five quarters. However, nonperforming loans increased 26.3% sequentially in the third quarter, to 3.18% of total loans. This rate of increase was well above peers, but much lower than PNC had recorded in the previous two quarters. Therefore, we see 2009 loan loss provisions of about $3.74 billion, based on our forecast of $2.52 billion of annualized net chargeoffs plus reserve building of $1.22 billion.

► Our 2009, 2010 and 2011 EPS estimates are $2.93, $3.53 and $5.03, respectively.

Investment Rationale/Risk

► PNC's acquisition of National City appears to be on track in terms of integration efforts, cost savings, and accretion to earnings. We see a continuation of PNC's vast and low-cost funding base, and we expect loan growth to improve as the recession ends. In addition, we see PNC's loan loss reserve coverage ratio, as a percentage of nonperforming loans, as well above peers, and we expect strong fee income and net interest income growth to continue in 2009 and beyond, offsetting credit costs during this time span. We see current valuation on earnings as in line with peers at about 15.7X our 2010 EPS estimate of $3.53, and about 11.0X our 2011 EPS estimate of $5.03.

► Risks to our opinion and target price include higher than expected credit losses from PNC's commercial lending and securities portfolios.

► Our 12-month target price of $60 implies an above-peers multiple of 17X our 2010 EPS estimate. This equates to a well-above-peers 2.48X our December 31 tangible book value per share estimate of $24.22, reflecting PNC's substantial and relatively stable noninterest income.

Qualitative Risk Assessment

LOW	MEDIUM	HIGH

Our risk assessment reflects our view of PNC's large-cap valuation and history of profitability, offset by the possibility of worsening credit quality following the late 2008 acquisition of National City Corp.

Quantitative Evaluations

S&P Quality Ranking B+

D	C	B-	B	B+	A-	A	A+

Relative Strength Rank STRONG

91

LOWEST = 1   HIGHEST = 99

Revenue/Earnings Data

Revenue (Million $)

	1Q	2Q	3Q	4Q	Year
2009	4,826	4,806	4,714	--	--
2008	2,586	2,639	2,228	2,227	9,680
2007	2,306	1,721	1,757	1,634	10,083
2006	2,251	2,356	4,146	2,186	10,939
2005	1,777	1,826	2,108	2,185	7,896
2004	1,577	1,395	1,523	1,413	6,315

Earnings Per Share ($)

	1Q	2Q	3Q	4Q	Year
2009	1.03	0.14	1.01	E0.73	E2.93
2008	1.09	1.45	0.71	-0.77	2.46
2007	1.46	1.22	1.19	0.51	4.35
2006	1.19	1.28	5.01	1.27	8.73
2005	1.24	0.98	1.14	1.20	4.55
2004	1.15	1.07	0.91	1.08	4.21

Fiscal year ended Dec. 31. Next earnings report expected: Early February. EPS Estimates based on S&P Operating Earnings; historical GAAP earnings are as reported.

Dividend Data (Dates: mm/dd Payment Date: mm/dd/yy)

Amount ($)	Date Decl.	Ex-Div. Date	Stk. of Record	Payment Date
0.660	01/08	01/14	01/16	01/24/09
0.100	04/02	04/08	04/13	04/24/09
0.100	07/02	07/09	07/13	07/24/09
0.100	10/01	10/08	10/13	10/24/09

Dividends have been paid since 1865. Source: Company reports.

Please read the Required Disclosures and Analyst Certification on the last page of this report.

PNC Financial Services Group Inc.

STANDARD
&POOR'S

Business Summary November 23, 2009

CORPORATE OVERVIEW. PNC Financial Services Group is a bank holding company that operates businesses engaged in retail banking, corporate and institutional banking, asset management, and global fund processing services. On December 31, 2008, PNC acquired Ohio-based National City Corp. (NCC) for $6.1 billion. The company now has seven primary reportable business segments: Retail Banking, Corporate and Institutional Banking, Asset Management, Residential Mortgage Banking, Global Investment Servicing, Distressed Assets Portfolio, and Other.

Retail Banking generated about 49% of PNC's earnings in 2008, down from about 60% in 2007, due to the cost of loan loss provisioning. Retail Banking provides deposit, lending, brokerage, trust, investment management and cash management services to consumers and small businesses. Corporate and Institutional Banking, which contributed about 25% of PNC's earnings in 2008,

down from about 29% in 2007, offers lending, treasury management and capital markets products and services to mid-sized corporations, government entities and selectively to large corporations. BlackRock and Other generated about 12% of earnings in 2008, up from about 2% in 2007, and includes 18.9%-owned BlackRock, Inc. (BLK 229, Hold), which provides diversified investment management services to institutional and individual investors worldwide through a variety of fixed income, cash management, equity and alternative investment products. Global Investment Servicing, which provided the remaining 14% of earnings in 2008, up from about 9% in 2007, offers mutual fund transfer agency and accounting and administration services.

Company Financials Fiscal Year Ended Dec. 31

Per Share Data ($)	2008	2007	2006	2005	2004	2003	2002	2001	2000	1999
Tangible Book Value	13.13	15.55	23.02	13.98	14.55	14.22	14.78	12.19	13.37	12.07
Earnings	2.46	4.35	8.73	4.55	4.21	3.65	4.20	1.26	4.09	4.15
S&P Core Earnings	1.83	4.47	8.63	4.43	4.00	3.53	3.83	0.92	NA	NA
Dividends	2.61	2.44	2.15	2.00	2.00	1.94	1.92	1.92	1.83	1.68
Payout Ratio	106%	56%	25%	44%	48%	53%	46%	152%	45%	40%
Prices:High	87.99	76.41	75.15	65.66	59.79	55.55	62.80	75.81	75.00	62.00
Prices:Low	39.09	63.54	61.78	49.35	48.90	41.63	32.70	51.14	36.00	43.00
P/E Ratio:High	36	18	9	14	14	15	15	60	18	15
P/E Ratio:Low	16	15	7	11	12	11	8	41	9	10

Income Statement Analysis (Million $)										
Net Interest Income	3,823	2,915	2,245	2,154	1,969	1,996	2,197	2,262	2,164	2,433
Tax Equivalent Adjustment	36.0	27.0	25.0	33.0	NA	NA	NA	NA	18.0	22.0
Non Interest Income	3,306	3,795	6,534	4,203	3,508	3,141	3,108	2,412	2,871	2,723
Loan Loss Provision	1,517	315	124	21.0	52.0	177	309	903	136	163
% Expense/Operating Revenue	62.0%	64.0%	50.5%	48.6%	68.2%	67.7%	60.8%	71.4%	60.8%	60.3%
Pretax Income	1,243	2,094	4,005	1,962	1,745	1,600	1,858	564	1,848	1,891
Effective Tax Rate	29.0%	29.9%	34.0%	30.8%	30.8%	33.7%	33.4%	33.2%	34.3%	33.2%
Net Income	882	1,467	2,595	1,325	1,197	1,029	1,200	377	1,214	1,264
% Net Interest Margin	3.37	3.00	2.92	3.00	3.22	3.64	3.99	3.84	3.64	3.68
S&P Core Earnings	639	1,503	2,565	1,294	1,134	993	1,093	270	NA	NA

Balance Sheet & Other Financial Data (Million $)										
Money Market Assets	1,856	2,729	1,763	350	1,635	50.0	3,658	1,335	1,151	1,148
Investment Securities	43,473	30,225	31,651	23,253	18,609	16,409	17,421	15,243	7,053	8,759
Commercial Loans	99,516	39,956	27,672	26,115	19,418	15,987	22,335	23,134	28,635	24,198
Other Loans	75,973	28,363	22,433	23,821	24,077	18,093	13,115	14,840	21,966	26,572
Total Assets	291,081	138,920	101,820	91,954	79,723	68,168	66,377	69,568	69,844	75,413
Demand Deposits	43,212	19,440	16,070	14,988	12,915	11,505	9,538	10,124	8,490	8,441
Time Deposits	149,653	63,256	50,231	45,287	40,354	33,736	35,444	37,180	39,174	38,227
Long Term Debt	47,087	21,157	10,266	6,797	8,684	7,667	9,112	8,922	7,266	9,395
Common Equity	17,504	14,854	10,788	8,563	7,548	6,735	6,943	5,822	6,649	5,939
% Return on Assets	0.4	1.2	2.7	1.5	1.6	1.5	1.8	0.5	1.7	1.7
% Return on Equity	5.5	11.4	26.8	16.5	16.8	15.0	18.7	5.9	19.0	20.8
% Loan Loss Reserve	2.2	1.2	1.1	1.2	1.3	1.8	1.8	1.5	1.3	1.2
% Loans/Deposits	91.0	79.5	79.1	123.7	84.8	78.4	82.4	89.1	109.6	119.7
% Equity to Assets	7.5	10.7	10.0	9.3	9.7	10.2	9.4	8.9	9.0	7.8

Data as orig reptd.; bef. results of disc opers/spec. items. Per share data adj. for stk. divs.; EPS diluted. E-Estimated. NA-Not Available. NM-Not Meaningful. NR-Not Ranked. UR-Under Review.

Office: 249 5th Ave, 1 PNC Plz, Pittsburgh, PA 15222-2707.
Telephone: 412-762-2000.
Email: corporate.communiations@pncbank.com
Website: http://www.pnc.com

Chrmn & CEO: J.E. Rohr
Pres: J.C. Guyaux
Vice Chrmn: T.G. Shack
EVP & CFO: R.J. Johnson

EVP & Chief Admin Officer: T.K. Whitford
Investor Contact: W. Callihan (800-843-2206)
Board Members: R. O. Berndt, C. E. Bunch, P. W. Chellgren, R. N. Clay, K. C. James, R. B. Kelson, B. C. Lindsay, A. A. Massaro, J. G. Pepper, J. E. Rohr, T. G. Shack, D. J. Shepard, L. K. Steffes, D. F. Strigl, S. G. Thieke, T. J. Usher, G. H. Walls, Jr., H. H. Wehmeier

Founded: 1922
Domicile: Pennsylvania
Employees: 59,595

The McGraw-Hill Companies

Polo Ralph Lauren Corp

STANDARD &POOR'S

S&P Recommendation **STRONG BUY** ★★★★★	Price $77.11 (as of Nov 27, 2009)	12-Mo. Target Price $95.00	Investment Style Large-Cap Growth

GICS Sector Consumer Discretionary
Sub-Industry Apparel, Accessories & Luxury Goods

Summary This company designs, markets and distributes men's and women's clothing and other premium lifestyle products.

Key Stock Statistics (Source S&P, Vickers, company reports)

52-Wk Range	$83.50– 31.64	S&P Oper. EPS 2010**E**	4.30	Market Capitalization(B)	$4.355	Beta	1.70
Trailing 12-Month EPS	$4.01	S&P Oper. EPS 2011**E**	4.80	Yield (%)	0.52	S&P 3-Yr. Proj. EPS CAGR(%)	10
Trailing 12-Month P/E	19.2	P/E on S&P Oper. EPS 2010**E**	17.9	Dividend Rate/Share	$0.40	S&P Credit Rating	NA
$10K Invested 5 Yrs Ago	$19,400	Common Shares Outstg. (M)	99.1	Institutional Ownership (%)	NM		

Price Performance

30-Week Mov. Avg. · · ·   10-Week Mov. Avg. – –   **GAAP Earnings vs. Previous Year**   Volume Above Avg. ‖‖‖   STARS
12-Mo. Target Price —   Relative Strength —   ▲ Up   ▼ Down   ► No Change   Below Avg. ‖‖‖   ★

Options: ASE, CBOE, Ph

Analysis prepared by **Marie Driscoll, CFA** on November 13, 2009, when the stock traded at **$ 80.84**.

Highlights

► While luxury demand remains materially weaker than during the heyday of 2007, we are beginning to see signs of stabilization and modest improvement as we lap the sharp deceleration of the final months of 2008. We regard RL as best able to navigate the current economic malaise with its superior brand positioning in virtually all channels and categories in which it participates. We note its relatively strong September-quarter results, with sales off 4%, but operating profits up 1%.

► We see FY 10 (Mar.) sales of $4.9 billion, down 3%. We are encouraged by quarterly comp improvement: -16% in March, -11% in June and -6% in September. Comparisons should ease in the second half of FY 10, and we look for flat retail sales at $1.9 billion, including a 10% e-commerce gain. We estimate a 4% drop in RL's wholesale business in tandem with reduced inventory at retail. We project a 5% sales gain in FY 11.

► We see about 30 basis points of EBIT margin contraction in FY 10, to 13.5%, but we see 70 bps of expansion in FY 11. Supply chain and sourcing initiatives should mitigate margin pressure in FY 10 and beyond.

Investment Rationale/Risk

► Geographic expansion, a more favorable merchandise mix and strong brand positioning provide RL with attractive long-term growth opportunities, in our view. RL's assumption of direct control of its Southeast Asia (including China) business in January 2010 should provide substantial long-term growth opportunities with strong demographic underpinnings as RL seeks to grow this region to a third of sales, from an estimated $150 million. Near term, a cautious consumer, in both the affluent luxury and moderate channels, concerns us.

► Risks to our recommendation and target price include integration risk from recent licensee acquisitions, execution risk in Asia and a sharp decline in consumer discretionary spending. Regarding corporate governance, we are concerned that chairman, CEO and founder Ralph Lauren controls approximately 86% of the voting shares.

► Our 12-month target price of $95 is about 20X our FY 10 EPS estimate of $4.80, in line with peers. RL recently doubled its dividend and added $225 million to its existing share repurchase program.

Qualitative Risk Assessment

LOW	MEDIUM	HIGH

Our risk assessment reflects our view of RL's strong balance sheet, with $925 million in cash and equivalents as of September 30, offset by its exposure to the consolidating and contracting department store channel.

Quantitative Evaluations

S&P Quality Ranking   A-

D	C	B-	B	B+	A-	A	A+

Relative Strength Rank   MODERATE
69
LOWEST = 1   HIGHEST = 99

Revenue/Earnings Data

Revenue (Million $)

	1Q	2Q	3Q	4Q	Year
2010	1,024	1,374	--	--	--
2009	1,114	1,429	1,252	1,224	5,019
2008	1,070	1,299	1,270	1,241	4,880
2007	953.6	1,167	1,144	1,031	4,295
2006	751.9	964.8	995.5	971.6	3,746
2005	535.8	821.5	888.0	834.5	3,305

Earnings Per Share ($)

	1Q	2Q	3Q	4Q	Year
2010	0.76	1.75	E0.95	E0.85	E4.30
2009	0.93	1.58	1.05	0.44	4.01
2008	0.82	1.09	1.08	1.00	3.99
2007	0.74	1.28	1.03	0.68	3.73
2006	0.48	0.97	0.84	0.58	2.87
2005	0.13	0.78	0.72	0.22	1.83

Fiscal year ended Mar. 31. Next earnings report expected: Early February. EPS Estimates based on S&P Operating Earnings; historical GAAP earnings are as reported.

Dividend Data (Dates: mm/dd Payment Date: mm/dd/yy)

Amount ($)	Date Decl.	Ex-Div. Date	Stk. of Record	Payment Date
0.050	03/17	03/25	03/27	04/10/09
0.050	06/16	06/24	06/26	07/10/09
0.050	09/15	09/23	09/25	10/09/09
0.100	11/04	12/22	12/24	01/08/10

Dividends have been paid since 2003. Source: Company reports.

STANDARD &POOR'S

Polo Ralph Lauren Corp

Business Summary November 13, 2009

CORPORATE OVERVIEW. Since its modest beginnings in men's ties in 1967, Polo Ralph Lauren has grown into one of America's leading lifestyle brands encompassing multiple permutations targeted at specific demographics, usage occasions and price points, with merchandise available at approximately 6,100 retail locations throughout the world. Licensor relationships extend the brand to fragrance, eyewear, leather goods, jewelry, and an extensive home merchandise offering. All told, we believe the Polo Ralph Lauren brand generates about $12 billion at retail worldwide.

MARKET PROFILE. The domestic men's, women's and children's apparel market represented an estimated $199 billion at retail in 2008, according to NPD Fashionworld consumer estimated data. S&P forecasts a 6% to 8% decline in 2009 apparel sales, which compares with a 4% decline in 2008 and 4% increments in both 2006 and 2007. The apparel market is fragmented, with national brands marketed by 20 companies accounting for about 30% of total apparel sales, and the remaining 70% comprised of smaller and/or private label "store" brands. The market is mature, and subject to pricing pressure due to channel competition and production steadily moving offshore to low-cost producers in India, Asia and China.

COMPETITIVE LANDSCAPE. By channel, specialty stores account for the largest share of apparel sales (31% in 2008, according to NPD). Mass merchants (Wal-Mart and Target) came in second, at 21%, and department stores, RL's primary channel, came in third, at 15%, and down 500 basis points since 2003. National chains (Sears and JC Penney) captured 14% of 2008 apparel sales, and off-price retailers (TJX and Ross Stores) 9%. The remaining 10% is divided among factory outlets and direct and e-mail pure plays. RL holds leading market shares in department stores with seven key department stores accounting for about 50% of its wholesale volume and Macy's the largest wholesale account at 19%. RL competes with Jones Apparel Group, Liz Claiborne and VF Corp., as well as private label offerings, which garner about a third of total apparel purchases and are an important differentiator for retailers. RL also sells directly to consumers through 328 specialty retail locations spanning the luxury, mid-market and factory channels and at RalphLauren.com and Rugby.com.

Company Financials Fiscal Year Ended Mar. 31

Per Share Data ($)	2009	2008	2007	2006	2005	2004	2003	2002	2001	2000
Tangible Book Value	14.41	10.71	11.99	10.35	10.38	10.56	8.93	7.38	5.76	5.08
Cash Flow	5.83	5.90	5.07	4.06	2.83	2.52	2.55	2.60	1.41	2.16
Earnings	4.01	3.99	3.73	2.87	1.83	1.69	1.76	1.75	0.61	1.49
S&P Core Earnings	4.01	3.99	3.75	2.80	2.32	1.53	1.55	1.54	0.44	NA
Dividends	0.20	0.20	0.20	0.20	0.20	Nil	Nil	Nil	Nil	Nil
Payout Ratio	5%	5%	5%	7%	11%	Nil	Nil	Nil	Nil	Nil
Calendar Year	2008	2007	2006	2005	2004	2003	2002	2001	2000	1999
Prices:High	82.02	102.58	83.15	56.84	42.83	31.52	30.82	31.34	23.25	25.38
Prices:Low	31.22	60.41	45.65	34.19	27.28	19.30	16.49	17.80	12.75	16.06
P/E Ratio:High	20	26	22	20	23	11	9	10	21	11
P/E Ratio:Low	8	15	12	12	15	11	9	10	38	17

Income Statement Analysis (Million $)										
Revenue	5,019	4,880	4,295	3,746	3,305	2,650	2,439	2,364	2,226	1,956
Operating Income	859	860	802	663	406	377	382	393	319	330
Depreciation	184	201	145	127	104	83.2	78.6	83.9	78.6	66.3
Interest Expense	26.6	25.1	21.6	12.5	11.0	10.0	13.5	19.0	25.1	15.0
Pretax Income	588	644	659	516	298	266	274	276	98.0	249
Effective Tax Rate	30.9%	34.5%	36.8%	37.7%	36.0%	35.7%	36.5%	37.5%	39.5%	40.8%
Net Income	406	420	401	308	190	171	174	173	59.3	147
S&P Core Earnings	406	420	403	299	242	154	154	151	43.1	NA

Balance Sheet & Other Financial Data (Million $)										
Cash	820	626	564	286	350	343	344	239	102	165
Current Assets	2,057	1,894	1,686	1,379	1,414	1,271	1,166	1,008	902	853
Total Assets	4,357	4,366	3,758	2,089	2,727	2,270	2,039	1,749	1,626	1,621
Current Liabilities	674	909	640	844	622	501	500	392	440	406
Long Term Debt	406	546	399	Nil	291	277	248	285	297	343
Common Equity	2,735	2,390	2,335	2,050	1,676	1,422	1,209	998	1,106	1,115
Total Capital	3,142	2,966	2,734	2,070	1,967	1,699	1,457	1,284	1,106	1,115
Capital Expenditures	185	217	184	159	174	123	98.7	88.0	105	122
Cash Flow	590	621	546	435	294	254	253	256	138	214
Current Ratio	3.1	2.1	2.6	1.6	2.3	2.5	2.3	2.6	2.1	2.1
% Long Term Debt of Capitalization	12.9	18.4	14.6	Nil	14.8	16.3	17.1	22.2	26.8	30.7
% Net Income of Revenue	8.1	8.6	9.3	8.2	5.8	6.5	7.1	7.3	2.7	7.5
% Return on Assets	9.3	10.3	11.7	12.8	7.6	7.9	9.2	10.2	3.7	10.8
% Return on Equity	15.8	17.8	18.3	16.5	12.3	13.0	15.8	19.1	7.5	20.6

Data as orig reptd.; bef. results of disc opers/spec. items. Per share data adj. for stk. divs.; EPS diluted. E-Estimated. NA-Not Available. NM-Not Meaningful. NR-Not Ranked. UR-Under Review.

Office: 650 Madison Ave, New York, NY 10022-1062.
Telephone: 212-318-7000.
Website: http://www.ralphlauren.com
Chrmn & CEO: R. Lauren

Pres & COO: R.N. Farah
SVP, CFO & Chief Acctg Officer: T.T. Travis
SVP, Secy & General Counsel: J.D. Drucker
Investor Contact: J. Hurley (212-318-7000)

Board Members: J. R. Alchin, A. H. Aronson, F. A. Bennack, Jr., J. F. Brown, R. N. Farah, J. L. Fleishman, H. Joly, R. Lauren, S. P. Murphy, J. Nemerov, R. C. Wright

Founded: 1967
Domicile: Delaware
Employees: 17,000

The McGraw-Hill Companies

PPG Industries Inc.

STANDARD &POOR'S

S&P Recommendation	**STRONG BUY** ★ ★ ★ ★ ★	Price	12-Mo. Target Price	Investment Style
		$59.33 (as of Nov 27, 2009)	$70.00	Large-Cap Blend

GICS Sector Materials
Sub-Industry Diversified Chemicals

Summary PPG is a leading manufacturer of coatings and resins, flat and fiber glass, and industrial and specialty chemicals.

Key Stock Statistics (Source S&P, Vickers, company reports)

52-Wk Range	$62.31–28.16	S&P Oper. EPS 2009**E**	2.80	Market Capitalization(B)	$9.907	Beta		1.25
Trailing 12-Month EPS	$1.61	S&P Oper. EPS 2010**E**	3.25	Yield (%)	3.64	S&P 3-Yr. Proj. EPS CAGR(%)		10
Trailing 12-Month P/E	36.9	P/E on S&P Oper. EPS 2009**E**	21.2	Dividend Rate/Share	$2.16	S&P Credit Rating		BBB+
$10K Invested 5 Yrs Ago	$10,338	Common Shares Outstg. (M)	167.0	Institutional Ownership (%)	72			

Price Performance

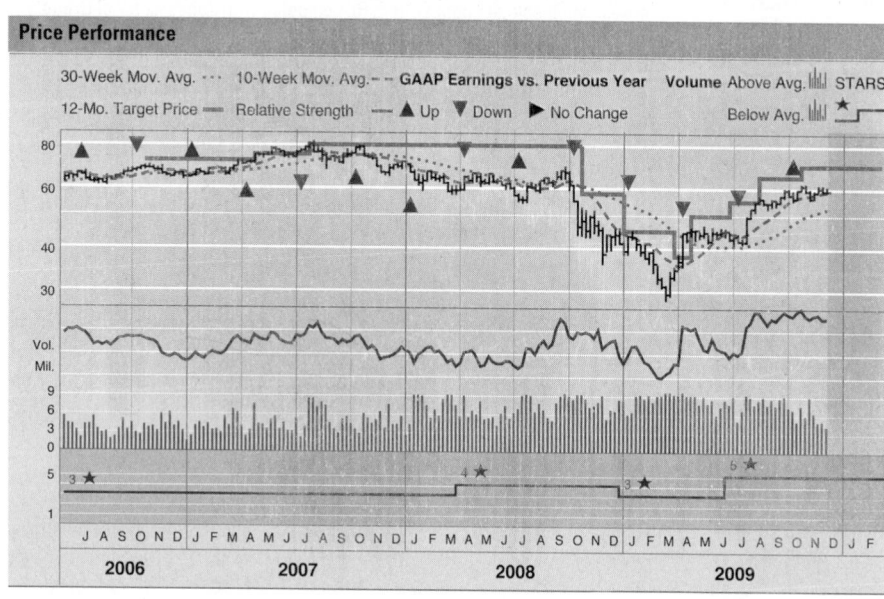

- 30-Week Mov. Avg. · · ·
- 10-Week Mov. Avg. – –
- **GAAP Earnings vs. Previous Year**
- Volume Above Avg. STARS
- 12-Mo. Target Price —
- Relative Strength
- ▲ Up ▼ Down ► No Change
- Below Avg. ★

J A S O N D J F M A M J J A S O N D J F M A M J J A S O N D J F M A M J J A S O N D J F
2006 · 2007 · 2008 · 2009

Options: ASE, CBOE, Ph

Analysis prepared by **Richard O'Reilly, CFA** on October 16, 2009, when the stock traded at **$ 61.66**.

Highlights

► We expect sales in 2010 to rise about 8% after an expected 22% decline in 2009, which includes unfavorable currency rates and the sale in September 2008 of 60% of the auto glass businesses (sales of $724 million in 2008). We think the coatings and silicas businesses in 2010 will be aided by stronger auto, industrial and housing related markets, while currency rates could become a tailwind.

► We forecast that margins for the coatings units will be helped by completion in early 2010 of restructuring programs announced since September 2008. Optical products sales should rebound after a drop in 2009, assuming better consumer spending. While overall chlor-alkali prices may have bottomed in the 2009 third quarter, we expect chemicals profits to remain below early 2009 levels as a result of a drop in caustic soda selling prices in 2009.

► We expect overall raw materials and energy costs to be lower in 2010, and we see the effective tax rate, before special items, at 33.0%. Our EPS forecast for 2009 is $2.80 before special charges of at least $0.86, down from $3.25 in 2008, which included total special charges of $1.21.

Investment Rationale/Risk

► Our strong buy opinion on the shares is based on our expectation that business conditions will begin to recover by 2010. The purchase of SigmaKalon greatly expanded PPG's coatings business in both size and geographical diversity, while the sale in 2008 of a majority of the auto glass business significantly reduced its exposure to the domestic auto market.

► Risks to our recommendation and target price include slower-than-projected industrial activity, unplanned production outages and interruptions, exposure to domestic auto makers, and unexpected weakness in selling prices for commodity chemicals.

► Our 12-month target price of $70 assumes that the stock's P/E multiple, based on our 2010 operating EPS estimate, will expand closer to its historical average high level of 22X as a result of the cyclical recovery in earnings that we foresee. The dividend has been increased for 38 consecutive years, and the yield is well above that of the S&P 500. We think PPG's liquidity is healthy, as the balance sheet showed about $900 million of cash at the end of September 2009.

Qualitative Risk Assessment

LOW	**MEDIUM**	HIGH

Our risk assessment reflects the company's diversified business mix, large market shares in key products, and what we see as its healthy balance sheet, offset by the cyclical nature of the commodity chemicals business and the auto and construction-related end markets.

Quantitative Evaluations

S&P Quality Ranking — B+

D	C	B-	B	**B+**	A-	A	A+

Relative Strength Rank — MODERATE

63

LOWEST = 1 · HIGHEST = 99

Revenue/Earnings Data

Revenue (Million $)

	1Q	2Q	3Q	4Q	Year
2009	2,783	3,115	3,225	--	--
2008	3,962	4,474	4,225	3,188	15,849
2007	2,917	3,173	2,823	2,874	11,206
2006	2,638	2,824	2,802	2,773	11,037
2005	2,493	2,656	2,547	2,505	10,201
2004	2,264	2,429	2,409	2,411	9,513

Earnings Per Share ($)

2009	-0.68	0.89	0.96	E0.77	E2.80
2008	0.53	1.51	0.70	0.43	3.25
2007	1.17	1.50	1.29	1.17	4.91
2006	1.11	1.68	0.54	0.94	4.27
2005	0.55	1.34	0.92	0.68	3.49
2004	0.69	1.08	1.12	1.06	3.95

Fiscal year ended Dec. 31. Next earnings report expected: Mid January. EPS Estimates based on S&P Operating Earnings; historical GAAP earnings are as reported.

Dividend Data (Dates: mm/dd Payment Date: mm/dd/yy)

Amount ($)	Date Decl.	Ex-Div. Date	Stk. of Record	Payment Date
0.530	01/16	02/18	02/20	03/12/09
0.530	04/16	05/07	05/11	06/12/09
0.530	07/16	08/06	08/10	09/11/09
0.540	10/16	11/06	11/10	12/11/09

Dividends have been paid since 1899. Source: Company reports.

Please read the Required Disclosures and Analyst Certification on the last page of this report.

The **McGraw·Hill** Companies

PPG Industries Inc.

Business Summary October 16, 2009

CORPORATE OVERVIEW. PPG Industries is a diversified producer of coatings, chemicals and glass products. International operations contributed 55% of sales and 43% of operating profits in 2008.

PPG Industries is one of the world's leading producers of protective and decorative coatings. Industrial coatings (25% of sales in 2008 and 13% of operating profits) is comprised of original automotive, industrial (used in appliance and industrial equipment), and packaging (container) coatings. PPG also produces adhesives and sealants for the automotive industry and metal pretreatments.

Performance coatings (30%, 37%) consists of automotive and industrial refinish coatings, aerospace coatings, marine and specialty industrial coatings, and a major North American supplier of architectural coatings (Pittsburgh, Olympic, Porter and Lucite brands). The architectural finishes business at the end of 2008 operated 410 company-owned service centers in North America and 50 stores in Australia. The company is a global supplier of aircraft coatings, sealants, and transparencies to OEM, maintenance and aftermarket customers. The European Architectural coatings (14%, 9%) segment consists of the majority of the sales of the former SigmaKalon acquired in January 2008. The coatings industry is highly competitive and consists of a few large firms

with a global presence and many smaller firms serving local or regional markets.

PPG's commodity chemicals business (12%, 21%) is the fourth largest U.S. producer of chlorine and caustic soda (used in a wide variety of industrial applications), vinyl chloride monomer (for use in polyvinyl chloride resins), calcium hypochlorite, and chlorinated solvents. These commodity chemicals are highly cyclical; PPG volumes rose 9% and 1% in 2007 and 2008, respectively, following two consecutive years of modest declines. The company's electro-chemical unit (ECU) average price rose 28% in 2008.

Optical and specialty materials (7%, 15%) consists of optical resins (Transitions photochromic lenses, sun lenses, and polarized film), silica compounds, and Teslin synthetic printing sheet. A fine chemicals business was sold in late 2007 (reported as discontinued operations). The optical products business grew 11% in 2008, aided by the introduction of the newest version of Transitions in early 2008.

Company Financials Fiscal Year Ended Dec. 31

Per Share Data ($)	2008	2007	2006	2005	2004	2003	2002	2001	2000	1999
Tangible Book Value	NM	55.71	7.59	8.46	10.81	7.36	3.49	9.10	8.57	8.30
Cash Flow	6.55	7.20	6.61	5.66	6.19	5.23	1.99	4.93	6.20	12.99
Earnings	3.25	4.91	4.27	3.49	3.95	2.92	-0.36	2.29	3.57	3.23
S&P Core Earnings	2.62	5.28	4.78	4.57	4.42	3.48	1.76	1.17	NA	NA
Dividends	2.09	2.04	1.91	1.86	1.79	1.73	1.70	1.68	1.60	1.52
Payout Ratio	64%	42%	45%	53%	45%	59%	NM	73%	45%	47%
Prices:High	71.00	82.42	69.80	74.73	68.79	64.42	62.86	59.75	65.06	70.75
Prices:Low	35.94	64.01	56.53	55.64	54.81	42.61	41.39	38.99	36.00	47.94
P/E Ratio:High	22	17	16	21	17	22	NM	26	18	22
P/E Ratio:Low	11	13	13	16	14	15	NM	17	10	15

Income Statement Analysis (Million $)										
Revenue	15,849	11,206	11,037	10,201	9,513	8,756	8,067	8,169	8,629	7,757
Operating Income	1,924	1,698	1,703	1,648	1,496	1,367	1,309	1,371	1,649	1,528
Depreciation	546	380	380	372	388	394	398	447	447	419
Interest Expense	262	104	83.0	81.0	90.0	107	128	169	161	133
Pretax Income	908	1,243	1,060	947	1,063	843	-28.0	666	1,017	973
Effective Tax Rate	31.3%	28.6%	26.2%	29.8%	30.3%	34.8%	NM	37.1%	36.3%	38.7%
Net Income	538	815	711	596	683	500	-60.0	387	620	568
S&P Core Earnings	434	877	797	780	765	597	300	197	NA	NA

Balance Sheet & Other Financial Data (Million $)										
Cash	1,021	2,232	455	466	709	499	117	108	111	158
Current Assets	6,348	7,136	4,592	4,019	4,054	3,537	2,945	2,703	3,093	3,062
Total Assets	14,698	12,629	10,021	8,681	8,932	8,424	7,863	8,452	9,125	8,914
Current Liabilities	4,210	4,661	2,787	2,349	2,221	2,139	1,920	1,955	2,543	2,384
Long Term Debt	3,009	1,201	1,155	1,169	1,184	1,339	1,699	1,699	1,810	1,836
Common Equity	3,333	4,151	3,234	3,053	3,572	2,911	2,150	3,080	3,097	3,106
Total Capital	6,923	5,649	4,673	4,420	4,997	4,475	4,044	5,453	5,578	5,560
Capital Expenditures	383	353	372	288	244	217	238	291	561	490
Cash Flow	1,084	1,195	1,091	968	1,071	894	338	834	1,067	987
Current Ratio	1.5	1.5	1.6	1.7	1.8	1.7	1.5	1.4	1.2	1.3
% Long Term Debt of Capitalization	43.5	21.3	24.7	26.4	23.7	29.9	42.0	31.2	32.4	33.0
% Net Income of Revenue	3.4	7.8	6.4	5.8	7.2	5.7	NM	4.7	7.2	7.3
% Return on Assets	3.9	7.2	7.6	6.8	7.9	6.1	NM	4.4	6.9	7.0
% Return on Equity	14.4	22.1	22.6	18.0	21.1	19.8	NM	12.5	20.0	19.0

Data as orig reptd.; bef. results of disc opers/spec. items. Per share data adj. for stk. divs.; EPS diluted. E-Estimated. NA-Not Available. NM-Not Meaningful. NR-Not Ranked. UR-Under Review.

Office: 1 PPG Pl, Pittsburgh, PA 15272.
Telephone: 412-434-3131.
Website: http://www.ppg.com
Chrmn & CEO: C.E. Bunch

SVP & CFO: R.J. Dellinger
SVP & General Counsel: J.C. Diggs
CTO: C.F. Kahle, II
Treas: A.S. Giga

Investor Contact: V. Morales (412-434-3740)
Board Members: J. G. Berges, C. E. Bunch, H. Grant, V. F. Haynes, M. J. Hooper, R. Mehrabian, M. H. Richenhagen, R. Ripp, T. J. Usher, D. R. Whitwam

Founded: 1883
Domicile: Pennsylvania
Employees: 44,900

PPL Corp

STANDARD &POOR'S

S&P Recommendation	HOLD ★★★☆☆	Price	12-Mo. Target Price	Investment Style
		$30.46 (as of Nov 27, 2009)	$34.00	Large-Cap Blend

GICS Sector Utilities
Sub-Industry Electric Utilities

Summary This holding company for PPL Utilities also has holdings in the U.K.

Key Stock Statistics (Source S&P, Vickers, company reports)

52-Wk Range	$34.42– 24.25	S&P Oper. EPS 2009E	1.78	Market Capitalization(B)	$11.485	Beta	0.52
Trailing 12-Month EPS	$1.41	S&P Oper. EPS 2010E	3.30	Yield (%)	4.53	S&P 3-Yr. Proj. EPS CAGR(%)	24
Trailing 12-Month P/E	21.6	P/E on S&P Oper. EPS 2009E	17.1	Dividend Rate/Share	$1.38	S&P Credit Rating	NA
$10K Invested 5 Yrs Ago	$13,508	Common Shares Outstg. (M)	377.1	Institutional Ownership (%)	62		

Price Performance

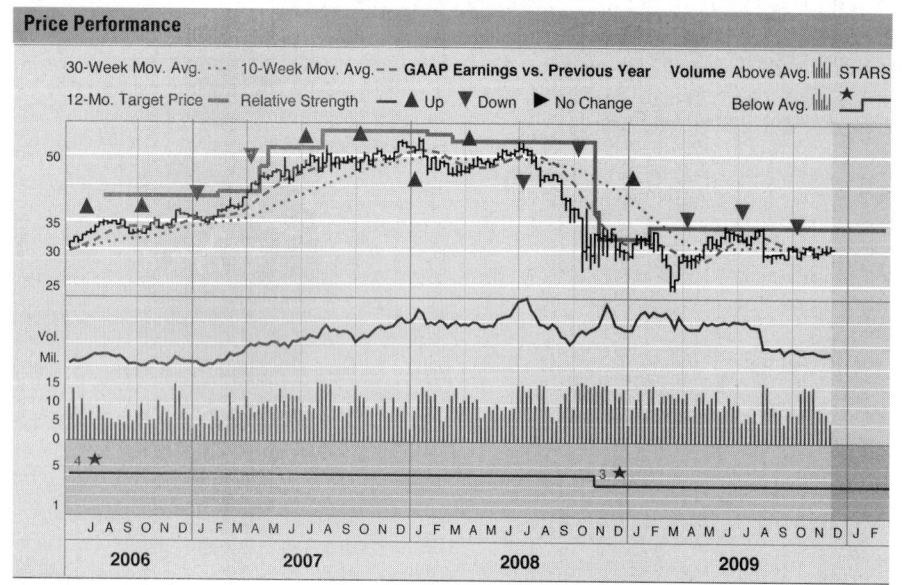

30-Week Mov. Avg. · · · 10-Week Mov. Avg. – – GAAP Earnings vs. Previous Year Volume Above Avg. STARS
12-Mo. Target Price — Relative Strength — ▲ Up ▼ Down ► No Change Below Avg.

2006 2007 2008 2009

Options: CBOE, P, Ph

Analysis prepared by **Justin McCann** on September 08, 2009, when the stock traded at **$ 29.29**.

Highlights

► Excluding $0.29 in net one-time charges, we expect operating EPS in 2009 to decline about 13% from 2008's $2.02. In addition to the impact of the weak economy, the sharp decline also reflects our expectation of higher financing, coal commodity, and transportation costs, the completion of the company's scrubber construction program, the fall in sulfur dioxide allowance prices, and less favorable currency exchange rates for the international operations.

► For 2010, we expect operating EPS to nearly double from anticipated results in 2009 as expired energy contracts are replaced by much higher-margin contracts. However, the sharp rise is expected to be less than previously projected due to lower customer demand, the decline in natural gas and power prices and, due to reduced activity and volatility in the energy markets, lower anticipated margins from the marketing and trading operations.

► Under the rate stabilization plan approved by the Pennsylvania's Public Utility Commission, residential and small-business customers were able to pay slightly higher bills in 2009 so as to lessen the very sharp increase expected in 2010 when the current rate cap expires.

Investment Rationale/Risk

► With the shares having recovered more than 20% from their multi-year low reached in March, they are down less than 4% year to date. The stock had been hurt, in our view, by the crisis in the credit markets, the drop in wholesale power prices, the weak economy, and the sharp decline in projected earnings for 2009. In addition to the recovery in the broader market, we believe the rebound in the stock has reflected increased market focus on the strong earnings advance projected for 2010. The stock's dividend yield (recently 4.7%) remains below the peer average (5.0%), while the effective payout ratio (78% of our 2009 operating EPS estimate) is well above that of peers (66%).

► Risks to our recommendation and target price include potentially unfavorable regulatory rulings, significantly lower results from the unregulated operations, and a major shift in the average P/E multiple of the peer group as a whole.

► Our 12-month target price is $34. While we expect PPL's earnings to significantly improve in 2010, we believe the shares will continue to reflect the still depressed state of the wholesale power markets and trade at a discount-to-peers P/E of 10.1X our 2010 EPS estimate.

Qualitative Risk Assessment

LOW	MEDIUM	HIGH

Our risk assessment reflects the steady cash flow we expect from the regulated Pennsylvania and U.K. distribution segments, which operate within supportive regulatory environments. This is offset by the highly profitable but less predictable earnings and cash flow from the power supply segment, as well as the currency risks related to the U.K. and Latin American businesses.

Quantitative Evaluations

S&P Quality Ranking B+

D	C	B-	B	B+	A-	A	A+

Relative Strength Rank MODERATE

54

LOWEST = 1 HIGHEST = 99

Revenue/Earnings Data

Revenue (Million $)

	1Q	2Q	3Q	4Q	Year
2009	2,359	1,673	1,805	--	--
2008	1,526	1,024	2,981	2,513	8,044
2007	1,638	1,613	1,763	1,606	6,498
2006	1,781	1,642	1,752	1,724	6,899
2005	1,602	1,476	1,643	1,498	6,219
2004	1,520	1,362	1,465	1,465	5,812

Earnings Per Share ($)

2009	0.64	0.07	0.12	E0.34	E1.78
2008	0.65	0.50	0.55	0.74	2.45
2007	0.58	0.63	0.72	0.57	2.63
2006	0.73	0.52	0.58	0.47	2.29
2005	0.44	0.47	0.51	0.50	1.92
2004	0.50	0.41	0.52	0.47	1.89

Fiscal year ended Dec. 31. Next earnings report expected: Early February. EPS Estimates based on S&P Operating Earnings; historical GAAP earnings are as reported.

Dividend Data (Dates: mm/dd Payment Date: mm/dd/yy)

Amount ($)	Date Decl.	Ex-Div. Date	Stk. of Record	Payment Date
0.345	02/27	03/06	03/10	04/01/09
0.345	05/20	06/08	06/10	07/01/09
0.345	08/28	09/08	09/10	10/01/09
0.345	11/20	12/08	12/10	01/01/10

Dividends have been paid since 1946. Source: Company reports.

PPL Corp

Business Summary September 08, 2009

CORPORATE OVERVIEW. PPL Corporation is an energy and utility holding company organized into three operating segments: the supply segment, the Pennsylvania delivery segment, and the international delivery segment. PPL's subsidiaries PPL Generation and PPL EnergyPlus comprise the supply segment. These units are involved in electricity generation and marketing of electricity and other power purchases to deregulated wholesale and retail markets. The Pennsylvania delivery segment operates through its PPL Electric subsidiary, which provides electric utility services in the regulated Pennsylvania market. In October 2008, PPL completed the sale of its natural gas distribution unit PPL Gas Utilities and its propane unit Penn Fuel Propane for proceeds of $303 million.

CORPORATE STRATEGY. The company's business strategy is to achieve stable growth in the regulated delivery business. It plans to earn long-term growth in delivery through efficient and low-cost operations while working to enhance strong customer and regulatory relations. In the unregulated supply business, PPL intends to reduce the volatility in both its cash flows and earnings and to ensure disciplined growth. The company's strategy for its electric-

ity generation and marketing business is to build an effective risk management framework to handle energy price risk and counterparty risk. It will work to reduce risk by entering into supply contracts of varying duration, which should reflect fluctuations in demand.

MARKET PROFILE. PPL provides electricity delivery service to 1.4 million customers in a 10,000-square mile territory covering 29 counties of eastern and central Pennsylvania. In 2008, about 45% of electricity revenues were from residential customers, 36% from commercial customers, 18% from industrial customers, and 1% from other customer classes. PPL Generation owned or controlled 12,002 megawatts (mw) of generating capacity at the end of 2008, with 9,785 mw at its plants in Pennsylvania and 1,287 mw in Montana. In the U.K., PPL operates two distribution companies that serve 2.6 million customers.

Company Financials Fiscal Year Ended Dec. 31

Per Share Data ($)	2008	2007	2006	2005	2004	2003	2002	2001	2000	1999
Tangible Book Value	9.93	11.33	9.35	7.73	7.50	5.53	5.87	6.98	6.65	5.60
Earnings	2.45	2.63	2.29	1.92	1.89	2.08	1.17	0.58	1.68	1.57
S&P Core Earnings	1.86	2.61	2.33	1.87	1.74	1.95	0.79	0.90	NA	NA
Dividends	1.34	1.22	1.10	1.21	0.82	0.77	0.68	0.53	0.53	0.50
Payout Ratio	55%	47%	48%	63%	43%	37%	57%	92%	32%	32%
Prices:High	55.23	54.58	37.34	33.68	27.08	22.17	19.98	31.18	23.06	16.00
Prices:Low	26.84	34.43	27.83	25.52	19.92	15.83	13.00	15.50	9.19	10.19
P/E Ratio:High	23	21	16	18	14	11	17	54	14	10
P/E Ratio:Low	11	13	12	13	11	8	11	27	5	6

Income Statement Analysis (Million $)	2008	2007	2006	2005	2004	2003	2002	2001	2000	1999
Revenue	8,044	6,498	6,899	6,219	5,812	5,587	5,429	5,725	5,683	4,590
Depreciation	551	756	446	420	412	380	367	254	261	257
Maintenance	NA	NA	NA	NA	NA	NA	314	269	261	215
Fixed Charges Coverage	3.86	3.61	3.46	2.70	2.72	2.72	2.49	3.08	2.95	3.20
Construction Credits	NA	NA	NA	NA	NA	NA	NA	NA	NA	NA
Effective Tax Rate	32.3%	20.7%	23.5%	14.0%	21.6%	18.5%	29.5%	54.4%	36.3%	26.1%
Net Income	922	1,013	885	737	700	748	425	221	513	478
S&P Core Earnings	705	1,007	897	716	645	674	240	262	NA	NA

Balance Sheet & Other Financial Data (Million $)	2008	2007	2006	2005	2004	2003	2002	2001	2000	1999
Gross Property	20,299	20,377	20,079	18,615	18,692	17,775	16,406	12,477	11,418	10,717
Capital Expenditures	1,429	1,685	1,394	811	703	771	648	565	460	318
Net Property	12,416	12,605	12,069	10,916	11,209	10,446	9,566	6,135	5,948	5,644
Capitalization:Long Term Debt	7,151	6,890	6,728	6,044	6,881	8,145	6,562	5,906	4,717	4,103
Capitalization:% Long Term Debt	57.1	54.1	55.4	57.5	61.6	71.1	74.0	75.3	69.1	71.8
Capitalization:Preferred	301	301	301	51.0	51.0	51.0	82.0	82.0	97.0	Nil
Capitalization:% Preferred	2.40	2.40	2.50	0.50	0.46	0.45	0.92	1.05	1.42	Nil
Capitalization:Common	5,077	5,556	5,122	4,418	4,239	3,259	2,224	1,857	2,012	1,613
Capitalization:% Common	40.5	43.5	42.1	42.0	37.9	28.5	25.1	23.7	29.5	28.2
Total Capital	14,311	14,958	14,241	12,766	13,653	13,710	11,274	9,332	6,880	7,328
% Operating Ratio	82.9	78.3	80.8	80.3	79.5	78.9	76.8	81.1	84.0	84.8
% Earned on Net Property	14.5	13.6	13.9	12.2	12.7	13.4	17.5	14.2	28.6	22.3
% Return on Revenue	11.5	15.6	12.8	11.9	12.0	13.4	7.8	3.9	9.0	10.4
% Return on Invested Capital	9.6	12.1	10.3	9.5	9.0	10.0	12.6	12.4	14.3	11.3
% Return on Common Equity	17.3	19.0	18.6	17.0	18.6	26.2	17.5	8.7	28.3	28.1

Data as orig reptd.; bef. results of disc opers/spec. items. Per share data adj. for stk. divs.; EPS diluted. E-Estimated. NA-Not Available. NM-Not Meaningful. NR-Not Ranked. UR-Under Review.

Office: 2 N 9th St, Allentown, PA, USA 18101-1170.
Telephone: 610-774-5151.
Email: invrel@pplweb.com
Website: http://www.pplweb.com

Chrmn, Pres & CEO: J.H. Miller
COO & EVP: W.H. Spence
EVP & CFO: P. Farr
SVP, Secy & General Counsel: R.J. Grey

Treas: J.E. Abel
Investor Contact: T.J. Paukovits (610-774-4124)
Board Members: F. Bernthal, J. W. Conway, E. A. Deaver, L. Goeser, S. E. Graham, S. Heydt, J. H. Miller, C. A. Rogerson, W. K. Smith, K. H. Williamson

Founded: 1920
Domicile: Pennsylvania
Employees: 10,554

Praxair Inc.

STANDARD & POOR'S

S&P Recommendation HOLD ★★★☆☆

Price	12-Mo. Target Price	Investment Style
$81.51 (as of Nov 27, 2009)	$84.00	Large-Cap Growth

GICS Sector Materials
Sub-Industry Industrial Gases

Summary This company is the largest producer of industrial gases in North and South America, and the second largest worldwide. It also provides ceramic and metallic coatings.

Key Stock Statistics (Source S&P, Vickers, company reports)

52-Wk Range	$85.24– 49.82	S&P Oper. EPS 2009E	3.98	Market Capitalization(B)	$25.008	Beta		0.85
Trailing 12-Month EPS	$3.57	S&P Oper. EPS 2010E	4.40	Yield (%)	1.96	S&P 3-Yr. Proj. EPS CAGR(%)		10
Trailing 12-Month P/E	22.8	P/E on S&P Oper. EPS 2009E	20.5	Dividend Rate/Share	$1.60	S&P Credit Rating		A
$10K Invested 5 Yrs Ago	$19,725	Common Shares Outstg. (M)	306.8	Institutional Ownership (%)	83			

Price Performance

30-Week Mov. Avg. ···· 10-Week Mov. Avg. --- **GAAP Earnings vs. Previous Year** Volume Above Avg. STARS
12-Mo. Target Price — Relative Strength — ▲ Up ▼ Down ▶ No Change Below Avg. ★

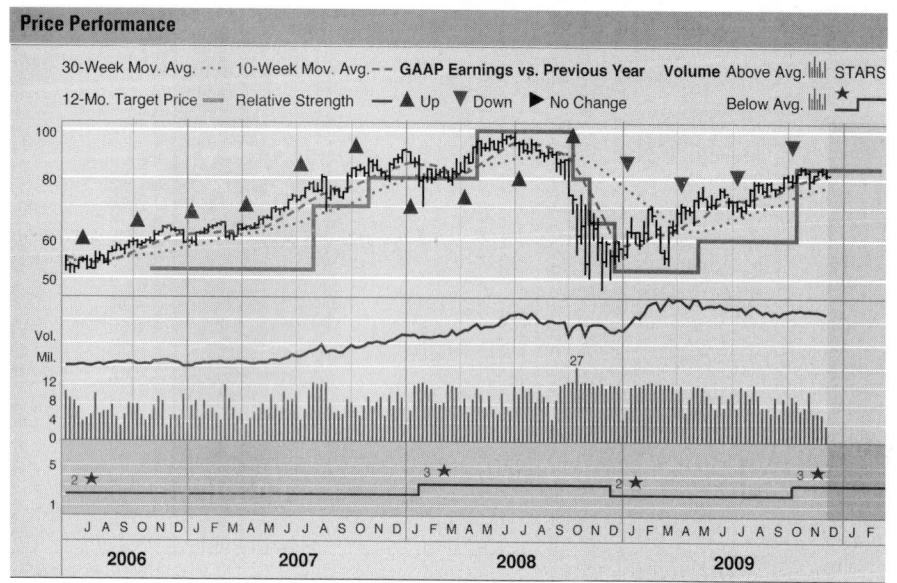

Analysis prepared by **Richard O'Reilly, CFA** on October 07, 2009, when the stock traded at **$80.72**.

Options: ASE, CBOE, Ph

Highlights

▶ We project that sales will decline about 17% in 2009, assuming unfavorable exchange rates and the pass-through of lower energy costs to customers. We expect underlying sales to be almost 10% lower, versus 9% growth in 2008, as reduced demand from manufacturing markets outweighs the start-up of new projects and applications. After a volume drop of 13% in the first half of 2009, we expect demand to be stronger beginning in late 2009 and 2010 assuming the restart of some customers' operations.

▶ We look for Surface Technologies' sales to also recover modestly on an expected rebound in demand in coatings services for industrial equipment and OEM aircraft engines.

▶ We forecast that 2009 operating profit margins will widen to almost 21%, from 19.2% in 2008, reflecting $80 million less overhead costs resulting from a work force reduction in late 2008, and the positive impact from the pass-through of lower natural gas costs. We look for an effective tax rate of 28%, while a stock buyback program in 2008 should help boost EPS comparisons. Reported EPS for 2008 includes charges totaling $0.40.

Investment Rationale/Risk

▶ We recently raised our recommendation on the shares to hold, from sell. While, earlier in the year, we had lowered our 2009 sales and EPS forecasts three times amid reduced industrial activity, we believe that the manufacturing sector will now show sequential improvement, which should result in strengthening demand for industrial gases.

▶ Risks to our recommendation and target price include an unexpected decline in industrial activity, especially in general manufacturing and metal-related markets; higher-than-projected power and natural gas costs; and an inability to rapidly develop and successfully introduce new products and applications for industrial gases.

▶ The shares were recently trading at 18.4X our 2010 EPS estimate of $4.40, a premium to peers. Our 12-month target price of $84 assumes a modest widening of the multiple to an above-peers 19X, reflecting what we see as an improved demand outlook for industrial gases. The quarterly dividend was raised in early 2009 for the 16th consecutive year.

Qualitative Risk Assessment

LOW	**MEDIUM**	HIGH

Our risk assessment reflects the relatively stable growth and cash flow of the industrial gases industry versus commodity chemicals, and PX's superior S&P Quality Ranking of A+, offset by the company's exposure to volatile energy costs.

Quantitative Evaluations

S&P Quality Ranking A+

D	C	B-	B	B+	A-	A	**A+**

Relative Strength Rank MODERATE

55

LOWEST = 1 HIGHEST = 99

Revenue/Earnings Data

Revenue (Million $)

	1Q	2Q	3Q	4Q	Year
2009	2,123	2,138	2,288	--	--
2008	2,663	2,878	2,852	2,403	10,796
2007	2,175	2,332	2,372	2,523	9,402
2006	2,026	2,076	2,099	2,123	8,324
2005	1,827	1,919	1,890	2,020	7,656
2004	1,531	1,603	1,674	1,786	6,594

Earnings Per Share ($)

2009	0.93	0.96	1.04	E1.07	E3.98
2008	0.96	1.08	1.11	0.64	3.80
2007	0.81	0.89	0.94	0.98	3.62
2006	0.68	0.75	0.75	0.82	3.00
2005	0.59	0.63	0.33	0.67	2.22
2004	0.49	0.53	0.53	0.55	2.10

Fiscal year ended Dec. 31. Next earnings report expected: Late January. EPS Estimates based on S&P Operating Earnings; historical GAAP earnings are as reported.

Dividend Data (Dates: mm/dd Payment Date: mm/dd/yy)

Amount ($)	Date Decl.	Ex-Div. Date	Stk. of Record	Payment Date
0.400	01/28	03/04	03/06	03/16/09
0.400	04/29	06/03	06/05	06/15/09
0.400	07/29	09/02	09/07	09/15/09
0.400	10/28	12/03	12/07	12/15/09

Dividends have been paid since 1992. Source: Company reports.

Please read the Required Disclosures and Analyst Certification on the last page of this report.

The McGraw-Hill Companies

Praxair Inc.

STANDARD &POOR'S

Business Summary October 07, 2009

CORPORATE OVERVIEW. Since its 1992 spin-off from Union Carbide Corp., Praxair Inc. (PX), the largest producer of industrial gases in North and South America, has expanded its operations to 40 countries. Foreign sales accounted for 56% of the total in 2008, with Brazil alone providing 15%.

PX conducts its industrial gases business through four operating segments: North America (55% of sales and 52% of profits in 2008); South America (18%, 19%); Europe (14%,17%); and Asia (8%, 7%). The capital-intensive industrial gases business involves the production, distribution and sale of atmospheric gases (oxygen, nitrogen, argon and rare gases), carbon dioxide, hydrogen, helium, acetylene, and specialty and electronic gases. Atmospheric gases are produced through air separation processes, primarily cryogenic, while other gases are produced by various methods. PX also produces specialty products (sputtering targets, mechanical planarization slurries and polishing pads, and coatings) for use in semiconductor manufacturing. In addition, the business includes the construction and sale of equipment to produce industrial gases.

Industrial gases are supplied to customers through three basic methods: on-

site/pipeline (26% of total 2008 sales, sold under long-term contracts), merchant (28%, with three- to five-year contracts) and packaged (32%). At the end of 2008, the company had 250 major production facilities (air separation, hydrogen and carbon dioxide plants) in North America and five major pipeline complexes; more than 50 facilities and three pipeline complexes in Europe; more than 40 plants in South America, primarily in Brazil; and more than 25 plants in Asia, mainly in China, Korea and India. S.A. White Martins is the largest producer of industrial gases in South America.

The Surface Technologies business (5%, 5%) applies metallic and ceramic coatings and powders to parts and equipment provided by customers, including aircraft engine, printing, power generation and other industrial markets, and manufactures electric arc, plasma and oxygen fuel spray equipment. In July 2006, PX sold its aviation services business (annual sales of $80 million).

Company Financials Fiscal Year Ended Dec. 31

Per Share Data ($)	2008	2007	2006	2005	2004	2003	2002	2001	2000	1999
Tangible Book Value	6.45	9.64	8.91	7.05	6.08	6.00	4.03	7.59	3.97	3.70
Cash Flow	6.48	6.01	5.12	4.23	3.85	3.33	3.12	2.84	2.59	2.73
Earnings	3.80	3.62	3.00	2.22	2.10	1.77	1.66	1.32	1.13	1.37
S&P Core Earnings	3.60	3.55	2.99	2.16	2.02	1.67	1.38	1.04	NA	NA
Dividends	1.50	1.20	1.00	0.72	0.60	0.46	0.38	0.34	0.31	0.28
Payout Ratio	39%	33%	33%	32%	29%	26%	23%	26%	28%	21%
Prices:High	99.74	92.12	63.70	54.31	46.25	38.26	30.56	27.96	27.47	29.06
Prices:Low	4740	57.97	50.36	41.06	34.52	25.02	22.28	18.25	15.16	16.00
P/E Ratio:High	26	25	21	24	22	22	18	21	24	21
P/E Ratio:Low	12	16	17	18	16	14	13	14	13	12

Income Statement Analysis (Million $)										
Revenue	10,796	9,402	8,324	7,656	6,594	5,613	5,128	5,158	5,043	4,639
Operating Income	2,892	2,557	2,183	1,948	1,681	1,444	1,358	1,333	1,220	1,199
Depreciation	850	774	696	665	578	517	483	499	471	445
Interest Expense	247	208	155	163	155	151	206	224	224	204
Pretax Income	1,721	1,639	1,312	1,145	959	735	726	585	493	638
Effective Tax Rate	27.0%	25.6%	27.1%	32.8%	24.2%	23.7%	21.8%	23.1%	20.9%	23.8%
Net Income	1,211	1,177	988	732	697	585	548	432	363	441
S&P Core Earnings	1,145	1,154	983	711	671	552	454	343	NA	NA

Balance Sheet & Other Financial Data (Million $)										
Cash	32.0	17.0	36.0	173	25.0	50.0	39.0	39.0	31.0	76.0
Current Assets	2,301	2,408	2,059	2,133	1,744	1,449	1,286	1,276	1,361	1,335
Total Assets	13,054	13,382	11,102	10,491	9,878	8,305	7,401	7,715	7,762	7,722
Current Liabilities	2,979	2,650	1,758	2,001	1,875	1,117	1,100	1,194	1,439	1,725
Long Term Debt	3,709	3,364	2,981	2,926	2,876	2,661	2,510	2,725	2,641	2,111
Common Equity	4,009	5,142	4,554	3,902	3,608	3,088	2,340	2,477	2,357	2,290
Total Capital	8,551	8,506	7,757	6,828	6,709	5,944	5,014	5,363	5,156	4,835
Capital Expenditures	1,611	1,376	1,100	877	668	983	498	595	704	653
Cash Flow	2,061	1,951	1,684	1,397	1,275	1,102	1,031	931	834	886
Current Ratio	0.8	0.9	1.2	1.1	0.9	1.3	1.2	1.1	0.9	0.8
% Long Term Debt of Capitalization	43.4	39.5	38.4	42.9	42.9	44.8	50.1	50.8	51.2	43.7
% Net Income of Revenue	11.2	12.5	11.9	9.6	10.6	10.4	10.7	8.4	7.2	9.5
% Return on Assets	9.2	9.6	9.2	7.2	7.7	7.4	7.3	5.6	4.7	5.6
% Return on Equity	26.5	24.3	23.4	19.5	20.8	21.6	22.8	17.9	15.6	19.1

Data as orig reptd.; bef. results of disc opers/spec. items. Per share data adj. for stk. divs.; EPS diluted. E-Estimated. NA-Not Available. NM-Not Meaningful. NR-Not Ranked. UR-Under Review.

Office: 39 Old Ridgebury Rd, Danbury, CT 06810-5109.
Telephone: 203-837-2000.
Website: http://www.praxair.com
Chrmn, Pres & CEO: S.F. Angel

EVP & CFO: J.S. Sawyer
SVP & CTO: R.P. Roberge
SVP, Secy & General Counsel: J.T. Breedlove
Treas: M.J. Allan

Investor Contact: E.T. Hirsch (203-837-2354)
Board Members: S. F. Angel, N. K. Dicciani, E. G. Galante, C. W. Gargalli, I. D. Hall, R. W. Leboeuf, L. D. McVay, W. T. Smith, H. M. Watson, Jr., R. L. Wood

Founded: 1988
Domicile: Delaware
Employees: 26,936

Precision Castparts Corp.

S&P Recommendation	BUY ★★★★☆	Price $105.27 (as of Nov 27, 2009)	12-Mo. Target Price $110.00	Investment Style Large-Cap Growth

GICS Sector Industrials
Sub-Industry Aerospace & Defense

Summary This company is a provider of complex metal components used primarily in the manufacture of jet engines and industrial gas turbines, and in the oil and gas industry.

Key Stock Statistics (Source S&P, Vickers, company reports)

52-Wk Range	$107.27– 47.71	S&P Oper. EPS 2010E	6.70	Market Capitalization(B)	$14.814	Beta	1.49
Trailing 12-Month EPS	$6.72	S&P Oper. EPS 2011E	7.45	Yield (%)	0.11	S&P 3-Yr. Proj. EPS CAGR(%)	7
Trailing 12-Month P/E	15.7	P/E on S&P Oper. EPS 2010E	15.7	Dividend Rate/Share	$0.12	S&P Credit Rating	BBB+
$10K Invested 5 Yrs Ago	$32,425	Common Shares Outstg. (M)	140.7	Institutional Ownership (%)	85		

Price Performance

30-Week Mov. Avg. ···   10-Week Mov. Avg.- - **GAAP Earnings vs. Previous Year**   Volume Above Avg. STARS
12-Mo. Target Price — Relative Strength — ▲ Up ▼ Down ▶ No Change   Below Avg. ★

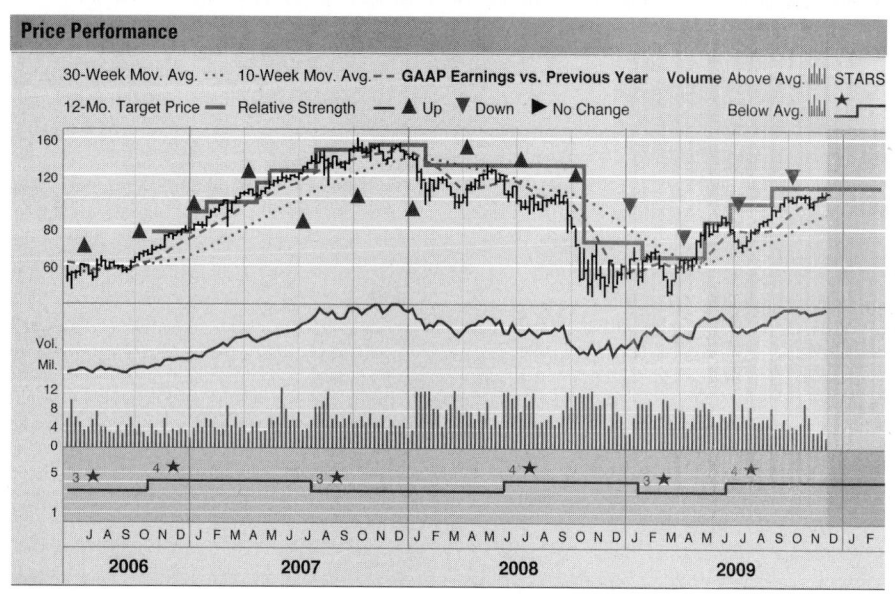

Options: ASE, CBOE, Ph

Analysis prepared by **Richard Tortoriello** on October 26, 2009, when the stock traded at **$ 100.00**.

Highlights

► We look for sales to decline 18% in FY 10 (Mar.), but project 7% growth in FY 11. Aerospace OEMs are currently reducing inventories by ordering less parts than needed to meet current production. We expect an increase in sales at PCP as parts inventories are depleted. Aftermarket demand in aerospace has slowed significantly as airlines are hoarding cash. We also expect some bounce back in the aftermarket as air traffic increases. We think industrial gas turbine demand will improve in 2010, along with general industrial demand, which PCP believes has bottomed out as of its September quarter.

► We estimate an operating margin of 26.4% for FY 10, well above FY 09's 23.4%, due to strong productivity programs. We project further margin improvement, to over 27%, in FY 11, as PCP continues to strengthen its efficiency in areas such as scrap metal management.

► We estimate EPS of $6.70 in FY 10, down about 9% from FY 09, but project growth to $7.45 in FY 10. We expect free cash flow (cash from operating activities minus capital expenditures) per share in FY 10 to be about 80% of EPS.

Investment Rationale/Risk

► Although we see the possibility of moderate further production cuts at Boeing and Airbus in 2010, as airlines continue to defer or cancel contracts due to the global economic downturn, we believe that current large backlogs at both aircraft makers will largely be maintained as airlines seek to modernize their fleets and increase fleet sizes, particularly in emerging economies. We also see a large opportunity for PCP with the 787, which we expect to fly for the first time before the end of 2009. PCP's revenues per 787 are four to five times those it receives from narrow-body aircraft. We expect production of the 787 to eventually reach a level of near 10 planes per month.

► Risks to our recommendation and target price include a steeper-than-anticipated slowdown in aerospace or gas turbine demand, and operational or other difficulties.

► Our 12-month target price of $110 is based on an enterprise value to estimated FY 11 EBITDA multiple of 8.5X, below the 20-year average for PCP of 9.1X. We believe that signs of economic stabilization in the U.S. and likely entry into production of the 787 warrant a near average multiple for the shares.

Qualitative Risk Assessment

LOW	MEDIUM	HIGH

Precision Castparts operates in a cyclical and capital-intensive industry and is subject to swings in commodity prices. However, due to PCP's large market share in most markets, we believe the company has significant pricing power for its products. We also consider its financial condition to be solid, including a relatively low debt level.

Quantitative Evaluations

S&P Quality Ranking B

D	C	B-	B	B+	A-	A	A+

Relative Strength Rank STRONG

82

LOWEST = 1   HIGHEST = 99

Revenue/Earnings Data

Revenue (Million $)

	1Q	2Q	3Q	4Q	Year
2010	1,380	1,302	--	--	--
2009	1,810	1,799	1,615	1,604	6,828
2008	1,660	1,727	1,697	1,791	6,852
2007	1,112	1,318	1,385	1,547	5,361
2006	854.6	874.9	864.4	952.6	3,546
2005	738.8	697.5	743.9	809.5	2,919

Earnings Per Share ($)

2010	1.70	1.54	E1.52	E1.94	E6.70
2009	1.94	1.88	1.69	1.87	7.38
2008	1.61	1.67	1.73	1.88	6.89
2007	0.83	1.03	1.15	1.44	4.45
2006	0.58	0.60	0.67	0.74	2.57
2005	0.40	0.43	0.47	0.52	1.80

Fiscal year ended Mar. 31. Next earnings report expected: Late January. EPS Estimates based on S&P Operating Earnings; historical GAAP earnings are as reported.

Dividend Data (Dates: mm/dd Payment Date: mm/dd/yy)

Amount ($)	Date Decl.	Ex-Div. Date	Stk. of Record	Payment Date
0.030	02/12	03/04	03/06	03/30/09
0.030	05/27	06/03	06/05	06/29/09
0.030	08/12	09/02	09/04	09/28/09
0.030	11/12	12/02	12/04	12/28/09

Dividends have been paid since 1978. Source: Company reports.

Please read the Required Disclosures and Analyst Certification on the last page of this report.

Precision Castparts Corp.

**STANDARD
&POOR'S**

Business Summary October 26, 2009

COMPANY OVERVIEW. Precision Castparts, a manufacturer of jet engine and industrial gas turbine (IGT) engine components, conducts business through three operating units. The aerospace market accounted for 53% of FY 09 (Mar.) sales, power generation for 25%, and general industrial and automotive for the remaining 22%. General Electric accounted for 12% of FY 09 sales. Although no other customer accounted for more than 10% of sales, United Technologies, Rolls-Royce and Boeing are all key customers.

PCP's Investment Cast Products segment (33% and 35% of FY 09 revenues and operating earnings, respectively) includes PCC Structurals, PCC Airfoils, and the Specialty Materials and Alloys Group (SMAG). These operations manufacture investment castings for aircraft engines, IGT engines, airframes, medical prostheses, armament and other industrial applications. Investment casting involves a technical, multi-step process that uses ceramic molds in the manufacture of metal components with more complex shapes, closer tolerances, and finer surface finishes than parts manufactured using other casting methods. PCP is the world's largest maker of jet engine structural castings used to strengthen sections of a jet engine. It also believes it is the leading supplier of investment casts for industrial gas turbine (IGT) engines, used in power generation. The company emphasizes low-cost, high-quality products and timely delivery. SMAG principally provides alloys and waxes to the company's investment casting operations, as well as other companies with investment casting or other foundry operations.

The Forged Products segment (44% of sales and 38% of operating profits) is a large maker of forged components for the aerospace and power generation markets. Forged Products segment aerospace and IGT sales are primarily derived from the same large engine customers served by the Investment Cast segment, with additional aerospace sales to manufacturers of landing gear and airframes. In addition, Forged Products manufactures high performance nickel-based alloys used to produce forged components for aerospace and non-aerospace markets, which includes products for oil and gas, chemical processing, and pollution control applications. Forging involves heating high-temperature nickel alloys, titanium or steel and then shaping them through pressing or extrusion, using hydraulic and mechanical presses. Through the May 2006 acquisition of Special Metals, PCP became the world's largest producer of high-performance, nickel-based alloys and superalloys used in the forging process.

Company Financials Fiscal Year Ended Mar. 31

Per Share Data ($)	2009	2008	2007	2006	2005	2004	2003	2002	2001	2000
Tangible Book Value	16.42	12.28	5.37	3.56	1.51	0.62	0.74	NM	NM	NM
Cash Flow	8.37	7.81	5.27	3.30	2.53	1.73	2.28	1.37	2.23	1.62
Earnings	7.38	6.89	4.45	2.57	1.80	1.18	1.51	0.41	1.23	0.87
S&P Core Earnings	6.95	6.87	4.47	2.51	1.79	1.21	1.17	0.63	1.22	NA
Dividends	0.12	0.12	0.11	0.06	0.06	0.06	0.06	0.06	0.06	0.06
Payout Ratio	2%	2%	2%	2%	3%	5%	4%	15%	5%	7%
Calendar Year	2008	2007	2006	2005	2004	2003	2002	2001	2000	1999
Prices:High	142.94	160.73	80.90	53.91	34.19	22.97	19.00	24.75	22.78	11.81
Prices:Low	47.08	77.51	48.80	31.15	20.68	10.61	8.43	9.00	5.92	5.86
P/E Ratio:High	19	23	18	21	19	19	13	61	19	14
P/E Ratio:Low	6	11	11	12	11	9	6	22	5	7

Income Statement Analysis (Million $)										
Revenue	6,828	6,852	5,361	3,546	2,919	2,175	2,117	2,557	2,326	1,674
Operating Income	1,739	1,639	1,086	656	517	380	390	448	401	267
Depreciation	139	128	113	99.2	97.0	88.2	82.5	101	102	74.2
Interest Expense	18.1	81.0	52.2	41.4	56.6	54.1	56.4	66.2	81.0	47.1
Pretax Income	1,578	1,463	918	513	360	212	242	135	209	139
Effective Tax Rate	34.2%	33.9%	33.2%	31.6%	33.7%	35.7%	34.5%	68.6%	40.1%	38.5%
Net Income	1,038	966	615	349	240	136	159	42.4	125	85.3
S&P Core Earnings	978	963	618	341	237	140	123	65.4	124	NA

Balance Sheet & Other Financial Data (Million $)										
Cash	554	221	150	59.9	154	80.3	28.7	38.1	40.1	17.6
Current Assets	2,785	2,372	2,037	1,234	1,213	1,188	786	878	863	752
Total Assets	6,721	6,050	5,259	3,751	3,625	3,756	2,467	2,565	2,573	2,416
Current Liabilities	1,061	1,205	1,658	768	780	913	625	727	657	592
Long Term Debt	251	335	319	600	799	823	532	697	838	884
Common Equity	4,860	4,045	2,836	2,244	1,780	1,715	1,062	952	902	774
Total Capital	5,222	4,400	3,182	2,844	2,579	2,538	1,594	1,649	1,740	1,658
Capital Expenditures	205	226	222	99.2	61.7	65.5	70.5	125	90.2	49.3
Cash Flow	1,177	1,094	727	448	337	224	242	143	227	160
Current Ratio	2.6	2.0	1.2	1.6	1.6	1.3	1.3	1.2	1.3	1.3
% Long Term Debt of Capitalization	4.8	7.6	10.0	21.1	31.0	32.4	33.4	42.3	48.2	53.3
% Net Income of Revenue	15.2	14.1	11.5	9.8	8.2	6.2	7.5	1.7	5.4	5.1
% Return on Assets	16.3	17.1	13.6	9.5	6.5	4.4	6.3	1.7	5.0	4.4
% Return on Equity	23.3	28.1	24.7	17.0	13.7	9.8	15.8	4.6	14.9	11.6

Data as orig reptd.; bef. results of disc opers/spec. items. Per share data adj. for stk. divs.; EPS diluted. E-Estimated. NA-Not Available. NM-Not Meaningful. NR-Not Ranked. UR-Under Review.

Office: 4650 SW Macadam Ave Ste 400, Portland, OR 97239-4262.
Telephone: 503-417-4850.
Email: info@precastcorp.com
Website: http://www.precast.com

Chrmn, Pres & CEO: M. Donegan
SVP, CFO & Chief Acctg Officer: S.R. Hagel
SVP, Secy & General Counsel: R.A. Cooke
Treas: S.C. Blackmore

Investor Contact: W.D. Larsson
Board Members: P. R. Bridenbaugh, M. Donegan, D. R. Graber, L. L. Lyles, D. J. Murphy, Jr., V. E. Oechsle, S. G. Rothmeier, U. Schmidt

Founded: 1949
Domicile: Oregon
Employees: 20,400

priceline.com Inc

S&P Recommendation	HOLD ★★★☆☆	Price $208.21 (as of Nov 27, 2009)	12-Mo. Target Price $200.00	Investment Style Large-Cap Growth

GICS Sector Consumer Discretionary
Sub-Industry Internet Retail

Summary This company is a leading provider of online travel services, primarily in the U.S. and Europe.

Key Stock Statistics (Source S&P, Vickers, company reports)

52-Wk Range	$214.47– 55.35	S&P Oper. EPS 2009**E**	7.15	Market Capitalization(B)	$9.151	Beta	0.74
Trailing 12-Month EPS	$9.46	S&P Oper. EPS 2010**E**	8.50	Yield (%)	Nil	S&P 3-Yr. Proj. EPS CAGR(%)	23
Trailing 12-Month P/E	22.0	P/E on S&P Oper. EPS 2009**E**	29.1	Dividend Rate/Share	Nil	S&P Credit Rating	BB-
$10K Invested 5 Yrs Ago	$86,430	Common Shares Outstg. (M)	44.0	Institutional Ownership (%)	NM		

Price Performance

30-Week Mov. Avg. · · · · 10-Week Mov. Avg. – – **GAAP Earnings vs. Previous Year** Volume Above Avg. ▮▮▮ STARS
12-Mo. Target Price — Relative Strength — ▲ Up ▼ Down ▶ No Change Below Avg. ▮▮▮ ★

Options: ASE, CBOE, P, Ph

Analysis prepared by **Scott H. Kessler** on November 12, 2009, when the stock traded at **$ 199.00**.

Highlights

▶ We project that revenues will rise 25% in 2009 and 15% in 2010, due to market share gains, healthy volumes, and improving pricing, offset by economic challenges. We expect international and merchant operations to drive growth, reflecting PCLN's past acquisitions of Active Hotels and Bookings B.V., providers of Internet hotel reservation services in Europe, which have enabled the company to become an over-seas leader in online hotel reservations.

▶ We believe PCLN will continue to build on its user and supplier bases in Europe, largely reflecting the benefits of efficient marketing efforts and the Network Effect (where more users beget more suppliers, etc.). In particular, we see PCLN's opaque travel offerings (where some details are not disclosed until the transaction is completed), especially in the U.S., as attractive in light of relatively high retail pricing.

▶ PCLN has reined in stock compensation expenses versus prior years, but we still expect the expense to detract from EPS. In the 2006 third quarter, PCLN authorized a $150 million stock buyback and we estimate that some $50 million remains available.

Investment Rationale/Risk

▶ While we believe PCLN has established itself as a global leader in online travel services, we do not think it is widely known that more than half of PCLN's gross bookings and revenues are derived from international businesses (mostly focused on Europe). Although we have concerns about European economies, we think positive secular trends are intact, such as a growing percentage of travel purchases being effected online. PCLN hopes that it can repli-cate its European success in Asia, with the ac-quisition of Agoda. Given current conditions and uncertainties, we believe the stock is ap-propriately valued at recent levels.

▶ Risks to our recommendation and target price include possible negative impacts from global economic weakness and leisure travel demand, and less success than we expect with regard to new offerings and/or acquisitions.

▶ Our DCF model (which assumes a WACC of 10.4%, annual free cash flow growth averaging 19% from 2008 to 2012, and a terminal growth rate of 3%) yields an intrinsic value of roughly $200, which is our 12-month target price. We view PCLN as a relatively volatile stock.

Qualitative Risk Assessment

LOW	MEDIUM	HIGH

Our risk assessment reflects our view of a very competitive online travel segment, relatively low barriers to entry, and the stock's notable volatility.

Quantitative Evaluations

S&P Quality Ranking B-

D	C	B-	B	B+	A-	A	A+

Relative Strength Rank STRONG

95

LOWEST = 1 HIGHEST = 99

Revenue/Earnings Data

Revenue (Million $)

	1Q	2Q	3Q	4Q	Year
2009	462.1	603.7	730.7	--	--
2008	403.2	514.0	561.6	406.0	1,885
2007	301.4	355.9	417.3	334.9	1,409
2006	241.9	307.7	313.5	260.1	1,123
2005	233.4	266.6	258.8	203.9	962.7
2004	224.1	259.4	235.9	195.0	914.4

Earnings Per Share ($)

2009	0.53	1.38	6.42	E1.28	E7.15
2008	0.37	1.08	1.81	0.73	3.98
2007	-0.44	0.79	2.27	0.68	3.42
2006	-0.02	0.28	1.05	0.33	1.68
2005	0.21	0.29	3.71	0.09	4.21
2004	0.11	0.28	0.23	0.22	0.96

Fiscal year ended Dec. 31. Next earnings report expected: Mid February. EPS Estimates based on S&P Operating Earnings; historical GAAP earnings are as reported.

Dividend Data

No cash dividends have been paid.

Please read the Required Disclosures and Analyst Certification on the last page of this report.

STANDARD &POOR'S

priceline.com Inc

Business Summary November 12, 2009

COMPANY OVERVIEW. Priceline.com is an online travel company that provides a broad range of travel services, including airline tickets, hotel rooms, car rentals, vacation packages, cruises, and destination services. PCLN offers customers a choice of purchasing certain travel services in a traditional, price-disclosed manner (retail products), or of using its proprietary Name Your Own Price service, which allows users to make offers for travel services at discounted prices (opaque products). Internationally, PCLN offers hotel room reservations in over 75 countries and 27 languages.

PCLN enables customers to make hotel reservations on a worldwide basis primarily under the Booking.com and Agoda brands internationally, and the priceline.com brand in the U.S. In the U.S., PCLN also allows users to purchase many other types of travel offerings. Interestingly, even though PCLN is best known in the U.S. for its Name Your Own Price system, 58% of its gross bookings and more than two-thirds of its operating income in 2008 were derived from its European operations. PCLN expects these percentages to in-

crease in 2009 and beyond.

The U.S. business consists of Name Your Own Price offerings (provided via a unique e-commerce pricing system intended to enable consumers to use the Internet to save money on products and services, while allowing sellers to generate incremental revenue and retail offerings) and retail services (whereby customers can choose specific suppliers and/or itineraries when making purchases of airline tickets and hotel and rental car reservations, and travel packages). The company has provided retail offerings since 2003, and believes that offering both opaque and retail products enables it to serve a broad array of value-conscious travelers, while providing diversified revenues.

Company Financials Fiscal Year Ended Dec. 31

Per Share Data ($)	2008	2007	2006	2005	2004	2003	2002	2001	2000	1999
Tangible Book Value	5.13	3.43	NM	0.53	0.79	3.44	3.12	3.30	NM	14.77
Cash Flow	4.86	4.24	2.41	4.70	1.03	0.56	-0.09	0.02	-10.71	-46.82
Earnings	3.98	3.42	1.68	4.21	0.96	0.27	-0.54	-0.48	-11.82	-47.42
S&P Core Earnings	3.99	4.19	1.70	4.13	0.53	-0.49	-2.94	-4.62	NA	NA
Dividends	Nil	Nil	Nil	Nil	Nil	Nil	Nil	Nil	Nil	Nil
Payout Ratio	Nil	Nil	Nil	Nil	Nil	Nil	Nil	Nil	Nil	Nil
Prices:High	144.34	120.67	44.28	27.08	29.52	39.81	41.36	62.12	625.75	990.40
Prices:Low	45.15	41.80	21.06	18.20	17.42	6.78	6.30	7.88	6.38	96.04
P/E Ratio:High	36	35	26	6	31	NM	NM	NM	NM	NM
P/E Ratio:Low	11	12	13	4	18	NM	NM	NM	NM	NM
Income Statement Analysis (Million $)										
Revenue	1,885	1,409	1,123	963	914	864	1,004	1,172	1,235	482
Operating Income	333	175	95.6	64.9	43.9	26.0	22.7	23.3	-40.5	-1,057
Depreciation	43.2	37.5	33.4	27.3	13.5	11.5	18.3	16.6	17.4	5.30
Interest Expense	9.38	10.4	7.06	5.07	3.72	0.91	Nil	Nil	Nil	Nil
Pretax Income	292	145	62.1	36.5	31.3	11.9	-19.2	-7.30	-315	-1,055
Effective Tax Rate	33.7%	NM	NM	NM	NM	NM	NM	NM	NM	NM
Net Income	193	157	74.5	193	31.5	11.9	-19.2	-7.30	-315	-1,055
S&P Core Earnings	194	191	73.3	187	20.3	-18.6	-111	-157	NA	NA
Balance Sheet & Other Financial Data (Million $)										
Cash	463	509	424	80.3	101	93.7	85.4	115	90.6	133
Current Assets	624	613	503	224	273	284	170	185	131	212
Total Assets	1,344	1,351	1,106	754	542	338	211	262	195	442
Current Liabilities	547	695	101	71.0	74.4	49.6	65.3	87.3	79.3	39.3
Long Term Debt	Nil	Nil	569	224	224	125	Nil	Nil	Nil	Nil
Common Equity	730	579	349	369	199	149	132	147	-249	403
Total Capital	779	643	953	672	467	287	145	172	111	403
Capital Expenditures	18.3	16.0	12.9	11.0	6.94	6.58	9.13	9.42	37.3	27.4
Cash Flow	237	193	108	218	43.5	22.0	-3.26	0.71	-298	-1,050
Current Ratio	1.1	0.9	5.0	3.1	3.7	5.7	2.6	2.1	1.7	5.4
% Long Term Debt of Capitalization	Nil	Nil	59.7	33.3	48.1	43.4	Nil	Nil	Nil	Nil
% Net Income of Revenue	10.3	11.1	6.6	20.0	3.4	1.4	NM	NM	NM	NM
% Return on Assets	14.4	12.7	8.0	29.7	7.2	4.3	NM	NM	NM	NM
% Return on Equity	29.6	33.5	20.8	67.2	17.2	7.4	NM	NM	NM	NM

Data as orig reptd.; bef. results of disc opers/spec. items. Per share data adj. for stk. divs.; EPS diluted. E-Estimated. NA-Not Available. NM-Not Meaningful. NR-Not Ranked. UR-Under Review.

Office: 800 Connecticut Ave, Norwalk, CT 06854-1625.
Telephone: 203-299-8000.
Website: http://www.priceline.com
Chrmn: R.M. Bahna

Pres & CEO: J.H. Boyd
Vice Chrmn: R.J. Mylod, Jr.
COO: L. Gillingham
EVP, Secy & General Counsel: P.J. Millones

Investor Contact: D.J. Finnegan (203-299-8000)
Board Members: R. M. Bahna, H. W. Barker, Jr., J. H. Boyd, J. L. Docter, J. Epstein, J. M. Guyette, R. J. Mylod, Jr., N. Peretsman, C. W. Rydin

Founded: 1997
Domicile: Delaware
Employees: 1,780

The McGraw-Hill Companies

Principal Financial Group Inc.

STANDARD &POOR'S

S&P Recommendation	HOLD ★★★☆☆	Price	12-Mo. Target Price	Investment Style
		$25.00 (as of Nov 27, 2009)	$26.00	Large-Cap Blend

GICS Sector Financials
Sub-Industry Life & Health Insurance

Summary This company offers businesses, individuals and other clients various financial products and services, including insurance, retirement and investment services.

Key Stock Statistics (Source S&P, Vickers, company reports)

52-Wk Range	$30.87–5.41	S&P Oper. EPS 2009**E**	2.70	Market Capitalization(B)	$7.974	Beta	3.11
Trailing 12-Month EPS	$1.55	S&P Oper. EPS 2010**E**	2.98	Yield (%)	2.00	S&P 3-Yr. Proj. EPS CAGR(%)	-19
Trailing 12-Month P/E	16.1	P/E on S&P Oper. EPS 2009**E**	9.3	Dividend Rate/Share	$0.50	S&P Credit Rating	BBB+
$10K Invested 5 Yrs Ago	$7,113	Common Shares Outstg. (M)	318.9	Institutional Ownership (%)	62		

Price Performance

30-Week Mov. Avg. ···· 10-Week Mov. Avg. – – **GAAP Earnings vs. Previous Year** Volume Above Avg. STARS
12-Mo. Target Price — Relative Strength ▲ Up ▼ Down ▶ No Change Below Avg. ★

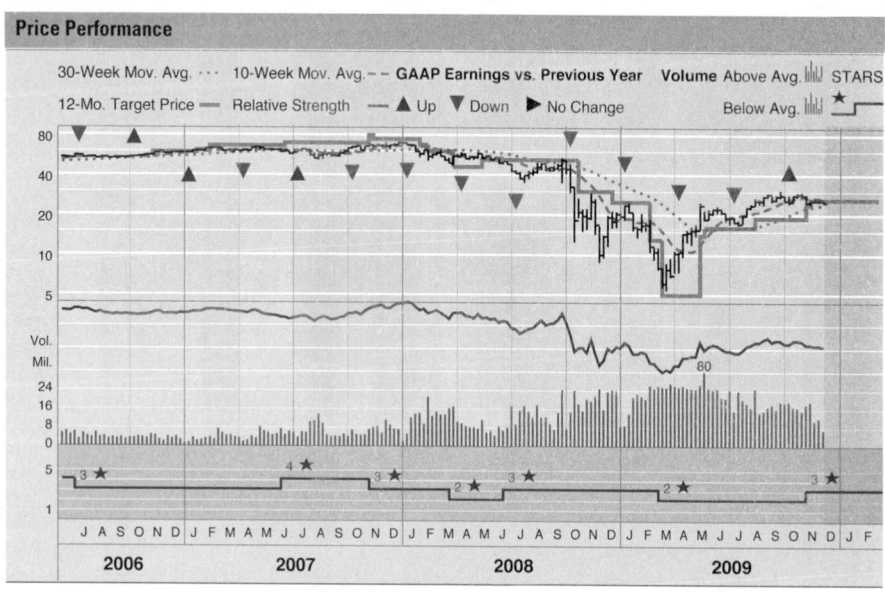

Options: CBOE

Analysis prepared by **Bret Howlett** on November 16, 2009, when the stock traded at **$ 26.65**.

Highlights

▶ We forecast that operating earnings for the U.S. Asset Management and Accumulation (USAMA) segment will increase 10% in 2010, based on higher assets under management (AUMs), as average account balances have increased following the rebound in the equity markets. We also expect a lower expense base to boost profits. However, we believe the weakened U.S. economy and high unemployment rate will pressure PFG's 401k plans through a decline in organic sales, increased withdrawals, lower participation and deferral rates, and a reduction in sponsor matching.

▶ We expect operating earnings to increase by double digits in the International Asset Management and Accumulation segment due to higher AUMs and the weakened U.S. dollar, partially offset by the deflationary environment in Latin America, and lower investment income. We believe Global Asset Management profits will be up on the improved equity and credit markets and a rebound in real estate associated income.

▶ We forecast operating EPS of $2.70 for 2009 and $2.98 for 2010, excluding realized investment gains or losses.

Investment Rationale/Risk

▶ While we believe PFG's economy-sensitive businesses still face headwinds, we have become more optimistic about its prospects given the improving macro environment. Although we think multiple expansion will be held back by sluggish top-line growth and elevated credit and mortgage loan losses, we believe this is reflected in PFG's shares. PFG trades at a premium to the group, but we believe this is warranted since its businesses are less capital-intensive and generate a higher return on equity versus peers. We are concerned about PFG's exposure to commercial real estate since we think impairments have yet to peak in this asset class. We think future losses are manageable, though, based on PFG's solid statutory capital position and recent equity and debt raises.

▶ Risks to our recommendation and target price include a significant decline in the equity markets, narrowing margins in the company's health insurance business, outflows in its US-AMA business, and deteriorating credit and economic conditions.

▶ Our 12-month target price of $26 is 1.1X our 2010 year-end book value forecast, below historical multiples.

Qualitative Risk Assessment

LOW	MEDIUM	HIGH

Our risk assessment reflects our view of PFG's significant exposure to the equity markets and potential for further investment losses, especially considering its exposure to commercial real estate. We believe PFG's capital position could come under strain if the economic environment and capital markets worsen. However, we believe PFG's financial position has improved following recent capital raises.

Quantitative Evaluations

S&P Quality Ranking NR

D	C	B-	B	B+	A-	A	A+

Relative Strength Rank MODERATE

30

LOWEST = 1   HIGHEST = 99

Revenue/Earnings Data

Revenue (Million $)

	1Q	2Q	3Q	4Q	Year
2009	2,189	2,158	2,270	--	--
2008	2,501	2,658	2,498	2,279	9,936
2007	2,661	2,832	2,850	2,564	10,907
2006	2,402	2,460	2,450	2,559	9,871
2005	2,144	2,200	2,218	2,445	9,008
2004	1,997	1,980	2,089	2,239	8,304

Earnings Per Share ($)

	1Q	2Q	3Q	4Q	Year
2009	0.43	0.52	0.57	E0.70	E2.70
2008	0.67	0.64	0.35	-0.03	1.63
2007	0.95	1.14	0.88	0.05	3.01
2006	1.01	0.76	0.92	0.93	3.63
2005	0.68	0.77	0.74	0.83	3.02
2004	0.62	0.40	0.62	0.71	2.23

Fiscal year ended Dec. 31. Next earnings report expected: Early February. EPS Estimates based on S&P Operating Earnings; historical GAAP earnings are as reported.

Dividend Data (Dates: mm/dd Payment Date: mm/dd/yy)

Amount ($)	Date Decl.	Ex-Div. Date	Stk. of Record	Payment Date
0.450	10/13	11/12	11/14	12/05/08
0.500	10/26	11/10	11/13	12/04/09

Dividends have been paid since 2002. Source: Company reports.

Please read the Required Disclosures and Analyst Certification on the last page of this report.

The McGraw-Hill Companies

Principal Financial Group Inc.

STANDARD
&POOR'S

Business Summary November 16, 2009

CORPORATE OVERVIEW. The Principal Financial Group is a leading provider of retirement savings, investment and insurance products and services, with approximately $247 billion in assets under management at December 31, 2008. The focus of the company is to provide retirement and employment products and services, specifically 401(k) plans, to small and medium-sized businesses. According to Spectrem Group, a consulting and market research firm, PFG is a leading corporate defined contributions plan provider with over 33,000 plans.

PFG's businesses are organized into five operating segments. The U.S. Asset Management and Accumulation segment (USAMA), which accounted for 43% of operating revenues excluding corporate and other in 2008, provides retirement savings and related investment products and services, and asset management operations, with a concentration on small and medium-sized businesses with fewer than 1,000 employees. At year-end 2008, USAMA account values totaled $146 billion.

The Global Asset Management segment includes Principal Global Investors and its affiliates, and focuses on providing a range of asset management ser-

vices. The segment accounted for 6.7% of operating revenues excluding corporate and other in 2008.

The International Asset Management and Accumulation segment (IAMA) consists of Principal International and offers retirement products and services, annuities, mutual funds and life insurance through operations in Brazil, Chile, Mexico, China, Hong Kong and India. IAMA accounted for 5.7% of operating revenues from continuing operations in 2008.

The Life and Health Insurance segment, which accounted for 45% of operating revenues from continuing operations in 2008, offers individual and group life and disability insurance, as well as group health, dental and vision insurance. The Corporate and Other segment includes, among other things, inter-segment eliminations, income on capital not allocated to other segments, and the company's financing activities.

Company Financials Fiscal Year Ended Dec. 31

Per Share Data ($)	2008	2007	2006	2005	2004	2003	2002	2001	2000	1999
Tangible Book Value	4.41	22.35	22.24	24.14	23.67	22.12	19.32	10.59	14.89	NA
Operating Earnings	NA	NA	NA	NA	NA	NA	2.46	1.96	NA	NA
Earnings	1.63	3.01	3.63	3.02	2.23	2.23	1.77	1.02	1.74	NA
S&P Core Earnings	2.77	3.69	3.45	3.02	2.36	2.38	1.85	1.69	NA	NA
Dividends	0.45	0.90	0.80	0.65	0.55	0.45	0.25	Nil	NA	NA
Payout Ratio	28%	30%	22%	22%	25%	20%	14%	Nil	NA	NA
Prices:High	68.94	70.85	59.40	52.00	41.26	34.67	31.50	24.75	NA	NA
Prices:Low	8.78	51.52	45.91	36.80	32.00	25.21	22.00	18.50	NA	NA
P/E Ratio:High	42	24	16	17	19	16	18	24	NA	NA
P/E Ratio:Low	5	17	13	12	14	11	12	18	NA	NA

Income Statement Analysis (Million $)

	2008	2007	2006	2005	2004	2003	2002	2001	2000	1999
Life Insurance in Force	246,329	243,119	218,947	197,690	180,344	136,530	137,794	62,309	60,389	NA
Premium Income:Life	1,564	1,827	1,560	1,546	1,477	1,500	1,824	2,089	1,792	NA
Premium Income:A & H	2,646	2,808	2,745	2,429	2,233	2,135	2,058	2,033	2,205	NA
Net Investment Income	3,994	3,967	3,618	3,361	3,227	3,420	3,305	3,395	3,172	NA
Total Revenue	9,936	10,907	9,871	9,008	8,304	9,404	9,223	8,818	8,885	7,660
Pretax Income	454	1,048	1,329	1,124	882	954	666	449	872	1,066
Net Operating Income	NA	NA	NA	NA	NA	NA	864	711	NA	NA
Net Income	458	840	1,034	892	702	728	620	370	627	742
S&P Core Earnings	722	991	951	871	742	778	647	608	NA	NA

Balance Sheet & Other Financial Data (Million $)

	2008	2007	2006	2005	2004	2003	2002	2001	2000	1999
Cash & Equivalent	3,359	2,119	2,314	2,324	1,131	2,344	1,685	1,218	940	NA
Premiums Due	988	951	1,252	593	628	720	460	531	572	NA
Investment Assets:Bonds	40,961	47,268	44,727	42,117	40,916	37,553	34,287	30,030	29,328	NA
Investment Assets:Stocks	401	586	848	815	763	712	379	834	579	NA
Investment Assets:Loans	14,010	13,522	12,515	12,312	12,529	14,312	11,900	11,898	12,359	NA
Investment Assets:Total	56,969	64,365	60,367	57,583	57,012	55,578	48,996	44,773	44,403	37,772
Deferred Policy Costs	4,153	2,810	2,419	2,174	1,838	1,572	1,414	1,373	1,338	NA
Total Assets	128,182	154,520	143,658	127,035	113,798	107,754	89,861	88,351	86,838	82,086
Debt	1,291	1,399	1,554	899	844	2,767	1,333	1,378	1,391	NA
Common Equity	2,473	7,422	7,861	7,807	7,544	7,400	13,314	6,820	6,624	5,553
% Return on Revenue	4.6	7.7	10.5	9.9	8.5	7.7	7.0	4.2	7.1	9.7
% Return on Assets	0.3	0.6	0.8	0.7	0.6	0.7	0.7	0.4	0.8	1.0
% Return on Equity	9.3	10.6	12.8	11.4	9.4	10.4	4.6	5.7	10.5	13.2
% Investment Yield	6.7	6.4	6.1	5.9	5.8	6.5	7.0	7.8	7.9	7.5

Data as orig reptd.; bef. results of disc opers/spec. items. Per share data adj. for stk. divs.; EPS diluted. E-Estimated. NA-Not Available. NM-Not Meaningful. NR-Not Ranked. UR-Under Review.

Office: 711 High Street, Des Moines, IA 50392-9992.
Telephone: 515-247-5111.
Website: http://www.principal.com
Chrmn, Pres & CEO: L.D. Zimpleman

EVP & General Counsel: K.E. Shaff
SVP, CFO & Chief Acctg Officer: T.J. Lillis
SVP & Secy: J.N. Hoffman
SVP & Cntlr: G. Elming

Investor Contact: T. Graf (515-235-9500)
Board Members: B. J. Bernard, J. E. Carter-Miller, G. E. Costley, M. T. Dan, C. Gelatt, Jr., J. B. Griswell, S. L. Helton, W. T. Kerr, R. L. Keyser, A. K. Mathrani, D. M. Stewart, E. E. Tallett, L. D. Zimpleman

Founded: 1998
Domicile: Delaware
Employees: 16,234

Procter & Gamble Co (The)

STANDARD &POOR'S

S&P Recommendation	BUY ★★★★☆	Price $62.48 (as of Nov 27, 2009)	12-Mo. Target Price $65.00	Investment Style Large-Cap Growth

GICS Sector Consumer Staples
Sub-Industry Household Products

Summary This leading consumer products company markets household and personal care products in more than 180 countries.

Key Stock Statistics (Source S&P, Vickers, company reports)

52-Wk Range	$64.00– 43.93	S&P Oper. EPS 2010E	3.61	Market Capitalization(B)	$182.550	Beta	0.60
Trailing 12-Month EPS	$4.29	S&P Oper. EPS 2011E	NA	Yield (%)	2.82	S&P 3-Yr. Proj. EPS CAGR(%)	7
Trailing 12-Month P/E	14.6	P/E on S&P Oper. EPS 2010E	17.3	Dividend Rate/Share	$1.76	S&P Credit Rating	AA-
$10K Invested 5 Yrs Ago	$13,086	Common Shares Outstg. (M)	2,921.7	Institutional Ownership (%)	57		

Price Performance

30-Week Mov. Avg. · · · 10-Week Mov. Avg. – – GAAP Earnings vs. Previous Year   Volume Above Avg. STARS
12-Mo. Target Price — Relative Strength — ▲ Up ▼ Down ▶ No Change   Below Avg.

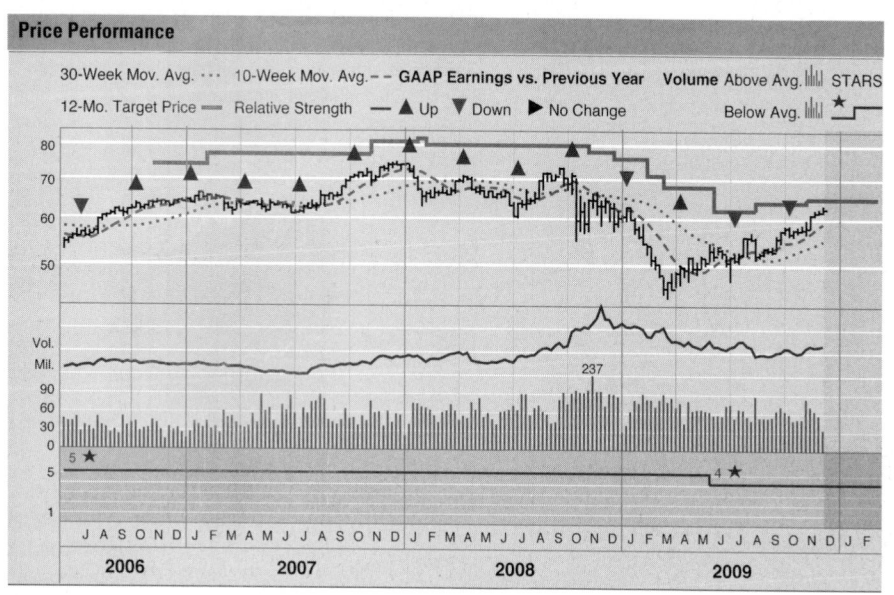

Options: ASE, CBOE, P, Ph

Analysis prepared by **Loran Braverman, CFA** on October 30, 2009, when the stock traded at **$ 59.54**.

Highlights

▶ Sales fell 3% in FY 09 (Jun.), including -4% from foreign exchange and -1% from divestitures. Despite slowing organic growth during FY 09, we think PG benefited from its tiered portfolio, which offers products at different price points, from new products that command higher pricing through innovation, and its broad geographic reach. We see modest sales growth in FY 10, with more emphasis on the value segment.

▶ The operating margin was flat in FY 09, with benefits from price increases, volume leveraging, and cost-saving programs that offset increases in commodity costs, "ongoing" restructuring charges, and about $0.12 per share of "temporary" restructuring charges from programs designed to offset the earnings dilution from the loss of the Folgers business and related stranded overhead costs. We look for a similar operating margin in FY 10, with benefits from moderating commodity costs offset by increased marketing expenses.

▶ We see FY 10 EPS of $3.61, excluding a discontinued health care business. FY 09's $3.58 excludes a $0.63 gain from the Folgers divestiture in the December 2008 quarter and $0.05 of Folgers earnings before the divestiture.

Investment Rationale/Risk

▶ Our buy opinion reflects our confidence that PG will continue to deliver relatively consistent operating results (excluding foreign currency impact), benefiting from the Gillette acquisition and its growth prospects in new markets and categories. In our view, PG's competitive strengths in developing markets include its broad product portfolio and sizable distribution network.

▶ Risks to our recommendation and target price include heightened competition, a worsening consumer spending environment, unfavorable currency translation, greater commodity cost pressures, higher promotional spending, and low consumer acceptance of new products.

▶ Our 12-month target price of $65 is based on a blended valuation. Our historical P/E analysis uses an 18.7X multiple, near the 10-year low, while our peer analysis, based on PG's strong earnings track record and leading market positions, uses 15.0X, the peer average. These multiples imply values, based on our $3.81 calendar 2010 EPS estimate, of $71 and $57, respectively. Our DCF model implies a $67 intrinsic value, assuming a WACC of 8.9% and a 3% terminal growth rate.

Qualitative Risk Assessment

LOW	MEDIUM	HIGH

Our risk assessment reflects that demand for household and personal care products is generally stable and not affected by changes in the economy or geopolitical factors, except for select categories such as fragrances.

Quantitative Evaluations

S&P Quality Ranking A+

D	C	B-	B	B+	A-	A	A+

Relative Strength Rank STRONG

82

LOWEST = 1   HIGHEST = 99

Revenue/Earnings Data

Revenue (Million $)

	1Q	2Q	3Q	4Q	Year
2010	19,807	--	--		--
2009	21,582	20,368	18,417	18,662	79,029
2008	20,199	21,575	20,463	21,266	83,503
2007	18,785	19,725	18,694	19,272	76,476
2006	14,793	18,337	17,250	17,842	68,222
2005	13,744	14,452	14,287	14,258	56,741

Earnings Per Share ($)

2010	0.97	E0.93	E0.84	E0.86	E3.61
2009	1.03	0.94	0.83	0.80	3.58
2008	0.92	0.98	0.82	0.92	3.64
2007	0.79	0.84	0.74	0.67	3.04
2006	0.77	0.72	0.63	0.55	2.64
2005	0.73	0.74	0.63	0.56	2.66

Fiscal year ended Jun. 30. Next earnings report expected: Early February. EPS Estimates based on S&P Operating Earnings; historical GAAP earnings are as reported.

Dividend Data (Dates: mm/dd Payment Date: mm/dd/yy)

Amount ($)	Date Decl.	Ex-Div. Date	Stk. of Record	Payment Date
0.400	01/23	01/21	01/23	02/17/09
0.440	04/14	04/22	04/24	05/15/09
0.440	07/13	07/22	07/24	08/17/09
0.440	10/13	10/21	10/23	11/16/09

Dividends have been paid since 1891. Source: Company reports.

Please read the Required Disclosures and Analyst Certification on the last page of this report.

The McGraw-Hill Companies

Procter & Gamble Co (The)

STANDARD &POOR'S

Business Summary October 30, 2009

CORPORATE OVERVIEW. Procter & Gamble's business is focused on providing branded products of what it considers superior quality and value to improve the lives of the world's consumers. By doing so successfully, the company believes this will result in leadership sales, profits, and value creation for employees, shareholders and the communities in which it operates. PG's products are sold in more than 180 countries. In FY 09 (Jun.), North America accounted for 43% of total sales, Western Europe 21%, Northeast Asia 4%, and developing markets 32%.

PG's customers include mass merchandisers, grocery stores, membership club stores, drug stores and high-frequency stores. Sales to Wal-Mart Stores, Inc. and its affiliates represented 15% of total FY 09 revenue. The top 10 customers accounted for 30% of total unit volume.

As of June 30, 2009, PG's business was structured in three Global Business Units (GBUs) and six reportable segments. The Beauty Unit consisted of the Beauty segment (23% of FY 09 sales and 22% of net earnings) and the Grooming segment (9%, 13%); the Household Care Unit had the Fabric Care and

Home Care segment (29%, 26%) and the Baby Care and Family Care Segment (18%, 16%); and the Health and Well-Being Unit had the Healthcare segment (17%, 21%) and the Snacks and Pet Care segment (4%, 2%).

IMPACT OF MAJOR DEVELOPMENTS. On October 1, 2005, PG acquired The Gillette Company for about $54 billion. Gillette is the world leader in the male and female grooming categories and holds the number one position worldwide in alkaline batteries and toothbrushes. We expect the acquisition to add to increased shareholder value over time through cost synergies and sales growth opportunities, following the initial two years of dilution. On November 6, 2008, PG's Folgers coffee business merged with The J.M. Smucker Company in a reverse Morris Trust transaction. P&G reported a gain of $0.63 per share from the transaction.

Company Financials Fiscal Year Ended Jun. 30

Per Share Data ($)	2009	2008	2007	2006	2005	2004	2003	2002	2001	2000
Tangible Book Value	NM	NM	NM	NM	NM	NM	0.43	NM	0.78	0.68
Cash Flow	4.50	4.54	4.30	3.56	3.30	2.90	2.41	2.11	1.85	2.01
Earnings	3.58	3.64	3.04	2.64	2.66	2.32	1.85	1.54	1.04	1.24
S&P Core Earnings	3.38	3.24	2.96	2.60	2.45	2.17	1.58	1.28	0.81	NA
Dividends	1.64	1.45	1.28	1.15	1.03	0.93	0.82	0.76	0.70	0.64
Payout Ratio	46%	40%	42%	44%	39%	40%	44%	49%	68%	52%
Prices:High	63.48	73.81	75.18	64.73	59.70	57.40	49.97	47.38	40.86	59.19
Prices:Low	43.93	54.92	60.42	52.75	51.16	48.89	39.79	37.04	27.98	26.38
P/E Ratio:High	18	20	25	25	22	25	27	31	39	48
P/E Ratio:Low	12	15	20	20	19	21	22	24	27	21

Income Statement Analysis (Million $)

	2009	2008	2007	2006	2005	2004	2003	2002	2001	2000
Revenue	79,029	83,503	76,476	68,222	56,741	51,407	43,377	40,238	39,244	39,951
Operating Income	19,205	20,249	18,580	15,876	12,811	11,560	9,556	8,371	7,007	8,145
Depreciation	3,082	3,166	3,130	2,627	1,884	1,733	1,703	1,693	2,271	2,191
Interest Expense	1,358	1,467	1,304	1,119	834	629	561	603	794	722
Pretax Income	15,325	16,078	14,710	12,413	10,439	9,350	7,530	6,383	4,616	5,536
Effective Tax Rate	26.3%	24.9%	29.7%	30.0%	30.5%	30.7%	31.1%	31.8%	36.7%	36.0%
Net Income	11,293	12,075	10,340	8,684	7,257	6,481	5,186	4,352	2,922	3,542
S&P Core Earnings	10,467	10,575	9,917	8,420	6,552	5,922	4,313	3,486	2,165	NA

Balance Sheet & Other Financial Data (Million $)

	2009	2008	2007	2006	2005	2004	2003	2002	2001	2000
Cash	4,781	3,541	5,354	6,693	6,389	5,469	5,912	3,427	2,306	1,415
Current Assets	21,905	24,515	24,031	24,329	20,329	17,115	15,220	12,166	10,889	10,146
Total Assets	134,833	143,992	138,014	135,695	61,527	57,048	43,706	40,776	34,387	34,366
Current Liabilities	30,901	30,958	30,717	19,985	25,039	22,147	12,358	12,704	9,846	10,141
Long Term Debt	20,652	23,581	23,375	35,976	12,887	12,554	11,475	11,201	9,792	8,916
Common Equity	63,099	69,494	65,354	61,457	15,994	15,752	14,606	12,072	10,309	10,550
Total Capital	95,827	104,880	102,150	111,238	33,258	32,093	29,057	25,984	22,696	21,828
Capital Expenditures	3,238	3,046	2,945	2,667	2,181	2,024	1,482	1,679	2,486	3,018
Cash Flow	14,183	15,065	13,470	11,311	9,005	8,083	6,764	5,921	5,193	5,733
Current Ratio	0.7	0.8	0.8	1.2	0.8	0.8	1.2	1.0	1.1	1.0
% Long Term Debt of Capitalization	21.6	22.5	22.9	32.3	38.7	39.1	39.5	43.1	43.1	40.8
% Net Income of Revenue	14.3	14.5	13.5	12.7	12.8	12.6	12.0	10.8	7.4	8.9
% Return on Assets	8.1	8.6	7.6	8.8	12.2	12.9	12.3	11.6	8.5	10.7
% Return on Equity	17.2	17.9	16.3	22.1	45.7	41.8	37.9	37.8	28.0	34.0

Data as orig reptd.; bef. results of disc opers/spec. items. Per share data adj. for stk. divs.; EPS diluted. E-Estimated. NA-Not Available. NM-Not Meaningful. NR-Not Ranked. UR-Under Review.

Office: One Procter & Gamble Plaza, Cincinnati, OH 45202.
Telephone: 513-983-1100.
Website: http://www.pg.com
Chrmn: A. Lafley

Pres & CEO: R.A. McDonald
SVP, Chief Acctg Officer & Cntlr: V.L. Sheppard
SVP & Treas: T.L. List
CFO: J.R. Moeller

Investor Contact: M. Erceg (800-742-6253)
Board Members: K. I. Chenault, S. D. Cook, R. K. Gupta, A. Lafley, C. R. Lee, L. M. Martin, R. A. McDonald, W. J. McNerney, Jr., J. A. Rodgers, R. Snyderman, M. Wilderotter, P. Woertz, E. Zedillo

Founded: 1837
Domicile: Ohio
Employees: 135,000

The McGraw-Hill Companies

Progressive Corp (The)

STANDARD &POOR'S

S&P Recommendation	HOLD ★★★☆☆	Price $16.61 (as of Nov 27, 2009)	12-Mo. Target Price $18.00	Investment Style Large-Cap Growth

GICS Sector Financials
Sub-Industry Property & Casualty Insurance

Summary This leading underwriter of nonstandard auto and other lines of coverage has expanded its product line and has evolved into a full-service auto insurer.

Key Stock Statistics (Source S&P, Vickers, company reports)

52-Wk Range	$17.50– 9.76	S&P Oper. EPS 2009**E**	1.50	Market Capitalization(B)	$11.199	Beta	0.81
Trailing 12-Month EPS	$1.36	S&P Oper. EPS 2010**E**	1.53	Yield (%)	Nil	S&P 3-Yr. Proj. EPS CAGR(%)	-1
Trailing 12-Month P/E	12.2	P/E on S&P Oper. EPS 2009**E**	11.1	Dividend Rate/Share	Nil	S&P Credit Rating	A+
$10K Invested 5 Yrs Ago	$8,028	Common Shares Outstg. (M)	674.2	Institutional Ownership (%)	68		

Price Performance

30-Week Mov. Avg. · · · · 10-Week Mov. Avg. – – GAAP Earnings vs. Previous Year Volume Above Avg. ▙▟ STARS
12-Mo. Target Price — Relative Strength — ▲ Up ▼ Down ▶ No Change Below Avg. ▙▟ ★

Options: ASE, CBOE, P, Ph

Analysis prepared by **Cathy A. Seifert** on November 20, 2009, when the stock traded at **$ 16.78.**

Highlights

► We believe earned premiums in 2009 and 2010 will rise almost 1%, reflecting likely market share gains, partly offset by continued price competition. Earned premiums declined 2% in 2007, were flat in 2008 and rose 1% in the first six months of 2009. This followed several years of growth.

► Barring a surge in catastrophe losses, we expect underwriting results to remain profitable in coming periods. Nine-month 2009 underwriting results were aided by a 3% decline in loss costs and a 2% drop in policy acquisition expenses. As a result, the combined (loss and expense) ratio improved to 91.6% in the 2009 interim, from 94.4% in the year-ago period. The combined ratio equaled 94.6% in 2008.

► We estimate operating EPS of $1.50 in 2009, and $1.53 in 2010, versus the $1.18 in operating EPS posted for 2008. Our estimates assume that a flat to modestly higher earned premium base and profitable underwriting results will be slightly offset by a decline in investment income in 2009 (and a slight year-to-year rise in 2010) in a more challenging investment environment.

Investment Rationale/Risk

► We view PGR's technology and marketing capabilities as superior to many peers. However, at recent levels, the shares traded at a premium to most peers on both a forward price/earnings and price/tangible book value basis. We view the shares as appropriately valued, but acknowledge that the favorable loss cost trends that have emerged year to date through September 30, 2009, will aid operating profitability and may help buoy the stock. We remain concerned, however, that PGR is still being impacted by ongoing competitive pressures. These pressures may force PGR to lower its underwriting standards to gain market share, in our view.

► Risks to our recommendation and target price include a greater-than-expected deterioration in premium revenues, higher-than-expected claim cost inflation and erosion in claim trends, and greater-that-expected erosion in the company's investment portfolio.

► Our 12-month target price of $18 assumes that the shares will continue to trade at a premium to their property-casualty insurance peers, albeit a smaller one, on a forward price/tangible book basis and a forward price/earnings basis.

Qualitative Risk Assessment

LOW	MEDIUM	HIGH

Our risk assessment reflects our view of PGR's position as a leading underwriter of personal lines coverage. As primarily an auto insurer, PGR is less exposed to catastrophe losses than a number of peers. However, exposure to catastrophe losses always exists.

Quantitative Evaluations

S&P Quality Ranking B+

D	C	B-	B	B+	A-	A	A+

Relative Strength Rank MODERATE

52

LOWEST = 1 HIGHEST = 99

Revenue/Earnings Data

Revenue (Million $)

	1Q	2Q	3Q	4Q	Year
2009	3,468	3,584	3,611	--	--
2008	3,586	3,537	2,210	3,508	12,840
2007	3,687	3,671	3,710	3,615	14,687
2006	3,661	3,708	3,724	3,694	14,786
2005	3,492	3,590	3,623	3,599	14,303
2004	3,280	3,367	3,438	3,696	13,782

Earnings Per Share ($)

2009	0.35	0.37	0.40	E0.36	E1.50
2008	0.35	0.32	-1.03	0.24	-0.10
2007	0.49	0.39	0.42	0.34	1.65
2006	0.55	0.51	0.53	0.53	2.10
2005	0.51	0.49	0.39	0.36	1.75
2004	0.52	0.44	0.44	0.50	1.91

Fiscal year ended Dec. 31. Next earnings report expected: Mid December. EPS Estimates based on S&P Operating Earnings; historical GAAP earnings are as reported.

Dividend Data

No cash dividends have been paid since 2006.

Progressive Corp (The)

Business Summary November 20, 2009

CORPORATE OVERVIEW. Progressive underwrites an array of personal and commercial lines insurance. Net written premiums totaled $13.6 billion in 2008, of which personal lines accounted for 87% and commercial and other lines 13%.

PGR's core business (90% of 2008's $11.9 billion in personal lines net premiums written) is underwriting private passenger automobile insurance. Based on year-end 2007 industry net written premium data (latest available), the company was the fourth largest private U.S. passenger auto insurer, a position that PGR believes it retained in 2008. PGR's other lines of business include recreational vehicle, motorcycle and small commercial vehicle insurance, and, to a lesser degree, commercial indemnity insurance.

Personal lines products are distributed through a network of more than 30,000, including independent agents, as well as brokers in New York and California, and strategic alliance business relationships with an array of financial institu-

tions. During 2008, 62% of total personal lines net written premiums were distributed through the agency channel (63% in 2007). Distribution through direct channels, including a toll free telephone line and the Internet, accounted for 38% of net written premiums in 2008 (37% in 2007).

PGR conducts its personal lines business in 50 states and in the District of Columbia. Commercial auto policies are written in every state except Hawaii; and not in the District of Columbia.

The commercial auto business (13% of net written premiums in 2008) writes primarily liability and physical damage insurance for automobiles and trucks owned by small businesses.

Company Financials Fiscal Year Ended Dec. 31

Per Share Data ($)	2008	2007	2006	2005	2004	2003	2002	2001	2000	1999
Tangible Book Value	6.23	7.26	9.15	7.74	6.43	5.85	4.32	3.69	3.25	3.14
Operating Earnings	NA	NA	NA	NA	NA	NA	0.81	0.54	0.06	0.30
Earnings	-0.10	1.65	2.10	1.75	1.91	1.42	0.75	0.46	0.05	0.33
S&P Core Earnings	1.29	1.55	2.11	1.77	1.85	1.40	0.79	0.52	NA	NA
Dividends	Nil	Nil	0.06	0.03	0.04	0.03	0.02	0.02	0.02	0.02
Payout Ratio	Nil	Nil	3%	2%	2%	2%	3%	5%	44%	7%
Prices:High	21.31	25.16	30.09	31.23	24.32	21.17	15.12	12.65	9.25	14.52
Prices:Low	10.29	17.26	22.18	20.34	18.28	11.56	11.19	6.84	3.75	5.71
P/E Ratio:High	NM	15	14	18	13	15	20	28	NM	44
P/E Ratio:Low	NM	10	11	12	10	8	15	15	NM	17

Income Statement Analysis (Million $)	2008	2007	2006	2005	2004	2003	2002	2001	2000	1999
Premium Income	13,631	13,877	14,118	13,764	13,170	11,341	8,884	7,162	6,348	5,684
Net Investment Income	638	681	648	537	484	465	455	414	385	341
Other Revenue	-1,429	116	20.7	539	612	54.5	34.3	24.7	37.4	99.0
Total Revenue	12,840	14,687	14,786	14,303	13,782	11,892	9,373	7,488	6,771	6,124
Pretax Income	-222	1,693	2,433	2,059	2,451	1,860	981	588	31.8	412
Net Operating Income	NA	NA	NA	NA	NA	NA	718	486	55.4	267
Net Income	-70.0	1,183	1,648	1,394	1,649	1,255	667	411	46.1	295
S&P Core Earnings	869	1,113	1,654	1,415	1,591	1,234	702	469	NA	NA

Balance Sheet & Other Financial Data (Million $)	2008	2007	2006	2005	2004	2003	2002	2001	2000	1999
Cash & Equivalent	2.90	148	140	139	124	110	94.8	86.4	73.1	68.2
Premiums Due	3,645	2,730	2,932	2,906	2,669	2,351	1,959	1,497	1,567	1,761
Investment Assets:Bonds	9,559	9,185	9,959	10,222	9,084	9,133	7,713	5,949	4,784	4,533
Investment Assets:Stocks	2,266	4,598	4,149	3,279	2,621	2,751	2,004	2,050	2,012	1,666
Investment Assets:Loans	Nil	Nil	Nil	Nil	Nil	Nil	Nil	Nil	Nil	Nil
Investment Assets:Total	12,978	14,165	14,689	14,275	13,082	12,532	10,284	8,226	6,983	6,428
Deferred Policy Costs	414	426	441	445	432	412	364	317	310	343
Total Assets	18,251	18,843	19,482	18,899	17,184	16,282	13,564	11,122	10,052	9,705
Debt	2,176	2,174	1,186	1,285	1,284	1,490	1,489	1,096	749	1,049
Common Equity	4,215	4,936	6,847	6,108	5,155	5,060	3,768	3,251	2,870	2,753
Property & Casualty:Loss Ratio	NA	71.5	66.6	68.1	65.0	67.4	70.9	73.6	83.2	75.0
Property & Casualty:Expense Ratio	21.1	21.1	19.9	87.4	19.6	18.8	20.4	21.0	21.0	22.1
Property & Casualty Combined Ratio	94.6	92.6	86.5	19.3	84.6	86.2	91.3	94.7	104.2	97.1
% Return on Revenue	NM	8.1	11.1	9.7	12.0	10.6	7.1	5.4	0.7	4.8
% Return on Equity	NM	20.1	25.4	24.8	32.4	28.4	19.3	13.4	1.6	11.1

Data as orig reptd.; bef. results of disc opers/spec. items. Per share data adj. for stk. divs.; EPS diluted. E-Estimated. NA-Not Available. NM-Not Meaningful. NR-Not Ranked. UR-Under Review.

Office: 6300 Wilson Mills Road, Mayfield Village, OH 44143.
Telephone: 440-461-5000.
Website: http://www.progressive.com
Chrmn: P.B. Lewis

Pres & CEO: G.M. Renwick
CFO: B. Domeck
Chief Acctg Officer: J.W. Basch
Treas: T.A. King

Investor Contact: P. Brennan (440-395-2370)
Board Members: C. A. Davis, R. N. Farah, L. W. Fitt, S. R. Hardis, B. P. Healy, A. F. Kohnstamm, P. B. Lewis, N. S. Matthews, P. H. Nettles, G. M. Renwick, D. B. Shackelford, B. T. Sheares

Founded: 1965
Domicile: Ohio
Employees: 25,929

Progress Energy Inc.

S&P Recommendation BUY ★★★★☆

Price $38.80 (as of Nov 27, 2009)	**12-Mo. Target Price** $42.00	**Investment Style** Large-Cap Blend

GICS Sector Utilities
Sub-Industry Electric Utilities

Summary This diversified energy company owns two electric utilities serving approximately 3.1 million customers in North Carolina, South Carolina and Florida.

Key Stock Statistics (Source S&P, Vickers, company reports)

52-Wk Range	$40.85–31.35	S&P Oper. EPS 2009**E**	3.05	Market Capitalization(B)	$10.786	Beta		0.41
Trailing 12-Month EPS	$2.59	S&P Oper. EPS 2010**E**	3.20	Yield (%)	6.39	S&P 3-Yr. Proj. EPS CAGR(%)		4
Trailing 12-Month P/E	15.0	P/E on S&P Oper. EPS 2009**E**	12.7	Dividend Rate/Share	$2.48	S&P Credit Rating		BBB+
$10K Invested 5 Yrs Ago	$11,610	Common Shares Outstg. (M)	278.0	Institutional Ownership (%)	59			

Price Performance

30-Week Mov. Avg. ···   10-Week Mov. Avg. -- ◼ **GAAP Earnings vs. Previous Year**   Volume Above Avg. ▮▮▮ STARS
12-Mo. Target Price ▬ Relative Strength ▬ ▲ Up ▼ Down ► No Change   Below Avg. ▮▮▮ ★

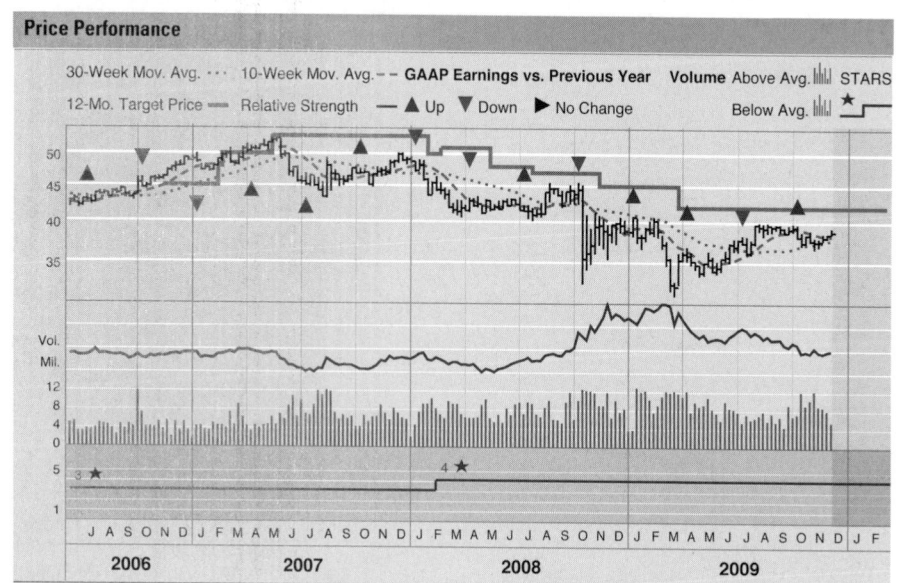

Options: ASE, CBOE, Ph

Analysis prepared by **Justin McCann** on November 11, 2009, when the stock traded at **$38.23**.

Highlights

► Excluding net one-time charges of $0.37, we expect EPS from ongoing operations in 2009 to increase about 2% from 2008's $2.98, with growth restricted by a weak economy, higher interest expense, and more shares outstanding. Results in the first nine months of 2009 were aided by more favorable weather in both the Carolinas and Florida, partially offset by a decline in industrial demand and reduced rates at a major customer in the Carolinas, and higher interest expense and the impact of the recession and housing downturn in Florida.

► For 2010, we project operating EPS to increase nearly 5% from anticipated results in 2009, aided by an expected rate increase in Florida. While we believe the economy and customer growth in Florida will remain weak, we think this will be partially offset by reduced operating costs. We expect customer growth in the Carolinas to stay positive.

► On October 28, 2009, the company announced that the U.S. Department of Energy had awarded it a grant of $200 million in federal infrastructure funds in support of its "Smart Grid" investments in both the Carolinas and Florida.

Investment Rationale/Risk

► The stock has rebounded approximately 22% from its year to date low, recovering nearly all of its earlier decline in 2009. The shares had been hurt, in our view, by the weakness of the housing market and economy in Florida, and concerns about the safety of PGN's dividend. As the situation in Florida appears to be improving, we expect the stock to recover further. While the 83% payout ratio on 2008 operating EPS is high relative to peers, we believe the company is strongly committed to at least maintaining the current dividend. Aided by a well-above-peers yield from the dividend (recently 6.5%), we believe the shares are attractive for above-average total return.

► Risks to our recommendation and target price include the possibility of unfavorable regulatory rulings as well as a sharp decline in the average P/E of the group as a whole.

► Our 12-month target price of $42 represents a premium-to-peers multiple of 13X our EPS estimate for 2010, and reflects the contraction of the average peer P/E for electric utility stocks. We believe the stock will be partly supported by its well-above-peers dividend yield.

Qualitative Risk Assessment

LOW	MEDIUM	HIGH

With the higher risk synthetic fuel business having been discontinued, our risk assessment reflects the strong and steady cash flow we forecast from the regulated utilities in both the Carolinas and Florida, which we believe have well above-average customer growth and operate within a generally supportive regulatory environment.

Quantitative Evaluations

S&P Quality Ranking   B

D	C	B-	B	B+	A-	A	A+

Relative Strength Rank   MODERATE

59

LOWEST = 1   HIGHEST = 99

Revenue/Earnings Data

Revenue (Million $)

	1Q	2Q	3Q	4Q	Year
2009	2,442	2,312	2,824	--	--
2008	2,066	2,244	2,696	2,161	9,167
2007	2,072	2,129	2,750	2,202	9,153
2006	2,433	2,499	2,913	2,273	9,570
2005	2,198	2,333	3,097	2,578	10,108
2004	2,234	2,430	2,775	2,358	9,772

Earnings Per Share ($)

	1Q	2Q	3Q	4Q	Year
2009	0.66	0.62	1.25	E0.54	E3.05
2008	0.58	0.77	1.18	0.44	2.96
2007	0.62	0.41	1.27	0.09	2.70
2006	0.19	0.06	0.97	0.51	2.05
2005	0.43	0.02	1.81	0.63	2.94
2004	0.45	0.63	1.24	0.78	3.10

Fiscal year ended Dec. 31. Next earnings report expected: Mid February. EPS Estimates based on S&P Operating Earnings; historical GAAP earnings are as reported.

Dividend Data (Dates: mm/dd Payment Date: mm/dd/yy)

Amount ($)	Date Decl.	Ex-Div. Date	Stk. of Record	Payment Date
0.620	12/10	01/08	01/12	02/02/09
0.620	03/18	04/08	04/13	05/01/09
0.620	05/13	07/08	07/10	08/03/09
0.620	09/18	10/07	10/12	11/02/09

Dividends have been paid since 1937. Source: Company reports.

Please read the Required Disclosures and Analyst Certification on the last page of this report.

Progress Energy Inc.

Business Summary November 11, 2009

CORPORATE OVERVIEW. Headquartered in Raleigh, NC, Progress Energy operates in retail utility markets in the southeastern U.S., and in competitive electricity, gas and other fuel markets in the eastern U.S. It is the holding company for the fully integrated regulated utilities Progress Energy Carolinas (PEC) and Progress Energy Florida (PEF), which together serve approximately 3.1 million retail electric customers. In 2008, PEC contributed about 58% of utility income (61% in 2007), and PEF 42% (39%).

CORPORATE STRATEGY. As an integrated energy company, PGN has stated that its primary focus will be on the end-use and wholesale electricity markets in its service territory and region. However, the company has experienced the adverse impact of the current economic recession and the downturns in the housing and consumer credit markets. PGN has attempted to offset this im-

pact through its ongoing cost management initiatives, and to mitigate its fuel costs through its diverse generation mix, staggered fuel contracts and hedging, as well as through supplier and transportation diversity. Despite the company's expectation of a challenging economic environment in 2009 and 2010, it remains intent on enhancing its operational excellence, strengthening its financial flexibility and growth, preparing for future power generating capacity, and to continue its record of having increased its dividend for 21 consecutive years.

Company Financials Fiscal Year Ended Dec. 31

Per Share Data ($)	2008	2007	2006	2005	2004	2003	2002	2001	2000	1999
Tangible Book Value	19.15	18.33	18.09	15.94	14.48	13.78	12.43	10.58	7.48	19.43
Earnings	2.96	2.70	2.05	2.94	3.10	3.40	2.53	2.64	3.03	2.55
S&P Core Earnings	2.59	2.67	1.95	2.94	2.93	3.44	2.04	2.59	NA	NA
Dividends	2.46	2.44	2.42	2.36	2.30	2.24	2.18	2.12	2.06	2.00
Payout Ratio	83%	90%	118%	80%	74%	66%	86%	80%	68%	78%
Prices:High	49.16	52.75	49.55	46.00	47.95	48.00	52.70	49.25	49.38	47.88
Prices:Low	32.60	43.12	40.27	40.19	40.09	37.45	32.84	38.78	28.25	29.25
P/E Ratio:High	17	20	24	16	15	14	21	19	16	19
P/E Ratio:Low	11	16	20	14	13	11	13	15	9	11

Income Statement Analysis (Million $)										
Revenue	9,167	9,153	9,570	10,108	9,772	8,743	7,945	8,461	4,119	3,358
Depreciation	957	905	1,032	1,074	1,068	1,040	820	1,090	740	496
Maintenance	NA	NA	NA	NA	NA	NA	NA	NA	NA	NA
Fixed Charges Coverage	2.84	2.76	2.28	1.93	2.21	2.16	1.64	1.75	2.60	4.23
Construction Credits	162	17.0	7.00	13.0	6.00	7.00	8.13	18.0	20.7	11.5
Effective Tax Rate	33.7%	32.2%	28.1%	NM	13.5%	NM	NM	NM	29.8%	40.3%
Net Income	773	693	514	727	753	811	552	542	478	382
S&P Core Earnings	677	685	487	726	712	819	445	532	NA	NA

Balance Sheet & Other Financial Data (Million $)										
Gross Property	29,591	27,500	25,796	26,401	25,602	25,172	23,021	22,541	21,028	12,233
Capital Expenditures	2,333	2,201	1,423	1,286	998	1,018	2,109	1,216	950	765
Net Property	18,293	16,605	15,732	16,799	16,819	17,056	12,541	12,445	11,677	7,257
Capitalization:Long Term Debt	10,983	9,069	8,928	10,539	9,650	10,027	9,840	9,577	5,983	3,029
Capitalization:% Long Term Debt	55.8	51.8	51.9	56.7	55.8	57.4	59.6	61.5	52.4	46.6
Capitalization:Preferred	Nil	Nil	Nil	Nil	Nil	Nil	Nil	Nil	Nil	59.4
Capitalization:% Preferred	Nil	Nil	Nil	Nil	Nil	Nil	Nil	Nil	Nil	0.91
Capitalization:Common	8,687	8,422	8,286	8,038	7,633	7,444	6,677	6,004	5,424	3,413
Capitalization:% Common	44.2	48.2	48.1	43.3	44.2	42.6	40.4	38.5	47.6	52.5
Total Capital	19,803	17,714	17,681	19,061	18,058	18,398	17,656	17,241	13,476	8,337
% Operating Ratio	85.9	86.8	87.5	87.2	86.7	66.8	85.4	83.5	87.1	82.4
% Earned on Net Property	9.6	9.7	8.5	7.7	8.8	8.2	8.3	10.3	7.6	12.1
% Return on Revenue	8.4	7.6	5.4	7.2	7.7	9.3	6.9	6.4	11.6	11.4
% Return on Invested Capital	7.6	7.4	6.8	7.3	7.6	8.2	7.2	9.2	7.1	7.3
% Return on Common Equity	9.0	8.3	6.3	9.3	10.0	11.5	8.7	9.4	10.8	11.9

Data as orig reptd.; bef. results of disc opers/spec. items. Per share data adj. for stk. divs.; EPS diluted. E-Estimated. NA-Not Available. NM-Not Meaningful. NR-Not Ranked. UR-Under Review.

Office: 410 S Wilmington St, Raleigh, NC 27601-1849.
Telephone: 919-546-6111.
Email: shareholder.relations@progress-energy.com
Website: http://www.progress-energy.com

Chrmn, Pres & CEO: W.D. Johnson
EVP, Chief Admin Officer & Secy: J. McArthur
SVP & CFO: M.F. Mulhern
SVP & General Counsel: F.A. Schiller

CFO: S.A. Allaire
Investor Contact: B. Drennan (919-546-7474)
Board Members: J. D. Baker, II, J. E. Bostic, Jr., H. E. DeLoach, Jr., J. B. Hyler, Jr., W. D. Johnson, R. W. Jones, W. S. Jones, E. M. McKee, J. H. Mullin, III, C. W. Pryor, Jr., C. A. Saladrigas, T. M. Stone, A. C. Tollison, Jr.

Founded: 1926
Domicile: North Carolina
Employees: 11,000

ProLogis

STANDARD &POOR'S

S&P Recommendation BUY ★★★★☆

Price
$12.63 (as of Nov 27, 2009)

12-Mo. Target Price
$14.00

GICS Sector Financials
Sub-Industry Industrial REITS

Summary This real estate investment trust is a major global provider of distribution facilities to manufacturers, retailers, transportation, third-party logistics companies across North America, Europe and Asia.

Key Stock Statistics (Source S&P, Vickers, company reports)

52-Wk Range	$16.68– 2.45	S&P FFO/Sh. 2009E	1.34	Market Capitalization(B)	$5.977	Beta	3.02
Trailing 12-Month FFO/Share	NA	S&P FFO/Sh. 2010E	0.95	Yield (%)	4.75	S&P 3-Yr. FFO/Sh. Proj. CAGR(%)	-26
Trailing 12-Month P/FFO	NA	P/FFO on S&P FFO/Sh. 2009E	9.4	Dividend Rate/Share	$0.60	S&P Credit Rating	BBB-
$10K Invested 5 Yrs Ago	$4,054	Common Shares Outstg. (M)	473.2	Institutional Ownership (%)	NM		

Price Performance

30-Week Mov. Avg. · · · · 10-Week Mov. Avg. – – GAAP Earnings vs. Previous Year · Volume Above Avg. ||| STARS
12-Mo. Target Price — Relative Strength — ▲ Up ▼ Down ▶ No Change · Below Avg. ||| ★

Options: ASE, CBOE, P, Ph

Analysis prepared by **Robert McMillan** on October 23, 2009, when the stock traded at **$ 12.79**.

Highlights

▶ We expect rental income, after falling 8.6% in 2008, to decline about 77% in 2009 on softer demand for space in PLD's industrial properties, sharply lower property disposition proceeds, and fewer properties in the portfolio, and to decline 5.3% in 2010 on the absence of property disposition proceeds.

▶ We see a gradual rebound in global trade stimulating demand for PLD's properties. At the end of the 2009 third quarter, the trust's directly owned non-development portfolio was 92.7% leased, up from 92.5% in the prior quarter, marking the first increase in occupancy in two years. We expect re-leasing spreads, which declined almost 15% in the third quarter, to become positive in mid-2010. Developers, such as PLD, have sharply reduced new development over the past year, helping to limit supply, which we believe will allow rents to increase once demand accelerates. We also believe management's de-leveraging efforts have reduced the company's risk profile.

▶ We project funds from operations (FFO) per share of $1.34 in 2009 (or $1.60 including non-cash items) and $0.95 in 2010.

Investment Rationale/Risk

▶ Long term, we see shareholders benefiting from PLD's position as one of the largest owners of global distribution facilities, which are increasingly important, in our view, to global companies looking to increase efficiency. In the short term, however, lingering concerns about PLD's debt burden may weigh on the shares.

▶ Risks to our recommendation and target price include a sharp drop in demand and rental rates for industrial space, a sharper-than-expected downturn in development activity, and higher interest rates.

▶ The stock recently traded at about 8.7X PLD's trailing 12-month FFO per share. Our 12-month target price of $14 is 15X our forward 12-month FFO estimate of $0.97. We attribute recent volatility in the shares in part to weakness in PLD's development business. Over the next 12 months, we expect the valuation multiple to widen to what we view as a very moderate level that is slightly above PLD's recent historical level, but warranted, in our opinion, as PLD likely demonstrates that its core property business is improving and as it de-levers its balance sheet and enhances liquidity.

Qualitative Risk Assessment

LOW	MEDIUM	HIGH

Our risk assessment reflects our view of PLD's position as one of the largest owners of industrial space in the world, and its broad geographic and customer diversification. However, it has sizable debt maturities in 2009 and especially in 2010 that it must address amid turmoil in the capital markets.

Quantitative Evaluations

S&P Quality Ranking B+

D	C	B-	B	B+	A-	A	A+

Relative Strength Rank STRONG

79

LOWEST = 1   HIGHEST = 99

Revenue/FFO Data

Revenue (Million $)

	1Q	2Q	3Q	4Q	Year
2009	459.4	282.2	284.9	--	--
2008	1,637	1,515	1,122	1,388	5,599
2007	955.9	989.4	3,461	799.9	6,205
2006	571.1	687.4	580.5	624.9	2,464
2005	431.9	469.6	532.0	434.6	1,868
2004	151.0	150.1	148.8	150.0	598.1

FFO Per Share ($)

	1Q	2Q	3Q	4Q	Year
2009	0.86	0.34	0.21	E0.23	E1.34
2008	1.38	1.06	0.63	0.61	3.68
2007	1.25	1.16	1.41	0.79	4.61
2006	0.90	0.90	0.79	1.11	3.69
2005	0.90	0.90	0.79	0.58	2.51
2004	0.63	0.67	0.74	0.56	2.11

Fiscal year ended Dec. 31. Next earnings report expected: Early February. FFO Estimates based on S&P Funds From Operations Est..

Dividend Data (Dates: mm/dd Payment Date: mm/dd/yy)

Amount ($)	Date Decl.	Ex-Div. Date	Stk. of Record	Payment Date
0.250	02/09	02/17	02/19	02/27/09
0.150	04/29	05/13	05/15	05/29/09
0.150	08/03	08/12	08/14	08/31/09
0.150	11/02	11/12	11/16	11/30/09

Dividends have been paid since 1994. Source: Company reports.

Please read the Required Disclosures and Analyst Certification on the last page of this report.

ProLogis

STANDARD
&POOR'S

Business Summary October 23, 2009

ProLogis (formerly ProLogis Trust, and prior to that Security Capital Industrial Trust) is a real estate investment trust that owns and operates industrial distribution and temperature-controlled distribution facilities in North America, Europe and Japan. The trust's investment strategy focuses on generic industrial distribution facilities in markets that PLD thinks offer attractive long-term growth prospects, and in which it believes it can achieve a strong market position by acquiring and developing flexible facilities for warehousing and light manufacturing uses.

PLD's business is organized into three main operating segments: direct owned, investment management, and corporate distribution facilities services and other (CDFS). The direct owned segment (about 47% of 2008 operating income) is involved in long-term ownership, management and leasing of industrial distribution facilities, usually adaptable for both distribution and light manufacturing or assembly uses. The trust earns income from rents and reimbursement of property operating expenses from unaffiliated customers, and management fees from entities in which it has an ownership interest. At December 31, 2008, PLD's direct owned segment consisted of 1,396 operating properties aggregating about 217 million square feet in North America, Europe

and Asia. The properties are primarily distribution properties, although it owns 34 retail and mixed-use properties aggregating 1.4 million square feet.

The investment management segment (5% of 2008 operating income) is involved in the long-term investment management of unconsolidated property funds, and the properties they own, with the objective of generating a high level of return for PLD and its fund partners. It allows PLD, as the manager of the property funds, to maintain the market presence and customer relationships that are the key drivers of the ProLogis Operating System, and it enables the trust to realize a portion of the development profits from its CDFS business activities by contributing its stabilized development properties to property funds. It also allows PLD to earn fees and incentives for providing services to the property funds and enables it to maintain a long-term ownership position in the properties. At the end of 2008, this segment had 1,339 industrial properties under management, aggregating 298 million square feet.

Company Financials Fiscal Year Ended Dec. 31

Per Share Data ($)	2008	2007	2006	2005	2004	2003	2002	2001	2000	1999
Tangible Book Value	21.27	25.44	23.09	21.08	14.82	14.35	13.96	12.94	13.53	13.86
Earnings	-0.85	3.61	2.71	1.39	1.09	1.16	1.20	0.52	0.96	0.81
S&P Core Earnings	-0.85	3.61	2.71	1.39	1.06	1.14	1.17	0.49	NA	NA
Dividends	2.07	1.84	1.60	1.48	1.46	1.44	1.42	1.38	1.34	1.30
Payout Ratio	NM	51%	59%	106%	134%	124%	118%	NM	140%	160%
Prices:High	66.58	73.35	67.52	47.62	43.33	32.62	26.00	23.30	24.69	22.19
Prices:Low	2.20	51.64	46.29	36.50	27.62	23.63	20.96	19.35	17.56	16.75
P/E Ratio:High	NM	20	25	34	40	28	22	45	26	27
P/E Ratio:Low	NM	14	17	26	25	20	17	37	18	20

Income Statement Analysis (Million $)										
Rental Income	1,002	1,068	928	635	527	Nil	449	466	480	492
Mortgage Income	Nil	Nil	Nil	Nil	Nil	Nil	Nil	Nil	Nil	Nil
Total Income	5,599	6,205	2,464	1,868	598	734	675	574	644	567
General Expenses	4,692	4,760	1,403	1,210	224	210	91.0	83.0	78.0	76.7
Interest Expense	341	368	294	178	153	155	153	164	172	172
Provision for Losses	Nil	Nil	Nil	Nil	Nil	Nil	Nil	Nil	Nil	Nil
Depreciation	339	309	293	199	172	165	153	143	151	152
Net Income	-195	987	718	318	234	251	249	128	214	182
S&P Core Earnings	-221	962	692	292	199	208	210	86.8	NA	NA

Balance Sheet & Other Financial Data (Million $)										
Cash	175	419	1,775	1,241	1,145	1,009	111	28.0	57.9	69.3
Total Assets	19,252	19,724	15,904	13,114	7,098	6,369	5,924	5,604	5,946	5,848
Real Estate Investment	15,706	16,579	13,954	11,875	6,334	5,854	5,396	4,588	4,689	4,975
Loss Reserve	Nil	Nil	Nil	Nil	Nil	Nil	Nil	Nil	Nil	Nil
Net Investment	14,123	15,210	12,674	10,757	5,345	5,007	4,683	4,013	4,213	4,608
Short Term Debt	Nil	Nil	Nil	Nil	Nil	Nil	222	49.3	69.7	43.5
Capitalization:Debt	11,008	9,650	7,844	6,678	3,414	2,991	2,510	2,529	2,555	2,413
Capitalization:Equity	6,075	7,086	6,049	5,138	2,752	2,586	2,486	2,276	2,236	2,243
Capitalization:Total	17,453	17,165	14,295	12,225	6,583	6,089	5,439	5,251	5,574	5,428
% Earnings & Depreciation/Assets	7.4	7.3	4.7	5.1	6.0	6.8	7.0	4.7	6.2	6.6
Price Times Book Value:High	3.1	2.9	2.9	2.3	2.9	2.3	1.9	1.8	1.8	1.6
Price Times Book Value:Low	0.1	2.0	2.0	1.7	1.9	1.6	1.5	1.5	1.3	1.2

Data as orig reptd.; bef. results of disc opers/spec. items. Per share data adj. for stk. divs.; EPS diluted. E-Estimated. NA-Not Available. NM-Not Meaningful. NR-Not Ranked. UR-Under Review.

Prudential Financial Inc

STANDARD &POOR'S

S&P Recommendation BUY ★★★★☆

Price	**12-Mo. Target Price**	**Investment Style**
$48.20 (as of Nov 27, 2009)	$54.00	Large-Cap Value

GICS Sector Financials
Sub-Industry Life & Health Insurance

Summary This company provides a wide range of insurance, investment management and other financial products and services to customers in the U.S. and overseas.

Key Stock Statistics (Source S&P, Vickers, company reports)

52-Wk Range	$55.99–10.63	S&P Oper. EPS 2009**E**	5.52	Market Capitalization(B)	$22.365	Beta	2.66
Trailing 12-Month EPS	$-0.60	S&P Oper. EPS 2010**E**	5.77	Yield (%)	1.45	S&P 3-Yr. Proj. EPS CAGR(%)	-6
Trailing 12-Month P/E	NM	P/E on S&P Oper. EPS 2009**E**	8.7	Dividend Rate/Share	$0.70	S&P Credit Rating	A
$10K Invested 5 Yrs Ago	$10,684	Common Shares Outstg. (M)	464.0	Institutional Ownership (%)	54		

Price Performance

30-Week Mov. Avg. · · · 10-Week Mov. Avg. - - - GAAP Earnings vs. Previous Year   Volume Above Avg. STARS
12-Mo. Target Price — Relative Strength — ▲ Up ▼ Down ▶ No Change   Below Avg. ★

Options: ASE, CBOE, Ph

Analysis prepared by **Bret Howlett** on November 10, 2009, when the stock traded at **$ 47.68**.

Highlights

▶ We see double-digit earnings growth in PRU's annuity business in 2010 due to strong sales and flows of variable annuities, an area where we expect market share gains. In retirement, we forecast solid earnings growth primarily from increased customer account values. We expect solid net flows in full service, boosted by strong persistency and case wins. We forecast earnings in insurance to increase in the mid-single digits, driven by robust sales of universal and term life products and higher investment income, partially offset by lower sales and a higher claims experience in group life.

▶ We expect double-digit earnings growth for the international division, on strong premium growth at Gibraltar Life, fueled by robust sales of protection-oriented products in the bank channel. We also see strong results at Life Planner on increased sales of variable life and retirement products, expanded distribution and acquisitions, and increased productivity of agents.

▶ We forecast 2009 operating EPS of $5.52, rising to $5.77 in 2010. Our earnings estimates exclude realized investment gains or losses.

Investment Rationale/Risk

▶ Our buy recommendation is based on our view of PRU's collection of high-growth businesses and its superior financial flexibility. We believe PRU will expand earnings and return on equity (ROE) at a faster rate than many of its peers and is well positioned to gain market share in many product areas. Despite our forecast for elevated investment losses in 2010, we believe PRU maintains a strong capital position, and we think it should be able to absorb these losses without the need to raise additional capital. We believe PRU's stock warrants a higher valuation versus peers due to its broad business mix, distribution capabilities, and its rapidly growing international division, which has benefited from its exposure to the lucrative insurance markets in Asia. We consider PRU undervalued at current levels.

▶ Risks to our recommendation and target price include currency risk; reserving risks for new guaranteed minimum benefits; integration risk from acquisitions; credit risk; and exposure to a sharp decline in the equity markets.

▶ Our 12-month target price is $54, or roughly 1.0X our 2010 book value estimate, below PRU's historical multiple.

Qualitative Risk Assessment

LOW	MEDIUM	**HIGH**

Our risk assessment reflects PRU's exposure to the equity markets and the risk for further asset impairments on its balance sheet. This is only partly offset by our view of PRU's varied product offerings, geographic diversification, and prominent market position.

Quantitative Evaluations

S&P Quality Ranking   NR

D	C	B-	B	B+	A-	A	A+

Relative Strength Rank   MODERATE

53

LOWEST = 1   HIGHEST = 99

Revenue/Earnings Data

Revenue (Million $)

	1Q	2Q	3Q	4Q	Year
2009	8,563	6,906	8,564	--	--
2008	7,564	7,709	7,036	6,966	29,275
2007	8,775	8,425	8,383	8,808	34,401
2006	7,850	7,373	8,408	8,857	32,488
2005	7,721	8,318	7,787	7,882	31,708
2004	6,743	6,904	7,346	7,355	28,348

Earnings Per Share ($)

2009	0.01	1.22	2.36	E1.00	E5.52
2008	0.20	1.35	-0.24	-3.91	-2.49
2007	2.10	1.86	1.89	1.89	7.58
2006	1.39	0.92	2.24	1.85	6.37
2005	1.47	1.56	2.61	0.78	6.46
2004	0.72	0.98	1.09	0.64	3.45

Fiscal year ended Dec. 31. Next earnings report expected: Early February. EPS Estimates based on S&P Operating Earnings; historical GAAP earnings are as reported.

Dividend Data (Dates: mm/dd Payment Date: mm/dd/yy)

Amount ($)	Date Decl.	Ex-Div. Date	Stk. of Record	Payment Date
0.580	11/11	11/20	11/24	12/19/08
0.700	11/10	11/20	11/24	12/18/09

Dividends have been paid since 2002. Source: Company reports.

Please read the Required Disclosures and Analyst Certification on the last page of this report.

The McGraw-Hill Companies

Prudential Financial Inc

STANDARD
&POOR'S

Business Summary November 10, 2009

CORPORATE OVERVIEW. Prudential Financial is one of the largest U.S. financial services companies, with $5.58 billion in assets under management and $2.5 trillion in life insurance in force at year-end 2008, and customers in roughly 37 other countries.

The financial services business operates through four divisions: retirement and investments (33% of 2008 operating revenues, 28% in 2007), insurance (30%, 37%), international insurance and investments (36%, 33%), and corporate and other (1.3%, 2.0%). The insurance division consists of the individual life unit (35.7% of the division's 2008 operating revenues) and the group insurance unit (64.3%), which distributes group life, disability and related insurance products through employee and member benefit plans.

The asset management unit (19.8% of the division's 2008 operating revenues), the individual annuities unit (23.4%) and the retirement services unit (56.8%) comprise the retirement and investment division. International insurance and investments consists of insurance (97% of the division's 2008 operating revenues) and investments (3.0%). PRU distributes life insurance products to the mass affluent markets mostly in Japan and Korea through its Life Planner operations. Additionally, the company's Life Advisor agents market insurance products to the middle-class in Japan through its Gibraltar Life subsidiary.

The closed block businesses represent some insurance products no longer offered, including certain participating insurance and annuity policies. At December 31, 2008, PRU had reinsurance agreements covering about 73% of the closed block policies.

CORPORATE STRATEGY. We believe PRU is focused on two prime areas of growth: international businesses and domestic retirement and savings. Prudential has made strategic acquisitions to enhance these opportunities.

As a consequence of the A.G. Edwards and Wachovia merger that was completed in 2007, Prudential Financial was allowed to have a "lookback" put option associated with its joint venture (JV) with Wachovia. If exercised, it required Wachovia to purchase Prudential's stake in the JV at an appraised value on January 1, 2008. The purchase price generally would have been $1 billion plus PRU's share of the joint venture's transition costs, adjusted for additional investments. On December 4, 2008, PRU announced it would exercise the put option and sell its 38% interest in the Wachovia JV for an estimated $5 billion. The transaction is scheduled to be completed on January 1, 2010.

Company Financials Fiscal Year Ended Dec. 31

Per Share Data ($)	2008	2007	2006	2005	2004	2003	2002	2001	2000	1999
Tangible Book Value	31.18	52.43	46.32	45.53	42.40	39.65	37.89	34.90	NA	NA
Operating Earnings	NA	NA	NA	NA	NA	NA	NA	NA	NA	NA
Earnings	-2.49	7.58	6.37	6.46	3.45	2.06	1.36	0.07	0.82	NA
S&P Core Earnings	2.77	6.18	5.41	4.96	1.91	1.79	1.13	NA	NA	NA
Dividends	0.58	1.15	0.95	0.78	0.63	0.50	0.40	Nil	NA	NA
Payout Ratio	NM	15%	15%	12%	18%	24%	29%	Nil	NA	NA
Prices:High	93.14	103.27	87.18	78.62	55.62	42.21	36.00	33.74	NA	NA
Prices:Low	13.10	81.61	71.28	52.07	40.14	27.03	25.25	27.50	NA	NA
P/E Ratio:High	NM	14	14	12	16	20	26	NM	NA	NA
P/E Ratio:Low	NM	11	11	8	12	13	19	NM	NA	NA

Income Statement Analysis (Million $)										
Life Insurance in Force	NA	NA	NA	NA	NA	1,928,650	1,800,788	1,768,038	NA	NA
Premium Income:Life	15,468	14,351	13,908	13,685	12,580	10,972	10,897	10,078	NA	NA
Premium Income:A & H	NA	NA	NA	NA	NA	806	586	515	NA	NA
Net Investment Income	11,883	12,017	11,354	10,560	9,079	8,681	8,832	9,151	9,467	NA
Total Revenue	29,275	34,401	32,488	31,708	28,348	27,907	26,675	27,177	26,514	26,568
Pretax Income	-1,565	4,932	4,611	4,471	3,287	1,958	64.0	-227	525	2,255
Net Operating Income	NA	NA	NA	NA	NA	NA	NA	NA	NA	NA
Net Income	-1,104	3,687	3,363	3,602	2,332	1,308	256	-170	304	1,213
S&P Core Earnings	1,189	2,899	2,675	2,580	1,022	981	650	-403	NA	NA

Balance Sheet & Other Financial Data (Million $)										
Cash & Equivalent	33,239	13,234	10,731	9,866	10,100	9,746	11,688	20,364	19,994	16,168
Premiums Due	1,558	2,119	1,958	3,548	32,790	Nil	Nil	Nil	NA	NA
Investment Assets:Bonds	161,864	165,710	166,285	158,515	153,715	132,011	128,075	110,316	NA	NA
Investment Assets:Stocks	24,276	26,216	24,574	18,792	4,283	6,703	2,807	2,272	NA	NA
Investment Assets:Loans	42,817	39,384	34,626	32,811	32,761	27,621	22,094	28,299	NA	NA
Investment Assets:Total	242,025	243,107	245,349	221,401	216,624	181,041	183,094	165,834	169,251	151,804
Deferred Policy Costs	15,126	12,339	10,863	9,438	8,847	7,826	7,031	6,868	6,751	NA
Total Assets	445,011	485,814	454,266	417,776	401,058	321,274	292,746	293,030	298,414	285,094
Debt	20,290	14,101	11,423	8,270	7,627	5,610	4,757	5,304	14,812	NA
Common Equity	13,422	23,457	22,892	22,763	22,344	21,292	21,330	20,453	20,692	19,291
% Return on Revenue	NM	10.7	10.4	11.4	8.2	4.7	1.0	NM	1.1	4.6
% Return on Assets	NM	0.8	0.8	0.9	0.6	0.4	0.1	NM	NA	NA
% Return on Equity	NA	15.9	14.7	16.0	10.7	6.1	1.2	NM	NA	NA
% Investment Yield	4.9	5.0	4.8	4.8	4.6	4.8	5.1	5.8	NA	12.3

Data as orig reptd.; bef. results of disc opers/spec. items. Per share data adj. for stk. divs.; EPS diluted. E-Estimated. NA-Not Available. NM-Not Meaningful. NR-Not Ranked. UR-Under Review.

Office: 751 Broad St, Newark, NJ 07102.
Telephone: 973-802-6000.
Email: investor.relations@prudential.com
Website: http://www.investor.prudential.com

Chrmn, Pres & CEO: J.R. Strangfeld, Jr.
Vice Chrmn: M.B. Grier
COO & SVP: J.R. Leibowtiz
EVP & CFO: R.J. Carbone

SVP, Chief Acctg Officer & Cntlr: P. Sayre
Board Members: T. J. Baltimore, Jr., F. K. Becker, G. Bethune, G. Caperton, III, G. F. Casellas, W. H. Gray, III, M. B. Grier, J. F. Hanson, C. J. Horner, K. J. Krapek, C. A. Poon, J. R. Strangfeld, Jr., J. A. Unruh

Founded: 1875
Domicile: New Jersey
Employees: 41,844

Public Storage

STANDARD
&POOR'S

S&P Recommendation	HOLD ★★★☆☆	Price	12-Mo. Target Price	Investment Style
		$76.44 (as of Nov 27, 2009)	$83.00	Large-Cap Blend

GICS Sector Financials
Sub-Industry Specialized REITS

Summary This real estate investment trust invests primarily in self-service storage facilities (mini-warehouses), but also in commercial and industrial properties.

Key Stock Statistics (Source S&P, Vickers, company reports)

52-Wk Range	$82.02–45.35	S&P FFO/Sh. 2009E	5.50	Market Capitalization(B)	$13.512	Beta	0.96
Trailing 12-Month FFO/Share	NA	S&P FFO/Sh. 2010E	5.00	Yield (%)	2.88	S&P 3-Yr. FFO/Sh. Proj. CAGR(%)	1
Trailing 12-Month P/FFO	NA	P/FFO on S&P FFO/Sh. 2009E	13.9	Dividend Rate/Share	$2.20	S&P Credit Rating	A-
$10K Invested 5 Yrs Ago	$16,452	Common Shares Outstg. (M)	176.8	Institutional Ownership (%)	76		

Price Performance

30-Week Mov. Avg. · · · · 10-Week Mov. Avg. - - GAAP Earnings vs. Previous Year Volume Above Avg. STARS
12-Mo. Target Price — Relative Strength ▲ Up ▼ Down ▶ No Change Below Avg.

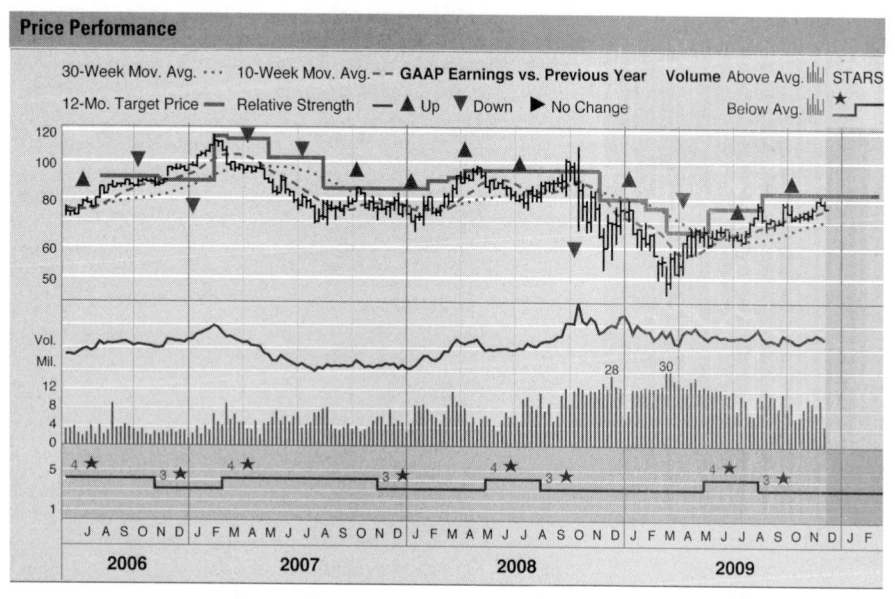

Options: ASE, Ph

Analysis prepared by **Robert McMillan** on November 09, 2009, when the stock traded at **$ 79.15**.

Highlights

▶ After revenue growth of about 34% in 2007, driven largely by contributions from the August 2006 acquisition of Shurgard Storage Centers, revenues fell 3.9% in 2008, reflecting the partial disposition of that business and tepid growth in demand for storage space. We expect revenues to decline 8.4% in 2009, on increased promotional activity as well the sale of the majority interest in Shurgard Europe, before rising fractionally in 2010 on improving occupancy and rent trends.

▶ As the economy strengthens, we expect that management will gradually need to use fewer incentives and discounts to retain existing customers and attract new customers. Same-store domestic occupancy declined to 88.7% during the third quarter, from 89.4% last year; rents per available square foot fell 4.0%. However, trends in early November seem to point to stabilization, and operations in Europe appear to be improving. Given the trust's healthy liquidity with very little debt, we look for it to make small opportunistic property acquisitions.

▶ We look for per share funds from operations (FFO) of $5.50 for 2009 and $5.00 in 2010.

Investment Rationale/Risk

▶ We see PSA benefiting from its ability to continue gaining share at the expense of smaller competitors by creating customer awareness in its markets and by offering an array of customer services that many small competitors cannot provide. Also, given its size versus the competition, the trust has significant pricing power as well as the funds to launch advertising campaigns to create public awareness, which many smaller competitors cannot afford.

▶ Risks to our recommendation and target price include slower-than-expected growth in rental rates and occupancy levels, a sharp drop in moving activity, and higher interest rates.

▶ The stock recently traded at about 13.0X trailing 12-month FFO per share. The shares and the valuation multiple have been volatile lately on concerns, in our view, about the state of the economy and the housing market. Our 12-month target price of $83 is equal to about 16.8X our forward four-quarter FFO estimate of $4.92. We expect a widening of the valuation multiple to be driven by continued improvement in operating results.

Qualitative Risk Assessment

LOW	MEDIUM	HIGH

Our risk assessment reflects PSA's position as one of the largest providers of self-storage space in a consolidating industry. In our opinion, the trust has a very strong balance sheet.

Quantitative Evaluations

S&P Quality Ranking B+

D	C	B-	B	B+	A-	A	A+

Relative Strength Rank MODERATE

62

LOWEST = 1   HIGHEST = 99

Revenue/FFO Data

Revenue (Million $)

	1Q	2Q	3Q	4Q	Year
2009	420.2	407.1	414.8	--	--
2008	462.8	428.8	443.2	428.5	1,766
2007	434.4	449.2	469.0	464.4	1,829
2006	278.5	297.9	371.4	433.9	1,382
2005	243.8	254.3	264.9	273.6	1,061
2004	222.7	231.6	237.2	240.3	928.0

FFO Per Share ($)

	1Q	2Q	3Q	4Q	Year
2009	1.51	1.40	1.44	E1.15	E5.50
2008	1.39	1.10	1.09	1.49	5.07
2007	1.05	1.10	1.43	1.40	4.97
2006	0.94	0.99	0.77	0.89	3.57
2005	0.79	0.90	0.97	0.96	3.61
2004	0.58	0.77	0.76	0.82	2.93

Fiscal year ended Dec. 31. Next earnings report expected: Early March. FFO Estimates based on S&P Funds From Operations Est..

Dividend Data (Dates: mm/dd Payment Date: mm/dd/yy)

Amount ($)	Date Decl.	Ex-Div. Date	Stk. of Record	Payment Date
0.60 Spl.	11/06	11/11	11/15	12/30/08
0.550	02/26	03/12	03/16	03/31/09
0.550	05/07	06/11	06/15	06/30/09
0.550	08/06	09/11	09/15	09/30/09

Dividends have been paid since 1981. Source: Company reports.

Please read the Required Disclosures and Analyst Certification on the last page of this report.

The McGraw-Hill Companies

Public Storage

STANDARD &POOR'S

Business Summary November 09, 2009

Public Storage is an equity real estate investment trust that was organized as a corporation under the laws of California on July 10, 1980. It is a fully integrated, self-administered and self-managed REIT that acquires, develops, owns and operates storage facilities.

PSA is the largest U.S. owner and operator of storage space, with direct and indirect equity investments in 2,012 self-storage facilities located in 38 states within the U.S. operating under the Public Storage name at the end of 2008. The facilities contain approximately 127 million net rentable square feet of space, and 181 self-storage facilities are located in seven Western European countries, which operate under the Shurgard Storage Centers name, containing approximately nine million net rentable square feet of space. PSA also has direct and indirect equity interests in approximately 21 million net rentable square feet of commercial space located in 11 states in the U.S. operated under the PS Business Parks and Public Storage, Inc. brands. PSA has a 46% ownership interest in PS Business Parks, Inc. (PSB: hold, $41), which, as of December 31, 2008, owned and operated commercial properties containing about 19.6 million net rentable sq. ft. of space.

PSA's growth strategies consist of improving the operating performance of stabilized existing traditional self-storage properties; acquiring additional interests in entities that own properties operated by the trust; purchasing interests in properties that are owned or operated by others; developing properties in selected markets; improving the operating performance of the container-

ized storage operations; and participating in the growth of PS Business Parks, Inc.

The trust's storage facilities are designed to offer accessible storage space for personal and business use at a relatively low cost. Individuals usually obtain this space for storage of furniture, household appliances, personal belongings, motor vehicles, boats, campers, motorcycles and other household goods. Businesses normally employ this space for storage of excess inventory, business records, seasonal goods, equipment and fixtures. A user rents a fully enclosed space that is for the user's exclusive use and that only the user has access to on an unrestricted basis during business hours. Some storage facilities also include rentable uncovered parking areas for vehicle storage, as well as space for portable storage containers. Leases for storage facility space may be on a long-term or short-term basis, although typically spaces are rented on a month-to-month basis. Rental rates vary according to the location of the property, the size of the storage space and the length of stay. PSA's self-storage facilities generally consist of three to seven buildings containing an aggregate of between 350 and 750 storage spaces, most of which have between 25 and 400 square feet and an interior height of approximately eight to 12 feet.

Company Financials Fiscal Year Ended Dec. 31

Per Share Data ($)	2008	2007	2006	2005	2004	2003	2002	2001	2000	1999
Tangible Book Value	30.21	28.85	28.16	16.72	16.69	17.03	16.16	28.37	18.24	21.43
Earnings	4.20	1.17	0.32	1.92	1.39	1.27	1.28	1.51	1.41	1.52
S&P Core Earnings	4.20	1.15	0.32	1.91	1.38	1.25	1.26	1.48	NA	NA
Dividends	2.20	2.00	2.00	1.85	1.80	1.80	1.80	1.69	1.48	0.88
Payout Ratio	52%	171%	NM	97%	129%	142%	1%	112%	105%	58%
Prices:High	110.00	117.16	98.05	72.02	57.64	45.81	39.29	35.15	26.93	29.38
Prices:Low	52.52	68.09	67.72	51.50	39.50	28.25	27.98	24.13	20.87	20.81
P/E Ratio:High	26	NM	NM	38	41	36	33	23	19	19
P/E Ratio:Low	13	NM	NM	27	28	22	24	16	15	14

Income Statement Analysis (Million $)										
Rental Income	1,581	1,663	1,240	980	894	844	813	782	703	628
Mortgage Income	Nil	Nil	Nil	Nil	Nil	Nil	Nil	Nil	Nil	Nil
Total Income	1,766	1,829	1,382	1,061	928	875	841	835	757	677
General Expenses	644	712	585	400	349	336	311	297	273	229
Interest Expense	44.0	64.0	33.1	8.22	0.76	1.12	3.81	3.23	3.29	7.97
Provision for Losses	Nil	Nil	Nil	Nil	Nil	Nil	Nil	Nil	Nil	Nil
Depreciation	414	622	438	196	183	186	180	168	149	138
Net Income	936	458	312	450	367	335	319	324	297	288
S&P Core Earnings	710	197	44.7	247	179	157	156	183	NA	NA

Balance Sheet & Other Financial Data (Million $)										
Cash	681	245	857	329	708	205	103	49.3	89.5	55.1
Total Assets	9,936	10,643	11,198	5,552	5,205	4,968	4,844	4,626	4,514	4,214
Real Estate Investment	10,227	11,719	11,262	6,314	5,908	5,544	5,424	5,062	4,822	4,421
Loss Reserve	Nil	Nil	Nil	Nil	Nil	Nil	Nil	Nil	Nil	Nil
Net Investment	7,822	9,591	9,507	4,814	4,588	4,391	4,436	4,242	4,154	3,887
Short Term Debt	13.0	216	Nil	Nil	Nil	Nil	39.8	Nil	Nil	Nil
Capitalization:Debt	631	808	1,848	134	130	76.0	76.1	144	156	167
Capitalization:Equity	5,291	5,236	5,353	2,319	2,328	2,353	2,342	2,369	2,569	2,534
Capitalization:Total	9,710	9,270	8,785	5,205	4,989	4,722	4,675	4,508	4,413	4,043
% Earnings & Depreciation/Assets	13.1	9.8	8.9	12.0	10.8	10.6	10.5	7.1	10.2	11.2
Price Times Book Value:High	3.6	4.1	3.5	4.3	3.5	2.7	2.4	1.2	1.5	1.4
Price Times Book Value:Low	1.7	2.4	2.4	3.1	2.4	1.7	1.7	0.9	1.1	1.0

Data as orig reptd.; bef. results of disc opers/spec. items. Per share data adj. for stk. divs.; EPS diluted. E-Estimated. NA-Not Available. NM-Not Meaningful. NR-Not Ranked. UR-Under Review.

Office: 701 Western Ave, Glendale, CA 91201-2349.
Telephone: 818-244-8080.
Email: investor@publicstorage.com
Website: http://www.publicstorage.com

Chrmn: B. Hughes
Pres, Vice Chrmn & CEO: R.L. Havner, Jr.
COO & SVP: M.C. Good
SVP, CFO & Chief Acctg Officer: J. Reyes

Secy: S.G. Heim
Investor Contact: C. Teng (818-244-8080)
Board Members: D. V. Angeloff, W. C. Baker, J. T. Evans, T. H. Gustavson, U. P. Harkham, R. L. Havner, Jr., B. Hughes, B. W. Hughes, Jr., H. Lenkin, G. Pruitt, D. C. Staton

Founded: 1980
Domicile: Maryland
Employees: 5,200

Public Service Enterprise Group Inc

STANDARD &POOR'S

S&P Recommendation **BUY** ★★★★☆	Price $30.90 (as of Nov 27, 2009)	12-Mo. Target Price $38.00	Investment Style Large-Cap Blend

GICS Sector Utilities
Sub-Industry Multi-Utilities

Summary PEG is the holding company for Public Service Electric and Gas (PSE&G), with a service area that encompasses 70% of New Jersey.

Key Stock Statistics (Source S&P, Vickers, company reports)

52-Wk Range	$34.02– 23.65	S&P Oper. EPS 2009E	3.10	Market Capitalization(B)	$15.635	Beta	0.55
Trailing 12-Month EPS	$2.91	S&P Oper. EPS 2010E	3.21	Yield (%)	4.30	S&P 3-Yr. Proj. EPS CAGR(%)	5
Trailing 12-Month P/E	10.6	P/E on S&P Oper. EPS 2009E	10.0	Dividend Rate/Share	$1.33	S&P Credit Rating	BBB
$10K Invested 5 Yrs Ago	$16,474	Common Shares Outstg. (M)	506.0	Institutional Ownership (%)	61		

Price Performance

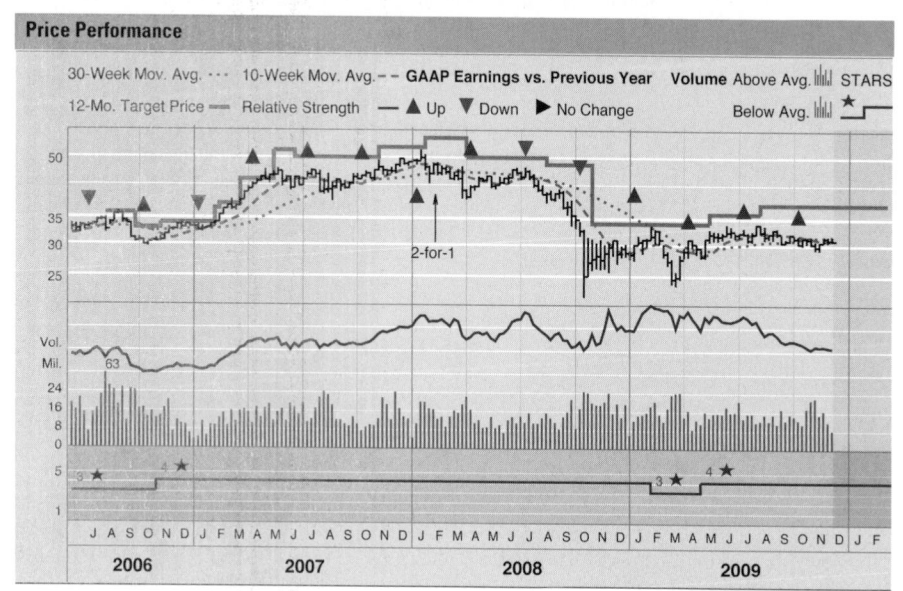

30-Week Mov. Avg. · · · 10-Week Mov. Avg. – – GAAP Earnings vs. Previous Year Volume Above Avg. STARS
12-Mo. Target Price — Relative Strength — ▲ Up ▼ Down ► No Change Below Avg.

2006 2007 2008 2009

Options: ASE, CBOE, Ph

Analysis prepared by **Justin McCann** on October 19, 2009, when the stock traded at **$ 31.14**.

Highlights

► Excluding net one-time charges of $0.09, we expect operating EPS in 2009 to rise about 6% from 2008 operating EPS of $2.92. We see earnings growth being driven by higher power margins, reflecting already contracted renewals of expired power contracts. However, this is seen partially offset by lower earnings at the utility, due to higher operating expenses and milder than normal weather. We also expect PEG's pension expense in 2009 to increase by about $0.15 a share, due to the decline in the market value of the company's pension assets.

► For 2010, we expect operating EPS to increase 3% to 4% from anticipated results in 2009. Our projection assumes a return to normal weather and a gradual recovery in the economy and the power markets.

► In the first half of 2009, PEG's Energy Holdings unit sold its interest in nine leveraged leases with a combined book value of $369 million, including seven international leases for which the IRS disallowed deductions taken in prior years. Total proceeds were about $460 million, and are being used to reduce the related tax exposure of $360 million to $780 million. PEG plans to litigate for the recovery of these taxes.

Investment Rationale/Risk

► While the shares have rebounded approximately 30% from their 2009 low, we believe the stock is still attractive at its recent trading level and we continue to recommend it for above-average total return over the next 12 months. Year to date, the shares are up nearly 7% (after a 40% drop in 2008), and while we expect near-term earnings to be restricted due to the downturn in the economy, we believe the company's cost-control efforts and its effective management of its power supply operations will leave it well positioned for an economic recovery.

► Risks to our recommendation and target price include a decline in the company's wholesale power margins, as well as weakness in the broader market and/or a reduction in the average P/E of the group as a whole.

► With the strong rebound in the shares, the dividend yield has declined from its 2009 peak of about 5.6% (reached in March) to about 4.3%. While this is below the recent peer average of about 4.9%, it is in line with the yields of other utility holding companies with large wholesale power operations. Our 12-month target price of $38 reflects an approximate peer P/E of 11.8X our EPS estimate for 2010.

Qualitative Risk Assessment

LOW	MEDIUM	HIGH

Our risk assessment reflects our view of the strong and steady cash flows from the regulated electric and gas utility operations of PSE&G, as well as the strong albeit less predictable earnings and cash flows from the non-regulated power generating operations. It also reflects what we see as a lowering of PEG's risk profile through the divestiture of non-core international investments.

Quantitative Evaluations

S&P Quality Ranking B+

D	C	B-	B	B+	A-	A	A+

Relative Strength Rank MODERATE

47

LOWEST = 1   HIGHEST = 99

Revenue/Earnings Data

Revenue (Million $)

	1Q	2Q	3Q	4Q	Year
2009	3,921	2,561	3,039	--	--
2008	3,803	2,561	3,718	3,262	13,322
2007	3,508	2,718	3,356	3,271	12,853
2006	3,461	2,556	3,212	2,935	12,164
2005	3,310	2,442	3,376	3,472	12,430
2004	3,221	2,290	2,747	2,731	10,996

Earnings Per Share ($)

2009	0.88	0.61	0.96	E0.67	E3.10
2008	0.85	-0.33	0.94	0.47	1.93
2007	0.64	0.56	0.96	0.44	2.59
2006	0.41	Nil	0.75	0.35	1.49
2005	0.59	0.21	0.53	0.45	1.76
2004	0.57	0.25	0.52	0.19	1.52

Fiscal year ended Dec. 31. Next earnings report expected: Early February. EPS Estimates based on S&P Operating Earnings; historical GAAP earnings are as reported.

Dividend Data (Dates: mm/dd Payment Date: mm/dd/yy)

Amount ($)	Date Decl.	Ex-Div. Date	Stk. of Record	Payment Date
0.333	02/17	03/06	03/10	03/31/09
0.333	04/21	06/05	06/09	06/30/09
0.333	07/21	09/04	09/09	09/30/09
0.333	11/17	12/07	12/09	12/31/09

Dividends have been paid since 1907. Source: Company reports.

Please read the Required Disclosures and Analyst Certification on the last page of this report.

The McGraw-Hill Companies

Public Service Enterprise Group Inc

STANDARD &POOR'S

Business Summary October 19, 2009

CORPORATE OVERVIEW. Headquartered in Newark, NJ, Public Service Enterprise Group has three primary operating units: Public Service Electric and Gas Co. - PSE&G ($364 million of net income in 2008), Power ($1.050 billion), and Energy Holdings (a loss of $403 million). The parent company and intersegment eliminations accounted for a loss of $28 million. PEG has sought to minimize its earnings and cash flow volatility through the divestiture of its international operations, and by entering into long-term contracts for most of its competitive wholesale power generation.

MARKET PROFILE. At the end of 2008, the company's New Jersey utility operations served about 2.1 million electric customers and 1.7 million natural gas customers. PSE&G earns income from the delivery of electricity and gas, with the cost of the gas passed through to ratepayers. In 2008, commercial customers accounted for 57% of total electric customers (36% of gas customers), residential 31% (60%), and industrial 12% (4%). As part of New Jersey's utility

deregulation, PSE&G transferred its power generating and gas supply operations to PEG's unregulated Power division in 2000 and 2002, respectively. Based on the proximity of its plants to PSE&G's customer base, Power has been able to win competitive bids for a significant portion of the utility's electricity supply obligations. Power's generating fleet, which had 13,576 megawatts (MW) of owned generating capacity as of December 31, 2008, is concentrated in the Pennsylvania, New Jersey and Maryland Interconnection (known as PJM), but it also has plants in Connecticut and New York. In addition to its electric business, Power provides PSE&G with all of the utility's gas supply needs under a contract that was extended from March 31, 2007, to March 31, 2012, and year to year thereafter.

Company Financials Fiscal Year Ended Dec. 31

Per Share Data ($)	2008	2007	2006	2005	2004	2003	2002	2001	2000	1999
Tangible Book Value	15.22	14.23	12.23	10.79	10.71	10.42	7.39	8.47	9.60	9.25
Earnings	1.93	2.59	1.49	1.76	1.52	1.86	1.00	1.84	1.78	1.65
S&P Core Earnings	1.85	2.59	1.92	1.70	1.49	2.02	1.53	1.58	NA	NA
Dividends	1.29	1.17	1.14	1.12	1.10	1.08	1.08	1.08	1.08	1.08
Payout Ratio	67%	45%	77%	64%	73%	58%	109%	59%	61%	66%
Prices:High	52.30	49.88	36.31	34.24	26.32	22.25	23.63	25.78	25.00	21.31
Prices:Low	22.09	32.16	29.50	24.66	19.05	16.05	10.00	18.44	12.84	16.00
P/E Ratio:High	27	19	24	20	17	12	24	14	14	13
P/E Ratio:Low	11	12	20	14	13	9	10	10	7	10

Income Statement Analysis (Million $)										
Revenue	13,322	12,853	12,164	12,430	10,996	11,116	8,390	9,815	6,848	6,497
Depreciation	792	783	832	748	719	527	571	522	362	536
Maintenance	NA	NA	NA	NA	NA	NA	NA	NA	NA	NA
Fixed Charges Coverage	4.18	4.10	2.73	2.55	2.21	2.43	2.38	2.46	2.88	3.20
Construction Credits	NA	NA	NA	NA	NA	NA	NA	NA	NA	NA
Effective Tax Rate	48.5%	44.5%	NM	38.7%	38.2%	35.3%	37.3%	NM	39.1%	43.8%
Net Income	983	1,319	752	858	721	852	416	763	764	723
S&P Core Earnings	945	1,316	967	834	708	925	638	656	NA	NA

Balance Sheet & Other Financial Data (Million $)										
Gross Property	20,818	19,310	18,851	18,896	19,121	17,406	16,562	14,886	11,968	11,156
Capital Expenditures	1,771	1,348	1,015	1,024	1,255	1,351	1,814	2,053	959	582
Net Property	14,433	13,275	13,002	13,336	13,750	12,422	11,449	10,064	7,702	7,078
Capitalization:Long Term Debt	8,085	8,742	10,450	11,359	13,005	13,025	12,391	11,061	6,505	5,783
Capitalization:% Long Term Debt	51.0	54.5	60.8	65.4	69.4	70.2	75.7	72.8	60.2	59.1
Capitalization:Preferred	Nil	Nil	Nil	Nil	Nil	Nil	Nil	Nil	Nil	Nil
Capitalization:% Preferred	Nil	Nil	Nil	Nil	Nil	Nil	Nil	Nil	Nil	Nil
Capitalization:Common	7,771	7,299	6,747	6,022	5,739	5,529	3,987	4,137	4,294	3,996
Capitalization:% Common	49.0	45.5	39.2	34.6	30.6	29.8	24.3	27.2	39.8	40.9
Total Capital	19,721	20,495	21,659	21,629	23,091	22,750	19,302	18,403	13,906	12,707
% Operating Ratio	87.3	85.0	78.7	88.6	87.5	86.5	78.8	76.9	79.6	80.4
% Earned on Net Property	18.9	23.3	15.1	15.9	14.9	17.3	14.3	21.3	18.9	20.4
% Return on Revenue	7.4	10.3	6.2	6.9	6.6	7.7	5.0	7.8	11.2	11.1
% Return on Invested Capital	7.8	9.3	9.3	7.6	6.9	8.1	9.3	9.6	10.8	9.5
% Return on Common Equity	13.0	18.8	11.8	14.6	12.8	18.1	10.2	18.8	18.4	15.9

Data as orig reptd.; bef. results of disc opers/spec. items. Per share data adj. for stk. divs.; EPS diluted. E-Estimated. NA-Not Available. NM-Not Meaningful. NR-Not Ranked. UR-Under Review.

Office: 80 Park Plaza, Newark, NJ 07102-4109.
Telephone: 973-430-7000.
Email: stkserv@pseg.com
Website: http://www.pseg.com

Chrmn, Pres & CEO: R. Izzo
EVP & CFO: C. Dorsa
EVP & General Counsel: R.E. Selover
Chief Acctg Officer & Cntlr: D.M. Dirisio

Treas: M.A. Plawner
Investor Contact: K.A. Lally
Board Members: A. R. Gamper, Jr., C. K. Harper, W. V. Hickey, R. Izzo, S. A. Jackson, D. Lilley, T. A. Renyi, H. C. Shin, R. J. Swift

Founded: 1985
Domicile: New Jersey
Employees: 9,849

The McGraw-Hill Companies

Pulte Homes Inc.

STANDARD &POOR'S

S&P Recommendation BUY ★★★★☆

Price	**12-Mo. Target Price**	**Investment Style**
$9.11 (as of Nov 27, 2009)	$14.00	Large-Cap Blend

GICS Sector Consumer Discretionary
Sub-Industry Homebuilding

Summary This builder of a wide range of single-family homes and condominiums throughout the country is the leading U.S. developer of active adult communities. It recently acquired rival Centex Corp.

Key Stock Statistics (Source S&P, Vickers, company reports)

52-Wk Range	$13.59– 7.71	S&P Oper. EPS 2009E	-6.50	Market Capitalization(B)	$3.465	Beta		0.93
Trailing 12-Month EPS	$-5.21	S&P Oper. EPS 2010E	-1.30	Yield (%)	Nil	S&P 3-Yr. Proj. EPS CAGR(%)		NM
Trailing 12-Month P/E	NM	P/E on S&P Oper. EPS 2009E	NM	Dividend Rate/Share	Nil	S&P Credit Rating		BB
$10K Invested 5 Yrs Ago	$3,265	Common Shares Outstg. (M)	380.4	Institutional Ownership (%)	74			

Price Performance

30-Week Mov. Avg. · · · · 10-Week Mov. Avg. – – **GAAP Earnings vs. Previous Year** Volume Above Avg. STARS
12-Mo. Target Price — Relative Strength — ▲ Up ▼ Down ► No Change Below Avg.

Options: ASE, CBOE, P, Ph

Analysis prepared by **Kenneth M. Leon, CPA** on November 04, 2009, when the stock traded at **$ 9.67**.

Qualitative Risk Assessment

LOW	MEDIUM	HIGH

Our risk assessment reflects execution risks for the new company in integrating the recently acquired Centex operations, which requires a full review of the combined home communities and the streamlining of sales and marketing and support services. While PHM enjoys greater scale post-merger, market risks remain should there be a delay in the recovery of the U.S. housing market.

Quantitative Evaluations

S&P Quality Ranking A-

D	C	B-	B	B+	A-	A	A+

Relative Strength Rank WEAK

16

LOWEST = 1 HIGHEST = 99

Highlights

► After further review of the August 2009 Centex merger and third quarter results reported by the new company, we have updated our financial model assumptions. Following an estimated 57% revenue decline in 2009 and with a contract backlog of $2.2 billion and 8,383 units, we forecast revenue growth of 10% in 2010 and 12% in 2011. With scale advantages over peers, we believe PHM can gain market share as the housing market recovers.

► We estimate that homebuilding gross margins will be -7.4% in 2009, 11.6% in 2010 and 16.5% in 2011, compared to 3.8% in 2008, assuming no asset writedowns. We expect SG&A costs to be 20% of revenues in 2009, compared to 15% in 2008, reverting to a more normalized 17% level in 2010 and 2011.

► Our 2009 net loss forecast includes asset charges booked in the first nine months, although with post-merger streamlining of the company, we believe new merger transition charges are likely for the next two quarters. We estimate losses per share of $6.50 for 2009, $1.30 for 2010, and $0.60 for 2011.

Investment Rationale/Risk

► In April 2009, PHM agreed to acquire rival Centex Corp. via a stock swap valued at around $1.3 billion, with CTX shareholders receiving 0.975 of a share of PHM common for each CTX share. The merger was finalized in August 2009, and we believe PHM can realize $250 million in operating cost savings and $100 million in interest cost savings from early debt retirements.

► Risks to our recommendation and target price include problems integrating Centex operations, further weakening of housing demand, a deepening recession, tighter mortgage lending, and future downward revisions of PHM's land inventory. Asset impairment charges and contract cancellations may also be significantly higher in coming quarters.

► We believe PHM has a strong balance sheet and ample cash to build new and existing communities from 176,727 total lots, of which 87% are owned and the rest are under contract option. Our 12-month target price of $14 is derived by applying a target price-to-book multiple of just over 1.3X -- toward the middle of the historical range, and below peers -- to our forward book value per share estimate of $10.60.

Revenue/Earnings Data

Revenue (Million $)

	1Q	2Q	3Q	4Q	Year
2009	583.9	678.6	1,091	--	--
2008	1,442	1,619	1,565	1,644	6,263
2007	1,871	2,021	2,472	2,899	9,257
2006	2,963	3,359	3,564	4,389	14,274
2005	2,518	3,251	3,794	5,132	14,695
2004	2,032	2,515	2,960	4,205	11,711

Earnings Per Share ($)

	1Q	2Q	3Q	4Q	Year
2009	-2.02	-0.74	-1.15	E-0.71	E-6.50
2008	-2.75	-0.62	-1.11	-1.33	-5.81
2007	-0.34	-2.01	-3.12	-3.54	-9.02
2006	1.01	0.94	0.74	-0.03	2.67
2005	0.83	1.16	1.45	2.03	5.47
2004	0.51	0.73	1.00	1.60	3.84

Fiscal year ended Dec. 31. Next earnings report expected: Early February. EPS Estimates based on S&P Operating Earnings; historical GAAP earnings are as reported.

Dividend Data (Dates: mm/dd Payment Date: mm/dd/yy)

Amount ($)	Date Decl.	Ex-Div. Date	Stk. of Record	Payment Date
0.040	11/24	12/18	12/22	01/02/09

Dividends have been paid since 1977. Source: Company reports.

Please read the Required Disclosures and Analyst Certification on the last page of this report.

The McGraw-Hill Companies

Pulte Homes Inc.

STANDARD &POOR'S

Business Summary November 04, 2009

CORPORATE OVERVIEW. As of September 30, 2009, after the merger with Centex, the new Pulte had 957 home communities, with 469 from the old Pulte and 488 from Centex. Average selling price was $253,000 as of September 30, 2009, compared to the old Pulte's averages of $284,000 in 2008 and $322,000 in 2007.

PHM targets buyers in nearly all home categories, but has recently concentrated its expansion efforts on affordable housing and on mature buyers (age 50 and over). In July 2001, it acquired Del Webb Corp., the leading U.S. builder of active adult communities, for a total of $1.9 billion in stock, cash, and the assumption of debt. Growth in this active adult segment and among first-time buyers, two groups that often prefer townhouses, condominiums or duplexes, helps to explain the decrease in single-family homes in PHM's product mix over the past five years.

CORPORATE STRATEGY. As of September 30, 2009, the new company controlled 176,727 lots, of which 153,618 were owned and 23,109 were under option agreements. Land is generally purchased after it is properly zoned and developed or is ready for development. In addition, PHM will dispose of owned land not required in the business through sales to appropriate end

users. Where the company develops land, its engages directly in many phases of the development process, including land and site planning, and obtaining environmental and other regulatory approvals, as well as constructing roads, sewers, water and drainage facilities, and other amenities.

To assist its home sales effort, PHM offers mortgage banking and title insurance services through Pulte Mortgage and other units mainly for the benefit of its domestic home buyers, but it also services the general public. In addition, it engages in the sale of loans and related servicing rights. Mortgage underwriting, processing and closing functions are centralized in Denver, CO, and Charlotte, NC, using a mortgage operations center concept.

In December 2005, the company sold Pulte Mexico, sharply reducing its international presence, and realized cash proceeds of $131.5 million. In the fourth quarter of 2005, PHM reported these results as discontinued operations.

Company Financials Fiscal Year Ended Dec. 31

Per Share Data ($)	2008	2007	2006	2005	2004	2003	2002	2001	2000	1999
Tangible Book Value	10.59	16.35	23.82	21.49	15.95	12.13	9.41	7.64	7.51	6.32
Cash Flow	-5.52	-8.69	2.99	5.70	4.01	2.61	1.92	1.67	1.38	1.09
Earnings	-5.81	-9.02	2.67	5.47	3.84	2.46	1.80	1.50	1.30	1.02
S&P Core Earnings	-5.80	-7.69	2.59	5.46	3.82	2.45	1.76	1.43	NA	NA
Dividends	0.16	0.16	0.16	0.09	0.10	0.04	0.04	0.04	0.04	0.04
Payout Ratio	NM	NM	6%	2%	3%	2%	2%	3%	3%	4%
Prices:High	23.24	35.56	44.70	48.23	32.50	24.71	14.94	12.56	11.25	7.81
Prices:Low	6.49	8.78	26.02	30.01	20.00	11.36	9.05	6.53	3.81	4.19
P/E Ratio:High	NM	NM	17	9	8	10	8	8	9	8
P/E Ratio:Low	NM	NM	10	5	5	5	5	4	3	4

Income Statement Analysis (Million $)	2008	2007	2006	2005	2004	2003	2002	2001	2000	1999
Revenue	6,263	9,263	14,274	14,695	11,711	9,049	7,472	5,382	4,159	3,730
Operating Income	-1,496	-1,800	2,678	244	1,587	997	746	601	429	350
Depreciation	74.0	83.9	83.7	62.0	46.3	40.2	29.8	32.9	14.2	13.5
Interest Expense	229	260	256	43.3	56.4	Nil	Nil	81.6	65.1	56.8
Pretax Income	-1,683	-2,497	1,083	2,277	1,601	996	729	492	355	286
Effective Tax Rate	NM	NM	36.3%	36.8%	37.6%	38.0%	39.0%	38.5%	38.5%	37.8%
Net Income	-1,473	-2,274	690	1,437	998	617	445	302	218	178
S&P Core Earnings	-1,469	-1,939	670	1,435	993	615	436	288	NA	NA

Balance Sheet & Other Financial Data (Million $)	2008	2007	2006	2005	2004	2003	2002	2001	2000	1999
Cash	1,655	1,060	551	1,002	315	404	613	72.1	184	51.7
Current Assets	NA	NA	NA	NA	NA	NA	NA	NA	NA	NA
Total Assets	7,708	10,226	13,177	13,048	10,407	8,063	6,888	5,714	2,886	2,597
Current Liabilities	NA	NA	NA	NA	NA	NA	NA	NA	NA	NA
Long Term Debt	3,143	3,478	3,538	3,387	2,737	1,962	1,913	1,738	678	526
Common Equity	2,836	4,320	6,577	5,957	4,522	3,448	2,760	2,277	1,248	1,093
Total Capital	5,978	7,798	10,115	9,352	7,274	5,418	4,674	4,015	1,926	1,619
Capital Expenditures	18.9	70.1	98.6	88.9	75.2	39.1	NA	NA	NA	NA
Cash Flow	-1,399	-2,191	773	1,499	1,044	657	474	335	233	192
Current Ratio	3.9	3.9	4.1	3.3	3.2	2.8	2.5	2.6	2.5	2.3
% Long Term Debt of Capitalization	52.6	44.6	35.0	36.2	37.6	36.2	40.9	43.3	35.2	32.5
% Net Income of Revenue	NM	NM	4.8	9.7	8.5	6.8	6.0	5.6	5.3	4.8
% Return on Assets	NM	NM	5.3	12.2	10.8	8.3	7.1	7.0	8.1	7.2
% Return on Equity	NM	NM	11.0	27.4	25.0	19.9	17.7	17.2	18.7	17.7

Data as orig reptd.; bef. results of disc opers/spec. items. Per share data adj. for stk. divs.; EPS diluted. E-Estimated. NA-Not Available. NM-Not Meaningful. NR-Not Ranked. UR-Under Review.

Office: 100 Bloomfield Hills Pkwy Ste 300, Bloomfield Hills, MI 48304-2950.
Telephone: 248-647-2750.
Website: http://www.pulte.com
Chrmn, Pres & CEO: R.J. Dugas, Jr.

Vice Chrmn: T.R. Eller
COO & EVP: S.C. Petruska
EVP & CFO: R.A. Cregg
SVP, Secy & General Counsel: S.M. Cook

Investor Contact: C. Boyd (248-647-2750)
Board Members: B. P. Anderson, R. J. Dugas, Jr., T. R. Eller, C. W. Grise, D. J. Kelly-Ennis, D. N. McCammon, C. W. Murchison, III, P. J. O'Leary, J. J. Postl, W. J. Pulte, B. W. Reznicek, T. M. Schoewe

Founded: 1969
Domicile: Michigan
Employees: 5,300

The McGraw-Hill Companies

QLogic Corp

STANDARD &POOR'S

| **S&P Recommendation** SELL ★ ☆ ☆ ☆ ☆ | **Price** $18.19 (as of Nov 27, 2009) | **12-Mo. Target Price** $17.00 | **Investment Style** Large-Cap Growth |

GICS Sector Information Technology
Sub-Industry Computer Storage & Peripherals

Summary This company supplies storage networking and network infrastructure solutions primarily to original equipment manufacturers and distributors.

Key Stock Statistics (Source S&P, Vickers, company reports)

52-Wk Range	$19.62–8.82	S&P Oper. EPS 2010E	0.89	Market Capitalization(B)	$2.085	Beta	1.56
Trailing 12-Month EPS	$0.67	S&P Oper. EPS 2011E	1.08	Yield (%)	Nil	S&P 3-Yr. Proj. EPS CAGR(%)	10
Trailing 12-Month P/E	27.2	P/E on S&P Oper. EPS 2010E	20.4	Dividend Rate/Share	Nil	S&P Credit Rating	NA
$10K Invested 5 Yrs Ago	$10,424	Common Shares Outstg. (M)	114.6	Institutional Ownership (%)	96		

Price Performance

Options: ASE, CBOE, P, Ph

Analysis prepared by **Jim Yin** on October 28, 2009, when the stock traded at **$ 18.19**.

Highlights

► We expect revenues to increase 11% in FY 11 (Mar.), following a 17% decline we see for FY 10. Our forecast is based on our outlook for a modest economic recovery in 2010. Besides a stronger economy, we believe enterprises have underinvested in data storage and network infrastructure solutions during the downturn. We also think sales will benefit from new products, in particular those related to Fibre Channel over Ethernet.

► We project gross margins of 65% and 66% in FY 10 and FY 11, respectively, down from 67% in FY 09. We believe QLGC will keep a tight control over employee headcount in FY 11. As a result, we see non-GAAP operating margins widening to 29% in FY 11 from a projected 26% for FY 10.

► We estimate operating EPS of $0.89 in FY 10 and $1.08 in FY 11, compared to $1.20 in FY 09, which excludes $0.35 in one-time items. Our estimates exclude $0.29 and $0.28 of amortization of intangibles and other one-time charges in FY 10 and FY 11, respectively. The lower earnings we see in the next two fiscal years reflects our projection for reduced revenues despite our outlook for an economic recovery in 2010.

Investment Rationale/Risk

► Our sell recommendation is based largely on valuation, following significant price appreciation. Even though we believe the global economy will recover in 2010, we project that QLGC will have lower revenues in FY 11 than in FY 09. In our view, QLGC lost market share during the economic downturn as customers sought vendors that provide more comprehensive solutions. We also think operating margins will be pressured due to higher development costs as the industry increases adoption of Fibre Channel over Ethernet technology.

► Risks to our recommendation and target price include an increase in end-market demand, lower-than-expected operating expenses, and a significant number of design wins from Tier 1 original equipment manufacturers.

► Our 12-month target price of $17 is based on a blend of our relative value and discounted cash flow (DCF) analyses. We apply an enterprise value-to-sales ratio of 2.6X, near the company's historical average, to our FY 11 sales estimate of $583 million to derive a $16 valuation. Our DCF model assumes a weighted average cost of capital of 12% and 3% terminal growth, yielding an intrinsic value of $18.

Qualitative Risk Assessment

| LOW | MEDIUM | HIGH |

Our risk assessment reflects the volatile nature of the data storage industry and the rapid pace of technological change. Offsetting these factors is our view of the company's significant market share and strong financial position.

Quantitative Evaluations

S&P Quality Ranking B+

| D | C | B- | B | B+ | A- | A | A+ |

Relative Strength Rank MODERATE
68
LOWEST = 1   HIGHEST = 99

Revenue/Earnings Data

Revenue (Million $)

	1Q	2Q	3Q	4Q	Year
2010	122.8	131.5	--	--	--
2009	168.4	171.2	163.7	130.6	633.9
2008	139.8	140.3	158.0	159.7	597.9
2007	136.7	145.3	157.6	147.1	586.7
2006	158.8	119.0	129.2	130.5	494.1
2005	129.8	134.6	150.3	157.2	571.9

Earnings Per Share ($)

	1Q	2Q	3Q	4Q	Year
2010	0.13	0.14	E0.24	E0.24	E0.89
2009	0.24	0.20	0.24	0.16	0.85
2008	0.12	0.16	0.23	0.17	0.67
2007	0.13	0.19	0.22	0.12	0.66
2006	0.23	0.17	0.20	0.19	0.70
2005	0.17	0.19	0.23	0.25	0.84

Fiscal year ended Mar. 31. Next earnings report expected: Late January. EPS Estimates based on S&P Operating Earnings; historical GAAP earnings are as reported.

Dividend Data

No cash dividends have been paid.

The McGraw-Hill Companies

QLogic Corp

STANDARD &POOR'S

Business Summary October 28, 2009

CORPORATE OVERVIEW. QLogic Corp. designs and develops storage networking infrastructure components sold to OEMs and distributors. QLGC produces host bus adapters (HBAs), fabric switches and management controller chips that provide the connectivity infrastructure for storage networks. The company serves customers with solutions based on various storage connectivity technologies, including Small Computer Systems Interface (SCSI), Internet SCSI (iSCSI), Fibre Channel, Fibre Channel over Ethernet (FCoE), Infiniband and intelligent Ethernet.

International revenues accounted for 52% of net revenues in FY 09 (Mar.), up from 49% in FY 08. IBM, Hewlett-Packard and Sun Microsystems each accounted for over 10% of FY 09 sales. The 10 largest customers accounted for 84% of FY 09 revenues, down from 85% in FY 08. QLGC works closely with independent hardware and software vendors, as well as with developers and integrators who create, test and evaluate complementary storage networking

products. Other key alliance partners include Cisco Systems, Dell, and EMC.

MARKET PROFILE. According to research firm IDC, growing server virtualization is driving an increase in storage area network (SAN) connectivity levels, partially offset by moderating server unit growth rates. IDC predicts worldwide HBA port shipments will increase from 4.5 million to 7.5 million between 2008 and 2013, resulting in a compound annual growth rate (CAGR) of 10.9% for the period. IDC expects single-port and multiport Fiber Channel (FC) HBA unit shipments to grow somewhat slower (a 2008-2013 CAGR of 4%), with 2013 shipments reaching 5.4 million.

Company Financials Fiscal Year Ended Mar. 31

Per Share Data ($)	2009	2008	2007	2006	2005	2004	2003	2002	2001	2000
Tangible Book Value	4.09	3.79	4.61	5.10	5.19	4.61	4.00	3.33	2.84	1.64
Cash Flow	1.22	1.01	0.83	0.81	0.92	0.77	0.62	0.44	0.42	0.38
Earnings	0.85	0.67	0.66	0.70	0.84	0.70	0.55	0.37	0.36	0.35
S&P Core Earnings	0.90	0.70	0.70	0.49	0.67	0.52	0.35	0.22	0.16	NA
Dividends	Nil	Nil	Nil	Nil	Nil	Nil	Nil	Nil	Nil	Nil
Payout Ratio	Nil	Nil	Nil	Nil	Nil	Nil	Nil	Nil	Nil	Nil
Calendar Year	2008	2007	2006	2005	2004	2003	2002	2001	2000	1999
Prices:High	20.21	22.46	22.94	21.83	26.57	29.36	28.55	49.56	101.63	41.88
Prices:Low	8.69	11.46	15.86	14.10	10.72	16.07	9.83	8.60	19.84	5.81
P/E Ratio:High	24	34	35	31	32	42	52	NM	NM	NM
P/E Ratio:Low	10	17	24	20	13	23	18	NM	NM	NM

Income Statement Analysis (Million $)										
Revenue	634	598	587	494	572	524	441	344	358	203
Operating Income	219	190	169	196	240	214	157	99.5	132	78.8
Depreciation	48.4	48.4	27.6	17.9	15.6	14.8	14.7	13.0	10.8	4.80
Interest Expense	Nil	Nil	Nil	Nil	Nil	Nil	Nil	Nil	Nil	0.02
Pretax Income	169	148	155	200	242	216	159	106	117	81.7
Effective Tax Rate	35.6%	34.9%	31.9%	39.2%	35.0%	38.0%	35.0%	33.0%	41.2%	34.0%
Net Income	109	96.2	105	122	158	134	103	70.7	68.8	54.0
S&P Core Earnings	115	100	112	85.6	126	99.4	67.0	42.1	30.5	NA

Balance Sheet & Other Financial Data (Million $)										
Cash	343	321	544	125	166	157	138	76.1	128	64.1
Current Assets	482	471	697	819	940	854	748	587	490	177
Total Assets	780	811	971	938	1,026	929	817	670	571	267
Current Liabilities	93.3	86.7	94.5	78.4	68.8	60.8	66.7	51.0	47.8	24.2
Long Term Debt	Nil	Nil	Nil	Nil	Nil	Nil	Nil	Nil	Nil	Nil
Common Equity	627	666	875	859	956	868	751	619	524	243
Total Capital	627	666	877	859	958	868	751	619	524	243
Capital Expenditures	30.7	30.0	31.7	28.3	25.7	22.3	15.7	14.5	16.7	40.0
Cash Flow	157	145	133	140	173	149	118	83.7	79.6	58.8
Current Ratio	5.2	5.4	7.4	10.5	13.7	14.0	11.2	11.5	10.3	7.3
% Long Term Debt of Capitalization	Nil	Nil	Nil	Nil	Nil	Nil	Nil	Nil	Nil	Nil
% Net Income of Revenue	17.2	16.1	18.0	24.7	27.6	25.5	23.5	20.5	19.2	26.6
% Return on Assets	13.7	10.8	11.0	12.4	16.1	15.3	13.9	11.4	14.2	24.5
% Return on Equity	16.8	12.5	12.2	13.4	17.3	16.5	15.1	12.4	15.6	27.3

Data as orig reptd.; bef. results of disc opers/spec. items. Per share data adj. for stk. divs.; EPS diluted. E-Estimated. NA-Not Available. NM-Not Meaningful. NR-Not Ranked. UR-Under Review.

Office: 26650 Aliso Viejo Pkwy, Aliso Viejo, CA 92656-2674.
Telephone: 949-389-6000.
Website: http://www.qlogic.com
Chrmn & CEO: H.K. Desai

COO: P.M. Mulligan
SVP, CFO & Chief Acctg Officer: S. Biddiscombe
Secy & General Counsel: M.L. Hawkins
Investor Contact: J.D. Herbert (949-389-6343)

Board Members: J. S. Birnbaum, H. K. Desai, J. R. Fiebiger, B. S. Iyer, K. B. Lewis, G. Wells

Founded: 1992
Domicile: Delaware
Employees: 1,031

QUALCOMM Inc

STANDARD &POOR'S

S&P Recommendation	**SELL** ★ ★ ☆ ☆ ☆	Price	12-Mo. Target Price	Investment Style
		$44.99 (as of Nov 27, 2009)	$40.00	Large-Cap Growth

GICS Sector Information Technology
Sub-Industry Communications Equipment

Summary This company focuses on developing products and services based on its advanced wireless broadband technology.

Key Stock Statistics (Source S&P, Vickers, company reports)

52-Wk Range	$48.72–29.34	S&P Oper. EPS 2010E	1.78	Market Capitalization(B)	$75.147	Beta	0.92
Trailing 12-Month EPS	$0.95	S&P Oper. EPS 2011E	NA	Yield (%)	1.51	S&P 3-Yr. Proj. EPS CAGR(%)	10
Trailing 12-Month P/E	47.4	P/E on S&P Oper. EPS 2010E	25.3	Dividend Rate/Share	$0.68	S&P Credit Rating	NA
$10K Invested 5 Yrs Ago	$11,594	Common Shares Outstg. (M)	1,670.3	Institutional Ownership (%)	82		

Price Performance

30-Week Mov. Avg. · · ·   10-Week Mov. Avg. - -   **GAAP Earnings vs. Previous Year**   Volume Above Avg. ▌▐▐ STARS
12-Mo. Target Price ▬   Relative Strength ▬   ▲ Up ▼ Down ▶ No Change   Below Avg. ▖▗▖ ★ ▬

Options: ASE, CBOE, P, Ph

Analysis prepared by **James Moorman, CFA** on November 10, 2009, when the stock traded at **$ 44.35**.

Qualitative Risk Assessment

LOW	**MEDIUM**	HIGH

We believe QCOM's intellectual property rights and strong service provider relations give it a solid position in the industry. With our view of its healthy cash flow, we think the company's cash balance can support potentially weaker demand from customers and litigation risks related to its CDMA patents.

Quantitative Evaluations

S&P Quality Ranking   **B**

D	C	B-	**B**	B+	A-	A	A+

Relative Strength Rank   **MODERATE**

64

LOWEST = 1   HIGHEST = 99

Revenue/Earnings Data

Revenue (Million $)

	1Q	2Q	3Q	4Q	Year
2009	2,517	2,455	2,753	2,690	10,416
2008	2,440	2,606	2,762	3,334	11,142
2007	2,019	2,221	2,325	2,306	8,871
2006	1,741	1,834	1,951	1,999	7,526
2005	1,390	1,365	1,358	1,560	5,673
2004	1,207	1,216	1,341	1,118	4,880

Earnings Per Share ($)

2009	0.20	-0.18	0.44	0.49	0.95
2008	0.46	0.47	0.45	0.52	1.90
2007	0.38	0.43	0.47	0.67	1.95
2006	0.36	0.34	0.37	0.36	1.44
2005	0.30	0.31	0.33	0.32	1.26
2004	0.25	0.26	0.29	0.23	1.03

Fiscal year ended Sep. 30. Next earnings report expected: Late January. EPS Estimates based on S&P Operating Earnings; historical GAAP earnings are as reported.

Highlights

► We forecast a 7.7% revenue increase for FY 10 (Sep.), following a 6.5% decline in FY 09 and a 26% rise in FY 08, inclusive of an unusually high royalty payment from Nokia in the fourth quarter of FY 08. We expect pressure on QCOM's chipset segment to abate following a period in which customers reduced orders to deplete inventories amid the macroeconomic slowdown. While we see stronger growth for its royalty business, we look for this to be tempered by a lower overall royalty rate.

► We expect growth in the WCDMA handset market, which supports QCOM's high-margin royalty business. We believe this will help margins remain stable, despite price declines, as more growth comes from emerging markets and royalty rates decline. We look for gross margins to remain flat at 69.5% in FY 10, versus 69.5% in FY 09 and 69.4% in FY 08, as handset and chipset sales begin to reaccelerate, but are offset by lower chipset prices and a lower royalty rate.

► We estimate that EPS will increase to $1.78 in FY 10, following $1.52 in FY 09 (excluding $1 billion of one-time charges, including the settlement charge with Broadcom) and $1.91 in FY 08.

Investment Rationale/Risk

► Regarding our earnings outlook, we believe QCOM could see increasing chipset sales throughout the year as the economy begins to improve, but we are still cautious as the consumer may not be out of the woods yet. While we think QCOM's investments in R&D will support longer-term prospects, we think this will further limit earnings over the next 12 months. By our analysis, QCOM has a strong balance sheet and will continue to generate sizable cash flow, but with near-term challenges and a premium valuation to peers, our recommendation is sell.

► Risks to our recommendation and target price include stronger demand in the replacement rate expected for more advanced CDMA handsets; higher selling prices for handsets; a faster recovery in orders to replace low inventory levels; and share repurchases.

► Applying a multiple of 22.5X to our FY 10 EPS estimate -- a premium to peers, reflecting QCOM's above-average margins and cash flow generation -- we arrive at our 12-month target price of $40.

Dividend Data (Dates: mm/dd Payment Date: mm/dd/yy)

Amount ($)	Date Decl.	Ex-Div. Date	Stk. of Record	Payment Date
0.160	01/16	02/25	02/27	03/27/09
0.170	04/08	05/27	05/29	06/26/09
0.170	07/08	08/26	08/28	09/25/09
0.170	10/02	11/23	11/25	12/23/09

Dividends have been paid since 2003. Source: Company reports.

Please read the Required Disclosures and Analyst Certification on the last page of this report.

The McGraw-Hill Companies

QUALCOMM Inc

Business Summary November 10, 2009

CORPORATE OVERVIEW. QUALCOMM Inc. is organized by these operating segments: CDMA technology (QCT), technology licensing (QTL), wireless and Internet (QWI), and strategic initiatives (QSI). The equipment and services unit, which is mostly from QCT, accounted for about 66% of total sales in the fourth quarter of FY 09 (Sep.) by providing integrated circuits and system software solutions to top wireless handset and infrastructure manufacturers. QCOM uses a fabless business model, employing several independent semiconductor foundries to manufacture its semiconductor products. Approximately 91 million model station modem (MSM) integrated circuits were sold during the fourth quarter of FY 09, compared to approximately 86 million a year earlier. QCOM expects to sell between 89 million to 92 million MSM circuits in the first quarter of FY 10 as the contraction in channel inventory begins to abate.

The license and royalty fee segment (QTL) accounted for about 34% of total sales, with 83% operating margins. QCOM holds a number of patents related to CDMA, and derives royalties from licensing its technology. Royalties are paid when manufacturers earn revenue from the sale of CDMA-based equipment, including CDMA and WCDMA handsets made by customers Samsung, LG Electronics, Motorola, and others. QCOM expects 20% growth in CDMA

and WCDMA handsets in calendar 2010 with the majority from of the gains from WCDMA handsets. In September 2009, QCOM estimated that the average selling price of a handset was $200 in FY 09, and projected it to decline to $189 in FY 10, limiting the growth of its royalty revenues.

LEGAL/REGULATORY ISSUES. QCOM has been involved in various legal issues involving patents on its chipsets and on competitors' chipsets. The company's multiple disputes with Nokia included litigation over Nokia's obligation to pay royalties for the use of certain of QCOM's patents. Without a license contract with QCOM, Nokia had opted to cancel its CDMA-related handset division. However, in July 2008, QCOM and Nokia signed a new 15-year agreement covering various second, third and fourth-generation technology standards that we believe keeps QCOM's royalty pipeline active beyond supporting current handset offerings. In addition to a lump-sum cash payment that helped boost fourth-quarter FY 08 revenues by $580 million, Nokia returned to being a royalty customer of QCOM in late FY 08.

Company Financials Fiscal Year Ended Sep. 30

Per Share Data ($)	2009	2008	2007	2006	2005	2004	2003	2002	2001	2000
Tangible Book Value	9.44	8.05	8.82	7.37	6.43	5.69	4.54	2.77	2.82	3.14
Cash Flow	NA	2.18	2.18	1.60	1.38	1.13	0.62	0.47	-0.14	0.57
Earnings	0.95	1.90	1.95	1.44	1.26	1.03	0.51	0.22	-0.36	0.43
S&P Core Earnings	1.64	2.05	1.86	1.40	1.03	0.83	0.74	0.34	-0.68	NA
Dividends	0.66	0.60	0.54	0.42	0.32	0.19	0.09	Nil	Nil	Nil
Payout Ratio	69%	32%	28%	29%	25%	18%	17%	Nil	Nil	Nil
Prices:High	48.72	56.88	47.72	53.01	46.60	44.99	27.43	26.67	44.69	100.00
Prices:Low	32.64	28.16	35.23	32.76	32.08	26.67	14.79	11.61	19.16	25.75
P/E Ratio:High	51	30	24	37	37	44	54	NM	NM	NM
P/E Ratio:Low	34	15	18	23	25	26	29	NM	NM	NM

Income Statement Analysis (Million $)	2009	2008	2007	2006	2005	2004	2003	2002	2001	2000
Revenue	10,416	11,142	8,871	7,526	5,673	4,880	3,971	3,040	2,680	3,197
Operating Income	NA	4,200	3,266	2,962	2,586	2,266	1,684	1,068	877	1,105
Depreciation	635	456	383	272	200	163	180	394	320	244
Interest Expense	NA	22.0	Nil	Nil	3.00	2.00	30.7	25.7	10.2	4.92
Pretax Income	2,076	3,826	3,626	3,156	2,809	2,313	1,285	461	-426	1,197
Effective Tax Rate	23.3%	17.4%	8.90%	21.7%	23.7%	25.4%	35.6%	22.0%	NM	44.0%
Net Income	1,592	3,160	3,303	2,470	2,143	1,725	827	360	-531	670
S&P Core Earnings	2,744	3,407	3,148	2,397	1,733	1,395	610	274	-512	NA

Balance Sheet & Other Financial Data (Million $)	2009	2008	2007	2006	2005	2004	2003	2002	2001	2000
Cash	11,069	6,411	6,581	5,721	6,548	5,982	4,561	2,795	2,283	1,772
Current Assets	NA	11,723	8,821	7,049	7,791	7,227	5,949	3,941	3,055	2,730
Total Assets	27,445	24,563	18,495	15,208	12,479	10,820	8,822	6,510	5,747	6,063
Current Liabilities	NA	2,291	2,258	1,422	1,070	894	808	675	521	472
Long Term Debt	NA	142	Nil	Nil	Nil	Nil	123	94.3	Nil	Nil
Common Equity	20,316	17,944	15,835	13,406	11,119	9,664	7,599	5,392	4,890	5,516
Total Capital	20,316	18,087	15,835	13,406	11,119	9,664	7,722	5,530	4,896	5,563
Capital Expenditures	761	1,397	818	685	576	332	231	142	114	163
Cash Flow	NA	3,616	3,686	2,742	2,343	1,888	1,007	754	-211	914
Current Ratio	4.5	5.1	3.9	5.0	7.3	8.1	7.4	5.8	5.9	5.8
% Long Term Debt of Capitalization	Nil	0.8	Nil	Nil	Nil	Nil	1.6	1.7	Nil	Nil
% Net Income of Revenue	15.3	28.4	37.2	32.8	37.8	35.3	20.8	11.8	NM	21.0
% Return on Assets	6.1	14.7	19.6	17.8	18.4	17.6	10.8	5.9	NM	12.6
% Return on Equity	8.3	18.7	22.5	20.1	20.6	20.0	12.7	7.1	NM	16.0

Data as orig reptd.; bef. results of disc opers/spec. items. Per share data adj. for stk. divs.; EPS diluted. E-Estimated. NA-Not Available. NM-Not Meaningful. NR-Not Ranked. UR-Under Review.

Office: 5775 Morehouse Drive, San Diego, CA 92121-1714.
Telephone: 858-587-1121.
Email: ir@qualcomm.com
Website: http://www.qualcomm.com

Chrmn & CEO: P.E. Jacobs
Pres: S.R. Altman
COO & EVP: L.J. Lauer
EVP, CFO & Chief Acctg Officer: W.E. Keitel

EVP & CTO: R. Padovani
Investor Contact: J. Gilbert (858-658-4813)
Board Members: B. T. Alexander, S. M. Bennett, D. G. Cruickshank, R. V. Dittamore, T. Horton, I. M. Jacobs, P. E. Jacobs, R. E. Kahn, S. Lansing, D. A. Nelles, P. M. Sacerdote, B. Scowcroft, M. I. Stern

Founded: 1985
Domicile: Delaware
Employees: 16,100

Quanta Services Inc.

STANDARD &POOR'S

S&P Recommendation HOLD ★★★☆☆

Price	**12-Mo. Target Price**	**Investment Style**
$18.96 (as of Nov 27, 2009)	$23.00	Large-Cap Blend

GICS Sector Industrials
Sub-Industry Construction & Engineering

Summary This company provides specialized contracting services, offering end-to-end network solutions to the electric power, gas, telecommunications and cable television industries.

Key Stock Statistics (Source S&P, Vickers, company reports)

52-Wk Range	$25.80–14.00	S&P Oper. EPS 2009**E**	0.72	Market Capitalization(B)	$3.966	Beta	1.42
Trailing 12-Month EPS	$0.84	S&P Oper. EPS 2010**E**	1.19	Yield (%)	Nil	S&P 3-Yr. Proj. EPS CAGR(%)	21
Trailing 12-Month P/E	22.6	P/E on S&P Oper. EPS 2009**E**	26.3	Dividend Rate/Share	Nil	S&P Credit Rating	NR
$10K Invested 5 Yrs Ago	$24,560	Common Shares Outstg. (M)	209.8	Institutional Ownership (%)	96		

Price Performance

30-Week Mov. Avg. · · · ·   10-Week Mov. Avg. – –   **GAAP Earnings vs. Previous Year**   **Volume** Above Avg.   STARS
12-Mo. Target Price —   Relative Strength —   ▲ Up ▼ Down ► No Change   Below Avg.   ★

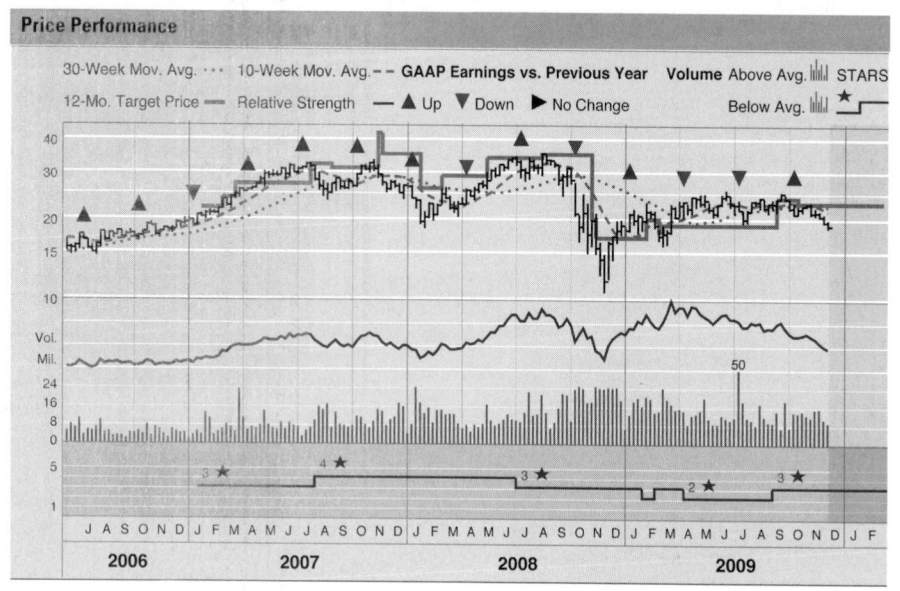

Options: ASE, CBOE, P, Ph

Analysis prepared by **Mathew Christy, CFA** on November 10, 2009, when the stock traded at **$ 21.19**.

Highlights

► We expect sales to decline nearly 14% in 2009, as weaker spending by gas, telecom and cable companies should more than offset improved utility spending later in the year. Our estimates are also based on PWR's 12-month backlog of $2 billion, and total backlog of $5.5 billion, reflecting recent major contract wins including Northeast Utilities, Nebraska Public Power and Light, and Duke Power. In addition, we base our estimates on continued contract wins, such as the recent National Grid award. In 2010, we see revenues advancing 45% on organic revenue growth and acquisitions.

► We estimate that PWR will experience a 0.8% improvement in 2009 gross margin, as we expect weaker margins in the first half to be offset by improved margin results in the second half. However, we expect higher overhead expenses to lead to flat operating margins. In 2010, we see somewhat better operating margins on higher operating leverage.

► On a 39% expected tax rate in both years, we estimate EPS of $0.72 for 2009 and $1.19 for 2010.

Investment Rationale/Risk

► We expect PWR to experience lower results in 2009, due to a contraction in capital spending by customers. In addition, we believe benefits from the long-term trend toward increased spending to maintain and upgrade aging transmission and distribution networks will take many years, given regulatory constraints. However, we expect much higher revenue and earnings in 2010 on improving end-market demand and acquisitions.

► Risks to our recommendation and target price include lower-than-expected capital spending levels by utilities and gas, telecommunications and cable companies, and a prolonged downturn in the economy.

► Our target price of $23 is based on two valuation metrics. Our discounted cash flow model, which assumes a 3% perpetuity growth rate and a 10.9% discount rate, indicates an intrinsic value of $23. In terms of relative valuation, we apply a target EV/EBITDA multiple of 8.3X to our 2010 EBITDA estimate, ahead of peers due to the company's historical premium valuation, and this also implies a value of $23.

Qualitative Risk Assessment

LOW	MEDIUM	**HIGH**

Our risk assessment reflects PWR's dependence on just a few industries, erratic spending patterns of the company's major customers, the lack of minimum service volumes in most contracts, the ability of customers to terminate agreements on short notice, the volatility of the storm restoration service business, and a large portion of revenue derived from fixed-price agreements.

Quantitative Evaluations

S&P Quality Ranking   B-

D	C	**B-**	B	B+	A-	A	A+

Relative Strength Rank   **WEAK**

15

LOWEST = 1   HIGHEST = 99

Revenue/Earnings Data

Revenue (Million $)

	1Q	2Q	3Q	4Q	Year
2009	738.5	813.4	780.8	--	--
2008	844.4	960.9	1,053	921.5	3,780
2007	574.9	557.6	655.9	879.0	2,656
2006	496.5	514.1	528.5	592.0	2,131
2005	372.5	439.3	523.3	523.5	1,859
2004	355.0	389.2	463.1	419.2	1,627

Earnings Per Share ($)

	1Q	2Q	3Q	4Q	Year
2009	0.11	0.17	0.32	E0.23	E0.72
2008	0.14	0.22	0.29	0.24	0.88
2007	0.23	0.17	0.30	0.18	0.87
2006	0.07	0.14	0.17	-0.26	0.15
2005	-0.04	0.03	0.11	0.15	0.25
2004	-0.10	-0.03	0.04	0.02	-0.08

Fiscal year ended Dec. 31. Next earnings report expected: Late February. EPS Estimates based on S&P Operating Earnings; historical GAAP earnings are as reported.

Dividend Data

No cash dividends have been paid.

Please read the Required Disclosures and Analyst Certification on the last page of this report.

The McGraw-Hill Companies

Quanta Services Inc.

STANDARD &POOR'S

Business Summary November 10, 2009

CORPORATE OVERVIEW. Quanta Services, Inc. (PWR) is a provider of specialty contracting services that designs, installs and maintains the infrastructure and networks for three primary industries: electric power and gas, telecommunications and cable television, and governmental and commercial entities. PWR had over 14,000 employees in 2008, of which approximately 45% were covered by collective bargaining agreements, primarily with the International Brotherhood of Electrical Workers (IBEW). The company believes it is the largest contractor serving the transmission and distribution sector of the U.S. electric utility industry. The electric power and gas network services segment (78% of PWR's 2008 revenues) installs, repairs and maintains electric power distribution networks and transmission lines with capacity up to 765,000 volts. The telecommunications and cable network segment (14%) designs, installs and maintains fiber optic, coaxial and copper cable for video, data and voice transmission, and builds wireless communications towers and installs switching systems for telecommunications carriers. The remaining revenues (8%) came from ancillary services such as inside electrical wiring, intelligent traffic networks, cable and control systems for light rail lines, airports and highways, and specialty rock trenching, directional boring and road milling for industrial, commercial and governmental customers, along with PWR's dark fiber leasing revenue.

MARKET PROFILE. We think that longer-term demand for infrastructure services in the electric, gas, telecom and cable industries is powered by the need to maintain and upgrade networks, while keeping costs low by outsourcing these services to third parties. Due to the Energy Policy Act of 2005 and the American Recovery and Reinvestment Act of 2009, which both promote investment in aging U.S. energy infrastructure, we expect many utilities to continue spending on the upgrade of their power transmission and distribution networks. However, we expect the downturn in the economy and the lack of available credit to dampen current demand dynamics, offsetting some of the positive aspects described above. For instance, several large telecom customers, including Verizon and AT&T, have slowed spending on their fiber optic build-out initiatives such as fiber to the premises (FTTP) and fiber to the node (FTTN), while the utility industry reduces or defers capital expenditures that were slated for 2009.

Company Financials Fiscal Year Ended Dec. 31

Per Share Data ($)	2008	2007	2006	2005	2004	2003	2002	2001	2000	1999
Tangible Book Value	5.87	4.01	3.36	2.67	2.34	2.35	3.05	2.79	2.76	2.41
Cash Flow	1.39	1.24	0.63	0.73	0.45	0.23	-1.41	2.10	2.12	1.58
Earnings	0.88	0.87	0.15	0.25	-0.08	-0.30	-2.26	1.10	1.42	1.00
S&P Core Earnings	0.88	0.88	0.61	0.26	-0.09	-0.30	-1.91	0.83	NA	NA
Dividends	Nil	Nil	Nil	Nil	Nil	Nil	Nil	Nil	Nil	Nil
Payout Ratio	Nil	Nil	Nil	Nil	Nil	Nil	Nil	Nil	Nil	Nil
Prices:High	35.39	33.42	20.05	14.97	9.52	9.87	18.90	37.50	63.13	29.58
Prices:Low	10.56	18.66	12.24	7.18	4.83	2.80	1.75	9.94	17.92	13.42
P/E Ratio:High	40	38	NM	60	NM	NM	NM	34	44	30
P/E Ratio:Low	12	21	NM	29	NM	NM	NM	9	13	13

Income Statement Analysis (Million $)										
Revenue	3,780	2,656	2,131	1,859	1,627	1,643	1,751	2,015	1,793	926
Operating Income	403	250	189	124	70.2	83.1	71.6	273	308	169
Depreciation	114	74.7	56.2	55.4	60.4	60.1	60.6	79.4	57.3	35.2
Interest Expense	17.5	21.5	26.8	23.9	25.1	31.8	35.9	36.1	25.7	15.2
Pretax Income	282	167	65.1	52.2	-12.6	-53.1	-194	157	200	103
Effective Tax Rate	40.8%	20.5%	73.2%	43.4%	NM	NM	NM	45.4%	47.0%	47.6%
Net Income	167	133	17.5	29.6	-9.19	-35.0	-174	85.8	106	53.9
S&P Core Earnings	167	134	74.1	30.3	-10.2	-33.9	-96.4	64.5	NA	NA

Balance Sheet & Other Financial Data (Million $)										
Cash	438	407	384	304	266	180	27.9	6.29	17.3	10.8
Current Assets	1,381	1,305	991	831	700	676	529	577	602	335
Total Assets	3,555	3,388	1,639	1,555	1,460	1,466	1,365	2,043	1,874	1,160
Current Liabilities	452	757	334	258	221	199	212	242	253	171
Long Term Debt	144	144	414	450	464	501	386	500	491	200
Common Equity	2,658	2,185	729	704	663	663	612	1,207	1,069	757
Total Capital	2,803	2,430	1,143	1,154	1,128	1,164	1,153	1,801	1,560	957
Capital Expenditures	186	128	48.5	42.6	39.0	35.9	49.5	85.0	89.6	61.1
Cash Flow	281	208	73.7	85.0	51.2	25.1	-114	164	162	88.8
Current Ratio	3.1	1.7	3.0	3.2	3.2	3.4	2.5	2.4	2.4	2.0
% Long Term Debt of Capitalization	5.1	5.9	36.2	39.0	41.2	43.0	33.5	27.8	31.5	20.9
% Net Income of Revenue	4.4	5.0	0.8	1.6	NM	NM	NM	4.3	5.9	5.8
% Return on Assets	4.8	5.3	1.1	2.0	NM	NM	NM	4.4	7.0	7.2
% Return on Equity	6.9	9.1	2.4	4.3	NM	NM	NM	7.5	11.5	11.6

Data as orig reptd.; bef. results of disc opers/spec. items. Per share data adj. for stk. divs.; EPS diluted. E-Estimated. NA-Not Available. NM-Not Meaningful. NR-Not Ranked. UR-Under Review.

Office: 1360 Post Oak Boulevard, Houston, TX 77056.
Telephone: 713-629-7600.
Email: headquarters@quantaservices.com
Website: http://www.quantaservices.com

Chrmn & CEO: J.R. Colson
Pres & COO: J.F. O'Neil, III
CFO: J.H. Haddox
Chief Admin Officer: D.B. Miller

Chief Acctg Officer: D.A. Jensen
Investor Contact: K. Dennard (713-529-6600)
Board Members: J. R. Ball, J. R. Colson, J. M. Conaway, R. R. DiSibio, V. D. Foster, B. Fried, L. Golm, W. F. Jackman, B. Ranck, J. R. Wilson, P. Wood, III

Founded: 1997
Domicile: Delaware
Employees: 14,751

The McGraw-Hill Companies

Questar Corp

STANDARD &POOR'S

S&P Recommendation HOLD ★★★☆☆

Price	12-Mo. Target Price	Investment Style
$39.35 (as of Nov 27, 2009)	$43.00	Large-Cap Growth

GICS Sector Utilities
Sub-Industry Gas Utilities

Summary This integrated natural gas holding company is engaged in gas and oil exploration, energy marketing, gas gathering, transportation and storage, and retail gas distribution.

Key Stock Statistics (Source S&P, Vickers, company reports)

52-Wk Range	$43.46– 24.26	S&P Oper. EPS 2009E	2.50	Market Capitalization(B)	$6.861	Beta	0.84
Trailing 12-Month EPS	$2.07	S&P Oper. EPS 2010E	2.40	Yield (%)	1.32	S&P 3-Yr. Proj. EPS CAGR(%)	-8
Trailing 12-Month P/E	19.0	P/E on S&P Oper. EPS 2009E	15.7	Dividend Rate/Share	$0.52	S&P Credit Rating	NR
$10K Invested 5 Yrs Ago	$16,359	Common Shares Outstg. (M)	174.4	Institutional Ownership (%)	75		

Price Performance

30-Week Mov. Avg. · · · 10-Week Mov. Avg. – – GAAP Earnings vs. Previous Year Volume Above Avg. STARS
12-Mo. Target Price — Relative Strength — ▲ Up ▼ Down ▶ No Change Below Avg.

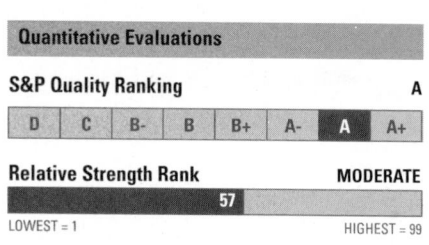

Options: ASE, CBOE, Ph

Analysis prepared by **Christopher B. Muir** on November 10, 2009, when the stock traded at **$ 42.66**.

Highlights

► We estimate a 15% revenue drop in 2009 on lower commodity prices and utility volumes. We believe STR's E&P segment will face lower prices, partly offset by higher production volumes. We think the pipeline will be hurt by a sharp decline in commodity prices, despite its continuing shift to fee based contracts. We think declines in utility revenues will reflect lower gas prices. We see revenues rising 0.2% in 2010, helped by higher volumes.

► We forecast operating margins of 29.9% in 2009 and 27.6% in 2010, versus 33.6% in 2008. In 2009, we see most per-revenue non-cost of sales expenses rising, partly offset by lower per-revenue cost of sales and abandonment costs. We see pretax profit margins falling faster to 26.5% in 2009 and 23.4% in 2010, from 31.0%, as we expect rising interest expense in both years.

► We estimate operating EPS of $2.50, excluding $0.01 in nonrecurring gains, in 2009, versus 2008's $3.65, which excludes $0.24 in nonrecurring gains. Our 2010 EPS forecast is $2.40. Mark-to-market loss estimates for 2008, 2009 and 2010 of $0.29, $0.33, and $0.06 are included above.

Investment Rationale/Risk

► STR has posted steady production gains through an aggressive drilling program at its Rockies and Midcontinent assets. In 2008, production increased 22% to 171.4 billion cubic feet equivalent (Bcfe), and we estimate a 7% rise for 2009 to 183 Bcfe and a 15% gain in 2010 to 210 Bcfe. In a higher price commodity environment, we expect strong drilling activity by others to help drive growth at STR's gas gathering and processing operations, where we see increasing fee-based volumes. We like STR's strong hedging program, which we believe will significantly reduce exposure to oil and gas price changes.

► Risks to our recommendation and target price include a prolonged drop in natural gas and oil prices, unusually mild winter weather, weaker-than-expected economic growth, and sharply higher interest rates.

► The stock recently traded at 17.6X our 2010 EPS estimate, a 24% premium to gas utility peers. Our 12-month target price of $43 is 17.9X our 2010 estimate, or a 14% premium to our peer target. We think this premium is warranted by our expectation of faster than peers EPS growth, partly offset by higher EPS volatility.

Qualitative Risk Assessment

LOW	MEDIUM	HIGH

Our risk assessment is based on our view that the company's higher risk exploration and production and energy marketing operations are balanced by its lower-risk regulated gas transmission and distribution businesses.

Quantitative Evaluations

S&P Quality Ranking   A

D	C	B-	B	B+	A-	A	A+

Relative Strength Rank   MODERATE

57

LOWEST = 1   HIGHEST = 99

Revenue/Earnings Data

Revenue (Million $)

	1Q	2Q	3Q	4Q	Year
2009	919.1	613.1	599.8	--	--
2008	1,001	825.8	760.0	878.8	3,465
2007	872.1	556.7	497.4	800.4	2,727
2006	911.4	596.2	555.1	772.9	2,836
2005	680.3	520.2	582.9	941.5	2,725
2004	563.6	369.5	360.2	608.1	1,901

Earnings Per Share ($)

2009	0.38	0.44	0.56	E1.12	E2.50
2008	1.05	0.98	1.16	0.69	3.88
2007	0.86	0.64	0.64	0.74	2.89
2006	0.79	0.52	0.54	0.70	2.54
2005	0.55	0.35	0.38	0.60	1.87
2004	0.45	0.25	0.22	0.43	1.34

Fiscal year ended Dec. 31. Next earnings report expected: Mid February. EPS Estimates based on S&P Operating Earnings; historical GAAP earnings are as reported.

Dividend Data (Dates: mm/dd Payment Date: mm/dd/yy)

Amount ($)	Date Decl.	Ex-Div. Date	Stk. of Record	Payment Date
0.125	02/10	02/18	02/20	03/16/09
0.125	05/19	05/27	05/29	06/15/09
0.125	08/11	08/19	08/21	09/14/09
0.130	10/27	11/18	11/20	12/14/09

Dividends have been paid since 1935. Source: Company reports.

The McGraw-Hill Companies

Questar Corp

STANDARD &POOR'S

Business Summary November 10, 2009

CORPORATE OVERVIEW. Questar Corp. (STR) is a natural gas energy entity operating three divisions: Questar Market Resources (QMR), Questar Gas Company (QGC), and Questar Pipeline Company (QPC). QMR, which is engaged in natural gas and oil exploration and production (E&P), energy marketing, gas gathering and processing services, contributed 86% of net income in 2008; QGC, which distributes natural gas as a public utility in Utah, southwestern Wyoming and a small portion of southeastern Idaho, contributed 6%; and QPC, an interstate pipeline company that provides natural gas transportation and underground storage services in Utah, Wyoming and Colorado, contributed 8%.

CORPORATE STRATEGY. STR's integrated model spans the entire natural gas value chain. The unregulated QMR businesses are the primary growth drivers for STR. The company believes these businesses -- which include E&P, gas gathering, and processing services -- have the potential to offer higher returns than the regulated utility and pipeline operations. QMR's hedging strategy attempts to smooth out the effects of commodity price peaks and valleys on earnings. QMR also says that it is more likely to make acquisitions and reduce hedging activity when commodity prices are low. STR's properties in the Rockies and mid-continent are expected to be a major contributor to growth. The utility and pipeline operations are less sensitive to commodity prices and

help fund dividend payouts. QPC has a role of eliminating pipeline bottlenecks within QMR's Rockies basins. It is also investing in a $5.0 billion pipeline to bring gas from the Rockies to Chicago.

MARKET PROFILE. QMR operates E&P properties, primarily natural gas, in the Rockies region of Wyoming, Utah and Colorado, and the Midcontinent region of Oklahoma, Texas and Louisiana. It has reported an estimated 2,218 Bcfe of proved reserves, with 72% of the proved reserves in the Rockies and the remainder in the Midcontinent region. As of 2008, QMR had developed 57% of the proved reserves, with most of the undeveloped reserves in the Pinedale Anticline property. Wexpro, a division of QMR, develops certain properties owned by QGC, and had proved reserves of 674 Bcfe as of year-end 2008. Wexpro charges the utility for costs plus a specified return, which averaged 19.9% (after tax) during 2008. Gas Management owns 1,598 miles of gathering pipelines in Utah, Wyoming and Colorado. Energy Trading also owns an underground storage reservoir in Wyoming.

Company Financials Fiscal Year Ended Dec. 31

Per Share Data ($)	2008	2007	2006	2005	2004	2003	2002	2001	2000	1999
Tangible Book Value	19.38	14.51	12.43	8.60	8.03	7.06	6.41	6.07	6.01	5.69
Cash Flow	7.03	5.05	4.34	3.34	2.66	3.41	2.21	1.90	1.85	1.43
Earnings	3.88	2.88	2.54	1.87	1.34	1.07	1.04	0.97	0.97	0.60
S&P Core Earnings	3.56	2.93	2.49	1.88	1.37	1.08	0.77	0.82	NA	NA
Dividends	0.49	0.49	0.47	0.45	0.43	0.39	0.36	0.35	0.34	0.34
Payout Ratio	13%	17%	18%	24%	32%	37%	35%	36%	35%	56%
Prices:High	74.87	58.75	45.51	44.80	26.06	17.75	14.73	16.88	15.94	9.97
Prices:Low	20.66	37.98	33.69	23.37	16.91	13.02	9.01	9.29	6.78	7.38
P/E Ratio:High	19	20	18	24	20	17	14	17	16	17
P/E Ratio:Low	5	13	13	12	13	12	9	10	7	12

Income Statement Analysis (Million $)										
Revenue	3,465	2,727	2,836	2,725	1,901	1,463	1,201	1,439	1,266	924
Operating Income	1,740	1,223	1,156	841	646	557	524	482	453	180
Depreciation	554	380	316	256	226	394	194	152	142	138
Interest Expense	120	80.2	73.6	69.3	68.4	70.7	81.1	64.8	63.5	53.9
Pretax Income	1,071	798	700	514	359	282	262	246	242	147
Effective Tax Rate	35.3%	36.4%	36.5%	36.6%	36.1%	36.4%	34.8%	35.8%	35.3%	32.6%
Net Income	684	507	444	326	229	179	171	158	157	98.8
S&P Core Earnings	628	516	438	327	234	182	125	132	NA	NA

Balance Sheet & Other Financial Data (Million $)										
Cash	23.9	14.2	24.6	13.4	3.68	13.9	21.6	11.3	14.8	45.0
Current Assets	1,185	659	753	756	480	345	280	344	427	239
Total Assets	8,636	5,944	5,065	4,357	3,647	3,309	3,068	3,236	2,539	2,238
Current Liabilities	1,132	999	679	874	544	483	301	781	535	324
Long Term Debt	2,079	1,021	1,022	983	933	950	1,145	997	715	735
Common Equity	3,418	2,578	2,206	1,550	1,440	1,261	1,139	1,081	991	926
Total Capital	6,861	4,542	3,992	3,157	2,906	2,666	2,676	2,422	1,971	1,878
Capital Expenditures	2,486	1,398	910	716	442	335	358	871	314	268
Cash Flow	1,238	888	760	581	455	573	365	310	299	237
Current Ratio	1.1	0.7	1.1	0.9	0.9	0.7	0.9	0.4	0.8	0.7
% Long Term Debt of Capitalization	30.3	22.5	25.6	31.1	32.1	35.6	42.8	41.2	36.3	39.1
% Net Income of Revenue	19.7	18.6	15.7	12.0	12.1	12.2	14.2	11.0	12.4	10.7
% Return on Assets	9.4	9.2	9.4	8.1	6.6	5.6	5.4	5.5	6.6	4.5
% Return on Equity	22.8	21.2	23.7	21.8	17.0	14.9	15.4	15.6	16.4	11.0

Data as orig reptd.; bef. results of disc opers/spec. items. Per share data adj. for stk. divs.; EPS diluted. E-Estimated. NA-Not Available. NM-Not Meaningful. NR-Not Ranked. UR-Under Review.

Office: 180 E 100 S, Salt Lake City, UT 84139-1500.
Telephone: 801-324-5699.
Website: http://www.questar.com
Chrmn, Pres & CEO: K.O. Rattie

COO & EVP: C.B. Stanley
EVP & CFO: R.J. Doleshek
Treas: M.H. Craven
Secy: A.L. Jones

Investor Contact: M. Craven (801-324-5077)
Board Members: P. S. Baker, Jr., T. Beck, R. D. Cash, L. R. Flury, J. A. Harmon, R. E. McKee, III, G. G. Michael, K. O. Rattie, M. W. Scoggins, H. H. Simmons, C. B. Stanley, B. A. Williamson

Founded: 1935
Domicile: Utah
Employees: 2,457

The McGraw-Hill Companies

Quest Diagnostics Inc

STANDARD &POOR'S

S&P Recommendation BUY ★★★★☆

Price	12-Mo. Target Price	Investment Style
$58.27 (as of Nov 27, 2009)	$70.00	Large-Cap Growth

GICS Sector Health Care
Sub-Industry Health Care Services

Summary This company provides diagnostic testing, information and services to physicians, hospitals, managed care organizations, employers and government agencies.

Key Stock Statistics (Source S&P, Vickers, company reports)

52-Wk Range	$59.57– 42.36	S&P Oper. EPS 2009E	3.83	Market Capitalization(B)	$10.774	Beta	0.40
Trailing 12-Month EPS	$3.77	S&P Oper. EPS 2010E	4.15	Yield (%)	0.69	S&P 3-Yr. Proj. EPS CAGR(%)	13
Trailing 12-Month P/E	15.5	P/E on S&P Oper. EPS 2009E	15.2	Dividend Rate/Share	$0.40	S&P Credit Rating	BBB+
$10K Invested 5 Yrs Ago	$13,132	Common Shares Outstg. (M)	184.9	Institutional Ownership (%)	73		

Price Performance

30-Week Mov. Avg. · · · 10-Week Mov. Avg. – – GAAP Earnings vs. Previous Year   Volume Above Avg. ▮▮▮ STARS
12-Mo. Target Price — Relative Strength — ▲ Up ▼ Down ► No Change   Below Avg. ▮▮▮ ★

Options: ASE, CBOE, Ph

Analysis prepared by **Jeffrey Loo, CFA** on October 22, 2009, when the stock traded at **$ 56.74**.

Highlights

► We see 2009 and 2010 sales increasing 3% and 4%, to $7.47 and $7.76 billion, respectively. We look for a continued increase in esoteric testing and tests per requisition, resulting in higher revenue per requisition, but we expect an adverse impact from the withdrawal of lab management deals and a continued decline in drug testing. We believe the decline in drug testing has stabilized and volume should improve by early 2010; we also note that drug testing is a lower-margin business. We see 2009 operating margins rising 140 basis points (bps), but see only a 10 bps rise in 2010 on a reduced benefit from DGX's years-long cost-cutting efforts.

► Historically, DGX has been a prolific acquirer, and we believe the current environment may present attractive opportunities. However, DGX is highly leveraged, with $2.73 billion of net debt as of September 30, 2009, and we think it will pay down debt and resume stock buybacks. In January 2009, DGX announced a $500 million buyback plan and repurchased 4.5 million shares from GlaxoSmithKline. As of September 2009, $150 million of the buyback remained.

► Our 2009 and 2010 EPS estimates are $3.83 and $4.15, respectively.

Investment Rationale/Risk

► We believe the shares are undervalued, recently trading at 13.5X our 2010 EPS estimate, below historical levels. Although we have some concerns about economic challenges and significantly lower pre-employment drug testing, we think DGX's core lab testing business is fundamentally sound and believe it should be able to maintain stable growth and margin expansion through improved efficiency and cost cutting. We believe diagnostic testing remains an essential health care service. We see two important metrics -- revenue per requisition and tests per requisition -- continuing to increase. We also expect better pricing stability as the majority of DGX's managed care contracts have been signed.

► Risks to our recommendation and target price include larger-than-expected declines in drug testing, the loss of managed care contracts and greater pricing pressure from third-party payors.

► Our 12-month target price of $70 is based on a P/E-to-growth ratio of about 1.3X applied to our 2010 EPS estimate and assuming a three-year EPS growth rate of 13%, in line with peers.

Qualitative Risk Assessment

LOW	MEDIUM	HIGH

Our risk assessment reflects our view of DGX's leadership position in the large and mature diagnostic testing industry; the company's broad geographic service area; its diverse and balanced payor mix; and the growing recognition of the importance and significance of diagnostic testing.

Quantitative Evaluations

S&P Quality Ranking B+

D	C	B-	B	B+	A-	A	A+

Relative Strength Rank STRONG

73

LOWEST = 1   HIGHEST = 99

Revenue/Earnings Data

Revenue (Million $)

	1Q	2Q	3Q	4Q	Year
2009	1,808	1,902	1,897	--	--
2008	1,785	1,838	1,827	1,800	7,249
2007	1,526	1,641	1,767	1,770	6,705
2006	1,553	1,583	1,583	1,549	6,269
2005	1,319	1,378	1,372	1,435	5,504
2004	1,256	1,298	1,290	1,283	5,127

Earnings Per Share ($)

2009	0.86	1.00	1.02	E0.95	E3.83
2008	0.72	0.83	0.81	0.87	3.23
2007	0.55	0.73	0.77	0.79	2.84
2006	0.77	0.78	0.82	0.77	3.14
2005	0.64	0.72	0.66	0.64	2.66
2004	0.54	0.59	0.62	0.60	2.35

Fiscal year ended Dec. 31. Next earnings report expected: Late January. EPS Estimates based on S&P Operating Earnings; historical GAAP earnings are as reported.

Dividend Data (Dates: mm/dd Payment Date: mm/dd/yy)

Amount ($)	Date Decl.	Ex-Div. Date	Stk. of Record	Payment Date
0.100	12/18	01/07	01/09	01/26/09
0.100	02/11	04/02	04/06	04/20/09
0.100	05/14	07/01	07/06	07/20/09
0.100	08/12	09/30	10/02	10/19/09

Dividends have been paid since 2004. Source: Company reports.

Please read the Required Disclosures and Analyst Certification on the last page of this report.

Quest Diagnostics Inc

STANDARD
&POOR'S

Business Summary October 22, 2009

CORPORATE OVERVIEW. Quest Diagnostics is the largest independent U.S. clinical lab provider. The clinical lab market is estimated to be about a $45 billion market, with hospital-based labs accounting for about 60% of the market, independent commercial labs, such as DGX, accounting for 33%, and physician-office labs the rest. DGX offers a broad range of clinical laboratory testing services used by physicians in the detection, diagnosis, and treatment of diseases and other medical conditions. Tests range from routine (such as blood cholesterol tests) to highly complex esoteric (such as gene-based testing and molecular diagnostics testing). At the end of 2008, DGX had a network of 35 principal laboratories throughout the U.S., 150 smaller "rapid response" (STAT) laboratories, and over 2,100 patient service centers, along with facilities in Mexico, Puerto Rico, and England. In 2008, DGX has started clinical lab services in India.

DGX processes more than 150 million requisitions (order forms completed by physicians indicating tests to be performed) annually. Routine testing and anatomic pathology generated 68% of net sales in 2008 (73% in 2007), esoteric testing 20% (18% in 2007), clinical trials and risk assessment services from LabOne (acquired in November 2005) 9% (9%), and 3% from overseas operations. Routine tests measure important health parameters such as the function of the kidney, heart, liver, thyroid and other organs. Esoteric tests are performed less frequently than routine tests, and/or require more sophisticated equipment and materials, professional hands-on attention, and more highly skilled personnel. As a result, they are generally priced substantially higher than routine tests.

Company Financials Fiscal Year Ended Dec. 31

Per Share Data ($)	2008	2007	2006	2005	2004	2003	2002	2001	2000	1999
Tangible Book Value	NM	NM	NM	NM	NM	NM	NM	NM	NM	NM
Cash Flow	4.58	4.06	4.24	3.51	3.12	2.79	2.31	1.70	1.27	0.64
Earnings	3.23	2.84	3.14	2.66	2.35	2.06	1.62	0.94	0.56	-0.01
S&P Core Earnings	3.29	2.85	3.17	2.57	2.13	1.80	1.42	0.83	NA	NA
Dividends	0.40	0.40	0.39	0.26	0.30	Nil	Nil	Nil	Nil	Nil
Payout Ratio	12%	14%	12%	10%	13%	Nil	Nil	Nil	Nil	Nil
Prices:High	59.95	58.63	64.69	54.80	48.41	37.50	48.07	37.88	36.56	8.23
Prices:Low	38.66	47.98	48.59	44.32	35.94	23.68	24.55	18.30	7.28	4.44
P/E Ratio:High	19	21	21	21	21	18	30	40	66	NM
P/E Ratio:Low	12	17	15	17	15	11	15	19	13	NM

Income Statement Analysis (Million $)										
Revenue	7,249	6,705	6,269	5,504	5,127	4,738	4,108	3,628	3,421	2,205
Operating Income	1,508	1,350	1,325	1,144	1,060	950	724	559	452	243
Depreciation	265	238	197	176	169	154	131	148	134	90.8
Interest Expense	185	186	96.5	61.4	57.9	59.8	53.7	70.5	120	69.8
Pretax Income	1,051	939	1,057	930	854	755	557	343	210	19.8
Effective Tax Rate	36.8%	38.2%	38.6%	39.2%	39.3%	39.9%	39.5%	43.4%	45.7%	NM
Net Income	632	554	626	546	499	437	322	184	105	-1.27
S&P Core Earnings	644	556	632	531	456	377	279	162	NA	NA

Balance Sheet & Other Financial Data (Million $)										
Cash	254	168	150	92.1	73.3	155	96.8	122	171	27.3
Current Assets	1,497	1,374	1,191	1,069	931	996	824	877	981	873
Total Assets	8,404	8,566	5,661	5,306	4,204	4,301	3,324	2,931	2,865	2,878
Current Liabilities	1,225	1,288	1,151	1,101	1,044	724	636	659	955	701
Long Term Debt	3,078	3,377	1,239	1,255	724	1,029	797	820	761	1,171
Common Equity	3,605	3,324	3,019	2,763	2,289	2,397	1,769	1,336	1,031	862
Total Capital	6,873	6,911	4,258	4,018	3,013	3,426	2,565	2,156	1,793	2,046
Capital Expenditures	213	219	193	224	176	175	155	149	116	76.0
Cash Flow	897	792	823	722	668	591	454	332	239	89.6
Current Ratio	1.2	1.1	1.0	1.0	0.9	1.4	1.3	1.3	1.0	1.2
% Long Term Debt of Capitalization	44.8	48.9	29.1	31.2	24.0	30.0	31.0	38.0	42.4	57.6
% Net Income of Revenue	8.7	8.3	10.0	9.9	9.7	9.2	7.8	5.1	3.1	NM
% Return on Assets	7.5	7.8	11.4	11.5	11.7	11.5	10.3	6.3	3.7	NM
% Return on Equity	18.3	17.5	21.6	21.6	21.3	20.9	20.8	15.5	11.1	NM

Data as orig reptd.; bef. results of disc opers/spec. items. Per share data adj. for stk. divs.; EPS diluted. E-Estimated. NA-Not Available. NM-Not Meaningful. NR-Not Ranked. UR-Under Review.

Office: Three Giralda Farms, Madison, NJ 07940.
Telephone: 973-520-2700.
Email: investor@questdiagnostics.com
Website: http://www.questdiagnostics.com

Chrmn, Pres & CEO: S.N. Mohapatra
COO: W.R. Simmons
SVP & CFO: R.A. Hagemann
SVP & General Counsel: M.E. Prevoznik

Chief Acctg Officer & Cntlr: T.F. Bongiorno
Investor Contact: L. Park (973-520-2900)
Board Members: J. C. Baldwin, J. K. Britell, W. F. Buehler, R. Haggerty, S. N. Mohapatra, G. M. Pfeiffer, D. C. Stanzione, G. Wilensky, J. Ziegler

Founded: 1967
Domicile: Delaware
Employees: 42,800

Qwest Communications International Inc.

STANDARD
&POOR'S

S&P Recommendation	HOLD ★★★☆☆	Price	12-Mo. Target Price	Investment Style
		$3.80 (as of Nov 27, 2009)	$4.00	Large-Cap Blend

GICS Sector Telecommunication Services
Sub-Industry Integrated Telecommunication Services

Summary This company offers consumer and corporate wireline and wireless services, primarily serving customers in 14 western and midwestern U.S. states.

Key Stock Statistics (Source S&P, Vickers, company reports)

52-Wk Range	$4.87– 2.63	S&P Oper. EPS 2009E	0.42	Market Capitalization(B)	$6.561	Beta	0.92
Trailing 12-Month EPS	$0.44	S&P Oper. EPS 2010E	0.32	Yield (%)	8.42	S&P 3-Yr. Proj. EPS CAGR(%)	4
Trailing 12-Month P/E	8.6	P/E on S&P Oper. EPS 2009E	9.0	Dividend Rate/Share	$0.32	S&P Credit Rating	BB
$10K Invested 5 Yrs Ago	$11,845	Common Shares Outstg. (M)	1,726.6	Institutional Ownership (%)	90		

Price Performance

30-Week Mov. Avg. · · · · 10-Week Mov. Avg. – – **GAAP Earnings vs. Previous Year** Volume Above Avg. STARS
12-Mo. Target Price — Relative Strength — ▲ Up ▼ Down ► No Change Below Avg.

Options: ASE, CBOE, P, Ph

Analysis prepared by **Todd Rosenbluth** on October 30, 2009, when the stock traded at **$ 3.64.**

Highlights

► We see a 7.6% decline in 2009 revenues, followed by a smaller 2.7% decline in 2010. We forecast pressure on voice services from access line losses, due to competition and still slow housing sales, and from wholesale weakness amid prior customer consolidation. In addition, in 2010 Q will not have wireless revenues as it has migrated customers off its service. We expect broadband additions and modest gains in the enterprise segment from new contracts to provide an offset.

► Despite revenue pressure, we look for EBITDA margins to be relatively stable at 34% in 2010, down from 35% projected for 2009. We believe cost reductions stemming from a smaller work force and network cost savings will help lower operating expenses and outweigh pension expense. We expect depreciation charges to be relatively flat.

► We estimate EPS of $0.42 in 2009 and, despite slightly lower interest expense, we forecast $0.32 in 2010. Second quarter 2009 EPS were boosted by about $0.04 by an abnormally low tax rate. Our forward estimates reflect a normal high-30% rate.

Investment Rationale/Risk

► We believe Q generates sufficient cash flow to support both its dividend policy and capital spending efforts geared toward offsetting competition. However, we still see increased access line pressure and weakness in wholesale revenues limiting the impact of cost savings to keep EBITDA relatively stable. With our forecast of limited growth, given competitive pressures and increased difficulty enacting further cost savings, we believe a discounted valuation is warranted.

► Risks to our recommendation and target price include greater-than-expected line losses, lower demand for Q's bundled services, which would hurt margins, an inability to access the credit market, and a dividend cut.

► With the operational challenges we foresee, we believe Q warrants a discounted valuation to peers. We apply a 4.5X peer group multiple to our 2010 EBITDA estimate and blend it with a P/E multiple of 10.5X, below our forecast for faster-growing peers, to arrive at our 12-month target price of $4.00. We believe Q's dividend yield, recently near 9%, adds support.

Qualitative Risk Assessment

LOW	MEDIUM	HIGH

Our risk assessment reflects the highly competitive nature of the industry and our view of the above-average debt load Q carries, offset by our view of steady operating cash flow that supports the dividend.

Quantitative Evaluations

S&P Quality Ranking B-

D	C	B-	B	B+	A-	A	A+

Relative Strength Rank MODERATE

65

LOWEST = 1   HIGHEST = 99

Revenue/Earnings Data

Revenue (Million $)

	1Q	2Q	3Q	4Q	Year
2009	3,173	3,090	3,054	--	--
2008	3,399	3,382	3,379	3,315	13,475
2007	3,446	3,463	3,434	3,435	13,778
2006	3,476	3,472	3,487	3,488	13,923
2005	3,449	3,470	3,504	3,480	13,903
2004	3,481	3,442	3,449	3,437	13,809

Earnings Per Share ($)

2009	0.12	0.12	0.07	E0.08	E0.42
2008	0.09	0.11	0.09	0.11	0.39
2007	0.12	0.13	1.08	0.20	1.52
2006	0.05	0.06	0.09	0.10	0.30
2005	0.03	-0.09	-0.08	-0.27	-0.41
2004	-0.17	-0.43	-0.31	-0.09	-1.00

Fiscal year ended Dec. 31. Next earnings report expected: Mid February. EPS Estimates based on S&P Operating Earnings; historical GAAP earnings are as reported.

Dividend Data (Dates: mm/dd Payment Date: mm/dd/yy)

Amount ($)	Date Decl.	Ex-Div. Date	Stk. of Record	Payment Date
0.080	12/11	02/11	02/13	03/06/09
0.080	04/16	05/20	05/22	06/12/09
0.080	07/27	08/19	08/21	09/11/09
0.080	10/15	11/18	11/20	12/11/09

Dividends have been paid since 2008. Source: Company reports.

Please read the Required Disclosures and Analyst Certification on the last page of this report.

The McGraw·Hill Companies

Qwest Communications International Inc.

Business Summary October 30, 2009

CORPORATE OVERVIEW. Qwest Communications International (Q) provides telecommunications services in 14 midwestern and western states. As of September 2009, Q had 10.6 million local access lines for consumers and businesses and 2.95 million DSL broadband customers (up 6% from a year earlier), with approximately 80% of its access lines in its eight largest markets, including Denver, Portland and Seattle. In March 2004, Q began offering wireless services using Sprint's network but retained control of all marketing, customer service, pricing and promotional offerings. In May 2008, the company announced plans to switch to using Verizon Wireless as part of a service bundle, and at the end of October 2009 had migrated all customers. In the third quarter of 2009, Q's revenues were pressured in its wholesale segment (23% of overall revenues) and in the mass markets segment (40%), but revenues in the business markets segment (34%) were barely lower.

COMPETITIVE LANDSCAPE. We believe Q faces competitive challenges partly due to low barriers to entry and characteristics unique to the company. As of September 2009, Q's access line count was 11% lower than a year earlier, as wireless and to a lesser extent cable telephony substitution was intense, and we believe fewer housing sales in core markets limited new customer additions. Q competes with cable providers such as Cox Communications and Comcast that offer broadband services and telephony products that were ag-

gressively marketed during 2008. To offset possible customer migration to cable, Q is offering a triple-play package of voice, data and video services through a partnership with satellite provider Direct TV (858,000 customers); 16% of its primary mass markets lines were subscribing to the service.

CORPORATE STRATEGY. During 2009, Q has been focused on reducing its operating expenses, aiming to improve its EBITDA margin. Q's headcount was reduced by 10% in the 12 months ended June 2009, and the company lowered its facility costs. Unlike large telecom peers such as Verizon and AT&T that have invested in their own video offerings to offset competitive pressure, Qwest long pursued a wholesale strategy to offer bundled services. However, Q has deployed fiber broadband services that reached nearly 3 million homes as of September 2009, and had achieved 11% penetration (340,000 subscribers). In addition, Q initially rolled out a lower-priced broadband offering in the third quarter of 2008 in hopes of restarting customer growth. Within its wholesale segment, Q aims to shift its focus to data and IP services, from legacy voice services.

Company Financials Fiscal Year Ended Dec. 31

Per Share Data ($)	2008	2007	2006	2005	2004	2003	2002	2001	2000	1999
Tangible Book Value	NM	0.32	NM	NM	NM	NM	NM	1.28	5.37	4.95
Cash Flow	1.72	2.80	1.51	1.26	0.74	1.07	-7.65	0.83	2.56	1.13
Earnings	0.39	1.52	0.30	-0.41	-1.00	-0.76	-10.48	-2.38	-0.06	0.60
S&P Core Earnings	0.07	1.58	0.25	-0.68	-0.81	-0.81	-7.38	-1.39	NA	NA
Dividends	0.32	Nil	Nil	Nil	Nil	Nil	Nil	0.05	Nil	Nil
Payout Ratio	82%	Nil	Nil	Nil	Nil	Nil	Nil	NM	Nil	Nil
Prices:High	7.07	10.45	9.22	5.95	5.00	6.15	15.19	48.19	66.00	52.38
Prices:Low	2.05	6.23	5.10	3.30	2.56	3.01	1.07	11.08	32.13	25.03
P/E Ratio:High	18	7	31	NM	NM	NM	NM	NM	NM	87
P/E Ratio:Low	5	4	17	NM	NM	NM	NM	NM	NM	42

Income Statement Analysis (Million $)										
Revenue	13,475	13,778	13,923	13,903	13,809	14,288	15,385	19,695	16,610	3,928
Depreciation	2,314	2,459	2,381	3,065	3,123	3,167	3,847	5,335	3,342	404
Maintenance	NA	NA	NA	NA	NA	NA	NA	NA	NA	NA
Construction Credits	NA	NA	NA	NA	NA	NA	NA	NA	NA	NA
Effective Tax Rate	38.0%	NM	NM	NM	NM	NM	NM	NM	NM	21.4%
Net Income	681	2,917	593	-757	-1,794	-1,313	-17,625	-3,958	-81.0	459
S&P Core Earnings	124	3,037	492	-1,154	-1,465	-1,382	-12,411	-2,327	NA	NA

Balance Sheet & Other Financial Data (Million $)										
Gross Property	46,770	46,646	46,374	45,954	45,428	45,094	44,580	55,099	48,318	4,469
Net Property	13,045	13,671	14,579	15,568	16,853	18,149	18,995	29,977	25,583	4,109
Capital Expenditures	1,777	1,669	1,632	1,613	1,731	2,088	2,764	8,543	6,597	1,900
Total Capital	11,390	14,213	11,761	11,751	14,078	14,744	16,924	59,046	58,493	9,370
Fixed Charges Coverage	2.2	1.6	1.4	0.6	NM	NM	0.2	1.3	2.5	4.9
Capitalization:Long Term Debt	12,839	13,650	13,206	14,968	16,690	15,639	19,754	20,197	15,421	2,368
Capitalization:Preferred	Nil	Nil	Nil	Nil	Nil	Nil	Nil	Nil	Nil	Nil
Capitalization:Common	-1,449	563	-1,445	-3,217	-2,612	-1,016	-2,830	36,655	41,304	7,001
% Return on Revenue	5.1	21.2	4.3	NM	NM	NM	NM	NM	NM	11.7
% Return on Invested Capital	14.1	31.0	15.0	8.1	NM	NM	12.4	NM	7.6	9.3
% Return on Common Equity	NM	NM	NM	NM	NM	NM	NM	NM	NM	8.2
% Earned on Net Property	16.6	12.4	10.3	5.3	NM	17.5	16.9	26.4	32.9	22.4
% Long Term Debt of Capitalization	NM	96.0	112.3	127.4	118.6	106.9	116.7	34.2	27.2	25.3
Capital % Preferred	Nil	Nil	Nil	Nil	Nil	Nil	Nil	Nil	Nil	Nil
Capitalization:% Common	NM	4.0	-12.3	-27.4	-18.6	-6.9	-16.7	62.0	72.8	74.7

Data as orig reptd.; bef. results of disc opers/spec. items. Per share data adj. for stk. divs.; EPS diluted. E-Estimated. NA-Not Available. NM-Not Meaningful. NR-Not Ranked. UR-Under Review.

Office: 1801 California St, Denver, CO 80202-2658.
Telephone: 303-992-1400.
Email: investor.relations@qwest.com
Website: http://www.qwest.com

Chrmn & CEO: E.A. Mueller
COO: T.A. Taylor
EVP & CFO: J.J. Euteneuer
EVP, Chief Admin Officer & General Counsel: R. Baer

SVP, Chief Acctg Officer & Cntlr: R.W. Johnston
Board Members: L. G. Alvarado, C. L. Biggs, K. D. Brooksher, P. S. Hellman, R. D. Hoover, P. J. Martin, C. S. Mathews, E. A. Mueller, W. Murdy, J. L. Murley, M. J. Roberts, J. A. Unruh, A. Welters

Founded: 1983
Domicile: Delaware
Employees: 32,937

The McGraw-Hill Companies

RadioShack Corp

STANDARD &POOR'S

S&P Recommendation **SELL** ★★☆☆☆	Price $18.38 (as of Nov 27, 2009)	12-Mo. Target Price $15.00	Investment Style Large-Cap Blend

GICS Sector Consumer Discretionary
Sub-Industry Computer & Electronics Retail

Summary This consumer electronics retailer operates the RadioShack chain, which has about 7,000 outlets (including dealers/franchises).

Key Stock Statistics (Source S&P, Vickers, company reports)

52-Wk Range	$20.57– 6.47	S&P Oper. EPS 2009**E**	1.49	Market Capitalization(B)	$2.301	Beta	1.84
Trailing 12-Month EPS	$1.53	S&P Oper. EPS 2010**E**	1.43	Yield (%)	1.36	S&P 3-Yr. Proj. EPS CAGR(%)	3
Trailing 12-Month P/E	12.0	P/E on S&P Oper. EPS 2009**E**	12.3	Dividend Rate/Share	$0.25	S&P Credit Rating	BB
$10K Invested 5 Yrs Ago	$6,031	Common Shares Outstg. (M)	125.2	Institutional Ownership (%)	98		

Price Performance

30-Week Mov. Avg. · · · 10-Week Mov. Avg. - - **GAAP Earnings vs. Previous Year** Volume Above Avg. STARS
12-Mo. Target Price — Relative Strength ▲ Up ▼ Down ▶ No Change Below Avg. ★

Options: ASE, CBOE, P

Analysis prepared by **Michael Souers** on October 28, 2009, when the stock traded at **$ 17.35**.

Highlights

▶ We see sales declining fractionally in 2010, following a projected 1.0% rise in 2009. We expect RSH to continue to focus on increasing profitability by opportunistically closing underperforming stores and kiosks. We also look for the company to increase its focus on selling prepaid wireless handsets and airtime, and also expect a sales lift from netbooks, offsetting anticipated sales declines in GPS devices, digital converter boxes and laptops. We see comp-store sales declining in the low single digits, driven by the challenging macroenvironment.

▶ We expect a slight narrowing of operating margins reflecting mix shift and the de-leveraging of fixed costs due to a slight decline in comparable store sales. We think RSH will struggle to achieve historical gross margins due to increased competitive pressures and the company's focus on faster-moving, lower-margin categories.

▶ After taxes that we forecast at 37.5% and flat net interest expense, we estimate EPS of $1.43 in 2010, a 4.0% decline from the $1.49 we project the company to earn in 2009.

Investment Rationale/Risk

▶ We see the company in the middle stages of its turnaround plan, which is focused on increasing average unit volume, rationalizing its cost structure, and growing profitable square footage. While RSH's CEO has extensive retail experience with turnarounds, we think the longer-term outlook for the company is uncertain, due to the highly competitive environment for electronics products. Given our view of the company's lackluster longer-term sales outlook and lack of earnings visibility, we believe the risk/reward quotient for owning the shares is negative, with the shares recently trading at about 13X our 2010 EPS estimate, a slight discount to peers.

▶ Risks to our recommendation and target price include the potential that management can rapidly execute its turnaround plan, and macroeconomic factors that could result in stronger-than-anticipated consumer spending levels.

▶ Our 12-month target price of $15, or about 10X our 2010 EPS estimate, is derived from our discounted cash flow analysis. Our DCF model assumes a weighted average cost of capital of 10.1% and a terminal growth rate of 3.0%.

Qualitative Risk Assessment

LOW	MEDIUM	HIGH

The company is a relatively large player in a fragmented industry, with numerous suppliers and buyers, and a history of profitability. However, we view consumer electronics retailing as highly competitive, with numerous rivals and strong price competition.

Quantitative Evaluations

S&P Quality Ranking B

D	C	B-	B	B+	A-	A	A+

Relative Strength Rank STRONG

83

LOWEST = 1 HIGHEST = 99

Revenue/Earnings Data

Revenue (Million $)

	1Q	2Q	3Q	4Q	Year
2009	1,002	965.7	990.0	--	--
2008	949.0	994.9	1,022	1,259	4,225
2007	992.3	934.8	960.3	1,364	4,252
2006	1,160	1,100	1,060	1,458	4,778
2005	1,123	1,092	1,195	1,672	5,082
2004	1,093	1,054	1,102	1,593	4,841

Earnings Per Share ($)

2009	0.34	0.39	0.30	E0.46	E1.49
2008	0.30	0.32	0.39	0.50	1.49
2007	0.31	0.34	0.34	0.77	1.74
2006	0.06	-0.02	-0.12	0.62	0.54
2005	0.34	0.33	0.75	0.40	1.81
2004	0.41	0.42	0.43	0.81	2.08

Fiscal year ended Dec. 31. Next earnings report expected: Late February. EPS Estimates based on S&P Operating Earnings; historical GAAP earnings are as reported.

Dividend Data (Dates: mm/dd Payment Date: mm/dd/yy)

Amount ($)	Date Decl.	Ex-Div. Date	Stk. of Record	Payment Date
0.250	11/07	11/25	11/28	12/17/08
0.250	11/09	11/24	11/27	12/16/09

Dividends have been paid since 1987. Source: Company reports.

Stock Report | November 28, 2009 | NYS Symbol: **RSH**

RadioShack Corp

STANDARD &POOR'S

Business Summary October 28, 2009

CORPORATE OVERVIEW. As of December 31, 2008, this consumer electronics retailer had 4,453 company-operated stores located through the U.S., including Puerto Rico and the U.S. Virgin Islands. RSH also had a network of 1,394 dealer/franchise stores, including 36 located outside the U.S. At the end of 2008, RSH operated 688 non-RadioShack branded kiosks, which offer product lines such as wireless phones and associated accessories. In addition, in December 2008, RadioShack acquired the remaining interest in its Mexican joint venture, RadioShack de Mexico, S.A. de C.V., RadioShack de Mexico had 200 stores and 14 dealers throughout Mexico at December 31, 2008.

Each store carries a broad assortment of electronics products, including batteries and accessories; wireless phones and communication devices such as scanners and GPS units; flat panel televisions; DVD players; direct-to-home (DTH) satellite systems; PCs; home entertainment, wireless and other computer accessories; wire, cable and connectivity products; digital cameras; and specialized products such as radio-controlled cars and other toys. RSH also provides access to third-party services, such as wireless telephone and DTH satellite activation, satellite radio service, prepaid wireless airtime and extended service plans. We believe that RSH is focusing on revamping its product offerings in order to enhance its competitive position within the consumer electronics industry. In the second half of 2005, RSH began dedicating floor space to Apple's iPod and accessories, a rapidly growing consumer electronics category, and the company made a concerted push to sell video gaming products in 2007, another hot product category.

Company Financials Fiscal Year Ended Dec. 31

Per Share Data ($)	2008	2007	2006	2005	2004	2003	2002	2001	2000	1999
Tangible Book Value	6.24	5.88	4.81	4.36	5.83	4.73	4.24	4.04	4.46	3.70
Cash Flow	2.26	2.57	1.48	2.65	2.70	2.31	1.97	1.41	2.38	1.87
Earnings	1.49	1.74	0.54	1.81	2.08	1.77	1.45	0.85	1.84	1.43
S&P Core Earnings	1.49	1.74	0.67	1.69	1.94	1.49	1.18	1.06	NA	NA
Dividends	0.25	0.25	0.25	0.25	0.25	0.25	0.22	0.22	0.22	0.15
Payout Ratio	17%	14%	46%	14%	12%	14%	15%	25%	12%	10%
Prices:High	19.90	35.00	23.37	34.48	36.24	32.48	36.21	56.50	72.94	79.50
Prices:Low	8.06	16.69	13.73	20.55	26.04	18.74	16.99	20.10	35.06	20.59
P/E Ratio:High	13	20	43	19	17	18	25	66	40	56
P/E Ratio:Low	5	10	25	11	13	11	12	24	19	14

Income Statement Analysis (Million $)										
Revenue	4,225	4,252	4,778	5,082	4,841	4,649	4,577	4,776	4,795	4,126
Operating Income	428	464	329	474	660	576	510	583	736	597
Depreciation	99.3	113	128	124	101	92.0	94.7	108	107	90.2
Interest Expense	29.9	38.8	44.3	44.5	29.6	35.7	43.4	50.8	53.9	37.2
Pretax Income	304	367	111	322	542	473	425	292	594	481
Effective Tax Rate	36.8%	35.4%	34.1%	16.0%	37.8%	36.9%	38.0%	42.8%	38.0%	38.0%
Net Income	192	237	73.4	270	337	299	263	167	368	298
S&P Core Earnings	192	236	92.3	251	315	252	211	200	NA	NA

Balance Sheet & Other Financial Data (Million $)										
Cash	815	510	472	224	438	635	447	401	131	165
Current Assets	1,792	1,567	1,600	1,627	1,775	1,667	1,707	1,714	1,818	1,403
Total Assets	2,284	1,990	2,070	2,205	2,517	2,244	1,707	2,245	2,577	2,142
Current Liabilities	637	748	984	986	957	858	829	826	1,232	925
Long Term Debt	732	348	346	495	507	541	591	565	303	319
Common Equity	817	770	654	589	922	769	729	714	812	758
Total Capital	1,550	1,118	1,000	1,084	1,429	1,311	1,320	1,344	1,284	1,150
Capital Expenditures	85.6	45.3	91.0	171	229	190	107	139	120	102
Cash Flow	292	350	202	394	439	391	354	270	470	383
Current Ratio	2.8	2.1	1.6	1.6	1.9	1.9	2.1	2.1	1.5	1.5
% Long Term Debt of Capitalization	47.3	31.1	34.6	45.7	35.5	41.3	44.8	42.1	23.6	27.8
% Net Income of Revenue	4.6	5.6	1.5	5.3	7.0	6.4	5.8	3.5	7.7	7.2
% Return on Assets	9.0	11.7	3.4	11.4	14.2	13.4	13.3	6.9	15.6	14.4
% Return on Equity	24.3	33.3	11.8	35.7	39.9	39.9	35.9	21.2	46.2	38.8

Data as orig reptd.; bef. results of disc opers/spec. items. Per share data adj. for stk. divs.; EPS diluted. E-Estimated. NA-Not Available. NM-Not Meaningful. NR-Not Ranked. UR-Under Review.

Office: 300 Radioshack Cir, Fort Worth, TX 76102-1964.
Telephone: 817-415-3011.
Email: investor.relations@radioshack.com
Website: http://www.radioshack.com

Chrmn & CEO: J.C. Day
COO: M. Carter
EVP & CFO: J.F. Gooch
SVP & CIO: S.S. Stufflebeme

Chief Acctg Officer, Treas & Cntlr: M.O. Moad
Investor Contact: P. Proffer (817-415-3189)
Board Members: F. J. Belatti, J. C. Day, D. R. Feehan, H. Lockhart, J. L. Messman, T. G. Plaskett, E. D. Woodbury

Founded: 1899
Domicile: Delaware
Employees: 36,800

Range Resources Corp.

STANDARD
&POOR'S

S&P Recommendation	HOLD ★★★☆☆	Price $47.93 (as of Nov 27, 2009)	12-Mo. Target Price $58.00	Investment Style Large-Cap Growth

GICS Sector Energy
Sub-Industry Oil & Gas Exploration & Production

Summary This company explores, develops and acquires oil and gas properties, primarily in the Southwest, Appalachian and Gulf Coast regions of the U.S.

Key Stock Statistics (Source S&P, Vickers, company reports)

52-Wk Range	$60.13– 28.05	S&P Oper. EPS 2009**E**	0.95	Market Capitalization(B)	$75.602	Beta	0.60
Trailing 12-Month EPS	$0.33	S&P Oper. EPS 2010**E**	0.90	Yield (%)	0.33	S&P 3-Yr. Proj. EPS CAGR(%)	-19
Trailing 12-Month P/E	NM	P/E on S&P Oper. EPS 2009**E**	50.5	Dividend Rate/Share	$0.16	S&P Credit Rating	BB
$10K Invested 5 Yrs Ago	$35,630	Common Shares Outstg. (M)	1,577.3	Institutional Ownership (%)	8		

Price Performance

30-Week Mov. Avg. · · · 10-Week Mov. Avg. - - GAAP Earnings vs. Previous Year Volume Above Avg. ▐▐▌ STARS
12-Mo. Target Price — Relative Strength ▲ Up ▼ Down ▶ No Change Below Avg. ▐▌ ★

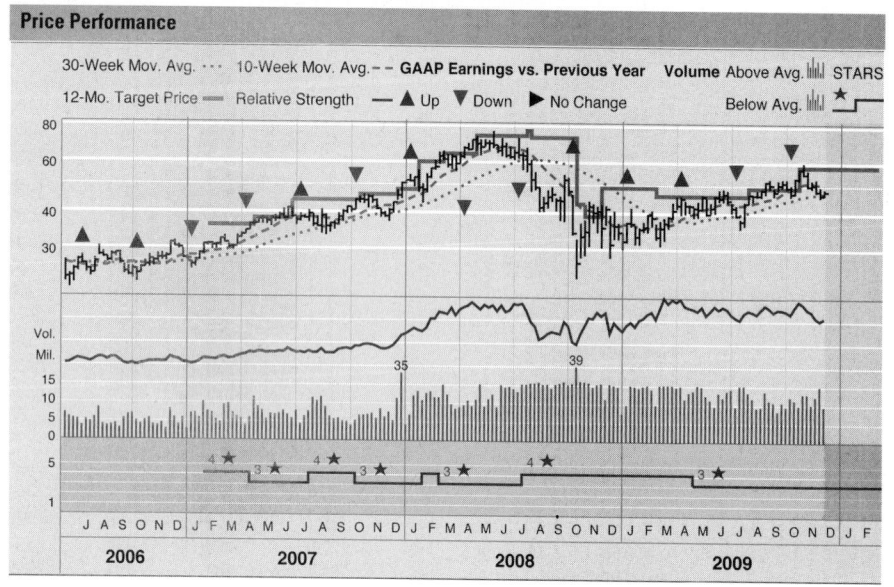

Options: ASE, CBOE, P, Ph

Analysis prepared by **Michael Kay** on October 20, 2009, when the stock traded at **$58.06**.

Highlights

▶ After production growth of 18% in 2008, we see boosts of 13% and 9% in 2009 and 2010, driven by the Devonian Shale play in the Nora field coal-bed methane (CBM) project in Virginia, an encouraging horizontal program at the Marcellus Shale, and a significantly increased acreage position in the Barnett Shale. We see most growth at Marcellus, where RRC sees its highest returns. RRC is running 15 total rigs versus 30 last year. Second quarter volumes beat expectations and we see a 12% year-over-year boost in third quarter production.

▶ Cost controls remain encouraging, as lease operating expense in 2008 was $1.40 per Mcfe, up slightly, and we see it down 11% and DD&A flat in 2009. We expect EBITDA to decline 37% in 2009 on an estimated 58% decline in natural gas prices.

▶ After EPS of $2.32 (with $0.29 of non-cash gain) in 2008, we see $1.14 (with $0.22 non-cash gain) in 2009 on lower prices. RRC's sees 2009 capex at $800 million, down from $1.27 billion. It plans to drill more than 70 Marcellus wells in 2009 and expand its processing capacity in the region. RRC has lowered its rig count in the Barnett Shale to two rigs.

Investment Rationale/Risk

▶ From 2005-2008, RRC had a three-year reserve CAGR of 24% with a reserve life of 19 years. Average three-year reserve replacement of 461% (363% organic) and three-year finding and development costs of $2.43/Mcf demonstrate its ability to replace reserves at attractive prices, in our view. Most reserves are based in Appalachia, where economics appear attractive. With the acceleration of development in the Marcellus Shale, and a new processing facility, RRC is producing 50 MMcfe/d and estimates production from the play of 80-100 MMcfe/d by year-end 2009. RRC has hedged 80% of forecast 2009 production at a floor of $7.49 per Mcf.

▶ Risks to our recommendation and target price include a sustained decline in oil and gas prices, an inability to replace reserves at reasonable costs, and production declines.

▶ Our 12-month target price of $58 blends our proven NAV per share estimate ($54), a target enterprise value to 2010 EBITDA ratio of 14X, and our DCF model ($59, assuming an 8.9% WACC, 3% terminal growth). We are positive on RRC's operations, especially at Marcellus Shale, but we see an appropriate valuation after 65% appreciation in the shares year-to-date.

Qualitative Risk Assessment

LOW	MEDIUM	HIGH

Our risk assessment reflects the company's operations in a capital intensive industry that is cyclical and derives value from producing a commodity whose price is very volatile.

Quantitative Evaluations

S&P Quality Ranking B+

D	C	B-	B	B+	A-	A	A+

Relative Strength Rank MODERATE

31

LOWEST = 1   HIGHEST = 99

Revenue/Earnings Data

Revenue (Million $)

	1Q	2Q	3Q	4Q	Year
2009	276.4	180.4	203.6	--	--
2008	205.3	150.1	622.7	344.9	1,323
2007	152.8	243.5	242.4	223.4	868.9
2006	189.2	177.6	228.9	184.1	779.7
2005	108.0	119.7	141.9	166.5	536.0
2004	63.53	68.70	86.21	102.3	320.7

Earnings Per Share ($)

2009	0.21	-0.26	-0.19	E0.25	E0.95
2008	0.01	-0.23	1.81	0.60	2.22
2007	0.06	0.43	0.39	0.22	1.11
2006	0.41	0.37	0.46	0.19	1.42
2005	0.18	0.17	0.19	0.32	0.86
2004	0.07	0.08	0.11	0.11	0.38

Fiscal year ended Dec. 31. Next earnings report expected: Late January. EPS Estimates based on S&P Operating Earnings; historical GAAP earnings are as reported.

Dividend Data (Dates: mm/dd Payment Date: mm/dd/yy)

Amount ($)	Date Decl.	Ex-Div. Date	Stk. of Record	Payment Date
0.040	12/01	12/11	12/15	12/31/08
0.040	03/03	03/13	03/17	03/31/09
0.040	06/01	06/11	06/15	06/30/09
0.040	09/01	09/11	09/15	09/30/09

Dividends have been paid since 2004. Source: Company reports.

Range Resources Corp.

STANDARD
&POOR'S

Business Summary October 20, 2009

CORPORATE OVERVIEW. Range Resources Corp. is an independent oil and gas company primarily engaged in acquiring, developing, exploring and producing oil and gas properties. RRC has established three core operating areas in the Appalachian, Southwestern and Gulf Coast regions of the U.S. The Southwest business unit encompasses operations in East Texas, West Texas, New Mexico, and the Mid-continent region of Oklahoma and the Texas Panhandle.

As of December 31, 2008, RRC had estimated proved reserves of 2.65 Tcfe, of which 82% was natural gas and 64% was proved developed. This compares with estimated proved reserves of 2.23 Tcfe, 82% natural gas and 64% proved developed, at the end of 2007, a 19% increase. We forecast RRC's reserve life to be 18.8 years, compared to 17.7 years at the end of 2007.

RRC estimates that it replaced 405% (537% in 2007) of production in 2008, including 337% (424%) from drilling. We estimate finding and development costs (exclude acquisitions) in 2008 were $3.20 per Mcfe versus a three-year average of $2.43 per Mcfe. Total reserve replacement costs (including acquisitions) in 2008 were $3.11 per Mcfe, versus a three-year average of $2.35 per Mcfe.

CORPORATE STRATEGY. RRC pursues what we consider a balanced growth strategy that targets the exploitation of its inventory of development drilling locations, higher potential exploration projects, and acquisitions. RRC focuses on acquisition opportunities within its core operating areas to capitalize on regional expertise and drive down costs.

In June 2006, RRC completed the acquisition of Stroud Energy for $465.2 million, including $278 million in cash. RRC purchased 171 Bcfe of proved reserves located primarily in the Barnett Shale play of North Texas, the Cotton Valley play of East Texas and the Austin Chalk play of Central Texas. RRC has a goal of doubling production in this region over the next 12 months.

IMPACT OF MAJOR DEVELOPMENTS. In February 2007, RRC completed the sale of its Austin Chalk assets acquired in the Stroud Energy transaction in 2006 for $82 million. RRC originally stated its intention to sell the assets In late July 2006, just as natural gas prices fell into a fairly steep decline, and RRC had difficulty selling the assets.

Company Financials Fiscal Year Ended Dec. 31

Per Share Data ($)	2008	2007	2006	2005	2004	2003	2002	2001	2000	1999
Tangible Book Value	15.82	11.57	9.04	5.36	4.65	3.24	2.50	3.11	2.43	1.73
Cash Flow	4.45	2.59	2.65	1.84	1.43	1.34	1.23	1.05	1.23	1.15
Earnings	2.22	1.11	1.42	0.86	0.38	0.35	0.29	0.07	0.38	-0.23
S&P Core Earnings	2.14	1.11	1.42	0.82	0.29	0.33	0.29	0.18	NA	NA
Dividends	0.16	0.13	0.09	0.07	0.03	Nil	Nil	Nil	Nil	0.02
Payout Ratio	7%	12%	6%	8%	9%	Nil	Nil	Nil	Nil	NM
Prices:High	76.81	51.88	31.77	28.37	14.43	6.57	3.97	4.75	4.67	4.75
Prices:Low	23.77	25.29	21.74	12.34	6.25	3.33	2.69	2.62	0.96	1.04
P/E Ratio:High	35	47	22	33	38	19	14	65	12	NM
P/E Ratio:Low	11	23	15	14	16	9	9	36	3	NM

Income Statement Analysis (Million $)										
Revenue	1,233	857	780	536	321	230	195	219	188	161
Operating Income	968	560	549	344	193	140	119	152	132	102
Depreciation, Depletion and Amortization	348	221	170	128	103	86.5	76.8	77.8	72.2	76.4
Interest Expense	99.8	77.7	57.6	38.8	23.1	22.2	23.2	30.7	40.0	47.1
Pretax Income	543	266	321	177	66.8	49.4	19.3	4.99	18.6	-8.62
Effective Tax Rate	36.2%	37.2%	38.5%	37.4%	36.8%	37.4%	NM	NM	NM	NM
Net Income	346	167	198	111	42.2	30.9	23.8	5.05	20.2	-10.2
S&P Core Earnings	333	167	198	105	27.9	27.3	23.5	14.1	NA	NA

Balance Sheet & Other Financial Data (Million $)										
Cash	0.75	4.02	2.38	4.75	18.4	0.63	1.33	3.25	2.48	15.1
Current Assets	404	262	320	208	136	66.1	37.4	78.6	62.1	72.9
Total Assets	5,563	4,017	3,188	2,019	1,595	830	658	692	689	752
Current Liabilities	354	305	232	322	177	107	67.2	44.0	45.9	53.6
Long Term Debt	1,791	1,151	1,049	616	621	358	368	392	458	572
Common Equity	2,458	1,728	1,346	770	566	224	206	246	185	126
Total Capital	5,032	3,470	2,864	1,561	1,305	643	574	648	643	699
Capital Expenditures	918	808	517	277	175	2.62	2.82	2.33	2.26	0.66
Cash Flow	694	388	367	239	140	117	101	82.9	91.0	63.9
Current Ratio	1.1	0.9	1.4	0.6	0.8	0.6	0.6	1.8	1.4	1.4
% Long Term Debt of Capitalization	35.6	33.1	36.6	39.5	47.6	55.7	64.1	60.6	71.2	81.8
% Return on Assets	7.2	4.7	7.6	6.1	3.5	4.2	3.5	0.7	2.8	NM
% Return on Equity	16.5	10.9	18.7	16.1	9.4	14.0	10.8	2.3	12.1	NM

Data as orig reptd.; bef. results of disc opers/spec. items. Per share data adj. for stk. divs.; EPS diluted. E-Estimated. NA-Not Available. NM-Not Meaningful. NR-Not Ranked. UR-Under Review.

Office: 100 Throckmorton St Ste 1200, Fort Worth, TX 76102-2842.
Telephone: 817-870-2601.
Website: http://www.rangeresources.com
Chrmn & CEO: J.H. Pinkerton

Pres & COO: J.L. Ventura
EVP & CFO: R.S. Manny
SVP, Secy & General Counsel: D.P. Poole
Investor Contact: R.L. Waller (817-870-2601)

Board Members: C. L. Blackburn, A. V. Dub, V. R. Eales, A. Finkelson, J. Funk, J. S. Linker, K. S. McCarthy, J. H. Pinkerton, J. L. Ventura

Founded: 1976
Domicile: Delaware
Employees: 835

Raytheon Co.

STANDARD &POOR'S

S&P Recommendation HOLD ★★★☆☆

Price	12-Mo. Target Price	Investment Style
$51.63 (as of Nov 27, 2009)	$50.00	Large-Cap Value

GICS Sector Industrials
Sub-Industry Aerospace & Defense

Summary Raytheon, the world's sixth largest military contractor, specializes in making high-tech missiles and electronics.

Key Stock Statistics (Source S&P, Vickers, company reports)

52-Wk Range	$53.00–33.20	S&P Oper. EPS 2009**E**	4.81	Market Capitalization(B)	$19.785	Beta	0.68
Trailing 12-Month EPS	$4.63	S&P Oper. EPS 2010**E**	5.00	Yield (%)	2.40	S&P 3-Yr. Proj. EPS CAGR(%)	6
Trailing 12-Month P/E	11.2	P/E on S&P Oper. EPS 2009**E**	10.7	Dividend Rate/Share	$1.24	S&P Credit Rating	A-
$10K Invested 5 Yrs Ago	$14,426	Common Shares Outstg. (M)	383.2	Institutional Ownership (%)	83		

Price Performance

30-Week Mov. Avg. · · · 10-Week Mov. Avg. - - GAAP Earnings vs. Previous Year   Volume Above Avg. STARS
12-Mo. Target Price — Relative Strength — ▲ Up ▼ Down ▶ No Change   Below Avg. ★

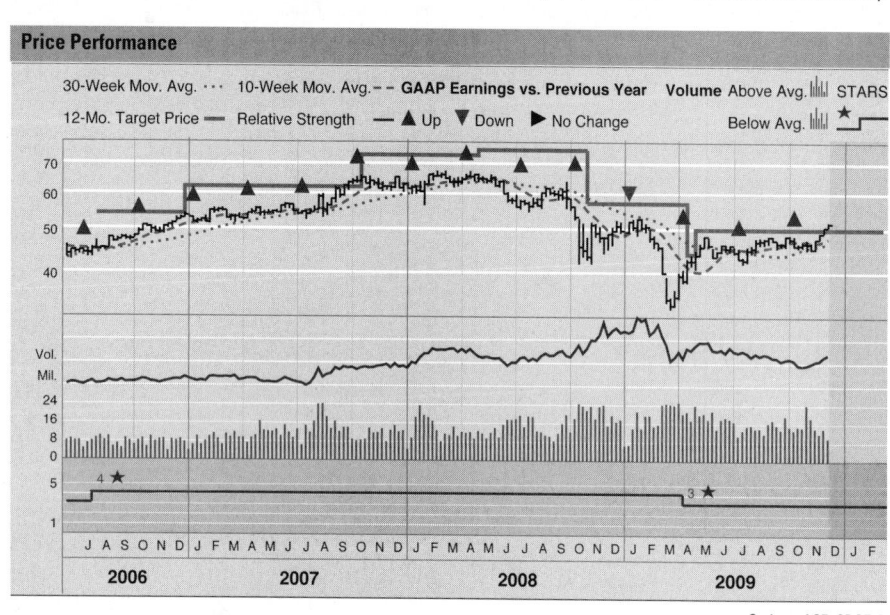

Options: ASE, CBOE, P

Analysis prepared by **Richard Tortoriello** on October 29, 2009, when the stock traded at **$45.40**.

Highlights

▶ We estimate revenue growth of 6.9% in 2009, and project 5.5% growth in 2010. The company's book-to-bill ratio was 1.20 in 2007 and 1.16 in 2008. Book to bill for the first nine months of 2009 was 0.99, and funded backlog as of September 2009 was $23.7 billion (up 12%), a little less than one year of sales. We see 2010 revenue driven by Integrated Defense (which includes Patriot), Space/Air Systems (classified projects), and Technical Services (training programs).

▶ We see operating profit margins expanding to 12.0% in 2009, from 11.2% in 2008, primarily on a pension gain versus pension expense in 2008 and lower general corporate expenses. We are modeling lower margins (11%) for 2010, primarily on our view of increased pension expense.

▶ We project EPS of $4.81 in 2009, with growth to $5.00 in 2010. We look for free cash flow (cash generated from operations less capital expenditures) of about $2.0 billion, or about $5.00 per share, in 2009, up from $1.7 billion, or $4.00, in 2008.

Investment Rationale/Risk

▶ Although we have a favorable view of RTN's order rates and backlog growth over the past two-plus years, we expect defense spending to flatten out with the government's fiscal 2010 budget, and to decline going forward, as we see very large budget deficits in coming years, increased social spending, and an emphasis on equipment for fighting guerilla warfare, versus heavy military equipment, putting very strong pressure on the U.S. defense budget. As a result, we would not add to positions, despite our view of RTN's historically low current valuation.

▶ Risks to our recommendation and target price include the potential for delays and/or cuts in military contracts and the failure to perform well on existing contracts or to win new business.

▶ Our 12-month target price of $50 is based on an enterprise value-to-EBITDA multiple of 6X, using our 2010 EBITDA estimate of about $3.3 billion. This compares to a 20-year low EV/EBITDA multiple for RTN of 3.5X and a 20-year average of 8.8X. We believe the shares deserve a below-average valuation, due to our view of projected weak defense spending.

Qualitative Risk Assessment

LOW	MEDIUM	HIGH

Our risk assessment reflects RTN's exposure to changes in defense spending and historically below-average earnings stability, offset by its relatively low long-term debt to capital ratio of 19%, as of September 2009, its leading defense contractor status, and its large project backlog.

Quantitative Evaluations

S&P Quality Ranking B

D	C	B-	B	B+	A-	A	A+

Relative Strength Rank STRONG

85

LOWEST = 1   HIGHEST = 99

Revenue/Earnings Data

Revenue (Million $)

	1Q	2Q	3Q	4Q	Year
2009	5,884	6,125	6,205	--	--
2008	5,354	5,870	5,864	6,086	23,174
2007	4,928	5,419	5,355	6,000	21,301
2006	4,660	4,973	4,936	5,722	20,291
2005	4,944	5,409	5,331	6,210	21,894
2004	4,676	4,929	4,936	5,704	20,245

Earnings Per Share ($)

	1Q	2Q	3Q	4Q	Year
2009	1.11	1.24	1.25	E1.19	E4.81
2008	0.93	1.00	1.01	1.02	3.95
2007	0.69	0.79	0.69	1.45	3.80
2006	0.61	0.61	0.59	0.81	2.46
2005	0.43	0.51	0.51	0.63	2.08
2004	0.24	-0.22	0.41	0.54	0.99

Fiscal year ended Dec. 31. Next earnings report expected: Late January. EPS Estimates based on S&P Operating Earnings; historical GAAP earnings are as reported.

Dividend Data (Dates: mm/dd Payment Date: mm/dd/yy)

Amount ($)	Date Decl.	Ex-Div. Date	Stk. of Record	Payment Date
0.280	12/10	12/30	01/02	01/30/09
0.310	03/25	04/03	04/07	05/01/09
0.310	05/28	07/02	07/07	08/04/09
0.310	09/24	10/02	10/06	11/05/09

Dividends have been paid since 1964. Source: Company reports.

The McGraw-Hill Companies

Raytheon Co.

Business Summary October 29, 2009

CORPORATE OVERVIEW. Raytheon, the world's fifth largest military contractor and a leading maker of missiles, conducts business through six business segments.

Integrated Defense Systems (21% of sales and 29% of operating profits in 2008) is a leading provider of integrated joint battlespace (e.g., space, air, surface, and subsurface) and homeland security solutions. Customers include the U.S. Missile Defense Agency (MDA), the U.S. Armed Forces, the Dept. of Homeland Security, as well as key international customers. Main product lines include seapower capability systems, focusing on the DDG-1000, the Navy's next-generation naval destroyer; national & theater security programs, including the X-band radars and missile defense systems; Patriot programs, principally the Patriot Air & Missile Defense System; global operations; and civil security and response programs.

Intelligence & Information Systems (13% of sales and 9% of profits) provides systems, subsystems, and software engineering services for national and tactical intelligence systems, as well as for homeland security and information technology (IT) solutions. Areas of concentration include signals and image processing, geospatial intelligence, air and space borne command & control, weather and environmental management, information technology, information assurance, and homeland security.

Missile Systems (21% of sales and 19% of profits) makes and supports a broad range of leading-edge missile systems for the armed forces of the U.S. and other countries. Business areas include naval weapon systems, which provides defensive missiles and guided projectiles to the navies of over 30 countries; air warfare systems, with products focused on air and ground-based targets, including the Tomahawk cruise missile; land combat, which includes the Javelin anti-tank missile; and other programs.

Network Centric Systems (18% of sales and 18% of profits) makes mission solutions for networking, command and control, battle space awareness, and transportation management. Business areas include combat systems, which provides ground-based surveillance systems; integrated communication systems; command and control systems; Thales-Raytheon Systems, a joint venture between the two companies; and precision technologies and components, which provides a broad range of imaging capabilities.

Company Financials Fiscal Year Ended Dec. 31

Per Share Data ($)	2008	2007	2006	2005	2004	2003	2002	2001	2000	1999
Tangible Book Value	NM	2.15	NM	NM	NM	NM	NM	NM	NM	NM
Cash Flow	4.69	4.63	3.28	3.19	1.93	2.22	2.74	2.03	3.50	3.46
Earnings	3.95	3.80	2.46	2.08	0.99	1.29	1.85	0.01	1.46	1.34
S&P Core Earnings	2.50	4.15	3.10	2.61	1.96	1.11	-0.25	-2.68	NA	NA
Dividends	1.12	1.02	0.96	0.86	0.80	0.80	0.80	0.80	0.80	0.80
Payout Ratio	28%	27%	34%	41%	81%	62%	43%	NM	55%	60%
Prices:High	67.49	65.94	54.17	40.57	41.89	33.97	45.70	37.44	35.81	76.56
Prices:Low	41.81	50.96	39.43	35.96	29.28	24.31	26.30	23.95	17.50	22.19
P/E Ratio:High	17	17	19	21	42	26	25	NM	25	57
P/E Ratio:Low	11	13	14	19	30	19	14	NM	12	17

Income Statement Analysis (Million $)										
Revenue	23,174	21,301	20,291	21,894	20,245	18,109	16,760	16,867	16,895	19,841
Operating Income	2,907	2,700	2,213	2,131	1,822	1,709	2,118	1,488	2,319	2,251
Depreciation	311	372	373	444	434	393	364	729	694	724
Interest Expense	129	196	273	312	418	537	497	660	736	713
Pretax Income	2,498	2,225	1,688	1,440	579	762	1,074	117	877	828
Effective Tax Rate	33.0%	23.9%	34.4%	34.6%	24.2%	29.8%	29.7%	95.7%	43.2%	44.8%
Net Income	1,674	1,693	1,107	942	439	535	755	5.00	498	457
S&P Core Earnings	1,059	1,848	1,392	1,180	866	460	-105	-970	NA	NA

Balance Sheet & Other Financial Data (Million $)										
Cash	2,259	2,655	2,460	1,202	556	661	544	1,214	871	230
Current Assets	7,417	7,616	9,517	7,567	7,124	6,585	7,190	8,362	8,013	8,931
Total Assets	23,296	23,281	25,491	24,381	24,153	23,668	23,946	26,636	26,777	28,110
Current Liabilities	5,149	4,788	6,715	5,900	5,644	3,849	5,107	5,753	4,865	7,886
Long Term Debt	2,309	2,268	3,278	3,969	4,637	7,376	7,138	6,875	9,054	7,298
Common Equity	9,087	12,542	11,101	10,798	10,611	9,162	8,870	11,290	10,823	10,959
Total Capital	11,659	15,261	14,544	15,011	15,345	16,538	16,008	18,743	20,650	18,810
Capital Expenditures	304	313	295	75.0	363	428	458	486	431	532
Cash Flow	1,985	2,065	1,480	1,386	873	928	1,119	734	1,192	1,181
Current Ratio	1.4	1.6	1.4	1.3	1.3	1.7	1.4	1.5	1.6	1.1
% Long Term Debt of Capitalization	19.8	14.9	22.5	26.4	30.2	44.6	44.6	36.7	43.8	38.8
% Net Income of Revenue	7.2	8.0	5.5	4.3	2.2	3.0	4.5	0.0	2.9	2.3
% Return on Assets	7.2	19.8	4.4	3.9	1.8	2.2	3.0	0.0	1.8	1.6
% Return on Equity	15.5	14.3	10.2	8.8	4.4	5.9	7.5	0.0	4.6	4.2

Data as orig reptd.; bef. results of disc opers/spec. items. Per share data adj. for stk. divs.; EPS diluted. E-Estimated. NA-Not Available. NM-Not Meaningful. NR-Not Ranked. UR-Under Review.

Office: 870 Winter St, Waltham, MA 02451-1449.
Telephone: 781-522-3000.
Email: invest@raytheon.com
Website: http://www.raytheon.com

Chrmn & CEO: W.H. Swanson
Pres: J.R. Harbison
SVP & CFO: D.C. Wajsgras
SVP, Secy & General Counsel: J.B. Stephens

CFO: D.E. Smith
Investor Contact: M. Kaplan (781-522-5141)
Board Members: V. E. Clark, J. M. Deutch, S. J. Hadley, F. M. Poses, M. Ruettgers, R. L. Skates, W. R. Spivey, L. G. Stuntz, W. H. Swanson

Founded: 1928
Domicile: Delaware
Employees: 72,800

Red Hat Inc

STANDARD &POOR'S

| S&P Recommendation | HOLD ★★★☆☆ | Price $26.80 (as of Nov 27, 2009) | 12-Mo. Target Price $27.00 | Investment Style Large-Cap Growth |

GICS Sector Information Technology
Sub-Industry Systems Software

Summary This company is a leading provider of Linux operating system software for enterprises.

Key Stock Statistics (Source S&P, Vickers, company reports)

52-Wk Range	$28.94– 8.30	S&P Oper. EPS 2010**E**	0.49	Market Capitalization(B)	$5.032	Beta	1.44
Trailing 12-Month EPS	$0.46	S&P Oper. EPS 2011**E**	0.57	Yield (%)	Nil	S&P 3-Yr. Proj. EPS CAGR(%)	20
Trailing 12-Month P/E	58.3	P/E on S&P Oper. EPS 2010**E**	54.7	Dividend Rate/Share	Nil	S&P Credit Rating	BB+
$10K Invested 5 Yrs Ago	$20,105	Common Shares Outstg. (M)	187.8	Institutional Ownership (%)	90		

Price Performance

30-Week Mov. Avg. · · · 10-Week Mov. Avg. - - - **GAAP Earnings vs. Previous Year** Volume Above Avg. STARS
12-Mo. Target Price — Relative Strength ▲ Up ▼ Down ▶ No Change Below Avg.

Options: CBOE, P, Ph

Analysis prepared by **Jim Yin** on September 24, 2009, when the stock traded at **$ 27.72**.

Highlights

► We estimate that total revenue in FY 10 (Feb.) will rise 11%, following 25% growth in FY 09. Our forecast for a deceleration in revenue growth, despite contributions from recent acquisitions, reflects our view of a sluggish economic recovery. However, we believe the company is gaining market share with its value proposition. Additionally, we see a higher long-term growth opportunity in server virtualization and increased adoption for RHT's JBoss middleware products.

► We expect the gross margin in FY 10 to be 85%, up from 84% in FY 09. We see operating expenses increasing 10% in FY 10, as RHT improves product and service offerings, but we expect a decrease to 69% of revenues, from 71% in FY 09, due to economies of scale. We project that operating margins in FY 10 will widen to 16%, from 13% in FY 09, reflecting better operating efficiency.

► Our EPS estimate for FY 10 is $0.49, versus $0.37 in FY 09. The projected rise reflects our expectations for higher revenues, improved operating margins, and a 9% decline in the number of shares outstanding. RHT repurchased $570 million of convertible debt in FY 09.

Investment Rationale/Risk

► We recently upgraded our recommendation to hold from sell. We remain concerned about weak IT spending amid a weak global economy. Forrester Research, an independent research firm, predicts IT spending will decline 5% in 2009. However, the economy is recovering, and we see IT spending rising 4% in 2010. Additionally, we believe RHT is gaining market share given its lower total cost of ownership. We also think the virtualization market segment represents a significant long-term growth opportunity.

► Risks to our recommendation and target price include a slower-than-expected recovery in the global economy, lower corporate IT spending, and increased competition.

► Our 12-month target price of $27 is based on a blend of our DCF and enterprise value (EV)-to-sales analyses. Our DCF model assumes a 12% weighted average cost of capital and a 3% terminal growth rate, yielding an intrinsic value of $27. From our EV-to-sales analysis, we derive a value of $26, based on an EV-to-sales ratio of 4.8X, a premium to the industry's average of 2.4X, reflecting RHT's higher growth potential.

Qualitative Risk Assessment

| LOW | MEDIUM | HIGH |

Our risk assessment reflects our view that growth will slow over the next few years due to increased competition and a slowdown in the global economy.

Quantitative Evaluations

S&P Quality Ranking B-

| D | C | B- | B | B+ | A- | A | A+ |

Relative Strength Rank MODERATE

59

LOWEST = 1   HIGHEST = 99

Revenue/Earnings Data

Revenue (Million $)

	1Q	2Q	3Q	4Q	Year
2010	174.4	183.6	--	--	--
2009	156.6	164.4	165.3	166.2	652.6
2008	118.9	127.3	135.4	141.5	523.0
2007	84.00	99.67	105.8	111.1	400.6
2006	60.78	65.72	73.11	78.72	278.3
2005	41.76	46.32	50.93	57.45	196.5

Earnings Per Share ($)

	1Q	2Q	3Q	4Q	Year
2010	0.10	0.15	E0.12	E0.12	E0.49
2009	0.08	0.10	0.12	0.08	0.39
2008	0.08	0.09	0.10	0.10	0.36
2007	0.07	0.05	0.07	0.10	0.29
2006	0.07	0.09	0.12	0.13	0.41
2005	0.06	0.06	0.06	0.06	0.24

Fiscal year ended Feb. 28. Next earnings report expected: Late December. EPS Estimates based on S&P Operating Earnings; historical GAAP earnings are as reported.

Dividend Data

No cash dividends have been paid.

Please read the Required Disclosures and Analyst Certification on the last page of this report.

The McGraw-Hill Companies

Red Hat Inc

STANDARD & POOR'S

Business Summary September 24, 2009

CORPORATE OVERVIEW. RHT is the leading provider of Linux operating systems and subsystems, capturing 62% of the market in terms of new license and maintenance revenues in 2007, according to IDC, a technology research firm, followed by Novell (NOVL $5, Hold), with 29%. The company introduced its core operating system -- Red Hat Enterprise Linux (RHEL) -- in 2002. RHT also offers enterprise middleware software -- JBoss Enterprise Middleware. Both software packages utilize an open source software development model, which provides users and developers access to the source code and permits them to copy, modify and redistribute the software. RHT enhances the open source software and delivers the technologies and related services in the form of annual or multi-year subscriptions, which accounted for 83% of revenues in FY 09 (Feb.). The remaining 17% of revenues came from services, primarily customization, implementation and training.

CORPORATE STRATEGY. RHT is focused on increasing the adoption of RHEL by large enterprises and growing sales of services to its customers. To drive increased adoption, RHT has formed partnerships and strategic relationships with BEA, BMC Software, Computer Associates, IBM, Oracle, SAP, Sybase, Symantec, HP, Dell, Fujitsu, Fujitsu Siemens, NEC and VMware. These part-

ners and others generally contribute between 50% and 60% of bookings in any given quarter, with the balance coming from direct sales. We believe this heavy reliance on the indirect channel will enable RHT to maintain higher operating margins than would be possible with an entirely in-house sales team, but we believe this will come at the cost of control over this portion of its business.

RHT will continue to expand its capabilities through strategic acquisitions. In June 2006, the company acquired JBoss, a provider of open source middleware, and the remaining minority interest in the Indian joint venture. In 2007, RHT acquired MetaMatrix, a leading provider of enterprise data management software. In September 2008, RHT acquired Qumranet, Inc. for $107 million in cash. Qumranet is a provider of virtualization software for managing Microsoft desktops.

Company Financials Fiscal Year Ended Feb. 28

Per Share Data ($)	2009	2008	2007	2006	2005	2004	2003	2002	2001	2000
Tangible Book Value	2.87	2.94	2.06	2.12	1.54	1.79	1.73	1.76	1.88	2.19
Cash Flow	0.56	0.50	0.38	0.46	0.26	0.11	Nil	-0.35	-0.19	-0.34
Earnings	0.39	0.36	0.29	0.41	0.24	0.08	-0.04	-0.71	-0.53	-0.40
S&P Core Earnings	0.39	0.35	0.29	0.28	0.06	-0.37	-0.20	-0.75	-1.07	NA
Dividends	Nil	Nil	Nil	Nil	Nil	Nil	Nil	Nil	Nil	Nil
Payout Ratio	Nil	Nil	Nil	Nil	Nil	Nil	Nil	Nil	Nil	Nil
Calendar Year	2008	2007	2006	2005	2004	2003	2002	2001	2000	1999
Prices:High	24.84	25.25	32.48	28.65	29.06	19.98	9.50	10.12	148.00	151.31
Prices:Low	7.50	18.04	13.70	10.37	11.21	4.95	3.46	2.40	5.00	20.00
P/E Ratio:High	64	70	NM	70	NM	NM	NM	NM	NM	NM
P/E Ratio:Low	19	50	NM	25	NM	NM	NM	NM	NM	NM

Income Statement Analysis (Million $)										
Revenue	653	523	401	278	196	126	90.9	78.9	103	42.4
Operating Income	123	103	76.1	73.5	39.5	10.1	-8.38	-17.7	-52.5	-25.2
Depreciation	40.3	33.0	23.9	15.4	10.9	6.87	6.52	59.7	55.0	5.94
Interest Expense	4.80	6.25	6.02	6.12	6.44	Nil	Nil	Nil	0.35	0.56
Pretax Income	122	125	89.6	82.0	44.9	14.0	-6.34	-120	-86.4	-39.5
Effective Tax Rate	35.2%	38.4%	33.1%	2.84%	NM	NM	NM	NM	NM	NM
Net Income	78.7	76.7	59.9	79.7	45.4	14.0	-6.34	-120	-86.7	-39.8
S&P Core Earnings	78.7	73.5	59.9	53.1	6.25	-63.8	-34.4	-126	-176	NA

Balance Sheet & Other Financial Data (Million $)										
Cash	663	990	527	268	140	545	45.3	55.5	85.2	242
Current Assets	891	1,192	1,007	881	385	658	120	119	180	280
Total Assets	1,754	2,080	1,786	1,314	1,134	1,110	390	370	505	424
Current Liabilities	447	970	300	201	139	83.6	47.1	37.0	40.7	29.9
Long Term Debt	Nil	Nil	570	570	600	601	1.39	1.56	0.28	0.23
Common Equity	1,106	951	821	477	361	409	336	327	464	393
Total Capital	1,106	951	1,391	1,048	962	1,010	338	329	465	394
Capital Expenditures	24.5	41.8	22.6	16.8	14.9	13.2	6.77	6.75	11.1	6.66
Cash Flow	119	110	83.8	95.1	56.3	20.9	0.18	-59.8	-31.7	-33.9
Current Ratio	2.0	1.2	3.4	4.4	2.8	7.9	2.6	3.2	4.4	9.4
% Long Term Debt of Capitalization	Nil	Nil	41.0	54.4	62.4	59.5	0.4	0.5	0.1	0.1
% Net Income of Revenue	12.1	14.7	15.0	28.6	23.1	11.1	NM	NM	NM	NM
% Return on Assets	4.1	4.0	3.9	6.5	4.0	1.9	NM	NM	NM	NM
% Return on Equity	7.7	8.7	9.2	19.0	11.8	3.8	NM	NM	NM	NM

Data as orig reptd.; bef. results of disc opers/spec. items. Per share data adj. for stk. divs.; EPS diluted. E-Estimated. NA-Not Available. NM-Not Meaningful. NR-Not Ranked. UR-Under Review.

Office: 1801 Varsity Drive, Raleigh, NC 27606.
Telephone: 919-754-3700.
Email: investors@redhat.com
Website: http://www.redhat.com

Chrmn: M.J. Szulik
Pres & CEO: J. Whitehurst
EVP & CFO: C.E. Peters, Jr.
EVP, Secy & General Counsel: M.R. Cunningham

CTO: B. Stevens
Investor Contact: L. Brewton (919-754-4476)
Board Members: M. Chau, J. J. Clarke, R. A. DiPentima, M. A. Fox, N. K. Gupta, W. S. Kaiser, D. H. Livingstone, H. H. Shelton, M. J. Szulik, J. Whitehurst

Founded: 1993
Domicile: Delaware
Employees: 2,800

The McGraw-Hill Companies

Regions Financial Corp

STANDARD &POOR'S

S&P Recommendation **BUY** ★★★★☆	Price $5.58 (as of Nov 27, 2009)	12-Mo. Target Price $7.00	Investment Style Large-Cap Value

GICS Sector Financials
Sub-Industry Regional Banks

Summary This major southeastern bank holding company has over 1,900 offices in 16 mostly Sunbelt states.

Key Stock Statistics (Source S&P, Vickers, company reports)

52-Wk Range	$10.49– 2.35	S&P Oper. EPS 2009**E**	-1.02	Market Capitalization(B)	$6.629	Beta	0.94
Trailing 12-Month EPS	$-7.99	S&P Oper. EPS 2010**E**	-1.37	Yield (%)	0.72	S&P 3-Yr. Proj. EPS CAGR(%)	17
Trailing 12-Month P/E	NM	P/E on S&P Oper. EPS 2009**E**	NM	Dividend Rate/Share	$0.04	S&P Credit Rating	BBB
$10K Invested 5 Yrs Ago	$2,013	Common Shares Outstg. (M)	1,188.0	Institutional Ownership (%)	60		

Price Performance

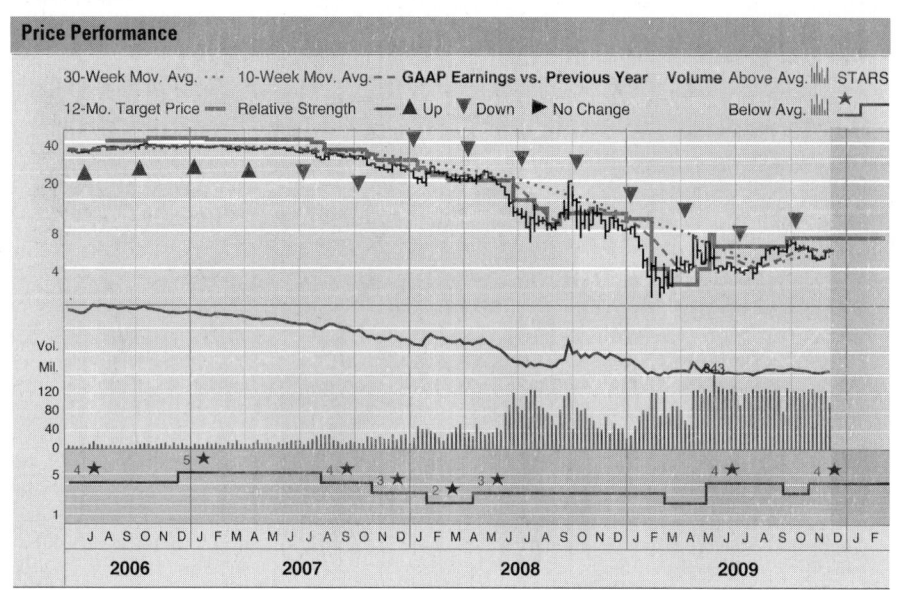

30-Week Mov. Avg. ··· 10-Week Mov. Avg. - - GAAP Earnings vs. Previous Year   Volume Above Avg. ▮▮▮ STARS
12-Mo. Target Price ▬ Relative Strength ▲ Up ▼ Down ► No Change   Below Avg. ▮▮▮

Options: C, Ph

Analysis prepared by **Stuart Plesser** on October 27, 2009, when the stock traded at **$ 5.11**.

Highlights

► Loans outstanding decreased 14% in the third quarter on a sequential annualized basis, reflecting a weakened economy. For 2010, we forecast a modest increase in loans reflecting an improvement in the economy offset by more stringent lending standards. Our net interest margin assumption for 2010 is 2.80%, versus a projected 2.69% in 2009, as RF's balance sheet is asset-sensitive and should benefit if interest rates rise. Excluding one-time items, we expect non-interest income to be up slightly in 2010, assuming higher fees and service charges, reflecting an improvement in the economy and a higher level of assets under management.

► We look for expenses to be higher in 2010, at 72% of revenues, reflecting the cost of asset disposals. We expect credit quality to continue to deteriorate through at least the first half of 2010, largely due to RF's construction and commercial loans, which should result in loan loss provisions of $3.9 billion in 2010, versus a projected $3.3 billion in 2009.

► Assuming share accretion of roughly 43%, we estimate a 2009 loss of $1.02 a share. In 2010, we look for a per share loss of $1.37.

Investment Rationale/Risk

► We think chargeoff levels will pick up in the coming quarters, with particular stress on RF's construction and commercial portfolios. We look for net chargeoffs to total roughly 2.5% of average loans in 2009, and to rise to 4.0% in 2010, with RF looking to aggressively sell its loans. We think RF's net interest margin will rise to about 2.8% as higher deposit yields reprice. RF recently raised roughly $1.85 billion via a common and mandatory preferred offering, and we think capital levels are now adequate. Even assuming the government's cumulative loss estimate of $9 billion proves correct, we do not think RF will need to raise additional capital. Under our loss assumptions, RF's TBV will drop to $5.60 by the end of 2010, from the current $7.40 level.

► Risks to our recommendation and target price include significant deterioration in credit trends, a lower-than-expected net interest margin, and operational performance below our expectations.

► Our 12-month target price of $7.00 reflects a below historical multiple of 1.25X our estimate of RF's TBV per share of $5.60 at the end of 2010.

Qualitative Risk Assessment

LOW	MEDIUM	HIGH

Our risk assessment reflects our view of the deteriorating credit quality of the company's loan portfolio coupled with the company's declining capital levels.

Quantitative Evaluations

S&P Quality Ranking   **B**

D	C	B-	**B**	B+	A-	A	A+

Relative Strength Rank   **STRONG**

74

LOWEST = 1   HIGHEST = 99

Revenue/Earnings Data

Revenue (Million $)

	1Q	2Q	3Q	4Q	Year
2009	2,445	2,550	2,079	--	--
2008	1,935	2,360	2,288	2,283	9,587
2007	2,797	2,724	2,742	2,667	10,925
2006	1,666	1,756	1,806	2,529	7,756
2005	1,423	1,565	1,564	1,572	6,124
2004	893.7	868.8	1,432	1,416	4,610

Earnings Per Share ($)

2009	0.04	-0.28	-0.37	E-0.41	E-1.02
2008	0.48	0.30	0.13	-8.97	-8.03
2007	0.65	0.63	0.56	0.10	1.96
2006	0.64	0.75	0.77	0.56	2.67
2005	0.51	0.53	0.55	0.55	2.15
2004	0.61	0.58	0.55	0.50	2.19

Fiscal year ended Dec. 31. Next earnings report expected: Late January. EPS Estimates based on S&P Operating Earnings; historical GAAP earnings are as reported.

Dividend Data (Dates: mm/dd Payment Date: mm/dd/yy)

Amount ($)	Date Decl.	Ex-Div. Date	Stk. of Record	Payment Date
0.100	01/15	03/16	03/18	04/01/09
0.010	04/16	06/15	06/17	07/01/09
0.010	07/16	09/15	09/17	10/01/09
0.010	10/15	12/14	12/16	01/04/10

Dividends have been paid since 1968. Source: Company reports.

Please read the Required Disclosures and Analyst Certification on the last page of this report.

The McGraw-Hill Companies

Regions Financial Corp

STANDARD &POOR'S

Business Summary October 27, 2009

CORPORATE OVERVIEW. Regions Financial is a bank holding company that operates primarily in the southeastern U.S., with operations consisting of banking, brokerage and investment services, mortgage banking, insurance brokerage, credit life insurance, commercial accounts receivable factoring and specialty financing. RF conducts its banking operations through Regions Bank, an Alabama-chartered commercial bank that is a member of the Federal Reserve System.

Banking operations also include Regions Mortgage (RMI). RMI's primary business is the origination and servicing of mortgage loans for long-term investors. RMI generally provides services in the same states in which RF has banking operations. Financial services operations include Morgan Keegan, a regional full-service brokerage and investment bank, which was acquired in 2001.

Other subsidiaries include Regions Insurance Group, Inc., Regions Agency Inc., Regions Life Insurance Company, Regions Interstate Billings Service Inc., and Regions Equipment Finance Corporation, providing all lines of personal and commercial insurance, credit-related insurance products, and other financial services.

MARKET PROFILE. As of June 30, 2008, which is the latest available FDIC data, RF had 1,924 branches and $86.2 billion in deposits. About 55% of its deposits and 52% of branches were concentrated in the adjoining states of Tennessee, Alabama and Florida, by our calculations.

Company Financials Fiscal Year Ended Dec. 31

Per Share Data ($)	2008	2007	2006	2005	2004	2003	2002	2001	2000	1999
Tangible Book Value	10.35	10.45	11.74	11.55	11.58	16.25	15.29	10.58	11.00	9.75
Earnings	-8.03	1.96	2.67	2.15	2.19	2.35	2.20	1.81	1.93	1.90
S&P Core Earnings	0.39	1.97	2.67	2.11	2.17	2.32	2.11	1.63	NA	NA
Dividends	0.96	1.46	2.11	1.36	0.93	1.00	0.94	0.91	0.87	0.79
Payout Ratio	NM	74%	79%	63%	43%	43%	43%	50%	45%	42%
Prices:High	25.84	38.17	39.15	35.54	35.97	30.70	31.10	26.72	22.68	33.72
Prices:Low	6.41	22.84	32.37	29.16	27.26	24.16	21.95	20.84	14.83	18.78
P/E Ratio:High	NM	19	15	17	16	13	14	15	12	18
P/E Ratio:Low	NM	12	12	14	12	10	10	11	8	10

Income Statement Analysis (Million $)										
Net Interest Income	3,843	4,398	3,353	2,821	2,113	1,475	1,498	1,425	1,389	1,426
Tax Equivalent Adjustment	36.7	38.1	NA	NA	NA	NA	NA	NA	NA	NA
Non Interest Income	3,021	2,864	2,054	1,832	1,591	1,373	1,207	950	641	537
Loan Loss Provision	2,057	555	143	165	129	122	128	165	127	114
% Expense/Operating Revenue	66.4%	64.2%	61.3%	65.5%	66.5%	64.6%	65.1%	64.2%	55.2%	54.2%
Pretax Income	-5,932	2,039	1,959	1,422	1,176	912	869	718	742	785
Effective Tax Rate	NM	31.7%	30.9%	29.6%	29.9%	28.5%	28.7%	29.1%	28.9%	33.1%
Net Income	-5,584	1,393	1,353	1,001	824	652	620	509	528	525
% Net Interest Margin	3.23	3.79	4.17	3.91	3.66	3.49	3.73	3.66	3.55	3.94
S&P Core Earnings	272	1,405	1,355	983	811	647	592	458	NA	NA

Balance Sheet & Other Financial Data (Million $)										
Money Market Assets	9,380	2,116	2,610	1,794	1,761	1,491	1,424	1,502	112	90.3
Investment Securities	18,896	17,369	18,562	11,979	12,617	9,088	8,995	7,847	8,994	10,913
Commercial Loans	23,595	20,907	24,145	14,728	15,180	9,914	10,842	9,912	9,070	8,230
Other Loans	73,823	74,472	70,360	43,677	42,556	22,501	20,144	21,225	22,402	19,992
Total Assets	146,248	141,042	143,369	84,786	84,106	48,598	47,939	45,383	43,688	42,714
Demand Deposits	33,479	18,417	20,709	13,699	11,424	5,718	5,148	5,085	4,513	4,420
Time Deposits	72,447	76,358	80,519	46,679	47,243	27,015	27,779	26,463	27,510	25,569
Long Term Debt	19,231	11,325	8,643	11,938	7,240	5,712	5,386	4,748	4,478	1,751
Common Equity	13,505	19,823	20,701	10,614	10,749	4,452	4,178	4,036	3,458	3,065
% Return on Assets	NM	1.0	1.2	1.2	1.2	1.4	1.3	1.1	1.2	1.3
% Return on Equity	NM	6.9	8.6	9.4	10.8	15.1	15.1	13.6	16.2	17.3
% Loan Loss Reserve	1.9	1.4	1.1	1.3	1.3	1.4	1.3	1.3	1.2	1.2
% Loans/Deposits	107.2	97.0	98.3	99.3	101.1	102.1	98.7	100.7	98.7	95.7
% Equity to Assets	11.6	14.3	13.7	12.6	11.5	8.9	8.8	8.4	7.5	7.6

Data as orig reptd.; bef. results of disc opers/spec. items. Per share data adj. for stk. divs.; EPS diluted. E-Estimated. NA-Not Available. NM-Not Meaningful. NR-Not Ranked. UR-Under Review.

Office: 1900 5th Ave N, Birmingham, AL 35203-2610.
Telephone: 205-944-1300.
Email: askus@regionsbank.com
Website: http://www.regions.com

Chrmn & CEO: C.D. Ritter
Pres, Vice Chrmn & COO: O.B. Hall, Jr.
EVP & CFO: I.M. Esteves
EVP, Secy & General Counsel: J.D. Buchanan

CTO: C. Rogers
Investor Contact: L. Underwood (205-801-0265)
Board Members: S. W. Bartholomew, Jr., G. W. Bryan, D. J. Cooper, D. DeFosset, Jr., E. W. Deavenport, Jr., O. B. Hall, Jr., J. R. Malone, S. W. Matlock, J. E. Maupin, Jr., C. D. McCrary, C. B. Nielsen, C. D. Ritter, J. R. Roberts, L. J. Styslinger, Jr.

Founded: 1970
Domicile: Delaware
Employees: 30,784

The McGraw-Hill Companies

Republic Services Inc.

STANDARD &POOR'S

S&P Recommendation BUY ★★★★☆	Price	12-Mo. Target Price	Investment Style
	$28.03 (as of Nov 27, 2009)	$31.00	Large-Cap Growth

GICS Sector Industrials
Sub-Industry Environmental & Facilities Services

Summary This company became the second largest U.S. provider of solid waste services in North America when it acquired Allied Waste Industries in December 2008.

Key Stock Statistics (Source S&P, Vickers, company reports)

52-Wk Range	$28.44– 15.05	S&P Oper. EPS 2009**E**	1.48	Market Capitalization(B)	$10.655	Beta		0.90
Trailing 12-Month EPS	$0.95	S&P Oper. EPS 2010**E**	1.75	Yield (%)	2.71	S&P 3-Yr. Proj. EPS CAGR(%)		5
Trailing 12-Month P/E	29.5	P/E on S&P Oper. EPS 2009**E**	18.9	Dividend Rate/Share	$0.76	S&P Credit Rating		BBB
$10K Invested 5 Yrs Ago	$14,666	Common Shares Outstg. (M)	380.1	Institutional Ownership (%)	91			

Price Performance

30-Week Mov. Avg. · · · · 10-Week Mov. Avg. - - - **GAAP Earnings vs. Previous Year** **Volume** Above Avg. ▌▌▌ STARS
12-Mo. Target Price — Relative Strength — ▲ Up ▼ Down ▶ No Change Below Avg. ▌▌▌ ★

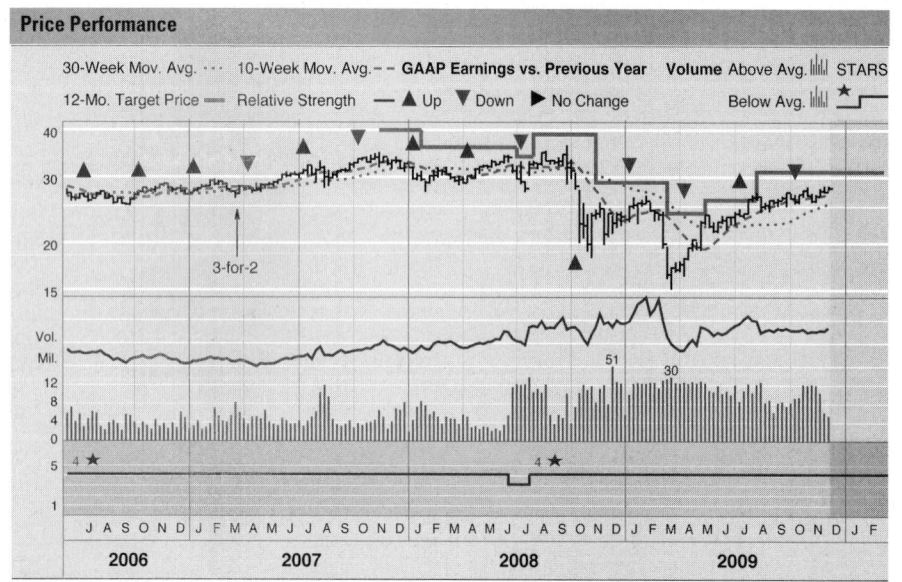

Options: CBOE, Ph

Analysis prepared by **Stewart Scharf** on November 11, 2009, when the stock traded at **$ 27.47**.

Highlights

► We expect pro forma core organic revenues to decline close to 6% in 2009, driven by lower temporary roll-off and landfill C&D (construction and demolition) volumes. Total revenue should drop at least 11%, as lower fuel surcharge and commodity prices offset higher core pricing. We see a gradual recovery during 2010, with volume growth returning later in the year.

► In our view, gross margins in 2009 will widen to about 41%, from near 38% in 2008 (pro forma), with further expansion seen in 2010, based on pricing initiatives, a better mix, and more stable fuel and commodity costs. Adjusted EBITDA before merger-related costs should also widen in 2010, from our projected 200-basis point improvement to 31% in 2009, as RSG leverages its health insurance costs, focusing on safety, training and systems. Run rate synergies should reach $145 million by the end of 2009, with about $170 million by the end of 2010.

► We expect a lower tax rate of 42.5% for 2009, and estimate pro forma operating EPS of $1.48 (before restructuring and merger-related costs), advancing to $1.75 in 2010.

Investment Rationale/Risk

► Our Buy opinion is based on our valuation metrics, and RSG's strong cash generation, balance sheet and return on invested capital. We also expect projected synergies from the Allied Waste merger to create long-term value as RSG boosts its position in the solid waste industry.

► Risks to our recommendation and target price include a prolonged housing and economic downturn, a decline in the customer retention rate, and any possible problems arising from the integration of Allied Waste. We also have corporate governance concerns related to compensation and board issues.

► Our DCF model, assuming a 3.5% perpetual growth rate and a weighted average cost of capital of 7%, results in an intrinsic value for RSG of $33. Applying a premium-to-peers forward P/E of 16.5X our 2010 EPS estimate, warranted, given our view of RSG's superior operating margins, strong cash position and higher ROIC, results in a value of $29. Blending these metrics, our 12-month target price is $31.

Qualitative Risk Assessment

LOW	MEDIUM	HIGH

Our risk assessment reflects our view of the company's strong balance sheet and focus on cash generation mainly for debt paydowns and dividend payments, as well as synergies and asset divestiture gains resulting from the Allied Waste acquisition.

Quantitative Evaluations

S&P Quality Ranking B+

D	C	B-	B	B+	A-	A	A+

Relative Strength Rank STRONG

76

LOWEST = 1   HIGHEST = 99

Revenue/Earnings Data

Revenue (Million $)

	1Q	2Q	3Q	4Q	Year
2009	2,061	2,066	2,074	--	--
2008	779.2	827.5	834.0	1,244	3,685
2007	765.6	808.4	806.2	796.0	3,176
2006	737.5	779.8	787.1	766.2	3,071
2005	677.2	718.6	730.0	738.1	2,864
2004	637.3	683.2	699.9	687.7	2,708

Earnings Per Share ($)

	1Q	2Q	3Q	4Q	Year
2009	0.30	0.60	0.32	E0.33	E1.48
2008	0.41	0.34	0.48	-0.55	0.37
2007	0.28	0.45	0.35	0.44	1.51
2006	0.31	0.35	0.39	0.34	1.38
2005	0.29	0.29	0.30	0.29	1.17
2004	0.24	0.26	0.27	0.25	1.02

Fiscal year ended Dec. 31. Next earnings report expected: Early March. EPS Estimates based on S&P Operating Earnings; historical GAAP earnings are as reported.

Dividend Data (Dates: mm/dd Payment Date: mm/dd/yy)

Amount ($)	Date Decl.	Ex-Div. Date	Stk. of Record	Payment Date
0.190	02/27	03/30	04/01	04/15/09
0.190	04/30	06/29	07/01	07/15/09
0.190	07/29	09/29	10/01	10/15/09
0.190	11/02	12/30	01/04	01/18/10

Dividends have been paid since 2003. Source: Company reports.

Please read the Required Disclosures and Analyst Certification on the last page of this report.

Republic Services Inc.

Business Summary November 11, 2009

CORPORATE OVERVIEW. Republic Services is the third largest U.S. provider of services in the non-hazardous solid waste industry. It provides collection services to commercial, industrial, municipal and residential customers through 380 collection companies in 40 states and Puerto Rico, and operates 236 transfer stations, 199 solid waste landfills and 78 recycling facilities. At the end of 2008, operations were divided into five regions: eastern, central, southern, southwestern and western. Collection revenues accounted for 76% of the total at September 30, 2009, while 19% was derived from net transfer and disposal revenues, and 4.4% from other. The estimated landfill life is 42 years (includes 23 sites with expansion airspace with an estimated remaining life of 32 years). RSG's internalization rate at September 30, 2009, was about 69%, up from 68% at 2008 year end. The average age of the company's truck fleet is about seven years. As of late 2009, we believe the customer churn rate was near 8%. The industry tends to lag economic swings by six to nine months.

In the third quarter of 2009, the fuel recovery fee fell 3.6% based on lower fuel costs. The average wholesale price of diesel fuel per gallon in the quarter dropped 40% to $2.60, from $4.34 a year earlier. As of early November 2009, fuel prices were $2.80 per gallon. RSG notes that a $0.01 change in the price of diesel fuel changes its fuel costs by about $1.7 million on an annual basis, partially offset by a smaller change in the fuel recovery fees charged to its customers. Commodity recycling prices dropped 32% in the third quarter of 2009,

to an average of $95 a ton, from $141 a ton a year earlier, but rose sequentially from $72.

In 2008, RSG bought back 4.6 million of its shares for $138 million, or $30.34 each, including 1.4 million shares in the second quarter. As of late 2009, the buyback program was still suspended, with $248 million of stock authorized for repurchase. Since 2000, stock buybacks totaled nearly $2.3 billion, or 44% of the shares outstanding. RSG plans to use free cash for debt paydowns and dividends.

In the first nine months of 2009, RSG recorded a net gain of $0.23 a share on the disposition of assets, restructuring charges of $0.09 a share, loss on the extinguishment of debt of $0.05 a share, costs to achieve synergies of $0.05 a share, and a $0.01 gain from insurance recoveries related to remediation activities.

As of late 2009, Bill Gates's investment firm, Cascade Investments LLC, owned about 15% of RSG's common stock.

Company Financials Fiscal Year Ended Dec. 31

Per Share Data ($)	2008	2007	2006	2005	2004	2003	2002	2001	2000	1999
Tangible Book Value	NM	NM	NM	0.07	1.24	1.36	1.27	0.80	0.91	0.78
Cash Flow	2.28	3.08	2.84	2.45	2.13	1.87	1.76	1.33	1.59	1.38
Earnings	0.37	1.51	1.38	1.17	1.02	0.89	0.96	0.49	0.84	0.76
S&P Core Earnings	0.44	1.47	1.38	1.10	0.99	0.85	0.90	0.45	NA	NA
Dividends	0.72	0.55	0.40	0.35	0.24	0.08	Nil	Nil	Nil	Nil
Payout Ratio	195%	37%	29%	30%	24%	9%	Nil	Nil	Nil	Nil
Prices:High	36.52	35.00	29.47	25.56	22.65	17.39	14.84	13.93	11.67	17.00
Prices:Low	18.25	26.22	24.47	20.07	16.33	12.17	10.84	9.17	6.42	5.92
P/E Ratio:High	99	23	21	22	22	19	15	29	14	22
P/E Ratio:Low	49	17	18	17	16	14	11	19	8	8
Income Statement Analysis (Million $)										
Revenue	3,685	3,176	3,071	2,864	2,708	2,518	2,365	2,258	2,103	1,839
Operating Income	1,017	892	816	756	712	1,077	654	598	638	554
Depreciation	378	302	296	279	259	239	200	215	197	163
Interest Expense	135	97.8	95.8	81.0	76.7	78.0	77.0	80.1	81.6	64.2
Pretax Income	159	468	444	409	384	347	387	209	356	327
Effective Tax Rate	53.6%	38.0%	37.0%	38.0%	38.0%	38.0%	38.0%	40.0%	38.0%	38.5%
Net Income	73.8	290	280	254	238	215	240	126	221	201
S&P Core Earnings	87.8	282	280	240	229	206	225	114	NA	NA
Balance Sheet & Other Financial Data (Million $)										
Cash	68.7	21.8	29.1	132	142	334	317	158	86.3	23.4
Current Assets	1,326	414	393	482	497	556	452	325	406	332
Total Assets	19,921	4,468	4,429	4,551	4,465	4,554	4,209	3,856	3,562	3,288
Current Liabilities	2,566	629	602	667	447	672	392	386	382	385
Long Term Debt	7,199	1,566	1,545	1,472	1,352	1,289	1,439	1,334	1,200	1,152
Common Equity	7,281	1,304	1,422	1,606	1,873	3,809	1,881	1,756	1,675	1,503
Total Capital	14,985	2,869	3,386	3,468	3,631	5,452	3,515	3,209	3,002	2,749
Capital Expenditures	387	293	338	329	284	273	259	249	208	290
Cash Flow	452	592	576	533	497	455	439	341	418	364
Current Ratio	0.5	0.7	0.7	0.7	1.1	0.8	1.2	0.8	1.1	0.9
% Long Term Debt of Capitalization	48.0	54.6	45.6	42.4	37.2	23.6	40.9	41.6	40.0	41.9
% Net Income of Revenue	2.0	9.1	9.1	8.9	8.8	8.6	10.1	5.6	10.5	10.9
% Return on Assets	0.6	6.5	6.2	5.6	5.3	4.9	5.9	3.4	6.5	6.6
% Return on Equity	1.7	21.3	18.5	14.6	12.6	5.7	13.2	7.3	13.9	14.3

Data as orig reptd.; bef. results of disc opers/spec. items. Per share data adj. for stk. divs.; EPS diluted. E-Estimated. NA-Not Available. NM-Not Meaningful. NR-Not Ranked. UR-Under Review.

Office: 18500 N Allied Way, Phoenix, AZ 85054-6164.
Telephone: 480-627-2700.
Website: http://www.republicservices.com
Chrmn & CEO: J.E. O'Connor

Pres & COO: D.W. Slager
Investor Contact: T.C. Holmes
EVP & CFO: T.C. Holmes
EVP, Secy & General Counsel: M.P. Rissman

Board Members: J. W. Croghan, J. W. Crownover, J. W. Crownover, W. J. Flynn, D. I. Foley, M. Larson, N. Lehmann, W. L. Nutter, J. E. O'Connor, R. A. Rodriguez, A. Sorensen, J. M. Trani, M. Wickham

Founded: 1996
Domicile: Delaware
Employees: 35,000

Reynolds American Inc

STANDARD &POOR'S

S&P Recommendation **BUY** ★★★★☆	Price	12-Mo. Target Price	Investment Style
	$51.32 (as of Nov 27, 2009)	$51.00	Large-Cap Value

GICS Sector Consumer Staples
Sub-Industry Tobacco

Summary Reynolds American, the second largest U.S. cigarette manufacturer, was formed via the mid-2004 merger of R.J. Reynolds and Brown & Williamson.

Key Stock Statistics (Source S&P, Vickers, company reports)

52-Wk Range	$51.78– 31.55	S&P Oper. EPS 2009**E**	4.69	Market Capitalization(B)	$14.953	Beta	0.67
Trailing 12-Month EPS	$3.45	S&P Oper. EPS 2010**E**	4.96	Yield (%)	7.01	S&P 3-Yr. Proj. EPS CAGR(%)	5
Trailing 12-Month P/E	14.9	P/E on S&P Oper. EPS 2009**E**	10.9	Dividend Rate/Share	$3.60	S&P Credit Rating	BBB-
$10K Invested 5 Yrs Ago	$18,218	Common Shares Outstg. (M)	291.4	Institutional Ownership (%)	46		

Price Performance

30-Week Mov. Avg. · · ·   10-Week Mov. Avg. – –   **GAAP Earnings vs. Previous Year**   Volume Above Avg. STARS
12-Mo. Target Price —   Relative Strength —   ▲ Up   ▼ Down   ► No Change   Below Avg. ★

Options: ASE, CBOE, P, Ph

Analysis prepared by **Esther Y. Kwon, CFA** on October 15, 2009, when the stock traded at **$ 47.68**.

Highlights

▶ We estimate that RAI's revenues in 2009 will fall at a mid-single digit rate, with a favorable product mix shift, price increases and new product introductions offset by a shipment decline of over 5%. We believe growth brands Camel, Pall Mall and American Spirit will see gains, with other brands suffering declines as marketing efforts were reduced. In 2010, we forecast revenues slipping 2%.

▶ We see operating margins up in 2009 as gross margins benefit from the rationalization of non-core brands and brand styles, higher pricing and lower promotions, while SG&A spending should remain well controlled as the company benefits from recent cost-saving actions. In September 2008, RAI announced a restructuring that included the elimination of 16% of its work force, which the company says could generate $35 million in annual savings.

▶ In 2009, we see slightly lower interest expense, and estimate a higher effective tax rate of about 38%, compared to 37%, on the termination of the joint venture with Gallaher Group. We expect EPS of $4.77, excluding a $458 million pretax impairment charge. In 2010, we forecast EPS of $5.00.

Investment Rationale/Risk

▶ We think leading smokeless tobacco company Conwood, which RAI acquired in mid-2006 for $3.5 billion, could continue to drive profits as higher-margin smokeless tobacco growth offsets declining cigarette sales. While we were somewhat cautious on potential heightened competition from Altria's recently acquired UST unit, as Altria extended its price cuts on Copenhagen and Skoal to additional markets through 2009, we see the impact remaining somewhat subdued. We also see continued good performance out of Pall Mall as consumers trade down in a weak economic environment in the United States. With an indicated dividend yield over 7%, we find the shares attractive on a total return basis.

▶ Risks to our recommendation and target price include additional regulation and taxation of tobacco products, in addition to near-term pressure on trading multiples due to ongoing litigation.

▶ Applying a forward P/E multiple of 10.5X, a discount to the peer average, to our 2010 EPS estimate of $5.00, we arrive at a relative valuation of $51, which is our 12-month target price.

Qualitative Risk Assessment

LOW	MEDIUM	HIGH

The domestic tobacco industry typically produces stable revenue streams and strong cash flow. While the industry is involved in significant litigation, recent rulings have led to an improvement in the litigation environment. However, we think RAI's "poison pill" anti-takeover provision is not in shareholders' best interests.

Quantitative Evaluations

S&P Quality Ranking   B+

D	C	B-	B	B+	A-	A	A+

Relative Strength Rank   STRONG

84

LOWEST = 1   HIGHEST = 99

Revenue/Earnings Data

Revenue (Million $)

	1Q	2Q	3Q	4Q	Year
2009	1,921	1,003	2,152	--	--
2008	2,057	2,339	2,272	2,177	8,845
2007	2,148	2,348	2,297	2,230	9,023
2006	1,960	2,291	2,190	2,069	8,510
2005	1,957	2,103	2,149	2,047	8,256
2004	1,218	1,352	1,866	2,001	6,437

Earnings Per Share ($)

	1Q	2Q	3Q	4Q	Year
2009	0.03	1.29	1.24	E1.16	E4.69
2008	1.71	1.24	0.72	0.89	4.57
2007	1.11	1.10	1.21	1.01	4.43
2006	0.95	1.24	1.05	0.61	3.85
2005	0.95	0.85	0.72	0.82	3.34
2004	0.72	0.88	1.14	0.22	2.81

Fiscal year ended Dec. 31. Next earnings report expected: NA. EPS Estimates based on S&P Operating Earnings; historical GAAP earnings are as reported.

Dividend Data (Dates: mm/dd Payment Date: mm/dd/yy)

Amount ($)	Date Decl.	Ex-Div. Date	Stk. of Record	Payment Date
0.850	02/03	03/06	03/10	04/01/09
0.850	05/06	06/08	06/10	07/01/09
0.850	07/16	09/08	09/10	10/01/09
0.900	10/06	12/08	12/10	01/04/10

Dividends have been paid since 1999. Source: Company reports.

Please read the Required Disclosures and Analyst Certification on the last page of this report.

The McGraw-Hill Companies

Reynolds American Inc

STANDARD
&POOR'S

Business Summary October 15, 2009

CORPORATE OVERVIEW. On July 30, 2004, R.J. Reynolds Tobacco Co. (RJRT) merged with Brown & Williamson (B&W), the U.S. operations of British American Tobacco (BTI), to form a new publicly traded company, Reynolds American, Inc. Combining RJRT and B&W, the second and third largest players, RAI is the second largest U.S. cigarette manufacturer, having a combined market share of 28.1% in 2008, down from 29% in 2007.

RAI is the parent company of RJRT, Santa Fe Natural Tobacco, which RJRT acquired in 2002, and Lane Limited, which was purchased from BTI for $400 million as part of the merger. In 2003, prior to the merger, RJRT began a significant restructuring plan, targeting cost savings of $1 billion by the end of 2005 through a significant work force reduction, asset divestitures and associated exit activities. Full integration of RJRT and B&W was expected to be completed in 2006, but realization of cost savings continued into 2007. The business combination was expected to result in approximately $600 million in annualized savings, including headcount reductions and operations consolidation, when compared with a separate entity basis.

In May 2006, RAI completed the acquisition of Conwood, the second largest manufacturer of smokeless tobacco products in the U.S., for $3.5 billion. RAI combined Conwood with its Lane Limited subsidiary into an Other Tobacco Products division in 2007. RAI's reportable segments are RJRT and Conwood.

The company's leading products are its Camel, Kool, Pall Mall, Doral and Winston brand cigarettes. The company's other brands include Salem, Misty and Capri. RAI also manages and contract manufactures cigarettes and tobacco products through its relationship with BAT affiliates.

Conwood's primary brands included Grizzly and Kodiak moist snuff.

CORPORATE STRATEGY. RAI's management has stated that its strategy is to generate sustainable earnings growth and strong cash flow in order to maximize shareholder value. To that end, RAI implemented a new portfolio strategy, designed to improve profitability, which established three categories for the combined brands of RJRT and B&W. The investment brand category, which includes premium brand Camel and value brand Pall Mall, receive the majority of resources to promote market share growth. The selective support brands, which include Kool, Winston, Salem, Capri and value brands Doral and Misty, receive limited support to optimize profitability; and the remaining brands are called non-support brands, which are managed to maximize profitability.

Company Financials Fiscal Year Ended Dec. 31

Per Share Data ($)	2008	2007	2006	2005	2004	2003	2002	2001	2000	1999
Tangible Book Value	NM	NM	NM	NM	NM	NM	NM	NM	NM	NM
Cash Flow	5.05	4.92	4.39	4.00	2.65	-20.81	3.34	4.72	4.10	3.11
Earnings	4.57	4.43	3.85	3.34	2.81	-22.04	2.32	2.24	1.73	0.90
S&P Core Earnings	3.63	4.41	3.95	3.96	3.59	2.13	1.73	1.52	NA	NA
Dividends	3.40	3.20	1.38	2.10	0.95	1.90	1.86	1.65	1.55	0.39
Payout Ratio	74%	72%	36%	63%	34%	NM	80%	74%	90%	43%
Prices:High	72.00	71.72	67.09	51.19	40.27	30.07	35.95	31.35	25.13	17.00
Prices:Low	37.21	58.55	47.48	38.24	26.69	13.76	17.42	22.09	7.88	8.00
P/E Ratio:High	16	16	17	15	14	NM	15	14	15	19
P/E Ratio:Low	8	13	12	11	9	NM	8	10	5	9

Income Statement Analysis (Million $)										
Revenue	6,955	9,023	8,510	8,256	6,437	5,267	6,211	8,585	8,167	7,567
Operating Income	2,602	2,496	2,183	1,880	1,239	873	1,200	1,409	1,399	1,368
Depreciation	142	143	162	195	153	151	184	491	485	482
Interest Expense	275	338	270	113	85.0	111	147	150	168	268
Pretax Income	2,128	2,073	1,809	1,416	829	-3,918	683	892	748	510
Effective Tax Rate	37.1%	37.0%	37.2%	30.4%	24.4%	NM	38.8%	50.2%	52.9%	61.8%
Net Income	1,338	1,307	1,136	985	627	-3,689	418	444	352	195
S&P Core Earnings	1,063	1,302	1,167	1,167	800	357	313	301	NA	NA

Balance Sheet & Other Financial Data (Million $)										
Cash	2,601	2,592	1,433	1,333	1,499	1,523	1,584	2,020	2,543	1,177
Current Assets	5,019	4,992	4,935	5,065	4,624	3,331	3,992	3,856	3,871	2,468
Total Assets	18,154	18,629	18,178	14,519	14,428	9,677	14,651	15,050	15,554	14,377
Current Liabilities	3,923	3,903	4,092	4,149	4,055	2,865	3,427	2,792	2,776	3,068
Long Term Debt	4,486	4,515	4,389	1,558	1,595	1,671	1,755	1,631	1,674	1,653
Common Equity	6,237	7,466	7,043	6,553	6,176	3,057	6,716	8,026	8,436	7,064
Total Capital	11,005	13,165	12,599	8,750	8,576	5,534	9,707	11,383	11,966	10,347
Capital Expenditures	113	142	136	105	92.0	70.0	111	74.0	60.0	55.0
Cash Flow	1,480	1,450	1,298	1,180	780	-3,538	602	935	837	677
Current Ratio	1.3	1.3	1.2	1.2	1.1	1.2	1.2	1.4	1.4	0.8
% Long Term Debt of Capitalization	40.8	34.3	34.8	17.8	18.6	30.2	18.1	14.3	14.0	16.0
% Net Income of Revenue	19.2	14.5	13.3	11.9	9.7	NM	6.7	5.2	4.3	2.6
% Return on Assets	7.3	7.1	6.9	6.8	5.2	NM	2.8	2.9	2.4	1.2
% Return on Equity	19.5	18.0	16.7	15.5	13.6	NM	5.7	5.4	4.5	2.3

Data as orig reptd.; bef. results of disc opers/spec. items. Per share data adj. for stk. divs.; EPS diluted. E-Estimated. NA-Not Available. NM-Not Meaningful. NR-Not Ranked. UR-Under Review.

Office: 401 North Main Street, Winston-Salem, NC 27102-2866.
Telephone: 336-741-2000.
Email: talktorjrt@rjrt.com
Website: http://www.reynoldsamerican.com

Chrmn, Pres & CEO: S.M. Ivey
Pres: J.B. O'Brien
EVP & CFO: T.R. Adams
EVP & General Counsel: E.J. Lambeth

EVP & CIO: D.I. Lamonds
Board Members: B. S. Atkins, N. Durante, M. Feinstein, S. M. Ivey, L. Jobin, H. Koeppel, N. Mensah, L. L. Nowell, III, H. G. Powell, T. C. Wajnert, N. R. Withington, J. Zillmer

Auditor: KPMG, Greensboro
Founded: 1875
Domicile: Delaware
Employees: 6,900

Robert Half International Inc.

STANDARD &POOR'S

S&P Recommendation	HOLD ★★★☆☆	Price	12-Mo. Target Price	Investment Style
		$22.19 (as of Nov 27, 2009)	$28.00	Large-Cap Blend

GICS Sector Industrials
Sub-Industry Human Resource & Employment Services

Summary This company is the world's largest specialized provider of temporary and permanent personnel in the fields of accounting and finance.

Key Stock Statistics (Source S&P, Vickers, company reports)

52-Wk Range	$28.06–14.06	S&P Oper. EPS 2009E	0.25	Market Capitalization(B)	$3.350	Beta	1.05
Trailing 12-Month EPS	$0.45	S&P Oper. EPS 2010E	0.50	Yield (%)	2.16	S&P 3-Yr. Proj. EPS CAGR(%)	-15
Trailing 12-Month P/E	49.3	P/E on S&P Oper. EPS 2009E	88.8	Dividend Rate/Share	$0.48	S&P Credit Rating	NA
$10K Invested 5 Yrs Ago	$8,750	Common Shares Outstg. (M)	151.0	Institutional Ownership (%)	91		

Price Performance

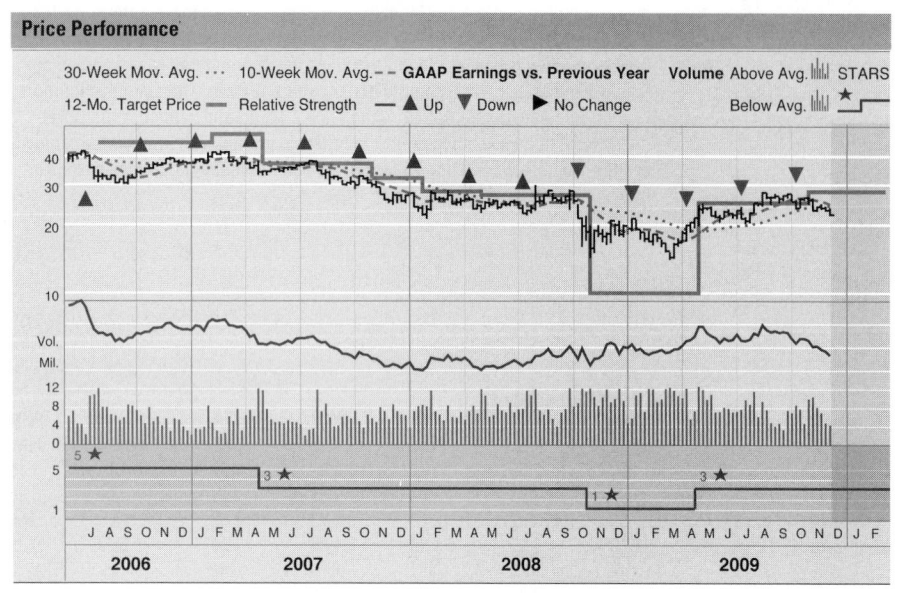

30-Week Mov. Avg. · · · 10-Week Mov. Avg. - - GAAP Earnings vs. Previous Year Volume Above Avg. STARS
12-Mo. Target Price — Relative Strength — ▲ Up ▼ Down ► No Change Below Avg. ★

Options: ASE, CBOE, Ph

Analysis prepared by **Michael W. Jaffe** on October 26, 2009, when the stock traded at **$ 25.76**.

Qualitative Risk Assessment

LOW	**MEDIUM**	HIGH

Our risk assessment reflects what we view as RHI's strong position in accounting and finance placements and a healthy balance sheet. This is offset by the highly cyclical nature of the company's business, which is largely dependent on the U.S. economy and the health of labor markets.

Quantitative Evaluations

S&P Quality Ranking B

D	C	B-	**B**	B+	A-	A	A+

Relative Strength Rank WEAK

19

LOWEST = 1   HIGHEST = 99

Highlights

► We forecast a 3% gain in revenues in 2010. Revenues have been much weaker over the past year, as they have been limited by very challenging economic conditions throughout the world. RHI's permanent placement business has been particularly hard hit. Moreover, while RHI's primary focus areas of accounting and finance stayed stronger than most non-professional areas for a good part of the labor downturn, their performance weakened considerably in recent quarters. However, based on our outlook for a modest recovery in global economies over the next year, we see a small upturn in RHI's top line in 2010.

► We see improved revenue trends aiding margins in 2010. We also see cost control efforts continuing to assist results. RHI's margins have been very weak over the past year, on the negative impact from very soft demand for its services. It has also been hurt by the cost of investments at the Protiviti consulting unit, which has also been experiencing sluggish demand.

► Our 2009 EPS forecast excludes $0.04 a share of one-time charges in the first quarter, with the largest part from staff reductions at Protiviti.

Investment Rationale/Risk

► We expect RHI's results to remain soft for a while longer, in light of the weak U.S. and global economies and their corresponding very soft labor markets. Although it will likely take some time before RHI's business makes a true recovery, it has started to exhibit what we believe are initial signs of stabilization. Based on these factors and valuation considerations, we think the shares are near a fair valuation.

► Risks to our recommendation and target price include an even longer-than-expected period of economic weakness in the U.S. and Western Europe, and less favorable-than-expected results from RHI's cost-cutting efforts.

► Based on our forecast of still depressed, but improving levels of earnings over the next year, we think price-to-sales analysis is the best method to currently value RHI. The shares recently traded at about 1.3X our 2010 sales per share estimate (based on our forecast of $3.1 billion of sales), which is somewhat above the low-end of RHI's valuation over the past two decades. We believe this valuation is merited, based on our view that the company's business is in the process of stabilizing. Our 12-month target price is $28.

Revenue/Earnings Data

Revenue (Million $)

	1Q	2Q	3Q	4Q	Year
2009	823.3	749.9	725.9	--	--
2008	1,226	1,225	1,160	989.8	4,601
2007	1,097	1,149	1,179	1,220	4,646
2006	943.9	981.8	1,028	1,060	4,014
2005	770.0	816.7	867.0	884.8	3,338
2004	572.3	641.2	708.0	754.2	2,676

Earnings Per Share ($)

2009	0.06	0.03	0.06	E0.06	E0.25
2008	0.45	0.48	0.43	0.26	1.63
2007	0.42	0.44	0.46	0.50	1.81
2006	0.38	0.39	0.43	0.45	1.65
2005	0.29	0.33	0.37	0.37	1.36
2004	0.09	0.18	0.24	0.28	0.79

Fiscal year ended Dec. 31. Next earnings report expected: Late January. EPS Estimates based on S&P Operating Earnings; historical GAAP earnings are as reported.

Dividend Data (Dates: mm/dd Payment Date: mm/dd/yy)

Amount ($)	Date Decl.	Ex-Div. Date	Stk. of Record	Payment Date
0.120	02/12	02/23	02/25	03/16/09
0.120	05/05	05/21	05/26	06/15/09
0.120	07/28	08/21	08/25	09/15/09
0.120	10/27	11/23	11/25	12/15/09

Dividends have been paid since 2004. Source: Company reports.

Robert Half International Inc.

STANDARD &POOR'S

Business Summary October 26, 2009

CORPORATE OVERVIEW. Robert Half International is the world's largest specialized staffing service in the fields of accounting and finance. In May 2002, RHI expanded its offerings to include risk consulting and internal audit services through its Protiviti unit. In 2008, the company derived 79% of its revenues from activities in temporary and consultant staffing, 9% from permanent placement staffing, and 12% from risk consulting and internal audit services. We calculate that foreign operations accounted for about 28% of RHI's revenues in 2008. As of year-end 2008, the company's staffing businesses had more than 370 offices in 42 states, the District of Columbia and 20 foreign countries, while Protiviti had more than 60 offices in 23 states and 17 foreign countries.

RHI's Accountemps temporary services division offers customers an economical means of dealing with uneven or peak work loads for accounting, tax and finance personnel. The temporary workers are employees of Accountemps, and are paid by Accountemps only when working on customer assignments. The customer pays a fixed rate for hours worked. If the client converts the temporary hire to a permanent worker, it typically pays a one-time fee for the conversion.

RHI offers permanent placement services through Robert Half Finance & Ac-

counting, which specializes in accounting, financial, tax and banking personnel. Fees for successful permanent placements are paid only by the employer and are usually a percentage of the new employee's annual salary.

Since the early 1990s, the company has expanded into additional specialty fields. OfficeTeam, formed in 1991, provides skilled temporary and full-time administrative and office personnel. In 1992, RHI acquired Robert Half Legal (formerly The Affiliates), which places temporary and regular employees in attorney, paralegal, legal administrative and other legal support positions. In 1994, Robert Half Technology (formerly RHI Consulting) was created to concentrate on the placement of contract and full-time information technology consultants. In 1997, the company established Robert Half Management Resources (formerly RHI Management Resources) to provide senior level project professionals specializing in the accounting and finance fields. The Creative Group, which started up in 1999, provides project staffing in the advertising, marketing and Web design fields. In 2008, Accountemps provided 38% of revenues, OfficeTeam 18%, other placement businesses 32%, and Protiviti 12%.

Company Financials Fiscal Year Ended Dec. 31

Per Share Data ($)	2008	2007	2006	2005	2004	2003	2002	2001	2000	1999
Tangible Book Value	5.26	4.99	5.15	4.72	4.30	3.65	3.41	3.69	3.13	2.28
Cash Flow	2.11	2.25	2.00	1.66	1.07	0.42	0.42	1.07	1.30	0.98
Earnings	1.63	1.81	1.65	1.36	0.79	0.04	0.01	0.67	1.00	0.77
S&P Core Earnings	1.63	1.81	1.65	1.29	0.71	-0.11	-0.17	0.51	NA	NA
Dividends	0.44	0.40	0.32	0.28	0.18	Nil	Nil	Nil	Nil	Nil
Payout Ratio	27%	22%	19%	21%	23%	Nil	Nil	Nil	Nil	Nil
Prices:High	29.99	42.21	43.94	39.86	30.98	25.18	30.90	30.90	38.63	24.19
Prices:Low	14.31	24.41	29.91	23.95	20.69	11.44	11.94	18.50	12.34	10.22
P/E Ratio:High	18	23	27	29	39	NM	NM	46	39	32
P/E Ratio:Low	9	13	18	18	26	NM	NM	28	12	13

Income Statement Analysis (Million $)	2008	2007	2006	2005	2004	2003	2002	2001	2000	1999
Revenue	4,601	4,646	4,014	3,338	2,676	1,975	1,905	2,453	2,699	2,081
Operating Income	487	549	511	433	280	75.0	71.2	261	348	268
Depreciation	73.2	71.4	61.1	51.3	49.1	65.9	72.3	73.1	56.6	39.1
Interest Expense	5.30	4.10	Nil	Nil	Nil	Nil	Nil	Nil	Nil	Nil
Pretax Income	419	490	466	392	235	11.7	3.50	196	302	235
Effective Tax Rate	40.3%	39.6%	39.3%	39.3%	40.1%	45.5%	38.0%	38.3%	38.3%	39.7%
Net Income	250	296	283	238	141	6.39	2.17	121	186	141
S&P Core Earnings	250	296	283	224	125	-18.4	-30.2	91.1	NA	NA

Balance Sheet & Other Financial Data (Million $)	2008	2007	2006	2005	2004	2003	2002	2001	2000	1999
Cash	355	310	447	458	437	377	317	347	239	151
Current Assets	1,033	1,060	1,112	1,017	916	699	643	686	672	491
Total Assets	1,412	1,450	1,459	1,319	1,199	980	936	994	971	777
Current Liabilities	413	448	403	337	280	189	184	177	237	176
Long Term Debt	1.89	3.75	3.83	2.70	2.27	2.34	2.40	2.48	2.54	2.60
Common Equity	984	984	1,043	971	912	789	745	806	719	576
Total Capital	986	988	1,047	974	914	791	747	808	721	601
Capital Expenditures	73.4	83.8	80.4	61.8	32.9	36.5	48.3	84.7	74.0	52.6
Cash Flow	323	368	344	289	190	72.3	74.5	194	243	181
Current Ratio	2.5	2.4	2.8	3.0	3.3	3.7	3.5	3.9	2.8	2.8
% Long Term Debt of Capitalization	0.2	0.4	0.4	0.3	0.2	0.3	0.3	0.3	0.4	0.4
% Net Income of Revenue	5.4	6.4	7.1	7.1	5.3	0.3	0.1	4.9	6.9	6.8
% Return on Assets	17.5	20.4	20.4	18.9	12.9	0.7	0.2	12.3	21.3	19.1
% Return on Equity	25.4	29.2	28.1	25.3	16.5	0.8	0.3	15.9	28.7	25.7

Data as orig reptd.; bef. results of disc opers/spec. items. Per share data adj. for stk. divs.; EPS diluted. E-Estimated. NA-Not Available. NM-Not Meaningful. NR-Not Ranked. UR-Under Review.

Office: 2884 Sand Hill Rd, Menlo Park, CA 94025-7072.
Telephone: 650-234-6000.
Website: http://www.rhi.com
Chrmn & CEO: H.M. Messmer, Jr.

Pres, Vice Chrmn & CFO: M.K. Waddell
EVP, Chief Admin Officer, Chief Acctg Officer & Treas: M.C. Buckley
SVP, Secy & General Counsel: S. Karel
CIO: K. White

Board Members: A. S. Berwick, Jr., F. P. Furth, E. W. Gibbons, H. M. Messmer, Jr., B. J. Novogradac, R. J. Pace, F. A. Richman, J. S. Schaub, M. K. Waddell

Founded: 1967
Domicile: Delaware
Employees: 235,300

The McGraw-Hill Companies

Rockwell Automation Inc.

STANDARD &POOR'S

S&P Recommendation	HOLD ★★★★★	Price $43.51 (as of Nov 27, 2009)	12-Mo. Target Price $48.00	Investment Style Large-Cap Blend

GICS Sector Industrials
Sub-Industry Electrical Components & Equipment

Summary This former aerospace and defense contractor (formerly Rockwell International) now primarily manufactures automated industrial equipment and power generators.

Key Stock Statistics (Source S&P, Vickers, company reports)

52-Wk Range	$46.72–17.50	S&P Oper. EPS 2010**E**	1.70	Market Capitalization(B)	$6.189	Beta		1.79
Trailing 12-Month EPS	$1.55	S&P Oper. EPS 2011**E**	2.39	Yield (%)	2.67	S&P 3-Yr. Proj. EPS CAGR(%)		6
Trailing 12-Month P/E	28.1	P/E on S&P Oper. EPS 2010**E**	25.6	Dividend Rate/Share	$1.16	S&P Credit Rating		A
$10K Invested 5 Yrs Ago	$10,504	Common Shares Outstg. (M)	142.3	Institutional Ownership (%)	73			

Price Performance

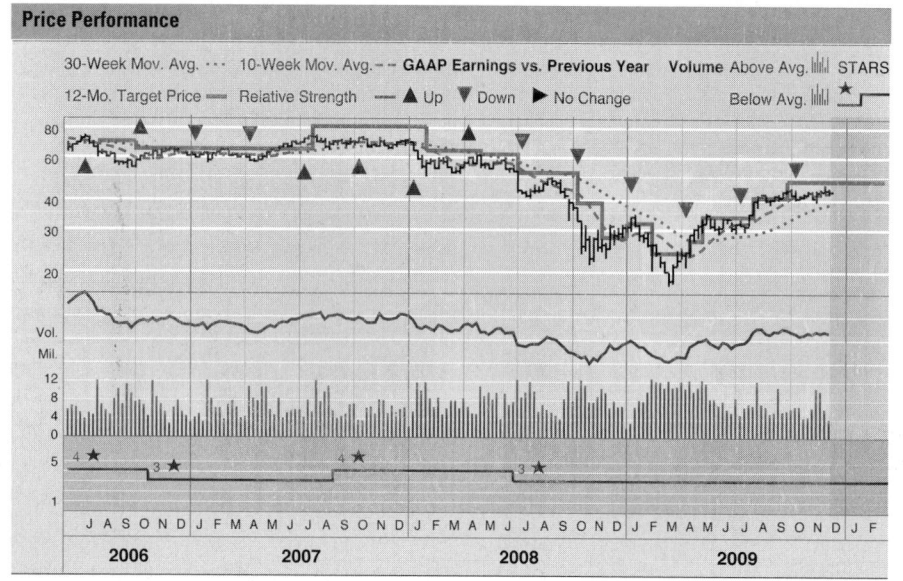

30-Week Mov. Avg. · · · · 10-Week Mov. Avg. – – GAAP Earnings vs. Previous Year   Volume Above Avg. STARS
12-Mo. Target Price ── Relative Strength ── ▲ Up ▼ Down ► No Change   Below Avg.

Options: ASE, CBOE, Ph

Analysis prepared by **Mathew Christy, CFA** on November 13, 2009, when the stock traded at **$ 43.04**.

Highlights

► After declining 24% in FY 09 (Sep), we expect revenues to fall about 2.5% in FY 10. This forecast is despite what we see as an improving economic environment, noting that both industrial production and capacity utilization rates have improved in recent months. Our forecast primarily reflects reduced orders at both the Control Products and Architecture & Software segments, as manufacturers await signs of a sustained economic recovery before increasing capital spending. However, we believe that the economic recovery will persist and see FY 11 gaining 8%.

► In our opinion, operating margins are likely to remain relatively flat in FY 10, despite a projected decline in revenue, as the company benefits from restructuring efforts that offsets somewhat lower operating leverage. In FY 11, we expect operating margins will expand as the company benefits from greater operating leverage and operating rates.

► Assuming an effective tax rate of 25% in both years and excluding earnings from discontinued operations, we project operating EPS of $1.70 for FY 10 and $2.39 for FY 11.

Investment Rationale/Risk

► We believe that shares are appropriately valued, recently trading at about 25X our FY 10 EPS estimate. This multiple is above those of peers, but more in line with historical multiples when results emerge from a downturn. In addition, we find positive the recent gains in capacity utilization rates, as reported by the Federal Reserve, as we believe they indicate a stabilization in the business spending environment.

► Risks to our recommendation and target price include weaker-than-expected global economic growth, rising raw material costs, and lower-than-forecast benefits from rationalization plans.

► Our 12-month target price of $48 is based on our relative peer valuation. We apply a target P/E multiple of 28X, above ROK's peers, to our FY 10 EPS per share estimate, implying a value of $48. We believe an above-peer average multiple is appropriate due to our expectation that earnings have bottomed and remain below more normal results, along with what we see as ROK's strong balance sheet.

Qualitative Risk Assessment

LOW	MEDIUM	HIGH

Our risk assessment reflects the highly cyclical end-market demand for the company's products, offset by corporate governance practices that we view as favorable, an S&P Quality Ranking of B+, reflecting average stability in earnings and dividend growth, and low capital requirements.

Quantitative Evaluations

S&P Quality Ranking B+

D	C	B-	B	B+	A-	A	A+

Relative Strength Rank MODERATE

68

LOWEST = 1   HIGHEST = 99

Revenue/Earnings Data

Revenue (Million $)

	1Q	2Q	3Q	4Q	Year
2009	1,189	1,058	1,011	1,074	4,333
2008	1,332	1,407	1,475	1,484	5,698
2007	1,146	1,207	1,281	1,371	5,004
2006	1,301	1,378	1,428	1,454	5,561
2005	1,185	1,218	1,265	1,335	5,003
2004	990.3	1,080	1,135	1,206	4,411

Earnings Per Share ($)

2009	0.81	0.29	0.23	0.20	1.53
2008	1.04	0.96	1.03	0.87	3.90
2007	0.76	0.65	1.07	1.07	3.53
2006	0.80	0.83	0.83	1.04	3.49
2005	0.65	0.75	0.68	0.69	2.77
2004	0.30	0.39	0.66	0.51	1.85

Fiscal year ended Sep. 30. Next earnings report expected: Early February. EPS Estimates based on S&P Operating Earnings; historical GAAP earnings are as reported.

Dividend Data (Dates: mm/dd Payment Date: mm/dd/yy)

Amount ($)	Date Decl.	Ex-Div. Date	Stk. of Record	Payment Date
0.290	02/04	02/12	02/17	03/10/09
0.290	04/08	05/14	05/18	06/10/09
0.290	06/04	08/13	08/17	09/10/09
0.290	11/04	11/12	11/16	12/10/09

Dividends have been paid since 1948. Source: Company reports.

Please read the Required Disclosures and Analyst Certification on the last page of this report.

The **McGraw·Hill** Companies

Rockwell Automation Inc.

STANDARD
&POOR'S

Business Summary November 13, 2009

CORPORATE OVERVIEW. In the early 1990s, Rockwell Automation (formerly Rockwell International) operated a broad range of manufacturing businesses. Following a series of divestitures that included the 2001 spin-off of Rockwell Collins, the 2006 divestitures of ElectroCraft Engineered Solutions, the sale of 50% interest in Rockwell Scientific, and the 2007 divestiture of Dodge mechanical and Reliance Electric motors, it now operates two business segments: Control Products and Solutions and Architecture and Software.

The Control Products and Solutions (CS) segment accounted for 57.5% of FY 08 (Sep.) total revenues and 43% of total operating profits, with 13.4% profit margins. CS supplies industrial control products and services focused on helping customers control, monitor and improve manufacturing processes. Products include industrial controls, variable frequency drives, smart motor controls, electronic overload controls, power control and motor control centers, drive systems, custom OEM panels, information systems and systems integration. Major markets served include consumer products, food and bever-

age, transportation, metals, mining, pulp and paper, and oil and gas. Competitors include Emerson Electric, GE, and Schneider Electric.

The Architecture and Software (A&S) segment generated 42.5% of FY 08 sales and 57% of operating profits, with 24.1% operating margins. The division offers control platforms and software as well as bundled automation products for enterprise business systems, distribution and supply chains. Control offerings include controllers, electronic interface devices, communications and network products, motor control sensors, programmable logic controllers (PLCs), input/output devices, sensors, and safety components. Software product offerings include configuration and visualization software, control platforms, and other manufacturing control software.

Company Financials Fiscal Year Ended Sep. 30

Per Share Data ($)	2009	2008	2007	2006	2005	2004	2003	2002	2001	2000
Tangible Book Value	1.21	3.65	4.29	4.40	2.95	3.95	2.41	2.61	2.23	6.90
Cash Flow	NA	4.72	4.26	4.35	3.68	2.83	2.53	2.29	5.39	4.80
Earnings	1.53	3.90	3.53	3.49	2.77	1.85	1.49	1.20	0.68	3.35
S&P Core Earnings	0.71	3.03	3.45	3.48	2.68	1.88	1.16	0.75	-0.06	NA
Dividends	1.16	1.16	1.16	0.90	0.78	0.66	0.66	0.66	0.93	1.02
Payout Ratio	76%	30%	33%	26%	28%	36%	44%	55%	137%	30%
Prices:High	46.72	69.72	75.60	799.47	63.30	49.97	36.10	22.79	49.45	54.50
Prices:Low	17.50	21.51	56.73	53.49	45.40	28.45	18.75	14.71	11.78	27.69
P/E Ratio:High	31	18	21	23	23	27	24	19	73	16
P/E Ratio:Low	11	6	16	15	16	15	13	12	17	8

Income Statement Analysis (Million $)	2009	2008	2007	2006	2005	2004	2003	2002	2001	2000
Revenue	4,333	5,698	5,004	5,561	5,003	4,411	4,104	3,909	4,279	7,151
Operating Income	NA	1,021	937	1,073	944	691	543	488	1,079	1,223
Depreciation	134	122	118	154	171	187	198	206	872	276
Interest Expense	NA	68.2	63.4	58.4	45.8	41.7	52.0	66.0	83.0	73.0
Pretax Income	274	809	789	365	737	438	299	233	168	943
Effective Tax Rate	20.5%	28.6%	27.8%	NM	29.7%	19.2%	5.69%	3.00%	25.6%	32.6%
Net Income	218	578	569	628	518	354	282	226	125	636
S&P Core Earnings	102	449	556	628	498	361	221	142	-12.0	NA

Balance Sheet & Other Financial Data (Million $)	2009	2008	2007	2006	2005	2004	2003	2002	2001	2000
Cash	644	582	624	415	464	474	226	289	121	190
Current Assets	NA	2,437	2,382	2,188	2,187	2,026	1,736	1,775	1,697	3,206
Total Assets	4,306	4,594	4,546	4,735	4,525	4,201	3,986	4,024	4,074	6,390
Current Liabilities	NA	1,303	1,745	1,293	941	864	820	966	867	1,820
Long Term Debt	905	904	406	748	748	758	764	767	922	924
Common Equity	1,316	1,689	1,743	1,918	1,649	1,861	1,587	1,609	1,600	2,669
Total Capital	2,221	2,593	2,149	2,822	2,397	2,708	2,388	2,534	2,693	3,593
Capital Expenditures	98.0	151	131	150	124	98.0	109	104	157	315
Cash Flow	NA	700	687	782	690	541	480	432	997	912
Current Ratio	5.8	1.9	1.4	1.7	2.3	2.3	2.1	1.8	2.0	1.8
% Long Term Debt of Capitalization	40.7	34.9	18.9	26.5	31.2	28.0	32.0	30.3	34.2	25.7
% Net Income of Revenue	5.0	10.1	11.4	11.3	10.4	8.0	6.9	5.8	2.9	8.9
% Return on Assets	4.9	12.6	12.3	13.6	11.9	8.7	7.1	5.6	2.7	9.8
% Return on Equity	14.5	33.7	31.1	35.2	29.5	20.5	17.6	14.1	5.9	24.4

Data as orig reptd.; bef. results of disc opers/spec. items. Per share data adj. for stk. divs.; EPS diluted. E-Estimated. NA-Not Available. NM-Not Meaningful. NR-Not Ranked. UR-Under Review.

Office: 1201 S 2nd St, Milwaukee, WI 53204-2498.
Telephone: 414-382-2000.
Website: http://www.rockwellautomation.com
Chrmn, Pres & CEO: K.D. Nosbusch

COO: M. Thomas
SVP & CFO: T.D. Crandall
SVP & CTO: S. Chand
SVP, Secy & General Counsel: D.M. Hagerman

Board Members: B. C. Alewine, V. G. Istock, B. C. Johnson, W. T. McCormick, Jr., K. D. Nosbusch, D. R. Parfet, B. M. Rockwell, D. B. Speer, J. F. Toot, Jr.

Founded: 1928
Domicile: Delaware
Employees: 19,000

The McGraw-Hill Companies

Rockwell Collins Inc.

STANDARD &POOR'S

S&P Recommendation **BUY** ★★★★☆	Price **$53.70** (as of Nov 27, 2009)	12-Mo. Target Price **$56.00**	Investment Style Large-Cap Growth

GICS Sector Industrials
Sub-Industry Aerospace & Defense

Summary This company is one of the world's largest makers of military and commercial avionics and electronics, including cockpit controls, communications and navigation systems, and in-flight entertainment systems.

Key Stock Statistics (Source S&P, Vickers, company reports)

52-Wk Range	$54.60–27.67	S&P Oper. EPS 2010**E**	3.50	Market Capitalization(B)	$8.443	Beta	1.32
Trailing 12-Month EPS	$3.73	S&P Oper. EPS 2011**E**	3.80	Yield (%)	1.79	S&P 3-Yr. Proj. EPS CAGR(%)	4
Trailing 12-Month P/E	14.4	P/E on S&P Oper. EPS 2010**E**	15.3	Dividend Rate/Share	$0.96	S&P Credit Rating	A
$10K Invested 5 Yrs Ago	$14,739	Common Shares Outstg. (M)	157.2	Institutional Ownership (%)	68		

Price Performance

- 30-Week Mov. Avg. · · ·
- 10-Week Mov. Avg. – –
- 12-Mo. Target Price —
- Relative Strength —
- GAAP Earnings vs. Previous Year
- ▲ Up ▼ Down ▶ No Change
- Volume Above Avg. / Below Avg.
- STARS ★

Options: ASE, CBOE, Ph

Analysis prepared by **Richard Tortoriello** on November 09, 2009, when the stock traded at **$ 52.65**.

Highlights

► We project that sales will rise about 4% in FY 10 (Sep.), following a 6% decline in FY 09, as we see significant sales growth in Government Systems partially offset by a large sales decline in Commercial Systems. We estimate that Commercial Systems revenues will decrease by 7% in FY 10, primarily due to reduced demand from business jet makers, which we see partially offset by increasing aftermarket demand, as business jet and commercial flight hours begin to recover. We project strong growth of about 12% in Government Systems, due to sales of aircraft display and control systems and defense communication systems.

► We expect operating margins to decline to 19.5% in FY 10, from 21.4% in FY 09, due to continued pressure on Commercial Systems margins, along with lower Government Systems margins, as a result of the dilutive effect of acquisitions on margins.

► We see EPS of $3.50 for FY 10 and $3.80 for FY 11. We project free cash flow (cash flow from operating activities less capital expenditures) of about 90% of net income in FY 10.

Investment Rationale/Risk

► Although we expect slowing business jet demand and aftermarket sales to constrain earnings, we look for a bounce-back in aftermarket demand in calendar 2010, due to a variety of factors, including depleted inventories at air carriers and our view of an uptick in air travel. We see the company generating returns on invested capital (ROIC) of well over 25%, despite the current economic downturn. We also see COL conserving cash for attractive acquisitions, which we think would favorably expand its market position. At the same time, we see COL's valuations below historical averages.

► Risks to our recommendation and target price include an unanticipated large number of cancellations in 2009 on commercial aerospace projects, failure to gain new contracts, and operational or other missteps.

► Our 12-month target price of $56 is based on an enterprise value to FY 10 estimated EBITDA multiple of 9.5X. Over its seven-year operating history COL has recorded EV-to-EBITDA multiples ranging from 5X to 15X. Given this stage of the economic recovery, we believe a multiple near the middle of this range is appropriate.

Qualitative Risk Assessment

LOW	MEDIUM	HIGH

Our risk assessment reflects the company's exposure to the airline industry, dependence on U.S. military procurement and R&D budgets, and high fixed-cost structure, offset by what we view as a solid balance sheet and strong returns.

Quantitative Evaluations

S&P Quality Ranking A

D	C	B-	B	B+	A-	**A**	A+

Relative Strength Rank STRONG

82

LOWEST = 1   HIGHEST = 99

Revenue/Earnings Data

Revenue (Million $)

	1Q	2Q	3Q	4Q	Year
2009	1,058	1,138	1,084	1,190	4,470
2008	1,112	1,186	1,194	1,277	4,769
2007	993.0	1,083	1,113	1,226	4,415
2006	881.0	957.0	964.0	1,061	3,863
2005	763.0	829.0	890.0	963.0	3,445
2004	628.0	719.0	744.0	839.0	2,930

Earnings Per Share ($)

2009	0.95	1.03	0.91	0.84	3.73
2008	0.93	1.03	1.07	1.13	4.16
2007	0.84	0.82	0.86	0.93	3.45
2006	0.59	0.65	0.70	0.79	2.73
2005	0.50	0.52	0.56	0.62	2.20
2004	0.38	0.39	0.42	0.48	1.67

Fiscal year ended Sep. 30. Next earnings report expected: NA. EPS Estimates based on S&P Operating Earnings; historical GAAP earnings are as reported.

Dividend Data (Dates: mm/dd Payment Date: mm/dd/yy)

Amount ($)	Date Decl.	Ex-Div. Date	Stk. of Record	Payment Date
0.240	01/20	02/11	02/16	03/09/09
0.240	04/22	05/14	05/18	06/08/09
0.240	07/28	08/13	08/17	09/08/09
0.240	10/26	11/12	11/16	12/07/09

Dividends have been paid since 2001. Source: Company reports.

Please read the Required Disclosures and Analyst Certification on the last page of this report.

The **McGraw-Hill** Companies

Rockwell Collins Inc.

STANDARD &POOR'S

Business Summary November 09, 2009

CORPORATE OVERVIEW. This global $4.8 billion revenue aircraft electronics (avionics) maker conducts its business through two segments: Commercial Systems (CS) and Government Systems (GS). CS (50% of revenues and 54% of segment operating earnings, and segment operating margins of 23.3% in FY 08 (Sep.)) primarily makes flight deck electronic systems. CS also provides a range of repair and overhaul services. GS (50%; 46%; 20.5%) primarily makes communication radios and cockpit displays installed in military jets. GS also makes navigation equipment embedded in guided missiles.

Commercial Systems products include integrated avionics systems, which include liquid crystal flight displays, flight management, integrated flight control, automatic flight controls, engine indications, and crew alerts; cabin electronics, including passenger connectivity and entertainment, business support systems, networks, and environmental controls; communications products and systems; navigation products and systems; situational awareness and surveillance products and systems, such as Heads-Up Guidance Systems, weather radar, and collision avoidance systems; flight deck systems, including liquid crystal, cathode ray tube, and heads-up displays; information management systems; electro-mechanical pilot controls and stabilization systems; simulation and training systems; and maintenance, repair, parts, and support

services. Customers include large commercial airplane, regional jet, and business jet makers; commercial airlines; regional airlines; fractional jet operators; and business jet operators.

Government Systems products include communications systems and products; military data link products; navigation systems and products, including radio navigation systems, global positioning systems (GPS), handheld navigation systems, and multi-mode receivers; subsystems for the flight deck that combine flight operations with navigation and guidance functions; cockpit display systems, including flat panel, helmet-mounted and other displays for fighter/attack aircraft; integrated computer systems for the Army's FCS initiative; simulation and training systems; and maintenance, repair, parts, and support services. Customers include the U.S. Department of Defense, other government agencies, civil agencies, defense contractors, and foreign ministries of defense. Products are used for airborne, ground, and shipboard applications.

Company Financials Fiscal Year Ended Sep. 30

Per Share Data ($)	2009	2008	2007	2006	2005	2004	2003	2002	2001	2000
Tangible Book Value	2.09	3.79	5.97	3.30	2.13	3.29	2.21	2.93	4.48	NA
Cash Flow	NA	4.95	4.14	3.34	2.86	2.28	2.02	1.85	1.47	1.87
Earnings	3.73	4.16	3.45	2.73	2.20	1.67	1.43	1.28	0.72	1.35
S&P Core Earnings	NA	3.39	3.35	2.66	2.04	1.47	0.82	0.46	NA	NA
Dividends	0.96	0.88	0.64	0.56	0.48	0.39	0.36	0.36	Nil	NA
Payout Ratio	26%	21%	19%	21%	22%	23%	25%	28%	Nil	NA
Prices:High	54.60	72.41	76.00	64.31	49.80	40.94	30.10	28.00	27.12	NA
Prices:Low	27.67	27.76	61.25	43.49	37.22	29.16	17.20	18.50	11.80	NA
P/E Ratio:High	15	17	22	24	23	17	21	14	16	NA
P/E Ratio:Low	7	7	18	16	17	17	12	14	16	NA

Income Statement Analysis (Million $)										
Revenue	4,470	4,769	4,415	3,863	3,445	2,930	2,542	2,492	2,820	2,510
Operating Income	NA	1,090	959	776	660	539	440	427	492	492
Depreciation	144	129	118	106	119	109	105	105	131	99.0
Interest Expense	NA	21.0	13.0	13.0	11.0	8.00	3.00	6.00	3.00	20.0
Pretax Income	867	953	843	689	547	430	368	341	224	381
Effective Tax Rate	31.5%	28.9%	30.6%	30.8%	27.6%	30.0%	29.9%	30.8%	37.9%	32.5%
Net Income	594	678	585	477	396	301	258	236	139	257
S&P Core Earnings	NA	552	568	465	367	264	148	86.8	59.2	NA

Balance Sheet & Other Financial Data (Million $)										
Cash	235	175	231	144	145	196	66.0	49.0	60.0	20.0
Current Assets	NA	2,338	2,169	1,927	1,775	1,663	1,427	1,438	1,639	1,531
Total Assets	4,645	4,144	3,750	3,278	3,140	2,874	2,591	2,560	2,628	2,628
Current Liabilities	NA	1,740	1,459	1,324	1,177	964	901	1,043	1,135	1,073
Long Term Debt	532	228	223	245	200	201	Nil	Nil	Nil	Nil
Common Equity	1,292	1,408	1,573	1,206	939	1,133	833	987	1,110	1,086
Total Capital	1,824	1,646	1,840	1,451	1,139	1,334	833	987	1,110	1,086
Capital Expenditures	153	171	125	144	111	94.0	72.0	62.0	110	NA
Cash Flow	NA	807	703	583	515	410	363	341	270	356
Current Ratio	1.7	1.3	1.5	1.5	1.5	1.7	1.6	1.4	1.4	1.4
% Long Term Debt of Capitalization	29.2	13.9	12.1	16.9	17.6	15.1	Nil	Nil	Nil	Nil
% Net Income of Revenue	13.3	14.2	13.3	12.3	11.5	10.3	10.1	9.5	4.9	10.2
% Return on Assets	13.5	17.2	16.7	14.8	13.2	11.0	10.0	9.1	5.9	NA
% Return on Equity	44.0	45.5	42.1	44.5	38.2	30.6	28.4	22.5	13.8	NA

Data as orig reptd.; bef. results of disc opers/spec. items. Per share data adj. for stk. divs.; EPS diluted. E-Estimated. NA-Not Available. NM-Not Meaningful. NR-Not Ranked. UR-Under Review.

Office: 400 Collins Rd NE, Cedar Rapids, IA 52498-0503.
Telephone: 319-295-1000.
Email: investorrelations@rockwellcollins.com
Website: http://www.rockwellcollins.com

Chrmn, Pres & CEO: C.M. Jones
COO: J.A. Moore
SVP & CFO: P.E. Allen
SVP & CTO: N. Mattai

SVP, Secy & General Counsel: G.R. Chadick
Investor Contact: D. Crookshank (319-295-7575)
Board Members: D. R. Beall, A. J. Carbone, C. A. Davis, M. Donegan, R. E. Eberhart, C. M. Jones, D. Lilley, A. J. Policano, C. L. Shavers

Employees: 19,300

The McGraw-Hill Companies

Rowan Companies Inc.

STANDARD &POOR'S

S&P Recommendation HOLD ★★★☆☆	Price $24.69 (as of Nov 30, 2009)	12-Mo. Target Price $25.00	Investment Style Large-Cap Value

GICS Sector Energy
Sub-Industry Oil & Gas Drilling

Summary This company performs contract oil and natural gas drilling, and builds heavy equipment and offshore drilling rigs.

Key Stock Statistics (Source S&P, Vickers, company reports)

52-Wk Range	$27.54–10.28	S&P Oper. EPS 2009E	3.29	Market Capitalization(B)	$2.809	Beta	1.55
Trailing 12-Month EPS	$3.54	S&P Oper. EPS 2010E	2.13	Yield (%)	Nil	S&P 3-Yr. Proj. EPS CAGR(%)	-21
Trailing 12-Month P/E	7.0	P/E on S&P Oper. EPS 2009E	7.5	Dividend Rate/Share	Nil	S&P Credit Rating	BBB-
$10K Invested 5 Yrs Ago	$9,798	Common Shares Outstg. (M)	113.8	Institutional Ownership (%)	89		

Price Performance

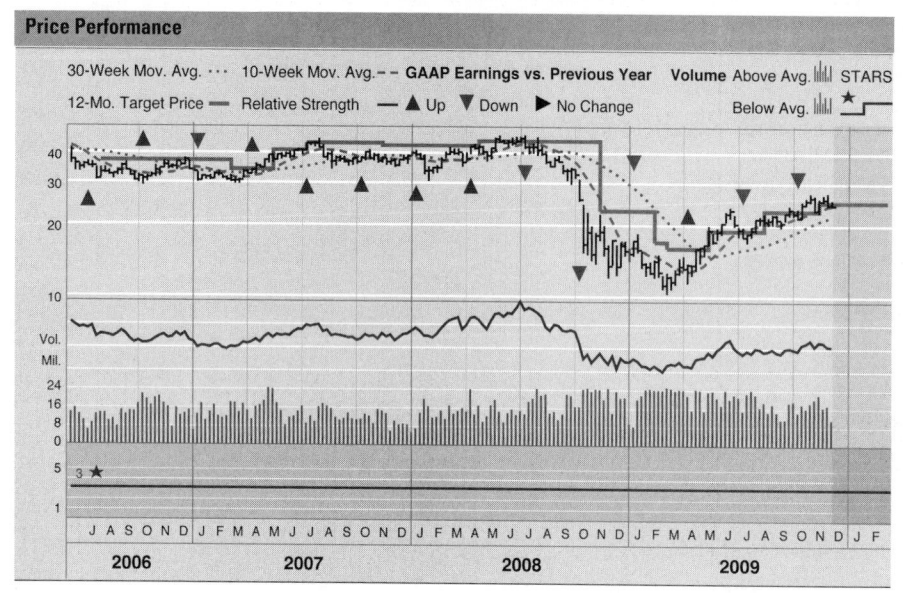

- 30-Week Mov. Avg. · · · 10-Week Mov. Avg. – – GAAP Earnings vs. Previous Year Volume Above Avg. | | | STARS
- 12-Mo. Target Price — Relative Strength — ▲ Up ▼ Down ► No Change Below Avg. | | | ★

J A S O N D J F M A M J J A S O N D J F M A M J J A S O N D J F M A M J J A S O N D J F
2006 · 2007 · 2008 · 2009

Options: ASE, CBOE, P

Analysis prepared by **Stewart Glickman, CFA** on November 30, 2009, when the stock traded at **$ 24.41**.

Highlights

▶ RDC has restarted plans to construct two high-specification jackups (in addition to four other jackups also under construction) which, upon completion, will raise RDC's offshore rig fleet to 28 units from 22. We interpret this decision by RDC management as expectation that these relatively premium units will be able to find term work despite the high number of jackups being built globally (66 in total, of which only 10 currently have contracts in place). We note that these two incremental units are due for delivery in late 2011/early 2012, providing ample time for the company to obtain term work. For 2010, we project cash from operations of $380 million, in excess of our estimate for RDC's capital spending needs.

▶ For 2010, we expect recent weakness in jackup utilization and dayrates to continue, although Mexico and Saudi Arabia remain wild cards and could provide incremental tender activity. Still, any such tenders are likely to see fierce bidding interest by competitors. We see RDC's offshore rig utilization dropping to about 70% in 2009 and 2010, versus 95% in 2008.

▶ We see EPS of $3.29 in 2009, declining to $2.13 in 2010.

Investment Rationale/Risk

▶ While we typically prefer drillers with greater deepwater exposure, we think RDC's high-spec jackup strategy offers a good value proposition to customers, although near-term prospects may be choppy as demand is absorbed by a rising supply of newbuild jackups. Credit constraints may also cause delays on receivables for its LTI subsidiary contract backlog; at the end of September, LTI's backlog stood at $440 million, versus $593 million at the end of March, and backlog at risk has crept back up to 12%, versus 7% at the end of June (still considerably better than the 42% mark at the end of 2008).

▶ Risks to our recommendation and target price include lower dayrates and utilization; shipyard delays; and, risk of contract cancellations at LTI.

▶ Our net asset valuation model, assuming terminal growth of 3% per year and a weighted average cost of capital of 11.1%, indicates that the shares have an intrinsic value of $21. Assuming relative multiples of 6X estimated 2010 EBITDA and 7X projected 2010 cash flow (discounts to peers, warranted, we think, by a below-peers ROIC), and blending these values with our NAV model, our 12-month target price is $25.

Qualitative Risk Assessment

LOW	MEDIUM	HIGH

Our risk assessment reflects RDC's exposure to volatile crude oil and natural gas prices, capital spending decisions made by its oil and gas producing customers, and risks associated with operating in frontier regions. Offsetting these risks is the company's relatively higher specification jackup rig fleet than peers.

Quantitative Evaluations

S&P Quality Ranking B

D	C	B-	B	B+	A-	A	A+

Relative Strength Rank MODERATE

63

LOWEST = 1 · HIGHEST = 99

Revenue/Earnings Data

Revenue (Million $)

	1Q	2Q	3Q	4Q	Year
2009	494.8	482.2	393.4	--	--
2008	485.5	587.1	527.1	613.0	2,213
2007	465.3	507.0	502.2	623.6	2,095
2006	299.8	382.9	417.1	411.0	1,511
2005	222.4	244.6	284.4	317.4	1,069
2004	170.5	190.9	234.6	202.2	708.5

Earnings Per Share ($)

2009	1.16	0.85	0.69	E0.59	E3.29
2008	0.88	1.06	1.00	0.81	3.77
2007	0.77	1.14	1.16	1.23	4.31
2006	0.53	0.98	0.77	0.56	2.84
2005	0.28	0.39	0.67	0.63	1.97
2004	-0.11	-0.02	0.09	0.15	0.25

Fiscal year ended Dec. 31. Next earnings report expected: Late February. EPS Estimates based on S&P Operating Earnings; historical GAAP earnings are as reported.

Dividend Data (Dates: mm/dd Payment Date: mm/dd/yy)

Amount ($)	Date Decl.	Ex-Div. Date	Stk. of Record	Payment Date
0.100	10/31	11/12	11/14	11/28/08
Div Suspended	01/26	--	--	01/26/09

Dividends have been paid since 2005. Source: Company reports.

Rowan Companies Inc.

Business Summary November 30, 2009

CORPORATE OVERVIEW. Rowan Companies is a major provider of international and domestic contract drilling services, and also has manufacturing operations. As of February 2009, RDC operated 22 jackup rigs (comprised of 19 cantilever jackups and three conventional jackups), and a fleet of 31 land rigs. Of the 22 active jackups in the fleet, ten were in the Gulf of Mexico (GOM), nine were in the Middle East, two were in the North Sea, and one was in West Africa. RDC's jackup rigs perform both exploratory and development drilling and, in certain areas, well workover operations. Its larger jackups can drill to depths of 20,000 ft. to 30,000 ft. in maximum water depths of 250 ft. to 490 ft.

RDC conducts business via two main operations. In 2008, Drilling Services operations, which includes the offshore rigs and land rigs, contributed $1.45 billion in revenues (up 5% from 2007), and accounted for 66% of RDC's total 2008 revenues (55% offshore, 11% land). Manufacturing operations contributed $761 million in net revenues in 2008 (up 6.8% from 2007), accounting for the remaining 34% of total revenues. Manufacturing operations are further subdivided into two business segments; the Drilling Products and Services segment (DPS), which provides equipment, parts and services for the drilling industry including jack-up rigs, rig kits and component packages. DPS generated $876 million in gross revenues in 2008 (before eliminations), up 76% from 2007. The Mining, Forestry and Steel Products segment (MFS), which produces large-wheeled mining and timber equipment and related parts and carbon and alloy steel, generated $268 million in gross revenues in 2008, up 25% from 2007. Af-

ter factoring in eliminations, net revenues in Manufacturing were $876 million in 2008.

IMPACT OF MAJOR DEVELOPMENTS. In late 2008, RDC took a charge of $81.9 million in the DPS segment, due in part to a dramatic weakening in business prospects. Due to this charge, the DPS segment generated a loss from operations of $44.6 million in 2008, versus operating income of $43.0 million in 2007. Absent this charge, operating income in DPS would have been $37.3 million in 2008. With MFS segment operating income of $32.6 million in 2008, up 12%, overall Manufacturing operations generated an operating loss of $12.0 million in 2008, versus operating income of $72.0 million. In March 2008, the company said it would explore strategic alternatives for its LTI business, including a potential spin-off to RDC shareholders. In November 2008, however, RDC said that due to financial market and industry conditions, it would not pursue further negotiations toward sale of LTI, although it will continue to review all strategic options. In September 2008, RDC lost the jackup rig Rowan Anchorage during a hurricane in the U.S. Gulf of Mexico. The rig was insured for $60 million, less a $17.5 million windstorm deductible, and had a carrying value of $4.5 million.

Company Financials Fiscal Year Ended Dec. 31

Per Share Data ($)	2008	2007	2006	2005	2004	2003	2002	2001	2000	1999
Tangible Book Value	23.52	20.99	16.97	14.75	12.97	11.95	12.09	11.84	11.17	8.69
Cash Flow	5.02	5.37	3.64	2.71	1.14	0.84	1.72	1.52	1.36	0.54
Earnings	3.77	4.31	2.84	1.97	0.25	-0.08	0.90	0.80	0.74	-0.12
S&P Core Earnings	3.22	4.10	2.76	1.63	0.28	-0.05	-0.31	0.65	NA	NA
Dividends	0.40	0.40	0.30	Nil	Nil	Nil	Nil	Nil	Nil	Nil
Payout Ratio	11%	9%	11%	Nil	Nil	Nil	Nil	Nil	Nil	Nil
Prices:High	47.94	46.16	48.15	39.50	27.26	26.72	27.03	33.89	34.25	21.69
Prices:Low	12.00	29.48	29.03	24.53	20.44	17.70	16.04	11.10	19.06	8.50
P/E Ratio:High	13	11	17	20	NM	NM	30	42	46	NM
P/E Ratio:Low	3	7	10	12	NM	NM	18	14	26	NM

Income Statement Analysis (Million $)										
Revenue	2,213	2,095	1,511	1,069	709	679	617	731	646	461
Operating Income	843	812	555	355	152	89.0	65.1	193	170	45.1
Depreciation, Depletion and Amortization	141	119	90.0	81.3	95.7	86.9	78.1	68.5	58.9	54.7
Interest Expense	4.00	25.9	20.6	22.0	18.7	15.9	15.9	13.1	12.1	11.5
Pretax Income	654	739	493	345	42.8	-12.0	133	120	111	-14.5
Effective Tax Rate	34.6%	34.5%	35.8%	36.9%	38.4%	NM	35.0%	35.9%	36.7%	NM
Net Income	428	484	317	218	26.4	-7.77	86.3	77.0	70.2	-9.67
S&P Core Earnings	366	460	308	181	28.9	-4.74	-30.2	62.8	NA	NA

Balance Sheet & Other Financial Data (Million $)										
Cash	222	284	258	676	466	58.2	179	237	193	87.1
Current Assets	1,369	1,303	1,103	1,208	815	444	470	507	483	325
Total Assets	4,549	3,875	3,435	2,975	2,492	2,191	2,055	1,939	1,678	1,356
Current Liabilities	745	496	517	341	235	150	116	201	104	202
Long Term Debt	356	420	485	550	574	569	513	438	372	297
Common Equity	2,660	2,348	1,874	1,620	1,409	1,137	1,132	1,108	1,053	724
Total Capital	3,442	3,182	2,707	2,485	2,147	1,924	1,811	1,674	1,516	1,099
Capital Expenditures	829	463	479	200	137	250	243	305	216	205
Cash Flow	569	603	407	299	122	79.1	164	145	129	45.0
Current Ratio	1.8	2.6	2.1	3.5	3.5	3.0	4.1	2.5	4.6	1.6
% Long Term Debt of Capitalization	10.3	13.2	17.9	22.1	26.8	29.6	28.3	26.2	24.5	27.0
% Return on Assets	10.2	13.2	9.9	8.0	1.1	NM	4.3	4.3	4.6	NM
% Return on Equity	17.1	22.9	18.1	14.4	2.1	NM	7.7	7.1	7.9	NM

Data as orig reptd.; bef. results of disc opers/spec. items. Per share data adj. for stk. divs.; EPS diluted. E-Estimated. NA-Not Available. NM-Not Meaningful. NR-Not Ranked. UR-Under Review.

Office: 2800 Post Oak Blvd Ste 5450, Houston, TX 77056-6189.
Telephone: 713-621-7800.
Email: ir@rowancompanies.com
Website: http://www.rowancompanies.com

Chrmn: H.E. Lentz, Jr.
Pres & CEO: W.M. Ralls
CFO: W.H. Wells
Chief Acctg Officer & Cntlr: G.M. Hatfield

Secy: M.M. Trent
Investor Contact: S.M. McLeod (713-960-7517)
Board Members: R. G. Croyle, W. T. Fox, III, G. Hearne, T. R. Hix, R. E. Kramek, F. R. Lausen, H. E. Lentz, Jr., C. B. Moynihan, P. D. Peacock, J. J. Quicke, W. M. Ralls

Founded: 1923
Domicile: Delaware
Employees: 6,023

Ryder System Inc

STANDARD &POOR'S

S&P Recommendation	HOLD ★★★☆☆	Price	12-Mo. Target Price	Investment Style
		$40.60 (as of Nov 27, 2009)	$45.00	Large-Cap Value

GICS Sector Industrials
Sub-Industry Trucking

Summary This company provides truck leasing and rental, logistics and supply chain management solutions worldwide.

Key Stock Statistics (Source S&P, Vickers, company reports)

52-Wk Range	$46.58– 19.00	S&P Oper. EPS 2009E	1.84	Market Capitalization(B)	$2.276	Beta	1.39
Trailing 12-Month EPS	$1.18	S&P Oper. EPS 2010E	2.16	Yield (%)	2.46	S&P 3-Yr. Proj. EPS CAGR(%)	5
Trailing 12-Month P/E	34.4	P/E on S&P Oper. EPS 2009E	22.1	Dividend Rate/Share	$1.00	S&P Credit Rating	BBB+
$10K Invested 5 Yrs Ago	$8,357	Common Shares Outstg. (M)	56.1	Institutional Ownership (%)	99		

Price Performance

30-Week Mov. Avg. · · · ·   10-Week Mov. Avg. - - - **GAAP Earnings vs. Previous Year**   **Volume** Above Avg. STARS

12-Mo. Target Price —   Relative Strength —   ▲ Up   ▼ Down   ▶ No Change   Below Avg.   ★

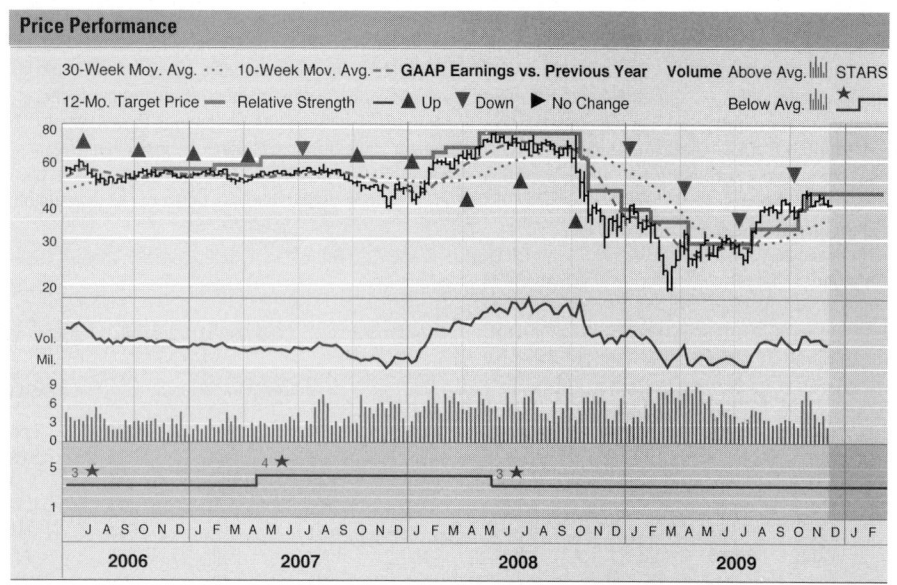

Options: ASE, CBOE, P

Analysis prepared by **Kevin Kirkeby** on October 29, 2009, when the stock traded at **$ 41.39.**

Highlights

► We forecast operating revenue, excluding fuel and subcontracted transportation, to increase 2% in 2010. This follows an expected 7% decline in 2009, during which time R exited certain international markets and scaled back its fleet of trucks in response to poor freight market conditions. While we expect the economy to gradually improve over the course of 2010, we think there are additional contracts, underutilized by the customer, that will be canceled as they come up for renewal. This will mute any early expansion in revenues, in our view.

► We see margins widening in 2010 as cost-cutting measures take hold, and customer shipping schedules stabilize, allowing for more effective fleet positioning. We expect pension expenses to remain near 2009 levels, but revaluations that are embedded in the depreciation charge should begin to come back down as fewer trucks are put up for sale. We note that pension expenses were the equivalent of $0.58 per share in the first nine months of 2009, compared with just $0.02 in the prior-year period.

► Our EPS estimate for 2009 of $1.80 excludes $0.07 in net special charges. We forecast EPS of $2.16 in 2010.

Investment Rationale/Risk

► Economic weakness is contributing to sizable declines in R's commercial rental and supply chain services operations. It has also weighed upon the leasing operations, which are contract-based and generally slower to respond to changes in the economy. We believe R will generally be a beneficiary from plant restarts over the course of 2010. Still, with the economy appearing to stabilize, and R using its free cash flows to pay down debt, we think valuations above the 10-year average are justified.

► Risks to our recommendation and target price include renewed weakness in the economy; deeper-than-expected declines in lease rates; increased competition from traditional truckload providers; higher interest rates, to which R is exposed in light of its financial leverage; and declining used vehicle prices.

► Our DCF model assumes a 12.0% cost of equity and terminal growth of 3.5%, and calculates intrinsic value near $43. Using a 0.70X multiple, which is slightly ahead of the historical average, in our price-to-invested capital model yields a $47 value. Blending these two metrics, we arrive at our 12-month target price of $45.

Qualitative Risk Assessment

LOW	MEDIUM	HIGH

Our risk assessment reflects our view of the company's financial leverage, exposure to low-margin businesses, and heavy capital spending needs to maintain its rental fleet, offset by its strong market position in truck leasing and what we see as steady cash flow generated by multi-year lease contracts.

Quantitative Evaluations

S&P Quality Ranking B+

D	C	B-	B	B+	A-	A	A+

Relative Strength Rank MODERATE

47

LOWEST = 1   HIGHEST = 99

Revenue/Earnings Data

Revenue (Million $)

	1Q	2Q	3Q	4Q	Year
2009	1,203	1,243	1,257	--	--
2008	1,544	1,660	1,626	1,374	6,204
2007	1,594	1,658	1,648	1,666	6,566
2006	1,496	1,596	1,621	1,594	6,307
2005	1,316	1,390	1,491	1,545	5,741
2004	1,212	1,269	1,306	1,363	5,150

Earnings Per Share ($)

2009	0.12	0.41	0.51	E0.56	E1.84
2008	0.96	1.10	1.25	0.19	3.52
2007	0.84	1.07	1.11	1.24	4.24
2006	0.77	1.13	1.06	1.08	4.04
2005	0.64	0.98	0.98	0.93	3.53
2004	0.53	0.97	0.83	0.96	3.28

Fiscal year ended Dec. 31. Next earnings report expected: Early February. EPS Estimates based on S&P Operating Earnings; historical GAAP earnings are as reported.

Dividend Data (Dates: mm/dd Payment Date: mm/dd/yy)

Amount ($)	Date Decl.	Ex-Div. Date	Stk. of Record	Payment Date
0.230	02/06	02/12	02/17	03/13/09
0.230	05/01	05/14	05/18	06/12/09
0.250	07/16	08/20	08/24	09/18/09
0.250	10/09	11/12	11/16	12/11/09

Dividends have been paid since 1976. Source: Company reports.

Please read the Required Disclosures and Analyst Certification on the last page of this report.

Ryder System Inc

STANDARD &POOR'S

Business Summary October 29, 2009

CORPORATE OVERVIEW. Ryder System is primarily a provider of transportation services and equipment to third parties. In 2008, the company generated over 89% of revenues in the United States and Canada, with the remainder spread across Europe, Asia and Latin America. The company serves a broad array of industries, with clients in the automotive, electronics, paper and paper products, food and beverage and retailing industries, among others. For reporting purposes, operations are divided into three segments: Fleet Management Solutions (FMS), Supply Chain Solutions (SCS), and Dedicated Contract Carriage (DCC).

FMS (67% of revenues and 81% of operating profits before eliminations and unallocated costs in 2008) provides full-service truck leasing to customers worldwide. Under a typical full-service lease, R provides customers with vehicles, maintenance, supplies and related equipment necessary for operation, while customers furnish and supervise their own drivers, as well as dispatch and exercise control over the vehicles. R leased approximately 120,400 vehicles under full-service leases at December 31, 2008. FMS also provides short-term truck rental to commercial customers that need to supplement their fleets during peak periods. About 13% of FMS revenue in 2008 was generated through commercial rentals. At December 31, 2008, the commercial rental fleet had about 32,300 units, down from about 38,400 at the end of 2005, re-

flecting the company's focus on the longer-term, contractual portions of its business rather than the more cyclical rental market.

SCS (25%, 9%) provides logistics support and transportation along the entire supply chain for its customers. This includes managing inbound raw materials all the way through to distribution of finished goods. Services include combinations of logistics systems and information technology design, the provision of vehicles and equipment (including maintenance and drivers), warehouse and transportation management, vehicle dispatch, and just-in-time delivery. The company said that its business with auto manufacturers, as well as parts suppliers, represented about 48% of SCS revenue in 2008. We believe General Motors is one of the unit's largest customers, at 17% of SCS revenues (and 4% of total company-wide revenues). R has said it supports 12 of General Motors plants, four of which were scheduled to be shut down as part of that company's reorganization plan. In the first half of 2009, these four plants represented about 1% of the SCS revenue, and utilized about 200 of R's vehicles.

Company Financials Fiscal Year Ended Dec. 31

Per Share Data ($)	2008	2007	2006	2005	2004	2003	2002	2001	2000	1999
Tangible Book Value	19.95	29.32	25.48	21.81	20.65	18.09	14.97	17.51	17.43	16.87
Cash Flow	18.38	17.89	10.57	15.65	14.03	11.90	10.65	9.30	11.20	10.12
Earnings	3.52	4.24	4.04	3.53	3.28	2.12	1.80	0.31	1.49	1.06
S&P Core Earnings	1.93	3.43	3.72	3.09	2.80	2.26	0.84	-0.76	NA	NA
Dividends	0.92	0.84	0.72	0.64	0.60	0.60	0.60	0.60	0.60	0.60
Payout Ratio	26%	20%	18%	18%	18%	28%	33%	194%	40%	57%
Prices:High	76.64	57.70	59.93	47.82	55.55	34.65	31.09	23.19	25.13	28.75
Prices:Low	27.71	38.95	39.61	32.00	33.61	20.00	21.05	16.06	14.81	18.81
P/E Ratio:High	22	14	15	14	17	16	17	75	17	27
P/E Ratio:Low	8	9	10	9	10	9	12	52	10	18

Income Statement Analysis (Million $)	2008	2007	2006	2005	2004	2003	2002	2001	2000	1999
Revenue	6,204	6,566	6,307	5,741	5,150	4,802	4,776	5,006	5,337	4,952
Operating Income	1,384	1,336	1,218	1,165	1,076	905	854	798	906	997
Depreciation	844	817	743	740	706	625	552	545	580	623
Interest Expense	157	160	141	120	100	96.2	91.7	119	154	184
Pretax Income	350	405	786	357	331	212	176	30.7	141	117
Effective Tax Rate	42.9%	37.4%	18.3%	36.3%	34.9%	36.2%	36.0%	39.2%	37.0%	37.9%
Net Income	200	254	642	228	216	136	113	18.7	89.0	72.9
S&P Core Earnings	110	206	229	200	184	145	53.1	-46.3	NA	NA

Balance Sheet & Other Financial Data (Million $)	2008	2007	2006	2005	2004	2003	2002	2001	2000	1999
Cash	120	200	129	129	101	141	104	118	122	113
Current Assets	951	1,222	1,262	1,164	1,228	1,107	1,024	982	928	1,209
Total Assets	6,690	6,855	6,829	6,033	5,638	5,279	4,767	4,924	5,475	5,770
Current Liabilities	1,111	1,019	1,268	1,253	1,455	1,074	862	1,014	1,302	1,450
Long Term Debt	2,479	2,553	2,484	1,916	1,394	1,449	1,389	1,392	1,604	1,819
Common Equity	1,345	1,888	1,721	1,527	1,510	1,344	1,108	1,231	1,253	1,205
Total Capital	4,741	5,425	5,112	4,293	3,775	3,688	3,431	3,625	3,874	4,035
Capital Expenditures	1,234	1,317	1,695	1,399	1,092	725	600	657	1,289	1,734
Cash Flow	1,044	1,071	642	968	922	760	665	564	669	696
Current Ratio	0.9	1.2	1.0	0.9	0.8	1.0	1.2	1.0	0.7	0.8
% Long Term Debt of Capitalization	52.3	47.1	48.6	44.6	36.9	39.3	40.5	38.4	41.4	45.1
% Net Income of Revenue	3.2	3.9	10.2	4.0	4.2	2.8	2.4	0.4	1.7	1.5
% Return on Assets	3.0	3.7	10.0	3.9	3.9	2.7	2.3	0.4	1.6	1.3
% Return on Equity	12.4	14.1	39.5	15.0	15.1	11.1	9.6	1.5	7.2	1.1

Data as orig reptd.; bef. results of disc opers/spec. items. Per share data adj. for stk. divs.; EPS diluted. E-Estimated. NA-Not Available. NM-Not Meaningful. NR-Not Ranked. UR-Under Review.

Office: 11690 NW 105th St, Miami, FL 33178.
Telephone: 305-593-3726.
Email: ryderforinvestor@ryder.com
Website: http://www.ryder.com

Chrmn & CEO: G.T. Swienton
EVP & CFO: R.E. Sanchez
EVP, Secy & General Counsel: R.D. Fatovic
SVP, Chief Acctg Officer & Cntlr: A.A. Garcia

SVP & CIO: K. Bott
Investor Contact: B. Brunn (305-500-4053)
Board Members: J. S. Beard, J. M. Berra, D. I. Fuente, J. A. Georges, L. P. Hassey, L. M. Martin, L. P. Nieto, Jr., E. A. Renna, A. J. Smith, E. F. Smith, G. T. Swienton, H. E. Tookes, II

Founded: 1933
Domicile: Florida
Employees: 28,000

The McGraw-Hill Companies

Safeway Inc

STANDARD &POOR'S

S&P Recommendation **SELL** ★★★★★	Price $22.44 (as of Nov 27, 2009)	12-Mo. Target Price $20.00	Investment Style Large-Cap Blend

GICS Sector Consumer Staples
Sub-Industry Food Retail

Summary This major food retailer operates about 1,750 stores in the U.S. and Canada.

Key Stock Statistics (Source S&P, Vickers, company reports)

52-Wk Range	$24.32–17.19	S&P Oper. EPS 2009**E**	1.75	Market Capitalization(B)	$9.120	Beta		0.70
Trailing 12-Month EPS	$2.01	S&P Oper. EPS 2010**E**	1.95	Yield (%)	1.78	S&P 3-Yr. Proj. EPS CAGR(%)		10
Trailing 12-Month P/E	11.2	P/E on S&P Oper. EPS 2009**E**	12.8	Dividend Rate/Share	$0.40	S&P Credit Rating		BBB
$10K Invested 5 Yrs Ago	$12,030	Common Shares Outstg. (M)	406.4	Institutional Ownership (%)	88			

Price Performance

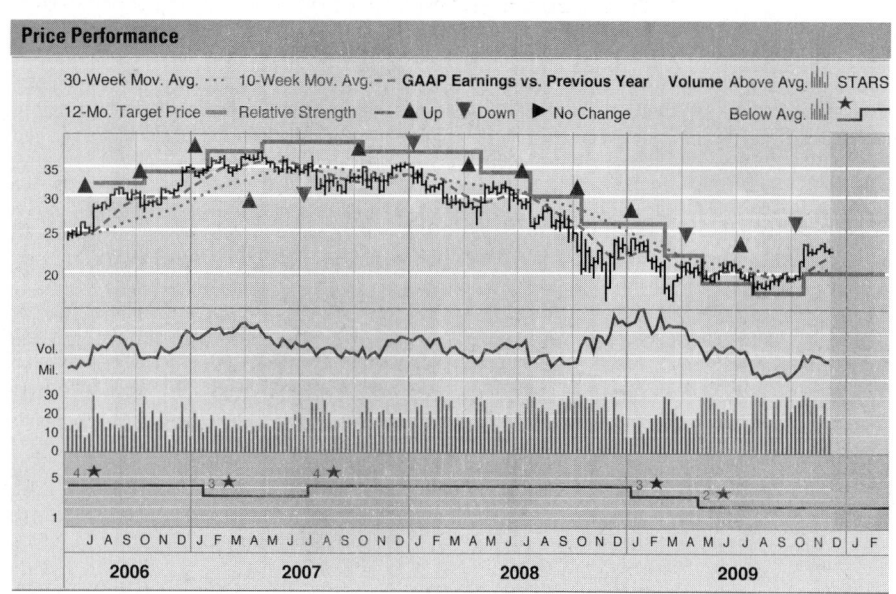

- 30-Week Mov. Avg. · · · 10-Week Mov. Avg. - - **GAAP Earnings vs. Previous Year**   Volume Above Avg. STARS
- 12-Mo. Target Price — Relative Strength — ▲ Up ▼ Down ► No Change   Below Avg.

2006   2007   2008   2009

Options: ASE, CBOE, P

Analysis prepared by **Joseph Agnese** on October 26, 2009, when the stock traded at **$ 22.52**.

Highlights

► We expect growth to be flat in 2010, following a projected decline of 5.3% in 2009, to $41.7 billion from $44.1 billion in 2008, reflecting slightly negative identical-store sales growth excluding fuel and unfavorable foreign currency exchange rates. We project that square footage will increase about 1%, reflecting new store openings and store remodels.

► We expect gross margins to stabilize in 2010 as a shift in product mix with increased sales of wider margin private label goods, improved shrink control, and a more inflationary competitive pricing environment should lead to a less aggressive pricing strategy in the second half of 2010. We look for operating margins to widen on improved sales leverage in 2010, despite increased healthcare costs and higher pension expense.

► Interest expense will likely be lower, in our opinion, on a reduction in debt levels, despite higher interest rates. We project 2010 EPS of $1.95, up 11% from our estimate of $1.75 in 2009, excluding $0.18 in one-time tax benefits.

Investment Rationale/Risk

► We see revenues hampered in the near term by deflationary pricing pressures in dairy and produce and increased pricing competition from peers. However, we expect an easing in the second half of 2010 as lessening deflationary pressures and a more stable macroeconomic environment leads to increased sales leverage.

► Risks to our recommendation and target price include a less competitive environment than we anticipate with moderate food inflation and stronger than expected economic growth.

► Due to our expectation for near-term earnings pressure from increased industry pricing competition and food deflation, we believe the shares should trade below their historical 26% discount to the forward 12-month P/E for the S&P 500. On our view of high earnings risk, reflecting potential margin compression in an adverse economic environment, we apply a P/E multiple of 10X, representing a 35% discount to the S&P 500's forward P/E multiple and near historical lows for relative P/E to the market, to our 2010 EPS estimate of $1.95, resulting in our 12-month target price of $20.

Qualitative Risk Assessment

LOW	MEDIUM	HIGH

Our risk assessment reflects our view of an improved shopping experience associated with new Lifestyle store remodelings. This is offset by a continued intense competitive environment as high unemployment rates and reduced consumer spending results in increased pricing pressure and trading down by consumers.

Quantitative Evaluations

S&P Quality Ranking   B

D	C	B-	B	B+	A-	A	A+

Relative Strength Rank   STRONG

71

LOWEST = 1   HIGHEST = 99

Revenue/Earnings Data

Revenue (Million $)

	1Q	2Q	3Q	4Q	Year
2009	9,236	9,462	9,458	--	--
2008	9,999	10,120	10,169	13,816	44,104
2007	9,322	9,823	9,785	13,356	42,286
2006	8,895	9,367	9,420	12,504	40,185
2005	8,621	8,803	8,946	12,046	38,416
2004	7,639	8,361	8,297	11,390	35,823

Earnings Per Share ($)

	1Q	2Q	3Q	4Q	Year
2009	0.34	0.57	0.31	E0.71	E1.75
2008	0.44	0.53	0.46	0.79	2.21
2007	0.39	0.49	0.44	0.68	1.99
2006	0.32	0.55	0.39	0.69	1.94
2005	0.29	0.30	0.27	0.39	1.25
2004	0.10	0.35	0.35	0.45	1.25

Fiscal year ended Dec. 31. Next earnings report expected: Late February. EPS Estimates based on S&P Operating Earnings; historical GAAP earnings are as reported.

Dividend Data (Dates: mm/dd Payment Date: mm/dd/yy)

Amount ($)	Date Decl.	Ex-Div. Date	Stk. of Record	Payment Date
0.083	12/12	12/22	12/24	01/14/09
0.083	03/06	03/24	03/26	04/16/09
0.100	04/30	06/23	06/25	07/16/09
0.100	08/26	09/22	09/24	10/15/09

Dividends have been paid since 2005. Source: Company reports.

Please read the Required Disclosures and Analyst Certification on the last page of this report.

The McGraw-Hill Companies

Safeway Inc

STANDARD &POOR'S

Business Summary October 26, 2009

CORPORATE OVERVIEW. Safeway is one of the largest U.S. food and drug re-tailers, operating about 1,750 stores principally in California, Oregon, Washington, Alaska, Colorado, Arizona, Texas, the Chicago metropolitan area, and the Mid-Atlantic region in the U.S., and in British Columbia, Alberta and Manitoba/Saskatchewan in Canada. To support its store network, SWY has a network of distribution, manufacturing and food processing facilities. The company seeks to provide value to customers by maintaining high store standards while differentiating its offerings with a wide selection of high-quality produce and meat at competitive prices. The company also provides third-party gift cards, prepaid cards and sports and entertainment cards to retailers for sales to customers in North America and the U.K. through its Blackhawk subsidiary.

MARKET PROFILE. The U.S. grocery industry was a $964 billion business in 2007, according to Progressive Grocer. Supermarkets generated $535 billion, or 56% of total grocery industry sales, followed by convenience stores ($307 billion, 32%) and warehouse clubs ($102 billion, 11%). When supermarkets are broken down by format, conventional supermarkets have the largest market share, holding 67% of the supermarket category, with $357 billion in sales. However, supercenters are quickly gaining market share, and generated a 26% market share in 2007 ($142 billion in sales).

With $42.3 billion in sales in 2007, Safeway held about an 8% market share within the supermarket category and 4.4% of total grocery sales. The average size of Safeway's stores (about 46,000 square feet) exceeded the industry average (33,300 square feet). Additionally, the company's sales per square foot ($527 per square foot) is higher than the supermarket average of $460 per square foot in 2007.

Company Financials Fiscal Year Ended Dec. 31

Per Share Data ($)	2008	2007	2006	2005	2004	2003	2002	2001	2000	1999
Tangible Book Value	10.25	9.76	7.44	5.60	4.24	2.79	1.77	1.67	1.35	NM
Cash Flow	4.83	4.40	4.16	3.32	3.24	1.57	2.91	4.29	3.77	3.24
Earnings	2.21	1.99	1.94	1.25	1.25	-0.38	1.20	2.44	2.13	1.88
S&P Core Earnings	2.03	1.87	1.91	1.26	1.15	1.21	2.42	2.19	NA	NA
Dividends	0.32	0.26	0.22	0.15	Nil	Nil	Nil	Nil	Nil	Nil
Payout Ratio	14%	13%	11%	12%	Nil	Nil	Nil	Nil	Nil	Nil
Prices:High	34.87	38.31	35.61	26.46	25.64	25.83	46.90	61.38	62.69	62.44
Prices:Low	17.19	30.10	22.23	17.85	17.26	16.20	18.45	37.44	30.75	29.31
P/E Ratio:High	16	19	18	21	21	NM	39	25	29	33
P/E Ratio:Low	8	15	11	14	14	NM	15	15	14	16

Income Statement Analysis (Million $)										
Revenue	44,104	42,286	40,185	38,416	35,823	35,553	32,399	34,301	31,977	28,860
Operating Income	2,994	2,816	2,591	2,147	2,067	2,167	3,190	3,535	3,119	2,698
Depreciation	1,141	1,071	991	933	895	864	812	946	838	700
Interest Expense	371	405	396	403	411	442	369	447	457	362
Pretax Income	1,505	1,404	1,240	849	794	141	1,320	2,095	1,867	1,674
Effective Tax Rate	35.8%	36.7%	29.8%	33.9%	29.4%	NM	56.9%	40.1%	41.5%	42.0%
Net Income	965	888	871	561	560	-170	568	1,254	1,092	971
S&P Core Earnings	888	835	859	566	517	538	1,140	1,122	NA	NA

Balance Sheet & Other Financial Data (Million $)										
Cash	383	278	217	373	267	175	73.7	68.5	91.7	106
Current Assets	3,976	4,008	3,566	3,702	3,598	3,508	4,259	3,312	3,224	3,052
Total Assets	17,485	17,651	16,274	15,757	15,377	15,097	16,047	17,463	15,965	14,900
Current Liabilities	4,499	5,136	4,601	4,264	3,792	3,464	3,936	3,883	3,780	3,583
Long Term Debt	4,184	4,658	5,037	5,605	6,124	7,072	7,522	6,712	5,822	6,357
Common Equity	6,786	6,702	5,667	4,920	4,307	3,644	3,628	5,890	5,390	4,086
Total Capital	11,729	11,614	10,821	10,748	10,894	11,139	11,727	13,100	11,721	10,822
Capital Expenditures	1,596	1,769	1,674	1,384	1,213	936	1,371	1,793	1,573	1,334
Cash Flow	2,106	1,960	1,862	1,494	1,455	694	1,381	2,200	1,930	1,671
Current Ratio	0.9	0.8	0.8	0.9	0.9	1.0	1.1	0.9	0.9	0.9
% Long Term Debt of Capitalization	35.7	40.1	46.5	52.2	56.2	63.5	64.1	51.2	49.7	58.7
% Net Income of Revenue	2.2	2.1	2.2	1.5	1.6	NM	1.8	3.7	3.4	3.4
% Return on Assets	5.5	5.2	5.4	3.6	3.7	NM	3.4	7.5	7.1	7.4
% Return on Equity	14.3	14.4	16.4	12.2	14.1	NM	11.9	22.2	23.0	27.1

Data as orig reptd.; bef. results of disc opers/spec. items. Per share data adj. for stk. divs.; EPS diluted. E-Estimated. NA-Not Available. NM-Not Meaningful. NR-Not Ranked. UR-Under Review.

Office: 5918 Stoneridge Mall Road, Pleasanton, CA 94588-3229.
Telephone: 925-467-3000.
Website: http://www.safeway.com
Chrmn, Pres & CEO: S. Burd

Co-Chrmn: G. Charters
EVP & CFO: R.L. Edwards
EVP & Chief Admin Officer: L.M. Renda
SVP & Chief Acctg Officer: D.F. Bond

Investor Contact: M.C. Plaisance (925-467-3136)
Board Members: S. Burd, J. Grove, M. Gyani, P. M. Hazen, F. C. Herringer, R. I. MacDonnell, K. W. Oder, A. Sarin, M. S. Shannon, R. Stirn, W. Tauscher, R. Viault

Founded: 1915
Domicile: Delaware
Employees: 197,000

St. Jude Medical Inc.

STANDARD &POOR'S

S&P Recommendation HOLD ★★★☆☆	Price $36.41 (as of Nov 27, 2009)	12-Mo. Target Price $37.00	Investment Style Large-Cap Growth

GICS Sector Health Care
Sub-Industry Health Care Equipment

Summary St. Jude, the leading maker of mechanical heart valves, also produces pacemakers, defibrillators, and other cardiac devices. In July 2008, STJ acquired EP Medsystems Inc. for $91 million in a deal that expanded its capabilities in the atrial fibrillation market.

Key Stock Statistics (Source S&P, Vickers, company reports)

52-Wk Range	$41.96– 25.00	S&P Oper. EPS 2009**E**	2.40	Market Capitalization(B)	$12.170	Beta	0.54
Trailing 12-Month EPS	$1.20	S&P Oper. EPS 2010**E**	2.69	Yield (%)	Nil	S&P 3-Yr. Proj. EPS CAGR(%)	13
Trailing 12-Month P/E	30.3	P/E on S&P Oper. EPS 2009**E**	15.2	Dividend Rate/Share	Nil	S&P Credit Rating	A
$10K Invested 5 Yrs Ago	$9,418	Common Shares Outstg. (M)	334.3	Institutional Ownership (%)	82		

Price Performance

30-Week Mov. Avg. · · · 10-Week Mov. Avg. – – **GAAP Earnings vs. Previous Year** Volume Above Avg. STARS

12-Mo. Target Price — Relative Strength ▲ Up ▼ Down ► No Change Below Avg. ★

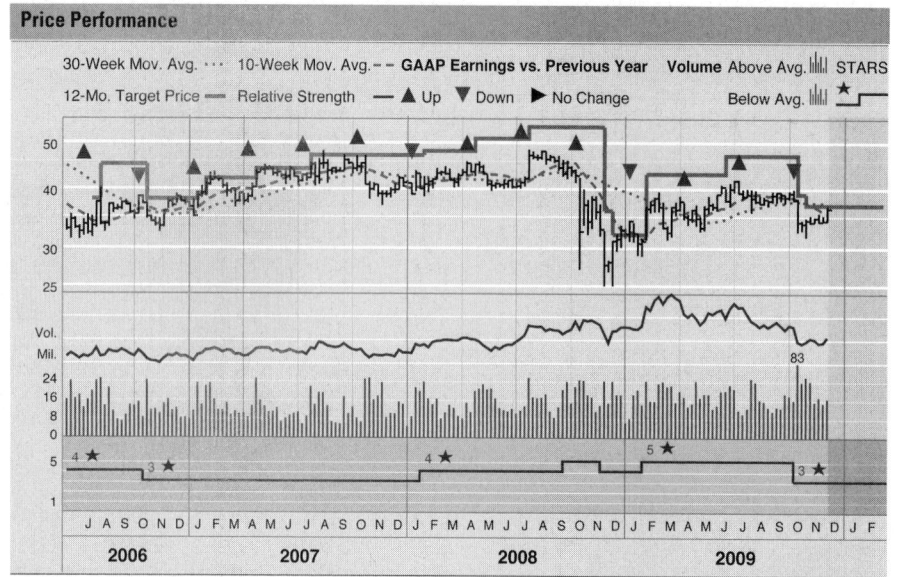

Options: ASE, CBOE

Analysis prepared by **Jeffrey Englander, CFA** on November 04, 2009, when the stock traded at **$ 34.65**.

Highlights

► While we believe STJ is well positioned for the long term to capture share in the market for implantable cardioverter defibrillators (ICDs) as the market expands based on results of the MADIT-CRT trials, in the near term we expect market share gains to be relatively challenging. We look for 2009 revenues to rise approximately 6% versus 2008, and about 9% in 2010.

► For 2009, we anticipate that gross margins will decline from 2008 levels due to expected lower unit pricing, expansion of neuromodulation manufacturing capabilities, as well as adverse currency impacts. We see SG&A expenses declining while R&D is flat, both as a percentage of sales compared to the prior year. For 2010, we look for gross margins to widen modestly and SG&A to decline slightly as STJ trims payroll, while R&D should remain flat, all relative to sales.

► Our 2009 EPS estimate is $2.40 (excluding $1.21 in one-time charges), up about 6% from 2008, excluding the impact of foreign currency translations. For 2010, we look for EPS of $2.69.

Investment Rationale/Risk

► Although we see STJ solidifying market share gains in the ICD market, near term the ICD market could remain challenging as hospital capital spending remains tight. We view STJ as a defensive health care name with strong and largely recession-resistant revenue growth characteristics. We see the majority of 2009 sales continuing to be from the CRM division, but believe the emerging neuromodulation and atrial fibrillation categories will also be significant growth drivers over time. We think STJ remains a possible takeover target due to our view of its defensive growth profile, strong cash flow, and conservatively managed balance sheet.

► Risks to our recommendation and target price include the failure to successfully commercialize new products, reimbursement rate cuts, and adverse foreign currency fluctuations.

► Our $37 target price applies a P/E of about 14X to our 2010 operating EPS estimate, a discount to STJ's historical levels due to some of the company's near-term challenges.

Qualitative Risk Assessment

LOW	MEDIUM	HIGH

The company operates in a highly competitive industry characterized by relatively short product life cycles and volatile market share fluctuations. However, there are significant barriers to entry in the company's core markets, as products must obtain FDA approval prior to launch, and they require a large investment in research and development and sales efforts.

Quantitative Evaluations

S&P Quality Ranking B+

D	C	B-	B	B+	A-	A	A+

Relative Strength Rank MODERATE

61

LOWEST = 1   HIGHEST = 99

Revenue/Earnings Data

Revenue (Million $)

	1Q	2Q	3Q	4Q	Year
2009	1,134	1,184	1,160	--	--
2008	1,011	1,136	1,084	1,133	4,363
2007	887.0	947.3	926.8	1,018	3,779
2006	784.4	832.9	821.3	863.8	3,302
2005	663.9	723.7	737.8	789.9	2,915
2004	548.6	556.6	578.3	610.7	2,294

Earnings Per Share ($)

	1Q	2Q	3Q	4Q	Year
2009	0.58	0.63	0.48	E0.62	E2.40
2008	0.53	0.58	0.55	-0.56	1.10
2007	0.41	0.39	0.46	0.34	1.59
2006	0.36	0.38	0.32	0.42	1.47
2005	0.32	0.27	0.44	0.01	1.04
2004	0.26	0.27	0.25	0.33	1.10

Fiscal year ended Dec. 31. Next earnings report expected: Late January. EPS Estimates based on S&P Operating Earnings; historical GAAP earnings are as reported.

Dividend Data

No cash dividends have been paid since 1994.

St. Jude Medical Inc.

STANDARD &POOR'S

Business Summary November 04, 2009

CORPORATE OVERVIEW. St. Jude Medical sells medical devices in the cardiac rhythm management (CRM), cardiac surgery, atrial fibrillation, and pain management categories. Although the company has a diversified product line, the principal driver of growth in recent years has been the CRM segment, where it sells pacemakers and defibrillators.

CRM products (62% of 2008 sales) include implantable cardioverter defibrillators (ICDs) that are used to treat hearts that beat too fast (tachycardia) by monitoring the heartbeat and delivering high energy electrical impulses to terminate ventricular tachycardia and ventricular fibrillation. ICD products include the Atlas, Photon, and Contour lines, as well as the Epic HF and Atlas+ HF ICDs with the ventricle-to-ventricle (V-to-V) timing feature.

Also within the CRM division, pacemakers and related systems are sold to treat patients with hearts that beat too slowly (bradycardia). Current pacemakers include the Victory and Victory XL models, which offer automatic P-wave and R-wave measurements with trends, lead monitoring and automatic polarity switch, follow-up electrograms, and Ventricular Intrinsic Preference to reduce right ventricle pacing and a ventricular rate during an automatic mode switch histogram.

Other pacemakers offer features such as AF Suppression Pacing Algorithm and the beat-by-beat Autocapture pacing system that lets the pacemaker monitor each paced beat to verify heart stimulation, deliver a back-up pulse in the event of non-stimulation, continuously measure the threshold, and adjust energy output to match changing patient needs. The Identity pacemaker line expands the feature set to include a suite of arrhythmia diagnostics. Outside the U.S., STJ sells the Genesis System, a device-based ventricular resynchronization system designed to treat congestive heart failure and suppress atrial fibrillation.

The company also offers low voltage device-based ventricular resynchronization systems (bi-ventricular) designed to treat heart failure and suppress atrial fibrillation. In the U.S., the company's pacemakers are the only bi-ventricular pacing devices indicated for use in patients with chronic atrial fibrillation who have been treated with atrioventricular nodal ablation.

Company Financials Fiscal Year Ended Dec. 31

Per Share Data ($)	2008	2007	2006	2005	2004	2003	2002	2001	2000	1999
Tangible Book Value	2.19	2.25	2.23	1.84	4.27	3.02	3.27	2.28	1.50	1.02
Cash Flow	1.63	2.08	1.92	1.38	1.34	1.12	0.96	0.74	0.65	0.32
Earnings	1.10	1.59	1.47	1.04	1.10	0.92	0.76	0.48	0.38	0.07
S&P Core Earnings	1.12	1.64	1.47	0.90	1.03	0.82	0.63	0.38	NA	NA
Dividends	Nil	Nil	Nil	Nil	Nil	Nil	Nil	Nil	Nil	Nil
Payout Ratio	Nil	Nil	Nil	Nil	Nil	Nil	Nil	Nil	Nil	Nil
Prices:High	48.49	48.10	54.75	52.80	42.90	32.00	21.56	19.52	15.63	10.19
Prices:Low	24.98	34.90	31.20	34.48	29.90	19.38	15.26	11.11	5.91	5.73
P/E Ratio:High	44	30	37	51	39	35	29	41	41	NM
P/E Ratio:Low	23	22	21	33	27	21	20	23	16	NM

Income Statement Analysis (Million $)										
Revenue	4,363	3,779	3,302	2,915	2,294	1,933	1,590	1,347	1,179	1,115
Operating Income	1,275	1,093	945	911	672	533	445	347	326	300
Depreciation	186	176	167	130	85.8	76.7	74.9	90.3	92.3	85.7
Interest Expense	22.6	38.2	33.9	Nil	Nil	Nil	Nil	Nil	Nil	Nil
Pretax Income	631	744	721	621	537	459	373	228	177	67.0
Effective Tax Rate	39.1%	24.9%	23.9%	36.7%	23.7%	26.0%	26.0%	24.3%	27.2%	63.8%
Net Income	384	559	548	393	410	339	276	173	129	24.2
S&P Core Earnings	392	576	548	341	377	302	231	136	NA	NA

Balance Sheet & Other Financial Data (Million $)										
Cash	136	389	79.9	535	688	461	402	148	108	88.9
Current Assets	2,080	2,128	1,690	1,941	1,863	1,492	1,114	798	705	690
Total Assets	5,724	5,329	4,790	4,845	3,231	2,556	1,951	1,629	1,533	1,554
Current Liabilities	1,029	1,849	676	1,534	605	510	375	322	297	283
Long Term Debt	1,126	182	859	177	235	352	Nil	123	295	477
Common Equity	3,236	2,928	2,969	2,883	2,334	1,604	1,577	1,184	941	794
Total Capital	4,476	3,217	3,992	3,217	2,625	2,046	1,577	1,307	1,235	1,272
Capital Expenditures	344	287	268	159	89.5	49.6	62.2	63.1	39.7	69.4
Cash Flow	570	735	715	524	496	416	351	263	221	110
Current Ratio	2.0	1.2	2.5	1.3	3.1	2.9	3.0	2.5	2.4	2.4
% Long Term Debt of Capitalization	25.2	5.7	21.5	5.5	8.9	17.2	Nil	9.4	23.8	37.6
% Net Income of Revenue	8.8	14.8	16.6	13.5	17.9	17.6	17.4	12.8	11.0	2.2
% Return on Assets	7.0	29.3	11.4	9.7	14.2	15.1	15.4	10.9	8.4	1.6
% Return on Equity	12.5	19.0	18.7	15.1	20.8	21.3	20.0	16.2	14.9	3.0

Data as orig reptd.; bef. results of disc opers/spec. items. Per share data adj. for stk. divs.; EPS diluted. E-Estimated. NA-Not Available. NM-Not Meaningful. NR-Not Ranked. UR-Under Review.

Office: One Lillehei Plaza, St. Paul, MN 55117.
Telephone: 651-483-2000.
Website: http://www.sjm.com
Chrmn, Pres & CEO: D.J. Starks.

EVP, CFO & Chief Acctg Officer: J.C. Heinmiller
Secy & General Counsel: P. Krop
Investor Contact: A. Craig (651-481-7789)
Cntlr: D. Zurbay

Board Members: J. W. Brown, R. R. Devenuti, S. M. Essig, T. H. Garrett, III, B. B. Hill, M. A. Rocca, D. J. Starks, S. Widensohler, W. L. Yarno

Founded: 1976
Domicile: Minnesota
Employees: 14,000

salesforce.com inc

STANDARD &POOR'S

S&P Recommendation	HOLD ★★★☆☆	Price $63.25 (as of Nov 27, 2009)	12-Mo. Target Price $66.00	Investment Style Large-Cap Growth

GICS Sector Information Technology
Sub-Industry Application Software

Summary This San Francisco-based company is a leading provider of on-demand customer relationship management applications.

Key Stock Statistics (Source S&P, Vickers, company reports)

52-Wk Range	$67.72– 25.19	S&P Oper. EPS 2010E	0.62	Market Capitalization(B)	$7.843	Beta	1.94
Trailing 12-Month EPS	$0.59	S&P Oper. EPS 2011E	0.86	Yield (%)	Nil	S&P 3-Yr. Proj. EPS CAGR(%)	35
Trailing 12-Month P/E	NM	P/E on S&P Oper. EPS 2010E	NM	Dividend Rate/Share	Nil	S&P Credit Rating	NA
$10K Invested 5 Yrs Ago	$35,674	Common Shares Outstg. (M)	124.0	Institutional Ownership (%)	93		

Price Performance

30-Week Mov. Avg. ···· 10-Week Mov. Avg. – – **GAAP Earnings vs. Previous Year** Volume Above Avg. STARS
12-Mo. Target Price — Relative Strength — ▲ Up ▼ Down ▶ No Change Below Avg.

Options: CBOE, Ph

Analysis prepared by **Zaineb Bokhari** on November 19, 2009, when the stock traded at **$ 62.58**.

Highlights

► We see sales rising 20% in FY 10 (Jan.) (following a 44% increase in FY 09), reflecting tough year-to-year comparisons and our outlook for slowing growth amid a weak economy. We expect sales to be driven by a 22% rise in subscription and support sales during FY 10. We think clients will slow implementations to control costs, and we look for attrition rates to be higher due to lower employment trends and clients' caution about the macro-economy. Slowing growth for bookings and deferred revenues lead us to expect a 16% advance in FY 11 sales to $1.5 billion.

► We expect gross margins to improve slightly in both FY 10 and FY 11, as we look for professional services to decline as a percentage of revenues. We forecast operating margins of about 9% in FY 10, versus 6% in FY 08. Our outlook includes higher stock-based compensation expense, which we believe will rise to $86 million in FY 10, from $77 million in FY 09. We anticipate wider operating margins again in FY 11.

► We forecast EPS of $0.62 in FY 10, up from $0.35 in FY 09. We expect some variability in CRM's effective tax rate, which we project at 42%. We estimate EPS of $0.86 in FY 11.

Investment Rationale/Risk

► We remain cautious in our outlook for enterprise IT spending in calendar 2009 and see modest improvements in 2010, in view of the global macro-economy. We think this will affect bookings, which are becoming more seasonal. We expect tougher comparisons in future periods, and we see sales growth slowing as well. As CRM continues to add scale in its business, however, we look for profitability to improve sharply from modest current levels. We continue to see competitive offerings from traditional vendors in future periods, in an effort to capitalize on strong growth prospects for on-demand software delivery, but we think CRM enjoys a considerable market lead. We think the company's on-demand model will have strong appeal in the current economic environment.

► Risks to our recommendation and target price include a further deterioration in the global economy, a sharper slowdown in sales or bookings growth from anticipated levels, and increased competition.

► Our 12-month target price of $66 applies a 5.5X enterprise value-to-sales multiple to our FY 11 sales estimate, within CRM's 2.6X-6.7X historical average range.

Qualitative Risk Assessment

LOW	MEDIUM	HIGH

Our risk assessment reflects the company's early dominance in an emerging area of the software market. We think growing competition from traditional software vendors and increasingly difficult annual comparisons may result in lower future reported growth relative to historical rates.

Quantitative Evaluations

S&P Quality Ranking NR

D	C	B-	B	B+	A-	A	A+

Relative Strength Rank STRONG
84
LOWEST = 1 HIGHEST = 99

Revenue/Earnings Data

Revenue (Million $)

	1Q	2Q	3Q	4Q	Year
2010	304.9	316.1	330.6	--	--
2009	247.6	263.1	276.5	289.6	1,077
2008	162.4	176.6	192.8	216.9	748.7
2007	104.7	118.1	130.1	144.2	497.1
2006	64.18	71.94	82.67	91.06	309.9
2005	34.84	40.58	46.36	54.59	176.4

Earnings Per Share ($)

2010	0.15	0.17	0.16	E0.14	E0.62
2009	0.08	0.08	0.08	0.11	0.35
2008	0.01	0.08	0.05	0.06	0.15
2007	Nil	Nil	Nil	Nil	Nil
2006	0.04	0.04	0.11	0.05	0.24
2005	Nil	0.01	0.02	0.03	0.07

Fiscal year ended Jan. 31. Next earnings report expected: Late February. EPS Estimates based on S&P Operating Earnings; historical GAAP earnings are as reported.

Dividend Data

No cash dividends have been paid.

Please read the Required Disclosures and Analyst Certification on the last page of this report.

salesforce.com inc

STANDARD
&POOR'S

Business Summary November 19, 2009

CORPORATE OVERVIEW. Salesforce.com is a leading provider of "on-demand" customer relationship management software. On demand refers to the delivery of application services over the Internet as needed. Under this delivery model, customers access a software provider's applications via the Web, with minor implementation and customization and no on-premise installation or maintenance of software. Payment for this "service" is generally on a per-seat per-user basis over an agreed-upon term.

In our view, the delivery of software on demand offers unique benefits to customers, including lower upfront investment, increased vendor accountability and risk sharing, greater awareness of customer needs due to the constant feedback from customers, and flexible subscription pricing, which can be tailored to customer requirements. This model offers benefits to the software vendor, including improved visibility into customers' needs and potentially higher customer satisfaction and retention levels. Another benefit we see is lower development and support costs arising from the use of a single version of software across a vendor's installed base.

CRM experienced service outages in late December 2005 and in early 2006. We believe these service issues have been addressed, since they have not resurfaced. The company moved to increase transparency regarding the performance, uptime, and security of its system, in our view. Since the delivery of its service over the Web is a key point of differentiation, we expect the company to continue to invest in infrastructure in future quarters. The low upfront cost of CRM's products has significant appeal to small- and mid-sized businesses, in our view; we estimate that the average customer had 25 to 26 subscribers in FY 09 (Jan.), up from 18 to 20 subscribers we calculated for FY 06. While the company no longer provides regular details on subscribers, we think average number of subscribers per customer has continue to rise. CRM also continues to sign a number of large customers, including ADP, EMC, Cisco Systems, Dell, and Thomson Reuters, among others.

Company Financials Fiscal Year Ended Jan. 31

Per Share Data ($)	2009	2008	2007	2006	2005	2004	2003	2002	2001	2000
Tangible Book Value	4.78	3.71	2.40	1.78	1.38	1.13	NA	NA	NA	NA
Cash Flow	0.51	0.29	0.11	0.29	0.09	0.06	-0.27	-1.25	NA	NA
Earnings	0.35	0.15	Nil	0.24	0.07	0.04	-0.37	-1.36	-2.38	NA
S&P Core Earnings	0.36	0.14	Nil	0.07	-0.04	-0.02	-0.43	NA	NA	NA
Dividends	Nil	Nil	Nil	Nil	Nil	NA	NA	NA	NA	NA
Payout Ratio	Nil	Nil	Nil	Nil	Nil	NA	NA	NA	NA	NA
Calendar Year	2008	2007	2006	2005	2004	2003	2002	2001	2000	1999
Prices:High	75.21	65.52	44.58	36.19	22.70	NA	NA	NA	NA	NA
Prices:Low	20.82	35.55	21.64	12.96	9.00	NA	NA	NA	NA	NA
P/E Ratio:High	NM	NM	NM	NM	NM	NA	NA	NA	NA	NA
P/E Ratio:Low	NM	NM	NM	NM	NM	NA	NA	NA	NA	NA

Income Statement Analysis (Million $)										
Revenue	1,077	749	497	310	176	96.0	51.0	22.4	5.43	NA
Operating Income	84.7	37.1	8.91	25.8	9.67	2.86	-7.84	-19.5	NA	NA
Depreciation	21.0	16.8	12.5	6.03	3.15	2.59	2.66	2.40	0.86	NA
Interest Expense	0.11	0.05	0.19	0.07	0.04	0.02	0.08	0.27	NA	NA
Pretax Income	85.6	46.2	12.5	28.2	9.15	4.24	-10.0	-29.0	-31.9	NA
Effective Tax Rate	43.9%	50.6%	78.4%	NM	13.3%	12.8%	Nil	Nil	NA	NA
Net Income	43.4	18.4	0.48	28.5	7.35	3.51	-9.72	-28.6	-31.7	NA
S&P Core Earnings	44.4	17.5	0.48	8.59	-3.26	-0.61	-11.4	NA	NA	NA

Balance Sheet & Other Financial Data (Million $)										
Cash	698	451	252	208	119	142	16.0	11.7	NA	NA
Current Assets	1,069	741	419	303	179	NA	NA	NA	NA	NA
Total Assets	1,480	1,090	665	435	280	191	39.4	29.1	NA	NA
Current Liabilities	767	606	377	235	132	NA	NA	NA	NA	NA
Long Term Debt	4.05	Nil	0.01	0.18	0.72	Nil	NA	NA	NA	NA
Common Equity	672	452	282	196	145	115	-56.1	-52.0	NA	NA
Total Capital	687	461	286	199	147	115	5.42	9.47	NA	NA
Capital Expenditures	61.1	43.6	22.1	23.4	4.31	NA	2.37	0.71	5.87	NA
Cash Flow	64.4	35.2	13.0	34.5	10.5	6.11	-7.06	-26.2	NA	NA
Current Ratio	1.4	1.2	1.1	1.3	1.4	NA	1.1	1.5	NA	NA
% Long Term Debt of Capitalization	0.6	Nil	0.0	0.1	0.5	Nil	Nil	Nil	NA	NA
% Net Income of Revenue	4.0	2.5	0.1	9.2	4.2	3.7	NM	NM	NM	NA
% Return on Assets	3.4	2.1	0.1	8.0	4.0	NA	NM	NA	NA	NA
% Return on Equity	7.7	5.0	0.2	16.7	14.9	NA	NM	NA	NA	NA

Data as orig reptd.; bef. results of disc opers/spec. items. Per share data adj. for stk. divs.; EPS diluted. E-Estimated. NA-Not Available. NM-Not Meaningful. NR-Not Ranked. UR-Under Review.

Office: The Landmark @ One Market, San Francisco, CA 94105.
Telephone: 415-901-7000.
Website: http://www.salesforce.com
Chrmn & CEO: M. Benioff

Pres: P.A. Sumner
EVP, CFO & Chief Acctg Officer: G.V. Smith
SVP, Secy & General Counsel: D. Schellhase
CTO: B. Pech

Board Members: M. Benioff, C. Conway, A. G. Hassenfeld, C. Ramsey, S. R. Robertson, S. Sclavos, L. J. Tomlinson, M. Webb, Jr., S. Young

Founded: 1999
Domicile: Delaware
Employees: 3,566

SanDisk Corp

STANDARD &POOR'S

S&P Recommendation	HOLD ★★★☆☆	Price $19.66 (as of Nov 27, 2009)	12-Mo. Target Price $27.00	Investment Style Large-Cap Growth

GICS Sector Information Technology
Sub-Industry Computer Storage & Peripherals

Summary This company designs, makes and markets flash memory storage products used in a wide variety of electronic systems.

Key Stock Statistics (Source S&P, Vickers, company reports)

52-Wk Range	$24.61– 6.79	S&P Oper. EPS 2009E	1.15	Market Capitalization(B)	$4.487	Beta	1.93
Trailing 12-Month EPS	$-7.72	S&P Oper. EPS 2010E	1.20	Yield (%)	Nil	S&P 3-Yr. Proj. EPS CAGR(%)	NM
Trailing 12-Month P/E	NM	P/E on S&P Oper. EPS 2009E	17.1	Dividend Rate/Share	Nil	S&P Credit Rating	B
$10K Invested 5 Yrs Ago	$8,533	Common Shares Outstg. (M)	228.2	Institutional Ownership (%)	80		

Price Performance

- 30-Week Mov. Avg. · · · ·   10-Week Mov. Avg. – – ·   **GAAP Earnings vs. Previous Year**   Volume Above Avg.   STARS
- 12-Mo. Target Price —   Relative Strength —   ▲ Up   ▼ Down   ▶ No Change   Below Avg.   ★

Options: ASE, CBOE, P, Ph

Analysis prepared by **Angelo Zino** on October 21, 2009, when the stock traded at **$ 23.90**.

Highlights

► We project that sales will increase 7.1% in 2009 and see an additional 6.4% rise in 2010, as we see growth in megabytes partially offset by average price deflation. We see demand for SNDK's products increasing at a modest pace, with growth primarily from OEM mobile customers. We expect inventories across the supply chain to be at reasonable levels near-term. We anticipate pricing for NAND memory to remain relatively flat.

► We forecast an annual gross margin of 32% in 2009, which includes the benefit of the sale of previously reserved inventory, and 31% in 2010. We think SNDK will benefit from higher growth in megabytes going forward, but expect some pricing pressure in 2010 despite a relatively healthy supply and demand picture. We think restructuring initiatives will lower the company's cost structure and aid margins. We believe SNDK is running at near full capacity and expect it to ramp to 32nm technology over the next few quarters.

► We forecast GAAP EPS of $1.15 in 2009 and $1.20 for 2010. We believe that SNDK can see sustained profitability through 2010 as long as industry supply tracks demand.

Investment Rationale/Risk

► Over the long term, we see restructuring initiatives, lower capital expenditures, and the recently renewed licensing and royalty agreement with Samsung aiding profitability. We believe that inventory levels across the supply chain are healthy, but remain cautious of uncertain end-market demand over the next few quarters. While we see opportunities for growth in its SSD business, recent NAND price increases have limited adoption as its target markets are highly price elastic. We expect the mobile market to be SNDK's highest growth business, and see the stock partly supported by net cash per share of over $7 at the end of September 2009.

► Risks to our recommendation and target price include the potential for more aggressive price erosion than we forecast, and more weakening in end-market demand than we foresee.

► Our 12-month target price of $27 is based on our price-to-sales analysis (P/S). We apply a P/S multiple of 1.7X to our 2010 sales per share estimate of $16.26, near SNDK's three-year historical average of 1.85X. However, the ratio is well below SNDK's five- and ten-year averages of 2.6X and 3.9X, respectively.

Qualitative Risk Assessment

LOW	MEDIUM	HIGH

Our risk assessment reflects the volatile nature of the flash memory space, an intensifying competitive environment, and what we deem to be significant price erosion within the industry.

Quantitative Evaluations

S&P Quality Ranking   B-

D	C	B-	B	B+	A-	A	A+

Relative Strength Rank   MODERATE

32

LOWEST = 1   HIGHEST = 99

Revenue/Earnings Data

Revenue (Million $)

	1Q	2Q	3Q	4Q	Year
2009	659.5	730.6	935.2	--	--
2008	850.0	816.0	821.5	863.9	3,351
2007	786.1	827.0	1,037	1,246	3,896
2006	623.3	719.2	751.4	1,164	3,258
2005	451.0	514.9	589.6	750.6	2,306
2004	386.9	433.3	408.0	548.9	1,777

Earnings Per Share ($)

2009	-0.92	0.23	0.99	E0.81	E1.15
2008	0.08	-0.30	-0.69	-8.25	-9.19
2007	Nil	0.12	0.36	0.45	0.93
2006	0.17	0.47	0.51	-0.17	0.96
2005	0.39	0.37	0.55	0.68	2.00
2004	0.34	0.38	0.29	0.42	1.44

Fiscal year ended Dec. 31. Next earnings report expected: Early February. EPS Estimates based on S&P Operating Earnings; historical GAAP earnings are as reported.

Dividend Data

No cash dividends have been paid.

SanDisk Corp

STANDARD
&POOR'S

Business Summary October 21, 2009

CORPORATE OVERVIEW. SanDisk Corp. (SNDK) designs, makes and markets flash storage card products used in a wide variety of consumer electronics products such as digital cameras, mobile phones, laptops, Universal Serial Bus, or USB, drives, gaming devices and MP3 players. Flash storage technology allows data to be stored in a durable, compact format that retains the digital information even after the power has been switched off. SNDK also provides high-speed and high-capacity storage solutions, known as solid-state drives, or SSDs, that can be used in lieu of hard disk drives in a variety of computing devices, including personal computers and enterprise servers.

The company's strategy focuses on identifying and developing current and emerging mass consumer markets for flash storage products and -- through its vertical integration supply strategy -- selling all major card formats in high volumes. SNDK sources the vast majority of its flash memory supply through its flash venture relationships with Toshiba, which provide SNDK with leading-edge, low-cost memory wafers.

CORPORATE STRATEGY. SNDK focuses primarily on four primary markets: consumer, mobile phones, digital audio and video players, computing. In the imaging market, the company makes cards used in all major brands of digital cameras. For mobile phones, SNDK's cards are experiencing increasing demand as multimedia features such as video and Internet access become more prevalent. Finally, SNDK offers a number of digital audio players, which allow consumers to download, store and play music.

Products are available to end users at approximately 222,000 retail storefronts around the globe and as data storage cards bundled with host products by SNDK's OEM customers. In 2008, the retail market accounted for 64% of product revenues, compared to 63% in 2007, while the OEM channel comprised 36% (37%). SNDK's top 10 customers and licensees in 2008 accounted for 48% of total revenues, up from 46% in 2007. Samsung accounted for 13% of total revenues in 2008. Product revenues from outside of North America made up 65% of the total in 2008 versus 65% in 2007 and 57% in 2006.

SNDK develops and owns leading-edge technology and patents for flash memory and data storage cards. The company has an extensive patent portfolio that has been licensed by several leading semiconductor companies. Over the past three years, on a cumulative basis, SNDK's license and royalty revenues exceeded $1 billion.

Company Financials Fiscal Year Ended Dec. 31

Per Share Data ($)	2008	2007	2006	2005	2004	2003	2002	2001	2000	1999
Tangible Book Value	13.76	16.94	15.31	13.41	10.78	9.32	4.54	4.93	6.40	4.38
Cash Flow	-8.00	1.97	1.61	2.34	1.62	1.12	0.40	-2.04	2.17	0.26
Earnings	-9.19	0.93	0.96	2.00	1.44	1.02	0.26	-2.19	2.06	0.22
S&P Core Earnings	-5.06	0.96	0.94	1.76	1.29	0.89	0.18	-1.05	NA	NA
Dividends	Nil	Nil	Nil	Nil	Nil	Nil	Nil	Nil	Nil	Nil
Payout Ratio	Nil	Nil	Nil	Nil	Nil	Nil	Nil	Nil	Nil	Nil
Prices:High	33.73	59.75	79.80	65.49	36.35	43.15	14.60	24.34	84.81	25.16
Prices:Low	5.07	32.74	37.34	20.25	19.28	7.39	4.80	4.30	13.75	3.31
P/E Ratio:High	NM	64	83	33	25	42	57	NM	41	NM
P/E Ratio:Low	NM	35	39	10	13	7	19	NM	7	NM

Income Statement Analysis (Million $)										
Revenue	3,351	3,896	3,258	2,306	1,777	1,080	541	366	602	247
Operating Income	-569	536	688	642	457	280	79.5	-124	141	37.2
Depreciation	254	246	136	65.8	38.9	23.0	21.3	20.5	15.9	7.15
Interest Expense	16.5	16.9	Nil	0.57	5.95	6.75	6.70	Nil	Nil	Nil
Pretax Income	-1,903	398	431	613	423	242	40.0	-442	492	39.6
Effective Tax Rate	NM	43.9%	53.4%	37.0%	37.0%	30.2%	9.35%	NM	39.3%	33.0%
Net Income	-2,070	218	199	386	267	169	36.2	-298	299	26.6
S&P Core Earnings	-1,138	225	195	339	239	149	25.7	-144	NA	NA

Balance Sheet & Other Financial Data (Million $)										
Cash	1,439	1,835	1,581	762	464	734	267	254	106	146
Current Assets	2,703	3,300	4,242	2,576	1,880	1,725	757	542	697	568
Total Assets	5,879	7,235	6,968	3,120	2,320	2,024	976	932	1,108	658
Current Liabilities	1,263	914	896	571	353	347	173	127	171	85.6
Long Term Debt	1,225	1,225	1,225	Nil	Nil	150	150	125	Nil	Nil
Common Equity	3,162	4,960	4,768	2,524	1,940	1,501	628	675	863	572
Total Capital	4,400	6,200	5,999	2,524	1,940	1,651	778	800	863	572
Capital Expenditures	184	259	176	134	126	52.5	16.6	26.2	26.6	21.4
Cash Flow	-1,803	464	334	452	305	192	57.6	-277	315	33.7
Current Ratio	2.1	3.6	4.7	4.5	5.3	5.0	4.4	4.3	4.1	6.6
% Long Term Debt of Capitalization	27.9	19.8	20.4	Nil	Nil	9.1	19.3	15.6	Nil	Nil
% Net Income of Revenue	NM	5.6	6.1	16.8	15.0	15.6	6.7	NM	49.6	10.7
% Return on Assets	NM	3.1	3.9	14.2	12.2	11.3	3.8	NM	33.8	5.8
% Return on Equity	NM	4.5	5.5	17.3	15.4	15.9	5.6	NM	41.6	6.8

Data as orig reptd.; bef. results of disc opers/spec. items. Per share data adj. for stk. divs.; EPS diluted. E-Estimated. NA-Not Available. NM-Not Meaningful. NR-Not Ranked. UR-Under Review.

Office: 601 McCarthy Blvd, Milpitas, CA 95035-7932.
Telephone: 408-801-1000.
Email: investor_relations@sandisk.com
Website: http://www.sandisk.com

Chrmn & CEO: E. Harari
Pres & COO: S. Mehrotra
Vice Chrmn: I. Federman
SVP, Secy & General Counsel: J. Brelsford

Investor Contact: J. Bruner
Board Members: K. A. DeNuccio, I. Federman, S. Gomo, E. Harari, E. W. Hartenstein, C. C. Hu, C. P. Lego, M. E. Marks, J. D. Meindl

Founded: 1988
Domicile: Delaware
Employees: 3,565

The McGraw-Hill Companies

Sara Lee Corp

STANDARD &POOR'S

S&P Recommendation	HOLD ★★★☆☆	Price $12.14 (as of Nov 27, 2009)	12-Mo. Target Price $12.00	Investment Style Large-Cap Blend

GICS Sector Consumer Staples
Sub-Industry Packaged Foods & Meats

Summary This diversified provider of branded food products (e.g., meats, fresh and frozen baked goods, and coffee) also sells household and body care products.

Key Stock Statistics (Source S&P, Vickers, company reports)

52-Wk Range	$12.61 – 6.80	S&P Oper. EPS 2010E	0.67	Market Capitalization(B)	$8.465	Beta	0.91
Trailing 12-Month EPS	$0.61	S&P Oper. EPS 2011E	UR	Yield (%)	3.62	S&P 3-Yr. Proj. EPS CAGR(%)	7
Trailing 12-Month P/E	19.9	P/E on S&P Oper. EPS 2010E	18.1	Dividend Rate/Share	$0.44	S&P Credit Rating	BBB+
$10K Invested 5 Yrs Ago	NA	Common Shares Outstg. (M)	697.3	Institutional Ownership (%)	74		

Price Performance

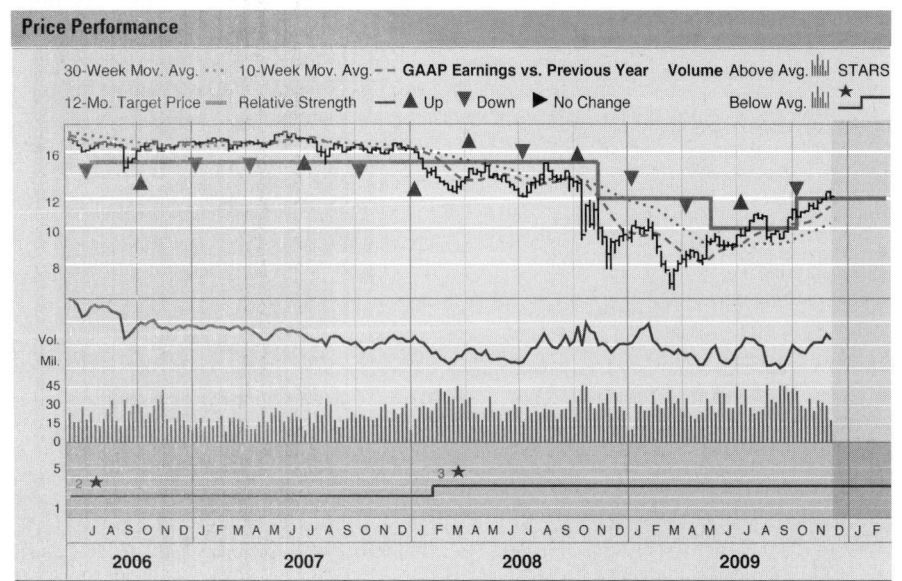

30-Week Mov. Avg. · · · · 10-Week Mov. Avg. – – **GAAP Earnings vs. Previous Year** Volume Above Avg. ⅢⅢ STARS
12-Mo. Target Price — Relative Strength — ▲ Up ▼ Down ▶ No Change Below Avg. ⅢⅢ ★

Options: ASE, CBOE, P

Analysis prepared by **Tom Graves, CFA** on October 02, 2009, when the stock traded at **$ 10.71**.

Highlights

▶ In September 2009, SLE said it had received a binding offer of EUR1.275 billion from Unilever (UL 28, Hold) to acquire SLE's global body care and European detergents businesses. At a recent currency exchange rate, we value the offer at about $1.9 billion. Subject to approvals, we look for the transaction to be completed in 2010. SLE said it planned to use proceeds from the divestiture to invest for growth in core businesses and to repurchase stock. SLE said it was also pursuing divestiture options for the remainder of its household business.

▶ In FY 10 (Jun.), which has an extra week, for the company as currently constituted, we look for sales to increase modestly from the $12.9 billion reported for FY 09, with strength of the U.S. dollar being less of a negative for growth comparisons.

▶ Excluding special items, but including the prospect of higher pension expense, we forecast FY 10 EPS of $0.90, up from $0.84 in FY 09, which excludes a net negative impact of $0.32 from special items.

Investment Rationale/Risk

▶ For SLE, we were pleased by Unilever's offer price for roughly half of SLE's international household and body care business. Longer term, we look for a multi-year improvement program called Project Accelerate to incur costs, but also to lead to substantial expense savings between now and the end of FY 12.

▶ Risks to our recommendation and target price include divestiture activity proceeding less favorably than expected, and weaker than expected sales resulting from disappointing demand or currency translation.

▶ Our 12-month target price of $12 reflects our view that SLE received a higher-than-anticipated offer for the businesses that Unilever has offered to acquire. As a result of the prospective price, we now think that SLE shares should trade at a P/E, on an FY 10 pro forma basis, that is closer to what we expect from a group of other packaged food stocks. Following the Hanesbrands spinoff in 2006, SLE reduced its dividend by about 49%. We expect at least four more quarters of $0.11 dividends. At the current dividend rate, the stock recently had an indicated dividend yield of 4.1%.

Qualitative Risk Assessment

LOW	MEDIUM	HIGH

Our risk assessment for Sara Lee reflects the relatively stable nature of the company's end markets, what we expect to be sizable cash flow from operating activities, and corporate governance practices that we view as favorable relative to peers.

Quantitative Evaluations

S&P Quality Ranking B

D	C	B-	B	B+	A-	A	A+

Relative Strength Rank STRONG

84

LOWEST = 1 HIGHEST = 99

Revenue/Earnings Data

Revenue (Million $)

	1Q	2Q	3Q	4Q	Year
2010	2,588	--	--	--	--
2009	3,349	3,340	3,028	3,164	12,881
2008	3,054	3,408	3,243	3,507	13,212
2007	2,891	3,182	3,006	3,199	12,278
2006	3,900	2,974	3,789	4,100	15,944
2005	4,861	5,199	4,785	4,754	19,254

Earnings Per Share ($)

2010	0.27	E0.15	E0.15	E0.24	E0.67
2009	0.32	-0.02	0.24	-0.02	0.52
2008	0.28	0.25	0.33	-0.96	-0.06
2007	0.34	-0.08	0.15	0.16	0.57
2006	0.25	-0.06	0.18	-0.15	0.53
2005	0.44	0.41	0.24	-0.14	0.92

Fiscal year ended Jun. 30. Next earnings report expected: Early February. EPS Estimates based on S&P Operating Earnings; historical GAAP earnings are as reported.

Dividend Data (Dates: mm/dd Payment Date: mm/dd/yy)

Amount ($)	Date Decl.	Ex-Div. Date	Stk. of Record	Payment Date
0.110	01/29	02/26	03/02	04/07/09
0.110	04/30	05/28	06/01	07/08/09
0.110	06/25	09/03	09/08	10/07/09
0.110	10/29	11/27	12/01	01/08/10

Dividends have been paid since 1946. Source: Company reports.

Sara Lee Corp

STANDARD &POOR'S

Business Summary October 02, 2009

CORPORATE OVERVIEW. Sara Lee, best known for its baked goods, also has various other branded food and non-food businesses. In North America, this includes Jimmy Dean and Hillshire Farm meat products, while outside the U.S., it includes coffee and tea, and household and body care products. In North America, in addition to providing products to retailers, SLE provides coffee, meats and bakery products to foodservice operators.

In FY 09 (Jun.), before intersegment eliminations, North American Retail (e.g., packaged meat, frozen bakery products, U.S. Senseo retail coffee business) represented 21% of total sales; North American Fresh Bakery accounted for 17%; North American Foodservice 16%; International Beverage 24%; International Bakery 6%; and International Household and Body Care 16%. SLE's Branded Apparel business, which had sales of $4.5 billion in FY 06, was spun off in September 2006.

CORPORATE STRATEGY. In September 2009, SLE said it had received a binding offer of EUR1.275 billion from Unilever (UL 28, Hold) to acquire SLE's global body care and European detergents businesses. In FY 09, these businesses had annual sales of about EUR750 million and an operating profit, before special items, of about $139 million. At a recent currency exchange rate, we value the acquisition offer at about $1.9 billion. Subject to approvals, we look for the transaction to be completed in 2010. SLE said it planned to use proceeds from

the divestiture to invest for growth in core businesses and to repurchase stock. Also, SLE said it had received significant interest in the remainder of its household business, and was pursuing divestiture options for this business, which includes air care, shoe care, insecticides and non-European cleaning brands.

In FY 09, as part of efforts to improve operational performance and reduce costs, SLE initiated Project Accelerate, which is expected to include outsourcing pieces of transaction processing, Global Information Services, and procurement activities. We expect Project Accelerate to incur costs, but also to lead to substantial expense savings between now and the end of FY 12.

In February 2005, the company announced a comprehensive restructuring program, involving a reorganization of business units and plans to dispose of various businesses. The key components of this plan were to transform the company's portfolio, reorganize continuing operations, improve operational efficiency, and consolidate the North American and European headquarters.

Company Financials Fiscal Year Ended Jun. 30

Per Share Data ($)	2009	2008	2007	2006	2005	2004	2003	2002	2001	2000
Tangible Book Value	NM	NM	NM	NM	NM	NM	NM	NM	NM	NM
Cash Flow	1.22	0.51	1.33	1.46	1.87	2.53	2.44	1.94	2.80	1.92
Earnings	0.52	-0.06	0.57	0.53	0.92	1.59	1.50	1.23	1.87	1.27
S&P Core Earnings	0.47	0.69	0.50	0.44	0.86	1.67	1.30	1.00	0.92	NA
Dividends	0.44	0.42	0.50	0.79	0.78	0.60	0.62	0.60	0.57	0.54
Payout Ratio	84%	NM	88%	149%	85%	38%	41%	48%	30%	43%
Prices:High	12.61	16.08	18.15	19.64	25.00	24.49	23.13	23.84	24.75	25.31
Prices:Low	6.80	7.74	14.75	14.08	17.31	20.17	16.25	16.15	18.26	13.38
P/E Ratio:High	24	NM	32	37	27	15	15	19	13	20
P/E Ratio:Low	13	NM	26	27	19	13	11	13	10	11

Income Statement Analysis (Million $)										
Revenue	12,881	13,212	12,278	15,944	19,254	19,566	18,291	17,628	17,747	17,511
Operating Income	1,488	1,484	1,242	1,779	2,183	2,386	2,345	2,138	2,191	2,345
Depreciation	497	403	539	701	737	734	674	582	599	602
Interest Expense	170	205	265	308	290	271	276	304	270	252
Pretax Income	588	137	419	683	934	1,542	1,484	1,185	1,851	1,567
Effective Tax Rate	38.1%	146.7%	NM	40.0%	21.7%	17.5%	17.7%	14.8%	13.4%	26.1%
Net Income	364	-64.0	426	410	731	1,272	1,221	1,010	1,603	1,158
S&P Core Earnings	327	501	385	339	684	1,336	1,047	806	768	NA

Balance Sheet & Other Financial Data (Million $)										
Cash	959	1,284	2,520	2,231	545	638	942	298	548	314
Current Assets	3,830	4,467	5,643	6,774	5,811	5,746	5,953	4,986	5,083	5,974
Total Assets	9,417	10,830	12,190	14,522	14,412	14,883	15,084	13,753	10,167	11,611
Current Liabilities	2,846	3,841	4,301	6,277	4,968	5,423	5,199	5,463	4,958	6,759
Long Term Debt	2,704	2,340	2,803	3,807	4,115	4,171	5,157	4,326	2,640	2,248
Common Equity	2,036	2,811	2,615	2,449	2,938	2,948	1,870	1,534	899	1,007
Total Capital	4,872	5,347	6,066	6,324	7,134	7,194	7,806	7,252	4,646	4,271
Capital Expenditures	357	454	529	625	538	530	746	669	532	647
Cash Flow	861	362	965	1,111	1,468	2,006	1,895	1,592	2,191	1,748
Current Ratio	1.4	1.2	1.3	1.1	1.2	1.1	1.1	0.9	1.0	0.9
% Long Term Debt of Capitalization	55.5	43.8	46.2	60.2	57.6	58.0	66.1	59.7	56.8	52.6
% Net Income of Revenue	2.8	NM	3.5	2.6	3.8	6.5	6.7	5.7	9.0	6.6
% Return on Assets	3.6	NM	3.2	2.8	5.0	8.4	8.5	8.4	14.7	10.6
% Return on Equity	15.0	NM	16.8	15.2	24.7	52.8	71.7	83.0	167.1	112.3

Data as orig reptd.; bef. results of disc opers/spec. items. Per share data adj. for stk. divs.; EPS diluted. E-Estimated. NA-Not Available. NM-Not Meaningful. NR-Not Ranked. UR-Under Review.

Office: 3500 Lacey Rd, Downers Grove, IL 60515-5424.
Telephone: 630-598-6000.
Website: http://www.saralee.com
Chrmn & CEO: B.C. Barnes

EVP & CFO: M.H. Smits
EVP, Secy & General Counsel: B.J. Hart
SVP, Chief Acctg Officer & Cntlr: T.S. Shilen, Jr.
Treas: S. Gupta

Investor Contact: L.M. de Kool
Board Members: B. C. Barnes, C. B. Begley, C. C. Bowles, V. W. Colbert, J. S. Crown, L. T. Koellner, J. D. McAdam, I. Prosser, N. Sorensen, J. W. Ubben, J. Ward, C. J. van Lede

Founded: 1941
Domicile: Maryland
Employees: 41,000

The McGraw-Hill Companies

SCANA Corp

STANDARD
&POOR'S

S&P Recommendation HOLD ★★★☆☆	Price $34.94 (as of Nov 27, 2009)	12-Mo. Target Price $36.00	Investment Style Large-Cap Blend

GICS Sector Utilities
Sub-Industry Multi-Utilities

Summary Through its subsidiaries, this energy-based holding company provides electric, natural gas, and telecommunications services.

Key Stock Statistics (Source S&P, Vickers, company reports)

52-Wk Range	$37.62– 26.01	S&P Oper. EPS 2009E	2.86	Market Capitalization(B)	$4.302	Beta	0.56
Trailing 12-Month EPS	$2.97	S&P Oper. EPS 2010E	3.04	Yield (%)	5.38	S&P 3-Yr. Proj. EPS CAGR(%)	4
Trailing 12-Month P/E	11.8	P/E on S&P Oper. EPS 2009E	12.2	Dividend Rate/Share	$1.88	S&P Credit Rating	BBB+
$10K Invested 5 Yrs Ago	$11,202	Common Shares Outstg. (M)	123.1	Institutional Ownership (%)	46		

Price Performance

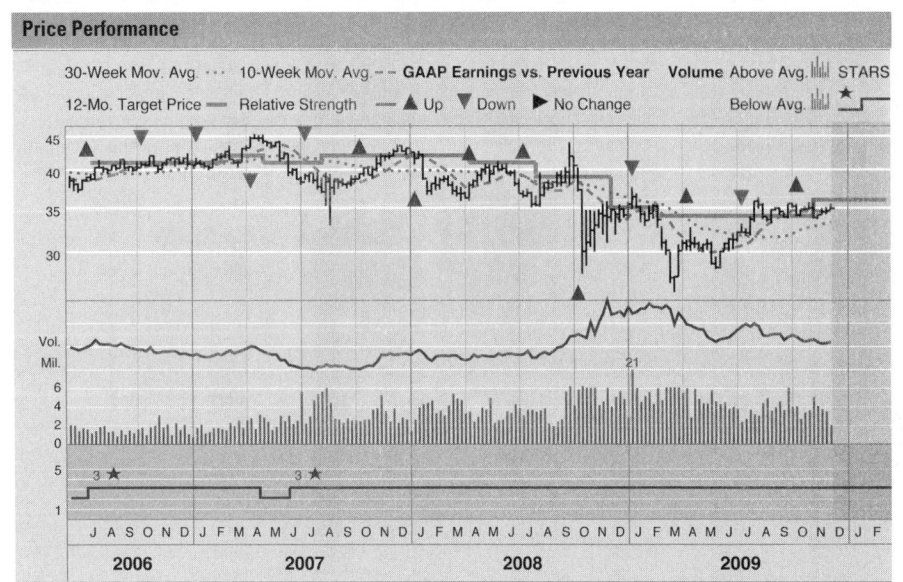

30-Week Mov. Avg. ···· 10-Week Mov. Avg. − − GAAP Earnings vs. Previous Year   Volume Above Avg. STARS
12-Mo. Target Price — Relative Strength — ▲ Up ▼ Down ► No Change   Below Avg.

Options: Ph

Analysis prepared by **Christopher B. Muir** on October 28, 2009, when the stock traded at **$ 34.40**.

Highlights

► We expect a 2009 revenue contraction of 18%. We believe the contraction will stem from lower gas prices and reduced industrial volumes, partly offset by growth in residential and commercial categories. SCG's gas and electric distribution territories should provide the utility with steady annual customer growth. In 2010, we see revenues rising 2.4% as we expect a stabilizing economy and more stable to slightly rising gas prices, but we continue to see pressure on industrial sales.

► We expect operating margins of 16.3% in 2009 and 17.1% in 2010, versus 13.4% in 2008. We expect per-revenue fuel costs to drop, partly offset by rising per-revenue non-fuel operating costs. We see pretax margins of 12.4% in 2009 and 13.2% in 2010, up from 10.1% in 2008, less than the improvement in operating margins as we see lower nonoperating income partly offset by lower interest expense.

► Assuming an effective tax rate of 35.0% and continued upward share drift related to compensation, we estimate 2009 EPS of $2.86, down 3.4% from 2008's $2.96. Our 2010 EPS estimate is $3.04, up 6.3%.

Investment Rationale/Risk

► We think above-average population growth in SCG's service areas will provide solid opportunities for further rate and rate base increases. SCG's cash flow generation has been solid, in our view. We see the unregulated gas business in Georgia providing more growth than the regulated businesses. However, with our expectation for 4% EPS growth in each of the next three years, we think the stock is fairly valued.

► Risks to our recommendation and target price include a sharp increase in interest rates, prolonged mild temperatures, unfavorable regulatory actions, and weaker-than-expected economic growth in the utility's service area.

► The stock recently traded at 11.4X our 2010 EPS estimate, or a 2% discount to its multi-utility peers. Our 12-month target price of $36 is 11.8X our 2010 estimate, a small premium to our peer target. We believe this valuation is warranted by what we see as a relatively strong balance sheet, partly offset by our expectation of slower than peers EPS growth and little improvement in the capital structure over the next three years.

Qualitative Risk Assessment

LOW	MEDIUM	HIGH

We think the largely regulated nature of SCG's operations provides a stable source of cash flow and earnings. In addition, the company has a less leveraged balance sheet than peers.

Quantitative Evaluations

S&P Quality Ranking   B

D	C	B-	B	B+	A-	A	A+

Relative Strength Rank   MODERATE

58

LOWEST = 1   HIGHEST = 99

Revenue/Earnings Data

Revenue (Million $)

	1Q	2Q	3Q	4Q	Year
2009	1,343	878.0	921.0	--	--
2008	1,533	1,218	1,266	1,301	5,319
2007	1,363	1,007	1,079	1,172	4,621
2006	1,389	944.0	1,062	1,168	4,563
2005	1,266	891.0	1,127	1,492	4,777
2004	1,136	846.0	857.0	1,053	3,885

Earnings Per Share ($)

2009	0.94	0.45	0.84	E0.75	E2.86
2008	0.93	0.49	0.80	0.73	2.96
2007	0.73	0.47	0.79	0.75	2.74
2006	0.80	0.50	0.76	0.57	2.63
2005	0.89	0.39	0.88	0.65	2.81
2004	0.91	0.54	0.48	0.37	2.30

Fiscal year ended Dec. 31. Next earnings report expected: Mid February. EPS Estimates based on S&P Operating Earnings; historical GAAP earnings are as reported.

Dividend Data (Dates: mm/dd Payment Date: mm/dd/yy)

Amount ($)	Date Decl.	Ex-Div. Date	Stk. of Record	Payment Date
0.470	02/19	03/06	03/10	04/01/09
0.470	04/23	06/08	06/10	07/01/09
0.470	07/30	09/08	09/10	10/01/09
0.470	10/28	12/08	12/10	01/01/10

Dividends have been paid since 1946. Source: Company reports.

SCANA Corp

STANDARD &POOR'S

Business Summary October 28, 2009

CORPORATE OVERVIEW. SCG's primary operating businesses are South Carolina Electric & Gas (SCE&G), Public Service of North Carolina (PSNC), SCANA Energy, and an intrastate pipeline operation in South Carolina. As of December 31, 2008, SCE&G had 649,600 electric customers and 307,200 natural gas customers. PSNC had 467,800 gas utility customers. SCANA Energy served over 30% of the 1.5 million customers in Georgia's competitive natural gas supply market, with about 90,000 of its 460,000 gas customers receiving regulated services. The company projects that its consolidated regulated base of more than 1.4 million electric and gas customers will grow 2.5% annually.

In 2008, 42% of SCG's external revenues were derived from electric operations (42% in 2007), 23% (24%) from natural gas distribution, 23% (21%) from energy marketing, and 12% (13%) from retail gas marketing. SCE&G owned 5,616 megawatt (MW) of generating plants as of December 2008. This capacity consisted of 46% coal, 29% oil/gas, 14% hydro and 11% nuclear. In 2008, 65% of SCE&G's power was generated by coal plants, 18% by nuclear, 13% by natural gas and oil, and 4% by hydroelectric.

CORPORATE STRATEGY. SCG sees reserve margins falling in its service territory over the next several years and believes that new baseload power will be needed. As a result, it plans to invest in nuclear generation to fill the gap.

SCE&G submitted a joint application to the NRC on March 31, 2008, with Santee Cooper, a state-owned utility, for a combined construction and operating license (COL) that covers two nuclear units. SCE&G has said that the companies have elected to use a 1,000 MW design, which would be built at the existing VC Summer nuclear station, if the economic need still exists after the approximately three-year COL application process. If the companies decide to move ahead with the project, SCG said the first plant could be built by 2016. SCE&G operates the VC Summer nuclear station and would remain the operator for all units after completion. Financially, SCG aims to increase earnings at a rate of 4%-6% annually and maintain a dividend payout ratio in the 55%-60% range.

SCG's energy investments over the past several years included the construction of a $450 million, 875 MW power plant in Jasper, SC (completed in May 2004); a $25 million, 38-mile gas pipeline, dubbed the South System Loop, that connects to the interstate pipeline (completed in May 2004); and a back-up dam at Lake Murray costing $275 million (completed in June 2005). The company also expects to add new natural gas peaking capacity by 2009.

Company Financials Fiscal Year Ended Dec. 31

Per Share Data ($)	2008	2007	2006	2005	2004	2003	2002	2001	2000	1999
Tangible Book Value	23.86	23.33	24.32	23.28	21.69	20.77	19.61	20.90	19.51	20.15
Earnings	2.96	2.74	2.63	2.81	2.30	2.54	0.83	5.15	2.12	1.73
S&P Core Earnings	2.55	2.52	2.44	2.60	2.51	2.40	1.93	1.59	NA	NA
Dividends	1.84	1.76	1.68	1.56	1.46	1.38	1.30	1.20	1.15	1.43
Payout Ratio	62%	64%	64%	56%	63%	54%	157%	23%	54%	83%
Prices:High	44.06	45.49	42.43	43.65	39.71	35.70	32.15	30.00	31.13	32.56
Prices:Low	27.75	32.93	36.92	36.56	32.82	28.10	23.50	24.25	22.00	21.13
P/E Ratio:High	15	17	16	16	17	14	39	6	15	19
P/E Ratio:Low	9	12	14	13	14	11	28	5	10	12

Income Statement Analysis (Million $)										
Revenue	5,319	4,621	4,563	4,777	3,885	3,416	2,954	3,451	3,433	1,650
Depreciation	344	324	333	510	265	238	220	224	217	168
Maintenance	NA	NA	NA	NA	NA	558	522	482	NA	90.0
Fixed Charges Coverage	3.25	3.18	3.02	2.18	2.83	2.81	2.68	2.49	2.47	2.55
Construction Credits	NA	NA	NA	3.00	26.0	11.0	NA	NA	7.00	7.00
Effective Tax Rate	35.3%	30.0%	28.1%	NM	32.4%	32.4%	29.0%	36.1%	39.0%	38.1%
Net Income	346	320	304	320	257	282	88.0	539	221	179
S&P Core Earnings	299	294	282	296	280	268	204	167	NA	NA

Balance Sheet & Other Financial Data (Million $)										
Gross Property	11,645	10,650	9,954	9,540	9,181	9,025	7,777	7,215	7,413	6,679
Capital Expenditures	904	712	485	366	498	738	675	523	334	238
Net Property	8,499	7,669	7,139	6,842	6,866	6,745	5,301	4,851	5,201	4,850
Capitalization:Long Term Debt	4,361	2,879	3,067	3,062	3,301	3,340	2,999	2,812	3,016	1,730
Capitalization:% Long Term Debt	58.0	48.4	50.9	53.4	58.3	59.2	57.9	56.2	59.7	45.2
Capitalization:Preferred	113	113	114	Nil	Nil	Nil	Nil	Nil	Nil	NA
Capitalization:% Preferred	1.50	1.90	1.89	Nil	Nil	Nil	Nil	Nil	Nil	NA
Capitalization:Common	3,045	2,960	2,846	2,677	2,357	2,306	2,177	2,194	2,032	2,099
Capitalization:% Common	40.5	49.7	47.2	46.6	41.7	40.8	42.1	43.8	40.3	54.8
Total Capital	8,631	7,000	7,094	6,800	6,658	6,550	6,041	5,844	5,888	4,750
% Operating Ratio	90.2	89.3	89.4	88.4	87.8	87.8	83.8	93.5	88.0	81.2
% Earned on Net Property	8.8	8.5	8.6	6.4	8.9	8.5	10.1	11.3	11.0	6.8
% Return on Revenue	6.5	6.9	6.7	6.7	6.6	8.3	3.0	15.6	6.4	10.8
% Return on Invested Capital	7.3	9.8	8.8	10.9	7.6	8.8	9.9	14.2	8.7	7.4
% Return on Common Equity	11.5	11.0	11.0	12.5	10.8	12.3	4.0	25.5	10.7	9.3

Data as orig reptd.; bef. results of disc opers/spec. items. Per share data adj. for stk. divs.; EPS diluted. E-Estimated. NA-Not Available. NM-Not Meaningful. NR-Not Ranked. UR-Under Review.

Office: 1426 Main Street, Columbia, SC 29201.
Telephone: 803-217-9000.
Email: invrel@scana.com
Website: http://www.scana.com

Chrmn, Pres & CEO: W.B. Timmerman
SVP & CFO: J.E. Addison
SVP & General Counsel: R.T. Lindsay
Chief Acctg Officer & Cntlr: J.E. Swan, IV

Secy: G. Champion
Investor Contact: J. Winn (803-217-9240)
Board Members: B. Amick, J. A. Bennett, S. A. Decker, D. M. Hagood, J. W. Martin, III, J. M. Micali, L. M. Miller, J. W. Roquemore, M. K. Sloan, H. C. Stowe, W. B. Timmerman, G. S. York

Founded: 1924
Domicile: South Carolina
Employees: 5,786

The McGraw-Hill Companies

Schlumberger Ltd

STANDARD &POOR'S

S&P Recommendation	**SELL** ★★☆☆☆	Price $63.14 (as of Nov 27, 2009)	12-Mo. Target Price $61.00	Investment Style Large-Cap Blend

GICS Sector Energy
Sub-Industry Oil & Gas Equipment & Services

Summary This leading oilfield services company provides equipment and technology to the oil and gas industry worldwide.

Key Stock Statistics (Source S&P, Vickers, company reports)

52-Wk Range	$71.10–35.05	S&P Oper. EPS 2009**E**	2.62	Market Capitalization(B)	$75.816	Beta	1.24
Trailing 12-Month EPS	$2.88	S&P Oper. EPS 2010**E**	2.92	Yield (%)	1.33	S&P 3-Yr. Proj. EPS CAGR(%)	-11
Trailing 12-Month P/E	21.9	P/E on S&P Oper. EPS 2009**E**	24.1	Dividend Rate/Share	$0.84	S&P Credit Rating	A+
$10K Invested 5 Yrs Ago	$19,868	Common Shares Outstg. (M)	1,200.8	Institutional Ownership (%)	76		

Price Performance

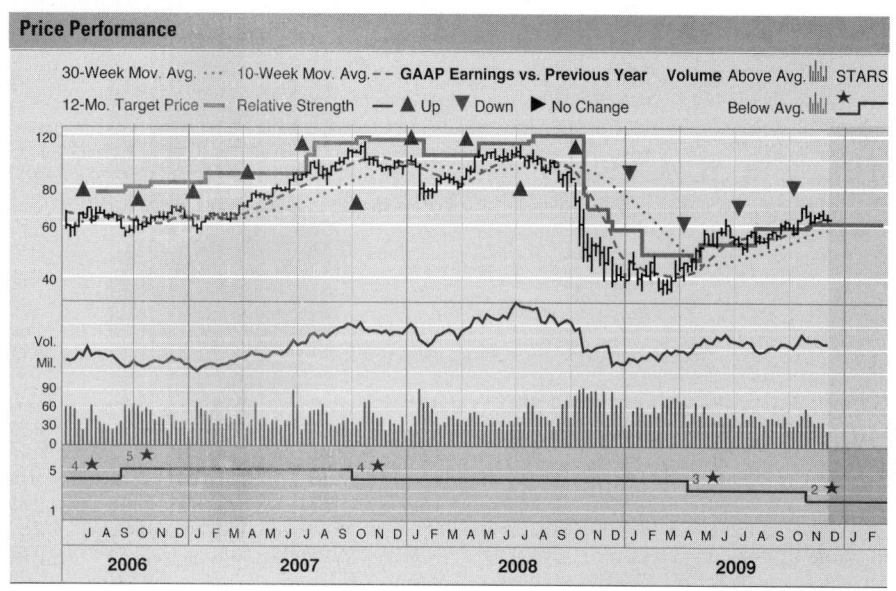

30-Week Mov. Avg. · · · 10-Week Mov. Avg. - - GAAP Earnings vs. Previous Year Volume Above Avg. STARS
12-Mo. Target Price — Relative Strength ▲ Up ▼ Down ► No Change Below Avg.

Options: ASE, CBOE, P, Ph

Analysis prepared by **Stewart Glickman, CFA** on October 27, 2009, when the stock traded at **$ 64.30**.

Highlights

► In October, SLB said that the negative impact of recent oilfield service price concessions might outweigh the positive impact of cost cutting measures, in terms of anticipated operating margin performance, particularly in the Eastern Hemisphere (which represented 60% of YTD revenues). While rising volumes could go a long way towards restoring margin performance (third quarter oilfield services operating margins of 20.4% were down 790 basis points from the year-ago quarter), we remain wary on the timing of a strong demand recovery. SLB also said in October that the state of the general economy in this cyclical downturn is, in their estimation, considerably worse than in the prior downturns in 2001, 1999 and 1986.

► Long term, we think energy demand will make a solid recovery, and recent stabilization of crude oil prices in the $70-80 per barrel range could boost customer confidence to increase upstream spending. Current bright spots, in our view, include deepwater development, and Latin America.

► On lower revenues and narrower operating margins, we see EPS of $2.62 in 2009 (a 41% drop from 2008), recovering to $2.92 in 2010.

Investment Rationale/Risk

► We recently downgraded our opinion to sell, from hold on valuation, given our concerns over near-term growth prospects. Long term, we see SLB as a best-of-breed oilfield services company, well positioned to benefit from an increasing trend toward new oil and gas development opportunities that require higher levels of technology content, especially in emerging markets, which we believe plays to the benefit of larger oilfield service providers. We also note SLB's attractive geographic footprint, with less exposure than peers to North America.

► Risks to our recommendation and target price include higher activity volumes; higher demand for integrated systems in oilfield services; and reduced political risk in emerging markets.

► Our DCF model, assuming free cash flow growth of 14% per year for 10 years and 3% thereafter, and a WACC of 11.5%, shows an intrinsic value of about $57 per share. Applying an enterprise value of 11X to our 2010 EBITDA estimate, a multiple of 12.5X projected 2010 cash flow (slightly above peer averages, we think merited by above-average ROIC), and blending these values with our DCF model, our 12-month target price is $61.

Qualitative Risk Assessment

LOW	MEDIUM	HIGH

Our risk assessment reflects the company's exposure to volatile crude oil and natural gas prices; its dependence on capital spending decisions by its oil and gas producing customers; and political risk associated with operating in frontier regions around the world. This is offset by the company's leading industry position.

Quantitative Evaluations

S&P Quality Ranking NR

D	C	B-	B	B+	A-	A	A+

Relative Strength Rank MODERATE

55

LOWEST = 1   HIGHEST = 99

Revenue/Earnings Data

Revenue (Million $)

	1Q	2Q	3Q	4Q	Year
2009	6,000	5,528	5,430	--	--
2008	6,290	6,746	7,259	6,868	27,163
2007	5,464	5,639	5,926	6,248	23,277
2006	4,239	4,687	4,955	5,350	19,230
2005	3,159	3,429	3,698	4,023	14,309
2004	2,673	2,833	2,906	3,068	11,480

Earnings Per Share ($)

2009	0.78	0.51	0.65	E0.69	E2.62
2008	1.06	1.16	1.25	0.95	4.42
2007	0.96	1.02	1.09	1.12	4.20
2006	0.59	0.69	0.81	0.92	3.01
2005	0.44	0.39	0.45	0.54	1.81
2004	0.09	0.22	0.25	0.29	0.85

Fiscal year ended Dec. 31. Next earnings report expected: Late January. EPS Estimates based on S&P Operating Earnings; historical GAAP earnings are as reported.

Dividend Data (Dates: mm/dd Payment Date: mm/dd/yy)

Amount ($)	Date Decl.	Ex-Div. Date	Stk. of Record	Payment Date
0.210	01/22	02/13	02/18	04/03/09
0.210	04/23	06/01	06/03	07/10/09
0.210	07/23	08/31	09/02	10/02/09
0.210	10/22	11/30	12/02	01/08/10

Dividends have been paid since 1957. Source: Company reports.

Please read the Required Disclosures and Analyst Certification on the last page of this report.

The McGraw·Hill Companies

Schlumberger Ltd

Business Summary October 27, 2009

CORPORATE OVERVIEW. As a global oilfield and information services company with major activity in the energy industry, Schlumberger operates in two primary business segments: Oilfield Services (89% of 2008 revenues; 87% of 2007 revenues), and WesternGeco (11%, 13%). Oilfield Services provides exploration and production services, solutions and technology to the petroleum industry. It is managed through four geographic areas (North America, South America, Europe/CIS/Africa, and the Middle East/Asia).

The company is largely focused on international operations; North America generated only 24% of Oilfield Services' total revenues in 2008, and 21% of the segment's 2008 pretax operating income. The Middle East/Asia region generated the highest operating margins in 2008, at 35.1%, with Europe/CIS/West Africa second, at 27.4%.

Operations within Oilfield Services are organized into eight technology segments: (1) wireline services, providing information technology to evaluate the reservoir, plan and monitor wells, and evaluate and monitor production; (2) drilling and measurements, including directional drilling, measurement while drilling and logging while drilling services; (3) well testing; (4) well services, which includes pressure pumping, coiled tubing, well cementing and stimulation; (5) completions, which includes gas-lift and safety valves, and a range of intelligent well completions technology and equipment; (6) artificial lift, which offers production optimization services using electric submersible pumps and other equipment; (7) data and consulting services; and (8) Schlumberger Infor-

mation Solutions. Supporting these eight technologies are 20 R&D centers.

In addition, SLB operates its WesternGeco seismic segment. WesternGeco provides worldwide comprehensive reservoir imaging, monitoring and development services, with seismic crews and data processing centers, as well as a large multiclient seismic library. Services include 3D and time-lapse (4D) seismic surveys, and multi-component surveys for delineating prospects and reservoir management.

CORPORATE STRATEGY. SLB has made a strategic focus of improving its research and development of advanced oilfield technologies, with the goal of enhancing oilfield efficiency, reducing finding and development (F&D) costs, improving productivity, maximizing reserve recovery, and increasing asset values. We believe that advanced technology will become increasingly important, as existing oilfields mature and new oilfields are developed in harsh environments and challenging geological conditions. We anticipate that most new major oilfield developments are likely to be found in the Eastern Hemisphere, given relatively lower F&D costs and higher growth reservoir potential.

Company Financials Fiscal Year Ended Dec. 31

Per Share Data ($)	2008	2007	2006	2005	2004	2003	2002	2001	2000	1999
Tangible Book Value	8.85	7.23	3.84	3.63	2.54	1.87	0.70	1.14	5.87	5.65
Cash Flow	5.97	5.41	4.24	2.89	1.89	1.74	-0.75	2.08	1.73	1.20
Earnings	4.42	4.20	3.01	1.81	0.85	0.41	-2.09	0.46	0.64	0.29
Dividends	0.84	0.70	0.50	0.42	0.38	0.38	0.38	0.38	0.38	0.38
Payout Ratio	19%	17%	17%	23%	44%	93%	NM	82%	59%	129%
Prices:High	111.95	114.84	74.75	51.49	34.95	28.12	31.22	41.41	44.44	35.34
Prices:Low	37.07	55.68	49.20	31.57	26.27	17.81	16.70	20.42	26.75	22.72
P/E Ratio:High	25	27	25	28	41	69	NM	91	70	NM
P/E Ratio:Low	8	13	16	17	31	44	NM	45	42	NM

Income Statement Analysis (Million $)										
Revenue	27,163	23,277	19,230	14,309	11,480	14,059	13,474	13,746	9,611	8,395
Operating Income	8,602	7,994	6,458	4,520	2,895	2,474	-456	3,165	2,084	1,327
Depreciation, Depletion and Amortization	1,904	1,526	1,561	1,351	1,308	1,571	1,545	1,896	1,271	1,021
Interest Expense	247	275	235	197	272	334	368	385	276	193
Pretax Income	6,852	6,624	4,948	2,972	1,327	568	-2,230	1,126	959	470
Effective Tax Rate	20.9%	21.9%	24.0%	22.9%	20.9%	36.9%	NM	51.1%	23.8%	29.9%
Net Income	5,397	5,177	3,710	2,199	1,014	473	-2,418	522	733	329

Balance Sheet & Other Financial Data (Million $)										
Cash	3,692	3,169	166	191	224	234	168	178	3,040	4,390
Current Assets	12,894	11,055	9,186	8,554	7,060	10,369	7,185	7,705	7,493	8,606
Total Assets	31,991	27,853	22,832	18,077	16,001	20,041	19,435	22,326	17,173	15,081
Current Liabilities	8,125	7,505	6,455	5,515	4,701	6,795	6,451	6,218	3,991	3,474
Long Term Debt	3,694	3,794	4,664	3,591	3,944	6,097	6,029	6,216	3,573	3,183
Common Equity	16,862	14,876	10,420	7,592	6,117	5,881	5,606	8,378	8,295	7,721
Total Capital	20,628	18,732	15,084	11,688	10,477	12,376	12,188	15,231	12,474	10,904
Capital Expenditures	3,723	3,191	2,457	1,593	1,216	1,025	1,366	2,053	1,323	792
Cash Flow	7,301	6,703	5,271	3,550	2,322	2,044	-872	2,418	2,003	1,350
Current Ratio	1.6	1.5	1.4	1.6	1.5	1.5	1.1	1.2	1.9	2.5
% Long Term Debt of Capitalization	17.9	20.3	30.9	30.7	37.6	49.3	49.5	40.8	28.6	29.2
% Return on Assets	18.0	20.4	18.1	12.9	5.6	2.4	NM	2.6	4.5	2.1
% Return on Equity	34.0	40.9	41.2	32.1	16.9	8.2	NM	6.3	9.1	4.2

Data as orig reptd.; bef. results of disc opers/spec. items. Per share data adj. for stk. divs.; EPS diluted. E-Estimated. NA-Not Available. NM-Not Meaningful. NR-Not Ranked. UR-Under Review.

Office: 5599 San Felipe St 17th Fl, Houston, TX 77056-2724.
Telephone: 713-513-2000.
Email: irsupport@slb.com
Website: http://www.slb.com

Chrmn & CEO: A. Gould
EVP & CFO: S. Ayat
CTO: A. Belani
Chief Acctg Officer: H. Guild

Treas: H.S. Oyinlola
Investor Contact: M. Theobald (713-375-3535)
Board Members: P. Camus, J. S. Gorelick, A. Gould, A. E. Isaac, N. Kudryavtsev, A. Lajous, M. E. Marks, L. R. Reif, R. C. Ross, T. Sandvold, H. Seydoux, L. G. Stuntz

Founded: 1926
Domicile: Netherlands Antilles
Employees: 87,000

Schwab (Charles) Corp

STANDARD &POOR'S

S&P Recommendation **SELL** ★☆☆☆☆	Price $17.74 (as of Nov 27, 2009)	12-Mo. Target Price $17.00	Investment Style Large-Cap Blend

GICS Sector Financials
Sub-Industry Investment Banking & Brokerage

Summary This company's subsidiary, Charles Schwab & Co., is among the largest brokerage firms in the U.S., primarily serving retail clients.

Key Stock Statistics (Source S&P, Vickers, company reports)

52-Wk Range	$19.87–11.00	S&P Oper. EPS 2009E	0.73	Market Capitalization(B)	$20.616	Beta	1.33
Trailing 12-Month EPS	$0.80	S&P Oper. EPS 2010E	0.90	Yield (%)	1.35	S&P 3-Yr. Proj. EPS CAGR(%)	4
Trailing 12-Month P/E	22.2	P/E on S&P Oper. EPS 2009E	24.3	Dividend Rate/Share	$0.24	S&P Credit Rating	A
$10K Invested 5 Yrs Ago	$17,956	Common Shares Outstg. (M)	1,162.1	Institutional Ownership (%)	67		

Price Performance

30-Week Mov. Avg. · · · 10-Week Mov. Avg. - - GAAP Earnings vs. Previous Year   Volume Above Avg. STARS
12-Mo. Target Price — Relative Strength — ▲ Up ▼ Down ► No Change   Below Avg.

Options: ASE, CBOE, P, Ph

Analysis prepared by **Matthew Albrecht** on October 20, 2009, when the stock traded at **$18.53**.

Highlights

► We expect revenues to decline 18% in 2009, reflecting lower fee-based client assets as a result of equity market declines over the past year and money market fee waivers. Also, with the federal funds rate close to zero, yields on SCHW's interest-earning assets are falling, which is the basis for our expectation of a 30% drop in net interest income. We see trading commissions declining slightly. Nevertheless, we view SCHW as an excellent asset gatherer, which we think will help the company emerge stronger once markets stabilize. In the September quarter, SCHW attracted $19.9 billion of net new assets, an improvement over the second quarter.

► We expect revenue compression to be partially offset by SCHW's cost-cutting efforts, led by our forecast of a 7.2% reduction in compensation costs in 2009. All told, we expect operating costs to be cut by 6.5% this year.

► We forecast EPS of $0.73 in 2009, a 31% decline from $1.06 in 2008. We forecast EPS of $0.90 in 2010, based on higher asset management fees and net interest revenues, particularly in the second half.

Investment Rationale/Risk

► Although we think a premium multiple afforded the shares versus peers is appropriate given SCHW's high proportion of recurring asset-based fees and strong brand recognition, we believe near-term challenges are likely to persist through 2009. In particular, although recent trading volume has been strong, a reduction in volatility in the fourth quarter and into 2010 could negatively impact revenues. Accordingly, we do not expect trading commissions to offset interest and asset management revenue declines in the near term. Nevertheless, we think SCHW's revenue streams are better diversified than other discount brokers, and will be situated to benefit from an economic recovery.

► Risks to our recommendation and target price include increased trading volumes, equity market appreciation, and a faster than expected rise in short-term interest rates.

► Our 12-month target price of $17 is 18.9X our 2010 EPS estimate of $0.90, a premium to discount brokerage peers, but at the low end of SCHW's historical range, reflecting ongoing uncertainties.

Qualitative Risk Assessment

LOW	**MEDIUM**	HIGH

Our risk assessment reflects our view of the company's strong competitive position, brand recognition and affluent client base, offset by industry cyclicality and our concerns about corporate governance.

Quantitative Evaluations

S&P Quality Ranking B+

D	C	B-	B	**B+**	A-	A	A+

Relative Strength Rank MODERATE

39

LOWEST = 1   HIGHEST = 99

Revenue/Earnings Data

Revenue (Million $)

	1Q	2Q	3Q	4Q	Year
2009	40.00	59.00	62.00	--	--
2008	1,307	1,308	1,251	51.00	5,150
2007	1,153	1,205	1,291	1,345	4,994
2006	1,054	1,093	1,066	1,096	4,309
2005	1,059	1,087	1,138	1,180	4,464
2004	1,108	1,034	1,000	1,060	4,202

Earnings Per Share ($)

	1Q	2Q	3Q	4Q	Year
2009	0.19	0.18	0.17	E0.19	E0.73
2008	0.26	0.26	0.26	0.27	1.06
2007	0.19	0.23	0.27	0.26	0.92
2006	0.19	0.19	0.21	0.37	0.69
2005	0.11	0.14	0.16	0.14	0.56
2004	0.12	0.08	-0.03	0.04	0.30

Fiscal year ended Dec. 31. Next earnings report expected: Mid January. EPS Estimates based on S&P Operating Earnings; historical GAAP earnings are as reported.

Dividend Data (Dates: mm/dd Payment Date: mm/dd/yy)

Amount ($)	Date Decl.	Ex-Div. Date	Stk. of Record	Payment Date
0.060	01/27	02/11	02/13	02/27/09
0.060	04/28	05/06	05/08	05/22/09
0.060	07/28	08/12	08/14	08/28/09
0.060	10/22	11/10	11/13	11/27/09

Dividends have been paid since 1989. Source: Company reports.

Schwab (Charles) Corp

STANDARD &POOR'S

Business Summary October 20, 2009

CORPORATE OVERVIEW. Charles Schwab Corp. (SCHW) is a financial holding company that provides securities brokerage and related financial services through three segments, Schwab Investor Services, Schwab Institutional and Schwab Corporate and Retirement Services. Another subsidiary, Charles Schwab Investment Management, is the investment adviser for Schwab's proprietary mutual funds. In December 2007, CyberTrader, Inc., formerly a subsidiary of SCHW, which provides electronic trading and brokerage services to highly active, online traders, was merged into Schwab.

Through the Schwab Investor Services segment (66% of 2008 net revenue), the company provides retail brokerage and banking services. Through various types of brokerage accounts, Schwab offers the purchase and sale of securities, including NASDAQ, exchange-listed and other equity securities, options, mutual funds, unit investment trusts, variable annuities and fixed-income investments. At the end of 2008, the company, through subsidiaries, served nearly 9 million active client accounts, and held client assets of $1.1 trillion.

Through its Schwab Advisor services segment (24%), SCHW provides custodi-

al, trade execution and support services to investment advisers, serves company 401(k) plan sponsors and third-party administrators, and supports company stock option plans. The company's Advisor services segment had some $477.2 billion in assets under management as of December 31, 2008. The Schwab Advisor Network (launched in 2002) refers affluent investors to local investment advisers.

Through the Schwab Corporate & Retirement Services segment (10%), SCHW provides retirement plan services, plan administrator services, stock plan services and mutual fund clearing services, and supports the availability of Schwab proprietary mutual funds on third-party platforms. This division services all aspects of employer sponsored plans: equity compensation, defined contribution plans, defined benefit plans, and other investment related benefit plans. At year-end 2008, assets under management exceeded $177.2 billion.

Company Financials Fiscal Year Ended Dec. 31

Per Share Data ($)	2008	2007	2006	2005	2004	2003	2002	2001	2000	1999
Tangible Book Value	3.03	2.76	3.63	2.71	2.57	2.56	0.55	2.58	2.69	1.81
Cash Flow	1.19	1.04	0.81	0.72	0.47	0.35	0.30	0.30	0.70	0.59
Earnings	1.06	0.92	0.69	0.56	0.30	0.35	0.07	0.06	0.51	0.47
S&P Core Earnings	1.08	0.92	0.68	0.53	0.23	0.27	-0.02	-0.09	NA	NA
Dividends	0.22	0.20	0.14	0.09	0.07	0.05	0.04	0.04	0.04	0.04
Payout Ratio	21%	22%	14%	16%	25%	14%	63%	73%	8%	8%
Prices:High	28.75	25.72	19.49	16.14	13.92	14.20	19.00	33.00	44.75	51.67
Prices:Low	14.28	17.41	14.00	9.65	8.25	6.25	7.22	8.13	22.46	16.96
P/E Ratio:High	27	28	21	29	46	41	NM	NM	88	NM
P/E Ratio:Low	13	19	15	17	28	18	NM	NM	44	NM

Income Statement Analysis (Million $)										
Commissions	1,080	860	785	779	936	1,207	1,206	1,355	2,294	1,863
Interest Income	1,908	2,270	2,113	1,944	1,213	970	1,186	1,857	2,589	1,471
Total Revenue	5,393	5,617	4,988	5,151	4,479	4,328	4,480	5,281	7,139	4,713
Interest Expense	243	623	679	687	277	241	345	928	1,352	768
Pretax Income	2,028	1,853	1,476	1,185	645	710	168	135	1,231	971
Effective Tax Rate	39.4%	39.6%	39.6%	38.4%	35.8%	33.5%	42.3%	42.2%	41.7%	39.4%
Net Income	1,230	1,120	891	730	414	472	97.0	78.0	718	589
S&P Core Earnings	1,247	1,117	875	678	314	357	-31.5	-131	NA	NA

Balance Sheet & Other Financial Data (Million $)										
Total Assets	51,675	42,286	48,992	47,351	47,133	45,866	39,705	40,464	38,154	29,299
Cash Items	20,127	15,567	15,369	17,589	21,797	24,175	24,119	22,148	14,300	10,547
Receivables	13,932	16,482	11,577	11,600	10,323	9,137	7,067	10,066	16,680	17,543
Securities Owned	15,072	8,201	6,386	6,857	5,335	4,023	1,716	1,700	1,603	340
Securities Borrowed	Nil	Nil	Nil	Nil	Nil	Nil	Nil	Nil	Nil	Nil
Due Brokers & Customers	21,356	22,212	22,119	25,994	28,622	29,845	27,877	27,822	26,785	25,171
Other Liabilities	25,375	15,441	21,477	NA	NA	NA	NA	NA	NA	NA
Capitalization:Debt	883	899	388	514	585	772	642	730	770	455
Capitalization:Equity	4,061	3,732	5,008	4,450	4,386	4,461	4,011	4,163	4,230	2,274
Capitalization:Total	4,944	4,631	5,396	4,964	4,971	5,233	4,653	4,893	5,000	2,729
% Return on Revenue	22.8	19.9	17.9	14.2	9.2	15.1	3.0	2.0	14.8	20.7
% Return on Assets	2.6	2.5	1.8	1.5	0.9	1.1	0.2	0.2	2.0	2.3
% Return on Equity	31.6	25.6	18.8	16.5	9.4	11.1	2.4	1.9	21.1	31.8

Data as orig reptd.; bef. results of disc opers/spec. items. Per share data adj. for stk. divs.; EPS diluted. Quarterly revs. excl. interest expense. E-Estimated. NA-Not Available. NM-Not Meaningful. NR-Not Ranked. UR-Under Review.

Office: 211 Main St, San Francisco, CA 94105.
Telephone: 415-636-7000.
Email: investor.relations@schwab.com
Website: http://www.aboutschwab.com

Chrmn: C.R. Schwab, Jr.
Pres & CEO: W.W. Bettinger, II
EVP, CFO & Chief Acctg Officer: J.R. Martinetto
EVP, Secy & General Counsel: C.E. Dwyer

EVP & CIO: J. Hier-King
Investor Contact: R.G. Fowler (415-636-9869)
Board Members: W. F. Aldinger, III, N. H. Bechtle, W. W. Bettinger, II, C. P. Butcher, F. C. Herringer, S. T. McLin, A. Sarin, C. R. Schwab, Jr., P. A. Sneed, R. O. Walther, R. N. Wilson

Founded: 1971
Domicile: Delaware
Employees: 13,400

Scripps Networks Interactive Inc

STANDARD & POOR'S

S&P Recommendation	STRONG BUY ★★★★★	Price $39.94 (as of Nov 27, 2009)	12-Mo. Target Price $48.00	Investment Style Large-Cap Value

GICS Sector Consumer Discretionary
Sub-Industry Cable & Satellite

Summary SNI, spun off by E.W. Scripps, owns and operates lifestyle properties including HGTV, Food Network, Fine Living, DIY Network and GAC, and has online search businesses.

Key Stock Statistics (Source S&P, Vickers, company reports)

52-Wk Range	$41.41– 18.10	S&P Oper. EPS 2009**E**	1.77	Market Capitalization(B)	$5.086	Beta	NA
Trailing 12-Month EPS	$0.31	S&P Oper. EPS 2010**E**	2.16	Yield (%)	0.75	S&P 3-Yr. Proj. EPS CAGR(%)	NM
Trailing 12-Month P/E	NM	P/E on S&P Oper. EPS 2009**E**	22.6	Dividend Rate/Share	$0.30	S&P Credit Rating	NA
$10K Invested 5 Yrs Ago	NA	Common Shares Outstg. (M)	165.6	Institutional Ownership (%)	61		

Price Performance

30-Week Mov. Avg. ··· 10-Week Mov. Avg. – · GAAP Earnings vs. Previous Year   Volume Above Avg. STARS
12-Mo. Target Price — Relative Strength — ▲ Up ▼ Down ► No Change   Below Avg. ★

Options: Ph

Analysis prepared by **Erik Kolb** on November 19, 2009, when the stock traded at **$ 40.01**.

Highlights

► We expect SNI, spun off from E.W. Scripps (SSP 5, hold) on July 1, 2008, to see a revenue decline of 4.3% in 2009 to $1.52 billion, versus a 10% increase in 2008, on a pro forma basis. Although it is still depressed, we think the ad market is showing modest signs of improvement, and believe that SNI fared better than most in the recent upfront bazaar. Additionally, SNI should realize higher pricing on withheld inventory in the scatter market. In 2010, we see total revenue growth of nearly 12%, to $1.70 billion, on continued ad improvements as well as high affiliate fees. We see growth returning to the Interactive segment next year.

► We look for 2009 EBITDA margins to decrease about 50 basis points, to 41.1%, primarily on lower advertising levels, as well as difficult comparisons against heavy political advertising in 2008. However, most of SNI's programming is low cost due to its unscripted nature, which we think leads to better margins than most peers. We see a 150 basis point improvement in 2010, to 42.6%.

► Our 2009 and 2010 EPS estimates are $1.77 and $2.16, respectively.

Investment Rationale/Risk

► We view SNI's niche television networks positively, and we think they will garner attractive ratings and attention from advertisers. The focused content of SNI's networks should also generate consistent advertising from specialty retailers, which should help provide a baseline advertising level. In the near term, we see higher affiliate fees as SNI renegotiates key contracts, especially for the Food Network. We see the beleaguered Interactive Services segment improving modestly in 2010. SNI's networks may be an acquisition target, but we note this is unlikely before July 2010 as it would jeopardize the tax-free status of the SNI spin-off for SSP shareholders.

► Risks to our recommendation and target price include a greater-than-expected slowdown in advertising, a decline in ratings for SNI's television networks, and a drop in visitors resulting in lower market share for the Interactive Services segment's comparison shopping websites.

► Our 12-month target price of $48 is derived by applying an 10.6X enterprise value multiple, slightly higher than peers in our coverage universe, to our 2010 EBITDA estimate.

Qualitative Risk Assessment

LOW	MEDIUM	HIGH

Our risk assessment reflects SNI's leading TV properties and our view of the company's solid ratings and advertising revenue growth. This is offset by a soft advertising market and higher volatility in the Interactive Services segment.

Quantitative Evaluations

S&P Quality Ranking   NR

D	C	B-	B	B+	A-	A	A+

Relative Strength Rank   **STRONG**

80

LOWEST = 1   HIGHEST = 99

Revenue/Earnings Data

Revenue (Million $)

	1Q	2Q	3Q	4Q	Year
2009	361.2	391.3	364.5	--	--
2008	388.3	416.1	374.7	411.5	1,591
2007	332.4	367.2	344.0	397.7	1,441
2006	--	--	--	--	1,323
2005	--	--	--	--	1,002
2004	--	--	--	--	--

Earnings Per Share ($)

2009	0.37	0.49	0.39	E0.51	E1.77
2008	0.41	0.33	0.35	-0.94	0.14
2007	--	0.43	0.35	-1.83	-0.72
2006	--	--	--	--	--
2005	--	--	--	--	--
2004	--	--	--	--	--

Fiscal year ended Dec. 31. Next earnings report expected: Early February. EPS Estimates based on S&P Operating Earnings; historical GAAP earnings are as reported.

Dividend Data (Dates: mm/dd Payment Date: mm/dd/yy)

Amount ($)	Date Decl.	Ex-Div. Date	Stk. of Record	Payment Date
0.075	02/19	02/25	02/27	03/10/09
0.075	05/21	05/27	05/29	06/10/09
0.075	08/20	08/27	08/31	09/10/09
0.075	11/18	11/25	11/30	12/10/09

Dividends have been paid since 2008. Source: Company reports.

Please read the Required Disclosures and Analyst Certification on the last page of this report.

Scripps Networks Interactive Inc

STANDARD
&POOR'S

Business Summary November 19, 2009

CORPORATE OVERVIEW. Scripps Networks Interactive is a lifestyle content and Internet search company with national television networks and interactive brands. SNI manages its operations through the Lifestyle Media (formerly Scripps Networks) and Interactive Services (formerly Interactive Media) segments. Lifestyle Media includes HGTV, Food Network, DIY, Fine Living, Great American Country, a minority interest in Fox-BRV South Sports Holdings, and Internet-based businesses, including RecipeZaar.com, HGTVPro.com, and FrontDoor.com. Interactive Media includes online comparison shopping and consumer information services, including Shopzilla, BizRate, uSwitch and UpMyStreet.

The Lifestyle Media segment derives revenues principally from advertising sales, affiliate fees, and ancillary sales, including the sale and licensing of consumer products. Revenues from the Interactive Media segment are gener-

ated primarily from referral fees and commissions paid by merchants and service providers for online leads generated by its websites. Lifestyle Media and Interactive Services accounted for 82% and 18% of 2008 revenue, respectively, compared to 83% and 17% in 2007, 80% and 20% in 2006, and 90% and 10% in 2005.

In 2008, HGTV accounted for 45.5% of operating revenue, Food Network for 37.0%, DIY for 4.9%, Fine Living for 4.0%, GAC for 1.9%, and SN Digital at 6.2%. In 2008, the HGTV network reached 97,700 homes, according to Nielsen; Food Network 97,900; DIY 49,400; Fine Living 53,900; and GAC 55,100.

Company Financials Fiscal Year Ended Dec. 31

Per Share Data ($)	2008	2007	2006	2005	2004	2003	2002	2001	2000	1999
Tangible Book Value	2.26	2.25	NA	NA	NA	NA	NA	NA	NA	NA
Cash Flow	0.59	-0.19	NA	NA	NA	NA	NA	NA	NA	NA
Earnings	0.14	-0.72	NA	NA	NA	NA	NA	NA	NA	NA
S&P Core Earnings	1.63	1.11	1.44	NA	NA	NA	NA	NA	NA	NA
Dividends	0.15	NA	NA	NA	NA	NA	NA	NA	NA	NA
Payout Ratio	107%	NA	NA	NA	NA	NA	NA	NA	NA	NA
Prices:High	44.98	NA	NA	NA	NA	NA	NA	NA	NA	NA
Prices:Low	20.00	NA	NA	NA	NA	NA	NA	NA	NA	NA
P/E Ratio:High	NM	NA	NA	NA	NA	NA	NA	NA	NA	NA
P/E Ratio:Low	NM	NA	NA	NA	NA	NA	NA	NA	NA	NA

Income Statement Analysis (Million $)	2008	2007	2006	2005	2004	2003	2002	2001	2000	1999
Revenue	1,591	1,441	1,323	1,002	NA	NA	NA	NA	NA	NA
Operating Income	651	591	NA	NA	NA	NA	NA	NA	NA	NA
Depreciation	73.9	86.7	101	67.0	NA	NA	NA	NA	NA	NA
Interest Expense	14.2	15.2	54.0	37.0	NA	NA	NA	NA	NA	NA
Pretax Income	309	98.7	427	343	NA	NA	NA	NA	NA	NA
Effective Tax Rate	62.5%	NM	28.3%	32.8%	NA	NA	NA	NA	NA	NA
Net Income	23.6	-118	234	176	NA	NA	NA	NA	NA	NA
S&P Core Earnings	267	183	235	NA	NA	NA	NA	NA	NA	NA

Balance Sheet & Other Financial Data (Million $)	2008	2007	2006	2005	2004	2003	2002	2001	2000	1999
Cash	12.7	44.2	19.0	NA	NA	NA	NA	NA	NA	NA
Current Assets	638	658	NA	NA	NA	NA	NA	NA	NA	NA
Total Assets	1,773	2,064	2,385	NA	NA	NA	NA	NA	NA	NA
Current Liabilities	166	124	NA	NA	NA	NA	NA	NA	NA	NA
Long Term Debt	80.0	450	765	NA	NA	NA	NA	NA	NA	NA
Common Equity	1,135	1,157	1,186	NA	NA	NA	NA	NA	NA	NA
Total Capital	1,368	1,391	2,069	NA	NA	NA	NA	NA	NA	NA
Capital Expenditures	77.4	NA	40.4	29.0	NA	NA	NA	NA	NA	NA
Cash Flow	97.5	-31.0	NA	NA	NA	NA	NA	NA	NA	NA
Current Ratio	3.8	5.3	3.5	NA	NA	NA	NA	NA	NA	NA
% Long Term Debt of Capitalization	5.8	32.3	39.2	Nil	NA	NA	NA	NA	NA	NA
% Net Income of Revenue	1.5	NM	17.7	17.5	NA	NA	NA	NA	NA	NA
% Return on Assets	1.2	NM	NA	NA	NA	NA	NA	NA	NA	NA
% Return on Equity	2.2	NM	NA	NA	NA	NA	NA	NA	NA	NA

Data as orig reptd.; bef. results of disc opers/spec. items. Per share data adj. for stk. divs.; EPS diluted. Data for 2007 pro forma; bal. sheet & book val. as of March 31, 2008. E-Estimated. NA-Not Available. NM-Not Meaningful. NR-Not Ranked. UR-Under Review.

Office: 312 Walnut Street, Cincinnati, OH 45202.
Telephone: 513-824-3200.
Website:
http://www.scrippsnetworksinteractive.com
Chrmn, Pres & CEO: K.W. Lowe

COO: R. Boehne
EVP & CFO: J.G. NeCastro
EVP, Secy & General Counsel: A.B. Cruz, III
SVP & CTO: M.S. Hale

Board Members: J. H. Burlingame, M. R. Costa, D. A. Galloway, K. W. Lowe, J. Mohn, N. B. Paumgarten, M. M. Peirce, D. Pond, J. Sagansky, N. E. Scagliotti, R. W. Tysoe

Founded: 2007
Domicile: Ohio
Employees: 1,900

The McGraw·Hill Companies

Sealed Air Corp

STANDARD &POOR'S

S&P Recommendation **BUY** ★★★★☆	Price $22.31 (as of Nov 27, 2009)	12-Mo. Target Price $25.00	Investment Style Large-Cap Growth

GICS Sector Materials
Sub-Industry Paper Packaging

Summary This company is a leading global manufacturer of a wide range of food and protective packaging materials and systems.

Key Stock Statistics (Source S&P, Vickers, company reports)

52-Wk Range	$22.82– 10.38	S&P Oper. EPS 2009**E**	1.45	Market Capitalization(B)	$3.546	Beta	1.42
Trailing 12-Month EPS	$1.25	S&P Oper. EPS 2010**E**	1.65	Yield (%)	2.15	S&P 3-Yr. Proj. EPS CAGR(%)	0
Trailing 12-Month P/E	17.9	P/E on S&P Oper. EPS 2009**E**	15.4	Dividend Rate/Share	$0.48	S&P Credit Rating	BB+
$10K Invested 5 Yrs Ago	$9,258	Common Shares Outstg. (M)	159.0	Institutional Ownership (%)	88		

Price Performance

30-Week Mov. Avg. · · · 10-Week Mov. Avg. - - **GAAP Earnings vs. Previous Year**   Volume Above Avg. STARS
12-Mo. Target Price ─── Relative Strength ─── ▲ Up ▼ Down ► No Change   Below Avg. ★

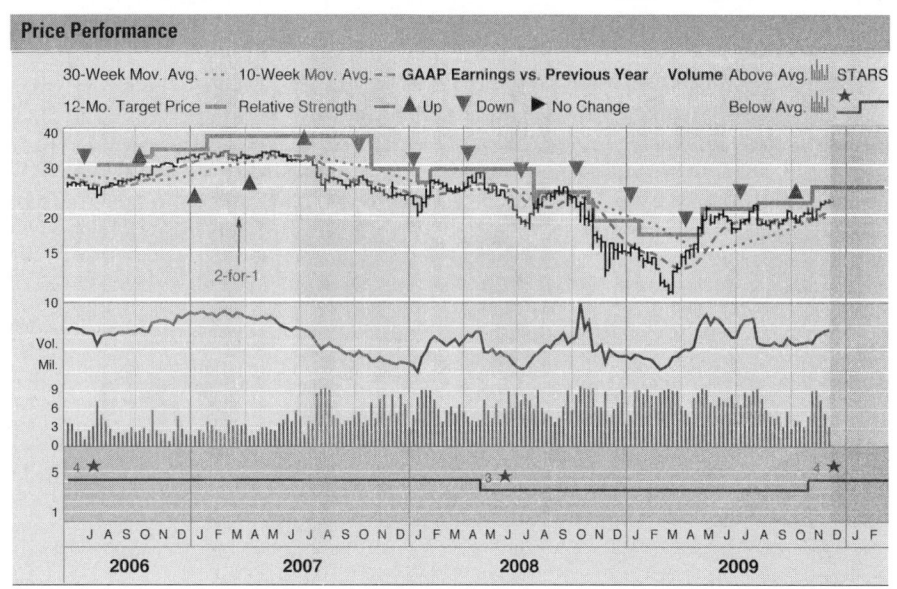

Options: CBOE, P, Ph

Analysis prepared by **Stewart Scharf** on November 02, 2009, when the stock traded at **$ 19.77**.

Highlights

► We expect net sales to decline roughly 12% in 2009 (about 5% before negative foreign exchange), driven by weak protective packaging and food solutions unit volume. We project a smaller foreign currency effect going forward, as the U.S. dollar has weakened, and see favorable trends for new food packaging and solutions products in parts of Latin America and Asia/Pacific. In our view, more consumers will continue to dine at home and buy lower-priced meat products.

► We look for gross margins to widen to about 28% in 2009, from 25.6% in 2008, with further expansion in 2010, reflecting contractual pricing pass-throughs, a better product mix and improved supply chain efficiencies. We expect EBITDA margins to expand by about 200 basis points in 2009, from 14.5% in 2008, due to a cost-reduction program and global manufacturing strategy, which included a shift in production overseas and a workforce reduction.

► We estimate a higher tax rate of about 26% for 2009, and operating EPS of $1.45 (before $0.08 of restructuring charges and a $0.02 tax-related charge), advancing 14% in 2010 to $1.65.

Investment Rationale/Risk

► We recently upgraded our recommendation on the shares to Buy, from Hold, based on our view that global market conditions will gradually recover during 2010. We expect the company to focus on generating strong free cash, controlling inventories, and developing new technologies and innovative products. Our valuation models also suggest the shares are undervalued at recent levels.

► Risks to our recommendation and target price include a prolonged global economic downturn, another significant increase in resin costs, a strengthening U.S. dollar, and a new "mad cow" type disease scare. We have some concern regarding corporate governance issues, since at least one former CEO serves on the board of directors.

► Applying a P/E of 14.5X to our 2010 EPS estimate -- a discount to historical levels but on par with the S&P Paper Packaging sub-industry group multiple -- we arrive at a value of $24. Our discounted cash flow model, which assumes a perpetual growth rate of 3.5% and a weighted average cost of capital of 9%, leads to an intrinsic value of $26. Our 12-month target price of $25 is a blend of these two metrics.

Qualitative Risk Assessment

LOW	**MEDIUM**	HIGH

Our risk assessment reflects tight global credit markets, food-related health issues that could lead to restrictions on imports and exports, and some corporate governance concerns. This is offset by our view of the company's sound balance sheet and cash flow generation.

Quantitative Evaluations

S&P Quality Ranking   B

D	C	B-	**B**	B+	A-	A	A+

Relative Strength Rank   STRONG

85

LOWEST = 1   HIGHEST = 99

Revenue/Earnings Data

Revenue (Million $)

	1Q	2Q	3Q	4Q	Year
2009	988.5	1,028	1,080	--	--
2008	1,177	1,279	1,219	1,168	4,844
2007	1,095	1,145	1,161	1,250	4,651
2006	1,019	1,082	1,081	1,146	4,328
2005	969.8	1,020	1,020	1,076	4,085
2004	913.1	923.7	944.2	1,017	3,798

Earnings Per Share ($)

2009	0.32	0.33	0.34	E0.40	E1.45
2008	0.33	0.34	0.05	0.26	0.99
2007	0.67	0.40	0.39	0.43	1.89
2006	0.30	0.31	0.41	0.45	1.47
2005	0.29	0.33	0.34	0.39	1.35
2004	0.31	0.32	0.35	0.17	1.13

Fiscal year ended Dec. 31. Next earnings report expected: Late January. EPS Estimates based on S&P Operating Earnings; historical GAAP earnings as are reported.

Dividend Data (Dates: mm/dd Payment Date: mm/dd/yy)

Amount ($)	Date Decl.	Ex-Div. Date	Stk. of Record	Payment Date
0.120	02/20	03/04	03/06	03/20/09
0.120	04/16	06/03	06/05	06/19/09
0.120	07/23	09/02	09/04	09/18/09
0.120	10/22	12/02	12/04	12/18/09

Dividends have been paid since 2006. Source: Company reports.

Please read the Required Disclosures and Analyst Certification on the last page of this report.

The **McGraw-Hill** Companies

Sealed Air Corp

STANDARD &POOR'S

Business Summary November 02, 2009

CORPORATE OVERVIEW. Sealed Air Corp., a leading protective and specialty packaging company, expects an increasing proportion of sales to come from outside the U.S. Foreign operations (excluding Canada, with about 3%) accounted for about 52% of sales in 2008, with Europe accounting for 30% of total sales, Latin America 8.6%, and Asia/Pacific 13%.

As of the second quarter of 2007, the company realigned its segment reporting to reflect its growth strategies in core markets and new business opportunities, as it focuses on long-term global trends, including higher living standards in emerging markets, conservation and energy efficiency, convenience and longevity. The food packaging segment (41% of net sales in 2008; $218 million of operating income) focuses on industrial products and new technologies that enable food processors to package and ship fresh and processed meats and cheeses through their supply chain. Food Solutions (20%; $80 million) targets advancements in food packaging technologies that provide consumers with fresh meals from food service outlets or expanding retail cases at grocery stores. Protective Packaging (31%; $169 million) includes core packaging technologies and solutions slated for traditional industrial applications while emphasizing consumer-oriented packaging solutions. Other sales accounted for 8.4% ($15 million).

Food packaging products primarily consist of flexible materials and related systems marketed mainly under the Cryovac trademark for a broad range of perishable food applications. The segment also manufactures polystyrene foam trays that are used by supermarkets and food processors to protect and display fresh meat, poultry and produce. The U.S. Department of Agriculture (USDA) projects increases in U.S. protein consumption. Case-ready packaging sales exceeded $480 million in 2008. The protective packaging products segment includes surface protection and other cushioning products such as air cellular packaging materials, and plastic sheets containing encapsulated air bubbles that protect products from damage during shipment, under the Bubble Wrap and Air Cap brand names. The new "Other" segment focuses on newer markets, including specialty materials for non-packaging applications such as insulation and products for value-added medical applications, as well as new ventures that include products sourced from renewable materials.

In 2008, SEE incurred restructuring charges of $0.33 per share.

Company Financials Fiscal Year Ended Dec. 31

Per Share Data ($)	2008	2007	2006	2005	2004	2003	2002	2001	2000	1999
Tangible Book Value	NM	NM	NM	NM	NM	NM	NM	NM	NM	NM
Cash Flow	1.77	2.62	2.30	2.64	1.99	1.95	-1.17	1.92	2.16	1.70
Earnings	0.99	1.89	1.47	1.35	1.13	1.00	-2.15	0.61	0.97	0.84
S&P Core Earnings	1.06	1.78	1.49	1.37	1.14	1.03	1.29	0.63	NA	NA
Dividends	0.48	0.40	0.30	Nil	Nil	Nil	Nil	Nil	Nil	Nil
Payout Ratio	48%	21%	20%	Nil	Nil	Nil	Nil	Nil	Nil	Nil
Prices:High	28.32	33.87	32.88	28.32	27.45	27.24	24.20	23.55	30.94	34.22
Prices:Low	12.01	22.41	22.81	22.78	22.03	17.50	6.35	14.40	13.19	22.25
P/E Ratio:High	29	18	22	21	24	27	NM	39	32	41
P/E Ratio:Low	12	12	16	17	20	17	NM	24	14	26

Income Statement Analysis (Million $)										
Revenue	4,844	4,651	4,328	4,085	3,798	3,532	3,204	3,067	3,068	2,840
Operating Income	642	712	707	687	716	693	1,766	641	687	648
Depreciation	155	149	168	175	180	154	166	221	220	147
Interest Expense	137	150	148	150	154	134	65.3	76.4	64.5	58.1
Pretax Income	222	456	400	377	323	377	-392	297	413	396
Effective Tax Rate	19.1%	22.6%	31.5%	32.1%	33.2%	36.2%	NM	47.3%	45.5%	46.6%
Net Income	180	353	274	256	216	240	-309	157	225	211
S&P Core Earnings	193	333	278	259	219	192	227	111	NA	NA

Balance Sheet & Other Financial Data (Million $)										
Cash	129	430	407	456	412	365	127	13.8	11.2	13.7
Current Assets	1,673	1,936	1,757	1,695	1,611	1,428	1,056	776	877	803
Total Assets	4,978	5,438	5,021	4,864	4,855	4,704	4,261	3,908	4,048	3,855
Current Liabilities	1,622	1,742	1,406	1,534	1,304	1,190	1,153	627	675	582
Long Term Debt	1,290	1,532	1,827	1,813	2,088	2,260	868	788	944	665
Common Equity	1,942	2,020	1,530	1,392	1,334	1,124	813	850	753	551
Total Capital	3,220	3,561	3,364	3,229	3,448	3,418	3,039	3,215	3,301	3,193
Capital Expenditures	181	211	168	96.9	103	124	91.6	146	114	75.1
Cash Flow	335	502	442	430	395	366	-197	322	381	287
Current Ratio	1.0	1.1	1.2	1.1	1.2	1.2	0.9	1.2	1.3	1.4
% Long Term Debt of Capitalization	40.1	43.0	54.3	56.1	60.5	66.1	28.6	24.5	28.6	20.8
% Net Income of Revenue	3.7	7.6	6.3	6.3	5.7	6.8	NM	5.1	7.3	7.4
% Return on Assets	3.5	6.8	5.5	5.3	4.5	5.4	NM	3.9	5.7	5.3
% Return on Equity	9.1	19.2	19.9	18.8	17.5	21.9	NM	12.7	24.7	28.3

Data as orig reptd.; bef. results of disc opers/spec. items. Per share data adj. for stk. divs.; EPS diluted. E-Estimated. NA-Not Available. NM-Not Meaningful. NR-Not Ranked. UR-Under Review.

Office: 200 Riverfront Blvd, Elmwood Park, NJ 07407-1033.
Telephone: 201-791-7600.
Website: http://www.sealedair.com
Pres & CEO: W.V. Hickey

SVP & CFO: D.H. Kelsey
VP, Secy & General Counsel: H.K. White
Chief Acctg Officer & Cntlr: J.S. Warren
Treas: T.S. Christie

Investor Contact: A. Butler (201-703-4210)
Board Members: H. Brown, M. Chu, L. R. Codey, D. T. Dunphy, C. F. Farrell, Jr., W. V. Hickey, J. Kosecoff, K. P. Manning, W. J. Marino

Founded: 1996
Domicile: Delaware
Employees: 17,000

Sears Holdings Corp

STANDARD
&POOR'S

S&P Recommendation	SELL ★★★★★	Price	12-Mo. Target Price	Investment Style
		$71.94 (as of Nov 27, 2009)	$68.00	Large-Cap Blend

GICS Sector Consumer Discretionary
Sub-Industry Department Stores

Summary Through its wholly owned Sears and Kmart subsidiaries, Sears Holdings is among the largest broadline retailers in the U.S.

Key Stock Statistics (Source S&P, Vickers, company reports)

52-Wk Range	$79.75–31.56	S&P Oper. EPS 2010**E**	1.65	Market Capitalization(B)	$8.314	Beta	1.44
Trailing 12-Month EPS	$-0.04	S&P Oper. EPS 2011**E**	1.75	Yield (%)	Nil	S&P 3-Yr. Proj. EPS CAGR(%)	2
Trailing 12-Month P/E	NM	P/E on S&P Oper. EPS 2010**E**	43.6	Dividend Rate/Share	Nil	S&P Credit Rating	BB-
$10K Invested 5 Yrs Ago	$6,699	Common Shares Outstg. (M)	115.6	Institutional Ownership (%)	NM		

Price Performance

30-Week Mov. Avg. · · · 10-Week Mov. Avg. - - **GAAP Earnings vs. Previous Year** Volume Above Avg. STARS
12-Mo. Target Price ── Relative Strength ── ▲ Up ▼ Down ▶ No Change Below Avg.

Options: ASE, CBOE, P, Ph

Analysis prepared by **Jason N. Asaeda** on November 25, 2009, when the stock traded at **$ 71.68**.

Highlights

▶ On a consolidated basis, we expect same-store sales to decline 6% in FY 10 (Jan.) and 3% in FY 11. By division, we look for Kmart to outperform Sears (domestic) as we perceive consumer demand being more stable for basic goods, including food, personal care products, and household cleaners, than for fashion apparel and accessories, fine jewelry, and home furnishings during an economic downturn. We also think a weak U.S. housing market will hurt sales in the tools, lawn & garden, and home appliance categories at Sears. Coupled with SHLD's planned closure of underperforming stores, we expect net sales to fall to $43.49 billion in FY 10 and $42.15 billion in FY 11.

▶ We look for SHLD to tightly manage inventory to reduce its markdown risk and to drive gross margin expansion annually. We also expect the company to realize expense reductions through cost savings initiatives and store closures.

▶ Factoring in likely share buybacks, we see EPS of $1.65 (excluding a $44 million asset sales gain, $34 million in mark-to-market losses on Sears Canada hedge transactions, and a $88 million charge for store closings through the fiscal third) in FY 10 and $1.75 in FY 11.

Investment Rationale/Risk

▶ Our Sell recommendation is based on valuation. We look for SHLD to aggressively manage its flow of goods, which should help keep inventories in line with demand, and to maintain a low cost structure to limit margin erosion. However, we expect Sears to lose market share in FY 10 as we see significant room for improvement in merchandising and the in-store shopping experience relative to peers such as Kohl's (KSS 56, Buy). By comparison, we perceive less downside risk for Kmart given its strong value proposition on basic goods, and a layaway program that enables cash-strapped customers to purchase higher-margin discretionary categories. Our corporate governance concerns include cash-only payments to directors and the non-disclosure of specific hurdle rates for performance-based equity awards.

▶ Risks to our recommendation and target price include better-than-expected sales due to favorable customer response to Sears's remerchandising and brand marketing efforts.

▶ Our 12-month target price of $68 reflects a peer-median EV/EBITDA multiple of 7.1X applied to our FY 11 EBITDA estimate of $1.44 billion.

Qualitative Risk Assessment

LOW	MEDIUM	HIGH

Our risk assessment reflects what we consider Kmart's and Sears's long records of inconsistent sales and earnings. This is partially offset by our view of SHLD's opportunity to leverage the two units' best practices and brands to strengthen its competitive positioning.

Quantitative Evaluations

S&P Quality Ranking   NR

D	C	B-	B	B+	A-	A	A+

Relative Strength Rank   STRONG

72

LOWEST = 1   HIGHEST = 99

Revenue/Earnings Data

Revenue (Million $)

	1Q	2Q	3Q	4Q	Year
2010	10,055	10,551	10,190	--	--
2009	11,068	11,762	10,660	13,280	46,770
2008	11,702	12,239	11,548	1,507	50,703
2007	11,998	12,785	11,941	16,288	53,012
2006	7,626	13,192	12,202	16,086	49,124
2005	4,615	4,785	4,392	5,909	19,701

Earnings Per Share ($)

2010	-0.22	-0.79	-1.09	E2.89	E1.65
2009	-0.42	0.50	-1.16	1.55	0.42
2008	1.40	0.51	0.01	3.21	5.70
2007	1.14	1.88	1.27	5.33	9.57
2006	0.65	0.98	0.35	4.03	6.17
2005	0.94	1.54	5.45	3.09	11.00

Fiscal year ended Jan. 31. Next earnings report expected: Late February. EPS Estimates based on S&P Operating Earnings; historical GAAP earnings are as reported.

Dividend Data

No cash dividends have been paid.

Please read the Required Disclosures and Analyst Certification on the last page of this report.

The McGraw-Hill Companies

Sears Holdings Corp

Business Summary November 25, 2009

CORPORATE OVERVIEW. Through the March 2005 merger of Kmart Holding Corp. and Sears, Roebuck and Co., which continue to operate under their separate brand names, Sears Holdings has emerged as one of the largest broad-line retailers in the U.S. based on FY 09 (Jan.) reported revenues. As of October 31, 2009, the company operated 2,571 Sears-branded full line and specialty stores in the U.S. and Canada (operated by Sears Canada), and 1,343 Kmart-branded discount stores and supercenters across the U.S. SHLD completed the integration of the Sears and Kmart supply chain, IT, finance, legal, human resources, marketing, and merchandising functions during FY 06, and the combination of store operations in February 2006.

CORPORATE STRATEGY. SHLD believes it has an opportunity to leverage Kmart's off-mall locations to expand the distribution of Sears products and services at a more rapid pace and at a lower cost than Sears would have been able to accomplish on its own. The company also sees the potential for Kmart to improve its value proposition and competitive positioning through the addition of Sears-owned brands and services (cross-selling).

SHLD initially planned to convert about 400 Kmart stores to a new mid-size

store format called Sears Essentials, which combines convenience items found in Kmart stores with Sears's more destination-focused purchase categories. However, based on what we believe were disappointing results from 50 Sears Essentials stores opened during FY 06, SHLD decided to focus on its other off-mall format, Sears Grand.

In response to declining sales trends, the company is attempting to raise productivity of its Sears and Kmart businesses through aggressive closure of underperforming stores in FY 10. During the second quarter, SHLD closed 24 stores (13 Kmart stores, four full-line Sears stores, and seven Sears Grand/Essentials stores) and announced plans to close an additional 28 stores (22 Kmart stores, two Sears full-line stores, one Sears Grand store, and three Sears specialty stores) by the end of the fiscal year. The company recorded a charge for costs associated with store closings and severance of $88 million through the third quarter of FY 10.

Company Financials Fiscal Year Ended Jan. 31

Per Share Data ($)	2009	2008	2007	2006	2005	2004	2003	2002	2001	2000
Tangible Book Value	38.57	42.64	49.25	41.80	50.21	24.36	NA	NA	NA	NA
Cash Flow	8.14	12.95	16.90	12.24	11.59	2.81	NA	NA	NA	NA
Earnings	0.42	5.70	9.57	6.17	11.00	2.52	-5.47	-5.24	-0.48	1.22
S&P Core Earnings	-0.99	4.44	9.24	4.53	4.51	-4.53	-6.80	-5.74	-0.55	NA
Dividends	Nil	Nil	Nil	Nil	Nil	Nil	Nil	NA	NA	NA
Payout Ratio	Nil	Nil	Nil	Nil	Nil	Nil	NA	NA	NA	NA
Calendar Year	2008	2007	2006	2005	2004	2003	2002	2001	2000	1999
Prices:High	114.00	195.18	182.38	163.50	119.69	34.55	NA	NA	NA	NA
Prices:Low	26.80	98.25	114.90	84.51	22.41	12.00	NA	NA	NA	NA
P/E Ratio:High	NM	34	19	26	11	14	NA	NA	NA	NA
P/E Ratio:Low	NM	17	12	14	2	5	NA	NA	NA	NA

Income Statement Analysis (Million $)										
Revenue	46,770	50,703	53,012	49,124	19,701	17,072	30,762	36,151	37,028	35,925
Operating Income	1,530	2,542	3,611	2,901	944	442	-1,303	NA	NA	NA
Depreciation	981	1,049	1,142	932	69.0	31.0	737	824	777	770
Interest Expense	272	286	337	322	146	105	155	NA	NA	NA
Pretax Income	184	1,452	2,464	1,965	1,775	400	-3,286	-2,702	-378	970
Effective Tax Rate	46.2%	37.9%	37.7%	36.4%	37.7%	38.0%	NM	4.26%	35.5%	34.7%
Net Income	53.0	826	1,490	948	1,106	248	-3,262	-2,587	-244	633
S&P Core Earnings	-126	645	1,439	696	448	-405	-3,439	-2,840	-260	NA

Balance Sheet & Other Financial Data (Million $)										
Cash	1,173	1,622	3,968	4,440	3,435	2,088	613	1,245	401	344
Current Assets	11,416	12,802	15,406	15,207	7,541	5,811	6,102	NA	NA	NA
Total Assets	25,342	27,397	30,066	30,573	8,651	6,084	11,238	14,298	14,630	15,104
Current Liabilities	8,512	9,562	10,052	10,350	2,086	1,776	2,120	NA	NA	NA
Long Term Debt	1,527	2,606	2,849	3,268	661	819	623	4,565	2,971	2,745
Common Equity	9,380	10,667	12,714	11,611	4,469	2,192	-301	3,459	6,083	6,304
Total Capital	14,168	13,586	15,563	14,879	5,130	3,011	322	8,024	9,122	9,115
Capital Expenditures	497	570	513	546	230	108	252	1,456	1,087	1,277
Cash Flow	1,034	1,875	2,632	1,880	1,175	279	-2,525	NA	NA	NA
Current Ratio	1.3	1.3	1.5	1.5	3.6	3.3	2.9	12.6	2.0	2.0
% Long Term Debt of Capitalization	10.8	19.2	18.3	22.0	12.9	27.2	NM	56.9	32.6	30.1
% Net Income of Revenue	0.1	1.6	2.8	1.9	5.6	1.5	NM	NM	NM	1.8
% Return on Assets	0.2	2.9	4.9	4.8	15.0	3.9	NM	NM	NM	4.3
% Return on Equity	0.5	7.1	12.3	11.8	33.1	12.7	NM	NM	NM	10.3

Data as orig reptd.; bef. results of disc opers/spec. items. Per share data adj. for stk. divs.; EPS diluted. E-Estimated. NA-Not Available. NM-Not Meaningful. NR-Not Ranked. UR-Under Review.

Office: 3333 Beverly Rd, Hoffman Estates, IL 60179-0001.
Telephone: 847-286-2500.
Website: http://www.searsholdings.com
Chrmn: E.S. Lampert

Pres & CEO: W.B. Johnson
EVP & Chief Admin Officer: W.C. Crowley
SVP & CFO: M.D. Collins
SVP, Chief Acctg Officer & Cntlr: W.K. Phelan

Board Members: W. C. Crowley, W. C. Kunkler, III, E. S. Lampert, S. T. Mnuchin, R. C. Perry, A. N. Reese, K. B. Rollins, E. Scott, T. J. Tisch

Founded: 1899
Domicile: Delaware
Employees: 324,000

Sempra Energy

STANDARD & POOR'S

S&P Recommendation	STRONG BUY ★★★★★	Price	12-Mo. Target Price	Investment Style
		$52.68 (as of Nov 27, 2009)	$63.00	Large-Cap Blend

GICS Sector Utilities
Sub-Industry Multi-Utilities

Summary This gas and electric utility is also engaged in unregulated power, liquefied natural gas and international energy projects.

Key Stock Statistics (Source S&P, Vickers, company reports)

52-Wk Range	$54.00–36.43	S&P Oper. EPS 2009E	4.71	Market Capitalization(B)	$12.983	Beta	0.60
Trailing 12-Month EPS	$4.67	S&P Oper. EPS 2010E	5.18	Yield (%)	2.96	S&P 3-Yr. Proj. EPS CAGR(%)	9
Trailing 12-Month P/E	11.3	P/E on S&P Oper. EPS 2009E	11.2	Dividend Rate/Share	$1.56	S&P Credit Rating	BBB+
$10K Invested 5 Yrs Ago	$15,919	Common Shares Outstg. (M)	246.4	Institutional Ownership (%)	66		

Price Performance

30-Week Mov. Avg. · · · 10-Week Mov. Avg. - - **GAAP Earnings vs. Previous Year** Volume Above Avg. STARS
12-Mo. Target Price — Relative Strength — ▲ Up ▼ Down ► No Change Below Avg.

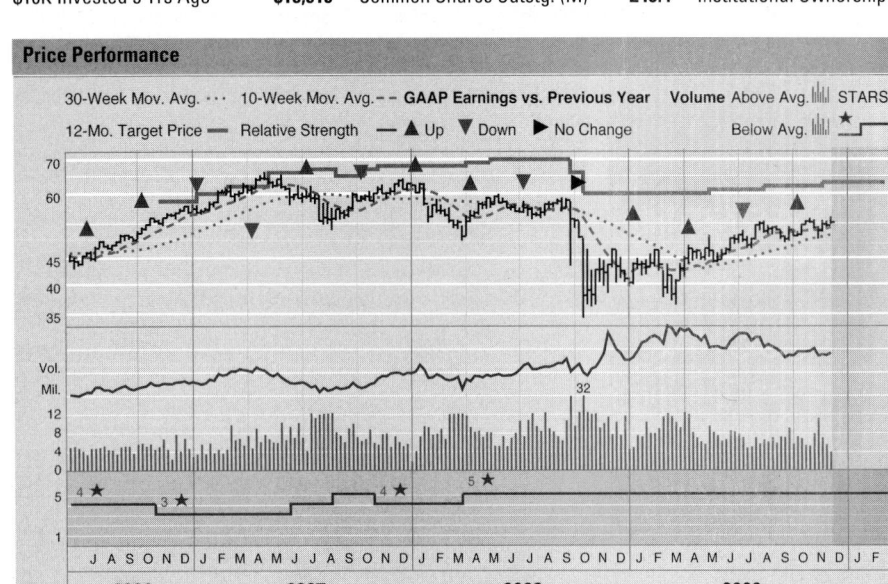

Options: CBOE

Analysis prepared by **Christopher B. Muir** on November 17, 2009, when the stock traded at **$52.96**.

Highlights

► We see revenues falling 26% in 2009 and rising 6.7% in 2010. Outside of a decline in revenues due to the spin-off of the commodities business into a joint venture in 2008 and lower gas prices at the utility, growth should accelerate due to the addition of one fully contracted LNG facility that opened in May 2008 and one that opened in late 2009, as well as the March 2008 completion of Rockies Express (REX)-West. We see additional projects being completed in late 2009 and in 2010 boosting 2010 revenues.

► We expect operating margins to widen to 15.3% in 2009 and 16.3% in 2010, from 11.9% in 2008, as we forecast lower per-revenue fuel and gas costs to more than offset higher per-revenue operations and maintenance expenses. We see pretax margins rising to 21.2% in 2009 and 22.3% in 2010, from 13.9% in 2008, as we expect earnings from the RBS Sempra Commodities joint venture to more than offset higher interest expense.

► We forecast operating EPS of $4.71, excluding a net nonrecurring charge of $0.26, up 10% from 2008's $4.28, which excludes a net nonrecurring gain of $0.15. Our 2010 forecast is $5.18, an additional 10% increase.

Investment Rationale/Risk

► We view the RBS Sempra Commodities joint venture structure very favorably. We think the placement of SRE's commodities business in a joint venture has substantially lowered SRE's risk profile, while still allowing SRE to participate in the upside of the business through a unique profit-sharing mechanism. We believe this mechanism provides incentive for its joint venture partner to give its full support to the business. Separately, Cameron LNG and significant portions of the REX-East pipeline started operating in mid-2009. We see growth opportunities in all of SRE's businesses.

► Risks to our recommendation and target price include a failure to complete LNG projects, declining wholesale power margins, potential losses from energy and metals trading, and a weaker-than-expected economy.

► The stock recently traded at a P/E of 10.3X our 2010 EPS estimate, a 15% discount to multi-utility peers. Our 12-month target price of $63 is about 12.3X our 2010 EPS estimate, a 3% premium to our peer P/E forecast, warranted, we believe, by SRE's prospects for slightly stronger-than-peers EPS and dividend growth beyond 2009.

Qualitative Risk Assessment

LOW	MEDIUM	HIGH

Our risk assessment reflects a balance between stable and steady earnings provided by SRE's regulated gas and electric utility operations and cyclical and volatile earnings from unregulated businesses, including power generation, energy marketing and trading, and international energy investments.

Quantitative Evaluations

S&P Quality Ranking B+

D	C	B-	B	B+	A-	A	A+

Relative Strength Rank MODERATE

65

LOWEST = 1   HIGHEST = 99

Revenue/Earnings Data

Revenue (Million $)

	1Q	2Q	3Q	4Q	Year
2009	2,108	1,689	1,853	--	--
2008	3,270	2,503	2,692	2,293	10,758
2007	3,004	2,661	2,663	3,110	11,438
2006	3,336	2,486	2,694	3,245	11,761
2005	2,697	2,276	2,770	3,994	11,737
2004	2,360	1,996	2,165	2,889	9,410

Earnings Per Share ($)

	1Q	2Q	3Q	4Q	Year
2009	1.29	0.80	1.28	E1.08	E4.71
2008	0.92	0.98	1.24	1.31	4.43
2007	0.86	1.06	1.24	1.10	4.26
2006	0.90	0.71	2.07	0.49	4.17
2005	0.92	0.49	0.86	1.40	3.69
2004	0.96	0.55	0.98	1.43	3.93

Fiscal year ended Dec. 31. Next earnings report expected: Late February. EPS Estimates based on S&P Operating Earnings; historical GAAP earnings are as reported.

Dividend Data (Dates: mm/dd Payment Date: mm/dd/yy)

Amount ($)	Date Decl.	Ex-Div. Date	Stk. of Record	Payment Date
0.350	12/12	12/19	12/23	01/15/09
0.390	02/20	03/17	03/19	04/15/09
0.390	06/09	06/17	06/19	07/15/09
0.390	09/11	09/22	09/24	10/15/09

Dividends have been paid since 1998. Source: Company reports.

Please read the Required Disclosures and Analyst Certification on the last page of this report.

The **McGraw-Hill** Companies

Sempra Energy

**STANDARD
&POOR'S**

Business Summary November 17, 2009

CORPORATE OVERVIEW. Sempra Energy is a holding company that operates five segments divided into California Utilities (CU -- 74% of 2008 revenue) and Sempra Global and parent (26%). The CU segment includes regulated public utilities Southern California Gas (SCG) and San Diego Gas & Electric (SDGE), which provide electricity and natural gas services in the Southern California. Sempra Global includes Sempra Generation, which develops and operates power plants and energy infrastructure; RBS Sempra Commodities, a joint venture that provides marketing and risk management services for energy products and base metals; Sempra LNG, which constructs and operates LNG receipt terminals in North America; and Sempra Pipelines & Storage, which operates in Mexico, the U.S. and South America.

CORPORATE STRATEGY. Sempra seeks to increase EPS through faster growth in its unregulated businesses through both acquisitions and organic growth. In the utility segment, the company focuses on managing regulatory risk as well as operating and capital expenditures. Recently, SRE has focused on new construction in most of its segments. Starting in 2006, the company changed course related to generation, selling ownership interests in some plants, but it has focused recently on developing renewable generation initia-

tives. In 2008, we believe the company reduced its risk profile and enhanced its growth prospects by placing its commodities trading business into a joint venture with a partner that has a stronger credit profile, which should allow for faster growth with less capital.

In July 2007, the company announced a deal with the Royal Bank of Scotland (RBS 13, Hold) that placed its commodity trading business in a joint venture. At closing, on April 1, 2008, SRE received about $1 billion in cash that had been used as collateral. Earnings from the joint venture will be divided into tranches so that each partner receives a 15% pretax return on capital. SRE is to receive 70% of the first $500 million in pretax income above that threshold and then 30% of any pretax income above the latter level. We think this structure gives RBS a huge incentive to commit its substantial resources to growing the business.

Company Financials Fiscal Year Ended Dec. 31

Per Share Data ($)	2008	2007	2006	2005	2004	2003	2002	2001	2000	1999
Tangible Book Value	30.54	31.27	28.67	23.97	20.79	17.14	13.78	13.17	12.27	12.60
Cash Flow	7.17	6.86	6.70	6.25	6.59	6.12	5.68	5.35	NA	NA
Earnings	4.43	4.26	4.17	3.69	3.93	3.24	2.79	2.52	2.06	1.66
S&P Core Earnings	3.59	4.26	4.19	3.44	3.65	3.29	2.16	1.76	NA	NA
Dividends	1.37	1.24	1.20	1.16	1.00	1.00	1.00	1.00	1.00	1.56
Payout Ratio	31%	29%	29%	31%	25%	31%	36%	40%	49%	94%
Prices:High	63.00	66.38	57.35	47.86	37.93	30.90	26.25	28.61	24.88	26.00
Prices:Low	34.29	50.95	42.90	35.53	29.51	22.25	15.50	17.31	16.19	17.13
P/E Ratio:High	14	16	14	13	10	10	9	11	12	16
P/E Ratio:Low	8	12	10	10	8	7	6	7	8	10

Income Statement Analysis (Million $)										
Revenue	10,758	11,438	11,761	11,737	9,410	7,887	6,020	8,029	7,143	5,360
Operating Income	2,027	2,365	1,785	1,111	1,272	939	987	993	NA	1,617
Depreciation	687	686	657	646	621	615	596	579	563	879
Interest Expense	263	381	361	321	332	327	323	352	301	229
Pretax Income	1,551	1,659	1,732	971	1,113	742	721	731	699	573
Effective Tax Rate	28.2%	31.6%	37.0%	4.33%	17.3%	6.33%	20.2%	29.1%	38.6%	31.2%
Net Income	1,113	1,135	1,091	929	920	695	575	518	429	394
S&P Core Earnings	904	1,124	1,096	866	855	708	445	362	NA	NA

Balance Sheet & Other Financial Data (Million $)										
Cash	507	669	920	772	419	432	455	605	637	487
Current Assets	2,476	11,338	12,016	13,318	8,776	7,886	7,010	4,808	NA	NA
Total Assets	26,400	30,091	28,949	29,213	23,643	22,009	17,757	15,156	15,612	11,270
Current Liabilities	3,612	10,394	10,349	12,157	9,082	8,348	7,247	5,524	NA	NA
Long Term Debt	6,646	4,655	4,704	5,002	4,371	4,199	4,487	3,840	3,468	2,902
Common Equity	7,969	8,339	7,511	6,160	4,865	3,890	2,825	2,692	2,494	2,986
Total Capital	15,980	13,852	12,694	11,480	9,734	8,807	8,202	7,474	7,093	6,813
Capital Expenditures	2,061	2,011	1,907	1,404	1,083	1,049	1,214	1,068	759	589
Cash Flow	1,800	1,811	1,748	1,575	1,541	1,310	1,171	1,097	NA	NA
Current Ratio	0.7	1.1	1.2	1.1	1.0	0.9	1.0	0.9	0.9	0.9
% Long Term Debt of Capitalization	41.6	33.6	37.1	43.6	44.9	47.7	54.7	51.4	54.8	48.0
% Net Income of Revenue	10.4	9.9	9.3	7.9	9.8	8.8	9.6	6.5	6.1	7.4
% Return on Assets	3.9	3.8	3.7	3.5	4.0	3.3	3.5	3.4	3.2	3.6
% Return on Equity	13.7	14.2	16.0	16.9	21.0	20.7	20.8	20.0	15.7	13.4

Data as orig reptd.; bef. results of disc opers/spec. items. Per share data adj. for stk. divs.; EPS diluted. E-Estimated. NA-Not Available. NM-Not Meaningful. NR-Not Ranked. UR-Under Review.

Office: 101 Ash Street, San Diego, CA 92101-3017.
Telephone: 619-696-2034.
Email: investor@sempra.com
Website: http://www.sempra.com

Chrmn & CEO: D.E. Felsinger
Pres & COO: N.E. Schmale
COO: M.R. Niggli
EVP & CFO: M.A. Snell

EVP & General Counsel: J. Chaudhri
Investor Contact: J. Martin (619-696-2901)
Board Members: J. G. Brocksmith, Jr., R. A. Collato, D. E. Felsinger, W. D. Godbold, Jr., W. D. Jones, R. G. Newman, W. G. Ouchi, T. A. Page, W. C. Rusnack, W. P. Rutledge, C. R. Sacristan, L. Schenk, N. E. Schmale

Founded: 1998
Domicile: California
Employees: 13,673

Sherwin-Williams Co (The)

STANDARD &POOR'S

| S&P Recommendation | **SELL** ★★☆☆☆ | Price
$61.13 (as of Nov 27, 2009) | 12-Mo. Target Price
$52.00 | Investment Style
Large-Cap Growth |

GICS Sector Consumer Discretionary
Sub-Industry Home Improvement Retail

Summary This company, the largest U.S. producer of paints, is also a major seller of wallcoverings and related products.

Key Stock Statistics (Source S&P, Vickers, company reports)

52-Wk Range	$64.13– 42.19	S&P Oper. EPS 2009E	3.69	Market Capitalization(B)	$6.929	Beta	0.70
Trailing 12-Month EPS	$3.59	S&P Oper. EPS 2010E	3.86	Yield (%)	2.32	S&P 3-Yr. Proj. EPS CAGR(%)	1
Trailing 12-Month P/E	17.0	P/E on S&P Oper. EPS 2009E	16.6	Dividend Rate/Share	$1.42	S&P Credit Rating	A-
$10K Invested 5 Yrs Ago	$15,076	Common Shares Outstg. (M)	113.3	Institutional Ownership (%)	73		

Price Performance

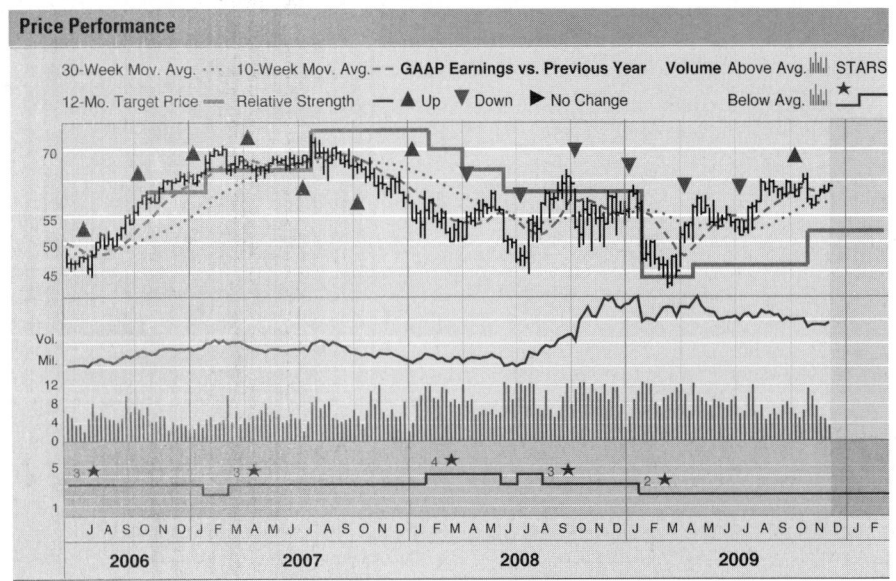

30-Week Mov. Avg. · · · 10-Week Mov. Avg. – – **GAAP Earnings vs. Previous Year** Volume Above Avg. STARS
12-Mo. Target Price — Relative Strength — ▲ Up ▼ Down ▶ No Change Below Avg. ★

Options: CBOE

Analysis prepared by **Michael Souers** on October 21, 2009, when the stock traded at **$ 58.46.**

Highlights

► We expect sales to increase 2.3% in 2010, following a projected 12% decline in 2009. We forecast a slight pickup in residential construction, which should positively affect architectural and Do-It-Yourself (DIY) sales, but we continue to see severe weakness in non-residential construction in 2010. We believe Paint Stores segment sales will increase slightly, as a projected 20 net new stores will help boost flat projected same-store-sales results. We expect SHW to make several small acquisitions throughout the year.

► We project a modest narrowing in gross margins in 2010, as slightly inflationary raw material cost pressure are only partially offset by improved pricing and product mix. We anticipate a 20 basis point narrowing of operating margins, as expenses are de-leveraged due to flat projected same-store sales results.

► With a projected 32.5% effective tax rate and a diluted share count that is seen about 3% lower, reflecting SHW's active share repurchase program, we estimate 2010 EPS of $3.86, a 4.6% increase from the $3.69 we project the company to earn in 2009.

Investment Rationale/Risk

► We continue to have a positive outlook with regard to the company's balance sheet and generation of free cash flow. In addition, we think the ruling by the Rhode Island Supreme Court, which overturned a negative verdict against SHW over the manufacturing and selling of lead paint, makes future negative rulings far less likely. However, we remain concerned that a weak housing market and deteriorating commercial real estate market will limit sales and earnings growth over the medium term. We think the shares lack a positive near-term catalyst and are overvalued at over 15X our 2010 EPS estimate.

► Risks to our recommendation and target price include a significant increase in economic growth; a rapid recovery in the housing market; and declines in raw material costs, which would ease pressure on gross margins.

► At over 15X our 2010 EPS estimate, the stock recently traded at a slight premium to the S&P 500 and a modest premium to SHW's historical average. Our 12-month target price of $52 is based on our DCF analysis, which assumes a weighted average cost of capital of 9.8% and a terminal growth rate of 3.0%.

Qualitative Risk Assessment

| LOW | **MEDIUM** | HIGH |

Our risk assessment for Sherwin-Williams reflects the cyclical nature of the company's business, which is reliant on new housing starts and remodeling, and lead pigment litigation risk, offset by an above-average S&P Quality Ranking of A.

Quantitative Evaluations

S&P Quality Ranking   A

| D | C | B- | B | B+ | A- | **A** | A+ |

Relative Strength Rank   MODERATE

66

LOWEST = 1   HIGHEST = 99

Revenue/Earnings Data

Revenue (Million $)

	1Q	2Q	3Q	4Q	Year
2009	1,551	1,948	1,997	--	--
2008	1,782	2,230	2,269	1,700	7,980
2007	1,756	2,198	2,197	1,854	8,005
2006	1,769	2,130	2,117	1,795	7,810
2005	1,539	1,965	1,977	1,710	7,191
2004	1,320	1,618	1,677	1,499	6,114

Earnings Per Share ($)

2009	0.32	1.35	1.51	E0.52	E3.69
2008	0.64	1.45	1.50	0.42	4.00
2007	0.83	1.52	1.55	0.80	4.70
2006	0.82	1.33	1.30	0.73	4.19
2005	0.58	1.08	1.07	0.54	3.28
2004	0.35	0.87	0.92	0.57	2.72

Fiscal year ended Dec. 31. Next earnings report expected: Late January. EPS Estimates based on S&P Operating Earnings; historical GAAP earnings are as reported.

Dividend Data (Dates: mm/dd Payment Date: mm/dd/yy)

Amount ($)	Date Decl.	Ex-Div. Date	Stk. of Record	Payment Date
0.355	02/18	02/25	02/27	03/13/09
0.355	04/15	05/13	05/15	06/05/09
0.355	07/16	08/19	08/21	09/11/09
0.355	10/16	11/10	11/13	12/04/09

Dividends have been paid since 1979. Source: Company reports.

The McGraw-Hill Companies

Sherwin-Williams Co (The)

STANDARD &POOR'S

Business Summary October 21, 2009

CORPORATE PROFILE. Sherwin-Williams manufactures, distributes and sells paints, coatings and related products to professional, industrial, commercial and retail customers primarily in North and South America. The company is structured into three reportable segments: Paint Stores, Consumer and Global.

The Paint Stores segment (61% of revenues in 2008) offers Sherwin-Williams branded architectural and industrial paints, stains and related products. Its diverse customer base includes architectural and industrial painting contractors, residential and commercial builders, property owners and managers, OEM product finishers and do-it-yourself (DIY) homeowners. In 2008, SHW opened 21 net new stores, bringing the North America Paint Stores store count to 3,346.

The Consumer segment (16%) develops, manufactures and distributes architectural paints, stains, varnishes, industrial maintenance products, wood finishing products, paint applicators, corrosion inhibitors and paint-related products. Brands include Dutch Boy, Krylon, Minwax, Thompson's Water Seal,

Purdy and Pratt & Lambert, as well as private label brands.

The Global segment (23%) develops, licenses, manufactures, distributes and sells paints, stains, coatings, varnishes, industrial products, wood finishing products, applicators, aerosols, high performance interior and exterior coatings for the automotive, aviation, fleet and heavy truck markets, OEM product finishes and related products. SHW sells these products through 541 company-operated architectural, automotive, industrial and chemical coatings branches and other operations in the United States, Argentina, Brazil, Canada, Chile, China, France, India, Ireland, Italy, Malaysia, Mexico, Peru, Philippines, Portugal, Singapore, United Kingdom, Uruguay and Vietnam. It also distributes these products to 16 other countries through wholly owned subsidiaries, joint ventures and licensees of technology, trademarks and tradenames.

Company Financials Fiscal Year Ended Dec. 31

Per Share Data ($)	2008	2007	2006	2005	2004	2003	2002	2001	2000	1999
Tangible Book Value	2.55	23.99	2.67	3.83	3.12	2.95	4.05	3.69	3.18	2.32
Cash Flow	5.20	5.76	5.41	4.30	3.59	3.13	2.86	2.39	0.77	2.42
Earnings	4.00	4.70	4.19	3.28	2.72	2.26	2.04	1.68	0.10	1.80
S&P Core Earnings	4.06	4.59	4.11	3.24	2.60	2.15	1.81	1.62	NA	NA
Dividends	1.40	1.58	1.00	0.82	0.68	0.62	0.60	0.58	0.54	0.48
Payout Ratio	35%	34%	24%	25%	25%	27%	29%	35%	NM	27%
Prices:High	65.00	73.96	64.76	48.84	45.61	34.77	33.24	28.23	27.63	32.88
Prices:Low	44.51	56.75	37.40	40.47	32.95	24.42	21.75	19.73	17.13	18.75
P/E Ratio:High	16	16	15	15	17	15	16	17	NM	18
P/E Ratio:Low	11	12	9	12	12	11	11	12	NM	10

Income Statement Analysis (Million $)										
Revenue	7,980	8,005	7,810	7,191	6,114	5,408	5,185	5,067	5,212	5,004
Operating Income	998	1,145	1,024	898	758	690	670	599	676	680
Depreciation	143	139	146	144	126	117	116	109	109	105
Interest Expense	65.7	71.6	67.2	49.6	39.9	38.7	40.5	54.6	62.0	61.2
Pretax Income	714	913	834	656	580	523	497	424	143	490
Effective Tax Rate	33.3%	32.6%	31.0%	29.2%	32.0%	36.5%	37.5%	38.0%	88.8%	38.0%
Net Income	477	616	576	463	393	332	311	263	16.0	304
S&P Core Earnings	483	602	564	458	376	317	276	254	NA	NA

Balance Sheet & Other Financial Data (Million $)										
Cash	26.2	27.3	469	36.0	45.9	303	164	119	2.90	18.6
Current Assets	1,909	2,070	2,450	1,891	1,782	1,715	1,506	1,507	1,552	1,597
Total Assets	4,416	4,855	4,995	4,369	4,274	3,683	3,432	3,628	3,751	4,052
Current Liabilities	1,937	2,141	2,075	1,554	1,520	1,154	1,083	1,141	1,115	1,190
Long Term Debt	304	293	292	487	488	503	507	504	624	624
Common Equity	1,606	1,461	1,559	1,696	1,475	1,174	1,300	1,319	1,472	1,699
Total Capital	1,923	2,079	2,284	2,218	2,139	1,962	1,849	1,991	2,095	2,323
Capital Expenditures	117	166	210	143	107	117	127	82.6	133	134
Cash Flow	620	755	722	607	519	449	426	372	125	409
Current Ratio	1.0	1.0	1.2	1.2	1.2	1.5	1.4	1.3	1.4	1.3
% Long Term Debt of Capitalization	15.7	14.0	12.8	22.0	22.8	25.6	27.4	25.3	29.8	26.9
% Net Income of Revenue	6.0	7.7	7.4	6.4	6.4	6.1	6.0	5.2	0.3	6.1
% Return on Assets	10.3	12.5	12.3	10.7	9.9	9.3	8.8	7.1	0.4	7.5
% Return on Equity	31.1	32.6	35.4	29.2	29.7	26.8	23.7	18.9	1.0	17.8

Data as orig reptd.; bef. results of disc opers/spec. items. Per share data adj. for stk. divs.; EPS diluted. E-Estimated. NA-Not Available. NM-Not Meaningful. NR-Not Ranked. UR-Under Review.

Office: 101 Prospect Avenue N.W., Cleveland, OH 44115-1075.
Telephone: 216-566-2000.
Website: http://www.sherwin.com
Chrmn & CEO: C.M. Connor

Pres & COO: J.G. Morikis
SVP & CFO: S.P. Hennessy
SVP, Secy & General Counsel: L.E. Stellato
Chief Admin Officer: R.M. Weaver

Investor Contact: R.J. Wells (216-566-2244)
Board Members: A. F. Anton, J. C. Boland, C. M. Connor, D. F. Hodnik, T. G. Kadien, S. J. Kropf, G. E. McCullough, A. Mixon, III, C. E. Moll, R. K. Smucker, J. M. Stropki, Jr.

Founded: 1866
Domicile: Ohio
Employees: 30,677

The McGraw-Hill Companies

Sigma Aldrich Corporation

STANDARD &POOR'S

S&P Recommendation HOLD ★★★☆☆	Price $53.06 (as of Nov 27, 2009)	12-Mo. Target Price $56.00	Investment Style Large-Cap Growth

GICS Sector Materials
Sub-Industry Specialty Chemicals

Summary This company makes and sells a wide range of biochemicals, organic chemicals, and chromatography products.

Key Stock Statistics (Source S&P, Vickers, company reports)

52-Wk Range	$56.29– 31.45	S&P Oper. EPS 2009E	2.76	Market Capitalization(B)	$6.457	Beta	0.78
Trailing 12-Month EPS	$2.73	S&P Oper. EPS 2010E	3.06	Yield (%)	1.09	S&P 3-Yr. Proj. EPS CAGR(%)	12
Trailing 12-Month P/E	19.4	P/E on S&P Oper. EPS 2009E	19.2	Dividend Rate/Share	$0.58	S&P Credit Rating	A
$10K Invested 5 Yrs Ago	$18,937	Common Shares Outstg. (M)	121.7	Institutional Ownership (%)	77		

Price Performance

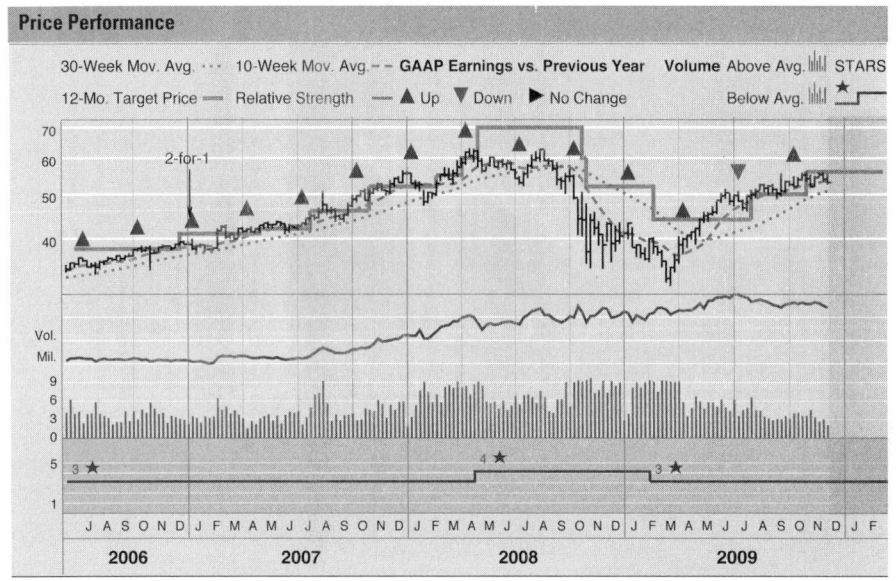

30-Week Mov. Avg. · · · 10-Week Mov. Avg. - - **GAAP Earnings vs. Previous Year** Volume Above Avg. STARS
12-Mo. Target Price — Relative Strength — ▲ Up ▼ Down ▶ No Change Below Avg. ★

Options: ASE, CBOE

Analysis prepared by **Jeffrey Loo, CFA** on October 29, 2009, when the stock traded at **$ 52.85.**

Qualitative Risk Assessment

LOW	MEDIUM	HIGH

Our risk assessment reflects the stable nature of the company's laboratory chemicals business, its broad geographic sales mix, and our view of its strong balance sheet.

Quantitative Evaluations

S&P Quality Ranking A+

D	C	B-	B	B+	A-	A	A+

Relative Strength Rank MODERATE

46

LOWEST = 1   HIGHEST = 99

Revenue/Earnings Data

Revenue (Million $)

	1Q	2Q	3Q	4Q	Year
2009	519.3	522.0	533.8	--	--
2008	569.6	580.7	540.6	509.8	2,201
2007	495.9	507.5	503.2	532.1	2,039
2006	443.1	448.5	441.4	464.5	1,798
2005	399.8	444.0	412.2	410.5	1,667
2004	368.1	348.6	340.6	351.9	1,409

Earnings Per Share ($)

2009	0.69	0.68	0.70	E0.69	E2.76
2008	0.64	0.70	0.64	0.68	2.65
2007	0.56	0.60	0.54	0.64	2.34
2006	0.49	0.52	0.51	0.53	2.05
2005	0.54	0.46	0.47	0.42	1.88
2004	0.45	0.43	0.41	0.40	1.67

Fiscal year ended Dec. 31. Next earnings report expected: Mid February. EPS Estimates based on S&P Operating Earnings; historical GAAP earnings are as reported.

Highlights

► We expect organic sales growth of 2% in 2009, but forecast adverse foreign currency exchange of 4%, resulting in an overall sales decline of 2%, to $2.15 billion. We see organic growth of 3% in Research Essentials, 3% in Research Specialties, and flat sales in Research Biotech, and in SAFC, the Fine Chemicals unit as second half 2009 sales rebound from soft sales over the past four quarters. We see 2010 sales growing 7%, to $2.3 billion. We think SIAL's efforts to increase international sales are paying off, and we project robust growth in the low double digits in Canada, Asia Pacific and Latin America, and we see slow but improving growth in Europe.

► We project flat 2009 gross margins, aided by SIAL's supply chain initiative, and we see operating margins improving 60 basis points on leverage and increased web-based ordering. Web-based sales now account for 52% of sales to U.S. customers and 46% worldwide.

► We think EPS should benefit from more share repurchases. We forecast 2009 EPS of $2.76 and estimate EPS of $3.06 for 2010.

Investment Rationale/Risk

► We see improved stability in SIAL's end markets following a challenging first half and believe demand trends are improving in its research and SAFC units. We also think the life sciences market is relatively stable and should continue to grow. We think the shares, trading at 17.0X our 2010 EPS forecast, in line with peers, are fairly valued. We are encouraged by SIAL's five-year supply chain initiative, which began in 2007, and believe it will lead to improved margins, but we only see a slight margin improvement of 60 bps in 2009. Also, marketing initiatives and an expanded sales force have increased operating expenses. We believe the company needs to improve efficiency and take advantage of leverage to improve its margins.

► Risks to our recommendation and target price include greater than expected weakness in key markets such as pharmaceuticals and academia, greater price competition, and an inability to successfully introduce new products.

► Our 12-month target price of $56 is based on an in-line-with-peers P/E-to-growth ratio of about 1.5X, based on our 2010 EPS estimate and assuming a three-year growth rate of 12%.

Dividend Data (Dates: mm/dd Payment Date: mm/dd/yy)

Amount ($)	Date Decl.	Ex-Div. Date	Stk. of Record	Payment Date
0.145	02/11	02/26	03/02	03/16/09
0.145	05/05	05/28	06/01	06/15/09
0.145	08/11	08/28	09/01	09/15/09
0.145	11/10	11/27	12/01	12/15/09

Dividends have been paid since 1970. Source: Company reports.

Please read the Required Disclosures and Analyst Certification on the last page of this report.

Sigma Aldrich Corporation

STANDARD &POOR'S

Business Summary October 29, 2009

CORPORATE OVERVIEW. Sigma-Aldrich, well known for its extensive catalog business, is one of the world's largest providers of research chemicals, reagents, chromatography products, and related products.

Foreign sales accounted for 64% of the total in 2008, up from 63% in 2007.

SIAL distributes more than 100,000 chemical products, under the Sigma, Aldrich, Fluka and Supelco brands names, for use primarily in research and development, diagnosis of disease, and as specialty chemicals for manufacturing. About 75% of sales are to customers in the life sciences, with the remaining 25% used in high-technology applications. Customer sectors include pharmaceutical (40% of sales), academia and government (30%), chemical industry (20%), and hospitals and commercial laboratories (10%). The company itself produces about 46,000 products, accounting for 61% of 2008 net sales of chemical products. Remaining products are purchased from outside sources. The company also supplies 30,000 equipment products.

The Research Essentials unit, 19% of sales in 2008 (19% in 2007), sells biological buffers, cell culture reagents, biochemicals, chemicals, solvents, and other reagents and kits. The Research Specialties unit, 37% of sales in 2008 (37%), sells organic chemicals, biochemicals, analytical reagents, chromatog-

raphy consumables, reference materials and high-purity products. The Research Biotech unit, 15% of sales in 2008 (15%), supplies immunochemical, molecular biology, cell signaling and neuroscience biochemicals and kits used in biotechnology, genomic, proteomic and other life science research applications. Sigma-Genosys (acquired in 1998) is a major maker of custom synthetic DNA products, synthetic peptides and genes to the life science product categories. SIAL believes it is the leading supplier of products used in cell signaling and neuroscience. The SAFC (Fine Chemicals) unit, 29% of sales in 2008 (29%), is a top 10 supplier of large-scale organic chemicals and biochemicals used in development and production by pharmaceutical, biotechnology, industrial and diagnostic companies. The February 2007 purchase of Epichem Group (annual sales of $40 million) greatly expanded SAFC's high technology sales.

SIAL also offers about 80,000 esoteric chemicals (less than 1% of total sales) as a special service to customers that screen them for potential applications.

Company Financials Fiscal Year Ended Dec. 31

Per Share Data ($)	2008	2007	2006	2005	2004	2003	2002	2001	2000	1999
Tangible Book Value	7.13	8.19	7.00	5.71	7.67	6.42	5.45	3.38	3.67	5.79
Cash Flow	3.42	3.07	1.37	2.54	2.19	1.83	1.72	1.41	1.24	1.07
Earnings	2.65	2.34	2.05	1.88	1.67	1.34	0.89	0.94	0.83	0.74
S&P Core Earnings	2.56	2.34	2.05	1.81	1.58	1.28	1.05	0.88	NA	NA
Dividends	0.52	0.46	0.42	0.38	0.34	0.25	0.17	0.17	0.16	0.15
Payout Ratio	20%	20%	20%	20%	20%	19%	19%	18%	19%	20%
Prices:High	63.04	56.59	39.68	33.55	30.81	28.96	26.40	25.75	20.44	17.63
Prices:Low	34.33	37.40	31.27	27.67	26.61	20.47	19.08	18.13	10.09	12.25
P/E Ratio:High	24	24	19	18	18	22	30	28	25	24
P/E Ratio:Low	13	16	15	15	16	15	21	19	12	17

Income Statement Analysis (Million $)										
Revenue	2,201	2,039	1,798	1,667	1,409	1,298	1,207	1,179	1,096	1,038
Operating Income	602	557	494	452	392	353	323	291	284	275
Depreciation	98.6	97.8	90.9	90.1	73.4	69.3	66.3	71.4	67.6	66.9
Interest Expense	21.0	28.9	24.0	18.1	7.20	10.1	13.8	18.2	10.2	Nil
Pretax Income	490	438	379	343	312	273	272	202	203	204
Effective Tax Rate	30.2%	28.9%	26.9%	24.8%	25.3%	30.2%	31.4%	30.2%	31.5%	27.1%
Net Income	342	311	277	258	233	190	187	141	139	149
S&P Core Earnings	331	310	276	249	221	180	155	133	NA	NA

Balance Sheet & Other Financial Data (Million $)										
Cash	252	238	174	98.6	169	128	52.4	37.6	31.1	43.8
Current Assets	1,309	1,283	1,113	950	893	815	695	727	714	775
Total Assets	2,557	2,629	2,334	2,131	1,745	1,548	1,390	1,440	1,348	1,432
Current Liabilities	794	635	443	461	231	257	266	398	335	106
Long Term Debt	200	207	338	283	177	176	177	178	101	0.21
Common Equity	1,379	1,617	1,411	1,233	1,212	999	882	810	859	1,259
Total Capital	1,598	1,866	1,797	1,597	1,389	1,176	1,059	987	960	1,260
Capital Expenditures	89.9	79.7	74.5	92.2	70.3	57.7	60.7	110	69.2	91.8
Cash Flow	440	409	368	348	306	260	253	212	207	216
Current Ratio	1.7	2.0	2.5	2.1	3.9	3.2	2.6	1.8	2.1	7.3
% Long Term Debt of Capitalization	12.5	11.1	18.8	17.7	12.8	15.0	16.7	18.0	10.5	0.0
% Net Income of Revenue	15.5	15.3	15.4	15.5	16.5	14.7	15.5	11.9	12.7	14.3
% Return on Assets	13.2	12.5	12.4	13.3	14.1	12.7	13.2	10.1	10.0	10.4
% Return on Equity	22.8	20.6	20.9	21.1	21.1	20.2	22.1	16.9	13.1	12.0

Data as orig reptd.; bef. results of disc opers/spec. items. Per share data adj. for stk. divs.; EPS diluted. E-Estimated. NA-Not Available. NM-Not Meaningful. NR-Not Ranked. UR-Under Review.

Office: 3050 Spruce Street, St. Louis, MO 63103.
Telephone: 314-771-5765.
Website: http://www.sigma-aldrich.com
Chrmn, Pres & CEO: J.P. Nagarkatti

Pres: J.P. Porwoll
SVP, Secy & General Counsel: G. Miller
CFO: R. Sachdev
Investor Contact: K.A. Richter (314-286-8004)

Board Members: R. M. Bergman, G. M. Church, D. R. Harvey, W. L. McCollum, J. P. Nagarkatti, A. M. Nash, S. M. Paul, J. P. Reinhard, T. R. Sear, D. D. Spatz, B. Toan

Founded: 1951
Domicile: Delaware
Employees: 7,925

Simon Property Group Inc.

STANDARD &POOR'S

S&P Recommendation	STRONG BUY ★★★★★	Price $69.73 (as of Nov 27, 2009)	12-Mo. Target Price $87.00	Investment Style Large-Cap Blend

GICS Sector Financials
Sub-Industry Retail REITS

Summary This real estate investment trust owns, develops, and manages retail real estate, primarily regional malls, outlet centers, and community/lifestyle centers, across the U.S.

Key Stock Statistics (Source S&P, Vickers, company reports)

52-Wk Range	$76.05–24.27	S&P FFO/Sh. 2009E	5.42	Market Capitalization(B)	$19.755	Beta	1.81
Trailing 12-Month FFO/Share	NA	S&P FFO/Sh. 2010E	5.64	Yield (%)	3.44	S&P 3-Yr. FFO/Sh. Proj. CAGR(%)	-2
Trailing 12-Month P/FFO	NA	P/FFO on S&P FFO/Sh. 2009E	12.9	Dividend Rate/Share	$2.40	S&P Credit Rating	A-
$10K Invested 5 Yrs Ago	$13,934	Common Shares Outstg. (M)	283.3	Institutional Ownership (%)	96		

Price Performance

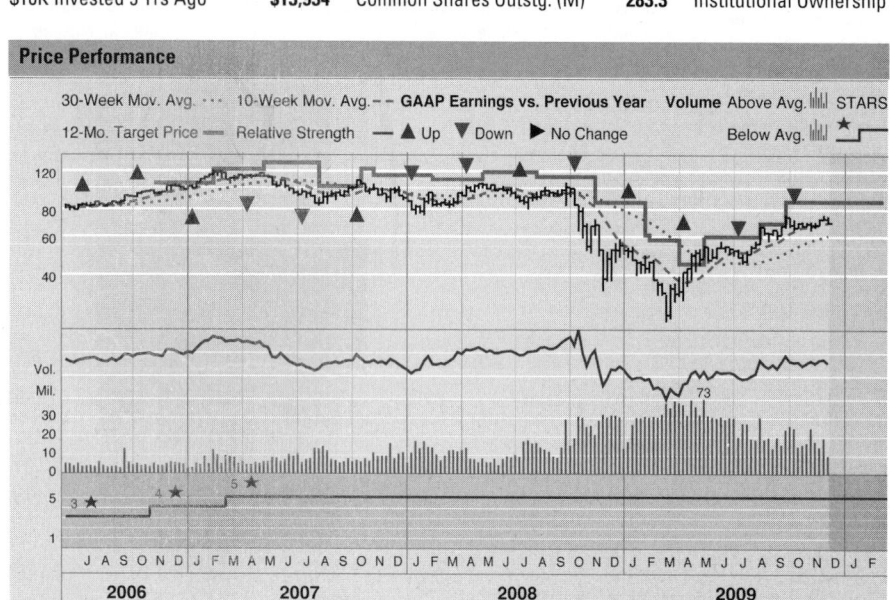

30-Week Mov. Avg. · · · 10-Week Mov. Avg. – – GAAP Earnings vs. Previous Year   Volume Above Avg. STARS
12-Mo. Target Price — Relative Strength — ▲ Up ▼ Down ► No Change   Below Avg. ★

Options: ASE, CBOE, Ph

Analysis prepared by **Robert McMillan** on November 03, 2009, when the stock traded at **$68.53**.

Highlights

► We expect the company to continue to benefit from what we view as a successful strategy of operating large and strategically located regional malls and shopping centers in major metropolitan markets.

► We look for total revenues to advance fractionally in 2009 and 4.3% in 2010 on higher rents and tenant reimbursements, after increasing 3.6% in 2008. Although occupancy and comparable sales per square foot declined across SPG's portfolio in the third quarter of 2009, they increased sequentially suggesting that trends are stabilizing. We were encouraged that management is seeing renewed retailer interest in new retail space, which we think bodes well for 2010 and 2011. Releasing spreads rose 10.6% for the regional malls, 32% for the outlet centers, but declined 4.7% for the community and lifestyle centers. Once the economy strengthens, we think a gradual pick-up in retailer expansions, combined with a prolonged drop in new construction activity, due to more stringent lending terms as well as ongoing cost reductions, will benefit SPG.

► We see FFO per share of $5.42 in 2009 (including impairments) and $5.64 in 2010.

Investment Rationale/Risk

► We think SPG's position as one of the largest owners and managers of shopping centers in the U.S. and its established relationships with numerous retailers will allow it to continue to generate solid growth long term. We also view the geographic, customer and format diversity of SPG's portfolio and management's acquisitions and developments in both the U.S. and overseas as positive factors in our valuation.

► Risks to our recommendation and target price include slower-than-expected growth in retailer expansion, higher-than-normal retailer bankruptcies, and a rise in interest rates.

► The shares recently traded at 10.4X SPG's trailing 12-month FFO. We believe the stock and valuation multiple have been volatile on concerns about the economy and consumer spending. Our 12-month target price of $87 is equal to 15.7X our forward 12-month FFO estimate of $5.53. We believe the multiple will expand based on improvements in the trust's operating performance long term, and a gradual easing of concerns about the impact of the economy on SPG's retailer-dependent business, which is anchored by long-term leases.

Qualitative Risk Assessment

LOW	MEDIUM	HIGH

Our risk assessment reflects SPG's position as one of the largest owners of shopping centers with a diverse tenant and geographic mix and variety of shopping center formats. The majority of SPG's customers are under long-term leases, which helps lessen short-term volatility. Although the trust has sizable debt maturing, we think recent equity and debt offerings enhance its liquidity.

Quantitative Evaluations

S&P Quality Ranking B+

D	C	B-	B	B+	A-	A	A+

Relative Strength Rank MODERATE

65

LOWEST = 1   HIGHEST = 99

Revenue/FFO Data

Revenue (Million $)

	1Q	2Q	3Q	4Q	Year
2009	918.5	903.6	924.9	--	--
2008	895.3	913.5	932.2	1,029	3,783
2007	852.1	855.9	907.2	1,036	3,632
2006	787.7	798.7	818.7	927.0	3,332
2005	756.9	756.3	786.8	889.8	3,167
2004	582.1	600.6	623.0	836.1	2,642

FFO Per Share ($)

2009	1.61	0.96	1.38	E1.50	E5.42
2008	1.46	1.49	1.61	1.86	6.42
2007	1.37	1.31	1.46	1.76	5.90
2006	1.26	1.26	1.30	1.57	5.39
2005	1.12	1.18	1.19	1.47	4.96
2004	0.96	1.01	1.04	1.36	4.39

Fiscal year ended Dec. 31. Next earnings report expected: Early February. FFO Estimates based on S&P Funds From Operations Est..

Dividend Data (Dates: mm/dd Payment Date: mm/dd/yy)

Amount ($)	Date Decl.	Ex-Div. Date	Stk. of Record	Payment Date
0.900	01/30	02/10	02/12	03/18/09
0.600	05/01	05/12	05/14	06/19/09
0.600	08/04	08/13	08/17	09/18/09
0.600	10/30	11/12	11/16	12/18/09

Dividends have been paid since 1994. Source: Company reports.

Simon Property Group Inc.

STANDARD &POOR'S

Business Summary November 03, 2009

CORPORATE OVERVIEW. Simon Property Group is a real estate investment trust that owns, develops, manages, leases and acquires primarily regional malls and community shopping centers. It is one of the largest owners of shopping centers in the world. At December 31, 2008, SPG owned or held an interest in 324 income-producing properties in the U.S. SPG also had ownership interests in 52 European shopping centers and nine premium outlet centers in Japan, Mexico and South Korea, and one shopping center in China.

SPG's regional malls typically contain at least one traditional department store anchor or a combination of anchors and big box retailers with a wide variety of smaller stores located in enclosed malls connecting the anchors. Additional freestanding stores are usually located along the perimeter of the parking area. SPG's 164 regional malls range in size from approximately 400,000 to 2.3 million square feet of gross leasable area (GLA) and contain more than 19,300 occupied stores, including approximately 740 anchors, which are mostly national retailers. SPG's 40 premium outlet centers, ranging in size from 200,000 to 850,000 square feet of GLA, contain a wide variety of retailers located in open-air manufacturers' outlet centers near metropolitan areas .

SPG's 70 community and lifestyle shopping centers are generally unenclosed and smaller than its regional malls. The community and lifestyle centers usually range in size from approximately 100,000 to 900,000 square feet of GLA and are designed to serve a larger trade area, and typically contain at least two anchors and other tenants that are usually national retailers among the leaders in their markets. These tenants generally occupy a significant portion of the GLA of the center. The company also owns traditional community shopping centers that focus primarily on value-oriented and convenience goods and services. These centers are usually anchored by a supermarket, discount retailer, or drugstore and are designed to service a neighborhood area. The trust also owns open-air centers adjacent to its regional malls designed to take advantage of the drawing power of the mall.

The Mills portfolio, which SPG acquired in 2007 with Farallon Capital Management, consists of Mills centers, regional malls, and community centers. The Mills centers, ranging from 1.0 million to 2.3 million square feet of GLA, are located in major metropolitan areas and have a combination of traditional mall, outlet center, and big box retailers and entertainment uses. The 16 regional malls generally range in size from 700,000 to 1.3 million square feet of GLA and contain a wide variety of national retailers. The four community centers are adjacent to Mills centers, and contain a mix of big box and other local and national retail tenants.

Company Financials Fiscal Year Ended Dec. 31

Per Share Data ($)	2008	2007	2006	2005	2004	2003	2002	2001	2000	1999
Tangible Book Value	10.93	12.40	13.98	14.64	16.21	14.66	13.87	13.00	14.29	15.36
Earnings	1.77	2.08	2.19	1.27	1.44	1.53	1.93	0.87	1.13	1.00
S&P Core Earnings	1.87	2.20	2.19	1.12	1.44	1.55	2.07	0.97	NA	NA
Dividends	3.60	3.36	3.04	2.80	2.60	2.40	2.18	2.08	2.02	2.02
Payout Ratio	203%	162%	139%	NM	181%	157%	113%	NM	179%	202%
Prices:High	106.43	123.96	104.08	80.97	65.87	48.59	36.95	30.97	27.13	30.94
Prices:Low	33.78	82.60	76.14	58.29	44.39	31.70	28.80	23.75	21.50	20.44
P/E Ratio:High	60	60	48	64	46	32	19	36	24	31
P/E Ratio:Low	19	40	35	46	31	21	15	27	19	20

Income Statement Analysis (Million $)										
Rental Income	3,458	3,288	3,063	2,920	2,411	1,423	1,386	1,320	1,284	1,207
Mortgage Income	Nil	Nil	Nil	Nil	Nil	Nil	Nil	Nil	Nil	Nil
Total Income	3,783	3,651	3,332	3,167	2,642	2,314	2,186	2,045	2,013	1,895
General Expenses	1,191	1,210	856	820	675	611	788	712	674	655
Interest Expense	965	1,535	822	799	662	615	603	622	667	580
Provision for Losses	24.0	9.56	9.50	8.10	17.7	Nil	8.97	8.41	9.64	8.50
Depreciation	970	906	856	850	623	498	423	453	420	382
Net Income	464	519	563	457	450	339	1,109	201	242	210
S&P Core Earnings	423	491	486	247	301	288	371	169	NA	NA

Balance Sheet & Other Financial Data (Million $)										
Cash	774	502	929	929	520	536	397	255	214	155
Total Assets	23,597	23,606	22,084	21,131	22,070	15,685	14,905	13,794	13,911	14,199
Real Estate Investment	25,206	24,415	24,390	23,307	23,175	14,972	14,250	13,187	13,038	12,794
Loss Reserve	Nil	Nil	Nil	Nil	Nil	Nil	20.5	24.7	20.1	14.6
Net Investment	19,021	19,103	19,784	19,499	20,012	12,415	12,027	11,311	11,558	11,697
Short Term Debt	1,476	810	NA	NA	NA	1,481	940	665	1,164	1,162
Capitalization:Debt	16,567	16,409	13,711	14,106	13,044	8,786	8,606	8,176	7,904	9,109
Capitalization:Equity	2,615	2,817	3,095	3,227	3,580	2,971	2,653	2,327	2,515	3,246
Capitalization:Total	19,607	21,821	18,885	19,681	19,065	13,241	12,074	11,381	10,958	12,355
% Earnings & Depreciation/Assets	6.1	6.2	6.7	6.0	5.7	5.5	10.7	4.7	4.7	4.3
Price Times Book Value:High	9.7	10.0	7.4	5.5	4.1	3.3	2.7	2.4	1.9	2.0
Price Times Book Value:Low	3.1	6.7	5.4	4.0	2.7	2.2	2.1	1.8	1.5	1.3

Data as orig reptd.; bef. results of disc opers/spec. items. Per share data adj. for stk. divs.; EPS diluted. E-Estimated. NA-Not Available. NM-Not Meaningful. NR-Not Ranked. UR-Under Review.

Office: 225 W Washington St, Indianapolis, IN 46204-3438.
Telephone: 317-636-1600.
Website: http://www.simon.com
Chrmn & CEO: D.E. Simon

Pres & COO: R.S. Sokolov
EVP & CFO: S.E. Sterrett
EVP & Chief Admin Officer: J. Rulli
EVP & Treas: A.A. Juster

Investor Contact: S.J. Doran (317-685-7330)
Board Members: M. E. Bergstein, L. W. Bynoe, K. N. Horn, A. Hubbard, R. S. Leibowitz, H. C. Mautner, H. C. Mautner, D. E. Simon, H. Simon, D. C. Smith, J. A. Smith, Jr., R. S. Sokolov

Founded: 1993
Domicile: Delaware
Employees: 5,300

The McGraw-Hill Companies

SLM Corp

STANDARD &POOR'S

S&P Recommendation BUY ★★★★☆	**Price** $10.72 (as of Nov 27, 2009)	**12-Mo. Target Price** $14.00	**Investment Style** Large-Cap Growth

GICS Sector Financials
Sub-Industry Consumer Finance

Summary This company (formerly USA Education) is a leading U.S. provider of post-secondary educational financial services.

Key Stock Statistics (Source S&P, Vickers, company reports)

52-Wk Range	$12.43– 3.11	S&P Oper. EPS 2009E	0.84	Market Capitalization(B)	$5.088	Beta	1.38
Trailing 12-Month EPS	$-0.69	S&P Oper. EPS 2010E	1.51	Yield (%)	Nil	S&P 3-Yr. Proj. EPS CAGR(%)	34
Trailing 12-Month P/E	NM	P/E on S&P Oper. EPS 2009E	12.8	Dividend Rate/Share	Nil	S&P Credit Rating	BBB-
$10K Invested 5 Yrs Ago	$2,214	Common Shares Outstg. (M)	474.6	Institutional Ownership (%)	NM		

Price Performance

30-Week Mov. Avg. · · · 10-Week Mov. Avg. - - **GAAP Earnings vs. Previous Year** Volume Above Avg. STARS
12-Mo. Target Price — Relative Strength — ▲ Up ▼ Down ► No Change Below Avg.

Options: ASE, CBOE, P

Analysis prepared by **Kevin Cole, CFA** on October 26, 2009, when the stock traded at **$ 11.00**.

Highlights

► We forecast that the loan portfolio mix will slightly shift towards private student loans in 2009 and then further increase in 2010, reflecting Congressional proposals to eliminate student loan subsidies for government-sponsored loans. In recent quarters, SLM's net interest margin was hurt by a dislocation in the three-month LIBOR/commercial paper spread, which narrowed to traditional levels by the end of the third quarter, and we expect SLM's net interest margin to widen from 0.90% in the first half of 2009 to over 1.50% for 2010.

► We believe loan loss provisions peaked in the third quarter of 2009, and we see delinquencies leveling off near 15% of loans in repayment in the fourth quarter of 2009, before falling in 2010. We expect that other income will nearly double in 2009, before falling slightly in 2010, reflecting our outlook for continuing improvement in credit spreads. We see other expenses declining approximately 13% in 2009, before flattening in 2010, based on much lower restructuring charges.

► Assuming a 37% effective tax rate, we estimate operating EPS of $0.84 in 2009 and $1.51 in 2010.

Investment Rationale/Risk

► Our Buy opinion is primarily based on valuation, as shares are trading at a discount to the historical average at approximately 7.3X our 2010 operating EPS estimate. In addition, student loan spreads returned to profitable levels in the third quarter of this year, and we expect credit spreads to continue to improve for the rest of the year. However, we believe private student loan losses have not peaked, and if private loan volumes do not return to levels seen earlier this decade, we think SLM's ability to increase assets in the long-term will be greatly hindered.

► Risks to our recommendation and target price include worse-than-expected credit deterioration, and a prolonged period of high unemployment.

► Our 12-month target price of $14 is based on a multiple of 9.3X our 2010 operating EPS estimate of $1.51. This multiple is a discount to the historical average to reflect the potential for loss of future federal subsides, and the deterioration we expect in SLM's loan portfolio.

Qualitative Risk Assessment

LOW	**MEDIUM**	HIGH

Our risk assessment reflect the effects of rising unemployment on the ability of former students to pay back student loans, offset by the return to historical credit spread levels and potentially higher net interest margin.

Quantitative Evaluations

S&P Quality Ranking B-

D	C	**B-**	B	B+	A-	A	A+

Relative Strength Rank STRONG

87

LOWEST = 1   HIGHEST = 99

Revenue/Earnings Data

Revenue (Million $)

	1Q	2Q	3Q	4Q	Year
2009	1,530	1,248	1,551	--	--
2008	1,963	2,331	1,697	631.2	7,689
2007	2,466	2,495	2,119	1,270	9,171
2006	1,766	2,695	2,252	2,038	8,751
2005	1,285	1,506	1,715	2,012	6,518
2004	915.1	1,509	1,047	1,525	4,997

Earnings Per Share ($)

2009	-0.10	-0.32	0.25	E0.30	E0.84
2008	-0.28	0.50	-0.40	-0.52	-0.69
2007	0.26	1.03	-0.85	-3.98	-2.26
2006	0.34	1.52	0.60	0.02	2.63
2005	0.49	0.66	0.95	0.96	3.05
2004	0.64	1.36	0.80	1.40	4.04

Fiscal year ended Dec. 31. Next earnings report expected: Late January. EPS Estimates based on S&P Operating Earnings; historical GAAP earnings are as reported.

Dividend Data

Dividends were omitted in April 2007.

SLM Corp

STANDARD &POOR'S

Business Summary October 26, 2009

CORPORATE OVERVIEW. SLM Corp., formerly USA Education Inc., is the largest U.S. private source of funding, delivery and service support for higher education loans, primarily through its participation in the Federal Family Education Loan Program (FFELP). The company's main business is to originate, acquire and hold student loans with the net interest income and gains on the sales of student loans in securitization, the primary source of earnings. The company funds its operation through student loan asset-backed securities and unsecured debt securities. SLM was chartered by an Act of Congress in 1972, but in 1996 it was rechartered as a private sector corporation and completed its privatization process in December 2004.

The company is divided into two business segments: Lending and Asset Performance Group (APG). According to the company, the SLM Lending segment manages the largest portfolio of FFELP and Private Education Loans in the student loan industry. As of December 31, 2008, the company served nearly 10 million borrowers, and managed $180.4 billion of student loans, of which 81% were federally insured.

PRIMARY BUSINESS DYNAMICS. There are two competing programs that divide student loans where the ultimate risk lies with the federal government: the FFELP and the Federal Direct Lending program (FDLP). FFELP loans are provided by private sector institutions, such as SLM, and are ultimately guaranteed by the U.S. Department of Education (ED). FDLP loans are funded by taxpayers and provided to borrowers directly by ED. Private Education Loans are originated by financial institutions where the lender assumes the credit risk of the borrower.

The company acquires student loans from three principal sources: SLM's Preferred Channel, which consists of the company's own brand of loans and loans originated by lenders with commitments to SLM; Consolidation Loans, which earn a lower yield than FFELP Loans due to a Consolidation Rebate Fee; and strategic acquisitions.

Company Financials Fiscal Year Ended Dec. 31

Per Share Data ($)	2008	2007	2006	2005	2004	2003	2002	2001	2000	1999
Tangible Book Value	4.37	5.93	5.90	5.13	4.81	4.55	3.08	3.59	2.54	1.43
Earnings	-0.69	-2.26	2.63	3.05	4.04	3.01	1.64	0.76	0.92	1.02
S&P Core Earnings	-0.70	-2.24	2.62	2.98	3.95	2.75	1.40	0.53	NA	NA
Dividends	Nil	0.25	0.97	0.85	0.74	0.59	0.28	0.24	0.22	0.20
Payout Ratio	Nil	NM	37%	28%	18%	20%	17%	32%	24%	20%
Prices:High	23.05	58.00	58.35	56.48	54.44	42.92	35.65	29.33	22.75	17.98
Prices:Low	4.19	18.68	44.65	45.56	36.43	33.73	25.67	18.63	9.27	13.17
P/E Ratio:High	NM	NM	22	19	13	14	22	39	25	18
P/E Ratio:Low	NM	NM	17	15	9	11	16	25	10	13

Income Statement Analysis (Million $)	2008	2007	2006	2005	2004	2003	2002	2001	2000	1999
Interest on:Mortgages	6,994	7,966	6,074	4,233	2,500	2,197	2,124	2,625	2,977	2,569
Interest on:Investment	276	708	503	277	233	151	87.9	373	501	240
Interest Expense	5,905	7,086	5,123	3,059	1,434	1,022	1,203	2,124	2,837	2,115
Guaranty Fees	Nil	Nil	Nil	Nil	Nil	Nil	Nil	Nil	Nil	Nil
Loan Loss Provision	720	1,015	287	203	111	147	117	66.0	32.1	34.4
Administration Expenses	1,357	1,529	1,346	1,138	895	808	690	708	586	359
Pretax Income	-376	-482	1,995	2,117	2,557	2,183	1,223	617	712	752
Effective Tax Rate	NM	NM	41.8%	34.4%	25.1%	35.7%	35.3%	36.2%	33.1%	31.9%
Net Income	-213	-896	1,157	1,382	1,913	1,404	792	384	465	501
S&P Core Earnings	-327	-923	1,119	1,324	1,853	1,276	664	261	NA	NA

Balance Sheet & Other Financial Data (Million $)	2008	2007	2006	2005	2004	2003	2002	2001	2000	1999
Mortgages	145,532	125,327	97,228	83,980	66,161	51,078	43,541	42,037	38,635	34,852
Investment	3,242	6,008	5,986	4,775	3,579	5,268	4,231	5,072	5,206	5,185
Cash & Equivalent	4,070	7,582	2,621	2,499	3,395	1,652	758	715	734	590
Total Assets	168,768	155,565	116,136	99,339	84,094	64,611	53,175	52,874	48,792	44,025
Short Term Debt	41,933	35,947	3.50	3,810	2,208	18,735	25,619	31,065	30,464	37,491
Long Term Debt	118,225	111,098	104,559	88,119	75,915	23,211	22,242	17,285	14,911	4,496
Equity	3,284	3,659	3,795	3,226	2,937	3,564	1,833	1,507	1,250	676
% Return on Assets	NM	NM	1.1	1.5	2.6	2.4	1.5	0.8	1.0	1.2
% Return on Equity	NM	NM	31.9	44.1	70.4	25.8	47.4	27.8	48.2	75.1
Equity/Assets Ratio	2.1	2.7	3.3	3.4	4.4	4.6	3.1	2.7	2.1	1.6
Price Times Book Value:High	5.7	9.8	9.9	11.0	11.3	9.4	11.6	8.2	8.9	12.6
Price Times Book Value:Low	1.0	3.2	7.6	8.9	7.6	7.4	8.3	5.2	3.6	9.2

Data as orig reptd.; bef. results of disc opers/spec. items. Per share data adj. for stk. divs.; EPS diluted. E-Estimated. NA-Not Available. NM-Not Meaningful. NR-Not Ranked. UR-Under Review.

Office: 12061 Bluemont Way, Reston, VA 20190-5684.
Telephone: 703-810-3000.
Website: http://www.salliemae.com
Chrmn: A.P. Terracciano

Chrmn: D.W. Acklie
Vice Chrmn & CEO: A.L. Lord
Vice Chrmn, CFO & Chief Acctg Officer: J.F. Remondi
EVP & Treas: J.C. Clark

Investor Contact: S. McGarry (703-810-7746)
Board Members: A. T. Bates, W. M. Diefenderfer, III, D. S. Gilleland, E. A. Goode, R. F. Hunt, A. L. Lord, M. E. Martin, B. Munitz, H. H. Newman, A. Porter, Jr., F. C. Puleo, J. F. Remondi, W. Schoellkopf, S. L. Shapiro, J. T. Strange, A. P. Terracciano, B. L. Williams

Founded: 1972
Domicile: Delaware
Employees: 8,000

The McGraw·Hill Companies

Smith International Inc.

STANDARD
&POOR'S

S&P Recommendation	SELL ★★☆☆☆	Price $26.54 (as of Nov 27, 2009)	12-Mo. Target Price $26.00	Investment Style Large-Cap Growth

GICS Sector Energy
Sub-Industry Oil & Gas Equipment & Services

Summary This company is an international supplier of products and services primarily used in drilling of oil and gas.

Key Stock Statistics (Source S&P, Vickers, company reports)

52-Wk Range	$34.46– 18.23	S&P Oper. EPS 2009**E**	0.76	Market Capitalization(B)	$5.823	Beta	1.32
Trailing 12-Month EPS	$1.49	S&P Oper. EPS 2010**E**	1.16	Yield (%)	1.81	S&P 3-Yr. Proj. EPS CAGR(%)	-29
Trailing 12-Month P/E	17.8	P/E on S&P Oper. EPS 2009**E**	34.9	Dividend Rate/Share	$0.48	S&P Credit Rating	BBB+
$10K Invested 5 Yrs Ago	$9,051	Common Shares Outstg. (M)	219.4	Institutional Ownership (%)	87		

Price Performance

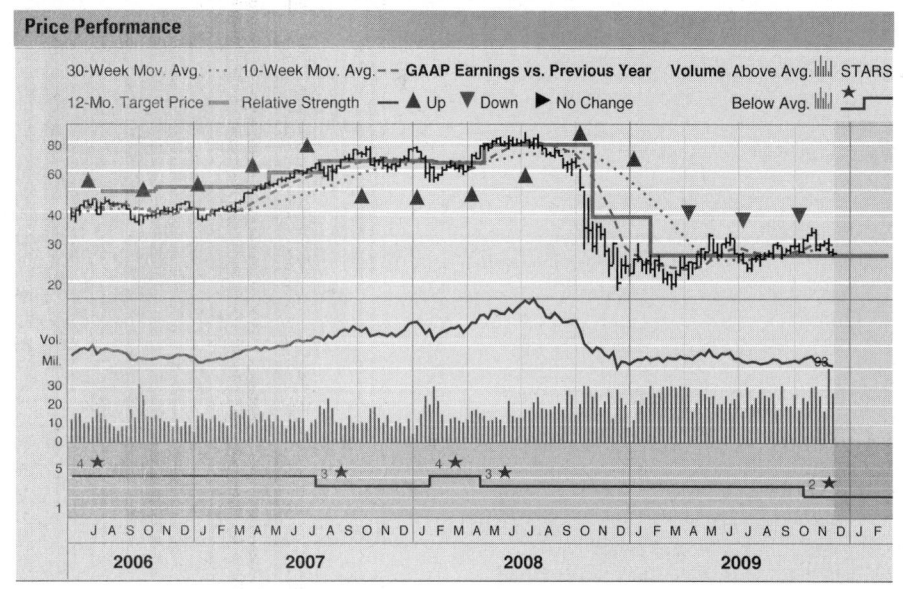

30-Week Mov. Avg. · · · 10-Week Mov. Avg. – – GAAP Earnings vs. Previous Year Volume Above Avg. STARS
12-Mo. Target Price — Relative Strength — ▲ Up ▼ Down ▶ No Change Below Avg.

Options: ASE, CBOE, P, Ph

Analysis prepared by **Stewart Glickman, CFA** on October 16, 2009, when the stock traded at **$ 31.39**.

Highlights

► We view SII as a beneficiary of a strong position in drilling fluids and drill bit technology. Typically, deepwater drilling and completion projects demand more advanced equipment, reflecting the relatively harsh environments found in such projects.

► While 2009 revenues are likely to be down significantly (similar to expectations for other oilfield services companies), we see 2010 as a recovery year for capital spending, which augurs well for such providers. We expect current deepwater projects to continue, which should provide SII with some protection given its relatively robust market share in deepwater developments; however, we think 2010 margins will be at best moderately above those of 2009. We see the greatest impact on margins in U.S. land and shallow U.S. Gulf of Mexico operations, which are very sensitive to persistently weak natural gas prices.

► Overall, we see revenues falling 26% in 2009 and EPS of $1.01 (a drop of 73% versus 2008). For 2010, we project revenues down only 2.5%, but with modest margin expansion, EPS rising 30%, to $1.31.

Investment Rationale/Risk

► We recently downgraded the shares on valuation, as we estimate SII is trading at or above peers on relative multiples, despite our projection of below-peer ROIC. Longer term, we believe SII is well positioned to benefit from secular trends in oil and gas exploration and production toward deeper, more challenging plays. We also view the August 2008 W-H Energy Services acquisition as a strategic positive for SII, enabling it to compete in directional drilling, complementing SII's franchise in drill bits.

► Risks to our recommendation and target price include reduced political risk in frontier regions; higher demand for drilling fluids and drill bits; and, less competition from larger companies in the drilling fluids business.

► Our DCF model, assuming free cash flow growth of 19%, a WACC of 10.5%, and 3% terminal growth, indicates intrinsic value of about $26. Given projected 2010 ROIC that is below peers, we think a modest multiple discount is merited. Assuming a 9.5X multiple on projected 2010 EBITDA and an 11.5X multiple on estimated 2010 cash flow (below peers), and blending these values with our DCF model, we derive our 12-month target price of $26.

Qualitative Risk Assessment

LOW	MEDIUM	HIGH

Our risk assessment reflects SII's exposure to volatile crude oil and natural gas prices, capital spending decisions made by its oil and gas producing customers, and political risk associated with operating in frontier regions. Offsetting these risks is SII's strong position in drill bits and drilling fluids.

Quantitative Evaluations

S&P Quality Ranking B+

D	C	B-	B	B+	A-	A	A+

Relative Strength Rank WEAK

23

LOWEST = 1   HIGHEST = 99

Revenue/Earnings Data

Revenue (Million $)

	1Q	2Q	3Q	4Q	Year
2009	2,411	1,944	1,879	--	--
2008	2,371	2,494	2,849	3,056	10,771
2007	2,108	2,114	2,245	2,297	8,764
2006	1,682	1,738	1,914	1,999	7,334
2005	1,288	1,350	1,410	1,530	5,579
2004	1,018	1,064	1,119	1,218	4,419

Earnings Per Share ($)

2009	0.44	0.11	0.03	E0.18	E0.76
2008	0.87	0.91	1.00	0.91	3.68
2007	0.80	0.76	0.83	0.83	3.20
2006	0.53	0.59	0.66	0.71	2.49
2005	0.33	0.33	0.39	0.44	1.48
2004	0.22	0.14	0.26	0.29	0.89

Fiscal year ended Dec. 31. Next earnings report expected: Late January. EPS Estimates based on S&P Operating Earnings; historical GAAP earnings are as reported.

Dividend Data (Dates: mm/dd Payment Date: mm/dd/yy)

Amount ($)	Date Decl.	Ex-Div. Date	Stk. of Record	Payment Date
0.120	02/06	03/11	03/13	04/13/09
0.120	04/28	06/10	06/12	07/13/09
0.120	07/22	09/09	09/11	10/13/09
0.120	10/23	12/09	12/11	01/11/10

Dividends have been paid since 2005. Source: Company reports.

Please read the Required Disclosures and Analyst Certification on the last page of this report.

The McGraw·Hill Companies

Smith International Inc.

STANDARD
&POOR'S

Business Summary October 16, 2009

CORPORATE OVERVIEW. Driven by exploration and production activities worldwide, Smith International manufactures and markets technologically advanced products and services to the oil and gas industry. Approximately 53% of total 2008 revenues were derived from equipment sold or services provided to customers outside the United States (versus 55% in 2007). In 2008, top non-U.S. regions included Europe/Africa (24%), Canada (8%), Middle East/Asia (12%), and Latin America (9%). The company's businesses are comprised of three operating segments: M-I Swaco, Smith Oilfield, and Distribution.

M-I SWACO (48% of 2008 revenues, and 48% of 2008 operating income before general corporate expenses) provides drilling and completion fluid systems and services, solids control equipment and waste management services. Drilling fluid products and systems are used to cool and lubricate the bit during drilling, contain formation pressures, remove rock cuttings, and maintain the stability of the wellbore. Engineering services ensure that products are applied to optimize operations. M-I Swaco is a joint venture with Schlumberger Limited, in which SII is the majority partner.

Smith Oilfield (27%, 42%) is a leading supplier of drill bits and borehole enlargement systems, drilling tools and services, tubulars, completion services and other related downhole solutions. SII broadened its capabilities in these areas with the August 2008 acquisition of W-H Energy Services, which added directional drilling and other complementary offerings. This segment's offerings are strategically oriented to premium products and services. This segment was created in mid-2008 by combining two formerly distinct segments, Smith Technologies and Smith Services.

The Distribution segment (26%, 10%) consists of Wilson, a supply-chain management company that markets pipe, valves, fittings, and mill and safety products, and a majority-owned interest in C.E. Franklin, a Canadian distribution company.

Company Financials Fiscal Year Ended Dec. 31

Per Share Data ($)	2008	2007	2006	2005	2004	2003	2002	2001	2000	1999
Tangible Book Value	NA	7.82	4.89	3.40	3.06	2.72	2.23	1.90	1.83	1.89
Cash Flow	4.94	4.00	3.23	2.05	1.41	1.12	0.91	1.22	0.76	0.67
Earnings	3.68	3.20	2.49	1.48	0.89	0.62	0.47	0.76	0.36	0.29
S&P Core Earnings	3.67	3.20	2.49	1.41	0.94	0.57	0.42	0.72	NA	NA
Dividends	0.48	0.40	0.32	0.24	Nil	Nil	Nil	Nil	Nil	Nil
Payout Ratio	13%	13%	13%	16%	Nil	Nil	Nil	Nil	Nil	Nil
Prices:High	88.40	76.99	46.48	40.08	31.49	21.59	19.36	21.13	22.13	13.02
Prices:Low	18.23	36.13	34.87	25.80	20.03	14.75	11.60	8.08	11.25	5.89
P/E Ratio:High	24	24	19	27	35	35	42	28	61	45
P/E Ratio:Low	5	11	14	17	23	24	25	11	31	20

Income Statement Analysis (Million $)										
Revenue	10,771	8,764	7,334	5,579	4,419	3,595	3,170	3,551	2,761	1,806
Operating Income	1,910	1,531	1,230	788	545	430	345	464	280	310
Depreciation, Depletion and Amortization	263	162	150	118	106	102	89.3	92.9	80.7	76.0
Interest Expense	89.8	70.0	63.0	44.4	38.8	41.0	40.9	45.4	36.8	40.8
Pretax Income	1,556	1,304	1,020	628	401	290	218	329	164	111
Effective Tax Rate	32.5%	31.3%	32.0%	32.3%	32.3%	32.2%	30.6%	32.3%	33.5%	43.2%
Net Income	767	647	502	302	182	125	93.2	152	72.8	56.7
S&P Core Earnings	766	646	503	290	192	115	84.6	145	NA	NA

Balance Sheet & Other Financial Data (Million $)										
Cash	163	158	80.4	62.5	53.6	51.3	86.8	44.7	36.5	24.1
Current Assets	5,086	3,728	3,271	2,437	2,020	1,680	1,427	1,523	1,310	1,055
Total Assets	10,819	6,062	5,335	4,060	3,507	3,097	2,750	2,736	2,295	1,895
Current Liabilities	2,933	1,173	1,379	933	887	631	595	666	643	457
Long Term Debt	1,441	846	801	611	388	489	442	539	375	347
Common Equity	4,549	2,595	1,987	1,365	1,401	1,236	1,064	949	817	720
Total Capital	7,730	4,732	3,710	2,827	2,537	2,392	2,087	2,019	1,615	1,422
Capital Expenditures	443	356	308	178	111	98.9	97.1	128	94.6	57.2
Cash Flow	1,030	809	652	420	289	226	183	245	153	133
Current Ratio	1.7	3.2	2.4	2.6	2.3	2.7	2.4	2.3	2.0	2.3
% Long Term Debt of Capitalization	18.6	17.9	21.6	21.6	15.3	20.4	21.2	26.7	23.2	24.4
% Return on Assets	4.1	11.4	10.7	8.0	5.5	4.3	3.4	6.0	3.5	3.1
% Return on Equity	21.5	28.2	28.2	21.9	13.8	10.8	9.3	17.2	9.5	8.4

Data as orig reptd.; bef. results of disc opers/spec. items. Per share data adj. for stk. divs.; EPS diluted. E-Estimated. NA-Not Available. NM-Not Meaningful. NR-Not Ranked. UR-Under Review.

Office: 16740 E Hardy Rd, Houston, TX 77032-1125.
Telephone: 281-443-3370.
Website: http://www.smith.com
Chrmn: D. Rock

Pres, CEO & COO: J. Yearwood
SVP, Secy & General Counsel: R.E. Chandler, Jr.
CFO & Treas: W. Restrepo
Investor Contact: M.K. Dorman (281-443-3370)

Board Members: L. Carroll, D. A. Fraser, J. R. Gibbs, R. Kelley, L. R. Machado, D. C. Radtke, D. Rock, J. Yearwood

Founded: 1937
Domicile: Delaware
Employees: 25,709

The McGraw-Hill Companies

J.M. Smucker Co (The)

STANDARD &POOR'S

S&P Recommendation	STRONG BUY ★★★★★	Price $58.49 (as of Nov 27, 2009)	12-Mo. Target Price $64.00	Investment Style Large-Cap Blend

GICS Sector Consumer Staples
Sub-Industry Packaged Foods & Meats

Summary This company's products include coffee, fruit spreads, peanut butter, shortening and oils, ice cream toppings, health and natural foods, and beverages. The Folgers coffee business was acquired in November 2008.

Key Stock Statistics (Source S&P, Vickers, company reports)

52-Wk Range	$59.30– 34.09	S&P Oper. EPS 2010**E**	4.05	Market Capitalization(B)	$6.957	Beta	0.67
Trailing 12-Month EPS	$3.50	S&P Oper. EPS 2011**E**	4.10	Yield (%)	2.39	S&P 3-Yr. Proj. EPS CAGR(%)	5
Trailing 12-Month P/E	16.7	P/E on S&P Oper. EPS 2010**E**	14.4	Dividend Rate/Share	$1.40	S&P Credit Rating	NA
$10K Invested 5 Yrs Ago	$16,231	Common Shares Outstg. (M)	118.9	Institutional Ownership (%)	78		

Price Performance

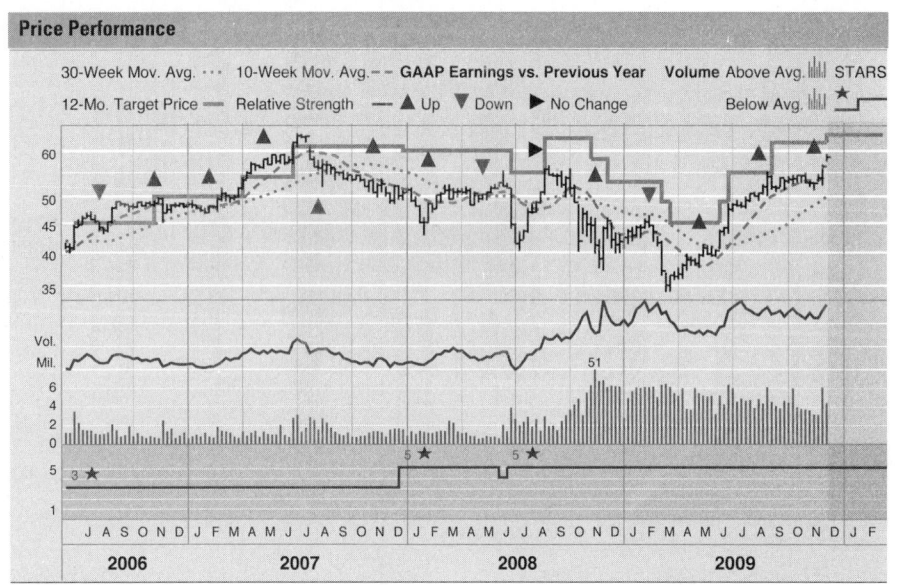

30-Week Mov. Avg. · · · 10-Week Mov. Avg. - - **GAAP Earnings vs. Previous Year** Volume Above Avg. STARS
12-Mo. Target Price — Relative Strength — ▲ Up ▼ Down ▶ No Change Below Avg. ★

Options: ASE, CBOE, Ph

Highlights

► The 12-month target price for SJM has recently been changed to $64.00 from $62.00. The Highlights section of this Stock Report will be updated accordingly.

Investment Rationale/Risk

► The Investment Rationale/Risk section of this Stock Report will be updated shortly. For the latest News story on SJM from MarketScope, see below.

► 11/20/09 10:56 am ET ... S&P REITERATES STRONG BUY OPINION ON SHARES OF J.M. SMUCKER (SJM 56.15*****): Before some special items, Oct-Q EPS of $1.22 vs. $1.01 is $0.07 above our est. We are pleased by strength of the U.S. retail coffee business. Before some special items, we raise our FY 10 (Apr) EPS estimate to $4.05 from $3.85, and FY 11's to $4.10 from $4.00. Both years have about $0.40 annual non-cash amortization. We see prospect of higher coffee commodity costs in FY 11. We are upping our target price to $64 from $62, on about a 10% expected P/E premium to other packaged food stocks. Indicated dividend yield is 2.5%. We expect the dividend to be raised in '10. /T.Graves-CFA

Qualitative Risk Assessment

LOW	MEDIUM	HIGH

Our risk assessment reflects the relative stability of the company's end markets, our view of its relatively strong balance sheet, and an S&P Quality Ranking of A+, which reflects S&P's appraisal of historical growth and stability of earnings and dividends.

Quantitative Evaluations

S&P Quality Ranking A+

D	C	B-	B	B+	A-	A	A+

Relative Strength Rank STRONG

88

LOWEST = 1 HIGHEST = 99

Revenue/Earnings Data

Revenue (Million $)

	1Q	2Q	3Q	4Q	Year
2010	1,052	1,279	--	--	--
2009	663.7	843.1	1,183	1,069	3,758
2008	561.5	707.9	665.4	590.0	2,525
2007	526.5	605.0	523.1	493.5	2,148
2006	510.3	606.3	536.5	501.7	2,155
2005	415.8	588.9	550.2	491.5	2,044

Earnings Per Share ($)

	1Q	2Q	3Q	4Q	Year
2010	0.83	1.18	E1.02	E0.89	E4.05
2009	0.77	0.94	0.68	0.80	3.12
2008	0.77	0.87	0.75	0.67	3.00
2007	0.50	0.80	0.71	0.75	2.76
2006	0.51	0.79	0.54	0.62	2.45
2005	0.50	0.69	0.60	0.45	2.26

Fiscal year ended Apr. 30. Next earnings report expected: Late February. EPS Estimates based on S&P Operating Earnings; historical GAAP earnings are as reported.

Dividend Data (Dates: mm/dd Payment Date: mm/dd/yy)

Amount ($)	Date Decl.	Ex-Div. Date	Stk. of Record	Payment Date
0.320	01/27	02/11	02/13	03/02/09
0.350	04/21	05/13	05/15	06/01/09
0.350	07/17	08/12	08/14	09/01/09
0.350	10/27	11/10	11/13	12/01/09

Dividends have been paid since 1949. Source: Company reports.

J.M. Smucker Co (The)

STANDARD &POOR'S

Business Summary August 31, 2009

CORPORATE PROFILE. From its origins in 1897, when Jerome M. Smucker first pressed cider at a mill that he opened in that year, the J. M. Smucker Co. has become a leading U.S. producer of such products as fruit spreads, peanut butter, shortening, ice cream toppings, and coffee.

In November 2008, SJM completed the acquisition of the Folgers coffee business from Procter & Gamble. PG shareholders received about 63 million SJM shares (about 53.5% of the total shares now outstanding) in exchange for the Folgers business. The Folgers transaction was preceded by SJM paying a one-time special dividend of $5 a share to SJM shareholders of record on September 30, 2008. On a pro forma basis, Folgers would have accounted for about 42% of SJM's total sales in FY 08 (assuming $1.8 billion from the Folgers business).

SJM is now reporting four business segments. The U.S. retail consumer market segment (29% of FY 09 (Apr.) net sales) includes such items as Smucker's fruit spreads and toppings, Jif peanut butter, and various products carrying the Hungry Jack and Smucker's Uncrustables brands. The U.S. retail oils and baking market segment (26%) includes baking mixes, frostings, flour, private label canned milk, and oils. The U.S. retail coffee market segment (23%) includes much of the Folgers business, and the special markets segment (21%) includes the Canada, foodservice, natural foods (formerly beverage), and international strategic business areas.

SJM's international business accounted for 11% of net sales in FY 09. Also, sales to Wal-Mart Stores, Inc. and its subsidiaries accounted for about 24% of net sales.

SJM product categories include coffee (25% of FY 09 sales), peanut butter (14%), shortening and oils (11%), fruit spreads (9%), baking mixes and frostings (8%), canned milk (7%), flour and baking ingredients (7%), portion control 4%, juices and beverages (3%, Uncrustables frozen sandwiches (3%), toppings and syrups (3%, and other (6%).

Company Financials Fiscal Year Ended Apr. 30

Per Share Data ($)	2009	2008	2007	2006	2005	2004	2003	2002	2001	2000
Tangible Book Value	NM	0.98	5.75	5.52	4.61	7.10	5.58	9.32	8.27	9.29
Cash Flow	4.50	4.11	3.81	3.77	3.19	3.01	2.81	2.39	2.40	1.83
Earnings	3.12	3.00	2.76	2.45	2.26	2.21	2.02	1.24	1.23	0.92
S&P Core Earnings	2.98	2.55	2.70	2.30	2.16	2.20	1.89	1.10	1.19	NA
Dividends	1.28	1.12	1.08	1.00	0.92	0.76	0.76	0.64	0.60	0.59
Payout Ratio	41%	37%	39%	41%	41%	34%	38%	52%	49%	64%
Calendar Year	2008	2007	2006	2005	2004	2003	2002	2001	2000	1999
Prices:High	56.69	64.32	49.98	51.65	53.50	46.75	40.42	37.73	29.00	25.75
Prices:Low	37.22	46.57	37.15	43.64	40.80	33.00	28.71	22.61	15.00	18.38
P/E Ratio:High	18	21	18	21	24	21	20	30	24	28
P/E Ratio:Low	12	16	13	18	18	15	14	18	12	20

Income Statement Analysis (Million $)	2009	2008	2007	2006	2005	2004	2003	2002	2001	2000
Revenue	3,758	2,525	2,148	2,155	2,044	1,417	1,312	687	651	632
Operating Income	655	354	318	325	526	227	214	88.4	83.7	81.9
Depreciation	118	62.6	58.9	71.1	56.0	39.9	37.8	28.6	26.9	26.2
Interest Expense	62.5	42.1	23.4	24.0	22.6	6.37	8.75	9.21	0.78	3.11
Pretax Income	396	255	241	216	205	179	155	50.2	50.0	41.5
Effective Tax Rate	32.9%	33.1%	34.8%	33.5%	36.2%	37.7%	38.0%	38.5%	36.6%	36.5%
Net Income	266	170	157	143	130	111	96.3	30.9	31.7	26.4
S&P Core Earnings	254	144	154	134	126	111	90.5	25.9	28.9	NA

Balance Sheet & Other Financial Data (Million $)	2009	2008	2007	2006	2005	2004	2003	2002	2001	2000
Cash	457	184	200	121	75.8	163	181	91.9	51.1	33.1
Current Assets	1,399	776	639	571	556	425	467	280	229	229
Total Assets	8,192	3,130	2,694	2,650	2,636	1,684	1,615	525	470	475
Current Liabilities	1,061	239	236	235	308	175	167	80.4	67.1	68.2
Long Term Debt	910	790	393	429	432	135	135	135	135	75.0
Common Equity	4,940	1,800	1,796	1,728	1,691	1,211	1,124	280	247	313
Total Capital	6,127	2,765	2,347	2,312	2,233	1,482	1,393	419	387	392
Capital Expenditures	109	76.4	57.0	63.2	87.6	100	49.5	23.5	29.4	32.2
Cash Flow	384	233	216	214	187	151	134	59.4	58.6	52.6
Current Ratio	1.3	3.2	2.7	2.4	1.8	2.4	2.8	3.5	3.4	3.4
% Long Term Debt of Capitalization	14.9	28.6	16.7	18.5	19.3	9.1	9.7	32.2	34.9	19.1
% Net Income of Revenue	7.1	6.8	7.3	6.7	6.4	7.9	7.3	4.5	4.9	4.2
% Return on Assets	4.7	5.9	5.9	5.4	6.0	6.7	9.0	6.1	6.8	5.8
% Return on Equity	7.9	9.5	8.9	8.4	9.0	9.5	13.7	11.6	11.3	8.3

Data as orig reptd.; bef. results of disc opers/spec. items. Per share data adj. for stk. divs.; EPS diluted. E-Estimated. NA-Not Available. NM-Not Meaningful. NR-Not Ranked. UR-Under Review.

Office: 1 Strawberry Ln, Orrville, OH 44667-0280.
Telephone: 330-682-3000.
Email: investor.relations@jmsmucker.com
Website: http://www.smuckers.com

Co-Chrmn, Pres & Co-CEO: R.K. Smucker
Co-Chrmn & Co-CEO: T. Smucker
CFO: M.R. Belgya
Chief Acctg Officer & Cntlr: J.W. Denman

Treas: D.A. Marthey
Investor Contact: S. Robinson (330-684-3440)
Board Members: V. C. Byrd, R. D. Cowan, K. W. Dindo, P. Dolan, N. L. Knight, E. V. Long, G. A. Oatey, A. Shumate, M. Smucker, R. K. Smucker, T. Smucker, W. H. Steinbrink, P. S. Wagstaff

Founded: 1897
Domicile: Ohio
Employees: 4,700

Snap-On Inc

STANDARD &POOR'S

S&P Recommendation	BUY ★★★★☆	Price $36.44 (as of Nov 27, 2009)	12-Mo. Target Price $43.00	Investment Style Large-Cap Value

GICS Sector Industrials
Sub-Industry Industrial Machinery

Summary This company is the largest manufacturer and distributor of hand tools, storage units and diagnostic equipment for professional mechanics.

Key Stock Statistics (Source S&P, Vickers, company reports)

52-Wk Range	$41.65– 20.51	S&P Oper. EPS 2009E	2.27	Market Capitalization(B)	$2.104	Beta	1.57
Trailing 12-Month EPS	$2.70	S&P Oper. EPS 2010E	2.90	Yield (%)	3.29	S&P 3-Yr. Proj. EPS CAGR(%)	12
Trailing 12-Month P/E	13.5	P/E on S&P Oper. EPS 2009E	16.1	Dividend Rate/Share	$1.20	S&P Credit Rating	A-
$10K Invested 5 Yrs Ago	$13,381	Common Shares Outstg. (M)	57.7	Institutional Ownership (%)	94		

Price Performance

30-Week Mov. Avg. · · · · 10-Week Mov. Avg. - - GAAP Earnings vs. Previous Year   Volume Above Avg. STARS
12-Mo. Target Price — Relative Strength — ▲ Up ▼ Down ► No Change   Below Avg. ★

Options: ASE, Ph

Analysis prepared by **Mathew Christy, CFA** on November 04, 2009, when the stock traded at **$ 37.87**.

Highlights

► After nearly flat revenue growth in 2008, we expect sales to decrease about 17% in 2009, followed by a 5% rebound in 2010. SNA continues to focus on improving its dealer business, which we think will benefit future sales. We forecast 2009 sales declines of nearly 6% for the Snap-on Tools Group and about 28% for the Commercial & Industrial Group, while we see a 12% sales decline for the Diagnostics & Information Group.

► In our opinion, SNA will experience lower gross and operating margins in 2009 due to reduced volumes and lower pricing, all leading to lower operating leverage along with the fixed-cost absorption of SNA's consolidation of its financing subsidiary in the second half of 2009. In 2010, we project somewhat better gross and operating margins on higher operating leverage and moderate profits in SNA's finance subsidiary.

► Assuming an effective tax rate of about 30% in 2009 and 2010, we estimate EPS will decline nearly 46% in 2009, to $2.27, followed by growth of about 28%, to $2.90, in 2010.

Investment Rationale/Risk

► We believe SNA is undergoing a transformation to become a leaner organization, with a high priority on bettering customer responsiveness and top-line growth. We expect these ongoing improvements to ultimately restore margins to prior levels when economies rebound. We believe the company's diversified products and customer base around the globe will buffer some of its exposure to a U.S. and European recession better than its peers. We believe the shares are attractively valued at 12.4X our 2010 EPS estimate, a 25% discount to the peer average and a nearly 20% discount to SNA's historical average.

► Risks to our recommendation and target price include weaker-than-expected results in SNA's major markets, failure to successfully introduce new products, and any negative effects from a deeper global recession.

► Our 12-month target price of $43 is based on our relative peer valuation analysis. We apply a P/E multiple of about 15X, a discount to SNA's peer group but in line with its five-year historical average, to our 2010 EPS estimate.

Qualitative Risk Assessment

LOW	MEDIUM	HIGH

Our risk assessment is based on our view of SNA's strong brand equity and healthy balance sheet, offset by intense competition and weaker economies in the U.S. and Europe. We believe an improved global supply chain and cost reduction initiatives will offset rising raw material and delivery costs.

Quantitative Evaluations

S&P Quality Ranking   B+

D	C	B-	B	B+	A-	A	A+

Relative Strength Rank   MODERATE

46

LOWEST = 1   HIGHEST = 99

Revenue/Earnings Data

Revenue (Million $)

	1Q	2Q	3Q	4Q	Year
2009	592.6	615.6	587.8	--	--
2008	747.0	784.4	713.8	687.5	2,935
2007	705.7	711.9	680.7	742.9	2,841
2006	593.5	624.4	599.5	656.0	2,522
2005	612.8	608.6	567.2	573.6	2,362
2004	616.3	612.1	568.8	610.0	2,407

Earnings Per Share ($)

2009	0.60	0.65	0.44	E0.58	E2.27
2008	0.97	1.15	0.94	1.01	4.07
2007	0.66	0.90	0.70	0.99	3.23
2006	0.37	0.20	0.48	0.64	1.69
2005	0.31	0.46	0.36	0.47	1.59
2004	0.22	0.38	0.39	0.42	1.40

Fiscal year ended Dec. 31. Next earnings report expected: Early February. EPS Estimates based on S&P Operating Earnings; historical GAAP earnings are as reported.

Dividend Data (Dates: mm/dd Payment Date: mm/dd/yy)

Amount ($)	Date Decl.	Ex-Div. Date	Stk. of Record	Payment Date
0.300	02/11	02/19	02/23	03/09/09
0.300	04/23	05/14	05/18	06/08/09
0.300	08/06	08/13	08/17	09/08/09
0.300	11/05	11/12	11/16	12/07/09

Dividends have been paid since 1939. Source: Company reports.

Snap-On Inc

STANDARD &POOR'S

Business Summary November 04, 2009

CORPORATE OVERVIEW. Snap-on Inc. is a major global manufacturer and marketer of high-quality tool, diagnostic, service and equipment solutions for professional tool and equipment users under various brands and trade names. Product lines include a broad range of hand and power tools, tool storage, saws and cutting tools, pruning tools, vehicle service diagnostics equipment, vehicle service equipment, including wheel service, safety testing and collision repair equipment, vehicle service information, business management systems, equipment repair services, and other tool and equipment solutions. SNA's customers include automotive technicians, vehicle service centers, manufacturers, industrial tool and equipment users, and those involved in commercial applications such as construction, electrical and agriculture. SNA services these customers through three primary channels of distribution: the mobile dealer van channel, including the company's technical representatives; company direct sales; and distributors.

SNA has four reportable business segments. The Snap-on Tools Group, formerly the Dealer Group (38% of 2008 sales, 38% of 2007 sales) consists of SNA's business operations serving the worldwide franchised dealer van channel. The Commercial & Industrial Group (48%, 47%) provides tools, equip-

ment products and equipment repair services to industrial and commercial customers worldwide through direct, distributor and other non-franchised distribution channels. The Diagnostics & Information Group (21%, 22%) provides diagnostic equipment, vehicle service information, business management systems and other solutions for customers in the vehicle service and repair marketplace. Financial Services (3%, 2%) is a relatively new business segment, which was originated in 2004. It consists of Snap-on Credit LLC, a consolidated 50%-owned joint venture between SNA and The CIT Group, and SNA's wholly owned finance subsidiaries in international markets where SNA has dealer operations. Segment eliminations as a percentage of total sales consist of negative 10% in 2008 and 9% in 2007. In regard to global reach, more than 45% of total sales in the fourth quarter of 2007 (latest available) were outside the U.S. market with margins widening in most of its operations overseas, in our opinion.

Company Financials Fiscal Year Ended Dec. 31

Per Share Data ($)	2008	2007	2006	2005	2004	2003	2002	2001	2000	1999
Tangible Book Value	2.90	3.94	0.72	8.17	9.67	8.29	6.27	6.01	6.53	6.69
Cash Flow	5.17	4.52	2.57	2.48	2.45	2.38	2.65	1.54	3.23	3.10
Earnings	4.07	3.23	1.69	1.59	1.40	1.35	1.76	0.37	2.10	2.16
S&P Core Earnings	3.31	3.15	2.07	1.56	1.35	1.31	0.92	0.09	NA	NA
Dividends	1.20	1.11	1.08	1.00	1.00	1.00	0.97	0.96	0.94	0.90
Payout Ratio	29%	34%	64%	63%	71%	74%	55%	NM	45%	42%
Prices:High	62.21	57.81	48.65	38.71	34.67	32.38	35.15	34.40	32.44	37.81
Prices:Low	27.70	44.58	36.38	30.57	27.15	22.60	20.71	21.15	20.88	26.44
P/E Ratio:High	15	18	29	24	25	24	20	93	15	18
P/E Ratio:Low	7	14	22	19	19	17	12	57	10	12

Income Statement Analysis (Million $)										
Revenue	2,935	2,841	2,522	2,362	2,407	2,233	2,109	2,096	2,176	1,946
Operating Income	467	401	217	220	203	167	217	168	270	228
Depreciation	63.8	76.0	51.9	52.2	61.0	60.3	51.7	68.0	66.2	55.4
Interest Expense	33.8	46.0	20.6	21.7	23.0	24.4	28.7	35.5	40.7	27.4
Pretax Income	355	284	146	148	120	117	161	47.6	193	198
Effective Tax Rate	33.2%	32.5%	31.4%	37.2%	32.1%	32.6%	36.0%	54.8%	36.1%	35.7%
Net Income	237	189	100	92.9	81.7	78.7	103	21.5	123	127
S&P Core Earnings	193	184	123	91.6	78.3	76.6	53.9	5.49	NA	NA

Balance Sheet & Other Financial Data (Million $)										
Cash	116	93.0	63.4	170	150	96.1	18.4	6.70	6.10	17.6
Current Assets	1,141	1,187	1,113	1,073	1,193	1,132	1,051	1,139	1,186	1,206
Total Assets	2,710	2,765	2,655	2,008	2,290	2,139	1,994	1,974	2,050	2,150
Current Liabilities	548	639	682	506	674	567	552	549	538	453
Long Term Debt	530	502	506	202	203	303	304	446	473	247
Common Equity	1,187	1,280	1,076	962	1,111	1,011	830	868	844	825
Total Capital	1,834	1,873	1,671	1,239	1,390	1,348	1,168	1,339	1,342	1,099
Capital Expenditures	73.9	62.0	50.5	40.1	38.7	29.4	45.8	53.6	57.6	35.4
Cash Flow	301	265	152	145	143	139	155	89.5	189	183
Current Ratio	2.1	1.9	1.6	2.1	1.8	2.0	1.9	2.1	2.2	2.7
% Long Term Debt of Capitalization	28.9	26.8	30.3	16.3	14.6	22.5	26.0	33.3	35.3	22.4
% Net Income of Revenue	8.1	6.6	4.0	3.9	3.4	3.5	4.9	1.0	5.7	6.5
% Return on Assets	8.7	6.9	4.3	4.3	3.7	3.8	5.2	1.1	5.9	6.7
% Return on Equity	19.2	16.0	9.8	9.0	7.7	8.5	12.9	2.4	14.7	16.0

Data as orig reptd.; bef. results of disc opers/spec. items. Per share data adj. for stk. divs.; EPS diluted. E-Estimated. NA-Not Available. NM-Not Meaningful. NR-Not Ranked. UR-Under Review.

Office: 2801 80th St, Kenosha, WI 53143-5656.
Telephone: 262-656-5200.
Website: http://www.snapon.com
Chrmn, Pres & CEO: N.T. Pinchuk

Investor Contact: M.M. Ellen (262-656-6462)
SVP & CFO: M.M. Ellen
Chief Acctg Officer & Cntlr: C.R. Johnsen
Secy & General Counsel: I.M. Shur

Board Members: B. S. Chelberg, K. L. Daniel, R. Decyk, J. F. Fiedler, J. P. Holden, N. J. Jones, A. L. Kelly, W. D. Lehman, N. T. Pinchuk, E. H. Rensi, R. F. Teerlink

Founded: 1920
Domicile: Delaware
Employees: 11,500

Southern Co (The)

STANDARD &POOR'S

S&P Recommendation HOLD ★★★☆☆	**Price** $31.61 (as of Nov 27, 2009)	**12-Mo. Target Price** $33.00	**Investment Style** Large-Cap Value

GICS Sector Utilities
Sub-Industry Electric Utilities

Summary This Atlanta-based energy holding company is one of the largest producers of electricity in the U.S.

Key Stock Statistics (Source S&P, Vickers, company reports)

52-Wk Range	$37.62– 26.48	S&P Oper. EPS 2009**E**	2.32	Market Capitalization(B)	$25.295	Beta	0.34
Trailing 12-Month EPS	$2.01	S&P Oper. EPS 2010**E**	2.43	Yield (%)	5.54	S&P 3-Yr. Proj. EPS CAGR(%)	4
Trailing 12-Month P/E	15.7	P/E on S&P Oper. EPS 2009**E**	13.6	Dividend Rate/Share	$1.75	S&P Credit Rating	A
$10K Invested 5 Yrs Ago	$11,808	Common Shares Outstg. (M)	800.2	Institutional Ownership (%)	41		

Price Performance

30-Week Mov. Avg. · · · ·   10-Week Mov. Avg. - - -   **GAAP Earnings vs. Previous Year**   Volume Above Avg. ▮▮▮▮ STARS
12-Mo. Target Price —   Relative Strength —   ▲ Up ▼ Down ▶ No Change   Below Avg. ▮▮▮▮ ★

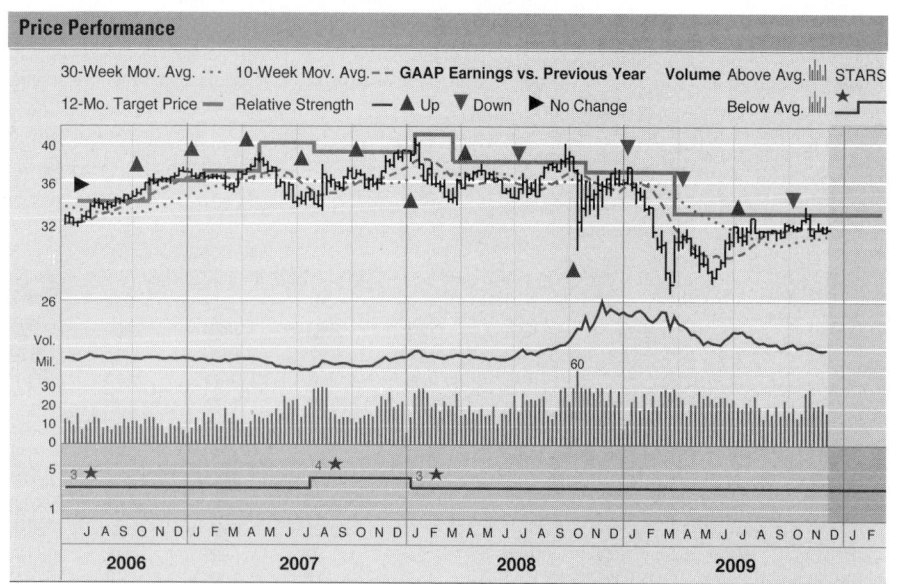

Options: ASE, CBOE, P, Ph

Analysis prepared by **Justin McCann** on November 10, 2009, when the stock traded at **$ 32.20**.

Highlights

▶ Excluding a one-time charge of $0.25, we expect operating EPS in 2009 to decline about 2% from 2008 EPS from ongoing operations of $2.37. Operating results in 2009 are expected to be restricted by the economic slowdown in SO's service territory, particularly in the industrial sector, where demand was down nearly 15% in the first nine months. Since SO's territory did not experience the housing bubble that occurred in other areas of the country, it has been less affected by the housing market decline.

▶ For 2010, we expect operating EPS to increase nearly 5% from anticipated results in 2009, as lower fuel and purchased power costs help to compensate for an expected slow economic recovery in SO's service territory. For the longer term, we expect the company to post average annual EPS growth of 4% to 6%, with the utilities returning to annual customer growth of about 1.7% and demand growth of around 2%.

▶ We expect the company to have total construction expenditures of about $16.6 billion in the 2009 through 2011 period, with $5.7 billion in 2009 (including $1.4 billion for environmental expenditures), $5.1 billion in 2011 ($737 million), and $5.8 billion in 2011 ($871 million).

Investment Rationale/Risk

▶ The stock is down nearly 13% year to date, but it has rebounded around 20% from its 2009 low and we expect further recovery over the next 12 months. We believe the decline in the housing market in SO's service territory has been milder than in other areas and that the economic downturn may be nearing a bottom. However, we think the weakness in the industrial sector may take time to recover. Given the above-peers yield from the dividend (recently 5.5%), we expect SO's shares to trade at a premium to peers, reflecting the relative predictability of the company's earnings and dividend stream.

▶ Risks to our recommendation and target price include a more severe economic downturn than expected in the company's service territory, and a significant decline in the average P/E of the electric utility group as a whole.

▶ We expect future dividends to increase at around a 4% annual rate. With the current dividend payout ratio at 71% of SO's 2008 operating EPS, such an increase would fall within the company's targeted payout range of 70% to 75%. We see the shares trading at a premium-to-peers P/E of about 13.6X our EPS estimate for 2010. Our 12-month target price is $33.

Qualitative Risk Assessment

LOW	MEDIUM	HIGH

Our risk assessment reflects our view of the company's strong and steady cash flow from its regulated electric utility operations, its solid balance sheet, and a generally supportive regulatory environment, partially offset by a slowing economy in its service territories.

Quantitative Evaluations

S&P Quality Ranking   A-

D	C	B-	B	B+	A-	A	A+

Relative Strength Rank   MODERATE

47

LOWEST = 1   HIGHEST = 99

Revenue/Earnings Data

Revenue (Million $)

	1Q	2Q	3Q	4Q	Year
2009	3,666	3,885	4,682	--	--
2008	3,683	4,215	5,426	3,802	17,127
2007	3,409	3,772	4,832	3,340	15,353
2006	3,063	3,592	4,549	3,152	14,356
2005	2,864	3,144	4,378	3,287	13,554
2004	2,732	3,009	3,441	2,720	11,902

Earnings Per Share ($)

2009	0.18	0.60	0.99	E0.30	E2.32
2008	0.47	0.55	1.01	0.24	2.26
2007	0.45	0.57	1.00	0.27	2.28
2006	0.35	0.52	0.99	0.25	2.10
2005	0.43	0.52	0.97	0.21	2.14
2004	0.45	0.47	0.87	0.27	2.06

Fiscal year ended Dec. 31. Next earnings report expected: Late January. EPS Estimates based on S&P Operating Earnings; historical GAAP earnings are as reported.

Dividend Data (Dates: mm/dd Payment Date: mm/dd/yy)

Amount ($)	Date Decl.	Ex-Div. Date	Stk. of Record	Payment Date
0.420	01/16	01/29	02/02	03/06/09
0.438	04/20	04/30	05/04	06/06/09
0.438	07/20	07/30	08/03	09/05/09
0.438	10/19	10/29	11/02	12/05/09

Dividends have been paid since 1948. Source: Company reports.

Please read the Required Disclosures and Analyst Certification on the last page of this report.

Southern Co (The)

STANDARD &POOR'S

Business Summary November 10, 2009

CORPORATE OVERVIEW. The Southern Company is one of the largest producers of electricity in the U.S. Based in Atlanta, GA, this utility holding company has approximately 42,607 megawatts of generating capacity and provides electricity to around 4.3 million customers in the Southeast through the following integrated utilities: Alabama Power, Georgia Power, Gulf Power (located in the northwestern portion of Florida), and Mississippi Power. Savannah Electric & Power was merged into Georgia Power on July 1, 2006.

MARKET PROFILE. Southern Power Company (SPC) was formed by SO in January 2001 to own, manage and finance wholesale generating assets in the Southeast. It serves both the utility units and the wholesale power market. Energy from SPC's assets, which included 7,555 megawatts of generating capacity at the end of 2008, was to be marketed to wholesale customers through the Southern Company Generation and Energy Marketing unit. SPC and the

utility units enter into contracts for power purchases, sales and exchanges among themselves, as well as with other utilities in the Southeast. Although Southern Power is not subject to state regulation, it is subject to regulation by the Federal Energy Regulatory Commission.

SO is also the parent company for SouthernLINC Wireless, which provides digital, wireless communications services to SO's four utility units, as well as to non-affiliates within the Southeast. It also provides wholesale fiber optic solutions to telecommunication providers in the Southeast.

Company Financials Fiscal Year Ended Dec. 31

Per Share Data ($)	2008	2007	2006	2005	2004	2003	2002	2001	2000	1999
Tangible Book Value	17.08	16.23	15.00	14.19	13.65	12.92	11.56	10.87	15.12	6.14
Earnings	2.26	2.28	2.10	2.14	2.06	2.02	1.85	1.61	1.52	1.86
S&P Core Earnings	1.83	2.26	2.06	2.04	1.93	1.85	1.35	1.12	NA	NA
Dividends	1.66	1.60	1.54	1.48	1.77	1.39	1.36	1.34	1.34	1.34
Payout Ratio	74%	70%	72%	69%	86%	69%	74%	83%	88%	72%
Prices:High	40.60	39.35	37.40	36.47	33.96	32.00	31.14	35.72	35.00	29.63
Prices:Low	29.82	33.16	30.48	31.14	27.44	27.00	23.22	20.89	20.38	22.06
P/E Ratio:High	18	17	18	17	16	16	17	22	23	16
P/E Ratio:Low	13	15	14	15	13	13	13	13	13	12

Income Statement Analysis (Million $)

	2008	2007	2006	2005	2004	2003	2002	2001	2000	1999
Revenue	17,127	15,353	14,356	13,554	11,902	11,251	10,549	10,155	10,066	11,585
Depreciation	1,704	1,245	1,200	1,176	955	1,027	1,047	1,173	1,171	1,307
Maintenance	NA	1,175	1,096	1,116	1,027	937	961	909	852	945
Fixed Charges Coverage	3.84	3.73	3.73	3.90	4.11	4.21	3.80	3.25	2.87	2.71
Construction Credits	152	106	50.0	51.0	47.0	25.0	22.0	NA	NA	NA
Effective Tax Rate	34.4%	31.9%	33.2%	27.2%	27.7%	29.3%	28.6%	33.3%	37.2%	33.2%
Net Income	1,742	1,734	1,574	1,591	1,532	1,474	1,318	1,119	994	1,276
S&P Core Earnings	1,412	1,720	1,551	1,532	1,436	1,351	964	776	NA	NA

Balance Sheet & Other Financial Data (Million $)

	2008	2007	2006	2005	2004	2003	2002	2001	2000	1999
Gross Property	56,152	53,094	50,167	47,580	45,585	43,722	41,764	38,104	35,972	38,620
Capital Expenditures	3,961	3,545	2,994	2,370	2,110	2,002	2,717	2,617	2,225	2,560
Net Property	37,866	35,681	33,585	31,853	30,634	29,418	26,315	23,084	21,622	24,544
Capitalization:Long Term Debt	17,898	15,223	13,247	13,442	13,010	10,587	8,956	10,941	10,457	14,443
Capitalization:% Long Term Debt	57.4	55.1	53.8	55.7	55.9	52.3	50.7	57.8	49.4	60.8
Capitalization:Preferred	Nil	Nil	Nil	Nil	Nil	Nil	Nil	Nil	Nil	Nil
Capitalization:% Preferred	Nil	Nil	Nil	Nil	Nil	Nil	Nil	Nil	Nil	Nil
Capitalization:Common	13,276	12,385	11,371	10,689	10,278	9,648	8,710	7,984	10,690	9,296
Capitalization:% Common	42.6	44.9	46.2	44.3	44.1	47.7	49.3	42.2	50.6	39.2
Total Capital	37,968	34,198	31,110	30,394	29,077	25,809	22,937	24,147	26,436	29,662
% Operating Ratio	84.9	83.8	83.0	82.5	81.2	79.7	80.5	81.9	82.0	81.7
% Earned on Net Property	9.5	9.6	9.9	9.5	9.4	10.0	10.1	10.7	11.4	8.5
% Return on Revenue	10.2	11.3	11.0	11.7	12.9	13.1	12.5	11.0	9.9	11.0
% Return on Invested Capital	7.4	8.3	8.0	8.0	7.9	8.9	8.5	7.4	7.3	9.6
% Return on Common Equity	13.6	14.6	14.3	15.2	15.4	16.1	15.8	12.0	10.0	13.4

Data as orig reptd.; bef. results of disc opers/spec. items. Per share data adj. for stk. divs.; EPS diluted. E-Estimated. NA-Not Available. NM-Not Meaningful. NR-Not Ranked. UR-Under Review.

Office: 30 Ivan Allen Jr Blvd NW, Atlanta, GA 30308-3003.
Telephone: 404-506-5000.
Email: investors@southerncompany.com
Website: http://www.southernco.com

Chrmn, Pres & CEO: D.M. Ratcliffe
COO & EVP: T.A. Fanning
EVP & CFO: W.P. Bowers
EVP, Secy & General Counsel: G.E. Holland, Jr.

Chief Acctg Officer & Cntlr: W.R. Hinson
Investor Contact: G. Kundert (404-506-5135)
Board Members: J. P. Baranco, J. A. Boscia, T. F. Chapman, H. A. Clark, III, H. W. Habermeyer, Jr., V. M. Hagen, W. A. Hood, Jr., D. M. James, G. J. Pe', J. N. Purcell, D. M. Ratcliffe, W. G. Smith, Jr.

Founded: 1945
Domicile: Delaware
Employees: 27,276

Southwestern Energy Co

STANDARD &POOR'S

| S&P Recommendation HOLD ★★★☆☆ | Price $43.86 (as of Nov 27, 2009) | 12-Mo. Target Price $51.00 | Investment Style Large-Cap Growth |

GICS Sector Energy
Sub-Industry Oil & Gas Exploration & Production

Summary Southwestern Energy is engaged in natural gas and crude oil exploration and production in the Arkoma Basin, East Texas, the Permian Basin, and onshore Gulf Coast. It also has natural gas gathering and marketing activities located in core market areas.

Key Stock Statistics (Source S&P, Vickers, company reports)

52-Wk Range	$50.61– 22.76	S&P Oper. EPS 2009**E**	1.46	Market Capitalization(B)	$15.145	Beta	0.72
Trailing 12-Month EPS	$-0.26	S&P Oper. EPS 2010**E**	1.94	Yield (%)	Nil	S&P 3-Yr. Proj. EPS CAGR(%)	44
Trailing 12-Month P/E	NM	P/E on S&P Oper. EPS 2009**E**	30.0	Dividend Rate/Share	Nil	S&P Credit Rating	BB+
$10K Invested 5 Yrs Ago	$64,738	Common Shares Outstg. (M)	345.3	Institutional Ownership (%)	87		

Price Performance

- 30-Week Mov. Avg. ··· 10-Week Mov. Avg. - - GAAP Earnings vs. Previous Year Volume Above Avg. STARS
- 12-Mo. Target Price — Relative Strength ▲ Up ▼ Down ▶ No Change Below Avg.

2-for-1

2006 2007 2008 2009

Options: ASE, CBOE, Ph

Analysis prepared by **Michael Kay** on October 20, 2009, when the stock traded at **$ 49.47**.

Highlights

▶ Production of 195 Bcfe in 2008, up 71%, reflects 600 MMcfe/day from the Fayetteville Shale, up 250%. On estimated production growth of 70% at Fayetteville, currently producing over 1 Bcfe/day, we see 47% production growth in 2009. SWN's Fayetteville properties are also showing impressive well results, with production rates up more than 75% since 2007. In addition, we believe SWN holds attractive acreage in the Marcellus and Haynesville Shales.

▶ SWN is a low-cost producer, in our view, with average finding and development costs of $1.53 per Mcfe in 2008. Lease operating expense (LOE) of $0.70 per Mcfe fell 26% in 2008, on Fayetteville operations, despite an industry rise in service costs. We see LOE down 27% in 2009.

▶ Operating EPS of $1.53 (before $0.10 gain in utility asset sales) in 2008 rose from $0.65 in 2007. We see attractive hedges on 58% of targeted 2009 production, and EPS of $1.44 (before a $1.62 impairment charge in the first three months) in 2009 and $1.87 in 2010, while peers have seen more pronounced declines. SWN's capex budget for 2009 is $1.8 billion, up from 2008, in contrast to major cutbacks by peers.

Investment Rationale/Risk

▶ SWN spent about $1.3 billion in the Fayetteville Shale in 2008, 76% of its total budget, and plans $1.5 billion (70%) in 2009, providing production and reserve growth visibility. We are positive on SWN's growth prospects at Fayetteville and its low-cost operations, and we view SWN as well positioned to boost earnings and cash flow in coming years. SWN holds significant leasehold acreage that it was able to acquire at attractive costs because of the limited attention paid to the region before 2004. We believe additional acreage in Marcellus and Haynesville should add value over the next several years.

▶ Risks to our opinion and target price include a sustained drop in oil and gas prices and further deterioration in global economic conditions resulting in lower-than-expected energy demand.

▶ We see markets discounting most probable and possible reserve estimates, and we now value companies on our proved reserve NAV estimates. We blend our proved NAV estimate of $44 with a target of 12X our 2010 EBITDA estimate, above peers on our view of impressive growth rates, to arrive at a 12-month target price of $51.

Qualitative Risk Assessment

| LOW | MEDIUM | HIGH |

Our risk assessment reflects SWN's operations in a capital-intensive industry that is competitive and cyclical and derives value from producing a commodity whose price is very volatile.

Quantitative Evaluations

S&P Quality Ranking B

| D | C | B- | B | B+ | A- | A | A+ |

Relative Strength Rank MODERATE

57

LOWEST = 1   HIGHEST = 99

Revenue/Earnings Data

Revenue (Million $)

	1Q	2Q	3Q	4Q	Year
2009	540.8	477.5	503.0	--	--
2008	524.1	604.5	683.0	500.1	2,312
2007	284.7	270.1	297.6	402.8	1,255
2006	226.7	154.0	168.4	214.0	763.1
2005	161.1	132.5	162.1	220.7	676.3
2004	119.8	96.43	111.4	149.5	477.1

Earnings Per Share ($)

	1Q	2Q	3Q	4Q	Year
2009	-1.26	0.35	0.34	E0.41	E1.46
2008	0.31	0.39	0.63	0.30	1.64
2007	0.15	0.14	0.15	0.21	0.64
2006	0.17	0.11	0.10	0.10	0.48
2005	0.11	0.09	0.13	0.15	0.48
2004	0.08	0.07	0.09	0.11	0.35

Fiscal year ended Dec. 31. Next earnings report expected: Late February. EPS Estimates based on S&P Operating Earnings; historical GAAP earnings are as reported.

Dividend Data

Cash dividends have not been paid since 2000.

Southwestern Energy Co

STANDARD &POOR'S

Business Summary October 20, 2009

CORPORATE OVERVIEW. Southwestern Energy Company (SWN) is primarily focused on the exploration and production of natural gas. SWN is engaged in natural gas and crude oil exploration and production (E&P) in the Arkoma Basin, East Texas, the Permian Basin, and the onshore Gulf Coast. SWN also has natural gas gathering and marketing activities located in core market areas. With the recent sale of its wholly owned subsidiary, Arkansas Western Gas Company (AWG), for about $230 million, SWN exited the natural gas distribution business and now operates in two segments: Exploration & Production, and Midstream Services.

As of December 31, 2008, SWN had estimated proved reserves of 2.19 Tcfe, of which 100% was natural gas and 62% was proved developed. This compares with estimated proved reserves of 1.45 Tcfe, 96% natural gas and 64% proved developed, at the end of 2007, a 51% increase. We forecast SWN's reserve life to be 11.2 years.

We estimate that SWN replaced 523% of production in 2008 (474% in 2007). As of the end of 2008, SWN's three-year average reserve replacement ratio was 483%. During 2008, SWN invested a total of $1.6 billion in the E&P business and participated in drilling 750 wells, of which 479 were successful, 11 were dry and 260 were in progress at year end. Capital spending focused primarily

on active drilling programs in the Fayetteville Shale (76%), East Texas (10%), the conventional Arkoma Basin (8%) and other (6%).

CORPORATE STRATEGY. SWN is focused on promoting long-term growth in the net asset value of its business. The key elements of SWN's E&P business strategy are to exploit and develop its existing asset base, control operations and costs, hedge production to stabilize cash flow, and achieve growth through new exploration and development activities.

SWN's primary business is natural gas and oil exploration, development and production, with operations primarily located in Arkansas, Oklahoma and Texas. These operations are conducted through its wholly owned subsidiaries, SEECO, Inc., and Southwestern Energy Production Company (SEPCO). Diamond M, also wholly owned, has interests in properties in the Permian Basin of Texas. DeSoto Drilling, Inc. (DDI), a wholly owned subsidiary of SEPCO, operates drilling rigs in the Fayetteville Shale play and in East Texas.

Company Financials Fiscal Year Ended Dec. 31

Per Share Data ($)	2008	2007	2006	2005	2004	2003	2002	2001	2000	1999
Tangible Book Value	7.30	4.82	4.25	3.32	1.54	1.19	0.86	0.91	0.71	0.95
Cash Flow	2.84	1.49	0.92	0.78	0.60	0.39	0.33	0.43	0.00	0.26
Earnings	1.64	0.64	0.48	0.48	0.35	0.19	0.07	0.17	-0.23	0.05
S&P Core Earnings	1.54	0.63	0.46	0.46	0.33	0.17	0.05	0.15	NA	NA
Dividends	Nil	Nil	Nil	Nil	Nil	Nil	Nil	Nil	0.02	0.03
Payout Ratio	Nil	Nil	Nil	Nil	Nil	Nil	Nil	Nil	NM	60%
Prices:High	52.69	28.50	22.14	20.90	6.93	3.19	1.91	2.04	1.30	1.38
Prices:Low	19.05	15.57	11.83	5.51	2.42	1.36	1.19	1.10	0.68	0.65
P/E Ratio:High	32	45	47	44	20	17	28	12	NM	27
P/E Ratio:Low	12	24	25	12	7	7	17	6	NM	13

Income Statement Analysis (Million $)

	2008	2007	2006	2005	2004	2003	2002	2001	2000	1999
Revenue	2,312	1,255	763	676	477	327	262	345	364	280
Operating Income	1,301	969	246	246	182	97.3	111	145	112	36.1
Depreciation	414	294	151	96.2	73.7	55.9	54.0	52.9	45.9	41.6
Interest Expense	28.9	37.7	12.4	21.0	19.8	19.1	21.5	24.0	23.2	17.4
Pretax Income	920	357	262	234	163	78.6	23.0	57.2	-74.7	16.4
Effective Tax Rate	38.2%	38.1%	38.0%	36.7%	36.2%	35.8%	35.6%	38.3%	NM	39.3%
Net Income	568	221	163	148	104	49.8	14.3	35.3	-45.8	9.90
S&P Core Earnings	533	217	157	143	98.6	46.6	10.3	30.8	NA	NA

Balance Sheet & Other Financial Data (Million $)

	2008	2007	2006	2005	2004	2003	2002	2001	2000	1999
Cash	196	0.73	43.0	224	1.20	1.30	1.69	3.64	2.39	1.20
Current Assets	889	363	324	461	131	100	76.1	93.2	113	70.2
Total Assets	4,760	3,623	2,379	1,869	1,146	891	740	743	705	671
Current Liabilities	793	431	379	302	134	95.1	74.6	71.5	240	56.3
Long Term Debt	674	978	136	100	325	279	342	350	225	295
Common Equity	2,508	1,647	1,434	1,110	448	342	177	183	141	190
Total Capital	3,253	103	1,953	1,477	989	780	649	668	464	612
Capital Expenditures	1,756	1,519	851	454	291	167	92.1	106	75.7	66.9
Cash Flow	982	515	314	244	177	106	68.3	88.2	0.07	56.6
Current Ratio	1.1	0.8	0.9	1.5	1.0	1.1	1.0	1.3	0.5	1.3
% Long Term Debt of Capitalization	20.7	31.5	6.9	6.7	32.9	35.7	52.8	52.4	48.5	48.1
% Net Income of Revenue	24.6	17.6	21.3	21.8	21.7	15.2	5.5	10.2	NM	3.5
% Return on Assets	13.6	7.4	7.6	9.8	10.2	6.1	1.9	4.9	NM	1.5
% Return on Equity	27.3	14.3	12.7	18.9	26.2	19.2	7.9	21.8	NM	5.2

Data as orig reptd.; bef. results of disc opers/spec. items. Per share data adj. for stk. divs.; EPS diluted. E-Estimated. NA-Not Available. NM-Not Meaningful. NR-Not Ranked. UR-Under Review.

Office: 2350 N Sam Houston Pkwy E Ste 125, Houston , TX 77032-3132.
Telephone: 281-618-4700.
Website: http://www.swn.com
Chrmn: H.M. Korell

Pres & CEO: S.L. Mueller
COO: J.L. Bolander, Jr.
EVP & CFO: G.D. Kerley
EVP, Secy & General Counsel: M.K. Boling

Investor Contact: B.D. Sylvester (281-618-4897)
Board Members: L. E. Epley, Jr., R. L. Howard, H. M. Korell, V. A. Kuuskraa, K. R. Mourton, S. L. Mueller, C. E. Scharlau
Founded: 1929
Domicile: Delaware
Employees: 1,367

Southwest Airlines Co.

STANDARD &POOR'S

| S&P Recommendation | **BUY** ★★★★☆ | Price $8.99 (as of Nov 27, 2009) | 12-Mo. Target Price $12.00 |

GICS Sector Industrials
Sub-Industry Airlines

Summary As the fifth largest U.S. airline, Southwest offers discounted fares, primarily for short-haul, point-to-point flights.

Key Stock Statistics (Source S&P, Vickers, company reports)

52-Wk Range	$10.20–4.95	S&P Oper. EPS 2009**E**	0.03	Market Capitalization(B)	$6.670	Beta	0.97
Trailing 12-Month EPS	$-0.10	S&P Oper. EPS 2010**E**	0.50	Yield (%)	0.20	S&P 3-Yr. Proj. EPS CAGR(%)	5
Trailing 12-Month P/E	NM	P/E on S&P Oper. EPS 2009**E**	NM	Dividend Rate/Share	$0.02	S&P Credit Rating	BBB
$10K Invested 5 Yrs Ago	$5,768	Common Shares Outstg. (M)	741.9	Institutional Ownership (%)	83		

Price Performance

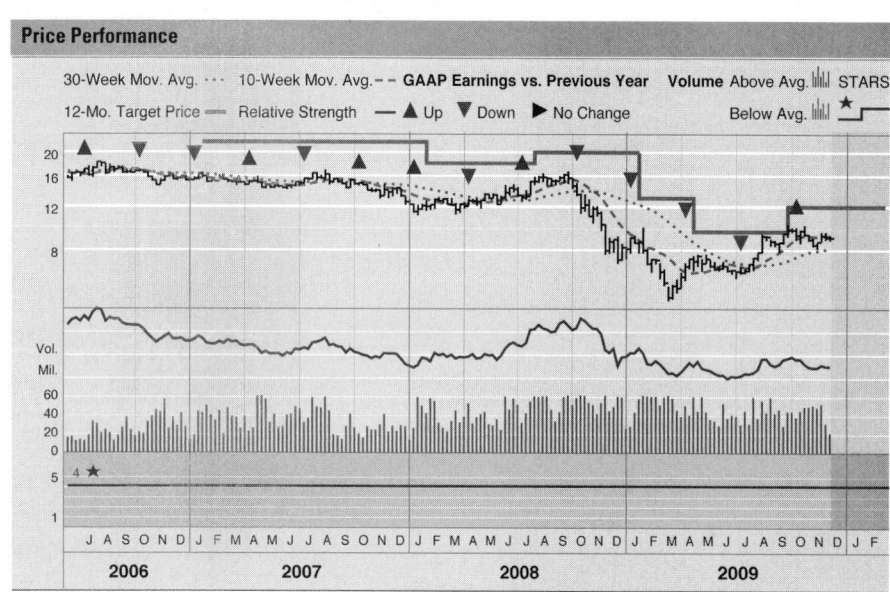

30-Week Mov. Avg. · · · 10-Week Mov. Avg. – – GAAP Earnings vs. Previous Year   Volume Above Avg. STARS
12-Mo. Target Price — Relative Strength   ▲ Up ▼ Down ▶ No Change   Below Avg. ★

Options: ASE, CBOE, P, Ph

Analysis prepared by **Jim Corridore** on October 19, 2009, when the stock traded at **$ 9.20**.

Highlights

▶ We look for 2009 revenues to fall 7%, based on our forecast of a 5% cut in capacity, a 6% drop in yields, and a one percentage point reduction in passenger load factor. For 2010, we see revenue growth of 6% on flat capacity, a two percentage point improvement in loads and 4% higher yields. We expect incremental revenues in both periods from the sale of assigned boarding slots, a more sophisticated revenue management system, and other ancillary revenue generating initiatives.

▶ We see margins impacted in 2009 by non fuel unit cost pressures driven by leveraging costs over a fewer number of available seat miles from reductions in capacity. Partly offsetting this, we expect jet fuel costs to drop about 20% in 2009. For 2010, we see margins rebounding, aided by revenue and mix improvement from LUV's recent initiative to redeploy flights to more profitable markets, coupled with our view of a modest rebound in business travel demand coupled with stronger leisure demand. We currently see jet fuel costs rising about 5% in 2010.

▶ We estimate 2009 EPS of $0.03, versus 2008 operating EPS of $0.40 ($0.24 after special items). For 2010, we see EPS of $0.50.

Investment Rationale/Risk

▶ We believe LUV is the financially strongest U.S. airline. It has posted 36 consecutive years of profitable operations, and we see the quality of those earnings as high. In addition, LUV has ample cash, and its debt to total capitalization is significantly below peer levels, by our analysis. We think these measures warrant a premium valuation to peers and the S&P 500. We believe LUV has the ability to participate in industry consolidation, should that occur, as the company has the capability to fund potential asset purchases.

▶ Risks to our recommendation and target price include a possible price war with one or more competitors, and further weakening of air travel demand. We are concerned about LUV's corporate governance relating to its use of affiliated outsiders on its board of directors' nominating and compensation committees.

▶ Our 12-month target price of $12 values the shares at an enterprise value-to-EBITDAR (EBITDA plus aircraft rent) multiple of 8.5X our 2010 EBITDAR estimate, a premium to peers. We expect the shares to be volatile due to difficult industry conditions and fluctuating oil prices, but less so than peers.

Qualitative Risk Assessment

| LOW | MEDIUM | HIGH |

Even though Southwest participates in the highly volatile airline industry, we think its conservative balance sheet, with low debt to total capitalization, and its track record of more than 35 consecutive years of profitability mitigate this risk.

Quantitative Evaluations

S&P Quality Ranking   **B**

| D | C | B- | B | B+ | A- | A | A+ |

Relative Strength Rank   **MODERATE**

59

LOWEST = 1   HIGHEST = 99

Revenue/Earnings Data

Revenue (Million $)

	1Q	2Q	3Q	4Q	Year
2009	2,357	2,616	2,666	--	--
2008	2,530	2,869	2,891	2,734	11,023
2007	2,198	2,583	2,588	2,492	9,861
2006	2,019	2,449	2,342	2,276	9,086
2005	1,663	1,944	1,989	1,987	7,584
2004	1,484	1,716	1,674	1,633	6,530

Earnings Per Share ($)

	1Q	2Q	3Q	4Q	Year
2009	-0.12	0.07	-0.02	E0.05	E0.03
2008	0.05	0.44	-0.16	-0.08	0.24
2007	0.12	0.36	0.22	0.15	0.84
2006	0.07	0.40	0.06	0.07	0.61
2005	0.09	0.20	0.28	0.10	0.67
2004	0.03	0.14	0.15	0.07	0.38

Fiscal year ended Dec. 31. Next earnings report expected: Mid December. EPS Estimates based on S&P Operating Earnings; historical GAAP earnings are as reported.

Dividend Data (Dates: mm/dd Payment Date: mm/dd/yy)

Amount ($)	Date Decl.	Ex-Div. Date	Stk. of Record	Payment Date
0.005	01/15	02/24	02/26	03/19/09
0.005	05/20	06/08	06/10	06/24/09
0.005	07/23	09/01	09/03	09/24/09
0.005	11/19	12/08	12/10	01/07/10

Dividends have been paid since 1976. Source: Company reports.

Please read the Required Disclosures and Analyst Certification on the last page of this report.

The McGraw-Hill Companies

Southwest Airlines Co.

STANDARD &POOR'S

Business Summary October 19, 2009

CORPORATE OVERVIEW. Southwest Airlines was the largest provider of scheduled domestic passenger air travel in the U.S. in 2008. Overall, the airline ranks as the fifth largest in U.S., based on total revenue passenger miles (RPMs). At December 31, 2008, it served 64 cities in 32 states. LUV specializes in low-fare, point-to-point, short-haul, high-frequency service. Although 80% of its work force belongs to unions, the company believes that it has generally enjoyed harmonious labor relations. LUV began service to Washington D.C. (Dulles) in October 2006, started Minneapolis-St. Paul in March 2009 and has received approval to acquire 14 take-off and landing slots at LaGuardia airport in New York from ATA Airlines.

MARKET PROFILE. The U.S. airline industry is a $173 billion market, according to 2007 data (latest available) from the U.S. Department of Transportation. With 2007 revenues of $9.9 billion (which grew 12%, to $11.0 billion, in 2008), LUV comprised around 5.7% of total industry revenues. Southwest also has an approximate 9.3% market share when measured by RPMs, as of September 2008. Southwest was profitable in 2008 for the 36th consecutive year and was profitable throughout the industry downturn that took place after 9/11/01, with net income totaling $2.1 billion in 2001-2005. Over the same period, S&P be-

lieves the 10 largest U.S. airlines lost about $58.6 billion.

COMPETITIVE LANDSCAPE. The industry consists of about 43 mainline commercial passenger airlines, of which about 11 are considered major airlines, defined as airlines with annual revenues in excess of $1.0 billion. Major competitors include AMR Corp.'s American Airlines (16.8% market share, as measured by RPMs, as of September 2008), UAL Corp.'s United Airlines (14.2%), Delta Air Lines (13.4%), Northwest Airlines (9.2%), Continental (10.7%), US Airways (7.8%) and JetBlue Airways (3.4%). Delta merged in 2008 with Northwest, and now has about a 22.6% combined market share. The U.S. airline industry is fragmented, and highly competitive. Barriers to entry are high, and there are highly entrenched competitors. Pricing is extremely competitive. Fuel costs, the second largest cost category for Southwest, have risen sharply over the past three years, although Southwest is partly protected by a fuel hedging position that we think is by far the best in the industry.

Company Financials Fiscal Year Ended Dec. 31

Per Share Data ($)	2008	2007	2006	2005	2004	2003	2002	2001	2000	1999
Tangible Book Value	6.69	10.49	8.23	8.38	7.04	6.40	5.69	5.23	4.57	3.79
Cash Flow	1.05	1.56	1.23	1.25	0.91	1.00	0.74	1.03	1.14	0.90
Earnings	0.24	0.84	0.61	0.67	0.38	0.54	0.30	0.63	0.79	0.59
S&P Core Earnings	0.23	0.83	0.60	0.62	0.30	0.48	0.23	0.61	NA	NA
Dividends	0.02	0.02	0.02	0.02	0.02	0.02	0.02	0.01	0.01	0.01
Payout Ratio	8%	2%	3%	3%	5%	3%	6%	2%	1%	2%
Prices:High	16.77	16.96	18.20	16.95	17.06	19.69	22.00	23.32	23.32	15.72
Prices:Low	7.05	12.12	14.61	13.05	12.88	11.72	10.90	11.25	10.00	9.58
P/E Ratio:High	70	20	30	25	45	36	73	37	30	26
P/E Ratio:Low	29	14	24	19	34	22	36	18	13	16
Income Statement Analysis (Million $)										
Revenue	11,023	9,861	9,086	7,584	6,530	5,937	5,522	5,555	5,650	4,736
Operating Income	1,058	1,371	1,449	1,289	985	867	774	949	1,302	1,030
Depreciation	599	555	515	469	431	384	356	318	281	249
Interest Expense	130	119	77.0	83.0	49.0	58.0	89.3	49.3	42.3	22.9
Pretax Income	278	1,058	790	874	489	708	393	828	1,017	774
Effective Tax Rate	36.0%	39.0%	36.8%	37.3%	36.0%	37.6%	38.6%	38.2%	38.5%	38.7%
Net Income	178	645	499	548	313	442	241	511	625	474
S&P Core Earnings	169	635	489	504	236	385	188	486	NA	NA
Balance Sheet & Other Financial Data (Million $)										
Cash	1,803	2,779	1,390	2,280	1,305	1,865	1,815	2,280	523	419
Current Assets	2,893	4,443	2,601	3,620	2,172	2,313	2,232	2,520	832	631
Total Assets	14,308	16,772	13,460	14,218	11,337	9,878	8,954	8,997	6,670	5,652
Current Liabilities	2,806	4,838	2,887	3,848	2,142	172	1,434	2,239	1,298	960
Long Term Debt	3,498	2,050	1,567	1,394	1,700	1,332	1,553	1,327	761	872
Common Equity	4,953	6,941	6,449	6,675	5,524	5,052	4,422	4,014	3,451	2,836
Total Capital	10,355	11,526	10,120	9,965	8,834	7,804	7,202	6,399	5,065	4,400
Capital Expenditures	923	1,331	1,399	1,210	1,775	1,238	603	998	1,135	1,168
Cash Flow	777	1,200	1,014	1,017	744	826	597	829	906	723
Current Ratio	1.0	0.9	0.9	0.9	1.0	13.4	1.6	1.1	0.6	0.7
% Long Term Debt of Capitalization	33.8	17.8	15.5	14.0	19.2	17.1	21.6	20.7	15.0	19.8
% Net Income of Revenue	1.6	6.5	5.5	7.2	4.8	7.4	4.4	9.2	11.1	10.0
% Return on Assets	1.2	4.3	3.6	4.3	3.0	4.7	2.7	6.5	10.1	9.2
% Return on Equity	3.0	9.6	7.6	9.0	5.9	9.3	5.7	13.7	19.9	18.1

Data as orig reptd.; bef. results of disc opers/spec. items. Per share data adj. for stk. divs.; EPS diluted. E-Estimated. NA-Not Available. NM-Not Meaningful. NR-Not Ranked. UR-Under Review.

Office: P.O. Box 36611, Dallas, TX 75235-1611.
Telephone: 214-792-4000.
Website: http://www.southwest.com
Chrmn, Pres & CEO: G.C. Kelly

COO & EVP: M.G. Van De Ven
EVP & Secy: R. Ricks
SVP, CFO & Chief Acctg Officer: L.H. Wright
Chief Admin Officer: J. Lamb

Investor Contact: L. Wright (214-792-4415)
Board Members: D. W. Biegler, C. W. Crockett, W. H. Cunningham, J. G. Denison, T. C. Johnson, G. C. Kelly, N. B. Loeffler, J. Montford, D. D. Villanueva

Founded: 1967
Domicile: Texas
Employees: 35,499

The McGraw·Hill Companies

Spectra Energy Corp

STANDARD &POOR'S

S&P Recommendation HOLD ★★★☆☆	Price $19.31 (as of Nov 27, 2009)	12-Mo. Target Price $22.00	Investment Style Large-Cap Blend

GICS Sector Energy
Sub-Industry Oil & Gas Storage & Transportation

Summary This integrated natural gas holding company is engaged in gas gathering and processing and gas transportation and storage in the U.S. and Canada, and retail gas distribution to 1.3 million customers in Ontario, Canada.

Key Stock Statistics (Source S&P, Vickers, company reports)

52-Wk Range	$20.55–11.21	S&P Oper. EPS 2009**E**	1.31	Market Capitalization(B)	$12.489	Beta	0.92
Trailing 12-Month EPS	$1.26	S&P Oper. EPS 2010**E**	1.32	Yield (%)	5.18	S&P 3-Yr. Proj. EPS CAGR(%)	-4
Trailing 12-Month P/E	15.3	P/E on S&P Oper. EPS 2009**E**	14.7	Dividend Rate/Share	$1.00	S&P Credit Rating	NA
$10K Invested 5 Yrs Ago	NA	Common Shares Outstg. (M)	646.8	Institutional Ownership (%)	64		

Price Performance

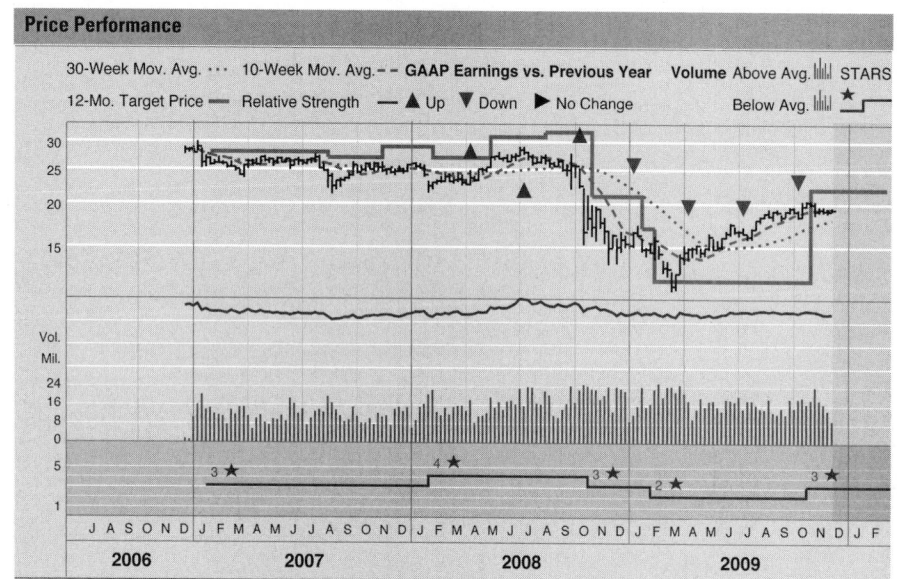

- 30-Week Mov. Avg. · · · 10-Week Mov. Avg. - - **GAAP Earnings vs. Previous Year**   Volume Above Avg. STARS
- 12-Mo. Target Price — Relative Strength ▲ Up ▼ Down ▶ No Change   Below Avg.

Options: ASE, CBOE, Ph

Analysis prepared by **Tanjila Shafi** on October 21, 2009, when the stock traded at **$ 20.30**.

Highlights

▶ We expect revenues in 2009 to decline due to lower volume, reflecting recessionary headwinds. We believe that earnings will be limited by lower commodity prices and weaker foreign exchange.

▶ The company allocated approximately $1.8 billion for expansion capital expenditures during 2008. We believe it will incur $600 million in capital expenditures in 2009. By the end of 2009, 10 expansion projects are expected to be placed into service, including the South Peace Pipeline, Sarnia Storage, Heritage Storage, and Egan Storage Cavern 3. We expect the new projects to add $35 million to EBIT in 2009 and $45 million in 2010.

▶ SE declared a cash distribution of $0.25 per unit for the third-quarter of 2009, unchanged from the 2008 third quarter and the 2009 second quarter. For the full year, we see distributions of $1.00.

Investment Rationale/Risk

▶ We recently upgraded our recommendation on the shares to hold, from sell, reflecting our expectations for improving fundamentals for the company. We believe that the company's fee-based businesses and expansion projects will improve earnings growth in 2010. However, we see volumes moderating in 2009 due to the recessionary environment. SE was formed on January 2, 2007, after Duke Energy spun off its natural gas businesses. SE operates a large and diverse portfolio of natural gas transportation and storage assets in the U.S. and Canada. In July 2007, SE spun off some assets into Spectra Energy Partners L.P. (SEP 26, NR) and received $345 million.

▶ Risks to our opinion and target price include slower natural gas production growth, lower natural gas prices, and a less favorable credit environment.

▶ Our 12-month target price of $22 is based on our revised 9.3X multiple of enterprise value to our 2009 EBITDA estimate, in line with peers.

Qualitative Risk Assessment

LOW	MEDIUM	HIGH

Our risk assessment reflects the company's large market capitalization and the lower risk inherent in its regulated gas transmission and distribution businesses, offset by its investments in higher-risk gas gathering and processing businesses.

Quantitative Evaluations

S&P Quality Ranking NR

D	C	B-	B	B+	A-	A	A+

Relative Strength Rank MODERATE

55

LOWEST = 1   HIGHEST = 99

Revenue/Earnings Data

Revenue (Million $)

	1Q	2Q	3Q	4Q	Year
2009	1,384	937.0	933.0	--	--
2008	1,608	1,141	1,080	1,261	5,074
2007	1,401	985.0	959.0	1,397	4,742
2006	NA	NA	NA	--	4,532
2005	--	--	--	--	4,132
2004	--	--	--	--	13,255

Earnings Per Share ($)

2009	0.47	0.22	0.29	E0.32	E1.31
2008	0.58	0.47	0.49	0.27	1.81
2007	0.37	0.29	0.38	0.45	1.49
2006	NA	NA	NA	--	NA
2005	--	--	--	--	1.07
2004	--	--	--	--	--

Fiscal year ended Dec. 31. Next earnings report expected: Early February. EPS Estimates based on S&P Operating Earnings; historical GAAP earnings are as reported.

Dividend Data (Dates: mm/dd Payment Date: mm/dd/yy)

Amount ($)	Date Decl.	Ex-Div. Date	Stk. of Record	Payment Date
0.250	01/05	02/11	02/13	03/16/09
0.250	04/03	05/13	05/15	06/15/09
0.250	06/23	08/12	08/14	09/14/09
0.250	10/20	11/10	11/13	12/14/09

Dividends have been paid since 2007. Source: Company reports.

Please read the Required Disclosures and Analyst Certification on the last page of this report.

The McGraw-Hill Companies

**STANDARD
&POOR'S**

Spectra Energy Corp

Business Summary October 21, 2009

CORPORATE OVERVIEW. SE owns and operates a diversified portfolio of natural gas-related energy assets and is primarily a natural gas midstream company. The company operates in three areas of the natural gas industry: transmission and storage, distribution, and gathering and processing. SE also owns a natural gas distribution company, Union Gas, and participates in a 50%-owned joint venture, DCP Midstream.

MARKET PROFILE. The company manages its business in four segments: U.S. Transmission, Distribution, Western Canada Transmission and Processing, and Field Services.

The U.S. Transmission segment provides transportation and storage of natural gas for customers in the eastern and southeastern U.S. and the Maritime provinces of Canada. The segment has 13,800 miles of natural gas pipelines and 265 billion cubic feet (bcf) of storage capacity. The company's largest pipeline, Texas Eastern Transmission, is 8,700 miles, has a capacity of 6.7 billion cubic feet per day (bcf/d), and has 75.1 bcf of storage capacity. The pipeline connects Gulf Coast gas supply to demand centers in the Northeast, as well as to the East Tennessee Natural Gas and Algonquin Gas Transmission pipelines. The Algonquin pipeline can transport 2.2 bcf/d and connects to

both the Texas Eastern and Maritimes and Northeast pipelines to provide gas to areas between Boston, MA, and northern New Jersey. The East Tennessee pipeline brings gas from the Texas Eastern pipeline through eastern Tennessee as far as Roanoke, VA. The 46%-owned Gulfstream pipeline brings natural gas into the fast growing state of Florida. The Maritimes and Northeast pipeline provides Sable Island area Canadian natural gas down into the Boston area and helps to supply the Algonquin pipeline. The segment also operates other pipeline interconnection assets and storage assets.

The Distribution segment provides retail natural gas distribution in Ontario, Canada, as well as natural gas transportation and storage services to other utilities and energy market participants in Ontario, Quebec and the U.S. Union Gas is the company's regulated transmission and distribution subsidiary, serving 1.3 million customers in communities throughout Ontario. Union Gas distributes its gas through 37,000 miles of distribution pipelines and owns 3,000 miles of transmission pipelines and 155 bcf of high deliverability storage.

Company Financials Fiscal Year Ended Dec. 31

Per Share Data ($)	2008	2007	2006	2005	2004	2003	2002	2001	2000	1999
Tangible Book Value	3.53	4.60	NM	NA	NA	NA	NA	NA	NA	NA
Cash Flow	2.72	2.31	NA	2.04	NA	NA	NA	NA	NA	NA
Earnings	1.81	1.49	NA	1.07	NA	NA	NA	NA	NA	NA
S&P Core Earnings	1.71	1.46	NA	NA	NA	NA	NA	NA	NA	NA
Dividends	0.96	0.88	Nil	Nil	NA	NA	NA	NA	NA	NA
Payout Ratio	53%	59%	Nil	Nil	NA	NA	NA	NA	NA	NA
Prices:High	29.18	30.00	29.00	NA	NA	NA	NA	NA	NA	NA
Prices:Low	13.36	21.24	27.50	NA	NA	NA	NA	NA	NA	NA
P/E Ratio:High	16	20	NA	NA	NA	NA	NA	NA	NA	NA
P/E Ratio:Low	7	14	NA	NA	NA	NA	NA	NA	NA	NA
Income Statement Analysis (Million $)										
Revenue	5,074	4,742	4,532	4,132	13,255	10,784	NA	NA	NA	NA
Operating Income	2,061	1,967	1,804	1,697	NA	NA	NA	NA	NA	NA
Depreciation	569	525	606	458	NA	NA	NA	NA	NA	NA
Interest Expense	636	651	605	607	744	806	NA	NA	NA	NA
Pretax Income	1,688	1,458	1,376	862	1,156	719	NA	NA	NA	NA
Effective Tax Rate	29.4%	30.4%	28.7%	41.7%	123.8%	29.2%	NA	NA	NA	NA
Net Income	1,129	944	936	502	-489	404	NA	NA	NA	NA
S&P Core Earnings	1,060	928	926	NA	NA	NA	NA	NA	NA	NA
Balance Sheet & Other Financial Data (Million $)										
Cash	214	94.0	299	NA	NA	NA	NA	NA	NA	NA
Current Assets	1,450	1,379	1,625	18,601	NA	NA	NA	NA	NA	NA
Total Assets	21,924	22,970	20,345	21,442	NA	NA	NA	NA	NA	NA
Current Liabilities	3,044	2,422	2,358	2,052	NA	NA	NA	NA	NA	NA
Long Term Debt	8,290	8,345	7,726	7,957	NA	NA	NA	NA	NA	NA
Common Equity	5,540	6,857	5,639	5,225	NA	NA	NA	NA	NA	NA
Total Capital	15,346	16,008	16,910	16,100	NA	NA	NA	NA	NA	NA
Capital Expenditures	2,030	1,202	987	NA	NA	NA	NA	NA	NA	NA
Cash Flow	1,698	1,469	1,542	960	NA	NA	NA	NA	NA	NA
Current Ratio	0.5	0.6	0.7	NA	NA	NA	NA	NA	NA	NA
% Long Term Debt of Capitalization	54.0	52.1	45.7	Nil	Nil	Nil	NA	NA	NA	NA
% Net Income of Revenue	22.3	19.9	20.7	12.2	NM	3.8	NA	NA	NA	NA
% Return on Assets	5.0	4.4	3.4	NA	NA	NA	NA	NA	NA	NA
% Return on Equity	18.2	15.1	10.9	NA	NA	NA	NA	NA	NA	NA

Data as orig reptd.; bef. results of disc opers/spec. items. Per share data adj. for stk. divs.; EPS diluted. E-Estimated. NA-Not Available. NM-Not Meaningful. NR-Not Ranked. UR-Under Review.

Office: 5400 Westheimer Court, Houston, TX 77056-5310.
Telephone: 713-627-5400 .
Website: http://www.spectraenergy.com
Chrmn: W.T. Esrey

Pres & CEO: G.L. Ebel
COO: A.N. Harris
CFO: J.P. Reddy
Chief Admin Officer: D.M. Ables

Investor Contact: J. Arensdorf (713-627-4600)
Board Members: A. A. Adams, P. M. Anderson, P. L. Carter, F. A. Comper, G. L. Ebel, W. T. Esrey, P. B. Hamilton, D. R. Hendrix, M. McShane, M. E. Phelps

Founded: 2006
Domicile: Delaware
Employees: 5,200

The McGraw·Hill Companies

Sprint Nextel Corp

STANDARD &POOR'S

S&P Recommendation	BUY ★★★★☆	Price $3.75 (as of Nov 27, 2009)	12-Mo. Target Price $6.00	Investment Style Large-Cap Value

GICS Sector Telecommunication Services
Sub-Industry Wireless Telecommunication Services

Summary This leading provider of wireless and other telecommunications services was formed in August 2005 through the merger of Sprint Corp. and Nextel Communications, Inc.

Key Stock Statistics (Source S&P, Vickers, company reports)

52-Wk Range	$5.94– 1.57	S&P Oper. EPS 2009**E**	-0.18	Market Capitalization(B)	$10.789	Beta	1.11
Trailing 12-Month EPS	$-1.07	S&P Oper. EPS 2010**E**	-0.20	Yield (%)	Nil	S&P 3-Yr. Proj. EPS CAGR(%)	6
Trailing 12-Month P/E	NM	P/E on S&P Oper. EPS 2009**E**	NM	Dividend Rate/Share	Nil	S&P Credit Rating	BB
$10K Invested 5 Yrs Ago	NA	Common Shares Outstg. (M)	2,877.1	Institutional Ownership (%)	90		

Price Performance

30-Week Mov. Avg. · · · 10-Week Mov. Avg. - - **GAAP Earnings vs. Previous Year** Volume Above Avg. STARS
12-Mo. Target Price — Relative Strength — ▲ Up ▼ Down ▶ No Change Below Avg. ★

Options: ASE, CBOE, P, Ph

Analysis prepared by **James Moorman, CFA** on November 02, 2009, when the stock traded at **$ 2.98.**

Highlights

► Following 11% lower revenues in 2008, we expect declines of 9.1% for 2009 and 1.9% for 2010, as S continues to work on maintaining its subscriber base in its wireless business (83% of projected revenues), while attracting new subscribers. We believe the company is beginning to make progress in improving its network quality and customer satisfaction, but it is still losing subscribers at a high rate. Within global markets, we see revenues declining roughly 10% in 2009 due to competitive pressures.

► We estimate total EBITDA margins of 20.2% in 2009 and 18.9% in 2010, versus 21.5% in 2008, as we believe cost-cutting measures will begin to show benefits later in 2009, and we think this should be offset by handset subsidies and pre-paid becoming a larger part of the subscriber base. We believe margins will be supported somewhat by cost reductions in the global markets segment. The proposed acquisition of Virgin Mobile is not included in our estimates.

► We estimate operating losses per share of $0.18 in 2009 and $0.20 per share in 2010, following operating EPS of $0.10 in 2008.

Investment Rationale/Risk

► In our opinion, the company is in a transition, trying to regain favor with customers as competitors take market share. We believe cost-cutting measures are bearing fruit, but S also plans to introduce several new handsets that could drive up the cost of acquiring new customers. We believe that the new handsets, such as the Pre, will have an impact and, combined with attractive price plans such as Boost Unlimited, could begin to turn the tide in subscriber losses. While we think S has a long way to go in turning its operations around, we believe the shares are nonetheless attractive at recent levels.

► Risks to our recommendation and target price include higher capital spending to deploy new services, liquidity issues relating to declining cash flow, and increased competition from nationwide peers that could lead to delayed growth in subscriber additions.

► Our 12-month target price of $6 assumes an enterprise value of 5.5X our 2010 EBITDA estimate, slightly below larger-cap telecom peers, to reflect S's subscriber losses, and below smaller pure-play wireless carriers that we think have stronger growth prospects.

Qualitative Risk Assessment

LOW	MEDIUM	HIGH

As we think S is one of the weakest national wireless carriers, its free cash flow could continue to be pressured in the near term, in our view. We believe this risk is partly offset by our view of the company's strong balance sheet and operating expense reductions.

Quantitative Evaluations

S&P Quality Ranking B

D	C	B-	**B**	B+	A-	A	A+

Relative Strength Rank STRONG

73

LOWEST = 1   HIGHEST = 99

Revenue/Earnings Data

Revenue (Million $)

	1Q	2Q	3Q	4Q	Year
2009	8,209	8,141	8,042	--	--
2008	9,334	9,055	8,816	8,430	35,635
2007	10,092	10,163	10,044	9,847	40,146
2006	11,548	10,014	10,496	10,444	41,028
2005	6,936	7,113	9,335	11,296	34,680
2004	6,707	6,869	6,922	6,930	27,428

Earnings Per Share ($)

2009	-0.21	-0.13	-0.17	E-0.10	E-0.18
2008	-0.18	-0.12	-0.11	-0.57	-0.98
2007	-0.07	0.01	0.02	-10.36	-10.31
2006	0.14	0.10	0.08	0.09	0.34
2005	0.32	0.40	0.23	0.07	0.87
2004	0.16	0.16	-1.32	0.29	-0.71

Fiscal year ended Dec. 31. Next earnings report expected: Mid February. EPS Estimates based on S&P Operating Earnings; historical GAAP earnings are as reported.

Dividend Data

No Dividend Data Available

Please read the Required Disclosures and Analyst Certification on the last page of this report.

Sprint Nextel Corp

Business Summary November 02, 2009

CORPORATE OVERVIEW. Sprint Nextel, a leading provider of wireless and other telecommunications services was formed in August 2005 through the merger of Sprint Corp. and Nextel Communications, Inc. The company has a balanced mix of consumer, business and government wireless customers. S spun off to shareholders the local telephone business in May 2006. As of the end of the third quarter of 2009, S provided service to roughly 48.3 million wireless subscribers, with 70% of them direct post-paid customers, while 12% were prepaid (Boost Mobile), and 18% were wholesale customers (from Virgin Mobile and others). S also generates revenues from wireline voice and data communication services and services to the cable multiple systems operators that use S's network and back-office capabilities.

COMPETITIVE LANDSCAPE. In most major U.S. metropolitan markets, four national carriers offer competing wireless services to customers along with some regional carriers. Wireless carriers such as S have adjusted to potential substitutes by integrating the service features into the handsets. Until recently, S had a unique service with push-to-talk service through Nextel's iDEN network, but AT&T (formerly Cingular) has launched a competing nationwide service aimed at the consumer segment, in contrast to S's dominant position with small business and enterprise firms.

Wireless services are very price elastic. For the consumer market, service rate plans have taken on new features such as $9.99 for each family member added to the account. S realized 2.17% post-paid churn in the third quarter of 2009, above that of its larger peers, but generated $56 in average revenue per user (ARPU). Pre-paid customers had a 6.7% churn rate and generated $35 in ARPU. The company has simplified its pricing with plans that include a $100 plan with unlimited voice, data, text and others, as well as a $90 plan for unlimited voice and texting. We believe this translates to roughly $80 for unlimited voice and compares to recent offers by the other three major wireless companies of $100 for unlimited voice alone. In our view, this is a good move that will help change S's image, but we do not expect the plans to drive big changes in customer growth. S also launched a $50 unlimited prepaid plan under its Boost Mobile brand on its iDEN network during the first quarter that we believe was very successful and led to the large prepaid gain in the quarter.

Company Financials Fiscal Year Ended Dec. 31

Per Share Data ($)	2008	2007	2006	2005	2004	2003	2002	2001	2000	1999
Tangible Book Value	NM	NM	NM	0.88	3.85	14.40	11.45	11.41	13.95	10.42
Cash Flow	1.96	-7.17	3.67	3.93	2.56	3.12	4.14	2.60	4.00	-4.35
Earnings	-0.98	-10.31	0.34	0.87	-0.71	0.33	1.18	-0.16	1.45	1.97
S&P Core Earnings	-0.66	-0.05	0.30	0.86	-0.72	1.20	1.26	-0.12	NA	NA
Dividends	Nil	0.10	0.13	0.30	0.50	0.50	0.50	0.50	0.50	0.50
Payout Ratio	Nil	NM	37%	34%	NM	152%	42%	NM	34%	25%
Prices:High	13.16	23.42	26.89	27.20	25.80	16.76	20.47	29.31	67.81	75.94
Prices:Low	1.35	12.96	15.92	21.57	15.74	10.22	6.65	18.50	19.63	36.88
P/E Ratio:High	NM	NM	79	31	NM	51	17	NM	47	39
P/E Ratio:Low	NM	NM	47	25	NM	31	6	NM	14	19

Income Statement Analysis (Million $)										
Revenue	35,635	40,146	41,028	34,680	27,428	14,185	15,182	16,924	17,688	17,016
Operating Income	7,664	10,282	12,283	10,220	8,148	4,376	4,488	4,238	5,101	-5,059
Depreciation	8,396	9,023	9,592	6,269	4,720	2,519	2,645	2,449	2,267	2,129
Interest Expense	1,362	1,433	1,533	1,351	1,248	236	295	57.0	76.0	182
Pretax Income	-4,060	-29,945	1,817	2,906	-1,603	434	1,453	-129	2,170	-2,797
Effective Tax Rate	NM	NM	26.9%	38.0%	NM	32.3%	28.0%	NM	40.5%	37.9%
Net Income	-2,796	-29,580	1,329	1,801	-1,012	294	1,046	-146	1,292	-1,736
S&P Core Earnings	-1,864	-155	849	1,772	-1,036	1,096	1,132	-112	NA	NA

Balance Sheet & Other Financial Data (Million $)										
Cash	3,719	2,440	2,061	10,665	4,556	1,635	641	134	122	104
Current Assets	8,344	8,661	10,304	19,092	9,975	4,378	3,327	3,485	4,512	4,282
Total Assets	58,252	64,109	97,161	102,580	41,321	21,862	23,043	24,164	23,649	21,803
Current Liabilities	6,281	9,104	9,798	14,050	6,902	2,359	4,320	6,298	5,004	4,301
Long Term Debt	20,992	20,469	21,011	Nil	15,916	2,627	2,736	3,258	3,482	4,531
Common Equity	19,605	21,999	53,131	51,937	13,521	13,372	11,814	11,704	12,343	10,514
Total Capital	47,793	51,157	84,237	52,184	29,684	17,632	16,385	16,514	17,101	15,980
Capital Expenditures	3,882	6,322	7,556	5,057	3,980	1,674	2,181	5,295	4,105	3,534
Cash Flow	5,600	-20,557	10,919	8,063	3,701	2,821	3,698	2,310	3,566	-3,858
Current Ratio	1.3	1.0	1.1	1.4	1.4	1.9	0.8	0.6	0.9	1.0
% Long Term Debt of Capitalization	43.9	40.0	24.9	Nil	53.6	14.9	16.7	19.7	20.4	28.4
% Net Income of Revenue	NM	NM	3.2	5.2	NM	2.1	6.9	NM	7.3	10.2
% Return on Assets	NM	NM	1.3	2.5	NM	1.3	4.4	NM	5.7	8.5
% Return on Equity	NM	NM	2.5	5.5	NM	2.3	8.8	NM	11.2	17.7

Data as orig reptd.; bef. results of disc opers/spec. items. Per share data adj. for stk. divs.; EPS diluted. E-Estimated. NA-Not Available. NM-Not Meaningful. NR-Not Ranked. UR-Under Review.

Office: 6200 Sprint Pkwy, Overland Park, KS 66251-6117.
Telephone: 800-829-0965.
Email: investorrelation.sprintcom@mail.sprint.com
Website: http://www.sprint.com

Chrmn: J.H. Hance, Jr.
Chrmn: P.H. Henson
Pres & CEO: D.R. Hesse
SVP & Treas: R.S. Lindahl

CFO: R.H. Brust
Board Members: R. R. Bennett, G. Bethune, L. C. Glasscock, J. H. Hance, Jr., D. R. Hesse, V. J. Hill, F. Ianna, S. Nilsson, W. Nuti, R. O'Neal

Founded: 1925
Domicile: Kansas
Employees: 56,000

Stanley Works (The)

STANDARD &POOR'S

| S&P Recommendation **HOLD** ★★★☆☆ | Price $48.73 (as of Nov 27, 2009) | 12-Mo. Target Price $51.00 | Investment Style Large-Cap Blend |

GICS Sector Industrials
Sub-Industry Industrial Machinery

Summary This worldwide producer of tools, hardware and specialty hardware for home improvement, consumer, industrial and professional use has agreed to acquire Black & Decker for stock.

Key Stock Statistics (Source S&P, Vickers, company reports)

52-Wk Range	$51.20– 22.61	S&P Oper. EPS 2009E	2.52	Market Capitalization(B)	$3.919	Beta	1.28
Trailing 12-Month EPS	$2.17	S&P Oper. EPS 2010E	2.88	Yield (%)	2.71	S&P 3-Yr. Proj. EPS CAGR(%)	12
Trailing 12-Month P/E	22.5	P/E on S&P Oper. EPS 2009E	19.3	Dividend Rate/Share	$1.32	S&P Credit Rating	A
$10K Invested 5 Yrs Ago	$11,831	Common Shares Outstg. (M)	80.4	Institutional Ownership (%)	76		

Price Performance

30-Week Mov. Avg. ···   10-Week Mov. Avg. ‑‑   GAAP Earnings vs. Previous Year   Volume Above Avg. STARS
12-Mo. Target Price   Relative Strength   ▲ Up ▼ Down ► No Change   Below Avg. ★

Options: P

Analysis prepared by **Mathew Christy, CFA** on November 11, 2009, when the stock traded at **$ 50.30**.

Highlights

▶ We project that total sales will decline nearly 16% in 2009, following flat sales in 2008 and a 12% increase in 2007 that stemmed from volume growth, price increases and acquisitions. Our 2009 forecast is based on a 23% decrease in sales at the Consumer Products segment, a 33% decline in Industrial Tools segment sales, and a slight increase at the Security Solutions segment. For 2010, we project low single digit sales growth.

▶ Our sales outlook takes into account very weak European and North American economies along with slackening to flat sales growth in Asia and other emerging markets seen in 2009. On lower sales volumes, we expect SWK to experience reduced operating leverage, and we look for operating margins to narrow to 9.5% in 2009, from 10.4% in 2008. In 2010, we project overall higher operating margins on improved sales volumes and operating leverage.

▶ After taxes at an effective rate we forecast near 30%, we project EPS of $2.52 in 2009, a 22% decline from 2008, and $2.88 in 2010, including $0.16 of one-time charges reflected in our 2009 GAAP earnings estimate.

Investment Rationale/Risk

▶ Despite challenging market conditions in consumer and industrial tools markets, we are positive on SWK's ability to manage its diversified businesses. While the company is reducing manufacturing plant capacity and staffing, we believe it is well positioned to gain market share in its three customer markets, especially if the major economies begin to recover in 2010.

▶ Risks to our recommendation and target price include the possibility of prolonged recessions in SWK's European and North American markets, lower-than-projected synergies from recent acquisitions, an inability to achieve the Security Solutions segment's target margin, and intense pricing pressure.

▶ Our 12-month target price of $51 is based on a blend of two valuation metrics. On a relative valuation basis, we apply a P/E multiple of 17.5X, in line with the peer average, to our 2010 EPS estimate, suggesting a value of $50. Our DCF valuation analysis, assuming terminal growth of 3% and a discount rate of 9.8%, results in an intrinsic value of $52.

Qualitative Risk Assessment

| LOW | **MEDIUM** | HIGH |

Our risk assessment takes into account our positive view of SWK's strong brand name and solid competitive position, offset by our negative view of industry cyclicality.

Quantitative Evaluations

S&P Quality Ranking   B+

| D | C | B- | B | **B+** | A- | A | A+ |

Relative Strength Rank   STRONG

81

LOWEST = 1   HIGHEST = 99

Revenue/Earnings Data

Revenue (Million $)

	1Q	2Q	3Q	4Q	Year
2009	913.0	919.2	935.5	--	--
2008	1,097	1,154	1,120	1,086	4,426
2007	1,062	1,123	1,131	1,167	4,484
2006	968.7	1,018	1,013	1,019	4,019
2005	796.3	814.7	834.9	839.4	3,285
2004	734.8	753.9	751.8	802.9	3,043

Earnings Per Share ($)

2009	0.48	0.89	0.77	E0.72	E2.52
2008	0.85	0.95	0.98	0.07	2.82
2007	0.80	1.01	1.09	1.11	4.00
2006	0.45	0.90	1.09	1.04	3.47
2005	0.78	0.77	0.89	0.75	3.18
2004	0.66	0.70	0.73	0.77	2.85

Fiscal year ended Dec. 31. Next earnings report expected: Late January. EPS Estimates based on S&P Operating Earnings; historical GAAP earnings are as reported.

Dividend Data (Dates: mm/dd Payment Date: mm/dd/yy)

Amount ($)	Date Decl.	Ex-Div. Date	Stk. of Record	Payment Date
0.320	02/17	03/02	03/04	03/24/09
0.320	04/23	06/01	06/03	06/23/09
0.330	07/20	09/02	09/04	09/22/09
0.330	10/16	12/02	12/04	12/15/09

Dividends have been paid since 1877. Source: Company reports.

Please read the Required Disclosures and Analyst Certification on the last page of this report.

The McGraw-Hill Companies

Stanley Works (The)

STANDARD
&POOR'S

Business Summary November 11, 2009

CORPORATE OVERVIEW. The Stanley Works is a worldwide supplier of industrial tools and security solutions for professional, industrial and consumer use. The company offers a broad line of hand tools and has many well-known brands. SWK's operations are classified into three business segments: Consumer Products (37.5% of 2008 sales), Industrial Tools (28.6%), and Security Solutions (33.8%).

MARKET PROFILE. In Consumer Products, SWK manufactures and markets hand tools, consumer mechanics tools and storage units, and hardware. Products are distributed directly to retailers (including home centers, mass merchants, hardware stores, and retail lumber yards) as well as third-party distributors, and include measuring instruments, hammers, knives and blades, screwdrivers, sockets and tool boxes. Among the company's brands are Stanley, FatMax, Powerlock, IntelliTools, ZAG, and National.

The Industrial Tools segment manufactures and markets professional mechanics tools and storage systems, pneumatic tools and fasteners, hydraulic tools and accessories, assembly tools and systems, and electronic measuring tools. Products are distributed primarily through third-party distributors. Brands include Stanley, Proto, Facom, USAG, MAC, Jensen, Bostich, Virax, David White, and Rolatape.

The Security Solutions segment is a provider of access and security solutions primarily for retailers, educational and healthcare institutions, government, financial institutions, and commercial and industrial customers. Products include security integration systems, software, related installation and maintenance services, automatic doors, and locking mechanisms, and are sold on a direct sales basis. Brands include Stanley, Blick, Frisco Bay, PAC, ISR, WanderGuard, StanVision, Sargent and Greenleaf, BEST and Xmark.

About 57% of 2008 sales were made in the U.S., 10% in Other Americas, 13% in France, 15% in Other Europe, and 5% in Asia. A large portion of SWK's products in the Consumer Products and Industrial Tools segments are sold through home centers and mass merchant distribution channels in the U.S. market.

Company Financials Fiscal Year Ended Dec. 31

Per Share Data ($)	2008	2007	2006	2005	2004	2003	2002	2001	2000	1999
Tangible Book Value	NM	NM	NM	4.59	3.56	2.65	5.05	7.05	6.59	6.18
Cash Flow	5.11	5.94	4.92	4.40	4.07	2.16	2.90	2.76	3.17	2.62
Earnings	2.82	4.00	3.47	3.18	2.85	1.14	2.10	1.81	2.22	1.67
S&P Core Earnings	2.63	4.08	3.57	3.16	2.49	1.12	1.43	1.30	NA	NA
Dividends	1.26	1.22	1.18	1.14	1.08	1.03	0.99	0.94	0.90	0.87
Payout Ratio	45%	30%	34%	36%	38%	90%	47%	52%	41%	52%
Prices:High	52.18	64.25	54.59	51.75	49.33	37.87	52.00	46.97	31.88	35.00
Prices:Low	24.19	47.01	41.60	41.51	36.42	20.84	27.31	28.06	18.44	22.00
P/E Ratio:High	19	16	16	16	17	33	25	26	14	21
P/E Ratio:Low	9	12	12	13	13	18	13	16	8	13

Income Statement Analysis (Million $)	2008	2007	2006	2005	2004	2003	2002	2001	2000	1999
Revenue	4,426	4,484	4,019	3,285	3,043	2,678	2,594	2,624	2,749	2,752
Operating Income	747	800	567	493	513	342	360	412	424	321
Depreciation	183	162	121	96.5	95.0	86.5	71.2	82.9	83.3	86.0
Interest Expense	82.0	85.2	69.3	40.4	38.6	34.2	28.5	18.9	34.6	33.0
Pretax Income	301	451	367	358	329	133	273	237	294	231
Effective Tax Rate	25.2%	25.4%	20.8%	24.1%	27.0%	27.3%	32.1%	33.1%	33.8%	35.1%
Net Income	225	337	291	272	240	96.7	185	158	194	150
S&P Core Earnings	211	343	299	270	209	94.7	127	113	NA	NA

Balance Sheet & Other Financial Data (Million $)	2008	2007	2006	2005	2004	2003	2002	2001	2000	1999
Cash	212	240	177	658	250	204	122	115	93.6	88.0
Current Assets	1,499	1,768	1,639	1,826	1,372	1,201	1,190	1,141	1,094	1,091
Total Assets	4,879	4,780	3,935	3,545	2,851	2,424	2,418	2,056	1,885	1,891
Current Liabilities	1,197	1,278	1,251	875	819	754	681	826	707	693
Long Term Debt	1,420	1,212	679	895	482	535	564	197	249	290
Common Equity	1,688	1,729	1,552	1,946	1,388	1,032	1,165	844	933	737
Total Capital	3,121	3,022	2,298	2,925	1,960	1,567	1,729	1,041	1,181	1,027
Capital Expenditures	141	65.5	59.6	53.3	47.6	31.4	37.2	55.7	59.8	78.0
Cash Flow	408	499	412	368	335	183	256	241	278	236
Current Ratio	1.3	1.4	1.3	2.1	1.7	1.6	1.7	1.4	1.5	1.6
% Long Term Debt of Capitalization	45.7	40.1	29.6	30.6	24.6	34.1	32.6	18.9	21.1	28.2
% Net Income of Revenue	5.1	7.5	7.2	8.3	7.9	3.6	7.1	6.0	7.1	5.5
% Return on Assets	4.7	7.7	7.8	8.5	9.1	4.0	8.3	8.0	10.3	7.8
% Return on Equity	13.2	20.5	19.4	14.4	19.8	8.8	16.9	20.0	20.8	20.8

Data as orig reptd.; bef. results of disc opers/spec. items. Per share data adj. for stk. divs.; EPS diluted. E-Estimated. NA-Not Available. NM-Not Meaningful. NR-Not Ranked. UR-Under Review.

Office: 1000 Stanley Dr, New Britain, CT 06053.
Telephone: 860-225-5111.
Website: http://www.stanleyworks.com
Chrmn & CEO: J.F. Lundgren

COO & EVP: J.M. Loree
SVP & CIO: H.W. Davis, Jr.
CFO: D. Allan, Jr.
CTO: D.E. Bither

Investor Contact: K. White (860-827-3833)
Board Members: J. G. Breen, P. D. Campbell, C. M. Cardoso, V. W. Colbert, R. B. Coutts, E. S. Kraus, J. F. Lundgren, M. M. Parrs, L. Zimmerman

Founded: 1843
Domicile: Connecticut
Employees: 18,225

Staples Inc

STANDARD &POOR'S

S&P Recommendation	SELL ★★☆☆☆	Price $23.32 (as of Nov 27, 2009)	12-Mo. Target Price $21.00	Investment Style Large-Cap Growth

GICS Sector Consumer Discretionary
Sub-Industry Specialty Stores

Summary This leading operator of office products superstores has over 2,000 units in the U.S. and internationally.

Key Stock Statistics (Source S&P, Vickers, company reports)

52-Wk Range	$23.65– 14.35	S&P Oper. EPS 2010E	1.10	Market Capitalization(B)	$16.845	Beta		0.79
Trailing 12-Month EPS	$0.95	S&P Oper. EPS 2011E	1.26	Yield (%)	1.59	S&P 3-Yr. Proj. EPS CAGR(%)		9
Trailing 12-Month P/E	24.6	P/E on S&P Oper. EPS 2010E	21.2	Dividend Rate/Share	$0.37	S&P Credit Rating		BBB
$10K Invested 5 Yrs Ago	$11,468	Common Shares Outstg. (M)	722.3	Institutional Ownership (%)	90			

Price Performance

30-Week Mov. Avg. · · · ·   10-Week Mov. Avg. – –   **GAAP Earnings vs. Previous Year**   Volume Above Avg. ▮▮▮ STARS
12-Mo. Target Price —   Relative Strength —   ▲ Up ▼ Down ▶ No Change   Below Avg. ▮▮▮ ★

Options: ASE, CBOE, P, Ph

Analysis prepared by **Michael Souers** on August 26, 2009, when the stock traded at **$ 21.99.**

Highlights

▶ We estimate sales growth of 3.7% in FY 10 (Jan.), following a 19% advance in FY 09. Sales growth should be aided by the acquisition of Corporate Express, which closed in July 2008, continued international penetration, and about 55 net new store additions in North America. We expect same-store sales in North American Retail to decline 5%, as customer traffic continues to weaken -- a byproduct of the overall slowdown in consumer spending.

▶ We expect a modest narrowing of gross margins due to the timing of the acquisition of Corporate Express, which carries lower margins, partially offset by benefits from a growing private label business, supply chain initiatives, and lower sourcing costs. However, we anticipate only a slight decline in operating margins, as the de-leveraging of fixed costs due to weak same-store sales results is partially offset by cost synergies from the acquisition.

▶ Following a significant increase in net interest expense, we estimate FY 10 operating EPS of $1.10, a 15% decrease from the $1.29 the company earned in FY 09, excluding integration and restructuring charges. We see FY 11 EPS of $1.26.

Investment Rationale/Risk

▶ We recently lowered our recommendation on the shares to sell, from hold, based on valuation, as SPLS recently traded at over 17X our FY 11 EPS estimate, a significant premium to the S&P 500. Although we anticipate strong results for SPLS's North American Delivery division over the longer term, we were disappointed in the severity of the recent slowdown, as well as the shift in mix, which will likely continue to pressure margins over the near term. While we favor SPLS' strong balance sheet, significant free cash flow generation and cost synergies from the Corporate Express acquisition that should accrue over the next few years, we think the office supply industry is extremely mature and growth potential rather limited.

▶ Risks to our recommendation and target price include a sharp recovery in economic growth and stronger-than-expected capital spending and hiring by businesses. International risks include favorable currency movements.

▶ Our 12-month target price of $21, about 17X our FY 11 EPS projection, is derived from our discounted cash flow model, which assumes a weighted average cost of capital of 9.6% and a terminal growth rate of 3.0%.

Qualitative Risk Assessment

LOW	MEDIUM	HIGH

Our risk assessment reflects the rather cyclical nature of the company, which relies on consumer as well as business spending, and investments in emerging markets for future growth. This is offset by untapped growth areas in major domestic metro markets.

Quantitative Evaluations

S&P Quality Ranking   B+

D	C	B-	B	B+	A-	A	A+

Relative Strength Rank   STRONG

73

LOWEST = 1   HIGHEST = 99

Revenue/Earnings Data

Revenue (Million $)

	1Q	2Q	3Q	4Q	Year
2010	5,818	5,534	--	--	--
2009	4,885	5,075	6,951	6,174	23,084
2008	4,589	4,290	5,168	5,324	19,373
2007	4,238	3,881	4,757	5,286	18,161
2006	3,899	3,472	4,246	4,462	16,079
2005	3,452	3,089	3,830	4,077	14,448

Earnings Per Share ($)

2010	0.20	0.13	E0.38	E0.34	E1.10
2009	0.30	0.21	0.22	0.40	1.13
2008	0.29	0.21	0.38	0.47	1.38
2007	0.25	0.22	0.39	0.46	1.32
2006	0.20	0.20	0.32	0.39	1.12
2005	0.17	0.16	0.27	0.33	0.93

Fiscal year ended Jan. 31. Next earnings report expected: Early December. EPS Estimates based on S&P Operating Earnings; historical GAAP earnings are as reported.

Dividend Data (Dates: mm/dd Payment Date: mm/dd/yy)

Amount ($)	Date Decl.	Ex-Div. Date	Stk. of Record	Payment Date
0.083	03/11	03/25	03/27	04/16/09
0.083	06/09	06/24	06/26	07/16/09
0.083	09/15	09/23	09/25	10/15/09

Dividends have been paid since 2004. Source: Company reports.

Staples Inc

STANDARD &POOR'S

Business Summary August 26, 2009

CORPORATE OVERVIEW. Staples is the world's leading office products company, with net sales of nearly $23.1 billion in FY 09 (Jan.). Staples operates under three segments: North American Retail (41% of total revenues in FY 09); North American Delivery (39%); and International Operations (20%). Sales by product line were: office supplies and services 47%; business machines and related products 28%; computers and related products 18%; and office furniture 7%.

At January 31, 2009, SPLS operated 2,218 superstores, mostly in the United States (1,523 stores) and Canada (312 stores), but also in a number of other countries, including: the U.K. (137), Germany (63), the Netherlands (47), Portugal (31), Sweden (28), China (26), Norway (21), Australia (20), Belgium (5), Denmark (2), Argentina (2) and Ireland (1).

SPLS has approximately 8,000 stock keeping units (SKUs) stocked in each of its typical North American retail stores and approximately 15,000 SKUs stocked in its North American Delivery fulfillment centers. On Staples.com,

the company's Internet site, approximately 50,000 SKUs are available to customers.

CORPORATE STRATEGY. Staples seeks to maintain its leadership position in the office products industry by differentiating itself from the competition, delivering industry-best execution and expanding its market share. In FY 10, it plans to add about 55 new stores in North America, filling in existing markets along with expansion into untapped metro markets. Approximately 10 of the new stores will be stand-alone copy and print shops, which average 4,000 square feet with 1,800 SKUs in supplies. We believe significant growth opportunities remain in other metropolitan markets where SPLS has yet to venture, and we expect the company to establish a strong Midwest presence over the next several years.

Company Financials Fiscal Year Ended Jan. 31

Per Share Data ($)	2009	2008	2007	2006	2005	2004	2003	2002	2001	2000
Tangible Book Value	1.51	5.28	4.64	3.84	3.45	3.01	1.74	2.63	2.19	1.99
Cash Flow	1.90	1.92	1.78	1.56	1.33	1.03	1.01	0.73	0.42	0.67
Earnings	1.13	1.38	1.32	1.12	0.93	0.66	0.63	0.42	0.10	0.45
S&P Core Earnings	1.20	1.42	1.32	1.05	0.88	0.61	0.58	0.32	0.21	NA
Dividends	0.29	0.22	0.17	0.17	0.13	Nil	Nil	Nil	Nil	Nil
Payout Ratio	26%	16%	13%	15%	14%	Nil	Nil	Nil	Nil	Nil
Calendar Year	2008	2007	2006	2005	2004	2003	2002	2001	2000	1999
Prices:High	26.57	27.66	28.00	24.14	22.57	18.58	14.97	12.97	19.17	23.96
Prices:Low	13.57	19.69	21.08	18.64	15.79	10.49	7.79	7.35	6.83	10.96
P/E Ratio:High	24	20	21	22	24	28	24	31	NM	54
P/E Ratio:Low	12	14	16	17	17	16	12	17	NM	25

Income Statement Analysis (Million $)										
Revenue	23,084	19,373	18,161	16,079	14,448	13,181	11,596	10,744	10,674	8,937
Operating Income	2,094	1,975	1,802	1,617	1,405	1,081	950	768	719	708
Depreciation	549	389	339	304	279	283	267	249	231	174
Interest Expense	150	38.3	47.8	56.8	39.9	20.2	20.6	27.2	45.2	17.1
Pretax Income	1,243	1,554	1,471	1,314	1,116	778	662	431	244	516
Effective Tax Rate	34.5%	36.0%	33.8%	36.5%	36.5%	37.0%	32.6%	38.5%	75.5%	39.0%
Net Income	805	996	974	834	708	490	446	265	59.7	315
S&P Core Earnings	857	1,020	974	784	667	450	413	221	147	NA

Balance Sheet & Other Financial Data (Million $)										
Cash	634	1,272	1,018	978	997	457	596	395	264	110
Current Assets	5,730	4,555	4,431	4,145	3,782	3,479	2,717	2,403	2,356	2,192
Total Assets	13,006	9,036	8,397	7,677	7,071	6,503	5,721	4,093	3,989	3,814
Current Liabilities	4,778	2,610	2,788	2,480	2,197	2,123	2,175	1,596	1,711	1,455
Long Term Debt	1,969	342	569	528	558	567	732	350	441	501
Common Equity	5,564	5,718	5,022	4,425	4,115	3,663	2,659	2,054	1,764	1,829
Total Capital	7,591	6,094	5,600	4,963	4,696	4,230	3,441	2,411	2,205	2,330
Capital Expenditures	378	470	528	456	335	278	265	340	450	355
Cash Flow	1,354	1,385	1,313	1,138	987	773	713	514	291	489
Current Ratio	1.2	1.8	1.6	1.7	1.7	1.6	1.2	1.5	1.4	1.5
% Long Term Debt of Capitalization	25.9	5.6	10.2	10.6	11.9	13.4	21.3	14.5	20.0	21.5
% Net Income of Revenue	3.5	5.1	5.4	5.2	4.9	3.7	3.8	2.5	0.6	3.5
% Return on Assets	7.3	11.4	12.1	11.3	10.4	8.0	9.1	6.6	1.5	9.0
% Return on Equity	14.3	18.5	20.5	19.5	18.2	15.5	18.9	13.9	3.3	18.1

Data as orig reptd.; bef. results of disc opers/spec. items. Per share data adj. for stk. divs.; EPS diluted. E-Estimated. NA-Not Available. NM-Not Meaningful. NR-Not Ranked. UR-Under Review.

Office: Five Hundred Staples Dr, Framingham , MA 01702.
Telephone: 508-253-5000.
Email: investor@staples.com
Website: http://www.staples.com

Chrmn & CEO: R.L. Sargent
Pres & COO: M. Miles, Jr.
EVP & CIO: B.T. Light
SVP, Chief Acctg Officer & Cntlr: C.T. Komola

SVP & Treas: N.P. Hotchkin
Investor Contact: N. Hotchkin (800-468-7751)
Board Members: B. L. Anderson, A. M. Blank, M. E. Burton, J. M. King, C. M. Meyrowitz, R. T. Moriarty, R. C. Nakasone, R. L. Sargent, E. Smith, R. E. Sulentic, V. Vishwanath, P. F. Walsh

Founded: 1985
Domicile: Delaware
Employees: 91,125

The McGraw-Hill Companies

Starbucks Corp

STANDARD &POOR'S

S&P Recommendation	SELL ★★☆☆☆	Price $21.43 (as of Nov 27, 2009)	12-Mo. Target Price $16.00	Investment Style Large-Cap Growth

GICS Sector Consumer Discretionary
Sub-Industry Restaurants

Summary Starbucks is the leading coffee roaster and retailer of high-quality coffee products in the world, which it sells through its approximately 16,600 retail stores globally, as well as increasingly through multiple retail channels.

Key Stock Statistics (Source S&P, Vickers, company reports)

52-Wk Range	$22.10– 7.93	S&P Oper. EPS 2010**E**	0.92	Market Capitalization(B)	$15.862	Beta		1.36
Trailing 12-Month EPS	$0.52	S&P Oper. EPS 2011**E**	0.98	Yield (%)	Nil	S&P 3-Yr. Proj. EPS CAGR(%)		8
Trailing 12-Month P/E	41.2	P/E on S&P Oper. EPS 2010**E**	23.3	Dividend Rate/Share	Nil	S&P Credit Rating		BBB
$10K Invested 5 Yrs Ago	$7,572	Common Shares Outstg. (M)	740.2	Institutional Ownership (%)	71			

Price Performance

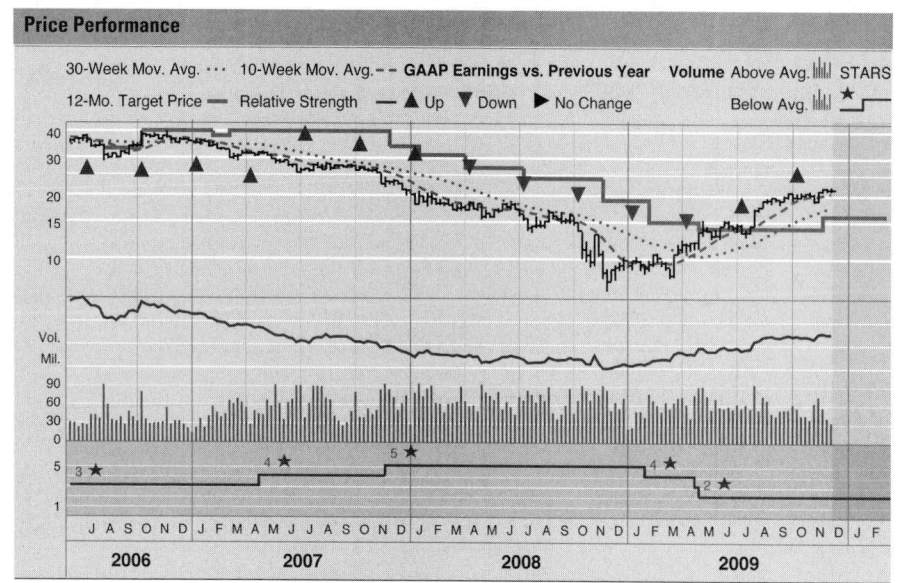

30-Week Mov. Avg. · · · 10-Week Mov. Avg. - - **GAAP Earnings vs. Previous Year** Volume Above Avg. STARS
12-Mo. Target Price — Relative Strength — ▲ Up ▼ Down ► No Change Below Avg. ★

Options: ASE, CBOE, P, Ph

Analysis prepared by **Mark S. Basham** on November 10, 2009, when the stock traded at **$ 21.41**.

Highlights

► In FY 09 (Sep.), Starbucks continued a restructuring plan and closed unprofitable stores and reduced new store openings as part of a plan to revitalize the company. Domestically, 439 (net) stores were closed, while 394 (net) were opened in international markets. Savings from the closings and other cost initiatives were $590 million, $40 million more than previously estimated by the company. FY 09 operating EPS rose to $0.80 from $0.71 in FY 08, excluding charges related to the closures and cost initiatives of $0.28 in both fiscal years.

► For FY 10, we expect new product initiatives, such as VIA instant coffee offerings through a number of retail channels, as well as a 53rd week, to result in a 2% increase in revenues. The effect of prior store closings will diminish as the fiscal year progresses.

► Effects of previous cost initiatives will likely continue to accrue in FY 10. We expect operating margins will widen by about 200 basis points. Including incremental EPS of about $0.02 from the 53rd week, we see EPS rising to $0.92.

Investment Rationale/Risk

► Although we think the company's revitalization agenda is on the right track, we expect any material improvement in business conditions to take several years. We see risks outweighing potential gains in the shares at recent price levels, as earnings improvement is still being nearly entirely driven by cost cuts.

► Risks to our recommendation and target price include the potentially positive impact of price decreases on customer traffic, enthusiastic customer acceptance of SBUX's new product initiatives, and potential recapture of market share from competitors.

► Our 12-month target price of $16 is largely derived from our DCF model, which assumes an initial weighted average cost of capital of 10.5% and reflects a substantial FY 09 cash flow increase over FY 08 levels. We also assume average annual cash flow increases of 7% through FY 14, then moderation to a perpetuity growth rate of 3%. We also use a premium-to-peers P/E of 17X our FY 10 estimate, which is reflective of SBUX's recent conservative bent in its capital structure, to derive a value of $16.

Qualitative Risk Assessment

LOW	MEDIUM	HIGH

Our risk assessment reflects uncertainties of ongoing steps to reinvigorate the Starbucks brand. We also see a threat from specialty coffee offerings by competitors. Partly offsetting these concerns, we think the company has significant financial strength, affording it the capacity to potentially return to moderate growth. Recent cost cutting has further bolstered the company's finances.

Quantitative Evaluations

S&P Quality Ranking   B+

D	C	B-	B	B+	A-	A	A+

Relative Strength Rank   STRONG
81
LOWEST = 1   HIGHEST = 99

Revenue/Earnings Data

Revenue (Million $)

	1Q	2Q	3Q	4Q	Year
2009	2,615	2,333	2,404	2,422	9,775
2008	2,768	2,526	2,574	2,515	10,383
2007	2,356	2,256	2,359	2,441	9,411
2006	1,934	1,886	1,964	2,003	7,787
2005	1,590	1,519	1,602	1,659	6,369
2004	1,281	1,241	1,319	1,453	5,294

Earnings Per Share ($)

2009	0.09	0.03	0.20	0.20	0.52
2008	0.28	0.15	-0.01	0.01	0.43
2007	0.26	0.19	0.21	0.21	0.87
2006	0.22	0.16	0.18	0.17	0.73
2005	0.17	0.12	0.16	0.16	0.61
2004	0.14	0.10	0.12	0.13	0.48

Fiscal year ended Sep. 30. Next earnings report expected: Late January. EPS Estimates based on S&P Operating Earnings; historical GAAP earnings are as reported.

Dividend Data

No cash dividends have been paid.

Please read the Required Disclosures and Analyst Certification on the last page of this report.

The **McGraw·Hill** Companies

Starbucks Corp

STANDARD &POOR'S

Business Summary November 10, 2009

CORPORATE OVERVIEW. The Starbucks brand is nearly synonymous with specialty coffee. However, a slowing economy and over-expansion under prior management led the company, beginning in FY 08 (Sep.) under returning CEO H. Schultz, to dramatically reduce expansion and begin to evolve the brand.

The number of Starbucks retail stores fell slightly, by 45, to 16,635 at September 30, 2009, from a year earlier. However, this decline gains a somewhat different perspective when compared to the 165 stores open at the end of FY 92. Company-operated retail stores accounted for 84% of net sales in both FY 09 and FY 08. Stores are typically clustered in high-traffic, high-visibility locations in each market. They are located in office buildings, downtown and suburban retail centers, and kiosks placed in building lobbies, airport terminals and supermarkets. In FY 08 (latest available), the retail store sales mix by product type was 76% beverages, 17% food items, 3% whole bean coffees, and 4% coffee-related hardware items.

At September 30, 2009, SBUX owned and operated 6,764 (7,238 as of September 30, 2008) of its stores in the U.S., and 2,068 (1,979) stores in international markets. It closed a net 385 company stores in FY 09, compared to a net total of 681 company-owned stores opened in FY 08, which was down substantially from 1,351 in FY 07.

There were also 4,364 (4,329) licensed retail stores in the U.S. and 3,439 (3,134) in international markets at September 30, 2009. A net 340 licensed store opened in FY 09, compared to 988 opened in FY 08. Revenue from retail licensees was approximately 13% of total revenues in FY 09 (11% in FY 08). The Global Consumer Products Group and a number of foodservice accounts were 3.8% of total revenues in FY 09 (4.2% in FY 08).

IMPACT OF MAJOR DEVELOPMENTS. At the time of the January 2008 reappointment of Howard Schultz as CEO, the company outlined a five-point agenda: 1) improve the U.S. business by focusing on the customer experience and other factors affecting store operations; 2) slow the pace of U.S. expansion and close underperforming U.S. locations; 3) re-energize the Starbucks brand and create an emotional connection to the brand with customers and employees; 4) realign and streamline management and back-end functions to better support customer-focused initiatives; and 5) accelerate expansion outside the U.S. and drive profit margins higher at international operations.

Company Financials Fiscal Year Ended Sep. 30

Per Share Data ($)	2009	2008	2007	2006	2005	2004	2003	2002	2001	2000
Tangible Book Value	3.66	2.93	2.74	2.68	2.56	3.00	2.52	2.20	1.78	1.50
Cash Flow	NA	1.17	1.51	1.25	1.06	0.85	0.66	0.55	0.45	0.48
Earnings	0.52	0.43	0.87	0.73	0.61	0.48	0.34	0.27	0.23	0.12
S&P Core Earnings	NA	0.44	0.86	0.73	0.53	0.42	0.29	0.23	0.18	NA
Dividends	Nil	Nil	Nil	Nil	Nil	Nil	Nil	Nil	Nil	Nil
Payout Ratio	Nil	Nil	Nil	Nil	Nil	Nil	Nil	Nil	Nil	Nil
Prices:High	22.10	21.01	36.61	40.01	32.46	32.13	16.72	12.85	12.83	12.70
Prices:Low	8.12	7.06	19.89	28.72	22.29	16.45	9.81	9.22	6.73	5.78
P/E Ratio:High	43	49	42	55	53	68	50	48	56	NM
P/E Ratio:Low	16	16	23	39	37	35	29	34	29	NM

Income Statement Analysis (Million $)	2009	2008	2007	2006	2005	2004	2003	2002	2001	2000
Revenue	9,775	10,383	9,411	7,787	6,369	5,294	4,076	3,289	2,649	2,169
Operating Income	NA	1,279	1,437	1,213	1,071	854	646	504	430	334
Depreciation	563	549	491	413	367	305	259	221	177	142
Interest Expense	NA	60.6	Nil	Nil	Nil	Nil	Nil	Nil	Nil	Nil
Pretax Income	559	460	1,056	906	796	624	436	341	289	161
Effective Tax Rate	30.1%	31.3%	36.3%	35.8%	37.9%	37.2%	38.5%	37.0%	37.3%	41.1%
Net Income	391	316	673	581	494	392	268	215	181	94.6
S&P Core Earnings	NA	325	668	579	437	346	231	181	143	NA

Balance Sheet & Other Financial Data (Million $)	2009	2008	2007	2006	2005	2004	2003	2002	2001	2000
Cash	666	322	281	313	174	299	201	175	113	70.8
Current Assets	NA	1,748	1,696	1,530	1,209	1,368	924	848	594	460
Total Assets	5,577	5,673	5,344	4,429	3,514	3,328	2,730	2,293	1,851	1,493
Current Liabilities	NA	2,190	2,156	1,936	1,227	783	609	537	445	313
Long Term Debt	549	550	550	1.96	2.87	3.62	4.35	5.08	5.79	6.48
Common Equity	3,046	2,491	2,284	2,229	2,091	2,487	2,082	1,727	1,376	1,148
Total Capital	3,595	3,059	2,834	2,230	2,094	2,537	2,120	1,754	1,406	1,180
Capital Expenditures	446	984	1,080	771	644	386	357	375	384	316
Cash Flow	NA	865	1,164	994	862	697	528	436	358	367
Current Ratio	1.3	0.8	0.8	0.8	1.0	1.7	1.5	1.6	1.3	1.5
% Long Term Debt of Capitalization	15.3	18.0	19.4	0.1	0.1	0.1	0.2	0.3	0.4	0.5
% Net Income of Revenue	4.0	3.0	7.1	7.5	7.8	7.4	6.6	6.5	6.8	4.4
% Return on Assets	7.0	5.7	13.8	14.6	14.3	12.9	10.9	10.4	10.8	6.9
% Return on Equity	14.1	13.2	29.8	26.9	21.7	17.1	14.1	13.9	14.4	9.0

Data as orig reptd.; bef. results of disc opers/spec. items. Per share data adj. for stk. divs.; EPS diluted. E-Estimated. NA-Not Available. NM-Not Meaningful. NR-Not Ranked. UR-Under Review.

Office: 2401 Utah Avenue South, Seattle, WA 98134.
Telephone: 206-447-1575.
Email: investorrelations@starbucks.com
Website: http://www.starbucks.com

Chrmn, Pres & CEO: H.D. Schultz
EVP, CFO & Chief Admin Officer: T. Alstead
EVP, Secy & General Counsel: P.E. Boggs
SVP & CIO: S. Gillett

Board Members: B. Bass, W. W. Bradley, M. L. Hobson, K. R. Johnson, O. C. Lee, S. Sandberg, H. D. Schultz, J. G. Shennan, Jr., J. G. Teruel, M. E. Ullman, III, C. Weatherup

Founded: 1985
Domicile: Washington
Employees: 176,000

Starwood Hotels & Resorts Worldwide Inc.

STANDARD &POOR'S

S&P Recommendation	STRONG SELL ★☆☆☆☆	Price	12-Mo. Target Price	Investment Style
		$31.60 (as of Nov 27, 2009)	$16.00	Large-Cap Blend

GICS Sector Consumer Discretionary
Sub-Industry Hotels, Resorts & Cruise Lines

Summary Starwood is one of the world's largest lodging companies, with about 1,000 hotels in approximately 100 countries operating under nine brands.

Key Stock Statistics (Source S&P, Vickers, company reports)

52-Wk Range	$36.45– 8.99	S&P Oper. EPS 2009E	0.25	Market Capitalization(B)	$5.910	Beta	1.93
Trailing 12-Month EPS	$1.42	S&P Oper. EPS 2010E	0.55	Yield (%)	0.63	S&P 3-Yr. Proj. EPS CAGR(%)	-39
Trailing 12-Month P/E	22.3	P/E on S&P Oper. EPS 2009E	NM	Dividend Rate/Share	$0.20	S&P Credit Rating	BB
$10K Invested 5 Yrs Ago	$8,446	Common Shares Outstg. (M)	187.0	Institutional Ownership (%)	96		

Price Performance

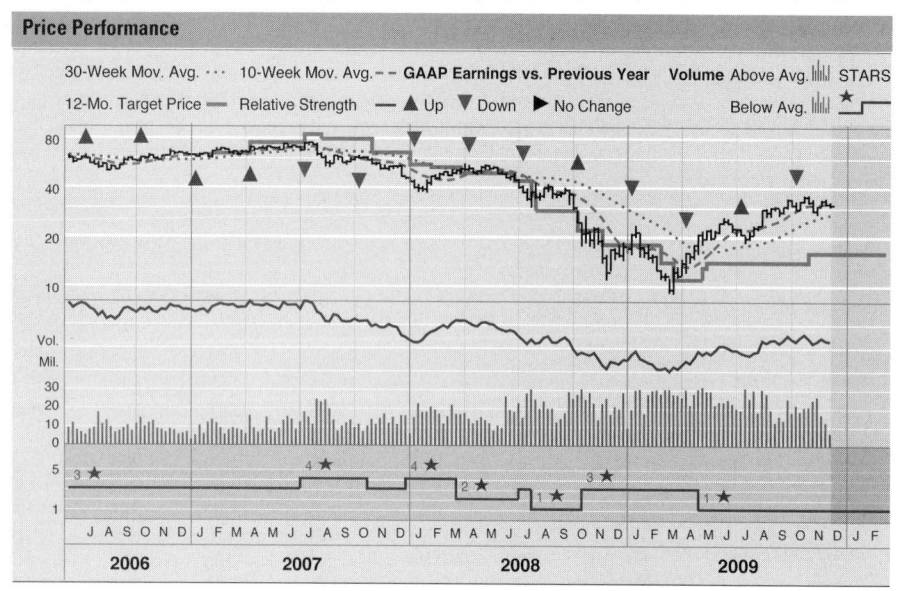

Options: CBOE, Ph

Analysis prepared by **Mark S. Basham** on November 03, 2009, when the stock traded at **$ 29.25**.

Highlights

► Although the first nine months 2009 decline in systemwide RevPAR of 24.3% was worse than we had forecast, we have maintained our forecast for systemwide RevPAR in 2009 of a decline of 18%, as Q4 comparisons get much easier. In North America, we expect rates to fall about 13%, with occupancy down 6%. Elsewhere, we forecast a decline in occupancy of about 7%, and 12% lower rates. We expect vacation ownership revenues to fall 33%.

► Despite significant cost reductions, we anticipate that EPS will decline 82% in 2009, to $0.25, from $1.37 in 2008. Results in 2008 included restructuring and other charges of $0.82 a share, while about $0.50 a share of such charges are included in 2009. HOT management's position that these charges should be excluded from operating results is controversial, in our view, as the charges relate to HOT's property portfolio, an activity inherent to its business of managing hotels. EPS in 2009 excludes $0.66 from a tax incentive program in Italy.

► In 2010, despite lingering weakness, we forecast that HOT will benefit further from cost cuts. We expect revenues to be flat, with EPS of $0.55.

Investment Rationale/Risk

► Our strong sell recommendation reflects our view that the rally from March to September in HOT shares, along with the industry and the S&P 500 in general, discounts a substantially greater improvement in HOT fundamentals through 2012 than is likely. We do not expect the hotel industry to stage a full recovery back to pre-2008 levels until at least 2012. In addition, the company does not expect to maintain its annual dividend at the $0.90 per share level paid in 2007 and 2008.

► Risks to our recommendation and target price include the potential for industry conditions to improve quicker than we currently foresee should the global economy recover sooner than S&P expects. Access to capital for some of the unfunded projects in the development pipeline may be more available under one of several government programs.

► Our 12-month target price of $16 is based on an enterprise value multiple of 10.0 our 2010 EBITDA projection of $640-$650 million, which is on par with peer valuations. Our 2010 EBITDA estimate is about flat with our estimate of $650 million for 2009.

Qualitative Risk Assessment

LOW	MEDIUM	HIGH

In our view, Starwood's financial flexibility has been substantially constrained by the current industry downturn. This was due in part to its decision to use cash and increase leverage to repurchase just over a quarter of its outstanding shares since 2006. We think this reduced flexibility not only limits its ability to acquire properties during the downturn at reduced prices, but has also led it to sell select properties to raise cash.

Quantitative Evaluations

S&P Quality Ranking NR

D	C	B-	B	B+	A-	A	A+

Relative Strength Rank MODERATE

56

LOWEST = 1   HIGHEST = 99

Revenue/Earnings Data

Revenue (Million $)

	1Q	2Q	3Q	4Q	Year
2009	1,118	1,205	1,218	--	--
2008	1,466	1,573	1,535	1,333	5,907
2007	1,431	1,572	1,540	1,610	6,153
2006	1,441	1,505	1,461	1,572	5,979
2005	1,406	1,559	1,496	1,516	5,977
2004	1,227	1,363	1,336	1,442	5,368

Earnings Per Share ($)

2009	0.04	0.72	0.22	E0.16	E0.25
2008	0.42	0.57	0.62	-0.25	1.37
2007	0.56	0.67	0.61	0.74	2.57
2006	0.34	3.01	0.71	0.94	5.01
2005	0.36	0.65	0.18	0.72	1.88
2004	0.16	0.56	0.49	0.51	1.72

Fiscal year ended Dec. 31. Next earnings report expected: Late January. EPS Estimates based on S&P Operating Earnings; historical GAAP earnings are as reported.

Dividend Data (Dates: mm/dd Payment Date: mm/dd/yy)

Amount ($)	Date Decl.	Ex-Div. Date	Stk. of Record	Payment Date
0.200	11/08	12/29	12/31	01/14/10

Dividends have been paid since 1995. Source: Company reports.

Please read the Required Disclosures and Analyst Certification on the last page of this report.

Starwood Hotels & Resorts Worldwide Inc.

STANDARD &POOR'S

Business Summary November 03, 2009

CORPORATE OVERVIEW. Starwood Hotels & Resorts (HOT) is one of the world's largest hotel companies, with owned, leased, managed, or franchised hotels in approximately 100 countries. At September 30, 2009, the company's business included 982 hotels, with 296,951 rooms, vs. 942 properties with 284,800 rooms as of December 31, 2008. Approximately 57% of management and franchise fees in 2008 were generated outside North America.

HOT's business includes owned, managed, and franchised properties. Its brands include St. Regis (luxury full-service hotels and resorts), The Luxury Collection (luxury full-service hotels and resorts), Westin (luxury and upscale full-service hotels and resorts), Sheraton (full-service hotels and resorts), W (boutique full-service urban hotels), and Four Points (moderately priced full-service hotels). At December 31, 2008, the company's hotel business included 409 Sheratons (143,278 rooms), 162 Westins (64,426 rooms), 76 properties (13,219 rooms) in the St. Regis and Luxury Collection groups, 134 Four Points (23,498 rooms), 26 hotels (7,742 rooms) in the W chain, 107 Le Meridien properties (27,686 rooms), 17 hotels with 2,505 rooms in HOT's new boutique hotel brand, aloft, the first two hotels in its new green brand, element (246 rooms) and nine other hotels (2,200 rooms).

The company's top six domestic markets by percentage of total owned EBITDA during 2008 were: New York (14%), Hawaii (7%), Phoenix (7%), Chicago (5%), and Atlanta and San Francisco/SanMateo (tied 4%). The top six international markets were Italy (9%), Canada (9%), Mexico (9%), Australia (5%), and Argentina and United Kingdom (both 4%). Worldwide operating statistics for the 59 owned hotels operating in both 2007 and 2008 were: average daily rate of $237.45 in 2008, up 1.0% from $235.18 in 2007, occupancy of 71.1% vs. 72.7%, and RevPAR of $168.93, down 1.2% from $171.01.

In addition, the company had 26 vacation ownership resorts as of December 31, 2008, including 21 in operations and 21 in active sales. There were 4,658 completed units, with 374 additional units under development. A potential additional 2,152 units were possible, based on land owned and average unit densities in existing markets. In total and assuming 52 intervals per unit, HOT had inventory of 375,648 vacation ownership intervals.

Company Financials Fiscal Year Ended Dec. 31

Per Share Data ($)	2008	2007	2006	2005	2004	2003	2002	2001	2000	1999
Tangible Book Value	NM	NM	3.31	13.59	10.73	4.55	3.57	2.35	2.50	2.16
Cash Flow	3.12	4.02	6.37	3.69	3.72	2.58	2.28	3.29	4.30	-0.86
Earnings	1.37	2.57	5.01	1.88	1.72	0.51	1.20	0.73	1.96	-3.41
S&P Core Earnings	1.31	2.69	4.87	1.66	1.37	0.12	0.77	0.52	NA	NA
Dividends	0.90	0.90	0.84	0.84	0.84	0.84	0.84	0.80	0.69	0.60
Payout Ratio	66%	35%	17%	45%	49%	165%	70%	110%	35%	NM
Prices:High	56.00	75.45	68.87	65.22	59.50	37.60	39.94	40.89	37.50	37.75
Prices:Low	10.97	42.78	49.68	51.50	34.81	21.68	19.00	17.10	19.75	19.50
P/E Ratio:High	41	29	14	35	35	74	33	56	19	NM
P/E Ratio:Low	8	17	10	27	20	43	16	23	10	NM
Income Statement Analysis (Million $)										
Revenue	5,907	6,153	5,979	5,977	5,368	4,630	4,659	3,967	4,345	3,862
Operating Income	1,083	1,217	1,145	1,242	1,047	1,698	1,856	1,191	1,509	1,329
Depreciation	323	306	306	407	431	429	222	526	481	476
Interest Expense	245	215	244	258	257	287	338	369	439	516
Pretax Income	330	733	682	642	412	-5.00	252	200	610	533
Effective Tax Rate	23.0%	25.8%	NM	34.1%	10.4%	NM	1.59%	23.0%	33.0%	NM
Net Income	254	543	1,115	423	369	105	246	151	401	-638
S&P Core Earnings	241	570	1,084	376	291	27.7	157	107	NA	NA
Balance Sheet & Other Financial Data (Million $)										
Cash	389	358	183	897	326	508	216	157	189	436
Current Assets	2,166	1,824	1,810	2,283	1,683	1,245	950	897	1,048	1,176
Total Assets	9,703	9,622	9,280	12,454	12,298	11,894	12,259	12,461	12,660	12,923
Current Liabilities	2,688	2,101	2,461	2,879	2,128	1,644	2,199	1,587	1,805	2,303
Long Term Debt	3,502	3,590	1,827	2,926	3,823	4,393	4,449	5,269	5,074	4,779
Common Equity	1,621	2,076	3,008	5,211	4,788	4,326	6,357	3,756	3,851	3,690
Total Capital	5,652	5,720	4,891	8,724	9,518	9,676	11,882	10,380	10,417	10,167
Capital Expenditures	476	384	371	464	333	307	82.0	477	544	521
Cash Flow	577	849	1,421	830	800	534	468	677	882	-162
Current Ratio	0.8	0.9	0.7	0.8	0.8	0.8	0.4	0.6	0.6	0.5
% Long Term Debt of Capitalization	61.9	62.8	37.4	33.5	40.2	45.4	37.4	50.8	48.7	47.0
% Net Income of Revenue	4.3	8.8	18.6	7.1	6.9	NM	5.3	3.8	9.2	NM
% Return on Assets	2.6	5.8	10.2	3.4	3.1	NM	2.0	1.2	3.1	NM
% Return on Equity	13.7	21.4	27.1	8.5	8.1	NM	3.9	4.0	10.6	NM

Data as orig reptd.; bef. results of disc opers/spec. items. Per share data adj. for stk. divs.; EPS diluted. E-Estimated. NA-Not Available. NM-Not Meaningful. NR-Not Ranked. UR-Under Review.

Office: 1111 Westchester Avenue, White Plains, NY 10604.
Telephone: 914-640-8100.
Website: http://www.starwoodhotels.com
Chrmn: B.W. Duncan

Pres & CEO: F. van Paasschen
Investor Contact: V.M. Prabhu (914-640-8100)
EVP & CFO: V.M. Prabhu
EVP, Chief Admin Officer, Secy & General Counsel: K.S. Siegel

Board Members: A. M. Aron, C. Barshefsky, J. Chapus, T. E. Clarke, C. C. Daley, Jr., B. W. Duncan, L. Galbreath, E. C. Hippeau, S. R. Quazzo, T. O. Ryder, K. C. Youngblood, F. van Paasschen

Founded: 1969
Domicile: Maryland
Employees: 145,000

State Street Corp

STANDARD &POOR'S

S&P Recommendation	STRONG BUY ★★★★★	Price $40.20 (as of Nov 27, 2009)	12-Mo. Target Price $62.00	Investment Style Large-Cap Growth

GICS Sector Financials
Sub-Industry Asset Management & Custody Banks

Summary This bank holding company, with about $11 trillion in assets under custody, is a leading servicer of financial assets worldwide.

Key Stock Statistics (Source S&P, Vickers, company reports)

52-Wk Range	$55.87–14.43	S&P Oper. EPS 2009E	3.86	Market Capitalization(B)	$19.886	Beta	1.31
Trailing 12-Month EPS	$-5.07	S&P Oper. EPS 2010E	4.41	Yield (%)	0.10	S&P 3-Yr. Proj. EPS CAGR(%)	1
Trailing 12-Month P/E	NM	P/E on S&P Oper. EPS 2009E	10.4	Dividend Rate/Share	$0.04	S&P Credit Rating	A+
$10K Invested 5 Yrs Ago	$9,539	Common Shares Outstg. (M)	494.7	Institutional Ownership (%)	85		

Price Performance

30-Week Mov. Avg. · · · 10-Week Mov. Avg. — GAAP Earnings vs. Previous Year   Volume Above Avg. STARS
12-Mo. Target Price — Relative Strength ▲ Up ▼ Down ► No Change   Below Avg. ★

Options: Ph

Analysis prepared by **Stuart Plesser** on October 28, 2009, when the stock traded at **$ 42.98**.

Highlights

► Following a projected 16.5% decline in 2009, we expect revenue to advance 10.0% in 2010, as STT's fee business will likely grow as business conditions improve and assets under management increase. We also think that net interest revenue will improve, as we project higher interest rates in 2010, which should result in higher average earning assets and investment in higher-yielding securities. We believe long-term favorable macro trends remain intact, including the outsourcing of custody services, growth in worldwide pension systems, the development of more complex investment vehicles, consolidation among financial processing providers, and increasing pressure on public retirement systems.

► We forecast expenses at roughly 64.5% of revenue in 2010, slightly worse than the 64.1% projected for 2009, due to higher performance fees. We forecast that the operating margin will be 35.7% in 2010, slightly higher than our projection for 2009.

► Excluding an extraordinary loss of $7.91 reflecting the addition of conduits to STT's balance sheet, we project operating EPS of $3.86 for 2009. In 2010, we forecast EPS of $4.41.

Investment Rationale/Risk

► STT has recently addressed our major concern -- low capital levels -- with a roughly $1.5 billion public equity offering. It also recently moved $22.7 billion of its conduits from off-balance sheet onto its balance sheet, removing another overhang on the stock, in our view. After the capital raise, its tangible common equity ratio now totals 5.7% and should improve further in the coming quarters based on profitability, by our analysis. We find further comfort that the government's stress test determined the company does not need to raise capital, even under an adverse economic scenario. With our view that most of STT's major risks have been removed, we look for its trading multiple to expand closer to historical levels of roughly 17.5X forward 12-month estimated earnings.

► Risks to our recommendation and target price include a significant slowdown in capital markets; further securities write-downs; and litigation.

► Our 12-month target price is $62, or 14.0X our 2010 EPS estimate of $4.41, a discount to the historical average that we view as warranted by the possibility of further securities losses.

Qualitative Risk Assessment

LOW	MEDIUM	HIGH

Our risk assessment reflects our view of solid fundamentals coupled with a strong customer base, good diversification and healthy earnings growth, offset by STT's lower-than-peer capital ratios combined with what we view as a risky securities book.

Quantitative Evaluations

S&P Quality Ranking   A

D	C	B-	B	B+	A-	A	A+

Relative Strength Rank   WEAK

14

LOWEST = 1   HIGHEST = 99

Revenue/Earnings Data

Revenue (Million $)

	1Q	2Q	3Q	4Q	Year
2009	2,002	--	--	--	--
2008	2,577	2,672	2,771	2,673	10,693
2007	1,696	2,740	3,165	2,479	11,818
2006	2,218	2,409	2,349	2,531	9,510
2005	1,699	1,837	1,925	2,035	7,496
2004	1,400	1,469	1,424	1,604	5,897

Earnings Per Share ($)

2009	1.02	0.79	1.04	E1.01	E3.86
2008	1.35	1.35	1.09	0.54	4.30
2007	0.93	1.07	0.91	0.57	3.45
2006	0.84	0.68	0.83	0.91	3.26
2005	0.67	0.66	0.75	0.74	2.82
2004	0.63	0.65	0.52	0.55	2.35

Fiscal year ended Dec. 31. Next earnings report expected: Late January. EPS Estimates based on S&P Operating Earnings; historical GAAP earnings are as reported.

Dividend Data (Dates: mm/dd Payment Date: mm/dd/yy)

Amount ($)	Date Decl.	Ex-Div. Date	Stk. of Record	Payment Date
0.240	12/18	12/30	01/02	01/15/09
0.010	02/26	03/30	04/01	04/15/09
0.010	06/18	06/29	07/01	07/15/09
0.010	09/17	09/29	10/01	10/15/09

Dividends have been paid since 1910. Source: Company reports.

Please read the Required Disclosures and Analyst Certification on the last page of this report.

State Street Corp

STANDARD &POOR'S

Business Summary October 28, 2009

CORPORATE OVERVIEW. STT is a leading specialist in meeting the needs of institutional investors worldwide. Its customers include mutual funds, collective investment funds and other investment pools, corporate and public retirement plans, insurance companies, foundations, endowments and investment managers. STT operates in 27 countries and more than 100 geographic markets worldwide including the U.S., Australia, Austria, Belgium, Canada, the Cayman Islands, Chile, France, Germany, India, Ireland, Italy, Japan, Luxembourg, Mauritius, the Netherlands, New Zealand, China, Singapore, South Africa, South Korea, Switzerland, Taiwan, Thailand, the United Arab Emirates and the United Kingdom.

STT reports two lines of business: Investment Servicing and Investment Management. Investment Servicing provides services for U.S. mutual funds, collective investment funds and other investment pools, corporate and public retirement plans, insurance companies, foundations and endowments worldwide. Products include custody, product- and participant-level accounting,

daily pricing and administration; master trust and master custody; record keeping; foreign exchange, brokerage and other trading services; securities finance; deposit and short-term investment facilities; loans and lease financing; investment manager and hedge fund manager operations outsourcing; and performance, risk and compliance analytics to support institutional investors.

Investment Management offers a broad array of services for managing financial assets, including investment management and investment research services, primarily for institutional investors worldwide. These services include passive and active U.S. and non-U.S. equity and fixed income strategies, and other related services, such as securities finance.

Company Financials Fiscal Year Ended Dec. 31

Per Share Data ($)	2008	2007	2006	2005	2004	2003	2002	2001	2000	1999
Tangible Book Value	10.46	12.67	16.37	13.73	12.49	11.66	12.92	11.87	10.13	8.31
Earnings	4.30	3.45	3.26	2.82	2.35	2.15	3.10	1.90	1.82	1.89
S&P Core Earnings	3.73	3.47	3.30	2.80	2.30	1.41	2.01	1.83	NA	NA
Dividends	0.95	0.88	0.80	0.72	0.64	0.56	0.48	0.41	0.35	0.29
Payout Ratio	22%	26%	25%	26%	27%	26%	15%	21%	19%	15%
Prices:High	86.55	82.53	68.56	59.80	56.90	53.63	58.36	63.93	68.40	47.63
Prices:Low	28.06	59.13	54.39	40.62	39.91	30.37	32.11	36.25	31.22	27.75
P/E Ratio:High	20	24	21	21	24	25	19	34	38	25
P/E Ratio:Low	7	17	17	14	17	14	10	19	17	15

Income Statement Analysis (Million $)	2008	2007	2006	2005	2004	2003	2002	2001	2000	1999
Net Interest Income	2,650	1,730	1,110	907	859	810	979	1,025	894	781
Tax Equivalent Adjustment	104	58.0	NA	42.0	45.0	51.0	61.0	67.0	65.0	40.0
Non Interest Income	7,693	6,599	5,201	4,566	4,074	3,925	3,421	2,782	2,665	2,255
Loan Loss Provision	Nil	Nil	Nil	Nil	-18.0	Nil	4.00	10.0	9.00	80.0
% Expense/Operating Revenue	38.5%	77.2%	71.9%	73.8%	76.2%	76.5%	64.6%	75.3%	74.3%	76.9%
Pretax Income	2,564	1,903	1,771	1,432	1,192	1,112	1,555	930	906	968
Effective Tax Rate	36.0%	33.7%	38.1%	34.0%	33.1%	35.1%	34.7%	32.5%	34.3%	36.1%
Net Income	1,642	1,261	1,096	945	798	722	1,015	628	595	619
% Net Interest Margin	2.08	1.71	1.25	1.08	1.08	1.17	1.42	1.66	1.66	1.66
S&P Core Earnings	1,549	1,269	1,107	939	782	473	658	604	NA	NA

Balance Sheet & Other Financial Data (Million $)	2008	2007	2006	2005	2004	2003	2002	2001	2000	1999
Money Market Assets	56,548	29,841	20,699	12,039	26,829	31,694	46,342	37,991	44,083	35,616
Investment Securities	76,017	74,559	64,992	59,870	37,571	38,215	28,071	20,781	13,740	14,703
Commercial Loans	6,397	13,822	6,617	4,152	2,352	2,768	2,052	3,289	3,476	2,326
Other Loans	NA	1,980	2,329	2,312	2,277	2,253	2,122	2,052	1,797	1,967
Total Assets	173,631	142,543	107,353	97,968	94,040	87,534	85,794	69,896	69,298	60,896
Demand Deposits	32,785	15,039	10,194	9,402	13,671	7,893	7,279	9,390	10,009	8,943
Time Deposits	79,440	80,750	55,452	50,244	41,458	39,623	38,189	29,169	27,928	25,202
Long Term Debt	4,419	3,636	2,616	2,659	2,458	2,222	1,270	1,217	1,219	921
Common Equity	10,721	11,299	7,252	6,367	6,159	5,747	4,787	3,845	3,262	2,652
% Return on Assets	1.0	1.0	1.1	1.0	0.9	0.8	1.3	0.9	0.9	1.1
% Return on Equity	14.9	13.6	16.1	15.1	13.4	13.7	23.5	17.7	20.1	24.9
% Loan Loss Reserve	0.2	0.1	0.2	0.3	0.4	1.2	1.5	1.1	1.1	1.1
% Loans/Deposits	9.2	15.3	13.6	10.9	8.4	10.6	9.2	13.9	13.9	12.6
% Equity to Assets	7.0	7.4	6.6	6.5	6.6	6.1	5.5	5.1	4.5	4.6

Data as orig reptd.; bef. results of disc opers/spec. items. Per share data adj. for stk. divs.; EPS diluted. E-Estimated. NA-Not Available. NM-Not Meaningful. NR-Not Ranked. UR-Under Review.

Office: 1 Lincoln St, Boston, MA 02111-2900.
Telephone: 617-786-3000.
Email: ir@statestreet.com
Website: http://www.statestreet.com

Chrmn & CEO: R.E. Logue
Pres & COO: J.L. Hooley
EVP & CFO: E.J. Resch
EVP & Chief Admin Officer: J.W. Chow

EVP, Chief Acctg Officer & Cntlr: J.J. Malerba
Investor Contact: S.K. MacDonald (617-786-3000)
Board Members: K. F. Burnes, P. Coym, P. De Saint-aignan, A. Fawcett, D. P. Gruber, L. A. Hill, R. Kaplan, C. R. Lamantia, R. E. Logue, R. P. Sergel, R. L. Skates, G. L. Summe, R. E. Weissman

Founded: 1832
Domicile: Massachusetts
Employees: 28,475

Stericycle Inc

STANDARD &POOR'S

S&P Recommendation	BUY ★★★★☆	Price $54.13 (as of Nov 27, 2009)	12-Mo. Target Price $61.00	Investment Style Large-Cap Growth

GICS Sector Industrials
Sub-Industry Environmental & Facilities Services

Summary SRCL provides medical waste collection, transportation, treatment, and disposal services and safety and compliance programs to health care companies throughout the U.S.

Key Stock Statistics (Source S&P, Vickers, company reports)

52-Wk Range	$57.15– 44.36	S&P Oper. EPS 2009E	2.08	Market Capitalization(B)	$4.559	Beta	0.30
Trailing 12-Month EPS	$1.96	S&P Oper. EPS 2010E	2.35	Yield (%)	Nil	S&P 3-Yr. Proj. EPS CAGR(%)	21
Trailing 12-Month P/E	27.6	P/E on S&P Oper. EPS 2009E	26.0	Dividend Rate/Share	Nil	S&P Credit Rating	NR
$10K Invested 5 Yrs Ago	$25,306	Common Shares Outstg. (M)	84.2	Institutional Ownership (%)	81		

Price Performance

30-Week Mov. Avg. · · · 10-Week Mov. Avg. - - GAAP Earnings vs. Previous Year Volume Above Avg. STARS
12-Mo. Target Price — Relative Strength ▲ Up ▼ Down ► No Change Below Avg. ★

Options: CBOE, P, Ph

Analysis prepared by **Stewart Scharf** on November 02, 2009, when the stock traded at **$ 52.79.**

Highlights

► We project about 8% revenue growth in 2009 (before 3% negative foreign exchange), with near 10% growth seen for 2010, driven primarily by increased small-quantity volume led by SR-CL's regulatory compliance program (Steri-Safe), as well as large-quantity growth from the sharps waste management service (Bio Systems) and new medical waste contracts. We expect near 10% small customer internal growth and 7% from large customers, with 8% domestic and 7% international.

► In our view, gross margins should expand further in 2010, from our 47% projection for 2009 (44.8% in 2008), based on price hikes and a better mix of higher-margin small quantity (SQ) customer accounts, and assuming stable energy costs. We believe operating margins (EBITDA) will widen by more than 200 basis points in 2009, from 29.5% in 2008, and continue to expand in 2010, on synergies from integrating acquisitions and well controlled SG&A expenses.

► We see an effective tax rate of about 37% through 2010, and project operating EPS in 2009 of $2.08 (before $0.04 of net charges), advancing by 13% to $2.35 in 2010.

Investment Rationale/Risk

► Our buy recommendation is based on favorable domestic and international trends in what we view as the recession-resistant medical waste business, as well as the stock's low beta, and our view of the company's highly consistent operating model with solid cash flow generation.

► Risks to our recommendation and target price include potential new competitors, significant changes in environmental regulations for medical waste disposal, a rebound in fuel and energy costs, and problems integrating acquisitions.

► We attribute the stock's above peer and S&P 500 forward P/E of 23X our 2010 EPS estimate to the company's broad medical services network, expanding market reach, and accretive acquisition strategy. Using historical and projected price-to-sales, P/E to three-year EPS growth (PEG) and price to EBITDA ratios, we derive a relative valuation of $59. Based on our DCF analysis, assuming 4% terminal growth and 8% cost of capital, our intrinsic valuation estimate is $64. Blending these metrics, we arrive at our 12-month target price of $61.

Qualitative Risk Assessment

LOW	MEDIUM	HIGH

Our risk assessment reflects our view that the regulated medical waste industry is relatively recession resistant, debt levels are reasonable, cash flow generation is sufficient, and ROIC is strong.

Quantitative Evaluations

S&P Quality Ranking B+

D	C	B-	B	B+	A-	A	A+

Relative Strength Rank STRONG

72

LOWEST = 1   HIGHEST = 99

Revenue/Earnings Data

Revenue (Million $)

	1Q	2Q	3Q	4Q	Year
2009	277.1	289.3	297.8	--	--
2008	254.8	277.8	277.1	274.0	1,084
2007	211.1	232.9	237.3	251.6	932.8
2006	179.3	198.4	203.3	208.7	789.6
2005	140.6	149.2	153.2	166.6	609.5
2004	117.6	123.8	136.0	138.9	516.2

Earnings Per Share ($)

2009	0.47	0.51	0.54	E0.54	E2.08
2008	0.35	0.44	0.45	0.45	1.68
2007	0.33	0.36	0.37	0.27	1.32
2006	0.26	0.28	0.31	0.32	1.17
2005	0.24	0.26	0.26	-0.01	0.74
2004	0.21	0.21	0.23	0.21	0.85

Fiscal year ended Dec. 31. Next earnings report expected: Early February. EPS Estimates based on S&P Operating Earnings; historical GAAP earnings are as reported.

Dividend Data

No cash dividends have been paid.

Stericycle Inc

Business Summary November 02, 2009

CORPORATE OVERVIEW. Stericycle, North America's largest regulated medical waste management company, serves customers throughout the U.S., Canada, Mexico, the United Kingdom, Ireland and Argentina. In addition to waste collection, transfer and disposal, the company provides OSHA compliance services, accreditation readiness monitoring software, hospital-acquired infection monitoring software, and expired medications return services. It entered the U.K. market through the June 2004 acquisition of White Rose Environmental Ltd., and the February 2006 purchase of Sterile Technologies Group Limited (STG).

SRCL's global network includes 78 treatment/collection centers and 98 additional transfer and collection sites. The company uses its network to provide the industry's broadest service offering, including medical waste collection, transportation and treatment, and related consulting, training and education services and products. SRCL's treatment technologies include its proprietary electro-thermal deactivation system (ETD), as well as traditional methods, such as autoclaving and incineration.

The company's two principal groups had over 440,000 customers as of September 30, 2009, including 429,000 small medical waste generators, such as

outpatient clinics, medical and dental offices, and long-term and sub-acute care facilities; and about 11,000 large medical waste generators, such as hospitals, blood banks, and pharmaceutical manufacturers. In the U.K., the mix is about 80% large-quantity (LQ) and 20% small-quantity (SQ) customers. Small-quantity customers accounted for 63% of domestic medical waste revenues at 2008 year end, up from 33% in late 1996, with gross margin of 45.7%, up from 21% in 1996. Foreign revenues accounted for 23% of the total in 2008, with Europe responsible for 14%.

MARKET PROFILE. SRCL estimates that annual revenues in the U.S. regulated medical waste services market are $3 billion, and greater than $10 billion globally. The company believes its global market share rose to 11% in 2008, up from 9.3% in 2007 and 7.9% in 2006. Waste generators outsource medical waste handling to reduce costs. Compliance issues have historically grown more complex, which has led to a shift toward more outsourcing.

Company Financials Fiscal Year Ended Dec. 31

Per Share Data ($)	2008	2007	2006	2005	2004	2003	2002	2001	2000	1999
Tangible Book Value	NM	NM	NM	NM	NM	NM	NM	NM	NM	NM
Cash Flow	2.08	1.66	1.47	0.98	1.08	0.90	0.67	0.56	0.47	0.41
Earnings	1.68	1.32	1.17	0.74	0.85	0.72	0.51	0.26	0.18	0.23
S&P Core Earnings	1.72	1.39	1.16	0.98	0.79	0.65	0.45	0.20	NA	NA
Dividends	Nil	Nil	Nil	Nil	Nil	Nil	Nil	Nil	Nil	Nil
Payout Ratio	Nil	Nil	Nil	Nil	Nil	Nil	Nil	Nil	Nil	Nil
Prices:High	66.15	62.56	38.22	31.80	26.61	26.01	20.27	15.71	10.56	4.94
Prices:Low	46.45	36.52	28.33	21.38	20.85	16.03	12.50	6.50	3.80	2.38
P/E Ratio:High	39	47	33	43	31	36	40	60	59	21
P/E Ratio:Low	28	28	24	29	25	22	25	25	21	10

Income Statement Analysis (Million $)	2008	2007	2006	2005	2004	2003	2002	2001	2000	1999
Revenue	1,084	933	790	610	516	453	402	359	324	133
Operating Income	316	272	233	191	169	144	119	102	91.4	30.1
Depreciation	34.2	31.1	27.0	21.4	21.8	17.3	15.0	25.2	23.5	9.88
Interest Expense	33.1	34.0	28.4	13.0	11.2	12.8	21.5	35.4	39.8	6.20
Pretax Income	239	191	173	112	129	109	75.6	36.7	23.8	7.80
Effective Tax Rate	37.8%	38.1%	39.0%	40.0%	39.2%	39.5%	39.5%	40.1%	39.1%	NM
Net Income	149	118	105	67.2	78.2	65.8	45.7	22.0	14.5	14.0
S&P Core Earnings	152	124	105	87.6	71.8	59.0	39.7	14.0	NA	NA

Balance Sheet & Other Financial Data (Million $)	2008	2007	2006	2005	2004	2003	2002	2001	2000	1999
Cash	10.5	18.4	13.5	7.83	7.85	7.24	8.38	12.7	2.67	19.3
Current Assets	224	210	219	144	115	97.7	94.4	98.0	91.0	77.5
Total Assets	1,759	1,608	1,328	1,048	834	707	667	615	598	596
Current Liabilities	180	150	142	98.8	83.2	69.0	53.8	63.4	43.1	50.7
Long Term Debt	754	614	443	349	190	163	224	267	345	355
Common Equity	670	714	625	522	495	408	327	233	135	118
Total Capital	1,571	1,453	1,174	942	743	634	610	545	551	543
Capital Expenditures	47.5	48.4	36.4	26.3	21.0	21.0	14.8	15.4	11.6	3.80
Cash Flow	183	150	132	88.6	100.0	83.0	60.7	47.3	38.0	23.5
Current Ratio	1.3	1.4	1.5	1.5	1.4	1.4	1.8	1.5	2.1	1.5
% Long Term Debt of Capitalization	48.0	42.3	37.8	37.0	25.6	25.7	36.8	49.1	62.6	65.5
% Net Income of Revenue	13.7	12.7	13.3	11.0	15.1	14.5	11.4	6.1	4.5	10.5
% Return on Assets	8.8	8.1	8.9	7.1	10.1	9.6	7.1	3.6	2.4	4.0
% Return on Equity	21.5	17.7	18.4	13.2	17.3	17.9	16.4	12.0	11.5	15.9

Data as orig reptd.; bef. results of disc opers/spec. items. Per share data adj. for stk. divs.; EPS diluted. E-Estimated. NA-Not Available. NM-Not Meaningful. NR-Not Ranked. UR-Under Review.

Office: 28161 North Keith Drive, Lake Forest, IL 60045.
Telephone: 847-367-5910.
Email: investor@stericycle.com
Website: http://www.stericycle.com

Chrmn, Pres & CEO: M.C. Miller
COO & EVP: R. Kogler
EVP, CFO & Chief Acctg Officer: F.J. ten Brink

Board Members: T. D. Brown, R. F. Dammeyer, W. Hall, J. T. Lord, M. C. Miller, J. Patience, J. Reid-Anderson, J. Schuler, R. G. Spaeth

Founded: 1989
Domicile: Delaware
Employees: 6,883

Stryker Corp

STANDARD &POOR'S

| S&P Recommendation **BUY** ★★★★☆ | Price $50.40 (as of Nov 30, 2009) | 12-Mo. Target Price $56.00 | Investment Style Large-Cap Growth |

GICS Sector Health Care
Sub-Industry Health Care Equipment

Summary This company makes specialty surgical and medical products such as orthopedic implants, endoscopic items, and hospital beds.

Key Stock Statistics (Source S&P, Vickers, company reports)

52-Wk Range	$51.32– 30.82	S&P Oper. EPS 2009**E**	2.95	Market Capitalization(B)	$20.046	Beta	0.96
Trailing 12-Month EPS	$2.70	S&P Oper. EPS 2010**E**	3.30	Yield (%)	0.79	S&P 3-Yr. Proj. EPS CAGR(%)	9
Trailing 12-Month P/E	18.7	P/E on S&P Oper. EPS 2009**E**	17.1	Dividend Rate/Share	$0.40	S&P Credit Rating	A+
$10K Invested 5 Yrs Ago	$11,462	Common Shares Outstg. (M)	397.7	Institutional Ownership (%)	61		

Price Performance

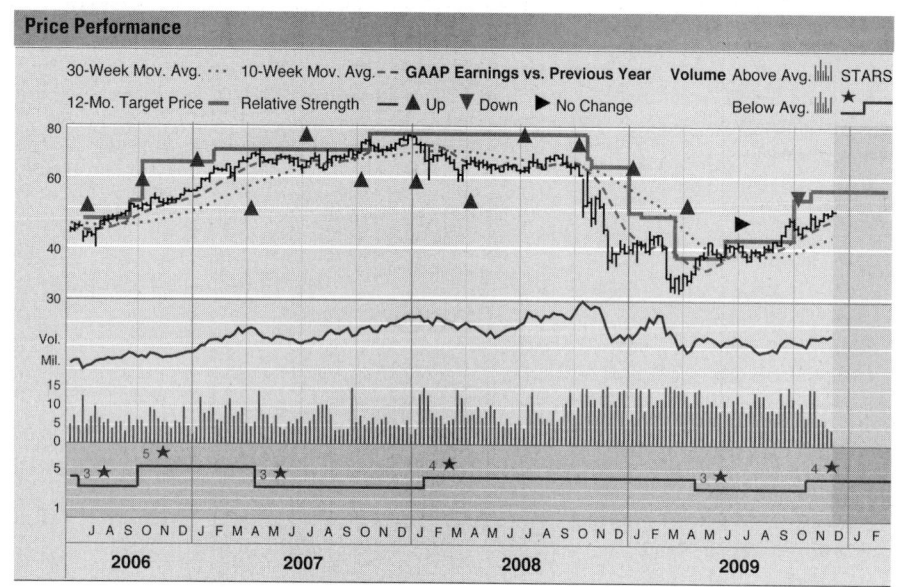

30-Week Mov. Avg. ···   10-Week Mov. Avg.─ ─   **GAAP Earnings vs. Previous Year**   Volume Above Avg. STARS
12-Mo. Target Price ─   Relative Strength   ▲ Up ▼ Down ► No Change   Below Avg.

Options: ASE, CBOE, Ph

Analysis prepared by **Phillip M. Seligman** on October 27, 2009, when the stock traded at **$ 47.92**.

Highlights

▶ We expect 2009 sales to approximate $6.7 billion, with low single digit global growth in the orthopedic implant business offset by a 6% decline in medical/surgical equipment sales and unfavorable currency exchange. For 2010, we forecast almost $7.2 billion in sales, assuming a recovery in orthopedic implant sales seen in 2009's third quarter is sustainable, and while we expect hospitals to remain cautious in their capital spending, we see med-surg equipment sales benefiting from weak comparisons.

▶ In our view, gross margin pressures stemming from investments in compliance initiatives, the slowdown of some of SYK's manufacturing plants, and pricing pressures will be only partially offset by an improving product mix and upgrades in quality. Hence, we anticipate that 2009 gross margins will be slightly under 68%, down modestly from 2008, but expect them to recover slightly in 2010. However, we forecast SG&A costs to continue to decline as a percentage of sales, on cost controls and despite a sales force expansion, while R&D costs continues to consume about 5% of sales.

▶ We estimate EPS of $2.95 in 2009 and look for an advance of 11% in 2010, to $3.30.

Investment Rationale/Risk

▶ We recently upgraded the shares to buy from hold, as SYK's third-quarter 2009 orthopedic implant sales growth was better than we expected, and while we do not see med-surg shipments revitalizing soon, we think the market has stabilized. We are also encouraged that the FDA has lifted one warning letter and see the three others lifted over time, lessening the overhang. Meanwhile, we continue to see long-term growth opportunities for SYK enabled by its active R&D and demographic trends. We see procedure deferrals lessening over time and but still see overall growth constrained by hospital spending cuts. We view cash flow as healthy, providing financial flexibility.

▶ Risks to our recommendation and target price include Medicare reimbursement rate reductions, rejection of a promising product by the FDA, and an unfavorable outcome from a probe into SYK's business practices.

▶ Our 12-month target price of $56 reflects a P/E of 17X our 2010 EPS estimate. In our view, Stryker's superior projected growth rate relative to peers justifies a premium valuation, but we apply a premium below historical levels to reflect the headwinds we see.

Qualitative Risk Assessment

| LOW | **MEDIUM** | HIGH |

Stryker operates in very competitive areas of the global medical device industry, characterized by rapid technological innovation and market share volatility. We believe the medical/surgical supplies unit may be vulnerable to reductions in hospital capital equipment spending, but we think demand for its orthopedic products is largely immune from economic cycles.

Quantitative Evaluations

S&P Quality Ranking A+

| D | C | B- | B | B+ | A- | A | **A+** |

Relative Strength Rank **STRONG**

86

LOWEST = 1   HIGHEST = 99

Revenue/Earnings Data

Revenue (Million $)

	1Q	2Q	3Q	4Q	Year
2009	1,601	1,634	1,653	--	--
2008	1,634	1,713	1,653	1,718	6,718
2007	1,426	1,464	1,453	1,658	6,001
2006	1,321	1,328	1,294	1,463	5,406
2005	1,203	1,219	1,172	1,279	4,872
2004	1,035	1,043	1,029	1,156	4,262

Earnings Per Share ($)

	1Q	2Q	3Q	4Q	Year
2009	0.71	0.73	0.57	E0.82	E2.95
2008	0.70	0.73	0.66	0.69	2.78
2007	0.58	0.58	0.55	0.66	2.37
2006	0.36	0.52	0.46	0.55	1.89
2005	0.42	0.45	0.32	0.45	1.64
2004	0.33	0.37	0.04	0.40	1.14

Fiscal year ended Dec. 31. Next earnings report expected: Late January. EPS Estimates based on S&P Operating Earnings; historical GAAP earnings are as reported.

Dividend Data (Dates: mm/dd Payment Date: mm/dd/yy)

Amount ($)	Date Decl.	Ex-Div. Date	Stk. of Record	Payment Date
0.400	12/03	12/29	12/31	01/30/09
.10 Spl.	10/30	11/16	11/19	12/16/09

Dividends have been paid since 1992. Source: Company reports.

Please read the Required Disclosures and Analyst Certification on the last page of this report.

The McGraw·Hill Companies

Stryker Corp

Business Summary October 27, 2009

Stryker Corp. traces its origins to a business founded in 1941 by Dr. Homer H. Stryker, a leading orthopedic surgeon and the inventor of several orthopedic products. The company has significant exposure to the artificial hip, prosthetic knee and trauma product areas. International sales accounted for 36% of the total in 2008.

Orthopedic implants (59% of 2008 sales) consist of products such as hip, knee, shoulder and spinal implants, associated implant instrumentation, trauma-related products, and bone cement. Artificial joints are made of cobalt chromium, titanium alloys, ceramics, or ultra-high molecular weight polyethylene, and are implanted in patients whose natural joints have been damaged by arthritis, osteoporosis, other diseases, or injury. SYK also sells trauma-related products, used primarily in the fixation of fractures resulting from sudden injury, including internal fixation devices such as nails, plates and screws, and external fixation devices such as pins, wires and connection bars. In addition, the division sells Simplex bone cement, a material used to secure cemented implants to bone, and the OP-1 Bone Growth Device. Composed of recombinant human osteogenic protein-1 and a bioresorbable collagen matrix, the product induces the formation of new bone when implanted into existing bone, and is approved to treat long bone fractures in patients in whom use of autograft treatments has failed or is not a feasible option. Stryker continues to develop OP-1 for spinal indications, including spinal stenosis, and is working with the FDA to obtain U.S. marketing clearance. In 2006, SYK began the initial

launch of a hip resurfacing product in certain international markets.

During 2006, Stryker acquired Sightline Inc., a privately held developer of flexible endoscopes for gastrointestinal and other markets, with a technology that is believed to improve insertion and sterilization during colonoscopy procedures. In August 2004, Stryker bought SpineCore Inc., a developer of artificial lumbar and cervical spinal discs.

The medical and surgical equipment unit (41%) operates through four units. Stryker Instruments sells powered surgical drills, saws, fixation and reaming equipment, as well as other instruments used for drilling, burring, rasping or cutting bone, wiring or pinning bone fractures, and preparing hip or knee surfaces for the placement of artificial hip or knee joints. Stryker Endoscopy offers medical video cameras, light sources, arthroscopes, laparascopes, powered surgical instruments, and disposable suction/irrigation devices. Stryker Medical produces 30 types of specialty stretchers customized for acute care and specialty surgical facilities. Stryker Leibinger makes plate and screw systems for craniomaxillofacial surgery to repair small bones in the hands, face and head, and sells a proprietary bone substitute material, BoneSource.

Company Financials Fiscal Year Ended Dec. 31

Per Share Data ($)	2008	2007	2006	2005	2004	2003	2002	2001	2000	1999
Tangible Book Value	11.28	10.84	7.98	5.75	4.44	2.98	1.42	0.65	0.04	NM
Cash Flow	3.25	2.79	2.69	2.34	1.78	1.71	1.30	1.09	0.97	0.46
Earnings	2.78	2.37	1.89	1.64	1.14	1.12	0.85	0.67	0.55	0.05
S&P Core Earnings	2.76	2.37	1.89	1.57	1.08	1.08	0.80	0.63	NA	NA
Dividends	14.00	0.33	0.22	0.11	0.09	0.07	0.06	0.05	0.03	0.03
Payout Ratio	NA	14%	12%	7%	8%	6%	7%	7%	5%	60%
Prices:High	74.94	76.89	55.92	56.32	57.66	42.68	33.74	31.60	28.88	18.31
Prices:Low	35.38	54.89	39.77	39.74	40.30	29.83	21.93	21.65	12.22	11.11
P/E Ratio:High	27	32	30	34	51	38	40	47	52	NM
P/E Ratio:Low	13	23	21	24	35	27	26	32	22	NM

Income Statement Analysis (Million $)										
Revenue	6,718	6,001	5,406	4,872	4,262	3,625	3,012	2,602	2,289	2,104
Operating Income	1,749	1,506	1,459	1,305	1,092	901	751	645	600	329
Depreciation	195	179	332	290	251	230	186	172	169	163
Interest Expense	30.5	22.2	Nil	7.70	6.80	22.6	40.3	67.9	96.6	123
Pretax Income	1,580	1,370	1,104	1,003	717	652	507	406	335	29.8
Effective Tax Rate	27.4%	28.0%	29.5%	32.7%	35.0%	30.5%	31.8%	33.0%	34.0%	34.9%
Net Income	1,148	987	778	675	466	454	346	272	221	19.4
S&P Core Earnings	1,141	987	779	645	441	436	324	257	NA	NA

Balance Sheet & Other Financial Data (Million $)										
Cash	2,196	2,411	1,415	1,057	349	65.9	37.8	50.1	54.0	80.0
Current Assets	4,979	4,905	3,534	2,870	2,143	1,398	1,151	993	997	1,110
Total Assets	7,603	7,354	5,874	4,944	4,084	3,159	2,816	2,424	2,431	2,581
Current Liabilities	1,462	1,333	1,352	1,249	1,114	850	708	533	617	670
Long Term Debt	Nil	Nil	Nil	184	0.70	18.8	491	721	876	1,181
Common Equity	5,407	5,379	4,191	3,252	2,752	2,155	1,498	1,056	855	672
Total Capital	5,568	5,524	4,191	3,436	2,753	2,174	1,989	1,777	1,731	1,853
Capital Expenditures	155	188	218	272	188	145	139	162	80.7	76.2
Cash Flow	1,343	1,165	1,110	965	717	683	532	444	390	182
Current Ratio	3.4	3.7	2.6	2.3	1.9	1.6	1.6	1.9	1.6	1.7
% Long Term Debt of Capitalization	Nil	Nil	Nil	5.4	0.0	0.9	24.7	40.6	50.6	63.8
% Net Income of Revenue	17.1	16.4	14.4	13.9	10.9	12.5	11.5	10.4	9.7	0.9
% Return on Assets	15.4	14.9	14.3	15.0	12.9	15.2	13.2	11.2	8.8	0.7
% Return on Equity	21.3	20.6	20.8	22.5	19.0	24.8	27.1	28.4	29.0	2.9

Data as orig reptd.; bef. results of disc opers/spec. items. Per share data adj. for stk. divs.; EPS diluted. E-Estimated. NA-Not Available. NM-Not Meaningful. NR-Not Ranked. UR-Under Review.

Office: 2825 Airview Blvd, Portage, MI 49002-1802.
Telephone: 269-385-2600.
Website: http://www.stryker.com
Chrmn: J.W. Brown

Pres & CEO: S.P. MacMillan
CFO: C.R. Hartman
Chief Acctg Officer: T.M. McKinney
Treas: J. Blondia

Investor Contact: K.A. Owen (269-385-2600)
Board Members: J. W. Brown, H. E. Cox, Jr., S. M. Datar, D. M. Engelman, L. L. Francesconi, H. L. Lance, S. P. MacMillan, W. U. Parfet, R. E. Stryker

Founded: 1946
Domicile: Michigan
Employees: 17,594

Sunoco Inc.

STANDARD &POOR'S

S&P Recommendation	HOLD ★★★☆☆	Price	12-Mo. Target Price	Investment Style
		$25.43 (as of Nov 27, 2009)	$30.00	Large-Cap Blend

GICS Sector Energy
Sub-Industry Oil & Gas Refining & Marketing

Summary One of the largest independent refiners in the U.S., this company has diversified operations in refining, marketing, chemicals, logistics and cokemaking.

Key Stock Statistics (Source S&P, Vickers, company reports)

52-Wk Range	$47.40– 21.45	S&P Oper. EPS 2009E	0.20	Market Capitalization(B)	$2.973	Beta	0.73
Trailing 12-Month EPS	$-1.30	S&P Oper. EPS 2010E	2.61	Yield (%)	2.36	S&P 3-Yr. Proj. EPS CAGR(%)	-16
Trailing 12-Month P/E	NM	P/E on S&P Oper. EPS 2009E	NM	Dividend Rate/Share	$0.60	S&P Credit Rating	BBB
$10K Invested 5 Yrs Ago	$6,850	Common Shares Outstg. (M)	116.9	Institutional Ownership (%)	79		

Price Performance

30-Week Mov. Avg. ··· 10-Week Mov. Avg. – – **GAAP Earnings vs. Previous Year** Volume Above Avg. STARS
12-Mo. Target Price — Relative Strength — ▲ Up ▼ Down ► No Change Below Avg.

Options: CBOE, Ph

Analysis prepared by **Tina J. Vital** on November 12, 2009, when the stock traded at **$ 27.53**.

Highlights

▶ Slowed global economies have reduced the demand for refined petroleum products. As a result, we estimate U.S. Gulf Coast 3-2-1 crack spreads will narrow about 16% in 2009 before widening about 7% in 2010. In response, U.S. refiners have trimmed throughput rates -- SUN's third-quarter throughputs declined 17%, to 679,700 b/d -- and, we expect 2009 volumes to contract about 18%. Also, SUN has initiated spending cuts, and in November, it was on track to achieve $300 million in annual cost saving.

▶ We expect SUN's Coke and Logistics segments will provide solid results over the next 12 months. We believe Coke earnings will be supported by 15-year, fixed-return take-or-pay contracts (renewal expected in 2012) with the steel industry, and, we look for Logistics to be supported by single-digit sales growth in its distribution business.

▶ First nine months operating EPS excluded $3.10 of net special charges related to restructurings. We look for EBITDA (earnings before interest, taxes and depreciation) to drop 62% in 2009 on reduced demand, but rise 69% in 2010 on an improved economic outlook.

Investment Rationale/Risk

▶ While SUN's focus on light sweet crude oil feedstocks has limited its ability to take advantage of the historically wide sour crude discounts, it has permitted a relatively high volume of higher-grade products. We believe its strong East Coast and Midwest retail distribution provides long-term earnings stability, and its stake in Sunoco Logistics Partners L.P. is a stable source of distribution. We expect SUN to continue to rationalize its refining and chemical business, pursue a possible oil sands joint venture for its Toledo refinery, and focus on expanding its logistics and coke operations.

▶ Risks to our recommendation and target price include unfavorable changes in economic, industry and operating conditions that would lead to a narrowing of operating margins, or overpaying for an acquisition.

▶ A blend of our discounted cash flow analysis ($29 per share, assuming a weighted average cost of capital of 7.3% and a terminal growth rate of 3%) and relative valuations leads to our 12-month target price of $30. This represents an expected enterprise value of about 5.2X our 2010 EBITDA estimate, a discount to peers.

Qualitative Risk Assessment

LOW	MEDIUM	HIGH

Our risk assessment reflects the company's solid business profile in the volatile and competitive refining industry, and diversification into retail marketing, chemicals, logistics and cokemaking.

Quantitative Evaluations

S&P Quality Ranking   A-

D	C	B-	B	B+	A-	A	A+

Relative Strength Rank   WEAK

19

LOWEST = 1   HIGHEST = 99

Revenue/Earnings Data

Revenue (Million $)

	1Q	2Q	3Q	4Q	Year
2009	6,441	6,877	8,695	--	--
2008	12,813	15,426	15,447	8,479	51,558
2007	9,305	10,764	11,497	13,162	44,728
2006	8,593	10,590	10,496	9,036	38,715
2005	7,209	7,990	9,295	9,270	33,764
2004	5,245	6,276	6,558	7,429	25,508

Earnings Per Share ($)

2009	0.10	-0.59	-2.67	E0.25	E0.20
2008	-0.50	0.70	4.70	1.74	6.63
2007	1.44	4.20	1.81	-0.08	7.43
2006	0.59	3.22	2.76	1.00	7.59
2005	0.84	1.75	2.39	2.12	7.08
2004	0.58	1.54	0.70	1.24	4.04

Fiscal year ended Dec. 31. Next earnings report expected: Early February. EPS Estimates based on S&P Operating Earnings; historical GAAP earnings are as reported.

Dividend Data (Dates: mm/dd Payment Date: mm/dd/yy)

Amount ($)	Date Decl.	Ex-Div. Date	Stk. of Record	Payment Date
0.300	01/02	02/05	02/09	03/10/09
0.300	04/02	05/07	05/11	06/10/09
0.300	07/02	08/07	08/11	09/10/09
0.300	09/03	11/06	11/10	12/10/09

Dividends have been paid since 1904. Source: Company reports.

Please read the Required Disclosures and Analyst Certification on the last page of this report.

The McGraw-Hill Companies

Sunoco Inc.

STANDARD &POOR'S

Business Summary November 12, 2009

CORPORATE OVERVIEW. Sunoco Inc. (SUN) has been active in the petroleum industry since 1886, and conducts its business through five operating segments: Refining and Supply (49% of 2008 revenues; 55% of 2008 segment income); Retail Marketing (30%; 21%); Chemicals (5%; 4%); Logistics (14%; 9%); and Coke (2%; 11%).

Refining and Supply manufactures refined petroleum products and commodity petrochemicals. As of December 31, 2008, SUN owned and operated five refineries with a crude unit capacity of about 910,000 barrels per day (b/d), located in the Northeast (655,000 b/d; in Marcus Hook, PA, Philadelphia, PA, and "Eagle Point" in Westville, NJ), and the MidContinent (255,000 b/d; Toledo, OH, and Tulsa, OK). Production available for sale declined 5.1%, to 860,000 b/d, in 2008 (gasoline 45%, middle distillates 35%, residual fuels 8%, petrochemicals 4%, and other 8%). SUN intends to convert an idle hydrocracker at its Philadelphia refinery into a hydrotreater for ultra-low-sulfur-diesel production (project completion slated for mid-2009).

SUN meets all of its crude oil requirements through purchases from third parties. Approximately 56% of SUN's 2008 crude oil supply came from West

Africa (25% from Nigeria), 18% from the U.S., 10% from Canada, 9% from Central Asia, 1% from the North Sea, 4% from South and Central America, 1% from Australia, and 1% from lubes extracted from gasoil/naphtha intermediate feedstock. In the 2004 second half, the company began processing limited amounts of lower value high acid sweet crude oils in some of its Northeast refineries; during 2008, about 71,000 b/d of high acid crude oil was processed.

The Chemicals segment manufactures, distributes and markets commodity and intermediate petrochemicals, consisting of aromatic derivatives (cumene, phenol, acetone and bispenol-A) and polypropylene. In early 2009, SUN shut down its Bayport, TX polypropylene plant, which had become uneconomic to run. As of October 2009, SUN was in discussions with various interested parties to sell its chemicals business; a decision is expected during the 2009 third quarter.

Company Financials Fiscal Year Ended Dec. 31

Per Share Data ($)	2008	2007	2006	2005	2004	2003	2002	2001	2000	1999
Tangible Book Value	22.30	19.12	17.01	15.42	11.65	10.23	9.05	10.88	10.03	8.37
Cash Flow	11.03	11.43	11.15	10.20	9.50	4.35	1.85	4.38	4.05	2.05
Earnings	6.63	7.43	7.59	7.08	4.04	2.02	-0.31	2.43	2.35	0.54
S&P Core Earnings	6.23	6.74	7.63	7.56	4.19	2.13	-0.70	1.88	NA	NA
Dividends	1.17	1.08	0.95	0.75	0.58	0.51	0.50	0.50	0.50	0.50
Payout Ratio	18%	14%	13%	11%	14%	25%	NM	21%	21%	93%
Prices:High	73.68	86.40	97.25	85.29	42.26	26.30	21.13	21.37	17.28	19.72
Prices:Low	21.30	56.68	57.50	38.10	25.26	14.84	13.51	14.56	10.97	11.44
P/E Ratio:High	11	12	13	12	10	13	NM	9	7	37
P/E Ratio:Low	3	8	8	5	6	7	NM	6	5	21

Income Statement Analysis (Million $)										
Revenue	51,558	44,728	38,715	33,764	25,508	17,929	14,384	14,063	14,300	10,068
Operating Income	1,988	1,835	2,049	2,078	1,501	934	313	954	948	331
Depreciation, Depletion and Amortization	515	480	459	429	818	363	329	321	298	276
Interest Expense	72.0	127	89.0	69.0	97.0	111	108	103	78.0	82.0
Pretax Income	1,173	1,476	1,580	1,580	995	495	-73.0	587	596	150
Effective Tax Rate	33.8%	35.1%	38.0%	38.4%	39.2%	37.0%	NM	32.2%	31.0%	35.3%
Net Income	776	891	979	974	605	312	-47.0	398	411	97.0
S&P Core Earnings	729	808	984	1,040	626	330	-106	307	NA	NA

Balance Sheet & Other Financial Data (Million $)										
Cash	240	648	263	919	405	431	390	42.0	239	87.0
Current Assets	2,835	4,638	4,015	3,687	2,551	2,068	1,898	1,510	1,683	1,456
Total Assets	11,150	12,426	10,982	9,931	8,079	6,922	6,441	5,932	5,426	5,196
Current Liabilities	3,937	5,640	4,755	4,210	3,022	2,170	1,776	1,778	1,646	1,766
Long Term Debt	1,705	1,724	1,705	1,234	1,379	1,350	1,453	1,142	933	878
Common Equity	2,842	2,533	2,075	2,051	1,607	1,556	1,394	1,642	1,702	4,782
Total Capital	5,844	5,723	5,227	4,749	4,271	3,940	3,816	3,335	2,885	5,897
Capital Expenditures	1,286	1,179	1,019	970	832	425	385	331	465	374
Cash Flow	1,291	1,371	1,438	1,403	1,423	675	282	719	709	373
Current Ratio	0.7	0.8	0.8	0.9	0.8	1.0	1.1	0.8	1.0	0.8
% Long Term Debt of Capitalization	29.2	30.1	32.6	26.0	32.3	34.3	38.1	34.2	32.3	14.9
% Return on Assets	6.6	7.6	9.4	10.8	8.0	4.7	NM	7.0	7.7	1.9
% Return on Equity	28.9	38.7	47.5	53.3	38.3	21.2	NM	23.8	25.6	2.0

Data as orig reptd.; bef. results of disc opers/spec. items. Per share data adj. for stk. divs.; EPS diluted. E-Estimated. NA-Not Available. NM-Not Meaningful. NR-Not Ranked. UR-Under Review.

Office: 1735 Market St Ste LL, Philadelphia, PA 19103-7583.
Telephone: 215-977-3000.
Email: sunocoonline@sunocoinc.com
Website: http://www.sunocoinc.com

Chrmn, Pres & CEO: L.L. Elsenhans
SVP & CFO: B.P. MacDonald
SVP & General Counsel: M.S. Kuritzkes
CTO: V.J. Kelley

Chief Acctg Officer & Cntlr: J.P. Krott
Investor Contact: T. Harr (215-977-6764)
Investor Contact: T.P. Delaney
Board Members: R. J. Darnall, G. W. Edwards, L. L. Elsenhans, U. O. Fairbairn, T. P. Gerrity, R. B. Greco, J. P. Jones, III, J. G. Kaiser, J. W. Rowe, J. K. Wulff

Founded: 1886
Domicile: Pennsylvania
Employees: 13,700

Sun Microsystems Inc

STANDARD &POOR'S

S&P Recommendation	HOLD ★★★☆☆	Price	12-Mo. Target Price	Investment Style
		$8.52 (as of Nov 27, 2009)	$9.50	Large-Cap Blend

GICS Sector Information Technology
Sub-Industry Computer Hardware

Summary Sun Microsystems has agreed to be acquired by Oracle Corporation for $9.50 cash per share, subject to regulatory and other approvals.

Key Stock Statistics (Source S&P, Vickers, company reports)

52-Wk Range	$9.37–2.83	S&P Oper. EPS 2010**E**	0.01	Market Capitalization(B)	$6.424	Beta	1.64
Trailing 12-Month EPS	$-0.90	S&P Oper. EPS 2011**E**	-0.05	Yield (%)	Nil	S&P 3-Yr. Proj. EPS CAGR(%)	NM
Trailing 12-Month P/E	NM	P/E on S&P Oper. EPS 2010**E**	NM	Dividend Rate/Share	Nil	S&P Credit Rating	BB+
$10K Invested 5 Yrs Ago	$4,049	Common Shares Outstg. (M)	753.9	Institutional Ownership (%)	72		

Price Performance

30-Week Mov. Avg. · · · 10-Week Mov. Avg. — **GAAP Earnings vs. Previous Year**   Volume Above Avg. ▥ STARS
12-Mo. Target Price — Relative Strength   ▲ Up ▼ Down ► No Change   Below Avg. ▥ ★

Options: ASE, CBOE, P, Ph

Analysis prepared by **Thomas W. Smith, CFA** on November 10, 2009, when the stock traded at **$8.15**.

Highlights

► For JAVA as a stand-alone operation, we project a revenue decrease of 14% for FY 10 (Jun.), and an increase of 2% for FY 11. We believe that weakness in enterprise IT spending, combined with delays and uncertainty in the pending acquisition by Oracle (ORCL 22, Hold), are outweighing the positive forces of partnerships and new products. The company took restructuring charges of $45 million in the first quarter of FY 10, following $395 million of restructuring charges in FY 09. On October 20, 2009, it announced further restructuring plans, including 3,000 job cuts.

► We look for strong pricing competition to be partly offset by manufacturing efficiencies from restructuring. We expect spending on R&D in FY 10 to decrease about $200 million, which should help contain costs but might hinder product development.

► We estimate per-share operating EPS, excluding restructuring charges but including stock option expense, of $0.01 for FY 10, and a loss of $0.05 per share in FY 11.

Investment Rationale/Risk

► On April 20, JAVA agreed to be acquired by Oracle Corp. (ORCL 22, Hold) for $9.50 in cash per JAVA common share. The company values the transaction at about $7.4 billion, or $5.6 billion net of JAVA's cash and debt. The U.S. Justice Dept. has cleared the deal, but on November 9, European regulators issued an objection to it based on the potential for reduced competition in the database market. JAVA shareholders had voted in favor of the transaction on July 16. As a stand-alone company, we see JAVA with a high risk profile resulting from intensifying competition in servers amid an industry downturn.

► Risks to our recommendation and target price include the possibility of the proposed acquisition by Oracle failing to proceed as planned, and the possibilities of server market share losses and a slow pace of customer spending on information technology equipment.

► Our 12-month target price of $9.50 is in line with the cash acquisition price offered by Oracle Corp. as part of the pending transaction.

Qualitative Risk Assessment

LOW	MEDIUM	**HIGH**

Our risk assessment of JAVA as a stand-alone operation reflects the spotty earnings record the company has compiled over the past several years, our view of its reliance on high-end systems sales, and the pricing pressures we see in the computer hardware industry.

Quantitative Evaluations

S&P Quality Ranking   C

D	**C**	B-	B	B+	A-	A	A+

Relative Strength Rank   **MODERATE**

38

LOWEST = 1   HIGHEST = 99

Revenue/Earnings Data

Revenue (Million $)

	1Q	2Q	3Q	4Q	Year
2010	2,243	--	--	--	--
2009	2,990	3,220	2,614	2,625	11,449
2008	3,219	3,615	3,266	3,780	13,880
2007	3,189	3,566	3,283	3,835	13,873
2006	2,726	3,337	3,177	3,828	13,068
2005	2,628	2,841	2,627	2,974	11,070

Earnings Per Share ($)

	1Q	2Q	3Q	4Q	Year
2010	-0.16	E0.04	E-0.05	E0.03	E0.01
2009	-2.24	-0.28	-0.27	-0.20	-2.99
2008	0.12	0.32	-0.04	0.11	0.49
2007	-0.08	0.16	0.08	0.36	0.52
2006	-0.16	-0.28	-0.24	-0.36	-1.00
2005	-0.16	Nil	-0.04	0.04	-0.12

Fiscal year ended Jun. 30. Next earnings report expected: Late January. EPS Estimates based on S&P Operating Earnings; historical GAAP earnings are as reported.

Dividend Data

No cash dividends have been paid.

Sun Microsystems Inc

STANDARD &POOR'S

Business Summary November 10, 2009

CORPORATE OVERVIEW. On April 20, 2009, Sun Microsystems (JAVA) agreed to be acquired by Oracle Corp. (ORCL 22, Hold) for $9.50 in cash per JAVA common share. The company valued the transaction at about $7.4 billion, or $5.6 billion net of JAVA's cash and debt. The JAVA board unanimously approved the transaction. JAVA shareholders approved the deal on July 16, and it was approved by the U.S. Department of Justice on August 20. On November 9, the European Commission issued a statement of objections that focused on the potential negative effects of combining Sun's open source MySQL database products with Oracle's products. We expect EU antitrust authorities to continue their assessment into January 2010. We still expect the deal to be completed at the proposed price, but there is some risk that it could be altered to address the MySQL issue.

Sun Microsystems, founded in 1982, operates in over 100 countries and serves a variety of markets including financial services, government, manufacturing, retail and telecommunications, as it continues to focus on a single vision -- that the network is the computer.

Sun is a primary supplier of networked computing products, including work-

stations, servers and storage products -- which had primarily used the company's own Scaleable Processor Architecture (SPARC) microprocessors and its Solaris software -- but this has been expanded to include other chips and operating system software. Other core brands include the Java technology platform, the MySQL database management system, and Sun StorageTek storage. Computer systems accounted for 42% of net revenues in FY 09 (Jun.) (45% in FY 08), storage 16% (17%), support services 32% (29%), and professional and educational services 10% (9%). In FY 09, electronics distributor Avnet accounted for 13% of total revenue, up from 11% in FY 08.

Sun generates the majority of its business from overseas markets. In FY 09, 63% of net revenues were from outside the U.S., similar to the level in FY 08. By region, the contributions to sales in FY 09 were U.S. 37%, Canada and Latin America 3%, Europe 33%, Emerging Markets 16%, and Asia Pacific 12%, allowing for rounding.

Company Financials Fiscal Year Ended Jun. 30

Per Share Data ($)	2009	2008	2007	2006	2005	2004	2003	2002	2001	2000
Tangible Book Value	1.78	2.40	4.56	3.20	7.20	7.08	7.52	9.28	10.52	8.90
Cash Flow	-1.96	1.33	1.45	-0.34	0.67	0.42	-3.15	0.47	2.59	3.11
Earnings	-2.99	0.49	0.52	-1.00	-0.12	-0.48	-4.28	-0.72	1.16	2.20
S&P Core Earnings	-1.80	0.39	0.48	-1.04	-1.00	-2.68	-3.24	-1.52	0.56	NA
Dividends	Nil	Nil	Nil	Nil	Nil	Nil	Nil	Nil	Nil	Nil
Payout Ratio	Nil	Nil	Nil	Nil	Nil	Nil	Nil	Nil	Nil	Nil
Prices:High	9.37	18.14	27.12	23.52	21.04	23.72	22.56	57.64	140.50	258.63
Prices:Low	3.45	2.60	17.96	14.96	13.68	13.16	12.08	9.36	30.08	100.50
P/E Ratio:High	NM	37	52	NM	NM	NM	NM	NM	NM	NM
P/E Ratio:Low	NM	5	35	NM	NM	NM	NM	NM	26	46

Income Statement Analysis (Million $)										
Revenue	11,449	13,880	13,873	13,068	11,070	11,185	11,434	12,496	18,250	15,721
Operating Income	392	1,331	1,236	119	556	3.00	694	239	2,617	3,181
Depreciation	770	687	830	575	671	730	918	970	1,229	776
Interest Expense	17.0	30.0	Nil	55.0	49.0	37.0	43.0	58.0	100	84.0
Pretax Income	-2,183	610	583	-675	-184	437	-2,653	-1,048	1,584	2,771
Effective Tax Rate	NM	33.9%	18.9%	NM	NM	NM	NM	NM	38.1%	33.1%
Net Income	-2,234	403	473	-864	-107	-388	-3,429	-587	981	1,854
S&P Core Earnings	-1,353	328	426	-904	-864	-2,166	-2,581	-1,253	471	NA

Balance Sheet & Other Financial Data (Million $)										
Cash	2,857	2,701	4,582	4,065	3,396	3,601	3,062	2,885	1,472	1,849
Current Assets	6,864	7,834	9,328	8,273	7,191	7,303	6,779	7,777	7,934	6,877
Total Assets	11,232	14,468	15,838	15,082	14,190	14,503	12,985	16,522	18,181	14,152
Current Liabilities	5,621	5,668	5,451	6,165	4,766	5,113	4,129	5,057	5,146	4,759
Long Term Debt	695	1,265	1,264	575	1,123	1,175	1,531	1,449	1,705	1,720
Common Equity	3,305	5,588	7,179	6,344	6,674	6,438	6,491	9,801	10,586	7,309
Total Capital	4,000	6,853	8,443	6,919	7,797	7,613	8,022	11,250	13,035	9,393
Capital Expenditures	466	520	488	315	257	249	373	559	1,292	982
Cash Flow	-1,464	1,090	1,303	-289	564	342	-2,511	383	2,210	2,630
Current Ratio	1.2	1.4	1.7	1.3	1.5	1.4	1.6	1.5	1.5	1.4
% Long Term Debt of Capitalization	17.4	18.5	15.0	8.3	14.4	15.4	19.1	12.8	13.1	18.3
% Net Income of Revenue	NM	2.9	3.4	NM	NM	NM	NM	NM	5.4	11.8
% Return on Assets	NM	2.7	3.1	NM	NM	NM	NM	NM	6.1	16.4
% Return on Equity	NM	6.3	7.0	NM	NM	NM	NM	NM	11.0	30.5

Data as orig reptd.; bef. results of disc opers/spec. items. Per share data adj. for stk. divs.; EPS diluted. E-Estimated. NA-Not Available. NM-Not Meaningful. NR-Not Ranked. UR-Under Review.

Office: 4150 Network Circle, Santa Clara, CA 95054.
Telephone: 650-960-1300.
Email: investor-relations@sun.com
Website: http://www.sun.com

Chrmn: S.G. McNealy
Pres & CEO: J.I. Schwartz
COO: C. Resse
EVP & CFO: M.E. Lehman

EVP & CTO: G.M. Papadopoulos
Investor Contact: P. Ziots
Board Members: J. L. Barksdale, S. M. Bennett, P. L. Currie, R. J. Finocchio, Jr., J. H. Greene, Jr., J. Marcus, M. E. Marks, S. G. McNealy, R. N. Merchant, P. E. Mitchell, M. Oshman, P. Ridder, J. I. Schwartz, A. Spence

Founded: 1982
Domicile: Delaware
Employees: 29,000

SunTrust Banks Inc.

STANDARD &POOR'S

S&P Recommendation HOLD ★★★☆☆	Price $22.59 (as of Nov 27, 2009)	12-Mo. Target Price $21.00	Investment Style Large-Cap Blend

GICS Sector Financials
Sub-Industry Regional Banks

Summary This bank holding company, which has $172.7 billion in assets and $119.3 billion in deposits, operates mostly in the southeastern U.S.

Key Stock Statistics (Source S&P, Vickers, company reports)

52-Wk Range	$34.12– 6.00	S&P Oper. EPS 2009**E**	-3.81	Market Capitalization(B)	$11.276	Beta	1.18
Trailing 12-Month EPS	$-4.47	S&P Oper. EPS 2010**E**	0.01	Yield (%)	0.18	S&P 3-Yr. Proj. EPS CAGR(%)	NM
Trailing 12-Month P/E	NM	P/E on S&P Oper. EPS 2009**E**	NM	Dividend Rate/Share	$0.04	S&P Credit Rating	BBB+
$10K Invested 5 Yrs Ago	$3,777	Common Shares Outstg. (M)	499.2	Institutional Ownership (%)	74		

Price Performance

30-Week Mov. Avg. · · · · 10-Week Mov. Avg. - - **GAAP Earnings vs. Previous Year** Volume Above Avg. ▮▮▮ STARS
12-Mo. Target Price — Relative Strength — ▲ Up ▼ Down ▶ No Change Below Avg. ▮▮▮ ★

Options: CBOE, P, Ph

Analysis prepared by **Erik Oja** on November 13, 2009, when the stock traded at **$ 20.23**.

Highlights

► In the third quarter, STI's net interest margin increased again to 3.10%, from 2.94% in the second quarter, as loan yields remained firm and deposit costs fell. This offset a large decrease in loans outstanding and increased levels of non-performing loans. We see a good net interest spread environment, currently offsetting the negative impacts of nonperforming loans and weak loan growth. We expect each of these effects to reverse at different times in 2010, beginning with the relatively wide spread, followed by improvements in loan growth and credit quality, and we are forecasting net interest income of $4.35 billion in 2010, down 1.1%, from our 2009 estimate of $4.40 billion.

► We are modeling 2009 loan loss provisions of about $4.1 billion, up from about $2.5 billion in 2008, based on our forecast of $3.3 billion net chargeoffs plus reserve building of about $800 million. For 2010, we expect net chargeoffs and loan loss provisions of $2.0 billion. For 2011, we expect net chargeoffs and provisions to equal $950 million, leading to significantly positive earnings in 2011.

► We see losses per share of $3.81 in 2009, and EPS of $0.01 in 2010, and $1.57 in 2011.

Investment Rationale/Risk

► In the third quarter, STI's nonperforming loans declined from second quarter levels, in Commercial, Home Equity Lines, Real Estate Construction, Consumer Loans, and they registered only modest increases in Residential Mortgages and Commercial Real Estate. Net chargeoffs, though, increased substantially from the second quarter. However, at this later stage of the credit cycle, we prefer to see a reduction in nonperforming loans, than net chargeoffs, if we had to choose between the two. Overall, nonperforming loans decreased slightly over 1.0% from the second quarter. Capital levels, considering STI's size, are relatively high. We also see STI as having more tools to maintain capital at its disposal than many of its peers.

► Risks to our opinion and target price include a longer than expected economic recovery, a downturn in credit quality, and a further dividend cut.

► Our 12-month target price of $21 is based on a peer equivalent 13.3X multiple on our 2011 EPS estimate of $1.57, and a slight discount to peers 1.05X multiple on our estimate of December 31 tangible book value per share of $20.00.

Qualitative Risk Assessment

LOW	MEDIUM	HIGH

Our risk assessment reflects SunTrust's large-cap valuation and history of profitability, offset by its exposure to possible further declines in residential and commercial lending credit quality.

Quantitative Evaluations

S&P Quality Ranking A-

D	C	B-	B	B+	A-	A	A+

Relative Strength Rank STRONG

84

LOWEST = 1 HIGHEST = 99

Revenue/Earnings Data

Revenue (Million $)

	1Q	2Q	3Q	4Q	Year
2009	2,851	2,765	2,433	--	--
2008	3,316	3,479	3,303	2,683	12,801
2007	3,407	3,698	3,334	3,025	13,313
2006	3,130	3,299	3,384	3,447	13,260
2005	2,470	2,614	2,829	2,973	10,886
2004	1,769	1,811	1,880	2,363	7,823

Earnings Per Share ($)

2009	-2.49	-0.41	-0.76	E-0.46	E-3.81
2008	0.82	1.53	0.88	-1.08	2.13
2007	1.44	1.89	1.18	0.01	4.55
2006	1.46	1.49	1.47	1.39	5.82
2005	1.36	1.28	1.40	1.43	5.47
2004	1.26	1.29	1.30	1.26	5.19

Fiscal year ended Dec. 31. Next earnings report expected: Late January. EPS Estimates based on S&P Operating Earnings; historical GAAP earnings are as reported.

Dividend Data (Dates: mm/dd Payment Date: mm/dd/yy)

Amount ($)	Date Decl.	Ex-Div. Date	Stk. of Record	Payment Date
0.100	02/10	02/26	03/02	03/16/09
0.100	04/28	05/28	06/01	06/15/09
0.010	08/11	08/28	09/01	09/15/09
0.010	11/10	11/27	12/01	12/15/09

Dividends have been paid since 1985. Source: Company reports.

The **McGraw·Hill** Companies

SunTrust Banks Inc.

Business Summary November 13, 2009

CORPORATE OVERVIEW. SunTrust Banks Inc. (STI) owns SunTrust Bank, an organization aligned as follows by geographic region: the Carolinas Group (North and South Carolina), the Central Group (Georgia, Tennessee), the Florida Group, and the Mid-Atlantic Group (D.C., Maryland, Virginia and West Virginia). The company has five lines of business: Retail Banking, Commercial Banking, Corporate and Investment Banking, Mortgage Banking, and Wealth and Investment Management.

The Retail and Commercial Banking segments generate about 55% of total segment net income. Retail Banking (35%) provides lending and deposit gathering as well as other banking-related products and services to consumers and small businesses with sales up to $10 million. Commercial Banking (20%) offers financial products and services, including commercial lending, treasury management, financial risk management, and corporate bankcard services, to enterprises with sales up to $250 million.

The Corporate and Investment Banking segment (10%) houses the company's corporate banking, investment banking, capital markets, commercial leasing and merchant banking activities. This segment focuses on companies with sales in excess of $250 million, and concentrates on small-cap and mid-cap

growth companies, raising public and private equity, and providing merger and acquisition advisory services for investment banking.

The Mortgage Banking segment (12%) offers residential mortgage products nationally through its retail, broker and correspondent channels. The Wealth and Investment Management segment (13%) provides wealth management products and professional services to individual and institutional clients. The remaining 10% of segment net income is allocated to corporate, other, treasury, and reconciling items.

The company has adopted an enterprise risk management model, which seeks to synthesize, assess, report and mitigate the full set of risks at the enterprise level and to provide management with an overall picture of the company's risk profile. The model incorporates an analysis of credit risk, organizational risk, market risk from trading activities, market risk from non-trading activities, and market liquidity risk.

Company Financials Fiscal Year Ended Dec. 31

Per Share Data ($)	2008	2007	2006	2005	2004	2003	2002	2001	2000	1999
Tangible Book Value	33.72	28.41	26.04	24.67	23.13	29.73	25.46	26.67	25.07	22.13
Earnings	2.13	4.55	5.82	5.47	5.19	4.73	4.66	4.70	4.30	3.50
S&P Core Earnings	1.32	4.37	5.64	5.39	5.17	4.80	4.38	4.50	NA	NA
Dividends	2.85	2.92	2.44	2.20	2.00	1.80	1.72	1.60	1.48	1.38
Payout Ratio	134%	64%	42%	40%	39%	38%	37%	34%	34%	39%
Prices:High	70.00	94.18	85.64	75.77	76.65	71.73	70.20	72.35	68.06	79.81
Prices:Low	19.75	60.02	69.68	65.32	61.27	51.44	51.48	57.29	41.63	60.44
P/E Ratio:High	33	21	15	14	15	15	15	15	16	23
P/E Ratio:Low	7	13	12	12	12	11	11	12	10	17

Income Statement Analysis (Million $)										
Net Interest Income	4,620	4,720	4,660	4,579	3,685	3,320	3,244	3,253	3,108	3,145
Tax Equivalent Adjustment	118	103	87.9	75.5	NA	45.0	39.5	40.8	40.4	42.5
Non Interest Income	4,010	3,186	3,519	3,162	2,646	2,179	2,187	2,003	1,767	1,769
Loan Loss Provision	2,552	683	263	177	136	314	470	275	134	170
% Expense/Operating Revenue	62.6%	66.2%	59.0%	60.6%	67.3%	68.4%	61.5%	59.2%	58.0%	59.3%
Pretax Income	728	2,250	2,986	2,866	2,257	1,909	1,823	2,020	1,920	1,696
Effective Tax Rate	NM	27.4%	29.1%	30.7%	30.3%	30.2%	27.0%	32.2%	32.6%	33.7%
Net Income	796	1,634	2,117	1,987	1,573	1,332	1,332	1,369	1,294	1,124
% Net Interest Margin	3.10	3.11	3.00	3.16	3.15	3.08	3.41	3.58	3.55	3.88
S&P Core Earnings	463	1,542	2,045	1,957	1,570	1,351	1,253	1,310	NA	NA

Balance Sheet & Other Financial Data (Million $)										
Money Market Assets	11,411	11,890	3,849	4,457	3,796	3,243	2,820	3,025	2,223	1,869
Investment Securities	19,697	16,264	25,102	26,526	28,941	25,607	23,445	19,656	18,810	18,317
Commercial Loans	27,926	48,539	47,182	33,764	31,824	30,682	28,694	28,946	30,781	26,933
Other Loans	96,721	73,780	74,273	80,791	69,602	50,050	44,474	40,013	41,459	39,069
Total Assets	189,289	179,574	182,162	179,714	158,870	125,393	117,323	104,741	103,496	95,390
Demand Deposits	11,361	21,083	22,887	41,973	30,979	24,185	21,250	19,200	15,064	14,201
Time Deposits	96,759	80,787	101,134	80,081	72,382	57,004	58,456	48,337	54,469	45,900
Long Term Debt	26,812	22,957	18,993	20,779	22,127	15,314	11,880	12,661	8,945	6,017
Common Equity	19,502	17,553	17,314	16,887	15,987	9,731	16,030	15,064	14,536	13,691
% Return on Assets	0.4	0.9	1.2	1.2	1.1	1.1	1.2	1.3	1.3	1.2
% Return on Equity	4.6	9.2	12.3	12.1	12.2	14.4	8.6	9.3	9.2	8.0
% Loan Loss Reserve	1.9	1.0	0.8	0.5	1.0	1.1	1.1	1.2	1.2	1.3
% Loans/Deposits	112.0	100.4	107.4	171.3	104.5	106.3	101.5	108.5	106.4	112.4
% Equity to Assets	9.4	9.6	9.5	9.7	9.1	7.6	14.0	14.2	14.2	14.8

Data as orig reptd.; bef. results of disc opers/spec. items. Per share data adj. for stk. divs.; EPS diluted. E-Estimated. NA-Not Available. NM-Not Meaningful. NR-Not Ranked. UR-Under Review.

Office: 303 Peachtree St NE, Atlanta, GA 30308-3201.
Telephone: 404-588-7711.
Website: http://www.suntrust.com
Chrmn & CEO: J.M. Wells, III

Pres: W.H. Rogers, Jr.
Investor Contact: M.A. Chancy (800-568-3476)
EVP & CFO: M.A. Chancy
EVP & Chief Admin Officer: D.F. Dierker

Board Members: R. Beall, II, A. D. Correll, J. C. Crowe, P. C. Frist, B. P. Garrett, Jr., D. H. Hughes, M. Ivester, J. H. Lanier, G. G. Minor, III, L. L. Prince, F. S. Royal, J. M. Wells, III, K. H. Williams, P. Wynn, Jr.

Founded: 1891
Domicile: Georgia
Employees: 29,333

SUPERVALU INC.

STANDARD &POOR'S

S&P Recommendation	SELL ★★☆☆☆	Price	12-Mo. Target Price	Investment Style
		$14.42 (as of Nov 27, 2009)	$15.00	Large-Cap Blend

GICS Sector Consumer Staples
Sub-Industry Food Retail

Summary One of the largest U.S. food wholesalers, this company is also one of the biggest supermarket retailers in the U.S.

Key Stock Statistics (Source S&P, Vickers, company reports)

52-Wk Range	$20.38– 10.52	S&P Oper. EPS 2010E	1.98	Market Capitalization(B)	$3.057	Beta	1.21
Trailing 12-Month EPS	$-13.99	S&P Oper. EPS 2011E	1.98	Yield (%)	2.43	S&P 3-Yr. Proj. EPS CAGR(%)	0
Trailing 12-Month P/E	NM	P/E on S&P Oper. EPS 2010E	7.3	Dividend Rate/Share	$0.35	S&P Credit Rating	BB-
$10K Invested 5 Yrs Ago	$5,209	Common Shares Outstg. (M)	212.0	Institutional Ownership (%)	92		

Price Performance

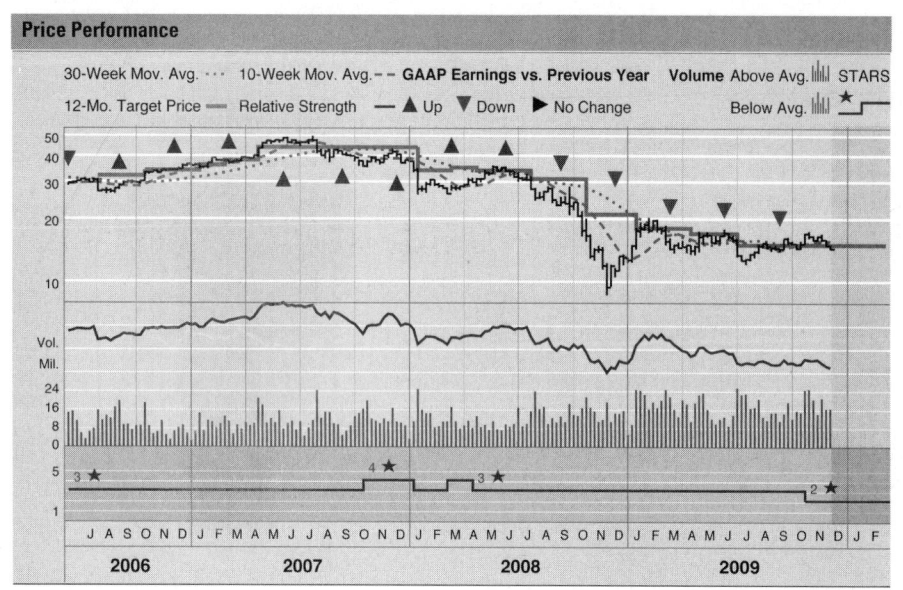

Options: CBOE, P, Ph

Analysis prepared by **Joseph Agnese** on October 27, 2009, when the stock traded at **$ 16.12.**

Highlights

▸ We see FY 11 (Feb.) revenues declining 1.1%, to about $40.8 billion, from our estimate of $41.2 billion in FY 10, reflecting retail store closures and a 2% decline in identical store sales (excluding fuel), partially offset by about 1.5% new square footage growth. We expect store traffic to be flat and average transaction sizes to be negative as consumers remain price sensitive, with U.S. unemployment rates seen peaking In FY 11.

▸ We project margins will be flat as a more aggressive pricing strategy, increased promotional spending and an unfavorable change in product mix offsets benefits from purchasing initiatives designed to better leverage its large scale, labor and shrink savings from a reduction in stock keeping units in stores, and improved sales leverage. We expect interest expense to decline due to lower interest rates and as the company pays off debt, which rose significantly as a result of the Albertson's acquisition in June 2006.

▸ We look for FY 11 operating EPS of $1.98, in line with our estimate of $1.98 for FY 10.

Investment Rationale/Risk

▸ Through the first three quarters of FY 10, the company has been experiencing identical store sales growth below its closest peers in FY 10, despite what we see as strong regional market share positions. We remain cautious on the shares, with pricing competition intensifying and consumer pressures mounting as we expect the unemployment rate to continue rising into FY 11.

▸ Risks to our recommendation and target price include better than expected identical store sales growth due to increased consumer demand or food inflation, and decreased pricing competition from an improved macroeconomic environment.

▸ The shares traded recently at an enterprise value of 4.9X our estimated FY 10 EBITDA of $2.3 billion, below its peers' average of 5.9X. Due to what we view as its weak balance sheet and high risks associated with the turnaround of its underperforming stores, we believe the shares should trade below the peer average. Applying an enterprise value to EBITDA multiple of 4.7X, about a 15% discount to peers, to our FY 11 EBITDA estimate of $2.2 billion, we arrive at our 12-month target price of $15.

Qualitative Risk Assessment

LOW	MEDIUM	HIGH

Our risk assessment reflects the intensely competitive environment in which the company operates, and threats of new entrants into its markets, partially offset by SVU's strong market share positions.

Quantitative Evaluations

S&P Quality Ranking B+

D	C	B-	B	B+	A-	A	A+

Relative Strength Rank WEAK

23

LOWEST = 1   HIGHEST = 99

Revenue/Earnings Data

Revenue (Million $)

	1Q	2Q	3Q	4Q	Year
2010	12,715	9,461	--	--	--
2009	13,347	10,226	10,171	10,820	44,564
2008	13,292	10,159	10,211	10,386	44,048
2007	5,783	10,666	10,657	10,301	37,406
2006	5,972	4,556	4,695	4,640	19,864
2005	5,911	4,487	4,555	4,591	19,543

Earnings Per Share ($)

2010	0.53	0.35	E0.47	E0.63	E1.98
2009	0.76	0.60	-13.95	-0.95	-13.51
2008	0.69	0.69	0.66	0.73	2.76
2007	0.57	0.61	0.54	0.57	2.32
2006	0.64	0.24	0.53	0.04	1.46
2005	1.04	0.55	0.46	0.65	2.71

Fiscal year ended Feb. 28. Next earnings report expected: Early January. EPS Estimates based on S&P Operating Earnings; historical GAAP earnings are as reported.

Dividend Data (Dates: mm/dd Payment Date: mm/dd/yy)

Amount ($)	Date Decl.	Ex-Div. Date	Stk. of Record	Payment Date
0.175	08/07	08/28	09/01	09/15/09
0.173	08/07	08/28	09/01	09/15/09
0.175	10/07	11/27	12/01	12/15/09

Dividends have been paid since 1936. Source: Company reports.

Please read the Required Disclosures and Analyst Certification on the last page of this report.

The McGraw-Hill Companies

SUPERVALU INC.

STANDARD &POOR'S

Business Summary October 27, 2009

CORPORATE OVERVIEW. SUPERVALU, organized in 1925 as the successor to two wholesale grocery concerns established in the 1870s, has grown into the largest U.S. food distributor to supermarkets, and the second largest conventional food retailer in the U.S. Retail operations are conducted through limited assortment stores, food stores, and combination food and drug stores. As of October 2009, the company operated about 2,400 multi-format retail food stores and was the primary grocery supplier to approximately 1,900 stores in addition to its own retail operations.

CORPORATE STRATEGY. The company aims to leverage its retail food and supply chain services by benefiting from economies of scale and its low-cost supply chain network. The company operated 874 combination stores, 369 food stores, and 316 limited assortment food stores through 69.3 million square feet of space as of February 2009. Combination food store banners (bigg's, Sav-On and Jewel-Osco, for example) typically carry 50,000 items and average 60,000 square feet. Food store banners (Bristol Farms, Jewel, Hornbacher's, Acme Markets, and Lucky) typically carry 40,000 items and average

approximately 40,000 square feet. Other major banners that operate both combination food store and food stores include Albertson's, Shaw's Supermarkets, Cub Foods, Shoppers Food & Pharmacy, Farm Fresh, Shop n' Save, and Star Market banners.

Limited assortment food stores include Save-A-Lot stores. The company licenses 862 Save-A-Lot stores to independent operators. Save-A-Lot food stores are typically 15,000 square feet and stock 1,400 high volume food items as well as a limited number of general merchandise items. The majority of food products offered for sale are private label products. The company positions itself to offer low prices by carrying a limited selection of the most frequently purchased goods. The majority of Save-A-Lot stores are found in small town/rural communities as opposed to urban and suburban locations.

Company Financials Fiscal Year Ended Feb. 28

Per Share Data ($)	2009	2008	2007	2006	2005	2004	2003	2002	2001	2000
Tangible Book Value	NM	NM	NM	7.37	6.52	4.84	3.24	2.54	1.43	1.40
Cash Flow	-8.43	7.55	6.79	3.55	4.75	4.34	4.14	4.08	3.20	4.03
Earnings	-13.51	2.76	2.32	1.46	2.71	2.07	1.91	1.53	0.62	1.87
S&P Core Earnings	1.85	2.42	2.45	1.90	2.21	2.03	1.61	1.24	0.39	NA
Dividends	0.68	0.66	0.64	0.60	0.58	0.57	0.56	0.55	0.54	0.54
Payout Ratio	NM	24%	28%	41%	21%	27%	29%	36%	87%	29%
Calendar Year	2008	2007	2006	2005	2004	2003	2002	2001	2000	1999
Prices:High	37.46	49.78	36.59	35.88	35.15	28.84	30.81	24.10	22.88	28.88
Prices:Low	8.59	34.46	26.14	29.55	25.70	12.60	14.75	12.60	11.75	16.81
P/E Ratio:High	NM	18	16	25	13	14	16	16	37	15
P/E Ratio:Low	NM	12	11	20	9	6	8	8	19	9

Income Statement Analysis (Million $)										
Revenue	44,564	44,048	37,406	19,864	19,543	20,210	19,160	20,909	23,194	20,339
Operating Income	2,682	2,788	2,058	750	936	919	870	904	860	800
Depreciation	1,077	1,030	879	311	303	302	297	341	344	277
Interest Expense	647	733	600	139	138	166	182	194	213	154
Pretax Income	-2,779	977	747	329	601	455	408	344	154	448
Effective Tax Rate	NM	39.3%	39.5%	37.4%	35.8%	38.4%	37.0%	40.1%	46.8%	45.8%
Net Income	-2,855	593	452	206	386	280	257	206	82.0	243
S&P Core Earnings	396	518	477	269	313	276	217	166	51.2	NA

Balance Sheet & Other Financial Data (Million $)										
Cash	240	243	285	686	464	292	29.2	12.0	11.0	11.0
Current Assets	4,105	4,147	4,460	2,168	2,127	2,037	1,647	1,604	2,092	2,178
Total Assets	17,604	21,062	21,702	6,038	6,278	6,153	5,896	5,825	6,407	6,495
Current Liabilities	4,472	4,607	4,705	1,507	1,632	1,872	1,525	1,701	2,341	2,510
Long Term Debt	7,968	8,502	9,192	1,406	1,579	1,634	2,020	1,875	2,008	1,954
Common Equity	2,581	5,953	5,306	2,619	2,511	2,210	2,009	1,918	1,793	1,821
Total Capital	10,549	14,455	15,006	4,079	4,240	3,986	4,146	3,873	3,831	3,778
Capital Expenditures	1,186	1,191	837	308	233	328	383	293	398	408
Cash Flow	-1,778	1,623	1,331	517	689	582	554	547	426	520
Current Ratio	0.9	0.9	0.9	1.4	1.3	1.1	1.1	0.9	0.9	0.9
% Long Term Debt of Capitalization	75.5	58.8	61.3	34.5	37.2	41.0	48.7	48.4	52.4	51.7
% Net Income of Revenue	NM	1.4	1.2	1.0	2.0	1.4	1.3	1.0	0.4	1.2
% Return on Assets	NM	2.8	3.2	3.3	6.2	4.6	4.4	3.4	1.3	4.5
% Return on Equity	NM	10.5	11.4	8.0	16.3	13.3	13.2	11.1	4.5	15.6

Data as orig reptd.; bef. results of disc opers/spec. items. Per share data adj. for stk. divs.; EPS diluted. E-Estimated. NA-Not Available. NM-Not Meaningful. NR-Not Ranked. UR-Under Review.

Office: 11840 Valley View Road, Eden Prairie, MN 55344.
Telephone: 952-828-4000.
Website: http://www.supervalu.com
Chrmn: J. Noddle

Pres & CEO: C. Herkert
EVP & CFO: P.K. Knous
SVP & CIO: P.L. Singer
Chief Acctg Officer: S.M. Smith

Investor Contact: Y. Scharton (952-828-4540)
Board Members: A. G. Ames, I. Cohen, R. E. Daly, L. A. Del Santo, S. E. Engel, P. Francis, E. C. Gage, C. Herkert, G. L. Keith, Jr., C. M. Lillis, J. Noddle, M. T. Peterson, S. S. Rogers, W. C. Sales, K. P. Seifert

Founded: 1871
Domicile: Delaware
Employees: 178,000

Symantec Corp

STANDARD &POOR'S

S&P Recommendation	HOLD ★★★☆☆	Price $17.69 (as of Nov 27, 2009)	12-Mo. Target Price $19.00	Investment Style Large-Cap Blend

GICS Sector Information Technology
Sub-Industry Systems Software

Summary This company provides software solutions that enable customers to protect their network infrastructure from potential threats and to store their data.

Key Stock Statistics (Source S&P, Vickers, company reports)

52-Wk Range	$18.19– 10.94	S&P Oper. EPS 2010E	0.72	Market Capitalization(B)	$14.339	Beta	0.94
Trailing 12-Month EPS	$-8.31	S&P Oper. EPS 2011E	0.92	Yield (%)	Nil	S&P 3-Yr. Proj. EPS CAGR(%)	10
Trailing 12-Month P/E	NM	P/E on S&P Oper. EPS 2010E	24.6	Dividend Rate/Share	Nil	S&P Credit Rating	NR
$10K Invested 5 Yrs Ago	$5,531	Common Shares Outstg. (M)	810.6	Institutional Ownership (%)	95		

Price Performance

Legend:
30-Week Mov. Avg. · · · 10-Week Mov. Avg. - - **GAAP Earnings vs. Previous Year** Volume Above Avg. STARS
12-Mo. Target Price — Relative Strength — ▲ Up ▼ Down ► No Change Below Avg.

Options: ASE, CBOE, P, Ph

Analysis prepared by **Jim Yin** on November 02, 2009, when the stock traded at **$ 17.58**.

Highlights

▶ We see total revenues rising 2.8% in FY 11 (Mar.), compared to a 4.0% decline we see for FY 10. Our forecast of revenue growth in FY 11 reflects our view of 4% growth in overall IT spending in 2010. We think SYMC will grow slower than the industry average due to a further loss in market share in the consumer market. We also think growth will be hurt by longer sales cycles on large contracts, as customers negotiate for more favorable terms. However, we see stronger growth in endpoint management and think SYMC will benefit from vendor consolidation, as customers prefer better-capitalized vendors during economic uncertainty.

▶ We project gross margins in FY 11 of 80%, the same level seen in FY 10. We look for operating expenses at 62.7% of revenues in FY 11, down from 63.3% expected in FY 10, reflecting higher revenues and better cost containment. We forecast FY 11 operating margins of 17%, up from 15% seen in FY 10.

▶ Our FY 11 EPS estimate is $0.92, compared to $0.72 projected for FY 10. The increase reflects slightly higher revenues and effective cost control.

Investment Rationale/Risk

▶ Our hold recommendation reflects our view of a sluggish recovery in IT spending in 2010. Overall, we think SYMC will grow slower than the industry's average due to loss in market share and its reliance on large contracts, which we think will remain difficult to close. However, we are positive on the company's cost-savings efforts and see wider operating margins in 2010. We also think the security software sector will be less affected than other IT sectors if the economy falters because of security software's mission-critical nature.

▶ Risks to our recommendation and target price include weaker than expected recovery in the global economy, lower enterprise IT spending, and integration problems associated with recent acquisitions.

▶ Our 12-month target price of $19 is based on a blend of our discounted cash flow (DCF) and P/ E analyses. Our DCF model assumes a 12% WACC and 3% terminal growth, yielding an intrinsic value of $21. From our P/E analysis, we derive a value of $17 based on an industry P/ E-to-growth ratio of 1.85X, or 18.5X our FY 11 EPS estimate of $0.92.

Qualitative Risk Assessment

LOW	MEDIUM	HIGH

Our risk assessment for Symantec reflects the highly competitive market in which the company operates and integration risks from recent acquisitions.

Quantitative Evaluations

S&P Quality Ranking B

D	C	B-	B	B+	A-	A	A+

Relative Strength Rank STRONG

77

LOWEST = 1   HIGHEST = 99

Revenue/Earnings Data

Revenue (Million $)

	1Q	2Q	3Q	4Q	Year
2010	1,432	1,474	--	--	--
2009	1,650	1,518	1,514	1,468	6,150
2008	1,400	1,419	1,515	1,540	5,874
2007	1,259	1,262	1,313	1,357	5,199
2006	699.9	1,056	1,149	1,239	4,143
2005	556.6	618.3	695.2	712.7	2,583

Earnings Per Share ($)

2010	0.09	0.18	E0.23	E0.22	E0.72
2009	0.22	0.16	-8.23	-0.30	-8.10
2008	0.10	0.06	0.15	0.22	0.53
2007	0.09	0.12	0.12	0.07	0.41
2006	0.27	-0.21	0.08	0.11	0.15
2005	0.16	0.19	0.22	0.16	0.74

Fiscal year ended Mar. 31. Next earnings report expected: Late January. EPS Estimates based on S&P Operating Earnings; historical GAAP earnings are as reported.

Dividend Data

No cash dividends have been paid.

Please read the Required Disclosures and Analyst Certification on the last page of this report.

The McGraw-Hill Companies

Symantec Corp

STANDARD
&POOR'S

Business Summary November 02, 2009

CORPORATE OVERVIEW. Symantec Corp. (SYMC) is a provider of security, storage and systems management solutions that enable enterprises and consumers to protect their network infrastructure from potential threats and to archive and recover their data. Its products include virus protection, firewall, virtual private network, data protection, compliance, vulnerability management, intrusion detection, remote management technologies, and security services.

The company is organized into five operating segments:

Consumer Products -- focuses on Internet security. Key products include Norton 360 and Norton Internet Security, which protect against viruses, worms and other security risks; Norton AntiVirus, which removes viruses, Trojan horses and worms; and Norton SystemWorks, which enables users to maintain and optimize their computers. The Consumer Products segment accounted for 30% and 29% of total revenue in FY 08 (Mar.) and FY 09, respectively.

Security and Compliance -- provides security throughout the network, including behind the gateway and at the client level including servers, desktop PCs, laptops and other mobile devices. Its Information Risk Management solutions enforce data security policies on email, storage systems, and archiving. The

company's enterprise security solutions address the following areas: Antivirus, Antispam, Compliance, and Managed Security Services. The Security and Compliance segment accounted for 27% and 26% of total revenue in FY 08 and FY 09, respectively.

Storage and Server Management -- provides software solutions designed to protect, back up, archive and restore data across the enterprise. It also helps customers manage heterogeneous storage and server environments. This segment accounted for 37% and 37% of total revenue in FY 08 and FY 09, respectively.

Services -- assists SYMC's customers in implementing, supporting and maintaining their security, storage and infrastructure software solutions. Services accounted for 6% and 8% of total revenues in FY 08 and FY 09, respectively.

The Other segment is comprised of products nearing the end of their life cycle. Revenues were insignificant during FY 08 and FY 09.

Company Financials Fiscal Year Ended Mar. 31

Per Share Data ($)	2009	2008	2007	2006	2005	2004	2003	2002	2001	2000
Tangible Book Value	NM	NM	NM	0.63	3.07	1.97	2.89	1.26	0.97	1.11
Cash Flow	-7.09	1.46	1.24	0.48	0.86	0.62	0.45	0.37	0.18	0.43
Earnings	-8.10	0.53	0.41	0.15	0.74	0.54	0.38	-0.05	0.12	0.34
S&P Core Earnings	NA	0.55	0.40	-0.06	0.59	0.43	0.26	-0.19	0.03	NA
Dividends	Nil	Nil	Nil	Nil	Nil	Nil	Nil	Nil	Nil	Nil
Payout Ratio	Nil	Nil	Nil	Nil	Nil	Nil	Nil	Nil	Nil	Nil
Calendar Year	2008	2007	2006	2005	2004	2003	2002	2001	2000	1999
Prices:High	22.80	21.86	22.19	26.60	34.05	17.50	11.55	9.19	10.20	8.66
Prices:Low	10.05	15.97	14.78	16.32	17.27	9.09	6.80	3.90	3.42	1.56
P/E Ratio:High	NM	41	54	NM	46	33	30	78	NM	25
P/E Ratio:Low	NM	30	36	NM	23	17	18	33	NM	5

Income Statement Analysis (Million $)	2009	2008	2007	2006	2005	2004	2003	2002	2001	2000
Revenue	6,150	5,874	5,199	4,143	2,583	1,870	1,407	1,071	854	746
Operating Income	1,918	1,597	1,402	942	926	611	417	269	240	191
Depreciation	837	824	811	340	96.3	78.8	59.6	238	105	42.9
Interest Expense	29.7	29.5	27.2	18.0	12.3	21.2	21.2	9.17	Nil	0.02
Pretax Income	-6,507	713	632	363	858	542	364	45.5	141	257
Effective Tax Rate	NM	34.9%	36.0%	56.8%	37.5%	31.6%	31.7%	NM	54.6%	33.9%
Net Income	-6,729	464	404	157	536	371	248	-28.2	63.9	170
S&P Core Earnings	NA	488	393	-51.0	423	284	157	-106	14.8	NA

Balance Sheet & Other Financial Data (Million $)	2009	2008	2007	2006	2005	2004	2003	2002	2001	2000
Cash	1,991	2,427	2,559	2,316	1,091	2,410	1,706	1,375	557	432
Current Assets	3,300	3,730	4,071	3,908	3,688	2,842	1,988	1,563	782	546
Total Assets	10,645	18,092	17,751	17,913	5,614	4,456	3,266	2,503	1,792	846
Current Liabilities	3,514	3,800	3,318	3,478	1,701	1,287	895	579	413	227
Long Term Debt	2,100	2,100	2,100	24.9	4.41	606	607	604	2.36	1.55
Common Equity	3,948	10,973	11,602	13,668	3,705	2,426	1,764	1,320	1,377	618
Total Capital	6,100	13,293	14,045	14,187	3,798	3,077	2,371	1,924	1,379	620
Capital Expenditures	272	274	420	267	91.5	111	192	141	61.2	28.5
Cash Flow	-5,892	1,288	1,216	497	633	453	308	210	95.9	213
Current Ratio	0.9	1.0	1.2	1.1	2.2	2.2	2.2	31.3	1.9	2.4
% Long Term Debt of Capitalization	34.4	15.8	15.0	0.2	0.1	19.7	25.6	0.3	0.2	0.3
% Net Income of Revenue	NM	7.9	7.8	3.8	20.8	19.8	17.7	NM	7.5	22.8
% Return on Assets	NM	2.6	2.3	1.3	10.6	9.6	8.6	NM	4.8	24.1
% Return on Equity	NM	4.1	3.2	1.8	17.5	17.7	16.1	NM	6.4	35.3

Data as orig reptd.; bef. results of disc opers/spec. items. Per share data adj. for stk. divs.; EPS diluted. E-Estimated. NA-Not Available. NM-Not Meaningful. NR-Not Ranked. UR-Under Review.

Office: 20330 Stevens Creek Boulevard, Cupertino, CA 95014-2132.
Telephone: 408-517-8000.
Email: investor-relations@symantec.com
Website: http://www.symantec.com

Chrmn: J. Thompson
Pres & CEO: E. Salem
EVP & CFO: J. Beer
EVP & CTO: M.F. Bregman

EVP, Secy & General Counsel: S.C. Taylor
Investor Contact: H. Corcos (408-517-8324)
Board Members: M. Brown, W. T. Coleman, III, F. E. Dangeard, G. B. Laybourne, D. L. Mahoney, R. S. Miller, Jr., E. Salem, D. H. Schulman, J. Thompson, V. Unruh

Founded: 1983
Domicile: Delaware
Employees: 17,400

Sysco Corp

STANDARD &POOR'S

S&P Recommendation HOLD ★★★☆☆	Price $26.83 (as of Nov 27, 2009)	12-Mo. Target Price $29.00	Investment Style Large-Cap Blend

GICS Sector Consumer Staples
Sub-Industry Food Distributors

Summary This company is the largest U.S. marketer and distributor of foodservice products.

Key Stock Statistics (Source S&P, Vickers, company reports)

52-Wk Range	$27.85– 19.39	S&P Oper. EPS 2010E	1.92	Market Capitalization(B)	$15.879	Beta	0.78
Trailing 12-Month EPS	$1.87	S&P Oper. EPS 2011E	NA	Yield (%)	3.73	S&P 3-Yr. Proj. EPS CAGR(%)	5
Trailing 12-Month P/E	14.4	P/E on S&P Oper. EPS 2010E	14.0	Dividend Rate/Share	$1.00	S&P Credit Rating	AA-
$10K Invested 5 Yrs Ago	$8,631	Common Shares Outstg. (M)	591.8	Institutional Ownership (%)	75		

Price Performance

- 30-Week Mov. Avg.   · · · 10-Week Mov. Avg. – – **GAAP Earnings vs. Previous Year**   **Volume** Above Avg. STARS
- 12-Mo. Target Price — Relative Strength ▲ Up ▼ Down ► No Change   Below Avg. ★

Options: ASE, CBOE, P

Analysis prepared by **Loran Braverman, CFA** on November 03, 2009, when the stock traded at **$ 26.50.**

Highlights

► With SYY's most important end market - restaurants - under pressure from weak consumer discretionary spending, total company sales fell 1.8% in FY 09 (Jun.), including about a 4.7% contribution from inflation. For 53-week FY 10, we expect the extra week to allow sales to be close to flat. SYY's food cost inflation trended lower throughout FY 09, and, according to management, turned negative in early FY 10. We think SYY is maintaining its market share.

► The operating margin was slightly higher in FY 09, with productivity gains compensating for the lack of sales leverage and higher bad debt expense. We look for productivity gains to allow again for a slightly higher operating margin in FY 10. Over time, we look for SYY's profitability to benefit from more consolidated purchasing, the addition of regional distribution centers, improved management of freight costs, and better inventory management.

► Our 53-week FY 10 EPS estimate is $1.92, vs. 52-week FY 09's $1.77. Our FY 10 estimate includes a $0.05 tax benefit and $0.04 benefit from a change in the value of corporate-owned life insurance.

Investment Rationale/Risk

► Longer term, we expect SYY to experience internal growth and to make additional acquisitions. We think that SYY is probably maintaining market share during the current difficult period for restaurant sales, which we believe is being caused by the weak consumer discretionary environment. Restaurants accounted for 62% of SYY's FY 09 sales.

► Risks to our recommendation and target price include a slowing of growth rates given SYY's significant size and reach, sharp increases in gasoline prices, and a potential prolonged slowdown in restaurant sales.

► Our 12-month target price of $29 is a blend of our historical and relative analyses. Our historical analysis applies an 18.0X multiple, towards the low end of the 10-year forward P/E range, to our calendar 2010 EPS estimate of $1.94, implying a value of $35. Our target multiple reflects what we see as the decreased likelihood of SYY consistently achieving its former sales growth rates, given its size and S&P's negative outlook for the restaurant industry. Our peer analysis applies a P/E of 12.3X, near the average of a small group of other food distributor stocks, suggesting a value of $24.

Qualitative Risk Assessment

LOW	MEDIUM	HIGH

Our risk assessment reflects SYY's operations in a relatively stable industry, in which we believe it has the largest market share.

Quantitative Evaluations

S&P Quality Ranking   A+

D	C	B-	B	B+	A-	A	A+

Relative Strength Rank   MODERATE

65

LOWEST = 1   HIGHEST = 99

Revenue/Earnings Data

Revenue (Million $)

	1Q	2Q	3Q	4Q	Year
2010	9,081	--	--	--	--
2009	9,877	9,150	8,739	9,087	36,853
2008	9,406	9,240	9,147	9,730	37,522
2007	8,672	8,569	8,573	9,228	35,042
2006	8,010	7,971	8,138	8,509	32,628
2005	7,532	7,331	7,437	7,981	30,282

Earnings Per Share ($)

2010	0.55	E0.41	E0.39	E0.57	E1.92
2009	0.46	0.40	0.38	0.53	1.77
2008	0.43	0.43	0.40	0.55	1.81
2007	0.37	0.39	0.35	0.49	1.60
2006	0.31	0.33	0.30	0.41	1.35
2005	0.35	0.36	0.34	0.44	1.47

Fiscal year ended Jun. 30. Next earnings report expected: Early February. EPS Estimates based on S&P Operating Earnings; historical GAAP earnings are as reported.

Dividend Data (Dates: mm/dd Payment Date: mm/dd/yy)

Amount ($)	Date Decl.	Ex-Div. Date	Stk. of Record	Payment Date
0.240	02/13	04/01	04/03	04/24/09
0.240	05/15	06/30	07/02	07/24/09
0.240	09/25	10/06	10/08	10/23/09
0.250	11/17	12/29	12/31	01/22/10

Dividends have been paid since 1970. Source: Company reports.

Please read the Required Disclosures and Analyst Certification on the last page of this report.

The McGraw-Hill Companies

Sysco Corp

Business Summary November 03, 2009

CORPORATE OVERVIEW. Sysco is the largest distributor of foodservice products in the U.S. and Canada. As of June 2009, it operated 186 distribution facilities in the U.S., Canada and Ireland. The company provides products and services to approximately 400,000 customers, including restaurants (62% of FY 09 sales), hospitals and nursing homes (11%), schools and colleges (5%), hotels and motels (6%), and others (16%).

Sysco distributes food products, including frozen foods such as meats, fully prepared entrees, fruits, vegetables and desserts; canned and dry foods; fresh meats; imported specialties; and fresh produce. The company also distributes non-food products. These include paper products, tableware such as china and silverware, cookware, restaurant and kitchen equipment and supplies, and cleaning supplies. The company stresses prompt and accurate delivery of orders, and close contact with customers, and also provides customers with ancillary services, such as providing product usage reports, menu-planning advice, food safety training, and assistance in inventory control. No single customer accounted for 10% or more of sales in FY 09.

CORPORATE STRATEGY. SYY seeks to expand its business by garnering an increased share of products purchased by existing customers, the development of new customers, the use of foldouts (new facilities built in established markets), and an acquisition program. SYY distributes nationally branded merchandise, as well as products packaged under SYY private brands. We believe that Sysco-branded products typically carry wider profit margins than other branded products distributed by the company. From its inception through the end of FY 09, the company had acquired about 150 companies or divisions of companies. At June 27, 2009, SYY's balance sheet included $1.511 billion of goodwill.

Over time, we look for SYY's profitability to benefit from an increased amount of consolidated purchasing, the addition of regional distribution centers, improved management of freight costs, and better inventory management. Among SYY's supply chain initiatives are (1) the construction of regional distribution centers (RDCs); SYY expects to build five to seven of these centers, with two already operational; and (2) improving the capability to view and manage all of SYY's inbound freight, both to RDCs and the operating companies, as a network and not as individual locations. FY 08 was the first full year SYY operated under this initiative. During FY 09, SYY began the design of an enterprise-wide project to implement an integrated software system to support the majority of its business processes.

Company Financials Fiscal Year Ended Jun. 30

Per Share Data ($)	2009	2008	2007	2006	2005	2004	2003	2002	2001	2000
Tangible Book Value	3.08	3.17	2.99	2.67	2.35	2.11	1.68	1.85	2.07	1.90
Cash Flow	2.41	2.41	2.23	1.89	1.96	1.80	1.59	1.47	1.27	1.02
Earnings	1.77	1.81	1.60	1.35	1.47	1.37	1.18	1.01	0.88	0.68
S&P Core Earnings	1.65	1.68	1.59	1.38	1.39	1.31	1.08	0.92	0.82	NA
Dividends	1.16	0.82	0.72	0.64	0.56	0.48	0.40	0.32	0.23	0.22
Payout Ratio	66%	45%	45%	47%	38%	35%	34%	32%	26%	32%
Prices:High	27.85	35.00	36.74	37.04	38.04	41.27	37.57	32.58	30.12	30.44
Prices:Low	19.39	20.74	29.90	26.50	29.98	29.48	22.90	21.25	21.75	13.06
P/E Ratio:High	16	19	23	27	26	30	32	32	34	45
P/E Ratio:Low	11	11	19	20	20	22	19	21	25	19

Income Statement Analysis (Million $)										
Revenue	36,853	37,522	35,042	32,628	30,282	29,335	26,140	23,351	21,784	19,303
Operating Income	2,255	2,246	2,071	1,840	1,906	1,816	1,597	1,439	1,286	1,030
Depreciation	382	366	363	345	317	284	273	278	248	220
Interest Expense	116	118	105	109	75.0	69.9	72.2	62.9	71.0	71.0
Pretax Income	1,771	1,791	1,621	1,395	1,525	1,475	1,260	1,101	967	738
Effective Tax Rate	40.4%	38.3%	38.3%	39.3%	37.0%	38.5%	38.3%	38.3%	38.3%	38.5%
Net Income	1,056	1,106	1,001	846	961	907	778	680	597	454
S&P Core Earnings	987	1,022	995	866	890	868	710	618	559	NA

Balance Sheet & Other Financial Data (Million $)										
Cash	1,087	552	208	202	192	200	421	230	136	159
Current Assets	5,271	5,175	4,676	4,400	4,002	3,851	3,630	3,185	2,985	2,733
Total Assets	10,322	10,082	9,519	8,992	8,268	7,848	6,937	5,990	5,469	4,814
Current Liabilities	3,150	3,499	3,415	3,226	3,458	3,127	2,701	2,239	2,090	1,783
Long Term Debt	2,467	1,975	1,758	1,627	956	1,231	1,249	1,176	961	1,024
Common Equity	3,450	3,409	3,278	3,052	2,759	2,565	2,198	2,133	2,148	1,762
Total Capital	6,444	5,925	5,037	5,403	4,440	4,483	3,945	3,750	3,379	3,032
Capital Expenditures	465	516	603	515	390	530	436	416	341	266
Cash Flow	1,438	1,473	1,364	1,191	1,278	1,191	1,051	958	845	674
Current Ratio	1.7	1.5	1.4	1.4	1.2	1.2	1.3	1.4	1.4	1.5
% Long Term Debt of Capitalization	38.3	33.3	34.9	30.1	21.5	27.4	31.7	31.4	28.4	33.8
% Net Income of Revenue	2.9	3.0	2.9	2.6	3.2	3.1	3.0	2.9	2.7	2.4
% Return on Assets	10.4	11.3	10.8	9.8	11.9	12.3	12.0	12.0	11.6	10.2
% Return on Equity	30.8	33.1	31.6	29.1	36.1	38.1	35.9	32.1	30.5	28.5

Data as orig reptd.; bef. results of disc opers/spec. items. Per share data adj. for stk. divs.; EPS diluted. E-Estimated. NA-Not Available. NM-Not Meaningful. NR-Not Ranked. UR-Under Review.

Office: 1390 Enclave Parkway, Houston, TX, USA 77077-2099.
Telephone: 281-584-1390.
Website: http://www.sysco.com
Chrmn: M.A. Fernandez

Pres, Vice Chrmn & COO: K.F. Spitler
CEO: W.J. DeLaney, III
EVP & CFO: R.C. Kreidler
SVP, Chief Acctg Officer & Cntlr: G.M. Elmer

Board Members: J. M. Cassaday, J. L. Craven, W. J. DeLaney, III, M. A. Fernandez, J. Golden, J. A. Hafner, Jr., H. Koerber, N. S. Newcomb, P. S. Sewell, K. F. Spitler, R. G. Tilghman, J. M. Ward

Founded: 1969
Domicile: Delaware
Employees: 47,000

Target Corp

S&P Recommendation HOLD ★★★☆☆

Price	12-Mo. Target Price	Investment Style
$46.56 (as of Nov 30, 2009)	$53.00	Large-Cap Growth

GICS Sector Consumer Discretionary
Sub-Industry General Merchandise Stores

Summary This company operates about 1,490 Target and 250 SuperTarget general merchandise stores across the U.S.

Key Stock Statistics (Source S&P, Vickers, company reports)

52-Wk Range	$51.77–25.00	S&P Oper. EPS 2010E	3.17	Market Capitalization(B)	$35.007	Beta	1.16
Trailing 12-Month EPS	$2.87	S&P Oper. EPS 2011E	3.50	Yield (%)	1.46	S&P 3-Yr. Proj. EPS CAGR(%)	11
Trailing 12-Month P/E	16.2	P/E on S&P Oper. EPS 2010E	14.7	Dividend Rate/Share	$0.68	S&P Credit Rating	A+
$10K Invested 5 Yrs Ago	$9,646	Common Shares Outstg. (M)	751.9	Institutional Ownership (%)	89		

Price Performance

30-Week Mov. Avg. · · · 10-Week Mov. Avg. – – **GAAP Earnings vs. Previous Year** Volume Above Avg. STARS
12-Mo. Target Price — Relative Strength — ▲ Up ▼ Down ▶ No Change Below Avg.

Options: ASE, CBOE, Ph

Analysis prepared by **Jason N. Asaeda** on November 30, 2009, when the stock traded at **$46.18**.

Highlights

► In recent months, we think TGT has been communicating a stronger value proposition to consumers through marketing changes and lower opening price points. However, we still perceive risk of the company losing market share to main competitor Wal-Mart Stores (WMT 55, Strong Buy). We look for about a 3% decline in FY 10 (Jan.) same-store sales on weak consumer demand for more discretionary purchase merchandise. Also factoring in our expectations of lower credit revenues and 61 net new store openings, we project flat revenues in FY 10. In FY 11, we see revenues reaching $65.5 billion on a 1% same-store sales increase and the addition of up to 10 net new stores.

► We look for faster sales growth in lower-margin consumables/perishables to be annually offset by higher merchandise markups, supported by direct imports and better inventory management, and well-controlled dollar expense growth. However, we anticipate operating margin pressure in FY 10 from higher bad debt expense and negative operating leverage on same-store sales declines we see.

► Assuming limited share repurchase activity, we forecast EPS of $3.17 in FY 10 and $3.50 in FY 11.

Investment Rationale/Risk

► Our Hold recommendation is based on valuation. We see TGT weathering a challenging retail environment with its growing assortment of value-priced consumables, including new "up & up" private label merchandise (encompassing about 800 items across 40 categories). And while we perceive an absence of major destination brands within the company's more discretionary-purchase categories, we are encouraged by steps TGT is taking to better align store assortments with customer preferences and in matching competitors' pricing. We also think the company is doing a good job of managing its flow of goods, which is limiting markdown risk, and we note that TGT faces easier same-store sales comparisons in the second half of FY 10.

► Risks to our recommendation and target price include a loss of business due to changes in consumer confidence, spending habits, and buying preferences, as well as increased promotional activity by competitors.

► Our 12-month target price of $53 is based on a peer-average forward P/E multiple of 15.1X applied to our FY 11 EPS estimate.

Qualitative Risk Assessment

LOW	MEDIUM	HIGH

Our risk assessment reflects our view of TGT's fairly consistent earnings track record, and its healthy balance sheet and cash flow, offset by our concerns over potential loss of market share as a result of lackluster merchandising and aggressive pricing by competitors.

Quantitative Evaluations

S&P Quality Ranking A+

D	C	B-	B	B+	A-	A	A+

Relative Strength Rank MODERATE

38

LOWEST = 1 HIGHEST = 99

Revenue/Earnings Data

Revenue (Million $)

	1Q	2Q	3Q	4Q	Year
2010	14,833	15,067	15,276	--	--
2009	14,302	15,472	15,114	19,560	64,948
2008	14,041	14,620	14,835	19,872	63,367
2007	12,863	13,347	13,570	19,710	59,490
2006	11,477	11,990	12,206	16,947	52,620
2005	11,587	10,556	10,909	15,194	46,839

Earnings Per Share ($)

2010	0.69	0.79	0.58	E1.11	E3.17
2009	0.74	0.82	0.49	0.81	2.86
2008	0.75	0.82	0.56	1.23	3.33
2007	0.63	0.70	0.59	1.29	3.21
2006	0.55	0.61	0.49	1.06	2.71
2005	0.48	0.40	0.37	0.90	2.07

Fiscal year ended Jan. 31. Next earnings report expected: Late February. EPS Estimates based on S&P Operating Earnings; historical GAAP earnings are as reported.

Dividend Data (Dates: mm/dd Payment Date: mm/dd/yy)

Amount ($)	Date Decl.	Ex-Div. Date	Stk. of Record	Payment Date
0.160	01/15	02/18	02/20	03/10/09
0.160	03/12	05/18	05/20	06/10/09
0.170	06/11	08/18	08/20	09/10/09
0.170	09/10	11/18	11/20	12/10/09

Dividends have been paid since 1965. Source: Company reports.

Please read the Required Disclosures and Analyst Certification on the last page of this report.

Target Corp

Business Summary November 30, 2009

CORPORATE PROFILE. In FY 05 (Jan.), Target Corp. (TGT) shed its non-core legacy department store operations, retaining only its eponymous chain of up-scale general merchandise stores that cater to middle- and upper-income consumers. As of October 31, 2009, the company operated 1,491 Target locations, and 252 SuperTarget stores. SuperTarget stores combine a full line of groceries with fashion apparel, electronics, home furnishings and other general merchandise found in Target stores. TGT's Web site serves as both a sales driver and a marketing vehicle. Target.com offers a more extensive selection of merchandise than the company's physical stores, including exclusive online products. To support sales and earnings growth, TGT offers credit to qualified customers. In FY 09, its credit card operations contributed nearly $2.1 billion of revenues.

PRIMARY BUSINESS DYNAMICS. TGT's primary growth drivers are new store openings and same-store sales (sales results for stores open for over one year). From FY 04 through FY 09, the company increased its retail square footage at a compound annual growth rate (CAGR) of 6.6%, as its store count rose from 1,225 to 1,682. At the end of FY 09, only 14% of TGT's store base was comprised of SuperTargets (239 stores). As a result, we believe consumers still do not associate the term "supercenter" with the company. TGT added a net of 62 Target and 29 SuperTarget locations to its store base in FY 09. As of October 2009, the company completed its expansion plan for FY 10, opening 76 new stores (61 net of relocations and closings), including its first two stores in Hawaii. TGT expects to open approximately 12 new stores (up to 10 net of relocations and closings) in FY 11.

Company Financials Fiscal Year Ended Jan. 31

Per Share Data ($)	2009	2008	2007	2006	2005	2004	2003	2002	2001	2000
Tangible Book Value	18.10	18.44	18.17	16.25	14.63	12.14	10.38	8.68	7.27	6.43
Cash Flow	5.22	5.30	4.93	4.29	3.45	3.45	3.14	2.70	2.41	2.19
Earnings	2.86	3.33	3.21	2.71	2.07	2.01	1.81	1.51	1.38	1.27
S&P Core Earnings	2.73	3.32	3.21	2.68	2.06	1.95	1.70	1.42	1.37	NA
Dividends	0.52	0.44	0.36	0.30	0.26	0.26	0.24	0.21	0.20	0.20
Payout Ratio	18%	13%	11%	11%	13%	13%	13%	14%	14%	16%
Calendar Year	2008	2007	2006	2005	2004	2003	2002	2001	2000	1999
Prices:High	59.55	70.75	60.34	60.00	54.14	41.80	46.15	41.74	39.19	38.50
Prices:Low	25.60	48.85	44.70	45.55	36.63	25.60	24.90	26.00	21.63	25.03
P/E Ratio:High	21	21	19	22	26	21	25	28	28	30
P/E Ratio:Low	9	15	14	17	18	13	14	17	16	20

Income Statement Analysis (Million $)

	2009	2008	2007	2006	2005	2004	2003	2002	2001	2000
Revenue	64,948	63,367	59,490	52,620	46,839	48,163	43,917	39,888	36,903	33,702
Operating Income	6,228	6,931	6,565	5,732	4,860	4,839	4,476	3,759	3,418	3,183
Depreciation	1,826	1,659	1,496	1,409	1,259	1,320	1,212	1,079	940	854
Interest Expense	894	747	597	532	674	559	588	464	425	393
Pretax Income	3,536	4,625	4,497	3,860	3,031	2,960	2,676	2,216	2,053	1,936
Effective Tax Rate	37.4%	38.4%	38.0%	37.6%	37.8%	37.8%	38.2%	38.0%	38.4%	38.8%
Net Income	2,214	2,849	2,787	2,408	1,885	1,841	1,654	1,374	1,264	1,185
S&P Core Earnings	2,117	2,841	2,784	2,383	1,876	1,791	1,553	1,289	1,247	NA

Balance Sheet & Other Financial Data (Million $)

	2009	2008	2007	2006	2005	2004	2003	2002	2001	2000
Cash	864	2,450	813	1,648	2,245	716	758	499	356	220
Current Assets	17,488	18,906	14,706	14,405	13,922	12,928	11,935	9,648	7,304	6,483
Total Assets	44,106	44,560	37,349	34,995	32,293	31,392	28,603	24,154	19,490	17,143
Current Liabilities	10,512	11,782	11,117	9,588	8,220	8,314	7,523	7,054	6,301	5,850
Long Term Debt	17,371	15,126	8,675	9,119	9,034	10,217	10,186	8,088	5,634	4,521
Common Equity	13,712	15,307	15,633	14,205	13,029	11,065	9,443	7,860	6,519	5,862
Total Capital	31,538	30,903	24,885	24,175	23,036	21,282	21,080	15,948	12,153	10,383
Capital Expenditures	3,547	4,369	3,928	3,388	3,068	3,004	3,221	3,163	2,528	1,918
Cash Flow	4,040	4,508	4,283	3,817	3,144	3,161	2,866	2,453	2,204	2,039
Current Ratio	1.7	1.6	1.3	1.5	1.7	1.6	1.6	1.4	1.2	1.1
% Long Term Debt of Capitalization	55.1	49.0	34.9	37.7	39.2	48.0	48.3	50.7	46.4	43.5
% Net Income of Revenue	3.4	4.5	4.7	4.5	4.0	3.8	3.8	3.4	3.4	3.5
% Return on Assets	5.0	7.0	7.7	7.1	5.9	6.1	6.3	6.3	6.9	7.2
% Return on Equity	15.3	18.4	18.7	17.6	15.6	18.0	19.1	19.1	20.4	21.7

Data as orig reptd.; bef. results of disc opers/spec. items. Per share data adj. for stk. divs.; EPS diluted. E-Estimated. NA-Not Available. NM-Not Meaningful. NR-Not Ranked. UR-Under Review.

Office: 1000 Nicollet Mall, Minneapolis, MN 55403-2467.
Telephone: 612-304-6073.
Website: http://www.target.com
Chrmn, Pres & CEO: G.W. Steinhafel

Investor Contact: D.A. Scovanner
EVP, CFO & Chief Acctg Officer: D.A. Scovanner
EVP, Secy & General Counsel: T.R. Baer
CTO & CIO: B.M. Jacob

Board Members: R. S. Austin, C. Darden, M. N. Dillon, J. A. Johnson, R. M. Kovacevich, M. E. Minnick, D. W. Rice, S. W. Sanger, G. W. Steinhafel, G. W. Tamke
Founded: 1902
Domicile: Minnesota
Employees: 351,000

TECO Energy Inc.

STANDARD &POOR'S

S&P Recommendation	HOLD ★★★☆☆	Price $14.53 (as of Nov 27, 2009)	12-Mo. Target Price $15.00	Investment Style Large-Cap Value

GICS Sector Utilities
Sub-Industry Multi-Utilities

Summary This company owns Tampa Electric Co., which serves the Tampa Bay region in west central Florida and has significant diversified operations related to its core business.

Key Stock Statistics (Source S&P, Vickers, company reports)

52-Wk Range	$15.17– 8.41	S&P Oper. EPS 2009**E**	1.10	Market Capitalization(B)	$3.106	Beta	0.88
Trailing 12-Month EPS	$0.86	S&P Oper. EPS 2010**E**	1.23	Yield (%)	5.51	S&P 3-Yr. Proj. EPS CAGR(%)	7
Trailing 12-Month P/E	16.9	P/E on S&P Oper. EPS 2009**E**	13.2	Dividend Rate/Share	$0.80	S&P Credit Rating	BBB
$10K Invested 5 Yrs Ago	$12,170	Common Shares Outstg. (M)	213.8	Institutional Ownership (%)	54		

Price Performance

30-Week Mov. Avg. · · · 10-Week Mov. Avg. – – **GAAP Earnings vs. Previous Year** Volume Above Avg. STARS
12-Mo. Target Price — Relative Strength ▲ Up ▼ Down ► No Change Below Avg.

Options: Ph

Analysis prepared by **Justin McCann** on September 23, 2009, when the stock traded at **$ 14.34**.

Highlights

► Excluding $0.02 in net one-time gains, we expect operating EPS in 2009 to rise about 25% from 2008 operating EPS of $0.87, which excludes $0.10 for a special one-time tax. We project that this increase will be driven primarily by improved earnings for TECO Coal, due to the renewal of below-market contracts with contracts that reflect the sharp increase in coal prices. However, we expect this to be partially offset by higher coal production costs and a slowdown in both domestic and international demand.

► We project only modest improvement at the utilities in 2009, as the recent rate increases for Tampa Electric and Peoples Gas are expected to be largely offset by the continuing weakness in the Florida economy and housing market. In the first half of 2009, retail energy sales were down 2.4% and there was a 0.2% decline in the average number of customers.

► For 2010, we project operating EPS will increase about 12% from anticipated results in 2009, reflecting an improvement in the economy and housing market, as well as a full year of the rate increases implemented in May 2009, and an additional rate increase expected in 2010.

Investment Rationale/Risk

► With the shares having rebounded about 70% from their multi-year low reached in March, we believe the stock has become fairly valued at recent levels. In addition to the weakness in the Florida economy and housing market, we think the sharp decline in the stock had reflected the rise in the coal operation's production costs and the slowing of international demand. We think the rebound in the shares has reflected an expected recovery in these situations and a well above peers yield from a dividend we have viewed as secure. The recent dividend yield of 5.5% was above the recent average yield (4.8%) of the company's electric and gas utility peers.

► Risks to our recommendation and target price include prolonged weakness in the housing market, a sharp decrease in the average P/E of the electric utility group as a whole, and much lower than anticipated earnings from the nonregulated coal operations.

► While TE's dividend represents 92% of 2008 EPS, it represents only 73% and 66% of our respective EPS estimates for 2009 and 2010. Our 12-month target price is $15, a slight premium-to-peers P/E of 12.3X our 2010 forecast.

Qualitative Risk Assessment

LOW	MEDIUM	HIGH

Our risk assessment reflects the steady cash flow we expect from the regulated electric and gas utilities, which operate within a generally supportive regulatory environment, offset by our view of the much less predictable earnings and cash flow from the unregulated coal and transport operations, particularly given uncertainties concerning tax credits related to the synthetic fuel operations.

Quantitative Evaluations

S&P Quality Ranking B

D	C	B-	B	B+	A-	A	A+

Relative Strength Rank MODERATE

67

LOWEST = 1   HIGHEST = 99

Revenue/Earnings Data

Revenue (Million $)

	1Q	2Q	3Q	4Q	Year
2009	824.0	825.2	896.3	--	--
2008	791.7	887.2	926.1	770.3	3,375
2007	821.3	866.5	990.0	858.3	3,536
2006	836.4	862.6	922.9	826.2	3,448
2005	684.7	719.0	836.4	770.0	3,010
2004	642.3	713.0	742.3	660.2	2,669

Earnings Per Share ($)

	1Q	2Q	3Q	4Q	Year
2009	0.16	0.29	0.30	E0.28	E1.10
2008	0.15	0.24	0.27	0.10	0.77
2007	0.35	0.28	0.44	0.83	1.90
2006	0.26	0.29	0.38	0.23	1.17
2005	0.25	0.04	0.45	0.24	1.00
2004	0.15	-0.44	0.27	-2.05	-2.10

Fiscal year ended Dec. 31. Next earnings report expected: Early February. EPS Estimates based on S&P Operating Earnings; historical GAAP earnings are as reported.

Dividend Data (Dates: mm/dd Payment Date: mm/dd/yy)

Amount ($)	Date Decl.	Ex-Div. Date	Stk. of Record	Payment Date
0.200	02/04	02/12	02/17	02/27/09
0.200	04/29	05/13	05/15	05/28/09
0.200	07/29	08/12	08/14	08/28/09
0.200	10/29	11/12	11/16	11/27/09

Dividends have been paid since 1900. Source: Company reports.

Please read the Required Disclosures and Analyst Certification on the last page of this report.

The McGraw-Hill Companies

TECO Energy Inc.

STANDARD
&POOR'S

Business Summary September 23, 2009

CORPORATE OVERVIEW. TECO Energy (TE) is a holding company for a diverse set of energy companies including the regulated utility subsidiary Tampa Electric Company, which provides retail electric service in west central Florida. TE's other regulated utility is Peoples Gas System, which distributes natural gas in Florida's metropolitan areas. TE's unregulated businesses include TECO Coal, which has coal-mining operations; and TECO Guatemala, which participates in independent power projects and electric distribution in Guatemala. In December 2007, TE completed the sale of TECO Transport, which provided shipping and storage services for coal and other dry-bulk commodities. In 2008, Tampa Electric accounted for 61.9% of TE's consolidated revenues; Peoples Gas System 20.4%; TECO Coal 17.4%; and TECO Guatemala 0.2%.

CORPORATE STRATEGY. Despite the challenges and uncertainties related to the current state of the economy and housing market in Florida, TECO Energy plans to continue its strategy of investment in Tampa Electric. The company intends to remain focused on the reduction of its debt and to improve its already investment-grade status so as to ensure access to the credit markets and to meet its growing level of necessary capital investment. TE expects to continue its investment in the Peoples Gas infrastructure to serve more customers and to maintain its compliance with federal pipeline standards. The company also intends to increase the output of TECO Coal in 2009 and has already contracted over 90% of its expected production at prices significantly higher than in 2008. While production costs are expected to rise, the company believes it will be at a slower rate than the rise in 2008.

Company Financials Fiscal Year Ended Dec. 31

Per Share Data ($)	2008	2007	2006	2005	2004	2003	2002	2001	2000	1999
Tangible Book Value	9.15	9.28	7.97	7.36	6.13	8.55	13.75	12.94	11.93	11.19
Earnings	0.77	1.90	1.17	1.00	-2.10	-0.08	1.95	2.24	1.97	1.53
S&P Core Earnings	0.67	1.25	1.19	1.00	-1.58	0.24	1.75	2.04	NA	NA
Dividends	0.80	0.78	0.76	0.76	0.76	0.93	1.41	1.37	1.33	1.29
Payout Ratio	103%	41%	65%	76%	NM	NM	72%	61%	68%	84%
Prices:High	21.99	18.58	17.73	19.30	15.49	17.00	29.05	32.97	33.19	28.00
Prices:Low	10.50	14.84	14.40	14.87	11.30	9.47	10.02	24.75	17.25	18.38
P/E Ratio:High	29	10	15	19	NM	NM	15	15	17	18
P/E Ratio:Low	14	8	12	15	NM	NM	5	11	9	12

Income Statement Analysis (Million $)										
Revenue	3,375	3,536	3,448	3,010	2,669	2,740	2,676	2,649	2,295	1,983
Depreciation	266	264	282	282	282	326	303	298	268	232
Maintenance	174	184	183	168	141	152	162	151	140	125
Fixed Charges Coverage	1.80	2.06	1.42	1.25	1.26	2.30	2.43	2.51	2.59	3.30
Construction Credits	8.70	6.20	3.80	Nil	1.00	27.4	9.60	2.60	0.70	0.50
Effective Tax Rate	36.8%	40.4%	40.2%	45.1%	NM	NM	NM	NM	6.87%	30.2%
Net Income	162	399	246	211	-404	-14.7	298	304	251	201
S&P Core Earnings	143	260	248	212	-306	44.4	267	277	NA	NA

Balance Sheet & Other Financial Data (Million $)										
Gross Property	7,311	6,894	7,084	6,755	6,723	8,040	8,215	7,544	6,560	8,501
Capital Expenditures	583	494	456	295	273	591	1,065	966	688	426
Net Property	5,221	4,888	4,767	4,567	4,658	5,679	5,464	4,838	3,970	6,064
Capitalization:Long Term Debt	3,207	3,158	3,213	3,709	3,880	4,393	3,973	2,043	1,575	1,208
Capitalization:% Long Term Debt	61.5	61.0	65.0	70.0	75.1	73.0	43.2	50.9	51.1	46.0
Capitalization:Preferred	Nil	Nil	Nil	Nil	Nil	Nil	Nil	Nil	Nil	Nil
Capitalization:% Preferred	Nil	Nil	Nil	Nil	Nil	Nil	Nil	Nil	Nil	Nil
Capitalization:Common	2,008	2,017	1,729	1,592	1,284	1,622	5,223	1,972	1,507	1,418
Capitalization:% Common	38.5	39.0	35.0	30.0	24.9	27.0	56.8	49.1	48.9	54.0
Total Capital	5,226	5,188	4,957	5,318	5,691	6,537	9,719	4,545	3,564	3,284
% Operating Ratio	91.4	94.3	91.9	91.4	80.2	83.7	84.0	83.7	82.8	83.0
% Earned on Net Property	5.7	8.6	9.0	7.7	NA	0.3	7.6	9.6	10.9	7.3
% Return on Revenue	4.8	11.3	7.1	7.0	NM	NM	11.1	11.5	10.9	10.1
% Return on Invested Capital	6.1	6.3	8.5	9.3	14.2	9.6	6.4	11.9	12.4	9.7
% Return on Common Equity	8.1	21.3	14.8	14.7	NM	NM	6.5	17.5	17.2	13.7

Data as orig reptd.; bef. results of disc opers/spec. items. Per share data adj. for stk. divs.; EPS diluted. E-Estimated. NA-Not Available. NM-Not Meaningful. NR-Not Ranked. UR-Under Review.

Office: 702 N Franklin St, Tampa, FL 33602.
Telephone: 813-228-1111.
Website: http://www.tecoenergy.com
Chrmn & CEO: S.W. Hudson

Pres: T.A. Smith
Pres & COO: J.B. Ramil
SVP & General Counsel: C. Attal, III
CFO, Chief Acctg Officer & Treas: S.W. Callahan

Investor Contact: M.M. Kane (813-228-1772)
Board Members: D. Ausley, J. L. Ferman, Jr., S. W. Hudson, J. P. Lacher, L. A. Penn, J. B. Ramil, T. L. Rankin, W. Rockford, J. T. Touchton, P. L. Whiting

Founded: 1899
Domicile: Florida
Employees: 4,400

The McGraw-Hill Companies

Tellabs Inc

STANDARD &POOR'S

S&P Recommendation	HOLD ★★★☆☆	Price	12-Mo. Target Price
		$5.61 (as of Nov 27, 2009)	$7.00

GICS Sector Information Technology
Sub-Industry Communications Equipment

Summary This company manufactures voice and data equipment used in public and private communications networks worldwide.

Key Stock Statistics (Source S&P, Vickers, company reports)

52-Wk Range	$7.70–3.51	S&P Oper. EPS 2009**E**	0.22	Market Capitalization(B)	$2.166	Beta	0.82
Trailing 12-Month EPS	$0.16	S&P Oper. EPS 2010**E**	0.28	Yield (%)	Nil	S&P 3-Yr. Proj. EPS CAGR(%)	7
Trailing 12-Month P/E	35.1	P/E on S&P Oper. EPS 2009**E**	25.5	Dividend Rate/Share	Nil	S&P Credit Rating	NA
$10K Invested 5 Yrs Ago	$6,501	Common Shares Outstg. (M)	386.2	Institutional Ownership (%)	79		

Price Performance

30-Week Mov. Avg. · · · 10-Week Mov. Avg. - - **GAAP Earnings vs. Previous Year** Volume Above Avg. STARS
12-Mo. Target Price — Relative Strength — ▲ Up ▼ Down ► No Change Below Avg. ★

Options: ASE, CBOE, P, Ph

Analysis prepared by **Ari Bensinger** on October 19, 2009, when the stock traded at **$ 6.92.**

Highlights

► Following an estimated 10% decline in 2009, we see sales advancing roughly 1% in 2010, as improving customer demand for new products, such as the 7100 optical transport, 8600 managed edge and 8800 multiservice router systems, is largely offset by a continued decline in demand for legacy products, particularly for the mature core 5500 cross connect solution.

► We see 2010 gross margins widening roughly 1,000 basis points from 2009, to 44%, aided by a favorable product mix shift and the benefits of cost reduction on new products. We expect 2010 operating expenses on an absolute basis to decline from the prior period, on aggressive restructuring initiatives.

► We forecast 2010 operating margins at 11%, up from 9% in 2009, but below the peer mean, hurt by high research and development costs. After factoring in our projection for continued share repurchases, we look for 2010 EPS of $0.28, versus the $0.22 that we estimate for 2009. Estimates for both years include projected stock option expense of $0.07.

Investment Rationale/Risk

► While near-term visibility remains limited, we are positive on TLAB's long-term market position, given its focus on broadband products, which are gaining an increasing portion of carrier spending. We are encouraged by the improving demand for TLAB's new growth products, and we forecast further customer traction throughout 2010. Even so, we believe the company's large legacy product base, which still represents roughly 50% of total sales, will hamper overall sales growth rates.

► Risks to our recommendation and target price include the loss of a major customer, slowing market penetration for the company's new broadband products, and a sales downtick for its core transport products.

► Our 12-month target price of $7 is based on 2X our 2010 sales estimate and 1.5X book value, multiples that are both in line with the peer mean. We view the company's balance sheet as strong, with $3 cash per share and no long-term debt as of July 2009. Operationally, we think TLAB is making good progress on aligning its cost structure closer to peer average profitability metrics.

Qualitative Risk Assessment

LOW	MEDIUM	HIGH

Our risk assessment reflects the competitive pressure the company faces, and its dependence on a consolidating telecom industry.

Quantitative Evaluations

S&P Quality Ranking B-

D	C	B-	B	B+	A-	A	A+

Relative Strength Rank WEAK

18

LOWEST = 1 HIGHEST = 99

Revenue/Earnings Data

Revenue (Million $)

	1Q	2Q	3Q	4Q	Year
2009	361.7	385.4	389.3	--	--
2008	464.1	432.5	424.1	408.3	1,729
2007	451.9	534.5	457.9	469.1	1,913
2006	514.7	549.3	522.5	454.7	2,041
2005	435.6	462.5	463.9	521.4	1,883
2004	263.8	304.3	284.3	379.4	1,232

Earnings Per Share ($)

2009	0.02	0.04	0.07	E0.07	E0.22
2008	0.04	-0.10	-2.51	0.03	-2.32
2007	0.06	0.07	0.01	0.02	0.15
2006	0.11	0.12	0.13	0.07	0.43
2005	Nil	0.09	0.09	0.20	0.39
2004	0.03	0.12	0.11	-0.32	-0.07

Fiscal year ended Dec. 31. Next earnings report expected: Late January. EPS Estimates based on S&P Operating Earnings; historical GAAP earnings are as reported.

Dividend Data

No cash dividends have been paid.

The McGraw-Hill Companies

Tellabs Inc

Business Summary October 19, 2009

CORPORATE OVERVIEW. Tellabs designs, manufactures, markets and services optical networking, next-generation switching and broadband access solutions. The company's products enable the delivery of wireline and wireless voice, data and video services. Solutions are primarily focused on the last mile of the communications network, the part of the network that is closest to homes and businesses. International sales represented 32% of total sales in 2008, up from 26% during 2007. Results are reported in three business segments; broadband, transport and services.

The broadband segment, which accounts for just over 50% of total sales, enables service providers to deliver bundled voice, video and high-speed Internet data services over copper or fiber networks. Broadband access products include digital loop carriers, digital subscriber line access multiplexers, fiber-to-the-premise (FTTP) optical line terminals for broadband passive optical networks, and voice gateways for voice over Internet protocol (VoIP). Managed access products include aggregation and transport products that deliver wireless and business services outside of the United States. Data products include next-generation packet-switched products that enable wireline and wireless carriers to deliver business services and next-generation wireless services to their customers.

The transport segment, which represents one-third of total sales, enables service providers to transport services and manage bandwidth by adding capacity when and where it is needed. Wireline and wireless providers use these to support wireless services, business services for enterprises, and triple-play voice, video and data services for consumers. Products include the company's core digital cross-connect systems, voice-quality enhancement products, and optical transport systems.

The services segment delivers deployment, training, support services and professional consulting to customers. Services in the planning phase include network architecture and design, network and applications planning, network management design, migration planning and others. Building services include applications integration, program and project management, installation, testing, network integration, third-party systems integration and others.

Company Financials Fiscal Year Ended Dec. 31

Per Share Data ($)	2008	2007	2006	2005	2004	2003	2002	2001	2000	1999
Tangible Book Value	4.25	4.14	3.97	3.53	3.34	3.76	4.45	5.55	6.26	4.85
Cash Flow	-2.11	0.35	0.66	0.66	0.12	-0.32	-0.41	-0.06	2.09	1.56
Earnings	-2.32	0.15	0.43	0.39	-0.07	-0.58	-0.76	-0.44	1.82	1.36
S&P Core Earnings	-0.69	0.16	0.44	0.38	-0.14	-0.71	-1.03	-0.68	NA	NA
Dividends	Nil	Nil	Nil	Nil	Nil	Nil	Nil	Nil	Nil	Nil
Payout Ratio	Nil	Nil	Nil	Nil	Nil	Nil	Nil	Nil	Nil	Nil
Prices:High	7.21	13.67	17.28	11.49	11.37	9.73	17.47	67.13	76.94	77.25
Prices:Low	3.10	6.52	8.84	6.56	7.40	5.07	4.00	8.98	37.63	32.38
P/E Ratio:High	NM	91	40	29	NM	NM	NM	NM	42	57
P/E Ratio:Low	NM	43	21	17	NM	NM	NM	NM	21	24

Income Statement Analysis (Million $)	2008	2007	2006	2005	2004	2003	2002	2001	2000	1999
Revenue	1,729	1,913	2,041	1,883	1,232	980	1,317	2,200	3,387	2,319
Operating Income	147	124	358	330	152	-77.1	-12.7	70.9	1,117	832
Depreciation	87.4	90.7	104	126	82.3	110	143	158	116	84.6
Interest Expense	Nil	Nil	Nil	Nil	Nil	0.70	0.90	0.51	0.63	0.58
Pretax Income	-952	70.2	285	213	-10.2	-245	-328	-245	1,109	816
Effective Tax Rate	NM	7.41%	31.8%	17.5%	NM	NM	NM	NM	31.5%	31.5%
Net Income	-930	65.0	194	176	-29.8	-242	-313	-182	760	559
S&P Core Earnings	-279	68.7	198	171	-58.9	-295	-427	-277	NA	NA

Balance Sheet & Other Financial Data (Million $)	2008	2007	2006	2005	2004	2003	2002	2001	2000	1999
Cash	1,331	1,510	154	1,371	293	246	1,019	1,102	1,022	966
Current Assets	1,936	2,112	2,233	1,873	1,819	1,499	1,534	1,945	2,322	1,786
Total Assets	2,508	3,747	3,922	3,515	3,523	2,608	2,623	2,866	3,073	2,353
Current Liabilities	541	673	762	525	524	208	257	320	412	274
Long Term Debt	Nil	Nil	Nil	Nil	Nil	Nil	Nil	3.39	2.85	2.85
Common Equity	1,847	2,913	2,938	2,815	2,797	2,219	2,290	2,466	2,628	2,048
Total Capital	1,847	2,992	2,938	2,815	2,797	2,319	2,290	2,490	2,637	2,058
Capital Expenditures	50.1	57.7	67.2	61.8	41.4	9.50	34.1	208	208	98.9
Cash Flow	-843	156	298	302	52.5	-131	-171	-24.5	876	644
Current Ratio	3.6	3.1	2.9	3.6	3.5	7.2	6.0	6.1	5.6	6.5
% Long Term Debt of Capitalization	Nil	Nil	Nil	Nil	Nil	Nil	Nil	0.1	0.1	0.1
% Net Income of Revenue	NM	3.4	9.5	9.3	NM	NM	NM	NM	22.4	24.1
% Return on Assets	NM	1.7	5.2	5.0	NM	NM	NM	NM	28.0	28.0
% Return on Equity	NM	2.2	6.7	6.3	NM	NM	NM	NM	32.5	32.5

Data as orig reptd.; bef. results of disc opers/spec. items. Per share data adj. for stk. divs.; EPS diluted. E-Estimated. NA-Not Available. NM-Not Meaningful. NR-Not Ranked. UR-Under Review.

Office: 1415 W Diehl Rd, Naperville, IL 60563-2349.
Telephone: 630-798-8800.
Website: http://www.tellabs.com
Chrmn: M.J. Birck

Pres & CEO: R.W. Pullen
COO: J.M. Brots
EVP & CFO: T.J. Wiggins
EVP, Chief Admin Officer & General Counsel: J.M. Sheehan

Investor Contact: T. Scottino (630-798-3602)
Board Members: L. W. Beck, M. J. Birck, B. C. Hedfors, F. Ianna, F. A. Krehbiel, M. E. Lavin, S. P. Marshall, R. W. Pullen, J. A. Schofield, W. F. Souders, J. H. Suwinski

Founded: 1974
Domicile: Delaware
Employees: 3,228

Tenet Healthcare Corp

STANDARD &POOR'S

S&P Recommendation HOLD ★★★☆☆	Price $4.95 (as of Nov 27, 2009)	12-Mo. Target Price $5.50	Investment Style Large-Cap Value

GICS Sector Health Care
Sub-Industry Health Care Facilities

Summary This company is the second largest U.S. for-profit hospital manager.

Key Stock Statistics (Source S&P, Vickers, company reports)

52-Wk Range	$6.39– 0.78	S&P Oper. EPS 2009**E**	0.12	Market Capitalization(B)	$2.382	Beta	2.19
Trailing 12-Month EPS	$0.26	S&P Oper. EPS 2010**E**	0.16	Yield (%)	Nil	S&P 3-Yr. Proj. EPS CAGR(%)	NM
Trailing 12-Month P/E	19.0	P/E on S&P Oper. EPS 2009**E**	41.3	Dividend Rate/Share	Nil	S&P Credit Rating	B
$10K Invested 5 Yrs Ago	$4,630	Common Shares Outstg. (M)	481.1	Institutional Ownership (%)	84		

Price Performance

30-Week Mov. Avg. ··· 10-Week Mov. Avg. – – GAAP Earnings vs. Previous Year Volume Above Avg. STARS
12-Mo. Target Price — Relative Strength — ▲ Up ▼ Down ▶ No Change Below Avg. ★

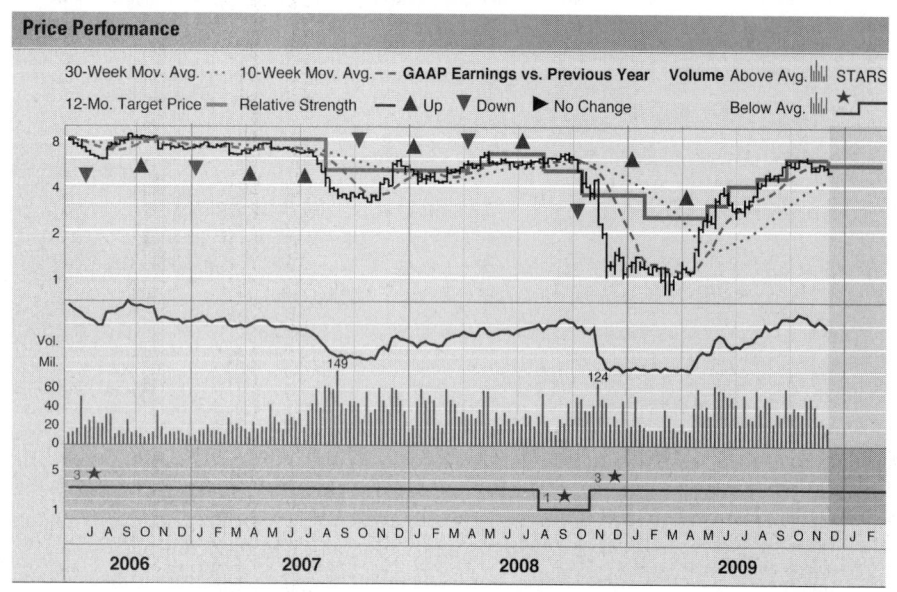

Options: ASE, CBOE, P

Analysis prepared by **Jeffrey Englander, CFA** on November 25, 2009, when the stock traded at **$5.07**.

Highlights

▶ We see revenues rising about 6% in both 2009 and 2010, as THC continues its turnaround efforts in a difficult market environment and challenges from weak employment in its key markets. In the near term, we expect THC to continue to struggle with lower managed care admissions for the remainder of the year and into 2010. Also, while we think health care reform is likely to pass this year, we expect pressure on pricing and margins to be felt before volume gains from implementation are seen.

▶ We see EBITDA margins widening in 2009 and 2010, as cost controls on most operating expenses offset large increases in bad debt reflecting the weaker economy, all as a percentage of sales. Despite the positive bad debt experience in the 2009 first half, compared to the 2008 fourth quarter, we expect bad debt to reach almost 8% of revenues in 2009 and just over 8.5% in 2010, from about 7.3% in 2008. In addition, we anticipate it may not be until late 2009 before the results of THC's Targeted Growth Initiative reach the bottom line.

▶ We see adjusted earnings per share of $0.12 in 2009 and $0.16 in 2010, excluding one-time items.

Investment Rationale/Risk

▶ Our hold opinion reflects valuation. We view 2009 as a transformative period for THC as it struggles with volume growth, particularly in commercial admits which have been under pressure recently. While signs are emerging that management's steps to improve service quality and relationships with physicians and managed care payors are beginning to have an impact, we look for more consistency in quarterly results. We think the strategic steps taken by THC have put it in a better position to meet recently raised EBITDA targets, and we think the company's recently completed debt exchange offer gives it time to return to positive operating cash flow.

▶ Risks to our recommendation and target price include a less favorable government or third-party reimbursement environment and slower physician recruitment than anticipated. In addition, higher self-pay volumes could negatively affect bad debt expense more than we expect.

▶ Our $5.50 target price assumes an EV/EBITDA multiple of about 6.25X our 2010 EBITDA estimate, in line with the peer group, as THC's turnaround efforts are offset in part by weak admissions growth.

Qualitative Risk Assessment

LOW	MEDIUM	HIGH

Our risk assessment for THC reflects our view of its high level of debt and ongoing negative operating cash flow position. In addition, we are concerned by the company's strong dependence on third-party reimbursements, including Medicare and Medicaid, which can be unpredictable.

Quantitative Evaluations

S&P Quality Ranking   C

D	**C**	B-	B	B+	A-	A	A+

Relative Strength Rank   **WEAK**

28

LOWEST = 1   HIGHEST = 99

Revenue/Earnings Data

Revenue (Million $)

	1Q	2Q	3Q	4Q	Year
2009	2,279	2,229	2,262	--	--
2008	2,178	2,132	2,158	2,195	8,663
2007	2,218	2,171	2,212	2,251	8,852
2006	2,414	2,195	2,117	2,179	8,701
2005	2,501	2,420	2,394	2,299	9,614
2004	2,574	2,505	2,428	2,412	9,919

Earnings Per Share ($)

	1Q	2Q	3Q	4Q	Year
2009	0.39	E-0.06	E-0.04	E-0.02	E0.12
2008	-0.02	-0.04	-0.24	-0.07	-0.13
2007	0.20	-0.06	-0.07	-0.18	-0.10
2006	-0.03	-0.95	-0.06	-0.83	-1.85
2005	0.04	Nil	-0.82	-0.54	-1.32
2004	-0.04	-0.45	-0.11	-3.43	-3.85

Fiscal year ended Dec. 31. Next earnings report expected: Late February. EPS Estimates based on S&P Operating Earnings; historical GAAP earnings are as reported.

Dividend Data

Dividends, initiated in 1973, were omitted beginning in 1993. A special dividend of $0.01 a share was paid in March 2000.

Please read the Required Disclosures and Analyst Certification on the last page of this report.

The McGraw·Hill Companies

Tenet Healthcare Corp

STANDARD
&POOR'S

Business Summary November 25, 2009

CORPORATE OVERVIEW. Tenet Healthcare ranks as the second largest U.S. for-profit hospital manager. At December 31, 2008, it owned or operated 53 hospitals (including three hospitals not yet divested but classified as discontinued operations), with 14,352 licensed beds. The largest concentrations of hospital beds were in California, Florida and Texas. THC also owns and operates a small number of rehabilitation hospitals, a specialty hospital, skilled nursing facilities, and medical office buildings located on or near the general hospital properties.

In January 2003, THC was sued by the U.S. Justice Department for allegedly submitting false claims to Medicare. In October 2003, the Justice Department served THC with a subpoena related to its investigation of Medicare outlier payments. In September 2003, the U.S. Senate launched an investigation into the company's corporate governance practices with respect to federal health care programs. In October 2004, additional investigations were announced into THC's medical directorship arrangements and physician relocation agreements.

In January 2006, THC reached an agreement to settle federal securities class

action lawsuits as well as shareholder derivative litigation for $215 million in cash; insurance proceeds covered $75 million of the this amount. The lawsuits were filed against the company beginning in 2002 and were consolidated in January 2003. In June 2006, THC and the U.S. Department of Justice reached an agreement to settle the ongoing investigation into Medicare outlier billing. The company agreed to pay $725 million over a period of four years, plus interest, and to waive its right to collect $175 million in Medicare payments for past services. In order to fund the settlement, at that time THC announced it would sell 11 hospitals. The settlement does not involve the Securities and Exchange Commission, which is investigating THC's financial disclosures surrounding the Medicare outlier payments. In our view, the Justice Department settlement removes some risk from the stock, but we expect its valuation to continue to be driven by the company's underlying operating fundamentals.

Company Financials Fiscal Year Ended Dec. 31

Per Share Data ($)	2008	2007	2006	2005	2004	2003	2002	2001	2000	1999
Tangible Book Value	NM	NM	NM	NM	1.63	4.85	4.40	4.40	3.45	1.57
Cash Flow	0.83	0.59	-1.12	-0.51	-3.02	-2.00	1.54	3.24	2.51	1.85
Earnings	-0.13	-0.10	-1.85	-1.32	-3.85	-3.01	0.93	2.04	1.39	0.72
S&P Core Earnings	NA	-0.11	-0.34	-1.14	-2.28	0.27	1.54	1.24	NA	NA
Dividends	Nil	Nil	Nil	Nil	Nil	Nil	Nil	Nil	Nil	0.01
Payout Ratio	Nil	Nil	Nil	Nil	Nil	Nil	Nil	Nil	Nil	1%
Prices:High	6.88	7.80	9.27	13.06	18.73	19.25	52.50	41.85	30.50	18.12
Prices:Low	0.99	3.06	5.77	7.27	9.15	11.32	13.70	24.67	11.29	10.25
P/E Ratio:High	NM	NM	NM	NM	NM	NM	56	21	22	25
P/E Ratio:Low	NM	NM	NM	NM	NM	NM	15	12	8	14

Income Statement Analysis (Million $)										
Revenue	8,663	8,852	8,701	9,614	9,919	13,212	8,743	13,913	12,053	11,414
Operating Income	694	669	687	571	434	1,072	1,676	2,797	2,244	1,935
Depreciation	335	330	342	382	388	471	302	604	554	533
Interest Expense	428	430	409	405	333	296	147	327	456	479
Pretax Income	43.0	-103	-1,129	-701	-1,616	-1,829	777	1,799	1,156	639
Effective Tax Rate	NM	56.3%	NM	NM	NM	NM	38.5%	40.9%	40.1%	43.5%
Net Income	62.0	-49.0	-871	-621	-1,797	-1,404	459	1,025	678	340
S&P Core Earnings	-1.05	-52.3	-159	-561	-1,061	123	760	607	NA	NA

Balance Sheet & Other Financial Data (Million $)										
Cash	523	592	784	1,373	654	619	210	38.0	62.0	135
Current Assets	2,709	2,560	3,025	3,508	3,992	4,248	3,792	3,394	3,226	3,594
Total Assets	8,174	8,393	8,539	9,812	10,078	12,298	13,780	13,814	12,995	13,161
Current Liabilities	1,949	2,048	1,925	2,292	2,130	2,394	2,381	2,584	2,166	1,912
Long Term Debt	4,778	4,771	4,760	4,784	4,395	4,039	3,872	3,919	4,202	5,668
Common Equity	103	54.0	995	1,760	2,460	4,361	5,723	5,619	5,079	4,066
Total Capital	4,982	4,944	5,862	6,756	7,166	8,404	10,121	10,227	9,835	10,225
Capital Expenditures	527	729	631	568	454	753	490	889	601	619
Cash Flow	397	281	-529	-239	-1,409	-933	761	1,629	1,232	873
Current Ratio	1.4	1.3	1.6	1.5	1.9	1.8	1.6	1.3	1.5	1.9
% Long Term Debt of Capitalization	95.9	96.5	81.2	70.8	61.3	48.1	38.3	38.3	42.7	55.4
% Net Income of Revenue	0.7	NM	NM	NM	NM	NM	5.2	7.4	5.6	3.0
% Return on Assets	0.8	NM	NM	NM	NM	NM	NM	7.6	5.2	2.5
% Return on Equity	79.0	NM	NM	NM	NM	NM	NM	19.2	14.8	8.6

Data as orig reptd.; bef. results of disc opers/spec. items. Per share data adj. for stk. divs.; EPS diluted. E-Estimated. NA-Not Available. NM-Not Meaningful. NR-Not Ranked. UR-Under Review.

Office: 13737 Noel Rd, Dallas, TX 75240-1331.
Telephone: 469-893-2200.
Email: feedback@tenethealth.com
Website: http://www.tenethealth.com

Chrmn: E.A. Kangas
Pres: T. Fetter
CEO: G.S. Manis
COO: S.L. Newman

EVP & CIO: S.F. Brown
Investor Contact: T. Rice (469-893-2522)
Board Members: J. E. Bush, T. Fetter, B. J. Gaines, K. M. Garrison, E. A. Kangas, J. R. Kerrey, F. D. Loop, R. R. Pettingill, J. A. Unruh, J. M. Williams

Founded: 1967
Domicile: Nevada
Employees: 60,297

The McGraw-Hill Companies

STANDARD
&POOR'S

Teradata Corp

S&P Recommendation	HOLD ★★★☆☆	Price $28.83 (as of Nov 27, 2009)	12-Mo. Target Price $29.00	Investment Style Large-Cap Blend

GICS Sector Information Technology
Sub-Industry Computer Hardware

Summary This Ohio-based company has global operations focused on data warehousing and enterprise analytics. Teradata was spun off from NCR Corporation in 2007.

Key Stock Statistics (Source S&P, Vickers, company reports)

52-Wk Range	$31.24– 12.62	S&P Oper. EPS 2009**E**	1.37	Market Capitalization(B)	$4.936	Beta	NA
Trailing 12-Month EPS	$1.43	S&P Oper. EPS 2010**E**	1.47	Yield (%)	Nil	S&P 3-Yr. Proj. EPS CAGR(%)	7
Trailing 12-Month P/E	20.2	P/E on S&P Oper. EPS 2009**E**	21.0	Dividend Rate/Share	Nil	S&P Credit Rating	NA
$10K Invested 5 Yrs Ago	NA	Common Shares Outstg. (M)	171.2	Institutional Ownership (%)	75		

Price Performance

30-Week Mov. Avg. · · · · 10-Week Mov. Avg. – – **GAAP Earnings vs. Previous Year** Volume Above Avg. STARS
12-Mo. Target Price — Relative Strength — ▲ Up ▼ Down ▶ No Change Below Avg. ★

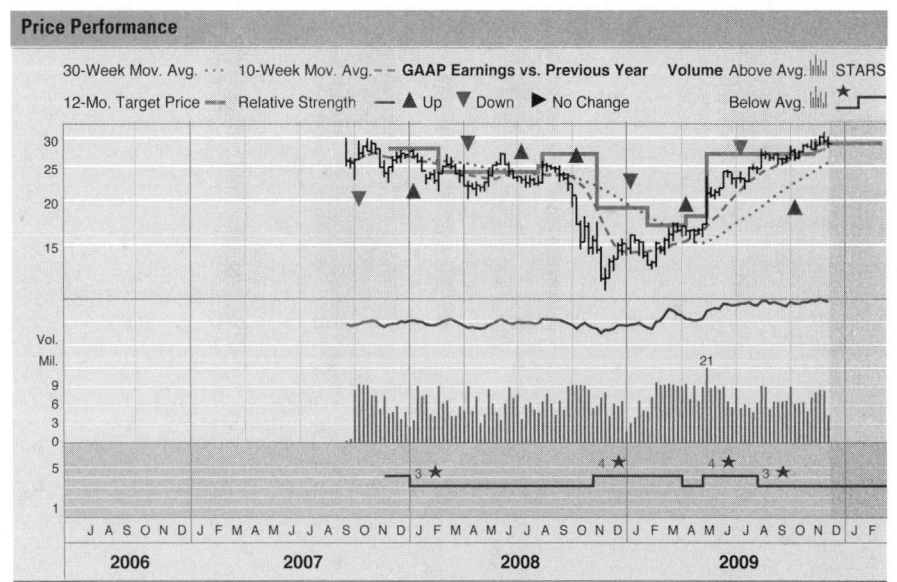

Options: CBOE, Ph

Analysis prepared by **Zaineb Bokhari** on November 10, 2009, when the stock traded at **$ 30.28**.

Highlights

▶ We project revenues will decrease 4% in 2009 to $1.69 billion reflecting a projected slowdown in information technology spending. We expect negative currency translation effects to dampen reported revenues for 2009, but we think the impact will moderate late in the year. We see revenues rising approximately 7% in 2010, aided by easier year-to-year comparisons and an anticipated improvement in the global economic environment.

▶ We forecast that the gross margin will widen slightly in 2009 and 2010 as the company seeks efficiencies as a stand-alone operation. We expect second half 2009 gross margins to narrow from the first half due to higher amortization of software development costs. We think operating margins will remain near 19%, unchanged from 2008, due to investment in R&D and sales. A lack of long-term debt and the establishment of a $300 million credit facility indicates to us that currently negligible interest expense could rise.

▶ We estimate operating EPS of $1.37 for 2009 and $1.47 for 2010. We expect share repurchases to continue to lend support to per-share results.

Investment Rationale/Risk

▶ We view Teradata as operating in a large niche of the information technology sector. A primary sales driver is rising interest among enterprises in using their transaction data to study and improve patterns of operation. The company aims to expand by entering new sales territories, and we believe has the potential to do well based on its one-stop shopping approach to offering business intelligence hardware, software, and consulting. Despite this, we think competition remains intense, and will contribute to unpredictable and lengthy sales cycles. Based on our forward P/E analysis, we view TDC's valuation as reasonable.

▶ Risks to our recommendation and target price include slowdowns in the general pace of spending on information technology for businesses, any failure to keep pace with rapidly evolving computer and analytical technology, and competition on price and quality of products and services.

▶ Applying a target P/E multiple of 20X, in line with the recent average for peers, to our 2010 EPS estimate of $1.47, we arrive at our 12-month target price of $29.

Qualitative Risk Assessment

LOW	MEDIUM	HIGH

Teradata participates in a large and growing global market we see for storing, retrieving, and analyzing data produced by businesses. While competition is high for technology and pricing, we believe a stream of revenue from services, and a lack of debt, lends some stability.

Quantitative Evaluations

S&P Quality Ranking NR

D	C	B-	B	B+	A-	A	A+

Relative Strength Rank MODERATE

67

LOWEST = 1   HIGHEST = 99

Revenue/Earnings Data

Revenue (Million $)

	1Q	2Q	3Q	4Q	Year
2009	367.0	421.0	425.0	--	--
2008	375.0	455.0	439.0	493.0	1,762
2007	367.0	430.0	439.0	466.0	1,702
2006	323.0	396.0	375.0	466.0	1,560
2005	347.0	357.0	358.0	405.0	1,467
2004	--	--	--	--	1,349

Earnings Per Share ($)

2009	0.26	0.36	0.36	E0.37	E1.37
2008	0.23	0.38	0.33	0.45	1.39
2007	0.24	0.27	0.16	0.46	1.10
2006	0.20	0.28	0.31	0.31	1.09
2005	--	--	--	--	1.14
2004	--	--	--	--	0.76

Fiscal year ended Dec. 31. Next earnings report expected: Mid February. EPS Estimates based on S&P Operating Earnings; historical GAAP earnings are as reported.

Dividend Data

No cash dividends have been paid.

Please read the Required Disclosures and Analyst Certification on the last page of this report.

The McGraw-Hill Companies

Teradata Corp

STANDARD
&POOR'S

Business Summary November 10, 2009

CORPORATE OVERVIEW. Teradata Corporation aims to help its enterprise customers make smarter and faster use of their stored data to improve decision-making. It views itself as a global leader in data warehousing and enterprise analytic technologies. The company offers hardware and software, as well as services including consulting, customer support and training. In 2008, almost 48% of revenues were derived from products (52% for 2007), and 52% (48%) came from services.

Headquartered in Dayton, Ohio, the company has offices throughout the Americas and operates in 60 countries worldwide. It earned 49% of its revenues outside the U.S. in 2008. Teradata has a broad customer base, in our view, with the top 10 customers in 2008 representing only about 20% of sales. In 2008, revenue came 56% from the Americas, 26% from EMEA (Europe, Middle East, Africa), and 18% from APJ (Asia Pacific/Japan), similar to the 2007 breakout. Gross margins have typically been widest for the Americas region, near 57% compared to a company average of 54% in 2008.

Data warehousing is the process of capturing, storing and analyzing data to gain insight, according to the company. This activity can be a significant

source of intelligence for the enterprise and become a competitive advantage. Beyond mere storage of data, modern solutions allow for near real-time information access and analysis. Predictive analytics on customer or business activity may be run. Both long-term strategic and short-term tactical inquiries may be pursued.

In one example of active data warehousing, a business's call center could produce raw data on call attributes (e.g., number of calls, duration, agent, customer, dropped calls, results), which could be a starting point for mapping and analyzing overall interactions with customers, including Internet communications, which could then become the basis for a plan to improve customer satisfaction. The company serves many large clients in the communications industry, as well as in media and entertainment, financial services, government, health care, manufacturing, retail, and transportation.

Company Financials Fiscal Year Ended Dec. 31

Per Share Data ($)	2008	2007	2006	2005	2004	2003	2002	2001	2000	1999
Tangible Book Value	3.30	2.91	2.15	NA	NA	NA	NA	NA	NA	NA
Cash Flow	1.72	1.48	1.40	1.44	1.03	NA	NA	NA	NA	NA
Earnings	1.39	1.10	1.09	1.14	0.76	NA	NA	NA	NA	NA
S&P Core Earnings	1.40	1.18	1.09	1.10	NA	NA	NA	NA	NA	NA
Dividends	Nil	Nil	NA	NA	NA	NA	NA	NA	NA	NA
Payout Ratio	Nil	Nil	NA	NA	NA	NA	NA	NA	NA	NA
Prices:High	27.90	30.08	NA	NA	NA	NA	NA	NA	NA	NA
Prices:Low	11.11	22.35	NA	NA	NA	NA	NA	NA	NA	NA
P/E Ratio:High	20	27	NA	NA	NA	NA	NA	NA	NA	NA
P/E Ratio:Low	8	20	NA	NA	NA	NA	NA	NA	NA	NA

Income Statement Analysis (Million $)										
Revenue	1,762	1,702	1,560	1,467	1,349	NA	NA	NA	NA	NA
Operating Income	393	405	367	339	247	NA	NA	NA	NA	NA
Depreciation	60.0	68.0	55.0	55.0	48.0	NA	NA	NA	NA	NA
Interest Expense	Nil	Nil	Nil	Nil	Nil	NA	NA	NA	NA	NA
Pretax Income	338	322	312	284	199	NA	NA	NA	NA	NA
Effective Tax Rate	26.0%	37.9%	36.5%	27.5%	30.7%	NA	NA	NA	NA	NA
Net Income	250	200	198	206	138	NA	NA	NA	NA	NA
S&P Core Earnings	252	213	198	200	NA	NA	NA	NA	NA	NA

Balance Sheet & Other Financial Data (Million $)										
Cash	442	270	200	NA	NA	NA	NA	NA	NA	NA
Current Assets	1,015	873	645	NA	NA	NA	NA	NA	NA	NA
Total Assets	1,445	1,295	983	911	NA	NA	NA	NA	NA	NA
Current Liabilities	540	572	428	NA	NA	NA	NA	NA	NA	NA
Long Term Debt	Nil	Nil	Nil	NA	NA	NA	NA	NA	NA	NA
Common Equity	782	631	477	517	NA	NA	NA	NA	NA	NA
Total Capital	777	631	477	517	NA	NA	NA	NA	NA	NA
Capital Expenditures	19.0	50.0	20.0	18.0	14.0	NA	NA	NA	NA	NA
Cash Flow	310	268	253	261	186	NA	NA	NA	NA	NA
Current Ratio	1.9	1.5	1.5	1.2	NA	NA	NA	NA	NA	NA
% Long Term Debt of Capitalization	Nil	Nil	Nil	Nil	10.2	NA	NA	NA	NA	NA
% Net Income of Revenue	14.2	11.8	12.7	14.0	10.2	NA	NA	NA	NA	NA
% Return on Assets	18.3	17.4	NM	NM	NA	NA	NA	NA	NA	NA
% Return on Equity	35.4	32.6	NM	NM	NA	NA	NA	NA	NA	NA

Data as orig reptd.; bef. results of disc opers/spec. items. Per share data adj. for stk. divs.; EPS diluted. E-Estimated. NA-Not Available. NM-Not Meaningful. NR-Not Ranked. UR-Under Review.

Office: 1700 S. Patterson Blvd., Dayton, OH 45479.
Telephone: 937-445-5000.
Website: http://www.teradata.com
Chrmn: J.M. Ringler

Pres & CEO: M.F. Koehler
COO: B.A. Langos
EVP, CFO & Chief Acctg Officer: S.M. Scheppmann
Chief Admin Officer: R.A. Young

Investor Contact: S. Scheppmann (888-261-6779)
Board Members: E. P. Boykin, N. E. Cooper, P. L. Fiore, C. T. Fu, D. E. Kepler, II, M. F. Koehler, V. L. Lund, J. M. Ringler, W. S. Stavropoulos

Auditor: PricewaterhouseCoopers
Founded: 1979
Domicile: Delaware
Employees: 6,400

The McGraw-Hill Companies

Teradyne Inc.

STANDARD &POOR'S

S&P Recommendation BUY ★★★★☆

Price	12-Mo. Target Price	Investment Style
$8.83 (as of Nov 27, 2009)	$12.00	Large-Cap Blend

GICS Sector Information Technology
Sub-Industry Semiconductor Equipment

Summary This company makes automatic test equipment used primarily by the semiconductor and telecommunications industries.

Key Stock Statistics (Source S&P, Vickers, company reports)

52-Wk Range	$10.67– 3.20	S&P Oper. EPS 2009**E**	-0.28	Market Capitalization(B)	$1.544	Beta	1.83
Trailing 12-Month EPS	$-3.13	S&P Oper. EPS 2010**E**	0.83	Yield (%)	Nil	S&P 3-Yr. Proj. EPS CAGR(%)	NM
Trailing 12-Month P/E	NM	P/E on S&P Oper. EPS 2009**E**	NM	Dividend Rate/Share	Nil	S&P Credit Rating	NR
$10K Invested 5 Yrs Ago	$5,011	Common Shares Outstg. (M)	174.9	Institutional Ownership (%)	NM		

Price Performance

30-Week Mov. Avg. · · · 10-Week Mov. Avg. – – **GAAP Earnings vs. Previous Year** Volume Above Avg. STARS
12-Mo. Target Price — Relative Strength ▲ Up ▼ Down ▶ No Change Below Avg. ★

Options: ASE, CBOE, P, Ph

Analysis prepared by **Angelo Zino** on October 29, 2009, when the stock traded at **$ 9.09**.

Highlights

► We expect revenues to decline 26% in 2009 and then rise 37% in 2010, as we see a rebound in the system-on-chip (SOC) test equipment market. We project SOC bookings to improve, on higher demand in wireless and power management as well as technology buys from outsourced assembly and packaging customers. We look for NAND flash memory test sales to increase from current levels, driven by rising utilization levels and stabilizing sales from customers. TER recently realized initial sales for its hard disk drive tester and we think it will generate orders for DRAM testers during 2010.

► We project annual gross margins of 38% in 2009 and 49% for 2010. Despite low production volume, we expect margins to widen going forward, benefiting from higher sales and recent cost reduction efforts. We see TER continuing initiatives to reduce costs through outsourcing more of its manufacturing processes to low-cost countries.

► We project a per-share operating loss of $0.28 in 2009, which excludes $0.48 in non-recurring charges, and EPS of $0.83 for 2010. We anticipate TER will focus on cash preservation amid current economic conditions.

Investment Rationale/Risk

► Our buy recommendation reflects our view of improving back-end equipment industry conditions, momentum from new product releases, and a compelling valuation. We think new product releases and TER's expansion into adjacent markets, such as Dynamic Random Access Memory (DRAM), will aid long-term growth and allow for potential market share gains. TER's leadership position in the business and what we view as its strong cash position, offset in part by the competitive and low-growth environment for testers, are incorporated into our opinion.

► Risks to our recommendation and target price include intensified pricing pressures, technological obsolescence, weakness in the global economy, and competitive threats.

► We derive our 12-month target price of $12 by applying a price-to-sales (P/S) multiple of 1.9X to our 2010 sales per share forecast of $6.17, above comparable back-end equipment manufacturers, which we view as warranted by TER's leading market share position in the SOC market. The ratio is above the historical three- and five-year P/S averages of 1.4X and 1.8X, given our outlook for robust sales growth.

Qualitative Risk Assessment

LOW	MEDIUM	HIGH

Our risk assessment reflects the historical cyclicality of the semiconductor equipment industry, the lack of visibility in the medium term, and intense competition, which we think are only partially offset by Teradyne's market position and financial strength.

Quantitative Evaluations

S&P Quality Ranking B-

D	C	B-	B	B+	A-	A	A+

Relative Strength Rank MODERATE

52

LOWEST = 1   HIGHEST = 99

Revenue/Earnings Data

Revenue (Million $)

	1Q	2Q	3Q	4Q	Year
2009	120.6	169.6	262.2	--	--
2008	297.3	317.7	297.3	194.8	1,107
2007	258.1	288.7	299.5	260.4	1,102
2006	362.9	391.6	359.1	263.2	1,377
2005	210.4	226.2	293.6	345.2	1,075
2004	430.6	526.5	457.8	377.0	1,792

Earnings Per Share ($)

	1Q	2Q	3Q	4Q	Year
2009	-0.53	-0.39	0.04	E0.15	E-0.28
2008	0.01	0.06	-0.14	-0.33	-0.38
2007	-0.04	0.14	0.19	0.10	0.39
2006	0.23	0.40	0.33	0.06	1.03
2005	-0.28	-0.26	-0.22	0.44	-0.31
2004	0.20	0.39	0.21	0.02	0.84

Fiscal year ended Dec. 31. Next earnings report expected: Late January. EPS Estimates based on S&P Operating Earnings; historical GAAP earnings are as reported.

Dividend Data

No cash dividends have been paid.

Teradyne Inc.

STANDARD &POOR'S

Business Summary October 29, 2009

CORPORATE OVERVIEW. Founded in 1960, Teradyne is a leading global supplier of automatic test equipment (ATE) for the electronics industry. As electronic systems have become more complex, the need for products to test the systems has grown dramatically. TER's product segments include Semiconductor Test (81% of 2008 revenue, 80% in 2007) and Systems Test Group (19%, 20%).

Semiconductor Test products test system on a chip (SOC) semiconductor devices during the manufacturing process. These systems are used for wafer level and device packaging testing and span a broad range of end users and functionality. TER's systems help customers improve and control quality, reduce time to market, increase production yields, and improve product performance. TER's FLEX Test platform is designed for scalability and allows for simultaneous parallel testing, reducing costs. The J750 platform is designed to address the highest volume semiconductor devices such as microcontrollers, with a single circuit board providing up to 64 digital input/output channels. The J750 platform technology has been extended to create the IP 750 Image Sensor test system, which focuses on testing image sensor devices used in digital cameras and other imaging products. The J750 platform has been expanded to include critical new devices that include high-end microcontroller, LCD drivers, and the latest generation of cameras.

TER's acquisition of Nextest expanded its product base to include the Magnum test platform. The Magnum platform offers memory test products for the flash memory and dynamic random access memory (DRAM) markets. TER's Eagle Test acquisition expanded its product offerings to include the ETS platform. The ETS platform is used by chipmaker's and assembly and test subcontractors, primarily in the low pin count analog/mixed signal discrete markets that cover more cost sensitive applications. Its SmartPin technology enables multiple semiconductor devices to be tested simultaneously, or in parallel, on an individual test system, permitting greater test throughput.

Company Financials Fiscal Year Ended Dec. 31

Per Share Data ($)	2008	2007	2006	2005	2004	2003	2002	2001	2000	1999
Tangible Book Value	3.16	6.70	6.84	5.75	5.00	4.33	4.97	8.69	9.89	6.77
Cash Flow	-1.92	0.71	1.35	0.16	1.47	-0.22	-3.06	-0.36	3.42	1.56
Earnings	-0.38	0.39	1.03	-0.31	0.84	-1.03	-3.93	-1.15	2.86	1.07
S&P Core Earnings	-1.21	0.37	0.92	-0.80	0.37	-1.44	-4.25	-1.65	NA	NA
Dividends	Nil	Nil	Nil	Nil	Nil	Nil	Nil	Nil	Nil	Nil
Payout Ratio	Nil	Nil	Nil	Nil	Nil	Nil	Nil	Nil	Nil	Nil
Prices:High	14.50	18.53	18.08	17.33	30.70	26.31	40.20	47.21	115.44	66.00
Prices:Low	2.80	10.02	11.50	10.80	12.53	8.75	7.10	18.43	23.00	20.63
P/E Ratio:High	NM	48	18	NM	37	NM	NM	NM	40	62
P/E Ratio:Low	NM	26	11	NM	15	NM	NM	NM	8	19

Income Statement Analysis (Million $)	2008	2007	2006	2005	2004	2003	2002	2001	2000	1999
Revenue	1,107	1,102	1,377	1,075	1,792	1,353	1,222	1,441	3,044	1,791
Operating Income	89.6	117	236	27.1	318	47.3	-192	-1.54	813	345
Depreciation	71.3	59.4	73.5	91.2	124	152	160	139	102	86.4
Interest Expense	NA	0.69	11.1	16.2	18.8	20.9	21.8	4.09	1.84	1.66
Pretax Income	-52.7	79.2	230	-80.1	188	-186	-561	-326	740	274
Effective Tax Rate	NM	9.29%	12.0%	NM	12.1%	NM	NM	NM	30.0%	30.0%
Net Income	-65.3	71.9	203	-60.5	165	-194	-718	-202	518	192
S&P Core Earnings	-206	68.3	179	-161	73.3	-270	-777	-290	NA	NA

Balance Sheet & Other Financial Data (Million $)	2008	2007	2006	2005	2004	2003	2002	2001	2000	1999
Cash	323	638	945	695	285	586	541	586	464	387
Current Assets	679	945	889	1,095	806	769	809	1,207	1,378	908
Total Assets	1,560	1,555	1,721	1,860	1,923	1,785	1,895	2,542	2,356	1,568
Current Liabilities	367	223	260	515	277	281	279	296	619	392
Long Term Debt	Nil	Nil	Nil	1.82	399	408	451	452	8.35	8.95
Common Equity	1,039	1,229	1,361	1,243	1,134	950	1,028	1,764	1,707	1,153
Total Capital	706	1,229	1,361	1,244	1,532	1,357	1,479	2,216	1,737	1,176
Capital Expenditures	87.2	86.1	110	113	165	30.8	46.4	198	235	120
Cash Flow	-327	131	276	30.7	290	-41.5	-559	-63.5	620	278
Current Ratio	1.9	4.2	3.4	2.1	2.9	2.7	2.9	4.1	2.2	2.3
% Long Term Debt of Capitalization	Nil	Nil	Nil	0.1	26.0	30.0	30.5	20.4	0.5	0.8
% Net Income of Revenue	NM	6.5	14.7	NM	9.2	NM	NM	NM	17.0	10.7
% Return on Assets	NM	4.4	11.3	NM	8.9	NM	NM	NM	26.4	13.3
% Return on Equity	NM	5.6	15.6	NM	15.9	NM	NM	NM	36.2	17.6

Data as orig reptd.; bef. results of disc opers/spec. items. Per share data adj. for stk. divs.; EPS diluted. E-Estimated. NA-Not Available. NM-Not Meaningful. NR-Not Ranked. UR-Under Review.

Office: 600 Riverpark Dr, North Reading, MA 01864-2634.
Telephone: 978-370-2700.
Email: investorrelations@teradyne.com
Website: http://www.teradyne.com

Chrmn: P.S. Wolpert
Pres & CEO: M.A. Bradley
CFO, Chief Acctg Officer & Treas: G.R. Beecher
Secy & General Counsel: C. Gray

Investor Contact: A. Blanchard (978-370-2425)
Board Members: J. W. Bageley, M. A. Bradley, A. Carnesale, E. Gillis, V. M. O'Reilly, P. Tufano, R. Vallee, P. S. Wolpert

Founded: 1960
Domicile: Massachusetts
Employees: 3,800

Tesoro Corp

S&P Recommendation	HOLD ★★★☆☆	Price $12.69 (as of Nov 27, 2009)	12-Mo. Target Price $16.00	Investment Style Large-Cap Blend

GICS Sector Energy
Sub-Industry Oil & Gas Refining & Marketing

Summary Tesoro is one of the largest independent refiners and marketers of petroleum products in the U.S., with operations focused on the West Coast.

Key Stock Statistics (Source S&P, Vickers, company reports)

52-Wk Range	$19.16–7.22	S&P Oper. EPS 2009E	0.28	Market Capitalization(B)	$1.779	Beta	1.31
Trailing 12-Month EPS	$0.98	S&P Oper. EPS 2010E	1.08	Yield (%)	1.58	S&P 3-Yr. Proj. EPS CAGR(%)	-3
Trailing 12-Month P/E	13.0	P/E on S&P Oper. EPS 2009E	45.3	Dividend Rate/Share	$0.20	S&P Credit Rating	BB+
$10K Invested 5 Yrs Ago	$8,019	Common Shares Outstg. (M)	140.2	Institutional Ownership (%)	86		

Price Performance

30-Week Mov. Avg. · · · 10-Week Mov. Avg. — — GAAP Earnings vs. Previous Year   Volume Above Avg. STARS
12-Mo. Target Price — Relative Strength ▲ Up ▼ Down ► No Change   Below Avg.

2-for-1

Options: ASE, CBOE, Ph

Analysis prepared by **Tina J. Vital** on November 12, 2009, when the stock traded at **$ 13.20**.

Highlights

▶ TSO's third-quarter 2009 refining throughputs declined 9.3%, to 564,000 b/d, below our expectations, reflecting maintenance and reduced demand. Taking guidance into consideration, we look for fourth-quarter throughputs to drop 5.8% sequentially.

▶ TSO estimates its 2009 EBITDA will see an incremental benefit about $450 million over 2008 on cost initiatives. Third-quarter refining manufacturing costs (before depreciation and amortization) fell 8.6% to $4.79 per throughput barrel, within the range of our expectations; however, we look for fourth-quarter manufacturing costs to rise about 17% sequentially on higher crude costs.

▶ First nine months operating EPS excluded $0.05 of special losses. We expect after-tax operating earnings to fall 87% in 2009 on narrowed refining margins, before rebounding 275% in 2010 on widened margins due to cost initiatives and increased demand. We project U.S. Gulf Coast 3-2-1 crack spreads will narrow about 16% in 2009 before widening about 7% in 2010 on our expectations of improved economic growth.

Investment Rationale/Risk

▶ We believe TSO's exposure to an above U.S. average refining margin environment on the West Coast enhances its earnings potential. While a significant portion of TSO's refining capacity is of lower complexity, we believe its facilities are strategically sited to benefit from local markets, and expect TSO will achieve enhanced operational efficiencies from recent refining upgrades.

▶ Risks to our recommendation and target price include unfavorable changes in economic, industry and operating conditions that would lead to narrowed refining margins or reduced refining volumes. About 58% of TSO's refining capacity is concentrated in three refineries (Martinez and Los Angeles, CA, and Anacortes, WA), which exposes the company to operational risk, in our view.

▶ A blend of our discounted cash flow, (intrinsic value of $17 per share, assuming a WACC of 10.2% and terminal growth of 3%) and relative valuations factoring in overall equity market conditions, leads to our 12-month target price of $16 per share. This represents an expected enterprise value of about 4.4X our 2010 EBITDA estimate, a discount to U.S. refining peers.

Qualitative Risk Assessment

LOW	MEDIUM	HIGH

Our risk assessment reflects our view of TSO's solid business profile in a competitive and volatile refining industry. We believe the company has strong asset quality and solid liquidity.

Quantitative Evaluations

S&P Quality Ranking   B

D	C	B-	B	B+	A-	A	A+

Relative Strength Rank   WEAK

18

LOWEST = 1   HIGHEST = 99

Revenue/Earnings Data

Revenue (Million $)

	1Q	2Q	3Q	4Q	Year
2009	3,280	4,181	4,670	--	--
2008	6,531	8,754	8,698	4,326	28,309
2007	3,876	5,604	5,902	6,533	21,915
2006	3,877	4,929	5,278	4,020	18,104
2005	3,171	4,033	5,017	4,360	16,581
2004	2,430	3,155	3,289	3,389	12,262

Earnings Per Share ($)

2009	0.37	-0.33	-0.24	E-0.05	E0.28
2008	-0.60	-0.03	1.86	0.70	2.00
2007	0.84	3.17	0.34	-0.29	4.06
2006	0.31	2.33	1.96	1.14	5.73
2005	0.20	1.31	1.60	0.49	3.60
2004	0.38	1.56	0.47	Nil	2.38

Fiscal year ended Dec. 31. Next earnings report expected: Mid February. EPS Estimates based on S&P Operating Earnings; historical GAAP earnings are as reported.

Dividend Data (Dates: mm/dd Payment Date: mm/dd/yy)

Amount ($)	Date Decl.	Ex-Div. Date	Stk. of Record	Payment Date
0.100	02/19	02/26	03/02	03/16/09
0.100	05/06	05/28	06/01	06/15/09
0.100	07/29	08/28	09/01	09/15/09
0.050	11/09	11/27	12/01	12/15/09

Dividends have been paid since 2005. Source: Company reports.

Please read the Required Disclosures and Analyst Certification on the last page of this report.

Tesoro Corp

STANDARD &POOR'S

Business Summary November 12, 2009

CORPORATE OVERVIEW. Tesoro Corp. (TSO; formerly Tesoro Petroleum Corp.) is one of the largest independent refiners and marketers of petroleum products in the U.S. The company operates in two business segments: Refining (86% of 2008 revenues; 93% of 2008 operating income) and Retail (14%; 7%).

The Refining segment refines crude oil and other feedstocks at its seven refineries (total refining capacity 664,500 b/d, as of December 31, 2008) in the U.S. West and Mid-Continent: California ("Wilmington" in Los Angeles, CA, 97,000 b/d; "Golden Eagle" in Martinez, CA, 166,000 b/d), the Pacific Northwest (Anacortes, WA, 120,000 b/d; and Kenai, AK, 72,000 b/d), the Mid-Pacific (Kapolei, HI, 93,500 b/d) and the Mid-Continent (Mandan, ND, 58,000 b/d; and Salt Lake City, UT, 58,000 b/d). Refining yields rose about 1%, to 625,000 b/d, in 2008, and included gasoline 44%, jet fuel 12%, diesel fuel 23%, and heavy oils, residual products and other 21%.

The company purchases its crude oil and other feedstocks for its refineries from various domestic (about 56% of its 2008 crude oil, with a significant amount from Alaska's North Slope) and foreign (around 44%, with a significant amount from Canada) sources through term agreements (34%), which are mainly short term, and in the spot market. TSO charters tankers to ship crude oil from foreign and domestic sources to its California, Mid-Pacific and Pacific

Northwest refineries. About 32% of its total refining throughput was heavy oil (API specific gravity of 24 or less) in 2008, up from 27% in 2007.

TSO's crude pipeline system in North Dakota and in Alaska are common carriers subject to regulation by various federal, state and local agencies, including the FERC under the Interstate Commerce Act.

MARKET PROFILE. TSO is one of the largest independent refiners in the U.S. The company operates the largest refineries in Hawaii and Utah, and the second largest refineries in northern California and Alaska. Through its network of retail stations, TSO sells gasoline and diesel fuel in the western and mid-continental U.S. As of December 31, 2008, TSO's retail segment included 879 branded retail stations (under the Tesoro, Mirastar, Shell and USA Gasoline brands), comprising 389 company-operated retail gasoline stations and 490 jobber/dealer stations. Reflecting recent acquisitions, retail fuel sales climbed 23%, to 1.35 billion gallons in 2008.

Company Financials Fiscal Year Ended Dec. 31

Per Share Data ($)	2008	2007	2006	2005	2004	2003	2002	2001	2000	1999
Tangible Book Value	20.78	19.48	17.09	12.12	8.31	5.70	5.00	6.75	7.17	8.57
Cash Flow	3.97	5.82	7.50	4.92	3.50	1.72	0.11	2.07	1.28	0.96
Earnings	2.00	4.06	5.73	3.60	2.38	0.58	-0.97	1.05	0.88	0.31
S&P Core Earnings	1.72	4.12	5.73	3.65	2.42	0.78	-0.97	1.00	NA	NA
Dividends	0.40	0.35	0.20	0.10	Nil	Nil	Nil	Nil	Nil	Nil
Payout Ratio	20%	9%	3%	3%	Nil	Nil	Nil	Nil	Nil	Nil
Prices:High	48.35	65.98	38.40	35.91	17.33	7.56	7.65	8.25	6.50	9.41
Prices:Low	6.71	31.47	26.48	14.13	7.00	1.69	0.62	4.85	4.47	3.72
P/E Ratio:High	24	16	7	10	7	13	NM	8	7	30
P/E Ratio:Low	3	8	5	4	3	3	NM	5	5	12

Income Statement Analysis (Million $)										
Revenue	28,309	21,915	18,104	16,581	12,262	8,846	7,119	5,218	5,104	3,000
Operating Income	787	1,473	1,614	1,232	881	638	120	290	205	140
Depreciation, Depletion and Amortization	274	246	247	186	154	148	131	91.2	45.5	42.9
Interest Expense	111	125	77.0	211	167	212	166	52.8	32.7	37.6
Pretax Income	429	905	1,286	831	547	123	-181	147	124	51.2
Effective Tax Rate	35.2%	37.5%	37.7%	39.0%	40.0%	38.2%	NM	40.1%	40.6%	37.1%
Net Income	278	566	801	507	328	76.1	-117	88.0	73.3	32.2
S&P Core Earnings	239	574	800	514	333	101	-117	77.2	NA	NA

Balance Sheet & Other Financial Data (Million $)										
Cash	20.0	23.0	986	440	185	77.2	110	51.9	14.1	142
Current Assets	1,646	2,600	2,811	2,215	1,393	1,024	1,054	878	630	612
Total Assets	7,433	8,128	5,904	5,097	4,075	3,661	3,759	2,662	1,544	1,487
Current Liabilities	1,441	2,494	1,672	1,502	993	687	608	538	382	322
Long Term Debt	1,609	1,657	1,029	1,044	1,215	1,605	1,907	1,113	307	390
Common Equity	3,218	3,052	2,502	1,887	1,327	965	888	757	505	463
Total Capital	5,243	5,097	3,908	3,320	2,835	2,750	2,923	2,006	1,084	1,099
Capital Expenditures	650	747	436	258	179	101	204	210	94.0	84.7
Cash Flow	552	812	1,048	693	482	224	13.7	173	107	63.1
Current Ratio	1.1	1.0	1.7	1.5	1.4	1.5	1.7	1.6	1.6	1.9
% Long Term Debt of Capitalization	30.7	32.5	26.3	31.4	42.9	58.4	65.2	55.4	28.3	35.5
% Return on Assets	3.6	8.1	14.6	11.1	8.5	2.1	NM	4.2	4.8	2.2
% Return on Equity	16.5	20.4	36.5	31.5	28.6	8.2	NM	13.0	12.7	4.7

Data as orig reptd.; bef. results of disc opers/spec. items. Per share data adj. for stk. divs.; EPS diluted. E-Estimated. NA-Not Available. NM-Not Meaningful. NR-Not Ranked. UR-Under Review.

Office: 300 Concord Plaza Drive, San Antonio, TX 78216-6999 .
Telephone: 210-828-8484.
Email: investor_relations@tesoropetroleum.com
Website: http://www.tsocorp.com

Chrmn, Pres & CEO: B.A. Smith
COO & EVP: E.D. Lewis
EVP & CFO: G.A. Wright
SVP, Secy & General Counsel: C.S. Parrish

Chief Acctg Officer & Cntlr: A.O. Glenewinkel, Jr.
Investor Contact: S. Phipps (210-283-2882)
Auditor: ERNST & YOUNG LLP
Board Members: J. F. Bookout, III, R. F. Chase, R. W. Goldman, S. H. Grapstein, W. J. Johnson, J. W. Nokes, D. H. Schmude, B. A. Smith, M. E. Wiley

Founded: 1939
Domicile: Delaware
Employees: 5,620

The McGraw-Hill Companies

Texas Instruments Inc

STANDARD &POOR'S

S&P Recommendation	BUY ★★★★☆	Price $25.25 (as of Nov 27, 2009)	12-Mo. Target Price $29.00	Investment Style Large-Cap Growth

GICS Sector Information Technology
Sub-Industry Semiconductors

Summary One of the world's largest manufacturers of semiconductors, this company also produces handheld graphing and scientific calculator products.

Key Stock Statistics (Source S&P, Vickers, company reports)

52-Wk Range	$26.08– 13.38	S&P Oper. EPS 2009**E**	1.11	Market Capitalization(B)	$31.635	Beta	1.10
Trailing 12-Month EPS	$0.72	S&P Oper. EPS 2010**E**	1.76	Yield (%)	1.90	S&P 3-Yr. Proj. EPS CAGR(%)	4
Trailing 12-Month P/E	35.1	P/E on S&P Oper. EPS 2009**E**	22.7	Dividend Rate/Share	$0.48	S&P Credit Rating	A
$10K Invested 5 Yrs Ago	$10,872	Common Shares Outstg. (M)	1,252.9	Institutional Ownership (%)	79		

Price Performance

30-Week Mov. Avg. · · · · 10-Week Mov. Avg. - - **GAAP Earnings vs. Previous Year** **Volume** Above Avg. STARS
12-Mo. Target Price — Relative Strength — ▲ Up ▼ Down ► No Change   Below Avg.

Options: ASE, CBOE, P, Ph

Analysis prepared by **Clyde Montevirgen** on October 21, 2009, when the stock traded at **$ 23.19**.

Qualitative Risk Assessment

LOW	MEDIUM	HIGH

Our risk assessment reflects the cyclicality of the industry in which TXN operates, offset by the large number of company operations, TXN's diverse line of semiconductor products with exposure to many end markets and customers, our view of its low debt levels, and its long corporate history.

Quantitative Evaluations

S&P Quality Ranking B

D	C	B-	B	B+	A-	A	A+

Relative Strength Rank STRONG

77

LOWEST = 1   HIGHEST = 99

Revenue/Earnings Data

Revenue (Million $)

	1Q	2Q	3Q	4Q	Year
2009	2,086	2,457	2,880	--	--
2008	3,272	3,351	3,387	2,491	12,501
2007	3,191	3,424	3,663	3,556	13,835
2006	3,334	3,697	3,761	3,463	14,255
2005	2,972	3,239	3,590	3,591	13,392
2004	2,936	3,241	3,250	3,153	12,580

Earnings Per Share ($)

	1Q	2Q	3Q	4Q	Year
2009	0.01	0.20	0.42	E0.47	E1.11
2008	0.49	0.44	0.43	0.08	1.45
2007	0.35	0.42	0.52	0.54	1.83
2006	0.33	0.47	0.45	0.45	1.69
2005	0.24	0.38	0.38	0.40	1.39
2004	0.21	0.25	0.32	0.28	1.05

Fiscal year ended Dec. 31. Next earnings report expected: Late January. EPS Estimates based on S&P Operating Earnings; historical GAAP earnings are as reported.

Highlights

► We forecast sales to rise 14% in 2010, after a projected 18% decline in 2009. Although we see economic uncertainty leading to a relatively slow rebound and expect top-line results to be limited by share losses in its baseband business, we believe that share gains for its higher-margin analog and embedded businesses will help support growth. Over the near-to mid-term, we look for sales to be aided by the telecom build-out in China and healthy computer and consumer electronics demand.

► We expect gross margins to widen to around 52% for 2010 from an anticipated 48% for 2009, reflecting our view of improving volume and plant utilization, and a more favorable sales mix. TXN has recently adjusted its cost base by reducing headcount and investments in its baseband business. We think that operating margins will expand to 27% for 2010 from an estimated 19% for 2009, largely due to more favorable operating leverage.

► Our 2009 EPS estimate assumes an effective tax rate of 29%, over $200 million in non-recurring expenses, and a 4% drop in the diluted share count.

Investment Rationale/Risk

► Our buy opinion reflects our view of improving profitability. We believe that TXN's dedication to the analog and embedded markets will benefit its long-term growth through market share gains and present a clearer path to wider margins. With the better profitability that we foresee, we expect improving return metrics, such as return on invested capital and return on equity, to support the company's valuations.

► Risks to our recommendation and target price include a longer-than-expected downturn, accelerated share losses in the wireless handset chip market, and increased competition.

► Our 12-month target price of $29 is based on our DCF and price-to-earnings (P/E) analyses. Our DCF model, which assumes a weighted average cost of capital of about 11% and a terminal growth rate of 4%, implies an intrinsic value of $30. Applying a P/E ratio of 16X our 2010 EPS estimate of $1.60, a bit below peer average to account for our view of more modest earnings growth relative to the industry, derives a value of $29.

Dividend Data (Dates: mm/dd Payment Date: mm/dd/yy)

Amount ($)	Date Decl.	Ex-Div. Date	Stk. of Record	Payment Date
0.110	01/15	01/28	01/30	02/09/09
0.110	04/15	04/28	04/30	05/18/09
0.110	07/16	07/29	07/31	08/17/09
0.120	09/17	10/28	10/30	11/16/09

Dividends have been paid since 1962. Source: Company reports.

Please read the Required Disclosures and Analyst Certification on the last page of this report.

The McGraw-Hill Companies

Texas Instruments Inc

STANDARD
&POOR'S

Business Summary October 21, 2009

CORPORATE OVERVIEW. Texas Instruments is the world's fourth largest semi-conductor company, based on 2008 revenues. The company's semiconductors are used for various functions including: converting and amplifying signals, in-terfacing with other devices, managing and distributing power, processing data, canceling noise and improving signal resolution. TXN's product portfolio includes the types of products that are integral to almost all electronic equip-ment. It offers either custom or standard products. A custom product is de-signed for a specific customer for a specific application, is sold only to that customer, and is typically sold directly to the customer. A standard product is designed for use by many customers and/or many applications and is general-ly sold through both distribution and direct channels. Standard products in-clude both proprietary and commodity products. TXN's product segments are analog (40% of sales in 2008), embedded processing (15%), wireless (25%), and other (20%).

Analog semiconductors change real-world signals - such as sound, tempera-ture, pressure or images - by conditioning them, amplifying them, and often converting them to a stream of digital data so the signals can be processed by other semiconductors. Analog products can be further divided by high perfor-mance and high volume. High-performance analog products include standard

analog semiconductors, such as amplifiers, data converters, low-power radio frequency devices, and interface and power management semiconductors. High-performance analog products generally have long life cycles, often 10 to 20 years. The high-volume products include two product types. The first, high-volume analog, includes products for specific applications, including custom products for specific customers. The life cycles of TXN's high-volume analog products are generally shorter than those of its high-performance analog products. The second product type, standard linear and logic, includes com-modity products marketed to many different customers for many different ap-plications. TXN had a 12% share of the $28 billion analog market in 2008.

Embedded processing include digital signal processors (DSPs) and microcon-trollers. DSPs perform mathematical computations almost instantaneously to process and improve digital data. Microcontrollers are microprocessors that are designed to control a set of specific tasks for electronic equipment. TXN had a 10% share of the $17 billion embedded processor market in 2008.

Company Financials Fiscal Year Ended Dec. 31

Per Share Data ($)	2008	2007	2006	2005	2004	2003	2002	2001	2000	1999
Tangible Book Value	6.43	6.72	7.08	6.99	7.13	6.35	5.73	6.42	6.71	5.39
Cash Flow	2.25	2.57	2.37	2.32	1.93	1.54	0.78	0.94	2.49	1.47
Earnings	1.45	1.83	1.69	1.39	1.05	0.68	-0.20	-0.12	1.73	0.84
S&P Core Earnings	1.40	1.81	1.68	1.26	0.86	0.40	-0.16	-0.34	NA	NA
Dividends	0.41	0.30	0.13	0.11	0.09	0.09	0.09	0.09	0.09	0.09
Payout Ratio	28%	16%	8%	8%	9%	13%	NM	NM	5%	10%
Prices:High	33.24	39.63	36.40	34.68	33.98	31.67	35.94	54.69	99.78	55.75
Prices:Low	13.38	28.24	26.77	20.70	18.06	13.90	13.10	20.10	35.00	21.50
P/E Ratio:High	23	22	22	25	32	47	NM	NM	58	66
P/E Ratio:Low	9	15	16	15	17	20	NM	NM	20	26

Income Statement Analysis (Million $)										
Revenue	12,501	13,835	14,255	13,392	12,580	9,834	8,383	8,201	11,875	9,468
Operating Income	3,794	4,580	4,419	4,222	3,756	2,493	1,977	1,246	3,715	2,751
Depreciation	1,059	1,070	1,052	1,431	1,549	1,528	1,689	1,828	1,376	1,055
Interest Expense	Nil	1.00	7.00	9.00	21.0	39.0	57.0	61.0	75.0	75.0
Pretax Income	2,481	3,692	3,625	2,988	2,421	1,250	-346	-426	4,578	2,019
Effective Tax Rate	22.6%	28.5%	27.2%	22.2%	23.1%	4.16%	NM	NM	32.6%	30.4%
Net Income	1,920	2,641	2,638	2,324	1,861	1,198	-344	-201	3,087	1,406
S&P Core Earnings	1,855	2,609	2,614	2,110	1,516	701	-275	-587	NA	NA

Balance Sheet & Other Financial Data (Million $)										
Cash	2,540	2,924	1,183	1,219	2,668	1,818	949	431	745	662
Current Assets	5,790	6,918	7,854	9,185	10,190	7,709	6,126	5,775	8,115	6,055
Total Assets	11,923	12,667	13,930	15,063	16,299	15,510	14,679	15,779	17,720	15,028
Current Liabilities	1,532	2,025	2,078	2,346	1,925	2,200	1,934	1,580	2,813	2,628
Long Term Debt	Nil	Nil	Nil	360	368	395	833	1,211	1,216	1,097
Common Equity	9,326	9,975	11,711	11,937	13,063	11,864	10,734	11,879	12,588	9,255
Total Capital	9,385	10,024	11,734	12,320	13,471	12,318	11,696	13,421	14,273	11,346
Capital Expenditures	763	686	1,272	1,330	1,298	800	802	1,790	2,762	1,373
Cash Flow	2,979	3,711	3,690	3,882	3,410	2,726	1,345	1,627	4,463	2,461
Current Ratio	3.8	3.4	3.8	3.9	5.3	3.5	3.2	3.7	2.9	2.3
% Long Term Debt of Capitalization	Nil	Nil	Nil	2.9	2.7	3.2	7.1	9.0	8.5	9.7
% Net Income of Revenue	15.4	19.1	18.5	17.4	14.8	12.2	NM	NM	26.0	14.9
% Return on Assets	15.6	19.9	18.2	14.8	11.7	7.9	NM	NM	18.6	10.6
% Return on Equity	19.9	24.8	22.2	18.6	14.9	10.6	NM	NM	27.9	17.6

Data as orig reptd.; bef. results of disc opers/spec. items. Per share data adj. for stk. divs.; EPS diluted. E-Estimated. NA-Not Available. NM-Not Meaningful. NR-Not Ranked. UR-Under Review.

Office: PO Box 660199, Dallas, TX 75266-0199.
Telephone: 972-995-3773.
Website: http://www.ti.com
Chrmn, Pres & CEO: R.K. Templeton

SVP, CFO & Chief Acctg Officer: K.P. March
SVP, Secy & General Counsel: J.F. Hubach
Investor Contact: R. Slaymaker (972-995-3773)

Board Members: J. R. Adams, D. L. Boren, D. A. Carp, C.
S. Cox, D. Goode, S. P. MacMillan, P. H. Patsley, W. R.
Sanders, R. J. Simmons, R. K. Templeton, C. T. Whitman

Founded: 1930
Domicile: Delaware
Employees: 29,537

Textron Inc.

STANDARD &POOR'S

S&P Recommendation **BUY** ★★★★☆	Price $20.08 (as of Nov 27, 2009)	12-Mo. Target Price $25.00	Investment Style Large-Cap Value

GICS Sector Industrials
Sub-Industry Industrial Conglomerates

Summary This aerospace and industrial conglomerate makes Cessna business jets, Bell helicopters, and industrial equipment and components. It also operates a diversified commercial finance company.

Key Stock Statistics (Source S&P, Vickers, company reports)

52-Wk Range	$21.00– 3.57	S&P Oper. EPS 2009E	-0.03	Market Capitalization(B)	$5.444	Beta	2.92
Trailing 12-Month EPS	$-0.69	S&P Oper. EPS 2010E	0.60	Yield (%)	0.40	S&P 3-Yr. Proj. EPS CAGR(%)	NM
Trailing 12-Month P/E	NM	P/E on S&P Oper. EPS 2009E	NM	Dividend Rate/Share	$0.08	S&P Credit Rating	BBB-
$10K Invested 5 Yrs Ago	$6,023	Common Shares Outstg. (M)	271.1	Institutional Ownership (%)	75		

Price Performance

30-Week Mov. Avg. · · · · 10-Week Mov. Avg. - - - **GAAP Earnings vs. Previous Year** Volume Above Avg. ▉▎ STARS
12-Mo. Target Price — Relative Strength — ▲ Up ▼ Down ► No Change Below Avg. ▉▎ ★

Options: ASE, CBOE, P, Ph

Analysis prepared by **Richard Tortoriello** on October 30, 2009, when the stock traded at **$ 17.91**.

Highlights

► We project a decline in sales of about 27% in 2009, due primarily to significant production cuts at Cessna as customers cancel or defer deliveries amid the global economic crisis, as well as a sharp decline in volume in the Industrial segment. For 2010, we expect sales to rebound slightly, by about 1.5%. We see moderate sales growth (3% to 4%) at Cessna, Bell and Textron Systems, with Bell revenues driven by military helicopters, and a 4% decline at Industrial. We expect large declines in both 2009 and 2010 in Finance, where TXT is liquidating its non-captive finance portfolio.

► We expect segment operating margins to narrow sharply to 4.5% in 2009, from 10.4% in 2008, on significant losses in Finance due to increased reserves for loan losses, and substantial volume declines at Cessna and Industrial. We project an increase to 6.5% in 2010, primarily on reduced loan loss provisions.

► We project a loss per share of $0.03 in 2009, including restructuring costs, with growth to EPS of $0.60 in 2010, as we expect significantly reduced restructuring spending.

Investment Rationale/Risk

► Based on its third-quarter conference call, we see TXT making significant progress toward generating liquidity to meet its obligations and extend its debt maturities. In particular, we note that, as of September, TXT's 2009 obligations of $6,631 million (including estimated debt payments and a small dividend) were 74% funded, that it had cash of $2,576 million, that it has generated $317 million in manufacturing cash flow so far in 2009, and that it appears on track to pay an estimated $2,200 million of debt due in 2010. Given our view of lower liquidity risk and world-class brand names, we view the shares as undervalued.

► Risks to our recommendation and target price include the risk that TXT could default on its financial obligations as a result of a liquidity crunch, and the risk of worse-than-anticipated performance at Bell or Cessna.

► Our 12-month target price of $25 is based on a 8X multiple of TXT's average EBITDA over the past eight years. We believe this average represents TXT's earnings power. The 8X multiple is in line with forward EBITDA multiples for commercial aerospace peers.

Qualitative Risk Assessment

LOW	MEDIUM	HIGH

Our risk assessment reflects our view of TXT's recent close match between its obligations to creditors in 2009 and 2010 and its projected sources of cash in those same years.

Quantitative Evaluations

S&P Quality Ranking B

D	C	B-	B	B+	A-	A	A+

Relative Strength Rank STRONG

86

LOWEST = 1 HIGHEST = 99

Revenue/Earnings Data

Revenue (Million $)

	1Q	2Q	3Q	4Q	Year
2009	2,526	2,612	2,549	--	--
2008	3,518	3,919	3,533	3,606	14,246
2007	2,964	3,235	3,263	3,763	13,225
2006	2,632	2,820	2,837	3,201	11,490
2005	2,791	3,188	2,862	2,701	10,043
2004	2,354	2,547	2,569	2,833	10,242

Earnings Per Share ($)

	1Q	2Q	3Q	4Q	Year
2009	0.18	-0.23	0.02	E0.02	E-0.03
2008	0.93	1.03	0.85	-1.44	1.38
2007	0.78	0.85	0.95	1.02	3.59
2006	0.60	0.67	0.68	0.77	2.72
2005	0.29	0.47	-0.63	0.63	1.89
2004	0.13	0.36	0.37	0.44	1.33

Fiscal year ended Dec. 31. Next earnings report expected: Late January. EPS Estimates based on S&P Operating Earnings; historical GAAP earnings are as reported.

Dividend Data (Dates: mm/dd Payment Date: mm/dd/yy)

Amount ($)	Date Decl.	Ex-Div. Date	Stk. of Record	Payment Date
0.020	02/25	03/11	03/13	04/01/09
0.020	04/22	06/10	06/12	07/01/09
0.020	07/22	09/09	09/11	10/01/09
0.020	10/21	12/09	12/11	01/01/10

Dividends have been paid since 1942. Source: Company reports.

Please read the Required Disclosures and Analyst Certification on the last page of this report.

The McGraw·Hill Companies

Textron Inc.

STANDARD &POOR'S

Business Summary October 30, 2009

CORPORATE OVERVIEW. Textron, a $13 billion in estimated 2009 revenue aerospace and industrial conglomerate, conducts business through five operating segments.

Bell Helicopter (20% of 2008 sales and 19% of operating profits) is the world's third largest rotary-wing aircraft maker, behind United Technologies' Sikorsky Unit and EADS's Eurocopter unit. Bell makes helicopters and tiltrotor aircraft (the V-22 Osprey) for both military and commercial applications, and provides spare parts and service. Bell supplies advanced military helicopters and support (including spare parts, support equipment, technical data, trainers, etc.) to the U.S. government and to military customers outside the U.S. Bell is also a leading supplier of commercially certified helicopters to corporate, offshore petroleum exploration and development, utility, charter, police, fire, rescue and emergency medical helicopter operators. The V-22 Osprey is a military tiltrotor aircraft built in conjunction with Boeing, with contracts for 285 units (98 of which had been delivered as of year-end 2008). Bell also makes the Marine Corps. H-1 helicopter (AH-1Z and UH-1Z), with a program of record that calls for 285 production units.

The Textron Systems segment (15% of sales and 19% of profits) principal strategy is to address the U.S. Defense Department's emphasis on precision engagement and network-centric warfare, by leveraging information technology in the development of networked sensors, weapons, and associated algorithms and software. TS makes precision weapons, airborne and ground-based surveillance systems, sophisticated intelligence and situational awareness software, armored vehicles and turrets, reciprocating piston aircraft engines, and aircraft and missile control actuators, valves and related components. As of March 2009, TS had produced about 1,875 armored security vehicles for the U.S. Army since 2005. The contract calls for more than 780 additional units through July 2010, with options for 164 units through year-end 2010. TS is also a tier-one supplier of unattended ground sensors and intelligent munition systems for the U.S. Army's Future Combat System program.

The Cessna segment (40% of sales and 61% of profits) primarily makes the Cessna brand aircraft. Business lines include Citation business jets, Caravan single engine turboprops, Cessna single-engine piston aircraft, and aftermarket services. Based on revenues, Cessna is the world's fourth largest corporate jet maker, behind Canada's Bombardier, General Dynamics' Gulfstream division, and France's Dassault aviation; however, it is the world's largest business jet maker in unit volume.

Company Financials Fiscal Year Ended Dec. 31

Per Share Data ($)	2008	2007	2006	2005	2004	2003	2002	2001	2000	1999
Tangible Book Value	2.06	2.77	4.86	8.02	7.35	8.09	6.46	6.20	5.80	5.28
Cash Flow	2.81	4.91	3.95	3.15	2.69	2.32	2.61	2.38	2.64	3.45
Earnings	1.38	3.59	2.72	1.89	1.33	1.03	1.30	0.58	0.95	2.03
S&P Core Earnings	1.11	3.51	2.66	2.06	1.01	0.59	0.14	-0.70	NA	NA
Dividends	0.92	0.85	0.78	0.70	0.66	0.65	0.65	0.65	0.65	0.63
Payout Ratio	67%	24%	29%	37%	50%	63%	50%	NM	68%	9%
Prices:High	70.14	74.40	49.48	40.36	37.46	29.00	26.80	30.24	38.75	49.00
Prices:Low	10.09	43.60	37.76	32.60	25.30	13.00	16.10	15.65	20.34	32.94
P/E Ratio:High	51	21	18	21	28	28	21	52	41	24
P/E Ratio:Low	7	12	14	17	19	13	12	27	21	16

Income Statement Analysis (Million $)

	2008	2007	2006	2005	2004	2003	2002	2001	2000	1999
Revenue	14,246	13,225	11,490	10,043	10,242	9,859	10,658	12,321	13,090	11,579
Operating Income	1,974	2,120	1,703	1,450	1,260	1,171	1,285	1,461	2,074	1,702
Depreciation	358	336	290	303	353	356	368	514	494	440
Interest Expense	432	484	438	290	248	283	330	459	492	260
Pretax Income	658	1,300	437	739	528	388	464	393	585	1,004
Effective Tax Rate	47.7%	29.6%	NM	30.2%	29.4%	27.6%	21.6%	57.8%	52.6%	37.9%
Net Income	344	915	706	516	373	281	364	166	277	623
S&P Core Earnings	272	895	690	565	282	161	38.6	-202	NA	NA

Balance Sheet & Other Financial Data (Million $)

	2008	2007	2006	2005	2004	2003	2002	2001	2000	1999
Cash	531	531	780	796	732	843	307	260	289	209
Current Assets	4,766	4,846	4,287	4,975	4,168	3,592	3,887	4,017	3,914	3,735
Total Assets	20,020	19,956	17,550	16,499	15,875	15,090	15,505	16,052	16,370	16,393
Current Liabilities	NA	7,248	2,994	3,147	2,975	2,256	2,239	3,075	3,263	3,256
Long Term Debt	6,779	6,384	6,150	7,079	6,141	6,144	7,038	5,962	6,648	6,142
Common Equity	2,366	3,505	2,639	3,266	3,642	3,680	3,395	3,923	3,982	4,365
Total Capital	3,924	10,363	8,799	10,816	10,246	10,224	10,842	10,253	10,957	10,826
Capital Expenditures	550	401	431	365	302	301	296	532	527	532
Cash Flow	702	1,251	996	819	726	637	732	680	771	1,062
Current Ratio	1.8	1.2	1.4	1.6	1.4	1.6	1.7	1.3	1.2	1.1
% Long Term Debt of Capitalization	172.7	61.6	69.9	65.4	59.9	60.1	64.9	58.1	60.7	56.7
% Net Income of Revenue	2.4	6.9	6.1	5.1	3.6	2.9	3.4	1.3	2.1	5.4
% Return on Assets	1.7	4.9	4.1	3.2	2.4	1.8	2.3	1.0	1.7	4.1
% Return on Equity	11.7	29.8	23.9	14.9	10.2	7.9	9.9	4.2	6.6	16.9

Data as orig reptd.; bef. results of disc opers/spec. items. Per share data adj. for stk. divs.; EPS diluted. E-Estimated. NA-Not Available. NM-Not Meaningful. NR-Not Ranked. UR-Under Review.

Office: 40 Westminster Street, Providence, RI 02903-2525.
Telephone: 401-421-2800.
Website: http://www.textron.com
Chrmn & CEO: L.B. Campbell

Pres & COO: S. Donnelly
EVP & CFO: F.T. Connor
EVP & General Counsel: T. O'Donnell
SVP, Chief Acctg Officer & Cntlr: D. Yates

Investor Contact: D.R. Wilburne (401-457-2353)
Board Members: K. M. Bader, L. B. Campbell, R. K. Clark, S. Donnelly, I. J. Evans, L. Fish, J. T. Ford, P. E. Gagne, D. M. Hancock, C. D. Powell, L. G. Trotter, T. B. Wheeler, J. Ziemer

Founded: 1928
Domicile: Delaware
Employees: 43,000

The McGraw-Hill Companies

Thermo Fisher Scientific Inc

STANDARD &POOR'S

S&P Recommendation	HOLD ★★★☆☆	Price $47.48 (as of Nov 27, 2009)	12-Mo. Target Price $50.00	Investment Style Large-Cap Growth

GICS Sector Health Care
Sub-Industry Life Sciences Tools & Services

Summary Formed through the November 2006 merger of Thermo Electron and Fisher Scientific, TMO is a leading manufacturer and developer of analytical and laboratory instruments and supplies for life science, drug discovery and industrial applications.

Key Stock Statistics (Source S&P, Vickers, company reports)

52-Wk Range	$48.51–28.52	S&P Oper. EPS 2009E	3.03	Market Capitalization(B)	$19.387	Beta		0.87
Trailing 12-Month EPS	$2.07	S&P Oper. EPS 2010E	3.34	Yield (%)	Nil	S&P 3-Yr. Proj. EPS CAGR(%)		13
Trailing 12-Month P/E	22.9	P/E on S&P Oper. EPS 2009E	15.7	Dividend Rate/Share	Nil	S&P Credit Rating		A-
$10K Invested 5 Yrs Ago	$15,790	Common Shares Outstg. (M)	408.3	Institutional Ownership (%)	94			

Price Performance

30-Week Mov. Avg. ··· 10-Week Mov. Avg. - - GAAP Earnings vs. Previous Year   Volume Above Avg. ‖‖ STARS
12-Mo. Target Price — Relative Strength — ▲ Up ▼ Down ▶ No Change   Below Avg. ‖‖ ★

Options: ASE, CBOE, Ph

Analysis prepared by **Jeffrey Loo, CFA** on November 02, 2009, when the stock traded at **$ 44.60**.

Highlights

▶ We expect 2009 sales, inclusive of a 3% adverse foreign exchange impact, to fall 5%, to $10.0 billion. Instrument sales in 2009 have been soft particularly in the pharmaceutical end-market, but we see improvement in 2010. However, we still expect softness within the industrial end-market to continue into early 2010. Consumable and services sales, which represent about 70% of total sales, have stabilized and should continue to improve in late 2009 and 2010, in our view. We also expect TMO to quickly rollout products in the U.S. from its BRAHMS acquisition, aiding consumable sales. We see gross margins narrowing 10 basis points in 2009 despite better pricing from sourcing initiatives and lower instrument sales, and operating margins declining 30 basis points, as TMO continues to make strategic investments. We expect 2010 sales to rise 4% to $10.4 billion.

▶ In September, COO Marc Casper was appointed CEO to replace Marijn Dekkers, who resigned to become CEO of Bayer AG.

▶ We see EPS of $3.03 in 2009 and $3.34 in 2010, before amortization of intangible assets.

Investment Rationale/Risk

▶ We believe the shares, recently trading at 13.6X our 2010 EPS forecast and at a P/E-to-growth (PEG) ratio of 1.05X, in line with peers, are fairly valued. While we believe the economic challenges affecting some of TMO's end-markets will continue into late 2009, we look for gradual improvement in key end-markets such as pharmaceuticals and see benefits from the economic stimulus package in 2010. We still view TMO as the industry leader, and we think its comprehensive product offering and broad geographic coverage should help retain its client base and potentially increase its market share as we think clients continue to seek efficiency and consolidate suppliers. In our view, the challenging environment has adversely affected TMO's smaller peers to a greater extent.

▶ Risks to our recommendation and target price include a prolonged slowdown in pharma R&D spending and TMO losing market share.

▶ Our 12-month target price of $50 assumes a PEG ratio of 1.15X, in line with peers, based on our 2010 EPS estimate of $3.34 and a three-year EPS growth rate of 13%.

Qualitative Risk Assessment

LOW	MEDIUM	HIGH

Our risk assessment reflects TMO's broad product lines and geographic coverage, spread across the life sciences, health care and industrial markets, which we believe reduces risk. However, TMO has a proactive acquisition strategy that we believe raises its risk profile.

Quantitative Evaluations

S&P Quality Ranking B-

D	C	B-	B	B+	A-	A	A+

Relative Strength Rank STRONG

76

LOWEST = 1   HIGHEST = 99

Revenue/Earnings Data

Revenue (Million $)

	1Q	2Q	3Q	4Q	Year
2009	2,255	2,484	2,531	--	--
2008	2,554	2,710	2,588	2,646	10,498
2007	2,338	2,386	2,401	2,621	9,746
2006	684.3	713.5	725.0	1,669	3,792
2005	559.2	653.6	679.4	740.8	2,633
2004	525.0	525.3	542.3	613.3	2,206

Earnings Per Share ($)

2009	0.35	0.49	0.53	E0.89	E3.03
2008	0.54	0.56	0.50	0.68	2.27
2007	0.31	0.42	0.51	0.53	1.76
2006	0.26	0.30	0.30	0.08	0.82
2005	0.28	0.35	0.25	0.34	1.21
2004	0.24	0.30	0.26	0.52	1.31

Fiscal year ended Dec. 31. Next earnings report expected: Early February. EPS Estimates based on S&P Operating Earnings; historical GAAP earnings are as reported.

Dividend Data

No cash dividends have been paid.

Please read the Required Disclosures and Analyst Certification on the last page of this report.

The McGraw-Hill Companies

Thermo Fisher Scientific Inc

STANDARD &POOR'S

Business Summary November 02, 2009

CORPORATE OVERVIEW. In November 2006, Thermo Electron Corp. and Fisher Scientific completed a stock-for-stock merger. The combined company was renamed Thermo Fisher Scientific (TMO) and is a leading provider of life science and laboratory analytical instruments, equipment, reagents and consumables, software and services for research, analysis, discovery and diagnosis. We expect annual revenues in excess of $9 billion, with over 30,000 employees in 38 countries providing services and sales in over 150 countries. Major end-markets served include drug discovery, proteomics research, biopharma services, molecular diagnostics, immunohistochemistry, cell screening, environmental regulatory compliance, and food safety. TMO believes these markets represent a combined $70 billion to $80 billion annual marketplace. We believe TMO is the largest company within its marketplace, with the broadest product offering and geographic coverage.

The legacy Thermo Electron business focuses primarily on the development and manufacture of analytical systems, instruments and components and provides solutions to monitor, collect and analyze data. These instruments are used primarily in life science, drug discovery, clinical, environmental and industrial laboratory applications. The legacy Fisher Scientific business focuses on providing a broad range of over 600,000 scientific research, health care and safety-related products and services. Customers included pharmaceutical and biotechnology companies, colleges and universities, medical research institutions, hospitals and reference labs, and research and development labs.

The company now reports through two business segments: Analytical Technologies and Laboratory Products and Services. Analytical Technologies should account for about 40% of sales and focuses on scientific instruments, bioscience reagents, lab informatics and automation, diagnostics, environmental monitoring instruments and industrial process instruments. Analytical Technologies is comprised primarily of the legacy Thermo Electron business. Laboratory Products and Services, comprised primarily of legacy Fisher Scientific business should account for about 60% of sales and focuses on lab equipment and consumables and biopharma outsourcing services.

Company Financials Fiscal Year Ended Dec. 31

Per Share Data ($)	2008	2007	2006	2005	2004	2003	2002	2001	2000	1999
Tangible Book Value	NM	NM	NM	2.32	6.19	5.00	3.79	1.33	6.34	5.03
Cash Flow	4.10	3.46	2.00	1.95	1.70	1.35	1.35	0.81	0.94	0.63
Earnings	2.27	1.76	0.82	1.21	1.31	1.04	1.12	0.27	0.36	-0.11
S&P Core Earnings	2.16	1.78	0.83	1.01	1.18	0.79	0.50	0.02	NA	NA
Dividends	Nil	Nil	Nil	Nil	Nil	Nil	Nil	Nil	Nil	Nil
Payout Ratio	Nil	Nil	Nil	Nil	Nil	Nil	Nil	Nil	Nil	Nil
Prices:High	62.77	62.02	46.34	31.87	31.40	25.40	24.60	30.62	31.24	20.25
Prices:Low	26.65	43.60	29.95	23.94	24.00	16.89	14.33	16.55	14.00	12.50
P/E Ratio:High	28	35	57	26	24	24	22	NM	87	NM
P/E Ratio:Low	12	25	37	20	18	16	13	NM	39	NM

Income Statement Analysis (Million $)	2008	2007	2006	2005	2004	2003	2002	2001	2000	1999
Revenue	10,498	9,746	3,792	2,633	2,206	2,097	2,086	2,188	2,281	2,471
Operating Income	2,059	1,823	528	404	319	292	264	265	296	362
Depreciation	793	757	241	123	66.1	58.5	56.4	98.5	97.5	114
Interest Expense	130	140	51.9	26.7	11.0	18.7	Nil	71.8	Nil	Nil
Pretax Income	1,150	881	209	286	259	219	288	70.7	185	37.5
Effective Tax Rate	14.0%	11.5%	20.6%	30.6%	15.8%	21.0%	32.3%	38.1%	60.7%	NM
Net Income	989	780	166	198	218	173	195	49.6	62.0	-14.6
S&P Core Earnings	941	785	169	164	196	131	79.3	5.63	NA	NA

Balance Sheet & Other Financial Data (Million $)	2008	2007	2006	2005	2004	2003	2002	2001	2000	1999
Cash	1,288	639	667	214	327	304	339	298	506	282
Current Assets	4,346	3,665	3,660	1,354	1,470	1,395	1,772	1,965	2,466	2,517
Total Assets	21,090	21,207	21,262	4,252	3,577	3,389	3,647	3,825	4,863	5,182
Current Liabilities	1,540	1,902	2,152	792	579	685	1,104	1,142	729	1,066
Long Term Debt	2,044	2,046	2,181	469	226	230	451	728	1,528	1,566
Common Equity	14,927	14,488	13,912	2,793	2,666	2,383	2,033	1,908	2,534	2,014
Total Capital	16,979	18,814	18,650	3,327	2,907	2,624	2,495	2,650	4,098	4,026
Capital Expenditures	264	176	76.8	43.5	50.0	46.1	51.2	84.8	74.0	87.2
Cash Flow	1,781	1,536	407	322	285	231	252	148	160	99.1
Current Ratio	2.8	1.9	1.7	1.7	2.5	2.0	1.6	1.7	3.4	2.4
% Long Term Debt of Capitalization	12.0	10.9	11.7	14.1	7.8	8.7	18.1	27.4	37.3	38.9
% Net Income of Revenue	9.4	8.0	4.4	7.5	9.9	8.2	9.4	2.3	2.7	NM
% Return on Assets	4.7	3.7	1.3	5.1	6.3	4.9	5.2	1.1	1.2	NM
% Return on Equity	6.7	5.5	2.0	7.3	8.7	7.8	9.9	2.2	2.7	NM

Data as orig reptd.; bef. results of disc opers/spec. items. Per share data adj. for stk. divs.; EPS diluted. E-Estimated. NA-Not Available. NM-Not Meaningful. NR-Not Ranked. UR-Under Review.

Office: 81 Wyman St PO Box 9046, Waltham, MA 02254-9046.
Telephone: 781-622-1000.
Website: http://www.fishersci.com
Chrmn: J.P. Manzi
Pres & CEO: M.N. Casper
SVP & CFO: P.M. Wilver
SVP, Secy & General Counsel: S.H. Hoogasian
Chief Acctg Officer: P.E. Hornstra
Investor Contact: K.J. Apicerno (781-622-1111)
Board Members: M. A. Bell, M. N. Casper, T. Jacks, S. Kaufman, J. C. Lewent, T. J. Lynch, P. J. Manning, J. P. Manzi, W. G. Parrett, M. E. Porter, S. M. Sperling, E. S. Ullian
Founded: 1956
Domicile: Delaware
Employees: 34,500

The McGraw-Hill Companies

3M Co

STANDARD &POOR'S

S&P Recommendation	**BUY** ★★★★☆	Price $76.75 (as of Nov 27, 2009)	12-Mo. Target Price $86.00	Investment Style Large-Cap Growth

GICS Sector Industrials
Sub-Industry Industrial Conglomerates

Summary This diversified global company has operations in electronics, health care, industrial, consumer, and office, telecommunications, safety and security, and other markets.

Key Stock Statistics (Source S&P, Vickers, company reports)

52-Wk Range	$79.25–40.87	S&P Oper. EPS 2009**E**	4.60	Market Capitalization(B)	$54.336	Beta		0.77
Trailing 12-Month EPS	$3.99	S&P Oper. EPS 2010**E**	4.99	Yield (%)	2.66	S&P 3-Yr. Proj. EPS CAGR(%)		6
Trailing 12-Month P/E	19.2	P/E on S&P Oper. EPS 2009**E**	16.7	Dividend Rate/Share	$2.04	S&P Credit Rating		AA-
$10K Invested 5 Yrs Ago	$10,903	Common Shares Outstg. (M)	708.0	Institutional Ownership (%)	65			

Price Performance

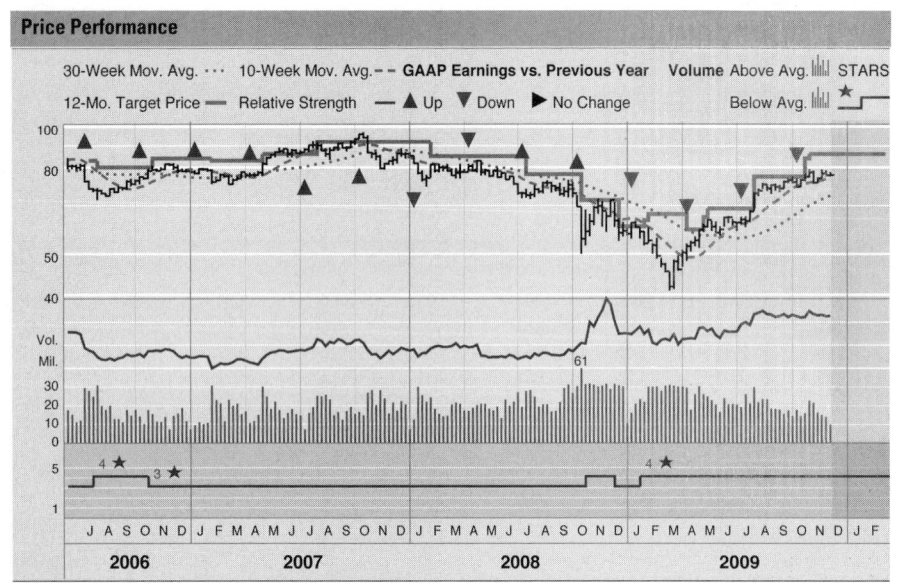

30-Week Mov. Avg. ··· 10-Week Mov. Avg. - - **GAAP Earnings vs. Previous Year** Volume Above Avg. ▮▮▮ STARS
12-Mo. Target Price — Relative Strength — ▲ Up ▼ Down ▶ No Change Below Avg. ▮▮▮ ★

Options: ASE, CBOE, P, Ph

Analysis prepared by **Mathew Christy, CFA** on October 28, 2009, when the stock traded at **$ 75.35**.

Highlights

▶ We see 2009 sales falling 10%, as declining revenues across all business segments should be led by the Industrial & Transportation, the Display & Graphics, Electro-Communications, and Safety units, due to the negative effects of currency and lower overall global volumes. This should more than offset favorable contributions from acquisitions. We expect revenue to be higher in the final quarter of year. In 2010, we project revenues will increase about 5%, on moderate volume and pricing gains.

▶ In 2009, we expect operating margins to narrow, despite benefits from Six Sigma and cost-cutting efforts, due mainly to lower operating leverage and weaker results from the optical unit. However, we believe continued efforts to streamline this diverse company will enable 3M to maintain above-average profitability, and we look for somewhat improved margin results in 2010.

▶ Assuming a steady 30% effective tax rate, we estimate 3M's operating EPS, excluding restructuring charges, for 2009 and 2010 at $4.60 and $4.99, respectively.

Investment Rationale/Risk

▶ We expect lower results for 2009 amid revenue declines across all of 3M's business units, especially the Industrial & Transportation and the Electro-Communications segments, due to the weak economy. In addition, we see results being pressured by continued declines in the optical unit. However, we view positively 3M's ability to generate strong returns on capital and free cash flows. In addition, we like the company's early cycle business mix. We view the shares, recently trading at nearly 15.2X our 2010 EPS estimate, and a 11% discount to the peer average, as attractively valued.

▶ Risks to our recommendation and target price include slower global economic growth, lower-than-projected growth in the optical display business, and execution risk associated with acquisitions and/or cost-saving initiatives.

▶ Our 12-month target price of $86 is based on a blend of valuations. Our DCF model, which assumes 3% growth in perpetuity and a 9% discount rate, indicates intrinsic value of about $79. In terms of relative valuation, we apply a P/E multiple of about 18.5X, ahead of peers, to our 2010 EPS estimate, suggesting a value of $92.

Qualitative Risk Assessment

LOW	MEDIUM	HIGH

Our risk assessment reflects our view of the company's strong historical earnings and dividend growth, its leading position in many of the markets it serves, its strong balance sheet with a relatively low amount of debt, and free cash flow that has averaged about 95% of net income over the past 10 years.

Quantitative Evaluations

S&P Quality Ranking A+

D	C	B-	B	B+	A-	A	A+

Relative Strength Rank MODERATE

68

LOWEST = 1 HIGHEST = 99

Revenue/Earnings Data

Revenue (Million $)

	1Q	2Q	3Q	4Q	Year
2009	5,089	5,719	6,193	--	--
2008	6,463	6,739	6,558	5,509	25,269
2007	5,937	6,142	6,177	6,206	24,462
2006	5,595	5,688	5,858	5,782	22,923
2005	5,166	5,294	5,382	5,325	21,167
2004	4,939	5,012	4,969	5,091	20,011

Earnings Per Share ($)

	1Q	2Q	3Q	4Q	Year
2009	0.74	1.12	1.35	E1.22	E4.60
2008	1.38	1.33	1.41	0.77	4.89
2007	1.85	1.25	1.32	1.17	5.60
2006	1.17	1.15	1.18	1.57	5.06
2005	1.03	1.00	1.10	1.04	4.16
2004	0.90	0.97	0.97	0.91	3.75

Fiscal year ended Dec. 31. Next earnings report expected: Late January. EPS Estimates based on S&P Operating Earnings; historical GAAP earnings are as reported.

Dividend Data (Dates: mm/dd Payment Date: mm/dd/yy)

Amount ($)	Date Decl.	Ex-Div. Date	Stk. of Record	Payment Date
0.510	02/10	02/18	02/20	03/12/09
0.510	05/12	05/20	05/22	06/12/09
0.510	08/10	08/19	08/21	09/12/09
0.510	11/10	11/18	11/20	12/12/09

Dividends have been paid since 1916. Source: Company reports.

3M Co

Business Summary October 28, 2009

CORPORATE OVERVIEW. 3M reports its business in six reportable segments -- Industrial and Transportation, Health Care, Display and Graphics, Consumer and Office, Electro and Communications, and Safety, Security and Protection Services. Most 3M products involve expertise in product development, manufacturing and marketing. As of the end of 2008, the company employed over 79,000 people.

The Industrial and Transportation segment (31% of 2008 revenues, with a 19.4% operating margin) serves a broad range of markets, from appliances and electronics to paper and packaging, food and beverages, automotive, automotive aftermarket, aerospace and marine, and other transportation-related industries. Products include pressure-sensitive tapes, abrasives, adhesives, specialty materials, supply chain management software and solutions, insulation components, films, masking tapes, fasteners, and adhesives and abrasives used in the repair and maintenance of automotive, marine, aircraft and other specialty vehicles.

The Health Care segment (17% and 28.5%) serves markets worldwide, including medical and surgical, pharmaceutical, dental, health information systems and personal care, with a variety of medical and surgical, infection prevention, pharmaceutical, drug delivery, dental, personal care and other products and systems.

The Display and Graphics segment (13% and 18.5%) serves markets that include electronic display, touch screen, commercial graphics and traffic control materials. Optical products include Vikkuiti display enhancement films for electronic displays, lens systems for projection televisions, and 3M Micro-Touch touch screens and touch monitors. Other products include 3M Scotchlite reflective sheeting for transportation safety and Scotchprint commercial graphics systems.

Company Financials Fiscal Year Ended Dec. 31

Per Share Data ($)	2008	2007	2006	2005	2004	2003	2002	2001	2000	1999
Tangible Book Value	3.93	13.40	7.04	8.13	9.62	6.62	4.91	6.23	7.17	7.06
Cash Flow	6.52	7.06	6.48	5.43	5.01	4.23	3.70	3.15	3.60	3.28
Earnings	4.89	5.60	5.06	4.16	3.75	3.02	2.49	1.79	2.32	2.17
S&P Core Earnings	3.77	4.68	4.26	4.13	3.66	2.91	1.71	0.94	NA	NA
Dividends	2.00	1.92	1.84	1.68	1.44	1.32	1.24	1.20	1.16	1.12
Payout Ratio	41%	34%	36%	40%	38%	44%	50%	67%	50%	52%
Prices:High	84.76	97.00	88.35	87.45	90.29	85.40	65.78	63.50	61.47	51.69
Prices:Low	50.10	72.90	67.05	69.71	73.31	59.73	50.00	42.93	39.09	34.66
P/E Ratio:High	17	17	17	21	24	28	26	35	26	24
P/E Ratio:Low	10	13	13	17	20	20	20	24	17	16

Income Statement Analysis (Million $)	2008	2007	2006	2005	2004	2003	2002	2001	2000	1999
Revenue	25,269	24,462	22,923	21,167	20,011	18,232	16,332	16,079	16,724	15,659
Operating Income	6,640	6,584	6,252	5,995	5,577	4,677	4,000	3,274	3,898	3,828
Depreciation	1,153	1,072	1,079	986	999	964	954	1,089	1,025	900
Interest Expense	215	210	122	82.0	69.0	84.0	80.0	124	111	109
Pretax Income	5,108	6,115	5,625	4,983	4,555	3,657	3,005	2,186	2,974	2,880
Effective Tax Rate	31.1%	32.1%	30.6%	34.0%	33.0%	32.9%	32.1%	32.1%	34.5%	35.8%
Net Income	3,460	4,096	3,851	3,234	2,990	2,403	1,974	1,430	1,857	1,763
S&P Core Earnings	2,672	3,418	3,242	3,227	2,918	2,319	1,356	750	NA	NA

Balance Sheet & Other Financial Data (Million $)	2008	2007	2006	2005	2004	2003	2002	2001	2000	1999
Cash	2,222	2,475	1,918	1,072	2,757	1,836	618	616	302	387
Current Assets	9,598	9,838	8,946	7,115	8,720	7,720	6,059	6,296	6,379	6,066
Total Assets	25,646	24,694	21,294	20,513	20,708	17,600	15,329	14,606	14,522	13,896
Current Liabilities	5,839	5,362	7,323	5,238	6,071	5,082	4,457	4,509	4,754	3,819
Long Term Debt	5,224	4,088	1,047	1,309	727	1,735	2,140	1,520	971	1,480
Common Equity	9,879	11,747	10,097	10,100	10,378	7,885	5,993	6,086	6,531	6,289
Total Capital	15,548	16,515	11,433	11,409	11,105	9,620	8,133	7,606	7,502	7,769
Capital Expenditures	1,471	1,422	1,168	943	937	677	763	980	1,115	1,039
Cash Flow	4,613	5,168	4,930	4,220	3,989	3,367	2,928	2,519	2,882	2,663
Current Ratio	1.6	1.8	1.2	1.4	1.4	1.5	1.4	1.4	1.3	1.6
% Long Term Debt of Capitalization	33.6	24.8	9.4	11.5	6.5	18.0	26.3	20.0	12.9	19.1
% Net Income of Revenue	13.7	16.7	16.8	15.3	14.9	13.2	12.1	8.9	11.1	11.3
% Return on Assets	13.8	17.8	18.4	15.7	15.6	14.6	13.2	9.8	13.1	12.6
% Return on Equity	32.0	37.7	37.3	31.6	32.7	34.6	32.7	22.7	29.0	28.8

Data as orig reptd.; bef. results of disc opers/spec. items. Per share data adj. for stk. divs.; EPS diluted. E-Estimated. NA-Not Available. NM-Not Meaningful. NR-Not Ranked. UR-Under Review.

Office: 3M Center, St. Paul, MN 55144-1000.
Telephone: 651-733-1110.
Email: innovation@mmm.com
Website: http://www.3m.com

Chrmn, Pres & CEO: G.W. Buckley
COO: I.G. Thulin
EVP & CTO: F.J. Palensky
SVP & CFO: P.D. Campbell

SVP & General Counsel: M.I. Smith
Investor Contact: M. Colin (651-733-8206)
Board Members: L. G. Alvarado, G. W. Buckley, V. D. Coffman, M. L. Eskew, W. J. Farrell, H. L. Henkel, E. M. Liddy, R. S. Morrison, A. L. Peters, R. J. Ulrich

Founded: 1902
Domicile: Delaware
Employees: 79,183

Tiffany & Co.

STANDARD &POOR'S

S&P Recommendation	HOLD ★★★☆☆	Price	12-Mo. Target Price	Investment Style
		$43.21 (as of Nov 27, 2009)	$45.00	Large-Cap Growth

GICS Sector Consumer Discretionary
Sub-Industry Specialty Stores

Summary Tiffany is a leading international retailer, designer, manufacturer, and distributor of fine jewelry and gift items.

Key Stock Statistics (Source S&P, Vickers, company reports)

52-Wk Range	$44.04– 16.70	S&P Oper. EPS 2010**E**	1.91	Market Capitalization(B)	$5.363	Beta	1.73
Trailing 12-Month EPS	$1.25	S&P Oper. EPS 2011**E**	2.11	Yield (%)	1.57	S&P 3-Yr. Proj. EPS CAGR(%)	10
Trailing 12-Month P/E	34.6	P/E on S&P Oper. EPS 2010**E**	22.6	Dividend Rate/Share	$0.68	S&P Credit Rating	NR
$10K Invested 5 Yrs Ago	$14,377	Common Shares Outstg. (M)	124.1	Institutional Ownership (%)	NM		

Price Performance

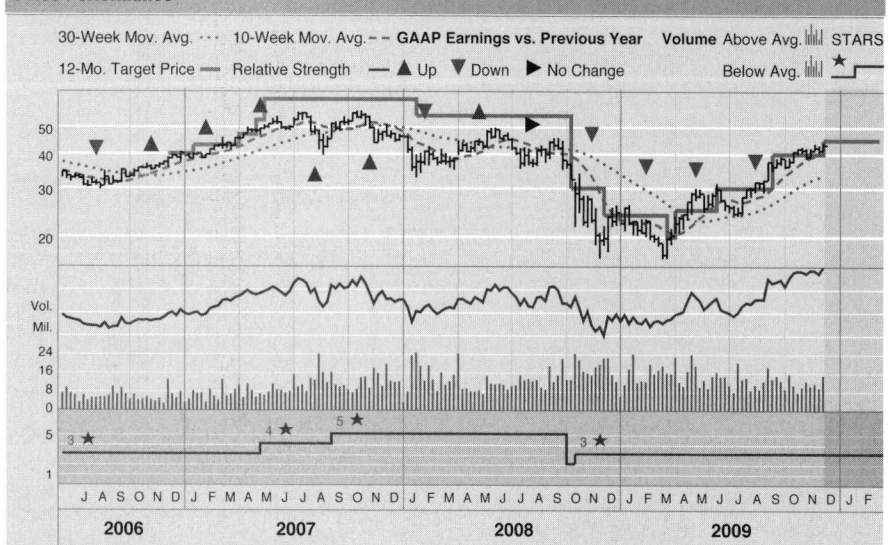

30-Week Mov. Avg. · · · · 10-Week Mov. Avg. – – **GAAP Earnings vs. Previous Year** Volume Above Avg. STARS
12-Mo. Target Price — Relative Strength — ▲ Up ▼ Down ▶ No Change Below Avg. ★

2006 2007 2008 2009

Options: CBOE, P, Ph

Qualitative Risk Assessment

LOW	MEDIUM	HIGH

Our risk assessment reflects TIF's favorable market position as a premier global luxury brand, offset by the weak outlook for U.S. consumer discretionary spending.

Quantitative Evaluations

S&P Quality Ranking　　　　　　　　　A-

D	C	B-	B	B+	A-	A	A+

Relative Strength Rank　　　　　　**STRONG**

88

LOWEST = 1　　　　　　　　　　　HIGHEST = 99

Revenue/Earnings Data

Revenue (Million $)

	1Q	2Q	3Q	4Q	Year
2010	523.1	612.5	--	--	--
2009	668.2	732.4	618.2	841.2	2,860
2008	595.7	662.6	627.3	1,053	2,939
2007	539.2	574.9	547.8	986.4	2,648
2006	509.9	526.7	500.1	858.5	2,395
2005	457.0	476.6	461.2	810.1	2,205

Earnings Per Share ($)

	1Q	2Q	3Q	4Q	Year
2010	0.20	0.46	E0.23	E0.91	E1.91
2009	0.50	0.63	0.35	0.25	1.74
2008	0.36	0.63	0.73	0.89	2.40
2007	0.30	0.29	0.21	1.02	1.80
2006	0.27	0.35	0.16	0.97	1.75
2005	0.25	0.22	0.12	1.48	2.05

Fiscal year ended Jan. 31. Next earnings report expected: Early December. EPS Estimates based on S&P Operating Earnings; historical GAAP earnings are as reported.

Highlights

▸ The 12-month target price for TIF has recently been changed to $45.00 from $40.00. The Highlights section of this Stock Report will be updated accordingly.

Investment Rationale/Risk

▸ The Investment Rationale/Risk section of this Stock Report will be updated shortly. For the latest News story on TIF from MarketScope, see below.

▸ 11/25/09 11:16 am ET ... S&P MAINTAINS HOLD RECOMMENDATION ON SHARES OF TIFFANY & CO (TIF 43.55***): TIF beats our $0.23 Oct-Q EPS view, at $0.34 vs. $0.36, on better than expected U.S. and European sales, with total sales down 3% vs. our -6% estimate. A lower tax rate aided EPS by $0.04. We see modest worldwide sales growth through FY 11 (Jan) on easy comparisons and market share opportunities in Europe and China. In the U.S., we see TIF's new smaller store format providing additional growth opportunity. We lift our FY '10 and '11 EPS estimates to $1.91 and $2.11 from $1.70 and $1.95 and our target price by $5 to $45, 21X our '11 estimate, in line with global luxury peers. /M.Driscoll-CFA

Dividend Data (Dates: mm/dd Payment Date: mm/dd/yy)

Amount ($)	Date Decl.	Ex-Div. Date	Stk. of Record	Payment Date
0.170	02/19	03/18	03/20	04/10/09
0.170	05/21	06/18	06/22	07/10/09
0.170	08/20	09/17	09/21	10/12/09
0.170	11/19	12/17	12/21	01/11/10

Dividends have been paid since 1988. Source: Company reports.

The McGraw-Hill Companies

Tiffany & Co.

STANDARD &POOR'S

Business Summary September 01, 2009

CORPORATE OVERVIEW. Charles Lewis Tiffany founded Tiffany & Co. in 1837. Jewelry is the company's primary sales driver, accounting for 86% of FY 08 (Jan.) net sales. The Tiffany & Co. brand also encompasses timepieces, sterling silver merchandise, china, crystal, stationery, fragrances, and personal accessories. TIF additionally sells other brands of timepieces and tableware in its U.S. stores.

Products are sold via four distribution channels: U.S. retail, comprised of company-owned stores and non-Internet, business-to-business sales (50% of FY 08 net sales); international retail (41%), including both retail and wholesale sales and a limited amount of business-to-business and Internet sales; U.S. direct marketing (6%), consisting of Internet, direct mail catalog and business-to-business Internet sales; and other (3%), which reflects sales transacted under trademarks and trade names other than Tiffany & Co., as well as wholesale sales of diamonds that do not meet the company's quality standards.

CORPORATE STRATEGY. Diamonds are at the heart of TIF's merchandise offering, which also includes colored gemstones and silver and gold fashion jewelry. In FY 08, the company produced 59% of its jewelry merchandise,

based on cost, and purchased almost all non-jewelry merchandise from third-party vendors. To drive sales, TIF introduces new products annually. In FY 07 architect Frank Gehry was added to TIF's list of outside designers and his designs accounted for 2% of FY 07 and FY 08 sales. Other outside designers whose jewelry is licensed and sold exclusively under the Tiffany & Co. brand include Jean Schlumberger, Elsa Peretti (11% of FY 08 sales) and Paloma Picasso (3%).

TIF believes that its multi-channel distribution represents a competitive advantage in a large and fragmented industry. In recent years, the company has expanded its direct marketing business, with a focus on e-commerce. TIF offers over 3,500 products through its U.S. consumer Web site, www.tiffany.com, which was launched in FY 00. The company extended e-commerce purchase capabilities to the U.K. in FY 02 and to both Japan and Canada in FY 06, and launched an informational Web site for China in FY 07.

Company Financials Fiscal Year Ended Jan. 31

Per Share Data ($)	2009	2008	2007	2006	2005	2004	2003	2002	2001	2000
Tangible Book Value	12.70	12.92	13.28	12.85	11.77	10.01	8.34	7.15	6.34	5.23
Cash Flow	2.83	3.28	2.64	2.50	2.79	2.06	1.80	1.58	1.56	1.25
Earnings	1.74	2.40	1.80	1.75	2.05	1.45	1.28	1.15	1.26	0.98
S&P Core Earnings	1.99	1.95	1.84	1.80	1.22	1.37	1.16	1.09	1.20	NA
Dividends	0.52	0.38	0.38	0.30	0.23	0.19	0.16	0.16	0.15	0.11
Payout Ratio	30%	16%	16%	17%	11%	13%	13%	14%	12%	11%
Calendar Year	2008	2007	2006	2005	2004	2003	2002	2001	2000	1999
Prices:High	49.98	57.34	41.29	43.80	45.22	49.45	41.00	38.25	45.38	45.00
Prices:Low	16.75	38.17	29.63	28.60	27.00	21.60	19.40	19.90	27.09	12.63
P/E Ratio:High	29	24	23	25	22	34	32	33	36	46
P/E Ratio:Low	10	16	16	16	13	15	15	17	22	13

Income Statement Analysis (Million $)										
Revenue	2,860	2,939	2,648	2,395	2,205	2,000	1,707	1,607	1,668	1,462
Operating Income	633	640	533	492	403	446	397	375	374	298
Depreciation	138	122	118	109	108	90.4	78.0	64.6	46.7	41.5
Interest Expense	29.0	16.2	26.1	23.1	22.0	14.9	15.1	19.8	16.2	15.0
Pretax Income	346	522	404	368	472	343	300	289	318	248
Effective Tax Rate	36.4%	36.6%	37.2%	30.8%	35.6%	37.1%	36.6%	40.0%	40.0%	41.3%
Net Income	220	331	254	255	304	216	190	174	191	146
S&P Core Earnings	252	269	260	261	181	204	173	164	181	NA

Balance Sheet & Other Financial Data (Million $)										
Cash	160	247	177	394	188	276	156	174	196	217
Current Assets	2,049	1,844	1,707	1,699	1,608	1,348	1,070	954	1,005	892
Total Assets	3,102	2,922	2,846	2,777	2,666	2,391	1,924	1,630	1,568	1,344
Current Liabilities	602	585	453	365	400	395	300	341	337	281
Long Term Debt	425	343	406	427	398	393	297	179	242	250
Common Equity	1,588	1,637	1,805	1,831	1,701	1,468	1,208	1,037	925	757
Total Capital	2,014	2,046	2,211	2,257	2,132	1,884	1,505	1,216	1,168	1,007
Capital Expenditures	154	186	182	157	142	273	220	171	108	171
Cash Flow	358	453	372	364	412	306	268	238	237	187
Current Ratio	3.4	3.2	3.8	4.7	4.0	3.4	3.6	2.8	3.0	3.2
% Long Term Debt of Capitalization	21.1	16.8	18.4	18.9	18.7	20.9	19.7	14.7	20.7	24.8
% Net Income of Revenue	7.7	11.3	9.6	10.6	13.8	10.8	11.1	10.8	11.4	10.0
% Return on Assets	7.3	11.5	9.0	9.4	12.0	10.0	10.7	10.9	13.1	12.1
% Return on Equity	13.6	19.3	14.0	14.4	19.2	16.1	16.9	17.7	22.7	22.9

Data as orig reptd.; bef. results of disc opers/spec. items. Per share data adj. for stk. divs.; EPS diluted. E-Estimated. NA-Not Available. NM-Not Meaningful. NR-Not Ranked. UR-Under Review.

Office: 727 Fifth Avenue, New York, NY 10022.
Telephone: 212-755-8000.
Website: http://www.tiffany.com
Chrmn & CEO: M.J. Kowalski

Pres: J.E. Quinn
COO: J.S. Petterson
EVP & CFO: J.N. Fernandez
SVP, Secy & General Counsel: P.B. Dorsey

Investor Contact: M.L. Aaron (212-230-5301)
Board Members: R. M. Bravo, G. E. Costley, L. Fish, A. F. Kohnstamm, M. J. Kowalski, C. K. Marquis, P. W. May, J. T. Presby, W. A. Shutzer

Auditor: PricewaterhouseCoopers LLP
Founded: 1837
Domicile: Delaware
Employees: 9,000

The McGraw-Hill Companies

Time Warner Cable Inc

STANDARD
&POOR'S

S&P Recommendation	STRONG BUY ★★★★★	Price $42.42 (as of Nov 27, 2009)	12-Mo. Target Price $51.00	Investment Style Large-Cap Growth

GICS Sector Consumer Discretionary
Sub-Industry Cable & Satellite

Summary As the second largest U.S. cable operator and a majority-owned subsidiary of media conglomerate Time Warner, TWC completed a structural separation from its parent company in early 2009.

Key Stock Statistics (Source S&P, Vickers, company reports)

52-Wk Range	$68.23– 20.19	S&P Oper. EPS 2009**E**	3.34	Market Capitalization(B)	$14.950	Beta		0.51
Trailing 12-Month EPS	$-21.66	S&P Oper. EPS 2010**E**	3.83	Yield (%)	Nil	S&P 3-Yr. Proj. EPS CAGR(%)		8
Trailing 12-Month P/E	NM	P/E on S&P Oper. EPS 2009**E**	12.7	Dividend Rate/Share	Nil	S&P Credit Rating		BBB
$10K Invested 5 Yrs Ago	NA	Common Shares Outstg. (M)	352.4	Institutional Ownership (%)	87			

Price Performance

30-Week Mov. Avg. · · · 10-Week Mov. Avg. – – **GAAP Earnings vs. Previous Year** Volume Above Avg. STARS
12-Mo. Target Price — Relative Strength — ▲ Up ▼ Down ▶ No Change Below Avg. ★

Analysis prepared by **Tuna N. Amobi, CFA, CPA** on November 23, 2009, when the stock traded at **$ 43.49.**

Highlights

▶ From about $17.9 billion in consolidated revenues in 2009, we expect a 2010 advance of about 6.0%, reaching almost $19.0 billion, mainly on further penetration of bundled residential (and increasingly commercial) high-speed data and digital phone products. We project relatively modest gains in video revenues, with the potential benefits of annual rate hikes and higher average pricing on advanced video offerings (HD and DVR), while assuming relatively moderate levels of basic subscriber losses. We forecast the relatively small ad revenues area to improve in 2010, after a sharp 2009 drop.

▶ We see relatively modest margin improvement on lower head count and further savings on programming costs per subscriber (on Adelphia's integration), partly offset by potential constraints to operating leverage on higher marketing and promotional spending. We see 2009 adjusted EBITDA of more than $6.4 billion, reaching nearly $6.9 billion in 2010.

▶ After D&A, significantly higher interest expense on higher debt on TWC's spin-off, and 40%-41% effective taxes, we forecast 2009 and 2010 operating EPS of $3.34 and $3.83, respectively.

Investment Rationale/Risk

▶ We are somewhat concerned by relatively weak subscriber growth through the 2009 third quarter -- evidently on the economic slowdown and competitive pressures -- which TWC suggested continued into the fourth quarter. With a likely tradeoff on profitable unit growth, however, margins seem to be holding up. We see continued traction for the nascent commercial business -- likely the next growth engine -- with TWC also set for an imminent launch its 4G wireless broadband product in several markets (under the Sprint/Clearwire JV). We see TWC on track for its near-term deleveraging goal of 3.25X leverage ratio by March 2010 -- with likely free cash flow acceleration thereafter.

▶ Risks to our recommendation and target price include a slower-than-expected economic recovery; increased competition from satellite TV/telcos (including wireless substitution); dilutive acquisitions; and, regulatory risk factors.

▶ Our 12-month target price of $51 reflects 5.8X 2010E EV/EBITDA, or $2,900 per subscriber, which we view as attractive relative to cable peers -- given TWC's position as the largest U.S. pure-play cable provider.

Qualitative Risk Assessment

LOW	MEDIUM	HIGH

Our risk assessment reflects what we view as the company's strong leadership position in a highly consolidated pay TV industry and a relatively strong balance sheet, combined with increased flexibility after a separation from its parent company, offset by increased competition and regulatory risk factors.

Quantitative Evaluations

S&P Quality Ranking NR

D	C	B-	B	B+	A-	A	A+

Relative Strength Rank STRONG

76

LOWEST = 1 HIGHEST = 99

Revenue/Earnings Data

Revenue (Million $)

	1Q	2Q	3Q	4Q	Year
2009	4,364	4,474	4,498	--	--
2008	4,160	4,298	4,340	4,402	17,200
2007	3,851	4,014	4,001	4,089	15,955
2006	2,385	2,721	3,209	3,651	11,767
2005	2,302	2,357	2,227	2,315	9,498
2004	--	--	--	--	8,484

Earnings Per Share ($)

2009	0.48	0.89	0.76	E0.87	E3.34
2008	0.75	0.84	0.93	-25.08	-22.56
2007	0.84	0.84	0.75	0.99	3.45
2006	0.60	0.87	0.69	0.75	2.85
2005	0.90	1.29	0.60	1.20	3.75
2004	--	--	--	--	2.19

Fiscal year ended Dec. 31. Next earnings report expected: Early February. EPS Estimates based on S&P Operating Earnings; historical GAAP earnings are as reported.

Dividend Data (Dates: mm/dd Payment Date: mm/dd/yy)

Amount ($)	Date Decl.	Ex-Div. Date	Stk. of Record	Payment Date
10.27 Spl.	02/26	03/09	03/11	03/12/09
1-for-3 REV.	--	03/12	--	03/12/09

Source: Company reports.

The McGraw-Hill Companies

Time Warner Cable Inc

STANDARD &POOR'S

Business Summary November 23, 2009

CORPORATE OVERVIEW. Time Warner Cable Inc. (TWC) is the second largest cable operator in the U.S., with 13.0 million basic subscribers as of September 30, 2009. After its July 2006 acquisition of Adelphia Communications (for about $8.9 billion in cash plus 16% of its common stock) -- which added a net 3.2 million subscribers) -- TWC became a public company on February 13, 2007 (effective date of Adelphia's reorganization plan), and its Class A shares began trading as of March 1, 2007 (the non-trading Class B shares are held by its parent). In March 2009, TWC was spun off from its former 84% equity owner Time Warner (TWX 32, Hold).

As of September 30, 2009, TWC's cable systems passed nearly 29.0 million U.S. homes (including the distribution on January 1, 2007, of the Texas/Kansas City JV), nearly 85% of which were located in New York, the Carolinas, Ohio, Southern California and Texas. Nearly 8.9 million (33% of basic customers) of TWC's homes passed subscribed to a residential high-speed data service such as Road Runner, and almost 4.1 million (or 15.0%) to residential digital phone. Also, there were 351,000 commercial customers (293,000 for data and 58,000 for digital phone). Nearly all of the homes passed in its legacy systems and more than 94% in the acquired systems were served by a system with at least 750 MHz of capacity.

CORPORATE STRATEGY. After its 2004 initial launch of digital phone service, TWC now offers the triple-play bundle substantially across its footprint, while it is in the relatively early stages of launching data and digital phone services to small to medium-sized businesses. In May 2008, TWC invested $550 million in a JV to build a nationwide WiMAX network with Sprint, Clearwire and others. In 2006, a cable consortium including TWC won 137 Advanced Wireless Spectrum (AWS) licenses from an FCC auction. An industry leader in advanced digital services (so-called Enhanced TV offerings), TWC is also pursuing a number of network-bandwidth reclamation initiatives (e.g., all-digital, switched digital video etc.), while adding a growing number of HD channels (now up to 100 in some of its systems). In August 2009, TWX unveiled pilot testing of its Web TV authentication technology with about a dozen TV programmers under the TV Everywhere initiative.

Company Financials Fiscal Year Ended Dec. 31

Per Share Data ($)	2008	2007	2006	2005	2004	2003	2002	2001	2000	1999
Tangible Book Value	NM	NM	NM	NA	NA	NA	NA	NA	NA	NA
Cash Flow	-2.32	12.60	9.05	NA	NA	NA	NA	NA	NA	NA
Earnings	-22.56	3.45	2.85	3.75	2.19	1.71	NA	NA	NA	NA
S&P Core Earnings	7.68	3.12	2.88	NA	NA	NA	NA	NA	NA	NA
Dividends	Nil	Nil	NA	NA	NA	NA	NA	NA	NA	NA
Payout Ratio	Nil	Nil	NA	NA	NA	NA	NA	NA	NA	NA
Prices:High	94.68	126.34	NA	NA	NA	NA	NA	NA	NA	NA
Prices:Low	48.90	70.81	NA	NA	NA	NA	NA	NA	NA	NA
P/E Ratio:High	NM	37	NA	NA	NA	NA	NA	NA	NA	NA
P/E Ratio:Low	NM	21	NA	NA	NA	NA	NA	NA	NA	NA

Income Statement Analysis (Million $)										
Revenue	17,200	15,955	11,767	9,498	8,484	7,699	NA	NA	NA	NA
Operating Income	76.0	5,765	4,285	NA	NA	NA	NA	NA	NA	NA
Depreciation	33.5	2,976	2,050	1,664	1,514	1,461	NA	NA	NA	NA
Interest Expense	25.8	907	646	501	491	514	NA	NA	NA	NA
Pretax Income	-13,072	2,028	1,664	1,535	1,305	987	NA	NA	NA	NA
Effective Tax Rate	NM	36.5%	37.3%	13.8%	39.6%	38.9%	NA	NA	NA	NA
Net Income	-7,344	1,123	936	1,253	726	541	NA	NA	NA	NA
S&P Core Earnings	2,511	1,019	945	NA	NA	NA	NA	NA	NA	NA

Balance Sheet & Other Financial Data (Million $)										
Cash	5,552	232	51.0	12.0	102	NA	NA	NA	NA	NA
Current Assets	57.1	1,163	910	NA	NA	NA	NA	NA	NA	NA
Total Assets	47,889	56,600	55,743	43,677	43,138	NA	NA	NA	NA	NA
Current Liabilities	387	2,536	2,490	NA	NA	NA	NA	NA	NA	NA
Long Term Debt	17,727	13,877	300	4,455	4,898	NA	NA	NA	NA	NA
Common Equity	17,164	24,706	23,564	21,331	20,039	NA	NA	NA	NA	NA
Total Capital	36,301	53,598	38,390	29,193	28,304	NA	NA	NA	NA	NA
Capital Expenditures	3,522	3,433	2,718	1,975	1,712	1,637	NA	NA	NA	NA
Cash Flow	-59.1	4,099	2,986	NA	NA	NA	NA	NA	NA	NA
Current Ratio	2.3	0.5	0.4	0.3	0.3	NA	NA	NA	NA	NA
% Long Term Debt of Capitalization	48.8	25.9	0.8	17.3	19.6	Nil	NA	NA	NA	NA
% Net Income of Revenue	NM	7.0	8.0	13.2	8.6	7.0	NA	NA	NA	NA
% Return on Assets	NM	2.0	1.9	2.9	NA	NA	NA	NA	NA	NA
% Return on Equity	NM	4.7	4.2	6.1	NA	NA	NA	NA	NA	NA

Data as orig reptd.; bef. results of disc opers/spec. items. Per share data adj. for stk. divs.; EPS diluted. E-Estimated. NA-Not Available. NM-Not Meaningful. NR-Not Ranked. UR-Under Review.

Office: 60 Columbus Cir, New York, NY 10023-5802.
Telephone: 212-364-8200.
Website: http://www.timewarnercable.com
Chrmn, Pres & CEO: G.A. Britt

COO: L. Hobbs
EVP & CFO: R.D. Marcus
EVP & CTO: M.L. LaJoie
EVP, Secy & General Counsel: M. Lawrence-Apfelbaum

Investor Contact: W. Osbourn, Jr. (203-351-2015)
Board Members: C. Black, G. A. Britt, T. H. Castro, D. C. Chang, J. Copeland, Jr., P. R. Haje, D. A. James, D. Logan, N. J. Nicholas, Jr., W. H. Pace, E. D. Shirley, J. E. Sununu

Founded: 2003
Domicile: Delaware
Employees: 46,600

Time Warner Inc.

STANDARD &POOR'S

S&P Recommendation HOLD ★★★☆☆	Price $30.85 (as of Nov 27, 2009)	12-Mo. Target Price $32.00	Investment Style Large-Cap Blend

GICS Sector Consumer Discretionary
Sub-Industry Movies & Entertainment

Summary One of the world's leading media companies, TWX has diversified interests in web properties, filmed entertainment content, television networks, and publishing.

Key Stock Statistics (Source S&P, Vickers, company reports)

52-Wk Range	$33.45– 17.81	S&P Oper. EPS 2009**E** 2.08	Market Capitalization(B) $36.020	Beta	1.12
Trailing 12-Month EPS	$-11.91	S&P Oper. EPS 2010**E** 2.35	Yield (%) 2.43	S&P 3-Yr. Proj. EPS CAGR(%)	7
Trailing 12-Month P/E	NM	P/E on S&P Oper. EPS 2009**E** 14.8	Dividend Rate/Share $0.75	S&P Credit Rating	BBB
$10K Invested 5 Yrs Ago	NA	Common Shares Outstg. (M) 1,167.6	Institutional Ownership (%) 82		

Price Performance

30-Week Mov. Avg. ··· 10-Week Mov. Avg. - - **GAAP Earnings vs. Previous Year**   Volume Above Avg. STARS
12-Mo. Target Price — Relative Strength — ▲ Up ▼ Down ► No Change   Below Avg. ★

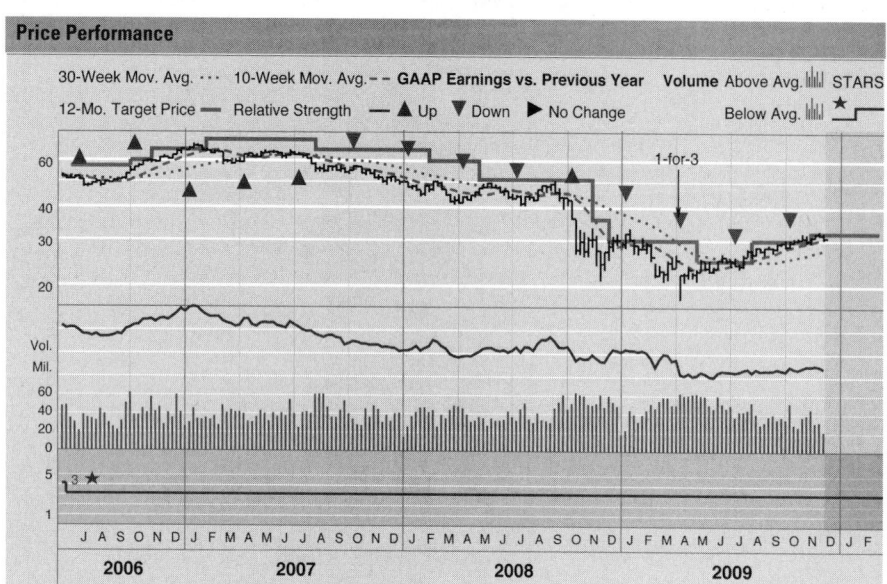

Options: ASE, CBOE, P, Ph

Analysis prepared by **Tuna N. Amobi, CFA, CPA** on November 12, 2009, when the stock traded at **$ 31.91.**

Highlights

▸ For the company as presently constituted (including AOL but excluding the spun-off cable systems business), we expect 2009 consolidated revenues to decline a little more than 6%, before edging up 1% in 2010 to about $28.9 billion. We see stronger contributions from cable TV networks (Turner and HBO), versus continued sharp revenue declines for AOL and the publishing divisions, and mixed comparisons for the film/TV studio businesses (mainly theatrical, DVD and syndication sales).

▸ We see relatively limited overall margin expansion in 2009 -- with gains in the networks and film businesses mostly offset by the impact of continued AOL subscriber erosion (and a sharp decline in online ads), as well as declining print ads and circulation. In 2010, however, we expect somewhat improved operating leverage, with further benefits from recent restructuring steps across most businesses, and an increase in higher-margin digital revenues.

▸ After D&A and lower net interest expense (on debt paydown and ample cash), we forecast 2009 and 2010 EPS of $2.08 and $2.35, respectively, with further share buybacks under a $5 billion program ($1.3 billion recently remaining).

Investment Rationale/Risk

▸ We are somewhat encouraged by a sequential improvement in 2009 third quarter results over a relatively more challenging first half, upon which management slightly raised its full year EPS target. An imminent AOL spin-off in 2009 should leave TWX as a purer-play content company -- with several leading film and TV franchises, and the publishing division perhaps poised to become the next strategic challenge. Still, with over $7 billion in cash, we see continued ample financial capacity (post AOL spin-off) for share buybacks, as well as possible acquisitions and a potential dividend increase.

▸ Risks to our recommendation and target price include a slower-than-expected economic and advertising recovery; lower ratings for the Turner networks; a sharp slowdown in the home video market; potentially dilutive acquisitions; secular challenges for the publishing unit; and high earnings volatility.

▸ Our 12-month target price of $32 implies a relatively ample 7.0X 2010 EV/EBITDA, with a blended sum-of-the-parts valuation. As presently constituted, we expect TWX to generate free cash flow of over $4.5 billion and nearly $5.0 billion in 2009 and 2010, respectively.

Qualitative Risk Assessment

LOW	MEDIUM	HIGH

Our risk assessment reflects our view of the company's leading content-oriented businesses, ample financial flexibility, and what we view as an adequate governance framework, offset by cyclical and secular pressures and a relatively volatile earnings stream.

Quantitative Evaluations

S&P Quality Ranking   B-

D	C	B-	B	B+	A-	A	A+

Relative Strength Rank   MODERATE

62

LOWEST = 1   HIGHEST = 99

Revenue/Earnings Data

Revenue (Million $)

	1Q	2Q	3Q	4Q	Year
2009	6,945	6,809	7,135	--	--
2008	11,417	11,555	11,706	12,306	46,984
2007	11,184	10,980	11,676	12,642	46,482
2006	10,327	10,519	10,912	12,466	44,224
2005	10,483	10,744	10,538	11,887	43,652
2004	10,178	10,858	9,936	11,109	42,081

Earnings Per Share ($)

2009	0.46	0.43	0.55	E0.57	E2.08
2008	0.63	0.66	0.90	-13.41	-11.22
2007	0.90	0.75	0.72	0.84	3.24
2006	0.78	0.60	0.99	1.29	3.63
2005	0.60	-0.21	0.57	0.87	1.86
2004	0.45	0.57	0.33	0.72	2.07

Fiscal year ended Dec. 31. Next earnings report expected: Early February. EPS Estimates based on S&P Operating Earnings; historical GAAP earnings are as reported.

Dividend Data (Dates: mm/dd Payment Date: mm/dd/yy)

Amount ($)	Date Decl.	Ex-Div. Date	Stk. of Record	Payment Date
1-for-3 REV.	--	03/27	--	03/27/09
0.188	04/22	11/24	11/27	12/09/09
Stk.	11/16	12/10	11/27	12/09/09
Stk.	02/27	--	03/12	03/27/09

Dividends have been paid since 2005. Source: Company reports.

Please read the Required Disclosures and Analyst Certification on the last page of this report.

The McGraw-Hill Companies

Time Warner Inc.

STANDARD
&POOR'S

Business Summary November 12, 2009

CORPORATE OVERVIEW. In January 2001, online access and content company America Online (AOL) merged with cable systems and media concern Time Warner, forming AOL Time Warner (later changed to Time Warner in October 2003), in a $106 billion transaction. Revenues are derived from subscriptions (55% of 2008 revenues), content (19%), advertising (24%), and other (2%).

AOL had nearly 5.4 million U.S. access subscribers at September 30, 2009. It owns the AOL, CompuServe and Netscape access brands, and the AOL.com, AIM and MapQuest portals and Websites. In March 2009, TWX spun off its formerly 84%-owned Time Warner Cable (TWC 42, Strong Buy) subsidiary.

Filmed Entertainment includes the Warner Bros. and New Line Cinema (independent) studios and home entertainment businesses, with key franchises such as Harry Potter, Lord of the Rings and Batman. The Networks segment includes cable networks CNN, HBO/Cinemax and Turner (TNT, TBS). In September 2006, TWX's WB broadcast network merged with CBS's UPN to create the CW network. Publishing includes Time Inc., with over 130 magazine titles worldwide, including Time, People, Sports Illustrated and Fortune.

CORPORATE STRATEGY. CEO Jeffrey Bewkes recently articulated several key priorities, including continued delivery of quality content, improved operating efficiency, international expansion, and exploiting advances in digital technology for new business opportunities.

AOL has made a number of recent acquisitions, notably including social networking site Bebo purchased in May 2008 for $850 million in cash. The company is on track to spin off its AOL division in December 2009.

Separately, in May 2009, TWX invested $241.5 million in Central European Media Enterprises (CETV 30, Strong Sell) for about a 31% equity stake in the European broadcaster.

Company Financials Fiscal Year Ended Dec. 31

Per Share Data ($)	2008	2007	2006	2005	2004	2003	2002	2001	2000	1999
Tangible Book Value	NM	NM	NM	NM	NM	NM	NM	NM	7.53	7.32
Cash Flow	-2.46	11.58	8.57	6.18	6.39	6.00	NA	NA	1.85	1.84
Earnings	-11.22	3.24	3.63	1.86	2.07	2.04	-28.29	-3.60	1.35	1.44
S&P Core Earnings	-6.72	2.85	3.21	2.49	1.86	1.26	-10.32	-3.24	NA	NA
Dividends	0.75	0.71	0.63	0.30	Nil	Nil	Nil	Nil	Nil	Nil
Payout Ratio	NM	22%	17%	16%	Nil	Nil	Nil	Nil	Nil	Nil
Prices:High	50.70	69.46	66.76	58.93	59.71	54.97	98.77	175.55	250.15	250.15
Prices:Low	21.00	48.51	47.10	48.30	46.23	29.70	26.10	82.21	98.26	98.26
P/E Ratio:High	NM	21	18	32	29	27	NM	NM	NM	NM
P/E Ratio:Low	NM	15	13	26	22	15	NM	NM	NM	NM

Income Statement Analysis (Million $)	2008	2007	2006	2005	2004	2003	2002	2001	2000	1999
Revenue	46,984	46,482	44,224	43,652	42,081	39,496	36,955	33,765	7,703	6,886
Operating Income	19,229	19,217	14,837	14,312	13,535	11,839	NA	NA	2,271	1,776
Depreciation	10,481	10,488	6,953	6,781	6,743	6,086	NA	NA	444	363
Interest Expense	2,275	2,509	1,971	1,622	1,754	1,926	1,900	1,576	55.0	40.0
Pretax Income	-18,623	6,795	6,826	4,007	5,206	4,763	-44,156	-4,465	1,884	2,014
Effective Tax Rate	NM	34.4%	19.6%	27.2%	33.0%	29.0%	NM	NM	38.9%	38.8%
Net Income	-13,402	4,051	5,114	2,921	3,239	3,164	-42,003	-5,313	1,152	1,232
S&P Core Earnings	-7,981	3,579	4,551	3,929	2,938	1,999	-15,240	-4,771	NA	NA

Balance Sheet & Other Financial Data (Million $)	2008	2007	2006	2005	2004	2003	2002	2001	2000	1999
Cash	6,682	1,516	1,549	4,220	6,139	3,040	1,730	771	2,610	2,490
Current Assets	16,602	12,451	10,851	13,463	14,639	12,268	11,155	10,274	4,671	4,428
Total Assets	113,896	133,830	131,669	122,745	123,149	121,748	115,508	209,429	10,827	10,673
Current Liabilities	13,976	12,193	12,780	12,608	14,673	NA	NA	NA	2,328	2,395
Long Term Debt	37,916	37,304	35,233	20,238	20,703	23,458	27,354	22,792	1,411	1,630
Common Equity	42,288	58,536	60,389	62,679	60,719	56,131	52,891	150,667	6,778	6,161
Total Capital	92,379	113,898	112,857	103,760	103,285	NA	NA	NA	8,189	7,791
Capital Expenditures	4,377	4,430	4,085	3,246	3,024	2,761	3,023	3,634	485	642
Cash Flow	-2,921	14,539	12,067	9,702	9,982	9,250	NA	NA	1,596	1,595
Current Ratio	1.2	1.0	0.8	1.1	1.0	0.8	0.8	0.8	2.0	1.8
% Long Term Debt of Capitalization	41.0	32.8	31.2	19.5	20.0	NA	NA	NA	17.2	20.9
% Net Income of Revenue	NM	8.7	11.6	6.7	7.7	8.0	NM	NM	15.0	17.9
% Return on Assets	NM	3.1	4.0	2.4	2.6	2.7	NM	NM	10.9	15.3
% Return on Equity	NM	6.8	8.2	4.7	5.5	5.8	NM	NM	17.6	26.6

Data as orig reptd.; bef. results of disc opers/spec. items. Per share data adj. for stk. divs.; EPS diluted. E-Estimated. NA-Not Available. NM-Not Meaningful. NR-Not Ranked. UR-Under Review.

Office: 1 Time Warner Ctr, New York, NY 10019-6038.
Telephone: 212-484-8000.
Email: aoltwir@aoltw.com
Website: http://www.timewarner.com

Chrmn & CEO: J. Bewkes
EVP & CFO: J. Martin, Jr.
EVP & General Counsel: P.T. Cappuccio
SVP, Chief Acctg Officer & Cntlr: P. Desroches

SVP & Treas: E.B. Ruggiero
Investor Contact: J.E. Burton
Board Members: J. L. Barksdale, W. P. Barr, J. Bewkes, S. F. Bollenbach, F. J. Caufield, R. C. Clark, M. Dopfner, J. P. Einhorn, F. Hassan, J. V. Kimsey, M. A. Miles, K. J. Novack, D. C. Wright

Founded: 1985
Domicile: Delaware
Employees: 87,000

The McGraw-Hill Companies

Titanium Metals Corp

STANDARD &POOR'S

| S&P Recommendation | SELL ★★☆☆☆ | Price $9.85 (as of Nov 27, 2009) | 12-Mo. Target Price $9.00 | Investment Style Large-Cap Blend |

GICS Sector Materials
Sub-Industry Diversified Metals & Mining

Summary This company is a worldwide integrated producer of titanium metal products.

Key Stock Statistics (Source S&P, Vickers, company reports)

52-Wk Range	$11.52– 4.04	S&P Oper. EPS 2009**E**	0.17	Market Capitalization(B)	$1.773	Beta	1.74
Trailing 12-Month EPS	$0.35	S&P Oper. EPS 2010**E**	0.29	Yield (%)	Nil	S&P 3-Yr. Proj. EPS CAGR(%)	0
Trailing 12-Month P/E	28.1	P/E on S&P Oper. EPS 2009**E**	57.9	Dividend Rate/Share	Nil	S&P Credit Rating	NR
$10K Invested 5 Yrs Ago	$35,680	Common Shares Outstg. (M)	180.0	Institutional Ownership (%)	24		

Price Performance

30-Week Mov. Avg. · · · 10-Week Mov. Avg. – – **GAAP Earnings vs. Previous Year** Volume Above Avg. STARS
12-Mo. Target Price — Relative Strength — ▲ Up ▼ Down ▶ No Change Below Avg. ★

Options: ASE, CBOE, Ph

Analysis prepared by **Leo J. Larkin** on October 23, 2009, when the stock traded at **$ 9.65**.

Highlights

▶ Following a 10% sales decline in 2008, we look for a sales decrease of 34% in 2009, reflecting another drop in volume and another decrease in the average realized price of both melted and mill products. We see demand being adversely affected by high customer inventories and the lingering effect from the delay of Boeing's 787 airplane project. We assume that GDP will decline by 2.7% in 2009, versus GDP growth of 0.4% in 2008. In our view, declining GDP will depress demand for durable goods.

▶ We look for margin contraction, as a combination of lower volume of shipments and reduced selling prices should offset lower raw material costs. Following minimal interest expense and a flat tax rate, we estimate that EPS will decline in 2009 to $0.21, from operating EPS of $0.82 in 2008, which excludes unusual gains totaling $0.07 in 2008's fourth quarter.

▶ Longer term, we look for higher EPS on an eventual rebound in the commercial aerospace industry, resumption of share repurchases, and increased use of titanium in other industrial applications and rising consumption in Asia.

Investment Rationale/Risk

▶ We believe TIE shares are overvalued, recently at 33.6X our 2010 estimate. While cyclical companies often carry very high multiples at an EPS trough, we think the P/E is excessive relative to its historical range. Long-term, we have a favorable view of TIE as a beneficiary of a recovery in commercial aerospace, growing acceptance of titanium in other industrial markets, and rising Asian demand for titanium. While we see another EPS decline in 2009, we expect that TIE will remain free cash flow positive, reflecting lower capital spending and reduced working capital. That, combined with its low debt levels should enable TIE to capitalize on a cyclical upturn in titanium demand.

▶ Risks to our recommendation and target price include an increase in volume and pricing in 2010 in excess of the gain we project.

▶ We project a P/E for the stock on our 2010 estimate of 31X, which would match the high end of the historical range. On our target P/E, TIE would sell at a premium to the P/E we apply to one its peers and at a discount to P/E we apply to another. On a price to tangible book value basis, TIE would sell at a discount to both rivals. On that basis, our 12-month target price is $9.

Qualitative Risk Assessment

| LOW | MEDIUM | HIGH |

Our risk assessment reflects the company's low debt levels and its large share of the markets it serves. Partly offsetting this is its heavy reliance on aerospace industry demand and the volatility of raw material costs.

Quantitative Evaluations

S&P Quality Ranking B-

| D | C | B- | B | B+ | A- | A | A+ |

Relative Strength Rank STRONG

73

LOWEST = 1 HIGHEST = 99

Revenue/Earnings Data

Revenue (Million $)

	1Q	2Q	3Q	4Q	Year
2009	203.4	205.7	181.4	--	--
2008	293.7	297.3	295.4	265.2	1,152
2007	341.7	341.2	297.3	298.6	1,279
2006	286.9	300.9	271.8	323.5	1,183
2005	155.2	183.8	190.0	220.8	749.8
2004	120.5	124.1	120.3	137.0	501.8

Earnings Per Share ($)

2009	0.11	0.05	0.01	E0.01	E0.17
2008	0.22	0.26	0.22	0.19	0.89
2007	0.41	0.42	0.29	0.61	1.46
2006	0.32	0.31	0.29	0.61	1.53
2005	0.23	0.21	0.20	0.23	0.86
2004	-0.01	0.02	0.17	0.08	0.28

Fiscal year ended Dec. 31. Next earnings report expected: Late February. EPS Estimates based on S&P Operating Earnings; historical GAAP earnings are as reported.

Dividend Data (Dates: mm/dd Payment Date: mm/dd/yy)

Amount ($)	Date Decl.	Ex-Div. Date	Stk. of Record	Payment Date
0.075	10/30	12/08	12/10	12/24/08

Source: Company reports.

Please read the Required Disclosures and Analyst Certification on the last page of this report.

The **McGraw-Hill** Companies

Titanium Metals Corp

Business Summary October 23, 2009

CORPORATE OVERVIEW. Titanium Metals Corp. is the one of the world's largest producers of titanium melted and mill products and the largest U.S. producer of titanium sponge (the raw material for titanium). TIE estimates that it accounted for some 15% of global industry shipments of titanium mill products in 2008 and 6% of worldwide sponge production. Melted and mill products and sponge are sold principally to the commercial aerospace industry. Other sources of product demand include the military, industrial and emerging markets. As of December 31, 2008, 27.9% of TIE's common shares were held by Contran Corporation and its subsidiaries, and an additional 8.5% of TIE's shares were held by a trust sponsored by Contran.

Products include titanium sponge; melted products (ingot, electrodes and slab); mill products, including billet and bar, plate, strip and pipe; and fabricated products such as spools, pipe fittings, manifolds and vessels. In 2008, mill products accounted for 79% of sales, melted products 10%, and other prod-

ucts (titanium fabrications, titanium scrap and titanium tetrachloride), 11%.

Sales by market sector in 2008 were: aerospace, 59%; military, 16%; industrial and emerging markets, 15%; and other, 10%.

In 2008, North America accounted for 56% of sales, Europe for 33% and other regions for 11%.

CORPORATE STRATEGY. The company's long-term strategy is to maximize the value of its core aerospace business while expanding its presence in non-aerospace markets. Additionally, the company seeks to develop new applications for its products.

Company Financials Fiscal Year Ended Dec. 31

Per Share Data ($)	2008	2007	2006	2005	2004	2003	2002	2001	2000	1999
Tangible Book Value	5.94	6.16	4.92	2.91	1.41	1.20	1.18	1.92	2.32	2.69
Cash Flow	1.15	1.65	1.68	0.96	0.47	0.19	-0.24	-0.01	0.03	0.08
Earnings	0.89	1.46	1.53	0.86	0.28	-0.11	-0.53	-0.33	-0.30	-0.25
S&P Core Earnings	0.80	1.35	1.29	0.82	0.29	-0.08	-0.37	-0.41	NA	NA
Dividends	0.30	0.08	Nil	Nil	Nil	Nil	Nil	Nil	Nil	0.03
Payout Ratio	34%	5%	Nil	Nil	Nil	Nil	Nil	Nil	Nil	13%
Prices:High	26.79	39.80	47.63	19.86	3.33	1.51	1.35	3.60	2.23	3.31
Prices:Low	5.31	25.26	15.96	2.91	1.06	0.39	0.23	0.59	0.78	0.89
P/E Ratio:High	30	27	31	23	12	NM	NM	NM	NM	NM
P/E Ratio:Low	6	17	10	3	4	NM	NM	NM	NM	NM

Income Statement Analysis (Million $)	2008	2007	2006	2005	2004	2003	2002	2001	2000	1999
Revenue	1,152	1,279	1,183	750	502	385	367	487	427	480
Operating Income	269	420	403	177	43.8	17.2	-9.02	28.2	1.81	19.6
Depreciation	47.7	41.1	34.1	31.5	32.8	36.6	37.1	40.1	41.9	42.7
Interest Expense	1.80	2.60	3.43	3.96	12.5	16.4	3.38	4.06	7.70	7.09
Pretax Income	237	394	418	185	39.0	-11.3	-54.5	4.47	-43.1	-33.7
Effective Tax Rate	29.1%	29.7%	30.7%	13.2%	NM	NM	NM	NM	NM	NM
Net Income	163	268	281	156	39.9	-12.9	-67.2	-41.8	-38.0	-31.4
S&P Core Earnings	145	243	230	136	37.9	-9.92	-46.4	-51.7	NA	NA

Balance Sheet & Other Financial Data (Million $)	2008	2007	2006	2005	2004	2003	2002	2001	2000	1999
Cash	45.0	90.0	86.2	17.6	54.4	35.0	6.21	24.5	9.80	20.7
Current Assets	789	898	758	550	344	276	263	309	248	343
Total Assets	1,368	1,420	1,217	907	666	567	564	699	759	883
Current Liabilities	152	178	211	167	162	78.5	92.6	122	116	194
Long Term Debt	0.20	0.50	Nil	57.2	12.2	9.77	217	221	229	233
Common Equity	1,076	1,129	804	430	206	159	159	298	357	408
Total Capital	1,101	1,168	918	660	404	180	388	533	604	662
Capital Expenditures	121	101	101	61.1	23.6	12.5	7.77	16.1	11.2	24.8
Cash Flow	210	304	309	175	68.4	23.7	-30.1	-1.63	3.91	11.3
Current Ratio	5.2	5.1	3.6	3.3	2.1	3.5	2.8	2.5	2.1	1.8
% Long Term Debt of Capitalization	Nil	Nil	Nil	8.7	3.0	5.4	56.0	41.4	37.9	35.3
% Net Income of Revenue	14.1	21.0	23.8	20.8	8.0	NM	NM	NM	NM	NM
% Return on Assets	11.7	20.3	26.5	19.4	6.5	NM	NM	NM	NM	NM
% Return on Equity	14.7	27.2	44.5	43.4	19.5	NM	NM	NM	NM	NM

Data as orig reptd.; bef. results of disc opers/spec. items. Per share data adj. for stk. divs.; EPS diluted. E-Estimated. NA-Not Available. NM-Not Meaningful. NR-Not Ranked. UR-Under Review.

Office: 5430 Lbj Fwy Ste 1700, Dallas, TX 75240-2620.
Telephone: 972-233-1700.
Website: http://www.timet.com
Chrmn: H.C. Simmons

Pres: B.D. O'Brien
Vice Chrmn & CEO: S.L. Watson
CFO: J.W. Brown
CTO: M.W. Kearns

Board Members: K. R. Coogan, G. R. Simmons, H. C. Simmons, T. P. Stafford, S. L. Watson, T. N. Worrell, P. J. Zucconi

Founded: 1950
Domicile: Delaware
Employees: 2,670

TJX Companies Inc. (The)

STANDARD &POOR'S

S&P Recommendation BUY ★★★★☆

Price	12-Mo. Target Price	Investment Style
$38.62 (as of Nov 27, 2009)	$44.00	Large-Cap Growth

GICS Sector Consumer Discretionary
Sub-Industry Apparel Retail

Summary TJX operates eight chains of off-price apparel and home fashion specialty stores in the U.S., Canada, Germany, Ireland and the U.K.

Key Stock Statistics (Source S&P, Vickers, company reports)

52-Wk Range	$40.64– 18.02	S&P Oper. EPS 2010**E**	2.62	Market Capitalization(B)	$16.369	Beta		0.62
Trailing 12-Month EPS	$2.49	S&P Oper. EPS 2011**E**	2.93	Yield (%)	1.24	S&P 3-Yr. Proj. EPS CAGR(%)		17
Trailing 12-Month P/E	15.5	P/E on S&P Oper. EPS 2010**E**	14.7	Dividend Rate/Share	$0.48	S&P Credit Rating		A
$10K Invested 5 Yrs Ago	$16,697	Common Shares Outstg. (M)	423.9	Institutional Ownership (%)	91			

Price Performance

30-Week Mov. Avg. · · · 10-Week Mov. Avg. – - **GAAP Earnings vs. Previous Year**   Volume Above Avg. ▮▮▮ STARS
12-Mo. Target Price — Relative Strength — ▲ Up ▼ Down ▶ No Change   Below Avg. ▮▮▮ ★

Options: ASE, CBOE

Analysis prepared by **Jason N. Asaeda** on October 20, 2009, when the stock traded at **$ 38.70**.

Highlights

► On a constant currency basis, we project consolidated same-store sales to increase 5% in FY 10 (Jan.) and 2% in FY 11. Across TJX's divisions, we believe that a continued focus on off-price buys (purchases made opportunistically and closer to need during a season), as well as moderate to better brands, will drive improved sales productivity. We also anticipate strengthening sales of home fashions at the company's Marmaxx and HomeGoods divisions, reflecting improved merchandising. Coupled with planned expansion in the U.S., Canada and Europe, we expect net sales to reach $20.2 billion in FY 10 and $21.1 billion in FY 11.

► Despite foreign currency headwinds in FY 10 and new store expenses, we forecast annual operating margin expansion supported by an increase in off-price buys, which carry higher mark-ups than upfront buys (purchases made before or early in a season), lower markdowns as a result of improved inventory management, and cost controls. TJX is targeting $150 million in FY 10 expense reductions.

► Factoring in likely share repurchase activity, we see EPS of $2.60 in FY 10 and $2.90 in FY 11.

Investment Rationale/Risk

► Our buy recommendation on the shares is based on valuation. We think TJX, with what we view as its compelling values on brand-name merchandise, is gaining marketshare at a time when consumers are growing increasingly cost-conscious. We also see the company's core Marmaxx division generating ample operating cash flow to fund various growth initiatives such as expansion of T.K. Maxx in Germany and HomeSense in the U.K.; further testing of the Marshalls Shoe Mega Shop (U.S.) and StyleSense (Canada) family footwear and accessories retail concepts; investments in infrastructure; and about $625 million in additional share buybacks in FY 10.

► Risks to our recommendation and target price include sales shortfalls due to changes in consumer spending habits and buying preferences; merchandise availability; increased promotional activity by competitors, particularly bankruptcy-related clearance sales in the U.S.; and further declines in both the Canadian dollar and the British pound.

► Our 12-month target price of $44 applies a forward P/E multiple of 15.2X, TJX's 10-year historical average, to our FY 11 EPS estimate.

Qualitative Risk Assessment

LOW	MEDIUM	HIGH

Our risk assessment reflects our view of TJX's leadership position in off-price retail and promising new merchandising and productivity initiatives that could boost sales and profit margins. This is offset by what we see as an inconsistent earnings track record and an uncertain outlook for consumer discretionary spending.

Quantitative Evaluations

S&P Quality Ranking   A+

D	C	B-	B	B+	A-	A	A+

Relative Strength Rank   MODERATE

64

LOWEST = 1   HIGHEST = 99

Revenue/Earnings Data

Revenue (Million $)

	1Q	2Q	3Q	4Q	Year
2010	4,354	4,748	5,245	--	--
2009	4,364	4,621	4,762	5,380	19,000
2008	4,108	4,313	4,737	5,488	18,647
2007	3,871	3,964	4,473	5,097	17,405
2006	3,652	3,648	4,042	4,716	16,058
2005	3,353	3,414	3,817	4,329	14,913

Earnings Per Share ($)

2010	0.49	0.61	0.81	E0.71	E2.62
2009	0.43	0.45	0.58	0.58	2.07
2008	0.34	0.45	0.54	0.66	1.66
2007	0.34	0.29	0.48	0.51	1.63
2006	0.28	0.23	0.32	0.60	1.41
2005	0.32	0.23	0.40	0.35	1.30

Fiscal year ended Jan. 31. Next earnings report expected: Late February. EPS Estimates based on S&P Operating Earnings; historical GAAP earnings are as reported.

Dividend Data (Dates: mm/dd Payment Date: mm/dd/yy)

Amount ($)	Date Decl.	Ex-Div. Date	Stk. of Record	Payment Date
0.110	12/02	02/10	02/12	03/05/09
0.120	04/07	05/12	05/14	06/04/09
0.120	06/02	08/11	08/13	09/03/09
0.120	09/21	11/09	11/12	12/03/09

Dividends have been paid since 1980. Source: Company reports.

Please read the Required Disclosures and Analyst Certification on the last page of this report.

TJX Companies Inc. (The)

STANDARD &POOR'S

Business Summary October 20, 2009

COMPANY PROFILE. With about $19 billion in annual revenues, TJX Companies is the largest U.S. off-price family apparel and home fashion retailer via its eight retail concepts. As of October 8, 2009, the company's core Marmaxx Group division operated 885 T.J. Maxx and 816 Marshalls stores. TJX also operated 147 A.J. Wright units and 323 HomeGoods stores in the U.S.; 12 HomeSense and 249 T.K. Maxx stores in Europe; and 77 HomeSense, 207 Winners and three StyleSense (a new family footwear and accessories test concept) stores in Canada. The company sold its 34-store Bob's Store chain to private equity firms Versa Capital Management and Crystal Capital in August 2008.

TJX believes it derives a competitive advantage by offering rapidly changing assortments of affordable, quality brand name and designer merchandise. Prices at T.J. Maxx and Marshalls are usually 20% to 60% below department and specialty store regular prices. With over 2,500 stores, the company has substantial buying power with more than 10,000 vendors worldwide. TJX purchases later in the buying cycle than department and specialty stores. Generally, purchases are for current selling seasons, with a limited quantity of packaway inventory intended for a future selling season. A combination of opportunistic buying, an expansive distribution infrastructure, and a low expense structure enable the company to offer everyday savings to its customers.

PRIMARY BUSINESS DYNAMICS. TJX's primary growth drivers are new store openings and same-store sales (sales results for stores open for all or a portion of two consecutive fiscal years). From FY 00 through FY 06 (Jan.), the company increased its consolidated store count from 1,493 to 2,381 at a compound annual growth rate (CAGR) of about 8%. TJX reported a 7.1% increase in FY 06, down from 7.8% in FY 05, and an 11% run rate from FY 00 through FY 04. Growth slowed during this period with the maturing of the core Marmaxx division. From FY 07 through FY 09, the company targeted 4% to 5% annual unit growth as it implemented changes at A.J. Wright and HomeGoods to improve store operations. TJX grew its consolidated store count by 3.6% in FY 07, to 2,466, by 3.9% in FY 08, to 2,563, and by 3.5% in FY 09, to 2,652. Given a challenging retail environment, the company sees opportunities to negotiate more favorable leases and to relocate stores to better locations in FY 10. As a result, TJX has committed to fewer locations for FY 10, allowing the company to be very opportunistic.

Company Financials Fiscal Year Ended Jan. 31

Per Share Data ($)	2009	2008	2007	2006	2005	2004	2003	2002	2001	2000
Tangible Book Value	4.74	4.55	4.65	3.71	3.06	2.74	2.36	2.14	1.85	1.55
Cash Flow	2.97	2.43	2.35	2.23	1.86	1.75	1.46	1.34	1.23	1.08
Earnings	2.07	1.66	1.63	1.41	1.30	1.28	1.08	0.97	0.93	0.83
S&P Core Earnings	2.03	1.63	1.64	1.40	1.22	1.21	1.01	0.91	0.90	NA
Dividends	0.34	0.27	0.23	0.17	0.14	0.13	0.12	0.11	0.07	0.07
Payout Ratio	16%	16%	14%	12%	10%	10%	11%	11%	7%	8%
Calendar Year	2008	2007	2006	2005	2004	2003	2002	2001	2000	1999
Prices:High	37.52	32.46	29.84	25.96	26.82	23.70	22.45	20.30	15.75	18.50
Prices:Low	17.80	25.74	22.16	19.95	20.64	15.54	15.30	13.56	6.97	8.25
P/E Ratio:High	18	20	18	18	21	19	21	21	17	22
P/E Ratio:Low	9	16	14	14	16	12	14	14	7	10

Income Statement Analysis (Million $)

	2009	2008	2007	2006	2005	2004	2003	2002	2001	2000
Revenue	19,000	18,647	17,405	16,058	14,913	13,328	11,981	10,709	9,579	8,795
Operating Income	1,833	1,811	1,616	1,444	1,394	1,334	1,171	1,104	1,064	1,022
Depreciation	398	365	353	405	288	238	208	204	176	160
Interest Expense	38.1	39.9	39.2	39.0	33.5	27.3	25.4	25.6	34.7	20.4
Pretax Income	1,451	1,243	1,247	1,009	1,080	1,068	938	874	865	854
Effective Tax Rate	37.0%	37.9%	37.7%	31.6%	38.5%	38.4%	38.3%	38.2%	37.8%	38.3%
Net Income	915	772	777	690	664	658	578	540	538	527
S&P Core Earnings	893	756	778	687	615	619	546	506	519	NA

Balance Sheet & Other Financial Data (Million $)

	2009	2008	2007	2006	2005	2004	2003	2002	2001	2000
Cash	454	733	857	466	307	246	492	493	133	372
Current Assets	3,626	3,992	3,749	3,140	2,905	2,452	2,241	2,116	1,722	1,701
Total Assets	6,178	6,600	6,086	5,496	5,075	4,397	3,940	3,596	2,932	2,805
Current Liabilities	2,768	2,761	2,383	2,252	2,204	1,691	1,566	1,315	1,229	1,366
Long Term Debt	384	853	808	807	599	692	694	702	319	319
Common Equity	2,135	2,131	2,290	1,893	1,653	1,552	1,409	1,341	1,219	1,119
Total Capital	2,646	3,028	3,120	2,700	2,405	2,369	2,145	2,043	1,538	1,439
Capital Expenditures	583	527	378	496	429	409	397	449	257	239
Cash Flow	1,313	1,137	1,130	1,096	953	897	786	744	714	687
Current Ratio	1.3	1.5	1.6	1.4	1.3	1.5	1.4	1.6	1.4	1.2
% Long Term Debt of Capitalization	14.5	28.2	25.9	29.9	24.9	29.2	32.3	34.4	20.8	22.2
% Net Income of Revenue	4.8	4.1	4.5	4.3	4.5	4.9	4.8	5.0	5.6	6.0
% Return on Assets	14.3	12.2	13.4	13.1	14.0	15.8	15.3	16.6	18.8	19.0
% Return on Equity	42.9	34.9	37.1	37.9	41.4	44.5	42.1	42.2	46.0	45.0

Data as orig reptd.; bef. results of disc opers/spec. items. Per share data adj. for stk. divs.; EPS diluted. E-Estimated. NA-Not Available. NM-Not Meaningful. NR-Not Ranked. UR-Under Review.

Office: 770 Cochituate Road, Framingham, MA 01701-4666.
Telephone: 508-390-1000.
Website: http://www.tjx.com
Chrmn: B. Cammarata

Pres & CEO: C.M. Meyrowitz
EVP, CFO, Chief Admin Officer & Chief Acctg Officer: J.G. Naylor
EVP, Secy & General Counsel: A. McCauley
Investor Contact: S. Lang (508-390-2323)

Board Members: J. B. Alvarez, A. Bennett, D. A. Brandon, B. Cammarata, D. T. Ching, M. Hines, A. B. Lane, C. M. Meyrowitz, J. F. O'Brien, R. F. Shapiro, W. B. Shire, F. H. Wiley

Founded: 1956
Domicile: Delaware
Employees: 133,000

The McGraw·Hill Companies

Torchmark Corp

STANDARD &POOR'S

S&P Recommendation SELL ★★☆☆☆

Price	12-Mo. Target Price	Investment Style
$42.62 (as of Nov 27, 2009)	$38.00	Large-Cap Blend

GICS Sector Financials
Sub-Industry Life & Health Insurance

Summary This financial services company derives most of its earnings from life and health insurance operations.

Key Stock Statistics (Source S&P, Vickers, company reports)

52-Wk Range	$47.25– 16.16	S&P Oper. EPS 2009**E**	5.93	Market Capitalization(B)	$3.528	Beta		1.70
Trailing 12-Month EPS	$5.13	S&P Oper. EPS 2010**E**	6.10	Yield (%)	1.41	S&P 3-Yr. Proj. EPS CAGR(%)		4
Trailing 12-Month P/E	8.3	P/E on S&P Oper. EPS 2009**E**	7.2	Dividend Rate/Share	$0.60	S&P Credit Rating		A
$10K Invested 5 Yrs Ago	$8,057	Common Shares Outstg. (M)	82.8	Institutional Ownership (%)	75			

Price Performance

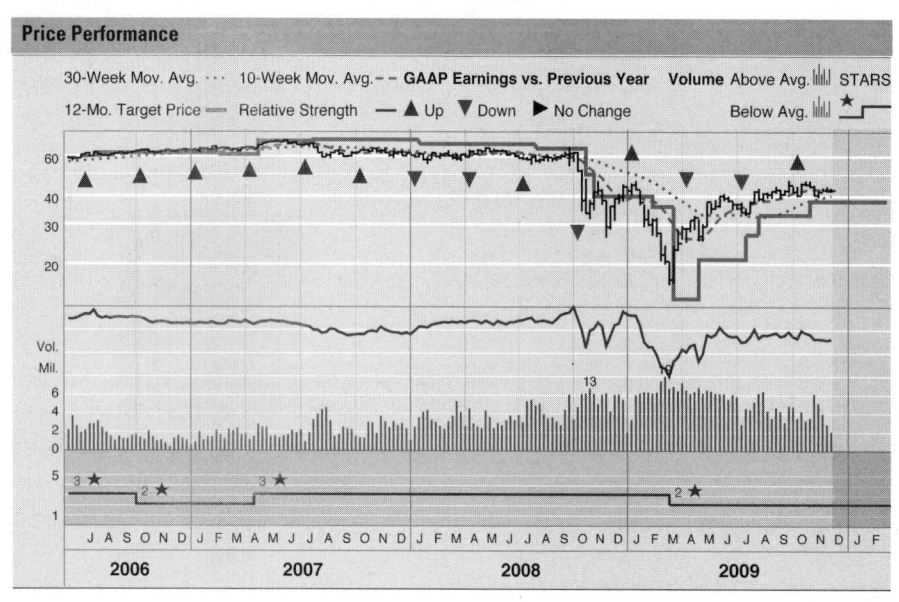

30-Week Mov. Avg. ···· 10-Week Mov. Avg. − − **GAAP Earnings vs. Previous Year** Volume Above Avg. ▐▐▌ STARS

12-Mo. Target Price — Relative Strength — ▲ Up ▼ Down ▶ No Change Below Avg. ▐▌ ★

Options: ASE

Analysis prepared by **Bret Howlett** on November 23, 2009, when the stock traded at **$ 42.32**.

Highlights

▸ We expect life underwriting margins to increase 7% in 2010 on solid premium growth and lower commissions, although we see a decline in health underwriting margins. We forecast total net sales growth will slow to the mid single-digits, helped by double-digit increases in life sales and higher agent productivity at American Income, partly offset by a significant drop in sales in health operations. We also forecast sales to fall slightly at the LNL Agency, due to agent retention issues and low persistency. We forecast sales will rise 5% at Direct Response, as the economy recovers.

▸ We forecast lower earnings at TMK's health business as the company focuses more on its life operations. The Health business fundamentals continue to be poor, in our opinion, due to intense competition and potential government regulation, and TMK believes its life products are more profitable. We forecast sales of TMK's Medicare Part-D business to be weak, although sales should improve in the second-half of the year.

▸ We estimate 2009 operating EPS of $5.93, and see EPS of $6.10 for 2010. Our estimates exclude realized investment gains or losses.

Investment Rationale/Risk

▸ Although TMK generates solid cash flow and statutory earnings, we think the company's financial position is weaker than many of its peers based on its above average exposure to lower quality corporate bonds. While we view positively the company reducing its below investment grade bonds to 10% of total fixed maturities, down from 15% at the end of the second-quarter, we continue to expect elevated investment losses, and capital charges stemming from adverse credit migration, to weigh on TMK's stock. In addition, we believe fundamentals in the Health business are poor and expect lower health income to remain a drag on earning. At current levels, we believe the shares are overvalued as they trade at a sizable premium to the group on a price-to-book value basis.

▸ Risks to our recommendation and target price include lower than expected investment losses, declines in competition for some products, lower loss ratios for TMK's Medicare Part D business, and a favorable mortality experience.

▸ Our 12-month target price of $38 is based on 0.9X our 2010 book value estimate, in line with the peer group average, but below historical levels.

Qualitative Risk Assessment

LOW	MEDIUM	HIGH

Our risk assessment reflects our view of the company's below peer average capital cushion and potential for further investment losses in its fixed income portfolio. This is offset by TMK's varied product lineup and limited exposure to the equity markets. Also, we think TMK generates strong cash flows and statutory earnings and uses excess cash flow to pay its dividend.

Quantitative Evaluations

S&P Quality Ranking A

D	C	B-	B	B+	A-	A	A+

Relative Strength Rank MODERATE

50

LOWEST = 1 HIGHEST = 99

Revenue/Earnings Data

Revenue (Million $)

	1Q	2Q	3Q	4Q	Year
2009	809.6	819.7	784.9	--	--
2008	872.4	860.5	753.4	840.6	2,758
2007	906.0	876.6	863.6	840.5	3,487
2006	857.0	869.1	837.9	857.1	3,421
2005	783.0	804.8	769.0	769.1	3,126
2004	772.5	764.0	774.2	760.8	3,072

Earnings Per Share ($)

	1Q	2Q	3Q	4Q	Year
2009	0.91	1.38	1.22	E1.45	E5.93
2008	1.29	1.47	0.72	1.61	5.11
2007	1.37	1.32	1.41	1.41	5.50
2006	1.16	1.26	1.28	1.43	5.13
2005	1.09	1.25	1.14	1.21	4.68
2004	1.05	1.04	1.12	1.05	4.25

Fiscal year ended Dec. 31. Next earnings report expected: Early February. EPS Estimates based on S&P Operating Earnings; historical GAAP earnings are as reported.

Dividend Data (Dates: mm/dd Payment Date: mm/dd/yy)

Amount ($)	Date Decl.	Ex-Div. Date	Stk. of Record	Payment Date
0.140	03/02	04/01	04/03	05/01/09
0.140	05/04	07/01	07/06	07/31/09
0.140	09/24	09/30	10/02	10/30/09
0.150	10/23	01/04	01/06	02/01/10

Dividends have been paid since 1933. Source: Company reports.

Please read the Required Disclosures and Analyst Certification on the last page of this report.

The **McGraw-Hill** Companies

Torchmark Corp

Business Summary November 23, 2009

CORPORATE OVERVIEW. TMK's subsidiaries offer a full line of nonparticipating ordinary individual life products and health insurance, as well as fixed and variable annuities. Traditional whole life insurance constituted 61% of life insurance in force at the end of 2008 as measured by annualized premiums, interest-sensitive whole life 6.6%, term life 29%, and other life products 3.2%. Medicare supplemental insurance accounted for 44% of supplemental health insurance in force at the end of 2008, as measured by annualized premiums, limited-benefit plans 39%, and Medicare Part D 17%. The number of individual health policies in force (excluding Medicare Part D) was 1.54 million at December 31, 2008, versus 1.56 million at prior year-end. Medicare Part D enrollees to begin the 2008 plan year were 158,000 at December 31, 2007, and the company believes enrollees are not expected to increase for the 2009 plan. Annuity separate account assets totaled $758.0 million at December 31, 2008, down nearly 47% from the year-earlier level.

Life segment premium revenue accounted for 59% of total premium revenue in 2008 (56% in 2007), the health segment 41% (44%), and the annuity segment 0.5% (0.7%).

CORPORATE STRATEGY. A key corporate strategy for TMK is to improve its distribution system. Distribution is through direct solicitation, independent agents, and exclusive agents. The Liberty National exclusive agency markets products to middle-income families in the Southeastern U.S. through full-time sales representatives. The American Income exclusive agency focuses on members of labor unions, credit unions, and other associations in the U.S., Canada and New Zealand. The United Investors agency markets to middle-income Americans through independent agents. The military agency consists of a nationwide independent agency comprised of former commissioned and noncommissioned military officers who sell exclusively to military officers and their families. The United American independent agency focuses primarily on health insurance in the U.S. and Canada to individuals over the age of 50. The United American branch office agency also focuses on health insurance to over-age-50 individuals through exclusive producing agents.

Company Financials Fiscal Year Ended Dec. 31

Per Share Data ($)	2008	2007	2006	2005	2004	2003	2002	2001	2000	1999
Tangible Book Value	19.52	31.74	31.39	29.49	28.16	25.39	20.91	17.24	14.34	12.05
Operating Earnings	NA	NA	NA	NA	NA	3.87	3.51	3.12	2.85	2.45
Earnings	5.11	5.50	5.13	4.68	4.25	3.73	3.18	3.11	2.82	1.93
S&P Core Earnings	5.81	5.35	5.07	4.29	4.03	3.68	3.39	2.73	NA	NA
Dividends	0.69	0.52	0.48	0.44	0.44	0.38	0.36	0.36	0.36	0.36
Payout Ratio	14%	9%	9%	9%	10%	10%	11%	12%	13%	19%
Prices:High	66.00	70.54	64.59	57.50	57.57	45.75	42.17	43.25	41.19	38.00
Prices:Low	26.27	58.50	53.91	50.05	44.61	33.00	30.02	32.56	18.75	24.56
P/E Ratio:High	13	13	13	12	14	12	13	14	15	20
P/E Ratio:Low	5	11	11	11	10	9	9	10	7	13

Income Statement Analysis (Million $)										
Life Insurance in Force	147,780	145,349	141,134	139,233	134,640	126,737	118,660	113,055	108,319	101,846
Premium Income:Life	1,617	1,570	1,524	1,468	1,396	1,246	1,221	1,144	1,082	1,018
Premium Income:A & H	1,127	1,237	1,238	1,015	1,049	1,034	1,019	1,011	911	825
Net Investment Income	671	649	629	603	577	557	519	492	472	447
Total Revenue	3,327	3,487	3,421	3,126	3,072	2,931	2,738	2,707	2,516	2,220
Pretax Income	715	797	774	732	721	655	580	597	553	393
Net Operating Income	NA	NA	NA	NA	NA	446	424	393	365	328
Net Income	452	528	519	495	476	430	383	391	362	259
S&P Core Earnings	514	514	512	455	452	424	408	343	NA	NA

Balance Sheet & Other Financial Data (Million $)										
Cash & Equivalent	223	193	185	178	164	155	140	129	154	127
Premiums Due	152	96.8	78.8	67.3	73.4	80.7	70.4	67.5	75.0	53.5
Investment Assets:Bonds	7,817	9,226	9,127	8,837	8,715	8,103	7,194	6,526	5,950	5,680
Investment Assets:Stocks	16.3	21.3	41.2	48.0	36.9	57.4	24.5	0.57	0.54	29.0
Investment Assets:Loans	360	344	329	317	338	704	401	393	374	245
Investment Assets:Total	8,489	9,772	9,703	9,649	9,405	8,795	7,784	7,154	6,471	6,399
Deferred Policy Costs	3,395	3,159	2,956	2,768	2,506	2,330	2,184	2,066	1,942	1,742
Total Assets	13,529	15,241	14,980	14,769	14,252	13,461	12,361	12,428	12,963	12,132
Debt	499	598	598	353	540	693	552	681	366	372
Common Equity	2,223	3,325	3,459	3,433	6,840	3,240	2,851	2,497	2,202	1,993
% Return on Revenue	13.6	15.1	15.2	15.8	15.5	14.7	14.0	14.4	14.4	11.7
% Return on Assets	3.1	3.5	3.5	3.4	3.4	3.3	3.1	3.1	2.9	2.2
% Return on Equity	16.2	15.6	15.1	14.5	7.1	14.1	14.3	16.6	17.2	12.2
% Investment Yield	7.3	6.7	6.5	6.3	6.4	6.7	7.0	7.2	7.5	6.8

Data as orig reptd.; bef. results of disc opers/spec. items. Per share data adj. for stk. divs.; EPS diluted. E-Estimated. NA-Not Available. NM-Not Meaningful. NR-Not Ranked. UR-Under Review.

Office: 3700 S Stonebridge Dr, McKinney, TX 75070-5934.
Telephone: 972-569-4000.
Website: http://www.torchmarkcorp.com
Chrmn & CEO: M.S. McAndrew

EVP & CFO: G.L. Coleman
EVP & Chief Admin Officer: V.D. Herbel
EVP & General Counsel: L.M. Hutchison
Chief Acctg Officer: D.H. Almond

Investor Contact: J.L. Lane (972-569-3627)
Board Members: C. E. Adair, D. L. Boren, J. M. Buchan, R. W. Ingram, J. L. Lanier, Jr., M. S. McAndrew, L. W. Newton, S. R. Perry, L. Smith, P. J. Zucconi

Auditor: DELOITTE & TOUCHE LLP
Founded: 1900
Domicile: Delaware
Employees: 3,605

Total System Services Inc.

STANDARD &POOR'S

S&P Recommendation	HOLD ★★★☆☆	Price $17.15 (as of Nov 27, 2009)	12-Mo. Target Price $17.00	Investment Style Large-Cap Growth

GICS Sector Information Technology
Sub-Industry Data Processing & Outsourced Services

Summary This company processes data, transactions, and payments for domestic and international issuers of credit, debit, commercial, and private-label cards.

Key Stock Statistics (Source S&P, Vickers, company reports)

52-Wk Range	$17.64–11.33	S&P Oper. EPS 2009**E**	1.11	Market Capitalization(B)	$3.382	Beta	0.87
Trailing 12-Month EPS	$1.13	S&P Oper. EPS 2010**E**	1.21	Yield (%)	1.63	S&P 3-Yr. Proj. EPS CAGR(%)	10
Trailing 12-Month P/E	15.2	P/E on S&P Oper. EPS 2009**E**	15.5	Dividend Rate/Share	$0.28	S&P Credit Rating	NA
$10K Invested 5 Yrs Ago	$7,852	Common Shares Outstg. (M)	197.2	Institutional Ownership (%)	58		

Price Performance

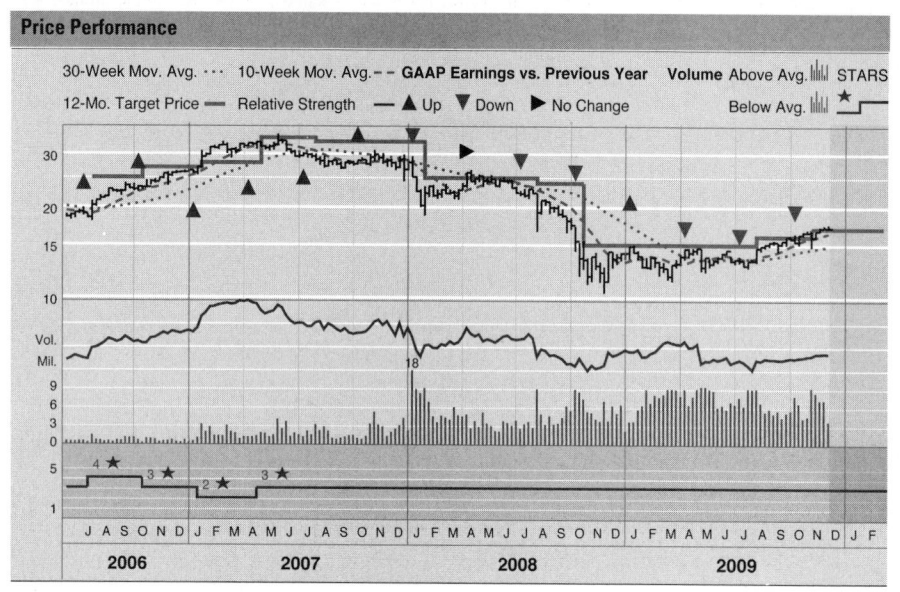

30-Week Mov. Avg. · · · 10-Week Mov. Avg. - - **GAAP Earnings vs. Previous Year** Volume Above Avg. |||| STARS
12-Mo. Target Price — Relative Strength — ▲ Up ▼ Down ► No Change Below Avg. |||| ★

Options: CBOE, Ph

Analysis prepared by **Zaineb Bokhari** on November 02, 2009, when the stock traded at **$ 16.35**.

Highlights

► We expect operating revenues (before reimbursable items) of approximately $1.4 billion in 2009, 3% lower than the previous year. We think TSS will see revenue growth in international markets, but we look for this to be offset by year-over-year declines at TSS's domestic customers and price erosion, attributable to customer loss, domestic economic weakness and a negative impact from fluctuations in foreign exchange rates. We expect total revenues to decline 5% to $1.69 billion in 2009. We forecast growth of 2% for operating and 5% for total revenues in 2010, with the difference due to higher expected reimbursable revenues.

► We look for operating margins of 24% in 2009, narrowing from 26% in 2008 (excluding items), reflecting our outlook for lower revenues and anticipated shifts in TSS's customer base, which the company is responding to with ongoing expense management measures. We expect slightly wider operating margins in 2010 reflecting our outlook for modest revenue growth.

► We estimate 2009 GAAP EPS of $1.11, down from $1.27 in 2008. Our 2010 EPS estimate is $1.21.

Investment Rationale/Risk

► TSS continues to navigate through a difficult period for its financial institution customers, some of whom have experienced considerable financial losses amid weak economic growth and tight credit markets. In this environment, card issuance has declined and issuers have been purging inactive consumer card accounts in an effort to trim expenses. Clients, also cautious about impending financial regulation, have delayed contracts. TSS continues to add new customers, but we expect the pace of account deconversions and purges to remain at high levels. We see TSS continuing to manage costs until the environment improves, but as it expands overseas, we expect investment.

► Risks to our recommendation and target price include greater competition from other payment processors, and an increased potential for business disruptions or loss due to ongoing industry consolidation. We expect the weak U.S. economy and tight credit markets to impact card growth.

► We derive our 12-month target price of $17 by applying a 14X P/E to our 2010 estimate, toward the lower end of the three-year forward P/E range for TSS shares of 13.5X-22.1X.

Qualitative Risk Assessment

LOW	MEDIUM	HIGH

Our risk assessment reflects our view that the company has managed itself through a difficult period of sizable customer losses. We continue to view TSS as a leading provider of card processing services, but we expect the company's account base to decline in 2009 given purges as customers remove inactive or undesirable accounts and issue fewer cards. We also expect price erosion in future quarters.

Quantitative Evaluations

S&P Quality Ranking   A

D	C	B-	B	B+	A-	A	A+

Relative Strength Rank   STRONG

78

LOWEST = 1   HIGHEST = 99

Revenue/Earnings Data

Revenue (Million $)

	1Q	2Q	3Q	4Q	Year
2009	408.9	412.0	432.3	--	--
2008	461.7	483.1	500.4	493.4	1,939
2007	429.6	460.2	457.6	458.5	1,806
2006	412.3	429.2	441.8	503.9	1,787
2005	350.0	410.2	422.0	420.7	1,603
2004	285.2	289.6	305.0	307.2	1,187

Earnings Per Share ($)

	1Q	2Q	3Q	4Q	Year
2009	0.26	0.27	0.29	E0.32	E1.11
2008	0.29	0.32	0.33	0.34	1.27
2007	0.29	0.33	0.35	0.23	1.20
2006	0.26	0.29	0.28	0.44	1.26
2005	0.23	0.26	0.24	0.25	0.99
2004	0.17	0.18	0.20	0.22	0.76

Fiscal year ended Dec. 31. Next earnings report expected: Late January. EPS Estimates based on S&P Operating Earnings; historical GAAP earnings are as reported.

Dividend Data (Dates: mm/dd Payment Date: mm/dd/yy)

Amount ($)	Date Decl.	Ex-Div. Date	Stk. of Record	Payment Date
0.070	12/03	12/16	12/18	01/02/09
0.070	02/25	03/17	03/19	04/01/09
0.070	06/02	06/16	06/18	07/01/09
0.070	09/03	09/15	09/17	10/01/09

Dividends have been paid since 1990. Source: Company reports.

Please read the Required Disclosures and Analyst Certification on the last page of this report.

The McGraw-Hill Companies

Total System Services Inc.

STANDARD
&POOR'S

Business Summary November 02, 2009

CORPORATE PROFILE. Total System Services provides electronic payment processing and associated services to financial and non-financial institutions in the U.S., Canada, Mexico, Honduras, Puerto Rico and Europe. Electronic payment processing services (which accounted for 65% of operating revenue in 2008, versus 67% in 2007) are generated primarily from charges based on the number of accounts on file, transactions and authorizations processed, statements mailed, and other processing services for cardholder accounts on file. As of December 2008, TSS had 347.6 million accounts on file, down from 375.5 million in 2007 and 461.4 million in 2006. Synovus Financial Corp., which owned an 80.7% interest in TSS in October 2007, completed its spin-off of TSS in December 2007. Services provided include processing for consumer, debit, commercial, stored value and retail cards, as well as for student loans. The company divides its services into three operating segments: North America Services (68.7% of 2008 revenues), Global Services (16.2%), and Merchant Services (15.2%).

PRIMARY BUSINESS DYNAMICS. TSS serves large financial institutions under long-term contracts. This results in revenue concentration that we view as a risk, since these large customers can be acquired, move to a competitor, or in some case, move processing of transactions in-house. In 2008, 2007 and 2006, the company's three largest customers contributed 32.4%, 32.4% and

39.2%, respectively, of total revenues. In 2006, Bank of America moved processing on its consumer card portfolio of about 46 million accounts in-house. In 2007, customer JPMorgan Chase ended its outsourcing agreement with TSS and moved its processing in-house, using a system licensed from TSS. Recent consolidation among financial institutions involving TSS clients include JPMorgan's acquisition of Washington Mutual Bank and Wells Fargo's acquisition of TSS client Wachovia.

MARKET PROFILE. The domestic market for third-party card processing is fairly concentrated, with three vendors serving most of the national market. In 2008, TSS believed that 42% of the domestic credit card processing was done using its systems. The company includes cards that are processed in-house, but using software licensed from TSS in this assessment of market share. On a comparable basis, this market share was unchanged from 2007, but up from 39% in 2006 and 2005 and 21% in 2004. The company's share of Visa and MasterCard U.S. commercial card processing fell to 85% in 2008, from 87% in 2007 and 86% in 2006.

Company Financials Fiscal Year Ended Dec. 31

Per Share Data ($)	2008	2007	2006	2005	2004	2003	2002	2001	2000	1999
Tangible Book Value	3.07	3.51	5.40	4.49	4.01	3.57	3.06	2.57	2.10	1.72
Cash Flow	1.53	1.44	2.20	1.75	1.31	1.21	1.01	0.82	0.70	0.61
Earnings	1.27	1.20	1.26	0.99	0.76	0.71	0.64	0.53	0.44	0.35
S&P Core Earnings	1.27	1.20	1.26	0.95	0.74	0.69	0.60	0.51	NA	NA
Dividends	0.28	3.31	0.27	0.22	0.14	0.08	0.07	0.06	0.05	0.04
Payout Ratio	22%	NM	21%	22%	18%	11%	11%	11%	11%	11%
Prices:High	28.19	35.05	26.61	25.88	31.27	31.50	29.44	35.84	22.75	26.25
Prices:Low	10.36	24.35	17.87	17.76	19.47	13.25	11.01	18.91	14.88	14.13
P/E Ratio:High	22	29	21	26	41	44	46	68	52	75
P/E Ratio:Low	8	20	14	18	26	19	17	36	34	40

Income Statement Analysis (Million $)										
Revenue	1,939	1,806	1,787	1,603	1,187	1,053	955	650	601	534
Operating Income	433	415	542	438	311	289	232	193	164	138
Depreciation	50.5	47.1	185	151	109	98.4	74.5	57.4	51.6	50.2
Interest Expense	11.3	3.13	0.57	0.37	0.94	Nil	1.10	Nil	Nil	Nil
Pretax Income	383	383	376	298	228	212	184	156	132	104
Effective Tax Rate	34.4%	37.5%	33.6%	34.7%	33.9%	33.4%	31.5%	33.9%	35.0%	33.8%
Net Income	250	237	249	195	151	141	126	103	85.6	68.6
S&P Core Earnings	250	237	249	188	145	136	119	99.5	NA	NA

Balance Sheet & Other Financial Data (Million $)										
Cash	220	240	389	238	232	123	113	56.0	80.1	54.9
Current Assets	625	587	745	512	448	274	266	206	211	180
Total Assets	1,539	1,479	1,634	1,411	1,282	1,001	783	652	604	457
Current Liabilities	249	274	296	277	278	147	114	103	147	103
Long Term Debt	210	257	3.63	3.56	4.51	29.7	0.07	Nil	Nil	0.16
Common Equity	989	844	1,217	1,013	865	733	602	501	409	334
Total Capital	1,260	1,177	1,296	1,106	1,004	854	668	550	446	354
Capital Expenditures	48.0	55.3	26.5	40.9	53.9	125	14.8	30.8	31.8	19.8
Cash Flow	301	285	434	346	259	239	200	160	137	119
Current Ratio	2.5	2.1	2.5	1.8	1.6	1.9	2.3	2.0	1.4	1.7
% Long Term Debt of Capitalization	16.7	21.8	0.3	0.3	0.4	3.5	0.0	Nil	Nil	0.0
% Net Income of Revenue	12.9	13.2	13.9	12.1	12.7	13.4	13.2	15.8	14.2	12.8
% Return on Assets	16.6	15.3	16.4	14.4	13.2	15.8	17.5	16.4	16.0	17.0
% Return on Equity	27.3	23.0	22.3	20.7	18.9	21.1	22.7	22.6	23.0	22.7

Data as orig reptd.; bef. results of disc opers/spec. items. Per share data adj. for stk. divs.; EPS diluted. E-Estimated. NA-Not Available. NM-Not Meaningful. NR-Not Ranked. UR-Under Review.

Office: One TSYS Wy, Columbus, GA 31902.
Telephone: 706-649-2267.
Email: ir@tsys.com
Website: http://www.tsys.com

Chrmn & CEO: P.W. Tomlinson
Pres & COO: M.T. Woods
EVP & CFO: J.B. Lipham
EVP & CTO: S.W. Humber

EVP, Chief Acctg Officer & Cntlr: D.K. Weaver
Investor Contact: S. Roberts (706-644-6081)
Board Members: R. E. Anthony, J. H. Blanchard, R. Y. Bradley, K. Cloninger, III, W. W. Driver, Jr., G. W. Garrard, Jr., S. E. Harris, M. H. Lampton, W. W. Miller, Jr., H. L. Page, P. W. Tomlinson, J. T. Turner, R. W. Ussery, M. T. Woods, J. D. Yancey, R. K. Yarbrough

Founded: 1982
Domicile: Georgia
Employees: 8,110

The McGraw-Hill Companies

Travelers Companies Inc (The)

STANDARD &POOR'S

S&P Recommendation	Price	12-Mo. Target Price	Investment Style
STRONG BUY ★★★★★	$51.65 (as of Nov 27, 2009)	$60.00	Large-Cap Value

GICS Sector Financials
Sub-Industry Property & Casualty Insurance

Summary Formed via the 2004 merger of Travelers Property Casualty Corp. and Saint Paul Cos., TRV is a leading provider of commercial property-liability and homeowners and auto insurance.

Key Stock Statistics (Source S&P, Vickers, company reports)

52-Wk Range	$54.47– 33.07	S&P Oper. EPS 2009**E**	5.50	Market Capitalization(B)	$28.220	Beta	0.69
Trailing 12-Month EPS	$5.38	S&P Oper. EPS 2010**E**	5.63	Yield (%)	2.56	S&P 3-Yr. Proj. EPS CAGR(%)	3
Trailing 12-Month P/E	9.6	P/E on S&P Oper. EPS 2009**E**	9.4	Dividend Rate/Share	$1.32	S&P Credit Rating	A-
$10K Invested 5 Yrs Ago	$15,118	Common Shares Outstg. (M)	546.4	Institutional Ownership (%)	86		

Price Performance

30-Week Mov. Avg. · · · 10-Week Mov. Avg. - - GAAP Earnings vs. Previous Year Volume Above Avg. STARS
12-Mo. Target Price — Relative Strength — ▲ Up ▼ Down ▶ No Change   Below Avg.

Options: ASE, CBOE, Ph

Analysis prepared by **Cathy A. Seifert** on November 06, 2009, when the stock traded at **$ 51.70**.

Highlights

▶ We expect earned premium growth of 1% to 3% in 2010, versus a fractional decline in earned premiums we see for 2009. This reflects our view of ongoing price competition in many core lines and the impact of a weak economic climate that we see affecting results in 2009. Our forecast of modestly higher premiums in 2010 is predicated on a modest economic recovery in the latter half of 2010, coupled with TRV's ability to leverage new business opportunities.

▶ We believe net investment income will advance about 8% to 10% in 2009, and more than 10% in 2010, versus a 21% decline reported for 2008, as improved claim trends enhanced cash flow trends.

▶ We estimate operating EPS of $5.50 in 2009 and $5.63 in 2010, versus operating EPS of $5.27 reported for 2008. Our 2009 estimate assumes that underwriting results will be aided by an unusually low level of catastrophe claims. Our forecast for 2010 assumes that catastrophe claims return to "normal" levels, and that prior-year loss reserve releases moderate, but that underwriting results remain profitable.

Investment Rationale/Risk

▶ Although our outlook remains tempered by concerns we have that both the underwriting and investment environments will remain challenging in 2009, we believe TRV's shares do not adequately reflect the actions the company has taken in recent years to improve its underwriting results and to better capitalize on what we see as a flight to quality within the property-casualty insurance market. We also view TRV as a prudent underwriter with an above-average quality balance sheet.

▶ Risks to our recommendation and target price include a deterioration in asbestos and environmental claims and reserve development, an erosion in underwriting trends, a surge in catastrophe losses, and an erosion in the credit quality of TRV's investment portfolio.

▶ Our 12-month target price of $60 assumes a forward price/earnings multiple of 10.7X our 2010 operating earnings per share estimate. This target multiple assumes TRV shares will trade at the lower end of their historical valuation range, but at a premium to some peers.

Qualitative Risk Assessment

LOW	MEDIUM	HIGH

Our risk assessment reflects our view of TRV as a leading property-casualty underwriter with a diversified mix of business and sound capital management practices. Offsetting this is our view that TRV may have to add to loss reserves for certain "long tail" liability lines of coverage, and could see impairments to its fixed income investment portfolio.

Quantitative Evaluations

S&P Quality Ranking   NR

D	C	B-	B	B+	A-	A	A+

Relative Strength Rank   MODERATE

69

LOWEST = 1   HIGHEST = 99

Revenue/Earnings Data

Revenue (Million $)

	1Q	2Q	3Q	4Q	Year
2009	5,735	6,162	6,327	--	--
2008	6,232	6,295	6,145	5,805	24,477
2007	6,427	6,612	6,526	6,491	26,017
2006	6,050	6,255	6,316	6,469	25,090
2005	6,105	6,037	6,042	6,181	24,365
2004	4,128	6,181	6,261	6,365	22,934

Earnings Per Share ($)

2009	1.11	1.27	1.65	E1.30	E5.50
2008	1.54	1.54	0.36	1.35	4.82
2007	1.56	1.86	1.81	1.64	6.86
2006	1.41	1.36	1.47	1.68	5.91
2005	1.25	1.33	0.11	0.26	2.95
2004	1.34	-0.42	0.50	0.44	1.53

Fiscal year ended Dec. 31. Next earnings report expected: Late January. EPS Estimates based on S&P Operating Earnings; historical GAAP earnings are as reported.

Dividend Data (Dates: mm/dd Payment Date: mm/dd/yy)

Amount ($)	Date Decl.	Ex-Div. Date	Stk. of Record	Payment Date
0.300	02/04	03/06	03/10	03/31/09
0.300	05/06	06/08	06/10	06/30/09
0.300	08/05	09/08	09/10	09/30/09
0.330	10/22	12/08	12/10	12/31/09

Dividends have been paid since 2003. Source: Company reports.

Travelers Companies Inc (The)

STANDARD &POOR'S

Business Summary November 06, 2009

CORPORATE OVERVIEW. The Travelers Companies (TRV) is a leading property-casualty underwriter. Net written premiums of $21.7 billion in 2008 (versus $21.6 billion in 2007) were divided as follows: business insurance 52%; personal lines 32%; and financial, professional and international lines 16% (all of which were unchanged from the business mix in 2007).

The business insurance lines segment offers a broad array of coverages distributed through about 6,300 independent brokers and agencies in the U.S. Business insurance net written premiums of $11.2 billion in 2008 were divided as follows: commercial multi-peril 26%, workers' compensation 22%, commercial automobile 17%, commercial property 17%, and general liability and other 18%. This segment's underwriting results in 2008 deteriorated slightly amid a slight increase in losses and a rise in underwriting expenses. The combined loss and expense ratio rose to 90.2% in 2008, from 87.8% in 2007.

The financial, professional and international lines segment underwrites a number of specialized lines of business, including lines of coverage related to the surety bond business, the construction industry, and certain types of professional and managerial liability. This unit operates throughout the U.S. and in the U.K., Canada and Ireland. Net written premiums of $3.5 billion in 2008

were divided as follows: general liability 26%, fidelity and surety 34%, international 36%, and other 4%. Underwriting results in this segment improved in 2008, largely due to well controlled underwriting expenses. As a result, the combined (loss and expense) ratio equaled 87.2% in 2008, versus 87.6% in 2007.

The personal lines segment underwrites an array of coverage for personal risks (primarily personal automobile and homeowners' coverage) via a network of independent agencies. Net premiums written of $7.0 billion in 2008 were divided as follows: personal auto 52%, and homeowners' and other 48%. At year-end 2008, the personal lines segment had approximately 7.4 million policies in force (consisting primarily of personal auto and homeowners' insurance policies). Underwriting results in 2008 deteriorated, reflecting higher catastrophe losses and a rise in loss costs (other than those associated with catastrophes) and an uptick in underwriting expenses. As a result, the combined ratio in 2008 was 97.0%, versus 86.8% in 2007.

Company Financials Fiscal Year Ended Dec. 31

Per Share Data ($)	2008	2007	2006	2005	2004	2003	2002	2001	2000	1999
Tangible Book Value	36.08	35.56	31.85	25.66	20.93	9.52	10.29	6.66	NA	NA
Operating Earnings	NA	NA	NA	NA	NA	NA	NA	NA	NA	NA
Earnings	4.82	6.86	5.91	2.95	1.53	1.68	0.23	1.06	1.71	1.48
S&P Core Earnings	5.10	6.67	5.87	2.87	1.50	3.71	0.14	2.42	NA	NA
Dividends	1.19	1.13	1.01	0.91	0.74	0.28	Nil	NA	NA	NA
Payout Ratio	25%	16%	17%	31%	48%	17%	Nil	NA	NA	NA
Prices:High	58.57	56.99	55.00	46.97	43.31	17.42	19.50	NA	NA	NA
Prices:Low	28.91	47.26	40.23	33.70	16.55	12.98	12.09	NA	NA	NA
P/E Ratio:High	12	8	9	16	28	10	85	NA	NA	NA
P/E Ratio:Low	6	7	7	11	11	8	53	NA	NA	NA

Income Statement Analysis (Million $)										
Premium Income	21,579	21,470	20,760	20,341	19,038	12,545	11,155	9,411	NA	NA
Net Investment Income	2,792	3,761	3,517	3,165	2,663	1,869	1,881	2,034	NA	NA
Other Revenue	106	825	813	859	20,271	725	1,234	786	NA	NA
Total Revenue	24,477	26,017	25,090	24,365	22,934	15,139	14,270	12,231	11,071	10,573
Pretax Income	3,716	6,216	5,725	2,671	1,128	2,229	-260	1,389	1,864	1,839
Net Operating Income	NA	NA	NA	NA	NA	NA	NA	NA	NA	NA
Net Income	2,924	4,601	4,208	2,061	955	1,696	216	1,062	1,312	1,136
S&P Core Earnings	3,087	4,464	4,171	2,001	937	1,615	41.1	803	NA	NA

Balance Sheet & Other Financial Data (Million $)										
Cash & Equivalent	369	1,132	1,286	1,098	933	714	432	865	196	NA
Premiums Due	5,954	6,142	6,181	6,124	6,201	4,090	3,861	NA	NA	NA
Investment Assets:Bonds	61,275	64,920	62,666	58,983	54,256	33,046	30,003	NA	NA	NA
Investment Assets:Stocks	379	488	476	579	791	733	852	NA	NA	NA
Investment Assets:Loans	Nil	Nil	Nil	145	191	211	258	32,843	NA	NA
Investment Assets:Total	70,199	74,818	72,268	68,287	64,710	38,652	38,425	32,619	30,754	NA
Deferred Policy Costs	1,774	1,809	1,615	1,527	1,559	925	873	NA	NA	NA
Total Assets	109,751	115,224	113,761	113,187	111,815	64,872	64,138	57,599	53,850	NA
Debt	6,181	6,242	4,588	5,850	5,709	2,675	2,744	3,755	NA	NA
Common Equity	25,230	26,504	25,006	33,077	32,323	11,987	10,137	9,729	9,214	NA
Property & Casualty:Loss Ratio	NA	56.6	57.5	71.9	NA	NA	NA	80.7	NA	NA
Property & Casualty:Expense Ratio	32.5	30.8	30.6	29.4	NA	NA	NA	27.3	NA	NA
Property & Casualty Combined Ratio	91.9	87.4	88.1	101.3	107.7	96.9	117.4	108.0	100.2	101.9
% Return on Revenue	12.0	17.8	20.3	8.5	4.2	11.2	1.6	8.7	11.9	10.7
% Return on Equity	11.3	17.9	17.8	6.3	3.7	15.3	NA	10.7	NA	NA

Data as orig reptd.; bef. results of disc opers/spec. items. Per share data adj. for stk. divs.; EPS diluted. E-Estimated. NA-Not Available. NM-Not Meaningful. NR-Not Ranked. UR-Under Review.

Office: 385 Washington Street, Saint Paul, MN 55102.
Telephone: 651-310-7911.
Website: http://www.stpaultravelers.com
Chrmn & CEO: J.S. Fishman

Pres & COO: B.W. MacLean
EVP & Chief Admin Officer: A. Bessette
EVP & Treas: M. Olivo
EVP & General Counsel: A.D. Schnitzer

Investor Contact: M. Parr (860-277-0779)
Board Members: A. L. Beller, J. H. Dasburg, J. M. Dolan, K. M. Duberstein, J. S. Fishman, L. G. Graev, P. L. Higgins, T. R. Hodgson, C. L. Killingsworth, Jr., R. I. Lipp, B. J. McGarvie, L. J. Thomsen

Auditor: KPMG
Founded: 1853
Domicile: Minnesota
Employees: 33,300

The McGraw-Hill Companies

STANDARD &POOR'S

T. Rowe Price Group Inc

S&P Recommendation HOLD ★★★☆☆	Price $47.37 (as of Nov 27, 2009)	12-Mo. Target Price $58.00	Investment Style Large-Cap Growth

GICS Sector Financials
Sub-Industry Asset Management & Custody Banks

Summary This company (formerly T. Rowe Price Associates) operates one of the largest no-load mutual fund complexes in the United States.

Key Stock Statistics (Source S&P, Vickers, company reports)

52-Wk Range	$55.48– 20.09	S&P Oper. EPS 2009**E**	1.60	Market Capitalization(B)	$12.198	Beta	1.79
Trailing 12-Month EPS	$1.17	S&P Oper. EPS 2010**E**	2.32	Yield (%)	2.11	S&P 3-Yr. Proj. EPS CAGR(%)	9
Trailing 12-Month P/E	40.5	P/E on S&P Oper. EPS 2009**E**	29.6	Dividend Rate/Share	$1.00	S&P Credit Rating	NA
$10K Invested 5 Yrs Ago	$17,456	Common Shares Outstg. (M)	257.5	Institutional Ownership (%)	73		

Price Performance

30-Week Mov. Avg. · · · 10-Week Mov. Avg. — GAAP Earnings vs. Previous Year   Volume Above Avg. STARS
12-Mo. Target Price — Relative Strength   ▲ Up   ▼ Down   ► No Change   Below Avg.   ★

Options: ASE, CBOE, P, Ph

Analysis prepared by **Matthew Albrecht** on October 29, 2009, when the stock traded at **$ 50.48**.

Highlights

► Equity markets have rebounded sharply since March lows, with the S&P 500 up more than 50% since that time. We look for relatively strong flows to TROW's target-date retirement funds to continue, and sales have again outpaced redemptions in its mutual funds overall. However, we expect an unfavorable asset mix will continue to pressure management fee income, as will lower average asset balances. Still, with more than 70% of assets in equity products, TROW should benefit more than peers from the market rebound. We think revenues will slide more than 11% in 2009 before better than 20% growth in 2010, helped by higher average assets and an improving product mix.

► We expect the pretax margin to contract in 2009 before improving in 2010. We look for most operating costs to rise on a relative basis compressing margins. And while compensation will likely be elevated on a relative basis, headcount reductions should help to mitigate the impact on margins. We also expect a return to investment gains, helping non-operating income.

► We see EPS of $1.60 in 2009 and $2.32 in 2010.

Investment Rationale/Risk

► We believe TROW's relative investment performance is strong, and we think this will drive net client inflows into its mutual funds and separately managed accounts as market conditions improve. We also view favorably its low debt levels, consistent dividend payout and continued share repurchases. Regarding corporate governance, we view stock option grants as generous, especially given reductions at competitors, and we would like to see more independent directors on the board.

► Risks to our recommendation and target price include stock and bond market depreciation, heightened regulatory scrutiny, and increased competition.

► The shares recently traded at 31.4X our 2009 EPS estimate. Our 12-month target price of $58 is equal to 25.9X our forward 12-months earnings estimate of $2.24, which is a premium-to-peers multiple to reflect our view of TROW's well-capitalized balance sheet and strong relative fund performance.

Qualitative Risk Assessment

LOW	MEDIUM	HIGH

Our risk assessment reflects the company's strong market share and our view of its consistent net client inflows and impressive relative investment performance, taking into account industry cyclicality.

Quantitative Evaluations

S&P Quality Ranking   A-

D	C	B-	B	B+	A-	A	A+

Relative Strength Rank   MODERATE

44

LOWEST = 1   HIGHEST = 99

Revenue/Earnings Data

Revenue (Million $)

	1Q	2Q	3Q	4Q	Year
2009	384.5	442.2	498.1	--	--
2008	560.4	587.7	555.9	417.3	2,121
2007	508.4	551.1	571.0	597.8	2,233
2006	429.3	446.0	450.6	489.1	1,819
2005	358.0	364.5	389.6	403.8	1,516
2004	306.5	310.5	317.0	346.4	1,280

Earnings Per Share ($)

2009	0.19	0.38	0.50	E0.53	E1.60
2008	0.55	0.60	0.56	0.09	1.82
2007	0.51	0.58	0.63	0.68	2.40
2006	0.42	0.49	0.46	0.53	1.90
2005	0.35	0.38	0.43	0.43	1.58
2004	0.29	0.30	0.31	0.36	1.26

Fiscal year ended Dec. 31. Next earnings report expected: Late January. EPS Estimates based on S&P Operating Earnings; historical GAAP earnings are as reported.

Dividend Data (Dates: mm/dd Payment Date: mm/dd/yy)

Amount ($)	Date Decl.	Ex-Div. Date	Stk. of Record	Payment Date
0.250	02/12	03/12	03/16	03/30/09
0.250	06/04	06/11	06/15	06/29/09
0.250	09/03	09/10	09/14	09/28/09
0.250	10/19	12/11	12/15	12/29/09

Dividends have been paid since 1986. Source: Company reports.

Please read the Required Disclosures and Analyst Certification on the last page of this report.

The **McGraw·Hill** Companies

T. Rowe Price Group Inc

STANDARD &POOR'S

Business Summary October 29, 2009

CORPORATE OVERVIEW. T. Rowe Price Group (TROW) is the successor to an investment counseling business formed by the late Thomas Rowe Price, Jr. in 1937. It is now the investment adviser to the T. Rowe Price family of no-load mutual funds, and is one of the largest publicly held U.S. mutual fund complexes. At the end of 2008, TROW had about $276 billion in assets under management, down from $400 billion at the end of 2007. As of year-end 2008, 71% of assets under management were invested in stock and blended asset portfolios, and 29% were invested in bond and money market portfolios.

T. Rowe Price offers mutual funds that employ a broad range of investment styles, including growth, value, sector-focused, tax-efficient, and quantitative index-oriented approaches. The company's investment approach is based upon a strong commitment to proprietary research, sophisticated risk-management processes, and a strict adherence to stated investment objectives. The company employs both fundamental and quantitative methods in performing security analyses, using internal equity and fixed income investment research capabilities. We believe T. Rowe Price's broad line of no-load mutual funds makes it easy for investors to reallocate assets among funds (which is not the case at some smaller fund companies), contributing to in-creased client retention.

All of the company's funds are sold without a sales commission, known as no-load funds. TROW also manages private accounts for individuals and institutions. At the end of 2007 (latest available), assets under management were sourced about 20%-30% from each of the following: individual U.S. investors, U.S. defined contribution retirement plans, third-party distributors, and institutional investors. Revenues primarily come from investment advisory fees for managing portfolios, which depend largely on the total value and composition of assets under management. At December 31, 2007 (latest available), the six largest Price funds--Equity Income, Mid-Cap Growth, Growth Stock, Blue Chip Growth, Capital Appreciation and Equity Index 500---accounted for 25% of assets under management and nearly 28% of 2007 investment advisory revenues.

Company Financials Fiscal Year Ended Dec. 31

Per Share Data ($)	2008	2007	2006	2005	2004	2003	2002	2001	2000	1999
Tangible Book Value	7.09	7.97	6.63	5.21	3.98	2.66	1.91	1.68	1.21	3.18
Cash Flow	2.05	2.60	2.07	1.80	1.48	1.11	0.96	20.71	1.33	1.13
Earnings	1.82	2.40	1.90	1.58	1.26	0.89	0.76	0.76	1.04	0.93
S&P Core Earnings	2.03	2.40	1.90	1.43	1.16	0.78	0.67	0.65	NA	NA
Dividends	0.96	0.75	0.59	0.49	0.40	0.35	0.33	0.31	0.27	0.20
Payout Ratio	53%	31%	31%	31%	32%	40%	43%	40%	26%	22%
Prices:High	70.20	65.46	48.50	37.70	31.70	23.80	21.35	21.97	24.97	21.63
Prices:Low	24.26	44.59	34.87	27.10	21.92	19.19	10.63	11.72	15.03	12.94
P/E Ratio:High	39	27	26	24	25	27	28	29	24	23
P/E Ratio:Low	13	19	18	17	17	22	14	15	14	14

Income Statement Analysis (Million $)	2008	2007	2006	2005	2004	2003	2002	2001	2000	1999
Income Interest	6.40	5.90	5.40	4.28	3.78	3.91	3.06	32.8	59.1	37.5
Income Other	2,115	2,227	1,814	1,512	1,277	995	923	995	1,153	999
Total Income	2,121	2,233	1,819	1,516	1,280	999	926	1,028	1,212	1,036
General Expenses	1,206	1,179	982	814	638	585	552	603	690	589
Interest Expense	5.00	4.80	4.30	4.03	3.30	3.29	4.96	12.7	9.72	Nil
Depreciation	61.7	54.0	47.0	42.0	40.0	45.3	50.6	80.5	53.7	32.6
Net Income	491	671	530	431	337	227	194	196	269	239
S&P Core Earnings	548	671	530	391	309	198	169	167	NA	NA

Balance Sheet & Other Financial Data (Million $)	2008	2007	2006	2005	2004	2003	2002	2001	2000	1999
Cash	619	785	773	804	500	237	111	79.7	80.5	358
Receivables	177	265	224	175	158	121	96.8	104	131	122
Cost of Investments	721	1,002	762	378	329	273	216	154	250	279
Total Assets	2,819	3,177	2,765	2,311	1,929	1,547	1,370	1,313	1,469	998
Loss Reserve	Nil	Nil	Nil	Nil	Nil	Nil	Nil	Nil	Nil	Nil
Short Term Debt	Nil	Nil	Nil	Nil	Nil	Nil	Nil	Nil	Nil	Nil
Capitalization:Debt	Nil	Nil	Nil	Nil	Nil	Nil	Nil	104	312	17.7
Capitalization:Equity	2,489	2,777	2,427	2,036	1,697	1,329	1,189	1,078	991	770
Capitalization:Total	2,489	2,777	2,427	2,036	1,697	1,329	1,189	1,181	1,304	848
Price Times Book Value:High	9.0	8.2	7.3	7.2	7.9	9.0	11.2	13.1	20.6	6.8
Price Times Book Value:Low	3.4	5.6	5.3	5.2	5.5	7.2	5.6	7.0	12.4	4.1
Cash Flow	553	725	577	473	377	273	245	276	323	272
% Expense/Operating Revenue	56.8	55.4	52.3	56.7	63.8	65.8	65.7	67.8	62.2	60.0
% Earnings & Depreciation/Assets	18.4	24.4	22.7	22.3	21.7	18.7	18.3	19.9	26.2	30.3

Data as orig reptd.; bef. results of disc opers/spec. items. Per share data adj. for stk. divs.; EPS diluted. E-Estimated. NA-Not Available. NM-Not Meaningful. NR-Not Ranked. UR-Under Review.

Office: 100 East Pratt Street, Baltimore, MD 21202.
Telephone: 410-345-2000.
Email: info@troweprice.com
Website: http://www.troweprice.com

Chrmn: B.C. Rogers
Pres & CEO: J.A. Kennedy
Vice Chrmn: E.C. Bernard
CFO: K.V. Moreland

Chief Acctg Officer & Treas: J.P. Croteau
Board Members: E. C. Bernard, J. T. Brady, J. A. Broaddus, Jr., D. B. Hebb, Jr., J. A. Kennedy, B. C. Rogers, A. Sommer, D. S. Taylor, A. M. Whittemore

Founded: 1937
Domicile: Maryland
Employees: 5,385

The McGraw-Hill Companies

Tyson Foods Inc.

STANDARD &POOR'S

S&P Recommendation BUY ★★★★☆

Price	12-Mo. Target Price	Investment Style
$12.29 (as of Nov 27, 2009)	$15.00	Large-Cap Blend

GICS Sector Consumer Staples
Sub-Industry Packaged Foods & Meats

Summary Tyson is the world's largest supplier of beef, chicken and pork products.

Key Stock Statistics (Source S&P, Vickers, company reports)

52-Wk Range	$14.25– 5.21	S&P Oper. EPS 2010**E**	0.95	Market Capitalization(B)	$3.769	Beta	1.24
Trailing 12-Month EPS	$-1.44	S&P Oper. EPS 2011**E**	NA	Yield (%)	1.30	S&P 3-Yr. Proj. EPS CAGR(%)	16
Trailing 12-Month P/E	NM	P/E on S&P Oper. EPS 2010**E**	12.9	Dividend Rate/Share	$0.16	S&P Credit Rating	BB
$10K Invested 5 Yrs Ago	$7,812	Common Shares Outstg. (M)	376.7	Institutional Ownership (%)	84		

Price Performance

30-Week Mov. Avg. · · · 10-Week Mov. Avg. – – **GAAP Earnings vs. Previous Year** Volume Above Avg. STARS
12-Mo. Target Price — Relative Strength — ▲ Up ▼ Down ► No Change Below Avg. ★

Options: ASE, CBOE, P

Qualitative Risk Assessment

LOW	MEDIUM	HIGH

Our risk assessment reflects the company's cyclical operations, which are significantly affected by exposure to commodity crop and meat markets, and regulations related to international trade.

Quantitative Evaluations

S&P Quality Ranking B-

D	C	B-	B	B+	A-	A	A+

Relative Strength Rank MODERATE

39

LOWEST = 1   HIGHEST = 99

Revenue/Earnings Data

Revenue (Million $)

	1Q	2Q	3Q	4Q	Year
2009	6,521	6,307	66,620	7,214	26,704
2008	6,766	6,612	6,849	7,201	26,862
2007	6,558	6,501	6,958	6,883	26,900
2006	6,454	6,251	6,383	6,471	25,559
2005	6,452	6,359	6,708	6,495	26,014
2004	6,505	6,153	6,634	7,149	26,441

Earnings Per Share ($)

2009	-0.30	-0.24	0.37	-1.22	-1.47
2008	0.10	-0.01	-0.01	0.13	0.24
2007	0.16	0.20	0.31	0.09	0.75
2006	0.11	-0.37	-0.15	-0.15	-0.56
2005	0.14	0.21	0.36	0.28	0.99
2004	0.16	0.33	0.45	0.19	1.13

Fiscal year ended Sep. 30. Next earnings report expected: Late January. EPS Estimates based on S&P Operating Earnings; historical GAAP earnings are as reported.

Highlights

► The 12-month target price for TSN has recently been changed to $15.00 from $14.00. The Highlights section of this Stock Report will be updated accordingly.

Investment Rationale/Risk

► The Investment Rationale/Risk section of this Stock Report will be updated shortly. For the latest News story on TSN from MarketScope, see below.

► 11/23/09 11:48 am ET ... S&P REITERATES BUY OPINION ON SHARES OF TYSON FOODS (TSN 12.99****): Before a special item, Sep-Q EPS from continuing operations of $0.28 vs. $0.12 exceeds our view by $0.04. Also, although we are increasing our projections for interest expense and tax rate in FY 10 (Sep.), we are keeping our FY 10 EPS estimate at $0.95. We expect FY 10 to benefit from an improving global economic environment. We look for stronger export demand to help bolster some product pricing. We are raising our 12-month target price to $15 from $14, which reflects a target P/E closer to a historic median. The shares have an indicated dividend yield of 1.2%. /T.Graves-CFA

Dividend Data (Dates: mm/dd Payment Date: mm/dd/yy)

Amount ($)	Date Decl.	Ex-Div. Date	Stk. of Record	Payment Date
0.040	02/06	05/28	06/01	06/15/09
0.040	05/08	08/28	09/01	09/15/09
0.040	07/31	11/27	12/01	12/15/09
0.040	11/23	02/25	03/01	03/15/10

Dividends have been paid since 1976. Source: Company reports.

Please read the Required Disclosures and Analyst Certification on the last page of this report.

Tyson Foods Inc.

STANDARD &POOR'S

Business Summary November 06, 2009

CORPORATE OVERVIEW. Tyson Foods is the world's largest producer of beef and one of the largest chicken and pork producers in the world. The company holds about 22% of the U.S. beef market, 20% of the chicken production market, and 17% of the pork market. Its goal is to become the primary protein provider for its customers. The company exports to more than 90 countries including Canada, China, Europe, Japan, Mexico, Russia and South Korea.

CORPORATE STRATEGY. The company's strategy is to discover and sell market leading products and services to grow the Tyson Foods brand. It opened a discovery center in early 2007 in which it operates 19 test kitchens. These kitchens are used to develop new products for direct shipment to stores for testing. As of February 2008, 41 new products and concepts were either in testing or had been launched. The company utilizes its scale and diversified product mix as a competitive advantage to gain additional market share in each of the product categories in which it operates. Its major operational segments include beef, chicken, pork and prepared foods.

The beef segment (43% of FY 08 (Sep.) revenues) includes the slaughter of live cattle and fabrication into primal and sub-primal meat cuts and case-ready products. Operations reduce live cattle to dressed carcasses and allied prod-

ucts for sales to further processors. The company markets its products to food retailers, distributors, wholesalers, restaurants and hotel chains, and other food processors. Allied products are marketed to manufacturers of pharmaceuticals and animal feeds. The company's primary supply of live cattle is purchased on a daily basis.

The chicken segment (33%) includes fresh, frozen and value-added chicken products sold through domestic foodservice, domestic retail markets for at-home consumption, wholesale club markets targeted to small food service operations, and individuals and distributors that deliver to restaurants, schools and international markets throughout the world. Also included in this segment are sales from allied products and TSN's chicken breeding stock subsidiary. The segment's primary raw material is live chickens that are raised by independent contractors. Profitability is partially dependent on corn and soybean meal, which represents about 40% of the cost of growing a chicken.

Company Financials Fiscal Year Ended Sep. 30

Per Share Data ($)	2009	2008	2007	2006	2005	2004	2003	2002	2001	2000
Tangible Book Value	5.98	6.30	5.96	5.05	5.66	4.49	3.17	2.92	1.71	NM
Cash Flow	NA	1.57	2.20	1.31	2.39	2.50	2.26	2.39	1.91	-1.97
Earnings	-1.47	0.24	0.75	-0.56	0.99	1.13	0.96	1.08	0.40	0.68
S&P Core Earnings	0.05	0.20	0.64	-0.56	1.06	1.10	0.64	1.02	0.39	NA
Dividends	0.16	0.16	0.16	0.16	0.16	0.16	0.16	0.16	0.16	0.16
Payout Ratio	NM	67%	21%	NM	16%	14%	17%	15%	40%	24%
Prices:High	14.25	67.00	24.32	17.33	19.91	21.28	15.10	15.71	14.20	17.38
Prices:Low	7.51	4.40	13.50	12.57	12.50	12.97	7.25	9.27	8.10	8.50
P/E Ratio:High	NM	81	32	NM	20	19	16	15	35	26
P/E Ratio:Low	NM	18	18	NM	13	11	8	9	20	13

Income Statement Analysis (Million $)										
Revenue	26,704	26,862	26,900	25,559	26,014	26,441	24,549	23,367	10,751	7,268
Operating Income	NA	878	1,130	510	1,266	1,415	837	1,407	650	643
Depreciation	496	471	514	517	501	490	458	467	335	294
Interest Expense	NA	218	232	268	227	275	592	305	144	116
Pretax Income	-526	154	410	-293	528	635	523	593	165	234
Effective Tax Rate	NM	44.2%	34.6%	NM	33.1%	36.5%	35.6%	35.4%	35.2%	35.5%
Net Income	-536	86.0	268	-191	353	403	337	383	88.0	151
S&P Core Earnings	21.4	71.1	228	-190	379	392	224	365	87.5	NA

Balance Sheet & Other Financial Data (Million $)										
Cash	1,004	250	42.0	28.0	40.0	33.0	25.0	51.0	70.0	43.0
Current Assets	NA	4,361	3,596	4,187	3,485	3,532	3,371	3,144	3,290	1,576
Total Assets	10,595	10,850	10,227	11,121	10,504	10,464	10,486	10,372	10,632	4,854
Current Liabilities	NA	2,103	2,115	2,846	2,157	2,293	2,475	2,093	2,416	886
Long Term Debt	3,333	2,888	2,642	2,987	2,869	3,024	3,114	3,733	4,016	1,357
Common Equity	4,352	5,014	4,731	4,900	4,615	4,912	3,954	3,662	3,354	2,175
Total Capital	8,002	8,193	7,740	8,382	8,141	8,631	7,790	8,038	7,979	3,917
Capital Expenditures	368	425	285	531	571	486	402	433	261	196
Cash Flow	NA	557	782	326	854	893	795	850	423	445
Current Ratio	2.2	2.1	1.7	1.5	1.6	1.5	1.4	1.5	1.4	1.8
% Long Term Debt of Capitalization	41.7	35.3	34.1	35.6	35.2	35.0	40.0	46.4	50.3	34.6
% Net Income of Revenue	NM	0.3	1.0	NM	1.4	1.5	1.4	1.6	0.8	2.1
% Return on Assets	NM	0.8	2.5	NM	3.4	3.8	3.2	3.6	1.1	3.0
% Return on Equity	NM	1.8	5.6	NM	7.9	8.5	8.8	10.9	3.2	7.0

Data as orig reptd.; bef. results of disc opers/spec. items. Per share data adj. for stk. divs.; EPS diluted. E-Estimated. NA-Not Available. NM-Not Meaningful. NR-Not Ranked. UR-Under Review.

Office: 2200 Don Tyson Pkwy, Springdale, AR 72762-6999.
Telephone: 479-290-4000.
Email: tysonir@tyson.com
Website: http://www.tyson.com

Chrmn: J.H. Tyson
Pres & CEO: D. Smith
COO: J.V. Lochner
EVP & CFO: D. Leatherby

EVP & General Counsel: D.L. Van Bebber
Investor Contact: R. Wisener
Board Members: L. V. Hackley, J. D. Kever, K. M. McNamara, B. T. Sauer, J. A. Smith, R. C. Thurber, B. A. Tyson, D. Tyson, J. H. Tyson, A. C. Zapanta

Founded: 1935
Domicile: Delaware
Employees: 117,000

Union Pacific Corp

STANDARD &POOR'S

S&P Recommendation HOLD ★★★☆☆	Price $63.19 (as of Nov 27, 2009)	12-Mo. Target Price $65.00	Investment Style Large-Cap Blend

GICS Sector Industrials
Sub-Industry Railroads

Summary Union Pacific operates the largest U.S. railroad, with over 32,200 miles of rail serving the western two-thirds of the country.

Key Stock Statistics (Source S&P, Vickers, company reports)

52-Wk Range	$66.73– 33.28	S&P Oper. EPS 2009**E**	3.57	Market Capitalization(B)	$31.882	Beta	1.18
Trailing 12-Month EPS	$3.97	S&P Oper. EPS 2010**E**	4.30	Yield (%)	1.71	S&P 3-Yr. Proj. EPS CAGR(%)	9
Trailing 12-Month P/E	15.9	P/E on S&P Oper. EPS 2009**E**	17.7	Dividend Rate/Share	$1.08	S&P Credit Rating	BBB
$10K Invested 5 Yrs Ago	$21,712	Common Shares Outstg. (M)	504.5	Institutional Ownership (%)	84		

Price Performance

30-Week Mov. Avg. · · · 10-Week Mov. Avg. - - **GAAP Earnings vs. Previous Year** Volume Above Avg. STARS
12-Mo. Target Price — Relative Strength — ▲ Up ▼ Down ▶ No Change Below Avg.

Options: CBOE, Ph

Analysis prepared by **Kevin Kirkeby** on October 26, 2009, when the stock traded at **$ 58.12**.

Highlights

▶ Traffic on UNP's network appears to have bottomed in June, partly on seasonal factors and partly from improved intermodal and auto shipments. Following an expected 21% decline in 2009, we look for revenues to rise 9% in 2010. This incorporates relatively stable mix and fuel surcharges, an 8% increase in volumes, and a modest improvement in core pricing. We expect the volume gains we see in 2010 to come mostly in intermodal, from new customers and new service offerings, as well as from the industrial and fertilizer categories. UNP's utility customers in early October had coal inventories well above historical averages.

▶ Margins, in our view, will widen during 2010 due to improved levels of traffic and the termination of contracts on certain parked railcars currently on lease. Opportunities for additional contract repricings, by our analysis, are limited, with about 3% of contracts up for renewal over the course of 2010. We think UNP's focus on fuel efficiency and distributed power will reduce overall fuel consumption.

▶ Our EPS estimate for 2009 of $3.57 excludes a $0.16 per share benefit from a large Colorado land sale.

Investment Rationale/Risk

▶ Recent economic data suggest that the economy is reaching a trough, which we expect will lead to a turnaround in UNP's more economically sensitive freight categories. At this point, we think a valuation above the historical average is warranted, as we balance the potential for economic recovery with UNP's above peer-average investment requirements over the next several years.

▶ Risks to our recommendation and target price include a slower-than-expected recovery in general economic growth, reduced coal consumption by utilities as a result of government efforts to control carbon dioxide emissions, and more regulatory oversight of railroad pricing.

▶ Our relative valuation model suggests an enterprise value to EBITDA multiple, using our 2010 estimate, of about 7.9X, which is above the 10-year average, and a value of $71. Our discounted cash flow model, which assumes a 10.5% cost of equity and a 3.5% terminal growth rate, estimates an intrinsic value near $59. Blending these models, we arrive at our 12-month target price of $65.

Qualitative Risk Assessment

LOW	MEDIUM	HIGH

Our risk assessment reflects UNP's exposure to economic cycles, regulations, and labor and fuel costs, coupled with significant capital expenditure requirements, offset by our view of the company's historically positive cash flow generation and moderate financial leverage.

Quantitative Evaluations

S&P Quality Ranking A

D	C	B-	B	B+	A-	A	A+

Relative Strength Rank STRONG

72

LOWEST = 1   HIGHEST = 99

Revenue/Earnings Data

Revenue (Million $)

	1Q	2Q	3Q	4Q	Year
2009	3,415	3,303	3,671	--	--
2008	4,270	4,568	4,846	4,286	17,970
2007	3,849	4,046	4,191	4,197	16,283
2006	3,710	3,923	3,983	3,962	15,578
2005	3,152	3,344	3,461	3,621	13,578
2004	2,893	3,029	3,076	3,217	12,215

Earnings Per Share ($)

	1Q	2Q	3Q	4Q	Year
2009	0.72	0.92	1.02	E1.05	E3.57
2008	0.85	1.02	1.38	1.31	4.54
2007	0.71	0.83	1.00	0.93	3.46
2006	0.58	0.72	0.77	0.89	2.96
2005	0.24	0.44	0.69	0.55	1.93
2004	0.32	0.30	0.39	0.15	1.15

Fiscal year ended Dec. 31. Next earnings report expected: Late January. EPS Estimates based on S&P Operating Earnings; historical GAAP earnings are as reported.

Dividend Data (Dates: mm/dd Payment Date: mm/dd/yy)

Amount ($)	Date Decl.	Ex-Div. Date	Stk. of Record	Payment Date
0.270	02/05	02/25	02/27	04/01/09
0.270	05/14	05/27	05/29	07/01/09
0.270	07/30	08/27	08/31	10/01/09
0.270	11/19	11/25	11/30	01/04/10

Dividends have been paid since 1900. Source: Company reports.

Please read the Required Disclosures and Analyst Certification on the last page of this report.

The *McGraw-Hill* Companies

Union Pacific Corp

STANDARD &POOR'S

Business Summary October 26, 2009

CORPORATE OVERVIEW. Union Pacific operates the largest U.S. railroad, with a network that spans about 32,200 miles, linking Pacific Coast and Gulf Coast ports to midwestern and eastern gateways. The rail lines touch 23 states, as well as the Mexican and Canadian borders. Energy accounted for 22% of freight revenues and 25% of carloadings in 2008. UNP is a major transporter of low-sulfur coal, with about 67% of its energy traffic consisting of coal originating in the Powder River Basin of Wyoming and Montana, primarily delivered to power utilities. In 2008, UNP's intermodal business represented 18% of freight revenue, and accounted for a much larger 37% of total carloads. The industrial products category represented another 19% of freight revenues, while chemicals, agricultural products, and automotive contributed 15%, 18%, and 8% of 2008 freight revenues.

COMPETITIVE LANDSCAPE. The U.S. rail industry has an oligopoly-like structure, with over 80% of revenues generated by the four largest railroads: UNP and Burlington Northern Santa Fe Corp. operating on the West Coast, and CSX Corp. and Norfolk Southern Corp. operating on the East Coast. Railroads simultaneously compete for customers while cooperating by sharing assets, interfacing systems, and completing customer movements. Railroads also com-

pete with trucking, shipping, and pipeline transportation. Rail rates are generally lower than trucking rates, as service is slower and less flexible, in our view, than trucking, which provides most U.S. transportation. We believe the rising price of fuel increases the cost attractiveness of railroads over less fuel-efficient trucking, which should help support industry volumes over the next five years. While large freight integrators, coal and utility companies may exert more pricing power than smaller customers, there has been an increase in shippers across the rail industry filing complaints with the Surface Transportation Board (STB) alleging excessive pricing. In a July 2009 ruling, the STB determined that UNP was seeking rate increases from Oklahoma Gas & Electric that exceeded permissible levels. The STB ordered UNP to reimburse the shipper for amounts already collected, and effectively capped the rate on those particular moves through 2018. We note that 50% of UNP's contracts that have not been repriced since 2004 are in the energy (coal) category.

Company Financials Fiscal Year Ended Dec. 31

Per Share Data ($)	2008	2007	2006	2005	2004	2003	2002	2001	2000	1999
Tangible Book Value	30.70	31.73	28.34	25.58	24.25	23.93	21.00	19.15	17.54	16.15
Cash Flow	7.23	5.92	5.23	4.13	3.27	3.96	4.60	3.93	3.67	3.46
Earnings	4.54	3.46	2.96	1.93	1.15	2.04	2.53	1.89	1.67	1.56
S&P Core Earnings	4.29	3.37	2.86	1.66	1.05	1.88	1.92	1.41	NA	NA
Dividends	0.98	0.75	0.60	0.60	0.60	0.50	0.42	0.40	0.40	0.40
Payout Ratio	22%	22%	20%	31%	52%	24%	16%	21%	24%	26%
Prices:High	85.80	68.78	48.75	40.63	34.78	34.75	32.58	30.35	26.41	33.94
Prices:Low	41.84	44.79	38.81	29.09	27.40	25.45	26.50	21.88	17.13	19.50
P/E Ratio:High	19	20	16	21	30	17	13	16	16	22
P/E Ratio:Low	9	13	13	15	24	13	10	12	10	13
Income Statement Analysis (Million $)										
Revenue	17,970	16,283	15,578	13,578	12,215	11,551	12,491	11,973	11,878	11,273
Operating Income	5,462	4,696	4,121	2,970	2,406	3,200	3,530	2,072	2,043	2,887
Depreciation	1,387	1,321	1,237	1,175	1,111	1,067	1,206	1,174	1,140	1,083
Interest Expense	511	482	477	504	527	574	633	701	723	733
Pretax Income	3,656	3,009	2,525	1,436	856	1,637	2,016	1,533	1,310	1,202
Effective Tax Rate	36.1%	38.4%	36.4%	28.6%	29.4%	35.5%	33.5%	37.0%	35.7%	34.9%
Net Income	2,338	1,855	1,606	1,026	604	1,056	1,341	966	842	783
S&P Core Earnings	2,209	1,808	1,553	886	551	972	1,003	708	NA	NA
Balance Sheet & Other Financial Data (Million $)										
Cash	1,249	878	827	773	977	527	369	113	105	175
Current Assets	2,813	2,594	2,411	2,325	2,290	2,089	2,152	1,542	1,285	1,314
Total Assets	39,722	38,033	36,515	35,620	34,589	33,460	32,764	31,551	30,499	29,888
Current Liabilities	2,880	3,041	3,539	3,384	2,516	2,456	2,701	2,692	2,962	2,885
Long Term Debt	8,607	7,543	6,000	6,760	7,981	7,822	8,928	9,386	9,644	9,926
Common Equity	15,447	15,585	15,312	13,707	12,655	12,354	10,651	9,575	8,662	8,001
Total Capital	34,336	33,178	31,008	29,949	29,816	29,345	28,057	26,843	25,449	24,642
Capital Expenditures	2,780	2,496	2,242	2,169	1,876	1,752	1,887	1,736	1,783	1,834
Cash Flow	3,725	3,176	2,843	2,201	1,715	2,123	2,547	2,140	1,982	1,866
Current Ratio	1.0	0.9	0.7	0.7	0.9	0.9	0.8	0.6	0.4	0.5
% Long Term Debt of Capitalization	25.1	22.7	19.3	22.6	26.8	26.7	31.8	35.0	37.9	40.3
% Net Income of Revenue	13.0	11.4	10.3	7.6	4.9	9.1	10.7	8.1	7.1	6.9
% Return on Assets	6.0	5.0	4.5	2.9	1.8	3.2	4.2	3.1	2.8	2.6
% Return on Equity	15.1	12.0	11.1	7.8	4.8	9.2	13.3	10.6	10.1	10.2

Data as orig reptd.; bef. results of disc opers/spec. items. Per share data adj. for stk. divs.; EPS diluted. E-Estimated. NA-Not Available. NM-Not Meaningful. NR-Not Ranked. UR-Under Review.

Office: 1400 Douglas St, Omaha, NE 68179-0002.
Telephone: 402-544-5000.
Website: http://www.up.com
Chrmn, Pres & CEO: J.R. Young

EVP & CFO: R.M. Knight, Jr.
SVP & Secy: B.W. Schaefer
SVP & General Counsel: J.M. Hemmer
SVP & CIO: L. Tennison

Investor Contact: J. Hamann (402-544-4227)
Board Members: A. H. Card, Jr., E. B. Davis, Jr., T. J. Donohue, Jr., A. W. Dunham, J. R. Hope, C. C. Krulak, M. R. McCarthy, M. W. McConnell, T. F. McLarty, III, S. R. Rogel, J. H. Villarreal, J. R. Young

Founded: 1862
Domicile: Utah
Employees: 48,242

The McGraw-Hill Companies

UnitedHealth Group Inc

STANDARD
&POOR'S

S&P Recommendation **BUY** ★★★★☆	Price $29.44 (as of Nov 27, 2009)	12-Mo. Target Price $32.00	Investment Style Large-Cap Growth

GICS Sector Health Care
Sub-Industry Managed Health Care

Summary This leading health care services company provided health benefit services to over 32 million individuals across the U.S. as of June 30, 2009.

Key Stock Statistics (Source S&P, Vickers, company reports)

52-Wk Range	$30.25– 16.18	S&P Oper. EPS 2009**E**	3.15	Market Capitalization(B)	$34.210	Beta	1.07
Trailing 12-Month EPS	$3.03	S&P Oper. EPS 2010**E**	3.10	Yield (%)	0.10	S&P 3-Yr. Proj. EPS CAGR(%)	6
Trailing 12-Month P/E	9.7	P/E on S&P Oper. EPS 2009**E**	9.3	Dividend Rate/Share	$0.03	S&P Credit Rating	A-
$10K Invested 5 Yrs Ago	$7,046	Common Shares Outstg. (M)	1,162.0	Institutional Ownership (%)	85		

Price Performance

30-Week Mov. Avg. · · · 10-Week Mov. Avg. – – GAAP Earnings vs. Previous Year   Volume Above Avg. |||| STARS
12-Mo. Target Price — Relative Strength — ▲ Up ▼ Down ▶ No Change   Below Avg. |||| ★

Options: ASE, CBOE, P

Analysis prepared by **Phillip M. Seligman** on October 26, 2009, when the stock traded at **$ 25.56**.

Highlights

► We look for operating revenues to rise 7.3% in 2009, to $86.3 billion. Drivers we see include higher premium pricing, about 300,000 additional Medicare Advantage (MA) members, 300,000 more Medicaid members, and non-health plan business growth. Partly offsetting these gains, we see 1.6 million fewer commercial members, mainly due to the soft economy. For 2010, we forecast operating revenues to rise 3.4%, assuming 400,000 fewer commercial members by year end. We also expect 100,000 more MA and 150,000 more Medicaid members, but premium rate hikes for both programs will be lower.

► We expect the consolidated medical loss ratio (MLR) to grow by 70 basis points (bps) in 2009, to 82.7%, mainly on changes in the enrollment mix and H1N1 flu costs. We see the consolidated MLR expanding another 90 bps in 2010, assuming margin pressure in the MA, Medicaid and pharmacy benefit management businesses. However, we expect the SG&A cost ratio to continue to decline, while investment income rises in 2010 after declining in 2009.

► We estimate operating EPS of $3.15 in 2009, versus 2008's $2.95 (before $0.55 of one-time items), and $3.10 in 2010.

Investment Rationale/Risk

► We recently upgraded our opinion on the shares to buy, from hold, mainly on valuation. In our view, UNH has been executing well in a weak economic environment with a higher medical cost trend, and we expect it to continue to exhibit disciplined pricing and operational improvements through 2010. We also believe UNH's overall diversification has tempered the margin pressure from the less-favorable enrollment mix we see and should enable the company to fare better than other managed care providers amid health care reform, assuming it occurs. For example, we see reform enabling enrollment to increase, offsetting margin pressures that may well arise, in our view. Meanwhile, we like UNH's conservative reserving policy, SG&A cost controls, and our view of strong cash flow, providing financial flexibility.

► Risks to our recommendation and target price include a sharp rise in medical costs and unfavorable rulings in remaining government probes of UNH's past stock option grants.

► Our 12-month target price of $32 assumes a target multiple of 10.3X our 2010 EPS estimate, slightly above peers, on our view of UNH's diversification and improved execution.

Qualitative Risk Assessment

LOW	MEDIUM	HIGH

Our risk assessment reflects UNH's leadership in the highly fragmented managed care market and its wide geographic, market and product diversity, which we believe permits stable operational performance even during periods of economic downturn. However, we see commercial enrollment growth slowing from an expanding base and from intensifying competition.

Quantitative Evaluations

S&P Quality Ranking A+

D	C	B-	B	B+	A-	A	A+

Relative Strength Rank STRONG

84

LOWEST = 1   HIGHEST = 99

Revenue/Earnings Data

Revenue (Million $)

	1Q	2Q	3Q	4Q	Year
2009	22,004	21,655	21,695	--	--
2008	20,304	20,272	20,156	20,454	81,186
2007	19,047	18,926	18,679	18,705	75,431
2006	17,581	17,863	17,970	18,128	71,542
2005	10,887	11,111	11,322	12,045	45,365
2004	8,144	8,704	9,859	10,511	37,218

Earnings Per Share ($)

2009	0.81	0.73	0.89	E0.72	E3.15
2008	0.78	0.27	0.75	0.60	2.40
2007	0.66	0.87	0.95	0.92	3.42
2006	0.63	0.70	0.80	0.84	2.97
2005	0.58	0.61	0.64	0.65	2.48
2004	0.44	0.47	0.52	0.55	1.97

Fiscal year ended Dec. 31. Next earnings report expected: Late January. EPS Estimates based on S&P Operating Earnings; historical GAAP earnings are as reported.

Dividend Data (Dates: mm/dd Payment Date: mm/dd/yy)

Amount ($)	Date Decl.	Ex-Div. Date	Stk. of Record	Payment Date
0.030	02/05	03/31	04/02	04/16/09

Dividends have been paid since 1990. Source: Company reports.

Please read the Required Disclosures and Analyst Certification on the last page of this report.

The McGraw-Hill Companies

UnitedHealth Group Inc

STANDARD
&POOR'S

Business Summary October 26, 2009

CORPORATE OVERVIEW. UnitedHealth Group, a U.S. leader in health care management, provides a broad range of health care products and services, including health maintenance organizations (HMOs), point of service (POS) plans, preferred provider organizations (PPOs), and managed fee for service programs.

The company reports results in four business segments, organized by product basis:

The Health Care Services segment (80% of 2008 revenues and 79% of operating earnings before eliminations) consists of the following business units: UnitedHealthcare coordinates network-based health and well-being services on behalf of multistate mid-sized and local employers and for individuals. Uniprise provides these services to large, self-insured accounts in return for administrative fees; it generally assumes no responsibility for health care costs. AmeriChoice facilitates and manages health care services for state Medicaid programs and their beneficiaries. Ovations delivers health and well-being services to Americans over the age of 50. At September 30, 2009, risk and fee-based Health Care Services enrollment totaled 31,980,000, versus 32,895,000 at December 31, 2008, including commercial risk-based (9,460,000 versus 10,360,000), commercial fee-based (15,295,000 versus 15,985,000),

Medicare Advantage (1,770,000 versus 1,495,000), Medicaid (2,795,000 versus 2,515,000), and Standardized Medicare Supplement (2,660,000 versus 2,540,000).

OptumHealth (5% and 11%) provides specialized benefits such as behavioral, dental and vision offerings, and financial services.

Ingenix (2% and 4%) is a leader in the field of health care data, analysis and application, serving pharmaceutical companies, health insurers and other payers, physicians and other health care providers, large employers and governments. We view Ingenix as key to the other segments' competitive strengths.

Prescription Solutions (13% and 6%) offers pharmacy benefit management and specialty pharmacy management services to employer groups, union trusts, seniors -- through Medicare prescription drug plans, and commercial health plans.

Company Financials Fiscal Year Ended Dec. 31

Per Share Data ($)	2008	2007	2006	2005	2004	2003	2002	2001	2000	1999
Tangible Book Value	NM	1.18	1.55	NM	0.04	1.24	0.79	0.88	0.61	0.75
Cash Flow	3.19	4.00	3.44	2.82	2.26	1.72	1.26	0.90	0.73	0.56
Earnings	2.40	3.42	2.97	2.48	1.97	1.48	1.07	0.70	0.55	0.40
S&P Core Earnings	2.95	3.40	2.94	2.36	1.86	1.37	0.99	0.62	NA	NA
Dividends	0.03	0.03	0.03	0.02	0.02	0.01	0.01	0.01	0.00	0.00
Payout Ratio	1%	1%	1%	1%	1%	1%	1%	1%	1%	1%
Prices:High	57.86	59.46	62.93	64.61	44.38	29.34	25.25	18.20	15.86	8.75
Prices:Low	14.51	45.82	41.44	42.63	27.73	19.60	16.96	12.63	5.80	4.92
P/E Ratio:High	24	17	21	26	23	20	24	26	29	22
P/E Ratio:Low	6	13	14	17	14	13	16	18	11	12

Income Statement Analysis (Million $)	2008	2007	2006	2005	2004	2003	2002	2001	2000	1999
Revenue	81,186	75,431	71,542	45,365	37,218	28,823	25,020	23,454	21,122	19,343
Operating Income	7,281	8,821	6,783	5,826	4,475	3,234	2,441	1,831	1,215	957
Depreciation	981	796	670	453	374	299	255	265	247	233
Interest Expense	639	544	456	241	128	95.0	90.0	94.0	72.0	49.0
Pretax Income	4,624	7,305	6,528	5,132	3,973	2,840	2,096	1,472	1,155	894
Effective Tax Rate	35.6%	36.3%	36.3%	35.7%	34.9%	35.7%	35.5%	38.0%	36.3%	36.5%
Net Income	2,977	4,654	4,159	3,300	2,587	1,825	1,352	913	736	568
S&P Core Earnings	3,655	4,629	4,108	3,137	2,443	1,689	1,260	812	NA	NA

Balance Sheet & Other Financial Data (Million $)	2008	2007	2006	2005	2004	2003	2002	2001	2000	1999
Cash	7,426	9,619	10,940	5,421	3,991	2,262	1,130	1,540	1,419	1,605
Current Assets	14,990	15,544	16,044	10,640	8,241	6,120	5,174	4,946	4,405	4,568
Total Assets	55,815	50,899	48,320	41,374	27,879	17,634	14,164	12,486	11,053	10,273
Current Liabilities	19,761	18,492	18,497	16,644	11,329	8,768	8,379	7,491	6,570	5,892
Long Term Debt	11,338	9,063	5,973	3,850	3,350	1,750	950	900	650	400
Common Equity	20,780	20,063	20,810	17,733	10,717	5,128	4,428	3,891	3,688	3,863
Total Capital	33,473	29,126	26,783	21,583	14,067	6,878	5,378	4,791	4,338	4,263
Capital Expenditures	791	871	728	5,876	350	352	419	425	245	196
Cash Flow	3,958	5,450	4,829	3,753	2,961	2,124	1,607	1,178	983	801
Current Ratio	0.8	0.8	0.9	0.6	0.7	0.7	0.6	0.7	0.7	0.8
% Long Term Debt of Capitalization	33.9	31.1	22.3	17.8	23.8	25.4	17.7	18.8	15.0	9.4
% Net Income of Revenue	3.7	6.2	5.9	7.3	7.0	6.3	5.4	3.9	3.5	2.9
% Return on Assets	5.6	9.4	9.3	9.5	11.4	11.5	10.1	7.8	6.9	5.7
% Return on Equity	14.6	22.8	21.5	23.2	32.7	38.2	32.5	24.1	19.5	14.4

Data as orig reptd.; bef. results of disc opers/spec. items. Per share data adj. for stk. divs.; EPS diluted. E-Estimated. NA-Not Available. NM-Not Meaningful. NR-Not Ranked. UR-Under Review.

Office: 9900 Bren Rd E, Minnetonka, MN 55343.
Telephone: 952-936-1300.
Website: http://www.unitedhealthgroup.com
Chrmn: R.T. Burke

Pres & CEO: S.J. Hemsley
COO & EVP: D.S. Wichmann
EVP & CFO: G.L. Mikan, III
EVP & General Counsel: C.J. Walsh

Board Members: W. C. Ballard, Jr., R. T. Burke, R. J. Darretta, S. J. Hemsley, M. J. Hooper, D. W. Leatherdale, G. M. Renwick, K. I. Shine, G. Wilensky

Founded: 1974
Domicile: Minnesota
Employees: 75,000

United Parcel Service Inc.

STANDARD &POOR'S

S&P Recommendation	HOLD ★★★☆☆	Price $57.43 (as of Nov 27, 2009)	12-Mo. Target Price $65.00	Investment Style Large-Cap Growth

GICS Sector Industrials
Sub-Industry Air Freight & Logistics

Summary UPS is the world's largest express delivery company, and has established itself as a facilitator of e-commerce.

Key Stock Statistics (Source S&P, Vickers, company reports)

52-Wk Range	$59.63–37.99	S&P Oper. EPS 2009E	2.16	Market Capitalization(B)	$40.559	Beta	0.80
Trailing 12-Month EPS	$1.64	S&P Oper. EPS 2010E	2.50	Yield (%)	3.13	S&P 3-Yr. Proj. EPS CAGR(%)	10
Trailing 12-Month P/E	35.0	P/E on S&P Oper. EPS 2009E	26.6	Dividend Rate/Share	$1.80	S&P Credit Rating	AA-
$10K Invested 5 Yrs Ago	$7,768	Common Shares Outstg. (M)	992.8	Institutional Ownership (%)	72		

Price Performance

30-Week Mov. Avg. · · ·   10-Week Mov. Avg. - -   **GAAP Earnings vs. Previous Year**   Volume Above Avg. ⃦⃦⃦ STARS
12-Mo. Target Price —   Relative Strength —   ▲ Up   ▼ Down   ▶ No Change   Below Avg. ⃦⃦⃦ ★

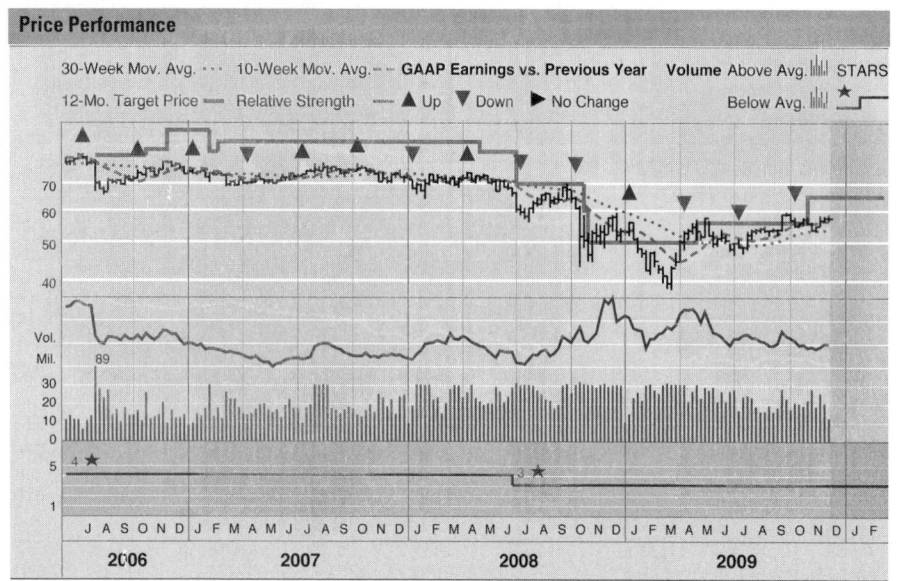

Options: ASE, CBOE, P, Ph

Analysis prepared by **Jim Corridore** on October 26, 2009, when the stock traded at **$ 55.95.**

Highlights

▶ We expect 2009 revenues to fall 14%, reflecting our forecast of a 6% volume decline and a 6% drop in yields on weak demand. Fuel surcharges are likely to be a drag on revenues as well, since fuel prices have come down sharply. We foresee a 20% decline in supply chain and freight revenues in 2009. We expect revenues to rise about 8% in 2010 on improved volumes and pricing into a strengthening U.S. economy.

▶ We see operating margins in 2009 being hurt by a weaker package mix. We also think productivity gains from new technology could be more than offset by inefficiencies created by pushing a lower volume of packages through the network. In 2009, UPS announced several rounds of cost-saving initiatives targeted to save about $1.0 billion annually. The company also froze management salaries and suspended its 401k matching program. For 2010, we see margins benefiting from improving volumes and realized savings from its cost cutting actions in 2009.

▶ We estimate 2009 EPS of $2.16, down 38% from 2008 operating EPS of $3.50. For 2010, we see EPS of $2.50.

Investment Rationale/Risk

▶ We think UPS will likely see increased international and domestic volumes and higher pricing once the economy starts to show material improvement. We think the company is a strong generator of cash, and we like that it has historically used its cash to pay dividends and repurchase stock. These positives support our hold opinion on the stock, despite a valuation trading toward the higher end of UPS's historical P/E range. We expect share repurchases to continue, and believe they will be accretive to earnings and provide support for the stock.

▶ Risks to our recommendation and target price include a more severe economic slowdown than we expect, a much slower improvement in the economy than we project, and a possible price war with competitors. Regarding corporate governance, we are concerned that Class A shareholders have 10 votes per share on many matters.

▶ Our 12-month target price of $65 values the stock at 26X our 2010 EPS estimate, toward the high end of UPS's five-year historical P/E range. We view positively return on assets and cash flow from operations.

Qualitative Risk Assessment

LOW	MEDIUM	HIGH

Our risk assessment reflects what we see as UPS's geographically diversified and increasing revenue base, a strong balance sheet with ample cash and low debt relative to total capitalization, and a track record of earnings and cash flow growth.

Quantitative Evaluations

S&P Quality Ranking   B+

D	C	B-	B	B+	A-	A	A+

Relative Strength Rank   MODERATE

67

LOWEST = 1   HIGHEST = 99

Revenue/Earnings Data

Revenue (Million $)

	1Q	2Q	3Q	4Q	Year
2009	10,938	10,829	11,153	--	--
2008	12,675	13,001	13,113	12,697	51,486
2007	11,906	12,189	12,205	13,392	49,692
2006	11,521	11,736	11,662	12,628	47,547
2005	9,886	10,191	10,550	11,954	42,581
2004	8,919	8,871	8,952	9,840	36,582

Earnings Per Share ($)

2009	0.40	0.44	0.55	E0.65	E2.16
2008	0.87	0.85	0.96	0.25	2.94
2007	0.78	1.04	1.02	-2.52	0.36
2006	0.89	0.97	0.96	1.04	3.86
2005	0.78	0.88	0.86	0.95	3.47
2004	0.67	0.72	0.78	0.76	2.93

Fiscal year ended Dec. 31. Next earnings report expected: Early February. EPS Estimates based on S&P Operating Earnings; historical GAAP earnings are as reported.

Dividend Data (Dates: mm/dd Payment Date: mm/dd/yy)

Amount ($)	Date Decl.	Ex-Div. Date	Stk. of Record	Payment Date
0.450	02/11	02/19	02/23	03/10/09
0.450	05/07	05/14	05/18	06/03/09
0.450	08/13	08/20	08/24	09/09/09
0.450	11/05	11/12	11/16	12/03/09

Dividends have been paid since 2000. Source: Company reports.

Please read the Required Disclosures and Analyst Certification on the last page of this report.

The McGraw-Hill Companies

STANDARD
&POOR'S

United Parcel Service Inc.

Business Summary October 26, 2009

United Parcel Service is the world's largest express and package delivery company. It is also a leading commerce facilitator, offering various logistics and financial services. The company, which was privately held since its founding in 1907, had its IPO of Class B stock in November 1999.

The company seeks to position itself as the primary coordinator of the flow of goods, information and funds throughout the entire supply chain (the movement from the raw materials and parts stage through final consumption of the finished product).

Domestic package delivery services accounted for 61% of revenues in 2008, down from 62% in 2007. About 84% of the 13.6 million daily domestic shipments handled by the company in 2008 were moved by its ground delivery service, which is available to every address in the 48 contiguous states in the U.S. Domestic air delivery is provided throughout the U.S., including next-day air, which is guaranteed by 10:30 a.m. to more than 75% of the U.S. population, and by noon to an additional 15% of the population.

UPS entered the international arena in 1975. In 2008, it handled 2.0 million international shipments per day. Its international package delivery service (22% of total revenues in 2008) is growing faster than its domestic business. UPS delivers international shipments to more than 200 countries and territories worldwide and provides delivery within one to two business days to the world's major business centers. Services include export (packages that cross national borders) and domestic (packages that stay within a single country's boundaries). UPS has a portfolio of domestic services in 20 major countries. Transborder services within the European Union are expected to continue to be a growth engine for the company. Asia continues to be an area in which UPS is investing in infrastructure and technology.

Company Financials Fiscal Year Ended Dec. 31

Per Share Data ($)	2008	2007	2006	2005	2004	2003	2002	2001	2000	1999
Tangible Book Value	4.29	9.04	11.46	12.44	12.84	12.03	11.09	9.14	8.58	10.31
Cash Flow	4.71	2.00	5.46	4.94	4.33	3.91	4.20	3.41	3.50	1.77
Earnings	2.94	0.36	3.86	3.47	2.93	2.55	2.87	2.12	2.50	0.77
S&P Core Earnings	2.61	0.20	3.78	3.40	2.87	2.46	2.48	1.70	NA	NA
Dividends	1.80	1.68	1.52	1.32	1.12	0.92	0.76	0.76	0.81	Nil
Payout Ratio	61%	NM	39%	38%	38%	36%	26%	36%	32%	Nil
Prices:High	75.08	78.99	83.99	85.84	89.11	74.87	67.10	62.50	69.75	76.94
Prices:Low	43.32	68.66	65.50	66.10	67.51	53.00	54.25	46.15	49.50	50.00
P/E Ratio:High	26	NM	22	25	30	29	23	29	28	NM
P/E Ratio:Low	15	NM	17	19	23	21	19	22	20	NM

Income Statement Analysis (Million $)										
Revenue	51,486	49,692	47,547	42,581	36,582	33,485	31,272	30,646	29,771	27,052
Operating Income	7,771	8,758	8,383	7,787	6,532	5,994	5,560	5,358	5,685	5,127
Depreciation	1,814	1,745	1,748	1,644	1,543	1,549	1,464	1,396	1,173	1,139
Interest Expense	490	313	211	172	149	121	173	184	205	228
Pretax Income	5,015	431	6,510	6,075	4,922	4,370	5,009	3,937	4,834	2,088
Effective Tax Rate	40.1%	11.4%	35.5%	36.3%	32.3%	33.7%	35.0%	38.4%	39.3%	57.7%
Net Income	3,003	382	4,202	3,870	3,333	2,898	3,254	2,425	2,934	883
S&P Core Earnings	2,664	212	4,109	3,784	3,261	2,790	2,820	1,948	NA	NA

Balance Sheet & Other Financial Data (Million $)										
Cash	1,049	2,604	794	1,369	5,197	2,951	2,211	1,616	1,952	6,278
Current Assets	8,845	11,760	9,377	11,003	12,605	9,853	8,738	7,597	7,124	11,138
Total Assets	31,879	39,042	33,210	35,222	33,026	28,909	26,357	24,636	21,662	23,043
Current Liabilities	7,817	9,840	6,719	6,793	6,483	5,518	5,555	4,629	4,501	4,198
Long Term Debt	7,797	7,506	3,133	3,159	3,261	3,149	3,495	4,648	2,981	1,912
Common Equity	6,780	12,183	15,482	16,884	16,384	14,852	12,455	10,248	9,735	12,474
Total Capital	16,231	22,309	21,144	20,043	25,027	18,001	15,950	14,896	12,716	14,386
Capital Expenditures	2,636	2,820	3,085	2,187	2,127	1,947	1,658	2,372	2,147	1,476
Cash Flow	4,817	2,127	5,950	5,514	4,876	4,447	4,718	3,821	4,107	2,022
Current Ratio	1.1	1.2	1.4	1.6	1.9	1.8	1.6	1.6	1.6	2.7
% Long Term Debt of Capitalization	48.0	33.7	14.8	15.8	13.0	17.5	21.9	31.2	23.4	13.3
% Net Income of Revenue	5.8	0.8	8.8	9.1	9.1	8.7	10.4	7.9	9.9	3.3
% Return on Assets	8.5	1.1	12.3	11.3	10.6	10.5	12.8	10.5	13.1	4.4
% Return on Equity	31.7	2.8	26.0	23.3	21.3	21.2	28.7	24.3	26.4	8.8

Data as orig reptd.; bef. results of disc opers/spec. items. Per share data adj. for stk. divs.; EPS diluted. E-Estimated. NA-Not Available. NM-Not Meaningful. NR-Not Ranked. UR-Under Review.

Office: 55 Glenlake Parkway N.E., Atlanta, GA 30328.
Telephone: 404-828-6000.
Website: http://www.shareholder.com/ups
Chrmn & CEO: D.S. Davis

COO & SVP: D. Abney
SVP, CFO, Chief Acctg Officer & Treas: K. Kuehn
SVP, Secy & General Counsel: T.P. McClure
SVP & CIO: D. Barnes

Investor Contact: M. Vale (404-828-6703)
Board Members: F. D. Ackerman, M. J. Burns, D. S. Davis, S. E. Eizenstat, M. L. Eskew, W. R. Johnson, A. M. Livermore, R. Markham, J. Thompson, C. B. Tome

Founded: 1907
Domicile: Delaware
Employees: 426,000

The McGraw-Hill Companies

U.S. Bancorp

STANDARD &POOR'S

S&P Recommendation	HOLD ★★★☆☆	Price $22.95 (as of Nov 27, 2009)	12-Mo. Target Price $27.00	Investment Style Large-Cap Blend

GICS Sector Financials
Sub-Industry Diversified Banks

Summary This bank holding company was formed through the February 2001 merger of Minneapolis-based U.S. Bancorp and Milwaukee-based Firstar Corp.

Key Stock Statistics (Source S&P, Vickers, company reports)

52-Wk Range	$29.90–8.06	S&P Oper. EPS 2009**E**	1.00	Market Capitalization(B)	$43.890	Beta	1.05
Trailing 12-Month EPS	$0.82	S&P Oper. EPS 2010**E**	1.46	Yield (%)	0.87	S&P 3-Yr. Proj. EPS CAGR(%)	4
Trailing 12-Month P/E	28.0	P/E on S&P Oper. EPS 2009**E**	23.0	Dividend Rate/Share	$0.20	S&P Credit Rating	A+
$10K Invested 5 Yrs Ago	$9,438	Common Shares Outstg. (M)	1,912.4	Institutional Ownership (%)	65		

Price Performance

- 30-Week Mov. Avg. · · ·
- 10-Week Mov. Avg. – –
- GAAP Earnings vs. Previous Year
- Volume Above Avg. STARS
- 12-Mo. Target Price —
- Relative Strength —
- ▲ Up ▼ Down ▶ No Change
- Below Avg. ★

Options: ASE, CBOE, Ph

Analysis prepared by **Stuart Plesser** on October 23, 2009, when the stock traded at **$ 24.86**.

Highlights

► We look for revenues to increase modestly in 2010, helped by the acquisition of Downey Savings and Loan and higher fee income. Specifically, we look for USB's revenue to increase 5.5% from a projected $16.5 billion in 2009. Although we believe USB will gain market share at the expense of the competition, loan growth will likely decline due to higher credit standards and a slowdown in the economy.

► We forecast a net interest margin of around 3.57% in 2010, versus a projected 3.63% in 2009, assuming a rate hike sometime in 2010. Although USB is well reserved for its non-performing loans, we believe chargeoffs will continue to increase in 2010, peaking in the middle of the year. Based on higher unemployment rates, we think chargeoffs will spread to more credit conscious customers. USB's reserve to non-performing loans seems adequate, by our analysis. We view USB's Tier 1 capital ratio of 9.55% as adequate and it will likely climb higher should earnings grow into 2010.

► We expect operating EPS of $1.00 in 2009, with minimal share repurchases. For 2010, we forecast EPS of $1.46.

Investment Rationale/Risk

► USB's loan book has held up better than peers throughout the credit downturn. Indeed, we expect annualized chargeoffs to only increase to 1.25% of loans by mid- 2010. We are encouraged by a slowdown in the sequential growth of chargeoffs and nonperforming loans, and think provisions should ease in the second half of 2010. Although loan growth will likely remain weak for the next several quarters, USB appears to be growing its loan book at a higher rate than peers. With the shares recently trading at an above-historical 16.9X our 2010 EPS estimate of $1.46, we think they are fairly valued.

► Risks to our recommendation and target price include deterioration in the economy, consumer spending, and credit quality, and a tightening of the credit markets.

► Our 12-month target price of $27 is about 18.5X our 2010 EPS estimate, above USB's historical average as we think 2009 will be a trough year in its earnings cycle. We think this valuation is justified as we believe USB will be one of the first banks to start to realize normalized earnings.

Qualitative Risk Assessment

LOW	MEDIUM	HIGH

Our risk assessment for U.S. Bancorp reflects our view of the company's solid fundamentals, along with good geographic and product diversification. We think USB is positioned to weather a downturn in the U.S. economy better than many peers.

Quantitative Evaluations

S&P Quality Ranking B+

D	C	B-	B	B+	A-	A	A+

Relative Strength Rank MODERATE

52

LOWEST = 1   HIGHEST = 99

Revenue/Earnings Data

Revenue (Million $)

	1Q	2Q	3Q	4Q	Year
2009	4,655	4,895	4,950	--	--
2008	5,249	4,907	4,469	4,604	19,229
2007	4,883	5,091	5,178	5,156	20,308
2006	4,505	4,773	4,897	4,934	19,109
2005	3,817	4,106	4,294	4,379	16,596
2004	3,576	3,478	3,827	3,825	14,706

Earnings Per Share ($)

	1Q	2Q	3Q	4Q	Year
2009	0.24	0.12	0.30	E0.34	E1.00
2008	0.62	0.53	0.32	0.15	1.61
2007	0.63	0.65	0.62	0.53	2.43
2006	0.63	0.66	0.66	0.66	2.61
2005	0.57	0.60	0.62	0.62	2.42
2004	0.52	0.54	0.56	0.56	2.18

Fiscal year ended Dec. 31. Next earnings report expected: Late January. EPS Estimates based on S&P Operating Earnings; historical GAAP earnings are as reported.

Dividend Data (Dates: mm/dd Payment Date: mm/dd/yy)

Amount ($)	Date Decl.	Ex-Div. Date	Stk. of Record	Payment Date
0.425	12/09	12/29	12/31	01/15/09
0.050	03/04	03/27	03/31	04/15/09
0.050	06/16	06/26	06/30	07/15/09
0.050	09/15	09/28	09/30	10/15/09

Dividends have been paid since 1863. Source: Company reports.

Please read the Required Disclosures and Analyst Certification on the last page of this report.

The McGraw-Hill Companies

U.S. Bancorp

STANDARD
&POOR'S

Business Summary October 23, 2009

CORPORATE OVERVIEW. USB consists of several major lines of business, which include wholesale banking, consumer banking, wealth management & securities services, payment services, and treasury and corporate support. Wholesale banking offers lending, equipment finance and small ticket leasing, depository, treasury management, capital markets, foreign exchange, international trade services and other financial services to middle-market, large corporate and public sector clients. Consumer banking delivers products and services through banking offices, telephone servicing and sales, online services, direct mail and ATMs. It encompasses community banking, metropolitan banking, in-store banking, small business banking, including lending guaranteed by the Small Business Administration, consumer lending, mortgage banking, consumer finance, workplace banking, student banking, and 24-hour banking.

Wealth management & securities services provides trust, custody, private banking, financial advisory, investment management, retail brokerage services, insurance, custody and mutual fund servicing through five businesses:

wealth management, corporate trust, FAF Advisors, institutional trust and custody, and fund services. Payment services includes consumer and business credit cards, stored-value cards, debit cards, corporate and purchasing card services, consumer lines of credit, and merchant processing.

CORPORATE STRATEGY. USB has several goals in order to achieve long-term success, including: 10%-plus EPS growth, a 20%-plus ROE, reducing credit and earnings volatility, providing high-quality customer service, investing in future growth, and targeting an 80% return on earnings to shareholders. In banking, USB is maintaining what we view as its low-cost, highly efficient model and plans to grow organically and through smaller, fill-in acquisitions in higher-growth markets.

Company Financials Fiscal Year Ended Dec. 31

Per Share Data ($)	2008	2007	2006	2005	2004	2003	2002	2001	2000	1999
Tangible Book Value	3.97	6.31	5.34	5.62	5.87	5.77	4.93	4.64	7.11	4.66
Earnings	1.61	2.43	2.61	2.42	2.18	1.92	1.73	0.88	1.32	0.87
S&P Core Earnings	1.49	2.54	2.59	2.41	2.16	1.89	1.59	0.66	NA	NA
Dividends	1.70	1.63	1.39	1.23	1.02	0.86	0.78	0.75	0.65	0.40
Payout Ratio	106%	67%	53%	51%	47%	45%	45%	85%	49%	46%
Prices:High	42.23	36.84	36.85	31.36	31.65	30.00	24.50	26.06	28.00	35.33
Prices:Low	20.22	29.09	28.99	26.80	24.89	18.56	16.05	16.50	15.38	19.56
P/E Ratio:High	26	15	14	13	15	16	14	30	21	41
P/E Ratio:Low	13	12	11	11	11	10	9	19	12	22

Income Statement Analysis (Million $)	2008	2007	2006	2005	2004	2003	2002	2001	2000	1999
Net Interest Income	7,732	6,689	6,741	7,055	7,111	7,189	6,840	6,409	2,699	2,643
Tax Equivalent Adjustment	134	75.0	49.0	33.0	28.6	28.2	36.6	55.9	45.1	54.3
Non Interest Income	6,811	7,157	6,832	6,151	5,624	5,068	5,569	5,030	1,505	1,388
Loan Loss Provision	3,096	792	544	666	670	1,254	1,349	2,529	222	187
% Expense/Operating Revenue	47.4%	49.6%	45.4%	44.3%	45.3%	45.7%	83.7%	57.5%	55.0%	59.9%
Pretax Income	4,033	6,207	6,863	6,571	6,176	5,651	5,103	2,634	1,927	1,413
Effective Tax Rate	27.0%	30.3%	30.8%	31.7%	32.5%	34.4%	34.8%	35.2%	31.4%	38.0%
Net Income	2,946	4,324	4,751	4,489	4,167	3,710	3,326	1,707	1,284	875
% Net Interest Margin	3.66	3.47	3.65	3.97	4.25	4.49	4.61	4.45	4.73	4.83
S&P Core Earnings	2,606	4,470	4,674	4,470	4,135	3,655	3,062	1,280	NA	NA

Balance Sheet & Other Financial Data (Million $)	2008	2007	2006	2005	2004	2003	2002	2001	2000	1999
Money Market Assets	Nil	Nil	Nil	Nil	Nil	Nil	1,332	1,607	200	897
Investment Securities	39,521	43,116	40,117	39,768	41,481	43,334	28,488	26,608	13,866	13,114
Commercial Loans	56,618	80,281	74,835	71,405	67,758	65,768	68,811	71,703	28,498	26,198
Other Loans	125,097	73,546	68,762	66,401	58,557	52,467	47,440	42,702	25,208	24,428
Total Assets	265,912	237,615	219,232	209,465	195,104	189,286	180,027	171,390	77,585	72,788
Demand Deposits	37,494	33,334	32,128	32,214	30,756	32,470	35,106	31,212	10,980	10,300
Time Deposits	121,856	98,111	92,754	92,495	89,985	86,582	80,428	74,007	45,298	41,586
Long Term Debt	38,359	43,440	37,602	37,069	22,807	33,816	31,582	28,542	3,877	5,038
Common Equity	18,369	20,046	20,197	20,086	19,539	19,242	18,101	16,461	6,528	6,309
% Return on Assets	1.2	1.9	2.2	2.2	2.2	2.0	1.9	1.0	1.7	1.2
% Return on Equity	15.3	21.2	23.6	22.7	21.5	19.7	19.2	10.8	20.0	13.6
% Loan Loss Reserve	1.9	1.3	1.4	1.5	1.6	2.0	2.0	2.1	1.3	1.4
% Loans/Deposits	116.2	118.1	117.6	111.9	105.8	100.5	100.6	111.4	95.4	98.8
% Equity to Assets	7.6	8.8	9.4	9.8	10.1	10.2	9.8	9.4	8.5	8.8

Data as orig reptd.; bef. results of disc opers/spec. items. Per share data adj. for stk. divs.; EPS diluted. E-Estimated. NA-Not Available. NM-Not Meaningful. NR-Not Ranked. UR-Under Review.

Office: 800 Nicollet Mall, Minneapolis, MN 55402-7000.
Telephone: 651-466-3000.
Website: http://www.usbank.com
Chrmn: T.H. Jacobsen

Chrmn, Pres & CEO: R. Davis
Vice Chrmn: M.C. Wheeler, Jr.
EVP, Chief Acctg Officer & Cntlr: T.R. Dolan
EVP & Treas: K.D. Nelson

Investor Contact: J.T. Murphy (612-303-0783)
Board Members: D. M. Baker, Jr., Y. M. Belton, G. B. Cameron, A. D. Collins, Jr., R. Davis, D. Garvin, V. B. Gluckman, J. F. Hladky, T. H. Jacobsen, J. W. Johnson, O. F. Kirtley, J. W. Levin, S. B. Lubar, F. Lyon, Jr., D. F. McKeithan, Jr., D. B. O'Maley, O. M. Owens, R. G. Reiten, C. D. Schnuck, P. T. Stokes, M. C. Wheeler, Jr., W. W. Wirtz

Founded: 1929
Domicile: Delaware
Employees: 57,904

The *McGraw-Hill* Companies

United States Steel Corp

STANDARD &POOR'S

S&P Recommendation HOLD ★★★☆☆

Price	12-Mo. Target Price	Investment Style
$43.05 (as of Nov 27, 2009)	$43.00	Large-Cap Value

GICS Sector Materials
Sub-Industry Steel

Summary This company manufactures and sells a wide variety of steel sheet, plate, tubular and tin products, coke, and taconite pellets.

Key Stock Statistics (Source S&P, Vickers, company reports)

52-Wk Range	$51.65–16.66	S&P Oper. EPS 2009**E**	-10.72	Market Capitalization(B)	$6.171	Beta	2.76
Trailing 12-Month EPS	$-6.61	S&P Oper. EPS 2010**E**	3.22	Yield (%)	0.46	S&P 3-Yr. Proj. EPS CAGR(%)	-26
Trailing 12-Month P/E	NM	P/E on S&P Oper. EPS 2009**E**	NM	Dividend Rate/Share	$0.20	S&P Credit Rating	BB
$10K Invested 5 Yrs Ago	$8,875	Common Shares Outstg. (M)	143.4	Institutional Ownership (%)	85		

Price Performance

30-Week Mov. Avg. · · · 10-Week Mov. Avg. – – **GAAP Earnings vs. Previous Year** Volume Above Avg. STARS
12-Mo. Target Price — Relative Strength — ▲ Up ▼ Down ▶ No Change Below Avg.

Options: ASE, CBOE

Analysis prepared by **Leo J. Larkin** on November 17, 2009, when the stock traded at **$ 41.86.**

Highlights

▶ Following an estimated decrease of 56% in 2009, we look for a 25% sales rise in 2010, on an anticipated rebound in tons shipped and steel prices. Our forecast rests on several assumptions. First, S&P forecasts GDP growth of 1.9% in 2010, versus a 2.5% decrease in GDP estimated for 2009. We see a resumption of GDP growth leading to rising demand for durable goods. Second, we think demand for oil country tubular goods will rise from 2009's depressed levels as drilling activity picks up. Third, we see distributors adding to inventory in 2010 after de-stocking through most of 2009. Fourth, we expect that demand for durable goods in Europe will recover from 2009's depressed levels.

▶ Aided by increased volume and higher revenue per ton, we look for a return to operating profit in 2010. After interest expense and taxes, and with more shares outstanding, we estimate EPS of $3.22, versus a per share loss of $10.72 projected for 2009.

▶ We think earnings over the long term will increase on industry consolidation, rising demand for oil country tubular goods, and a gradual decline in costs for employee pensions and health care.

Investment Rationale/Risk

▶ Over the long term, we see X's earnings rising on a gradual decline in pension and health care costs, further acquisitions, well controlled raw material costs in domestic operations, consolidation of the global steel industry, and a secular increase in demand for oil country tubular goods used for oil and gas exploration. Also, we believe that as X begins to generate higher EPS and free cash flow, it will be in a position to engage in share repurchases and thereby reduce some of the dilution from its 2009 stock offering. However, with the shares recently trading with just modest upside potential to our target price, we would not add to positions.

▶ Risks to our recommendation and target price include declines in shipment volume and average realized price per ton in 2010 instead of the increases we project.

▶ Our 12-month target price of $43 is based on our view that the shares will trade at a multiple of about 13.4X our 2010 EPS estimate. On this projected multiple, X's valuation would exceed the high end of the P/E range in which it traded in 2004, the first year of an earnings recovery following a loss in 2003, and would be about in line with the P/E we apply to peers.

Qualitative Risk Assessment

LOW	MEDIUM	HIGH

Our risk assessment reflects the company's exposure to highly cyclical industries such as autos and construction along with what we view as its high ratio of liabilities to assets and its unfunded pension and health care liabilities of $5.1 billion at the end of 2008.

Quantitative Evaluations

S&P Quality Ranking   B

D	C	B-	B	B+	A-	A	A+

Relative Strength Rank   STRONG

77

LOWEST = 1   HIGHEST = 99

Revenue/Earnings Data

Revenue (Million $)

	1Q	2Q	3Q	4Q	Year
2009	2,750	3,127	2,817	--	--
2008	5,196	6,744	7,312	4,502	23,754
2007	3,756	4,228	4,354	4,535	16,873
2006	3,728	4,107	4,106	3,774	15,715
2005	3,787	3,582	3,200	3,470	14,039
2004	2,963	3,466	3,729	3,932	14,108

Earnings Per Share ($)

	1Q	2Q	3Q	4Q	Year
2009	-3.78	-2.92	-2.11	E-1.91	E-10.72
2008	1.98	5.65	7.79	2.50	17.96
2007	2.30	2.54	2.27	0.30	7.40
2006	2.04	3.22	3.42	2.50	11.18
2005	3.51	1.91	0.71	0.85	7.00
2004	0.36	1.62	2.72	3.59	8.37

Fiscal year ended Dec. 31. Next earnings report expected: Late January. EPS Estimates based on S&P Operating Earnings; historical GAAP earnings are as reported.

Dividend Data (Dates: mm/dd Payment Date: mm/dd/yy)

Amount ($)	Date Decl.	Ex-Div. Date	Stk. of Record	Payment Date
0.300	01/27	02/09	02/11	03/10/09
0.050	04/27	05/11	05/13	06/10/09
0.050	07/28	08/10	08/12	09/10/09
0.050	10/27	11/06	11/11	12/10/09

Dividends have been paid since 1991. Source: Company reports.

Please read the Required Disclosures and Analyst Certification on the last page of this report.

The **McGraw·Hill** *Companies*

United States Steel Corp

Business Summary November 17, 2009

CORPORATE OVERVIEW. Following its acquisition of Stelco Inc. and Lone Star Technologies in 2007, U.S. Steel is the fifth largest steel producer in the world, the largest integrated steel producer headquartered in North America, and one of the largest integrated flat-rolled producers in Central Europe. X ended 2008 with raw steelmaking capacity of 31.7 million tons, consisting of 24.3 million tons in North America and 7.4 million tons in Europe. In 2008, X produced 19.2 million tons of steel in North America and 6.4 million tons in Europe.

The company's other business activities include the production of coke in both North America and Central Europe; and the production of iron ore pellets from taconite, transportation services (railroad and barge operations), real estate operations, and engineering and consulting services in North America.

CORPORATE STRATEGY. The company seeks to boost its revenues and earnings by expanding its value-added product mix, becoming a prime supplier of steel to growing European markets, strengthening its balance sheet, and becoming more cost competitive.

MARKET PROFILE. The primary factor affecting demand for steel products is economic growth in general, and growth in demand for durable goods in particular. The two largest end markets for steel products in the U.S. are autos and construction, which together accounted for 35.1% of shipments in 2007. Other end markets include appliances, containers, machinery, and oil and gas. Distributors, also known as service centers, accounted for 24.9% of industry shipments in the U.S. in 2007. Distributors are the largest single market for the steel industry in the U.S. Because distributors sell to a wide variety of OEMs, it is impossible to trace the final destination of much of the industry's shipments. Consequently, consumption of steel by the auto, construction and other industries may be higher than the shipment data would suggest. U.S. production was 100.7 million tons in 2008. X's largest end markets in 2008 were distributors (21% of revenues), appliances (7%), converters (23%), construction (13%), automotive (13%), containers (8%), oil and gas (7%), and other (8%). U.S. consumption decreased at a compound annual rate (CAGR) of 1.8% from 1999 through 2008. Global steel consumption rose at a CAGR of 6.4% from 1998 through 2007.

Company Financials Fiscal Year Ended Dec. 31

Per Share Data ($)	2008	2007	2006	2005	2004	2003	2002	2001	2000	1999
Tangible Book Value	25.85	28.81	36.82	25.63	32.30	7.98	15.81	28.16	21.54	23.22
Cash Flow	23.26	11.66	14.69	11.54	11.17	-0.57	4.24	1.42	3.72	3.93
Earnings	17.96	7.40	11.18	7.00	8.37	-4.09	0.62	-2.45	-0.33	0.48
S&P Core Earnings	14.34	7.42	11.76	6.64	8.74	-1.06	-4.10	-8.47	NA	NA
Dividends	1.10	0.60	0.25	0.28	0.20	0.20	0.20	0.55	1.00	1.00
Payout Ratio	6%	8%	2%	4%	2%	NM	32%	NM	NM	NM
Prices:High	196.00	127.26	79.01	63.90	54.06	37.05	22.00	22.00	32.94	34.25
Prices:Low	20.71	68.83	48.05	33.59	25.22	9.61	10.66	13.00	12.69	21.75
P/E Ratio:High	11	17	7	9	6	NM	35	NM	NM	71
P/E Ratio:Low	1	9	4	5	3	NM	17	NM	NM	45

Income Statement Analysis (Million $)	2008	2007	2006	2005	2004	2003	2002	2001	2000	1999
Revenue	23,817	16,873	15,715	14,039	14,108	9,458	7,054	6,375	6,090	5,380
Operating Income	3,406	1,804	2,143	1,740	1,964	316	478	-61.0	422	520
Depreciation	605	506	441	366	382	363	350	344	360	304
Interest Expense	176	163	117	107	138	148	136	153	115	75.0
Pretax Income	3,007	1,108	1,723	1,312	1,461	-860	13.0	-546	-1.00	76.0
Effective Tax Rate	28.4%	19.7%	18.8%	27.8%	24.0%	NM	NM	NM	NM	32.9%
Net Income	2,112	879	1,374	910	1,077	-406	61.0	-218	-21.0	51.0
S&P Core Earnings	1,686	882	1,438	847	1,104	-109	-398	-755	NA	NA

Balance Sheet & Other Financial Data (Million $)	2008	2007	2006	2005	2004	2003	2002	2001	2000	1999
Cash	724	401	1,422	1,479	1,037	316	243	147	219	22.0
Current Assets	5,732	4,959	5,196	4,831	4,243	3,107	2,440	2,073	2,717	1,981
Total Assets	16,087	15,632	10,586	9,822	10,956	7,838	7,977	8,337	8,711	7,525
Current Liabilities	2,778	3,003	2,702	2,749	2,531	2,130	1,372	1,259	1,391	1,266
Long Term Debt	3,064	3,147	943	1,363	1,363	1,890	1,408	1,434	2,485	1,151
Common Equity	4,895	5,531	4,365	3,108	3,754	867	2,027	2,506	1,917	2,053
Total Capital	8,132	8,736	5,346	4,719	5,959	2,989	3,658	4,672	5,070	3,555
Capital Expenditures	896	692	612	741	579	316	258	287	244	287
Cash Flow	2,735	1,385	1,807	1,258	1,441	-59.0	411	126	331	346
Current Ratio	2.1	1.7	1.9	1.8	1.7	1.5	1.8	1.6	2.0	1.6
% Long Term Debt of Capitalization	37.7	36.0	17.6	28.9	22.9	63.2	38.5	30.7	49.0	32.4
% Net Income of Revenue	8.9	5.2	8.7	6.5	7.8	NM	0.9	NM	NM	0.9
% Return on Assets	13.3	6.7	13.5	8.7	11.5	NM	0.7	NM	NM	0.7
% Return on Equity	40.5	17.8	36.6	25.6	45.8	NM	2.7	NM	NM	2.0

Data as orig reptd.; bef. results of disc opers/spec. items. Per share data adj. for stk. divs.; EPS diluted. E-Estimated. NA-Not Available. NM-Not Meaningful. NR-Not Ranked. UR-Under Review.

Office: 600 Grant Street, Pittsburgh, PA 15219-2702.
Telephone: 412-433-1121.
Email: shareholderservices@uss.com
Website: http://www.ussteel.com

Chrmn & CEO: J. Surma, Jr.
COO & EVP: J.H. Goodish
EVP & CFO: G.R. Haggerty
SVP & Chief Admin Officer: D.H. Lohr

SVP & General Counsel: J.D. Garraux
Investor Contact: N. Harper (412-433-1184)
Board Members: R. J. Darnall, J. G. Drosdick, R. A. Gephardt, C. R. Lee, J. M. Lipton, F. J. Lucchino, G. G. McNeal, S. E. Schofield, G. B. Spanier, J. Surma, Jr., D. S. Sutherland, P. A. Tracey

Founded: 2001
Domicile: Delaware
Employees: 49,000

United Technologies Corp

STANDARD &POOR'S

S&P Recommendation BUY ★★★★☆

Price $67.20 (as of Nov 27, 2009)	**12-Mo. Target Price** $70.00	**Investment Style** Large-Cap Growth

GICS Sector Industrials
Sub-Industry Aerospace & Defense

Summary This aerospace-industrial conglomerate's portfolio includes Pratt & Whitney jet engines, Sikorsky helicopters, Otis elevators, and Carrier air conditioners, among other products.

Key Stock Statistics (Source S&P, Vickers, company reports)

52-Wk Range	$69.96– 37.40	S&P Oper. EPS 2009**E**	4.10	Market Capitalization(B)	$63.003	Beta	0.96
Trailing 12-Month EPS	$4.20	S&P Oper. EPS 2010**E**	4.40	Yield (%)	2.29	S&P 3-Yr. Proj. EPS CAGR(%)	4
Trailing 12-Month P/E	16.0	P/E on S&P Oper. EPS 2009**E**	16.4	Dividend Rate/Share	$1.54	S&P Credit Rating	A
$10K Invested 5 Yrs Ago	$15,281	Common Shares Outstg. (M)	937.5	Institutional Ownership (%)	80		

Price Performance

30-Week Mov. Avg. ···   10-Week Mov. Avg. - -   **GAAP Earnings vs. Previous Year**   **Volume** Above Avg.   **STARS**
12-Mo. Target Price —   Relative Strength —   ▲ Up ▼ Down ▶ No Change   Below Avg.   ★

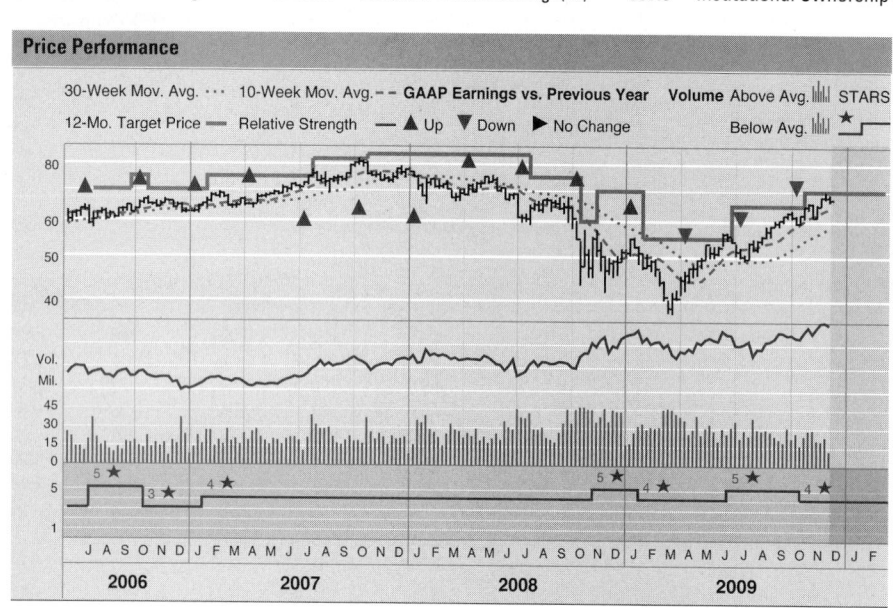

Options: ASE, CBOE, P, Ph

Analysis prepared by **Richard Tortoriello** on October 26, 2009, when the stock traded at **$ 65.81**.

Highlights

► We expect sales to decline by 11% in 2009, and see a turnaround in 2010 to 3% growth. For 2010, we expect continued strong growth at Sikorsky (9%) on military helicopter demand, with lower growth (2% to 3%) in all other segments, due to improvement in the global economy and government stimulus packages in the U.S. and China. We see current improvement in residential construction, and expect improvement in commercial construction to occur later in 2010 or 2011. We also expect some increase in air traffic in 2010 to aid aftermarket revenues in aerospace.

► We estimate 2009 operating margins of 12.5%, down from 13.0% in 2008, on increased restructuring spending to lower costs. We expect a significant rebound in operating margins, to 13.6%, in 2010, as volume improves and benefits from prior restructuring efforts take effect.

► We estimate EPS of $4.10 in 2009, and project growth to $4.40 in 2010. For 2009, we expect free cash flow (cash from operating activities less capital expenditures) of over $4 billion, well in excess of estimated dividend payments of $1.4 billion.

Investment Rationale/Risk

► We see the following trends positively affecting UTX's business: large backlogs of commercial aircraft at both Airbus and Boeing, which we view as providing good production levels through 2010; economic stimulus spending in the U.S., China, and elsewhere, which we expect to affect UTX in late 2009 and 2010; an improved residential housing market; and strong demand for military helicopters. We also see the possibility of a declining U.S. dollar, which aids profitability at UTX. We expect these positives to be offset in 2010 by very weak commercial construction markets, and slow global growth. However, we think recent valuations make the shares attractive for purchase.

► Risks to our recommendation and target price include a severe and prolonged global recession, operational issues within UTX's business segments, and a sustained rise in the dollar.

► Our 12-month target price of $70 is based on an enterprise value-to-estimated 2010 EBITDA multiple of about 9X, slightly above the 20-year historical average multiple of 8X, reflecting our view that signs of global economic recovery merit an average valuation for the shares.

Qualitative Risk Assessment

LOW	MEDIUM	HIGH

Our risk assessment is based on our view of UTX's history of steady growth in both earnings and dividends over the past 10 years, as reflected in its S&P Quality Ranking of A+. We also consider UTX's balance sheet strong, with long-term debt at 28% of total capital and cash at 7% of assets as of September 2009.

Quantitative Evaluations

S&P Quality Ranking   A+

D	C	B-	B	B+	A-	A	A+

Relative Strength Rank   STRONG

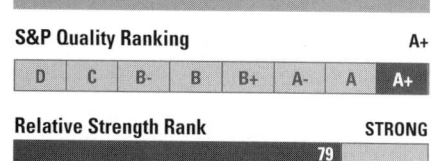

79

LOWEST = 1   HIGHEST = 99

Revenue/Earnings Data

Revenue (Million $)

	1Q	2Q	3Q	4Q	Year
2009	12,249	13,196	13,358	--	--
2008	13,577	15,535	14,702	14,299	58,681
2007	12,278	13,904	13,863	14,714	54,759
2006	10,446	12,046	11,972	12,654	47,829
2005	9,309	10,974	10,832	11,172	42,725
2004	8,646	9,622	9,339	8,938	37,445

Earnings Per Share ($)

2009	0.78	1.05	1.14	E1.13	E4.10
2008	1.03	1.32	1.33	1.23	4.90
2007	0.82	1.16	1.21	1.08	4.27
2006	0.76	1.09	0.99	0.87	3.71
2005	0.64	0.95	0.81	0.71	3.12
2004	0.57	0.83	0.72	0.65	2.76

Fiscal year ended Dec. 31. Next earnings report expected: Late January. EPS Estimates based on S&P Operating Earnings; historical GAAP earnings are as reported.

Dividend Data (Dates: mm/dd Payment Date: mm/dd/yy)

Amount ($)	Date Decl.	Ex-Div. Date	Stk. of Record	Payment Date
0.385	02/09	02/18	02/20	03/10/09
0.385	04/08	05/13	05/15	06/10/09
0.385	06/10	08/19	08/21	09/10/09
0.385	10/14	11/18	11/20	12/10/09

Dividends have been paid since 1936. Source: Company reports.

Please read the Required Disclosures and Analyst Certification on the last page of this report.

United Technologies Corp

STANDARD &POOR'S

Business Summary October 26, 2009

CORPORATE OVERVIEW. United Technologies is a multi-industry holding company that conducts business through six business segments: Carrier, Otis, Pratt & Whitney, UTC Fire & Security, Hamilton Sundstrand, and Sikorsky.

Carrier (25% of sales and 16% of operating profits in 2008) is the world's largest maker of heating, ventilating and air-conditioning (HVAC) and refrigeration systems. It offers HVAC, refrigeration systems and food service equipment, and refrigeration-related controls for residential, commercial, industrial and transportation applications. In addition, Carrier provides installation, retrofit, and parts and services for its products, as well as those of other HVAC and refrigeration makers. International sales, including U.S. export sales, accounted for 60% of segment sales in 2008.

Otis (22% of sales and 31% of operating profits) is the world's largest maker of elevators and escalators. Otis designs, manufactures, sells, installs, maintains and modernizes a wide range of passenger and freight elevators for low-, medium- and high-speed applications, as well as a broad line of escalators and moving walkways. International revenues were 80% of total segment revenues in 2008.

Pratt & Whitney (22% and 26%) is a major supplier of jet engines for commercial, general aviation and military aircraft. P&W also sells industrial gas turbines (for industrial power generation) and space propulsion systems. P&W's Global Services provides maintenance, repair and overhaul services, and fleet management services. Boeing and Airbus accounted for 12% and 7%, respectively, of segment sales in 2008, and the U.S. government accounted for 27%. International revenues were 60% of total segment revenues in 2008.

UTC Fire & Security (11% and 7%), created in 2005 with the purchase of Kidde, is a global provider of security and fire safety products and services, including fire and special hazard detection and supression systems; fire fighting equipment; electronic security, monitoring and rapid response systems; and, service and security personnel services. International sales accounted for 83% of total segment sales in 2008.

Company Financials Fiscal Year Ended Dec. 31

Per Share Data ($)	2008	2007	2006	2005	2004	2003	2002	2001	2000	1999
Tangible Book Value	NM	2.45	NM	0.91	1.84	2.32	1.46	1.66	0.95	0.80
Cash Flow	6.19	5.38	4.74	4.09	3.73	3.14	2.93	2.81	2.63	1.66
Earnings	4.90	4.27	3.71	3.12	2.76	2.35	2.21	1.92	1.78	0.83
S&P Core Earnings	3.81	4.17	3.64	3.05	2.59	2.16	1.32	1.14	NA	NA
Dividends	1.35	1.17	1.02	0.88	0.70	0.57	0.49	0.45	0.41	0.38
Payout Ratio	27%	27%	27%	28%	25%	24%	22%	23%	23%	46%
Prices:High	77.14	82.50	67.47	58.89	53.14	48.38	38.88	43.75	39.88	37.98
Prices:Low	41.76	61.85	54.20	48.43	40.34	26.76	24.42	20.05	23.25	25.81
P/E Ratio:High	16	19	18	19	19	21	18	23	22	46
P/E Ratio:Low	9	14	15	16	15	11	11	10	13	31

Income Statement Analysis (Million $)	2008	2007	2006	2005	2004	2003	2002	2001	2000	1999
Revenue	58,681	54,759	47,829	42,725	37,445	31,034	28,212	27,897	26,583	23,844
Operating Income	9,031	8,223	7,131	6,166	5,448	4,644	4,384	4,138	3,999	2,361
Depreciation	1,228	1,173	1,033	984	978	799	727	905	859	844
Interest Expense	689	666	606	498	363	375	381	426	382	260
Pretax Income	6,936	6,384	5,492	4,684	4,107	3,470	3,276	2,807	2,758	1,257
Effective Tax Rate	27.2%	28.8%	27.2%	26.8%	26.4%	27.1%	27.1%	26.9%	30.9%	25.9%
Net Income	4,689	4,224	3,732	3,164	2,788	2,361	2,236	1,938	1,808	841
S&P Core Earnings	3,648	4,125	3,653	3,089	2,619	2,147	1,298	1,113	NA	NA

Balance Sheet & Other Financial Data (Million $)	2008	2007	2006	2005	2004	2003	2002	2001	2000	1999
Cash	4,327	2,904	2,546	2,247	2,265	1,623	2,080	1,558	748	957
Current Assets	24,099	22,071	18,844	17,206	15,522	12,364	11,751	11,263	10,662	10,627
Total Assets	56,469	54,575	47,141	45,925	40,035	34,648	29,090	26,969	25,364	24,366
Current Liabilities	19,434	17,469	15,208	15,345	12,947	10,295	7,903	8,371	9,344	9,215
Long Term Debt	9,337	8,015	7,037	5,935	4,231	4,257	4,632	4,237	3,476	3,086
Common Equity	15,917	21,355	17,297	16,991	14,008	11,707	10,506	8,369	7,662	7,117
Total Capital	27,379	30,282	25,170	23,704	19,149	16,673	16,445	13,899	12,514	11,664
Capital Expenditures	1,216	1,153	954	929	795	530	586	793	937	762
Cash Flow	5,917	5,319	4,765	4,148	3,766	3,160	2,963	2,843	2,667	1,685
Current Ratio	1.2	1.3	1.2	1.1	1.2	1.2	1.5	1.3	1.1	1.2
% Long Term Debt of Capitalization	35.6	26.5	28.0	25.0	22.1	25.5	28.2	30.5	27.8	26.5
% Net Income of Revenue	8.0	7.7	7.8	7.4	7.4	7.6	7.9	6.9	6.8	3.5
% Return on Assets	8.5	8.3	8.0	7.3	7.4	7.4	8.0	7.4	7.3	4.0
% Return on Equity	25.2	21.9	21.8	20.2	21.7	23.9	23.0	24.2	24.5	14.6

Data as orig reptd.; bef. results of disc opers/spec. items. Per share data adj. for stk. divs.; EPS diluted. E-Estimated. NA-Not Available. NM-Not Meaningful. NR-Not Ranked. UR-Under Review.

Office: 1 Financial Plz, Hartford, CT 06103.
Telephone: 860-728-7000.
Email: invrelations@corphq.utc.com
Website: http://www.utc.com

Chrmn: G. David
Pres & CEO: L.R. Chenevert
COO: E. Drake
SVP & CFO: G.J. Hayes

SVP & General Counsel: C.D. Gill
Investor Contact: J. Moran (860-728-7062)
Board Members: L. R. Chenevert, G. David, J. V. Faraci, J. P. Garnier, J. S. Gorelick, C. M. Gutierrez, E. A. Kangas, C. R. Lee, R. D. McCormick, H. McGraw, III, R. B. Myers, H. P. Swygert, A. H. Villeneuve, C. T. Whitman

Founded: 1934
Domicile: Delaware
Employees: 223,100

Unum Group

STANDARD &POOR'S

S&P Recommendation HOLD ★★★☆☆	Price $18.90 (as of Nov 27, 2009)	12-Mo. Target Price $20.00	Investment Style Large-Cap Value

GICS Sector Financials
Sub-Industry Life & Health Insurance

Summary This leading provider of individual and group disability coverage was formed through the June 1999 merger of Provident Cos. and UNUM Corp.

Key Stock Statistics (Source S&P, Vickers, company reports)

52-Wk Range	$23.25– 7.61	S&P Oper. EPS 2009**E**	2.59	Market Capitalization(B)	$6.270	Beta	1.93
Trailing 12-Month EPS	$2.10	S&P Oper. EPS 2010**E**	2.72	Yield (%)	1.75	S&P 3-Yr. Proj. EPS CAGR(%)	11
Trailing 12-Month P/E	9.0	P/E on S&P Oper. EPS 2009**E**	7.3	Dividend Rate/Share	$0.33	S&P Credit Rating	BBB-
$10K Invested 5 Yrs Ago	$13,270	Common Shares Outstg. (M)	331.8	Institutional Ownership (%)	93		

Price Performance

30-Week Mov. Avg. · · · 10-Week Mov. Avg. - - GAAP Earnings vs. Previous Year   Volume Above Avg. STARS
12-Mo. Target Price — Relative Strength   ▲ Up ▼ Down ► No Change   Below Avg. ★

Options: ASE, CBOE, P

Analysis prepared by **Bret Howlett** on November 10, 2009, when the stock traded at **$ 20.31**.

Qualitative Risk Assessment

LOW	MEDIUM	HIGH

Our risk assessment reflects regulatory scrutiny surrounding certain claims practices. Although the largest suits have been settled, UNM faces the possibility of additional suits and increased reserving for benefit costs in its claims reassessment. Our risk assessment also reflects the poor macro environment and possible increased claims in UNM's product portfolios. We are also concerned about elevated investment losses, although we believe UNM maintains a strong financial position relative to peers.

Quantitative Evaluations

S&P Quality Ranking — B

D	C	B-	B	B+	A-	A	A+

Relative Strength Rank — WEAK

24

LOWEST = 1   HIGHEST = 99

Highlights

► We expect earnings for Unum US to increase slightly in 2010, as premium growth should be tempered by the weak economy. We expect solid persistency and stable margins, as we do not believe high unemployment will lead to a deterioration in the benefit ratio for most products. We forecast mid-single digit sales growth in the core market, but we believe sales will decline in the large case market due to intense competition and lower new business production. We expect earnings to decline in the mid-single digits in supplemental and voluntary lines, as we believe these products are more economically sensitive, and we expect the benefit ratio to top 80% on a higher claims experience.

► We look for flat earnings at Colonial, as favorable agent recruitment trends and stable persistency offset poor risk results in accident, sickness and disability lines. We expect operating earnings at Unum UK to increase in the single digits on an improvement in the benefit ratio and higher sales.

► We project operating EPS of $2.59 in 2009 and $2.72 in 2010. Our estimates exclude realized investment gains or losses.

Investment Rationale/Risk

► While we are encouraged by the underwriting results in Unum U.S. in 2009, we are concerned that rising unemployment may temper sales growth and restrict disability margins and enrollment levels. However, UNM's benefit ratio continues to improve, reflecting solid risk results, changes in sales mix, and underwriting discipline. We believe UNM will continue to experience a decline in sales and poor risk results in the large case market, which should slow premium growth. However, UNM has not been exposed to the magnitude of investment losses that have affected other life insurers, and it maintains a strong risk-based capital ratio. We believe UNM's low leverage and ample liquidity are positives in this environment.

► Risks to our recommendation and target price include worse-than-expected client retention and sales following income protection product price increases; unfavorable claims handling in the group income protection area; higher-than-forecast costs for reassessed claims; and investment losses.

► Our 12-month target price of $20 is 1.0X our 2010 book value per share estimate, below UNM's historical multiple.

Revenue/Earnings Data

Revenue (Million $)

	1Q	2Q	3Q	4Q	Year
2009	2,449	2,628	2,518	--	--
2008	2,541	2,675	2,443	2,324	9,982
2007	2,601	2,666	2,610	2,644	10,520
2006	2,600	2,622	2,617	2,696	10,535
2005	2,572	2,657	2,544	2,665	10,437
2004	2,624	2,509	2,655	2,677	10,465

Earnings Per Share ($)

2009	0.50	0.80	0.67	E0.67	E2.59
2008	0.46	0.69	0.32	0.13	1.62
2007	0.49	0.43	0.52	0.45	1.89
2006	0.23	0.37	-0.19	0.79	1.21
2005	0.49	0.55	0.17	0.43	1.64
2004	-1.93	0.25	0.55	0.45	-0.65

Fiscal year ended Dec. 31. Next earnings report expected: Early February. EPS Estimates based on S&P Operating Earnings; historical GAAP earnings are as reported.

Dividend Data (Dates: mm/dd Payment Date: mm/dd/yy)

Amount ($)	Date Decl.	Ex-Div. Date	Stk. of Record	Payment Date
0.075	01/12	01/22	01/26	02/20/09
0.075	04/13	04/23	04/27	05/15/09
0.083	07/16	07/29	07/31	08/21/09
0.083	10/05	10/22	10/26	11/20/09

Dividends have been paid since 1925. Source: Company reports.

Please read the Required Disclosures and Analyst Certification on the last page of this report.

The McGraw·Hill Companies

Unum Group

STANDARD &POOR'S

Business Summary November 10, 2009

CORPORATE OVERVIEW. UNM provides group and individual income protection insurance in North America and the U.K. through its subsidiaries. The company offers other products, including long-term care insurance, life insurance, group benefits, and related services.

The company has six operating segments: Unum US, Unum UK, Colonial, individual income protection - closed block, other, and corporate. Unum US accounted for 60% of operating revenue in 2008, Unum UK 10%, Colonial 10%, individual income protection - closed block 17%, and other and corporate 2.3%. In 2008, premium income for Unum US declined 1.0%, Unum UK premium income declined roughly 8.2%, and Colonial premium income increased 7.7%.

The Unum US segment includes group income protection insurance, group life and accidental death and dismemberment products, and supplemental and voluntary lines of business. The Unum UK segment includes group long-term income protection insurance, group life products, and individual income protection products issued by Unum Limited and sold primarily in the U.K. through field sales personnel and independent brokers and consultants. The Colonial segment includes a broad line of products sold mainly to employees at their

workplaces, including income protection, life, and cancer and critical illness products. The other segment includes products that are no longer actively marketed, with the exception of the closed block business, including individual life and corporate-owned life insurance, reinsurance pools and management operations, group pension, health insurance, and individual annuities. The corporate segment includes investment income on unallocated corporate assets, interest expense, and certain unallocated corporate income and expense items.

The individual income protection - closed block segment mainly includes individual income protection insurance written on a noncancelable basis with a fixed annual premium. Generally, the policies are individual disability insurance policies designed to be distributed to individuals in a non-workplace setting and written prior to UNM's restructuring of its individual disability business, where the focus was changed to workplace distribution.

Company Financials Fiscal Year Ended Dec. 31

Per Share Data ($)	2008	2007	2006	2005	2004	2003	2002	2001	2000	1999
Tangible Book Value	18.34	21.72	21.93	23.76	23.45	22.94	25.58	21.74	20.29	17.82
Operating Earnings	NA	NA	NA	NA	NA	NA	2.52	2.44	2.37	-1.00
Earnings	1.62	1.89	1.21	1.64	-0.65	-0.96	1.68	2.39	2.33	-0.77
S&P Core Earnings	2.43	2.10	1.29	1.81	-0.26	-0.54	2.35	2.30	NA	NA
Dividends	0.30	0.30	0.30	0.30	0.30	0.37	0.59	0.59	0.59	0.35
Payout Ratio	19%	16%	25%	18%	NM	NM	35%	25%	25%	NM
Prices:High	27.50	28.20	24.44	22.90	18.25	19.54	29.70	33.75	31.94	56.88
Prices:Low	9.33	19.79	16.15	15.50	11.41	5.91	16.30	22.25	11.94	26.00
P/E Ratio:High	17	15	20	14	NM	NM	18	14	14	NM
P/E Ratio:Low	6	10	13	9	NM	NM	10	9	5	NM

Income Statement Analysis (Million $)

	2008	2007	2006	2005	2004	2003	2002	2001	2000	1999
Life Insurance in Force	629,069	692,012	773,070	833,363	908,034	787,199	712,826	642,988	583,848	567,215
Premium Income:Life	1,620	1,641	1,761	7,816	5,985	1,800	1,683	1,554	1,448	1,452
Premium Income:A & H	6,163	6,261	6,187	1,787	1,855	5,816	5,770	5,524	5,608	5,391
Net Investment Income	2,389	2,410	2,321	2,188	2,159	2,158	2,086	2,003	2,060	2,060
Total Revenue	9,982	10,520	10,535	10,437	10,465	9,992	9,613	9,395	9,432	9,330
Pretax Income	824	997	465	710	-260	-435	1,019	825	866	-166
Net Operating Income	NA	NA	NA	NA	NA	NA	614	593	NA	NA
Net Income	553	672	404	514	-192	-265	817	582	564	-183
S&P Core Earnings	824	748	428	570	-77.1	-150	568	564	NA	NA

Balance Sheet & Other Financial Data (Million $)

	2008	2007	2006	2005	2004	2003	2002	2001	2000	1999
Cash & Equivalent	49.9	791	768	688	719	663	734	2,515	NA	836
Premiums Due	1,785	1,915	2,057	NA	NA	NA	NA	NA	NA	NA
Investment Assets:Bonds	31,926	35,655	35,002	34,857	32,488	31,187	27,486	24,393	22,589	22,357
Investment Assets:Stocks	208	Nil	Nil	13.6	12.9	39.1	27.9	10.9	24.5	38.0
Investment Assets:Loans	4,029	3,705	944	3,941	3,572	3,353	3,344	3,510	3,679	3,595
Investment Assets:Total	37,866	40,951	40,163	39,357	36,588	35,028	31,152	28,324	26,604	26,549
Deferred Policy Costs	2,472	2,381	2,983	2,913	2,883	3,052	2,982	2,675	2,424	2,391
Total Assets	49,417	52,433	52,823	51,867	50,832	49,718	45,260	42,443	40,364	38,448
Debt	2,259	2,515	2,660	3,262	2,862	2,789	1,914	2,304	1,915	1,467
Common Equity	6,398	8,040	7,719	7,364	7,224	7,271	9,398	5,940	5,576	4,983
% Return on Revenue	5.5	6.4	3.9	4.9	NM	NM	8.5	6.2	6.0	NM
% Return on Assets	1.1	1.3	0.8	1.0	NM	NM	1.9	1.4	1.4	NM
% Return on Equity	7.7	8.5	5.4	7.0	NM	NM	9.1	10.1	10.7	NM
% Investment Yield	6.1	5.9	5.8	5.8	6.0	6.5	7.0	7.3	7.8	NM

Data as orig reptd.; bef. results of disc opers/spec. items. Per share data adj. for stk. divs.; EPS diluted. E-Estimated. NA-Not Available. NM-Not Meaningful. NR-Not Ranked. UR-Under Review.

Office: 1 Fountain Square, Chattanooga, TN 37402-1307.
Telephone: 423-294-1011.
Website: http://www.unum.com
Chrmn: J.S. Fossel

Pres & CEO: S. Hall
Pres & CEO: T. Watjen
EVP & CFO: R.P. McKenney
EVP & General Counsel: E.L. Bishop, III

Investor Contact: T.A. White (423-294-8996)
Board Members: E. M. Caulfield, J. S. Fossel, P. H. Godwin, R. E. Goldsberry, K. T. Kabat, T. A. Kinser, G. C. Larson, A. MacMillan, Jr., M. McCaig, E. J. Muhl, M. J. Passarella, W. J. Ryan, T. Watjen

Founded: 1887
Domicile: Delaware
Employees: 9,800

The McGraw-Hill Companies

Valero Energy Corp

STANDARD &POOR'S

S&P Recommendation HOLD ★ ★ ★ ☆ ☆

Price	**12-Mo. Target Price**	**Investment Style**
$16.00 (as of Nov 27, 2009)	$23.00	Large-Cap Blend

GICS Sector Energy
Sub-Industry Oil & Gas Refining & Marketing

Summary Valero is the largest oil refiner in North America, one of the largest independent U.S. refined petroleum products retailers, and operates refineries that can process sour and acidic crude oils.

Key Stock Statistics (Source S&P, Vickers, company reports)

52-Wk Range	$26.20– 15.10	S&P Oper. EPS 2009**E**	-0.43	Market Capitalization(B)	$9.030	Beta	1.25
Trailing 12-Month EPS	$-7.26	S&P Oper. EPS 2010**E**	1.80	Yield (%)	3.75	S&P 3-Yr. Proj. EPS CAGR(%)	-16
Trailing 12-Month P/E	NM	P/E on S&P Oper. EPS 2009**E**	NM	Dividend Rate/Share	$0.60	S&P Credit Rating	BBB
$10K Invested 5 Yrs Ago	$7,174	Common Shares Outstg. (M)	564.4	Institutional Ownership (%)	76		

Price Performance

30-Week Mov. Avg. · · · 10-Week Mov. Avg. - - GAAP Earnings vs. Previous Year Volume Above Avg. ⅢⅢ STARS
12-Mo. Target Price — Relative Strength — ▲ Up ▼ Down ▶ No Change Below Avg. ⅢⅢ ★

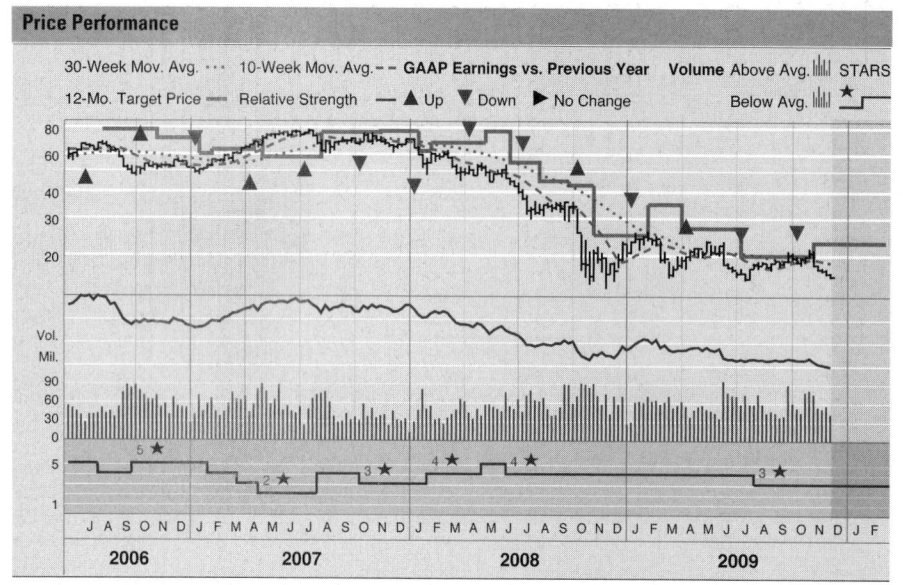

Options: ASE, CBOE, P, Ph

Analysis prepared by **Tina J. Vital** on October 29, 2009, when the stock traded at **$ 18.70.**

Highlights

► Demand for refined products has dropped on an economic slowdown, and industry-wide refining margins have narrowed. We project that U.S. industrywide refining margins will narrow about 16% in 2009 before widening about 7% in 2010 on an improved economic outlook. As a result, refiners have cut production rates. VLO's third-quarter throughputs dropped 8%, to 2.38 million b/d; we expect fourth-quarter rates will decline about 4.6% from third-quarter levels.

► VLO has rationalized its operations to improve its profitability. It shut down its entire refinery at Aruba, is in the process of shutting down a coker and fluid catalytic cracking unit at Corpus Christi, and intends to shut down a gasifer and coker complex in Delaware City. In addition, fourth and first quarter turnarounds are slated at its St. Charles, Port Arthur, Memphis and Wilmington refineries.

► After-tax operating earnings exclude $0.47 of net special charges in the 2009 first nine months. We look for an after-tax operating loss for VLO in 2009, but we expect earnings to rebound to positive ground in 2010 on our expectations for increased product demand.

Investment Rationale/Risk

► VLO is the largest independent refiner in North America, focused on the refining of heavy and sour crudes. As a result, we believe narrowed sour crude discounts and light-heavy crude differentials pose significant challenges for the company over the next 12 months. Offsets include its retail fuel marketing and investments in alternative energy. Over the long term, we believe VLO's size and ability to refine these lower quality oils offer strategic and economic advantages. In December 2008, VLO estimated its complexity-adjusted capacity at 2.64 million b/d, with a Nelson factor of 11.3.

► Risks to our recommendation and target price include weaker economic growth, excess industry refining capacity, or changes in operating conditions that lead to a narrowing of margins or reduced throughput rates.

► A blend of our DCF ($24 per share intrinsic value assuming a WACC of 9.1% and terminal growth of 3%) and relative valuations leads to our 12-month target price of $23. This represents an expected enterprise value of about 5.2X our 2010 EBITDA estimate, a discount to peers.

Qualitative Risk Assessment

LOW	MEDIUM	HIGH

Our risk assessment reflects our view of VLO's strong business profile in the volatile and competitive oil refining industry. The company is the largest oil refiner in the U.S. and possesses above-average refining complexity, which allows it to process a large amount of lower-cost heavy and sour crudes.

Quantitative Evaluations

S&P Quality Ranking   B+

D	C	B-	B	B+	A-	A	A+

Relative Strength Rank   WEAK

16

LOWEST = 1   HIGHEST = 99

Revenue/Earnings Data

Revenue (Million $)

	1Q	2Q	3Q	4Q	Year
2009	13,824	17,696	19,489	--	--
2008	27,945	36,436	35,753	18,358	118,298
2007	18,755	24,202	23,699	28,671	95,327
2006	20,941	26,781	24,319	19,792	91,833
2005	14,943	18,032	23,283	25,894	82,162
2004	11,082	13,808	14,339	15,390	54,619

Earnings Per Share ($)

2009	0.59	-0.48	-1.12	E-0.15	E-0.43
2008	0.48	1.38	2.18	-6.36	-2.16
2007	1.86	3.57	1.34	1.02	7.72
2006	1.32	2.98	2.55	1.80	8.64
2005	0.96	1.53	1.47	2.06	6.10
2004	0.46	1.14	0.79	0.88	3.27

Fiscal year ended Dec. 31. Next earnings report expected: Late January. EPS Estimates based on S&P Operating Earnings; historical GAAP earnings are as reported.

Dividend Data (Dates: mm/dd Payment Date: mm/dd/yy)

Amount ($)	Date Decl.	Ex-Div. Date	Stk. of Record	Payment Date
0.150	01/20	02/09	02/11	03/11/09
0.150	04/30	05/22	05/27	06/17/09
0.150	07/30	08/10	08/12	09/16/09
0.150	10/15	11/06	11/11	12/09/09

Dividends have been paid since 1997. Source: Company reports.

Please read the Required Disclosures and Analyst Certification on the last page of this report.

Valero Energy Corp

STANDARD &POOR'S

Business Summary October 29, 2009

CORPORATE OVERVIEW. Incorporated in 1981 under the name Valero Refining and Marketing Co., the company changed its name to Valero Energy Co. (VLO) in 1997. In 2001, VLO merged with Ultramar Diamond Shamrock, and in 2005 with Premcor Inc., creating the largest refiner in North America, based on atmospheric distillation capacity.

The company operates in two business segments: Refining (91% of 2008 operating revenues, 68% of 2008 operating income), and Retail (9%, 32%). VLO serves customers in the U.S. (85% of 2008 revenues), Canada (8%), and other countries (7%); no single customer accounted for over 10% of consolidated operating revenues.

The Refining segment includes refining operations, wholesale marketing, product supply and distribution, and transportation operations. As of year-end 2008, the company owned and operated 16 refineries in the U.S., Canada and Aruba, with a combined throughput capacity of 2.99 million barrels per day (b/d). These capacities by region include: Gulf Coast (eight refineries, 54% of 2008 throughput capacity), the Mid-Continent (three, 15%), the West Coast

(two, 10%), and the Northeast (three, 21%).

During 2008, sour crude oils, acidic sweet crude oils and residuals represented 60% of VLO's throughput volumes; sweet crude oil 23%, and blendstocks and other feedstocks 17%. About 65% of VLO's current crude oil feedstock requirements were purchased through term contracts, with the remainder generally purchased on the spot market. About 80% of these 2008 crude oil feedstocks were imported from foreign sources, and around 20% were domestic.

VLO is one of the largest independent retailers of refined products in the central and southwest U.S. and eastern Canada. Its retail operations are segregated geographically into two groups: Retail-U.S. System (1,010 company operated sites - 79% owned, 21% leased - in 2008) and Retail-Canada (412 retail stores, owned or leased).

Company Financials Fiscal Year Ended Dec. 31

Per Share Data ($)	2008	2007	2006	2005	2004	2003	2002	2001	2000	1999
Tangible Book Value	29.82	31.75	23.33	15.82	9.55	5.86	3.24	3.90	6.28	4.84
Cash Flow	0.18	9.55	10.47	7.57	3.24	2.31	1.23	2.75	1.86	0.47
Earnings	-2.16	7.72	8.64	6.10	3.27	1.27	0.21	2.21	1.40	0.06
S&P Core Earnings	2.32	7.73	8.32	6.02	3.25	1.25	0.14	2.14	NA	NA
Dividends	0.57	0.48	0.30	0.19	0.15	0.15	0.10	0.09	0.08	0.08
Payout Ratio	NM	6%	3%	3%	4%	11%	48%	4%	6%	128%
Prices:High	71.12	78.68	70.75	58.63	23.91	11.77	12.49	13.15	9.66	6.33
Prices:Low	13.94	47.66	46.84	21.01	11.43	8.05	5.79	7.88	4.63	4.17
P/E Ratio:High	NM	10	8	10	7	9	60	6	7	NM
P/E Ratio:Low	NM	6	5	3	3	6	28	4	3	NM

Income Statement Analysis (Million $)										
Revenue	118,298	95,327	91,833	82,162	54,619	37,969	26,976	14,988	14,671	7,961
Operating Income	20.4	8,278	9,165	6,334	2,979	1,733	920	1,139	723	162
Depreciation, Depletion and Amortization	1,038	1,360	1,155	875	618	511	449	138	112	92.4
Interest Expense	340	466	210	266	260	278	256	102	83.0	55.4
Pretax Income	336	6,726	8,196	5,287	2,710	989	164	895	528	20.2
Effective Tax Rate	NM	32.1%	33.3%	32.1%	33.4%	36.9%	35.5%	37.0%	35.8%	29.2%
Net Income	-1,131	4,565	5,463	3,590	1,804	622	91.5	564	339	14.3
S&P Core Earnings	1,212	4,572	5,258	3,534	1,785	604	60.0	547	NA	NA

Balance Sheet & Other Financial Data (Million $)										
Cash	940	2,495	1,590	436	864	369	409	346	14.6	60.1
Current Assets	9,450	14,792	10,760	8,276	5,264	3,817	3,536	4,113	1,285	829
Total Assets	34,417	42,722	37,753	32,728	19,392	15,664	14,465	14,337	4,308	2,979
Current Liabilities	6,209	11,914	8,822	7,305	4,534	3,064	3,007	4,730	1,039	719
Long Term Debt	6,264	6,470	4,657	5,156	3,901	4,245	4,867	2,805	1,042	785
Common Equity	15,620	18,507	18,605	14,982	7,590	5,535	4,308	4,203	1,527	1,085
Total Capital	26,047	28,998	27,309	20,206	13,710	11,585	10,592	8,884	3,149	2,146
Capital Expenditures	2,790	2,260	3,187	2,133	1,292	976	628	394	195	101
Cash Flow	93.0	5,529	6,616	4,452	1,791	1,128	541	701	451	107
Current Ratio	1.5	1.2	1.2	1.1	1.2	1.2	1.2	0.9	1.2	1.2
% Long Term Debt of Capitalization	24.0	22.3	17.1	25.5	28.5	36.6	45.9	31.6	33.0	36.5
% Return on Assets	NM	11.4	15.5	13.8	10.3	4.1	0.6	6.0	9.3	0.5
% Return on Equity	NM	24.6	32.5	31.7	27.3	12.5	2.2	19.7	26.0	1.3

Data as orig reptd.; bef. results of disc opers/spec. items. Per share data adj. for stk. divs.; EPS diluted. E-Estimated. NA-Not Available. NM-Not Meaningful. NR-Not Ranked. UR-Under Review.

Office: 1 Valero Way, San Antonio, TX 78249-1616.
Telephone: 210-345-2000.
Email: investorrelations@valero.com
Website: http://www.valero.com

Chrmn, Pres & CEO: W.R. Klesse
COO & EVP: R.J. Marcogliese
Investor Contact: M.S. Ciskowski (210-345-2000)
EVP, CFO & Chief Acctg Officer: M.S. Ciskowski

EVP & General Counsel: K.S. Bowers
Board Members: W. E. Bradford, R. K. Calgaard, J. D. Choate, I. F. Engelhardt, R. M. Escobedo, W. R. Klesse, B. Marbut, D. L. Nickles, R. Profusek, S. K. Purcell, S. M. Waters

Founded: 1955
Domicile: Delaware
Employees: 21,765

The McGraw-Hill Companies

Varian Medical Systems Inc

STANDARD &POOR'S

S&P Recommendation	HOLD ★★★☆☆	Price $46.83 (as of Nov 27, 2009)	12-Mo. Target Price $46.00	Investment Style Large-Cap Growth

GICS Sector Health Care
Sub-Industry Health Care Equipment

Summary This leading maker of radiotherapy cancer systems also supplies X-ray tubes and flat-panel digital subsystems for imaging in medical, scientific and industrial applications.

Key Stock Statistics (Source S&P, Vickers, company reports)

52-Wk Range	$47.78–27.10	S&P Oper. EPS 2010**E**	2.70	Market Capitalization(B)	$5.879	Beta	0.77
Trailing 12-Month EPS	$2.55	S&P Oper. EPS 2011**E**	2.90	Yield (%)	Nil	S&P 3-Yr. Proj. EPS CAGR(%)	6
Trailing 12-Month P/E	18.4	P/E on S&P Oper. EPS 2010**E**	17.3	Dividend Rate/Share	Nil	S&P Credit Rating	NA
$10K Invested 5 Yrs Ago	$11,325	Common Shares Outstg. (M)	125.5	Institutional Ownership (%)	91		

Price Performance

30-Week Mov. Avg. · · · 10-Week Mov. Avg. – – **GAAP Earnings vs. Previous Year** Volume Above Avg. STARS
12-Mo. Target Price — Relative Strength — ▲ Up ▼ Down ▶ No Change Below Avg. ★

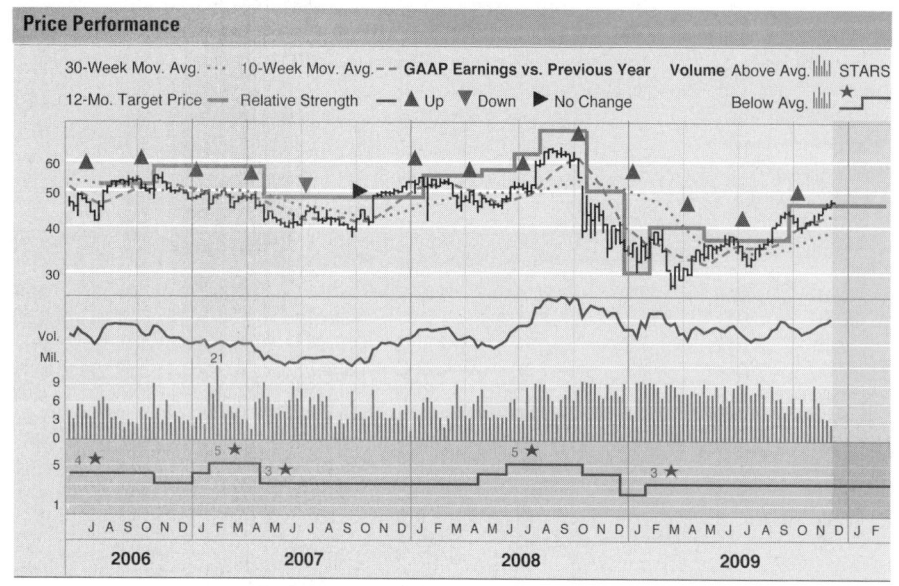

Options: ASE

Analysis prepared by **Phillip M. Seligman** on November 17, 2009, when the stock traded at **$ 46.36**.

Highlights

▶ We look for total sales in FY 10 (Sep.) to increase 4.5%, on reasonably strong demand for RapidArc products and for services, particularly outside the U.S., and a recent recovery in X-ray revenues, reflecting stronger demand for VAR's new digital radiography panels and after-market X-ray tubes that we view as sustainable. We also assume top-line benefits from the lapping of the unfavorable currency exchange experienced in FY 09. While we view long-term prospects as favorable for cargo-screening systems, we expect orders for such systems to remain weak as governments continue to focus on more-immediate spending priorities.

▶ We see gross margins narrowing in FY 10, mainly on pricing pressures and a less-favorable geographic mix, assuming a greater proportion of ex-U.S. sales, which have tended to focus more on lower-priced, lower-margin products. We expect SG&A costs to decline as a percentage of sales on revenue leverage, but the R&D cost ratio to rise by 20 basis points, reflecting VAR's intention to boost R&D spending.

▶ Our FY 10 and FY 11 EPS estimates for continuing operations are $2.70 and $2.90, respectively.

Investment Rationale/Risk

▶ VAR's order rates have been hurt almost across the board by U.S. hospitals facing tightened capital budgets. Still, we see more U.S. hospitals prioritizing radiation oncology modernization assuming their budgets eventually expand. Although Medicare recently increased its reimbursement rate for Intensity Modulation Radiation Therapy (IMRT) in hospital outpatient settings by 16.0% for calendar 2010, not much below its proposed 16.8% increase, we do not think this will positively impact purchase decisions. In addition, we do not view Medicare's decision to cut its reimbursement rate for IMRT in free-standing clinics by 23.7%, compared to its proposed 43.7% cut, as enhancing the prospects for more orders for VAR. Meanwhile, we are encouraged by VAR's overseas gains.

▶ Risks to our recommendation and target price include unfavorable changes in Medicare reimbursements, competitive pricing, and further deterioration in the outlook for hospital spending plans in 2010.

▶ Our 12-month target price of $46 is 16.8X our calendar 2010 EPS estimate of $2.74, reflecting recent peerwide valuation expansion but still below historical averages.

Qualitative Risk Assessment

LOW	MEDIUM	HIGH

Our risk assessment reflects that while Varian offers some of the more technologically advanced products in the oncology equipment industry, the company operates in a competitive industry characterized by technological innovation and new product entrants. In addition, although we believe radiation therapy will continue to be an integral component of global cancer treatment protocols, the continued development of drug-based oncology treatments represents a substantial threat to the company's radiation therapy equipment business. In our view, tight credit market conditions globally could also negatively affect capital expenditure decisions by Varian's customers.

Quantitative Evaluations

S&P Quality Ranking B+

D	C	B-	B	B+	A-	A	A+

Relative Strength Rank STRONG

88

LOWEST = 1 HIGHEST = 99

Revenue/Earnings Data

Revenue (Million $)

	1Q	2Q	3Q	4Q	Year
2009	508.7	553.6	509.8	642.0	2,214
2008	451.2	518.4	507.4	592.7	2,070
2007	387.9	442.6	423.7	522.4	1,777
2006	334.2	413.9	395.7	454.0	1,598
2005	299.0	350.8	346.5	386.2	1,383
2004	267.0	320.6	303.1	344.8	1,236

Earnings Per Share ($)

2009	0.56	0.64	0.68	0.78	2.65
2008	0.46	0.57	0.61	0.68	2.31
2007	0.37	0.46	0.39	0.61	1.83
2006	0.30	0.41	0.49	0.61	1.80
2005	0.29	0.39	0.37	0.45	1.50
2004	0.21	0.30	0.30	0.37	1.18

Fiscal year ended Sep. 30. Next earnings report expected: Late January. EPS Estimates based on S&P Operating Earnings; historical GAAP earnings are as reported.

Dividend Data

Cash dividends were last paid in 1999.

The **McGraw·Hill** Companies

Varian Medical Systems Inc

STANDARD & POOR'S

Business Summary November 17, 2009

CORPORATE OVERVIEW. Varian is one of the largest manufacturers of oncology diagnostic products, X-ray tubes, and imaging subsystems. The company is focused primarily on capturing share in the global oncology radiation therapy markets. Cancer rates are expected to increase 50% by 2020.

MARKET PROFILE. Driven by an aging global population and improved diagnostic methods, the number of newly diagnosed cancer cases continues to increase. According to estimates published in February 2005 by the Annals of Oncology, nearly 2.9 million new cancer cases were diagnosed during 2004, and the U.S. National Cancer Institute estimates that cancer diagnoses will rise 1.6 million per year by 2010, a 23% increase from the 1.3 million cancers per year seen in 2000. Radiation therapy is commonly used in the treatment of cancer, alone or in combination with surgery or chemotherapy. The most common type of radiotherapy uses X-rays delivered by external beams, and is administered using linear accelerators. In addition to external radiation, radioactive seeds, wires or ribbons are sometimes inserted into a tumor or into a body cavity (brachytherapy), a modality that does not require radiation to pass through healthy tissues.

Varian's oncology systems group (81% of FY 09 (Sep.) revenues) designs, markets and services hardware and software products for cancer radiation treatment, including linear accelerators, treatment simulators and verification products, and software systems for planning cancer treatment and managing information and images for radiation oncology. Products focus on enabling a new therapy that delivers high doses of radiation to tumors while reducing risk to surrounding tissues. This three-dimensional conformal radiation therapy, called Intensity Modulation Radiation Therapy (IMRT), links treatment planning, information management and driver software to the treatment delivery device, the linear accelerator. This is designed to allow clinicians to determine and deliver a clinically optimized plan of radiation for each patient. IMRT is used to treat head and neck, breast, prostate, pancreatic, lung, liver, gynecological and central nervous system cancers. VAR has also developed image-guided radiation therapy (IGRT), which improves radiation therapy precision by using technologies that compensate for tumor changes and movements during and between treatments.

Company Financials Fiscal Year Ended Sep. 30

Per Share Data ($)	2009	2008	2007	2006	2005	2004	2003	2002	2001	2000
Tangible Book Value	NA	6.43	4.92	5.21	4.11	3.74	3.71	3.05	2.93	2.13
Cash Flow	NA	2.60	2.08	2.02	1.70	1.32	1.06	0.81	0.64	0.55
Earnings	2.65	2.31	1.83	1.80	1.50	1.18	0.92	0.66	0.50	0.41
S&P Core Earnings	NA	2.28	1.83	1.80	1.34	1.04	0.78	0.54	0.40	NA
Dividends	Nil	Nil	Nil	Nil	Nil	Nil	Nil	Nil	Nil	Nil
Payout Ratio	Nil	Nil	Nil	Nil	Nil	Nil	Nil	Nil	Nil	Nil
Prices:High	47.78	65.84	53.22	61.70	52.92	46.49	35.65	25.66	19.31	17.75
Prices:Low	27.10	33.12	37.30	41.10	31.65	29.63	23.70	15.80	13.50	6.88
P/E Ratio:High	18	29	29	34	35	39	39	39	39	43
P/E Ratio:Low	10	14	20	23	21	25	26	24	27	17

Income Statement Analysis (Million $)	2009	2008	2007	2006	2005	2004	2003	2002	2001	2000
Revenue	2,214	2,070	1,777	1,598	1,383	1,236	1,042	873	774	690
Operating Income	NA	456	367	339	332	277	219	165	129	108
Depreciation	NA	36.7	32.2	29.6	27.1	20.8	20.3	20.4	19.3	17.8
Interest Expense	NA	4.88	4.79	4.65	4.70	4.67	4.38	4.49	4.13	5.16
Pretax Income	475	426	343	319	308	257	201	146	107	84.9
Effective Tax Rate	30.2%	30.7%	30.1%	23.6%	33.0%	35.0%	35.0%	36.0%	36.5%	37.5%
Net Income	332	295	239	244	207	167	131	93.6	68.0	53.0
S&P Core Earnings	NA	292	240	245	184	148	111	75.9	54.2	NA

Balance Sheet & Other Financial Data (Million $)	2009	2008	2007	2006	2005	2004	2003	2002	2001	2000
Cash	554	397	263	366	378	352	323	299	219	83.3
Current Assets	NA	1,394	1,160	1,156	1,017	885	806	651	620	451
Total Assets	2,308	1,976	1,684	1,512	1,317	1,170	1,053	910	759	603
Current Liabilities	NA	782	782	644	544	461	409	358	285	250
Long Term Debt	23.4	32.4	40.4	49.4	57.3	53.3	58.5	58.5	58.5	58.5
Common Equity	1,312	1,027	821	797	659	614	564	504	418	270
Total Capital	1,344	1,060	862	847	716	667	622	562	477	329
Capital Expenditures	NA	81.4	64.1	41.4	43.9	24.2	18.9	25.9	16.5	19.2
Cash Flow	NA	332	272	273	234	188	151	114	87.3	70.8
Current Ratio	2.0	1.8	1.5	1.8	1.9	1.9	2.0	1.8	2.2	1.8
% Long Term Debt of Capitalization	1.7	3.1	4.7	5.8	8.0	8.0	9.4	10.4	12.3	17.8
% Net Income of Revenue	15.0	14.3	13.5	15.2	14.9	13.5	12.6	10.7	8.8	7.7
% Return on Assets	15.5	16.1	15.0	17.2	16.5	15.0	13.3	11.2	10.0	9.3
% Return on Equity	28.4	32.0	29.6	33.4	32.2	28.4	25.3	20.3	19.2	23.3

Data as orig reptd.; bef. results of disc opers/spec. items. Per share data adj. for stk. divs.; EPS diluted. E-Estimated. NA-Not Available. NM-Not Meaningful. NR-Not Ranked. UR-Under Review.

Office: 3100 Hansen Way, Palo Alto, CA 94304-1030.
Telephone: 650-493-4000.
Website: http://www.varian.com
Chrmn: R.M. Levy

Pres & CEO: T.E. Guertin
SVP & CFO: E.W. Finney
CTO: G.A. Zdasiuk
Chief Acctg Officer & Cntlr: T. Chen

Investor Contact: S. Sias (650-424-5782)
Board Members: S. L. Bostrom, J. S. Brown, R. A. Eckert, T. E. Guertin, M. R. Laret, R. M. Levy, D. W. Martin, Jr., R. Naumann-Etienne, V. Thyagarajan

Founded: 1976
Domicile: Delaware
Employees: 4,900

Ventas Inc.

STANDARD &POOR'S

S&P Recommendation HOLD ★★★☆☆

Price	12-Mo. Target Price	Investment Style
$41.00 (as of Nov 27, 2009)	$44.00	Large-Cap Blend

GICS Sector Financials
Sub-Industry Specialized REITS

Summary This real estate investment trust invests in health care facilities, including senior housing, specialty care facilities, hospitals, and medical office buildings.

Key Stock Statistics (Source S&P, Vickers, company reports)

52-Wk Range	$42.82– 17.97	S&P FFO/Sh. 2009E	2.62	Market Capitalization(B)	$6.421	Beta		1.56
Trailing 12-Month FFO/Share	NA	S&P FFO/Sh. 2010E	2.72	Yield (%)	5.00	S&P 3-Yr. FFO/Sh. Proj. CAGR(%)		-4
Trailing 12-Month P/FFO	NA	P/FFO on S&P FFO/Sh. 2009E	15.6	Dividend Rate/Share	$2.05	S&P Credit Rating		BBB-
$10K Invested 5 Yrs Ago	$19,413	Common Shares Outstg. (M)	156.6	Institutional Ownership (%)	NM			

Price Performance

30-Week Mov. Avg. · · · · 10-Week Mov. Avg. – – GAAP Earnings vs. Previous Year   Volume Above Avg. STARS
12-Mo. Target Price — Relative Strength ▲ Up ▼ Down ▶ No Change   Below Avg. ★

Analysis prepared by **Robert McMillan** on November 02, 2009, when the stock traded at **$ 40.13**.

Highlights

▶ We believe VTR has assembled a portfolio of health care properties that is well diversified in terms of asset type, geography, and tenant base. With its core focus on senior housing, we think VTR will benefit from increased demand driven by the aging baby boomer population. However, we see economic uncertainty and a still weak residential real estate market straining those consumers looking to transition into senior housing.

▶ After rising 23% in 2008 on acquisitions, we see revenue growth in VTR's need-based businesses slowing to a more normal 1.2% in 2009 and 1.7% in 2010. In VTR's senior housing portfolio, average occupancy in the 2009 third quarter fell to 88.1% from 91.5% a year earlier, while the average daily rate (ADR) rose 1.2%. Occupancy fell to 94.0% from 94.5% in the medical office portfolio, while average annual rents jumped 7.4%. We look for continued expense reductions to also help results.

▶ We forecast per-share funds from operations (FFO) of $2.62 (or $2.71 on a normalized basis which excludes non-recurring items) in 2009 and $2.72 in 2010.

Investment Rationale/Risk

▶ We like the predictable nature of VTR's long-term triple net lease revenue stream, and believe the stock correlates less with macroeconomic trends than most other REITs. Amid economic uncertainty, we favor what we see as VTR's stable revenue stream with minimal short-term lease expirations, solid balance sheet, and relatively secure dividend payout. We view the shares as fairly valued.

▶ Risks to our recommendation and target price include a faster-than-expected decline in senior housing occupancy, and an decrease in government reimbursement rates.

▶ The stock recently traded at about 15.1X trailing 12-month FFO per share. Our 12-month target price of $44 is about 16.2X our forward four-quarter FFO per share estimate of $2.70, a modest multiple by historical standards, but reasonable, we believe, given VTR's portfolio and operating performance. We expect a widening of the valuation multiple to be driven by continued improvement in operating results. We think VTR's recent decision to commence a tender offer for some of its outstanding debt will further help reduce leverage.

Qualitative Risk Assessment

LOW	MEDIUM	HIGH

Our risk assessment reflects VTR's position as the owner of a large and diversified portfolio of health care-related properties that provide what we see as a steady and predictable stream of income.

Quantitative Evaluations

S&P Quality Ranking   B+

D	C	B-	B	B+	A-	A	A+

Relative Strength Rank   STRONG

74

LOWEST = 1   HIGHEST = 99

Revenue/FFO Data

Revenue (Million $)

	1Q	2Q	3Q	4Q	Year
2009	230.9	232.0	235.8	--	--
2008	231.8	233.5	238.6	234.0	929.8
2007	119.2	193.8	226.3	232.6	771.8
2006	97.81	100.3	109.7	120.6	428.4
2005	63.80	74.95	95.93	98.30	333.0
2004	53.94	59.43	61.26	62.23	236.9

FFO Per Share ($)

	1Q	2Q	3Q	4Q	Year
2009	0.66	0.68	0.66	E0.70	E2.62
2008	0.75	0.73	0.81	0.69	2.74
2007	0.68	0.70	0.66	0.66	2.69
2006	0.55	0.57	0.64	0.69	2.44
2005	0.48	0.51	0.54	0.55	2.09
2004	0.41	0.45	0.47	0.47	1.80

Fiscal year ended Dec. 31. Next earnings report expected: Mid February. FFO Estimates based on S&P Funds From Operations Est..

Dividend Data (Dates: mm/dd Payment Date: mm/dd/yy)

Amount ($)	Date Decl.	Ex-Div. Date	Stk. of Record	Payment Date
0.513	12/08	12/17	12/19	12/30/08
0.513	02/12	03/16	03/18	03/31/09
0.513	05/07	06/05	06/09	06/30/09
0.513	08/31	09/09	09/11	09/30/09

Dividends have been paid since 1999. Source: Company reports.

The McGraw·Hill Companies

Ventas Inc.

Business Summary November 02, 2009

CORPORATE OVERVIEW. Ventas Inc. is a health care REIT that specializes in senior housing (248 facilities), skilled nursing (192), hospitals (41), and medical office buildings (32). In 2008, approximately 78% of VTR's owned property annualized net operating income came from triple-net lease properties, where VTR receives rents, and tenants receive all property level revenues and pay all property level expenses. Properties under triple-net lease agreements include hospitals, skilled nursing, and independent and assisted living facilities. The remaining 22% came from operating agreements under which VTR is responsible for property level expenses and collects property level revenues. This includes a senior housing management agreement with Sunrise Senior Living, and VTR's medical office buildings.

VTR's independent and assisted living facilities (68% of 2008 total revenues) are a combination of housing, personalized supportive services, and health care designed to meet the needs of those who require help with the activities of daily living. Occupancy at such facilities is on a month-to-month basis, and revenues come from private pay sources. Skilled nursing facilities (19%) provide inpatient skilled nursing and personal care services as well as rehabilitative, restorative and transitional medical services. The company's hospital facilities (10%) include mostly long-term acute care hospitals specializing in treating patients that have a length of stay greater than 25 days and suffer from chronically ill patients with medically complex ailments. Medical office buildings (3%) are office and clinical facilities designed for the use of physicians and other health care professionals.

As of December 31, 2008, VTR had about $5.74 billion in gross real estate investments and $207 million in loan receivables. VTR's stated business strategy is to maintain a diversified portfolio, have stable earnings and growth, and manage a balance sheet with strong liquidity.

PRIMARY BUSINESS DYNAMICS. We think the key issue facing the health care facility operations industry is changing government reimbursement rates for Medicare and Medicaid programs. These government programs tend to account for the majority of revenue for health care facility operators, and have come under pressure in recent years as the government attempts to deal with rising health care costs. While we believe the reimbursement environment has stabilized, we see the uncertainty around future reimbursement levels as the largest risk factor for both facility operators and health care facility owners, whose revenue is dependent on the ability of operators to make their lease and mortgage payments. We expect the $87 billion in additional Medicaid funding under the recent federal stimulus package to remove some of the uncertainty surrounding Medicaid reimbursement cuts in skilled nursing, but since Medicaid is directly related to unemployment levels, we believe the worsening jobs outlook may offset much of the law's effect.

Company Financials Fiscal Year Ended Dec. 31

Per Share Data ($)	2008	2007	2006	2005	2004	2003	2002	2001	2000	1999
Tangible Book Value	14.99	13.65	6.51	6.28	1.73	0.53	NM	NM	NM	0.04
Earnings	1.30	1.15	1.25	1.31	1.19	1.21	0.75	0.75	-0.90	0.63
S&P Core Earnings	1.30	1.15	1.25	1.14	1.18	1.08	0.70	0.56	NA	NA
Dividends	2.05	2.05	1.58	1.44	1.30	1.07	0.95	0.92	0.62	0.39
Payout Ratio	158%	105%	126%	110%	109%	88%	127%	123%	NM	62%
Prices:High	52.00	47.97	42.40	32.71	29.48	22.98	13.76	12.85	5.81	13.75
Prices:Low	17.31	23.98	29.54	24.43	20.56	11.08	10.06	5.56	2.68	3.19
P/E Ratio:High	40	42	34	25	25	19	18	17	NM	22
P/E Ratio:Low	13	21	24	19	17	9	13	7	NM	5

Income Statement Analysis (Million $)										
Rental Income	487	484	418	NA	NA	191	190	185	233	229
Mortgage Income	Nil	Nil	Nil	NA	NA	Nil	Nil	Nil	Nil	Nil
Total Income	930	772	428	333	237	205	197	205	242	233
General Expenses	348	234	36.7	115	18.3	15.2	54.9	16.6	20.5	20.3
Interest Expense	203	204	141	106	66.8	66.7	82.0	91.6	95.3	88.8
Provision for Losses	Nil	Nil	Nil	NA	NA	Nil	Nil	Nil	Nil	Nil
Depreciation	232	234	120	91.9	49.0	81.7	42.1	42.0	43.5	44.0
Net Income	182	147	131	125	100	96.7	53.0	51.9	-61.2	42.5
S&P Core Earnings	182	141	131	108	99.3	87.4	49.1	38.6	NA	NA

Balance Sheet & Other Financial Data (Million $)										
Cash	177	82.4	1.25	2,528	3.37	82.1	39.1	880	114	140
Total Assets	5,770	5,717	3,254	2,639	1,127	813	896	942	981	1,071
Real Estate Investment	NA	6,290	6,161	NA	NA	1,090	1,221	1,231	1,176	1,183
Loss Reserve	Nil	Nil	Nil	NA	NA	Nil	Nil	Nil	Nil	Nil
Net Investment	5,173	5,494	3,084	2,526	1,058	681	829	861	849	895
Short Term Debt	118	Nil	Nil	NA	NA	Nil	Nil	Nil	Nil	Nil
Capitalization:Debt	3,030	3,360	2,199	1,803	843	641	708	848	886	974
Capitalization:Equity	2,148	1,824	710	667	160	56.3	78.3	-91.1	-118	162
Capitalization:Total	5,456	5,320	2,939	2,470	1,034	56.3	816	788	799	1,167
% Earnings & Depreciation/Assets	7.2	8.4	8.5	NA	NA	20.9	10.4	9.8	NM	8.5
Price Times Book Value:High	3.5	3.5	6.5	NA	NA	43.3	NM	NM	NM	NM
Price Times Book Value:Low	1.2	1.8	4.5	NA	NA	20.9	NM	NM	NM	NM

Data as orig reptd.; bef. results of disc opers/spec. items. Per share data adj. for stk. divs.; EPS diluted. E-Estimated. NA-Not Available. NM-Not Meaningful. NR-Not Ranked. UR-Under Review.

Office: 111 S Wacker Dr Ste 4800, Chicago, IL 60606-4302.
Telephone: 877-483-6827.
Email: info@ventasreit.com
Website: http://www.ventasreit.com

Chrmn, Pres & CEO: D.A. Cafaro
EVP & CFO: R.A. Schweinhart
EVP, Chief Admin Officer, Secy & General Counsel: T.R. Riney
Chief Acctg Officer & Cntlr: R.J. Brehl

Investor Contact: L. Weiner (312-765-0390)
Board Members: D. A. Cafaro, D. Crocker, II, R. G. Geary, J. M. Gellert, R. D. Reed, S. Z. Rosenberg, J. D. Shelton, T. C. Theobald

Founded: 1983
Domicile: Delaware
Employees: 63

VeriSign Inc

STANDARD &POOR'S

S&P Recommendation	STRONG BUY ★★★★☆	Price $22.30 (as of Nov 27, 2009)	12-Mo. Target Price $27.00	Investment Style Large-Cap Blend

GICS Sector Information Technology
Sub-Industry Internet Software & Services

Summary This leading provider of infrastructure services that enable secure digital communications and commerce has recently sold many of its businesses to focus on core operations.

Key Stock Statistics (Source S&P, Vickers, company reports)

52-Wk Range	$24.99– 16.89	S&P Oper. EPS 2009**E**	0.98	Market Capitalization(B)	$4.289	Beta	0.97
Trailing 12-Month EPS	$0.30	S&P Oper. EPS 2010**E**	1.38	Yield (%)	Nil	S&P 3-Yr. Proj. EPS CAGR(%)	25
Trailing 12-Month P/E	74.3	P/E on S&P Oper. EPS 2009**E**	22.8	Dividend Rate/Share	Nil	S&P Credit Rating	NA
$10K Invested 5 Yrs Ago	$7,075	Common Shares Outstg. (M)	192.3	Institutional Ownership (%)	NM		

Price Performance

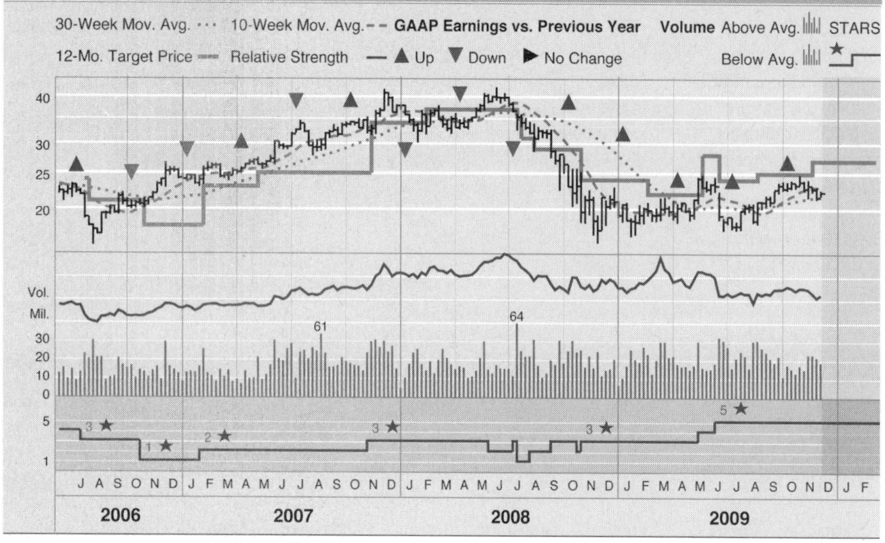

30-Week Mov. Avg. ···· 10-Week Mov. Avg. --- **GAAP Earnings vs. Previous Year** Volume Above Avg. �!!!! STARS
12-Mo. Target Price — Relative Strength — ▲ Up ▼ Down ▶ No Change Below Avg. !!!! ★

Options: ASE, CBOE, P, Ph

Analysis prepared by **Scott H. Kessler** on November 10, 2009, when the stock traded at **$ 23.02**.

Highlights

▶ We project that revenues from continuing operations will rise 6% in 2009, reflecting the adverse affect of the global recession, including some pricing pressures. We project growth of 9% in 2010. Our forecasts exclude material communications-related and other businesses that were sold in 2009.

▶ We believe annual margins will bottom in 2009, reflecting a challenging economic backdrop and expenses related to notable divestiture activity. We believe a more focused VRSN will also be able to more effectively pursue sales opportunities and efficiencies.

▶ In February 2008, VRSN announced a new $800 million buyback plan, and in August 2008, announced it had $1 billion authorized for repurchases (adding $680 million). VRSN has pursued notable divestitures in recent years, including the late 2008 sale of a joint venture stake for some $200 million and the May 2009 sale of its communications unit for some $230 million. With the proceeds, we expect VRSN to continue active stock repurchases and look to make smaller strategic acquisitions.

Investment Rationale/Risk

▶ A mostly new management team was installed in late 2006 and 2007, focused on realigning and repositioning VRSN and divesting a number of businesses. Four high level executives left in 2008, including former CEO Bill Roper. Former VRSN executive Mark McLaughlin re-joined VRSN as president and COO in early 2009 and was announced as CEO in August 2009. We see VRSN as a more focused and profitable market leader in multiple businesses, with a compelling valuation.

▶ Risks to our opinion and target price include sustained weakness or pricing pressures in its core businesses, less successful actions intended to generate shareholder value than we foresee, and adverse legal developments perhaps related to VRSN's .com contract.

▶ Our DCF model includes assumptions such as a WACC of 10.4% and a substantial decline in FCF reflecting notable divestiture activity, followed by average annual growth of 12% from 2010 to 2014 and a perpetuity growth rate of 3%. These inputs lead to an intrinsic value calculation of $27, which is our 12-month target price.

Qualitative Risk Assessment

LOW	MEDIUM	HIGH

Our risk assessment reflects what we consider the emerging nature of, and notable competition in, many of the company's businesses, substantial corporate transactional activity since 2004, and numerous one-time items appearing in the company's recent financials.

Quantitative Evaluations

S&P Quality Ranking B-

D	C	B-	B	B+	A-	A	A+

Relative Strength Rank MODERATE

43

LOWEST = 1 HIGHEST = 99

Revenue/Earnings Data

Revenue (Million $)

	1Q	2Q	3Q	4Q	Year
2009	255.0	256.6	258.0	--	--
2008	232.5	239.2	243.0	247.0	961.7
2007	373.1	363.2	373.6	386.4	1,496
2006	372.8	390.7	399.5	412.2	1,575
2005	401.0	444.8	414.8	392.1	1,609
2004	229.1	256.1	325.3	356.0	1,166

Earnings Per Share ($)

2009	0.24	0.22	0.25	E0.27	E0.98
2008	0.08	-0.07	0.21	0.24	0.46
2007	0.24	-0.02	0.07	-0.88	-0.61
2006	0.06	1.52	0.06	-0.12	1.53
2005	0.17	0.14	0.17	0.07	0.53
2004	0.04	0.09	0.16	0.43	0.72

Fiscal year ended Dec. 31. Next earnings report expected: Early February. EPS Estimates based on S&P Operating Earnings; historical GAAP earnings are as reported.

Dividend Data

No cash dividends have been paid.

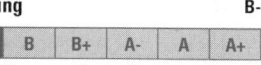

The **McGraw·Hill** Companies

VeriSign Inc

STANDARD &POOR'S

Business Summary November 10, 2009

CORPORATE OVERVIEW. VeriSign, Inc. provides Internet infrastructure services for the networked world, offering products and services that help organizations communicate and conduct commerce. After notable divestiture activity, as of December 2008, VRSN's had two operating segments: Internet Infrastructure and Identity Services (3IS) and Other Services.

3IS consists of Naming Services, SSL Certificate Services, Identity and Authentication Services (IAS) and VeriSign Japan. Other Services includes continuing operations of non-core businesses and legacy products and services from divested businesses.

Naming Services is the directory provider for all .com, .net, .cc., .tv, .name and .jobs domain names. SSL Certificate Services enables enterprises and online merchants to implement and operate secure networks and websites, allowing customers to authenticate themselves and encrypt communications. IAS includes identity protection services, fraud detection services, managed public key infrastructure (PKI) services, and unified authentication services, all of which are intended to help enterprises secure intranets, extranets and other applications and devices, and provide for authentication. VeriSign Japan is a majority-owned subsidiary with offerings similar to SSL Certificate Services and IAS.

In June 2009, an antitrust suit filed against the company in 2005 was essential-

ly reinstated, in our view. It challenges VRSN's .com contract, and we think that even though the company will retain this key business, this development could result in restrained price increases or even reductions.

CORPORATE STRATEGY. With its areas of focus established a number of years ago, VRSN expanded via regular acquisitions. The companies VRSN purchased generally had proprietary offerings and technology that VRSN leveraged with its expansive geographic footprint, customer base, and corporate alliances. We believe this was a good strategy, particularly because many of the applications and areas that VRSN had been emphasizing were significantly fragmented, by our analysis. VRSN's challenge was to purchase the best companies at attractive valuations, and to integrate them successfully.

In 2004, VRSN acquired two companies in transactions valued at $401 million in cash and stock. In 2005, it bought five companies in deals worth $423 million in cash and stock. In 2006, it purchased six companies for some $589 million. We believe the increasing frequency and magnitude of this acquisition activity raised its risk profile.

Company Financials Fiscal Year Ended Dec. 31

Per Share Data ($)	2008	2007	2006	2005	2004	2003	2002	2001	2000	1999
Tangible Book Value	NM	2.17	2.44	2.98	2.92	3.16	1.89	3.50	4.15	2.88
Cash Flow	1.10	0.36	2.47	1.25	1.05	-0.61	0.16	1.63	0.64	0.08
Earnings	0.46	-0.61	1.53	0.53	0.72	-1.08	-20.97	-65.64	-19.57	0.03
S&P Core Earnings	0.73	-0.30	1.45	NA	0.01	-1.75	-8.79	-35.05	NA	NA
Dividends	Nil	Nil	Nil	Nil	Nil	Nil	Nil	Nil	Nil	Nil
Payout Ratio	Nil	Nil	Nil	Nil	Nil	Nil	Nil	Nil	Nil	Nil
Prices:High	42.50	41.96	26.77	33.67	36.09	17.55	39.23	97.75	258.50	212.00
Prices:Low	16.23	22.92	15.95	19.01	14.94	6.55	3.92	26.25	65.38	13.50
P/E Ratio:High	92	NM	17	64	50	NM	NM	NM	NM	NM
P/E Ratio:Low	35	NM	10	36	21	NM	NM	NM	NM	NM

Income Statement Analysis (Million $)										
Revenue	962	1,496	1,575	1,609	1,166	1,055	1,222	984	475	84.8
Operating Income	387	309	340	416	242	304	287	277	70.0	2.09
Depreciation	128	231	232	191	85.6	114	5,000	13,687	3,217	5.40
Interest Expense	41.1	18.3	Nil	Nil	Nil	Nil	149	20.7	Nil	Nil
Pretax Income	119	-130	140	248	214	-237	-4,951	-13,433	-3,114	3.12
Effective Tax Rate	39.5%	NM	NM	42.2%	12.9%	NM	NM	NM	NM	NM
Net Income	88.3	-145	378	139	186	-260	-4,961	-13,356	-3,115	3.96
S&P Core Earnings	146	-72.0	359	-1.39	2.76	-421	-2,080	-7,134	NA	NA

Balance Sheet & Other Financial Data (Million $)										
Cash	789	1,378	501	477	331	394	282	306	460	70.4
Current Assets	1,625	1,750	1,332	1,228	1,006	880	604	1,091	1,186	183
Total Assets	2,726	4,023	3,974	3,173	2,593	2,100	2,391	7,538	19,195	341
Current Liabilities	977	946	1,359	938	700	555	665	834	665	42.7
Long Term Debt	1,262	1,265	Nil	Nil	Nil	Nil	Nil	Nil	Nil	Nil
Common Equity	169	1,528	2,377	2,032	1,692	1,414	1,579	6,506	18,471	299
Total Capital	1,362	2,851	2,449	2,092	1,728	1,443	1,579	6,533	18,471	299
Capital Expenditures	104	152	182	140	92.5	108	176	380	58.8	6.02
Cash Flow	221	85.9	609	330	272	-145	38.9	331	101	9.36
Current Ratio	1.7	1.9	1.0	1.3	1.4	1.6	0.9	1.3	1.8	4.3
% Long Term Debt of Capitalization	92.6	44.4	Nil	Nil	Nil	Nil	Nil	Nil	Nil	Nil
% Net Income of Revenue	9.2	NM	24.0	8.6	16.0	NM	NM	NM	NM	4.7
% Return on Assets	2.6	NM	10.6	4.8	7.9	NM	NM	NM	NM	2.0
% Return on Equity	10.4	NM	17.1	7.4	12.1	NM	NM	NM	NM	2.3

Data as orig reptd.; bef. results of disc opers/spec. items. Per share data adj. for stk. divs.; EPS diluted. E-Estimated. NA-Not Available. NM-Not Meaningful. NR-Not Ranked. UR-Under Review.

Office: 487 East Middlefield Road, Mountain View, CA 94043.
Telephone: 650-961-7500.
Website: http://www.verisign.com
Chrmn: D.J. Bidzos

Pres, CEO & COO: M. McLaughlin
EVP, CFO & Chief Acctg Officer: B.G. Robins
SVP & Chief Admin Officer: G.L. Clark
SVP & CTO: K.J. Silva

Investor Contact: K. Bond (650-426-3744)
Board Members: D. J. Bidzos, B. Chenevich, K. A. Cote, M. McLaughlin, R. H. Moore, J. D. Roach, L. A. Simpson, T. Tomlinson

Founded: 1995
Domicile: Delaware
Employees: 3,297

The **McGraw-Hill** Companies

Verizon Communications Inc

STANDARD &POOR'S

S&P Recommendation BUY ★★★★☆

Price	12-Mo. Target Price	Investment Style
$31.63 (as of Nov 27, 2009)	$34.00	Large-Cap Value

GICS Sector Telecommunication Services
Sub-Industry Integrated Telecommunication Services

Summary VZ offers wireline, wireless and broadband services primarily in the northeastern United States. It acquired MCI Inc in 2006 and has since sold or spun off non-core assets. Alltel was acquired in early 2009.

Key Stock Statistics (Source S&P, Vickers, company reports)

52-Wk Range	$34.90–26.10	S&P Oper. EPS 2009E	2.49	Market Capitalization(B)	$89.850	Beta	0.60
Trailing 12-Month EPS	$1.95	S&P Oper. EPS 2010E	2.59	Yield (%)	6.01	S&P 3-Yr. Proj. EPS CAGR(%)	6
Trailing 12-Month P/E	16.2	P/E on S&P Oper. EPS 2009E	12.7	Dividend Rate/Share	$1.90	S&P Credit Rating	A
$10K Invested 5 Yrs Ago	NA	Common Shares Outstg. (M)	2,840.6	Institutional Ownership (%)	58		

Price Performance

30-Week Mov. Avg. · · · 10-Week Mov. Avg. – – GAAP Earnings vs. Previous Year   Volume Above Avg. STARS
12-Mo. Target Price — Relative Strength   ▲ Up ▼ Down ► No Change   Below Avg. ★

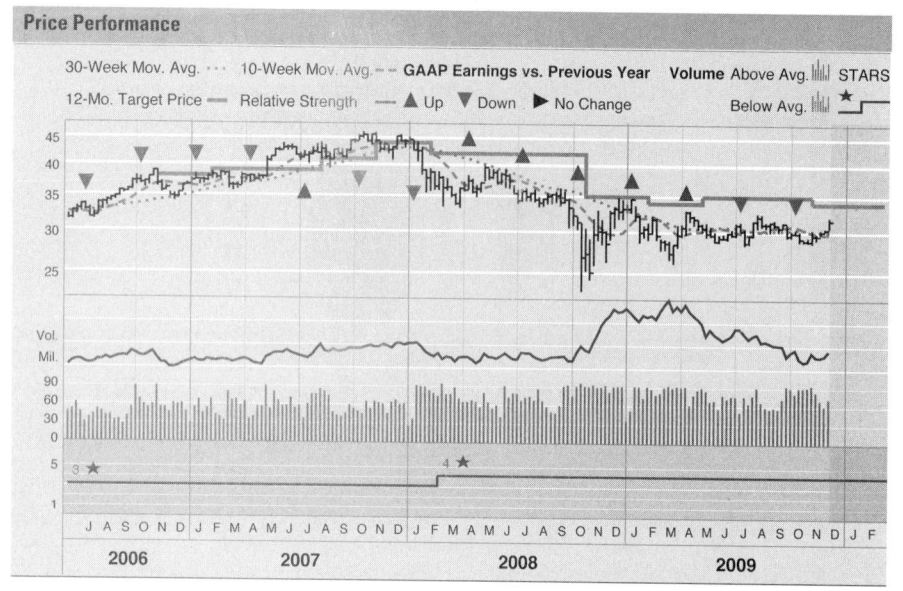

Options: ASE, CBOE, P, Ph

Analysis prepared by **Todd Rosenbluth** on October 27, 2009, when the stock traded at **$ 29.18.**

Highlights

▶ We see total revenues of $108 billion in 2009 and $110 billion in 2010, with gains stemming in part from the Alltel deal. On an organic basis, we expect strong wireless revenue growth in 2010, driven by customer growth and data services. On the wireline side, we think the penetration of FiOS services should be outweighed by a decline in the domestic telecom unit's voice revenues, with weakness in VZ's enterprise segment and, to a lesser extent, its consumer operations.

▶ We estimate the EBITDA margin will widen back to 34% in 2010 from a projected 33% in 2009, consistent with the 34% achieved in 2008. We expect higher pension expenses, due to weakness in VZ's investments during 2008, but believe cost synergies in wireless and work force reduction benefits will provide an offset.

▶ Our operating EPS estimate is $2.49 for 2009 and $2.59 in 2010, compared to operating EPS of $2.54 in 2008, excluding one-time items related to past merger activity. We exclude the impact of a pending asset spin-off.

Investment Rationale/Risk

▶ We believe VZ's wireless customer additions have remained ahead of peers, despite competitive and economic pressure. While the global enterprise segment is facing some macroeconomic pressure and should lag a broader market recovery, we are encouraged by FiOS gains as a partial offset. We believe VZ's recently raised dividend is secure and well supported by its cash flow and capital spending discipline. We see VZ's pending asset spin-off as in line with its wireless and broadband expansion plans.

▶ Risks to our recommendation and target price include a greater impact from a depressed economy, pricing pressures, a weaker balance sheet, and the cost and level of success of fiber-based services.

▶ Our blended 12-month target price of $33 is based on a P/E multiple of 13X, a slight premiums to peers based on stronger growth, but a discount to the broader market. VZ's dividend yield of about 6.5% adds support to the shares, in our view. At a P/E of about 11X, VZ recently traded near the low end of its historical range.

Qualitative Risk Assessment

LOW	MEDIUM	HIGH

Our risk assessment reflects our view of VZ's strong cash flow generation and the pricing power it has over its suppliers, offset by the competitive conditions it faces offering telecom services.

Quantitative Evaluations

S&P Quality Ranking B

D	C	B-	**B**	B+	A-	A	A+

Relative Strength Rank STRONG
77
LOWEST = 1   HIGHEST = 99

Revenue/Earnings Data

Revenue (Million $)

	1Q	2Q	3Q	4Q	Year
2009	26,591	26,861	27,265	--	--
2008	23,833	24,124	24,752	24,645	97,354
2007	22,584	23,273	23,772	23,840	93,469
2006	21,221	21,876	22,449	22,598	88,144
2005	18,179	18,569	19,038	19,326	75,112
2004	17,056	17,758	18,206	18,263	71,283

Earnings Per Share ($)

	1Q	2Q	3Q	4Q	Year
2009	0.58	0.52	0.41	E0.63	E2.49
2008	0.57	0.65	0.59	0.43	2.26
2007	0.51	0.58	0.44	0.37	1.90
2006	0.57	0.43	0.53	0.48	1.87
2005	0.63	0.75	0.67	0.59	2.65
2004	0.42	0.64	0.64	0.90	2.59

Fiscal year ended Dec. 31. Next earnings report expected: Late January. EPS Estimates based on S&P Operating Earnings; historical GAAP earnings are as reported.

Dividend Data (Dates: mm/dd Payment Date: mm/dd/yy)

Amount ($)	Date Decl.	Ex-Div. Date	Stk. of Record	Payment Date
0.460	12/04	01/07	01/09	02/02/09
0.460	03/04	04/07	04/09	05/01/09
0.460	06/04	07/08	07/10	08/03/09
0.475	09/03	10/07	10/09	11/02/09

Dividends have been paid since 1984. Source: Company reports.

Please read the Required Disclosures and Analyst Certification on the last page of this report.

The McGraw-Hill Companies

Verizon Communications Inc

STANDARD &POOR'S

Business Summary October 27, 2009

CORPORATE OVERVIEW. As of September 2009, Verizon Communications (VZ) provided wireline service to 33.4 million access lines (down 10% from a year earlier), and, through its joint venture with the Vodafone Group, was the largest wireless carrier, with 89 million wireless customers. In January 2009, VZ closed on its $28 billion acquisition of wireless carrier Alltel, which contributed 13 million subscribers.

MARKET PROFILE. Verizon Wireless added more than 6 million net subscribers (including 650,000 from acquisitions) in 2008 and, together with peer AT&T, continued to capture market share in the first nine months of 2009. Strong wireless rivalry has raised the level of competition, in our view, with new service plans and data-equipped devices. As of September 2009, Verizon Wireless had a better-than-average 1.4% monthly churn rate, and monthly service revenue per user was $51. Wireless data average revenue per user rose 17% in the third quarter of 2009 and comprised more than 30% of service revenues. The EBITDA service margin of 46% in the third quarter of 2009 for Verizon Wireless was the best in the industry. As of September 2009, 23% of VZ's retail post-paid customers had a smartphone or similar data-centric device, up from 12% a year earlier.

Verizon serves the Internet market through its broadband offerings (9.2 million connections) and has increased the speed of its connectivity in what we view as an effort to upgrade dial-up and DSL subscribers. However, beginning in early 2009, the traditional DSL customer base declined modestly, slowed by the effects of the economy and new, faster fiber offerings by Verizon gained traction.

In the third quarter of 2009, revenues at VZ's global enterprise segment declined 5% from a year earlier. In October 2009, VZ said increased U.S. unemployment was hampering the segment, and we believe the segment will lag an economic recovery.

COMPETITIVE LANDSCAPE. VZ's wireline segment competes for broadband and now telephony customers against cable companies Cablevision and Comcast. At the end of September 2009, 14.5 million homes and businesses had access to VZ's advanced fiber-based broadband services (FiOS), many of which also had access to FiOS video. As of September 2009, VZ had a 28% penetration rate (3.3 million customers) with its FiOS broadband service and a 25% penetration rate for the video service (2.7 million).

Company Financials Fiscal Year Ended Dec. 31

Per Share Data ($)	2008	2007	2006	2005	2004	2003	2002	2001	2000	1999
Tangible Book Value	NM	NM	NM	NM	NM	NM	NM	NM	12.79	10.22
Cash Flow	7.37	6.85	1.87	7.61	7.67	6.14	6.56	5.22	8.43	6.59
Earnings	2.26	1.90	1.87	2.65	2.59	1.27	1.67	0.22	3.95	2.66
S&P Core Earnings	1.72	1.85	1.87	2.42	2.76	1.76	1.91	0.58	NA	NA
Dividends	1.75	1.65	1.62	1.60	1.54	1.54	1.54	1.54	1.54	1.54
Payout Ratio	77%	88%	86%	60%	60%	121%	92%	NM	39%	58%
Prices:High	44.32	46.24	38.95	41.06	42.27	44.31	51.09	57.40	66.00	69.50
Prices:Low	23.07	35.60	30.04	29.13	34.13	31.10	26.01	43.80	39.06	50.63
P/E Ratio:High	20	25	21	15	16	35	31	NM	17	26
P/E Ratio:Low	10	19	16	11	13	24	16	NM	10	19

Income Statement Analysis (Million $)	2008	2007	2006	2005	2004	2003	2002	2001	2000	1999
Revenue	97,354	93,469	88,144	75,112	71,283	67,752	67,625	67,190	64,707	33,174
Depreciation	14,565	14,377	14,545	14,047	13,910	13,617	13,423	13,657	12,261	6,221
Maintenance	NA	NA	NA	NA	NA	NA	NA	NA	NA	NA
Construction Credits	NA	NA	NA	NA	NA	NA	NA	NA	NA	NA
Effective Tax Rate	20.9%	27.4%	21.9%	23.5%	22.8%	19.7%	21.7%	64.2%	38.9%	37.8%
Net Income	6,428	5,510	5,480	7,397	7,261	3,509	4,584	590	10,810	4,208
S&P Core Earnings	4,893	5,370	5,467	6,774	7,724	4,859	5,250	1,557	NA	NA

Balance Sheet & Other Financial Data (Million $)	2008	2007	2006	2005	2004	2003	2002	2001	2000	1999
Gross Property	215,605	213,994	204,109	193,610	185,522	180,975	178,028	169,586	158,957	89,238
Net Property	86,546	85,294	82,356	75,305	74,124	75,316	74,496	74,419	69,504	39,299
Capital Expenditures	17,238	17,538	17,101	15,324	13,259	11,884	11,984	17,371	17,633	8,675
Total Capital	137,633	125,856	121,788	120,714	120,819	118,935	122,120	116,888	115,923	39,091
Fixed Charges Coverage	9.4	8.6	5.9	6.7	5.1	2.5	5.5	3.6	3.7	6.9
Capitalization:Long Term Debt	46,959	28,203	28,646	31,869	35,674	39,413	44,791	45,657	42,491	18,664
Capitalization:Preferred	Nil	Nil	Nil	Nil	Nil	Nil	Nil	Nil	Nil	Nil
Capitalization:Common	41,706	50,581	48,535	39,680	37,560	33,466	33,720	32,539	36,342	15,880
% Return on Revenue	6.6	5.9	6.2	9.8	10.2	5.2	6.8	0.9	16.7	12.7
% Return on Invested Capital	10.5	9.5	9.8	10.5	8.6	5.1	7.6	4.0	15.4	16.9
% Return on Common Equity	13.9	11.1	12.4	19.2	20.4	10.6	13.5	1.8	33.5	29.1
% Earned on Net Property	19.7	18.6	17.2	37.9	36.2	28.1	34.5	50.5	38.3	22.3
% Long Term Debt of Capitalization	53.0	35.8	37.1	44.5	48.7	54.1	36.6	58.4	53.9	54.0
Capital % Preferred	Nil	Nil	Nil	Nil	Nil	Nil	Nil	Nil	Nil	Nil
Capitalization:% Common	47.0	64.2	62.9	55.5	51.3	45.9	42.9	41.6	46.1	46.0

Data as orig reptd.; bef. results of disc opers/spec. items. Per share data adj. for stk. divs.; EPS diluted. E-Estimated. NA-Not Available. NM-Not Meaningful. NR-Not Ranked. UR-Under Review.

Office: 1095 Avenue of the Americas, New York, NY 10036.
Telephone: 212-395-2121.
Website: http://www.verizon.com
Chrmn & CEO: I.G. Seidenberg

Pres: D.F. Strigl
EVP & CFO: J.F. Killian
EVP & CTO: R.J. Lynch
EVP & General Counsel: R.S. Milch

Investor Contact: C. Webster (212-395-1000)
Board Members: R. L. Carrion, M. F. Keeth, R. W. Lane, S. O. Moose, J. Neubauer, D. T. Nicolaisen, T. H. O'Brien, Jr., C. Otis, Jr., H. B. Price, I. G. Seidenberg, J. W. Snow, J. R. Stafford

Founded: 1983
Domicile: Delaware
Employees: 223,880

The McGraw·Hill Companies

V.F. Corp

STANDARD &POOR'S

S&P Recommendation HOLD ★★★☆☆

Price	12-Mo. Target Price	Investment Style
$72.32 (as of Nov 27, 2009)	$75.00	Large-Cap Blend

GICS Sector Consumer Discretionary
Sub-Industry Apparel, Accessories & Luxury Goods

Summary This global apparel company, with leading shares in denim and daypacks, is transforming into a designer and marketer of lifestyle apparel brands.

Key Stock Statistics (Source S&P, Vickers, company reports)

52-Wk Range	$79.79– 46.06	S&P Oper. EPS 2009**E**	4.87	Market Capitalization(B)	$8.027	Beta	0.92
Trailing 12-Month EPS	$4.58	S&P Oper. EPS 2010**E**	5.10	Yield (%)	3.32	S&P 3-Yr. Proj. EPS CAGR(%)	8
Trailing 12-Month P/E	15.8	P/E on S&P Oper. EPS 2009**E**	14.9	Dividend Rate/Share	$2.40	S&P Credit Rating	A-
$10K Invested 5 Yrs Ago	$15,442	Common Shares Outstg. (M)	111.0	Institutional Ownership (%)	88		

Price Performance

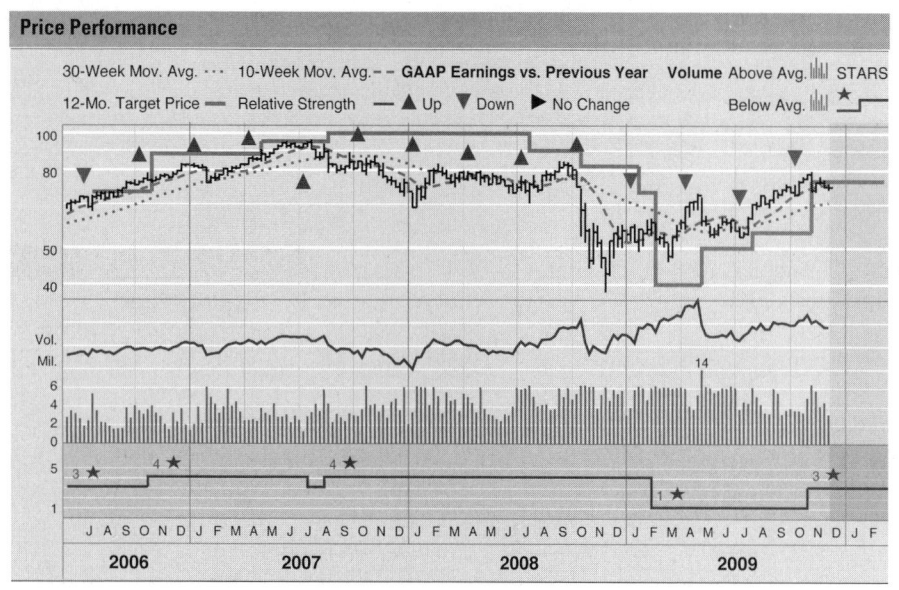

30-Week Mov. Avg. · · · 10-Week Mov. Avg. — — **GAAP Earnings vs. Previous Year**   Volume Above Avg. STARS
12-Mo. Target Price — Relative Strength — ▲ Up ▼ Down ► No Change   Below Avg. ★

Options: CBOE

Analysis prepared by **Marie Driscoll, CFA** on October 28, 2009, when the stock traded at **$ 73.35**.

Highlights

► VFC reported a 7% revenue decline for the first nine months of 2009 (down 4% excluding foreign exchange impact) as Vans and The North Face continue to report growth but all coalitions reported sales declines, albeit not as bad as in the first half pf 2009. We expect easier comparisons going forward, but with unemployment and discretionary income trends still negative, we believe top line growth will be difficult. We view Asia, new store growth and VFC's power brands, Vans and The North Face, as 2010 growth drivers.

► We see 2009 sales down 6% with foreign exchange trimming 2%-3% from sales, but we project a 5% sales gain for 2010. We project 70 bps of EBIT margin erosion in 2009 to 11.7%, following the 90 bps contraction in 2008. A $90 million pension expense is expected to drive about 130 bps of the EBIT margin contraction, offset by inventory management and improved profitability in the sportswear coalition. We see margin expansion in 2010.

► After taxes at a 27% rate, we estimate EPS of $4.87 for 2009 and $5.10 in 2010.

Investment Rationale/Risk

► We assume deteriorating employment and consumer spending trends will continue to penalize VFC's results in 2009 into 2010, by impacting demand for VFC's popular lifestyle and contemporary branded products, and will drive retailers to curtail inventory investment for the 2009 holiday season. While we believe a number of VFC's recent acquisitions have superior growth potential, and think the company has the potential to penetrate international markets, we see these as opportunities for 2010 and beyond.

► Risks to our recommendation and target price include worse than expected and/or slower economic and consumer rebounds.

► Our 12-month target price of $75 is derived by applying an 14.7X multiple to our 2010 EPS estimate of $5.10, in line with the forward multiple of VFC's apparel and footwear peers. We also note the company's dividend has more than doubled since 2005, and recently yielded about 3%.

Qualitative Risk Assessment

LOW	MEDIUM	HIGH

Our risk assessment reflects our view of VFC's strong cash flow, offset by integration risk as VFC pursues growth via acquisitions.

Quantitative Evaluations

S&P Quality Ranking A

D	C	B-	B	B+	A-	A	A+

Relative Strength Rank MODERATE

51

LOWEST = 1   HIGHEST = 99

Revenue/Earnings Data

Revenue (Million $)

	1Q	2Q	3Q	4Q	Year
2009	1,725	1,486	2,094	--	--
2008	1,846	1,677	2,207	1,912	7,643
2007	1,674	1,517	2,073	1,955	7,219
2006	1,456	1,351	1,810	1,599	6,216
2005	1,582	1,452	1,822	1,646	6,502
2004	1,433	1,270	1,793	1,560	6,055

Earnings Per Share ($)

	1Q	2Q	3Q	4Q	Year
2009	0.91	0.68	1.94	E1.34	E4.87
2008	1.33	0.94	2.10	1.05	5.42
2007	1.17	0.93	1.86	1.46	5.41
2006	1.05	0.80	1.64	1.24	4.73
2005	1.00	0.85	1.57	1.13	4.54
2004	0.93	0.80	1.38	1.10	4.21

Fiscal year ended Dec. 31. Next earnings report expected: Mid February. EPS Estimates based on S&P Operating Earnings; historical GAAP earnings are as reported.

Dividend Data (Dates: mm/dd Payment Date: mm/dd/yy)

Amount ($)	Date Decl.	Ex-Div. Date	Stk. of Record	Payment Date
0.590	02/10	03/06	03/10	03/20/09
0.590	04/28	06/05	06/09	06/19/09
0.590	07/21	09/03	09/08	09/18/09
0.600	10/26	12/04	12/08	12/18/09

Dividends have been paid since 1941. Source: Company reports.

Please read the Required Disclosures and Analyst Certification on the last page of this report.

The McGraw-Hill Companies

V.F. Corp

STANDARD &POOR'S

Business Summary October 28, 2009

CORPORATE OVERVIEW. VF Corp. is the world's largest apparel manufacturer, and holds the leading position in several market categories, including jean-swear, workwear and daypacks. In early 2004, VFC developed a growth plan to support its long-term sales growth target of 8%-10% annually, its 15% operating margin goal, and a 17% return on invested capital goal. The growth strategy consists of six drivers: building new, growing lifestyle brands; expanding share with successful retailers; growing internationally; leveraging supply chain and information technology; identifying, developing and recruiting qualified leaders; and expanding its direct to consumer business.

MARKET PROFILE. VFC participates in the broad apparel market, spanning product categories from women's activewear to denim, as well as the outdoor market for apparel and accessories via its lifestyle brands. Apparel is a mature market, with demand mirroring population growth and a modicum related to fashion; it is fragmented, with national brands marketed by 20 companies accounting for about 30% of total apparel sales and the remaining 70% comprised of smaller and/or private label "store" brands. Deflationary pricing pressure is, we think, a function of channel competition and production steadily

moving offshore to low-cost producers in Asia, especially India and China. S&P forecasts an 8% decrease in 2009 apparel sales, following the 4% decline in 2008 and 4% gains in 2007 and 2006.

According to the SGMA (Sporting Goods Manufacturers Association), sports apparel equipment and sportswear wholesale revenues were $66.3 billion in 2008, a 3.5% decline with a like decline projected for 2009. In 2007, this broad category experienced a 3% gain; it has been growing since 2004. Apparel represents about 44% of the mix, footwear 19%, and equipment 37%. Sports apparel and footwear brands more frequently serve a fashion market than a true athletic or active sports market; generally only a third of sports apparel and footwear is purchased with the intent that it will be used in an active sport, according to the NPD Group.

Company Financials Fiscal Year Ended Dec. 31

Per Share Data ($)	2008	2007	2006	2005	2004	2003	2002	2001	2000	1999
Tangible Book Value	7.54	7.86	13.18	8.78	7.56	8.61	10.91	9.97	9.71	10.08
Cash Flow	6.72	6.48	5.74	5.56	5.53	4.64	4.35	0.00	3.73	5.71
Earnings	5.42	5.41	4.73	4.54	4.21	3.61	3.24	1.19	2.27	2.99
S&P Core Earnings	4.98	5.31	4.82	4.67	4.36	3.70	2.75	0.77	NA	NA
Dividends	2.33	2.23	1.94	1.10	1.05	1.01	0.97	0.93	0.89	0.85
Payout Ratio	43%	41%	41%	24%	25%	28%	30%	78%	39%	28%
Prices:High	84.60	96.20	83.10	61.61	55.61	44.08	45.64	42.70	36.90	55.00
Prices:Low	38.22	68.15	53.25	50.44	42.06	32.62	31.50	28.15	20.94	27.44
P/E Ratio:High	16	18	18	14	13	12	14	36	16	18
P/E Ratio:Low	7	13	11	11	10	9	10	24	9	9

Income Statement Analysis (Million $)										
Revenue	7,643	7,219	6,216	6,502	6,055	5,207	5,084	5,519	5,748	5,552
Operating Income	1,124	1,081	935	944	874	718	729	516	683	820
Depreciation	144	122	108	116	141	104	107	169	173	335
Interest Expense	94.1	72.1	57.3	70.6	76.1	61.4	71.3	93.4	88.7	71.4
Pretax Income	848	906	777	771	712	599	562	263	432	596
Effective Tax Rate	28.9%	32.3%	31.2%	32.7%	33.3%	33.5%	35.1%	47.6%	38.1%	38.5%
Net Income	603	613	535	519	475	398	364	138	267	366
S&P Core Earnings	554	602	544	532	490	406	303	84.6	NA	NA

Balance Sheet & Other Financial Data (Million $)										
Cash	382	322	343	297	486	515	496	332	119	79.9
Current Assets	2,653	2,645	2,578	2,365	2,379	2,209	2,075	2,031	2,110	1,877
Total Assets	6,434	6,447	5,466	5,171	5,004	4,246	3,503	4,103	4,358	4,027
Current Liabilities	1,012	1,134	1,015	1,152	1,372	872	875	814	1,006	1,113
Long Term Debt	1,104	1,145	635	648	557	956	602	904	905	518
Common Equity	3,556	3,577	3,265	2,808	2,513	1,951	1,658	2,113	2,192	2,164
Total Capital	4,662	4,722	3,901	3,479	3,096	2,938	2,297	3,062	3,145	2,733
Capital Expenditures	124	114	127	110	81.4	86.6	64.5	81.6	125	150
Cash Flow	747	735	643	635	615	502	472	304	437	698
Current Ratio	2.6	2.3	2.5	2.1	1.7	2.5	2.4	2.5	2.1	1.7
% Long Term Debt of Capitalization	24.3	24.2	16.3	18.6	18.0	32.6	26.2	29.5	28.8	18.9
% Net Income of Revenue	7.9	8.5	8.6	7.9	7.8	7.6	7.2	2.5	4.6	6.6
% Return on Assets	9.4	10.3	10.1	10.2	10.3	10.3	9.6	3.3	6.4	9.3
% Return on Equity	16.9	17.9	17.6	19.5	21.3	22.1	19.3	6.3	12.1	17.1

Data as orig reptd.; bef. results of disc opers/spec. items. Per share data adj. for stk. divs.; EPS diluted. E-Estimated. NA-Not Available. NM-Not Meaningful. NR-Not Ranked. UR-Under Review.

Office: 105 Corporate Center Boulevard , Greensboro, NC 27408.
Telephone: 336-424-6000.
Email: irrequest@vfc.com
Website: http://www.vfc.com

Chrmn, Pres & CEO: E.C. Wiseman
SVP & CFO: R.K. Shearer
Chief Admin Officer, Secy & General Counsel: C.S. Cummings
Chief Acctg Officer & Cntlr: B.W. Batten

Treas: F.C. Pickard, III
Investor Contact: C. Knoebel (336-424-6189)
Board Members: C. V. Bergh, R. T. Carucci, J. L. Chugg, U. O. Fairbairn, B. S. Feigin, G. Fellows, R. J. Hurst, W. A. McCollough, C. Otis, Jr., M. R. Sharp, R. Viault, E. C. Wiseman, J. E. de Bedout

Founded: 1899
Domicile: Pennsylvania
Employees: 46,600

The McGraw-Hill Companies

Viacom Inc

STANDARD &POOR'S

S&P Recommendation	HOLD ★★★☆☆	Price	12-Mo. Target Price	Investment Style
		$30.03 (as of Nov 27, 2009)	$33.00	Large-Cap Blend

GICS Sector Consumer Discretionary
Sub-Industry Movies & Entertainment

Summary Emerging from a January 2006 separation from CBS Corp., this branded entertainment content provider owns and operates key properties such as MTV (cable networks) and Paramount Pictures (film studio), as well as the Rock Band (casual gaming) franchise.

Key Stock Statistics (Source S&P, Vickers, company reports)

52-Wk Range	$31.56– 13.15	S&P Oper. EPS 2009**E**	2.33	Market Capitalization(B)	$16.657	Beta	1.26
Trailing 12-Month EPS	$1.79	S&P Oper. EPS 2010**E**	2.61	Yield (%)	Nil	S&P 3-Yr. Proj. EPS CAGR(%)	7
Trailing 12-Month P/E	16.8	P/E on S&P Oper. EPS 2009**E**	12.9	Dividend Rate/Share	Nil	S&P Credit Rating	BBB
$10K Invested 5 Yrs Ago	NA	Common Shares Outstg. (M)	607.0	Institutional Ownership (%)	86		

Price Performance

- 30-Week Mov. Avg. · · · 10-Week Mov. Avg. - - **GAAP Earnings vs. Previous Year**   Volume Above Avg. ▮▮▮ STARS
- 12-Mo. Target Price — Relative Strength — ▲ Up ▼ Down ▶ No Change   Below Avg. ▮▮▮ ★

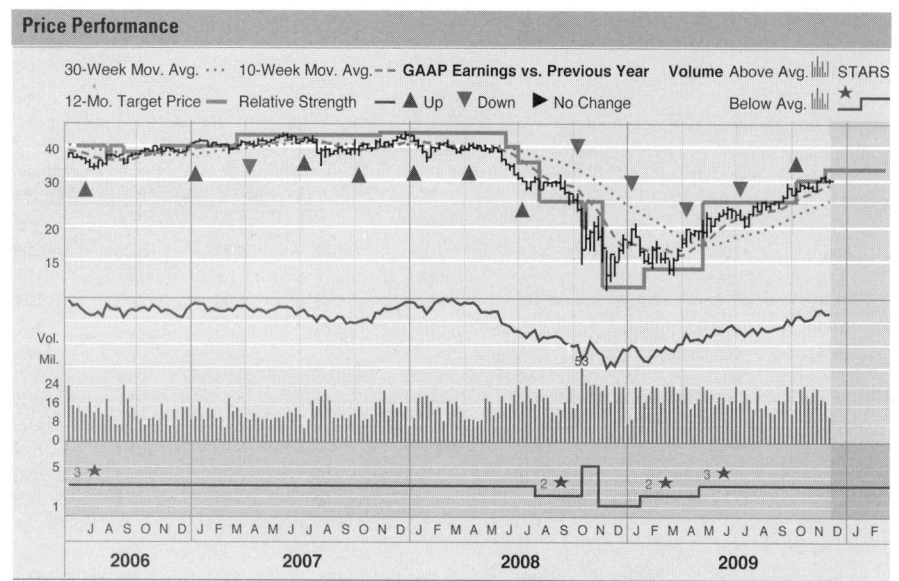

Options: ASE, CBOE, P, Ph

Analysis prepared by **Tuna N. Amobi, CFA, CPA** on November 19, 2009, when the stock traded at **$ 29.96**.

Highlights

▶ After a projected 6% decline in Viacom's consolidated revenues in 2009 (on a challenging advertising and home video environment, lower ancillary revenues, and absent contributions from DreamWorks studio), we expect a rebound of some 5% in 2010, to almost $14.5 billion. Our 2010 outlook reflects an improved ad environment and continued strong gains in worldwide affiliate fees, as well as higher ancillary revenues (including sales of the Rock Band video games franchise, consumer products/merchandise licensing) and digital revenues.

▶ Margins should significantly improve in the 2009 fourth quarter, as the Rock Band franchise edges to break-even profitability, after higher MTV programming costs. We expect further improvements in 2010 operating leverage, with the benefit of restructuring-related cost savings for the networks and film divisions.

▶ We estimate total EBIT of about $2.8 billion in 2009, and $3.1 billion in 2010. After interest and taxes, we forecast operating EPS of $2.33 and $2.61 in the respective years, with minimal share buybacks under a $4 billion plan.

Investment Rationale/Risk

▶ We think Viacom's 2009 third-quarter sequential improvements reflected some business stabilization and the benefits of certain actions to position the company for an economic recovery. The company alluded to an improving ads scatter market but kept a somewhat cautious tone for the fourth quarter. We see several blockbuster DVD titles (Transformers 2, Star Trek, G.I. Joe) for the crucial holiday season. A new Beatles version could help create longer-term upside for Rock Band. We see a strong balance sheet with ample financial flexibility for modest acquisitions -- exemplified by the recent Teenage Mutant Ninja Turtles deal.

▶ Risks to our recommendation and target price include a weaker-than-expected ads recovery; sharp ratings declines at MTV; a sharp slowdown in DVD and/or Rock Band sales; potential distribution hurdles for the new Epix channel; and adverse currency exposure.

▶ Based on 2010 estimates, our 12-month target price is $33, blending sum-of-the-parts analysis, 7.8X total EV/EBITDA, and 1.8X P/E-to-growth, in line with large media peers and the S&P 500.

Qualitative Risk Assessment

LOW	MEDIUM	HIGH

Our risk assessment reflects the company's leading demographically targeted brands, as well as our view of relatively encouraging but recently decelerating growth prospects and ample financial flexibility, offset by exposure to cyclical advertising and a volatile, hit-driven filmed entertainment business.

Quantitative Evaluations

S&P Quality Ranking NR

D	C	B-	B	B+	A-	A	A+

Relative Strength Rank STRONG

80

LOWEST = 1   HIGHEST = 99

Revenue/Earnings Data

Revenue (Million $)

	1Q	2Q	3Q	4Q	Year
2009	2,905	3,299	3,317	--	--
2008	3,117	3,857	3,408	4,243	14,625
2007	2,746	3,186	3,271	4,248	13,423
2006	2,368	2,847	2,660	3,593	11,467
2005	2,107	2,302	2,478	2,724	9,610
2004	1,829	1,829	1,970	2,504	8,132

Earnings Per Share ($)

2009	0.29	0.46	0.73	E0.86	E2.33
2008	0.42	0.64	0.62	0.28	1.97
2007	0.29	0.63	0.67	0.84	2.41
2006	0.43	0.58	0.50	0.69	2.19
2005	0.48	0.48	--	0.29	1.73
2004	--	--	--	0.52	1.48

Fiscal year ended Dec. 31. Next earnings report expected: Mid February. EPS Estimates based on S&P Operating Earnings; historical GAAP earnings are as reported.

Dividend Data

No cash dividends have been paid.

Please read the Required Disclosures and Analyst Certification on the last page of this report.

The **McGraw·Hill** Companies

Viacom Inc

STANDARD &POOR'S

Business Summary November 19, 2009

CORPORATE OVERVIEW. In its present form, the "new" Viacom is one of the two public companies created after the January 2006 separation of the "old" Viacom into two independent public entities (the "old" Viacom was renamed CBS Corp.). Each Class A and B shareholder of the "old" Viacom received 0.5 of a share of the corresponding A or B stock of each of the new entities. We believe that the company is the faster growing of the two companies resulting from the separation, and is specifically targeted to growth-oriented investors.

The company's media networks segment (60% of 2008 revenues) is mainly comprised of MTV Networks (including MTV, Nickelodeon, VH1, Comedy Central, Country Music Television, Spike TV, TV Land, Logo, Neopets, Xfire and VIVA) and BET Networks. Epix pay TV channel -- a joint venture with Lions Gate and MGM -- was launched in October 2009. In November 2007, Viacom launched its Rock Band music video games franchise (which had passed $1 billion in sales as of March 2009). The entertainment segment (41%) mainly comprises Paramount Pictures film studio (and home entertainment).

About 32% of 2008 revenues were derived from ad sales, 30% from feature films, 18% from affiliate fees, 9% from TV licensing, and 11% from other ancillary sources (including merchandise licensing).

CORPORATE STRATEGY. We see various digital initiatives, aided by partnerships with Internet and technology companies, such as pacts with Microsoft, Yahoo, Comcast/Fancast, AOL, Bebo, Dailymotion, Veoh, GoFish, and MeeVee. Since the start of 2006, the company has made selective digital acquisitions (mostly in online gaming and films), including Xfire, Y2M, Atom Entertainment, Harmonic Music and Quizilla. The company's global footprint traverses Europe and emerging markets (India and China), with nearly 130 channels (including MTV channels) across 169 territories in 28 languages, reaching nearly 450 million homes. The company recently had more than 300 web sites, and launched a social networking site, Flux.

Company Financials Fiscal Year Ended Dec. 31

Per Share Data ($)	2008	2007	2006	2005	2004	2003	2002	2001	2000	1999
Tangible Book Value	NM	NM	NM	NM	NM	NA	NA	NA	NA	NA
Cash Flow	2.55	2.99	2.70	2.08	1.78	NA	NA	NA	NA	NA
Earnings	1.97	2.41	2.19	1.73	1.48	NA	NA	NA	NA	NA
S&P Core Earnings	2.01	2.34	2.22	1.46	1.47	NA	NA	NA	NA	NA
Dividends	Nil	Nil	Nil	Nil	NA	NA	NA	NA	NA	NA
Payout Ratio	Nil	Nil	Nil	Nil	NA	NA	NA	NA	NA	NA
Prices:High	44.19	45.40	43.90	44.95	NA	NA	NA	NA	NA	NA
Prices:Low	11.60	33.74	32.42	39.78	NA	NA	NA	NA	NA	NA
P/E Ratio:High	22	19	20	26	NA	NA	NA	NA	NA	NA
P/E Ratio:Low	6	14	15	23	NA	NA	NA	NA	NA	NA

Income Statement Analysis (Million $)	2008	2007	2006	2005	2004	2003	2002	2001	2000	1999
Revenue	14,625	13,423	11,467	9,610	8,132	7,304	6,051	NA	NA	NA
Operating Income	3,341	3,404	3,137	2,625	2,534	NA	NA	NA	NA	NA
Depreciation	364	393	366	259	2,522	198	195	NA	NA	NA
Interest Expense	514	487	472	23.0	20.0	NA	NA	NA	NA	NA
Pretax Income	1,855	2,579	2,322	2,328	2,017	1,938	1,641	NA	NA	NA
Effective Tax Rate	32.6%	36.0%	31.8%	43.8%	36.4%	40.6%	39.3%	NA	NA	NA
Net Income	1,233	1,630	1,570	1,304	1,281	1,147	994	NA	NA	NA
S&P Core Earnings	1,257	1,588	1,592	1,165	1,282	NA	NA	NA	NA	NA

Balance Sheet & Other Financial Data (Million $)	2008	2007	2006	2005	2004	2003	2002	2001	2000	1999
Cash	792	920	706	361	99.2	58.3	NA	NA	NA	NA
Current Assets	4,502	4,833	4,211	3,513	2,384	NA	NA	NA	NA	NA
Total Assets	22,487	22,904	21,797	19,116	18,400	22,304	NA	NA	NA	NA
Current Liabilities	4,842	5,273	4,617	3,269	2,617	NA	NA	NA	NA	NA
Long Term Debt	7,897	8,060	7,584	5,702	3,718	NA	NA	NA	NA	NA
Common Equity	7,033	7,111	7,166	7,788	9,905	15,816	NA	NA	NA	NA
Total Capital	14,980	15,312	14,932	13,534	13,623	16,441	NA	NA	NA	NA
Capital Expenditures	288	237	210	193	NA	114	122	NA	NA	NA
Cash Flow	1,597	2,023	1,936	1,563	1,533	NA	NA	NA	NA	NA
Current Ratio	0.9	0.9	0.9	1.1	0.9	0.9	NA	NA	NA	NA
% Long Term Debt of Capitalization	52.7	52.6	50.8	42.1	27.3	Nil	Nil	NA	NA	NA
% Net Income of Revenue	8.4	12.2	13.7	13.6	15.8	15.7	16.4	NA	NA	NA
% Return on Assets	5.4	7.3	7.7	6.9	NA	NA	NA	NA	NA	NA
% Return on Equity	17.4	22.8	21.0	12.3	NA	NA	NA	NA	NA	NA

Data as orig reptd.; bef. results of disc opers/spec. items. Per share data adj. for stk. divs.; EPS diluted. E-Estimated. NA-Not Available. NM-Not Meaningful. NR-Not Ranked. UR-Under Review.

Office: 1515 Broadway, New York, NY 10036-5794.
Telephone: 212-258-6000.
Website: http://www.viacom.com
Chrmn: S.M. Redstone

Pres & CEO: P.P. Dauman
Vice Chrmn: S.E. Redstone
EVP, CFO & Chief Admin Officer: T. Dooley
EVP, Secy & General Counsel: M.D. Fricklas

Investor Contact: J. Bombassei (212-258-6700)
Board Members: G. S. Abrams, P. P. Dauman, T. Dooley, A. C. Greenberg, R. K. Kraft, B. J. McGarvie, C. E. Phillips, Jr., S. E. Redstone, S. M. Redstone, F. V. Salerno, W. Schwartz

Founded: 2005
Domicile: Delaware
Employees: 11,500

Vornado Realty Trust

STANDARD &POOR'S

S&P Recommendation	HOLD ★★★☆☆	Price $62.05 (as of Nov 27, 2009)	12-Mo. Target Price $63.00	Investment Style Large-Cap Blend

GICS Sector Financials
Sub-Industry Diversified REITS

Summary This real estate investment trust owns a diverse group of properties, including Northeast retail properties, New York City office buildings, and other interests.

Key Stock Statistics (Source S&P, Vickers, company reports)

52-Wk Range	$70.23–27.01	S&P FFO/Sh. 2009E	5.05	Market Capitalization(B)	$11.139	Beta	1.81
Trailing 12-Month FFO/Share	NA	S&P FFO/Sh. 2010E	5.00	Yield (%)	2.45	S&P 3-Yr. FFO/Sh. Proj. CAGR(%)	3
Trailing 12-Month P/FFO	NA	P/FFO on S&P FFO/Sh. 2009E	12.3	Dividend Rate/Share	$1.52	S&P Credit Rating	BBB+
$10K Invested 5 Yrs Ago	$10,585	Common Shares Outstg. (M)	179.5	Institutional Ownership (%)	91		

Price Performance

Analysis prepared by **Royal F. Shepard, CFA** on November 11, 2009, when the stock traded at **$64.64**.

Highlights

▶ We expect a challenging economic environment to limit the opportunity to sign new office tenants through calendar 2010. However, the trust's long-term leases in New York City and a relatively strong job picture in Washington, DC, should keep occupancy levels close to 95%, in our view. VNO's retail portfolio, which is weighted toward strip centers, will likely compete with space vacated by a rising list of bankrupt retailers. Retail occupancy fell 240 basis points year over year in the third quarter to 91.6%, and we see further erosion as we enter 2010.

▶ We think VNO's large scale has given it better access to capital markets than most of its office REIT peers. As of September 30, 2009, it had $2.6 billion in cash, due, in part, to an April equity offering of 17.25 million common shares and September's offering of $460 million in unsecured notes.

▶ In order to preserve cash, VNO plans to pay up to 60% of regular 2009 dividends in common stock. In view of the trust's strong balance sheet position, we think VNO will return to an all cash payout in 2010.

Investment Rationale/Risk

▶ We think VNO has the financial resources to expand a strong portfolio of office and retail assets in supply-limited markets. We would like to see the trust put excess cash balances to work in buying select assets from distressed sellers. In our view, new development opportunities could produce positive returns once the economy recovers. In the near term, we think a well diversified operating platform will produce a steady stream of cash flow. With the shares recently trading at a premium to diversified peers based on price to estimated 2010 FFO, we think they appropriately reflect VNO's long-term growth prospects.

▶ Risks to our opinion and target price include rising interest rates, and economic declines in New York and/or Washington, DC. We also have corporate governance concerns related to anti-takeover defenses, including a classified board and blank check preferred stock.

▶ Our 12-month target price of $63 represents a multiple of 12.6X our 2010 FFO per share forecast, a moderate premium to peers. We arrive at an intrinsic value of $62 using our dividend discount model, which assumes an 8.5% discount rate and a terminal growth rate of 3%.

Qualitative Risk Assessment

LOW	MEDIUM	HIGH

Our risk assessment of VNO reflects its large market capitalization, and what we see as its financial strength, diversified asset portfolio, and low stock volatility.

Quantitative Evaluations

S&P Quality Ranking   B+

D	C	B-	B	B+	A-	A	A+

Relative Strength Rank   MODERATE

57

LOWEST = 1   HIGHEST = 99

Revenue/FFO Data

Revenue (Million $)

	1Q	2Q	3Q	4Q	Year
2009	788.1	678.4	694.2	--	--
2008	649.3	674.4	677.2	696.3	2,697
2007	736.3	792.8	853.0	888.5	3,271
2006	647.3	663.0	678.5	723.3	2,712
2005	598.7	594.8	657.0	697.2	2,548
2004	391.4	397.8	413.4	504.7	1,707

FFO Per Share ($)

	1Q	2Q	3Q	4Q	Year
2009	1.63	0.54	E1.18	E1.07	E5.05
2008	3.27	1.27	1.06	-0.50	5.16
2007	1.65	1.72	1.35	1.18	5.89
2006	1.37	1.49	1.31	1.34	5.51
2005	1.84	1.51	0.65	1.26	5.21
2004	1.01	1.22	1.18	2.22	5.63

Fiscal year ended Dec. 31. Next earnings report expected: Late February. FFO Estimates based on S&P Funds From Operations Est..

Dividend Data (Dates: mm/dd Payment Date: mm/dd/yy)

Amount ($)	Date Decl.	Ex-Div. Date	Stk. of Record	Payment Date
0.950	01/14	02/03	02/05	03/12/09
0.950	04/30	05/07	05/11	06/12/09
0.650	07/30	08/07	08/11	09/14/09
0.650	10/29	11/06	11/10	12/14/09

Dividends have been paid since 1990. Source: Company reports.

The **McGraw-Hill** Companies

Vornado Realty Trust

Business Summary November 11, 2009

CORPORATE OVERVIEW. Vornado Realty Trust is a diversified REIT that has interests in a wide range of properties, including office buildings, retail properties, refrigerated warehouses, a hotel, and dry warehouses, among others, primarily in the Northeast. The company conducts its business through, was the sole general partner of, and, as of December 31, 2008, owned 90.6% of the limited partnership interests in, Vornado Realty L.P.

MARKET PROFILE. During 2008, VNO derived 60% of operating segment EBITDA from office properties. The market for office leases is inherently cyclical. The U.S. office market tends to track the overall economy on a lagged basis. At year-end 2008, we believe the national vacancy rate was about 14.0%, reflecting deterioration since its cyclical low of about 12.5% at the end of 2007.

Local economic conditions, particularly the employment level, play an important role in determining competitive dynamics. In our opinion, VNO's principal target markets, the New York City metropolitan area and Washington DC, have among the lowest vacancy rates in the nation at less than 10%. In addition, unlike many markets, rates on new or renewed leases are often at higher rates than those previously in place. At December 31, 2008, VNO owned or had an interest in 115 office properties totaling 35.6 million sq. ft. The New York portfolio was 96.7% occupied at December 31, 2008; the Washington, DC, portfolio was 95.0% occupied.

In 2008, VNO derived about 19% of EBITDA from its retail segment. As of December 31, 2008, the retail portfolio included about 21.9 million sq. ft. in 21 states, Washington DC, and Puerto Rico. For VNO, as well as other retail oriented REITs, location and the financial health and growth of its retail tenants are among the most important factors affecting the success of its portfolio. Further, the companies in this industry enjoy relatively high barriers to entry, since developing new shopping centers requires large amounts of capital as well as time-consuming regulatory approvals which have been difficult to obtain in the recent past amid concerns about traffic and pollution. We expect VNO to focus on the re-development of recently acquired properties, including the Manhattan Mall, in New York City, and shopping centers acquired in Northern New Jersey and Long Island, New York.

Company Financials Fiscal Year Ended Dec. 31

Per Share Data ($)	2008	2007	2006	2005	2004	2003	2002	2001	2000	1999
Tangible Book Value	27.79	34.57	35.22	31.38	26.86	24.15	21.68	21.15	18.31	18.14
Earnings	1.16	2.86	3.13	3.27	3.75	2.29	2.18	2.50	2.21	1.94
S&P Core Earnings	1.13	2.69	2.62	3.09	3.62	3.63	2.15	2.58	NA	NA
Dividends	3.65	3.45	3.25	3.85	2.89	2.91	2.97	2.31	1.97	1.81
Payout Ratio	NM	107%	104%	118%	77%	127%	136%	92%	89%	93%
Prices:High	108.15	136.55	131.35	89.70	76.99	55.84	47.20	42.03	40.75	40.00
Prices:Low	36.66	82.82	83.28	68.25	47.00	33.25	33.20	34.47	29.87	29.69
P/E Ratio:High	93	42	42	27	21	24	22	17	18	21
P/E Ratio:Low	32	26	27	21	13	15	15	14	14	15

Income Statement Analysis (Million $)										
Rental Income	2,211	1,989	1,568	1,397	1,345	1,261	1,249	842	695	591
Mortgage Income	Nil	Nil	Nil	Nil	Nil	Nil	Nil	Nil	Nil	Nil
Total Income	2,697	3,271	2,712	2,548	1,707	1,503	1,435	986	827	697
General Expenses	1,264	2,935	1,588	1,488	825	706	668	472	366	322
Interest Expense	608	635	478	341	242	230	240	173	170	142
Provision for Losses	Nil	Nil	Nil	Nil	Nil	Nil	Nil	Nil	Nil	Nil
Depreciation	537	530	397	335	243	215	206	124	99.8	83.6
Net Income	241	510	607	507	514	285	263	267	235	203
S&P Core Earnings	178	426	393	435	476	421	236	238	NA	NA

Balance Sheet & Other Financial Data (Million $)										
Cash	1,527	1,858	2,690	763	NA	NA	NA	NA	NA	NA
Total Assets	21,418	22,479	17,954	13,637	11,581	9,519	9,018	6,777	6,370	5,479
Real Estate Investment	17,870	18,972	13,553	11,449	9,757	7,748	7,560	4,690	4,295	3,922
Loss Reserve	Nil	Nil	Nil	Nil	Nil	Nil	Nil	Nil	Nil	Nil
Net Investment	15,709	16,565	11,585	9,776	8,349	6,879	6,822	4,184	3,901	3,613
Short Term Debt	357	527	778	398	Nil	Nil	Nil	Nil	425	681
Capitalization:Debt	12,292	12,426	9,056	5,857	4,937	3,768	3,622	1,643	2,232	1,368
Capitalization:Equity	4,841	5,293	5,322	4,260	3,301	2,827	2,362	2,101	1,597	1,577
Capitalization:Total	19,567	20,038	16,335	12,208	8,238	8,767	8,287	5,693	5,767	4,645
% Earnings & Depreciation/Assets	3.5	5.1	6.3	6.6	7.1	5.4	5.9	5.9	5.6	5.8
Price Times Book Value:High	3.9	3.9	3.7	2.9	2.9	2.3	2.2	2.0	2.2	2.2
Price Times Book Value:Low	1.3	2.4	2.4	2.2	1.7	1.4	1.5	1.6	1.6	1.6

Data as orig reptd.; bef. results of disc opers/spec. items. Per share data adj. for stk. divs.; EPS diluted. E-Estimated. NA-Not Available. NM-Not Meaningful. NR-Not Ranked. UR-Under Review.

Vulcan Materials Co

STANDARD &POOR'S

S&P Recommendation SELL ★★☆☆☆	**Price** $48.69 (as of Nov 27, 2009)	**12-Mo. Target Price** $40.00	**Investment Style** Large-Cap Growth

GICS Sector Materials
Sub-Industry Construction Materials

Summary This company is a major producer of aggregates and concrete used in road construction and the building of commercial, residential and public buildings and infrastructure.

Key Stock Statistics (Source S&P, Vickers, company reports)

52-Wk Range	$77.95– 34.30	S&P Oper. EPS 2009**E**	0.50	Market Capitalization(B)	$6.106	Beta		1.31
Trailing 12-Month EPS	$-1.51	S&P Oper. EPS 2010**E**	1.50	Yield (%)	2.05	S&P 3-Yr. Proj. EPS CAGR(%)		5
Trailing 12-Month P/E	NM	P/E on S&P Oper. EPS 2009**E**	97.4	Dividend Rate/Share	$1.00	S&P Credit Rating		BBB
$10K Invested 5 Yrs Ago	$10,567	Common Shares Outstg. (M)	125.4	Institutional Ownership (%)	88			

Price Performance

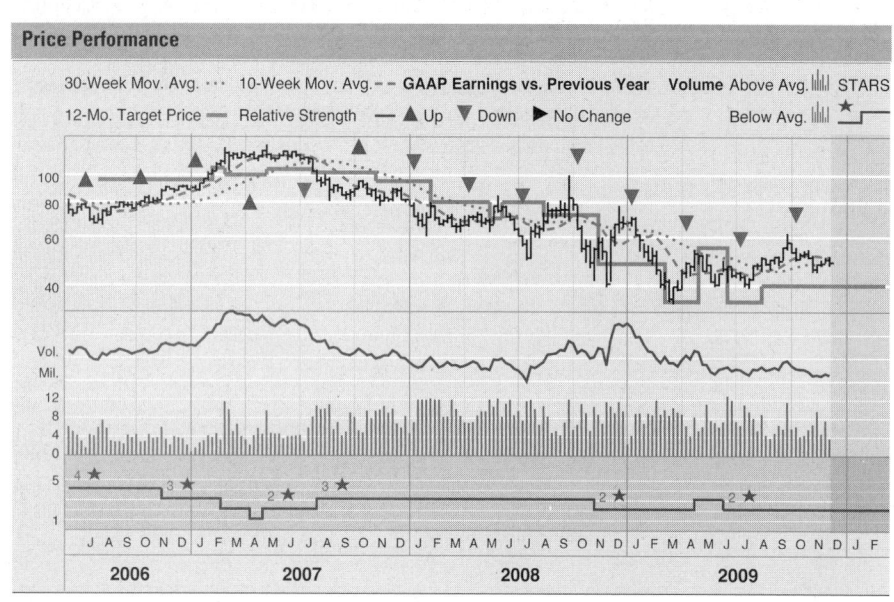

30-Week Mov. Avg. · · · 10-Week Mov. Avg. - - **GAAP Earnings vs. Previous Year** Volume Above Avg. STARS
12-Mo. Target Price — Relative Strength — ▲ Up ▼ Down ► No Change Below Avg.

Options: P

Analysis prepared by **Stuart J. Benway, CFA** on November 11, 2009, when the stock traded at **$ 48.85.**

Highlights

► We expect revenues to fall 20%-25% in 2009, followed by a modest recovery of about 10% in 2010. Demand for construction aggregates is likely to be weak, as we expect housing starts to decline 37% in 2009. We forecast that housing starts will rebound by nearly 50% in 2010, although commercial construction is likely to remain very weak. Spending on highways and other public infrastructure is expected to rise due to increased federal spending, and weak demand should be partially offset by price increases.

► We see operating margins falling nearly 300 basis points in 2009, to 9.4%. Despite significant progress on reducing administrative costs and a relatively flexible cost structure, margins at VMC are likely to suffer from significantly underutilized capacity. The volume recovery that we expect in 2010, coupled with the lower cost base, should lead to a 400-500 basis point increase in operating margins.

► We project EPS of $0.50 in 2009, which would mark the lowest level of earnings in more than a decade. In 2010, we expect a modest recovery to $1.50.

Investment Rationale/Risk

► We expect conditions in most of Vulcan's markets to remain weak into early 2010. Our forecast is for a further decline in new home starts and a significant drop in commercial construction in 2009 before a modest recovery in 2010. Industrial markets should provide some stability as they are more long term in nature. We look for an increase in government infrastructure spending to moderately boost demand for construction aggregates.

► Risks to our recommendation and target price include demand being stronger than we project due to higher residential construction activity and public infrastructure spending being boosted more than expected by a government-sponsored stimulus plan.

► Our DCF model, which assumes a 9.8% weighted average cost of capital, lower free cash flow generation in 2010, and 3% cash flow growth in perpetuity, indicates intrinsic value of $45. The shares have historically traded at a P/E of about 20X. Applying this ratio to our 2010 EPS forecast yields a value of $30. Our 12-month target price of $40 is a blend of these two measures.

Qualitative Risk Assessment

LOW	MEDIUM	HIGH

Our risk assessment reflects that while VMC's earnings are exposed to the construction industry, about 44% of the aggregates volume comes from public construction, which is more stable than commercial construction. In addition, we view VMC's free cash flow generation as strong.

Quantitative Evaluations

S&P Quality Ranking   B+

D	C	B-	B	B+	A-	A	A+

Relative Strength Rank   MODERATE

38

LOWEST = 1   HIGHEST = 99

Revenue/Earnings Data

Revenue (Million $)

	1Q	2Q	3Q	4Q	Year
2009	600.3	721.9	778.2	--	--
2008	817.3	1,022	1,013	799.2	3,651
2007	687.2	878.8	904.9	856.9	3,328
2006	708.7	888.2	929.3	816.3	3,342
2005	528.6	782.1	830.0	754.6	2,895
2004	617.5	816.3	891.2	608.7	2,454

Earnings Per Share ($)

2009	-0.29	0.14	0.38	E0.23	E0.50
2008	0.13	1.27	0.54	0.14	2.08
2007	0.91	1.46	1.47	0.83	4.66
2006	0.70	1.47	1.45	1.19	4.79
2005	0.21	0.98	1.23	0.89	3.30
2004	0.14	0.85	0.96	0.62	2.52

Fiscal year ended Dec. 31. Next earnings report expected: Mid February. EPS Estimates based on S&P Operating Earnings; historical GAAP earnings are as reported.

Dividend Data (Dates: mm/dd Payment Date: mm/dd/yy)

Amount ($)	Date Decl.	Ex-Div. Date	Stk. of Record	Payment Date
0.490	02/13	02/25	02/27	03/10/09
0.490	05/08	05/21	05/26	06/10/09
0.250	07/10	08/24	08/26	09/10/09
0.250	10/09	11/23	11/25	12/10/09

Dividends have been paid since 1934. Source: Company reports.

Vulcan Materials Co

STANDARD
&POOR'S

Business Summary November 11, 2009

CORPORATE OVERVIEW. Vulcan Materials is the largest U.S. producer of construction aggregates, a major producer of asphalt and concrete, and a leading producer of cement in Florida. Proven and probable reserves of aggregates were estimated at 13.3 billion tons at the end of 2008, representing a reserve life of 52 years based on current production rates. Vulcan shipped 204 million tons of aggregates in 2008 to 23 states, the District of Columbia, Mexico, the Bahamas, Canada, the Cayman Islands and Chile from 331 production facilities and distribution points. Construction aggregates were 65% of sales in 2008, asphalt mix and concrete 32%, and cement was 3%. VMC estimates that 45% of its aggregates shipments in 2008 went to publicly funded construction projects and 55% was used for privately funded residential and nonresidential construction.

PRIMARY BUSINESS DYNAMICS. Public sector construction spending is generally more stable than in the private sector, in part because public sector spending is less sensitive to interest rates and is often supported by multi-year legislation and programs. Public construction is typically funded through a combination of federal state and local sources. The federal transportation bill is the principal source of federal funding for public infrastructure and transportation projects. Federal highway spending is primarily determined by

a six-year authorization bill and annual budget appropriations suing funds largely taken from the Federal Highway Trust Fund, which receives taxes on gasoline and other levies. State highway and bridge projects supplement federal funding with state fuel taxes and vehicle registration fees. Although historically over 40% of VMC's sales have on average gone into publicly funded construction, insignificant sales are made directly to federal, state, county or municipal governments. Therefore, the company's business is not directly subject to renegotiation of profits or termination of contract as a result of state or federal government elections. Private nonresidential construction includes a wide array of project types and generally is more aggregates intensive than residential construction but less so than public construction. Demand in private nonresidential construction is driven by job growth, vacancy rates, private infrastructure needs, and demographic trends. The majority of residential construction activity is for single-family houses with the remainder consisting of multifamily construction. Household formation is a primary driver of housing demand along with mortgage rates.

Company Financials Fiscal Year Ended Dec. 31

Per Share Data ($)	2008	2007	2006	2005	2004	2003	2002	2001	2000	1999
Tangible Book Value	NM	NM	14.60	15.05	13.77	12.01	11.04	10.02	9.00	8.63
Cash Flow	3.53	7.33	7.04	5.43	4.88	4.87	4.47	4.89	4.43	4.37
Earnings	2.08	4.66	4.79	3.30	2.52	2.18	1.86	2.17	2.29	2.35
S&P Core Earnings	1.20	4.22	4.53	3.17	2.29	1.89	1.51	1.81	NA	NA
Dividends	1.96	1.84	1.48	1.16	1.04	0.97	0.94	0.90	0.84	0.78
Payout Ratio	94%	39%	31%	35%	41%	44%	51%	41%	37%	33%
Prices:High	100.25	128.62	93.85	76.31	55.53	48.60	49.95	55.30	48.88	51.25
Prices:Low	39.52	77.04	65.85	52.36	41.94	28.75	32.35	37.50	36.50	34.31
P/E Ratio:High	48	28	20	23	22	22	27	25	21	22
P/E Ratio:Low	19	17	14	16	17	13	17	17	16	15

Income Statement Analysis (Million $)	2008	2007	2006	2005	2004	2003	2002	2001	2000	1999
Revenue	3,651	3,328	3,342	2,895	2,454	2,892	2,797	3,020	2,492	2,356
Operating Income	814	954	914	690	623	618	560	649	573	565
Depreciation	389	266	225	221	245	277	268	278	232	207
Interest Expense	187	53.4	26.3	37.1	40.3	54.1	55.0	61.3	48.1	48.6
Pretax Income	327	668	703	480	376	311	260	324	312	352
Effective Tax Rate	29.5%	30.6%	32.1%	28.4%	30.4%	28.3%	25.8%	31.3%	29.6%	31.8%
Net Income	231	463	477	344	261	223	190	223	220	240
S&P Core Earnings	132	419	452	328	236	194	155	186	NA	NA

Balance Sheet & Other Financial Data (Million $)	2008	2007	2006	2005	2004	2003	2002	2001	2000	1999
Cash	46.9	34.9	55.2	275	271	417	171	101	55.3	52.8
Current Assets	894	1,157	731	1,165	1,418	1,050	790	730	695	625
Total Assets	9,176	8,936	3,424	3,589	3,665	3,637	3,448	3,398	3,229	2,839
Current Liabilities	1,663	2,528	494	579	427	543	298	344	572	387
Long Term Debt	2,154	1,530	322	323	605	339	858	906	685	699
Common Equity	3,784	3,760	2,001	2,127	2,014	1,803	1,697	1,604	1,471	1,324
Total Capital	6,626	5,961	2,611	2,725	2,967	2,573	2,993	2,829	2,426	2,273
Capital Expenditures	401	483	435	216	204	194	249	287	340	315
Cash Flow	387	729	702	565	506	501	458	501	452	447
Current Ratio	0.5	0.5	1.5	2.0	3.3	1.9	2.7	2.1	1.2	1.6
% Long Term Debt of Capitalization	32.5	25.7	12.3	11.9	20.4	13.2	28.7	32.0	28.3	30.7
% Net Income of Revenue	6.3	13.9	14.3	11.9	10.6	7.7	6.8	7.4	8.8	10.2
% Return on Assets	2.6	7.5	13.6	9.5	7.2	6.3	5.6	6.7	7.2	10.7
% Return on Equity	6.1	16.1	23.1	16.6	13.7	12.8	11.5	14.5	15.7	19.4

Data as orig reptd.; bef. results of disc opers/spec. items. Per share data adj. for stk. divs.; EPS diluted. E-Estimated. NA-Not Available. NM-Not Meaningful. NR-Not Ranked. UR-Under Review.

Office: 1200 Urban Center Drive, Birmingham, AL 35242.
Telephone: 205-298-3000.
Email: ir@vmcmail.com
Website: http://www.vulcanmaterials.com

CEO: D.M. James
SVP & CFO: D.F. Sansone
SVP & General Counsel: R.A. Wason, IV
Chief Acctg Officer, Cntlr & CIO: E.A. Khan

Treas: J.P. Alford
Investor Contact: M. Warren (205-298-3220)
Board Members: P. J. Carroll, Jr., P. W. Farmer, H. A. Franklin, D. M. James, A. M. Korologos, D. J. McGregor, J. V. Napier, R. T. O'Brien, D. B. Rice, V. J. Trosino

Founded: 1910
Domicile: New Jersey
Employees: 9,320

Walgreen Co

STANDARD &POOR'S

S&P Recommendation HOLD ★★★☆☆	**Price** $39.01 (as of Nov 27, 2009)	**12-Mo. Target Price** $41.00	**Investment Style** Large-Cap Growth

GICS Sector Consumer Staples
Sub-Industry Drug Retail

Summary The largest U.S. retail drug chain in terms of revenues, this company operates about 7,000 drug stores throughout the U.S. and Puerto Rico.

Key Stock Statistics (Source S&P, Vickers, company reports)

52-Wk Range	$40.69–21.39	S&P Oper. EPS 2010**E**	2.39	Market Capitalization(B)	$38.574	Beta	0.77
Trailing 12-Month EPS	$2.02	S&P Oper. EPS 2011**E**	2.74	Yield (%)	1.41	S&P 3-Yr. Proj. EPS CAGR(%)	15
Trailing 12-Month P/E	19.3	P/E on S&P Oper. EPS 2010**E**	16.3	Dividend Rate/Share	$0.55	S&P Credit Rating	A+
$10K Invested 5 Yrs Ago	$10,602	Common Shares Outstg. (M)	988.8	Institutional Ownership (%)	67		

Price Performance

30-Week Mov. Avg. · · · 10-Week Mov. Avg. - - **GAAP Earnings vs. Previous Year** Volume Above Avg. STARS
12-Mo. Target Price — Relative Strength — ▲ Up ▼ Down ► No Change Below Avg.

Options: ASE, CBOE, P

Analysis prepared by **Joseph Agnese** on November 04, 2009, when the stock traded at **$ 39.55**.

Highlights

► We see sales advancing 8.9% in FY 10 (Aug.), to roughly $69.0 billion, from $63.3 billion in FY 09, fueled by about 300 net new store openings (approximately 4% square footage growth), a pharmacy same-store sales gain of about 6%, and front-end same-store sales growth of about 5%. We see front-end growth benefiting from better traffic trends as the company improves merchandise assortments through the rollout of new store remodelings across a majority of its stores by the end of FY 10.

► We expect margins to expand on benefits from increased sales of wider-margin generic drugs, reduced inventory markdowns in the second half of the year, lower labor costs and benefits from a more mature store base, partially offset by a shift in the mix toward the pharmacy segment. We think costs associated with WAG's investment in health clinics will continue to negatively affect margins in FY 10, and we expect interest expense to rise, reflecting higher debt levels.

► We look for EPS to increase 18% in FY 10, to $2.39, from $2.02 in FY 09, and another 15% in FY 11, to $2.74.

Investment Rationale/Risk

► We believe the company is well positioned to benefit over the long term from favorable demographics, improved non-pharmacy merchandising, and increased generic drug sales, despite decreased prescription and discretionary product demand we see in the near term due to an adverse economic environment.

► Risks to our recommendation and target price include a weaker than expected economy, increased competition from peers and other retail formats, and legislative changes that may affect drug reimbursements.

► The stock recently traded at about 16.2X our FY 10 operating EPS estimate of $2.39, about a 10% premium to peers. We believe the shares should trade at a premium as the company makes progress on initiatives to cut costs, improve merchandising and slow new store expansion, leading to an acceleration of earnings growth, and on WAG's long history of consistent earnings growth and what we view as its strong balance sheet. Applying a multiple of 15X to our FY 11 EPS estimate of $2.74, a 10% premium to the average of our target prices for peers, results in a value of $41, which is our 12-month target price.

Qualitative Risk Assessment

LOW	**MEDIUM**	HIGH

Our risk assessment reflects the company's strong market share positions in the relatively stable U.S. retail drug industry, offset by growth of non-traditional competitors and potential adverse legislation.

Quantitative Evaluations

S&P Quality Ranking A+

D	C	B-	B	B+	A-	A	**A+**

Relative Strength Rank STRONG

75

LOWEST = 1   HIGHEST = 99

Revenue/Earnings Data

Revenue (Million $)

	1Q	2Q	3Q	4Q	Year
2009	14,947	16,475	16,210	15,703	63,335
2008	14,028	15,394	15,016	14,597	59,034
2007	12,709	13,934	13,698	13,422	53,762
2006	10,900	12,163	12,175	12,170	47,409
2005	9,889	10,987	10,831	10,495	42,202
2004	8,721	9,782	9,579	9,427	37,508

Earnings Per Share ($)

2009	0.41	0.65	0.53	0.44	2.02
2008	0.46	0.69	0.58	0.45	2.17
2007	0.43	0.65	0.56	0.40	2.03
2006	0.34	0.51	0.46	0.41	1.72
2005	0.32	0.48	0.40	0.32	1.52
2004	0.25	0.42	0.33	0.32	1.32

Fiscal year ended Aug. 31. Next earnings report expected: Late December. EPS Estimates based on S&P Operating Earnings; historical GAAP earnings are as reported.

Dividend Data (Dates: mm/dd Payment Date: mm/dd/yy)

Amount ($)	Date Decl.	Ex-Div. Date	Stk. of Record	Payment Date
0.113	01/15	02/13	02/18	03/12/09
0.113	04/08	05/19	05/21	06/12/09
0.138	07/08	08/19	08/21	09/12/09
0.138	10/15	11/12	11/16	12/12/09

Dividends have been paid since 1933. Source: Company reports.

Please read the Required Disclosures and Analyst Certification on the last page of this report.

The McGraw·Hill Companies

Walgreen Co

STANDARD
&POOR'S

Business Summary November 04, 2009

CORPORATE OVERVIEW. Walgreen Co. is one of the largest drug store chains in the U.S., based on sales and store count. In 1909, the company's founder, Charles Rudolph Walgreen Sr., purchased one of the busiest drug stores on Chicago's South Side, and transformed it by constructing an ice cream fountain that featured his own brand of ice cream. The ice cream fountain was the forerunner of the famous Walgreen's soda fountain, which became the main attraction for customers from the 1920s through the 1950s. People lined up to buy a product that WAG invented in the early 1920s: the milkshake. The company continued to be innovative by pioneering computerized pharmacies connected by satellite in 1981, completing chain wide point-of-sale scanning in 1991, and introducing freestanding stores with drive-thru pharmacies in 1992. It also operates worksite health centers, home care facilities and specialty, institutional and mail service pharmacies. Its Take Care Health Systems subsidiary manages convenient care clinics at Walgreen's drug stores.

MARKET PROFILE. Walgreen operates the largest U.S. drugstore chain based on sales, generating $63.3 billion in sales in FY 09 (Aug.). According to our analysis, the company filled about 650 million prescriptions in FY 09, accounting for about 18% of the U.S. retail market. The company experienced a 6.9% growth rate in prescription volume in FY 09, outpacing our estimate of a low single digit growth rate for the industry. On a dollar basis, WAG pharmacy sales rose 7.8% in FY 09, to about $42 billion, versus our estimate of a low single digit growth rate for the total industry, on comparable prescription sales growth of 3.5%. Sales of non-pharmacy items outperformed competitors, with the company increasing market share in most of its core categories versus drug store, grocery and mass merchant competition. Based on store count, Walgreen is the second largest chain store operator in the U.S. As of October 2009, the company operated 7,000 drug stores throughout the U.S. and Puerto Rico and about 500 worksite, home care, specialty pharmacy and mail service facilities.

Company Financials Fiscal Year Ended Aug. 31

Per Share Data ($)	2009	2008	2007	2006	2005	2004	2003	2002	2001	2000
Tangible Book Value	13.06	11.56	10.13	9.61	8.69	8.04	7.02	6.08	5.11	4.19
Cash Flow	NA	3.01	2.70	2.28	1.99	1.71	1.47	1.29	1.12	0.99
Earnings	2.02	2.17	2.03	1.72	1.52	1.32	1.14	0.99	0.86	0.76
S&P Core Earnings	2.01	2.17	2.03	1.71	1.44	1.27	1.07	0.93	0.80	NA
Dividends	0.48	0.40	0.33	0.27	0.22	0.22	0.18	0.16	0.15	0.14
Payout Ratio	24%	18%	16%	16%	15%	14%	14%	15%	16%	18%
Prices:High	40.69	39.00	49.10	51.60	49.01	39.51	37.42	40.70	45.29	45.75
Prices:Low	21.39	21.28	35.80	39.55	39.66	32.00	26.90	27.70	28.70	22.06
P/E Ratio:High	20	18	24	30	32	30	33	41	53	60
P/E Ratio:Low	11	10	18	23	26	24	24	28	33	29

Income Statement Analysis (Million $)										
Revenue	63,335	59,034	53,762	47,409	42,202	37,508	32,505	28,681	24,623	21,207
Operating Income	NA	4,202	3,827	3,274	2,906	2,546	2,194	1,932	1,668	1,454
Depreciation	975	840	676	572	482	403	346	307	269	230
Interest Expense	NA	30.0	Nil	Nil	Nil	Nil	Nil	Nil	3.10	0.40
Pretax Income	3,164	3,430	3,189	2,754	2,456	2,176	1,889	1,637	1,423	1,263
Effective Tax Rate	36.6%	37.1%	36.0%	36.4%	36.5%	37.5%	37.8%	37.8%	37.8%	38.5%
Net Income	2,006	2,157	2,041	1,751	1,560	1,360	1,176	1,019	886	777
S&P Core Earnings	1,997	2,158	2,042	1,754	1,478	1,302	1,104	955	820	NA

Balance Sheet & Other Financial Data (Million $)										
Cash	2,587	443	255	920	577	1,696	1,017	450	16.9	12.8
Current Assets	NA	10,433	9,511	9,705	8,317	7,764	6,358	5,167	4,394	3,550
Total Assets	25,142	22,410	19,314	17,131	14,609	13,342	11,406	9,879	8,834	7,104
Current Liabilities	NA	6,644	6,744	5,755	4,481	4,078	3,421	2,955	3,012	2,304
Long Term Debt	2,336	1,377	Nil	Nil	Nil	Nil	Nil	Nil	Nil	Nil
Common Equity	14,376	12,869	11,104	10,116	8,890	8,228	7,196	6,230	5,207	4,234
Total Capital	16,712	14,396	11,263	10,257	9,130	8,556	7,424	6,407	5,344	4,336
Capital Expenditures	1,927	2,225	1,785	1,338	1,238	940	795	934	1,237	1,119
Cash Flow	NA	2,997	2,717	2,323	2,042	1,763	1,522	1,327	1,155	1,007
Current Ratio	1.8	1.6	1.4	1.7	1.9	1.9	1.9	1.7	1.5	1.5
% Long Term Debt of Capitalization	14.0	9.6	Nil	Nil	Nil	Nil	Nil	Nil	Nil	Nil
% Net Income of Revenue	3.2	3.7	3.8	3.7	3.7	3.6	3.6	3.6	3.6	3.7
% Return on Assets	8.4	10.3	11.2	11.0	11.2	10.9	11.0	10.9	11.1	11.9
% Return on Equity	14.7	18.0	19.2	18.4	18.3	17.6	17.5	17.8	18.8	20.1

Data as orig reptd.; bef. results of disc opers/spec. items. Per share data adj. for stk. divs.; EPS diluted. E-Estimated. NA-Not Available. NM-Not Meaningful. NR-Not Ranked. UR-Under Review.

Office: 200 Wilmot Road, Deerfield, IL 60015.
Telephone: 847-940-2500.
Email: investor.relations@walgreens.com
Website: http://www.walgreens.com

Chrmn: A.G. McNally
Pres, CEO & COO: G.D. Wasson
EVP & CFO: W.D. Miquelon
SVP, Secy & General Counsel: D.I. Green

SVP & CIO: T.J. Theriault
Investor Contact: R.J. Hans (847-940-2500)
Board Members: S. A. Davis, W. C. Foote, M. P. Frissora, A. G. McNally, C. Reed, N. M. Schlichting, D. Y. Schwartz, A. Silva, J. A. Skinner, M. M. Von Ferstel, C. R. Walgreen, III, G. D. Wasson

Founded: 1901
Domicile: Illinois
Employees: 238,000

Wal-Mart Stores Inc

STANDARD &POOR'S

S&P Recommendation	**STRONG BUY** ★★★★☆	Price $54.63 (as of Nov 27, 2009)	12-Mo. Target Price $62.00	Investment Style Large-Cap Blend

GICS Sector Consumer Staples
Sub-Industry Hypermarkets & Super Centers

Summary The largest retailer in North America, WMT operates a chain of discount department stores, wholesale clubs, and combination discount stores and supermarkets.

Key Stock Statistics (Source S&P, Vickers, company reports)

52-Wk Range	$59.23– 46.25	S&P Oper. EPS 2010E	3.61	Market Capitalization(B)	$210.698	Beta	0.20
Trailing 12-Month EPS	$3.45	S&P Oper. EPS 2011E	3.95	Yield (%)	2.00	S&P 3-Yr. Proj. EPS CAGR(%)	9
Trailing 12-Month P/E	15.8	P/E on S&P Oper. EPS 2010E	15.1	Dividend Rate/Share	$1.09	S&P Credit Rating	AA
$10K Invested 5 Yrs Ago	$10,722	Common Shares Outstg. (M)	3,856.8	Institutional Ownership (%)	36		

Price Performance

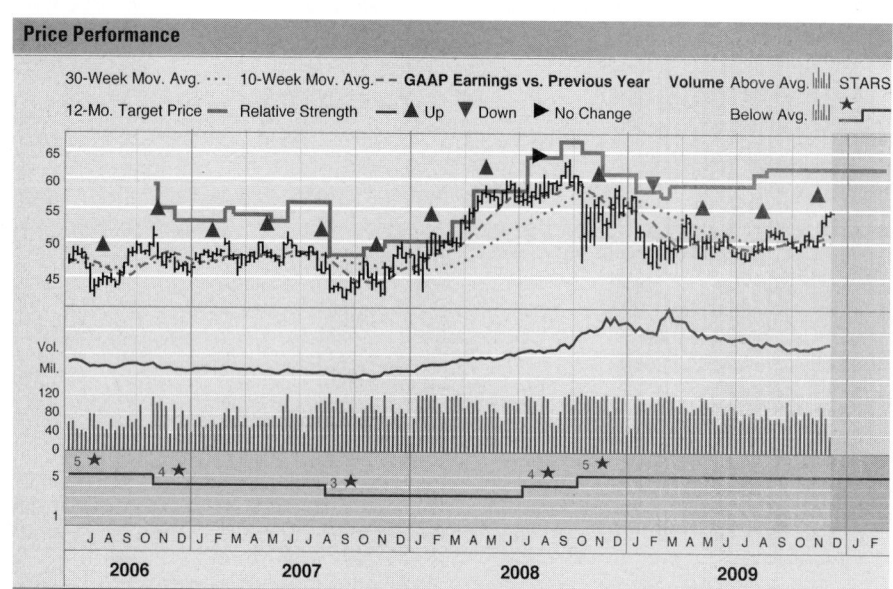

30-Week Mov. Avg. · · · 10-Week Mov. Avg. - - **GAAP Earnings vs. Previous Year** Volume Above Avg. STARS
12-Mo. Target Price — Relative Strength — ▲ Up ▼ Down ► No Change Below Avg. ★

Options: ASE, CBOE, P, Ph

Analysis prepared by **Joseph Agnese** on November 16, 2009, when the stock traded at **$ 53.42**.

Qualitative Risk Assessment

LOW	MEDIUM	HIGH

Our risk assessment of Wal-Mart Stores, Inc. reflects our view of the company's high-quality earnings, as reflected in its S&P Quality Ranking of A+, its dominant market share positions, continued price leadership and strong cash flow generation.

Quantitative Evaluations

S&P Quality Ranking A+

D	C	B-	B	B+	A-	A	A+

Relative Strength Rank STRONG

80

LOWEST = 1   HIGHEST = 99

Revenue/Earnings Data

Revenue (Million $)

	1Q	2Q	3Q	4Q	Year
2010	94,242	100,910	99,411	--	--
2009	94,070	101,544	97,634	107,996	405,607
2008	85,387	91,990	90,880	106,269	378,799
2007	79,613	85,430	84,467	99,078	348,650
2006	71,680	76,811	75,436	89,273	312,427
2005	64,763	69,722	68,520	82,216	285,222

Earnings Per Share ($)

	1Q	2Q	3Q	4Q	Year
2010	0.77	0.88	0.84	E1.12	E3.61
2009	0.76	0.86	0.77	0.96	3.35
2008	0.68	0.86	0.70	1.03	3.16
2007	0.64	0.72	0.62	0.95	2.92
2006	0.58	0.67	0.57	0.86	2.68
2005	0.50	0.62	0.54	0.75	2.41

Fiscal year ended Jan. 31. Next earnings report expected: Late January. EPS Estimates based on S&P Operating Earnings; historical GAAP earnings are as reported.

Highlights

▶ We expect net revenues to increase 6.5% in FY 11 (Jan.), to $436.3 billion, from our estimate of $409.5 billion in FY 10, driven by low single digit U.S. same-store sales and the addition of around 4% in square footage of new retail space, with square footage growth (excluding acquisitions) shifting toward international markets (25 million square feet) from domestic expansion (12 million square feet), partially offset by store closures and unfavorable foreign currency exchange rates. We expect foreign exchange rates to be favorable and food inflation to accelerate throughout FY 11.

▶ We estimate that EBITDA margins will widen slightly, reflecting increased sales leverage and well controlled inventory levels, partially offset by a shift in the product mix due to higher sales of food and pharmacy products and slow sales growth in discretionary categories such as apparel and home departments. Additionally, we see continued benefits from improved labor productivity due to the rollout of scheduling software.

▶ We project EPS of $3.95 for FY 11, up 9.4% from our estimate of $3.61 in FY 10.

Investment Rationale/Risk

▶ We believe the company is well positioned to gain market share in an adverse economic environment, as we think consumers will continue to trade down from higher-cost competitors and take advantage of its one-stop shopping convenience. We believe WMT's significant staples product offerings and basics discretionary offerings position it well despite weak consumer spending.

▶ Risks to our recommendation and target price include economic pressures such as rising unemployment or lower consumer confidence, which we think would negatively affect WMT's core customers and the company's results, and unfavorable foreign currency exchange rates.

▶ Our 12-month target price of $62 reflects our analysis of relative P/E ratios. Based on our expectation for market share gains in a weak economic environment, we believe the shares should trade above the forward 12-month P/E multiple of the S&P 500. Applying a multiple of 15.7X, a 3.0% discount to WMT's five-year median P/E but an 11% premium to the forward 12-month P/E for the S&P 500, to our FY 11 EPS estimate of $3.95 implies a value of $62.

Dividend Data (Dates: mm/dd Payment Date: mm/dd/yy)

Amount ($)	Date Decl.	Ex-Div. Date	Stk. of Record	Payment Date
0.273	03/05	03/11	03/13	04/06/09
0.273	03/05	05/13	05/15	06/01/09
0.273	03/05	08/12	08/14	09/08/09
0.273	03/05	12/09	12/11	01/04/10

Dividends have been paid since 1973. Source: Company reports.

Please read the Required Disclosures and Analyst Certification on the last page of this report.

The McGraw-Hill Companies

Wal-Mart Stores Inc

STANDARD
&POOR'S

Business Summary November 16, 2009

CORPORATE OVERVIEW. Walmart, the largest retailer in North America, has set its sights on other parts of the world. The company's operations are divided into three divisions: Walmart U.S. (FY 09 (Jan.) sales $255.7 billion), Sam's Club ($46.9 billion), and Walmart International ($98.6 billion). Internationally, WMT recently operated 28 units in Argentina, 345 in Brazil, 318 in Canada, 502 in Central America,197 in Chile, 243 in China (through joint ventures), 371 in Japan, 1,197 in Mexico, 56 in Puerto Rico, and 358 in the U.K.

MARKET PROFILE. With over 100 million people walking into Walmart stores every week, the company is a dominant player in many of the markets in which it competes. With FY 09 sales of about $150 billion within supermarket-related categories (grocery, health & wellness), the Walmart U.S. division is the

largest supermarket operator in the U.S., commanding over 25% market share of the $500+ billion supermarket industry. Other major product categories within the Walmart division include entertainment ($33 billion in estimated sales in FY 09), hardlines ($31 billion), apparel ($28 billion), and home ($13 billion). Sam's Club is the second largest warehouse club in the U.S., with sales of $46.9 billion in FY 09. About 67% of Sam's Club sales were generated from sundries and food categories.

Company Financials Fiscal Year Ended Jan. 31

Per Share Data ($)	2009	2008	2007	2006	2005	2004	2003	2002	2001	2000
Tangible Book Value	12.75	12.22	11.57	9.84	9.12	7.83	6.78	5.95	4.99	3.69
Cash Flow	5.06	4.72	4.23	3.81	3.44	2.91	2.58	2.22	2.04	1.78
Earnings	3.35	3.16	2.92	2.68	2.41	2.03	1.81	1.50	1.40	1.25
S&P Core Earnings	3.42	3.16	2.92	2.66	2.41	2.03	1.79	1.47	1.39	NA
Dividends	0.88	0.67	0.67	0.60	0.52	0.36	0.30	0.28	0.24	0.20
Payout Ratio	26%	21%	23%	22%	22%	18%	17%	19%	17%	16%
Calendar Year	2008	2007	2006	2005	2004	2003	2002	2001	2000	1999
Prices:High	63.85	51.44	52.15	54.60	61.31	60.20	63.94	58.75	69.00	70.25
Prices:Low	43.11	42.09	42.31	42.31	51.08	46.25	43.72	42.00	41.44	38.68
P/E Ratio:High	19	16	18	20	25	30	35	39	49	56
P/E Ratio:Low	13	13	14	16	21	23	24	28	30	31

Income Statement Analysis (Million $)

	2009	2008	2007	2006	2005	2004	2003	2002	2001	2000
Revenue	405,607	378,799	348,650	312,427	285,222	256,329	244,524	217,799	191,329	165,013
Operating Income	26,580	24,784	22,298	23,247	18,729	16,525	15,075	15,367	12,392	10,684
Depreciation	6,739	6,317	5,459	4,717	4,405	3,852	3,432	3,290	2,868	2,375
Interest Expense	2,272	1,467	1,809	1,420	1,187	996	1,063	1,326	1,374	1,022
Pretax Income	20,898	20,198	18,968	17,358	16,105	14,193	12,719	10,751	10,116	9,083
Effective Tax Rate	34.2%	34.2%	33.6%	33.4%	34.7%	36.1%	35.3%	36.2%	36.5%	36.8%
Net Income	13,254	12,884	12,178	11,231	10,267	8,861	8,039	6,671	6,295	5,575
S&P Core Earnings	13,505	12,880	12,178	11,134	10,267	8,861	7,955	6,592	6,235	NA

Balance Sheet & Other Financial Data (Million $)

	2009	2008	2007	2006	2005	2004	2003	2002	2001	2000
Cash	7,275	5,569	7,373	6,414	5,488	5,199	2,758	2,161	2,054	1,856
Current Assets	48,949	47,585	46,588	43,824	38,491	34,421	30,483	28,246	26,555	24,356
Total Assets	163,429	163,514	151,193	138,187	120,223	104,912	94,685	83,451	78,130	70,349
Current Liabilities	55,390	58,454	51,754	48,826	42,888	37,418	32,617	27,282	28,949	25,803
Long Term Debt	31,349	29,799	30,735	30,171	23,669	20,099	19,608	18,732	15,655	16,674
Common Equity	65,285	64,608	61,573	53,171	49,396	43,623	39,337	35,102	31,343	25,834
Total Capital	104,673	102,259	94,468	84,809	74,388	65,206	60,307	55,041	48,138	43,987
Capital Expenditures	11,499	14,937	15,666	14,563	12,893	10,308	9,355	8,383	8,042	6,183
Cash Flow	19,993	19,201	17,637	15,948	14,672	12,713	11,471	9,961	9,163	7,950
Current Ratio	0.9	0.8	0.9	0.9	0.9	0.9	0.9	1.0	0.9	0.9
% Long Term Debt of Capitalization	30.0	29.1	32.5	35.6	31.8	30.8	32.5	34.0	32.5	38.0
% Net Income of Revenue	3.3	3.4	3.5	3.5	3.6	3.5	3.3	3.1	3.3	3.4
% Return on Assets	8.1	8.2	8.4	8.7	9.1	8.9	9.0	8.3	8.5	9.3
% Return on Equity	20.4	20.4	21.2	21.9	22.1	21.3	21.6	20.1	22.0	23.8

Data as orig reptd.; bef. results of disc opers/spec. items. Per share data adj. for stk. divs.; EPS diluted. E-Estimated. NA-Not Available. NM-Not Meaningful. NR-Not Ranked. UR-Under Review.

Office: 702 S.W. 8th Street, Bentonville, AR 72716.
Telephone: 479-273-4000.
Website: http://www.walmartstores.com
Chrmn: S.R. Walton

Pres & CEO: M. Duke
Pres & CEO: L. Scott
Vice Chrmn: E. Castro-Wright
EVP & CFO: T.M. Schoewe

Investor Contact: M. Beckstead (479-277-9558)
Board Members: A. M. Alvarez, J. W. Breyer, M. M. Burns, J. I. Cash, Jr., E. Castro-Wright, R. C. Corbett, D. N. Daft, M. Duke, G. B. Penner, A. I. Questrom, H. L. Scott, Jr., A. M. Sorenson, J. Walton, S. R. Walton, C. J. Williams, L. S. Wolf

Founded: 1945
Domicile: Delaware
Employees: 2,100,000

Washington Post Co (The)

**STANDARD
&POOR'S**

S&P Recommendation	HOLD ★★★☆☆	Price	12-Mo. Target Price	Investment Style
		$410.42 (as of Nov 27, 2009)	$502.00	Large-Cap Growth

GICS Sector Consumer Discretionary
Sub-Industry Publishing

Summary WPO publishes The Washington Post newspaper and Newsweek magazine, operates TV stations and cable systems, and provides education and database services.

Key Stock Statistics (Source S&P, Vickers, company reports)

52-Wk Range	$495.60–300.16	S&P Oper. EPS 2009**E**	21.49	Market Capitalization(B)	$3.328	Beta		0.87
Trailing 12-Month EPS	$3.09	S&P Oper. EPS 2010**E**	27.94	Yield (%)	2.10	S&P 3-Yr. Proj. EPS CAGR(%)		30
Trailing 12-Month P/E	NM	P/E on S&P Oper. EPS 2009**E**	19.1	Dividend Rate/Share	$8.60	S&P Credit Rating		A
$10K Invested 5 Yrs Ago	$4,608	Common Shares Outstg. (M)	9.4	Institutional Ownership (%)	80			

Price Performance

- 30-Week Mov. Avg. · · · 10-Week Mov. Avg. - - **GAAP Earnings vs. Previous Year** Volume Above Avg. STARS
- 12-Mo. Target Price — Relative Strength — ▲ Up ▼ Down ▶ No Change Below Avg.

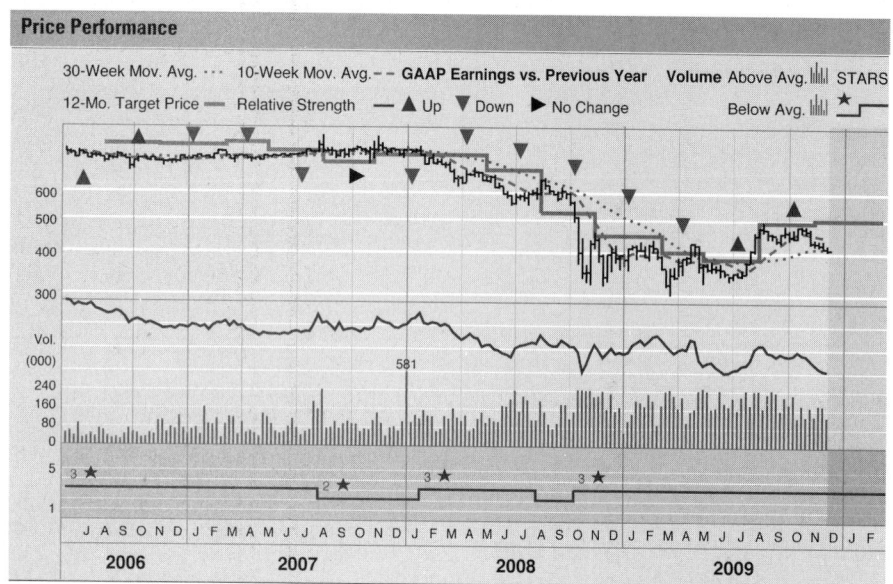

| | 2006 | 2007 | 2008 | 2009 |

Analysis prepared by **Joseph Agnese** on November 03, 2009, when the stock traded at **$ 429.00**.

Highlights

► We look for revenues to rise about 4.6% in 2010, to $4.7 billion, from our estimate of $4.5 billion in 2009. We project growth in education segment (Kaplan, Inc.) revenues, driven by a mix of organic gains and acquisitions. We forecast a healthy increase in cable segment revenues from the addition of new cable modem, telephone and digital video subscribers. We expect television segment revenues to improve in 2010 on easier comparisons and more stable advertising demand. Although we see declines in the magazine and newspaper segments amid persisting secular challenges, we see cyclical challenges easing.

► We expect operating margins widening in 2010. We see margin improvements in the cable division, coupled with less severe losses in the company's publishing businesses, offsetting a shift in mix toward lower margin education business. We expect publishing margins to be supported by more stable advertising demand and benefits from cost cutting efforts.

► We see EPS of $27.94 in 2010, up from our estimate of operating EPS of $21.49 in 2009, excluding restructuring and early retirement charges of $10.59.

Investment Rationale/Risk

► Our hold recommendation is based on valuation. In recent years, the education segment has grown revenues steadily through numerous acquisitions and has helped WPO diversify away from traditional media businesses. However, investments in new businesses have contributed to this segment's record of inconsistent earnings. While restructuring actions and cost cuts led to improved profitability in 2008, we expect the education segment to remain a low-margin business for the foreseeable future. We also see a recessionary U.S. economy hurting revenues and profitability for the company's publishing operations.

► Risks to our recommendation and target price include revenue shortfalls in WPO's education and cable operations. Regarding corporate governance, 28 holders of non-publicly traded Class A shares (as of January 29, 2009) have the right to elect a majority of the directors, which we believe may not be in the best interests of common (Class B) stockholders.

► Our 12-month target price of $502 is based on a peer-median EV/EBITDA multiple of 7.3X applied to our 2009 EBITDA estimate of $600 million.

Qualitative Risk Assessment

LOW	MEDIUM	HIGH

Our risk assessment incorporates our view of a highly competitive environment for advertising among publishers and other media, and a significant downward trend in print advertising and circulation, partially offset by the recurring nature of a significant portion of company revenues.

Quantitative Evaluations

S&P Quality Ranking B+

D	C	B-	B	B+	A-	A	A+

Relative Strength Rank WEAK

26

LOWEST = 1 HIGHEST = 99

Revenue/Earnings Data

Revenue (Million $)

	1Q	2Q	3Q	4Q	Year
2009	1,054	1,128	1,149	--	--
2008	1,063	1,106	1,129	1,164	4,462
2007	985.6	1,047	1,023	1,126	4,180
2006	948.3	969.0	946.9	1,041	3,905
2005	833.9	897.6	873.7	948.7	3,554
2004	759.0	818.4	820.0	902.7	3,300

Earnings Per Share ($)

2009	-2.05	1.30	1.81	E7.81	E21.49
2008	4.08	-0.31	1.08	2.01	6.87
2007	6.70	7.19	7.60	8.72	30.19
2006	8.48	8.17	7.60	9.97	34.21
2005	6.87	8.16	6.89	10.65	32.59
2004	6.15	8.82	8.57	11.03	34.59

Fiscal year ended Dec. 31. Next earnings report expected: Late February. EPS Estimates based on S&P Operating Earnings; historical GAAP earnings are as reported.

Dividend Data (Dates: mm/dd Payment Date: mm/dd/yy)

Amount ($)	Date Decl.	Ex-Div. Date	Stk. of Record	Payment Date
2.150	01/15	01/22	01/26	02/06/09
2.150	02/24	04/23	04/27	05/08/09
2.150	06/25	07/23	07/27	08/07/09
2.150	09/10	10/22	10/26	11/06/09

Dividends have been paid since 1956. Source: Company reports.

Please read the Required Disclosures and Analyst Certification on the last page of this report.

The McGraw-Hill Companies

Washington Post Co (The)

STANDARD &POOR'S

Business Summary November 03, 2009

CORPORATE OVERVIEW. The Washington Post operates principally in four areas of the media business: newspaper publishing, television broadcasting, magazine publishing, and cable television. Through its subsidiary Kaplan, Inc., the company also provides educational services for individuals, schools and businesses. In 2008, about 87% of the company's revenues was derived from the United States, down from 88% and 91% in 2007 and 2006, respectively.

The company divides Kaplan's various educational businesses (52% of 2008 revenues) into three categories: higher education (55% of segment revenues), test preparation and admissions (25%), and professional (20%). Higher education includes Kaplan's domestic and international post-secondary education businesses, including fixed facility colleges and online post-secondary and career programs. We note that approximately 71% of Kaplan's higher education revenues came from Title IV (federal financial aid) programs in 2008, and thus we believe the segment is vulnerable to budget cuts for education spending. Test prep includes standardized test prep and English-language courses, as well as the K12 and Score! businesses. Professional includes the

domestic and overseas professional businesses, including study programs for the CFA and CPA exams. Part of the company's strategy in the education business is to grow through acquisition; along those lines, Kaplan made nine acquisitions in both 2008 and 2007.

The Newspaper division (18%) includes The Washington Post, The Washington Post National Weekly Edition, Express (a free weekly tabloid), Washingtonpost.Newsweek Interactive (WPNI), and other publications. WPNI holds a 16.5% interest in Classified Ventures, a company that provides online classified advertising databases for cars, apartment rentals and residential real estate. Newspaper segment online revenues grew about 7% to $123 million in 2008, down from 11% growth in 2007 and 28% growth in 2006.

Company Financials Fiscal Year Ended Dec. 31

Per Share Data ($)	2008	2007	2006	2005	2004	2003	2002	2001	2000	1999
Tangible Book Value	89.89	NM	143.64	103.66	92.76	64.70	59.82	50.31	50.03	51.03
Cash Flow	37.42	55.26	57.76	53.26	54.04	43.38	40.93	38.62	26.79	38.45
Earnings	6.87	30.19	34.21	32.59	34.59	25.12	22.61	24.06	14.32	22.30
S&P Core Earnings	15.82	25.02	30.53	26.50	29.88	15.68	12.98	-1.24	NA	NA
Dividends	8.60	8.20	7.80	7.40	7.00	5.80	5.60	5.60	5.40	5.20
Payout Ratio	125%	27%	23%	23%	20%	23%	25%	23%	38%	23%
Prices:High	823.25	885.23	815.00	982.03	999.50	819.50	743.00	651.50	628.75	594.50
Prices:Low	320.00	726.93	690.00	716.00	790.21	650.03	516.00	470.00	467.25	490.13
P/E Ratio:High	NM	29	24	30	29	33	33	27	44	27
P/E Ratio:Low	NM	24	20	22	23	26	23	20	33	22

Income Statement Analysis (Million $)	2008	2007	2006	2005	2004	2003	2002	2001	2000	1999
Revenue	4,462	4,180	3,905	3,554	3,300	2,839	2,584	2,417	2,412	2,216
Operating Income	598	716	682	713	748	497	549	358	458	551
Depreciation	288	239	222	198	185	174	172	138	118	163
Interest Expense	24.7	24.1	25.3	26.8	28.0	27.8	33.8	49.6	54.7	26.8
Pretax Income	145	481	519	500	542	383	354	388	230	375
Effective Tax Rate	54.7%	40.0%	36.5%	37.1%	38.7%	37.0%	38.8%	40.7%	40.6%	39.9%
Net Income	65.7	289	330	314	333	241	216	230	136	226
S&P Core Earnings	148	238	293	255	287	150	124	-13.4	NA	NA

Balance Sheet & Other Financial Data (Million $)	2008	2007	2006	2005	2004	2003	2002	2001	2000	1999
Cash	748	373	348	216	119	87.4	28.8	31.5	20.3	75.5
Current Assets	1,352	995	935	818	754	496	383	397	405	476
Total Assets	5,158	6,005	5,381	4,585	4,317	3,902	3,584	3,559	3,201	2,987
Current Liabilities	1,094	1,013	803	695	688	712	736	434	409	823
Long Term Debt	400	401	402	404	426	422	406	1,862	873	398
Common Equity	2,858	3,461	3,160	2,638	2,412	2,075	1,837	1,683	1,481	1,368
Total Capital	3,630	4,583	4,173	3,477	3,254	2,814	2,517	3,781	2,485	1,891
Capital Expenditures	289	290	284	238	205	126	153	224	130	130
Cash Flow	353	526	551	511	518	414	387	367	253	388
Current Ratio	1.2	1.0	1.2	1.2	1.1	0.7	0.5	0.9	1.0	0.6
% Long Term Debt of Capitalization	11.0	8.7	9.6	11.6	13.1	15.0	16.1	49.3	35.1	21.0
% Net Income of Revenue	1.5	6.9	8.4	8.8	10.1	8.5	8.4	9.5	5.7	10.2
% Return on Assets	1.2	5.1	6.6	7.1	8.0	6.4	6.1	6.8	4.4	7.9
% Return on Equity	2.1	8.7	11.3	12.4	14.9	12.3	12.2	14.4	9.5	15.2

Data as orig reptd.; bef. results of disc opers/spec. items. Per share data adj. for stk. divs.; EPS diluted. E-Estimated. NA-Not Available. NM-Not Meaningful. NR-Not Ranked. UR-Under Review.

Office: 1150 15th Street N.W., Washington, DC 20071-0002.
Telephone: 202-334-6000.
Website: http://www.washpostco.com
Chrmn & CEO: D.E. Graham

SVP & CFO: H. Jones
SVP, Secy & General Counsel: V. Dillon
CTO: R.S. Terkowitz
CTO: Y. Kochar

Investor Contact: J.B. Morse, Jr. (202-334-6662)
Board Members: L. C. Bollinger, W. E. Buffett, C. C. Davis, B. Diller, J. L. Dotson, Jr., M. F. Gates, T. S. Gayner, D. E. Graham, A. M. Mulcahy, R. L. Olson

Founded: 1947
Domicile: Delaware
Employees: 20,000

The McGraw-Hill Companies

Waste Management Inc.

STANDARD &POOR'S

S&P Recommendation **BUY** ★★★★☆	Price $33.06 (as of Nov 27, 2009)	12-Mo. Target Price $35.00	Investment Style Large-Cap Blend

GICS Sector Industrials
Sub-Industry Environmental & Facilities Services

Summary This Houston-based company is the largest U.S. trash hauling/disposal concern.

Key Stock Statistics (Source S&P, Vickers, company reports)

52-Wk Range	$33.99–22.10	S&P Oper. EPS 2009E	1.98	Market Capitalization(B)	$16.188	Beta	0.52
Trailing 12-Month EPS	$1.82	S&P Oper. EPS 2010E	2.20	Yield (%)	3.51	S&P 3-Yr. Proj. EPS CAGR(%)	2
Trailing 12-Month P/E	18.2	P/E on S&P Oper. EPS 2009E	16.7	Dividend Rate/Share	$1.16	S&P Credit Rating	BBB
$10K Invested 5 Yrs Ago	$12,855	Common Shares Outstg. (M)	489.7	Institutional Ownership (%)	79		

Price Performance

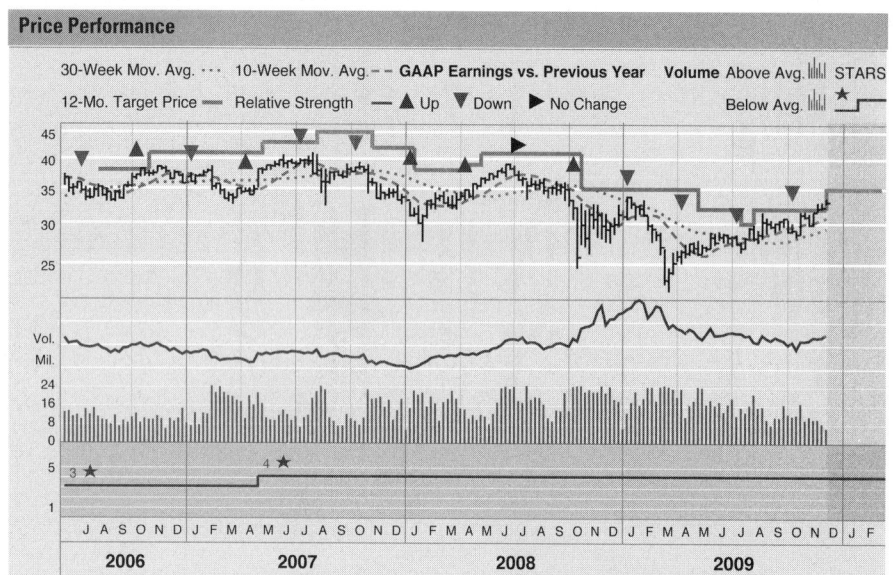

- 30-Week Mov. Avg. ···
- 10-Week Mov. Avg. - -
- GAAP Earnings vs. Previous Year
- Volume Above Avg. STARS
- 12-Mo. Target Price —
- Relative Strength —
- ▲ Up ▼ Down ► No Change
- Below Avg.

Options: ASE, CBOE, P, Ph

Analysis prepared by **Stewart Scharf** on November 04, 2009, when the stock traded at **$ 30.67**.

Highlights

► We expect organic revenues to decline at least 4% in 2009, reflecting weak roll-off volume in the C&D (construction and demolition) and special waste business lines, and lower fuel surcharges and recycling commodity prices, which should outweigh higher pricing. We expect some sequential improvement over the next few periods, with volume growth possibly resuming later in 2010 as market conditions recover.

► In our view, gross margins (before D&A) will widen by more than 200 basis points in 2009, from 36.8% in 2008, with further expansion likely in 2010, based on cost savings from routing initiatives, and further price hikes. We see the EBITDA margin widening in 2010 from our projected 27.5% in 2009 (25.7% in 2008), reflecting restructuring efforts, improved productivity, and lower maintenance and safety costs. We believe SG&A expenses will remain well controlled at near 11% of sales.

► We project a virtually unchanged tax rate of about 37% for 2009, with a slight rise in 2010, and see operating EPS of $1.98 (before at least $0.13 of charges), advancing 11% in 2010 to $2.20.

Investment Rationale/Risk

► Our buy recommendation is based on our valuation metrics and WM's pricing and divestiture strategy. We expect WM to use its strong free cash generation for niche acquisitions, growth prospects in alternative energy, dividends and share repurchases.

► Risks to our opinion and target price include a significant rise in fuel costs, a prolonged downturn in the U.S. economy, a sharp drop in recycling prices and demand, a lower customer retention rate, and an inability to raise prices enough to meet return on invested capital (ROIC) goals.

► We view the stock's recent dividend yield of 3.8%, above the 2% yield of the S&P 500, as attractive. Correlating various relative metrics, including its historical five-year average P/E multiple, we believe WM should trade at an above-peer average P/E of about 16.5X our EPS estimate for 2010, valuing the stock at $36. Based on our discounted cash flow model, assuming a 7.5% weighted average cost of capital and 3% terminal growth, our intrinsic value estimate is $34. Blending these metrics, we derive our 12-month target price of $35.

Qualitative Risk Assessment

LOW	MEDIUM	HIGH

Our risk assessment reflects some market share loss due to ongoing pricing initiatives in a soft economic environment, and volatile commodity recycling prices, offset by our view of a solid balance sheet, strong cash generation for dividends, debt paydowns and share buybacks, and a favorable interest rate environment. In addition, we view WM's corporate governance practices as sound.

Quantitative Evaluations

S&P Quality Ranking B+

D	C	B-	B	B+	A-	A	A+

Relative Strength Rank STRONG

82

LOWEST = 1   HIGHEST = 99

Revenue/Earnings Data

Revenue (Million $)

	1Q	2Q	3Q	4Q	Year
2009	2,810	2,952	3,023	--	--
2008	3,266	3,489	3,525	3,108	13,388
2007	3,188	3,358	3,403	3,361	13,310
2006	3,229	3,410	3,441	3,283	13,363
2005	3,038	3,289	3,375	3,372	13,074
2004	2,896	3,138	3,274	3,208	12,516

Earnings Per Share ($)

2009	0.31	0.50	0.56	E0.50	E1.98
2008	0.48	0.64	0.63	0.44	2.19
2007	0.42	0.64	0.54	0.61	2.23
2006	0.34	0.76	0.55	0.46	2.10
2005	0.26	0.92	0.38	0.52	2.09
2004	0.25	0.37	0.52	0.47	1.60

Fiscal year ended Dec. 31. Next earnings report expected: Mid February. EPS Estimates based on S&P Operating Earnings; historical GAAP earnings are as reported.

Dividend Data (Dates: mm/dd Payment Date: mm/dd/yy)

Amount ($)	Date Decl.	Ex-Div. Date	Stk. of Record	Payment Date
0.290	02/25	03/05	03/09	03/20/09
0.290	05/08	05/28	06/01	06/19/09
0.290	08/25	09/03	09/08	09/25/09
0.290	11/10	11/30	12/02	12/18/09

Dividends have been paid since 1998. Source: Company reports.

Please read the Required Disclosures and Analyst Certification on the last page of this report.

The McGraw-Hill Companies

Waste Management Inc.

STANDARD
&POOR'S

Business Summary November 04, 2009

CORPORATE OVERVIEW. Waste Management, the largest waste disposal company in North America, provides collection, transfer, recycling and resource recovery, as well as disposal services. It also owns U.S. waste-to-energy facilities. As of December 31, 2008, it served nearly 20 million customers through 355 transfer stations and 267 owned or operated landfills (six hazardous waste landfills), 16 waste-to-energy plants, 105 recycling plants, and 108 beneficial-use landfill gas projects. In 2008, revenues from the North American solid waste (NASW) business were: 56% collection; 19% landfill; 5.8% waste-to-energy (Wheelabrator Technologies unit); 10% transfer; 7.6% recycling; and 1.3% other. WM's average remaining landfill life at December 31, 2008, was 32 years, and 39 years when considering remaining permitted capacity and projected annual disposal volume. WM's internalization rate was 69.2% at September 30, 2009, up from 67.5% a year earlier. WM believes that for every 1% reduction in its "churn" ratio (customer turnover), it adds $25 million to EBIT (earnings before interest and taxes). On August 5, 2009, the company changed its ticker symbol to WM from WMI.

We project free cash flow of about $1.3 billion for 2009, down from $1.47 billion in 2008. WM bought back nearly 12.7 million shares in 2008 for $410 million, down from 40 million shares for $1.4 billion in 2007. Following a year of inactivity, WM resumed its repurchase program in the third quarter of 2009, and through October 2009, had bought back $100 million of stock. It is targeting

$400 million in buybacks. The company sees a strong acquisition pipeline and more attractive valuations over the next 12 to 18 months, targeting $250 million for solid waste deals and $200 million in landfill gas-to-energy, while also looking to expand its medical waste operations both internally and via acquisitions. We believe capital spending for 2009 will near $1.1 billion, versus $1.2 billion in 2008. Additionally, the company noted that although for every 1% price increase it can lose 3% to 5% of volume, it believes this method still boosts profit.

CORPORATE STRATEGY. In our view, WM will use its strong cash generation primarily for acquisitions, dividends and share buybacks, with favorable acquisition multiples leading to more acquired revenues than divestitures. In October 2007, the company announced an environmental initiative, under which it plans to invest in waste-based energy production, recycling and new waste technologies, including up to $500 million a year for 10 years to increase the fuel efficiency of its fleet. We view this as a positive long-term environmental strategy as more methane in landfills is converted into energy.

Company Financials Fiscal Year Ended Dec. 31

Per Share Data ($)	2008	2007	2006	2005	2004	2003	2002	2001	2000	1999
Tangible Book Value	0.57	0.52	1.52	1.10	0.91	0.24	0.21	0.43	NM	NM
Cash Flow	4.87	4.64	4.66	4.50	3.90	3.44	5.29	2.97	2.14	1.99
Earnings	2.19	2.23	2.10	2.09	1.60	1.21	1.33	0.80	-0.16	-0.64
S&P Core Earnings	2.15	2.18	2.08	1.90	1.48	1.09	1.17	1.04	NA	NA
Dividends	1.08	0.96	0.88	0.80	0.75	0.01	0.01	0.01	0.01	0.02
Payout Ratio	49%	43%	42%	38%	47%	1%	1%	1%	NM	NM
Prices:High	39.25	41.19	38.64	31.03	31.42	29.72	31.25	32.50	28.31	60.00
Prices:Low	24.51	32.40	30.08	26.80	25.67	19.39	20.20	22.51	13.00	14.00
P/E Ratio:High	18	18	18	15	20	25	23	41	NM	NM
P/E Ratio:Low	11	15	14	13	16	16	15	28	NM	NM

Income Statement Analysis (Million $)										
Revenue	13,388	13,310	13,363	13,074	12,516	11,574	11,142	11,322	12,492	13,127
Operating Income	3,577	3,746	3,388	3,167	3,021	2,841	2,870	3,034	3,216	2,154
Depreciation	1,323	1,259	1,334	1,361	1,336	1,265	2,444	1,371	1,429	1,614
Interest Expense	472	521	545	496	455	439	462	541	748	770
Pretax Income	1,797	1,784	1,518	1,140	1,214	1,129	1,240	792	344	-139
Effective Tax Rate	37.2%	30.2%	21.4%	NM	20.3%	35.8%	34.2%	35.9%	NM	NM
Net Income	1,087	1,163	1,149	1,182	931	719	823	503	-97.0	-395
S&P Core Earnings	1,066	1,133	1,139	1,072	864	643	725	653	NA	NA

Balance Sheet & Other Financial Data (Million $)										
Cash	480	348	614	666	443	135	264	730	94.0	181
Current Assets	2,335	2,480	3,182	3,451	2,819	2,588	2,700	3,124	2,457	6,221
Total Assets	20,227	20,175	20,600	21,135	20,905	20,656	19,631	19,490	18,565	22,681
Current Liabilities	3,036	2,598	3,268	3,257	3,205	3,332	3,173	3,721	2,937	7,489
Long Term Debt	7,491	8,008	7,495	8,165	8,182	7,997	8,062	7,709	8,372	8,399
Common Equity	5,902	5,792	6,222	6,121	5,971	5,563	5,308	5,392	4,801	4,403
Total Capital	15,160	15,521	15,357	15,931	14,435	15,473	13,389	14,241	14,067	13,540
Capital Expenditures	1,221	1,211	1,329	1,180	1,258	1,200	1,287	1,328	1,313	1,327
Cash Flow	2,410	2,422	2,483	2,543	2,267	1,984	3,267	1,874	1,332	1,219
Current Ratio	0.8	1.0	1.0	1.1	0.9	0.8	0.9	0.8	0.8	0.8
% Long Term Debt of Capitalization	49.4	51.5	48.8	51.3	56.7	51.7	60.2	54.1	59.5	62.0
% Net Income of Revenue	8.1	8.7	8.6	9.0	7.4	6.2	7.4	4.4	NM	NM
% Return on Assets	5.4	5.7	5.5	5.6	4.5	3.5	4.2	2.6	NM	NM
% Return on Equity	18.6	19.3	18.6	19.6	16.1	13.2	15.4	9.9	NM	NM

Data as orig reptd.; bef. results of disc opers/spec. items. Per share data adj. for stk. divs.; EPS diluted. E-Estimated. NA-Not Available. NM-Not Meaningful. NR-Not Ranked. UR-Under Review.

Office: 1001 Fannin Street, Houston, TX 77002.
Telephone: 713-512-6200.
Website: http://www.wm.com
Chrmn: J.C. Pope

Pres & COO: L. O'Donnell, III
CEO: D.P. Steiner
SVP & CFO: R.G. Simpson
SVP & General Counsel: R.L. Wittenbraker

Investor Contact: J. Alderson (713-394-2281)
Board Members: P. S. Cafferty, F. M. Clark, Jr., P. W. Gross, J. C. Pope, W. R. Reum, S. G. Rothmeier, D. P. Steiner, T. H. Weidemeyer

Founded: 1894
Domicile: Delaware
Employees: 45,900

The McGraw-Hill Companies

Waters Corp

S&P Recommendation	HOLD ★★★☆☆	Price $59.02 (as of Nov 27, 2009)	12-Mo. Target Price $60.00	Investment Style Large-Cap Growth

GICS Sector Health Care
Sub-Industry Life Sciences Tools & Services

Summary This company manufactures scientific and industrial analytical equipment such as liquid chromatography, thermal analysis and mass spectrometry products.

Key Stock Statistics (Source S&P, Vickers, company reports)

52-Wk Range	$61.45–30.00	S&P Oper. EPS 2009**E**	3.42	Market Capitalization(B)	$5.589	Beta	1.14
Trailing 12-Month EPS	$3.27	S&P Oper. EPS 2010**E**	3.64	Yield (%)	Nil	S&P 3-Yr. Proj. EPS CAGR(%)	13
Trailing 12-Month P/E	18.1	P/E on S&P Oper. EPS 2009**E**	17.3	Dividend Rate/Share	Nil	S&P Credit Rating	NA
$10K Invested 5 Yrs Ago	$12,517	Common Shares Outstg. (M)	94.7	Institutional Ownership (%)	93		

Price Performance

30-Week Mov. Avg. · · · 10-Week Mov. Avg. - - **GAAP Earnings vs. Previous Year** Volume Above Avg. STARS
12-Mo. Target Price — Relative Strength — ▲ Up ▼ Down ► No Change Below Avg.

Options: ASE, CBOE, Ph

Analysis prepared by **Jeffrey Loo, CFA** on November 03, 2009, when the stock traded at **$ 58.00**.

Highlights

► We see sales, including 3% adverse foreign currency exchange, declining 4% in 2009, to $1.5 billion, as we expect the challenging global economic environment to constrain equipment sales, particularly in the industrial end-markets, throughout 2009. However, we think instrument sales to the pharmaceutical and life sciences end-markets should stabilize by year end and improve in 2010, aided by the $10 billion in additional NIH funding from the economic stimulus package. We expect instrument sales by the Thermal Analysis unit to the industrial end-market to fall 11%, primarily on lower sales to the chemical industry, but we see growth in food safety demand. We forecast WAT's large installed client base to contribute to high single digit growth for consumables and services, which account for over 50% of sales. We see 2010 sales growing 6% to $1.58 billion.

► We see gross margins improving 280 basis points (bps), aided by foreign currency translation and product mix, and operating margins increasing 300 bps, helped by lower costs.

► We estimate 2009 and 2010 EPS at $3.42 and $3.64, aided by a lower share count due to stock buybacks.

Investment Rationale/Risk

► We believe the shares, recently trading at 15.9X our 2010 EPS estimate and at a 1.2X P/E-to-growth ratio, both in line with peers, are fairly valued. We see some stability in various end-markets, particularly life sciences and pharmaceutical, and we look for continued solid growth in consumables and services sales. However, we anticipate continued uncertainty in WAT's industrial end-market amid tight credit conditions and a challenging global economic environment, continuing to pressure sales and resulting in limited sales visibility. That said, we maintain our favorable view of WAT's systems integration approach and new products such as the Synapt High Definition MS and tandem quadrupole devices.

► Risks to our recommendation and target price include weaker-than-expected equipment sales to the life sciences and pharmaceutical end-markets.

► Based on our P/E-to-growth (PEG) analysis, using our 2010 EPS forecast, a PEG ratio of 1.25X, in line with peers, and a 13% projected three-year growth rate, our 12-month target price is $60.

Qualitative Risk Assessment

LOW	MEDIUM	HIGH

Our risk assessment reflects WAT's strong market share in the liquid chromatography and mass spectrometry markets, offset by a highly competitive marketplace and a reliance on customer demand for expensive instruments.

Quantitative Evaluations

S&P Quality Ranking B+

D	C	B-	B	B+	A-	A	A+

Relative Strength Rank STRONG

73

LOWEST = 1 · · · HIGHEST = 99

Revenue/Earnings Data

Revenue (Million $)

	1Q	2Q	3Q	4Q	Year
2009	333.1	362.8	374.0	--	--
2008	371.7	398.8	386.3	418.3	1,575
2007	330.8	352.6	352.6	437.0	1,473
2006	290.2	301.9	301.2	386.9	1,280
2005	268.3	284.6	273.0	332.3	1,158
2004	255.1	260.5	264.8	324.2	1,105

Earnings Per Share ($)

	1Q	2Q	3Q	4Q	Year
2009	0.75	0.72	0.79	E1.09	E3.42
2008	0.67	0.82	0.71	1.01	3.21
2007	0.54	0.59	0.52	0.96	2.62
2006	0.42	0.46	0.49	0.78	2.13
2005	0.38	0.46	0.22	0.71	1.74
2004	0.33	0.49	0.42	0.58	1.82

Fiscal year ended Dec. 31. Next earnings report expected: Late January. EPS Estimates based on S&P Operating Earnings; historical GAAP earnings are as reported.

Dividend Data

No cash dividends have been paid.

Please read the Required Disclosures and Analyst Certification on the last page of this report.

The **McGraw·Hill** Companies

Waters Corp

STANDARD & POOR'S

Business Summary November 03, 2009

CORPORATE OVERVIEW. Waters manufactures, distributes, and services analytical instruments to the pharmaceutical, life sciences, biochemical, industrial, academic, and government end-markets. Analytical instruments and components manufactured include high-performance liquid chromatography (HPLC) instruments, columns and other consumables, mass spectrometry (MS) instruments that can be integrated with other analytical instruments, and thermal analysis (TA) and rheology instruments. HPLC is the standard technique to identify and analyze constituent components of various chemicals and materials. Its unique performance capabilities let it separate and identify 80% of known chemicals and materials. HPLC is used to analyze substances in a variety of industries for R&D, quality control, and process engineering applications. Pharmaceutical and life science industries use HPLC primarily to identify new drugs.

In March 2004, WAT introduced a novel technology that it describes as Ultra Performance Chromatography, the Acquity UPLC. WAT believes the Acquity UPLC provides more comprehensive chemical separation and faster analysis times compared to the HPLC. MS is an analytical technique used to identify unknown compounds, quantify known materials, and elucidate the structural and chemical properties of molecules by measuring the masses of individual molecules that have been converted into ions. These products serve diverse markets, including pharmaceutical and environmental industries. The TA In-

struments division makes and services thermal analysis and rheology instruments used for the physical characterization of polymers and related materials. Thermal analysis measures physical characteristics of materials as a function of temperature. Changes in temperature affect several characteristics of materials, such as their physical state, weight, dimension and mechanical and electrical properties, which may be measured using thermal analysis techniques. As a result, thermal analysis is widely used to develop, produce and characterize materials in industries such as plastics, chemicals and pharmaceuticals.

WAT has supplemented its internal growth with various strategic acquisitions. In March 2004, it acquired NuGenesis Technologies Corp. for about $43 million. NuGenesis and Creon Lab formed the company's new Lab Informatics market segment. In March 2006, WAT acquired VICAM, a provider of bioseparation and rapid detection instruments for food safety. In August 2006, WAT acquired Thermometric AB, and in November 2006, it acquired Environmental Resource Associates, a provider of environmental testing and services. In 2007 WAT acquired Calorimetry Sciences Corporation.

Company Financials Fiscal Year Ended Dec. 31

Per Share Data ($)	2008	2007	2006	2005	2004	2003	2002	2001	2000	1999
Tangible Book Value	2.48	5.71	NM	NM	3.05	2.67	NM	3.19	2.21	0.98
Cash Flow	3.50	2.88	2.57	2.12	2.16	1.60	1.40	1.08	1.36	1.14
Earnings	3.21	2.62	2.13	1.74	1.82	1.34	1.12	0.84	1.14	0.92
S&P Core Earnings	3.21	2.62	2.18	1.57	1.45	1.18	0.99	1.07	NA	NA
Dividends	Nil	Nil	Nil	Nil	Nil	Nil	Nil	Nil	Nil	Nil
Payout Ratio	Nil	Nil	Nil	Nil	Nil	Nil	Nil	Nil	Nil	Nil
Prices:High	81.84	81.53	51.64	51.57	49.80	33.42	39.25	85.38	90.94	33.84
Prices:Low	32.21	48.55	37.06	33.99	33.10	19.79	17.86	22.33	21.97	18.13
P/E Ratio:High	25	31	24	30	27	25	35	NM	80	37
P/E Ratio:Low	10	19	17	20	18	15	16	NM	19	20

Income Statement Analysis (Million $)	2008	2007	2006	2005	2004	2003	2002	2001	2000	1999
Revenue	1,575	1,473	1,280	1,158	1,105	958	890	859	795	704
Operating Income	436	389	355	330	321	271	251	258	240	205
Depreciation	29.1	27.5	46.2	43.7	41.9	33.8	37.2	34.0	29.4	28.9
Interest Expense	38.5	56.5	51.7	24.7	10.1	2.37	2.48	1.26	Nil	8.95
Pretax Income	372	323	263	275	286	224	195	147	211	168
Effective Tax Rate	13.4%	17.1%	15.5%	26.4%	21.6%	23.6%	22.1%	22.3%	26.0%	27.0%
Net Income	322	268	222	202	224	171	152	115	156	122
S&P Core Earnings	322	268	227	183	179	150	134	147	NA	NA

Balance Sheet & Other Financial Data (Million $)	2008	2007	2006	2005	2004	2003	2002	2001	2000	1999
Cash	429	693	514	494	539	357	313	227	75.5	3.80
Current Assets	956	1,237	1,000	913	974	715	636	523	344	247
Total Assets	1,623	1,881	1,617	1,429	1,460	1,131	1,011	887	692	584
Current Liabilities	290	658	686	604	493	379	320	281	221	198
Long Term Debt	500	500	500	500	250	125	Nil	Nil	Nil	81.1
Common Equity	661	586	362	284	679	590	665	582	452	292
Total Capital	1,161	1,086	862	784	929	715	665	582	452	373
Capital Expenditures	69.1	60.3	51.4	51.0	66.2	34.6	37.9	42.4	35.4	19.4
Cash Flow	352	296	268	246	266	205	189	148	186	151
Current Ratio	3.3	1.9	1.5	1.5	2.0	1.9	2.0	1.9	1.6	1.3
% Long Term Debt of Capitalization	43.1	46.0	58.0	63.8	26.9	17.5	Nil	Nil	Nil	21.7
% Net Income of Revenue	20.5	18.2	17.4	17.4	20.3	17.8	17.1	13.3	19.6	17.4
% Return on Assets	18.4	15.3	14.6	14.0	17.3	15.9	16.0	14.5	24.4	21.1
% Return on Equity	51.7	56.5	68.8	42.0	35.3	27.2	24.3	22.2	42.0	55.3

Data as orig reptd.; bef. results of disc opers/spec. items. Per share data adj. for stk. divs.; EPS diluted. E-Estimated. NA-Not Available. NM-Not Meaningful. NR-Not Ranked. UR-Under Review.

Office: 34 Maple Street, Milford, MA 01757-3696.
Telephone: 508-478-2000.
Email: info@waters.com
Website: http://www.waters.com

Chrmn, Pres & CEO: D.A. Berthiaume
CFO, Chief Admin Officer & Chief Acctg Officer: J.A. Ornell
Secy & General Counsel: M.T. Beaudouin
Cntlr: W. Curry

Auditor: PricewaterhouseCoopers LLP, Boston, MA
Board Members: M. J. Berendt, D. A. Berthiaume, L. H. Glimcher, C. A. Kuebler, W. J. Miller, J. A. Reed, T. P. Salice

Founded: 1991
Domicile: Delaware
Employees: 5,033

Watson Pharmaceuticals Inc.

STANDARD &POOR'S

S&P Recommendation `HOLD` ★ ★ ★ ☆ ☆

Price	12-Mo. Target Price	Investment Style
$36.96 (as of Nov 27, 2009)	$37.00	Large-Cap Blend

GICS Sector Health Care
Sub-Industry Pharmaceuticals

Summary This company produces generic and branded drugs. In November 2006, Watson acquired rival generic drugmaker Andrx Corp. for $1.9 billion in cash.

Key Stock Statistics (Source S&P, Vickers, company reports)

52-Wk Range	$38.48– 22.16	S&P Oper. EPS 2009**E**	2.55	Market Capitalization(B)	$3.923	Beta	0.57
Trailing 12-Month EPS	$1.94	S&P Oper. EPS 2010**E**	2.65	Yield (%)	Nil	S&P 3-Yr. Proj. EPS CAGR(%)	5
Trailing 12-Month P/E	19.1	P/E on S&P Oper. EPS 2009**E**	14.5	Dividend Rate/Share	Nil	S&P Credit Rating	BBB-
$10K Invested 5 Yrs Ago	$12,666	Common Shares Outstg. (M)	106.1	Institutional Ownership (%)	87		

Price Performance

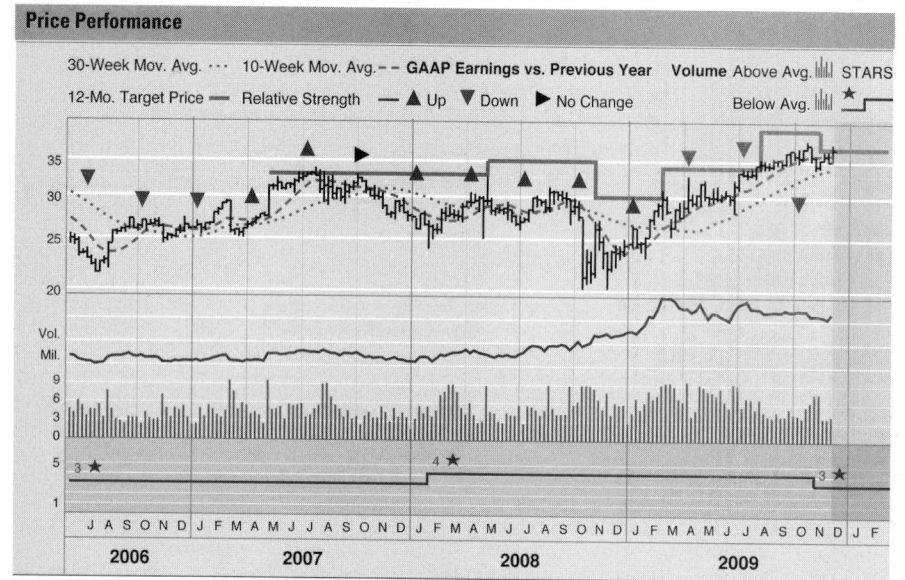

30-Week Mov. Avg. · · ·   10-Week Mov. Avg. - -   **GAAP Earnings vs. Previous Year**   Volume Above Avg. 📊   STARS
12-Mo. Target Price —   Relative Strength —   ▲ Up   ▼ Down   ▶ No Change   Below Avg. 📊   ★

2006   2007   2008   2009

Options: ASE, CBOE, Ph

Analysis prepared by **Herman B. Saftlas** on November 05, 2009, when the stock traded at **$ 35.01**.

Highlights

▶ We project a modest advance in 2010 revenues, from the $2.7 billion that we forecast for 2009 (excluding sales from the planned acquisition of Arrow Group). Despite the likelihood of a more competitive pricing environment in the generics market, we see volume helped by new generic versions of Toprol XL, metoprolol XR and certain oral contraceptives, and possibly, Concerta and Lovenox. Volume should also reflect increased production from new facilities in India, and from the Davie, FL, plant. Distribution revenues are likely to increase, but sales on the branded side are expected to decline sharply, reflecting the absence of Ferrlecit.

▶ We expect gross margins to hold up relatively well, largely from manufacturing efficiencies, and other supply chain improvements. However, we see SG&A and R&D spending increasing as a percentage of sales. Amortization is expected to be about 10% higher.

▶ After estimated taxes at an effective rate of about 37% (similar to our projected rate for 2009), we see operating EPS of $2.65 for 2010, up from the $2.55 that we forecast for 2009.

Investment Rationale/Risk

▶ We believe that WPI's diversified business platform, which comprises growing positions in generics, branded drugs and drug distribution, coupled with ongoing cost streamlining measures, will provide the underpinnings for earnings growth over the coming years. While we see the planned purchase of Arrow Group a key strategic move, expanding WPI's generic lines and geographic base, we think WPI faces integration risks with Arrow, as well as increased competitive pressures in the generics industry. In addition, WPI loses rights to market branded Ferrlecit, a treatment for anemia in hemodialysis patients (12% of gross profits in 2008), at the end of 2009.

▶ Risks to our recommendation and target price include greater-than-expected competitive pressures in principal generic and branded product lines, as well as possible R&D pipeline disappointments.

▶ Our 12-month target price of $37 applies a near peer P/E of 13.9X to our 2010 EPS estimate. This is supported by our DCF model, which assumes decelerating cash flow growth over the next 10 years, a WACC of 7.0%, and perpetuity growth of 1%, indicating intrinsic value of $37.

Qualitative Risk Assessment

LOW	MEDIUM	HIGH

Our risk assessment reflects risks common to the generic pharmaceutical business, which include the need to successfully develop generic products, obtain regulatory approvals and legally challenge branded patents. However, we believe these risks are offset by the company's wide and diverse generic portfolio and the balance afforded by WPI's branded drug business.

Quantitative Evaluations

S&P Quality Ranking   B-

D	C	B-	B	B+	A-	A	A+

Relative Strength Rank   **STRONG**

71

LOWEST = 1   HIGHEST = 99

Revenue/Earnings Data

Revenue (Million $)

	1Q	2Q	3Q	4Q	Year
2009	667.4	677.8	662.1	--	--
2008	627.0	622.6	640.7	645.2	2,536
2007	671.6	603.0	594.7	627.3	2,497
2006	407.2	510.4	440.5	621.2	1,979
2005	400.8	416.3	410.3	418.8	1,646
2004	409.7	399.4	408.0	423.5	1,641

Earnings Per Share ($)

	1Q	2Q	3Q	4Q	Year
2009	0.43	0.46	0.55	E0.70	E2.55
2008	0.45	0.53	0.62	0.50	2.09
2007	0.29	0.33	0.31	0.34	1.27
2006	0.23	-0.15	0.31	-4.80	-4.37
2005	0.32	0.35	0.35	0.19	1.21
2004	0.39	0.29	0.13	0.46	1.27

Fiscal year ended Dec. 31. Next earnings report expected: Mid February. EPS Estimates based on S&P Operating Earnings; historical GAAP earnings are as reported.

Dividend Data

No cash dividends have been paid.

The McGraw-Hill Companies

Watson Pharmaceuticals Inc.

STANDARD &POOR'S

Business Summary November 05, 2009

CORPORATE PROFILE. Watson Pharmaceuticals is a leading maker of generic pharmaceuticals that targets difficult to produce niche off-patent drugs. WPI significantly expanded its generic business with the acquisition of Andrx Corp. It also offers a line of specialty branded pharmaceuticals, largely in the areas of urology and nephrology.

Many WPI pharmaceuticals incorporate the company's novel proprietary drug delivery systems, such as transmucosal, vaginal and transdermal systems that allow for defined rates of drug release. Total revenues in 2008 were 58% from generic drugs, 18% from branded drugs, and 24% from distributed products. Drugs produced by third-party manufacturers represented about 58% of WPI's revenues in 2008.

WPI markets over 150 generic drug products, which comprise a broad cross section of therapeutic categories. Key segments include oral contraceptives, analgesics, antihypertensives, diuretics, antiulcers, antipsychotics, anti-inflammatories, analgesics, hormone replacements, antispasmodics and antidiarrheals.

During 2008, WPI launched 11 new generic products. Key launches in 2008 included generic versions of Wellbutrin XL, Prilosec, Marinol, Biaxin XL and

Reminyl. In total, Watson has about 60 ANDAs pending at the FDA.

Branded pharmaceuticals comprise specialty drugs and nephrology products. Specialty drugs includes urology; antihypertensive, psychiatry, pain management and dermatology products; and a genital warts treatment. Key products include Trelstar, a treatment for prostate cancer; Oxytrol oxybutynin transdermal patch and Gelnique oxytrol gel to treat urinary incontinence; Androderm, a testosterone transdermal patch; and Rapaflo, a treatment for enlarged prostates.

The nephrology product line consists of products used to treat iron deficiency anemia. The primary product is Ferrlecit, which is indicated for patients undergoing hemodialysis in conjunction with erythropoietin therapy. Ferrlecit accounted for about 12% of gross profits in 2008. WPI's rights to branded Ferrlecit end at December 31, 2009. However, WPI plans to market a generic version Ferrlecit. Branded products are marketed to urologists, primary care physicians, endocrinologists, obstetricians and gynecologists.

Company Financials Fiscal Year Ended Dec. 31

Per Share Data ($)	2008	2007	2006	2005	2004	2003	2002	2001	2000	1999
Tangible Book Value	6.51	3.56	0.09	8.81	7.97	5.54	4.33	3.79	0.98	5.00
Cash Flow	3.48	3.37	-2.23	2.87	2.07	2.78	2.45	2.01	2.34	2.28
Earnings	2.09	1.27	-4.37	1.21	1.27	1.86	1.64	1.07	1.65	1.83
S&P Core Earnings	1.96	1.24	-4.32	1.09	1.16	1.64	1.36	0.52	NA	NA
Dividends	Nil	Nil	Nil	Nil	Nil	Nil	Nil	Nil	Nil	Nil
Payout Ratio	Nil	Nil	Nil	Nil	Nil	Nil	Nil	Nil	Nil	Nil
Prices:High	32.70	33.91	35.27	36.93	49.19	50.12	33.25	66.39	71.50	62.94
Prices:Low	20.17	25.02	21.35	27.99	24.50	26.90	17.95	26.50	33.69	26.50
P/E Ratio:High	16	27	NM	31	39	27	20	62	43	34
P/E Ratio:Low	10	20	NM	23	19	14	11	25	20	14

Income Statement Analysis (Million $)										
Revenue	2,536	2,497	1,979	1,646	1,641	1,458	1,223	1,161	812	689
Operating Income	539	515	364	450	419	439	386	404	227	281
Depreciation	171	254	218	207	107	100	86.6	101	71.4	44.0
Interest Expense	28.2	44.5	22.1	14.5	13.3	25.8	22.1	27.8	24.3	11.1
Pretax Income	358	224	-411	219	237	318	279	199	355	273
Effective Tax Rate	33.5%	37.1%	NM	37.0%	36.1%	36.2%	37.0%	41.5%	52.0%	34.4%
Net Income	238	141	-445	138	151	203	176	116	171	179
S&P Core Earnings	222	138	-441	123	137	178	146	56.3	NA	NA

Balance Sheet & Other Financial Data (Million $)										
Cash	521	216	161	630	680	574	273	329	238	116
Current Assets	1,458	1,174	1,262	1,360	1,370	1,323	921	890	831	435
Total Assets	3,678	3,472	3,761	3,080	3,244	3,283	2,663	2,528	2,580	1,439
Current Liabilities	482	445	690	246	256	339	375	245	280	129
Long Term Debt	825	899	1,124	588	588	723	332	416	438	150
Common Equity	2,109	1,849	1,680	2,104	2,243	2,057	1,798	1,672	1,548	1,055
Total Capital	3,108	2,928	3,008	2,692	2,831	2,924	2,282	2,274	2,242	1,292
Capital Expenditures	100	75.1	44.4	78.8	69.2	151	87.5	62.0	34.3	26.8
Cash Flow	409	395	-227	345	258	303	262	218	242	223
Current Ratio	3.0	2.6	1.8	5.5	5.4	3.9	2.5	3.6	3.0	3.4
% Long Term Debt of Capitalization	26.5	30.7	37.4	21.8	20.8	24.7	14.5	18.3	19.6	11.6
% Net Income of Revenue	9.4	5.7	NM	8.4	9.2	13.9	14.4	10.0	21.0	26.0
% Return on Assets	6.7	3.9	NM	4.4	4.6	6.8	6.8	4.6	8.4	13.9
% Return on Equity	12.1	8.0	NM	6.4	7.0	10.5	10.1	7.2	13.1	19.3

Data as orig reptd.; bef. results of disc opers/spec. items. Per share data adj. for stk. divs.; EPS diluted. E-Estimated. NA-Not Available. NM-Not Meaningful. NR-Not Ranked. UR-Under Review.

Office: 311 Bonnie Circle, Corona, CA 92880-2882.
Telephone: 951-493-5300.
Website: http://www.watson.com
Chrmn: A.L. Turner

Pres & CEO: P.M. Bisaro
SVP, CFO, Chief Acctg Officer & Treas: R.T. Joyce
SVP, Secy & General Counsel: D.A. Buchen
SVP & CIO: T.R. Giordano

Investor Contact: P. Eisenhaur (951-493-5611)
Board Members: P. M. Bisaro, C. W. Bodine, M. Fedida, M. J. Feldman, A. F. Hummel, C. M. Klema, J. Michelson, R. Taylor, A. L. Turner, F. G. Weiss

Founded: 1983
Domicile: Nevada
Employees: 5,070

WellPoint Inc

STANDARD &POOR'S

S&P Recommendation	BUY ★★★★☆		Price $54.24 (as of Nov 27, 2009)	12-Mo. Target Price $57.00	Investment Style Large-Cap Growth

GICS Sector Health Care
Sub-Industry Managed Health Care

Summary This managed health organization is the largest in the U.S., serving 34 million members mainly under the Blue Cross and/or Blue Shield license in 14 states.

Key Stock Statistics (Source S&P, Vickers, company reports)

52-Wk Range	$55.73–29.32	S&P Oper. EPS 2009E	5.92	Market Capitalization(B)	$24.861	Beta	1.09
Trailing 12-Month EPS	$4.74	S&P Oper. EPS 2010E	5.95	Yield (%)	Nil	S&P 3-Yr. Proj. EPS CAGR(%)	7
Trailing 12-Month P/E	11.4	P/E on S&P Oper. EPS 2009E	9.2	Dividend Rate/Share	Nil	S&P Credit Rating	A-
$10K Invested 5 Yrs Ago	$10,952	Common Shares Outstg. (M)	458.3	Institutional Ownership (%)	89		

Price Performance

- 30-Week Mov. Avg. · · ·
- 10-Week Mov. Avg. – –
- GAAP Earnings vs. Previous Year
- Volume Above Avg.
- STARS
- 12-Mo. Target Price —
- Relative Strength —
- ▲ Up ▼ Down ▶ No Change
- Below Avg. ★

Options: ASE, CBOE, Ph

Analysis prepared by **Phillip M. Seligman** on November 05, 2009, when the stock traded at **$ 50.59**.

Highlights

▶ We look for 2009 operating revenues to decline by about 1%, to $60.6 billion, from 2008's $61.6 billion, on 1.2 million fewer commercial members, reflecting the rising unemployment rate, WLP's elimination of an unprofitable Senior plan, and its state Medicaid program exits. Looking at 2010, we expect operating revenue to decline by 2% to 3% on further risk-based commercial member losses and the pending Medicare Advantage (MA) rate cuts.

▶ We forecast that the firmwide medical loss ratio (MLR) will decline by 70 basis points in 2009 as the benefit from higher prices and the exit of higher-cost Medicare and Medicaid members is tempered by an increase in high-cost COBRA members and H1N1 flu virus costs. However, we expect it to rise 100 bps in 2010, partly on continued flu and COBRA costs, pending MA rate cuts, and a less-favorable membership mix. Elsewhere, we see a higher SG&A cost ratio in 2009, partly on higher premium taxes and compensation expense, but a lower one in 2010, partly on cost control.

▶ We look for EPS of $5.92 in 2009, before $0.46 of net realized investment losses, versus 2008's comparable $5.53, and we see $5.95 in 2010.

Investment Rationale/Risk

▶ We like WLP's execution in the challenging economic environment. It has exited underperforming markets, eliminated 1,500 positions, and hiked prices. While it expects further commercial membership attrition into 2010 assuming unemployment continues to climb, it is enjoying a strong national accounts selling season. Elsewhere, we like what we view as WLP's conservative reserving for estimated future medical costs, and we see its cash flow providing financial flexibility. We also expect the planned sale of its pharmacy benefit management (PBM) unit, NextRx, to Express Scripts (ESRX 84, Strong Buy), subject to closing conditions, and its ESRX tie to be increasingly accretive to EPS over time. Our earnings model does not reflect any use of the expected proceeds until the transaction is complete.

▶ Risks to our recommendation and target price include enrollment losses above our expectations, higher medical costs, unfavorable regulatory changes, and failure of the PBM sale.

▶ Our 12-month target price of $57 reflects a forward P/E of 9.5X applied to our 2010 EPS estimate. This multiple matches peers and also reflects recent groupwide valuation expansion.

Qualitative Risk Assessment

LOW	MEDIUM	HIGH

Our risk assessment reflects WLP's leadership in the highly fragmented managed care market. We believe that its geographic, market and product diversity and its Blue Cross/Blue Shield tie are competitive strengths. However, we think that enrollment growth going forward will be limited by heightened competition that we see following consolidation in the managed care industry and by the difficult economic environment.

Quantitative Evaluations

S&P Quality Ranking NR

D	C	B-	B	B+	A-	A	A+

Relative Strength Rank STRONG

84

LOWEST = 1   HIGHEST = 99

Revenue/Earnings Data

Revenue (Million $)

	1Q	2Q	3Q	4Q	Year
2009	15,143	15,413	15,425	--	--
2008	15,554	15,667	14,961	15,070	61,251
2007	15,079	15,260	15,234	15,561	61,134
2006	13,820	14,152	14,426	14,556	56,953
2005	11,100	11,299	11,305	11,432	45,136
2004	4,574	4,608	4,807	6,826	20,815

Earnings Per Share ($)

	1Q	2Q	3Q	4Q	Year
2009	1.16	1.43	1.53	E1.02	E5.92
2008	1.07	1.44	1.60	0.65	4.76
2007	1.26	1.35	1.45	1.51	5.56
2006	1.09	1.17	1.29	1.28	4.82
2005	0.98	0.90	1.02	1.04	3.94
2004	1.04	0.83	0.85	0.46	3.05

Fiscal year ended Dec. 31. Next earnings report expected: Late January. EPS Estimates based on S&P Operating Earnings; historical GAAP earnings are as reported.

Dividend Data

No cash dividends have been paid.

The McGraw·Hill Companies

WellPoint Inc

STANDARD &POOR'S

Business Summary November 05, 2009

CORPORATE OVERVIEW. WellPoint, Inc. was formed by the merger consummated on November 30, 2004, between publicly traded managed care giants Anthem, Inc. and WellPoint Health Networks Inc. (WHN). All prior historical data in this report are for Anthem. WLP is the largest publicly traded commercial health benefits company in the U.S., serving 33.9 million members as of September 30, 2009 (versus 35.0 million at December 31, 2008), and an independent licensee of the Blue Cross and Blue Shield Association. It serves members as the Blue Cross licensee for California and the Blue Cross or Blue Cross and Blue Shield (BCBS) licensee in all or parts of 13 other states. WLP also serves members in various parts of the U.S. as UniCare and conducts insurance operations in all 50 states and Puerto Rico through an affiliate.

WLP's network-based managed care plans include preferred provider organizations (PPOs), health maintenance organizations (HMOs), point-of-service plans (POS), traditional indemnity plans and other hybrid plans, including consumer-driven health plans (CDHPs), hospital only, and limited benefit products. It also provides managed care services to self-funded customers. In addition, WLP provides specialty and other products and services, including

pharmacy benefit management, group life and disability insurance, dental, vision, behavioral health, workers compensation and long-term care insurance. Approximately 93% of 2008 operating revenue was derived from premium income and 7% from administrative services and other revenues.

The customer base includes local groups (15,717,000 members as of September 30, 2009, versus 16,632,000 as of December 31, 2008); individuals under age 65 (2,173,000 versus 2,272,000); National Accounts (multi-state employers primarily headquartered in WLP's service area with 1,000 or more eligible employees, with 5% or more located outside headquarters state, 6,857,000 versus 6,720,000); BlueCard (enrollees of non-owned BCBS plans who receive benefits in WLP's BCBS markets, 4,779,000 versus 4,736,000); Senior (1,225,000 versus 1,304,000); State Sponsored (1,717,000 versus 1,968,000); and, Federal Employee Program (1,387,000 versus 1,393,000).

Company Financials Fiscal Year Ended Dec. 31

Per Share Data ($)	2008	2007	2006	2005	2004	2003	2002	2001	2000	1999
Tangible Book Value	NM	0.60	2.92	2.78	2.03	8.44	5.76	7.71	7.66	NA
Cash Flow	5.84	6.24	4.82	3.94	2.05	3.59	2.90	2.23	1.55	NA
Earnings	4.76	5.56	4.82	3.94	3.05	2.73	2.26	1.65	1.05	NA
S&P Core Earnings	6.00	5.50	4.79	3.82	2.69	2.49	1.93	1.16	NA	NA
Dividends	Nil	Nil	Nil	Nil	Nil	Nil	Nil	Nil	Nil	NA
Payout Ratio	Nil	Nil	Nil	Nil	Nil	Nil	Nil	Nil	Nil	NA
Prices:High	90.00	89.95	80.37	80.40	58.88	41.45	37.75	25.95	NA	NA
Prices:Low	27.50	72.90	65.50	54.58	36.10	26.50	23.20	18.00	NA	NA
P/E Ratio:High	19	16	17	20	19	15	17	16	NA	NA
P/E Ratio:Low	6	13	14	14	12	10	10	11	NA	NA

Income Statement Analysis (Million $)	2008	2007	2006	2005	2004	2003	2002	2001	2000	1999
Revenue	61,251	61,134	56,953	45,136	20,815	16,771	13,282	10,445	8,771	6,270
Operating Income	4,297	6,117	5,748	4,750	2,072	1,595	1,093	733	487	NA
Depreciation	564	411	430	634	279	245	157	121	102	61.8
Interest Expense	470	448	404	226	142	131	98.5	60.2	69.6	NA
Pretax Income	3,122	5,258	4,914	3,890	1,443	1,219	808	525	315	60.8
Effective Tax Rate	20.2%	36.4%	37.0%	36.7%	33.5%	36.1%	31.6%	35.0%	30.8%	16.8%
Net Income	2,491	3,345	3,095	2,464	960	774	549	342	216	50.9
S&P Core Earnings	3,143	3,308	3,077	2,402	842	708	467	240	NA	NA

Balance Sheet & Other Financial Data (Million $)	2008	2007	2006	2005	2004	2003	2002	2001	2000	1999
Cash	2,208	6,535	2,602	2,897	1,457	523	744	406	421	204
Current Assets	12,130	13,032	11,807	25,945	19,358	8,865	7,877	5,300	5,025	NA
Total Assets	48,403	52,060	51,760	51,405	39,738	13,439	12,293	6,277	6,021	4,816
Current Liabilities	15,020	14,388	15,323	14,857	11,571	4,772	4,449	2,963	2,784	NA
Long Term Debt	7,834	9,024	6,493	6,325	4,277	1,663	1,659	818	789	522
Common Equity	21,432	22,990	25,299	25,755	20,331	6,000	5,362	2,060	2,055	1,661
Total Capital	31,365	35,018	35,142	35,386	27,204	8,188	7,412	2,878	2,844	2,183
Capital Expenditures	346	322	194	162	137	111	123	70.4	73.3	96.7
Cash Flow	3,054	3,756	3,095	2,464	1,239	1,019	706	463	318	NA
Current Ratio	0.8	0.9	0.8	1.7	1.7	1.9	1.8	1.8	1.8	1.7
% Long Term Debt of Capitalization	25.0	25.8	18.5	17.9	15.7	20.3	22.4	28.4	27.7	23.9
% Net Income of Revenue	4.1	5.5	62.1	5.5	4.7	4.6	50.8	35.6	2.5	0.8
% Return on Assets	5.0	6.5	6.0	5.4	3.6	6.0	5.9	5.7	4.3	NA
% Return on Equity	11.2	14.1	12.1	10.7	7.2	13.6	14.8	17.2	12.6	NA

Data as orig reptd.; bef. results of disc opers/spec. items. Per share data adj. for stk. divs.; EPS diluted. E-Estimated. NA-Not Available. NM-Not Meaningful. NR-Not Ranked. UR-Under Review.

Office: 120 Monument Circle, Indianapolis, IN 46204-4903.
Telephone: 317-488-6000.
Email: anthem.corporate.communications@anthem.com
Website: http://www.wellpoint.com

Chrmn: L.C. Glasscock
Pres & CEO: A.F. Braly
Investor Contact: W.S. Deveydt (317-488-6390)
EVP & CFO: W.S. Deveydt

EVP, Secy & General Counsel: J. Cannon, III
Board Members: L. D. Baker, Jr., S. B. Bayh, A. F. Braly, S. P. Burke, W. H. Bush, L. C. Glasscock, J. A. Hill, W. Y. Jobe, V. S. Liss, W. G. Mays, R. G. Peru, J. G. Pisano, D. W. Riegle, Jr., W. J. Ryan, G. A. Schaefer, Jr., J. M. Ward, J. E. Zuccotti

Founded: 1944
Domicile: Indiana
Employees: 42,900

The McGraw-Hill Companies

Wells Fargo & Co

STANDARD &POOR'S

S&P Recommendation HOLD ★★★☆☆	Price $27.14 (as of Nov 27, 2009)	12-Mo. Target Price $33.00	Investment Style Large-Cap Blend

GICS Sector Financials
Sub-Industry Diversified Banks

Summary This bank holding company provides banking, insurance, investment, mortgage, and consumer finance services throughout North America.

Key Stock Statistics (Source S&P, Vickers, company reports)

52-Wk Range	$32.76– 7.80	S&P Oper. EPS 2009E	2.11	Market Capitalization(B)	$127.153	Beta	1.33
Trailing 12-Month EPS	$1.07	S&P Oper. EPS 2010E	1.70	Yield (%)	0.74	S&P 3-Yr. Proj. EPS CAGR(%)	20
Trailing 12-Month P/E	25.4	P/E on S&P Oper. EPS 2009E	12.9	Dividend Rate/Share	$0.20	S&P Credit Rating	AA-
$10K Invested 5 Yrs Ago	$10,253	Common Shares Outstg. (M)	4,685.1	Institutional Ownership (%)	74		

Price Performance

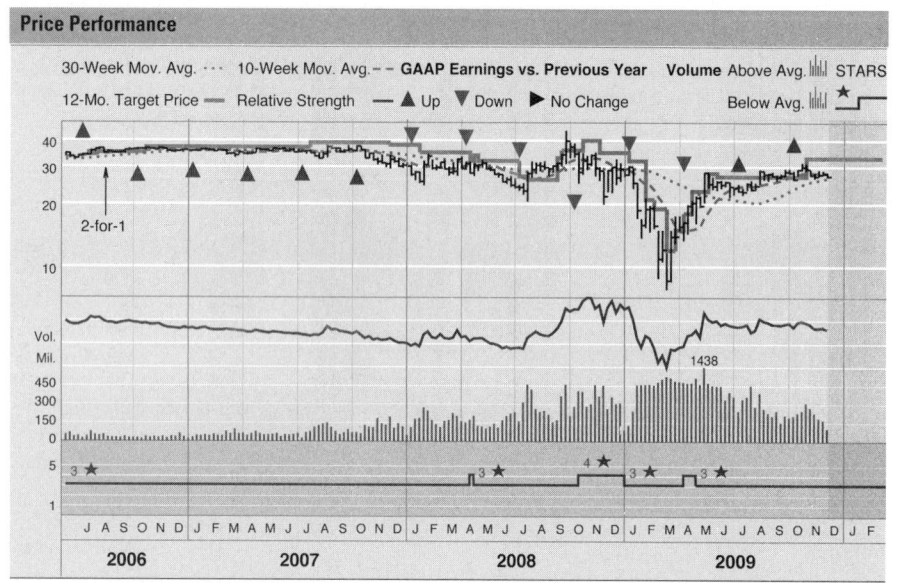

Options: ASE, CBOE, P, Ph

Analysis prepared by **Stuart Plesser** on October 28, 2009, when the stock traded at **$ 27.86**.

Highlights

► We think WFC is taking advantage of weaker players exiting the market, and believe it will continue to increase its loan book by gaining market share. However, given constraints in the economy, we look for average earning assets to decline modestly in 2010, after projected double-digit gains in 2009. While WFC should benefit from the low interest rate environment, we look for its net interest margin to narrow to 4.25% in 2010, from 4.28% projected for 2009, assuming that short-term interest rates will begin to rise sometime in 2010.

► We expect non-interest income to be up modestly, even assuming a decline in mortgage banking revenue. We see expenses totaling 54.0% of revenue in 2010, versus projected 54.5% for 2009, as we see further expense synergies from the Wachovia (WB) acquisition. We expect continued deterioration in WFC's loan portfolio on a combination of stress in its option-arm and commercial mortgage portfolios, and we look for total 2010 loan loss provisions to rise to $26 billion versus projected $22 billion in 2009.

► On 35% share accretion, we project EPS of $2.11 for 2009. In 2010, we look for $1.70.

Investment Rationale/Risk

► WFC consummated its purchase of Wachovia in late 2008. We think WB fits nicely and adds significantly to WFC's footprint, particularly in the Northeast. Although the acquisition should add significantly to WFC's fee revenue, we think it will also result in elevated chargeoffs. Due to the nature of WFC's loan portfolio, we think its ability to post normalized earnings will be more protracted than some peers. Although non performing loans remain elevated, it's difficult to tell the percentage that will be written down as chargeoffs. Positively, however, capital levels, although historically low, should continue to be built up.

► Risks to our recommendation and target price include a more severe economic downturn than we expect; shareholder dilution; and, litigation and regulatory risks.

► Our 12-month target price of $33 is based on an above-historical 19.4X our 2010 EPS estimate, warranted, in our view, as we think 2010 will be the trough year in WFC's earnings cycle, and chargeoffs peak in mid 2010.

Qualitative Risk Assessment

LOW	MEDIUM	HIGH

Our risk assessment reflects what we see as solid business fundamentals and a strong customer base, offset by increased risk stemming from the Wachovia acquisition combined with declining tangible capital levels.

Quantitative Evaluations

S&P Quality Ranking A-

D	C	B-	B	B+	A-	A	A+

Relative Strength Rank MODERATE

36

LOWEST = 1   HIGHEST = 99

Revenue/Earnings Data

Revenue (Million $)

	1Q	2Q	3Q	4Q	Year
2009	23,954	25,044	24,750	--	--
2008	13,652	13,728	12,772	11,828	51,980
2007	12,570	13,268	13,796	13,959	53,596
2006	11,217	11,882	12,286	12,594	47,979
2005	9,509	9,529	10,427	10,897	40,407
2004	7,955	8,269	8,305	9,347	33,876

Earnings Per Share ($)

	1Q	2Q	3Q	4Q	Year
2009	0.56	0.57	0.56	E0.42	E2.11
2008	0.60	0.53	0.49	-0.79	0.75
2007	0.66	0.67	0.68	0.37	2.38
2006	0.60	0.61	0.64	0.64	2.49
2005	0.54	0.56	0.58	0.57	2.25
2004	0.52	0.50	0.51	0.52	2.05

Fiscal year ended Dec. 31. Next earnings report expected: Late January. EPS Estimates based on S&P Operating Earnings; historical GAAP earnings are as reported.

Dividend Data (Dates: mm/dd Payment Date: mm/dd/yy)

Amount ($)	Date Decl.	Ex-Div. Date	Stk. of Record	Payment Date
0.340	01/28	02/04	02/06	03/01/09
0.050	04/28	05/06	05/08	06/01/09
0.050	07/28	08/05	08/07	09/01/09
0.050	10/27	11/04	11/06	12/01/09

Dividends have been paid since 1939. Source: Company reports.

Please read the Required Disclosures and Analyst Certification on the last page of this report.

The **McGraw-Hill** Companies

Wells Fargo & Co

STANDARD
&POOR'S

Business Summary October 28, 2009

CORPORATE OVERVIEW. Wells Fargo & Co. (WFC) has three lines of business for management reporting: community banking, wholesale banking, and Wells Fargo Financial. The community banking group offers a complete line of banking and diversified financial products and services to consumers and small businesses with annual sales generally up to $20 million, in which the owner generally is the financial decision maker. Community banking also offers investment management and other services to retail customers and high-net-worth individuals, insurance, securities brokerage through affiliates, and venture capital financing.

Community banking serves customers through a wide range of channels, including traditional banking stores, in-store banking centers, business centers and ATMs. In addition, Phone Bank centers and the National Business Banking Center provide 24-hour telephone service.

The wholesale banking group serves businesses across the U.S. with annual sales generally in excess of $10 million. Wholesale banking provides a complete line of commercial, corporate and real estate banking products and ser-

vices. These include traditional commercial loans and lines of credit; letters of credit; asset-based lending; equipment leasing; mezzanine financing; high-yield debt; international trade facilities; foreign exchange services; treasury management; investment management; institutional fixed income and equity sales; interest rate, commodity and equity risk management; online/electronic products; insurance, corporate trust fiduciary and agency services and investment banking services.

Wholesale banking manages and administers institutional investments, employee benefit trusts and mutual funds, including the Wells Fargo Advantage Funds. Wholesale banking includes the majority ownership interest in the Wells Fargo SC Trade Bank, which provides trade financing, letters of credit, and collection services, and is sometimes supported by the Export-Import Bank of the United States.

Company Financials Fiscal Year Ended Dec. 31

Per Share Data ($)	2008	2007	2006	2005	2004	2003	2002	2001	2000	1999
Tangible Book Value	3.31	5.55	10.13	8.76	7.95	7.04	6.11	4.90	4.59	3.96
Earnings	0.75	2.38	2.49	2.25	2.05	1.83	1.66	0.99	1.17	1.12
S&P Core Earnings	0.57	2.39	2.47	2.18	1.96	1.78	1.57	0.84	NA	NA
Dividends	1.30	1.18	1.08	1.00	0.93	0.75	0.55	0.50	0.45	0.39
Payout Ratio	173%	50%	43%	44%	45%	41%	33%	51%	39%	35%
Prices:High	44.69	37.99	36.99	32.35	32.02	29.59	26.72	27.41	28.19	24.97
Prices:Low	19.89	29.29	30.31	28.81	27.16	21.64	21.65	19.13	15.69	16.09
P/E Ratio:High	63	16	15	14	16	16	16	28	24	22
P/E Ratio:Low	27	12	12	13	13	12	13	19	13	14

Income Statement Analysis (Million $)										
Net Interest Income	25,143	20,974	19,951	18,504	17,150	16,007	14,855	12,460	10,865	9,355
Tax Equivalent Adjustment	321	146	116	110	104	NA	NA	NA	65.0	64.0
Non Interest Income	16,776	17,473	15,021	14,054	12,530	12,323	9,348	7,227	9,565	6,653
Loan Loss Provision	15,979	4,939	2,204	2,383	1,717	1,722	1,733	1,780	1,329	1,045
% Expense/Operating Revenue	54.1%	59.4%	59.3%	58.2%	64.8%	60.7%	52.2%	65.5%	57.7%	60.9%
Pretax Income	3,585	11,627	12,745	11,548	10,769	9,477	8,854	5,479	6,549	5,948
Effective Tax Rate	20.7%	30.7%	33.4%	33.6%	34.9%	34.6%	35.5%	37.5%	38.5%	37.0%
Net Income	2,842	8,057	8,482	7,671	7,014	6,202	5,710	3,423	4,026	3,747
% Net Interest Margin	4.83	4.74	4.83	4.86	4.89	5.08	5.57	5.36	5.35	5.66
S&P Core Earnings	1,937	8,099	8,401	7,423	6,722	6,055	5,374	2,894	NA	NA

Balance Sheet & Other Financial Data (Million $)										
Money Market Assets	104,317	10,481	11,685	16,211	14,020	2,745	3,174	2,530	1,598	1,554
Investment Securities	151,569	72,951	42,629	41,834	33,717	32,953	27,947	40,308	38,655	38,518
Commercial Loans	218,298	152,841	122,065	108,903	98,515	48,729	47,292	47,547	60,541	46,538
Other Loans	625,519	229,354	273,069	201,934	189,071	204,344	149,342	124,952	10,583	72,926
Total Assets	1,309,639	575,442	481,996	481,741	427,849	387,798	349,259	307,569	272,426	218,102
Demand Deposits	630,565	84,348	89,119	87,712	81,082	74,387	74,094	65,362	55,096	42,916
Time Deposits	NA	260,112	221,124	226,738	193,776	173,140	142,822	121,904	114,463	89,792
Long Term Debt	267,158	99,393	72,404	79,668	73,580	63,642	50,205	38,530	32,981	24,160
Common Equity	68,307	47,660	45,492	40,335	37,596	34,255	30,107	26,996	26,103	21,860
% Return on Assets	0.3	1.5	1.8	1.7	1.7	1.7	1.7	1.2	1.6	1.8
% Return on Equity	4.9	17.2	19.8	19.7	19.5	19.3	20.0	12.8	16.2	17.6
% Loan Loss Reserve	2.4	1.4	1.1	1.1	1.2	1.3	1.5	1.8	2.1	2.5
% Loans/Deposits	110.7	107.1	113.8	111.9	118.6	117.0	117.3	110.9	104.7	93.8
% Equity to Assets	6.2	8.9	8.9	8.6	8.8	8.7	8.7	9.2	9.7	10.0

Data as orig reptd.; bef. results of disc opers/spec. items. Per share data adj. for stk. divs.; EPS diluted. E-Estimated. NA-Not Available. NM-Not Meaningful. NR-Not Ranked. UR-Under Review.

Office: 420 Montgomery St, San Francisco, CA 94163.
Telephone: 1-866-878-5865.
Website: http://www.wellsfargo.com
Chrmn: R.M. Kovacevich

Pres & CEO: J.G. Stumpf
COO & CTO: A. Modjtabai
EVP & CFO: H.I. Atkins
EVP, Chief Acctg Officer & Cntlr: R.D. Levy

Board Members: J. D. Baker, II, J. S. Chen, L. H. Dean, S. E. Engel, E. Hernandez, Jr., D. M. James, R. M. Kovacevich, R. D. McCormick, M. J. Mcdonald, C. H. Milligan, N. G. Moore, P. J. Quigley, D. B. Rice, J. M. Runstad, S. W. Sanger, R. K. Steel, J. G. Stumpf, S. G. Swenson, M. W. Wright

Founded: 1929
Domicile: Delaware
Employees: 281,000

Western Digital Corp

STANDARD &POOR'S

S&P Recommendation	BUY ★★★★☆	Price $37.50 (as of Nov 27, 2009)	12-Mo. Target Price $49.00	Investment Style Large-Cap Blend

GICS Sector Information Technology
Sub-Industry Computer Storage & Peripherals

Summary This company designs and manufactures hard disk drives for personal computing.

Key Stock Statistics (Source S&P, Vickers, company reports)

52-Wk Range	$39.38– 10.65	S&P Oper. EPS 2010**E**	4.82	Market Capitalization(B)	$8.452	Beta	1.50
Trailing 12-Month EPS	$2.41	S&P Oper. EPS 2011**E**	4.76	Yield (%)	Nil	S&P 3-Yr. Proj. EPS CAGR(%)	7
Trailing 12-Month P/E	15.6	P/E on S&P Oper. EPS 2010**E**	7.8	Dividend Rate/Share	Nil	S&P Credit Rating	NA
$10K Invested 5 Yrs Ago	$39,185	Common Shares Outstg. (M)	225.4	Institutional Ownership (%)	95		

Price Performance

30-Week Mov. Avg. ··· 10-Week Mov. Avg. -- **GAAP Earnings vs. Previous Year** Volume Above Avg. STARS
12-Mo. Target Price — Relative Strength ▲ Up ▼ Down ► No Change Below Avg. ★

Options: ASE, CBOE, P

Analysis prepared by **Jim Yin** on October 27, 2009, when the stock traded at **$ 34.86**.

Highlights

► We expect revenues to increase 19% and 7% in FY 10 (Jun.) and FY 11, respectively. Our forecast is based on our outlook for a rebound in PC demand, compounded by lower-than-average price deflation. Although we expect sales of desktop PCs to remain soft near term, we think we are at the beginning of an upgrade cycle given the growing age of corporate PCs. We see stronger growth in notebooks, netbooks and branded products. We anticipate that non-PC sales will be more than 60% of total revenues in FY 10.

► We project gross margins will widen to 23% and 22% in FY 10 and FY 11, respectively, from 18% in FY 09, reflecting our outlook for a benign pricing environment and improved manufacturing productivity. We believe the company's restructuring initiatives will help lower its cost structure, especially employee head count, in FY 10. As a result, we forecast operating margins will widen to 13.8% in FY 10 and 12.7% in FY 11, from 7.0% in FY 09.

► We estimate EPS of $4.82 in FY 10 and $4.76 in FY 11, compared to $2.08 in FY 09. The increases in earnings reflect our view of stronger PC demand and cost savings from restructuring.

Investment Rationale/Risk

► We recently upgraded our recommendation to buy, from hold, based on our view of improving end-user demand, as the world economy recovers from a severe recession. We think WDC will benefit from an inventory restocking near term, as OEMs ramp up production for the Christmas shopping season. We are positive on recent cost reductions and see expanding operating margins. We believe the company is financially well positioned, given its $1.8 billion in cash and investments ($7.90 per share) and what we view as minimal debt of $482 million as of June 2009.

► Risks to our recommendation and target price include a weaker-than-expected economic recovery and significant loss in market share.

► Our 12-month target price of $49 is based on a blend of price-to-sales (P/S) and DCF analyses. We apply a peer-discount P/S ratio of 1.1X to our 2010 revenue per share estimate to derive a $49 valuation. We think WDC warrants a peer discount due to what we see as earnings growth potential below the industry. Our DCF model assumes a weighted average cost of capital of 13.3% and 3% terminal growth, and yields an intrinsic value of $50.

Qualitative Risk Assessment

LOW	MEDIUM	HIGH

Our risk assessment reflects our view of the volatile nature of the disk drive industry, which includes significant exposure to the PC sector and ongoing erosion of average selling prices.

Quantitative Evaluations

S&P Quality Ranking   B

D	C	B-	**B**	B+	A-	A	A+

Relative Strength Rank   **STRONG**

78

LOWEST = 1   HIGHEST = 99

Revenue/Earnings Data

Revenue (Million $)

	1Q	2Q	3Q	4Q	Year
2010	2,208	--	--	--	--
2009	2,109	1,823	1,592	1,928	7,453
2008	1,766	2,204	2,111	1,993	8,074
2007	1,264	1,428	1,410	1,367	5,468
2006	1,010	1,117	1,129	1,086	4,341
2005	823.6	954.9	919.9	940.4	3,639

Earnings Per Share ($)

2010	1.25	E1.36	E1.04	E1.17	E4.82
2009	0.93	0.06	0.22	0.86	2.08
2008	0.31	1.39	1.23	0.94	3.84
2007	0.46	0.57	0.53	0.94	2.50
2006	0.31	0.47	0.45	0.53	1.76
2005	0.14	0.26	0.32	0.19	0.91

Fiscal year ended Jun. 30. Next earnings report expected: Late January. EPS Estimates based on S&P Operating Earnings; historical GAAP earnings are as reported.

Dividend Data

No cash dividends have been paid.

The McGraw-Hill Companies

Western Digital Corp

STANDARD
&POOR'S

Business Summary October 27, 2009

CORPORATE OVERVIEW. Western Digital designs, develops, manufactures and markets hard disk drives. The company's hard drives are used in desktop PC, notebook computers, enterprise servers, network attached storage devices, and consumer electronics products such as personal/digital video recorders, and satellite and cable set-top boxes. WDC's hard drive products include 3.5- and 2.5-inch form factor drives with capacities ranging from 40 gigabytes to 2 terabyte and rotation speeds up to 10,000 revolutions per minute. The company believes that these form factors represent its major growth areas, with 3.5-inch form factor hard drives used in the desktop, enterprise, consumer electronic and external storage markets, and 2.5-inch form factor hard drives serving the mobile PC/laptop, consumer electronic and external storage markets.

WDC entered the solid-state drive market by acquiring SiliconSystems in the first quarter of 2009. A solid-state drive is a storage device that uses semiconductor rather than magnetic disks and heads to store data and is more commonly used in notebooks because of its lighter weight and higher durability. We expect the solid-state drive market segment to grow faster than the rest of the industry given the rapid growth of netbooks. However, we think solid-

state drives will represent less than 3% of WDC's FY 10 (Jun.) total sales.

Drives are sold globally to OEMs, distributors and retailers. Sales to OEMs accounted for 54% of revenues in FY 09, up from 51% in FY 08. Distributors made up 26% (31%) and retailers 20% (18%).

MARKET PROFILE. The hard drive industry is highly competitive. Key competitors include Fujitsu, Hitachi Global Storage Technologies, Samsung Electronics, Seagate Technology and Toshiba. Because hard drives manufactured by different competitors are highly substitutable, hard drive manufacturers often compete on the basis of price along with product quality, performance and storage capacity. As technology advances, storage density and drive speed continue to increase, resulting in price erosion of older drive models. The industry is characterized by periods of intense pricing pressure following new technological innovations.

Company Financials Fiscal Year Ended Jun. 30

Per Share Data ($)	2009	2008	2007	2006	2005	2004	2003	2002	2001	2000
Tangible Book Value	13.17	11.16	7.73	5.24	3.29	2.36	1.61	0.54	0.04	NM
Cash Flow	4.20	5.66	3.42	2.48	1.54	1.17	1.13	0.51	-0.21	-2.25
Earnings	2.08	3.84	2.50	1.76	0.91	0.70	0.88	0.28	-0.71	2.89
S&P Core Earnings	2.01	3.88	2.50	1.82	0.87	0.58	0.81	0.14	-0.69	NA
Dividends	Nil	Nil	Nil	Nil	Nil	Nil	Nil	Nil	Nil	Nil
Payout Ratio	Nil	Nil	Nil	Nil	Nil	Nil	Nil	Nil	Nil	Nil
Prices:High	39.38	40.00	31.70	24.70	19.15	13.55	14.95	8.96	6.79	8.81
Prices:Low	11.49	9.48	16.21	15.90	9.84	6.39	6.44	2.98	1.95	2.19
P/E Ratio:High	19	10	13	14	21	19	17	32	NM	3
P/E Ratio:Low	6	2	6	9	11	9	7	11	NM	1

Income Statement Analysis (Million $)	2009	2008	2007	2006	2005	2004	2003	2002	2001	2000
Revenue	7,453	8,074	5,468	4,341	3,639	3,047	2,719	2,151	1,953	1,958
Operating Income	1,106	1,468	625	526	332	257	237	96.5	18.0	-215
Depreciation	479	413	210	160	135	102	50.4	45.8	51.9	78.5
Interest Expense	NA	52.0	4.00	3.70	Nil	Nil	Nil	8.13	8.94	19.2
Pretax Income	501	981	443	382	202	155	188	52.1	-88.3	-374
Effective Tax Rate	6.19%	11.6%	NM	NM	1.93%	2.51%	4.03%	NM	NM	NM
Net Income	470	867	564	395	198	151	181	53.2	-87.1	-355
S&P Core Earnings	454	875	564	407	186	125	166	27.0	-117	NA

Balance Sheet & Other Financial Data (Million $)	2009	2008	2007	2006	2005	2004	2003	2002	2001	2000
Cash	1,794	1,107	700	551	485	378	393	224	168	184
Current Assets	3,230	2,731	2,029	1,492	1,181	857	744	528	386	451
Total Assets	5,291	4,871	2,901	2,073	1,589	1,159	866	637	508	616
Current Liabilities	1,525	1,564	1,130	859	818	587	506	493	340	445
Long Term Debt	400	482	10.0	19.4	32.6	52.7	Nil	Nil	112	225
Common Equity	3,192	2,696	1,716	1,157	702	488	327	103	6.80	-110
Total Capital	3,592	3,205	1,726	1,177	735	540	327	103	129	126
Capital Expenditures	519	615	324	302	233	132	61.9	47.7	50.7	22.0
Cash Flow	949	1,280	774	554	333	253	231	99.0	-35.2	-276
Current Ratio	2.1	1.8	1.8	1.7	1.4	1.5	1.5	1.1	1.1	1.0
% Long Term Debt of Capitalization	11.1	15.0	0.6	1.6	4.4	9.8	Nil	Nil	87.4	179.4
% Net Income of Revenue	6.3	10.7	10.3	9.1	5.5	5.0	6.7	2.5	NM	NM
% Return on Assets	9.3	22.3	22.6	21.6	14.4	14.9	24.1	9.3	NM	NM
% Return on Equity	16.0	39.3	39.3	42.5	33.4	37.1	84.0	97.1	NM	NM

Data as orig reptd.; bef. results of disc opers/spec. items. Per share data adj. for stk. divs.; EPS diluted. E-Estimated. NA-Not Available. NM-Not Meaningful. NR-Not Ranked. UR-Under Review.

Office: 20511 Lake Forest Drive, Lake Forest, CA 92630.
Telephone: 949-672-7000.
Website: http://www.westerndigital.com
Chrmn: T.E. Pardun

Pres & CEO: J.F. Coyne
COO: M.W. Finkbeiner
EVP & CFO: T.M. Leyden
SVP & CTO: H.M. Moghadam

Investor Contact: R. Blair
Board Members: P. D. Behrendt, K. A. Cote, J. F. Coyne, H. T. DeNero, W. L. Kimsey, M. D. Lambert, M. E. Massengill, R. H. Moore, T. E. Pardun, A. Shakeel

Founded: 1970
Domicile: Delaware
Employees: 45,991

Western Union Co

STANDARD &POOR'S

S&P Recommendation	HOLD ★★★☆☆	Price $18.50 (as of Nov 27, 2009)	12-Mo. Target Price $22.00	Investment Style Large-Cap Blend

GICS Sector Information Technology
Sub-Industry Data Processing & Outsourced Services

Summary Spun off from First Data Corp. in September 2006, Western Union is a leading independent provider of consumer money transfer services.

Key Stock Statistics (Source S&P, Vickers, company reports)

52-Wk Range	$20.64– 10.05	S&P Oper. EPS 2009**E**	1.28	Market Capitalization(B)	$12.804	Beta	1.59
Trailing 12-Month EPS	$1.23	S&P Oper. EPS 2010**E**	1.42	Yield (%)	0.22	S&P 3-Yr. Proj. EPS CAGR(%)	12
Trailing 12-Month P/E	15.0	P/E on S&P Oper. EPS 2009**E**	14.5	Dividend Rate/Share	$0.04	S&P Credit Rating	A-
$10K Invested 5 Yrs Ago	NA	Common Shares Outstg. (M)	692.1	Institutional Ownership (%)	92		

Price Performance

30-Week Mov. Avg. · · · 10-Week Mov. Avg. - - **GAAP Earnings vs. Previous Year** Volume Above Avg. STARS
12-Mo. Target Price — Relative Strength — ▲ Up ▼ Down ▶ No Change Below Avg. ★

Options: ASE, CBOE, P, Ph

Analysis prepared by **Zaineb Bokhari** on October 29, 2009, when the stock traded at **$ 18.65.**

Highlights

▶ We expect revenue to fall 5% to $5 billion in 2009. Domestic consumer money transfer remains challenged by the macro-economy, and the slowdown has impacted global markets as well, although recently, Asia has shown more resilience. While a portion of transactions are non-discretionary, transaction growth has slowed and there has been a decline in the amount of principal sent per transaction, hurting revenue. We also note that unfavorable currency movements have penalized reported growth rates. We see a 5% rise in revenues in 2010, reflecting our outlook for an improving economic outlook, and easier year-ago comparisons.

▶ We look for gross margins to widen modestly in 2009, reflecting our outlook for below-average consumer money transfer price declines. We expect operating margins to stay near 27% in 2009 and 2010, as an ongoing shift in mix from higher-margin U.S.-originated money transfers to lower-margin international business is offset by internal cost management. We note that changes in geographic mix can impact results.

▶ We estimate EPS of $1.28 in 2009, rising to $1.42 in 2010.

Investment Rationale/Risk

▶ We expect the weak global economy to negatively impact transaction volumes, fees and foreign exchange revenues per transaction, resulting in lower 2009 sales. Still, we believe WU will benefit from a recent restructuring and continue to focus on costs, and we think the company is investing prudently ahead of any recovery. We view favorably agreements through which WU provides consumer money transfer services through banks, thus expanding the distribution of its services. We think WU, with more than $1.1 billion in cash from operations estimated for 2009, has adequate near-term liquidity, although we look for somewhat more conservative share buybacks given the tight credit markets.

▶ Risks to our recommendation and target price include worsening global economic trends, accelerating consumer adoption of digital alternatives to WU's money transfer offerings, and competition from traditional financial institutions and money transfer peers.

▶ We derive our 12-month target price of $22 by applying a 15.6X P/E multiple to our 2010 EPS estimate, within the historical average P/E range for the shares of 10.5X-19.4X.

Qualitative Risk Assessment

LOW	MEDIUM	HIGH

Our risk assessment reflects the ongoing weakness in the global macro-economy, which we expect will impact transaction volumes, partly offset by what we see as relatively high barriers to entry in WU's businesses and potential for operating margin expansion.

Quantitative Evaluations

S&P Quality Ranking NR

D	C	B-	B	B+	A-	A	A+

Relative Strength Rank MODERATE

40

LOWEST = 1 HIGHEST = 99

Revenue/Earnings Data

Revenue (Million $)

	1Q	2Q	3Q	4Q	Year
2009	1,201	1,254	1,314	--	--
2008	1,266	1,347	1,377	1,292	5,282
2007	1,131	1,203	1,257	1,309	4,900
2006	1,043	1,114	1,140	1,173	4,470
2005	919.6	980.8	1,019	1,068	3,988
2004	--	--	--	--	3,524

Earnings Per Share ($)

2009	0.32	0.31	0.26	E0.32	E1.28
2008	0.27	0.31	0.33	0.34	1.24
2007	0.25	0.26	0.28	0.32	1.11
2006	0.29	0.29	0.34	0.28	1.19
2005	--	--	0.32	0.31	0.96
2004	--	--	--	--	--

Fiscal year ended Dec. 31. Next earnings report expected: Early February. EPS Estimates based on S&P Operating Earnings; historical GAAP earnings are as reported.

Dividend Data (Dates: mm/dd Payment Date: mm/dd/yy)

Amount ($)	Date Decl.	Ex-Div. Date	Stk. of Record	Payment Date
0.040	12/11	12/18	12/22	12/31/08

Dividends have been paid since 2006. Source: Company reports.

Please read the Required Disclosures and Analyst Certification on the last page of this report.

Western Union Co

STANDARD &POOR'S

Business Summary October 29, 2009

CORPORATE OVERVIEW. Western Union is a leading independent provider of consumer money transfer services. WU offers its services through a network of more than 400,000 agent locations (at September 30, 2009) spanning more than 200 countries and territories. The company provides its services globally, mainly under the Western Union brand name and also under the Orlandi Valuta and Vigo brands. WU derives the majority of revenues from fees that consumers pay when they send money. The company's main segments include consumer-to-consumer (C2C; 85% of 2008 revenues) and global payments (formerly consumer-to-business or C2B; 14%).

WU's core C2C services allow customers to transfer money to other individuals. The majority of these transfers are originated in cash at Western Union agent locations, although consumers can also send money via the Internet, telephone, credit or debit card and, in some cases, through bank debits. In 2008, C2C transactions increased 12%, to 188 million, while C2C transaction fees rose about 7%.

Through its C2B segment, consumers can make payments to businesses electronically, over the telephone, via the Internet, or at one of WU's agent locations. The company has long-standing relationships with billers such as utilities, auto finance companies, mortgage servicers, financial service providers and government agencies who accept such payments. In 2008, WU's C2B

transactions increased 2%, to 412.3 million, while C2B transaction fees rose less than 1%.

CORPORATE STRATEGY. The pursuit of growth through international expansion is a key tenet of Western Union's growth strategy. The company believes that a majority of its C2C transactions involve at least one non-U.S. location. Domestic transactions (within the U.S. and Canada) accounted for 10% of 2008 consolidated revenues, while Mexico accounted for 7%. Outside of these two geographies, WU's revenue base is well-diversified geographically. Building on and maintaining its well-recognized consumer brand is another key element to the company's strategy. WU spent approximately 5% of revenues on marketing, advertising and developing customer loyalty programs in 2008, down from 6% in 2007. The company also invested about 3% of annual revenues in selective price reductions on its C2C services in individual markets depending on the dynamics within those markets in 2006 and 2007; in 2008, such reductions accounted for 1% of revenues. We think the difference in growth between transaction fees and transaction volumes is evidence of this strategy.

Company Financials Fiscal Year Ended Dec. 31

Per Share Data ($)	2008	2007	2006	2005	2004	2003	2002	2001	2000	1999
Tangible Book Value	NM	NM	NM	NM	NA	NA	NA	NA	NA	NA
Cash Flow	1.33	1.17	1.32	NA	NA	NA	NA	NA	NA	NA
Earnings	1.24	1.11	1.19	0.96	NA	NA	NA	NA	NA	NA
S&P Core Earnings	1.22	1.11	1.18	1.10	0.95	NA	NA	NA	NA	NA
Dividends	0.04	0.04	0.01	NA	NA	NA	NA	NA	NA	NA
Payout Ratio	3%	4%	1%	NA	NA	NA	NA	NA	NA	NA
Prices:High	28.62	24.83	24.14	NA	NA	NA	NA	NA	NA	NA
Prices:Low	10.48	15.00	16.85	NA	NA	NA	NA	NA	NA	NA
P/E Ratio:High	23	22	20	NA	NA	NA	NA	NA	NA	NA
P/E Ratio:Low	8	14	14	NA	NA	NA	NA	NA	NA	NA

Income Statement Analysis (Million $)										
Revenue	5,282	4,900	4,470	3,988	3,524	3,121	NA	NA	NA	NA
Operating Income	1,500	1,393	1,415	NA	NA	NA	NA	NA	NA	NA
Depreciation	61.7	49.1	104	NA	79.2	78.4	NA	NA	NA	NA
Interest Expense	171	189	53.0	202	NA	NA	NA	NA	NA	NA
Pretax Income	1,239	1,222	1,335	1,063	1,098	970	NA	NA	NA	NA
Effective Tax Rate	25.8%	29.9%	31.5%	29.5%	31.5%	34.1%	NA	NA	NA	NA
Net Income	919	857	914	749	752	639	NA	NA	NA	NA
S&P Core Earnings	908	857	913	859	734	NA	NA	NA	NA	NA

Balance Sheet & Other Financial Data (Million $)										
Cash	1,296	2,030	1,422	1,186	470	NA	NA	NA	NA	NA
Current Assets	NA	NA	NA	NA	NA	NA	NA	NA	NA	NA
Total Assets	5,578	5,784	5,321	4,659	3,307	NA	NA	NA	NA	NA
Current Liabilities	NA	NA	NA	NA	NA	NA	NA	NA	NA	NA
Long Term Debt	2,561	2,500	2,996	3,500	9.90	NA	NA	NA	NA	NA
Common Equity	-8.10	50.7	-315	-687	1,909	NA	NA	NA	NA	NA
Total Capital	2,823	2,814	2,681	2,183	1,919	NA	NA	NA	NA	NA
Capital Expenditures	53.9	83.5	64.0	NA	26.5	23.6	NA	NA	NA	NA
Cash Flow	981	906	1,018	NA	NA	NA	NA	NA	NA	NA
Current Ratio	2.1	1.3	1.9	NA	7.0	NA	NA	NA	NA	NA
% Long Term Debt of Capitalization	90.7	88.8	112.0	160.3	0.5	Nil	NA	NA	NA	NA
% Net Income of Revenue	17.4	17.5	20.4	18.8	21.3	20.5	NA	NA	NA	NA
% Return on Assets	16.2	15.4	18.3	NA	NA	NA	NA	NA	NA	NA
% Return on Equity	NM	NM	NM	NA	NA	NA	NA	NA	NA	NA

Data as orig reptd.; bef. results of disc opers/spec. items. Per share data adj. for stk. divs.; EPS diluted. Pro forma data in 2005, balance sheet and book value as of Jun. 30, 2006. E-Estimated. NA-Not Available. NM-Not Meaningful. NR-Not Ranked. UR-Under Review.

Office: 12500 East Belford Avenue, Englewood, CO 80112.
Telephone: 866-405-5012.
Website: http://www.westernunion.com
Chrmn: J.M. Greenberg

Pres & CEO: C.A. Gold
COO & CTO: R. Heller
EVP & CFO: S.T. Scheirman
EVP, Secy & General Counsel: D.L. Schlapbach

Investor Contact: G. Kohn (720-332-8276)
Board Members: D. S. Devitre, C. A. Gold, J. M. Greenberg, B. D. Holden, A. J. Lacy, R. Mendoza, M. Miles, Jr., D. Stevenson, W. Von Schimmelmann, L. F. levinson

Founded: 1851
Domicile: Delaware
Employees: 5,900

The McGraw-Hill Companies

Weyerhaeuser Co

STANDARD &POOR'S

S&P Recommendation **HOLD** ★★★☆☆	Price $37.69 (as of Nov 27, 2009)	12-Mo. Target Price $38.00	Investment Style Large-Cap Blend

GICS Sector Materials
Sub-Industry Forest Products

Summary One of the world's largest integrated forest products companies, WY grows timber; makes and sells forest products, and pulp; and engages in real estate construction and development.

Key Stock Statistics (Source S&P, Vickers, company reports)

52-Wk Range	$41.28– 18.67	S&P Oper. EPS 2009E	-1.40	Market Capitalization(B)	$7.966	Beta	1.38
Trailing 12-Month EPS	$-7.49	S&P Oper. EPS 2010E	-0.50	Yield (%)	0.53	S&P 3-Yr. Proj. EPS CAGR(%)	-50
Trailing 12-Month P/E	NM	P/E on S&P Oper. EPS 2009E	NM	Dividend Rate/Share	$0.20	S&P Credit Rating	BBB-
$10K Invested 5 Yrs Ago	$6,839	Common Shares Outstg. (M)	211.4	Institutional Ownership (%)	82		

Price Performance

- 30-Week Mov. Avg. ··· 10-Week Mov. Avg. - - GAAP Earnings vs. Previous Year Volume Above Avg. ▮▮▮ STARS
- 12-Mo. Target Price — Relative Strength ▲ Up ▼ Down ▶ No Change Below Avg. ▮▮▮ ★

Options: CBOE, P

Analysis prepared by **Stuart J. Benway, CFA** on November 04, 2009, when the stock traded at **$ 37.19**.

Highlights

▶ We look for as much as a 30% decline in revenues in 2009 from continuing operations. Divestitures have reduced WY's revenue base by a third over the past two years. S&P expects housing starts to fall 37% in 2009, which we think will prevent a recovery in prices for lumber and panels and lead to lower closings and sale prices in homebuilding. We see sales rising about 10% in 2010 as we expect the housing market to begin to recover. Pulp prices should also be higher in 2010.

▶ We believe planned cost reductions and lower prices for raw material and energy will be more than offset by lower selling prices and underutilized capacity in 2009. Conditions should improve somewhat in 2010, with both demand and prices for wood products likely to add to margin expansion. We estimate that operating margins will be negative in 2009, before turning positive again in 2010.

▶ For 2009, we see an operating loss of $1.40 per share, excluding unusual items but including land sales gains. We look for improvement in 2010, but still project a loss of $0.50.

Investment Rationale/Risk

▶ WY has divested major assets to focus on its timber, wood products, real estate, and fiber businesses. Although these sales generated significant proceeds, its lumber and homebuilding businesses have been hurt badly by the downturn in residential real estate. The company has reduced its annual dividend by over 90%. However, WY is considering adopting the REIT form of corporate structure, which could result in a large distribution.

▶ Risks to our recommendation and target price include a further drop in wood product prices, continued contraction of the credit markets, and a lack of recovery in the housing market.

▶ Given the company's recent and potential corporate repositioning moves, we believe it is appropriate to value WY shares on a sum-of-the-parts basis. Our model recognizes the cyclical characteristics of the wood products and real estate businesses, the relative stability of the fibers unit, and what we view as the significant value of the timberlands. Considering these factors, we derive a value of $38, which is our 12-month target price.

Qualitative Risk Assessment

LOW	**MEDIUM**	HIGH

Our risk assessment reflects that Weyerhaeuser operates in a cyclical industry, with large capital requirements and significant variability in both costs and prices. However, the company is one of the largest companies in the industry, and we believe it has a major base of assets and modest debt levels.

Quantitative Evaluations

S&P Quality Ranking B-

D	C	**B-**	B	B+	A-	A	A+

Relative Strength Rank MODERATE

51

LOWEST = 1 HIGHEST = 99

Revenue/Earnings Data

Revenue (Million $)

	1Q	2Q	3Q	4Q	Year
2009	1,275	1,391	1,407	--	--
2008	2,096	2,174	2,107	1,760	8,018
2007	3,891	4,334	4,146	3,937	16,308
2006	5,256	5,657	5,328	5,655	21,896
2005	5,404	5,838	5,604	5,868	22,629
2004	5,037	5,893	5,849	5,886	22,665

Earnings Per Share ($)

	1Q	2Q	3Q	4Q	Year
2009	-1.25	-0.50	E0.20	E-0.33	E-1.40
2008	-1.08	-0.98	-0.95	-5.67	-8.61
2007	-0.07	0.17	0.34	-0.21	0.23
2006	-2.36	1.20	0.75	1.67	1.44
2005	0.98	1.22	1.16	-1.00	2.36
2004	0.54	1.57	2.45	0.82	5.43

Fiscal year ended Dec. 31. Next earnings report expected: Early February. EPS Estimates based on S&P Operating Earnings; historical GAAP earnings are as reported.

Dividend Data (Dates: mm/dd Payment Date: mm/dd/yy)

Amount ($)	Date Decl.	Ex-Div. Date	Stk. of Record	Payment Date
0.250	12/19	01/28	01/30	03/02/09
0.250	04/16	04/29	05/01	06/01/09
0.050	07/07	07/29	07/31	08/31/09
0.050	10/08	11/04	11/06	11/30/09

Dividends have been paid since 1933. Source: Company reports.

Please read the Required Disclosures and Analyst Certification on the last page of this report.

The **McGraw·Hill** Companies

Weyerhaeuser Co

STANDARD
&POOR'S

Business Summary November 04, 2009

CORPORATE OVERVIEW. Weyerhaeuser, one of the world's largest integrated forest products companies, is primarily engaged in growing and harvesting timber; the production, distribution and sale of wood and paper products; and real estate development. Through its timberlands segment (11% of 2008 sales), WY manages 22 million acres of forestland through company-owned or leased property in eight states and Canada. The wood products businesses (48%) produce and sell softwood and hardwood lumber, plywood and veneer, composite panels, oriented strand board, and engineered lumber. Products made by the pulp and paper unit (23%) include paper grade, absorbent, dissolving and specialty pulp grades. Paper products include coated papers, which are used in the printing and publishing industries. Through Weyerhaeuser Real Estate Company (18%), the company is involved in the development of single-family housing and residential lots, including the development of master-planned communities. The containerboard, packaging and recycling segment, which manufactures corrugating medium, linerboard and kraft paper, was sold in August 2008.

MARKET PROFILE. Weyerhaeuser operates in a highly cyclical and capital-intensive industry. Demand for the company's products is dependent on a number of factors including consumer spending, white collar employment levels, domestic and Japanese new home construction and repair and remodeling activity, and movements in currency exchange rates. Historical prices for paper and wood products have been volatile, and, despite its size, Weyerhaeuser has had only a limited direct influence over the timing and extent of price changes for its products. Pricing is significantly affected by the relationship between supply and demand, and supply is influenced primarily by fluctuations in available manufacturing capacity.

Company Financials Fiscal Year Ended Dec. 31

Per Share Data ($)	2008	2007	2006	2005	2004	2003	2002	2001	2000	1999
Tangible Book Value	22.58	27.35	28.92	27.81	24.84	17.44	15.80	25.45	25.95	27.15
Cash Flow	-5.80	4.43	6.88	7.80	10.76	7.23	6.63	5.94	7.52	6.07
Earnings	-8.61	0.23	1.44	2.36	5.43	1.30	1.09	1.61	3.72	2.98
S&P Core Earnings	-7.30	-0.25	2.97	1.79	4.37	0.70	-0.75	NA	NA	NA
Dividends	2.40	2.40	2.20	1.90	1.60	1.60	1.60	1.60	1.60	1.60
Payout Ratio	NM	NM	182%	81%	29%	123%	147%	99%	43%	54%
Prices:High	73.75	87.09	75.50	71.85	68.59	64.70	68.09	63.50	74.50	73.94
Prices:Low	28.68	59.67	54.25	60.62	55.06	45.40	37.35	42.77	36.06	49.56
P/E Ratio:High	NM	NM	62	30	13	50	62	39	20	25
P/E Ratio:Low	NM	NM	45	26	10	35	34	27	10	17

Income Statement Analysis (Million $)										
Revenue	8,018	16,308	21,896	22,629	22,665	19,873	18,521	14,545	15,980	12,262
Operating Income	38.0	1,628	2,914	3,443	4,028	2,716	2,455	1,689	2,536	1,902
Depreciation	593	925	1,283	1,337	1,322	1,318	1,225	876	859	640
Interest Expense	550	586	531	730	829	796	771	344	351	277
Pretax Income	-2,707	59.0	826	906	1,945	436	371	516	1,323	970
Effective Tax Rate	NM	13.6%	57.0%	35.8%	34.0%	33.9%	35.0%	31.4%	36.5%	36.5%
Net Income	-1,819	51.0	355	582	1,283	288	241	354	840	616
S&P Core Earnings	-1,542	-53.0	728	444	1,029	156	-168	2.35	NA	NA

Balance Sheet & Other Financial Data (Million $)										
Cash	2,432	114	243	1,104	1,197	202	122	204	123	1,643
Current Assets	NA	NA	4,121	4,876	5,293	4,021	3,888	3,061	3,288	4,543
Total Assets	16,735	23,806	26,862	28,229	29,954	28,109	28,219	18,293	18,195	18,339
Current Liabilities	NA	NA	3,129	3,255	3,149	2,525	2,994	1,863	2,704	2,934
Long Term Debt	5,557	6,522	7,675	8,262	10,144	12,397	12,721	5,715	5,114	4,453
Common Equity	4,814	7,981	9,095	9,800	9,255	7,109	6,623	6,695	6,832	7,173
Total Capital	12,228	17,830	20,461	22,097	23,932	23,800	23,400	14,787	14,323	13,611
Capital Expenditures	608	880	837	861	492	608	930	660	848	487
Cash Flow	-1,226	976	1,638	1,919	2,605	1,606	1,466	1,230	1,699	1,256
Current Ratio	3.4	2.1	1.3	1.5	1.7	1.6	1.3	1.6	1.2	1.5
% Long Term Debt of Capitalization	45.4	36.6	37.5	37.4	42.4	52.1	54.4	38.6	35.7	32.7
% Net Income of Revenue	NM	0.3	1.6	2.6	5.7	1.4	1.3	2.4	5.3	5.0
% Return on Assets	NM	0.2	1.3	2.0	4.4	1.0	1.0	1.9	4.6	4.0
% Return on Equity	NM	0.6	3.8	6.1	15.7	4.2	3.6	5.2	12.0	10.5

Data as orig reptd.; bef. results of disc opers/spec. items. Per share data adj. for stk. divs.; EPS diluted. E-Estimated. NA-Not Available. NM-Not Meaningful. NR-Not Ranked. UR-Under Review.

Office: 33663 Weyerhaeuser Way South, Federal Way, WA 98003.
Telephone: 253-924-2345.
Email: invrelations@weyerhaeuser.com
Website: http://www.weyerhaeuser.com

Chrmn: C.R. Williamson
Pres & CEO: D.S. Fulton
EVP & CFO: P.M. Bedient
SVP & CTO: M.P. Drake

SVP & General Counsel: S.D. McDade
Investor Contact: K.F. McAuley (253-924-2058)
Board Members: D. A. Cafaro, M. A. Emmert, D. S. Fulton, J. I. Kieckhefer, A. G. Langbo, W. Murdy, N. Piasecki, R. H. Sinkfield, D. M. Steuert, J. N. Sullivan, K. Williams, C. R. Williamson

Founded: 1900
Domicile: Washington
Employees: 19,843

Whirlpool Corp

STANDARD
&POOR'S

S&P Recommendation	HOLD ★★★☆☆	Price $74.60 (as of Nov 27, 2009)	12-Mo. Target Price $80.00	Investment Style Large-Cap Blend

GICS Sector Consumer Discretionary
Sub-Industry Household Appliances

Summary Whirlpool, which acquired Maytag in 2006, is the world's largest manufacturer of home appliances. Sears, Roebuck is its biggest customer.

Key Stock Statistics (Source S&P, Vickers, company reports)

52-Wk Range	$80.41– 19.19	S&P Oper. EPS 2009**E**	4.40	Market Capitalization(B)	$5.541	Beta	2.18
Trailing 12-Month EPS	$3.69	S&P Oper. EPS 2010**E**	5.00	Yield (%)	2.31	S&P 3-Yr. Proj. EPS CAGR(%)	14
Trailing 12-Month P/E	20.2	P/E on S&P Oper. EPS 2009**E**	17.0	Dividend Rate/Share	$1.72	S&P Credit Rating	BBB-
$10K Invested 5 Yrs Ago	$13,102	Common Shares Outstg. (M)	74.3	Institutional Ownership (%)	NM		

Price Performance

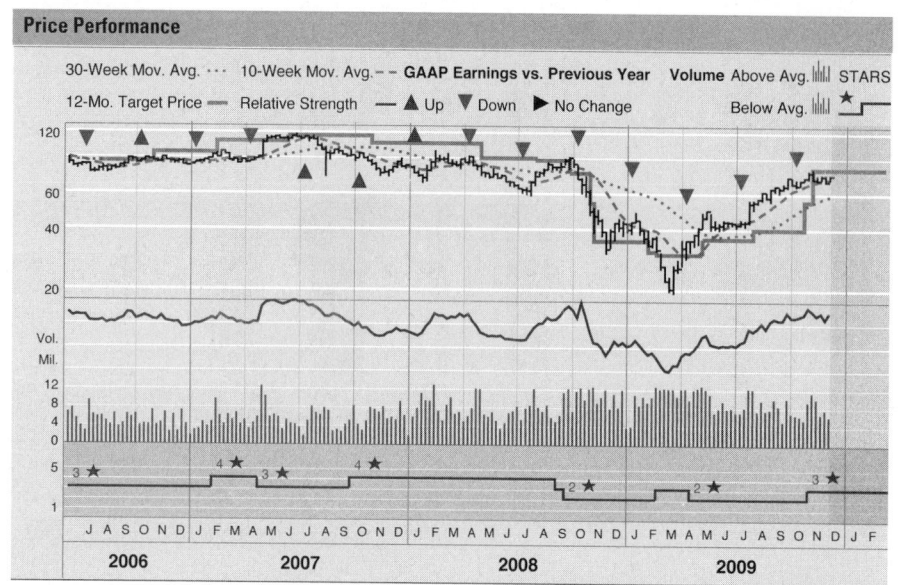

30-Week Mov. Avg. · · ·   10-Week Mov. Avg. - -   **GAAP Earnings vs. Previous Year**   Volume Above Avg. STARS
12-Mo. Target Price —   Relative Strength   ▲ Up ▼ Down ▶ No Change   Below Avg.

2006   2007   2008   2009

Options: CBOE, P

Analysis prepared by **Kenneth M. Leon, CPA** on October 23, 2009, when the stock traded at **$ 76.35**.

Highlights

▶ Following an estimated sales decline of 11% in 2009, we forecast increases of 4.5% in 2010 and 8% in 2011 as the general economy rebounds. In 2009, the company estimates industry unit shipments will be off 10% to 15% in emerging markets, compared to a 10% to 12% decline in the U.S. market and a 13% drop in Europe. We believe customer demand for large kitchen and laundry appliances remains challenging.

▶ We think WHR's addressable markets for appliances will begin to improve in 2010, but will still trail total sales reported for 2008. With improved cost controls, we think WHR will widen its gross margins to 13.7% in 2009, from 13.3% in 2008, staying at 13.5% to 14% in 2010 and 2011.

▶ WHR's operating margin widened to 5.8% in 2007, from 5.0% in 2006, but narrowed to 3.4% in 2008. We forecast 4.4%% margins in 2009, staying at 4% to 4.5% in the next two years. Longer term, we believe WHR will benefit from its larger scale and purchasing power. With material federal energy tax credits, we see operating EPS of $4.40 in 2009, $5.00 in 2010 and $5.70 in 2011.

Investment Rationale/Risk

▶ Lack of visibility in demand for WHR's products remains a concern to us, as the industry association for appliances continues to report weak monthly major appliance shipments. However with the global economy seen improving in 2010, we believe the company can gain market share from smaller appliance makers that do not have WHR's scale advantages to price competitively without hurting margins.

▶ Risks to our opinion and target price include a prolonged recession that further weakens business conditions or growth prospects in WHR's major markets, particularly in the Americas and Europe; less competition and/or market share losses; and narrower margins resulting from higher raw material costs.

▶ Despite a cautious outlook for household appliances, our 12-month target price of $80 is based on a target P/E of about 16X, near the mid-point of the historical range for WHR and peers, applied to our 2010 EPS projection of $5.00, which excludes one-time benefits. With the shares priced near our view of appropriate value assuming an economic recovery, our recommendation is hold.

Qualitative Risk Assessment

LOW	MEDIUM	HIGH

Our risk assessment reflects WHR's leading market share across many brands, offset by intense industry rivalry and heightened competition from foreign companies. While WHR benefits from its scale advantages, sales have weakened from a global recession negatively affecting household appliance demand.

Quantitative Evaluations

S&P Quality Ranking   B+

D	C	B-	B	B+	A-	A	A+

Relative Strength Rank   STRONG

83

LOWEST = 1   HIGHEST = 99

Revenue/Earnings Data

Revenue (Million $)

	1Q	2Q	3Q	4Q	Year
2009	3,569	4,169	4,497	--	--
2008	4,614	5,076	4,902	4,315	18,907
2007	4,389	4,854	4,840	5,325	19,408
2006	3,536	4,747	4,843	4,954	18,080
2005	3,208	3,556	3,599	3,954	14,317
2004	3,007	3,264	3,318	3,632	13,220

Earnings Per Share ($)

2009	-0.91	1.04	1.15	E0.90	E4.40
2008	1.22	1.53	2.15	0.60	5.50
2007	1.55	2.00	2.20	2.39	8.10
2006	1.70	1.26	1.68	1.67	6.35
2005	1.26	1.42	1.66	1.83	6.19
2004	1.43	1.53	1.50	1.44	5.90

Fiscal year ended Dec. 31. Next earnings report expected: Early February. EPS Estimates based on S&P Operating Earnings; historical GAAP earnings are as reported.

Dividend Data (Dates: mm/dd Payment Date: mm/dd/yy)

Amount ($)	Date Decl.	Ex-Div. Date	Stk. of Record	Payment Date
0.430	02/17	02/25	02/27	03/15/09
0.430	04/21	05/27	05/29	06/15/09
0.430	08/18	08/26	08/28	09/15/09
0.430	10/19	11/18	11/20	12/15/09

Dividends have been paid since 1929. Source: Company reports.

Whirlpool Corp

Business Summary October 23, 2009

CORPORATE OVERVIEW. Whirlpool Corp. (WHR) manufactures and markets a full line of major appliances and related products, primarily for home use. Products are manufactured in 12 countries and marketed worldwide under 13 main brand names. The company's growth strategy over the past several years has been to introduce innovative new products, strengthen customer loyalty, expand its global footprint, enhance distribution channels, and make strategic acquisitions where appropriate.

MARKET PROFILE. WHR's total sales in 2008 were 57% from North America. As the market leader, its major product brands in the U.S. include Whirlpool, Maytag, KitchenAid, Jenn-Air, Roper, Estate, Admiral, Magic Chef, Amana, and Inglis. In Europe, which generated 21% of sales, products are marketed under the Whirlpool, Maytag, Amana, Bauknecht, Ignis, Laden, Polar and KitchenAid brand names. Markets also include Latin America and Asia. About 20% of total sales in 2008 were from Latin America, where WHR distributes its major home appliances under the Whirlpool, Brastemp, Consul and Eslabon de Lugo brand names. About 2% of sales were from Asia.

COMPETITIVE LANDSCAPE. The company has been able to retain a number one position in brand and market share in most global regions. Combined with high reliability, WHR has developed strong customer loyalty. Competitors in the appliance industry include long-time incumbents Electrolux and General Electric, as well as expanding foreign operations such as LG Electronics, Bosch Siemens, Samsung, Fisher & Paykel, and Haier.

Net sales in 2008 decreased 2.6%, due to weak domestic and international sales, and lower global average unit prices. Excluding currency fluctuations and the impact of the acquisition of Maytag, sales decreased 7%. WHR's international businesses experienced strong performance in 2007 driven by an 8.8% increase in units sold. It experienced a 5.1% decrease in unit sales during 2008 in North America, primarily resulting from a decline in appliance industry demand, lower original equipment manufacturer sales and lower share within the value and Maytag brands.

Company Financials Fiscal Year Ended Dec. 31

Per Share Data ($)	2008	2007	2006	2005	2004	2003	2002	2001	2000	1999
Tangible Book Value	NM	6.06	NM	21.49	19.85	15.23	5.82	11.10	13.97	14.29
Cash Flow	13.36	15.52	13.54	12.65	12.35	12.00	9.62	6.32	10.39	9.64
Earnings	5.50	8.10	6.35	6.19	5.90	5.91	3.78	0.50	5.20	4.56
S&P Core Earnings	3.17	7.33	6.33	5.99	5.58	5.71	2.12	-1.91	NA	NA
Dividends	1.72	1.72	2.15	1.72	1.72	1.36	1.36	1.02	1.36	1.36
Payout Ratio	31%	21%	34%	28%	29%	23%	36%	NM	26%	30%
Prices:High	98.00	118.00	96.00	86.52	80.00	73.35	79.80	74.20	68.31	78.25
Prices:Low	30.19	72.10	74.07	60.78	54.53	42.80	39.23	45.88	31.50	40.94
P/E Ratio:High	18	15	15	14	14	12	21	NM	13	17
P/E Ratio:Low	5	9	12	10	9	7	10	NM	6	9

Income Statement Analysis (Million $)	2008	2007	2006	2005	2004	2003	2002	2001	2000	1999
Revenue	18,907	19,408	18,080	14,317	13,220	12,176	11,016	10,343	10,325	10,511
Operating Income	1,347	1,717	1,428	1,291	1,218	1,219	1,207	1,147	1,178	1,261
Depreciation	597	593	550	442	445	427	405	396	371	386
Interest Expense	203	203	202	130	128	137	143	162	180	166
Pretax Income	246	786	620	598	615	652	468	89.0	580	510
Effective Tax Rate	NM	14.9%	20.3%	28.6%	34.0%	35.0%	41.2%	48.3%	34.5%	38.6%
Net Income	418	647	486	422	406	414	262	34.0	367	347
S&P Core Earnings	241	587	484	408	384	401	147	-130	NA	NA

Balance Sheet & Other Financial Data (Million $)	2008	2007	2006	2005	2004	2003	2002	2001	2000	1999
Cash	146	201	262	524	243	249	192	316	114	261
Current Assets	6,044	6,555	6,476	4,710	4,514	3,865	3,327	3,311	3,237	3,177
Total Assets	13,532	14,009	13,878	8,248	8,181	7,361	6,631	6,967	6,902	6,826
Current Liabilities	5,563	5,893	6,002	4,301	3,985	3,589	3,505	3,082	3,303	2,892
Long Term Debt	2,002	1,668	1,798	745	1,160	1,134	1,092	1,295	795	714
Common Equity	3,006	3,911	3,283	1,745	1,606	1,301	796	2,126	1,684	1,867
Total Capital	5,277	5,648	5,481	2,749	3,074	2,734	2,083	3,725	2,801	2,738
Capital Expenditures	547	536	576	484	511	423	430	378	375	437
Cash Flow	1,015	1,240	1,036	864	851	841	667	430	738	733
Current Ratio	1.1	1.1	1.1	1.1	1.1	1.1	0.9	1.1	1.0	1.1
% Long Term Debt of Capitalization	37.9	29.5	32.8	27.1	37.8	41.5	52.4	34.8	28.4	26.1
% Net Income of Revenue	2.2	3.3	2.7	2.9	3.1	3.4	2.4	0.3	3.6	3.3
% Return on Assets	3.0	4.6	4.4	5.1	5.2	5.9	3.9	0.5	5.3	4.7
% Return on Equity	12.1	18.0	19.3	25.2	27.9	40.6	22.8	1.5	20.7	17.9

Data as orig reptd.; bef. results of disc opers/spec. items. Per share data adj. for stk. divs.; EPS diluted. E-Estimated. NA-Not Available. NM-Not Meaningful. NR-Not Ranked. UR-Under Review.

Office: 2000 N M 63, Benton Harbor, MI 49022-2692.
Telephone: 269-923-5000.
Email: info@whirlpool.com
Website: http://www.whirlpool.com

Chrmn & CEO: J.M. Fettig
EVP & CFO: R. Templin
SVP, Secy & General Counsel: D.F. Hopp
CTO: S. Sarraf

Chief Acctg Officer & Cntlr: A.B. Petitt
Investor Contact: G. Fritz (269-923-2641)
Board Members: H. Cain, G. T. DiCamillo, J. M. Fettig, K. J. Hempel, M. F. Johnston, W. T. Kerr, A. G. Langbo, M. L. Marsh, P. G. Stern, J. D. Stoney, M. A. Todman, M. D. White

Founded: 1906
Domicile: Delaware
Employees: 69,612

Whole Foods Market Inc

S&P Recommendation **SELL** ★★☆☆☆	Price $25.90 (as of Nov 27, 2009)	12-Mo. Target Price $27.00	Investment Style Large-Cap Blend

GICS Sector Consumer Staples
Sub-Industry Food Retail

Summary This company owns and operates the largest U.S. chain of natural and organic foods supermarkets.

Key Stock Statistics (Source S&P, Vickers, company reports)

52-Wk Range	$34.40 – 8.68	S&P Oper. EPS 2010**E**	1.00	Market Capitalization(B)	$3.638	Beta	1.33
Trailing 12-Month EPS	$0.85	S&P Oper. EPS 2011**E**	1.15	Yield (%)	Nil	S&P 3-Yr. Proj. EPS CAGR(%)	15
Trailing 12-Month P/E	30.5	P/E on S&P Oper. EPS 2010**E**	25.9	Dividend Rate/Share	Nil	S&P Credit Rating	BB-
$10K Invested 5 Yrs Ago	$6,034	Common Shares Outstg. (M)	140.5	Institutional Ownership (%)	87		

Price Performance

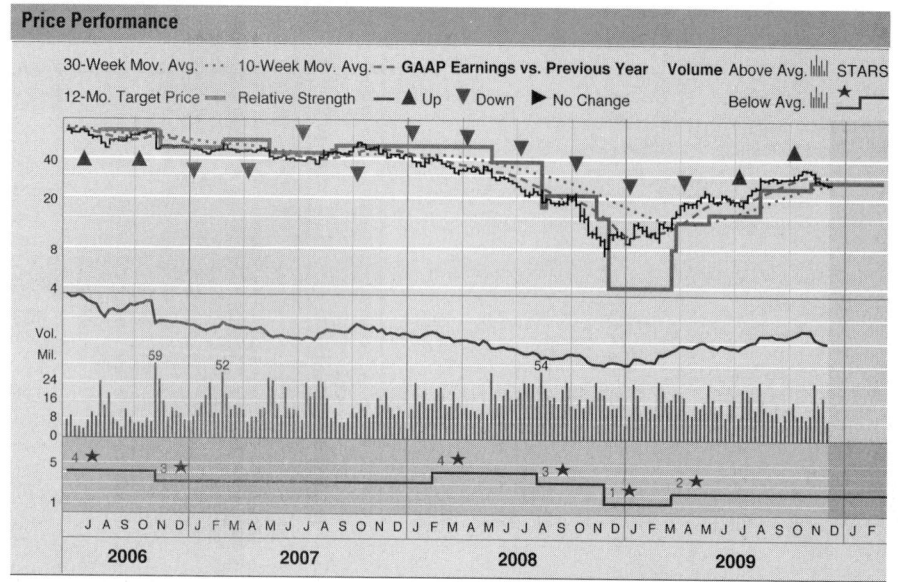

30-Week Mov. Avg. · · · 10-Week Mov. Avg. – – **GAAP Earnings vs. Previous Year** Volume Above Avg. STARS
12-Mo. Target Price — Relative Strength — ▲ Up ▼ Down ► No Change Below Avg. ★

Options: ASE

Analysis prepared by **Joseph Agnese** on November 16, 2009, when the stock traded at **$ 27.09**.

Highlights

► We expect FY 10 (Sep.) sales to increase about 6.8% to $8.6 billion, from $8.0 billion in FY 09, reflecting square footage growth of 6.5% from the opening of 13 new stores, and a projected comparable-store sales increase of about 3.0%. We believe comparable store sales will benefit from easier comparisons, an increased selection of low-priced products, and from our expectation of rising food inflation throughout the year.

► We believe margins will expand slightly, reflecting lower new store opening costs and a favorable shift in product mix as consumers trade down to private label goods, partially offset by increased competitive pricing pressure in an effort to drive traffic. We estimate that pre-opening and relocation expenses will decline significantly as a percentage of sales as square footage growth slows. We expect net interest expense to decline due to higher investment income.

► We project that FY 10 EPS will increase 18%, to $1.00, up from $0.85 in FY 09 (including $0.08 in FTC-related legal costs and a $0.20 negative impact from the issuance of preferred shares).

Investment Rationale/Risk

► We believe the company is poorly positioned in an adverse economic environment as we see negative impacts from increased consumer pricing sensitivity and as consumers trade down to lower-priced retailing alternatives. However, we view the issuance of preferred shares in FY 09, the pay down of debt and a slowdown in square footage growth as beneficial in helping strengthen the company's balance sheet in an adverse environment, although negatively impacting EPS.

► Risks to our recommendation and target price include better-than-expected comparable store sales growth on stronger-than-expected consumer demand.

► Despite our projection for near-term earnings risks due to an adverse economic environment, we believe the shares should trade in line with the broader consumer staples sector, reflecting our expectations for revived growth over the next three years. Assuming the shares trade in line with their historical median P/E premium of 1.75X with the S&P 500, we apply a P/E multiple of 27.1X to our FY 10 EPS estimate of $1.00, or 1.8X our estimated 15% three-year growth rate, to reach our 12-month target price of $27.

Qualitative Risk Assessment

LOW	MEDIUM	**HIGH**

Our risk assessment reflects the intensely competitive environment in the retail food industry, partly offset by our view of WFMI's strong balance sheet and growing natural and organic food industry sales momentum.

Quantitative Evaluations

S&P Quality Ranking B

D	C	B-	**B**	B+	A-	A	A+

Relative Strength Rank WEAK

18

LOWEST = 1   HIGHEST = 99

Revenue/Earnings Data

Revenue (Million $)

	1Q	2Q	3Q	4Q	Year
2009	2,467	1,858	1,878	1,829	8,032
2008	2,457	1,866	1,841	1,789	7,954
2007	1,871	1,463	1,514	1,743	6,592
2006	1,667	1,312	1,338	1,291	5,607
2005	1,368	1,085	1,133	1,115	4,701
2004	1,118	902.1	917.4	927.3	3,865

Earnings Per Share ($)

2009	0.20	0.19	0.25	0.20	0.85
2008	0.28	0.29	0.24	0.01	0.82
2007	0.38	0.32	0.35	0.24	1.29
2006	0.40	0.36	0.37	0.28	1.41
2005	0.35	0.29	0.29	0.07	0.99
2004	0.30	0.27	0.25	0.23	1.05

Fiscal year ended Sep. 30. Next earnings report expected: Mid February. EPS Estimates based on S&P Operating Earnings; historical GAAP earnings are as reported.

Dividend Data

No Dividend Data Available

Please read the Required Disclosures and Analyst Certification on the last page of this report.

Whole Foods Market Inc

Business Summary November 16, 2009

CORPORATE OVERVIEW. Whole Foods Market, established in 1980, has grown into the largest U.S. retailer of natural and organic foods, with $8.0 billion in sales in FY 09 (Sep.). Reflecting a series of store openings and acquisitions, the company has expanded from a single Austin, TX, store in 1980 to a chain of more than 280 stores in 37 states plus Washington, DC; six stores in Canada; and five stores in the United Kingdom. The company strives to differentiate its stores from those of its competitors by tailoring its product mix, customer service attitude and store environment to appeal to health conscious and gourmet customers.

CORPORATE STRATEGY. The company opens or acquires stores in existing regions, and in metropolitan areas in which it believes it can become the leading natural foods supermarket retailer. In developing new stores, WFMI seeks to open large format units of 35,000 sq. ft. to 50,000 sq. ft., located on premium sites, often in urban, highly populated areas. Although approximately 32% of its store base consists of acquired stores, the company expects more of its future growth to come from developing new stores. As of October 2009, WFMI had signed leases for 53 stores averaging approximately 44,800 square feet in size, which is about 120% larger than its existing store base average. It oper-

ated about 10.6 million square feet of retail space, with about 2.4 million square feet (23% of existing sq. ft.) of retail space that were under development at that time.

Stores average about 37,200 sq. ft., and offer a selection of some 30,000 food and non-food products. Each store contributes an average of almost $29 million in annual sales and average about 7.4 years old. Products sold include natural and organic foods and beverages; dietary supplements; natural personal care products; natural household goods; and educational products. Natural foods can be defined as foods that are minimally processed, largely or completely free of artificial ingredients, preservatives and other non-naturally occurring chemicals, and as near as possible to their whole, natural state. Organic foods are based on the minimal use of off-farm inputs and on management practices that restore, maintain and enhance the ecology.

Company Financials Fiscal Year Ended Sep. 30

Per Share Data ($)	2009	2008	2007	2006	2005	2004	2003	2002	2001	2000
Tangible Book Value	NA	5.47	4.97	9.00	9.06	6.82	5.57	4.21	2.98	2.11
Cash Flow	NA	2.49	2.60	2.48	1.93	1.84	1.54	1.34	1.16	0.85
Earnings	0.85	0.82	1.29	1.41	0.99	1.05	0.83	0.70	0.61	0.26
S&P Core Earnings	NA	0.82	1.29	1.40	-0.21	0.85	0.70	0.58	0.38	NA
Dividends	Nil	0.78	0.69	0.88	0.42	0.23	Nil	Nil	Nil	Nil
Payout Ratio	Nil	95%	53%	62%	42%	22%	Nil	Nil	Nil	Nil
Prices:High	34.40	42.48	53.65	78.27	79.90	48.74	33.81	27.30	23.25	15.94
Prices:Low	9.06	7.04	36.00	45.56	44.14	32.96	22.39	17.74	9.73	8.59
P/E Ratio:High	40	52	42	56	81	47	41	39	38	60
P/E Ratio:Low	11	9	28	32	45	32	27	25	16	32

Income Statement Analysis (Million $)	2009	2008	2007	2006	2005	2004	2003	2002	2001	2000
Revenue	8,032	7,954	6,592	5,607	4,701	3,865	3,149	2,690	2,272	1,839
Operating Income	NA	470	484	475	363	341	285	248	209	181
Depreciation	267	234	186	156	134	112	98.0	85.9	78.8	63.9
Interest Expense	NA	42.4	4.21	0.03	2.22	7.25	8.11	10.4	17.9	15.1
Pretax Income	251	207	305	340	237	229	173	141	89.8	63.5
Effective Tax Rate	41.5%	44.6%	40.0%	40.0%	42.5%	40.0%	40.0%	40.0%	42.5%	54.5%
Net Income	147	115	183	204	136	137	104	84.5	51.6	28.9
S&P Core Earnings	NA	115	183	202	-28.0	109	85.0	70.4	43.0	NA

Balance Sheet & Other Financial Data (Million $)	2009	2008	2007	2006	2005	2004	2003	2002	2001	2000
Cash	430	30.5	Nil	2.25	309	198	166	12.6	1.84	0.40
Current Assets	NA	623	668	624	673	485	364	172	145	152
Total Assets	3,783	3,381	3,213	2,043	1,889	1,520	1,197	943	829	760
Current Liabilities	NA	666	785	510	418	331	240	176	156	143
Long Term Debt	739	929	736	8.61	12.9	165	163	162	251	298
Common Equity	1,628	1,506	1,459	1,404	1,366	988	776	589	409	307
Total Capital	2,780	2,435	2,195	1,413	1,379	1,173	942	751	660	605
Capital Expenditures	315	522	140	132	116	110	84.1	61.4	49.0	111
Cash Flow	NA	348	369	360	270	249	202	170	130	92.8
Current Ratio	1.5	0.9	0.9	1.2	1.6	1.5	1.5	1.0	0.9	1.1
% Long Term Debt of Capitalization	26.6	38.2	33.5	0.6	0.9	14.0	17.3	21.6	38.0	49.2
% Net Income of Revenue	1.8	1.4	2.8	3.6	2.9	3.5	3.3	3.1	2.3	1.6
% Return on Assets	4.1	3.5	7.0	10.4	8.0	10.1	9.7	9.5	6.5	4.1
% Return on Equity	9.4	7.7	12.8	14.7	11.8	15.5	15.2	16.9	14.4	9.4

Data as orig reptd.; bef. results of disc opers/spec. items. Per share data adj. for stk. divs.; EPS diluted. E-Estimated. NA-Not Available. NM-Not Meaningful. NR-Not Ranked. UR-Under Review.

Office: 550 Bowie St, Austin, TX 78703-4644.
Telephone: 512-477-4455.
Website: http://www.wholefoods.com
Chrmn & CEO: J.P. Mackey

COO & Co-Pres: W. Robb
COO & Co-Pres: A.C. Gallo
EVP, CFO, Chief Acctg Officer & Secy: G.J. Chamberlain
General Counsel: R. Lang

Investor Contact: C. McCann (512-477-4455)
Board Members: J. B. Elstrott, G. E. Greene, S. M. Hassan, S. Kugelman, J. P. Mackey, J. A. Seiffer, M. Siegel, J. D. Sokoloff, R. Sorenson, W. A. Tindell, III

Founded: 1978
Domicile: Texas
Employees: 52,900

Williams Cos Inc. (The)

STANDARD &POOR'S

S&P Recommendation BUY ★★★★★

Price $19.97 (as of Nov 27, 2009)

12-Mo. Target Price $23.00

Investment Style Large-Cap Blend

GICS Sector Energy
Sub-Industry Oil & Gas Storage & Transportation

Summary This company, which primarily finds, produces, gathers, processes and transports natural gas, also manages a wholesale power business.

Key Stock Statistics (Source S&P, Vickers, company reports)

52-Wk Range	**$20.66–9.52**	S&P Oper. EPS 2009**E**	**0.95**	Market Capitalization(B)	**$11.645**	Beta	**1.28**
Trailing 12-Month EPS	**$0.39**	S&P Oper. EPS 2010**E**	**1.13**	Yield (%)	**2.20**	S&P 3-Yr. Proj. EPS CAGR(%)	**-13**
Trailing 12-Month P/E	**51.2**	P/E on S&P Oper. EPS 2009**E**	**21.0**	Dividend Rate/Share	**$0.44**	S&P Credit Rating	**BBB-**
$10K Invested 5 Yrs Ago	**$12,967**	Common Shares Outstg. (M)	**583.1**	Institutional Ownership (%)	**78**		

Price Performance

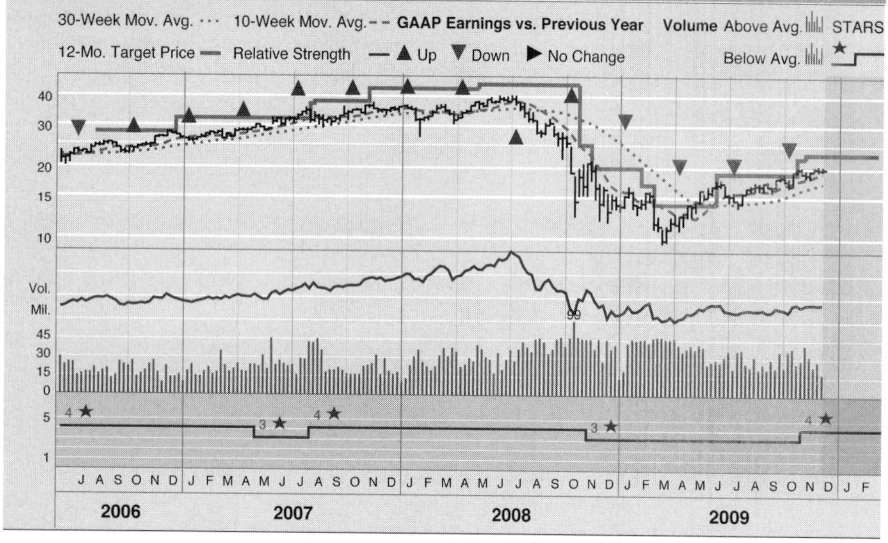
30-Week Mov. Avg. ··· 10-Week Mov. Avg. - - GAAP Earnings vs. Previous Year Volume Above Avg. STARS
12-Mo. Target Price — Relative Strength — ▲ Up ▼ Down ▶ No Change Below Avg.
Vol. Mil.
2006
2007
2008
2009

Options: ASE, CBOE, P

Analysis prepared by **Michael Kay** on November 02, 2009, when the stock traded at **$ 18.90**.

Highlights

- After production growth of 19% in 2008, lower natural gas prices have reduced 2009 forecasts, and we see flat production on a 25%-32% decline in capital spending. In 2009, WMB completed a bolt-on acquisition in the Piceance Basin for $258 million, likely to contribute 150 Bcfe in proved reserves and current production of 24 MMcfe/day. WMB expects the deal to be accretive to EPS by $0.04 in 2010 and $0.15 in 2011. Long term, we look for E&P to benefit from the development of drilling prospects, especially in the Piceance and Powder River Basins, but we see lower prices impeding segment profits in 2009.

- Given volatile markets, we expect WMB to limit asset dropdowns into master limited partnerships Williams Partners (WPZ 26, NR) and Williams Pipeline Partners (WMZ 20, NR). Its capital budget is $2.450-$2.675 billion for 2009, down from $3.59 billion in 2008, then $1.9-$2.7 billion in 2010 and $2.3-$3.8 billion in 2011.

- In 2008, EPS was $2.15, up 27%, on higher natural gas prices and NGL margins, and we see a 56% drop in 2009 to $0.95 (before impairments), increasing to $1.13 in 2010. WMB sees 2009 cash flow of $1.9-$2.1 billion, down 35%-43%.

Investment Rationale/Risk

- WMB has expanded drilling in the Piceance and Powder River basins, which, if developed, could provide major boosts to proven reserves. After a review earlier in the year, WMB plans no structural changes, a positive, in our view, as we see three major pipelines and growing fee-based and regulated midstream natural gas businesses providing steady cash flows. We project WMB to overspend cash flow in 2009 by $200 million, which is expected to be funded by cash on hand. We are encouraged by WMB's early entry into the Marcellus Shale.

- Risks to our recommendation and target price include sharply higher interest rates, slower-than-projected economic growth, a sustained decline in natural gas prices, and lower rates for FERC regulated pipelines.

- For 2009, we see lower cash flow, earnings and capex plans on a decline in natural gas prices. Our 12-month target price of $23 reflects a blend of above-peer relative metrics, given our view of high-quality pipelines and a strong asset base in E&P, including an enterprise value to projected 2010 EBITDA multiple of 7X, a target P/E of 20X 2010 EPS forecast and our proved-reserve NAV of $20.

Qualitative Risk Assessment

LOW | MEDIUM | **HIGH**

Our risk assessment reflects our belief that although WMB has an E&P segment that can be very volatile, its business portfolio is overweighted in regulated industries with largely fixed returns.

Quantitative Evaluations

S&P Quality Ranking **B**

D | C | B- | **B** | B+ | A- | A | A+

Relative Strength Rank **STRONG**

78

LOWEST = 1 HIGHEST = 99

Revenue/Earnings Data

Revenue (Million $)

	1Q	2Q	3Q	4Q	Year
2009	2,128	1,909	2,098	--	--
2008	3,204	3,701	3,245	2,202	12,352
2007	2,368	2,824	2,860	2,506	10,558
2006	3,028	2,715	3,300	2,770	11,813
2005	2,954	2,871	3,082	3,676	12,584
2004	3,070	3,052	3,375	2,964	12,461

Earnings Per Share ($)

	1Q	2Q	3Q	4Q	Year
2009	-0.29	0.21	0.24	**E**0.28	**E**0.95
2008	0.70	0.70	0.62	0.23	2.26
2007	0.28	0.40	0.38	0.34	1.39
2006	0.22	-0.11	0.19	0.25	0.55
2005	0.34	0.07	0.01	0.12	0.53
2004	Nil	-0.03	0.03	0.17	0.18

Fiscal year ended Dec. 31. Next earnings report expected: Mid February. EPS Estimates based on S&P Operating Earnings; historical GAAP earnings are as reported.

Dividend Data (Dates: mm/dd Payment Date: mm/dd/yy)

Amount ($)	Date Decl.	Ex-Div. Date	Stk. of Record	Payment Date
0.110	01/22	03/11	03/13	03/30/09
0.110	05/21	06/10	06/12	06/29/09
0.110	07/14	08/26	08/28	09/14/09
0.110	11/19	12/09	12/11	12/28/09

Dividends have been paid since 1974. Source: Company reports.

Please read the Required Disclosures and Analyst Certification on the last page of this report.
Redistribution or reproduction is prohibited without written permission. Copyright ©2009 The McGraw-Hill Companies, Inc.

The McGraw-Hill Companies

Williams Cos Inc. (The)

STANDARD
&POOR'S

Business Summary November 02, 2009

CORPORATE OVERVIEW. WMB primarily finds, produces, gathers, and processes and transports natural gas. Operations are concentrated in the Pacific Northwest, Rocky Mountains, Gulf Coast, Southern California and Eastern Seaboard.

In February 2003, WMB announced a business strategy focused on migrating to an integrated natural gas business comprised of a smaller portfolio of natural gas businesses, reducing debt and increasing liquidity via asset sales, strategic levels of financing, and reductions in operating costs.

CORPORATE STRATEGY. WMB has transitioned its corporate strategy toward aggressively focusing on the market in the segments in which it perceives a sustainable competitive advantage, primarily its exploration and production (E&P) segment and its midstream segment. WMB has about 4.5 Tcfe of proved reserves, with natural gas produced from tight sands formations and coal bed methane reserves in the Piceance (71% of year-end 2008), San Juan (12%), Powder River (9%), Midcontinent (5%) and other basins (3%). Proved reserves are up 5% from 2007.

The midstream division provides natural gas gathering, processing and treating, and natural gas liquid fractionation, storage and marketing, with primary service areas concentrated in the western states of Wyoming, Colorado and

New Mexico, and the onshore and offshore shelf and deepwater areas in and around the Gulf Coast states of Texas, Louisiana, Mississippi and Alabama. Geographically, midstream natural gas assets are positioned to maximize commercial and operational synergies with other WMB assets (e.g., offshore gathering and processing assets attach and process or condition natural gas supplies delivered to the Transco pipeline; WMB gathering and processing facilities in the San Juan basin handle about 80% of the group's wellhead production in the basin).

The gas pipeline division has 15,000 miles of pipeline, with total annual throughput of 2,700 trillion BTUs, including the Transcontinental Gas Pipeline (Transco) and the Northwest Pipeline. Each pipeline system operates under Federal Energy Regulatory Commission (FERC) approved tariffs that establish rates, cost recovery mechanisms, and service terms and conditions. The established rates are a function of WMB's cost of providing services, including a "reasonable" return on invested capital (ROIC).

Company Financials Fiscal Year Ended Dec. 31

Per Share Data ($)	2008	2007	2006	2005	2004	2003	2002	2001	2000	1999
Tangible Book Value	12.85	9.51	8.48	7.70	7.06	5.96	7.15	9.43	13.26	11.69
Cash Flow	4.46	3.16	1.97	1.75	1.37	1.27	0.53	3.17	3.80	2.04
Earnings	2.26	1.39	0.55	0.53	0.18	-0.03	-1.14	1.67	1.95	0.36
S&P Core Earnings	2.14	1.41	0.78	0.64	0.05	-0.26	-1.34	1.40	NA	NA
Dividends	0.43	0.39	0.35	0.25	0.08	0.04	0.42	0.68	0.60	0.60
Payout Ratio	19%	28%	63%	47%	44%	NM	NM	41%	31%	167%
Prices:High	40.75	37.74	28.32	25.72	17.18	10.73	26.35	46.44	49.75	53.75
Prices:Low	11.69	25.17	19.35	15.18	8.49	2.51	0.78	20.80	29.50	28.00
P/E Ratio:High	18	27	51	49	95	NM	NM	28	26	NM
P/E Ratio:Low	5	18	35	29	47	NM	NM	12	15	NM

Income Statement Analysis (Million $)										
Revenue	12,352	10,558	11,813	12,584	12,461	16,834	5,608	11,035	10,398	8,593
Operating Income	3,853	2,938	2,124	1,972	1,903	1,849	1,566	3,389	2,602	1,591
Depreciation	1,310	1,082	866	740	668	671	775	798	832	742
Interest Expense	594	685	659	664	833	1,241	1,325	747	1,010	668
Pretax Income	2,221	1,461	579	557	246	71.0	-617	1,533	1,415	316
Effective Tax Rate	32.1%	35.9%	35.6%	38.4%	53.4%	51.3%	NM	41.1%	39.1%	51.0%
Net Income	1,334	847	333	317	93.2	15.2	-502	835	873	162
S&P Core Earnings	1,266	852	480	388	27.3	-144	-699	703	NA	NA

Balance Sheet & Other Financial Data (Million $)										
Cash	800	1,699	2,269	1,597	930	2,316	2,019	1,301	1,211	1,092
Current Assets	4,411	5,538	6,322	9,697	6,044	8,795	12,886	12,938	15,477	6,517
Total Assets	26,006	25,061	25,402	29,443	23,993	27,022	34,989	38,906	40,197	25,289
Current Liabilities	3,519	4,431	4,694	8,450	5,146	6,270	11,309	13,495	16,804	5,772
Long Term Debt	7,683	7,757	7,622	7,591	7,712	11,040	11,896	10,621	10,532	9,746
Common Equity	8,440	6,375	6,073	5,428	4,956	4,102	4,778	6,044	5,892	5,585
Total Capital	20,127	18,558	17,656	15,741	15,238	17,595	20,723	21,532	20,693	18,475
Capital Expenditures	3,475	2,816	-2,509	1,299	787	957	1,824	1,922	4,904	3,513
Cash Flow	2,644	1,929	1,198	1,057	762	657	274	1,633	1,705	901
Current Ratio	1.3	1.3	1.3	1.1	1.2	1.4	1.1	1.0	0.9	1.1
% Long Term Debt of Capitalization	38.2	41.8	43.2	48.2	50.6	62.7	57.4	49.3	50.9	52.8
% Net Income of Revenue	10.8	8.0	2.8	2.5	0.7	0.1	NM	7.6	8.4	1.9
% Return on Assets	5.2	3.4	1.2	1.2	0.4	0.0	NM	2.3	2.7	0.7
% Return on Equity	18.0	13.6	5.8	6.1	2.1	0.0	NM	14.0	15.2	3.3

Data as orig reptd.; bef. results of disc opers/spec. items. Per share data adj. for stk. divs.; EPS diluted. E-Estimated. NA-Not Available. NM-Not Meaningful. NR-Not Ranked. UR-Under Review.

Office: 1 Williams Ctr, Tulsa, OK 74172-0140.
Telephone: 918-573-2000.
Website: http://www.williams.com
Chrmn, Pres & CEO: S.J. Malcolm

Pres: J.C. Bumgarner, Jr.
SVP & CFO: D.R. Chappel
SVP & Chief Admin Officer: R.L. Ewing
SVP & General Counsel: J.J. Bender

Investor Contact: T.N. Campbell (918-573-2944)
Board Members: J. R. Cleveland, K. B. Cooper, I. F. Engelhardt, W. R. Granberry, W. E. Green, J. H. Hinshaw, W. R. Howell, G. A. Lorch, W. G. Lowrie, F. T. MacInnis, S. J. Malcolm, J. D. Stoney

Founded: 1908
Domicile: Delaware
Employees: 4,704

Windstream Corp

STANDARD
&POOR'S

S&P Recommendation	STRONG BUY ★★★★★	Price $10.12 (as of Nov 27, 2009)	12-Mo. Target Price $12.00	Investment Style Large-Cap Value

GICS Sector Telecommunication Services
Sub-Industry Integrated Telecommunication Services

Summary This company was formed through the combination of former Alltel wireline assets and Valor Communications in July 2006. It provides telephone service to nearly 3 million lines in rural markets.

Key Stock Statistics (Source S&P, Vickers, company reports)

52-Wk Range	$10.39–6.28	S&P Oper. EPS 2009**E**	0.86	Market Capitalization(B)	$4.325	Beta	0.98
Trailing 12-Month EPS	$0.78	S&P Oper. EPS 2010**E**	0.90	Yield (%)	9.88	S&P 3-Yr. Proj. EPS CAGR(%)	3
Trailing 12-Month P/E	13.0	P/E on S&P Oper. EPS 2009**E**	11.8	Dividend Rate/Share	$1.00	S&P Credit Rating	BB
$10K Invested 5 Yrs Ago	NA	Common Shares Outstg. (M)	427.4	Institutional Ownership (%)	63		

Price Performance

30-Week Mov. Avg. ⋯ 10-Week Mov. Avg. - - GAAP Earnings vs. Previous Year Volume Above Avg. ⅢⅢ STARS
12-Mo. Target Price — Relative Strength ▲ Up ▼ Down ► No Change Below Avg. ⅢⅢ ★

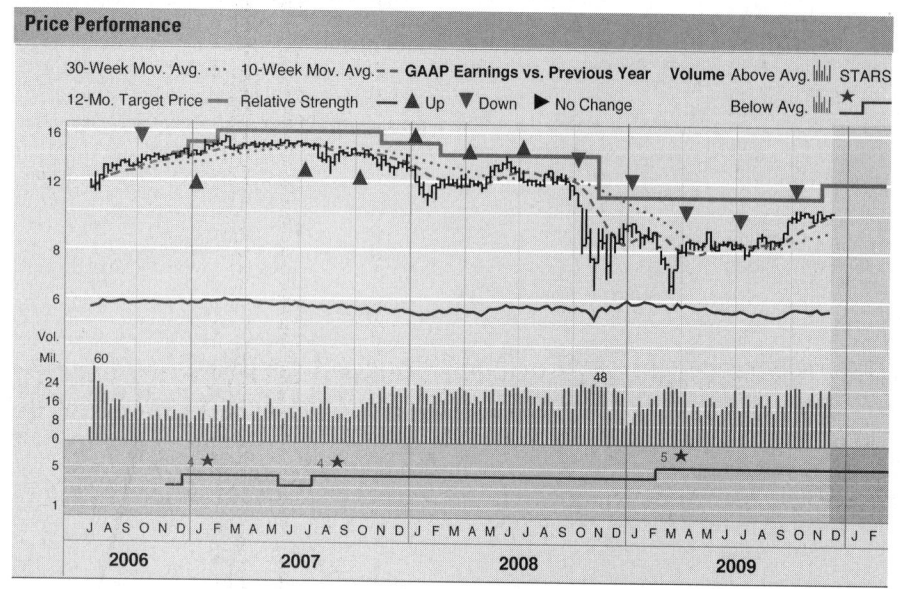

Analysis prepared by **Todd Rosenbluth** on November 12, 2009, when the stock traded at **$ 9.87**.

Options: CBOE, Ph

Highlights

▶ We project revenues of $3 billion in 2009 with a fractional increase in 2010 aided by completed acquisitions. On an organic basis, we see broadband customer additions nearly offsetting the impact of increasing access line losses, although growth will likely slow due to an above-average penetration rate. We expect lower universal service funding due to the loss of access lines putting pressure on revenues.

▶ We expect WIN to generate EBITDA of $1.51 billion in 2009 and $1.54 billion in 2010, down from $1.64 billion in 2008. We forecast that EBITDA margins will widen fractionally in 2010 with the benefit of cost synergies from acquisitions. This should be partially offset by the loss of higher-margin voice revenues.

▶ We look for interest expenses to be up slightly in 2010. We forecast operating EPS of $0.86 in 2009 and $0.90 in 2010, with modest share repurchases that took place in late 2009 being offset by the stock issuance component of merger activity.

Investment Rationale/Risk

▶ With a low estimated 60% of WIN's free cash flow in 2009 being used to support its dividend, helped by expense controls, we see the telco's dividend as stable. In our view, due to its rural operations and high broadband penetration, WIN's access-line base has been less volatile than peers, and we expect improved demand from business customers when the economy becomes stronger. While we see risks due to the company's acquisition strategy, we see little impact from its dependence on intercarrier compensation that, in our view, undeservedly pressured the stock in late 2008.

▶ Risks to our recommendation and target price include increased cable telephony competition, federal or state regulatory changes that pressure cash flow, and inability to support the dividend.

▶ Using a projected P/E of 12.5X our 2010 EPS estimate and an enterprise value/EBITDA multiple of 6.4X, in line with rural telecom peers with similar operating structures, we have a 12-month target price of $12. At our target price, WIN's dividend yield would still be an above-average 8.3%.

Qualitative Risk Assessment

LOW	MEDIUM	HIGH

Our risk assessment reflects the stable rural markets that WIN serves and our view of its lower-than-peer debt leverage, offset by potential risks in integrating acquisitions.

Quantitative Evaluations

S&P Quality Ranking NR

D	C	B-	B	B+	A-	A	A+

Relative Strength Rank STRONG
74
LOWEST = 1   HIGHEST = 99

Revenue/Earnings Data

Revenue (Million $)

	1Q	2Q	3Q	4Q	Year
2009	755.0	752.9	734.3	--	--
2008	811.7	799.9	794.1	777.5	3,172
2007	783.7	826.7	822.6	827.8	3,261
2006	703.0	125.5	771.4	827.6	3,033
2005	712.6	736.5	728.9	745.5	3,414
2004	--	--	--	--	2,934

Earnings Per Share ($)

2009	0.20	0.21	0.18	E0.22	E0.86
2008	0.28	0.27	0.24	0.21	0.98
2007	0.21	0.24	0.25	1.25	1.94
2006	--	0.22	0.21	0.25	1.02
2005	--	--	0.27	0.23	0.83
2004	--	--	--	--	0.96

Fiscal year ended Dec. 31. Next earnings report expected: Early February. EPS Estimates based on S&P Operating Earnings; historical GAAP earnings are as reported.

Dividend Data (Dates: mm/dd Payment Date: mm/dd/yy)

Amount ($)	Date Decl.	Ex-Div. Date	Stk. of Record	Payment Date
0.250	02/03	03/27	03/31	04/15/09
0.250	05/06	06/26	06/30	07/15/09
0.250	08/05	09/28	09/30	10/15/09
0.250	11/04	12/29	12/31	01/15/10

Dividends have been paid since 2006. Source: Company reports.

Please read the Required Disclosures and Analyst Certification on the last page of this report.

The McGraw-Hill Companies

Windstream Corp

STANDARD
&POOR'S

Business Summary November 12, 2009

CORPORATE OVERVIEW. In July 2006, Alltel Corp spun off its wireline operations into a separate entity. Immediately after the consummation of the tax free spin-off, the entity merged with Valor Communications, and the resulting company was renamed Windstream Corporation. As of September 2009, WIN had 2.9 million access lines, including lines that were previously part of CT Communications, which was acquired in August 2007. The company also had just under 2 million long distance customers and 1.1 million broadband customers (36% of total access lines and 53% of primarily residential lines), up 9% from a year earlier. WIN operates primarily in rural markets in the southern U.S., such as Lexington, KY, and Lincoln, NE, with an average of about 20 access lines per square mile.

During most of 2007, WIN operated a directory publication business. In November 2007, it completed the sale of its directory operations to a private equity firm for $525 million in a tax-free transaction that led to $210 million in debt retirement.

CORPORATE STRATEGY. Since becoming a public company, WIN has looked to make small acquisitions and benefit from expense savings (consolidating call centers and IT systems) and expanding service bundles via broadband and digital TV. In addition to CT Communications, WIN completed its acquisition of D&E Communications (114,000 incumbent access lines) in November 2009. Also during the second half of 2009, WIN announced deals, pending

necessary approvals, to acquire Lexcom Inc. (23,0000 lines) and NuVox, which offers phone services to business customers.

WIN provides a wholesale satellite TV product from Echostar with 322,000 customers (up 28% from a year earlier), to retain its wireline customers and improve revenue per customer. During 2009, WIN also has had success in upgrading existing DSL customers with higher-speed offerings and was offering 12 Mbps of broadband service, 10 times the speed of traditional DSL service, in certain markets. At the end of September 2009, WIN's average monthly revenue per household was $80, up fractionally from a year earlier. In 2008, WIN also began to target customers who did not have a wireline phone and recommended its broadband product.

COMPETITIVE LANDSCAPE. We believe that WIN's access lines count, which fell 5.1% in the 12 months ended September 2009, has declined amid increased competition. Wireless coverage in rural markets has improved over the past couple of years, and we think that many of these customers have dropped their landlines. However, the line loss has improved since earlier in 2009 and is less severe than peers.

Company Financials Fiscal Year Ended Dec. 31

Per Share Data ($)	2008	2007	2006	2005	2004	2003	2002	2001	2000	1999
Tangible Book Value	NM	NM	NM	NM	NA	NA	NA	NA	NA	NA
Cash Flow	2.10	3.08	1.88	2.08	NA	NA	NA	NA	NA	NA
Earnings	0.98	1.94	1.02	0.83	0.96	NA	NA	NA	NA	NA
S&P Core Earnings	0.87	0.98	0.95	0.80	0.80	NA	NA	NA	NA	NA
Dividends	1.00	1.00	0.38	NA	NA	NA	NA	NA	NA	NA
Payout Ratio	102%	52%	37%	NA	NA	NA	NA	NA	NA	NA
Prices:High	14.05	15.63	14.43	NA	NA	NA	NA	NA	NA	NA
Prices:Low	6.37	12.38	11.13	NA	NA	NA	NA	NA	NA	NA
P/E Ratio:High	14	8	14	NA	NA	NA	NA	NA	NA	NA
P/E Ratio:Low	7	6	11	NA	NA	NA	NA	NA	NA	NA

Income Statement Analysis (Million $)										
Revenue	3,172	3,261	3,033	3,414	2,934	NA	NA	NA	NA	NA
Operating Income	1,646	1,705	1,398	1,617	NA	NA	NA	NA	NA	NA
Depreciation	493	540	450	593	509	NA	NA	NA	NA	NA
Interest Expense	416	443	210	391	35.6	NA	NA	NA	NA	NA
Pretax Income	718	1,169	722	662	646	NA	NA	NA	NA	NA
Effective Tax Rate	39.4%	21.6%	38.3%	40.5%	40.2%	NA	NA	NA	NA	NA
Net Income	435	917	446	394	386	NA	NA	NA	NA	NA
S&P Core Earnings	385	462	451	382	382	NA	NA	NA	NA	NA

Balance Sheet & Other Financial Data (Million $)										
Cash	297	72.0	387	119	NA	NA	NA	NA	NA	NA
Current Assets	709	498	877	533	NA	NA	NA	NA	NA	NA
Total Assets	8,009	8,211	8,031	7,751	NA	NA	NA	NA	NA	NA
Current Liabilities	665	641	685	459	NA	NA	NA	NA	NA	NA
Long Term Debt	5,358	5,331	5,456	5,525	NA	NA	NA	NA	NA	NA
Common Equity	252	700	470	533	NA	NA	NA	NA	NA	NA
Total Capital	6,681	7,137	6,917	7,064	NA	NA	NA	NA	NA	NA
Capital Expenditures	318	366	374	NA	338	NA	NA	NA	NA	NA
Cash Flow	928	1,457	895	987	NA	NA	NA	NA	NA	NA
Current Ratio	1.1	0.8	1.3	1.2	NA	NA	NA	NA	NA	NA
% Long Term Debt of Capitalization	80.2	74.7	78.9	78.2	Nil	NA	NA	NA	NA	NA
% Net Income of Revenue	13.7	28.1	14.7	11.5	13.2	NA	NA	NA	NA	NA
% Return on Assets	5.4	11.3	6.9	NA	NA	NA	NA	NA	NA	NA
% Return on Equity	91.4	156.8	22.5	NA	NA	NA	NA	NA	NA	NA

Data as orig reptd.; bef. results of disc opers/spec. items. Per share data adj. for stk. divs.; EPS diluted. E-Estimated. NA-Not Available. NM-Not Meaningful. NR-Not Ranked. UR-Under Review.

Office: 4001 N Rodney Parham Rd, Little Rock, AR 72212-2442.
Telephone: 501-748-7000.
Website: http://www.windstream.com
Chrmn: F.X. Frantz

Pres & CEO: J. Gardner
COO: B.K. Whittington
EVP, Secy & General Counsel: J.P. Fletcher
SVP & CIO: C.B. Nash

Investor Contact: M. Michaels (501-748-7578)
Board Members: C. Armitage, S. E. Beall, III, D. E. Foster, F. X. Frantz, J. Gardner, J. T. Hinson, J. K. Jones, W. A. Montgomery, F. E. Reed

Founded: 2000
Domicile: Delaware
Employees: 7,349

Wisconsin Energy Corp

S&P Recommendation HOLD ★★★☆☆	Price $45.02 (as of Nov 27, 2009)	12-Mo. Target Price $45.00	Investment Style Large-Cap Blend

GICS Sector Utilities
Sub-Industry Multi-Utilities

Summary This energy company serves more than 1.1 million electric customers in Wisconsin and Michigan's Upper Peninsula, and more than 1 million natural gas customers in Wisconsin.

Key Stock Statistics (Source S&P, Vickers, company reports)

52-Wk Range	$46.50– 36.31	S&P Oper. EPS 2009E	3.08	Market Capitalization(B)	$5.263	Beta	0.38
Trailing 12-Month EPS	$3.09	S&P Oper. EPS 2010E	3.73	Yield (%)	3.00	S&P 3-Yr. Proj. EPS CAGR(%)	8
Trailing 12-Month P/E	14.6	P/E on S&P Oper. EPS 2009E	14.6	Dividend Rate/Share	$1.35	S&P Credit Rating	BBB+
$10K Invested 5 Yrs Ago	$14,816	Common Shares Outstg. (M)	116.9	Institutional Ownership (%)	68		

Price Performance

30-Week Mov. Avg. · · · · 10-Week Mov. Avg. – – GAAP Earnings vs. Previous Year   Volume Above Avg. STARS
12-Mo. Target Price — Relative Strength — ▲ Up ▼ Down ▶ No Change   Below Avg. ★

Analysis prepared by **Justin McCann** on November 20, 2009, when the stock traded at **$ 44.62**.

Qualitative Risk Assessment

LOW	MEDIUM	HIGH

Our risk assessment reflects our view of the company's strong and steady cash flow from the regulated electric and gas utility operations, and a regulatory environment that has historically been supportive. We believe this is only partially offset by the higher risk profile of the company's non-regulated power generating subsidiary, as well as by the high level of capital expenditures the company expects to incur over the next five years.

Quantitative Evaluations

S&P Quality Ranking B+

D	C	B-	B	B+	A-	A	A+

Relative Strength Rank MODERATE

58

LOWEST = 1   HIGHEST = 99

Highlights

► We expect operating EPS in 2009 to increase only slightly from 2008's $3.03. Operating results in 2009 should benefit from a full year of the Port Washington generating unit and the Blue Sky wind farm, each of which went into operation in May 2008. Although we expect earnings to be restricted by a decline in electric sales to commercial and industrial customers due to a very mild summer and the downturn in the economy, this should be partially offset by a decline in fuel and purchased power costs, and other operating expenses.

► For 2010, we expect operating EPS to grow about 20% from projected results for 2009, due to anticipated increases in electric and gas rates, and the new power plants that are expected to come on line at the end of 2009 and in August 2010. We also expect results to benefit from a gradual recovery in the local economy.

► Under WEC's revised dividend policy, approved by directors in December 2008, the company plans to target a dividend payout ratio of between 40% and 45% of earnings for the years 2009 through 2011. After 2011, directors plan to target a payout ratio of 45% to 50%.

Investment Rationale/Risk

► With the shares up nearly 7% year to date, the stock has outperformed WEC's electric utility peers, but underperformed the company's gas utility peers. The yield from WEC's recently increased dividend (3.0%) and its dividend payout ratio (45% of 2008 operating EPS) are still well below those of peers (4.8% and 60%, respectively), but we expect that the company's new dividend policy will result in dividend increases in the next couple of years. We would hold the shares for their total return potential.

► Risks to our investment recommendation and target price include significant delays in bringing the new power plants into operation, which could result in sharply higher costs, and unfavorable regulatory rulings.

► The company increased its dividend 25% with the March 2009 payment, and has announced a new policy under which it plans to raise the annual dividend at a rate of about half that of its EPS growth. Our 12-month target price is $45, reflecting a modest premium-to-peers P/E of 12X our EPS estimate for 2010.

Revenue/Earnings Data

Revenue (Million $)

	1Q	2Q	3Q	4Q	Year
2009	1,396	842.5	821.9	--	--
2008	1,432	946.1	852.5	1,201	4,431
2007	1,301	906.5	881.5	1,149	4,238
2006	1,247	814.4	839.8	1,095	3,996
2005	1,095	788.5	797.3	1,135	3,816
2004	1,066	716.4	696.6	952.0	3,431

Earnings Per Share ($)

	1Q	2Q	3Q	4Q	Year
2009	1.20	0.54	0.50	E0.84	E3.08
2008	1.04	0.49	0.65	0.85	3.03
2007	0.85	0.49	0.70	0.80	2.84
2006	0.88	0.50	0.60	0.65	2.64
2005	0.76	0.48	0.56	0.77	2.56
2004	0.69	0.17	-0.56	0.73	1.03

Fiscal year ended Dec. 31. Next earnings report expected: Early February. EPS Estimates based on S&P Operating Earnings; historical GAAP earnings are as reported.

Dividend Data (Dates: mm/dd Payment Date: mm/dd/yy)

Amount ($)	Date Decl.	Ex-Div. Date	Stk. of Record	Payment Date
0.338	12/04	02/11	02/13	03/01/09
0.338	04/23	05/12	05/14	06/01/09
0.338	07/23	08/12	08/14	09/01/09
0.338	10/15	11/10	11/13	12/01/09

Dividends have been paid since 1939. Source: Company reports.

Please read the Required Disclosures and Analyst Certification on the last page of this report.

Wisconsin Energy Corp

Business Summary November 20, 2009

CORPORATE OVERVIEW. Wisconsin Energy Corporation (WEC) is a holding company that primarily operates in two segments: utility energy and non-utility energy. The principal utilities (under the trade name We Energies) are Wisconsin Electric Power Company and Wisconsin Gas LLC). On October 29, 2009, WEC announced that it had reached a definitive agreement to sell the Edison Sault Electric Company for $61.5 million. WEC's non-regulated segment consists primarily of We Power, which was formed to design, construct, own and lease to Wisconsin Electric the new generating capacity included in the company's "Power the Future" strategy. In 2008, utility operations contributed 99.85% of total operating revenues.

CORPORATE STRATEGY. WEC's goal is to strengthen its utility business through the development of a reliable power supply and the upgrade of its infrastructure, and to continue the divestiture of its non-energy and real estate operations. The company has initiated its "Power the Future" strategy, which is expected to significantly improve the supply and reliability of power. The company has invested in four new electric generation facilities (two of which have been completed) and is also upgrading the existing ones. The strategy also includes an upgrade of existing distribution facilities. WEC is working to achieve operational synergies by integrating the businesses of Wisconsin Electric and Wisconsin Gas, which it believes will result in improved customer satisfaction.

MARKET PROFILE. In 2008, We Energies served nearly 1.14 million electric customers in Wisconsin and (through its Edison Sault unit) the Upper Peninsula of Michigan, nearly 1.06 million gas customers in Wisconsin, around 3,060 water customers in Milwaukee, and about 465 steam customers in Milwaukee. Over the next five years, WEC estimates that the utility energy segment in the service territories will grow at an annual rate of 0.25% to 0.75%; annual peak electric demand is projected to grow at a rate of 1.0% to 1.5%. In 2008, residential customers accounted for 36.4% of electric utility revenues; small commercial/industrial customers 33.2%; large commercial and industrial users 24.5%; other retail 0.8%; other wholesale 2.2%; resale-utilities 1.4%; and other 1.5%. Residential customers accounted for 62.4% of gas utility revenues in 2008; commercial/industrial customers, 33.8%; transported gas, 2.8%; and other, 0.9%. In 2008, coal accounted for 56.7% of the company's total fuel sources; purchased power 35.8%; natural gas 5.5%; hydroelectric 1.4%; and wind 0.6%.

Company Financials Fiscal Year Ended Dec. 31

Per Share Data ($)	2008	2007	2006	2005	2004	2003	2002	2001	2000	1999
Tangible Book Value	24.76	22.72	20.92	0.71	17.53	12.86	11.26	10.61	10.03	16.89
Earnings	3.03	2.84	2.64	2.56	1.03	2.06	1.44	1.77	1.27	1.79
S&P Core Earnings	-0.16	2.70	2.70	2.55	0.84	1.97	0.93	1.19	NA	NA
Dividends	1.08	1.00	0.92	0.88	0.83	0.80	0.80	0.80	1.37	1.56
Payout Ratio	36%	35%	35%	34%	81%	39%	56%	45%	108%	87%
Prices:High	49.61	50.48	48.70	40.83	34.60	33.68	26.48	24.62	23.56	31.56
Prices:Low	34.89	41.06	38.16	33.35	29.50	22.56	20.17	19.13	16.81	19.06
P/E Ratio:High	16	18	18	16	34	16	18	14	19	18
P/E Ratio:Low	12	14	14	13	29	11	14	11	13	11

Income Statement Analysis (Million $)										
Revenue	4,431	4,238	3,996	3,816	3,431	4,054	3,736	3,929	3,355	2,273
Depreciation	332	328	326	332	327	332	321	342	336	270
Maintenance	NA	NA	NA	NA	NA	NA	NA	NA	NA	NA
Fixed Charges Coverage	4.41	4.00	3.60	3.61	2.64	2.68	2.03	2.17	1.64	2.68
Construction Credits	NA	NA	NA	NA	2.80	18.6	11.2	15.2	16.2	13.3
Effective Tax Rate	37.7%	39.1%	35.9%	33.0%	39.7%	35.6%	38.8%	41.9%	44.9%	34.7%
Net Income	359	337	313	304	122	244	167	209	154	209
S&P Core Earnings	-18.7	320	319	302	98.5	233	108	142	NA	NA

Balance Sheet & Other Financial Data (Million $)										
Gross Property	11,832	10,805	10,476	9,651	9,025	9,017	8,406	8,014	8,065	6,969
Capital Expenditures	1,137	1,212	929	745	637	659	557	672	611	518
Net Property	8,517	7,681	7,053	6,363	5,903	5,926	4,399	4,188	4,152	3,719
Capitalization:Long Term Debt	4,105	3,203	3,104	3,061	3,270	3,605	3,261	3,468	2,933	2,365
Capitalization:% Long Term Debt	55.2	50.8	51.8	50.9	55.3	60.1	60.4	62.8	59.3	54.1
Capitalization:Preferred	Nil	Nil	Nil	Nil	Nil	Nil	Nil	Nil	Nil	Nil
Capitalization:% Preferred	Nil	Nil	Nil	Nil	Nil	Nil	Nil	Nil	Nil	Nil
Capitalization:Common	3,337	3,099	2,889	2,955	2,645	2,393	2,139	2,056	2,017	2,008
Capitalization:% Common	44.8	49.2	48.2	49.1	44.7	39.9	39.6	37.2	40.7	45.9
Total Capital	8,298	6,902	6,618	6,666	6,507	6,712	6,039	6,147	5,617	5,078
% Operating Ratio	90.0	90.4	90.2	89.2	86.9	88.6	86.8	88.4	90.5	84.8
% Earned on Net Property	8.2	8.4	8.5	9.2	6.5	9.6	10.7	14.5	11.1	9.7
% Return on Revenue	8.1	7.9	7.8	8.0	3.6	6.0	4.5	5.3	4.6	9.2
% Return on Invested Capital	6.1	6.8	7.5	7.2	7.1	8.1	13.6	8.0	7.9	7.9
% Return on Common Equity	11.1	11.2	11.2	10.8	4.9	10.5	8.0	10.2	7.7	10.7

Data as orig reptd.; bef. results of disc opers/spec. items. Per share data adj. for stk. divs.; EPS diluted. E-Estimated. NA-Not Available. NM-Not Meaningful. NR-Not Ranked. UR-Under Review.

Office: 231 West Michigan Street, Milwaukee, WI 53201.
Telephone: 414-221-2345.
Website: http://www.wisconsinenergy.com
Chrmn, Pres & CEO: G.E. Klappa

EVP & CFO: A.L. Leverett
EVP & General Counsel: J. Fleming
SVP & Chief Admin Officer: K.A. Rappe
Chief Acctg Officer & Cntlr: S.P. Dickson

Investor Contact: C.F. Henderson (414-221-2592)
Board Members: J. F. Bergstrom, B. L. Bowles, P. W. Chadwick, R. A. Cornog, C. S. Culver, T. Fischer, G. E. Klappa, U. Payne, C. P. Stratton, Jr.

Founded: 1981
Domicile: Wisconsin
Employees: 4,935

Wyndham Worldwide Corp

STANDARD &POOR'S

S&P Recommendation	**STRONG SELL** ★☆☆☆☆	Price	12-Mo. Target Price	Investment Style
		$18.56 (as of Nov 27, 2009)	$8.00	Large-Cap Blend

GICS Sector Consumer Discretionary
Sub-Industry Hotels, Resorts & Cruise Lines

Summary This company's operations include the sale of interests in vacation ownership resorts; facilitating the exchange and rental of access to vacation properties; and the franchising of hotels.

Key Stock Statistics (Source S&P, Vickers, company reports)

52-Wk Range	$19.98–2.77	S&P Oper. EPS 2009E	1.45	Market Capitalization(B)	$3.315	Beta	3.61
Trailing 12-Month EPS	$-6.40	S&P Oper. EPS 2010E	1.00	Yield (%)	0.86	S&P 3-Yr. Proj. EPS CAGR(%)	-23
Trailing 12-Month P/E	NM	P/E on S&P Oper. EPS 2009E	12.8	Dividend Rate/Share	$0.16	S&P Credit Rating	BBB-
$10K Invested 5 Yrs Ago	NA	Common Shares Outstg. (M)	178.6	Institutional Ownership (%)	NM		

Price Performance

30-Week Mov. Avg. · · · 10-Week Mov. Avg. – – **GAAP Earnings vs. Previous Year** Volume Above Avg. STARS
12-Mo. Target Price — Relative Strength — ▲ Up ▼ Down ► No Change Below Avg. ★

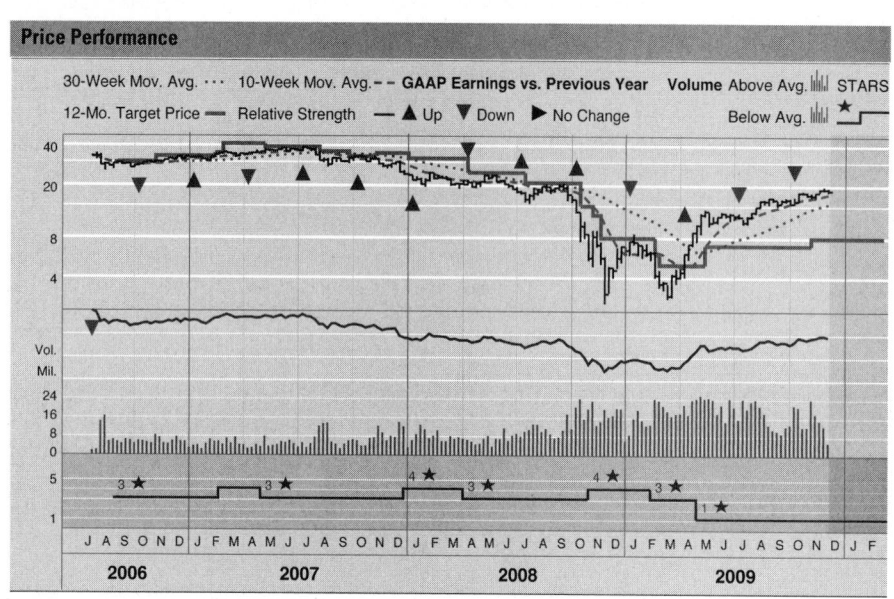

Options: CBOE, Ph

Analysis prepared by **Mark S. Basham** on November 10, 2009, when the stock traded at **$ 18.61**.

Highlights

▶ We believe trends across all operating segments will remain weak into 2010. For 2009, we see gross timeshare contract sales falling 38%, but expect net timeshare segment revenues to decline 17%, reflecting recognition of $190 million of deferred revenues. Consumer financing income will likely be 2% higher, due to higher interest rates offset by greater loan losses. Revenues in the exchange and rental segment are likely to fall 11%, by our analysis. In the lodging segment, we project a 13% decline.

▶ We estimate that even after personnel and other cost cuts, operating EPS will decline to $1.45 in 2009 from $1.78 in 2008. Results for 2008 exclude impairments of $1.4 billion, or $7.83 a share. Our estimates are not adjusted to exclude certain legacy items, forex conversion, and other items that are of a recurring nature.

▶ We expect 2010 to be a year in which all three segments are more likely than not to experience more stable operations. Because we expect WYN to recognize a smaller amount of deferred timeshare revenues, but a greater amount of interest expense, we look for EPS to decline to $1.00.

Investment Rationale/Risk

▶ Our Strong Sell opinion reflects our view that the stock is overvalued after the share price rise since the S&P 500 bottomed in early March. We believe that lodging industry fundamentals will likely deteriorate modestly in 2010, with a recovery not until 2012 at the earliest. Although the cost reductions WYN has achieved may serve it well through the downturn, we think substantial operating and financial risks remain.

▶ Risks to our recommendation and target price include a quick positive turnaround in consumer confidence and a related boost to vacation spending. Also, future travel activity could be aided by lower fuel costs compared to 2008.

▶ We believe the stock should have a slightly lower P/E and enterprise value-to-EBITDA multiple than some lodging industry peers in our coverage universe given the company's higher revenue mix of vacation exchange, ownership sales and financing, as well as legacy tax liabilities. Our 12-month target price of $8 reflects an enterprise value/EBITDA multiple of 8.5X applied to our 2010 EBITDA estimate of $595 million.

Qualitative Risk Assessment

LOW	MEDIUM	HIGH

Our risk assessment reflects our view that the company's business is sensitive to changes in consumer confidence and hotel room demand, as well as the receptivity of credit markets to its securitized vacation ownership receivables.

Quantitative Evaluations

S&P Quality Ranking NR

D	C	B-	B	B+	A-	A	A+

Relative Strength Rank STRONG

85

LOWEST = 1 HIGHEST = 99

Revenue/Earnings Data

Revenue (Million $)

	1Q	2Q	3Q	4Q	Year
2009	901.0	920.0	1,016	--	--
2008	1,012	1,132	1,226	911.0	4,281
2007	1,012	1,100	1,216	1,032	4,360
2006	870.0	955.0	1,047	970.0	3,842
2005	795.0	867.0	948.0	861.0	3,471
2004	--	--	--	--	3,014

Earnings Per Share ($)

	1Q	2Q	3Q	4Q	Year
2009	0.25	0.39	0.57	E0.24	E1.45
2008	0.24	0.55	0.80	-7.62	-6.03
2007	0.45	0.52	0.65	0.59	2.20
2006	0.46	0.37	0.45	0.48	1.77
2005	--	0.44	0.61	0.46	1.73
2004	--	--	--	--	--

Fiscal year ended Dec. 31. Next earnings report expected: Mid February. EPS Estimates based on S&P Operating Earnings; historical GAAP earnings are as reported.

Dividend Data (Dates: mm/dd Payment Date: mm/dd/yy)

Amount ($)	Date Decl.	Ex-Div. Date	Stk. of Record	Payment Date
0.040	02/19	02/24	02/26	03/13/09
0.040	05/13	05/26	05/28	06/12/09
0.040	07/24	08/25	08/27	09/11/09
0.040	10/22	11/20	11/24	12/10/09

Dividends have been paid since 2007. Source: Company reports.

Please read the Required Disclosures and Analyst Certification on the last page of this report.

The **McGraw-Hill** Companies

Wyndham Worldwide Corp

STANDARD &POOR'S

Business Summary November 10, 2009

CORPORATE OVERVIEW. Wyndham Worldwide (WYN) operates lodging, vacation exchange and rental, and vacation ownership businesses.

The Wyndham Hotel Group franchises hotels in various segments of the lodging industry under brands such as Super 8, Days Inn, Ramada, Travelodge, and Wyndham Hotels. As of December 31, 2008, WYN's lodging business had 7,043 franchised hotels with 592,900 rooms in operation. As of December 31, 2008, there were also about 990 hotels with about 111,000 rooms in the development pipeline, of which 55% represented new construction and 42% were in international markets.

On July 21, 2008, WYN acquired U.S. Franchise Systems, Inc. for $131 million. Previously part of the Hyatt hotel business, U.S. Franchise Systems includes the Microtel Inns & Suites and Hawthorn Suites brands. At the time of purchase, the Microtel system included 298 all new construction economy hotels with 35 more under construction, and the Hawthorn chain was comprised of 91, all-suites, extended-stay hotels.

Wyndham Exchange and Rentals (previously Group RCI) provides vacation exchange products and services to developers, managers and owners of intervals of vacation ownership interests, and markets vacation rental properties.

WYN's vacation exchange and rental business has access for specified periods, often on an exclusive basis, to about 73,000 vacation properties located in 100 countries. Membership as of December 31, 2008, was nearly 3.7 million.

Wyndham Vacation Ownership markets and sells vacation ownership interests, provides consumer financing in connection with the purchase by individuals of vacation ownership interests, manages properties for property owners' associations, and develops and acquires vacation ownership resorts. It operates principally under its two primary brands, Wyndham Vacation Resorts and WorldMark by Wyndham. WYN has developed or acquired just over 150 vacation ownership resorts in North America, the Caribbean and the South Pacific that serve over 830,000 owners of vacation ownership and other real estate interests. WYN's sales of vacation ownership interests totaled $2.0 billion in 2008, unchanged from 2007. Inventory of unsold interests was approximately $1.3 billion as of December 31, 2008.

Company Financials Fiscal Year Ended Dec. 31

Per Share Data ($)	2008	2007	2006	2005	2004	2003	2002	2001	2000	1999
Tangible Book Value	NM	NM	NM	NM	NA	NA	NA	NA	NA	NA
Cash Flow	-5.00	2.96	2.63	2.37	NA	NA	NA	NA	NA	NA
Earnings	-6.03	2.20	1.77	1.73	NA	NA	NA	NA	NA	NA
S&P Core Earnings	1.47	2.20	1.75	1.97	NA	NA	NA	NA	NA	NA
Dividends	0.16	0.08	Nil	Nil	NA	NA	NA	NA	NA	NA
Payout Ratio	NM	4%	Nil	Nil	NA	NA	NA	NA	NA	NA
Prices:High	25.00	39.40	34.87	NA	NA	NA	NA	NA	NA	NA
Prices:Low	2.55	23.28	25.48	NA	NA	NA	NA	NA	NA	NA
P/E Ratio:High	NM	18	20	NA	NA	NA	NA	NA	NA	NA
P/E Ratio:Low	NM	11	14	NA	NA	NA	NA	NA	NA	NA

Income Statement Analysis (Million $)	2008	2007	2006	2005	2004	2003	2002	2001	2000	1999
Revenue	4,281	4,360	3,842	3,471	3,014	2,652	NA	NA	NA	NA
Operating Income	865	821	824	699	NA	NA	NA	NA	NA	NA
Depreciation	184	139	148	135	119	107	NA	NA	NA	NA
Interest Expense	99.0	96.0	67.0	41.0	NA	NA	NA	NA	NA	NA
Pretax Income	-887	655	542	523	587	500	NA	NA	NA	NA
Effective Tax Rate	NM	38.5%	35.1%	29.8%	39.9%	37.2%	NA	NA	NA	NA
Net Income	-1,074	403	352	367	349	299	NA	NA	NA	NA
S&P Core Earnings	261	404	352	419	NA	NA	NA	NA	NA	NA

Balance Sheet & Other Financial Data (Million $)	2008	2007	2006	2005	2004	2003	2002	2001	2000	1999
Cash	136	276	269	106	94.0	NA	NA	NA	NA	NA
Current Assets	1,914	2,056	2,052	1,874	NA	NA	NA	NA	NA	NA
Total Assets	9,573	10,459	9,520	8,590	8,343	NA	NA	NA	NA	NA
Current Liabilities	2,169	2,180	1,977	2,212	NA	NA	NA	NA	NA	NA
Long Term Debt	3,331	3,195	1,322	1,733	1,478	NA	NA	NA	NA	NA
Common Equity	2,342	3,516	3,559	3,464	4,679	NA	NA	NA	NA	NA
Total Capital	6,136	7,638	5,663	5,987	6,447	NA	NA	NA	NA	NA
Capital Expenditures	187	194	191	134	116	102	NA	NA	NA	NA
Cash Flow	-890	542	500	502	NA	NA	NA	NA	NA	NA
Current Ratio	0.9	0.9	1.0	0.9	1.8	NA	NA	NA	NA	NA
% Long Term Debt of Capitalization	54.3	41.8	23.3	28.9	22.9	Nil	NA	NA	NA	NA
% Net Income of Revenue	NM	9.2	9.2	10.5	11.6	11.3	NA	NA	NA	NA
% Return on Assets	NM	4.0	3.8	NA	NA	NA	NA	NA	NA	NA
% Return on Equity	NM	11.4	8.2	NA	NA	NA	NA	NA	NA	NA

Data as orig reptd.; bef. results of disc opers/spec. items. Per share data adj. for stk. divs.; EPS diluted. E-Estimated. NA-Not Available. NM-Not Meaningful. NR-Not Ranked. UR-Under Review.

Office: 22 Sylvan Wy, Parsippany, NJ 07054.
Telephone: 973-753-6000.
Website: http://www.wyndhamworldwide.com
Chrmn & CEO: S.P. Holmes

EVP & CFO: T.G. Conforti
EVP & General Counsel: S.G. McLester
SVP & Chief Acctg Officer: N. Rossi
SVP & Secy: L.A. Feldman

Investor Contact: M. Happer (973-753-5500)
Board Members: M. J. Biblowit, J. E. Buckman, G. Herrera, S. P. Holmes, B. R. Mulroney, P. Richards, M. H. Wargotz

Founded: 2003
Domicile: Delaware
Employees: 27,000

The McGraw-Hill Companies

Wynn Resorts Ltd

STANDARD &POOR'S

S&P Recommendation	HOLD ★★★☆☆	Price $62.98 (as of Nov 27, 2009)	12-Mo. Target Price $61.00	Investment Style Large-Cap Growth

GICS Sector Consumer Discretionary
Sub-Industry Casinos & Gaming

Summary This company is involved in the design, development, financing and construction of gaming projects in Las Vegas and Macau.

Key Stock Statistics (Source S&P, Vickers, company reports)

52-Wk Range	$74.90– 14.50	S&P Oper. EPS 2009**E**	0.30	Market Capitalization(B)	$7.754	Beta	2.89
Trailing 12-Month EPS	$-1.15	S&P Oper. EPS 2010**E**	0.76	Yield (%)	1.27	S&P 3-Yr. Proj. EPS CAGR(%)	NM
Trailing 12-Month P/E	NM	P/E on S&P Oper. EPS 2009**E**	NM	Dividend Rate/Share	$0.80	S&P Credit Rating	BB
$10K Invested 5 Yrs Ago	$12,582	Common Shares Outstg. (M)	123.1	Institutional Ownership (%)	70		

Price Performance

30-Week Mov. Avg. · · · 10-Week Mov. Avg. - - **GAAP Earnings vs. Previous Year** Volume Above Avg. STARS
12-Mo. Target Price — Relative Strength — ▲ Up ▼ Down ► No Change Below Avg.

Options: ASE, CBOE, P, Ph

Analysis prepared by **Esther Y. Kwon, CFA** on October 27, 2009, when the stock traded at **$ 56.34**.

Highlights

▸ We look for net revenue in 2009 to be up slightly from the $3.0 billion reported for 2008, including a full year's results from the Encore Las Vegas, which opened in late 2008, with a 2,034-room all-suite hotel, an approximately 72,000 square foot casino, and 12 food and beverage outlets. Domestically, we project revenue to be pressured by increased price competition and lower spend per visit. In Macau, we forecast revenue declines with stabilization late in 2009. In 2010, we project revenue growth of about 7%.

▸ On cost reduction initiatives, such as pay, work weeks, elimination of bonus accruals, and suspension of 401(k) matches, we project savings of about $90 million on an annual basis. We estimate approximately $40 million in savings on similar moves in Macau. We see EBITDA about flat as strong second half improvement offsets weak results in the first half of 2009. In 2010, we estimate higher EBITDA, driven by the opening of the Encore in Macau.

▸ Before special items, with more shares outstanding and higher depreciation charges, we see EPS of $0.30 in 2009, down significantly from 2008's EPS of $2.49. In 2010, we forecast EPS of $0.76.

Investment Rationale/Risk

▸ We see WYNN's results benefiting from strength in its Macau operations, which we estimate will account for over 60% of 2010 total property EBITDA. With easing travel restrictions and easier comparisons in the second half of 2009 in Macau, we believe the Macau segment results will more than offset lackluster Las Vegas performance. We view favorably the relative strength of WYNN's balance sheet, which we saw further strengthened by a successful Hong Kong share listing in October.

▸ Risks to our opinion and target price include the possibility that expected profit contributions from Macau will be less favorable than we anticipate, or that Las Vegas properties experience an accelerated decline in room revenue or gaming handle.

▸ Our 12-month target price of $61 is based on an EV/EBITDA multiple of about 16X our 2010 EBITDA estimate, a premium to gaming peers and to the historical average. We believe a higher than peer multiple is warranted based on WYNN's large exposure to the Macau market, which we see as having better prospects over the long term, and what we view as its solid balance sheet compared to peers.

Qualitative Risk Assessment

LOW	MEDIUM	HIGH

In our view, there is likely to be an opportunity for additional expansion by WYNN in Macau. However, we see uncertainty surrounding the regulatory environment there and the extent to which demand in that market will develop, adding to risk.

Quantitative Evaluations

S&P Quality Ranking NR

D	C	B-	B	B+	A-	A	A+

Relative Strength Rank MODERATE

65

LOWEST = 1   HIGHEST = 99

Revenue/Earnings Data

Revenue (Million $)

	1Q	2Q	3Q	4Q	Year
2009	740.0	723.3	773.1	--	--
2008	778.7	825.2	769.2	614.3	2,987
2007	635.3	687.5	653.4	711.3	2,688
2006	277.2	273.4	318.1	563.6	1,432
2005	Nil	201.1	251.4	269.4	722.0
2004	0.14	0.06	Nil	Nil	0.20

Earnings Per Share ($)

2009	-0.30	0.21	0.28	E0.15	E0.30
2008	0.41	2.42	0.49	-1.49	1.92
2007	0.54	0.82	0.41	0.57	2.34
2006	-0.12	-0.20	6.43	-0.51	6.24
2005	-0.30	-0.43	-0.09	-0.10	-0.92
2004	-0.16	-0.49	-0.26	-1.31	-2.37

Fiscal year ended Dec. 31. Next earnings report expected: Late February. EPS Estimates based on S&P Operating Earnings; historical GAAP earnings are as reported.

Dividend Data (Dates: mm/dd Payment Date: mm/dd/yy)

Amount ($)	Date Decl.	Ex-Div. Date	Stk. of Record	Payment Date
4.0 Spl.	11/09	11/17	11/19	12/08/09

Dividends have been paid since 2006. Source: Company reports.

Please read the Required Disclosures and Analyst Certification on the last page of this report.

The McGraw-Hill Companies

Wynn Resorts Ltd

STANDARD
&POOR'S

Business Summary October 27, 2009

CORPORATE OVERVIEW. Wynn Resorts is involved in the design, development, financing and construction of gaming projects in Las Vegas and Macau. The company's first such project, Wynn Las Vegas, opened in April 2005. We believe that the cost of this project was about $2.7 billion.

Wynn Las Vegas, which occupies about 215 acres of land, includes about 2,716 guest rooms and suites, an approximate 111,000 sq. ft. casino, 22 food and beverage outlets, an 18-hole golf course, about 223,000 sq. ft. of meeting space, a Ferrari and Maserati dealership, and about 76,000 sq. ft. of retail space.

The company also operates the Encore at Wynn Las Vegas, which includes about 2,034 guest rooms, suites or villas, plus additional gaming, entertainment and other facilities. In February 2007, WYNN said that the Encore project had an estimated cost of about $2.1 billion.

In China, the company is operating Wynn Macau under a 20-year concession agreement with the government of Macau. The initial stage of Wynn Macau opened in September 2006, and included about 600 hotel rooms or suites, about 100,000 sq. ft. of gaming space, seven restaurants, and additional facilities. A second phase included additional casino space and other facilities. We believe that Wynn Macau, including the second phase, had a project budget of about $1.2 billion. This excludes Wynn Diamond Suites, a resort hotel for which WYNN is developing plans, which is expected to be a further expansion of Wynn Macau. Also, the company has submitted an application for a land concession on 52 acres in Macau's Cotai Strip area, where we expect additional WYNN-related development could occur. There are a limited number of companies with casino operating rights in Macau.

Company Financials Fiscal Year Ended Dec. 31

Per Share Data ($)	2008	2007	2006	2005	2004	2003	2002	2001	2000	1999
Tangible Book Value	13.75	16.79	14.75	14.16	15.64	11.38	11.70	12.92	NA	NA
Cash Flow	4.32	4.24	7.20	0.13	-2.29	-0.54	-0.49	-0.25	NA	NA
Earnings	1.92	2.34	6.24	-0.92	-2.37	-0.62	-0.68	-0.45	-79.62	NA
S&P Core Earnings	1.92	2.29	1.00	-1.00	-2.41	-0.64	-0.69	-84.35	NA	NA
Dividends	Nil	6.00	6.00	Nil	Nil	Nil	Nil	NA	NA	NA
Payout Ratio	Nil	256%	96%	Nil	Nil	Nil	Nil	NA	NA	NA
Prices:High	124.77	176.14	98.45	76.45	72.99	28.61	14.39	NA	NA	NA
Prices:Low	28.06	85.53	52.44	42.06	27.50	12.76	10.76	NA	NA	NA
P/E Ratio:High	65	75	16	NM	NM	NM	NM	NA	NA	NA
P/E Ratio:Low	15	37	8	NM	NM	NM	NM	NA	NA	NA

Income Statement Analysis (Million $)										
Revenue	2,987	2,688	1,432	722	0.20	1.02	1.16	1.16	0.13	NA
Operating Income	608	708	249	77.5	-81.5	-46.9	-24.8	0.73	NA	NA
Depreciation	263	220	175	103	6.98	5.74	8.93	8.16	6.07	NA
Interest Expense	260	188	206	103	2.69	9.03	1.90	NA	NA	NA
Pretax Income	149	327	799	-90.8	-207	-45.8	-30.8	-17.7	-15.9	NA
Effective Tax Rate	NM	21.1%	21.3%	NM	NM	NM	NM	NM	NA	NA
Net Income	210	258	629	-90.8	-206	-48.9	-31.7	-17.7	-15.9	NA
S&P Core Earnings	210	252	44.1	-98.6	-210	-50.9	-32.0	-17.3	NA	NA

Balance Sheet & Other Financial Data (Million $)										
Cash	1,134	1,275	789	434	330	342	110	39.3	54.4	NA
Current Assets	1,411	1,582	1,096	685	451	402	112	NA	NA	NA
Total Assets	6,743	6,299	4,660	3,945	3,464	1,733	1,399	389	387	NA
Current Liabilities	724	585	511	270	170	71.2	20.7	NA	NA	NA
Long Term Debt	4,290	3,539	2,381	2,091	1,628	730	382	1,501	0.33	NA
Common Equity	1,593	1,948	1,646	1,563	1,644	1,002	992	972	382	NA
Total Capital	5,886	5,640	4,123	3,654	3,272	1,733	1,378	2,473	382	NA
Capital Expenditures	1,333	1,007	643	877	1,008	415	66.3	29.1	85.7	NA
Cash Flow	473	478	804	12.5	-199	-43.1	-22.8	-9.56	NA	NA
Current Ratio	2.0	2.7	2.1	2.5	2.7	5.7	5.4	10.4	11.8	NA
% Long Term Debt of Capitalization	72.9	62.8	57.7	57.2	49.8	42.1	27.7	0.1	0.1	NA
% Net Income of Revenue	7.0	9.6	43.9	NM	NM	NM	NM	NM	NM	NA
% Return on Assets	3.2	4.7	14.6	NM	NM	NM	NM	NM	NA	NA
% Return on Equity	11.9	14.4	39.2	NM	NM	NM	NM	NM	NA	NA

Data as orig reptd.; bef. results of disc opers/spec. items. Per share data adj. for stk. divs.; EPS diluted. E-Estimated. NA-Not Available. NM-Not Meaningful. NR-Not Ranked. UR-Under Review.

Office: 3131 Las Vegas Blvd S, Las Vegas, NV 89109.
Telephone: 702-733-4444.
Email: investorrelations@wynnresorts.com
Website: http://www.wynnresorts.com

Chrmn & CEO: S.A. Wynn
Vice Chrmn: K. Okada
COO: M.D. Schorr
Investor Contact: J. Strzemp (702-770-7555)

EVP & Chief Admin Officer: J. Strzemp
Board Members: L. Chen, R. Goldsmith, R. R. Irani, R. J. Miller, J. A. Moran, K. Okada, A. V. Shoemaker, D. B. Wayson, E. P. Wynn, S. A. Wynn, A. Zeman

Founded: 2002
Domicile: Nevada
Employees: 20,600

Xcel Energy Inc.

STANDARD & POOR'S

S&P Recommendation	**BUY** ★★★★☆	Price $20.19 (as of Nov 27, 2009)	12-Mo. Target Price $22.00	Investment Style Large-Cap Value

GICS Sector Utilities
Sub-Industry Multi-Utilities

Summary This energy holding company was created through the August 2000 merger of Northern States Power and New Century Energies.

Key Stock Statistics (Source S&P, Vickers, company reports)

52-Wk Range	$20.61–16.01	S&P Oper. EPS 2009E	1.47	Market Capitalization(B)	$9.220	Beta	0.43
Trailing 12-Month EPS	$1.48	S&P Oper. EPS 2010E	1.63	Yield (%)	4.85	S&P 3-Yr. Proj. EPS CAGR(%)	5
Trailing 12-Month P/E	13.6	P/E on S&P Oper. EPS 2009E	13.7	Dividend Rate/Share	$0.98	S&P Credit Rating	BBB+
$10K Invested 5 Yrs Ago	$13,868	Common Shares Outstg. (M)	456.6	Institutional Ownership (%)	58		

Price Performance

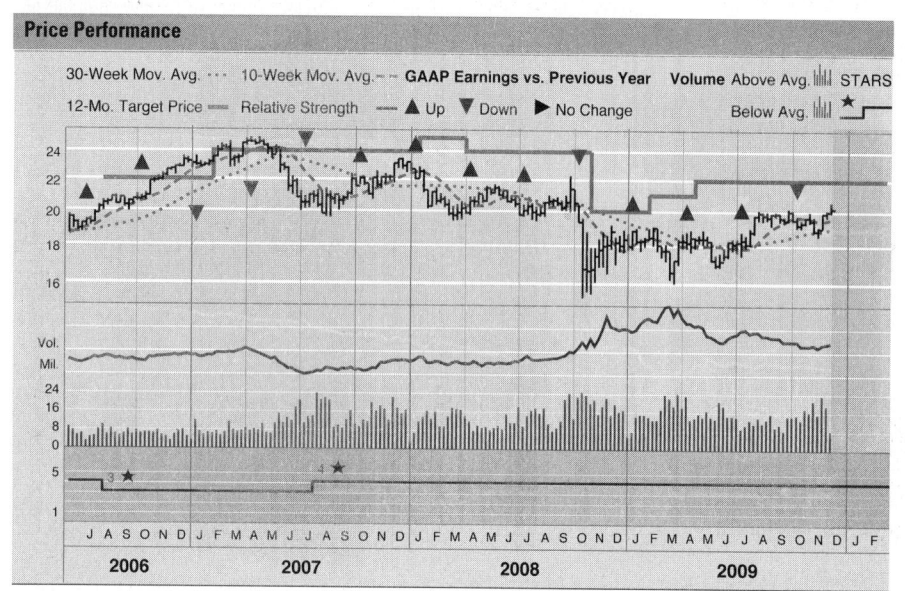

30-Week Mov. Avg. · · · 10-Week Mov. Avg. · · · **GAAP Earnings vs. Previous Year** Volume Above Avg. STARS
12-Mo. Target Price — Relative Strength — ▲ Up ▼ Down ► No Change Below Avg.

Options: ASE, CBOE

Analysis prepared by **Justin McCann** on September 10, 2009, when the stock traded at **$ 19.37**.

Highlights

► We expect 2009 operating EPS to increase about 3% from 2008's $1.45. The projected results would reflect electric rate increases in Texas, New Mexico and Minnesota, as well as lower interest expense, partially offset by higher operating and depreciation expenses. While the economic slowdown in XEL's territory has been less severe than elsewhere, we believe it will result in a decline in electric retail sales and an increase in uncollected accounts.

► For 2010, we believe operating EPS will grow approximately 8% from projected results for 2009, reflecting anticipated electric rate increases in Colorado, Wisconsin and South Dakota, as well as a full year of the increases that were implemented in 2009.

► On June 30, 2009, Northern States Power (NSP) Minnesota filed to increase its South Dakota electric rates by $18.6 million, while on June 1, 2009, NSP Wisconsin filed to increase its electric rates by $30.4 million. Earlier, on May 1, 2009, Public Service of Colorado filed to increase its electric rates by $180 million. The rates ultimately approved by the respective regulatory commissions are all expected to become effective in January 2010.

Investment Rationale/Risk

► Having rebounded more than 20% from its 2009 low, the stock is up more than 4% year to date. We think the nearly 14% drop in the first nine weeks of 2009 reflected the steep decline in both the broader market and the utility sector, but, despite the strong recovery, we believe the shares remain attractive for above-average total return over the next 12 months. As of July 21, 2009, XEL had available credit lines of $1.749 billion and cash of $65 million. We believe this $1.814 billion of total liquidity is more than adequate for XEL's near-term requirements.

► Risks to our recommendation and target price include the possibility of a severe economic downturn in the company's service territory, unfavorable legislative or regulatory decisions, and a major decline in the average P/E of the electric and gas utility sectors.

► With the recent yield from its dividend approximately in line with peers (4.9%, versus an average peer yield of 5.0%), we believe the stock remains attractive for total return potential. We expect the dividend to be increased at a rate of 2% to 4% a year. Our 12-month target price is $22, which reflects a premium-to-peers P/E of 13.5X our operating EPS estimate for 2010.

Qualitative Risk Assessment

LOW	MEDIUM	HIGH

Our risk assessment reflects the steady cash flow that we expect from the regulated electric and gas utility operations, which have a relatively low-cost power supply, our view of a relatively healthy economy in most of the company's service territories, and a generally supportive regulatory environment.

Quantitative Evaluations

S&P Quality Ranking   **B**

D	C	B-	B	B+	A-	A	A+

Relative Strength Rank   **MODERATE**

70

LOWEST = 1   HIGHEST = 99

Revenue/Earnings Data

Revenue (Million $)

	1Q	2Q	3Q	4Q	Year
2009	2,696	2,016	2,315	--	--
2008	3,028	2,616	2,852	2,708	11,203
2007	2,764	2,267	2,400	2,603	10,034
2006	2,888	2,074	2,412	2,467	9,840
2005	2,381	2,074	2,289	2,882	9,625
2004	2,280	1,797	2,009	2,259	8,345

Earnings Per Share ($)

	1Q	2Q	3Q	4Q	Year
2009	0.38	0.25	0.48	E0.35	E1.47
2008	0.35	0.24	0.51	0.36	1.46
2007	0.28	0.16	0.59	0.31	1.34
2006	0.36	0.24	0.53	0.23	1.35
2005	0.31	0.18	0.47	0.24	1.20
2004	0.35	0.21	0.40	0.30	1.27

Fiscal year ended Dec. 31. Next earnings report expected: Late January. EPS Estimates based on S&P Operating Earnings; historical GAAP earnings are as reported.

Dividend Data (Dates: mm/dd Payment Date: mm/dd/yy)

Amount ($)	Date Decl.	Ex-Div. Date	Stk. of Record	Payment Date
0.238	12/10	12/24	12/29	01/20/09
0.238	02/25	03/24	03/26	04/20/09
0.245	05/20	06/23	06/25	07/20/09
0.245	08/26	09/22	09/24	10/20/09

Dividends have been paid since 1910. Source: Company reports.

Please read the Required Disclosures and Analyst Certification on the last page of this report.

The **McGraw·Hill** Companies

Xcel Energy Inc.

STANDARD &POOR'S

Business Summary September 10, 2009

CORPORATE OVERVIEW. Xcel Energy Inc. (XEL) is a holding company with a diverse portfolio of regulated and nonregulated subsidiaries. The company's utility subsidiaries are Northern States Power Company of Minnesota and Wisconsin (NSPM and NSPW, respectively), Public Service Company of Colorado (PSCo), and Southwestern Public Service Co. (SPS), which provide electric and gas services in eight western and midwestern states, and West-Gas Interstate Inc. (WGI), an interstate natural gas pipeline. XEL's nonregulated subsidiaries include Eloigne Co., which operates rental housing projects. The electric utility operations accounted for 77.5% of operating revenues in 2008; the natural gas utility operations for 21.8%; and non-regulated and other for 0.7%.

CORPORATE STRATEGY. XEL's strategy is to continue investing in the core utility business and to earn the authorized returns, and to divest those businesses not linked to the electric and natural gas operations. In its most significant transaction, the company divested its ownership interest in NRG Energy, which was involved in independent power projects in the U.S. and internation-

ally, in December 2003. XEL had divested its ownership interest in nearly all of its non-utility subsidiaries as of December 31, 2005. XEL's other remaining non-utility businesses are WGI, a small interstate national gas pipeline company, and Eloigne, which invests in projects qualifying for low income housing tax credits. The company also has a strong focus on system reliability and continues to invest in transmission and distribution systems. To recover the cost without the delay caused by the filing of rate cases, XEL gets regulatory approval for rate riders. This ensures fair returns on the company's investment. Given the current economic environment, the company remains committed to maintaining a strong balance sheet, which will provide it with the financial flexibility to respond appropriately to the challenges and opportunities it will face.

Company Financials Fiscal Year Ended Dec. 31

Per Share Data ($)	2008	2007	2006	2005	2004	2003	2002	2001	2000	1999
Tangible Book Value	15.35	14.70	14.28	13.11	12.99	12.95	11.44	17.91	15.79	15.67
Earnings	1.46	1.34	1.35	1.20	1.27	1.23	-4.36	2.27	1.54	1.43
S&P Core Earnings	1.11	1.31	1.35	1.15	1.21	1.03	-4.57	1.68	NA	NA
Dividends	0.94	0.91	0.88	0.85	0.81	0.75	1.13	1.50	1.47	1.44
Payout Ratio	65%	68%	65%	71%	64%	61%	NM	66%	96%	101%
Prices:High	22.90	25.03	23.63	20.19	18.78	17.40	28.49	31.85	30.00	27.94
Prices:Low	15.32	19.59	17.80	16.50	15.48	10.40	5.12	24.19	16.13	19.31
P/E Ratio:High	16	19	18	17	15	14	NM	14	19	20
P/E Ratio:Low	10	15	13	14	12	8	NM	11	10	14

Income Statement Analysis (Million $)	2008	2007	2006	2005	2004	2003	2002	2001	2000	1999
Revenue	11,203	10,034	9,840	9,625	8,345	7,938	9,524	15,028	11,592	2,869
Depreciation	948	827	822	782	708	756	1,037	949	792	356
Maintenance	NA	NA	NA	NA	NA	NA	NA	NA	NA	179
Fixed Charges Coverage	2.92	2.62	2.43	2.43	2.36	2.50	1.54	2.37	2.54	1.86
Construction Credits	103	71.8	56.0	0.88	33.6	NA	NA	NA	NA	7.00
Effective Tax Rate	34.4%	33.8%	24.2%	25.8%	23.2%	23.7%	NM	28.2%	34.2%	22.8%
Net Income	646	576	569	499	527	510	-1,661	785	546	224
S&P Core Earnings	487	554	566	472	498	417	-1,745	579	NA	NA

Balance Sheet & Other Financial Data (Million $)	2008	2007	2006	2005	2004	2003	2002	2001	2000	1999
Gross Property	29,546	26,726	25,219	24,054	23,160	22,371	29,119	31,770	25,000	13,478
Capital Expenditures	2,050	2,096	1,626	1,304	1,274	951	1,503	5,366	2,196	462
Net Property	17,689	16,676	15,549	14,696	14,096	13,667	18,816	21,165	15,273	8,146
Capitalization:Long Term Debt	7,732	6,342	6,450	5,898	6,493	6,519	7,044	12,612	8,060	3,653
Capitalization:% Long Term Debt	52.2	49.8	52.1	51.3	55.0	55.0	59.6	66.7	58.7	57.8
Capitalization:Preferred	105	105	105	105	105	105	105	105	105	104
Capitalization:% Preferred	0.70	0.80	0.85	0.91	0.89	0.89	0.89	0.56	0.76	1.65
Capitalization:Common	6,964	6,301	5,817	5,484	5,203	5,222	4,665	6,194	5,562	2,558
Capitalization:% Common	47.1	49.4	47.0	47.7	44.1	44.1	39.5	32.8	40.5	40.5
Total Capital	17,699	15,415	14,751	13,813	14,019	14,017	13,303	22,040	15,996	7,246
% Operating Ratio	90.6	89.5	89.9	98.6	88.8	88.1	78.0	87.1	87.0	85.9
% Earned on Net Property	8.1	8.4	7.8	13.0	7.8	8.0	13.0	10.7	11.2	4.8
% Return on Revenue	5.8	5.7	5.8	5.2	6.3	6.4	NM	5.2	4.7	7.8
% Return on Invested Capital	7.0	7.4	7.4	6.9	7.0	7.3	12.4	10.9	10.3	7.5
% Return on Common Equity	9.7	9.4	10.1	9.2	10.1	10.1	NM	13.5	10.0	8.7

Data as orig reptd.; bef. results of disc opers/spec. items. Per share data adj. for stk. divs.; EPS diluted. E-Estimated. NA-Not Available. NM-Not Meaningful. NR-Not Ranked. UR-Under Review.

Office: 414 Nicollet Mall, Minneapolis, MN 55401-1993.
Telephone: 612-330-5500.
Website: http://www.xcelenergy.com
Chrmn & CEO: R.C. Kelly

Pres & COO: B.G. Fowke, III
CFO: D.M. Sparby
Chief Admin Officer: M. McDaniel
Treas: G.E. Tyson, II

Investor Contact: P. Johnson (612-215-4535)
Board Members: C. C. Burgess, F. W. Corrigan, R. Davis, R. C. Kelly, A. F. Moreno, M. R. Preska, A. P. Sampson, R. Truly, D. A. Westerlund, T. V. Wolf

Founded: 1909
Domicile: Minnesota
Employees: 11,223

Xerox Corp

STANDARD &POOR'S

| S&P Recommendation **BUY** ★★★★☆ | Price $7.79 (as of Nov 27, 2009) | 12-Mo. Target Price $10.00 | Investment Style Large-Cap Blend |

GICS Sector Information Technology
Sub-Industry Office Electronics

Summary This company serves the worldwide document processing market, offering a complete line of copiers, electronic printers, and other office and computer equipment.

Key Stock Statistics (Source S&P, Vickers, company reports)

52-Wk Range	$9.75– 4.12	S&P Oper. EPS 2009**E**	0.57	Market Capitalization(B)	$6.771	Beta	1.50
Trailing 12-Month EPS	$0.35	S&P Oper. EPS 2010**E**	0.75	Yield (%)	2.18	S&P 3-Yr. Proj. EPS CAGR(%)	51
Trailing 12-Month P/E	22.3	P/E on S&P Oper. EPS 2009**E**	13.7	Dividend Rate/Share	$0.17	S&P Credit Rating	BBB
$10K Invested 5 Yrs Ago	$5,106	Common Shares Outstg. (M)	869.2	Institutional Ownership (%)	82		

Price Performance

30-Week Mov. Avg. ···· 10-Week Mov. Avg. --- **GAAP Earnings vs. Previous Year** Volume Above Avg. |ılıl STARS
12-Mo. Target Price — Relative Strength — ▲ Up ▼ Down ▶ No Change Below Avg. |ılıl ★

Options: ASE, CBOE, P, Ph

Analysis prepared by **Thomas W. Smith, CFA** on October 22, 2009, when the stock traded at **$ 8.00.**

Highlights

► For XRX as a stand-alone company, we expect revenues to decrease 16% in 2009 and then rise 1% in 2010 and 3% in 2011. On September 28, 2009, the company agreed to acquire information services provider Affiliated Computer Services (ACS 54, Hold) in a stock and cash deal valued at $6.4 billion plus $2 billion in assumed debt. The company plans to close the proposed transaction in the first quarter of 2010, subject to regulatory and other approvals. We believe the combination could broaden geographic sales territories for ACS services via XRX's global sales network, and help smooth revenue flows for XRX.

► We see the company benefiting from a printer industry rebound that we project for 2010, following a deep industry downturn in 2009. We expect gross margins to improve in 2010 as unit volumes rise and cost control initiatives remain in place.

► As a stand-alone operation, we estimate operating EPS of $0.57 in 2009, down from non-GAAP EPS of $1.10 in 2008, as adjusted for restructuring, litigation and other charges. We see EPS of $0.75 in 2010 and $0.90 in 2011.

Investment Rationale/Risk

► We believe XRX as a stand-alone company will gradually recover from lower demand for printers seen in 2009, in line with trends for information technology hardware. We view the results so far in 2009 as delivering on some of the potential savings from several rounds of restructuring and from sales of new color printing products. In the context of a tough industry recession that we foresee continuing for a few more quarters, we view the shares as attractively valued.

► Risks to our recommendation and target price include a more aggressive pricing environment, longer sales cycles, and slower deployment of new products than we project. The company's cost efficiency efforts could prove less effective than we project.

► We apply a target P/E multiple of 14X, a discount to the level of Information Technology Sector peers in the S&P 500 Index to reflect a slow market that we foresee for office electronics, to our 12-month forward operating EPS estimate of $0.72 to obtain a value of $10, which is our 12-month target price.

Qualitative Risk Assessment

| LOW | MEDIUM | **HIGH** |

Xerox operates in a cyclical industry marked by lively price and marketing competition for often commoditized printer and copier products. We observe a trend toward lackluster organic revenue growth, but note XRX's efforts to improve profitability through strategic marketing and cost control efforts.

Quantitative Evaluations

S&P Quality Ranking   B

| D | C | B- | **B** | B+ | A- | A | A+ |

Relative Strength Rank   MODERATE

41

LOWEST = 1   HIGHEST = 99

Revenue/Earnings Data

Revenue (Million $)

	1Q	2Q	3Q	4Q	Year
2009	3,554	3,731	3,675	--	--
2008	4,335	4,533	4,370	4,370	17,608
2007	3,836	4,208	4,302	4,882	17,228
2006	3,695	3,977	3,844	4,379	15,895
2005	3,771	3,921	3,759	4,250	15,701
2004	3,827	3,853	3,716	4,326	15,722

Earnings Per Share ($)

	1Q	2Q	3Q	4Q	Year
2009	0.05	0.16	0.14	E0.22	E0.57
2008	-0.27	0.24	0.29	Nil	0.26
2007	0.24	0.28	0.27	0.41	1.19
2006	0.20	0.26	0.54	0.22	1.22
2005	0.20	0.35	0.06	0.27	0.90
2004	0.17	0.21	0.17	0.24	0.78

Fiscal year ended Dec. 31. Next earnings report expected: Late January. EPS Estimates based on S&P Operating Earnings; historical GAAP earnings are as reported.

Dividend Data (Dates: mm/dd Payment Date: mm/dd/yy)

Amount ($)	Date Decl.	Ex-Div. Date	Stk. of Record	Payment Date
0.043	02/12	03/27	03/31	04/30/09
0.043	05/21	06/26	06/30	07/31/09
0.043	07/16	09/28	09/30	10/30/09
0.043	10/15	12/29	12/31	01/29/10

Dividends have been paid since 2008. Source: Company reports.

Xerox Corp

Business Summary October 22, 2009

CORPORATE OVERVIEW: Xerox is a global manufacturer of document equipment such as document equipment printing and publishing systems; digital copiers; laser and solid ink printers; fax machines; and digital multifunctional devices, which can print, copy, scan and fax. Equipment sales represented 27% of sales in 2008 (28% of sales in 2007), with the remaining 73% (72%) coming from post-sale operations including maintenance, services, supplies, and financing.

Since early 2008, the company reports in three operating segments, which are grouped according to the type of customer they serve. Production represented 30% of 2008 revenues (31% of 2007 revenues), Office 56% (55%), and Other 14% (14%). Production provides large enterprises and companies in the graphic communications industry with high-end devices that enable digital on-demand printing, digital full-color printing, digital monochrome printing, and enterprise printing. Office serves global, national and small- to medium-size commercial customers with a lineup of digital printers, and copiers. Lastly, Other includes revenue from paper sales, value-added services, wide-format systems and GIS network integration solutions and electronic presentations systems.

The company operates in over 160 countries and derived 52% of revenues in 2008 (53% of revenues in 2007) from the U.S., 34% (34%) from Europe, and 14% (13%) from other areas. The company's manufacturing operations include plants in Rochester, NY, Wilsonville, OR, and Dunwalk, Ireland. The company also outsources some manufacturing operations, and in 2007 entered a multi-year master supply agreement with Flextronics, a large electronic manufacturing services company that accounts for about 15% of XRX's worldwide production.

MARKET PROFILE: Xerox believes it can address an overall market opportunity of about $132 billion. Xerox faces larger and smaller competitors, including Hewlett-Packard, Canon, Ricoh, and others.

Company Financials Fiscal Year Ended Dec. 31

Per Share Data ($)	2008	2007	2006	2005	2004	2003	2002	2001	2000	1999
Tangible Book Value	2.50	4.93	5.04	4.68	4.29	1.57	NM	0.52	2.86	4.79
Cash Flow	0.94	1.88	1.95	1.62	1.45	1.25	1.38	1.72	0.96	3.13
Earnings	0.26	1.19	1.22	0.90	0.78	0.36	0.10	-0.17	-0.44	1.96
S&P Core Earnings	0.73	1.16	1.27	0.88	0.75	0.53	-0.17	-1.33	NA	NA
Dividends	0.17	0.17	Nil	Nil	Nil	Nil	Nil	0.05	0.65	0.78
Payout Ratio	65%	4%	Nil	Nil	Nil	Nil	Nil	NM	NM	40%
Prices:High	16.43	20.18	17.31	17.02	17.24	13.89	11.45	11.35	29.31	63.94
Prices:Low	4.83	15.26	13.16	12.40	12.55	7.90	4.20	4.69	3.75	19.00
P/E Ratio:High	63	17	14	19	22	39	NM	NM	NM	33
P/E Ratio:Low	19	13	11	14	16	22	NM	NM	NM	10

Income Statement Analysis (Million $)	2008	2007	2006	2005	2004	2003	2002	2001	2000	1999
Revenue	17,608	17,228	15,895	15,701	15,722	15,701	15,849	17,008	18,701	19,228
Operating Income	2,340	2,699	2,165	2,159	2,451	2,585	2,803	3,011	1,946	3,815
Depreciation	613	656	636	637	686	748	1,035	1,332	948	935
Interest Expense	567	316	305	231	708	362	401	457	605	547
Pretax Income	-1.00	1,535	922	928	1,116	494	306	418	-323	2,104
Effective Tax Rate	NM	26.0%	NM	NM	30.5%	27.1%	19.6%	NM	NM	30.0%
Net Income	230	1,135	1,210	933	776	360	154	-109	-257	1,424
S&P Core Earnings	670	1,101	1,235	862	666	434	-128	-931	NA	NA

Balance Sheet & Other Financial Data (Million $)	2008	2007	2006	2005	2004	2003	2002	2001	2000	1999
Cash	1,229	1,099	1,399	1,322	3,218	2,477	2,887	3,990	1,741	126
Current Assets	8,150	8,540	8,754	8,736	10,928	10,335	11,019	12,600	13,022	11,985
Total Assets	22,447	23,543	21,709	21,953	24,884	24,591	25,458	27,689	29,475	28,814
Current Liabilities	5,450	4,077	4,698	4,346	6,300	7,569	7,787	10,260	6,268	7,950
Long Term Debt	7,422	7,571	6,284	6,765	7,767	8,739	11,485	11,815	16,042	11,632
Common Equity	6,238	8,588	7,080	6,319	6,244	3,291	1,893	1,820	3,493	4,911
Total Capital	15,329	16,159	13,364	13,973	14,900	13,418	14,001	14,313	20,323	17,339
Capital Expenditures	206	236	215	181	204	197	146	219	452	594
Cash Flow	843	1,791	1,846	1,512	1,389	1,037	1,116	1,209	638	2,305
Current Ratio	1.5	2.1	1.9	2.0	1.7	1.4	1.4	1.2	2.1	1.5
% Long Term Debt of Capitalization	48.4	46.8	47.0	48.4	52.1	65.1	82.0	82.5	78.9	67.1
% Net Income of Revenue	1.3	6.5	7.6	5.9	4.9	2.3	1.0	NM	NM	7.4
% Return on Assets	1.0	5.0	5.5	4.0	3.1	1.4	0.6	NM	NM	4.8
% Return on Equity	3.1	14.4	18.1	13.9	14.7	11.1	4.4	NM	NM	28.1

Data as orig reptd.; bef. results of disc opers/spec. items. Per share data adj. for stk. divs.; EPS diluted. E-Estimated. NA-Not Available. NM-Not Meaningful. NR-Not Ranked. UR-Under Review.

Office: 45 Glover Ave, Norwalk, CT 06850-1203.
Telephone: 203-968-3000.
Website: http://www.xerox.com
Chrmn: A.M. Mulcahy

Pres: J. Guers
Vice Chrmn & CFO: L. Zimmerman
CEO: U.M. Burns
SVP, Secy & General Counsel: D.H. Liu

Investor Contact: J.H. Lesko (800-828-6396)
Board Members: G. A. Britt, U. M. Burns, R. J. Harrington, W. C. Hunter, R. A. McDonald, A. M. Mulcahy, N. J. Nicholas, Jr., C. Prince, III, A. N. Reese, M. Wilderotter, L. Zimmerman

Founded: 1906
Domicile: New York
Employees: 57,100

Xilinx Inc

STANDARD &POOR'S

S&P Recommendation HOLD ★★★☆☆	Price $22.63 (as of Nov 27, 2009)	12-Mo. Target Price $26.00	Investment Style Large-Cap Growth

GICS Sector Information Technology
Sub-Industry Semiconductors

Summary This company is the world's largest supplier of programmable logic chips and related development system software.

Key Stock Statistics (Source S&P, Vickers, company reports)

52-Wk Range	$24.49– 14.78	S&P Oper. EPS 2010**E**	0.92	Market Capitalization(B)	$6.265	Beta	0.97
Trailing 12-Month EPS	$1.14	S&P Oper. EPS 2011**E**	1.21	Yield (%)	2.83	S&P 3-Yr. Proj. EPS CAGR(%)	-5
Trailing 12-Month P/E	19.9	P/E on S&P Oper. EPS 2010**E**	24.6	Dividend Rate/Share	$0.64	S&P Credit Rating	BBB-
$10K Invested 5 Yrs Ago	$7,753	Common Shares Outstg. (M)	276.9	Institutional Ownership (%)	88		

Price Performance

30-Week Mov. Avg. · · · · 10-Week Mov. Avg. - - **GAAP Earnings vs. Previous Year** Volume Above Avg. ▮▮▮ STARS
12-Mo. Target Price — Relative Strength — ▲ Up ▼ Down ▶ No Change Below Avg. ▮▮▮ ★

Options: ASE, CBOE, P

Analysis prepared by **Clyde Montevirgen** on October 16, 2009, when the stock traded at **$ 23.41**.

Qualitative Risk Assessment

LOW	MEDIUM	HIGH

Our risk assessment reflects the cyclicality of the semiconductor industry, offset by the company's position as the largest competitor in a fast-growing niche, its diverse end markets, and its sharing of factory operations risk with chip foundry partners.

Quantitative Evaluations

S&P Quality Ranking B

D	C	B-	B	B+	A-	A	A+

Relative Strength Rank MODERATE

52

LOWEST = 1   HIGHEST = 99

Revenue/Earnings Data

Revenue (Million $)

	1Q	2Q	3Q	4Q	Year
2010	376.2	415.0	--	--	--
2009	488.3	483.5	458.4	395.0	1,825
2008	445.9	444.9	474.8	475.8	1,841
2007	481.4	467.2	450.7	443.5	1,843
2006	405.4	398.9	449.6	472.3	1,726
2005	423.6	403.3	355.4	391.0	1,573

Earnings Per Share ($)

2010	0.14	0.23	E0.26	E0.29	E0.92
2009	0.30	0.29	0.51	0.26	1.36
2008	0.28	0.30	0.35	0.34	1.25
2007	0.24	0.27	0.26	0.27	1.02
2006	0.21	0.24	0.23	0.32	1.00
2005	0.26	0.24	0.18	0.19	0.87

Fiscal year ended Mar. 31. Next earnings report expected: Mid January. EPS Estimates based on S&P Operating Earnings; historical GAAP earnings are as reported.

Highlights

▶ We project that revenues will fall 7% in FY 10 (Mar.), compared to a 1% decline in FY 09, reflecting economic weakness and supply delays due to production problems. We expect orders to remain relatively soft until economic conditions improve, and we are modeling only a modest rebound in coming quarters. But we view favorably XLNX's exposure to the less cyclical defense and wireless markets, the proprietary nature of its products, and their long product cycles, which should provide a reliable sales base until demand from the more cyclical markets returns.

▶ We think XLNX will be able to maintain fairly steady gross margins in the low 60% area due to what we view as its cost effective manufacturing partnerships with chip foundries and its product portfolio of higher-margin programmable devices. However, we see minor fluctuations based on varying customer and sales mixes. We look for operating margins to narrow to about 20% in FY 10, from 24% in FY 09, as sales decline faster than expenses.

▶ Our EPS projections assume an effective tax rate of 19% and an essentially flat share count.

Investment Rationale/Risk

▶ Our hold recommendation reflects our view of declining earnings balanced by a fair valuation. Having improved its cost structure, XLNX has enough design wins with its 65nm and 90nm offerings to experience healthy long-term sales and margins, in our opinion. The company boasts above industry profitability and returns, and also has what we see as a strong balance sheet and cash flows. Also, XLNX has steadily increased dividend payouts, and the yield is currently near 3%. But we believe competitive offerings from its main rival Altera will pose a threat to XLNX's market share, and we think Altera could take the lead in the next generation of devices. Therefore, we are forecasting healthy yet below-peer growth in future quarters.

▶ Risks to our recommendation and target price include a worse than expected economic downturn, dependence on chip foundry partners, and fluctuations in chip inventories.

▶ Our 12-month target price of $26 is based on our discounted cash flow analysis, which assumes a weighted average cost of capital around 9% and a terminal growth rate of 4%.

Dividend Data (Dates: mm/dd Payment Date: mm/dd/yy)

Amount ($)	Date Decl.	Ex-Div. Date	Stk. of Record	Payment Date
0.140	01/14	02/02	02/04	02/25/09
0.140	04/22	05/11	05/13	06/03/09
0.140	07/15	08/03	08/05	08/26/09
0.160	10/14	11/02	11/04	11/24/09

Dividends have been paid since 2004. Source: Company reports.

Please read the Required Disclosures and Analyst Certification on the last page of this report.

The **McGraw·Hill** Companies

Xilinx Inc

Business Summary October 16, 2009

CORPORATE OVERVIEW. Founded in 1984, Xilinx is the world's leading supplier of programmable logic devices (PLDs) based on market share. These devices include field programmable gate arrays (FPGAs) and complex programmable logic devices (CPLDs). They are standard integrated circuits (ICs) that are programmed by customers to perform desired logic operations. The company believes it provides high levels of integration and creates significant time and cost savings for electronic equipment manufacturers in the telecommunications, networking, computing and industrial markets.

Xilinx's FPGAs are proprietary ICs designed by the company; they provide a combination of the high logic density usually associated with custom gate arrays, the time-to-market advantages of programmable logic, and the availability of a standard product. Like other chipmakers, Xilinx utilizes manufacturing process technologies that enable the PLD to increase functionality. Generally, the smaller the process technology, the higher the chip's performance and density and the lower the power consumption. XLNX has several product families, including the Virtex, Spartan and CoolRunner lines. The Virtex-5 is the latest generation FPGA produced on 65 nanometer (nm) process technology.

Older generations include the Virtex-4 (90nm) and Virtex II Pro (150nm).

Products are classified as new, mainstream, base and support. New products accounted for 33% of FY 08 (Mar.) sales (23% in FY 07), mainstream products 46% (54%), base products 15% (17%), and support products 6% (6%). Revenue by end market in FY 08 broke down as follows: 43% (45% in FY 07) communications, 32% (29%) industrial and other, 17% (16%) consumer and automotive, and 8% (10%) data processing.

Xilinx sells its products globally to OEMs and to electronic components distributors that resell them. Avnet distributes the majority of the company's products worldwide and accounted for 83% of XLNX's accounts receivable in FY 08. However, no single end customer accounted for more than 10% of Xilinx's revenues.

Company Financials Fiscal Year Ended Mar. 31

Per Share Data ($)	2009	2008	2007	2006	2005	2004	2003	2002	2001	2000
Tangible Book Value	5.74	5.45	5.54	7.53	7.24	6.79	5.44	5.26	5.82	5.68
Cash Flow	1.58	1.46	1.24	1.19	1.05	1.05	0.57	-0.02	0.36	2.03
Earnings	1.36	1.25	1.02	1.00	0.87	0.85	0.36	-0.34	0.10	1.90
S&P Core Earnings	1.48	1.28	1.01	0.78	0.58	0.57	0.05	-0.31	0.35	NA
Dividends	0.48	0.36	0.36	0.28	0.20	Nil	Nil	Nil	Nil	Nil
Payout Ratio	35%	29%	35%	28%	23%	Nil	Nil	Nil	Nil	Nil
Calendar Year	2008	2007	2006	2005	2004	2003	2002	2001	2000	1999
Prices:High	28.21	30.50	29.98	32.30	45.40	39.20	47.15	59.25	98.31	48.56
Prices:Low	14.28	21.14	18.35	21.25	25.21	18.50	13.50	19.52	35.25	15.31
P/E Ratio:High	21	24	29	32	47	46	NM	NM	NM	26
P/E Ratio:Low	10	17	18	21	26	22	NM	NM	NM	8

Income Statement Analysis (Million $)										
Revenue	1,825	1,841	1,843	1,726	1,573	1,398	1,156	1,016	1,659	1,021
Operating Income	513	485	424	489	442	412	283	87.3	568	371
Depreciation	61.0	61.0	73.9	69.5	63.1	67.9	72.5	106	93.5	44.2
Interest Expense	29.0	0.17	Nil	Nil	Nil	Nil	Nil	0.06	0.17	Nil
Pretax Income	498	474	431	457	401	351	170	-193	61.1	1,030
Effective Tax Rate	24.6%	21.1%	18.7%	22.4%	21.9%	13.6%	26.0%	NM	42.3%	36.7%
Net Income	376	374	351	354	313	303	126	-114	35.3	652
S&P Core Earnings	409	382	348	277	205	204	18.1	-103	132	NA

Balance Sheet & Other Financial Data (Million $)										
Cash	1,325	1,296	636	783	449	337	214	230	209	85.5
Current Assets	1,752	1,820	1,700	1,648	1,466	1,302	1,175	999	1,102	1,041
Total Assets	2,826	3,137	3,179	3,174	3,039	2,937	2,422	2,335	2,502	2,349
Current Liabilities	233	341	303	345	298	381	314	196	350	245
Long Term Debt	690	1,000	1,000	Nil	Nil	Nil	Nil	Nil	Nil	Nil
Common Equity	1,738	1,672	1,773	2,729	2,674	2,483	1,951	1,904	1,918	1,777
Total Capital	2,511	2,756	2,875	2,821	2,741	2,556	2,108	2,140	2,152	2,104
Capital Expenditures	39.1	45.6	111	67.0	61.4	41.0	46.0	94.9	223	144
Cash Flow	437	435	425	424	376	371	198	-7.51	129	697
Current Ratio	7.5	5.3	5.6	4.8	4.9	3.4	3.7	5.1	3.1	4.3
% Long Term Debt of Capitalization	27.5	36.3	34.8	Nil	Nil	Nil	Nil	Nil	Nil	Nil
% Net Income of Revenue	20.6	20.3	19.0	20.5	19.8	21.7	10.9	NM	2.1	63.9
% Return on Assets	12.6	11.8	11.0	11.4	10.5	11.3	5.3	NM	1.5	38.2
% Return on Equity	22.0	21.7	15.6	13.1	12.1	13.7	6.5	NM	1.9	49.1

Data as orig reptd.; bef. results of disc opers/spec. items. Per share data adj. for stk. divs.; EPS diluted. E-Estimated. NA-Not Available. NM-Not Meaningful. NR-Not Ranked. UR-Under Review.

Office: 2100 Logic Drive, San Jose, CA, USA 95124-3400.
Telephone: 408-559-7778.
Email: ir@xilinx.com
Website: http://www.xilinx.com

Chrmn: P.T. Gianos
Pres & CEO: M.N. Gavrielov
COO: R.G. Petrakian
Investor Contact: J.A. Olson (408-559-7778)

SVP, CFO & Chief Acctg Officer: J.A. Olson
Board Members: J. L. Doyle, J. G. Fishman, M. N. Gavrielov, P. T. Gianos, W. G. Howard, Jr., J. M. Patterson, M. Turner, Jr., E. W. Vanderslice

Founded: 1984
Domicile: Delaware
Employees: 3,145

XL Capital Ltd

STANDARD &POOR'S

S&P Recommendation HOLD ★★★☆☆

Price	12-Mo. Target Price	Investment Style
$17.70 (as of Nov 27, 2009)	$19.00	Large-Cap Blend

GICS Sector Financials
Sub-Industry Property & Casualty Insurance

Summary Bermuda-based XL, which originally provided excess liability coverage, has expanded into providing a broad array of commercial lines insurance, reinsurance, and other risk management services.

Key Stock Statistics (Source S&P, Vickers, company reports)

52-Wk Range	$18.65–2.56	S&P Oper. EPS 2009**E**	2.66	Market Capitalization(B)	$6.056	Beta		2.93
Trailing 12-Month EPS	$-3.54	S&P Oper. EPS 2010**E**	2.80	Yield (%)	2.26	S&P 3-Yr. Proj. EPS CAGR(%)		-20
Trailing 12-Month P/E	NM	P/E on S&P Oper. EPS 2009**E**	6.7	Dividend Rate/Share	$0.40	S&P Credit Rating		NA
$10K Invested 5 Yrs Ago	$2,841	Common Shares Outstg. (M)	342.1	Institutional Ownership (%)	99			

Price Performance

30-Week Mov. Avg. ··· 10-Week Mov. Avg. – – GAAP Earnings vs. Previous Year Volume Above Avg. STARS
12-Mo. Target Price — Relative Strength — ▲ Up ▼ Down ► No Change Below Avg. ★

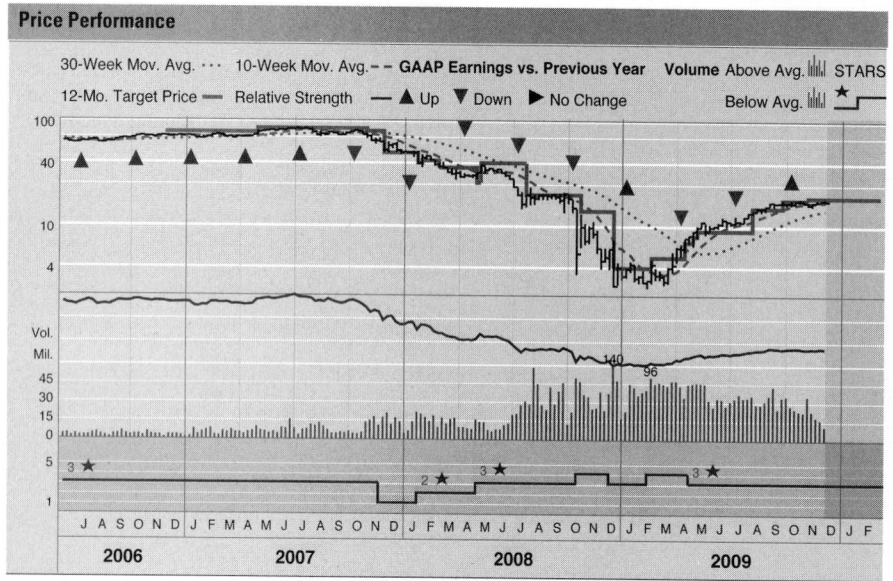

Options: CBOE, P, Ph

Analysis prepared by **Cathy A. Seifert** on November 24, 2009, when the stock traded at **$18.37**.

Highlights

▶ We expect earned premiums to decline 12% to 15% in 2009, following a 7.8% decrease in 2008, reflecting the impact of competitive pricing in the core property casualty line, coupled with reduced writings in the life insurance and financial guarantee lines. We expect earned premiums to remain under pressure in 2010, reflecting a competitive pricing environment and steps XL is taking to pare certain writings. Net written premiums declined 21%, year to year, in the first nine months of 2009.

▶ We anticipate net investment income in 2009 will likely decline by more than 20%, reflecting a challenging investment environment and steps XL is taking to lower the risk profile of its investment portfolio. We expect net investment income to rise modestly in 2010.

▶ We estimate operating EPS of $2.66 for 2009 and $2.80 for 2010, versus $3.51 of operating EPS in 2008. Our estimates exclude realized investment gains/losses. XL reported a 2008 net loss of $11.02 a share, due mainly to a $1.4 billion charge taken to (among other things) terminate a reinsurance agreement with Syncora Holdings (formerly Security Capital Assurance).

Investment Rationale/Risk

▶ Our hold recommendation reflects our view that, after significant appreciation since February, the shares are now fairly valued. At recent levels, the stock was trading at just under 1X September 30, 2009, tangible common equity. This represents a discount to some peers, reflecting concerns, in our view, over the quality of XL's balance sheet. We believe this discount is warranted in light of our belief that XL may incur additional writedowns as it seeks to restructure its balance sheet.

▶ Risks to our recommendation and target price include a greater-than-anticipated decline in premium rates and underwriting margins; a more significant deterioration in the credit quality of XL's investment portfolio; and not executing on its balance sheet restructuring.

▶ Our 12-month target price of $19 assumes that the shares will trade at approximately 1X our estimate of year-end 2009 tangible book value. This represents a discount (albeit less of one than before) to most of XL's peers and to XL's historical valuation range.

Qualitative Risk Assessment

LOW	MEDIUM	**HIGH**

Our risk assessment reflects our concerns about XL's exposure to catastrophe losses and the adequacy of its loss reserves in certain liability lines of business, and our view that XL could face writedowns of its fixed income investment portfolio and certain other investments. This is only partially offset by our view of XL as an opportunistic underwriter seeking to leverage opportunities for growth.

Quantitative Evaluations

S&P Quality Ranking   NR

D	C	B-	B	B+	A-	A	A+

Relative Strength Rank   STRONG

76

LOWEST = 1   HIGHEST = 99

Revenue/Earnings Data

Revenue (Million $)

	1Q	2Q	3Q	4Q	Year
2009	1,531	1,725	1,486	--	--
2008	2,174	2,125	1,744	1,106	7,148
2007	2,483	2,597	2,153	1,902	9,136
2006	2,473	2,499	2,364	2,496	9,833
2005	2,401	4,108	2,296	2,479	11,285
2004	2,157	3,179	2,370	2,390	10,028

Earnings Per Share ($)

2009	0.53	0.23	-0.03	E0.67	E2.66
2008	1.20	1.34	-6.09	-4.36	-11.02
2007	3.06	3.00	1.82	-6.88	1.15
2006	2.56	2.10	2.32	2.62	9.60
2005	3.18	0.97	-7.53	-5.51	-9.14
2004	3.25	2.62	0.16	2.07	8.13

Fiscal year ended Dec. 31. Next earnings report expected: Mid February. EPS Estimates based on S&P Operating Earnings; historical GAAP earnings are as reported.

Dividend Data (Dates: mm/dd Payment Date: mm/dd/yy)

Amount ($)	Date Decl.	Ex-Div. Date	Stk. of Record	Payment Date
0.100	02/11	03/11	03/13	03/31/09
0.100	04/24	06/11	06/15	06/30/09
0.100	07/24	09/11	09/15	09/30/09
0.100	10/23	12/11	12/15	12/31/09

Dividends have been paid since 1992. Source: Company reports.

Please read the Required Disclosures and Analyst Certification on the last page of this report.

The McGraw·Hill Companies

XL Capital Ltd

STANDARD
&POOR'S

Business Summary November 24, 2009

CORPORATE OVERVIEW. Bermuda-based XL Capital was formed in 1986 by a consortium of Fortune 500 companies to provide excess liability coverage. Since then, XL has expanded (mostly via acquisitions) to include insurance, reinsurance, and other financial services. Gross written premiums of nearly $8.3 billion in 2008 (down 7.8% from $9.0 billion in 2007) were divided: insurance 64%, reinsurance 28%, and life operations 8%.

Insurance business written includes general liability, as well as other specialized types of liability coverage, such as directors' and officers' liability and professional and employment practices liability coverage. An array of property coverage, as well as marine and aviation coverage, is also offered. Insurance net written premiums of $3.98 billion in 2008 were divided: professional liability 34%, casualty 20%, property 12%, marine/energy/aviation/satellite 15%, other specialty lines 18%, and other lines of coverage 1%.

Reinsurance business written includes treaty and facultative reinsurance to primary insurers of casualty risk. Reinsurance net written premiums totaled $1.75 billion in 2008 and were divided: property 34%, casualty 20%, property catastrophe 17%, professional lines 12%, marine, energy aviation and satellite 6%, and other lines (which include political risk, surety and structured indemnity) 11%.

Life operations include reinsurance written from other life insurers, principally to help in managing mortality, morbidity, survivorship, investment, and lapse risks. Net written premiums totaled $649.8 million in 2008 and were divided: annuity risks 24%, life insurance 76%. In August 2008, XL announced its intention to "review strategic opportunities" related to its life insurance business. To that end, the company sold the renewal rights to certain short-term life, accident and health business in late 2008.

In July 2001, the company acquired Winterthur International, for about $330.2 million in cash (as adjusted). As part of the transaction, XL received certain post-closing arrangements protecting it against (among other things) certain types of adverse loss development. XL valued the post-closing payment at $1.45 billion, and Winterthur Swiss Insurance Co. (the seller) believed the post-closing payment was $541 million. In December 2005, an independent actuarial review concluded that Winterthur's estimate was closer than the estimate submitted by XL. As a result of this difference, XL recorded a fourth-quarter 2005 after-tax charge of $834.2 million.

Company Financials Fiscal Year Ended Dec. 31

Per Share Data ($)	2008	2007	2006	2005	2004	2003	2002	2001	2000	1999
Tangible Book Value	16.74	39.95	45.93	37.08	42.55	37.07	36.13	28.35	31.86	30.91
Operating Earnings	NA	NA	NA	NA	NA	NA	5.10	-3.67	4.52	3.63
Earnings	-11.02	1.15	9.60	-9.14	8.13	2.69	2.88	-4.55	4.03	3.62
Dividends	1.14	1.52	1.52	2.00	1.96	1.92	1.88	1.84	1.80	1.76
Payout Ratio	NM	76%	16%	NM	24%	71%	65%	NM	45%	49%
Prices:High	52.26	85.67	72.90	79.80	82.00	88.87	98.48	96.50	89.25	75.75
Prices:Low	2.65	48.16	59.82	60.03	66.70	63.49	58.45	61.50	39.00	41.94
P/E Ratio:High	NM	43	8	NM	10	33	34	NM	22	21
P/E Ratio:Low	NM	24	6	NM	8	24	20	NM	10	12

Income Statement Analysis (Million $)	2008	2007	2006	2005	2004	2003	2002	2001	2000	1999
Premium Income	6,640	7,205	7,570	2,238	1,406	6,969	5,990	3,476	2,035	1,750
Net Investment Income	1,769	2,249	1,978	1,475	995	780	735	563	542	525
Other Revenue	-1,261	-318	8,904	8,864	7,426	268	-147	18.0	140	236
Total Revenue	7,148	9,136	9,833	11,285	10,028	8,017	6,578	4,057	2,717	2,511
Pretax Income	-2,331	534	2,007	-1,194	1,260	451	442	-764	451	431
Net Operating Income	NA	NA	NA	NA	NA	NA	701	-465	NA	NA
Net Income	-2,554	276	1,763	-1,252	1,167	412	406	-576	506	471

Balance Sheet & Other Financial Data (Million $)	2008	2007	2006	2005	2004	2003	2002	2001	2000	1999
Cash & Equivalent	4,717	4,328	2,656	4,085	2,631	2,698	3,785	2,044	1,074	669
Premiums Due	4,273	4,455	4,698	4,842	4,934	4,847	4,833	2,182	1,120	1,126
Investment Assets:Bonds	25,636	33,608	36,121	32,310	25,100	19,494	14,483	10,832	8,605	7,581
Investment Assets:Stocks	361	855	891	869	963	583	575	548	557	1,136
Investment Assets:Loans	Nil	Nil	Nil	Nil	Nil	Nil	Nil	Nil	Nil	Nil
Investment Assets:Total	29,017	39,585	42,137	38,171	30,066	22,821	17,956	13,741	10,472	9,768
Deferred Policy Costs	714	755	870	866	845	778	688	394	309	276
Total Assets	45,682	57,762	59,309	58,455	49,015	40,764	35,647	27,963	16,942	15,091
Debt	3,190	2,869	3,368	3,413	2,721	1,905	1,878	1,605	450	411
Common Equity	6,615	9,948	16,422	14,078	12,286	10,171	6,569	5,437	5,574	5,577
Property & Casualty:Loss Ratio	66.1	59.8	60.7	107.1	68.6	75.3	68.0	105.0	70.4	69.1
Property & Casualty:Expense Ratio	29.6	29.0	27.8	25.8	27.4	27.3	29.0	34.9	36.4	34.3
Property & Casualty Combined Ratio	95.7	88.8	88.5	132.9	96.0	102.6	97.0	139.9	106.8	103.4
% Return on Revenue	NM	3.0	18.6	NM	11.9	5.2	6.0	NM	18.6	19.9
% Return on Equity	NM	2.1	11.3	NM	10.0	3.9	6.6	NM	9.1	8.4

Data as orig reptd.; bef. results of disc opers/spec. items. Per share data adj. for stk. divs.; EPS diluted. E-Estimated. NA-Not Available. NM-Not Meaningful. NR-Not Ranked. UR-Under Review.

Office: XL House, 1 Bermudiana Rd, Hamilton, Bermuda HM 11.
Telephone: 441-292-8515.
Website: http://www.xlcapital.com
Chrmn: R.R. Glauber

Pres & CEO: M.S. McGavick
EVP, CFO & Chief Acctg Officer: B.W. Nocco
EVP, Secy & General Counsel: K.R. Gould
SVP & Treas: F. Muldoon

Investor Contact: D.R. Radulski (441-292-8515)
Board Members: D. R. Comey, R. R. Glauber, H. N. Haag, G. T. Hutton, J. Mauriello, M. S. McGavick, E. M. McQuade, R. S. Parker, A. Z. Senter, E. E. Thrower, J. M. Vereker

Founded: 1986
Domicile: Cayman Islands
Employees: 4,000

XTO Energy Inc.

STANDARD
&POOR'S

S&P Recommendation	BUY ★★★★☆	Price $42.15 (as of Nov 27, 2009)	12-Mo. Target Price $50.00	Investment Style Large-Cap Growth

GICS Sector Energy
Sub-Industry Oil & Gas Exploration & Production

Summary This independent oil and gas producer is highly leveraged to unconventional natural gas resources (such as tight gas, shale gas and coal bed methane) in the U.S.

Key Stock Statistics (Source S&P, Vickers, company reports)

52-Wk Range	$46.49–28.64	S&P Oper. EPS 2009E	3.38	Market Capitalization(B)	$24.461	Beta	0.79
Trailing 12-Month EPS	$3.14	S&P Oper. EPS 2010E	2.41	Yield (%)	1.19	S&P 3-Yr. Proj. EPS CAGR(%)	-12
Trailing 12-Month P/E	13.4	P/E on S&P Oper. EPS 2009E	12.5	Dividend Rate/Share	$0.50	S&P Credit Rating	BBB
$10K Invested 5 Yrs Ago	NA	Common Shares Outstg. (M)	580.3	Institutional Ownership (%)	77		

Price Performance

30-Week Mov. Avg. ···· 10-Week Mov. Avg. – — **GAAP Earnings vs. Previous Year** Volume Above Avg. ▌▌▌ STARS
12-Mo. Target Price — Relative Strength ▲ Up ▼ Down ► No Change Below Avg. ▌▌▌ ★

Options: ASE, CBOE, P, Ph

Analysis prepared by **Michael Kay** on November 02, 2009, when the stock traded at **$ 41.52**.

Highlights

► Oil and gas production climbed 28% in 2008, mainly from ongoing success in tight-sand and shale basins. Given the recent drop in oil and gas prices, we project growth of 21% and 9% in 2009 and 2010, respectively, on the development of projects in the East Texas Freestone Trend, Barnett Shale, Permian Basin, San Juan Region, Woodford and Fayetteville Shale plays. We expect XTO to manage production growth in 2009 and 2010 to maximize economic returns as operating costs are expected to decline.

► In 2008, XTO continued to pursue 'bolt-on' acquisitions for its best development fields, as evidenced by the $800 million Barnett Shale acquisition. XTO estimates it holds 1.25 million net acres of shale potential, with its largest acreage position in the Fayetteville Shale. XTO also has acreage in the Marcellus, Woodford and Haynesville shales. In the Barnett, XTO is one of the top three producers.

► After-tax earnings rose 13% in 2008, and we see 2009 and 2010 EPS of $3.48 and $2.38, respectively, as hedges fall off. XTO's 2009 capital budget was raised to $3.6 billion, and it hedged 78% of second half 2009 forecasted natural gas volumes at $10.69/Mcf.

Investment Rationale/Risk

► We expect XTO to seek production growth through developments, and we see a more conservative approach to acquisitions given the credit crunch and XTO's above-peer debt levels. XTO has an inventory of largely undeveloped unconventional assets. In May 2008, XTO entered the Bakken Shale with a $1.85 billion purchase for acreage from Headington Oil Co. In September 2008, it purchased privately held Hunt Petroleum for $4.2 billion. In 2008, it raised $3.3 billion in stock and debt offerings to fund acquisitions. XTO grew year-end 2008 proved reserves by 23%.

► Risks to our opinion and target price include unfavorable changes in economic, industrial and operating conditions such as rising operating costs, difficulties in replacing reserves, aggressively priced and financed acquisitions, and sustained declines in oil and gas prices.

► We see markets discounting probable or possible reserves, and we value XTO on proved-reserve NAV estimates. We blend our NAV of $48, which discounts significant shale play potential, with our DCF ($52; WACC 8%, terminal growth 3%) and relative valuations to arrive at our 12-month target price of $50.

Qualitative Risk Assessment

LOW	MEDIUM	HIGH

Our risk assessment for XTO reflects our view of its position as a large independent exploration and production company focused on unconventional natural gas resources with sizable acreage positions in low-risk drilling opportunities in the U.S. This is offset by our view of XTO's relatively high debt leverage, reflecting its aggressive growth through acquisition strategy.

Quantitative Evaluations

S&P Quality Ranking — B+

D	C	B-	B	B+	A-	A	A+

Relative Strength Rank — MODERATE

49

LOWEST = 1   HIGHEST = 99

Revenue/Earnings Data

Revenue (Million $)

	1Q	2Q	3Q	4Q	Year
2009	2,161	2,273	2,288	--	--
2008	1,673	1,936	2,125	1,961	7,695
2007	1,169	1,329	1,421	1,594	5,513
2006	1,215	1,066	1,096	1,199	4,576
2005	628.9	748.7	964.2	1,177	3,519
2004	394.8	444.8	507.4	600.7	1,948

Earnings Per Share ($)

	1Q	2Q	3Q	4Q	Year
2009	0.83	0.85	0.86	E0.85	E3.38
2008	0.92	1.11	0.94	0.61	3.56
2007	0.82	0.91	0.84	0.95	3.53
2006	1.01	1.30	0.79	0.93	4.02
2005	0.38	0.48	0.68	0.98	2.52
2004	0.24	0.24	0.32	0.40	1.21

Fiscal year ended Dec. 31. Next earnings report expected: Mid February. EPS Estimates based on S&P Operating Earnings; historical GAAP earnings are as reported.

Dividend Data (Dates: mm/dd Payment Date: mm/dd/yy)

Amount ($)	Date Decl.	Ex-Div. Date	Stk. of Record	Payment Date
0.125	02/17	03/27	03/31	04/15/09
0.125	05/19	06/26	06/30	07/15/09
0.125	08/18	09/28	09/30	10/15/09
0.125	11/17	12/29	12/31	01/15/10

Dividends have been paid since 1993. Source: Company reports.

STANDARD
&POOR'S

XTO Energy Inc.

Business Summary November 02, 2009

CORPORATE OVERVIEW. XTO Energy Inc. (formerly Cross Timbers Oil Co.) is engaged in the acquisition, development, exploitation and exploration of producing oil and gas properties, and in the production, processing and marketing and transportation of oil and natural gas. The company operates in the U.S. and is focused on the following areas: Eastern Region (East Texas Basin, northwestern Louisiana and Mississippi); North Texas Region (including the Barnett Shale); San Juan Region; Permian and South Texas Region; and the Mid-Continent and Rocky Mountain Region (including the Fayetteville and Woodford Shales).

Proved oil and gas reserves rose 23% to 13.86 trillion cubic feet equivalent (Tcfe; 64% developed, 88% natural gas) in 2008. Oil and gas production rose 28% to 2.3 Bcfe per day in 2008 (83% natural gas). We estimate XTO's 2008 organic reserve replacement at 168%. Using data from John S. Herold, we estimate XTO's three-year (2005-07) reserve replacement at 435%, in-line with the peer average; its three-year proved acquisition costs at $12.75 per boe, in line with peers; and its three-year finding & development costs at $9.76 per boe, well-below the peer average. In February 2009, XTO estimated it had replaced 401% of its 2008 production (168% through developments).

COMPETITIVE LANDSCAPE. XTO's operations are highly leveraged to unconventional natural gas plays, and it has build sizable acreage positions in tight gas, shale gas and coalbed methane (CBM) basins in the U.S. As a result of its large acreage position, XTO has a solid inventory of low-risk drilling opportunities, by our analysis. Although these basins can be technically challenging and entail complex drilling and fracturing techniques, we believe XTO has proved itself a competent operator. Over the years, we believe XTO has built a solid track record of finding, developing and producing reserves in a generally consistent and cost efficient manner.

IMPACT OF MAJOR DEVELOPMENTS. Acquisitions have played a key role in XTO's growth strategy. In 2007, the company was particularly active, and acquired proved and unproved reserves for a total of $4.03 billion. In 2008, XTO acquired proved and unproved reserves for a total of over $11 billion. We expect XTO to be less aggressive with respect to acquisitions in 2009 as debt and equity markets remain uncertain.

Company Financials Fiscal Year Ended Dec. 31

Per Share Data ($)	2008	2007	2006	2005	2004	2003	2002	2001	2000	1999
Tangible Book Value	27.25	15.92	12.20	8.81	4.49	3.76	2.57	2.39	1.45	0.82
Cash Flow	7.38	6.01	6.00	4.03	1.65	1.52	1.12	1.32	1.26	0.51
Earnings	3.56	3.53	4.02	2.52	1.21	0.76	0.53	0.85	0.37	0.15
S&P Core Earnings	3.56	3.53	3.38	2.41	1.13	0.73	0.52	0.72	NA	NA
Dividends	0.48	0.41	0.25	0.19	0.07	0.02	0.01	0.01	0.01	0.01
Payout Ratio	13%	12%	6%	8%	6%	3%	3%	2%	2%	7%
Prices:High	73.74	53.99	40.99	38.09	22.13	14.06	9.50	7.82	6.96	2.42
Prices:Low	23.80	35.09	29.21	19.09	12.28	8.17	5.29	4.43	1.21	0.73
P/E Ratio:High	21	15	10	15	18	19	18	9	19	16
P/E Ratio:Low	7	10	7	8	10	11	10	5	3	5

Income Statement Analysis (Million $)										
Revenue	7,695	5,513	4,576	3,519	1,948	1,190	810	839	601	341
Operating Income	5,479	4,068	3,445	2,198	1,338	801	550	611	398	208
Depreciation, Depletion and Amortization	2,056	1,187	875	655	407	284	204	154	260	112
Interest Expense	482	297	180	153	93.7	63.8	53.6	55.6	78.9	64.2
Pretax Income	3,026	2,642	2,961	1,810	826	445	287	455	176	70.6
Effective Tax Rate	36.8%	36.0%	37.2%	36.4%	38.5%	35.5%	35.1%	35.6%	33.7%	33.9%
Net Income	1,912	1,691	1,860	1,152	508	287	186	293	117	46.7
S&P Core Earnings	1,912	1,691	1,565	1,098	476	275	183	249	NA	NA

Balance Sheet & Other Financial Data (Million $)										
Cash	25.0	Nil	5.00	2.00	9.70	7.00	15.0	6.81	7.44	5.73
Current Assets	4,258	1,287	1,585	943	437	261	245	239	193	113
Total Assets	38,254	18,922	12,885	9,857	6,110	3,611	2,648	2,132	1,592	1,477
Current Liabilities	2,930	1,537	1,240	884	501	321	286	202	219	74.2
Long Term Debt	11,959	6,320	3,451	3,109	2,043	1,252	1,118	856	769	991
Common Equity	17,347	7,941	5,865	4,209	2,599	1,466	908	821	470	249
Total Capital	34,506	16,871	11,294	7,318	5,398	3,144	2,312	1,876	1,349	1,395
Capital Expenditures	13,030	7,346	616	1,621	1,905	654	358	225	45.6	270
Cash Flow	3,968	2,878	2,735	1,807	915	571	390	448	375	157
Current Ratio	1.5	0.8	1.3	1.1	0.9	0.8	0.9	1.2	0.9	1.5
% Long Term Debt of Capitalization	34.7	37.5	30.6	42.5	37.8	39.8	48.4	45.6	57.0	71.1
% Return on Assets	6.7	10.6	16.4	14.4	10.4	9.2	7.8	15.8	7.6	3.5
% Return on Equity	15.1	24.5	36.9	33.8	25.0	24.1	21.5	45.4	32.0	21.3

Data as orig reptd.; bef. results of disc opers/spec. items. Per share data adj. for stk. divs.; EPS diluted. E-Estimated. NA-Not Available. NM-Not Meaningful. NR-Not Ranked. UR-Under Review.

Office: 810 Houston St, Fort Worth, TX 76102.
Telephone: 817-870-2800.
Email: investor_relations@xtoenergy.com
Website: http://www.xtoenergy.com

Chrmn: B.R. Simpson
Pres: V.O. Vennerberg, II
CEO: K.A. Hutton
COO: K.A. Carwile

EVP & CFO: L.G. Baldwin
Investor Contact: G.D. Simpson (817-870-2800)
Board Members: W. H. Adams, III, M. Arntzen, L. G. Baldwin, L. G. Collins, K. A. Hutton, P. R. Kevil, T. L. Petrus, J. P. Randall, S. Sherman, H. D. Simons, B. R. Simpson, G. D. Simpson, V. O. Vennerberg, II

Founded: 1986
Domicile: Delaware
Employees: 3,129

The McGraw-Hill Companies

Yahoo! Inc

STANDARD &POOR'S

S&P Recommendation	**STRONG BUY** ★★★★★	Price	12-Mo. Target Price	Investment Style
		$15.00 (as of Nov 27, 2009)	$24.00	Large-Cap Growth

GICS Sector Information Technology
Sub-Industry Internet Software & Services

Summary This company is one of the world's largest providers of online content and services.

Key Stock Statistics (Source S&P, Vickers, company reports)

52-Wk Range	$18.02– 10.50	S&P Oper. EPS 2009E	0.42	Market Capitalization(B)	$21.016	Beta	0.77
Trailing 12-Month EPS	$0.10	S&P Oper. EPS 2010E	0.58	Yield (%)	Nil	S&P 3-Yr. Proj. EPS CAGR(%)	20
Trailing 12-Month P/E	NM	P/E on S&P Oper. EPS 2009E	35.7	Dividend Rate/Share	Nil	S&P Credit Rating	NR
$10K Invested 5 Yrs Ago	$3,967	Common Shares Outstg. (M)	1,401.1	Institutional Ownership (%)	72		

Price Performance

30-Week Mov. Avg. · · · 10-Week Mov. Avg. – – GAAP Earnings vs. Previous Year Volume Above Avg. STARS
12-Mo. Target Price — Relative Strength ▲ Up ▼ Down ► No Change Below Avg. ★

Options: ASE, CBOE, P, Ph

Analysis prepared by **Scott H. Kessler** on October 21, 2009, when the stock traded at **$ 17.99.**

Highlights

► We see revenues excluding traffic acquisition costs falling 14% in 2009, reflecting a significant global economic slowdown and revised broadband relationships. We project 7% gains for 2010 and 2011.

► We believe revenues will continue to benefit from secular growth in online advertising. We think annual operating margins bottomed in 2008, reflecting changed broadband alliances and aggressive investment in new initiatives, and we see improvements through 2011.

► After nearly 18 months of on-again, off-again negotiations about some kind of business combination or partnership, YHOO announced a search technology and advertising agreement with Microsoft (MSFT 27, Hold) in July 2009. MSFT would power YHOO's search results and non-premium related advertising, and YHOO would sell the companies' premium search inventory. Although the deal (which we expect to be consummated in the first half of 2010 pending approvals) was perceived by some as disappointing for YHOO, we think it should enable the company to better focus and invest in its core media operations.

Investment Rationale/Risk

► We think increasing percentages of advertising budgets are being spent online. We also see multiple potential positive catalysts, including consummation of the MSFT deal, additional streamlining actions, and divestiture activity.

► Risks to our opinion and target price include the possible delay/cancellation of the pending search partnership with MSFT, and the potential worsening of the global recession. Our estimates and assumptions exclude the pending MSFT deal.

► After excluding the value of YHOO's Asia-based equity investments and cash/equivalents, relative P/E analysis yields a value of $12 to $13, and peer P/E-to-growth comparisons lead to a value of $13 to $14. Our DCF analysis, with assumptions including a WACC of 13.3%, projected annual FCF growth of 11% from 2009 to 2013, and a perpetuity growth rate of 3%, results in an intrinsic value of $15. We estimate the value of YHOO's Asian investments at $8 and cash/investments at $3. Weighing these assessments, and adding the value of the investments and cash/equivalents, results in our 12-month target price of $24.

Qualitative Risk Assessment

LOW	MEDIUM	**HIGH**

The company is a large and well-capitalized leader in a number of areas related to Internet content and services. However, in our view, the markets in which it participates change rapidly and have relatively low barriers to entry, which has contributed to the notable competition and inconsistent financial execution that we have observed.

Quantitative Evaluations

S&P Quality Ranking B-

D	C	**B-**	B	B+	A-	A	A+

Relative Strength Rank WEAK

25

LOWEST = 1 HIGHEST = 99

Revenue/Earnings Data

Revenue (Million $)

	1Q	2Q	3Q	4Q	Year
2009	1,580	1,573	1,575	--	--
2008	1,818	1,798	1,786	1,806	7,209
2007	1,672	1,698	1,768	1,832	6,969
2006	1,567	1,576	1,580	1,702	6,426
2005	1,174	1,253	1,330	1,501	5,258
2004	757.8	832.3	906.7	1,078	3,575

Earnings Per Share ($)

2009	0.08	0.10	0.13	E0.11	E0.42
2008	0.37	0.09	0.04	-0.22	0.29
2007	0.10	0.11	0.11	0.15	0.47
2006	0.11	0.11	0.11	0.19	0.52
2005	0.14	0.51	0.17	0.46	1.28
2004	0.07	0.08	0.17	0.25	0.58

Fiscal year ended Dec. 31. Next earnings report expected: Late January. EPS Estimates based on S&P Operating Earnings; historical GAAP earnings are as reported.

Dividend Data

No cash dividends have been paid.

The McGraw·Hill Companies

Yahoo! Inc

STANDARD
&POOR'S

Business Summary October 21, 2009

CORPORATE OVERVIEW. Yahoo! is one of the world's largest Internet companies. Primary categories for its properties and services are Front Doors (including the Yahoo front page, My Yahoo and the Yahoo Toolbar), Search (consisting of offerings related to search, yellow pages, maps, local, shopping, travel, and personals, and Yahoo Answers), Communications and Communities (including mail and messaging offerings, and Yahoo Groups, Yahoo 360 and Flickr), Media (consisting of information/entertainment offerings related to news, finance, sports (including Rivals.com), music, movies, television, games, autos, real estate, food, consumer technology, kids and health), and Connected Life (including Yahoo Mobile, Yahoo Digital Home, and Yahoo Desktop). YHOO has more than 500 million worldwide registered users (excluding the 34% stake in Yahoo! Japan, 44% interest in Alibaba Group, 1% holding in Alibaba.com, and 10% share of Gmarket as of December 2008). Gmarket was acquired in June 2009 the Alibaba.com stake was sold in September 2009.

Blake Jorgensen became CFO in June 2007. Soon thereafter, co-founder Jerry Yang replaced Terry Semel as CEO, and long-time CFO Sue Decker became President and COO. One-time COO Dan Rosensweig, CTO and Technology Group leader Farzad Nazem, and Chief Sales Officer Wenda Millard left in the first half of 2007. Many other important executives have also left YHOO since early 2007, and the pace and magnitude of these departures increased around mid-2008, in our view. Carol Bartz replaced Jerry Yang as CEO and Sue Decker left in January 2009, and Tim Morse replaced Jorgensen as CFO in July 2009.

Company Financials Fiscal Year Ended Dec. 31

Per Share Data ($)	2008	2007	2006	2005	2004	2003	2002	2001	2000	1999
Tangible Book Value	5.26	3.70	4.25	3.59	2.94	1.64	1.47	1.52	1.69	1.11
Cash Flow	0.87	0.94	0.89	1.54	0.79	0.31	0.18	0.03	0.11	0.09
Earnings	0.29	0.47	0.52	1.28	0.58	0.19	0.09	-0.08	0.06	0.05
S&P Core Earnings	0.33	0.46	0.51	0.56	0.24	0.03	-0.32	-0.85	NA	NA
Dividends	Nil	Nil	Nil	Nil	Nil	Nil	Nil	Nil	Nil	Nil
Payout Ratio	Nil	Nil	Nil	Nil	Nil	Nil	Nil	Nil	Nil	Nil
Prices:High	30.25	34.08	43.66	43.45	39.79	22.74	10.68	21.69	125.03	112.00
Prices:Low	8.94	22.27	22.65	30.30	20.57	8.25	4.47	4.01	12.53	27.50
P/E Ratio:High	NM	73	84	34	69	NM	NM	NM	NM	NM
P/E Ratio:Low	NM	47	44	24	35	NM	NM	NM	NM	NM

Income Statement Analysis (Million $)										
Revenue	7,209	6,969	6,426	5,258	3,575	1,625	953	717	1,110	589
Operating Income	1,477	1,355	1,481	1,505	1,000	455	198	34.5	390	197
Depreciation	790	659	540	397	311	160	109	131	69.1	42.3
Interest Expense	NA	Nil	Nil	Nil	Nil	Nil	Nil	Nil	Nil	Nil
Pretax Income	693	1,000	293	2,672	1,280	391	180	-81.1	264	104
Effective Tax Rate	37.9%	33.7%	NM	28.7%	34.2%	37.6%	39.7%	NM	71.2%	39.0%
Net Income	424	660	751	1,896	840	238	107	-92.8	70.8	61.1
S&P Core Earnings	464	651	744	840	353	35.5	-377	-966	NA	NA

Balance Sheet & Other Financial Data (Million $)										
Cash	3,452	2,001	2,601	2,561	3,512	1,310	774	926	1,120	872
Current Assets	4,746	3,238	3,750	3,450	4,090	1,722	970	1,052	1,291	946
Total Assets	13,690	12,230	11,514	10,832	9,178	5,932	2,790	2,379	2,270	1,470
Current Liabilities	1,705	2,300	1,474	1,204	1,181	708	412	359	311	192
Long Term Debt	43.0	Nil	750	750	750	750	Nil	Nil	Nil	Nil
Common Equity	11,242	9,533	9,161	8,566	7,101	4,363	2,262	1,967	1,897	1,261
Total Capital	11,269	9,545	9,919	9,316	7,896	5,151	2,294	1,997	1,926	1,265
Capital Expenditures	675	602	689	409	246	117	51.6	86.2	94.4	49.5
Cash Flow	1,214	1,319	1,291	2,293	1,151	398	216	37.8	140	103
Current Ratio	2.8	1.4	2.5	2.9	3.5	2.4	2.4	2.9	4.1	4.9
% Long Term Debt of Capitalization	0.4	Nil	7.6	8.0	9.5	14.6	Nil	Nil	Nil	Nil
% Net Income of Revenue	5.9	9.5	11.7	36.0	23.5	14.6	11.2	NM	6.4	10.3
% Return on Assets	3.3	5.6	6.7	18.9	11.1	5.5	4.1	NM	3.7	5.4
% Return on Equity	4.1	7.1	8.5	24.2	14.6	7.2	5.1	NM	4.5	6.3

Data as orig reptd.; bef. results of disc opers/spec. items. Per share data adj. for stk. divs.; EPS diluted. E-Estimated. NA-Not Available. NM-Not Meaningful. NR-Not Ranked. UR-Under Review.

Office: 701 First Avenue, Sunnyvale, CA 94089.
Telephone: 408-349-3300.
Email: investor_relations@yahoo-inc.com
Website: http://www.yahoo.com

Chrmn: R.J. Bostock
CEO: C.A. Bartz
COO: J. Marcom, Jr.
EVP, CFO & Chief Acctg Officer: T.R. Morse

EVP & CTO: A. Balogh
Board Members: C. A. Bartz, F. J. Biondi, Jr., R. J. Bostock, R. W. Burkle, J. H. Chapple, E. C. Hippeau, V. I. Joshi, A. Kern, J. F. Miller, P. B. Toms, Jr., M. Wilderotter, G. L. Wilson, J. Yang

Founded: 1995
Domicile: Delaware
Employees: 13,600

The McGraw-Hill Companies

YUM! Brands Inc.

STANDARD &POOR'S

S&P Recommendation SELL ★★☆☆☆

Price	$35.40 (as of Nov 27, 2009)
12-Mo. Target Price	$31.00
Investment Style	Large-Cap Growth

GICS Sector Consumer Discretionary
Sub-Industry Restaurants

Summary This company operates, franchises, has interests in or licenses the largest number of fast food restaurants in the world, with nearly 37,000 units in 110 countries, including the KFC, Pizza Hut, and Taco Bell chains.

Key Stock Statistics (Source S&P, Vickers, company reports)

52-Wk Range	$36.96– 23.37	S&P Oper. EPS 2009**E**	2.14	Market Capitalization(B)	$16.557	Beta	1.06
Trailing 12-Month EPS	$2.20	S&P Oper. EPS 2010**E**	2.35	Yield (%)	2.37	S&P 3-Yr. Proj. EPS CAGR(%)	11
Trailing 12-Month P/E	16.1	P/E on S&P Oper. EPS 2009**E**	16.5	Dividend Rate/Share	$0.84	S&P Credit Rating	BBB-
$10K Invested 5 Yrs Ago	$16,759	Common Shares Outstg. (M)	467.7	Institutional Ownership (%)	73		

Price Performance

30-Week Mov. Avg. ···   10-Week Mov. Avg. ---   **GAAP Earnings vs. Previous Year**   Volume Above Avg. STARS
12-Mo. Target Price —   Relative Strength —   ▲ Up ▼ Down ► No Change   Below Avg.

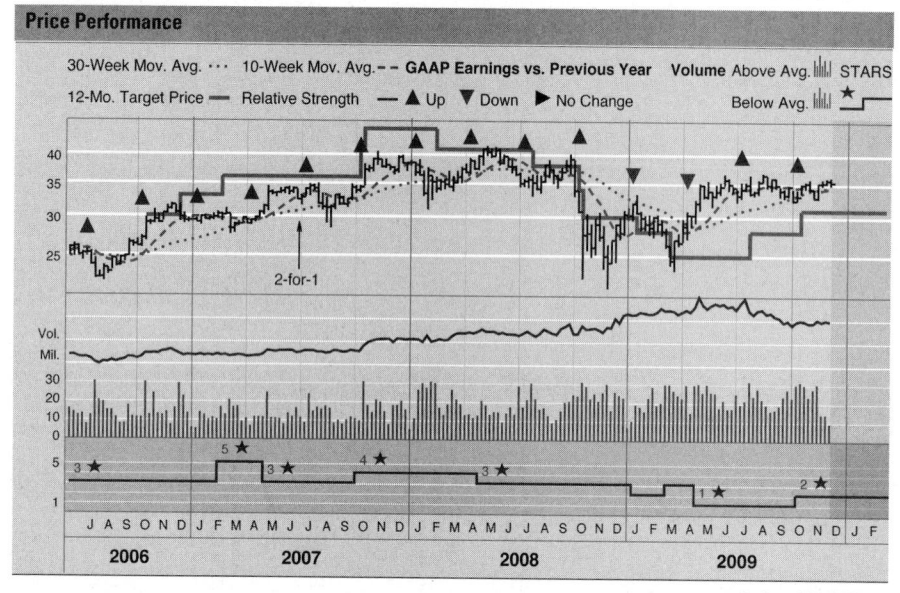

Options: ASE, CBOE, Ph

Analysis prepared by **Mark S. Basham** on October 09, 2009, when the stock traded at **$ 34.52**.

Highlights

▶ YUM's growth strategy is focused primarily on developing markets. YUM in 2009 expects to open at least 500 new units in its China division and about 900 in the Yum Restaurants International division (YRI). In the U.S., YUM expects about 200 openings, offset by a similar number of closings. In early October, YUM provided 2010 new restaurant guidance for each division that is approximately similar to 2009.

▶ We expect 2009 to be a difficult year for the restaurant industry. We see revenue growth in local currencies of 10% in China vs. expectations for 17% at the beginning of the year. U.S. results will be down due to about 3% lower systemwide comparable sales. In YRI, we see comparable sales about flat, but expect about a 10% negative forex effect.

▶ For 2009, we expect about a 200 basis point improvement in margins due to deflation in food costs. We estimate 2009 EPS of $2.14 versus operating EPS of $1.88 in 2008. For 2010, we see EPS rising to $2.35 on global revenue growth of 4.5%, overhead cost reductions, lower interest expense, and a lower effective tax rate.

Investment Rationale/Risk

▶ Our sell recommendation reflects the stock's overvaluation relative to our target price as YUM's share price has risen sharply since the S&P 500's recent low on March 9. Our fundamental outlook since that time has also improved as food cost deflation has been greater than we anticipated. Lower costs are more than offsetting weak sales in U.S. and certain European markets. While China growth remains relatively strong, it has slowed somewhat in 2009 from prior years.

▶ Risks to our recommendation and target price include more favorable energy, food and labor costs, currency exchange rate risk should the dollar weaken materially (making foreign profits worth more in dollars), and a faster return to expansion in fast-growing emerging economies.

▶ Our 12-month target price of $31 is based on our discounted cash flow analysis, which assumes a weighted average cost of capital of 10.7%, and free cash flow increases averaging 6% to 8% annually for the next five years, then gradually slowing to a terminal rate of 2%.

Qualitative Risk Assessment

LOW	MEDIUM	HIGH

YUM competes in the fast food industry, in which its concepts possess a very strong brand name presence domestically and in certain foreign markets. However, operating margins can vary widely due to fluctuations in food costs. Furthermore, YUM's profits can be affected by changing currency exchange rates due to its large and fast-growing international business.

Quantitative Evaluations

S&P Quality Ranking   A-

D	C	B-	B	B+	A-	A	A+

Relative Strength Rank   MODERATE

63

LOWEST = 1   HIGHEST = 99

Revenue/Earnings Data

Revenue (Million $)

	1Q	2Q	3Q	4Q	Year
2009	2,217	2,476	2,778	--	--
2008	2,408	2,653	2,835	3,383	11,279
2007	2,223	2,367	2,564	3,262	10,416
2006	2,085	2,182	2,278	3,016	9,561
2005	2,054	2,153	2,243	2,899	9,349
2004	1,970	2,077	2,179	2,785	9,011

Earnings Per Share ($)

	1Q	2Q	3Q	4Q	Year
2009	0.46	0.63	0.69	E0.50	E2.14
2008	0.50	0.45	0.58	0.43	1.96
2007	0.35	0.39	0.50	0.44	1.68
2006	0.29	0.34	0.42	0.42	1.46
2005	0.24	0.29	0.35	0.39	1.28
2004	0.24	0.29	0.31	0.39	1.21

Fiscal year ended Dec. 31. Next earnings report expected: Early February. EPS Estimates based on S&P Operating Earnings; historical GAAP earnings are as reported.

Dividend Data (Dates: mm/dd Payment Date: mm/dd/yy)

Amount ($)	Date Decl.	Ex-Div. Date	Stk. of Record	Payment Date
0.190	03/27	04/07	04/10	05/01/09
0.190	05/28	07/15	07/17	08/07/09
0.210	09/30	10/14	10/16	11/06/09
0.210	11/20	01/13	01/15	02/05/10

Dividends have been paid since 2004. Source: Company reports.

Please read the Required Disclosures and Analyst Certification on the last page of this report.

The McGraw-Hill Companies

YUM! Brands Inc.

STANDARD &POOR'S

Business Summary October 09, 2009

CORPORATE PROFILE. Yum! Brands has the world's largest quick service restaurant (QSR) system, with approximately 36,600 restaurants, including licensee units, in more than 110 countries and territories. The company operates and franchises restaurants under the KFC, Pizza Hut, Taco Bell, Long John Silver's and A&W All American Food concepts. In 2008, the company's brands generated approximately $36 billion in systemwide sales (up 7% in constant currencies) and $11.3 billion in worldwide revenues, up 8.3% from 2007.

KFC (originally Kentucky Fried Chicken) is the leader in the U.S. chicken QSR segment, with about a 44% market share at 2008 year end (45% in 2007), according to NPD Group CREST. At the end of 2008, there were 5,253 units in the U.S. and 10,327 units internationally.

Pizza Hut is the world's largest restaurant chain specializing in ready-to-eat pizza products. At December 31, 2008, it led the U.S. pizza QSR segment with about a 15% market share (15%). As of December 2008, there were 7,564 units in the U.S. and 5,611 units internationally.

Taco Bell is the leader in the U.S. Mexican food QSR segment, with about a 54% market share (58%). At the end of 2008, it had 5,588 units in the U.S. and

245 units internationally.

Long John Silver's operates mostly in the U.S., with 1,060 restaurants in total. A&W operates in 10 countries and territories with 363 units in the U.S. and 264 outside the U.S.

In each concept, units are operated by the company as well as by independent franchisees, licensees, or unconsolidated affiliates. The company intends to refranchise restaurants as part of a long range plan to reduce company ownership of U.S. restaurants to below 10% of the total by 2010. During 2008, it reduced company ownership in the U.S. to about 17%, from 22% at the end of 2007. During 2008, 775 company-owned restaurants worldwide were sold to franchisees.

For financial reporting purposes, YUM has three business segments: the U.S. division, the China division, and the Yum Restaurants International (YRI) division.

Company Financials Fiscal Year Ended Dec. 31

Per Share Data ($)	2008	2007	2006	2005	2004	2003	2002	2001	2000	1999
Tangible Book Value	NM	0.27	0.81	1.04	1.20	0.42	NM	NM	NM	NM
Cash Flow	3.10	2.67	2.46	2.07	1.95	1.67	1.54	1.39	1.29	1.58
Earnings	1.96	1.68	1.46	1.28	1.21	1.01	0.94	0.81	0.69	0.98
S&P Core Earnings	1.76	1.69	1.51	1.26	1.15	1.04	0.80	0.68	NA	NA
Dividends	0.68	0.52	0.26	0.22	0.10	Nil	Nil	Nil	Nil	Nil
Payout Ratio	35%	31%	18%	17%	8%	Nil	Nil	Nil	Nil	Nil
Prices:High	41.73	40.60	31.84	26.90	23.74	17.71	16.58	13.33	9.64	18.47
Prices:Low	21.50	27.51	22.11	22.37	16.07	10.77	10.18	7.89	5.89	8.75
P/E Ratio:High	21	24	22	21	20	18	18	16	14	19
P/E Ratio:Low	11	16	15	18	13	11	11	10	9	9
Income Statement Analysis (Million $)										
Revenue	11,279	10,416	9,561	9,349	9,011	8,380	7,757	6,953	7,093	7,822
Operating Income	1,971	1,808	1,724	1,538	1,518	1,471	1,375	1,220	1,217	1,280
Depreciation	560	533	479	469	448	401	370	354	354	386
Interest Expense	253	199	154	127	129	173	172	158	176	202
Pretax Income	1,280	1,191	1,108	1,026	1,026	886	858	733	684	1,038
Effective Tax Rate	24.7%	23.7%	25.6%	25.7%	27.9%	30.2%	32.1%	32.9%	39.6%	39.6%
Net Income	964	909	824	762	740	618	583	492	413	627
S&P Core Earnings	863	913	849	754	704	635	494	416	NA	NA
Balance Sheet & Other Financial Data (Million $)										
Cash	164	789	319	158	62.0	192	130	110	133	89.0
Current Assets	951	1,481	901	837	747	806	730	547	688	486
Total Assets	6,506	7,242	6,353	5,698	5,696	5,620	5,400	4,388	4,149	3,961
Current Liabilities	1,722	2,062	1,724	1,605	1,376	1,461	1,520	1,805	1,216	1,298
Long Term Debt	3,564	2,924	2,045	1,649	1,731	2,056	2,299	1,552	2,397	2,391
Common Equity	-112	1,139	1,437	1,449	1,595	1,120	594	104	-322	-560
Total Capital	3,509	4,063	3,482	3,098	3,326	3,176	2,893	1,656	2,085	1,838
Capital Expenditures	935	742	614	609	645	663	760	636	572	470
Cash Flow	1,524	1,442	1,303	1,231	1,188	1,019	953	846	767	1,013
Current Ratio	0.6	0.7	0.5	0.5	0.5	0.6	0.5	0.3	0.6	0.4
% Long Term Debt of Capitalization	101.6	71.9	58.7	53.2	52.0	64.7	79.5	93.7	115.0	130.1
% Net Income of Revenue	8.6	8.7	8.6	8.2	8.2	7.4	7.5	7.1	5.8	8.0
% Return on Assets	14.0	13.4	13.6	13.4	13.1	11.2	11.9	11.5	10.2	14.8
% Return on Equity	NM	70.6	57.1	50.1	54.5	72.1	167.0	NM	NM	NM

Data as orig reptd.; bef. results of disc opers/spec. items. Per share data adj. for stk. divs.; EPS diluted. E-Estimated. NA-Not Available. NM-Not Meaningful. NR-Not Ranked. UR-Under Review.

Office: 1441 Gardiner Lane, Louisville, KY 40213.
Telephone: 502-874-8300.
Email: yum.investors@yum.com
Website: http://www.yum.com

Chrmn, Pres & CEO: D.C. Novak
Vice Chrmn: J.S. Su
COO: E.J. Brolick
SVP, Chief Acctg Officer & Cntlr: T.F. Knopf

SVP, Secy & General Counsel: C.L. Campbell
Investor Contact: B. Bishop (502-874-8905)
Board Members: D. W. Dorman, M. Ferragamo, J. D. Grissom, B. Hill, R. Holland, Jr., K. G. Langone, J. S. Linen, T. C. Nelson, D. C. Novak, T. M. Ryan, J. S. Su, J. Trujillo, R. D. Walter

Founded: 1997
Domicile: North Carolina
Employees: 336,000

The McGraw·Hill Companies

Zimmer Holdings Inc.

STANDARD &POOR'S

S&P Recommendation	BUY ★★★★☆	Price $58.52 (as of Nov 27, 2009)	12-Mo. Target Price $61.00	Investment Style Large-Cap Growth

GICS Sector Health Care
Sub-Industry Health Care Equipment

Summary This company, spun off by Bristol-Myers Squibb in August 2001, manufactures orthopedic reconstructive implants, fracture management products and dental implants.

Key Stock Statistics (Source S&P, Vickers, company reports)

52-Wk Range	$59.31–30.67	S&P Oper. EPS 2009E	3.90	Market Capitalization(B)	$12.464	Beta	1.07
Trailing 12-Month EPS	$3.33	S&P Oper. EPS 2010E	4.30	Yield (%)	Nil	S&P 3-Yr. Proj. EPS CAGR(%)	5
Trailing 12-Month P/E	17.6	P/E on S&P Oper. EPS 2009E	15.0	Dividend Rate/Share	Nil	S&P Credit Rating	A-
$10K Invested 5 Yrs Ago	$7,356	Common Shares Outstg. (M)	213.0	Institutional Ownership (%)	NM		

Price Performance

30-Week Mov. Avg. · · · 10-Week Mov. Avg. — **GAAP Earnings vs. Previous Year** Volume Above Avg. STARS
12-Mo. Target Price — Relative Strength — ▲ Up ▼ Down ▶ No Change Below Avg. ★

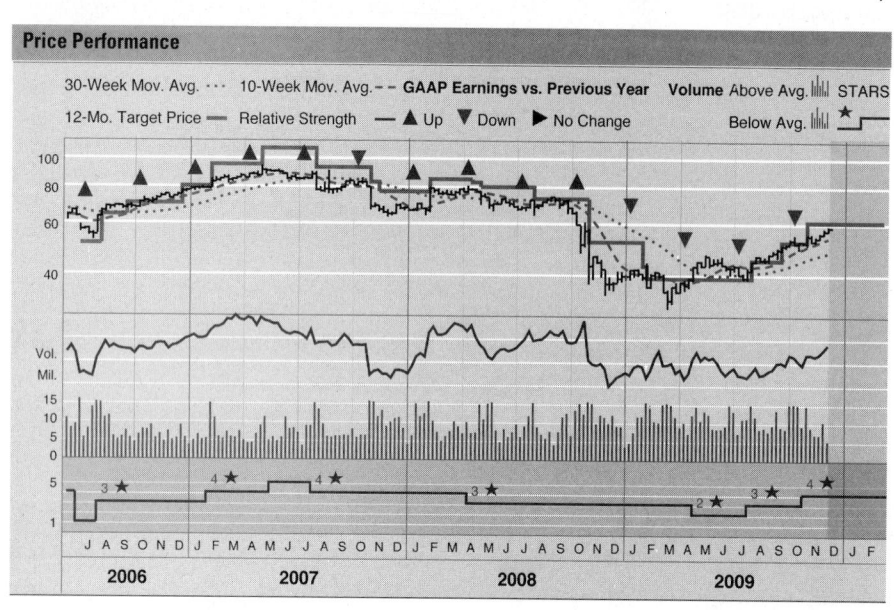

Options: ASE, CBOE, P, Ph

Analysis prepared by **Phillip M. Seligman** on October 28, 2009, when the stock traded at **$ 53.45.**

Highlights

▶ We expect revenues to decline 0.5% in 2009 to about $4.1 billion, with knee implant sales of over $1.7 billion, hip implant sales of over $1.2 billion, other reconstructive sales of $340 million, spinal sales of about $270 million, fracture management sales of over $230 million, and other surgical product sales of $280 million. We expect the 2009 top line to be affected by the first half's unfavorable foreign exchange. Assuming a modest orthopedic market recovery and the recent more favorable foreign exchange environment, we look for revenues to grow by 7% in 2010.

▶ We believe gross margins will widen modestly in 2009, with higher margins in the first half on foreign currency hedge gains, followed by lower margins in the second half, on slower plant throughput and the drawdown of higher cost inventory. We expect foreign exchange and more stable throughput to help widen 2010's gross margins. We see a higher SG&A cost ratio in 2009 partly on increased spending on medical training programs, followed by a decline in 2010 on revenue leverage.

▶ We see 2009 EPS of $3.90, and we believe EPS in 2010 will reach $4.30.

Investment Rationale/Risk

▶ We recently upgraded the shares to buy, from hold. We think ZMH's hip and knee, spine and trauma businesses have stabilized, and ZMH is seeing positive, albeit modest, momentum, which we expect will strengthen over time on new products and assuming the continued easing of procedure deferrals. Moreover, we think the longer-term demand drivers for ZMH's orthopedic implants remain intact, given demographic trends, a promising product pipeline, and an upgraded medical training program for surgeons. Meanwhile, we are encouraged that ZMH views implant price trends as not having worsened. We also view cash flow as healthy, providing financial flexibility.

▶ Risks to our recommendation and target price include lower Medicare reimbursement and significant device reimbursement cuts in key overseas markets, notably Japan.

▶ Our 12-month target price is $61, or about 14X our 2010 EPS estimate. The forward P/E multiple we apply reflects recent peerwide valuation expansion and a narrower discount to the stock's historical levels to reflect our view of ZMH's turnaround progress.

Qualitative Risk Assessment

LOW	MEDIUM	HIGH

Our risk assessment reflects Zimmer's operations in a highly competitive industry characterized by relatively short product life cycles, requiring a significant number of new product introductions to maintain market share and gross profit margins. Many of the company's customers are reimbursed by the federal government through Medicare, and a more restrictive budgetary environment could result in lower prices paid to medical device suppliers such as Zimmer. However, this is offset by the company's position as one of the dominant manufacturers in the orthopedic device industry, with substantial global sales force capabilities and an expansive product line.

Quantitative Evaluations

S&P Quality Ranking NR

D	C	B-	B	B+	A-	A	A+

Relative Strength Rank STRONG
89
LOWEST = 1 HIGHEST = 99

Revenue/Earnings Data

Revenue (Million $)

	1Q	2Q	3Q	4Q	Year
2009	992.6	1,020	975.6	--	--
2008	1,059	1,080	952.2	1,030	4,121
2007	950.2	970.6	903.2	1,074	3,898
2006	860.4	881.6	819.8	933.6	3,495
2005	828.5	846.8	762.5	848.3	3,286
2004	742.2	737.4	700.2	801.1	2,981

Earnings Per Share ($)

2009	0.91	0.98	0.70	E1.08	E3.90
2008	1.02	0.99	0.95	0.75	3.72
2007	0.98	0.97	0.19	1.12	3.26
2006	0.82	0.81	0.76	1.02	3.40
2005	0.70	0.76	0.67	0.80	2.93
2004	0.40	0.47	0.52	0.81	2.19

Fiscal year ended Dec. 31. Next earnings report expected: Late January. EPS Estimates based on S&P Operating Earnings; historical GAAP earnings are as reported.

Dividend Data

No cash dividends have been paid.

Zimmer Holdings Inc.

STANDARD &POOR'S

Business Summary October 28, 2009

CORPORATE OVERVIEW. Zimmer Holdings primarily designs, develops, manufactures and markets orthopedic reconstructive implants and fracture management products. The former division of Bristol-Myers Squibb was spun off to BMY shareholders in August 2001.

Zimmer's reconstructive implants (82% of 2008 sales) are used to restore function lost due to disease or trauma in joints such as knees, hips, shoulders and elbows. The company offers a wide range of products for specialized knee procedures, including The NexGen Complete Knee Solution, NexGen Legacy, NexGen Revision Knee, Innex Total Knee System, M/G Unicompartmental Knee System, and Prolong Highly Crosslinked Polyethylene Articular Surface material. Hip replacement products include the VerSys Hip System, the ZMR Hip System, the Trilogy Acetabular System and a line of specialty hip products. The company also continues to develop a portfolio of minimally invasive hip replacement procedures. ZMH sells the Coonrad/Morrey product line of elbow replacement implant products, along with a line of restorative dental products.

In the spine/trauma area (11%), the company sells devices used to reattach or

stabilize damaged bone and tissue to support the body's natural healing process. The most common stabilization of bone fractures concerns the internal fixation of bone fragments, which can involve the use of an assortment of plates, screws, rods, wires and pins. ZMH offers a line of products designed for use in fracture fixation. In October 2008, the company acquired the spinal business of Abbott Labs for $360 million in cash.

ZMH makes and markets other orthopedic surgical products (6%) used by surgeons for orthopedic as well as non-orthopedic procedures. Products include tourniquets, blood management systems, wound debridement products, powered surgical instruments, pain management devices, and orthopedic soft goods that provide support and/or heat retention and compression for trauma of the knee, ankle, back and upper extremities, including the shoulder, elbow, neck and wrist.

Company Financials Fiscal Year Ended Dec. 31

Per Share Data ($)	2008	2007	2006	2005	2004	2003	2002	2001	2000	1999
Tangible Book Value	8.96	9.76	7.15	7.94	2.52	0.38	1.88	0.41	NM	NA
Cash Flow	4.92	4.22	4.21	3.68	2.92	1.87	1.43	0.89	0.92	NA
Earnings	3.72	3.26	3.40	2.93	2.19	1.38	1.31	0.77	0.81	0.78
S&P Core Earnings	3.56	3.94	3.36	2.73	2.08	1.31	1.24	0.70	NA	NA
Dividends	Nil	Nil	Nil	Nil	Nil	Nil	Nil	Nil	NA	NA
Payout Ratio	Nil	Nil	Nil	Nil	Nil	Nil	Nil	Nil	NA	NA
Prices:High	80.92	94.38	79.11	89.10	89.44	71.85	43.00	33.30	NA	NA
Prices:Low	34.10	63.00	52.20	60.19	64.40	38.02	28.00	24.70	NA	NA
P/E Ratio:High	22	29	23	30	41	52	33	43	NA	NA
P/E Ratio:Low	9	19	15	21	29	28	21	32	NA	NA

Income Statement Analysis (Million $)	2008	2007	2006	2005	2004	2003	2002	2001	2000	1999
Revenue	4,121	3,898	3,495	3,286	2,981	1,901	1,372	1,179	1,041	939
Operating Income	1,510	1,553	1,369	1,297	1,026	633	426	272	291	NA
Depreciation	275	230	197	186	181	103	25.0	23.4	23.0	22.0
Interest Expense	NA	NA	4.00	14.0	32.0	13.0	12.0	7.40	29.0	NA
Pretax Income	1,122	1,132	1,169	1,040	732	438	389	241	239	231
Effective Tax Rate	24.3%	31.6%	28.5%	29.5%	25.9%	33.6%	33.7%	37.8%	34.3%	35.1%
Net Income	849	773	835	733	542	291	258	150	157	150
S&P Core Earnings	812	936	823	682	515	277	244	137	NA	NA

Balance Sheet & Other Financial Data (Million $)	2008	2007	2006	2005	2004	2003	2002	2001	2000	1999
Cash	213	466	266	233	155	78.0	16.0	18.4	50.0	NA
Current Assets	2,179	2,083	1,746	1,576	1,561	1,339	612	509	487	NA
Total Assets	7,239	6,634	5,974	5,722	5,696	5,156	859	745	669	606
Current Liabilities	771	749	628	607	701	645	401	373	217	NA
Long Term Debt	460	104	100	82.0	624	1,008	Nil	214	500	NA
Common Equity	5,650	5,450	4,921	4,683	3,943	3,143	366	78.7	-48.0	391
Total Capital	6,114	5,554	5,024	4,767	4,574	4,158	366	293	452	391
Capital Expenditures	488	331	142	105	101	45.0	34.0	54.7	NA	33.0
Cash Flow	1,124	1,003	1,032	919	723	394	283	173	180	NA
Current Ratio	2.8	2.8	2.8	2.6	2.2	2.1	1.5	1.4	2.2	2.0
% Long Term Debt of Capitalization	7.5	1.8	1.9	1.7	13.6	24.2	Nil	73.0	110.6	Nil
% Net Income of Revenue	20.6	19.8	23.8	22.3	18.1	15.3	18.9	12.7	15.1	16.0
% Return on Assets	12.2	12.3	14.2	12.8	9.9	9.7	32.1	22.4	NA	NA
% Return on Equity	15.3	14.9	17.3	16.9	15.2	10.6	115.0	NM	NA	NA

Data as orig reptd.; bef. results of disc opers/spec. items. Per share data adj. for stk. divs.; EPS diluted. E-Estimated. NA-Not Available. NM-Not Meaningful. NR-Not Ranked. UR-Under Review.

Office: 345 East Main Street, Warsaw, IN 46580.
Telephone: 574-267-6131.
Email: zimmer.infoperson@zimmer.com
Website: http://www.zimmer.com

Chrmn: J.L. McGoldrick
Pres & CEO: D. Dvorak
COO: R.C. Stair
EVP & CFO: J.T. Crines

SVP & CSO: C.R. Blanchard
Investor Contact: P. Blair (574-371-8042)
Board Members: B. J. Bernard, M. N. Casper, D. Dvorak, L. C. Glasscock, R. A. Hagemann, A. J. Higgins, J. L. McGoldrick, C. B. Pickett, A. A. White, III

Founded: 1927
Domicile: Delaware
Employees: 8,500

Zions BanCorp

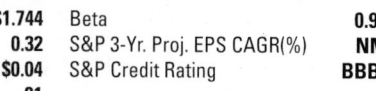

S&P Recommendation	HOLD ★★★☆☆		Price $12.62 (as of Nov 27, 2009)	12-Mo. Target Price $15.00	Investment Style Large-Cap Blend

GICS Sector Financials
Sub-Industry Regional Banks

Summary ZION has more than 500 full-service banking offices in 10 western states. As of September 30, 2009, it had assets of $53.4 billion and deposits of $43.0 billion.

Key Stock Statistics (Source S&P, Vickers, company reports)

52-Wk Range	$31.38– 5.90	S&P Oper. EPS 2009**E**	-10.37	Market Capitalization(B)	$1.744	Beta	0.98
Trailing 12-Month EPS	$-13.31	S&P Oper. EPS 2010**E**	-1.73	Yield (%)	0.32	S&P 3-Yr. Proj. EPS CAGR(%)	NM
Trailing 12-Month P/E	NM	P/E on S&P Oper. EPS 2009**E**	NM	Dividend Rate/Share	$0.04	S&P Credit Rating	BBB-
$10K Invested 5 Yrs Ago	$2,093	Common Shares Outstg. (M)	138.2	Institutional Ownership (%)	81		

Price Performance

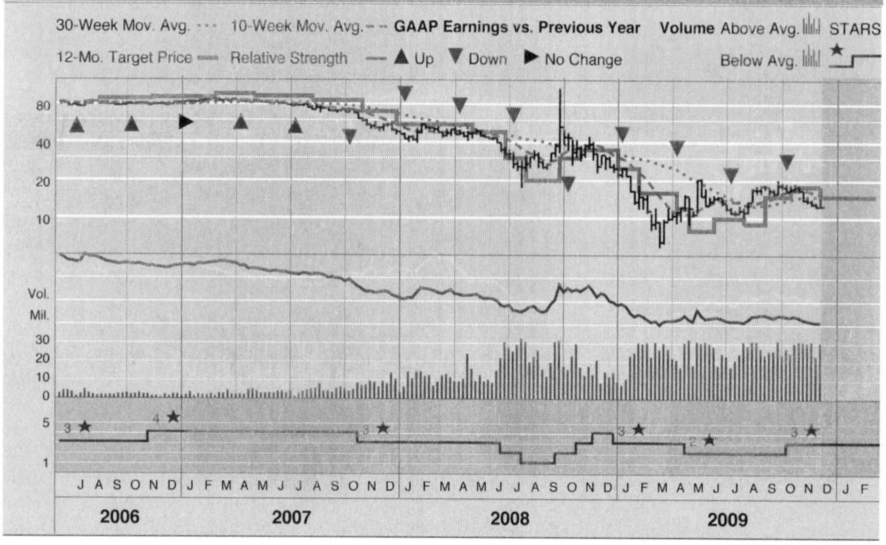

30-Week Mov. Avg. · · · 10-Week Mov. Avg. – – **GAAP Earnings vs. Previous Year** Volume Above Avg. STARS
12-Mo. Target Price — Relative Strength — ▲ Up ▼ Down ► No Change Below Avg. ★

[Price performance chart showing stock price, volume, and STARS from 2006 through 2009 into 2010]

Options: CBOE, Ph

Analysis prepared by **Erik Oja** on November 24, 2009, when the stock traded at **$ 14.12.**

Highlights

► We expect ZION to earn $1.90 billion of net interest income in 2009, down 3.5%. We see a good net interest spread environment, currently offsetting the negative impacts of nonperforming loans and weak loan growth. We expect each of these effects to reverse at different times in 2010, beginning with the relatively wide spread, followed by improvements in loan growth and credit quality, and we are forecasting net interest income of $1.8 billion in 2010, down 6.5%.

► Provisions fell to $566 million in the third quarter of 2009, from the previous all-time high of roughly $763 million in the second quarter. While we believe provisions will now decline, we expect continued elevated levels through 2010, averaging over $280 million, driven by weakness in ZION's relatively large commercial loan portfolio. We see ZION taking at least $150 million in securities impairments over the same period, and we do not rule out the possibility of more goodwill write-downs.

► We project losses per share of $10.37 in 2009 and $1.73 in 2010. We expect earnings to finally turn positive in 2011, at $0.30 per share.

Investment Rationale/Risk

► Nonperforming loan growth moderated in the third quarter, and they were up 11% from the level at the end of the second quarter. Nonperforming loans, excluding FDIC-covered assets, were about $1.81 billion, about 4.35% of loans, slightly higher than peers. This suggests to us that net chargeoffs will run at a rate of about $250 million per quarter for at least the next five quarters, through the end of 2010. At September 30, ZION had $2.86 billion of tangible equity, including $1.5 billion of TARP preferred stock, equal to 8.39% of tangible assets. In addition, ZION recently offered to convert $140 million of preferred stock to common equity, so as to bolster equity capital. However, we think ZION will still need to raise additional equity capital in 2010. ZION recently traded at about 0.65X tangible book value per share, and we see other banks, which have similar levels of nonperforming loans, at this valuation.

► Risks to our recommendation and target price include larger-than-expected securities write-downs, and declining economic conditions.

► Our 12-month target price of $15 reflects a below-peers multiple of 0.64X tangible book value per share of $23.40.

Qualitative Risk Assessment

LOW	MEDIUM	**HIGH**

Our risk assessment reflects the company's credit exposure to housing and commercial real estate in California, Arizona, and Nevada.

Quantitative Evaluations

S&P Quality Ranking   A-

D	C	B-	B	B+	**A-**	A	A+

Relative Strength Rank   WEAK

11

LOWEST = 1   HIGHEST = 99

Revenue/Earnings Data

Revenue (Million $)

	1Q	2Q	3Q	4Q	Year
2009	528.1	733.7	756.4	--	--
2008	901.1	795.3	825.3	642.9	3,165
2007	915.9	931.0	963.6	807.3	3,776
2006	767.1	824.1	876.9	901.2	3,369
2005	525.8	562.3	594.5	666.5	2,349
2004	457.4	469.8	492.6	503.3	1,923

Earnings Per Share ($)

2009	-7.29	-0.35	-1.41	E-1.02	E-10.37
2008	0.98	0.65	0.31	-4.37	-2.66
2007	1.36	1.43	1.22	0.40	4.42
2006	1.28	1.35	1.42	1.32	5.36
2005	1.20	1.30	1.34	1.32	5.16
2004	1.10	1.09	1.13	1.15	4.47

Fiscal year ended Dec. 31. Next earnings report expected: Late January. EPS Estimates based on S&P Operating Earnings; historical GAAP earnings are as reported.

Dividend Data (Dates: mm/dd Payment Date: mm/dd/yy)

Amount ($)	Date Decl.	Ex-Div. Date	Stk. of Record	Payment Date
0.040	01/26	02/09	02/11	02/25/09
0.040	04/23	05/11	05/13	05/27/09
0.010	07/22	08/10	08/12	08/26/09
0.010	10/30	11/09	11/12	11/20/09

Dividends have been paid since 1966. Source: Company reports.

Please read the Required Disclosures and Analyst Certification on the last page of this report.

The **McGraw-Hill** Companies

Zions BanCorp

STANDARD &POOR'S

Business Summary November 24, 2009

CORPORATE OVERVIEW. Zions Bancorp. is a financial holding company that operates eight different banks in 10 western states, with each bank operating as an individual segment under a different name and management. In addition, the company's Other segment contains the parent company operations, certain nonbank subsidiaries and operating units, The Commerce Bank of Oregon, and eliminations of transactions between segments.

The company's largest bank, Zions First National Bank, serves Utah and Idaho and accounted for 35% of loans and 39% of deposits at year-end 2008. ZFNB also houses the company's capital markets and wealth management operations. California Bank & Trust (19% of loans and 18% of deposits) serves California and has loan production offices in Arizona, Colorado, Florida, Georgia, Illinois, Michigan, Missouri, Nevada, Ohio, Oregon and Washington. Amegy Corporation (21% of loans and 20% of deposits), acquired in December 2005, serves Houston and Dallas, Texas. National Bank of Arizona (10% of loans and

9% of deposits) serves the Phoenix and Tucson metropolitan areas. Nevada State Bank (8% of loans and 8% of deposits) serves the state of Nevada. Vectra Bank Colorado (5% of loans and 5% of deposits) serves Colorado. The Commerce Bank of Washington (2% of loans and 1% of deposits) has one office in the Seattle area serving businesses, executives and professionals.

The company tries to control risks by maintaining formal loan policies and procedures, independent compliance examinations of adherence to the policies and procedures, performing portfolio risk analysis, using financial instruments to reduce interest rate risk, and by pursuing a loan portfolio diversification strategy.

Company Financials Fiscal Year Ended Dec. 31

Per Share Data ($)	2008	2007	2006	2005	2004	2003	2002	2001	2000	1999
Tangible Book Value	27.24	27.02	25.15	20.45	23.29	20.96	17.21	15.19	13.06	11.61
Earnings	-2.67	4.42	5.36	5.16	4.47	3.74	3.44	3.15	1.86	2.26
S&P Core Earnings	-0.67	4.46	5.36	5.04	4.33	4.42	3.17	2.42	NA	NA
Dividends	1.61	1.68	1.47	1.44	1.26	1.02	0.80	0.80	0.89	0.86
Payout Ratio	NM	38%	27%	28%	28%	27%	23%	25%	48%	38%
Prices:High	57.05	88.56	85.25	77.67	69.29	63.86	59.65	64.00	62.88	75.88
Prices:Low	21.07	45.70	75.13	63.33	54.08	39.31	34.14	42.30	32.00	48.25
P/E Ratio:High	NM	20	16	15	16	17	17	20	34	34
P/E Ratio:Low	NM	10	14	12	12	11	10	13	17	21

Income Statement Analysis (Million $)										
Net Interest Income	1,972	1,882	1,765	1,361	1,174	1,095	1,035	950	803	741
Tax Equivalent Adjustment	23.7	26.1	24.3	21.1	NA	NA	NA	NA	NA	16.2
Non Interest Income	191	395	527	439	425	426	402	388	274	270
Loan Loss Provision	650	152	72.6	43.0	44.1	69.9	71.9	73.2	31.8	18.0
% Expense/Operating Revenue	58.9%	61.7%	57.4%	56.4%	57.8%	63.7%	59.8%	63.9%	75.9%	66.4%
Pretax Income	-315	738	913	742	624	546	481	440	243	309
Effective Tax Rate	NM	32.0%	34.8%	35.5%	35.3%	39.1%	34.9%	35.8%	32.8%	35.5%
Net Income	-266	494	583	480	406	340	317	290	162	194
% Net Interest Margin	4.18	4.43	4.63	4.58	4.32	4.45	4.56	4.64	4.27	4.31
S&P Core Earnings	-73.1	483	579	469	394	402	292	223	NA	NA

Balance Sheet & Other Financial Data (Million $)										
Money Market Assets	2,703	1,500	369	667	593	569	543	280	528	525
Investment Securities	4,509	6,895	6,790	6,996	5,786	5,402	4,238	3,463	4,188	4,437
Commercial Loans	34,333	31,508	27,559	23,122	16,337	10,404	13,648	4,110	3,615	3,311
Other Loans	7,659	7,744	7,260	7,131	6,395	9,613	5,195	13,304	10,843	9,133
Total Assets	55,093	52,947	46,970	42,780	31,470	28,558	26,566	24,304	21,939	20,281
Demand Deposits	9,683	9,618	25,869	9,954	6,822	5,883	5,117	4,481	3,586	3,277
Time Deposits	31,633	27,305	9,113	22,689	16,471	15,014	15,015	13,361	11,484	10,786
Long Term Debt	2,657	2,815	2,495	2,746	1,919	1,843	1,310	781	420	453
Common Equity	4,920	5,053	4,747	4,237	2,790	2,540	2,374	2,281	1,779	1,660
% Return on Assets	NM	1.0	1.3	1.3	2.0	1.2	1.2	1.3	0.8	1.0
% Return on Equity	NM	9.8	12.9	13.7	15.2	13.8	13.6	14.3	9.4	12.5
% Loan Loss Reserve	1.6	1.2	1.1	1.1	1.2	0.9	1.4	1.5	1.3	1.6
% Loans/Deposits	101.2	103.1	99.1	92.3	97.1	142.6	96.0	97.0	96.6	91.0
% Equity to Assets	9.2	9.8	10.0	9.5	13.3	8.9	9.2	8.8	8.1	8.1

Data as orig reptd.; bef. results of disc opers/spec. items. Per share data adj. for stk. divs.; EPS diluted. E-Estimated. NA-Not Available. NM-Not Meaningful. NR-Not Ranked. UR-Under Review.

Office: 1 S Main St 15th Fl, Salt Lake City, UT, USA 84133.
Telephone: 801-524-4787.
Website: http://www.zionsbancorporation.com
Chrmn, Pres & CEO: H.H. Simmons

Vice Chrmn, EVP & CFO: D.L. Arnold
EVP, Secy & General Counsel: T.E. Laursen
EVP & CIO: J.T. Itokazu
SVP, Chief Acctg Officer & Cntlr: N.X. Bellon

Investor Contact: C.B. Hinckley (801-524-4787)
Board Members: D. L. Arnold, J. C. Atkin, R. D. Cash, P. Frobes, J. D. Heaney, R. B. Porter, S. D. Quinn, H. H. Simmons, L. E. Simmons, S. Wheelwright, S. T. Williams

Founded: 1961
Domicile: Utah
Employees: 11,011

The McGraw-Hill Companies